D1243683

COMPARATIVE CONSTITUTIONAL LAW

by

VICKI C. JACKSON
Professor of Law
Georgetown University Law Center

MARK TUSHNET
Carmack Waterhouse Professor of Constitutional Law
Georgetown University Law Center

NEW YORK, NEW YORK
FOUNDATION PRESS

1999

 TEXT IS PRINTED ON 10% POST CONSUMER RECYCLED PAPER

Professor Jackson dedicates her work on this book to her parents,
Harriet Burstein Jackson and Theodore R. Jackson,
her husband, Robert S. Taylor, and her children
Jacob, Michael and Sophie.

Professor Tushnet dedicates his work on this book
to the memory of his grandparents.

*

PREFACE

Comparative constitutional law is both a very old and a relatively new subject. Centuries ago scholars and political activists ranging from Aristotle to James Madison compared and analyzed systems of government to determine how best to constitute polities. But until the post-World War II era, only a small number of nations had sustained experience in living under governments constituted by written constitutions. Moreover, until the recent spread of communications technology, access to foreign legal materials has been limited. Since World War II, and with renewed vigor since the fall of the Soviet Union, nations across the world are engaged in constitutionmaking, and constitutional courts with constitution interpreting.

Being able to think systematically about different structures for organizing a government, and different approaches to establishing just, effective, and stable forms of government while providing the flexibility for the future that is required to meet changing needs and ensure continued stability are general benefits of studying these materials. Further, the better informed a person is about the world, the more he or she can bring to the legal profession, and the more he or she can enjoy and appreciate life. Comparison also provides opportunities to discover that aspects of the system with which our students are most familiar are not inevitable even for those who, in the words of the U.S. Constitution's Preamble, seek "to form a more perfect Union, establish Justice, insure domestic Tranquility, . . . and secure the Blessings of Liberty to ourselves and our Posterity."

Earlier efforts, both of comparativists generally and particularly of scholars of comparative constitutional law, have been invaluable to us. Donald Kommers' more than two decades of work in translating and explaining the German Constitutional Court and its jurisprudence, Mauro Cappelletti's work on comparative judicial processes, and the Cappelletti & Cohen casebook (1979) have been fundamental to our work. Political scientists, those represented in these materials and others, have played an important role in furthering the comparative study of constitutional systems and constitutional law.

Our approach differs from that in the work of those on whom we build and to whom we are enormously indebted. Immersion in a single, or selected few constitutional systems, can yield depth and particularity of knowledge and insight. In contrast, we have chosen to draw on the expertise of others to provide foundations for a more structural approach to constitutions, constitution-making, and constitution-interpreting. We deal with questions like these: Why have constitutions? What is the relationship between constitutionalism and written constitutions? Through whose perspectives, in what categories, should questions about constitutions and constitutionalism be asked? Are there lessons—positive or negative—to be learned from comparing constitutional experiences in different countries and times? Or are lessons from one culture to another always hobbled by the possibility that constitutional experience is particularized by context and culture?

Our approach also differs in its use of scholarly works in addition to case materials and constitutional texts. Traditional casebooks use "primary" materials to allow the student to derive the broader themes and narratives of a legal system. Again in contrast, the wide scope of the materials we draw from requires use of scholarly works to explain and describe. (In addition, since neither of us was in a position to translate foreign works directly, our selection of materials outside the English-using court systems of the world was limited to works translated by others. For a helpful discussion of research tools in comparative law, see Rudolf B. Schlesinger, Hans W. Baade, Peter E. Herzog, and Edward M. Wise, COMPARATIVE LAW 999-1004 (6th ed. 1998).) The questions with which our book is concerned have been the subject of so much thoughtful writing and research by academics in law and political theory around the world that it seems valuable and important to introduce students to such works. We recognize the importance of context in understanding and evaluating constitutional structures and decisions, and thus seek to provide relevant background material, both through our introductions and through lengthy excerpts from scholars with particular expertise in the various countries' constitutional systems.

We have spent time considering what is lost by this approach: deep knowledge of a single other constitutional system; appreciation of details; and, perhaps, students' ability independently to evaluate characterizations of particular other systems through presentation of a wide range of material. We are aware of the materials' limitations, and of our own experience, so we recurrently direct attention to the risks (and benefits) of borrowing solutions from one or another constitutional system, and more generally to the risks of ethnocentricity in the design and evaluation of constitutional systems. We compare the enthusiasm of some that comparative constitutional study will help identify transcendental principles of justice with more skeptical views of our ability to get beyond the categories of legal thought that prevail within our legal culture. (These problems of comparative constitutional study are in some respects a specific example of more general problems and questions in comparative law. For useful discussion, see Alan Watson, LEGAL TRANSPLANTS: AN APPROACH TO COMPARATIVE LAW 10-15 (2d ed. 1993); Rudolf B. Schlesinger, Hans W. Baade, Peter E. Herzog, and Edward M. Wise, COMPARATIVE LAW 974-98 (6th ed. 1998) (describing "language, classificatory and practical difficulties" as part of a "caveat" on "the special hazards of comparative law").) What is gained by our approach, however, is the ability to identify a broader range of questions and concepts, that can be brought to bear on the tasks of the reader as lawyer, as political theorist, and as public citizen, in thinking about both the design of constitutions and of how to interpret their ambiguous provisions.

We begin with readings from three different constitutional systems on a common issue—the regulation of abortions. Chapter I poses a recurrent question—whether discovery that constitutional law or structure in other polities differs from that with which the reader is familiar makes it possible to transfer other systems' solutions to the reader's polity, or whether these differences are inextricably entwined with other differences so that comparison does not justify borrowing or transplantation.

Chapter II provides a more theoretical framework for considering the nature of comparative constitutional law. We provide alternative perspectives on the value of comparative constitutional law, and raise a number of claims about its possibilities and limits for students to consider. We also seek to draw more generally on comparative law literature to raise cautions about the possible limitations of comparison and comparative law. The chapter closes with a description of the Irish experience with abortion, in part to concretize for students the need to be intellectually aware of and healthily skeptical about the ordering, and cataloguing, of categories for comparisons in constitutional law.

Chapters III and IV expand on the conceptual issues raised in the first two chapters. Chapter III pursues more systematically what the functions of constitutions are, and how constitutions can be understood either to facilitate constitutionalism or in some cases to obstruct constitutionalism. Chapter IV considers the problem of constitutional transitions, amendments, and regime changes. What is the relationship between the processes of constitutional change and the substance of the constitution? The stability and workability of the constitutional product? Are "constitutional moments" required to produce lasting constitutions? What is the value and possibility of more evolutionary approaches?

Chapter V focuses on the decades-long debate in Great Britain over whether to adopt a constitutional bill of rights, and poses questions about the connection between constitutionalism and judicial review. It concludes with a section on Australia's recent caselaw deriving individual constitutional freedoms from a constitution that contemplates representative democratic government but that lacks a bill of rights.

These first five chapters deal with broad and general questions of the role of constitutions. The next three chapters focus on particular questions of constitutional structure.

Chapter VI looks at the role and structure of constitutional courts, examining the various forms in which judicial review of constitutional claims is carried out and identifying positive and negative claims about the effects of judicial review. Many constitutional scholars believe that courts are needed to secure the enforcement of constitutions in the western liberal tradition, though others question how large or definitive a role courts, as compared to legislatures, should play in defining the legal environment. Is "juridification" of politics through influence of constitutional law decisions a good or bad development? Is there any relationship between the substantive outcome of judicial review and the institutional structures and procedures through which it is carried out?

Introducing the range of structures by which representative democracies have organized their central governments, Chapter VII considers "separation of powers" issues, the relationship between executive, legislative and judicial functions in systems in different parts of the world. Focusing on foreign affairs and the relationship between representative structures of government and commitment of military force, the materials also reconsider the role of constitutional courts in policing or enforcing boundaries of power. Because of "justiciability" limitations in the U.S. and strong deference to other branches in other constitutional systems, much of the "law" of separation of powers in military and foreign affairs is developed outside the courts. Yet, control of the military is a basic requisite for western liberal constitututionalism, and thus worthy of comparative study.

Chapter VIII explores "federalism" as a structural feature of many governments. This chapter focuses on three kinds of questions: What are the relations between federalism and the exercise of regulatory powers? What, if anything, can federalism contribute to protecting individual rights, or the interests of minority groups? And to what extent can constitutions, and constitutional courts, enforce or promote the power-sharing and/or individual-protecting goals of federalism? More broadly, can federalism be understood from the perspective of political or constitutional theory, or do federalist arrangements result more from pragmatic, historical factors? Is federalism, to the extent that it involves decentralized decisionmaking, in tension with the modern social welfare state? And what do we mean when we speak of a successful "federalism"?

Chapter IX bridges the middle third of the book's focus on government structure with the last third's focus on "rights" by exploring pluralistic approaches to some of the problems of diverse populations to which federalism is sometimes addressed. Examining affirmative action in India and the United States, it explores what might be called substantive efforts to accommodate pluralism and democracy through constitutional rules concerning rights for members of particular groups to equality of treatment and/or social advancement.

The final three chapters build on the prior materials to address other individual and group "rights"-based problems in constitutional law. Chapter X focuses on religious pluralism, and constitutional approaches to religious accommodation, religious tolerance and public expressions of religion in several countries. Chapter XI concerns freedom of speech and the state action problem, revisiting as well some of the questions first raised in Chapter I about what substantive norms are needed for constitutional systems to work. To what extent are freedoms of speech and political association normatively required by concepts of constitutionalism? Can such questions be answered across different constitutional cultures?

Our final Chapter addresses the question of constitutional social welfare rights, rights commonly found in European constitutions and constitutions adopted after World War II, but not found in the bare text of the U.S. Constitution. The readings raise a number of questions: Are there conflicts between social welfare rights and "first generation" political and civil rights? Can courts effectively enforce social welfare rights? Why might constitutional designers include social welfare rights in constitutions even if such rights are not judicially enforceable?

Like any coursebook in a broad field, this book does not cover everything that we would have wanted to include. For example, instead of one chapter focused on affirmative action, more could have been included on equality issues across a variety of dimensions. Whole Chapters (instead of one Note) could have been written on gender discrimination and gender equality in comparative constitutional law. In the separation of powers chapter, use of the no confidence vote and the timing of parliamentary elections, as well as constitutional constraints on voting methods in different polities, could have been more substantially developed. Limitations of time and knowledge, and limited availability of materials in translation played roles in our selections, as well as the ever-present tension between inclusion and manageability. (For the most part the research for this book ended in late 1997, although we have noted some developments in 1998.) In the future, and as more materials become available, we might seek to include more as well on such topics as constitutionalism and Islamic cultures, and on constitutional developments in Latin America, Asia and Africa. We hope that readers and users will point out mistakes, omissions, or other materials they would find useful.

We have tried to be clear in acknowledging our debt to the work of other scholars. We hope that this book will prove useful both in law and political science classrooms, and in prompting additional work by other scholars on the rich range of questions that comparative study of constitutional law and constitutional systems presents.

VICKI C. JACKSON
MARK TUSHNET

December, 1998

*

ACKNOWLEDGMENTS

We are indebted to more people than could possibly be listed. Apart from those whose work is listed below, we want to thank the following academics and jurists for invaluable guidance and suggestions, in reviewing material and in discussions about various problems of comparative constitutionalism: Justice Albie Sachs, Professors Bruce Ackerman, T. Alexander Aleinikoff, Winfried Bruegger, James Feinerman, Charles Gustafson, John Jackson, Daniel Meltzer, Judith Resnik, Susan Deller Ross, Peter Schuck, L. Michael Seidman, Jane Stromseth, Robin West, Edith Brown Weiss, Carlos Vázquez, and other legal academics with whom we have discussed this work over the years. Our law librarians, including Barbara Rainwater and Ellen Schaffer, provided helpful guidance on research materials. A work of this magnitude requires assistance from many, and we are grateful for the help provided over several years by Georgetown University Law Center students who served as Research Assistants, including Amy Bowler, Elaine Combs, John Cuddihy, Florence Davis, Tom Heineman, Elizabeth Heinold, Adam Lewis, Alice Pellegrino, J.C. Scott, Tuan Samahon, and Heather Walker. We could not have prepared these materials without the patience, insight, and enthusiasm of several classes of Georgetown University Law Center students, both in upper class seminars and in a first year elective, who studied from earlier, and much bulkier, versions of these materials. Wonderful technical support was provided by the superb administrative staff of the GULC, including Mary Ann De Rosa, Toni Patterson, Brenda Greenfield, and June Hardesty. We want to express our deep gratitude for the support that GULC has provided to this project over several years, including through summer research grants, and a willingness to pay for permissions for classroom use of materials, and our thanks to The Foundation Press, for its willingness to support these materials as a book. For their moral support and intellectual contributions, finally, we want to thank our families, first, last and always.

Foundation Press and the authors gratefully acknowledge the authors and publishers that permitted us to reprint excerpts of copyrighted works. They are

Ackerman, Bruce, The Future of Liberal Revolution (1992), pages 46-68. Reprint permission granted by Yale University Press.

Assemblée Nationale, French Constitution of 1958, excerpts in English translation, **Declaration of the Rights of Man and of the Citizen,** copyright Assemblée Nationale/Ministere des Affaires Étrangeres; The

English translation was prepared under the joint responsibility of the Press, Information and Communication Directorate of the Ministry of Foreign Affairs and the European Affairs Department of the National Assembly. The French original is the sole authentic.

Beatty, David, The Last Generation, in David Beatty Ed., Human Rights and Judicial Review, (published by Martinus Nijhoff Publishers) (1994), 347-54, with kind permission from Kluwer Law International.

Bell, John, French Constitutional Law (1992), 26 pages. Reprinted by permission of Oxford University Press.

Brewer-Carias, Allan-Randolph, Judicial Review in Comparative Law (1989), pages 128-35, 186-94. Reprinted with the permission of Cambridge University Press.

Bulgaria Report vol. 5 (1996), page 8. Reprint permission granted by East European Constitutional Review.

Burley, Anne-Marie Slaughter, Are Foreign Affairs Different?, vol. 106 (1993), pages 1983-94. Reprint permission granted by Harvard Law Review.

Berman, Harold, Religious Rights in Russia at a Time of Tumultuous Transition, in Johan van der Vyver & John Witte Jr., Religious Human Rights, Global Perspective (published by Martinus Nijhoff Publishers) (1996), pages 302-03, with kind permission from Kluwer Law International.

Cappelletti, Mauro, The Judicial Process in Comparative Perspective (1989), 2 pages. Reprint permission granted by Oxford University Press.

Cassels, Jamie, Judicial activism and Public Interest Litigation in India, vol. 37 (1989). Reprint permission granted by American Journal of Comparative Law.

Cullen, Richard, Adaptive Federal in Belgium, vol. 13 (1990), pages 346-58. Reprinted by Permission of University of New South Wales Law Journal.

Damrosch, Lori Fisler, Constitutional Control Over War Powers, vol. 50 (1995), pages 182-99. Reprint permission granted by University of Miami Law Review who owns copyright to the article.

Durham, Cole W., Perspectives on Religious Liberty, in Johan van der Vyver & John Witte Jr., Religious Human Rights in Global Perspective (published by Martinus Nijhoff Publishers) (1996), pages 12-25, with kind permission from Kluwer Law International.

Dworkin, Ronald, Bill of Rights for Britain (1990), pages 1-12,24-38, 41-56, Chatto & Windus, publisher.

Elster, Jon, Forces and Mechanisms in the Constitution-Making Process, vol. 45 (1995), pages 364, 370-82, 384-88, 393-95. Reprint permission granted by Duke Law Journal.

Epstein, Lee, A Better Way to Appoint Justices, March 17, 1992.

Favoreu, Louis, Constitutional Review in Europe, From Louis Henkin & Albert Rosenthal eds., Constitutionalism and Rights (1990), pages 38-59, from ©1968, Columbia University Press. Reprinted with the permission of the publisher.

Field, Martha, The Differing Federalism of Canada and the United States, 55 (1992), pages 107-20. Reprint permission granted by Law and Contemporary Problems, Duke University Law School.

Finer, S.E. et al, Comparing Constitutions (1995), 13 pages. Reprinted by permission of Oxford University Press.

Fleiner, Thomas, Comment on Swiss Federalism, in Robert Goldwin et al. Eds., Forging Unity Out of Diversity (1985), pages 245-47. Reprint permission granted by American Enterprise Institute.

Franck, Thomas, Political Questions/Judicial Answers (1992), pages 107-28, Reprinted by permission of Princeton University Press.

Frankenberg, Gunter, Critical Comparisons vol. 26 (1985), pages 411-12, 414-15, 422-26, 430-33,435-43,445-47,452-53. Permission granted by the Harvard International Law Journal © 1985 by the President and Fellows of Harvard College.

Franklin, Daniel & Michael Baun, (eds), Political Culture and Constitutionalism: A Comparative Approach, 1994, pages 4-10, 219-229. Reprinted by permission from M.E. Sharpe, Inc., Armonk, NY 10504.

Fried, Charles, A New First Amendment Jurisprudence, vol. 59 (1992), pages 245-46. Reprint permission granted by University of Chicago Law Review.

Galanter, Marc, Competing Equalities (1984), pages 562-67.

Galanter, Marc, Law and Society in Modern India (1989), pages 185-87, 192-97, 203-07, 259-78, Reprinted by permission of Oxford University Press, New Delhi.

Graber, Mark, Old Wine in New Bottles, vol. 48 (1995), pages 367-68, 371-72. Reprint permission granted by Vanderbilt Law Review.

Greenawalt, Kent, Free Speech in the United States and Canada, 55 (1992), pages 5-33. Reprint permission granted by Law and Contemporary Problems, Duke University Law School.

Hausmaninger, Herbert, Towards a New Russian Constitutional Court, vol. 28 (1995), pages 349-65, 367-86. Reprint permission granted by Cornell International Law Journal © Copyright 1995 by Cornell University All Rights Reserved.

Holmes, Stephen & Sunstein, Cass, The Politics of Constitutional Revision in Eastern Europe, from Sanford Levinson ed., Responding to Imperfection (1995). pages 275-306. Reprinted by permission of Princeton University Press.

Howard, Dick A.E., The Indeterminacy of Constitutions, vol. 31 (1996), pages 383, 402-04, 405-06. Reprint permission granted by Wake Forest Law Review.

Hueglin, Thomas O., New Wine in Old Bottles? This excerpt is reprinted with permission of the publisher from Thomas O. Hueglin, New Wine in Old Bottles? In Rethinking Federalism: Citizens, Markets and Governments in a Changing World. Edited by Karen Knop, Sylvia Ostry, Richard Simeon and Katherine Swinton © University of British Columbia Press 1995. All rights reserved by the Publisher.

Hungarian Benefits Case (English translation). Reprinted from East European Case Reporter of Constitutional Law, vol. 4 (1997), with the permission of Book World Publications and Dr. Anton C. Van de Plas, Publisher.

Itoh, Hiroshi & Beer, Lawrence Ward, The Constitutional Case Law of Japan: Selected Supreme Court Decisions, 1961-70 (1978), pages 134-37. Reprinted by permission of the University of Washington Press.

Itoh, Hiroshi & Beer, Lawrence Ward, The Constitutional Case Law of Japan, 1970 through 1990 (1996), pages 479-91. Reprinted by permission of the University of Washington Press.

Jacobsohn, Gary, Apple of Gold (1993), pages 95, 98-135. Reprinted by permission of Princeton University Press.

Jackson, Vicki, Federalism and the Uses and Limits of Law, pages 2219-20, 2221-22. Reprinted by permission of Harvard Law Review.

Jeffrey, Anthea, The Danger of Direct Horizontal Application, from Human Rights and Constitutional Law Journal of South Africa, vol. 1 (Feb. 1997), page 13. Reprinted by Permission of Heinemann Publishers (pty) Lyd.

Jonas and Gorby, translators, West German Abortion Decision. vol. 9 (1976), pages 605-84. Reprint permission granted by John Marshall Journal of Practice and Procedure.

Katz, Stanley, Constitutionalism in East Central Europe (December 1993).

Kaufman, Otto, Swiss Federalism, Robert Goldwin et al. Eds., Forging Unity Out of Diversity (1985), pages 209-32. Reprint permission granted by American Enterprise Institute.

Knesset Gov Il., paragraphs were taken from the Knesset web site Israel Parliament, The Knesset.

Kommers, Donald, Judicial Politics in West Germany (1976).

Kommers, Donald, The Constitutional Jurisprudence of the Federal Republic of Germany, 1 ed. Copyright 1989. Reprinted with permission Duke University Press.

Kommers, Donald, The Constitutional Jurisprudence of the Federal Republic of Germany, 2 ed. Copyright 1997. Reprinted with permission by Duke University Press.

Kommers, Donald, The Value of Comparative Constitutional Law, vol. 9 (1976), pages 685-95. Reprint permission granted by John Marshall Journal of Practice and Procedure.

Kritz, Neal, Transitional Justice, vol. 3 (1995), pages 620-27, by the Endowment of the United States Institute of Peace. Reprinted with permission by the United States Institute of Peace, Washington DC.

Krotoszynski, Ronald, Brink and Rust v. Sullivan, vol. 22 (1994), pages 2-4, 7-18, 34. Reprint permission granted by Florida State University Law Review, original publisher and holder of copyright.

Kumer, Christopher B., translator, Case Translation, Pershing II and Cruise Missile Case, from Notre Dame International and Comparative Law Journal, vol. 2 (1984), pages 202-07.

Mahoney, Kathleen, The Canadian Approach to Freedom of Expression, 55 (1992), pages 77-105. Reprint permission granted by Law and Contemporary Problems, Duke University Law School.

Mandel, Michael, The Charter of Rights and the Legalization of Politics (1989), pages 61-71. Reprinted with permission by Thompson Educational Publishing, Inc.

Maoz, Asher, Religious Human Rights in the State of Israel, in Johan van der Vyver & John Witte Jr., Religious Human Rights in Global Perspective (published by Maartinus Nijhoff Publishers) (1996), pages 366-71, with kind permission from Kluwer Law International.

McWhinney, Edward, Constitution-Making: Principles, Process, Practice (1981), pages 6-9, 127-32. Reprinted with permission by University of Toronto Press, Inc.

Minow, Martha, Putting Up and Putting Down, from Mark Tushnet ed., Comparative Constitutuional Federalism (1990), pages 77-79, 95-103. Reproduced with permission of Greenwood Publishing Group.

Monaghan, Henry, The Confirmation Process, vol. 101 (1988), pages 1203, 1208-13. Permission granted by The Harvard Law Review Assoc. and Henry Monaghan.

Murphy, Alexander, Belgium's Regional Divergence, from Graham Smith ed., Federalism: The Multiethnic Challenge (1995), pages 74-96. Reprinted by permission of Addison Wesley Longman Ltd.

Murphy, Walter & Tanenhaus, Joseph, Comparative Constitutional Law (1977), pages 208-12, 212-15, 227-29. Reprinted with permission of Bedford/St. Martin's Press, Inc.

Murphy, Walter F., Consent and Constitutional Change from James O'Reilly ed., Human Rights and Constitutional Law (1992), pages 123-46, Reprinted by permission of Round Hall Sweet & Maxwell and Walter Murphy.

Murphy, Walter, Constitutions, Constitutionalism, and Democracy, from Douglas Greenberg et al. Eds., Constitutionalism and Democracy: Transitions in the Contemporary World (1993), pages 3-25, Permission granted by Oxford University Press, Inc.

Nariman, Fali Sam, The Indian Constitution, in Robert Goldwin et al. Eds., Forging Unity Out of Diversity (1985), pages 8-31, Reprint permission granted by American Enterprise Institute.

Nathan, Courtney, British and United States Hate Speech Legislation, vol.19 (1993), pages 727-48, 759-64-769, permission granted by Brooklyn Journal of International Law.

Neuman, Gerald, Casey in the Mirror, vol. 43 (1995), pages 279-89, Reprint permission granted by American Journal of Comparative Law.

Nino, Carlos Santiago, Transition to Democracy, Corporatism and Presidentialism with Special Reference to Latin America, from Douglas Greenberg et al. eds., Constitutionalism and Democracy: Transitions in the Contemporary World (1993), pages 46-63, Permission granted by Oxford University Press.

Okoth-Ogendo, H.W.O., Constitutions Without Constitutionalism, from Douglas Greenberg et al. Eds., Constitutionalism and Democracy: Transitions in the Contemporary World (1993), pages 65-80. Reprinted by permission of Oxford University Press.

Osiatynski, Wiktor, The Constitution-Making Process in Poland, vol. 13 (1991), pages 125-33. Permission granted by Blackwell Publishers.

Osiatynski, Wiktor, Perspectives on the Current Constitutional Situation in Poland, from Douglas Greenberg et al. Eds., Constitutionalism and Democracy: Transitions in the Contemporary World (1993), pages 312-20, Permission granted by Oxford University Press.

Osiatynski, Wiktor, Social and Economic Rights in a New Constitution for Poland, in Andras Sajo eds. Western Rights? Post-communist Application (1996), pages 233-39, 241-42, 248-49, 252-57, 262-67. With kind permission from Kluwer Law International.

Parekh, Bhikku, India's Diversity, Dissent (Summer 1996), pages 145-48, Permission granted by Foundation for the Study of Independent Social Idea.

Rehnquist, William, Constitutional Courts—Comparative Remarks, from Paul Kirchof & Donald Kommers eds., Germany and Its Basic Law (1993), pages 412, Reprint permission granted by Nomos Verlagsgesellschaft.

Rubin, Edward & Feeley, Malcolm, Federalism: Some Notes on a National Neurosis, vol. 41 (1994), pages 908-09, Orginally published in 41 UCLA L. Rev. 903. Copyright 1994, The Regents of the University of California. All rights Reserved. Permission granted by UCLA Law Review and Fred B. Rothman & Co.

Russell, Peter et al. eds., Federalism and the Charter (1989), pages 243-51, 273, 557-59. Reprint permission granted by Carleton University Press.

Sajo, Andras, How the Rule of Law Killed Hungarian Welfare Reform, vol. 5 (1996), pages 31-41. Reprint permission granted by East European Constitutional Review.

Sajó, András & Losonci, Vera, Rule by Law in East Central Europe, from Douglas Greenberg et al. eds., Constitutionalism and Democracy: Transitions in the Contemporary World (1993), pages 321-34. Permission granted by Oxford University Press.

Seidman, Louis Michael & Tushnet, Mark, Remnants of Belief (1996), pages 70-71. Reprint permission granted by Oxford University Press.

Sharfman, Dafna, Living Without a Constitution: Civil Rights in Israel, 1993, pages 138-145, Reprinted by permission from M.E. Sharpe, Inc., NY Armonk, NY 10504.

Simeon, Richard, Canada and the United States. This excerpt is reprinted with permission of the publisher from Richard Simeon, Canada and the United States, in Rethinking Federalism: Citizens, Markets and Governments, a Changing World. Edited by Karen Knop, Sylvia Ostry, Richard Simeon and Katherine Swinton © University of British Columbia Press 1995. All rights reserved by the Publisher.

Stone, Alec, The Birth of Judicial Politics in France (1992), pages 46-53, 57-59, 64-69, 257-60. Reprint granted by Oxford University Press.

Shamir, Ronen, Landmark Cases and the Reproduction of Legitimacy, vol. 24 (1990), pages 784-89, 795-99. Reprinted by permission of the Law and Society Association.

Sharlet, Robert, Chief Justice as Judicial Politician vol. 2 (1993), pages 32-37. Reprint permission granted by East European Constitutional Review.

Smith, Graham, Federalism: The Multiethinic Challenge. Reprinted by permission of Addison Wesley Longman Ltd.

Solyom, Laszlo, The Hungarian Constitutional Court and Social Change, vol. 19 (1994), pages 223-27. Reprinted by permission of Yale Journal of International Law.

Sowell, Thomas, Preferential Policies (1990), pages 91-95, 97-103,163-65. Reprinted by Permission of William Morrow and Company, Inc.

Strayer, Barry, The Canadian Constitution and Diversity, in Robert Goldwin et al. Eds., Forging Unity Out of Diversity (1985), pages 157-81. Reprint permission granted by American Enterprise Institute.

Stone, Alec, Abstract Constitutional Review and Policy Making, in Donald Jackson & Neal Tate Eds., Comparative Judicial Review and Public Policy (1992), pages 41-55. Reproduced with permission of Greenwood Publishing Group.

Sullivan, Winnifred Fallers, Paying the Words Extra (1994), pages 109-12, Permission granted by Harvard Center for the Study of World Religions.

Sunstein, Cass, Against Positive Rights in Andras Sajo eds. Western Rights? Post-Communist Application (1996), pages 225-32, with kind permission from Kluwer Law International.

Sunstein, Cass, Constitutionalism and Secession, vol 58 (1991), pages 636-42. Permission granted by University of Chicago Law Review.

Teitel, Ruti, Paradoxes in the Revolution of the Rule of Law, vol. 19 (1994), pages 239-40. Reprinted by permission of Yale Journal of International Law.

Tomkins, Adam and Gearty, Colin, Understanding Human Rights, excerpts from Living with a Bill of Rights, by Mark Tushnet (1996); permission granted by Mansell, a Cassell imprint, Wellington House, 125 Strand, London, WC2R 0BB, England.

Tully, James, Strange Multiplicity (1995), pages 169-76. Reprinted with the permission of Cambridge University Press.

Tushnet, Mark, Civil Rights and Social Rights, vol. 25 (1992), pages 1211-19.

Tushnet, Mark, Federalism and Liberalism, vol. 4 (1996), pages 329-44. Reprint permission granted by Cardozo Journal of International and Comparative Law.

Tushnet, Mark, Policy Distortion and Democratic Debilitation vol. 94 (1995), pages 275-300. Reprint permission granted by The Michigan Law Review Association.

Wa Mutua, Makua, Limitations on Religious Rights, in Johan van der Vyver & John Witte Jr., Religious Human Rights in Global Perspective (published by Martinus Nijhoff Publishers) (1996), pages 417, 437-40, with kind permission from Kluwer Law International.

Weaver, Russell & Knechtle, John, Constitutional Drafting in the Former Soviet Union, vol. 12 (1994), pages 29-30, 34, 3-40. Reprint permission granted by Winsconsin International Law Journal.

Williams, Colin, A Requiem for Canada, from Graham Smith ed., Federalism: The Multiethnic Challenge (1995), page 66. Reprinted by permission of Addison Wesley Longman Ltd.

Zander, Michael, A Bill of Rights, 3rd edition (1985), pages 47-67. Reprinted with permission by Sweet & Maxwell.

SUMMARY OF CONTENTS

*

TABLE OF CONTENTS

*

TABLE OF CASES

Principal cases are in bold type. Non-principal cases are in roman type. References are to Pages.

*

TABLE OF AUTHORITIES

References are to Pages.

EDITORIAL NOTICE

In the excerpted materials, citations (including internal references) and footnotes are generally omitted. Other textual material that is omitted is indicated by ellipses; textual material that we have added (or slightly modified) is indicated by brackets. In editing material in translation we have tried to use a light hand so as to intrude as little as possible on the voice of the piece. Footnotes by the editors are identified by lower case letters or by asterisks; footnotes included from excerpted materials retain their original numbering.

*

COMPARATIVE CONSTITUTIONAL LAW

*

CHAPTER I

INTRODUCTION: REPRODUCTIVE RIGHTS AND COMPARATIVE CONSTITUTIONAL LAW

We begin with an issue familiar to students of U.S. constitutional law—government regulation of abortion. We do so in part because most American students have some familiarity with the U.S. Supreme Court's decisions in Roe v. Wade and Planned Parenthood v. Casey. We begin here as well because of the availability of familiar kinds of materials (judicial decisions concerning the constitutional validity of abortion laws) in English or English translations. And we begin here because these materials raise a set of questions—about constitutions and their purposes, about "constitutionalism," about the roles of courts, legislatures and popular initiative in defining a nation's constitution, and about the values and limitations of comparative study—that pervade the materials.

As you read through the materials on abortion decisions by courts in the U.S., Canada and Germany, consider the following questions:

1. What role does constitutional text play in these decisions?

2. Does "constitutionalism" necessarily embrace substantive norms? If so, what are those norms in the context of abortion?

3. What roles are and should be played in constitutional decision-making by legislators and legislative bodies, by other members of the government, and by popular majorities?

4. In what voice, or voices, do constitutional tribunals speak? What, if anything, does this suggest about the relationship(s) of judging to constitutional interpretation?

5. What significance, if any, do constitutional practices in other nations, or other international influences, have in the resolution of constitutional issues concerning abortion in the U.S., Canada, Germany and (in chapter II) Ireland? What significance should they have?

6. Does the procedural posture of adjudication (e.g., whether the constitutional issue is raised in defense of a criminal prosecution as compared with "abstract" review) affect analysis or outcome?

A. THE U.S. SUPREME COURT'S ABORTION DECISIONS

Early in the 20th century, the Supreme Court held that the "liberty" protected by the Due Process Clause of the 14th Amendment included not only the freedom to contract unencumbered by state regulation of working conditions, Lochner v. New York, 198 U.S. 45 (1905), but also parents' decisions to educate their children. See Meyer v. Nebraska, 262 U.S. 390 (1923) (holding unconstitutional a state law prohibiting any public or private school from teaching any modern language other than English); Pierce v. Society of Sisters, 268 U.S. 510 (1925) (invalidating state law requiring all students to attend public, rather than private, schools). While the *Lochner* Court's constitutional opposition to government regulation of wages, hours and working conditions was largely abandoned by the New Deal and subsequent Courts, see, e.g., United States v. Darby, 312 U.S. 100 (1941) (rejecting substantive due process challenge to Fair Labor Standards Act), the *Meyer* and *Pierce* view of "liberty" as including parental rights to make decisions for their families survived to form the doctrinal basis for the Court's approach to issues concerning reproductive decisions.[a]

In Griswold v. Connecticut, 381 U.S. 479 (1965), the Court struck down as a violation of the Due Process Clause Connecticut's statute barring any person from using a drug or medical device to prevent conception. Physicians who sought to give advice to married couples as to birth control challenged the statute. The physicians were permitted to assert the rights of their married patients. The majority opinion found that specific guarantees of the Bill of Rights have "penumbras, formed by emanations from those guarantees that help give them life and substance.... Various guarantees create zones of privacy [referring to the right of association protected by First Amendment cases, the Third Amendment's prohibition of quartering soldiers in homes, the Fourth Amendment's declaration that the right of the people to be secure in their persons, houses, papers and effects against unreasonable searches and seizures, as well as the Fifth and Ninth Amendments]." It found the marital relationship to lie within a zone of privacy created by several fundamental constitutional guarantees. The Connecticut statute was too intrusive on the marital relationship—"Would we allow the police to search the sacred precincts of marital bedrooms for telltale signs of the use of contraceptives? The very idea is repulsive...."

In a concurring opinion Justice Goldberg relied more heavily on the Ninth Amendment, as lending support to the view that the liberty protect-

---

a. See also Skinner v. Oklahoma, 316 U.S. 535 (1942) (state law providing for the sterilization of some but not all of those who commit repetitive economic crimes violates Equal Protection Clause of 14th amendment; the legislation involved "one of the basic civil rights of man ... [that] [m]arriage and procreation are fundamental to the very existence and survival of the race," and that the "power to sterilize, if exercised, may have subtle, far-reaching and devastating effects [i]n evil or reckless hands....").

ed by the 14th Amendment is not restricted to rights specifically mentioned in the first eight amendments. He wrote, "In determining which rights are fundamental, judges are not left at large to decide cases in light of their personal and private notions. Rather they must look to the 'traditions and [collective] conscience of our people' to determine whether a principle is 'so rooted [there] . . . as to be ranked as fundamental.' The inquiry is whether a right involved 'is of such a character that it cannot be denied without violating those 'fundamental principles of liberty and justice which lie at the base of all our civil and political institutions'. . . .' " . . .

"The entire fabric of the Constitution and the purposes that clearly underlie its specific guarantees demonstrate that the rights to marital privacy and to marry and raise a family are of similar order and magnitude as the fundamental rights specifically protected."

"Although the Constitution does not speak in so many words of the right of privacy in marriage, I cannot believe that it offers these fundamental rights no protection. The fact that no particular provision of the Constitution explicitly forbids the State from disrupting the traditional relation of the family—a relation as old and as fundamental as our entire civilization—surely does not show that the Government was meant to have the power to do so."

Justice Goldberg went on to reject the dissent's conclusion that there is no constitutional protection of the marital right to bear children, because that position would permit government to require forced sterilization. He also rejected the state's claim of a rational relation between the statute and the concededly legitimate goal of discouraging extra-marital relations.

Justice Harlan concurred in the judgment. He argued, consistent with his view expressed in a wide range of cases, that the Due Process Clause protects "basic values implicit in the concept of ordered liberty," an inquiry aided but not governed by the scope of the first eight amendments. Justice Harlan's view was developed in contrast to Justice Black's argument that the Due Process Clause of the 14th amendment "incorporated" all of the provisions of the first eight amendments against the states. Harlan believed Black's theory to be historically unfounded. In defending his own theory against attacks that it would lead to unprincipled, personal decisions by judges, he argued that judicial restraint would be achieved "by continual insistence upon respect for the teachings of history, solid recognition of the basic values that underlie our society, and wise appreciation of the great roles that the doctrines of federalism and separation of powers have played in establishing and preserving American freedoms."

Justice Harlan's dissent in Poe v. Ullman, 367 U.S. 497 (1961) from the Court's dismissal, on justiciability grounds, of an earlier challenge to the Connecticut statute invalidated in *Griswold*, had described the statute as an "intolerable and unjustifiable invasion of privacy in the conduct of the most intimate concerns of an individual's personal life, insofar as it applied to married couples' use of contraceptives. The liberty guaranteed by the Due Process Clause is not a series of isolated points [i.e. those rights specified by the Bill of Rights]. . . . It is a rational continuum which . . .

includes freedom from all substantial arbitrary impositions and purposeless restraints ... and which also recognizes, what a reasonable and sensitive judgment must, that certain interests require particularly careful scrutiny of the state needs asserted to justify their abridgement." While agreeing that Connecticut had much latitude in making moral judgments, Harlan asserted a judicial obligation to review the choice of state means. He agreed with Justice Goldberg in *Griswold* that the means used—involving intrusions on marital life with the full power of the criminal law—could not be sustained, and were inconsistent with principles of privacy of the home and home life suggested by the Third and Fourth Amendments.

Justice White concurred in the judgment, relying on *Meyer*, *Pierce* and *Skinner* to establish that there is a realm of family life which the state cannot enter without substantial justification, justification that was lacking here.

Justice Black with Justice Stewart dissented, on the ground that there is no general constitutional right of privacy. Black argued that the Due Process and Ninth Amendment arguments "turn out to be the same thing—merely using different words to claim for this Court and the federal judiciary power to invalidate any legislative act which the judges find irrational, unreasonable or offensive.... If these formulas based on 'natural justice' prevail, they require judges to determine what is or is not constitutional on the basis of their own appraisal of what laws are unwise or unnecessary. The power to make such decisions is of course that of a legislative body.... I realize that many good and able men have eloquently spoken and written ... about the duty of this Court to keep the Constitution in tune with the times.... I must with all deference reject that philosophy. The Constitution makers knew the need for change and provided for it. The Due Process Clause ... was liberally used by this Court to strike down economic legislation in the early decades of this century, threatening, many people thought, the tranquility and stability of the Nation. [This practice] ... is no less dangerous when used to enforce this Court's views about personal rights than those about economic rights...."

Justice Stewart dissented as well, joined by Justice Black: "I think this is an uncommonly silly law [but not unconstitutional].... What provision of the Constitution ... make[s]this state law invalid? The Court says it is the right of privacy 'created by several fundamental constitutional guarantees.' With all deference, I can find no such general right of privacy in the Bill of Rights, in any other part of the Constitution, or in any case ever before decided by this Court...."

In 1972, *Griswold* was extended in Eisenstadt v. Baird, 405 U.S. 438 (1972), which invalidated under the Equal Protection Clause a law forbidding the distribution of contraceptives to unmarried couples. Abandoning the marital privacy emphasis that played so prominent a role in the *Griswold* opinions, the Court reformulated the right as an individual right to be free from unwarranted government interference "into matters so fundamentally affecting a person as [the] decision whether to bear or beget a child."

A year later, the Court for the first time struck down a state abortion statute as unconstitutional. An edited version of Roe v. Wade and a brief description of Doe v. Bolton follow.

Roe v. Wade

410 U.S. 113 (1973).

Mr. Justice Blackmun delivered the opinion of the Court.

This Texas federal appeal and its Georgia companion, Doe v. Bolton, present constitutional challenges to state criminal abortion legislation. The Texas statutes under attack here are typical of those that have been in effect in many States for approximately a century. The Georgia statutes, in contrast, have a modern cast and are a legislative product that, to an extent at least, obviously reflects the influences of recent attitudinal change, of advancing medical knowledge and techniques, and of new thinking about an old issue.

We forthwith acknowledge our awareness of the sensitive and emotional nature of the abortion controversy, of the vigorous opposing views, even among physicians, and of the deep and seemingly absolute convictions that the subject inspires. One's philosophy, one's experiences, one's exposure to the raw edges of human existence, one's religious training, one's attitudes toward life and family and their values, and the moral standards one establishes and seeks to observe, are all likely to influence and to color one's thinking and conclusions about abortion.

In addition, population growth, pollution, poverty, and racial overtones tend to complicate and not to simplify the problem.

Our task, of course, is to resolve the issue by constitutional measurement, free of emotion and of predilection. We seek earnestly to do this, and, because we do, we have inquired into, and in this opinion place some emphasis upon, medical and medical-legal history and what that history reveals about man's attitudes toward the abortion procedure over the centuries. We bear in mind, too, Mr. Justice Holmes' admonition in his now-vindicated dissent in Lochner v. New York, 198 U.S. 45, 76 (1905):

> "[The Constitution] is made for people of fundamentally differing views, and the accident of our finding certain opinions natural and familiar, or novel, and even shocking, ought not to conclude our judgment upon the question whether statutes embodying them conflict with the Constitution of the United States."

I

The Texas statutes ... make it a crime to "procure an abortion," as therein defined, or to attempt one, except with respect to "an abortion procured or attempted by medical advice for the purpose of saving the life of the mother." Similar statutes are in existence in a majority of the States.

Texas first enacted a criminal abortion statute in 1854. This was soon modified into language that has remained substantially unchanged to the present time. The final article in each of these compilations provided the same exception, as does the present Article 1196, for an abortion by "medical advice for the purpose of saving the life of the mother."

II

Jane Roe, a single woman who was residing in Dallas County, Texas, instituted this federal action in March 1970 against the District Attorney of the county. She sought a declaratory judgment that the Texas criminal abortion statutes were unconstitutional on their face, and an injunction restraining the defendant from enforcing the statutes.

Roe alleged that she was unmarried and pregnant; that she wished to terminate her pregnancy by an abortion "performed by a competent, licensed physician, under safe, clinical conditions"; that she was unable to get a "legal" abortion in Texas because her life did not appear to be threatened by the continuation of her pregnancy; and that she could not afford to travel to another jurisdiction in order to secure a legal abortion under safe conditions. She claimed that the Texas statutes were unconstitutionally vague and that they abridged her right of personal privacy, protected by the First, Fourth, Fifth, Ninth, and Fourteenth Amendments. By an amendment to her complaint Roe purported to sue "on behalf of herself and all other women" similarly situated.

James Hubert Hallford, a licensed physician, sought and was granted leave to intervene in Roe's action. In his complaint he alleged that he had been arrested previously for violations of the Texas abortion statutes and that two such prosecutions were pending against him. He described conditions of patients who came to him seeking abortions, and he claimed that for many cases he, as a physician, was unable to determine whether they fell within or outside the exception recognized by Article 1196. He alleged that, as a consequence, the statutes were vague and uncertain, in violation of the Fourteenth Amendment, and that they violated his own and his patients' rights to privacy in the doctor-patient relationship and his own right to practice medicine, rights he claimed were guaranteed by the First, Fourth, Fifth, Ninth, and Fourteenth Amendments.

John and Mary Doe, a married couple, filed a companion complaint to that of Roe.... The Does alleged that they were a childless couple; that Mrs. Doe was suffering from a "neural-chemical" disorder; that her physician had "advised her to avoid pregnancy until such time as her condition has materially improved" (although a pregnancy at the present time would not present "a serious risk" to her life); that, pursuant to medical advice, she had discontinued use of birth control pills; and that if she should become pregnant, she would want to terminate the pregnancy by an abortion performed by a competent, licensed physician under safe, clinical conditions. By an amendment to their complaint, the Does purported to sue "on behalf of themselves and all couples similarly situated."

The two actions were consolidated and heard together by a duly convened three-judge district court. The suits thus presented the situations of the pregnant single woman, the childless couple, with the wife not pregnant, and the licensed practicing physician, all joining in the attack on the Texas criminal abortion statutes....

IV

We are ... confronted with issues of justiciability, standing, and abstention. Have Roe and the Does established that "personal stake in the outcome of the controversy," Baker v. Carr, 369 U.S. 186, 204 (1962), that insures that "the dispute sought to be adjudicated will be presented in an adversary context and in a form historically viewed as capable of judicial resolution," Flast v. Cohen, 392 U.S. 83, 101 (1968) ... ?

A.   Jane Roe. Despite the use of the pseudonym, no suggestion is made that Roe is a fictitious person. For purposes of her case, we accept as true, and as established, her existence; her pregnant state, as of the inception of her suit in March 1970 and as late as May 21 of that year when she filed an alias affidavit with the District Court; and her inability to obtain a legal abortion in Texas.

Viewing Roe's case as of the time of its filing and thereafter until as late as May, there can be little dispute that it then presented a case or controversy and that, wholly apart from the class aspects, she, as a pregnant single woman thwarted by the Texas criminal abortion laws, had standing to challenge those statutes. Indeed, we do not read the appellee's brief as really asserting anything to the contrary. The "logical nexus between the status asserted and the claim sought to be adjudicated," and the necessary degree of contentiousness are both present.

The appellee notes, however, that the record does not disclose that Roe was pregnant at the time of the District Court hearing on May 22, 1970, or on the following June 17 when the court's opinion and judgment were filed. And he suggests that Roe's case must now be moot because she and all other members of her class are no longer subject to any 1970 pregnancy.

The usual rule in federal cases is that an actual controversy must exist at stages of appellate or certiorari review, and not simply at the date the action is initiated.

But when, as here, pregnancy is a significant fact in the litigation, the normal 266-day human gestation period is so short that the pregnancy will come to term before the usual appellate process is complete. If that termination makes a case moot, pregnancy litigation seldom will survive much beyond the trial stage, and appellate review will be effectively denied. Our law should not be that rigid. Pregnancy often comes more than once to the same woman, and in the general population, if man is to survive, it will always be with us. Pregnancy provides a classic justification for a conclusion of nonmootness. It truly could be "capable of repetition, yet evading review."

We, therefore, agree with the District Court that Jane Roe had standing to undertake this litigation, that she presented a justiciable controversy, and that the termination of her 1970 pregnancy has not rendered her case moot.

B. Dr. Hallford. The doctor's position is different.... Dr. Hallford is ... in the position of seeking, in a federal court, declaratory and injunctive relief with respect to the same statutes under which he stands charged in criminal prosecutions simultaneously pending in state court. Although he stated that he has been arrested in the past for violating the State's abortion laws, he makes no allegation of any substantial and immediate threat to any federally protected right that cannot be asserted in his defense against the state prosecutions. Neither is there any allegation of harassment or bad-faith prosecution ... [The court holds that Dr. Hallford's complaint must be dismissed.]

C. The Does....

We ... have as plaintiffs a married couple who have, as their asserted immediate and present injury, only an alleged "detrimental effect upon [their] marital happiness" because they are forced to "the choice of refraining from normal sexual relations or of endangering Mary Doe's health through a possible pregnancy." Their claim is that sometime in the future Mrs. Doe might become pregnant because of possible failure of contraceptive measures, and at that time in the future she might want an abortion that might then be illegal under the Texas statutes.

This very phrasing of the Does' position reveals its speculative character. Their alleged injury rests on possible future contraceptive failure, possible future pregnancy, possible future unpreparedness for parenthood, and possible future impairment of health. Any one or more of these several possibilities may not take place and all may not combine. In the Does' estimation, these possibilities might have some real or imagined impact upon their marital happiness. But we are not prepared to say that the bare allegation of so indirect an injury is sufficient to present an actual case or controversy....

The Does therefore are not appropriate plaintiffs in this litigation. Their complaint was properly dismissed by the District Court....

V

The principal thrust of appellant's attack on the Texas statutes is that they improperly invade a right, said to be possessed by the pregnant woman, to choose to terminate her pregnancy. Appellant would discover this right in the concept of personal "liberty" embodied in the Fourteenth Amendment's Due Process Clause; or in personal, marital, familial, and sexual privacy said to be protected by the Bill of Rights or its penumbras, see Griswold v. Connecticut, 381 U.S. 479 (1965); Eisenstadt v. Baird, 405 U.S. 438 (1972); or among those rights reserved to the people by the Ninth Amendment, Griswold v. Connecticut, 381 U.S., at 486, (Goldberg, J., concurring). Before addressing this claim, we feel it desirable briefly to survey, in several aspects, the history of abortion, for such insight as that history may afford us, and then to examine the state purposes and interests behind the criminal abortion laws.

VI

It perhaps is not generally appreciated that the restrictive criminal abortion laws in effect in a majority of States today are of relatively recent vintage. Those laws, generally proscribing abortion or its attempt at any time during pregnancy except when necessary to preserve the pregnant woman's life, are not of ancient or even of common-law origin. Instead, they derive from statutory changes effected, for the most part, in the latter half of the 19th century.

1.   Ancient attitudes. These are not capable of precise determination. We are told that at the time of the Persian Empire abortifacients were known and that criminal abortions were severely punished. We are also told, however, that abortion was practiced in Greek times as well as in the Roman Era,[9] and that "it was resorted to without scruple." The Ephesian, Soranos, often described as the greatest of the ancient gynecologists, appears to have been generally opposed to Rome's prevailing free-abortion practices. He found it necessary to think first of the life of the mother, and he resorted to abortion when, upon this standard, he felt the procedure advisable. Greek and Roman law afforded little protection to the unborn. If abortion was prosecuted in some places, it seems to have been based on a concept of a violation of the father's right to his offspring. Ancient religion did not bar abortion.

2.   The Hippocratic Oath. What then of the famous Oath that has stood so long as the ethical guide of the medical profession and that bears the name of the great Greek (460(?)–377(?) B.C.), who has been described as the Father of Medicine, the "wisest and the greatest practitioner of his art," . . . who dominated the medical schools of his time, and who typified the sum of the medical knowledge of the past? The Oath varies somewhat according to the particular translation, but in any translation the content is clear: "I will give no deadly medicine to anyone if asked, nor suggest any such counsel; and in like manner I will not give to a woman a pessary to produce abortion," or "I will neither give a deadly drug to anybody if asked for it, nor will I make a suggestion to this effect. Similarly, I will not give to a woman an abortive remedy."

Although the Oath is not mentioned in any of the principal briefs in this case or in Doe v. Bolton . . . it represents the apex of the development of strict ethical concepts in medicine, and its influence endures to this day.

---

9.   J. Ricci, The Genealogy of Gynaecology 52, 84, 113, 149 (2d ed. 1950) (hereinafter Ricci); L. Lader, Abortion 75–77 (1966) (hereinafter Lader); K. Niswander, Medical Abortion Practices in the United States, in Abortion and the Law 37, 38–40 (D. Smith ed. 1967); G. Williams, The Sanctity of Life and the Criminal Law 148 (1957) (hereinafter Williams); J. Noonan, An Almost Absolute Value in History, in The Morality of Abortion 1, 3–7 (J. Noonan ed. 1970) (hereinafter Noonan); Quay, Justifiable Abortion-Medical and Legal Foundations, (pt. 2), 49 Geo.L.J. 395, 406–422 (1961) (hereinafter Quay).

Why did not the authority of Hippocrates dissuade abortion practice in his time and that of Rome? The late Dr. Edelstein provides us with a theory: The Oath was not uncontested even in Hippocrates' day; only the Pythagorean school of philosophers frowned upon the related act of suicide. Most Greek thinkers, on the other hand, commended abortion, at least prior to viability. See Plato, Republic, V, 461; Aristotle, Politics, VII, 1335b 25. For the Pythagoreans, however, it was a matter of dogma. For them the embryo was animate from the moment of conception, and abortion meant destruction of a living being. The abortion clause of the Oath, therefore, "echoes Pythagorean doctrines," and "(i)n no other stratum of Greek opinion were such views held or proposed in the same spirit of uncompromising austerity."

Dr. Edelstein then concludes that the Oath originated in a group representing only a small segment of Greek opinion and that it certainly was not accepted by all ancient physicians. He points out that medical writings down to Galen (A.D. 130–200) "give evidence of the violation of almost every one of its injunctions." But with the end of antiquity a decided change took place. Resistance against suicide and against abortion became common. The Oath came to be popular. The emerging teachings of Christianity were in agreement with the Pythagorean ethic. The Oath "became the nucleus of all medical ethics" and "was applauded as the embodiment of truth." Thus, suggests Dr. Edelstein, it is "a Pythagorean manifesto and not the expression of an absolute standard of medical conduct."

This, it seems to us, is a satisfactory and acceptable explanation of the Hippocratic Oath's apparent rigidity. It enables us to understand, in historical context, a long-accepted an revered statement of medical ethics.

3. The common law. It is undisputed that at common law, abortion performed *before* "quickening"—the first recognizable movement of the fetus in utero, appearing usually from the 16th to the 18th week of pregnancy[20]—was not an indictable offense.[21] The absence of a common-law crime for pre-quickening abortion appears to have developed from a confluence of earlier philosophical, theological, and civil and canon law concepts of when life begins. These disciplines variously approached the question in terms of the point at which the embryo or fetus became "formed" or recognizably human, or in terms of when a "person" came into being, that is, infused with a "soul" or "animated." A loose consensus evolved in early English law that these events occurred at some point between conception

20. Dorland's Illustrated Medical Dictionary 1261 (24th ed. 1965).

21. E. Coke, Institutes III *50; 1 W. Hawkins, Pleas of the Crown, c. 31, § 16 (4th ed. 1762); 1 W. Blackstone, Commentaries *129–130; M. Hale, Pleas of the Crown 433 (1st Amer. ed. 1847). For discussions of the role of the quickening concept in English common law, see Lader 78; Noonan 223–226; Means, The Law of New York Concerning Abortion and the Status of the Foetus, 1664–1968: A Case of Cessation of Constitutionality (pt. 1), 14 N.Y.L.F. 411, 418–428 (1968) (hereinafter Means I); Stern, Abortion: Reform and the Law, 59 J.Crim.L.C. & P.S. 84 (1968) (hereinafter Stern); Quay 430–432; Williams 152.

and live birth.[22] This was "mediate animation." Although Christian theology and the canon law came to fix the point of animation at 40 days for a male and 80 days for a female, a view that persisted until the 19th century, there was otherwise little agreement about the precise time of formation or animation. There was agreement, however, that prior to this point the fetus was to be regarded as part of the mother, and its destruction, therefore, was not homicide. Due to continued uncertainty about the precise time when animation occurred, to the lack of any empirical basis for the 40–80–day view, and perhaps to Aquinas' definition of movement as one of the two first principles of life, Bracton focused upon quickening as the critical point. The significance of quickening was echoed by later common-law scholars and found its way into the received common law in this country.

Whether abortion of a *quick* fetus was a felony at common law, or even a lesser crime, is still disputed. Bracton, writing early in the 13th century, thought it homicide. But the later and predominant view, following the great common-law scholars, has been that it was, at most, a lesser offense. In a frequently cited passage, Coke took the position that abortion of a woman "quick with childe" is "a great misprision, and no murder." Blackstone followed, saying that while abortion after quickening had once been considered manslaughter (though not murder), "modern law" took a less severe view. A recent review of the common-law precedents argues, however, that those precedents contradict Coke and that even post-quickening abortion was never established as a common-law crime. This is of some importance because while most American courts ruled, in holding or dictum, that abortion of an unquickened fetus was not criminal under their received common law, others followed Coke in stating that abortion of a

---

22. Early philosophers believed that the embryo or fetus did not become formed and begin to live until at least 40 days after conception for a male, and 80 to 90 days for a female. See, for example, Aristotle, Hist. Anim. 7.3.583b; Gen.Anim. 2.3.736, 2.5.741; Hippocrates, Lib. de Nat.Puer., No. 10. Aristotle's thinking derived from his three-stage theory of life: vegetable, animal, rational. The vegetable stage was reached at conception, the animal at "animation," and the rational soon after live birth. This theory, together with the 40/80 day view, came to be accepted by early Christian thinkers.

The theological debate was reflected in the writings of St. Augustine, who made a distinction between embryo inanimatus, not yet endowed with a soul, and embryo animatus. He may have drawn upon Exodus 21:22. At one point, however, he expressed the view that human powers cannot determine the point during fetal development at which the critical change occurs. See Augustine, De Origine Animae 4.4 (Pub.Law 44.527). See also W. Reany, The Creation of the Human Soul, c. 2 and 83–86 (1932); Huser, The Crime of Abortion in Canon Law 15 (Catholic Univ. of America, Canon Law Studies No. 162, Washington, D.C., 1942).

Galen, in three treatises related to embryology, accepted the thinking of Aristotle and his followers. Quay 426–427. Later, Augustine on abortion was incorporated by Gratian into the Decretum, published about 1140. Decretum Magistri Gratiani 2.32.2.7 to 2.32.2.10, in 1 Corpus Juris Canonici 1122, 1123 (A. Friedberg, 2d ed. 1879). This Decretal and the Decretals that followed were recognized as the definitive body of canon law until the new Code of 1917. For discussions of the canon-law treatment, see Means I, pp. 411–412; Noonan 20–26; Quay 426–430; see also J. Noonan, Contraception: A History of Its Treatment by the Catholic Theologians and Canonists 18–29 (1965).

quick fetus was a "misprision," a term they translated to mean "misdemeanor." That their reliance on Coke on this aspect of the law was uncritical and, apparently in all the reported cases, dictum (due probably to the paucity of common-law prosecutions for post-quickening abortion), makes it now appear doubtful that abortion was ever firmly established as a common-law crime even with respect to the destruction of a quick fetus.

4. The English statutory law. England's first criminal abortion statute, Lord Ellenborough's Act, came in 1803. It made abortion of a quick fetus, a capital crime, but ... provided lesser penalties for the felony of abortion before quickening, and thus preserved the "quickening" distinction. This contrast was continued in the general revision of 1828. It disappeared, however, together with the death penalty, in 1837, and did not reappear in the Offenses Against the Person Act of 1861 that formed the core of English anti-abortion law until the liberalizing reforms of 1967. In 1929, the Infant Life (Preservation) Act came into being. Its emphasis was upon the destruction of "the life of a child capable of being born alive." It made a willful act performed with the necessary intent a felony. It contained a proviso that one was not to be found guilty of the offense "unless it is proved that the act which caused the death of the child was not done in good faith for the purpose only of preserving the life of the mother."

A seemingly notable development in the English law was the case of Rex v. Bourne, (1939) 1 K.B. 687. This case apparently answered in the affirmative the question whether an abortion necessary to preserve the life of the pregnant woman was excepted from the criminal penalties of the 1861 Act. In his instructions to the jury, Judge MacNaghten referred to the 1929 Act, and observed that that Act related to "the case where a child is killed by a willful act at the time when it is being delivered in the ordinary course of nature." He concluded that the 1861 Act's use of the word "unlawfully," imported the same meaning expressed by the specific proviso in the 1929 Act, even though there was no mention of preserving the mother's life in the 1861 Act. He then construed the phrase "preserving the life of the mother" broadly, that is, "in a reasonable sense," to include a serious and permanent threat to the mother's *health*, and instructed the jury to acquit Dr. Bourne if it found he had acted in a good-faith belief that the abortion was necessary for this purpose. The jury did acquit.

Recently, Parliament enacted a new abortion law. This is the Abortion Act of 1967. The Act permits a licensed physician to perform an abortion where two other licensed physicians agree (a) "that the continuance of the pregnancy would involve risk to the life of the pregnant woman, or of injury to the physical or mental health of the pregnant woman or any existing children of her family, greater than if the pregnancy were terminated," or (b) "that there is a substantial risk that if the child were born it would suffer from such physical or mental abnormalities as to be seriously handicapped." The Act also provides that, in making this determination, "account may be taken of the pregnant woman's actual or reasonably foreseeable environment." It also permits a physician, without the concurrence of others, to terminate a pregnancy where he is of the good-faith opinion that the abortion "is immediately necessary to save the life or to prevent grave permanent injury to the physical or mental health of the pregnant woman."

5.   The American law. In this country, the law in effect in all but a few States until mid–19th century was the pre-existing English common law. Connecticut, the first State to enact abortion legislation, adopted in 1821 that part of Lord Ellenborough's Act that related to a woman "quick with child." The death penalty was not imposed. Abortion before quickening was made a crime in that State only in 1860. In 1828, New York enacted legislation that, in two respects, was to serve as a model for early anti-abortion statutes. First, while barring destruction of an unquickened fetus as well as a quick fetus, it made the former only a misdemeanor, but the latter second-degree manslaughter. Second, it incorporated a concept of therapeutic abortion by providing that an abortion was excused if it "shall have been necessary to preserve the life of such mother, or shall have been advised by two physicians to be necessary for such purpose." By 1840, when Texas had received the common law, only eight American States had statutes dealing with abortion. It was not until after the War Between the States that legislation began generally to replace the common law. Most of these initial statutes dealt severely with abortion after quickening but were lenient with it before quickening. Most punished attempts equally with completed abortions. While many statutes included the exception for an abortion thought by one or more physicians to be necessary to save the mother's life, that provision soon disappeared and the typical law required that the procedure actually be necessary for that purpose.

Gradually, in the middle and late 19th century the quickening distinction disappeared from the statutory law of most States and the degree of the offense and the penalties were increased. By the end of the 1950's a large majority of the jurisdictions banned abortion, however and whenever performed, unless done to save or preserve the life of the mother. The exceptions, Alabama and the District of Columbia, permitted abortion to preserve the mother's health. Three States permitted abortions that were not "unlawfully" performed or that were not "without lawful justification," leaving interpretation of those standards to the courts. In the past several years, however, a trend toward liberalization of abortion statutes has resulted in adoption, by about one-third of the States, of less stringent laws, most of them patterned after the ALI Model Penal Code.

It is thus apparent that at common law, at the time of the adoption of our Constitution, and throughout the major portion of the 19th century, abortion was viewed with less disfavor than under most American statutes currently in effect. Phrasing it another way, a woman enjoyed a substantially broader right to terminate a pregnancy than she does in most States today. At least with respect to the early stage of pregnancy, and very possibly without such a limitation, the opportunity to make this choice was present in this country well into the 19th century. Even later, the law continued for some time to treat less punitively an abortion procured in early pregnancy.

6.   The position of the American Medical Association. The anti-abortion mood prevalent in this country in the late 19th century was shared by the medical profession. Indeed, the attitude of the profession may have played a significant role in the enactment of stringent criminal abortion legislation during that period.

An AMA Committee on Criminal Abortion was appointed in May 1857. It presented its report, 12 Trans. of the Am. Med. Assn. 73–78 (1859), to the Twelfth Annual Meeting. That report observed that the Committee had been appointed to investigate criminal abortion "with a view to its general suppression." It deplored abortion and its frequency and it listed three causes of "this general demoralization":

"The first of these causes is a wide-spread popular ignorance of the true character of the crime—a belief, even among mothers themselves, that the foetus is not alive till after the period of quickening.

"The second of the agents alluded to is the fact that the profession themselves are frequently supposed careless of foetal life. . . .

"The third reason of the frightful extent of this crime is found in the grave defects of our laws, both common and statute, as regards the independent and actual existence of the child before birth, as a living being. These errors, which are sufficient in most instances to prevent conviction, are based, and only based, upon mistaken and exploded medical dogmas. With strange inconsistency, the law fully acknowledges the foetus in utero and its inherent rights, for civil purposes; while personally and as criminally affected, it fails to recognize it, and to its life as yet denies all protection."

The Committee then offered, and the Association adopted, resolutions protesting "against such unwarrantable destruction of human life," calling upon state legislatures to revise their abortion laws, and requesting the cooperation of state medical societies "in pressing the subject."

In 1871 a long and vivid report was submitted by the Committee on Criminal Abortion. It ended with the observation, "We had to deal with human life. In a matter of less importance we could entertain no compromise. An honest judge on the bench would call things by their proper names. We could do no less." It proffered resolutions, adopted by the Association, recommending, among other things, that it "be unlawful and unprofessional for any physician to induce abortion or premature labor, without the concurrent opinion of at least one respectable consulting physician, and then always with a view to the safety of the child—if that be possible," and calling "the attention of the clergy of all denominations to the perverted views of morality entertained by a large class of females—aye, and men also, on this important question."

Except for periodic condemnation of the criminal abortionist, no further formal AMA action took place until 1967. In that year, the Committee on Human Reproduction urged the adoption of a stated policy of opposition to induced abortion, except when there is "documented medical evidence" of a threat to the health or life of the mother, or that the child "may be born with incapacitating physical deformity or mental deficiency," or that a pregnancy "resulting from legally established statutory or forcible rape or incest may constitute a threat to the mental or physical health of the patient," two other physicians "chosen because of their recognized professional competency have examined the patient and have concurred in writing," and the procedure "is performed in a hospital accredited by the Joint Commission on Accreditation of Hospitals." The providing of medical information by physicians to state legislatures in their consideration of legislation regarding therapeutic abortion was "to be considered consistent with the principles of ethics of the American Medical Association." This recommendation was adopted by the House of Delegates. Proceedings of the AMA House of Delegates 40–51 (June 1967).

In 1970, after the introduction of a variety of proposed resolutions, and of a report from its Board of Trustees, a reference committee noted "polarization of the medical profession on this controversial issue"; division among those who had testified; a difference of opinion among AMA councils and committees; "the remarkable shift in testimony" in six months, felt to be influenced "by the rapid changes in state laws and by the judicial decisions which tend to make abortion more freely available;" and a feeling "that this trend will continue." On June 25, 1970, the House of Delegates adopted preambles and most of the resolutions proposed by the reference committee. The preambles emphasized "the best interests of the patient," "sound clinical judgment," and "informed patient consent," in contrast to "mere acquiescence to the patient's demand." The resolutions asserted that abortion is a medical procedure that should be performed by a licensed physician in an accredited hospital only after consultation with two other physicians and in conformity with state law, and that no party to the procedure should be required to violate personally held moral principles.[38] Proceedings of the AMA House of Delegates 220 (June 1970). The AMA Judicial Council rendered a complementary opinion.[39]

---

38. "Whereas, Abortion, like any other medical procedure, should not be performed when contrary to the best interests of the patient since good medical practice requires due consideration for the patient's welfare and not mere acquiescence to the patient's demand; and

"Whereas, The standards of sound clinical judgment, which, together with informed patient consent should be determinative according to the merits of each individual case; therefore be it

"RESOLVED, That abortion is a medical procedure and should be performed only by a duly licensed physician and surgeon in an accredited hospital acting only after consultation with two other physicians chosen because of their professional competency and in conformance with standards of good medical practice and the Medical Practice Act of his State; and be it further

"RESOLVED, That no physician or other professional personnel shall be compelled to perform any act which violates his good medical judgment. Neither physician, hospital, nor hospital personnel shall be required to perform any act violative of personally-held moral principles. In these circumstances good medical practice requires only that the physician or other professional personnel withdraw from the case so long as the withdrawal is consistent with good medical practice." Proceedings of the AMA House of Delegates 220 (June 1970).

39. "The Principles of Medical Ethics of the AMA do not prohibit a physician from performing an abortion that is performed in accordance with good medical practice and

7. The position of the American Public Health Association. In October 1970, the Executive Board of the APHA adopted Standards for Abortion Services. These were five in number:

"a. Rapid and simple abortion referral must be readily available through state and local public health departments, medical societies, or other non-profit organizations.

"b. An important function of counseling should be to simplify and expedite the provision of abortion services; it should not delay the obtaining of these services.

"c. Psychiatric consultation should not be mandatory. As in the case of other specialized medical services, psychiatric consultation should be sought for definite indications and not on a routine basis.

"d. A wide range of individuals from appropriately trained, sympathetic volunteers to highly skilled physicians may qualify as abortion counselors.

"e. Contraception and/or sterilization should be discussed with each abortion patient." Recommended Standards for Abortion Services, 61 Am.J.Pub.Health 396 (1971).

Among factors pertinent to life and health risks associated with abortion were three that "are recognized as important:"

"a. the skill of the physician,

"b. the environment in which the abortion is performed, and above all

"c. The duration of pregnancy, as determined by uterine size and confirmed by menstrual history."

It was said that "a well-equipped hospital" offers more protection "to cope with unforeseen difficulties than an office or clinic without such resources.... The factor of gestational age is of overriding importance." Thus, it was recommended that abortions in the second trimester and early abortions in the presence of existing medical complications be performed in hospitals as inpatient procedures. For pregnancies in the first trimester, abortion in the hospital with or without overnight stay "is probably the safest practice." An abortion in an extramural facility, however, is an acceptable alternative "provided arrangements exist in advance to admit patients promptly if unforeseen complications develop." Standards for an abortion facility were listed. It was said that at present abortions should be performed by physicians or osteopaths who are licensed to practice and who have "adequate training."

8. The position of the American Bar Association. At its meeting in February 1972 the ABA House of Delegates approved, with 17 opposing votes, the Uniform Abortion Act that had been drafted and approved the

under circumstances that do not violate the laws of the community in which he practices.

"In the matter of abortions, as of any other medical procedure, the Judicial Council becomes involved whenever there is alleged violation of the Principles of Medical Ethics as established by the House of Delegates."

preceding August by the Conference of Commissioners on Uniform State Laws 58 A.B.A.J. 380 (1972). [The Court's opinion included the full Act.] . . .

VII

Three reasons have been advanced to explain historically the enactment of criminal abortion laws in the 19th century and to justify their continued existence.

It has been argued occasionally that these laws were the product of a Victorian social concern to discourage illicit sexual conduct. Texas, however, does not advance this justification in the present case, and it appears that no court or commentator has taken the argument seriously. . . .

A second reason is concerned with abortion as a medical procedure. When most criminal abortion laws were first enacted, the procedure was a hazardous one for the woman. This was particularly true prior to the development of antisepsis. Antiseptic techniques, of course, were based on discoveries by Lister, Pasteur, and others first announced in 1867, but were not generally accepted and employed until about the turn of the century. Abortion mortality was high. Even after 1900, and perhaps until as late as the development of antibiotics in the 1940's, standard modern techniques such as dilation and curettage were not nearly so safe as they are today. Thus, it has been argued that a State's real concern in enacting a criminal abortion law was to protect the pregnant woman, that is, to restrain her from submitting to a procedure that placed her life in serious jeopardy.

Modern medical techniques have altered this situation. Appellants and various amici refer to medical data indicating that abortion in early pregnancy, that is, prior to the end of the first trimester, although not without its risk, is now relatively safe. Mortality rates for women undergoing early abortions, where the procedure is legal, appear to be as low as or lower than the rates for normal childbirth.[44] Consequently, any interest of the State in protecting the woman from an inherently hazardous procedure, except when it would be equally dangerous for her to forgo it, has largely disappeared. Of course, important state interests in the areas of health and medical standards do remain. The State has a legitimate interest in seeing to it that abortion, like any other medical procedure, is performed under circumstances that insure maximum safety for the patient. This interest obviously extends at least to the performing physician and his staff, to the facilities involved, to the availability of after-care, and to adequate provision for any complication or emergency that might arise.

---

44. Potts, Postconceptive Control of Fertility, 8 Int'l J. of G. & O. 957, 967 (1970) (England and Wales); Abortion Mortality, 20 Morbidity and Mortality 208, 209 (June 12, 1971) (U.S. Dept. of HEW, Public Health Service) (New York City); Tietze, United States: Therapeutic Abortions, 1963–1968, 59 Studies in Family Planning 5, 7 (1970); Tietze, Mortality with Contraception and Induced Abortion, 45 Studies in Family Planning 6 (1969) (Japan, Czechoslovakia, Hungary); Tietze & Lehfeldt, Legal Abortion in Eastern Europe, 175 J.A.M.A. 1149, 1152 (April 1961). Other sources are discussed in Lader 17–23.

The prevalence of high mortality rates at illegal "abortion mills" strengthens, rather than weakens, the State's interest in regulating the conditions under which abortions are performed. Moreover, the risk to the woman increases as her pregnancy continues. Thus, the State retains a definite interest in protecting the woman's own health and safety when an abortion is proposed at a late stage of pregnancy.

The third reason is the State's interest—some phrase it in terms of duty—in protecting prenatal life. Some of the argument for this justification rests on the theory that a new human life is present from the moment of conception.[45] The State's interest and general obligation to protect life then extends, it is argued, to prenatal life. Only when the life of the pregnant mother herself is at stake, balanced against the life she carries within her, should the interest of the embryo or fetus not prevail. Logically, of course, a legitimate state interest in this area need not stand or fall on acceptance of the belief that life begins at conception or at some other point prior to live birth. In assessing the State's interest, recognition may be given to the less rigid claim that as long as at least *potential* life is involved, the State may assert interests beyond the protection of the pregnant woman alone.

Parties challenging state abortion laws have sharply disputed in some courts the contention that a purpose of these laws, when enacted, was to protect prenatal life. Pointing to the absence of legislative history to support the contention, they claim that most state laws were designed solely to protect the woman. Because medical advances have lessened this concern, at least with respect to abortion in early pregnancy, they argue that with respect to such abortions the laws can no longer be justified by any state interest. There is some scholarly support for this view of original purpose. The few state courts called upon to interpret their laws in the late 19th and early 20th centuries did focus on the State's interest in protecting the woman's health rather than in preserving the embryo and fetus. Proponents of this view point out that in many States, including Texas, by statute or judicial interpretation, the pregnant woman herself could not be prosecuted for self-abortion or for cooperating in an abortion performed upon her by another. They claim that adoption of the "quickening" distinction through received common law and state statutes tacitly recognizes the greater health hazards inherent in late abortion and impliedly repudiates the theory that life begins at conception.

It is with these interests, and the weight to be attached to them, that this case is concerned.

VIII

The Constitution does not explicitly mention any right of privacy.... [But] the Court has recognized that a right of personal privacy, or a

---

45. See Brief of Amicus National Right to Life Committee; R. Drinan, The Inviolability of the Right to Be Born, in Abortion and the Law 107 (D. Smith ed. 1967); Louisell, Abortion, The Practice of Medicine and the Due Process of Law, 16 U.C.L.A. L.Rev. 233 (1969); Noonan 1.

guarantee of certain areas or zones of privacy, does exist under the Constitution. In varying contexts, the Court or individual Justices have, indeed, found at least the roots of that right in the First Amendment, Stanley v. Georgia, 394 U.S. 557, 564, (1969); in the Fourth and Fifth Amendments, Terry v. Ohio, 392 U.S. 1, 8–9 (1968), Katz v. United States, 389 U.S. 347, 350 (1967), Boyd v. United States, 116 U.S. 616 (1886), see Olmstead v. United States, 277 U.S. 438, 478 (1928) (Brandeis, J., dissenting); in the penumbras of the Bill of Rights, Griswold v. Connecticut, 381 U.S., at 484–485; in the Ninth Amendment, id., at 486 (Goldberg, J., concurring); or in the concept of liberty guaranteed by the first section of the Fourteenth Amendment, see Meyer v. Nebraska, 262 U.S. 390, 399 (1923). These decisions make it clear that only personal rights that can be deemed "fundamental" or "implicit in the concept of ordered liberty," Palko v. Connecticut, 302 U.S. 319, 325 (1937), are included in this guarantee of personal privacy. They also make it clear that the right has some extension to activities relating to marriage, Loving v. Virginia, 388 U.S. 1, 12 (1967); procreation, Skinner v. Oklahoma, 316 U.S. 535, 541–542 (1942); contraception, Eisenstadt v. Baird, 405 U.S., at 453–454; family relationships, Prince v. Massachusetts, 321 U.S. 158, 166 (1944); and child rearing and education, Pierce v. Society of Sisters, 268 U.S. 510, 535 (1925), Meyer v. Nebraska, supra.

This right of privacy, whether it be founded in the Fourteenth Amendment's concept of personal liberty and restrictions upon state action, as we feel it is, or, as the District Court determined, in the Ninth Amendment's reservation of rights to the people, is broad enough to encompass a woman's decision whether or not to terminate her pregnancy. The detriment that the State would impose upon the pregnant woman by denying this choice altogether is apparent. Specific and direct harm medically diagnosable even in early pregnancy may be involved. Maternity, or additional offspring, may force upon the woman a distressful life and future. Psychological harm may be imminent. Mental and physical health may be taxed by child care. There is also the distress, for all concerned, associated with the unwanted child, and there is the problem of bringing a child into a family already unable, psychologically and otherwise, to care for it. In other cases, as in this one, the additional difficulties and continuing stigma of unwed motherhood may be involved. All these are factors the woman and her responsible physician necessarily will consider in consultation.

On the basis of elements such as these, appellant and some amici argue that the woman's right is absolute and that she is entitled to terminate her pregnancy at whatever time, in whatever way, and for whatever reason she alone chooses. With this we do not agree.... The Court's decisions recognizing a right of privacy also acknowledge that some state regulation in areas protected by that right is appropriate. As noted above, a State may properly assert important interests in safeguarding health, in maintaining medical standards, and in protecting potential life. At some point in pregnancy, these respective interests become sufficiently compelling to sustain regulation of the factors that govern the abortion decision. The privacy right involved, therefore, cannot be said to be absolute. In fact, it is not clear to us that the claim asserted by some amici that one has an unlimited right to do with one's body as one pleases bears a close relationship to the right of privacy previously articulated in the Court's decisions. The Court has refused to recognize an unlimited right of this kind in the past. Jacobson v. Massachusetts, 197 U.S. 11 (1905) (vaccination); Buck v. Bell, 274 U.S. 200 (1927) (sterilization).

We, therefore, conclude that the right of personal privacy includes the abortion decision, but that this right is not unqualified and must be considered against important state interests in regulation.

We note that those federal and state courts that have recently considered abortion law challenges have reached the same conclusion. . . .

Where certain "fundamental rights" are involved, the Court has held that regulation limiting these rights may be justified only by a "compelling state interest," and that legislative enactments must be narrowly drawn to express only the legitimate state interests at stake. Griswold v. Connecticut, 381 U.S., at 485; see Eisenstadt v. Baird, 405 U.S., at 460, 463–464, (White, J., concurring in result).

In the recent abortion cases, [lower] courts have recognized these principles. Those striking down state laws have generally scrutinized the State's interests in protecting health and potential life, and have concluded that neither interest justified broad limitations on the reasons for which a physician and his pregnant patient might decide that she should have an abortion in the early stages of pregnancy. Courts sustaining state laws have held that the State's determinations to protect health or prenatal life are dominant and constitutionally justifiable.

IX

The District Court held that the appellee failed to meet his burden of demonstrating that the Texas statute's infringement upon Roe's rights was necessary to support a compelling state interest, and that, although the appellee presented "several compelling justifications for state presence in the area of abortions," the statutes outstripped these justifications and swept "far beyond any areas of compelling state interest." Appellant and appellee both contest that holding. Appellant, as has been indicated, claims an absolute right that bars any state imposition of criminal penalties in the area. Appellee argues that the State's determination to recognize and protect prenatal life from and after conception constitutes a compelling state interest. As noted above, we do not agree fully with either formulation.

A. The appellee and certain amici argue that the fetus is a "person" within the language and meaning of the Fourteenth Amendment. In support of this, they outline at length and in detail the well-known facts of fetal development. If this suggestion of personhood is established, the appellant's case, of course, collapses, for the fetus' right to life would then be guaranteed specifically by the Amendment. The appellant conceded as much on reargument. On the other hand, the appellee conceded on reargument that no case could be cited that holds that a fetus is a person within the meaning of the Fourteenth Amendment.

The Constitution does not define "person" in so many words. Section 1 of the Fourteenth Amendment contains three references to "person." The first, in defining "citizens," speaks of "persons born or naturalized in the United States." The word also appears both in the Due Process Clause and in the Equal Protection Clause. "Person" is used in other places in the Constitution: in the listing of qualifications for Representatives and Senators, Art. I, § 2, cl. 2, and § 3, cl. 3; in the Apportionment Clause, Art. I, § 2, cl. 3; [53] in the Migration and Importation provision, Art. I, § 9, cl. 1; in the Emolument Clause, Art. I, § 9, cl. 8; in the Electors provisions, Art. II, § 1, cl. 2, and the superseded cl. 3; in the provision outlining qualifications for the office of President, Art. II, § 1, cl. 5; in the Extradition provisions, Art. IV, § 2, cl. 2, and the superseded Fugitive Slave Clause 3; and in the Fifth, Twelfth, and Twenty-second Amendments, as well as in §§ 2 and 3 of the Fourteenth Amendment. But in nearly all these instances, the use of the word is such that it has application only postnatally. None indicates, with any assurance, that it has any possible pre-natal application. [54]

All this, together with our observation that throughout the major portion of the 19th century prevailing legal abortion practices were far freer than they are today, persuades us that the word "person," as used in the Fourteenth Amendment, does not include the unborn. This is in accord with the results reached in those few cases where the issue has been squarely presented. Indeed, our decision in United States v. Vuitch, 402 U.S. 62, (1971), inferentially is to the same effect, for we there would not have indulged in statutory interpretation favorable to abortion in specified circumstances if the necessary consequence was the termination of life entitled to Fourteenth Amendment protection.

This conclusion, however, does not of itself fully answer the contentions raised by Texas, and we pass on to other considerations.

B. The pregnant woman cannot be isolated in her privacy. She carries an embryo and, later, a fetus, if one accepts the medical definitions of the

---

53. We are not aware that in the taking of any census under this clause, a fetus has ever been counted.

54. When Texas urges that a fetus is entitled to Fourteenth Amendment protection as a person, it faces a dilemma. Neither in Texas nor in any other State are all abortions prohibited. Despite broad proscription, an exception always exists. The exception contained in Art. 1196, for an abortion procured or attempted by medical advice for the purpose of saving the life of the mother, is typical. But if the fetus is a person who is not to be deprived of life without due process of law, and if the mother's condition is the sole determinant, does not the Texas exception

appear to be out of line with the Amendment's command?

There are other inconsistencies between Fourteenth Amendment status and the typical abortion statute. It has already been pointed out that in Texas the woman is not a principal or an accomplice with respect to an abortion upon her. If the fetus is a person, why is the woman not a principal or an accomplice? Further, the penalty for criminal abortion specified by Art. 1195 is significantly less than the maximum penalty for murder prescribed by Art. 1257 of the Texas Penal Code. If the fetus is a person, may the penalties be different?

developing young in the human uterus. See Dorland's Illustrated Medical Dictionary 478–479, 547 (24th ed. 1965). The situation therefore is inherently different from marital intimacy, or bedroom possession of obscene material, or marriage, or procreation, or education, with which *Eisenstadt* and *Griswold*, *Stanley*, *Loving*, *Skinner* and *Pierce* and *Meyer* were respectively concerned. As we have intimated above, it is reasonable and appropriate for a State to decide that at some point in time another interest, that of health of the mother or that of potential human life, becomes significantly involved. The woman's privacy is no longer sole and any right of privacy she possesses must be measured accordingly.

Texas urges that, apart from the Fourteenth Amendment, life begins at conception and is present throughout pregnancy, and that, therefore, the State has a compelling interest in protecting that life from and after conception. We need not resolve the difficult question of when life begins. When those trained in the respective disciplines of medicine, philosophy, and theology are unable to arrive at any consensus, the judiciary, at this point in the development of man's knowledge, is not in a position to speculate as to the answer.

It should be sufficient to note briefly the wide divergence of thinking on this most sensitive and difficult question. There has always been strong support for the view that life does not begin until live birth. This was the belief of the Stoics. It appears to be the predominant, though not the unanimous, attitude of the Jewish faith. It may be taken to represent also the position of a large segment of the Protestant community, insofar as that can be ascertained; organized groups that have taken a formal position on the abortion issue have generally regarded abortion as a matter for the conscience of the individual and her family. As we have noted, the common law found greater significance in quickening. Physicians . . . have tended to focus either upon conception, upon live birth, or upon the interim point at which the fetus becomes "viable," that is, potentially able to live outside the mother's womb, albeit with artificial aid. Viability is usually placed at about seven months (28 weeks) but may occur earlier, even at 24 weeks. The Aristotelian theory of "mediate animation," that held sway throughout the Middle Ages and the Renaissance in Europe, continued to be official Roman Catholic dogma until the 19th century, despite opposition to this "ensoulment" theory from those in the Church who would recognize the existence of life from the moment of conception. The latter is now, of course, the official belief of the Catholic Church. As one brief amicus discloses, this is a view strongly held by many non-Catholics as well, and by many physicians. Substantial problems for precise definition of this view are posed, however, by new embryological data that purport to indicate that conception is a "process" over time, rather than an event, and by new medical techniques such as menstrual extraction, the "morning-after" pill, implantation of embryos, artificial insemination, and even artificial wombs.

In areas other than criminal abortion, the law has been reluctant to endorse any theory that life, as we recognize it, begins before live birth or to accord legal rights to the unborn except in narrowly defined situations and except when the rights are contingent upon live birth. For example, the traditional rule of tort law denied recovery for prenatal injuries even though the child was born alive. That rule has been changed in almost every jurisdiction. In most States, recovery is said to be permitted only if the fetus was viable, or at least quick, when the injuries were sustained, though few courts have squarely so held. In a recent development, generally opposed by the commentators, some States permit the parents of a stillborn child to maintain an action for wrongful death because of prenatal injuries. Such an action, however, would appear to be one to vindicate the parents' interest and is thus consistent with the view that the fetus, at most, represents only the potentiality of life. Similarly, unborn children have been recognized as acquiring rights or interests by way of inheritance or other devolution of property, and have been represented by guardians ad litem. Perfection of the interests involved, again, has generally been contingent upon live birth. In short, the unborn have never been recognized in the law as persons in the whole sense.

X

In view of all this, we do not agree that, by adopting one theory of life, Texas may override the rights of the pregnant woman that are at stake. We repeat, however, that the State does have an important and legitimate interest in preserving and protecting the health of the pregnant woman, whether she be a resident of the State or a non-resident who seeks medical consultation and treatment there, and that it has still *another* important and legitimate interest in protecting the potentiality of human life. These interests are separate and distinct. Each grows in substantiality as the woman approaches term and, at a point during pregnancy, each becomes "compelling."

With respect to the State's important and legitimate interest in the health of the mother, the "compelling" point, in the light of present medical knowledge, is at approximately the end of the first trimester. This is so because of the now-established medical fact that until the end of the first trimester mortality in abortion may be less than mortality in normal childbirth. It follows that, from and after this point, a State may regulate the abortion procedure to the extent that the regulation reasonably relates to the preservation and protection of maternal health. Examples of permissible state regulation in this area are requirements as to the qualifications of the person who is to perform the abortion; as to the licensure of that person; as to the facility in which the procedure is to be performed, that is, whether it must be a hospital or may be a clinic or some other place of less-than-hospital status; as to the licensing of the facility; and the like.

This means, on the other hand, that, for the period of pregnancy prior to this "compelling" point, the attending physician, in consultation with his patient, is free to determine, without regulation by the State, that, in his medical judgment, the patient's pregnancy should be terminated. If that decision is reached, the judgment may be effectuated by an abortion free of interference by the State.

With respect to the State's important and legitimate interest in potential life, the "compelling" point is at viability. This is so because the fetus then presumably has the capability of meaningful life outside the mother's womb. State regulation protective of fetal life after viability thus has both logical and biological justifications. If the State is interested in protecting fetal life after viability, it may go so far as to proscribe abortion during that period, except when it is necessary to preserve the life or health of the mother.

Measured against these standards, Art. 1196 of the Texas Penal Code, in restricting legal abortions to those "procured or attempted by medical advice for the purpose of saving the life of the mother," sweeps too broadly. The statute makes no distinction between abortions performed early in pregnancy and those performed later, and it limits to a single reason, "saving" the mother's life, the legal justification for the procedure. The statute, therefore, cannot survive the constitutional attack made upon it here. . . .

XI

To summarize and to repeat:

1. A state criminal abortion statute of the current Texas type, that excepts from criminality only a *life-saving* procedure on behalf of the mother, without regard to pregnancy stage and without recognition of the other interests involved, is violative of the Due Process Clause of the Fourteenth Amendment.

> (a) For the stage prior to approximately the end of the first trimester, the abortion decision and its effectuation must be left to the medical judgment of the pregnant woman's attending physician.

> (b) For the stage subsequent to approximately the end of the first trimester, the State, in promoting its interest in the health of the mother, may, if it chooses, regulate the abortion procedure in ways that are reasonably related to maternal health.

> (c) For the stage subsequent to viability, the State in promoting its interest in the potentiality of human life may, if it chooses, regulate, and even proscribe, abortion except where it is necessary, in appropriate medical judgment, for the preservation of the life or health of the mother.

2. The State may define the term "physician," as it has been employed in the preceding paragraphs of this Part XI of this opinion, to mean only a physician currently licensed by the State, and may proscribe any abortion by a person who is not a physician as so defined. . . .

This holding, we feel, is consistent with the relative weights of the respective interests involved, with the lessons and examples of medical and legal history, with the lenity of the common law, and with the demands of the profound problems of the present day. The decision leaves the State free to place increasing restrictions on abortion as the period of pregnancy lengthens, so long as those restrictions are tailored to the recognized state interests. The decision vindicates the right of the physician to administer medical treatment according to his professional judgment up to the points where important state interests provide compelling justifications for intervention. Up to those points, the abortion decision in all its aspects is inherently, and primarily, a medical decision, and basic responsibility for it must rest with the physician. If an individual practitioner abuses the privilege of exercising proper medical judgment, the usual remedies, judicial and intra-professional, are available.

. . .

[Concurring opinions by MR. CHIEF JUSTICE BURGER, MR. JUSTICE DOUGLAS, and MR. JUSTICE STEWART and dissenting opinions of MR. JUSTICE WHITE and MR. JUSTICE REHNQUIST omitted.]

Note on Doe v. Bolton

Doe v. Bolton, 410 U.S. 179 (1973) was a companion case to *Roe*, involving a challenge to the Georgia abortion statute by an indigent, married woman who was denied an abortion after eight weeks of pregnancy. The Court upheld that portion of the statute permitting a physician to perform an abortion only if it was necessary, in the physician's best clinical judgment, in light of all of the circumstances.[b] The Court struck down portions requiring (1) that first trimester abortions be conducted in hospitals, (2) that hospitals in which abortions were performed be specially accredited, and (3) that permission from a hospital abortion committee and concurrence of two other physicians in the recommendation of the pregnant woman's own doctor be obtained. The Court also invalidated a provision limiting abortions to Georgia residents. The last holding, invalidating the residency requirement, rested on the Privileges and Immunities Clause, Art IV, Section 2; the others rested on the 14th Amendment's Due Process Clause.

Questions and Comments on *Roe* and *Doe*

1.   These cases have generated enormous controversy, both in scholarly and political circles. Critics of *Roe* regard it as an illegitimate judicial creation of a right, analogous to the liberty of contract protected by the Court in *Lochner*. See, e.g., John Hart Ely, *The Wages of Crying Wolf: A Comment on Roe v. Wade*, 82 Yale L. J. 920 (1973). Others defend *Roe* as a principled extension of the 14th Amendment's conception of liberty, sup-

---

b.   The lower federal courts had found unconstitutional a further limit, requiring the physician to find the abortion necessary either because of danger to the life or health of the mother, or the fetus would be born with permanent and serious defects, or the pregnancy resulted from rape. The lower court concluded that limiting the abortion decision to these three reasons unduly limited the pregnant woman's right of privacy. *Doe*, 410 U.S. at 186.

ported in part by tradition and moral philosophy. See, e.g., Laurence Tribe, American Constitutional Law 1308–12 (2d ed 1988). Consider what interpretations of the text of the Due Process Clause seem plausible, and identify what interpretation the majority relied on.

2. Other criticism has focussed on the Court's analysis of the nature and scope of the state's interests in regulating the abortion decision. After reading the next case, *Casey*, consider which treatment of the state's interests, as to protecting the potential life of the fetus and protecting maternal health, is (i) more persuasive, and (ii) more justified by constitutionally relevant criteria.

3. In part VI of the opinion, the *Roe* Court describes in some detail the treatment of abortion in ancient Greece, in the British common law, in the development of religious theologies, in English statutory law, and in the American states from the 19th century through the present, as well as the evolution of the positions of the American Medical Association and the American Bar Association. Why are these relevant? What purpose(s) are served by this discussion? Later in this chapter you will read decisions from the Canadian and German constitutional courts on abortion; consider whether these opinions contain material with a similar purpose.

Planned Parenthood of Southeastern Pennsylvania v. Casey

505 U.S. 833 (1992).

JUSTICE O'CONNOR, JUSTICE KENNEDY, and JUSTICE SOUTER announced the judgment of the Court and delivered the opinion of the Court with respect to Parts I, II, III, V–A, V–C, and VI, an opinion with respect to Part V–E, in which JUSTICE STEVENS joins, and an opinion with respect to Parts IV, V–B, and V–D.

I

Liberty finds no refuge in a jurisprudence of doubt. Yet 19 years after our holding that the Constitution protects a woman's right to terminate her pregnancy in its early stages, Roe v. Wade, 410 U.S. 113 (1973), that definition of liberty is still questioned. Joining the respondents as amicus curiae, the United States, as it has done in five other cases in the last decade, again asks us to overrule *Roe*. . . .

At issue in these cases are five provisions of the Pennsylvania Abortion Control Act of 1982. . . . The Act requires that a woman seeking an abortion give her informed consent prior to the abortion procedure, and specifies that she be provided with certain information at least 24 hours before the abortion is performed. For a minor to obtain an abortion, the Act requires the informed consent of one of her parents, but provides for a judicial bypass option if the minor does not wish to or cannot obtain a parent's consent. Another provision of the Act requires that, unless certain exceptions apply, a married woman seeking an abortion must sign a statement indicating that she has notified her husband of her intended abortion. The Act exempts compliance with these three requirements in the event of a "medical emergency," which is defined in § 3203 of the Act. In addition to the above provisions regulating the performance of abortions, the Act imposes certain reporting requirements on facilities that provide abortion services.

Before any of these provisions took effect, the petitioners, who are five abortion clinics and one physician representing himself as well as a class of physicians who provide abortion services, brought this suit seeking declaratory and injunctive relief. Each provision was challenged as unconstitutional on its face. The District Court entered a preliminary injunction against the enforcement of the regulations, and, after a 3-day bench trial, held all the provisions at issue here unconstitutional, entering a permanent injunction against Pennsylvania's enforcement of them. The Court of Appeals for the Third Circuit affirmed in part and reversed in part, upholding all of the regulations except for the husband notification requirement. We granted certiorari.

The Court of Appeals found it necessary to follow an elaborate course of reasoning even to identify the first premise to use to determine whether the statute enacted by Pennsylvania meets constitutional standards. And at oral argument in this Court, the attorney for the parties challenging the statute took the position that none of the enactments can be upheld without overruling Roe v. Wade. We disagree with that analysis; but we acknowledge that our decisions after *Roe* cast doubt upon the meaning and reach of its holding. Further, the Chief Justice admits that he would overrule the central holding of *Roe* and adopt the rational relationship test as the sole criterion of constitutionality. State and federal courts as well as legislatures throughout the Union must have guidance as they seek to address this subject in conformance with the Constitution. Given these premises, we find it imperative to review once more the principles that define the rights of the woman and the legitimate authority of the State respecting the termination of pregnancies by abortion procedures.

After considering the fundamental constitutional questions resolved by *Roe*, principles of institutional integrity, and the rule of stare decisis, we are led to conclude this: the essential holding of Roe v. Wade should be retained and once again reaffirmed.

It must be stated at the outset and with clarity that *Roe's* essential holding, the holding we reaffirm, has three parts. First is a recognition of the right of the woman to choose to have an abortion before viability and to obtain it without undue interference from the State. Before viability, the State's interests are not strong enough to support a prohibition of abortion or the imposition of a substantial obstacle to the woman's effective right to elect the procedure. Second is a confirmation of the State's power to restrict abortions after fetal viability, if the law contains exceptions for pregnancies which endanger the woman's life or health. And third is the principle that the State has legitimate interests from the outset of the pregnancy in protecting the health of the woman and the life of the fetus that may become a child. These principles do not contradict one another; and we adhere to each.

II

Constitutional protection of the woman's decision to terminate her pregnancy derives from the Due Process Clause of the Fourteenth Amendment.... Although a literal reading of the Clause might suggest that it governs only the procedures by which a State may deprive persons of liberty, for at least 105 years ... the Clause has been understood to contain a substantive component as well, one "barring certain government actions regardless of the fairness of the procedures used to implement them." Daniels v. Williams, 474 U.S. 327, 331 (1986). ...

The most familiar of the substantive liberties protected by the Fourteenth Amendment are those recognized by the Bill of Rights. We have held that the Due Process Clause of the Fourteenth Amendment incorporates most of the Bill of Rights against the States. It is tempting, as a means of curbing the discretion of federal judges, to suppose that liberty encompasses no more than those rights already guaranteed to the individual against federal interference by the express provisions of the first eight Amendments to the Constitution. See Adamson v. California, 332 U.S. 46, 68–92 (1947) (Black, J., dissenting). But of course this Court has never accepted that view.

It is also tempting, for the same reason, to suppose that the Due Process Clause protects only those practices, defined at the most specific level, that were protected against government interference by other rules of law when the Fourteenth Amendment was ratified. See Michael H. v. Gerald D., 491 U.S. 110, 127–128, n. 6 (1989) (opinion of Scalia, J.). But such a view would be inconsistent with our law. It is a promise of the Constitution that there is a realm of personal liberty which the government may not enter. We have vindicated this principle before. Marriage is mentioned nowhere in the Bill of Rights and interracial marriage was illegal in most States in the 19th century, but the Court was no doubt correct in finding it to be an aspect of liberty protected against state interference by the substantive component of the Due Process Clause in Loving v. Virginia, 388 U.S. 1, 12 (1967) (relying, in an opinion for eight Justices, on the Due Process Clause). ...

Neither the Bill of Rights nor the specific practices of States at the time of the adoption of the Fourteenth Amendment marks the outer limits of the substantive sphere of liberty which the Fourteenth Amendment protects. See U.S. Const., Amdt. 9. As the second Justice Harlan recognized:

> "[T]he full scope of the liberty guaranteed by the Due Process Clause cannot be found in or limited by the precise terms of the specific guarantees elsewhere provided in the Constitution. This 'liberty' is not a series of isolated points pricked out in terms of the taking of property; the freedom of speech, press, and religion; ... and so on. It is

a rational continuum which, broadly speaking, includes a freedom from all substantial arbitrary impositions and purposeless restraints, ... and which also recognizes, what a reasonable and sensitive judgment must, that certain interests require particularly careful scrutiny of the state needs asserted to justify their abridgment." Poe v. Ullman, supra, 367 U.S., at 543 (opinion dissenting from dismissal on jurisdictional grounds).

Justice Harlan wrote these words in addressing an issue the full Court did not reach in Poe v. Ullman, but the Court adopted his position four Terms later in *Griswold*. In *Griswold*, we held that the Constitution does not permit a State to forbid a married couple to use contraceptives. That same freedom was later guaranteed, under the Equal Protection Clause, for unmarried couples. See Eisenstadt v. Baird, 405 U.S. 438 (1972). Constitutional protection was extended to the sale and distribution of contraceptives in Carey v. Population Services International, 431 U.S 678 (1977). It is settled now, as it was when the Court heard arguments in Roe v. Wade, that the Constitution places limits on a State's right to interfere with a person's most basic decisions about family and parenthood, as well as bodily integrity.

The inescapable fact is that adjudication of substantive due process claims may call upon the Court in interpreting the Constitution to exercise that same capacity which by tradition courts always have exercised: reasoned judgment. Its boundaries are not susceptible of expression as a simple rule. That does not mean we are free to invalidate state policy choices with which we disagree; yet neither does it permit us to shrink from the duties of our office. As Justice Harlan observed:

"Due process has not been reduced to any formula; its content cannot be determined by reference to any code. The best that can be said is that through the course of this Court's decisions it has represented the balance which our Nation, built upon postulates of respect for the liberty of the individual, has struck between that liberty and the demands of organized society. If the supplying of content to this Constitutional concept has of necessity been a rational process, it certainly has not been one where judges have felt free to roam where unguided speculation might take them. The balance of which I speak is the balance struck by this country, having regard to what history teaches are the traditions from which it developed as well as the traditions from which it broke. That tradition is a living thing. A decision of this Court which radically departs from it could not long survive, while a decision which builds on what has survived is likely to be sound. No formula could serve as a substitute, in this area, for judgment and restraint." Poe v. Ullman, 367 U.S., at 542 (opinion dissenting from dismissal on jurisdictional grounds).

Men and women of good conscience can disagree, and ... always shall disagree about the profound moral and spiritual implications of terminating a pregnancy, even in its earliest stage. Some of us as individuals find abortion offensive to our most basic principles of morality, but that cannot control our decision. Our obligation is to define the liberty of all, not to mandate our own moral code. The underlying constitutional issue is whether the State can resolve these philosophic questions in such a definitive way that a woman lacks all choice in the matter, except perhaps in those rare circumstances in which the pregnancy is itself a danger to her own life or health, or is the result of rape or incest. . . .

Our law affords constitutional protection to personal decisions relating to marriage, procreation, contraception, family relationships, child rearing, and education. . . . These matters, involving the most intimate and personal choices a person may make in a lifetime, choices central to personal dignity and autonomy, are central to the liberty protected by the Fourteenth Amendment. At the heart of liberty is the right to define one's own concept of existence, of meaning, of the universe, and of the mystery of human life. Beliefs about these matters could not define the attributes of personhood were they formed under compulsion of the State.

These considerations begin our analysis of the woman's interest in terminating her pregnancy but cannot end it, for this reason: though the abortion decision may originate within the zone of conscience and belief, it is more than a philosophic exercise. Abortion is a unique act. It is an act fraught with consequences for others: for the woman who must live with the implications of her decision; for the persons who perform and assist in the procedure; for the spouse, family, and society which must confront the knowledge that these procedures exist, procedures some deem nothing short of an act of violence against innocent human life; and, depending on one's beliefs, for the life or potential life that is aborted. Though abortion is conduct, it does not follow that the State is entitled to proscribe it in all instances. That is because the liberty of the woman is at stake in a sense unique to the human condition and so unique to the law. The mother who carries a child to full term is subject to anxieties, to physical constraints, to pain that only she must bear. That these sacrifices have from the beginning of the human race been endured by woman with a pride that ennobles her in the eyes of others and gives to the infant a bond of love cannot alone be grounds for the State to insist she make the sacrifice. Her suffering is too intimate and personal for the State to insist, without more, upon its own vision of the woman's role, however dominant that vision has been in the course of our history and our culture. The destiny of the woman must be shaped to a large extent on her own conception of her spiritual imperatives and her place in society.

It should be recognized, moreover, that in some critical respects the abortion decision is of the same character as the decision to use contraception, to which Griswold v. Connecticut, Eisenstadt v. Baird, and Carey v. Population Services International afford constitutional protection. We have no doubt as to the correctness of those decisions. They support the reasoning in *Roe* relating to the woman's liberty because they involve personal decisions concerning not only the meaning of procreation but also human responsibility and respect for it. As with abortion, reasonable people will have differences of opinion about these matters. One view is based on such reverence for the wonder of creation that any pregnancy ought to be welcomed and carried to full term no matter how difficult it will be to provide for the child and ensure its well-being. Another is that the inability to provide for the nurture and care of the infant is a cruelty to the child and an anguish to the parent. These are intimate views with infinite variations, and their deep, personal character underlay our decisions in *Griswold, Eisenstadt,* and *Carey.* The same concerns are present when the woman confronts the reality that, perhaps despite her attempts to avoid it, she has become pregnant. . . .

While we appreciate the weight of the arguments made on behalf of the State in the cases before us, arguments which in their ultimate formulation conclude that *Roe* should be overruled, the reservations any of us may have in reaffirming the central holding of *Roe* are outweighed by the explication of individual liberty we have given combined with the force of stare decisis. We turn now to that doctrine.

III

A.   The obligation to follow precedent begins with necessity, and a contrary necessity marks its outer limit. With Cardozo, we recognize that no judicial system could do society's work if it eyed each issue afresh in every case that raised it. Indeed, the very concept of the rule of law underlying our own Constitution requires such continuity over time that a respect for precedent is, by definition, indispensable. At the other extreme, a different necessity would make itself felt if a prior judicial ruling should come to be seen so clearly as error that its enforcement was for that very reason doomed.

Even when the decision to overrule a prior case is not, as in the rare, latter instance, virtually foreordained, it is common wisdom that the rule of stare decisis is not an "inexorable command," and certainly it is not such in every constitutional case, Rather, when this Court reexamines a prior holding, its judgment is customarily informed by a series of prudential and pragmatic considerations designed to test the consistency of overruling a prior decision with the ideal of the rule of law, and to gauge the respective costs of reaffirming and overruling a prior case. Thus, for example, we may ask whether the rule has proven to be intolerable simply in defying practical workability; whether the rule is subject to a kind of reliance that would lend a special hardship to the consequences of overruling and add inequity to the cost of repudiation; whether related principles of law have so far developed as to have left the old rule no more than a remnant of abandoned doctrine; or whether facts have so changed, or come to be seen so differently, as to have robbed the old rule of significant application or justification.

So in this case we may enquire whether *Roe's* central rule has been found unworkable; whether the rule's limitation on state power could be removed without serious inequity to those who have relied upon it or significant damage to the stability of the society governed by it; whether the law's growth in the intervening years has left *Roe's* central rule a doctrinal anachronism discounted by society; and whether *Roe's* premises of fact have so far changed in the ensuing two decades as to render its central holding somehow irrelevant or unjustifiable in dealing with the issue it addressed.

1. Although *Roe* has engendered opposition, it has in no sense proven "unworkable," representing as it does a simple limitation beyond which a state law is unenforceable. . . .

2. The inquiry into reliance counts the cost of a rule's repudiation as it would fall on those who have relied reasonably on the rule's continued application. Since the classic case for weighing reliance heavily in favor of following the earlier rule occurs in the commercial context, where advance planning of great precision is most obviously a necessity, . . . some would find no reliance worthy of consideration in support of *Roe*.

. . . Abortion is customarily chosen as an unplanned response to the consequence of unplanned activity or to the failure of conventional birth control, and except on the assumption that no intercourse would have occurred but for *Roe's* holding, such behavior may appear to justify no reliance claim. Even if reliance could be claimed on that unrealistic assumption, the argument might run, any reliance interest would be de minimis . . . [because] reproductive planning could take virtually immediate account of any sudden restoration of state authority to ban abortions.

To eliminate the issue of reliance that easily, however, one would need to limit cognizable reliance to specific instances of sexual activity. But to do this would be simply to refuse to face the fact that for two decades of economic and social developments, people have organized intimate relationships and made choices that define their views of themselves and their places in society, in reliance on the availability of abortion in the event that contraception should fail. The ability of women to participate equally in the economic and social life of the Nation has been facilitated by their ability to control their reproductive lives. The Constitution serves human values, and while the effect of reliance on *Roe* cannot be exactly measured, neither can the certain cost of overruling *Roe* for people who have ordered their thinking and living around that case be dismissed.

3. No evolution of legal principle has left *Roe's* doctrinal footings weaker than they were in 1973. No development of constitutional law since the case was decided has implicitly or explicitly left *Roe* behind as a mere survivor of obsolete constitutional thinking. . . .

The original holding resting on the concurrence of seven Members of the Court in 1973 was expressly affirmed by a majority of six in 1983, see Akron v. Akron Center for Reproductive Health, Inc., 462 U.S. 416 (Akron I), and by a majority of five in 1986, see Thornburgh v. American College of Obstetricians and Gynecologists, 476 U.S. 747, expressing adherence to the constitutional ruling despite legislative efforts in some States to test its limits. More recently, in Webster v. Reproductive Health Services, 492 U.S. 490 (1989), although two of the present authors questioned the trimester framework in a way consistent with our judgment today, a majority of the

Court either decided to reaffirm or declined to address the constitutional validity of the central holding of *Roe*.

Nor will courts building upon *Roe* be likely to hand down erroneous decisions as a consequence. Even on the assumption that the central holding of *Roe* was in error, that error would go only to the strength of the state interest in fetal protection, not to the recognition afforded by the Constitution to the woman's liberty. The latter aspect of the decision fits comfortably within the framework of the Court's prior decisions, the holdings of which are "not a series of isolated points," but mark a "rational continuum." . . .

The soundness of this prong of the *Roe* analysis is apparent from a consideration of the alternative. If indeed the woman's interest in deciding whether to bear and beget a child had not been recognized as in *Roe*, the State might as readily restrict a woman's right to choose to carry a pregnancy to term as to terminate it, to further asserted state interests in population control, or eugenics, for example. Yet *Roe* has been sensibly relied upon to counter any such suggestions. E.g., Arnold v. Board of Education of Escambia County, Ala., 880 F.2d 305, 311 (C.A.11 1989) (relying upon *Roe* and concluding that government officials violate the Constitution by coercing a minor to have an abortion). . . . In any event, because *Roe's* scope is confined by the fact of its concern with postconception potential life, a concern otherwise likely to be implicated only by some forms of contraception protected independently under *Griswold* and later cases, any error in *Roe* is unlikely to have serious ramifications in future cases.

4. We have seen how time has overtaken some of *Roe's* factual assumptions: advances in maternal health care allow for abortions safe to the mother later in pregnancy than was true in 1973, and advances in neonatal care have advanced viability to a point somewhat earlier. But these facts go only to the scheme of time limits on the realization of competing interests, and the divergences from the factual premises of 1973 have no bearing on the validity of *Roe's* central holding, that viability marks the earliest point at which the State's interest in fetal life is constitutionally adequate to justify a legislative ban on nontherapeutic abortions. The soundness or unsoundness of that constitutional judgment in no sense turns on whether viability occurs at approximately 28 weeks, as was usual at the time of *Roe*, at 23 to 24 weeks, as it sometimes does today, or at some moment even slightly earlier in pregnancy, as it may if fetal respiratory capacity can somehow be enhanced in the future. Whenever it may occur, the attainment of viability may continue to serve as the critical fact, just as it has done since *Roe* was decided; which is to say that no change in *Roe's* factual underpinning has left its central holding obsolete, and none supports an argument for overruling it.

5. The sum of the precedential enquiry to this point shows *Roe's* underpinnings unweakened in any way affecting its central holding. While it has engendered disapproval, it has not been unworkable. An entire generation has come of age free to assume *Roe's* concept of liberty in

defining the capacity of women to act in society, and to make reproductive decisions....

B. In a less significant case, stare decisis analysis could, and would, stop at the point we have reached. But the sustained and widespread debate *Roe* has provoked calls for some comparison between that case and others of comparable dimension that have responded to national controversies and taken on the impress of the controversies addressed. Only two such decisional lines from the past century present themselves for examination, and in each instance the result reached by the Court accorded with the principles we apply today.

The first example is that line of cases identified with Lochner v. New York, 198 U.S. 45 (1905), which imposed substantive limitations on legislation limiting economic autonomy in favor of health and welfare regulation, adopting, in Justice Holmes's view, the theory of laissez-faire. Id., at 75 (dissenting opinion). The *Lochner* decisions were exemplified by Adkins v. Children's Hospital of District of Columbia, 261 U.S. 525 (1923), in which this Court held it to be an infringement of constitutionally protected liberty of contract to require the employers of adult women to satisfy minimum wage standards. Fourteen years later, West Coast Hotel Co. v. Parrish, 300 U.S. 379 (1937), signaled the demise of *Lochner* by overruling *Adkins*. In the meantime, the Depression had come and, with it, the lesson that seemed unmistakable to most people by 1937, that the interpretation of contractual freedom protected in *Adkins* rested on fundamentally false factual assumptions about the capacity of a relatively unregulated market to satisfy minimal levels of human welfare.... The facts upon which the earlier case had premised a constitutional resolution of social controversy had proven to be untrue, and history's demonstration of their untruth not only justified but required the new choice of constitutional principle that *West Coast Hotel* announced....

The second comparison that 20th century history invites is with the cases employing the separate-but-equal rule for applying the Fourteenth Amendment's equal protection guarantee. They began with Plessy v. Ferguson, 163 U.S. 537 (1896), holding that legislatively mandated racial segregation in public transportation works no denial of equal protection, rejecting the argument that racial separation enforced by the legal machinery of American society treats the black race as inferior. The *Plessy* Court considered "the underlying fallacy of the plaintiff's argument to consist in the assumption that the enforced separation of the two races stamps the colored race with a badge of inferiority. If this be so, it is not by reason of anything found in the act, but solely because the colored race chooses to put that construction upon it." Id., at 551. Whether, as a matter of historical fact, the Justices in the *Plessy* majority believed this or not, see id., at 557, 562 (Harlan, J., dissenting), this understanding of the implication of segregation was the stated justification for the Court's opinion. But this understanding of the facts and the rule it was stated to justify were repudiated in Brown v. Board of Education, 347 U.S. 483 (1954) (Brown I). As one commentator observed, the question before the Court in *Brown* was "whether discrimination inheres in that segregation which is imposed by law in the twentieth century in certain specific states in the American Union. And that question has meaning and can find an answer only on the ground of history and of common knowledge about the facts of life in the times and places aforesaid." Black, The Lawfulness of the Segregation Decisions, 69 Yale L.J. 421, 427 (1960).

The Court in *Brown* addressed these facts of life by observing that whatever may have been the understanding in *Plessy's* time of the power of segregation to stigmatize those who were segregated with a "badge of inferiority," it was clear by 1954 that legally sanctioned segregation had just such an effect, to the point that racially separate public educational facilities were deemed inherently unequal. Society's understanding of the facts upon which a constitutional ruling was sought in 1954 was thus fundamentally different from the basis claimed for the decision in 1896. While we think *Plessy* was wrong the day it was decided, see *Plessy*, supra, 163 U.S. at 552–564 (Harlan, J., dissenting), we must also recognize that the *Plessy* Court's explanation for its decision was so clearly at odds with the facts apparent to the Court in 1954 that the decision to reexamine *Plessy* was on this ground alone not only justified but required.

West Coast Hotel and *Brown* each rested on facts, or an understanding of facts, changed from those which furnished the claimed justifications for the earlier constitutional resolutions. Each case was comprehensible as the Court's response to facts that the country could understand, or had come to understand already, but which the Court of an earlier day, as its own declarations disclosed, had not been able to perceive. As the decisions were thus comprehensible they were also defensible, not merely as the victories of one doctrinal school over another by dint of numbers (victories though they were), but as applications of constitutional principle to facts as they had not been seen by the Court before. In constitutional adjudication as elsewhere in life, changed circumstances may impose new obligations, and the thoughtful part of the Nation could accept each decision to overrule a prior case as a response to the Court's constitutional duty.

Because the cases before us present no such occasion it could be seen as no such response. Because neither the factual underpinnings of Roe's central holding nor our understanding of it has changed..., the Court could not pretend to be reexamining the prior law with any justification beyond a present doctrinal disposition to come out differently from the Court of 1973. To overrule prior law for no other reason than that would run counter to the view repeated in our cases, that a decision to overrule should rest on some special reason over and above the belief that a prior case was wrongly decided.

C. ... [T]he conditions justifying the repudiation of *Adkins* by *West Coast Hotel* and *Plessy* by *Brown* ... suggest the terrible price that would have been paid if the Court had not overruled as it did. In the present cases, however, as our analysis to this point makes clear, the terrible price would be paid for overruling. Our analysis would not be complete, however, without explaining why overruling *Roe's* central holding would not only reach an unjustifiable result under principles of stare decisis, but would seriously weaken the Court's capacity to exercise the judicial power and to function as the Supreme Court of a Nation dedicated to the rule of law. To understand why this would be so it is necessary to understand the source of this Court's authority, the conditions necessary for its preservation, and its relationship to the country's understanding of itself as a constitutional Republic.

The root of American governmental power is revealed most clearly in the instance of the power conferred by the Constitution upon the Judiciary of the United States and specifically upon this Court. As Americans of each succeeding generation are rightly told, the Court cannot buy support for its decisions by spending money and, except to a minor degree, it cannot independently coerce obedience to its decrees. The Court's power lies, rather, in its legitimacy, a product of substance and perception that shows itself in the people's acceptance of the Judiciary as fit to determine what the Nation's law means and to declare what it demands. . . .

. . . The Court must take care to speak and act in ways that allow people to accept its decisions on the terms the Court claims for them, as grounded truly in principle, not as compromises with social and political pressures having, as such, no bearing on the principled choices that the Court is obliged to make. Thus, the Court's legitimacy depends on making legally principled decisions under circumstances in which their principled character is sufficiently plausible to be accepted by the Nation.

The need for principled action to be perceived as such is implicated to some degree whenever this, or any other appellate court, overrules a prior case. . . . [But] the country can accept some correction of error without necessarily questioning the legitimacy of the Court.

In two circumstances, however, the Court would almost certainly fail to receive the benefit of the doubt in overruling prior cases. There is, first, a point beyond which frequent overruling would overtax the country's belief in the Court's good faith. . . . There is a limit to the amount of error that can plausibly be imputed to prior Courts. If that limit should be exceeded, disturbance of prior rulings would be taken as evidence that justifiable reexamination of principle had given way to drives for particular results in the short term. The legitimacy of the Court would fade with the frequency of its vacillation.

That first circumstance . . . [is] hypothetical; the second is to the point here and now. Where, in the performance of its judicial duties, the Court decides a case in such a way as to resolve the sort of intensely divisive controversy reflected in *Roe* and those rare, comparable cases, its decision has a dimension that the resolution of the normal case does not carry. It is the dimension present whenever the Court's interpretation of the Constitution calls the contending sides of a national controversy to end their national division by accepting a common mandate rooted in the Constitution.

The Court is not asked to do this very often, having thus addressed the Nation only twice in our lifetime, in the decisions of *Brown* and *Roe*. But when the Court does act in this way, its decision requires an equally rare precedential force to counter the inevitable efforts to overturn it and to thwart its implementation. Some of those efforts may be mere unprincipled emotional reactions; others may proceed from principles worthy of profound respect. But whatever the premises of opposition may be, only the most convincing justification under accepted standards of precedent could suffice to demonstrate that a later decision overruling the first was anything but a surrender to political pressure, and an unjustified repudiation of the principle on which the Court staked its authority in the first instance. So to overrule under fire in the absence of the most compelling reason to reexamine a watershed decision would subvert the Court's legitimacy beyond any serious question.

The country's loss of confidence in the Judiciary would be underscored by ... another failing.... Some cost will be paid by anyone who approves or implements a constitutional decision where it is unpopular.... To all those who will be so tested by following, the Court implicitly undertakes to remain steadfast, lest in the end a price be paid for nothing. The promise of constancy, once given, binds its maker for as long as the power to stand by the decision survives and the understanding of the issue has not changed so fundamentally as to render the commitment obsolete. From the obligation of this promise this Court cannot and should not assume any exemption when duty requires it to decide a case in conformance with the Constitution. A willing breach of it would be nothing less than a breach of faith, and no Court that broke its faith with the people could sensibly expect credit for principle in the decision by which it did that.

... Unlike the political branches, a Court thus weakened could not seek to regain its position with a new mandate from the voters.... Like the character of an individual, the legitimacy of the Court must be earned over time. So, indeed, must be the character of a Nation of people who aspire to live according to the rule of law. Their belief in themselves as such a people is not readily separable from their understanding of the Court invested with the authority to decide their constitutional cases and speak before all others for their constitutional ideals. If the Court's legitimacy should be undermined, then, so would the country be in its very ability to see itself through its constitutional ideals. The Court's concern with legitimacy is not for the sake of the Court, but for the sake of the Nation to which it is responsible.

The Court's duty in the present cases is clear. In 1973, it confronted the already-divisive issue of governmental power to limit personal choice to undergo abortion, for which it provided a new resolution based on the due process guaranteed by the Fourteenth Amendment. Whether or not a new social consensus is developing on that issue, its divisiveness is no less today than in 1973, and pressure to overrule the decision, like pressure to retain it, has grown only more intense. A decision to overrule *Roe's* essential holding under the existing circumstances would address error, if error there was, at the cost of both profound and unnecessary damage to the Court's legitimacy, and to the Nation's commitment to the rule of law. It is therefore imperative to adhere to the essence of *Roe's* original decision, and we do so today.

IV

... Liberty must not be extinguished for want of a line that is clear. And it falls to us to give some real substance to the woman's liberty to determine whether to carry her pregnancy to full term.

We conclude the line should be drawn at viability, so that before that time the woman has a right to choose to terminate her pregnancy. We adhere to this principle for two reasons. First, as we have said, is the doctrine of stare decisis. Any judicial act of line-drawing may seem somewhat arbitrary, but *Roe* was a reasoned statement, elaborated with great care.... Although we must overrule those parts of *Thornburgh* and *Akron I* which, in our view, are inconsistent with *Roe's* statement that the State has a legitimate interest in promoting the life or potential life of the unborn, the central premise of those cases represents an unbroken commitment by this Court to the essential holding of *Roe*. It is that premise which we reaffirm today.

The second reason is that the concept of viability, as we noted in *Roe*, is the time at which there is a realistic possibility of maintaining and nourishing a life outside the womb, so that the independent existence of the second life can in reason and all fairness be the object of state protection that now overrides the rights of the woman.... [Courts] must justify the lines we draw. And there is no line other than viability which is more workable....

The woman's right to terminate her pregnancy before viability is the most central principle of Roe v. Wade. It is a rule of law and a component of liberty we cannot renounce.

On the other side of the equation is the interest of the State in the protection of potential life. The *Roe* Court recognized the State's "important and legitimate interest in protecting the potentiality of human life."

... Roe v. Wade speaks with clarity in establishing not only the woman's liberty but also the State's "important and legitimate interest in potential life." That portion of the decision in *Roe* has been given too little acknowledgment and implementation by the Court in its subsequent cases. ... [W]e choose to rely upon *Roe*, as against the later cases.

Roe established a trimester framework to govern abortion regulations. Under this elaborate but rigid construct, almost no regulation at all is permitted during the first trimester of pregnancy; regulations designed to protect the woman's health, but not to further the State's interest in potential life, are permitted during the second trimester; and during the third trimester, when the fetus is viable, prohibitions are permitted provided the life or health of the mother is not at stake. Most of our cases since

Roe have involved the application of rules derived from the trimester framework.

The trimester framework no doubt was erected to ensure that the woman's right to choose not become so subordinate to the State's interest in promoting fetal life that her choice exists in theory but not in fact. We do not agree, however, that the trimester approach is necessary to accomplish this objective....

... Even in the earliest stages of pregnancy, the State may enact rules and regulations designed to encourage her to know that there are philosophic and social arguments of great weight that can be brought to bear in favor of continuing the pregnancy to full term and that there are procedures and institutions to allow adoption of unwanted children as well as a certain degree of state assistance if the mother chooses to raise the child herself. "[T]he Constitution does not forbid a State or city, pursuant to democratic processes, from expressing a preference for normal childbirth." Webster v. Reproductive Health Services, 492 U.S. at 511. It follows that States are free to enact laws to provide a reasonable framework for a woman to make a decision that has such profound and lasting meaning. This, too, we find consistent with *Roe's* central premises, and indeed the inevitable consequence of our holding that the State has an interest in protecting the life of the unborn.

We reject the trimester framework, which we do not consider to be part of the essential holding of *Roe*. Measures aimed at ensuring that a woman's choice contemplates the consequences for the fetus do not necessarily interfere with the right recognized in *Roe*, although those measures have been found to be inconsistent with the rigid trimester framework announced in that case. A logical reading of the central holding in *Roe* itself, and a necessary reconciliation of the liberty of the woman and the interest of the State in promoting prenatal life, require, in our view, that we abandon the trimester framework as a rigid prohibition on all previability regulation aimed at the protection of fetal life. The trimester framework suffers from these basic flaws: in its formulation it misconceives the nature of the pregnant woman's interest; and in practice it undervalues the State's interest in potential life, as recognized in *Roe*....

... Numerous forms of state regulation might have the incidental effect of increasing the cost or decreasing the availability of medical care, whether for abortion or any other medical procedure. The fact that a law which serves a valid purpose, one not designed to strike at the right itself, has the incidental effect of making it more difficult or more expensive to procure an abortion cannot be enough to invalidate it. Only where state regulation imposes an undue burden on a woman's ability to make this decision does the power of the State reach into the heart of the liberty protected by the Due Process Clause.

For the most part, the Court's early abortion cases adhered to this view. In Maher v. Roe, 432 U.S. 464, 473–474 (1977), the Court explained: "*Roe* did not declare an unqualified 'constitutional right to an abortion,' as the District Court seemed to think. Rather, the right protects the woman from unduly burdensome interference with her freedom to decide whether to terminate her pregnancy."

These considerations of the nature of the abortion right illustrate that it is an overstatement to describe it as a right to decide whether to have an abortion "without interference from the State." Planned Parenthood of Central Mo. v. Danforth, 428 U.S. 52 (1976). All abortion regulations interfere to some degree with a woman's ability to decide whether to terminate her pregnancy. It is, as a consequence, not surprising that despite the protestations contained in the original *Roe* opinion to the effect that the Court was not recognizing an absolute right, the Court's experience applying the trimester framework has led to the striking down of some abortion regulations which in no real sense deprived women of the ultimate decision.... Not all governmental intrusion is of necessity unwarranted; and that brings us to the other basic flaw in the trimester framework: even in *Roe's* terms, in practice it undervalues the State's interest in the potential life within the woman.

... Before viability, *Roe* and subsequent cases treat all governmental attempts to influence a woman's decision on behalf of the potential life within her as unwarranted. This treatment is, in our judgment, incompatible with the recognition that there is a substantial state interest in potential life throughout pregnancy.

The very notion that the State has a substantial interest in potential life leads to the conclusion that not all regulations must be deemed unwarranted. Not all burdens on the right to decide whether to terminate a pregnancy will be undue. In our view, the undue burden standard is the appropriate means of reconciling the State's interest with the woman's constitutionally protected liberty....

A finding of an undue burden is a shorthand for the conclusion that a state regulation has the purpose or effect of placing a substantial obstacle in the path of a woman seeking an abortion of a nonviable fetus. A statute with this purpose is invalid because the means chosen by the State to further the interest in potential life must be calculated to inform the woman's free choice, not hinder it. And a statute which, while furthering the interest in potential life or some other valid state interest, has the effect of placing a substantial obstacle in the path of a woman's choice cannot be considered a permissible means of serving its legitimate ends....

... What is at stake is the woman's right to make the ultimate decision, not a right to be insulated from all others in doing so. Regulations which do no more than create a structural mechanism by which the State, or the parent or guardian of a minor, may express profound respect for the life of the unborn are permitted, if they are not a substantial obstacle to the woman's exercise of the right to choose. Unless it has that effect on her right of choice, a state measure designed to persuade her to choose childbirth over abortion will be upheld if reasonably related to that goal. Regulations designed to foster the health of a woman seeking an abortion are valid if they do not constitute an undue burden.

... We give this summary:

(a) To protect the central right recognized by Roe v. Wade while at the same time accommodating the State's profound interest in potential life, we will employ the undue burden analysis as explained in this opinion. An undue burden exists, and therefore a provision of law is invalid, if its purpose or effect is to place a substantial obstacle in the path of a woman seeking an abortion before the fetus attains viability.

(b) We reject the rigid trimester framework of Roe v. Wade. To promote the State's profound interest in potential life, throughout pregnancy the State may take measures to ensure that the woman's choice is informed, and measures designed to advance this interest will not be invalidated as long as their purpose is to persuade the woman to choose childbirth over abortion. These measures must not be an undue burden on the right.

(c) As with any medical procedure, the State may enact regulations to further the health or safety of a woman seeking an abortion. Unnecessary health regulations that have the purpose or effect of presenting a substantial obstacle to a woman seeking an abortion impose an undue burden on the right.

(d) Our adoption of the undue burden analysis does not disturb the central holding of Roe v. Wade, and we reaffirm that holding. Regardless of whether exceptions are made for particular circumstances, a State may not prohibit any woman from making the ultimate decision to terminate her pregnancy before viability.

(e) We also reaffirm *Roe's* holding that "subsequent to viability, the State in promoting its interest in the potentiality of human life may, if it chooses, regulate, and even proscribe, abortion except where it is necessary, in appropriate medical judgment, for the preservation of the life or health of the mother." Roe v. Wade, 410 U.S., at 164–165....

V

A. [The Court upholds the definition of a "medical emergency" permitting an immediate abortion based on the Court of Appeal's construction of the definition.]

B. We next consider the informed consent requirement. Except in a medical emergency, the statute requires that at least 24 hours before performing an abortion a physician inform the woman of the nature of the procedure, the health risks of the abortion and of childbirth, and the "probable gestational age of the unborn child." The physician or a qualified nonphysician must inform the woman of the availability of printed materials published by the State describing the fetus and providing information about medical assistance for childbirth, information about child support from the father, and a list of agencies which provide adoption and other services as alternatives to abortion. An abortion may not be performed unless the woman certifies in writing that she has been informed of the availability of these printed materials and has been provided them if she chooses to view them.

Our prior decisions establish that as with any medical procedure, the State may require a woman to give her written informed consent to an abortion. In this respect, the statute is unexceptional. Petitioners challenge the statute's definition of informed consent because it includes the provision of specific information by the doctor and the mandatory 24–hour waiting period. The conclusions reached by a majority of the Justices in the separate opinions filed today and the undue burden standard adopted in this opinion require us to overrule in part some of the Court's past decisions, decisions driven by the trimester framework's prohibition of all previability regulations designed to further the State's interest in fetal life.

In *Akron I*, we invalidated an ordinance which required that a woman seeking an abortion be provided by her physician with specific information "designed to influence the woman's informed choice between abortion or childbirth." ...

To the extent *Akron I* and *Thornburgh* find a constitutional violation when the government requires, as it does here, the giving of truthful, nonmisleading information about the nature of the procedure, the attendant health risks and those of childbirth, and the "probable gestational age" of the fetus, those cases go too far, are inconsistent with *Roe's* acknowledgment of an important interest in potential life, and are overruled.... If the information the State requires to be made available to the woman is truthful and not misleading, the requirement may be permissible.

We also see no reason why the State may not require doctors to inform a woman seeking an abortion of the availability of materials relating to the consequences to the fetus, even when those consequences have no direct relation to her health. An example illustrates the point. We would think it constitutional for the State to require that in order for there to be informed consent to a kidney transplant operation the recipient must be supplied with information about risks to the donor as well as risks to himself or herself. A requirement that the physician make available information similar to that mandated by the statute here was described in *Thornburgh* as "an outright attempt to wedge the Commonwealth's message discouraging abortion into the privacy of the informed-consent dialogue between the woman and her physician." We conclude, however, that informed choice need not be defined in such narrow terms that all considerations of the effect on the fetus are made irrelevant.... [R]equiring that the woman be informed of the availability of information relating to fetal development and the assistance available should she decide to carry the pregnancy to full term is a reasonable measure to ensure an informed choice, one which might cause the woman to choose childbirth over abortion. This requirement cannot be considered a substantial obstacle to obtaining an abortion, and, it follows, there is no undue burden....

All that is left of petitioners' argument is an asserted First Amendment right of a physician not to provide information about the risks of abortion, and childbirth, in a manner mandated by the State. To be sure, the physician's First Amendment rights not to speak are implicated, but only as part of the practice of medicine, subject to reasonable licensing and regulation by the State. We see no constitutional infirmity in the requirement that the physician provide the information mandated by the State here. . . .

Our analysis of Pennsylvania's 24–hour waiting period between the provision of the information deemed necessary to informed consent and the performance of an abortion under the undue burden standard requires us to reconsider the premise behind the decision in *Akron I* invalidating a parallel requirement. In *Akron I* we said: "Nor are we convinced that the State's legitimate concern that the woman's decision be informed is reasonably served by requiring a 24–hour delay as a matter of course." We consider that conclusion to be wrong. The idea that important decisions will be more informed and deliberate if they follow some period of reflection does not strike us as unreasonable, particularly where the statute directs that important information become part of the background of the decision. The statute, as construed by the Court of Appeals, permits avoidance of the waiting period in the event of a medical emergency and the record evidence shows that in the vast majority of cases, a 24–hour delay does not create any appreciable health risk. In theory, at least, the waiting period is a reasonable measure to implement the State's interest in protecting the life of the unborn, a measure that does not amount to an undue burden.

Whether the mandatory 24–hour waiting period is nonetheless invalid because in practice it is a substantial obstacle to a woman's choice to terminate her pregnancy is a closer question. The findings of fact by the District Court indicate that because of the distances many women must travel to reach an abortion provider, the practical effect will often be a delay of much more than a day because the waiting period requires that a woman seeking an abortion make at least two visits to the doctor. The District Court also found that in many instances this will increase the exposure of women seeking abortions to "the harassment and hostility of anti-abortion protestors demonstrating outside a clinic." As a result, the District Court found that for those women who have the fewest financial resources, those who must travel long distances, and those who have difficulty explaining their whereabouts to husbands, employers, or others, the 24–hour waiting period will be "particularly burdensome."

These findings are troubling in some respects, but they do not demonstrate that the waiting period constitutes an undue burden. We do not doubt that, as the District Court held, the waiting period has the effect of "increasing the cost and risk of delay of abortions," but the District Court did not conclude that the increased costs and potential delays amount to substantial obstacles. Rather, applying the trimester framework's strict prohibition of all regulation designed to promote the State's interest in potential life before viability, the District Court concluded that the waiting period does not further the state "interest in maternal health" and "infringes the physician's discretion to exercise sound medical judgment." Yet, as we have stated, under the undue burden standard a State is permitted to enact persuasive measures which favor childbirth over abortion, even if those measures do not further a health interest. . . .

We also disagree with the District Court's conclusion that the "particularly burdensome" effects of the waiting period on some women require its invalidation. A particular burden is not of necessity a substantial obstacle. Whether a burden falls on a particular group is a distinct inquiry from whether it is a substantial obstacle even as to the women in that group. And the District Court did not conclude that the waiting period is such an obstacle even for the women who are most burdened by it. Hence, on the record before us, and in the context of this facial challenge, we are not convinced that the 24–hour waiting period constitutes an undue burden. . . .

C. Section 3209 of Pennsylvania's abortion law provides, except in cases of medical emergency, that no physician shall perform an abortion on a married woman without receiving a signed statement from the woman that she has notified her spouse that she is about to undergo an abortion. The woman has the option of providing an alternative signed statement certifying that her husband is not the man who impregnated her; that her husband could not be located; that the pregnancy is the result of spousal sexual assault which she has reported; or that the woman believes that notifying her husband will cause him or someone else to inflict bodily injury upon her. A physician who performs an abortion on a married woman without receiving the appropriate signed statement will have his or her license revoked, and is liable to the husband for damages.

The District Court heard the testimony of numerous expert witnesses, and made detailed findings of fact regarding the effect of this statute. These included:

"273. The vast majority of women consult their husbands prior to deciding to terminate their pregnancy. . . .

"279. The 'bodily injury' exception could not be invoked by a married woman whose husband, if notified, would, in her reasonable belief, threaten to (a) publicize her intent to have an abortion to family, friends or acquaintances; (b) retaliate against her in future child custody or divorce proceedings; (c) inflict psychological intimidation or emotional harm upon her, her children or other persons; (d) inflict bodily harm on other persons such as children, family members or other loved ones; or (e) use his control over finances to deprive [her] of necessary monies for herself or her children. . . .

"281. Studies reveal that family violence occurs in two million families in the United States. This figure, however, is a conservative one that substantially understates (because battering is usually not reported until it reaches life-threatening proportions) the actual number of families affected by domestic violence. In fact, researchers estimate that one of every two women will be battered at some time in their life. . . .

"282. A wife may not elect to notify her husband of her intention to have an abortion for a variety of reasons, including the husband's illness, concern about her own health, the imminent failure of the marriage, or the husband's absolute opposition to the abortion....

"283. The required filing of the spousal consent form would require plaintiff-clinics to change their counseling procedures and force women to reveal their most intimate decision-making on pain of criminal sanctions. The confidentiality of these revelations could not be guaranteed, since the woman's records are not immune from subpoena....

"284. Women of all class levels, educational backgrounds, and racial, ethnic and religious groups are battered....

"285. Wife-battering or abuse can take on many physical and psychological forms. The nature and scope of the battering can cover a broad range of actions and be gruesome and torturous....

"286. Married women, victims of battering, have been killed in Pennsylvania and throughout the United States....

"287. Battering can often involve a substantial amount of sexual abuse, including marital rape and sexual mutilation....

"288. In a domestic abuse situation, it is common for the battering husband to also abuse the children in an attempt to coerce the wife....

"289. Mere notification of pregnancy is frequently a flashpoint for battering and violence within the family. The number of battering incidents is high during the pregnancy and often the worst abuse can be associated with pregnancy.... The battering husband may deny parentage and use the pregnancy as an excuse for abuse....

"290. Secrecy typically shrouds abusive families. Family members are instructed not to tell anyone, especially police or doctors, about the abuse and violence. Battering husbands often threaten their wives or her children with further abuse if she tells an outsider of the violence and tells her that nobody will believe her. A battered woman, therefore, is highly unlikely to disclose the violence against her for fear of retaliation by the abuser....

"291. Even when confronted directly by medical personnel or other helping professionals, battered women often will not admit to the battering because they have not admitted to themselves that they are battered....

"294. A woman in a shelter or a safe house unknown to her husband is not 'reasonably likely' to have bodily harm inflicted upon her by her batterer, however her attempt to notify her husband pursuant to section 3209 could accidentally disclose her whereabouts to her husband. Her fear of future ramifications would be realistic under the circumstances.

"295. Marital rape is rarely discussed with others or reported to law enforcement authorities, and of those reported only few are prosecuted. . . .

"296. It is common for battered women to have sexual intercourse with their husbands to avoid being battered. While this type of coercive sexual activity would be spousal sexual assault as defined by the Act, many women may not consider it to be so and others would fear disbelief. . . .

"297. The marital rape exception to section 3209 cannot be claimed by women who are victims of coercive sexual behavior other than penetration. The 90–day reporting requirement of the spousal sexual assault statute, 18 Pa.Con.Stat.Ann. § 3218(c), further narrows the class of sexually abused wives who can claim the exception, since many of these women may be psychologically unable to discuss or report the rape for several years after the incident. . . .

"298. Because of the nature of the battering relationship, battered women are unlikely to avail themselves of the exceptions to section 3209 of the Act, regardless of whether the section applies to them." 744 F.Supp., at 1360–1362 (footnote omitted).

These findings are supported by studies of domestic violence. The American Medical Association (AMA) has published a summary of the recent research in this field, which indicates that in an average 12–month period in this country, approximately two million women are the victims of severe assaults by their male partners. In a 1985 survey, women reported that nearly one of every eight husbands had assaulted their wives during the past year. The AMA views these figures as "marked underestimates," because the nature of these incidents discourages women from reporting them, and because surveys typically exclude the very poor, those who do not speak English well, and women who are homeless or in institutions or hospitals when the survey is conducted. According to the AMA, "[r]esearchers on family violence agree that the true incidence of partner violence is probably double the above estimates; or four million severely assaulted women per year. Studies on prevalence suggest that from one-fifth to one-third of all women will be physically assaulted by a partner or ex-partner during their lifetime." AMA Council on Scientific Affairs, Violence Against Women 7 (1991) (emphasis in original). Thus on an average day in the United States, nearly 11,000 women are severely assaulted by their male partners. Many of these incidents involve sexual assault. Id., at 3–4; Shields & Hanneke, Battered Wives' Reactions to Marital Rape, in The Dark Side of Families: Current Family Violence Research 131, 144 (D. Finkelhor, R. Gelles, G. Hataling, & M. Straus eds. 1983). In families where wifebeating takes place, moreover, child abuse is often present as well.

Other studies fill in the rest of this troubling picture. Physical violence is only the most visible form of abuse. Psychological abuse, particularly forced social and economic isolation of women, is also common. L. Walker, The Battered Woman Syndrome 27–28 (1984). Many victims of domestic violence remain with their abusers, perhaps because they perceive no superior alternative. Many abused women who find temporary refuge in shelters return to their husbands, in large part because they have no other source of income. Returning to one's abuser can be dangerous. Recent Federal Bureau of Investigation statistics disclose that 8.8 percent of all homicide victims in the United States are killed by their spouses. Mercy & Saltzman, Fatal Violence Among Spouses in the United States, 1976–85, 79 Am.J.Public Health 595 (1989). Thirty percent of female homicide victims are killed by their male partners. Domestic Violence: Terrorism in the Home, Hearing before the Subcommittee on Children, Family, Drugs and Alcoholism of the Senate Committee on Labor and Human Resources, 101st Cong., 2d Sess., 3 (1990).

The limited research that has been conducted with respect to notifying one's husband about an abortion, although involving samples too small to be representative, also supports the District Court's findings of fact. The vast majority of women notify their male partners of their decision to obtain an abortion. In many cases in which married women do not notify their husbands, the pregnancy is the result of an extramarital affair. Where the husband is the father, the primary reason women do not notify their husbands is that the husband and wife are experiencing marital difficulties, often accompanied by incidents of violence.

This information and the District Court's findings reinforce what common sense would suggest. In well-functioning marriages, spouses discuss important intimate decisions such as whether to bear a child. But there are millions of women in this country who are the victims of regular physical and psychological abuse at the hands of their husbands. Should these women become pregnant, they may have very good reasons for not wishing to inform their husbands of their decision to obtain an abortion. Many may have justifiable fears of physical abuse, but may be no less fearful of the consequences of reporting prior abuse to the Commonwealth of Pennsylvania. Many may have a reasonable fear that notifying their husbands will provoke further instances of child abuse; these women are not exempt from § 3209's notification requirement. Many may fear devastating forms of psychological abuse from their husbands . . . [that] may act as even more of a deterrent to notification than the possibility of physical violence, but women who are the victims of the abuse are not exempt from § 3209's notification requirement. And many women who are pregnant as a result of sexual assaults by their husbands will be unable to avail themselves of the exception for spousal sexual assault, because the exception requires that the woman have notified law enforcement authorities within 90 days of the assault, and her husband will be notified of her report once an investigation begins. If anything in this field is certain, it is that victims of spousal sexual assault are extremely reluctant to report the abuse to the government; hence, a great many spousal rape victims will not be exempt from the notification requirement imposed by § 3209.

The spousal notification requirement is thus likely to prevent a significant number of women from obtaining an abortion. It does not merely make abortions a little more difficult or expensive to obtain; for many women, it will impose a substantial obstacle. We must not blind ourselves to the fact that the significant number of women who fear for their safety and the safety of their children are likely to be deterred from procuring an abortion as surely as if the Commonwealth had outlawed abortion in all cases.

Respondents attempt to avoid the conclusion that § 3209 is invalid by pointing out that it imposes almost no burden at all for the vast majority of women seeking abortions.... [O]nly about 20 percent of the women who obtain abortions are married.... [O]f these women about 95 percent notify their husbands of their own volition. Thus, respondents argue, the effects of § 3209 are felt by only one percent of the women who obtain abortions. Respondents argue that since some of these women will be able to notify their husbands without adverse consequences or will qualify for one of the exceptions, the statute affects fewer than one percent of women seeking abortions. For this reason, it is asserted, the statute cannot be invalid on its face....We disagree....

The analysis does not end with the one percent of women upon whom the statute operates; it begins there. Legislation is measured for consistency with the Constitution by its impact on those whose conduct it affects.... The proper focus of constitutional inquiry is the group for whom the law is a restriction, not the group for whom the law is irrelevant....

We recognize that a husband has a "deep and proper concern and interest ... in his wife's pregnancy and in the growth and development of the fetus she is carrying." [Planned Parenthood of Central Missouri v. Danforth, 428 U.S. 52, 69 (1976).] With regard to the children he has fathered and raised, the Court has recognized his "cognizable and substantial" interest in their custody. If these cases concerned a State's ability to require the mother to notify the father before taking some action with respect to a living child raised by both, therefore, it would be reasonable to conclude ... that the father's interest in the welfare of the child and the mother's interest are equal.

... [H]owever, ... [i]t is an inescapable biological fact that state regulation with respect to the child a woman is carrying will have a far greater impact on the mother's liberty than on the father's. The effect of state regulation on a woman's protected liberty is doubly deserving of scrutiny in such a case, as the State has touched not only upon the private sphere of the family but upon the very bodily integrity of the pregnant woman. The Court has held that "when the wife and the husband disagree on this decision, the view of only one of the two marriage partners can prevail. Inasmuch as it is the woman who physically bears the child and who is the more directly and immediately affected by the pregnancy, as between the two, the balance weighs in her favor." [Planned Parenthood of Central Missouri v. Danforth, 428 U.S. 52, 71 (1976)]. This conclusion rests upon the basic nature of marriage and the nature of our Constitution: "[T]he marital couple is not an independent entity with a mind and heart of its own, but an association of two individuals each with a separate intellectual and emotional makeup. If the right of privacy means anything, it is the right of the *individual*, married or single, to be free from unwarranted governmental intrusion into matters so fundamentally affecting a person as the decision whether to bear or beget a child." Eisenstadt v. Baird, 405 U.S., at 453 (emphasis in original). The Constitution protects individuals, men and women alike, from unjustified state interference, even when that interference is enacted into law for the benefit of their spouses.

There was a time, not so long ago, when a different understanding of the family and of the Constitution prevailed. In Bradwell v. State, 16 Wall. 130 (1873), three Members of this Court reaffirmed the common-law principle that "a woman had no legal existence separate from her husband, who was regarded as her head and representative in the social state; and, notwithstanding some recent modifications of this civil status, many of the special rules of law flowing from and dependent upon this cardinal principle still exist in full force in most States." Only one generation has passed since this Court observed that "woman is still regarded as the center of home and family life," with attendant "special responsibilities" that precluded full and independent legal status under the Constitution. Hoyt v. Florida, 368 U.S. 57, 62 (1961). These views, of course, are no longer consistent with our understanding of the family, the individual, or the Constitution.

In keeping with our rejection of the common-law understanding of a woman's role within the family, the Court held in *Danforth* that the Constitution does not permit a State to require a married woman to obtain her husband's consent before undergoing an abortion. 428 U.S., at 69. The principles that guided the Court in *Danforth* should be our guides today. . . .

The husband's interest in the life of the child his wife is carrying does not permit the State to empower him with this troubling degree of authority over his wife. The contrary view leads to consequences reminiscent of the common law. . . . A State may not give to a man the kind of dominion over his wife that parents exercise over their children.

Section 3209 embodies a view of marriage consonant with the common-law status of married women but repugnant to our present understanding of marriage and of the nature of the rights secured by the Constitution. Women do not lose their constitutionally protected liberty when they marry. . . .

[The opinion's discussion of the parental consent provision for minors and of the record keeping and reporting requirements of the statute is omitted].

VI

Our Constitution is a covenant running from the first generation of Americans to us and then to future generations. It is a coherent succession. Each generation must learn anew that the Constitution's written terms embody ideas and aspirations that must survive more ages than one. We accept our responsibility not to retreat from interpreting the full meaning of the covenant in light of all of our precedents. We invoke it once again to define the freedom guaranteed by the Constitution's own promise, the promise of liberty. . . .

JUSTICE STEVENS, concurring in part and dissenting in part.

The portions of the Court's opinion that I have joined are more important than those with which I disagree. . . .

I

The Court is unquestionably correct in concluding that the doctrine of stare decisis has controlling significance in a case of this kind, notwithstanding an individual Justice's concerns about the merits. The central holding of Roe v. Wade, has been a "part of our law" for almost two decades. It was a natural sequel to the protection of individual liberty established in Griswold v. Connecticut. The societal costs of overruling *Roe* at this late date would be enormous. *Roe* is an integral part of a correct understanding of both the concept of liberty and the basic equality of men and women. . . .

II

My disagreement with the joint opinion begins with its understanding of the trimester framework established in *Roe*. Contrary to the suggestion of the joint opinion, it is not a "contradiction" to recognize that the State may have a legitimate interest in potential human life and, at the same time, to conclude that that interest does not justify the regulation of abortion before viability. . . .

First, it is clear that, in order to be legitimate, the State's interest must be secular; consistent with the First Amendment the State may not promote a theological or sectarian interest. Moreover, . . . the state interest in potential human life is not an interest in loco parentis, for the fetus is not a person. . . .

Weighing the State's interest in potential life and the woman's liberty interest, I agree with the joint opinion that the State may " ' " expres[s] a preference for normal childbirth," that the State may take steps to ensure that a woman's choice "is thoughtful and informed," ' " and that "States are free to enact laws to provide a reasonable framework for a woman to make a decision that has such profound and lasting meaning." Serious questions arise, however, when a State attempts to "persuade the woman to choose childbirth over abortion." Decisional autonomy must limit the State's power to inject into a woman's most personal deliberations its own views of what is best. . . .

. . . Pa.Cons.Stat. §§ 3205(a)(2)(i)-(iii) (1990) of the Pennsylvania statute are unconstitutional. Those sections require a physician or counselor to provide the woman with a range of materials clearly designed to persuade her to choose not to undergo the abortion. While the Commonwealth is free, pursuant to § 3208 of the Pennsylvania law, to produce and disseminate such material, the Commonwealth may not inject such information into the woman's deliberations just as she is weighing such an important choice.

Under this same analysis, §§ 3205(a)(1)(i) and (iii) of the Pennsylvania statute are constitutional. Those sections, which require the physician to inform a woman of the nature and risks of the abortion procedure and the medical risks of carrying to term, are neutral requirements comparable to those imposed in other medical procedures. Those sections indicate no effort by the Commonwealth to influence the woman's choice in any way. If anything, such requirements enhance, rather than skew, the woman's decisionmaking.

III

The 24–hour waiting period required by §§ 3205(a)(1)-(2) of the Pennsylvania statute raises even more serious concerns. Such a requirement arguably furthers the Commonwealth's interests in two ways, neither of which is constitutionally permissible.

First, it may be argued that the 24–hour delay is justified by the mere fact that it is likely to reduce the number of abortions, thus furthering the Commonwealth's interest in potential life. But such an argument would justify any form of coercion that placed an obstacle in the woman's path. The Commonwealth cannot further its interests by simply wearing down the ability of the pregnant woman to exercise her constitutional right.

Second, it can more reasonably be argued that the 24–hour delay furthers the Commonwealth's interest in ensuring that the woman's decision is informed and thoughtful. But there is no evidence that the mandated delay benefits women or that it is necessary to enable the physician to convey any relevant information to the patient. The mandatory delay thus appears to rest on outmoded and unacceptable assumptions about the decisionmaking capacity of women. While there are well-established and consistently maintained reasons for the Commonwealth to view with skepticism the ability of minors to make decisions, none of those reasons applies to an adult woman's decisionmaking ability. . . .

In the alternative, the delay requirement may be premised on the belief that the decision to terminate a pregnancy is presumptively wrong. This premise is illegitimate. Those who disagree vehemently about the legality and morality of abortion agree about one thing: The decision to terminate a pregnancy is profound and difficult. No person undertakes such a decision lightly—and States may not presume that a woman has failed to reflect adequately merely because her conclusion differs from the State's preference. A woman who has, in the privacy of her thoughts and conscience, weighed the options and made her decision cannot be forced to reconsider all, simply because the State believes she has come to the wrong conclusion.

Part of the constitutional liberty to choose is the equal dignity to which each of us is entitled. A woman who decides to terminate her pregnancy is entitled to the same respect as a woman who decides to carry the fetus to term. The mandatory waiting period denies women that equal respect.

IV

In my opinion, a correct application of the "undue burden" standard leads to the same conclusion concerning the constitutionality of these requirements. A state-imposed burden on the exercise of a constitutional right is measured both by its effects and by its character....

The 24–hour delay requirement fails both parts of this test. The findings of the District Court establish the severity of the burden that the 24–hour delay imposes on many pregnant women. Yet even in those cases in which the delay is not especially onerous, it is, in my opinion, "undue" because there is no evidence that such a delay serves a useful and legitimate purpose....

The counseling provisions are similarly infirm....

JUSTICE BLACKMUN, concurring in part, concurring in the judgment in part, and dissenting in part.

I join Parts I, II, III, V–A, V–C, and VI of the joint opinion of JUSTICES O'CONNOR, KENNEDY, AND SOUTER, ante.

Three years ago, in *Webster*, four Members of this Court appeared poised to "cas[t] into darkness the hopes and visions of every woman in this country" who had come to believe that the Constitution guaranteed her the right to reproductive choice. Id., at 557 (Blackmun, J., dissenting). All that remained between the promise of *Roe* and the darkness of the plurality was a single, flickering flame. Decisions since *Webster* gave little reason to hope that this flame would cast much light. But now, just when so many expected the darkness to fall, the flame has grown bright.

I do not underestimate the significance of today's joint opinion. Yet I remain steadfast in my belief that the right to reproductive choice is entitled to the full protection afforded by this Court before *Webster*. And I fear for the darkness as four Justices anxiously await the single vote necessary to extinguish the light.

I

Make no mistake, the joint opinion of Justices O'Connor, Kennedy, and Souter is an act of personal courage and constitutional principle. In contrast to previous decisions in which Justices O'Connor and Kennedy postponed reconsideration of *Roe*, the authors of the joint opinion today join Justice Stevens and me in concluding that "the essential holding of Roe v. Wade should be retained and once again reaffirmed." In brief, five Members of this Court today recognize that "the Constitution protects a woman's right to terminate her pregnancy in its early stages." ...

In striking down the Pennsylvania statute's spousal notification requirement, the Court has established a framework for evaluating abortion regulations that responds to the social context of women facing issues of reproductive choice. . . .

Lastly, while I believe that the joint opinion errs in failing to invalidate the other regulations, I am pleased that the joint opinion has not ruled out the possibility that these regulations may be shown to impose an unconstitutional burden. The joint opinion makes clear that its specific holdings are based on the insufficiency of the record before it. I am confident that in the future evidence will be produced to show that "in a large fraction of the cases in which [these regulations are] relevant, [they] will operate as a substantial obstacle to a woman's choice to undergo an abortion."

II . . .

A . . .

State restrictions on abortion violate a woman's right of privacy in two ways. First, compelled continuation of a pregnancy infringes upon a woman's right to bodily integrity by imposing substantial physical intrusions and significant risks of physical harm. . . .

Further, when the State restricts a woman's right to terminate her pregnancy, it deprives a woman of the right to make her own decision about reproduction and family planning—critical life choices that this Court long has deemed central to the right to privacy. . . . Because motherhood has a dramatic impact on a woman's educational prospects, employment opportunities, and self-determination, restrictive abortion laws deprive her of basic control over her life. For these reasons, "the decision whether or not to beget or bear a child" lies at "the very heart of this cluster of constitutionally protected choices." [*Carey*, 431 U.S. at 685].

A State's restrictions on a woman's right to terminate her pregnancy also implicate constitutional guarantees of gender equality. State restrictions on abortion compel women to continue pregnancies they otherwise might terminate. By restricting the right to terminate pregnancies, the State conscripts women's bodies into its service, forcing women to continue their pregnancies, suffer the pains of childbirth, and in most instances, provide years of maternal care. The State does not compensate women for their services; instead, it assumes that they owe this duty as a matter of course. This assumption—that women can simply be forced to accept the "natural" status and incidents of motherhood—appears to rest upon a conception of women's role that has triggered the protection of the Equal Protection Clause. The joint opinion recognizes that these assumptions about women's place in society "are no longer consistent with our understanding of the family, the individual, or the Constitution."

B . . .

In my view, application of [*Roe's*] analytical framework is no less warranted than when it was approved by seven Members of this Court in *Roe*. Strict scrutiny of state limitations on reproductive choice still offers the most secure protection of the woman's right to make her own reproductive decisions, free from state coercion. No majority of this Court has ever agreed upon an alternative approach. The factual premises of the trimester framework have not been undermined, and the *Roe* framework is far more administrable, and far less manipulable, than the "undue burden" standard adopted by the joint opinion.

Nonetheless, three criticisms of the trimester framework continue to be uttered. First, the trimester framework is attacked because its key elements do not appear in the text of the Constitution. My response to this attack ... [is the same as in *Webster*, 492 U.S. at 548:]

> "Were this a true concern, we would have to abandon most of our constitutional jurisprudence. [T]he 'critical elements' of countless constitutional doctrines nowhere appear in the Constitution's text.... The Constitution makes no mention, for example, of the First Amendment's 'actual malice' standard for proving certain libels, see New York Times Co. v. Sullivan, 376 U.S. 254 (1964).... Similarly, the Constitution makes no mention of the rational-basis test, or the specific verbal formulations of intermediate and strict scrutiny by which this Court evaluates claims under the Equal Protection Clause. The reason is simple. Like the *Roe* framework, these tests or standards are not, and do not purport to be, rights protected by the Constitution. Rather, they are judge-made methods for evaluating and measuring the strength and scope of constitutional rights or for balancing the constitutional rights of individuals against the competing interests of government."

The second criticism is that the framework more closely resembles a regulatory code than a body of constitutional doctrine. Again, my answer remains the same....

The final, and more genuine, criticism of the trimester framework is that it fails to find the State's interest in potential human life compelling throughout pregnancy. No Member of this Court—nor for that matter, the Solicitor General, Tr. of Oral Arg. 42—has ever questioned our holding in *Roe* that an abortion is not "the termination of life entitled to Fourteenth Amendment protection." 410 U.S., at 159. Accordingly, a State's interest in protecting fetal life is not grounded in the Constitution. Nor, consistent with our Establishment Clause, can it be a theological or sectarian interest. It is, instead, a legitimate interest grounded in humanitarian or pragmatic concerns.

But while a State has "legitimate interests from the outset of the pregnancy in protecting the health of the woman and the life of the fetus that may become a child," legitimate interests are not enough. To overcome the burden of strict scrutiny, the interests must be compelling.... Again, I stand by [my views in] *Webster*:

> "... The viability line reflects the biological facts and truths of fetal development; it marks that threshold moment prior to which a fetus cannot survive separate from the woman and cannot reasonably and objectively be regarded as a subject of rights or interests distinct from, or paramount to, those of the pregnant woman. At the same

time, the viability standard takes account of the undeniable fact that as the fetus evolves into its postnatal form, and as it loses its dependence on the uterine environment, the State's interest in the fetus' potential human life, and in fostering a regard for human life in general, becomes compelling. . . ."

C. Application of the strict scrutiny standard results in the invalidation of all the challenged provisions. Indeed, as this Court has invalidated virtually identical provisions in prior cases, stare decisis requires that we again strike them down. . . .

III

At long last, the Chief Justice and those who have joined him admit it. Gone are the contentions that the issue need not be (or has not been) considered. There, on the first page, for all to see, is what was expected: "We believe that *Roe* was wrongly decided, and that it can and should be overruled consistently with our traditional approach to stare decisis in constitutional cases." If there is much reason to applaud the advances made by the joint opinion today, there is far more to fear from the Chief Justice's opinion.

The Chief Justice's criticism of *Roe* follows from his stunted conception of individual liberty. . . . [H]e . . . construe[s] this Court's personal-liberty cases as establishing only a laundry list of particular rights, rather than a principled account of how these particular rights are grounded in a more general right of privacy. This constricted view is reinforced by the Chief Justice's exclusive reliance on tradition as a source of fundamental rights. . . . In the Chief Justice's world, a woman considering whether to terminate a pregnancy is entitled to no more protection than adulterers, murderers, and so-called sexual deviates.[11] Given the Chief Justice's exclusive reliance on tradition, people using contraceptives seem the next likely candidate for his list of outcasts

Even more shocking than the Chief Justice's cramped notion of individual liberty is his complete omission of any discussion of the effects that compelled childbirth and motherhood have on women's lives. . . . The Chief Justice's view of the State's compelling interest in maternal health has less to do with health than it does with compelling women to be maternal. . . .

Under his standard, States can ban abortion if that ban is rationally related to a legitimate state interest—a standard which the United States calls "deferential, but not toothless." Yet when pressed at oral argument to describe the teeth, the best protection that the Solicitor General could offer to women was that a prohibition, enforced by criminal penalties, *with no exception for the life of the mother*, "could raise very serious questions." . . .

Even if it is somehow "irrational" for a State to require a woman to risk her life for her child, what protection is offered for women who become pregnant through rape or incest? Is there anything arbitrary or capricious

---

11. Obviously, I do not share the Chief Justice's views of homosexuality as sexual deviance. See Bowers, 478 U.S., at 202–203 n. 2 (Blackmun, J., dissenting).

about a State's prohibiting the sins of the father from being visited upon his offspring?[12]

But, we are reassured, there is always the protection of the democratic process. While there is much to be praised about our democracy, our country since its founding has recognized that there are certain fundamental liberties that are not to be left to the whims of an election. A woman's right to reproductive choice is one of those fundamental liberties. Accordingly, that liberty need not seek refuge at the ballot box.

IV

In one sense, the Court's approach is worlds apart from that of the Chief Justice and Justice Scalia. And yet, in another sense, the distance between the two approaches is short—the distance is but a single vote.

I am 83 years old. I cannot remain on this Court forever, and when I do step down, the confirmation process for my successor well may focus on the issue before us today. That, I regret, may be exactly where the choice between the two worlds will be made.

CHIEF JUSTICE REHNQUIST, with whom JUSTICE WHITE, JUSTICE SCALIA, and JUSTICE THOMAS join, concurring in the judgment in part and dissenting in part.

The joint opinion, following its newly minted variation on stare decisis, retains the outer shell of Roe v. Wade, 410 U.S. 113 (1973), but beats a wholesale retreat from the substance of that case. We believe that *Roe* was wrongly decided, and . . . should be overruled. . . . We would . . . uphold the challenged provisions of the Pennsylvania statute in their entirety.

I . . .

In arguing that this Court should invalidate each of the provisions at issue, petitioners insist that we reaffirm our decision in Roe v. Wade, supra, in which we held unconstitutional a Texas statute making it a crime to procure an abortion except to save the life of the mother.[1] . . . [A]s the

---

12. Justice Scalia urges the Court to "get out of this area," and leave questions regarding abortion entirely to the States. Putting aside the fact that what he advocates is nothing short of an abdication by the Court of its constitutional responsibilities, Justice Scalia is uncharacteristically naive if he thinks that overruling *Roe* and holding that restrictions on a woman's right to an abortion are subject only to rational-basis review will enable the Court henceforth to avoid reviewing abortion-related issues. State efforts to regulate and prohibit abortion in a post-*Roe* world undoubtedly would raise a host of distinct and important constitutional questions meriting review by this Court. For

example, does the Eighth Amendment impose any limits on the degree or kind of punishment a State can inflict upon physicians who perform, or women who undergo, abortions? What effect would differences among States in their approaches to abortion have on a woman's right to engage in interstate travel? Does the First Amendment permit States that choose not to criminalize abortion to ban all advertising providing information about where and how to obtain abortions?

1. Two years after *Roe*, the West German constitutional court, by contrast, struck down a law liberalizing access to abortion on the grounds that life developing within the

Court of Appeals found, the state of our post-*Roe* decisional law dealing with the regulation of abortion is confusing and uncertain, indicating that a reexamination of that line of cases is in order. Unfortunately for those who must apply this Court's decisions, the reexamination undertaken today leaves the Court no less divided than beforehand. Although they reject the trimester framework that formed the underpinning of *Roe*, Justices O'Connor, Kennedy, and Souter adopt a revised undue burden standard to analyze the challenged regulations. We conclude, however, that such an outcome is an unjustified constitutional compromise, one which leaves the Court in a position to closely scrutinize all types of abortion regulations despite the fact that it lacks the power to do so under the Constitution.

In *Roe*, the Court opined that the State "does have an important and legitimate interest in preserving and protecting the health of the pregnant woman, ... and that it has still another important and legitimate interest in protecting the potentiality of human life." 410 U.S., at 162 (emphasis omitted).... But while the language and holdings of these cases appeared to leave States free to regulate abortion procedures in a variety of ways, later decisions based on them have found considerably less latitude for such regulations than might have been expected.

For example, after *Roe*, many States have sought to protect their young citizens by requiring that a minor seeking an abortion involve her parents in the decision ... In a number of decisions, however, the Court has substantially limited the States in their ability to impose such requirements....

We have treated parental *consent* provisions even more harshly. Three years after *Roe*, we invalidated a Missouri regulation requiring that an unmarried woman under the age of 18 obtain the consent of one of her parents before proceeding with an abortion.... In light of Bellotti [v. Baird, 443 U.S. 622 (1979),] we have upheld one parental consent regulation which incorporated a judicial bypass option we viewed as sufficient, see Planned Parenthood Assn. of Kansas City, Mo., Inc. v. Ashcroft, 462 U.S. 476 (1983), but have invalidated another because of our belief that the judicial procedure did not satisfy the dictates of *Bellotti*....

States have also regularly tried to ensure that a woman's decision to have an abortion is an informed and well-considered one. In *Danforth*, we upheld a requirement that a woman sign a consent form prior to her abortion, and observed that "it is desirable and imperative that [the decision] be made with full knowledge of its nature and consequences." Since that case, however, we have twice invalidated state statutes designed to impart such knowledge to a woman seeking an abortion....

womb is constitutionally protected. Judgment of February 25, 1975, 39 BVerfGE 1 (translated in Jonas & Gorby, West German Abortion Decision: A Contrast to Roe v. Wade, 9 John Marshall J.Prac. & Proc. 605 (1976)). In 1988, the Canadian Supreme Court followed reasoning similar to that of *Roe* in striking down a law that restricted abortion. Morgentaler v. Queen, 1 S.C.R. 30, 44 D.L.R. 4th 385 (1988).

We have not allowed States much leeway to regulate even the actual abortion procedure. Although a State can require that second-trimester abortions be performed in outpatient clinics, see Simopoulos v. Virginia, 462 U.S. 506 (1983), we concluded in *Akron* and *Ashcroft* that a State could not require that such abortions be performed only in hospitals. . . .

Although *Roe* allowed state regulation after the point of viability to protect the potential life of the fetus, the Court subsequently rejected attempts to regulate in this manner. In Colautti v. Franklin, 439 U.S. 379 (1979), the Court struck down a statute that governed the determination of viability. In the process, we made clear that the trimester framework incorporated only one definition of viability—ours—as we forbade States to decide that a certain objective indicator—"be it weeks of gestation or fetal weight or any other single factor"—should govern the definition of viability. . . .

Dissents in these cases expressed the view that the Court was expanding upon *Roe* in imposing ever greater restrictions on the States. And, when confronted with state regulations of this type in past years, the Court has become increasingly more divided: The three most recent abortion cases have not commanded a Court opinion. See Ohio v. Akron Center for Reproductive Health, 497 U.S. 502 (1990); Hodgson v. Minnesota, 497 U.S. 417 (1990); Webster v. Reproductive Health Services, 492 U.S. 490 (1989).

. . . This state of confusion and disagreement warrants reexamination of the "fundamental right" accorded to a woman's decision to abort a fetus in *Roe*, with its concomitant requirement that any state regulation of abortion survive "strict scrutiny." See Payne v. Tennessee, 501 U.S. 808, 827–828 (1991) (observing that reexamination of constitutional decisions is appropriate when those decisions have generated uncertainty and failed to provide clear guidance, because "correction through legislative action is practically impossible" (internal quotation marks omitted)). . . .

In construing the phrase "liberty" incorporated in the Due Process Clause of the Fourteenth Amendment, we have recognized that its meaning extends beyond freedom from physical restraint. In Pierce v. Society of Sisters, we held that it included a parent's right to send a child to private school; in Meyer v. Nebraska, we held that it included a right to teach a foreign language in a parochial school. Building on these cases, we have held that the term "liberty" includes a right to marry, *Loving*; a right to procreate, *Skinner*; and a right to use contraceptives, *Griswold*; *Eisenstadt*. But a reading of these opinions makes clear that they do not endorse any all-encompassing "right of privacy."

In Roe v. Wade, the Court recognized a "guarantee of personal privacy" which "is broad enough to encompass a woman's decision whether or not to terminate her pregnancy." We are now of the view that, in terming this right fundamental, the Court in *Roe* read the earlier opinions upon which it based its decision much too broadly. Unlike marriage, procreation, and contraception, abortion "involves the purposeful termination of a potential life." Harris v. McRae, 448 U.S. 297, 325 (1980). The abortion decision must therefore "be recognized as sui generis, different in kind from the others that the Court has protected under the rubric of personal or family privacy and autonomy." *Thornburgh*, at 792 (White, J., dissenting).... One cannot ignore the fact that a woman is not isolated in her pregnancy, and that the decision to abort necessarily involves the destruction of a fetus.

Nor do the historical traditions of the American people support the view that the right to terminate one's pregnancy is "fundamental." The common law which we inherited from England made abortion after "quickening" an offense. At the time of the adoption of the Fourteenth Amendment, statutory prohibitions or restrictions on abortion were commonplace; in 1868, at least 28 of the then–37 States and 8 Territories had statutes banning or limiting abortion. J. Mohr, Abortion in America 200 (1978). By the turn of the century virtually every State had a law prohibiting or restricting abortion on its books. By the middle of the present century, a liberalization trend had set in. But 21 of the restrictive abortion laws in effect in 1868 were still in effect in 1973 when *Roe* was decided, and an overwhelming majority of the States prohibited abortion unless necessary to preserve the life or health of the mother. On this record, it can scarcely be said that any deeply rooted tradition of relatively unrestricted abortion in our history supported the classification of the right to abortion as "fundamental" under the Due Process Clause of the Fourteenth Amendment.

We think, therefore, both in view of this history and of our decided cases dealing with substantive liberty under the Due Process Clause, that the Court was mistaken in *Roe* when it classified a woman's decision to terminate her pregnancy as a "fundamental right" that could be abridged only in a manner which withstood "strict scrutiny." ...

We believe that the sort of constitutionally imposed abortion code of the type illustrated by our decisions following *Roe* is inconsistent "with the notion of a Constitution cast in general terms, as ours is, and usually speaking in general principles, as ours does." Webster, 492 U.S. at 578 (plurality opinion). The Court in *Roe* reached too far when it analogized the right to abort a fetus to the rights involved in *Pierce, Meyer, Loving,* and *Griswold.*...

II

The joint opinion of Justices O'Connor, Kennedy, and Souter ... contains an elaborate discussion of stare decisis. This discussion of the principle of stare decisis appears to be almost entirely dicta, because the joint opinion does not apply that principle in dealing with *Roe. Roe* decided that a woman had a fundamental right to an abortion. The joint opinion rejects that view.... *Roe* analyzed abortion regulation under a rigid trimester framework, a framework which has guided this Court's decision-making for 19 years. The joint opinion rejects that framework.

Stare decisis is defined in Black's Law Dictionary as meaning "to abide by, or adhere to, decided cases." Black's Law Dictionary 1406 (6th ed. 1990). Whatever the "central holding" of *Roe* that is left after the joint opinion finishes dissecting it is surely not the result of that principle. While purporting to adhere to precedent, the joint opinion instead revises it. *Roe* continues to exist, but only in the way a storefront on a western movie set exists: a mere facade to give the illusion of reality. Decisions following *Roe* ... are frankly overruled in part under the "undue burden" standard expounded in the joint opinion.

In our view, authentic principles of stare decisis do not require that any portion of the reasoning in *Roe* be kept intact.... Erroneous decisions in ... constitutional cases are uniquely durable, because correction through legislative action, save for constitutional amendment, is impossible. It is therefore our duty to reconsider constitutional interpretations that "depar[t] from a proper understanding" of the Constitution.... [W]hen it becomes clear that a prior constitutional interpretation is unsound we are obliged to reexamine the question.

The joint opinion discusses several stare decisis factors which, it asserts, point toward retaining a portion of *Roe*. Two of these factors are that the main "factual underpinning" of *Roe* has remained the same, and that its doctrinal foundation is no weaker now than it was in 1973. Of course, what might be called the basic facts which gave rise to *Roe* have remained the same—women become pregnant, there is a point somewhere, depending on medical technology, where a fetus becomes viable, and women give birth to children. But this is only to say that the same facts which gave rise to *Roe* will continue to give rise to similar cases. It is not a reason, in and of itself, why those cases must be decided in the same incorrect manner as was the first case to deal with the question. And surely there is no requirement, in considering whether to depart from stare decisis in a constitutional case, that a decision be more wrong now than it was at the time it was rendered. If that were true, the most outlandish constitutional decision could survive forever, based simply on the fact that it was no more outlandish later than it was when originally rendered.

Nor does the joint opinion faithfully follow this alleged requirement. The opinion frankly concludes that *Roe* and its progeny were wrong in failing to recognize that the State's interests in maternal health and in the protection of unborn human life exist throughout pregnancy. But there is no indication that these components of *Roe* are any more incorrect at this juncture than they were at its inception.

The joint opinion also points to the reliance interests involved in this context.... [A]ny traditional notion of reliance is not applicable here....

The joint opinion thus turns to what can only be described as an unconventional—and unconvincing—notion of reliance, a view based on the surmise that the availability of abortion since *Roe* has led to "two decades of economic and social developments" that would be undercut if the error of *Roe* were recognized. The joint opinion's assertion of this fact is undeveloped and totally conclusory. In fact, one cannot be sure to what economic and social developments the opinion is referring. Surely it is dubious to suggest that women have reached their "places in society" in reliance upon *Roe*, rather than as a result of their determination to obtain higher education and compete with men in the job market, and of society's increasing recognition of their ability to fill positions that were previously thought to be reserved only for men.

In the end, having failed to put forth any evidence to prove any true reliance, the joint opinion's argument is based solely on generalized assertions about the national psyche, on a belief that the people of this country have grown accustomed to the *Roe* decision over the last 19 years and have "ordered their thinking and living around" it. As an initial matter, one might inquire how the joint opinion can view the "central holding" of *Roe* as so deeply rooted in our constitutional culture, when it so casually uproots and disposes of that same decision's trimester framework. Furthermore, at various points in the past, the same could have been said about this Court's erroneous decisions that the Constitution allowed "separate but equal" treatment of minorities, see Plessy v. Ferguson, 163 U.S. 537 (1896), or that "liberty" under the Due Process Clause protected "freedom of contract," see Adkins v. Children's Hospital of District of Columbia, 261 U.S. 525 (1923); Lochner v. New York, 198 U.S. 45 (1905). The "separate but equal" doctrine lasted 58 years after *Plessy*, and *Lochner's* protection of contractual freedom lasted 32 years. However, the simple fact that a generation or more had grown used to these major decisions did not prevent the Court from correcting its errors in those cases, nor should it prevent us from correctly interpreting the Constitution here. See Brown v. Board of Education, 347 U.S. 483 (1954) (rejecting the "separate but equal" doctrine); West Coast Hotel Co. v. Parrish, 300 U.S. 379 (1937) (overruling Adkins v. Children's Hospital, supra, in upholding Washington's minimum wage law).

Apparently realizing that conventional stare decisis principles do not support its position, the joint opinion advances a belief that retaining a portion of *Roe* is necessary to protect the "legitimacy" of this Court.... [T]he joint opinion properly declares it to be this Court's duty to ignore the public criticism and protest that may arise as a result of a decision. Few would quarrel with this statement, although it may be doubted that Members of this Court, holding their tenure as they do during constitutional "good behavior," are at all likely to be intimidated by such public protests.

But the joint opinion goes on to state that when the Court "resolve[s] the sort of intensely divisive controversy reflected in *Roe* and those rare, comparable cases," its decision is exempt from reconsideration under established principles of stare decisis in constitutional cases. This is so, the joint opinion contends, because in those "intensely divisive" cases the Court has "call[ed] the contending sides of a national controversy to end their national division by accepting a common mandate rooted in the Constitution," and must therefore take special care not to be perceived as "surrender[ing] to political pressure" and continued opposition. This is a truly novel principle, one which is contrary to both the Court's historical practice and to the Court's traditional willingness to tolerate criticism of its opinions. Under this principle, when the Court has ruled on a divisive issue, it is apparently prevented from overruling that decision for the sole reason that it was incorrect, *unless opposition to the original decision has died away.*

The first difficulty with this principle lies in its assumption that cases that are "intensely divisive" can be readily distinguished from those that are not. . . .

The joint opinion picks out and discusses two prior Court rulings that it believes are of the "intensely divisive" variety, and concludes that they are of comparable dimension to *Roe*. It appears to us very odd indeed that the joint opinion chooses as benchmarks two cases in which the Court chose *not* to adhere to erroneous constitutional precedent, but instead enhanced its stature by acknowledging and correcting its error, apparently in violation of the joint opinion's "legitimacy" principle. One might also wonder how it is that the joint opinion puts these, and not others, in the "intensely divisive" category. . . . There is no reason to think that either *Plessy* or *Lochner* produced the sort of public protest when they were decided that *Roe* did. There were undoubtedly large segments of the bench and bar who agreed with the dissenting views in those cases, but surely that cannot be what the Court means when it uses the term "intensely divisive," or many other cases would have to be added to the list. In terms of public protest, however, Roe, so far as we know, was unique. But just as the Court should not respond to that sort of protest by retreating from the decision simply to allay the concerns of the protesters, it should likewise not respond by determining to adhere to the decision at all costs lest it *seem* to be retreating under fire. Public protests should not alter the normal application of stare decisis, lest perfectly lawful protest activity be penalized by the Court itself.

Taking the joint opinion on its own terms, we doubt that its distinction between *Roe*, on the one hand, and *Plessy* and *Lochner*, on the other, withstands analysis. . . . [T]he Court improved its stature by overruling *Plessy* in *Brown* on a deeply divisive issue. And our decision in *West Coast Hotel*, which overruled Adkins v. Children's Hospital, and *Lochner*, was rendered at a time when Congress was considering President Franklin Roosevelt's proposal to "reorganize" this Court and enable him to name six additional Justices in the event that any Member of the Court over the age of 70 did not elect to retire. It is difficult to imagine a situation in which the Court would face more intense opposition to a prior ruling than it did at that time, and, under the general principle proclaimed in the joint opinion, the Court seemingly should have responded to this opposition by stubbornly refusing to reexamine the *Lochner* rationale, lest it lose legitimacy by appearing to "overrule under fire."

The joint opinion agrees that the Court's stature would have been seriously damaged if in *Brown* and *West Coast Hotel* it had dug in its heels and refused to apply normal principles of stare decisis to the earlier decisions. But the opinion contends that the Court was entitled to overrule *Plessy* and *Lochner* in those cases, despite the existence of opposition to the original decisions, only because both the Nation and the Court had learned new lessons in the interim. This is at best ... feebly supported....

For example, the opinion asserts that the Court could justifiably overrule its decision in *Lochner* only because the Depression had convinced "most people" that constitutional protection of contractual freedom contributed to an economy that failed to protect the welfare of all. Surely the joint opinion does not mean to suggest that people saw this Court's failure to uphold minimum wage statutes as the cause of the Great Depression! In any event, the *Lochner* Court did not base its rule upon the policy judgment that an unregulated market was fundamental to a stable economy; it simply believed, erroneously, that "liberty" under the Due Process Clause protected the "right to make a contract." Lochner v. New York, 198 U.S., at 53. Nor is it the case that the people of this Nation only discovered the dangers of extreme laissez-faire economics because of the Depression. State laws regulating maximum hours and minimum wages were in existence well before that time....

... [I]n *West Coast Hotel*, ...[a]lthough the Court did acknowledge in the last paragraph of its opinion the state of affairs during the then-current Depression, the theme of the opinion is that the Court had been mistaken as a matter of constitutional law when it embraced "freedom of contract" 32 years previously.

The joint opinion also agrees that the Court acted properly in rejecting the doctrine of "separate but equal" in *Brown*. In fact, the opinion lauds *Brown* in comparing it to *Roe*. This is strange, in that under the opinion's "legitimacy" principle the Court would seemingly have been forced to adhere to its erroneous decision in *Plessy* because of its "intensely divisive" character. To us, adherence to *Roe* today under the guise of "legitimacy" would seem to resemble more closely adherence to *Plessy* on the same ground. Fortunately, the Court did not choose that option in *Brown*, and instead frankly repudiated *Plessy*. The joint opinion concludes that such repudiation was justified only because of newly discovered evidence that segregation had the effect of treating one race as inferior to another. But it can hardly be argued that this was not urged upon those who decided *Plessy*, as Justice Harlan observed in his dissent that the law at issue "puts the brand of servitude and degradation upon a large class of our fellow-citizens, our equals before the law." Plessy v. Ferguson, 163 U.S., at 562. It is clear that the same arguments made before the Court in *Brown* were made in *Plessy* as well. The Court in *Brown* simply recognized, as Justice Harlan had recognized beforehand, that the Fourteenth Amendment does not permit racial segregation. The rule of *Brown* is not tied to popular opinion about the evils of segregation; it is a judgment that the Equal Protection Clause does not permit racial segregation, no matter whether the public might come to believe that it is beneficial....

There is also a suggestion in the joint opinion that the propriety of overruling a "divisive" decision depends in part on whether "most people" would now agree that it should be overruled. Either the demise of opposition or its progression to substantial popular agreement apparently is required to allow the Court to reconsider a divisive decision. How such agreement would be ascertained, short of a public opinion poll, the joint opinion does not say. But surely even the suggestion is totally at war with the idea of "legitimacy" in whose name it is invoked. The Judicial Branch derives its legitimacy, not from following public opinion, but from deciding by its best lights whether legislative enactments of the popular branches of Government comport with the Constitution. The doctrine of stare decisis is an adjunct of this duty, and should be no more subject to the vagaries of public opinion than is the basic judicial task. . . .

Roe is not this Court's only decision to generate conflict. Our decisions in some recent capital cases, and in Bowers v. Hardwick, 478 U.S. 186 (1986), have also engendered demonstrations in opposition. The joint opinion's message to such protesters appears to be that they must cease their activities in order to serve their cause, because their protests will only cement in place a decision which by normal standards of stare decisis should be reconsidered. Nearly a century ago, Justice David J. Brewer of this Court, in an article discussing criticism of its decisions, observed that "many criticisms may be, like their authors, devoid of good taste, but better all sorts of criticism than no criticism at all." Justice Brewer on "The Nation's Anchor," 57 Albany L.J. 166, 169 (1898). This was good advice to the Court then, as it is today. Strong and often misguided criticism of a decision should not render the decision immune from reconsideration, lest a fetish for legitimacy penalize freedom of expression.

The end result of the joint opinion's paeans of praise for legitimacy is the enunciation of a brand new standard for evaluating state regulation of a woman's right to abortion—the "undue burden" standard. As indicated above, Roe v. Wade adopted a "fundamental right" standard under which state regulations could survive only if they met the requirement of "strict scrutiny." While we disagree with that standard, it at least had a recognized basis in constitutional law at the time *Roe* was decided. The same cannot be said for the "undue burden" standard, which is created largely out of whole cloth by the authors of the joint opinion. It is a standard which even today does not command the support of a majority of this Court. . . .

In evaluating abortion regulations under that standard, judges will have to decide whether they place a "substantial obstacle" in the path of a woman seeking an abortion. In that this standard is based even more on a judge's subjective determinations than was the trimester framework, the standard will do nothing to prevent "judges from roaming at large in the constitutional field" guided only by their personal views. Griswold v. Connecticut, 381 U.S., at 502 (Harlan, J., concurring in judgment). Because the undue burden standard is plucked from nowhere, the question of what is a "substantial obstacle" to abortion will undoubtedly engender a variety of conflicting views. For example, in the very matter before us now, the authors of the joint opinion would uphold Pennsylvania's 24–hour waiting period, concluding that a "particular burden" on some women is not a substantial obstacle. But the authors would at the same time strike down

Pennsylvania's spousal notice provision, after finding that in a "large fraction" of cases the provision will be a substantial obstacle....

Furthermore, while striking down the spousal *notice* regulation, the joint opinion would uphold a parental *consent* restriction that certainly places very substantial obstacles in the path of a minor's abortion choice. The joint opinion is forthright in admitting that it draws this distinction based on a policy judgment that parents will have the best interests of their children at heart, while the same is not necessarily true of husbands as to their wives. This may or may not be a correct judgment, but it is quintessentially a legislative one. The "undue burden" inquiry does not in any way supply the distinction between parental consent and spousal consent which the joint opinion adopts. Despite the efforts of the joint opinion, the undue burden standard presents nothing more workable than the trimester framework which it discards today. Under the guise of the Constitution, this Court will still impart its own preferences on the States in the form of a complex abortion code.

The sum of the joint opinion's labors in the name of stare decisis and "legitimacy" is this: Roe v. Wade stands as a sort of judicial Potemkin Village, which may be pointed out to passers-by as a monument to the importance of adhering to precedent. But behind the facade, an entirely new method of analysis, without any roots in constitutional law, is imported to decide the constitutionality of state laws regulating abortion. Neither stare decisis nor "legitimacy" are truly served by such an effort.

... Accordingly, we think that the correct analysis is [that] ... [a] woman's interest in having an abortion is a form of liberty protected by the Due Process Clause, but States may regulate abortion procedures in ways rationally related to a legitimate state interest. With this rule in mind, we examine each of the challenged provisions.

III ...

C ...

We first emphasize that Pennsylvania has not imposed a spousal consent requirement of the type the Court struck down in Planned Parenthood of Central Mo. v. Danforth. Missouri's spousal consent provision was invalidated in that case because of the Court's view that it unconstitutionally granted to the husband "a veto power exercisable for any reason whatsoever or for no reason at all." But the provision here involves a much less intrusive requirement of spousal *notification*, not consent. Such a law requiring only notice to the husband "does not give any third party the legal right to make the [woman's] decision for her, or to prevent her from obtaining an abortion should she choose to have one performed." ... The District Court indeed found that the notification provision created a risk that some woman who would otherwise have an abortion will be prevented from having one. For example, petitioners argue, many notified husbands will prevent abortions through physical force, psychological coercion, and other types of threats. But Pennsylvania has incorporated exceptions in the notice provision in an attempt to deal with these problems. For instance, a woman need not notify her husband if the pregnancy is the result of a reported sexual assault, or if she has reason to believe that she would suffer bodily injury as a result of the notification. 18 Pa.Cons.Stat. § 3209(b) (1990). Furthermore, because this is a facial challenge to the Act, it is insufficient for petitioners to show that the notification provision "might operate unconstitutionally under some conceivable set of circumstances." United States v. Salerno, 481 U.S. 739, 745 (1987). Thus, it is not enough for petitioners to show that, in some "worst case" circumstances, the notice provision will operate as a grant of veto power to husbands. Because they are making a facial challenge to the provision, they must "show that no set of circumstances exists under which the [provision] would be valid." This they have failed to do.

The question before us is therefore whether the spousal notification requirement rationally furthers any legitimate state interests. We conclude that it does. First, a husband's interests in procreation within marriage and in the potential life of his unborn child are certainly substantial ones. The State itself has legitimate interests both in protecting these interests of the father and in protecting the potential life of the fetus, and the spousal notification requirement is reasonably related to advancing those state interests. By providing that a husband will usually know of his spouse's intent to have an abortion, the provision makes it more likely that the husband will participate in deciding the fate of his unborn child, a possibility that might otherwise have been denied him. This participation might in some cases result in a decision to proceed with the pregnancy. As Judge Alito observed in his dissent below, "[t]he Pennsylvania legislature could have rationally believed that some married women are initially inclined to obtain an abortion without their husbands' knowledge because of perceived problems—such as economic constraints, future plans, or the husbands' previously expressed opposition—that may be obviated by discussion prior to the abortion." 947 F.2d, at 726.

The State also has a legitimate interest in promoting "the integrity of the marital relationship." 18 Pa.Cons.Stat. § 3209(a) (1990). This Court has previously recognized "the importance of the marital relationship in our society." In our view, the spousal notice requirement is a rational attempt by the State to improve truthful communication between spouses and encourage collaborative decisionmaking, and thereby fosters marital integrity. Petitioners argue that the notification requirement does not further any such interest; they assert that the majority of wives already notify their husbands of their abortion decisions, and the remainder have excellent reasons for keeping their decisions a secret. In the first case, they argue, the law is unnecessary, and in the second case it will only serve to foster marital discord and threats of harm. Thus, petitioners see the law as a totally irrational means of furthering whatever legitimate interest the State might have. But, in our view, it is unrealistic to assume that every husband-wife relationship is either (1) so perfect that this type of truthful and important communication will take place as a matter of course, or (2) so imperfect that, upon notice, the husband will react selfishly, violently, or contrary to the best interests of his wife.... The Pennsylvania Legislature was in a position to weigh the likely benefits of the provision against its likely adverse effects, and presumably concluded, on balance, that the provision would be beneficial. Whether this was a wise decision or not, we cannot say that it was irrational. We therefore conclude that the spousal notice provision comports with the Constitution. . . .

IV

For the reasons stated, we therefore would hold that each of the challenged provisions of the Pennsylvania statute is consistent with the Constitution. It bears emphasis that our conclusion in this regard does not carry with it any necessary approval of these regulations. Our task is, as always, to decide only whether the challenged provisions of a law comport with the United States Constitution. If, as we believe, these do, their wisdom as a matter of public policy is for the people of Pennsylvania to decide.

JUSTICE SCALIA, with whom THE CHIEF JUSTICE, JUSTICE WHITE, and JUSTICE THOMAS join, concurring in the judgment in part and dissenting in part.

. . . The States may, if they wish, permit abortion on demand, but the Constitution does not require them to do so. The permissibility of abortion, and the limitations upon it, are to be resolved like most important questions in our democracy: by citizens trying to persuade one another and then voting. . . . A State's choice between two positions on which reasonable people can disagree is constitutional even when (as is often the case) it intrudes upon a "liberty" in the absolute sense. Laws against bigamy, for example—with which entire societies of reasonable people disagree—intrude upon men and women's liberty to marry and live with one another. But bigamy happens not to be a liberty specially "protected" by the Constitution.

That is, quite simply, the issue in these cases: not whether the power of a woman to abort her unborn child is a "liberty" in the absolute sense; or even whether it is a liberty of great importance to many women. Of course it is both. The issue is whether it is a liberty protected by the Constitution of the United States. I am sure it is not. I reach that conclusion not because of anything so exalted as my views concerning the "concept of existence, of meaning, of the universe, and of the mystery of human life." Rather, I reach it for the same reason I reach the conclusion that bigamy is not constitutionally protected—because of two simple facts: (1) the Constitution says absolutely nothing about it, and (2) the longstanding traditions of American society have permitted it to be legally proscribed.[1]

1. The Court's suggestion that adherence to tradition would require us to uphold laws against interracial marriage is entirely wrong. Any tradition in that case was contradicted by a text—an Equal Protection Clause that explicitly establishes racial equality as a constitutional value. The enterprise launched in Roe v. Wade, by contrast, sought to *establish*—in the teeth of a clear, contrary tradi-

The Court destroys the proposition, evidently meant to represent my position, that "liberty" includes "only those practices, defined at the most specific level, that were protected against government interference by other rules of law when the Fourteenth Amendment was ratified." That is not, however, what *Michael H.* says; it merely observes that, in defining "liberty," we may not disregard a specific, "relevant tradition protecting, or denying protection to, the asserted right." ...

Beyond that brief summary of the essence of my position, I will not swell the United States Reports with repetition of what I have said before; and applying the rational basis test, I would uphold the Pennsylvania statute in its entirety. I must, however, respond to a few of the more outrageous arguments in today's opinion, which it is beyond human nature to leave unanswered. I shall discuss each of them under a quotation from the Court's opinion to which they pertain.

"The inescapable fact is that adjudication of substantive due process claims may call upon the Court in interpreting the Constitution to exercise that same capacity which by tradition courts always have exercised: reasoned judgment."

Assuming that the question before us is to be resolved at such a level of philosophical abstraction, in such isolation from the traditions of American society, as by simply applying "reasoned judgment," I do not see how that could possibly have produced the answer the Court arrived at in Roe v. Wade. Today's opinion describes the methodology of *Roe*, quite accurately, as weighing against the woman's interest the State's " 'important and legitimate interest in protecting the potentiality of human life.' " But "reasoned judgment" does not begin by begging the question, as *Roe* and subsequent cases unquestionably did by assuming that what the State is protecting is the mere "potentiality of human life." The whole argument of abortion opponents is that what the Court calls the fetus and what others call the unborn child *is a human life*. Thus, whatever answer *Roe* came up with after conducting its "balancing" is bound to be wrong, unless it is correct that the human fetus is in some critical sense merely potentially human. There is of course no way to determine that as a legal matter; it is in fact a value judgment. Some societies have considered newborn children not yet human, or the incompetent elderly no longer so.

The authors of the joint opinion, of course, do not squarely contend that Roe v. Wade was a *correct* application of "reasoned judgment"; merely that it must be followed, because of stare decisis. But in their exhaustive discussion of all the factors that go into the determination of when stare

tion—a value found nowhere in the constitutional text.

There is, of course, no comparable tradition barring recognition of a "liberty interest" in carrying one's child to term free from state efforts to kill it. For that reason, it does not follow that the Constitution does not protect childbirth simply because it does not protect abortion. The Court's contention, that the only way to protect childbirth is to protect abortion shows the utter bankruptcy of constitutional analysis deprived of tradition as a validating factor. It drives one to say that the only way to protect the right to eat is to acknowledge the constitutional right to starve oneself to death.

decisis should be observed and when disregarded, they never mention "how wrong was the decision on its face?" Surely, if "[t]he Court's power lies . . . in its legitimacy, a product of substance and perception," the "substance" part of the equation demands that plain error be acknowledged and eliminated. *Roe* was plainly wrong—even on the Court's methodology of "reasoned judgment," and even more so (of course) if the proper criteria of text and tradition are applied.

. . . It is not reasoned judgment that supports the Court's decision; only personal predilection. Justice Curtis's warning is as timely today as it was 135 years ago:

> "[W]hen a strict interpretation of the Constitution, according to the fixed rules which govern the interpretation of laws, is abandoned, and the theoretical opinions of individuals are allowed to control its meaning, we have no longer a Constitution; we are under the government of individual men, who for the time being have power to declare what the Constitution is, according to their own views of what it ought to mean." Dred Scott v. Sandford, 19 How. 393, 621 (1857) (dissenting opinion).

"Liberty finds no refuge in a jurisprudence of doubt."

One might have feared to encounter this august and sonorous phrase in an opinion defending the real Roe v. Wade, rather than the revised version fabricated today by the authors of the joint opinion. The shortcomings of *Roe* did not include lack of clarity: Virtually all regulation of abortion before the third trimester was invalid. But to come across this phrase in the joint opinion—which calls upon federal district judges to apply an "undue burden" standard as doubtful in application as it is unprincipled in origin—is really more than one should have to bear. . . .

The joint opinion explains that a state regulation imposes an "undue burden" if it "has the purpose or effect of placing a substantial obstacle in the path of a woman seeking an abortion of a nonviable fetus." An obstacle is "substantial," we are told, if it is "calculated[,] [not] to inform the woman's free choice, [but to] hinder it." This latter statement cannot possibly mean what it says. *Any* regulation of abortion that is intended to advance what the joint opinion concedes is the State's "substantial" interest in protecting unborn life will be "calculated [to] hinder" a decision to have an abortion. It thus seems more accurate to say that the joint opinion would uphold abortion regulations only if they do not *unduly* hinder the woman's decision. That, of course, brings us right back to square one. . . . Consciously or not, the joint opinion's verbal shell game will conceal raw judicial policy choices concerning what is "appropriate" abortion legislation.

The ultimately standardless nature of the "undue burden" inquiry is a reflection of the underlying fact that the concept has no principled or coherent legal basis. . . . The appropriate analogy . . . is that of a state law requiring purchasers of religious books to endure a 24–hour waiting period, or to pay a nominal additional tax of 1 cents. The joint opinion cannot possibly be correct in suggesting that we would uphold such legislation on the ground that it does not impose a "substantial obstacle" to the exercise of First Amendment rights. The "undue burden" standard is not at all the generally applicable principle the joint opinion pretends it to be; rather, it is a unique concept created specially for these cases, to preserve some judicial foothold in this ill-gotten territory. . . .

I do not, of course, have any objection to the notion that, in applying legal principles, one should rely only upon the facts that are contained in the record or that are properly subject to judicial notice.[6] But what is remarkable about the joint opinion's fact-intensive analysis is that it does not result in any measurable clarification of the "undue burden" standard. Rather, the approach of the joint opinion is, for the most part, simply to highlight certain facts in the record that apparently strike the three Justices as particularly significant in establishing (or refuting) the existence of an undue burden; after describing these facts, the opinion then simply announces that the provision either does or does not impose a "substantial obstacle" or an "undue burden." We do not know whether the same conclusions could have been reached on a different record. . . . The inherently standardless nature of this inquiry invites the district judge to give effect to his personal preferences about abortion. By finding and relying upon the right facts, he can invalidate, it would seem, almost any abortion restriction that strikes him as "undue"—subject, of course, to the possibility of being reversed by a court of appeals or Supreme Court that is as unconstrained in reviewing his decision as he was in making it.

To the extent I can discern *any* meaningful content in the "undue burden" standard as applied in the joint opinion, it appears to be that a State may not regulate abortion in such a way as to reduce significantly its incidence. . . . We are not told, however, what forms of "deterrence" are impermissible or what degree of success in deterrence is too much to be tolerated. If, for example, a State required a woman to read a pamphlet describing, with illustrations, the facts of fetal development before she could obtain an abortion, the effect of such legislation might be to "deter" a "significant number of women" from procuring abortions, thereby seemingly allowing a district judge to invalidate it as an undue burden. Thus, despite flowery rhetoric about the State's "substantial" and "profound" interest in "potential human life," and criticism of *Roe* for undervaluing that interest, the joint opinion permits the State to pursue that interest only so long as it is not too successful. As Justice Blackmun recognizes (with evident hope), the "undue burden" standard may ultimately require the invalidation of each provision upheld today if it can be shown, on a better record, that the State is too effectively "express[ing] a preference for

---

6. The joint opinion is not entirely faithful to this principle, however. In approving the District Court's factual findings with respect to the spousal notice provision, it relies extensively on nonrecord materials, and in reliance upon them adds a number of factual conclusions of its own. . . . [If] a court can find an undue burden simply by selectively string-citing the right social science articles, I do not see the point of emphasizing or requiring "detailed factual findings" in the District Court.

childbirth over abortion." Reason finds no refuge in this jurisprudence of confusion.

> **"While we appreciate the weight of the arguments ... that** **_Roe_ should be overruled, the reservations any of us may have** **in reaffirming the central holding of _Roe_ are outweighed by** **the explication of individual liberty we have given combined** **with the force of stare decisis."**

The Court's reliance upon stare decisis can best be described as contrived. It insists upon the necessity of adhering not to all of _Roe_, but only to what it calls the "central holding." It seems to me that stare decisis ought to be applied even to the doctrine of stare decisis, and I confess never to have heard of this new, keep-what-you-want-and-throw-away-the-rest version. . . .

I have always thought, and I think a lot of other people have always thought, that the arbitrary trimester framework, which the Court today discards, was quite as central to _Roe_ as the arbitrary viability test, which the Court today retains. It seems particularly ungrateful to carve the trimester framework out of the core of _Roe_, since its very rigidity (in sharp contrast to the utter indeterminability of the "undue burden" test) is probably the only reason the Court is able to say, in urging stare decisis, that _Roe_ "has in no sense proven 'unworkable' ".... I thought I might note, however, that the following portions of _Roe_ have not been saved:

• Under _Roe_, requiring that a woman seeking an abortion be provided truthful information about abortion before giving informed written consent is unconstitutional, if the information is designed to influence her choice. _Thornburgh_; _Akron I_. Under the joint opinion's "undue burden" regime (as applied today, at least) such a requirement is constitutional.

• Under _Roe_, requiring that information be provided by a doctor, rather than by nonphysician counselors, is unconstitutional, _Akron I_. Under the "undue burden" regime (as applied today, at least) it is not.

• Under _Roe_, requiring a 24–hour waiting period between the time the woman gives her informed consent and the time of the abortion is unconstitutional. _Akron I_. Under the "undue burden" regime (as applied today, at least) it is not. . . .

> **"Where, in the performance of its judicial duties, the Court** **decides a case in such a way as to resolve the sort of intensely** **divisive controversy reflected in _Roe_ ..., its decision has a** **dimension that the resolution of the normal case does not** **carry. It is the dimension present whenever the Court's inter-** **pretation of the Constitution calls the contending sides of a** **national controversy to end their national division by accept-** **ing a common mandate rooted in the Constitution."**

The Court's description of the place of _Roe_ in the social history of the United States is unrecognizable. Not only did _Roe_ not, as the Court suggests, resolve the deeply divisive issue of abortion; it did more than anything else to nourish it, by elevating it to the national level where it is infinitely more difficult to resolve. National politics were not plagued by abortion protests, national abortion lobbying, or abortion marches on Congress before Roe v. Wade was decided. Profound disagreement existed among our citizens over the issue—as it does over other issues, such as the death penalty—but that disagreement was being worked out at the state level. As with many other issues, the division of sentiment within each State was not as closely balanced as it was among the population of the Nation as a whole, meaning not only that more people would be satisfied with the results of state-by-state resolution, but also that those results would be more stable. Pre-*Roe*, moreover, political compromise was possible.

Roe's mandate for abortion on demand destroyed the compromises of the past, rendered compromise impossible for the future, and required the entire issue to be resolved uniformly, at the national level. At the same time, *Roe* created a vast new class of abortion consumers and abortion proponents by eliminating the moral opprobrium that had attached to the act. ("If the Constitution guarantees abortion, how can it be bad?"—not an accurate line of thought, but a natural one.) Many favor all of those developments, and it is not for me to say that they are wrong. But to portray *Roe* as the statesmanlike "settlement" of a divisive issue, a jurisprudential Peace of Westphalia that is worth preserving, is nothing less than Orwellian. *Roe* fanned into life an issue that has inflamed our national politics in general, and has obscured with its smoke the selection of Justices to this Court in particular, ever since. And by keeping us in the abortion-umpiring business, it is the perpetuation of that disruption, rather than of any Pax Roeana, that the Court's new majority decrees.

> **"[T]o overrule under fire ... would subvert the Court's legitimacy....**
>
> **"... To all those who will be ... tested by following, the Court implicitly undertakes to remain steadfast.... The promise of constancy, once given, binds its maker for as long as the power to stand by the decision survives and ... the commitment [is not] obsolete....**
>
> **"[The American people's] belief in themselves as ... a people [who aspire to live according to the rule of law] is not readily separable from their understanding of the Court invested with the authority to decide their constitutional cases and speak before all others for their constitutional ideals. If the Court's legitimacy should be undermined, then, so would the country be in its very ability to see itself through its constitutional ideals."**

The Imperial Judiciary lives. It is instructive to compare this Nietzschean vision of us unelected, life-tenured judges—leading a Volk who will be "tested by following," and whose very "belief in themselves" is mystically bound up in their "understanding" of a Court that "speak[s] before all others for their constitutional ideals"—with the somewhat more modest role envisioned for these lawyers by the Founders.

"The judiciary . . . has . . . no direction either of the strength or of the wealth of the society, and can take no active resolution whatever. It may truly be said to have neither Force nor Will, but merely judgment. . . ." The Federalist No. 78, pp. 393–394 (G. Wills ed. 1982).

· · ·

It is particularly difficult . . . to sit still for the Court's lengthy lecture upon the virtues of "constancy," of "remain[ing] steadfast," of adhering to "principle." Among the five Justices who purportedly adhere to *Roe*, at most three agree upon the *principle* that constitutes adherence (the joint opinion's "undue burden" standard)—and that principle is inconsistent with *Roe*. . . . It is beyond me how the Court expects these accommodations to be accepted "as grounded truly in principle, not as compromises with social and political pressures having, as such, no bearing on the principled choices that the Court is obliged to make." The only principle the Court "adheres" to, it seems to me, is the principle that the Court must be seen as standing by *Roe*. That is not a principle of law (which is what I thought the Court was talking about), but a principle of *Realpolitik*—and a wrong one at that.

I cannot agree with, indeed I am appalled by, the Court's suggestion that the decision whether to stand by an erroneous constitutional decision must be strongly influenced—*against* overruling, no less—by the substantial and continuing public opposition the decision has generated. . . .

. . . [W]hether it would "subvert the Court's legitimacy" or not, the notion that we would decide a case differently from the way we otherwise would have in order to show that we can stand firm against public disapproval is frightening. It is a bad enough idea, even in the head of someone like me, who believes that the text of the Constitution, and our traditions, say what they say and there is no fiddling with them. But when it is in the mind of a Court that believes the Constitution has an evolving meaning; that the Ninth Amendment's reference to "othe[r]" rights is not a disclaimer, but a charter for action; and that the function of this Court is to "speak before all others for [the people's] constitutional ideals" unrestrained by meaningful text or tradition—then the notion that the Court must adhere to a decision for as long as the decision faces "great opposition" and the Court is "under fire" acquires a character of almost czarist arrogance. . . .

Of course, as the Chief Justice points out, we have been subjected to what the Court calls "political pressure" by *both* sides of this issue. Maybe today's decision not to overrule *Roe* will be seen as buckling to pressure from *that* direction. Instead of engaging in the hopeless task of predicting public perception—a job not for lawyers but for political campaign managers—the Justices should do what is *legally* right by asking two questions: (1) Was *Roe* correctly decided? (2) Has *Roe* succeeded in producing a settled body of law? If the answer to both questions is no, *Roe* should undoubtedly be overruled.

In truth, I am as distressed as the Court is . . . about the "political pressure" directed to the Court: the marches, the mail, the protests aimed at inducing us to change our opinions. How upsetting it is, that so many of our citizens (good people, not lawless ones, on both sides of this abortion issue, and on various sides of other issues as well) think that we Justices should properly take into account their views, as though we were engaged not in ascertaining an objective law but in determining some kind of social consensus. The Court would profit, I think, from giving less attention to the *fact* of this distressing phenomenon, and more attention to the *cause* of it. That cause permeates today's opinion: a new mode of constitutional adjudication that relies not upon text and traditional practice to determine the law, but upon what the Court calls "reasoned judgment," which turns out to be nothing but philosophical predilection and moral intuition. . . .

What makes all this relevant to the bothersome application of "political pressure" against the Court are the twin facts that the American people love democracy and the American people are not fools. As long as this Court thought (and the people thought) that we Justices were doing essentially lawyers' work up here—reading text and discerning our society's traditional understanding of that text—the public pretty much left us alone. Texts and traditions are facts to study, not convictions to demonstrate about. But if in reality our process of constitutional adjudication consists primarily of making *value judgments*; if we can ignore a long and clear tradition clarifying an ambiguous text, as we did, for example, five days ago in declaring unconstitutional invocations and benedictions at public high school graduation ceremonies, Lee v. Weisman, 505 U.S. 577 (1992); if, as I say, our pronouncement of constitutional law rests primarily on value judgments, then a free and intelligent people's attitude towards us can be expected to be (*ought* to be) quite different. The people know that their value judgments are quite as good as those taught in any law school—maybe better. If, indeed, the "liberties" protected by the Constitution are, as the Court says, undefined and unbounded, then the people *should* demonstrate, to protest that we do not implement *their* values instead of *ours*. Not only that, but confirmation hearings for new Justices *should* deteriorate into question-and-answer sessions in which Senators go through a list of their constituents' most favored and most disfavored alleged constitutional rights, and seek the nominee's commitment to support or oppose them. Value judgments, after all, should be voted on, not dictated; and if our Constitution has somehow accidently committed them to the Supreme Court, at least we can have a sort of plebiscite each time a new nominee to that body is put forward. Justice Blackmun not only regards this prospect with equanimity, he solicits it.

* * *

There is a poignant aspect to today's opinion. Its length, and what might be called its epic tone, suggest that its authors believe they are bringing to an end a troublesome era in the history of our Nation and of our Court. . . .

There comes vividly to mind a portrait by Emanuel Leutze that hangs in the Harvard Law School: Roger Brooke Taney, painted in 1859, the 82nd year of his life, the 24th of his Chief Justiceship, the second after his opinion in *Dred Scott*. He is all in black, sitting in a shadowed red armchair, left hand resting upon a pad of paper in his lap, right hand hanging limply, almost lifelessly, beside the inner arm of the chair. He sits facing the viewer and staring straight out. There seems to be on his face, and in his deep-set eyes, an expression of profound sadness and disillusionment. Perhaps he always looked that way, even when dwelling upon the happiest of thoughts. But those of us who know how the lustre of his great Chief Justiceship came to be eclipsed by *Dred Scott* cannot help believing that he had that case—its already apparent consequences for the Court and its soon-to-be-played-out consequences for the Nation—burning on his mind. I expect that two years earlier he, too, had thought himself "call[ing] the contending sides of national controversy to end their national division by accepting a common mandate rooted in the Constitution."

It is no more realistic for us in this litigation, than it was for him in that, to think that an issue of the sort they both involved—an issue involving life and death, freedom and subjugation—can be "speedily and finally settled" by the Supreme Court, as President James Buchanan in his inaugural address said the issue of slavery in the territories would be. Quite to the contrary, by foreclosing all democratic outlet for the deep passions this issue arouses, by banishing the issue from the political forum that gives all participants, even the losers, the satisfaction of a fair hearing and an honest fight, by continuing the imposition of a rigid national rule instead of allowing for regional differences, the Court merely prolongs and intensifies the anguish.

We should get out of this area, where we have no right to be, and where we do neither ourselves nor the country any good by remaining.

Questions and Comments on *Casey*

1. After reading *Casey,* are you any more, or any less, convinced of the correctness of *Roe*'s conclusion that the decision whether to abort is an aspect of liberty protected by the Due Process Clause?

2. For what audience(s) do you think Part I of the plurality opinion is written?

3. Is stare decisis a constitutionally required doctrine? How would formally abandoning the doctrine of stare decisis affect constitutional adjudication in the U.S.? If, as the plurality argued, stare decisis required adherence to *Roe*'s "essential holding," why did it not require adherence to *Roe*'s trimester framework and to decisions following *Roe* that had invalidated waiting period requirements?

4. Why does Justice Blackmun refer to the plurality opinion as an act of courage?

B. ABORTION AND CONSTITUTIONAL LAW IN CANADA AND GERMANY

Consider as you read the major abortion decisions from Canada and Germany below the role played by constitutional text, history and tradition, moral principle or moral consensus.

1. THE MORGENTALER DECISION: SOME BACKGROUND NOTES ON ABORTION AND THE CONSTITUTION IN CANADA[c]

Canada gained its independence from Britain in 1867, under the British North America Act of 1867, inheriting from Britain a tradition of parliamentary supremacy. Sections 91 and 92 of that Act (now called the Constitution Act of 1867) defined the division of power between the provincial and federal governments, and formed an early basis for judicial review of legislation on federalism grounds by the Canadian Supreme Court (and from there, until well into this century, to the Privy Council). Individual rights, however, remained essentially unprotected under constitutional law until more recently. Peter W. Hogg, Constitutional Law of Canada 639 (2d ed. 1985).

Under the British North America Act, Canada inherited an 1861 statute from England called the "Offenses Against the Person Act." This Act, and its codification in the Canadian criminal code, completely prohibited abortion, even to save the life of the mother, and made it punishable by life imprisonment.

In 1969, section 251 of the Criminal Code, at issue in *Morgentaler*, replaced the old abortion law. It continued to treat abortion as a crime, but created an exception: the "therapeutic abortion committee" procedure, by which women could obtain legal abortions in limited circumstances. Under this procedure, a woman wanting an abortion was required to consult with a hospital-appointed panel of three doctors. The doctors were to decide if "the continuation of the pregnancy of such female person would or would be likely to endanger her life or health." If so, a legal abortion could be performed. Section 251 was not satisfactory to either pro-life or pro-choice advocates. It was not impossible to obtain abortions on mental health grounds, but the standards applied were inconsistent, and delays inherent in the committee procedure posed serious obstacles to many women seeking abortions.

Henry Morgentaler, a doctor and abortion rights advocate, repeatedly challenged section 251. In 1975, he claimed that the Section was invalid under the British North America Act and the (statutory) Canadian Bill of Rights, R. v. Morgentaler [1975] 1 S.C.R. 616. These arguments faced an

c. We gratefully acknowledge the research assistance of Tom Heinemann, J.D. Georgetown 1995, in the preparation of these materials.

uphill battle, in large part because of the tradition of legislative supremacy in Canada. In 1960, the Canadian Parliament had passed a statutory Bill of Rights. The Canadian Bill of Rights, S.C. 1960, c. 44. Almost ten years passed before the Supreme Court decided, in R. v. Drybones [1970] S.C.R. 282, that the Bill of Rights granted power to the courts to strike down legislation not in conformity with the rights it enumerated. *Drybones* was the only case in which the Canadian Supreme Court relied on the statutory Bill of Rights to invalidate legislation. Dr. Morgentaler's claim under the statutory Bill of Rights in 1975 was not successful.

In 1982, Canada adopted a constitutional Charter of Rights and Freedoms. Canadian Charter of Rights and Freedoms, part I of the Constitution Act of 1982, schedule B to the Canada Act of 1982, c. 11 (U.K.). The Charter, unlike the earlier statutory bill of rights, can only be modified through constitutional amendment procedures, and applies at both the federal and provincial levels. The Charter, moreover, fairly explicitly contemplates judicial review. Section 52(1) states that the constitution is "the supreme law of Canada, and any law that is inconsistent with the provisions of the Constitution is, to the extent of the inconsistency, of no force or effect." While Section 52 does not state that it is the courts that will decide on the inconsistency, that appears to be implied in Section 24, which states that anyone whose Charter rights are violated shall have access to a court to obtain a remedy. And the Canadian Supreme Court early on interpreted the Charter of Rights to mean that its own power of judicial review had been expanded. Attorney General of Quebec v. Quebec Assn of Protestant School Boards [1984] 2 S.C.R. 66, 68.

In 1988, the validity of the abortion law came before the Supreme Court again, but this time, under the new Charter of Rights. The decision, as edited, follows.

Morgentaler, Smoling and Scott v. The Queen

[1988] 1 S.C.R. 30. (Supreme Court of Canada)

The judgment of DICKSON, C.J., and LAMER, J., was delivered by THE CHIEF JUSTICE (DICKSON).:—The principal issue raised by this appeal is whether the abortion provisions of the Criminal Code infringe the "right to life, liberty and security of the person and the right not to be deprived thereof except in accordance with the principles of fundamental justice" as formulated in s. 7 of the Canadian Charter of Rights and Freedoms. The appellants, Dr. Henry Morgentaler, Dr. Leslie Frank Smoling and Dr. Robert Scott, have raised thirteen distinct grounds of appeal. During oral submissions, however, it became apparent that the primary focus of the case was upon the s. 7 argument. It is submitted by the appellants that s. 251 of the Criminal Code, [R.S.C. 1970, c. C-34] contravenes s. 7 of the Canadian Charter of Rights and Freedoms and that s. 251 should be struck down. Counsel for the Crown admitted during the course of her submissions that s. 7 of the Charter was indeed "the key" to the entire appeal....

Although no doubt it is still fair to say that courts are not the appropriate forum for articulating complex and controversial programmes of public policy, Canadian courts are now charged with the crucial obligation of ensuring that the legislative initiatives pursued by our Parliament and legislatures conform to the democratic values expressed in the Canadian Charter of Rights and Freedoms. As Justice McIntyre states in his reasons for judgment, "the task of the court in this case is not to solve nor seek to solve what might be called the abortion issue, but simply to measure the content of s. 251 against the Charter". It is in this latter sense that the current Morgentaler appeal differs from the one we heard a decade ago. . . .

II.   Relevant Statutory and Constitutional Provisions

Criminal Code

251(1) Every one who, with intent to procure the miscarriage of a female person, whether or not she is pregnant, uses any means for the purpose of carrying out his intention is guilty of an indictable offence and is liable to imprisonment for life.

(2) Every female person who, being pregnant, with intent to procure her own miscarriage, uses any means or permits any means to be used for the purpose of carrying out her intention is guilty of an indictable offence and is liable to imprisonment for two years. . . .

(4) Subsections (1) and (2) do not apply to

(a) a qualified medical practitioner, other than a member of a therapeutic abortion committee for any hospital, who in good faith uses in an accredited or approved hospital any means for the purpose of carrying out his intention to procure the miscarriage of a female person, or

(b) a female person who, being pregnant, permits a qualified medical practitioner to use in an accredited or approved hospital any means described in paragraph (a) for the purpose of carrying out her intention to procure her own miscarriage,

if, before the use of those means, the therapeutic abortion committee for that accredited or approved hospital, by a majority of the members of the committee and at a meeting of the committee at which the case of such female person has been reviewed,

(c) has by certificate in writing stated that in its opinion the continuation of the pregnancy of such female person would or would be likely to endanger her life or health, and

(d) has caused a copy of such certificate to be given to the qualified medical practitioner. . . .

The Canadian Charter of Rights and Freedoms

1.   The Canadian Charter of Rights and Freedoms guarantees the rights and freedoms set out in it subject only to such reasonable limits

prescribed by law as can be demonstrably justified in a free and democratic society.

.   .   .

7.   Everyone has the right to life, liberty and security of the person and the right not to be deprived thereof except in accordance with the principles of fundamental justice.

III.   Procedural History

The three appellants are all duly qualified medical practitioners who together set up a clinic in Toronto to perform abortions upon women who had not obtained a certificate from a therapeutic abortion committee of an accredited or approved hospital as required by s. 251(4). The doctors had made public statements questioning the wisdom of the abortion laws in Canada and asserting that a woman has an unfettered right to choose whether or not an abortion is appropriate in her individual circumstances.

Indictments were preferred against the appellants charging that they conspired with each other between November, 1982, and July, 1983, with intent to procure the miscarriage of female persons, using an induced suction technique to carry out that intent, contrary to ss. 423(1)(d) and 251(1) of the Criminal Code.

[After unsuccessfully moving to dismiss the indictment on the grounds that s. 251 violated, *inter alia*, section 7 of the Canadian Charter of Rights and Freedoms, the defendants were acquitted by a jury. As permitted under Canadian law, the government appealed, and the defendants cross-appealed; the intermediate appellate court again rejected the defendants' constitutional challenge, and ordered a new trial. The defendants then took this appeal to the highest court in Canada.]

IV.   Section 7 of the Charter

In his submissions, counsel for the appellants argued that the court should recognize a very wide ambit for the rights protected under s. 7 of the Charter. Basing his argument largely on American constitutional theories and authorities, Mr. Manning submitted that the right to "life, liberty and security of the person" is a wide-ranging right to control one's own life and to promote one's individual autonomy. The right would therefore include a right to privacy and a right to make unfettered decisions about one's own life.

In my opinion, it is neither necessary nor wise in this appeal to explore the broadest implications of s. 7 as counsel would wish us to do. I prefer to rest my conclusions on a narrower analysis than that put forward on behalf of the appellants. I do not think it would be appropriate to attempt an all-encompassing explication of so important a provision as s. 7 so early in the history of Charter interpretation. The court should be presented with a wide variety of claims and factual situations before articulating the full range of s. 7 rights. I will therefore limit my comments to some interpretive principles already set down by the court and to an analysis of only two aspects of s. 7, the right to "security of the person" and "the principles of fundamental justice".

A. Interpreting s. 7

The goal of Charter interpretation is to secure for all people "the full benefit of the Charter's protection".... To attain that goal, this Court has held consistently that the proper technique for the interpretation of Charter provisions is to pursue a "purposive" analysis of the right guaranteed. A right recognized in the Charter is "to be understood, in other words, in the light of the interests it was meant to protect".

... [T]here are three distinct elements to the s. 7 right, [and] "life, liberty, and security of the person" are independent interests, each of which must be given independent significance by the Court....

With respect to the second part of s. 7, in early academic commentary one of the principal concerns was whether the reference to "principles of fundamental justice" enables the courts to review the substance of legislation ... [A]ny attempt to draw a sharp line between procedure and substance would be ill-conceived ... [I]t would not be beneficial in Canada to allow a debate which is rooted in United States constitutional dilemmas to shape our interpretation of s. 7 ... [T]he principles of fundamental justice referred to in § 7 can relate both to procedure and to substance, depending upon the circumstances presented before the Court.

I have no doubt that s. 7 does impose upon courts the duty to review the substance of legislation once it has been determined that the legislation infringes an individual's right to "life, liberty and security of the person". The section states clearly that those interests may only be impaired if the principles of fundamental justice are respected. Lamer J. emphasized, however, that the courts should avoid "adjudication of the merits of public policy". In the present case, I do not believe that it is necessary for the court to tread the fine line between substantive review and the adjudication of public policy ... [I]t will be sufficient to investigate whether or not the impugned legislative provisions meet the procedural standards of fundamental justice. First it is necessary to determine whether s. 251 of the Criminal Code impairs the security of the person.

B. Security of the person

The law has long recognized that the human body ought to be protected from interference by others. At common law, for example, any medical procedure carried out on a person without that person's consent is an assault. Only in emergency circumstances does the law allow others to make decisions of this nature. Similarly, art. 19 of the Civil Code of Lower Canada* provides that "The human person is inviolable" and that "No person may cause harm to the person of another without his consent or

---

* [Editors' Note: Lower Canada is now Quebec Province. "Common law" and "civil code" refer to the background legal systems inherited by, respectively, the English-speaking and the French-speaking parts of Canada.]

without being authorized by law to do so". "Security of the person", in other words, is not a value alien to our legal landscape. With the advent of the Charter, security of the person has been elevated to the status of a constitutional norm. This is not to say that the various forms of protection accorded to the human body by the common and civil law occupy a similar status. "Security of the person" must be given content in a manner sensitive to its constitutional position. The above examples are simply illustrative of our respect for individual physical integrity. Nor is it to say that the state can never impair personal security interests. There may well be valid reasons for interfering with security of the person. It is to say, however, that if the state does interfere with security of the person, the Charter requires such interference to conform with the principles of fundamental justice.

The appellants submitted that the "security of the person" protected by the Charter is an explicit right to control one's body and to make fundamental decisions about one's life. The Crown contended that "security of the person" is a more circumscribed interest and that, like all of the elements of s. 7, it at most relates to the concept of physical control, simply protecting the individual's interest in his or her bodily integrity.

... The Ontario Court of Appeal has held that the right to life, liberty and security of the person "would appear to relate to one's physical or mental integrity and one's control over these ..."

That conclusion is consonant with the holding of Justice Lamer in Mills v. The Queen ...: " ... security of the person is not restricted to physical integrity;" rather, it encompasses protection against " 'overlong subjection to vexations and vicissitudes of a pending criminal accusation'.... These include stigmatization of the accused, loss of privacy, stress and anxiety resulting from a multitude of factors, including possible disruption of family, social life and work, legal costs, uncertainty as to the outcome and sanction."

I note also that the Court has held in other contexts that the psychological effect of state action is relevant in assessing whether or not a Charter right has been infringed. In R. v. Therens, at p. 644 S.C.R., Le Dain J. held that "The element of psychological compulsion, in the form of a reasonable perception of suspension of freedom of choice, is enough to make the restraint of liberty involuntary" for the purposes of defining "detention" in s. 10 of the Charter. A majority of the Court accepted the conclusions of Le Dain, J. on this issue.

It may well be that constitutional protection of the above interests is specific to, and is only triggered by, the invocation of our system of criminal justice. It must not be forgotten, however, that s. 251 of the Code, subject to s-s. (4), makes it an indictable offence for a person to procure the miscarriage and provides a maximum sentence of two years in the case of the woman herself, and a maximum sentence of life imprisonment in the cases of another person. Like Justice Beetz, I do not find it necessary to decide how s. 7 would apply in other cases.

The caselaw leads me to the conclusion that state interference with bodily integrity and serious state-imposed psychological stress, at least in the criminal law context, constitute a breach of security of the person. It is not necessary in this case to determine whether the right extends further, to protect either interests central to personal autonomy, such as a right to privacy, or interests unrelated to criminal justice.

I wish to reiterate that finding a violation of security of the person does not end the s. 7 inquiry. Parliament could choose to infringe security of the person if it did so in a manner consistent with the principles of fundamental justice. The present discussion should therefore be seen as a threshold inquiry and the conclusions do not dispose definitively of all the issues relevant to s. 7. With that caution, I have no difficulty in concluding that the encyclopedic factual submissions addressed to us by counsel in the present appeal establish beyond any doubt that s. 251 of the Criminal Code is prima facie a violation of the security of the person of thousands of Canadian women who have made the difficult decision that they do not wish to continue with a pregnancy.

At the most basic, physical and emotional level, every pregnant woman is told by the section that she cannot submit to a generally safe medical procedure that might be of clear benefit to her unless she meets criteria entirely unrelated to her own priorities and aspirations. Not only does the removal of decision-making power threaten women in a physical sense; the indecision of knowing whether an abortion will be granted inflicts emotional stress. Section 251 clearly interferes with a woman's bodily integrity in both a physical and emotional sense. Forcing a woman, by threat of criminal sanction, to carry a foetus to term unless she meets certain criteria unrelated to her own priorities and aspirations, is a profound interference with a woman's body and thus a violation of security of the person. Section 251, therefore, is required by the Charter to comport with the principles of fundamental justice.

Although this interference with physical and emotional integrity is sufficient in itself to trigger a review of s. 251 against the principles of fundamental justice, the operation of the decision-making mechanism set out in s. 251 creates additional glaring breaches of security of the person. The evidence indicates that s. 251 causes a certain amount of delay for women who are successful in meeting its criteria. In the context of abortion, any unnecessary delay can have profound consequences on the woman's physical and emotional well-being.

More specifically, in 1977, the Report of the Committee on the Operation of the Abortion Law (the Badgley report) revealed that the average delay between a pregnant woman's first contact with a physician and a subsequent therapeutic abortion was eight weeks. Although the situation appears to have improved since 1977, the extent at the improvement is not clear. The intervener, the Attorney-General of Canada, submitted that the average delay in Ontario between the first visit to a physician and a therapeutic abortion was now between one and three weeks. Yet the respondent Crown admitted in a supplementary factum filed on November 27, 1986, with the permission of the court that:

> ".... the evidence discloses that some women may find it very difficult to obtain an abortion: by necessity, abortion services are limited, since hospitals have budgetary, time, space and staff constraints as well as many medical responsibilities. As a result of these problems a woman may have to apply to several hospitals."

If forced to apply to several different therapeutic abortion committees, there can be no doubt that a woman will experience serious delay in obtaining a therapeutic abortion.... [S]tudies showed that in Quebec the waiting time for a therapeutic abortion in hospital varied between one and six weeks.

These periods of delay may not seem unduly long, but in the case of abortion, the implications of any delay, according to the evidence, are potentially devastating. The first factor to consider is that different medical techniques are employed to perform abortions at different stages of pregnancy. The testimony of expert doctors at trial indicated that in the first twelve weeks of pregnancy, the relatively safe and simple suction dilation and curettage method of abortion is typically used in North America. From the thirteenth to the sixteenth week, the more dangerous dilation and evacuation procedure is performed, although much less often in Canada than in the United States. From the sixteenth week of pregnancy, the instillation method is commonly employed in Canada. This method requires the intra-amniotic introduction of prostoglandin, urea, or a saline solution, which causes a woman to go into labour, giving birth to a foetus which is usually dead, but not invariably so. The uncontroverted evidence showed that each method of abortion progressively increases risks to the woman....

The second consideration is that even within the periods appropriate to each method of abortion, the evidence indicated that the earlier the abortion was performed, the fewer the complications and the lower the risk of mortality.... Even more revealing were the overall mortality statistics evaluated by Drs. Cates and Grimes. They concluded from their study of the relevant data that: "Anything that contributes to delay in performing abortions increases the complication rates by 15% to 30%, and the chance of dying by 50% for each week of delay." These statistics indicate clearly that even if the average delay caused by s. 251 per arguendo is of only a couple of weeks' duration, the effects upon any particular woman can be serious and, occasionally, fatal.

It is no doubt true that the over-all complication and mortality rates for women who undergo abortions are very low, but the increasing risks caused by delay are so clearly established that I have no difficulty in concluding that the delay in obtaining therapeutic abortions caused by the mandatory procedures of s. 251 is an infringement of the purely physical aspect of the individual's right to security of the person. I should stress that the marked contrast between the relative speed with which abortions can be obtained at the government-sponsored community clinics in Quebec and in hospitals under the s. 251 procedure was established at trial. The evidence indicated that at the government-sponsored clinics in Quebec, the maximum delay was less than a week. One must conclude, and perhaps underline, that the delay experienced by many women seeking a therapeutic abortion, be it of one, two, four, or six weeks duration, is caused in large measure by the requirements of s. 251 itself.

The above physical interference caused by the delays created by s. 251, involving a clear risk of damage to the physical well-being of a woman, is sufficient, in my view, to warrant inquiring whether s. 251 comports with the principles of fundamental justice. However, there is yet another infringement of security of the person. It is clear from the evidence that s. 251 harms the psychological integrity of women seeking abortions. A 1985 report of the Canadian Medical Association, discussed in the Powell report, [Report on Therapeutic Abortion Services in Ontario (1987)] at p. 15, emphasized that the procedure involved in s. 251, with the concomitant delays, greatly increases the stress levels of patients and that this can lead to more physical complications associated with abortion. A specialist in fertility control, Dr. Henry David, was qualified as an expert witness at trial on the psychological impact upon women of delay in the process of obtaining an abortion. He testified that his own studies had demonstrated that there is increased psychological stress imposed upon women who are forced to wait for abortions, and that this stress is compounded by the uncertainty whether or not a therapeutic abortion committee will actually grant approval. . . .

In its supplementary factum and in oral submissions, the Crown argued that evidence of what could be termed "administrative inefficiency" is not relevant to the evaluation of legislation for the purposes of s. 7 of the Charter. The Crown argued that only evidence regarding the purpose of legislation is relevant. The assumption, of course, is that any impairment to the physical or psychological interests of individuals caused by s. 251 of the Criminal Code does not amount to an infringement of security of the person because the injury is caused by practical difficulties and is not intended by the legislator.

The submission is faulty on two counts. First, as a practical matter it is not possible in the case of s. 251 to erect a rigid barrier between the purposes of the section and the administrative procedures established to carry those purposes into effect. For example, although it may be true that Parliament did not enact s. 251 intending to create delays in obtaining therapeutic abortions, the evidence demonstrates that the system established by the section for obtaining a therapeutic abortion certificate inevitably does create significant delays. It is not possible to say that delay results only from administrative constraints, such as limited budgets or lack of qualified persons to sit on therapeutic abortion committees. Delay results from the cumbersome operating requirements of s. 251. Although the mandate given to the courts under the Charter does not, generally speaking, enable the judiciary to provide remedies for administrative inefficiencies, when denial of a right as basic as security of the person is infringed by the procedure and administrative structures created by the law itself, the courts are empowered to act.

Secondly, were it nevertheless possible in this case to dissociate purpose and administration, this court has already held as a matter of law that purpose is not the only appropriate criterion in evaluating the constitutionality of legislation under the Charter. In R. v. Big M Drug Mart, Ltd., [[1985] 1 S.C.R. 295], the Court stated that " . . . both purpose and effect are relevant in determining constitutionality; either an unconstitutional purpose or an unconstitutional effect can invalidate legislation." Even if the purpose of legislation is unobjectionable, the administrative procedures created by law to bring that purpose into operation may produce unconstitutional effects, and the legislation should then be struck down . . .

In summary, s. 251 is a law which forces women to carry a foetus to term contrary to their own priorities and aspirations and which imposes serious delay causing increased physical and psychological trauma to those women who meet its criteria. It must, therefore, be determined whether that infringement is accomplished in accordance with the principles of fundamental justice, thereby saving s. 251 under the second part of s. 7.

C.   The principles of fundamental justice . . .

. . . In outline, s. 251 operates in the following manner. Subsection (1) creates an indictable offence for any person to use any means with the intent "to procure the miscarriage of a female person". Subsection (2) establishes a parallel indictable offence for any pregnant woman to use or to permit any means to be used with the intent "to procure her own miscarriage". . . . The crucial provision for the purposes of the present appeal is s-s. (4) which states that the offences created in s-ss. (1) and (2) "do not apply" in certain circumstances. The Ontario Court of Appeal in the proceedings below characterized s. 251(4) as an "exculpatory provision" . . . In Morgentaler (1975), a majority of this court held that the effect of s. 251(4) was to afford "a complete answer and defence to those who respect its terms".

The procedure surrounding the defence is rather complex. A pregnant woman who desires to have an abortion must apply to the "therapeutic abortion committee" of an "accredited or approved hospital". Such a committee is empowered to issue a certificate in writing stating that in the opinion of a majority of the committee, the continuation of the pregnancy would be likely to endanger the pregnant woman's life or health. Once a copy of the certificate is given to a qualified medical practitioner who is not a member of the therapeutic abortion committee, he or she is permitted to perform an abortion on the pregnant woman and both the doctor and the woman are freed from any criminal liability.

A number of definitions are provided in s-s. (6) which have a bearing on the disposition of this appeal. An "accredited hospital" is described as a hospital accredited by the Canadian Council on Hospital Accreditation "in which diagnostic services and medical, surgical and obstetrical treatment" are provided. An "approved hospital" is a hospital "approved for the purposes of this section by the Minister of Health" of a province. A "therapeutic abortion committee" must be "comprised of not less than three members each of whom is a qualified medical practitioner" who is appointed by a hospital's administrative board. Interestingly, the term "health" is not defined for the purposes of s. 251, so it would appear that the therapeutic abortion committees are free to develop their own theories as to when a potential impairment of a woman's "health" would justify the granting of a therapeutic abortion certificate.

As is so often the case in matters of interpretation, however, the straightforward reading of this statutory scheme is not fully revealing. In order to understand the true nature and scope of s. 251, it is necessary to investigate the practical operation of the provisions. The court has been provided with a myriad of factual submissions in this area . . .

The Badgley Report . . . demonstrates that many of the most serious problems with the functioning of s. 251 are created by procedural and administrative requirements established in the law. For example, . . .

> the Abortion Law implicitly establishes a minimum requirement of three qualified physicians to serve on a therapeutic abortion committee, plus a qualified medical practitioner who is not a member of the therapeutic abortion committee, to perform the procedure . . .

> Of the 1,348 civilian hospitals in operation in 1976, at least 331 hospitals had less than four physicians on their medical staff. In terms of the distribution of physicians, 24.6 percent of hospitals in Canada did not have a medical staff which was large enough to establish a therapeutic abortion committee and to perform the abortion procedure.

In other words, the seemingly neutral requirement of s. 251(4) that at least four physicians be available to authorize and to perform an abortion meant in practice that abortions would be absolutely unavailable in almost one quarter of all hospitals in Canada.

Other administrative and procedural requirements of s. 251(4) reduce the availability of therapeutic abortions even further. For the purposes of s. 251, therapeutic abortions can only be performed in "accredited" or "approved" hospitals . . . [A]n "accredited" hospital must not only be accredited by the Canadian Council on Hospital Accreditation, it must also provide specified services. Many Canadian hospitals do not provide all of the required services, thereby being automatically disqualified from undertaking therapeutic abortions. The Badgley Report stressed the remarkable limitations created by these requirements, especially when linked with the four-physician rule discussed above:

> Of the total of 1,348 non-military hospitals in Canada in 1976, 789 hospitals, or 58.5 percent, were ineligible in terms of their major treatment functions, the size of their medical staff, or their type of facility to establish therapeutic abortion committees.

Moreover, even if a hospital is eligible to create a therapeutic abortion committee, there is no requirement in s. 251 that the hospital need do so. The Badgley Committee discovered that in 1976, of the 559 general hospitals which met the procedural requirements of s. 251, only 271 hospitals in Canada, or only 20.1% of the total, had actually established a therapeutic abortion committee (p. 105) . . .

The Powell Report reveals another serious difficulty with s. 251 procedures. The requirement that therapeutic abortions be performed only in "accredited" or "approved" hospitals effectively means that the practical availability of the exculpatory provisions of s-s. (4) may be heavily restricted, even denied, through provincial regulation. In Ontario, for example, the provincial government promulgated O. Reg. 248/70 under the Public Hospitals Act, R.S.O. 1960, c. 322, now R.R.O. 1980, Reg. 865. This regulation provides that therapeutic abortion committees can only be established where there are 10 or more members on the active medical staff. A Minister of Health is not prevented from imposing harsher restrictions. During argument, it was noted that it would even be possible for a provincial government, exercising its legislative authority over public hospitals, to distribute funding for treatment facilities in such a way that no hospital would meet the procedural requirements of s. 251(4). Because of the administrative structure established in s. 251(4) and the related definitions, the "defence" created in the section could be completely wiped out.

A further flaw with the administrative system established in s. 251(4) is the failure to provide an adequate standard for therapeutic abortion committees which must determine when a therapeutic abortion should, as a matter of law, be granted. Subsection (4) states simply that a therapeutic abortion committee may grant a certificate when it determines that a continuation of a pregnancy would be likely to endanger the "life or health" of the pregnant woman. It was noted above that "health" is not defined for the purposes of the section. The Crown admitted in its supplementary factum that the medical witnesses at trial testified uniformly that the "health" standard was ambiguous, but the Crown derives comfort from the fact that "the medical witnesses were unanimous in their approval of the broad World Health Organization definition of health". The World Health Organization defines "health" not merely as the absence of disease or infirmity, but as a state of physical, mental and social well-being.

I do not understand how the mere existence of a workable definition of "health" can make the use of the word in s. 251(4) any less ambiguous when that definition is nowhere referred to in the section. There is no evidence that therapeutic abortion committees are commonly applying the World Health Organization definition. Indeed, the Badgley Report indicates that the situation is quite the contrary (p. 20):

> There has been no sustained or firm effort in Canada to develop an explicit and operational definition of health, or to apply such a concept directly to the operation of induced abortion. In the absence of such a definition, each physician and each hospital reaches an individual decision on this matter. How the concept of health is variably defined leads to considerable inequity in the distribution and the accessibility of the abortion procedure.

Various expert doctors testified at trial that therapeutic abortion committees apply widely differing definitions of health. For some committees, psychological health is a justification for therapeutic abortion; for others it is not. Some committees routinely refuse abortions to married women unless they are in physical danger, while for other committees it is possible for a married woman to show that she would suffer psychological harm if she continued with a pregnancy, thereby justifying an abortion. It is not typically possible for women to know in advance what standard of health will be applied by any given committee ...

When the decision of the therapeutic abortion committee is so directly laden with legal consequences, the absence of any clear legal standard to be applied by the committee in reaching its decision is a serious procedural flaw.

The combined effect of all of these problems with the procedure stipulated in s. 251 for access to therapeutic abortions is a failure to comply with the principles of fundamental justice ... One of the basic tenets of our system of criminal justice is that when Parliament creates a defence to a criminal charge, the defence should not be illusory or so difficult to attain as to be practically illusory. The criminal law is a very special form of governmental regulation, for it seeks to express our society's collective disapprobation of certain acts and omissions. When a defence is provided, especially a specifically-tailored defence to a particular charge, it is because the legislator has determined that the disapprobation of society is not warranted when the conditions of the defence are met.

Consider then the case of a pregnant married woman who wishes to apply for a therapeutic abortion certificate because she fears that her psychological health would be impaired seriously if she carried the foetus to term. The uncontroverted evidence reveals that there are many areas in Canada where such a woman would simply not have access to a therapeutic abortion. She may live in an area where no hospital has four doctors; no therapeutic abortion committee can be created. Equally, she may live in a place where the treatment functions of the nearby hospitals do not satisfy the definition of "accredited hospital" in s. 251(6). Or she may live in a province where the provincial government has imposed such stringent requirements on hospitals seeking to create therapeutic abortion committees that no hospital can qualify. Alternatively, our hypothetical woman may confront a therapeutic abortion committee in her local hospital which defines "health" in purely physical terms or which refuses to countenance abortions for married women. In each of these cases, it is the administrative structures and procedures established by s. 251 itself that would in practice prevent the woman from gaining the benefit of the defence held out to her in s. 251(4).

The facts indicate that many women do indeed confront these problems. Doctors from the Chedoke-McMaster Hospital in Hamilton testified that they received telephone calls from women throughout Ontario who had applied for therapeutic abortions at local hospitals and been refused....

The Crown argues in its supplementary factum that women who face difficulties in obtaining abortions at home can simply travel elsewhere in Canada to procure a therapeutic abortion. That submission would not be especially troubling if the difficulties facing women were not in large measure created by the procedural requirements of s. 251 itself. If women were seeking anonymity outside their home town or were simply confronting the reality that it is often difficult to obtain medical services in rural areas, it might be appropriate to say "let them travel". But the evidence establishes convincingly that it is the law itself which in many ways prevents access to local therapeutic abortion facilities. The enormous emotional and financial burden placed upon women who must travel long distances from home to obtain an abortion is a burden created in many instances by Parliament. Moreover, it is not accurate to say to women who would seem to qualify under s. 251(4) that they can get a therapeutic abortion as long as they are willing to travel. . . .

Parliament must be given room to design an appropriate administrative and procedural structure for bringing into operation a particular defence to criminal liability. But if that structure is "so manifestly unfair, having regard to the decisions it is called upon to make, as to violate the principles of fundamental justice", that structure must be struck down. In the present case, the structure—the system regulating access to therapeutic abortions—is manifestly unfair. It contains so many potential barriers to its own operation that the defence it creates will in many circumstances be practically unavailable to women who would prima facie qualify for the defence, or at least would force such women to travel great distances at substantial expense and inconvenience in order to benefit from a defence that is held out to be generally available.

I conclude that the procedures created in s. 251 of the Criminal Code for obtaining a therapeutic abortion do not comport with the principles of fundamental justice. It is not necessary to determine whether s. 7 also contains a substantive content leading to the conclusion that, in some circumstances at least, the deprivation of a pregnant woman's right to security of the person can never comport with fundamental justice. Simply put, assuming Parliament can act, it must do so properly. For the reasons given earlier, the deprivation of security of the person caused by s. 251 as a whole is not in accordance with the second clause of s. 7. It remains to be seen whether s. 251 can be justified for the purposes of s. 1 of the Charter.

V.   Section 1 Analysis

Section 1 of the Charter can potentially be used to "salvage" a legislative provision which breaches s. 7. . . . [Under the Supreme Court's decision in R. v. Oakes, [1986] 1 S.C.R. 103,] [a] statutory provision which infringes any section of the Charter can only be saved under s. 1 if the party seeking to uphold the provision can demonstrate first, that the objective of the provision is "of sufficient importance to warrant overriding a constitutionally protected right or freedom" . . . and secondly, that the means chosen in overriding the right or freedom are reasonable and demonstrably justified in a free and democratic society. This second aspect ensures that the legislative means are proportional to the legislative ends.... [T]hree considerations ... are typically useful in assessing the proportionality of means to ends. First, the means chosen to achieve an important objective should be rational, fair and not arbitrary. Secondly, the legislative means should impair as little as possible the right or freedom under consideration. Third, the effects of the limitation upon the relevant right or freedom should not be out of proportion to the objective sought to be achieved.

The appellants contended that the sole purpose of s. 251 of the Criminal Code is to protect the life and health of pregnant women. The respondent Crown submitted that s. 251 seeks to protect not only the life and health of pregnant women, but also the interests of the foetus. On the other hand, the Crown conceded that the court is not called upon in this appeal to evaluate any claim to "foetal rights" or to assess the meaning of "the right to life". I expressly refrain from so doing. In my view, it is unnecessary for the purpose of deciding this appeal to evaluate or assess "foetal rights" as an independent constitutional value. Nor are we required to measure the full extent of the state's interest in establishing criteria unrelated to the pregnant woman's own priorities and aspirations. What we must do is evaluate the particular balance struck by Parliament in s. 251, as it relates to the priorities and aspirations of pregnant women and the government's interests in the protection of the foetus.

Section 251 provides that foetal interests are not to be protected where the "life or health" of the woman is threatened. Thus, Parliament itself has expressly stated in s. 251 that the "life or health" of pregnant women is paramount. The procedures of s. 251(4) are clearly related to the pregnant woman's "life or health" for that is the very phrase used by the subsection. As McIntyre J. states in his reasons, the aim of s. 251(4) is "to restrict abortion to cases where the continuation of the pregnancy would, or would likely, be injurious to the life or health of the woman concerned, not to provide unrestricted access to abortion". I have no difficulty in concluding that the objective of s. 251 as a whole, namely, to balance the competing interests identified by Parliament, is sufficiently important to meet the requirements of the first step in the *Oakes* inquiry under s. 1. I think the protection of the interests of pregnant women is a valid governmental objective, where life and health can be jeopardized by criminal sanctions. Like Beetz and Wilson JJ., I agree that protection of foetal interests by Parliament is also a valid governmental objective. It follows that balancing these interests, with the lives and health of women a major factor, is clearly an important governmental objective....

I am equally convinced, however, that the means chosen to advance the legislative objectives of s. 251 do not satisfy any of the three elements of the proportionality component of R. v. Oakes. The evidence has led me to conclude that the infringement of the security of the person of pregnant women caused by s. 251 is not accomplished in accordance with the principles of fundamental justice. It has been demonstrated that the procedures and administrative structures created by s. 251 are often arbitrary and unfair. The procedures established to implement the policy of s. 251 impair s. 7 rights far more than is necessary because they hold out an illusory defence to many women who would prima facie qualify under the exculpatory provisions of s. 251(4). In other words, many women whom Parliament professes not to wish to subject to criminal liability will nevertheless be forced by the practical unavailability of the supposed defence to risk liability or to suffer other harm such as a traumatic late abortion caused by the delay inherent in the s. 251 system. Finally, the effects of the limitation upon the s. 7 rights of many pregnant women are out of proportion to the objective sought to be achieved. Indeed, to the extent that s. 251(4) is designed to protect the life and health of women, the procedures it establishes may actually defeat that objective. The administrative structures of s. 251(4) are so cumbersome that women whose health is endangered by pregnancy may not be able to gain a therapeutic abortion, at least without great trauma, expense and inconvenience.

I conclude, therefore, that the cumbersome structure of s-s. (4) not only unduly subordinates the s. 7 rights of pregnant women but may also defeat the value Parliament itself has established as paramount, namely, the life and health of the mother. As I have noted, counsel for the Crown did contend that one purpose of the procedures required by s-s. (4) is to protect the interests of the foetus. State protection of foetal interests may well be deserving of constitutional recognition under s. 1. Still, there can be no escape from the fact that Parliament has failed to establish either a standard or a procedure whereby any such interests might prevail over those of the woman in a fair and non-arbitrary fashion.

Section 251 of the Criminal Code cannot be saved, therefore, under s. 1 of the Charter....

VII. Conclusion

Section 251 of the Criminal Code infringes the right to security of the person of many pregnant women. The procedures and administrative structures established in the section to provide for therapeutic abortions do not comply with the principles of fundamental justice. Section 7 of the Charter is infringed and that infringement cannot be saved under s. 1.

In oral argument, counsel for the Crown submitted that if the court were to hold that procedural aspects of s. 251 infringed the Charter, only the procedures set out in the section should be struck down, that is s-ss. (4) and (5). After being pressed with questions from the bench, Ms. Wein conceded that the whole of s. 251 should fall if it infringed s. 7. Mr. Blacklock for the Attorney-General of Canada took the same position. This was a wise approach, for in Morgentaler (1975) the court held that "s. 251 contains a comprehensive code on the subject of abortions, unitary and complete within itself". Having found that this "comprehensive code" infringes the Charter, it is not the role of the court to pick and choose among the various aspects of s. 251 so as effectively to re-draft the section.

The appeal should therefore be allowed and s. 251 as a whole struck down under s. 52(1) of the Constitution Act, 1982 . . .

The reasons of BEETZ and ESTEY, JJ. were delivered by

BEETZ J.:—I have had the advantage of reading the reasons for judgment written by the Chief Justice, as well as the reasons written by Mr. Justice McIntyre and Justice Wilson. . . .

Like the Chief Justice and Wilson J., I would allow the appeal and answer the first constitutional question in the affirmative and the second constitutional question in the negative. This, however, is a result which I reach for reasons which differ from those of the Chief Justice and those of Wilson J.

I find it convenient to outline at the outset the steps which lead me to this result:

I—Before the advent of the Charter, Parliament recognized, in adopting s. 251(4) of the Criminal Code, that the interest in the life or health of the pregnant woman takes precedence over the interest in prohibiting abortions, including the interest of the state in the protection of the foetus, when "the continuation of the pregnancy of such female person would or would be likely to endanger her life or health". In my view, this standard in s. 251(4) became entrenched at least as a minimum when the "right to life, liberty and security of the person" was enshrined in the Canadian Charter of Rights and Freedoms at s. 7.

II—"Security of the person" within the meaning of s. 7 of the Charter must include a right of access to medical treatment for a condition representing a danger to life or health without fear of criminal sanction. If an Act of Parliament forces a pregnant woman whose life or health is in danger to choose between, on the one hand, the commission of a crime to obtain effective and timely medical treatment and, on the other hand, inadequate treatment or no treatment at all, her right to security of the person has been violated.

III—According to the evidence, the procedural requirements of s. 251 of the Criminal Code significantly delay pregnant women's access to medical treatment resulting in an additional danger to their health, thereby depriving them of their right to security of the person.

IV—The deprivation referred to in the preceding proposition does not accord with the principles of fundamental justice. While Parliament is justified in requiring a reliable, independent and medically sound opinion as to the "life or health" of the pregnant woman in order to protect the state interest in the foetus, and while any such statutory mechanism will inevitably result in some delay, certain of the procedural requirements of s. 251 of the Criminal Code are nevertheless manifestly unfair. These requirements are manifestly unfair in that they are unnecessary in respect of Parliament's objectives in establishing the administrative structure and that they result in additional risks to the health of pregnant women.

V—The primary objective of s. 251 of the Criminal Code is the protection of the foetus. The protection of the life and health of the pregnant woman is an ancillary objective. The primary objective does relate to concerns which are pressing and substantial in a free and democratic society and which, pursuant to s. 1 of the Charter, justify reasonable limits to be put on a woman's right. However, rules unnecessary in respect of the primary and ancillary objectives which they are designed to serve, such as some of the rules contained in s. 251, cannot be said to be rationally connected to these objectives under s. 1 of the Charter. Consequently, s. 251 does not constitute a reasonable limit to the security of the person.

It is not necessary to decide whether there is a proportionality between the effects of s. 251 and the objective of protecting the foetus, nor is it necessary to answer the question concerning the circumstances in which there is a proportionality between the effects of s. 251 which limit the right of pregnant women to security of the person and the objective of the protection of the foetus. But I feel bound to observe that the objective of protecting the foetus would not justify the severity of the breach of pregnant women's right to security of the person which would result if the exculpatory provision of s. 251 was <u>completely</u> removed from the Criminal Code. However, a rule that would require a higher degree of danger to health in the latter months of pregnancy, as opposed to the early months, for an abortion to be lawful, could possibly achieve a proportionality which would be acceptable under s. 1 of the Charter....

I. Section 251 of the Criminal Code ...

What is important, for our purposes, in considering s-s. (4) is not, of course, the name we give to the exculpatory rule but the rule itself: Parliament has recognized that circumstances exist in which an abortion can be procured lawfully. The Court of Appeal observed ...: "A woman's only right to an abortion at the time the Charter came into force would accordingly appear to be that given to s-s. (4) of s. 251." Given that it appears in a criminal law statute, s. 251(4) cannot be said to create a "right", much less a constitutional right, but it does represent an exception decreed by Parliament pursuant to what the Court of Appeal aptly called "the contemporary view that abortion is not always socially undesirable behaviour". Examining the content of the rule by which Parliament decriminalizes abortion is the most appropriate first step in considering the validity of s. 251 as against the constitutional right to abortion alleged by the appellants in argument.

By enacting s-s. (4), (5), (6) and (7) of s. 251 in 1969, Parliament endeavoured to decriminalize abortion in one circumstance, described in substantive terms in s. 251(4)(c): when the continuation of the pregnancy of the woman would or would be likely to endanger her life or health. This is the crux of the exception ...

The remaining provisions of s-s. (4), (5), (6) and (7) of s. 251 are designed to ascertain whether the standard has been met in a given case....

. . . These other rules are a means to an end and not an end unto themselves. As a whole, s-s. (4), (5), (6) and (7) of s. 251 seek to make therapeutic abortions lawful and available but also to ensure that the excuse of therapy will not be abused and that lawful abortions be safe.

That abortions are recognized as lawful by Parliament based on a specific standard under its ordinary laws is important, I think, to a proper understanding of the existence of a right of access to abortion founded on rights guaranteed by s. 7 of the Charter. The constitutional right does not have its source in the Criminal Code, but, in my view, the content of the standard in s. 251(4) that Parliament recognized in the Criminal Law Amendment Act, 1969 was for all intents and purposes entrenched at least as a minimum in 1982 when a distinct right in s. 7 became part of Canadian constitutional law.

II—The right to security of the person in s. 7 of the Charter

. . . [T]he minimum content which I attribute to s. 7 does not preclude, or for that matter assure, the finding of a wider constitutional right when the courts will be faced with this or other issues in other contexts. As we shall see, the content of the "security of the person" element of the s. 7 right is sufficient in itself to invalidate s. 251 of the Criminal Code and consequently dispose of the appeal.

. . . Enjoying "security of the person" free from criminal sanction is central to understanding the violation of the Charter right which I describe herein. It is not necessary to decide whether s. 7 would apply in other circumstances.

A pregnant woman's person cannot be said to be secure if, when her life or health is in danger, she is faced with a rule of criminal law which precludes her from obtaining effective and timely medical treatment.

Generally speaking, the constitutional right to security of the person must include some protection from state interference when a person's life or health is in danger. The Charter does not, needless to say, protect men and women from even the most serious misfortunes of nature. Section 7 cannot be invoked simply because a person's life or health is in danger. The state can obviously not be said to have violated, for example, a pregnant woman's security of the person simply on the basis that her pregnancy in and of itself represents a danger to her life or health. There must be state intervention for "security of the person" in s. 7 to be violated.

If a rule of criminal law precludes a person from obtaining appropriate medical treatment when his or her life or health is in danger, then the state has intervened and this intervention constitutes a violation of that man's or that woman's security of the person. "Security of the person" must include a right of access to medical treatment for a condition representing a danger to life or health without fear of criminal sanction. If an Act of Parliament forces a person whose life or health is in danger to choose between, on the one hand, the commission of a crime to obtain effective and timely medical treatment and, on the other hand, inadequate treatment or no treatment at all, the right to security of the person has been violated....

III—Delays caused by s. 251 procedure in violation of security of the person....

A hospital with a dormant committee is no more useful to a pregnant woman seeking a therapeutic abortion than a hospital without a committee or no hospital at all. The delay suffered by a pregnant woman because her local hospital has a dormant committee is perhaps more the result of internal hospital policy than of s. 251 of the Criminal Code, but s. 251 is at least indirectly the cause of the delay in requiring an opinion from the therapeutic abortion committee of that hospital before a lawful abortion can be performed there.

Delays result not only from the absence or inactivity of therapeutic abortion committees. The evidence discloses that some hospitals with committees impose quotas on the number of therapeutic abortions which they perform while others place quotas on patients depending on their place of residence.... These quotas are inevitable given that s. 251 requires that therapeutic abortions be performed only in eligible hospitals and that there is a lack of hospitals with committees in some parts of the country. The quotas cannot, therefore, be said to reflect simple administrative or budgetary constraints. In this respect, the s. 251 procedure is again the source of delays in medical treatment....

The delays which a pregnant woman may have to suffer as a result of the requirements of s. 251(4) must undermine the security of her person in order that there be a violation of this element of s. 7 of the Charter. As I said earlier, s. 7 cannot be invoked simply because a woman's pregnancy amounts to a medically dangerous condition. If, however, the delays occasioned by s. 251(4) of the Criminal Code result in an additional danger to the pregnant woman's health, then the state has intervened and this intervention constitutes a violation of that woman's security of the person. By creating this additional risk, s. 251 prevents access to effective and timely medical treatment for the continued pregnancy which would or would be likely to endanger her life or health. If an effective and timely therapeutic abortion may only be obtained by committing a crime, then s. 251 violates the pregnant woman's right to security of the person.

The evidence reveals that the delays caused by s. 251(4) result in at least three broad types of additional medical risks. The risk of post-operative complications increases with delay. Secondly, there is a risk that the pregnant woman require a more dangerous means of procuring a miscarriage because of the delay. Finally, since a pregnant woman knows her life or health is in danger, the delay created by the s. 251(4) procedure may result in an additional psychological trauma.

IV—The principles of fundamental justice

I turn now to a consideration of the manner in which pregnant women are deprived of their right to security of the person by s. 251. Section 7 of the Charter states that everyone has the right not to be deprived of security of the person except in accordance with the principles of fundamental justice. As I will endeavour to demonstrate, s. 251(4) does not accord with the principles of fundamental justice.

I am of the view, however, that certain elements of the procedure for obtaining a therapeutic abortion which counsel for the appellants argued could not be saved by the second part of s. 7 are in fact in accordance with the principles of fundamental justice. The expression of the standard in s. 251(4)(c), and the requirement for some independent medical opinion to ascertain that the standard has been met as well as the consequential necessity of some period of delay to ascertain the standard are not in breach of s. 7 of the Charter.

Counsel for the appellants argued that the expression of the standard in s. 251(4)(c) is so imprecise that it offends the principles of fundamental justice. He submits that pregnant women are arbitrarily deprived of their s. 7 right by reason of the different meanings that can be given to the word "health" in s. 251(4)(c) by therapeutic abortion committees. . . .

I [believe] that the standard is manageable because it is addressed to a panel of doctors exercising medical judgment on a medical question. . . . With the greatest of respect, I cannot agree with the view that the therapeutic abortion committee is a "strange hybrid, part medical committee and part legal committee" as the Chief Justice characterizes it. In s. 251(4) Parliament has only given the committee the authority to make a medical determination regarding the pregnant woman's life or health. The committee is not called upon to evaluate the sufficiency of the state interest in the foetus as against the woman's health. . . .

In Jones v. The Queen, [1986] 2 S.C.R. 284 at p. 304, 31 D.L.R. (4th) 569 at p. 598, 28 C.C.C. (3d) 513 at p. 541.* La Forest J. explained that the legislator must be accorded a certain latitude to make choices regarding the type of administrative structure that will suit its needs unless the use of such structure is in itself "so manifestly unfair, *having regard to the decisions it is called upon to make* [my emphasis], as to violate the principles of *fundamental* justice". An administrative structure made up of unnecessary rules, which result in an additional risk to the health of pregnant women, is manifestly unfair and does not conform to the principles of fundamental justice. Section 251(4), taken as a whole, does not accord with the principles of fundamental justice in that certain of the procedural requirements of s. 251 create unnecessary delays. As will be seen, some of these requirements are manifestly unfair because they have no connection whatsoever with Parliament's objectives in establishing the administrative structure in s. 251(4). Although connected to Parliament's objectives, other rules in s. 251(4) are manifestly unfair because they are not necessary to assure that the objectives are met. . . .

* [Editors' Note: These are parallel citations to decisions of the Supreme Court of Canada. The official report is Supreme Court Reports (S.C.R.).]

Parliament is justified in requiring a reliable, independent and medically sound opinion in order to protect the state interest in the foetus. This is undoubtedly the objective of a rule which requires an independent verification of the practising physician's opinion that the life or health of the pregnant woman is in danger. It cannot be said to be simply a mechanism designed to protect the health of the pregnant woman. While this latter objective clearly explains the requirement that the practising physician be a "qualified medical practitioner" and that the abortion take place in a safe place, it cannot explain the necessary intercession of an in-hospital committee of three physicians from which is excluded the practising physician. . . .

I do not believe it to be unreasonable to seek independent medical confirmation of the threat to the woman's life or health when such an important and distinct interest hangs in the balance. I note with interest that in a number of foreign jurisdictions, laws which decriminalize abortions require an opinion as to the state of health of the woman independent from the opinion of her own physician. The Crown, in its book of authorities, cited the following statutes which included such a mechanism: United Kingdom, Abortion Act, 1967, c. 87, s. 1(1)(a); Australian Northern Territory, Criminal Law Consolidation Act, s. 79 A(3)(a); South Australia, Criminal Law Consolidation Act, 1935-1975, s. 82a(1)(a); West Germany, Criminal Code, as amended by the Fifteenth Criminal Law Amendment Act (1976), s. 219; Israel, Penal Law, 5737-1977 (as amended), s. 315; New Zealand, Crimes Act 1961, as amended by the Crimes Amendment Act 1977 and the Crimes Amendment Act 1978, s. 187A(4); Code penal suisse, art. 120(1). . . .

The assertion that an independent medical opinion, distinct from that of the pregnant woman and her practising physician, does not offend the principles of fundamental justice would need to be reevaluated if a right of access to abortion is founded upon the right to "liberty" in s. 7 of the Charter. I am of the view that there would still be circumstances in which the state interest in the protection of the foetus would require an independent medical opinion as to the danger to the life or health of the pregnant woman. Assuming without deciding that a right of access to abortion can be founded upon the right to "liberty", there would be a point in time at which the state interest in the foetus would become compelling. From this point in time, Parliament would be entitled to limit abortions to those required by therapeutic reasons and therefore require an independent opinion as to the health exception. The case law reveals a substantial difference of opinion as to the state interest in the protection of the foetus as against the pregnant woman's right to liberty. . . . As I indicated at the outset of my reasons, it is nevertheless possible to resolve this appeal without attempting to delineate the right to "liberty" in s. 7 of the Charter. The violation of the right to "security of the person" and the relevant principles of fundamental justice are sufficient to invalidate s. 251 of the Criminal Code.

Some delay is inevitable in connection with any system which purports to limit to therapeutic reasons the grounds upon which an abortion can be performed lawfully. Any statutory mechanism for ensuring an independent confirmation as to the state of the woman's life or health, adopted pursuant to the objective of assuring the protection of the foetus, will inevitably result in a delay which would exceed whatever delay would be encountered if an independent opinion was not required. Furthermore, rules promoting the safety of abortions designed to protect the interest of the pregnant woman will also cause some unavoidable delay. It is only insofar as the administrative structure creates delays which are unnecessary that the structure can be considered to violate the principles of fundamental justice. Indeed, an examination of the delays caused by certain of the procedural requirements in s. 251(4) reveals that they are unnecessary, given Parliament's objectives in establishing the administrative structure. I note parenthetically that it is not sufficient to argue that the structure would operate in a fair manner but for the applications from women who do not qualify in respect of the standard in s. 251(4)(c). A fair structure, put in place to decide between those women who qualify for a therapeutic abortion and those who do not, should be designed with a view to efficiently meeting the demands which it must necessarily serve.

One such example of a rule which is unnecessary is the requirement in s. 251(4) that therapeutic abortions must take place in an eligible hospital to be lawful. I have observed that s. 251(4) directs that therapeutic abortions take place in accredited or approved hospitals, with at least four physicians, and that, because of the lack of such hospitals in many parts of Canada, this often causes delay for women seeking treatment. As I noted earlier, this requirement was plainly adopted to assure the safety of the abortion procedure generally, and particularly the safety of the pregnant woman, after the standard of s. 251(4) has been met and after the certificate to this effect has been issued enabling the woman to have a lawful abortion. The objective in respect of which the in-hospital rule was adopted is safety and not the state interest in the protection of the foetus. As the rule stands in s. 251(4), however, no exception is currently possible. The evidence discloses that there is no justification for the requirement that all therapeutic abortions take place in hospitals eligible under the Criminal Code. In this sense, the delays which result from the hospital requirement are unnecessary and, consequently, in this respect, the administrative structure for therapeutic abortions is manifestly unfair and offends the principles of fundamental justice.

Experts testified at trial that the principal justification for the in-hospital rule is the problem of post-operative complications....

In many cases, however, there is no medical justification that the therapeutic abortion take place in a hospital. Experts testified at trial, that many first trimester therapeutic abortions may be safely performed in specialized clinics outside of hospitals because the possible complications can be handled, and in some cases better handled, by the facilities of a specialized clinic....

The substantial increase in the percentage of abortions performed on an out-patient basis since 1975 underscores the view that the in-hospital requirement, which may have been justified when it was first adopted, has become exorbitant. One suspects that the number of out-patient abortions would be even higher if the Criminal Code did not prevent women in many parts of Canada from obtaining timely and effective treatment by requiring them to travel to places where eligible hospital facilities were available. Furthermore, these figures do not include out-patient abortions which may have qualified as therapeutic under the standard in s. 251(4)(c) which were performed on Canadian women in the United States and in clinics currently operating in Canada outside the s. 251(4) exception. . . .

The presence of legislation in other jurisdictions permitting certain abortions to be performed outside of hospitals is especially revealing as to the safety of the procedure in those circumstances and of the necessity to provide alternative means given the limited resources of hospitals. . . . In the Powell Report, it was observed that:

> In a number of European countries, including the Netherlands, Poland and West Germany, approximately half of the abortions are performed in non-hospital facilities. In France in 1982, 53 percent of abortions were performed in 90 "centres d' interruption volontaire de grossesse" which were administered by hospitals but were in practice separate abortion clinics. The French government ordered all public hospitals that could not meet the demand for abortions to provide such clinics.

Particularly striking is the United States experience in respect of the in-hospital rule. The Powell Report noted that 82% of abortions performed in the United States in 1982 were done outside of hospitals. . . .

Whatever the eventual solution may be, it is plain that the in-hospital requirement is not justified in all cases. Although the protection of health of the woman is the objective which the in-hospital rule is intended to serve, the requirement that all therapeutic abortions be performed in eligible hospitals is unnecessary to meet that objective in all cases. In this sense, the rule is manifestly unfair and offends the principles of fundamental justice. . . .

An objection can also be raised in respect of the requirement that the committee come from the accredited or approved hospital in which the abortion is to be performed. It is difficult to see a connection between this requirement and any of the practical purposes for which s. 251(4) was enacted. . . .

The Law Reform Commission's Working Group raises the possibility of regional abortion committees to replace the current rule. The Powell Report proposals include a model whereby a central therapeutic abortion committee could serve several hospitals.

Whatever solution is finally retained, it is plain that the requirement that the therapeutic abortion committee come from the hospital in which the abortion will be performed serves no real purpose. The risk resulting from the delay caused by s. 251(4) in this respect is unnecessary. Consequently, this requirement violates the principles of fundamental justice.

Other aspects of the committee requirement in s. 251(4) add to the manifest unfairness of the administrative structure. . . . Allowing a board to increase the number of members above a statutory minimum of three members does not add to the integrity of the independent opinion. This aspect of the current rule is unnecessary and, since it can result in increased risks, offends the principles of fundamental justice.

Similarly, the exclusion of all physicians who practise therapeutic abortions from the committees is exorbitant. This rule was no doubt included in s. 251(4) to promote the independence of the therapeutic abortion committees' appreciation of the standard. As I have said, the exclusion of the practising physician, although it diverges from usual medical practice, is appropriate in the criminal context to ensure the independent opinion with respect to the life or health of that physician's patient. The exclusion of all physicians who perform therapeutic abortions from committees, even when they have no connection with the patient in question, is not only unnecessary but potentially counterproductive. There are no reasonable grounds to suspect bias from a physician who has no connection with the patient simply because, in the course of his or her medical practice, he or she performs <u>lawful</u> abortions. Furthermore, physicians who perform therapeutic abortions have useful expertise which would add to the precision and the integrity of the independent opinion itself. Some state control is appropriate to ensure the independence of the opinion. However, this rule as it now stands is excessive and can increase the risk of delay because fewer physicians are qualified to serve on the committees.

The foregoing analysis of the administrative structure of s. 251(4) is by no means a complete catalogue of all the current systems' strengths and failings. It demonstrates, however, that the administrative structure put in place by Parliament has enough shortcomings so that s. 251(4), when considered as a whole, violates the principles of fundamental justice. These shortcomings stem from rules which are not necessary to the purposes for which s. 251(4) was established. These unnecessary rules, because they impose delays which result in an additional risk to women's health, are manifestly unfair.

V—Section 1 of the Charter

I agree with the view that s. 1 of the Charter can be used to save a legislative provision which breaches s. 7 in the manner which s. 251 of the Criminal Code violates s. 7 in this case. . . .

. . . Those seeking to uphold s. 251 of the Criminal Code must demonstrate the following:

(1) the objective which s. 251 is designed to serve must "relate to concerns which are pressing and substantial", and

(2) "once a sufficiently significant objective is recognized, then the party invoking s. 1 must show that the means chosen are reasonable

and demonstrably justified. This involves a 'form of proportionality test' ".

I shall consider each of these two criteria which must be met if the limit on the s. 7 right is to be found reasonable. . . .

. . . [A]s federal legislation in respect of Parliament's jurisdiction over the criminal law in s. 91(27) of the Constitution Act, 1867, s. 251 cannot be said to have as its sole or principal objective, as the appellants argue, the protection of the life or health of the pregnant women. Legislation which in its pith and substance is related to the life or health of pregnant women, depending of course on its precise terms, would be characterized as in relation to one of the provincial heads of power. The exculpatory provision in s. 251(4) cannot stand on its own as a valid exercise of Parliament's criminal law power.

Does the objective of protecting the foetus in s. 251 relate to concerns which are pressing and substantial in a free and democratic society? The answer to the first step of the *Oakes* test is yes. I am of the view that the protection of the foetus is and, as the Court of Appeal observed, always has been, a valid objective in Canadian criminal law. I have already elaborated on this objective in my discussion of the principles of fundamental justice. I think s. 1 of the Charter authorizes reasonable limits to be put on a woman's right having regard to the state interest in the protection of the foetus.

I turn now to the second test in *Oakes*. The Crown must show that the means chosen in s. 251 are reasonable and demonstrably justified . . . [and meet] the proportionality test.

. . . A rule which is unnecessary in respect of Parliament's objectives cannot be said to be "rationally connected" thereto or to be "carefully designed to achieve the objective in question". Furthermore, not only are some of the rules in s. 251 unnecessary to the primary objective of the protection of the foetus and the ancillary objective of the protection of the pregnant woman's life or health, but their practical effect is to undermine the health of the woman which Parliament purports to consider so important. Consequently, s. 251 does not meet the proportionality test in *Oakes*. . . .

Given my conclusion in respect of the first component of the proportionality test, it is not necessary to address the questions as to whether the means in s. 251 "impair as little as possible" the s. 7 Charter right and whether there is a proportionality between the effects of s. 251 and the objective of protecting the foetus. Thus, I am not required to answer the difficult question concerning the circumstances in which there is a proportionality between the effects of s. 251 which limit the right of pregnant women to security of the person and the objective of the protection of the foetus. I do feel bound, however, to comment . . . [that] [t]he objective of protecting the foetus would not justify, in my view, the severity of the breach of pregnant women's right to security which would result if the exculpatory provision was completely removed from the Criminal Code. . . .

... This decision of the Canadian Parliament to the effect that the life or health of the pregnant woman takes precedence over the state interest in the foetus is also reflected in legislation in other free and democratic societies....

Finally, I wish to stress that we have not been asked to decide nor is it necessary, given my own conclusion that s. 251 contains rules unnecessary to the protection of the foetus, to decide whether a foetus is included in the word "everyone" in s. 7 so as to have a right to "life, liberty and security of the person" under the Charter....

The reasons of McINTYRE and LaFOREST JJ. were delivered by

McINTYRE J. (dissenting):— ... There is no female person involved in the case who has been denied a therapeutic abortion and, as a result, the whole argument on the right to security of the person, under s. 7 of the Charter, has been on a hypothetical basis. The case, however, was addressed by all the parties on that basis and the court has accepted that position.... [According to the Attorney General of Canada]

> The evidence of opinion surveys indicates that [r]oughly 21 to 23% of people at one end of the spectrum are of the view, on the one hand, that abortion is a matter solely for the decision of the pregnant woman and that any legislation on this subject is an unwarranted interference with a woman's right to deal with her own body, while about 19 to 20% are of the view, on the other hand, that destruction of the living fetus is the killing of human life and tantamount to murder. The remainder of the population (about 60%) are of the view that abortion should be prohibited in some circumstances.

Parliament has heeded neither extreme. Instead, an attempt has been made to balance the competing interests of the unborn child and the pregnant woman. Where the provisions of s. 251(4) are met, the abortion may be performed without legal sanction. Where they are not, abortion is deemed to be socially undesirable and is punished as a crime....

Scope of judicial review under the Charter

Before the adoption of the Charter, there was little question of the limits of judicial review of the criminal law. For all practical purposes it was limited to a determination of whether the impugned enactment dealt with a subject which could fall within the criminal law power in s. 91(27) of the Constitution Act, 1867. There was no doubt of the power of Parliament to say what was and what was not criminal and to prohibit criminal conduct with penal sanctions, although from 1960 onwards legislation was subject to review under the Canadian Bill of Rights: see Morgentaler, supra. The adoption of the Charter brought a significant change. The power of judicial review of legislation acquired greater scope but, in my view, that scope is not unlimited and should be carefully confined to that which is ordained by the Charter. I am well aware that there will be disagreement about what was ordained by the Charter and, of course, a measure of interpretation of the Charter will be required in order to give substance and reality to its provisions. But the courts must not, in the guise of interpretation, postulate rights and freedoms which do not have a firm and a reasonably identifiable base in the Charter.... I would suggest that in "ensuring that the legislative initiatives pursued by our Parliament and legislatures conform to the democratic values expressed in the Canadian Charter of Rights and Freedoms" the courts must confine themselves to such democratic values as are clearly found and expressed in the Charter and refrain from imposing or creating other values not so based....

I adopt the words of Holmes J., which were referred to in Ferguson v. Skrupa, 372 U.S. 726 at pp. 729-30 (1963):

> There was a time when the Due Process Clause was used by this Court to strike down laws which were thought unreasonable, that is, unwise or incompatible with some particular economic or social philosophy. In this manner the Due Process Clause was used, for example, to nullify laws prescribing maximum hours for work in bakeries, Lochner v. New York, 198 U.S. 45 (1905), outlawing "yellow dog" contracts, Coppage v. Kansas, 236 U.S. 1 (1915), setting minimum wages for women, Adkins v. Children's Hospital, 261 U.S. 525 (1923), and fixing the weight of loaves of bread, Jay Burns Baking Co. v. Bryan, 264 U.S. 504 (1924). This intrusion by the judiciary into the realm of legislative value judgments was strongly objected to at the time, particularly by Mr. Justice Holmes and Mr. Justice Brandeis. Dissenting from the Court's invalidating a state statute which regulated the resale price of theatre and other tickets, Mr. Justice Holmes said:
>
> > "I think the proper course is to recognize that a state legislature can do whatever it sees fit to do unless it is restrained by some express prohibition in the Constitution of the United States or of the State, and that Courts should be careful not to extend such prohibitions beyond their obvious meaning by reading into them conceptions of public policy that the particular Court may happen to entertain".
>
> And in an earlier case he had emphasized that, "The criterion of constitutionality is not whether we believe the law to be for the public good." ...

[T]he courts should interpret the Charter in a manner calculated to give effect to its provisions, not to the idiosyncratic view of the judge who is writing. This approach marks out the limits of appropriate Charter adjudication. It confines the content of Charter guaranteed rights and freedoms to the purposes given expression in the Charter. Consequently, while the courts must continue to give a fair, large and liberal construction to the Charter provisions, this approach prevents the court from abandoning its traditional adjudicatory function in order to formulate its own conclusions on questions of public policy, a step which this court has said on numerous occasions it must not take....

It is not for the courts to manufacture a constitutional right out of whole cloth. I conclude on this question by citing and adopting the following words, although spoken in dissent, from the judgment of Harlan J. in Reynolds v. Sims, 377 U.S. 533 (1964), which, in my view, while stemming from the American experience, are equally applicable in a consideration of the Canadian position. Harlan J. commented, at pp. 624-5, on the:

> ... current mistaken view of the Constitution and the constitutional function of this Court. This view, in a nutshell, is that every major social ill in this country can find its cure in some constitutional "principle," and that this Court should "take the lead" in promoting reform when other branches of government fail to act. The Constitution is not a panacea for every blot upon the public welfare, nor should this Court, ordained as a judicial body, be thought of as a general haven for reform movements. The Constitution is an instrument of government, fundamental to which is the premise that in a diffusion of governmental authority lies the greatest promise that this Nation will realize liberty for all its citizens. This Court, limited in function in accordance with that premise, does not serve its high purpose when it exceeds its authority, even to satisfy justified impatience with the slow workings of the political process. For when, in the name of constitutional interpretation, the Court adds something to the Constitution that was deliberately excluded from it, the Court in reality substitutes its view of what should be so for the amending process.

The right to abortion and s. 7 of the Charter

The judgment of my colleague, Wilson J., is based upon the proposition that a pregnant woman has a right, under s. 7 of the Charter, to have an abortion. The same concept underlies the judgment of the Chief Justice. He reached the conclusion that a law which forces a woman to carry a foetus to term, unless certain criteria are met which are unrelated to her own priorities and aspirations, impairs the security of her person. That, in his view, is the effect of s. 251 of the Criminal Code. He has not said in specific terms that the pregnant woman has the right to an abortion, whether therapeutic or otherwise. In my view, however, his whole position depends for its validity upon that proposition and that interference with the right constitutes an infringement of her right to security of the person. It is said that a law which forces a woman to carry a foetus to term unless she meets certain criteria unrelated to her own priorities and aspirations interferes with security of her person. If compelling a woman to complete her pregnancy interferes with security of her person, it can only be because the concept of security of her person includes a right not to be compelled to carry the child to completion of her pregnancy. This, then, is simply to say that she has a right to have an abortion. It follows, then, that if no such right can be shown, it cannot be said that security of her person has been infringed by state action or otherwise. . . .

The proposition that women enjoy a constitutional right to have an abortion is devoid of support in the language of s. 7 of the Charter or any other section. While some human rights documents, such as the American Convention on Human Rights, 1969 (art. 4(1)), expressly address the question of abortion, the Charter is entirely silent on the point. It may be of some significance that the Charter uses specific language in dealing with other topics, such as voting rights, religion, expression and such controversial matters as mobility rights, language rights and minority rights, but remains silent on the question of abortion which, at the time the Charter was under consideration, was as much a subject of public controversy as it is today. . . .

The historical review of the legal approach in Canada taken from the judgment of the Court of Appeal serves, as well, to cast light on the underlying philosophies of our society and establishes that there has never been a general right to abortion in Canada. There has always been clear recognition of a public interest in the protection of the unborn and there has been no evidence or indication of any general acceptance of the concept of abortion at will in our society. It is to be observed as well that at the time of adoption of the Charter the sole provision--for an abortion in Canadian law was that to be found in s. 251 of the Criminal Code. It follows then, in my view, that the interpretive approach to the Charter, which has been accepted in this court, affords no support for the entrenchment of a constitutional right of abortion.

As to an asserted right to be free from any state interference with bodily integrity and serious state-imposed psychological stress, I would say that to be accepted, as a constitutional right, it would have to be based on something more than the mere imposition, by the State, of such stress and anxiety. It must, surely, be evident that many forms of government action deemed to be reasonable, and even necessary in our society, will cause stress and anxiety to many, while at the same time being acceptable exercises of government power in pursuit of socially desirable goals. The very facts of life in a modern society would preclude the entrenchment of such a constitutional right. . . . It is hard to imagine a governmental policy or initiative which will not create significant stress or anxiety for some and, frequently, for many members of the community. Governments must have the power to expropriate land, to zone land, to regulate its use and the rights and conditions of its occupation. The exercise of these powers is frequently the cause of serious stress and anxiety. . . . At the present time there is great pressure on governments to restrict—and even forbid—the use of tobacco. Government action in this field will produce much stress and anxiety among smokers and growers of tobacco, but it cannot be said that this will render unconstitutional control and regulatory measures adopted by governments. Other illustrations abound to make the point.

To invade the s. 7 right of security of the person, there would have to be more than state-imposed stress or strain. A breach of the right would have to be based upon an infringement of some interest which would be of such nature and such importance as to warrant constitutional protection.

This, it would seem to me, would be limited to cases where the state-action complained of, in addition to imposing stress and strain, also infringed another right, freedom or interest which was deserving of protection under the concept of security of the person. For the reasons outlined above, the right to have an abortion—given the language, structure and history of the Charter and given the history, traditions and underlying philosophies of our society—is not such an interest. . . .

. . . [S]ave for the provisions of the Criminal Code, which permit abortion where the life or health of the woman is at risk, no right of abortion can be found in Canadian law, custom or tradition, and . . . the Charter, including s. 7, creates no further right. Accordingly, it is my view that s. 251 of the Code does not in its terms violate s. 7 of the Charter. Even accepting the assumption that the concept of security of the person would extend to vitiating a law which would require a woman to carry a child to the completion of her pregnancy at the risk of her life or health, it must be observed that this is not our case. As has been pointed out, s. 251 of the Code already provides for abortion in such circumstances.

Procedural fairness

I now turn to the appellant's argument regarding the procedural fairness of s. 251 of the Criminal Code. The basis of the argument is that the exemption provisions of s-s. (4) are such as to render illusory or practically illusory any defence arising from the subsection for many women who seek abortions. . . .

It would seem to me that a defence created by Parliament could only be said to be illusory or practically so when the defence is not available in the circumstances in which it is held out as being available. The very nature of the test assumes, of course, that it is for Parliament to define the defence and, in so doing, to designate the terms and conditions upon which it may be available. . . . I would suggest it is apparent that the court's role is not to second-guess Parliament's policy choice as to how broad or how narrow the defence should be. The determination of when "the disapprobation of society is not warranted" is in Parliament's hands. . . .

In my opinion, then, the contention that the defence provided in s. 251(4) of the Criminal Code is illusory cannot be supported. From evidence adduced by the appellants, it may be said that many women seeking abortions have been unable to get them in Canada because s. 251(4) fails to respond to this need. This cannot serve as an argument supporting the claim that s-s. (4) is procedurally unfair. Section 251(4) was designed to meet specific circumstances. Its aim is to restrict abortion to cases where the continuation of the pregnancy would, or would likely, be injurious to the life or health of the woman concerned, not to provide unrestricted access to abortion. It was to meet this requirement that Parliament provided for the administrative procedures to invoke the defence in s-s. (4). This machinery was considered adequate to deal with the type of abortion Parliament had envisaged. When, however, as the evidence would indicate, many more would seek abortions on a basis far wider than that contemplated by Parliament, any system would come under stress and possibly fail.... It is not open to a court, in my view, to strike down a statutory provision on this basis....

I would adopt as clearly expressive of the proper approach to be taken by the courts in dealing with Charter issues the words of Taylor, J., ...:

> It is, of course, true that the function of the courts has been extended. In many cases in which the meaning or proper application of the Charter is in doubt the courts must decide whether or not a legislative, administrative or other act complained of requires constitutional sanction, and such decisions may well have social or economic consequences. As has been emphasized by Mr. Justice Lamer in Reference re Section 94(2) of the Motor Vehicle Act [1985] 2 S.C.R. 486 at pp. 496-7, 24 D.L.R. (4th) 536 at pp. 544-5, this imposes on the courts a new and onerous duty. In carrying out that task, however, the courts can be concerned with social or economic implications only to the extent that they assist in answering the question whether or not the right claimed is one entitled to constitutional protection. The rights to which the Charter grants protection are those fundamental to the free and democratic society.

This approach is applicable to the abortion question. The solution to this question in this country must be left to Parliament. It is for Parliament to pronounce on and to direct social policy. This is not because Parliament can claim all wisdom and knowledge but simply because Parliament is elected for that purpose in a free democracy and, in addition, has the facilities—the exposure to public opinion and information—as well as the political power to make effective its decisions. I refer with full approval to a further comment by Taylor J., at p. 210 D.L.R.:

> The present case may serve, perhaps, to emphasize that the courts lack both the exposure to public opinion required in order to discharge the essentially "political" task of weighing social or economic interests and deciding between them, and also the ability to gather the information they would need for that task. When it has run its course the litigation may also have served to demonstrate—if demonstration be needed—that the judicial system of necessity lacks the capacity of parliamentary bodies to act promptly when economic or social considerations indicate that a change in the law is desirable and, of equal importance, to react promptly when results show either that a change made for that purpose has not achieved its objective or that the objective is no longer desirable....

Opinion of Wilson J.

Wilson J.:—At the heart of this appeal is the question whether a pregnant woman can, as a constitutional matter, be compelled by law to carry the foetus to term. The legislature has proceeded on the basis that she can be so compelled and, indeed, has made it a criminal offence punishable by imprisonment under s. 251 of the Criminal Code, for her or her physician to terminate the pregnancy unless the procedural requirements of the section are complied with.

My colleagues, the Chief Justice and Beetz J., ... have found that the requirements do not comport with the principles of fundamental justice in the procedural sense and have concluded that, since they cannot be severed from the provisions creating the substantive offence, the whole of s. 251 must fall.

With all due respect, I think that the court must tackle the primary issue first. A consideration as to whether or not the procedural requirements for obtaining or performing an abortion comport with fundamental justice is purely academic if such requirements cannot as a constitutional matter be imposed at all. If a pregnant woman cannot, as a constitutional matter, be compelled by law to carry the foetus to term against her will, a review of the procedural requirements by which she may be compelled to do so seems pointless. Moreover, it would, in my opinion, be an exercise in futility for the legislature to expend its time and energy in attempting to remedy the defects in the procedural requirements unless it has some assurance that this process will, at the end of the day, result in the creation of a valid criminal offence. I turn, therefore, to what I believe is the central issue that must be addressed. . . .

[Discussing Section 7 of the Charter]

... If either the right to liberty or the right to security of the person or a combination of both confers on the pregnant woman the right to decide for herself (with the guidance of her physician) whether or not to have an abortion, then we have to examine the legislative scheme not only from the point of view of fundamental justice in the procedural sense but in the substantive sense as well. I think, therefore, that we must answer the question: what is meant by the right to liberty in the context of the abortion issue? Does it, as Mr. Manning suggests, give the pregnant woman control over decisions affecting her own body? If not, does her right to security of the person give her such control? I turn first to the right to liberty.

(a) The Right to Liberty ...

The Charter is predicated on a particular conception of the place of the individual in society. An individual is not a totally independent entity disconnected from the society in which he or she lives. Neither, however, is the individual a mere cog in an impersonal machine in which his or her values, goals and aspirations are subordinated to those of the collectivity. The individual is a bit of both. The Charter reflects this reality by leaving a wide range of activities and decisions open to legitimate government control while at the same time placing limits on the proper scope of that control. Thus, the rights guaranteed in the Charter erect around each individual, metaphorically speaking, an invisible fence over which the state will not be allowed to trespass. The role of the courts is to map out, piece by piece, the parameters of the fence.

The Charter and the right to individual liberty guaranteed under it are inextricably tied to the concept of human dignity.... Professor Neal MacCormick, Regius Professor of Public Law [,] University of Edinburgh, ...[states]:

> To be able to decide what to do and how to do it, to carry out one's own decisions and accept their consequences, seems to me essential to one's self-respect as a human being, and essential to the possibility of that contentment. Such self-respect and contentment are in my judgment fundamental goods for human beings, the worth of life itself being on condition of having or striving for them. If a person were deliberately denied the opportunity of self-respect and that contentment, he would suffer deprivation of his essential humanity....

According to *Oakes*,

> A second contextual element of interpretation of s. 1 is provided by the words "free and democratic society". Inclusion of these words as the final standard of justification for limits on rights and freedoms refers the court to the very purpose for which the Charter was originally entrenched in the Constitution: Canadian society is to be free and democratic. The court must be guided by the values and principles essential to a free and democratic society which I believe embody, to name but a few, respect for the inherent dignity of the human person, commitment to social justice and equality, accommodation of a wide variety of beliefs, respect for cultural and group identity, and faith in social and political institutions which enhance the participation of individuals and groups in society. The underlying values and principles of a free and democratic society are the genesis of the rights and freedoms guaranteed by the Charter and the ultimate standard against which a limit on a right or freedom must be shown, despite its effect, to be reasonable and demonstrably justified....

... [A]n aspect of the respect for human dignity on which the Charter is founded is the right to make fundamental personal decisions without interference from the state. This right is a critical component of the right to liberty. Liberty ... is a phrase capable of a broad range of meaning. In my view, this right, properly construed, grants the individual a degree of autonomy in making decisions of fundamental personal importance....

Liberty in a free and democratic society does not require the state to approve the personal decisions made by its citizens; it does, however, require the state to respect them.

This conception of the proper ambit of the right to liberty under our Charter is consistent with the American jurisprudence on the subject....

... [B]y a process of accretion the scope of the right of individuals to make fundamental decisions affecting their private lives was elaborated in the United States on a case by case basis. The parameters of the fence were being progressively defined.

For our purposes the most interesting development in this area of American law are the decisions of the Supreme Court in Roe v. Wade, 410 U.S. 113 (1973), and its sister case Doe v. Bolton, 410 U.S. 179 (1973)....

The decision in Roe v. Wade was reaffirmed by the Supreme Court in City of Akron v. Akron Center for Reproductive Health Inc., 462 U.S. 416 (1983), and again, though by a bare majority, in Thornburgh v. American College of Obstetricians and Gynecologists, 106 S.Ct. 2169 (1986)....

In my opinion, the respect for individual decision-making in matters of fundamental personal importance reflected in the American jurisprudence also informs the Canadian Charter.... [T]he right to liberty contained in s. 7 guarantees to every individual a degree of personal autonomy over important decisions intimately affecting their private lives.

The question then becomes whether the decision of a woman to terminate her pregnancy falls within this class of protected decisions. I have no doubt that it does. This decision is one that will have profound psychological, economic and social consequences for the pregnant woman. The circumstances giving rise to it can be complex and varied and there may be, and usually are, powerful considerations militating in opposite directions. It is a decision that deeply reflects the way the woman thinks about herself and her relationship to others and to society at large. It is not just a medical decision; it is a profound social and ethical one as well. Her response to it will be the response of the whole person.

It is probably impossible for a man to respond, even imaginatively, to such a dilemma not just because it is outside the realm of his personal experience (although this is, of course, the case) but because he can relate to it only by objectifying it, thereby eliminating the subjective elements of the female psyche which are at the heart of the dilemma ... [T]he history of the struggle for human rights from the 18th century on has been the history of men struggling to assert their dignity and common humanity against an overbearing state apparatus. The more recent struggle for women's rights has been a struggle to eliminate discrimination, to achieve a place for women in a man's world, to develop a set of legislative reforms in order to place women in the same position as men.... It has not been a struggle to define the rights of women in relation to their special place in the societal structure and in relation to the biological distinction between the two sexes. Thus, women's needs and aspirations are only now being translated into protected rights. The right to reproduce or not to reproduce which is in issue in this case is one such right and is properly perceived as an integral part of modern woman's struggle to assert her dignity and worth as a human being.

Given then that the right to liberty guaranteed by s. 7 of the Charter gives a women the right to decide for herself whether or not to terminate her pregnancy, does s. 251 of the Criminal Code violate this right? Clearly it does. The purpose of the section is to take the decision away from the woman and give it to a committee. Furthermore, as the Chief Justice correctly points out, the committee bases its decision on "criteria entirely unrelated to [the pregnant woman's] priorities and aspirations". The fact that the decision whether a woman will be allowed to terminate her pregnancy is in the hands of a committee is just as great a violation of the woman's right to personal autonomy in decisions of an intimate and private nature as it would be if a committee were established to decide whether a woman should be allowed to continue her pregnancy. Both these arrangements violate the woman's right to liberty by deciding for her something that she has the right to decide for herself.

(b) The right to security of the person . . .

I agree with the Chief Justice and with Beetz J. that the right to "security of the person" under s. 7 of the Charter protects both the physical and psychological integrity of the individual . . .

[Discussing the scope of the right under s. 7]

(a) The principles of fundamental justice

Does s. 251 deprive women of their right to liberty and to security of the person "in accordance with the principles of fundamental justice"? . . .

In my view, the deprivation of the s. 7 right with which we are concerned in this case offends s. 2(a) of the Charter. I say this because I believe that the decision whether or not to terminate a pregnancy is essentially a moral decision, a matter of conscience. I do not think there is or can be any dispute about that. The question is: whose conscience? Is the conscience of the woman to be paramount or the conscience of the state? I believe, for the reasons I gave in discussing the right to liberty, that in a free and democratic society it must be the conscience of the individual. Indeed, s. 2(a) makes it clear that this freedom belongs to "everyone", i.e., to each of us individually. I quote the section for convenience:

2.   Everyone has the following fundamental freedoms:

(a) freedom of conscience and religion . . .

In R. v. Big M Drug Mart, Ltd., Dickson, C.J. made some very insightful comments . . . :

What unites enunciated freedoms in the American First Amendment, s. 2(a) of the Charter and in the provisions of other human rights documents in which they are associated is the notion of the centrality of individual conscience and the inappropriateness of governmental intervention to compel or to constrain its manifestation. In Hunter v. Southam, supra, the purpose of the Charter was identified, at p. 649, 11 DLR (4th) 641 (1984), as "the unremitting protection of individual rights and liberties". It is easy to see the relationship between respect for individual conscience and the valuation of human dignity that motivates such unremitting protection. . . .

It seems to me . . . that in a free and democratic society "freedom of conscience and religion" should be broadly construed to extend to conscientiously-held beliefs, whether grounded in religion or in a secular morality. Indeed, as a matter of statutory interpretation, "conscience" and "religion" should not be treated as tautologous if capable of independent, although related, meaning. Accordingly, for the state to take sides on the issue of abortion, as it does in the impugned legislation by making it a criminal offence for the pregnant woman to exercise one of her options, is not only to endorse but also to enforce, on pain of a further loss of liberty through actual imprisonment, one conscientiously-held view at the expense of another. It is to deny freedom of conscience to some, to treat them as means to an end, to deprive them, as Professor MacCormick puts it, of their "essential humanity". Can this comport with fundamental justice? Was Blackmun J. not correct when he said in Thornburgh, supra, at p. 2185: "A woman's right to make that choice freely is fundamental. Any other result . . . would protect inadequately a central part of the sphere of liberty that our law guarantees equally to all."

Legislation which violates freedom of conscience in this manner cannot, in my view, be in accordance with the principles of fundamental justice within the meaning of s. 7. . . .

(b) Section 1 of the Charter . . .

Section 251 of the Criminal Code takes the decision away from the woman at all stages of her pregnancy. It is a complete denial of the woman's constitutionally protected right under s. 7, not merely a limitation on it. It cannot, in my opinion, meet the proportionality test in *Oakes*. It is not sufficiently tailored to the legislative objective and does not impair the woman's right "as little as possible". It cannot be saved under s. 1. Accordingly, even if the section were to be amended to remedy the purely procedural defects in the legislative scheme referred to by the Chief Justice and Beetz J. it would, in my opinion, still not be constitutionally valid.

One final word. I wish to emphasize that in these reasons I have dealt with the existence of the developing foetus merely as a factor to be considered in assessing the importance of the legislative objective under s. 1 of the Charter. I have not dealt with the entirely separate question whether a foetus is covered by the word "everyone" in s. 7 so as to have an independent right to life under that section. The Crown did not argue it and it is not necessary to decide it in order to dispose of the issues on this appeal.

Appeal allowed; acquittals restored.

Questions and Comments on *Morgentaler*

1. Does the holding in *Morgentaler* differ from that in *Roe*? If so, how?

2. How did the text of the Canadian Charter affect the justices' decisions? Note that the Canadian Charter of Rights was adopted in 1982—9 years after *Roe*. Why do you think the subject was not addressed more specifically in the Charter?

3. What use did the justices make of the fact that the validity of the abortion statute arose in the context of a criminal prosecution? Consider whether any of the issues in *Casey* might have been decided differently in a different procedural setting.

4. *A Cautious Opinion?* According to some, the Canadian Supreme Court proceeded with "far more caution" than its U.S. counterpart did in *Roe*. Daniel O. Conkle, *Canada's Roe: The Canadian Abortion Decision and Its Implications for American Constitutional Law and Theory*, 6 Constitutional Commentary 299, 315–16 (1989). Conkle suggests that the Canadian Court acted commendably by avoiding final constitutional decision on the abortion question by opening a dialogue with Parliament, leaving largely for Parliament to decide how the interests of the mother and the interest in preserving fetal life should be resolved in the adoption of any new abortion statute. According to Conkle, the *Roe* court overreached, trying to provide a "final" answer, polarizing debate, and inhibiting political debate over the basic moral questions. Should constitutional courts strive for narrow, limited decisions on important constitutional issues, at least where the decision is to invalidate a law, as Conkle's argument suggests? (It may be relevant to note that protests, sometimes violent, over abortion policy and against abortion providers have occurred in Canada as well as in the United States in recent years, and that one effort to reinstate federal criminal regulation of abortion failed to pass the Parliament in 1991 on a tie vote.)

5. *Using U.S. Law:* Consider the use of U.S. constitutional cases in the opinions. One Canadian scholar has criticized Justice Wilson for "fail[ing] to note the controversy surrounding the conceptual foundation of this [U.S. abortion] case law and the precarious nature of its current hold" in the U.S., thereby losing "an opportunity to examine the extent to which American jurisprudence can reliably inform ... our understanding of the Charter." Lorraine Eisenstat Weinrib, *The Morgentaler Judgment: Constitutional Rights, Legislative Intention and Institutional Design*, 12 U. Toronto Law J. 1, 50 (1992). Professor Weinrib is also critical of dissenting Justice McIntyre, who relied on U.S. cases to suggest the perils of judicial activism, but then argued that Section 7 of the Charter fails to refer to (and thus does not protect rights to) abortion without, as Weinrib puts it, referring to "the troubled textual foundation of the American Supreme Court's recognition of a right against criminalization of abortion." Weinrib also criticizes Justice McIntyre for arguing that the silence of the text should be read to permit continued criminal regulation of abortion because during the Charter's formation the minister of justice had indicated that the Canadian Justice Department's view was that Section 7 would not interfere with Parliament's regulation of abortion. After noting that the Justice failed to consider portions of the Charter added after this comment, Weinrib says that, with respect to "[t]his kind of 'historical' analysis ... [i]f there is a morass one can choose to avoid by reflecting upon American experience, this is it." What, if any, are the lessons of the U.S. constitutional experience?

2.   INTRODUCTION TO THE GERMAN ABORTION DECISIONS

The German Constitutional Court, created by Article 94 of the Basic Law (the German constitution), has the exclusive power to invalidate laws on federal constitutional grounds. Cases can be brought before the Constitutional Court in several ways:

(1) through review of a law which a lower court has found is not compatible with the Basic Law;[d]

(2) through a constitutional complaint, which can be brought by any person, asserting a violation of certain basic rights, provided all other means of legal recourse have been exhausted;[e] and

(3) through abstract judicial review, provided for in Article 93(1). Under this form of review, the federal government, a *land* (state) government, or one-third of the Bundestag may ask the Constitutional Court to determine the compatibility of a federal or *land* law with the Basic Law, or the compatibility of a *land* law with any other federal law. As noted below, the first German Abortion Case was an abstract judicial review proceeding, initiated by Christian Democratic legislators. (Consider, as you read the following materials, whether the difference between "abstract" and "incidental" judicial review appears to have any discernible effect on the various courts' opinions you have read.)

The German experience with abortion prior to 1975 included a liberalization effort in the 1920s, culminating with a 1927 decision recognizing an abortion necessary for the mother's health and life as an "extra-statutory necessity."[f] In the 1930s, Nazi laws on heredity established a "eugenic test" designed to promote the purification of the German race. According to Eser, when the "eugenic test was repudiated at the end of World War II, the legality of abortion once again depended exclusively on medical criteria." The new Criminal Code of 1962 essentially endorsed the "medical test," under which approach the number of legal abortions rose from 2,858 in 1968 to 17,814 in 1974, while the number of those convicted for illegal abortions fell from 596 to 94 in the same period.

The 1960s saw further work on reform of abortion laws. Two alternative models were developed by a group of German and Swiss law professors. The first, or "indications model," went beyond the medical test in allowing abortion "when the carrying to term of the pregnancy cannot be expected of the mother considering all the aspects of her situation." Under this plan, abortion would be permitted for such reasons as where an additional child would jeopardize the well-being of existing children, or if the mother was a

d. The Basic Law refers to the German constitution. The lower courts in Germany may engage in incidental judicial review of constitutional challenges to laws, and have power to find such laws to be constitutional. If, however, a lower court concludes that a law passed by the national legislature is not constitutional, then under Article 100(1) the lower court must discontinue its proceedings and direct the question of constitutionality to the Federal Constitutional Court.

e. This is the most numerous category of cases filed before the Constitutional Court; however, screening committees of three judges dismiss most of these cases (i.e., 96–97%). The exhaustion requirement is strictly interpreted, as well.

f. The German experience with abortion is summarized in Albin Eser, *Reform of German Abortion Law: First Experiences*, 34 Am. J. Comp. L. 369, 370–73 (1986) on which this description relies.

minor at the time of conception. The second, more influential alternative was the so-called "periodic model," which would legalize abortion in the first three months provided that the woman consulted a counselling service beforehand. This model in some respects gave more priority to the mother's right to decide, but also sought, by requiring counseling, to limit abortions to severe situations.

The 1974 legislation at issue in the first German Abortion Decision was based largely on the periodic model, and was immediately challenged by a group of legislators (some of whom might have accepted an indications model). As you will see below, the Court rejected the 1974 version of the "periodic model."

West German Abortion Decision: A Contrast to Roe v. Wade, translated by Robert E. Jonas and John D. Gorby, in 9 John Marshall J. of Prac. & Proc. 605 (1978):

Guiding Principles applicable to the judgment of the First Senate of the 25th of February, 1975:

1.   The life which is developing itself in the womb of the mother is an independent legal value which enjoys the protection of the constitution (Article 2, Paragraph 2, Sentence 1; Article 1, Paragraph 1 of the Basic Law).

The State's duty to protect forbids not only direct state attacks against life developing itself, but also requires the state to protect and foster this life.

2.   The obligation of the state to protect the life developing itself exists, even against the mother.

3.   The protection of life of the child *en ventre sa mere* takes precedence as a matter of principle for the entire duration of the pregnancy over the right of the pregnant woman to self-determination and may not be placed in question for any particular time.

4.   The legislature may express the legal condemnation of the interruption of pregnancy required by the Basic Law through measures other than the threat of punishment. The decisive factor is whether the totality of the measures serving the protection of the unborn life guarantees an actual protection which in fact corresponds to the importance of the legal value to be guaranteed. In the extreme case, if the protection required by the constitution cannot be realized in any other manner, the legislature is obligated to employ the criminal law to secure the life developing itself.

5.   A continuation of the pregnancy is not to be exacted (legally) if the termination is necessary to avert from the pregnant woman a danger to her life or the danger of a serious impairment of her health. Beyond that the legislature is at liberty to designate as non-exactable other extraordinary

burdens for the pregnant woman, which are of similar gravity and, in these cases, to leave the interruption of pregnancy free of punishment.

6. The Fifth Statute to Reform the Penal Law of the 18th of June, 1974, (Federal Law Reporter I, p. 1297) has not in the required extent done justice to the constitutional obligation to protect prenatal life.

The Federal Constitutional Court—First Senate—President of the Court Dr. Benda, presiding, and Justices Ritterspach, Dr. Haager, Rupp von Brünneck, Dr. Böhmer, Dr. Faller, Dr. Brox, Dr. Simon, participating,

on the basis of the oral argument of the 18th and 19th of November 1974, recognizes as law by this opinion:

HOLDING

I. Section 218a of the Penal Code in the version of the Fifth Statute to Reform the Penal Law (5 PLRS) of June 18, 1974, is incompatible with Article 2, Paragraph 2, Sentence 1, in conjunction with Article 1, Paragraph 1, of the Basic Law and is null insofar as it excepts the interruption of pregnancy from criminal liability when no reasons are present which, in the sense of the reasons for this decision, have validity in the ordering of values of the Basic Law....

[The statutes at issue were as follows]

s. 218

Interruption of Pregnancy

(1) Anyone who interrupts a pregnancy after the 13th day following conception shall be punished by incarceration up to three years or fined.

. . .

s. 218a

Freedom from Punishment for Interruption of Pregnancy in the First Twelve Weeks

An interruption of pregnancy performed by a physician with the consent of the pregnant woman is not punishable under § 218 if no more than twelve weeks have elapsed since conception.

s. 218b

Indications for Interruption of Pregnancy After Twelve Weeks

An interruption of pregnancy performed by a physician with the consent of the pregnant woman after the expiration of twelve weeks after conception is not punishable under s. 218 if, according to the judgment of medical science:

1. The interruption of pregnancy is indicated in order to avert from the pregnant woman a danger to her life or the danger of a serious impairment to the condition of her health insofar as the danger

cannot be averted in a manner that is otherwise exactable (reasonably expected) from her, or

2.   Compelling reasons require the assumption that the child will suffer from an impairment of its health which cannot be remedied on account of an hereditary disposition or injurious prenatal influences which is so serious that a continuation of the pregnancy cannot be exacted (reasonably expected) of the pregnant woman; and not more than 22 weeks have elapsed since conception.

s. 218c

Interruption of Pregnancy Without Instruction
and Counseling of the Pregnant Woman

(1) He who interrupts a pregnancy without the pregnant woman:

1.   first having, on account of the question of the interruption of her pregnancy, presented herself to a physician or to a counseling center empowered for the purpose and there been instructed about the public and private assistance available for the pregnant women, mothers and children, especially such assistance which facilitates the continuation of the pregnancy and eases the condition of mother and child, and

2.   having been counseled by a physician, shall be punished up to one year incarceration or by a fine if the act is not punishable under s. 218.

(2) The woman upon whom the operation is performed is not subject to punishment under Paragraph one.

.   .   .

C

The question of the legal treatment of the interruption of pregnancy has been discussed publicly for decades from various points of view. . . . It is the task of the legislature to evaluate the many sided and often opposing arguments which develop from these various ways of viewing the question, to supplement them through considerations which are specifically legal and political as well as through the practical experiences of the life of the law, and, on this basis, to arrive at a decision as to the manner in which the legal order should respond to this social process. The statutory regulation in the Fifth Statute to Reform the Penal Law which was decided upon after extraordinarily comprehensive preparatory work can be examined by the Constitutional Court only from the viewpoint of whether it is compatible with the Basic Law, which is the highest valid law in the Federal Republic. The gravity and the seriousness of the constitutional question posed becomes clear, if it is considered that what is involved here is the protection of human life, one of the central values of every legal order. The decision regarding the standards and limits of legislative freedom of decision demands a total view of the constitutional norms and the hierarchy of values contained therein.

I

1. Article 2, Paragraph 2, Sentence 1, of the Basic Law also protects the life developing itself in the womb of the mother as an intrinsic legal value.

a) The express incorporation into the Basic Law of the self-evident right to life—in contrast to the Weimar Constitution—may be explained principally as a reaction to the "destruction of life unworthy of life," to the "final solution" and "liquidations," which were carried out by the National Socialistic Regime as measures of state. Article 2, Paragraph 2, Sentence 1, of the Basic Law, just as it contains the abolition of the death penalty in Article 102, includes "a declaration of the fundamental worth of human life and of a concept of the state which stands, in emphatic contrast to the philosophies of a political regime to which the individual life meant little and which therefore practiced limitless abuse with its presumed right over life and death of the citizen."

b) In construing Article 2, Paragraph 2, Sentence 1, of the Basic Law, one should begin with its language: "Everyone has a right to life ...". Life, in the sense of historical existence of a human individual, exists according to definite biological-physiological knowledge, in any case, from the 14th day after conception (nidation, individuation). The process of development which has begun at that point is a continuing process which exhibits no sharp demarcation and does not allow a precise division of the various steps of development of the human life. The process does not end even with birth; the phenomena of consciousness which are specific to the human personality, for example, appear for the first time a rather long time after birth. Therefore, the protection of Article 2, Paragraph 2, Sentence 1, of the Basic Law cannot be limited either to the "completed" human being after birth or to the child about to be born which is independently capable of living. The right to life is guaranteed to everyone who "lives"; no distinction can be made here between various stages of the life developing itself before birth, or between unborn and born life. "Everyone" in the sense of Article 2, Paragraph 2, Sentence 1, of the Basic Law is "everyone living"; expressed in another way: every life possessing human individuality; "everyone" also includes the yet unborn human being....

c) ... The security of human existence against encroachments by the state would be incomplete if it did not also embrace the prior step of "completed life," unborn life.

This extensive interpretation corresponds to the principle established in the opinions of the Federal Constitutional Court, "according to which, in doubtful cases, that interpretation is to be selected which develops to the highest degree the judicial effectiveness of the fundamental legal norm" (Decisions of the Federal Constitutional Court. 32, 54 71; 6, 55 72).

d) In support of this result the legislative history of Article 2, Paragraph 2, Sentence 1, of the Basic Law ... suggests that the formulation "everyone has the right to life" should also include "germinating" life. In any case, even less can be concluded from the materials on behalf of the contrary point of view. On the other hand, no evidence is found in the legislative history for answering the question whether unborn life must be protected by the penal law....

2.   The duty of the state to protect every human life may therefore be directly deduced from Article 2, Paragraph 2, Sentence I, of the Basic Law. In addition to that, the duty also results from the explicit provision of Article 1, Paragraph 1, Sentence 2, of the Basic Law since developing life participates in the protection which Article 1, Paragraph 1, of the Basic Law guarantees to human dignity. Where human life exists, human dignity is present to it; it is not decisive that the bearer of this dignity himself be conscious of it and know personally how to preserve it. The potential faculties present in the human being from the beginning suffice to establish human dignity....

3.   ... According to the constant judicial utterances of the Federal Constitutional Court, the fundamental legal norms contain not only subjective rights of defense of the individual against the state but embody, at the same time, an objective ordering of values, which is valid as a constitutionally fundamental decision for all areas of the law and which provides direction and impetus for legislation, administration, and judicial opinions....

II

1.   The duty of the state to protect is comprehensive. It forbids not only—self-evidently—direct state attacks on the life developing itself but also requires the state to take a position protecting and promoting this life, that is to say, it must, above all, preserve it even against illegal attacks by others. It is for the individual areas of the legal order, each according to its special function, to effectuate this requirement. The degree of seriousness with which the state must take its obligation to protect increases as the rank of the legal value in question increases in importance within the order of values of the Basic Law. Human life represents, within the order of the Basic Law, an ultimate value, the particulars of which need not be established; it is the living foundation of human dignity and the prerequisite for all other fundamental rights.

2.   The obligation of the state to take the life developing itself under protection exists, as a matter of principle, even against the mother. Without doubt, the natural connection of unborn life with that of the mother establishes an especially unique relationship, for which there is no parallel in other circumstances of life. Pregnancy belongs to the sphere of intimacy of the woman, the protection of which is constitutionally guaranteed through Article 2, Paragraph 1, in connection with Article 1, Paragraph 1, of the Basic Law. Were the embryo to be considered only as a part of the maternal organism the interruption of pregnancy would remain in the area

of the private structuring of one's life, where the legislature is forbidden to encroach. Since, however, the one about to be born is an independent human being who stands under the protection of the constitution, there is a social dimension to the interruption of pregnancy which makes it amenable to and in need of regulation by the state. The right of the woman to the free development of her personality, which has as its content the freedom of behavior in a comprehensive sense and accordingly embraces the personal responsibility of the woman to decide against parenthood and the responsibilities flowing from it, can also, it is true, likewise demand recognition and protection. This right, however, is not guaranteed without limits—the rights of others, the constitutional order, and the moral law limit it. *A priori*, this right can never include the authorization to intrude upon the protected sphere of right of another without justifying reason or much less to destroy that sphere along with the life itself; this is even less so, if, according to the nature of the case, a special responsibility exists precisely for this life.

A compromise which guarantees the protection of the life of the one about to be born and permits the pregnant woman the freedom of abortion is not possible since the interruption of pregnancy always means the destruction of the unborn life. In the required balancing, "both constitutional values are to be viewed in their relationship to human dignity, the center of the value system of the constitution" (Decisions of the Federal Constitutional Court, 35, 202, 225). A decision oriented to Article 1, Paragraph 1, of the Basic Law must come down in favor of the precedence of the protection of life for the child *en ventre sa mere* over the right of the pregnant woman to self-determination. Regarding many opportunities for development of personality, she can be adversely affected through pregnancy, birth and the education of her children. On the other hand, the unborn life is destroyed through the interruption of pregnancy. According to the principle of the balance which preserves most of competing constitutionally protected positions in view of the fundamental idea of Article 19, Paragraph 2, of the Basic Law; precedence must be given to the protection of the life of the child about to be born. This precedence exists as a matter of principle for the entire duration of pregnancy and may not be placed in question for any particular time. . . .

3.   From this point, the fundamental attitude of the legal order which is required by the constitution with regard to the interruption of pregnancy becomes clear: the legal order may not make the woman's right to self-determination the sole guideline of its rulemaking. The state must proceed, as a matter of principle, from a duty to carry the pregnancy to term and therefore to view, as a matter of principle, its interruption as an injustice. The condemnation of abortion must be clearly expressed in the legal order. The false impression must be avoided that the interruption of pregnancy is the same social process as, for example, approaching a physician for healing an illness or indeed a legally irrelevant alternative for the prevention of conception. . . .

III . . .

1.   . . . It is . . . the task of the state to employ, in the first instance, social, political, and welfare means for securing developing life. . . . [H]ow the assistance measures are to be structured in their particulars is largely left to the legislature and is generally beyond judgment by the Constitutional Court. [T]he primary concern is to strengthen readiness of the expectant mother to accept the pregnancy as her own responsibility and to bring the child *en ventre sa mere* to full life. Regardless of how the state fulfills its obligation to protect, it should not be forgotten that developing life itself is entrusted by nature in the first place to the protection of the mother. To reawaken and, if required, to strengthen the maternal duty to protect, where it is lost, should be the principal goal of the endeavors of the state for the protection of life. . . .

2.   The question of the extent to which the state is obligated under the constitution to employ, even for the protection of unborn life, the penal law, the sharpest weapon standing at its disposal, cannot be answered by the simplified posing of the question whether the state must punish certain acts. . . .

The legislature is not obligated, as a matter of principle, to employ the same penal measures for the protection of the unborn life as it considers required and expedient for born life. As a look at legal history shows, this was never the case in the application of penal sanctions and is also true for the situation in the law up to the Fifth Statute to Reform the Penal Law.

a) The task of penal law from the beginning has been to protect the elementary values of community life. That the life of every individual human being is among the most important legal values has been established above. The interruption of pregnancy irrevocably destroys an existing human life. Abortion is an act of killing. . . . [T]he employment of penal law for the requital of "acts of abortion" is to be seen as legitimate without a doubt; it is valid law in most cultural states— under prerequisites of various kinds—and especially corresponds to the German legal tradition. . . .

b) Punishment, however, can never be an end in itself. Its employment is in principle subject to the decision of the legislature. The legislature is not prohibited . . . from expressing the legal condemnation of abortion required by the Basic Law in ways other than the threat of punishment. The decisive factor is whether the totality of the measures serving the protection of the unborn life, whether they be in civil law or in public law, especially of a social-legal or of a penal nature, guarantees an actual protection corresponding to the importance of the legal value to be secured. . . .

On the other hand, the objection that a political duty to punish can never be deduced from a norm of the Basic Law which guarantees freedom is not decisive. . . . The elementary value of human life requires criminal law punishment for its destruction.

3.   The obligation of the state to protect the developing life exists—as shown—against the mother as well. Here, however, the employment of the penal law may give rise to special problems which result from the unique situation of the pregnant woman. The incisive effects of a pregnancy on the physical and emotional condition of the woman are immediately evident and need not be set forth in greater detail. . . . In individual cases, difficult, even life-threatening situations of conflict may arise. The right to life of the unborn can lead to a burdening of the woman which essentially goes beyond that normally associated with pregnancy. The result is the question of exactability, or, in other words, the question of whether the state, even in such cases, may compel the bearing of the child to term with the means of the penal law. Respect for the unborn life and the right of the woman not to be compelled to sacrifice the values in her own life in excess of an exactable measure in the interest of respecting this legal value are in conflict with each other. In such a situation of conflict which, in general, does not allow an unequivocal moral judgment and in which the decision for an interruption of pregnancy can attain the rank of a decision of conscience worthy of consideration, the legislature is obligated to exercise special restraint. If, in these cases, it views the conduct of the pregnant woman as not deserving punishment and forgoes the use of penal sanctions, the result, at any rate, is to be constitutionally accepted as a balancing incumbent upon the legislature. . . .

A continuation of the pregnancy appears to be non-exactable especially when it is proven that the interruption is required "to avert" from the pregnant woman "a danger for her life or the danger of a grave impairment of her condition of health" (s. 218b, No. 1, of the Penal Code in the version of the Fifth Statute to Reform the Penal Law). In this case her own "right to life and bodily inviolability" (Article 2, Paragraph 2, Sentence 1, of the Basic Law) is at stake, the sacrifice of which cannot be expected of her for the unborn life. Beyond that, the legislature has a free hand to leave the interruption of pregnancy free of punishment in the case of other extraordinary burdens for the pregnant woman, which, from the point of view of non-exactability, are as weighty as those referred to in s. 218b, No. 1. In this category can be counted, especially, the cases of the eugenic (*cf.* Section 218b, No. 2, of the Penal Code), ethical (criminological), and of the social or emergency indication for abortion which were contained in the draft proposed by the Federal Government in the sixth election period of the Federal Parliament and were discussed both in the public debate as well as in the course of the legislative proceedings. During the deliberations of the Special Committee for the Reform of the Penal Law (Seventh Election Period, 25th Session, Stenographic Reports, p. 1470 ff), the representative of the Federal Government explained in detail and with convincing reasons why, in these four cases of indication, the bearing of the child to term does not appear to be exactable. The decisive viewpoint is that in all of these cases another interest equally worthy of protection, from the standpoint of the constitution, asserts its validity with such urgency that the state's legal order cannot require that the pregnant woman must, under all circumstances, concede precedence to the right of the unborn.

... Finally, the general social situation of the pregnant woman and her family can produce conflicts of such difficulty that, beyond a definite measure, a sacrifice by the pregnant woman in favor of the unborn life cannot be compelled with the means of the penal law. In regulating this case, the legislature must so formulate the elements of the indication which is to remain free of punishment that the gravity of the social conflict presupposed will be clearly recognizable and, considered from the point of view of non-exactability, the congruence of this indication with the other cases of indication remains guaranteed. If the legislature removes genuine cases of conflict of this kind from the protection of the penal law, it does not violate its duty to protect life. Even in these cases the state may not be content merely to examine, and if the occasion arises, to certify that the statutory prerequisites for an abortion free of punishment are present. Rather, the state will also be expected to offer counseling and assistance with the goal of reminding pregnant women of the fundamental duty to respect the right to life of the unborn, to encourage her to continue the pregnancy and—especially in cases of social need—to support her through practical measures of assistance.

In all other cases the interruption of pregnancy remains a wrong deserving punishment since, in these cases, the destruction of a value of the law of the highest rank is subjected to the unrestricted pleasure of another and is not motivated by an emergency. If the legislature wants to dispense (even in this case) with penal law punishment, this would be compatible with the requirement to protect of Article 2, Paragraph 2, Sentence 1, of the Basic Law, only on the condition that another equally effective legal sanction stands at its command which would clearly bring out the unjust character of the act (the condemnation by the legal order) and likewise prevent the interruptions of pregnancy as effectively as a penal provision. . . .

D . . .

II

It is generally recognized that the previous § 218 of the Penal Code, precisely because it threatened punishment without distinction for nearly all cases of the interruption of pregnancy, has, as a result, only insufficiently protected developing life. . . .

. . . The [1974] statute is based upon the idea that developing life would be better protected through individual counseling of the pregnant woman than through a threat of punishment, which would remove the one determined upon the abortion from every possible means of influence, which from a criminological point of view would be mistaken and, in addition, has proven itself without effect. On this basis the legislature has reached the decision to abandon the criminal penalty entirely for the first twelve weeks of pregnancy under definite prerequisites and, in its place, to introduce the preventive counseling and instruction (§s. 218a and 218c).

It is constitutionally permissible and to be approved if the legislature attempts to fulfill its duty to improve protection of unborn life through preventive measures, including counseling to strengthen the personal responsibility of the woman. The regulation in question, however, encounters decisive constitutional problems in several respects.

1. The legal condemnation of the interruption of pregnancy required by the constitution must clearly appear in the legal order existing under the constitution. Therefore, as shown, only those cases can be excepted in which the continuation of the pregnancy is not exactable from the woman in consideration of the value decision made in Article 2, Paragraph 2, Sentence 1, of the Basic Law. This absolute condemnation is not expressed in the provisions of the Fifth Statute to Reform the Penal Law with regard to the interruption of pregnancy during the first twelve weeks because the statute leaves unclear whether an interruption of pregnancy which is not "indicated" is legal or illegal after the repeal of the criminal penalty through s. 218a of the Penal Code.... With the unbiased reader of the statute the impression must arise that s. 218a completely removes, through the absolute repeal of punishability, the legal condemnation—without consideration of the reasons—and legally allows the interruption of pregnancy under the prerequisites listed therein. The elements of s. 218 of the Penal Code recede into the background since by far most interruptions of pregnancy, experience shows, are performed in the first twelve weeks—over $9/10$ —according to the statements of the representative of the government. The picture which results is of a nearly complete decriminalization of the interruption of pregnancy....

... The proposed regulation, as a whole, can therefore only be interpreted to mean that an interruption of pregnancy performed by a physician in the first twelve weeks of pregnancy is not illegal and therefore should be allowed (under law)....

2. ... Through the complete repeal of punishability ... a gap in the protection has resulted which completely destroys the security of the developing life in a not insignificant number of cases by handing this life over to the completely unrestricted power of disposition of the woman. There are many women who have previously decided upon an interruption of pregnancy without having a reason which is worthy of esteem within the value order of the constitution and who are not accessible to a counseling such as s. 218c, Par. 1, proposes. These women find themselves neither in material distress nor in a grave situation of emotional conflict. They decline pregnancy because they are not willing to take on the renunciation and the natural motherly duties bound up with it. They have serious reasons for their conduct with respect to the developing life; there are, however, no reasons which can endure against the command to protect human life. For these women, pregnancy is exactable in line with the principles reiterated above [i.e. the woman may reasonably be expected to continue the pregnancy.] ...

The objection against this is that women not subject to influence understand best from experience how to avoid punishment so that the penal sanction is often ineffective.... At the same time, according to this objection, the threat of punishment, by discouraging counseling of women susceptible of influence, impedes saving life in other cases because it is precisely women in whose cases the prerequisites of an indication are absent and, beyond that, also those who do not trust the ... procedure to determine an indication who will, in the face of a penal threat, [keep the pregnancy secret and avoid counselling.] On the basis of such an analysis, there could not be a defense of unborn life ... free of gaps ... [and] the Legislature would not have transgressed its constitutionally drawn boundaries with the regulation of terms.

a) ... [T]his concept does not do justice to the essence and function of the penal law.... [T]he task of the penal law [is] the protection of especially important legal values and values of the community.... No doubt, the mere existence of such a penal sanction has influence on the conceptions of value and the ... behavior of the populace (cf. the report of the Special Committee for the Penal Law Reform, Federal Parliamentary Press, 7/1981 new p. 10).... An opposite effect will result if, through a general repeal of punishability, even doubtlessly punishable behavior is declared to be legally free from objection.... The purely theoretical announcement that the interruption of pregnancy is "tolerated," but not "approved," must remain without effect so long as no legal sanction is recognizable which clearly segregates the justified cases of abortion from the reprehensible. If the threat of punishment disappears in its entirety, ... [t]he "dangerous inference of moral permissibility from a legal absence of sanction" (Engisch, In the Quest for Justice, 1971, p. 104) is too near not to be drawn by a large number of those subject to the law....

b) ... The weighing in bulk of life against life which leads to the allowance of the destruction of a supposedly smaller number in the interest of the preservation of an allegedly larger number is not reconcilable with the obligation of an individual protection of each single concrete life....

... The fundamental legal protection in individual cases may not be sacrificed to the efficiency of the regulation as a whole. The statute is not only an instrument to steer social processes according to sociological judgments and prognoses but is also the enduring expression of socio-ethical—and as a consequence—legal evaluation of human acts; it should say what is right and wrong for the individual.

c) A dependable factual foundation is lacking for "a total accounting"—which is to be rejected on principle. A sufficient basis is lacking for the conclusion that the number of interruptions of pregnancy in the future will be significantly less than with the previous statutory regulation....

The available statistics from other countries ... allow no certain conclusion that there will be a substantial decline in abortions. Experiments ... are not permissible considering the great worth of the legal value to be protected.

... [A]n increase in abortions is to be counted on because—as shown—the mere existence of the penal norm of s. 218 of the Penal Code has exerted influence on the value conceptions and manner of behavior of the populace. . . .

3. The counseling and instruction of the pregnant woman provided under s. 218c, Par. 1, of the Penal Code cannot, considered by itself, be viewed as suitable to effectuate a continuation of the pregnancy. . . .

b) It is especially questionable that the instruction about social assistance can be undertaken by the same physician who will perform the interruption of pregnancy. Since, according to the result of the previous inquiries and according to the position statements of representative medical professional panels, it must be assumed that the majority of physicians decline to perform interruptions of pregnancy which are not indicated, only those physicians will make themselves available who either see in the interruption of pregnancy a money-making business or who are inclined to comply with every wish of a woman for interruption of pregnancy because they see in it merely a manifestation of the right to self-determination or a means to the emancipation of women. In both cases, an influence by the physician on the pregnant woman for the continuation at the pregnancy is highly improbable.

The experiences in England show this. . . .

c) Furthermore, the prospects for success are poor since the interruption of pregnancy can immediately follow the instruction and counseling. . . . For the woman decided upon an interruption of pregnancy it is only necessary to find an obliging physician. Since he may undertake the social as well as the medical counseling and finally even carry out the operation, a serious attempt to dissuade the pregnant woman from her decision is not to be expected from him. . . .

IV

The regulation encountered in the Fifth Statute to Reform the Penal Law at times is defended with the argument that in other democratic countries of the Western World in recent times the penal provisions regulating the interruption of pregnancy have been "liberalized" or "modernized" in a similar or an even more extensive fashion; this would be, as the argument goes, an indication that the new regulation corresponds, in any case, to the general development of theories in this area and is not inconsistent with fundamental socio-ethical and legal principles.

These considerations cannot influence the decision to be made here. Disregarding the fact that all of these foreign laws in their respective countries are sharply controverted, the legal standards which are applicable there for the acts of the legislature are essentially different from those of the Federal Republic of Germany.

Underlying the Basic Law are principles for the structuring of the state that may be understood only in light of the historical experience and the spiritual-moral confrontation with the previous system of National Socialism. In opposition to the omnipotence of the totalitarian state which claimed for itself limitless dominion over all areas of social life and which, in the prosecution of its goals of state, consideration for the life of the individual fundamentally meant nothing, the Basic Law of the Federal Republic of Germany has erected an order bound together by values which places the individual human being and his dignity at the focal point of all of its ordinances. At its basis lies the concept ... that human beings possess an inherent worth as individuals in order of creation which uncompromisingly demands unconditional respect for the life of every individual human being, even for the apparently socially "worthless," and which therefore excludes the destruction of such life without legally justifiable grounds. This fundamental constitutional decision determines the structure and the interpretation of the entire legal order....

Dissenting Opinion of Justice Rupp von Brünneck and Justice Dr. Simon....

The life of each individual human being is self-evidently a central value of the legal order. It is uncontested that the constitutional duty to protect this life also includes its preliminary stages before birth. The debates in Parliament and before the Federal Constitutional Court dealt not with the *whether* but rather only the *how* of this protection. This decision is a matter of legislative responsibility. Under no circumstances can the duty of the state to prescribe punishment for abortion in every stage of pregnancy be derived from the constitution. The legislature should be able to determine the regulations for counseling and the term solution as well as for the indications solution....

A–I

The authority of the Federal Constitutional Court to annul the decisions of the legislature demands sparing use, if an imbalance between the constitutional organs is to be avoided. The requirement of judicial self-restraint, which is designated as the "elixir of life" of the jurisprudence of the Federal Constitutional Court, is especially valid when [what is] involved is not a defense from overreaching by state power but rather the making, via constitutional judicial control, of provisions for the positive structuring of the social order for the legislature which is directly legitimatized by the people. The Federal Constitutional Court must not succumb to the temptation to take over for itself the function of a controlling organ and shall not in the long run endanger the authority to judicially review constitutionality.

1.   The test proposed in this proceeding departs from the basis of classical judicial control. The fundamental legal norms standing in the central part of our constitution guarantee as rights of defense to the citizen in relation to the state a sphere of unrestricted structuring of one's life based on personal responsibility. The classical function of the Federal

Constitutional Court lies in defending against injuries to this sphere of freedom from excessive infringement by the state power. On the scale of possible infringements by the state, penal provisions are foremost: they demand of a citizen a definite behavior and subdue him in the case of a violation with grievous restrictions of freedom or with financial burdens. Judicial control of the constitutionality of such provisions therefore means a determination whether the encroachment resulting either from the enactment or application of penal provisions into protected spheres of freedom is allowable; whether, therefore, the state, generally or to the extent provided, may punish.

In the present constitutional dispute, the inverse question is presented for the first time for examination, namely whether the state *must* punish, whether the abolition of punishment for the interruption of pregnancy in the first three months of pregnancy is compatible with fundamental rights. It is obvious, however, that the disregard of punishment is the opposite of state encroachment. Since the partial withdrawal of the penal provision did not occur to benefit interruptions of pregnancies but rather, because the previous penal sanction, according to the unrefuted assumption of the legislature which has been confirmed by experience, has thoroughly proved itself ineffective, an "attack" on the unborn life by the state is not even indirectly construable. Because no such infringement exists, the Austrian Constitutional Court has denied that the regulation of terms there violates the catalog of fundamental rights recognized by the law of Austria.

2. Since the fundamental rights as defense rights are from the beginning not suitable to prevent the legislature from eliminating penal provisions, the majority of this Court seeks to find the basis for this in the more extensive meaning of fundamental rights as *objective value decisions*. According to this, the fundamental rights not only establish rights of defense of the individual against the state, but also contain at the same time objective value decisions, the realization of which through affirmative action is a permanent task of state power. This idea has been developed by the Federal Constitutional Court in the laudable endeavor to lend greater effectiveness to the fundamental rights in their capacity to secure freedom and to strive for social justice. The majority of this Court insufficiently considers differences in the two aspects of fundamental rights, differences essential to the judicial control of constitutionality.

As defense rights the fundamental rights have a comparatively clear recognizable content; in their interpretation and application, the judicial opinions have developed practicable, generally recognized criteria for the control of state encroachments—for example, the principle of proportionality. On the other hand, it is regularly a most complex question, *how* a value decision is to be realized through affirmative measures of the legislature. The necessarily generally held value decisions can be perhaps characterized as constitutional mandates which, to be sure, are assigned to point the direction for all state dealings but are directed necessarily toward a transposition of binding regulations. Based upon the determination of the actual circumstances, of the concrete setting of goals and their priority and of the suitability of conceivable means and ways, very different solutions are possible. The decision, which frequently presupposes compromises and takes place in the course of trial and error, belongs, according to the principle of division of powers and to the democratic principle, to the responsibility of the legislature directly legitimatized by the people....

The idea of objective value decisions should however not become a vehicle to shift specifically legislative functions in the formation of social order onto the Federal Constitutional Court. Otherwise the Court will be forced into a role for which it is neither competent nor equipped....

II

1. Our strongest reservation is directed to the fact that for the first time in opinions of the Constitutional Court an objective value decision should function as a *duty* of the legislature to enact *penal norms,* therefore to postulate the strongest conceivable encroachment into the sphere of freedom of the citizen. This inverts the function of the fundamental rights into its contrary. If the objective value decision contained in a fundamental legal norm to protect a certain legal value should suffice to derive therefrom the duty to punish, the fundamental rights could underhandedly, on the pretext of securing freedom, become the basis for an abundance of regimentations which restrict freedom. What is valid for the protection of life can also be claimed for other legal values of high rank—for example, inviolability of the body, freedom, marriage, and family.

Quite obviously the constitution presupposes that the state can also resort to its power to punish to protect an orderly social life; the thrust of fundamental rights, however, does not go to the promotion of such a utilization but rather to the drawing of its boundaries. In this way the Supreme Court of the United States has even regarded punishment for the interruption of pregnancy, performed by a physician with the consent of the pregnant woman in the first third of pregnancy, as a violation of fundamental rights. This would, according to German constitutional law, go too far indeed. According to the liberal character of our constitution, however, the legislature needs a constitutional justification to punish, not to disregard punishment, because, according to its view, a threat of punishment promises no success or appears for other reasons to be an improper reaction....

2. ...

A contrary standpoint cannot be supported with the argument that the reception of Article 2, Paragraph 2, of the Basic Law unquestionably originated from the reaction to the inhumane ideology and practice of the National Socialist regime. This reaction refers to the mass destruction of human life by the state in concentration camps and, in the case of the mentally ill, sterilizations and forced abortions directed by authorities, to involuntary medical experiments on human beings, to disrespect of individual life and human dignity which was expressed by countless other measures of state.

Drawing conclusions concerning the constitutional assessment of the killing of a child *en ventre sa mere* by the pregnant woman herself or by a third party with her consent is less pertinent than drawing conclusions from such a killing by the state, as, for example, by the Nazi regime which had taken up a rigorous standpoint corresponding to its biologically oriented ideology towards population. Alongside of new provisions against advertising for abortions or abortion methods, a stricter application of penal provisions was worked out through corresponding state measures in contrast to the Weimar period. This penal sanction which was already severe was significantly sharpened in 1943. Until that time only imprisonment was provided for the pregnant woman and her non-professional helper; by this time, however, self-abortion, in especially aggravated cases, was punished with imprisonment in the penitentiary. The professional abortion was, apart from less serious cases, always punished with imprisonment in the penitentiary; and, even with the death penalty, if the perpetrator had "thereby continually injured the vitality of the German people." In the face of these provisions, which remained unchanged when the Basic Law was adopted and was mitigated solely through the Allied prohibition of cruel or excessively severe punishments, the reasons which led to the adoption of Article 2, Paragraph 2, of the Basic Law can by no means be adduced in favor of a constitutional duty to punish abortions. Rather, the decisive renunciation completed with the Basic Law of the totalitarian National Socialist state demands rather the reverse conclusion, that is, restraint in employing criminal punishment, the improper use of which in the history of mankind has caused endless suffering.

B

Even if one, contrary to our position, agrees with the majority that a constitutional duty to punish is conceivable, no constitutional violation can be charged to the legislature. Although it is not necessary to go into every detail, the majority reasoning encounters the following objections:

I . . .

1.   The immediately impressive statements about the undisputed high rank of the protection of life neglect the *uniqueness of the interruption of pregnancy* in relation to other dangers of human life. Involved here is not the academic question of whether it is proper to employ the power of the state to protect against murderers and killers, who can be deterred in no other way. In the European legal history, which has been influenced by the Church, a distinction has been constantly made between born and unborn life. . . .

The unusual circumstances that in the person of the pregnant woman there is a unique unity of "actor" and "victim" is of legal significance, because much more is demanded of the pregnant woman than mere omission—as opposed to the demands on the one addressed by penal provisions against homicide: she must not only tolerate the far-reaching changes in her health and well-being associated with carrying the child *en ventre sa mere* to term, but also submit to encroachments upon her way of life which result from pregnancy and birth, and especially accept the maternal responsibility for the further development of the child after birth. . . .

According to the view of the undersigned Madame Justice, the refusal of the pregnant woman to permit the child *en ventre sa mere* to become a human being is something essentially different from the killing of independently existing life, not only according to the natural sensitivities of the woman but also legally. For this reason the equating in principle of abortion in the first stage of pregnancy with murder or intentional killing is not allowable from the outset. . . . [F]or the legal consciousness of the pregnant woman as well as for the general legal consciousness, there is a difference between an interruption of pregnancy which takes place in the first stage of pregnancy and one which takes place in a later phase. This has resulted at all times in domestic and foreign legal systems in a different penal assessment which is tied to such stages which are based on time, as, for example, the Supreme Court of the United States impressively stated. . . .

2.   . . . In the reasoning of the majority, one finds only slight allusion to the complexity of this problem and—in connection with the regulation of indications—some discussion about the social causes of abortion[;] as a whole, however, because of the more dogmatic manner of consideration, there was insufficient appreciation, for a reform which was recognized on all sides as necessary, of the conditions found by the legislature and of the difficulties flowing therefrom.

a) These conditions are in the first place complicated by the enormous number of illegal abortions. . . .

Furthermore, the legislature cannot be indifferent to the fact that illegal interruptions of pregnancy lead even today to injuries of health. . . .

3.   . . . In the solution chosen the legislature was within its authority to proceed on the assumption that, in view of the failure of the penal sanction, the suitable means toward a remedy are to be sought in the social and community realm and that involved is, on the one hand, facilitating the bearing of the child to term by the mother through preventive psychological, social, and social-political promotional measures and strengthening her willingness to this end; and, on the other hand, decreasing the number of unwanted pregnancies through better information about the possibilities for preventing conception. . . .

. . . According to the conception of the legislature the pregnant woman shall thus—without fear of punishment—be brought out of her isolation; the surmounting of her difficulties shall be facilitated by open contacts with her environment and by an individual counseling addressed to her personal conflict situation. That the consultation provided should serve the protection of developing life, since it awakens and strengthens the willingness to carry the child *en ventre sa mere* to term. . . .

. . . [T]he success of the counseling regulation depends essentially on whether help can be offered to or arranged for the pregnant woman which opens for her ways out of her difficulties. If this fails, even the penal law is nothing other than an alibi for the deficit of effective help.... If, however, judicial self-restraint has validity, the Constitutional Court *a fortiori* should not compel the legislature to employ the power of punishment, which is the strongest means of state coercion, to compensate for the social neglect of duty with the threat of punishment. This certainly does not correspond to the function of penal law in a liberal social state....

II

The majority emphatically bases the maintenance of a—differentiated—penal sanction upon the idea that the constitutionally required "condemnation" of unindicated abortions must be clearly expressed.... [I]t demands, even independently of the desired actual effect, a condemnation as an expression of a social-ethical negative value judgment, which clearly characterizes unmotivated abortions as unjust....

1. ... Unmotivated interruptions of pregnancy obviously are ethically objectionable. With respect to the majority reasoning one questions whether disregarding of punishment here as elsewhere does not compel the conclusion that conduct no longer punishable would be approved....

2. Our most important objection is directed to the majority's failure to explain how the requirement of condemnation as an independent duty is constitutionally derived.... In a pluralistic, ideologically neutral and liberal democratic community, it is a task for the forces of society to codify the postulates of opinion. The state must practice abstention in this matter; its task is the protection of the legal values guaranteed and recognized by the constitution. For the constitutional decision it matters only whether the penal provision is imperatively required to secure an effective protection of developing life, having taken into consideration the interests of the woman which are deserving of protection.

III

That the decision of the German legislature for the regulation of terms and counseling neither arises from a fundamental attitude which is to be morally or legally condemned nor proceeds from apparently false premises in the determination of the circumstances of life is confirmed by identical or similar *provisions for reform in numerous foreign states*. In Austria, France, Denmark, and Sweden an interruption of pregnancy, performed during the first twelve weeks (in France, ten) of pregnancy by a physician with the consent of the pregnant woman, is not punishable; in Great Britain and in the Netherlands a regulation of indications is in effect which amounts to the same thing in its practical application. These states can boast that they are a part of an impressive constitutional tradition and all-in-all certainly do not lag behind the Federal Republic in unconditional respect for life of each individual human being; some of them likewise have historical experience with an inhuman system of injustice.... The Constitutional Court of Austria has expressly determined that the term solution of that country is compatible with the [European] Human Rights Convention, which in Austria enjoys constitutional rank....

Questions and Comments on the 1975 German Abortion Decision

1. In light of the Constitutional Court's decision, what would the West German legislature have needed to do if it wanted to adopt an abortion law consistent with the Court's decision?

2. Is the German court's decision any more, or less, "legislative" in character than that in *Roe*?

3. Note the agreement between the majority and the dissent that the Basic Law's right to life protects unborn children. Cf. David P. Currie, The Constitution of the Federal Republic of Germany 311 (1994)(reporting that the Court relied on reports of the drafting of the German Basic Law, including a committee report indicating that a provision explicitly protecting the unborn was defeated because of the prevailing understanding that such protection was encompassed by the right to life).

Abortion and Reunification in Germany

Following the 1975 decision excerpted above, abortion was permitted in the Federal Republic of Germany (West Germany) only where "indicated" in limited circumstances (e.g., where the mother's health was at risk or the pregnancy resulted from a criminal assault). The written opinion of a physician other than the physician performing the abortion as to the presence of a legal "indication" was required, as was counselling for the pregnant woman.

At the time of German unification in 1990, abortion on demand and at public expense in the first trimester was legal in the German Democratic Republic (East Germany). The Unification Treaty specifically permitted each portion of the united country to maintain its own practice on abortion until 1992, when a unified law was to be enacted.

The Bundestag's first effort at a unified law was struck down again by the Constitutional Court in 1993 (by a 6-2 vote), as explained in the following excerpts from Professor Neuman's article.

The 1993 Decision: Gerald L. Neuman, Casey *in the Mirror: Abortion, Abuse and The Right to Protection in the United States and Germany*, 43 Am. J. Comp. L. 273 (1995)

. . .

The Court delivered its opinion in May 1993, invalidating significant portions of the new statute but upholding some of its central features. The opinion is very long and complex, occupying 135 pages of the official reports.

1. Majority Opinion

The following attempts to summarize the major features of the majority's argument, not to replicate the structure of the opinion.

a.   The Duty of the State

The majority reaffirmed that the human fetus, at least from the moment of implantation, possessed human dignity, and that the state owed a duty to protect its life. The textual basis for this duty lay in Article 1(1) of the Constitution ("Human dignity is inviolable. To respect and protect it is the duty of all state authority."), and its content was more closely specified by Article 2(2)(1) ("Everyone has the right to life and bodily integrity."). The state owed this duty to each individual human life, not merely to human life in general.... Protection against the woman herself required that abortion be prohibited in principle, and that the state impose upon the woman in principle a legal duty to carry the child to term. The legal duty needed to be binding and needed to have legal consequences.

The duty of protection was not, however, absolute. The interest in fetal life conflicted with other constitutionally protected interests, including the human dignity of the pregnant woman, her own right to life and bodily integrity, and her right of personality.[40] In striking the balance between these conflicting interests, the legislature had some room for discretion, limited by several considerations. First, the right to life did not vary in strength with time; but rather was independent of the stage of fetal development.[41] Second, the balance had to recognize that abortion involved the total destruction of the fetus; thus, no opportunity for compensatory measures existed. Still, abortion could be legally permitted in certain exceptional circumstances where the pregnancy imposed hardship beyond the magnitude of the typical pregnancy (indeed, the constitution itself possibly required some of these exceptions).

----

40. The latter protected by GG Article 2(1) ("Everyone shall have the right to the free development of his personality in so far as he does not violate the rights of others or offend against the constitutional order or the moral code."). [GG here refers to the Basic Law, the German Constitution.]

41. 88 BVerfGE at 254. The dissenting justices Mahrenholz and Sommer disagreed, viewing the progression of fetal development as permitting different balances between the rights of the woman and of the fetus in different trimesters. The majority also viewed the first trimester as a distinctive time period, not because of any lesser right of the fetus, but because of the state's greater difficulty in preventing abortion during the first trimester.

The majority viewed the underlying constitutional standard for abortion as identical to the one described in the 1975 decision: abortion had to be forbidden unless continuation of the pregnancy involved a more intense sacrifice from the woman than the legal system could reasonably expect—a standard which I will translate as "unreasonable demands." As under the former indication system, continuation of the pregnancy would place unreasonable demands upon a woman if it created serious danger to her life or health (medical indication), if the pregnancy resulted from enumerated sex crimes (criminological indication), or if severe birth defects were expected (embryopathic indication). More generally, other situations of personal necessity (the "general situation of need" indication) could meet this standard if they were comparable in intensity to the foregoing indications. The majority made clear its belief that the "general situation of need" criterion had been too loosely applied in the intervening years.

The conclusion that a pregnant woman's situation involved unreasonable demands would not, however, relieve the state of its obligation to protect the fetus. Instead, the state must offer the woman advice and assistance, for the purpose of winning her over to voluntary continuation of the pregnancy.

The state's obligation to protect unborn life also required the state to take steps to prevent situations from arising in which a pregnancy would place unreasonable demands on the woman. In this respect the state's duty converged with its duties under Article 6 of the Constitution to protect the family.[45] The majority offered a wide-ranging survey of supportive measures that the state could take. Financial subsidies were appropriate so that women would not have to abort from fear of being unable to afford the child. The state was obliged to do more to protect women against educational and occupational disadvantages resulting from pregnancy and child rearing, especially considering the obligation under Article 3(2) of the Constitution to further the equal participation of men and women in working life.[46] Social security law needed to take account of periods spent

---

45. GG Art. 6 provides:

(1) Marriage and Family shall enjoy the special protection of the state.

(2) The care and upbringing of children are a natural right of, and a duty primarily incumbent on, the parents. The national community shall watch over their endeavours in this respect.

(3) Children may not be separated from their families against the will of the persons entitled to bring them up, except pursuant to a law, if those so entitled fail or the children are otherwise threatened with neglect.

(4) Every mother shall be entitled to the protection and care of the community.

(5) Illegitimate children shall be provided by legislation with the same opportunities for their physical and spiritual development and their place in society as are enjoyed by legitimate children.

The majority regarded pregnant women as "mothers" within the meaning of Article 6(4). 88 BVerfGE at 258.

46. 88 BVerfGE at 259-60. Article 3(2) is the gender equality clause, "Men and women shall have equal rights." The First Senate of the Federal Constitutional Court has recently been interpreting Article 3(2) as going beyond a nondiscrimination norm to require government action to bring about substantive equality. See Judgment of July 7, 1992, BVerfG, 87 BVerfGE 1, 42; Judgment of Jan. 28, 1992, BVerfG, 85 BVerfGE 191, 206-07.

in uncompensated childrearing. Landlords could be forbidden to terminate leases due to increase in family size. Credit laws could be reformed to ease repayment burdens after the birth of a child. The state needed to do more to create a "child-friendly society," recognizing that the raising of children was a service parents perform to the common benefit.... The state also had to reinforce the general public's consciousness of the claim of the unborn to protection—this duty obliged the schools, public information and counseling offices, and both public and private broadcasting.

The woman's legal duty to carry a fetus to term when this would not impose unreasonable demands upon her would ordinarily have been expressed through the criminal law. The state was permitted to express this legal duty in other ways, without threatening criminal punishment, only if it provided constitutionally sufficient protective measures. Criminal law categories continued to play a significant role in the analysis, however, because of the majority's reliance on the German criminal law doctrine of "justification." ... The majority held that only unreasonable demands could render an abortion "justified."[48] Even if abortion in the absence of unreasonable demands were decriminalized, it would still be an unjustified and unlawful action.

The constitutional sufficiency of the state's alternative protective measures was subject to judicial review. This evaluation involved an empirical estimate of the future effects of regulation, a matter that required deference to the legislature's judgment. Still, that judgment had to be at least reasonable, and to rest upon an adequate consideration of the character of the subject matter and the importance of the interests at stake. The prospect of the killing of the fetus led the majority to employ a particularly intense form of "reasonableness" analysis.

b. Review of the Legislation

Applying this standard, the majority concluded that the legislature had acted reasonably in changing over from the system based on third party determination of indications to a system based on counseling. A key element of its reasoning was the fact that in the early phase of pregnancy, outsiders could not perceive that a woman was pregnant.... A system that elicited the cooperation of the woman therefore had a greater chance of success in preventing abortion than a system that antagonized her and prompted evasion. The threat of criminal punishment and the subjection of

---

48. [Relocated] See Eser, "Justification and Excuse," 24 Am.J.Comp.L.621, 622-23, 629 (1976). Modern German criminal law distinguishes among (1) the elements that define a crime, (2) conditions that make conduct that otherwise meets that definition justified and hence lawful, and (3) conditions that make the conduct that meets that definition excused and hence unlawful but not blameworthy. Id. at 621-23; George P. Fletcher, Rethinking Criminal Law 454-59, 552-55 (1978).

The majority regarded unevaluated abortions as neither justified (lawful) nor excused (unlawful but not blameworthy) but rather as excluded from the definition of the crime by statute. In dissent, Justices Mahrenholz and Sommer criticized the majority for treating the question how decriminalized abortions should be classified within the doctrinal categories of criminal law as itself a matter of constitutional moment. 88 BVerfGE at 356.

the woman to third party evaluation of her need for an abortion had proved antagonizing. It would be more effective, as well as more respectful, to appeal to the woman's sense of responsibility through individual counseling. . . . The counselor had to explain to the woman that only unreasonable demands could justify an abortion, and had to explore frankly with her whether her situation corresponded to that standard. . . . [T]he majority noted that its approval of a system based on counseling depended on a prediction of future effects; the legislature had a continuing constitutional duty to monitor the operation of the new system and to improve it if necessary. . . .

The court was not satisfied with the legislature's specification of the content and organization of the counseling process. The legislation should have specified that the counseling must be directed toward the protection of the fetus, by helping the woman resolve her conflicted feelings through a decision to bear the child. . . .

. . . A majority of the court viewed the absence of a third party determination as having fateful consequences for the legal treatment of these "unevaluated abortions." The woman's own decision that continuation of the pregnancy would impose unreasonable demands upon her could not be treated as legally conclusive. To do so would make her a judge in her own case, and would violate the rule of law. People sometimes tended to place undue value on their own interests, and the counseling system could not be guaranteed to exclude this possibility. Therefore the legislature could decriminalize unevaluated abortions, but it could not define them as justified or lawful. This conclusion applied principally to abortions founded on the "general situation of need" criterion, because the medical, criminological and embryopathic criteria were susceptible to an objective third party verification that would not endanger the counseling process. Treating every unevaluated abortion as justified and lawful would violate the state's duty to protect every fetus. It would also undermine the public's sense of justice, increasing the danger that more women would choose to abort for constitutionally insufficient reasons.

The majority added a key qualification to its conclusion that an unevaluated abortion could not be treated as lawful. The state was forbidden to treat the abortion as lawful *except* in those contexts where treating the abortion as unlawful would impair the effectiveness of the counseling system as a means of protecting the fetus. Decriminalization was already one example of this exception: because the threat of criminal punishment could induce women to prevaricate in counseling or to avoid the counselors altogether, withdrawal of the criminal sanction was proper. The opinion addressed a variety of legal rules implicating aspects of abortion, and evaluated where the success of the counseling system required that unevaluated abortions be treated as if they were lawful, and where it did not.

The majority invalidated the new s. 218a(1) of the Criminal Code, because it declared that unevaluated abortions after counseling within the first twelve weeks of pregnancy were "not unlawful," rather than merely free of criminal sanction. The majority found that the success of the counseling system did not require that women be granted the solace of a favorable legal judgment on their decisions.

The success of the system did, however, require that women seeking abortions be able to form legal contractual relationships with physicians and hospitals, and that the usual tort sanctions for inadequate performance of the operation be available. Still, damages for a failed abortion had to be limited: the constitutional guarantee of human dignity precluded viewing the existence of a child or the duty of supporting a child as a source of damage.

The most controversial portion of the decision concerned the financing of unevaluated abortions. Five justices concluded that the public medical insurance system could not cover the cost of an unevaluated abortion if the woman had sufficient funds to pay for it herself. The state would be participating in unlawful killing if it paid for abortions without ascertaining that they were justified; this would violate the rule of law at its core. Such coverage was not necessary to the success of the counseling system, and it would tend to give the erroneous impression that the abortion was lawful.... If the woman did not personally have the means to pay for an abortion, however, state payment would be permissible, because it was necessary to the success of the counseling system: otherwise the woman might not obtain the services of a law-abiding physician, and then her health would be endangered and the physician's protective function would not be performed. The majority identified a provision of the welfare laws as supplying a current legal basis for financing abortions for needy women....

2. The Dissents

The decision prompted two dissenting opinions, a broad dissent by Justices Mahrenholz and Sommer, and a narrower dissent by Justice Böckenförde. Unlike the earlier case, in which the only woman on the court dissented, the majority in this case included the one female member of the Second Senate.

Justice Böckenförde dissented only from the majority's disallowance of payment. If the counseling system required the absence of a third party evaluation, then it was for the legislature to decide whether the indistinguishable category of unevaluated abortions, some of which were substantively lawful and some of which were not, should be treated as lawful for social insurance purposes. The majority's choice could not be defended as strengthening the public's sense of justice, which was more likely to be weakened if women whose conduct was normatively justified were treated as if they had acted unlawfully.

Justices Mahrenholz and Sommer offered a more sweeping critique of the majority's decision. They did not question the state's duty to protect the fetus from the beginning of the pregnancy. But the state's duty did not imply a legal duty of the woman to carry the fetus to term. The constitution did not specify the balance between the rights of the woman and the fetus. The legislature had discretion in choosing how to accommodate its duty to the fetus and its duty to respect the dignity and personality of the woman. Unlike the majority, they saw the progress of fetal development as providing a basis for a proportionate accommodation of both interests by giving the woman the right to decide early in the pregnancy, while requiring her to undergo counseling. The adoption of the counseling concept had resulted from a changed understanding of the personality and dignity of women.

Instead, the majority had inappropriately transplanted the standard of unreasonable demands from the prior decision on the indication system to the new counseling system. It made no sense to tell a woman confronting an unwanted pregnancy that she must decide whether the intensity of the demands it placed on her was comparable to situations of birth defects, rape, or endangered health. Moreover, this inappropriate standard led the majority to withhold legal justification from women who had complied with the system's own guidelines. This contradiction would undermine, rather than strengthen, a sense of justice, and came close to reducing the woman to the role of an object. Anyway, the majority was stretching the constitutional duty of protection too far by including a duty to form the public's sense of justice. The educative effect of laws was difficult to verify, and the majority's speculations contradicted expert opinion and the views expressed in the 1975 decision. The court should not substitute its evaluation for the legislature's. . . .

Questions and Comments on the 1993 German Abortion Decision

It is noteworthy that one of the Court's principal concerns was with the label of first trimester abortions as "not illegal" in the legislation. The Court's opinion permitted the government to label first trimester abortions as illegal but not prosecute those women who made the decision to abort after having counselling, on the theory that eliminating the punitive sanctions would encourage more women to seek counselling which might in turn reduce abortions more than criminal prosecution.

In August 1995 a new unified abortion law was enacted, designed to meet the Constitutional Court's objections to the 1992 statute and taking up its invitation to label abortions as illegal but assure nonprosecution of women who choose to have an abortion. The new law provides that (a) in general, abortions are illegal, (b) a woman who chooses to have an abortion will not be subject to criminal prosecution if (i) it occurs within the first 12 weeks of pregnancy and (ii) the woman attends compulsory counselling geared "to the protection of unborn life," and (c) abortions on medical grounds, or in cases of rape, are legal and, for these abortions, the national health system will pay the costs.[g]

g. For discussion, see Rosemarie Will, *German Unification and the Reform of Abor-* *tion Law,* 3 Cardozo Women's L. J. 399 (1996).

1. After *Casey* and the 1993 German abortion decision, how different are the U.S. and German formulations of (1) the nature of the problem in regulation of abortion, (2) the nature of government power, or obligation, to regulate abortion and (3) the nature of the pregnant woman's power to decide? Consider, for example, the *Casey* Court's upholding the 24 hour waiting period, reversing *Akron* to do so. Professor Neumann argues that the post-*Casey* situation in the U.S. is very close to that in Germany in essentially permitting first trimester abortions following counseling.[h]

2. To the extent that there are differences, do these differences invite normative judgments of which is "better"?

3. Is it possible to make such judgments outside of the particular legal system and time in which they were developed?

4. Is there a substantive aspect to constitutional governance implicated in the abortion controversy? Is the 1975 German abortion decision inconsistent with constitutional governance? Is *Roe*? Are each consistent with constitutionalism?

C. CONCLUDING NOTE ON COMPARISONS

You have now read major abortion decisions from three different western constitutional democracies—the U.S., Canada and Germany. What can be learned by such comparative readings? Would you describe the current state of the law in these three countries as dramatically different or basically similar? In what ways?

Prominent scholars have debated the utility of such comparisons for the development of U.S. constitutional law.

1. *Glendon's Argument*: In the 1980s Professor Mary Ann Glendon argued for U.S. adoption of the European approach, which she saw as more communal and as more respectful of the conflicting views of those who favor women's right to choose and those who oppose abortion as murder. In discussing the French abortion statute,[i] she argued that "the French

---

h. Waiting period provisions are common in many countries—six days in Belgium, 3 days in Portugal, 7 days in Italy, 5 days in the Netherlands, 1 week in Luxembourg and, in France, one week from the date of the woman's request and 2 days from the date of counselling. Charles Stanley Ross, *The Right of Privacy and Restraints on Abortion Under the Undue Burden Test: A Jurisprudential Comparison of Planned Parenthood v. Casey with European Practice and Italian Law*, 3 Ind. Int'l & Comp. L. Rev. 199 (1993).

i. The 1975 French law states that abortion is permissible in the first ten weeks of pregnancy if the mother is placed "in

distress" as a result of her pregnancy, and if the woman obtains counseling from a physician, a private interview with a government counselor with a view toward enabling her to keep the child, and a waiting period of one week from the woman's initial request for abortion and two days from the date of the counseling interview. Under this standard, women who want abortions in the first ten weeks will generally be able to have one; social security in France covers about 70 percent of the cost of a nonmedically necessary abortion. Glendon, 16–17. After the tenth week, abortion is permissible only (1) when the health of the mother is in danger or (2) when the child will likely have a birth defect

statute names the underlying problem as one involving human life, not as a conflict between a woman's individual liberty or privacy and a non-person. While showing great concern for the pregnant women, it tries, [through counselling provisions of a type that, at the time she wrote, had been struck down in a series of American cases] to make her aware of her alternatives without either frightening or unduly burdening her." Mary Ann Glendon, Abortion and Divorce Law in Western Law: American Failures, European Challenges 19 (1989). Glendon argued (pre-*Casey*), that U.S. abortion law is unique among Western nations

> "not only because it requires no protection of unborn life at any stage of pregnancy, in contrast to all the other countries with which we customarily compare ourselves, but also because our abortion policy was not worked out in the give and take of the legislative process. Our basic approach to, and our regulation of, abortion was established by the United States Supreme Court in a series of cases that rendered the abortion legislation of all states wholly or partly unconstitutional and severely limited the scope of future state regulation of abortion."

Far better, she argues, to have allowed the issue of abortion to be worked out in the state legislatures, 19 of which, in the seven years before *Roe*, had reformed or repealed abortion prohibitions; European experience suggests that ultimately most states would adopt schemes that permitted abortions provided appropriate medical findings or counselling were present, she suggests. Cf. Kim Scheppele, Constitutionalizing Abortion, in Abortion Politics: Public Policy in Cross–Cultural Perspective (Marianne Githens & Dorothy McBridie Stetson, eds., 1996) (arguing that constitutional law should not be used to resolve abortion controversy because it legalizes debate and thus diminishes the possibility for compromise solutions).

2. *Tribe's Response*: Professor Tribe disagrees with Glendon's assumption that a European approach would work in U.S. constitutionalism. The "codification of a truly empty promise . . . whose vision is belied by the people's day-to-day experience . . . can take an unacceptably high toll on confidence in the rule of law and the integrity of the legal system as a whole. The French solution, within an Anglo–American legal system that has long insisted that law be composed of enforceable norms, seems to teach mostly hypocrisy." Laurence H. Tribe, Abortion: The Clash of Absolutes 73–84 (1992). If Glendon's argument is that "it might be wise for us to denounce abortion in principle while we permit it in practice," Tribe doubts its effectiveness in validating the views of pro-lifers: "To anesthetize through rhetoric those who wish to protect fetal life . . . is a far cry from genuinely protecting fetal life or its value."

Tribe argues further that Glendon underestimates the strength and value of American commitment to individual rights, which he sees as at odds with regulations that empower government agents to affect abortion

or serious disease. See Bonnie L. Hertberg, Note, *Resolving the Abortion Debate: Compromise Legislation, An Analysis of the Abortion* *Policies of the United States, France and Germany*, Suffolk Transnational L. J. 513, 548 (1993).

decisions. He also raises concerns that at least in the U.S., regulatory schemes that afford substantial discretion to the government to ignore or not prosecute apparent violations of law—as may be the case in some European countries in which safe, but illegal, abortions are available—risk exercises of power that disadvantage minorities and other less privileged groups. Tribe notes that regional differences within apparently homogeneous European countries affect the practical availability of abortion. In Switzerland, for example, he notes that pregnant women from predominantly Catholic areas must travel to Protestant areas to obtain abortions, because the exception for "women's health" is read more broadly there. "Abortion by caprice," he argues, in which access to abortion depends on where one lives, "would not conform to American legal norms of equality." (Recall the District Court's finding in *Casey* that "because of distance many women must travel to reach an abortion provider").

In response to Glendon's argument for allowing democratic legislatures to work out compromises on the regulation of abortion, Tribe recognizes that such an approach might "soften the frustrations of those who oppose abortion rights." But, he concludes,

> "the gap between stated principle and actual practice that would be necessary for us to sustain the European approach would probably make such a solution too costly for us. And of course, urging a democratic solution just begs the question of whether or not the regulation of abortion is properly *for* the legislative arena...."

3. *Do Different Constitutional Regimes Matter?* A German scholar disagrees with the claim that there is now a significant difference between European and American approaches to abortion. Writing in 1996 (after both *Casey* and the 1993 German abortion decision), Udo Werner, *The Convergence of Abortion Regulation in Germany and the United States: A Critique of Glendon's Rights Talk Thesis*, 18 Loyola (L.A.) Int. & Comp. L.J. 571, 601 (1996), asserts: "[A] demand for abortion services existed in German society despite the pronouncements of the Constitutional Court. This demand proves to be relatively independent from the legal prohibition of abortion. After the Court's 1993 ruling, this demand is likely to be satisfied by the ability to obtain an illegal but unpunished abortion. Furthermore, the distinction between 'illegality' of a crime and its punishment represents a concept lawyers have difficulty understanding. This is more true of the average citizen. How illegal is an abortion that goes unpunished not only in exceptional cases but in principle? The illegality of abortion, stressed by the Constitutional Court, may be transformed in reality into an empty legalistic shell."

4. *Differences In Constitutional Consensus and Duties:* Note that the basis for the German court's abortion decisions lies in an affirmative conception of the state having a positive duty to protect the life of the fetus, and to do so not only through prohibiting abortion but through counselling. Even though Germany requires that the state say that most abortions are illegal, it also requires the state to pay for medically necessary abortions. Compare Maher v. Roe, 432 U.S. 464 (1977); Harris v. McRae, 448 US 297

(1980) (government has no obligation to provide financial assistance to women for abortions even where other medical services are provided, and even if the abortion is medically necessary). Can the U.S. and German abortion decisions be compared without taking into account differences in the two nation's commitments to "social welfare," e.g., medical and other support for pregnant women and for children?

Professor Kommers cautions that meaningful comparisons between U.S. and German abortion decisions are difficult because in Germany, "the most non-religious Social Democrat could agree with the most religious Christian Democrat" that the state has a duty to protect the fetus at all stages of pregnancy; no such consensus exists between pro-life and pro-choice advocates in the United States. Donald P. Kommers, *The Constitutional Law of Abortion in Germany: Should Americans Pay Attention?* 10 J. Contemp. Health L. & Pol'y 1, 28 (1993). Is Kommers correct about the U.S. consensus or lack thereof? If so, how is that relevant to evaluating constitutional decisionmaking?[j]

j. Note that constitutional questions about abortion laws have arisen in those countries of eastern Europe that engaged in constitution-making beginning in the late 1980s. For example, on May 28, 1997, the Polish Constitutional Tribunal ruled that a law allowing abortion for social reasons (such as economic inability to afford the child) was unconstitutional and in violation of the constitutional guarantee of the right to life. The decision came just before the Pope's visit to Poland, prompting proponents of the law to question the Court's motives. After parliamentary elections, the Sejm (a legislative body) in December 1997 by a substantial margin approved of the Tribunal's decision, reinstating the former regime of very restricted legal availability of abortion. For discussion of earlier legislation and litigation, concerning the permissible scope of abortion in Poland, see Mark Brzezinski & Leszek Garlicki, *Judicial Review in Post–Communist Poland: The Emergence of a Rechtsstaat?*, 31 Stan. J. Int'l L. 13, 50-53 (1995).

CHAPTER II

WHAT IS COMPARATIVE CONSTITUTIONAL LAW?

Our readings so far present several basic questions: What do we do when we "compare" decisions? What does the subject "comparative constitutional law" consist of? And why study comparative constitutional law?

Why study comparative constitutional law? Standard arguments involve the claim that more knowledge of other legal arrangements enhances one's general understanding of the world, and that understanding how other constitutional systems work may reveal as choices aspects of one's own legal system that appear simply to be "natural" or "necessary" practices. In addition, comparative study may help generate hypotheses about the structures of governance, and their effects in different settings, that are then testable. As the materials that appear below on the *Soering* case suggest, moreover, understanding something about comparative constitutional law may affect lawyers' practices, both before our domestic courts and in international law settings.

Comparing Decisions: We have read decisions concerning reproductive rights in several different countries. Has our discussion assumed that these decisions could be compared? Into what category did we place these decisions? What justified that choice? Why are we reading judicial decisions, rather than other legal texts or descriptions of law? More generally, what can be learned by comparing constitutional systems? Does anything unite "constitutions" in a way that makes comparative study meaningful?

Constitutions and Constitutionalism: What is "constitutionalism" and how, if at all, does it differ from "constitutions"? How closely is our concept of constitutionalism tied to a written constitution? To judicial review?

The readings in this chapter and in chapter III explore these questions in a more systematic way.

A. THE VALUE OF COMPARATIVE CONSTITUTIONAL STUDY: COMPETING PERSPECTIVES

Proponents of comparative legal studies often argue that they help dispel the sense a person embedded in a single legal system may have that his or her own system's legal arrangements are the only ones that could reasonably accomplish the legal system's goals. For example, U.S. law students are likely to think that a constitutional system could not possibly sustain a reasonable level of civil liberties without an independent judiciary enforcing constitutional restrictions on government power. Examining the protection of civil liberties in Great Britain or Israel, reasonably well-functioning democracies, may weaken the confidence that such a student would have in the statement that judicial review of statutes is necessary for protecting civil liberties.

By seeing how different constitutional systems handle the same or related questions, students may discover that the U.S courts, or the U.S. Constitution, simply fail to address adequately arguments that apparently sensible people in other nations have addressed. Recall here Glendon's argument about the relative merits of the U.S. and European approaches to the abortion issue.

But we must also think carefully about whether comparative study really can dispel a sense of "false necessity". True, different legal systems can accomplish roughly similar goals in quite different ways. But each system may be so closely tied up with its political, economic and cultural surroundings that each legal system's arrangements may be truly necessary as part of the "ensemble" of legal, political, cultural and other institutions. Thus, for example, a federal system in a nation with strong political parties organized nationally along distinctive ideological lines, as in Australia, is likely to be quite different from a federal system in a nation with relatively weak and non-ideological parties, as in the U.S. It may therefore be very difficult to support a claim that, with respect to any particular issue, the legal arrangements you are studying represent either "false" or "true" necessities.

In the first of two selections below, Professor Donald Kommers is quite enthusiastic about the benefits and values of comparative constitutional study, including the possibility of discovering universal truths about "principles of justice and political obligation that transcend the culture bound opinions and conventions of a particular political community." Donald Kommers, *The Value of Comparative Constitutional Law*, 9 J. Marshall J. of Practice & Procedure 685 (1976). Kommers also argues that by having to meet the challenge of responding to arguments found persuasive by other constitutional courts on similar issues, the quality of U. S. constitutional jurisprudence will be improved.

Günter Frankenberg offers a more skeptical view about the possibility of knowledge (and particularly any form of universal truth) from comparative study. While his article focuses on comparative law generally, his observations are pertinent to the study of comparative constitutional law. Frankenberg is concerned that knowledge about other legal systems is understood in categories formed by the perceiver's embeddedness in her own social and legal realities, creating obstacles to achieving critical understandings of multiple legal realities including our own. Efforts at objectivity can be no more than a "fictitious neutrality" which "destabiliz[e] the influence and authority of the comparativist's own perspective...." He argues that problems both of false neutrality and mindless relativism can be overcome by comparativists learning that they are inevitably "participant observers," and thus have to be prepared to question all of the categories—including "law"—with which they approach comparative study. He seeks a "liberating distance" that "takes nothing for granted, least of all the forms and rationality of law . . . "

————————

Donald P. Kommers, *The Value of Comparative Constitutional Law,* 9 J. Marshall J. of Practice & Procedure 685 (1976)

Since the end of the Second World War, several nations have created courts of judicial review modeled after the United States Supreme Court. Judicial review, once regarded as a unique mark of the American governmental system, has been explicitly provided for in the written constitutions of several newly independent nations, although in many of these places it has not evolved into a living principle of juridical democracy; that is particularly true of several emergent nations of Asia and Africa, where judicial review has succumbed to authoritarian rule. . . .

Judicial review is also known in various commonwealth countries, although it is not an articulate principle of their constitutions. . . .

As a mere accident of Empire, judicial review appears to lack a firm philosophical foundation in commonwealth legal theory, and some commonwealth courts are even uneasy with the very notion of "unconstitutionality" as applied to national legislation. . . .

The constitutional courts of the aforementioned countries have been the objects of considerable research in recent years. Legal scholars have tended to write analytical commentaries on selected decisions of these courts, dwelling mainly on certain "headline" cases—the atypical cases, it must be added—that have caused high political tension in the applicable countries. Judicial scholars in political science have . . . [not focused on constitutional interpretation but rather on] the political significance of constitutional courts in the totality of the governmental process. These studies express the belief of American scholars that a high level of comparability is to be achieved by relating the U.S. Supreme Court to the constitutional tribunals of Western European nations and the supreme courts of other countries heavily influenced by western models of politico-legal organization.

Yet it is possible to suggest that nations do differ to such an extent in the details of their political structure, legal culture, or the wording of their constitutions that no meaningful comparison of constitutional law across national boundaries is possible. That caveat might be made even in connection with the German and American abortion cases. Perhaps this matter should be addressed for a moment, using West Germany and the United States as examples. True, the structure of their governments differ. West Germany, following the parliamentary model, unites legislative and executive authority in a government with a chancellor, elected by Parliament, as its head. The United States follows the presidential model, with a popularly elected executive separated from the legislature. Judicial review also differs in operation. . . .

Finally, the German Court's organization differs from that of the U.S. Supreme Court's. Whereas the latter is a single collegial body of nine justices with life-time appointments, the former is divided into two senates with mutually exclusive jurisdiction; the eight justices on each senate are elected by Parliament and serve for a single, non-renewable term of twelve years.

But these differences would seem to be of minimal value in explaining variations in constitutional doctrine. . . .

Perhaps a more crucial explanation of variations in constitutional doctrine across national boundaries than any feature of governmental structure are the general philosophical values and historical traditions that inform the meaning of constitutions. Constitutional interpretation in West Germany and the United States would seem to depend more on these values and traditions than on any variation in the textual content of their constitutions. For instance, there was nothing inexorable about the abortion rulings in Germany and the United States; they might have gone the other way. The German Constitution states that "[e]veryone shall have the right to life and to inviolability of his person." . . . But whether "everyone" within the meaning of the Basic Law includes unborn persons is a point of hearty contention among German constitutional lawyers. The United States Constitution is less explicit about the right of persons to life. In addition, there is dispute over whether the fifth and fourteenth amendments impose an affirmative duty upon government to protect persons against encroachments upon their life or liberty by private individuals and institutions. The U.S. Supreme Court could very easily have found that the unborn fetus is a person. . . . The point to be underlined here is that the constitutions of the countries we would want to include in studies of comparative constitutional law are all adaptable to changing circumstances and flexible enough to spur the mind and imagination of creative judges.

In the final analysis, what really makes West Germany [and] the United States . . . fitting subjects for the study of comparative constitutional law is their commitment to political democracy and constitutional government, especially in the area of civil liberties and human rights. Equally relevant is the fact that these countries are secular political cultures; they are technologically sophisticated and pluralistic societies; socio-economically, they are advanced polities faced with similar problems of political order. . . . [T]hat . . . Germany and the United State[s] are also federal systems of government powered by competitive political parties is a further reason why these two countries along with Australia, Canada and perhaps India, are particularly good candidates for the study of comparative constitutional law. In addition, each of these countries feature courts with authority analogous to the U.S. Supreme Court. . . .

As noted earlier, several new courts of constitutional review have in the last quarter century produced a large body of jurisprudence. The case law of the West German Federal Constitutional Court alone is currently bound in forty volumes of *Entscheidungen des Bundesverfassungsgerichts* published since 1951. This excludes about 20,000 cases disposed of without opinion. The constitutional case law of other nations is equally rich, and it continues to multiply with each passing year as precedents accumulate and old constitutional principles gather new meaning....

... [T]rans-national studies of constitutional law should be more than mere statements of positive law or mechanical comparison. Useful teaching materials would include analytical commentaries and historical treatises on the uses of judicial review. The relation of constitutional doctrine to philosophy, history, tradition, and sociology—to resurrect Cardozo's terminology—would be a major focus of exploration. It would be the special task of the comparativist to explain the variations and similarities in constitutional doctrine from country to country. Successful achievement of this task would require complete familiarity with methods of constitutional interpretation used in the nations under study, together with knowledge of thought-forms predominant in varying legal cultures.

Now that the possibility of a systematic study of comparative constitutional law has been discussed, what then is the value of embarking upon such a study? First, comparative constitutional law can provide Americans with valuable insight into the experience of other constitutional democracies, including that of non-western cultures.... Straddling the line between jurisprudence and political theory, this body of case law has much to say about notions such as consent, contract, due process, equality under law, justice, representation, and fraternity, elements all inherent in the principle of constitutionalism. Men who call themselves free ought to be acquainted with the range of human experience expressed by these ideals in order to provide them with a greater sense of the community they share with the peoples of other constitutional democracies.

Second, comparative constitutional law can be helpful in the quest for a theory of the public good and right political order. It can represent a disinterested quest for a public philosophy and a statement of the rights and duties that would be assigned in a more perfect constitutional polity. Constitutional courts are reflective institutions. In a very real sense, they represent political man writ large and *thinking* about where to draw the troublesome line between liberty and order. It would therefore be interesting to know what constitutional values and ideas about man and his relationship to the state are commonly shared across national boundaries.... Thus, the study of comparative constitutional law can be a search for principles of justice and political obligation that transcend the culture-bound opinions and conventions of a particular political community. As such, it can lead men to the attainment of truth and a better understanding of man's political condition.

Third, comparative constitutional law can enrich the study of comparative politics. It could restore the linkage of constitutional norms to political ideologies, intra-governmental relations, and public policies.... In examining the values that inform the constitutional law of various nations, students might begin to explore the reasons for the similarities and differences in constitutional rulings. By scrutinizing the conditions and historical circumstances out of which these rulings emerge—some rulings may not represent long-range solutions to problems of governance, but rather temporary adjustments of conflicting interests—students might also begin to appreciate which constitutional doctrines or policies can be transferred across national lines and which cannot....

Fourth, the comparative perspective can enrich the study of American constitutional law. Such a perspective will provide critical standards for reviewing the work of the U.S. Supreme Court. It will require the student to come to terms with the force and merit of arguments found in the opinions of foreign constitutional courts.... [I]n looking at constitutional problems through the eyes of foreign courts, the student is able to draw upon traditions, insights, and values that transcend the American experience.... In the abortion cases, for example, the German Court frontally addressed and forthrightly answered questions—important questions of value—which the American Court consciously avoided.... That the highest tribunals of two nations equally respectful of the humanity and basic freedoms of their people have decided the question of the unborn child's right to life under their respective constitutions differently would give him pause for reflection. Upon reflection he might deepen his understanding of what the constitutional problem or issue is all about. For some this would be an intellectually liberating experience, challenging conventional wisdom and bringing into question old and new assumptions and preconceptions. For others, the comparative perspective would lead to a deeper appreciation of the meaning and wisdom of American constitutional values and practices.

Finally, the comparative perspective can contribute to the growth of American constitutional law.... In light of a full generation of constitutional governments in other countries, perhaps Americans can now in turn learn from these related constitutional experiences....

Many German justices have a close familiarity with American constitutional law. Indeed, a full set of the United States Supreme Court Reports is available in the library of the West German Federal Constitutional Court. Perhaps one day this manifest interest in our constitutional jurisprudence will be reciprocated by U.S. Supreme Court Justices....

Obviously, many German constitutional rulings could not be assimilated into American constitutional law. But in some areas, such as the right to vote and to political representation, German and American constitutional principles and theories could be blended fruitfully and seasonably to produce more equitable balances between rights and duties within the American political order. The day may possibly dawn when the high constitutional tribunals of the world's major industrial democracies will be citing each other's opinions and drawing from each other's jurisprudence with increasing frequency. The academic study of comparative constitutional law may hasten the arrival of that day.

Günter Frankenberg, *Critical Comparisons: Re-thinking Comparative Law,* 26 Harv. Int'l L. J. 411 (1985).

This essay will consider the aims of comparative law and focus on how the de-emphasized theoretical discussions and foundations of comparative work influence the various comparative approaches. It will argue that because of comparative legal scholarship's faith in an objectivity that allows culturally biased perspectives to be represented as "neutral" the practice of comparative law is inconsistent with the discipline's high principles and goals. In response, this essay will suggest a critical approach that recognizes the problems of perspective as a central and determinative element in the discourse of comparative law.

I.   Distance and Difference

Comparative Law is somewhat like traveling. The traveler and the comparatist are invited to break away from daily routines, to meet the unexpected and, perhaps, to get to know the unknown. Traveling promises opportunities for learning both about one's own country and culture and about other countries and cultures. Going places and gazing at a strange world do not, however, automatically open up new horizons. . . .

As long as we understand foreign places as like or unlike home, we cannot begin to fully appreciate them, or ourselves. We travel as if blindfolded: visiting only landmarks of our past, that restore confidences and banish fear. Only close attention to detail—variety and heterogeneity— can prevent our leveling others in images taken from our vision of the order of our own world.

Comparative law offers the same opportunities and risks. . . . I suggest that the dialectic of learning requires at least two operations that prevent the old categories and ways from being merely projected onto the world and that allow the new to speak for itself. These operations I call "distancing" and "differencing." Distance is needed to gain a vantage on who we are and what we are doing and thinking. Distancing can be described as an attempt to break away from firmly held beliefs and settled knowledge and as an attempt to resist the power of prejudice and ignorance. From a distance old knowledge can be reviewed and new knowledge can be distinguished as it is in its own right. Distance de-centers our world-view and thus establishes what might be called objectivity.

Mere distance, however, neither opens our eyes nor makes us see clearly. As long as foreign places only look like or unlike home . . . as long as they are treated as same or other, they do not speak for themselves. In order to break the unconscious spell that holds us to see others by the measure of ourselves without abandoning the benefits of criticism, traveling as well as comparison has to be an exercise in difference. By differencing we not only develop and practice a sharp sense for diversity and heterogeneity but, more importantly, we make a conscious effort to establish subjectivity, that is, the impact of the self, the observer's perspective and experience, is scrupulously taken into account. Differencing calls into question the neutrality and universality of all criteria; it rejects the notion ... [that] the categories and concepts with which new experiences are grasped, classified, and compared have nothing whatsoever to do with the socio-cultural context of those who see in terms of them. Differencing is necessary to prevent the observer-comparatist from confusing the present content of (Western) ideas and concepts with the criteria of a universal truth and logic. . . .

The dilemma of understanding foreign (legal) cultures and of transcending the domestic (legal) culture can neither be resolved by "going rational" nor by "going native." The rigorous rationalist who relies on conceptual or evolutionary functional universals is prone to give her worldview and norms, her language and biases only a different label. In the end, she may bring home from her comparative enterprise nothing but dead facts and living errors, the progeny of ethnocentrism. The rigorous relativist who naively deludes herself into believing that cultural baggage and identities can be dropped at will, is prone to oscillate between ventriloquism and mystification. As a cultural ventriloquist she would reproduce ethnocentrism under the guise of a pseudo-authentic understanding. As a cultural immigrant she might over-identify with the mystified new way and thereby be unable or unwilling to relate anything her sympathetic eye happens upon in travel to what she learns at home.

Both universalism and relativism tend to reproduce the dichotomy between the self and other; they are non-dialectical in the sense that they either come up with "bad" abstractions or with no abstractions at all. Comparison however presupposes that one abstract from a given context. . . .

The problem then is how to produce "good," that is, non-ethnocentric abstractions. . . .

[Frankenberg also describes efforts by comparative law scholars to achieve "cognitive control," which he asserts "is characterized by the formalist ordering and labeling and the ethnocentric interpretation of information, often randomly gleaned from limited data."]

Dichotomies measure the object in terms of inclusion in the category of one or the other extreme of two opposed terms, such as the civil law/common law dichotomy constituting the "relevant" legal world. This dichotomy implies the existence of less relevant or even irrelevant as well as legal or non-legal worlds. This dichotomy can be related to the dichotomy between the law in cultures sharing a "common core" and the law "in radically different cultures." This second dichotomy overlaps somewhat with the Western/Eastern dichotomy and the mature/immature, developed/developing, modern/primitive, parent/derivative dichotomies. Such dichotomies over-simplify complexity and almost invariably put the Western legal culture at the top of some implicit normative scale. Such self-confirming hierarchies threaten the comparatist's claim to non-ethnocentric, impartial research. . . .

The comparatist always returns to the original and prior conception, which is never exposed to criticism from the vantage the new conception allows. The foreign law is conceived of as like or, unlike, derivative or opposite. Strategic comparison confirms the antagonism between "capitalist" and "socialist" law; it idealizes modern law, for example, common law, as mature and rationally superior. . . .

Underlying these distinctions is the notion that law exists first and foremost as written text: statutes, court decisions and scholarly opinions. The texts and their normative commands have or do not have operative effects. In order to find, compare and evaluate these effects, the comparatist has to move back and forth between texts and their application. Although this procedure is certainly more complex than mere legal philology, . . . the law is located "out there." It can be grasped quite positively as text—written and practiced by legal officials and subjects. Hence law as a series of discrete legal events is given a life of its own. It can be distinguished from its socio-economic and politico-cultural "environment," with which it is said to interact causally. Though considered interdependent with other spheres of social life, the legal is analytically isolated from, and later added to, the non-legal reality of society and its sub-systems. This apartheid of law allows for situating it in a social vacuum and for stylizing it as a prism, allegedly enabling the legal scholar to look through it at reality and to detect and normatively criticize political ideologies.

Defining law as an additive to and not (as I shall later propose) as a constitutive element of social reality confirms the domination of the text (dead or alive) over social experience and makes it difficult if not impossible to analyze legal ideologies and the rituals pervading social life. . . .

Positioning the comparatist as pure spectator, objective analyst, and disinterested evaluator is the final mechanism of cognitive control.

[T]he fictitious neutrality stabilizes the influence and authority of the comparatist's own perspective, and nurtures the good conscience with which comparatists deploy their self-imposed dichotomies, distinctions and systemizations. The objective posture allows the comparatist to present and represent her own assumptions and what she observes in a scientific logic, with the balances and measures that project neutrality and conceal the weigher's complicity with both selection of the units on the scale and the objects to be measured. . . .

Consequently, comparison is not open-textured and infinite, self-critical and self-reflective, but a way of getting it straight—"it" being the "true" story of similarities and dissimilarities between legal cultures, traditions, systems, families, styles, origins, solutions and ideas.

Questions and Comments

1. Consider the extent to which our earlier discussion of the treatment of the abortion issue is subject to criticisms like those of Frankenberg.

2. Consider whether the "units" of comparing abortion rights should include more, or different, materials on (a) public financial support for abortion and for childbirth and (b) public financial support for child-care, upbringing, health care and education.

3. For further explication of Frankenberg's position, see below in this chapter, section B(7), (8).

B. Comparing Legal Decisions and the Concept of Borrowings

1. The Death Penalty: Stanford and Soering

Stanford v. Kentucky

492 U.S. 361 (1989).

Justice Scalia announced the judgment of the Court and delivered the opinion of the Court [in the sections included here].

These two consolidated cases require us to decide whether the imposition of capital punishment on an individual for a crime committed at 16 or 17 years of age constitutes cruel and unusual punishment under the Eighth Amendment.

I

The first case involves the shooting death of 20–year-old Barbel Poore in Jefferson County, Kentucky. Petitioner Kevin Stanford committed the murder on January 7, 1981, when he was approximately 17 years and 4 months of age. Stanford and his accomplice repeatedly raped and sodomized Poore during and after their commission of a robbery at a gas station where she worked as an attendant. They then drove her to a secluded area near the station, where Stanford shot her point-blank in the face and then in the back of her head. The proceeds from the robbery were roughly 300 cartons of cigarettes, two gallons of fuel, and a small amount of cash. A corrections officer testified that petitioner explained the murder as follows: " 'He said, I had to shoot her, [she] lived next door to me and she would recognize me.... I guess we could have tied her up or something or beat [her up] ... and tell her if she tells, we would kill her.... Then after he said that he started laughing.' " ...

Stanford was convicted of murder, first-degree sodomy, first-degree robbery, and receiving stolen property, and was sentenced to death and 45 years in prison. The Kentucky Supreme Court affirmed the death sentence, [stating] that petitioner's "age and the possibility that he might be rehabilitated were mitigating factors appropriately left to the consideration of the jury that tried him."

The second case before us today involves the stabbing death of Nancy Allen, a 26–year-old mother of two who was working behind the sales counter of the convenience store she and David Allen owned and operated in Avondale, Missouri. Petitioner Heath Wilkins committed the murder on July 27, 1985, when he was approximately 16 years and 6 months of age. The record reflects that Wilkins' plan was to rob the store and murder "whoever was behind the counter" because "a dead person can't talk." While Wilkins' accomplice, Patrick Stevens, held Allen, Wilkins stabbed her, causing her to fall to the floor. When Stevens had trouble operating the cash register, Allen spoke up to assist him, leading Wilkins to stab her three more times in her chest. Two of these wounds penetrated the victim's heart. When Allen began to beg for her life, Wilkins stabbed her four more times in the neck, opening her carotid artery. After helping themselves to liquor, cigarettes, rolling papers, and approximately $450 in cash and checks, Wilkins and Stevens left Allen to die on the floor . . . .

On mandatory review of Wilkins' death sentence, the Supreme Court of Missouri affirmed, rejecting the argument that the punishment violated the Eighth Amendment.

We granted certiorari in these cases to decide whether the Eighth Amendment precludes the death penalty for individuals who commit crimes at 16 or 17 years of age.

II

The thrust of both Wilkins' and Stanford's arguments is that imposition of the death penalty on those who were juveniles when they committed their crimes falls within the Eighth Amendment's prohibition against "cruel and unusual punishments." Wilkins would have us define juveniles as individuals 16 years of age and under; Stanford would draw the line at 17.

Neither petitioner asserts that his sentence constitutes one of "those modes or acts of punishment that had been considered cruel and unusual at the time that the Bill of Rights was adopted." Ford v. Wainwright, 477 U.S. 399, 405 (1986). Nor could they support such a contention. At that time, the common law set the rebuttable presumption of incapacity to commit any felony at the age of 14, and theoretically permitted capital punishment to be imposed on anyone over the age of 7. In accordance with the standards of this common-law tradition, at least 281 offenders under the age of 18 have been executed in this country, and at least 126 under the age of 17.

Thus petitioners are left to argue that their punishment is contrary to the "evolving standards of decency that mark the progress of a maturing society," Trop v. Dulles, 356 U.S. 86, 101 (1958) (plurality opinion). They are correct in asserting that this Court has "not confined the prohibition embodied in the Eighth Amendment to 'barbarous' methods that were generally outlawed in the 18th century," but instead has interpreted the Amendment "in a flexible and dynamic manner." Gregg v. Georgia, 428 U.S. 153, 171 (1976) (opinion of Stewart, Powell, and Stevens, JJ.). In determining what standards have "evolved," however, we have looked not to our own conceptions of decency, but to those of modern American society as a whole.[1] As we have said, "Eighth Amendment judgments should not be, or appear to be, merely the subjective views of individual Justices; judgment should be informed by objective factors to the maximum possible extent." Coker v. Georgia, 433 U.S. 584, 592 (1977) (plurality opinion). This approach is dictated both by the language of the Amendment—which proscribes only those punishments that are both "cruel and unusual"—and by the "deference we owe to the decisions of the state legislatures under our federal system," Gregg v. Georgia, at 176. . . .

III

"First" among the " 'objective indicia that reflect the public attitude toward a given sanction' " are statutes passed by society's elected representatives. McCleskey v. Kemp, 481 U.S. 279, 300 (1987), quoting Gregg v. Georgia, at 173. Of the 37 States whose laws permit capital punishment, 15 decline to impose it upon 16–year-old offenders and 12 decline to impose it on 17–year-old offenders. This does not establish the degree of national consensus this Court has previously thought sufficient to label a particular punishment cruel and unusual. In invalidating the death penalty for rape of an adult woman, we stressed that Georgia was the sole jurisdiction that authorized such a punishment. See Coker v. Georgia, at 595–596. In striking down capital punishment for participation in a robbery in which an accomplice takes a life, we emphasized that only eight jurisdictions authorized similar punishment. Enmund v. Florida, at 792. In finding that the Eighth Amendment precludes execution of the insane . . . we relied upon . . . the fact that "no State in the Union" permitted such punishment. Ford v. Wainwright, 477 U.S., at 408. And in striking down a life sentence without parole under a recidivist statute, we stressed that "it appears that [petitioner] was treated more severely than he would have been in any other State." Solem v. Helm, 463 U.S. 277, 300 (1983). . . .

V

Having failed to establish a consensus against capital punishment for 16–and 17–year-old offenders through state and federal statutes and the

---

1. We emphasize that it is *American* conceptions of decency that are dispositive, rejecting the contention of petitioners and their various amici (accepted by the dissent) that the sentencing practices of other countries are relevant. While "the practices of other nations, particularly other democracies, can be relevant to determining whether a practice uniform among our people is not merely an historical accident, but rather so 'implicit in the concept of ordered liberty' that it occupies a place not merely in our mores, but, text permitting, in our Constitution as well," Thompson v. Oklahoma, 487 U.S. 815, 868–869, n. 4 (1988) (Scalia, J., dissenting), quoting Palko v. Connecticut, 302 U.S. 319, 325 (1937) (Cardozo, J.), they cannot serve to establish the first Eighth Amendment prerequisite, that the practice is accepted among our people.

behavior of prosecutors and juries, petitioners seek to demonstrate it through other indicia, including public opinion polls, the views of interest groups, and the positions adopted by various professional associations. We decline the invitation to rest constitutional law upon such uncertain foundations. A revised national consensus so broad, so clear, and so enduring as to justify a permanent prohibition upon all units of democratic government must appear in the operative acts (laws and the application of laws) that the people have approved. . . .

Justice Brennan, with whom Justice Marshall, Justice Blackmun, and Justice Stevens join, dissenting.

I believe that to take the life of a person as punishment for a crime committed when below the age of 18 is cruel and unusual and hence is prohibited by the Eighth Amendment. . . .

I

Our judgment about the constitutionality of a punishment under the Eighth Amendment is informed, though not determined, by an examination of contemporary attitudes toward the punishment, as evidenced in the actions of legislatures and of juries. McCleskey v. Kemp, 481 U.S. 279, 300 (1987); Coker v. Georgia, 433 U.S. 584, 592 (1977)(plurality opinion). The views of organizations with expertise in relevant fields and the choices of governments elsewhere in the world also merit our attention as indicators whether a punishment is acceptable in a civilized society. . . .

C

. . . Where organizations with expertise in a relevant area have given careful consideration to the question of a punishment's appropriateness, there is no reason why that judgment should not be entitled to attention as an indicator of contemporary standards. There is no dearth of opinion from such groups that the state-sanctioned killing of minors is unjustified. A number, indeed, have filed briefs amicus curiae in these cases, in support of petitioners. The American Bar Association has adopted a resolution opposing the imposition of capital punishment upon any person for an offense committed while under age 18, as has the National Council of Juvenile and Family Court Judges. The American Law Institute's Model Penal Code similarly includes a lower age limit of 18 for the death sentence. And the National Commission on Reform of the Federal Criminal Laws also recommended that 18 be the minimum age.

Our cases recognize that objective indicators of contemporary standards of decency in the form of legislation in other countries is also of relevance to Eighth Amendment analysis. Thompson, at 830–831; Enmund, 458 U.S., at 796, n. 22; Coker, 433 U.S., at 596, n. 10; Trop v. Dulles, 356 U.S., at 102, and n. 35. Many countries, of course—over 50, including nearly all in Western Europe—have formally abolished the death penalty, or have limited its use to exceptional crimes such as treason. App. to Brief for Amnesty International as Amicus Curiae. Twenty-seven others do not in practice impose the penalty. Of the nations that retain capital punishment, a majority—65—prohibit the execution of juveniles. Sixty-one countries retain capital punishment and have no statutory provision exempting juveniles, though some of these nations are ratifiers of international treaties that do prohibit the execution of juveniles. Since 1979, Amnesty International has recorded only eight executions of offenders under 18 throughout the world, three of these in the United States. The other five executions were carried out in Pakistan, Bangladesh, Rwanda, and Barbados. In addition to national laws, three leading human rights treaties ratified or signed by the United States explicitly prohibit juvenile death penalties. Within the world community, the imposition of the death penalty for juvenile crimes appears to be overwhelmingly disapproved.

D

Together, the rejection of the death penalty for juveniles by a majority of the States, the rarity of the sentence for juveniles, both as an absolute and a comparative matter, the decisions of respected organizations in relevant fields that this punishment is unacceptable, and its rejection generally throughout the world, provide to my mind a strong grounding for the view that it is not constitutionally tolerable that certain States persist in authorizing the execution of adolescent offenders. . . .

V

. . . These indicators serve to confirm in my view my conclusion that the Eighth Amendment prohibits the execution of persons for offenses they committed while below the age of 18, because the death penalty is disproportionate when applied to such young offenders and fails measurably to serve the goals of capital punishment. I dissent.

Soering v. United Kingdom

European Court of Human Rights*
(1989) Publication of the European Court of Human Rights, Series A, Vol. 161 (Soering Case),
reprinted in 11 EHRR 439.

Panel: The President, Judge Ryssdal; Judges Cremona, Thór Vilhjálmsson, Golcüklü, Matscher, Pettiti, Walsh, Sir Vincent Evans, Macdonald,

* [Editors' Note: The European Court of Human Rights was established by the Convention for the Protection of Human Rights and Fundamental Freedoms signed in Rome in 1950 (generally referred to as the European Convention on Human Rights). As of 1997, 40 countries had ratified this Convention. Until recently, the European Commission on Human Rights, a quasi-judicial, quasi-investigative body, received petitions either from member states or from individuals asserting violations of the Convention. If the Commission found the petition "admissible," it attempted to settle the complaint, failing which, the Commission issued an opinion on whether a violation has been shown. Either the Commission or the defendant country could then appeal to the European Court of Human Rights, a judicial body staffed by judges from the different signatory countries, no two of whom may be from the same country. Its judgments are generally given legal effect by the signatory nations. For more detailed treatment, see Laurence R. Helfer &

Russo, Bernhardt, Spielmann, De Meyer, Carrillo Salcedo, Valticos, Martens, Palm, Foighel

. . .

Facts:

I. Particular circumstances of the case

11. The applicant, Mr Jens Soering, was born on 1 August 1966 and is a German national. He is currently detained in prison in England pending extradition to the United States of America to face charges of murder in the Commonwealth of Virginia.

12. The homicides in question were committed in Bedford County, Virginia, in March 1985. The victims, William Reginald Haysom (aged 72) and Nancy Astor Haysom (aged 53), were the parents of the applicant's girlfriend, Elizabeth Haysom, who is a Canadian national. Death in each case was the result of multiple and massive stab and slash wounds to the neck, throat and body. At the time the applicant and Elizabeth Haysom, aged 18 and 20 respectively, were students at the University of Virginia. They disappeared together from Virginia in October 1985, but were arrested in England in April 1986 in connection with cheque fraud.

13. The applicant was interviewed in England between 5 and 8 June 1986 by a police investigator from the Sheriff's Department of Bedford County. In a sworn affidavit dated 24 July 1986 the investigator recorded the applicant as having admitted the killings in his presence and in that of two United Kingdom police officers. The applicant had stated that he was in love with Miss Haysom but that her parents were opposed to the relationship. He and Miss Haysom had therefore planned to kill them. They rented a car in Charlottesville and travelled to Washington where they set up an alibi. The applicant then went to the parents' house, discussed the relationship with them and, when they told him they would do anything to prevent it, a row developed during which he killed them with a knife.

On 13 June 1986 a grand jury of the Circuit Court of Bedford County indicted him on charges of murdering the Haysom parents. The charges alleged capital murder of both of them and the separate non-capital murders of each.

14. On 11 August 1986 the Government of the United States of America requested the applicant's and Miss Haysom's extradition under the terms of the Extradition Treaty of 1972 between the United States and the United Kingdom. On 12 September a Magistrate at Bow Street Magistrates' Court was required by the Secretary of State for Home Affairs to issue a warrant for the applicant's arrest under the provisions of section 8 of the Extradition Act 1870. The applicant was subsequently arrested on 30 December at HM Prison Chelmsford after serving a prison sentence for cheque fraud.

Anne–Marie Slaughter, *Toward a Theory of Effective Supranational Adjudication*, 107 Yale L. J. 273 (1997); see also Mauro Cappel-letti & William Cohen, Comparative Constitutional Law: Cases and Materials 145–48 (1979)].

15.   On 29 October 1986 the British Embassy in Washington addressed a request to the United States' authorities in the following terms:

> "Because the death penalty has been abolished in Great Britain, the Embassy has been instructed to seek an assurance, in accordance with the terms of ... the Extradition Treaty, that, in the event of Mr Soering being surrendered and being convicted of the crimes for which he has been indicted ..., the death penalty, if imposed, will not be carried out.

> "Should it not be possible on constitutional grounds for the United States Government to give such an assurance, the United Kingdom authorities ask that the United States Government undertake to recommend to the appropriate authorities that the death penalty should not be imposed or, if imposed, should not be executed." ...

18.   On 8 May 1987 Elizabeth Haysom was surrendered for extradition to the United States. After pleading guilty on 22 August as an accessory to the murder of her parents, she was sentenced on 6 October to 90 years' imprisonment (45 years on each count of murder)....

20.   On 1 June 1987 Mr Updike swore an affidavit in his capacity as Attorney for Bedford County, in which he certified as follows:

> "I hereby certify that should Jens Soering be convicted of the offence of capital murder as charged in Bedford County, Virginia ... a representation will be made in the name of the United Kingdom to the judge at the time of sentencing that it is the wish of the United Kingdom that the death penalty should not be imposed or carried out."

This assurance was transmitted to the United Kingdom Government under cover of a diplomatic note on 8 June. It was repeated in the same terms in a further affidavit from Mr Updike sworn on 16 February 1988 and forwarded to the United Kingdom by diplomatic note on 17 May 1988. In the same note the Federal Government of the United States undertook to ensure that the commitment of the appropriate authorities of the Commonwealth of Virginia to make representations on behalf of the United Kingdom would be honoured.

During the course of the present proceedings the Virginia authorities have informed the United Kingdom Government that Mr Updike was not planning to provide any further assurances and intended to seek the death penalty in Mr Soering's case because the evidence, in his determination, supported such action.

21.   On 16 June 1987 at the Bow Street Magistrates' Court committal proceedings took place before the Chief Stipendiary Magistrate.

The Government of the United States adduced evidence that on the night of 30 March 1985 the applicant killed William and Nancy Haysom at their home in Bedford County, Virginia. In particular, evidence was given of the applicant's own admissions as recorded in the affidavit of the Bedford County police investigator.

On behalf of the applicant psychiatric evidence was adduced from a consultant forensic psychiatrist (report dated 15 December 1986 by Dr Henrietta Bullard) that he was immature and inexperienced and had lost his personal identity in a symbiotic relationship with his girlfriend—a powerful, persuasive and disturbed young woman. The psychiatric report concluded:

"There existed between Miss Haysom and Soering a 'folie a deux', in which the most disturbed partner was Miss Haysom. . . .

"At the time of the offence, it is my opinion that Jens Soering was suffering from [such] an abnormality of mind due to inherent causes as substantially impaired his mental responsibility for his acts. The psychiatric syndrome referred to as *'folie a deux'* is a well-recognised state of mind where one partner is suggestible to the extent that he or she believes in the psychotic delusions of the other. The degree of disturbance of Miss Haysom borders on the psychotic and, over the course of many months, she was able to persuade Soering that he might have to kill her parents for she and him to survive as a couple. . . . Miss Haysom had a stupefying and mesmeric effect on Soering which led to an abnormal psychological state in which he became unable to think rationally or question the absurdities in Miss Haysom's view of her life and the influence of her parents. . . .

In conclusion, it is my opinion that, at the time of the offences, Soering was suffering from an abnormality of mind which, in this country, would constitute a defence of 'not guilty to murder but guilty of manslaughter'. " . . .

The Chief Magistrate found that the evidence of Dr Bullard was not relevant to any issue that he had to decide and committed the applicant to await the Secretary of State's order for his return to the United States. . . .

24.   On 14 July 1988 the applicant petitioned the Secretary of State, requesting him to exercise his discretion not to make an order for the applicant's surrender under section 11 of the Extradition Act 1870.

This request was rejected, and on 3 August 1988 the Secretary of State signed a warrant ordering the applicant's surrender to the United States' authorities. However, the applicant has not been transferred to the United States by virtue of the interim measures indicated in the present proceedings firstly by the European Commission and then by the European Court. . . .

26.   By a declaration dated 20 March 1989 submitted to this Court, the applicant stated that should the United Kingdom Government require that he be deported to the Federal Republic of Germany he would consent to such requirement and would present no factual or legal opposition against the making or execution of an order to that effect.

[The Court reviewed United Kingdom and Virginia law and conditions in Virginia's prisons.] . . .

64. The applicant adduced much evidence of extreme stress, psychological deterioration and risk of homosexual abuse and physical attack undergone by prisoners on death row, including Mecklenburg Correctional Center. This evidence was strongly contested by the United Kingdom Government on the basis of affidavits sworn by administrators from the Virginia Department of Corrections. . . .

Proceedings Before the Commission

76. Mr Soering's application (no 14038/88) was lodged with the Commission on 8 July 1988. In his application Mr Soering stated his belief that, notwithstanding the assurance given to the United Kingdom Government, there was a serious likelihood that he would be sentenced to death if extradited to the United States of America. He maintained that in the circumstances and, in particular, having regard to the 'death row phenomenon' he would thereby be subjected to inhuman and degrading treatment and punishment contrary to Article 3 of the Convention. In his further submission his extradition to the United States would constitute a violation of Article 6(3)(c) because of the absence of legal aid in the State of Virginia to pursue various appeals. Finally, he claimed that, in breach of Article 13, he had no effective remedy under United Kingdom law in respect of his complaint under Article 3. . . .

[Decision] As to the Law

I.   Alleged breach of Article 3

80. The applicant alleged that the decision by the Secretary of State for the Home Department to surrender him to the authorities of the United States of America would, if implemented, give rise to a breach by the United Kingdom of Article 3 of the Convention, which provides:

> "No one shall be subjected to torture or to inhuman or degrading treatment or punishment."

A.   Applicability of Article 3 in cases of extradition

81. The alleged breach derives from the applicant's exposure to the so-called "death row phenomenon." This phenomenon may be described as consisting in a combination of circumstances to which the applicant would be exposed if, after having been extradited to Virginia to face a capital murder charge, he were sentenced to death.

82. . . . The applicant likewise submitted that Article 3 not only prohibits the Contracting States from causing inhuman or degrading treatment or punishment to occur within their jurisdiction but also embodies an associated obligation not to put a person in a position where he will or may suffer such treatment or punishment at the hands of other States. For the applicant, at least as far as Article 3 is concerned, an individual may not be surrendered out of the protective zone of the Convention without the certainty that the safeguards which he would enjoy are as effective as the Convention standard. . . .

84. The Court will approach the matter on the basis of the following considerations.

85. As results from Article 5 s. (1)(f), which permits "the lawful ... detention of a person against whom action is being taken with a view to ... extradition", no right not to be extradited is as such protected by the Convention. Nevertheless, in so far as a measure of extradition has consequences adversely affecting the enjoyment of a Convention right, it may, assuming that the consequences are not too remote, attract the obligations of a contracting State under the relevant Convention guarantee. (See, mutatis mutandis, Abdulaziz, Cabales and Balkkandali v. United Kingdom (1985) 7 EHRR 471, paras 59–60—in relation to rights in the field of immigration.) What is at issue in the present case is whether Article 3 can be applicable when the adverse consequences of extradition are, or may be, suffered outside the jurisdiction of the extraditing State as a result of treatment or punishment administered in the receiving State....

88. ... The question remains whether the extradition of a fugitive to another State where he would be subjected or be likely to be subjected to torture or to inhuman or degrading treatment or punishment would itself engage the responsibility of a Contracting State under Article 3. That the abhorrence of torture has such implications is recognised in Article 3 of the United Nations Convention Against Torture and Other Cruel, Inhuman or Degrading Treatment or Punishment, which provides that "no State Party shall ... extradite a person where there are substantial grounds for believing that he would be in danger of being subjected to torture". The fact that a specialised treaty should spell out in detail a specific obligation attaching to the prohibition of torture does not mean that an essentially similar obligation is not already inherent in the general terms of Article 3 of the European Convention. It would hardly be compatible with the underlying values of the Convention, that "common heritage of political traditions, ideals, freedom and the rule of law" to which the Preamble refers, were a Contracting State knowingly to surrender a fugitive to another State where there were substantial grounds for believing that he would be in danger of being subjected to torture, however heinous the crime allegedly committed. Extradition in such circumstances, while not explicitly referred to in the brief and general wording of Article 3, would plainly be contrary to the spirit and intendment of the Article, and in the Court's view this inherent obligation not to extradite also extends to cases in which the fugitive would be faced in the receiving State by a real risk of exposure to inhuman or degrading treatment or punishment proscribed by that Article.

89. What amounts to "inhuman or degrading treatment or punishment" depends on all the circumstances of the case. Furthermore, inherent in the whole of the Convention is a search for a fair balance between the demands of the general interest of the community and the requirements of the protection of the individual's fundamental rights. As movement about the world becomes easier and crime takes on a larger international dimension, it is increasingly in the interest of all nations that suspected offenders

who flee abroad should be brought to justice. Conversely, the establishment of safe havens for fugitives would not only result in danger for the State obliged to harbour the protected person but also tend to undermine the foundations of extradition. These considerations must also be included among the factors to be taken into account in the interpretation and application of the notions of inhuman and degrading treatment or punishment in extradition cases.

90.   It is not normally for the Convention institutions to pronounce on the existence or otherwise of potential violations of the Convention. However, where an applicant claims that a decision to extradite him would, if implemented, be contrary to Article 3 by reason of its foreseeable consequences in the requesting country, a departure from this principle is necessary, in view of the serious and irreparable nature of the alleged suffering risked, in order to ensure the effectiveness of the safeguard provided by that Article.

91.   In sum, the decision by a Contracting State to extradite a fugitive may give rise to an issue under Article 3, and hence engage the responsibility of that State under the Convention, where substantial grounds have been shown for believing that the person concerned, if extradited, faces a real risk of being subjected to torture or to inhuman or degrading treatment or punishment in the requesting country. The establishment of such responsibility inevitably involves an assessment of conditions in the requesting country against the standards of Article 3 of the Convention. Nonetheless, there is no question of adjudicating on or establishing the responsibility of the receiving country, whether under general international law, under the Convention or otherwise. In so far as any liability under the Convention is or may be incurred, it is liability incurred by the extraditing Contracting State by reason of its having taken action which has as a direct consequence the exposure of an individual to proscribed ill-treatment.

B.   Application of Article 3 in the particular circumstances of the present case . . .

[The Court concluded that Soering ran "a real risk of a death sentence and hence of exposure to the 'death row phenomenon.' "]

2.   Whether in the circumstances the risk of exposure to the "death row phenomenon" would make extradition a breach of Article 3.

(a) General considerations . . .

101.   Capital punishment is permitted under certain conditions by Article 2(1) of the Convention, which reads:

> "Everyone's right to life shall be protected by law. No one shall be deprived of his life intentionally save in the execution of a sentence of a court following his conviction of a crime for which this penalty is provided by law."

In view of this wording, the applicant did not suggest that the death penalty per se violated Article 3. He, like the two Government Parties, agreed with the Commission that the extradition of a person to a country where he risks the death penalty does not in itself raise an issue under either Article 2 or Article 3. On the other hand. Amnesty International in their written comments argued that the evolving standards in Western Europe regarding the existence and use of the death penalty required that the death penalty should now be considered as an inhuman and degrading punishment within the meaning of Article 3.

102. Certainly, "the Convention is a living instrument which ... must be interpreted in the light of present-day conditions"; and, in assessing whether a given treatment or punishment is to be regarded as inhuman or degrading for the purposes of Article 3, "the Court cannot but be influenced by the developments and commonly accepted standards in the penal policy of the member States of the Council of Europe in this field." (See Tyrer v. United Kingdom 2 EHRR 1, para 31.) De facto the death penalty no longer exists in time of peace in the Contracting States to the Convention. In the few Contracting States which retain the death penalty in law for some peacetime offences, death sentences, if ever imposed, are nowadays not carried out. This "virtual consensus in Western European legal systems that the death penalty is, under current circumstances, no longer consistent with regional standards of justice", to use the words of Amnesty International, is reflected in Protocol No 6 to the Convention, which provides for the abolition of the death penalty in time of peace. Protocol No 6 was opened for signature in April 1983, which in the practice of the Council of Europe indicates the absence of objection on the part of any of the Member States of the Organisation; it came into force in March 1985 and to date has been ratified by thirteen Contracting States to the Convention, not however including the United Kingdom.

Whether these marked changes have the effect of bringing the death penalty per se within the prohibition of ill-treatment under Article 3 must be determined on the principles governing the interpretation of the Convention.

103. The Convention is to be read as a whole and Article 3 should therefore be construed in harmony with the provisions of Article 2. (See, mutatis mutandis, Klass v. Germany 2 EHRR 214, 214, para 68.) On this basis Article 3 evidently cannot have been intended by the drafters of the Convention to include a general prohibition of the death penalty since that would nullify the clear wording of Article 2(1).

Subsequent practice in national penal policy, in the form of a generalised abolition of capital punishment, could be taken as establishing the agreement of the Contracting States to abrogate the exception provided for under Article 2(1) and hence to remove a textual limit on the scope for evolutive interpretation of Article 3. However, Protocol No 6, as a subsequent written agreement, shows that the intention of the Contracting Parties as recently as 1983 was to adopt the normal method of amendment of the text in order to introduce a new obligation to abolish capital punishment in time of peace and, what is more, to do so by an optional instrument allowing each State to choose the moment when to undertake such an engagement. In these conditions, notwithstanding the special character of the Convention, Article 3 cannot be interpreted as generally prohibiting the death penalty.

104. That does not mean however that circumstances relating to a death sentence can never give rise to an issue under Article 3. The manner in which it is imposed or executed, the personal circumstances of the condemned person and a disproportionality to the gravity of the crime committed, as well as the conditions of detention awaiting execution, are examples of factors capable of bringing the treatment or punishment received by the condemned person within the proscription under Article 3. Present-day attitudes in the Contracting States to capital punishment are relevant for the assessment whether the acceptable threshold of suffering or degradation has been exceeded.

(b) The particular circumstances

105. The applicant submitted that the circumstances to which he would be exposed as a consequence of the implementation of the Secretary of State's decision to return him to the United States, namely the "death row phenomenon", cumulatively constituted such serious treatment that his extradition would be contrary to Article 3. He cited in particular the delays in the appeal and review procedures following a death sentence, during which time he would be subject to increasing tension and psychological trauma; the fact, so he said, that the judge or jury in determining sentence is not obliged to take into account the defendant's age and mental state at the time of the offence; the extreme conditions of his future detention in "death row" in Mecklenburg Correctional Center, where he expects to be the victim of violence and sexual abuse because of his age, colour and nationality; and the constant spectre of the execution itself, including the ritual of execution. He also relied on the possibility of extradition or deportation, which he would not oppose, to the Federal Republic of Germany as accentuating the disproportionality of the Secretary of State's decision....

(c) Conclusion

111. For any prisoner condemned to death, some element of delay between imposition and execution of the sentence and the experience of severe stress in conditions necessary for strict incarceration are inevitable. The democratic character of the Virginia legal system in general and the positive features of Virginia trial, sentencing and appeal procedures in particular are beyond doubt. The Court agrees with the Commission that the machinery of justice to which the applicant would be subject in the United States is in itself neither arbitrary nor unreasonable, but, rather, respects the rule of law and affords not inconsiderable procedural safeguards to the defendant in a capital trial. Facilities are available on death row for the assistance of inmates, notably through provision of psychological and psychiatric services.

However, in the Court's view, having regard to the very long period of time spent on death row in such extreme conditions, with the ever-present and mounting anguish of awaiting execution of the death penalty, and to the personal circumstances of the applicant, especially his age and mental state at the time of the offence, the applicant's extradition to the United States would expose him to a real risk of treatment going beyond the threshold set by Article 3. A further consideration of relevance is that in the particular instance the legitimate purpose of extradition could be achieved by another means which would not involve suffering of such exceptional intensity or duration.

Accordingly, the Secretary of State's decision to extradite the applicant to the United States would, if implemented, give rise to a breach of Article 3....

Concurring Opinion Of Judge De Meyer

The applicant's extradition to the United States of America would not only expose him to inhuman or degrading treatment or punishment. It would also, and above all, violate his right to life.

Indeed, the most important issue in this case is not "the likelihood of the feared exposure of the applicant to the 'death row phenomenon,'" but the very simple fact that his life would be put in jeopardy by the extradition.

The second sentence of Article 2 §(1) of the Convention, as it was drafted in 1950, states that "no one shall be deprived of his life intentionally save in the execution of a sentence of a court following his conviction of a crime for which this penalty is provided by law".

In the circumstances of the present case, the applicant's extradition to the United States would subject him to the risk of being sentenced to death, and executed, in Virginia for a crime for which that penalty is not provided by the law of the United Kingdom.

When a person's right to life is involved, no requested State can be entitled to allow a requesting State to do what the requested State is not itself allowed to do.

If, as in the present case, the domestic law of a State does not provide the death penalty for the crime concerned, that State is not permitted to put the person concerned in a position where he may be deprived of his life for that crime at the hands of another State.

That consideration may already suffice to preclude the United Kingdom from surrendering the applicant to the United States.

There is also something more fundamental.

The second sentence of Article 2 s. (1) of the Convention was adopted, nearly forty years ago, in particular historical circumstances, shortly after the Second World War. In so far as it still may seem to permit, under certain conditions, capital punishment in time of peace, it does not reflect the contemporary situation, and is now overridden by the development of legal conscience and practice.[4]

Such punishment is not consistent with the present state of European civilisation.

De facto, it no longer exists in any State Party to the Convention.

---

4. See also Art. 6 §s. (2) and (6) of the International Covenant on Civil and Political Rights and Article 4 §§ (2) and (3) of the American Convention on Human Rights. The

Its unlawfulness was recognised by the Committee of Ministers of the Council of Europe when it adopted in December 1982, and opened for signature in April 1983, the Sixth Protocol to the Convention, which to date has been signed by sixteen, and ratified by thirteen, Contracting States.

No State party to the Convention can in that context, even if it has not yet ratified the Sixth Protocol, be allowed to extradite any person if that person thereby incurs the risk of being put to death in the requesting State. . . .

2.   The Relevance of Practical Concerns in the Study of Comparative Constitutional Law

The year *Stanford* was decided Chief Justice Rehnquist gave a speech in which he said:

> For nearly a century and a half, courts in the United States exercising the power of judicial review had no precedents to look to save their own, because our courts alone exercised this sort of authority. When many new constitutional courts were created after the Second World War, these courts naturally looked to decisions of the Supreme Court of the United States, among other sources, for developing their own law. But now that constitutional law is solidly grounded in so many countries, it is time that the United States courts begin looking to the decisions of other constitutional courts to aid in their own deliberative process. The United States courts, and legal scholarship in our country generally, have been somewhat laggard in relying on comparative law and decisions of other countries. But I predict that with so many thriving constitutional courts in the world today . . . that approach will be changed in the near future.

William Rehnquist, *Constitutional Courts—Comparative Remarks* (1989), in Germany and Its Basic Law: Past, Present and Future—A German–American Symposium 412 (Paul Kirchhof & Donald P. Kommers eds. 1993).

These comments focus on the courts, and suggest that lawyers in the United States could strengthen their arguments by incorporating material about comparative constitutional law.[a] But constitutional law is about constitutional structures, not simply about judicial review, and lawyers as policy-makers might consider insights available from comparative constitutional law as they consider revising domestic constitutional arrangements.

More mundanely, perhaps, comparative constitutional law may affect a lawyer's practice. After *Soering*, for example, U.S. prosecutors seeking

very wording of each of these provisions, adopted respectively in 1966 and in 1969, clearly reflects the evolution of legal conscience and practice towards the universal abolition of the death penalty.

a. A more recent debate between Justice Scalia and Justice Breyer over the utility of comparative constitutional knowledge sug-

extradition from European Union nations may have to make stronger representations of their intentions than the prosecutor there did. In Soering's case the Virginia prosecutor eventually agreed to refrain from seeking the death penalty. Soering was extradited, convicted, and sentenced to two life terms for the Haysom murders.

---

3.   THE RELEVANCE OF COMPARATIVE CONSTITUTIONAL LAW IN GENERATING PHILOSOPHICAL OR SOCIAL SCIENTIFIC "HYPOTHESES"

Comparative constitutional law shows different mid-level institutional arrangements designed to deal with enduring problems of social order.

gests both that some on the Court may now be open to such arguments and that others will be resistant. In Printz v. United States, 521 U.S. 98 (1997), the Court held a federal requirement that local law enforcement officers perform background checks on prospective gun buyers to be an unconstitutional federal "commandeering" of state employees to administer federal law. Justice Breyer, in dissent, argued that

"other countries, facing the same basic problem, have found that local control is better maintained through application of a principle that is the direct opposite of the principle that the majority derives from the silence of our Constitution. The federal systems of Switzerland, Germany and the European Union, for example, all provide that constituent states, not federal bureaucracies, will themselves implement many of the laws, rules, regulations or decrees enacted by the central, 'federal' body. They do so in part because they believe that such a system interferes less, not more, with the independent authority of the ... subsidiary government....

... "[T]heir experience may ... cast an empirical light on the consequences of different solutions to a common legal problem—in this case the problem of reconciling central authority with the need to preserve the liberty-enhancing autonomy of a smaller constituent government entity....

... "[C]omparative experience suggest[s] there is no need to interpret the Constitution as containing an absolute principle—forbidding the assignment of virtually any federal duty to any state official...."

Justice Scalia, writing for the Court, responded with his version of "American exceptionalism":

"[S]uch comparative analysis [is] inappropriate to the task of interpreting a constitution, though it was of course quite relevant to the task of writing one. The Framers were familiar with many federal systems, from classical antiquity down to their own time; ... Federalist 20, after an extended critique of the system of government established by the Union of Utrecht for the United Netherlands, concludes:

'I make no apology for having dwelt so long on the contemplation of these federal precedents. Experience is the oracle of truth; and where its responses are unequivocal, they ought to be conclusive and sacred. The important truth, which it unequivocally pronounces in the present case, is that a sovereignty over sovereigns, a government over governments, a legislation for communities as contradistinguished from individuals, as it is a solecism in theory, so in practice it is subversive of the order and ends of civil polity....'

"Antifederalists ... pointed specifically to Switzerland—and its then-400 years success as a 'confederate republic'—as proof that the proposed Constitution and its federal structure was unnecessary. The fact is that our federalism is not Europe's. It is the 'unique contribution of the Framers to political science and political theory.' United States v. Lo-

Philosophers and social scientists address those problems in their own ways. Comparative constitutional law might be able to illuminate their discussions. For example, Chapter VIII presents an argument that federalism may be an institutional arrangement that contributes to the developing of the overlapping consensus that philosopher John Rawls claims is essential to having stable liberal societies. Similarly, Chapter VIII presents an argument that federal systems have a tendency to centralize rather than disperse power over time. Neither argument may be correct, but both may help people think about the more general questions concerning liberalism and centralization that they deal with in other settings.

4. DISPELLING THE SENSE OF FALSE NECESSITY AND LEARNING ABOUT OTHER CULTURES

As noted earlier, comparative study can help dispel the sense of false necessity about the existing constitutional arrangements in one's home country, although it may be difficult on further reflection to distinguish false from true necessities within different systems of constitutionalism. Apart from the possibility of dispelling one's sense of "false necessity" about familiar legal arrangements, the study of comparative constitutional law may be justified on the simple ground that it exposes students to different ways of doing things, and thereby enhances your general education. But consider Frankenberg's critique of unreflective foreign travel.

5. NOTE ON CONSTITUTIONAL "BORROWING" AND OTHER TRANSNATIONAL INFLUENCES

Judge Guido Calabresi, noting that several post–1945 constitutions were modeled explicitly on the U.S. Constitution, has argued that experience with judicial review in those systems could inform our judgment about how judicial review should operate in the United States: "Wise parents," Judge Calabresi wrote, "learn from their children." United States v. Then, 56 F.3d 464, 469 (2d Cir.1995) (Calabresi, J., concurring). To what extent can constitutional solutions be "borrowed" from one system to another?

Consider these observations:

Borrowing constitutional ideas from other countries has its hazards.... Planting a proposition in a different cultural, historical, or traditional context may lead to results quite different from those one finds in the country from which the proposition was borrowed.... Liberal reformers in early nineteenth century Latin America ... often tried to copy the experience of the United States. Those transplants failed because the soil in which they were planted was simply not congenial; the conditions for constitutional democracy were not yet in existence.... The limits of imitation are suggested by an observation penned by Juan Bautista Alberdi, the father of Argentine constitutionalism:

pez, 514 U.S. 549, 575 (1995) (Kennedy, J., concurring)."

> All constitutions change or succumb when they are but children of imitation; the only one which does not change, the only one which moves and lives with the country, is the constitution which that country has received from the events of its history, that is to say, from those deeds which form the chain of its existence, from the day of its birth. . . .

Alberdi . . . seems to have underestimated the value of borrowing. . . . There are many examples of successful constitutional adaptations from one country's experience to another. . . . When India achieved its independence and drafted a constitution, there seemed widespread agreement on the Euro–American constitutional tradition as a source both of principles and often of specific provisions. But Alberdi's statement is still useful as a cautionary note: a constitution is unlikely to succeed if it is drafted without regard for a country's history, traditions, and political culture.

> Diverse or contending parties may well agree, in general, on the usefulness of a foreign model when they are at work drafting their own country's constitution. Such agreement, however, may only mask the essential ambiguity of the model to which they seem jointly to aspire. . . . Even among those countries sharing notions about constitutionalism, specific norms may play out quite differently, depending on the cultural assumptions that qualify a norm's interpretation. Consider, for example, freedom of expression. Every post-communist constitution has guaranteed for freedom of speech and press. One who examines the actual contours of free expression in those countries, however, will find striking differences between the way those principles are perceived in the United States, on the one hand, and in the emerging democracies, on the other.

A.E. Dick Howard, *The Indeterminacy of Constitutions*, 31 Wake Forest L.Rev. 383, 402–04 (1996).

Sometimes constitutions are imposed on nations. West Germany's Basic Law was the result of negotiations with the western occupying powers after World War II, and particularly with representatives of the U.S. armed forces. The Japanese post-war constitution was essentially written under the direction of General Douglas MacArthur and his staff. Most analysts regard the German and Japanese constitutions as "successes." In light of Alberdi's observations, what might account for that?

Howard also asks why constitutional drafters borrow from other countries:

> One reason for borrowing . . . is convenience: why reinvent the constitutional wheel when there are so many constitutions already available on which to draw? . . . Beyond matters of convenience stand other imperatives. Drafters of constitutions may be seeking—indeed, may feel compelled—to adopt principles found in international documents. . . . A country's leaders may see a new constitution as the means of achieving international acceptance. . . . Similarly, a country

may hope to achieve admission into a regional arrangement. . . . Moreover, a country, hoping to shore up its security interests, may seek to curry the favor [of] a powerful country o[r] patron. . . . Drafters might also see a constitution as a way of attracting western trade and investment.

Howard, at 405–06.

a. *Influences in Hungary?* The Hungarian Constitutional Court may have held the death penalty unconstitutional at least in part because Hungarian political and legal elites believed that doing so was a precondition for entry into association with the European Union, as the concurrence in *Soering* would suggest. For discussion, see George P. Fletcher, *Searching for the Rule of Law in the Wake of Communism*, 1992 Brigham Young U. L. Rev. 145, 159. In what ways would the motives for development of constitutional doctrine (e.g., constructing constitutional law in part to gain admission to international organizations, or other benefits) be important? Would external motives suggest the possible instability of such constitutional law, the possibility of expanding real commitments to particular doctrines through external incentives, or both?

b. *Influences in Turkey?* Turkey has been described as "the only state with a predominantly Muslim population that has achieved the status of a multi-party, constitutional democracy." Paul J. Magnarella, *The Comparative Constitutional Law Enterprise*, 30 Willamette L. Rev. 509, 516 (1994). (Consider Frankenberg's possible comment on "achieved the status of".) Magnarella argues that this resulted, not from the traditional values of the governed, but from the ruling elites' calculation that "Turkey's best prospects for economic development and security from Soviet aggression lay in alliances" with the West (including NATO, and the European Community). In order to become a member of these organizations, the Turkish elites had to commit to maintain constitutional democracy, human rights and the rule of law. EU officials, Magnarella reports, took the position that Turkey had to join the European Human Rights Convention and agree to the jurisdiction of the European Court of Justice in order to move towards EU membership. For a somewhat pessimistic evaluation of Turkey's prospects, see Ersin Kalaycioglu, *Constitutional Viability and Political Institutions in Turkish Democracy*, in Designs for Democratic Stability: Studies in Viable Constitutionalism 179–210 (1997) (Abdo I. Baaklini & Helen Desfosses, eds. 1997).

c. *U.S. Freedom Support Act.* The Freedom Support Act, 22 U.S.C. Sec. 5801 et seq (1992), directs that in allocating U.S. foreign assistance, the President "take into account" the extent to which the states of the former Soviet Union are "mak[ing] significant progress toward, and [are] committed to the comprehensive implementation of, a democratic system based on principles of the rule of law, individual freedoms, and representative government determined by free and fair elections" and are "mak[ing] significant progress in, and [are] committed to the comprehensive implementation of economic reform based on market principles, private ownership, and integration into the world economy, including implementation of the legal and policy frameworks necessary for such reform (including protection of intellectual property and respect for contracts)." Is this similar to the reported actions of the EC towards Turkey? What problems, if any, do you see with this Act's incentives to foreign constitutional change?

d. *Ethnocentricity*? In general, consider whether the preceding analyses of borrowing constitutions are subject to Frankenburg's criticisms of comparative constitutional law as potentially ethnocentric.

e. *Inevitability of borrowings*? Consider also Professor Alan Watson's work suggesting, in the context of comparative law generally, that borrowings (not always in the sense of conscious transplantation but also in the sense of influences) are pervasive and perhaps inevitable. See Alan Watson, *Legal Change: Sources of Law and Legal Culture*, 131 U. Pa. L. Rev. 1121 (1983) (summarizing his earlier work on comparative law and emphasizing the extent of "legal transplants"). Is there reason to think that constitutional law would differ from private law in this regard?

f. *Comparative constitutional law for domestic law purposes*: Constitutions may direct interpreters to examine the laws of other jurisdictions. The Interim Constitution of South Africa (1993) provided that in interpreting its provisions, courts shall "have regard to public international law applicable to the protection of the rights entrenched in this Chapter, and may have regard to comparable foreign case law." The Constitutional Court cited this provision in explaining its extensive consideration of international and foreign constitutional decisions when it held the death penalty unconstitutional. State v. Makwanyane, Case No. CCT/3/94 (June 6 1995), ¶ 34. The Final Constitution (1996) provides in s. 39 that when interpreting the Bill of Rights, courts, tribunals and other forums "must consider international law and may consider foreign law."[b]

In the death penalty case, the South African Constitutional Court noted the large numbers of countries that formally or practically forbid the death penalty. After a lengthy discussion of U. S. law, the South African Court concluded that its "jurisprudence has not resolved the dilemma arising from the fact that the Constitution prohibits cruel and unusual punishments but also ... contemplates that there will be capital punishment. The acceptance by the majority of the [U.S. Supreme Court] of the proposition that capital punishment is not per se unconstitutional, but that in certain circumstances it may be arbitrary, and thus unconstitutional, has led to endless litigation. ... The difficulties that have been experienced in following this path ... persuade [the Court] that we should not follow this route." ¶ 56.

b. Cf. Eric Stein, *Lawyers, Judges, and the Making of a Transnational Constitution*, 75 Am. J. Int'l L. 1, 15–16 (1981) (describing European Court of Justice decision in International Handelsgesellschaft case that it would apply fundamental unwritten general principles of law, " 'inspired by the constitutional traditions common to the Member States,' " including the " 'fundamental principles of national legal systems' forming 'a philosophical, political and legal substratum common to the Member States' ").

g. *Comparative experience and public opinion.* One study of the world-wide experience with abolishing capital punishment concludes that "[s]uccessful and sustained abolition has never been the result of great popular demand," and that "[i]n this context public opinion is invariably led, not followed." The authors conclude, "However, and whenever, the death penalty is abolished in the United States, that step will be taken with limited popular support and will be contrary to the manifest weight of public opinion." Franklin E. Zimring & Gordon Hawkins, Capital Punishment and the American Agenda 12, 22, 154 (1986). Is this information, if accurate, relevant to your assessment of the Supreme Court's analysis in *Stanford*? Should it be relevant to the court itself? In 1986 Zimring and Hawkins asserted that "[w]hen democratic countries cease to execute and subsequently repeal death penalty legislation, this is accomplished by institutions of representative democracy." Since they wrote, the constitutional courts in South Africa and Hungary have held the death penalty unconstitutional. How, if at all, do these events affect your evaluation of their argument about the importance of political leadership in successful abolition campaigns? Is it still to early to tell whether abolition in these countries will be "successful"? Do constitutional courts, in some settings, act as institutions of "representative democracy" in leading public opinion?

---

6. Note on Constitutionalism, Sovereignty and International Agreements

Note that *Soering* itself involved the application of an international agreement to a domestic British matter. It is not, then, a constitutional law case (as conventionally understood). But note as well the similarity between concurring Judge De Meyer's opinion and Justice Brennan's dissent in *Stanford*. Occasionally these materials deal with other treaty-based issues, which are dealt with in more detail in courses on international human rights and European Union law. Treaty-based issues do resemble constitutional ones in some important ways: Both raise questions that cannot be resolved merely by finding out what a contemporary political majority in a single nation wants to do. And both raise questions of what makes a judicial decision contravening judgments of governmental actors legitimate and effective in a legal order.

Although this book concentrates primarily on constitutions and constitutionalism within particular nation states, it occasionally includes material relating to supranational constitutional issues and design, including decisions of the European Court of Human Rights, the European Court of Justice and commentary on the design and operation of the European Union. In so doing, we implicitly indicate willingness to acknowledge constitutions and constitutionalism operating as constraints on the exercise of power at the international as well as at the national level. Consider whether recognizing constitutional aspects of international or supranational decisionmaking unduly expands the "category" of constitutions and constitutionalism. Consider whether a failure to include such materials would unduly constrain the appropriate category in an age of economic and political globalization.[c]

---

7.   NOTE ON THE UNITS OF COMPARISON: THE IRISH EXPERIENCE WITH REPRODUCTIVE FREEDOM AND POPULAR INITIATIVE

Ireland's laws, influenced by the nation's Catholic heritage, made abortions generally illegal.[d] In one widely reported 1938 case, a celebrated trial judge instructed a jury considering a criminal charge against a person who performed an abortion that a physician was *required* to perform an abortion if carrying the pregnancy to term would leave the woman a "physical and mental wreck." The jury then acquitted the defendant, who had performed the abortion on a fourteen-year-old rape victim. The "physical and mental wreck" standard might have made it relatively easy to obtain a legal abortion in Ireland. But Irish lawyers disagreed over whether the jury instruction accurately described Irish law, and Irish doctors almost uniformly refused to perform abortions. They adhered to Roman Catholic interpretations of the principle of double effect, and would not perform abortions where the destruction of the fetus was the directly intended effect.

c. There is a growing literature on constitutionalism in international law, treaties and organizations, and on the process by which international obligations come to be internalized as binding. Much of this literature discusses the "interpenetration" of domestic and international legal systems, and the dramatic change in the reach of international law and treaties in providing individuals direct rights against states, formerly the province of domestic public law. An introduction to some of this literature can be found in Harold Hongju Koh, *Why Do Nations Obey International Law?*, 106 Yale L. J. 2599 (1997) (reviewing Abram Chayes and Antonia Handler Chayes, The New Sovereignty: Compliance with International Regulatory Agreements (1995) and Thomas M. Franck, Fairness in International Law and Institutions (1995)); Harold Hongju Koh, *Transnational Legal Process*, 75 Neb. L. Rev. 181 (1996); and Ernst–Ulrich Petersmann, *Constitutionalism and International Organizations*, 17 Nw. J. Int'l L & Bus. 398 (1996–97). See also John H. Barton & Barry E. Carter, *International Law and Institutions for a New Age*, 81 Geo. L. J. 535 (1993); John Jackson, *Reflections on Constitutional Changes to the Global Trading System*, 72 Chi. Kent L. Rev. 511 (1996). Whether international law should be regarded as part of federal common law in

the U.S., and whether treaties are directly enforceable against the U.S. in domestic courts, remain subjects of debate. For varying perspectives, see Curtis A. Bradley & Jack L. Goldsmith, *The Current Illegitimacy of International Human Rights Litigation*, 66 Fordham L. Rev. 319 (1997); Curtis A. Bradley & Jack L. Goldsmith, *Customary International Law as Federal Common Law: A Critique of the Modern Position*, 110 Harv. L. Rev. 815 (1997); Gerald L. Neuman, *Sense and Nonsense About Customary International Law: A Response to Professors Bradley and Goldsmith*, 66 Fordham L. Rev. 371 (1997); Harold Hongju Koh, *Is International Law Really State Law?*, 111 Harv. L. Rev. 1824 (1998); Louis Henkin, *A Century of Chinese Exclusion and Its Progeny*, 100 Harv. L. Rev. 853 (1987); Peter Westen, *The Place of Foreign Treaties in the Constitution of the United States: A Reply to Louis Henkin*, 101 Harv. L. Rev. 511 (1987); Carlos Vazquez, *Treaty-Based Rights and Remedies of Individuals*, 92 Colum. L. Rev. 1082 (1992).

d. Ireland's Constitution has been described by leading jurists as avowedly "Christian" in content. See Gerard Sheehy, *The Right to Marry in the Irish Tradition of the Common Law*, in Human Rights and Constitutional Law: Essays in Honor of Brian Walsh 21 (James O'Reilly ed., 1992).

In 1974 the Irish Supreme Court decided the counterpart to Griswold v. Connecticut, holding that married persons had a constitutional right to privacy encompassing a right to obtain contraceptive devices. McGee v. Attorney General, [1974] Irish Rep. 284. The Irish Supreme Court's decision referred to *Griswold* and other U.S. cases. Those references alerted Irish pro-life groups to what they thought might be a real threat, even though the Irish Supreme Court rather clearly implied that the contraceptive case implicated different interests from abortion. Pro-life groups feared that, just as the U.S. Supreme Court had extended the right to privacy announced in *Griswold* to cover the right to choose in *Roe v. Wade*, so too the Irish Supreme Court might extend *its* decision in *McGee*.

After several years of organizing political support, pro-life groups in Ireland put a "right to life" constitutional amendment on the ballot. With 54% of those eligible voting, the Irish electorate approved the referendum in 1983 by a margin of approximately 2–1, thereby adding the Eighth Amendment (Article 40) to the Irish Constitution:

> "The State acknowledges the right to life of the unborn and, with due regard to the equal right to life of the mother, guarantees in its laws to respect and, as far as practicable, by its laws to defend and vindicate that right."

According to Kelly, "enactment of this paragraph was a unique example in the Irish experience of a constitutional amendment being proposed and pioneered outside the party political system ... [and] resembl[ed] the old device of initiative ... designed to allow the electorate to promote proposals for legislative and constitutional change."[e]

Because few Irish doctors had been performing abortions, the right-to-life amendment had no immediate direct effects. But Irish women had been able to obtain abortions by flying to Great Britain, where abortion was legal and available. Some estimates indicate that each year in the 1980s between five and ten thousand Irish women traveled to Great Britain to have abortions. A number of groups, many serving university communities, offered information about the availability of abortions in Great Britain. Pro-life groups, led by the Society for the Protection of the Unborn Child (SPUC), saw the amendment as an opportunity to restrict the operation of these counseling centers: Closing them down would "defend" the right to life of unborn Irish children, as Article 40 required.

The SPUC went to court and got orders requiring the counseling services to stop "assisting" abortions by making travel arrangements for women or by giving information about the availability of abortions at specific clinics outside Ireland. The counseling services then moved the controversy outside Ireland as well. They called on European international courts to overturn the Irish decisions.

e.   J.M. Kelly, The Irish Constitution 782 (3d ed., Gerard Hogan & Gerry White eds., 1994).

The European Convention on Human Rights, which Ireland has signed, protects a right of free expression "regardless of frontiers." The counseling services went to the European Court of Human Rights, claiming that the injunction against distributing information about abortions in Great Britain violated this guarantee. A majority of that court agreed that the injunction violated freedom of expression. Most of the judges relied on the technical ground that freedom of expression is violated when courts issue injunctions without a specific statute authorizing them to do so; they believed that Article 40 itself was not specific enough. Some of the judges, though, said that limiting freedom of expression regarding abortion information was excessive, even if the government had a right to prevent abortions. They noted that telling people not to distribute information was likely to be ineffective unless those who received the information could be barred from leaving Ireland. A few years later the court adopted that position, noting that information about abortions could be obtained not simply from counseling services but from magazines and telephone directories. Barring counseling services from providing information was, the court said, ineffective in protecting unborn life.

Another European court also disapproved Ireland's policy. As a member of the European Community (the Common Market, now known as the European Union), Ireland may not interfere with the provision of commercial services across national borders, or with international travel. The counseling services argued that banning distribution of information interfered with the commercial operations of abortion providers in Great Britain. This claim went to the European commercial court, the European Court of Justice. The counseling services lost on technical grounds. The Court of Justice agreed that injunctions against providing information interfered with commerce, but it pointed out that the counseling services in the case before the court were university student groups. Because they had no ties to commercial abortion providers, *their* rights to free commerce were not violated by the injunction against them.

The commercial decision was a victory for the Irish government in name only, because it clearly opened the door for foreign abortion service providers to advertise their services in Ireland. The Irish government therefore tried to protect its "right to life" amendment by renegotiating its international obligations. As these cases were proceeding, the members of the European Community were negotiating a new treaty to strengthen their commercial ties. The Irish government insisted that the new treaty, called the Maastricht Treaty, include a provision, Protocol 17, stating that nothing in the treaty would affect the application of the "right to life" amendment in Ireland. The government's goal was to ensure that the Irish courts could continue to bar the distribution of information about the availability of abortions in Great Britain, though it was not clear whether Protocol 17 would achieve that end.[f]

---

f. As a technical matter, it might not have. Some lawyers argued, for example, that the court's decision did not deal with the application of the amendment "in Ireland," but rather dealt with the effects of the amendment in Great Britain.

A more serious defeat for Irish pro-life groups lay ahead. A fourteen-year-old young woman, known throughout the litigation only as X, was sexually assaulted and made pregnant by the father of a friend whom she had been visiting. She and her parents decided they should go to Great Britain for an abortion. They were concerned, though, that the friend's father not escape punishment, so they went to the police and asked whether DNA test evidence taken from the aborted fetus would be admitted into evidence in an Irish prosecution of the father. The police said they would ask the public prosecutor. When the prosecutor learned of the plans being made by X and her parents, he went to court—not to prosecute the rapist, but to get an order barring X from leaving the country for nine months.[g]

In February 1992, ten days after the Maastricht Treaty was signed, the judge issued such an order. The judge said that the travel plans posed a "real and imminent danger to the life of the unborn," and that the risk that X would commit suicide was "much less" and was "of a different order of magnitude than the certainty that the life of the unborn will be terminated."

The judge's order created a huge public outcry. The Irish electorate had to ratify the Maastricht Treaty, and the X case became bound up in the ratification controversy. One-third of the public had opposed the "right to life" amendment, but many were able to live with it because women could at least go abroad for abortions. The European Union treaties ordinarily protected the right to travel. Right-to-life proponents argued, though, that the provision saying that the Union agreements did not affect the application of the "right to life" amendment in Ireland authorized a travel ban as well.

Claiming that the order violated her constitutional right to travel, X and her parents immediately appealed. After lifting the injunction against travel, in March the Irish court issued its opinion. Attorney General v. X, [1992] Irish Rep. 1. Two justices said that the order did *not* violate X's right to travel. As they saw it, the case presented a conflict of constitutional rights. On the one side there was X's right to travel, and on the other the fetus's right to life. These judges thought it easy to strike the balance: in favor of life. As the court's chief justice put it, "if there were a stark conflict between the right of a mother of an unborn child to travel and the right to life of the unborn child, the right to life would necessarily have to take precedence over the right to travel."

Two other justices, though, thought that the courts did not have to "balance" competing rights. If the woman had a right to travel abroad, she had the right to do whatever was lawful in Great Britain. They thought that she could not be said to be "conspiring" to violate any law, and therefore could not be barred from leaving Ireland.

g. Later the friend's father was convicted of criminal assault and was initially sentenced to fourteen years in prison; a judge reduced the sentence to 4 1/2 years.

Then, in an analysis that few observers had expected, these four justices said that X was nonetheless entitled to have an abortion *in Ireland*.[h] She had threatened to commit suicide and, the court held, that created a risk to her own life. The risk did not have to be "inevitable or immediate," but only "real and substantial." The chief justice noted that sometimes the woman's life was *physically* threatened by her pregnancy. In such cases the woman's physical condition could be monitored and, if "diagnostic warning signs" appeared an abortion could then be performed. In contrast, the chief justice said, it was impossible to monitor the woman to see if she was about to commit suicide. Another judge made the same point by saying that suicide threats meant that it was not "practicable" to protect the life of the unborn. Because the "right to life" amendment required the government to defend the fetus's right to life "as far as practicable," the amendment did not require the state to prohibit abortions in circumstances like X's.

Only one justice dissented. He argued that in making a "choice . . . between the certain death of the unborn life and a feared substantial danger of death but no degree of certainty of the mother by way of self-destruction," the courts should respond to the certainty of death rather than its probability. "If there is a suicidal tendency then this is something which has to be guarded against" by putting X under appropriate supervision with "loving and sympathetic care and professional counseling and all the protection which the State agencies can provide or furnish." He thought that "suicide threats can be contained." The dissenter also agreed that the woman's right to travel had to be subordinated to the fetus's right to life.

X's plight had caught the attention of the Irish public. The Supreme Court decision ended a major public controversy, but few were completely satisfied with the outcome. Right-to-life proponents believed that the X decision made abortions more freely available in Ireland than they thought proper. Pro-choice activists were worried about what a majority of the court had said about the right to travel. Three of the court's five judges said the right to travel *could* be overridden to protect the life of the unborn. That seemed to mean that the majority of women who went to Great Britain for abortions—who ordinarily did not face a "real and substantial" threat of death—might be barred from travel. Perhaps the same European commercial treaties that protected the distribution of information also protected the right to travel. The pending Maastricht Treaty, though, had Protocol 17 immunizing Irish abortion law from attack under the commercial treaties.

The Irish government tried to appease pro-choice objections by getting Protocol 17 amended, to make it clear that rights to information and travel were not affected. Unfortunately for the government, its treaty partners refused to amend the protocol. The Maastricht Treaty was controversial in many nations, and the governments feared that opening the treaty up to

h. As explained above, these four disagreed on whether, absent entitlement to an abortion in Ireland, the right to travel under the EU would control, or instead would need to be balanced against the obligation to protect the unborn under Article 40.

one change would open it up to others. Instead, all the governments that signed the Agreement issued a "Solemn Declaration" saying "it was and is their intention" that Protocol 17 would not limit freedom to travel or make information available in Ireland "relating to services lawfully available" elsewhere in Europe. They did this even though the Irish government had initially insisted on Protocol 17 *after* the European international courts had already protected the right to information; the "Solemn Declaration" apparently meant that Protocol 17 never really was intended to overcome the European courts' decisions.

Ireland's pro-life groups continued to have serious objections to the X decision. In its political campaign for ratification of the Maastricht Treaty, the Irish government promised to hold a referendum on abortion and the rights to travel and information. Three constitutional amendments were placed on the ballot in November 1992. Two would insert new language in the "right to life" amendment to protect the rights to travel and information. The third would have strengthened the ban on abortions,[i] repudiated the X decision, and placed in the Irish Constitution a stringent standard for determining when abortions would be lawful.

After another heated political campaign, the Irish voting public approved the amendments protecting the rights to travel and information, and rejected the stronger "right to life" proposal.[j] Approximately 68% of the electorate voted, and this time over 65% of the voters opposed that amendment. Pro-choice groups, and those satisfied with the X decision, opposed it; and, according to Irish political observers, even some pro-life voters did so as well, because they disagreed with its limited recognition that sometimes "direct" abortions—intended to kill the fetus in order to preserve the woman's life—would be legal.

Subsequently, the so-called "Information Bill," enacted to permit information about abortion services in other countries to be made available to women in Ireland, was submitted to the Irish Supreme Court pursuant to Article 26 of the Irish Constitution, which permits the President to refer a bill to the Supreme Court to determine if it is constitutional.[k] The Court

---

i. The third proposed amendment (not enacted) provided, "It shall be unlawful to terminate the life of an unborn unless such termination is necessary to save the life, as distinct from the health, of the mother where there is an illness or disorder of the mother giving rise to a real and substantial risk to her life, not being a risk of self-destruction."

j. The provisions added to Article 40.3.3 were as follows:

This subsection shall not limit freedom to travel between the State and another state.

This subsection shall not limit freedom to obtain, or make available, in the State, subject to such conditions as may be laid down by law, information relating to services lawfully available in another state.

k. Article 26 provides in part:

"1. (1) The President may, after consultation with the council of State, refer any Bill to which this Article applies to the Supreme Court for a decision on the question as to whether such Bill or any specified provisions or provision of such Bill is or are repugnant to this Constitution or any provision thereof.

* * *

"2. The decision of the majority of the judges of the Supreme Court shall, for the purposes of this Article, be the decision of the court and shall be pronounced by such one of

unanimously upheld the constitutionality of the law in May, 1995.[1]

For an overview of most of these Irish constitutional developments, see J.M. Kelly, The Irish Constitution 790–810 (3d ed., Gerard Hogan & Gerry White eds., 1994).

* * *

a. **Compared to what?**: With what should the foregoing material be compared? If we compare them to the U.S., Canadian and German materials in the prior chapter, does that imply (incorrectly?) that abortion and reproductive freedom are of similar importance, or function, or raise similar constitutional problems, in those societies?

i) *External Influences*: We might emphasize the influence of non-Irish institutions at several points, including Irish concern about borrowing *Griswold* and therefore *Roe* and the later role of the two European courts. The Irish Constitution was amended, following the *McGee* decision, because of fears that the Irish Supreme court would follow the path from *Griswold* to *Roe*. Subsequently, interpretation of the Eighth Amendment (Article 40) was influenced by decisions of two European international courts. And the Irish Constitution was again amended in response to both international judicial decisions and international treaties.

ii) *Influence of concrete facts and forms of review*: Or we might emphasize the apparent influence of the dramatic facts on the result in the X case. The dramatic predicament in which X was placed (because of her family's effort to assist in the prosecution of her assailant) was important in mobilizing Irish public opinion, in the decision the Supreme Court reached, and ultimately in securing passage of the referendum on the rights to travel and to information.

We might then raise questions about the impact of different forms of judicial review—abstract in Germany, concrete in the X case, and somewhere in between in most of the U.S. abortion cases—on outcomes. But in thinking about the possible effects of deciding "concrete cases" as compared with "abstract review," we might also include cases in which seemingly sympathetic facts did not persuade courts to recognize legal claims. Consider DeShaney v. Winnebago County Dept.

those judges as the Court shall direct, and no other opinion, whether assenting or dissenting, shall be pronounced nor shall the existence of any such other opinion be disclosed.

* * *

"3. (1) In every case in which the Supreme Court decides that any provision of a Bill the subject of a reference to the Supreme Court under this Article is repugnant to this constitution or to any provision thereof, the President shall decline to sign such Bill.

* * *

"(3) [Except where a reference to the people is required by article 27,] the President shall sign the Bill as soon as may be after the date on which the decision of the Supreme Court shall have been pronounced."

1. In re Article 26, 2 ILRM 81 (1995) (upholding constitutionality of the Regulation of Information (Services outside the State for Termination of Pregnancies) Bill, 1995), reprinted in Irish Times, May 13, 1995, at 8.

of Social Services, 489 U.S. 189 (1989): A Wyoming court awarded custody of Joshua DeShaney to his father Randy, who moved to Wisconsin. County social workers began receiving reports that Randy was abusing Joshua, and noted the reports (and some of Joshua's physical injuries), but did not attempt to remove him from Randy's custody. When Joshua was four years old, his father beat him so severely that he suffered permanent brain injuries. As a result Joshua became severely retarded and needed to reside in an institution. Joshua and his mother sued the state's social work department, alleging that their failure to act deprived Joshua of his liberty in violation of the Due Process Clause. The Supreme Court rejected their claim.

iii) *Role of popular initiatives*: Alternatively, we might consider the role of popular majorities and courts, respectively, in defining the contours of constitutional rights. One of the notable features of the provisions of the U.S. Constitution, the Canadian Charter, and the German Basic Law at issue in the abortion decisions of these countries is their generality (or, put in other words, their lack of specificity with respect to abortion). In Ireland, by contrast, a history which began (as did that of Canada) with the Offenses Against the Person Act of 1861 (prohibiting abortions), took a somewhat different turn following *McGee*. Consider what light the Irish experience casts on Professor Tribe's question whether abortion policy is properly for the legislative, or popular, arena. Note the complex interactions between popular initiatives, domestic judicial decisions, international decisions, economic incentives, and political interest groups in Ireland.

b. **Candidates for determining the units of comparison**: Deciding what part of one nation's constitutional law should be compared with some part of another nation's law, that is, requires choices. And each choice raises questions.

(i) *The problem of nominalism*: The simple fact that someone classifies two situations under a single heading, as we did in Chapter One, does not necessarily mean that the two situations are the same—even if they have the same name. You should always be alert to the possibility that what seems to you to be a single problem might actually be different problems when looked at within different legal systems. We have separated the discussion of the Irish experience with reproductive freedom from our treatment of abortion in part to drive this point home.

(ii) *The problem of "problems of governance"*: An attractive alternative might be to identify large- or medium-scale problems of governance that many constitutional regimes have to face—dealing with religious diversity, or creating a democratic nation after a revolution, for example—and compare the ways in which different systems address particular problems. Again, however, you should be alert to the possibility that the purportedly similar problems of governance may actually be different. The "problem" of dealing with religious diversity may be one thing in a nation with a long history of deep religious discord and another in a nation otherwise demographically similar, where conflicts have taken the form of ethnic rather than religious division.

(iii) *The problem of particularism*: Because nations differ along many dimensions, their use of constitutional forms, and the outcomes of specific constitutional disputes, may be determined as much by the particular arrays of facts—geography, demography, history, and the like—as by the nations' constitutions. Once again, this concern raises questions about the utility of the comparative enterprise.

c. **Frankenberg's critique of "functionalism"**: Frankenberg describes five "paradigms in comparative law." In addition to "Encyclopedic comparison," "Constructive Comparison" aimed at "updat[ing], unify[ing], and improv[ing] the international legal order through comparative legislation," and "Comparative Historical Reconstruction," he describes two other approaches of particular interest here. The first is "Juxtaposition-plus:"

> the juxtaposition, excerpts from cases, statutes, and doctrinal treatises, and the "pluses," a variety of interpretive and explanatory additions ranging from brief introductory remarks via descriptive sketches of historical backgrounds or systemic contexts to a more detailed analysis of similarities and contrasts. Depending on the author's choice and intentions, Juxtaposition-plus is meant to enhance a deeper knowledge of the domestic laws and their inherent foreign elements, or to open up foreign legal horizons, or to further insights into international law or conflicts of law. At first glance, Juxtaposition-plus appears to have the advantages of a fairly unobtrusive comparative method that clearly represents "the fact" and restrains evaluative comments, thus allowing the student to make up her mind independently about the old and the new law fashions.
>
> If we follow the paths of Juxtaposition-plus more closely, we can discern a pattern that is less objective and open than we may have originally thought. First, the comparatist selects the historical or national context ... which constitutes and limits the field and objects of comparison. This seems necessary and quite common-sensical, for nobody can compare everything in the world of laws. Generally and rather implicitly, however, the textbook authors assume that legal cultures are objects whose reality can be grasped adequately through texts and excerpts.... Which context is picked, not surprisingly, depends upon the author's field of study, area of competence and preconceptions about law and comparison. Surprisingly, however, comparatists rarely find it worth mentioning by which criteria they select their material ... Typically France and West Germany represent the civil law world, while the United States and England stand for the common law world....
>
> Which legal texts are selected to represent a system or culture again depends on the author's choice, approach, and (implicit) theory.... [Frankenberg distinguishes "three major variations" of Juxta-

position-plus: systematic identification of general characteristics and abstract concepts; a "factual focus of presentation," and a topical approach.] The selected materials are then juxtaposed accordingly. From a systematic perspective, the objects of comparison are classified on the basis of their likenesses and grouped in "families," "styles," or "traditions." On a lower level of abstraction the casuists juxtapose the various legal answers and concrete factual situations, thereby audaciously bridging time and space—especially once they leave the civil/common law world. The topical approach promises to overcome the random nature of the selected items by stressing the commonality of the problems in, say, Botswana, the People's Republic of China, Egypt, and California (representing the West). Thus, juxtaposition conveys the message that legal problems and solutions are universal and perennial. . . .

To set out from the law one is accustomed to and informed about seems plausible; indeed, simply ignoring it would be quite impossible. Yet, it is crucial how the domestic law and legal experience are introduced, and how the others are picked. Typically, comparison starts and ends on the legal home turf. Before the student is exposed to foreign systems, alternative visions and new ideas, her own "system" is posed as authoritative, influential, principal and natural, and so the measure of the other. . . .

. . . The comparatist travels strategically, always returning to the ever-present and idealized home system. Other societies or legal systems are "not yet" developed, but may be considered on their way. . . .

As a "method" of doctrinal jurisprudence, Juxtaposition-plus compares legal rules and statutes and theories of different systems in order to formulate or at least indicate the general principles and precepts, common cores or the constants of law. The implied adequacy of *law* to solve what appear to be the universal and perennial problems of life in society betrays and underscores not only how the comparatist's own country's approach is supposed and privileged, but more particularly . . . how [the United States, British, German, and French] notion of law is itself privileged. We can perhaps call this phenomenon the legocentrism of the discourse: the constant reaffirmation of a central notion of law in the avowed attempt to re-evaluate and re-imagine it. There is little outside the law a jurist has to think about when solving one of these problems. . . .

The final approach Frankenberg calls "Comparative Legal Functionalism":

Comparative Functionalists . . . analyze the living law in its two basic elements: in books and in action. Legal texts and institutions represent solutions for the problems of life in organized societies. The legal system in general and its institutions and norms answer to social needs or (organized) interests. Society constitutes the environment for law—law conceptualized as a sub-system of the social system. Broadly speaking, social life either determines the law or the law influences social development. . . .

In general, the functionalist's comparative activity begins with a question or a feeling, such as a feeling of dissatisfaction with, say, the way product liability is regulated in the domestic legal system. Comparison is then spurred on by the intuition that other legal systems may have produced something better. Functionality becomes the pivotal methodological principle determining the choice of laws to compare, the scope of the undertaking, the creation of a system of comparative law, and the evaluation of the findings. How to identify cross-cultural legal solutions that serve comparable functions is, of course, difficult.

In order to be able to compare, the functionalist has to assay either what "the law" is or what "the same function" could be. A minimal requirement of a strictly functionalist analysis would be an acknowledgment of this dilemma and then experimentation with a variety of possible cultural means involved in the resolution of particular social conflicts in different societies. Only then could hypothetical statements be made about "the law" or "legal system" and about "the same function." Comparative functionalists tend to disregard the basic problem of their theoretical strategy and typically offer two pseudosolutions. The first is an a priori notion of the "legal system" and the second is an assumption about the "essence" of what law is all about. . . . The sameness of the problems produces the relative sameness of results—whatever the legal means may look like. And if the same function cannot be identified, a similar function will do. Grand similarities and not differences in detail are what the functionalist is out for. Such synthetic vision is helped by the presumption that all practical results are similar. . . . ^m **[m]**

Furthermore, those areas of law have to be singled out which are "marked by strong political or moral views and values." Thus the functionalist reduces the law to a formal technique of conflict resolution, stripping it of its political and moral underpinnings, and tries to cope with the problem that social and economic conditions, apparently similar in relevant respects, have actually produced radically different legal solutions. The comparative functionalist may celebrate this analytical operation as a necessary reduction of complexity. Yet, it may be interpreted as a further vain attempt to escape the implications of the functionalist creed. Whether she believes that law is determined by social problems or social development is (co-)determined by law or whether law and society are interdependent entities, the functionalist

m. Frankenberg quotes the following text as an example of the presumption: " '[The] presumption acts as a means of checking our results: the comparatist can rest content if his researches through all the relevant material lead to the conclusion that the systems he has compared reach the same or similar practical results, but if he finds that there are great differences or indeed diametrically opposite results, he should be put on notice and go back to check again whether the terms in which he posed his original question were indeed purely functional, and whether he has spread the net of his researches quite wide enough.' "

has to account for the basic difficulty that apparently not all legal norms and doctrines are functionally related to social life because they run counter to any conceivable need or interest, or because they do not make a difference in social life.

. . . [T]he comparative legal functionalist entertains an evolutionary vision of legal development. Law progressively adapts to social needs or interests, or develops through interacting with its environment. The "modernizers" even grant law an activist role. It is understood to be a crucial instrument in bringing about social change. Both versions of evolutionism . . . are questionable. . . .

Typically, the evolutionist perspective focuses on the actions and decisions of certain specialized agencies, . . . negating or marginalizing the effects of legal forms and ideas in the realm of consciousness as ideologies and rituals. By stressing the production of "solutions" through legal regulations the functionalist dismisses as irrelevant or does not even recognize that law also produces and stocks interpretive patterns and visions of life which shape people's ways of organizing social experience, giving it meaning, qualifying it as normal and just or as deviant and unjust. That is why it is implausible to situate law vis-à-vis society and to separate the legal form from its social contents. The "interests" of social life that make demands upon the agencies and officials law are "not self-constituting pre-legal entities but owe important aspects of their identities, traits, organizational forms and sometimes their very existence to their legal constitution." The functionalist notion of law as a regulatory technique or as a bundle of techniques for the solution of social problems can also be criticized as legocentric. There is nothing outside legal texts and institutions for functionalists. Law as consciousness or cluster of beliefs is beyond a perspective that focuses on the instrumental efficiency of legal regulations. Functionalism has no eye and no sensitivity for what is not formalized and not regulated under a given legal regime. What started out as a fascinating hypothetical experiment has turned into a rather dry affirmation of legal formalism.

The functionalist assimilates herself to her object of study by positioning herself as a neutral analyst, who has to face neither hermeneutic difficulties nor the impact of perspective. . . . The functionalist assumes an objectivist stance, thus betraying the false modesty of her project. . . . Neutrality, or rather its guise, begins with terminology that translates the language of legal formalism into the language of universal problems. . . .

In order to be objective, the comparatist is basically asked to exercise sober self-restraint and is assured that the functionalist method guarantees both—objectivity and restraint. . . . The functionalist negates the interaction between legal institutions and provisions by stripping them from their systemic context and integrating them in an artificial universal typology of "solutions." In this way, "function" is reified as a principle of reality and not taken as an analytical principle that orders the real world. It becomes the magic carpet that shuttles us between the abstract and the concrete, that transcends the boundaries of national legal concepts, that builds the system of comparative law, the "universal" comparative legal science or "the general law." . . .

8.   CRITICAL COMPARISON?

Frankenberg offers an alternative for comparative legal studies, and provides an example of applying his approach to issues of abortion and reproduction.

Instead of continuing the endless search for a neutral stance and objective status, comparatists have to recognize that they are participant observers[;] therefore their studies have to be self-reflective and self-critical. Instead of presupposing the necessity, functionality, and universality of law, critical comparisons have to question "legocentrism." . . . Instead of "getting straight" the histories and diversities of laws, critical comparisons must call for a rigorous analysis of and tolerance for ambiguity. . . .

Perspective is not only a cognitive or emotional defect or disposition that can be manipulated or cured by a "right" ethic, attitude or reasoning. It is an integral aspect of every person's history of learning. Being socialized into a particular culture—or simply: growing up— means to become familiar with, to gain a particular perspective on and be biased toward that environment. Are we therefore victims to our culture? Can a Western head only think in Western terms? I do not think so. We can transcend perspective, we can learn about, understand and empathize with what we find "strange" or "foreign" or "exotic," provided that we always recognize that we are participants of one culture and observers of any other. To transcend perspective means to realize that we use our language, which is culture-based, to grasp what is new and seemingly other than us. While the self, our cognitive history and its baggage of assumptions and perspective, cannot be disposed of at will, we can still try to honestly and consciously account for it, exposing it to self-critical re-examination. . . .

Comparison has to be self-reflective. . . . Once the comparatist asks herself how she came to be what she is in terms of the law (an "individual" with "rights" and "duties," a "tenant," "taxpayer," "parent," "consumer," etc.) and how she comes to think as a "legal scholar" about her own law and the other laws the way she does, notions of normality and universality begin to blur. It becomes clearer then that any vision of the foreign laws is derived from and shaped by domestic assumptions and bias.

To cope with ethnocentrism, we have to analyze and unravel the cultural ties that bind us to the domestic legal regime. A practical . . . beginning could be a deviant reading of comparative legal literature focussing on the marginal stuff [in, e.g., prefaces] that is normally skipped for lack of relevance. . . .

... The deviant reading of marginal information would thus precede and prepare a critical reading of the "real" [material]....

... Once comparatists have made "hermeneutics" part of their vocabulary they will begin to feel uneasy about the distinction between comparison and evaluation, between understanding and interpreting, between facts and value judgments....

In order to be liberating, comparative legal studies would also have to overcome the legocentrism that characterizes the comparatists' as well as the non-comparatists' discourse. By legocentrism I mean that law is treated as a given and a necessity, as the natural path to ideal, rational, or optimal conflict resolutions and ultimately to a social order guaranteeing peace and harmony.... [T]he law is not immutable, but ... it is in constant flux.... [T]here are quite different paths to social conflicts, and more importantly, ... other societies seem to get by with little or no law of the type to which we are accustomed....

Legal realism and, to a lesser degree, sociological jurisprudence have undermined this legocentrist-formalist syndrome by connecting law with social purposes, political interest and problems of language/writing. They have challenged the idea of a politically neutral normative structure determined by legal reasoning and forming a coherent system. The realist message and, of course, its radicalization by critical legal scholars go to a large extent unnoticed in the discourses on comparative law. Mainstream comparatists, so it seems, try to escape from the critique of the legal order by comparing and affirming the relative determinacy, rationality and consistency of modern (civil and common) law....

... The formalized relationships ... of the law are only the frozen aspects of a social practice constituted by specific ways of thinking and acting alienated from immediate experience, by a specific normative imagery ("rule of law," "rights," "due process," etc.). Law teachers and students, legal practitioners as well as law-abiding, law-avoiding and law-breaking citizens are deeply involved in, sustain and develop this practice. Isn't it true that "legal gains" have been made? That "rights" when enforced have protected individuals and minorities? That freedom of speech is essential? A pervasive legal consciousness keeps us in a Kafkaesque and fascinating world of rights and duties, rules and standards, procedures and substances, crimes and punishments. It is not so much the law's institutional framework or symbolic representation, not so much courts ... or conscious use of the instruments of law. It is rather its hiddenness and pervasiveness as a social agenda ... that account for its mystique and magic spell.

What good can comparison do in this situation? ... A comparative perspective could be *one* of the methods for questioning and distancing oneself from the dominant legal consciousness.... Distance requires taking nothing for granted.... A liberating distance begins with investigating what the law does to us, to our world views, and to human relations. Intuitively we know or have a hunch that legal provisions and procedures—whatever their positive effects may be—also disempower by channelling conflicts to legal agencies, reify by turning personal relations into matters of law, and alienate by imposing an exclusive and excluding language and logic and by imposing a time-frame that abstracts from real persons and their life. A non-comparative approach might be more prone to discount these features and effects of law as necessary evils if not as rational mechanisms. I believe that the comparatist is in a privileged position by the very fact that she is confronted with different legal forms and categories, with alternative legal and non-legal strategies all of which may be more or less realistic, adequate, mystifying, reifying, alienating, and so forth....

Frankenberg concludes with an application of his suggested "non-legocentric" approach to the abortion issue, part of which follows:

A contrasting view from, say, the practice of coerced abortions in China after the first child for the sake of population control or the legal regulation of abortion in Western countries would allow for an experience of distance or difference. Such contrast brings to the fore the contours and peculiarities of the categories ("infanticide," "unborn life," "right") and of the sets of relationships ("individual"/"state," "private"/"public") of the domestic world as well as our own normative preferences and emotional reactions. It elucidates options and perspectives not allowed by the traditionally closed systems of comparison. Comparison can show that there are whole other issues, such as population control and other (not necessarily better) solutions. To turn in on the public and legal discourse on abortion in the United States, Canada, West Germany, and Italy from the vantage point of a "radically different" culture like China means to recognize alternatives, to recognize behind moral/legal debates the imposition of "modernization" on a traditional culture and the sustenance of patriarchy and state authority against women's movements and democratization here. Comparison can thus contribute to learning—beyond the conservative "infanticide"-discourse and the liberal "rights"-discourse on abortion and brings out that birth control is not an essentially legal issue [and] that [it] can be discussed more fully and adequately beyond the horizon of legal regulations and reasoning. This way critical comparisons call into question the formalist distinction of the "legal" and the "non-legal" and enhance alternative visions of how to resolve social conflicts and individual problems.

Questions and Comments

1. Frankenberg's "critical" approach clearly derives from post-modern thought, and shares some of that thought's difficulties. Assuming that his criticisms of existing comparative scholarship are accurate, do they establish that those studies are fundamentally misconceived, or only that they are badly executed?

2.   A much narrower question: Are there *any* "essentially legal" questions that comparative legal studies might deal with? What, if anything, is an "essentially legal" question associated with the abortion materials you have studied?

3.   Frankenberg argues that his critique is not intended to paralyze or forestall inquiry but to re-construct comparison. Consider his alternative treatment of abortion issues. Does it illustrate the possibilities and/or limitations (to be dichotomous for a moment) of critically reconstructed comparisons in law?

CHAPTER III

CONSTITUTIONS AND CONSTITUTIONALISM

A. GENERAL CONSIDERATIONS

What marks out "constitutional law" from other legal studies? The next set of readings offers a variety of perspectives relevant to this question. Consider the assumptions made by different writers on the importance of legal entrenchment, institutional structures, moral norms and political culture in defining constitutionalism.

Cass Sunstein, *Constitutionalism and Secession,* 58 U. Chi. L. Rev. 633 (1991)

[Sunstein's article is drawn from a longer one dealing with whether constitutions should acknowledge a right to secede. The excerpt we have given you asks the question, "Why have a constitution?" Sunstein summarizes some of the best recent answers to that question. Note particularly his discussion of the ways in which taking issues (of political structure and substantive rights) off the political agenda by constitutionalizing them may facilitate political decisionmaking.]

* * *

I. CONSTITUTIONS AS PRECOMMITMENT STRATEGIES

A. In General: Notes on Constitutionalism

It is often said that constitutionalism is in considerable tension with democracy. Thomas Jefferson was emphatic on the point, arguing that constitutions should be amended by each generation in order to ensure that the dead past would not the constrain the living present. Many contemporary observers echo the Jeffersonian position, claiming that constitutional constraints often amount to unjustified, antidemocratic limits on the power of the present and future. Responding to Jefferson, James Madison argued that a constitution subject to frequent amendment would promote factionalism and provide no firm basis for republican self-government.

Madison envisioned firm and lasting constitutional constraints as a precondition for democratic processes, rather than a check on them. This vision captures a central goal of American constitutionalism: to ensure the conditions for the peaceful, long-term operation of democracy in the face of often-persistent social differences and plurality along religious, ethnic, cultural, and other lines. This goal is highly relevant to constitutional developments in Eastern Europe, where religious and ethnic hostilities are especially intense. Madison saw differences and diversity as strengths rather than weaknesses, if channeled through constitutional structures that would promote deliberation and lead groups to check, rather than exploit, other groups. It may be possible for Eastern European countries to replicate this approach, although they face far more profound differences of language, ethnicity, history, and religion than those that confronted the Framers of our Constitution.

To approach the question of secession, it will be useful to provide a brief outline of some of the reasons for entrenching institutional arrangements and substantive rights.[13] On such questions, constitutional theory remains in a surprisingly primitive state.[14] I begin by examining what sorts of considerations might lead people forming a new government to place basic rights and arrangements beyond the reach of ordinary politics. The crucial idea here is that for various reasons, people in a newly formed nation might attempt to do so as part of a precommitment strategy.

Some rights are entrenched because of a belief that they are in some sense pre- or extra-political, that is, because individuals ought to be allowed to exercise them regardless of what majorities might think. Some of these rights are entrenched for reasons entirely independent of democracy. Here constitutionalism is indeed a self-conscious check on self-government, attempting to immunize a private sphere from public power. Plausible examples include the rights to private property,[15] freedom from self-incrimination, bodily integrity, protection against torture or cruel punishment, and privacy.

But many of the rights that are constitutionally entrenched actually derive from the principle of democracy itself. Their protection from majoritarian processes follows from and creates no tension with the goal of self-determination through politics. The precommitment strategy permits the people to protect democratic processes against their own potential excesses or misjudgments. The right to freedom of speech and the right to vote are familiar illustrations. Constitutional protection of these rights is not at odds with the commitment to self-government but instead a logical part of it.

Institutional arrangements can also be understood as an effort to protect a private sphere from majoritarianism. Often this effort stems from a fear of democratic processes. A decision to divide government among the

---

13. By using the word "entrenching" here and elsewhere, I refer to simple constitutionalization, not to a decision to immunize a constitutional provision from amendment. I assume throughout that constitutional provisions are much more difficult to change than ordinary statutes, but nonetheless amendable if there is a consensus that they should be.

14. For a valuable collection of essays on this topic, see Jon Elster and Rune Slagstad, eds, *Constitutionalism and Democracy* (Cambridge, 1988).

15. The right to property is an ambiguous case; it is a democratic right as well as a private one. Private property provides for security and independence from government, and these are preconditions for citizenship—a theme that played a large role in republican thought. See J.G.A. Pocock, ed., *The Political Works of James Harrington* 53-63, 67-68, 144-52 (Cambridge, 1977).

legislative, executive, and judicial branches might be regarded as an effort to check and limit government by requiring a consensus among all three before the state can interfere with the private sphere. Private liberty flourishes because government is partially disabled. So too, a federal system might ensure that the nation and its subunits will check each other, generating a friction that enables private liberty to flourish.

Structural provisions of this sort limit the political power of present majorities (or minorities), and in this sense raise difficulties for those who believe that the only or principal purpose of constitutionalism is to provide a framework for democratic governance. But if structural provisions are generally seen as precommitment strategies, some of them can be enabling as well as constraining. We can understand both individual rights and structural provisions in this way. Like the rules of grammar, such provisions set out the rules by which political discussion will occur, and in that sense free up the participants to conduct their discussions more easily.

The system of separation of powers, for example, does not merely constrain government, but also helps to energize it, and to make it more effective, by creating a healthy division of labor. This was a prominent argument during the framing period in America. A system in which the executive does not bear the burden of adjudication may well strengthen the executive by removing from it a task that frequently produces public opprobrium. Indeed, the entire framework might enable rather than constrain democracy, not only by creating an energetic executive but, more fundamentally, by allowing the sovereign people to pursue a strategy, against their government, of divide and conquer. So long as it is understood that no branch of government is actually "the people," a system of separation of powers can allow the citizenry to monitor and constrain their inevitably imperfect agents. In general, the entrenchment of established institutional arrangements enables rather than merely constrains present and future generations by creating a settled framework under which people may make decisions.

Thus far I have suggested that constitutions might create rights and institutions that follow from some independent theory of what individuals are owed, that are a natural corollary of the commitment to democracy, or that help to facilitate the democratic process by establishing the basic structures under which political arrangements can take place. Constitutional provisions may be facilitative in quite another sense: a decision to take certain issues off the ordinary political agenda may be indispensable to the political process.

For example, the initial decision to create a system of private property places severe constraints on the scope of any political deliberations on that fundamental issue, and often serves to keep issues of private property off the political agenda completely. Indeed, Madison understood the protection of rights of property largely as a mechanism for limiting factional conflict in government, not as a means of protecting "rights" and much less as a means of ensuring against redistribution.[23] The removal of the issue from politics serves, perhaps ironically, to ensure that politics may continue.

So too, a nation might protect questions of religion against resolution by democratic processes, not only because there is a right to freedom of religious conscience, but also because the democratic process works best if the fundamental and potentially explosive question of religion does not intrude into day-to-day decisions. More narrowly and no doubt more controversially, the decision to constitutionalize the right to abortion might be justified because it minimizes the chances that this intractable and polarizing question will intrude into and thus disable the political process.

Yet another set of facilitative constitutional precommitment strategies includes provisions that are designed to solve collective action problems or prisoners' dilemmas, that is, situations in which the pursuit of rational self-interest by each individual actor produces outcomes that are destructive to all actors considered together, and that could be avoided if all actors agreed in advance to coercion, assuring cooperation. People who are creating their government might voluntarily waive a right whose existence would rematerialize, and create serious risks, without the waiver. A decision to relinquish an otherwise available right advances the interests of all or most who are involved.

This idea has played a large role in the American constitutional experience. The leading example is the Full Faith and Credit Clause, which requires each state to enforce judgments rendered in other states. Every state might have an incentive to refuse to enforce the judgments of other states; if Massachusetts chooses not to honor the judgment of a New York court against a Massachusetts citizen, then Massachusetts receives a short-term gain because the resources its citizen needs to satisfy any judgment remain within the borders of Massachusetts. But all states would be better off if the law bound each of them to respect the judgments of others. The Full Faith and Credit Clause ensures precisely this outcome, effectively solving a conventional prisoners' dilemma.

Another illustration is the Commerce Clause. The Supreme Court has consistently interpreted the clause as disabling the states from regulating interstate commerce. In the period between the Articles of Confederation and the Constitution, battles among the states produced mutually destructive tariffs and other protectionist measures. The adoption of each of these measures may well have furthered the interest of each state considered in isolation. Collectively, this system proved disastrous.

Especially in light of the strong emotional attachments that fuel perceptions of state self-interest, a system in which each state can choose whether to initiate protectionist measures might well lead many states to

---

23. See Meyers, ed. *The Mind of the Founder* 502-09. In fact, the failure of the Framers to eliminate slavery in the original Constitution was attributable to ideas of this sort. The example reveals that the decision to take an issue off the political agenda is also a decision to resolve that issue one way rather than another. Such a decision may well be objectionable on democratic or other grounds.

do so. But an agreement by all states to refrain from protectionism, and thus to waive their antecedent right under the Articles of Confederation, should further the collective interest. The constitutional decision to remove control of interstate commerce from state authority solves the problem. In this case, as with the Full Faith and Credit Clause, a relinquishment of what appears to be state sovereignty very likely furthers the interest of all states concerned. . . .

Finally, constitutional precommitment strategies might serve to overcome myopia or weakness of will on the part of the collectivity, or to ensure that representatives follow the considered judgments of the people. Protection of freedom of speech, or from unreasonable searches and seizures, might represent an effort by the people themselves to provide safeguards against the impulsive behavior of majorities. Here the goal is to ensure that the deliberative sense of the community will prevail over momentary passions. Similarly, a constitution might represent a firm acknowledgement that the desires of the government, even in a well-functioning republic, do not always match those of the people. Constitutional limits, introduced by something like the people themselves, therefore respond to the agency problem created by a system in which government officials inevitably have interests of their own. This problem arises in all systems of government, including democracies. In countries emerging from communist rule, without established principles of democratic representation, it is likely to pose a special danger, against which constitutional provisions should guard.

In all of these cases, the decision to take certain questions off the political agenda might be understood as a means not of disabling but of protecting politics, by reducing the power of highly controversial questions to create factionalism, instability, impulsiveness, chaos, stalemate, collective action problems, myopia, strategic behavior, or hostilities so serious and fundamental as to endanger the governmental process itself. In this respect, the decision to use constitutionalism to remove certain issues from politics is often profoundly democratic.

We can also see many constitutional provisions as mechanisms for ensuring discussion and deliberation oriented toward agreement about the general good rather than factionalism and self-interested bargaining. The states' relinquishment of their preexisting sovereign right to control the entry and exit of goods is the most prominent example. But the institutions of representation and checks and balances have frequently been designed to promote general discussion and compromise, to diminish the influence of particular segments of society, and to produce the incentives for and possibility of agreement. These principles largely guided the development of the United States Constitution. They bear directly on the attempts of Eastern European countries to meld constitutionalism with democracy in the midst of extraordinary diversity and pluralism. . . .

Questions and Comments on Sunstein

1. Do Sunstein's examples of slavery and abortion support his general argument about the way in which constitutionalizing issues facilitates democratic decision-making by taking some issues off the table?

2. Consider also his argument that precommitting on the rules for political discussion and decisionmaking will "free up the participants to conduct their discussions more easily." Are there circumstances when this might threaten rather than facilitate democracy? Is it always desirable to entrench "established institutional arrangements" to create a "settled framework under which people" make decisions? Might it be desirable to have some method of unsettling established arrangements? For a discussion of whether constitutions should be easy or hard to amend, see Chapter IV (B) below.

3. Are constitutional commitments necessary to avoid the prisoners' dilemma problems he describes? Over the long run, what would happen if states refused to enforce judgments rendered in other states? If states adopted ruinous trade barriers?

4. How does protection of free expression protect the people against their own "impulsive" behavior? From whose perspective should we decide whether some behavior is impulsive: that of the constitution's framers? that of the people? in the long run or in the short run? On what basis can we choose among those perspectives?

Walter F. Murphy, *Constitutions, Constitutionalism, and Democracy*, in Constitutionalism and Democracy: Transitions in the Contemporary World (Douglas Greenberg, Stanley N. Katz, Melanie Beth Oliviero, and Steven C. Wheatley eds. 1993)

[Murphy provides a useful introduction to the relation between constitutionalism and democracy. Democracy's central values lie in participation in self-government, and depend most crucially on popular election of representatives who serve in institutions that actually govern; universal adult suffrage; limited terms; approximately equal-sized voting districts; liberal access for citizens to become candidates; and freedom of political speech and association. Democratic theory, according to Murphy, says that "what makes governmental decisions morally binding is process;" thus, "[d]emocratic theory tends to embrace both positivism and moral relativism."

Constitutionalism, in Murphy's terms, tends to be more pessimistic about human nature than democratic theory is. Constitutionalism tends to seek out "institutional restraints on substantive matters to prevent lapses into authoritarian or even totalitarian system cloaked with populist trappings." And while Murphy associates democratic theory with moral relativism, constitutionalism, he claims "turns to moral realism," and posits that "discoverable standards" exist to determine whether particular policies infringe on humane dignity. Legitimacy depends not simply on popular participation but on "substantive criteria."

In describing "Constitutional Democracy," Murphy argues that the two theories are in tension with and need each other. Constitutionalism can prevent a majority from effectively depriving minorities of participation rights, while democracy can prevent the paralysis that may be associated with rigid constitutionalism. He argues that both constitutionalism and democracy rest on respect for human worth and dignity, but, he points out, documents labelled "The Constitution" need not.

Murphy presents his own enumeration of the functions of a constitution. Note particularly his suggestion that constitutions may serve as "covenants, symbols and aspirations." What, if any, provisions of the U.S. constitution are best described with those terms?[a] Murphy points out that, in some constitutional systems, constitutional provisions themselves may be unconstitutional, and some constitutional provisions may be unamendable. Do you understand why?]

* * *

The Concept of a "Constitution"

Constitutionalism and democratic theory raise questions about the concept of a constitution and the relationship of any particular constitution to those theories as well as to constitutional democracy. One has to ask *what* the constitution is: What is its authority? Its functions? What does it include? How does it validly change over time?

What Is a Constitution?

What Is the Constitution's Authority?

To constitute means to make up, order, or form; thus a nation's constitution should pattern a political system. Some texts implicitly proclaim themselves to be supreme law, and many do so explicitly. Still, a document's bearing the label "a constitution" and declaring its own control over all other political acts proves nothing. We need to distinguish between the authority a text asserts and the authority it exerts.

Constitutional texts fall along a spectrum of authority. At one extreme are shams, such as those of Stalin and Mao. At the other extreme should be those whose provisions are fully operative; but no constitutional text operates with complete authority. Its description of processes may be misleading. For example, the British North America Act of 1867, which served for more than a century as Canada's principal constitutional document, asserted that the British Queen, not a Canadian Cabinet and Prime Minister responsible to a Canadian Parliament, in turn responsible to a Canadian electorate, governed. Seemingly conscientious officials may ignore or skew express commands and prohibitions: U.S. Presidents and legisla-

---

a. Consider at least the Preamble: "We the people of the United States, in order to   form a more Perfect Union...."

tors have never taken seriously their document's requirement that "a regular Statement and Account of the Receipts and Expenditures of all public Money shall be published from time to time." So, too, for almost a hundred years, legislators, presidents, judges, and the mass of voters pretended that states were fulfilling their obligation under the Fourteenth Amendment to accord "equal protection of the laws" to blacks and women.

The prevalence—perhaps inevitability—of deviations from the text indicates the complex nature of a constitution's authority. Thus, when we speak of "authoritative constitutions," we are talking about those that are only "reasonably authoritative."

What Are the Functions of a Constitution?

A Constitution as Sham, Cosmetic, or Reality. The principal function of a sham constitutional text is to deceive. Lest U.S. citizens revel in righteousness, they might recall that Charles A. Beard charged the framers of the U.S. text with hypocrisy, and the Conference of Critical Legal Studies still so accuses the entire American legal system. Whether Beard and the Critics have told the full story, they have reminded us that a constitutional document's representation of itself, its people, their values, and decisional processes is imperfect. Thus, even reasonably authoritative texts play a cosmetic role, allowing a nation to hide its failures behind idealistic rhetoric. But, insofar as a text is authoritative, its rhetoric also pushes a people to renew their better selves.

A Constitution as a Charter for Government. At minimum, an authoritative constitutional text must sketch the fundamental modes of legitimate governmental operations: who its officials are, how they are chosen, what their terms of office are, how authority is divided among them, what processes they must follow, and what rights, if any, are reserved to citizens. Such a text need not proclaim any substantive values, beyond obedience to itself; if it does proclaim values, they might be those of Naziism or Stalinism, anathema to constitutional democracy.

A Constitution as Guardian of Fundamental Rights. Thus the question immediately arises about the extent to which a constitutional text relies on or incorporates democratic and/or constitutionalist theories. Insofar as a text is authoritative and embodies democratic theory, it must protect rights to political participation. Insofar as it is authoritative and embodies constitutionalism, it must protect substantive rights by limiting the power of the people's freely chosen representatives.

The Constitution as Covenant, Symbol, and Aspiration. Insofar as a constitution is a covenant by which a group of people agree to (re)transform themselves into a nation, it may function for the founding generation like a marriage consummated through the pledging partners' positive, active consent to remain a nation for better or worse, through prosperity and poverty, in peace and war.

For later generations, a constitution may operate more as an arranged marriage in which consent is passive, for the degree of choice is then typically limited. Even where expatriation is a recognized right, exit from a society offers few citizens a viable alternative. Revolution becomes a legal right only if it succeeds and transforms revolutionaries into founders. And deeply reaching reform from within a constitutional framework tends to become progressively more difficult, for a system usually endures only by binding many groups to its terms.

The myth of a people's forming themselves into a nation presents a problem not unlike that between chicken and egg. To agree in their collective name to a political covenant, individuals must have already had some meaningful corporate identity *as a people*. Thus the notion of constitution as covenant must mean it formalizes or solidifies rather than invents an entity: it solemnizes a previous alliance into a more perfect union.

A constitution's formative force varies from country to country and time to time. The French, one can plausibly argue, have been the French under monarchies, military dictatorships, and assorted republics. It is also plausible, however, to contend that Germans have been a different people under the Kaiser, the Weimar Republic, the Third Reich, and the Federal Republic. In polyglotted societies such as Canada, India, and the United States or those riven by religious divisions and bleeding memories of civil war such as Ireland, "there may be no other basis for uniting a nation of so many disparate groups." A constitution may thus function as a uniting force, "the only principle of order," for there may be "no [other] shared moral or social vision that might bind together a nation." It is difficult to imagine what has united the supposedly United States more than the political ideas of the Declaration of Independence and the text of 1787.

Reverence for the constitution may transform it into a holy symbol of the people themselves. The creature they created can become their own mythical creator. This symbolism might turn a constitutional text into a semisacred covenant, serving "the unifying function of a civil religion." In America, "The Bible of verbal inspiration begat the constitution of unquestioned authority."

Religious allusions remind us, however, that this symbolic role may also have a dark side. Long histories of bitter and often murderous struggles among Christians and among Muslims demonstrate that a sacred text may foster division rather than cohesion, conflict rather than harmony. The "potential of a written constitution to serve as the source of fragmentation and disintegration" is nowhere more savagely illustrated than in the carnage of the U.S. Civil War. For, ultimately, that fratricidal struggle was over two visions of one constitutional document. The result was a gory war that wiped out more than 600,000 lives. Complicating analysis is the fact that when the blood of battle dried, the document of 1787, duly amended, resumed its unifying role.

In a related fashion, a constitution may serve as a binding statement of a people's aspirations for themselves as a nation. A text may silhouette the sort of community its authors/subjects are or would like to become: not only their governmental structures, procedures, and basic rights, but also their goals, ideals, and the moral standards by which they want others, including their own posterity, to judge the community. In short, a constitutional text may guide as well as express a people's hopes for themselves as a society. The ideals the words enshrine, the processes they describe, and the actions they legitimize must either help to change the citizenry or at least reflect their current values. If a constitutional text is not "congruent with" ideals that form or will reform its people and so express the political character they have or are willing to try to put on, it will quickly fade.

What Does "the Constitution" Include?

Almost every nation now has a document labeled a constitution; but to have a constitution a nation need not have a text or texts so titled. Britain, Israel, and New Zealand provide plausible examples. Nor does the existence of a constitutional document mean that any particular nation's constitution is coextensive with that text. What a constitution includes is a problem, not a datum. But where and how do we find the constitution beyond the text? Do subtexts control or mediate the text? How do we identify them? What about interpretations and practices? And what about political theories that inform and underpin the text?

The Text. The most obvious candidate is the whole text and nothing but the text. The late Justice Hugo Black and former Attorney General Edwin Meese III were among the more notable Americans to take that position. Such people stress the "writtenness" of the U.S. Constitution, though writtenness, literary, and biblical scholars would warn, sires as well as solves problems. Moreover, Black and Meese qualified their textualism with a commitment to "original intent" or "understanding"—additions to the text.

Less Than the Text. Anything less than the full text might seem a strange candidate, but every constitutional document drawn up in a free society is likely to reflect a bundle of compromises, necessary to obtain approval from the drafters and ratifiers but perhaps not always mutually compatible. As one solution, the German Constitutional Court has proposed reconciliation through structural interpretation:

> An individual constitutional provision cannot be considered as an isolated clause and interpreted alone. A constitution has an inner unity, and the meaning of any one part is linked to that of other provisions. Taken as a unit, a constitution reflects certain overarching principles and fundamental decisions to which individual provisions are subordinate.

The final sentence also looks to invalidation, and the Court made it clear that option was also open:

> That a constitutional provision itself may be null and void is not conceptually impossible just because it is part of the constitution. There are constitutional principles that are so fundamental and to such an extent an expression of a law that precedes even the constitution that they also bind the framer of the constitution, and other

constitutional provisions that do not rank so high may be null and void, because they contravene those principles.

On another occasion, the Constitutional Court divided 4-4 on the validity of an amendment; the Supreme Court in India has several times voided constitutional amendments; and the California Supreme Court has once done so. Moreover, many U.S. presidents, legislators, judges, and commentators have tried to exclude portions of their constitutional text from the canon. The Slaughter-House Cases in 1873, for instance, all but expunged the Fourteenth Amendment's clause forbidding states to abridge "the privileges or immunities" of citizens of the United States. And despite frequent avowals of textualism, Justice Black could not accept the Ninth Amendment's declaration: "The enumeration in the Constitution of certain rights, shall not be construed to deny or disparage others retained by the people." Furthermore, many commentators who assert that the text's principal function is to serve as a charter for government dismiss as empty rhetoric the Preamble's statement of purposes, especially its dedication to the establishment of "Justice."

Intent of the Framers. One might claim that a text can be understood only in light of certain "understandings" and "intentions" founders took for granted. To the extent that such unspoken thoughts control the text, they become a supertext. A quest for original understanding or intent raises enormous methodological, theoretical, and practical problems. After a few years have gone by, interpreters can pursue originalism only through documents, which are fraught with all the hermeneutic problems of the text itself.

Other Documents. Still other texts might have strong claims to canonicity. The Canadian Constitution Act, 1982, for example, explicitly bestows constitutional status on a number of documents. Probably most other nations have candidates with respectable pedigrees. In the United States, the two most robust would be the second paragraph of the Declaration of Independence and *The Federalist*. The Declaration justified the creation of a new nation and set out its founding principles:

> We hold these truths to be self-evident, that all men are created equal; that they are endowed by their Creator with certain unalienable rights, that among these are Life, Liberty and the Pursuit of Happiness. That to secure these rights, Governments are instituted among men, deriving their just powers from the consent of the governed. That whenever any form of Government becomes destructive of these ends, it is the Rights of the People to alter or abolish it....

As the definitive statement of the new nation's basic values, so the argument goes, the Declaration stands until explicitly repudiated, something neither the Philadelphia Convention nor the state ratifying conventions even suggested.

The case for *The Federalist*, essays by John Jay, James Madison, and Alexander Hamilton urging ratification of the newly drafted constitutional text, would be that those who ratified that document accepted these views as authoritative and, therefore, they form part of the original understanding.

Practices and Interpretations. Some practices might become so settled as to fuse into the constitution. One would expect common-law systems, with their sensitivity to prescription, the doctrine that long and unchallenged usage confers legal title, would be hospitable to such a concept. Canadian judges, however, have been ambivalent; and judges in the United States, though open to such ideas, have also recognized severe problems.

Most fundamentally, governmental practice often violates the basic text or its underlying principles. Does a long violation effect a constitutional change? If "the constitution" is devoid of normative content beyond obedience to specified procedures, the answer might well be yes. If, however, "the constitution" entails normative political theory, the issue becomes far more complex. Sotirios A. Barber proposes a distinction between practice, a country's history, and tradition, what the constitution's underlying theory says its people stand for. The minimum standard he would use to test a practice's legitimacy is congruence with both the document and tradition.

Interpretations trigger similar disputes. Although not every interpretation has a serious claim to be part of the canon, some interpretations meld into the larger constitution. The U.S. Supreme Court's divination of judicial review provides the most striking example. As one of Court's opponents asked at the time, "Is it not extraordinary that if the high power was intended, it should nowhere appear [in the text]?"

Political Theories. The case for inclusion of any theory in a particular constitution is empirical, and the mix between political theories may be complex. In the 1990s, democratic and constitutionalist theory are the prime candidates; but, in the recent past, versions of Fascism and Marxism have been successful contenders, and perhaps will be again in the future.

How Does a Constitution Validly Change over Time?

The spoken word evanesces as soon as it is uttered; the written word seems permanent. Centuries later, audiences can parse its sentences and explore its implications—thus the immense attractions of a "written constitution." Alas, even when embossed on parchment, words can suggest a variety of meanings; and readers necessarily impose their own frameworks of understanding on a text. "When the Almighty himself condescends to address mankind in their own language," Madison noted, "his meaning, luminous as it must be, is rendered dim and doubtful by the cloudy medium through which it is communicated."

Moreover, language evolves. New meanings sometimes replace old; sometimes the two (or three or four) live side by side. Rules of grammar, punctuation, and syntax may also mutate. And these changes may occur at different times or proceed at different paces across a polity.

Most important, the world and people's perceptions of the world change. Framers of the German or Japanese constitutional text could not have foreseen the economic miracles that would quickly restore those devastated nations. Thus, Japan's commitment never to maintain "land, sea, and air forces, as well as other war potential" has pulsed in response to domestic demands, international crises, and pressure from the United States. Even more dramatically, the pledge of reunification in West Germany's Basic Law had by 1976 turned to de facto acceptance of two Germanys; then, in 1989-1990, reunification suddenly changed from distant dream to joyous reality.

The constitutional text of every major nation explicitly provides for its own amendment. But even a superficial glance reveals other means to change a constitution, usage and interpretation being among the most common. Furthermore, it is often difficult to tell, except in a mechanical sense, when political actors move from one of these processes to another. Officials who begin a usage may have justified their action by interpreting the text, just as those who follow an older interpretation may unthinkingly accept it as a usage. And there can be little doubt that some legislative, executive, and judicial interpretations have affected the constitutional order far more radically than many formal amendments.

It is no wonder, then, that democratic theorists express concern about "constitutional interpretation," for it is potentially both creative and enormous in effect. I am tempted to add "especially when dealing with the broad terms of most constitutional texts"; but India's experience with a finely detailed document suggests it is the capacious nature of constitutional problems rather than the generality of language that implodes creativity into interpretive processes.

Accepting constitutional change as inevitable still leaves open questions of whether some paths can lead to legitimate change and whether there are limits to valid mutation. One might argue for a hierarchy of efforts at legitimate constitutional modification, from usage to interpretation to formal amendment: the more fundamental the change, the more weighty the reasons for resorting to formal processes and the more weighty the reasons for directly involving the people themselves, as do Australia, Ireland, and sometimes Italy.

The second question poses greater intellectual difficulty: Are there substantive limits to valid constitutional change? Under two circumstances, the case for such limits is very forceful. First, if the text is authoritative and specifies limits, they should be observed or changed only in accordance with the document's terms. And some texts do contain "unamendable" provisions. For example, Article V of the U.S. document forbids denying any state, without its consent, equal representation in the Senate. Article 79(3) of West Germany's Basic Law forbids amendments that would destroy the federal, democratic, or social nature of the nation, release legislation from the constitution's restraints or the executive or judiciary from those of "law and justice," lessen human dignity, or remove the right of the people to resist subversion of their constitutional order.

The second circumstance under which the case for restrictions on constitutional change is strong occurs when a constitutional text represents an agreement among a people, functions as a limitation on as well as a charter for government, states a people's goals and aspirations, and embodies normative political theory(ies). Then the very nature of the document itself may outlaw some kinds of amendment—for instance, those curtailing rights to political participation. As we have seen, some German, Indian, and even U.S. judges have directly addressed this issue: Certain principles bind those who would amend as well as those who would create constitutions in a democratic-constitutionalist mold. Provisions that violate those principles, even if lodged in the basic text itself, are void.

As applied to constitutional amendments, the gist of the argument is that "to amend" comes from the Latin "emendere," to correct. Thus an "amendment" corrects or modifies the system without fundamentally changing its nature: An "amendment" operates within the theoretical parameters of the existing constitution. A proposal to transform a central aspect of the compact to create another kind of system—for example, to change a constitutional democracy into an authoritarian state, as the Indian Court said Mrs. Gandhi tried to do—would not be an amendment at all, but a re-creation of both the covenant and its people. That deed would lie outside the authority of any set of governmental bodies, for all are creatures of the people's agreement. Insofar as officials destroy that compact, they destroy their own legitimacy.

This argument does not deny the legitimacy of radical constitutional reformation, but it does deny that such changes could find justification in the old text or in the compact that text reflects. Using extraconstitutional means, the people might reconstitute themselves; but it would be the people's exercising their constituent power, not the old constitution's benediction, that validates the new order.

Who Is/Are the Constitution's Authoritative Interpreter(s)?

The answer to *who* has interpretive authority is seldom easy. Let us take the simplest case: a constitution that is a grant from some higher authority functions merely as a charter for government, does not incorporate normative political theory, and includes only the text itself. The document's designation of interpretive agency(ies) and the processes it outlines settles the issue. If the text does not directly or clearly address the issue, one can request the grantor to decide the matter.

A more complex case occurs where the constitution claims to be a compact among a people. Then the polity must seek a solution through interpretation, raising serpentine problems of *how* to interpret. And that reliance poses yet other difficulties: If interpretation controls the text, will that interpretation become part of the constitution?

The most complex situation occurs where a constitution is an agreement among a people, functions as a charter for and a limitation on government, expresses its people's aspirations, includes certain usages and traditions, incorporates both democratic and constitutionalist theory, and does not directly or clearly address the issue of *who*. Resort to previous interpretations, traditions, or usages might well beg questions of *whose* interpretations, *whose* usages, and *whose* assessment of traditions.

Several solutions present themselves. The first is interpretation by the people themselves: As creators of the compact, they have authority to define its parameters. Elections may allow them to do so indirectly. Jefferson advocated a more direct role: "the people of the Union, assembled by their deputies in convention, at the call of Congress, or of two-thirds of the states." But "recurrence to the people" raises serious theoretical and practical difficulties, and Jefferson would have deployed a national convention only when government was deadlocked over competing interpretations. For day-to-day management, he preferred "departmentalism," under which coordinate institutions share interpretive responsibility.

Democratic theorists would lodge such authority with elected officials, while constitutionalists would place it in the hands of officials more insulated from public opinion. Many texts seem to point to a constitutionalist victory. Early on, judges in the United States interpreted their document—and made that interpretation stick—as allowing them to invalidate legislative or executive action they believed contrary to its provisions. Constitution makers around the world have adopted similar institutional arrangements. Canada, India, Ireland, and Japan have vested regular courts with interpretive power, while Civil-Law nations have tended to follow the model Hans Kelsen designed for Austria after World War I: a special tribunal exercising exclusive jurisdiction within the judiciary over constitutional interpretation.

Germany represents constitutionalism's greatest triumph in this respect. The Basic Law specifically establishes judicial review, vests it exclusively in the constitutional Court, and protects the Court's jurisdiction against diminution even in emergencies. Furthermore, in enacting the Court's primary jurisdictional statute, the Federal Constitutional Court Act of 1951, Parliament ceded the justices interpretive hegemony:

> The decisions of the Federal Constitutional Court shall be binding upon the constitutional bodies of the Federation and of the *Länder* as well as upon all law courts and public authorities.

And, in its first decision, the Court indicated it would broadly construe this broad acknowledgment of authority:

> [This] decision together with the main reasons for the decisions binds all constitutional organs of the Federation ... in such a way that no federal law with the same content can again be deliberated and enacted by the legislative bodies and promulgated by the federal president.

Britain represents almost total victory for democratic theory. Parliament is supposedly the authoritative creator, emendator, and interpreter of the constitution, restrained only by the ballot box and its collective conscience. Other officers, at least where the European Economic Community or the European Convention on Human Rights are not involved, have only what interpretive power Parliament chooses to delegate.

Most constitutional democracies, however, distribute interpretive power somewhat differently. Forms of departmentalism abound. And one could make a strong case that in reality, judges are neither omnipotent in Germany [63] nor impotent in Britain. Interpreting a constitution is something executives and legislators must often do. In deciding how to draft or vote on a bill or to make an inquiry—or protest—on behalf of a constituent, legislators commonly engage in informal constitutional interpretation. Even police, in deciding if they can arrest a suspect, what they can ask, and how long the suspect can be held, are engaging in this enterprise. That some officials do so mindlessly does not alter the fact that they are doing it.

Moreover, interpretation and usage may provide for a sharing of interpretive power. Even in the United States, the Supreme Court has been reluctant to claim the role of "ultimate constitutional interpreter" as far as other branches of the federal government are concerned. It has also created the "doctrine of political questions" to mark certain areas of interpretation (such as the federal government's obligation to guarantee each state "a republican form of government") that fall outside its competence, a doctrine that has cast shadows across German and Japanese jurisprudence. And judges of constitutional courts often repeat that they will usually presume legislation valid.

In addition, presidents and congresses have frequently and effectively asserted equal interpretive authority. The power to veto legislation gives the president a pulpit from which to expound his own constitutional doctrines. As President Andrew Jackson said in 1832:

> Each public officer who takes an oath to support the Constitution swears that he will support it as he understands it, and not as it is understood by others.... The opinion of the judges has no more authority over Congress than the opinion of Congress has over the judges, and on that point the President is independent of both.

Congress and the president also have an arsenal of weapons to persuade the justices to change their minds. The president may refuse to enforce judicial decrees and/or Congress may decline to appropriate money for such a purpose. Congress may also repass a controversial statute to appear to meet some of the justices' constitutional objections, alter the Supreme Court's appellate jurisdiction, or increase the number of justices and so permit appointment of people with differing views. Even without such tampering, a vacancy occurs on the Supreme Court about once every two to two and a half years, allowing presidents opportunities to shape that tribunal's constitutional interpretation.

63. Under Art. 93 of the Basic Law, each house of Parliament selects half the justices of the Constitutional Court. But beyond stipulating that the justices may not, when chosen, be members of parliament or cabinet, *Land* or Federal, the Basic Law does not set qualifications for membership, the number of justices, or the length of their terms. All these, like details of the Court's jurisdiction, are left to legislative discretion. And if Parliament disapproves of the Court's interpretations, it can try, when it chooses new judges, to select people who will undo the earlier work....

Nor are officials in other countries helpless when confronting judges. For instance, until Canada's adoption of a new constitutional text in 1982, judicial review rested only on a statute. Even now all federal courts are creatures of statutes;* and what Parliament may create, Parliament may destroy. Further, while judges seldom die, they must retire at 75, thus creating vacancies ruling parties can fill with "right thinking" jurists.

Some nations have made the sharing of interpretive authority explicit. Article 34 of the Irish text vests the Supreme Court with judicial review, but Article 28(3) excludes from this authority questions of the validity of any law "which is expressed to be for the purpose of securing the public safety and the preservation of the State in time of war or armed rebellion" as well as all acts done "in pursuance of such law." Furthermore, Article 45 announces principles of social policy to guide parliament but adds that these "shall not be cognizable by any Court under any of the provisions of this Constitution."

One of the compromises necessary to secure passage of Canada's Constitution Act, 1982, makes an elegant compromise between democratic and constitutionalist theory. This text entrenched a bill of rights and explicitly lodged enforcement, under ordinary circumstances, with the judiciary. But Article 33 allows the federal or a provincial parliament, for whatever reasons, to announce that a statute "shall operate notwithstanding a provision" protecting certain fundamental freedoms and more specific rights.[67] ...

Questions and Comments on Murphy

1. What does it mean to say that some constitutional provisions are unamendable? Should such provisions be confined to fundamental constitu-

----

* [Editors' Note: But cf. Constitution Act of 1982 Sections 41(d), 42 (1)(d) (providing that constitutional amendments relating to the Supreme Court of Canada must follow specified procedures); Peter W. Hogg, Constitutional Law of Canada 72, 79-80 (suggesting that because the Supreme Court is not provided for in the Constitution, Parliament still has control over Court through ordinary legislation, but noting that references to Supreme Court in amending provisions are "puzzling")].

67. There are at least two important checks on legislative power: The first is that an exemption, though renewable, can run for a maximum of 5 years. The second is that the legislature must "expressly declare" it means to violate a constitutionally protected right—a declaration that could, at the national level, destroy a Prime Minister and his party at the next election unless they can persuade the electorate that a serious case existed to negate a constitutionally guaranteed right. At the provincial level, however, those risks may be much smaller. Quebec has not only used Article 33 to "reverse" a decision regarding rights of Anglophones to display signs in English—*Allan Singer Ltd. v. Attorney General for Quebec*, [1988] S.C.R. 790—but has also tried to protect most of its code by retroactively cloaking its regulations under Article 33. Whatever difficulties the ruling party in Quebec has experienced, popular outrage at the government's restricting the rights of Anglophones or thumbing its nose at Ottawa has not been among them.

tional guarantees? Is it consistent with fundamental ideas about constitutionalism to insist that the allocation of two Senators to each state be unamendable (without the consent of the state being deprived of representation)?

2. Would an amendment to the U.S. Constitution giving legislatures authority to ban flag-burning as a means of political protest be unconstitutional (or anti-constitutional)? See Jeff Rosen, *Was the Flag Burning Amendment Unconstitutional?*, 100 Yale L.J. 1073 (1991) (arguing yes). Would an amendment eliminating the Establishment Clause be unconstitutional (or anti-constitutional)? See Bruce Ackerman, We the People 14 (1991) (arguing no).

Edward McWhinney, Constitution-Making: Principles, Process, Practice (1981)

[McWhinney's book raises the question whether Murphy's perspective on constitutionalism is ethnocentric: He asks whether the "very notion of a constitutional system is inherently ethnocentric." At the same time, McWhinney endorses the view that some "open society" values of Anglo–Saxon constitutionalism are transcendent and immutable. He also reminds us that there is a gap between the law on the books and the law in action. How far can the law in action depart from the law on the books before we should conclude that the constitution "really" is meaningless? Using one of McWhinney's examples, did the United States have a sham Constitution between the end of Reconstruction and the mid–1940s? McWhinney poses a set of questions about the relationship between economic conditions, elite preferences and experience, institutional structure, and successful constitutionalism that later readings address in more detail.]

* * *

The Ethnocentricity of Constitutionalism: Its Particular Space-Time Dimension

The 1958 constitution of the Fifth French Republic and the Bonn Constitution of 1949 represent, together with the British constitutional system and the American constitution, the principal alternative models or stereotypes for democratic constitution-making at the present time. Is it altogether by accident that they have so emerged as the textbook examples for study and application in communities other than their own, often differing very widely in terms of basic social and economic conditions and political history and experience? One first question that suggests itself is whether the very notion of a constitutional system is inherently ethnocentric and western in character. If a constitution is thought of as no more than a recording of the basic institutions of decision-making in the contemporary state, and an identification of the alternative instruments for achievement and application (concretization) of those decisions, then the term is no doubt value-neutral and can be applied to any particular ideological system with equal impartiality. If, however, we think of a constitutional system as meaning something more than the mere formal source of decision-making competence in the state but as implying, in addition, certain notions about the manner and quality of the decision-making act and its exercise, and perhaps, beyond that, even the substantive content of the actual decisions, then we are rooting our conceptions of constitutional law in ideas of the nature and quality of government itself; and our very definition of law does begin to take on a quality of historical particularism or ethnic-cultural relativism. The original Anglo-Saxon common law conceptions of equality of government official and private citizen before the law, and of basic fairness and absence of surprise in legal process and procedure—worked out especially in the constitutional battles of the seventeenth century between the common law courts and parliament on the one hand and royal prerogative power on the other—are refined, elaborated, and extended by the late nineteenth century so as to be codified, in legal-literary form, as Dicey's celebrated "Rule of Law" concept. Clearly, in substantive law terms, this is English constitutionalism quite as much as, or more than, the essentially institutions-based concept of the sovereignty of parliament. . . .

Most constitutional authorities today would say that the United States Supreme Court's development and application of substantive due process norms represented a very substantial and historically unwarranted and, in the end, politically dangerous extension of the notion of constitutionalism and of inherent constitutional values that the courts, qua institution of government, are obligated to defend. . . . But the more general notion of constitutional fairness which procedural due process in its common law historical origins implies remains, as does the concomitant notion of keeping the political processes open and unobstructed, and free from unnecessary clogs in their operation—leading on to the concept of freedom of speech and discussion as the constitutional "preferred freedom," and to fair and honest election laws as the basis of any constitutional government. These latter "open society" values are certainly rooted historically in nineteenth-century political liberalism, but they have a quality of permanence and immutability, nevertheless, that quite transcends issues of temporary economic advantage. In so far as the notion of constitutionalism has a meaning going beyond the positivism of a constitutional charter or constitutional texts, as written, it is this; and it seems common to all western European and western European derived constitutionalism, whether under the rubric of constitutional due process, "preferred freedoms," the rule of law, *le principe de la légalité*, or the *Rechtsstaat*, or some similar synonym.

The Law-in-Books and the Law-in-Action: Of the Necessary Distinction Between Nominal and Normative Constitutions

. . . Leaders of the sociological approach to law in the United States— the School of Sociological Jurisprudence, as it was called—distinguished between the law-in-books and the law-in-action: the positive law as originally enacted by the legislature and the de facto community attitudes and expectations, and hence practice, in regard to that law. The textbook example usually cited by American jurists was the 18th (Prohibition) Amendment to the United States Constitution, launched after the American entry into the First World War and ratified after the conclusion of that war in 1919, formally prohibiting the manufacture, sale, or consumption of alcoholic liquors in the United States. The 18th Amendment was a dead letter, almost from the date of its coming into legal effect, ignored alike by private citizens and the law enforcement officials sworn to apply it. The fate of the 18th Amendment raises interesting questions about the long-range utility and merits of trying to concretise transient community social or moral attitudes by putting them, in permanent form, into the constitutional charter itself. But, more important, in the immediate context, it underlines the importance of underlying community attitudes in regard to law, and the importance of having a certain minimum societal support for the positive law. Some degree of non-correspondence between the positive law, as written, and de facto community attitudes and practices, is no doubt inevitable and even desirable in order to permit and encourage administrative flexibility in the application of the law. But how big a gap is permissible for the positive law rules concerned still to deserve the accolade of law, and for us to be able to speak of the existence of a viable, operational legal system?

Certainly, in the case of the United States, with the adoption of the 13th, 14th, and 15th amendments to the constitution in the immediate aftermath of the American Civil War, the principle of racial equality, to which those amendments were specifically directed, remained largely a dead letter in many parts of the United States, in regard to basic social and economic rights, and even voting rights for almost three quarters of a century. It was not until a series of courageous, imaginative Supreme Court decisions in the 1940s and the 1950s that the gap between the constitutional law-in-books and the constitutional law-in-action could be narrowed to the point of more substantial correspondence with the historical intentions of the original drafters of the 13th, 14th, and 15th amendments, and the principle of racial equality accepted as a constitutional "living law" imperative.

This dichotomy between abstract constitutional principle, as drafted, and concrete governmental application of that principle exists, as we can see, even in regard to the classical constitutional systems where the constitution really is a going concern and has endured over a certain period of years. It is the more marked, however, in the case of some more recent ventures in constitution-making where the constitutional charter takes on a politically hortatory, programmatic character, and reads more in the nature of a statement of ideological principles than a practical blue-print for government. The constitution, in this case, has a symbolic rather than a functional quality and seems designed more for public relations at home or abroad than as a genuinely operational legal charter. The more rhetorical the formulations in the charter, the more it may appear that the constitution is intended to be nominal and not normative, and not in any case controlling as to the modalities of governmental decision-making, its procedural application in concrete cases, and its substantive content and compliance or otherwise with the postulated fundamental principles....

The Socio-Economic Limits to Constitutionalism

Is constitutionalism, which found its political apogee, in western society, during the predominance of political and economic laissez-faire ideas, inextricably linked with political liberalism to the point where it amounts to a barrier, today, to the effectuation of social democratic ideas, community planning, and the "welfare state[?]" Certainly, the supreme court jurisprudence of the main western federal systems, and also of non-western federal systems such as post-decolonization India that were strongly influenced by "received" western constitutional ideas, indicates a series of prolonged, last-ditch battles before the courts by economic special interest groups resisting governmental social and economic planning legislation, with the judges, in the earlier years at least, actively supporting the special interest groups and striking down the legislation trenching on their privileges. Those who could no longer control the legislatures did, indeed, look to the courts and the judges as guardians of their special interests.... The important thing, however, in relation to the jurisprudence of the "Old Court" majority on the United States Supreme Court up to 1937, or, for that matter, the "decentralized" weighting given by the Privy Council to the Canadian constitution from the close of the nineteenth century to the late 1930s, or the favouring of private property claims by the Indian supreme court majority in the first decade after decolonization and independence, is that it ended and was capable of being ended within the existing constitutional system and within the general context of the existing constitutional charter. The constitution was open-ended enough to allow of its continuing adaptation to changing societal conditions.... The openness of constitutional systems to societal change is a key element in liberal constitutionalism, and it is no barrier in itself to social democracy. Perhaps the process of community transition could be assisted, in the case of new ventures in constitution-making, by constitutional bill of rights provisions that identify the new social and economic claims to sharing of wealth and social opportunity in addition to the classical liberal, "open society," freedom of speech and association and communication values; though there is always the risk of jelling as timeless constitutional absolutes the purely passing, temporary political claims of today and so, ultimately, of acting as a brake on social change and social progress....

[McWhinney notes tendencies in more modern European constitutions to address economic and social welfare conditions, referring to the Weimar (1919) and Bonn (1949) constitutions in Germany, and the Constitutions of both the 4th (1946) and 5th (1958) French Republics. He concludes that at least the latter provisions cannot be seen as "constitutional law-in-action, bridging the gap between classical liberal constitutionalism and the claimed newer constitutional exigencies of the social welfare state."]

The Ethnocentric Limits to Constitutionalism

Is constitutionalism and the essentially western derived institutional models and practices in which it is historically rooted something that is peculiarly limited to western culture, in the sense that it cannot easily be exported to other, non-western societies with any reasonable prospects of its taking root there and becoming genuinely operational? All laws do reflect culture in certain measure, to the point that, within western constitutionalism itself, there are discernible differences of emphasis and degree between the English common law-derived and the continental European civil law-derived institutional models; and even within continental European civil law constitutionalism, the French experience shades off significantly from, for example, the German. We can meaningfully speak, therefore, of "Anglo-Saxon" and continental European constitutional models, and, within these categories, of "English" and "American" models, and "French," "German," "Swiss," and "Italian" models. The categories and sub-categories are the result of different national specialized legal and more general historical developments, and of differences in the timing and degree of "reception" of original foreign legal elements—the Roman law, for example. To speak of an ethnic-cultural aspect to constitutionalism thus becomes meaningful and rational in this particular context. What is also true and demonstrable, however, in the light of comparative constitutional law experience, is that there is no necessary and inevitable ethnic-cultural barrier to the successful reception or transfer of particular constitutional institutions developed in the one society to another society, so long as the special social and economic and other basic historical conditions under which those institutions developed in the first society are already present in reasonable degree or at least can be expected to be present within a reasonable period of time in the second society. The special intellectual skills and aptitudes of the political élite group in the second, "receiving" society are obviously crucial, of course. What is clear, in retrospect, is that some of the immediate, post-decolonization "receptions" of constitutional institutions in newly independent Third World countries from the "parent" European imperial powers—in the late 1940s, the 1950s, and the 1960s— were not particularly useful or scientific exercises in the sociology of law. Entered upon too hurriedly, perhaps, and undoubtedly in good faith, they sought to implant the institutions of essentially stable, politically bland, post-industrial societies in new countries that too often had not yet conquered the basic problems of mass education and that were still to go through even the earliest of stages of economic growth. There is something especially ironic in the attempt to export "classical" federal constitutionalism—which requires, above all, enormous skills of pragmatism and political compromise for its continuingly successful operation, as recent Canadian experience shows—to the new, post-independence, multiracial societies of Asia, Africa, and the Caribbean. Strong executive decision-making was clearly needed to overcome the massive social and economic problems of the post-decolonization era, and the reconciliation with the strains and tensions of multi-culturalism required some more imaginative ventures in plural-constitutional models.... It is not surprising perhaps that Indian government, under Nehru and Madame Gandhi, though maintaining a British styled prime minister as the official head of government, evolved increasingly, at the level of constitutional law-in-action, into a "strong executive," presidential-type regime; or that Nigeria, having ended the disastrous Biafran Civil War with a military solution, should wind up the long period of post-war reconstruction by the adoption, in 1979, of an American presidential model, federal state. The attempt is there, in any case, to reconcile in constitutional form the twin, often directly competing imperatives of a strong central executive and the deference to regionally based, ethnic-cultural particularism. It is a change from the authoritarian "Man-on-horseback" model of direct military rule; and the military leaders in Nigeria, in handing back civilian government on this basis, seem to have chosen a far more promising constitutional model for their present needs than the immediate post-decolonization, classical federal model (British Empire, polite export variety)....

[McWhinney also argues that the immediate post-colonization constitutions of new Asian and African countries placed too much weight on civil and political rights, and permitted too much constitutional litigation impeding executive and administrative decisionmaking, suggesting that "expensive and sophisticated, special interests groups-based, constitutional litigation ... is a trademark of contemporary American ... [and other] 'older' commonwealth" countries, but not appropriate to new nations.]...

The Political Limits to Constitutionalism

This question takes us back directly to the nature of the political élite in any society, and its inherent problem-solving capacities. Some of the problems of post-decolonization constitution-making, in the Third World countries, clearly stemmed from the character of the "succession" political élite to whom the parent European imperial state had handed over political sovereignty, and its representativeness, or lack of it, in nationwide terms, in the new succession state. Where the succession élite was drawn from only one geographical region of the new country, or from one dominant communal or tribal group, no amount of technical legal sophistication in constitutional drafting, and no federal charter, however carefully balanced in institutional terms, could expect to succeed in veiling the naked facts of power and to keep a basically non-representative constitutional system together in the face of all the centrifugal pressures....

The political limits to constitutionalism are thus a product of the two distinct elements, usually in mutual and reciprocal interaction: the constitutional system, as such—its degree of openness to new political ideas or ideologies, and also its intrinsic qualities of creative adjustment or change, without too much expenditure of energy or social cost, to rapidly changing societal expectations and demands—and the political élite—its ability to be seen as legitimate or representative, and also its inherent intellectual flexibility and ability to apprehend and respond to new problems in timely fashion. No constitutional charter could have ... saved Louis XVI or Marie Antoinette. On the other hand, no government, however intelligent and forward-looking and representatively established, can be expected to operate successfully with an archaic or rigid charter that imposes serious practical obstacles to much needed community decisions for change. Poland may well have been doomed, politically, in the late eighteenth century because of the pressures of external events, but the institution of the liberum veto certainly speeded it along the road to disaster.

A principal task and responsibility of a constitutional-governmental élite, therefore, becomes one of anticipating and correcting in advance the attrition or decay of the constitutional system. Constitutional systems must always include an in-built quality of change; and constitutionalism itself becomes not merely the substantive values written into the constitutional charter, but the actual processes of constitutional change themselves. That is why constitutional style—the respect for the constitutional rules of the game, and their respect in the spirit as well as in the letter—becomes so important in the ultimate evaluation of a constitutional system.

––––––––

Daniel P. Franklin & Michael J. Baun (eds.), Political Culture And Constitutionalism: A Comparative Approach (1994)

[Franklin and Baun consider several important questions: the role of what they call political culture in maintaining or establishing constitutionalism; the relationship between constitutionalism and cultural diversity; and whether the particular institutions of liberal democracy are required to provide for constitutional government. Consider, as you read these excerpts, drawn from introductory and concluding essays that refer to other chapters in the book, what constitutes "political culture."]

* * *

. . . [W]e can speak of the political culture or that portion of the *zeitgeist*—the moral, intellectual, and cultural climate in a state—that deals with public policy. The concept of political culture (as well as *zeitgeist*) also suggests a temporal component. The tenor of the times is a function not only of the past but also of the present. Therefore, it may be difficult to define exactly what it is to be a citizen of the United States in the twentieth century, but it is inherently obvious that there is something special about the culture in the United States that is unique to that land and to that time.

A political culture is capable of promoting constitutional or nonconstitutional public policy. Constitutionalism is the governmental component of a democratic culture. Every society, by definition, must make decisions concerning the distribution of scarce resources, and those decisions must be enforced. This being the case, the constitutional regime of a state requires not only the enumeration of rules of public behavior but the establishment of an institutional structure for the implementation of that law. Thus, the concept of constitutionalism rests on two pillars, a theory of justice and process.

By its very nature, a society can only be a society as long as there is some kind of consensus—a collection of shared values. The key to this definition is the word *shared*. For a society to remain cohesive, for a government to be capable and willing to protect the rights of all its citizens, there must be certain shared values. The most basic tenet of any constitutional society is the shared belief that by virtue of being citizens of a state, all persons are equal in the eyes of the law. Thus, we can identify the constitutional state as being one in which the rule of law prevails. The law is never arbitrarily applied in the constitutional state, and the only coercion exercised by government is guided by procedural guarantees and restraints.

It should be evident by now that we define constitutionalism in functional rather than structural terms. The forms of constitutionalism are not so important to us as is the fact that the constitutional state is governed by the rule of law. According to our definition, the prevailing theory of justice in any given state or procedural forms will vary enormously. Thus, we are loath even to equate a constitutional regime with a "democratic" state.

We are determined to redefine the debate concerning the path to democratization by allowing for regime building that is "constitutional" but not at the same time necessarily "democratic" in the Western, structural meaning of the term. For example, is it possible to speak of a constitutional regime in a Muslim state that is governed by Islamic law (*sharia*)? We think so. To deny this possibility is to lend an irrevocably Western bias to our analysis. After all, a people's willingness to surrender to the authority of the state (in the person of a king, or in the form of a particular philosophy or theology) is variable and culturally determined. We entertain the possibility (admittedly without much enthusiasm) that political modernization can take a path different from that of liberal democracy. Since elections do not a democracy make, we may need to search for other standards, not only for measuring political modernization but also for talking about democracy. It may well be that the establishment of the constitutional state is a preliminary step to the establishment of a full democracy. Alternatively, some completely different end point may be possible.

If underlying the establishment of the constitutional state is a shared or consensual theory of justice and reliance on procedural solutions for the settlement of disputes, we need to examine the underpinnings of *consensus* in society. How consensus develops within a society is the key to our discussion of the formation of the constitutional state. It is in trying to explain the source of consensus that we turn to the concept of *political culture*.

Political Culture

The study of culture as a factor shaping political outcomes has waxed and waned over the years. There was an upsurge of interest in cultural explanations of political phenomena in the 1960s following the publication of Gabriel Almond and Sidney Verba's *Civic Culture*. However, difficulties of measurement, the trend toward scientific behavioralism, and problems of cultural stereotyping eclipsed the interest in cultural explanations, which were replaced by a new institutional focus. This institutional focus had the great advantage for social scientists of being more conducive to empirical study. Structural determinants such as socioeconomic variables are fairly easily measured but may well miss the point. The difficulty and controversial nature of the study of cultural traits should not prevent us from factoring in this crucial determinant of the maturization of a state.

We do not deny the possibility that the success of the state in institution building may be an indicator of political modernization. However, we suspect that this explanation is dangerously incomplete. A strong state, in the absence of consensus, has the potential of exercising great violence against its people. We believe that the popular control of government is a necessary component of the constitutional state and that this control is either organic and consensual or external. The control of a state by an outside power is a topic we will address more completely [elsewhere]. The organic control of institutions, however, is in its essence a cultural phenomenon.

In his essay "The Nature of Social Action," Max Weber gives us some idea of his thinking on the nature of political culture:

> In interpreting action, the sociologist must take account of the fundamentally important fact that the collective concepts which we employ in our thinking, whether in legal or other specialist contexts or in everyday life, *represent* something: what they represent is something which in part actually exists and has a normative force in the minds of real men (not only judges and officials, but also the general public) whose actions take account of it. Because of this, they are of great, often absolutely vital, importance in giving a causal explanation of the way in which the actions of real human beings proceed.

For Weber these "collective concepts" are a vital determinant of the behavior of individuals in a given state. This collectivity or shared vision is the glue that binds a political culture. Without this collectivity, we argue, the constitutional state is impossible. How these "collective concepts" develop, therefore, is a key to our study of political modernization.

Concepts central to a collective political culture are *tolerance* and *trust*. Consensus can never be absolute. There are certain to be disagreements based on class, ideology, religion, or ethnicity in any society. A societal consensus must embrace an "agreement to disagree" based on the assumptions that other citizens have a right to different views and that the political process is a legitimate forum for resolving disputes resulting therefrom. For any procedural structure to endure, it is important that when decisions are made through the appropriate process, citizens, even losers in the political game, abide by the outcome. Beyond this central value—that of tolerance—there can be any number of variations on a theme.

We note, therefore, that theocracies, especially those that do not preach tolerance, are unlikely to develop into a constitutional state. Only under a very special set of conditions, basically the presence of a completely homogeneous population, will a theocracy be able to produce the kind of consensus integral to the constitutional state. Otherwise, only a secular state with a fairly strict prohibition and value placed on the separation of church and state will be able to develop into a constitutional regime and, ultimately, some form of participatory rule. . . .

Of one thing we are certain: a self-sustaining democracy cannot be imposed simply by overlaying an institutional structure similar to that which exists in a mature political system. A court system, parliament, elections, and a written constitution do not, themselves, constitute or necessarily lead to a democracy. In fact, inappropriate institutional arrangements can impede as well as advance political development. Institutional structures must be tailored to meet the needs and reflect the political culture of a particular state. Institutional schemes transplanted in their entirety from abroad will either bend or break. That is why the specifics of institution building are a concern secondary to the building of a constitutional regime.

In addition, certain types of structural arrangements can divide as well as unite. The formal recognition through law of cultural divisions in society, while a short-run "fix," can become a devastating long-run problem in the sense that such arrangements put off constitution building by deepening divisions. . . . As early as the 1920s, Rosa Luxemburg presaged the collapse of the Soviet Union under the pressure of nationality-based activism. This resurrected nationalism, long submerged, was apparently energized and sustained throughout the seventy-year history of the Soviet Union through the geographical principle endorsed by V.I. Lenin that ethnic groups would have a measure of self-determination.

The desire for self-determination is the Gordian knot of constitution building. On the one hand, demands for national self-determination require immediate attention and have been explicitly endorsed by the international community. On the other, the formal recognition of national self-determination sows the seeds of the destruction of the state and the collapse of democracy somewhere down the line. Can the aspirations of nationality be served through a process that involves less than the formal and permanent recognition of divisions in society? For this question we do not have an answer. To its elucidation we dedicate this effort. What of our collective expertise can we bring to bear for the solution of this seemingly intractable problem?

The trappings of democracy have little meaning without the foundation of a constitutional base. Much of the optimism following the collapse of the Soviet Union concerning the potential for the expansion of democracy was misplaced. Many Western clients during the cold war were not ripe for democracy and, in the absence of massive Western assistance, will slip back to the status of pre-constitutional, authoritarian regimes. Certainly the former clients of the Soviet Union will not automatically become democratic states. The absence of communism does not in itself guarantee a liberal democratic government. In fact, we believe that a large percentage of the world's states are still without a political culture appropriate to the establishment of a constitutional regime. Thus the first step in the establishment of a democracy should be the development of a constitutional state. This, we expect, will be the most difficult objective to achieve....

The Institutional Structure of Constitutionalism

A basic question concerns the institutional makeup or structure of constitutionalism. In other words, what types of political institutions provide the best possible framework or shell for constitutional government? On the surface, at least, the answer to this question appears obvious: the institutions of liberal democracy, including parliamentary or representative government, institutionalized checks on government power, and constitutional guarantees of individual rights and liberties. Nevertheless, the authors were open to the possibility that forms of constitutionalism other than a liberal democratic one could exist.

The results of this study seem to indicate, however, that there is indeed a close association between liberal democracy and constitutionalism. In most of the countries surveyed, the success of constitutionalism was intimately connected with the construction and functioning of liberal democratic institutions. By the same token, the failure of these institutions—most typically through military coups (Turkey, Egypt, Nigeria) or declarations of emergency by seated governments (India)—was synonymous with the failure of constitutionalism.

The one significant exception to this pattern is Mexico. While it has enjoyed relatively stable constitutional government over the past seven decades, Mexico is not classifiable as a liberal democracy. Instead it is a one-party state, with the Party of Revolutionary Institutions (PRI) exercising near complete political hegemony. Mexico also has an authoritarian, executive-dominated political system, with few institutionalized checks on government power. Finally, while basic individual and political rights are formally enumerated in the 1917 Constitution, they are often not observed by the state.

Nevertheless, a certain form of constitutionalism can be said to exist in Mexico. Most important, there are established "rules of the game" that have functioned fairly effectively over the years and have provided Mexico with a considerable degree of political stability. The secret, according to Howard J. Wiarda, is the fundamental legitimacy of the system, which is largely based on indigenous cultural values and institutions and widely regarded by Mexicans as "our democracy." At the same time, Wiarda argues that while Mexicans believe strongly in the ideals of constitutionalism and the rule of law, the Mexican version of constitutionalism is a "very malleable and open-ended concept." In this sense, the Mexican model of constitutionalism is culturally appropriate. Whether what passes for constitutionalism in Mexico can be properly regarded as such, however, remains open to question.

A second suggestion that some form of constitutionalism other than a liberal democratic one might be possible comes from the chapter on Egypt.

In their discussion of Egyptian political culture, Nathan J. Brown and Roni Amit assert that Islamic ideology is not necessarily opposed to the concept of constitutionalism *per se*, at least as far as it concerns defining the operation of government in a written document and the idea of the rule of law. In fact, they argue that constitutions themselves are no longer an exclusively Western concept and note that writing a constitution was among the first tasks undertaken by the revolutionary Islamic government of Iran. Nevertheless, Brown and Amit also recognize that the Islamic version of constitutionalism remains as of yet vaguely formulated, and they remark that Islamic "religious authorities have had much less to say about the process of governing than about the rights and duties of the ruler." Since constitutional government is all about process, however, this omission is crucial.

Ultimately, it would seem that a theocratic form of constitutionalism, whether Islamic or otherwise, is not very plausible. Any political order that derives its authority from essentially nonpolitical sources—that is, God—is subject more to the whims of divine interpretation than it is limited by earthbound constraints on the use of government or state power. The same would also appear to be the case for political orders, such as Marxism and communism, that derive their authority from supposedly inevitable historical processes.

Culture versus Institutions

While liberal democracy appears to be the best institutional shell for constitutionalism, it is also true that the mere existence of democratic institutions does not, by itself, guarantee constitutional government. Perhaps the classic example is Germany's Weimar Republic (1919-33), which collapsed and gave way to Nazi dictatorship despite having one of the most democratic constitutions ever designed. Formally democratic constitutions and institutional structures were also key features of the Soviet Union and many communist countries. Needless to say, they meant little in practice.

The experiences of several countries examined in this study also support the conclusion that democratic institutions do not ensure constitutional government. In Turkey, Egypt, and Nigeria, for example, the democratic principles contained in constitutions have often not reflected political reality or the actual practices of government. At the same time, the existence of written constitutions and formal democratic structures in these countries has not prevented the frequent resort to military coups as a means of establishing political order or bringing about political change. Indeed, Brown and Amit's description of Egypt as being rich in constitutions yet poor in constitutionalism appears to fit a number of other countries included in this survey.

This is not to argue that institutions do not matter. Clearly, they are an important part of the equation of constitutionalism. Nevertheless, institutions alone are not sufficient to produce stable and effective constitutional government. What is also necessary, it would appear, is a firm commitment to constitutionalism that is rooted in the national political culture. Once again, the Weimar experience serves as an instructive example, in this case of the likely fate of "republics without republicans," or of constitutional regimes without a cultural consensus on constitutionalism.

The political-cultural basis of constitutionalism is clearly obvious in the "evolutionary" democracies. In the United States, according to Daniel P. Franklin, constitutionalism has thrived despite the existence of serious flaws or contradictions in the basic constitutional order. Thus, while the U.S. Constitution has been a suitable and remarkably adaptable framework for government, constitutionalism in the United States appears to stem primarily from the unique values and beliefs of a consensual American political culture. . . .

What is distinctive about the "evolutionary" democracies is that the cultural commitment to constitutionalism is reflected in actual institutional performance and government practice. For many of the developing countries considered in this study, this has often not been the case. Nevertheless, it appears that in several of these countries a strong popular commitment to constitutionalism has been an important factor sustaining democratic development, even in the frequent instances in which institutions and leaders have failed. In her discussion of Turkey, for instance, Marcie J. Patton argues that widespread public support for the values of constitutionalism has kept the democratic project alive over the years and seen it through periodic impositions of military rule. In a similar fashion, Sankaran Krishna argues that the national culture of politics has become the main "bedrock of democracy" in India, even as that country's democratic institutions have decayed in recent years. . . .

Cultural Learning . . .

A number of factors appear capable of influencing cultural change. Interestingly enough, the least effective of these seems to be direct efforts by government to remake political values. This conclusion is indicated, for instance, by the failed attempts of the Nigerian Third Republic (1986-93) to shape a national political culture supportive of the country's new institutions, although admittedly this was an effort of short duration. Perhaps more successful in this regard were the intensive efforts of the postwar Federal Republic to eradicate vestiges of nazism and reform the traditionally authoritarian German political culture. As will be seen below, however, other factors, such as economic growth and effective system performance, may have been even more important in promoting the transformation of German political culture. Another useful lesson to ponder is the monumental failure of the Soviet regime to create a new communist human, which remains an enduring symbol of the general futility of such efforts at forced cultural change.

An important agent of political-cultural transformation is socioeconomic change resulting from economic development and modernization. These were particularly powerful factors supporting political democratization in Mexico and Turkey. In each of these semi-industrialized countries, economic modernization and socioeconomic change have fostered the growth of new demands for democracy, individual freedom, and human rights. A potential problem, in fact, is that political-cultural change stemming from economic modernization can outrun the capacity of established institutions to adjust. This seems to be the case in Mexico, for example, where, as Wiarda notes, the democratic demands of a more pluralistic society have gotten ahead of the process of institutional reform, increasing pressures and tension within that country's paternalist and statist political system.

It would be a mistake, however, to link the spread of democratic values too closely to processes of economic development and modernization. Indeed, in some of the countries studied, it seems that traditional cultural values are essentially democratic and the real threat to democracy may come, instead, from the forces of modernization and progress. In Nigeria, for instance, Suberu argues that the main barrier to democratic constitutionalism has not been the traditional political culture but the statist values of modernizing elites and regimes. Far from promoting democratization, the process of statist modernization threatens to undermine the democratic aspects of traditional popular culture in Nigeria. As Krishna notes in his chapter, a similar argument has been made about India. He cites Ashis Nandy's assertion that the indigenous political culture of India is inherently democratic, in the sense that it is essentially tolerant and pluralistic. As in Nigeria, though, Nandy believes that modernizing institutions and elites threaten to subvert this traditional political culture and thereby pose the greatest threat to Indian democracy.

The experiences of several countries also suggest that the very existence of democratic institutions can play a role in promoting cultural change. In India, for instance, Krishna concludes that there is a "dialectical" or mutually reinforcing relationship between democratic institutions and political culture. What has taken place in India over time, he argues, is a process of societal learning that is somewhat like a game, with society becoming better at it the more it plays. A similar process appears to have taken place in Turkey, where Patton argues that the existence of a democratic institutional infrastructure has facilitated the spread of democratic values.

The prospects for cultural learning are greatly enhanced, of course, when democratic institutions are successful in providing political stability and economic prosperity. Perhaps the best example of this is West Germany, where a process of societal learning appears to have taken place over a period of twenty years following the establishment of the Federal Republic in 1949. As a consequence, by the 1970s a new consensus held that the formerly authoritarian German political culture had become firmly democratic. A crucial factor in this learning process was that the experience with democratic institutions in the postwar decades had been almost wholly positive and proved that they could be effective and functional. This was the direct opposite of the negative experience with democracy in the Weimar years, when parliamentary institutions became associated in many minds with economic hardship and political chaos.

In sum, it appears that political culture can be democratized and that constitutionalist values can be promoted....

Constitutionalism and Cultural Diversity . . .

[While acknowledging the "successful constitutionalism" in the "multicultural societies" of the U.S. and Canada, the authors hypothesize that the success may result from the countries being populated through immigration over a period of time yielding a commitment to the idea of multiculturalism.]

The growth of ethnonationalism poses a serious problem for democracy and constitutional government in many European countries, especially as since the exclusionary sentiment of nationality is a direct contradiction of the universalistic norms of liberal constitutionalism. It also undermines the values of mutual tolerance and trust that are so vital as a basis for constitutionalism. Even in multicultural democracies such as the United States, of course, a constant tension between the opposing forces of nationalism and liberal universalism is evident. In many European countries, however, as well as in other traditional nation-states, membership in the political community has always been more closely linked to ethnicity or nationality. The epitome of this connection is Germany, with its strikingly ethnonationalist citizenship laws. The link between nationalism and citizenship has produced disastrous results in Europe in the past. Today, while no one predicts a return to fascism and nazism, it is nevertheless clear that a resurgence of ethnonationalism poses a major dilemma for European democracy. The future of democratic constitutionalism in many European countries, in fact, may well be tied to their capacity to accept that they are, or are increasingly becoming, multicultural societies and their ability to redefine nationhood in institutional rather than ethnic terms.

Ethnic or cultural conflict has also been a problem for many Third World countries. In many cases, problems have stemmed from the fact that the political borders drawn by the departing colonial powers did not coincide with the traditional territorial distribution of national and ethnic groups. As a consequence, included within the boundaries of many postcolonial countries were tribal or ethnic groups that had previously either been enemies or had little history of affiliation with one another. In other cases, the boundaries of new states divided particular ethnic groups among two or more countries. In this manner, the potential for ethnic conflict and upheaval in many postcolonial states has been considerable. In fact, it has been a major barrier to the construction of stable and effective governments in much of the Third World.

Surprisingly, therefore, the experiences of two postcolonial countries examined in this study seem to suggest that cultural heterogeneity or pluralism might be a factor actually supporting the establishment of constitutional government. This is the opposite, of course, of what has been traditionally asserted: that small, ethnically or culturally homogeneous societies are the most suitable for democracy, at least in its more pure Athenian or Rousseauean sense. . . .

The success of constitutionalism in ethnically or culturally diverse societies, however, appears to be closely linked to questions of institutional design. Here again, the experiences of India and Nigeria are instructive. In

India in particular, according to Krishna, federalist structures combine with ethnic pluralism to produce effective checks on government power.....

One reason why ethnic diversity and pluralism are supportive of democratic constitutionalism in Nigeria and India might be that in these countries no one group is dominant. Instead, a rough balance of power exists among different groups, or else there is so much fragmentation that no group can achieve dominance.....

B.   CONSTITUTIONS WITHOUT CONSTITUTIONALISM

Constitutions are often linked with ideas of constitutionalism—the rule of law applied to both people and government officers, judicial independence, and existence of basic human rights. Sunstein's article, moreover, assumes that a "constitution" is a kind of basic law more deeply entrenched—that is, more difficult to change—than other forms of law.

Many countries which have adopted written constitutions, however, do not have much in the way of "constitutionalism" in the senses described above. Why are constitutions adopted if not to promote constitutionalism? The readings below suggest some reasons.

As you read the next set of articles bear in mind Murphy's suggestion that constitutions may serve as symbols or aspirational models, and McWhinney's reminder that there is always some degree of distance between a written constitution and the operative realities of law, and that countries vary in the degree of that distance. How is a constitution as aspiration or symbol different from what Murphy calls a "sham" constitution?

Also consider the argument by Okoth-Ogendo that constitutions serve "constitutive" functions both internally, by establishing the structure for the exercise of government power, and externally, by establishing a convincing sovereign presence to other nations. Does his argument in favor of "autochthonous" constitutions suggest that some African constitutions were "shams" because they relied on forms of governance associated with external colonial powers and did not draw from indigenous traditions?

H.W.O. Okoth–Ogendo, *Constitutions Without Constitutionalism: Reflections on an African Political Paradox*, in Constitutionalism and Democracy: Transitions in the Contemporary World (Douglas Greenberg, Stanley N. Katz, Melanie Beth Oliviero, and Steven C. Wheatley, eds., 1993)

. . .

A number of perspectives have contributed to [a] distressing lack of interest in African constitutions. The first is primarily ideological and argues that the primary function of *a constitution* is to limit governmental authority and to regulate political processes in the state. This view, whose origin lies in the liberal democratic tradition, forms the backdrop of many arguments among politicians and academics about the "correct" exercise of power in Africa. According to this view, there can be no "constitutional" government unless mechanisms exist within the constitution for the supervision of these functions; further, such mechanisms must be erected on the doctrine of the separation of powers and the principle of limited government, both of which must conform to the theory that *government* itself ought, at all times, to conform to the *rule of law*.

A more important factor alluded to by Ghai and McAuslan is analytical: a totally inadequate conception of law and its relationship to power in Africa. To many scholars, the idea of law still connotes the existence of a determinate rule, founded on some perspective of value (whether individualist or communitarian), that provides a basis for predicting and evaluating authoritative decisions in specified circumstances. Constitutional *law*, concerned entirely (or so it is thought) with decisions that lie in the public domain, is, more than any other body of law, expected to be basic, rational, even *fundamental*, and therefore capable of withstanding pressures generated by the vicissitudes of political life.

Political developments in Africa since Ghana's independence in 1957 have demonstrated repeatedly, however, that not only have constitutions "failed" to regulate the exercise of power, but, devastatingly, they have not become as basic as the analytical tradition scholars predicted: "few African governments have valued them other than as rhetoric."

This situation has led to both a dilemma and a paradox. The dilemma is whether to abandon the study of constitutions altogether on the grounds that no body of *constitutional law or principles of constitutionalism* appears to be developing in Africa, and might well fail to do so; or to continue teaching and theorizing on the utility of constitutional values in the hope that state elites in Africa will eventually internalize and live by them. The paradox lies in the simultaneous existence of what appears as a clear commitment by African political elites to the idea of the constitution and an equally emphatic rejection of the classical or at any rate liberal democratic notion of constitutionalism.

The dilemma is, in my view, inconsequential, even false; the paradox, however, is both sufficiently manifest and intriguing to merit an examination to explain the contemporary patterns of constitutional development in Africa (or lack of them). Such an examination is all the more necessary since the paradox is essentially political, and not evidence as others think, of deliberate disregard of legal or "constitutional" processes stricto sensu . . . .

Constitutions as Organized Power

The analysis of the paradox begins with a simple but important assertion: *all law*, and *constitutional law* in particular, is concerned, not with abstract norms, but with the creation, distribution, exercise, legitimation, effects, and reproduction of *power*; it matters not whether that power lies with the state or in some other organized entity. From this perspective, therefore, the very idea of law, hence of *a constitution as a special body of law*, entails commitment or adherence to a theory of organized power, as appears evident in the historical experience and shared aspirations of all societies. The fact that in some societies the exercise of power has become more predictable, and even legal-rational in Weberian sense, merely records the complexity of the relationship between power and law in different contexts.

A useful model for the analysis of any constitution, therefore, is to regard it as a "power map" on which framers may delineate a wide range of concerns: an application of the Hobbesian concept of "covenant" as in the American constitution; a basic constitutive process, as in the Malawi constitution; a code of conduct to which public behavior should conform, as in the Liberian or French constitutions; a program of social, economic, and political transformations, as in the Ethiopian or Soviet constitutions; an authoritative affirmation of the basis of social, moral, political, or cultural existence, including the ideals toward which the polity is expected to strive, as in the Libyan constitution. The process of *constitution making*, which involves, inter alia, making choices as to which concerns should appear on that map, cannot be regarded as a simple reproduction of some basic principles that particular societies may have found operational. It is, as D. Elazar has noted, an "eminently political act," which must draw on past experiences and future aspirations. An analysis of the African constitutional paradox must start, therefore, with an examination of the *political origins of the idea of the constitution in the continent.*

The Nature of the Paradox

The precise form in which that paradox, *commitment to the idea of the constitution and rejection of the classical notation of constitutionalism*, has emerged over the last three decades requires a description.

The idea of and the necessity for a constitution appear fully established in the minds of state elites in Africa in at least two important senses. First, the constitution is an act without which the polity can have no legitimate or sovereign existence; it is of no small significance, for example, that the very first article of most African constitutions *declare* that each respective country is *sovereign*. In Africa, the idea that the constitution is "a means to demonstrate the sovereignty of the state" appears quite strong; in that sense, the constitutive value of some form of a constitution remains preeminent. It is notable that very few European and American constitutions make such declaration; sovereignty is assumed as the basis of constitution making.

Second, the idea of the constitution is firmly established as the *basic law of the state*. Since all African independence constitutions provide for some method of change, fundamental alteration, or even total abrogation (e.g., in the constitution of Swaziland 1968), *the notion of a basic law in the African context entails no element of sanctity*. What it does entail is minimum, and perhaps popular observance of the rules contained in the constitution.

The notion that a constitution is important as a basic law in the above sense underlies the amendments, the revisions, and the experimentation with non-Westminster models by civilian governments. When King Sobhuza II of Swaziland abrogated the constitution in 1973, he said that he had come to the conclusion inter alia,

> that the [independence] constitution has failed to provide the machinery for good government and for the maintenance of law and order, [and] that I and my people heartily ... desire to march forward progressively under *our own constitution* guaranteeing peace, order and good government. (emphasis added)

Sobhuza was seeking a basic law more relevant to traditional Swazi values than was the Westminster constitution that brought his country into sovereign status. In 1986, the Sotho King, faced with a military insurrection, proclaimed the need for basic law (Lesotho order 1986)

> to provide for the peace, order and good Government of Lesotho until such time as a new constitution better suited to the needs of the Basotho Nation shall have been agreed.

That law formally repealed the organs of civilian government and substituted for them bodies under the nominal supervision of the King but controlled by the military.

The essence of commitment in the second sense, then, is to an autochthonous (or socially relevant) basic law. Nyerere formulated this essence forcefully as follows:

> We refuse to adopt the institutions of other countries even where they have served those countries well because it is our conditions that have to be served by our institutions. We refuse to put ourselves in a straitjacket of constitutional devices—even of our own making. The constitution of Tanzania must serve the people of Tanzania. We do not intend that the people of Tanzania should serve the constitution.

This search for autochthony involves not only the rejection of external (specifically "western") institutions and constitutional "devices," but, more emphatically, the abandonment of the classical notion that the purposes of constitutions are to limit and control state power, not to facilitate it. A purely instrumental view of the purposes of constitutions, such as Nyerere's, has guided state elites' search for the formal means by which to preserve the integrity of the "constituted polity" without being embroiled in a maze of constitutional law whose function, in classical theory, is to control and supervise constitutionality....

The Nature of the Constitutional State and Power Realities

The origin of the paradox also lies in the nature of the state as "constituted" by the independence constitution, which was fundamentally different from anything the colonialists themselves had devised. This was particularly obvious in English-speaking Africa, where the constituted state was based on a remarkable distrust of *centralized* power ... based almost entirely on the need to *exclude* the state (as a centralized entity) from functions it had exercised before independence.

Two aspects of the constituted state were particularly disturbing. The first was the distribution of power in these constitutions; the second was the clear tension between that distribution and the rest of the legal order. . . .

In the case of English-speaking Africa, that "power map" was based on a severely modified version of the Westminster model, complete with bicameral legislatures, separation of powers, judicial review of legislative and executive action, and a Bill of Rights distilled from the Magna Charta. In the case of French-speaking Africa, that map was based on the principle of constitutional tripartism as developed in the eighteenth century by Montesquieu and incorporated the provisions of the French Revolution of the Rights of Man and the Citizen of 1789.

Provisions were made in Mauritius, Kenya, Nigeria, Swaziland, and Zimbabwe, for the separation of powers between the head of State (the President) and the head of government (the Prime Minister), but this arrangement quickly gave way to a hybrid form of presidentialism unknown to western constitutional jurisprudence. Further, it was assumed, even though this was not expressly stated, that the constituted state would operate on a multiparty style of "democracy," an assumption derived from provisions of the Bill of Rights guaranteeing freedom of association.

What was disturbing about the power maps described above was not that they were not "democratic": *in the western liberal sense they were.* It was, first, the *rationale* for them that was the problem. Whereas institutions such as federalism (Nigeria and Uganda), regionalism (Kenya), constitutional monarchy (Swaziland and Lesotho), chieftancy (Zambia and Zimbabwe), and of course Bills of Rights have been used throughout history in appropriate contexts as the primary media for the socialization of politics and power; no such value-specific function was the reason for their presence in independence constitutions. For at least a decade after independence, these institutions *essentially* were operated as mechanisms for the entrenchment of interest that had accrued by reason of the exploitative nature of the colonial process itself.

Having seen the efficiency with which control of state institutions had enabled the colonial elite to convert the "national" economy into *some kind of private estate*, the African elites regarded as sabotage any suggestion that there should be any "withering away" of state power in the domain of public (including economic) affairs. For some of these elites, control of the instrumentalities of state power was the key to development in the postcolonial state.

Another disturbing aspect of the new constitutions was their relation to the rest of the legal order. . . . Invariably the first or second Article of the Independence Constitution declared the former the supreme law of the land and stated that "if any other law is inconsistent with [the] constitution, that other law shall, to the extent of inconsistency, be void." The intriguing thing is that it was the rest of the legal order, not the constitutional order, that offered African elites real power and the bureaucratic machinery with which to exercise it effectively.

In these circumstances it was always tempting to "opt out" of the constitutional order, the more effectively to manipulate the legal order whenever exigencies demanded it. Indeed, the constitutional order often appeared precariously perched on the legal order and the actual power structure, without the creative and rationalizing normativity that Kelsenian positivists would have expected. The potential for subverting the constitutional order through "legitimate" exercise of bureaucrative power was present, *ab initio*, and almost limitless. (It is not in the least surprising that not a single African *military* regime has forgotten to provide for the continuance "with full force and effect" of the legal order even as the constitution was being abrogated.)

The Development of the Paradox

The actual process of "subverting" the constitutional order in the sense suggested above took a number of forms. The most notorious was the *coup d'état....* The more interesting for our analysis was the move by state elites in a number of African countries to *politicize* the constitution, *initially* by declaring it a liability, and subsequently by converting it into an instrument of political warfare.

The Constitution as a Liability

The argument that the independence constitutional order was the state's most serious liability was carried to the public in the rhetoric of the need for rapid economic development. It was argued that a fragmented power structure would pose severe drawbacks to central planning, financial coordination, and the formulation of policies on important matters such as health, education, and agriculture. It was also argued that the constitutional order sought to frustrate the goals of equity and faster delivery of services which the fact of independence, per se, was exposed to facilitate; by focusing mainly on the loci of power, it had failed to resolve the important ideological issue of how to locate people's expectations and aspirations within its compass and permitted the importation of "undesirable political practices alien to and incompatible with the [African] ... way of life."

The last of these arguments, although made most explicitly and forcefully by King Sobhuza II of Swaziland, has been echoed in Tanzania, Zambia, Zimbabwe, Lesotho, Kenya, and the Central African Republic over the last quarter of a century.

But prosecuting that argument under the new constitutions was difficult, not least because of the severe restrictions placed on mechanisms for reconstitution. Much rhetoric was spent on exposing the absurdity of the constitutional order; for example, it was often stated, with some justification, that structuring the apparatuses of the state around minority *protection* rather than majority *expectations* was inherently absurd. In Kenya and

Zimbabwe, state elites succeeded in convincing "minorities" that the popular will was by no means a dangerous externality. (In Zaire, Malawi, and Zambia, minorities, including opposition parties, were simply harassed into submission.) Once that happened, as it did in Kenya in 1964 and more recently in Zimbabwe, those elites moved swiftly toward the creation of a tidier political and *administrative* landscape by removing all restrictions placed on the ability of the center to change the constitution (amendment procedures et al.!) and by making prolific use of the resulting flexibility.

The Constitution as a Political Instrument

With a tidy landscape before them, state elites then proceeded to insert new devices whose purpose was to recentralize power as it had been under colonial rule. Four main devices were used; the first was the extension of appointive and dismissal authority of the chief executive to all offices in the *public service*: civil, military, and "constitutional," such as those of judges and attorneys-general. . . . The second was the subjection of political recruitment at all levels (local, municipal, and parliamentary) to strict party sponsorship, the more effectively to monitor commitment to regime values. In a large number of countries including Kenya, Tanzania, Malawi, Zaire, and Zimbabwe, this particular device has led to a rapid transition toward the dominant or one-party state. . . .

The third device was the expansion of the coercive powers of the state by allowing extensive derogation from Bills of Rights wherever these were justiciable. This expansion was usually accomplished by the removal (or weakening) of parliamentary supervision of emergency powers, and then, by so subjective a redefinition of the conditions under which those powers could be invoked that any meaningful inquiry into the bona fides of any particular action was excluded. The fourth, and perhaps most interesting device, was to ensure that the constitutional order conformed to the inherited legal order; this device was often preferred whenever conflicts arose between the provisions of the constitution and those of specific legislation. The most recent use of this device took place in Kenya, where the constitution [was] amended inter alia to reflect the full complement of powers already being exercised by the police under penal and public security legislations.

As these and other devices found their places within the "constitutional" framework, so did the view that the constitutional arena, if properly controlled by the state elite, offered a more efficient and effective environment for the resolution of *political* conflicts than even the party and certainly the electorate at large. Indeed, by translating a *political* option or decision into a *constitutional* device or norm, state elites gained the added advantage of passing on the problem of enforcement or supervision ultimately to the judicial arm of government. A *run to amend the constitution* to deal with a political crisis became increasingly attractive as a method of reestablishing equilibrium within the body politic.

No doubt the original intent behind the desire to "subvert" the constitutional order in any or these ways (at least in the 1960s) was substantially above board. This intent was to redesign the state to a form appropriate to the social conditions of independent Africa. In the event, however, it was not the *state* that was redesigned; it was the colonial power map that was *reconstituted*. In the course of that reconstitution, the constitutional order became not an arbiter in the power process, but a crucial element in political warfare, an instrument of and from the appropriation of power. The *Constitution lost most of its claim to being the basic law* of the land, that arbiter in the power process. State elites then revised the domain of administrative law so as to reserve to themselves full and unfettered discretion over public affairs; this was done, inter alia, by strengthening all aspects of public order law: security, meetings, police powers, processions and marches, and aspects of licensing. Thus, the coercive administrative law of the legal order continued to be strengthened even as the essence of constitutionalism was being drained from the reconstitution.

Reconstituted States

Three aspects of the reconstitutions of most African states stand out as the clearest evidence of that result. The first is the emergence and predominance of a form of imperial presidentialism, the second is a perceptible shrinkage of the political arena, and the third is the preeminence of discretion as the basis of "constitutional" power.

The Rise of the Imperial Presidency

The fusion of executive power in a *single individual* was perhaps inevitable in the historical process of redesigning the state in Africa.... [U]nlike the medieval monarchs of Europe, the African presidents do not claim any *divine* right to rule, do not demand obsequiousness from the public at large, and are, at least in point of theory, *constitutionally* subject to popular accreditation. However, the indices of imperium, the exclusive constitutional right to direct the affairs of state, are quite clear.

The first of these is the supremacy of the office of the President over all organs of government. The semblance of separation of powers that remains is, at best, of administrative significance only.... Although supremacy of the presidency over the legislature is usually indirect (the latter is not constituted by the former), its effectiveness is exercised through the (dominant) political party.

The second index is the immunity of the President from the legal process, civil and criminal, as long as he remains in office.... The purpose ... is the protection of the dignity of the office rather than of the holder per se. What is interesting, however, is the political interpretation that state elites in Africa have placed on this immunity: a President is "above" the law. He cannot be sued, nor can his decisions be challenged, in court or elsewhere. The second consequence is the protection of the President against abuse, slander, and other forms of disparagement.... [T]he ordinary law of libel and slander is irrelevant. The practice is to "criminalize" any utterance or conduct deemed to be disparaging to the reputation of the presidency or to its occupant; for this purpose most liberal use has been made of public order law, especially the inherited penal codes. Thus, the immunity of a President is safeguarded, and all criticism, whether legitimate or not, is censored.

The third index of *imperium* is the indefinite eligibility of a President for reelection; the reasons for it are several. The first has to do with the mystique and sanctity surrounding the public image of the *founder* president; although such figures are now few and far between, this attitude seems to have passed on to second or even third generation civilian and military leaders. The second reason involves elite perceptions of public expectations of leadership; as early as 1966, for example, the office of the President in Kenya was arguing that to be understood by the people, government must be personalized in one individual who is easily accessible, sympathetic, understanding, and authoritative. An essential element of that personalization was the individual's continuity in office.

The third reason inheres in the argument that political and economic stability requires continuity in leadership *at the top* . . . .

The fourth index of *imperium* is the high degree of paranoia that tends to surround the *exercise* of executive power in Africa, a special characteristic of military regimes, but not limited to them. This paranoia is perhaps most visible in the high attrition rate found among political functionaries and public service bureaucrats in many governments. This potential for attrition, a technique usually orchestrated from the presidency, has several important consequences: it creates tremendous uncertainty within the channels through which presidential power is exercised; it generates a concern for survival within those channels that translates easily into sycophantic behavior toward the presidency; and it identifies the presidency as the only source of final redress even for the simplest of problems. . . . [Thus, the] presidency in Africa usually tends to "overreach" itself, both in political decisions and in public utterances.

The Shrinking Political Arena

The arena of politics in any country ought, at least in theory, to be open to any citizen, especially if qualified, under the law, to vote. The mechanisms for participation in that arena may vary, but it is generally accepted in all known political systems that the most important is the political party. . . . In Africa, however, the reconstitutions have recast the political parties into different kinds of instruments; instead of expanding the arena of politics in any or all of the above ways, political parties have been used to shrink it ... [primarily] through constitutional and other legal instruments that confer supremacy in matters of public policy on a single political party; the most comprehensive statement is found in Article 3 of the constitution of the United Republic of Tanzania, 1977. Seventeen Article 3 of the 1984 Constitution appears to have relaxed somewhat this comprehensive submission of the Constitution to the Party by providing, inter alia, that the party exercises its jurisdiction in accordance also, with the state constitution. . . .

When, as often happens in one-party presidencies, the Chief Executive is also the *de jure* (or de facto) leader of the Party, the political arena may shrink even further. Skillful manipulation of the Party machinery can easily shift its entire mandate to the presidency. . . .

This power of the Party excludes the citizenry at large from any meaningful control over the conduct of government; with respect to the legislature, that shrinkage means that the electorate may be totally excluded from the determination of parliamentary (or similar assembly) membership or be subjected to a carefully orchestrated routine for that purpose. In the one-party presidencies, party membership has become essential for entry into and for maintenance of legislative roles at local and national levels; these roles can be terminated through simple expulsion from the Party. The electorate is then faced with the task, *under the supervision of the Party*, of finding a replacement. This is clearly a contest the electorate cannot win.

Discretion as the Basis of Power

The most liberal of jurists will concede that though the essence of constitutionalism may lie in the limitation of arbitrary power, "the limiting of government . . . is not to be the weakening of it. The problem is to maintain a proper balance between power and law."

The rise of an imperial presidency and the shrinkage of the political arena as a result of the entry of political parties in the constitutional process both point to the fact that in Africa, the issue of power and law has been resolved, for the time at least, in favor of power. Therefore the *legal* basis of executive power (if this must be found) is to be sought in the domain of administrative law, which, it is worth recalling, was and remains a complex maze of highly structured and coercive instruments. What the reconstitution added to this complex was a degree of discretion that even courts sometimes found difficult to circumscribe. Discretion as a basis of power is most visible in the ideology and operation of national or public security legislation.

The operative concept of national or public security was kept deliberately fuzzy. Such fuzziness is not only an African problem; what is peculiar to Africa is the breadth of that concept in security laws. A typical definition is to be found in Kenya's Preservation of Public Security Act (Cap. 57), which is so generous that one could say that the definition says no more than that "the preservation of public security *means* whatever the authority to invoke security powers says it is." Indeed, courts in some African countries have so decided. . . .

The most important point is that in an ever-increasing number of African countries, security powers can be and often are exercised *without* recourse to a declaration of emergency. All that is required in Kenya and Malawi, for example, is for the relevant authority to indicate by gazette notice that *in his own subjective judgment*, sufficient grounds exist for the exercise of those powers. As long as such a notice is in effect, a whole set of measures, ranging from indefinite detention without trial, restriction of movement including the imposition of curfews, press censorship, to suspension of any legislation (other than the Constitution and the enabling Act itself), may be taken; in practice, gazette notices are never withdrawn. As a result, security powers are permanently available *and* exercisable. An important consequence of this is that the boundaries between security powers, stricto sensu, and ordinary criminal law are often blurred.

Two main grounds have been used to defend this widespread use of discretionary power. The first is symbolic: the national (or public) security claim has a respectable history.... The second defense argues that as the constitution expressly permits the exercise of security powers, elites can regard that exercise as *legitimate*....

The formalism with which the need for security powers is argued to the public accords well with their primary function: the strengthening of the presidency at the expense of other organs of government....

The Military and the Idea of Constitutionalism

The preceding analysis suggests that in many parts of Africa, the idea of the constitution clearly *excludes* the notion of a basic (or fundamental) law other than in a purely "constitutive" sense. Civilian regimes have reached that position in fact or in law....

There can be [little] doubt that the *immediate reason* for the vast majority of military coups in Africa has been the failure of "constitutional" government and the desire "to wipe the political and constitutional slate clear." Some African scholars have [even] hailed military intervention as a "necessary tonic to decadent constitutionalism." The record of military government in Africa in the last three decades with the occurrences of more than seventy *coups d'état*, does not, in my view, disclose any ground for that optimism. That record indicates only that military regimes consider [t]he *constitutive value* of constitutions important. Virtually every announcement of suspension or abrogation of a constitution after a *coup d'état* in the 1960s was accompanied by commitment to the drawing up of a new one; these commitments were kept in some countries (Ghana, Nigeria, Sierra Leone). In the 1970s and 1980s, military rulers became even more organized; they began to suspend or abrogate only those constitutional provisions that formed the basis of their power: legislative, executive, and judicial powers, and provisions dealing with the protection of fundamental rights. The "constitutive" provisions remained virtually unscathed and survived many of changes in military and civilian government; in Uganda the 1967 document is still recognized as the constitution of the state.

The military attitude to governance appears to be no different from the civilian attitude described above.... In short, far from wiping the political and constitutional slate clean, the military have only reproduced the basic power structures operated by civilian regimes. While clinging to some notion of the constitution, they have advanced the issue of constitutionalism no further than civilian regimes have.

Some Reflections

This chapter set out to examine the condition of constitutional govern-ment in Africa; what we found is a situation *in which only the idea of the constitution* has survived. The most fundamental of the functions of a constitution, at least in liberal democratic theory, to regulate the use of executive power, is clearly not one that African constitutions that have survived military intervention now perform. It is important therefore that we conclude with some reflections on what that condition means for governance in the next century.

Do Constitutions Matter?

Perhaps the first issue one should reflect on is whether constitutions really matter? In the Preface to his study of a number of Western and Eastern constitutions, S.E. Finer warns that no one constitution is an entirely realistic description of what actually happens and precious few are one hundred percent unrealistic fictions bearing no relationship whatsoever to what goes on. His message is that even when constitutions are being violated, subverted, or otherwise ignored, it is important for scientists to examine them and practitioners to maintain faith in them. Constitutions therefore *do* matter. It is interesting in this respect that Swaziland, which abrogated its Independence Constitution in 1973, has had to reinstate a number of important provisions of that document over the years.

This issue becomes not whether constitutions matter, but what consti-tutional regime best fits the needs of particular societies? Here again Finer's observation is most apt. He says "Different historical contexts have generated different preoccupations: different preoccupations have generat-ed different emphases."

Constitutional arrangements look both to the past and to the future. Hence, although certain basic and cross-cultural functions are and should be expected of any constitution, one cannot say that a single model is good for all societies at all times. The falsity of that assumption has clearly been demonstrated in the historical experience of sub-Saharan Africa over the past 30 years. Autochthony is therefore an indispensable part of constitu-tional development. What appears to have gone drastically wrong in Africa is not the search for autochthony but rather the extreme disregard of constitutionalism that this process has assumed. . . .

Questions and Comments on Okoth-Ogendo

1. Consider why, according to Okoth-Ogendo, many African nations have adopted constitutions. Do they serve as symbols or aspirations? Are they intended to entrench legal norms? Consider the proposition that Okoth-Ogendo's arguments support Frankenberg's concerns about identifying the proper subjects of comparison. If the African constitutions discussed by Okoth-Ogendo are units comparable to those Sunstein discusses, Sunstein's arguments seem plainly incomplete, if not wrong. A defender of Sunstein might reply that he was discussing the functions of "true" constitutions. Consider the predominance of (and/or English-speakers' greater familiarity with) scholars from the U.S., U.K., Germany and other 'western' constitutional states as an explanation for what constitutions are considered to be at the core of the concept of constitutions.

2.   Consider also whether Okoth-Ogendo is at once critiquing understandings of constitutions as inadequate to describe and understand the functions of African constitutions and at the same time critiquing African failures to, e.g., constrain and harness presidential power facilitated through those constitutions. Does his critique raise questions of "legocentrism"—that is, whether the responses to the problems he identifies should be sought in law or elsewhere?

Carlos Santiago Nino, *Transition to Democracy, Corporatism and Presidentialism with Special Reference to Latin America*, in Constitutionalism and Democracy: Transitions in the Contemporary World (Douglas Greenberg, Stanley N. Katz, Melanie Beth Oliviero, Steven C. Wheatley, eds., 1993).

[Many writers have noted the expansive authority of presidents in Latin America. See, e.g., Claudio Grossman, *States of Emergency: Latin America and the United States*, in Constitutionalism and Rights: The Influence of the United States Constitution Abroad 185 (Louis Henkin and Albert J. Rosenthal eds., 1990) ("Presidential domination, supported by the political, cultural and socioeconomic structure of Latin American societies, is a general feature that has permeated Latin American systems since their inception.") (For additional materials on presidential as compared to parliamentary systems, see Chapter VII below.) This state of presidential dominance has constitutional support in Latin America as well. In many Latin American constitutions, the president has substantial powers to declare emergencies which, in turn, authorize substantial increases in presidential governance powers. Such limits as are provided for in constitutions have often been abused.

While writers like Grossman suggest that Latin American constitutions' recognition of a distinction between a state of peace and state of emergency contributes to human rights abuses and should be abolished or mitigated, Nino argues that the presidential form of governance itself should be abandoned because it stands in the way of the increased political participation he sees as essential to eliminate the deleterious effects of "corporatism" in Latin America. "Corporatism," as he describes it, is a condition in which powerful elite institutions, including but not limited to business corporations, control and interpenetrate the government, while the government itself, through interconnections with powerful elites, affects and strengthens the power of these elites.

Although not explicitly framed in constitutional terms, his argument, like Grossman's, suggests that a change in constitutional structure is needed to facilitate what other writers would call "constitutionalism." Thus, it offers the possibility that a written constitution can actually obstruct constitutionalism.]

* * *

This chapter seeks to connect the movement toward revision of the presidentialist system of government, perceptible in several Latin American countries, with some sociostructural variables with considerable impact on the process of consolidation of democracy. In particular, I intend to show that as the main threats to that consolidation of democracy are the pressures of so-called "corporative groups"—the military, the Church, the trade unions, and entrepreneurial conglomerates—it is necessary to develop mechanisms for wider popular participation and stronger political parties to counteract those pressures.... [and] ... to modify the presidential system of government to allow for the operation of mechanisms to contain the pressures of corporations, thus amplifying the space of the democratic process.

Transition to Democracy and Corporatism

As we all know, in the past decade a wave of democratization began to move in most of Latin America, finally reaching some islands of authoritarianism such as Chile. This process is often called "transition to democracy." ...

I want to argue that whatever their origins or modes, the main challenge faced by processes of transition in consolidating democratic institutions is the containment of the network of de facto power relationships that corporations weave, as they take advantage of the vacuum left by representatives of popular sovereignty....

For our purpose, it is ... important to mention how corporatism is linked with populist and authoritarian experiences in the context of Latin American political cycles. As James M. Mallo[y] says,

> It is now evident that populism was and is based on an implicit *corporatist* image of sociopolitical organization. With the exception of Vargas, the populist preference for a corporatist solution to the pressure of modernization was seldom stated explicitly, but there seems little gainsaying that populism has always shown a high affinity for corporatist principles of organizing the relations between state and society.

He adds that populism in its first phases emphasized mobilization in an "inclusionary" way, trying to broaden the set of actors in the political process while controlling them through organizations "formed, in sectoral and functional criteria thereby fragmenting their support groups into parallel primary organizational structures joined at the top by interlocking sectoral elites." ... [C]orporatism is a way of controlling and containing the social strata that populism seeks to promote, thus avoiding social conflicts.... [C]orporatism is not exclusively tied to populism but is a structural element of Latin American politics with different manifestations and cultural roots in the Spanish attitude toward hierarchical status, patronages, clientelism, etc.

The interlude between this connection between corporatism and populism and that between the corporatism and the bureaucratic-authoritarian State is the social situation that Samuel Huntington called "praetorianism." This is a system that combines a low degree of institutionalization with a high degree of participation of mobile social forces that penetrate the political spheres, resulting in confrontations between new active social forces and between them and the traditional establishment. Malloy describes the process in several countries of Latin America in the late 1950s and from the mid-1960s until the early 1970s:

> An important aspect of the praetorianization of Latin American politics during this period was the fact that although the formal state apparatuses [sic] in the region grew markedly, this was accompanied not by an increase in the power and efficiency of the State but rather by the reverse. The continuing reality of dependence was a critical factor in the development of states that were formally large and powerful but in practice weak. Another factor was a kind of *de facto* disaggregation of the state as various particularistic interest blocs in a sense captured relevant pieces of the state which they manipulated to their own benefit.

Of course, at its extreme, this process of disaggregation of the State affects also its monopoly of coercion, so that violence accompanies social confrontations.

... [T]his praetorianization of Latin American politics has led to a social "impasse" in which no sector has stable domination. The way out of this impasse [according to Guillermo O'Donnell] has been "the bureaucratic-authoritarian State, which is a system of political and economic exclusion of the popular sector and which emerges after a substantial degree of industrialization has been achieved, and also after and to a large extent as a consequence of substantial political activation of the popular sector." The popular sector is excluded by abolishing its channels of participation and by controlling its organization. The bureaucratic-authoritarian state is open to other corporations, the military, in some cases the Church, and an entrepreneurial bourgeoisie, partly connected with international capital and partly protected from it by its association with the state and its enjoyment of a system of privileges and shields....

Of course, when these bureaucratic-authoritarian regimes founder and are replaced by liberal democracies, as is happening in the present processes of transition to democracy in Latin America, the previously favored groups struggle to retain as much as possible of their privileges, competing hard with the popular sector as it reenters the scene. The popular sector's return to the practical field of course overcomes its illegitimate exclusion, but often organizations claiming the privileges that the populist ideology ascribe to them reactivate corporatism....

Corporatism, Popular Participation, and Political Parties

A Conception of a Deliberate Democracy. . . . [T]he first premise of my argument [is] that the main obstacle to be overcome by the process of transition to a consolidated democracy in Latin American countries is the interpenetration of corporative power relations, remnants of previous populist and authoritarian stages, within the political structure of a liberal democracy.

My second premise . . . conceives of democracy as an organization of the process of collective discussion about the right standards on which to organize public life. It assumes that the democratic process so conceived, insofar as it respects some structural requirements of the process of deliberation and decision making, enjoys some epistemological reliability, its internal mechanisms generating an inherent tendency toward impartiality that is the mark of moral validity in intersubjective issues. The premise asserts that the strengthening of the working of democracy against corporative powers requires the broadening of direct popular participation in decision making and control of governmental action, perfecting the mechanisms of representation, and strengthening political parties, which are themselves internally democratic and open, disciplined, and ideologically defined.

This view of democracy presupposes that individuals—who are basically moral persons—are its natural agents and that the freedom and quality of their intervention in the democratic process should be preserved and expanded, which is not the case when corporations intermediate. Besides, this conception of democracy as a regimentation of moral discourse presupposes that the primary objects of decision in the democratic process are, not *crude interests, but principles* that legitimize a certain balance of interests impartially. Therefore, corporations that bring people together around common interests rather than around moral views about how to deal with interests cannot be the protagonists of the democratic process. . . .

Popular Participation. Therefore, to strengthen the democratic power of common citizens against that of corporations, it is crucial to broaden and to deepen popular participation in discussion and decision. I believe that even the imposition of obligatory voting is justified as a piece of legitimate paternalism, given the problem that exists when many individuals in some sectors of society fail to vote because they are unaware of like-minded others, are not organized, and believe most individuals votes are of no account. Another factor to consider is that the mechanisms of representation necessary in large and complex societies are prone to subversion by corporative power because representatives are subject to corruption. . . . Therefore, it is essential to widen the ways of *direct* participation of the people whose interests are at stake, by general procedures such as plebiscites or popular consultations, or by decentralizing decisions into smaller ambits in which the people concerned can affect them. . . .

. . . Benjamin Barber asserts:

If the corporation is not to defeat democracy, then democracy must defeat the corporation—which is to say that the curbing of monopoly and the transformation of corporatism is a political, not an economic task. Democracy proclaims priority of the political over the economic, the modern corporation rebuts that claim by its very existence. But unitary democracy [meaning one which seeks consensus by process of a cohesive identification with the community] is too easily assimilated to the unitary aspects of corporatism, with possible results that can only be called Fascistic. And liberal democracy is too vulnerable—its citizens too passive and its ideas of freedom and individualism too illusory—to recognize, let alone to battle with the mammoth modern corporation that has assumed the identity and ideology of the traditional family firm. Strong democracy (that is participative democracy) has no qualms about inventing and transforming society in the name of a democratically achieved vision and it may be able to engage the multinational corporation in a meaningful struggle. Yet the corporate society and the corporate mentality stand in the way of the idea of active citizenship that is indispensable to strong democracy.

Additionally, direct participation of the population in the decisions that affect them may tend to diminish the social tensions associated with the so-called "crisis of democracy" and corporative struggles. In opposition to the recommendation of the Trilateral Commission that such crises should be countered by restraint of discussion and participation, and faithful to the idea pungently expressed by Al Smith that "the evils of democracy are cured with more democracy," I think that the broadening of direct participation operates as an escape valve for social pressures and helps limit them insofar as people acquire consciousness of the scarcity of the resources available to satisfy competing demands.

The Role of Political Parties. ... [O]rganizations that bring together people, not on the basis of crude interests, but of principles, ideologies, and moral outlooks ... are *political parties* when they are conceived of as the bearers of programs about the organization of society based on fundamental principles of political morality. They are indispensable in a modern and large society, not only because they train professional politicians who profess those principles and purport to put them in practice if duly elected, but because they exempt people from justifying their vote before each other on the basis of principles; it is enough to vote for a party that organizes its proposals on the basis of public and general principles.

Political parties are the main antibodies protecting democratic health against corporative power. Their reasons for being are exactly antithetic: to represent some particular interests in the case of corporations, and to defend principles that legitimate certain *composition* of interests from an impartial viewpoint, in the case of political parties. Therefore an inverse relation exists between their respective strengths....

The Centrality of Parliament. The deterioration of the role of political parties in favor of corporations also involves the erosion of the importance of the natural scene of those parties: parliament. Corporations naturally prefer to exert pressures and achieve agreements in the quiet of offices than in the noisy pluralistic and more public parliamentary corridors. Of course, the administration tends to follow suit, preserving some of the practices inherited from previous authoritarian governments (for instance, the Argentinean Central Bank has powers equivalent to those that the Constitution of the country grants to the National Congress, e.g., the power to concede special lines of credit, which amount to subsidies)....

However, even though the fortifying of political parties and of the parliamentary institutions contributes to protecting the democratic system from corporative power, this remains true only insofar as political parties and parliamentary bodies do not transform themselves into other corporations, developing elites with distinctive interests and prone to compromise with those of traditional corporative groups. This change occurs when parties weaken their ideological commitment, do not promote debates on essential questions of political morality, block channels of participation, operate through methods of patronage and clientelism, and resort to personalism and *"caudillism."* This situation is then reflected in parliament, by a lack of representativeness, by a discourse both ideologically vacuous and detached from the experiences and interests of the people represented, and by a general appearance of opacity and self-service.

For that reason, the strengthening of the political parties and parliament to contain corporative power requires the opening of parties to broad popular participation, the promotion of permanent political debates within them, the perfection of the internal democratic mechanism for choosing party authorities and candidates, and the openness of the management of funds....

Strong Democracy and Presidentialism

Methodological Remarks. After stating my first premise, that corporative political power is one of the greatest obstacles to the consolidation of democracy in Latin America, and the second, that two of the most important contributive factors to the containment of corporatism are the broadening and deepening of popular participation in decisions and control, and the strengthening of participative and ideologically committed political parties.... I am ready to defend my last two-fold premise: that strong democracy is functionally incompatible with the extreme forms of presidentialism typical of Latin American constitutions, and that when presidentialism is not accompanied by limited or conditioned forms of democracy, tensions are generated that often lead to the breakdown of the institutional system.

Before arguing for this premise, I must comment on a methodological point of great importance. There is a longstanding disagreement ... about the capacity of law and institutional design to influence social changes.... In the field of law this disagreement can be illustrated with the paradigmatic position of two great jurists: Friedrich Karl von Savigny and Jeremy Bentham. Savigny professed a historicist conception of law, according to which the true law is found and not made; it is found in the spirit of the people and in social customs; legislation and institutional design should be extremely cautious and follow, not promote social development. Bentham, a fervent believer in law as an instrument of social engineering, devoted his life to the writing of codes for different nations; his preaching influenced the modern conception of Parliament as an active body through which legislation can achieve social reforms.... Truth seems to be here between the extremes, since it is undeniable both that the law and institutional design have on many occasions considerable impact on social developments, and that society is not a malleable material that adapts plastically to deliberate legislation, subject as it is to causal factors other than the legal....

... Even when true that strong democracy is contributive to the containment of corporative power, a limited democracy does not always lead to corporatism and hence to conditioned democracy in the Latin American way (this is obviously true in the case of the United States where the power of corporations is a complex phenomenon not assimilable to Latin American corporatism). On the other hand, the adoption of the presidentialist system of government is undoubtedly correlated, when conjoined with some conditions to be studied, with the recurrence of specific social effects that lead to institutional disruptions.

In this respect a study by Prof. Fred W. Riggs, prefaced by the following remark, is extremely revealing:

> One starting point for analysis might be in the proposition that some 33 Third World countries (but none in the First or Second) have adopted presidentialist constitutions. Almost universally these polities have endured disruptive catastrophes usually in the form of one or more coups d'etat, whereby conspiratorial groups of military officers seize power, suspend the constitution, displace elected officials, impose martial law and promote authoritarian rule: recent examples in Korea, South Vietnam, Liberia, and many Latin American countries come to mind.... By contrast, almost two-thirds of the Third World countries which have adopted parliamentary constitutions, usually based upon British and French models have maintained their regimes and avoided the disruptions typical of all American-type systems.

Preconditions of a Stable Presidential System. .... [S]everal problems of a presidentialist regime—executive-legislative confrontations, paralysis of the assembly, weakness of the party system, and the politics of the court—... have led to collapse in more than 30 such regimes outside the United States....

... [F]or the presidential system to work smoothly ... parties ... must try to form coalitions prior to the elections in order to have some change of forming a majority; in a parliamentary system parties can go to elections supporting well-defined programs and try to form coalitions in parliament itself after the elections are over. A second factor (which allows presidentialism to work in the United States and involves a weakening of parties) is the lack of party discipline, which, according to Riggs, may be "a necessary condition for the success of a presidentialist regime, whereas if party discipline were enforced, the capacity of government to govern would be severely impaired whenever the president belonged to one party and the opposition party had a congressional majority." . . .

Another factor that weakens political parties within a presidentialist system is the effect on them of defeat in elections; many of the nonpolitical functions that parties perform in a parliamentary system cannot be carried out in a presidentialist one because parties are not tied to a more or less stable representation in Parliament. . . . Because parties in a presidential system cannot be ideologically committed but must present broad stances and make many compromises to win support for their presidential candidates from many social sectors, they awaken little enthusiasm in voters, most of whom do not identify themselves with any party but just choose the lesser evil. In sum, the presidential system faces the following dilemma with regard to political parties. Either the parties become weaker and weaker as a result of the nature of political competition under this system—which, given some other social and cultural conditions, may make ample room for the corporations' exercise of their political muscle; or else, if some other factors operate to preserve the parties' strength, as in Argentina, they help create the tensions that are typical of the presidentialist system, blockages between the powers, exhaustion of the figure of the president, etc., which will be commented on below.

The other variable that marks the U.S. system is directly connected with the above characterization of a strong democracy: that is popular participation, particularly with the propensity to vote. Riggs is explicit about this point:

> One of the limitations of a presidentialist system of government appears to be voter apathy. Despite its long history and the apparent commitment of Americans to representative democracy, voting turnout is notably less in the United States than in virtually all parliamentary governments. We normally assume, of course, that popular participation in elections is necessary for the health of democratic institutions. However, sad to say, a low voter turnout seems to be a cost entailed by various para-constitutional aspects of a presidential system. In addition, it could even be a para-constitutional feature. . . . The higher the level of popular participation in voting, the greater would be the contradiction between the interests of the voting majority. The presidentialist system, therefore, works most smoothly when voting participation remains fairly low. . . . A conspicuous reason for the skewed distribution of voters can be found in the substance of a party platform. In order to secure the support of a majority of voters, a majority required by the arithmetic of a winner-take-all presidential competition—these platforms have to take ambiguous stands on many issues that divide public opinion. But such issues are also likely to attract the greatest interest especially of poor people. . . . The price for high voter turnout is lively and divisive political controversy—whereas

low voter turnout is linked to apathy and indifference.... To put the negative case, mass participation is less threatening to the survival of parliamentary than of presidentialist regimes.

This comment underscores a point of great importance to the comparative study of the United States' presidential system and some unsuccessful ones, such as the Argentine. In the United States the low voting turnout has a feedback effect; presidential candidates address themselves to potential voters.... By contrast, in Argentina, for instance, a 1912 law introduced obligatory voting, which since 1916 has more than trebled the voting turnout in comparison with elections held under voluntary voting. This indicated that the middle class, mainly through Peronism, participated actively in the electoral process; those parties were at different times the only winners of free elections, permanently displacing the conservative parties that held power before 1916. Although candidates tend to be vague in their proposals and to compromise to get wider bases of support, a varying interest and even enthusiasm are preserved due in part to emotional factors, such as those involved in the Peronist-antiPeronist controversy. Rigg's suggestion about the threatening aspect of high levels of participation in a presidentialist system seems to be confirmed by the considerable political stability in Argentina prior to 1916 and the extreme instability afterward without obligatory voting. Obviously, those displaced by the results of massive voting sought other ways of acceding to power....

The Dysfunctionalities of Presidentialism ...

... In other words, the two features characteristic of democracy that serve to defend it against the phenomenon of corporatism (that has arisen in Latin America due to different and complex factors) are absent in the most successful presidentialist systems in the world and there are reasons to connect their absence with its success....

... [T]he presidential system divides the expression of popular sovereignty between the president and parliament, each of whom has a sort of veto power over some decisions of the other. When different political parties control the parliament and the presidency (a situation usually reflecting majorities that varied through time) the parties' dynamics of confrontation is mirrored in the relation between the powers of the state, leading to fights and stalemates. The United States avoids this danger as a result, as I said, to the weakness of the parties and the electoral system; the President is able to collect majorities outside the limits of his own party and to govern even when his party is the minority one in either or both of Houses of Congress. The situation is quite different in countries such as Argentina in which the traditional strength of the parties is enhanced by the discipline promoted by proportional representational. In that country several important initiatives of the present national government of the Radical Party were blocked or delayed by the opposition parties, not always by a majoritarian vote, but by parliamentary maneuvers, such as withholding a "quorum" for a session, which are sometimes addressed to obtaining unrelated advantages.... Of course, these confrontations between administration and Parliament are dangerous because in a presidentialist system the latter has no direct or indirect power to influence the course of the administration, thus the antagonism leads to complete stalemate.

In the third place, even when the parties are not seriously antagonistic, the presidential system makes it very difficult for them to collaborate in the same government, as is sometimes required in a national crisis, by an internal or external war, or by the threats of corporative power. . . .

In the fourth place, the confrontation between the parties often leads to the political exhaustion of the President's . . . popularity long before the expiration of his term, which usually coincides with the point of retraction of the economic cycles . . . to which Latin American countries have long been subject. The rigidity of the term of the government in the Presidential system means the political crisis cannot be vented through an escape valve. The President often reaches a point at which, though he still has an enormous set of formal powers, he has lost credibility, popularity, and parliamentary support. The only way to replace him, other than through his voluntary resignation, would be through impeachment. Impeachments are all but impossible to carry out; they require an accusation of misconduct and a qualified majority, which implies the support of the President's party, not usually willing to commit suicide. The President himself is not generally inclined to resign; he feels that he has a mandate for the whole period and does not want to become a historical failure. In Argentina this situation occurred in 1976; several people thought that the coup could have been avoided, or at least delayed, if Isabel Peron had been removed by resignation or impeachment, or if there had been another system of government, under which she could have been confined as head of state to more circumscribed functions and an acceptable head of government appointed.

. . . [Thus] the elements that may make democracy strong against corporatist pressures—wide popular participation and ideologically defined, disciplined, and broadly participative political parties—are ill suited to a presidentialist system because they generate tensions difficult to handle within it and they aggravate its inherent difficulties.

Conclusion: Toward a More Parliamentary System of Government for Latin America

My reasoning has had the following course: one of the main challenges facing the process of transition to a full consolidated democracy in Latin America is the need to overcome the entrenched network of power relations and privileges established by different corporations during earlier periods; corporations seek to preserve these power relations and privileges in the transition, generating distortions and crises, such as that provoked by inflation, that create pressures on the democratic system.

The best means to counter this corporative power is to recover a sense of a polity governed by universal and impersonal principles chosen in a process of public justification and dialogue by individual citizens, who, unidentified with any particular interests, preserve the capacity of adopting different ones. In practical terms, this requires the promotion of broad popular participation in voting, discussion, and direct decisions, and political parties organized on the basis of principles and programs, with active and participative members and with an internal democracy whose results are enforced in a disciplined way. But this kind of a strong democracy is functionally incompatible with a presidentialist system of government, which tends to weaken political parties; further, even if this weakening does not occur for diverse historical and cultural factors, the difficulties inherent in the presidentialist system—the erosion of the presidential figure, blockages between powers, the difficulties of forming coalitions—are serious and dangerous threats to the stability of the system.

This reasoning leads to an obvious conclusion: the presidentialist system of government, in Latin American conditions that include the phenomenon of corporatism, is an obstacle to the consolidation of democratic institutions. The transition to democracy would be considerably facilitated by constitutional reforms that incorporate parliamentary mechanisms.

Despite the setbacks mentioned above, many people and groups are deeply attached to the presidential system of government in Latin America. Some on the right argue for it on the basis of tradition and the widespread inclination to seek strong leaders, supposedly embedded in the Hispanic mentality. I think that these arguments are not serious enough; traditions are not above criticisms and have no automatic value, particularly when they lead to obviously evil results over a long stretch of history. It is also fair to say that the *côup d'état* is more of a tradition in Latin America than is the presidential system. As for the alleged Hispanic inclination for strong leaders, this would be in any case something to counteract institutionally rather than promote; further it is a rather dubious postulate given the easy adaptation of Spain, for example, to a parliamentary system after 40 years of a *caudillo's* rule, and the similar searches for strong leaders in the past by other nations with different traditions.

More serious is the argument of some conservatives that a parliamentary or mixed system of government would lead to unstable administrations in Latin America, given the climate of economic crisis, social strife, and political tensions. The answer to this argument is that there are mechanisms, e.g., the constructive vote of no-confidence, that considerably attenuate the risk of the collapse of governments, as has been shown in Germany and Spain. Besides, and more importantly, very often the circumstances that lead to a change of government in a parliamentary system are the same that in a presidential system lead to the exhausting of the presidential figure, to a stalemate between the administration and parliament, and to a hard confrontation between the parties, all of which often create the vacuum filled by corporative power, indirectly or through military rule.

The left also defends the presidential system. Recently the Brazilian Roberto Mangabeira Unger argued for the preservation of the presidential system in his country with some important modifications: the provision of power to the President to dissolve Congress and of power to Congress to call for a new presidential election. The kernel of his argument was that only the presidential candidate is apt to break the network of power binding conservative party leaders and to mobilize the masses after a program of structural transformation. But this argument touches precisely on the main weakness of the presidential system: if there is a wide consensus on specific program and a certain man or group to carry it on, any system would work; the presidential one would only add the risk of abuses against minorities. The problem occurs when, as often happens in Latin America, there is no such a consensus. The presidential system is the least likely to promote its formation; on the contrary, it promotes dissent, even between parties with similar views, because of the struggle for the presidency. If a president with a narrow electoral base tries to enforce a program of deep structural transformation, as president Salvador Allende tried to do in Chile, he is liable to be confronted by powerful forces of the opposition and conservative groups. As Arend Lijphart has argued, a parliamentary system is more suited to govern societies in which no definite majorities exist in support of a program and a consensus has to be worked out. I envisage that, for instance, in Argentina no program of deep structural transformation could be carried out without the support of the two majority parties that confront the corporative pressures maintaining the status quo, and that combined support is impossible to obtain within a presidential system. On the other hand, the progressive sector of both parties may well reach an agreement in Parliament to support a program of transformation through a collaborative government, if the struggle for the Presidency ceases. . . .

The crucial advantage of a more parliamentary system would be to make the formation itself of government as responsive as possible to the consensus of society. This consensus is better reflected in parliamentary elections than in presidential ones; the former are more frequent, more sensible to the differing hues of public opinion, and more adaptable to the need of the people to express themselves in situations of crisis. Of course, the mixed system of government allows both parliamentary and presidential elections to influence the formation of the government. That the government reflects flexibly the consensus of society enhances most of the values in the light of which a political system may be appraised. That coincidence between a government and its measures and social consensus deepens the *objective legitimacy* of the political system, under a deliberate conception of democracy; I have elaborated this topic elsewhere. The fact that the government is necessarily backed by popular consensus also strengthens the *stability* of the democratic system; as we have seen, the mixed system allows for the structural transformations necessary to contain corporative power, and provides a more direct barrier against that power, constituted by a more cohesive democratic front. Finally, the correlation between the formation of government and consensus contributes to the *efficacy* of the political system; the lack of political and popular support for a government (evidenced by the last period of Raoul Ricardo Alfonsin's government in Argentina) makes it incapable of effective measures, stymied as it is by blockages, criticisms, and lack of observance of its enactments, which are the consequences of the absence of consensus.

Of course, the inability of the presidential system of government to allow for the expression of a wider consensus than that represented by the party occupying the presidency is itself the main obstacle, in many countries of Latin America, to reaching the broad agreement between the parties necessary to move away from the presidential system.

Note on Constitutions as Obstacles to Constitutionalism

1. Nino's essay ends on a deeply pessimistic note, suggesting that the existing constitutional and social structures will prevent transition to the structure he has argued will improve constitutional government. But if presidentialism is a "constitutive" feature of constitutions in Latin America, does this favor a more modest approach to change, such as the elimination or curtailment of emergency powers provisions, argued for by Grossman?

2. How can presidentialism be an obstacle to constitutionalism? Has presidentialism "succeeded" in the United States? What are the criteria for answering that question?

3. Professor Minasse Haile has argued that the Ethiopian Constitution of 1994, "instead of solving the problems facing the country such as tribalism, denial of human rights and poverty, has exacerbated them." Minasse Haile, The *New Ethiopian Constitution: Its Impact Upon Unity, Human Rights and Development*, 20 Suffolk Transnat'l L. Rev. 1, 4–5, 20–22 (1996). Consider his argument on tribalism:

> [P]articularly recently, tribal conflict has been extant in Ethiopia. From 1936 to 1941, Mussolini's Fascists attempted to divide the Ethiopian people along ethnic lines to facilitate their rule of the country. In the 1970's, the Communist regime in Ethiopia, known as the Derg, meaning committee in Amharic, resuscitated the same tribal weapon to the same end. Later, liberation movements based on ethnic groups in the country expelled the Derg and established themselves as the government of Ethiopia. The consequences of these events were the intensification of tribal hostility throughout the country and the secession of Eritrea. These events should have impelled the drafters of the new Ethiopian Constitution to endeavor to lessen the problem of tribalism in the country. However, the makers of the constitution have entrenched and glorified ethnicity by establishing a "federal government" based on tribal affiliation and by granting to the subunits, styled as "states," such a disproportionate share of power as to make them almost sovereign entities. This non-sequitur of curing tribalism with even more institutionalized tribalism, represents the culmination

of efforts of the internal and external enemies of the Ethiopians, stretching over a millennium, to undermine the unity of the nation.

By dividing the country into 9 states whose boundaries are determined by the locations of the major tribal groups, authorizing each tribal state to determine the language it will use, devolving substantial power to the states and providing for a right of secession for "every nation, nationality and people in Ethiopia," he argues, the Constitution has "juridically extinguished" Ethiopia as a sovereign entity. Rather, he argues, Constitution drafters should have written a constitution based on "the common ties that exist among the people of Ethiopia," including religion and language, rather than using ethnicity as a basis for political affiliation. Haile attributes to the Constitution a force destructive of sovereignty, unity and rule of law. See id at 46–49 (arguing that constitution's authorization to ministers to suspend political and civil rights makes most human rights derogable).

For additional materials on the effects of federalism when subnational units reflect existing lines of linguistic, or ethnic division, see Chapter VIII (B) below.

4. Consider whether there are any provisions in the U.S. Constitution that could be seen as obstacles to what you understand "constitutionalism" to be. Some possibilities: the provisions in the 1787 Constitution prohibiting Congress until 1808 from prohibiting the "Importation of . . . Persons;" the "Three–Fifths" clause for counting slaves in determining the apportionment of the House of Representatives originally found in Article I; the provisions of Article I (retained by Amendment XVII) that each State have two Senators, regardless of population and of Article V that no state can be deprived of its equal representation in the Senate, even by constitutional amendment, without the consent of the state involved; the Second Amendment. Are there any *omissions* from the U.S. Constitution that are obstacles to constitutionalism? For a collection of short essays bearing on these questions, see William N. Eskridge, Jr., and Sanford Levinson eds., Constitutional Stupidities, Constitutional Tragedies (1998).

Note on the People's Republic of China

Between 1948 and the present the PRC has had at least 5 Constitutions.[b] The present Constitution of 1982 enumerates such rights as "freedom of speech, of the press, of assembly."[c] Yet the exercise of all rights under the Constitution are limited by article 51, which provides that

b. The 1949 Common Program of the Chinese People's Political Consultative Conference; the 1954 Constitution; the 1975 Constitution (the "Gang of Four" constitution); the 1978 Constitution; and the Constitution of 1982. In addition, a draft constitution was promulgated in 1970 but was not adopted. Hungdah Chiu, *The 1982 Chinese Constitution and the Rule of Law*, (Occasional Papers/Reprints in Contemporary Asian Studies, No. 4 (1985)).

c. Art. 35, 1982 Constitution.

"the exercise by citizens ... of their freedoms and rights may not infringe upon the interest of the state, of society and the collective , or upon the lawful freedoms and rights of other citizens ..."

As James Feinerman has argued, these provisions make it possible that any exercise of free speech or assembly rights could be deemed prohibited by other articles of the constitution, and the history of the PRC since 1982 reveals frequent persecution of those who exercised rights of speech in ways disapproved of by the government.[d]

The Chinese constitutions assume that the purpose of rights is to enable citizens to support the broader interests of the community. Correspondingly, the government's powers are not limited by the people's, but must be served by their exercise. According to one group of scholars, the Chinese Constitution is a

"manifesto, by the leaders to the people, describing the society that exists and its institutions, and proclaiming its values, goals and aspirations ... As regards individual rights ...the constitution appears not to prescribe the rights that government must observe but rather sets forth rights which the government claims to be providing and promises to provide."[e]

The 1982 Constitution goes further than its predecessors in identifying the Constitution as superior to other laws or decrees, i.e., in asserting the supremacy of the constitution. In addition, it provides, as had the 1954 constitution, for the "independence" of the people's courts (the judiciary) and the prosecutors' offices. 1982 Constitution, arts. 126, 131. See Hungdah Chiu, note b. at 8. However, there is no explicit jurisdiction in any court to review the constitutionality of laws, decrees or executive action; under 1982 Constitution, the National People's Congress [NPC] has power to "supervise the enforcement" of the Constitution and the NPC's Standing Committee has power to both "interpret the Constitution and supervise its enforcement." Cai Dingjian, *Constitutional Supervision and Interpretation in the People's Republic of China*, 9 Journal of Chinese Law 219 (1995). Cai Dingjian emphasizes use of the term "constitutional supervision" instead of "constitutional review" because of "vast differences between the organizing political principles" of China and West, and concludes that "in practice, constitutional supervision and interpretation has not effectively been carried out."

Commentators argue, convincingly, that the NPC's Standing Committee has disregarded clear constitutional limitations (e.g., on what courts can impose death sentences), and that "the Standing Committee of the NPC can do whatever it wants to interpret the Constitution." Hungdah Chiu, at 12–13; cf. Cai Dingjian (describing ongoing debate about whether to estab-

d. James Feinerman, The Constitution and Protection of Rights in the PRC, in Jones, Feinerman, and Clarke, Introduction to the Law of the People's Republic of China (forthcoming).

e. R. Randle Edwards, Louis Henkin, and Ander Nathan, Human Rights in Communist China 26–27 (Columbia University Press New York 1986).

lish "a constitutional supervisory organ" apart from the NPC Standing Committee but not inconsistent with principle of "democratic centralism" under which the NPC is highest organ of state power). Finally, there appears to be no clearly established procedure for individual citizens to challenge the constitutionality of legislation.[f]

In major respects, then, the Chinese Constitution bears little relationship to the "rule of law" aspects of constitutionalism discussed previously. Why, then, was it adopted? Consider these possibilities, several of which have been suggested by Professor Feinerman:

    1. To establish the internal structure for governance and to define the offices of government.

    2. To establish legality and/or sovereignty at the international level.

    3. To promote greater "rights consciousness" among the people to forestall repetition of an event like the Cultural Revolution.

    4. To protect the power of those currently holding it.

Is the Chinese constitution a "sham"? Is it simply based on a theory of constitutional legality that is much more collectivist than those of western nations? How would one judge the success of such a constitution?

Note on the Role of International (or Extra-national) Influences in Promoting Domestic Constitution–making or Interpretation

While the focus of these materials is on constitutions and constitutionalism within nations, we have already referred to several situations (some overlapping) in which extra-national events strongly influence domestic constitutional matters:

    i. Direct intervention by other nations to require adoption of particular forms of constitutions, as occurred in Germany and Japan following World War II;

    ii. Adoption of constitutions as part of independence movements away from colonial status but under the influence of the prior occupying power's legal regimes;

    iii. Requirements of particular forms or aspects of constitutionalism as conditions for coveted membership in international bodies, as was arguably the case in Turkey and in eastern European nations, or for receipt of international aid;

---

f. But see Cai Dingjian, at 233 (noting "one expert['s]" view that article 41 of the Constitution can be interpreted to mean that citizens have the right to make accusations of unconstitutionality, and that China therefore should establish a system of constitutional litigation). Since 1989 there has been a procedure to challenge the validity of certain administrative acts. See Ying Songnian, *China's Administrative Procedure System*, China Law 1995, no. 2 at 81-83.

iv. Adoption of constitutional provisions, or stances on particular constitutional matters, to achieve specific international goals, as was arguably the case in Ireland's response to "X" at the time the Maastricht Treaty ratification was pending;

v. Adoption of constitutions, or constitutional provisions, to enhance national stature in eyes of other nations (a) by demonstrating progress towards internationally acceptable legal norms and/or (b) by manifesting the full attributes of sovereignty.

vi. Direct application as law of international or extranational norms that constrain a domestic government's powers, both by domestic organs of government and in international tribunals (as in the Irish dispute over prohibiting information about abortion services elsewhere).

These phenomena raise several questions: Is the category of domestic, national constitutions an appropriate category for comparative study? Should the focus instead be on international norms and/or interventions in domestic constitution-formation? At a minimum, what we have encountered suggests the need to attend to international and extra-national influences and incentives as part of the multiple realities in which constitutions and legal systems are situated, created and recreated.[g] More speculatively, how does the idea of entrenchment—a common theme in U.S. constitutionalism—relate to the idea that constitutional development may itself need to respond to international pressures?

g. See, e.g., Eric Stein, International Law in Internal Law: Toward Internationalization of Central–Eastern European Constitutions?, 88 Am. J. Intl L. 427 (1994) (discussing incorporation of international treaties and international law in domestic constitutions).

CHAPTER IV

CONSTITUTIONAL MOMENTS AND TRANSITIONS

What is the relationship between crisis, extralegal behavior, and constitution-making? What is the relationship between coercive power and consent in establishing a constitution? And how is "consent" manifested, or determined? Consider U.S. experiences. Some would argue that several of our most transformative constitutional moments have been characterized by questionable legality, most notably in the formation of the Constitution of 1787 and in the procedures by which the Reconstruction Amendments to the Constitution were ratified.[a]

Among the perspectives offered in this chapter's readings, consider Murphy's argument that consent of the governed is not a sufficient basis for the legitimacy of a constitution or constitutional change; Ackerman's argument that constitutional change should take place in revolutionary moments; Elster's suggestion of a paradox between the crises that generate constitution-making and the conditions for good constitutional change; Jacobsohn's argument that constitutionalism is dependent on deep consensus on underlying values; and Katz's skepticism regarding the revolutionary tradition of American constitutionalism in Eastern Europe.

A. CONSTITUTIONAL CHANGE AND CONSTITUTIONAL LEGITIMACY

1. CONSENT AND LEGITIMACY

Walter F. Murphy, *Consent and Constitutional Change*, in Human Rights and Constitutional Law (James O'Reilly, ed., 1992)

Every viable political system must provide some means for innovation. . . .

---

a. Recall that the delegates to the Convention of 1787 were charged to amend and revise the Articles of Confederation, which required a unanimous vote of the states, and that what emerged was an entirely new constitution that provided it would become effective upon ratification by only 9 of the 13 states. Recall also that during the early years of Reconstruction, the representatives to Congress of many of the southern states were not seated, and that ratification of the 14th amendment was made a condition for readmission to the Union (after being initially rejected by many southern states). See Section 5, First Reconstruction Act (Mar. 2 1867)

251

Yet ... some constitutional texts do prohibit certain kinds of amendment, that of the United States, for instance, forbids denying any state equal representation in the Senate without that State's consent. Such textual interdictions present interesting problems for constitutional theory. Even more interesting and more difficult issues revolve around whether there are non-textually prescribed limits to valid constitutional change.

These problems are not merely academic. Germany's Federal Constitutional Court, following the reasoning of the Constitutional Court of Bavaria, has claimed authority to strike down not only an amendment but part of the original constitutional text itself as violative of the Basic Law's fundamental principles. The Supreme Court of India has on several occasions, though with differing rationales, declared constitutional amendments unconstitutional....

Objections to judicial invalidation of clauses in or added to a constitutional text are generally of two kinds. The first is ... based on fear of judicial oligarchy—in short, on constitutionalism's weakening democracy and corrupting itself in the process.

The second, related, objection is that the text of the constitution is what "the people" have consented to be ruled by. They have also agreed to certain procedures to change that basic compact and even the larger constitution that the text reflects and of which it is a part. Thus, *if* there is ground at all for any institution's invalidating a portion of that text, it can only be that the government did not secure the people's consent to the document in the first place or did not follow agreed upon procedures for change.

This paper deals only with the second objection. The reasoning behind that objection is straightforward. The people are sovereign and can accept any kind of political system that pleases them; it follows that they can transform the system as they wish, provided only that they observe the procedures they previously agreed to and, in fact, they and/or their representatives permit free and informed choice. In short, consent of the people is the great legitimator of government. With consent, any political system is legitimate; without it, no system is legitimate.

A weaker form of the claim would stipulate that consent is a necessary but not sufficient element in legitimation. This diluted variant is, I believe much more defensible, but it deprives consent of its supposed role as ultimate legitimator. I wish to challenge the stronger proposition, not for the joy of attacking a straw man, but because I think that in so doing I can both better explicate the nature of consent and offer a more convincing reason for the weaker version than its proponents do....

This paper argues that, insofar as the claim for consent as the great political legitimator has validity, it draws that validity from a concept of human nature. Because it is this underlying notion of what it means to be a human being that confers upon consent what legitimating power it has, this notion also places limits on consent's power to legitimate. Concern for consent demonstrates acceptance, however unreflective, of this more basic legitimator of a political system and, hence, of the limits it imposes on political (re)formation. . . .

POLITICAL LEGITIMACY

. . . Empirically, political legitimacy refers to a psychological bond between a people and their governmental system and/or its officials. It is a belief, which may not exist at all or may vary from very weak to very strong, among the people themselves that they have a moral obligation to conform to public regulations that are lawful under the regime's principles and rules. . . .

. . . [T]he second sense of legitimacy, [demands] an intellectually defensible [moral] argument for a people's being obligated to a political system. . . . It may be true, as John Adams wrote Thomas Jefferson, that "human Reason and human Conscience . . . are not a Match, for human Passions, human Imagination, and human Enthusiasm." Nevertheless, intelligent men and women should be able to explain why "consent" serves as the ultimate legitimator for their political system. To accept without reflection the legitimating function of consent and to substitute the myth of social contract for that of divine right of kings is to reject both the value of reason and the necessity of offering reasoned explanation for a political system. . . .[15]

The need to justify consent's alleged power is especially pressing for men and women who believe in constitutional democracy, for it is painfully obvious that consent does not necessarily lead to that sort of political system or even to unalloyed representative democracy. . . .

. . . The possibility of a sovereign people's choosing an evil political system is both real and irrelevant to the regime's legitimacy. The legitimating power of consent is "value free" in that it posits no limitations whatever on the people who confer it or on the rulers the people agree to, other than what the people themselves choose to impose.

This logic is hard but necessary if consent is to play the role of great legitimator. For, if consent is cabined by other considerations, for example, its capacity to yield "correct" political solutions, then it is the force of those considerations, the correctness of those solutions, not consent itself, that begets legitimacy.

---

15. . . . It is worth noting that John Rawls, the great contractarian of the twentieth century, used the notion of justice, not consent, to justify constitutional democracy:

> Even the rule of promising does not give rise to a moral obligation by itself. To account for fiduciary obligations we must take the principle of fairness as a prem-

ise. Thus along with most other ethical theories, justice as fairness holds that natural duties and obligations arise only in virtue of ethical principles. These principles are those that would be chosen in the original position. [*A Theory of Justice* (Cambridge, Mass., 1971), p. 348; see also pp. 112 and 343.].

THE MEANING OF CONSENT

Like "legitimacy" consent is a plastic concept. First are matters of recognition. Even if we agree on what consent truly means, how do we know when a people have, in fact, consented to a political system? Referenda and elections do not invariably provide authoritative anointing; besides, these processes are rather recent and still not universally used.

Definition poses another central problem. *Webster's Third International Dictionary* first defines consent as: "a: Compliance or approval, espec. of what is done or proposed by another. . . ." This usage seems too broad to convey moral commitment. Webster's second definition is more fitting: "b. Capable, deliberate, voluntary agreement to or concurrence in some act or purpose implying physical and mental power and free action. . . ." Now here are elements that might create moral obligation: capability, deliberation, voluntariness. But each raises immense analytical as well as practical problems.

"Capable" and "deliberate" indicate both freedom to choose and informed choice. As matters of practical politics, it is typically doubtful how much of either quality is present at the creation of a political order, even when we can put a specific date on a new system's coming into operation. Doubts increase when we speak of constitutional amendments.

Options, where they exist, are often unclear and always restricted; and public understanding of what choices are open may be small. One might extrapolate from studies of the political knowledge of voters in the United States to argue that, beyond the drafters of the text and a smattering of professional politicians, journalists, and academics, a level of comprehension necessary to make agreement informed as well as deliberate seldom if ever obtains. Indeed, drafters of a constitutional text are likely to realize that they operate behind what Buchanan calls "a veil of uncertainty". The document they foal is more likely to be a set of hopes than a self-executing blueprint for public affairs. On being congratulated on the constitutional text the American convention of 1787 produced, Gouverneur Morris, who had been largely responsible for drafting the final version, replied that its worth "depends on how it is interpreted." . . .

. . . And the present's capacity to bind the future to a choice that curtails or even removes those latter-day citizens' capacity to choose radically different political arrangements raises hard issues of justification.
. . .

ARGUMENTS FOR CONSENT AS LEGITIMATOR

For the purposes of analysis, let us assume that advocates of consent as the great legitimator have addressed and overcome problems of recognition and definition. What basic arguments can justify consent's claim?

1. *Conventionalism: It's Our System*

At least in the United States, conventionalism would offer the most forthright answer. "That's what we fought for. The American Revolution was all about government by consent. 'No taxation without representation' was a specific conception from this larger concept.'' Whatever the historicity of this reply—and surely it is simplistic—it does raise certain problems. First, it says nothing about whether the consent of the people of other nations is necessary to the legitimacy of their own regimes. . . . After World War II, for example, the United States imposed constitutional democracy on Japan; and the Western Allies insured that the Federal Republic of Germany would adopt such a political system. . . . At most, conventionalism offers an explanation of how a particular set of relationships came about, not a justification for those relationships—unless, of course, a people worship their ancestors.

Second, and more significant, this argument is essentially circular: Consent is the legitimator because the people consented to consent's playing that role. . . .

2. Consent as Resting on Power

A second explanation for the primacy of consent also relates to power and is both pragmatic and secular. Lord Bryce was not alone in arguing that, because the bulk of power rests with the mass of the people, all regimes that endure for any extended period, must rest on consent. Thus, the argument would go: The people ultimately possess power. Thus, where a regime is stable, it must, by definition, rest on consent. . . .

If it is power that justifies consent's legitimating role, then it is the groups with the most power whose consent legitimates a form of politics. We should, therefore, look with special care at the status of particular elites such as the military and police rather than to the people as a whole. These armed groups typically possess a huge share of the instruments of coercion: the weapons, training, and discipline to control others. . . .

. . . [E]ver since Thrasymachus debated Socrates the notion that justice is the interest of the stronger (and so it must be power that makes a regime just) has been in bad intellectual repute, pace Adolf Hitler, Joseph Stalin, and Mao Tse Tung. But, even if that historic judgment is wrong, it was certainly neither hastily arrived at nor unconnected with human experience. If, however, that judgment is correct, champions of consent who use this kind of argument must be wrong—and tragically so. . . .

3. Consent and Efficiency

An argument for consent as the most efficient way of governing is related to but subtly different from the claim about consent, power, and stability: Consent is the ultimate legitimator because a political system so based will be able drastically to reduce the costs of keeping order. This sort of reasoning makes moral claims only to the extent it incorporates the principle that, in a world of limited resources and practically unlimited human needs, justice demands that a political system employ resources efficiently. Thus to construct a political system that must use disproportionately more resources to keep public order than would other viable systems is inefficient and hence unjust. . . .

The crucial question here is not whether consent does or does not lower the probability that citizens will attempt to subvert the polity or decrease the need for governmental coercion in enforcing laws protecting personal safety. The real question is whether, if consent does those deeds, it would thereby earn the status of supreme legitimator. If success on these and related counts were the critical indicium of a claim to be the legitimator, then consent would have to trump competitors to win the crown. But free, mass distribution of drugs and alcohol, in the fashion of Huxley's *Brave New World,* might well accomplish the same tasks more cheaply and completely than consent given in a sober state. . . .

If . . . we want to measure efficiency in terms of limiting government, i.e., by guarding citizens' rights against threats from officials, consent to constitutional democracy does further that goal. On the other hand, consent to authoritarian government would not do so. Thus, consent would make it legitimate for a society to adopt or move closer toward constitutional democracy, but not a more authoritarian system. By its own terms, this conclusion tightly restricts consent's legitimating power.

CONSENT AND HUMAN DIGNITY

Alone or together, arguments based on conventionalism, power and efficiency do not offer sufficient support for judging consent to be the ultimate political legitimator. Those arguments indicate the prudence of government's obtaining the consent of the governed, but to act with prudence is not the same as to act with legitimacy. . . .

. . . Because people can perceive reality, analyze evidence, and draw reasonable conclusions, they can understand much, though probably never all, about themselves. One of the things they can grasp is that they are capable of reason and that capability constitutes a great good. For others to impose their choices on us, to force us to choose what our reason tells us we should not, lessens that good by destroying its chief function. Thus our capacity to reason entails moral autonomy as necessary to preserve our individual identity as reasoning beings.

Because people can comprehend their own capacity to reason, they can extrapolate that self-understanding to other humans and can realize that those others share the capacity to reason and the need for moral autonomy. Thus we can understand that it is equally as bad to impose our choices on others as it is for others to impose their choices on us.

Furthermore, people can understand that, when choices are their own, they bear responsibility for those selections, even when their choices entail costs, anticipated and unanticipated. Reason generates autonomy, and autonomy generates obligation. . . .

Consent can function as a legitimator only to the extent that the people agree as reasoning, morally autonomous, and responsible human beings. As Joseph Raz concludes, "to the extent that the validity of consent rest on the intrinsic value of autonomy it cannot extend to acts of consent that authorize another person to deprive people of their autonomy." Thus, what began as an argument for consent as the ultimate legitimator has turned into an argument for a closely related but more fundamental value, that of human dignity, based on a capacity to reason, a need for moral autonomy, and an ability to make morally binding commitments. Consent reflects that fundamental value; but, of itself, it does not, as Hamilton maintained, constitute "the pure, original foundation of all legitimate authority".

At this juncture, some proponents of consent as the great legitimator might assert that they had all along taken for granted such a view of human nature; they did not explain it because they thought it obvious. If, however, they do accept this argument about human nature, they must also accept the conclusion that consent can justify only certain kinds of regimes and, therefore, only certain kinds of changes in regimes. Thus it may be a proximate legitimator, but one needs to examine carefully what it produces to make sure. Such a role for consent offers a weak version of the weaker version of its legitimating function: Consent may provide a necessary but it cannot provide a sufficient condition for the legitimacy of a political system. . . .

CONCLUSION

The purpose of this paper was to defend the position that there are limits, shadowy but nonetheless real, to the sorts of constitutional change that consent may validate. The fact that "the people" freely and over-whelmingly consent to (re)design their political system is insufficient to legitimate (re)construction that would destroy or damage human dignity. For it is from this value and the corollary need for autonomy and the capacity to make binding commitments that consent derives whatever power it has to legitimate political systems for reflective, reasoning men and women.

Whether judges in a constitutional democracy are the proper officials to brand such a change invalid is a matter separate from the argument about the potentially defective nature of systemic transformations. Other officials might well have equally or even more important roles to play, for, no less solemnly than judges, they have sworn to uphold "the constitution". Nevertheless, where a polity has established judicial review, judges will bear a heavy responsibility to protect not merely the letter of the constitutional text but its essence.

Note on Murphy and the Intertemporal Problem

How can consent given at the time of framing a constitution bind people in a later generation? This is a classic problem in political theory. See, e.g., Jon Elster, Ulysses and the Sirens 36–111 (1979); Bruce A. Ackerman, *The Storrs Lectures: Discovering the Constitution*, 93 Yale L.J.

1013, 1058–60 (1984). Does constitutionalism require that we come up with a good answer to it?

Historical Note on Adoption of post-World War II Constitutions in Germany and Japan

Use of coercion by conquering powers to impose regimes of constitutionalism and respect for human rights may seem paradoxical. But the experience of the United States after the Civil War, in which the victorious Union forces denied the defeated southern states representation in Congress until after ratification of the 14th amendment had been secured, has parallels in this century.

At the end of World War II, the victorious Allied Powers (including the United States) required Germany to adopt a constitution establishing a federal structure of government, designed both to protect the rights of the länder (German states) and provide "adequate central authority," and to guarantee "individual rights and freedoms." Many scholars agree that these "minimal conditions ... coincided fully with the ideas of the Germans themselves."[b] At the demand of the Allied Powers, the new länder legislatures selected representatives to a Parliamentary Council that, working with a committee of German experts at Herrenchiemsee, drafted a new Basic Law. Allied powers interacted with the work of the Parliamentary Council, and posed objections in April 1949 to the draft in development because it provided " 'too much centralization of authority'. "[c] An acceptable compromise was worked out, that in the views of some German jurists drew sufficiently on prior German constitutional traditions that it was not regarded as an instrument "stained" by imposition from the outside.[d] The new Basic Law was submitted to the legislative bodies of the länder, and ratified by more than two-thirds of those legislatures in May, 1949.

Germany's Basic Law has been regarded as largely successful in structuring a modern, federal, constitutional democracy. Regular elections and orderly changes in elected leadership have prevailed. As you have

b. David P. Currie, The Constitution of the Federal Republic of Germany 9 (1994). For the view of a prominent German jurist, see Helmut Steinberger, *American and German Constitutional Development* 212–13, in Constitutionalism and Rights: The Influence of the United States Constitution Abroad (Louis Henkin and Albert J. Rosenthal eds. 1990) (arguing that after World War II, in Germany there was "continuous reflection on, comparisons with, and evaluation of American constitutional ideas and principles. [A]s a result, one finds many functionally equivalent solutions for and/or approaches to constitutional problems, rather than just a transplant or mechanical adoption of ideas. Functional equivalence does not necessarily imply causal relationships . . . .").

c. Currie, at 10, quoting Lucius Clay, Decision in Germany at 421–22 (1950). Lucius Clay was the general in charge of the American role in helping to re-establish constitutional democracy in Germany.

d. Currie, at 10, quoting Helmut Steinberger (who served as a Justice of the new German Constitutional Court). For similar expression of views see Steinberger, at 216.

already seen from the first chapter, the German Constitutional Court has not shied from declaring invalid laws enacted by the national legislature.

Japan adopted its constitution in 1947, also under pressure from American occupying forces. Here, however, there seems to be less evidence of a foundation in prior legal traditions for the Constitution that emerged, and the process involved more of a sudden, externally imposed departure from prior tradition. The initial draft of what became the Constitution was prepared by a small group of American lawyers in General Macarthur's office as Supreme Commander of Allied Powers (SCAP), under orders to establish human rights protected by the constitution, retain the emperor but make him subject to popular control, renounce belligerency and eliminate trappings of aristocracy.[e] This draft was then worked on and modified by the Shidehara government, with continued consultations and negotiations with SCAP. While the amendment procedures of the Meiji Constitution were followed, the legislative body that approved the new Constitution was elected under voting rules imposed by the Allies that broadened suffrage (e.g. to include women).

Professor Beer characterizes the process of constitution-drafting as "a binational product." He argues that the 1947 Constitution both embodies a "statement of the rights of an American, as envisioned by some American occupationnaires in the authentically idealistic months following World War II," and at the same time, "for most Japanese the Constitution has also become the most authoritative statement [of their rights] . . . and . . . the most sacred writ of the country's current civilization."[f] He notes as further evidence of the success of this Constitution the history since 1947 of peaceful electoral transitions, recognition of rights, and stability of the constitution itself.

Consider, in light of these brief and necessarily simplistic summaries of Japan and Germany, Walter Murphy's argument about the relationship of consent to constitutionalism. Note also the possible distinction between interventions by occupying forces that are themselves from liberal constitutional democracies (the U.S. in Japan and Germany) and interventions by less domestically-constrained occupying forces. See Franklin and Baun, in chapter II above.

---

e. Lawrence W. Beer, *Constitutionalism and Rights in Japan and Korea* in Constitutionalism and Rights: The Influence of the United States Constitution Abroad 232–33 (Louis Henkin and Albert Rosenthal eds., 1990).

f. Beer at 229. For a more restrained evaluation, see Masamito Ito, *The Modern Development of Law and Constitution in Japan*, in Constitutional Systems in Late Twentieth Century Asia 129–74 (Lawrence W. Beer, ed., 1992) (noting revisionist calls for amending the constitution, in part because it was forced on Japan, but concluding that this is very unlikely to occur.). For a useful collection of articles, see *Symposium, The Constitution of Japan—The Fifth Decade*, Percy R. Luney, Special Editor, 53 Law & Contemp. Prob. Nos. 1 & 2 (1990).

2.   CONSTITUTION–MAKING: CLEAN BREAKS OR EVOLUTIONARY CHANGE?

In the readings that follow, consider the contrasting concepts concerning the significance of formal constitutions and the possibility of transitions to constitutionalism without "constitutional moments."

Elster analyzes the process of creating a written constitution as a collective choice problem. He identifies the circumstances that create sufficient urgency to prompt political actors to put aside other matters to draft new constitutions, and argues that those circumstances are on a collision course with the conditions for disinterested, or even long term planning, that constitutions (in his view) require. Note the degree to which his analysis of constitution-making in history, and his recommendations of procedures (e.g. for isolation of the deliberators) to overcome collective action problems, are similar to Ackerman's. Consider the extent to which their assumptions about the interests of constitution-makers diverge.

Ackerman explores the connection between revolutionary movements and constitutional moments, arguing that at least for nations emerging from Communist regimes a clean break with the past through adoption of a formal constitution is important. Ackerman identifies some of the conditions for the successful constitution-making following the 18th century American Revolution that he believes should guide action by revolutionary elites in Eastern Europe. He also urges use of procedural devices such as constitutional conventions to mark and enhance the distinctiveness of constitution-making. Finally, he rejects "relativism" to argue that liberal values of Western constitutions are central to success in Eastern Europe.

In contrast to some of Ackerman's views, e.g., that at least in newly emerging states a formal written constitution is of value, and that a "constitutional moment" was lost at the inception of the modern state of Israel, Jacobsohn suggests that "small-c" constitutions may exist without a formal written constitution, and emphasizes that constitutions serve different functions in different settings. He suggests that the Israeli postponement of formal constitution-writing served important purposes to the construction of the Israeli polity and the integration of differing constitutional traditions (those of the Jewish "torah" and those of the modern liberal state). In accepting that a formal constitution may not be requisite to "constitutionalism," Jacobsohn also emphasizes the connections between a constitution and its political surroundings. Jacobsohn contrasts constitutions that embody a clear vision of a nation's fundamental commitments while simultaneously making some politically necessary compromises inconsistent with that vision (his view of the U.S. Constitution and its treatment of slavery),[g] and constitutions that fail to choose any clear vision at all (his view of the Israeli "small-c" constitution).

---

g. Compare Jacobsohn's view here with Sunstein's view that one of the functions of a constitution is to take morally divisive issues (such as slavery in 1787) out of the reach of politics.

Katz is more skeptical than Ackerman that American constitutionalism should be regarded as a universal concept. He argues that the "appropriate starting point for new European constitutions ... is to be found in local traditions, rather than in the history of the United States during the era of Enlightenment." In further contrast to Ackerman, Katz finds the Hungarian experience to suggest that a piecemeal approach to developing constitutionalism through gradual amendments may be associated with stronger popular legitimacy. Moreover, Katz argues for a more limited understanding of "constitutionalism" as "a process within a society by which the community commits itself to the rule of law, specifies its basic values, and agrees to abide by a legal/institutional structure which guarantees that formal social institutions will respect the agreed-on values."

* * *

Jon Elster, *Essay: Forces and Mechanisms in the Constitution–Making Process*, 45 Duke L. J. 364 (1995)

Creating a constitution involves making choices under constraints. In most of the cases that concern me, these are collective choices.... We must consider, therefore, both the goals of individual constitution-makers and the mechanisms by which these are aggregated into collective choices. These ... key notions ... [of] constraint, individual motivations, and systems of aggregation ... [shall be considered along with] the cognitive assumptions of the constitution-makers—their beliefs about what institutional arrangements will bring about which results....

WAVES OF CONSTITUTION–MAKING

[Elster limits his analysis to the development of written constitutions and electoral laws of comparable importance; surveys several waves of constitution-making from the late 18th century on; and indicates that his examples will come primarily from the American and French experiences of the 1780s and those of Eastern Europe in the 1990s.]

... [L]et me point to a large fact that may help us understand why constitutions occur in waves. The fact is that new constitutions almost always are written in the wake of a crisis or exceptional circumstances of some sort. There are some exceptions.... By and large, however, the link between crisis and constitution-making is quite robust....

... [A] number of circumstances ... induce constitution-making. First [there is] social and economic crisis, as in the making of the American Constitution of 1787 or the French Constitution of 1791; ... [T]he making of the first French constitution was not an effect of the French Revolution but rather its cause: The economic crisis caused the constitution-making process, which eventually turned into a political revolution. Second, there is revolution, as in the making of the 1830 charter in France or the French and German 1848 constitutions. Third, there is regime collapse, as in ... Eastern Europe in the early 1990s. Fourth, there is fear of regime collapse, as in the making of the French Constitution of 1958, which was imposed by de Gaulle under the shadow of military rebellion. Fifth, there is defeat in war.... Sixth, there is reconstruction after war, as in France in 1946. Seventh, there is the creation of a new state, as in Poland and Czechoslovakia after the First World War. Eighth and finally, there is liberation from colonial rule, as in the United States after 1776 and in many third world countries after 1945....

... [W]hat happens in one country may influence what happens elsewhere by the mechanism of upgrading beliefs.... [Take] the 1989–90 Round Table Talks in Eastern Europe.... The lack of Soviet intervention in Poland enabled the Hungarians to upgrade their beliefs about the likelihood of Soviet intervention in their country. For the Czechoslovaks, it was the Soviet nonintervention in East Germany that made them understand that there would not be a repetition of 1968....

CONSTRAINTS

[Elster distinguishes "upstream" and "downstream" constraints on constituent assemblies.]

Constituent assemblies are rarely self-created; rather they have ... external ... creators.... [T]here is the institution or individual that makes the decision to convene a constituent assembly [in the U.S. in 1787, the Continental Congress] ... [and] there is the institutional mechanism that selects delegates to the constituent assembly [in the U.S., state legislatures that selected delegates.] ...

... [T]hese upstream actors ... will often seek to impose constraints on the procedures of the assembly or on the substance of the constitution. The Continental Congress instructed the Federal Convention to propose changes to the Articles of Confederation, not to propose an entirely new Constitution. The delegates from Delaware came ... with instructions from the state legislature to insist on equality of voting power for all states in the new constitution.... In France, many delegates came with instructions ... to vote for an absolute veto for the King in the new constitution....

Downstream constraints arise from the process of ratification. If the framers know that the document they produce will have to be ratified by another body, knowledge of the preferences of that body will act as a constraint on what they can propose....

... Typically the downstream constraints are in fact imposed by the upstream authority.... [Elster points out that the relationship between constituent assemblies and downstream or upstream actors is complex, and that constituent assemblies have often departed from instructions by the upstream authorities.] Almost by definition, the old regime is part of the problem that a constituent assembly is convened to solve. There would be no need to have an assembly if the regime was not flawed. But if it is flawed, why should the assembly respect its instructions?

DESIRES AND BELIEFS

[Elster goes on to discuss the desires and beliefs of the framers in terms of "interest," "passion" and "reason."]

The personal interest of constitution-makers in specific constitutional clauses is a relatively marginal factor, although it does play a certain role in some cases. . . .

The most blatant example . . . is found in the making of the Czech Constitution of 1992. The decision . . . to create a bicameral parliament in the new constitution was widely seen as an incentive offered to the Czech Deputies in the Federal Assembly [of the Czech and Slovak Federation] to pass a constitutional law abolishing the federation in exchange for a place in the new [Czech] Senate*. . . .

Group interest is a much more important factor in the constitution-making process. At the [U.S.] Federal Convention the interest of the states were a crucial determinant of the outcome . . . reflected both in substantive and procedural provisions of the Constitution. . . .

In the French Assembly of 1789, the interests of the estates were an important factor in the initial procedural debates. The nobility and the clergy wanted the assembly to vote by estate, which would enable them to outvote the Third Estate. The Third Estate insisted on voting by heads, which would enable them, with the help of a few renegades, to outvote the other two estates. . . .

In Czechoslovakia [prior to its split] . . . Slovakia, with one third of the population, managed to ensure that half of the judges of the constitutional court would be Slovaks and that the chairmanship of the central bank would rotate annually between a Czech and a Slovak. . . .

. . . Even when groups act to promote their interest, they tend to argue publicly in terms of impartial values . . .

Although . . . self-serving arguments tend to dress themselves in public interest garb, the converse—that all impartial argument is nothing but self-interest in disguise—is invalid. . . . [T]he reductionist claim is internally incoherent. If nobody was ever moved by the public interest, nobody would have anything to gain by appealing to it. . . .

Institutional interest in the constitution-making process operates when a body that participates in that process writes an important role for itself into the constitution. . . .

[One implication is that] constituent assemblies that also serve as the ordinary legislature will give preponderant importance to the legislative branch at the expense of the executive . . . and the judiciary. . . .

A second implication is that unicameral and bicameral constituent assemblies will tend to create, respectively, unicameral and bicameral constitutions. . . .

---

* [Editors' Note: As Elster notes, this promise was not quickly fulfilled, since the Senate was not established and no elections for Senate were held until late 1996.]

A final implication is that constitution-making parliaments will give themselves large powers to amend the constitution. . . .

. . . Whereas group interest has strong explanatory power with regard to electoral laws, institutional interest is a stronger determinant of the machinery of government. Institutional interest fails, however to explain the creation of strong constitutional courts, an institution that was nowhere represented in the constitutionmaking process [in Eastern Europe] and that nevertheless did quite well. . . .

. . . Sometimes . . . reason can win out over passion as well as interest. . . .When the framers at the federal Convention decided to proceed behind closed doors, it was because their reason told them that otherwise they might yield to passion. . . .

Similarly, when the French delegates of 1789 adopted Robespierre's proposal for a law that would render them ineligible to the first ordinary legislature, it was because they wanted to shield themselves from institutional interests. . . .

From the Federal Convention . . . another discussion that pits interest against reason [concerned the number and status of new states to be admitted. Against arguments that the dominance of the Atlantic states should be preserved, Mason argued for admission of western states "as equals," on the grounds that this was "right in itself."] This argument . . . rest[s] . . . on a conception of intrinsic fairness.

AGGREGATION, TRANSFORMATION AND MISREPRESENTATION OF PREFERENCES . . .

It is not simply a question of aggregating given preferences by a given procedure. For one thing, the procedure itself has to be chosen by the delegates. . . .

For another thing, we cannot assume that delegates simply express given preferences or follow instructions from their constituencies. . . . [T]he delegates to the Federal Convention imposed secrecy on the debates to make it easier for them to change their minds through discussion. In the first French Assembly, imperative mandates were rejected for the same reason. . . .

[S]ecrecy . . . is likely to have two consequences. On the one hand, it will tend to shift the center of gravity from impartial discussion to interest-based bargaining . . . On the other hand, secrecy tends to improve the quality of whatever discussion does take place because it allows framers to change their mind when persuaded of the truth of an opponent's view. . . . [W]hile public debate drives out any appearance of bargaining, it also encourages stubbornness, overbidding and grandstanding in ways that are incompatible with genuine discussion. Rather than fostering transformation of preferences, the public setting encourages their misrepresentation.

The Federal Convention and the first French Assembly are polar cases in this respect. In Madison's notes from the Convention, we come across some exceptionally fine instances of rational discussion and some exceptionally hard bargains. In the records of the French Assembly we find neither. The speakers argue without exception in terms of the public interest. We know from other evidence, however, that because of publicity generated fears of sanctions, many of the constituents spoke and voted against their convictions. The radical delegates insisted on voting by roll call, a procedure that enabled members or spectators to identify those who opposed radical measures and to circulate lists with their names in Paris. The defeat of bicameralism and of an absolute veto for the King, in particular, owed much to the fear generated by this publicity.

[Elster then turns to logrolling, and the use of threats (e.g., foreign powers, police or military, terrorism, command over crowds) as mechanisms for aggregation.]

... In situations like those [e.g., prospects of military rebellion, mob riots], people do not always act rationally. Fear, anger, and enthusiasm often get the better of them. Nor can they easily estimate the likelihood of the various contingencies. In these situations, constitution-making has more of the opaqueness of battle than the calculability of parliamentary proceedings. Formal theory helps us to make more precise sense of some of the factors we can identify, but it hardly allows for complete explanation.

CONCLUSION

Let me conclude by underlining two basic paradoxes of constitution-making and then drawing some normative implications of the analysis. The first paradox arises from the fact that the task of constitution-making generally emerges in conditions that are likely to work against good constitution-making. Being written for the indefinite future, constitutions ought to be adopted in maximally calm and undisturbed conditions. Also, the intrinsic importance of constitution-making requires that procedures be based on rational, impartial argument. In ordinary legislatures, log-rolling and horsetrading may ensure that all groups realize some of their most strongly held goals. Constitution-makers, however, legislate mainly for future generations, which have no representatives in the constituent assembly. It is part of their task to look beyond their own horizons and interests. At the same time, the call for a new constitution usually arises in turbulent circumstances, which tend to foster passion rather than reason. Also the external circumstances of constitution-making invite procedures based on threat-based bargaining....

The second paradox stems from the fact that the public will to make major constitutional change is unlikely to be present unless a crisis is impending. Suppose, for example, that constitutional change is put on the agenda even though there are no dramatic external circumstances. In that case, no solution may be found at all.... In Canada after 1982 and in Poland after 1992, we can observe how constitution-making failed to get off the ground because there was no urgent need to reshape the basic institutions.... If people find themselves with all the time they need to find a good solution, no solution at all may emerge.

I conclude with some comments on the normative implications.... The most important is perhaps that to reduce the scope for institutional interests, constitutions ought to be written by specially convened assemblies and not by bodies that serve as ordinary legislatures. Nor should the legislature be given a central place in the process of ratification. In both respects, the Federal Convention can serve as a model. Another implication is that the process ought to contain both elements of secrecy (committee discussion) and of publicity (plenary assembly discussions). With total secrecy, partisan interest and logrolling come to the forefront, whereas full publicity encourages grandstanding and rhetorical overbidding. At the Federal Convention, there was too little publicity; in the French Assembly of 1789, too much....**

Bruce Ackerman, The Future of Liberal Revolution (1992)

Constitutionalizing Revolution

The present revolutionary cycle in Europe may be just beginning, but it is already sufficiently advanced to require thought about the way that revolutions end. Poland provides the best example. In many other areas in the East, the disintegration of Communism has not (yet) involved a full-blown revolution as I have defined the term. In contrast, Solidarity was a paradigmatic popular movement that self-consciously struggled long and hard for a new beginning in national political life. Moreover, its success in gaining power created a characteristic set of dilemmas. As we have seen, liberal revolutionaries detest the very notion of permanent revolution. They have not struggled so long merely to establish another grim period of party dictatorship. But how should they use their power? Are there good and bad ways of consolidating a liberal revolution?

I shall be arguing for setting one priority above all others. Neither the privatization of the economy nor the construction of civil society should preoccupy revolutionaries first and foremost. However much liberals may want to think about such things, the organization of state power deserves immediate concern. The window of opportunity for constitutionalizing liberal revolution is open for a shorter time than is generally recognized. Unless the constitutional moment is seized to advantage, it may be missed entirely. In contrast, constructing a liberal market economy, let alone a civil society, requires decades, perhaps generations, and the project can easily be undermined without the timely adoption of an appropriate constitutional framework.

To make my case, I must work around an embarrassing intellectual vacuum. A piece of paper calling itself a constitution can be many things:

** [Editors' Note: Elster makes other recommendations as well, e.g., that elections to the constituent assembly follow proportional rather than majority system, that to reduce threats the assembly not convene in a

an empty ideological gesture, a narrowly legalistic document, or a profound act of political self-definition. But we do not have a powerful literature describing the conditions under which constitutions of the third type come into being. I try to fill this gap, at least in part, by arguing that the dynamics of revolutionary activity and the processes of constitutional promulgation may have a synergistic effect—yielding a situation in which a constitutional text can become a potent political symbol of national identity, not another bit of legalistic mumbo jumbo.[1]

To gain perspective, I begin by looking back to the first great age of liberal transformation: How did the American revolutionaries manage to endow their Constitution with a formative political significance, one that shaped the terms of subsequent debate and decision for generations to come? Too often, the question provokes an uncritical celebration of the unique glories of eighteenth-century America. I believe, however, that generalizable lessons can be learned from the founding—lessons that alert us to analogous challenges in the present period of revolutionary possibility. We may glimpse important parallels between the situation confronting George Washington on the eve of the Constitutional Convention and the problem facing Lech Walesa as Solidarity took power in the aftermath of the Polish Revolution—parallels that point to the need for speedy action if Poland is to take constitutional leadership in the new revolutionary era.

Two other cases offer different perspectives. The first involves Russia, which may now be entering a constitutional moment of the kind that Poland is leaving. The second involves the establishment of the state of Israel a generation ago. A familiar pattern will begin to take shape, but this time, the window of opportunity for liberal constitutionalism slammed shut while revolutionaries busied themselves with other, seemingly more pressing matters.

Constitutional Moments

The problem of successful revolutionaries is paradoxical but real: they have won and, in winning, risk losing much of what they have fought to attain....

... [T]he existence of the old regime provided the typical movement with a common target, and having a common target served to suppress some crucial problems—notably, disagreements among the revolutionaries about important features of the political world they hoped to establish. "The enemy of my enemy is my friend"—this familiar logic made sense so long as the revolutionaries were in opposition. Why let disagreements detract from the imperative task of displacing the political regime?

major city, and that the assembly work with a time limit.]

1. I fill the gap only in part. A constitution can also win legitimation through evolutionary processes, in which elites build consent without the support of revolutionary mass mobilizations. The most recent success along these lines has been in Spain. See Andrea Bonime-Blanc, *Spain's Transition to Democracy* (1987). A systematic comparison of recent evolutionary and revolutionary exercises in constitutionalism should be high on the agenda of future research.

With victory, the restraints imposed by the common enemy disappear. Now the revolutionaries must decide what they are for, not merely what they are against. And they must do so under circumstances in which personal ambitions are whetted by the prospect of governmental office. Leaders and followers alike find themselves more and more often in a position to appreciate how the great principles proclaimed during the period of mobilization affect their concrete interests, sometimes in surprisingly adverse ways. At the same time, new political organizations form around these concrete interests and compete for the attention and allegiance of movement supporters.

Yet in spite of these formidable diversions of political energy and attention, the members of the movement remember their struggle in the political wilderness. Can they somehow hammer out the guiding principles of their movement into an enduring form that will shape political action in the years ahead? Or will they remain passive as the political centrality of these principles is lost in the swirl of special interests seeking to gain practical advantages within the emerging state structure?

These questions define the promise of a revolutionary constitution. Writing a constitutional text offers an opportunity for a victorious movement to make a collective effort both to frame their fundamental principles and to mobilize broad popular support for their crucial initiatives. So long as these steps are taken at the propitious moment created by a successful revolution, the democratically affirmed constitutional principles may prove remarkably resistant to change even as politics becomes very unrevolutionary. Without decisive action, the liberal dimension of the revolutionary achievement may suffer great erosion, even without a massive antiliberal backlash from the general population. . . .

The challenge is to describe the American case in terms that emphasize structural similarities to later revolutions, including those that catapulted down very different paths. First off, the Americans did not manage a peaceful revolution. On the contrary. George Washington is simply the first in a long line of guerrilla leaders who have conceded the major cities to the reactionary power while spending long years leading hit-and-run attacks from the countryside. The difference between General Washington and Marshall Giap or Chairman Mao is that Washington refused to use his military forces for political ends after the war. Rather than playing on the many grievances of his army, Washington disbanded the troops and went home to Virginia as a civilian.

Similarly, Jefferson and Madison head a very long list of intellectuals who have established their positions by writing political tracts—what else are the Declaration of Independence and the Federalist Papers?—and by serving as civilian leaders in revolutionary zones unoccupied by the reactionary power. Jefferson and Madison differed from future totalitarians in rejecting the legitimacy of an elite vanguard party. Instead of embracing such antidemocratic models, they grasped the possibility of using constitutional lawmaking to consolidate their revolutionary principles. Here I am less concerned with the substance of their Constitution than with two mechanisms they used to take advantage of their constitutional moment.

The first mechanism, the Constitutional Convention of 1787, is one of the most famous American contributions to the fund of Western political thought and practice. It involved a handful of revolutionary leaders from different parts of the country converging on Philadelphia to write a constitution four years after the peace treaty with England.

By establishing a convention apart from ordinary organs of government, the revolutionaries did more than isolate the problem of constitutional order from the many short-term issues that bulked large on the political agenda. The very creation of the separate forum created new and powerful political incentives for a successful conclusion of the experiment in constitutional formulation.

These incentives operated in a very personal way that all politicians can understand: quite simply, the revolutionary leaders risked making fools of themselves if the convention dissolved without achieving an acceptable constitutional text. Not surprisingly, this point was very clear to those with the most moral capital to lose—as any reader of the agonized correspondence between James Madison and George Washington can attest. It was absolutely crucial for Madison to persuade Washington to lend his enormous prestige to the constitutional project by chairing the convention. But why should the military hero be prepared to risk his public standing on the revolutionary intellectual's pipe dream?

We should not use twenty-twenty hindsight to belittle Washington's gamble. Modern revolutionaries with moral capital of Washingtonian dimension have yet to take similar risks. Once Washington and other leaders made their decision to go to Philadelphia, however, they were engaging in a self-fulfilling prophecy. They were self-consciously creating an incentive structure that maximized the chances of success by imposing new penalties for failure.

Their success should be assessed along three different dimensions. First, the revolutionaries at the convention had sacrificed much of their lives for certain fundamental principles, and a text that did not express those principles would be a failure in their eyes. Second, the delegates to the convention were perfectly aware that they lacked the resources to enact a constitution on their own authority. They could only propose a text and then campaign for its adoption by a majority of the voting population in each state. To win victory back home, delegates knew they had to protect their own region's basic interests—even when, as in the case of slavery, these interests offended the basic principles of the revolution. They could not afford the luxury of ideological purism; they would have to bargain with one another, as well as argue from first principles. Their task was to reach a sound political compromise of principles and interests through a complex process of argument and negotiation. The result hardly met with every delegate's satisfaction: one-fourth of them had quit in disgust before the convention reached agreement. Of the fifty-five who participated, only thirty-nine were willing to sign the final text, but these included many important revolutionary leaders.

This suggests a third measure of success: it was not enough for a revolutionary elite to reach a constitutional solution that they considered a sound political compromise. Their final text had to be sufficiently transparent and attractive to mobilize support throughout the country. Unless their proposed constitution could serve as a popular symbol of the revolutionary generation's achievement, the posturings of a few well-established leaders would lead nowhere.

Recognizing the importance of popular support, the revolutionary leadership took a second decisive step to exploit their moment of opportunity. They appealed for support from the People over the heads of existing governments. In spite of the requirements of preexisting constitutional law, the convention refused to allow state legislatures to veto its initiative. Instead, it designed a novel procedure for bringing the popular will more directly into play. Voters in each state were asked to select special delegates to ratifying conventions. These elections allowed competing candidates to concentrate on the merits of the constitutional proposal. By voting on delegates to the ratifying conventions, citizens could make a decision that was narrowly focused on the Constitution itself; they could ask themselves, Is this text an appropriate symbol of our generation's achievement? By winning these elections, the revolutionary elite could claim a special legitimacy for its constitutional text. Unlike normal legislation, the Constitution had won a "mandate from the People."

Indeed, we owe the device of the modern referendum to an analogous effort during the next great liberal revolution to exploit its own window of opportunity. Like the Americans, the French revolutionaries sought to consolidate their achievement through a constitutional text. And they are the ones who hit upon the device of the formal referendum to lend credibility to their talk of a democratic mandate from the People in support of their liberal breakthrough. Of course, legal forms alone never guarantee success: the French Revolution spun out of control, with tragic consequences for the next two centuries of European history.

Walesa and Washington

The question is whether Eastern Europeans are now able and willing to pick up the thread. The news coming out of Poland is not encouraging, at least when compared to the bright prospects of 1989. At that point, the similarities with the American experience seemed striking. Lech Walesa, like Washington, was a man of courage and insight. The Solidarity movement also contained a number of powerful liberal intellectuals capable of playing Madison to Walesa's Washington. We cannot know whether the same order of success might have occurred in 1990 if the task of constitutional construction had been given the highest priority. Unfortunately, the revolutionary leadership was easily diverted [and] revolutionary unity disintegrated in a blinding display of personal pettiness and intellectual hubris.

Not that anyone should expect revolutionary movements like Solidarity to sustain themselves forever. It is right and proper for revolutionary leadership to split into rival parties as new problems bring new issues to the fore. It is only natural for most ordinary people to lose interest in politics as time goes on and to attend to more personal dimensions of life. Constitutional moments in the aftermath of successful revolutions represent such precious opportunities precisely because liberals reject the idea of permanent revolution. The question is whether it is too late for Poland, whether the window of opportunity has slammed shut. . . .

. . . [T]he possibility, if it exits, will not be realized by treating constitutional formulation as one of many tasks confronting parliament. Instead, the damage that has been done may be repaired only by a gesture that emphasizes the crucial importance of seeking out a reasonable constitutional solution before the collective triumph of Solidarity becomes a bitter memory.

A special constitutional convention is urgently required—one that includes members of Parliament and representatives of the presidency. The constitutional proposal generated by this high-visibility group should be presented to Parliament for its approval. Then, if adopted there, it should be submitted to the People for ratification in a special referendum. As we have seen, the creation of a special constitutional forum creates new incentives for the participants to reach a sound constitutional compromise. But it is a mistake to evaluate the institutional innovation in terms of partisan self-interest. The call for a special constitutional forum symbolizes the present state of the revolution by asking, Is it still possible for men and women who sacrificed so much for a better Poland to transcend factionalism and clear solid constitutional ground for further democratic advance? As delegates enter the convention, they will know not only that the nation is watching them but—like it or not—that history will be judging them. Poland gave the modern world its second written constitution in 1791. Will it once again take constitutional leadership, this time with a more enduring result? By dramatizing such questions, the existence of the special forum may encourage participants to rise to the occasion and demonstrate that for all their differences, the spirit of the revolution lives on, at least in their constitutional text.

The American Constitution, it should be recalled, was not formulated in the first flush of revolutionary triumph. The Americans' first experiment in constitution writing—the Articles of Confederation of 1781—led to a pervasive political malaise comparable to the feeling in Poland today. Only after six years of dissatisfaction with this first constitutional experiment did Washington and his fellow leaders attempt a new beginning at the Philadelphia Convention of 1787. The chances for failure were as high then as they are now, but no one should underestimate the creativity of the human spirit. . . .

Is a Constitution Important?

But maybe I am exaggerating. Is it really so clear that every nation needs a Constitution-with-a-capital-C, a text that proclaims itself to be the fundamental law of the nation, with a higher status than all other statutes? After all, the English have been doing well enough without one for centuries. But it is one thing for a country with the liberal traditions of England to do without a constitution, quite another for nations attempting a new beginning through liberal revolution. Because these nations will characteristically find themselves with constitutions left behind by the displaced Communist regimes, the rising political elites have but two choices: to attempt a comprehensive statement of their revolutionary principles or to make do with a series of ad hoc modifications of the older Communist texts.

The second course has predictable consequences. Many authoritarian principles and practices inherited from the old regime may escape the process of ad hoc modification, even though they would have been rejected in a comprehensive revision. More important, the status of constitutional norms is grievously compromised. The old Communist texts were more propaganda symbols than serious operational realities. If the aim is to transform the very character of constitutional norms, a clean break seems desirable for two different, if related, reasons.

The first involves the role that a liberal constitution can play within the structure of political identity rising from the ashes of the old regime. If constitutional formulation and ratification are given the weight they deserve, the constitution can function for the wider public as the central symbol of its revolutionary achievement and become, over time, the center of an enlightened kind of patriotism. Although America serves as an obvious example of this process, modern Germany is closer to the present scene of action. Thus far at least, "patriotic constitutionalism" has provided Germany with an understanding of itself that can serve as a more humane and satisfying alternative to uglier possibilities. Surely the nations of Eastern Europe will require similar symbols as they strive to establish their political identity in the crises that lie ahead. When political partisans seek to exploit economic and spiritual discontent by appealing to xenophobic nationalism, the supporters of a more open society will sorely regret the opportunity they lost in failing to construct a constitutional symbol that might serve as a rallying point for a mobilized liberal politics.

My second reason for a clean break with the past concerns a narrower audience—the political elite that participates more directly in the bargaining and arguing that surrounds a constitutional compromise. Once these leaders sign the constitutional text, they will find it harder to play fast and loose with it to serve their short-run interests. Not only will they take pride in their achievement but they will have a vivid sense of the difficulty of regaining constitutional equilibrium once the original solution falls apart.

A very different situation obtains when the constitutional order emerges from ad hoc adaptation of norms inherited from the old regime. Why should either the political elite or the mass of ordinary citizens look upon brazen violations of such a text with grave concern? The question is even more pertinent when, as has been the case, ad hoc modifications are not made in a considered fashion and are not referred to the general electorate for ratification through a plebiscite. The resulting softness of the constitutional norms will have different effects, depending upon the structure of authority pieced together from the institutional debris of the old regime. On the one hand, the evolving system may be bipolar, with a president and a parliament sharing control. Because the constitutional norms that putatively determine power sharing lack strong political legitimacy, the scene is set for a struggle between president and parliament that emphasizes power plays and faits accomplis. This game will generally favor the president, especially one who has gained office through popular election. As a single person, the president can act swiftly and effectively, challenging the parliament to organize its multiple membership for a suitable counteraction against those unilateral decisions. As a final resort, the president can also take advantage of older authoritarian traditions and proclaim the existence of a state of emergency that justifies rule by executive decree. Whatever the outcome of this kind of unilateralism, one of the first casualties will be the idea of subjecting the conflicts between president and parliament to a rule of law that defines a stable separation of powers.

If, in contrast, a strong president does not arise in the process of ousting the Communist regime, soft constitutional norms will make it too easy for a parliamentary majority to run roughshod over fundamental rights. The short history of the state of Israel provides a cautionary tale. Turn back to the late 1940s, and you will find analogies to today's situation in Eastern Europe. After decades of revolutionary struggle, the Zionist leadership could credibly claim the support of a mobilized majority of the Jewish residents of Palestine, with men like David Ben-Gurion playing a symbolic role comparable to the one played by Washington in America, Walesa in Poland, Havel in Czechoslovakia, and Yeltsin in Russia. Moreover, the authors of the Israeli Declaration of Independence grasped the significance of a rapid formulation of a constitutional text. The declaration explicitly called for elections to a constituent assembly for this precise purpose. When the assembly convened, however, it ignored its instructions. Although strong majority support for a comprehensive constitution was within his grasp, Ben-Gurion refused to make this a top priority. Instead, the assembly deferred the task of constitutional formulation and transformed itself into the first Knesset, asserting plenary legislative powers in the manner of the British Parliament. Since this coup, subsequent Knessets have returned to constitution writing in fits and starts, never bringing it to completion. Forty years later, Israel has yet to promulgate a bill of rights.

Meanwhile, the constitutional moment passed into history. The men and women with the greatest moral standing died, leaving others who were less confident of their ability to take constitutional leadership. The broad-based revolutionary movement fractured into a multiplicity of parties and factions. As politicians became more accomplished in serving specific constituencies, they became less interested in uniting with one another in making an overarching constitutional statement of principle.

Within this second-generation setting, small parties of committed activists—in this case, religious groups of Orthodox Jews—could begin to set the ideological agenda. Although few in number, their representatives could play a strategic role in making a parliamentary majority. When other parties split apart, the ideologues could trade their support with the secular grouping that was more willing to advance their particular ideals. These tradeoffs have paid off in state support for laws that undermine liberal principles of religious toleration, enacted even though the overwhelming majority of Israelis continue to hold secular views. Similar scenarios—involving xenophobic nationalist groups exploiting their parliamentary position to impose antiliberal views that are not widely held—are all too easy to generate in the Eastern Europe of the future.

Another process of erosion is no less significant. It involves responses to crises, of which Israel has had more than its fair share. In a crisis, leaders are always tempted to ignore the long-run damage to individual rights. Indeed, one statutory assault on rights often serves as a precedent for another. Although the Israeli Supreme Court has tried to check the damage, its responses would have been more aggressive if the previous generation had ratified a formal bill of rights.... The long term costs of a short-term failure to act at the moment of revolutionary triumph are easy to underestimate.

[Ackerman considers whether he is wrong to think that the overthrow of Communism in 1989 opened up "liberal possibilities," because other factors—the Church in Poland, nationalism, interest in wealth acquisition—contributed to that overthrow. He argues that even if liberalism was only a small part of the events of 1989, "an emphasis on constitutionalism [will] tilt[ ] the public debate onto ... favorable terrain ...; if liberals succeed in pushing the constitutional project to the center of the political stage, this initial success will give a liberal spin to the evolving pattern of debate and decision[ ] [because] [l]iberal constitutional thought and practice is far more developed than its competitors." He goes on to argue that the number of deeply divisive issues in each polity is likely to be small, and that "many other dimensions of the constitution will affect the unpredictable crises ... that lie ahead. On these low-visibility matters of high importance, liberals will often find it surprisingly easy to use the constitution to crystallize widespread, but amorphous, commitments into legal forms that will have substantial influence upon the day after tomorrow." He goes on to acknowledge that liberals must be prepared to compromise, by finding common ground in making constitutions, lest a "liberal utopia ... be abandoned during the first crisis."]

This said, I want to resist the fashionable relativism that looks upon liberalism as a local prejudice of Anglo-American civilization or maybe even a few English-speaking universities inhabited by rootless cosmopolitans. Whatever else the Eastern Europeans have been rebelling against, their experience with Communist tyranny has impressed upon them the supreme value of the rule of law and personal freedom. We do not do justice to these insights by supposing them to be foreign imports from "the West." The

Eastern Europeans who have endured years of Communist tyranny are often far more alive to the importance of liberal values than the English or Americans who take them for granted. It is one thing, however, to affirm the enduring significance of freedom and the rule of law, quite another to translate these values into enduring political structures.

This is the reason I emphasize the dynamics of the process by which revolutions may—or may not—be constitutionalized. Given their protracted history of undemocratic rule, Eastern European revolutionaries desperately need to provide compelling models of a different kind of government—one in which the consent of the People is not merely a propaganda slogan but a lived reality. The effort to hammer out a sound constitutional compromise may fail: the revolutionary leadership may prove unequal to the task, or the broader population may look upon the entire exercise with cynical disbelief. Even the greatest success will be ambiguous; even the most committed will be uncertain whether they have, at long last, begun to master a legacy of arbitrary government. But the task will not be any easier if infinitely delayed. The moment to begin is when the promise of revolutionary renewal remains alive.

Gary Jeffrey Jacobsohn, Apple of Gold: Constitutionalism in Israel and the United States (1993)

Constituting the Polity

> Do we need a Constitution like the American? By all means let us profit from the experience of others and borrow laws and procedures from them, provided they match our needs.
>
> —*David Ben-Gurion*

A Constitution by Any Other Name?

A young Israeli attorney general, Haim Cohn, once paid a visit to the U.S. Supreme Court. His purpose was to speak with the members of the Court about constitutional matters. More specifically, he had been sent by his prime minister, David Ben-Gurion, to pursue the question of a constitution for the state of Israel, a document promised in that country's Declaration of Independence, but as yet unrealized. The prime minister had always been an outspoken opponent of such a charter, and he was hoping that his attorney general's visit would produce a report confirming him in his strongly held belief. In carrying out his assignment, Cohn proceeded from justice to justice, inquiring of each his views on the appropriate course of action for Israel. From Justice Black he received a recommendation that was unlikely to appeal to Ben-Gurion: "Make a constitution immediately, and make it so stringent that no Supreme Court can evade it." As he made his rounds, sentiments of this sort were regularly voiced by other justices as well. Until, that is, he got to Justice Frankfurter, who said, "Never write a constitution. What you need are independent judges, not a written constitution." When the prime minister received his attorney general's report he expressed satisfaction that his stance on the undesirability of a written constitution for Israel had found such impressive support on the U.S. Supreme Court.[1] . . .

. . . The Federalists had pointed out that the notion of a bill of rights developed in England, where there was no written constitution. But precisely because Americans had constructed a constitution of limited, enumerated powers, they had no need, the Federalists argued, for a list of enumerated rights. This did not satisfy their opponents. As one said, "Any system therefore which appoints a legislature, without any reservation of the rights of individuals, surrenders all power in every branch of legislation to the government." Ultimately such arguments proved persuasive; should they not be even more persuasive in Israel, where there is no comprehensive written constitution, where the supremacy of the Knesset is a fact of political life?

The answer to this question is a complicated one, which this chapter will seek to illuminate. Its complexity is in part related to assumptions embedded in the question itself. For example, while it is fair to say that Israel lacks a comprehensive written constitution, it is highly misleading to portray this as an absence of written constitutional rules. Recently a visiting French jurist [Robert Badinter] told his Israeli hosts, "Your problem is not that you are trying to adopt a constitution, but that you already have one and are trying to change it." By this he meant that efforts to reform the Israeli system in the direction of a single, unified fundamental charter should be evaluated in terms of the actual constitutional changes that would result from such a development, rather than in the erroneously conceived context of a sudden departure from a constitutional tradition characterized by the absence of written limits on the exercise of power. If the subject under consideration is the protection of individual rights, it surely matters if the status quo is described in a way that conveys the impression of a system of power unconstrained by constitutional checks.

But if parliamentary supremacy reigns, is there really any other way to convey a sense of the status quo? Yes would be the answer of many students of Great Britain; as Vernon Bogdanor observes, "The British Constitution is essentially a *political* constitution, one whose operation depends upon the strength of political factors and whose interpretation depends upon the will of its political leaders." It is frequently pointed out that a common historic political tradition of respect for law provides effective constitutional checks even in the face of a legislature that theoretically can do what it pleases. Is the same confidence justified, however, in the case of a society where tradition, demography, and culture do not follow the British example? Israel certainly differs significantly in these respects from Great Britain in spite of the enormous influence of the British legal tradition on Israeli institutions and practice. And yet, as we shall see,

---

1. This story is based on an interview by the author with Haim Cohn. Mr. Cohn, known for his iconoclastic opinions, acerbic wit, and commitment to liberal ideals, eventually served with great distinction as a member of the Israeli Supreme Court. . . .

practices are being established in Israel that cast doubt on the omnipotence of the legislative branch. For example, it is still a debatable proposition whether the Israeli Supreme Court has the authority to nullify a legislative act of the Knesset on constitutional grounds.

But the specific questions relating to the prospects for and desirability of constitutional reform in Israel, while interesting in themselves, are not the real concern of this chapter. Rather, the main focus is a broader one— the subject of constitutionalism itself, or how the concerns of Black, Frankfurter, Jefferson, and Hamilton get addressed in two constitutional contexts that share a language of constitutional discourse while differing so profoundly in many politically relevant ways. . . .

Binding the Future

The story of Israel's failure to fulfill its Declaration of Independence's prescription for "a Constitution to be drawn up by the Constitutuent Assembly" is an oft-told tale.[17] Quite properly it is frequently cast as a political story, in which considerations of partisan advantage receive ample attention. For historians and legal scholars, even those inclined to resist cynicism, it is relatively easy to accept the allegations of Menachem Begin, then the leader of the minority Herut movement, that Ben-Gurion's opposition to a constitution was fundamentally attributable to his fear of losing all or some of his power. As Begin expressed it in debate in the First Knesset, "If the Constituent Assembly legislates a constitution, then the government will not be free to do as it likes." The clear inference to be drawn from the tone and substance of the debates is that adherence to parliamentary supremacy is perfectly natural for the leader of the predominant political party, particularly a leader with no experience in the constitutional tradition of limited government.

Without losing sight of these obvious political calculations, we must still reflect on the arguments used by both sides to justify their respective positions. These justifications addressed genuine concerns, even if they also masked less principled considerations. One line of argument ... was pursued in the debate in the First Israeli Knesset by a member of the governing Mapai party, who urged delay with respect to the constitutional question: "One does not create a constitution at the beginning of a revolution, but when it is completed. All constitutions are an attempt to

---

17. The usual point of departure is the United Nations' 1947 partition resolution, stipulating that the new Jewish and Arab states were to adopt democratic constitutions. Subsequent to the adoption of the U.N. resolution, the Jewish Agency for Palestine commenced the drafting of such a document, although preparation for this task had been initiated prior to the U.N. action. In addition, the Declaration of Independence contained language consistent with the partition resolution, including the provision for a Constituent Assembly whose sole function was to adopt the constitution. This assembly was elected in January 1949 (several months after the deadline set in the Declaration), and it immediately assumed a legislative function as well, an indication that the intent of the Declaration would not in the end be implemented. The Constituent Assembly enacted the Transition Law, providing broadly for the nation's government institutions. The legislature was to be known as the Knesset, and the Constituent Assembly was officially designated the First Knesset. It never executed the specific task for which it was constituted.

'freeze' certain principles, to preserve them, inasmuch as it is possible to preserve any particular thing in the life of a nation." There were several additional reasons adduced for postponing the adoption of a constitution; this one, which followed Ben-Gurion's argument that the drafting of a constitution should not precede the "Ingathering of the Exiles," was arguably of lesser importance than some others in influencing the subsequent course of events. Yet it speaks to some unique aspects of the Israeli constitutional experience.[20]

The proponents of a formal constitution had made several arguments in support of their position: that a constitution would protect individual rights by establishing written limits on the power of the majority; that it would stand as a symbol of Israeli independence and status within the international community; and that it would serve the pedagogical purpose of educating a diverse population in the political principles of their regime. The opponents contended that the goals associated with the first two arguments did not require the "novelty" (Ben-Gurion's term) of a formal written constitution. These opponents, it is worth noting, represented an interesting alliance, consisting on the one hand of extreme secularists such as Ben-Gurion, and on the other of ultra-Orthodox Jews, who maintained that Israel had no need of *another* constitution, the Torah being a more than adequate fundamental law.[22] Indeed, it was the radically different understandings of the essence of the regime held by these alliance partners that explains why the third argument of the proponents was, from the opposition's perspective, flawed in its most basic assumptions.

Educating people in the principles of the regime assumes that such principles exist, or at least that they exist in a manner that can be inscribed coherently in constitutional form. But if the basic nature of the regime is in doubt (a Western state? a state of the Jewish people? a Jewish state? all of the above?), does it not make sense to postpone constitutionalizing, which is to say "freezing," a set of principles on which no consensus had yet congealed? To the extent that a consensus existed, it was that the state of Israel was to be a homeland for the Jewish people; but if this was the case, why not postpone the constitutional decision until such time as a much larger percentage (i.e., much more than 7 percent) of the Jewish people resided within its borders? "The constitution is created for that population which was in existence within the borders of the state.... Our population is fluid. We are not at the end of a revolutionary process but at its beginning."

During the debate, the American example was cited as one to be followed. After all, it took from 1776 to 1791 for the Americans to produce

---

20. As Ruth Gavison has observed, it is an "argument that would be inconceivable and clearly objectionable in almost any other country and it reveals one of the unique features of Israel." Ruth Gavison, The Controversy Over Israel's Bill of Rights, *Israel Yearbook on Human Rights* 15 (1985): 135.

22. Said one member of the ultra-Orthodox Agudat Israel, "Any Constitution created by man can have no place in Israel." Quoted in Norman Zucker, *The Coming Crisis in Israel: Private Faith and Public Policy* (Cambridge: MIT Press, 1973), p. 67.

their constitution; why then, it was asked, expect Israelis to be more expeditious? A reasonable question, to be sure, but there are serious limitations to the appropriateness of the analogy. The U.S. Constitution was written in 1777, ratified in 1781, and then rewritten and reratified beginning in 1787. The Americans did what most successful revolutionaries have done subsequently, seize the opportunity provided by the occasion to codify the fruits of their victory. In their case they quickly became dissatisfied with their creation and went back to the drawing board. But their more successful venture in 1787 was not attributable to any massive infusion of new members into their ranks; rather, it resulted from specific lessons learned from actual experience under the earlier constitutional structure. In fact, the document was eventually sold as an improvement over its predecessor not because it had discovered the true meaning of the Revolution, but because it represented a better prospect for realizing its aspirations.

In this regard it is worth recalling Ben-Gurion's observation . . . in which he sought to distinguish between the revolutionary experiences of Israel and other countries, including the United States: "There the people rose against the government and a change in government signified attainment of the people's aim. But not we. We rose against a destiny of the years, against exile and dispersion, against deprivation of language and culture." The observation is helpful in illuminating alternative understandings of nationhood, but in one respect, at least as applied to the United States, it is not quite accurate. While it is fair to say that the American Revolution was essentially political in nature, the claim that its success signified attainment of the people's aim is valid only if success is narrowly defined in terms of independence. But if the broader political goals of the Revolution, those announced to the world in the Declaration of Independence, are included among the aims of the people, then they were most assuredly not attained. One need look no further than to the existence of slavery to appreciate the magnitude of their unfulfilled aspirations.

Ben-Gurion might respond by saying that as far as the desirability of a constitution is concerned, this broader understanding alters nothing. He might say, for example, that the gap between reality and the principles that validated the Revolution required that a constitution be adopted in the United States as a means of closing the gap. In this he could appeal to . . . [Abraham Lincoln's belief] that those involved in the interpretation and enforcement of the Constitution were morally and legally obliged to pursue the aspirational content of the Declaration, and the legitimacy of their efforts in this regard hinged on their success. Essentially, then, it was the purpose of the regime's founders to bind the future, to "freeze" a set of political principles that would serve as developmental guidelines for the nation. In the case of Israel, however, binding the future should, according to Ben-Gurion, await the now feasible goal of undoing the historic injustice of "exile and dispersion."

Proponents of an Israeli constitution might have a different take on all of this. They might start by pointing out that while the Declaration of

Independence establishes an admirably high standard of political justice, the Constitution of 1787, with its recognition (if not endorsement) of slavery, manifests a clear set of moral compromises. It is thus obvious that the Americans adopted a constitution prior to their having resolved the greatest challenge to their professed principles, the presence on their soil of human bondage. The lesson to be learned, then, is that a consensus on critical questions of regime definition is not a prerequisite for constitution making. . . .

To this the following might be said. The American Declaration indicates clearly what direction constitutional evolution will have to take in order for the document to work itself pure. The constitutional compromises over slavery should, therefore, be seen as the pragmatic concession of principle to reality, namely that slavery was an existential fact that threatened to derail the entire experiment in popular government. As Herbert J. Storing explained, "Slavery was an evil to be tolerated, allowed to enter the Constitution only by the back door, grudgingly, unacknowledged, on the presumption that the house would be truly fit to live in only when it was gone, and that it would ultimately be gone." Even the major concession of Article I, section 9, involving the migration and importation of slaves (euphemistically referred to as "such persons"), was, as Storing noted, "not a guarantee of a right but a postponement of a power to prohibit." After 1808 Congress could regulate in a manner that would support what Lincoln later claimed was the true intent of the framers, to place slavery on the course of ultimate extinction. Or put another way, the compromise was accomplished in a constitutional form consistent with the goal of binding the future to the realization of universal principles of justice.

The Israeli Declaration, on the other hand, is, as we have seen, much more problematic as far as the consistency of its political vision is concerned. It is one thing to compromise principle in the face of political exigency; quite another to achieve a viable constitutional result in the face of competing, and potentially contradictory, visions. Moreover, where the definition of nationhood is straightforwardly understood in terms of a set of political ideals, binding the future through constitutional mandate becomes an intrinsic part of the self-understanding of the polity. Where, alternatively, the essence of the regime is so much bound up with the issue of *who* the majority of the citizens are, the adoption of a formal constitution may be seen as a less significant event in the inception of the postrevolutionary system. Indeed, the argument that the ingathering of the exiles, represented by the Law of Return, should precede the creation of a formal code of fundamental law is not without a certain compelling logic. It makes sense, that is, to want to leave the future relatively unfettered by principled constraints until more people can participate in defining the substance of the principles. Carried to the extreme this logic becomes a formula for indefinite postponement; and it may very well be that at a certain point (perhaps now) it is wise for the appropriate authority to make a more definitive constitutional declaration of its vision of the future. However,

Ben-Gurion's contention, politically motivated though it may have been, was not an unreasonable claim at the time it was made.

The ultimate outcome of the First Knesset's deliberations over the constitutional question was the passage of a compromise proposal, known as the "Harari Resolution," that prescribes a process of incremental accumulation of individual chapters—or basic laws—that when terminated will together form the state constitution. This vaguely worded and much criticized legislation left unclear the status of the basic laws, just as it was silent as to a timetable for completion of the constitution.[33] It provided formal commitment (sincere or otherwise) to the principle of the written constitution, while maintaining maximum flexibility in the Knesset's capacity to determine its realization. It was essentially a formula to proceed with "all deliberate speed," although it lacked any mechanism to enforce compliance. It left the state with an evolving constitution that conceivably possesses superior status to ordinary law, but which, predictably, coexists uneasily with the tradition of parliamentary supremacy.

This piecemeal approach, in which every Knesset in effect serves concurrently as a constituent assembly with the power to enact basic laws, represents an appealing solution from the Ben-Gurion point of view.... [If] a constitution is "a repository of society's hopes for its future," then it is prudent for a polity whose future cannot as yet be projected in the hopes of its highly conflicted people to retain flexibility in its constitution-making authority, which is to say, to ensure its capacity to revise its fundamental (or basic) law with relative ease. The Madisonian argument of *Federalist #49,* that "frequent appeals [to the people for constitutional change] would, in a great measure, deprive the government of that veneration which time bestows on every thing," did not apparently persuade Ben-Gurion. Indeed, he was a severe critic of the American amendment process, arguing that "only within the framework of laws that must be altered and improved from time to time as hurrying life demands ..., only therein is civic freedom truly alive and are the rights of every man upheld." ...

[T]he cautious nature of Madisonian concerns about veneration and stability applies to the process of constitutional amendment, not to the act of constitutional creation; indeed it was Madison himself who took the lead in the Continental Congress in arguing for the radical departure undertaken by the recently concluded Constitutional Convention. While the putative purpose of the Revolution—restoration of traditional rights of Englishmen—was not *revolutionary,* the specific constitutional solution for achieving this objective was profoundly innovative. And as the inaugural *Federalist* essay indicates, the novelty of the solution is importantly connected to

---

33. In fact it was claimed at the time by opponents of the constitution that the Declaration of Independence was not binding on the First Knesset, and consequently its members were under no obligation to adopt a written charter. Indirect support for this view may be found in the early Supreme Court's relegation of the Declaration to constitutional insignificance. On the subject of the tainted origins of the U.S. Constitution, see Richard S. Kay, "The Illegality of the American Constitution," *Constitutional Commentary* 4 (1987). [Footnote relocated—eds.]

the character of its creation. "It has been frequently remarked that it seems to have been reserved to the people of this country, by their conduct and example, to decide the important question, whether societies of men are really capable or not of establishing good government from reflection and choice, or whether they are forever destined to depend for their political constitutions on accident and force."

Reliance on reflection and choice, or what is the same, the imposition of a particular political vision on constitutional arrangements, is not incompatible with an account of the American founding that portrays the Constitution as the heir of a fully mature tradition.... The Constitution was essentially an indigenous outgrowth that, while drawing on foreign sources, manifested a uniquely American mix of political principles and practices. Yet to understand the 1787 document as the inevitable stage of a historical progression is to ignore the deliberative options available to the framers, particularly with respect to the creation of a national government....

Madison's conservatism regarding the amendment process is not unrelated to his boldness in constitution making. The latter activity did more than provide a set of rules for a new regime; it did, as Lincoln put it, culminate in the "picture of silver" that framed the "apple of gold." It constitutionalized the principles that gave to the people of the new regime the basis for a sense of nationhood. Not surprisingly, then, its leading advocate and intellectual benefactor would think it unwise to provide the people with unobstructed access to constitutional change. One is reminded of the advice not to mess with Mother Nature. In the case of the Constitution, the point would seem to be that when such a written document embodies principles that are the wellspring of the polity's national identity, it should not be altered for light and transient causes. Depriving "government of that veneration which time bestows on every thing" should therefore be especially avoided if the principles that animate and drive the government constitute the core of the society's collective sense of identity. Or as Lincoln later put it, "As a general rule, I think, we would [do] much better [to] let it [the Constitution] alone. No slight occasion should tempt us to touch it. Better not take the first step, which may lead to a habit of altering it. Better, rather, habituate ourselves to think of it, as unalterable.... The men who made it ... have passed away. Who shall improve, on what *they* did?"

In contrast, the Israeli experience displays greater conservatism in the initial phase of constitutional development, but less concern for the exalted place and survival of rooted constitutional norms. It is interesting, for example, that the Basic Law on the Judiciary specifically exempts the Supreme Court from any obligation to observe the principle of *stare decisis*.[37] And even if some basic laws have an entrenched character (itself a topic of considerable debate), in the sense that they take precedence over

---

37. Paragraph 20 reads: (a) A rule laid down by a court shall guide any lower courts. (b) A rule laid down by the Supreme Court shall bind any court other than the Supreme Court.

ordinary law, the process by which they may be altered or discarded is reflective of a much greater tolerance for constitutional innovation than is the case in the United States. To be sure, much of the early conservatism is attributable to a more complex legal environment confronting the founders of the new Israeli state in comparison with their American counterparts. But perhaps more fundamental is the different roles that the constitution serves in their respective politics. For the American founders, a written constitution was the final legitimation of their Revolution, a revolution that gave birth to a new people. They needed it to affirm their existence as a nation. "In other countries, one can abrogate the constitution without abrogating the nation. The United States does not have that choice." [Samuel P. Huntington]. Or in John M. Murrin's artful formulation, Americans are notable in the "architecture of nationhood" for having "erected their constitutional roof before they put up the national walls." The Israeli founders were architects confronting a different structural challenge. They were, as Daniel J. Elazar has aptly pointed out, in possession of an ancient traditional constitution rooted in history and religion, within which was contained their "national walls." Their problem was to erect a constitutional roof over these walls while also integrating features of the modern liberal democratic style into their architectural planning. In order to complete the roof they would have to determine what was as yet unclear—how the merging of these two traditions would affect the configuration of the structure they were erecting.

Stanley N. Katz, *Constitutionalism in East Central Europe: Some Negative Lessons from the American Experience* (1993)

Many American experts have urged East Central Europeans to adopt a particular kind of constitution ... A valid constitution, they argue, must be a written document [and] must include provisions for separation of powers and judicial review, as well as a bill of rights, and various other by now historic attributes of American constitutionalism. . . .

The real question . . . is what the appropriate starting point for new European constitutions might be. The answer, in my judgment, is to be found in local traditions rather than in the history of the United States during the era of the enlightenment. . . .

[Katz indicates that his participation in the mid–1980s in discussions of constitutionalism around the world, in developed and developing societies, socialist and capitalist regimes, had an impact on his current views.]

We heard from those who believed that constitutions must be written, legitimized by bodies other than ordinary legislatures, based on individual rights and conducted by rigorous formal limitations on the power of government. We also heard from those who believed that group rights were the essence of constitutionalism, and that the underlying purpose of constitutions was to empower governments to achieve popular ends.

It became obvious that there was no international consensus on the meaning of constitutionalism.... American and Western European universalistic constitutionalism were not persuasive in many parts of the world.... Meaningful approaches in different national contexts require the development of the core meaning of constitutionalism in terms of local cultures ... a more ethnographic approach [to comparative constitutionalism.] ...

[Based on a series of conferences in Warsaw, Budapest, Prague and Bratislava, funded by the Pew Charitable Trusts and organized by the American Council of Learned Societies, he concludes that] the most striking aspect ... was the degree to which national and local history, culture and politics influenced thinking about constitutionalism, even within such a relatively small geographic region.

[Katz argues that this diversity is analogous to the diversity among the American states in their state constitutions after the Revolutionary War, and that the Constitution of 1787 can be seen as] an attempt to mediate universal reason with local traditions, while, at the same time, accommodating local differences through the federal structure as well as through the intentional ambiguity of many of its substantive provisions [including those relating to slavery].... Individual liberty ... was not a universal principle for early American national constitutionalism.

[We must] view the nations of East Central Europe with a renewed sense of their different traditions and realities.

To take only a few examples, Hungary and Poland are in the process of developing new constitutional structures in piecemeal fashion, by amending formerly socialist constitutions, with changes driven by the force of the transformations taking place in their social and economic relations. The Czech Republic and Slovakia, on the other and, impelled by their separation into two nations, have drafted new constitutions. Yet paradoxically, the popular legitimacy of the Hungarian and Polish constitutional orders appears to be stronger than that of the Czech and Slovak regimes. It seems that, particularly in the Hungarian case, a more varied political landscape is better accommodated by this piecemeal approach. And, in any case, the difficulties and dangers of starting to write a new constitution from scratch have made constitutional accommodation a better approach.

Another example is the differing impact of history on constitutionalism. Hungarians tend to take their constitutional past for granted without public discourse.... Kalman Kulsra, the ... last socialist Minister of Justice, has argued that the precommunist Hungarian constitutional tradition makes the gradual resumption of constitutionalism a practical reality. For Poles, on the other hand, the question of their constitutional history and tradition seems to be self-consciously central to their constitutional legitimacy. For example, during one of our Warsaw conferences a lively and extended disagreement arose over the significance of the Polish Constitution of May 3, 1791, which was never implemented.... Several [speakers] pushed the discussion back even further, identifying a pre–1791 constitutional tradition involving obedience to the rule of law, as a basis for the current constitutional structure.

Slovaks are also concerned with history, but in a manner almost diametrically opposed to that of the Poles. Slovakia had no history of national autonomy prior to the formation of Czechoslovakia in the aftermath of World War I. Slovakia's only prior history of independent statehood came during World War II, when the Nazis established a fascist Slovakian puppet regime. The fact that the first Slovak constitution was promulgated during this period is a potential source of delegitimation for the current regime ... [particularly] given the absence of other historical antecedents for Slovak constitutionalism....

Once we acknowledge the fact that national, even local history, culture and politics are of central importance to the constitutional scheme that develops in a particular place, however, where does this leave us? That is to say, shorn of universals, what is constitutionalism? To my mind, if there is an essence of constitutionalism (and I believe that there is), it is not to be found in the constitutional arrangements and institutions that are established in a particular country. Rather, it is to be found in the *practice* of constitutionalism, in a form of politics that is based on the notion of respect for the rule of law, in which the government, however it is configured, reflects the basic values and aspirations of the community.

That is to say that generic constitutionalism consists in a process within a society by which the community commits itself to the rule of law, specifies its basic values, and agrees to abide by a legal/institutional structure which guarantees that formal social institutions will respect the agreed-upon values....

[Katz goes on to note important differences between American constitutionalism and "European varieties": 1. the U.S. tradition of dividing lawmaking authority between Congress and President vs. the civil law tradition of unitary parliamentary government; 2. the limitation of protected individual rights in the U.S. to "negative liberties" vs. the social and economic rights sought after in post-socialist countries; 3. the "political self-denial of the American military establishment"; 4. the practice of dual sovereignty in American federalism; 5. the rigorous separation of church and state; and 6. the U.S. adherence to a "consensual notion of citizenship with all of the pluralistic tolerance that implies for American political life."]

[Katz concludes that the American Constitution is] primarily a point of reference for the socio-political system.... Constitutionalism reflects the recognition by all political actors that a particular political process, established democratically, must be respected for valid political activity to take place. Whether this political process includes judicial review, whether it is grounded in notions of individual liberty or group solidarity, whether the constitution stresses political or social and economic rights, none of these is essential to constitutionalism. The crucial element is that, whatever the constitutional structure, it must reflect the will of the people and it must command sufficient respect from all political actors to serve as an effective limitation on the unprincipled exercise of public power.

... [A] primary concern expressed at each of our East Central European constitutionalism conferences was the unfamiliarity of the mass of the people ... with basic constitutional values and principles.... [I]n the Czech Republic, [speakers] ... lamented the pervasive influence of ... "legal nihilism" derived from the long Czechoslovak experience of a formal and unenforceable constitution, ineffective courts, and a near total rejection of the notion of individual civil and political rights.... [T]he failure of post communist governments to carry out constitutional mandates for upper houses of the legislature, constitutional courts and the like have reinforced these public attitudes skeptical towards law.

Another ominous note is the regional preoccupation with referenda—most of the constitutions provide for the possibility of referenda on legislation and on governments themselves ... [and many] fear the possibility of democratic rejection by referendum....

... [T]he greatest threats to constitutionalism in East Central Europe do not derive from the negativity of skepticism but rather from all too positive public sentiments of ethnic, religious and national identity. How to cope with the role of the Catholic Church in Poland, the Hungarian minority in Slovakia, or ideas of a "greater Hungary" are the urgent questions, and they are questions for which universal conceptions of constitutionalism provide neither answers nor possible courses of public action. Yugoslavia is the ghost at the table of constitutionalism....

... If the essence of constitutionalism is ... a specific national political process, really a cultural process, then the transition must be seen as a series of political struggles. Each "new" nation will undergo different forms of struggle which, ultimately, will produce different outcomes.... Hopefully ... [these will] reflect the will of the people and their own sense of the rule of law. But with free politics there are no guarantees, and no certain outcome....

As the course of lustration ["cleansing"] everywhere other than the Czech Republic and the German Democratic Republic shows, memory itself must be abolished if political development is to take place. And here is the rub. The post-colonial nations of Africa and Asia could at least find some degree of integrative vigor in their rejection of common enemies, but in East Central Europe too many of the enemies were domestic....

[Katz expresses cautious optimism about constitutionalism in East Central Europe, in contrast to contemporary Russia where, he argues,] historical experience is a crucial difference in that Russians have no history of democratic constitutionalism....

[Katz concludes by emphasizing that] what sympathetic foreigners must hope for is the development of self conscious and self-referential local processes in each country, designed to develop popular constitutional consciousness and commitment.... [by] nurturing their most promising local traditions and institutions....

Questions and Comments on Constitutional Transitions

1. What is a "constitutional moment"? Can one know it exists at the time it occurs, or is it only after the passage of time that such moments can be identified? Is it helpful, then, to think of "moments" of "constitutional opportunity"?

2. What is "constitutionalism"? Would Katz's definition include dictatorships initially agreed to by a people desiring "strong leaders"? What does "rule of law" mean?

3. Ackerman has elsewhere argued that the New Deal represented a "constitutional moment" in U.S. history, in that the broad understanding of the scope of federal power embodied in the Roosevelt administration's legislation was (ultimately) both accepted by the Supreme Court and ratified by "the people" in the election of 1936. If a "constitutional moment" can be identified without resort to formal modification of written constitutions in the U.S., why not in Israel, or in Eastern Europe?

4. Several writers discuss the relationship between "principle," and particularly revolutionary principles motivating armed conflict leading to substantial rupture with prior regime, and constitution-making. What is the relationship between "principle" and constitutional moments?

5. In any moment of constitution-making there are likely to be issues that are politically controversial and divisive: in the United States, slavery; in Israel, the secular or religious nature of the state; in Poland, the position of the church. What is the function of constitutions with respect to those issues? Is there some practical limit on the range and number of "hard" issues that constitutions can productively address?

6. Are some structures of constitutional governance inconsistent with stable constitutionalism? Reconsider here Nino's arguments about presidentialism in Latin America. Consider also Justice Albie Sachs' explanation of why South Africa chose to have a President elected by the Parliament, not the people: He argued that several South African traditions, including that of despotic government by strong, colonial governors appointed by the British, and the tradition of strong leadership imposed through a very hierarchical chain of command in clandestine organizations (like the ANC) battling apartheid (as well as certain authoritarian leadership traditions in tribal communities in South Africa) created too great a risk of an overly strong, authoritarian president were South Africa to follow a U.S. presidential model. Speech by Justice Albie Sachs, of the Constitutional Court of South Africa, at Georgetown University Law Center (October 8 1996). Instead, the President is selected by the national legislature, and chooses cabinet ministers largely from the legislature. See Constitution of the Republic of South Africa 1996, Sections 86, 91.

B. Modern Constitutional Regime Change: Principle and Compromise

The next set of readings describes processes of constitutional change in Eastern Europe after 1989. Osiatynski (1991) argues that while the "moment" for making a "constitution of principle" may have been lost, Poland still had the opportunity to create a constitution of compromise, that would result from what he called "the political process rather than ... moral reasoning." Osiatynski (1993) also argues that Polish traditions, including the absence of a strong commitment to protection of individual rights as well as the presence of traditions of both democracy and strong leaders, are challenges for creation of a Constitution committed to both democracy and freedom. Is the distinction between a "constitution of principle" and a "constitution of compromise" persuasive? Is it even plausible? What is the difference, and how can you tell? Where would you classify the U.S. constitution?

Sajó and Losonci emphasize the impact of the role of law under communist regimes (to support the state) and the absence of broad public acceptance of liberal traditions in Poland, Hungary and the Czech Republic as obstacles to the development of constitutionalism. They are skeptical of the ability of Eastern European nations to utilize constitutions to move toward rule of law, in part because of the ease with which, e.g. the Hungarian Constitution has been amended, and the difficulty of establishing independent judicial review. Both Osiatynksi and Sajó and Losonci thus implicitly hold up a model of constitutionalism based on practice in the United States and in Western Europe as a standard of measure.

Holmes and Sunstein suggest, contrary to the experience of U.S. constitutionalism, that relatively easy amendment procedures are important to establishing constitutionalism in Eastern Europe in the first decade after the fall of Communism. They urge more attention to the importance of encouraging representative politics to develop, and to the positive uses of constitutions to facilitate, rather than to restrain, effective governance. And they challenge the claim that, at least in Eastern Europe, "constitutional moments" for creating "constitutions of principle" must be seized, and entrenched, against future "ordinary politics."

For an innovative combination of elite decisionmaking, representative democracy, and judicial review in the constitution-making process, we include materials on the process by which the new South African Constitution was adopted.

1.   CONSTITUTIONS OF PRINCIPLE OR COMPROMISE: POLAND

Wiktor Osiatynski, *The Constitution–Making Process in Poland*, 13 Law & Policy 125 (1991) and *Perspectives on the Current Constitutional Situation in Poland,* in Constitutionalism and Democracy: Transitions in the Contemporary World (Douglas Greenberg, Stanley N. Katz, Melanie Beth Oliviero, and Steven C. Wheatley eds., 1993)

OSIATYNSKI (1991)

WIKTOR OSIATYŃSKI (WO): The constitution is at mid-stage in Poland. There are two drafts adopted by the former Parliament. There were two drafting committees, one in the Sejm, which is the lower house of Parliament, and one in the Senate, which is the upper house. The origin of the arrangement was related to the Round Table agreement and the legitimacy of the drafters. Many Solidarity politicians in the Senate held that the lower house had no legitimacy even to work on the constitution because the Sejm was elected in elections with predetermined results: sixty-five percent of the places in the Sejm were reserved for the Communists and their cronies and only thirty-five percent were open for free elections. The Senate was freely elected so the assumption was that the Senate might have the legitimacy to work on the constitution. Accordingly, two different constitutional committees were formed.

Initially, there was a hope that perhaps the freely-elected part of the Sejm would work with the Senate's Constitutional Commission and propose a joint version of the constitution. However, as time passed, a growing rift developed between the Sejm and the Senate, until eventually members of the two commissions stopped communicating altogether. I was actually witness to some provisions created in both chambers that were made just to be different from the proposal of the other chamber. This conflict really influenced the constitution-making process.

During 1989-91, there were seven drafts submitted to these two committees. Two of them were submitted or prepared by the former allies of the Communist party - the Peasant party and the so-called Democratic Alliance. There were also three proposals prepared by one group of authors. In addition, there were two drafts of the Bill of Rights, one prepared by three members of the Helsinki Foundation for Human Rights and one by the Center for Human Rights in Poznan.

The Sejm draft was heavily based on the Poznan project. One could feel a considerable influence in the lower house of the "social democrats," i.e., people who were more or less apologetic constitutional scholars under the Communists and who recently have been changing their ways of thinking, to move from socialist dogmas to some kind of the rule of law. These "social democrats" played the most important role in the preparation of the Sejm draft. The Senate draft drew on other types of experts: either very old professors of law who grew up before World War II and later did not support communism, or younger scholars who did not have time to become heralds of the Communist constitutionalism.

The final results of this process are two projects, one produced by the Sejm and one by the Senate. In my perception, they are so different that it would be impossible to combine them into something new now. Both projects are big steps towards the rule of law on the statutory level. However, they are short of constitutionalist principles. In both cases they are easily amendable; these constitutions can be relatively easily changed by the Parliament. Secondly, both drafts provide that the statutes passed by the Parliament can set general limits on individual rights. . . .

EM: Can you say a little more about the relationship between the Polish culture and the constitution that you are developing? Can you see distinctive influences of Polish culture on the evolving constitution?

WO: I think there may be some. We are now looking back to the pre-World War II traditions. These were traditions of some constitutional order: there were some rights, there were some mechanisms of protection, and rights were enforceable in courts. There was also a strong tradition, even before the war, of social and economic rights, not only political freedoms. These traditions influence our thinking today.

Another issue is the traditional attitude in Poland toward the constitution as such. I do not think it was ever perceived as the social contract. It was never perceived as the grant of power given to government by the free people. Instead there were two other concepts of constitutions: one derives from the nineteenth century when we had a number of constitutions given by the powers that partitioned Poland. In this conception, the constitution was the grant of privileges given by the sovereign state power to the population. I think that the constitutions between the two wars were embedded in this tradition: we the leaders, elites that represent the power of the state, are giving you, the people, the following rights and we hereby organize the state in the following way.

But there was another older, although often overlooked or misunderstood, constitutionalism which originated in the Polish noble republics of the sixteenth and seventeenth centuries. These constitutions were basically limits imposed by the nobility upon the power of the king. These constitutions can be exemplified by the Nihil Novi Constitution of 1505, which said that nothing new could be enacted by the king without the consent of the nobility. This constitutionalism took the form of a contract between the nominal power (the king) and the real power (the nobility). This contract, which was reaffirmed by every free election of a king, had two parts. One part was constant: it included the rights and immunities of the nobility that would never be violated by the king, and it had to be agreed to by every king that was freely elected. The second part prescribed what each individually elected king was to give to the nobility in return for his post. In any case it was the constitutionalism as a contract between the nominal power and the real power in the society. It was implied that if the balance of power between these two parties to the contract changed, the constitution could be renegotiated.

If we think about this tradition, we will be struck by its resemblance to the Round Table Agreement, which was signed at the inception of a new post-Communist Poland, but no one notices this. I think, however, that this older tradition of constitutionalism may be strongly - even if unconsciously - embedded in the policy-makers and the politicians. It may surface once in a while, in particular, when new post-Communist elites will inevitably become alienated from the society whose expectations have to be frustrated. Then, a new opposition will emerge, which will claim to represent the society and a new contract will be proposed. Hopefully it will take place within the Parliament rather than in the streets or in the factories.

Interestingly, in 1990, the Democratic Union suggested the need for the "Pact for Poland," a contract between major political forces which would limit the scope of political conflicts. Such a pact, signed outside of the Parliament, would have some characteristics of a constitution as a contract between major social forces.

ANDRÁS SAJÓ (AS): Aren't you afraid of losing the constitutional moment?

WO: We have already lost the constitutional moment. But I would be very cautious to judge it. I do not know if it is good or bad. The issue of constitutional moment has to do with two possible versions of constitution making. One is the constitution of principle, the other is the constitution of the compromise. The constitution of principle resembles the commitment or self-limitation in a moral sense. When an individual sometimes torn with guilt or hangover hits bottom, he or she may decide to make some commitments, to limit self-will for the future. It does not happen every day. The same is true with societies. In periods of crisis and massive change, leaders and people as well may want to learn from the past lessons, and limit the possibility of the abuse of power in the future. Such seemed to be the attitude in Poland immediately after the change, in late 1989, when the leaders of the change had not yet become the government politicians. They were still the conscience of the society and they thought in terms of highest values. However, they soon became politicians in the government or in the new opposition. And because all power changes people, they did change, even if they did not change their principles, they changed their way of thinking. People change with power, they have new responsibilities. Now they thought in terms of their immense tasks in the transformation of a society rather than constitutional limitation of power or they thought in terms of a new power struggle. Thus we definitely lost the moment for making a constitution of principles. But we still need a new constitution both as a plan of the government and as a limitation of the government. But the constitution we will have will now be a result of political process rather than of moral reasoning. It will most probably be enacted as a result of some political compromises. Then we will try it out in practice and learn by experience, as other societies have learned, of its mistakes and short-comings. In five or ten years we will probably realize the need to make the next step toward deeper (not more) constitutionalism. Such was the development in Western Europe. It was only in the mid-1950s when Western Europe really accepted the principle of constitutionalism, introducing the judicial review and making constitutions supreme to the power of parliaments.

EM: When you think of constitutions as contracts between the dominant powers in society, one dominant power you have not mentioned yet is the church or religion. And there is also religion as a cultural force. Does religion play a role? Will it play a role?

WO: Absolutely. However, besides the existing agreement between the church and the state, the Catholic Church will also influence the very process of constitution making. The impact of the church and the bishops on the Senate proceedings was clearly visible, and the church will probably continue trying to influence the process. Moreover, the church will influence both the society and the state to ensure its interests.

EM: What are its interests?

WO: I think there are two or three different kinds of church interests. I would try to distinguish between them, even though the church does not make such distinctions and puts everything in moral terms. I think that there are some constitutional interests which are vested in the moral principles of the church. These have to do with divorce law or with the abortion issue, where the church is defending its moral principles.

The second kind are the institutional interests of the church. These are clearly visible when the separation of the church and the state is involved. The bishops have their own concept of such separation. They say we should have the separation of the state from the church, but not vice versa. The state should be banned from interfering in the church's affairs, but the church should be able to act in the public sphere. That is how the bishops argued for the reintroduction of religious instruction in public schools. In general, the church wants to protect its institutional interests. Do not forget that under communism the Catholic Church was the most important institution in the society, since it was the only legally acknowledged institutional alternative to the Communists. Thus it had immense support. Now, when there are more alternatives, this support may wane. There is nothing strange in the church wanting to constitutionally protect its position and interests.

The third issue is the protection of the church's interests against too much change and modernism in general. Here the American type of culture is a more difficult adversary of the Catholic Church than anything else in the world, including communism. The hierarchical, paternalistic attitude of the church can hardly accept the permissiveness of a modern culture. Moral paternalism may have a hard time letting people learn by their own mistakes and sins. I interpret the insistence on the reintroduction of religion to schools as an attempt to stop permissiveness and bring back some moral guidance, very much needed, in reality.

Also, there is a natural tendency on the part of the church to "cut the coupons" to profit from the support the church gave to the opposition during communism and to petrify its dominant position in the society. Although now that may change with emerging pluralism, I think that the church will remain a very important power in Poland, but it will not be the only power, perhaps even not the dominant power.

EM: What are the other structures in Polish society that need to be reconciled in the new constitution?

WO: I do not know if the particular structures have to be reconciled. There must be openings for participation in mainstream politics by some institutions. What do you do with the unions, for instance? With Solidarity? Solidarity was pushing Communist power from the outside—from the streets, strikes in the factories and by other extra-constitutional means. How do you constitutionalize the position of the unions now? Should they exist on the basis of the provisions about unions or on the right to associate? Should they have their own representation in the Parliament or should they be represented by political parties? Should they create their own party? Not all of these questions demand answers in the constitution but all of them are very important.

The next interest is business. We do not have legitimate representation of business interests, although some parties began to attract newly emerging capitalists. Many people in Poland believe that this is the transition period and eventually the parties in general will represent different social interests. This may take some time, for, up to now, the parties are being created around the ideological programs, and leaders' ambitions rather than around the economic or other interests. The formation of a mature party system will take time as it did in older democracies. . . .

EM: The last thing I can think of that I would like you to speculate on is an issue we mentioned in discussing the church, that is the tension between modernity, or American-driven culture, and traditional culture. Do you have thoughts on how that is working itself out at the present time in Poland or where it might go?

WO: The division between American culture and the Catholic Church is very rough but let's stick to it for this purpose. American culture wins in the market. Market culture wins among the youth. American culture wins among the capitalists. Church values, on the other hand, are extremely strong among the peasants and among people in the small towns. The real issue is who will win the workers? If the economic situation gets worse and worse and if the powers for modernization in the direction of the market—the state and capitalism—lose the symbolic means of influencing or addressing the needs of the workers—then they will probably be absorbed by the church into some kind of conservative symbolism.

The realm of symbols is extremely important, especially in difficult times of transition. Unfortunately, perhaps with the exception of Lech Walesa, the two post-Communist governments in Poland almost totally discarded the importance of symbolic elements in politics. The church works in the realm of symbols. Therefore, if there is not another attractive proposition in this realm, the church with all their skepticism towards modernity, may win people's minds. I am not judging, I am not saying it is better or worse, I'm just saying that in the realm of symbols that is real power—and that also in this realm there is a need for power balance. This power, however, is almost totally extra-constitutional. [However,] the making of the constitution and including ordinary people in this process may by itself exert immense symbolic effect on the birth of democracy in Poland and other post-Communist countries as well.

* * *

OSIATYNSKI (1993) [Editors' summary]

In his article *Perspectives on the Current Constitutional Situation in Poland,* in Constitutionalism and Democracy: Transitions in the Contemporary World (Greenberg et al. eds. 1993), written in April 1990 and revised in early 1991, Osiatynski elaborated on the constitutional traditions of

Poland that situate what he saw as the relatively slow pace of Poland's transformation from communist control. First, as already noted, the history of constitutions in Poland was understood as a grant of privilege by the ruler to the people (or the nobles), not as a contract or bargain among the people to provide for limited government. Second, at least three of the six Polish Constitutions between 1791 and 1989 were imposed by foreign powers, "usually with an active participation of a part of the Polish political elites which collaborated with those powers."

Third, Poland has some tradition of governance by a single highly powerful leader. In 1921, Poland adopted a strong version of parliamentary supremacy in order to head off undue accumulation of power in the hands of Marshal Josef Pilsudski. This was followed in 1926 by a splintering of authority in parliament due to the presence of many conflicting parties, and Pilsudski essentially staged a coup. The new constitution adopted under Pilsudski in 1935 gave "full authority to the President, who was to be responsible before nobody but 'God and History.' Thus the principle of separation and above all balance of powers was never consolidated in this tradition." Indeed, Osiatynski argues, Poland lacks an understanding of separation of powers, misconstruing the U.S. presidency as an essentially unlimited Presidential model. Poland lacks, as well, any tradition of constitutional review of legislation.

Osiatynski argues that Poland lacks a tradition of a limited state, in part because it was the weakness of the Polish government that was seen to contribute to Poland's fall to first German and then Soviet occupation. In this light, "the Polish people appreciate the need for a strong state.... The Polish tradition is ... one of a benevolent, paternalistic authority figure that grants favors to the people rather than one in which people enjoy inalienable rights and have claims on the authorities based on those rights....

"In this conception of power and the state, found in the traditions of both Christian social ethics and the pre-Communist Social–Democratic Left, civil rights are closely related to duties toward society and state. These traditions attach an incomparably greater weight to the social rights than to liberties. What is more, they understood a strong state to be the instrument to provide social welfare; the constitution, in turn, was to create that very instrument.

"This interpretation of state and constitutionalism was a logical effect of the modern Polish history: the history of a weak state situated between two hostile powers; the history of a powerless society composed of a small class of lords and of masses of indigent peasants, without a strong middle class; the history created not by capitalists but by the intellectual elite derived from *declassé* nobility who aimed at retrieval of lost power and influence by political means."

Osiatynski goes on to suggest that at the time of his writing, the decline of Communist rule had led to a discrediting of the idea of the state as the means to achieve the good, but that in thinking about the new principles for public life, one needs to understand the fundamental attitudes of Polish society that will affect constitutional decisions. First, he considers the nature of political elites in Poland and expresses concern about whether these elites will be primarily "political" or intellectual elites, or will instead represent "specific economic" "interests" such as those of producers, investors, and workers. He argues that "theoretical constitutions [written by intellectual or purely political groups] tend to fail in practice," and that the key problem is how "various groups of interests, including those that now have no parliamentary representation, can secure influence in the preparing of the Constitution." He also cautions against writing a constitution "to solve specific . . . problems [such as 'parliament's apprehension about Walesa's power,' and as was the case in 1935 with Pilsudski] and urges instead attention to creating mechanisms for solutions to future social and political problems, by having the 'authors of the new Polish basic statute . . . rise above personal interests, prejudices and fears. . . .' "

Osiatynski believes that the "reforming elites" need to have greater appreciation for the benefits of "local democracy" in local government, whose "actual liveliness and responsibility . . . will depend on the Constitution. . . ." This responsibility requires that the local governments be granted independence and secured specific competences on which the state authority cannot encroach. Some have suggested that those spheres reserved for local governments should include care for the social problems of the inhabitants; state authorities would thus be relieved of the welfare duties that sometimes clash with the aims of economic reform toward a market economy and of political reform. The question here is would reforming intellectuals within the parliament and those connected with the government be willing to trust local governments and relinquish the desire for control over all issues and reforms in the State?"

With respect to separation of powers, he described debate over the American presidential as compared with the British parliamentary model, as well as debate over voting methods. At the time of his writing, the Sejm—the lower house of the Polish parliament—supported proportional voting and representation, which, he feared, might lead to a proliferation of small parties and inability to fashion governing coalitions.

Returning to his opening themes, Osiatynski argues that democracy has much stronger appeal to Poles than does the principle of limited government or of protection of individual rights. After the fall of communism, he notes a wave of local government action against HIV carriers. He asks, "Can we now accept the fact that human rights limit all authority, including (and perhaps in particular!) the democratic one? History demonstrates that democracies, particularly the local ones, are not too sensitive to the rights of minorities and of individuals who think differently. Thus, the greater the powers of local governments the more important it becomes to mark the exact limits of their power, that is, the rights that no authority may infringe." He urges that Poland go beyond its tradition (which, in the 20th century, was to declare human rights in the constitution but without provisions for individual remedies in the event of infringements) to establish mechanisms through which all can vindicate their rights.

He notes "conflicts between the economic and political reforms and the aspirations for social equality and safety . . . [including how to] squar[e] . . . the inviolability of property and transactions with the social sense of justice." Anticipating problems of transitional justice addressed below, he notes that a "large part of society would want the members of the Communist nomenklatura to return the wealth appropriated while they were in power, even if this would weaken the much needed process of the privatization of the economy and the creation of a capitalist class."

"A more serious problem is the squaring of contradictory economic and social values. A rather distinct conflict exists between the changes of the political system and reforms aimed at the market economy, on the one hand, and the trend to secure economic and social safety." He notes again the possibility of soothing this conflict by transferring to local governments responsibility for social welfare. But the problem is deeper. Poland has a tradition of guaranteeing social rights in its constitutions. "If, however, we are to treat human rights seriously today, we cannot grant rights in the Constitution that we will not be able to secure. . . . [T]oday's Poland cannot afford a state guarantee of the right to work or the right to rest, and perhaps not even the right to free medical care. If such vain declarations were to be included in the chapter on civil rights, it would result in a depreciation of all rights, including political rights and liberties. On the other hand, a removal of social rights from the Constitution would be an abandonment of the entire Polish social tradition."

To resolve this conflict, he makes two suggestions: inclusion of social rights in an aspirational preamble, and creation of a mechanism providing in the future for a given percentage of growth in national income, or in state and local budgets, to be reserved for implementing social and economic rights. In support of the latter, he observes that "[in developed countries] before they reached the level of development necessary to implement social rights, strong political and economic elites in all those countries resisted redistribution, because they themselves did not need such rights. The creation of a mechanism of future redistribution would be a serious attempt to provide for the rights that most citizens seem to be most particular about today."

In discussing the Constitution in the heirarchy of law, Osiatynski observes: "Poland has never had a strong tradition of constitutionalism that limited parliamentary authority. . . . What will the new Constitution be? As it was in the past, a mere plan of organization of power, and a charter of privileges granted by the authorities? Or a truly supreme law, binding on the citizens and on the authorities including the Parliament? Will it create a mechanism to secure review of the constitutionality of statutes? . . . .

"Connected to the question of the Constitution's rank is the very procedure of its passing. Obviously, society should participate in that process, the more so as the present Sejm and Senate were not elected but are the result of a political compromise negotiated during the 'Round Table' conference. Anyway, no parliament should have the right to decide singlehandedly about the Constitution by which it is granted a greater or smaller amount of power. . . .

"What does seem controversial is the actual form of expressing [society's] approval. Most deputies and senators . . . favor a national referendum. Another option [is] ratification of the Constitution by independent local communities; it is argued that this solution would encourage the formation of a civic society, which cannot be built from the top, that is by the Parliament. The grant of a right to ratify the Constitution to local governments would give those basic units of the civic society a sense of identity as independent and fully legitimate actors in Polish social and political life. . . . Ratification by this means might also provide a mechanism to link political elites with the masses, and an unprecedented opportunity for mass political education."

He concludes, "The difficult choices are the task of the authors of Poland's new Constitution—and of society as a whole. . . . [T]hose problems reflect the fundamental questions in Poland today. . . . How can the foundations of freedom be created in a country that lacks a strong class of businessmen independent of the state . . . without a middle class[?] . . .

And finally, how can the sense of responsibility for one's own life be developed in each Polish citizen? . . . The foundation of responsibility for one's own life is freedom: free choice of one's life path. The Constitutions that the post-Communist countries need today should provide the foundations for that freedom."

Questions and Comments on the Idea of a Constitution of Principle

1. What is a constitution of principle? How tightly is it linked to constitutional supremacy and constitutional review?

2. Would a transfer of power to the local governments resolve the conflict between political liberalism and market economies and social welfare, or simply defer it? Would deferring the conflict be a valuable constitutional function?

3. Is there a tension between Osiatynski's preference for "bottom up" involvement in constitution-making and his preference for a constitution of principle?

4. In 1992, Poland adopted a so-called "Little Constitution," having failed to resolve issues for a permanent constitution. In 1997 a new constitution was adopted through a national referendum. Osiatynski has attributed Poland's delay in adopting a new constitution to the difficulty of three simultaneous transitions—to democracy, to markets, and to constitutionalism. "[T]he process of democratizing the state began to obstruct the creation of the Constitution." Wiktor Osiatynski, *A Brief History of the*

Constitution, 6 E. Eur. Const. Rev. 66, 68 (1997). Osiatynski also expressed regret for his own part in the process of moving towards a new constitution in Poland, indicating that he had overestimated the degree to which the process could be one of public civic education and underestimated the degree to which most politicians lack a desire to educate the public and will attempt to enhance their own careers. Does Osiatynski's skepticism about the possibility of civic education warrant a more general caution about the possibilities of public understanding and mobilization in constitution-making?

5. After almost 10 years of drafting, the 1997 Constitution of Poland was approved by both houses of the national legislature in the spring of 1997 and was put to a national referendum on May 25, 1997. Voter turnout was only 42.9%. The Constitution was approved by 52.7% of those voting, with 45.9% of those voting opposed. Notwithstanding questions raised about the meaning of the vote in light of the low turnout, the Constitution came into force in October, 1997. Does this support the assertion that Poland missed a "constitutional moment" in 1989? Or is it possible that in 30 years, the period from 1989 through 1997 in Poland will be seen as the "constitutional moment"?

----

2. EASTERN EUROPE AND CONSTITUTIONAL CHANGE

Andraś Sajó and Vera Losonci, *Rule By Law in East Central Europe: Is the Emperor's New Suit a Straitjacket?*, in Constitutionalism and Democracy: Transitions in the Contemporary World (Douglas Greenberg, Stanley N. Katz, Melanie Beth Oliviero, and Steven C. Wheatley eds., 1993)

This chapter analyzes the new legalistic trends developing in east European socialist countries, considering events in Czechoslovakia, in Hungary, and in Poland....

...The new regimes tend to rely to a great extent on law to define the new societies in order to transform them. It is only a slight exaggeration to state that most of the efforts of social transformation focus on achieving the governance of these societies by impartial laws.

In the turmoil of the recent and ongoing changes and transformations in eastern Europe, the people of this region think of themselves as on their way to becoming central Europeans, which in their eyes equals being accepted or incorporated into a somewhat mystical Europe. This aspiration is particularly strong in Czechoslovakia and Hungary. In that process, emphasis lies on the rule of law and the *Rechtsstaat* legalism both for the protection of society and human rights against an all pervasive state (party) domination, and for the promotion of a market economy, believed to be the ultimate solution to the present economic crisis. However, when it comes to creating a positive legal framework for the functioning of a market economy (a more liberal contractual and property system, bankruptcy law, banking law, mortgage system, etc.), the process becomes slow and painful, partly because fundamental constitutional (and social) issues are unresolved.

As will be noted, these dominating ideas are generally simple negations of the former system and the idea of market is generally used as an attractive promise. There is little desire to pay the social price of a market-oriented transformation. I will try to point out that there is a similar reluctance when it comes to taking seriously law and the rule of law. These reluctances are related.

Further, to understand the meaning of "legalism" and the striving toward a market-supportive rule of law system in these countries, two circumstances should be taken into consideration. First, in these societies social oppression was, primarily, oppression by the state. The State and the Party controlled the society through a biased and discretionary legal system and through state ownership of the national economies. Liberation in these countries means the curtailment of the powers of the state and the bureaucracy; it is in this context that rule of law and privatization are to be understood. Second, there are indications within the present transformation of the survival instincts of the former ruling classes, who, in some countries, seek a compromise with new forces representing the "new" legitimate ideologies, for example, those presecular value systems that resisted socialism. Religion and nationalism are particularly important in this respect. In other countries, compromise is out of the question; these presecular forces tend simply to gain control of the old centers of domination.... The reluctance to change radically the economic and other (e.g., cultural) monopolies and the easy falling back on concepts of material justice indicate similar tendencies.

The *Rechtsstaat* Tradition and the Underdeveloped Constitutionalism of the Pre-Communist Period

The absence of a constitutional tradition of the pre-Communist period is a considerable factor in the present legal and constitutional transformation process. One of the great problems that the new regime ... faces is that members of the political elite and the judiciary were educated in the Communist system; therefore, little understanding of what constitutionalism entails exists even among members of the former opposition, not to mention the popular masses.... A prevailing concept in east central Europe is that after the past 40 years of usurpation, return to the traditional institutional and moral systems represents genuine national values and virtues, and that "return" is to a legitimate constitutional system. The idealization of the past is obviously an expression of national identity, a sense of which played a major role in the resistance to Communism. Modeling society on the traditional institutional and moral systems poses an obvious problem when it comes to the question of private property and redistribution.... [E]galitarianism make the prewar, often privilege-oriented private property system less attractive. Yet a reluctance to safeguard property dooms all constitutional efforts both politically and socially....

The Poles are proud of the progressive democratic nature of 1791 and, naturally, there is strong political interest after the election of Lech Walesa in believing that [a former pre-communist regime] fully m[e]t modern requirements of democracy....

Legality under State Socialism

According to the now defunct official ideology of the eastern European socialist states, law serves the building of socialism. To be an effective means of building socialism, law must conform to the ideals of socialist legality. The socialist systems of eastern Europe were legalistic societies to a surprising extent, although the meaning of law may have been quite different from what one generally conceives under this notion.... [T]he socialist theory boasted of the "superior nature" of socialist law precisely because it was not based on the concept of individual rights. Theory claimed the law to be a collective interest-oriented system that emphasized the reciprocity of rights and obligations, with social obligations as the source of rights.

... Lenin himself, in his struggle to regain central control over society, emphasized the importance of socialist legality. He defined socialist legality as a uniform country-wide application of the central commands versus the autonomous and capricious decision making of local bodies, including the revolutionary tribunals applying the standards of the revolutionary consciousness of the worker-judges. To promote the central control a former Czarist institution, the military organized *procurata*, received extended powers to review various decisions for the purposes of conformity to the law. This was an extraordinary power because it meant that no court decision was immune from review. The *procurata*'s powers were discretionary. As laws were extremely loosely worded, therefore, nearly all decisions could be reviewed for reasons of nonconformity with the law.

A second feature of the socialist legal system emphasized by Lenin is the predominance of public law over private law. ("We do not recognize anything private. For us all is public.") The statement clearly prioritizes public interest, understood as party and state interest.

In eastern Europe socialist law was interpreted as a system closely following the example of Soviet law. Nevertheless, because of the different legal traditions and the lesser degree of centralization of society, the legal systems of the people's democracies are much closer to the western, civil law tradition.... It would be an error, however, to overestimate the importance of these features, especially if one takes into consideration the amount of discretionary power built into the flexible texts of the laws, and the lack of sufficient and independent judicial review.

Law was understood as instrumental to social and economic planning; its legislative role was negligible in comparison with its regulatory function. Regulation by governmental decrees, some secret, was present to varying extents in all countries.... Judges and courts acted as bureaucrats, and fulfilled the expectation that they would promote centrally determined public interests. The courts were declared independent; however, the career of the judges was bureaucratic as was their remuneration and evaluation; all were based on political loyalty....

Lawyers ... played a subservient role in exchange for the privilege of *numerus clausus*.* Their university education and legal training were subject to party control. Their socialization made them vulnerable to external, nonlegal values and interests. They conceived their role as directly related to general social concerns and legal texts offered little possibility for independent action. Lawyers became increasingly dependent on their superiors and on political forces. The prestige of the legal professions declined. Under these circumstances not even the relative simplicity of access to justice and the relatively low cost of litigation are attractive to the public, since the achieved justice does not protect their interests (not to mention rights).

A closer look at the contents of laws and regulations reveals further consequences of the instrumentalist approach. Laws were intended to achieve set targets, partly by strict orders and partly by prohibitions and hidden constraints. In this area the law was hair-splittingly keen on precise details; in many other areas one cannot find any reasonable rule. The law promoted privileges simply by failing to regulate relations openly. The wide gap left to administrative discretion was filled by secret regulations granting privileges to the state and the members of the *nomenklatura*. In many cases no rules were set, but those who applied the law knew which departments of institutions, offices, local party organizations, and other local notables were to be obeyed when it came to decision making.

The system created for itself the advantage of keeping most of its participants (including the decision makers) in a dependent position. This dependence resulted from imprecision and the insecurity stemming from it. Anyone could be summoned to account under many pretexts; this possibility increased dependence and obedience to informed commands. On the other hand, the system managed to disguise under its legalistic facade a great number of built-in inequalities and modes of domination.

... In reality all actions had to originate from the state, and, therefore, had to have some appearance of legality. Consequently, law was bureaucratic and purposive; it denied individual rights, as rights might have resulted in independent social action. Social reliance on the state increased; independent organizations were considered suspect or were simply not tolerated. The state initiative remained the only or, at least the only admitted, active force in society. Projects of the central government were often arbitrary as they were based on external models of socialist modernization.

As the system did not tolerate self-interest, not even in its most enlightened version, it assumed that all participants in the realization of a centrally determined and therefore legally prescribed project should be controlled; law was to a great extent understood and used to control and supervise people who would have been otherwise unmotivated to comply. In

---

* [Editors' Note: *Numerous clausus* refers to restrictions on entry to the profession.]

the economies of shortage the motivation to cheat existed to meet the unrealistic centrally planned goals and the people's modest needs.

The legal system was further distorted by the influence of the Communist Party, though this was generally informal and/or to a certain extent illegal. The ways and means of the influence of the Party varied from country to country, but it was far-reaching everywhere with respect to the contents of the legislation and personnel policies. The Party often made the actual decisions of the local public administration . . . .

Lasting Consequences of the Socialist Legal System

In the Weberian sense, the legal systems of eastern and central eastern Europe were open to demands to substantive justice. . . . [I]n Poland, Hungary, and perhaps in Czechoslovakia, the ideas behind law making and application of the law were not contrary to legal formalism. Undermining this modest formal virtue of the legal system was, however, the nonlegal determination of the *Rechtsträger*—lawyers, legal scholars, and legislators; therefore, foreseeability was not expected of the system. Politically, the law became an overt means of repression of the political opposition. The general public was skeptical about the . . . legal system, an obstacle to be outmaneuvered for survival's sake.

The attitudes of the elites and the general public toward law will play an important, perhaps crucial role, in the shaping of the new legal and constitutional system. These attitudes were contradictory. Generally, the opposition in the east European countries felt that they were persecuted by the existing legal system. Their criticism was based less on the technical concepts or models of western constitutionalism and rule of law than on universal human rights. This position related to a tactical possibility offered by international conventions on human rights. Some east European countries ratified them or at least voiced their support for human rights to create a direct confrontation between the existing legal practice and the officially accepted standards. This position also resulted in a strange "legalism" by some opposition groups, which made attempts to force the authorities to take "their law" seriously. On the other hand, by rejecting the existing political system the opposition emphasized the importance of civil society. The autonomous bodies of civil society presuppose a legally bounded state, a kind of rule of law over the state.

The New Legalism

Legalism as Legitimation

Reformative and revolutionary forces considered the legal system one to be . . . conquered for their purposes. In Hungary, and to a certain extent in Poland, and in a different way in the Soviet Union, Communists were partly responsible for the beginning of reform. . . . In these countries, the transformation of the legal system was considered a proof of the good intentions of the reformists. It was an often-stated belief that a modernized legal system, which observed constitutionalism and promised a calculable legal environment for business, including a gradual transition to market economy, would grant legitimacy and credibility to the reform process both inside and outside the country. Furthermore, it was hoped that a system with more open rules would increase the efficiency of that system. The ruling elites hoped that once their system became constitutional, it would also be acceptable and, therefore, would continue to survive.

Given the nature of the system, the interests of the participants and the transition process, this proved to be a somewhat naive illusion....

. . . In the Soviet Union, Mikhail Gorbachev's rule partly destroyed the old inefficient but working network of illegal relations without replacing it with a system based on the rule of law. In Poland and Hungary, the spectacular changes in the public law contributed to democracy, but failed to instill respect for constitutionalism or to create the rule of law.

Both in the reform process and after the more or less revolutionary victories by the masses, the creation of a constitutional legal system with western types of liberal/formal solutions was a high priority. For the public this ideology was not self-legitimating. Religion, anticommunism, nationalism, and consumer values seem more important now to the masses. In any event, it was never made clear what was constitutional; nor were the fundamental differences between the American and the *Rechtstaat* model taken into consideration. There has only been a minimal common acceptance of the liberal tradition. Agreement exists on the importance of human rights, on the separation of powers (interpreted as denial of one-party rule), and on independent judiciary; but there is still no position of principle on welfare rights or on public interest priorities, in particular *vis-à-vis* private property. This level of acceptance obviously reflects the present political struggle for the control of the state, and more generally the slow emancipation of society from centralism.

Democratic legislation was thought to be a remedy for the malaise of the previous system. In this respect the east European transformation process follows the general pattern of revolutionary legal change: it is a denial of the previous solutions. The replacement of these solutions is, however, a matter of choice; there are many ways to part with the past. One group of possible choices is offered by the available western models (which are often little and selectively known or misunderstood, and are too sophisticated to be adapted). Another major choice consists of the pre-Communist legal solutions, which present linguistic barriers, and which are attractive because they can be legitimized as genuinely national solutions. The problem is that these solutions are often outdated; they did not meet criteria of democracy 50 or 60 years ago.... [But] nationalism and religion were important sources of resistance, and important conservative voices among the emerging leaders in the society supported this solution.

If the new ruling classes and elites manage to convince the population that they are offering them rights through the new legal system, their legitimacy will increase. This is not an easy task, as economic hardship and political instability make it imperative to pass unpopular measures through law. The inherent formalism of a legalistic system will be unpopular, too.

The possibility exists ... that the new political elites will seek popular support by disregarding legal formalism, its own "creation," claiming that it supports only the unjust *status quo ante*. The investigative special procedures against the former leaders aid in their discrediting; with these, however, the rule of law concept becomes fully instrumental or nonexistent: special tribunals are set up and retroactive force is acceptable. The extreme case is Rumania where due process is irrelevant when weighing needs for punishment and revenge....

Different Uses of Law

Constitutions

One of the first steps of the social and political transformation taken in all former socialist societies was the amendment of the Communist constitutions. These amendments abolished the privileges of the Communist Party. Moreover, in the case of Hungary, they institutionalized the protection of human rights and separation of powers. Nevertheless, in every case the amendments were the result of an elite agreement with the former Communist leadership. They were not intended to be expressions of the "will," values, or demands of the masses who to varying degrees participated in the process resulting in the collapse of Communist rule. The amendments, openly intended to be revised, reflected the provisional arrangements; revisions became routine procedures as new conflicts emerged. Such confrontations surfaced over presidential powers in Poland, Bulgaria, and Hungary, over federalism in Czechoslovakia, and over the constitutional powers of the executive (government) in all the countries of the region.

From the point of view of a rule of law system or any system that takes law (i.e., the meaning of words) seriously, utilizing the constitution to rewrite political agreements is counterproductive to the goal of creating respect and belief in constitutionalism. If a constitution is easy to amend it loses its majestic special role. The Hungarian Constitution of 1989 was amended six times in the first year of its existence; the changes amount to one-third of the text.... In that process law, including the text of the Constitution, easily becomes a matter of technicality. For instance, after the Hungarian Constitutional Court ruled unconstitutional an article of the Election law, the Parliament the next day amended the Constitution so as to make the article in question conform to the Election Law!

Public Interest Legislation

Legislation is still understood as a means to protect the public interest with the consequence that wide discriminatory powers are granted to public authorities. The amendment of the press law in Hungary is a typical case. The amended Act on Press established practically complete freedom of the press.... The change was, however, limited in its spirit. Freedom of the press did not include an understanding of what free speech means. In the case of libel, the journalist must pay a fine to the *state*, and not to the injured party (who would have to go through a civil process for damages). ... [T]he overwhelming majority of Parliament accepted a further provision which states that the libel fine applies in case of harm to *public morality*.

The extremely slow and contradictory process of privatization is also illuminating in this respect. After much hesitation, Hungary, Poland, and Czechoslovakia have committed themselves to some kind of privatization, and some kind of reprivatization. Rumania expressly denied reprivatization in the industrial sector, and discourages the reprivatization of land. Even where privatization appears to be a governmental policy, it is not construed as a legal question or as a constitutional issue. Public interest concerns prevail, resulting in the creation of new state bureaucracies or in the extension of the powers of the already existing bureaucracies, which can control privatization without judicial review, public liability, or a limit to administrative discretion. Xenophobia, nationalism, or simple government (bureaucratic) interests result in discriminatory measures against foreign investors, which is of course counterproductive. Economic dissatisfaction, on the other hand, results in granting to the government extraordinary unconstitutional power to deal with the economic hardships.

Some scholars do take Frederic Hayek more seriously and would limit government intervention to a minimum (after the destruction of the monopolies and regulations). Notwithstanding the popularity of Hayek as a brand name, most people are too afraid of the unforeseen consequences of liberalism. On the other hand, one can easily predict the consequences of public interest protection through regulatory agencies where there is no countervailing market force and where public interest protection means only the protection and survival of existing bureaucracies.

Given the predominance of public interest concern with obvious political overtones, it is hardly surprising that in Hungary there is little willingness to rely on impartial abstract rules operating within an independent judiciary. The Act on the Prosecutor's Office of 1953 often gives the public prosecutor special rights to review cases, although these rights are clearly part of the Stalinist legacy. Parliament sets up almost on a daily basis "independent" investigative commissions with undefined powers and without procedural rules. . . .

Juridification . . .

The contradictory nature of juridification is perhaps most obvious in the role attributed to the recently established Hungarian Constitutional Court. Citizens have a basically unlimited right to petition the Court, and the Court itself may refer cases to its own jurisdiction! In the first 60 days of its existence more than 50 laws were referred to the Court for nullification. The Government tried to use the Constitutional Court as a means to avoid politically embarrassing decisions. For example, the Prime Minister tried to avoid a conflict within the government coalition by asking the Court to give a preliminary advisory opinion on the restitution of private property confiscated by the Communists. When the Constitutional Court in May 1991 later declared unconstitutional the government's reprivatization Act, leading members of the majority parties started a campaign to curtail the powers of the Court. The Dred Scott case is an extreme, but in all respects instructive, example of the possible consequences of the juridification of politics.

Activism

Obviously, rule of law is not a system based on any kind of active interference, and certainly not on the active role of the judge.... Quite understandably, however, one might expect active intervention and shaping of liberal institutions in a society on the verge of economic collapse whose faculty of self-determination has been systematically destroyed.... [A]t least some of the elementary systems and institutional frames to promote market relations in such a society have to be created by the government.... It seems reasonable to regulate legally companies limited by shares ... if you want foreign investment or domestic transfer of capital, and some positive evidence exists to support governmental creation of stock markets. A great bulk of the east European legislation takes that direction.

However, a closer scrutiny of some of the market-creating laws yields controversial findings.... Evidence suggests that one of the crucial aims of these laws in Hungary was to make the head of governmental agencies (generally someone who served the Communist Party) unremovable. The laws creating the agencies do not set forth rules to govern their activities; there is only a general clause about protecting public interest and promoting the establishment of the market. The law creating the Agency for State Fund provided internal rules for the composition of governing bodies, but, notwithstanding repeated warnings by the World Bank and some domestic agencies, failed to set forth either clear policy criteria or due process requirements. The rule of law issue is settled simply by granting judicial review, without offering criteria for that review. In all countries, and in Poland in particular, there is a growing dissatisfaction with the existing business law structures, which seem only to guarantee in private business the privileged positions of the former Communist bureaucracy.

Political Justice

A major blow to the *Rechtsstaat* principle is expected from the "legalization" of political justice, intended to be used against former communist leaders. The scope, sanction system, and retroactivity of these tribunals vary from country to country, depending on the level of hatred, the legal culture, the number of supporters of the Communist Party, and the need for finding scapegoats.... [E]lements of unfairness are easily noticeable in the Ceausescu and Honecker cases.

Judicial Review and the Judiciary

Although judicial review ... in cases where actual individual decisions affected individual interests and rights[ ] was to be the cornerstone of the new legalism, it meets considerable resistance.... In Hungary, the Parliament failed to enact a law that would have institutionalized judicial review as required by the Constitution; the Constitutional Court declared administrative decisions concerning the fundamental rights of citizens to be subject to appeal, but there are simply no courts to review these appeals.

As we know, the east European judiciary was trained in a bureaucratic tradition open to extralegal considerations (the public interest) and with little interest in independence, though most of the judges believe that what they have is independence indeed. Practically all county court presidents in Hungary openly declared that they saw nothing wrong in summoning young judges who were about to pass sentence, as these "youngsters are not well prepared and thereby unfair and illegal decisions are avoided." In some countries judges are also the worst paid members of the legal field. . . . [S]ome of the judges and prosecutors were politically compromised by administering political justice or by simply having used their discretionary powers unfairly against the victors of today. . . . In the GDR, agreement was reached to dismiss, though not try, 10 to 15% of the former judges. In Hungary, a handful of compromised judges was quietly asked to retire. In Poland, however, there was a major replacement of judges with young lawyers who were partly schooled by Solidarity.

Changing the judiciary, even for a "good cause," is particularly problematic because it represents a departure from the idea of judicial independence. Nor is there trained personnel to replace judges in most of these countries. Mediation and other alternatives to justice are unpopular because of earlier abuses of informality; informal justice contradicts the strict legality that is to be reestablished.

In response to the demands of rule of law in Hungary, judges hurried to support the suggestion of the anti-Communist opposition at the Round Table talks that judges be barred from membership in any political party in exchange for an informal grant of immunity. Parliament and the Ministry of Justice also promised them self-government, which may maintain for their lifetimes the positions of Communist Party appointees. The contradiction is obvious: if you support judicial self-government as part of creating the *Rechtsstaat*, you will be aiding the position of people who seem to be unresponsive to ideas of fairness, are unfamiliar with judicial independence, and resist responsibility for creative precedents.

On the other hand, as is usual after revolutions, judges are not much trusted. And after so many years of imposed will, the doctrine of popular sovereignty identified with parliamentary majority rule fascinates the people. . . .

Little help can be expected from the bar. The lawyers enjoyed the privilege of *numerus clausus* and became wealthy partly through illegal activities or other privileges (in Hungary, real estate agency monopolies). Their interest lies in the preservation of the present system. . . .

Evaluation and Conclusions

It is certainly too early to make a definitive evaluation of . . . the changes in these societies from the point of view of rule of law or of a market-oriented liberal-democratic legal system. Before any evaluation, it should be stressed again that the differences among the countries discussed are enormous and nothing conclusive has been achieved.

First, under socialism, the role of law was understood in its relation to the state. Its purpose was to discipline people and create some kind of bureaucratic consistency in the administration of state affairs. Contrary to Weber's bureaucratic law model, this legal system was not predictable; bureaucratic discipline and the rules of jurisdiction served the irrational or only the Party-dictated politically rational decisions of the moment.

After the collapse of state socialism contradictory tendencies emerged. Party of the intelligentsia, which opposed Communism and now has some influence on legislation, supported the liberal tradition and maintained that law should be used to limit and govern government action. They considered the judiciary a key element in case of a state breach of its legal mandate *vis-a-vis* the citizen. In the short run, this assumption will be so exaggerated as to lead to the juridification of politics. No doubt this tendency is partly a result of the lack of confidence in traditional political organizations and private agreements. Further, with the collapse of other normative communication systems, law as communication has become particularly important.

The new political mechanism and the emerging power elite share this interest in legalism. The new governments hope to achieve internal and external (international) legitimation by making their actions more legalistic and basing their legalism on attractive formal criteria. They use law, and legislation in particular, as a symbolic means to create the *Rechtsstaat* system. The formal regulation of social relations, even if often accomplished in a liberal manner, presently does not have the dignity of law. Dignity of law in this respect requires built-in mechanisms that make the law relatively unalterable and self-reflecting. Since legislation plays a primary role in the process of creating a rule of law, or at least a rule by law system, and has extensive legitimizing functions, much less importance is given to the internal characteristics of law, or to use Lon Fuller's approach, the morality of law. Procedural legitimation, including both the democratic making of law and judicial review by constitutional courts, prevails over the internal structural components of the rule of law system, such as retroactive laws and the responsible use of and definitions as a protection against discretionary power.

These important elements in legislation and in the political culture, however, are not favorable to constitutionalism (in the rule of law tradition). In this connection we have already mentioned ... groups of former privilege. Too, the emerging sentiments of nationalism and religion are not particularly tolerant of some of the formal "impartial" criteria of law and constitutionalism. Other elements relate directly to the interests of the freely elected governments in maintaining the role of the state sector in the economy and perhaps in the welfare sector as well. Social groups for whom the reduction of the state sector means unemployment and poverty support these tendencies. The same social groups have less interest in and comprehension of individual rights and their protection through courts as their education, in a paternalistic tradition, has alienated them from law. Paternalism, in this context, means that they accept their role as clients and as more or less obedient servants of an uncontrolled state welfare system.

Political power factors also make the emergence of constitutionalism difficult. In all these societies at least part of the present ruling elite was involved in one way or another in the Communist system. Revision of the past through retroactive laws ... became crucial in one respect or another in all the countries of the region in 1990. Obviously, this is not the best education in constitutionalism. A contradictory situation emerged. "Rejecting the embourgeoisment of the old elite jeopardizes economic liberalism, but accepting it jeopardizes political liberalism.... Accepting the embourgeoisment of the nomenclature, however, allows liberalism to be perceived as representing the interests of the Communists." [David Ost].

Forms of intolerance, in addition to anti-Communism, present problems for constitutionalism. In general, there is little tolerance for minorities, and protection of them is not high on the priority lists of political organizations capable of shaping constitutions. Political forces do not incline to undertake the commitments necessary to write a constitution for the future that would require a firm stance on constitutional values that are unpopular or still debatable....

The emerging elites and the lack of constitutional legal culture are not the only factors responsible for these conceptual insufficiencies. Communist rule and the lack of a capitalist society and a civic culture contributed to the passive acceptance and mistrust of law. On the other hand, as the emergence of civil society and a nonstate ownership system that would make personal independence a possibility is very slow, there is little actual interest or urge to have a rule of law system. Of course, the failure to develop a constitutional framework and an impartial legal system will make the formation of a constitutionalism-hungry society extremely painful if not impossible in the coming years. There are social groups advocating their interests in the new-corporatist structures, which are ready to promote concepts of material justice. If there is not enough time left for the consolidation of formal structures, the inevitable result will be the maintenance of the present imperfect legalism where the law has mainly symbolic and legitimating functions.

Questions and Comments on Sajó and Losonci

1. Sajó and Losonci take a firm position against the easy amendability of constitutions. Re-evaluate their argument after reading the Holmes and Sunstein piece below.

2. What do Sajó and Losonci mean by the "juridification" of politics? In what sense is *Dred Scott* an example of its consequences?

3. The tension between "liberalism," understood as commitment to rule of law, and "democracy," understood as popular self-rule, is a theme in several of the readings in this chapter. Consider the proposal in the next section, for relatively easy amendment of constitutions in newly democratic countries of Eastern Europe, as one kind of resolution of that tension.

4. Does Eastern Europe face problems (of boundaries, political membership, property rights and redistribution of wealth) not easily solved by liberal principles, and which cannot be addressed judicially, but only politically? If so, should current constitution-writers attempt to entrench solutions in constitutions at this point? Consider the argument of Holmes and Sunstein that follows.

————————

Stephen Holmes and Cass R. Sunstein, *The Politics of Constitutional Revision in Eastern Europe,* in Responding to Imperfection: The Theory and Practice of Constitutional Amendment (Sanford Levinson, ed., 1995)

A CONSTITUTION, among other things, is a document that is unusually difficult to change. Constitutionalism hinges upon a distinction between the procedures governing ordinary legislation and the more onerous procedural hurdles that must be overcome in order to recast the ground rules of political life. To understand the amending power and its limits, therefore, is to understand the balance of rigidity and flexibility, of permanence and adaptability, that lies at the heart of constitutional government. To institutionalize a constitutional system, as post-Communist drafters from Tirana to Tallinn are now attempting to do, means, among other things, to establish clear rules for, and restraints upon, future constitutional change.

A seemingly simple, albeit important, practical question raised by all such attempts is what amending formula should be adopted by these particular countries during this particular phase of their dramatic economic, political, and social transformations. The amending power is not a legal technicality but may, in turn, color the political process as a whole. The answer that we propose and defend in this chapter can be stated succinctly. The procedure for constitutional modification best adapted to Eastern Europe today sets relatively lax conditions for amendment, keeps unamendable provisions to a minimal core of basic rights and institutions, and usually allows the process to be monopolized by parliament, without any obligatory recourse to popular referenda.

This arrangement, or so we will argue, should make possible necessary but legally channeled readjustments to swiftly changing circumstances without undermining the already weak legitimacy of democratically accountable assemblies. We urge this approach with some ambivalence. Under better conditions, a sharp split between constitutional law and ordinary law would be preferable. But the peculiar conditions of Eastern Europe do not make this a sensible solution.

Some Theoretical Issues

Before turning to recent experiences with constitutional revision in Eastern Europe and defending our recommendation, we introduce a few analytical points. An amending formula, first of all, provides a way for framers to share some of their authority over the constitution with subsequent generations. Because of this relationship to the initial framing power, the amending power trenches upon core issues of democracy and sovereignty. Constitutional revision raises the question of the source of law or "popular sovereignty" in its most institutionally concrete form. If all political agency must be authorized by the constitution, whence comes the authority to remake the constitution? If the amending power is conceived as wholly subordinate to the constitution, it presents an obvious anomaly.

... As Bruce Ackerman and others have argued, democracy would be incomplete if the citizenry could act only through periodic elections and public discussions of concrete policy alternatives conducted through a free press. To this must be added the right to change or not to change fundamental value commitments and the rules of the game. Political legitimacy in liberal systems ultimately depends upon the option to bring about change, used or held in reserve.

The legitimacy of a liberal constitution has a similar foundation, paradoxically, in its own liability to revision. It is accepted, or deserves to be accepted, partly because it could be changed.[6] ...

Amendability suggests, to put it crudely, that basic rights are ultimately at the mercy of interest-group politics, if some arbitrary electoral threshold is surpassed and amenders play by the book. Is this a correct way of understanding liberal democracy? ...

This question can be reformulated in practical terms. Does the political system of a specific country, say the United States or Germany, admit judicial review of procedurally correct constitutional amendments? The United States does not, on the ground that the constitution-remaking power is superior to the power of judicial review; but Germany does, on the ground that an amendment, even if passed in the formally correct manner, may be inconsistent with the core or fundamental features of the constitution. Germany entrenches certain rights in the sense that it places them beyond not only politics, but even the kind of revision represented by constitutional amendment.

The form taken by the amending power, in other words, sheds light on the variety of theories underlying different liberal democracies....

... Every functioning liberal democracy depends on a variety of techniques for introducing flexibility into the constitutional framework. The two usual methods are, first, amendment and, second, judicial interpretation in the light of evolving circumstances and social norms. There are

---

6. For Eastern Europe, as we will argue below, the crucial implication of this principle is that the more difficult it is to amend a constitution, the less plausible it becomes to infer "consent" from a failure to amend it.

intriguing interaction or mutual compensation effects of constitutional amendment and constitutional interpretation, and these can help us understand better the relationship between the judiciary and the political branches.... If amendments are relatively difficult, the legislature has a ready alibi for failure to give in to the electorate, and the court, in turn, will gain in prestige because it can pose as the guardian of the ark of the covenant.... As circumstances change over time, flexible interpretation also diminishes the pressure for frequent amendment....

The free availability of amendment may have a range of diverse effects on the courts. If it is easy to amend the Constitution, the stakes of constitutional decision are lowered, for an erroneous or unpopular judicial decision can be overridden. Moreover, the availability of the amendment option may embolden the court, since the judges will know that mistaken decisions can be corrected. For Eastern Europe, it is especially important to keep in mind the following point: Stringent amending formulas will allow parliaments faced with large social problems to deflect social disapprobation and to escape democratic accountability in difficult times.

Eastern Europe

How are these somewhat abstruse theoretical issues reflected in the constitutional politics now under way in Eastern Europe? When the Communist system collapsed in Albania, Bulgaria, Czechoslovakia, Estonia, Hungary, Latvia, Lithuania, Poland, Romania, Russia, and Ukraine, one of the first acts of the wobbly new regimes was a solemnly enacted constitutional amendment.... Such a beginning was meant by the actors involved to register or symbolize a commitment to a nonrevolutionary form of political change. The rule of law had begun. There was to be no more rumbling of tanks. Future transformations would come seriatim, could not be wholly planned in advance, and would be legal, public, and nonviolent....

Consider, as a first although admittedly untypical example, the Russian Federation. Ruslan Khasbulatov, before he was deposed by Boris Yeltsin from his position as Speaker of the Russian Supreme Soviet, had several constitutional lawyers on his staff whose job was to tell him when his legislative proposals conflicted with the constitution. When Khasbulatov learned of a possible conflict, he did not abandon his legislative proposal, of course, but with breathtaking nonchalance initiated the procedure whereby the constitution itself could be changed. Put succinctly, constitutional amendments have been used in contemporary Russia (by Yeltsin as well as by Khasbulatov) as just another technique for outmaneuvering one's political enemies of the moment. Or, in Jon Elster's words, the constitution is viewed as an instrument of action instead of a framework for action. The idea that constitutional revision represents some kind of "higher track of lawmaking," different from and superior to the elbowing and intrigues of ordinary political life, is dramatically belied by recent Russian experience. And while Russia lies on one extreme of the spectrum, the subordination of constitutional revision to everyday political antics and aims is a trend observable everywhere in the region.[16] It follows that the conception of constitutions as precommitment strategies—however helpful it may be for analyzing some constitutional processes and for conceiving of constitutionalism in general—is descriptively inaccurate for Eastern Europe.

The Politics of Constitutional Change

[The authors describe the collapse of "higher track" constitutional lawmaking into the " 'lower track' of ordinary politics" along several dimensions: the lack of time for founding myths to arise; the ignorance in which initial negotiations about constitutional structure were made; the rapid pace of change that these nations have confronted; and the role of legislative assemblies, frequently made of fragmented parties, in constitution-making.]

In general, no group of framers, given the universally acknowledged proneness of all actors to commit colossal blunders in turbulent circumstances, can plausibly monopolize authority over the constitutional framework, refusing to share this authority with subsequent generations, or even with the successor representative assembly. Amateurish drafting guarantees that numerous mistakes will become visible with benefit of hindsight. The personal domination of the drafting process by a tiny number of powerful deputies and their backroom constitutional experts means that some clauses will be smuggled into the constitution without anyone noticing, only to be discovered, to the consternation of some later on. A stringent amendment procedure, patented in the West, whereby constitutional provisions are cemented into the system, implies *deference* toward the decisions of the framers. Because such deference cannot be conjured magically out of the East European air, given who the framers are and the purposes they visibly pursue, a lax amending formula, one that will not saddle successors with the schemes and follies of predecessors, is unusually desirable....

... [T]he very creation of a constitutional culture in post-Communist societies depends upon a willingness to mix constitutional politics and ordinary politics. Perhaps the most fundamental part of any constitution is the elemental choice of regime type. Soviet-style constitutions did not explicitly forbid amendments that would transform the Communist system into a capitalist one. But we may safely infer that such a prohibition ... was implicit and understood by all. To change a communist constitution into a liberal-democratic one required something more drastic than modification, revision, or amendment. It required the wholesale destruction of the old and the creation, from ground zero, of the new. It required a *constitu-*

---

16. We do not deny that high principle plays a role in constitutional politics in Eastern Europe. For example, the elaborate catalogue of protected rights—building on Western examples and international human rights documents—tends to undermine the view that strategy and partisanship can explain everything. See the discussion in Cass R. Sunstein, "Something Old, Something New," *East European Constitutional Review* (1992): 18. With the new constitutions, as with new laws, there is a mixture of principled argument and strategic behavior. Our point is that, in general, there is no sharp split between constitution making and the ordinary processes of politics.

tional revolution, or new founding. Because the basic "choice of regime" is involved, as we already suggested, the legal transformations under way in Eastern Europe must be seen as constitutional revolutions rather than incremental constitutional revisions.

More precisely, they are constitutional revolutions *cloaked* as constitutional revisions. Most striking, from this perspective, is the discordance of content and form. A wholesale constitutional replacement was presented to domestic publics and the world at large as an act of constitutional tinkering. One of the most revolutionary changes of modern times was symbolically de-revolutionized. A total rupture with the past, all aspects of society being reformed simultaneously, was packaged as a piecemeal reform. This was unrealistic, of course. As Vaclav Havel said, commenting upon the Czecho-Slovak partition, "States do not begin and end in a constitutional fashion." But the aspiring liberal democracies of Eastern Europe have all *pretended* to begin and end in this way. The clause about the leading role of the party was revoked, presidencies created, constitutional courts put in place, bills of rights enacted, and so forth—all by sitting or newly elected legislatures. It probably had to happen in this manner.

Chicken Little

In every Eastern European country, including Poland, the basic choice of regime fell out of the sky. The transition from communism to a rudimentary form of democratic capitalism . . . was *not* achieved by mass mobilization, and thus cannot, even now, be viewed realistically as an expression of the national will. What occurred in 1989 was not only a revolution; it was also an unexpected act of decolonization. The Soviet patron went home. A large part of the revolution was precisely this exodus of what seemed like an occupying military force. Western observers have received the downfall of communism as a vindication of democratic liberty, of religious and political freedom, and of a certain conception of appropriate economic arrangements. Undoubtedly much of this is true. But we cannot overstate the extent to which the developments of 1989 represented a repudiation of the mere fact of foreign domination from the Soviets—in some ways a repudiation that was independent of the particular form that the domination took. . . .

. . . Wholly new political arrangements have been institutionalized throughout the region on the basis of a string of constitutional amendments passed by weakly legitimate parliaments, assemblies that are, in turn, fragmented into a chaos of small parties. . . . How could such a massive change be introduced by such a feeble institution deploying such feeble measures? The answer lies in the power vacuum left in the wake of Moscow's unexpected collapse. Power is relative, and the power of parliaments in Eastern Europe, however small, usually looms large in societies where all rival centers of power are (for the time being) even weaker. These parliaments, in any case, were suddenly charged with a monumental task for which they were monumentally ill prepared. Their members were and are inexperienced in governance and they do not enjoy high public prestige.

Their relative power, as a result, may be difficult to sustain. The absence of a historically anchored constitutional tradition is only one problem among many. Even if agreements between mutually suspicious and opportunist deputies, prone to conspiracy thinking and vulnerable to blackmail, could be hammered out, there is no way these assemblies could simply impose (*octroyer*) a constitution upon a passive citizenry and expect it to last or be obeyed.

These various considerations converge on a single conclusion: *Constitution making in Eastern Europe must be a long, drawn-out political act.* Only in this way can a revolution delivered on a platter be transformed into a basic choice of regime made, or rather *achieved,* by the countries themselves. The fundamental choice of liberal democracy, one that fell out of the sky, must now be brought down to earth and worked out politically, by trial and error, by consultation and debate, if it is to gain the public support it needs. This can be achieved best by vesting the parliament with full authority to frame a new constitution and with a flexible capacity for constitutional amendment (we offer details below).

To be sure, this *parliamentization* of constitution making has many drawbacks: false starts, half steps and missteps, interim arrangements based on myopic bargains, legislative deadlocks, interest-group pressures, the short-term stalling of economic reform, technically botched or amateurish constitutional provisions, and so forth. But this "collapse" of constitutional politics into ordinary politics has two great advantages that outweigh all the obvious disadvantages. First, it provides an opportunity for the political nation to be introduced, over time, to the large questions of constitutional government (presidentialism versus parliamentarism, proportional representation versus single-member districts, unicameralism versus bicameralism, legislative supremacy versus judicial review, and so forth) *while* such issues are being seriously debated. And, second, it provides a chance for opposition elites, trained in clandestine nonacquiescence and witness bearing (and therefore inclined to irony and "principled stands"), to learn the arts of public coalition formation and governance. And it achieves this constitutional education for both officials and citizens without undermining, as easy recourse to popular referenda might do, the still feeble legitimacy of representative institutions. (Note also that a significant risk of referenda, under current conditions, is that very few people will vote.)

Parliamentary fumbling, or trial and error, in the constitutional arena appears more desirable than deplorable when viewed from this perspective. To expect that societies that are so disorganized socially could establish a "higher track" of constitution making *outside* the parliament, moreover, is as unrealistic as to expect that the representative assembly will stay its hand and bypass the fundamental controversies dividing society. Neither the mobilized masses nor a commission of experts could do the job in question. Furthermore, to hand over the constitution modifying process to a special convention, separate from parliament, and operating in the pure legal air above the political fray, may seem plausible to visiting law professors; but it would be quixotic in the conditions in Eastern Europe today. Because the most fundamental questions—such as, What sort of regime do we want?—have not been answered by the citizenry, and since no organized forum for national political debate is about to develop outside of the assembly, ordinary parliamentary politics is necessarily *about* constitutional questions. In today's circumstances, constitutional choices are partisan choices and institutional arrangements are necessarily experimental. The rules of the game cannot be clearly distinguished from the content of the game....

As a result, we should not expect constitution drafting and modification in Eastern Europe to be untainted by political interests. Indeed, it would be futile to attempt to separate the currently inseparable, assigning the "lower track" of ordinary politics to one assembly and the "higher track" of constitutional politics to another.... [T]olerance for crisis, without resort to mass violence, seems much greater in Eastern Europe than most observers have predicted. The politicization of constitution making in Eastern Europe, in any case, is not fundamentally the result of confusion or a cultural deficit or a failure to understand the Western distinction between politics and law, or the difference between the instruments of action and the framework of action. It is the result of a need for public legitimation, difficult to achieve, of a constitutional revolution that was delivered unexpectedly from abroad.

Survey of the Amending Procedures in Eastern Europe

We now briefly describe amending procedures in existing Eastern European constitutions, actual or in draft. Our central contrast is between Bulgaria and Romania, on the one hand, and Poland and Hungary, on the other.

The Hungarian Parliament and the Polish Sejm enjoy a great deal of free authority to amend the constitution ... subject only to two procedural constraints, supermajorities of two-thirds and attendance requirements.

The Bulgarian and the Romanian assemblies are far more limited in their authority.... [B]oth face subject matter restrictions. The Romanian Parliament must also rely on a referendum.... While the Bulgarian National Assembly is granted the power to amend the Constitution on its own, and while the National Assembly cannot be bypassed by other bodies, its amending procedure is extremely cumbersome.... In order for amendment to proceed, a proposal must garner a three-fourths vote from all the members of the Assembly—the most stringent supermajoritarian requirement in Eastern Europe. Moreover, at least one month must pass between initiation and the first vote for ratification. Finally, the Bulgarian formula requires three different ballots on the three different days. While the Romanian Parliament is the weakest amending power, the Bulgarian National Assembly is the most tightly bound.

We choose these four countries to make an analytical point. Constitutionalists tend to favor a system of deep entrenchment of constitutional provisions (i.e., a stringent amending formula) and recourse to popular referenda. This may be desirable in Western democracies, but it is inappropriate, we argue, in Eastern Europe. The amending formula should be relatively lax, and it should be virtually monopolized by parliament, with no recourse to referenda....

... From a Western perspective, therefore, Bulgaria and Romania should be seen as having made greater strides toward establishing *sacralized constitutionalism* than Poland and Hungary. But this is not an adequate account. Stopgap constitutionalism—embodied in the Polish and Hungarian systems—is the most effective kind in Eastern Europe because, among other reasons, important choices can be tolerated more easily by losers if these choices are perceived as temporary and up for further consideration at a later date. The "deep entrenchment" of constitutional provisions, on the other hand, and the availability of referenda in south-eastern Europe, result from the dominance of ex-Communists, eager to "lock in" their privileges, over the constitution-drafting process there. Given the atomization of these societies, "going to the people" is not especially democratic. The "plebiscitary legitimacy" gained via referenda can be easily manipulated by political elites. In Eastern Europe, in any case, the harder it is to amend a constitution and the greater role granted to popular referenda and extraparliamentary authorities, the less constitutionalism matters as a political force.

Why should the least liberal leadership in the region have been the first to create liberal constitutional frameworks? The reason seems to be that old-regime elites, fighting a rear-guard action, have both a greater opportunity and a greater incentive to implement new constitutions than do post-Communist elites....

So much for the contrast between two different general conceptions of the appropriate amending formula; we are now prepared to offer more details. Several constitutions prohibit the amendment of certain provisions altogether.... Article 148(1) of the Romanian Constitution expressly prohibits any amendments that attempt to alter "the national, unitary and indivisible character of the Romanian State, *the Republican form of government,* territorial integrity, independence of the judiciary, [and] political pluralism." ... The Czech Constitution says, "An amendment to the *essential requirements for a democratic legal state shall be inadmissible.*" Other provisions placed beyond the reach of formal revision include those addressing "fundamental rights and freedoms" and those protecting "human rights."

The Bulgarian Constitution takes a different approach. Rather than prohibiting the revision of the protected provisions altogether, Bulgaria, as noted, offers an amending institution that is cumbersome and time-consuming: the amending convention. Among the new Eastern European constitutions, only the Bulgarian Constitution provides for an amending convention, called by the National Assembly upon a two-thirds vote of all its members. Moreover, the Constitution entrenches provisions that establish the form of state structure and government, preserve the inviolability of human rights, and define the territory of the republic.

Many of the Eastern European documents ban amendments during states of war and states of emergency....

The Eastern European documents allow for different agents of change. Under the Albanian draft constitution, the Albanian People's Assembly enjoys the greatest amending power in Eastern Europe. Article 78(2) mandates that the People's Assembly "approves and amends the Constitution." This is done "when the majority of the deputies present have voted for [the laws and other acts]." No other institution in Eastern Europe has the unilateral power to enact an amendment with an ordinary legislative plurality.

Other institutions of constitutional revision in Eastern Europe have the power of amendment. Article 24(3) of the Hungarian Constitution says that "for the amendment of the Constitution ... the affirmative votes of two-thirds of the Members of Parliament are required." The Hungarian Parliament's control is exclusive because no other institution has a claim to participate in the amending procedure.... The Polish Sejm has similar power....

We can ... identify four different systems for the allocation of amending powers among political institutions. First, some constitutions grant the assembly exclusive power over the amending process. Among this group are the Hungarian Parliament, the Polish Sejm, and the Czech Parliament. Second, some constitutions grant to the assembly both the necessary and the sufficient power to amend the constitution, but also grant other institutions the right of access to the amendment process. Third, the Romanian Constitution gives no institution the power to amend any part of the Constitution unilaterally. Finally, some constitutions give the assembly power to enact amendments, but do not make that power exclusive. In most instances, these constitutions allow direct popular participation, with the right of petition and referendum being granted to the citizenry. Ukraine, Slovakia, and Latvia are of this variety. In some of these cases, direct popular participation is at some point dependent upon the president or the assembly for approval. The Croatian and the Slovenian constitutions are examples....

There are also different procedural requirements in the various constitutions and drafts. The Albanian draft constitution gives the People's Assembly the power to determine its own amending procedure. No procedural hurdles hamper the Assembly's power to revise the constitution beyond normal legislative procedures.... The Polish Sejm has only two procedural requirements placed upon it. First, a constitutional revision requires a two-thirds plurality; second, at least half the members of the Sejm must vote to enact an amendment. The Hungarian Constitution is slightly more difficult to amend. Like the Polish, the Hungarian Constitution may be revised with a two-thirds plurality of Parliament. But in the Hungarian case, all the members of Parliament must cast a vote on an amendment proposal.

Supermajority requirements and turnout requirements are common in Eastern Europe. . . .

What Is to Be Done?

From the previous section, it should be clear that the amending formula reflects two basic choices: (1) is the procedure difficult or easy? and (2) is the procedure dominated by the established powers, or is a popular referendum involved? We argue, against the grain of most contemporary constitutional theory, for a lax procedure dominated by the assembly.

We begin by noting a reasonable fear—that under our proposal, the amending power will be overused, thus endangering stability and perhaps democracy itself. In the circumstances of Eastern Europe, the fear seems unrealistic. First, in highly fragmented parliaments, even a simple majority for amendment will be difficult to muster. Second, most East European politicians seem to recognize that imperfect or unimproved constitutional provisions are not wholly dysfunctional. Textual ambiguity provides useful room for maneuver. It is unlikely that there will be ready resort to constitutional change even if such change is relatively easy to bring about as a matter of technical law.

Our basic argument runs into the teeth of the old cliché: A "balance must be struck" between rigidity and flexibility in constitutional entrenchment. The reasoning behind this proverbial balancing approach can be easily stated. On the one hand, if a constitution is too difficult to amend, if it is excessively rigid, it is liable to break. An overly rigid constitution, based on a stringent amending formula, invites extraconstitutional solutions (or free-floating interpretation, which poses dangers of its own). On the other hand, if a constitution is too easy to amend, it will invite the constitutionalization of political life, or the collapse of constitutional politics into ordinary politics. A lax amending procedure, especially when monopolized by the assembly, will encourage legislators to attempt to outmaneuver their opponents of the moment by changing the rules of the game while in midstream. It will also make basic rights vulnerable to political winds and eliminate the kinds of stability and facilitation that are provided by agreement on basic institutional arrangements.

We believe that, in this context, we should abandon this balanced approach. More specifically, we urge a general presumption in favor of flexible amending procedures dominated by the established powers, especially the legislature. Let constitutional politics collapse into ordinary politics—for this "collapse" is not only inevitable but, under current circumstances in Eastern Europe, desirable. Let the constitutional process drag on, for several years, one pro tempore arrangement replacing another. The needs of the transition from state socialism, after all, are not the same as the needs of an established or incipient liberal democracy building on existing understandings and traditions (like the young United States[39] or,

---

39. As the countries of the former East bloc struggle to establish constitutional de-   mocracies in difficult circumstances today, we should ask ourselves again how the United

in quite a different way, postwar Germany). So why should the framework established for the former be bequeathed to those who will be grappling with the latter? Anyway, there is nothing particularly healthy about *la rage de vouloir conclure*. The postponement of permanence is not always foot dragging, but may also be the sage acknowledgment of an ongoing social earthquake, where foundation builders must trim their ambitions to create immortal works. The entrenchment gained by a stringent amending formula, moreover, will adversely affect the political process by raising the stakes of constitutional choice, increasing the perceived benefits of confrontation. Losers face the possibility of total frustration, which makes them less likely to accept compromise and more likely to risk deadlock. If no side sees a chance to entrench its partisan advantage permanently, by contrast, all parties may slowly develop a taste for concession making.

The assumption underlying this recommendation is the following. *The central task of the states of Eastern Europe today is the creation of legitimate democratic authority.* The fundamental challenge is less to restrict abusive authority—though this is also important—than to create accountable authority.[41] The collapse of Sovietism left East European societies with virtually no institutions to build upon. (What role does the Solidarity trade union now play in constructing Polish democracy?) Institution building, therefore, must not be forgotten in the race to prevent future abuses of power. Any arrangement that obstructs the creation of democratic authority, or undermines it once it has been created, is to be shunned.

Some commentators have deplored the fact that the new constitutions and constitutional drafts embody bargains among parliamentary forces

States managed to launch a stable liberal-republican regime at the end of the eighteenth century. The endurance of the Constitution written at Philadelphia in 1787 was not foreordained. The members of the Constituent Assembly in Paris in 1791, whose ideals were not radically discrepant from those of the American Founders, produced a respectable, if not perfect, liberal constitution that spattered to a swift and miserable end. Why did the Americans succeed and the French fail? There are many reasons, of course, stemming from the vastly different political, religious, economic, demographic, and military situations of the two countries. (While the French were saddled with Louis XVI, moreover, the United States was favored with George Washington.) But one additional reason deserves to be pointed out. Unlike their French contemporaries, the American Founders devised their Constitution *after a period of frustration with the weakness of the central government*. They aimed, therefore, not only to prevent tyranny, but also to create an energetic govern-ment with the capacity to govern, to rule effectively, and to "promote the general Welfare." This devotion to governmental effectiveness, this passion for state building, was virtually absent at the Paris Constituent Assembly. Framed in response to the unpredictable arbitrariness of monarchical rule, the French Constitution of 1791 proved so constricting that, when the first crisis struck, authorities were driven to slough it off and govern extraconstitutionally. By contrast, the desire simultaneously to limit and reinforce the state resulted, in the American case, in a stable constitutional regime that was neither tyrannical nor weak.

41. Constitutional lawyers tend to be poor political advisers in today's circumstances because *constitutional law assumes the preexistence of the political authority that needs to be limited.* Like many economists, most of them are professionally biased against constitutional techniques for state building or reinforcing the governing capacities of public authorities.

rather than high-minded legal principles. But this squeamishness about public bargaining is precisely one of the forces that must be overcome in order to consolidate the transition to constitutional democracy.

We do urge that Eastern European countries should experiment with different approaches for entrenching provisions. It would not make sense to offer a blueprint here, but our preferred approach is an innovation in constitutional practice: a three-tiered system of amendability. Under this approach, most of the Constitution would be easily amendable. But some provisions would not be amendable at all (as in the German Constitution), or could be changed only by a strong majority that has favored revision on two or more occasions. Still other provisions would be amendable with some difficulty, but without the severe obstacles facing the most entrenched provisions.

Under this approach, we suggest that two sets of rights should be most strongly entrenched. First, a specified list of individual rights should be made immune to revision. This list should include, first and foremost, rights that are indispensable to democratic legitimacy. We therefore suggest that freedom of speech, the right to vote, religious liberty, and freedom from discrimination on grounds of race, religion, ethnicity, and sex should be especially protected against politics, including constitutional politics. The category of entrenched rights should also include rights against abuse of the criminal justice system—including the basic right to fair hearing.

Second, we suggest that some of the broad outlines of the institutional arrangements might be safeguarded against too easy change. Thus, for example, the political process might be prevented from over-coming the judgment that there will be one president, or that there will be three separated powers within a system of checks and balances. So, too, the provisions that guarantee basic democratic arrangements—the right to free speech, democratic elections, the right to vote—should be made immune to constitutional revision.

By contrast, the social and economic rights that one finds spelled out in a number of actual and proposed Eastern European constitutions should be easily amendable, especially if they are considered fit for judicial enforcement and not simply aspirational goals. Consider, for example, the fact that the Hungarian Constitution protects not merely the right to equal pay for equal work, but also the right to an income conforming with the quantity and quality of work performed. What would it mean for the Hungarian Constitutional Court to take these provisions seriously? Similarly, the Slovak draft includes the right to a standard of living commensurate to each citizen's potential and that of society as a whole, as well as the right to just pay. One also finds in some constitutions such rights as food, shelter, and even recreation complementing more traditional rights of private property, free speech, and the like. We think that these former guarantees should be amendable through ordinary legislative processes.

So much for the basic issue of entrenchment. Who should be allowed to bring about constitutional change? From what we have said thus far, it follows that most issues of constitutional revision should be decided by the parliament.... What message is conveyed to the citizenry if popular referenda are given a central role in the amending process? Our answer is that such a provision implies that the voice of the people is not adequately expressed through the representative process. *In other words, referenda implicitly erode the legitimacy of democratically elected assemblies by expressing the seemingly reasonable belief that the most important choices should not be left up to politicians.* But this principle is less democratic than it first sounds. Since the parliaments in question have little enough legitimacy as it is, reliance on referenda may be the straw that breaks the camel's back....

... In its first stages, at least, democracy should be parliament- and not court-centered, and it should avoid ready resort to popular referenda. Any system that preempts the right of parliament to make the most vital decisions will ultimately damage the prospects of both democracy and limited government.

Does the Czecho-Slovak "divorce," engineered by politicians in Prague and Bratislava and supported by less than 40 percent of the electorate, provide an important counterexample to this thesis? Would a popular referendum, bypassing the federal and state parliaments, have been more democratic and led to a more satisfactory (as well as more legitimate) outcome? We doubt it. The reason is that liberal democracy must assign responsibility to officials to make decisions, and hold them accountable if the decisions turn out badly. Seen in this light, referenda seem as undemocratic as imperative mandates and immediate recall. Ultimately, the feasibility of the union would have depended upon the ability of the federal legislature to govern the country as a whole and to maintain authority over the two state assemblies. This is not a task that could have been fulfilled by an extraparliamentary appeal. If a government cannot govern, referenda will not help. Hence the failure to save the union registered a political incapacity that would probably have trivialized the federal government in a relatively short time....

We summarize here all the arguments about the need to provide for constant readjustments and "updating" in the fluid circumstances of Eastern Europe. Certainty and predictability cannot be produced by constitutional rigidity. On the contrary, rigid constitutions invite extra-constitutional solutions that cannot, in principle, be foreseen. The more difficult it is to amend a constitution, moreover, the less plausible it becomes to infer "consent" from the failure to amend it. That is acceptable in certain conditions—like those of the contemporary United States—but it is a terrible fault in circumstances where the principal need is to create both public confidence in representative institutions and political accountability of elected officials....

... The relatively high prestige of constitutional courts in the region (which advocates of a stringent amending formula unwisely hope to increase still further) may derive at least in part from the strange resemblance between this unelected body of people who make decisions in secret (without public bargaining) and the old Politburo (which also claimed to speak with the "higher voice" of the people).

Overconfidence in the judiciary and overemphasis on the bill of rights are especially problematic given the poor quality of the sitting judges and the embryonic condition of legal education. (We put to one side the case of Hungary, whose constitutional court has already established itself as one of the most authoritative in the world.) But a court-centered democracy is unlikely to last in any case. The greater power and prestige granted to the constitutional court, the more diminished may be the power and prestige of parliament, and the more difficult it may be to create legitimate and accountable authority through elections, especially in countries with a history of compulsory voting in fake elections. And if a military or presidential coup occurs, the only force capable of protecting the constitutional order will be the parliament. It will be unfortunate, in this event, if the constitutional drafters will have helped feed growing public disgust with politicians in general and the constitutional court will have contributed to a lowering of the assembly's already-damaged prestige.

We do not contend that a constitutional court is a bad idea, or that it cannot accomplish considerable good. On the contrary, we believe that such a court can help bring about the transition to democracy and constitutionalism. We mean only to suggest that the court is merely a part of the picture, and a secondary part at that. The point bears on the topic of constitutional amendment. If the court will play a secondary role, it cannot be counted on to furnish the sorts of creative interpretation (found in, say, Germany and the United States) that serve to keep the founding document consistent with changing circumstances and values. And if constitutional interpretation cannot accomplish this function, it becomes all the more important to allow relatively easy resort to constitutional amendment.

Concluding Points

... [S]ome constitutional lawyers believe that the central function of constitutionalism is to *prevent tyranny,* including especially *the tyranny of the majority* (i.e., oppression by democratically elected officials, accountable to a majority of the voters). As a result, they want to increase the power of constitutional courts and decrease the power of parliaments. As a general prescription, this is probably a strategic mistake, which will have the consequence of making a relapse into autocracy more rather than less likely.

A constitution is not simply a device for preventing tyranny. It has several other functions as well. For instance, constitutions do not only limit power and prevent tyranny; they also construct and guide power and prevent anarchy. More comprehensively, liberal constitutions are designed to help solve a whole range of political problems: tyranny, corruption, anarchy, immobilism, collective action problems, absence of deliberation, myopia, lack of accountability, instability, and the stupidity of politicians. Constitutions are multifunctional. It is a radical over-simplification to identify the constitutional function exclusively with the prevention of tyranny.

The identification is also excessively negative. The positive or facilitative dimensions of constitutionalism must also be taken into account, especially in countries shattered by a wholesale disintegration of state authority and involved in impromptu state building while trying to avoid scapegoating and campaigns for ethnic homogenization. A constitution can be an instrument of government. It can establish rules that help put democracy into effect. It can create an institutional framework that, if it functions properly, makes decision making more thoughtful and mistakes easier to learn from. It can prevent power wielders from invoking secrecy and shutting themselves off, as they naturally would do, from criticisms, counterarguments, and fresh ideas. At the same time, it can mobilize collective resources for solving collective problems.

This positive vision of constitutionalism is rare among constitutional specialists in Eastern Europe. Advocates of *negative constitutionalism* dominate the discussion and make it difficult to see the advantages for governmental effectiveness to be gained from constitutional channeling of sovereign power. This is unfortunate. If constitutions are designed with a primarily negative purpose, to prevent tyranny, they will probably lead to political deadlock, and thus invite tyranny. If the government cannot govern, if it cannot pass its reform program, for example, public pressure will mount to throw the hampering constitution off and govern extraconstitutionally. In short, the challenge of constitutional drafting in Eastern Europe is positive as well as negative. Theorists should therefore place greater emphasis than they have hitherto done on *positive constitutionalism*. The task is to create a limited government that is nevertheless fully capable of governing.

Constitutional lawyers and economists tend to share an unfriendly attitude toward state power. . . .

The fact is that political decision-making authority will eventually emerge in Eastern Europe. The questions are: on what basis and within which constraints? The danger is that nondemocratic forms of legitimacy will eclipse democratic ones. Charisma, nationalism, traditional Catholic or Orthodox Christianity, excessively efficacious marketization—all of these are, in principle, potentially nondemocratic sources of governmental legitimacy. . . . Hence, the basic problem in post-Communist societies is not to hamstring the autocratic state or to avoid the tyranny of the majority. On the contrary, *the crucial task is to create government that is simultaneously accountable and effective.* More specifically, the challenge is to create a parliamentary system that is capable of governing effectively and of integrating the more substantive or qualitative forms of legitimacy within itself (shutting down all rival claimants). . . .

This observation bears directly on the question of constitutional amendment. A stringent amending formula, we might say, registers what is under current circumstances an unwise attempt to codify a dual democratic legitimacy. The entrenched constitution is familiarly said to embody *the higher voice of the people*, a voice that can trump the elected legislature. In Eastern Europe, this would be a myth; it would amount in practice (at least in part) to the superiority of the unelected constitutional court over the parliament. Seen from the assembly's viewpoint, it could promote collective irresponsibility. Deputies have readily available an alibi for failure: We cannot do this or that because such actions are forbidden by the constitution as interpreted by the courts. That is a questionable arrangement, given the current weakness of public confidence in state institutions . . . because judges are notoriously less able to communicate with citizens than are politicians. The total superiority of a constitutional court over the parliament, in a situation where government as a whole is viewed as an establishment game having little relevance to the lives of most people, will simply exacerbate the problem of public alienation, making the creation and consolidation of democratic authority all the more difficult.

There is no clear evidence, incidentally, that constitutions based on low political bargains, rather than high legal principles, are particularly unstable. Such an "ignoble" source may be a great asset. To the extent that constitutions are publicly acknowledged as codified bargains, there will be less temptation to mythologize the constitutional framework and treat it unrealistically as the word of God (or "We the People"). The rational reason for a subsequent generation to respect the terms of the constitutional settlement, in any case, has less to do with the source than with the content of the constitution. If a constitution does not help current citizens to solve their problems and achieve their aims, it will and should have little appeal, no matter how great the supermajority that originally ratified it. The appropriateness of treating a constitution as "sacred" surely depends on what the constitution contains. . . .

. . . All that a democratic electorate needs to know to resist every whimsical impulse to "improve" the constitution is (1) that *all* rules, including the alternatives proposed, have defects and deplorable side effects, and (2) the costs of change are likely to outweigh the benefits. If the rules of the game are functioning fairly well, this is all that needs to be said to prevent endless tampering with the constitutional framework. No appeal need be made to a "higher track of lawmaking," implicit in the constitution, reserved to the "higher self" of the nation, and riding high above the lowly politics of ordinary lawmaking. Such an appeal also carries the risk of unjustified ancestor worship.

Finally, the complete subordination of ordinary politics to the constitution, treated as a sacred framework that cannot be changed and that governs in the last resort, is possible only under very specific historical conditions. Court-centered democracy worked wonderfully well in West Germany, a country that became *a political dependency* and was democratized on that basis alone. Many important choices were simply "off the agenda" for the politicians of the early Federal Republic. Because politics itself was strictly limited by postwar Germany's international situation, it was possible to develop a strict political style that strictly subordinated the legislature to the constitutional court. . . .

Questions and Comments on Entrenchment and Amendment

1. The Holmes and Sunstein argument implies that a danger of too rigidly entrenching a constitution in the fluid circumstances of Eastern Europe is that, by raising the stakes of constitution-making, losers may face such frustration that they become obstacles to both effective government and rule of law. This argument is grounded in their analysis of the economic, cultural and political situations in eastern Europe. At the same time, they caution against "ancestor worship" of a constitution simply because of its longevity or prior popular approval, and reject the claimed superiority of a constitution of principle over a constitution of compromise. On what basis do they draw these conclusions? What, if any, implications would their reasoning have for compliance with and interpretation of the U.S. Constitution?

2. Consider whether Holmes and Sunstein are really making as dramatic an argument in favor of ease of amendment as the beginning of their article might suggest. Are they instead searching for a way to distinguish social and economic rights from other "constitutional" provisions to avoid the supposed depreciation of constitutional legitimacy from nonenforcement of social rights alluded to by Osiatynski?

3. What role do revolutionary leaders play in "consolidating" the transition to constitutionalism? To the extent that you are aware of the facts, consider the different roles of George Washington in the U.S., Lech Walesa in Poland, and Vaclav Havel in the Czech Republic in the years immediately after their nations underwent constitutional transitions. Consider also the possibility that leaders may impede the process of stabilizing a new constitutional regime by forcing upon the public choices that could be avoided.

Note on South Africa's Procedure for Adopting a New Constitution and the Possibility of Unconstitutional Constitutions and Amendments

South Africa is in the process of one of the most dramatic political, social and constitutional transformations of this century. Generations of legal commitment to racial apartheid and institutionalized control by a white minority have been abandoned. Internal resistance and external pressure resulted in the 1990 release of Nelson Mandela after many years in prison and the onset of formal negotiations between the white government in power (the National Party), the African National Congress (ANC) and other political groups (including followers of KwaZulu Chief Minister

Buthelezi). (The negotiations are referred to as the Multi–Party Negotiating Process.) The background to these talks is summarized by the Constitutional Court of South Africa.

a.   *Historical and political context*

In re Certification of the Constitution of the R.S.A.

1996, (4) S.A. 744, 776–79 (Constitutional Court Sept. 6, 1996) (South Africa).

. . .

[5] South Africa's past has been aptly described as that of "a deeply divided society characterised by strife, conflict, untold suffering and injustice" which "generated gross violations of human rights, the transgression of humanitarian principles in violent conflicts and a legacy of hatred, fear, guilt and revenge". From the outset the country maintained a colonial heritage of racial discrimination: in most of the country the franchise was reserved for white males and a rigid system of economic and social segregation was enforced. The administration of African tribal territories through vassal "traditional authorities" passed smoothly from British colonial rule to the new government, which continued its predecessor's policy.

[6] At the same time the Montesquieuan principle of a threefold separation of State power—often but an aspirational ideal—did not flourish in a South Africa which, under the banner of adherence to the Westminster system of government, actively promoted parliamentary supremacy and domination by the executive. Multi-party democracy had always been the preserve of the white minority but even there it had languished since 1948. The rallying call of apartheid proved irresistible for a white electorate embattled by the spectre of decolonisation in Africa to the north.

[7] From time to time various forms of limited participation in government were devised by the minority for the majority, most notably the "homeland policy" which was central to the apartheid system. Fundamental to that system was a denial of socio-political and economic rights to the majority in the bulk of the country, which was identified as "white South Africa", coupled with a Balkanisation of tribal territories in which Africans would theoretically become entitled to enjoy all rights. Race was the basic, all-pervading and inescapable criterion for participation by a person in all aspects of political, economic and social life.

[8] As the apartheid system gathered momentum during the 1950s and came to be enforced with increasing rigour, resistance from the disenfranchised—and increasingly disadvantaged—majority intensified. Many (and eventually most) of them demanded non-discriminatory and wholly representative government in a non-racial unitary State, tenets diametrically opposed to those of apartheid. Although there were reappraisals and adaptations on both sides as time passed, the ideological chasm remained apparently unbridgeable until relatively recently.

[9] The clash of ideologies not only resulted in strife and conflict but, as the confrontation intensified, the South African government of the day—and some of the self-governing and "independent" territories spawned by apartheid—became more and more repressive. More particularly from 1976 onwards increasingly harsh security measures gravely eroded civil liberties. The administration of urban black residential areas and most "homeland" administrations fell into disarray during the following decade. The South African government, backed by a powerful security apparatus operating with sweeping emergency powers, assumed strongly centralised and authoritarian control of the country.

[10] Then, remarkably and in the course of but a few years, the country's political leaders managed to avoid a cataclysm by negotiating a largely peaceful transition from the rigidly controlled minority regime to a wholly democratic constitutional dispensation. After a long history of "deep conflict between a minority which reserved for itself all control over the political instruments of the state and a majority who sought to resist that domination", [quoting Azapo v. President of the Republic of South Africa, 1996 (4) S.A. 671, 676], the overwhelming majority of South Africans across the political divide realised that the country had to be urgently rescued from imminent disaster by a negotiated commitment to a fundamentally new constitutional order premised upon open and democratic government and the universal enjoyment of fundamental human rights. That commitment is expressed in the preamble to the Interim Constitution by an acknowledgement of the

> "... need to create a new order in which all South Africans will be entitled to a common South African citizenship in a sovereign and democratic constitutional State in which there is equality between men and women and people of all races so that all citizens shall be able to enjoy and exercise their fundamental rights and freedoms".

With this end in view the IC

> "... provides a historic bridge between the past of a deeply divided society characterised by strife, conflict, untold suffering and injustice, and a future founded on the recognition of human rights, democracy and peaceful co-existence and development opportunities for all South Africans, irrespective of colour, race, class, belief or sex".

[11] Following upon exploratory and confidential talks across the divide, the transitional process was formally inaugurated in February 1990, when the then government of the Republic of South Africa announced its willingness to engage in negotiations with the liberation movements. Negotiations duly ensued and persevered, despite many apparent deadlocks. Some of the "independent homeland" governments gave their support to the negotiation process. Others did not but were overtaken by the momentum of the ensuing political developments and became part of the overall transition, unwillingly or by default.

[12] One of the deadlocks, a crucial one on which the negotiations all but foundered, related to the formulation of a new constitution for the

country. All were agreed that such an instrument was necessary and would have to contain certain basic provisions. Those who negotiated this commitment were confronted, however, with two problems. The first arose from the fact that they were not elected to their positions in consequence of any free and verifiable elections and that it was therefore necessary to have this commitment articulated in a final constitution adopted by a credible body properly mandated to do so in consequence of free and fair elections based on universal adult suffrage. The second problem was the fear in some quarters that the constitution eventually favoured by such a body of elected representatives might not sufficiently address the anxieties and the insecurities of such constituencies and might therefore subvert the objectives of a negotiated settlement. The government and other minority groups were prepared to relinquish power to the majority but were determined to have a hand in drawing the framework for the future governance of the country. The liberation movements on the opposition side were equally adamant that only democratically elected representatives of the people could legitimately engage in forging a constitution: neither they, and certainly not the government of the day, had any claim to the requisite mandate from the electorate.

The impasse was resolved by a compromise which enabled both sides to attain their basic goals without sacrificing principle. What was no less important in the political climate of the time was that it enabled them to keep faith with their respective constituencies: those who feared engulfment by a black majority and those who were determined to eradicate apartheid once and for all. In essence the settlement was quite simple. Instead of an outright transmission of power from the old order to the new, there would be a programmed two-stage transition. An interim government, established and functioning under an interim constitution agreed to by the negotiating parties, would govern the country on a coalition basis while a final constitution was being drafted. A national Legislature, elected (directly and indirectly) by universal adult suffrage, would double as the constitution-making body and would draft the new constitution within a given time. But—and herein lies the key to the resolution of the deadlock— that text would have to comply with certain guidelines agreed upon in advance by the negotiating parties. What is more, an independent arbiter would have to ascertain and declare whether the new constitution indeed complied with the guidelines before it could come into force.

---

b. *The Multi-Party Negotiating Process, the Interim Constitution, and the Role of the Constitutional Court*

Over years of talks, largely between 1992 and 1994, the Multi–Party Negotiating Process resulted in an extraordinary agreement on the substance and process of developing a new South African Constitution.[h] In a

h. The following account is based on an Address by Justice Albie Sachs, a human rights scholar and member of the Constitutional Court, at the Georgetown University

compromise between those in the existing government who wanted the (largely unelected) negotiators to draft a Constitution to submit to the people, and the "liberationists" who wanted the drafting done by an elected and representative body, the negotiators agreed on a two-stage procedure of constitution-making. The Multi–Party Negotiating Process drafted an interim constitution, which included 34 basic principles which would have to be reflected in the new final constitution (e.g., human rights and freedoms provisions, no substantial reduction of the provincial powers agreed to for the interim Constitution). These principles were intended to establish a working government premised on respect for the human dignity of all persons in a multicultural, multi-linguistic federal union. The interim constitution was adopted by the existing government, which resulted, inter alia, in the immediate establishment of a Constitutional Court and a Bill of Rights. Elections based on universal non-racial suffrage were held in 1994 to select a new Parliament, which would also function as a Constitutional Assembly for purposes of proposing a new final constitution.

The newly elected legislature, which consisted of 400 directly elected members of the National Assembly as well as a Senate (composed of 10 representatives from each of the 9 provinces and chosen by the provincial legislatures), was charged by the interim Constitution with producing a final Constitution within two years—by May 1996. Under the interim constitution, the new constitution had to conform with the 34 basic Constitutional Principles, and the Constitutional Court had to so certify. During the two year period 1994–96, a massive public education campaign was conducted relating to the drafting of the Constitution, including circulating drafts of various provisions and seeking public input.[i]

The procedures agreed to in the earlier negotiations and embodied in the interim Constitution required that the new Constitution be passed by a two-thirds vote of the legislature and then reviewed by the Constitutional Court, to determine whether the new Constitution fully complied with the 34 basic principles. Constitution of the Republic of South Africa (Act 200 of 1993), ch. 5, sections 68, 71, 73.[j] In May 1996 a Constitution was adopted

Law Center (October 8, 1996); Dion A. Basson, South Africa's Interim Constitution: Text and Notes 96–106 (1994); Constitution of the Republic of South Africa 1996, as adopted by the Constitutional Assembly on 8 May 1996 with accompanying Explanatory Memorandum; Medard Rwelamira, South Africa: Introductory and Comparative Notes, in XVII Constitutions of the World (Gisbert H. Flanz ed., Nov. 1997); and In re Certification of the Constitution of the Republic of South Africa, 1996, (4) SA 744 (Sept. 6, 1996). For convenience, readers should note the Appendix, Schedule 4 of the Interim Constitution of the Republic of South Africa (Act 200 of 1993), reprinted in 41 St. Louis U. L. J. 1319 (1997) (the 34 basic principles).

i. See S. Afr. Const. of May 8 1996 (Explanatory Memorandum). Justice Sachs said in his Georgetown Address that survey research showed that the percentage of the public that understood the constitutional process increased from 30% to 70% as a result of this campaign, which included radio and television broadcasts, meetings, and pamphlets using cartoons and simple language.

j. The interim Constitution, Section 74(1) of Act 200 of 1993, prohibited amendment of the provisions of the 34 basic constitutional principles and of the requirement for the Constitutional Court to review and certify the new constitution as complying with

by the legislature by an 86% majority, and certified to the Constitutional Court for review.[k]

In early September 1996, after receiving substantial public comment concerning many aspects of the draft Constitution, the Constitutional Court issued its judgment, commending the draft as a "monumental achievement," the overwhelming majority of whose provisions complied with the 34 principles. However, it also found that in 9 respects the draft Constitution did not sufficiently comply with the 34 principles.[l] For example, it found that the Constitution's provisions permitting Parliament to amend bill of rights provisions by a two-thirds vote was not sufficient adequately to entrench those rights; something beyond a mere large majority in the ordinary Parliament was required. It also found that the provisions permitting removal by a majority vote of the Parliament of the "Public Protector," an entity designed to serve as something between an ombudsman and an Inspector General and protect the honesty and integrity of government, insufficiently assured the position of its needed impartiality and independence. Another area of concern was that the draft Constitution allocated too much power to the central and too little to the provincial governments.

Thus, the Constitutional Court found that the draft constitution was not constitutional and could not be certified as in all respects complying with the 34 Constitutional Principles. Resubmission of the proposed Constitution by Parliament to the Constitutional Court, took place quickly, with passage of an amended version of the new constitution on October 11, 1996. The newest draft left the constitution substantially similar but made about 40 revisions to address the Court's objections. For example, proce-

those principles. These provisions were thus fully entrenched against change, though a procedure for amending other parts of the interim constitution was provided for.

k. Alternative procedures were specified in the Interim Constitution: In the event that a constitution did not receive the requisite 2/3 vote, but was passed by a majority, Section 73 (3) of the interim constitution required that the draft be referred to a panel of "constitutional experts" for advice. If an amended text unanimously recommended by the experts passed by a 2/3 vote in the legislature, it would become the Constitution (subject, though, to Constitutional Court approval). If the experts failed to submit a unanimous text or it was not adopted by a 2/3 vote, "any proposed text" passed by a majority of the Constitutional Assembly would then be referred to the electorate for decision in a national referendum. If 60% of the votes cast were in favor, it would become the Constitution. The requirement that the Constitutional Court approve the constitu-

tion text as complying with the 34 Constitutional Principles appears to apply to all methods of enactment, see Basson, at 103, a moot point since the proposed constitution passed the legislature by the requisite 2/3 vote.

l. See In re Certification of the Constitution of the R.S.A., 1996, (4) S.A. 744, 785–86, 910–11 (Constitutional Court Sept. 6, 1996); see also Rwelamira (for a summary of the decision). The Court received objections from 5 political parties and on behalf of 84 private parties. The political parties and 27 others were allowed to appear in person and make argument to the Court, whose "underlying principle was to hear the widest spectrum of potentially relevant views." 4 S. A. at 783. Justice Sachs indicated that proceedings in the Constitutional Court, in receiving public comment and in rendering its decision, were televised—not for immediate public broadcast but to create a historical record of those aspects of the constitution-making process.

dures for amending the Constitution were made more rigorous, language assuring the entrenchment and judicial enforceability of fundamental rights and freedoms was added, and, in order to assure more independence and impartiality a provision was amended to require a two-thirds vote in the National Assembly to dismiss the Public Protector. After a public comment period, the Constitutional Court approved the new draft in late 1996. In January 1997 President Nelson Mandela issued a proclamation by which the Constitution was to come into effect beginning in February, 1997.[m]

Questions and Comments

1. How does Elster's analysis apply to the process of constitutional design created in South Africa? How are the "upstream" constraints different from the "downstream" constraints in this process? How would he explain the decision to give the Constitutional Court the final say?

2. What, if any, role did preexisting legal institutions play in the process of constitutional change? (Consider the effects of prior legal history as counter-examples. Note, too, that while South Africa had an existing court system, it chose to establish an entirely new Constitutional Court.)

3. Is there a "moment," or a particular step in the process, when one can say that South Africa created its new constitution? Once agreement to the 34 principles in the extra-legal negotiations between the white government and the ANC and other groups was reached? Once the Constitutional Court was created? When its decisions (i.e., invalidating the death penalty in 1995) were respected? When it declared unconstitutional some of the proposed constitution? Not quite yet because the process of fully implementing the new constitution (as of this writing) is ongoing?

4. Would Holmes and Sunstein recommend ease of amendment for South Africa's new constitution? Why or why not?

5. Reconsider Osiatynski's skepticism about the prospects for civic education. Are there reasons to think this problem would differ in South Africa than in Poland? Cf. S. Afr. Const. of May 8, 1996, Explanatory Memorandum (stating that "[t]he objective in drafting this text was to ensure that the final constitution is legitimate, credible and accepted by all South Africans. To this extent, the process of drafting this text involved many South Africans in the largest public participation programme ever carried out in South Africa."); Makau wa Mutua, *Hope and Despair for a New South Africa: The Limits of Rights Discourse*, 10 Harv. Hum. Rts. J. 63, 83 n. 110 (1997) (noting widespread public hearings and a national media

---

m. See Constitution of the Republic of South Africa, Act No. 108 of 1996, certified by the Court in In re Certification of the Amended Text of the Constitution of the R.S.A., 1996, (2) S.A. 97 (Constitutional Court Dec. 4, 1996), and entered into force February 4, 1997. Some provisions were not to come into effect until 1999. See e.g., Constitution of R.S.A., 1996, Schedule 6 Transitional Arrangements Section 6 (elections of new national assembly deferred until April, 1999).

campaign resulting in over 1.7. million public submissions to the constitutional assembly).

Note on Historical Context in Constitutionalism: Incrementalism and Clean Breaks

Several of the readings suggest that constitution-making tends to occur at a point of crisis, a revolutionary moment. Elster argues that, descriptively, constitutions generally do not get made absent a crisis. While Elster expresses skepticism that these conditions are conducive to rational, principled decisionmaking, Ackerman argues that in moments of revolutionary crisis the prospects for altruistic and principled constitution-making are greatest. The unfolding constitutional story in South Africa might be taken as illustrative of the seizing of a constitutional moment, marked by revolutionary change in the power structure of society, to make as clean (and reasoned) a break as possible from an oppressive and unjust past structure of governance.

Other writers, such as Stanley Katz, are more skeptical of universal claims about how constitutions should be made and constitutionalism established. Hungary's recent experience is sometimes referred to as a model of more incremental, or evolutionary, constitutional change in regimes. To the extent that Britain, or Israel, is viewed as a "constitutional" regime, its progress towards that state has strong elements of incremental, evolutionary development. Consider also Sunstein and Holmes' argument about the ease of amending post-cold war constitutions in Eastern Europe.

Are there circumstances in which one or the other (clean break or evolutionary) process is more likely to "work" in producing viable constitutionalism? One might start by assuming that the greater degree of "break" from the past that is required, the greater the likely resistance of those formally empowered by a regime. Clean breaks and sharp constitutional moments may thus be more possible in settings in which relatively segregated and small minorities are overthrown from power, or in which colonial powers are divested of control. In both of these cases, the ability of those formerly holding power to obstruct is limited—in one case by their isolated, minority status, in the other by their distance. Incremental change may be more associated with successful adaptations of constitutionalism in societies in which the controlling figures in a prior regime are more fully integrated with broader majoritarian social groupings; or, to put it differently, efforts in such societies to make a "clean break" with the past may involve greater social disruption and more risk of violence.

Consider, additionally or alternatively, the degree to which the new regime's leaders are, or are not, invested in the protection of aspects of the prior legal regime, as influencing the process by which the country moves towards constitutionalism. Finally, consider the impact of existing legal institutions and layers of law on the framework for decisionmaking. Was the "success" of the drafters of the 1787 Constitution of the United States conditioned in part by the very limited legal history of the colonies as a nation and by agreement to leave in place substantial aspects of existing state law regimes? How did the development of international human rights norms and of the drafting of bills of rights by those affiliated with or sympathetic to the ANC in the years leading up to South Africa's constitutional change affect South Africa's success in coming to agreement on a constitution to govern the transition to majority rule?

C. CONSTITUTIONAL TRANSITIONS AND THE PROBLEM OF "LUSTRATION"

When constitutional regimes change, some body of existing law is likely to continue in effect, even though changes are made to the constitution and to other particular laws. Consider here the views of Judge Aharon Barak of the Israeli Supreme Court, expressed in his 1988 opinion in a free speech case involving whether certain censorship was permitted by Defense Regulations originally enacted by the British in 1937 when they controlled Palestine and which became part of the State of Israel's legislation under the Law and Administration Ordinance of 1948. According to Barak, "This change from Mandatory law to Israeli law was not a purely technical matter. A change in the framework brings in its wake, by the nature of things, a change in content.... A colonial rule was replaced by political independence. Autocratic rule was replaced by democracy...." This change, he argued supported a change in the interpretation of the Censor's authority, in light of the values of the Israeli Declaration of Independence.[n]

Sometimes a regime replaced after a constitutional transition is seen as illegitimate and as having perpetrated injustices. A central problem in this setting, not so easily solved by changed interpretation of past laws, is how to develop a commitment to constitutionalism and rule of law while addressing past injustices that may have been "legal" under the prior regime's law. Claims to restoration of private property improperly taken, and efforts to identify and/or punish government officials who committed bad acts, are two major areas in which problems of justice, nonretroactivity, and the limits of law in constitutional transitions recur.

In the readings below, Teitel focuses on the difficulties of establishing the "rule of law" while at the same time according justice to those who

---

n. See Schnitzer v. Chief Military Censor (1988), 42 P.D. (4) 617, reproduced in 9 Selected Judgments of the Supreme Court of Israel, 1977–90 at 77, 85–89 (1995) (issuing order preventing Censor from interfering with publication of an article critical of the outgoing head of the Mossad). Another perspective emerges from Argentina, which has had several periods of "de facto" governments that seized power through means not set forth in its Constitution. Once a constitutional government is established, what is the status of the prior regime's "de facto" laws? See Tim Dockery, *The Rule of Law Over the Law of Rulers: The Treatment of De Facto Laws in Argentina*, 19 Fordham Int'l L. J. 1578 (1996) (arguing that legislative ratification of de facto laws best reconciles the need to protect expectations based on those laws and the idea that laws become laws only through constitutional processes).

were perpetrators, or victims, of injustice under prior regimes. She points out the necessarily paradoxical problem of addressing, in a legal forum, the "wrongs" that may have been committed by those who, under prior regimes, had the support of positive law for their actions, while at the same time developing adherence to the rule of law. The essay argues that the Hungarian Constitutional Court, by applying retroactivity principles to prohibit Parliament's effort to revive time-barred criminal prosecutions of former leaders, engaged in a "power grab" from the Parliament, "brilliant" because it appeared to reflect an advance towards the rule of law. Sólyom's account of the same problem suggests that international law provides a vehicle for resolution of at least some of this tension. Sólyom, President of the Hungarian Constitutional Court, provides a fascinating glimpse of the extraordinary first years of that Court, suggesting—contrary to the view implied by Sajó and Losonci—that the Court has made significant progress towards establishing the independence and significance of constitutional judicial review. By contrast, Czech and German decisions on retroactivity reach different results on the basic tension between substantive justice and the certainty and predictability of law. Consider, as you read the materials that follow, whether a commitment to constitutionalism provides guidance on this kind of choice.

---

1. Notes on the Problem of the Prior Regime in U.S. Constitutional History

As suggested earlier, those faced with drafting a constitution for the newly independent "United States" of America had the advantage that the prior regime was controlled from abroad. Once overthrown, its leaders were at some distance. Yet loyalist portions of the population with "tory" sympathies did remain. Many loyalists fled to Canada, but some remained in the United States. One of the difficulties encountered under the Articles of Confederation was the inadequacy of the national government's means to enforce obligations under the Treaty of Paris of 1783 applicable to the states. These included, for example, the provisions of Article VI of the Treaty, intended to prevent further "confiscations ... [or] prosecutions ... against any person or persons for, or by reason of the part which he ... may have taken in the present war," and further providing "that no person shall, on that account, suffer any future loss or damage, either in his person, liberty or property...." Treaty of Peace with Great Britain Art VI (Sept. 3 1783), reprinted in Henry Steele Commager, I Documents of American History 117, 110 (7th ed. 1963). Virginia's resistance to these portions of the treaty, and its refusal to recognize property rights held through British citizens, led to two landmark Supreme Court decisions. Fairfax's Devisee v. Hunter's Lessee, 7 Cranch 603 (1813) (Virginia's actions of escheating property of Lord Fairfax after 1783 violated Treaty and thus title remained in Fairfax and his devisees as against claims of those whose title derived from escheat to state); Martin v. Hunter's Lessee, 14 U.S. (1 Wheat.) 304 (1816) (upholding Supreme Court's jurisdiction to have reviewed question of title on appeal from Virginia state court in Fairfax's Devisee case).

Following the Civil War, the U.S. was again confronted with the problem of reconciling constitutional order with the misdeeds of and antipathy to those with whom it had battled, this time in the more complex situation of an unsuccessful secession effort. The southern states were governed for several years by federal military governors under "Reconstruction," whose constitutionality was placed in issue by the decision in Ex parte Milligan, 4 Wall. 2 (1866) (where civil courts are open, civilians cannot be tried by military tribunals). Congress essentially ignored the implications of this decision for Reconstruction, and deprived the Supreme Court of jurisdiction to hear a challenge to Congress' power to establish military government in the south. Ex parte McCardle, 74 U.S. (7 Wall.) 506 (1869). In addition, Congress addressed the problem of whether to permit those involved in the Confederacy to hold office following the war. See Amend. XIV (Sec. 3) (disqualification from federal office for those who, having "previously taken an oath.... to support the Constitution of the United States," took part in "insurrection or rebellion against the same, or [gave] aid or comfort to the enemies thereof."). At the same time, the Fourteenth Amendment, in Section 4, took the position that certain losses suffered by secessionists did not deserve to be and were not compensable. See Amend XIV, Sec. 4 (making void and nonpayable any debt incurred in aid of the rebellion or based on claim for loss from emancipation of slaves). Questions of qualification for office, and compensation for property taken by the Union armies, came before the Supreme Court. See Ex parte Garland, 4 Wall. 333 (1867) (invalidating law of Congress forbidding practice before Supreme Court unless lawyer could swear that he had never fought against the U.S., as applied to a lawyer who had received a full presidential pardon); United States v. Klein, 80 U.S. (13 Wall.) 128 (1872) (invalidating attempt to restrict jurisdiction of federal court so as to deprive pardoned claimants of compensation for property taken during the war). Both cases turn, at least in part, on interpretations of the President's pardon power; both uphold that power in the face of contrary or limiting legislation, and both, perhaps coincidentally, affirm a "conciliatory" approach to former "enemies."

---

2. RETROACTIVITY, THE RULE OF LAW, AND DOING JUSTICE IN EASTERN EUROPE

Ruti Teitel, *Paradoxes in the Revolution of the Rule of Law*, 19 Yale J. Int'l L. 239 (1994)

Perhaps it is in the nature of "velvet revolutions" that their rough undersides are revealed in public forums, such as courts of law, where debates rage about the normative content of changed political systems. In Eastern and Central Europe, courts are now defining the powers of new regimes committed to the rule of law. One of the most difficult issues faced by these courts is how to maintain a commitment to the rule of law while serving the principles of substantive justice. . . .

Two court cases highlight the dilemma. The first is the Hungarian Constitutional Court's consideration of the Zetenyi Law, which would have allowed prosecutions for treason and murder related to the brutal suppression of the 1956 coup attempt. The second is a "border guards" case, heard by the Berlin Trial Court, which involved the prosecution of several guards for shootings at the Berlin Wall. Both cases involve weighty symbols of freedom and repression: 1956 is thought of as the founding year of Hungary's revolution, while the Berlin Wall and its collapse were the central symbols of Soviet domination and its demise. Both cases also illustrate the problems involved in attempting to effect substantial change in a society through and within the law. Any resolution of the paradox is not merely a matter of jurisprudential interest, but one that could have political implications wherever transitions similar to those in Eastern and Central Europe take place.

I. Rule of Law in Hungary and Unified Germany

In 1991, Hungary's Parliament passed the Zetenyi Law, which authorized the lifting of statutes of limitations for treason, premeditated murder, and aggravated assault. The law, in effect, allowed prosecutions for crimes committed in suppressing the 1956 revolution, among other grave crimes of the past. In a landmark opinion, the Hungarian Constitutional Court held the law unconstitutional. The Court reasoned that, under the newly amended Hungarian Constitution, the rule-of-law principle of prospectivity in lawmaking overrode any *ex post* attempt to extend the statute of limitations, even if the worst offenses would thereby go unpunished.

The opinion begins with a statement of the Court's perception of its dilemma: "The Constitutional Court is the repository of the paradox of the 'revolution of the rule of law.' " Rule of law, the Constitutional Court asserted, means "predictability and foreseeability." Furthermore,

> certainty of the law demands of the state, and primarily the legislature, that the whole of the law ... be clear, unambiguous, its impact predictable and its consequences foreseeable by those whom the laws address. From the principle of predictability and foreseeability, the criminal law's prohibition of the use of retroactive legislation, especially ex post facto legislation ... directly follows. . . . Only by following formalized legal procedures can there be valid law, only by adherence to procedural norms can the administration of justice operate constitutionally.

According to the Court, the basic principle of the rule of law is "certainty of the law." This basic principle is juxtaposed against the principle of substantive justice implied in the law. For the court, however, "[t]he certainty of the law based on formal and objective principles is more important than necessarily partial and subjective justice." The choices seemed irreconcilable.

In a newly unified Germany, the trial of the border guards for shootings at the Berlin Wall offers another illustration of the dilemma. The Border Protections Law of the former German Democratic Republic (GDR) authorized soldiers to shoot in response to "act[s] of unlawful border crossing." Such acts were very broadly defined and included border crossings attempted by two people together or those committed with "particular intensity." The custom at the border was to enforce the law strictly: supervisors emphasized that "a breach of the border should be prevented at all costs."

In determining whether the GDR law provides border guards a defense against the charges, the Berlin Trial Court acknowledged the rule-of-law/justice dilemma:

> In analyzing the question of whether it is permissible to threaten with death a person who does not want to abide by the exit prohibition and—disregarding it—wants to cross the border, and whether, if necessary, it is permissible to kill him, we are confronted with the question of whether everything is just that was formally, or through interpretation, considered to be a law.

The tension between the "formal" and the "just" is at the heart of the problem. Holding the border guards accountable, the court rejected defenses based on the law as written:

> The basic principle that an act can be punished only if punishability was determined by law before the act was committed ... does not hinder punishment in this case.... Justice and humanity were portrayed as ideals also in the then GDR. In general, adequate ideas as to the basis of natural justice were indeed disseminated.

The court relied on precedents of the Federal Constitutional Court elevating the principle of material justice over the principle of the certainty of the law in certain circumstances. Thus, the Hungarian and German courts formulated the dilemma in a similar manner, but came down on opposite sides: the Hungarian court interpreted the rule of law to require certainty, whereas the Berlin court interpreted it to require substantive justice.

The dilemma of successor justice faced by the Hungarian and German courts forms part of a rich dialogue on the nature of law. H.L.A. Hart and Lon Fuller's debate on transitional justice wrestles with the relationship between law and morality, between positivism and natural law. Fuller rejected Hart's abstract formulation of the problem, and instead focused on postwar Germany. The "true nature of the dilemma confronted by Germany in seeking to rebuild her shattered legal institutions," he wrote, was "to restore both respect for law and respect for justice.... [P]ainful antinomies were encountered in attempting to restore both at once...." In a now well-known hypothetical, *The Problem of the Grudge Informer,* Fuller questioned whether a new government can bring a collaborator to justice if doing so would necessitate tampering with the laws in effect at the time when the acts were committed. Arguing that Hart's opposition to selective tampering elevates rule-of-law considerations over those of substantive criminal justice, Fuller justified selective tampering to preserve the morality of the law....

The judges in the two cases in question saw the problem as the pursuit of successor justice threatening certainty of the law. Their approach suggests that "procedural justice" has become detached from a more substantive understanding of the rule of law. Yet what is the independent content of the principle of prospectivity? How are we to make sense of a commitment to these principles separated from some other rule-of-law ideal? Were the two always in tension? Or was there a time when the prospectivity principle could not be understood apart from the principle of substantive justice? ...

In a democracy, a prospectivity requirement can be viewed as a way to make operational a principle of equal justice. The Greeks viewed majority lawmaking as a way to promote equal treatment under the law. But the tyranny or unequal-justice problem is not entirely remedied by democratic lawmaking; a majority may still tyrannize a minority. Here, a role for prospectivity arises: prospectivity is not an autonomous rule-of-law ideal, but rather a constraint designed to promote the rule of law understood as equal justice.

II. The Search for Neutral Principles and the Least Dangerous Branch

Probing the legal rhetoric of the Hungarian and German cases leads to a different explanation for the decisions involved. By framing the rule-of-law/justice dilemmas as *ex post facto* problems in ordinary constitutional times, the opinions avoid addressing the larger question of the authority of a transitional judiciary to decide the extent of legal continuity of a prior regime. What is the role of the judge and of judicial review where the regime itself, and not merely one piece of legislation, is of questionable legitimacy? To what extent are the questions confronted by the Berlin and Hungarian courts appropriate questions for the judiciary? Should they not instead be part of a vital political debate?

Returning first to the Berlin court in the border guards case, to what extent did acceptance or rejection of the guards' defenses imply evaluation of the validity of the past legal regime? According to the Unification Treaty, acts that took place prior to the treaty are subject to the provisions of the GDR's former criminal code. The Berlin court rejected the guards' defenses, even though they were grounded in prior law, and thus apparently ignored the Treaty's command. The court, however, was guided by past decisions concerning the Nazi regime. Relying on a doctrine established in a 1953 decision distinguishing positive law from justice, the court asserted, "The experience of the National Socialist regime in Germany, in particular, has taught that ... it must be possible *in extreme cases* to value the principle of material justice more highly than the principle of the certainty of the law." This response to World War II injustice constrains judicial decisionmaking in contemporary post-Communist controversies in unified Germany. The court's reference to "extreme cases" appears to equate the crimes of the national socialist period with the actions taken during the Communist period.

The Court's attempt to link its decision to the post-Nazi rule-of-law dilemma, however, cannot obscure the differences between the post-Nazi and present-day cases. In post-Nazi Germany, achieving the rule of law as equal justice, appeared to collide with achieving the rule of law as procedural regularity. In postwar Germany, legal institutions had no legitimacy. Simultaneously restoring society's confidence in law and in justice required some degree of compromise.

The post-Nazi dilemma does not arise in post-Communist Germany. East Germany was incorporated into a fully functioning legal order; in post-Nazi Germany, no such order existed. To the extent that the legal continuity problem arises at all in the border guards cases, it does so on a much smaller scale than in other post-Communist transitions....

Turning to the Hungarian Constitutional Court, the rule-of-law paradox can be better understood as a rhetorical device enabling the court to avoid explicitly addressing the related question of the extent of legal continuity with the prior regime. The court's conclusion that the Zetenyi Law was unconstitutional appears questionable when one considers that the amended Constitution lacked an express provision against *ex post facto* laws. The mandate for the rule of law is derived from one word in the Constitution: *jogallam*. It is from this one word, alternatively interpreted as promising a "rule of law" or "constitutional" state, that the court construed a mandate to prohibit the Parliament's revival of time-barred causes of action. In elevating the *ex post facto* principle above equal justice under the law, the court employed a formalist approach to halt Parliament's efforts to make perpetrators from previous regimes criminally accountable. This approach enables the court to operate in a counterrevolutionary fashion while increasing judicial power. In effect, the statute-of-limitations decision represents a controversial power grab by the court. It is a brilliant power grab in that it appears to represent a victory for the rule of law.

The question of legal continuity with the prior regime, so deftly skirted by the Hungarian Constitutional Court, lies at the heart of Fuller's hypothetical. Fuller offers some possible solutions: absolute legal continuity, absolute discontinuity, and selective discontinuity. The Hungarian Parliament, in effect, chose the route of selective discontinuity in the statute-of-limitations law. The Constitutional Court, however, ultimately denied Parliament the power to make this choice, striking down the law. In a profound challenge to Parliament's authority, the court limited Parliament's power to interpret the prior legal order and held that full continuity is required by the rule of law: "Certainty of the law demands ... the protection of rights previously conferred." It characterized Parliament's choice of selective discontinuity as a challenge to the legality of the new legal order:

> With respect to its validity, there is no distinction between "pre-constitution" and "post-constitution" law. The legitimacy of the differ-

ent [political] system during the past half century is a matter of indifference.... From the viewpoint of the constitutionality of laws it does not comprise a meaningful category.

The court justified its rejection of Parliament's selective discontinuity proposal on the basis of rule-of-law principles. Yet the court's emphasis on certainty of the law masked its own interpretive leaps and exercise of discretion.

Focusing exclusively on the content of the concept of the rule of law ignores the question of which governmental institutions should have the power to define its parameters. Does the power properly lie with the court or with Parliament? In its decision on the Zetenyi Law, the court asserted itself as the exclusive interpreter of the Constitution, and more broadly of the constitutional regime. Following this holding, the full burden of evaluating the past legal order lies on the court. The court's assertion of exclusive interpretive power is highly problematic; in a constitutional democracy, understandings of legality and constitutionality are best promoted not by judicial monopoly over constitutional interpretation, but by a system allowing for simultaneous and parallel interpretation by the political branches and by the people.

Although the court never acknowledged its own interpretive leaps, a general concern about illegality pervaded the opinion. Nagging questions underlie the court's formalism. What is the validity of the entire endeavor? What ensures the legitimacy of a constitutional court engaging in judicial review under an amended constitution in a transitional period? To what extent does a new constitutional system, and, as in Hungary, an entirely new constitutional court, imply a moment of illegality, a glitch in the rule of law as the court has defined it? The Hungarian court addressed these concerns by clinging to the fiction that a state under the rule of law cannot be—and was not in the case of Hungary—created by undermining rule of law:

> The politically revolutionary changes adopted by the [October 1989] Constitution and the fundamental laws were all enacted in a procedurally impeccable manner, in full compliance with the old legal system's regulation of the power to legislate, thereby gaining their binding force.

The court thus dismissed questions about its own legitimacy.

The *Zetenyi* case stands for the proposition that the authority to assess the legality of the prior regime does not lie with Parliament, but instead with the Constitutional Court. Perhaps this makes sense; after all, the Constitutional Court is an entirely new institution. New institutions carry with them the legitimacy of hope. In contrast, Parliament and the political process suffer from accumulated distrust. It is no wonder that there is fear of Parliament, when one considers the nature of its work in prior years: from 1980 to 1985, it met for a total of thirty-two days. In those thirty-two days, twenty-two acts were passed, with twenty-one of these unanimously approved. Distrust of parliaments and politics is not particular to Hungary;

it is pervasive in the region. Sadly, the distrust does not seem to be a function of post-changeover elections but seem to be more deeply, perhaps historically and institutionally, ingrained.

Consider the following hypothetical: what if the question of legal continuity had arisen, not in the context of new legislation, but instead in the case of an individual defendant? Would Hungary's Constitutional Court have reached the same decision? Or might the court have articulated a principle allowing the revival of statutes of limitations in cases of grave crimes committed in the course of political persecution? Perhaps it might have based such a decision on a more substantive conception of the rule of law as the promise of equal justice under law, regardless of political affiliation. If the court had come to such a decision, then the *Zetenyi* case would be less about the rule of law than about institutional distrust....

––––––––––

László Sólyom, *The Hungarian Constitutional Court and Social Change*, 19 Yale J. Int'l L. 223 (1994)

On January 1, 1990, the Hungarian Constitutional Court became the first institution created by Hungary's new Constitution to assume its responsibilities. The birth of a constitutional court can generate a complex set of problems in any society. A government must build public acceptance of, and support for, the institution and create an effective structure for its activities. A whole new set of problems arises when a constitutional court begins its work in a time of transition from an undemocratic state to a state based on the rule of law. This paper discusses some of the problems encountered by Hungary as well as Hungary's attempts to solve them.

I.   Continuity and a New Start

The new Hungarian Constitution went into effect on October 23, 1989. The first five judges of the Constitutional Court were elected by Parliament in November 1989; the first free parliamentary elections followed in April 1990. Because the Court was established before the elections, it was able to oversee events until the new government took office and issue opinions on the new election law and on the President's legal standing. The existence of the Constitutional Court during the transition thus allowed the transformation of political problems into legal questions that could be addressed with final, binding decisions. Furthermore, it gave the Court an opportunity to demonstrate its political independence and, thus, the possibility of separation of powers between governmental branches.

The Constitutional Court has played a major role in "harmonizing" pre-constitutional norms with the Constitution through a process of abstract judicial review. The new Constitution did not automatically suspend pre-existing laws. Instead, it required Parliament to review all pre-constitutional laws and regulations to insure that they would be consistent with the newly established Constitution. In the process, such old laws acquired validity in the new system....

Some observers, contending that the old legal norms caused many of the new regime's social problems, have criticized this piecemeal, gradual reorganization of the Hungarian legal order; they would dispense with the entire old legal order. The Constitutional Court has itself been criticized because of its support for legal continuity. Its response to pressures for a speedy transition from the old system to a new one has therefore been a critical issue in Hungary.

II. The Constitutional Court in the New System

Although the Constitution defines the scope of the authority of the Court and guarantees the independence of its judges, determining its position in the structure of the newly created constitutional state—that is, its relation to the other organs of the state—has raised fundamental issues of constitutional interpretation.

A. *Parliament*

Parliament has found, to some dismay, that its powers are limited by the Constitutional Court's oversight. Since the legislature under socialism had unlimited sovereignty, it is understandable that some members of Parliament would have difficulty accepting the existence of a Constitutional Court. The Court has been able to withstand their political attacks by responding with the legitimizing force of constitutional analysis....

B. *Other Courts*

The relationship between the Constitutional Court and other courts is also uncertain. As previously noted, anyone can submit a petition for abstract judicial review of a law or regulation. When an individual petitions the Court with a fact-based complaint—claiming that the law or regulation applied to her case violates one of her basic constitutional rights—the Court can issue whatever legal remedies [are] appropriate and quash the lower court's decision in order to open the way for a new lawsuit. Just as Parliament has found it difficult to accept judicial review of its laws, some judges of the ordinary courts think that the Constitutional Court is meddling with their jurisdiction....

C. *Public Opinion*

Just as the Court's position in the overall structure of government is somewhat ambiguous, its place in a representative democracy has been questioned. A number of the Court's decisions have been contrary to public opinion. For example, the Court held a law establishing the death penalty unconstitutional, although the vast majority of the Hungarian population view this punishment as acceptable and necessary. Many observers expected the Constitutional Court to strike down the Law Concerning the Compensation for Expropriated and Nationalized Property (Compensation Law) given the widespread public support for complete restitution to former property owners. The Court, however, did not mandate restitution or any other form of privatization. Rather, it focused on the constitutionality of the specific solution chosen by the legislature. In another case, the

Court considered the constitutionality of a law permitting the government to prosecute certain crimes that had not been prosecuted previously for political reasons, and that were then technically barred by the statute of limitations. Despite considerable public outcry, the Court found that the government could not prosecute the crimes. The Court, like similar institutions in other countries, strives not to be swayed by public opinion. Its position, however, is a precarious one. In a new democracy, one may expect the majority's opinion to rule. Some citizens may have difficulty reconciling this majoritarian vision of democracy with the significant authority of a counter-majoritarian body, albeit one whose members are elected by Parliament.

III.   The Development of Constitutional Rights and Doctrines

Hungary understandably lacks polished constitutional theories and doctrines. The Court must make up for forty years lost during Communist rule. From its first cases, the Court has required that the government demonstrate a compelling state interest and a proportional relationship between means and ends as preconditions to any limitations on constitutional rights. It has introduced the concept of *Wesensgehalt*, or "the core of a right," which stands for the principle that the essential content of a constitutional right cannot be limited by law. The Court has also set forth principles for interpreting the equality provisions of the Constitution. The Court has applied several of Ronald Dworkin's theories, first as a statement of basic principles, then as a detailed test for the constitutionality of discriminatory legislation. . . .

In the abortion case, the Court declared a ministerial decree regulating abortion unconstitutional on procedural grounds. Specifically, it ruled that a fundamental right cannot be regulated through non-statutory means. The Court, however, did not limit its discussion to this aspect of the case. It noted that the constitutionality of regulating abortion turns on whether the embryo is human in the legal sense—that is, whether the embryo is a legal subject. The Court then noted that Parliament has a duty to define the term "human." The relevant inquiry is whether the embryo can have fundamental rights at all. Parliament's decision is constrained only in that it cannot narrow the present legal definition of the human being. If the legislature declares the embryo a legal subject, pregnancy could be terminated only to save the mother's life. If the legislature does not deem the embryo a legal subject, the Court could weigh the mother's right to control her body against the state's duty to protect human life. Since such a balance must be struck, neither a complete prohibition of abortion nor a complete freedom of abortion would be constitutional.

IV.   Difficulties of Transition

The Constitutional Court has faced a number of complicated issues arising from the transition from a non-democratic to a democratic society. Most of these issues first surfaced in 1991, after the Constitutional Court had spent a year developing its procedures and building its legitimacy. Constitutional problems arose primarily in four areas: (1) the regulation of property relations, (2) the prosecution of politically motivated crimes committed during the previous regime, (3) the separation of powers and federalism, and (4) legal procedure and due process.

A. Property Relations

The Constitutional Court has played a major role in harmonizing the legal and political aspects of the new system of property. Under Communism, more than ninety percent of industrial and commercial enterprises was state-owned. The political and economic reorganization of the 1980s was intended to create a market economy based on private property. Privatization is a constitutional goal: the Preamble refers to the "social market economy" and Article 4 grants public and private property equal rank in a market economy.

One important issue was whether private property that was nationalized in the 1940s and 1950s should be returned to its original owners or whether those owners should be compensated. Those who favored the latter approach disagreed on whether compensation should be limited to property loss or whether it should include additional payments to those who were persecuted by the old regime. The largest party of the ruling coalition, the Hungarian Democratic Forum, wanted a policy of partial monetary compensation for property as well as certain additional damages for personal suffering. The Smallholders Party (representing former peasant landowners) sought the actual return of land, which would have required that land of agricultural cooperatives be expropriated without compensation. The ruling coalition drafted a bill that would have provided all those who had lost land with their original or similar plots, and all those who had lost personal property with payment. To determine the bill's constitutionality, the Prime Minister asked the Court to interpret the Constitution's provisions relating to equality and to the right of property.

The Court found that a scheme to compensate former real property owners and personal property owners by such significantly different means, would, in the absence of a compelling reason for the discrimination, violate the Constitution's equality provision. Furthermore, for the government to distribute governmental largess to some individuals (i.e., former property owners) and not others, it must demonstrate that the discrimination is necessary for fair competition in the marketplace. The Court also declared that the Constitution protects the property of agricultural cooperatives, and that this property cannot be taken away without prompt and complete compensation.

The Court disregarded the fact that the cooperatives' property rights had arisen through forced collectivization. It held that the Constitution protects property acquired through measures that were legal at the time, and that settled legal relationships must be respected and accepted. The Court's position on these questions reflects an acknowledgement of the complexity of compensation and restoration. Property may have changed hands a number of times between 1939 and 1989, sometimes through now-discredited governmental acts. For example, Germany, during its World

War II occupation of Hungary, expropriated the property of Jews. After the war, the Hungarian government expropriated property in the hands of ethnic Germans and redistributed it to ethnic Hungarian refugees. These lands were subsequently nationalized under Communist rule. In recent years the government has sold such nationalized property to private individuals. The question thus arises, if property is to revert to its former owner, to whom should it be restored? . . .

B. *Prosecution of Politically Motivated Crimes and General Legal Procedure*

The prosecution of acts of murder, manslaughter, and high treason committed between 1944 and 1990 has been a particularly controversial issue for the Court. For political reasons, some of these crimes were not prosecuted under the old regime, and the applicable statutes of limitations have long since expired. Parliament enacted a law that would have reset statutes of limitations, and the President referred it to the Court for pre-enactment review. The Court thus squarely confronted the question of whether Parliament could take action potentially inconsistent with the rule of law for the sake of prosecuting individuals affiliated with the old regime. It held unconstitutional attempts to punish criminal deeds already barred by a statute of limitations, attempts to extend the statute of limitations for the prosecution of crimes where the statute of limitations had not yet expired, and attempts to retroactively introduce new causes of action to bypass statutes of limitations. In effect, the Court's holding forestalls the passage of any retroactive criminal laws.

This ruling, however, did not end the Court's confrontation with Parliament over the issue of political crimes. In March 1992, Parliament passed an authoritative resolution on the interpretation of statutes of limitations, which excluded the period between 1944 and 1989 from such statutes of limitations. The Court declared the regulation unconstitutional on both procedural and substantive grounds. Since an authoritative parliamentary resolution does not qualify as a legislative act, it cannot regulate citizens' basic rights, and it violates the principles of legality, legal certainty, and judicial independence. Substantively, the Court found the resolution unconstitutional because it sought to make retroactive criminal prosecution possible.

In response to this ruling, Parliament enacted a bill in February 1993 amending the Criminal Procedural Act of 1973. By doing so, Parliament sought to oblige public prosecutors to bring charges in certain cases, even if trial would be barred by a statute of limitations. The President of the Republic did not sign the bill but turned to the Constitutional Court for a preliminary ruling on the bill's constitutionality. The Court rejected the bill, based on the same arguments used in the decision to strike down Parliament's interpretive resolution, stating that the bill violated the principles of the rule of law, legality, and legal certainty. Finally, in October 1993, on the President's motion, the Court reviewed a bill passed by Parliament concerning crimes committed during the 1956 revolution. The Court held that crimes defined by international law can be prosecuted without regard to domestic laws, including statutes of limitations.

These opinions have had a major impact on the debate over whether major transitions in Hungarian society can and should be accomplished strictly within the framework of the rule of law. The Court chose the appropriate course. A full transformation cannot take place through means inconsistent with the Constitution. The Court thus held that the rule of law must be respected under all circumstances.

The Court's approach can be questioned on two grounds. First, why should legal relationships that developed under unconstitutional legal norms be preserved? The Constitutional Court has answered simply that settled legal relationships are generally unaffected by a declaration that the underlying legal norms are invalid. Second, does Hungary's special historical situation weigh in favor of a more flexible application of the rule of law? According to the Court, while the historical situation may be important, it cannot justify violations of the underlying guarantee of the rule of law. A state governed by the rule of law cannot be realized through means incompatible with that rule of law. In cases of conflict, the Court will place legal stability, which is based on objective and formal principles, ahead of substantive justice, which is partial and subjective. . . .

V. Conclusion

Fortunate countries are blessed with time for organic development—time in which the principles of basic rights can evolve through the interaction of legal science and case law. Doctrines in such countries arise out of detailed analysis in a series of cases. In contrast, a country attempting to form a democratic government after a totalitarian regime does not have the benefits of time. The new Hungarian Constitutional Court, for instance, was confronted with momentous decisions shortly after its creation. Issues relating to abortion, the death penalty, separation of powers, individual rights, and property rights had to be resolved immediately.

The Court's decisions were made in an atmosphere characteristic of the regimes that emerged out of the collapse of the Eastern Bloc. The new regimes frequently attempted to incorporate idealized pre-communist arrangements. When confronted with difficult questions, the government and Parliament have tried to avoid unconventional solutions. The Court has realized, however, that important cases need not be decided in a traditional manner, and that the Court was not bound by the constitutional practice of other state organs. Because the Court has enjoyed relative insulation from certain political forces, it has been able to develop its own approach to the interpretation and contextualization of constitutional rights.

Decision on the Act on the Illegality of the Communist Regime

(Dec. 21, 1993)
(Constitutional Court of the Czech Republic)

Translation is in III Transitional Justice: How Emerging Democracies Reckon with Former Regimes 620 (Neil J. Kritz ed., 1995)

[The Court upholds a statute suspending limitations periods between 1948 and 1989 for criminal acts not prosecuted for "political reasons incompatible with the basic principles of the legal order of a democratic State," and in the portion excerpted below explains why it rejected the challenge filed by a group of deputies in the Czech Parliament.]

Reasoning

On 15 September 1993, a group of 41 Deputies of the Parliament of the Czech Republic submitted a petition requesting that the Constitutional Court, on the basis of Article 87, paragraph 1, letter (a) of the Constitution of the Czech Republic, annul Act No. 198/1993, on the Illegality of the Communist Regime and Resistance to It....

The main object of the group of Deputies' criticism is Article 5 of Act No. 198/1993, according to which "the period of time from 25 February 1948 until 29 December 1989 shall not be counted as part of the limitation period for criminal acts if, due to political reasons incompatible with the basic principles of the legal order of a democratic State, [a person] was not finally and validly convicted or the charges [against him] were dismissed."

According to the petitioners' view " ...the fact that State bodies, which no longer exist and formerly had competence over criminal matters, were, *for whatever reason*, inactive or ineffectual and brought on the termination of criminal liability for certain acts by virtue of the expiration of the limitations period, was not and is not a component of the subjective element [the *mens rea* or culpability requirement] of a criminal act, came about independently of the will of the offender, and therefore may not be to his detriment."

Thus, the Constitutional Court is, in the first place, concerned with the question why the "formerly competent State bodies [were] inactive and ineffectual," and further with the question whether the reasons for their failure to criminally prosecute politically shielded offenses, by their significance, their extent and their consequences to society, justify the measures in Article 5 of Act No. 198/1993.

At the same time, the Constitutional Court proceeds from the recognition that the constitutional law texts of the communist regime merely formulated a principle of legality that was general and equally applicable to all (or the so-called socialist legality). As early as the Constitution of 9 May (No. 150/1948), the duty to uphold the constitution and laws (Article 30) was imposed on every citizen regardless of office or official position.... However, these legal norms became fictional and hollow whenever the party recognized such to be advantageous for its political interests. Its monopoly on political and governmental power and the bureaucratically centralized organization of them were constructed upon this simple expedient.... The authorities in charge of the protection of legality thus became instruments of the central monopoly power.

In the period from 1948 to 1989, the regime of illegality that went unprosecuted attained a massive scope: starting with the purges in 1948, through the illegal way in which agriculture was collectivized, the transfer of 77,500 employees of administrative bodies to manufacturing work in

1951, the arrests and executions in the context of the so-called fight against agents of imperialism, to the preparations for invasion of the Warsaw Pact armies, the illegality of the so-called normalization process and the firings and prosecutions of political dissidents on a massive scale. . . .

Although the Deputies' petition seeking the annulment of the Act regarding the Illegality of the Communist Regime and Resistance to It does not generally dispute that, during the given period, illegal activities occurred and that the State did not prosecute them, even though it knew about them; however, it is clear from the type of arguments they make that, as regards the extent and implications of these cases, they do not consider them worthy of special attention or special resolution. Rather, the group of Deputies bases its arguments on juristically worded objections which can be summarized as follows:

(1) . . . By excluding the period from 25 February 1948 until 29 December 1989 from the running of the limitation period, [the Act] considerably extends the limitation period, leading to the destabilization of rights and an infringement of citizens' legal certainty;

(2) Paragraph 5 infringes a principle of law-based States, that criminal liability many not be revived once it has been extinguished by the expiration of the limitation period, and it introduces retroactive effect . . . of statutes, otherwise permissible only in instances where the subsequent statute is more favorable to the offender. According to the petitioners, this situation violates Article 40, paragraph 6 of the Charter of Fundamental Rights and Basic Freedoms, as well as the Czech Republic's international legal obligations;

(3) Alongside the preceding argument on the anti-constitutionality of retroactivity, the petition also raises its incompatibility with Article 1 of the Charter concerning the equality of all persons before the law and Article 40, paragraph 6 of the Charter, according to which the criminal liability of an act should be judged in accordance with the laws in force when the act was committed. . . .

The introduction of new legal impediments to the running of the statutory period limiting the right to bring a criminal prosecution is not, in and of itself, unconstitutional, which means that the Constitutional Court would not be required to deal with the matter at all. However, this claim relates to issues which affect the evaluation of the other objections raised against Article 5 of Act No. 198/1993, so that we can not pass over it.

Act No. 198/1993 itself does not alter the regulation of the legal institution of the limitation of criminal prosecutions. According to Article 67, paragraph 2 of the Criminal Act No. 140/1961, as subsequently amended, periods of time when it was not possible to bring an offender before a court due to legal impediments, as well as periods when he remained abroad, are not counted as part of the limitation period. Nor does the length of the limitation period set down in Article 67, paragraph 1 of the Criminal Act change. . . .

Therefore, in assessing Article 5 of Act No. 198/1993, we are not concerned either generally with the institution of the limitation of actions as such, or with the introduction of a new statutory impediment to the running of the limitation period, rather with the question whether the institution of the limitation of actions should be viewed as real or as fictional for a period when the infringement of legality in the entire sphere of legal life became a component of the politically as well as governmentally protected regime of illegality. Paragraph five of Act 198/1993 is not a constitutive norm, rather a declaratory norm. It is merely a declaration that during a certain stretch of time and for a certain type of criminal act the limitation period could not run, as well as the reason therefor. It is well-known that, apart from those areas of societal and individual life where the legal order from 1948 to 1989 retained a certain real significance and was based on legality, there were also spheres of the ruling class' political interest in which a condition of legal uncertainty existed and which the regime maintained as a measure of preventive self-defense and as an instrument for the manipulation of society.

The criminal behavior of person[s] in political and governmental positions [was] inspired or tolerated by the political regime when, in consideration of its actual or supposed interests, the governing class found it expedient to contravene even its own laws. The group of Deputies is not at all credible in its arguments that the limitation period was running during that era even for this category of governmental and political criminal behavior, that carried out entirely by the State.... The State became much rather a guarantor of their non-sanctionability and their actual criminal law immunity....

An indispensable component of the concept of the limitation of the right to bring a criminal prosecution is the intention, efforts and readiness on the part of the State to prosecute a criminal act. Without these prerequisites, the content of the concept is not complete, nor can the purpose of this legal institution be fulfilled. That happens only if there has been a long-term interaction of two elements: the intention and the efforts of the State to punish an offender and the ongoing danger to the offender that he may be punished, both giving a real meaning to the institution of the limitation of actions. If the State does not want to prosecute certain criminal acts or certain offenders, then the limitation of actions is pointless: in such cases, the running of the limitation period does not take place in reality and the limitation of actions, in and of itself, is fictitious. Written law is deprived of the possibility of being applied. In order for a criminal act to become statute-barred, it would be necessary for the process involved in the running of the limitation period to proceed, that is, a period of time during which the State makes efforts to criminally prosecute the offender is necessary. An action is barred at the end of the limitation period, only if at the time the ongoing efforts of the State to prosecute a criminal act remain futile. This prerequisite cannot be met for the category of politically protected offenses from 1948 until 1989. The condition of mass, State-protected illegal activities was not the consequence of individual errors, blunders, negligence or misdeeds, which would have left open some possibility for criminal prosecution, rather it was the consequence of the purposeful and collective behavior of the political and State authorities *as a whole,* which ruled out criminal prosecution in advance. By these means, the protection of offenders became as universal as the system of power.

Therefore, we cannot agree with the petitioners' position that an *a priori* awareness of the non-prosecutability of certain offenses was not a part of the subjective element of these criminal acts and that this "quasi limitation of actions" ran independently of the intent of the offender. The situation is different for the offenders under the political protection of the State. Their criminal act was *de facto* "statute-barred," even before it was committed. This fact sometimes functioned precisely as an incentive to additional criminal acts.... There was a type of "legal certainty" which the perpetrators of such criminal acts already had when they began their activities and which consists of State-assured immunity from criminal liability.

This "legal certainty" of offenders is, however, a source of legal uncertainty to citizens (and vice versa). In a contest of these two types of certainty, the Constitutional Court gives priority to the certainty of civil society, which is in keeping with the idea of a law-based State. Some other solution would mean conferring upon a totalitarian dictatorship a stamp of approval as a law-based State, a dangerous portent for the future: a sign that crime may become non-criminal, so long as it is organized on a massive scale and carried out over a long period of time under the protection of an organization empowered by the State. That would mean the loss of credibility of the present law-based State, as well as the current infringement of Article 9, paragraph 3 of the Constitution of the Czech Republic " ...legal norms may not be interpreted so as to justify eliminating or jeopardizing the foundations of a democratic State." ...

A requirement for a law-based State is the maintenance of a state of trust in the durability of legal rules. The perpetrators of this type of criminal activity do not have the continuity of written law in mind, rather that of unwritten practices. It would be an infringement of the continuity of written law, if the violation of law, which was committed under the protection of the State, could not even now be criminally prosecuted.

All of these individual points of view gain significance in direct proportion to the considerable extent of which this form of State-protected or tolerated political criminal behavior was committed. In forced labor camps and in the so-called auxiliary technical battalions alone, over 200,000 persons were held during this period of time. As is known, nearly a quarter of a million persons have already been rehabilitated on the basis of the Act on Legal Rehabilitation. In many of these cases of rehabilitation, the power apparatus' violation of its own legal principles was an important, if not the principal factor....

[I]t is necessary to assess to what extent the provision of Article 40, paragraph 6 of the Charter of Fundamental Rights and Basic Freedoms or Article 15 of the International Convention on Civil and Political Rights (No. 120/1976) prevents a subsequent amendment to the procedural rules, making possible the subsequent running of the limitation period in those special cases when the prior political regime prevented it from running.

Under Article 40, paragraph 6 of the Charter, criminal liability for an act should be judged and punishment imposed in accordance with the laws in effect when the act took place. A subsequent statute shall be applied if it is more favorable to the offender. Article 15 of the Convention is worded according to the same sense and, in addition, paragraph 2 makes it possible to punish acts in accordance with "the general principles of law recognized by the community of nations."

Article 40, paragraph 6 of the Charter of Fundamental Rights and Basic Freedoms defines and restricts the prohibition on the retroactive effect of statutes in two respects, namely:

(a) if a "criminal act" is concerned, or

(b) if the "imposition of punishment" is concerned. . . .

Article 40, paragraph 6 of the Charter manifestly does not permit the retroactivity of a statute where the definition of criminality or the severity of punishment is concerned. . . . Nothing more was intended by Article 40, paragraph 6 than what is stated, namely that the definition of individual criminal acts and of their criminal nature, which is effected under the Criminal Act by the designation of their specific characteristic features and the degree of danger which the individual acts pose to society; it may not be *ex post,* an amendment to the detriment of the offender adopted subsequently to the commission of an act. The same requirements are also set for the definition and setting of the length of punishment. The second sentence of paragraph 6 defines the prohibition of the retroactivity of law only in this sense and to this extent. . . .

Neither in the Czech Republic, nor in other democratic States does the issue of the procedural requirements for a criminal prosecution in general, and that of the limitation of actions in particular, rank among the principal fundamental rights and basic freedoms which, under Article 3 of the Constitution, form a part of the constitutional order of the Czech Republic and, thus take the place of the usual chapter in a constitution on fundamental rights and basic freedoms found in other constitutions.

The argument that the limitation of actions is an institution of substantive criminal law is not crucial to judgment in this matter, not only due to the fact that the issue is an ongoing subject of dispute in criminal law doctrine and that in several other democratic States it is considered, for the most part, as a procedural law institution, but first and foremost due to the fact that neither the Constitution nor the Charter of Fundamental (and not of other) Rights and Basic Freedoms resolve detailed issues of criminal law, but set down, in the first place, uncontested and basic constitutive principles of the State and of law. Article 40, paragraph 6 of the Charter of Fundamental Rights and Basic Freedoms deals with the issue of *which* criminal acts may in principle be prosecuted (namely those which were defined by law at the time the act was committed) and does not govern the issue of *for how long* these acts may be prosecuted. As a consequence, the regulations on the limitation of actions and on the limitation period, especially those setting the period during which an act which is declared to be criminal may be prosecuted, cannot be understood to be an area governed by Article 40, paragraph 6 of the Charter.... The procedural requirements for prosecution are not the subject of this reservation.

From among the European judicature, we can refer to the same point of view of the Federal Constitutional Court of the [Federal Republic of Germany], which in 1969 ruled that the prohibition on the retroactivity of statutes did not apply to the statute of limitations: the subsequent designation of criminality or of a higher possible punishment fall under this prohibition, but not the limitation of actions, governing the period of time during which an act which is declared to be criminal may be prosecuted and leaving the criminality of an act unaffected....[1]

The group of Deputies also detect in 5 of Act No. 198/1993 a violation of Article 1 of the Charter of Fundamental Rights and Basic Freedoms concerning the equality of all persons before the law because—as they assert—it involves discrimination against one segment of the citizenry because those who were not put on trial, for reasons that were not political, will still enjoy the right not to be prosecuted, while this right is denied to others, if [for] political reasons they were not convicted or the charges against them were dropped.

Equality before the law must always be judged in relation with the nature of the matter at issue. When assessing matters that are apparently, or even only in certain formal respects, identical, legislators must make efforts that they do not contradict the ideas of justice and reasonableness, which belong among the conceptual requirements of a law-based State.... In the case of Article 5 of Act No. 198/1993, it seems reasonable and just to extend the possibility of criminal prosecution for those criminal acts which, by the will of the political and State leadership, were earlier exempted from that possibility. In contrast to what the Deputies contend, this is the way to rectify the inequality with those who had already faced the possibility of being put on trial because, not only were they not under special political protection, but it was the State's wish and in its interest to prosecute them for the criminal acts which they committed....

With regard to the principle of the equality of citizens before the law, Article 5 of Act No. 198/1993 does not establish any special or extraordi-

---

1. The statute on the "tolling" of the limitation period for the unlawful acts of the SED (the Socialist Unity Party of East Germany) of March 1993 proceeds from the same point of view. Under this statute, in calculating the period of limitation for the prosecution of acts which were committed during the rule of the unlawful regime of the SED, but on the basis of the explicit or presumed wishes of the State or party leadership of the former GDR (German Democratic Republic), such acts were not prosecuted on political or other grounds incompatible with the free order of a law-based State, the period from 11 October 1949 until 2 October 1990 shall not be counted. Thus, a criminal prosecution may be instituted for acts which are already "statute-barred" before then. Later, a second statute regulated more precisely the running of the limitation period and excluded the criminal prosecution of acts which were statute-barred by a later deadline of 27 September 1993.

nary criminal law regime: Article 5 does not permit the principle of collective guilt or collective responsibility, nor does it alter the principle of the presumption of innocence or the prohibition of the retroactivity of statutes, which means that criminal prosecution is only possible for acts which were criminal at the time of their commission, and only on the basis of the law then in force, unless the subsequent statute is more favorable for the offender. Article 5 of Act No. 198/1993 merely alters the period of time during which a criminal prosecution may take place and defines only a certain category of such criminal acts for which this may be done, meaning those that the principle of the equality of citizens before the law makes necessary in order for a law-based State to maintain its credibility....

Questions and Comments on Transitional Justice

1. How convincing is Justice Sólyom's argument that adherence to rules against ex post facto applications is necessary to establish a rule of law? Is he worried about a slippery slope? Note that in 1996, the Hungarian Constitutional Court voided a 1993 law on proceedings in prosecutions for offenses committed during the 1956 revolution, but noted that crimes against humanity could be prosecuted and punished without a special law and that crimes under the Geneva Convention were not subject to statutes of limitations under Hungary's constitution.[o] Is the Hungarian Court trying to "have its cake and eat it too" (as the U.S. Court arguably did in *Marbury*) by voiding as unconstitutional a law while at the same time permitting the government to proceed against those involved in suppressing the 1956 uprising?

2. The Czech decision permitting suspension of the limitations period relied, in part, on decisions of the German Constitutional Court. It might thus be compared with the recent decision of the German Constitutional Court (November 12, 1996).[p] The Court upheld the convictions of former GDR officials who had helped hand down the shoot-on-sight policy that resulted in the deaths of 260 people trying to cross the border between East and West Germany, or East and West Berlin, between 1949 and 1989. It rejected the defense argument that the German constitution's provision that "[a]n act may be punishable only if it constituted a criminal offense under the law before the act was committed," Basic Law article 103, para. 2, prohibited such prosecutions. This article, the Court found, did not apply to a case such as this where a state (the GDR) had used its law to try to authorize clear violations of generally recognized human rights.

3. The problem addressed in the preceding articles and court decision in the context of criminal prosecutions occurs in several other arenas in which the felt demands of justice for past wrongs conflict with ongoing efforts to

o. MTI Euronews (Sept. 4, 1996) (LEX-IS, EUROPE LIBRARY, Hungary File).

p. This description is based on a report in German Information Center, The Week in Germany 2 (Nov. 15, 1996).

adopt and enforce predictable rules of law, raising problems of what might be called "transitional justice." See generally Neil J. Kritz, ed., Transitional Justice: How Emerging Democracies Reckon with Former Regimes (1995). For example, both Germany and the Czech Republic undertook a process of "lustration" to identify, and eliminate from important government positions, supporters of the old regime. Some advocate this as a relatively mild method (as compared with criminal prosecutions) of identifying the truth about past regimes, trying to assure that past abuses will not be repeated, and preventing wrongdoers from continuing to benefit from their wrongs by retaining their positions. Yet lustration may confront what Stephen Holmes calls "a socially diffuse sense of complicity," in which cooperators with the prior regime were pervasive. Stephen Holmes, *The End of Decommunization*, in I Transitional Justice at 116, 118. As he and others point out, lustration raises other difficulties: the problem of judging people unfairly by applying today's standards to the past; the high potential for inaccuracies in the secret police files relied on to carry out lustrations of those believed to have been "collaborators"; the pain of guilt by association and incorrect accusation; the inevitable discrimination between those who are and are not "lustrated"; and the need to devote attention to the future, not to purging the past. See Herman Schwartz, *Lustration in Eastern Europe*, in I Transitional Justice at 461. Consider how these arguments for and against lustration relate to the process of moving towards a constitutional regime, and how what Nino calls "retroactive justice" may be affected by the degree of continuity between displaced and new regimes.[q]

Another difficult problem for several regimes in Eastern Europe is that of compensation for past takings of property. Several countries have struggled with the question of what takings (e.g, those by the Communists; those by the Communists in accordance with their own law vs. those not in accordance with the then-law) by what governments (Nazi? communist?), should be treated as compensable; who should be eligible to claim compensation (only current residents; those outside the state with intent to return; heirs wherever located?); and how compensation is to be provided without impairing the financial integrity of the country (return of property itself, compensation at full value at the time of the taking; compensation in some form of government-issued instrument).

4. Yet another mechanism for reconciling the demands of justice for past wrongs with compliance with norms of law is the truth commission, which has been used in Latin America and, more recently, in South Africa. Recently, the South African Constitutional Court upheld the power of the

---

q. See Carlos Santiago Nino, Radical Evil on Trial 60–104, 120–121 (1996). Nino provides a compelling account of Argentina's legal efforts to come to terms with the atrocities (including the "disappearance" of thousands of citizens, including children) of the military regime of the 1970s and early 1980s, by a scholar who also acted as an advisor to President Alfonsin in his efforts to guide Argentina through complex processes of truth seeking, trial, blame assignment, punishment and amnesty for those involved in prior abuses, without inviting a successful military coup or Peronist-style authoritarian rule.

South African Truth Commission to grant amnesties that preclude criminal or civil liability for those who cooperate with its truth seeking efforts. See Azanian Peoples Organization (AZAPO) v. President of the Republic of South Africa, 1996 (4) S.A. 671 (Constitutional Court of South Africa, July 25, 1996)(reasoning inter alia that the Constitution's Epilogue contemplated a process of reconciliation that could embrace such broad amnesty to "facilitat[e] the constitutional journey from the shame of the past to the promise of the future" notwithstanding another constitutional provision that "every person" has a "right" to have court or independent forum settle "justiciable disputes;" noting reconciliation processes for human rights abusers in Chile, El Salvador and Argentina; also rejecting challenge to amnesty's extension to state liability for wrongful acts of former officers because Parliament was entitled to prefer present and future "claims of . . . school children and the poor and the homeless" to claims of those who had suffered torture under past regimes).

5.   Consider the competing arguments for pursuing, and not pursuing, various forms of "justice" against members of overthrown regimes in the context of an effort to establish "constitutionalism." How does your understanding of constitutionalism affect your answer?

CHAPTER V

CONSTITUTIONAL ENTRENCHMENT, COURTS AND DEMOCRACY

Many people (including legal scholars) in the United States and elsewhere believe that having a written and judicially enforceable bill of rights is a key aspect of constitutionalism. Constitutionalism, in these terms, is believed to rest on the idea of entrenchment—that is, that the constitution as law should be more difficult to change, more "entrenched," than "ordinary" law. Indeed, there is a strong tendency among constitutionalists to assume that constitutionalism means, in part, a fixing of some basic legal rules such that ordinary legislative processes cannot amend them.

As readings in earlier chapters suggest, some argue that in emerging constitutional systems the amendment process should be relatively easy. In this way, for example, Holmes and Sunstein argue that the forms of stable constitutional democracies can be better approached without yielding the flexibility to restructure or modify as conditions change, and without raising the stakes for constitution-making so high at the outset that no agreement is possible. Yet underlying this argument remains a notion that constitutions ultimately should be, as compared to ordinary law, relatively entrenched.

Entrenchment implies that an ordinary majority, utilizing ordinary processes of law-making, cannot change the entrenched rule. It is thus a form of "countermajoritarianism" closely related, but not identical, to the countermajoritarian concerns about judicial review prominent in U.S. constitutional discussion. The readings in this chapter, which begin with Great Britain and its debate over a Bill of Rights, raise a different set of concerns about entrenching constitutional rights: Can a more or less constitutional system operate without a clearly entrenched, written constitution specifying individual constitutional rights? Are there advantages to having a constitutional system that does not entrench individual rights? Is it possible? How would (do?) constitutional systems function without individual bill of rights provisions?

A. CONSTITUTIONALISM WITHOUT A CONSTITUTION?

Great Britain is sometimes described as lacking a constitution. As Finer, Bogdanor and Rudden suggest below, most British scholars would say that Great Britain has a constitution—but it is unwritten. With respect to entrenchment, they point out, part of the British constitution includes the strong convention of parliamentary supremacy—that is, that the courts cannot invalidate a law enacted by Parliament. Consider in what sense one could say that Great Britain nonetheless has a constitutional form of government. In this regard, compare Israel (discussed in the Jacobsohn reading in Chapter III).

In reflecting on the arguments for introducing a formal Bill of Rights in Britain, proponents argue for the benefits of having judges enforce written guarantees of rights to restrain parliamentary excesses. These arguments are thoroughly laid out in the essays by Michael Zander and Ronald Dworkin below. Consider whether, under current U.S. Supreme Court interpretation of the First and Fourth Amendments, some of the practices described in these articles would be found constitutionally prohibited here. Note also the form that the Labor Government in 1997 and Dworkin suggest that a Bill of Rights take and in particular, the role that the European Convention on Human Rights plays in Dworkin's argument. Does he think that a bill of rights should be entrenched—that is, permanently embedded in the law so that a future parliamentary majority cannot displace its provisions? Does he think that it can be? Recall our discussion of constitutional moments, and reconsider how the individual rights protecting provisions of the U.S. Constitution and its amendments were entrenched.

Mark Tushnet argues that U.S.-style bills of rights are double-edged swords that, for example, in protecting free speech rights, reinforce existing distributions of wealth and power towards the interests of the already powerful. As you read the Dworkin and Zander pieces, note what elements of the political spectrum have supported a bill of rights, and when. Consider carefully the bases for Tushnet's concerns about both the costs, and likely political direction, of having judicially enforceable bills of rights entrenched in a constitution.

---

1. The Constitution of the United Kingdom

S.E. Finer, Vernon Bogdanor & Bernard Rudden, *On the Constitution of the United Kingdom*, in Comparing Constitutions (1995)

[Unlike the constitutions of the United States, France or Germany, the authors write, the constitution of the United Kingdom "is marked by three striking features: it is indeterminate, indistinct, and unentrenched."]

4. *Indeterminate content.* Her Majesty's Stationery Office publishes the Official Revised Edition of the statutes in force. The two volumes devoted to "Constitutional Law" give the text of 138 Acts of Parliament (from the Tallage Act 1297 to the Welsh Language Act 1993), while a quite separate volume on "Rights of the Subject" gives another thirty-two (including what is left of Magna Carta). From these hundreds of pages, what is or is not "the Constitution" is a matter for scholars' individual judgements. Furthermore, many matters regulated with great precision in codified constitutions—such as the procedure on a finance bill, or that covering a vote of no confidence in the government—are in the UK governed entirely by custom, convention, or Standing Orders of the House.

There is no authoritative selection of statutes, conventions, common law rules, and the like which together comprise "the Constitution"; every author is free to make a personal selection and to affirm that this is the one, even the only one, that embraces all the most important rules and excludes all the unimportant ones—though nobody has ever been so foolish as to assert this. As Dicey put it, a writer on the Constitution "has good reason to envy professors who belong to countries such as France ... or the United States, endowed with Constitutions on which the terms are to be found in printed documents, known to all citizens and accessible to every man who is able to read".[1]

5.   Despite this indeterminacy at the edges, since we are concerned with the constitution of a "United Kingdom", all scholars must agree on the importance of the specific legal acts which constituted that entity. Great Britain was brought into being by a Treaty followed by two distinct Acts of two different legislators. The "Acts of Union" of 1707 are complex but fundamental. From 1603 the crowns of England and Scotland had been united in the same person, but the two countries remained distinct sovereign states each with its own parliament, laws, courts, and (customary) constitution. In 1706, commissioners for England and separate commissioners for Scotland agreed Articles of Union—also called a Treaty. As Queen of Scotland, Anne "with advice and consent of the estates of (the Scottish) Parliament" enacted a statute which established the Presbyterian Church in Scotland, declaring that it was to be inserted in any (Scottish) Act ratifying the Treaty of Union and was to be a fundamental and essential condition thereof. The Scottish Parliament then passed an "Act for the Union with England". The English Parliament with Anne as Queen of England then passed a lengthy Act for the Union with Scotland which recited and approved the Treaty of Union and the Scottish statutes. This process gave birth to an entity described in the Acts as "the United Kingdom of Great Britain". The Scottish Act for the Union with England (in a provision repeated in the English Act for a Union with Scotland) stated that henceforth Scots law was alterable by the Parliament of Great Britain but that no alteration could be made in private law "except for evident utility of the subjects within Scotland". It is therefore argued by some jurists that, by the very act of its creation, the UK Parliament is not empowered to alter Scots private law to the prejudice of the people there, and so is not absolutely supreme.[2] The issue has never been finally tested by litigation, although it is conceivable that English courts might take one view of the outcome and Scottish courts another.

6.   In 1800 the kingdoms of Great Britain and Ireland were united by similar legal procedures—Articles of Union followed by an Act of each

1. A. V. Dicey, *Introduction to the study of the Law of the Constitution* (10th edn., E.C.S. Wade (ed.), Macmillan, 1958), 4.

2. There are other provisions of the Scots Act of Union which may limit the powers of Parliament. See generally, Neil Mac-

Cormick, "Does the United Kingdom have a Constitution?" (1978) 29 *Northern Ireland Legal Quarterly* 1; Denis J. Edwards, "The Treaty of Union: more hints of constitutionalism" (1992) 12 *Legal Studies* 34; and *Pringle, Petitioner*, 1991 SLT 330.

parliament. In 1922 a UK Act recognized the "Irish Free State" comprising the island of Ireland minus six counties in the north-east, and gave force of law to an agreement between the UK government and an Irish delegation. The Ireland Act 1949 finally declared that Ireland had ceased to be part of His Majesty's dominions, though the statute also enacts that Ireland is not a foreign country (so its citizens are not aliens or foreigners for the purposes of UK law). Since 1922 legislation of the UK Parliament has in effect limited the United Kingdom to Great Britain and Northern Ireland (the latter is dealt with later).

7. *Indistinct structure*. The second striking feature of the UK position is that there is no special device to signal the repugnancy of "ordinary" laws to those we choose to regard as laws forming part of the constitution. The constitution is a rag-bag of statutes and judicial interpretations thereof, of conventions, of the Law and Custom of Parliament, of common law principle, and jurisprudence. Inside this miscellany all that we can assert with certainty is that statutes override non-statutory provisions, and that among statutes the latter overrides the earlier one. So if it be a statute relating to political practices that is being broken, this will be cognizable and dealt with by the ordinary courts and not by any specially constituted tribunal. And an infraction will be handled just like an infraction of, let us say, the Highways Act. If on the other hand the law being broken is not a law but a convention, the only way in which this is signalled is by private persons like the authors writing or making speeches on the subject, supported by some and opposed by others.

8. *Unentrenched*. One of the main reasons for the UK constitution's indistinct structure and indeterminate content is the absence of any special *formal* requirements for enacting or amending constitutional norms. Codified constitutions are adopted and can be altered only in certain way—by special voting requirements, by referendum, and the like. But in the UK, statutes relating to political practices, that is "constitutional law", are changed or repealed in exactly the same way as any other statute.

9. Now statutes are made, and made exclusively, by one organ. This is the Queen-in-Parliament. Often in this particular context this is simply called Parliament. The Queen-in-Parliament therefore becomes the starting-point for the exposition of the Constitution of Britain.

THE SUPREMACY (OR SOVEREIGNTY) OF PARLIAMENT

10. For present purposes Parliament is the Queen, the House of Lords, and the House of Commons combined. Except as when otherwise laid down by statute, a statute is made by the Queen assenting to a Bill which has been passed by each of the two Houses. The Parliament Acts of 1911 and 1949 lay down the circumstances in and the procedures by which a Bill can become law without the consent of the House of Lords, that is by being passed only by the Commons and thereafter receiving the Royal Assent.

11. Until recently, the law assumed that Parliament was omnicompetent and paramount. It could make or unmake law on any matter whatso-

ever and, indeed, it could do so with retrospective effect. No court in the kingdom was competent to question the legal validity of any Act of Parliament, that is of a statute. Every lawmaking body in the country was subordinate to it, since even if it did not derive its original authority from Parliament, it exerted this authority only as long as Parliament cared to suffer it. . . .

13. When, however, the United Kingdom entered the European Community in 1973, it was committing itself to the "new legal order" created by the Community Treaty,[5] a legal order which took precedence over rules of domestic law. . . .

14. It seems, however, that the UK constitution now recognizes the supremacy of Community law (within the latter's jurisdiction) together with the power of Community law to determine what matters do fall within its own jurisdiction—what the Germans call *die Kompetenz-kompetenz*. There are three sources of this rule of recognition: the UK Parliament, government statements, and court decisions. . . .

18. A simple example of the judicial recognition of the supremacy of Community law is to be found in its treatment of the Sex Discrimination Act 1975 which provided—in perfectly lucid English—that a compensation order must not exceed a specified limit (£6,250 at the material time). The discrimination in question was also a breach of Community law, and Community law requires adequate financial recompense so British courts, where necessary, disregard the upper limit which Parliament imposed on their powers.[8]

19 The possibility of conflict remains in the perhaps unlikely circumstance of Parliament deliberately legislating in breach of the European Community or Union Treaty by passing a statute which cannot be made compatible with Community law. It is not clear whether, in such circumstances, the courts would uphold the doctrine of the sovereignty of Parliament; or alternatively, whether, by striking down the statute in question, they would uphold the doctrine of the supremacy of Community law. Short of this extreme possibility, however, it seems difficult to deny that, by passing the European Communities Act 1972, a sovereign Parliament has voluntarily yielded its sovereignty. . . .

[In a description of what they call "the sovereign authority," the authors explain the concept of the "Queen-in-Parliament":]

THE SOVEREIGN AUTHORITY

46. The supreme legal authority in the United Kingdom, then, is the Queen-in-Parliament. In law, the Queen is the executive branch of government, so that the very expression, Queen-in-Parliament, suggests the

---

5. Case 26/62, *Van Gend en Loos v. Nederlandse Administratie der Belastingen* [1963] ECR 1.

8. Case C-271/91 *Marshall v. Southampton and South West Hampshire Area*

Health Authority (No. 2) [1993] 4 All ER 586 (ECJ) and [1994] 1 All ER 736 (HL); and *R. v. Secretary of State for Employment, ex p. Equal Opportunities Commission* [1994] 1 All ER 910 (HL).

fusion in one organ of the two traditional branches of government, namely the executive and the legislature. But the Queen-in-Parliament is also regarded, in law, as the High Court of Parliament; a court of record, whose record, the Parliament Roll, must be accepted as valid by all other courts in the kingdom which, *ex hypothesi*, are inferior to it. "Parliament" therefore is the supreme executive, legislative, and judicial authority all rolled into one, and this state of affairs, sometimes called the fusion of powers, stands in contrast to the USA, where there is a system of separated powers.

47. However, the concept of the "separation of powers" has been shown to be imprecise, confused, and confusing when closely examined. For our present purpose, it is more useful to use the related concept of "checks and balances", since this can be defined and evaluated by asking whether, how far, and in what respect any one of the three branches of government can either impose its will on the others or, alternatively, prevent them from taking action. The American Constitution goes furthest in this respect.... In practice it is very hard or even impossible for the incumbents of one branch to remove the incumbents of the others or to pressure them by threat of removal; yet each branch can seriously obstruct, even where it is not permitted to veto, the plans of the others. To speak very broadly, these three branches have co-ordinate status and in certain circumstances each can veto the others. In Britain, however, these three branches do not have co-ordinate status, since the Crown, whose origin is certainly independent of Parliament, must by law exercise most of its functions via ministers whose authority depends on Parliament. As to the judges, the effects of their judgments can be (and have been) altered retrospectively by Act of Parliament. The authority to veto a parliamentary Bill is still vested in the Queen, it is true, but it has not been used since 1707.

48. Thus authority ultimately rests in the legislature, on whose confidence the Ministers of the Crown depend, and although a prime minister may ask the Queen to dissolve Parliament and call a general election in the hope of securing such confidence, his Cabinet could not continue to govern if the election returned a hostile majority. A new prime minister and Cabinet would have to be installed, such as can command the confidence of the new parliamentary majority....

52. Apart from [having two houses], the British Parliament may be contrasted notably with the legislatures of the USA and of France in two different ways. It is unlike the former in that the executive authority resides in and is dependent upon the confidence of this legislature, instead of being independently elected, all but irremovable, and constitutionally endowed with a great number of powers in its own right. It is unlike the French Parliament in a different way: the British Parliament is omnicompetent, whereas the powers of its French equivalent are restricted to what the constitution stipulates, with the unspecified remainder of governmental authority inhering as of right in an autonomous executive power, that is to say, in the presidency, the prime ministership, and the ministers themselves. Thus, [in France] the domain of legislation is exceptional, while that of regulations constitutes, juridically, the common rule....

[After explaining the "perpetual and nonelective" composition of the House of Lords (hereditary and life peers) and elected membership of the House of Commons (elected at least as often as every 5 years), the authors discusses the "powers of the upper house", i.e., Lords:]

66.   *The Powers of the Upper House.* In the USA, neither of the two Houses of the legislature can overrule the other, which means that the Upper House has a full veto over the bills passed in the Lower House. In Germany the same is true for a range of items duly specified in the text as requiring the consent of the Upper House, which in that country is the Bundesrat, the Council of States, that is the House specifically charged with the protection of the interests of the Länder into which this federal republic is divided. On all other matters, however, the Lower House can override the Upper House provided it does so by a majority vote which is not less than that by which the Upper House made its decision....

69.   The relationship between the two Houses in Britain is regulated by the Parliament Acts 1911 and 1949. Money Bills, duly certified as such by the Speaker of the House of Commons, can become law without the assent of the Lords provided they are sent to this House for consideration at least one month before the end of the parliamentary session. With one important exception—a Bill to prolong the life of a parliament beyond the statutory five years—all other public Bills ... do not require the assent of the Lords provided that: (1) the Bill has been passed by the Commons in two successive sessions, whether of the same Parliament or not; and (2) one year has elapsed between the date of second reading of the Bill in the first of these two sessions and the final passing of the Bill in the second of these two sessions. This procedure has been used to pass only one bill, the War Crimes Bill 1991.[21] ...

[In describing the circumstances in which a government must resign and call for elections, the authors explain:]

79.   *The Cabinet's Responsibility to the Commons.* The meaning of the convention of collective responsibility will be considered below. Here we have to ask whether there exists in the constitution a definition of the circumstances in which a government, having suffered a defeat on the floor of the House, must resign. It seems fairly clear that if a government says in advance that it is treating a particular vote as a "matter of confidence", this is tantamount to its stating that, if defeated, it intends to resign. Accordingly, if defeated in these circumstances, we might confidently expect it to do so. If the Opposition puts down a motion of censure and carries it, then, too, we might expect the government to resign: but one cannot be absolutely sure that it will do so since it might argue that the vote was a "snap" vote, or freakish and unrepresentative of the government's majority in one or other of a number of ways. However, the

---

21. See Gabrielle Ganz, "The War Crimes Act 1991—Why No Constitutional Crisis?" (1992) 55 MLR 87.

probability that a government would resign after defeat on a censure motion is certainly very high indeed.

80.   However, apart from these two highly formal occasions, certain traditions concerning when a government ought and ought not constitutionally to resign used to exist in the past. A defeat in committee is not a confidence matter, since in principle this could always be reversed by the House as a whole. But defeats on the second reading of a Bill used to be regarded as a matter of confidence entailing the government's resignation. It is traditional also that snap votes and defeats by "ambush" might be disregarded by a government since, *ex hypothesi*, such defeats do not express the normal balance of votes in the House. These traditions worked well enough in the heyday of majority one-party governments but became more and more elastic under the minority governments of Wilson and Callaghan, between 1974 and 1979. Mr. Callaghan's government lost a Bill (the Redundancy Rebate Bill, on 7 February 1977) at its second reading, but ignored the defeat and simply carried on. It is increasingly clear that the usages governing the occasions on which it is requisite for a government to resign are much more flexible in the case of a minority government than where the government has an absolute majority in the House; and that such a minority government is allowed a good deal of latitude to disregard occasional defeats on the way. In such circumstances only a motion relating to "confidence", whether formulated by the Opposition or by the government itself, seems to be the appropriate mechanism for bringing such a minority government down. . . .

[With respect to the powers of the Prime Minister, Finer, Bogdanor and Rudden write,]

98.   *Powers.* The British prime minister is always, by convention, the First Lord of the Treasury (the Second Lord is always the Chancellor of the Exchequer), draws the salary and pension by virtue of holding that post, and, as First Lord, is also generally responsible for civil service matters, his approval being required in the appointment of Permanent Heads of the departments.

99.   For the rest, the powers depend wholly on convention and usage and derive from his position as leader of the government and, normally, party leader, not from any statutory powers. The prime minister recommends to the Queen, who must give her assent, the persons he or she wishes her to appoint as principal ministers, and from those he or she selects his Cabinet. . . . He or she can require a minister to resign at any time and for any reason, and if the minister chooses not to do so, he or she can advise the Queen to dismiss him, as occurred with a junior minister, Eric Heffer, in 1975, the only example of a dismissal in modern times. It is he or she who presides over the Cabinet, draws up its agenda, establishes its committees, and appoints their membership, presiding personally over the most important of them. Finally, if the prime minister resigns then the entire government must also resign.

100.   So influential is the prime minister today that the late Richard Crossman in 1963, before himself becoming a Cabinet minister, described

the British polity as being "Prime Ministerial Government". This it certainly is not, but neither is the prime minister only a "first among equals".

. . .

[On the Judicial Branch, here is the authors' description:]

121.   First, the British courts resemble those of [the USA, France, Germany, and Russia] in that they interpret the laws in force and their interpretation is the law until or unless it is altered by a higher court or by Parliament.

122.   Second, British courts resemble those of the USA in that they interpret such law as may be deemed "constitutional", that is relating to the distribution and allocation of public authority, as well as all other aspects of law. Another way of putting this is to say that in these two countries the interpretation of constitutional law vests in the "ordinary" courts of the land. In Germany, by contrast, the court that handles these matters is a specially constituted one, the Federal Constitutional Court or *Verfassungsgericht* (art. 93). In France only a limited number of "constitutional" issues are reviewable, principally, for our present purposes the compatibility of a Bill, already duly enacted by Parliament but not yet promulgated, with the constitution. Furthermore the body that reviews such a matter is not a court at all but a special tribunal called the Constitutional Council.

123.   Third, unlike the appropriate court or tribunal for constitutional laws in the USA, Germany, France, and Russia, and subject to what has been said about European Community law, the British law courts cannot set aside a duly enacted parliamentary statute.

124.   Fourth, the British arrangement resembles the American in that both these countries have but one set of courts to deal with all cases, whether these pertain to the executive branch or otherwise. Both France and Germany have a further set of special administrative courts in parallel to the "ordinary" courts of the country. However, in Britain there are administrative tribunals, separate from the courts, to deal with a wide range of miscellaneous activities.

125.   Fifth, Britain differs from France but not from the other countries concerned in that not one legal and judicial system obtains, as in France, but one for England and Wales, another for Scotland, and a third for Northern Ireland. . . .

129.   *The House of Lords as the Highest Court.* This body illustrates a characteristic feature of the UK constitution, namely the gap between form and function. Although bearing the same name as the Upper House of the legislature of which it is theoretically an advisory committee for lawsuits, in fact the House of Lords in its judicial capacity is quite a different entity. It hears civil and criminal appeals from England, Wales, and Northern Ireland, and also in civil (but not criminal) cases originating in Scotland. In theory any peer may sit, uninvited, to hear an appeal. This last happened in 1883, when the intrusive lay peer's opinion was superciliously ignored by

the lawyers. In practice its members consist of eleven judges appointed from the Bench of the superior courts or (occasionally) from among the ranks of senior barristers; normally at least two are Scots lawyers. The formal name for these judges is Lords of Appeal in Ordinary, and they are usually called "the Law Lords"; they are appointed to life peerages on elevation to the highest court. To them may be added the Lord Chancellor, ex-Lord Chancellors and other peers who have held high judicial office. Normally a hearing is held before five Law Lords. . . .

[The authors also describe the Judicial Committee of the Privy Council, whose jurisdiction includes giving "advisory" opinions to the Crown, which opinions are always followed. This body heard appeals from the courts of commonwealth nations.]

131. *Judicial Independence.* The independence of the judiciary from the pressures of both the legislative and the executive branches of government is a cardinal entailment of the doctrine of the separation of powers. . . . How then is the "independence" of the judiciary secured?

132. The answer lies in the respective provisions for payment and for removal. The principle seems to be that though a judge may be appointed by the executive, he or she shall not—or not easily—be removed by it. Thus the German Constitution provides (art. 97) that the judge cannot be dismissed "except by virtue of a judicial decision", and under this is subsumed removal by the process of impeachment (art. 98). The French Constitution declares that "Judges shall be irremovable" (art. 64) and that disciplinary proceedings must take place in the Conseil Supérieur de la Magistrature. It must be remembered, however, that in these two countries, as in all "civil law" countries, judges are civil servants. In the USA, a common law country like Britain, the judges are appointed during "good behaviour", their salaries may not be tampered with, but they may be impeached before the Senate for misconduct.

133. In Britain judges are not, or rather do not seem to be, Crown agents. Their independence is secured by the conventional and statutory provisions for their appointment, payment, and removal and for their judicial immunities. They are appointed by the Crown, which in practice means by the prime minister or the Lord Chancellor, depending on the status of the court in question. The possibility of appointing for primarily political reasons is mitigated by the statutory provision that only practising lawyers of many years' standing shall be appointed to the Bench. Once appointed, the judges' salaries are charged on the Consolidated Fund (which is not subject to annual review by the Commons) and, furthermore, if changed (which is done by Order in Council) can only be raised, and never lowered. While in office, judges enjoy judicial immunity for all acts said or done within their jurisdiction. They are disqualified from sitting in the House of Commons as MPs.

134. A High Court judge is indeed removable by the Crown but, by convention, only under the procedures laid down in the Act of Settlement (1701) as restated by the Appellate Jurisdiction Act 1875 and the Supreme Court Act 1981. These Acts require removal to take place only on an

address to the Crown presented by both Houses of Parliament. The last occasion on which a judge was removed was in 1830. He was an Irish judge, and the reason for his removal was emphatically not political.

· · ·

[For our purposes, perhaps the most interesting part of this essay's description is of the "rights and duties of citizens." Noting that the French have the 1789 Declaration of the Rights of Man and Citizens, the Americans have their Bill of Rights, and acknowledging that "[n]o such document exists among the laws of Britain," the authors continue:]

157. Yet the British unquestionably enjoy a large number of individual rights in their capacity as citizens of the country. As far as the application of the law is concerned it may fairly be argued that they enjoy much wider personal freedom than in some countries with Bills of Rights. But, while they may appear to enjoy freedoms comparable with those of their American, French, and German counterparts, in the constitutions of these countries the rights are expressed in the written constitution and are enforceable by a court or (in a limited range of circumstances) a specially appointed constitutional tribunal (as in the case of France).

158. The UK, like Germany and France, is a signatory of the European Convention on Human Rights (1950) and in 1966 accepted the compulsory jurisdiction of the European Commission and Court of Human Rights to which, therefore, an aggrieved individual can appeal. From this it may be inferred that the rights of the citizen in either Britain, France, or Germany are all subsumable under the Declaration of Human Rights, since the first seventeen articles of the European Convention are those of the Declaration. But Britain, unlike France or Germany and most of the other signatories, did not choose to incorporate the European Convention into her domestic law.

159. From these equivalences and differences we may deduce the following. First, it is possible to express the rights of British citizens in such general language and subject to so many qualifications and escape clauses that, at a certain level of abstraction, they may appear identical with those of their European neighbours. Second, the detailed and precise import of these generally expressed rights in Britain, *vis-à-vis* Germany and France, can be understood only by examining the specific laws and the judicial decisions thereon in Britain compared with these other countries. Such a task is beyond the scope of this introduction. A catalogue of rights such as freedom of expression, assembly, petition, association, and election would be too equivocal; a particularization would, conversely, be tantamount to a volume on civil liberties in Britain and would, indeed, take us beyond even that into the fields of judicial procedure, police powers, and of social and economic legislation. Third, the scope and effectiveness of the laws relating to civil liberty are not affected in principle by whether or not they are embodied in a charter which has the force of fundamental and superior law; witness the insubstantiality of rights in the former constitu-

tion of the USSR on the one hand and the practical effectiveness of the American Constitution's "Bill of Rights" on the other.

160.   The most that can be done here, therefore, is not to describe the substance of citizens' rights but their status. And the following observations may be made about this:

(1) The rights of the British citizen are not codified into statements of general principle like the clauses in the preamble to the French 1946 constitution, the first twenty articles of the German Constitution, or Amendments I-X, XIV, and XV of the American Constitution. Nor are they guaranteed any greater legal sanctity than that enjoyed by, for example, a Lotteries and Gaming Act. These liberties are founded in the common law of the kingdom, or in statutes, and in either case they are interpreted by the ordinary courts of the country; and both these and subsequent judicial decisions thereon can be overridden or altered by subsequent parliamentary statutes. In a word: the rights of the British citizen are not "entrenched".

(2) Furthermore, these rights are residual. To know one's rights is to know what matters or actions the law forbids. Thus citizens are free to express their opinion in speech or writing or other visual means, subject, however, to a long train of restrictions including, *inter alia*, the laws relating to treason, the Official Secrets Act, sedition, defamation, incitement to mutiny or to disaffection, obscene publication, or blasphemy; and to those also that relate to incitement to a criminal offence, or to provoking public discord or incitement to racial hatred. And each of these qualifying restrictions is defined by statute, common law, and the judicial decisions thereon.

(3) Finally, for every wrongful encroachment on the citizens' liberties, there exists a legal remedy, ascertainable and enforceable by the ordinary courts of the land.

161.   A number of eminent lawyers have increasingly found this situation unsatisfactory. They have called for a Bill of Rights enshrined in a codified constitution on lines similar to the American or the German constitution. Their dissatisfaction has arisen from recent developments in the parliamentary system. Parliament is sovereign; this is the key axiom of the constitution, and consequently Lord Scarman was able to write: "Its sovereign power [is] more often than not exercised at the will of an executive sustained by an impregnable majority ... The less internal control Parliament is prepared to accept, the greater the need for a constitutional settlement protecting entrenched provisions in the field of fundamental human rights".[27] But to establish such a "constitutional settlement" is far more easily said than done, especially in the light of the doctrine of the sovereignty of Parliament.

162.   It is sometimes argued that the desired result could be brought about by Parliament passing a statute which is, somehow, "entrenched".

27. Leslie Scarman, English Law: The
New Dimension (Stevens, 1974), 74-5.

That is to say, the statute would prescribe a procedure for altering itself which is more elaborate than that required for ordinary statutes, for example that it may be amended only by a two-thirds majority, or a two-thirds majority in each House, and/or by a popular referendum. But constitutional lawyers are divided as to whether such entrenchment is legally feasible, that is whether Parliament could not, under its ordinary procedure, simply wipe from the book the "entrenching" statute.

163. This argument can be taken more widely, too. On the one hand, it seems that the mechanism of the entrenched Bill of Rights plus judicial review operates effectively only in countries whose legislatures have long been habituated to the arrangement: the American experience dates from *Marbury v. Madison* (1803), while the German system takes up the centuries-old *Rechtsstaat* tradition. On the other hand, the absence of entrenched clauses in the Australian and Canadian constitutions did not restrict civil liberties in those countries as compared with, say, the USA or Germany, and has demonstrably restricted them far less than in the great majority of states which have such entrenched Bills of Rights. In short, there are more ways than one of negating civil liberties and more ways than one of guaranteeing them.

164. In his unpublished lectures on the Comparative Study of Constitutions, Dicey characterized the British constitution as a "historic" constitution. By this he meant not just that it was an ancient constitution but, more importantly, that it was original and spontaneous, the product not of deliberate design but of historical development. It is the long historical continuity of British institutions that gives the constitution its strength. Indeed, the most striking feature of the constitution is the way in which continuity in the form of institutions has masked a transformation of their function. The monarchy and the House of Lords, for example, have their origins in Anglo-Saxon times, while the House of Commons was born in the mediæval period. Their roles today, however, are quite different from those which they performed even 200 years ago. The Commons no longer makes and unmakes governments, while the House of Lords is now a revising chamber rather than an active legislative body, and the evolution of a limited monarchy has led to royal power being replaced by a constitutional monarchy. Evolutionary change within a framework of unchanging forms has, since the Restoration in 1660, been the hallmark of British constitutional development.

165. The constitution relies, however, more heavily than [the French, German, Russian, or U.S.] upon tacitly accepted and agreed conventions. British government, the political scientist Sidney Low declared at the beginning of this century, "is based upon a system of tacit understandings. But the understandings are not always understood". The stability of the constitution depends upon some common agreement as to what the conventions of the constitution actually are; it rests on what President de Gaulle, speaking in Westminster Hall in 1960, referred to as "an unchallengeable general consent". Were that consent to be withdrawn, then the perpetuation of an uncodified constitution might also come under threat. For, as

Gladstone once remarked, the British Constitution "presumes more boldly than any other, the good faith of those who work it". That remains as true today as it was when Gladstone wrote it, over 100 years ago.

Questions and Comments

1. The essay mentions the disagreement among British constitutional lawyers over whether Parliament can entrench a Bill of Rights. The problem is that Parliament at time–1 can enact a statute stating that its terms can be overridden only by a three-fifths majority, for example, but has no way of ensuring that Parliament at later time–2 will refrain from repealing that statute by a simple majority.

These lawyers' concerns raise more general questions about how any constitution can become entrenched. Can a constitution itself prescribe the provisions for its own entrenchment? Or must there be some extra-constitutional (or meta-constitutional) rule dealing with the process by which a constitution is entrenched? Addressing that question in the British context is particularly difficult because of the "indeterminate content" and "indistinct structure" of the British constitution.

For the United States, consider here Bruce Ackerman's argument that the process by which the Constitution of 1787 was adopted was illegal in the sense that it was inconsistent with the processes of constitutional change set out in the then-governing document, the Articles of Confederation. (The Articles provided for amendment only by unanimous agreement of the states; compare Article VII of the Constitution, stating that ratification by nine states "shall be sufficient for the Establishment of this Constitution" among those states). Ackerman's argument is developed in detail in Bruce Ackerman, We the People: Transformations (1998). Ackerman's account, including his suggestion of illegality, has not gone unchallenged, but one prominent challenger, Akhil Reed Amar himself argues that legitimate constitutional change in the United States does not require compliance with the procedures specified in Article V. Akhil Reed Amar, *The Consent of the Governed: Constitutional Amendment Outside of Article V*, 94 Colum. L. Rev. 457 (1994). If these accounts are right, do the constitutional moments of U.S. constitutionalism—periods of large-scale change in the constitutional regime—-differ that much from the accretion of unentrenched conventions in the British constitution?

2. What functions could be served or meanings intended in referring to unentrenched legal and political practices as a "constitution"?

---

2. INTRODUCTION TO THE HISTORY OF THE BILL OF RIGHTS DEBATE IN GREAT BRITAIN

As the prior reading indicates, recent years have seen increasing interest in the adoption of some form of entrenched protections of fundamental rights in Great Britain. Such a bill of rights would be enforceable in the courts, and its adoption would constitute a partial rejection of the principle of parliamentary supremacy. As the authors indicate states, some political theorists have questioned whether a single parliament could entrench rights against repudiation by later parliaments. The objection is that one parliament cannot bind a later one.

Note that some constitutions have been adopted by popular referenda or by constituent assemblies elected specifically for the task of drafting a constitution. Why are these mechanisms thought to overcome the theoretical objection? Consider the related objection that the people acting today cannot bind the people acting in the future, even by prescribing the methods by which the people may later amend their constitution. The Israeli parliament (or Knesset) sits in two capacities, as an ordinary legislature and as a constituent assembly to enact Basic Laws that, it is understood, will come to constitute the Israeli Constitution once all the Basic Laws have been enacted. (The degree to which that constitution will be entrenched is unclear, and controversial). Does allowing a single body elected by the people today to sit in two capacities offer a satisfactory solution to the theoretical problem? Is any solution satisfactory?

The Labor Party in Great Britain was historically hostile to the idea of a judicially enforceable bill of rights. In part that resulted from the Party's Marxist heritage, which led it to treat bills of rights as inevitably individualistic and anti-socialist; in part it resulted from experience with the administration of common law rules by courts hostile to labor's interests in the early twentieth century, which made the Labor Party suspicious of courts generally. Labor's hostility was fueled as well by its view that judges were drawn from a narrow social class and would regularly favor policies inconsistent with those advanced by the party of the working people. By the 1970s and 1980s, however, the Labor Party's position began to change, in part because of experience with parliamentary supremacy while Margaret Thatcher was Prime Minister. As Labor Party activists saw it, some of the government initiatives undertaken by the Thatcher government were incompatible with important British conventions but were vulnerable to being overridden in a system of parliamentary supremacy. They came to believe that the courts might be counted on to invalidate laws inconsistent with an entrenched bill of rights.

Conservatives also tended to oppose the adoption of a bill of rights, generally on the ground that enforcing its provisions would force the judges to take sides on controversial issues of public policy. One opponent called the United States Supreme Court a "dignified cauldron" in which essentially political issues were decided, and another suggested that, as in the United States, appointments to the bench would become highly politicized events. As Michael Zander, a bill of rights supporter, puts it in describing the British debate, "It is taken as axiomatic by virtually all English participants . . . that any system which produces the kind of public process for the selection of Supreme Court justices which takes place in the United States is self-evidently to be rejected." Michael Zander, *A Bill of Rights for the United Kingdom—Now*, 32 Texas International L.J. 441, 444 (1997). A bill of rights, according to another opponent, would deprive Great Britain of "constitutional flexibility and judicial nonpartisanship"; it would "dismantle the flexible system that, over the centuries, has so successfully adapted itself to changing circumstances and would transfer part of the sovereign power now vested in an elected Parliament to an unelected, unrepresentative judiciary. . . . The judiciary will become politicized as in the United States." Lord Browne–Wilkinson, *A Bill of Rights for the United Kingdom—The Case Against*, 32 Texas International L.J. 435, 437 (1997).

But the adherence of the United Kingdom to European treaties made the idea of judicial enforcement of "higher law" directives familiar to British lawyers. The European Court of Justice has held that a failure of domestic tribunals to provide effective remedies for violations of European Community (now European Union) law itself violated Community law. The effect of this holding is to make Community law enforceable in domestic courts, even, it appears, in the face of contrary parliamentary legislation. (Recall, though, Finer, Bogdanor and Rudden's caveat on this point.) Although most Community law deals with commercial matters, some, such as rules implicating equal pay, have human rights overtones. The United Kingdom is also a signatory of the European Convention on Human Rights. That Convention, in contrast to the Community treaties, is not directly enforceable in domestic courts unless a signatory state chooses to make it enforceable domestically, as have all signatories other than Great Britain. Great Britain is called before the European Court of Human Rights as a defendant, and judgments can be rendered against it in particular cases. Great Britain need not alter its law in response to such judgments, however. (Some British decisions suggest that decisions by the European Court of Human Rights might influence the development of the common law by British courts. They have not, however, suggested that such decisions would limit Parliament's power.)

Great Britain's experience in the European Court of Human Rights has been thought to be something of an embarrassment, as it lost a fair number of cases, including challenges to corporal punishment in the schools, Tyrer v. U.K., 26 Eur.Ct. H.R. (Ser. A) (1978), 2 EHRR 1(1979–80), treatment of suspected IRA terrorists, McCann et al. v. U.K., 324 Eur. Ct. H.R. (Ser. A) (1995), 21 EHRR 97 (1996), restrictions on discussion of pending cases, The Sunday Times v. U.K., 30 Eur.Ct. H.R. (Ser. A) (1979), 2 EHRR 245 (1979–80) and criminal laws against homosexual acts between consenting adults, Dudgeon v. U.K., 45 Eur.Ct. H.R. (Ser. A) (1981), 4 EHRR 149 (1982). Advocates of an entrenched bill of rights came to argue that adopting one would avoid this international embarrassment. Further, they argued that it was difficult to reconcile, in legal theory, these judgments criticizing British law with the proposition that Great Britain always adhered to the rule of law: In what sense was that so, they argued, when an international tribunal repeatedly found that British law violated a treaty to which Great Britain was a signatory?

The modern debate over adopting a bill of rights began with an important 1968 pamphlet written by Anthony Lester, a prominent lawyer associated with leaders of the Labor Party. Lester criticized episodes of popular hysteria against minorities, most recently in legislation restricting immigration to Great Britain from Commonwealth countries even by citizens of the United Kingdom. Lester also pointed to the growth of a potentially arbitrary government bureaucracy. In 1969 the House of Lords defeated, by a vote of 161 against to 137 in favor, a proposal by a Conservative member that would have enumerated some individual rights and would have required the Attorney–General to "check" all future legislation to ensure that it did not violate the enumerated rights. Shortly thereafter, three prominent Liberals echoed Lester's themes, and again the House of Lords debated the wisdom of adopting some form of a bill of rights. (The following account draws heavily on Chapter I of Michael Zander, A Bill of Rights? (4th ed. 1997) which provides detailed information and is the source of material quoted here.)

In 1970 Lord Hailsham, the Conservative Lord Chancellor, made a major speech rejecting the idea of a bill of rights. Although he had earlier thought that "the arbitrary rule of the modern Parliament ... needs consideration," in 1970 he argued that fundamental rights were protected better by general moral sentiments, and by specific statutory enactments, than by the illusion that a legal document could protect rights stated only in the most general terms.

Lord Scarman, a prominent sitting judge, reopened the debate in December 1974 with a speech that attracted a great deal of attention. Lord Scarman pointed to the pressures international human rights law was placing on the British system of common law and parliamentary supremacy: "The legal system must now ensure that the law of the land will itself meet the exacting standards of human rights declared by international instruments, to which the United Kingdom is a party, as inviolable. This calls for entrenched or fundamental laws protected by a Bill of Rights—a constitutional law which it is the duty of the courts to protect even against the power of Parliament." He also suggested that such protection would be particularly important as power was "devolved" to regional legislatures.

Conservatives also began to support the idea of a bill of rights, citing Labor Party legislation they believed violated fundamental rights. As Lord Hailsham said in 1975, the Labor government was proposing legislation that "would almost certainly be caught by any Bill of Rights legislation, however formulated."

By the summer of 1975 official Labor Party committees had developed a proposal for a "Charter of Human Rights," which would convert the European Convention on Human Rights into a regular, domestically enforceable statute. Proponents of this idea thought that it would be consistent with parliamentary supremacy because the statute could be changed by ordinary legislation. (In what sense, then, would this proposal entrench the Convention?)

Yet, although there appeared to be substantial momentum for the adoption of some form of bill of rights—typically by adopting the European Convention as domestic law in one form or another—, political forces made doing so impossible. While there was widespread agreement that any bill of rights should resemble the European Convention, there was substantial disagreement over whether any bill of rights was needed. For example, a Select Committee of the House of Lords reported in July 1978 that it divided 6–5 on the question of whether a bill of rights was desirable. Three Conservatives supported the idea, three Labor Party members rejected it, two Liberals divided, as did the two unaffiliated members. Responding to the Committee's report, the House of Lords voted 56–30 to urge the government to introduce bill of rights legislation that would "incorporate the European Convention on Human Rights into the domestic law of the United Kingdom." The Conservative Party took control of the government in 1979, and the movement to legislate a bill of rights lost ground, primarily because Conservative Party leaders who had endorsed the idea while they were in opposition became less enthusiastic once they controlled the government.

Proposals were sporadically advanced, but as late as 1987 the chief speakers on the issue for both major parties opposed adoption of a bill of rights. The Conservative Solicitor–General opposed the idea because it would damage the judiciary's reputation for impartiality by forcing them to make controversial policy decisions. The Labor speaker asserted that the judges were "drawn from a narrow atypical section of the population," and could not be trusted with the large law-making task that enforcing a bill of rights would require. Outside of Parliament, an impressive movement called Charter 88 developed to mobilize public opinion in favor of adopting a bill of rights. Other non-governmental organizations such as Liberty (roughly the British parallel to the American Civil Liberties Union) and some think tanks published detailed statements and analyses of the arguments for a bill of rights. A public opinion survey in 1991 showed 79% of the people surveyed favoring a bill of rights. (Similar results occurred in a 1995 survey.)

By 1993 the Labor Party had changed its position. John Smith, the party's leader, gave a major speech sponsored by Charter 88, in which he called for "a new constitutional settlement," shifting away from "an overpowering state to a citizen's democracy." Smith's speech referred explicitly to the experiences of the nation under Conservative government as evidence showing that something new needed to be done. "The quickest and simplest way of achieving democratic and legal recognition of a substantial package of human rights would be by incorporating into British law the European Convention on Human Rights." The Labor program of 1993 adopted Smith's position as well. Tony Blair's succession to Labor Party leadership did not change the party's position, which was embodied in the party's platform on which it was elected in 1997.

The government presented its Human Rights Bill in November 1997. The bill would direct courts to take the provisions on the European

Convention into account in their decisions. In addition, "[s]o far as it is possible to do so, primary legislation and subordinate legislation must be read and given effect in a way which is compatible with the Convention rights." The bill would also make it unlawful for public authorities "to act in a way which is incompatible with one or more of the Convention rights," unless their actions were required by primary legislation that could not be interpreted to remove the incompatibility. Courts could award "just and appropriate relief" for unlawful acts. The bill would not in itself make parliamentary legislation (referred to as "primary legislation") directly unlawful, nor would it provide remedies for harms caused by the implementation of primary legislation. Appeals courts could, however, make a declaration that a statute was incompatible with the Convention. The government's White Paper on its proposal, "Rights Brought Home: The Human Rights Bill" (October 1997), stated that a declaration of this sort "will almost certainly prompt the Government and Parliament to change the law." The bill would authorize ministers to amend statutes to remove the incompatibility, even to the point of repealing the statute. To do so, however, they would either have to have prior approval from Parliament for the amendment, or declare that amendment was "urgent," in which case the amendment would be placed on a forty-day "fast track" for parliamentary approval or disapproval.

Michael Zander, an academic supporter of adopting a bill of rights, addresses some important arguments against doing so in the following excerpts.

Michael Zander, A BILL OF RIGHTS? (3d ed. 1985)

. . .

A Bill of Rights is too powerful a tool to be entrusted to judges and is incompatible with democratic principles—especially where the government of the day is to the left of centre

This argument . . . is based on the view that in most modern democratic communities difficult, controversial or important issues ought to be decided by the legislature rather than the courts. . . .

This view is strengthened by the fact that judges tend, on average, to be slightly older than legislators and, therefore, arguably, less in touch with the conditions of contemporary society. Also, they tend to be drawn from a relatively narrow segment of the community, the upper middle classes, and insofar as they actually come from a lower economic or social class, they have frequently adopted the views and attitudes of the upper middle classes. Also, judges all over the world tend to be of conservative disposition. Finally, there is a strong feeling in some important groups in this country, notably the trade unions, that the judges are simply not to be trusted with any important issues affecting the fate of the ordinary man. There is a great deal of bitterness about what is felt to be a pronounced class bias amongst the judges against the interests of the unions and their members. . . . The belief that "English judges are the best in the world" is probably fairly broadly held amongst all social classes, but it seems to coexist, for some, with the apparently irreconcilable feeling that at least in certain fields judges as a class are irredeemably prejudiced.

The belief that "the judges cannot be trusted to get it right" is held not only by many in the trade unions, but, from a different vantage point, in the civil service. Administrators, perhaps understandably, mostly believe that they are best fitted to run things, to take account of and reconcile the various conflicting values and interests, to evolve the highest common denominator of agreement and to apply the most effective solutions to problems. Judges, by comparison, are largely ignorant of crucial matters such as the availability and disposition of resources, and the implications of choosing one solution over another.

A realistic assessment might conclude that, of all the problems, this could be the most difficult on which to reach a consensus in favour of a Bill of Rights. Suspicion of judges is almost an article of faith in certain quarters, especially on the Left. . . .

. . . [W]hatever system one has will give rise to *some* unsatisfactory results. The present system certainly does. The question, therefore, is not whether the courts will sometimes arrive at interpretations that are unacceptable to this or that group in the community—governors or governed—but whether any group or groups will be especially and consistently victimised. Will the overall balance be tolerably fair, or will it not? Will the benefits to be derived from a Bill of Rights outweigh the disadvantages? Will the judges persistently decide cases under the Bill of Rights to the disadvantage of minority interests? . . . Minority rights are uncongenial to judges, especially when they are those of groups who are thought to represent dissident or disaffected groups—squatters, demonstrators, prisoners, drug addicts, gypsies, students, even mental patients. If these fears were realised the position of such groups would be worse rather than better under a Bill of Rights. This would be more so since adverse decisions given in the course of interpreting a Bill of Rights would have even more than the usual authority—simply because of the special aura surrounding a Bill of Rights.

The pessimistic view that the judges should not be relied on as defenders of civil liberties was the main theme of John Griffith's book. He argued that careful analysis of the case law in fields such as police powers, race relations, immigration and deportation, industrial relations, conspiracy laws, students and property matters showed that the judges generally tended to take "the wrong side." He criticised the bench for its "strong adherence to the maintenance [of] order, distaste for minority opinions, demonstrations and protests, indifference to the promotion of better race relations[,] support of governmental secrecy, [and] concern for the preservation of the moral and social behaviour to which it is accustomed." This was not however because the judges were products of a capitalist system—rather it was a function of the role of judges in any society. . . . His thesis, he said, was that governments represent stability and had a considerable interest in preserving it. This was true of all governments of all political complexions, capitalist and communist alike. . . .

But this view may not pay sufficient regard to certain factors pointing in a different direction. For one thing it ignores the extent to which the record of the English judges is far from uniform. (The following section provides some evidence of the mixed record of the judges in at least some fields). Insofar as Professor Griffith's thesis is based on a view of the role of judges in *any* society it fails to explain the role of the United States federal judges in developing the constitution and the common law for the protection of many disadvantaged groups including blacks, the poor, prisoners, civil rights demonstrators and other minority interests. The record of the different levels of the United States judiciary in the past two or three decades in these fields though by no means uniform has nevertheless been impressive. No doubt the Supreme Court under Chief Justice Earl Warren was more "liberal" than that of Chief Justice Burger but even the Burger court is a good deal more liberal on many civil liberties issues than say the Court of Appeal or House of Lords. There is therefore some evidence that judges *per se* are not beyond redemption....A further safeguard is that if the judges *did* consistently decide Bill of Rights cases so as to benefit the strong against the weak it is certain that sooner or later the Bill of Rights would be scrapped. The experiment would have failed. What seems more likely is that if the pendulum swung in one direction at a given time, it would tend to correct itself in the next period. Corrective pressure would come from both outside and inside the system—from lay and professional criticism, appointment of new judges, test cases brought on behalf of the discontented and the general climate of opinion.

The Bill of Rights would be a means for educating the judges to the values implicit in a more "civil liberties" oriented approach to the law....Moreover, unfortunate decisions could be set right by the legislature by whatever method was prescribed for amendments to the Bill of Rights.

It should also be said that the suspicions of the Left are, to some extent, based on a view of the world which is simply inconsistent with the protection of human rights. This element in radical thinking proceeds on the basis that the individual must, if necessary, be sacrificed to the greater good of Society or the People—with a capital "S" or "P." Democracy, of course, recognises the potency of a majority. But the traditional liberal democratic view, if true to itself, should not countenance oppressive conduct by the majority against the minority....

Also, although a Bill of Rights would transfer significant power to the judges, it would leave much more significant powers in the legislature....

The European Convention on Human Rights, for instance, guarantees to all "the peaceful enjoyment of his possessions."

"No-one shall be deprived [of] his possessions except in the public interest and subject to the conditions provided for by the law and by the general principles of international law. The preceding provisions shall not, however, in any way impair the right of a State to enforce such laws as it deems necessary to control the use of property in accordance with the general interest or to secure the payment of taxes or other contributions or penal[ties]."

Sir Keith Joseph seems to believe that enactment of a Bill of Rights would prevent a Government from enacting legislation providing for, say, compulsory purchase of housing, or slum clearance or steep rates of taxation. But there is nothing to justify such expectations in the European Convention. There is ample protection for a government concerned to nationalise industries or redistribute income, say, by a wealth tax, to do so consistently with the Convention. What might not be permitted, however, is nationalisation of the property of aliens without compensation, or the seizure of accrued rights to social security payments at least under a system where contributions are related to benefits.

English judges are too executive or Establishment minded to be entrusted with a Bill of Rights

As has already been seen, there are those who criticise the judges as being too executive minded to be entrusted with the development of a Bill of Rights. . . .

In *Duncan* v. *Jones* in 1936, the Divisional Court held that the police were entitled to stop a public meeting, even though there was no obstruction or breach of the peace, if they reasonably thought that a breach of the peace might ensue. In *Thomas* v. *Sawkins* the Divisional Court held that the police were entitled to be present at a public meeting on private premises even when the organisers asked them to leave. It is unclear whether the basis of the decision was that the police must reasonably apprehend any offence, a breach of the peace, a seditious offence or some combination of these. But clearly the decision in practice gives extensive powers to the police.

In recent decisions of the Court of Appeal police powers of search and seizure were extended so far as seemingly to undermine the protection of the fundamental common law principle prohibiting the general ransacking of a man's house to search for incriminating evidence against him.

The House of Lords in 1961 ruled in favour of the vague offence of conspiracy to corrupt public morals, and in 1973 in favour of conspiracy to commit a trespass even though the trespass itself was not a crime.

In 1964, the House of Lords ruled that members of the Committee of 100 who conspired to incite others to enter an R.A.F. station committed the offence of conspiring to commit and to incite a breach of the Official Secrets Act. It said the accused were not permitted to give evidence that their intention was the peaceable one of protesting against nuclear weapons. It upheld the doctrine that what was Crown policy was necessarily in the interests of the State and the conduct of the accused was for a purpose prejudicial to the interests of the State if it interfered with dispositions of the armed forces.

The Divisional Court in the Paul Foot case invented a new principle of the law of contempt of court to cover publication of the name of a witness where the court had asked for anonymity. In the Vassal tribunal case in

1963 the Divisional Court ordered that two journalists who would not divulge their sources of information should be imprisoned.

The courts will admit evidence that has been illegally obtained and indeed their attitude to the exercise of this discretion has been normally to admit it. The interpretation by the courts of the Judges Rules increasingly denuded them of any real meaning. They are reluctant to quash jury decisions, to admit fresh evidence on appeal, to order retrials in criminal cases.

In war time, the executive was held to have powers of detention without trial which did not have to be justified in the courts—the onus of proof that the detention was for improper purposes lay on the applicant. The executive discretion to deport or to refuse permission for an alien to stay in the United Kingdom did not require the application of the rules of natural justice. In a clash between the freedom of the press to publish details concerning the conduct of a defendant in civil cases, and the principle of contempt of court, the House of Lords upheld the restrictive rather than the open policy.

There is therefore ample material from which to construct a case suggesting that Her Majesty's judges are hardly supporters of civil liberties and of minority causes. (See also the cases in John Griffiths, *The Politics of the Judiciary*.)

And yet, there are also a considerable number of cases which point in precisely the opposite direction. The judges have, for instance, at least until recently been insistent on the principle that an accused person's statement be voluntary to be admissible evidence against him. Their definition of "voluntary" in this context leant far in favour of the accused. The House of Lords has ruled that the courts rather than the executive are the arbiters of whether documents claimed to be covered by state privilege should be disclosed in the course of judicial proceedings. The House of Lords ruled in 1935 that the onus of proof in criminal cases is always on the prosecution and in 1947 that a person who has been arrested must be told the reasons for his detention. The Divisional Court held in 1966 that, with rare exceptions, a citizen has no duty to answer police questions. A High Court judge, in 1971, was so caustic about the Official Secrets Act as virtually to guarantee that a major political prosecution would end in an acquittal. The courts have made it clear they will not easily accept legislative attempts to deprive them of jurisdiction. Nor will they allow themselves to be excluded by a Minister's claim to an absolute or unfettered discretion. They have ruled that important decision-taking bodies must have a fair procedure and must observe the rules of natural justice. The House of Lords rejected the argument that an immigrant who landed surreptitiously at a point on the coast where there were no immigration officers had committed an offence under the Commonwealth Immigrants Act 1972. It was not an offence to do acts which were neither prohibited by Act of Parliament nor at common law merely because the object which Parliament hoped to achieve by the Act might thereby be thwarted. . . .

... The Lord Chief Justice Lord Widgery was responsible for the Practice Direction in 1973 which provided that an acquitted defendant ... should normally get his costs out of public funds. Lord Widgery was presiding in the Court of Appeal, Criminal Division, when it ruled that the courts should be prepared to quash a jury's verdict if, subjectively, it felt that there was some "lurking doubt" which made the court wonder whether an injustice had been done. It is difficult to imagine a more liberal statement of the court's duty in regard to this power, and although the court does not in practice always follow this test, it is nevertheless an important statement of principle. It was Lord Widgery's predecessor, Lord Parker, who laid down rules for the exercise by the judges of their responsibilities regarding plea bargaining. He disapproved the common practice whereby judges had secured guilty pleas by indicating that they would send the defendant to prison if he chose to plead not guilty, whereas he would get a non-custodial sentence if he pleaded guilty. In 1975, Lord Widgery ruled in favour of publication of the Crossman diaries. In 1978 the Court of Appeal ruled that Boards of Prison visitors were subject to the control of the courts in meting out punishments to prisoners. The decision meant that for the first time the courts would become involved in problems of prison disciplinary hearings. In 1982 in *Raymond* v. *Honey* the House of Lords held that a prison governor who stopped a prisoner from applying to a court to have him committed for contempt had himself committed a contempt of court. The prison governor had acted on the authority of the "prior ventilation rule" which required a prisoner to complain internally before taking the matter outside the prison service. The House of Lords said that this rule was contrary to the basic principle of allowing prisoners unimpeded access to the courts. The "prior ventilation rule" was modified by the Home Office to a "simultaneous ventilation rule." But this too was held unlawful by the Divisional Court in 1983. The court in *Anderson's* case said that it still impeded the prisoner's right to have free access to the courts and to lawyers for the purpose of advice about legal proceedings.

In 1980 the Lord Chief Justice ruled that it was not contempt of court for the *New Statesman* to publish an interview with a juror in the Jeremy Thorpe case. In 1981 Mr. Justice McNeil, to the annoyance of the Home Office, ordered it to produce classified documents relating to the development of the policy setting up "control units" in prisons. The Home Office claimed public interest immunity from disclosure of the documents in the course of proceedings brought by a prisoner who had been confined in such a unit. The judge rejected the claim for immunity.

In 1982 the Divisional Court held that the police had no right to enter the premises of a person arrested for attempted murder to search for the motorcar which it was alleged had been the weapon used. This was in spite of the fact that the arrest had been made on those premises and the police had merely come back to pursue their inquiries.

In another decision that certainly went against official policy the House of Lords held in 1982 that overseas students were entitled to mandatory grants to cover the expenses of university education even though they had come here for the purpose of study. The decision was almost immediately cancelled by legislative action. In the following year the House of Lords departed from its own previous decision in the *Zamir* case in which it had held that an immigrant owed a duty of candour so that non-disclosure of relevant facts constituted fraud which made him an illegal immigrant. In *Khawaja* the Law Lords in effect reversed their decision in *Zamir* and held that although silence as to a material fact coupled with conduct could in some circumstances amount to deception or fraud the 1971 Immigration Act did not impose a positive duty of candour on an applicant for admission to this country.

All of these were decisions that ran counter to official, Establishment or governmental policies. But neither these decisions nor those in the other direction *prove* the point either way. Nor is it easy to draw up a balance sheet as a whole. Clearly, there is much evidence in both directions and it must be a matter of individual judgment whether, on balance, the judges have been more executive minded than not.

At the least, it would seem fair to suggest that the case is far from wholly one sided.

Bills of Rights are only as good as those who interpret them and our judges are not equipped for the task

. . . A Bill of Rights demands a capacity to handle broad statements of principle. The tradition of English judges is to hug closely to the shores of literal meanings and to eschew the "unruly horse" of public policy. This objection is founded on a number of related arguments.

(*a*) English judges carry to extremes the tendency to write their judgments in such a way as to make it seem that the decision is the result either of inexorable logic or of the self-impelling momentum of the precedents. In either case, the judge seems to say he has had little or no control over the outcome.

(*b*) An English judge is still today apt to object if counsel before him tries to argue openly what the law should be ("We are here to decide what the law *is*, not what it ought to be.") Judges who put forward this view reveal their own ignorance of the nature of the judicial process. . . . [69]

(*c*) The English situation is made the worse because of the reluctance to go outside the narrow confines of the technical question. In interpreting statutes, for instance, the judges have traditionally refused to look not merely at Parliamentary debates, but even at the reports of law reform bodies which propose and often prepare the legislation. This attitude is slowly changing. . . .

---

69. The belief that judges do not *make* law was described by Austin over a hundred years ago as a childish fiction. Today it is impossible to sustain in the face of the statement in 1966 by the House of Lords that it will, in appropriate circumstances, decline to follow its own decisions. If the House of Lords changes its mind on a rule of law it must be because it has fashioned a new rule.

(*d*) The traditional, literal approach to interpretation is another example. The court, at least in the past, has been apt to construe an ambiguous provision (whether in a statute or a will, contract or other document) as if the use of language was like mathematics, capable of right and wrong answers. If the draftsman has been inept, the court will reject his effort and tell him to try to do better next time. ("It is not for the court to write the document." "We can see what was meant but the words used failed to give it expression." "If Parliament had meant that it would have said so.") In applying the literal approach, the court will often deny the existence of any ambiguity. This occurs even when the existence of an ambiguity is manifest from the very fact that there are two opposing parties before the court. Sometimes, even more absurdly, several judges say that the meaning of the words used is so clear as not to require interpretation—yet they disagree as to what the clear, obvious or literal meaning is.

(*e*) Another example is the virtual absence in English courts of arguments on points of law based on factual data—economic, social, or other relevant material. In the United States such argument has been a familiar part of legal disputation since the famous "Brandeis brief" in 1907. The later Supreme Court Justice argued the constitutionality of Oregon legislation limiting hours of work for women by producing data drawn from hundreds of reports designed to show that *as a matter of fact* long hours were dangerous to women's health, safety and morals and that shorter hours resulted in social and economic benefits. The strictly legal argument took less than two pages, the factual data occupied over a hundred pages of Brandeis' brief. The court accepted the argument and based its decision on his reasoning.

In English courts such argument would simply not be presented—partly because the court would deny its relevance, partly because counsel would in any event find it difficult to marshal the data. Argument in an English case is normally limited to discussion of the statutes and precedents, and what counsel on either side can add, through reasoning by analogy, "common sense" and assertion of the consequences of adopting alternative views. . . .

(*f*) A final example of the alleged inappropriateness of English judicial procedures to a Bill of Rights is the reluctance of English courts to accept argument save from the parties. It is a familiar part of United States judicial argument that interested and expert bodies may, with the permission of the Court, participate in litigation between third parties by submitting written arguments. The *amicus* brief from, say the National Association for the Advancement of Coloured Peoples, the American Civil Liberties Union, the American Legion or other similar groups has played a major seminal role in the development of the law. The concept of the *amicus* is known to English procedure mainly as a means of permitting the Attorney General to argue "the public interest" in rare cases, and then often at the instance of the court. Interested private bodies, however expert and however much they might be able to contribute to the court's understanding of the problem before it, are not normally permitted to intervene. . . . At least one reason is that the English courts have not yet understood the value (at least for certain purposes, and in addition to oral argument) of written argument. But the more fundamental reason is that litigation is seen principally as a way of resolving disputes between the parties. . . .

The above objections amount to a formidable case. . . .

To give English judges the responsibility for interpreting a broad Bill of Rights would be a considerable risk. There have been too many examples of their adopting a needlessly restrictive approach to legislation, even of the current style. Nevertheless, there are at least some reasons for thinking that a Bill of Rights may still be worth having even though it may not necessarily fulfil its entire promise in the short run.

First, a Bill of Rights has to be judged over the long run—decades or even centuries. What happens in the first few years, which is all one can hope to predict, is of *relatively* minor importance, save in so far as it determines the eventual course of events. Even in the United States it was a long time before the Supreme Court gave expression to many of the rights enshrined in the Bill of Rights. Judge Skelly Wright listed in 1981 the dates of the decision in which the Supreme Court vindicated some of the most significant express guarantees of the Bill of Rights—the free exercise of religion (1940); freedom of speech (1927); freedom of the press (1931); freedom of assembly (1937); freedom of petition (1939); speedy trial (1955); public trial (1948); right to counsel (1932), etc. Until the twentieth century the record of the United States judges under the Bill of Rights was less than distinguished.

Secondly, a Bill of Rights, by its very nature could have an effect in changing the traditional interpretative techniques of the judges. They would probably recognise this as a different kind of animal requiring a more generous approach. This tendency might be increased by actually putting in an admonition to this effect in the Bill (along the lines of the New Zealand Acts Interpretation Act 1924 which exhorts the judges to give statutes "such fair, large, and liberal construction and interpretation as will best ensure the attainment of the object of the Act and of such provision or enactment according to its true intent, meaning and spirit").

Another way of assisting the necessary broadening of approach would be to alter the procedure of the courts to permit intervention by qualified third parties (with the consent of the court), and by the admissibility of written arguments by parties and others. This would encourage the fuller development of argument on relevant aspects of problems. . . .

Thirdly, a Bill of Rights would inevitably increase participation in human rights matters by lawyers, politicians, the press, academic commentators as well as judges. . . .

The risks would also be limited by the fact that the European Commission and the European Court would remain as "long stops." It may be that in the long run the remedy of the European Commission and Court would be unnecessary since the local remedy would be more "human rights oriented" than anything offered by Strasburg. But it is reasonable to assume that it would take some, if not many, years for this to be achieved. For the first 10 or 20 years of an English Bill of Rights, it would be wise to assume that there might continue to be a need for the support of the European model. Whilst this continued to exist there would, in effect, be a right of appeal from the decisions of the English judges to Strasburg. Moreover, the English judges could look to the European jurisprudence both of the Commission and of the Court for guidance. . . .

The risks could, if desired, be further limited by restricting interpretation of the Bill of Rights to a specially constituted court with judges selected (hopefully) for their concern and sympathy for human rights. Or, at least the *final* court of appeal in Bills of Rights matters could be such a specially selected court. Some of its members could even be non-lawyers— such as senior administrators. . . .

In fact however, interpretation of Bills of Rights or written constitutions is not entirely unfamiliar to English judges. . . .

In 1965, the Privy Council had before it an appeal by 11 appellants charged with offences arising out of the abortive coup d'état in Ceylon in 1962. The appellants objected to retrospective criminal law passed specifically to deal with the named conspirators in the coup. They alleged that such legislation was contrary to the Constitution. This contention was upheld by the Judicial Committee on the ground that the intent of the legislation was to interfere with the judicial function. "Quite bluntly, their aim was to ensure that the judges in dealing with these particular persons on these particular charges were deprived of their normal discretion as respects appropriate sentences. . . . If such Acts as these were valid, the judicial power could be wholly absorbed by the legislature and taken out of the hands of the judges. It is appreciated that the legislature had no such general intention. It was beset by a grave situation and it took grave measures to deal with it, thinking, one must presume, that it had power to do so and was acting rightly; but that consideration is irrelevant, and gives no validity to acts which infringe the constitution. What is done once, if it be allowed, may be done again and in a lesser crisis and less serious circumstances; and thus judicial power may be eroded. Such an erosion is contrary to the clear intention of the constitution. In their lordship's view, the Acts were *ultra vires* and invalid."

In the following year, the Privy Council had to consider the allegation by the editor of a Malta Labour Party newspaper that a ministry circular banning his paper from government offices was in breach of the provisions in the Malta Constitution guaranteeing freedom of religion and freedom of expression. The circular prohibited papers such as that in question, which were "condemned by the ecclesiastical authorities." The Privy Council held that the prohibition was contrary to the constitution in that it went beyond reasonable orders regulating working conditions of government employees and constituted an infringement of the freedom of expression. . . . The cour[t] said where fundamental rights and freedoms of the individual were involved "a court should be cautious before accepting the view that some particular disregard of them is of minimal account."

In 1969, the Judicial Committee heard the appeal of someone born of an indigenous mother and a Lebanese father, who had lived in Sierra Leone for the previous 56 years. On Sierra Leone achieving independence in 1961, he became a citizen by virtue of the constitution. But in 1962, legislation was passed which purported retrospectively to deprive him of his citizenship by limiting citizenship to those of [N]egro-African descent. He claimed this legislation was unconstitutional in that it was discriminatory and contrary to the provisions of the constitution which prohibited laws that discriminated on grounds of race—save when there were special circumstances making it reasonably justifiable in a democratic society. The Board held that it was doubtful whether the measure was reasonably justifiable in a democratic society, but that in any event there were no special circumstances within the meaning of the exception. . . .

All these decisions exhibit a strong concern for fundamental rights and a willingness to defy legislative or Government authority in the name of higher principles of constitutionality. They suggest that those who prophecy that English judges are temperamentally not equipped to handle a Bill of Rights may be taking an unduly pessimistic view.

The English judges have equally shown their ability to handle effectively the broad and open textured phrases of European Community law in regard to equal pay and sex discrimination. . . .

. . . The conventional view, frequently espoused by the judges themselves, is indeed that they are the citizen's chief bulwark against the State. A Bill of Rights would take the judges at their word and give them better tools to do the job.

A Bill of Rights would "politicise" the judges

This argument is based on the fear that a Bill of Rights would necessarily involve the judges in controversial issues and would, to that extent, result in some loss of the reputation for impartiality which characterises the English judiciary. English judges do not take a full part in public life. They usually decline to appear on radio or television. They generally do not write in the newspapers. They only rarely write even in learned journals. If they speak in the House of Lords or on other public platforms, it is normally on issues of lawyers' law reform rather than general economic, social or political questions. This reluctance to get involved in political controversy is based on the conventional view that a judge's main task is to decide disputes in court between litigants and that it is important that the community should feel confidence in the fairness of such decision-making.

A Bill of Rights would require the judges to show themselves more openly as law-makers. It would be fairly apparent that the words of the Bill of Rights would permit alternative interpretations that might be associated with particular viewpoints. If the judges favoured one interpretation, they might be promoting the "conservative" approach; if they adopted the alternative, they might be thought to be following the "liberal" or "progressive" school. In either event, they would be subject to criticism from the supporters of the losing faction.

There can be no doubt that English judges do enjoy an unusually high reputation for impartiality and fairness. The one significant exception, perhaps, is in the field of industrial relations where, as has been seen, there is a significant body of opinion which holds, rightly or wrongly, that the judges are not free from bias. But apart from this area, judges are generally believed to be even-handed and apolitical in deciding cases.

Partly, this belief is based on an insufficient appreciation of the degree to which judges can and do exercise choice in their decision-making, on questions of law. Most judges spend most of their time deciding disputed questions of fact and in such cases they are usually impeccably fair. But when it comes to deciding a disputed point of law, as has been seen, there may be scope for the judge's own preferences to influence the way he marshals the precedents and the competing arguments. Even intelligent members of the public are probably unaware of the extent to which this does occur. . . .

In other words, the judges' reputation for impartiality is greater than the facts could justify.

If the full process of decision-making were exposed to the gaze of the populace, the public would have a more realistic view. Research, for instance, has shown the extent to which the leading nineteenth-century decisions in the field of landlord-tenant relations, tended to a marked degree to favour the landlord class. Conflicts between the revenue and the taxpayer tended to be resolved in favour of the taxpayer 50 years ago, where today the judges, being more sympathetic to the basic objectives of the welfare state, would decide the same cases the other way. In the nineteenth century male judges tended to rule that women were not persons within the meaning of statutes that gave persons the right to vote or to exercise other civic functions. In other words, in a variety of contexts the judge's "political" preconceptions may, and in fact do, influence his judicial decisions. The pretence that this does not occur is merely naive.

There can be no doubt that a Bill of Rights would increase this tendency. Moreover it would be somewhat more visible, since a Bill of Rights is cast in general terms which patently lend themselves to differing interpretations. The law-making functions of the judges in interpreting the Bill of Rights would be clearer to be seen. Would the greater scope for law-making in areas of controversy, combined with the greater visibility of the process, be harmful?

Fears that English judges would be politicised is usually made by reference to the experience of the United States and to the nature of the Supreme Court. But this example may be somewhat misleading. First, part of the Supreme Court's particular character is undoubtedly due to the fact that the court has the power to strike down legislation as unconstitutional. . . .[I]t is not suggested here that an English Bill of Rights should give it this overriding role. . . .

Secondly, differences between the two systems suggest why the Supreme Court is more political than would be likely of any English court even with a Bill of Rights. Judges in the United States are selected from more varied backgrounds—academics, politicians and office lawyers in addition to advocates. The doctrine of precedent is weaker than in this country and courts feel freer than ours to deviate from past decisions. Legal education in America produces lawyers who are more policy orientated than does our own. Lawyers are more dominant in society generally than in England and feel less diffident than here in offering their techniques to solve society's problems.

Thirdly, the belief that the American judiciary is political in the sense discussed here is not usually applied to the main body of the federal judges around the country. It applies principally to the Supreme Court. . . .

English judges are, by tradition, more conservative than most. It is likely that they would tend to under-use rather than to over-use powers of law-making implicit in a Bill of Rights. To the extent that the Bill of Rights produced greater public familiarity with the true nature of the judicial process and its scope for judicial law-making, this would in itself be a gain. If the emperor has fewer clothes than had previously been thought, it is not necessarily a bad thing for this to be understood. . . .

[In the following essay, Ronald Dworkin, the prominent Anglo–American legal philosopher, argues in favor of adopting a bill of rights. Dworkin's essay provides many of the arguments prominent in the British debates. Others include these: the traditional idea of complete parliamentary supremacy is today out of line with practices elsewhere in the world, where courts routinely enforce fundamental rights even against parliamentary legislation; a bill of rights would provide some support for legislative action to reform the law even if Parliament was not compelled by the bill of rights to do so; and a bill of rights would educate the public about its fundamental rights. As Harold Laski, a prominent Labor Party theorist, wrote, "Bills of Rights . . . warn us that certain popular powers have had to be fought for, and may have to be fought for again. The solemnity they embody serves to set the people on their guard. It acts as a rallying point . . . for all who care deeply for the ideals of freedom." Harold Laski, Liberty and the Modern State 75 (3d ed. 1948).]

* * *

Ronald Dworkin, A BILL OF RIGHTS FOR BRITAIN (1990)

Liberty is Ill in Britain

Great Britain was once a fortress for freedom. It claimed the great philosophers of liberty—Milton and Locke and Paine and Mill. Its legal tradition is irradiated with liberal ideas: that people accused of crime are presumed to be innocent, that no one owns another's conscience, that a man's home is his castle. But now Britain offers less formal legal protection to central freedoms than most of its neighbours in Europe. I do not mean that it has become a police state, of course. Citizens are free openly to criticise the government, and the government does not kidnap or torture or kill its opponents. But liberty is nevertheless under threat by a notable decline in the *culture* of liberty—the community's shared sense that individual privacy and dignity and freedom of speech and conscience are crucially important and that they are worth considerable sacrifices in official convenience or public expense to protect.

The erosion of liberty is not the doing of only one party or one government. Labour governments in the 1970s compromised the rights of immigrants, tried to stop publication of embarrassing political material, and tolerated an outrageous censorship and intimidation of journalists by the newspaper unions. But most of the worst examples of the attack on liberty have occurred in the last decade, and Margaret Thatcher and her government are more open in their indifference to liberty than their predecessors were.

Official Secrecy The list of liberties compromised or ignored in Britain in recent years is a long, sad one. Freedom of speech has consistently been sacrificed to liberty's most powerful enemy: official secrecy, the value rulers put on keeping their own acts and decisions dark. Censorship is no longer an isolated event accepted with great regret and keen sense of loss in the face of some emergency. On the contrary, censorship has become routine, an inexpensive way of the government's saving itself trouble or embarrassment.

Mrs. Thatcher's government has indiscriminately prosecuted civil servants and others who revealed information they thought the public should know. It brought contempt proceedings against Harriet Harman for turning over to the press official records that had already been made public in open court, and prosecuted Clive Ponting for leaking records of no importance to security but which he believed showed grave official misconduct. A jury acquitted Ponting; and the government, furious, changed the Official Secrets Act to make it plain that the public interest could be no defence to any such charge in the future.

Publishing The government made Britain look ridiculous throughout the world when it tried every conceivable legal strategy to stop people reading *Spycatcher*, an unpleasant but harmless book about British security services, written by a former employee of Britain's secret service in defiance of his promise of confidentiality. Even after *Spycatcher* had been published in the United States, Australia and elsewhere, and Britons who travelled abroad had flooded the country with copies they brought back, the government still sought and won an injunction forbidding the *Sunday Times* and other papers from printing excerpts here, all the time conceding that publication posed not the slightest security risk. The government finally lost its preposterous battle, even in Britain, when the courts held that there was no sense in stopping the publication here of what was common knowledge in the rest of the world.

Broadcasting Censorship by intimidation has become sadly common-place. Ministers now routinely denounce broadcasters as biased and unpatriotic. When Thames Television showed a film about the shooting of IRA members by British security officers in Gibraltar, called *Death on the Rock*, the Prime Minister and Home Secretary immediately attacked the programme as deceptive and substantially untrue, though (as an eminent commission chaired by Lord Windlesham later concluded) it was neither.

Officials have no hesitation, moreover, in using direct censorship of television when they believe indirect methods will not work. It is incredible but true that under the License Agreement with the BBC, and under a Broadcasting Act regulating independent television, the Home Secretary has the power at any time to stop the broadcast of any matter or classes of matter he specifies. In 1988 he invoked that power in a massive way, to prohibit any broadcast of any interviews with representatives of various Northern Ireland organisations on any subject whatsoever, including the re-broadcast of films made decades ago. The order included not only the IRA but Sinn Fein, which is a legal party with a Member of Parliament. That was an uncommonly silly and pointless decision—the order allowed actors to read lines spoken by members of the forbidden organisations. It is also a direct and savage example of political censorship; it strikes to the heart of a journalist's right to speak and the public's right to hear.

The government recently suggested that it will change, in the broadcasting Bill scheduled shortly to become law, the standards that require television companies to maintain impartiality about matters of political controversy. Its proposed changes have not yet been announced, but since the government has widely criticised the media as being biased against it, many editors and journalists are now fearful of what will come.

Privacy and Surveillance Police wiretapping, bugging and secret surveillance are for all practical purposes legally uncontrolled in Britain, and the police have a quite scandalous power to invade the privacy of individuals. Under the Interception of Communications Act of 1985, the police can tap anyone's phone or read his mail if they have the permission not of a judge, as in other countries, but of a politician—the Home Secretary. (In what the statute describes as "an urgent case", the Home Secretary himself need not even sign the order.)

The Act provides only an ineffective scheme of review of the Home Secretary's decisions. Different forms of review are conducted by a special tribunal of senior lawyers, who are appointed by the Prime Minister, and by a special Commissioner who is also appointed by the Prime Minister, and whose reports she can censor before publication. There are no effective sanctions against illegal wiretapping, and the Act expressly forbids the investigation, or even the *mention*, of wiretapping in court. Police use of bugging devices and secret video cameras is subject to no control at all, except Home Office guidelines and circulars which the police are free to ignore. All this would seem incredible in many other constitutional democracies.

Moralism Britain interferes much more with its citizen's private lives than it used to do, particularly about sex, which next to secrecy is the nation's chief obsession. The government's decision to implement Section 28 of the Local Government Act of 1988, which prohibits support for "the teaching in any maintained school of the acceptability of homosexuality as a pretended family relationship", sent a chilling message of intolerance that is explicable only on nasty political grounds, whatever the legal consequences of that bizarre language turn out to be.

Protest Britain is less tolerant of political protest than many other nations, and much readier to deny that right for reasons only of convenience or distaste. Other countries wrestle with the difficult problem of allowing the maximum freedom of political protest consistent with public order and safety. In Britain freedom of protest is permitted only when the cost to public convenience is minimal. There is no general right to protest, and the use of even traditional public places for protest requires the prior approval of the police. The Campaign for Nuclear Disarmament, the Save Greece from Fascism, and the Northern Ireland Civil Rights Movement have all been denied the use of Trafalgar Square.

The 1986 Public Order Act requires advance notice even for peaceful processions or marches which cause no obstruction, and that Act makes the leader criminally responsible if the march takes a somewhat different route or starts later than the notice specified. The Act gives the police power to issue any order, at a public meeting of 20 or more persons, that they deem necessary to prevent "serious disruption in the life of the community". They can order a meeting or march to move or to reduce its numbers, for example, and the protest's leaders may be sent to jail if those orders are disobeyed. If protesters challenge the orders in court, the judge must uphold them if he decides that the police thought them necessary to maintain order, whether they actually were necessary or not. It is hard to imagine a scheme of regulating demonstrations in a democracy more mean-spirited to liberty, more contemptuous of the importance and value of committed protest.

Rights of Suspects British justice led the world in insisting on criminal procedures which provide strong protection against convicting innocent people. But under the pressure of terrorist threats these procedures are being abandoned, and the president of Britain's Law Society recently warned, at that group's annual conference, that the delicate balance between prosecution and defence was being upset in favour of the former. Parliament continues to re-enact the detention provisions of the Prevention of Terrorism Act, which allow people suspected of that crime to be held incommunicado for two days, and then for a further five days with the permission of the Home Secretary, without being charged with any crime or being allowed to see a lawyer in private. (Only 7 per cent of people detained in that way have ever been charged with any crime at all; the rest were released having, in effect, served a week's jail sentence by the fiat of a politician.) In 1988 the European Court of Human Rights declared these rules a violation of the European Convention of Human Rights, which

Britain has signed, and ordered Britain to change them. The Thatcher government then argued that it had the right to derogate from its obligations under that Convention pursuant to Article 15, which allows a state to derogate in "time of war or other public emergency". The European Commission is now considering that claim.[*]

Since the seventeenth century British law has insisted that in a criminal trial the State must prove the suspect's guilt by its own evidence and not out of his or her mouth. So the common law gave defendants a right of silence, and that right has been copied and respected in the jurisprudence of many other nations and in the famous Fifth Amendment to the United States Constitution. But the ancient right is about to be extinguished in the nation that invented it. In 1988 Mrs. Thatcher's government announced that the principle would no longer hold in Northern Ireland, and might be curtailed in the rest of Britain soon. Under the Ulster rules, if a suspect refuses to answer questions put by the police that fact can count as evidence against him, even if the evidence was otherwise not sufficient to convict. If he refuses to testify at trial, the judge or jury is entitled to draw an inference of guilt. That is exactly what Senator Joe McCarthy proposed when he attacked the Fifth Amendment in the United States in the 1950s. The Supreme Court protected the ancient right of silence there, but no British court can now prevent it from being annihilated here.

The Tyranny of Convenience

The tory government calls itself conservative, but it is wrecking the best part of Britain's legal heritage. Thatcher's people are not despots. But they have a more mundane and corrupting insensitivity to liberty. Of course any democratic government must balance the interests and demands of different sections of the public and choose policies they think best for the community as a whole. It must therefore restrain people's freedom in various ways. It must lay down rules regulating how fast or in what direction people may drive, the size and character of the buildings they may build, the terms on which they may hire or fire employees, when and how they may merge or combine their businesses, and thousands of other matters.

In a culture of liberty, however, the public shares a sense, almost as a matter of secular religion, that certain freedoms are in principle exempt from this ordinary process of balancing and regulation. It insists that government may not dictate its citizens' convictions or tastes, or decide what they say or hear or read or write, or deny them a fair trial by historical standards, even when it believes, with however good reason, that infringing these liberties would on balance protect security or promote economy or efficiency or convenience. In a culture of liberty, these freedoms

---

* [Editors' Note: In 1993, the European Court of Human Rights upheld the claim that Article 15's "public emergency" provision authorized the derogation from Article 5's provisions. Blannigan & McBride v. U.K., 258-B Eur. Ct. H.R. (Ser. A) (1993), 17 EHRR 539 (1994)].

cannot be abridged except to prevent a clear and serious danger—a calamity—and even then only so far as is absolutely necessary to prevent it.

Of course difficult questions arise about exactly which activities should belong to the protected system of liberties, about how clear and present a particular danger is, and about when less stringent means of regulation than censorship or prohibition are available. People equally committed to freedom disagree about whether, for example, the dangers of tobacco advertising or the offensiveness of racial epithets justify withholding protection from these forms of speech. The essence of liberty is not agreement over particular hard cases, however, but an attitude: that the traditional liberties are so crucial to human dignity that hard questions should be decided in their favour as far as possible, that a fence should be constructed around and at some distance from the heartland of free expression, privacy and fair criminal process, that government should bear the onus of demonstrating that *any* interference with *any* part of the fundamental liberties is really necessary to secure some essential goal.

That is the spirit in which a culture of liberty approaches hard questions about speech and protest and the right to silence and the rights of minorities. It does not ask whether the public will be more or less pleased, on the whole, if there is less sex on television. Or whether the loss of valuable information to the public will outbalance the gain to the security system if television programmes about Gibraltar or Northern Ireland are censored, or whether government operates more smoothly and efficiently when public officials are prosecuted for leaking embarrassing information, or whether there will be less crime if suspects are henceforth denied the right of silence.

These questions are unfair to liberty, because the value of liberty cannot be measured piecemeal, in iotas of information sacrificed or imagination stifled or creativity impaired or innocent people convicted. Measured case-by-case against the immediate aims of ordinary politics, the value of liberty will always seem speculative and marginal; it will always seem academic, abstract, and dispensable. Liberty is already lost, whatever the outcome, as soon as old freedoms are put at risk in cost-benefit politics. A decent nation is committed to freedom in a different way. It knows that liberty's value lies on a different scale, that invading freedom is not a useful technique of government but a compromise of the nation's dignity and civilisation.

The [Thatcher] government rejects that view of liberty's value. It makes freedom just another commodity, to be enjoyed when there is no particular political or commercial or administrative price to be paid for it, but abandoned, with no evident grief, when the price begins to rise. That is not despotism. But it cheapens liberty and diminishes the nation.

How Could the Convention be Incorporated?

The European Convention is not a perfect Bill of Rights for Britain. It was a compromise drafted to accommodate a variety of nations with different legal systems and traditions; it is in many ways weaker than the

American Bill of Rights; and it is hedged about with vague limitations and powerful escape clauses of different sorts. The Convention does protect liberty better than it is now protected by Parliament alone, however, as recent history shows. It protects freedom of speech, religion and expression, privacy, and the most fundamental rights of accused criminals, and it grants in an indirect but effective way rights against discrimination. Since Britain is already subject to the Convention as a matter of both moral obligation and international law, it would plainly be easier to enact that charter into British law, substantially as it is, perhaps with clarifying changes and additions from other international covenants Britain has also signed, than to begin drafting and debating a wholly new Bill of Rights. Even if it were possible to adopt an entirely new set of rights, perhaps modelled on the American Constitution, the European Convention would remain law enforceable in Strasbourg, and the potential conflict between the two fundamental charters of rights would be a source of wasteful confusion.

So those who love liberty should unite in supporting the incorporation of the Convention. But how can this be done, and in what form should it be done? Suppose Parliament declared tomorrow that both its own past and future statutes and the acts of ministers and officials under them shall be null and void unless they are in conformity with the Convention's principles. Would not a future Parliament, tired of that constraint, have the power simply to repeal the incorporation? Indeed, would it not repeal the incorporation automatically whenever it enacted a statute inconsistent with the Convention, in which case incorporation would be a nonsense from the start? Suppose Parliament tomorrow both incorporated the Convention *and* provided that the incorporation could not be repealed by a future Parliament except by an extraordinary majority of, say, three-quarters of the members. Could not a future Parliament, by ordinary majority vote, simply repeal the provision requiring an extraordinary majority?

Many lawyers assume that it could. So does Roy Hattersley, the Deputy Leader of the Labour Party; he defends his opposition to a Bill of Rights on the ground, among others, that even if Parliament incorporated the European Convention unanimously, a future Parliament could simply repeal the incorporation any time it proved inconvenient....

In any case, I disagree with the judgment of law that Parliament cannot limit the power of a future Parliament. That judgment assumes that any Parliament has the legal power to do absolutely anything it wishes to do, notwithstanding what earlier Parliaments have done. What is the authority for that proposition? It plainly does not owe *its* authority to any parliamentary decision, because it would beg the question for Parliament to decide that its own power was unlimited.

British lawyers say that Parliament is an absolute sovereign because that seems (for most of them intuitively and unreflectively) the best interpretation of British legal history, practice and tradition. But legal history and practice can change with great speed. Suppose a national debate on constitutional principle took place, after which Parliament declared that the European Convention was incorporated into British law, and also declared that this decision could itself be repealed or amended only by a special procedure requiring an extraordinary majority of both Houses. Then British constitutional history would have been altered just by that decision having been made, understood and accepted by the public as a whole. Practice and tradition would have changed, and the old interpretation, which declares absolute parliamentary supremacy, would plainly no longer fit. Judges would have no legal or logical reason not to hold future Parliaments to the decision the nation had made. They would have no legal or logical reason not to insist that only an extraordinary majority could restore the present situation.

So the popular argument that there is no way Parliament can impose a constitutional Bill of Rights on a later Parliament is at least dubious. But notice that I have so far been discussing what might be called a *strong* form of incorporation, which provides that any statute inconsistent with the Convention is null and void. Several influential supporters of a Bill of Rights (including Lord Scarman, a former member of the House of Lords, who has been a pioneer in the argument for incorporation) have proposed that in the first instance incorporation should take what is technically a weaker form: the incorporating statute should provide that an inconsistent statute is null and void unless Parliament has expressly stated that it *intends* the statute to override the Convention. In practice this technically weaker version of incorporation would probably provide almost as much protection as the stronger one. If a government conceded that its statute violated the Convention, it would have no defence before the Commission or Court in Strasbourg. . . .

At least in the first instance, therefore, proponents should press for the weaker version of incorporation. If they succeed, then unless Parliament has expressly provided to the contrary any citizen will have the right in British courts to challenge a law or an official decision on the ground that it is offensive to the Convention's principles. . . .

Should Parliament be Supreme?

. . . Ministers and officials are rarely keen to justify themselves before judges, and constitutional rights often make important political objectives more difficult to achieve. These are the costs of a culture of liberty, and politicians, above all, hate to pay them. What is surprising, however, is the ineptness of the arguments politicians have deployed against incorporation. In the rest of this essay, I shall consider all the arguments of which I am aware.

The politicians say that the very idea of a Bill of Rights restricting the power of Parliament is hostile to the British tradition that Parliament and Parliament alone should be sovereign. That supposed tradition seems less appealing now, when a very powerful executive and well-disciplined political parties mean less effective power for backbench MPs than it did before these developments. The tradition has already been compromised in recent decades, moreover. It was altered by the European Communities Act, for example, under which judges have the power to override parliamentary decisions in order to enforce directly effective Community rules.

In any case, quite apart from these considerations, incorporating the European Convention would not diminish Parliament's present power in any way that could reasonably be thought objectionable. Parliament is *already* bound by international law to observe the terms of that Convention. If the Convention were incorporated in what I have called the strong form, under which a future Parliament would not have the legal power to violate the Convention even if it expressly said it intended to do so, then the power of Parliament might be somewhat more limited than it is now, because British judges might develop a special British interpretation of the Convention that in some cases recognised individual constitutional rights the Strasbourg Court would not.

It is hard to argue that this further limitation would be wrong in principle, however. Britain agreed when it accepted the European Convention and the jurisdiction of the European Court of Human Rights, that it would be bound by the principles laid down in the Convention as these principles were interpreted not by Parliament but by a group of judges. If that limitation on the power of Parliament is acceptable, how can it be unacceptable that the principles be interpreted not by mainly foreign judges but by British judges trained in the common law and in the legal and political traditions of their own country?

The argument for parliamentary supremacy would be irrelevant, moreover, if the Convention were incorporated in the weaker form I suggested should be the initial goal. For then Parliament could override the Convention by mere majority vote. . . . [F]orcing Parliament to make the choice between obeying its international obligations and admitting that it is violating them does not limit Parliament's supremacy, but only its capacity for duplicity. Candour is hardly inconsistent with sovereignty.

Is Incorporation Undemocratic?

The argument for parliamentary supremacy is often thought to rest on a more important and fundamental argument, however, according to which Britain should not have subscribed to the European Convention in the first place. This is the argument that it is undemocratic for appointed judges rather than an elected Parliament to have the last word about what the law is. People who take that view will resist incorporation, because incorporation enlarges the practical consequences of what they regard as the mistake of accepting the Convention. They will certainly resist the idea that domestic judges should have the power to read the Convention more liberally and so provide more protection than Strasbourg requires.

Their argument misunderstands what democracy is, however. In the first place, it confuses democracy with the power of elected officials. There is no genuine democracy, even though officials have been elected in otherwise fair elections, unless voters have had access to the information they need so that their votes can be knowledgeable choices rather than only manipulated responses to advertising campaigns. Citizens of a democracy must be able to participate in government not just spasmodically, in elections from time to time, but constantly through informed and free debate about their government's performance between elections. Those evident requirements suggest what other nations have long ago realised: that Parliament *must* be constrained in certain ways in order that democracy be genuine rather than sham. The argument that a Bill of Rights would be undemocratic is therefore not just wrong but the opposite of the truth.

The depressing story of the Thatcher government's concentrated assault on free speech is more than enough to prove that point. In the Harman, Ponting and *Spycatcher* cases, in denying a public interest exception in the new Official Secrets Act, in the broadcasting bans, in the *Death on the Rock* matter, government tried to censor information of the type citizens need in order to vote intelligently or criticise officials effectively. The officials who took these decisions acted out of various motives: out of concern for confidentiality, or to discourage views they thought dangerous, or to improve the morale of the police and security services, or sometimes just to protect themselves from political damage. But none of these reasons is good enough: in a democracy officials have no right to dictate what the voters should know or think. The politicians would very likely have acted differently in every one of these cases if Article 10 of the European Convention had been part of British law, and the prospect of judicial intervention had been immediate and certain rather than delayed and in doubt. British democracy would obviously have been strengthened not weakened as a result.

It is true, however, that the European Convention forbids governments to adopt or retain some laws that a majority of their citizens do want, and would continue to want even if they had all the information anyone might wish. The European Court struck down Northern Ireland's homosexuality law, for example, not because the Court doubted that a majority of the voters of Northern Ireland wanted that law, but because the Convention prohibits that form of discrimination whether the majority wishes it or not. If the European Convention were incorporated, British judges might strike down Britain's blasphemy law, which prohibits books or art deeply offensive to orthodox Christianity, even if a majority favoured retaining that law. The blasphemy law violates Articles 9 and 10 of the Convention, which protect freedom of conscience and free speech. In my view (although British courts have rejected the suggestion) the blasphemy law also violates Articles 9 and 14, which taken together prohibit religious discrimination, because that law discriminates in favour of Christianity. (Moslems said it was unjust that Salman Rushdie's book, *The Satanic Verses*, could not be prosecuted as blasphemous of their religion.) Of course the blasphemy law should not be extended to other religions, as they argued it should. It should instead be repealed, because it would violate the Convention even if it applied to religion in general.

Would it offend democracy if a British court had the power to strike down the blasphemy law as inconsistent with the Convention? No, because true democracy is not just *statistical* democracy, in which anything a majority or plurality wants is legitimate for that reason, but *communal* democracy, in which majority decision is legitimate only if it is a majority within a community of equals. That means not only that everyone must be allowed to participate in politics as an equal, through the vote and through freedom of speech and protest, but that political decisions must treat everyone with equal concern and respect, that each individual person must be guaranteed fundamental civil and political rights no combination of other citizens can take away, no matter how numerous they are or how much they despise his or her race or morals or way of life.

That view of what democracy means is at the heart of all the charters of human rights, including the European Convention. It is now the settled concept of democracy in Europe, the mature, principled concept that has now triumphed throughout Western Europe as well as in North America. It dominates the powerful movement towards democracy in Eastern Europe and Russia, and it was suppressed only with the most horrible tyranny in China. The rival, pure statistical concept of democracy, according to which democracy is consistent with oppressing minorities, was the concept proclaimed as justification by the Communist tyrannies after the Second World War: they said democracy meant government in the interests of the masses. The civilised world has recoiled from the totalitarian view, and it would be an appalling irony if Britain now embraced it as a reason for denying minorities constitutional rights.

This seems to me a decisive answer to the argument that incorporation would be undemocratic. I hope and believe that a different but equally decisive answer can also be made in Britain now: that the argument is self-defeating because the great majority of British people themselves rejects the crude statistical view of democracy on which the argument is based. . . . Even people who cannot imagine being isolated in [the] way [of, e.g. a religious minority] might prefer to live in a genuine political community, in which everyone's dignity as an equal is protected, rather than just in a state they control.

That attractive impulse lies dormant in day-to-day political argument about how to fight terrorism or whether tolerance for homosexuals should be promoted with taxpayers' money or when suspected criminals' telephones should be tapped. But it might well surface during a general constitutional debate, when the nation reflects about its traditions and its image of itself. A public opinion poll in Britain in 1986, taken before a parliamentary debate about incorporation, reported that twice as many of those questioned favoured incorporation as opposed it, and that 71 per cent thought a constitutional Bill of Rights would improve democracy. Such polls are unreliable in various ways, but the dramatic preference for incorporation is nevertheless impressive. Britain will not have a Bill of Rights, even in the relatively weak form we have been discussing, unless it turns out, after an intense period of public debate, that the preference is genuine, that the British people do share a constitutional sense of justice. If so, and if we assume that this sense of justice will be shared by their descendants, then the argument that incorporation is undemocratic will have been defeated on its own terms. . . .

Will the Judges Have to Work Too Hard?

The remaining objections I shall consider appeal not to philosophical principles about parliamentary supremacy or democracy or the superiority of ordinary legislation, but to more practical problems associated with the British judicial system. I begin with the most surprising of these. It is said that British judges are already overworked, and that asking them to consider constitutional questions as well as the ordinary legal claims they now entertain would impose far too great a burden on them. . . . [T]he fear of overwork is surely overstated. Canadian judges complained of overwork when the Canadian Charter of Human Rights was first adopted, but most of them now concede that the additional work is becoming manageable.

I do not doubt that if the Convention did become part of British internal law, enterprising lawyers would make constitutional claims in a wide variety of criminal and even civil proceedings. . . .

Judges would, of course, have to consider any such claim. But they would soon gain enough experience in constitutional matters quickly to see which of such claims had no merit. . . .

But suppose the fear of judicial overwork were well-founded. Suppose that even after plainly unmeritorious claims had been weeded out, constitutional issues took up so much judicial time that the overall legal system did suffer from clogging and lack of time for other matters. That would mean that the situation of freedom and justice in Britain is even worse than advocates of a Bill of Rights fear. It would then be preposterous to complain that it would have been better to save judges the work than to ask them to help defend the fundamental rights of British citizens. The appropriate solution—the only defensible solution—would then be to strengthen the judiciary.

If nothing else worked, then more judges could be appointed—there is no lack of qualified senior lawyers. But it is far from clear that new judges would be required. The British judicial system is famously under-financed and inefficient: even the most senior judges are given next to no secretarial, library or other assistance. In America every judge in the federal system, and almost every judge in the higher state courts, is assisted by at least one full-time paid clerk, and justices of the Supreme Court, which has the greatest burden of constitutional cases, each have exclusive use of four clerks. . . .

. . . Any problem of judicial overload could therefore be cured if the government were to spend more money on justice, by appointing new judges or allowing the present judges to use their time better. So the argument that incorporation would overwork the judges is actually an argument based on stinginess, a particularly debased form of the bad idea that rights should be denied when it is expensive or otherwise inconvenient to recognise them.

Are the Judges Up to the Job?

If even the weak version of incorporating the European Convention were adopted, judges would have more power than they do now....But the increase in the judges' role would be significant even if only quantitative, and that provokes an objection which is thought particularly powerful on the left of British politics.

It claims that British judges are, as a group, drawn from a very narrow and privileged section of the community, that they are insensitive or hostile to the interests and convictions of the rest of the nation, that they have for generations shown a collective bias for property and the middle class and against the trades-union movement, and that they therefore cannot be trusted with the increased political power that incorporation, even in a weak form, would give them. This view of British judges is, in my view, both exaggerated and dated, but it does have a foundation in truth. Judges are drawn from the bar, which remains an élitist profession, and an unconscionably high percentage of them are Oxbridge graduates....

[T]he argument that British judges cannot be trusted with constitutional rights makes an obviously untenable assumption: that judges will remain the same kind of people, and decide cases in the same kinds of way, whether or not they are asked to enforce a Bill of constitutional rights. If the Convention were incorporated into British law, even the most legally conservative judges would believe themselves bound to apply that decision in the spirit in which it was taken; in any case they would know they were obliged, by the act of incorporation, to have regard to decisions of the European Court. The legal culture would have changed around them: legal education and professional literature and debate would be based on new assumptions. In time, as I said earlier, the character of the bar and then the bench might well change in consequence. If the experiment worked, different men and women from different backgrounds would want to be lawyers, and these would include many who were attracted to law as an instrument of social justice. They would be trained differently, in a more international and cosmopolitan style, taught by a law faculty engaged in a different kind of research. Judges would soon begin to be drawn from a very different and much more diverse and exciting profession.

Suppose all this is wrong, however, and too many judges continue to be insensitive to the values of liberty and equality. How much would have been lost by incorporation then? Some writers suppose that bad judges armed with a Bill of Rights can wreck the nation. It is closer to the truth to say that they can merely disappoint it, as the Supreme Court now dominated by Reagan's ultra-conservative appointments is disappointing America. Conservative or unimaginative judges who refused to exercise their power to check ministers and officials or to set aside Parliamentary statutes would simply be leaving the legal world as it would have been *without* incorporation. At worst nothing substantial would have been lost, and it is extremely unlikely that nothing would have been gained. Some judges would exercise their new power well even if most did not, and the profession and the public would have a new basis for criticising and educating the laggards. Litigants who were denied their rights in decisions the profession criticised would be more likely to appeal to Strasbourg, and the European Court would hand down decisions that even the most conservative judges would then be obliged to follow in future cases.

It is odd how often all this is misunderstood. . . . [L]awyers point to the fact that the American Supreme Court did not prevent the American government from interning citizens of Japanese extraction after Pearl Harbor, or prevent Senator McCarthy's short reign of terror. These are indeed conspicuous failures in the Supreme Court's long and on the whole creditable record. But it is absurd to think that internment or McCarthyism would not have occurred if America had had no Bill of Rights at all.

Some lawyers worry, however, that judges really could make things worse if the Convention were incorporated, because judges could then stand in the way of a Labour government's reforms by declaring novel social regulations invalid. They cite the decisions of the Supreme Court in the early 1930s which held important parts of Franklin Roosevelt's social legislation unconstitutional, until the "Nine Old Men" of that Court gave way, by death and retirement, to new appointments. But a careful reading of the European Convention should reassure those who are worried by the analogy. The Convention was adopted by governments several of which had already embarked on welfare-state programmes. It contains a specific guarantee of the right to form and join trades unions, and no provision that any judge, no matter how conservative, could use to strike down legislation a responsible Labour government would sponsor.

The Supreme Court in its most conservative period cited the Fifth Amendment, which provides that Congress may not deprive anyone of liberty or property without due process, to hold progressive legislation unconstitutional. It held, for example, that a New York law limiting the number of hours bakers could be asked to work each week deprived both bakers and their employers of the "liberty" of contract. That use of the due process clause was legally indefensible, as even the most conservative American lawyers now almost all agree. But in any case there is no comparable clause in the European Convention.

The first protocol does provide that no one shall be deprived of "possessions" except in accordance with principles of international law, and that states must "respect the right of parents to secure . . . education and teaching in accordance with their own religious and philosophical convictions". It has already bean established, through decisions of the Strasbourg Court, that these provisions would not permit a British government to confiscate private property with no compensation, or to abolish independent schools. (Britain accepted an even clearer prohibition on abolishing independent schools when it ratified the International Covenant on Civil and Political Rights in 1976.) But the protocol leaves ample room for social legislation any responsible government would wish to enact; it insists, for example, that a state may "control the use of property in accordance with the public interest", and it does not oppose obvious measures that would decrease the unfair advantages of private schooling.

The risk is therefore inconsequential that after incorporation judges would be able to stop social and economic changes a future government of the left would actually want, and would otherwise be permitted to make.

Would Judges Become Politicians?

The last objection in my catalogue argues that if judges had the power to set aside legislation as unconstitutional, judicial appointments would become undesirably political, and judges would be thought politicians themselves.... They point to the political character of high judicial appointments in America, and they cite, in particular, the national debate and partisan contest over Reagan's nomination of Judge Robert Bork to the Supreme Court in 1987.

That nomination battle was most extraordinary even in America, and it was provoked by Reagan's decision to appoint a judge who had made himself a political figure already. Bork had for many years campaigned among right-wing groups for his own nomination, promising in articles and speeches that he would revolutionise constitutional law. He denounced, and suggested that he would vote to overrule, a great number of well-established Supreme Court decisions that Americans had come to think of as the core of civil rights and racial justice in the United States. When the Senate rejected his nomination, Reagan appointed Anthony Kennedy instead, and though Justice Kennedy's judicial record suggested he would be a conservative judge—his record since appointment has been extremely conservative—the Senate approved him with no difficulty or acrimony.

There are important differences between the way judicial appointments are made in Britain and the United States, moreover, which weaken the analogy. Though judges in Britain are largely drawn from a much too narrow sector of the population, and judicial appointments have tended to favour more conventional and conservative lawyers, these appointments are not regarded as political in a narrow, political-party, sense. Appointments are made by the Lord Chancellor, after consultation with senior judges, on a basis that seems to reflect a reasonably plausible combination of a candidate's seniority, success at the bar and esteem in the profession. Appointments are not reviewed in Parliament, as they are in the United States Senate.

Would it be necessary or desirable to change this system of appointment if judges had the power to strike down parliamentary statutes? If so, would the necessary changes make the process of appointment too political? It is far from clear that it would be either necessary or wise to make judicial appointments subject to parliamentary approval. In the United States the Senate's power to refuse a presidential nomination is a very real one. The Senate is never wholly controlled by the President, who makes nominations, and it is often controlled by the opposite party, as it was when Bork was rejected. So the process acts as a genuine check on presidential power. If a British Prime Minister began to control judicial appointments behind the scenes, however, a parliamentary check would be only a rubberstamp, because a Prime Minister with an adequate majority can generally have his or her way on almost anything.

It is true that a requirement of parliamentary approval would give the opposition a chance to examine a candidate's record and qualification, and to expose inadequacies or biases that might show the appointment to be a political or ideological one. But the same examination could be made at least as well in other ways. The public is already more aware than it used to be of the importance of a particular judge's judicial attitude and philosophy. . . . If judges had the additional powers that incorporating the European Convention would give them, the public would have even more interest in who the judges were, and the media would have that incentive for examining the qualifications of controversial appointees. So would academic lawyers, public interest groups and professional committees. A government whose judicial appointments did not follow the established pattern of selecting among barristers with the highest professional qualifications could expect the public to notice and strongly to disapprove.

It would therefore seem unwise, if the European Convention were incorporated, immediately to alter the traditional British process of judicial selection, which has so far raised no question of partisan party influence or executive tampering. If suspicion did begin to arise about judicial appointments, Britain could adopt other techniques of monitoring. As a matter of routine, the American Bar Association and other non-political professional groups publish their ratings of the legal ability of nominees to important courts, and Senators pay great attention to these ratings. The ABA has refused to endorse as qualified only one Supreme Court nominee in recent years—Judge Bork—but it has discouraged other judicial nominations by giving candidates relatively low ratings. If necessary, a committee with similar functions could be constituted in Britain (or could constitute itself) consisting of the officers from time to time of professional associations, law school deans or heads of faculties, and representatives of public interest legal groups. Such a group could call attention not only to doubtful appointees, but to other lawyers well-qualified according to traditional tests who were being passed over.

It might now be said, however, that if judges had more power over legislation, the traditional methods and standards for choosing them should change to make the bench deliberately more representative of the diverse groups and cultures within the British community. That is, in some ways, an appealing suggestion. But I think it should be resisted, at least until it becomes clear that adequate diversity will not be produced by the changes in the legal profession that are already underway and that incorporation would accelerate. The British public's sense that judges are not politicians gives Britain an important advantage over many other nations in making constitutional rights work. That sense would be jeopardised by a system of appointment which treated judges as representatives of sections of the population, because any such system would suggest that constitutional law is only politics in a different place.

Questions and Comments

1. If, as Dworkin suggests, liberty is ill, how can politics produce a bill of rights that would cure the ailment? If politics can produce a bill of rights, would this suggest that the polity has recovered from its illness?

2. Is Dworkin's account of the possibility that adoption of a bill of rights would change the legal culture too utopian? Does it adequately consider the possibilities that adopting a bill of rights would unduly impair democratic vitality? Dworkin refers to polls showing strong public support for a bill of rights. What if in the future public opinion polls run against a bill of rights, or strongly in favor of legislation courts would invalidate under the Bill of Rights? Dworkin suggests that the British constitution could change through public mobilization and debate over a bill of rights, which could entrench a bill of rights. If a later public mobilization resulted in a statute declaring the bill of rights capable of modification by ordinary legislation, would it follow that the "constitution" had again changed?

3. Do you agree with Zander that if judges were consistently to interpret a Bill of Rights to benefit "the strong against the weak it is certain that sooner or later the Bill of Rights would be scrapped"?

Mark Tushnet, *Living with a Bill of Rights*, in Understanding Human Rights (Connor Gearty and Adam Tomkins eds., 1995)

[Taking off from the debate in the U.K. over a judicially enforceable and entrenched bill of rights, Tushnet argues against their adoption, on the grounds that they are likely to have relatively conservative effects on political outcomes. He considers two different kinds of effects: the legitimation of intrusive government practices if they are approved under an entrenched constitution, and the obstruction of other government practices, e.g. wealth redistribution, campaign finance reform, that progressives might desire.]

. . . [A] nation with an entrenched and judicially enforceable bill of rights is not necessarily better off than a nation without one. By definition, entrenched bills of rights impede legislatures as they attempt to respond to changing social, economic and political circumstances. And, by definition, judicially enforceable bills of rights are enforced by an institution staffed by people with legal training whose specifically legal culture inevitably affects the way in which the bill of rights is interpreted.

Often, those who advocate and those who oppose adopting a bill of rights for the UK describe potentialities and possibilities: a bill of rights *might* do some good, advocates say; the judges who interpret the bill of rights *might* construe it to impose an undesirable rigidity and conservatism on legislation. Cast in such forms, the arguments are essentially unanswerable. What one would like to know are the relative chances of one or the other outcome.

I doubt that there is any assured method of determining those chances. Still, examining the experience in the USA with an entrenched and judicially enforceable bill of rights may be illuminating. That experience is probably the world's most extensive, and the reputation of the US Bill of Rights is quite high. In addition, the legal cultures of the USA and the UK are both based on the common law. That makes it more likely that a bill of rights in the UK would be enforced through the ordinary courts, as in the USA, rather than through the more political institutions [such as the French Constitutional Council] that provid[e] the main alternative model for enforcement of constitutional rights....

My general thesis, stated broadly, is that, if adopted today, an entrenched bill of rights enforced by a judiciary like that in the UK is likely to have a *relatively conservative* effect on political outcomes. I have inserted temporal and geographical qualifications in this formulation deliberately, because I do not want to be taken as arguing that there is something inherent in the concept of an entrenched bill of rights that makes it conservative. I do believe, however, that in the modern era those bills of rights that are likely to be adopted and enforced by the judiciaries in place at the time the bills are adopted will have a particular conservative form.[4]

. . .

...[P]rogressives may hope that by adopting a bill of rights they will encourage courts to intervene against repressive forces more readily than the courts would in the absence of a bill of rights. So, for example, if a bill of rights contains express guarantees of procedural protections against certain forms of police investigation that were common before the bill of rights was adopted, progressives might hope that courts would enforce those guarantees and thereby limit the activities of the police.

That hope might be realized, of course, but it also might be defeated. Deferring to the asserted expertise of the police and the perceived requirements of law and order, judges might interpret the new guarantees so that they do not restrict police activities. So, for example, in the USA the Fourth Amendment to the Constitution bars police from conducting "unreasonable" searches, but the Supreme Court has been willing to stamp nearly every troublesome form of police activity as either not a search or not unreasonable. Oddly enough, the Court has made the law in this area nearly unintelligible because—apparently out of concern that it has to take the Constitution seriously at least occasionally—it sometimes invalidates police practices that hardly seem bothersome. For example, the Supreme Court found a constitutional violation when police officers, lawfully present in a suspect's apartment, moved his stereo equipment slightly to check its serial number: it would have been all right if the police had been able to see the number without touching the stereo, but moving it shifted their inspection over the line.[5]

4. Things might be different if, in the sort of regime transformation we have recently seen elsewhere in Europe, there were a wholesale replacement of judges, but even in those countries that has proved hard to accomplish. The experience over the next decade in South Africa may prove quite instructive on these matters.

5. *Arizona v. Hicks,* 480 U.S. 321 (1987).

And yet, when more troublesome activities are involved, the Court has approved. The most notable example recently is *Florida v. Bostick*, in which the Supreme Court held that the Fourth Amendment was not violated by a police practice of "asking permission" of everyone on a bus to allow a search of their possessions. Anyone who objected, the Court said, could readily refuse the "request" and get off the bus. Because they could avoid being searched—or even answering the request for permission to search—by leaving the bus, they were not seized within the meaning of the Fourth Amendment: this notwithstanding the facts, obvious to everyone, that getting off the bus meant not taking the trip, that bus transportation is a preferred means of transit for the relatively poor, and that these so-called consent searches were targeted at racial minorities.

As troubling as this sort of decision is—and the examples could be multiplied, drawing from experience not only in the USA but also with the European Court of Human Rights—it is not what I want to focus on. For, in one sense, this sort of political outcome cannot be *attributed* to the bill of rights. Arguably, progressives are no worse off with a bill of rights than they were without one: in both situations the police are allowed to search—*without* a bill of rights because there are no judicially enforced limits on what they can do, and *with* a bill of rights because what they have done is found to be consistent with the bill of rights' guarantees.[7] Yet it is at least *possible* that, as a practical political matter, there is a difference between a decision saying that the police can do whatever they want because we do not have a bill of rights, and one saying that the police activity was consistent with the bill of rights we have. The latter decision might send a signal to the public—or to informed observers—not merely that the police activity was not prohibited, but that it was quite all right.[8]

Conceptually, the world of political activities in a system regulated by a bill of rights consists of three categories: actions that are unconstitutional, actions that are merely permissible under the bill of rights, and actions that are affirmatively desirable (and constitutionally permitted). A decision finding no violation of the bill of rights merely says, again on the conceptual level, that the activity does not fall in the first category. But the bill of rights may come to have such an exalted status in the public mind that the distinction between the two other categories may become blurred. A court decision that an action is merely "not unconstitutional" may be understood by the public as a decision determining that the action is affirmatively desirable. In the USA at least, that confusion sometimes arises. When it does, the existence of the Bill of Rights has affirmatively contributed to a

---

7. Of course, there may be limits on what the police can do that result from deeply embedded cultural assumptions not embodied in law. A bill of rights is unnecessary to ensure that such limitations are respected.

8. In addition, the protections afforded by the bill of rights, such as they are, may displace other protections. Having found that a practice does not violate the bill of rights, judges may find it easier to say that it is authorized by statute, or consistent with the common law. Without a bill of rights, the judges might give more thought to the possibility that the common law bars the practice, or that it is not authorized by statute.

progressive defeat: it has not merely failed to alter the situation as it existed before the Bill of Rights was adopted.[9]

Thus far I have discussed the possibility that progressives might not get what they hope for from a bill of rights. More important, I think, is that progressives will get *more than* they hope for. That is, progressives may find that courts enforce the bill of rights to *restrict* what progressives might be able to accomplish through ordinary political means.

A signal of the difficulty is that, under current US constitutional law, at least some of the restrictions on racist speech in UK and European Union law might well be violations of our free speech provision as interpreted by the Supreme Court—or, at least, they would be subject to serious constitutional challenges that would take a long time, and much expense, to resolve.[10] Many progressives in the USA and elsewhere regard such restrictions as good public policy. Other progressives disagree, citing concerns about whether such restrictions actually reduce the amount of racist expression in a society. In the USA, the decentralized political system means that a huge number of public officials would be empowered to enforce such restrictions, and among that number there are surely those who would abuse the power. Whether adopting such restrictions would in fact advance progressive political interests is a quite complex matter. Whether framing the discussion of their wisdom as a matter of fundamental rights is a good thing is, for me, a simpler one. I would far prefer to have the discussion about these proposals conducted purely on the ground of policy: would they actually advance their proponents' goals, for example, or are they likely to entrench rather than displace existing power centres? The difficulty a bill of rights creates is that discussion can too easily get diverted from these basic policy questions into unproductive and contentious controversies about what the "First Amendment means".

But I must again emphasize that the examples that follow do not rest on anything *inherent* in the very idea of having a bill of rights. Much of the story is historically and institutionally contingent. So, for example, early in this century, and through most of the 1930s, the US Supreme Court interpreted the Constitution to limit what it called "labor laws pure and simple". These included general minimum wage and maximum hours laws,

---

9. This argument depends on the proposition that, without a bill of rights, a court decision allowing the challenged police activity would *not* be taken as an endorsement of the activity. I am inclined to accept that proposition, because in a world where everything is permitted, it is unclear to me how a specific decision to uphold a particular activity could be understood to endorse it; on this view it is only the possibility that *some* activities might not be permitted—a possibility that arises only in the presence of a bill of rights—that makes it possible for people to interpret a holding of "not unconstitutional" as a determination of affirmative desirability.

I would not want to push this too hard, though, because I know that in no non-totalitarian regime is it really the case that "everything is permitted" to the government. Statutes and administrative regulations limit what police and other authorities can do, and it may be that judicial holdings that a police activity did not violate some statute or regulation would be interpreted by the public as an endorsement of the activity.

10. For a discussion, see M. Matsuda, Public response to racist speech: considering the victim's story (1989) 87 *Michigan Law Review* 2320.

which the Court understood to be the result of a pure political struggle by organized labour to capture from employers some of the employers' profits. I do not believe that any country adopting a bill of rights today will find its constitutional court making precisely the same rulings. More recently, the US Supreme Court has begun to place limits on regulations that governments adopt to protect the environment, finding the regulations to be "takings" of private property for which compensation must be paid. I do not believe that any country adopting a bill of rights today, even one with a requirement that takings of property be compensated, would find its constitutional court following precisely the same course. I am concerned here with overall tendencies, and I do believe that under present circumstances there will in fact be a tendency in systems that adopt bills of rights in the near future to enforce them in ways that obstruct progressive political changes.

My main example involves [campaign finance reform, which] many constitutional scholars believe to be the most important question in contemporary constitutional law in the USA. . . . [C]ampaign finance reform is an important part of the progressive political agenda in the USA, and progressives believe that the Supreme Court's interpretation of the Constitution stands in the way of an effective system of such reform. . . . [P]rogressives might think that allowing private wealth to dominate the campaign finance process is particularly pernicious because, roughly speaking, if only those who cater to the wealthy are able to raise enough money to campaign effectively, it is quite unlikely that, once elected, those same people will do anything that would significantly reduce the disparities of wealth that progressives typically are concerned about.

Here, then, is an example of a constitutional provision that obstructs progressive change. And, notably, I have not been dealing with some minor aspect of a bill of rights. The US Supreme Court has interpreted the free speech provision to bar important aspects of campaign finance reforms. . . .

Of course one might respond to [this] exampl[e] by suggesting that, whatever was the case in the USA, *here* (or wherever) we can count on the courts to interpret a bill of rights more sensibly. It is not a bill of rights that is a bad idea for progressives; it is a badly interpreted bill of rights. How, though, can progressives ensure that the bill of rights will be interpreted well rather than badly?

We might deal with the kinds of examples I have given in a number of ways. The bill of rights might itself provide a guide to interpretation, encouraging judges to interpret it in a direction consistent with progressive political wishes. Whether judges protected against political control would consistently do that over the long term is, as discussed below, a complex question.

A second method would be to [provide] in a bill of rights that the constitutional protections it affords simply do not apply in certain situations. . . . But there is a deeper problem, which arises from the conception of a bill of rights as limiting government power.

... [M]y central exampl[e]—campaign finance ... involve[s] [a] situatio[n] in which free speech principles are said to *limit* the power of government to regulate private property. And, I believe, conceiving of bill of rights restrictions in that way is almost natural. The point of having a bill of rights, many people think, is precisely to ensure that those who have the concentrated power of a government in their hands do not abuse the rest of us: bills of rights, that is, are designed exactly to limit *government* power. In one standard terminology, bills of rights are negative guarantees, barring governments from doing things.

Those who favour campaign finance regulation.... believe that concentrated government power is not the only thing we need to worry about. They are concerned that those who have the concentrated power of wealth in their hands might abuse the rest of us at least as much as the government can. If bills of rights are directed only at the possibilities of abusing government power, they might not only *allow* private abuses of power to continue, but, as my examples suggest, they might affirmatively *protect* the holders of private power against efforts to regulate them....

The key to understanding the views of bills of rights solely as restrictions on government power is that they take the background distributions of power and wealth as settled, not attributable to exercises of government power, and therefore unchallengeable through constitutional litigation. When people use their wealth and power to speak, by making contributions to political campaigns or by investing in the mass media, they are not, on this view, exercising public power and therefore are not subject to the controls that a bill of rights places on government power.

... [T]o deal with the problem posed by bills of rights that are conceptualized solely as restrictions on the exercise of government power[s] [o]ne strategy is represented in the various efforts, spread throughout the world, to ensure that "social charter" provisions are written into the constitution as well: guarantees of a minimum standard of subsistence, of housing and jobs, and the like....

I have serious doubts about whether modern constitutions are likely to adopt ... social charter provisions....

There is a standard argument against constitutionalizing affirmative rights. Consider a constitutional provision guaranteeing each able-bodied person a right to a job. Many critics of such provisions, and some supporters, argue that no government can actually implement such a right, considering the fiscal constraints that governments are under. So, the argument goes, no court can realistically enforce that guarantee. Then, however, consider what might happen. Suppose the court says that the affirmative right is merely an exhortation, stating a policy that elected legislatures should do their best to carry out but not creating an entitlement that courts will enforce as they enforce other legal entitlements. This creates two sets of constitutional rights, the "real" ones the courts enforce, and the "fake" ones they do not.

Having two sets of constitutional rights is a problem, for a number of reasons. First, if people believe that the affirmative rights are really important, and observe that they are not being enforced, they may conclude that the bill of rights as a whole really is not worth much. As I understand it, this was a widespread popular reaction to the constitutions of eastern Europe and the former Soviet Union. Second, those who would like to abuse government power will say, "Well, why should we treat the negative restrictions on our power differently from the affirmative rights? All we have to do to comply with the bill of affirmative rights is to do our best, so all we ought to have to do to comply with the bill of negative rights is to do our best as well—and that is what the challenged practice is." That is, treating affirmative rights as exhortations opens the way to treating negative guarantees as mere exhortations as well. All this leads people, including those who find the idea of affirmative rights attractive, to conclude that bills of rights ought not to include affirmative rights. . . .

Another set of reasons for my scepticism about bills of rights arises from a certain parochialism, but one that I think is likely to have some influence on the adoption of bills of rights in the modern era. I have little doubt but that the US experience with enforcing a bill of rights is widely regarded as the most successful example of bill of rights enforcement in the world. Nations that have recently adopted bills of rights typically emulate at least some aspects of US constitutional jurisprudence.

Now, if courts enforcing bills of rights elsewhere look to the US for guidance, they will find all the problems I have identified: a scepticism about the capacity of courts to enforce affirmative rights, coupled with a relatively vigorous sense that courts can and should enforce negative rights. That, however, is a formula for the frustration of progressive efforts to modify, through government action, the effects of existing distributions of wealth and power. This problem might be exacerbated by some aspects of what I call the legal-judicial culture. Here I have in mind the general cast of mind that a judge brings to the task of enforcing a written bill of rights. I want to distinguish between two ways of interpreting a bill of rights, which I call formalist and instrumentalist.

Formalists treat a bill of rights as ordinary, though supreme, law. They interpret it just as they would interpret any other legal document: primarily with an eye to its text, its structure, and the background against which it was adopted. They are relatively inattentive to the evils at which it was directed, although they do not disregard them. Instrumentalists, in contrast, pay most attention to those evils; in resolving a question of constitutional interpretation, instrumentalists will ask which of the competing interpretive alternatives is more likely to advance the purposes that the provision at issue is supposed to promote.

Instrumentalism and formalism pose different problems for bills of rights. Roughly speaking, the risk of instrumentalism is that it will fall to the pressures of the moment: precisely the same reasons that led legislatures to adopt constitutionally questionable acts—which seemed like good reasons for the legislature—will seem good enough reasons to believe that the purposes of the bill of rights are best served by interpreting the bill of rights to allow the legislature to do what seems sensible enough.[30] And the risk of formalism is that it will degenerate into an apparently purposeless enforcement of restrictions on government power to no apparent good end—or, even worse, that it will become the vehicle that obstructionist judges use to impede the enforcement of programmes that they simply disagree with.

These difficulties are more likely to appear over an extended period than they are in the immediate aftermath of the adoption of a bill of rights. I have little doubt that, immediately after a bill of rights is adopted, people will get pretty much what they expected from it: some restrictions on government action they had not had before, some impetus to government action that had been lacking earlier. That, however, should not lead us to conclude that these effects are attributable to the bill of rights itself.

After all, a bill of rights is always adopted as part of—and as the result of—a political mobilization. The people who advocate its adoption do so because they expect it to yield some results. And, ordinarily, it will. The results may occur because they are clearly written into the bill of rights. Or they may occur when judges take interpretative instructions written into the bill of rights seriously. Or, finally, they may occur when judges, interpreting ambiguous provisions, recall the political struggles that led to their adoption and, acting either as formalists or instrumentalists but in any event being prudent about these things, enforce the outcome of those political struggles.

The question, though, has to be: do these results occur because there is a bill of rights in place, or because there was a political mobilization that led to the adoption of the bill of rights? To put the point starkly, if you can pass a bill of rights that places substantial restrictions on police activity, why could you not have passed a statute that placed exactly those same restrictions on police activity?

Bruce Ackerman has recently suggested an answer, although I think that it is unsatisfactory.[31] Again roughly, Ackerman's response to my sceptical question is something like this: "Well, if you actually were able to mobilize people into political action, you might be able to get statutes that are effectively equivalent to the bill of rights that others are proposing. But, as a matter of sheer historical fact, it just turns out that you cannot get people to act politically in this way all that often. And it turns out that one way of getting people to mobilize—getting them to act politically—is to present their political choices to them in such fundamental packages as are represented by modern bills of rights."

---

30. As I noted earlier, the instrumentalist degeneration may not make society worse off than it would have been without a bill of rights. The instrumentalist degeneration means that courts approve what legislatures have done, just as they would in the absence of a bill of rights.

31. B. Ackerman, *We The People* (Cambridge, MA, 1991).

The idea here, then, is that there may not be a significant conceptual difference between passing a bill of rights and passing a statute, but there is a real political difference. The claim is that mobilizing around a platform of "We Need a Bill of Rights" is more likely to energize the people in a progressive direction than mobilizing around a platform of "Get the Police Under Control". In the USA, Shiffrin points out, campus radicals got things going at least in part by mobilizing what they called the Free Speech Movement, rather than the "Fight the Multiversity Movement"....

... [T]he political case for using "Enact a Bill of Rights" as a platform may be crucially dependent on the weak party structure that exists in the USA. If political parties had more coherent substantive platforms, perhaps "Elect Us" would do just as well in getting reforms adopted.

There is, however, a second question. Even if a political movement focused on entrenching a bill of rights is the only method of securing the rights presently available, what are the long-term effects of entrenching a bill of rights? Of course, precisely because the questions ask for speculation about effects over decades or even longer, they cannot be answered definitively. The US experience suggests, however, that the risks of both formalist and instrumentalist degeneration are not trivial.

Perhaps whatever enthusiasm there is for adopting a bill of rights in the UK results from the perception that the party system is not as coherent as it has been. If so, the "Enact a Bill of Rights" platform may be a decent substitute. It is not, however, a platform to lead progressives into the promised land.

Questions and Comments

1.   As Bogdanor and other British scholars describe it, the British constitution depends primarily on the "good faith" of those who "work it." Compare Learned Hand (a well-known and highly-regarded judge on the U.S. Court of Appeals for the Second Circuit): "A society so riven that the spirit of moderation is gone no court can save; a society where that spirit flourishes, no court need save; and in a society which evades its responsibilities by thrusting upon the courts the nurture of that spirit, that spirit in the end will perish." L. Hand, *The Contribution of an Independent Judiciary to Civilization*, in The Spirit Of Liberty 155, 164 (I. Dilliard ed. 1960), quoted in Stone, Seidman, Sunstein & Tushnet, Constitutional Law 71 (2d ed. 1991).

2.   Dworkin's arguments for a British Bill of Rights differ from Zander's primarily insofar as Dworkin emphasizes the relationship between law and culture. He perceives a decline in the culture of civil liberty in Britain, and argues that the process of instituting a Bill of Rights, together with the effects of such an enacted Bill of Rights, would help to restore the culture of liberty. Is Dworkin's argument in tension with, or consistent with, Judge Hand's observation above?

3. Zander and Dworkin address the primary opponent of a British Bill of Rights, J.A. G. Griffiths, some of whose arguments are echoed in Tushnet. What is the source of Griffith's and Tushnet's skepticism? How would Zander and Dworkin respond, particularly to the claim that a judicially enforceable bill of rights could, to the extent it were interpreted to permit, e.g., intrusive government conduct in criminal investigations, affirmatively worsen the environment for civil liberties than would otherwise exist without the bill of rights?

4. Does Tushnet's argument adequately answer Dworkin's point that judges, "armed with a Bill of Rights," cannot "wreck" but can merely "disappoint" a nation? How convincing is Dworkin's argument that judges' upholding laws (that some would regard as violating constitutional rights) leaves the polity no worse off than it would be without a Bill of Rights? Consider, in this regard, Korematsu v. United States, 323 U.S. 214 (1944). The Court there upheld Korematsu's conviction for refusing to leave his home to be moved to a "relocation center" under executive and military orders excluding persons of Japanese descent (including U.S. citizens) from a sizable area on the West Coast during World War II. Acknowledging that "legal restrictions which curtail the civil rights of a single racial group are immediately suspect," the Court nonetheless upheld the conviction, concluding that it was within "the war power of Congress and the Executive to exclude those of Japanese ancestry from the West Coast war area at the time they did." Because "[t]here was evidence of disloyalty on the part of some, the military authorities considered that the need for action was great, and the time was short," the exclusion order, in the Court's view, had "a definite and close relationship to the prevention of espionage and sabotage."

Justice Jackson, in dissent, wrote,

It would be impractical and dangerous idealism to expect or insist that each specific military command in an area of probable operations will conform to conventional tests of constitutionality. When an area is so beset that it must be put under military control at all, the paramount consideration is that its measures be successful, rather than legal. . . .

But if we cannot confine military expedients by the Constitution, neither would I distort the Constitution to approve all that the military may deem expedient. That is what the Court appears to be doing. . . .

Much is said of the danger to liberty from the Army program for deporting and detaining these citizens of Japanese extraction. But a judicial construction of the due process clause that will sustain this order is a far more subtle blow to liberty than the promulgation of the order itself. A military order, however unconstitutional, is not apt to last longer than the military emergency. . . . But once a judicial opinion rationalizes such an order to show that it conforms to the Constitution, or rather rationalizes the Constitution to show that the Constitution sanctions such an order, the Court for all time has validated the principle of racial discrimination in criminal procedure and of transplanting American citizens. The principle then lies about like a loaded weapon ready for the hand of any authority that can bring forward a plausible claim of an urgent need . . . .

Korematsu has not been deployed as the "loaded weapon" described by Justice Jackson. Instead, the majority's decision has been widely and harshly criticized. See Report of the Commission on Wartime Relocation and Internment of Civilians, Personal Justice Denied (originally published 1982, 1983; republished 1997); see also Korematsu v. United States, 584 F.Supp. 1406 (S.D.Cal.1984) (granting writ of coram nobis to vacate the conviction); Hirabayashi v. United States, 828 F.2d 591 (9th Cir.1987) (same). Do *Korematsu* and its aftermath support Dworkin's or Tushnet's claims about the legitimation effects of judicial review?

5. Consider the possibility that subconstitutional law—whether it be administrative law principles such as ultra vires rules requiring clear legislative authorization for actions that trench on human rights, or other similar statutory interpretation principles—might accomplish much that proponents of bills of rights seek to achieve. Consider, also, whether an independent court system is not required in order for such subconstitutional law to have this effect.

6. For a different perspective on the effects of judicial review, consider the argument suggested by Vivian Hart, *Righting wrongs: The normality of constitutional politics*, in Constitutionalism, Democracy and Sovereignty: American and European Perspectives 45 (Richard Bellamy ed., 1996)—that constitutional review may provide greater long-run benefits even when courts in the short run invalidate legislation. Drawing on the experience with minimum wage legislation in Great Britain and the United States, Hart argues that reformers in the United States had to engage in "creative search for new legally *and* politically acceptable ways forward" when their initial proposals were thwarted by the courts. Ultimately, she argues, their efforts produced more substantial political support for minimum wage laws than existed in Great Britain. There the laws were enacted quickly but were administered by specialist boards that had little independent political support. Consider, however, the possibility that the search for reforms that the courts would find constitutionally acceptable might distort or transform the reformers' initial vision, so that the statutes that are ultimately enacted and upheld embody a different program from the ones reformers originally sought. See Chapters VI, VII below (discussing Stone and Mandel).

7. For competing perspectives on the possible effects of incorporating judicially enforceable economic and social welfare rights as well as "negative" rights concerning political and civil liberties in constitutions, see below Chapter XII.

B.   CONSTITUTIONALISM WITHOUT ENTRENCHMENT?

Although discussion of constitutionalism is often closely tied to the idea that the constitution is "entrenched," that is, harder to change than ordinary law, a recurrent problem is the relationship between entrenching basic rules for society, on the one hand, and enhancing self-government and democratic decisionmaking, on the other. One approach is to provide, as many constitutions do, for the methods by which the constitution can be amended. In the U.S., an amendment is permitted only upon completion of supermajority requirements both in Congress and in the states: an amendment must be proposed, either by 2/3 of each House of Congress or by a convention called at the request of the legislatures of 2/3 of the states, and then the proposed amendment must be approved by the legislatures of or conventions in 3/4 of the states. This makes the U.S. constitution one of the most deeply entrenched. In Britain, as discussed above, the "constitution" is not formally entrenched by law. In Canada, under the 1982 Constitution Act, constitutional change can occur in several ways, depending on the subject matter: Generally, the constitution can be amended by resolutions of the Senate and House of Commons, and agreement by resolution of the legislatures of at least 2/3 of the provinces that also have in aggregate at least 50% of the population of all the provinces. Amendments that derogate from the legislative powers or rights of provincial governments require the consent of the provincial legislature to be effective in a province. Certain amendments require unanimous consent of the provinces, including amendments to the representation of the provinces in the House of Commons, the composition of the Supreme Court of Canada and amendments of the amending procedure. And Parliament alone can make amendments to the constitution that affect the executive government of Canada, or the Senate or the House (in some cases without the Senate's consent). Canada's Constitution Act, 1982, §§ 38, 41, 42, 44.

In the search for a balance between the stability supposed to be provided by an entrenched "constitution" and the flexibility to respond to changes over time, formal amendment of the Constitution itself is only one of many mechanisms of adjustment. Some nations have constitutions that specifically authorize legislative overrides of constitutional provisions. Canada's "notwithstanding clause" is the best known of these.

Canada's Charter—its constitution—provides that legislative majorities in the provinces, or in the national government, can "override" some of the Charter's guarantees of individual rights (free speech, for example, though not the right to vote.)[a] These overrides can last for no longer than five years, though they are renewable. (Note that legislative elections in Canada must occur at least once in any five year period). Consider whether the override provision solves the "problem" of entrenchment. Should the U.S. consider adopting something similar?

Mark Tushnet argues below that the apparent advantages of the override provision are illusory, and that its defects reflect the very unre-

---

a. Can. Const. (Constitution Act, 1982) pt. I (Canadian Charter of Rights and Freedoms), § 33 ("Parliament or the legislature of a province may expressly declare in an Act of Parliament or of the legislature ... that the Act or a provision thereof shall operate notwithstanding a provision included in" the Charter's rights and freedoms, with certain limited exceptions.)

solved compromises out of which it was born; he expresses pessimism on the capacity of such mechanisms to mediate the entrenchment problem. Consider whether a 14 year time span is adequate to evaluate the function played by such a provision, or whether Tushnet draws too broad a conclusion from particular developments in Canada.

Some aspects of U.S. constitutional law—flexible interpretation over time,[b] requirements for legislative 'clear statements' where legislation would raise serious constitutional questions,[c] or the doctrine of Katzenbach v. Morgan that Congress can, within limits, prohibit behavior that the Court has found not to violate the 14th amendment—can be seen as devices to engage legislatures in a dialogue with courts over the meaning of the Constitution. These approaches can thus be understood as efforts to mediate the problems of "entrenchment," problems that appear particularly acute as the polity moves further away in time from a consensus on how constitutional provisions should be interpreted to govern particular situations.

---

1. Legislative Override in Canada

Mark Tushnet, *Policy Distortion and Democratic Debilitation: Comparative Illumination of the Countermajoritarian Difficulty,* 94 Mich. L. Rev. 245 (1995)

[One problem with entrenching constitutional provisions, addressed by Mark Tushnet in this essay, is that of "democratic debilitation"—that is, "when the public and their democratically elected representatives cease to formulate and discuss constitutional norms, instead relying on the courts to address constitutional problems." This, in turn, may diminish public attachment to constitutional norms and may deprive courts of the benefit of public and legislative views on constitutional matters. Tushnet argues that the Section 33 override provisions of the Canadian Charter, despite their apparent appeal, have not provided a solution to the debilitative effects of entrenchment.

The origins of Section 33, quoted in note a above, lay in Prime Minister Pierre Trudeau's effort to fully "patriate" the Canadian Constitution—that

---

b. Given provisions for formal amendment in most constitutions, why not simply have a rule that a constitution means what the appropriate court says it means, with corrections through the amending process? Consider these responses: (1) The amending process may be too difficult to use to address important but technical issues; (2) the amending process may open things up too broadly and be too destabilizing; (3) reluctance to use the amending process would, absent other mechanisms for flexibility, give courts too much power. Could these objections be met by making it easier to amend a constitution? Would that be preferable to oth-er mechanisms, such as flexible judicial interpretation or legislative overrides?

c. See Gregory v. Ashcroft, 501 U.S. 452 (1991) (Congress would be presumed, absent very clear statement, not to impose obligation on state that would change the balance of federal-state power; thus, provisions of federal Age Discrimination in Employment Act that applied to state employees would not be construed to apply to state court judges and such judges were within statutory exception for elected officials or "appointee[s] on the policymaking level").

is, to have a system in which all questions concerning Canada's constitution would be finally resolved in Canada, without the need to obtain review or agreement by Britain. In response to provincial opposition to what was seen as a plan for aggrandizing national authority, the Supreme Court of Canada concluded that "as a matter of law the national government could request patriation without the consent of the provinces," but it also found that "doing so without a substantial—though not unanimous—measure of provincial consent would violate an apparently nonlegal constitutional convention."

Provincial leaders, concerned about whether amendments to the proposed Constitution would require unanimous consent from the provinces, were also reluctant to endorse the proposed bill of rights until, as Tushnet describes, "Saskatchewan's premier, a social democrat influenced by the traditional hostility toward entrenched bills of rights in the European and especially British left," suggested a legislative override provision. Trudeau accepted this, subject to a 5 year limit, thus "allaying enough concerns so that the Charter was adopted in 1982, although Quebec refused to accede to it at least in part because section 33 did not apply to language rights. . . . [T]he political setting in which section 33 developed meant that its theoretical underpinnings were not well-developed."]

* * *

As a textual matter, section 33 lent itself to a narrow reading. Two limitations immediately suggest themselves. First, in a system in which judicial review is routine, one might naturally read the clause to require that legislative overrides be retrospective. That is, the clause could be read to allow an override only with respect to a legislative provision that the courts had already held to be inconsistent with the Charter's rights-protecting provisions. Otherwise, the textual argument goes, the legislative provision does not operate "notwithstanding" the Charter's other provisions; where there is no prior declaration of unconstitutionality, the legislative provision operates, so far as the legislature knows, in a manner entirely consistent with the Charter.

Second, the clause rather naturally reads as if legislative overrides must be discrete. That is, in a single statute, a legislature can override only with respect to provisions of *that* very statute. The clause, after all, says that the legislature may declare "in *an* Act . . . that *the* Act . . . shall operate notwithstanding."

Further, these narrow readings seem to be consistent with the proposition that section 33 was designed to accommodate entrenched rights and parliamentary supremacy. The narrow construction would mean that [in Roger Tassé's words,] "the legislative decision to enact an override clause is taken with full knowledge at the facts, thereby encouraging public discussion of the issues raised by the use of such a clause." The public would know, that is, that its legislature was about to deprive it or some part of it of entrenched rights, and as a result, political opposition to overriding those rights or political support for the group to be disadvantaged might be mobilized. As Paul Weiler put it, "[i]n a society sufficiently enamored of fundamental rights to enshrine them in its constitution, invocation of the *non obstante* [notwithstanding] phrase is guaranteed to produce a lot of political flak." ...

The narrow interpretation of section 33 links the entrenched rights directly to the political process. Consider the implications of interpreting section 33 to require targeted and retrospective overrides, in the senses described [above]. A proposal to invoke section 33 would be tied to a single enactment, thus drawing public attention to the fact that the legislature proposed to enact a statute notwithstanding the individual rights provisions of the Charter. Further, the proposal would be a reaction to an authoritative decision specifying that its predecessor enactment did indeed violate one of those provisions.

Court invalidation of a proposal on the grounds that it violates entrenched rights creates important political considerations. Analysis of whether a statute violates Charter rights proceeds in two steps. First, the court must decide whether the statute constitutes a limitation on a protected right. If it does, the court must then decide whether the limitation is "demonstrably justified in a free and democratic society." That is, judicial invalidation implies that the court has concluded that the limitation is *not* demonstrably justified in a free and democratic society.

What does a proposal to override such an invalidation imply? It may be helpful to identify three possibilities. First, is *bolstering:* The legislature may attempt to bolster its prior enactment by providing a better "demonstration" of the statute's justification. It may, for example, compile a more extensive investigative record, attempting to provide the demonstration the court requires. Second, is *disagreement on justification:* The legislature may express its disagreement with the court's assessment of the adequacy of the already available demonstration. It may contend that the court failed to give proper weight to the considerations the court itself identified and that when those considerations are given appropriate weight, the enactment is demonstrably justified. Third, is *disagreement on democracy:* The legislature may express its disagreement with the court's characterization of what a "free and democratic" society is. That is, the legislature may agree that, given the court's characterization of a free and democratic society, the enactment is indeed not demonstrably justified, but it may conclude that the court's characterization was erroneous.

In all three situations, the public through its representatives has the opportunity to engage in a focused discussion of the characteristics of a free and democratic society. On this account, section 33 allows judicial review to coexist with majoritarian decisionmaking in a way that contributes to enhancing the public's understanding of democratic values and constitutional norms.

In addition, the mere existence of the section 33 power may strengthen judicial review. Michael Mandel, a severe critic of the Charter on the ground that it puts into legal form—and into the hands of lawyers— controversies that ought to be handled openly through politics, reported the comments of the clause's critics who begrudgingly acknowledged that "governments can be 'thrown out' for exercising" their powers under the clause and that invoking the clause "will be a red flag for opposition parties and the press . . . [which] will make it difficult for government to override the Charter." Or, as phrased more generously by John Whyte, it "means, first, that what were once political problems have been transformed into legal problems but, second, that when political interests are sufficiently compelling these issues can revert to being resolved through political choice."

A Charter enthusiast, in contrast, pointed out that the process has two faces. "It is probably true," according to Dale Gibson, "that a government would be taking a considerable political risk by introducing, in normal circumstances," overriding legislation, but the existence of the clause, particularly when it is interpreted narrowly, might strengthen judicial review by alleviating judicial concern about acting contrary to majority views. "[J]udges may safely assume . . . that their vigilance will not frustrate the democratic process," and they might therefore invalidate legislation more readily than they would if they knew that the only response available to the public was a constitutional amendment. For one who admires the political process but who thinks that some rights deserve greater protection than they are likely to get in ordinary politics, section 33 might seem to be a useful way of setting in motion an extraordinary sort of majoritarian politics in which the claims of the community and the claims of rights would both get their due.

Suppose a court invalidates a statute, and a legislative effort to override the decision fails. . . .[151] The political culture then can take the failure to override as an indication of popular support for the court decision. To adapt a phrase from Thomas Reed Powell, the failure to invoke section 33 is a way in which the people can be "silently vocal"; their inaction demonstrates their agreement with the court's decision. Without the section 33 power, the people have no way to express that agreement.

Section 33 thus appears to offer a method of creating a system of more-than-minimal judicial review while eliminating or reducing the problem of democratic debilitation. Section 33, on this account, might actually invigorate majoritarian politics by providing the people and their representatives with a way of engaging in direct discussion of constitutional values in the ordinary course of legislation. . . .

---

151. Peter Russell observes that after the Canadian Supreme Court invalidated the nation's criminal prohibitions on abortion, "the aroused and losing group went immediately to the parliamentary lobby to press for legislative redress" but there was no "inclination on the part of the politicians to use the override." Peter H. Russell, *Canadian Constraints on Judicialization from Without,* 15 Intl. Pol. Sci. Rev. 165, 171 (1994). Instead, the government proposed to amend the abortion statutes in a manner it contended would make them consistent with the court's decision. It was not able to muster sufficient support for the new statute, however, and the court decision stood unmodified. [See Chapter I, p. 113 above.]

As legislation and litigation proceeded under the Charter, section 33 did not overcome the problem of democratic debilitation in a system with vigorous judicial review. The retrospective interpretation, which, as I have argued, would have served to focus public debate on the invalidated policy and potential legislative override, was the first element of the limited interpretation to go. A lower court held that the Charter's guarantee of freedom of association protected the right of public employees to engage in a strike. Before the country's highest court had expressed its view on that question, the Saskatchewan government enacted a back-to-work law ending a strike and used section 33 to insulate the law from judicial review. According to Mandel, the government suffered no adverse political consequences from using section 33 in this prospective manner.

The reaction of the Quebec legislature, however, posed a more serious threat to the narrow interpretation of the clause. Nine weeks after the Charter was proclaimed, the Quebec parliament enacted a general "notwithstanding" statute. The technique was ingenious. The legislature repealed every statute in force and immediately reenacted every one, along with a statute that invoked section 33 with respect to them all and indeed with respect to all statutes that it would thereafter adopt. The validity of this approach to section 33 came before the Supreme Court of Canada in *Ford v. Quebec (Attorney General).*[165]

The case involved one of the province's more sweeping attempts to preserve its Francophone cultural identity: a statute, known throughout the litigation as Bill 101, requiring that all public signs and commercial advertising in the province be only in French. The Quebec legislature included an override provision in the statute when it was reenacted after the Charter's adoption. Businesses that wanted to post signs in French and English challenged the statute; Ford, the lead appellant in the Canadian Supreme Court case, ran a shop in which she sold wool and was told that she had to take down her sign that said "Laine—Wool" because it violated the statute. The challenge rested on Charter provisions guaranteeing the right of free expression, but such a provision would be unavailing if the override provision was upheld.

The plaintiff businesses argued that the override provision "did not sufficiently specify the guaranteed rights or freedoms which the legislation intended to override." Like other "clear statement" arguments, this one ultimately rested on the idea that when a legislature does something as serious as overriding otherwise applicable constitutional protections, it ought to follow procedures that are sufficient to bring into public view precisely what is at stake. In that way, the argument goes, the constitutional protections will be overridden only after the public duly considers precisely what is at stake.

The Supreme Court of Canada, however, rejected this argument, saying that section 33 "lays down requirements of form only." The court said that requiring the statute to specify the constitutional provisions to be

---

165. [1998] 2 S.C.R. 712 (Can.).

overridden would amount to a substantive requirement. It suggested that requiring specificity would be unreasonable in situations, likely to be common, where the legislature could not reasonably be expected to anticipate which of the Charter's many provisions might be invoked to challenge its statute.

Because of some procedural aspects of the case that are irrelevant to my discussion here,[169] the court went on to hold that the sign law did indeed violate constitutional guarantees of free expression: freedom to use one's language was encompassed by the guarantee of free expression. The court's analysis made it clear that the sign law would be unconstitutional under the Charter once the override's five-year term expired in February 1989, less than two months from the date the *Ford* decision was announced. Three days after the *Ford* decision was announced, Quebec premier Robert Bourassa announced his government's intention to introduce a new sign law that would incorporate a notwithstanding provision.

The Canadian Supreme Court's decision would appear to be inconsistent with one part of the political account of section 33 that I have offered, under which the point of the clause is to make it politically costly to override constitutional protections. Under the *Ford* decision, rather routine and indeed quite unfocused "notwithstanding" statutes satisfy the requirements of section 33. At this point, though, it is important to distinguish between the political costs of using the section 33 power and the political costs of adopting the substantive legislation. Even without constitutional protections of entrenched rights, some legislative proposals will be controversial on the merits because they infringe on the values that entrenched rights *would* protect if the system had such rights. If we add entrenched rights *and* the override power to the system, the same controversies will arise on the merits. The argument for section 33 is that legislatures will incur some special costs, beyond those associated with adopting controversial legislation, when they use their power to override constitutional protections. Anglophones in Quebec and elsewhere in Canada objected to the sign law on the merits; indeed, three anglophone members of the Quebec government resigned to protest the new law. The degree to which the protests were directed at section 33's invocation, as opposed to the statute's substance, though, is unclear.

Does the *Ford* interpretation of section 33 undermine the argument that special political costs will attend the invocation of an override? Perhaps it does. A provincial legislature is unlikely to incur serious marginal costs within the province for using its section 33 power because it can do so with the ordinary low-level public attention that occurs in connection

---

169. The court held that the sign law violated § 3 of the Quebec Charter of Human Rights and Freedoms, which states that "[e]very person is the possessor of the fundamental freedoms, including freedom of conscience ... [and] freedom of expression." R.S.Q., ch. C-12, § 3 (1988) (Can.). The parallel provision of the Canadian Charter provides that "everyone has the following fundamental freedoms: ... freedom of thought, belief, opinion and expression...." Can. Const. (Constitution Act, 1982) Pt. I (Canadian Charter of Rights and Freedoms), § 2(B). An override provision did not protect the sign law against the provisions of the Quebec Charter.

with every statute. Overriding court decisions may have been particularly easy in Quebec, which had its own judicially enforceable bill of rights nearly equivalent to the Charter. The people of Quebec thus could get almost all of the benefits of a bill of rights without feeling that one had been imposed on them from the outside.

Outside the province, however, the situation differed. Quebec's expansive use of the notwithstanding clause did draw public attention to the significance of overriding constitutional protections. It was not the Quebec public that noticed, though; it was the public in the rest of Canada.

Here the political context of the *Ford* litigation plays a central role. As the *Ford* litigation proceeded through the courts, the Canadian national government attempted to reach a new accommodation with Quebec in what was known as the Meech Lake Accord, the key—though in many ways largely symbolic—provision of which would have embedded in the Canadian constitution the statement that Quebec "constitutes within Canada a distinct society." By the time of the *Ford* decision, the national government, Quebec's legislature, and all but two provincial parliaments had agreed to the Accord's provisions.

Some thought that under the "distinct society" clause, Quebec's sign law would be constitutional without regard to the section 33 power. Under these circumstances, Quebec's use of a blanket override power, even if permissible under *Ford*, somehow seemed like a dirty pool. To those elsewhere in Canada who already had misgivings about the Meech Lake Accord, the override was just another example of Quebec's overreaching. The *Ford* decision and Bourassa's response affirmed that concern, and "from this point on 'there was virtually no chance that the Meech Lake Accord would be ratified.'" [P. Russell]

The Canadian provinces failed to adopt the Meech Lake Accord for many reasons, but one was surely that people elsewhere in Canada thought Quebec was pushing too hard for special rights. To the extent that its legislature's use of a blanket override was inconsistent with the expectations about how the power to override would be used, as expressed in the debates over the Charter's adoption, Quebec may indeed have incurred a distinctive political cost attributable to its use of override power, independent of the costs incurred by adopting the sign law itself. According to one observer, the invocation of section 33 "undermined political support for the Meech Lake Accord outside Quebec, dealing a fatal blow to its chances for ratification."[182] . . .

Perhaps the outcome of the experience with section 33 was predictable, as positive political theory might suggest. Consider the sequence of decisions in constitutional adjudication. (1) A legislature adopts a statute by a majority vote. (2) A court decides that the statute is unconstitutional. (3) Some process—constitutional amendment or a section 33 override—is available to override the court decision. If the decision-rule at stage 3 is no

---

182. [Christopher P. Manfredi, Judicial Power and the Charter: Canada and the Par-   adox of Liberal Constitutionalism 202 (1993)].

different from the decision-rule at stage 1 and—importantly—if there are no changes in preferences in the legislature between stage 1 and stage 3, we should expect that at the end of the day, the statute will be in effect; the same majority that enacted the statute in the first place will override the court's decision.

In contrast, if repudiating a judicial decision requires more than a majority, we can expect that some statutes that received a majority vote would not survive the supermajority requirement. The U.S. experience with anti-flag-burning statutes seems an obvious example. Substantial majorities in both the House of Representatives and the Senate voted for the Flag Protection Act of 1989. A proposal to amend the Constitution to override the Supreme Court's invalidation of the Act secured more than a majority but less than the required two-thirds vote in the House of Representatives.

On closer examination, the flag-burning episode illuminates the Canadian experience as well. After the Supreme Court's first flag-burning decision, the Republican administration proposed, not a new statute, but a constitutional amendment. The Democratic congressional leadership did not want to put the amendment to a vote and proposed a new statute as an alternative, holding out the possibility of a vote on an amendment if that proved necessary. Most observers believed that the Democratic leadership opposed a constitutional amendment but feared that, in the heat of the moment, it might receive the required supermajority. Apparently, the leadership hoped that by the time the Supreme Court rejected their proposed statute, if it did, passions would have cooled and the legislature would not adopt a constitutional amendment.

Why would the passage of time matter so much, though? Similarly, how could proponents of section 33 believe that it could make a difference in outcomes, given that a majority could enact a statute overriding a court decision? The answer is obvious: in both situations, proponents hoped that preferences would change between stage 1 and stage 3 . . . .

. . . [One] source of preference change worth noting [is] the court decision itself. Certainly proponents of section 33 believed that a court decision might educate the public in constitutional values, persuading some who supported the statute that it was indeed inconsistent with their commitment to more fundamental values. Similarly, in the flag-burning episode, the Democratic leadership may have hoped that passions would cool, not in the sense that other issues would displace flag burning, but rather in the sense that the public would reflect on the values of speech and nationhood at stake and would conclude that their sense of national unity could be sustained without infringing so severely on the values promoted by the First Amendment. Here the change in preferences between stage 1 and stage 3 occurs *because of* what happens at stage 2.

There are, of course, other techniques of educating the public . . . .

Perhaps the language issue in Quebec was so important that even an endogenous preference change induced by the Canadian Supreme Court's decision invalidating the sign law could not shift enough votes to prevent enactment of a statute overriding the decision. Or, perhaps, the ability of a constitutional court to educate is smaller than proponents of section 33 and other techniques of public education through judicial decision have hoped....

The story of the Canadian constitution continues to unfold and the precise arrangements that Quebec and what I have so far called the rest of Canada—but which might end up being called Canada *tout court*—will reach remain to be determined. After the Meech Lake Accord failed, Canada's prime minister attempted to blame its failure not on Quebec but on section 33 itself, the "fatal flaw of 1981, which reduces your individual rights and mine." No longer seen as a way of avoiding problems of democratic debilitation, section 33 came to be seen as inconsistent with the idea of judicially enforceable constitutional rights. Like the power to regulate jurisdiction in the U.S. Constitution, section 33 may no longer be a significant part of the Canadian Charter. Something like a convention against its use may have emerged, precisely because the political costs of invoking the power turned out to be too great. This is analogous to the convention in the United States against using the power to regulate jurisdiction to insulate significant constitutional issues from judicial review. Effectively, then, the Canadian system may include only the possibility of amending the constitution by a supermajority, not the possibility of majoritarian control of constitutional interpretation.

The reason for the apparent emergence of the convention in Canada may shed some light on broader issues at constitution making and the problem of democratic debilitation. As one commentator put it, "Canadians experienced a use of the notwithstanding clause that they found outrageous before they experienced a Supreme Court decision of equivalent political unpopularity."[197]...

... [T]he political setting in which section 33 emerged may mean that it did not become an element of Canadians' constitutional consciousness at all. It was inserted into the Charter as part of a compromise that papered over arguably the most important issue in Canadian constitutional life—the status of Quebec. It was discredited, at least in part, because it was used in connection with precisely that issue.

Canada's experience with the notwithstanding clause suggests that institutions designed to address the problem of democratic debilitation by making it possible to deal with that problem visibly may fail *because* of their visibility. The characteristic that makes the institution attractive may make it impossible to function effectively. As Paul Weiler has noted,

> By taking the initiative ... before the Charter had time to put down roots in Quebec political life, and by making use of the *non obstante* formula a matter of legislative routine, the Parti Québécois [which enacted Bill 101, the initial sign law] was able to remove the political hazard of invoking the formula for particular laws, thus frustrating the entire scheme of the Charter.

197. [Manfredi at 204].

This "accident of history" in the Canadian experience actually may be built into the institution of a *non obstante* formula in the following way.

Constitutions in general consist of institutional arrangements designed to provide a framework for the resolution of political issues over the long term. The outlines of those long-term issues may be only dimly discerned when the constitution is adopted, and constitution makers do their best to put in place institutions that will do the best that can be done with whatever problems arise. Simultaneously, however, constitution makers face ordinary political problems in the present day, and frequently they may have to address those problems as a condition for securing the constitution's adoption. They have three strategies for dealing with such pressing problems. First, they may simply resolve them, adopting the kind of political solution already available through the use of existing political institutions. Second, they may relegate those problems to the new institutions they create, hoping that those institutions will do no worse in resolving them than the preexisting institutions did. Third, they may defer their resolution, in the hope that time will make those particular problems go away.

Consider here ... the U.S. Constitution....Article I, Section 9 bars Congress from exercising its enumerated power over interstate and foreign commerce to prohibit "the migration or importation of such persons as any of the States now existing shall think proper to admit" until 1808 but authorizes Congress to impose a tax of up to $10 on each such person. This compromise represents the third approach. The controversy over congressional regulation of the interstate slave trade was deferred until 1808, by which time, the Framers apparently hoped, the issue would have changed so that it could be resolved through ordinary political means.

If the deferred issue does not change, as the slavery issue did not, or if it ends up not being deferred at all, as the language issue in Canada was not, the compromises on that issue, designed to secure adoption of the constitution, may well fail. A provision like a notwithstanding clause makes the overall process particularly vulnerable in dealing with those pressing political problems that have, under the second approach, simply been relegated to the new institutions. Such a provision allows politicians to take the issue *away from* the new institutions, leaving them to be handled by the process that did not resolve it in a satisfactory way before the constitutional revision....

If, however, the use of the notwithstanding power were delayed, a second problem would arise. As time passes, the notwithstanding clause or parallel institutions designed to address the problem of democratic debilitation would become less visible....[I]nvoking them might seem contrary to understandings of constitutionalism that would have developed during the period when these institutions were not utilized.

The preceding suggestions may be too bleak, however. In Canada, the drafters of the Charter explicitly embedded ordinary politics within their fundamental constitutional arrangements, expecting that ordinary politics would interact with constitutional concerns in ways that would ultimately benefit the society overall. In one dimension, their expectations seem to have been defeated. Section 33 did affect the politics of constitutional arrangements, though not in the way the drafters seem to have anticipated. Yet, the text and history of section 33 would have supported an interpretation different from the one the Canadian Supreme Court gave it in *Ford*. Had the court chosen a different interpretation, the course of constitutional development might have been different as well.

In another dimension, the drafters' expectations have neither been fulfilled nor defeated because the ultimate constitutional settlement involving Quebec remains to be reached. When it is, we may be able to decide whether section 33 and its attempt to make ordinary politics and constitutional law penetrate each other did indeed benefit the society.

That examination will then raise once again Thayer's concern about the impact of judicial review. He may have been correct in believing that more-than-minimal judicial review contributed to democratic debilitation. That is different from establishing that minimal judicial review will revitalize or enhance constitutional consciousness among the public. For, in the presence of minimal judicial review, the public and its representatives may simply enact what they know they can get away with doing. That is not a prospect that Thayer would have found encouraging. . . .

. . . Despite claims made for it, the Canadian notwithstanding clause did not prove to be a means by which democratic discussion of constitutional norms could be promoted within a system also authorizing judicial review. Thayer's alternative, of course, was to give judicial review a very narrow scope.

Minimal judicial review does, almost by definition, provide a wider domain within which legislators and the public have an opportunity to articulate constitutional norms. To the extent that they seize that opportunity, minimal judicial review is a successful response to the problem of democratic debilitation. It is not an entirely adequate response to the problem of policy distortion, however. If courts rarely invalidate statutes, they provide few focal points that might lead to bargaining breakdowns. But, by itself, giving judicial review a minimal scope cannot reduce misunderstanding as a source of policy distortion.

Experience with constitutions in other countries suggests that Thayer and Bickel were right in identifying problems associated with judicial review and not merely with the forms of U.S. constitutionalism. For democratic constitutionalists, the problems Thayer and Bickel placed on the agenda remain serious ones, perhaps so serious that their solution— giving judicial review a minimal scope—deserves renewed attention.

Questions and Comments

1. Tushnet suggests that the convention against invoking Section 33 that appears to have arisen in the wake of the sign controversy shows that

Section 33 has failed to provide a meaningful mechanism for democratic participation in decisionmaking about constitutional norms. Quebec's use of the override might be seen as evidence of democratic vigor in Quebec. Would a convention against the use of the override elsewhere in Canada be evidence of a lack of democratic vigor there? Or might the failure to use the override reflect a consensus on the norms expressed in the 1982 Charter, even when the Canadian Supreme Court invokes those norms to invalidate legislation supported, at least initially, by legislative majorities? The Supreme Court has invalidated restrictions on tobacco advertising, RJR–MacDonald Inc v. Canada (Attorney General) (1995), [1995] 3 S.C.R. 199 (declaring void large portions of the Tobacco Products Control Act of 1988, forbidding commercial advertisements of tobacco products in Canada). There was no serious effort to invoke the Section 33 procedure in response. Should that fact be taken as evidence of consensus on underlying norms and their application to specific cases, or as evidence of the failure of the Section 33 procedure as a mechanism for encouraging democratic participation in constitutional norm development?

2. "Override" provisions, or provisions for relatively easy amendment of constitutions, can be viewed both as positive contributions to democracy or as subversions of constitutionalism. For example, the Weimar Constitution of Germany (1919) was an attempt to establish democratic, representative parliamentary government. Several of its provisions have been criticized as contributing to the rise to power of the Nazis, including Art. 48, under which the president could exercise emergency legislative powers, and Art. 76, under which the Constitution itself could be amended by a 2/3 vote in the legislature. According to Professor Currie, under a practice known as "breaking the constitution," the legislature could, by passing a law by a two-thirds vote, effectively change the Constitution without an explicit amendment. David P. Currie, The Constitution of the Federal Republic of Germany 7 (1994). The "law" by which executive and legislative powers were transferred to Hitler in 1933 was enacted by the two-thirds vote contemplated by Art. 76 (a vote that may well have been influenced by the fact that the legislature was surrounded by storm troopers and that Communist Party deputies had been arrested to prevent their participation). See Peter Caldwell, *National Socialism and Constitutional Law: Carl Schmitt, Otto Koellreutter and the Debate over the Nature of the Nazi State*, 1933–37, 16 Cardozo L. Rev. 399 (1995); Gregory H. Fox & Georg Nolte, *Intolerant Democracies*, 36 Harv. Int'l L. J. 1, 10–13 (1995).

Does the connection between the Nazi consolidation of power and the provisions of Art. 76 suggest that legislative overrides of constitutions are generally not desirable? Does the practice of enacting laws by a two-thirds vote that can, without explicitly saying so, trump or change the constitution, differ from practice in the U.K.? In Israel? In the Canadian Section 33 override procedure (which, you will recall, is limited to 5 years)?

3. The quorum requirement for amending the constitution under Art. 76 of the Weimar Constitution was that 2/3 of the deputies had to be present; two-thirds of those present had to approve the amendment. As a result, amendments could occur with an affirmative vote of less than half the elected members. Would a differently designed procedure—for example, one requiring a two-thirds vote of the entire legislature—have different effects?[d] Consider whether you can answer this question without thinking through these other questions: How much of a connection is there between the Nazi rise to power and the provisions of the Weimar Constitution? Obviously, many factors other than constitutional structure contributed to Hitler's ability to gain power.[e] Does this limit the usefulness of these materials in introducing you to questions about comparative constitutional law? Or is it useful to consider the effects of different constitutional decision structures, even if their impact is limited and even if different structural balances between entrenchment rules and procedures for change in or avoidance of constitutional requirements may be needed in different polities?

2. CONSTITUTIONAL ENTRENCHMENT AND LEGISLATIVE OVERRIDES IN THE U.S

While many might initially be tempted to agree with the assertion that the U.S. Congress cannot overrule the Supreme Court on issues of constitutional law, on reflection Congress can override the Supreme Court in at least one area: the "dormant" Commerce Clause. If the Court finds that a particular state regulation is inconsistent with Congress's Commerce Clause power, Congress can subsequently authorize that action through national legislation. Compare Philadelphia v. New Jersey, 437 U.S. 617 (1978) (dormant Commerce Clause prohibits state from excluding waste products from other states) with New York v. United States, 505 U.S. 144 (1992) (Congress constitutionally authorized states complying with federal requirements for disposal of nuclear waste to exclude from their states waste generated in noncomplying states). The Commerce Clause, in its dormant effects, is not interpreted as entrenching a particular regime of prohibited state action. For a broad argument that Congress has competence to "remove constitutional limits on state power if those limits stem solely from divisions of power within the federal system," see William

d. Compare the contemporary German Basic Law, art. 79(2), specifying that the Basic Law can be "amended only by a law expressly modifying or supplementing its text," and requiring that "[s]uch law must be carried by two thirds of the Members of the Bundestag and two thirds of the votes of the Bundesrat," a more rigorous requirement than two-thirds of those present. (Art. 79 also prohibits amendments affecting länder participation in the legislative process or the fundamental rights principles of the first 20 articles.)

e. Does use of the legal procedure for relatively easy amendment of the Weimar Constitution suggest that the facade of legality that this afforded was helpful to the Nazis' rise to and retention of power? For different perspectives, see Ingo Müller, Hitler's Justice: The Courts of the Third Reich (Deborah Lucas Schneider trans. 1991); David Luban, *A Report on the Legality of Evil: The Case of the Nazi Judges*, 61 Brook L. Rev. 1121, 1139 (1995).

Cohen, *Congressional Power to Validate Unconstitutional State Laws: A Forgotten Solution to an Old Enigma*, 35 Stan. L. Rev. 387, 388 (1983).

How would it affect constitutionalism in the U.S. if the U.S. constitution could be changed as easily, or almost as easily, as an ordinary law? Think about whether you might answer this question differently with respect to different topics addressed by the Constitution—for example, the "dormant" Commerce Clause limitations on state powers, as compared to separation of powers between the President and Congress, or the First Amendment. Think also about the role interpretation plays in U.S. constitutionalism, and how they would be affected by more ready amendability.

Consider Congress's power to implement a different view from that of the Court concerning the "individual rights" protecting provisions of the Bill of Rights. In *Katzenbach v. Morgan*, the Court upheld a federal law that forbids states from using literacy tests, a practice that the Court previously had held not to violate the federal Constitution. However, in *Boerne v. Flores* the Court retreated from an interpretation of *Morgan* that would recognize a power in Congress under Section 5 of the Fourteenth Amendment to disagree with the Court about the substantive meaning of individual rights provisions as a basis for restricting state and local governments.

Katzenbach v. Morgan
384 U.S. 641 (1966)

[In Lassiter v. Northampton Election Board, 360 U.S. 45 (1959), the Court rejected 14th and 15th amendment challenges to the facial validity of a South Carolina English-literacy requirement for voting. Six years later, during floor debate on the Voting Rights Act of 1965, the two Senators from New York and one representative from New York sponsored what became Section 4(e) of that Act, which provides that no person who has completed the sixth grade in a school in Puerto Rico should be denied the right to vote because of his or her inability to read or write English. The intended effect of this provision was to override a New York law requiring that voters be literate in English, in order to enfranchise several hundred thousands of citizens who had migrated from Puerto Rico to New York. The Court upheld Section 4(e) of the Voting Rights Act, over constitutional objections by the State of New York, as an exercise of Congress' power under Section 5 of the 14th Amendment.]

MR. JUSTICE BRENNAN delivered the opinion of the Court. . . .

The Attorney General of the State of New York argues that an exercise of congressional power under § 5 of the Fourteenth Amendment that prohibits the enforcement of a state law can only be sustained if the judicial branch determines that the state law is prohibited by the provisions of the Amendment that Congress sought to enforce. More specifically, he urges that § 4(e) cannot be sustained as appropriate legislation to enforce the Equal Protection Clause unless the judiciary decides—even with the guidance of a congressional judgment—that the application of the English literacy requirement prohibited by § 4(e) is forbidden by the Equal Protection Clause itself. We disagree. Neither the language nor history of § 5 supports such a construction.[7] As was said with regard to § 5 in Ex parte Com. of Virginia, 100 U.S. 339, 345, "It is the power of Congress which has been enlarged. Congress is authorized to enforce the prohibitions by appropriate legislation. Some legislation is contemplated to make the amendments fully effective." A construction of § 5 that would require a judicial determination that the enforcement of the state law precluded by Congress violated the Amendment, as a condition of sustaining the congressional enactment, would depreciate both congressional resourcefulness and congressional responsibility for implementing the Amendment.[8] It would confine the legislative power in this context to the insignificant role of abrogating only those state laws that the judicial branch was prepared to adjudge unconstitutional, or of merely informing the judgment of the judiciary by particularizing the "majestic generalities" of § 1 of the Amendment.

Thus our task in this case is not to determine whether the New York English literacy requirement as applied to deny the right to vote to a person who successfully completed the sixth grade in a Puerto Rican school violates the Equal Protection Clause. Accordingly, our decision in *Lassiter* ... is inapposite. *Lassiter* did not present the question before us here: Without regard to whether the judiciary would find that the Equal Protection Clause itself nullifies New York's English literacy requirement as so applied, could Congress prohibit the enforcement of the state law by legislating under § 5 of the Fourteenth Amendment? In answering this question, our task is limited to determining whether such legislation is, as required by § 5, appropriate legislation to enforce the Equal Protection Clause.

By including § 5 the draftsmen sought to grant to Congress, by a specific provision applicable to the Fourteenth Amendment, the same broad powers expressed in the Necessary and Proper Clause, Art. I, § 8, cl. 18. The classic formulation of the reach of those powers was established by Chief Justice Marshall in McCulloch v. Maryland, 4 Wheat. 316, 421:

---

7. For the historical evidence suggesting that the sponsors and supporters of the Amendment were primarily interested in augmenting the power of Congress, rather than the judiciary, see generally Frantz, Congressional Power to Enforce the Fourteenth Amendment Against Private Acts, 73 Yale L.J. 1353, 1356-1357; Harris, The Quest for Equality, 33-56 (1960); tenBroek, The Antislavery Origins of the Fourteenth Amendment 187-217 (1951).

8. Senator Howard, in introducing the proposed Amendment to the Senate, described § 5 as "a direct affirmative delegation of power to Congress," and added:

"It casts upon Congress the responsibility of seeing to it, for the future, that all the sections of the amendment are carried out in good faith, and that no State infringes the rights of persons or property. I look upon this clause as indispensable for the reason that it thus imposes upon Congress this power and this duty. It enables Congress, in case the States shall enact laws in conflict with the principles of the amendment, to correct that legislation by a formal congressional enactment." Cong. Globe, 39th Cong., 1st Sess., 2766, 2768 (1866).

This statement of § 5's purpose was not questioned by anyone in the course of the debate.

"Let the end be legitimate, let it be within the scope of the constitution, and all means which are appropriate, which are plainly adapted to that end, which are not prohibited, but consist with the letter and spirit of the constitution, are constitutional."

Ex parte Com. of Virginia, 100 U.S., at 345-346, decided 12 years after the adoption of the Fourteenth Amendment, held that congressional power under § 5 had this same broad scope. . . . Thus the McCulloch v. Maryland standard is the measure of what constitutes "appropriate legislation" under § 5 of the Fourteenth Amendment. Correctly viewed, § 5 is a positive grant of legislative power authorizing Congress to exercise its discretion in determining whether and what legislation is needed to secure the guarantees of the Fourteenth Amendment.

We therefore proceed to the consideration whether § 4(e) is "appropriate legislation" to enforce the Equal Protection Clause, that is, under the McCulloch v. Maryland standard, whether § 4(e) may be regarded as an enactment to enforce the Equal Protection Clause, whether it is "plainly adapted to that end" and whether it is not prohibited by but is consistent with "the letter and spirit of the constitution."[10]

There can be no doubt that § 4(e) may be regarded as an enactment to enforce the Equal Protection Clause. Congress explicitly declared that it enacted § 4(e) "to secure the rights under the fourteenth amendment of persons educated in American-flag schools in which the predominant classroom language was other than English." The persons referred to include those who have migrated from the Commonwealth of Puerto Rico to New York and who have been denied the right to vote because of their inability to read and write English, and the Fourteenth Amendment rights referred to include those emanating from the Equal Protection Clause. More specifically, § 4(e) may be viewed as a measure to secure for the Puerto Rican community residing in New York nondiscriminatory treatment by government—both in the imposition of voting qualifications and the provision or administration of governmental services, such as public schools, public housing and law enforcement.

Section 4(e) may be readily seen as "plainly adapted" to furthering these aims of the Equal Protection Clause. The practical effect of § 4(e) is to prohibit New York from denying the right to vote to large segments of its Puerto Rican community. Congress has thus prohibited the State from denying to that community the right that is "preservative of all rights." Yick Wo v. Hopkins, 118 U.S. 356, 370. This enhanced political power will be helpful in gaining nondiscriminatory treatment in public services for the

---

10. Contrary to the suggestion of the dissent, § 5 does not grant Congress power to exercise discretion in the other direction and to enact "statutes so as in effect to dilute equal protection and due process decisions of this Court." We emphasize that Congress' power under § 5 is limited to adopting measures to enforce the guarantees of the Amendment; § 5 grants Congress no power to restrict, abrogate, or dilute these guarantees. Thus, for example, an enactment authorizing the States to establish racially segregated systems of education would not be—as required by § 5—a measure "to enforce" the Equal Protection Clause since that clause of its own force prohibits such state laws.

entire Puerto Rican community. Section 4(e) thereby enables the Puerto Rican minority better to obtain "perfect equality of civil rights and the equal protection of the laws." It was well within congressional authority to say that this need of the Puerto Rican minority for the vote warranted federal intrusion upon any state interests served by the English literacy requirement. It was for Congress, as the branch that made this judgment, to assess and weigh the various conflicting considerations—the risk or pervasiveness of the discrimination in governmental services, the effectiveness of eliminating the state restriction on the right to vote as a means of dealing with the evil, the adequacy or availability of alternative remedies, and the nature and significance of the state interests that would be affected by the nullification of the English literacy requirement as applied to residents who have successfully completed the sixth grade in a Puerto Rican school. It is not for us to review the congressional resolution of these factors. It is enough that we be able to perceive a basis upon which the Congress might resolve the conflict as it did. . . .

The result is no different if we confine our inquiry to the question whether § 4(e) was merely legislation aimed at the elimination of an invidious discrimination in establishing voter qualifications. We are told that New York's English literacy requirement originated in the desire to provide an incentive for non-English speaking immigrants to learn the English language and in order to assure the intelligent exercise of the franchise. Yet Congress might well have questioned, in light of the many exemptions provided, and some evidence suggesting that prejudice played a prominent role in the enactment of the requirement, whether these were actually the interests being served. Congress might have also questioned whether denial of a right deemed so precious and fundamental in our society was a necessary or appropriate means of encouraging persons to learn English, or of furthering the goal of an intelligent exercise of the franchise. Finally, Congress might well have concluded that as a means of furthering the intelligent exercise of the franchise, an ability to read or understand Spanish is as effective as ability to read English for those to whom Spanish-language newspapers and Spanish-language radio and television programs are available to inform them of election issues and governmental affairs. Since Congress undertook to legislate so as to preclude the enforcement of the state law, and did so in the context of a general appraisal of literacy requirements for voting to which it brought a specially informed legislative competence,[17] it was Congress' prerogative to weigh these competing considerations. Here again, it is enough that we perceive a basis upon which Congress might predicate a judgment that the application of New York's English literacy requirement to deny the right to vote to a

---

17. See, e.g., 111 Cong.Rec. 11061 (Senator Long of Louisiana and Senator Young), 11064 (Senator Holland), drawing on their experience with voters literate in a language other than English. See also an affidavit from Representative Willis of Louisiana expressing the view that on the basis of his thirty years' personal experience in politics he has "formed a definite opinion that French-speaking voters who are illiterate in English generally have as clear a grasp of the issues and an understanding of the candidates, as do people who read and write the English language."

person with a sixth grade education in Puerto Rican schools in which the language of instruction was other than English constituted an invidious discrimination in violation of the Equal Protection Clause....

Mr. Justice Harlan, whom Mr. Justice Stewart joins, dissenting.

Worthy as its purposes may be thought by many, I do not see how § 4(e) of the Voting Rights Act of 1965, can be sustained except at the sacrifice of fundamentals in the American constitutional system—the separation between the legislative and judicial function and the boundaries between federal and state political authority. By the same token I think that the validity of New York's literacy test, a question which the Court considers only in the context of the federal statute, must be upheld....

I . . .

In 1959, in *Lassiter*, this Court dealt with substantially the same question and resolved it unanimously in favor of the legitimacy of a state literacy qualification. . . .

. . . [T]he same interests recounted in *Lassiter* indubitably point toward upholding the rationality of the New York voting test. . . .

. . . New York may justifiably want its voters to be able to understand candidates directly rather than through possibly imprecise translations or summaries reported in a limited number of Spanish news media. . . . Given the State's legitimate concern with promoting and safeguarding the intelligent use of the ballot, and given also New York's long experience with the process of integrating non-English-speaking residents into the mainstream of American life, I do not see how it can be said that this qualification for suffrage is unconstitutional . . . .

II . . .

The pivotal question . . . is what effect the added factor of a congressional enactment has on the straight equal protection argument dealt with [in *Lassiter*]. The Court declares that since § 5 of the Fourteenth Amendment gives to the Congress power to "enforce" the prohibitions of the Amendment by "appropriate" legislation, the test for judicial review of any congressional determination in this area is simply one of rationality; that is, in effect, was Congress acting rationally in declaring that the New York statute is irrational? Although § 5 most certainly does give to the Congress wide powers in the field of devising remedial legislation to effectuate the Amendment's prohibition on arbitrary state action, Ex parte Virginia, 100 U.S. 339. I believe the Court has confused the issue of how much enforcement power Congress possesses under § 5 with the distinct issue of what questions are appropriate for congressional determination and what questions are essentially judicial in nature.

When recognized state violations of federal constitutional standards have occurred, Congress is of course empowered by § 5 to take appropriate remedial measures to redress and prevent the wrongs. But it is a judicial question whether the condition with which Congress has thus sought to deal is in truth an infringement of the Constitution, something that is the necessary prerequisite to bringing the § 5 power into play at all . . . .

. . . In State of South Carolina v. Katzenbach, 383 U.S. 301, decided earlier this Term, we held certain remedial sections of this Voting Rights Act of 1965 constitutional under the Fifteenth Amendment, which is directed against deprivations of the right to vote on account of race. In enacting those sections of the Voting Rights Act the Congress made a detailed investigation of various state practices that had been used to deprive Negroes of the franchise. In passing upon the remedial provisions, we reviewed first the "voluminous legislative history" as well as judicial precedents supporting the basic congressional finding that the clear commands of the Fifteenth Amendment had been infringed by various state subterfuges. Given the existence of the evil, we held the remedial steps taken by the legislature under the Enforcement Clause of the Fifteenth Amendment to be a justifiable exercise of congressional initiative.

Section 4(e), however, presents a significantly different type of congressional enactment. The question here is not whether the statute is appropriate remedial legislation to cure an established violation of a constitutional command, but whether there has in fact been an infringement of that constitutional command, that is, whether a particular state practice or, as here, a statute is so arbitrary or irrational as to offend the command of the Equal Protection Clause of the Fourteenth Amendment. That question is one for the judicial branch ultimately to determine. Were the rule otherwise, Congress would be able to qualify this Court's constitutional decisions under the Fourteenth and Fifteenth Amendments let alone those under other provisions of the Constitution, by resorting to congressional power under the Necessary and Proper Clause. . . .

I do not mean to suggest in what has been said that a legislative judgment of the type incorporated in § 4(e) is without any force whatsoever. Decisions on questions of equal protection and due process are based not on abstract logic, but on empirical foundations. To the extent "legislative facts" are relevant to a judicial determination, Congress is well equipped to investigate them, and such determinations are of course entitled to due respect. In State of South Carolina v. Katzenbach, such legislative findings were made to show that racial discrimination in voting was actually occurring. . . .

But no such factual data provide a legislative record supporting § 4(e).[9]

. . . Thus, we have here not a matter of giving deference to a congressional estimate, based on its determination of legislative facts, bearing upon

---

9. There were no committee hearings or reports referring to this section, which was introduced from the floor during debate on the full Voting Rights Act. See 111 Cong.Rec. 11027, 15666, 16234.

the validity vel non of a statute, but rather what can at most be called a legislative announcement that Congress believes a state law to entail an unconstitutional deprivation of equal protection....

In assessing the deference we should give to this kind of congressional expression of policy, it is relevant that the judiciary has always given to congressional enactments a presumption of validity....[A]lthough it has been suggested that this Court should give somewhat more deference to Congress than to a state legislature,[10] such a simple weighing of presumptions is hardly a satisfying way of resolving a matter that touches the distribution of state and federal power in an area so sensitive as that of the regulation of the franchise....

To deny the effectiveness of this congressional enactment is not of course to disparage Congress' exertion of authority in the field of civil rights; it is simply to recognize that the Legislative Branch like the other branches of federal authority is subject to the governmental boundaries set by the Constitution. To hold, on this record, that § 4(e) overrides the New York literacy requirement seems to me tantamount to allowing the Fourteenth Amendment to swallow the State's constitutionally ordained primary authority in this field....

City of Boerne v. Flores

521 U.S. 507 (1997)

[In Employment Division v. Smith, 494 U.S. 872 (1990), the Court rejected "Free Exercise" of religion arguments against the constitutionality of applying an Oregon criminal law prohibiting possession of peyote to the religiously motivated use of peyote by members of the Native American Church. The Court said that if a prohibition of conduct is not designed to suppress religious conduct, but merely has the incidental effect of doing so, and is contained in an otherwise valid law of general applicability, no violation of the Free Exercise clause exists. It rejected application of its own earlier decisions suggesting that the government needed some compelling or important reason to burden, even incidentally, religiously motivated conduct.

In response to concerns generated by *Smith*, Congress passed the Religious Freedom Restoration Act.]

JUSTICE KENNEDY delivered the opinion of the Court, in which REHNQUIST, C.J., and STEVENS, THOMAS, and GINSBURG, JJ., joined, and in all [portions of which are reprinted here] SCALIA, J., joined.

A decision by local zoning authorities to deny a church a building permit was challenged under the Religious Freedom Restoration Act of

------

10. See Thayer, The Origin and Scope of the American Doctrine of Constitutional Law, 7 Harv. L. Rev. 129, 154-155 (1893).

1993 (RFRA), 107 Stat. 1488, 42 U.S.C. § 2000bb et seq. The case calls into question the authority of Congress to enact RFRA. We conclude the statute exceeds Congress' power....

II

Congress enacted RFRA in direct response to the Court's decision in Employment Div., Dept. of Human Resources of Ore. v. Smith, [in which] we considered a Free Exercise Clause claim brought by members of the Native American Church who were denied unemployment benefits when they lost their jobs because they had used peyote. Their practice was to ingest peyote for sacramental purposes, and they challenged an Oregon statute of general applicability which made use of the drug criminal. In evaluating the claim, we declined to apply the balancing test set forth in Sherbert v. Verner, 374 U.S. 398 (1963), under which we would have asked whether Oregon's prohibition substantially burdened a religious practice and, if it did, whether the burden was justified by a compelling government interest. We stated:

> "Government's ability to enforce generally applicable prohibitions of socially harmful conduct ... cannot depend on measuring the effects of a governmental action on a religious objector's spiritual development. To make an individual's obligation to obey such a law contingent upon the law's coincidence with his religious beliefs, except where the State's interest is 'compelling' ... contradicts both constitutional tradition and common sense."

The application of the *Sherbert* test, the *Smith* decision explained, would have produced an anomaly in the law, a constitutional right to ignore neutral laws of general applicability. The anomaly would have been accentuated, the Court reasoned, by the difficulty of determining whether a particular practice was central to an individual's religion. We explained, moreover, that it "is not within the judicial ken to question the centrality of particular beliefs or practices to a faith, or the validity of particular litigants' interpretations of those creeds." ...

Four members of the court disagreed. They argued the law placed a substantial burden on the Native American Church members so that it could be upheld only if the law served a compelling state interest and was narrowly tailored to achieve that end....

These points of constitutional interpretation were debated by Members of Congress in hearings and floor debates. Many criticized the Court's reasoning, and this disagreement resulted in the passage of RFRA. Congress announced:

> "(1) [T]he framers of the Constitution, recognizing free exercise of religion as an unalienable right, secured its protection in the First Amendment to the Constitution;

> "(2) laws 'neutral' toward religion may burden religious exercise as surely as laws intended to interfere with religious exercise;

"(3) governments should not substantially burden religious exercise without compelling justification;

"(4) in Employment Division v. Smith, 494 U.S. 872 (1990), the Supreme Court virtually eliminated the requirement that the government justify burdens on religious exercise imposed by laws neutral toward religion; and

"(5) the compelling interest test as set forth in prior Federal court rulings is a workable test for striking sensible balances between religious liberty and competing prior governmental interests."

The Act's stated purposes are:

"(1) to restore the compelling interest test as set forth in Sherbert v. Verner, 374 U.S. 398 (1963) and Wisconsin v. Yoder, 406 U.S. 205 (1972) and to guarantee its application in all cases where free exercise of religion is substantially burdened; and

"(2) to provide a claim or defense to persons whose religious exercise is substantially burdened by government."

RFRA prohibits "[g]overnment" from "substantially burden[ing]" a person's exercise of religion even if the burden results from a rule of general applicability unless the government can demonstrate the burden "(1) is in furtherance of a compelling governmental interest; and (2) is the least restrictive means of furthering that compelling governmental interest." The Act's mandate applies to any "branch, department, agency, instrumentality, and official (or other person acting under color of law) of the United States," as well as to any "State, or . . . subdivision of a State." The Act's universal coverage is confirmed in § 2000bb–3(a), under which RFRA "applies to all Federal and State law, and the implementation of that law, whether statutory or otherwise, and whether adopted before or after [RFRA's enactment]." . . .

III

A . . .

Congress relied on its Fourteenth Amendment enforcement power in enacting the most far reaching and substantial of RFRA's provisions, those which impose its requirements on the States. . . . The parties disagree over whether RFRA is a proper exercise of Congress' § 5 power. . . .

In defense of the Act respondent contends . . . [that] Congress . . . is only protecting by legislation one of the liberties guaranteed by the Fourteenth Amendment's Due Process Clause, the free exercise of religion, beyond what is necessary under *Smith* . . . [and that the] congressional decision to dispense with proof of deliberate or overt discrimination and instead concentrate on a law's effects accords with the settled understanding that § 5 includes the power to enact legislation designed to prevent as well as remedy constitutional violations. It is further contended that Congress' § 5 power is not limited to remedial or preventive legislation. . . .

...Legislation which deters or remedies constitutional violations can fall within the sweep of Congress' enforcement power even if in the process it prohibits conduct which is not itself unconstitutional and intrudes into "legislative spheres of autonomy previously reserved to the States." For example, the Court upheld a suspension of literacy tests and similar voting requirements under Congress' parallel power to enforce the provisions of the Fifteenth Amendment, see U.S. Const., Amdt. 15, § 2, as a measure to combat racial discrimination in voting, South Carolina v. Katzenbach, 383 U.S. 301, 308 (1966), despite the facial constitutionality of the tests under Lassiter v. Northampton County Bd. of Elections, 360 U.S. 45 (1959)....

Congress' power under § 5, however, extends only to "enforc[ing]" the provisions of the Fourteenth Amendment. The Court has described this power as "remedial," South Carolina v. Katzenbach, at 326. The design of the Amendment and the text of § 5 are inconsistent with the suggestion that Congress has the power to decree the substance of the Fourteenth Amendment's restrictions on the States. Legislation which alters the meaning of the Free Exercise Clause cannot be said to be enforcing the Clause. Congress does not enforce a constitutional right by changing what the right is. It has been given the power "to enforce," not the power to determine what constitutes a constitutional violation. Were it not so, what Congress would be enforcing would no longer be, in any meaningful sense, the "provisions of [the Fourteenth Amendment]."

While the line between measures that remedy or prevent unconstitutional actions and measures that make a substantive change in the governing law is not easy to discern, and Congress must have wide latitude in determining where it lies, the distinction exists and must be observed. There must be a congruence and proportionality between the injury to be prevented or remedied and the means adopted to that end. Lacking such a connection, legislation may become substantive in operation and effect. History and our case law support drawing the distinction, one apparent from the text of the Amendment....

Recent cases have continued to revolve around the question of whether § 5 legislation can be considered remedial. In South Carolina v. Katzenbach, we emphasized that "the constitutional propriety of [legislation adopted under the Enforcement Clause] must be judged with reference to the historical experience ... it reflects." There we upheld various provisions of the Voting Rights Act of 1965, finding them to be "remedies aimed at areas where voting discrimination has been most flagrant," and necessary to "banish the blight of racial discrimination in voting, which has infected the electoral process in parts of our country for nearly a century." We noted evidence in the record reflecting the subsisting and pervasive discriminatory—and therefore unconstitutional—use of literacy tests. The Act's new remedies, which used the administrative resources of the Federal Government, included the suspension of both literacy tests and, pending federal review, all new voting regulations in covered jurisdictions, as well as the assignment of federal examiners to list qualified applicants enabling those listed to vote. The new, unprecedented remedies were deemed necessary given the ineffectiveness of the existing voting rights laws, and the slow costly character of case-by-case litigation.

After South Carolina v. Katzenbach, the Court continued to acknowledge the necessity of using strong remedial and preventive measures to respond to the widespread and persisting deprivation of constitutional rights resulting from this country's history of racial discrimination. See ... Morgan, 384 U.S. at 656 (Congress had a factual basis to conclude that New York's literacy requirement "constituted an invidious discrimination in violation of the Equal Protection Clause")....

Any suggestion that Congress has a substantive, non-remedial power under the Fourteenth Amendment is not supported by our case law....

There is language in our opinion in Katzenbach v. Morgan which could be interpreted as acknowledging a power in Congress to enact legislation that expands the rights contained in § 1 of the Fourteenth Amendment. This is not a necessary interpretation, however, or even the best one.... The Court provided two related rationales for its conclusion that § 4(e) could "be viewed as a measure to secure for the Puerto Rican community residing in New York nondiscriminatory treatment by government." Under the first rationale, Congress could prohibit New York from denying the right to vote to large segments of its Puerto Rican community, in order to give Puerto Ricans "enhanced political power" that would be "helpful in gaining nondiscriminatory treatment in public services for the entire Puerto Rican community." Section 4(e) thus could be justified as a remedial measure to deal with "discrimination in governmental services." The second rationale, an alternative holding, did not address discrimination in the provision of public services but "discrimination in establishing voter qualifications." The Court perceived a factual basis on which Congress could have concluded that New York's literacy requirement "constituted an invidious discrimination in violation of the Equal Protection Clause." Both rationales for upholding § 4(e) rested on unconstitutional discrimination by New York and Congress' reasonable attempt to combat it....

If Congress could define its own powers by altering the Fourteenth Amendment's meaning, no longer would the Constitution be "superior paramount law, unchangeable by ordinary means." It would be "on a level with ordinary legislative acts, and, like other acts, ... alterable when the legislature shall please to alter it." Marbury v. Madison. Under this approach, it is difficult to conceive of a principle that would limit congressional power. Shifting legislative majorities could change the Constitution and effectively circumvent the difficult and detailed amendment process contained in Article V....

B   ...

[The Court concluded that RFRA could not be regarded as a proper exercise of remedial or preventive power, in part because the legislative record did not reveal current instances of intentional discrimination against the free exercise of religion.]

Regardless of the state of the legislative record, RFRA cannot be considered remedial, preventive legislation, if those terms are to have any meaning. RFRA is so out of proportion to a supposed remedial or preventive object that it cannot be understood as responsive to, or designed to prevent, unconstitutional behavior. It appears, instead, to attempt a substantive change in constitutional protections. Preventive measures prohibiting certain types of laws may be appropriate when there is reason to believe that many of the laws affected by the congressional enactment have a significant likelihood of being unconstitutional.... Remedial legislation under § 5 "should be adapted to the mischief and wrong which the [Fourteenth] Amendment was intended to provide against." Civil Rights Cases, [109 U.S. 3, 13 (1883)].

RFRA is not so confined. Sweeping coverage ensures its intrusion at every level of government, displacing laws and prohibiting official actions of almost every description and regardless of subject matter. RFRA's restrictions apply to every agency and official of the Federal, State, and local Governments....Any law is subject to challenge at any time by any individual who alleges a substantial burden on his or her free exercise of religion.

The reach and scope of RFRA distinguish it from other measures passed under Congress' enforcement power, even in the area of voting rights....[The court discussed termination provisions of some voting rights preclearance legislation]. This is not to say, of course, that § 5 legislation requires termination dates, geographic restrictions or egregious predicates. Where, however, a congressional enactment pervasively prohibits constitutional state action in an effort to remedy or to prevent unconstitutional state action, limitations of this kind tend to ensure Congress' means are proportionate to ends legitimate under § 5.

The stringent test RFRA demands of state laws reflects a lack of proportionality or congruence between the means adopted and the legitimate end to be achieved. If an objector can show a substantial burden on his free exercise, the State must demonstrate a compelling governmental interest and show that the law is the least restrictive means of furthering its interest. Claims that a law substantially burdens someone's exercise of religion will often be difficult to contest....Requiring a State to demonstrate a compelling interest and show that it has adopted the least restrictive means of achieving that interest is the most demanding test known to constitutional law....Laws valid under *Smith* would fall under RFRA without regard to whether they had the object of stifling or punishing free exercise. We make these observations not to reargue the position of the majority in *Smith* but to illustrate the substantive alteration of its holding attempted by RFRA. Even assuming RFRA would be interpreted in effect to mandate some lesser test, say one equivalent to intermediate scrutiny, the statute nevertheless would require searching judicial scrutiny of state law with the attendant likelihood of invalidation. This is a considerable congressional intrusion into the States' traditional prerogatives and general authority to regulate for the health and welfare of their citizens.

The substantial costs RFRA exacts, both in practical terms of imposing a heavy litigation burden on the States and in terms of curtailing their traditional general regulatory power, far exceed any pattern or practice of unconstitutional conduct under the Free Exercise Clause as interpreted in *Smith*. Simply put, RFRA is not designed to identify and counteract state laws likely to be unconstitutional because of their treatment of religion. In most cases, the state laws to which RFRA applies are not ones which will have been motivated by religious bigotry.... It is a reality of the modern regulatory state that numerous state laws, such as the zoning regulations at issue here, impose a substantial burden on a large class of individuals. When the exercise of religion has been burdened in an incidental way by a law of general application, it does not follow that the persons affected have been burdened any more than other citizens, let alone burdened because of their religious beliefs. In addition, the Act imposes in every case a least restrictive means requirement—a requirement that was not used in the pre-*Smith* jurisprudence RFRA purported to codify—which also indicates that the legislation is broader than is appropriate if the goal is to prevent and remedy constitutional violations.

When Congress acts within its sphere of power and responsibilities, it has not just the right but the duty to make its own informed judgment on the meaning and force of the Constitution. This has been clear from the early days of the Republic. In 1789, when a Member of the House of Representatives objected to a debate on the constitutionality of legislation based on the theory that "it would be officious" to consider the constitutionality of a measure that did not affect the House, James Madison explained that "it is incontrovertibly of as much importance to this branch of the Government as to any other, that the constitution should be preserved entire. It is our duty." 1 Annals of Congress 500 (1789). Were it otherwise, we would not afford Congress the presumption of validity its enactments now enjoy.

Our national experience teaches that the Constitution is preserved best when each part of the government respects both the Constitution and the proper actions and determinations of the other branches. When the Court has interpreted the Constitution, it has acted within the province of the Judicial Branch, which embraces the duty to say what the law is. Marbury v. Madison, 1 Cranch at 177. When the political branches of the Government act against the background of a judicial interpretation of the Constitution already issued, it must be understood that in later cases and controversies the Court will treat its precedents with the respect due them under settled principles, including stare decisis, and contrary expectations must be disappointed. RFRA was designed to control cases and controversies, such as the one before us; but as the provisions of the federal statute here invoked are beyond congressional authority, it is this Court's precedent, not RFRA, which must control.

... Broad as the power of Congress is under the Enforcement Clause of the Fourteenth Amendment, RFRA contradicts vital principles necessary to maintain separation of powers and the federal balance. The judgment of the Court of Appeals sustaining the Act's constitutionality is reversed.

[A concurring opinion of JUSTICE SCALIA, joined by JUSTICE STEVENS, a separate concurring opinion by JUSTICE STEVENS, and dissenting opinions of JUSTICES O'CONNOR, BREYER and SOUTER are omitted]

Questions and Comments

1. *Katzenbach v. Morgan* can be read to assert that Congress has special competence to determine what conduct violates section 1 of the 14th amendment, or, alternatively, that Congress has power under section 5 to prohibit conduct that does not itself violate section 1 but whose prohibition will help avoid other conduct that would violate section 1. *Boerne v. Flores* rejects the first, more "substantive" interpretation. Under *Boerne v. Flores*, does Congress still retain power to prohibit otherwise lawful state conduct in order to prevent the occurrence of conduct that the Court would agree violates section 1? What standard does *Boerne* articulate for such a "preventative" use of the enforcement power?

2. Professor Cohen has suggested a distinction between "congressional competence to make 'liberty' and 'federalism' judgments." William Cohen, *Congressional Power to Interpret Due Process and Equal Protection*, 27 Stan L. Rev. 603, 614 (1975).

> "A congressional judgment rejecting a judicial interpretation of the due process or equal protection clauses—an interpretation that had given the individual procedural or substantive protection from state and federal government alike—is entitled to no more deference than the identical decision of a state legislature. Congress is no more immune to momentary passions of the majority than are the state legislatures. But a congressional judgment resolving at the national level an issue that could—without constitutional objection—be decided in the same way at the state level, ought normally to be binding on the courts, since Congress presumably reflects a balance between both national and state interests and hence is better able to adjust such conflicts."

Cohen treats expansions of individual rights through congressional action under Section 5 of the 14th amendment as an exercise of Congress' "federalism" competence (since states would be free to adopt greater protection of individual rights than the Constitution requires), and treats congressional attempts to restrict individual rights under Section 5 as a prohibited effort by Congress to substitute its judgment for the Court's on "liberty" questions. Is this argument more or less persuasive than those offered by Justice Brennan in support of the one-way ratchet described in note 7 of *Katzenbach v. Morgan*?

3. Is the possibility of legislative override of constitutional decisions healthy, or detrimental, to the development of constitutional law? On what would your answer depend?

4. The scope of Congress' section 5 power has important implications for current constitutional controversies in the United States. The Court recently held that Congress lacks power under the Commerce Clause, or other article I powers, to authorize federal courts to hear claims against States for violations of federal law. In Seminole Tribe v. Florida, 517 U.S. 44 (1996) the Court held that the sovereign immunity of the states from suits in federal courts could not be overcome by Congress acting under Article I. At the same time, the Court appeared to reaffirm earlier decisions upholding Congress' power under section 5 of the 14th amendment to authorize federal courts to hear claims against states. Thus, it becomes increasingly important to identify precisely the source of Congress' power in connection with efforts, fairly widespread, to subject state governments to the same legal regimes as apply to private entities, e.g., private employers (under the Fair Labor Standards Act), private invaders of copyright and patent rights, or private violators of environmental laws.

5. Earlier in this chapter you were asked how it would affect the U.S. Constitution if it could be more easily amended. In thinking about this question, you may want to reflect on the experience of the states. The constitutions of states in the United States are more easily[f] and frequently amended[g] than is the federal constitution.

C.   CONSTITUTIONAL REVIEW WITHOUT A BILL OF RIGHTS

The Australian Constitution does not have a free speech provision, which was deliberately omitted by the Constitution's drafters. In the following case, the Australian High Court nonetheless invalidated national campaign finance legislation because of concerns related to free speech and representative government.

f. As to the procedures for amendment, in 17 states the state legislature may propose an amendment by a simple majority vote; if the amendment is ratified by voters by a majority vote, it becomes effective. In other states, a super-majority vote of the legislature is required, followed by approval by a majority vote at an election. Only in New Hampshire must the voters approve by a super-majority of two-thirds. Eighteen states provide for constitutional amendment through citizen initiatives, and more than 40 states provide in their constitutions for the calling of constitutional conventions to make changes. Interestingly, 14 state constitutions require a periodic popular vote, ranging from every 20 years to every 9 years, on whether to convene a constitutional convention. This information is based on Janice C. May, *State*

Constitutions and Constitutional Revision, 1990–91, in 29 The Book of the States 1992–93, pp. 2–26 (Council of State Governments, 1992–93) and research by Adam Lewis, Georgetown J.D. 1998, which we gratefully acknowledge.

g. As to frequency of amendment, May reports that in each of the four years ending in 1990, more than 40 states considered constitutional amendments proposed by their state legislatures. The total numbers of amendments considered in each of those years ranged from 246 to 197. The number of amendments adopted in each of those years ranged from 188 to 134. Between 67% and 75% of the amendments proposed during this time period were adopted. May at Table A.

Australian Capital Television Pty. Ltd. v. Commonwealth of Australia

(1992) 177 CLR 106 (High Court of Australia).

[This case is a constitutional challenge to Australia's campaign finance laws. Those laws prohibited televised political advertising, broadly defined, during an election period. Broadcasters were required to make free time available to political parties and candidates. Incumbent candidates and parties got automatic access to the free time slots, whereas challengers had to apply to a Tribunal for the slots.]

* * *

JUDGEMENT–1: MASON C.J. . . . .

14. The effect of [the statute] is, as the plaintiffs submit, to exclude the use of radio and television during election periods as a medium of political campaigning and even as a medium for the dissemination of political information, comment and argument and as a forum of discussion except in so far as [it] . . . permits the broadcasting of news and current affairs items and talkback radio programmes; . . . permits free election broadcasts; and . . . permits the broadcasting of policy launches. . . .

16. The consequence is that Pt IIID severely impairs the freedoms previously enjoyed by citizens to discuss public and political affairs and to criticize federal institutions. Part IIID impairs those freedoms by restricting the broadcasters' freedom to broadcast and by restricting the access of political parties, groups, candidates and persons generally to express views with respect to public and political affairs on radio and television.

17. The Commonwealth's response is that the evident and principal purpose of Pt IIID is to safeguard the integrity of the political system by reducing, if not eliminating, pressure on political parties and candidates to raise substantial sums of money in order to engage in political campaigning on television and radio, a pressure which renders them vulnerable to corruption and to undue influence by those who donate to political campaign funds. . . .

[Chief Justice Mason describes experience in other constitutional systems, pointing out that paid political advertising is not permitted in the United Kingdom, France, Norway, Sweden, the Netherlands, Denmark, Austria, Israel, and Japan, and free time is allocated in Canada, France, New Zealand, Denmark, Austria, Israel, Japan, Germany, and the Netherlands.]

22. But, and this is the critical point, the overseas experience does not refute the proposition that Pt IIID impairs freedom of discussion of public and political affairs and freedom to criticize federal institutions in the respects previously mentioned. Thus, the Commonwealth's claim that Pt IIID introduces and maintains a "level playing field" cannot be supported if that claim is to be understood as offering equality of access to all in relation to television and radio. It is obvious that the provisions of Div.3 regulating the allocation of free time give preferential treatment to political parties represented in the preceding Parliament or legislature which are contesting the relevant election with at least the prescribed number of

candidates. Their entitlement amounts to 90 per cent of the total free time. Others must of necessity rely on the exercise of discretion by the Tribunal. As among the political parties, the principle of allocation to be applied will tend to favour the party or parties in government because it gives weight to the first preference voting in the preceding election. Furthermore, a senator who seeks re-election is given preferential treatment over a candidate, not being a senator, who stands for election to the Senate. The former, but not the latter, is entitled to a grant of free time. The latter must rely on an exercise of discretion by the Tribunal and the Act makes no attempt to enunciate the criteria according to which that discretion is to be exercised. The provisions of Pt IIID manifestly favour the status quo. More than that, the provisions regulating the allocation of free time allow no scope for participation in the election campaign by persons who are not candidates or by groups who are not putting forward candidates for election. Employers' organizations, trade unions, manufacturers' and farmers' organizations, social welfare groups and societies generally are excluded from participation otherwise than through the means protected by s.95A. The consequence is that freedom of speech or expression on electronic media in relation to public affairs and the political process is severely restricted by a regulatory regime which evidently favours the established political parties and their candidates without securing compensating advantages or benefits for others who wish to participate in the electoral process or in the political debate which is an integral part of that process.

The Issues ...

25. But, on the view which I take of these actions, Pt IIID contravenes an implied guarantee of freedom of communication, at least in relation to public and political discussion. I shall therefore confine my discussion of the issues to that aspect of the actions, without embarking upon the other issues which were argued.

Constitutional implications ...

29. It may not be right to say that no implication will be made unless it is necessary. In cases where the implication is sought to be derived from the actual terms of the Constitution it may be sufficient that the relevant intention is manifested according to the accepted principles of interpretation. However, where the implication is structural rather than textual it is no doubt correct to say that the term sought to be implied must be logically or practically necessary for the preservation of the integrity of that structure.

30. It is essential to keep steadily in mind the critical difference between an implication and an unexpressed assumption upon which the framers proceeded in drafting the Constitution ((62) Australian National Airways Pty. Ltd. v. The Commonwealth (1945) 71 CLR , per Dixon J. at p. 81). The former is a term or concept which inheres in the instrument and as such operates as part of the instrument, whereas an assumption stands outside the instrument. Thus, the founders assumed that the Senate would protect the States but in the result it did not do so. On the other hand, the

principle of responsible government—the system of government by which the executive is responsible to the legislature—is not merely an assumption upon which the actual provisions are based; it is an integral element in the Constitution (The Engineers' Case (1920) 28 CLR, per Knox C.J., Isaacs, Rich and Starke JJ. at p. 147). In the words of Isaacs J. in The Commonwealth v. Kreglinger and Fernau Ltd. and Bardsley ((1926) 37 CLR 393, at p. 413): "It is part of the fabric on which the written words of the Constitution are superimposed."

The implication of fundamental rights

31. The adoption by the framers of the Constitution of the principle of responsible government was perhaps the major reason for their disinclination to incorporate in the Constitution comprehensive guarantees of individual rights. They refused to adopt a counterpart to the Fourteenth Amendment to the Constitution of the United States. Sir Owen Dixon said (Sir Owen Dixon, "Two Constitutions Compared", Jesting Pilate, (1965), p. 102):

> "(they) were not prepared to place fetters upon legislative action, except and in so far as it might be necessary for the purpose of distributing between the States and the central government the full content of legislative power. The history of their country had not taught them the need of provisions directed to control of the legislature itself."

The framers of the Constitution accepted, in accordance with prevailing English thinking, that the citizen's rights were best left to the protection of the common law in association with the doctrine of parliamentary supremacy. . . .

33. In the light of this well recognized background, it is difficult, if not impossible, to establish a foundation for the implication of general guarantees of fundamental rights and freedoms. To make such an implication would run counter to the prevailing sentiment of the framers that there was no need to incorporate a comprehensive Bill of Rights in order to protect the rights and freedoms of citizens. That sentiment was one of the unexpressed assumptions on which the Constitution was drafted.

34. However, the existence of that sentiment when the Constitution was adopted and the influence which it had on the shaping of the Constitution are no answer to the case which the plaintiffs now present. Their case is that a guarantee of freedom of expression in relation to public and political affairs must necessarily be implied from the provision which the Constitution makes for a system of representative government. The plaintiffs say that, because such a freedom is an essential concomitant of representative government, it is necessarily implied in the prescription of that system.

Representative government . . .

37. The very concept of representative government and representative democracy signifies government by the people through their representatives. Translated into constitutional terms, it denotes that the sovereign

power which resides in the people is exercised on their behalf by their representatives.... The point is that the representatives who are members of Parliament and Ministers of State are not only chosen by the people but exercise their legislative and executive powers as representatives of the people. And in the exercise of those powers the representatives of necessity are accountable to the people for what they do and have a responsibility to take account of the views of the people on whose behalf they act.

Freedom of communication as an indispensable element in representative government

38.   Indispensable to that accountability and that responsibility is freedom of communication, at least in relation to public affairs and political discussion. Only by exercising that freedom can the citizen communicate his or her views on the wide range of matters that may call for, or are relevant to, political action or decision. Only by exercising that freedom can the citizen criticize government decisions and actions, seek to bring about change, call for action where none has been taken and in this way influence the elected representatives. By these means the elected representatives are equipped to discharge their role so that they may take account of and respond to the will of the people. Communication in the exercise of the freedom is by no means a one-way traffic, for the elected representatives have a responsibility not only to ascertain the views of the electorate but also to explain and account for their decisions and actions in government and to inform the people so that they may make informed judgments on relevant matters. Absent such a freedom of communication, representative government would fail to achieve its purpose, namely, government by the people through their elected representatives; government would cease to be responsive to the needs and wishes of the people and, in that sense, would cease to be truly representative.

39.   Freedom of communication in relation to public affairs and political discussion cannot be confined to communications between elected representatives and candidates for election on the one hand and the electorate on the other. The efficacy of representative government depends also upon free communication on such matters between all persons, groups and other bodies in the community. That is because individual judgment, whether that of the elector, the representative or the candidate, on so many issues turns upon free public discussion in the media of the views of all interested persons, groups and bodies and on public participation in, and access to, that discussion....

44.   The concept of freedom to communicate with respect to public affairs and political discussion does not lend itself to subdivision. Public affairs and political discussion are indivisible and cannot be subdivided into compartments that correspond with, or relate to, the various tiers of government in Australia. Unlike the legislative powers of the Commonwealth Parliament, there are no limits to the range of matters that may be relevant to debate in the Commonwealth Parliament or to its workings. The consequence is that the implied freedom of communication extends to

all matters of public affairs and political discussion, notwithstanding that a particular matter at a given time might appear to have a primary or immediate connection with the affairs of a State, a local authority or a Territory and little or no connection with Commonwealth affairs. Furthermore, there is a continuing inter-relationship between the various tiers of government. To take one example, the Parliament provides funding for the State governments, Territory governments and local governing bodies and enterprises. That continuing inter-relationship makes it inevitable that matters of local concern have the potential to become matters of national concern. That potential is in turn enhanced by the predominant financial power which the Commonwealth Parliament and the Commonwealth government enjoy in the Australian federal system.

[The remainder of the Chief Justice's opinion addresses the merits of the constitutional challenge and invalidates the statute.]

JUDGEMENT–4: DAWSON J . . . .

15. I have previously observed that the Australian Constitution, with few exceptions and in contrast with its American model, does not seek to establish personal liberty by constitutional restrictions upon the exercise of governmental power. The choice was deliberate and based upon a faith in the democratic process to protect Australian citizens against unwarranted incursions upon the freedoms which they enjoy. This was recognized by the majority in the Engineers' Case in the following passage ((186) (1920) 28 CLR , at pp. 151–152.):

> "(T)he extravagant use of the granted powers in the actual working of the Constitution is a matter to be guarded against by the constituencies and not by the Courts. When the people of Australia, to use the words of the Constitution itself, 'united in a Federal Commonwealth,' they took power to control by ordinary constitutional means any attempt on the part of the national Parliament to misuse its powers. If it be conceivable that the representatives of the people of Australia as a whole would ever proceed to use their national powers to injure the people of Australia considered sectionally, it is certainly within the power of the people themselves to resent and reverse what may be done. No protection of this Court in such a case is necessary or proper."

16. Thus the Australian Constitution, unlike the Constitution of the United States, does little to confer upon individuals by way of positive rights those basic freedoms which exist in a free and democratic society. They exist, not because they are provided for, but in the absence of any curtailment of them. Freedom of speech, for example, which is guaranteed in the United States by the First Amendment to the Constitution, is a concept which finds no expression in our Constitution, notwithstanding that it is as much the foundation of a free society here as it is there. The right to freedom of speech exists here because there is nothing to prevent its exercise and because governments recognize that if they attempt to limit it, save in accepted areas such as defamation or sedition, they must do so at

their peril. Not only that, but courts recognize the importance of the basic immunities and require the clearest expression of intention before construing legislation in such a way as to interfere with them. The fact, however, remains that in this country the guarantee of fundamental freedoms does not lie in any constitutional mandate but in the capacity of a democratic society to preserve for itself its own shared values....

24. ... [I]t must nevertheless be recognized that the Constitution provides for a Parliament the members of which are to be directly chosen by the people—in the case of the Senate by the people of the respective States and in the case of the House of Representatives by the people of the Commonwealth. Thus the Constitution provides for a choice and that must mean a true choice. It may be said—at all events in the context of an election—that a choice is not a true choice when it is made without an appreciation of the available alternatives or, at least, without an opportunity to gain an appreciation of the available alternatives. As Windeyer J. observed in Australian Consolidated Press Ltd. v. Uren (1966) 117 CLR 185, at p. 210: "(f)reedom at election time to praise the merits and policies of some candidates and to dispute and decry those of others is an essential of parliamentary democracy". Perhaps the freedom is one which must extend beyond the election time to the period between elections, but that is something which it is unnecessary to consider in this case. It is enough to recognize, as this Court did in Evans v. Crichton–Browne (1981) 147 CLR 169, at p. 206, the importance of ensuring that freedom of speech is not unduly restricted during an election period. Thus an election in which the electors are denied access to the information necessary for the exercise of a true choice is not the kind of election envisaged by the Constitution. Legislation which would have the effect of denying access to that information by the electors would therefore be incompatible with the Constitution....

26. The question, therefore, is whether the provisions of the Act which were introduced by the Political Broadcasts and Political Disclosures Act are incompatible with those sections of the Constitution which provide for the direct choice of members of the Parliament. The question is not whether the legislation ought be regarded as desirable or undesirable in the interests of free speech or even of representative democracy. [The remainder of the opinion concludes, contrary to the views of a majority of the judges, that the Act is consistent with the relevant constitutional provisions.]

JUDGEMENT–5: GAUDRON J....

21. The notion of a free society governed in accordance with the principles of representative parliamentary democracy may entail freedom of movement, freedom of association and, perhaps, freedom of speech generally. But, so far as free elections are an indispensible feature of a society of that kind, it necessarily entails, at the very least, freedom of political discourse. And that discourse is not limited to communication between candidates and electors, but extends to communication between the members of society

generally. . . . [Gaudron concludes that the challenged provisions are unconstitutional.]

JUDGEMENT–6: McHUGH J. . . .

17.   Representative government involves the conception of a legislative
chamber whose members are elected by the people. But, . . . to have a full
understanding of the concept of representative government, "we need to
add that the chamber must occupy a powerful position in the political
system and that the elections to it must be free, with all that this implies in
the way of freedom of speech and political organization". Furthermore,
responsible government involves the conception of a legislative chamber
where the Ministers of State are answerable ultimately to the electorate for
their policies. As Sir Samuel Griffith pointed out in his Notes on Australian
Federation, the effect of responsible government "is that the actual government of the State is conducted by officers who enjoy the confidence of the
people".

18.   It is not to be supposed, therefore, that, in conferring the right to
choose their representatives by voting at periodic elections, the Constitution intended to confer on the people of Australia no more than the right to
mark a ballot paper with a number, a cross or a tick, as the case may be.
The "share in the government which the Constitution ensures" would be
but a pious aspiration unless §§ 7 and 24 carried with them more than the
right to cast a vote. The guarantees embodied in §§ 7 and 24 could not be
satisfied by the Parliament requiring the people to select their representatives from a list of names drawn up by government officers.

19.   If the institutions of representative and responsible government are to
operate effectively and as the Constitution intended, the business of government must be examinable and the subject of scrutiny, debate and
ultimate accountability at the ballot box. The electors must be able to
ascertain and examine the performances of their elected representatives
and the capabilities and policies of all candidates for election. Before they
can cast an effective vote at election time, they must have access to the
information, ideas and arguments which are necessary to make an informed judgment as to how they have been governed and as to what
policies are in the interests of themselves, their communities and the
nation. As the Supreme Court of the United States pointed out in Buckley
v. Valeo,* the ability of the people to make informed choices among
candidates for political office is fundamental because the identity of those
who are elected will shape the nation's destiny.

20.   It follows that the electors must be able to communicate with the
candidates for election concerning election issues and must be able to
communicate their own arguments and opinions to other members of the

---

* [Editors' Note: Buckley v. Valeo, 424
U.S. 1 (1976), found unconstitutional key
provisions in the Federal Election Campaign
Act that would have limited expenditures (by
candidates, their campaigns, or independent
persons) in federal political campaigns as a
violation of fundamental First Amendment
rights, although it upheld a limit on contributions in excess of $1,000 from any person to
any candidate in an election.]

community concerning those issues. Only by the spread of information, opinions and arguments can electors make an effective and responsible choice in determining whether or not they should vote for a particular candidate or the party which that person represents. Few voters have the time or the capacity to make their own examination of the raw material concerning the business of government, the policies of candidates or the issues in elections even if they have access to that material. As Lord Simon of Glaisdale pointed out in Attorney–General v. Times Newspapers((1974) AC 273, at p. 315):

> "People cannot adequately influence the decisions which affect their lives unless they can be adequately informed on facts and arguments relevant to the decisions. Much of such fact-finding and argumentation necessarily has to be conducted vicariously, the public press being a principal instrument."

21. The words "directly chosen by the people" in §§ 7 and 24, interpreted against the background of the institutions of representative government and responsible government, are to be read, therefore, as referring to a process—the process which commences when an election is called and ends with the declaration of the poll. The process includes all those steps which are directed to the people electing their representatives—nominating, campaigning, advertising, debating, criticising and voting. In respect of such steps, the people possess the right to participate, the right to associate and the right to communicate. That means that, subject to necessary exceptions, the people have a constitutional right to convey and receive opinions, arguments and information concerning matter intended or likely to affect voting in an election for the Senate or the House of Representatives. Moreover, that right must extend to the use of all forms and methods of communication which are lawfully available for general use in the community. To fail to give effect to the rights of participation, association and communication identifiable in §§ 7 and 24 would be to sap and undermine the foundations of the Constitution.

22. It may be that the rights to convey and receive opinions, arguments and information conferred by §§ 7 and 24 are not confined to the period of an election for the Senate and House of Representatives. It may be that the rights inherent in those sections are simply part of a general right of freedom of communication in respect of the business of government of the Commonwealth.... [The opinion concludes that the relevant statutory provisions are invalid.]

[The judgments written by the remaining justices are omitted.]

Questions and Comments

1. How is the protection of free expression implied from the Australian Constitution? More recent cases suggest that the approach taken in the *ACTV* case has been limited. Implied freedoms, the cases suggest, must be

tied to specific constitutional provisions. See Lange v. Australian Broadcasting Corp., 145 Austral. L.R. 96 (1997) (High Court of Australia).

2. Consider the argument that constitutionalism can be secured by a few minimum conditions: (a) regular, open, and competitive elections; (b) freedoms of speech and press; and (c) well-functioning, relatively independent courts. Without regular elections, claims about the people's will are not readily testable. Without open elections—in the sense that the choice of candidates is not tightly constrained and in the sense that citizens can participate in elections on terms of reasonably equality—elections cannot provide the basis for government by consent. To effectuate the values associated with regular, open, and competitive elections, some freedoms of speech and press may be essential. Without public discussion facilitated by the press, information needed for public choice will not be sufficiently disseminated. When majorities choose intolerant or abusive policies, the possibility of dissent that can legally be expressed, particularly in open elections, may lead the system to correct itself. Independent courts provide means not only to enforce but also to interpret laws in ways that can check excesses of other branches. To the extent that the courts are perceived as relatively impartial, they provide an additional vehicle for those who "lose" in particular electoral contests to challenge, without violence, legal developments with which they disagree. Courts can also help to secure such consistency in the application of law as is associated with fairness.

Does this analysis suggest that the basic requirements of constitutionalism will be secured by the minimal preconditions we have described? (Note that Tushnet's concerns about vigorous judicial review of a Bill of Rights might be allayed by the more modest role accorded judicial review in this analysis.) Can *ACTV* be understood as resting on the proposition that judicial review must be available to secure these minimum preconditions?

3. Is it plausible that in a legal culture committed to human rights the minimal preconditions to constitutionalism will not be understood as part of law, either through incorporation in a written constitution or as a convention that courts can enforce? What does enacting a formal Bill of Rights add? One possibility is that the adoption of a Bill of Rights will change public understanding or commitments in the very process of adoption. (Another possibility may be that courts will take the Bill of Rights as the basis for enforcing a more complete—and more controversial—set of rights than those identified by the minimal preconditions of constitutionalism.)

4. For an interesting discussion of neutrality and the civil service in modern liberal democracies, see Adrian Ellis, *Neutrality and the Civil Service*, in Liberal Neutrality (Robert E. Goodin and Andrew Reeve eds. 1989). Ellis begins from the proposition that all modern liberal democracies need "a body of permanent officials to assist the elected leaders of the day in the formulation, presentation and execution of policies," a requirement that comes "from the complexity and size of the tasks undertaken on behalf of elected governments." The legitimacy of the civil service, he argues, depends on its being able to serve different administrations with equal, and maximum effectiveness, "corollaries of permanence ... best understood as encapsulating political loyalty and political neutrality." These two requirements—of loyalty and neutrality—in a polity lacking in strong political consensus come into tension with each other. Ellis argues that some of the mechanisms in Britain that reinforce the neutrality of civil servants—that is, their ability faithfully to serve the policies of differing governments—include anonymity; the requirement to provide nonpartisan advice to ministers; self regulation; and limits on involvement in overtly partisan activities. All four of these, he argues, have been undermined in recent years, with a corresponding increase in emphasis on the duties of loyalty to the current government, manifest in the 1980s, for example, in increased political influence in the selection of those holding positions of responsibility in the civil service.

Is an independent, impartial civil service (or government bureaucracy) a requirement of constitutionalism; if so, will it evolve from the minimal structures described in note 2 above?

Note on the Status of Basic Laws in Israel

As noted earlier, the Israeli Knesset has from its inception enacted a series of "Basic Laws." Although it was initially contemplated at the time of Israel's founding that the first elected assembly would function as a constitutional assembly, agreement could not be reached on a constitution. Instead, the assembly acted as a legislative body, the Knesset, under an approach (the Harari Proposal) that contemplated that the Basic Laws, once completed, would constitute the Constitution of Israel. The process of drafting and enacting Basic Laws is not yet complete. The relationship of these Basic Laws to other statutes is (surprisingly) unclear. The State of Israel's website provides the following description:

> Regarding the question of the superiority of the basic laws over other laws, there are differences of opinion. Some claim that the basic laws are not superior to an ordinary law, unless they include a specific stipulation to the contrary. They base their position on the argument that since a basic law is passed by an ordinary majority (i.e. a majority of those voting) such a majority cannot grant superior status to a piece of legislation. Others claim that the superiority of basic laws stem from the fact that they are the product of the Knesset acting as the *Constituent Assembly*, and that from their mere definition as "basic laws" one may conclude that they are constitutionally superior.

> What happens when there is a contradiction between a basic law and an ordinary law passed after the basic law was passed? The answer to this question hasn't yet been given in any law (the Basic Law: Legislation will deal with it). However, on September 24, 1997, the *High Court of Justice* with a make-up of 11 judges, canceled in a precedential ruling several instructions in the law for regulating the occupation of investment consultancy. In the opinion of the High

Court, they contradict the Basic law: Freedom of Occupation " 'to a degree which supercedes that required to realize the goal of the law.' " http://knesset.gov.il/knesset/knes/eng_mimshal_yesod1.htm.

While some Basic Laws purport to entrench their provisions by requiring special majorities in the Knesset for amendment, many do not, including the 1984 Basic Law on the Judiciary.[f] As discussed in more detail in the next chapter, the Israeli Supreme Court has, on at least one occasion prior to 1997, appeared to rely on a Basic Law to invalidate a subsequently enacted law, one relating to elections. (Is it of any significance that both the Australian and Israeli decisions noted here concern elections?)

According to one scholar, the Israeli Supreme Court, sitting as the High Court of Justice on original petitions to rectify official wrongs, was highly activist in enforcing basic human rights in the 1980s and early 1990s: substantially limiting censorship, protecting journalists' sources, requiring registration of a Reform Jewish convert and that women be included in certain religious councils and electoral bodies, overturning a military decision during the Gulf War not to distribute gas masks to Palestinians when they were given to Jews in the same area, and interpreting a work agreement to provide benefits to homosexual spouses on equal terms with married employees. Menachem Hofnung, *The Unintended Consequences of Unplanned Constitutional Reform: Constitutional Politics in Israel*, 44 Am. J. Comp. L. 585 (1996).[g] Hofnung argues, however, that while enactment of the Basic Law on Human Dignity and Liberty in 1992 increased the formal power of the Court to invalidate laws, it paradoxically decreased the Court's legitimacy. "Suddenly, the judges, and especially the new Supreme court President, Aharon Barak, were conceived of as pushing forward their own political agenda. The civil judicial system is now viewed by a considerable portion of the Israeli population as an active participant in political debate, an actor identified with the secular-liberal segment of Israeli society." His argument is that the Court, now being in a position to have to confront the government more routinely, has backed down from its earlier more human rights oriented decisions to take more politically cautious decisions, e.g., dealing with expulsion of Hamas activists. Hofnung

f. Combining a special majority rule with an approach similar in some respects to Canada's Section 33 override, Section 8 of the 1992 Basic Law on Freedom of Occupation, referred to above, authorizes the enactment of laws that violate freedom of occupation if the law is passed by a majority of the members of the Knesset (i.e., all members, not just those voting), expressly states that it shall be in effect notwithstanding the provisions of the Basic Law, and expires within 4 years.

g. See also The Jerusalem Post Law Reports 37 (ed. Asher Felix Landau 1993) (describing the Shoshana Miller case involving a convert to Judaism within the Reform movement and requiring that the Minister of Interior register her as "Jewish" without comment on her being converted); id. at 177 (describing Morcos v. Minister of Defense as holding that the military must distribute "defense kits" without discriminating against Arab inhabitants); 8 Selected Judgments of the Supreme Court of Israel, Constitutional Law Cases 1969–88 at 186 (reprinting Shakdiel vs. Minister of Religious Affairs, a 1987 decision finding that the exclusion of women because of gender from membership on a religious council performing administrative duties was contrary to fundamental principles of the legal system including those of the Declaration of Independence).

fears that in the future the Court's jurisdiction will be limited through new basic laws.[h] Is it possible that enactment of the unentrenched "constitutional" Basic Law will work against constitutionalism?

Some would characterize Israel as a constitutional democracy that has a form of constitutional judicial review, notwithstanding the uncertain status of the Basic Laws. Consider, as you read more about Israel in the next chapter, whether the examples of Great Britain, Australia, and Israel change your view of the relationship between a written constitution, constitutionalism and judicial review.

h. The Basic Law on Human Dignity and Liberty is not entrenched, and so can be amended by ordinary majority vote. Moreover, it authorizes invalidation of subsequently enacted laws, but not of laws enacted prior to the Basic Law. Finally, it is worth noting that the Basic Law on the Judiciary (1984) is not entrenched and it too can be changed by simple majority vote.

CHAPTER VI

COURTS AND CONSTITUTIONALISM

Does constitutionalism require judicial review of the constitutionality or lawfulness of the acts of governments and their officers? In the U.S., "law" and "courts" go together as seemingly natural companions. Whether law is seen as simply a prediction of the decisions courts will make, or as having some principled existence apart from particular decisions, courts are experienced as primary in the determination of the meaning and force of law. See the U.S. Constitution, Art. IV, Section 2 ("Supremacy Clause," declaring the Constitution and laws of the United States to be supreme over state law, followed by an admonition to state court *judges* to enforce federal law when it conflicts with state law).

Associated with the introduction of modern written constitutions has been the development of special institutions to enforce the constitution. Constitutions do not necessarily provide for *judicial* enforcement, as the readings in chapter III on the People's Republic of China suggest. Many constitutional scholars believe that courts are needed to secure the enforcement of constitutions in the western liberal tradition, though others question how large or definitive a role courts, as compared to legislatures, should play in defining the legal environment. Political scientists argue that the "growing influence of judicial institutions" and the accompanying "juridification" of politics is both a global phenomenon and a highly significant trend in governance for the end of this century and the beginning of the next.[a]

Most European constitutions provide for some form of judicial enforcement of the constitution, but create institutions that—at least formally—are quite different from the decentralized judicial review found in the United States. In this chapter we examine the various forms in which judicial review of constitutional claims is carried out, and consider both positive and negative claims about the effects of judicial review.

a. James L. Gibson, Gregory A. Caldeira & Vanessa Baird, *On the Legitimacy of National High Courts*, 92 Am. Poli. Sci. Rev. 343 (1998). This comparative study finds that the public support and legitimacy of the U.S. Supreme Court, while high, is not unique: "the high courts of the Netherlands, Denmark, Germany (among West Germans), Greece and even Poland have at least as much institutional legitimacy as the [U.S.] Supreme Court." Id. at 349.

A.   Structure and Function of Constitutional Courts: An Introduction

Two significant questions for students of comparative constitutional law are first, the relationship between judicial review and constitutionalism, and second, the relationship between the substantive outcomes of judicial review and the institutional structures and procedures through which it is carried out.

The U.S. Supreme Court represents just one mode of constitutional review in a range of choices made by other nations about judicial review of constitutional issues. It engages in judicial review of the constitutional acts of other branches and levels of government. So too do other federal and state courts in the United States. But this diffusion of authority to decide constitutional question is not universal even among legal systems that incorporate judicial review. The U.S. Supreme Court functions not only as a constitutional decisionmaker, but as an adjudicator of issues of statutory interpretation under federal law, and as the court of last resort for review of decisions in the lower federal courts. But in acting thus as a "generalist" court, and not primarily as a specialist in constitutional law, the U.S. Supreme Court differs from many European constitutional courts. For an argument that "constitutional review" is unnecessarily identified with the American form of "judicial review," see Louis Favoreu, *American and European Models of Constitutional Justice*, in Comparative and Private International Law: Essays in Honor of John Henry Merryman (David Clark ed., 1990). In the following materials, we highlight some differences between the United States Supreme Court and other high courts, in other nations, that engage in constitutional judicial review.

---

1.   Centralized v. Decentralized Review

There are at least two models for the organization of constitutional judicial review within a court system: the decentralized model and the centralized model. (For helpful treatments on which this discussion in part relies, see Mauro Cappelletti, The Judicial Process in Comparative Perspective 132 (1989); Favoreu, supra; see also Allan Randolph Brewer–Carias, Judicial Review in Comparative Law 91–93 (1989).)

The decentralized model (also known as the "American" or "diffuse" model involving "incidental" review) is represented by the organization of the United States judicial jurisdiction. A key characteristic of this model is that the jurisdiction to engage in constitutional interpretation is not limited to a single court. It can be exercised by many courts, state and federal, and is seen as inherent to and an ordinary incident of the more general process of case adjudication. It has been used in such countries as Argentina, Australia, Canada, India and Japan. In the United States, we might think of it as a model in which courts are "generalists" deciding common law, statutory and constitutional questions as the case demands.

The centralized model (also called the "Austrian" or "European" model) is characterized by the existence of a special court, with exclusive or close to exclusive jurisdiction over constitutional rulings. The Austrian Constitution of 1920 created such a court, and similar "constitutional courts" exist today in countries like Germany, France,[b] Italy and some of the eastern European nations as well. Often, in such legal systems, there is a "Constitutional Court" that decides, for example, on the constitutionality of legislation, and at least one separate "Supreme Court" with jurisdiction over matters of statutory interpretation and administrative law. Centralized constitutional courts are, in a sense, "specialists" in constitutional decisionmaking, that sit outside of, rather than on top of, the normal structure of judicial jurisdiction. See Favoreu at 111.

Centralized constitutional review is closely associated, philosophically, with notions of parliamentary supremacy and a corresponding suspicion of permitting judges to set aside laws. To the extent this philosophical tradition is strongly held in the legal culture, even proponents of constitutional review may think it better to limit the number and visibility of judges authorized to set aside legislative decisions, rather than to permit every judge in every court to exercise such power.

---

2. THE POSSIBLE SIGNIFICANCE OF CIVIL LAW VS. COMMON LAW TRADITIONS

a. *Civil Law Judges*: According to Professor Cappelletti, civil law judges in Europe are typically career judges, whose professional training emphasizes skills of technical interpretation, rather than the broader issues often involved in constitutional judicial review. This limitation in training is consistent with continental notions of parliamentary supremacy, and suspicion of according substantial power to judges.[c] (A standard epithet in France for the work of constitutional courts is "gouvernment des juges").[d] Cappelletti argues that constitutional adjudication "often demands a higher sense of discretion than the task of interpreting ordinary statutes," and that the ordinary training of civil law judges does not conduce to the task of constitutional interpretation. Favoreu suggests as well that the election or appointment of judges in the U.S. by political branches gives them a legitimacy in constitutional interpretation that continental career judges

b. Although nominally not a "court", the Conseil Constitutionnel functions in many respects like a constitutional court whose jurisdiction is limited to pre-promulgation abstract review of legislation. But cf. Alec Stone, The Birth of Judicial Politics in France: The Constitutional Council in Comparative Perspective 212–16 (1992) (disagreeing with Favoreu and arguing that the Council functions as a third legislative chamber).

c. For an argument that there is an "unofficial discourse" among French judges

that is less formalist and technical and more concerned with both doctrine and policy than the formal, reported discourse, see Mitchel de S-.D–I'E. Lasser, *Judicial (Self-) Portraits: Judicial Discourse in the French Legal System*, 104 Yale L. J. 1325 (1995). .

d. An oft-cited work is Edouard Lambert's, Gouvernment des Juges at La Lutte contre la Legislation Sociale aux Etas–Unis (1921), suggesting that American judicial review is conservative, and favorable to the political right.

lack. In civil law countries, then, establishing a special and separate Court, distinct from the ordinary judicial system, may be a way of calling into play different skills and aptitudes, and different qualifications to enhance the legitimacy of a court engaged in the "political" act of reviewing legislation.

In addition, many European nations adopted constitutional review at a time when their ordinary judicial systems were mature and complex; adding to the duties of existing court systems may have seemed a less satisfactory solution than the creation of the specialized "Constitutional Court." (Favoreu refers to this as the "absence of unity between the legal order and the judicial apparatus," and argues that where there are complicated and separate jurisdictions for dealing with most legal questions, it is more difficult to permit decentralized constitutional adjudication than in countries like the United States were there is a "unity of jurisdictions.") Moreover, it has been suggested that in countries in transition from authoritarian regimes, it would be very difficult to implement decentralized review, since the general corps of available judges would be unlikely to have either the training or the independence from prior regimes to function with legitimacy as constitutional adjudicators. Finding a small number of respected and untainted jurists, who might constitute a centralized and specialized constitutional court, is simply more doable.

b. *Stare Decisis*: In the United States, as in other common law countries, the doctrine of stare decisis extends the effect of rulings of law from the parties in the case before it to the broader legal community. The rationale for, and legal effect, of stare decisis in the Supreme Court's adjudication has been the subject of significant debate in recent years. But it is important to recognize that many constitutional courts function in civil code systems, which do not have the same tradition of stare decisis.

The absence of principles of stare decisis in civil law countries may have contributed to the tendency towards centralized judicial review. If all courts could decide constitutional questions without stare decisis effect, Cappelletti suggests, a chaotic situation with respect to the validity of laws would result.

The binding effect of decisions of the centralized constitutional courts may be set forth in the respective constitutions. Typically such decisions are binding on all, and European commentators frequently draw a contrast with U.S. decisions, often described as binding only upon the parties to the litigation. Such a description is, however, far too simplistic—and may not be accurate at all, cf. Cooper v. Aaron, 358 U.S. 1 (1958)—with respect to constitutional adjudication in the U.S. Supreme Court.

c. *Case or Controversy limitations*: The European model typically does not formally recognize the kinds of "case or controversy" limitations that are so important a part of United States' constitutional jurisprudence. Indeed, many European constitutions give dissenting members of the national legislature the right to challenge, on an "abstract" basis, the constitutional validity of laws. Such "abstract" review may form a more important part of the docket than individual or "concrete review" cases. Professor Cappelletti has argued that the make-up of European centralized constitutional courts recognize the political character of judicial review both in the nature of and qualifications for appointments, and in the types of cases they hear, more overtly than is the case in the United States.

d. *Convergence*: As many comparative scholars have also argued, the world's systems of constitutional review are in many respects "converging"—similarities in practice, procedure, and jurisprudential problems and methods have emerged in recent decades in notable respects. Consider, as you read the following descriptions of judicial review, one focussing on Europe and one including Latin America as well, the extent of the convergences as well as differences between the systems of judicial review.

Louis Favoreu, *Constitutional Review in Europe*, in Constitutionalism and Rights: The Influence of the United States Constitution Abroad (Louis Henkin & Albert J. Rosenthal eds., 1990)

For Europeans, the primary interest in United States constitutional jurisprudence is the idea of constitutional review and the protection it provides for fundamental rights. European states have tried to adopt similar institutions and practices. Until recently, especially in France, American-style "constitutional justice" had a mythic quality—its image was simplistic, and it was an ideal, unattainable system. The illusive representation of United States constitutional jurisprudence has sometimes influenced the actions of governments and the writings of European scholars. In France, for example, constitutional review is still studied and taught with reference to an ideal perception of the United States model, which in fact has never been incorporated in or applied under any of France's successive constitutions. Italy and Spain have established systems of constitutional review quite different from that which prevails in the United States.

From an historical viewpoint, the United States example undoubtedly has had a decisive impact on constitutional development and the protection of rights. The Founding Fathers had drawn upon the European intellectual background developed during the seventeenth and eighteenth centuries, but the United States was the first to elaborate a modern written constitution and a bill of rights.

The French 1789 *Déclaration des droits de l'homme et du citoyen* and the 1791 Constitution were a second instance of the constitutionalism initiated in the United States. It is significant to recall that the first draft of the United States Bill of Rights was presented in France to the Assemblée Constituante on July 11, 1789, by the Marquis de La Fayette, who was known for his appreciation of American ideas, developed in the course of his stay in the United States during the drafting of the fundamental texts. Furthermore, when on July 27, 1789, Champion de Cice reported to the Assemblée Constituante the works of the Constitutional Committee and the decision to have the proposed constitution for France preceded by a bill of rights, he said:

This noble idea coming from another hemisphere was to be implemented here first. We participated in the events which led North America to freedom: it shows us on which principles we should rely to keep ours. The New World on which we put chains in the past is today showing us how to protect ourselves from being chained.

So the United States exported to Europe the concept of a written constitution and a bill of rights . . .

United States contributions to constitutional theory include also the regime of separation of powers, often called the "presidential system" (the American type), and in particular constitutional review. As to the separation of powers, the United States experience has generated much academic interest, and still remains a theoretical model, but it has had little practical effect, as few European countries have adopted such a system. Attempts to imitate it, including several in France, failed. Most European countries have preferred a parliamentary system of the British type. On the other hand, constitutional review has had great impact both on political theory and on political practice. The practical impact, however, is often misconceived and must be studied with care. The idea of reviewing legislation to determine whether it conforms to a constitution is undoubtedly American, but the implementation of that idea in Europe has followed different paths.

The United States, then, contributed to the theory of European constitutional law the idea of a written constitution and a bill of rights obtained by the people's representatives, the idea of constitutional review, and the idea that the supremacy of constitutional rules is genuine only if it is guaranteed by an institution that is independent of the political authorities whose acts are being reviewed.

But for a long time, constitutional review was not established in Europe, whether for reasons of fundamental principle, the inconsistency of such review with the sovereignty of parliaments, or for a "technical reason," the unacceptability of entrusting such review to the courts. In his conclusion to an international colloquium on European constitutional courts, Jean Rivero suggested that "at that time (before World War II) constitutional review was for public law like Western and American comedy for movies—an American specialty."

An early attempt to establish American-style constitutional review met many obstacles, and the project was dropped. The "American way" proving unfeasible, another way appeared, beginning after World War I, first in Austria and then. After World War II, in several Western European countries. This model of constitutional justice—the Austrian or Kelsenian model—became the European model.

The essential difference between the United States and the European models is in the way constitutional review is organized. In the United States, constitutional review is exercised by the entire court system; in Europe it is exercised by a unique, specialized court. In other respects—

particularly regarding the function and impact of constitutional review—there are great similarities....

TWO MODELS OF CONSTITUTIONAL REVIEW

European and American models of constitutional review differ principally in how the system of constitutional review is organized....

In the American system, constitutional review is lodged in the judicial system as a whole, and is not distinct from the administration of justice generally. All disputes, whatever their nature, are decided by the same courts, by the same procedures, in essentially similar circumstances. Constitutional matters may be found in any case and do not receive special treatment. At bottom, then, there is no particular "constitutional litigation," anymore than there is administrative litigation; there is no reason to distinguish among cases or controversies raised before the same court. Moreover, in de Tocqueville's words, "An American court can only adjudicate when there is litigation; it deals only with a particular case, and it cannot act until its jurisdiction is invoked." Review by the court, therefore, leads to a judgment limited in principle to the case decided, although a decision by the Supreme Court has general authority for the lower courts.

In the European system, constitutional review is organized differently. It is common in Europe to differentiate among categories of litigation (administrative, civil, commercial, social, or criminal) and to have them decided by different courts. Constitutional litigation, too, is distinguished from other litigation and is dealt with separately. Constitutional issues are decided by a court specially established for this purpose and enjoying a monopoly on constitutional litigation. That means that, unlike United States courts, the ordinary German, Austrian, Italian, Spanish, or French courts cannot decide constitutional issues. At most they can refer an issue to the constitutional court for a decision; the decision of the constitutional court will be binding on the ordinary courts.

In Europe, moreover, in general, the constitutionality of a law is examined in the abstract, not, as in the United States, in the context of a specific case; therefore the lawfulness of legislation is considered in general, without taking into account the precise circumstances of any particular case. This is because in Europe constitutional issues are generally raised by a public authority (the government, members of Parliament, courts) and not by individuals.

As a consequence, the effect of the decision is *erga omnes*, i.e., applicable to all, absolute. When a European constitutional judge declares an act unconstitutional, his declaration has the effect of annulling the act, of making it disappear from the legal order. It is no longer in force; it has no further legal effect for anybody, and sometimes the ruling of unconstitutionality operates retroactively. Kelsen characterized the constitutional court as a "negative legislator," as distinguished from the "positive legislator," the parliament.

The United States model and the European model, however, are two means to the same end. Both have to fulfill the same tasks:

- Above all, the United States and the European systems protect fundamental rights against infringement by governmental authority, particularly the legislature. The means are different, but the ends are the same and the results similar.

- Both systems generally try to maintain a balance between the state and the entities of which it is composed. In a federal state, constitutional review serves that function whether the system of review follows the United States model or the European one. The United States Supreme Court and the German Constitutional Tribunal play a similar role in maintaining the balance between the federal government and the member states.

- United States and European constitutional courts perform the same tasks, as contemplated by their respective constitutions, when they protect the separation of powers—the division of authority between the various organs of the state, whether between the executive and the legislature, or between the chambers of Parliament.

- In Europe, as in the United States, constitutional courts may have to decide electoral disputes regarding the highest positions in the state, or the arraignment of the highest political authorities.

In both the United States and the European models, constitutional review is vested with an essential and delicate mission: to decide political issues in legal terms. In both the United States and Europe, it incurs the risk of displeasing both the executive and the legislature. In both systems, the Court is subject to the same criticism, sometimes for being too timid, sometimes, to the contrary, for being too "activist" or daring.

THE UNITED STATES MODEL IN EUROPE BETWEEN THE WARS

A different model of constitutional review emerged in Europe because in various European countries the United States model could not strike root. At the beginning of the twentieth century, several European states wished to adopt the American model, but, despite numerous efforts, the "graft" proved unsuccessful. In order to obtain the same results, the Europeans have established another model that did not encounter the same obstacles.

At the beginning of the twentieth century, and particularly between the two world wars, the United States model was very popular in Europe, especially in France, Germany, and Italy. In France, a campaign in favor of establishing the American model of constitutional review was initiated in 1902 by Dean Larnaude in the Société de Législation Comparée. Famous writers as well as politicians backed the idea, but this led a French specialist of the American system, Edouard Lambert, to write a famous book on "government by the judges" and their part in the struggle for social legislation in the United States. Because some jurists and some politicians of very different ideologies had "suddenly come to agree that it is necessary to introduce into our constitutional system judicial review as in the United States," Lambert deemed it necessary to show the French the results of the American experience. In effect, he indicted the Supreme Court for having curbed social progress and for being an instrument of conservatism generally.

Lambert's work did not slow down the momentum to implement the United States model. The campaign even spread to the newspapers. An inquiry was published in the November–December 1925 issue of *Le Temps*. In December 1925 a debate was held at the Académie des Sciences Morales et Politiques. The most renowned public law specialists—Professors Berthélémy, Duguit, Hauriou, Mestre, and Rolland—reached agreement—itself an unusual occurrence—to instigate the judges of the ordinary courts to "dare" to follow the American example. The results, however, were meager. In a few cases the Conseil d'État or the Cour de Cassation seemed to avoid giving effect to an unconstitutional law by interpreting it so as to bring it within constitutional limits; but there was no case in which either the Conseil d'État or the Cour formally declared a law unconstitutional. When a constitutional issue was raised before an ordinary court, whether an administrative or civil court, the judge took the position that he had to apply the law and could not consider whether the law was constitutional. That is the position today, and writers at present hardly support the United States system in principle. But bills in the legislature continue to propose adopting this system, or at least the mythical conception of the Supreme Court which has long found favor with politicians and some writers. France, we shall see, has introduced constitutional review by the Conseil Constitutionnel, but it is not the United States model.

In Germany, beginning with a decision of the Reich Tribunal on November 4, 1925, ordinary courts accepted the responsibility of reviewing the constitutionality of laws on the basis of Article 102 of the Weimar constitution. But ordinary courts did not decide concrete cases on constitutional grounds. They did not prevent "numerous early violations of the constitution by the Parliament." In particular, they did not do so to protect fundamental rights, although they did achieve improvements in some respects, particularly regarding respect for the principle of equality. The Weimar experience led the reformers after World War II to move toward the Austrian model, despite the fact that the American occupation might have made its influence felt in Germany, as it did in Japan.

Italy experienced the United States model after the war, before establishing its constitutional court. Constitutional review, and particularly judicial review of legislation by ordinary courts, had been debated in Italy for a long time, most extensively at the same time as it was debated in France and Germany (i.e., at the end of the 1920s). But Italy's first and only experiment with the United States model began with a decision by the Court of Cassation on July 28, 1947, and ended with the establishment of the Constitutional Court in 1956. One cannot say that it had been successful. As Cappelletti and Cohen emphasize:

The first phase—1948 to 1956—was still dominated by the strong resistance of those who could hardly adapt to a new conception of law and justice. The ordinary "career" judge, particularly the elderly judges of the Supreme Court of Cassation and the other appellate courts, did a very poor job in the implementation of a highly programmatic and progressive Constitution, strongly opposed to a stratification of either asocial or authoritarian legislation.

In any case, at the Constituent Assembly, those in favor of Kelsen's model prevailed, and the delay in implementing it only underlined how difficult it was to adapt the United States model to Italy. To be sure, the present Italian system is not without some similarities to the United States system, in that constitutional review can be launched by a constitutional objection in an ordinary proceeding. But there is an important difference, since in Italy the incidental proceeding develops independently from the main proceeding.

Why the Graft Failed to Work

The graft of the United States system onto the European legal and political order was not successful even in countries that appeared to have incorporated that system. All attempts to explain this failure emphasize that constitutional "engineering" does not work everywhere; technique has to be adapted to the institutional and sociological framework.

One explanation is the sovereignty of the law and its "sacred nature." Since the 1789 Revolution, Jean–Jacques Rousseau's statement that "law is the expression of the general will" has been regarded as imperative, both in France and in other European countries. The law therefore cannot be subject to outside review. Only the legislature can scrutinize or limit itself:

> The legislature when making law has to examine whether the law considered is consistent with the Constitution and resolve issues in that regard.... This means that interpretation of the Constitution is to be left to Parliament. Because it is exercising the powers of the sovereign, Parliament is the judge of the constitutionality of its own laws. Therefore courts are not to interpret the Constitution; at least they do not have that power in relation to the legislature.

This, as expressed by a famous public law theoretician [Raymond Carré de Malberg], is the official French doctrine, as well as the position held by most European countries between the two world wars. This is the exact opposite of the United States system. In Europe, the law is identified with legislation, whereas in the United States there is still a substantial common law and, in the past at least, legislation was seen as an exception to the common law. In Europe, courts cannot interpret the constitution and apply their interpretation to legislation, whereas in the United States the opposite attitude was established at the beginning by Chief Justice Marshall.

In the United States, the Constitution is sacred. In Europe, "the law"—legislation—is sacred.

A second reason for the failure of the graft is the inability of the ordinary European judge to exercise constitutional review. As Mauro Cappelletti stressed:

The bulk of Europe's judiciary seems psychologically incapable of the value-oriented, quasi-political functions involved in judicial review. It should be borne in mind that continental judges usually are "career" judges who enter the judiciary at a very early age and are promoted to the higher courts largely on the basis of seniority. Their professional training develops skills in technical rather than policy-oriented application of statutes. The exercise of judicial review, however, is rather different from [the] usual judicial function of applying the law. Modern Constitutions do not limit themselves to a fixed definition of what the law is, but contain broad programs for future action. Therefore the task of fulfilling the Constitution often demands a higher sense of discretion than the task of interpreting ordinary statutes. That is certainly one reason why Kelsen, Calamandrei, and others have considered it to be a legislative rather than a purely judicial activity.

The "weakness" and "timidity" of the Continental judge lies perhaps in his being a "career judge," and not, like the United States judge, selected for the task. Also, in the United States, federal judges, at least, after they are appointed, enjoy tenure for life and are largely immune from political pressures. In Germany, Italy, France, Spain, and Greece, the judge has not been immune from purging or other coercive measures, if only in times of emergency—which have not been frequent.

Another reason for the failure of the United States model in Europe is the lack of a unified system of courts. The duality or plurality of courts in European countries has weighed against the success of the graft. The United States system works well perhaps only where there is a single, unified judicial system under the authority of a supreme court, as in the United States (as far as constitutional issues are concerned) and in common law countries. Since such a system provides for ultimate resolution of constitutional issue by a supreme court, it can allow constitutional issues to be raised in any case in any court without requiring separate treatment. and without the risk of abiding differences of opinion as to the constitutionality of fundamental provisions. Constitutional review, I believe, cannot be divided: it can be diffused within a united court system if the system is under the final authority of a single supreme court, or it must be lodged in a special constitutional court.

Another reason why the United States model was rejected by some European countries between the two world wars was that constitutions, in those countries at that time, were not in fact supreme and binding on parliaments. This was clear with respect to France during the Third Republic:

In America a court decision declaring a law unconstitutional has the effect of raising an impassable barrier since the legislature is powerless by itself to modify the constitution. . . . In France, on the contrary, the Parliament, if confronted with a court decision of unconstitutionality, could rather easily overcome the resistance of the court: the parliamentary majorities that adopted the law paralyzed by the judicial action have only to reaffirm their original measure by a simple majority in order to make their will prevail ... *In such circumstances, it is likely that the judiciary would hesitate to refuse to apply a law on grounds of its unconstitutionality.* [Carré de Malberg]

Similarly, in Germany under the Weimar Constitution, laws passed with the special majority provided for in Article 76 of the Constitution could "materially depart" from the Constitution to the prejudice of fundamental rights.

MODELS OF REVIEW IN CONTEMPORARY EUROPE

After World War II, Western European countries rebuilt their political institutions, with particular concern to assure respect for fundamental rights. Inevitably, the influence of the United States was strongly felt, both for reasons of international politics and because the success of its constitutional system was commonly recognized. The influence of the ideas that the United States and France had developed and helped spread was reflected in new national constitutions and in international instruments—the Universal Declaration of Human Rights, and, in Europe, the European Convention on Human Rights. New European constitutions reflected also the appeal of United States institutions, especially judicial review. In time, countries of western and northern Europe (except Great Britain, the Netherlands, Finland, and Luxembourg) moved toward some system of constitutional review. Some—the Scandinavian countries, Greece, and Switzerland—adopted the United States model; others—Austria, the Federal Republic of Germany, Italy, and France—opted for the European model.

The United States Model

Constitutional review in the Scandinavian countries is lodged in courts of general jurisdiction, as in the United States. (In Sweden, the only one of the four countries without a unified judicial system, constitutional review is lodged in both judicial and administrative courts). Constitutional issues can be raised in any proceeding, but only by persons with standing; the judge is obliged to decide the constitutionality of a challenged law. Constitutional issues generally go up to the Supreme Court, which has the final say. The decision as to constitutionality in any case affects only the parties to the case, since the inapplicability of the statute is pronounced only for that case, but, as in the United States, all courts, and political authorities, respect a decision of unconstitutionality after it is rendered final by the Supreme Court.

NORWAY

Norway's system of judicial review, the oldest and most effective of the Scandinavian systems, had developed on the basis of the 1814 Constitution and has been confirmed in the jurisprudence of its Supreme Court since the 1890s.

There have been twenty to thirty cases in which the Supreme Court held a law to be unconstitutional; most of them occurred between 1885 and 1930. Since then, particularly since World War II, the Court has tended to be restrained, probably because of "the relative political and social stability in the country, for more than thirty years, and of the increasing influence within the Supreme Court of the 'social' ideology which is dominant today among the governing classes." [Eivind Smith]

The main difficulty with judicial review in Norway is the lack of a clear set of principles against which the constitutionality of laws can be evaluated. The 1814 Constitution includes a catalogue of fundamental liberties and rights, but this bill of rights, unlike the 1789 French Declaration, was drafted with an eye to solving the problems of the time; it did not attempt to formulate general principles and was not intended to last. However, there have been recent attempts to modernize the text. In 1980, Article 110 of the Constitution was modified to require the authorities to create conditions "which make it possible for every person who is able to work to earn his living by his work." In recent years, the Supreme Court has referred to unwritten principles as grounds for constitutional review. For example, in 1983 the Court referred to "unwritten principles which bind the legislature" as a basis for challenging the constitutionality of an abortion law. Many of the "unwritten principles" have been derived from international human rights documents, particularly the European Convention on Human Rights.

DENMARK

Constitutional review was accepted in Denmark in the 1920s. The first cases dealt with land reforms involving particularly disputes between former owners of large lands and their farmers. In a 1921 decision on the constitutionality of a law requiring full compensation for property taken for a public purpose, the Supreme Court—in a now-famous expression—declared that unlawfulness cannot be established "with the required certainty for the courts to be able to declare unlawful the provisions of a law which was passed according to the Constitution."

The Danish Supreme Court has remained very prudent, and one cannot cite a single decision declaring a law unconstitutional....

SWEDEN

Unlike the Constitutions of Norway and Denmark, the contemporary Swedish Constitution expressly provides for constitutional review.

Like Norway, Sweden had a nineteenth-century constitution (1809), but unlike their Norwegian counterparts, judges in Sweden did not exercise constitutional review until recently, following a 1963 Supreme Court decision. In 1975, the Constitution of 1809 was replaced by a new one, and during "the preparatory works the Constitution writers accepted the case law [supporting judicial review], but the text adopted by Parliament does not refer it." In 1978, the constitution was amended so as to include an express provision for constitutional review (Art. 14, ch. 11). Commenting on this amendment, Professor Torsten Bjerken stated that "the intent of the legislator was not, however, to change the law; it was just to transform constitutional convention into written law."

The final sentence of the amendment is most important: "[I]f the provision has been decided by the Riksdag or by the Government, the provision may be set aside *only if the inaccuracy is obvious and apparent*" (emphasis added). That appears to imply that judges, whether administrative or judicial, should exercise authority to rule on the constitutionality of laws, but only with caution.

That has been and continues to be the attitude of Sweden's judiciary. Neither before nor after the constitutional amendment has there been a case in which a conflict with the Constitution was acknowledged by the Supreme Court (Högsta domstolen) or by the Administrative Supreme Court (Regeringsrätten). The constitutionality of laws has been raised before the two courts since the 1979 amendment, but no law has been invalidated as unconstitutional. . . .

Why so much caution? There are, I believe, two principal reasons, like those that explain the rejection of the United States model by other European countries. As elsewhere in Europe, judges in Scandinavian countries are not elected. They are career judges who are unwilling to enter into conflict with Parliament, the highest political authority in those countries. This awe of Parliament is understandable, considering that Scandinavian parliaments consist of only one chamber, and that there is strong cohesion between the majority in Parliament and the executive. (This is particularly true in Sweden where the same Parliament has remained in power for over forty years). Furthermore, legal education in those countries emphasizes legislative and written sources of law, and rejects the lawmaking capacity of the judges that is accepted in the United States.

Thus, even in European countries that have adopted the United States model, the transfer has not been complete. . . .

SWITZERLAND

Switzerland is often included among states that have review on the United States model, but constitutional review in Switzerland is limited to nonfederal acts, i.e., to the acts of the cantonal authorities. In that respect, it differs greatly from the United States. Regarding federal laws, Article 113(3) of the Constitution states that "the Federal Tribunal shall apply the laws adopted by the Federal Assembly." The decision to bar judicial review of federal laws was justified as designed to prevent judicial supremacy over the legislature. . . .

Constitutional review of cantonal acts can be initiated in different circumstances by citizens or by public officials. A citizen can petition the Federal Tribunal by a "public law petition" if he feels his constitutional rights had been violated. A public official can raise a public law claim, i.e., an allegation of conflict between federal and cantonal acts or between various cantonal acts.

The exclusion of constitutional review of federal laws has been attributed to the historical context of the adoption of the 1874 constitution. At that time, the leading party, the Radicals, controlled all branches of the federal government. Naturally they felt it more important to have review of cantonal rather than federal acts. Also stressed is the democratic character of the federal legislative process: "The Constitution-makers of 1874, who were democrats before they were liberals, would not have wanted a group of judges to be able to undo the work of a parliamentary majority, and even of a popular majority." Thus Article 113(3) of the Constitution represented the victory of democracy over liberalism. . . .

The European Model

"It is impossible . . . to propose a uniform solution for all possible constitutions: constitutional review will have to be organized according to the specific characteristics of each of them." Kelsen's wise warning was followed by countries establishing systems of constitutional review. Although many countries have followed the European model, each has tailored its system to its own needs and circumstances.

Countries that have adopted the European model include: Austria (since 1970), the Federal Republic of Germany (1951), Italy (1956), France (1958), Cyprus (1960), Turkey (1961), Yugoslavia (1963), Portugal (1976 and 1983), Spain (1980), Belgium (1984), and Poland (1985). I consider the principal examples.

AUSTRIA

The Austrian High Constitutional Court, the oldest in Europe, was established in 1920 according to a plan developed by Hans Kelsen, who was a member of the Court and its general reporter until 1929. The Court was suppressed on March 13, 1938, when Germany invaded Austria, but was reestablished in the constitutional law of October 12, 1945.

The Court has jurisdiction over several matters: elections, conflicts between courts, and litigation between the federal state and the *Länder* (states). It acts as an administrative court to review administrative acts alleged to violate rights guaranteed by the constitution. It acts also as a high court of justice to bring to trial the head of state or ministers accused by the houses of Parliament.

The Court can exercise judicial review at the request of any of the following: a *Land* government, higher courts, a third of the members of the National Council (or a third of the members of a *Land* legislature), or, under some conditions, individuals. The Court may also raise constitutional issues on its own initiative. The Court's case law, developed over the last sixty years, is extensive, particularly in relation to fundamental rights. The impact of its decisions on the legal and political system is strong even though the Court's decisions are not binding on ordinary courts, unlike the decisions of the German and Spanish high courts.

About 90 percent of the registered or decided cases of the Court in 1982 dealt with the constitutionality of administrative acts. This is probably due to the fact that it is easier to challenge the constitutionality of an administrative act than to bring a case by direct petition.

THE FEDERAL REPUBLIC OF GERMANY

The German Federal Constitutional Tribunal was prescribed by the 1949 Constitution and established in 1951. It is surely the most powerful of the European constitutional courts since it has the widest jurisdiction. In addition to constitutional review of legislation, it has jurisdiction to review cases involving the election of members to Parliament; to decide cases brought against the President of the Republic; to adjudicate controversies between constitutional organs, and between the Federal Republic and the *Länder*, or between two *Länder*. Constitutional review can be initiated by the government of a *Land* or by a third of the members of the *Bundestag* in regard to a federal law (for review of a law on its face); by reference to the Court from lower courts (for review of a law as applied); or by an individual claiming that his fundamental rights have been violated by a judgment, by an administrative act, or (under certain conditions) by a statute.

Since 1951, the constitutional court has disposed of some 50,000 cases. About 90 percent of these were decided by panels of three judges. In recent years, of some 3,000 cases decided each year, about 97 percent came to the Court on individual petition, almost all of them challenging administrative acts or judicial judgments, not the constitutionality of a statute. . . .

ITALY

The Italian Constitutional Court was established by the 1947 Constitution, and came into force in 1956. The Court is composed of fifteen judges appointed equally by the Parliament, the President of the Republic, and the Supreme Courts (the Council of State, the Court of Cassation, and the Court of Auditors).

The Constitutional Court has jurisdiction over conflicts of jurisdiction between various state authorities and between regions; over allegations against the President of the Republic, the President of the Council of Ministers, and the ministers; the acceptance of abrogative referendums; and constitutional review of laws. This last area of jurisdiction is by far the most important. Constitutional issues regarding laws are referred to the Court by the ordinary civil, administrative, and commercial courts that would have had to apply them.

The number of cases submitted to the Court is noteworthy. In 1983, 1,100 issues were referred to the Court, which made 400 decisions as to the constitutionality of laws. In 1984, out of 1,489 cases registered, 1,384 (93 percent) were referred to the Court by ordinary courts. The other areas of jurisdiction appear less important. Since ordinary courts have a tendency to refer difficult cases to the Constitutional Court, the Court has been increasingly overwhelmed by these issues.

Clearly, the Court plays a large legal and political role.

FRANCE

The French Constitutional Council was established in 1958 and came into force in 1959. It is composed of nine judges—three appointed by the president of the Republic, three by the chairman of the Senate, and three by the chairman of the National Assembly. Former presidents of the Republic are *de jure* members, but since 1962 none has sat on the Constitutional Council.

The Constitutional Council has jurisdiction over electoral issues (elections to the National Assembly and Senate, election of the President, and referenda); conflicts regarding the division between the legislative domain and regulations (*lois* and *règlements*); the constitutionality of the rules of a chamber of Parliament; the constitutionality of international treaties; and the constitutionality of laws—upon request by one of the four highest authorities of the state (the president of the Republic, the chairmen of the National Assembly and of the Senate, and the prime minister), or by sixty members of the National Assembly or sixty members of the Senate.

The Constitutional Council has developed constitutional review of laws challenged as being beyond the authority of Parliament. But other nonconstitutional issues, particularly electoral issues, remain important. On the other hand, it is unnecessary for the council to ensure that the bureaucracy or the courts respect constitutional rules because the bureaucracy is subject to review by the Council of State (*Conseil d'Etat*), and the courts by the Court of Cassation. But the Council of State and the Court of Cassation have to respect the Constitutional Council's decisions; and they do.

During the past ten years, members of Parliament have often used their power to raise constitutional issues before the Constitutional Council, and its case law has therefore become an important factor in France's legal and political system.

SPAIN

The Spanish Constitutional Tribunal was established by the 1978 Constitution, and started its work in 1980. It is composed of twelve judges appointed by the king, four upon nomination by Congress, four by the Senate, two by the government, and two by the General Council of the Judicial Power.

The Constitutional Tribunal has jurisdiction over conflicts between state authorities; the petition of *amparo* against administrative acts and court decisions interfering with fundamental rights; the lawfulness of treaties in the light of the Constitution; and the constitutionality of laws. In this last category, issues can be raised by the President of the Government, by fifty deputies or fifty senators, by the authorities of autonomous communities, or by the people's defender (*defensor del pueblo*). Constitutional issues can be raised by courts when they are confronted with them during litigation. The Constitutional Tribunal's role already appears important, particularly concerning respect for the balance between the state and the autonomous communities.

The writ of *amparo*, the origins of which go back to the Kingdom of Aragon, is an institution that has been used since the nineteenth century in Latin America and was adopted in the Spanish Constitution of 1931. Under the present Spanish Constitution, an individual may invoke this writ to request the Constitutional Tribunal to assure the protection of his or her fundamental rights against an administrative act or a judgment of a court, when the ordinary courts have not provided such protection. (In fact, the writ of *amparo* is invoked particularly against judicial acts.) *Amparo* cannot be invoked directly for review of the constitutionality of a statute (unlike constitutional review in the Federal Republic of Germany), but the chamber of the Constitutional Tribunal that reviews writs of *amparo* may refer questions on the constitutionality of an underlying statute to the full court. The petition of *amparo* is the basis of 90 percent of the registered cases. This action is popular because claimants doubt the ability of ordinary courts to formulate proper constitutional principles.

Major Trends in the Evolution of the Courts

Today, the German, Italian, and Spanish constitutional courts resemble the United States Supreme Court. Indeed, German constitutional review mainly covers lower court decisions and often appears as a third- or fourth-level appellate court. Because of the issues referred by the judge *a quo*, the Italian Constitutional Court increasingly decides civil, criminal, and administrative cases. The Spanish writ of *amparo* is mostly used against judicial decisions. These courts, therefore, deal mostly with ordinary cases from which they extract and consider constitutional issues. German and Italian constitutional judges devote themselves essentially to [what Gustavo Zagrebelsky calls] "microconstitutional review": "They slide from reviewing for conformity to the constitution, to reviewing the implementation of the laws." One might ask whether this is their proper function or is it something of a diversion from their original function? By comparison, French and Austrian constitutional judges appear to fulfill a function closer to the one originally provided for in the Austrian, Kelsenian model.

The procedures for screening petitions to the German, Italian, Austrian, and Spanish high courts can be linked to the trend just noted. Because of their increasing numbers most of the cases go through committees or panels of judges. Thus they are decided, not by the court itself as constitutional review requires, but by "branches" of the court, by summary procedure. This clearly reduces the usually acknowledged advantages of open petition and of direct or indirect access of individuals to constitutional courts. This is particularly relevant when the delay is such that some petitions are not adjudicated until several years after they are made.

The overall problem, therefore, is controlling the flow of cases while ensuring that important issues are adjudicated within a reasonable period of time and with the required guarantees. In several countries, reforms are being considered, and some have already been implemented (e.g., in Austria in 1984).

THE SIGNIFICANCE OF THE DIFFERENCES BETWEEN THE TWO MODELS

Differences between the United States and European models of constitutional review are most clearly seen in the way such review is organized, which can be explained by differences in the institutions and political culture of the different countries. Are these differences merely technical, or do they have theoretical significance? Have they made a difference in practice? Are there convergences between the two systems? There has been no thorough study of these questions, but some preliminary observations are now in order.

The fact and the form of constitutional review pose the fundamental question—first addressed and resolved by the United States—of how to limit power, executive as well as legislative, and reduce confrontation between judge and legislature. The United States has resolved these problems in its own way by a diffused, or decentralized, system of constitutional review. Europe, unable to adopt the American system, has provided a solution by creating constitutional review that is concentrated or centralized. From a theoretical perspective, differences between the two systems may reflect different conceptions of the separation of powers. In the American model, limitations on executive and legislative power have been achieved by the progressive recognition of a third power, the judiciary, described as "the least dangerous branch." That third power does not exist in most European countries. European constitutional theory acknowledges only executive and legislative power. There is no recognition of a "judicial power" and judges do not enjoy the legitimacy and authority of their American counterparts.

It was therefore necessary to build—following Kelsen—a system in which constitutional review, entrusted to a single court, constitutes not a third parallel power but one above the others that is charged with monitoring the three essential functions of the state (executive, legislative, and judicial) to ensure that they are exercised within the limits set by the Constitution. That has been clearly explained [by Vezio Crisafulli] with reference to the Italian Constitutional Court:

> [The Court] is neither part of the judicial order, nor part of the judicial organization in its widest sense: ... [T]he Constitutional Court remains outside the traditional categories of state power. It is an independent power whose function consists in insuring that the Constitution is respected in all areas.

The impetus for constitutional courts in Europe owes much also to the increased concentration of political power. It is no longer accurate in most cases to refer to a "separation of powers." In most Western European countries with a parliamentary regime, the balance of powers between the executive and the legislature has been replaced by a concentration of power in a bloc composed of the government and its majority in the lower house and, in some cases (as in France and Portugal), also the President of the Republic. There is no longer a quest for a balance between the Government and the Parliament, but between the majority (government and Parliament) and the (parliamentary) opposition. Constitutional review therefore serves to assure a balance between the majority and the opposition.

The need for constitutional review as a counterweight to majority power has been expressed as follows:

> In the parliamentary system of government, the governing political party or coalitions of parties, displacing both the legislative and executive powers, becomes omnipotent. The popular belief in judicial review establishes the courts, on the one hand, as the guarantors of the basic consensus on which democracy is founded, and, on the other hand, as the arbitrators that adjudge how far the reforms of regulations dictating the social, economic, and cultural life conform with this consensus, without reversing it. [E. Spiliotopoulos]

Whatever the theoretical differences, the practical differences between the European and American models of constitutional review may be less significant than their similarities. There are many similarities between the United States Supreme Court and the European constitutional courts as regards the appointment and the qualifications of judges. In both cases, appointments are political—made by political authorities and taking into account the political inclinations of the judges. This is fully justified, since the democratic legitimacy of constitutional review rests upon the appointment of judges by elected authorities.

In this respect there is no great difference between the U.S. practice of having the president choose the members of the Supreme Court with the consent of the Senate, and the practice in various European countries. In every instance the appointing authorities choose persons who belong to, or are close to, the same political ideology, and are not necessarily legal experts or famous jurists. One might note, however, that in Europe a large proportion of the judges are university professors.

The two models are similar also in their judicial methodology. European constitutional courts resort to techniques used by the United States Supreme Court half a century earlier. One of these techniques, for example, used increasingly by German, Austrian, Italian and French courts, allows the judge to interpret a law so that it would not violate the constitution. Another technique complementing that one is "the rule of reasonableness," which was developed in the United States at the beginning of this century for interpreting antitrust laws. German and Italian courts, for the most part, began to use it by the early 1960s, but the French Constitutional Council has not yet resorted to it.

There are increasing similarities also in how the U.S. Supreme Court and the European constitutional courts conduct their business. The U.S. Supreme Court does not hear all of the cases referred to it. Like the constitutional courts, it chooses to pronounce only on selected important issues. Moreover, the fact that American judicial review is diffused or decentralized is balanced by restrictive procedures. These convergences between the two systems are clearly underlined by comparative law specialists:

Through the use of certiorari, the United States Supreme Court, with the growing number of cases in which review is sought each year, confines itself more to the most significant-mostly constitutionally grounded-questions. This is, of course, the exact role of the European constitutional courts which have no jurisdiction at all in "ordinary" cases.

[Cappelletti and Cohen] conclude:

> The Supreme Court is only in some ways an ordinary court of appeals; in others it is, like the European constitutional courts, "a special organ of constitutional review."

The two types of courts are also beginning to resemble each other in another way: some European constitutional courts, contrary to their original function, are turning into ordinary courts and becoming more like the United States Supreme Court. This is the case in Italy, for example, because of the increased number of cases referred to the Constitutional Court by ordinary courts; in the Federal Republic of Germany, because of the very large number of individual petitions; in Austria, because of the increasing number of constitutional "amendments"; and in Spain due to the success of the petition of *amparo*. This leads us to ask whether "too great a development of judicial review of laws and its efficacy, leading the constitutional judge to intervene directly or indirectly in many cases ... will not result in rendering this review commonplace and in transforming the constitutional court into the supreme court to which in fact all cases, even the most ordinary cases, can be referred?"

Another area in which the two models of constitutional review are converging is the protection of fundamental rights. Here the influence of United States case law would be greater if that jurisprudence were better known. For example, the U.S. Supreme Court's techniques regarding respect for the principle of equality, individual liberty, and freedom of opinion would be of great interest. Of course, each European constitutional court develops a jurisprudence appropriate to its own institutional and sociological environment, but when that jurisprudence is not yet firm, acquaintance with foreign, particularly United States precedents, would be very useful.

Finally, but not least, there is surely room for greater convergence concerning the relation between jurisprudence and politics and the influence that constitutional adjudication might have on political systems....

CONCLUSION: DOES CONSTITUTIONALISM "WORK WELL" IN EUROPE?

Is constitutionalism, the doctrine of constitutional supremacy which owes so much to the United States, well established in Europe—thanks, notably, to constitutional review?

One can say that constitutionalism has made great progress in countries that have established constitutional courts. Because of their decisions, constitutional courts have engendered respect for constitutions and for fundamental rights that did not exist previously and that are still absent in countries that lack an efficient system of constitutional review (e.g., the Scandinavian countries), even though these countries proclaim the supremacy of their constitutions. The recent Spanish, Portuguese, and Greek constitutions show that modern constitutions in democratic countries necessarily include constitutional supremacy and constitutional review. The effective supremacy of the constitution is always affirmed. It is a fundamental change from the situation that prevailed before World War II; one that cannot be reversed. The constitution has finally become "holy writ" in Europe as it is in the United States.

Can one compare the results of the American and European systems of judicial review? It is difficult, since their contexts are so different. First, in the United States state laws and regulations constitute a much larger part of the corpus of the laws of the country than in European countries, even in European federal states. In Europe, moreover, the legislature makes the law, whereas in the United States judges enjoy real lawmaking power. For these reasons, comparing figures is hardly meaningful. . . .

Comparing the systems nevertheless suggests some conclusions. First, the European system seems to have the advantage of isolating important constitutional issues for decision by a specialized court, which is free from other duties and can devote the time required for this delicate task. The constitutionality of a national law is taken immediately to the constitutional court and does not have to go through the various steps of the jurisdictional ladder. Is it not significant that, as in Canadian law, there has been thought of creating a United States federal court of appeals to reduce the Supreme Court's work load and limit its jurisdiction, so as to permit the Court to do better its job of judicial review?

On the other hand, one might ask whether—with a view to strengthening constitutionalism—the European system is as successful as is the American system in spreading constitutional rules throughout the various branches of law. In the European system the ordinary judge is excluded from the process of constitutional review, although he can sometimes set the process in motion (as in Italy, Spain, or Germany). If the judge later has to apply the decision of a constitutional court and follow its interpretation, he is not in the same position as are the lower courts in the United States in relation to the Supreme Court. In the European system, constitutional courts cannot even impose sanctions if their decisions are disregarded; only supreme courts in each order (the Council of State or Court of Cassation) can do this. Issues regarding the implementation of Constitutional Court decisions can sometimes be submitted to that Court (in Germany or Spain, for example) by means of a constitutional petition or a petition of *amparo*; but that would not be as effective or as efficient as the United States system.

Allan–Randolph Brewer–Carias, JUDICIAL REVIEW IN COMPARATIVE LAW (1989)

[The following excerpts sketch Brewer–Carias' argument that there is no necessary connection between the way constitutional review is organized (e.g., diffuse or centralized review) and the common law or civil law tradition of the nation.]

* * *

(b) The compatibility of the [diffuse] system with all legal systems

The diffuse system of judicial review of constitutionality of legislation is not a system peculiar to the common law system of law. It has existed since the last century in most Latin American countries, all of which belong to the roman law family of legal systems.

This is the case in Mexico, Argentina and Brazil, which followed the American model, and also of the mixed systems in Colombia and Venezuela. It has also existed in Europe in countries with a civil law tradition, like Switzerland, Portugal and Greece. In Switzerland, the diffuse system of judicial review was first established in the 1874 Constitution, although in a limited way. The Swiss system also currently allows the courts to review legislative acts of the Cantons on constitutional grounds, although this does not apply to federal laws. In the mixed system of Greece, the 1975 Constitution entrusts all courts with the power not to apply legal dispositions whose contents they consider to be contrary to the Constitution. in particular, Article 95 establishes that "The courts shall be bound not to apply laws, the contents of which are contrary to the Constitution." Although certain authors have commented on the suitability of a diffused system of judicial review to civil law systems, it appears as if the determining factor is not the system of law but the acceptance of constitutional supremacy.

If the principle of constitutional supremacy is adopted the logical and necessary consequence is that the courts must have the power to decide which norm is to be applied when a contradiction exists between a particular law and the Constitution. Regardless of whether the legal system of the country is the common law or roman law system, the courts are obliged to give priority to the Constitution,

Nevertheless, other criticisms have been made with regard to the practical effects of a diffuse system method of judicial review in a civil law system. For example, Hans Kelsen referred to the problems raised by the diffuse system for justifying the "centralization of the power to examine the regularity of general norms", stressing "the absence of unity in the solutions" and "the legal uncertainty" that results when a court "abstains from applying a regulation and even a law as irregular, while another court does the contrary". The argument is as follows:

> Under the Anglo–American doctrine of *stare decisis,* a decision by the highest court in any jurisdiction is binding on all lower courts in the same jurisdiction, and thus as soon as the court has declared a law unconstitutional, no other court can apply it. The court does not need a specific grant of the power to declare a law invalid, nor must it decide

anything beyond the applicability of the law in question to the concrete case; *stare decisis* does the rest by requiring other courts to follow the precedent in all succeeding cases. Thus. although the unconstitutional statute may remain on the book. it is a dead law ... *Stare decisis,* however, is not normally part of the Roman Law systems, and thus in these systems, the courts are not generally bound even by the decisions of the highest court.

Where the essence of the criticism is that the conflicting decisions of a diffuse system will result in uncertainty, the situation will be the same in common law or civil law countries. If it is true that the doctrine of *stare decisis* may be a correction of the problem, such correction will not be absolute since even in common law systems not all cases in which constitutional matters are decided upon by lower courts can go before a Supreme Court. In fact, that court usually has discretionary power to control the cases which may be brought to it on appeal.

Alternatively, although *stare decisis* is a common law concept, certain roman law countries have a related concept. For instance, the Mexican Constitution has adopted the principle that with regard to the particular law of *amparo*, the *jurisprudencia* or the precedents derived from previous decisions of the federal courts are to be considered obligatory for lower courts. This happens only after five consecutive decisions to the same effect, uninterrupted by any incompatible ruling, have been rendered. The effects of the *jurisprudencia* have been considered equivalent to those resulting from the role of *stare decisis.*

Similarly, in Argentina and Brazil an institution called the "extraordinary recourse of unconstitutionality" has been developed which can be brought before the Supreme Court against judicial decisions adopted at the last instance, when a federal law is considered as unconstitutional and inapplicable by a court. In these cases, the decision adopted by the Supreme Court has *in casu et inter partes* effects but, being adopted by the highest court, has factual binding effects upon inferior courts.

In the same sense, in some European countries with a roman law tradition but which have adopted the diffuse system of judicial review, special judicial mechanisms have been established to overcome the problems deriving from contradictory decisions of different courts on constitutional issues. This is the case in Greece under the 1975 Constitution where a Special Highest Court has powers to decide upon the unconstitutionality of laws when contradictory decisions on the matter have been adopted by the State Council, the Court of Cassation or the Auditory Court. In such cases, the decisions of the Special Highest Court have absolute and general effect regarding the constitutionality of laws.

Finally, in other countries with a roman law tradition, the corrections to the problems of uncertainty and conflictiveness have been established by adopting a mixed model of judicial review, that is to say, by having the diffuse and concentrated systems operate in parallel. This is the case in Guatemala, Colombia and Venezuela. Through the functioning of the concentrated system of judicial review, the Supreme Court is empowered to formally annul any law, on the grounds of unconstitutionality, with *erga omnes* effects. The action is usually initiated through a popular action which allows any inhabitant of the country to bring the constitutionality issue before the Supreme Court.

In the same sense, other European countries with a roman law tradition and a diffuse system of judicial review, have mixed certain features of the concentrated systems so as to give their Supreme Court the power to annul unconstitutional laws. This is the case with Switzerland with regard to the issue of constitutionality of Canton laws in cases of violations of fundamental rights.

Therefore, in order to resolve the problems of uncertainty and the possible conflictive character of judicial decisions taken by different courts upon the unconstitutionality of laws which the diffuse system of judicial review could bring about, some countries with a roman law tradition and a diffuse system of judicial review have developed various particular legal solutions, either by giving obligatory character to precedents or by granting the necessary powers to declare the unconstitutionality of statutes to their Supreme Court, in some cases even with general and binding effects.

The problems posed by the diffuse control of constitutionality of legislation, therefore, are common to countries with either common or roman law systems. This cannot of itself result in a conclusion that the diffuse system of judicial review and the civil or roman law system of law are incompatible. The compatibility which is consistent is that when the principle of the supremacy of the Constitution exists, the logical consequence is that all judges, who are charged with applying the law must have the power to decide upon the applicability of legislation to the Constitution.

While European countries with a roman law system have manifested their traditional distrust of judicial power with the establishment of the concentrated system of judicial review, this is merely a method of constitutional supremacy by other means. Yet this cannot lead one to consider the diffuse control of the constitutionality of legislation as being incompatible with the roman law legal system.

(c) The rationality of the system

As indicated earlier, the essence of the diffuse system of judicial review is the very notion of constitutional supremacy: if the Constitution is to be the supreme law of the land, prevailing over all other laws, no state act contrary to the Constitution can be an effective law. In the words of Chief Justice Marshall, if the Constitution is "the fundamental and paramount law of the nation . . . an act of the legislature, repugnant to the Constitution, is void". In this respect, the effective guarantee of the supremacy of the Constitution is that acts repugnant to it are in fact null and void, and as such have to be considered by the courts that are the state organs called upon to apply the laws. . . .

(iii) The incidental character of the system . . .

Therefore, a non-constitutional process must be initiated before a court on any matter or subject whatsoever, before the diffuse system of judicial review of unconstitutionality can operate. The question of the unconstitutionality of a law and of its inapplicability may be raised in such an instance so long as the issue of the validity of the law is considered to be, by the judge, relevant to the decision in the case.

(iv) The initiative power of the courts

If it is a duty of the judges to apply the Constitution in a concrete decision, and therefore to consider the constitutionality of the law, the rationality of the diffuse system must allow the judge to consider the constitutional question even on his own initiative, even when none of the parties in the particular process have raised the question of the constitutionality of the law before the judge. This is the direct consequence of the guarantee of the Constitution, established as an objective guarantee which means the nullity of laws contrary to its norms.

Although this aspect of the rationality of the diffuse system of judicial review is followed in many countries, as in the case of Venezuela and Greece, procedural rules in most countries forbid the courts to consider, on their own initiative, any questions of the constitutionality of laws.

(v) The *inter partes* effects of the court decision

The fifth and final aspect of the rationality of the diffuse system of judicial review concerns the effects of the decision adopted by the court in regard to the constitutionality or applicability of the law in the concrete process; and this aspect of the effect of the judicial decision refers to two questions: first, who does the decision affect? and, second, when do the effects of the decision begin?

In relation to the first question, the rationality of the diffuse system of judicial review is that the decision adopted by the court only has *in casu et inter partes* effects; that is, restricted to the concrete parties and the concrete process in which the decision is adopted. This is a direct consequence of ... the incidental character of the diffuse system of review as raised in a concrete process. Thus, if a law is considered unconstitutional in a judicial decision. this does not mean that the law has been invalidated and that it is not enforceable or applicable elsewhere.... [T]o avoid the uncertainty of the legal order and of contradictions in relation to the value of the laws, corrections have been made to these *inter partes* effects through the doctrine of *stare decisis* or through positive law, in instances when the decision has been given by a Supreme Court.

(vi) The declarative effects of the court decision....

The first and foremost fundamental aspect of the rationality of the diffuse system of judicial review is that of the supremacy of the Constitution over all state acts. Thus since the Constitution provides the authority for all state acts, any act which is created without the authority of the Constitution has no validity whatsoever. Consequently when a court decides upon the constitutionality of a law and declares it unconstitutional, it is because it considers the law null and void as if it had never existed.

Since the law has never had any validity, the court need not do any positive act in order to invalidate the law. They need only to declare that the law is unconstitutional and consequently, that it has been unconstitutional ever since its enactment. This law is considered by the court as never having been valid and as always having been null and void. That is why it is said that the decision of the court, as it is a declarative one, has *ex tunc, pro-praeterito* or retroactive effects in the sense that they go back to the moment of the enactment of the statute considered unconstitutional.

(d) Conclusion

In conclusion we can say that as a matter of principle the rationality of the diffuse system of judicial review works as follows.

The Constitution has a supreme character over the whole legal order so that acts contrary to the Constitution cannot have any effects and are considered null and void.

All courts have the power and duty of applying the Constitution and the laws, and therefore, to give preference to the Constitution over statutes which violate it, and to declare them unconstitutional and inapplicable to the concrete process developed before the court. This power and duty of the courts to consider a statute unconstitutional giving preference to the Constitution, can only be exercised in a particular process initiated by a party, where the constitutional question is only an incidental matter, and when its consideration is necessary to resolve the case. The court judgement regarding the unconstitutionality and inapplicability of a statute in a particular process can be taken by the judge on his own initiative because it is his duty to apply and respect the supremacy of the Constitution.

The decision adopted by the court concerning the unconstitutionality and inapplicability of a law only has *inter partes* effects regarding the concrete case in which it is made; and it is of a declarative effect in the sense that it only declares the *ab initio* nullity of the statute. Thus, when declaring the statute unconstitutional and inapplicable, in fact, the decision has *ex-tunc* and *pro praeterito* effects in the sense that they are retroactive to the moment of the enactment of the statute so that the statute is considered as not having produced any legal effect with regard to the concrete process and parties.

Of course, this logic of the diffuse system of judicial review is not always consistent. Each legal system has modified this pure form to its own particular specification. . . .

[Brewer–Carias then turns to the centralized systems.]

(b) The compatibility of the [centralized] system with all legal systems

The concentrated system should not be thought of as peculiar to the civil law system of law, and incompatible with the common law tradition. Instead. it must be considered in relation to its origin: a system that must be expressly established and regulated in a written Constitution. Accordingly, it can therefore indifferently exist in systems with a common law tradition or with a civil law basis, although it is most commonly found in civil law countries.

For instance, in Papua New Guinea, a country which gained its independence from Australia in 1975 and which therefore has a common law tradition, the Constitution gives the Supreme Court exclusive jurisdiction over questions of interpretation and application of constitutional law. Therefore, when such a question arises in any court or tribunal, it shall be referred to the Supreme Court. In a similar sense, the 1966 Constitution of Uganda also established an exclusive jurisdiction of the High Court on constitutional matters. . . .

Similarly, in the 1960, 1969 and 1979 Ghanaian Constitutions, the Supreme Court was vested with original and exclusive jurisdiction to exercise the power of judicial review. Article 42 of the 1960 Constitution and Article 106 of the 1969 Constitution stated:

> The Supreme Court shall have original jurisdiction in all matters where a question arises whether an enactment was made in excess of the powers conferred on Parliament by or under the Constitution, and if any such question arises in the High Court or an inferior court, the hearing shall be adjourned and the question referred to the Supreme Court for decision.

Additionally, Article 2 of the 1969 Constitution established a direct action that could be brought before the Supreme Court to seek judicial review, as follows:

> A person who alleges that an enactment or anything contained in or done under the authority of that or any other enactment is inconsistent with, or in contravention of, any provision of this Constitution may bring an action in the Supreme Court for a declaration to that effect. . . .

These provisions regarding judicial review were also adopted in the 1979 Constitution, but since 1971 were interpreted by the Supreme Court to reduce the referral of certain cases to the Supreme Court and to avoid referrals of frivolous submissions.

Although judicial review itself has not always functioned in some Commonwealth countries because of democratic instability, the concentrated system of judicial review exists and has functioned in legal systems with a common law tradition. While it is true that common law "practice has always been intolerant of the notion of specialised, expert, tribunals on the continental model", this must be understood as referring to the specialised Constitutional Court as in the European model, and not to a system "where jurisdiction is determined and limited in terms of subject matters".

The adoption of a system is always a constitutional option according to the concrete circumstances of each country. Many European countries have opted for Constitutional Courts, Tribunals or Councils for their exercise of the concentrated system of judicial review. This can only be seen as a concrete consequence of a peculiar constitutional tradition regarding the principles of the supremacy of the law, the separation of powers and the traditional fear of the judges to control legislative acts. Other countries with a civil law tradition have developed concentrated systems of judicial review by attributing the original and exclusive jurisdiction to annul statutes and other state acts with similar rank and effects to their Supreme Courts.

Three conclusions can be drawn from this: first, the concentrated system of judicial review can only exist when it is established *expressis verbis* in a Constitution, and it cannot be developed by interpretation of the principle of the supremacy of the Constitution; second, the concentrated system of judicial review is compatible with any legal system, whether common law or roman law legal systems; third, the concentrated system of judicial review does not imply the attribution of the functions of constitutional justice to a special Constitutional Court, Tribunal or Council created separate to the ordinary judicial organization. It may also exist when constitutional justice functions are attributed to the existing Supreme Court of the country, even though in the latter case the system generally tends to mix its trends with elements of the diffuse system of judicial review.

(c) The rationality of the system

Just as in the diffuse system of judicial review, the essence of the concentrated system of judicial review is based on the notion of the supremacy of the Constitution...

... The main element that leads to the differentiation between both systems of judicial review is the type of guarantee adopted in the constitution system to maintain that supremacy....

(i) The annullability of certain unconstitutional state acts

The first aspect that shows the rationality of the concentrated system of judicial review is the principle that when state acts are considered to be contrary to the Constitution, they may be annulled. This annullability of a state act, as an objective guarantee of the Constitution, means that a state act, even if it is irregular or unconstitutional, once issued by a public body it must be considered as valid and effective until it is repealed by the same organ which produced it or until it is annulled by another state organ with constitutional powers to do so. In the concentrated systems of judicial review, the Constitution assigns this power to annul unconstitutional state acts to only one state organ; either the existing Supreme Court or a special constitutional body created separately from the ordinary judiciary....

... In effect, with regard to state acts of lower levels in the hierarchy of norms, for instance administrative acts with normative effects, all judges in a concentrated system of judicial review normally have the power to consider them null and void when unconstitutional, with respect to the particular process in which they are questioned. In such cases, the guarantee of the Constitution is the nullity of the unconstitutional state act, even though only the courts can determine that.

What is peculiar to the concentrated system is that constitutional positive law establishes an additional limitation concerning the effects of the unconstitutionality of state acts. With regard to certain acts, the power to declare their unconstitutionality and invalidity has been exclusively reserved to one constitutional organ: the existing Supreme Court or a special Constitutional Court. In those cases, and regarding such certain acts. normally being legislative acts and other state acts enacted under the direct authority of the Constitution, the guarantee of the Constitution has been reduced to the annullability of unconstitutional state acts.

(ii) The power of a special constitutional body regarding the annulment of certain state acts on the grounds of unconstitutionality

The second aspect of the rationality of the concentrated system is that the power to declare the nullity of legislation is assigned to one single constitutional organ with jurisdictional functions. This modality of the concentrated system of judicial review, which consists of the establishment of a special constitutional body, has marked the development of constitutional law during the recent decades, since the first Constitutional Courts were established in Austria and Czechoslovakia in 1920. The system was later adopted in Germany and Italy, after the Second World War, and more recently in Spain and Portugal. It has also been adopted in some socialist countries (Yugoslavia, Czechoslovakia and Poland) and has been developed with particular trends in France. Under the influence of the European model, but in an incomplete way, the system was adopted in the early seventies in Chile where a Constitutional Tribunal was established, and more recently in Ecuador and Peru, where Constitutional Guarantees Tribunals have been created.

Although constitutionalism developed in the theory and practice of constitutional law since the beginning of the last century, a system of constitutional justice was not accepted in Europe until after the First World War, and then took place in two ways. One was established in the Weimar Constitution (1919)....

The second was the Austrian system, the personal masterpiece of Professor Hans Kelsen....

The incorporation of this system of constitutional justice in Europe was due to the influence of Hans Kelsen's pure theory of law, which conceived constitutional norms as the basis for the validity of all the norms, of a given legal order. This basic concept had a fundamental corollary: the need for a state body to guarantee the Constitution, that is to say, to settle disputes over the consistency of all legal norms, both specific and general, with the superior hierarchy on which they are based, and in the last instance with the Constitution....

Kelsen's conception of the concentrated system of judicial review, contrary to the diffuse system which implies that all judges are entitled to abstain from enforcing laws they deem contrary to the Constitution, results in an attribution of an exclusive power to declare the unconstitutionality of a law to a single state body. In this system, ordinary courts lack the power to refrain from enforcing unconstitutional laws on their own.

In its original theoretical conception, this concentrated system was conceived by Kelsen as being "a system of negative legislation". A Constitutional Court does not specifically decide upon the unconstitutionality of statutes on any assumption of a single fact; this is reserved for the *a quo* court raising the question of constitutionality. Its competence is normally limited to the purely abstract issue of the logical compatibility which must exist between the statute and the Constitution.... This led Kelsen to maintain that when the Constitutional Tribunal declares a statute unconstitutional, the decision with *erga omnes* effects was a typical legislative action. Hence the common assumption that the Constitutional Tribunal's decision had the force of law. Consequently, until a decision is adopted, the statute is valid and the judges of ordinary courts are obliged to enforce it.

This reasoning was developed by Kelsen in response to possible objections that the jurisdictional control of legislative action, based on the European concept of the supremacy of Parliament, could produce. By forbidding ordinary judges to abstain from enforcing the laws and granting the power to declare a statute unconstitutional with *erga omnes* effect to the Constitutional Court the judiciary was subject to the laws adopted by Parliament and at the same time the primacy of the Constitution over Parliament could be maintained. In this way, it was considered that the Constitutional Tribunal became Parliament's logical complement. Its function was reduced to judging the validity. of a statute with simple and rational logic, completely separate from the need to settle disputes in specific cases and acting as a negative legislator. In this way, legislative power was, for Kelsen, divided between two bodies: the first, Parliament, the holder of political initiative, the positive legislator; and the second, the Constitutional Tribunal, entrusted with the power to annul laws which violate the Constitution. Under this conception, of course, the Constitutional Court needed to be a constitutional body separate from all traditional state powers: thus it was not strictly a judicial body.

(iii) The principal and incidental character of the system

Under a concentrated system of judicial review, constitutional issues can be brought before the Constitutional Court either by virtue of a direct action or request or by referral from a lower court where the constitutional question has been raised in a concrete proceeding, either *ex officio* or through the initiative of a party. Thus the concentrated feature of the system does not imply that the constitutional question must only be raised either in a principal or in an incidental way. It can be either one form or the other, or through both in parallel, depending on the concrete positive law regulations. Consequently, the concentrated system of judicial review cannot be identified by the principal character of the method of reviewing the constitutional question although this may have been true in the original Austrian system established in 1920.

In the principal method, the constitutional issue regarding a statute is the only and principal question of the process initiated through the exercise of a direct action that can be brought before the Constitutional Court, either by someone through an *actio popularis* or within some *locus standi* rules or by specific public officials and authorities. In the incidental method the constitutional issue is raised before an ordinary court as an incidental question aspect of a process, or the court can raise it *ex officio*. This court is the one which must refer the constitutional question to the Constitutional Court, the suspension of the decision of the concrete case being necessary until the constitutional issue is resolved.

(iv) The initiative power of judicial review

The [older] Constitutional Court[s] including the Supreme Court [generally] d[o] not have any self-initiative to act as a constitutional judge.... But once a constitutional question has reached the court as a result of an action or of a lower court referral, ... [the Constitutional Court] has *ex officio* powers to consider questions of constitutionality other than those already submitted....

(v) The *erga omnes* effects of the court decision

The final aspect of the rationality of the concentrated system of judicial review can be considered under two issues: who the decision affects; and second, when do the effects of the decision begin.

In relation to the first issue, the decision adopted by a Constitutional Court has general effects so that it applies *erga omnes*....

[E]ven when judicial review is sought by incidental methods, the decision of the Constitutional Court must be concentrated on aspects regarding law only and not facts. Since the court in this case is not limited to a concrete process or to the parties in which the constitutional question was originally raised, the effects must also be *erga omnes*.

Accordingly, the constitutional judge in the concentrated system does not decide a concrete case, but only a question of constitutionality of a statute. The logic of the system, therefore, is that the decision must apply to everybody and to all state organs, thus the *erga omnes* effects. Thus if a law is considered unconstitutional by the Constitutional Court, the law thereof is annulled and cannot be enforceable or applicable anywhere or in any case.

(vi) The constitutive effects of the Constitutional Court decision

These *erga omnes* effects and the annullability aspect are closely related to the question as to when the declaration of unconstitutionality is to be effective. As indicated earlier, the fundamental aspect of the rationality of the concentrated system is that of the supremacy of the Constitution. In concentrated systems, the Constitution has restricted its own guarantee by reserving the appreciation and declaration of nullity of laws to only one single constitutional organ.

Consequently, when a constitutional judge decides upon the unconstitutionality of a law, the decision has a constitutive effect: it determines that the law is a nullity because of its unconstitutionality, the law having produced effects up to the moment in which its nullity is established, Thus the decision of the court has *ex-nunc, pro futuro* or prospective effects.

Nevertheless, this element of the logic of the concentrated system of judicial review is normally tempered by the constitutional system itself. Therefore a distinction is established between the absolute or relative nullity of the law. Thus certain constitutional errors may produce a statute with an absolute nullity, so that the decision of the court has *ex-tunc* effects, or the constitutional defects of the statute may be considered to be not so grave as to produce an absolute nullity but only a relative nullity. In this instance, the effects of the annulment of the statute are only *ex-nunc, pro futuro*.

Questions and Comments

1. Consider Professor Favoreu's suggestion that the European system permits the final constitutional court to do a "better job," but that the system of diffuse review, as in the United States, permits better distribution and reception of constitutional ideas. By what criteria do you measure how good a job a constitutional court does? Do any of those criteria relate to the ease of distributing constitutional ideas? Are there different audiences to whom or for whom dissemination of constitutional ideas is desirable? Might this be accomplished through different mechanisms of judicial review?

2. Even if Brewer–Carias is correct that there is no formal logical inconsistency between diffuse review and civil law traditions, are Cappelletti and Favoreu nonetheless persuasive that the traditions and customs of the judiciary in a civil law system make centralized review work better there?

3. Consider the consistency of Brewer–Carias' description of the limited "inter partes" effects of rulings in a diffuse system, on the one hand, and his description of the "declaratory effects," on the other. Consider whether this reflects a tension between the views of judicial review set forth in Marbury v. Madison, 5 U.S. 137 (1803), and Cooper v. Aaron, 358 U.S. 1 (1958).

4. Professor Brewer–Carias' argument is formalist in character, based largely upon the legally established aspects of the system for judicial review and on legal doctrine. It thus differs substantially from efforts, e.g., by Professor Dworkin in his essay in Chapter V concerning the culture of civil liberty in England, to describe law as reflected in, and interacting with, culture. But at the same time that Brewer–Carias can be seen to ascribe substantial importance to formal, institutional categories of law, his argument might be seen as a rejection of the claim that the formal elements of law tell you very much about more important aspects of the legal system since his claim is that there is no necessary connection between one, and another, formal element.

For different views of how to understand law (in the books and in action) in another constitutional culture, compare Jonathan M. Miller, "Ignoring Political Influences," Legal Times, p. 51 (Aug. 14 1995) (attacking recent analysis of Argentine Supreme Court decisions for failing to describe alleged corruption of Argentine Supreme Court, including incident in which one justice surreptitiously had removed from the court's files a decision approved by requisite majority and resubmitted a new decision, favoring the government, for signature to other judges) with William D. Rogers and Paolo Wright–Carozza, "Providing Independent Analysis," Legal Times, p. 51 (Aug. 14 1995) (defending their book against Miller's critique, emphasizing the "narrow scope" of the project of giving close analysis to legal precedents and a comparative analysis of Argentine and U.S. constitutional jurisprudence, and noting the inherent impossibility of drawing strong inferences about judicial independence from the published opinions of the court). For a detailed account of the Argentine Supreme Court and its decline in status since World War II, see Jonathan Miller, *Judicial Review and Constitutional Stability: A Sociology of the U.S. Model and Its Collapse in Argentina*, 21 Hast. Int'l & Comp. Law Rev 77, 151–66 (1997).

B.   STRUCTURE, COMPOSITION, APPOINTMENT AND JURISDICTION OF CONSTITUTIONAL COURTS: THE U.S., GERMANY, FRANCE, AND EASTERN EUROPE

The following materials provide some greater detail concerning the jurisdiction and composition of major constitutional courts. After the introductory chart, a brief description and some short excerpts on the composition of the U.S. Supreme Court are included, followed by a more detailed introduction to the system of constitutional review in France and Germany. These materials provide some history and background to the formation of constitutional courts in both France and Germany, and address the structure, composition and appointment methods of the judges of the courts charged with constitutional review. Finally, we briefly identify some of the issues and dynamics of constitution-making, insofar as it concerns judicial review, in Eastern Europe.

As you read this section, questions to think about include: (1) whether, and how, appointment mechanisms for judges and the composition of the constitutional courts relate to the types of jurisdiction exercised by the court; (2) what are the benefits and costs of life tenure for constitutional court judges, and what is its relationship to the independence of the judiciary; (3) whether there are different "packages" of provisions concerning appointment, advancement, tenure, salary, or retirement that will foster judicial independence, and (4) whether an independent judiciary is necessary for a constitutional system and, if not, what role an institutionally subordinate judiciary might play. . . .

1.   SURVEY OF CONSTITUTIONAL COURTS, JURISDICTION AND COMPOSITION.

As the following chart suggests, among the constitutional courts of western democracies that have had judicial review since at least the early 1980s, the U.S. is singular in its provisions for life tenure. India and Japan, whose constitutional courts have been in existence since shortly after World War II, likewise provide for mandatory retirement at a set age (65 or 70), while the justices of the of the new Constitutional Court of South Africa are appointed for nonrenewable twelve-year terms and must in any event retire by age 70.

Constitutional Courts and Judicial Appointments in Comparative Perspective

Court	# of Justices on High Court	Term/Age Limits	Appointing Authority	Legal Qualifications	Organizational Features	Other Facts	Concrete Judicial Review?	Abstract Judicial Review?
U.S. Supreme Court	Nine (set by statute)	Life, 'during good behavior'; subject to removal by impeachment	President, with advice and consent of the Senate	None required but justices typically are law-trained	Sits as plenary body	Highly public and political nomination process; nominees are "rated" by ABA; appointees are generally from private practice, government, or lower courts	Yes	No
Canadian Supreme Court	Nine (by statute); (composition of Court now seems to have constitutional status)	Mandatory retirement Age of 75; serve during good behavior; may be removed for dishonesty or incompetence	Cabinet & Prime minister; minister of Justice recommends to cabinet which appoints, subject to Prime Minister's final say; PM has more control over who is chief justice	3 must be from Quebec	Sits as plenary body	Informal, customary geographic and linguistic allocations (e.g., 1 of 3 from Quebec to be English-speaker). Govt solicits advice from Canadian Bar Assn., other sources. Many academic apptd recently	Yes	Yes, on issues referred by the federal government
Federal Constitutional Court of Germany	16 (set by statute)	Twelve year, non-renewable term, further limited by mandatory retirement age of 68	Each house of legislature selects one-half of the judges, based on but not ltd to lists submitted by fedl & state govts and political parties. Bundestag elects by 2/3 vote of Judicial Selection Comm. Bundesrat by 2/3 vote.	40 years old, eligible for political office, successfully passed both judicial exams; 6 of judges (3 in each "senate") to come from higher federal courts; may not hold other government positions	Sits in 2 different panels, or "senates," with differing jurisdictions	2 houses work together to protect party interests; multi-party system and qualified majority for selection fosters closed-door compromises	Yes	Yes; federal and lander (federated member state) legislation may be subject to review within 30 days following adoption
French Constitutional Council	Nine, plus any living former Presidents	Nine year, nonrenewable terms; staggered every 3 years, 3 members' terms expire	One-third by President of Republic; one-third by President of the Senate; one-third by National Assembly. President of Republic names Court's President	None	No public dissents	Most appointees active in public life prior to appointment	No	Yes; national legislation may be subject to review within 15 days following adoption
Italian Constitutional Court	Fifteen, but quorum of eleven enough to adjudicate	Nine year terms, not immediately renewable	One-third by President; one-third by Parliament (by a two-thirds vote) and one-third by "Senior Judiciary," which selects from its own ranks	Parliamentary and presidential nominees must be magistrates of superior courts, or attorneys of at least 20 years standing, or full law professors	When court hears criminal case against President or ministers of state, 16 lay judges are added to court from list prepared by Parliament		Yes	Yes, national and regional legislation may be subject to review within 30 days following adoption
Australian High Court	Seven members but only formal requirement is for at least 3 members	Mandatory retirement age of 70	Attorney General and cabinet after consulting with states, through Governor-General in Council	None	Plenary hearings not required	Bar association generally consulted on fitness	Yes	No

Court	# of Justices on High Court	Term/Age Limits	Appointing Authority	Legal Qualifications	Organizational Features	Other Facts	Concrete Judicial Review?	Abstract Judicial Review?
Spanish Constitutional Tribunal	Twelve	Nine year renewable terms	Appointed: two by federal government, two by judiciary; elected:four by Congress, four by Senate (by 3/5 majorities) (all nominally appointed by King)	May be judges, lawyers, law professors, or civil servants with at least 15 years experience and whose "judicial competence is well known"			Yes	Yes; national and regional legislation may be subject to review within 90 days following adoption
Portuguese Constitutional court	Thirteen	Six year terms	Ten appointed by the Assembly; three appointed by the Court itself	Six of the thirteen must be chosen from among judges of other courts; others must have legal training		President of court elected by other judges of that court	Yes	Yes

Sources:

"Comparative Analysis of the Constitutional Courts of Selected European Countries," prepared by the Central and East European Initiative for the Technical Legal Assistance Workshop on Romania's Draft Constitution (Washington, D.C. 1991).

Allan-Randolph Brewer-Carias, JUDICIAL REVIEW IN COMPARATIVE LAW (1989).

CONSTITUTIONS OF THE COUNTRIES OF THE WORLD (Albert B. Blaustein & Gisbert H. Flanz, eds., editions between 1991 and 1997 for most recently available texts).

Alec Stone, Governing With Judges: The New Constitutionalism, in GOVERNING THE NEW EUROPE (Jack Hayward and Edward Page, eds. 1995).

2.   THE UNITED STATES AND THE U.S. SUPREME COURT

Although judicial review was not explicitly provided for by the Constitution, it is well-accepted under the reasoning of Marbury v. Madison, 5 U.S. 137 (1803), that the government of the United States is one of limited powers, that the constitution is intended to act as law in enforcing those limits, that "[i]t is emphatically the province and duty of the judicial department to say what the law is," and to apply the constitution as superior to "any ordinary act of legislation" in cases in which they both apply and are in conflict. For a detailed description of the early history of the Court, see Julius Goebel, Antecedents and Beginnings to 1801, History of the Supreme Court of the United States (1971).

In the United States all judges, state and federal, can decide on constitutional issues. The Supreme Court has jurisdiction to review those decisions, however, and we therefore focus on it. The Supreme Court of the United States (like all federal Article III courts) has jurisdiction only over concrete "cases and controversies." The Court has therefore declined to provide "advisory opinions," beginning from when President Washington sought the justices' advice on the effects of certain treaties and laws on maintaining U.S. neutrality. See Opinion of the Justices (Aug. 8 1793), reproduced in Richard H. Fallon, Daniel J. Meltzer & David Shapiro, Hart & Wechsler's Federal Courts and the Federal System 92–93 (4th ed. 1996). The Justices explained their refusal to respond, in part, by noting that "[t]he lines of separation drawn by the Constitution between the three departments of the government ... being in certain respects checks upon each other—and our being judges of a court in the last resort—are considerations which afford strong arguments against the propriety of our extrajudicially deciding the questions alluded to. . . . "

The Supreme Court can review all questions of federal law (constitutional, statutory, relating to treaties or to federal common law or admiralty) that were dispositive in the lower courts, as well as any other matter decided by a lower federal court, e.g., in diversity cases. The Supreme Court's jurisdiction is largely discretionary; as a matter of statute, the Court gets to set its own agenda of cases that it decides on the merits. Most requests for review (called petitions for certiorari) are denied, with the denial having, as a formal matter, no implications for the Court's view of the merits, and no precedential effect. Its jurisdiction is primarily appellate (which is subject to regulation by Congress), though in a small number of cases (mostly litigation between two or more states) the matter is commenced originally in the Supreme Court.

There are nine justices on the Court. The number may be fixed by Congress but has not changed since the 1870s. Given public outrage at President Roosevelt's court-packing plan of 1937, the number may have become a fixture. (Is this an unwritten U.S. constitutional "convention"?) The Constitution provides no qualifications for Justices, who are nominated by the President but must be confirmed by majority vote of the Senate. They serve essentially for life, and they can be removed from office only by impeachment. No Supreme Court justice has been removed from office by impeachment.

The Senate has, however, refused to confirm presidential nominees—close to one-fifth of all presidential nominees to the Supreme Court have failed to be confirmed by the Senate. See Laurence H. Tribe, God Save This Honorable Court 78 (1985); see also Henry J. Abraham, Justices and Presidents: A Political History of Appointments to the Supreme Court (3d ed. 1992). Although no public hearings were held on nominees by the Senate until the 1930s, current practice is for a nominee to undergo investigation by the Senate, various interest groups and the media, and to answer questions in a public hearing, before being confirmed. Data suggest that Presidents facing a Senate controlled by another political party, and "lame duck" Presidents in their last term, are more likely to suffer defeat in the Senate on their proposed nominees.[e] In the last decade appointees have all served previously as judges, but this is a relatively recent phenomenon.[f] For a more detailed history of appointments to the Court, see Abraham.

In the excerpts below, Monaghan and Epstein, respectively, ask whether the nomination and confirmation process to the U.S. Supreme Court would be improved if (1) an age or year limit were placed on the service of such justices, or (2) a two-thirds vote in the Senate were required for confirmation. In thinking about these questions, consider as you read further in this chapter the experience of judicial selection in both France and Germany, as well as Germany's move towards a nonrenewability requirement for the judges of its constitutional court.

Henry Paul Monaghan, *The Confirmation Process: Law or Politics*, 101 Harv. L. Rev. 1202 (1988)

In this commentary, I want to submit two claims—one normative, the other empirical—and to raise one question. The normative claim is that the Senate's role in the appointment of Supreme Court judges is properly viewed as largely "political" in the broadest sense of the term: no significant affirmative constitutional compulsion exists to confirm any presidential nominee. So viewed, the Senate can serve as an important political check on the President's power to appoint. Moreover, the political nature of the Senate's role, like that of the President, helps ameliorate the "counter-

---

e. See Thomas Halper, *Senate Rejection of Supreme Court Nominees*, 22 Drake L. Rev. 102 (1972). For helpful discussion, see generally Susan Low Bloch and Thomas G. Krattenmaker, Supreme Court Politics: The Institution and Its Procedures (1994).

f. Earlier in this century, Charles Evans Hughes went to the Court from being Governor of New York; Hugo Black went from the Senate to the Court; Robert Jackson from being Attorney General; Earl Warren from being Governor of California and vice-presidential candidate to Chief Justice; Byron White was Deputy Attorney General in the Justice Department under President Kennedy; Lewis Powell came from private practice and active involvement in the American Bar Association; and William Rehnquist from Assistant Attorney General for the Office of Legal Counsel in the Justice Department.

majoritarian difficulty'': by increasing the likelihood that Supreme Court judges will hold views not too different from those of the people's representatives, the Senate can reduce the tension between the institution of judicial review and democratic government.

The empirical claim is that, at least for the foreseeable future, the overriding political power of the modern Presidency will continue to confine the Senate's actual role in the appointment process to its current dimensions. The Senate is incapable of systematically assuming any role greater than that of providing a check against the appointment of nominees perceived to be morally unworthy or too radical. In this respect, the unanimous confirmations of Judges Kennedy and Scalia reveal far more than does the rejection of Judge Bork.

Finally, the question I wish to raise is suggested by the nomination (not the withdrawal) of Judge Douglas Ginsburg. Should limits be imposed on the tenure of persons appointed judges of the Supreme Court? ...

II.

The Senate's actual role in the conformation process depended upon the shifting balance of political power between Congress and the President. The Senate's significant nineteenth-century role reflected the general congressional dominance of that era. Scarcely one hundred years ago, Woodrow Wilson argued that national government was congressional government— more precisely, "government by the chairmen of the Standing Committees of Congress." Wilson put aside the President with the dismissive observation that his "business ... occasionally great, is usually not much above routine." Although some such model of congressional government could be defended as late as the beginning of the New Deal, modern government is presidential government, at least in its most important aspects. Presidential ascendancy in the appointment process reflects this fact.

The modern Presidency, even a lame-duck Presidency facing a Senate controlled by the opposite party, has enormous resources for mobilizing support and for disciplining those senators who refuse to go along. Such resources—party discipline, ideology, and various carrots and sticks—can be concentrated on any issue of significant importance to the President. One could speculate extensively about why those resources failed in the case of Judge Bork. For us it suffices that the Bork proceedings themselves arose in a special context, one in which the administration's hard-line attitude on judicial nominations had left a bitter residue. Many parties were spoiling for a fight, and Judge Bork, who was perceived as far outside the mainstream of legal thinking, was the perfect catalyst to provoke one. Such a configuration is unlikely to be repeated frequently, suggesting Judge Bork's rejection portends no important institutional changes in the President's ability to win confirmation of nominees.

The institutionally important point is that it takes enormous energy for senators to unite in order to resist the President. Once undertaken, such conduct cannot easily be sustained, as evidenced by the relief with which the Senate greeted Judge Kennedy's nomination. The senators made every effort to see him as different from Judge Bork, regardless of whether he actually was. Commenting on Judge Kennedy's "smooth sailing" on his initial Senate visit, Senator John McCain, a conservative Republican from Arizona, put the point well: the Senate was simply "weary" of fighting. "Nobody wants to go through that again. There's just too much blood on the floor." At most, Judge Bork's hearings may have established a tradition of more probing Senate interrogation of a nominee, but the political background in which the entire confirmation process functions remains one with a powerful Presidency. To be sure, the rejection reminds us that periodically the American people seem to need a battle over a Supreme Court appointment. But symbolism aside, the hard fact is that the President's vision of what is proper judicial philosophy ultimately will prevail, as Judge Kennedy's confirmation demonstrates.

Nonetheless, some believe that Judge Bork's rejection shows that the Senate's role is less marginal than I have argued. The Senate's failure to confirm Judge Bork is said to reflect popular rejection of original understanding theory and popular acceptance of a general constitutional right to privacy. Although these contentions initially appear plausible, when carefully analyzed their flaws become apparent. In fact, Judge Bork did not avow original understanding as the sole basis for legitimate judicial decisionmaking. Moreover, the abortion cases, the most frequently cited illustration of Judge Bork's rejection of a constitutional right to privacy, actually involve autonomy or freedom from regulation, not privacy. Furthermore, the claim that, at least in exceptional circumstances, the Senate acts as a court of popular opinion endorsing or rejecting certain constitutional views is unpersuasive.[35] . . .

III.

The events surrounding President Reagan's efforts to fill the vacancy left by Justice Powell's retirement raise an additional question. When nominated, Judge Ginsburg was 41 years old. His relative youth cannot by itself be treated as a disqualification. Benjamin Curtis was 41 when nominated, and Judge Story only 32. Because confirmation effectively carries life tenure, Judge Ginsburg might well have served for four decades. The nomination for such a potentially lengthy period of service provides a singular occasion for reexamining the advisability of life tenure for Supreme Court judges. For some, the same premises that justify the free play of politics in the confirmation process might also weigh against life tenure.

---

35. Those who would argue otherwise must explain why Judge Bork's recent rejection implicitly endorses a liberal judicial philosophy, whereas the Senate's rejection of Justice Fortas as Chief Justice did not repudiate the same philosophy. Not surprisingly, claims of this nature tend to reflect the ideological commitments of their advocates. *Compare* Dworkin, *From Bork to Kennedy*, N.Y. Rev. of Books, Dec. 17, 1987, 38 *passim* (stating that liberals contend that Judge Bork's rejection was a declaration of popular will) *with* H. Abraham, *supra*, at 43–45 (arguing that the rejection of Justice Fortas' nomination as Chief Justice reflected a referendum on the Warren Court).

Also some limits on judicial tenure would help reconcile judicial review with democratic government. My concerns lie elsewhere, however.

The most common defenses of life tenure, contained in Hamilton's writing in The Federalist, are not fully persuasive. In Federalist No. 78, Hamilton argued that life tenure is indispensable to insulate the judiciary from the other branches of government, and thus to ensure its independence. But even assuming that such complete judicial independence is desirable, eliminating life tenure need not materially undermine it. Presumably, what relieves judges of the incentive to please is not the prospect of indefinite service, but the awareness that their continuation in office does not depend on securing the continuing approval of the political branches. Independence, therefore, could be achieved by mandating fixed, nonrenewable terms of service. Hamilton's objection in Federalist No. 79 to a state constitutional provision imposing mandatory retirement on judges at sixty is similarly unpersuasive. He stated that such a provision was unsound in "a republic, where fortunes are not affluent, and pensions not expedient." Given the current prevalence of pensions, however, Hamilton's argument no longer carries weight.

I propose the consideration of two kinds of limitations on judicial tenure. The first is an age limit. I think it quite astounding that a majority of Supreme Court judges bordered on eighty years of age before Chief Justice Burger and Justice Powell retired. The Court's workload is very heavy, and it is doubtful that many octogenarians would be able to devote the energy necessary to the task. As Aristotle said, "that judges of important causes should hold office for life is a disputable thing, for the mind grows old as well as the body." The graying of the Court can only work to ensure even greater delegation of responsibility to law clerks.

My second suggestion is premised on a distrust of relatively unaccountable powerholders. The suggestion is that no one be permitted to serve for more than some fixed and unrenewable term, such as fifteen or twenty years. Governor Winthrop once described judges as "gods upon earth," and that surely is true of the Supreme Court judges. It seems dubious policy to leave such power in any person's hands for too long. In light of these concerns, and of the defects in the original justifications for life tenure, the burden should be on those who favor the continuation of the present arrangement to come forth with their argument. Or is the short response to both of my suggestions, "If it ain't broke, don't fix it"?

Lee Epstein, "A BETTER WAY TO APPOINT JUSTICES," The Christian Science Monitor (Mar. 17 1992)

[This essay argues that the Clarence Thomas nomination shows that "something is seriously wrong" with the way justices are appointed. To secure the framers' goal of keeping "justices above partisan politics," Epstein proposes amending the Constitution to require a two-thirds vote of the Senate to confirm Supreme Court justices.]

A two-thirds vote would change, for the better, the political calculations of the president. Presidents—be they Democrats or Republicans—would have to rethink whom they nominated to the court. To gain approval of their nominees, they would need true bipartisan support, not just a few crossover votes. That would require them to place far more stock in candidates' legal credentials. It also would compel presidents to seek the advice of senators of both parties before making nominations.

A two-thirds vote would also change, for the better, thinking in the Senate. If presidents gave senators a greater role at the "advice" stage, it would help to eliminate the sort of proceedings we have experienced in recent years—unacceptable candidates would never make it that far. Confirmation hearings would serve as forums to discern nominees' legal qualifications to sit on the Supreme Court, rather than as showcases for senators on the Judiciary Committee.

A two-thirds vote is required for the approval of treaties (by the Senate) and the proposal of constitutional amendments (both Houses); who sits on the Supreme Court is today of similar importance. The framers required two-thirds votes for matters of great national importance. What has become more important—at least on domestic matters—than decisions of the US Supreme Court? Courts of the last three decades have enunciated public policy on reapportionment, affirmative action, and abortion.

A two-thirds vote would not eliminate qualified candidates. Since the emergence of the modern Supreme Court (a date scholars fix at around 1937), only one successful nominee to be an associate justice might have failed to gain 67 Senate votes—Mr. Thomas. William Rehnquist might still have attained confirmation as an associate justice (he had 68 votes in 1971), but he might not have been able to ascend to the chief justiceship (he received only 65 votes in 1986).

I stress the word "might," because a change in the rules would significantly alter the calculus of both the president and the Senate. With a two-thirds requirement, Ronald Reagan might not have sought to elevate Mr. Rehnquist (or pursued the confirmation of Robert Bork), nor might President Bush have nominated Thomas. Alternatively, Rehnquist might have received more votes from the Senate if it was operating under the constraints of a two-thirds rule.

My point is not to second-guess past votes; it is to suggest that a two-thirds requirement would not restrict the pool of serious candidates. It may, though, reduce it just enough to eliminate those who have no business sitting on the most important judicial body in our nation.

Questions and Comments

1. For an argument that the political dynamics of the appointments process in the U.S. mirrors the political dynamics of other issues, so that, for example, when interest group politics shape social security policy interest group politics likewise dominate judicial nomination politics, see Mark Silverstein, Judicious Choices (1994). Silverstein suggests that the increasingly public and interest-group dominated nature of the confirmation process will drive nominations to the center, with a focus on the nominee's technical skills, since these are the nominees who can get through the political minefields, a result he finds not unacceptable: "That a politicized system of selecting and confirming our judges may mean that people of stature, a Brandeis and a Holmes, a Marshall and a Warren, do not find their way to the Court is a consequence that must be measured against a paramount commitment to self-rule."

2. Has the political process, as described by Silverstein, come to approximate the effects of Epstein's proposed two-thirds rule?

---

3.   FRANCE AND THE CONSEIL CONSTITUTIONNEL

Because current French constitutional jurisprudence incorporates to some degree the Declaration of the Rights of Man and Citizen of 1789, this introduction begins with France in 1789. From then until 1958, sovereignty and power were located in elected assemblies, and/or strong rulers, with courts playing a decidedly subordinate role.

In the 1780s, France had accumulated substantial debts, and the reform and taxation efforts of its king, Louis XVI, were obstructed by clergy and nobility who controlled the local "parlements" or lawcourts; the "parlements" did not have power to legislate but their agreement was required to register laws or edicts promulgated by the King. In order to obtain assent to raise taxes, the King convened the "estates general," which had not met for 150 years and whose voting rules permitted the clergy and nobility to outvote all others. Soon, however, representatives of the so-called "third estate"—consisting of everyone other than the clergy or nobility—broke off and established the first National Assembly which, after being joined by some clergy and nobles, the King recognized as representative of France.

The National Assembly, which abolished the feudal privileges of the "ancien regime" and established the principle of civic equality, also promulgated the Declaration of the Rights of Man and Citizen, a foundational document still important in the French constitutional order. By 1791, France had been declared a constitutional monarchy, but in 1792 the National Convention declared France a Republic, without a king. The King's subsequent execution was part of the Reign of Terror, in which thousands suspected of being royalist, or having "unrepublican" sympathies, were executed. During the Reign of Terror, republican leaders sought to make a clean break with the past by, *inter alia*, creating a new calendar. In reaction to the excesses of this reign of terror, the "thermidorian reaction" began and led to the Constitution of the Year III, which established a 5–person directorate to head the government. Following military successes, Napoleon Bonaparte seized power in 1799 and issued a Constitution of the year VIII, establishing rule by "consul" and under which Napoleon was "first Consul." This form of government was soon abandoned, with Bonaparte declaring himself Emperor within 5 years.[g]

In the 19th century, after the rise and fall of Napoleon Bonaparte, France moved between republican, monarchical and imperial forms of government until 1870, when Prussia defeated France in the Franco–Prussian War. Napoleon III was overthrown, a National Assembly elected, and in 1875 a new constitution was a written. Under the constitution of this Third Republic, Parliament was extremely powerful and the President, Prime Minister and cabinet correspondingly weak.

Following World War II, France adopted another new constitution to govern the Fourth Republic.[h] DeGaulle, who had led the French resistance in World War II, formed the provisional government and became President in 1945. But he opposed the 1946 constitution of the Fourth Republic on the grounds that it did not provide sufficiently strong executive power. DeGaulle left the government, and it proved difficult to maintain an effective government under the 1946 Constitution, which gave parliament the power to dismiss the prime minister and cabinet, a power used on average more than once year.[i]

In the 1950s France's colonies in Indochina and Northern Africa began actively seeking their independence and in 1954, a revolution began in Algeria. While France gave up control of Morocco and Tunisia, it was reluctant to recognize the independence of Algeria, which had a substantial French population. By 1958, though, many in France had become persuaded that Algerian independence should be recognized. But French army leaders revolted and threatened to overthrow the government if it gave up Algeria. In order to avert this crisis, DeGaulle returned as prime minister, with emergency powers and authority to propose a new constitution. Under his government the present Constitution of the Fifth Republic—a very substantial departure from prior constitutions—was prepared and was approved by the voters in 1958.

Under the Constitution of 1958, parliament's powers were curtailed and those of the executive substantially expanded to include the power to issue "reglements" (rules) in areas of "executive legislative competence." Article 34 sets forth the areas in which parliament makes laws (lois),[j] while

---

g. For an overview of French history during the revolution, on which this summary is in part based, see Donald Kagan, Steven Ozment & Frank M. Turner, The Western Heritage 690–735 (5th ed. 1995); see also L. Neville Brown & John S. Bell, French Administrative Law 8–47 (4th ed. 1993). The contribution of Jacob L. Taylor to this section is gratefully acknowledged.

h. France is reported to have "had a total of fifteen constitutional instruments in the two hundred years since the Revolution

of 1789." John Bell, French Constitutional Law 1 (1992).

i. Bell reports that France had 23 governments in twelve years. Bell, at 11.

j. These include civil rights and civil liberties; nationality and capacity of person; matrimony and laws of inheritance; crimes and penalties; taxes; electoral law; public corporations; fundamental guarantees to civil and military employees; nationalizations and privatizations; the general organization of the national defense; the administration of

article 37 in essence confers legislative power on the executive to make "reglements" (decrees or rules). Laws generally require rules, made by the government, to be implemented. The president, moreover, can direct the order of proceeding on matters in Parliament. Thus the executive's authority in legislation is quite strong. Under this constitution, finally, Parliament's power to dismiss a government was substantially curtailed, and among the expanded powers of the President is the power to appoint the Prime Minister.

In the readings that follow, Bell and Stone give complementary accounts of the creation and development of the Conseil Constitutionnel. Initially designed to enforce the power of the president against parliamentary encroachments, the Conseil has proven to be an even more substantial innovation in French constitutional law.

John Bell, FRENCH CONSTITUTIONAL LAW (1992)

1.3   CONSTITUTIONAL REVIEW

The creation of the Conseil constitutionnel was originally intended as an additional mechanism to ensure a strong executive by keeping Parliament within its constitutional role. As will be seen later, this original intention has been departed from to a significant degree in subsequent years to create what is effectively a constitutional court.

Constitutional Review in French History

In presenting the Conseil constitutionnel to the Conseil d'État in 1958, Debré stated that "It is neither in the spirit of a parliamentary regime, nor in the French tradition, to give to the courts, that is to say, to each litigant, the right to examine the validity of a *loi*...." [A]lthough the rule of law quite quickly involved the subordination of the executive to the law and to bodies that could be called courts, Parliament, as the lawmaker and representative of the nation, was in a different position. This is reflected both in the history of institutions and in currents of ideas.

Institutions. In the *ancien régime* there was nothing quite like a modern national Parliament. The Estates General, composed of representatives of the three orders of society (nobility, clergy, and commoners), was the nearest equivalent to one, but it did not meet from 1614 until 1789. The regional *parlements* were lawcourts, membership of which was an office of profit to be bought and sold, and representatives were drawn from the nobility and the clergy. In order to be valid, a law made by the King

local authorities; education; regimes for property and commercial obligations; labor law and social security. Article 35 states that a "declaration of war shall be authorized by parliament." The parliament consists of a direct, popularly elected National Assembly, and a Senate elected by indirect suffrage which consists of representatives of local governments. All matters not included in article 34 belong, under Article 37, to the "regulatory" power of the Government.

had to be registered with the local *parlement,* from which grew up the view that it had the power to refuse to register laws made by the King. Although the King could impose his will by holding a *lit de justice,* remonstrances made by the *parlement* against a particular measure could ensure that it was altered. This power had been used in the years leading up to the Revolution of 1789 in order to block reforms introduced by Louis XVI. The clergy and nobility were thus able to resist change, and the *parlements* gained the reputation of being reactionary.

The separation of powers introduced by the revolutionary Constitutions sought to prevent the judiciary, being able to obstruct Parliament. Hence the *loi* of 16–24 August 1790 insisted in article 10 that the judiciary was not "to take part directly or indirectly in the exercise of legislative power", or to "obstruct or suspend the execution of the decrees of the legislative body". Article 127 of the Criminal Code backed this up by making it an offence for a judge to interfere with the legislative power. The Tribunal de cassation (as the highest ordinary court was known) decided as early as 1797 that "the absolute terms in which the prohibition on the courts to stop or suspend the implementation of *lois* is drafted can admit of no exception or excuse". Apart from two possibly aberrant decisions of the Cour de cassation (as the Tribunal de cassation had then become) in 1851, the ordinary judiciary has consistently refused to challenge the validity of *lois.*

This reaction to the *parlements* did not mean that the French were not aware of the need to keep Government and Parliament within the limits of the Constitution. The excesses of the Terror brought home the necessity for such control. In the debates on the *Directoire* Constitution of 1795 Sieyès suggested that there should be a *jurie constitutionnaire* that would ensure that the Constitution was obeyed by annulling acts of the legislature and the executive that were contrary to it. Rejected then, the idea was taken up at the adoption of the next Constitution in 1799. The Constitution of year VIII established a Sénat conservateur that had the function of considering the constitutionality of provisions, and even annulling decisions referred to it by the Tribune (Assembly) or by the Government (article 21); this included annulling *lois,* though only before their promulgation (article 37). In fact, this body was totally ineffective. Composed of persons appointed by the consuls, who were irremovable, it did nothing to prevent the excesses of the Napoleonic period. It only decided to quash legislative acts two days before the capitulation of Paris in 1814. The institution was revived under Louis Napoleon (soon to become Napoleon III) in the Constitution of 14 January, 1852. Again composed of persons appointed with security of tenure, it was intended as the guardian of liberties and other basic values. It could pronounce on the constitutionality of *lois* before promulgation, but it could also pronounce on any decision referred to it by the Government or on a petition of citizens. This was thought to open the way to review of *lois* even after they had been promulgated. But the provision was never put to the test, and the Sénat of the Second Empire was as ineffective as that of the First.

The contrary, and typically republican, tradition exhibited in other Constitutions before 1946 was that Parliament itself was the guardian of constitutionality. In the very first Constitution of 1791 the National Assembly was enjoined to refuse all proposals that infringed the Constitution. Self-limitation was the preferred institutional device for ensuring that the Constitution was respected, with an ultimate control exercised by the electorate.

It was the collapse of the Third Republic, and the actions of the Vichy regime that encouraged further consideration of institutional safeguards. The First Constituent Assembly of 1945–6 adhered to the predominant republican tradition, and did not even have a second chamber as a check on the National Assembly. Following the Second Constituent Assembly, the Constitution of 1946 established a Comité constitutionnel composed of the Presidents of the Republic, the National Assembly, and the Council of the Republic (as the Senate was called), and then seven persons nominated by the National Assembly and three by the Council of the Republic. The nominees appointed by the two Assemblies were to come from outside their membership. This body was designed to make prompt decisions on a limited range of matters concerned exclusively with the institutional provisions of the Constitution, and deliberately excluding the declarations of rights. It could examine *lois* before they were promulgated to see if a constitutional amendment was necessary. Since the procedures for such an amendment were cumbersome, this was, in theory, a serious obstacle to unconstitutional legislation. It was concerned merely to resolve conflicts between the two chambers, and was designed to redress the power of the National Assembly to override the Council of the Republic. It was called upon to make only one decision: in 1948, on the question of the time-limit within which the Council to the Republic had to vote on a bill when the National Assembly had classified it a matter of urgency. Other attempts to have matters referred were not successful. Notably, in 1957 the Gaullists tried to have the bill ratifying the Treaty of Rome referred to the Comité on the ground that it was incompatible with national sovereignty. Since there was no conflict between the two Assemblies on the issue, the Comité had no jurisdiction to consider the matter.

The self-limitation of Parliament was not very effective, in that blatantly abusive *lois* were passed both in terms of procedure—for example, the delegation of blanket legislative powers to the executive—and substance—the anticlerical legislation of the turn of the century. Even the Fourth Republic offered no check where both chambers were agreed on a measure. . . .

The Doctrinal Debate In the realm of ideas, constitutional review did not loom large as an issue in the public imagination. . . .

The main arguments used against constitutional review focused on the status of *loi* and the separation of powers.

Article 6 of the Declaration of 1789 stated that *loi* is the supreme expression of the *volonté générale*. This was interpreted as meaning that Parliament was the representative of the general will of the nation, and that its enactments thus enjoyed the status appropriate to the expression of the will of the sovereign. On this view, the State was the voice of the nation, and its authority was a pre-condition for liberty. In no sense was it argued that constitutional review was incompatible with the idea of sovereignty. The people could easily agree to restrict that authority, and Carré de Malberg considered that such limitations were very much expressions of sovereignty. All the same, the introduction of constitutional review would be a change in the way in which it was to be exercised.

The argument from the separation of powers has two elements. On the one hand there is the statement of the appropriate function of each organ; on the other, there is the appropriate deference that must be paid by other organs of government.

The function of the legislature was, according to Carré de Malberg, to be the continuing representative of the will of the nation, and, as such, to complete the task of making the Constitution. The French situation under the Third Republic was different from that in other countries, since Parliament had the power to alter the Constitution, and was not subordinated in this task to a prior or external institution or mechanism. In addition, the legislature was to be the interpreter of the Constitution; this was appropriate, since it was representative of the people who made it. Parliament was to interpret the Constitution when it came to passing legislation, and if it decided that its interpretation was compatible with the Constitution, this could not be gainsaid by any other organ:

> Nothing is more natural than to make interpretation an act of the very person who made the text ... In other words, it is for the legislature, at the very moment of making laws, to examine if the *loi* being considered is consistent with the Constitution, and to resolve the problems that may arise on this point. The legislature interprets in this way by virtue of its popular representation.

The appropriate role of the judiciary here was to defer to the decision of the legislature. The demarcation of powers was to be understood not as a separation of functions, as in the United States, but as a separation of organs of government. In making constitutional amendments, Parliament had to meet in a different way from when it passed ordinary legislation, but it was still Parliament that "was acting". For both ordinary and constitutional *lois,* the separation of powers required the judiciary to respect the actions of Parliament. To try to impose the will of Parliament constituted as constitutional legislator over Parliament constituted as ordinary legislator did not make sense. The revolutionary texts, attacked as outdated by the proponents of constitutional review, were seen as merely expressive of the appropriate separation of powers in a democracy, since judges could not stand in the way of the will of the people.

A significant concern of the writers was the conservative effect of providing constitutional review based on any declarations of rights. The authors like Duguit and Hauriou who proposed some form of substantive review envisaged that this would strike down measures such as the anti-clerical laws of 1905, the provisions on secrecy of tax returns (which enabled private settlements between the revenue and the taxpayer), the granting of judicial powers to parliamentary committees, and attacks on property. To Jèze, this would simply make the judiciary a block to social progress: "Against a democratic Parliament, product of universal suffrage, and against its possible will for reform, it is desired in reality to set up bourgeois judges for the defence and irreducible preservation of the possessing classes characterized as élites." This concern seemed to be supported by the highly influential study of the US Supreme Court published by Édouard Lambert in 1921. He described it as "doubtless the most perfected tool of social inertia to which one can currently resort to restrain workers' agitations and to hold back the legislator from the slippery slope of economic interventionism". Time and again the opponents of constitutional review would point to the experience of the United States in the 1910s as an illustration of what could happen in France.

Other arguments centred on the effect that this would have on the judiciary. Currently, this career civil service was strongly influenced in its appointments by the Government, and there was no strong, fearless independence equivalent to the Supreme Court of the United States. In any case, judges would inevitably be drawn into the political forum by constitutional review, and this would lead to attacks on them for their political views that would further reduce the reputation of the French judiciary.

In any case, if Jèze and Eisenmann were right about the nature of the Constitution of 1875, reduced to mere rules of procedure without any declarations of rights, an institution of constitutional review would have very little impact and importance, and would thus not be worth while.

The Intentions of the Drafters of the Constitution. As originally conceived, the Conseil constitutionnel was not to be a radical departure from what had gone before in terms of its institutional competence. The essential difference was the new view of parliamentary sovereignty as limited by the role accorded to the executive. The Conseil was merely one institutional mechanism to ensure that this new function of Parliament was adhered to. The Comité consultatif constitutionnel saw the Conseil as "a corset", "an essential element for the harmonious operation of public authorities", a body to keep Parliament and the executive within their proper limits. It was not to be some form of supreme court in constitutional matters, along the lines of the German Constitutional Court, a specialist body to which references can be made from all courts during litigation. As the *commissaire du gouvernement* (the civil servant representing the Government), Janot, stated:

> Such a system would be tempting intellectually, but it seemed to us that constitutional review through an action in the courts would conflict too much with the traditions of French public life. To give the members of the Conseil constitutionnel the power to oppose the promulgation of unconstitutional texts appeared sufficient to us. To go further would risk leading us into a kind of government by judges,

would reduce the legislative role of Parliament, and would hamper governmental action in a harmful way:

. . .

The longest debate in the Comité was on the question of who should be able to refer matters to the Conseil. The draft—as, indeed, the final text put to the people—only enabled the President of the Republic, and the Presidents of the Senate and the National Assembly, and the Prime Minister to do so. . . . Triboulet . . . moved an amendment . . . to allow one–third of the members of either assembly to refer a *loi* to the Conseil. The argument was one of protecting the position of minorities within the Parliament. Since the Presidents of the National Assembly and Senate were, on past experience, likely to belong to the majority, the opposition had no way of having a matter raised before the Conseil. Debré argued that this would be incompatible with parliamentary government. . . . Similarly, Teitgen argued, "Every time that a *loi* has given rise to an impassioned debate, the opposition will . . . refer it to the Conseil constitutionnel, and in the end effective government will be in the hands of the pensioners who will sit on the Conseil". . . .

The role of the Conseil constitutionnel has increased significantly since 1974, when members of Parliament were permitted to make references to it. . . .

The Functions of the Conseil constitutionnel The Conseil has five broad heads of jurisdiction, which are not necessarily related.

First, the Conseil is an election court and returning officer. It determines the existence of a presidential vacancy or incapacity, oversees the election process, and announces the results. It has a similar supervisory function in relation to referendums. With regard to parliamentary elections, it rules on disputed elections. It also rules on the ineligibility of members of Parliament. The case-load is quite considerable. As a result of the parliamentary elections of June 1988, some eighty-five decision on electoral matters are reported in the annual *Recueil* of decisions of the Conseil constitutionnel.

In the case of parliamentary elections, the Conseil will judge after the event, though it has recognized that it may be appropriate to rule on an issue before elections taken place, where this affects a large number of constituencies. Thus in *Delmas* it ruled on whether the duration of the election campaign was not too short, in breach of the Electoral Code. This affected all elections. In this area the Conseil is like any judge, seeing that the provisions of the Electoral Code have been obeyed. As an election court, it does not have jurisdiction to challenge the validity of the *lois* that set out the rules for elections.

Secondly, the Conseil also advises the President both when he seeks to use emergency powers under article 16 and on the rules made thereunder. Such advice is not binding, but it is of considerable authority all the same. The practice of 1961 would suggest that the Conseil's formal advice is preceded by informal advice. This may, however, be due to the particular personalities involved in the 1961 crisis, and might not be so easily repeated.

Thirdly, the Conseil may also be asked to rule on the constitutionality of treaties. Treaties are signed by the President, but require parliamentary legislation in most cases before they can be ratified. Once ratified, they have a status superior to *lois* (article 55). Although the Conseil constitutionnel will not strike down a *loi* for incompatibility with a treaty, other courts may refuse to apply it in such a case. Prior examination of the compatibility of a treaty and the Constitution is thus desirable.

The Presidents of the Republic, the National Assembly, and the Senate, or the Prime Minister or 60 deputies or senators may refer a treaty for consideration by the Conseil to determine whether it is contrary to the Constitution. If it is, then it can only be ratified after a constitutional amendment has been passed (article 54). This procedure is merely an extension of the competence of the Comité constitutionnel under the Fourth Republic, about which there was controversy when the EEC Treaty was ratified. The President of the Republic has been the only one to make use of it in relation to EEC taxation (1970), European elections (1976), the additional Protocol to the European Declaration on Human Rights on the death penalty (1985) and the Maastricht Treaty (1992).

Fourthly, the Conseil also examines the constitutionality of organic laws and parliamentary standing orders. Both are subject to compulsory review by the Conseil before they are promulgated (article 61 § 1).

Organic laws are required in a number of areas, such as on the judiciary, on the composition of Parliament, on finance laws, and on the procedure of the Conseil constitutionnel. The process for passing them is stricter than for ordinary *lois,* requiring the agreement of the Senate or an absolute majority of members of the National Assembly (article 46). Since these organic laws may be used subsequently as a basis for judging the constitutionality of *lois,* and may extend the body of constitutional rules, it is appropriate that the Conseil should review them before enactment.

The scrutiny of *parliamentary standing orders* is justified by the desire to ensure that Parliament does not overstep the boundaries set out for it in the Constitution. If Parliament were to adopt procedures that blocked the dominance of the executive, this could clearly upset the new arrangements of 1958. It may have been all right to leave such matters to the sole judgment of Parliament in an era of parliamentary sovereignty, but this could no longer be the case in the 1958 regime. . . .

Fifthly, the Conseil had, as its primary original function, to police the boundaries of the legislative competences of Parliament and of the executive. This is performed in any of three ways.

(1) Under article 37, the Government can only amend or repeal provisions in *lois* passed after 1958 by way of *règlement* if the Conseil constitutionnel has first declassified them, in other words, if it has ruled that the provision does fall within the domain of executive legislative competence. In this way, it ensures that the Government does not overstep

its competence. The Government must take the initiative, and refer provisions of *lois* to the Conseil if it wishes to have them declassified.

(2) When private members' bills or amendments are proposed in Parliament that stray into the area of the executive's legislative competence, the Government may seek to have the proposed provisions ruled out of order. Where the President of the relevant chamber of Parliament disputes the claim of the Government, either he or the Prime Minister may refer the dispute to the Conseil, which has to give a ruling within eight days (article 41). Since 1979, this procedure has rarely been used.

(3) Once a *loi* has been passed by Parliament, the Conseil has jurisdiction to rule on its constitutionality if a reference is made to it by the President of the Republic, the President of either the National Assembly or the Senate, the Prime Minister, or (since 1974) sixty members of either Assembly (article 61 §2). The reform of 1974 effectively gave the opposition a chance to challenge legislation, and it has become almost the only challenger to *lois*.

Although originally designed to keep Parliament within the competences set out in article 34, the reference of enacted *loi* to the Conseil has become a procedure for challenging them on wider, substantive grounds, particularly for breach of fundamental rights. The importance of this procedure can be seen from Table 1.1.

TABLE 1.1. *References to the* Conseil constitutional *under article 61 § 2 of the Constitution*

Period	References under art. 61 § 2	Number not consistent	Proportion not consistent (%)
1959–September 1974	9	7	77.0
October 1974–April 1981	47	13	28.0
May 1981–March 1986	66	33	50.0
April 1986–January1989	32	19	64.6

The Conseil only has jurisdiction to challenge a *loi* before it has been promulgated. In early decisions it stated that references cannot be used to challenge the validity of previously promulgated *loi*. But in 1985 the Conseil declared *obiter:* "though the validity with respect to the Constitution of a promulgated *loi* may properly be contested on the occasion of an examination of legislative provisions that amend it, complement it, or affect its scope, this is not the case when it is a matter of simply applying such a *loi....*"

Alec Stone, The Birth of Judicial Politics in France: The Constitutional Council in Comparative Perspective (1992) (excerpts from pp. 46–53, 57–59)

From Watchdog to Policymaker: Structure, Function, Mandate

[Stone describes the transition from the Fourth to the Fifth Republic:]

... The new constitution, drafted principally by *conseillers d'Etat* under the watchful eyes of de Gaulle, Michel Debré, and their associates, shifted effective power over the legislative process and over the form and content of legislation from parliament to the executive. In a word, the parliamentary system was *rationalized,* that is, placed under the management of a government detached from parliament (if left responsible). A special body, the Constitutional Council, was created to guarantee the viability of this new distribution of powers, and—not wholly unlike the Bonapartist Senates—the institution was expressly denied a judicial role, and its competence was limited entirely to parliamentary space. This chapter, first, examines the creation of the Council—with special attention paid to the intention of the founders—along with attributes of the body's jurisdiction, composition and recruitment.

The Council and Original Intent

After a nearly century-long period of unrivaled supremacy, parliament was mastered by the political settlement that gave birth to the Fifth Republic. The central objective of the founders was to "alter the status of parliament so that it would no longer be at the center of political life ... and ... permanently be incapable of obstructing government action. From this point of view, their success was complete." The settlement, as everyone knows, resulted in a "servile" legislature, in the famous words of François Mitterrand, in a "permanent *coup d'état.*" Without belaboring an overworked subject, the central features of the rationalized legislative process are worth recalling. First, and most important, the constitution distinguishes between statute—*la loi*—and a certain class of executive acts—*le règlement.* Whereas parliament was free to legislate on any subject during the Third and Fourth Republics, article 34 of the new constitution lists inclusively those legislative subject matters which together constitute what the constitution calls the "domain" of *la loi.* These subject matters include among others the "fixing of rules concerning" civil and fundamental rights of citizens; nationality, marriage, and inheritance; changes in the penal code and the code on penal procedure, amnesties, and the creation of new courts and the status of judges; electoral laws; the rights of the civil and military services; the creation of "public enterprises," the nationalization of industry, and the expropriation of private property; local administration and education; and labor laws and social security. It later, in article 40, forbids any member or group of parliament from proposing bills or amendments which would have the effect of either raising public expenditures or reducing public funds. All subject matters not listed in article 34 are expressly reserved to the executive by article 37. In sum, *la loi* was no longer to be defined by its form, an act of parliament, but by its content, the matter to be regulated. Second, the process itself was "streamlined" in favor of the government. The constitution grants to the executive alone control over the legislative calendar, and the means to control parliamentary discussion, the amending process, and voting procedures.

The function of the Council in this system was made explicit: to facilitate the centralization of executive authority, and to ensure that the system would not somehow revert to traditional parliamentary orthodoxy. Its primary role, as seen by the founders, was to police the frontiers of the domains of *la loi* and *le règlement,* to be a "watchdog on behalf of executive supremacy." As Debré put it, in [a speech in 1958] outlining the general contours of the new constitution to the *Conseil d'Etat:*

> We must ... suppress ... parliamentary arbitrariness, which—under the pretext of sovereignty, not of the nation (which is just), but of the Assemblies (which is fallacious)—has subverted without limit the status of the Constitution and of governmental authority. The creation of the Constitutional Council manifests the will to subordinate *la loi,* that is, the decision of the parliament, to the superior rule *[règle]* laid down by the Constitution. It is neither in the spirit of the parliamentary regime, nor in the French tradition, to give to judicial authorities ... the right to examine the status of *la loi.* The project therefore imagines a special institution to which only four authorities will have access.... The Constitution thus creates an arm against deviation from the [new] parliamentary regime.

... [A]lthough its role in reviewing legislation was that of a referee engaged in settling conflicts between the executive and the legislature, *the Council was not meant to be a fair or impartial referee* (any more than the constitution was designed to be fair or impartial). Its field of play was to be exclusively parliamentary space; it was to have jurisdiction only over legislative and *not* executive acts; and a proposal to balance the equation— to allow legislative authorities to refer executive acts to the Council—was not seriously considered. Moreover, the mode of recruitment proposed all but guaranteed that a majority of the Council's members would be active supporters of the government. Indeed, the government's working draft (as well as the final product) strictly limited access to the institution for rulings on constitutionality, of proposed legislation to four officials—the president of the Republic, the prime minister, the president of the Senate, and the president of the National Assembly....

Second, *neither the government nor the CCC* considered the Council to be a court,* if by that we mean a judicial or courtlike body. The constitution does not provide for any interaction between the Council and the judicial system, and unlike the constitutional provisions governing the recruitment of other constitutional courts on the continent, *no prerequisite of prior judicial service or minimum requirements of legal training was ever contemplated.* The 1958 constitution does not mention the Council in its chapter on "Judicial Authority," but instead sets it apart in its own chapter. Where the Council is mentioned, it is to grant authority, over aspects of legislative process. Perhaps even more important, its review powers were restricted to verifying that a statute or statutory provisions had not 1) been passed in violation of the procedures laid down by the constitution or, 2) trespassed on the domain of *le règlement.*

---

* [Editors' Note: The CCC is the Constitutional Consultative Committee, consisting of legislators and law professors from several political parties, asked by the government to comment on the Constitution during its final drafting.]

Discussion in the CCC on the *valeur constitutionnel* of the proposed preamble to the 1958 constitution is instructive on these points. As finally promulgated in October, the preamble is a simple two-line statement, the relevant part of which reads as follows:

The French People solemnly proclaim their attachment to the Rights of Man and to the principles of national sovereignty as defined by the Declaration of 1789, confirmed and completed by the preamble of the Constitution of 1946.

In July, a working group within the CCC had adopted an amendment to article 34 which would have required that legislation, in order to be valid, respect "the general principles of individual rights and liberties defined by the preamble." The government's spokesman *(commissaire du gouvernement)*, Raymond Janot, opposed the amendment on the grounds that "jurists would be tempted to invoke the mention of the preamble ... as a means of bestowing *valeur constitutionnel* to past declarations of the rights of man," and the following discussion ensued:

DEJEAN: ... I had asked if the preamble had, juridically, *valeur constitutionnel.*

JANOT: No, but if you refer to it in the Constitution itself, ... it will have. Do you really think that the rules laid down in 1789 still possess normative value in the 20th century, that they respond to the present structure of our society?

DEJEAN: For the authors of the draft, therefore, the preamble does not possess *valeur constitutionnel.*

JANOT: No, certainly not.

Waline protested, arguing that if the government's position was upheld and the amendment rejected, the *Conseil d'Etat's* jurisprudence of general principles would be undermined. Janot responded that such principles derived their source uniquely from jurisprudence, and not by virtue of their constitutional status: "As a practical matter, they do not limit the legislator."

The significance of the preamble's status for the future activity of the Council was a matter of crucial concern. After a member of the CCC asked if the amendment would require the Council to "determine if statutes conform to the preamble and the declaration of 1789," Janot answered in the affirmative, and warned that the CCC was flirting with instituting "a government of judges." Dejean then withdrew his support, and called successfully for the amendment to be quashed:

Would it be a good thing to give unquestioned *valeur constitutionnel* to the contents of the preamble ...? We would no longer be able to pass legislation without unhappy people referring it to the Council under the pretext that such and such a principle had been violated. We must be very prudent.

A similar move to strengthen the role of principles contained in the 1789 declaration was opposed by the government on the grounds that it might appear to "constitutionalize the capitalist system."

Composition and Recruitment

The constitutional provisions relevant to recruitment and composition are contained in article 56:

> The Constitutional Council is composed of 9 members who serve 9 year, non-renewable terms. The Constitutional Council is renewed in thirds every three years. Three of its members are named by the President of the Republic, three by the President of the National Assembly, three by the President of the Senate.

> In addition to the 9 members mentioned above, former Presidents of the Republic are members of the Constitutional Council for life.

Members need only be 18 years of age or older and in possession of their civil rights—there exist no other formal prerequisites for membership, no nomination or confirmation procedures, and no means to block appointments. Alone among former presidents of the Republic, Vincent Auriol and Rény Coty were seated in the 1959–62 period, and it is likely that they will be the last to do so. In July 1960, Auriol walked out in protest of what he called the Council's excessive deference to de Gaulle, which he linked to the institution's mode of recruitment, and referral mechanism.

In practice, the single most important criterion for appointment to the Council is political affiliation, and the Council has been dominated by professional politicians. This is the case for all five of the presidents of the Council, four of whom had also served as government ministers. Statistically, of the forty-one members who have been appointed to the Council from 1958 to 1988, 59 percent (twenty-four) were selected from the ranks of former parliamentarians and/or government ministers. This percentage has increased dramatically in the past two decades: every Council since that of 1968 has been composed of at least six (67 percent) such politicians, increasing to seven (78 percent) in 1983, and to eight (89 percent) in 1986. The second largest category, representing 24 percent (ten) of total membership, is made up of men who had served in staffs or as advisors to either politicians or political parties, but not as parliamentarians. Other categories are less coherent due to overlapping professional and political activities, but several points deserve to be noted. First, only three judges have been appointed (in 1958, 1969, and 1979), the first two of whom were recruited from the *Cour de cassation;* the last, a former deputy and minister, had served on the European Court of Justice. In addition, seven law professors have been named, some of whom had also been, perhaps more importantly, parliamentarians and/or ministers. . . .

The naming of the president of the Council (an important position not least because the Council president casts the deciding vote in the case of deadlock, and controls procedures, including the designation of the *rapporteur* for each decision) is also the prerogative of the president of the

Republic. There have been five presidents of the Council to date, two named by de Gaulle, one by Pompidou, and two by Mitterrand, and in each case, the appointment decision was treated as a matter of high politics. De Gaulle appointed men who had been members of his entourage during resistance days, and had later been instrumental in establishing the Fifth Republic: Léon Nöel, a member of the CCC, and Gaston Palewski, appointed by de Gaulle in compensation for his work on the 1962 referendum on the direct election of the president, and for organizing the office of the new presidency. Their ascribed role was no less than to ensure the subservience of the Council to the wishes of the general. As discussed later, they fulfilled this role, if on occasion with some regret. Pompidou's appointment in 1974 of Roger Frey, a "Baron of Gaullism," was made for a variety of political reasons: to guarantee continuity of Gaullist principles in the case of possible upcoming electoral defeat, and—it was speculated—to satisfy calls to avenge the president of the Senate's appointment, of the day before, of de Gaulle's and the Council's most powerful and persistent opponent, Gaston Monnerville (a longtime president of the Senate). Pompidou himself was said to have put it to Frey, a minister in every government from 1959 until his appointment to the presidency of the Council in 1974, and then secretary-general of the Gaullist party, in these terms: "I need you in this post because I have no one else to put there. The second reason is personal, very personal: I must fill the post very quickly." Pompidou died barely a month after the appointment, and the Gaullists did subsequently lose the presidency in the 1974 election. Pompidou's appointment was criticized in an article in the *Revue du droit public* as being analogous to the "entrenchment" of federalists in the U.S. Supreme Court at the turn of the eighteenth century, and the Left cited it as an important reason for their opposition to the 1974 amendment. Finally, Mitterrand's choices are of interest, not least because of his professed scorn for the Council—as late as 1978, for example, he had stated that:

> it is the institution that I indict, because the Constitutional Council is a political institution, the political instrument of the executive, nothing more, nothing less. We thought it servile, but it is actually only obedient.

His first appointee, Daniel Mayer, a minister in Léon Blum's 1946 government, a human rights activist, and an intimate of Mitterrand's, served only three years of his term as president, while retaining his seat on the Council. His resignation from the presidency, only weeks before the 1986 parliamentary elections, paved the way for Mitterrand to name Robert Badinter. Badinter at the time was minister of justice (1981–86), as well as a respected law professor and human rights advocate; this appointment thus combined formidable legal expertise and political loyalty. The maneuver was treated as a scandal: it was denounced by the future majority, and legal specialists debated its constitutionality, Duverger calling it a "constitutional fraud."

Appointments made by presidents of the National Assembly have been the most unambiguously "political," if political is understood to mean the appointment of full-time professional politicians. Of fifteen members named, ten had held national elected office before their appointment, including former ministers and a former president of the National Assembly; four others had served as chief of staffs or members of the personal staffs of prominent politicians, including those of General de Gaulle and Pierre Mendés France; the remaining appointee and also the most recent (1987), was recruited from the National Council of the present Gaullist party, Jacques Chirac's RPR. Francois Luchaire, a law professor and a former Council judge (1965–74) appointed by the president of the Senate, wrote in 1980 that traditionally the president of the National Assembly defers to the wishes of the president of the Republic in making these decisions. It can be inferred from appointments made since that the tradition remains a viable one; the one obvious exception to this rule occurred during the period of *cohabitation* (1987) when the president of the National Assembly was a Chirac Gaullist.

In contrast, presidents of the Senate have manifested great independence vis-à-vis the executive and have, overall, opted for higher standards of legal expertise. Of twelve members appointed, ten had been either professional lawyers (six), law professors (three), or judges (two) or a combination. Still the majority even of these had engaged in substantial political activities. Of the past six appointees—going back to 1968—all had been former parliamentarians, bringing the total to seven of twelve.

The Council's composition has been the subject of intense criticism by politicians and legal scholars, criticism which has been based on the partisan backgrounds of its members, and its oft-expressed corollary—that the Council's "acquaintance with public law is dubious, to say the least." Because of the high political profile of the great majority of Council members, the Council is vulnerable to charges that its function too is inherently "political." Its vulnerability is made more acute by the fact that many appointments are of men in advanced stages in their parliamentary careers. In the CCC debates on the drafting of the constitution, critics had predicted that the Council would be composed of retired politicians, and even warned of a *"gouvernement des retraires"* ("retirees"). They have not been proved wrong. Although the average age of Council members from 1958 to 1986 is 68 years, it has steadily increased: to 73 years from 1970 to 1986, and to more than 74 years in the 1980s. With very few exceptions (notably Badinter—the lone Council member to be appointed who was under the age of 60 years in the entire 1968–86 period), appointments have increasingly gone to politicians in the twilight of their careers and, it can be presumed, in compensation for long and distinguished service.

Until recently, criticism of the Council's composition has been framed in traditional Left/Right ideological terms. Until at least the early 1970s, the Council's Gaullist character was virtually an axiom, cited by the Left as a footnote, if an important one, to the history of an alleged *coup d'etat*. After the first *alernance* in 1981, the Council's composition became an affair of high politics. The Left appointed its first Council member in 1983, increased its share to four in 1986, and achieved its first majority in 1989. Since at least 1984, criticism of the Council has not centered so much on partisan make-up as on its jurisprudential activism and expanding influence over the legislative process....

Constitutional Review of Legislation

The most important responsibility of the Constitutional Council ... is its power of constitutional review of legislation. This power is spelled out by the constitution in articles 61 and 62, which read as follows:

> *Article 61:* ... ordinary laws may be referred to the Constitutional Council, before their promulgation, by the President of the Republic, the Prime Minister, the President of the National Assembly, the President of the Senate, or 60 deputies or 60 senators.
>
> In these cases, the Constitutional Council must decide within 1 month. At the demand of the Government, after a declaration of urgency, this time limit is reduced to 8 days.
>
> A referral of any law to the Constitutional Council suspends its promulgation.
>
> *Article 62*: A provision declared unconstitutional may not be promulgated nor may it enter into force.
>
> The decisions of the Constitutional Council may not be appealed....

It may be argued, however, that the Council does not possess a monopoly on constitutional interpretation. Article 5 reads, "the President of the Republic shall ensure the respect of the Constitution," and presidents have appealed to this provision on occasion as a justification for certain decisions, much to the chagrin at times of the legal community. Moreover, under certain conditions parliament too is empowered to render a definitive judgment on the constitutionality of bills before it, when it votes *motions d'irrecevabilité*.... In any event, the Constitutional Council had few opportunities to exercise its review authority until the mid–1970s. The increase in the number of instances of constitutional review since is positively correlated with two events: the 1974 constitutional amendment which expanded the right of referral to any sixty deputies or senators, and the electoral victories of the Left in 1981 which resulted in the use of referrals by the Right for purposes of opposition to Socialist reform. Table 2.1 shows the dramatic impact of the amendment on numbers of referrals in quantitative terms, from less than one referral per year from 1959 to 1974, to eighteen per year since 1981.

Table 2.1. Constitutional Review and the
Constitutional Council, 1958–1987*

	1959–1973	1974–1980	1981–1987
Number of Referrals	*9*	*66*	*136*
Referring Authority			
Pres. of the Republic	0	0	0
Prime Minister	6	2	0
Pres. of the National Assembly	0	2	0
Pres. of the Senate	3	0	2
Parliamentarians (total)	—	62	134
Deputies	—	49	77
Senators	—	13	57
Result			
Number of Decisions Rendered	9	46	92
Censuring referred text	7	14	49
Favorable to referred text	2	32	43

* This table includes all referral and Constitutional Council activity pursuant to the procedures provided by article 61.2. Due to multiple referrals, the number of referrals since 1974 is larger than the number of decisions.

Before 1974, review was dependent in practice on referrals by either the prime minister (largely to establish and then ensure executive dominance over policy processes) or the president of the Senate (as leader of the only anti-Gaullist institution in the early years of the Fifth Republic). Since 1974, 97 percent of all referrals have been of parliamentary origin, and it is unlikely that this percentage will decrease. Prime ministers have not referred a bill to the Council in this decade, precisely because only bills which the government supports are ever adopted definitively by parliament and are therefore eligible for referral. The presidents of the assemblies are just as unlikely to refer bills regularly today: they can rely on their friends in parliament to draft the petitions (which they too may sign as ordinary members of parliament) without putting the prestige of their offices at risk. During the *cohabitation* period, Mitterrand publicly threatened to refer matters to the Council during 1986 to 1988 but in the end did not.

Finally, it is worth noting that the Constitutional Council's constitutional review authority would have been substantially altered had a constitutional revision, first proposed by the Council's president, Badinter, and then taken up by Mitterrand and the Rocard government, been successfully adopted. Simplifying, the proposal would have allowed litigants in the ordinary and administrative courts systems to challenge the constitutionality of trial-relevant legislation on the grounds that the legislation had violated their fundamental rights. Once requested, the *Conseil d'Etat* and the *Cour de cassation*—the final appellate jurisdictions in the ordinary and administrative court systems respectively—would decide if the challenge was a serious one and, if so, to refer the matter to the Council. The Council then would have had three months to render a decision.

Parliament debated the proposal from late April to late June 1990; however, after substantially differing versions adopted by the National

Assembly and the Senate could not be harmonized, deliberations ended, and the government chose not to place the revision on the parliamentary calendar for 1991. Politically, Giscard and his allies in the center-Right parties strongly opposed the measure; Gaullists expressed discomfort with such a fundamental transformation of the general's document; and the entire Right knew well that expanding the power of the Council would play into the hands of Mitterrand's party, since its 1988 electoral victories mean that the Socialists will control a majority of the Council's seats until at least 1998. Last, the majority in the Senate worried about a further dilution of its self-proclaimed role as a protector of fundamental rights. The Right's control of the Senate proved crucial, since revision of the constitution requires that both chambers adopt identical texts.

Had the revision been successful, the Council's role and functioning may well have been transformed. The Council would have possessed a formal link to the judicial system and to individual litigants; and its status as *the* guarantor of rights and liberties would have been consolidated. Last, such a change might have provided the Constitutional Council with a more stable source of legitimacy. . . .

Questions and Comments

1. Note the transformation in the institutional role of the Conseil Constitutionnel. Should such a change have been anticipated by its original proponents?

2. Do Monaghan's concerns over the effects of life tenure for U.S. judges have any application to the judges of Conseil Constitutionnel, whose average age is reported to be 74?

3. In light of the strong French critique of the U.S. Supreme Court, particularly in the Lochner era, as a "gouvernement des juges" obstructing useful and democratically approved social welfare change, and the strength of the French opposition to constitutional review of laws, how did France come to adopt a constitutional court? Or would you agree with those who asserted, at least in the 1970s, that the Conseil Constitutionnel was not really a court? You may want to come back to this question after reading more about French constitutional law later in this chapter.

4.   GERMANY AND ITS FEDERAL CONSTITUTIONAL COURT

a.   *Historical Background*

In the early 19th century modern Germany did not exist; its constituent parts were ultimately pulled together, following the break up of the Holy Roman Empire. After the defeat of Napoleon Bonaparte in 1815, the German Confederation was established. This was a very loose union of independent states, described as "a largely defensive alliance among autonomous aristocrats" dominated by Austria. David P. Currie, The Constitution of the Federal Republic of Germany 2 (1994). The German Confederation did help consolidate the number of separate states from approximately 300 to about 40. In connection with the Confederation, the Bundestag—an assembly appointed by the rulers of the various states—was established. Federalism, and the roles of the constituent parts of Germany (called "länder"), are dominant themes in German constitutional development and in the development of the concept of a constitutional court.

In 1848 there was an unsuccessful attempt at revolution in many parts of Europe, including Prussia. While a new national parliament was elected to take over powers from the Bundestag in 1848, and a new constitution was written, it was not effective. This ineffective constitution provided for a bill of rights, enforceable by judges, based on the American model.[k]

By 1867 Prussia, the strongest of the different states that came to make up modern Germany, under the military leadership of Prime Minister Bismarck, organized the North German Confederation, leading to the defeat of France in the Franco–Prussian war and the establishment of the German Empire. Wilhelm I became "Kaiser", or emperor, and Bismarck continued to head the government as Chancellor. Under the Constitution of the Empire, there was a two-house parliament, consisting of the Reichstag (an elected body) and the Bundesrat (members appointed by the state governments). The legislative authority of the Reichstag was limited, however, and the Empire Constitution provided neither a bill of rights nor for judicial review of legislation.

Following the defeat of Germany in World War I, the Weimar Republic and Constitution were created. A national assembly was elected to write the constitution, that provided for a two-house parliament, a president and chancellor. The Weimar Constitution included a bill of rights, and was interpreted to permit judicial review. While the chancellor and the cabinet were appointed by the president, they could be removed from their offices by the Reichstag without the designation of a successor; conversely, the President could dissolve the Reichstag, and frequently did. Apart from formal amendments, the legislature could, by passing an unconstitutional law by a two-thirds vote, alter the constitution without explicit amendment; Professor Currie asserts that in this way, "the Constitution could be altered entirely by accident and ... no one could determine what the Constitution provided by reading it .... "

By the early 1930s the Nazis had obtained substantial representation in the parliament and in 1933, President Hindenberg appointed Hitler as Chancellor. Hitler immediately took advantage of emergency power provisions in the Weimar Constitution, declaring an emergency. His allies in the legislature extended those powers, authorizing essentially unlimited executive governance by decree and subordinating the länder (state) governments to federal control. All other political parties were suppressed. After

k. Currie, at 3. Prussia's own constitution, also adopted in response to the events of 1848, permitted some popular participation in lawmaking, and included a bill of rights.

Hindenberg died in 1934, Hitler declared himself the "Führer" (leader) and the government the "Third Reich." (The first two were the Holy Roman Empire and the German Empire.) For a popular historical account, see William L. Shirer, The Rise and Fall of the Third Reich (1959).

Following Germany's defeat in World War II, West Germany (the portion of Germany under the control of the western allies) adopted a new constitution, the Basic Law of 1949. When East and West Germany reunited in 1990, they did so under that Basic Law.

Under the Basic Law lawmaking authority is lodged primarily in the popularly elected Bundestag.[l] The Bundesrat is made up of members of the executive branches of the länder, and it can exercise a suspensive veto over legislation proposed by the Bundestag; in some cases agreement of the Bundesrat is required. While most laws are made at the federal level,[m] administration of most law is carried out by the länder. There is a President, but primary executive authority is vested in the Chancellor, and the Cabinet. The Chancellor is chosen by the Bundestag but can only be removed if a replacement is designated. The opening provisions of the Basic Law consist of a Bill of Rights, emphasizing their primacy. Constitutional amendments require a two-thirds vote by both houses, must be clearly stated, and cannot affect certain provisions of the Basic Law.[n]

b.   The German Constitutional Court: Creation, Jurisdiction, Status

A leading scholar of the German Constitutional Court is Professor Donald Kommers. His works provide useful accounts of the origins of judicial review in Germany, of the current operation of the Constitutional Court and of the history of appointments to that Court. The following summary is based largely on his text, The Constitutional Jurisprudence of the Federal Republic of Germany (2d ed. 1997).

Germany's decision to create a single, specialized constitutional court was influenced by such factors as the notion, advanced by Professor Cappelletti, that Europe's career judiciaries are not well suited to constitutional adjudication, and by what Kommers calls the "conservative reputation and public distrust" of the regular courts. Kommers also emphasizes the role of earlier traditions, including "constitutional review" and "judicial review" in Germany.

Pre–World War II History: Kommers traces "constitutional review" to the Holy Roman Empire, with a revival in the 19th century German Empire. "Constitutional review" provided a forum to resolve disputes

---

l. By statute, a mixed system of proportional representation and direct voting for candidates is used.

m. Although the residuary principle in Germany allots to the länder all competence not given to the federal government, art. 70(1), the federal government has both areas of exclusive jurisdiction (where it must specifically authorize the länder to act) and areas

of concurrent jurisdiction (where both are authorized to act). Federal law is supreme. Art. 31.

n. Art. 79 (3) prohibits amendments to the Bill of Rights provisions, to provisions for the division of the federation into länder, and to provisions dealing with the participation of the länder in the legislative process.

among and between the different states and also between the states and the central government. During the German Empire this function was performed by the legislative house in which the different states were represented. Under the Weimar Republic, the Staatsgerichtshof was a constitutional tribunal, or court, that assumed some of the jurisdiction previously exercised by that house. In addition to resolving conflicts between and among the different governments, the Staatsgerichtshof had jurisdiction over trial of impeachments against high executive officers for constitutional violations and over disputes involving the lander administration of national law. Kommers concludes that the structure of the Staatsgerichtshof influenced subsequent constitutional development in several respects: A tribunal separate from ordinary courts exercised constitutional review, taking cases as a matter of original jurisdiction and in a procedure simpler than that of an ordinary lawsuit, and had jurisdiction to settle disputes of a constitutional nature among and between the different levels of government.

What Kommers calls "judicial review"—a broader concept including the power to review the constitutionality of enacted laws—also had some history in Germany dating back to the unsuccessful Frankfurt Constitution of 1849. This tradition did not take root then, nor later in the 19th century when Robert von Mohl, a scholar familiar with the U.S. Supreme Court's practices, wrote a major legal treatise defending judicial review. At the time of the Weimar Constitution of 1919 (which was silent on whether the courts could review the constitutionality of laws) there was more support for this idea, both in the National Assembly and among German legal scholars, among whom the "free school" theory of judicial interpretation challenged the strong legal positivism that had been dominant. During the 1920s, several German courts, including the Supreme Court (the Reichsgericht) suggested that they had power to review the constitutionality of laws. At the lander level, one constitution authorized courts to review laws in light of the national and state constitutions (Bavaria) and one expressly forbad such review (Schaumburg–Lippe).

1945–51: Kommers emphasizes that "judicial review in Germany did not spring full-blown" from the Basic Law of 1949 and in particular, cannot be attributed to U.S. pressure (although the allied representatives did make clear that the new constitution would need to include judicial review in independent courts). He concludes that there was no reluctance to adopt judicial review, but rather that the Germans themselves decided to establish a specialized constitutional courts with power not only to decide intergovernmental disputes but also to review the constitutionality of laws and other government actions, relying principally on German traditions.

After World War II, it was the lander governments (not the federal government) that were first organized under constitutions, several of which specifically authorized review of the constitutionality of laws, though generally in a specialized court. The lander governments in the allied occupation zone organized a group of constitutional law experts (whose work product was called the "Herrenchiemsee" draft) to produce a draft federal constitution, reflecting the experience with the Weimar's "Staatsgerichtshof" in defining the powers of the proposed constitutional court, which was to have the powers of that court and in addition the power to hear constitutional complaints by citizens. The Herrenchiemsee proposal was that equal number of the judges should be chosen by the Bundestag (the popularly elected house) and the Bundesrat (the house representing the states), that both houses should together select the Court president, and that one half the judges should come from federal courts of appeals and high state courts. The drafters at this stage were divided on whether the court should be entirely separate from other courts, or created as part of one of the federal courts of appeals.

In the subsequent constitutional convention (called the Parliamentary Council), debate centered on whether the new court's jurisdiction should be limited to resolving disputes between governments (that is, a court of "constitutional review") or should also have jurisdiction to review the constitutionality of laws (in the terms used by Kommers, "judicial review"). After resolving that the new Federal Constitutional Court should be independent of other courts dealing with public law issues, delegates were still concerned with whether the single tribunal should exercise both forms of review. Some members of the convention favored having two different courts—one to deal with "political" disputes between governments and the other to deal with the constitutionality of laws. Others favored a single court with several different, specialized panels, exercising jurisdiction over many areas of public and constitutional law. Many German judges were concerned about such a mixing of "law" and "politics" in one forum.

The compromise that emerged was to have a single constitutional tribunal, with authority over all constitutional disputes including the validity of laws. The mandatory jurisdiction of the court could be invoked only by federal and state governments, political parties and in some cases other courts; but the initial Basic Law, while permitting the legislature to add to the Court's jurisdiction by statute, did not provide a constitutional right for private persons to petition the Constitutional Court, a decision influenced by practice in Weimar Germany. The political interests of the major parties were also served by the compromise: Kommers explains that the Social Democrats favored the limited access rules because political minorities would be protected and Christian Democrats thought they would be useful in preserving German federalism. This interest also was protected by the power of the Bundestag to choose half the judges, while the Social Democrats saw their interests supported by provisions that "federal judges *and others*" would be appointed to the court, which contemplated that persons in addition to federal judges would be appointed, thereby avoiding entrenched domination by professional judges in the largely conservative judiciary.

Once the Basic Law was adopted, it took almost another two years to enact the statute creating the Federal Constitutional Court. The competing perspectives of the central government, the Social Democrats and the

Bundesrat on judicial selection and tenure, the proportion of career judges to "other members," the size and structure of the court and the extent to which the Ministry of Justice controlled the courts were all subjects of debate. Months of negotiation resulted in a bill with substantial support from all major parties and all branches of government, and the Federal Constitutional Court Act (FCCA) was passed in March, 1951. According to Kommers, all participants felt that the court's political effectiveness and legitimacy would depend on the parties and the different governments reaching broad agreement on these matters. The FCCA provides for the qualifications and selection procedures for the Constitutional Court judges; establishes a two-senate tribunal and prescribes the jurisdiction of each; defines when the two senates sit together as a "plenum"; and provides for removal and retirement of the judges.

Major Categories of Jurisdiction:

Constitutional complaints: The Constitutional Court has jurisdiction over both "abstract review" of laws, and over "concrete" review that can arise out of ordinary litigation, both of which are invoked by government entities or officials. But roughly 95% of the Constitutional Court's docketed caseload has been generated from constitutional complaints, which may be filed by any person who claims that a government action has violated a right under the Basic Law if the person has exhausted other legal remedies.[o]

Initially authorized by statute, this provision became so important that in 1969 the Basic Law was amended to constitutionalize the right to file constitutional complaints. Even though the initial drafters declined to require the constitutional complaint procedure, by the late 1960s, Kommers reports, virtually no public official opposed amending the constitution to guarantee it. He quotes Wolfgang Zeilder, a former president of the Federal Constitutional Court as saying some time thereafter, that " 'the administration of justice in the Federal Republic of Germany would be unthinkable without the complaint of unconstitutionality'." About 95% of constitutional complaints are generated by judicial decisions; the constitutional complaint procedure permits dissatisfied litigants to refer questions of constitutional law to the Constitutional Court (even if the lower court judges did not make a referral for concrete review, discussed below). Kommers argues that the constitutional complaint is a "foundation" for the Court's high ratings in German public opinion polls and for the "rising constitutional consciousness among Germans generally."

Interestingly, the Court receives a large number of communications from citizens each year that do not fall within the categories of the Court's

---

o. Different time limits apply for different kinds of claims. Although exhaustion of remedies is required, a person threatened by enforcement of a criminal statute need not violate the law in order to challenge its validity, according to Kommers. A constitutional complaint can only be filed by one who suffers a clear injury directly from the government action complained of. For a more detailed description, see Kommers, at 14–15; see also Michael Singer, *The Constitutional Court of the German Federal Republic: Jurisdiction over Individual Complaints*, 31 Int'l & Comp. Law Q. 331 (1982).

jurisdiction; many are procedurally defective attempts at filing constitutional complaints. These communications are referred to a separate office, the General Register, from which civil servants respond to the writers advising them that their letter is misdirected or their complaint is without merit. If the writer responds and nonetheless requests review, these so-called "claims" are referred to one of the chambers of the courts.[p] In 1985, Kommers reports in the first edition of his book, approximately 10,000 informal notes were received, of which 728 (or 14%) ended up being referred on to chambers, where they were all rejected; in 1993, 1,441 claims went to the chambers and again, all were rejected. Although the General Register office performs a "nay-saying" function, it does provide some response to each person who writes.

Abstract Review of Laws: The Court can be asked to decide whether a law is constitutional by a federal, or state government, or by one third of the members of the Bundestag. Oral argument is rare in constitutional complaint cases, but abstract review cases always have oral argument as well as written briefs. If the Court decides against the constitutionality of the law, it is null and void. Although these cases are few in number compared to the constitutional complaints, many highly important decisions of the Constitutional Court, including the abortion decision in Chapter I and the Southwest decision that appears later in this chapter, occur in abstract review proceedings. Typically these cases are initiated by a minority political party that lost in the legislative process, or by a state or the federal government challenging the action of another government controlled by a different political party. Kommers reports that some have called for elimination of the abstract review procedure as permitting manipulation of the Court for political purposes. But he suggests this is unlikely, as the power to review the constitutionality of laws when they are enacted is central to the Court's functioning as guardian of the constitution, as understood both by legislators and by members of the court.

Concrete Judicial Review: This may be referred to as "collateral" review, and occurs during the course of ordinary litigation. A constitutional question of the validity of a federal or state law can be raised before ordinary German courts. If the court believes the law is valid, it can so decide. But if it believes the law is unconstitutional, it cannot so rule but must refer the question to the Federal Constitutional Court. A court may raise a question sua sponte, and on such a referral, the constitutional court offers the federal or state government, as appropriate, an opportunity to be heard in addition to the parties to the ordinary litigation. Kommers reports that the number of concrete review referrals is low (a total of 55 in 1994), relative to the number of lower courts, and suggests that the low number may reflect both the reluctance of courts steeped in the traditions of legal positivism to find a law unconstitutional and a degree of protectiveness of their own jurisdiction served by finding or interpreting a law to be constitutional.

p. For a discussion of the three judge "chambers" and their role in screening frivolous complaints and deciding cases where the law is clear, see below in this subsection.

Separation of Powers Disputes: Disputes between the highest branches of the federal government, called "Organstreit proceedings," require the Court to oversee the operations and even the internal procedures of both executive and legislative branches to maintain the required balance between them. In addition to the President, the federal government, and the two houses of the legislature, political parties may initiate proceedings; under the Basic Law, "political parties" are recognized to perform constitutional functions in organizing the will of the voters (see Basic Law, Art. 21(1)). The complaint must allege that the conduct complained of infringes a right or duty set forth in the Basic Law.

Federalism Conflicts: The Federal Constitutional Court has jurisdiction over disputes between the states and the central government, disputes which generally arise out of conflicts concerning state administration of federal law. The Court also has jurisdiction over disputes between different states. These proceedings, like those in the Organstreit jurisdiction, can be initiated only by certain governments or government parties, and must allege violation of rights or duties under the Basic Law.

Prohibiting Political Parties: As a substantive matter, the Basic Law provides that political parties that "seek to impair or do away with the free democratic basic order or threaten the existence of the Federal Republic of Germany shall be unconstitutional." Basic Law, Art. 21(2). The Basic Law also provides, however, that only the Federal Constitutional Court can declare parties unconstitutional, and only at the request of the Bundestag, the Bundesrat, or the federal government. According to Kommers, as of 1995, the federal government invoked this jurisdiction only three times— once to have the new Nazi Socialist Reich party banned in 1952, again in 1956, when the Communist Party was banned, and then, unsuccessfully, in 1994 when its petition (joined with the Bundesrat's) to outlaw one party, and a petition from the land of Hamburg to outlaw another party, were both denied by the Court on the grounds that the organizations, while advocating beliefs hostile to democracy, were not political parties.[q]

The Federal Constitutional Court as An Institution: Status, Structure, Appointments

Although the Basic Law specifically authorized judicial review, at its inception the status of the Constitutional Court in the governing structure was somewhat unclear, particularly given the parliament's authority to regulate the Court's organization and structure. Over the first two decades of the Court's existence, its status as a coordinate, independent constitutional arm of government, on a par with the Bundesrat, the Bundestag, the President, and the government (the Chancellor and Cabinet) has been confirmed. This was partly a result of the first justices on the Court

q. This discussion does not exhaust the jurisdiction of the Constitutional Court, which also extends, for example, to impeachment of judges (Art. 98(2)), certain international law disputes (Art. 100(2)), certain Bundestag election disputes (Art. 41(2)), proceedings for forfeiture of basic rights (Art. 18) and questions of the continuing validity of federal laws (Art. 126).

advancing measures to secure the autonomy and independence of their court.

In June, 1952, the Constitutional Court released a memorandum prepared by Justice Gerhard Leibholz, a highly regarded member, calling for an end to the Court's being under the supervisory authority and budget of the Ministry of Justice. The Court sought full control over internal administration, including the power to select and appoints its own officials and law clerks. The memo asserted that the Court was a supreme constitutional organ of coordinate rank with the Bundestag, Bundesrat, federal chancellor and president, that its members were neither civil servants nor ordinary judges but were the supreme guardians of the Basic Law, who had a greater duty than the other organs to assure that they observed the requirements of the basic law. This memorandum created a furor, and a political battle that lasted some years. Social democrats and the Bundesrat generally were hospitable to the memo, while the Bundestag and the Ministry of Justice opposed them. But by 1960, the demands of the Lieibholz Memo had all been met: By 1953 the Court had obtained independence from the Ministry of Justice and by 1960 the President of the Constitutional Court was the fifth-ranking official, following the president, chancellor and the presidents of the two houses of parliament. In 1968, the Basic Law was amended to prohibit impairments of the Constitutional Court even during states of emergency, and to prohibit amendments of the FCCA in emergencies unless the Court itself agreed that the amendment was required to maintain the Court's ability to function.

The two-senate structure of the Court did not work out as the drafters had anticipated. The senates are separate panels of 8 (originally twelve judges) of the Court that have separate jurisdiction and administrative support. A "plenum" of the two senates meets to resolve jurisdictional disputes between them and to decide on rules of judicial administration. When justices are chosen, they are chosen for either the First or Second Senate; interchange between them is strictly limited. The original distribution of authority reflected the compromise from which the senates were born and the initial intention that they act as very different fora. The Second Senate was to perform functions similar to those of the Staatsgerichtshof of the Weimar republic, deciding on abstract questions of law and resolving disputes between the different governments, ruling on the constitutionality of political parties and in impeachment proceedings. It thus was envisioned as a court of "constitutional review." The First Senate was given authority over concrete judicial review, involving constitutional questions that arose in ordinary litigation well as over constitutional complaints. The original understanding was that it would function as a less political, more "objective" court engaged in constitutional interpretation.

Due to the popularity of the constitutional complaint, this initial allocation caused a substantial imbalance in workload. In 1956 the FCCA was amended to distribute the work more evenly, with the Second Senate being given a substantial portion of the jurisdiction initially allocated to the First; the Plenum was authorized to reallocate authority to maintain rough equality in caseloads. The Second Senate was given jurisdiction over constitutional complaints and concrete review cases involving issues of civil and criminal procedure (in addition to its original docket of abstract review and more "political" cases). Professor David Currie describes the division of authority in the early 1990s as follows: "the allocation of cases between the two [Senates] is determined partly by the procedural posture of the case, partly by the substantive issues presented and partly by alphabetical order.... [T]he Second Senate is responsible ... for intergovernmental disputes and most abstract norm-control proceedings, for matters of criminal procedure, and for complaints filed by parties whose names begin with the letters L–Z in which questions of civil procedure predominate." David P. Currie, The Constitution of the Federal Republic of Germany 29–30 (1994).

Justices of the Federal Constitutional Court must meet certain minimum eligibility requirements. They must be at least 40 years old, eligible for election to the Bundestag, and must have passed the first and second state examinations in law (which are also qualifications for holding ordinary judicial office). Justices cannot hold other federal or state government offices; the only position that they may hold while serving on the Court is as a lecturer of law in a German university, a position they must subordinate to their judicial duties.

Unlike the U.S. Constitution, the Basic Law allows the legislature to modify the term of appointment for the Constitutional Court Justices. Early on the FCCA provided for life terms for the eight justices who were selected from existing federal judges, while the eight "other members" had renewable eight year terms. In 1970, the FCCA was modified to the current rule: all justices are appointed for single, nonrenewable twelve year terms, and at least three of the eight justices in each Senate must come from the federal judiciary. In addition, justices must retire at age 68, even if this cuts short the twelve year term. The change to single, nonrenewable 12 year terms also involved a debate, in 1970, concerning whether the justices should be permitted to publish dissents. There was concern that if the justices were dependent on the legislature for reappointment, they might feel less free to express dissenting opinions. Although a majority of the justices favored being allowed to dissent, they also favored lifetime appointments. The government introduced a bill providing for dissenting opinions and a twelve year term renewable once. The Social Democrats, however, were able to insist on a single twelve year term in exchange for supporting authorization of dissenting opinions. Both changes were approved.

Under the Basic Law, the Bundestag and the Bundesrat each select half the members of the Constitutional Court; and under the FCCA each house selects half the members of each Senate.[r] The Bundesrat (the council of länder) votes as a whole, with a two thirds vote required. Under the

---

r. The effort to balance the powers of the houses in the composition of the two Senates is quite detailed: the FCCA also provides that of the 3 federal judges chosen for each house, one should be selected from one house and two from the other, while of the 5 "other members," three should be selected by one house and two by the other.

FCCA, the Bundestag relies entirely on a special twelve person committee, the Judicial Selection Committee (JSC) to make its choice. The JSC is selected through a unique procedure in the Bundestag, resulting in party representation proportional to the party's representation in the entire body; the Bundestag votes for an entire list, or slate, of members of the Committee, to which changes from the floor are not permitted. Within the JSC, it takes eight votes to elect a justice.

The JSC's proceedings are closed, and its members are obligated by the FCCA to "keep secret the personal circumstances of candidates which became known to them as a result of their activities in the committee as well as discussions thereof in the committee and the voting." Kommers, quoting FCCA § 6(4). German advocates of a move towards U.S.-style more open process and public hearings have (at least thus far) not been successful in gathering support for their proposal, according to Kommers, because of concerns that inquiries into voting in particular issues would threaten the independence of the nominee and the institutional integrity of the Court, and that partisan lobbying before the legislators charged with selection would interfere with their independence in choosing the justices; moreover, the intense public exposure of personal aspects of the nominee's life would be regarded as an unwarranted invasion of privacy.

The law also requires the Minister of Justice to compile a list of all federal judges meeting the qualifications as well as the names if candidates submitted by political parties, or the federal or state governments. These lists are delivered to the JSC or Bundesrat, as appropriate. If after two months from the expiration of an existing justice's term no replacement has been named, then the Plenum of the Constitutional Court proposes a list of three candidates (or more, if there are multiple openings). The legislature is not obligated to choose from any of these lists, however.

Despite the secrecy in which the selection proceeds, it is, not surprisingly, highly political. The JSC membership is typically high party officials and legal experts; membership frequently overlaps with the Judiciary Committees, and members of the JSC themselves sometimes become candidates. The JSC members consult with party leaders, and informally with the Bundesrat. The two-thirds voting rule enables minority parties to exercise power and tends to promote compromise, both in the JSC and in the Bundesrat. In the Bundesrat, state (lander) governments and their justice ministers are the prime decisionmakers, and Bundesrat members may become candidates. This process of judicial selection, in the early years of the Court, is described in more detail in the following excerpt from Professor Kommers 1976 book.

c. The German Constitutional Court and the Appointments Process

Donald P. Kommers, JUDICIAL POLITICS IN WEST GERMANY (1976) (pp. 113–49)

...Partly because of the rule requiring a two-thirds vote for the election of a Justice, appointments to the Federal Constitutional Court are the subject of intensive bargaining. The selection system ensures that political parties will play the decisive role in the recruitment of Justices and that the Court will be widely representative of parliamentary interests.

Bundestag: Who are the choosers? Let us start with the *Wahlmän-nerauschuss,* or Judicial Selection Committee (JSC), of the Bundestag, which elects half the members of the Constitutional Court. This is no ordinary standing committee, but one staffed mainly by party leaders. If a committee member is not a party leader, he invariably is a person of prominence and influence in judicial matters or a person who enjoys high regard among his party associates and often among members of the opposition parties.

Ideally, the JSC functions as an independent decision-maker. But the parliamentary parties do seek to influence the selection of Justices through the lists they put forward when the committee is chosen by the whole house. The members of the committee in fact represent their respective parties, although the parties may not legally instruct the JSC members how to vote. Still there is close collaboration between party contingents on the JSC and the parliamentary party leadership. As just noted, this leadership actually dominates JSC membership. In fact, election to the JSC is now a signal that the committee member himself may be in line for a seat on the Constitutional Court.

Table 5* is an overview of the party alignment on the JSC at the beginning of each legislative period. In every period the parties in the governing coalition agreed on a common list of JSC candidates. Even so, no single party or governing coalition in the JSC has ever attained sufficient strength to elect a Justice over the objections of the opposition party. It is this situation which mandates negotiations among all parties in the JSC. Yet, if politics must direct the search for qualified Constitutional Court Justices it would be hard to find a group of twelve men anywhere who have as much negotiating skill or who combine as much political experience with as many legal qualifications as JSC members.

The elite character of the JSC is indicated by the concurrent positions held by the forty-four persons who have served on the committee since 1951. Eighteen were committee chairmen, nineteen were members of their party executive committees, thirty-two were members of the Judiciary Committee, and twenty-five were members of the Federal Judges' Committee. It is also noteworthy that thirty-five have been lawyers, many of whom have specialized in judicial and legal matters during their legislative careers. As Gerhard Loewenberg has observed, specialization is highly valued in the Bundestag, and the skilled lawyer is apt to end up on the "prestigious" Judiciary Committee. Thus, there seems to be a rather firm link between the Judiciary Committee and the JSC. The link is underscored by the fact that so far in each legislative period the chairman of the Judiciary Committee has also been a member of the JSC.

Equally interesting is the link between the JSC and the Bundestag's Federal Judges' Committee (FJC), which is responsible for recruiting all

* [Table omitted].

federal judges other than Constitutional Court Justices. The FJC, incidentally, is not made up exclusively of Bundestag members. Besides eleven members of the Bundestag, also chosen by proportional representation, its membership includes the federal and state ministers within whose competence a federal judge is being selected. Thus, if a judge of the Federal Labor Court is being chosen, the FJC includes the labor ministers of both federal and state governments. No fewer than eighteen members of the JSC have simultaneously been members of both the Judiciary Committee and FJC (usually as a full member of one and an alternate member of the other). . . .

Thus, the three committees are interlocked in membership. Their relationship in the selection of federal judges, including Constitutional Court Justices, is one of cooperation and mutual adjustment. Collaboration is of course necessary to avoid duplicate selections. But occasionally a person chosen as judge of one of the federal courts will beheaded eventually, by prearrangement, to the Constitutional Court. In 1971, the Federal Judges' Committee even elected a sitting Federal Constitutional Court Justice as president of the Federal Administrative Court. In this connection, incidentally, it is worth mentioning that among federal judgeships a seat on the Constitutional Court may no longer be as desirable as some positions on the other high federal courts. For one thing, the emoluments of a president or senate president of a high federal court are more attractive than an ordinary seat on the Constitutional Court. For another, tenure on the high federal courts expires when a judge reaches retirement at age 68. Ironically, Justices forced to leave the Federal Constitutional Court under the new twelve-year rule are, if not of retirement age, likely to be prime candidates for selection to some other high federal court. . . .

Bundesrat: The Basic Law provides for the direct election of Constitutional Court Justices in the Bundesrat. It has never quite worked this way, however. The role of the Bundesrat as a whole is one of ratifying choices made elsewhere. . . . For one thing, the Bundesrat must ensure that it is not about to designate a Justice already under consideration by the Bundestag. For another, the JSC and the Bundesrat alternate in choosing the Court's president and vice president from among Justices already appointed. Moreover, the Justice who becomes president or vice president is usually elected as Associate Justice by one electoral organ and then selected, simultaneously, to one of these offices by the other. The recent election of Ernst Benda exemplifies this. The JSC chose him as an Associate Justice while the Bundesrat, simultaneously, in an independent proceeding, elected him president. If the Bundesrat had made its own decision in the matter, it would not have selected Benda as president. Though it was the Bundesrat's turn to name the president, the JSC or, more accurately, the Christian Democrats in the Bundestag, wanted Benda. He was accepted by the Bundesrat, and by Social Democrats, as part of a package deal which we will discuss later, involving four new Justices of the Constitutional Court.

The Bundesrat, like the JSC, has elected only eleven new Justices since 1951. But it is essential to point out that in the Bundesrat the states, many of which have coalition governments, vote as a bloc. Thus, the votes themselves say little about the influence of the various parties.

. . . [N]o one party or governing coalition has come close to achieving two-thirds strength in the Bundesrat.

From the beginning the Bundesrat's negotiations with the JSC have been handled by a special *ad hoc* committee made up largely of the justice ministers of the individual states. The *ad hoc* committee is drawn mainly from members of the Bundesrat's Judiciary Committee. As a rule, the committee recruits Justices from the Bundesrat's own state constituencies. Moreover, the states, particularly the larger ones, have informally agreed to divide the judgeships among themselves. In any case, the recommendations of the *ad hoc* committee are usually unanimously accepted by the Bundesrat as a whole.

Yet it is open to question whether even the *ad hoc* committee makes its own decisions. Since each state casts a bloc vote, justice ministers invariably consult with their respective governments before "voting" in committee. In coalition governments, a decision may require consultation among the ruling parties. In some states, the minister-president takes full command of the selection process. Ministers-president have concluded informal pacts among themselves relative to the order in which their states shall claim a Constitutional Court judgeship. In these cases, the minister-president whose state is up for a judgeship can, if he wishes, usually name his own man to the Constitutional Court. . . .

. . . [N]o one person is in a position to control all electoral outcomes. Many interests have to be considered. Party interests are important, but state interests seem equally critical. Then, too, the Bundesrat has to deal with the JSC, the point at which negotiations are most likely to break down. Finally, the Bundesrat is itself made up of many powerful and distinguished men, several of whom may themselves be candidates for the Federal Constitutional Court. Erwin Stein (Hesse), Gebhart Müller (Baden–Württemberg), and Rudolf Katz (Schleswig–Holstein), to name just three, were chosen from the Bundesrat's own membership. No political party or single coalition of political parties has ever commanded enough votes . . . to name its own Justice. The partisan adjustments necessitated by this general situation are undoubtedly one reason why the Bundesrat has commonly looked to its own members as a principal source of judgeships.

Politics of Judicial Selection: 1951 . . .

The search for the original twenty-four Justices commenced when the Constitutional Court Act was being forged in Parliament. At that time, each party came forward with its own list of candidates for all available seats. The CDU's list reputedly included members of the coalition parties, but no member of the SPD*. The SPD list, while heavily weighted with

---

* [Editors' Note: CDU refers to the Christian Democratic Union; SPD to the So- cial Democratic Party; FDP to the Free Dem- ocratic Party; and DP to the German Party].

party faithful, included both Christian and Free Democrats. The FDP and DP also submitted candidate lists. The Court's presidency was first offered to Gebhart Müller, popular minister-president of Württemberg–Hohenzollern. Following his refusal and subsequent talks among Adenauer, Ollenhauer and FDP leaders, Hermann Höpker–Aschoff emerged as the unanimous choice to head the Court, but five months of further negotiation among the parliamentary parties failed to produce further agreement on a common list of candidates.

At an impasse, party leaders adopted the following formula in constructing the common list. The coalition parties and the SPD were each to select eight Justices; the remaining eight seats were to go to persons unaffiliated with any party. These "neutral" Justices, however, were also recruited by Bonn politicians and, like the other Justices, had to be acceptable to all parties. Still, it is interesting to note that even in the first years of the Court's existence these so-called neutral seats were rather easily identified, by the press and others, as being CDU or SPD "controlled." Besides partisan political parity, the recruiters sought to achieve religious equilibrium on the Court as well as some balance among Justices with centralistic, and those with federalistic views. In addition, three other criteria governed the selection process. First, and most importantly, the Justices had to be "clean," as some interviewees put it; they had to be untainted by Nazism. Second, they had to be persons with wide experience in public life; within this frame, the recruiters sought to achieve further balance among Justices drawn from state justice ministries, the general civil service, and the federal courts. Finally, a portion of the seats was to be assigned to persons of Jewish ancestry.

The job of recruiting such persons was assigned to a joint subcommittee composed of representatives of the Bundestag—all of whom were on the JSC—and the Bundesrat. The subcommittee worked in tandem with the government, which was represented mainly by Federal Justice Minister Dehler (FDP), who enjoyed the confidence of Adenauer. Federal Supreme Court President Hermann Weinkauff also appears to have played a critical role; he had strong ties to Christian Democrats in the Bundestag who sought his advice on Justices to be chosen from the high federal courts. Seven of the eight Justices ultimately recruited from the federal courts were chosen from his Court. . . .

[Kommers describes how the common subcommittee composed three lists—one of the candidates supported by the SPD, one of candidates supported by the coalition parties, and a third nonpartisan list, made up of former judges and law professors. One of the justices was actively Jewish, and four members of the original Court had been forced to leave Nazi Germany. Emphasizing the importance of " 'clean' backgrounds," Kommers notes also that "nine of the Justices had been dismissed from public service or hindered in their careers for opposition to Naziism," while "[t]hree . . . resigned from government service and sat out the Nazi period as private citizens." Most of the justices had experience in public life, "establish[ing] their reputations in the immediate postwar period, between 1945–51...."]

If the Bundestag had planned to pick a president who combined the splendor of Prussia's grand tradition of government service with an abiding faith in Bonn's new democracy it could scarcely have done better than its selection of Hermann Höpker–Aschoff. ... A German liberal and democrat, he participated in the creation of both the Weimar and Bonn Republics. ... [In] 1933 ... he withdrew altogether from public life. ... In 1946, he emerged as finance minister of North Rhine–Westfalia and ... was elected to the Bundestag. ... [Credited with drafting the financial provisions of the Basic Law relating to federalism,] Höpker–Aschoff also commanded the high respect of his colleagues on the Constitutional Court ... [giving] public defenses of the Court ... and ... identify[ing] the Court's work with the fate of German freedom.

Rudolf Katz, elected by the Bundesrat, had equally impressive credentials as vice president, in which capacity he presided over the Second Senate. He had personal attributes and political qualities that offset those of Höpker-Aschoff. He was Jewish, an emigree, and a leading figure in the Social Democratic Party. Active in SPD politics since 1924, he left Germany in 1933, served for a brief time as an adviser to the League of Nations, lectured at Columbia University from 1930 to 1938, and edited the New York German language newspaper *Neue Volkszeitung* from 1938 to 1946. He then returned to Germany, renewed his contracts with SPD leaders, became minister of justice in Schleswig-Holstein, was elected to the parliamentary council, and became chairman of the Judiciary Committee of the Bundesrat in 1949.

Katz was a man of immense charm, deep religious convictions (he was the son of a cantor), personal courage (he had defended many Communists in German courts during 1929–1933), and was respected for his intellectual capabilities. He renounced his membership in the SPD upon election to the Constitutional Court and skillfully led the Second Senate until his death in 1961. While a judicial pragmatist, he was uncompromising—like Höpker-Aschoff—in his defense of the Constitutional Court. He had no reservations about responding publicly to the Court's critics, even when they turned out to be former SPD colleagues.

The remaining twenty-two Justices were also recruited, for the most part, from high positions in German public life or were found to have had strong links to powerful politicians in Bonn or to state officials with influence in the Bundesrat. In surveying the recruitment of these Justices, we find that many of them emerged out of broadly identifiable groups—or loose friendship networks—allied to certain centers of power within or at the fringes of the major parties. We underscore the importance of these groups here because they continued to be principal sources of recruitment long after the first twenty-four Justices were selected.

The first group we shall call the "Zinn circle." Zinn's influence is attributable in part to his powerful position at the head of the largest and most powerful state. (Hesse) controlled by the Social Democratic Party and, in part, to the respect he commanded from all parties in the Bundesrat. . . .

A second group, which might be referred to as the "Bamberg circle," was dedicated to preserving Bavaria's interests on the Federal Constitutional Court. Primarily Catholic and largely conservative, it formed originally around Minister–President Hans Ehard. The group's influence was predominant in the Bundestag. . . .

Yet a third circle needs to be mentioned. . . . [I]t began to take shape with the selection of Leibholz and became increasingly influential in subsequent years. The group is not marked by the internal cohesion or self-consciousness of the other two groups, but it is no less real. To some extent it might be regarded as the Protestant equivalent of the Bamberg circle. Though mainly Christian Democratic in composition, it includes Social Democrats highly active in Evangelical affairs. . . . [This circle] had its origin in the Protestant resistance movement that included Leibholz's brother-in-law, the renowned Pastor Dietrich Bonhoeffer whom the Nazis executed in 1945. What we wish to suggest here, apart from this historical note, is that more than coincidence is involved in the selection of numerous Protestant Justices with strong Church affiliations. . . .

Politics of Judicial Selection: 1952–1972

It was not until after the Court had begun to function that politicians seemed actually to realize that it would become an extremely important factor in the life of the nation. That is one reason it is hard to separate the subsequent process of judicial recruitment from the actual work of the Court. . . .

[A] trend that in one respect helped to simplify judicial recruitment after 1951 [is that o]nce a political party had "possession" of a seat, the party held onto it. There has only been one real break in this pattern, and that was when Geller (CDU) succeeded Klass (SPD) in 1963. But that was an unusual year, as we shall see. There was no real break when Wintrich (CDU) succeeded Höpker-Aschoff (FDP). for it was generally understood in Bonn that the president's chair was the "property" of the CDU and when Wand (CDU) succeeded Kutschef (SPD) in 1970 it was also clear that the partisan balance on the Second Senate would be restored in 1971 by the CDU's concession to the SPD of both the Geller and Leibholz seats. In turn, the SPD conceded one of these to the FDP (Rottmann) as a reward for participation in the coalition government. In each case, however, agreement by the other party was necessary. In addition to all this, the recruitment process was simplified further by the practice of keeping sitting judges on the Court, obviating the necessity for renewed battle at the expiration of each term. . . .

. . .[A]fter the original twenty-four Justices were selected, there were no more pretensions about recruiting so-called nonpartisan Justices. In every case but one—Justice Karl Heck—it was relatively easy to position the Justices in one party camp or another. In recent years, actually, a rising crescendo of criticism has been directed toward the open political horsetrading involved in the selection process, many commentators feeling that the Court has undergone, as a consequence, a measurable decline in the quality of its personnel.

Despite the horse-trading, bitter fights have broken out periodically over the recruitment of Constitutional Court Justices. ... [T]he practice of assigning seats to "members" of certain political parties was not the product of a happy handshake following a gentlemen's agreement. It was a hard pill that the parties—especially the CDU/CSU—had to swallow if Germany was to have a Constitutional Court peopled with live Justices. ...

[Kommers describes how it took more than two years to fill the first vacancy in the First Senate, which arose when Kurt Zweigert (one of the CDU party appointees) resigned for financial reasons after only five months to become a judge of the Administrative Court of Appeals. The SPD opposed CDU efforts to replace him with a CDU–backed nominee, a battle in part over the outcome of a challenge to a pending treaty. In early 1954, death created a second vacancy on that Senate, and federal elections had increased the CDU–FDP majority in the Bundestag. The majority sought, unsuccessfully, to change the voting rule in the JSC, which at the time required a 9/12 vote to elect a justice. Ultimately the opposing parties agreed to nominate two "professional judges with no visible party ties."]

. . .

The first vacancy on the Second Senate was easy to fill, partly because the Bundesrat made the selection. Egon Schunck replaced Leusser, who resigned in 1952. ... The terms of several Justices, incidentally, were about to expire in 1955, at a time when the Bundestag was considering a bill to reduce the Court's membership. As a stop-gap measure, all these Justices were reelected, but only for a term of one year, pending the outcome of the bill. Other changes in the Constitutional Court Act were being considered against the background of the government's anger over the First Senate's reluctance to decide its petition for a declaration of unconstitutionality against the Communist Party (KPD).

Because of its problems with the Court, the federal government initiated a second major effort to change the method of judicial selection and to reorganize the Court. The Bundesrat, however, once again proved to be the stumbling block, as nearly all the ministers-president and state ministers of justice opposed any attempt to abolish or modify the principle of parliamentary selection. An earlier government proposal to reduce the Court's membership by almost half generated speculation that the Chancellor and his aides wanted to get rid of at least six Justices up for reelection in 1956, several of whom were believed to have opposed Adenauer on German rearmament. The Justices most frequently named in this connection were Drath, Friesenhahn, Leibholz, and Conrad Zweigert, all professors. Indeed, Friesenhahn had publicly rebuked Justice Minister Dehler for his attacks on the Court over the EDC affair. Leibholz, too, lashed out at the Court's critic, virtually identifying them as enemies of West Germany's new constitutional democracy. In the course of the following year, newspapers supporting the government wrote, occasionally disparagingly, about the

Court's "professorial contingent," while Arndt and the SPD leaped to the Justices' defense. The "cold war" between Bonn and Karlsruhe,* as *Die Zeit* described the fray, had turned hot.

It cooled down, as usual, with a compromise. The parties agreed to reduce the Court to ten Justices per senate—to reduce it still further to eight Justices in 1963—and to allow the JSC to elect Justices by eight votes, still short of what the coalition parties originally wanted or would need unilaterally to pack the Court. The likelihood of a purge in 1956 was reduced by several voluntary resignations. In the Second Senate, three Justices—Wolff, Fröhlich, and Roediger—resigned, because of age, as their terms expired. Konrad Zweigert of the First Senate also resigned, preferring to return to the university. Kutscher was reelected and, to even the senates at ten Justices each, transferred to the Second Senate. All other Justices whose terms had expired were reelected for full terms. Thus, something approaching a sitting judge tradition was beginning to establish itself.

From 1956 to 1963 a modus vivendi prevailed between the political parties. By now, seats on the Court were clearly labelled "SPD" or "CDU." These each party conceded to the other, reserving the right to veto the other party's choice. Moreover, tempers had a chance to cool owing to the lapse of two and a half years before another occasion arose to select a Justice. In any case, four new Justices were elected in the absence of any major frictions among the parties....

Round two: 1963. In the spring of 1963, new storm clouds gathered as the Court was scheduled for a further reduction in membership, effective September 1, coincident with the expiration of the terms of no less than nine Justices. The political context deepened the conflict. By now the Court had decided a large number of important and very controversial cases, some resulting in bitter defeats for the government. In Bonn's high circles, the air was heavy with talk about bringing the Court down to size and curtailing its jurisdiction if necessary. By this time, however, the Court's own power and prestige had reached the point of making any such frontal assault on the Court politically inadvisable. Thus, the battle was fought at the level of judicial recruitment.

Terms about to expire were those of Müller, Drath, Lehmann, and Scheffler on the First Senate, and those of Kutschef, Klaas, Leibholz, Friesenhahn, and Schunk on the Second. Scheffler and Schunck used the occasion to announce their retirement, while Friesenhahn decided to return to his chair at Bonn University. The remaining six let it be known that they were available for reelection, but there was only room for five. Müller, Leibholz, and Kutscher were reelected without difficulty. But Klaas, Lehmann, and Drath were removed and replaced by two new justices, Wiltraut von Brünneck and Gregor Geller. Drath['s removal] was controversial. ...

...[SPD representatives made public] an agreement between government and opposition that sitting Justices were customarily to be reelected

---

* [Editors' Note: The Constitutional Court sits in Karlsruhe.]

and that any reduction in the Court's membership would not be at the expense of a sitting Justice.

[Influential SPD member Adolf Arndt] noted that the pact was observed in 1956. But now he blamed the CDU for seeking to purge the Court of SPD members and for spreading false rumors about Drath. Two of these rumors ... were particularly damaging to Drath. First, ... President Müller himself [was accused] of trying to "dump" Drath for not doing his work on the Court. Second, ... [it was rumored] that a high official in the Bavarian Ministry of Justice had informed the Bundesrat that Drath had undertaken a lecture tour in East Germany and had held discussions with top communist officials in East Berlin. ... Drath might easily have been harmed by the latter rumor. Long a target of Germany's right-wing press, he was a man of strong leftward convictions. Active in the SPD since his youth, he was involved in the political reconstruction of Thuringia (in the East Zone) after the war. He taught law at Jena University and later in East Berlin, where he was alleged to have joined the Socialist Unity Party (SED) before joining the staff of West Berlin's new Free University. He had never been able to still whispers that his early ties in East Germany were more than mere accidents of time and circumstance. On top of all this, the question of his professional qualifications was once more resurrected. After his original appointment in 1951, mainly on Zinn's recommendation, questions of propriety were raised about his quick promotion to professor of law at Jena. Particularly damaging was the lack of any record showing that he had taken his major state examinations in law. Within this context, questions about his workmanship on the Court, not to mention those concerning his political links, proved fatal to his reelection, at least in Drath's own assessment of the situation. These rumors, which cast doubt upon his political reliability and judicial competence, reached the point where the Federal Constitutional Court itself felt impelled to speak out in his defense. On November 29, 1963, the Plenum made a brief statement that Drath enjoyed, during his tenure on the Court, the complete confidence of his colleagues, and that rumors of his political unreliability were totally false. The Court's statement came too late to do Drath any good, however, for he had already been denied reelection....

Not until 1971 was there to be another open controversy over judicial nominees. Eight new Justices were elected between 1963 and 1971, all filling vacancies left by an unusual number of retirements and resignations. The recruitment of these Justices proceeded without a hitch and followed a familiar pattern, reflecting partisan, religious, and geographical balances, except that now one witnesses also the beginning of a trend to recruit former assistants of Federal Constitutional Court Justices, in a few cases with the active support of the Justices themselves....

Round three: 1971. The first sign that there might be trouble in electing Justices in 1971 was the Bundesrat's failure to replace Stein, one of the original 1951 appointees, when his term expired in March. The Bundestag's JSC, however, held up the election, pending a package agreement with the Bundesrat on all Justices to be selected in 1971. Müller,

Geller, and Leibholz, like Stein, having reached the age of 68, would retire upon the expiration of their terms in August. Wand and von Brünneck, whose terms also expired in August, were eventually reelected out of respect for the sitting judge tradition. Round three was fought over the vacancies created by the four retiring Justices.

By 1971, the German political scene had changed significantly. Social Democrats, in coalition with the FDP, were at the helm in Bonn, with a slim parliamentary majority over the CDU/CSU. In the Bundesrat, as a result of similar shifts of power in several states, the Christian Democratic majority had been shaved to one vote.... Now that Social Democrats were on top in Bonn, speculation was adrift that the SPD would try to wrench the presidency away from the CDU.... Two Justices were to be selected by the Bundestag and two by the Bundesrat. In addition, the Bundesrat was this time to designate the president, which would require close collaboration with the Bundestag, since the JSC was to elect the Justice whom the Bundesrat would then, simultaneously, elect as president.

... At length, in late October ... the JSC appeared finally to have agreed on Ernst Benda (CDU) ... for president, while Martin Hirsch (SPD) was slated to succeed Leibholz and, eventually, after Seuffert's retirement in 1975, to attain the vice presidency itself. It bears notice that both Benda and Hirsch were members of the JSC. While such blatant cooperation by the JSC of its own members did not go unnoticed or uncriticized in the German press, both men were nevertheless widely recognized as the top lawyers in their respective parliamentary parties.

Following a JSC meeting on November 3, 1971, however, owing to what now appeared to be an FDP–SPD feud, the SPD announced its choice of Emmy Diemer–Nicolaus, the FDP's representative on the JSC, instead of Hirsch. The CDU immediately objected, accusing the SPD of breaking the covenant which produced the Benda–Hirsch combination. SPD leaders retaliated by announcing that they would block Benda's election if the CDU refused to accept Diemer–Nicolaus. The CDU held firm, and Benda's election as president remained a question mark for over a month.

The Diemer–Nicolaus case, to the embarrassment of the SPD, was reminiscent of the Carswell episode in the United States, although without the racial issue. Christian Democrats might eventually have opposed Diemer–Nicolaus on the basis of her extremely liberal views on social and cultural matters, but they chose to base their opposition on her qualifications, which were not manifestly impressive. Although she held a doctoral degree in law, she had published nothing since her dissertation, nor had she attained any real distinction as a practicing attorney, a role she combined with that of housewife. At 62 years of age, her clearest claim to recognition, besides her role in the Bundestag, was two decades of unstinting service to the Free Democratic Party. Wolfgang Mischnik, FDP parliamentary chief, ardently defended this "liberal personality and courageous woman," as he described her, but in the meantime the SPD's ardor for Diemer–Nicolaus had visibly shrunk. In mid-November Diemer–Nicolaus herself broke the logjam by withdrawing her name from consideration, whereupon Benda and Hirsch emerged again as the JSC's top choices to succeed Müller and Leibholz.

The Bundesrat's choice for the Geller seat was Joachim Rottmann (FDP), a high civil servant in the Interior Ministry whom the SPD had, all along, preferred over Diemer–Nicolaus. Rottmann was strongly supported by Federal Interior Minister Hans–Dieter Genscher (FDP). The remaining seat, "belonging" to the CDU, was a source of some friction between CDU Minister–President Hans Filbinger (Baden–Württemberg) who preferred the appointment of his aide, Paul Feuchte, and other Christian Democrats who preferred Hans Faller, a judge of the Federal Supreme Court. What finally tipped the scale in favor of Faller was the "intervention" of the Federal Constitutional Court itself. In a statement signed by a majority of the Justices, the Court noted that Stein's successor must be chosen from the federal bench, a highly dubious legal position in view of the fact that there were already three Justices on the First Senate who had been recruited directly from the federal courts. Nevertheless, the Bundesrat accepted the Court's view and Faller became the fourth former law clerk to be elected to the Federal Constitutional Court....

Background characteristics...

All Justices must be at least forty years old to be elected to the Constitutional Court. This rule and the practice of recruiting justices from high governmental positions means that they are well advanced in career, the median age being 53 at the time of election.

Close to half the Justices were born outside the territory of what is now West Germany. Birthplace is of some importance, since it is very often related to the Justices' religious affiliation and partisan background. Seventeen of twenty Justices born outside the Federal Republic are Protestant and, of these, eleven have been identified with the SPD and one with the FDP. Seuffert, whose father worked as a chemist for a German-owned company in New Jersey, was born in the United States, but at age four he returned to Germany with his parents shortly after the company's seizure by the American government at the outset of World War I. Like Seuffert, nearly all the Justices were born into middle- or upper-middle-class families. Their fathers, many of whom were among the privileged few with university training, were businessmen, landowners, teachers, or highly placed officials in public careers closely allied to law. In addition, two Justices were the sons of Protestant ministers, two of physicians, one of a high army officer, and one of a renowned professor of law. Only two Justices had working-class backgrounds.

Geographical residence seems to be a conscious factor in judicial recruitment, especially by the Bundesrat. The distribution of seats among the various states is in rough accord with their population and political importance. The large number of Justices recruited from Baden–Württemberg (with half the population of North Rhine–Westphalia) is explained by the presence there, in Karlsruhe, of the Federal Supreme Court, from which most of the "federal judges" on the Constitutional Court have been chosen....

...Judicial recruiters have attempted to achieve a balance between Catholic and Protestant representation on the Court. This has produced a deep philosophical cleavage among the Justices. Relative to their numbers in the population, however, Catholics are actually underrepresented on the Federal Constitutional Court. One reason for this is that Social Democrats have not sought to achieve a religious balance among the "members" of their party elected to the Court; as a consequence, vice president Seuffert is the only Catholic among Justices affiliated with the SPD. Hence, Catholics are recruited within the framework of the CDU. But here seats are shared by Catholics and Protestants. Even so, the large majority of CDU seats—sixteen out of twenty-three—have gone to Catholics....

Finally, what distinguishes Federal Constitutional Court Justices as a whole from other German judges is the wide variety of life experiences they represent. German judges generally ... are very much alike in attitude and background, and their experience is confined mainly to the conservative social milieu of the judicial establishment. Constitutional Court Justices, on the other hand, have been drawn from a variety of professions and career backgrounds. ... [D]ata in ... show ... the occupations in which the Justices were engaged immediately prior to their selection. The large number of those with judicial backgrounds stems partly from the requirement that one-fourth of the Justices be recruited from the federal courts. Of the thirteen federal judges so far chosen under this mandate, ten have been recruited from the Federal Supreme Court and one each from the Federal Administrative Court, the Federal Finance Court, and the Federal Labor Court. Six other justices have also been recruited from the courts, five from high state tribunals and one (Simon) from the Federal Supreme Court. Justices recruited from high civil service positions include two persons with substantial experience in foreign affairs, several high ministerial officials in Bonn, a number of state cabinet ministers, a minister-president, and a former director of the Federal Constitutional Court. ...

...Only twelve Justices have had careers confined exclusively to civil service or the judiciary. Twenty-eight have held high civil service positions in state or national government. Ten have had legislative experience. Nine Justices spent most of their professional lives practicing law. Five had careers as professors of law, while three others held professorships at one time or another. Many were involved in the work of the Parliamentary Council and in the constitutional conventions of the German states. A few served on state constitutional courts, while others authored authoritative commentaries on their state constitutions.

It is important to mention that at least ten Justices have had considerable experience traveling and studying abroad....

Questions and Comments

1. Does the German experience with its high constitutional court being divided into two permanent, separate senates, suggest different possibilities for thinking about (a) the qualifications of those who would serve on a federalism/separation of powers "senate" as compared to the qualifications of those who would serve on an individual rights, concrete review and constitutional complaint side, and (b) whether the U.S. Constitution should be interpreted, as some claim, to preclude the court's sitting in panels (or, a fortiori, being constituted as separate divisions)?

2. Does the number of judges to be selected at the same time, or the regularity of periodic selection, affect the selection process?

3. Consider how the German experience with the organization of its Constitutional Court bears on questions of (a) what should be in a constitution, and (b) how easy or hard it should be to amend the constitution.

4. Does the nonrenewability of a judge's term of office address issues of judicial independence that the U.S. provisions for life tenure seek to secure? Should former judges be barred from certain pursuits after retiring from the court?

5. The JSC (the Committee of the Bundestag that makes the Bundestag's judicial nominations for it) works under a two-thirds rule. This, together with the requirement for representation of parties in the JSC proportional to their representation in the Bundestag, tends to promote the need for compromise between majority and minority parties. After reading about the JSC, what do you think of Epstein's proposal that the U.S. Senate be required to approve by a two-thirds vote nominees to the U.S. Supreme Court?

---

5. The Constitutional Courts of Eastern Europe

As the former Soviet Union dissolved, many in the countries of Eastern Europe and in the former Soviet Union have been engaged in constitutional change, as well as economic transformation. Almost all of these countries have looked to variants of the European, rather than American, model of judicial review.

The struggles to establish these courts often reveal broader contests within their respective nations. For example the Czechoslovak Constitutional Court Act did not authorize the proposed court to subordinate Czech, or Slovak, law to Czechoslovak federal legislation, but only to the proposed new federal constitution; and it did not specify whether the subordinate unit's law was void if found to conflict with the proposed federal constitution. See Herman Schwartz, *The New East European Constitutional Courts*, 13 Mich. J. Intl. L. 741, 781 (1992). This silence on basic questions of the hierarchy of legal norms and the relationship between the whole nation to its constituent parts reflected the deepening division between Czechs and Slovaks that, by the end of 1992, led to the break up of Czechoslovakia into two separate nations.

In his 1992 study of six east European nations (Czechoslovakia, Romania, Bulgaria, Russia, Hungary and Poland), Professor Schwartz found that in all the constitutional court judges were selected "in whole or in part by the parliaments, sometimes by simple majority rule."[s] In none of those six did the constitutional court judges have life tenure, and generally they had limited nonrenewable terms. Hungary enacted nine year terms for its new Constitutional Court judges; the judges could be reappointed once.[t] In Russia, under the 1991 Constitutional Court Act, judges did not have limited terms, but were appointed to serve until age 65. After the Constitutional Court's activities had been suspended by President Yeltsin, see below at Section E(3), this provision was changed by the new Constitution of 1993 and the Constitutional Court Act of 1994 to limit newly-appointed judges to the constitutional court to a single, twelve year term (with mandatory retirement at age 70).

   a.   *Constitutional Transitions and Constitutional Judges.* Consider the relationship between the problem of transition, discussed in Chapter IV, and the structure and status of constitutional courts and their judges. For example, should minimum age requirements for members of constitutional courts be eliminated or made relatively low, in order to permit the infusion of younger jurists who are not inculcated in the former regime's norms? See Herbert Hausmaninger, *Towards a "New" Russian Constitutional Court*, 28 Cornell Int'l L. J. 349, 370 n. 150 (1995) (criticizing Russia for raising the minimum age for its constitutional court judges from 35 to 40 in view of need to "prevent legal petrification [that could result if all] sitting justices received their training under the Communist system").

   b.   *Term limits for constitutional judges*? From the same perspective, Hausmaninger praised Russia's move from unlimited terms (up to age 65) for its constitutional court justices to a 12–year nonrenewable term limit. Do long, nonrenewable terms provide an alternative to the U.S. life tenure system for promoting judicial independence in adjudication and at the same time a judiciary that is not (too) "legally petrifi[ed]"?

   c.   *Transitions and institutional capital.* Using Russia as an example, Owen Fiss has cautioned that, in studying these new constitutional courts, it is important to remember that in some of the countries, "there is uncertainty . . . whether or not a constitution exists in any but the most formal sense." Owen Fiss, *Introductory Remarks, Symposium*, 19 Yale J. Int. L. 219 (1994). In addition, Fiss observes,

---

   s. In Poland, for example, the twelve justices of the Tribunal were chosen by the Sejm (the lower house of the Parliament), Polish Const. art. 33 (a), to serve eight year, nonrenewable terms. See George Brunner, *Development of a Constitutional Judiciary in Eastern Europe*, 18 Rev. Cent. & E. Eur L. 535, 545–46 (1992). In the newly enacted Polish Constitution of 1997, the Constitutional Tribunal was expanded to fifteen judges, appointed by the Sejm to nine year nonrenewable terms; the President's powers now include authority to appoint the President and Vice President of the Tribunal from among those proposed by the judges. 1997 Polish Constitution, Art. 194 (2).

   t. The Hungarian Constitutional court was to be composed of fifteen judges, chosen by the parliament. Cheryl W. Gray, Rebecca J. Hanson, and Michael Heller, *Hungarian Legal Reform for the Private Sector*, 26 Geo. Wash. J. Int'l L. & Econom. 294, 300 (1992); Ethan Klingsberg, *Judicial Review and Hungary's Transition from Communism to De-*

the judiciaries of these new nations have very little institutional capital ... In the new democracies of the East ... the judiciary cannot take its authority for granted. Not only must it fashion a constitution, it often must give life and force to the idea of a constitutional court ... [to] convince their fellow citizens that law is distinct from politics, and that they are entitled to decide what the law is.

If Fiss' observations are correct, what (if any) implications would they have for the structure and membership of the new constitutional courts of eastern Europe?

d. *Countermajoritarianism and international norms.* The Constitutional Court of Hungary has attracted considerable attention with a series of boldly countermajoritarian rulings. See Justice Solyom's essay, excerpted in chapter IV, with its description of the Court's efforts to establish itself as a "countermajoritarian" institution, committed to the rule of law. In doing so, the court has self-consciously drawn on extra-national legal sources. Recall Justice Solyom's application of Dworkin's principles of jurisprudence. See also Hungarian Death Penalty Case, Alkotmanybirosag [Constitutional Law Court], 107 1990 M.K., U.T. 1, 1 (Hung. Oct. 31 1990) (underlying principle of human dignity would exist even without support in constitutional text as foundational part of "invisible constitution" supported by western constitutional conventions), described in Ethan Klingsberg, *Judicial Review and Hungary's Transition from Communism to Democracy,* 1992 Brigham Young U. L. Rev. 41, 79–80 and George P. Fletcher, *Searching for the Rule of Law in the Wake of Communism,* 1992 Brigham Young U. L. Rev. 145, 153 n. 5. To what extent is resort to international (or extra-national) legal norms likely to promote Fiss's project of convincing citizens that law is distinct from politics and that courts should say what the law is?

e. *Incrementalism in establishing constitutional tribunals.* In Poland a constitutional court was established in the mid–1980s, initially by an amendment to the Constitution in 1982 which some describe as a concession "for foreign consumption" by the Communist leadership of the country that the leadership did not intend to follow through on. Mark F. Brzezinski and Leszek Garlicki, *Judicial Review in Post–Communist Poland: The Emergence of a Rechtsstaat?,* 31 Stan J. Int'l L. 13, 23 n.50, 26 (1995) (citing Professor Izdebski).[u] By 1985, however, a constitutional court act had been passed, and in 1989, the jurisdiction of the court (the Constitutional Tribunal) was significantly expanded. Yet that Tribunal could not review laws passed before 1982, and a decision by the Tribunal holding national legislation unconstitutional could still be overturned by Parliament on a two-thirds vote, within six months of the Court's decision. Little Constitution of 1992 art. 33a. While the Polish Constitutional Tribunal was fairly activist in finding laws unconstitutional between 1989 and 1997, the Parliament also exercised its veto power over the Court's decisions on some occasions. On these developments, see generally Brzezinski

mocracy, 1992 Brigham Young U. L. Rev. 43, 53.

u. For a useful summary of Polish constitutional history, see Mark F. Brzezinski,

Note, *Constitutional Heritage and Renewal: The Case of Poland,* 77 Va. L. Rev. 49 (1991).

& Garlicki. In the 1997 Final Constitution adopted by the legislature and approved in a public referendum, the authority of the parliament to overturn the Tribunal's decisions was eliminated. See Art. 190 (1) ("Judgments of the Constitutional Tribunal shall be of universally binding application and shall be final.").[v]

f. *Incrementalism, social welfare rights and judicial review.* In a description of constitution-drafting in Poland in 1991, Professor Rapaczynski commented on the relationships between, and difficulties of determining, (a) what form of constitutional review to have, (b) whether the constitution should include positive welfare rights or not and (c) how easy or difficult it should be to amend the constitution. See Andrzej Rapaczynski, *Constitutional Politics in Poland: A Report on the Constitutional Committee of the Polish Parliament,* 58 U. Chi. L. Rev. 595, 608–31 (1991). The 1992 "little constitution," adopted as a provisional interim measure, did not address the structure of Constitutional Tribunal, though it did add to its jurisdiction a power of pre-enactment review at the request of the President.[w] In late 1995, the Constitutional Commission charged with attempting to draft a new constitution for Poland made proposals for an expanded, and more powerful, role for the Constitutional Tribunal,[x] many of which were ultimately enacted in the 1997 Constitution. However, art. 81 states that certain economic and social welfare rights "may be asserted subject to limitations specified by statute," and commentators suggest accordingly that the new constitutional complaint procedure provided by Art. 79 of this new Constitution does not provide much in the way of enforcement of economic welfare rights provided for in the Constitution. For detailed discussion of social welfare rights, see Chapter XII below.

C. CONSTITUTIONAL COURTS AND FOUNDATIONAL CASES

Most law students in the United States, if asked to identify a "foundational case" for the legitimacy of judicial review of the constitutionality of

v. An English translation is found at the following website maintained by the University of Wuerzburg: http://www.uni-wuerzburg.de/law/, and in 15 Constitutions of the Countries of the World 17 (Albert P. Blaustein and Gisbert H. Flanz, eds. 1997). One commentator notes that it is unclear whether the Tribunal may review judicial decisions involving constitutional challenges to judicial interpretations of a statute as distinguished from challenges to the statute itself. Ewa Letowksa, *A Constitution of Possibilities,* 6 East Eur. Const. Rev. 76, 80 (1997) (implicitly referring to arts. 79, 188, 193).

w. See *Interim Constitution Approved in Poland,* East European Constitutional Review 13 (summer 1992); "Little Constitution" of 1992, art. 18.4 (after Presidential veto and repassage by two-thirds, legislation may be referred by president for preenactment review by Constitutional Tribunal; if Tribunal finds law constitutional President must sign it).

x. The Commission proposed that the Tribunal's decisions be final and binding, and that the tribunal have authority to defer for a limited period of time the effective date of its invalidation of a law; it also proposed to expand the scope of its jurisdiction to, e.g., include citizen constitutional complaints. See Constitution Watch, East European Constitutional Rev. 20–21 (Fall 1995).

acts by the political branches of government, would answer, Marbury v. Madison. What makes *Marbury* a "foundational" case? Is McCulloch v. Maryland foundational in the way *Marbury* is? Do your answers have to do with the nature of the issue? the nature of the Court's reasoning? its consonance with principled/moral values of the polity? the political context in which the decisions were made? the response of other actors in the political system? how the decisions have been interpreted over time?

The materials in this section raise the question whether there are "foundational" cases in other functioning systems of constitutional judicial review. As you read the cases from Germany (the Southwest case), France (especially the 1971 decision) and Israel (especially Bergman and Elon Moreh) consider whether some or all of these cases should be regarded as "foundational." Is it important that most (all?) of these cases involve the court finding the act of another branch of government to be invalid? Why?

Consider, also, the possibility that the idea of "foundational cases" is an unhelpful construct. Why should we care about identifying foundational cases? Could a series of small decisions accomplish the same thing that foundational cases are said to accomplish?

---

1.   GERMANY AND THE SOUTHWEST CASE

In its very first case, the German Constitutional Court (1) found a law enacted by the federal legislature to violate the Basic Law, (2) asserted that its decision and reasons for invalidating the law were binding on all other branches and levels of government, and (3) raised the possibility that an amendment to the Basic Law would itself be unconstitutional.[y]

The following explanation and translation of the case is from Walter F. Murphy & Joseph Tanenhaus, COMPARATIVE CONSTITUTIONAL LAW: CASES AND COMMENTARIES 208–12 (1977):

y. The Southwest case you are about to read involved a challenge to federal government power to reorganize the boundaries of the länder and to the procedures used for doing so. As background, bear in mind that the Nazi rise to power was accompanied by a constitutional crisis involving, inter alia, federal suspension of länder governments. According to Professor McWhinney,

[i]n the major constitutional conflict of July 1932, when the federal president invoked Article 48 of the [Weimar] constitution and the constitutional doctrine of emergency powers to suspend the administration of the *Land* of Prussia and replace it by a federal administrator and to occupy the Prussian government offices by federal army units, the Staatsgerichtshof [the highest court] was, in fact, promptly seized of the matter by the deposed Prussian government and by another *Land*, Bavaria. The [court's] decision on this constitutional crisis ... was mixed: the court confirmed the removal of the Prussian ministers from the exercise of their office, but declared that a formal dismissal of them could not constitutionally be made by the federal president under Article 48(2) of the [Weimar] constitution. In the immediate result, the court decision changed nothing in the ... political situation [but provided a precedent on which the 1949 Basic Law built and went beyond to establish] judicial control of constitutionality.

Edward McWhinney, Constitution–Making: Principles, Process, Practice 115 (1981).

Southwest Case

I BVerfGE 14 (1951) (Federal Constitutional Court of Germany)

After World War II, the three Western occupying powers divided the two former states of Baden and Württemberg in southwest Germany into three areas for purposes of military and political administration: Baden, Baden–Württemberg, and Württemberg–Hohenzollern. When the Bonn Constitution came into operation in 1949, these three areas became Laender in the Federal Republic with their own Land constitutions. Art. 118 of the Basic Law, however, provided:

> The reorganization of the territory comprising the Laender of Baden, Württemberg–Baden, and Württemberg-Hohenzollern may be elected notwithstanding the provisions of Article 29, by agreement among the Laender concerned. If no agreement is reached, the reorganization shall be elected by federal legislation which must provide for a referendum.

The Laender were not able to agree on reorganizing themselves, and in 1951 the federal parliament passed a pair of statutes. The First Reorganization Law extended the lives of the Land legislatures of Baden and Württemberg–Hohenzollern until completion of reorganization. The Second Reorganization Law set out details for merging the three Laender into a single Land to be called Baden–Württemberg. The act conditioned operation on a referendum, as specified in Art. 118, to be held in the three Laender of the southwest area.

On the very first day the Constitutional Court sat, Baden brought suit challenging the validity of both acts as infringing on its constitutionally guaranteed status within the Federation.

JUDGMENT OF THE SECOND SENATE. . . .

D.   [FIRST REORGANIZATION LAW] . . . .

2. . . . An individual constitutional provision cannot be considered as an isolated clause and interpreted alone. A constitution has an inner unity, and the meaning of any one part is linked to that of other provisions. Taken as a unit, a constitution reflects certain overarching principles and fundamental decisions to which individual provisions are subordinate. Art. 79, par. 3, makes it clear that the Basic Law proceeds in this fashion. Thus this Court agrees with the statement of the Bavarian Constitutional Court:

> That a constitutional provision itself may be null and void, is not conceptually impossible just because it is a part of the constitution. There are constitutional principles that are so fundamental and to such an extent an expression of a law that precedes even the constitution that they also bind the framer of the constitution, and other constitutional provisions that do not rank so high may be null and void because they contravene these principles. . . .

From this rule of interpretation, it follows that any constitutional provision must be interpreted in such a way that it is compatible with those elementary principles and with the basic decisions of the framer of the constitution. This rule applies also to Art. 118, sent. 2.

3.   The Basic Law has decided in favor of a *democracy* as the basis for the governmental system (Arts. 20, 28): The Federal Republic is a democratic, federal state. The constitutional order in the Laender must conform to the principles of the democratic state based on the rule of law in the sense of the Basic Law. The Federation guarantees that the constitutional order of the Laender will conform to this political order.

As prescribed by the Basic Law, democracy requires not only that parliament control the Government, but also that the right to vote of eligible voters is not removed or impaired by unconstitutional means.... It is true that the democratic principle does not imply that the life of a Landtag must not exceed four years or that it cannot be extended for important reasons. But this principle does require that the term of a Landtag, whose length was set by the people in accepting their constitution, can only be extended through procedures prescribed in that constitution, i.e., only with the consent of the people.

If, without the consent of the people of the Land, the Federation prevents an election scheduled by the Land constitution, the Federation violates the fundamental right of a citizen in a democratic state, the right to vote, as protected by Art. 28, par. 3, of the Basic Law....

4.   Another fundamental principle of the Basic Law is that of federalism (Arts. 20, 28, 30). As members of the Federation, Laender are states with their own sovereign power which, even if limited as to subject matter, is not derived from the Federation, but recognized by it. A Land's constitutional order, as long as it stays within the framework of Art. 28, par. 1, falls within the Land's sphere of competency. In particular, determination of rules that govern formation of the Land's constitutional organs, their functions, and their competencies are exclusively concerns of the Land. This competence also includes regulations concerning how often and on what occasions citizens may vote and when and under what conditions the term of a Landtag expires....

This rule also applies to legislation pursuant to Art. 118, sent. 2. It is true that, in order to effect reorganization, the federal legislator has power to "retrench" the Laender of Baden, Württemberg-Baden and Württemberg-Hohenzollern. But he cannot disturb the constitutional orders of these Laender as long as they exist in full.

The argument that, by eliminating the three Landtags in the process of reorganization, the Federation shortens their terms of office and can consequently also extend them for a transition period, is legally erroneous....

... Elimination of the Landtags is a necessary consequence of elimination of the Laender; thus it does not constitute a curtailment of terms of office. Extension of the terms, however, applies to existing Landtags. This extension requires a special legislative act which the Federation cannot pass for the reasons already mentioned. A Land cannot dispose of its legislative competency. And the Federation cannot by consent of a Land obtain a legislative competency that is not granted by the Basic Law. Therefore approval by Württemberg-Hohenzollern of the measure taken by the Federation is without legal significance.

5.   Art. 118. sent. 2, only authorizes the federal legislator to regulate "reorganization" and thus draws constitutional limits.... The federal legislator could extend the lives of the Landtags only if ... the "matter cannot be effectively regulated by legislation of individual Laender" [Art. 72, par. 2, of the Basic Law]. This limitation precludes extending the terms of Landtags.... Such authority remains primarily a matter for the Laender....

6.   In view of these legal restraints, neither reasons of practicality, political necessity, nor similar considerations can confer unfettered choice on the federal legislator to enact, under the guise of reorganizing Laender, any regulations that seem reasonable and proper....

The fact that the First Reorganization Law was passed and promulgated at the same time as the Second Reorganization Law is also irrelevant to the question of its validity....

7.... The Federal Constitutional Court must hold a legal provision null and void if it is inconsistent with the Basic Law. Hence it must be declared that the First Reorganization Law ... is null and void.... This declaration has legal force. It is to be published in the Federal Law Gazette. The declaration together with the main reasons for the decision binds all constitutional organs of the Federation ... in such a way that no federal law with the same content can again be deliberated and enacted by the legislative bodies and promulgated by the federal president.

E.   [SECOND REORGANIZATION LAW] ...

2.   Whenever the compatibility of a federal law with the Basic Law is the subject of dispute ... the Federal Constitutional Court must examine the validity of the entire law and of each individual provision under *all* legal aspects, even if they have not been put forward by the participants....

8.... a) It has been claimed that in a federation, a member state cannot be eliminated against its population's will. As a rule a federal constitution does guarantee the existence and territory of member states. But the Basic Law expressly deviates from this rule. Art. 79, par. 3, guarantees as an inviolable principle only that the Federation must be divided "into Laender." The Basic Law does not contain any guarantee for presently existing Laender and their borders. On the contrary, it provides— as follows from Art. 29 and 118—for changes in territorial conditions of individual Laender as well as for a reorganization of federal territory which may entail elimination of one or several existing Laender. This reorganization may even be effected against the will of the population of the Land concerned.... The Basic Law thus decides in favor of a "changeable federal state." ...

b) It follows from Art. 29, par. 4, however, that the will of the population of a member state cannot be broken by an ordinary federal law, but only by a new Bundestag decision and a referendum of the entire federal population. Thus only the will of the population of the higher unit suffices, and not merely the will of the population of one or several neighboring Laender.

The question arises of whether or not this principle also applies to regulations pursuant to Art. 118, sent. 2. The provision that protects the existence of a Land is an outgrowth of the Basic Law's principle of federalism.... This principle ... might speak for the view that the principle contained in [Art. 29] also applies to regulations pursuant to Art. 118. On the other hand the framer of the Basic Law ... expressly declared in Art. 118, sent. 1, that reorganization may be effected "deviating from the provisions of Art. 29. ... But in particular it follows from the deliberations in the Parliamentary Council [that framed the Basic Law,"] from the public discussion in the past few years, and from consultations among the three Laender Governments that present public law conditions in the southwest area were in general considered as especially unsatisfactory and therefore ripe for immediate reorganization. A fast and simple reorganization was therefore desired. It must not be frustrated by the opposition of the population of one Land....

c) Baden claims that, aside from the principle contained in Art. 29, par. 4, other clauses of the Basic Law recognize the democratic principle (Arts. 20, 28).... Democracy means self-determination of the people. [The Second Reorganization Law, Baden argues,] deprives the people of Baden of this right because it forces them against their will to become part of a southwest state.

That a people themselves must on principle determine their basic order ... certainly follows from the notion of democracy.... The Land of Baden, as a member of the Federation, is a state to which necessarily belongs a state people. This state people—a term which must be well distinguished from the sociological-ethnological-political term of a people—possesses in a democracy the right of self-determination. It is decisive, however, that Baden as a member state of a federation is not autonomous and independent, but is part of a federal order that restricts its sovereign power in various aspects.... To a certain extent the principles of democracy and federalism conflict as far as a member state within the federation is concerned. A compromise between the two can only be found if both suffer certain restrictions. In the case of reorganization of federal territory ... it is in the nature of the matter that, in the interest of the more comprehensive unit, the right to self-determination of the Land's people be restricted. Within the scope of what is possible in a federal state, the democratic principle is safe–guarded by the Basic Law's provisions in Art. 29 that the entire people of the Federation and in Art. 118, sent. 2, that the population in the area to be reorganized will, in the final analysis, decide.

10.   Finally, objections have been raised that [the statute] violates the principle of equality (Art. 3; Art. 19, par. 3)....

a) On the one hand it is argued: If, under Art. 118, sent. 2, Baden can against the will of its population be forced by a majority decision in the two neighboring states to relinquish its existence, the status of Baden is ... weaker than that of the Laender whose will can be overcome only by a decision of the entire people. Thus, it is claimed, the federal law subjects Baden to unequal treatment....

Such an argument is misdirected—Its force runs not against the reorganization law, but against Art. 118, sent. 2, of the Basic Law, which authorizes unequal treatment. Besides, the principle of equality only prohibits essentially equal matters from being treated in an unequal manner....

Notes [by Murphy and Tanenhaus]: 1. The Court examined a number of other issues that the judges saw in the Second Reorganization Act and, with the exception of one provision dealing with delegation of power by the federal parliament to the federal executive, held the various sections met constitutional standards. The Court specifically rejected Baden's argument that rules of international law should govern Federation–Land relations. For a brief analysis of the case, see the article by one of the judges of the Second Senate of the Constitutional Court, Gerhard Leibholz, "The Federal Constitutional Court in Germany and the 'Southwest Case,' " 46 *Am. Pol. Sci. Rev.* 723 (1952).

2. In this, its first argued case, the Court carved out for itself a broad authority, especially in asserting: (a) it could find implicit in the Basic Law certain super constitutional norms that took precedence not only over ordinary political acts but also over specific clauses in the Basic Law itself; (b) not only its decision but also its reasoning bound the federal parliament and President; and (c) it had authority to answer questions that the judges thought the case presented even though the litigants did not raise them.

3. The referendum was held in December 1951, and the voters in the southwest area overwhelmingly approved the merger.

4. See the amendments to Art. 118 of the Basic Law adopted in 1969.

Selected Provisions of the Basic Law for the Federal Republic of Germany (promulgated by the Parliamentary Council on May 23, 1949, as amended through November 15, 1994) (Official Translation published by the Press and Information Office of the Federal Government of Germany):

Article 20 [Political and social structure, defence of the constitutional order]

(1) The Federal Republic of Germany shall be a democratic and social federal state.

(2) All public authority emanates from the people. It shall be exercised by the people through elections and referendums and by specific legislative, executive and judicial bodies.

(3) The legislature shall be bound by the constitutional order, the executive and the judiciary by law and justice.

(4) All Germans have the right to resist anybody attempting to do away with this constitutional order, should no other remedy be possible.

Article 28 [Federal guarantee of Land constitutions and local government]

(1) The constitutional order in the Länder shall conform to the principles of the republican, democratic and social state governed by the rule of law within the meaning of this Basic Law. In each of the Lander, counties and municipalities the people shall be represented by a body elected by general, direct, free, equal and secret ballots.. . .

(2) The municipalities shall be guaranteed the right to manage all the affairs of the local community on their own responsibility within the limits set by law. . . . The right of self-government shall include responsibility for financial matters.

(3) The Federation shall ensure that the constitutional order of the Lander conforms to the basic rights and the provisions of paragraphs (1) and (2) of this Article.

Article 79 [Amendments to the Basic Law]

(1) This Basic Law may be amended only by a law expressly modifying or supplementing its text. In respect of international treaties concerning a peace settlement, the preparation of a peace settlement, or the phasing out of an occupation regime, or serving the defence of the Federal Republic, it shall he sufficient, in order to make clear that the provisions of this Basic Law do not preclude the conclusion and entry into force of such treaties, to supplement the text of this Basic Law and to confine the supplement to such clarification.

(2) Such law must be carried by two thirds of the Members of the Bundestag and two thirds of the votes of the Bundesrat.

(3) Amendments to this Basic Law affecting the division of the Federation into Under, their participation in the legislative process, or the principles laid down in Articles I and 20 shall be prohibited.

CHAPTER IX: ADMINISTRATION OF JUSTICE

Article 92 [Judicial power]

Judicial power shall be vested in the judges; it shall be exercised by the Federal Constitutional Court, the federal courts provided for in this Basic Law, and the courts of the Lander.

Article 93 [The Federal Constitutional Court, jurisdiction]

(1) The Federal Constitutional Court shall rule:

1. on the interpretation of this Basic Law in disputes concerning the extent of the rights and obligations of a supreme federal institution or other institutions concerned who have been vested with rights of their own by this Basic Law Or by the rules of procedure of a supreme federal institution;

2. in case of disagreement or doubt as to the formal and material compatibility of federal or Land legislation with this Basic Law or as to the compatibility of Land legislation with other federal (legislation at the request of the Federal Government, a Land government or one third of the Members of the Bundestag);

[2a omitted]

3. in case of disagreement on the rights and obligations of the Federation and the Lander, particularly in the implementation of federal legislation by the Lander and in the exercise of federal supervision,

4. on other disputes involving public law between the Federation and the Lander, between Lander or within a Land, unless recourse to another court exists;

4a. on constitutional complaints which may be filed by anybody claiming that one of their basic rights or one of their rights under paragraph (4) of Article 20 or under Article 33, 38, 101, 103 or 104 has been violated by public authority;

4b. on constitutional complaints by municipalities or associations of municipalities alleging violation of their right of self-government under Article 28 by a (federal) law; in case of violation by a Land law, however, only where a complaint cannot be lodged with the Land constitutional court;

5. in the other cases provided for in this Basic Law.

(2) The Federal Constitutional Court shall also rule on any other cases referred to it by federal legislation.

Article 94 [The Federal Constitutional Court, composition]

(1) The Federal Constitutional Court shall be composed of federal judges and other members. Half of the members of the Federal Constitutional Court shall be elected by the Bundestag and half by the Bundesrat. They may not be members of the Bundestag, the Bundestat, the Federal Government, nor of any of the corresponding institutions of a Land.

(2) The constitution and procedure of the Federal Constitutional Court shall be governed by a federal law which shall specify the cases in which its, decisions have the force of law. Such law may make a complaint of unconstitutionality conditional upon the exhaustion of all other legal remedies and provide for a special admissibility procedure.

Article 95 [Supreme federal courts, joint panel]

(1) For the purposes of ordinary, administrative, financial, labour and social jurisdiction the Federation shall establish as supreme courts the

Federal Court of Justice, the Federal Administrative Court, the Federal Finance Court, the Federal Labour Court and the Federal Social Court.

(2) The judges of each of these courts shall be selected jointly by the appropriate Federal Minister and a selection committee composed of the appropriate Land ministers and an equal number of members elected by the Bundestag.

...[3] [omitted]

Article 97 [Independence of judges]

(1) Judges shall be independent and subject only to the law.

(2) Judges appointed to full-time, permanent posts cannot, against their will, be dismissed or permanently or temporarily suspended or transferred or retired before the expiration of their term of office except by virtue of a judicial decision and only on the grounds and in the form provided for by law. Legislation may set age limits for the retirement of judges appointed for life. In the event of changes in the structure of courts or their districts judges may be transferred to another court or removed from office, but only on full salary.

Article 98 [Status of federal and Land judges]

(1) The status of federal judges shall be the subject of a special federal law.

(2) Where a federal judge, in an official capacity or unofficially, infringes the principles of this Basic Law or the constitutional order of a Land the Federal Constitutional Court may, upon the request of the Bundestag and with a two-thirds majority, order the judge's transfer or retirement. If the infringement was deliberate it may order dismissal.

(3) The status of Land judges shall be governed by specific Land legislation....

(5) In respect of Land judges the Under may make provision corresponding to that described in paragraph (2) of this Article. Land constitutional law shall remain unaffected. The ruling in a case of impeachment of a judge shall rest with the Federal Constitutional Court.

Article 99 [Rulings of the Federal Constitutional Court and the supreme federal courts in disputes concerning Land legislation]

Rulings on constitutional disputes within a Land may be referred by Land legislation to the Federal Constitutional Court and rulings at last instance in matters involving the application of Land law to the supreme courts referred to in paragraph (1) of Article 95.

Article 100 [Compatibility of legislation and constitutional law]

(1) Where a court considers that a law on whose validity its ruling depends is unconstitutional it shall stay the proceedings and, if it holds the constitution of a Land to be violated, seek a ruling from the Land court with jurisdiction for constitutional disputes or, where it holds this Basic

Law to be violated, from the Federal Constitutional Court. This shall also apply where this Basic Law is held to be violated by Land law or where a Land law is held to be incompatible with a federal law.

(2) Where in the course of litigation doubt exists whether a rule of international law is an integral part of federal law and whether such rule directly establishes rights and obligations for the individual (Article 25), the court shall seek a ruling from the Federal Constitutional Court.

(3) Where in interpreting this Basic Law the constitutional court of a Land proposes to deviate from a ruling of the Federal Constitutional Court or of the constitutional court of another Land it shall seek a ruling from the Federal Constitutional Court.

Questions and Comments

1.   Are the two parts of the *Southwest* decision consistent with each other? If the court can find constitutional provisions unconstitutional, why did it not so find the provisions of art. 118? And why, if the First Reorganization Act violated principles of self-governance and representative democracy, did not the Second?

2.   In both Canada and South Africa, a large number of holdings of unconstitutionality in the early years of their most recent constitutions came in cases challenging statutory presumptions in criminal cases, which the courts found were violations of the government's constitutional obligation to prove guilt beyond a reasonable doubt. See, e.g., R. v. Oakes, 24 C.C.C. 3d 321 (Supreme Court of Canada, 1986); S. v. Coetzee, 1997 (4) B.C.L.R. 437 (CC), 1997 SACLR Lexis 4 (Constitutional Court of South Africa, June 30, 1997). What might account for this coincidence? Is there something about judicial review of criminal convictions that facilitates establishing the legitimacy of judicial review of laws? Is it possible for a series of small decisions, each accepted by the government, to establish the legitimacy of judicial review as effectively as "landmark" or foundational cases? Is it possible to avoid the reconstruction of one or more cases as "foundational" in successful constitutional states?

----

2.   FRANCE AND THE 1971 DECISION ON ASSOCIATIONS

As earlier readings set out, the French Conseil Constitutionnel was established in the 1958 Constitution in order to maintain the newly created limits on the powers of the parliament and to protect the broad executive authority (including executive lawmaking through "règlements") of the President and his government. Under the original terms of the 1958 Constitution, the Conseil Constitutionnel's power to review laws could be exercised only before a law had been promulgated, and only at the request of the President, the Prime Minister, the president of the National Assembly or of the Senate. Not until 1974 was the referral power broadened to include "sixty deputies or sixty senators," thus permitting an opposition party to challenge a law favored by the government and the parliament.

Because of the terse nature of the Conseil Constitutionnel's decisions, we include Alec Stone's description of the 1971 decisions and of the circumstances leading up to it. See also James E. Beardsley, *The Constitutional Council and Constitutional Liberties in France*, 20 Am. J. Comp. L. 431 (1972). Stone's description is followed by translations of the two principal decisions Stone discusses.

Alec Stone, The Birth of Judicial Politics in France (1992) (pp. 64–69, 257–60):

...[Between 1959-70, in] only one instance ... was the Council asked to rule *against* the executive, when in 1962 the president of the Senate, Gaston Monnerville, asked the Council to invalidate de Gaulle's attempt to amend the constitution by referendum—a procedure not provided for by the constitution. The subsequent decision put the Council on center stage, for one brief moment, but damaged the institution's public reputation for years thereafter.

In late September 1962, de Gaulle announced to a national television audience his plan to institute direct election to the office of the presidency by universal suffrage. Although such a change would require an amendment to the constitution, de Gaulle was unwilling to follow the only procedures providing for revision, those of article 89, which requires that constitutional amendments be adopted in "identical terms" by both houses of parliament. Instead, the government proposed that the revision be adopted by the people in a national referendum according to article 11, which allows legislating but not constitutional revision by referendum, thus bypassing a hostile parliament completely. The stakes of de Gaulle's gamble were high. If he were to succeed, the last argument for parliamentary sovereignty—namely, that the National Assembly was the sole institution elected by the people—would be silenced.

The proposal caused immediate and shrill protest from politicians, the print-media, and from constitutional scholars, including the editor of the *Revue du droit public,* largely to the effect that the procedure to be used was unconstitutional, and would result in a presidential system of government. The government, as required by the constitution, consulted with both the *Conseil d'Etat* and the Council, and *both* bodies ruled—in nonbinding opinions—that the procedure was unconstitutional. Several days later, the National Assembly brought down the Pompidou government, the first and only censure of a government in the Fifth Republic: "Mr. Prime Minister," Paul Reynaud told Pompidou, "go say to the Elysée ... that this Assembly is not so degenerate as to renounce the Republic."

The referendum passed on 28 October 62–38 percent, and the law was adopted. Days before it was promulgated, Monnerville appealed to the Council to determine if the referendum procedure, and therefore the law, was constitutional. In his referral, the President of the Senate argued that only article 89 could be employed to amend the constitution properly, and that to admit any other possibility would be to "make nonsense of the essential distinctions" between organic, constitutional, and ordinary laws. The president of the Senate argued further that even power exercised by the voters is "only legitimate if it respects the rules and procedures laid down by the Constitution"; to rule otherwise would be "ruinous for *le droit,* as well as for the stability of our institutions."

On 6 November the Council (by a 6–4 vote) ruled, first, that article 61 only grants the Council jurisdiction over ordinary legislation and not over legislation "adopted by the people following a referendum, which constitute the direct expression of national sovereignty," and second, that since nothing in the constitution gives the Council the competence to examine the constitutionality of referenda, it could not do so. Having been declared beyond the reach of control, the law was promulgated on 8 November.

"The Constitutional Council just committed suicide," Monnerville declared afterwards, and asked, "If the Council does not have the competence to judge a violation so patent and so serious of the constitution, who does in our country?" Monnerville's frustration is understandable: the answer to his question is: no one. For opponents—which included large segments of the parliamentary *majority*—the Council's argumentation leads to an absurdity: while the law is an executive proposal, it can not be legally challenged; after the law is adopted by referendum, it is virtually a superconstitutional law which no institution may contest; in between, no amount of protest could deter the government. Every competent institutional authority had declared itself against the plan, and de Gaulle and his government had simply ignored them all. While there is no shortage of compelling arguments which the Council might have used to claim jurisdiction, in the end it was the lack of political will of a majority of its members to stand up to de Gaulle, and not the power of legal arguments, which was crucial.

One remarkable, if on its face ironic, outcome of this affair was the unprecedented achievement of a consensus among parliamentarians for the principle of constitutional review. Gaullists, naturally enough, rallied behind the Council. *For those opposed to de Gaulle* and the presidentialization of the regime, including those otherwise affiliated with the Right, *the abolition of the Council and the establishment of a supreme court came to be viewed as necessary.* It was argued that a supreme court—replete with "real" judges granted the power to exercise a posteriori review of executive as well as legislative acts—was the indispensable means to ensure a proper balance of power between institutions. Between 1958 and 1970, seven bills to create a supreme court were introduced, although none was proposed by the Left. By 1972, the joint Socialist–Communist Common Program included a plan to abolish the Council and replace it with a supreme court.

1971–80: Raising the Preamble

The 1971–80 period was dominated by two events. First, a 1971 decision—characterized by some as France's *Marbury v. Madison*—answered in the affirmative an important question left over from the first period: would the Council ever annul a piece of legislation backed by the executive? Of far greater long-range importance, the 1971 decision affirmed the *valeur constitutionnel* of the texts contained in the 1946 preamble—the 1789 declaration, the FPRLR*, and the list of "political, economic, and social principles particularly necessary for our times" *[cited as the 1946 principles]*—opening up an unexplored area of *substantive* constraints on policymaking. Second, the 1974 amendment to the constitution expanding the power of referral to deputies and senators who, inspired by the new politics of the preamble, lead to greatly increased Council activity.

"A Revolution Made in Four Words"

The Constitutional Council's decision of 16 July 1971 capped the first parliamentary legislative process in which ordinary legislation *proposed by the executive* was threatened with referral to the Council. The events leading up to this decision . . . can be briefly summarized. In May 1970, the government, enabled by 1936 legislation outlawing private militias, banned *La gauche prolétarienne*, a leftist political party. In reaction, a group of concerned citizens including Jean–Paul Sartre and Simone de Beauvoir formed the *Association des amis de la cause du peuple*, taking the name of the group's newspaper. In an effort to establish legal personality, the group sought to register with the Paris prefecture, whereupon the minister of the Interior ordered the *préfet* to refuse to issue the requisite receipt, on the grounds that the two groups were one and the same. This order was reversed by a Paris administrative tribunal, conforming to a long-standing jurisprudence of the *Conseil d'Etat*. In June 1971, attempting to obviate such problems for the future, the government introduced into parliament a bill which would have amended a 1901 law on association, by empowering a *préfet* to withhold recognition from any association which "appeared to have an immoral or illicit purpose or to be trying to reconstitute an illegal association."

The bill generated a heated debate in the National Assembly, where a number of prominent opposition figures on the Left and even a Gaullist denounced the measure as an intolerable infringement on liberties long enshrined by the 1901 legislation, but the majority approved it nonetheless. In the Senate, Pierre Marcilhacy, a prominent independent-centrist and the leading constitutional specialist on that body, raised a *quéstion préalable* in which he argued that the bill abridged rights contained in article 4 of the constitution—which states that political parties and groups may "form and exercise their activities freely"—by allowing for the possibility of a priori suppression of free association. The motion was adopted, and discussion of the bill was aborted before it had begun. After the National Assembly overrode the Senate and passed the bill, the president of the Senate, Alain Poher, "acting dispassionately" and after "numerous hesitations," gave in

---

* [Editors' Note: The acronym FPRLR stands for "fundamental principles recognized by the laws of the Republic," a phrase found in the Preamble to the 1946 Constitution, reproduced below.]

to pressure exerted by Marcilhacy and others and referred the bill to the Council; "to throw some light on the matter," he declared.

Over the ensuing two weeks, the Council was subjected to an unprecedented and unrelenting lobby campaign for the annulment of the legislation. In addition to agitation by centrist senators and the opposition political parties, unions, small leftist groups, and other social formations publicly expressed their displeasure with the bill. Daniel Mayer, the president of the League of Human Rights (and future Council president) denounced the measure as a sign that French rights were being "eroded and ridiculed," and he was joined by other human rights organizations. Law professors, including Robert Badinter (another future Council president) and Olivier Dupéyroux, argued—in detailed and lengthy "briefs" published in *Le Monde*—that the bill was unconstitutional, was sanctionable by any reading of the Conseil d'Etat's jurisprudence, and constituted a direct challenge to the Council to escape its image of "mediocrity." "A child can see that this bill is unconstitutional," wrote Dupéyroux on the eve of the decision, and one which the Council "must strike down" if it is to fulfill "its historic responsibility" to protect fundamental rights, and thus "determine [its] destiny." *Le Monde's* cartoonist even got into the act, depicting the minister of the interior poised to crush with a huge rock a tiny fly which had lighted on a sleeping and undisturbed Marianne (the symbol of the Republic). Jean Foyer, a law professor, former Gaullist minister of justice, and the president of the powerful *Commission des lois* in the National Assembly, even felt compelled to protest against what he called "this effort of intoxication"—"the absolutely inadmissible political operation" which claims, "in essence, that if the Council is independent, if it is liberal, it will declare the bill unconstitutional."

On 16 July the Council did just that, amputating the bill's controversial provisions, and prompting *Le Monde's* banner headline: "The Constitutional Council checks [executive] power and affirms its independence." Far outweighing the importance of the annulment, the Council had, by a vote of 6–3 (dissenting was the Gaullist law professor, François Goguel and two former Gaullist ministers) chosen not only to censure the government, but to base its decision on the preamble generally and on the FPRLR specifically. The "liberty of association," which the Council found to be "recognized" in the same 1901 law which the government had attempted to modify, constituted a FPRLR. Because the freedom of association is not listed as a fundamental right in the 1946 preamble, and because the FPRLR are only mentioned and not enumerated, the Council's ruling constituted unabashed judicial creativity (as *any* ruling based on the FPRLR would have). The result is a curious one: the Council's decision enforces substantive constraints on parliamentary activity, constraints which it found in the work of parliament some seventy years before, when constitutional review did not exist! As disconcerting, because the Council had listed no other principles which might be contained in the corpus of the FPRLR, its discretionary power to discover more of them appeared virtually boundless.

For *le droit*, the decision was cause for general celebration, constituting no less than a judicial "revolution ... made in 4 words": "In view of the Constitution," the Council had written, *"and notably its preamble.... "* "With this single phrase," stated Rivéro, the declaration of 1789, the preamble of 1946, and the fundamental principles recognized by the laws of the Republic were incorporated into the constitution, which was thus "doubled in volume." Council members certainly understood the magnitude of their decision. As then-president Palewski remembered later:

> To justify our decision it was necessary to invoke the preamble of the 1958 Constitution, referring to the 1946 declaration and to that of 1789. We could thus create a veritable judicial bastion for the defense of the rights of citizens.

While the decision is inarguably an audacious one, a conjunction of favorable conditions might have led Palewski to believe that his Council could weather any political storm it might create. Several points deserve emphasis. First, *the Council's move had been well prepared for by doctrinal activity.* ... [T]he *valeur constitutionnel* of much of the preamble had been asserted by doctrinal authority long before ordinary and administrative courts went on to affirm it. It was not altogether surprising then for legal specialists like Badinter and Dupéyroux to direct similar arguments at the Council, which they did in high-profile, public advocacy. By invoking the preamble, the Council was also invoking the legitimacy of legal scholarship and the jurisprudence of the *Conseil d'Etat*. Second, while the FPRLR have the dubious distinction of being the least precise of the sources mentioned by the preamble, the *Conseil d'Etat* had already consecrated "freedom of association" during its Fourth Republic cataloguing of the "general principles of law"; the Council therefore had simply to "constitutionalize" this principle. Third, although Marcilhacy had argued in parliament that the bill violated rights guaranteed by article 4 of the constitution, the referral did *not* raise the article 4 argument, instead relying on the FPRLR via the 1901 legislation. The Council's defenders could therefore readily claim that its "activism" was carefully measured: its jurisprudential choices arose from a decision-making context constructed by "politics." (The president of the Senate was only formally the author of the 1971 referral; in fact, the petition was written by a law professor.) Last, the political environment in which constitutional politics were conducted had fundamentally changed. General de Gaulle's departure had, among other things, made the evolution of the French constitution a much more participatory process. The Council was asserting that a primary constituent element of this process would henceforth be constitutional review.

The decision also signaled to the opposition that constitutional review could be used to enshrine substantive rights important to it and to the detriment of the majority's legislative agenda. Of the Council's next three decisions, two had the effect of rebroadcasting, clarifying, and reinforcing this message. In the first, a decision of 27 December 1973, the Council again gave satisfaction to the president of the Senate in a legislative conflict with the government, consecrating the "general principles of equality before the law" found in the 1789 Declaration of the Rights of Man. Barely a year later, on 15 January 1975, the Council refused to annul any aspect of the government's bill to permit abortion where pregnancy puts a woman in a "situation of distress," ruling that the bill did not violate one of the "political, economic, or social principles particularly necessary to our times." Thus by January 1975, the Constitutional Council had formally spoken to each of the three texts contained in the preamble, thus legitimizing their use as sources of constitutional debate in parliament. . . .

The 1971 Decision on Freedom of Association, and the 1962 Decision on the Referendum, from John Bell, FRENCH CONSTITUTIONAL LAW 272–73, 301–02 (1992) (with his background comments)

CC decision no. 71–44 DC of 16 July 1971, *Associations Law, Rec.* 29, . . .

Background: This is the first decision of the Conseil constitutionnel that struck down a provision of a *loi* for breach of fundamental rights. Its justification appealed to the Preamble of the 1958 Constitution and to a fundamental principle recognized by the laws of the Republic, to be found in the *loi* of 1 July 1901 on associations. That *loi* provides that, before an association may be recognized as having legal status, it must file certain particulars with the prefect, who must then issue a certificate of registration.

In this case the National Assembly sought, against the opposition of the Senate, to pass a *loi* that would empower the prefect to refuse registration pending a reference to the courts over the legality of the objectives of a proposed association. The President of the Senate referred the *loi* to the Conseil. The principal issue was the constitutionality of prior restraint of the freedom of association.

DECISION

In the light of the Constitution and notably of its Preamble;

In the light of the *ordonnance* of 7 November 1958 creating the organic law on the Conseil constitutionnel, especially chapter 2 of title II of the said *ordonnance;*

In the light of the *loi* of 1 July 1901 (as amended) relating to associations;

In the light of the *loi* of 10 January. 1936 relating to combat groups and private militias;

1. Considering that the *loi* referred for scrutiny by the Conseil constitutionnel was put to the vote in both chambers, following one of the procedures provided for in the Constitution, during the parliamentary session beginning on 2 April 1971;

2. Considering that, among the fundamental principles recognized by the laws of the Republic and solemnly reaffirmed by the Constitution, is to

be found the freedom of association; that this principle underlies the general provisions of the *loi* of 1 July 1901; that, by virtue of this principle, associations may be formed freely and can be registered simply on condition of the deposition of a prior declaration; that, thus, with the exception of measures that may be taken against certain types of association, the validity of the creation of an association cannot be subordinated to the prior intervention of an administrative or judicial authority, even where the association appears to be invalid or to have an illegal purpose;

3. Considering that, even if they change nothing in respect of the creation of undeclared associations, the provisions of article 3 of the *loi*, the text of which is referred to the Conseil before its promulgation for scrutiny as to its compatibility with the Constitution, is intended to create a procedure whereby the acquisition of legal capacity by declared associations could be subordinated to a prior review by a court as to its compliance with the law;

4. Considering that, therefore, the provisions of article 3 of the *loi* are declared not to be compatible with the Constitution. . . .

* * *

CC decision no. 62–20 DC of 6 November 1962, *Referendum Law, Rec.* 27.
Background:

. . . The reference was made by the President of the Senate.

DECISION

1. Considering that the competence of the Conseil constitutionnel is strictly limited by the Constitution, as well as by the provisions of the organic law of 7 November 1958 on the Conseil constitutionnel . . . that the Conseil constitutionnel cannot be called upon to rule on matters other than the limited number for which those texts provide;

2. Considering that, even if article 61 of the Constitution gives the Conseil constitutionnel the task of assessing the compatibility with the Constitution of organic laws and ordinary laws, which, respectively, must be submitted to it for scrutiny, without stating whether this competence extends to all texts of legislative character, be they adopted by the people after a referendum or passed by Parliament, or whether, on the contrary, it is limited only to the latter category, it follows from the spirit of the Constitution, which made the Conseil constitutionnel a body regulating the activity of public authorities, that the laws to which the Constitution intended to refer in article 61 are only those *loi* passed by Parliament, and not those which, adopted by the people after a referendum, constitute a direct expression of national sovereignty;

3. Considering that this interpretation follows equally from the express provisions of the Constitution, especially article 60, which regulates the role of the Conseil constitutionnel in referendums, and from article 11, which does not provide for any formality between the adoption of a bill by the people and its promulgation by the President of the Republic;

4. Considering that, finally, this same interpretation is again expressly confirmed by the provisions of article 17 of the above-mentioned organic

law of 7 November 1958, which only mentions *"lois* passed by Parliament"', as well as article 23 of the said law, which provides that "when the Conseil constitutionnel declares that the *loi* of which it is seised contains a provision contrary to the Constitution, without finding at the same time that it is not severable from the rest of the *loi,* the President may promulgate it without this provision, or request a new reading from the chambers";

5.   Considering that it follows from what has been said that none of the provisions of the Constitution, nor of the above-mentioned organic law applying it, gives the Conseil constitutionnel the competence to rule on the request submitted by the President of the Senate, that it consider whether the bill adopted by the French people by way of referendum on 28 October 1962 is compatible with the Constitution . . .

Selected portions of French constitutional texts:

[The English translations of the 1958 Constitution and the 1946 Preamble were prepared under the joint responsibility of the Press and Information Communication Directorate of the Ministry of Foreign Affairs and the European Affairs Department of the National Assembly. © Minis-tère des Affaires étrangéres, Mai 1997 (French Ministry of Foreign Affairs, May 1997).]

1958 Constitution

PREAMBLE

The French people solemnly proclaim their attachment to the Rights of Man and the principles of national sovereignty as defined by the Declaration of 1789, confirmed and complemented by the Preamble to the Constitution of 1946.

By virtue of these principles and that of the self-determination of peoples, the Republic offers to the overseas territories that express the will to adhere to them new institutions founded on the common ideal of liberty, equality and fraternity and conceived with a view to their democratic development.

Article 1

France shall be an indivisible, secular, democratic and social Republic. It shall ensure the equality of all citizens before the law, without distinction of origin, race or religion. It shall respect all beliefs.

ON SOVEREIGNTY

Article 2

The language of the Republic shall be French.

The national emblem shall be the blue, white and red tricolour flag.

The national anthem shall be La Marseillaise.

The motto of the Republic shall be "Liberty, Equality, Fraternity".

Its principle shall be: government of the people, by the people and for the people.

Article 3

National sovereignty shall belong to the people, who shall exercise it through their representatives and by means of referendum.

No section of the people nor any individual may arrogate to itself, or to himself, the exercise thereof.

Suffrage may be direct or indirect as provided by the Constitution. It shall always be universal, equal and secret.

All French citizens of either sex who have reached their majority and are in possession of their civil and political rights may vote as provided by statute.

Article 4

Political parties and groups shall contribute to the exercise of suffrage. They shall be formed and carry on their activities freely. They must respect the principles of national sovereignty and democracy.

THE PRESIDENT OF THE REPUBLIC

Article 5

The President of the Republic shall see that the Constitution is observed. . . .

THE CONSTITUTIONAL COUNCIL

Article 56

The Constitutional Council shall consist of nine members, whose term of office shall be nine years and shall not be renewable. One third of the membership of the Constitutional Council shall be renewed every three years. Three of its members shall be appointed by the President of the Republic, three by the President of the National Assembly and three by the President of the Senate.

In addition to the nine members provided for above, former Presidents of the Republic shall be ex officio life members of the Constitutional Council.

The President shall be appointed by the President of the Republic. He shall have a casting vote in the event of a tie.

Article 57

The office of member of the Constitutional Council shall be incompatible with that of minister or Member of Parliament. Other incompatibilities shall be determined by an institutional Act.

Article 58

The Constitutional Council shall ensure the proper conduct of the election of the President of the Republic.

It shall examine complaints and shall declare the results of the vote.

Article 59

The Constitutional Council shall rule on the proper conduct of the election of deputies and senators in disputed cases.

Article 60

The Constitutional Council shall ensure the proper conduct of referendum proceedings and shall declare the results of the referendum.

Article 61

Institutional Acts, before their promulgation, and the rules of procedure of the parliamentary assemblies, before their entry into force, must be referred to the Constitutional Council, which shall rule on their conformity with the Constitution.

To the same end, Acts of Parliament may be referred to the Constitutional Council, before their promulgation, by the President of the Republic, the Prime Minister, the President of the National Assembly, the President of the Senate, or sixty deputies or sixty senators.

In the cases provided for in the two preceding paragraphs, the Constitutional Council must rule within one month. However, at the request of the Government, if the matter is urgent, this period shall be reduced to eight days.

In these same cases, reference to the Constitutional Council shall suspend the time limit for promulgation.

Article 62

A provision declared unconstitutional shall be neither promulgated nor implemented.

No appeal shall lie from the decisions of the Constitutional Council. They shall be binding on public authorities and on all administrative authorities and all courts.

Article 63

An institutional Act shall determine the rules of organization and operation of the Constitutional Council, the procedure to be followed before it and, in particular, the time limits allowed for referring disputes to it.

* * *

Preamble to the Constitution of 27 October 1946

On the morrow of the victory achieved by the free peoples over the regimes that had sought to enslave and degrade humanity, the people of

France proclaim anew that each human being, without distinction of race, religion or creed, possesses sacred and inalienable rights. They solemnly reaffirm the rights and freedoms of man and the citizen enshrined in the Declaration of Rights of 1789 and the fundamental principles acknowledged in the laws of the Republic.

They further proclaim, as being especially necessary to our times, the political, economic and social principles enumerated below:

The law guarantees women equal rights to those of men in all spheres.

Any man persecuted in virtue of his actions in favour of liberty may claim the right of asylum upon the territories of the Republic.

Each person has the duty to work and the right to employment. No person may suffer prejudice in his work or employment by virtue of his origins, opinions or beliefs.

All men may defend their rights and interests through union action and may belong to the union of their choice.

The right to strike shall be exercised within the framework of the laws governing it.

All workers shall, through the intermediary of their representatives, participate in the collective determination of their conditions of work and in the management of the work place.

All property and all enterprises that have or that may acquire the character of a public service or de facto monopoly shall become the property of society.

The Nation shall provide the individual and the family with the conditions necessary to their development.

It shall guarantee to all, notably to children, mothers and elderly workers, protection of their health, material security, rest and leisure. All people who, by virtue of their age, physical or mental condition, or economic situation, are incapable of working, shall have to the right to receive suitable means of existence from society.

The Nation proclaims the solidarity and equality of all French people in bearing the burden resulting from national calamities.

The Nation guarantees equal access for children and adults to instruction, vocational training and culture. The provision of free, public and secular education at all levels is a duty of the State.

The French Republic, faithful to its traditions, shall conform to the rules of international public law. It shall undertake no war aimed at conquest, nor shall it ever employ force against the freedom of any people.

Subject to reciprocity, France shall consent to the limitations upon its sovereignty necessary to the organization and preservation of peace.

France shall form with its overseas peoples a Union founded upon equal rights and duties, without distinction of race or religion.

The French Union shall be composed of nations and peoples who agree to pool or coordinate their resources and their efforts in order to develop their respective civilizations, increase their well-being, and ensure their security.

Faithful to its traditional mission, France desires to guide the peoples under its responsibility towards the freedom to administer themselves and to manage their own affairs democratically; eschewing all systems of colonization founded upon arbitrary rule, it guarantees to all equal access to public office and the individual or collective exercise of the rights and freedoms proclaimed or confirmed herein.

* * *

Declaration of the Rights of Man and of the Citizen (1789)

Preamble

The representatives of the French People, formed into a National Assembly, considering ignorance, forgetfulness or contempt of the rights of man to be the only causes of public misfortunes and the corruption of Governments, have resolved to set forth, in a solemn Declaration, the natural, unalienable and sacred rights of man, to the end that this Declaration, constantly present to all members of the body politic, may remind them unceasingly of their rights and their duties; to the end that the acts of the legislative power and those of the executive power, since they may be continually compared with the aim of every political institution, may thereby be the more respected; to the end that the demands of the citizens, founded henceforth on simple and incontestable principles, may always be directed toward the maintenance of the Constitution and the happiness of all.

In consequence whereof, the National Assembly recognizes and declares, in the presence and under the auspices of the Supreme Being, the following Rights of Man and of the Citizen.

Article first—Men are born and remain free and equal in rights. Social distinctions may be based only on considerations of the common good.

Article 2—The aim of every political association is the preservation of the natural and imprescriptible rights of man. These rights are Liberty, Property, Safety and Resistance to Oppression.

Article 3—The source of all sovereignty lies essentially in the Nation. No corporate body, no individual may exercise any authority that does not expressly emanate from it.

Article 4—Liberty consists in being able to do anything that does not harm others: thus, the exercise of the natural rights of every man has no bounds other than those that ensure to the other members of society the enjoyment of these same rights. These bounds may be determined only by Law.

Article 5—The Law has the right to forbid only those actions that are injurious to society. Nothing that is not forbidden by Law may be hindered, and no one may be compelled to do what the Law does not ordain.

Article 6—The Law is the expression of the general will. All citizens have the right to take part, personally or through their representatives, in its making. It must be the same for all, whether it protects or punishes. All citizens, being equal in its eyes, shall be equally eligible to all high offices, public positions and employments, according to their ability, and without other distinction than that of their virtues and talents.

Article 7—No man may be accused, arrested or detained except in the cases determined by the Law, and following the procedure that it has prescribed. Those who solicit, expedite, carry out, or cause to be carried out arbitrary orders must be punished; but any citizen summoned or apprehended by virtue of the Law, must give instant obedience; resistance makes him guilty.

Article 8—The Law must prescribe only the punishments that are strictly and evidently necessary; and no one may be punished except by virtue of a Law drawn up and promulgated before the offense is committed, and legally applied.

Article 9—As every man is presumed innocent until he has been declared guilty, if it should be considered necessary to arrest him, any undue harshness that is not required to secure his person must be severely curbed by Law.

Article 10—No one may be disturbed on account of his opinions, even religious ones, as long as the manifestation of such opinions does not interfere with the established Law and Order.

Article 11—The free communication of ideas and of opinions is one of the most precious rights of man. Any citizen may therefore speak, write and publish freely, except what is tantamount to the abuse of this liberty in the cases determined by Law.

Article 12—To guarantee the Rights of Man and of the Citizen a public force is necessary; this force is therefore established for the benefit of all, and not for the particular use of those to whom it is entrusted.

Article 13—For the maintenance of the public force, and for administrative expenses, a general tax is indispensable; it must be equally distributed among all citizens, in proportion to their ability to pay.

Article 14—All citizens have the right to ascertain, by themselves, or through their representatives, the need for a public tax, to consent to it freely, to watch over its use, and to determine its proportion, basis, collection and duration.

Article 15—Society has the right to ask a public official for an accounting of his administration.

Article 16—Any society in which no provision is made for guaranteeing rights or for the separation of powers, has no Constitution.

Article 17—Since the right to Property is inviolable and sacred, no one may be deprived thereof, unless public necessity, legally ascertained, obviously requires it, and just and prior indemnity has been paid.

---

3. ISRAEL, AND THE BERGMAN AND ELON MOREH DECISIONS

Martin Edelman, *The Changing Role of the Israeli Supreme Court,* in Comparative Judicial Systems: Challenging Frontiers in Conceptual and Empirical Analysis (John R. Schmidhauser, ed. 1987)

In the course of the 35 years of Israel's statehood, its Supreme Court has come to play an increasingly important political role. In 1948 it functioned very much like the House of Lords in the British system; its impact on the political process was on the margins rather than at the center. Now however the Israeli Supreme Court is beginning to exercise power akin to that of its American counterpart.

In its 1982–83 Term, the Court dealt with such issues as the religious-secular dispute involving the archeological dig at the City of David; the Government's limited suspension of publication of an East Jerusalem (Arab) newspaper; the continued validity of the 1948 eviction of the Arab residents of lkrit; and the right of Reform rabbis to perform marriages in Israel. When the Supreme Court decided these and similar issues it was obviously directly affecting public policy. Yet unlike its American counterpart, the Israeli Supreme Court is functioning as an important policymaker in the absence of a written constitution. How the Supreme Court came to play this role tells us much about the nature of Israeli society as well as judicial statecraft.

I ...

1. THE PRESENT ISRAELI "CONSTITUTION"

To this day, Israel functions without a formal written constitution. The Israeli leadership began with the belief that every modern state ought to have a written constitution. In addition they were seeking to comply with the terms of the UN Resolution which had called for the establishment of a Jewish state in Palestine.[1] Following Independence, the Provisional Government of Israel (14 May 1948–10 March 1949) called for an election of a Constituent Assembly to adopt a written constitution.

---

1. The Resolution on the Future Government of Palestine (The Partition Resolution) called for a constituent assembly in both the proposed Jewish and Arab states in order to draft written constitutions embodying protection for basic human rights. (U.N. General Assembly, Resolution 181, November 29, 1947; Part I, B. 10.)

The attempt to adopt a written constitution foundered on the division between religious and secular parties about the role of Jewish religious law in the new State. That issue could not be resolved without doing irreparable harm to the much-needed consensus of all elements in the community. Moreover, many Israeli leaders—most notably Prime Minister David Ben Gurion—saw political advantages in a constitutionally unrestricted supreme parliament. The move for a formal written constitution was tabled.

Because the Constituent Assembly was more representative than the Provisional Government, it was decided that the newly elected body would function as the supreme governing agency. Therefore the Constituent Assembly assumed the functions of a parliament; it became the First Knesset (Transition Act, 1949). Israel's constitutional arrangements are in large measure a product of the decisions of the Provisional Government and the 1949 Transition Law. Because of the stability of those institutional arrangements, it is possible to describe the country's "operative" constitution: Israel is a secular republic, with a theoretically supreme parliament (the Knesset), a powerful cabinet (the Government), a largely ceremonial president and an independent civil judiciary.*

2.   THE ISRAELI POLITICAL CULTURE

The key political institutions of Israel, however, are not the formal governmental agencies but the political parties. Israel is a highly politicized society. The reasons for this go back to the Zionist Movement where most existing parties had their origins. They were voluntary associations formed to help bring the Jewish State into existence. Each Zionist group sought to influence the course of events not only by direct political action in Palestine and within the World Zionist Organization but also by establishing a network of institutions reflecting its own ideology. . . .

Most parties still provide their members with a variety of ancillary services—youth movements, health insurance, recreation and vacation facilities. And some party institutions—like the kibbutzim—are still all-enveloping. Furthermore, the creation of government agencies did not entirely displace the parties; many Israeli bureaucracies show excessive partisanship. Professor Benjamin Azkin's (1955:509) statement is still accurate: political parties in Israel "occupy a more prominent place and exercise a more pervasive influence than in any other state, with the exception of some one-party states."

Moreover until May, 1977, Israeli politics was dominated by the Labor Party and its predecessor, Mapai. For the first 29 years of statehood, and indeed throughout most of the Mandate period (1918-1948), the Jewish community in Palestine was led by socialists. While the Mapai–Labor leadership were more pragmatic than doctrinaire . . . they were ideologically disposed to a state-run society. By design, the "House of Labor" permeated all aspects of Israeli society, the current Likud-led Government

* [Editors' Note: The most recent Israeli election, in 1996, was the first to use direct election to choose the prime minister, Benjamin Netanyahu.]

is seeking to change this pattern into a more liberal, market-oriented society. For the present, however, Israel remains a society thoroughly permeated by freely competing political parties.

In this political culture, overt partisan considerations are an inseparable element in the workings of the Knesset and the Government. Party discipline is exceptionally strong; the Knesset Member is expected to carry out faithfully the party's program as defined by its leadership bureau. The centralized, hierarchical nature of Israeli political parties all but insures a majority for a Government proposal. Despite the multi-party system, and despite the failure of any party list ever to obtain a parliamentary majority, decisions reached by the Government are rarely overturned by the Knesset. As a result, Israelis expect that public policies emanating from these institutions will reflect the partisan concerns of the ruling coalition.

3.   THE ISRAELI CIVIL COURT SYSTEM

With a keen awareness of their highly politicized society, the Israelis have taken great pains to insulate the judiciary from the political environment. The Judges Law (5713–1953) states that "A judge in judicial matters, is subject to no authority other than that of the law." The primary institutions of the civil court system are the Magistrates' Courts, the District Courts, and the Supreme Court. In addition to the usual concern for the quality of the judges, both the composition of the Nominations Committee,[4] and the formal qualifications for judicial office bespeak an overriding desire to avoid any taint of partisanship. Once appointed, the judges, of the Supreme and inferior courts, hold their offices until attaining the mandatory retirement age of 70.[6] Thus there was a decision early in the institution-building years of the State to protect the judges on the civil courts from outside influence. It was plainly a deliberate choice in a policy where virtually everything else was allotted on the basis of party affiliation.

This same concern has meant that judicial behavior is circumscribed by a series of informal norms designed to insure political neutrality and to project that image. The most obvious is the most rigidly observed: civil judges do not engage in politics. Individuals who find that prohibition is too constraining invariably resign their judicial appointments. When in 1983 Prime Minister Begin convinced Supreme Court Justice Menachem Elon to stand as the Likud-backed candidate for President of Israel, the Justice publicly announced his decision not to participate in court cases during the brief period preceding the presidential election. Justice Elon lost the election, and resumed his normal judicial duties, but even this did not

---

4. The Nominations Committee is chaired by the Minister of Justice, contains one other Minister selected by the Government, the President of the Supreme Court and two other Justices elected by the members of that Court, two Members of the Knesset selected by secret ballot (to mitigate the effects of party. discipline), and two practising advocates elected by the Chamber of Ad-vocates. The Nominations Committee decisions are by a majority vote and its selections are binding on the President of Israel who makes the actual appointments. (Judges Law, 5713–1953: section 5.)

6. There is a Disciplinary Committee to insure proper behavior during this life tenure.

satisfy all Israelis: "According to every accepted public test, and according to the sentence which Justice Elon imposed on himself during the campaign period, someone who has been proposed for such a high office by overtly political bodies should not serve on the Supreme Court." *(Ha 'aretz: 15 March 1983)*. As a result of deliberate political decisions and continuous judicial behavior patterns, the Israelis have succeeded in keeping their civil judiciary fully independent.

4. PUBLIC SUPPORT FOR THE CIVIL COURTS

The support for the civil courts in Israel, and hence their power and authority, is rooted in the public's respect for the "rule of law." From this perspective, law is seen as something quite distinct from politics. In politics, values and principles are perceived as instrumental tools for achieving certain results. Law is perceived as flowing from an impartial, objective analysis of principles. Law and politics are seen as distinct methods of conflict resolution. Functioning, observable judicial independence has meant that respect for the civil courts has become deeply implanted in the Israeli political culture. Although no survey data is available, all the indirect evidence supports this conclusion. Judges are frequently selected to perform tasks which are required to be non-partisan in both appearance and reality. They serve as presiding officers on a variety of special committees and tribunals such as the National Insurance Tribunal and Rent Tribunal. By law, a Justice of the Supreme Court, chosen by members of that Court, chairs the Elections Committee which supervises the fairness of Israeli elections.

Perhaps the best indication of the public's perception of the Supreme Court is the structure of the Israeli Commissions of Inquiry. They are created to investigate matters of current and vital public importance which require clarification. The most famous Inquiries were the Agranat (1974) and Kahan (1983) Commissions (named for the Presidents of the Supreme Court who chaired them). The Agranat Commission investigated the Government's actions before and during the 1973 Yom Kippur War. Largely as a result of its finding, Prime Minister Golda Meir and Defense Minister Moshe Dayan felt compelled to resign. The Kahan Commission investigated the Phalangist massacre of Palestinian civilians at the Shattila and Sabra refugee camps in Beirut. As a result of its finding that he did not exercise proper care (that he bore indirect responsibility), Defense Minister Ariel Sharon was forced to resign from that position.

The President of the Supreme Court appoints all the members of a Commission Inquiry and a sitting Supreme Court Justice must chair the Committee. Peter Elman (1971:405) explained why these politically important bodies are dominated by the non-partisan judiciary:

> In view of the nature of a Commission of Inquiry, its tasks and functions, which call for public confidence, as far as humanly possible, *in its neutrality and freedom from party pressures and considerations*, it is very, necessary, that its members should be of the highest integrity and reputation and therefore proper that the power of nomi-

nation should reside in *the traditional repository of independent, objective and impartial decision.* [Italics added]

Precisely because of the rampant partisanship of their society, Israelis see the utility of independent, objective and impartial decision-making. Because the civil judiciary are seen as the institutional repository of non-partisan judgment, authority has flowed to their courts. That authority gives the Israeli civil judiciary, particularly the Supreme Court, considerable political power.

5. THE JURISDICTION OF THE ISRAELI SUPREME COURT

The Israeli Supreme Court has both appellate and original jurisdiction. As an appellate court, its jurisdiction includes civil, criminal, administrative, fiscal matters. The Supreme Court hears appeals from the District Court and such other institutions as the labor courts, workers' compensation boards and rent tribunals. As a court of first instance, the Supreme Court sits as the High Court of Justice. In this capacity it deals with matters in which it may be necessary to grant relief in "the interest of justice" and which are not within the jurisdiction of any other court or tribunal. In both its appellate and general equity capacities, the Supreme Court can consider matters within the jurisdiction of the various religious court systems only with regard to the jurisdiction of those court systems to resolve a particular matter.[9] In all its functions, the Supreme Court is the final, authoritative interpreter of the law of the State of Israel. (Courts Law, 5717–1957; Judges Law, 5713–1953).

6. ACCESS TO THE SUPREME COURT

The Israeli citizen has direct easy access to the civil court system. In 1979, a total of 671,313 matters were entered in these courts. Of these, 4368 were entered in the Supreme Court. In the 23–year period from 1956 to 1979, number of matters entered on the Supreme Court's docket increased by a staggering 533% while the population of Israel increased by 209%. [Table omitted]

The growth in the Court's workload has accounted for the growth in the size of the Court itself. Cases are still usually heard by a panel of three Justices; only the more important issues are heard by a larger, uneven number of Justices (Courts Law, 5717–1957). But the larger case load noted above has required a gradual increase in the number of Justices. In the 35 years of statehood, the Supreme Court has gradually increased from 6 to 12 members.

No point of access to the Supreme Court is more important than its function as the High Court of Justice. In the exercise of its broad equity jurisdiction, the High Court is now receiving more than four times as many petitions as it did 23 years ago. In the highly centralized governmental system of Israel, and one that is highly politicized, the potential for

---

9. The religious courts of the 12 religions recognized by the State deal with divorce, alimony and certain other matters of personal status.

arbitrary action by public officials is obvious. The High Court of Justice, by emphasizing the rights of citizens and other residents who have come into conflict with governmental agencies, has enhanced the judiciary's reputation for fairness and objectivity. That reputation has encouraged still more petitions to the High Court of Justice.

7.   THE TREND OF SUPREME COURT DECISIONS: THE COURT AS POLICY–MAKER

In all its activities, the Court has extended its authority as policy-maker. As Jeffrey M. Albert (1969) noted:

> Yet despite the non-existence of a written constitution or bill of rights ... the Supreme Court has begun to assert a significant constitutional function. In a number of important cases it has asserted the right to read legislation in the light of supra-statutory principles which are said to exist independently of the legislative authority.... Rights to hearing and cross-examination have been required in statutory proceedings that did not provide such safeguards, and administrative discretion to deny licenses, to determine election lists, to register companies, and to censor newspapers has been substantially whittled down. When statutory language is equally susceptible to either of two readings, resort to a superstatutory standard is simply a technique of deducing the legislature's intent which does not involve wide use of the Court's creative power. But where a court adds requirements to a statutory scheme, as the Israeli court has done in the hearing and cross-examination cases, or when it bends language away from its ordinary meaning to conform to some superstatutory norm, as it has done in the administrative discretion cases, it has taken upon itself a much more significant function.

While the Israeli Supreme Court could use these means to extend its authority, there were obvious limits so long as it could not invalidate governmental actions for being unconstitutional. In the guise of "interpreting" legislative intent, the Court was bound by subsequent Knesset clarification....

In Israel, the authority of the Court, and its care in imposing only the most basic, most widely accepted values of natural justice has precluded Knesset reversal.[11] The Knesset's non-interference with the Court's judgments has been based on the perception of the Justices as neutral. impartial guardians of "the law." And this tradition of legislative respect for the judiciary had the practical political effect of adding still further to the Court's prestige and authority. Yet the Justices and commentators were well aware of the fragile political and legal base of the Court's actions.

---

11. The Knesset has indeed reversed Supreme Court interpretations which were not based on fundamental principles of natural justice. particularly on matters of major political concern to the coalition. Note, for example. the Knesset debates and actions on Supreme Court decisions touching upon the question of "Who is a Jew" in the State of Israel. (Kraines, 1976).

II

Because of the rampant partisanship within the political system of Israel, the demand for a written constitution had not died with the 1949 Constituent Assembly decision to transform itself into the First Knesset. A written constitution, by its very nature, would regularize procedures and define governmental powers. It would help ensure that the Government of the day would not simply act as it pleased. Moreover, a written constitution would undoubtedly contain a bill of rights articulating those fundamental human concerns which were to be beyond governmental authority in most circumstances. The support for a written constitution therefore transcended party interests; it was rooted in a concern for democracy itself.

Thus try as he might, Prime Minister Ben Gurion had not been able to kill the idea that a democratic Israel needed a written constitution. Towards the end of 1949 Ben Gurion's cabinet voted to postpone indefinitely the drafting of a constitution. Yet the Knesset's Constitution Law and Justice Committee continued to consider the issue. They were unable to resolve the matter, but it was too important to die in committee. The issue was referred to the full plenum where it was debated at great length. Ultimately, a compromise resolution was passed. On 13 June 1950, the Knesset agreed that a constitution would be built up, chapter by chapter, upon the enactment of Basic Laws.

Six Basic Laws—The Knesset (1958); Israel Land Administration (1960); The President (1964); The Government (1968); The State Economy (1976); The Armed Forces (1976)—were later enacted.* But their relationship to other laws enacted by the theoretically supreme Knesset was unsettled. Israeli scholars frequently discussed the operative nature of Israel's "piecemeal constitution." In *Bergman v. Minister of Finance* (1969) the Supreme Court forced the issue of Israel's constitution back onto its overt political agenda.

Dr. Aharon Bergman brought an action before the Supreme Court, sitting as the High Court of Justice, to block the implementation of the (Campaign) Financing Law of 1969. Dr. Bergman's complaint was that the law unfairly discriminated against new political parties because it provided governmental funds only for those parties represented in the outgoing Knesset. Specifically, he argued that the Financing Law violated the equality required by section 4 of The Basic Law: The Knesset. Moreover, that section expressly provided that its provisions "shall not be varied save by a majority of the Members of the Knesset." In 1959, the Knesset had entrenched that provision still further.[15] If Because the Financing Law had

---

* [Editors' Note: By late 1997, the following additional Basic Laws had been enacted: Jerusalem, the Capital of Israel (1980); The Judiciary (1984); the State Comptroller (1988); Human Dignity and Liberty (1992); The Government (1992); Freedom of Occupation (1994).]

15. "The Majority required by this law for a change of sections 4, 44 or 45 shall be required for decisions of the Knesset plenary at *every stage* of law-making except on a motion for the Knesset agenda. In this section 'change' means both an express or an implied change." (Basic Law: The Knesset, section 46).

passed its first reading in the Knesset by a vote of 24 to 2 (a majority of the plenum would consist of not less than 61 votes), Dr. Bergman also argued that it plainly could not be viewed as an amendment to section 4 of the Basic Law: The Knesset.

In his opinion for all five Justices who participated in the case, Justice Landau agreed that the Financing Law was in conflict with the equality required by section 4 of the Basic Law: The Knesset. The absolute denial of funds to a new list constituted a major violation of equal opportunity in the democratic electoral process. Justice Landau acknowledged the absence of any provision in Israel's law which expressly authorized the Court to construe statutes in terms of the natural justice principle of the equality of all before the law. "Nevertheless, this principle that is nowhere inscribed breathes the breath of life into our whole constitutional system." It was therefore right and just, Justice Landau argued, for the High Court to use it in interpreting the law. On this basis the Supreme Court declared an Act of the Knesset void for violating a Basic Law. In a state without a formal written constitution, its highest court had declared an Act of the "sovereign" parliament unconstitutional.

The Court's opinion was a skillful amalgam of the conventional and the radical. It purported to be doing nothing more than using the principle of natural justice to interpret a "borderline case," "open to two interpretations." As noted above, this had become familiar Israeli judicial practice. Actually, without so much as a single comment, the Court had decided the case on novel grounds. It had applied its natural justice approach to a Basic Law and then used its interpretation to block the implementation of the subsequently enacted Financing Law.

Normally, Israeli courts adhere to the principle of *lex posterior derogatat priori*. If the Knesset was the sovereign legal authority in Israel, each Knesset had the same unlimited authority as its predecessors. The duly enacted Financing Law, precisely because it was posterior in time, should have prevailed over any conflicting interpretation of an earlier law. Plainly, the Supreme Court had acted on the unarticulated premise that section 4 of the Basic Law had constitutional status and as such was superior to ordinary law.

The Court's silence left important theoretical issues unaddressed. Why were Basic Laws—which had been enacted by the same procedure as all other statutes—to be regarded as fundamental? Was their special status derived from their designation as Basic Laws? Was it derived from their lineage—the early debates about a constitution and the chapter by chapter compromise? Perhaps these questions gave the *Bergman* decision a "constitutional" dimension it did not warrant. Perhaps the key to that opinion was simply the fact that an entrenched provision had not been observed. If so, what gave one Knesset the authority to entrench provisions and thereby limit the freedom of action of its theoretically equal successors? The Justices had not attempted to resolve these issues.

As it stood, the *Bergman* opinion meant that the political leadership could only surmise the premises on which the Supreme Court Justices had operated. Yet to deal with the consequences of the *Bergman* decision—to replace the Financing Law held invalid—the Israeli political elite had to enter into serious discussion about the nature of a constitution for their poli[t]y.

Events proved that the *Bergman* decision was indeed a landmark case. It provided the catalyst for Israel accepting the principle that it ought to be governed within the parameters set by a written constitution authoritatively interpreted by its highest court. That theoretical consensus has not led to concrete action: Israel still functions with its same "piecemeal" constitution. Yet the agreement on principle has further enhanced the authority and hence the power of the Supreme Court. A series of events in the political arena indicates the transformation.

Two days before the High Court had rendered its decision in the *Bergman* case, the Minister of Justice had indicated that the time was approaching when the Knesset should complete the Israeli constitutional structure through its chapter by chapter approach. He indicated that his ministry was drafting Basic Laws on the Judiciary, on Human Rights, and on Legislation. Significantly, the Minister indicated that the completed constitution would not be superior, paramount law. The Ministry was acting on the premise that the Knesset, like the British Parliament, was the sovereign legal authority in Israel.

The Knesset too was operating on that theory. True, they amended the Financing Law to comply with the *Bergman* decision. Ignoring the decision was not possible in Israel. And the major Israeli political parties were simply unwilling to enter the forthcoming election campaign without public funds. Nor were politicians willing to re-enact the original law by the requisite majority specified by section 4 of the Basic Law: The Knesset: that would have made the major parties vulnerable to the charge that they favored playing with a stacked deck. So within two weeks of the *Bergman* decision the Knesset found a formula for providing campaign funds for new election lists as well as the established parties. Thus the Knesset once again complied with a Supreme Court's ruling.

Yet at the same time that the law was amended to bring itself into compliance with *Bergman,* the Knesset pointedly enacted a law by a 68–8 majority reasserting its *own* legal authority: "For the purpose of removing doubt it is hereby laid down that the provisions contained in Knesset Election Laws are from the date of their coming into effect valid for every legal proceeding and for every matter and purpose." (Elections (Ratification of Validity of Laws) Law, 5729–1969).

But within six years most members of the Israeli political and legal elites had changed their minds. In December 1975, the Government finally introduced the draft Basic Law: Legislation. It frankly acknowledged that it was proposing a "fundamental change." The "important innovation" related to the status of Basic Laws. Under the proposal, all Basic Laws were to be treated as superior to other Knesset legislation. The Supreme Court sitting as a special Constitutional Court, was to be authorized to nullify laws which conflicted with Basic Laws (draft Basic Law: Legislation, 1975,

Introduction.). After six years of study and much comment from Israeli and foreign experts, the Government had reversed its position.

While there were a number of factors involved in the Government's change of position, none was more important than *Bergman* itself. That decision meant that the existence of a legally sovereign Knesset, unfettered by judicial review, was no longer an unquestioned truism. As Attorney General (now Justice) Shamgar (1974) noted, "That case pointed out that in the absence of some contrary, legislative provision, the Supreme Court and perhaps every court of the country is bound to decide the question of the legality or validity of laws." It had become doubtful whether the legal *status quo* really safeguarded the continued acceptance of the principle of parliamentary sovereignty. "The developments accentuated by the *Bergman* case," the Attorney General maintained, "cast doubt on parliamentary supremacy and accelerated the readiness for legislative intervention in order to create more exact definitions."

In point of fact, the Government's draft would have resolved most of the remaining questions concerning the Israeli constitution and the Supreme Court's authority to interpret it.

The question—much discussed in the scholarly literature—about whether the Knesset could legitimately enact constitutional provisions was answered with a clear affirmative. The proposed Basic Law: Legislation explicitly authorized the Knesset to enact Basic Laws (draft Basic Law: Legislation, 1975: Chapter I, section 1). The source of that authority, however, was not discussed either in the text of the draft or in the official explanatory notes. The logical paradox created by giving one parliament the power to control the actions of its theoretically equal successors remained. But less than theoretically ideal resolutions are frequent occurrences when constitutions are established.[18] Moreover, because Knesset enactment of Basic Laws had become the established Israeli practice, investing the parliament with continuing constituent power was certainly an acceptable resolution.[19]

The proposed Basic Law: Legislation also resolved the ambiguous status of the six existing Basic Laws. The *Bergman* decision had involved an entrenched provision of the Basic Law: The Knesset. Therefore some Israeli scholars had argued that *only* such entrenched provisions were to be

---

18. For example, the Constitution of the United States of America, the oldest current written constitution, was adopted by procedures which by-passed the provisions of the then existing Articles of Consideration. Hans Kelsen (1967: 194–221) maintained that the validity of the final norm in a national legal order cannot be derived from a still higher legal norm: it is invariably a political act whose validity depends upon its acceptance and effectiveness.

19. Investing the Knesset with continuing constitutional power, however, might en-

able a temporary, parliamentary majority to entrench its particular policy objectives in the Basic Law. To guard against that potential abuse of power and to enhance the authority of all future Basic Laws, the proposal provided that all such laws must henceforth be enacted, at all stages of Knesset decision-making, by a majority of the full plenum. Ordinary laws require only a majority of those present and voting (and abstentions are not counted). . . .

regarded as superior to ordinary statutes. Other scholars had argued that only fundamental provisions within the Basic Laws were to be given constitutional status. The proposed Basic Law: Legislation explicitly conferred constitutional status on all provisions of all six prior Basic Laws as well as future Basic Laws.

The Governmental draft recognized the great status of the Supreme Court and sought to utilize it in constitutional matters. Under the proposal, the basic mechanism for applying the higher law embodied in the Basic Laws was to be vested in the Supreme Court functioning as a Constitutional Court. The Constitutional Court was to consist of a panel of at least seven Justices selected by the President of the Supreme Court. Only the Constitutional Court was authorized to rule on the question of a law's constitutional validity. A legal provision declared unconstitutional was to be null and void. In short, under the proposal, the Israeli Supreme Court, sitting as the Constitutional Court, was to be explicitly authorized to exercise judicial review like its American counterpart.

It was precisely on that point that most of the objections to the Government's proposal were focused. After the Draft was introduced by the Minister of Justice, the first to attack it was another leading figure of the Labor Party, the Speaker of the Knesset. In a letter to all Members of the Knesset, he criticized the proposal as an unwise denigration of parliament's legal sovereignty. The Speaker maintained that if the Draft were adopted, a group of non-elected judges would function as the Supreme Legislator instead of the 120 Members elected by—and politically responsible to—the people. According to the Speaker, the proposal would eliminate the distinction between law and politics and would lead to the eventual politicization of the Supreme Court itself. And in a special symposium arranged by the Speaker and held in the Knesset building, Supreme Court Justice Haim Cohn also asserted that the proposal would assign an essentially political non-judicial function upon the Court.

Despite such opposition, the bill proceeded through the legislative process with strong support. Even the change in Government in May 1977 from a Labor-led coalition to a Likud-led Cabinet did not affect this support. Thus by May, 1978 even Justice Cohn perceived further opposition to be futile; he expected that the draft Basic Law: Legislation would soon be promulgated.

That expectation has not materialized. The reasons do *not* concern the substance of the proposed Basic Law: Legislation. The support which developed during the last fifteen years remains. Rather, concern is now focused on the substantive provisions of the draft Basic Law on Human and Civil Rights. Sections of that proposal have become controversial in the extreme. The Israelis cannot envision a written constitution without a bill of rights. In fact, much of the impetus behind the drive for a written constitution is linked to the demand for a formal bill of rights. The Israelis are unwilling to adopt a written constitution (as envisioned by the proposed Basic Law: Legislation) until they are assured that a bill of rights would shortly be added to the existing Basic Laws.

Thirty-five years of statehood, therefore, have not removed all the obstacles to a written constitution. In light of *Bergman* and the consensus surrounding the draft Basic Law: Legislation, however, the ability of the Supreme Court to continue as an important policy-maker is assured. Nor have the justices been hesitant in exercising their power. The Justices are deciding matters which the first generation of Israeli leaders believed to be within the exclusive purview of the elected branches of government.

The Supreme Court's impact on national policy is well illustrated by the way it intervened in the ongoing debate about settlement policies in Judea and Samaria (the West Bank). Acting in its capacity as the High Court of Justice, it ordered the Government to dismantle Elon Moreh within 30 days. That settlement had been established on land seized from 17 Arabs. The Government of Prime Minister Begin had given specific approval to the project. The Israeli Defense Forces had seized the land. The Chief of Staff had testified that the settlement would enhance Israel's military position in the Administered Territories. Moreover, the project was also in accord with the West Bank settlement policies of the Cabinet majority. Nonetheless the Justices who heard the case had looked behind the national security argument and found it wanting *(Elon Moreh* case, 1979). The Court's decision was obeyed by the Government.

Thus the prescient comment that Tocqueville made a century and a half ago is now equally applicable to Israel: scarcely any political controversy arises that does not find its way, in some form, into the courts. The ensuing decisions in Israel, as in the United States, have important consequences.

III

In sum, in the highly politicized democracy that is Israel, authority has flowed towards its premier non-partisan institution—the Supreme Court built upon the tradition of respect for the "rule of law." The Justices began by insisting upon their role as interpreters—not creators—of law. Gradually the Justices began to use principles of natural justice to help them interpret the meaning of the Legislator. By carefully using that indirect form of judicial review only when abiding, consensual values were present, the Justices were not accused of abusing their discretion. They were not seen as using their positions to advance a special cause; they were perceived as the protectors of fundamental values. When at last, in *Bergman*, the Justices openly exercised judicial review, it became the occasion to confirm, rather than deny, their place in the political system. The boldness of the Justices' recent actions indicates that they well understand their stronger position.

Gary Jeffrey Jacobsohn, APPLE OF GOLD: CONSTITUTIONALISM IN ISRAEL AND THE UNITED STATES (1993) (pp. 110–35)

LOOKING ANEW AT JUDICIAL REVIEW

Conflict, Consensus, and the Role of the Court

In his most influential (and certainly most controversial) work, *The Liberal Tradition in America,* Louis Hartz introduced the concept of

"Hebraism" in order to convey a sense of American exceptionalism, of Americans as a "chosen people." His characterization followed the Tocquevillian insight that Americans possessed the distinct advantage of having "arrived at a state of democracy without having to endure a democratic revolution." This fortunate circumstance of having been "born equal, instead of becoming so" meant that their social and political development could proceed largely in the absence of the bitterly divisive ideological battles that prevailed in most other places. It also meant, according to Hartz, that the crusading spirit of Americans would likely be tempered by an appreciation of the uniqueness of their own society. While the principles that formed the basis of American "moral unanimity" were thought to be universally valid, their universal application was quite another thing. Thus Americans were a "chosen people" by virtue of having been blessed with ideal conditions for enjoying the blessings of liberty. Hartz quoted Gouveneur Morris as having given voice to this Hebraic sentiment when, as ambassador to France in 1789, he counseled the French against following the American example, declaiming in a snobbish sort of way, "They want an American constitution without realizing they have no Americans to uphold it."

Hartz exaggerated the modesty of American missionary pretensions, and Morris's comment would require major qualification in order accurately to capture the spirit of American involvement in subsequent efforts in constitution making abroad. More fundamentally, Hartz's thesis has long been subjected (mainly in the context of the mounting of a "republican" challenge to the presumed hegemony of his liberal paradigm) to torrents of criticism, focusing on what is seen as the Hartzian failure to take sufficient note of conflict, and the corollary inflation of the importance of John Locke ("He is a massive national cliche") to American political development. . . . [W]hile a good bit of the criticism is on target, Hartz's argument is, as one of his more sympathetic critics has written, "animated by a basic instinct that is historically far sounder than that of most books written under the influence of more recent fashions." Focusing on the centrality of the liberal theory of rights, even as one recognizes that it is at once more aspirational and more complex than Hartz might have had us believe, illuminates important aspects of constitutional development in the United States, including that "most puzzling of American cultural phenomena," judicial review.

As Hartz wisely pointed out, "Judicial review as it has worked in America would be inconceivable without the national acceptance of the Lockian creed, ultimately enshrined in the Constitution, since the removal of high policy to the realm of adjudication implies a prior recognition of the principles to be legally interpreted." The exalted position of the Supreme Court is not simply attributable to the fact that it happens to be the nation's highest court: rather, it rests significantly on the acceptance of its unique role in enforcing, and hence validating, the nation-defining principles of the regime. The power to restrain the majority through the exercise of judicial review presupposes the existence of a moral consensus that is embodied in a constitution, and that may be safely entrusted to an institution possessing "neither Force nor Will." ...

The argument that American experience with judicial review is in a profound way tied to the presence in the United States of a pervasive and dominant political creed (in Bickel's formulation. "enduring values") has obvious and important comparative implications... If Hartz and Bickel were correct, then a critical factor in any comparative assessment of the institution will be the extent to which a consensus may, be said to exist with respect to a society's defining political principles.

[Jacobsohn has earlier argued that Israel, unlike the U.S., lacks consensus on basic moral principles due to unresolved tension between the ideals of a democratic, and a Jewish, state.]

The contrast between the United States and Israel on this matter has been developed: it remains now to explore some of its ramifications for ... judicial review ... [consider] an argument that builds on a different assumption than the one suggested here, namely that there is "a common historical basis for the development of judicial review" in the United States and Israel. The argument is advanced in a provocative analysis by Robert A. Burt, who maintains that the emergence of judicial review in both countries is best understood as an institutional response to the presence of fundamental societal conflict. The "central truth" is that "deep-riven ideological disputes in a democratic society, provide the impetus for the development of the institution of judicial review." And so, according to Burt, the American and Israeli Supreme Courts have endeavored to transcend such divisions by invoking their nation's respective founding creeds in the context of bold and innovative assertions of judicial power.

... While most commentators cite the case of *Bergman v. Minister of Finance** (frequently in conjunction with *"Kol Ha'am" v. Minister of Interior*),** decided in 1969, as the critical legal event in the evolution of

---

* [Editors' Note: For an English translation of Bergman, see 8 Selected Judgments of the Supreme Court of Israel 13 (1992).]

** [Editors' Note: In Kol Ha'am the Israel Supreme Court held invalid the Interior Minister's suspension of a newspaper that had criticized a supposed government decision to send troops to Korea. The allegation that a decision had been made proved false. Analogizing to U.S. law, the Court held that a mere "tendency" to endanger the public peace was not sufficient to warrant the Minister in finding a likely endangerment of the public peace; unless the publication posed a "near certainty" or real probability of endangering the public peace, the suspension was unwarranted. See Kol Ha'am Co. Ltd. v. Minister of Justice, (1953), 7 P.D. 871, reproduced in English translation in Selected Judgments of the Supreme Court of Israel, 1948–53 at 90 (1962); Stephen Goldsmith, Protection of Human Rights by Judges: The Israeli Experience, 38 St. Louis U.L. J. 605, 611–12 (1994). *Kol Ha'am* has been applied in more recent cases. See Schnitzer v. Chief Military Censor, (1988), 42 P.D. (4) 617, reproduced in 9 Selected Judgments of the Supreme Court of Israel, 1977–90 at 77, 9394, 109–16 (1995) (issuing order preventing Censor from interfering with publication of an article critical of the outgoing head of the Mossad and indicating that a change in leadership of the Mossad was occurring, where the Censor's bases for acting did not meet the test of there being a "near certainty" of real danger to the security of the state).]

judicial review in Israel, Burt assigns greater significance to the landmark *Elon Moreh* case of 1979, in which the Supreme Court, following its initial steps of four years earlier, arguably embraced a role for itself as principal guardian of the constitutional system. It was a role thrust upon the Court by the 1967 Six–Day War, an event that had a transformative effect on Israeli society, including the impetus generated for the realization of an independent judiciary. "The political aftermath of the 1967 War raised profound and disquieting questions about the viability of democratic theory in Israeli society. The role that the Court has claimed for itself with progressively increasing clarity since 1979, as the independent embodiment of the rule of law, is in effect its answer to these questions." Similarly according to Burt, the partisan conflict that culminated in Jefferson's election in 1800 created the opportunity for John Marshall to establish and institutionalize the meliorative role of the judiciary. "The 1967 Six Day War and resulting military occupation had the same underlying implication for Israeli society that the partisan struggle and resulting Republican electoral victory had in 1800 for American society: Both events raised serious doubts about whether the divisions were so sharp among a populace ostensibly subject to a common government that brute force was the only possible source of unified governmental authority."

In the *Elon Moreh* decision, the Israeli Supreme Court did indeed venture into the thicket of intense ideological disputation. The case involved the seizure of Arab-owned land by the military commander of the occupied territories, followed shortly by civilian settlement by members of Gush Emunim, the religious nationalist group that views the West Bank (Judea and Samaria) as divinely promised land for the Jewish people. The seizure occurred under the justification of military necessity, but the Court, in its decision to order the eviction of the Jewish settlers, apprehended a political motive behind the initiative, one connected to a particular Zionist commitment to the settlement of Eretz–Israel in its entirety. Burt correctly highlights the boldness of a decision that directly challenged an important policy of a sitting government, although the extent of the challenge may be less than he suggests, and its comparability to two American cases— *Marbury v. Madison* and *Dred Scott v. Sandford*—may be questioned.

That the underlying issue in *Eton Moreh* bears directly on the democratic aspirations set out in the Declaration of Independence is indisputable. Thus a policy that implied eventual incorporation of a million or more Arabs into an enlarged Israeli state raises serious doubts about the long-term compatibility of the dual commitments of that country's founding document. What was always a tension would inevitably become an unabridgeable divide. To the extent, then, that the development of judicial review is seen as a response to this situation, a conflict-based theory of the origins of the practice appears eminently reasonable. Moreover, as a benchmark for comparative judgment, the very stark nature of the conflict involved in this political setting can serve to mitigate any tendency in other places to see political difference as evidence of deeply rooted conflict. Thomas Jefferson's famous pronouncement in his First Inaugural Address—"We are all Republicans, we are all Federalists"—is too easily dismissed as simply a rhetorical ploy to establish a foundation for governance in a bitterly divided young republic. ... [T]he differences between Jeffersonians and Hamiltonians, Federalists and Anti–Federalists, are ultimately reconcilable within a broader consensus of agreement on political fundamentals. However, as one reflects on the Israeli scene, it is just this sort of agreement that is absent in the political context surrounding a case like *Elon Moreh.*

It is therefore not just the seemingly trivial facts *of Marbury* that contrast so sharply with the portentous matters involved in the Israeli case; it is also the contrasting nature of the respective underlying political struggles. The election of 1800 was one of only a few critical elections in American history, but like other political realignments (with the exception perhaps of Lincoln's election), it did not, in the end, represent a triumph of principle. It was, to be sure, an exceptionally nasty partisan affair that, as Burt suggests, may very well have caused some to wonder about the viability of the Union.* Jefferson's victory, however, did not signal the repudiation of, or ascendance of any vital principle that was contestable at the time. Indeed, more revealing than the names each side called the other, was the fact that, as Richard Hofstadter noted, "each ... saw the other as having a political aspiration or commitment that lay outside the republican covenant of the Constitution."[56] Each, in other words, sought to delegitimize the other by appealing to a common base of principle. Subsequent history is also revealing: if the Jeffersonian–Hamiltonian contest conjures up great conflict over principle (for example, regarding the federal government's role in the development of the country), it is worth remembering *whose* purchase Louisiana was.

As far as *Marbury v. Madison* is concerned, and in particular Marshall's skillful navigation of highly charged political waters, Louis Hartz's point is well taken: "We say of the Supreme Court that it is courageous when it challenges Jefferson, but since in a liberal society the individualism of Hamilton is also a secret part of the Jeffersonian psyche, we make too much of this. The real test of the Court is when it faces the excitement

---

* [Editors' Note: Jacobsohn is referring to Robert A. Burt, *Inventing Judicial Review: Israel and America,* 10 Cardozo Law Rev. 2013 (1989)]

56. Richard Hofstadter, *The Idea of a Party System: The Rise of Legitimate Opposition in the United States, 1780–1840* (Berkeley: University of California Press. 1969), p. 90. More revealing, perhaps, than the parallel between *Marbury* and *Elon Moreh* is another one that might be made between the American case and an early Israeli case, *Jabotinsky v. Weizmann,* 5 P.D. 801 (1951), surely the most famous writ of mandamus case in Israeli constitutional history. Like *Marbury* it occurred in the setting of a political crisis, in this instance one engendered by the collapse of the first National Unity government. The justices rejected a petition that sought to have the Court order the president to extend an invitation to another member of the Knesset to form a government, after his first request of Ben–Gurion had failed to achieve that result. In both cases the Courts concluded that they lacked the authority to issue a writ of mandamus, and in both cases the decisions hinged on distinctions made between law and politics. But in Israel no ground was broken on the subject of judicial review. In my opinion. the politics of these cases presents more of a parallel than that which exists between *Marbury* and *Elon Moreh.*

both of Jefferson and Hamilton, when the Talmudic text itself is at stake, when the general will on which it feeds rises to the surface in anger." John Marshall did, as Burt emphasizes, use *Marbury* as an opportunity to affirm the primacy of the rule of law, but the immediate threat to that rule—the failure of a federal official to deliver some judicial commissions—was occasioned by partisan rather than principled considerations.[58] Very different from this was the threat to the rule of law presented in *Elon Moreh,* where individuals were deprived of their property rights on the basis of *who* they were rather than on the basis of *what* their partisan attachments were.

In this sense, then, a more fruitful comparison might be made between *Elon Moreh* and *Dred Scott.* In the latter decision it surely is the case that matters of high principle were at stake in a context where the denial of rights was directly related to circumstances of ascriptive status. It was also the first case since *Marbury* where the Court had exercised its power of judicial review to invalidate an act of Congress. And inasmuch as there is some evidence to suggest that the justices in the majority thought they were making a substantial contribution toward the resolution of the great conflict that was dividing the nation, support may be found for the Burt thesis about the origins and development of judicial review. All of this of course does not escape Burt's attention; in fact he refers to *Elon Moreh* as "Israel's *Dred Scott.*" "The same considerations evident in the background of the Israeli Supreme Court's actions around 1967 dominated the deliberations of the United States Supreme Court in 1857 when it decided *Dred Scott.*"

But there is also a great difference in these two cases, one that speaks directly to the contrasting constitutional environments within which judicial review must operate. It is inadvertently signaled by Burt, who says of *Dred Scott* that "the devisive [sic] underlying dispute in that case was between a conception of religiously based moral law that condemned slavery and the secular law of the Constitution that protected private property rights in slaves and thereby apparently ensured the continued political union of discordant peoples." This suggests a parallel to *Elon Moreh,* where property rights of Arabs were in conflict with the biblical

---

58. An Israeli political scientist, Allen Shapiro, also finds the political upheaval surrounding *Marbury* to have been decisive in the development of judicial review. But interestingly, he sees the parallel to the Israeli situation differently: for him the Court did not assume a role of Olympian detachment, but rather it became a player in the partisan battles. Thus it "became a bastion of power of forces that had lost hold of the political centres and a spokesman for a vision of the new republic that had been defeated at the polls." "This," he goes on, "may be the true parallel to Israel's present stage of constitutional development." *Jerusalem Post,* Decem- ber 2, 1988. In the United States, Leonard W. Levy has expressed the familiar view on this question: "The realities of political partisanship had as much to do with the growth of national judicial review as did abstract theories of constitutionalism." Leonard W. Levy, *Original Intent and the Framers' Constitution* (New York: Macmillan Publishing Co., 1988), p. 121. My argument is that Shapiro may be correct—that the Court is in the process of taking sides—but that its alignment should be viewed not so much as a partisan affair as a choice to emphasize one of the principled visions in the Declaration of Independence. . . .

claims of Jewish settlers, and where, as in the American case, the Supreme Court intervened on the side of the secular law. The difficulty with this comparison, however, is that it was not *only* a religiously based moral law that condemned slavery but also the secular law of the Constitution as interpreted in a particular way, namely as a document incorporating the natural rights commitments of the Declaration of Independence. To be sure, the radical abolitionists rejected the Constitution, a charter seen by them as a covenant with Hell, in favor of biblical scripture. But Lincoln's consistent view, what we might call the abolitionist position with the best chance of success, was that the Constitution (the "picture of silver") was itself committed to the ultimate extinction of slavery.

It was for this reason that Lincoln opposed the *Dred Scott* ruling, arguing that the decision did not create any politically binding obligations for the coordinate branches of the federal government. His position was distorted at the time by his political enemies, notably Stephen Douglas, and it has been much misunderstood in subsequent years; but in essence it amounts to this: that those sworn to uphold the Constitution have an obligation to advance the cause of constitutional principle, to the end of realizing the ideals of the Declaration of Independence. The Court's invalidation of the Missouri Compromise, accompanied by an opinion by Chief Justice Taney that Lincoln rightly saw as a repudiation of the substance of the Declaration, meant that a critical feature of the Constitution, its aspirational component, was being abandoned. "[The signers of the Declaration] meant simply to declare the *right,* so that the *enforcement* of it might follow as fast as circumstances should permit." Judicial review had to be consistent with the overriding obligation of all citizens—but especially governmental officials—to promote the progressive realization of those principles that gave definition to the nation.

Lincoln knew the Bible well, but his was a distinctly secular interpretation of the moral law incorporated into the Constitution. Taney had claimed that his opinion was in conformity with the Declaration, but in limiting its coverage only to white men, he effectively denuded it of its natural rights content. What so alarmed Lincoln in this was the real prospect that a general acceptance of the reasoning in Taney's opinion would *reconstitute* the nation in accordance with an alternative, and much inferior, set of principles. If this prospect was obscured by Taney's deceptive legal claims, it was evident in the more straightforward repudiations of the Declaration found in the writings of other apologists for slavery. It is, for example, apparent in John C. Calhoun's *A Disquisition on Government,* where he speaks of the "dangerous error" of supposing "that all men are born free and equal," of which "nothing can be more unfounded and false." The reason for this error, according to Calhoun, was the acceptance of "the assertion that all men are equal in the state of nature," a state that is totally "inconsistent with the preservation and perpetuation of the race." For a polity whose identity was bound up so closely in a particular set of ideas, Taney's opinion in *Dred Scott* was therefore a thoroughly subversive act, the toleration of which would further the preservation of the nation in name only.

Lincoln sought to counter this subversion by denying *Dred Scott* the finality that only a "fully settled" decision, that is, one consistent with constitutional aspiration, deserves. In so doing, he exemplified Bickel's understanding of the Court as the institutional voice of enduring values, but more important, he reminded us of the origins of judicial review in the United States, origins that played a part—albeit a symbolic one—in the birth of the nation. In his famous argument in the *Writs of Assistance Case,* James Otis exclaimed, "As to Acts of Parliament, an Act against the Constitution is void, an Act against natural Equity is void: and if an Act of Parliament should be made, in the very Words of this Petition, it would be void. The Executive Courts must pass such Acts into disuse." John Adams, who had been in the audience, noted many years later, "Then and there the child Independence was born." Or to put it differently: that an act of constitutional violation should be associated with the birth of a new nation (dedicated to a certain proposition) has both symbolic and real significance as far as the institution of judicial review is concerned, namely that its legitimacy, in the end, inheres in its furtherance of those ideas that nourish the American conception of nationhood. Thus it is clear from an important recent examination of the early American experience with judicial review that the *pre-Marbury* history is rich in establishing a vital connection between judicial review and the defense of first principles of natural justice.[69] To focus on *Marbury v. Madison* and the political conflict that brought it about is potentially to lose sight of the history that precedes it, a history in which judicial review emerges as an institutional expression of fundamental political agreement.

Fundamental agreement rarely, if ever, connotes universal assent; thus a critic of Lincoln might very well make a case that Lincoln simply got it wrong, that the founding documents mean something very different from what he said about them. So someone might say that it is inconceivable on the basis of what we know of human nature that "all men are created equal" in the sense intended by Lincoln. Or someone else might say that on the basis of our history—most importantly the fact that slavery was legal at the time the Declaration and the Constitution were written—it could not have been their authors' understanding of the self-evident fact of human equality that it applied to members of the black race. Both of these arguments are serious ones, even if, as I think is the case, Lincoln convincingly disposed of them by revealing their ultimately subversive purpose. But what is noteworthy is that, with respect to the Declaration of Independence, these contrary understandings are not the result of an appeal to different sections of a document in tension with itself. And herein lies a critical, perhaps *the* critical, difference with the Israeli constitutional scene, in which the source of interpretive disagreement over first principles is itself foundational.

69. Sylvia Snowiss, *Judicial Review*   Yale University, Press, 1990)....
and the Law of the Constitution (New Haven:

Let us, then, return to *Elon Moreh,* but before doing so directly, consider what the author of the Court's opinion, Justice Landau, has written elsewhere (and later) on the subject of judicial review: "I am worried about our adults, whether they know what the Declaration of Independence is about, both in embodying human rights and also in its opening passages; in affirming that the State of Israel is the state of the Jewish people, established by our founding fathers who were Zionists. How to bridge this tension between these two parts of the declaration is, of course, a question which has been with us for a long time and will continue to be with us for a long time to come, but this is a matter of living with the facts of life and is inescapable." As an outspoken proponent of judicial restraint, Landau's concern here is that the Supreme Court's considerable prestige will be jeopardized if the final settlement of political issues left unresolved by this tension becomes lodged in the Court. In *Shalit,** this concern prompted an important question: "What can the court contribute to the solution of an ideological dispute such as this which divides the public? The answer is—nothing, and whoever expects judges to produce a magic formula is merely deluding himself in his naivete." But in an opinion by Justice Landau in *Elon Moreh,* the Court *did,* according to Burt, contribute to the solution of perhaps the most divisive ideological dispute in Israel; moreover, it did so in part on the strength "of the existence of a creedal basis for national unity formulated at a specific founding moment."

What particularly impressed Burt was a passage in the Landau opinion in which the justice seemed to go out of his way to dispute the claims underlying the settlement policy implicated in the case at hand. He did so by appealing to "the authentic voice of Zionism which insists on the Jewish people's right of return to its land ... but which has never sought to deprive the residents of the country, members of other peoples, of their civil rights." This meant that Zionist principles were consistent with the international standards set out in the Hague Convention, standards that left the Court no choice (unlike the situation in *Shalit)* but to intervene on behalf of the rule of law. For Burt what is important is that this landmark case in the development of judicial review should be accompanied by a judicial pronouncement on Zionist principles, and that the Court should emerge as an agent of moral unity in the face of deep fissures in the body politic.

Landau was gently rebuked by one of his colleagues on the Court for unnecessarily entering into "political or ideological debate." But it is difficult to see how this entry—to the extent that it may be deemed political or ideological—rests on a creedal basis that can rightfully be construed as a source of fundamental political unity for the polity. The justice was doing what judges do best—asserting the primacy of the rule of

* [Editors' Note: *Shalit* (1970) was a 5:4 decision concerning the status of children of a Jewish, Israeli father and a non-Jewish, naturalized Israeli citizen mother; the controversial decision led to Knesset legislation precluding anyone from being registered as a Jew if, inter alia, they were not born of a Jewish mother or became converted to Judaism.]

law; it would be hard to imagine an Israeli judge *not* subscribing to a vision of Zionism that included protection for the civil rights of all people. But if, as Burt correctly, asserts, the founding creed of the Israeli polity is that Israel is to be a "national home for the Jewish people" ("in America the creed was political equality"), then Landau could not have intended his observation to mean that "the creed had a single discernible meaning that could be definitively invoked to transcend political conflict." That Justice Landau's intervention barely scratches the surface of fundamental political division becomes clear if one focuses on what is ultimately at the heart of the substantive issue in this case—Jewish ownership and control of land.

Indeed, it was toward the end of securing a "national home for the Jewish people" that the expropriation of Arab lands came to be associated with the Zionist movement. For example, in the 1950s and 1960s Arab land in the Galilee was expropriated by public authority, in order to construct the development towns of Upper Nazareth and Carmiel. One does not minimize the significance of the Court's ruling in *Elon Moreh* by suggesting that it does not really address the fundamental tension in the Declaration, the pursuit of equality for all people on the one hand, and as is manifest in this case, the development of the land of Israel for the Jewish people on the other. What distinguishes the taking of Arab land in the *Elon Moreh* case from other Jewish settlements (both in Israel proper and in the contested or occupied territories) was its blatant illegality, which the Court could not ignore (although it is possible that an earlier Court might have done so).[77] The 1967 war clearly exacerbated extremist tendencies in the Israeli polity,

---

77. A 1955 case, *Committee for the Protection of the Expropriated Nazareth Lands v. Minister of Finance*, 9 P.D. 1261, is revealing in this regard. It involved the expropriation of Arab land by the Development Authority for the purpose of establishing a *kiryah,* that is, governmental offices and housing for public servants. The petitioners claimed that the transferral of lands from their Arab owners to Jewish settlers constituted discrimination against the Arabs in favor of the Jews. The Court, however, upheld the expropriation, arguing, among other things, that it was not its function to inquire into whether the purpose for which the land was acquired was a public purpose as required by the relevant ordinance. But it did proceed to consider whether the choice of the lands acquired was an arbitrary, one. Interestingly, Justice Witkon's opinion relies in this regard on Justice Landau's discussion of discrimination in *Yosifof,* [a] bigamy decision.... Landau ... placed the issue of discrimination within the context of "the social realities of the country." Witkon's opinion is less candid, for in borrowing the idea that not all differentiation between categories of people is "discrimination," he

simply says, "In a sovereign state one does not recognize the autonomy of local residents, be they Jews or Arabs, to the extent that they are allowed to frustrate a plan that has been confirmed as a public purpose and decided upon for the benefit of the region and entire country. This concerns the priority of the central government over the will of the local people. No matter of discrimination is involved here." Ibid., V–24 (Barak et. al.) Translation by Carmel Shalev, in Barak, Goldstein, and Marshall, *Limits of Law.* While this may be technically correct, it neglects to mention that the benefits have mainly to do with the development of the nation as a homeland for the Jewish people. The case thus illustrates how a judicial decision that may very well be consistent with the rule of law may also be consistent with the special recognition given by the Declaration of Independence to the Jewish people. In the *Elon Moreh* decision, upholding the rule of law is consistent with the more egalitarian passages of the Declaration. In short, the principle of the rule of law does not, by itself, get at the underlying tensions in the Israeli constitutional system.

but it did not produce the deeply embedded societal divisions that generate them. These were always present and were implicit in the origins of the regime.

The war and its legacy may also have stimulated a number of justices to heighten the political profile of the Supreme Court by expanding the Court's powers of judicial review. In this sense, as Burt maintains, there may very well be a correlation between conflict and judicial review, or at least judicial activism. While in Israel the conflict may always have been present, at a certain point in its development its problematic character becomes so apparent and disturbing that many people—including judges—perceive the need to approach things differently. They may seek in fact to set into motion a process that holds out the hope of establishing a moral-political consensus that will eventually heal the increasingly dangerous rifts within the body politic. But my argument is that they will not be appealing to a foundational source of creedal unity; instead, whether acknowledged or not, they will be pursuing . . . the constitutional implications that flow from one side of a divided political inheritance. In response to this initiative, more skeptical judges, such as Justice Landau, will come forth to remind their countrymen and fellow jurists that there are definite limits to what the courts can do in the face of the tension embodied in the Declaration of Independence, and that the Court may be endangering what it *can* do by reaching too far.[78]

Bergman, Marbury, and Judicial Restraint

That such a message has come from Justice Landau is interesting, for in addition to his role in *Elon Moreh*, he is also the author of the Court's opinion in *Bergman v. Minister of Interior*, the Israeli decision most often compared to *Marbury v. Madison*. Decided in 1969, it has the potential for becoming what *Marbury* has become in American constitutional law, the leading precedent for a broadly based power of judicial review. Were that to occur within a time frame comparable to what has evolved in the United States, it would of course be many years before that potential (adjusting, as one would have to, for the absence of a formal written constitution) would be realized. And just as it is easy to imagine a surprised reaction from John Marshall in the face of how his opinion had been exaggerated with respect to the later claims made on its behalf, Moshe Landau could be expected to express a similar sense of wonderment at the inflated purposes to which his opinion had been put. . . .

The Court in *Cooper* [v. Aaron] made its argument for judicial supremacy on the basis of Marshall's famous declaration that "it is emphatically the province and duty of the judicial department to say what the law is." It is now largely taken for granted that the power of the Supreme Court to issue final and binding interpretations of the Constitution is a necessary corollary of judicial review. That Marshall's original formulation was writ-

---

78. In contrast, the U.S. Supreme Court, as its experience in *Dred Scott* reveals, threatens its legitimacy most when, in reaching too far, it fails to fulfill its role as institutional voice for those enduring values that constitute the American creed.

ten in the context of reviewing a section of a law that dealt specifically with the powers of the judiciary is long forgotten. And not only in the United States, as is illustrated in a recent Israeli case where the Marshall quote was used to make the point that "in a regime based on the separation of powers, the authority, to interpret legislative acts—ranging from basic laws to regulations and administrative orders—is vested in the Court." Furthermore, "Its interpretation is binding upon the parties, and . . . is binding upon the public in general." The case involved a decision by the chairman of the Knesset to preclude a one-member (Meir Kahane) party faction from submitting a proposal of nonconfidence in the government. The intervention by the Court in what has at least the appearance of an internal legislative matter is reminiscent of the American case *Powell v. McCormack,* in which the Court said, again relying on *Marbury,* "It is the responsibility of this Court to act as the ultimate interpreter of the Constitution."

This statement, too, was quoted in the Israeli opinion, accompanied by a reminder from its author, Justice Barak: "These words are not special to a legal system in which there is a formal constitution, and which recognizes judicial review of the lawfulness of legislation. These words are fundamental truths in every legal system in which there is an independent judicial branch." Israel may not have a normal constitution, but it does have documents that have come to enjoy constitutional status, and that, when interpreted by the Court, have done much to establish the independence of the judiciary. The indirect use of the Declaration of Independence in *"Kol Ha'am"* to invalidate an administrative action infringing on freedom of the press is perhaps the classic example. But despite its independence, the Court's authority to act as "ultimate interpreter" in constitutional matters involving the Knesset is far from being established, with the exception of legislation inconsistent with an entrenched clause of a basic law. *Bergman* is the basis for this exception: however, a close reading of the case reveals how it could support a considerably broader claim. In this respect it may very well parallel the history of *Marbury,* another case whose relatively narrow holding includes language with an alluringly expansive potential. [86]

In the *Bergman* case the Court responded favorably to the petition of Aharon Bergman, who had sought to enjoin the minister of finance from acting under the provisions of the Financing Law of 1969. That law provided for governmental financing of political parties in election campaigns, but only for those parties represented in the outgoing Knesset. Bergman claimed that this unequal treatment violated the principle of electoral equality incorporated in section 4 of Basic Law: The Knesset, which reads as follows: "The Knesset shall be elected by general, country-wide, direct, equal, secret and proportional elections, in accordance with the Knesset Elections Law: this section shall not be varied save by a

86. Elsewhere, for example, Justice Barak has written, "Our *Marbury v. Madison* is about to be pronounced—or maybe it was several years ago. It will probably be decided before our constitution is written." Barak, "Freedom of Speech in Israel: The Impact of the American Constitution," *Tel Aviv University Studies in Law* 8 (1988). . . .

majority of the members of the Knesset." The last clause gives to the section its "entrenched" character, distinguishing it from ordinary legislation and providing the Court, according to *Bergman*, with the authority to overturn the Financing Law, which had not been passed by the required special majority. This the Court did, without addressing "some very difficult preliminary constitutional questions with regard to the status of the Basic Laws and the justiciability before this court of the question whether in practice the Knesset observes any self-imposed restriction by way of 'entrenching' a statutory provision such as section 4 of the Basic Law that is being dealt with by us." The case was decided on the assumption that ordinary legislation of the Knesset can be struck down by the Court when it contravenes an entrenched provision of a basic law, but it is not, in itself, an authority for the correctness of that assumption.[88]

Opinions about what the Court actually did diverge markedly, ranging from the view that *"Bergman* is actually the least important basis for the Israeli Supreme Court's contemporary claims for increased judicial authority," to the view that it "revolutioniz[ed] the Israeli legal system by introducing *de facto* judicial supervision of the constitutionality of primary legislation." It did seem to mean that the Knesset could bind itself, but beyond that, its implications for judicial review were uncertain.[90] As in *Marbury*, where a narrow interpretation of its meaning for judicial review would confine the holding to matters of direct concern to the judiciary, and a broad view would see it as a basis for judicial supremacy in all constitutional questions, Justice Landau's opinion possesses similar alternative possibilities. This may be seen in his treatment of the conflict between the two Knesset laws.

The attorney general had argued that no conflict existed, in that the principle of equality in the Basic Law was to be narrowly construed to mean only that each voter shall have one vote of equal weight (i.e., one person, one vote). But by an alternative reading of the statute accepted by the Court, section 4 should not be confined to technical provisions regard-

---

88. This decision by the Court not to address the question of the Court's authority to invalidate a law inconsistent with an entrenched provision of a Basic Law has come in for some heavy criticism. For example: "Is ... a Basic Law ... 'superior' to an ordinary law? If so, then the court should have said so in clear terms and set the question at rest." Peter Elman, "Comment," *Israel Law Review* 4 (1969):568. Justice Landau's avoidance of the justiciability issue was based on the fact that the attorney general had not contested this issue, and further, that the case was one of extreme urgency and therefore precluded the thorough examination that the question deserved. Nevertheless, his postponement of the question inevitably gave rise to a comparison with *Marbury,* in that both opinions challenged a powerful branch of government without providing that branch with a very good opportunity to respond effectively.

90. This is not to say that at the time of the decision the power of the Knesset to bind future Knessets was a settled question. Indeed, it was a much debated question in Israeli legal circles, but as Ruth Gavison has noted, "In fact, the debate about the Knesset's *power* [to enact an entrenched bill of rights] would seem to have been well-nigh decided by the political system. The Knesset has enacted entrenched provisions of basic laws, and the courts have opted for some version of recognition of the power of the Knesset to bind itself." Gavison, "The Controversy Over Israel's Bill of Rights," p. 115.

ing the carrying out of elections, but should also cover the equal right to be elected, a right clearly denied by the Financing Law. Justice Landau acknowledged, however, that as an issue of statutory interpretation, this was a "borderline" call, an acknowledgment very different from Chief Justice Marshall's decisive (although much more dubious) interpretation of section 13 of the Judiciary Act of 1789. But according to Landau, any doubt as to the meaning of the provision was to be resolved by applying the general principle of the equality of all before the law to the specific area of electoral laws. In this he rejected the claim by the attorney general that because the equality principle was not embodied in a written constitution or a basic law, it could not hinder the legislature from deviating from it.

Although it "is nowhere inscribed [it is a principle that] breathes the breath of life into our whole constitutional system. It is therefore right that just in the border-line case, when the provision of the enacted Law is open to two interpretations. we should prefer that which preserves the equality of all before the law and does not set it at naught." That preference led the Court to invalidate the Financing Law despite the fact that "the first inclination of the court must ... be to uphold the law and not invalidate it, even when the contention against it is that it contradicts an 'entrenched' statutory provision." This, then, raises an obvious question: if the unwritten constitutional principles referred to by Justice Landau are clear and powerful enough to overcome this "first inclination," then is it not proper to infer as a general jurisprudential proposition that when there is a statute of questionable consistency with an entrenched Basic Law, its validity may be established by application of the unwritten constitution? Or even more, if a law passed by the Knesset repudiates one of the life-breathing principles of the constitutional system, is it even necessary that there be an entrenched Basic Law for the Supreme Court to invalidate it? In this respect is not *Bergman* considerably more sweeping than *Marbury?* As one commentator has put it, "Where Chief Justice Marshall declared an Act of Congress void because it was in conflict with the Constitution, Mr. Justice Landau ... declared an Act of the Knesset void despite the fact that Israel has not yet adopted a written constitution."[93]

In fact there is nothing in Justice Landau's opinion to indicate that he had such expansive possibilities in mind, that he intended anything more than that where there are two possible statutory interpretations, the interpretation that conforms to the principle of equality is to be preferred. There is certainly no clear warrant for supposing that a Knesset law may be overturned on the strength, standing alone, of any unwritten constitutional principle. Landau himself argued in a subsequent case that "apart

---

93. Melville B. Nimmer. "The Uses of Judicial Review in Israel's Quest for a Constitution," *Columbia Law Review* 70 (1970): 1218. The decision in *Bergman* might usefully be compared to an American decision, *American Party of Texas v. White,* 415 U.S. 767 (1974), in which the Court upheld a Texas statute that, among other things, de-nied ballot position to parties that failed to secure at least 2 percent of the vote in the previous election (although there were other routes for getting on the ballot). The decision may be seen as displaying more deference to the legislative branch than what occurred in the Israeli case, especially since the legislature was that of a state and not the Congress.

from the special problem of entrenched clauses, this Court does not assume for itself the jurisdiction to review the content of Knesset legislation." But that is no guarantee that in the future the Court will not assume such a power, and that in doing so it will not appeal to the unwritten principles adverted to by the justice in *Bergman*. In Justice Menachem Elon's words, *"For the moment* this court exercises self-restraint and does not use the power of judicial review it has over legislative proceedings of the Knesset."[95] A Court, however, that is moving in the direction of "ultimate interpreter" could quite easily (although at present it might not be very likely) appropriate the language in *Bergman* to conclude that primary legislation offensive to the fundamental principles of the constitutional system cannot stand.

As we have seen, Justice Landau's own reluctance to move in this direction is related to his concerns about the character of these fundamental principles. While the courts must enforce the principle of equality before the law in justiciable cases, there may be other principles (as well, perhaps, as this principle in certain situations) where enforcement by the Supreme Court would inappropriately enmesh the judiciary in controversies more amenable to political resolution. He has advocated a sort of bifurcated system for the exercise of judicial power, arguing that "the institutional part of the constitution should be entrenched and should be subject to judicial review," but that an entrenched bill of rights would lead to the unfortunate politicization of the Court. In the context of *Bergman,* the Court's intervention might therefore be understood as a proper assertion of judicial power in defense of a vital institutional concern, namely, the sanctity of the electoral process. But nothing in this intervention, Landau would no doubt claim, should be construed as necessarily legitimating interventions by the Court in other constitutional domains.

There is in this position an echo of the now arcane American doctrine of departmentalism, which denies that any one institution should possess final interpretive authority on all constitutional questions, and more particularly, that deference should be accorded each branch of government in matters concerning its own functions. Denying that the Supreme Court should be "ultimate arbiter of all constitutional questions," Thomas Jefferson maintained. "The constitution has erected no such single tribunal, knowing that to whatever hands confided, with the corruptions of time and party, its members would become despots. It has more wisely made all the departments co-equal and co-sovereign within themselves." While this is a view most frequently associated with Jefferson, some constitutional scholars make the argument that it is an essential component of Marshall's opinion in *Marbury v. Madison.* Marshall "claimed no more than that each department shall have final authority to pass on constitutional questions

---

95. ... [T]he Basic Law on the Judiciary contains language that could be interpreted to provide support for extensive judicial review over acts of the Knesset. Section 15(d)(2) reads: "The Supreme Court sitting as a High Court of Justice shall be competent to order state authorities and officials thereof *and other persons who carry out public duties under law* to do or refrain from doing any act in the lawful exercise of their duties, or if they were improperly elected or appointed to retain from acting" (emphasis added)....

affecting its own duties and responsibilities.'' This is not the claim found in most contemporary *Marbury* justifications of particular exercises of judicial review, but then, as has been said, "the mythic *Marbury* and the real *Marbury* inhabit different constitutional galaxies.'' It is, for example, noteworthy that prior to the late nineteenth century, Marshall's opinion was not cited as a precedent for judicial review; nor was it cited with any frequency in this regard until the 1950s. Its absence in *Dred Scott* is especially significant, because that case was the first post-*Marbury* instance in which judicial review was used to overturn a congressional enactment, and also the first instance in the Court's history when it struck down a law that concerned matters falling outside the immediate purview of the judicial department.

As plausible as this understanding *of Marbury* is, the eventual demise of departmentalism (at least in its most fully developed Jeffersonian version) is not without a logic of its own. Marshall may very well have intended that the Court exercise judicial review only over acts of a "judiciary nature,'' but the practical as well as theoretical difficulties of determining jurisdictional boundaries in individual cases make it clear why such an intent would likely not in the end be faithfully observed. In addition, the historic connection between judicial review and natural rights jurisprudence suggests that confining the Court to narrowly prescribed substantive questions would be difficult to maintain. Lincoln's opposition to *Dred Scott*—specifically his recommendation that the finality of the Court's judgment be withheld—did not flow from a sense that the Court had, in invalidating the Missouri Compromise, ventured inappropriately beyond the province of its own department. Rather, it reflected his deeply held belief that the Court's judgment was wrong; wrong, that is, in the most decisive way possible, because it repudiated the principles of the Declaration. For the same reason that he could not have endorsed judicial supremacy, he could not have endorsed the narrow view of *Marbury*; judicial finality is after all justified if it advances the aspirational goals of the Declaration and Constitution.

Justice Landau, on the other hand, *would* endorse what others might characterize as a narrow construction of *Bergman* if for no other reason than that it could not then become a precedent for an expansion of judicial review into more controversial areas of nonentrenched basic law provisions, to say nothing of principles yet to be embodied in any Basic Law. One might say of his position, that like the advocates of a narrow reading of *Marbury*, he would prefer to confine the activity of the Court, as far as its review of legislation is concerned, to things of a "judiciary nature.'' His opposition to an entrenched bill of rights does not mean that the Court should stay out of rights enforcement (as is obvious from his own record on these questions) only that its institutional health depends on minimizing opportunities for direct confrontation with the legislature over such issues. ... [In the U.S., judicial review has] become instrumental in putting into the hands of the judiciary many of the most divisive social and political issues confronting the American people. The judges have not, in other words, been "kept strictly to their own department," as Jefferson, perhaps unrealistically, thought they should.

That a similar evolution in Israel, where societal division cuts more deeply, might concern someone like Justice Landau, is understandable. One should of course question whether his own variant of a departmental solution, in which the judiciary is limited in its power by excluding from review legislative acts pertaining directly to individual rights, is any more realistic. Many would argue, for example, that Justice Landau has (to his considerable credit) done as much as anyone in Israel in creating a "judicial bill of rights," that, in other words, the Court has already become a principal player in the great issues that divide the body politic. While perhaps true, that may not be the best way to frame the issue. Developing a de facto bill of rights through statutory interpretation and administrative review does not entail the degree of certainty or finality, that is involved in judicial review of primary legislation. Prudence thus dictates judicial restraint. Or to put it another way: judicial restraint in Israel means avoiding judgments of finality in the absence of a final settlement of regime principles.

CONCLUSION

Walter F. Murphy has argued that the question of *who* should be the authoritative source for constitutional interpretation is directly connected to the more basic question of *what* the constitution is. For example, "Does a constitution point toward a vision or several visions of the good society?" "Does it bind a people together into a nation?" In this chapter I have proceeded in a similar fashion by considering the issue of judicial review in the context of the nature and role of the constitution in Israel and the United States. The fact that in the United States the Constitution assumes a more prominent role as a source for a shared political identity than it does in Israel has a bearing on how we should understand the act of constitutional interpretation. The *who* and the *what* of constitutional interpretation is in some manner related to the question of the *who* and the *what* of civic identity. If it is judicial review we are speaking about in this context, then the judges who perform this act, especially in the American system, are directly or indirectly engaged in a process of political legitimation.[106]

But this does not answer the question of ultimate interpretive responsibility. While Bickel and others are persuasive in showing why the Court is particularly well suited to articulate and defend "enduring values," it is Lincoln who demonstrated that the centrality of these principles precluded

---

106. I mean this in a deeper sense than what is implied in Charles L. Black's understanding of the Supreme Court as a legitimating agent in American politics. "The Court, through its history, has acted as the legitimator of the government. In a very real sense, the Government of the United States is based on the opinions of the Supreme Court." Charles L. Black, Jr., *The People and the Court: Judicial Review in a Democracy* (Englewood Cliffs, N.J.: Prentice-Hall, 1960), p. 52. While not disagreeing with this, my point is that the Court is a legitimator of the principles by which Americans derive their collective sense of identity.

a judicial monopoly over constitutional interpretation.[107] His position did not deny judicial finality; it did, however, accept nonjudicial participation in the process by which it was ultimately achieved. To the extent that all branches (and, we might add, citizens) were involved in the common enterprise of attempting to realize constitutional ideals, they all had a responsibility to defend, in appropriate ways, their best understanding of these ideals. *Dred Scott* was of course Lincoln's great lesson in judicial fallibility, a specific version of a lesson detailed in the opening essay of *The Federalist:* "So numerous indeed and so powerful are the causes which serve to give a false bias to the judgment, that we, upon many occasions, see wise and good men on the wrong as well as the right side of questions of the first magnitude to society. This circumstance, if duly attended to, would furnish a lesson in moderation to those who are ever so much persuaded of their being in the right, in any controversy.". . .

Thus it is that while the existence of a moral consensus embodied in a written constitution legitimates the exercise of judicial review by a counter-majoritarian institution, the possibility of error or willful distortion suggests the inappropriateness of an unqualified finality in constitutional interpretation. Regrettably, however, this is not a widely shared view: mainly because of a preference among many judges and scholars for constitutional theories that in one way or another embrace the teaching contained in the aphorism that the Constitution is what the judges say it is. Americans are in need of a Court that is vitally engaged in the process of clarifying and elaborating those meanings that give definition to the nation as a whole; but for that reason they must also see to it that that engagement be part of a collaborative enterprise in which the finality, of any constitutional judgment involving fundamental principle becomes more than a formalistic matter of determining who has the last word.

The Israeli example can illuminate this problem. There the notion of a court as ultimate constitutional interpreter is particularly problematic in the light of that polity's historic difficulty in achieving a unified constitutional vision or consensus, to say nothing of its longstanding tradition of parliamentary supremacy. Right and wrong, when applied in Israel to founding principles, will largely depend on the perceived correctness of a choice between particularistic and universal filaments in the existent constitutional constellation. The position of judicial restraint reflects, among other things an understandable desire to avoid making this choice. Indeed, such restraint is further justified if the alternative to it follows the American pattern of a ratcheting up of the practice of judicial review into a defense of judicial supremacy. But this should not be seen as inevitable; judicial review, or more broadly, constitutional interpretation by the Court, has a much greater potential than in the United States for retaining a relatively modest role in the development of constitutional understanding.

---

107. Bickel, it should be noted, was very much influenced by Lincoln in these matters. Speaking of these great issues of principle, he observed that "the functions [of the branches of government] cannot and need not be rigidly compartmentalized." Bickel, *The Least Dangerous Branch,* p. 261.

There is less reason for concern over an active judiciary if it is clearly understood that the specific results of its activity possess a politically tentative or intermediate status in the elaboration of regime principles. A Court pursuing the more libertarian aspirations of the nation's founding agenda can and ought to be checked by a Knesset that is more sensitive to the other parts of that agenda, as the latter in turn should be checked by the Court. If a genuine constitutional colloquy emerges from this process it may contain within it the possibility of achieving a greater unity of constitutional purpose. But it also contains within it a lesson for those polities that begin with this greater unity: they too can profit from a constitutional arrangement that allows them to achieve a higher level of clarity in the articulation, development, and application of constitutional principle.

Ronen Shamir, *"Landmark Cases" and the Reproduction of Legitimacy: The Case of Israel's High Court of Justice*, 24 Law & Society Rev. 781 (1990).

[In contrast to the views of Edelman, Jacobsohn and Burt, consider the following argument by Ronen Shamir: "judicial failure to uphold and sustain state actions can ... contribute to state legitimacy. By occasionally overruling or annulling governmental policies in some 'landmark cases,' the juridical apparatus asserts its independence from the polity. ... [T]he court can cast the cloak of legitimacy over the state as a whole by vindicating other decisions that uphold governmental action as right and reasonable." While recognizing that the court may not intend a legitimating effect, and indeed may find its anti-government decisions painful, he argues that landmark cases against government policy can reinforce the legitimacy of both the government as a whole and of the court, even though, courts tend generally to support and uphold state-sponsored policies. He elaborates this argument in connection with the occupied territories, and *Elon Moreh* specifically:]

* * *

The Israeli Supreme Court serves a dual function: as a high court of appeal, hearing appeals from district courts, and as a high court of justice (HCJ) with original jurisdiction over disputes between individuals and the state in matters that are not within the jurisdiction of other courts and tribunals. Since Israel lacks a written constitution, one of the court's primary objectives is to provide a constitutional means to ensure that public officials and agents of the state will not exceed or abuse their powers of discretion.

The Court is able to grant petitioners immediate relief and to issue orders and injunctions, either interim or absolute, which may compel the government to take a particular action or prevent it from taking an intended one. The court considers petitions rapidly and inexpensively. Any person who has reason to believe that a particular state action denies her legal rights may petition the court and ask it to issue an order *nisi*. A single judge reviews the petition and may issue an order requiring the relevant respondent to appear in court and show why a particular action should or should not be performed. A full hearing then takes place, and the court determines whether to annul its prior injunctions and to sustain the state's position or to order the respondents to act, or to refrain from acting, in a prescribed manner.

Since the beginning of Israel's occupation of the West Bank and Gaza Strip, the residents of these areas have been allowed to petition the HCJ. The petitions have asked the court to review the legality of a large variety of state actions and policies and to determine whether administrative officials exceeded their discretionary powers in their handling of particular affairs.

International legal standards do not give a population under occupation the right to petition the court of the occupying party. The Israeli authorities could have contested the court's jurisdiction to preside over matters that belonged to military rule in an occupied area. In fact, the court explicitly stated that had such arguments been raised, they might well have been sufficient to prevent further litigation (*Hilu et al v. Government of Israel* (1972)). Yet when the first petitions from the occupied territories were filed, the Israeli authorities did not object to the HCJ's jurisdiction, in a decision that was described as "unprecedented in international practice" (Shamgar, 1971). In the absence of arguments against its power to consider such a petition, the court accepted jurisdiction. The HCJ referred to the consent of the parties to litigate and later claimed that the court had an acquired right to rule in matters concerning actions taken by agents of the state, wherever they happened to operate *(El Masulia v. Army Commander* (1982)).

The HCJ's record shows that in the course of twenty years of occupation, from 1967 till 1986, residents of the occupied territories had submitted 557 petitions to the court. The cases the court heard during these years included matters of land and property confiscations and seizures, deportations, limits on the freedom of speech and the freedom of movement, demolition of houses, administrative detentions, and numerous other administrative decisions concerning taxation, permits of residency, and work permits. The overwhelming majority of these petitions were removed, compromised, or settled in one way or another.[4] Sixty-five petitions reached adjudication and were officially published as HCJ decisions in matters of dispute between the Israeli government and its agents (e.g., the military) and the residents of the territories. In deciding these cases, the court

---

4. These data are based on HCJ files. However, there might be slight inconsistencies due to inaccurate filing. Also, the number includes petitions of residents of East Jerusalem, which was annexed to Israel, but does not include petitions of prisoners. Although this article treats only officially published decisions, the larger body of unpublished decisions includes no cases in which the court favored the petitioners.

gradually established legal doctrines and judicial constructions that covered most of the debated issues.

Five of the sixty-five adjudicated cases upheld at least some of the arguments of the petitioners. All five were decided in 1979–80, over a time span of less than two years. Each of these cases dealt with a different issue. One, usually referred to as the *Elon Moreh* case, declared null and void a certain confiscation of land *(Dawikat et al v. Government of Israel* (1979)). A second decision, often cited as *Mt. Hebron Deportees*, ruled against the legality of the deportation of two Palestinian leaders *(Kawasme et al v. Minister of Defense* (1980)). In a third case, the court ordered the Minister of Interior to issue a newspaper permit he had previously declined to grant *(El Asad v. Minister of Interior* (1979)). In a fourth decision, the court overruled an official refusal to allow the petitioner to reunite with his family *(Samara v. Regional Commander of Judea and Samaria* (1979)). And a fifth ruling prevented an acquisition of a Palestinian electricity company *(Jerusalem District Electricity Co. v. Minister of Energy et al.* (1980)).

These cases unquestionably marked a direct confrontation between the government and the court concerned policies and actions in the occupied territories. By declaring certain governmental actions to be void, illegal, or improper, the court publicly embarrassed the government and appeared to endorse alternative courses of action. Since the government deferred to the court's injunctions,[5] these decisions demonstrated judicial boldness and provided evidence of the regime's accountability.

By placing these cases in a broader perspective and by reading the decisions more closely, I show that the significance of these landmark cases was primarily symbolic rather than substantive. The long-range outcome of these decisions legitimized governmental policies precisely because these decisions became symbols of democracy in action. To demonstrate these arguments, three cases that involved confiscation, deportation, and freedom of speech are considered at length. The two remaining cases of rulings against the state, which received less public attention, reveal similar patterns and are consistent with the argument.

B. Land Confiscations: The Elon-Moreh Case

The most publicized and discussed of the landmark decisions is the 1979 *Elon Moreh* case in which the court declared a land seizure order issued by the army to be null and void. As a result, a Jewish civilian settlement built on this land had to be evacuated and removed. The case stirred a heated debate in Israel, augmented the power and centrality of the HCJ and is often cited as an indicator of judicial supremacy.

---

5. In *Elon Moreh*, the government evacuated the settlement. In *Mt. Hebron Deportees*, Israel allowed two of the deportees to return. In *El Asad*, the newspaper obtained a permit. In *Samara,* the petitioner was permitted to reunite with his family. In *Jerusalem District Electricity Co.*, the decision to acquire the company was postponed.

This was not the first time the court had dealt with a (privately owned) land confiscation in the occupied territories. The first attempt to challenge the validity of a land seizure was made in 1973, when the court ruled that land seizures for military purposes were within the scope of the legal framework prevailing in the occupied territories and that such seizures did not violate the provisions of international law. Moreover, the court declined to question the validity of the security considerations that backed up the administrative decision: "[O]ne thing is clear, the scope of the court's intervention in the operations of military authorities in security matters is necessarily very narrow" (*Hilu et al, v. Government of Israel* (1972)[.])

In similar cases that followed, the court gradually expanded the limits of the "security reasons" and "military necessities" concepts, thereby expanding the justification of policies in military terms. This expansion became acute in 1977, with the establishment of a new government in Israel that had promised its constituency a wide-scale Jewish settlement in the occupied territories. Yet it was essential to justify the civilian settlements in the occupied territories in light of military necessities if Israel wished to abide by its earlier commitments to respect the relevant provisions of international law, namely, the Hague Regulations Respecting the Laws and Customs of War on Land and the Fourth Geneva Convention Relative to the Protection of Civil Persons in Time of War.[6] Thus, land seizures were reviewed in light of article 52 of the Hague regulations. The court interpreted the article as allowing a temporary seizure of land with compensation for military purposes.... The concept of the Hague regulations that allowed several specified actions when they were "imperatively demanded by the necessities of war" (art. 23) was liberally interpreted by the court, as was also article 49(6) of the IV Geneva Convention.

In December 1978 the court upheld the establishment of dwelling units for families of army personnel on confiscated land as part of the "military necessities" doctrine. The court also ruled that the temporary nature of the planned dwelling units was proof enough that international law had not been violated (*Salame et al v. Minister of Defense* (1978)). Two months later the court ruled that a civilian settlement built on confiscated land did not conflict with international law since it promoted the security of the state:

> [T]here is no doubt that the presence of civilian settlements ... contributes to national security and helps the army. One need not be a military expert to realize that terrorists can operate with more ease where the population is indifferent or supportive of them, than where part of the population observes them and informs the authorities about suspicious movements.... [A] Jewish settlement in an occupied area ... serves concrete security needs. (*Aioub et al v. Minister of Defense* (1978)).

6. Israel claims that its policies in the occupied territories do not violate the provisions of the Hague Regulations (Scott, 1915) and the IV Geneva Convention of 1949 (United National Treaty Series, 1950), although it claims that the latter is not binding on it. For a detailed discussion of the Israeli position with regard to international law, see Shamgar (1971); Dinstein (1983: 229–39).

The HCJ laid an additional brick of this doctrine in August 1978, when the petitioners in a new case recruited a former army general whose affidavit challenged the view that civilian settlements promoted the security of the state. The court decided that in such cases the official version would always prevail: "When a professional military controversy arises, in which the court does not have sufficient knowledge, he who speaks in the name of those responsible for the security of the administered territories ... will be considered to hold innocent considerations. Very strong evidence will be needed to contradict this presumption" (*Amira et al. v. Minister of Defense* (1979)).

Yet only two months later, in October 1979, the court dramatically ruled that the seizure order that allowed the settlement of Elon Moreh should be declared null and void. The court found that the settlement was intended to be a permanent one, not in line with international law, and not justified by military needs. Consequently, the government had to evacuate the area, using its armed forces to deal with the frustrated settlers. It was the first confiscation case ever won at court by Palestinian residents of the occupied territories, and it was "repeatedly referred to as proof of the effectiveness of the High Court in keeping the military within the parameters of the law" (Shehadeh, 1985: 22).

When the decision is studied more carefully, however, the reality appears to be different. The court did not rescind its previous decisions. The decision was not inspired by a novel set of considerations in assessing military necessities. Rather, the court confronted overwhelming evidence that undermined the government's security argument that the court had used as the touchstone to examine the legality of confiscations.

The court's doubts concerning the security reasoning arose from two facts. First, the Jewish settlers provided the court with an affidavit in which they explicitly denied that their settlement had been inspired by military considerations. They proclaimed that the settlement was "a Godly commandment to inherit the land promised to our ancestors," and that "[t]he act of settling ... is not inspired by security considerations and physical necessities, but by the destiny and the homecoming of the people of Israel." Second, Israel's minister of defense publicly expressed his opposition to the establishment of the settlement, in sharp contrast to the opinions of the army chief of staff and other members of the cabinet. Faced with these facts, one judge asserted: "[An] extraordinary situation is at hand. The respondents cannot agree among themselves about the issue." A second judge described the situation as "unprecedented in Israel's judicial history."

Under those circumstances, the court followed its own doctrine and ruled in favor of the petitioners. But at the same time it paved the way for future alternative forms of land-seizure. In its decision, the court suggested that future land-seizure orders could adopt the pattern of declaring lands as "state lands," and it promised that it would refuse to inquire into the validity of such declarations. In distinguishing between privately owned property and public property, the court ruled that land previously held by the former (Jordanian) government passed into the hands of Israel which, in accordance with international law, performed in the capacity of usufructuary (having a lawful right to make use of the land without a legal title of ownership).

Most of the lands in the occupied territories have been cultivated for generations by the residents but were not formally registered as private property. After the *Elon Moreh* case, the Israeli government ceased to consider these lands as private. Thus, in its isolated and well-differentiated decision, the court established new limitations on the ability of future petitioners to resist land seizures and provided a sounder legal basis for future takeovers. The court also ruled that in the future it would not intervene in matters of dispute concerning the ownership status of land and that such disputes would be heard before a military appeal board. Following the *Elon Moreh* case, therefore, the number of petitions regarding land seizures dropped significantly and those submitted were dismissed.

.   .   .

III.   THE LEGITIMATION EFFECT OF THE COURT'S RULINGS

The HCJ enjoyed a reputation for independence and impartiality prior to the cases discussed in this study. It role in protecting individual rights was already acknowledged in other spheres of public policy (e.g., decisions concerning freedom of press; see *Kol Ha'am Ltd. v. Minister of Interior* (1953)). But after the Israeli occupation of the West Bank and Gaza Strip, Israelis became especially attuned to policy issues concerning these areas and their inhabitants. Consequently, the court's decisions in matters of dispute between the Israeli government and the Palestinian petitioners placed the court at the center of public attention. The mere ability of Palestinian residents to petition the HCJ was regarded as a sign of the court's receptiveness and received local and international attention.

The landmark cases discussed here significantly contributed to the image of the court as an impartial body which boldly challenged the government in its pursuit of justice. This is most evident in the way these decisions were extensively reported in the news media and discussed by political observers and legal scholars.[9]

The *Elon Moreh* decision, for example, was printed verbatim over four pages in the daily *Ma'ariv* (23 October 1979, p. 17). Further, each landmark ruling was followed by a flood of commentaries and editorial that praised the court's contribution to the democratic character of Israel and the humane nature of Israeli rule in the occupied territories. One columnist wrote that the Elon Moreh decision was "a document which fills with pride everyone who considers Israel to respect not only the rule of law ... but also the celebrated spirit of Judaism" (Bartov, 1979). Another wrote that "[t]he High Court of Justice deserves a blessing and respect. It proved to be

---

9. The importance of the news media in conveying perceptions of legitimacy is particularly central given that Israel has only four major newspapers. Of the 78 percent of the population who read newspapers, 93 percent read these four (Ben-Ami, 1988).

a guardian of law and justice and demonstrated its independence" (Kol, 1979). Another claimed that "[t]he decision of the court in the case of *Elon Moreh* enhanced great respect towards Israel; it proved that 'there was justice' in Jerusalem and that Israel was indeed ruled by Law" (Peres, 1979). In short, as one observer put it: "The open mindedness of the court proves that Israel is a 'legitimate state' which is governed according to constitutional principles" (Evron, 1979).

The same enthusiastic response was expressed in scholarly writing about the court. Cohen (1985), a legal historian who studied the protection of human rights in the occupied territories, wrote that the HCJ "proved to be one of the most effective safeguards against abuses". Negbi (1981), a legal scholar who examined the overall record of the HCJ in the occupied territories, concluded: "It is due to the jurisdiction of the High Court over the territories that the humanitarian character of the military rule remained intact and the moral contamination of the Zionist undertaking and the State of Israel had been prevented". A report that sharply criticized Israel's policies of human rights singled out the HCJ:

> There is ample evidence that Supreme Court intervention restrains the potential arbitrariness of military government action, even when there are instances in which the Supreme Court is unable to help these residents. It may, therefore, be concluded that the existence of the Supreme Court in the background is to the benefit of the local population. (International Center for Peace in the Middle East, 1985: 15)[10]

The HCJ's legitimacy, then, was reinforced by the court's apparently antigovernment decisions. The impact of the landmark decisions on the legitimacy of the court cannot be exaggerated. Numerous writers repeatedly stress the invaluable importance of the HCJ to the image of Israel as a democratic state and point at the role of the court in securing humane policies. Most students of the court share the conclusion that the HCJ is "a solid defender of liberties" and rest their conclusion on the record of the court in the occupied territories (Rubinstein, 1987). These opinions are consistent with the finding of public opinion studies. One recent public opinion study reports that Israelis trust the integrity of the HCJ much more than they trust their elected parliament and their cabinet (Peres, 1987).

Israelis are not the only ones who acknowledge the decisions of the court as legally binding interpretations of Israeli and international law. Egypt's foreign minister welcomed the *Elon Moreh* decision and went as far as to conclude that the decision marked a shift in Israeli public opinion. Another daily newspaper reported enthusiastic responses by Palestinian leaders and American and British observers who saw the HCJ's *Elon Moreh* decision as an indication of Israel's moral strength. A recent U.S. State

---

10. I do not dispute the potential deterrent effect of the HCJ on state action. Yet I believe that any restraints imposed on the government are compensated for by the legitimation effect of the HCJ's presence.

Department report on human rights criticized Israel's deportation of Palestinian leaders, regarding the action as a violation of the Geneva Convention. The same report acknowledged that the Israeli Supreme Court held a different interpretation of the relevant provision. Such assertions suggest that the Israeli Court enjoys a high stature also in the eyes of foreign observers.

The analysis of cases decided by the Israeli Supreme Court suggests that the effect of the landmark cases was primarily symbolic. On the one hand, the cases reinforced the court's legitimacy as a solid defender of human rights. On the other hand, all these cases were isolated victories of Palestinian petitioners which were not followed by similar results in subsequent cases. None of the decisions had any significant effect on later policies, save the growing sophistication of the authorities in their implementation of legal procedures. Yet the significance of the cases was exaggerated, allowing them to appear as symbols of justice.

Such symbols appear when isolated court decisions are mistakenly identified as real breakthroughs, and as a result courts and litigation are perceived as effective means for obtaining rights and implementing them. Exaggerated expectations about the ability of the judicial system to impose a political change are created. Thus an effective "myth of rights" (Scheingold 1974) evolves, a belief that "litigation can evoke a declaration of rights from court; that it can, further, be used to assure the realization of these rights; and finally, that realization is tantamount to meaningful change". The Israeli Supreme Court created such a myth of rights in reacting to the actions taken by the israeli government in the occupied territories.

How does this impact come about? The bottom line of a decision, its immediate outcome, stripped of legal reasoning, can shape the image of the court. Justice Landoi, in his concluding remarks in *Elon Moreh,* was aware of this phenomenon of "selective memory": "I know perfectly well that the public is not interested in the legal reasoning but pays attention only to the final conclusion. Hence, the court risks its appropriate status as one which stands above the debates which divide the people" *(Dawikat et al. v. Government of Israel* (1979)). While the judge was concerned with the ability of the court to retain its legitimacy as a nonpolitical institution, his statement also hinted at the potential impact of a decision regardless of its long-term significance in judicial and political terms. The reputation of the HCJ as a "fortress of justice" (Negbi, 1981) obscured the fact that the judiciary supported the government in the overwhelming mass of circumstances. In the course of twenty years of occupation there were very few scholarly challenges to the image of the court as a defender of human rights.

Judicial decisions that failed to sustain the position of the state in some concrete cases has allowed Israel to appear as a determined guardian of human rights. The fact that the court established its authority above the rough and tumble of politics, and the fact that one could point to crucial moments when the court did not side with the government, allowed the Israeli administration to justify policies by falling back on those numerous rulings that were upheld at court. For example, following a particular seizure of land which was upheld in court, Israel's prime minister instructed Israeli diplomats to cite the judicial decision when explaining Israel's policies in the occupied territories; referring to the HCJ's decision, the prime minister said: "If someone will tell me that Jewish settlements in the Land of Israel are illegal ... I would reply: There are Justices presiding in Jerusalem".

Consequently, there was a growing tendency for Israeli officials to justify policies in legal terms. Rubinstein (1987) described the evolving political culture in which everything that was legal also became moral and ethical, a political culture often described as legalism: "The ethical attitude that holds moral conduct to be a matter of rule following" (Shklar, 1964). Thus, when an Israeli official was asked why a pregnant woman was being deported, he explained: "Because the High Court dismissed her petitions, removed the *order nisi* and determined that she did not have a right to permanent residency in Gaza" (Rubinstein, 1987).

Most important, the landmark cases provided reassurances that Israel's administrative and political institutions were responsive to constitutional values. In fact, the HCJ itself seemed aware of its legitimizing role. In *Mt. Hebron Deportees* it reminded the state: "[I]nsistence on following the letter of the law is not a nuisance but is a duty to be followed under all circumstances. It is the obligation of the authorities not only for the sake of the individual ... but also—and perhaps mainly—*in order to retain the image of the state as a lawful state for the sake of all its citizens*" (*Kawasme et al. v. Minister of Defense* (1980); emphasis added). Friedman (1989: 354) offered an insightful analysis of this phenomenon: "Why did Israelis insist on this pretense of law? Because without the mask of the law, the conflict between them and the Palestinians would be just a messy tribal feud, and that would not be consistent with how the Israelis see themselves and how they want the West to see them." ...

Questions and Comments

1. To what extent does a court's legitimacy, in constitutional or quasi constitutional cases like *Elon Moreh* or *Bergman*, turn on its legal reasoning? The result of the decision? The degree to which the opinion, or result, corresponds to what some see as first principles of natural justice? The degree to which the Court adheres to its decision in subsequent challenges? The results, or reasoning, of the entire body of the Court's decisions? The degree to which the immediate decision is accepted by the political branches?

2. How (if at all) do these factors relate to whether the decision of a court is viewed as "foundational?" To what extent does one need to rely on a theory of the purposes of judicial review in order to respond?

3. Shamir's analysis suggests that landmark decisions are more likely to reinforce what he and others have called "a myth of rights" than to represent substantive limits on government policy. See also George Bisharat, *Land, Law and Legislation in Israel and the Occupied Territories*, 43 Am. U. L. Rev. 467 (1994). Others treat cases like *Elon Moreh*, and the continued availability of judicial review in the High Court of Justice under the 1994 Self–Rule Accord in Gaza, as a basis for asserting and imposing limits on abuse of power by the Israeli government.[z] Jacobsohn envisions an ongoing dialogue between courts and other branches over the basic principles of the polity and how to administer them. Which of these ideas has most descriptive power in the legal systems with which you are familiar? How would you test their validity?

4. Do you agree with Shamir that the Israeli High Court of Justice performs a legitimating role for the regime (at least for the audiences of the Israeli non-Palestinian public and for foreign governments, like the U.S., friendly to Israel)? If so, how does that legitimating role compare with the legitimating role Justice Solyom has claimed for the Hungarian Constitutional Court? Consider in particular the role and traditions of the legislature.

5. Shamir concludes that the landmark cases in Israel should not be seen simply as the Court's disagreement with the substantive policy at stake but as an assertion of its own role in the balance of powers. He writes,

> ... In at least four of the five landmark cases I examined, the HCJ reacted to practices that seemed to restrict its own participation in decisionmaking or to limit its discretion: In *El Asad* the court rejected the governmental attempt to restrict its access to confidential evidence. In *Elon Moreh* it insisted on adhering to its previous judicial doctrines. In *Mt. Hebron Deportees*, it reacted to the attempt to exclude it from supervising the deportation process. And in *Samara* the HCJ rejected the attempt to deny its jurisdiction.
>
> It seems, therefore, that the petitions which were granted were not stimulated simply by the court's discomfort with the substance of the policies pursued by the state. Each time, the court reacted to practices that seemed to upset the division of authority within the power structure of the state and to narrow the HCJ's jurisdiction. I do not suggest that *all* cases of dispute between the judiciary and the government stem from struggles over issues of jurisdiction. Yet I believe that this line of inquiry may shed more light on the circumstances under which antigovernment decisions are reached. Jurisdictional struggles express the judiciary's independence, while permitting the judiciary to

z. See Mark Allison, *Note and Comment, The Hamas Deportation: Israel's Response to Terrorism During the Middle East Peace Process*, 10 Am. U. J. Intl L. & Pol'y 397 (1994); see also Adam Roberts, *Prolonged Military Occupation:The Israeli Occupied Territories Since 1967*, 84 Am. J. Intl Law 44, 63 (1990) (noting positive role of Israeli Supreme Court in accepting applicability of Hague Regulations and commendable if not total acceptance by Israel of relevance of international legal norms to govern occupation of the territories).

generally act in ways that support the interests of the government of the day.

Should *Marbury v. Madison* and *Cooper v. Aaron* be understood in these terms?

6. Is Jacobsohn's argument one for avoiding self consciously foundational decisions? For judicial humility in a regime conflicted about fundamental tenets? Compare Jacobsohn's view of the benefits of "avoiding judgments of finality in the absence of a final settlement of regime" with *Casey* and *Roe* in chapter I.

---

4. HUNGARY AND SOUTH AFRICA ON THE DEATH PENALTY

The new constitutional courts of Hungary and of South Africa each broke ground by declaring their country's respective death penalty laws unconstitutional as one of their earliest acts.

a. *South Africa's Makwanyane Decision*: The Constitutional Court of South Africa, created by the transitional constitutional provisions of 1993, unanimously held the death sentence to be unconstitutional under that constitution. State v. Makwanyane, Case No CCT/3/94, 1995 (3) S.A.391, 1195 (4) BCLR 665 (CC) (June 6 1995).[aa] According to the Court's decision, the death penalty was debated in discussions of the interim constitution, which was the product of the Multi–Party Negotiating Process, whose final draft was adopted by Parliament. The failure to address the death penalty specifically in the constitution was "not accidental," and reflected a "Solomonic decision" that the constitutional court decide whether the death penalty was consistent with the basic rights of the Constitution.

Section 11(2) of that interim constitution prohibited "cruel, unhuman, or degrading treatment or punishment," while section 9 provided that "every person shall have the right to life," and section 10 that "every person shall have the right to respect for and protection of his or her dignity." Section 33(1) provided, (in terms similar to those of Section 1 of the Canadian Charter), that "any limitation on rights must be justifiable in an open and democratic society based on freedom and equality[;] must be both reasonable and necessary[;] and must not negate the essential content of the right."

The Court's opinion extensively analyzed court decisions, constitutional provisions and treaties of nations around the world, including India, Germany, the United States, and other countries of Europe and Africa (referring, inter alia, to *Soering*). It addressed the relevance of public opinion, which the court assumed would support capital punishment for

---

aa. The federal government of South Africa (which, by the time the case was argued in early 1995 was led by Nelson Mandela) conceded the unconstitutionality of the death penalty. The death penalty was supported by the state of Witwatersrand, which had brought the prosecution.

murder in South Africa; but, the Court said, public opinion "is no substitute for the duty vested in the Courts to interpret the Constitution and to uphold its provisions with fear or favour." Finding that the death penalty infringes on fundamental rights, it evaluated the necessity and reasonableness of the limitation (relying, *inter alia*, on Canada's *Oakes* test).

Turning to justifications for the death penalty for murder, the Court found the evidence did not support the conclusion that the death penalty deterred murder more than life imprisonment did. The Court also noted evidence that the death penalty was imposed arbitrarily. With respect to retribution, the Court wrote that while "punishment must be to some extent commensurate with the offence ... there is no requirement that it be equivalent or identical to it .... The state does not need to engage in the cold and calculated killing of murderers in order to express moral outrage at their conduct." It found an impairment of the essential content of the right:

> The rights to life and dignity are the most important of all human rights .... By committing ourselves to a society founded on the recognition of human rights we are required to value these two rights above all others .... This is not achieved by objectifying murderers and putting them to death to serve as an example to others .... Retribution cannot be accorded the same weight under our Constitution as the rights to life and dignity ....

In the ongoing process of drafting an entrenched constitution for the new South Africa, despite public opposition to the death penalty decision, the drafters did not overrule the Court's decision, possibly because of the experiences of oppressive justice that many in the liberation movement had suffered under apartheid. Lecture by Justice Albie Sachs, Georgetown University Law Center (Oct. 1996); Final Constitution of South Africa (1996).

b. *Hungary's Death Penalty Decision*: In its very first decision, the Hungarian Constitutional Court struck down that country's death penalty, by a 9:1 vote. The Death Penalty Case, Alkotmanybirosag [Constitutional Law Court] 107 1990 M.K., U.T. 1, 1 (Hung. 1990), cited in George P. Fletcher, *Searching for the Rule of Law in the Wake of Communism*, 1992 Brigham Young U. L. Rev. 145, 153 n.5. The Court acted, not on review of a criminal conviction and sentence to death as in South Africa, but on a complaint filed by a Hungarian law professor. While the Court appointed three experts to opine on the question, all three spoke against capital punishment. After hearing the experts in the morning, the Court returned in the afternoon and declared the death penalty invalid. The lone dissent argued that the decision to abolish the death penalty was one for the Parliament, and not the Constitutional Court.

As in South Africa, there was no text specifically addressing the death penalty in the amended Hungarian Constitution. According to Professor Fletcher, article 54(1) at the time provided that in Hungary, "everyone has the inherent right to life and human dignity of which no one shall be arbitrarily deprived. And no one shall be subject to torture or to cruel and inhumane or degrading treatment or punishment.... " The majority took the view that unless the death penalty were soundly supported by good reason, it would result in the arbitrary deprivation of life and thereby violate section 54(1). Focussing primarily on the claimed deterrent effects of the death penalty, the Court found an inadequate basis to uphold its use. One judge addressed the question of retribution, but argued that long terms of imprisonment would be sufficient to meet retributive interests. And Chief Justice Solyom, in another concurrence, took the position that the right to life was absolute, precluding state imposition of the death penalty.

As noted earlier in the materials, many speculate that the decision was motivated in part to aid Hungary's effort to be accepted into the Council of Europe, which reportedly had demanded that Hungary (1) establish an independent judiciary, (2) protect freedom of the press, (3) reduce pretrial detention time prior to appearance before a magistrate, and (4) abolish capital punishment.

Can one see these as potential "foundational" cases for Hungary's and South Africa's constitutional courts? Is the death penalty so touched with international concern (both in terms of potential sources of law and in terms of the expressed interests of other nations) that these court decisions should be regarded in some sense as compelled? Can they be regarded as "anti-government," in the sense used by Shamir?

D. ADJUDICATORY PROCEDURES

In this section we explore divergences and similarities in adjudicatory procedures in different constitutional court systems, and consider how these may relate both to the kinds of decisions the courts make and to the role of the constitutional court in the governing structures of the nation. What are the procedures for constitutional adjudication in the various forms of constitutional review? How, if at all, do the procedures relate to or affect the nature of constitutional review? We will consider differences in how, when and by whom constitutional cases are brought; how the courts obtain information on which to decide the cases; how quickly they act on the cases before them; and in what form they render their decisions.

Standing: Consider the effect of rules concerning who can invoke the jurisdiction of constitutional courts. U.S. justiciability doctrine tends to link limited concepts of standing with core notions of the judicial function. Contrast this with the prevalence of "abstract" review in Europe and its use, e.g., in the German abortion decision, or the French decision on free association of 1971.

Kommers claims that a benefit of the German "constitutional complaint" is to increase a sense of constitutionalism among citizens. Is this plausible? Would such a procedure increase popular commitment to judicial review? If so, is this good, or is it an unwise diversion of popular energy away from democratic political processes? Consider the situation in France, where, Bell asserts, because no political party was willing to make a referral to the Court of a proposed law on racism and anti-semitism, and only designated government actors can refer a bill, important constitutional questions (especially concerning the penalty of loss of civil rights) may not be decided.[ab]

Reporters: The role of "reporters," particularly in France, does not seem to have direct analog to U.S. constitutional adjudicatory procedures. Note the free-ranging authority of French reporters to obtain information. Consider whether in a U.S. case like Bowsher v. Synar,[ac] adjudication would be improved if the Chief Justice's law clerk functioned like a French reporter and, for example, called up heads of congressional committees to inquire how often Comptroller Generals had been threatened with removal or actually removed by Congress.

Specialization of expertise: In Germany, note the specialization of judges by different subject areas. The "vota" prepared by individual judges play a significant role in resolution of cases, generally without oral argument. This might be thought to resemble the process by which certiorari petitions are decided in the U.S. Supreme Court (based on a single memo prepared and circulated to most of the justices by one law clerk), but does not have a close analog to how argued cases are decided.[ad] For cases in which certiorari is granted, the justices in the U.S. individually review briefs, in some cases based on memos prepared by their own law clerks; hear oral argument; then meet in conference for an initial vote on how to decide the case; only then does the senior justice in the majority assign the opinion for writing and circulation to the others.

Opinion-writing: Different courts opinions reflect different conventions of opinion-writing. In U.S. constitutional history, Chief Justice John Marshall is credited with abandoning the British practice (reflected in the Canadian abortion decision in Chapter I) of "seriatim" opinions in which each justice states his/her opinion separately, in favor of "opinions of the Court." Thomas Jefferson criticized this innovation on the grounds that it deprived the people of knowledge of the actual views of each justice, and contributed to judicial laziness and undue power on the part of the justice (in that case, usually Marshall) writing the opinions. You have now seen a range of practices: In France, the decisions of the Conseil Constitutionnel

---

ab. Some suggest that, to vindicate individual rights, a system of diffuse, decentralized review, with individual complainants having access to constitutional courts, maximizes effectiveness, while the enforcement of structural allocations of power within a government can adequately be enforced through a single, centralized court whose jurisdiction can be invoked only by limited governmental parties. See Robert F. Utter & David C. Lundsgaard, *Judicial Review in the New Nations of Central and Eastern Europe*, 54 Ohio St. L. J. 559, 601 (1993).

ac. 478 U.S. 714 (1986) (invalidating the Gramm–Rudman law on the grounds that the Comptroller General, who played a key role in carrying out its budget reduction goals, was controlled by Congress in part through existence of removal power through means other than impeachment).

ad. Consider the role which discretion (as to which cases to decide on a plenary basis) plays in both the U.S. and German constitutional review system.

are short, and almost always unanimous. The German court's decisions are lengthy and usually do not have published dissents (though the abortion case did include a published dissent). Do these differences reflect anything significant about constitutional adjudication in different settings?

Speed of Decision: The time frame for constitutional adjudication also varies. In France, decisions generally issue between 8 and 30 days after a bill is referred; the speed may be seen as necessary because the Conseil functions, in some ways, as part of the ongoing legislative process. In the United States Supreme Court, which generally hears constitutional cases only after they have been in litigation for several months to several years in the lower courts, the time from a case being accepted for decision and the decision actually issuing is usually less than one year. In rare instances, e.g, the steel seizure case,[ae] the Nixon tapes case,[af] or the Pentagon Papers case[ag]—the Court will act with great speed, sometimes granting certiorari before judgment in the court of appeals, and rendering decision within days, or a few weeks, after argument.

---

1.   THE UNITED STATES SUPREME COURT: PROCEDURE AND JUSTICIABILITY

In the 1990s, the United States Supreme Court has been receiving over 6,000 petitions for certiorari (essentially requests to review a lower federal or state court judgment) each year. Of these it will typically "grant"—that is, agree to decide the merits of the case—fewer than 300. And of those reviewed on the merits, it will hear full argument on anywhere from 75–125 cases per year.

The certiorari jurisdiction is discretionary—that is, the justices decide which cases to decide. They do so according to a "rule of 4"—if four of the nine justices vote to hear a case, the case will be heard. The Court generally does not give reasons for the denial of certiorari, and denials of certiorari do not represent decisions on the merits; as a formal matter this means only that the Court decided not to hear the case. The Court is more likely to agree to hear a case involving the presence of a conflict in interpretation of federal law between two or more federal circuits or state courts, or the development of lower court decisions significantly at variance from what the Supreme Court believes the law should be, or lower court decisions that are markedly inconsistent with controlling Supreme Court decisions, or when the Solicitor General of the United States requests review. Cases in which there may be procedural obstacles to considering the federal question, or in which unusual fact patterns predominate, are unlikely to be granted.[ah] Cases that are filed "in forma pauperis (ifp)",—that is, without

---

ae. Youngstown Sheet & Tube Co. v. Sawyer, 343 U.S. 579 (1952).

af. United States v. Nixon, 418 U.S. 683 (1974)

ag. New York Times Co. v. United States, 403 U.S. 713 (1971).

ah. While many of the Court's well-known decisions concern issues of federal constitutional law, a significant number of cases each term deal solely with interpretations of federal statutes.

payment of the filing fees due to indigency—are much less likely to be found certworthy than are "paid" cases, a fact at least in part related to the fact that a much higher portion of the "ifp" cases are filed "pro se," that is, without a lawyer's assistance.

Most of the justices now on the Court rely on a "cert memo," to make at least preliminary decisions on the certiorari petitions. This memo is prepared by one of the law clerks employed by the justices. Given the volume of petitions many believe that the justices are not capable of individually reviewing each petition, and that, the justices' law clerks exercise substantial influence over this process. While most of the justices "pool" their law clerks so that each clerk writes fewer cert memos and can give greater attention to each, in each chambers the cert memos from the pool can be examined by the justice or her or his law clerks for an independent determination. At least some justices can determine from the brief "Question presented" in the very front of the cert petition that the case is not one warranting the grant of certiorari. See William F. Brennan, *The National Court of Appeals: Another Dissent*, 40 U. Chi. L. Rev. 473, 477–83 (1973). Unless a justice affirmatively designates a petition for certiorari for discussion by the Court as a whole, certiorari is denied.

If the Court decides to hear a case, it will set the case for briefing and oral argument. Typically there will have been prior judicial decisions and briefing of the issue in the case, as well as papers filed in the Supreme Court in connection with the cert petition. The parties to the case, and any amici, file briefs on the merits. Each justice's chambers prepares separately for the hearing of each case, with many justices having their law clerks prepare "bench memos" involving an extensive analysis of the parties contentions and of the relevant legal materials. Oral argument is usually one hour per case. The justices frequently ask many questions of counsel, who rarely are allowed to deliver prepared arguments.

After the arguments, the justices confer in a private conference and reach tentative decisions. The most senior justice in the majority assigns the writing of the opinion, but justices are free to write dissents, or separate concurrences, and frequently do so. Majority opinion assignments are most often made by the Chief Justice, who is automatically the most senior in any majority. While a number of factors influence opinion assignment, expertise plays a relatively small role, while securing a majority by assignment to the justice best able to draft an opinion that will be joined by four others, and achieving equality in the number of opinions assigned, are relatively important factors. Draft opinions are circulated within the Court until all of the justices are ready to release the opinion or set of opinions in the case, subject to the very strong constraint that the Court finish its business, and issue opinions, on all cases heard each "term" within that term. For a helpful treatment of the Supreme Court as an institution, see Susan Low Bloch & Thomas G. Krattenmaker, Supreme Court Politics: The Institution and Its Procedures (1994).

The Supreme Court, like all federal "article III" courts, can only decide "cases and controversies" within the meaning of article III. The Court has, since its early days, construed article III to limit its jurisdiction to matters of a "judiciary" nature. Thus, the Court refuses to give "advisory opinions" as discussed earlier, or to decide issues that are not "ripe,"[ai] or that have become "moot."[aj] The federal courts will not hear a claim that presents a "political question," see below, Chapter VII, nor one brought by a party who lacks "standing." Citizens generally do not have standing to challenge governmental acts or expenditures simply because they believe them to be unconstitutional. Rather, as the following case illustrates, litigants involving the jurisdiction of a federal court must show a legally cognizable personal injury sufficiently directly caused by the government conduct complained of.

Allen v. Wright

468 U.S. 737 (1984).

O'CONNOR, J. delivered the opinion of the Court, in which BURGER, C.J., and WHITE, POWELL, and REHNQUIST, JJ., joined. BRENNAN, J., filed a dissenting opinion, STEVENS, J., filed a dissenting opinion, in which BLACKMUN, J., joined. MARSHALL, J., took no part in the decision of the cases.

JUSTICE O'CONNOR delivered the opinion of the Court.

Parents of black public school children allege in this nation-wide class action that the Internal Revenue Service (IRS) has not adopted sufficient standards and procedures to fulfill its obligation to deny tax-exempt status to racially discriminatory private schools. They assert that the IRS thereby harms them directly and interferes with the ability of their children to receive an education in desegregated public schools. The issue before us is whether plaintiffs have standing to bring this suit. We hold that they do not.

I

The IRS denies tax-exempt status under §§ 501(a) and (c)(3) of the Internal Revenue Code, 26 U.S.C. §§ 501(a) and (c)(3)—and hence eligibility to receive charitable contributions deductible from income taxes—... to racially discriminatory private schools. Rev.Rul. 71–447, 1971–2 Cum.Bull. 230. The IRS policy requires that a school applying for tax-exempt status show that it "admits the students of any race to all the rights, privileges, programs, and activities generally accorded or made available to students at that school and that the school does not discriminate on the basis of race in administration of its educational policies, admissions policies, scholarship and loan programs, and athletic and other school-administered programs."

---

ai. See Poe v. Ullman, 367 U.S. 497 (1961) (refusing to hear challenge to Connecticut statute, ultimately struck down in Griswold, prohibiting use of contraceptives because there was no allegation that the state had threatened to prosecute under the statute).

aj. A case is moot if the court's judgment would come too late to affect the parties' legal interests. But compare *Roe* (where the Court found that because the abortion issue was one capable of repetition, yet evading appellate review, it could be decided).

To carry out this policy, the IRS has established guidelines and procedures for determining whether a particular school is in fact racially nondiscriminatory. Failure to comply with the guidelines "will ordinarily result in the proposed revocation of" tax-exempt status....

In 1976 respondents challenged these guidelines and procedures in a suit filed in Federal District Court against the Secretary of the Treasury and the Commissioner of Internal Revenue. The plaintiffs named in the complaint are parents of black children who, at the time the complaint was filed, were attending public schools in seven States in school districts undergoing desegregation. They brought this nationwide class action "on behalf of themselves and their children, and ... on behalf of all other parents of black children attending public school systems undergoing, or which may in the future undergo, desegregation pursuant to court order [or] HEW regulations and guidelines, under state law, or voluntarily." They estimated that the class they seek to represent includes several million persons.

Respondents allege in their complaint that many racially segregated private schools were created or expanded in their communities at the time the public schools were undergoing desegregation. According to the complaint, many such private schools, including 17 schools or school systems identified by name in the complaint (perhaps some 30 schools in all), receive tax exemptions either directly or through the tax-exempt status of "umbrella" organizations that operate or support the schools. Respondents allege that, despite the IRS policy of denying tax-exempt status to racially discriminatory private schools and despite the IRS guidelines and procedures for implementing that policy, some of the tax-exempt racially segregated private schools created or expanded in desegregating districts in fact have racially discriminatory policies. ...Respondents allege that the IRS grant of tax exemptions to such racially discriminatory schools is unlawful.[12]

Respondents allege that the challenged Government conduct harms them in two ways. The challenged conduct

"(a) constitutes tangible federal financial aid and other support for racially segregated educational institutions, and

"(b) fosters and encourages the organization, operation and expansion of institutions providing racially segregated educational opportunities for white children avoiding attendance in desegregating public school districts and thereby interferes with the efforts of federal courts, HEW and local school authorities to desegregate public school districts which have been operating racially dual school systems."

Thus, respondents do not allege that their children have been the victims of discriminatory exclusion from the schools whose tax exemptions they challenge as unlawful. Indeed, they have not alleged at any stage of

---

12. ...Last Term, in Bob Jones University v. United States, 461 U.S. 574 (1983), the Court concluded that racially discriminatory private schools do not qualify for a tax exemption under § 501(c)(3) of the Internal Revenue Code.

this litigation that their children have ever applied or would ever apply to any private school. Rather, respondents claim a direct injury from the mere fact of the challenged Government conduct and, as indicated by the restriction of the plaintiff class to parents of children in desegregating school districts, injury to their children's opportunity to receive a desegregated education. The latter injury is traceable to the IRS grant of tax exemptions to racially discriminatory schools, respondents allege, chiefly because contributions to such schools are deductible from income taxes under §§ 170(a)(1) and (c)(2) of the Internal Revenue Code and the "deductions facilitate the raising of funds to organize new schools and expand existing schools in order to accommodate white students avoiding attendance in desegregating public school districts." . . .

II

A

Article III of the Constitution confines the federal courts to adjudicating actual "cases" and "controversies." As the Court explained in Valley Forge Christian College v. Americans United for Separation of Church and State, Inc., 454 U.S. 464, 471–476 (1982), the "case or controversy" requirement defines with respect to the Judicial Branch the idea of separation of powers on which the Federal Government is founded. The several doctrines that have grown up to elaborate that requirement are "founded in concern about the proper—and properly limited—role of the courts in a democratic society." Warth v. Seldin, 422 U.S. 490, 498 (1975).

> "All of the doctrines that cluster about Article III—not only standing but mootness, ripeness, political question, and the like—relate in part, and in different though overlapping ways, to an idea, which is more than an intuition but less than a rigorous and explicit theory, about the constitutional and prudential limits to the powers of an unelected, unrepresentative judiciary in our kind of government." Vander Jagt v. O'Neill, 699 F.2d 1166, 1178–1179 (1982) (Bork, J., concurring).

The case-or-controversy doctrines state fundamental limits on federal judicial power in our system of government.

The Art. III doctrine that requires a litigant to have "standing" to invoke the power of a federal court is perhaps the most important of these doctrines. "In essence the question of standing is whether the litigant is entitled to have the court decide the merits of the dispute or of particular issues." Warth v. Seldin, supra, at 498. Standing doctrine embraces several judicially self-imposed limits on the exercise of federal jurisdiction, such as the general prohibition on a litigant's raising another person's legal rights, the rule barring adjudication of generalized grievances more appropriately addressed in the representative branches, and the requirement that a plaintiff's complaint fall within the zone of interests protected by the law invoked. See *Valley Forge*, at 474–475. The requirement of standing, however, has a core component derived directly from the Constitution. A plaintiff must allege personal injury fairly traceable to the defendant's allegedly unlawful conduct and likely to be redressed by the requested relief. . . .

. . . [T]he standing inquiry requires careful judicial examination of a complaint's allegations to ascertain whether the particular plaintiff is entitled to an adjudication of the particular claims asserted. Is the injury too abstract, or otherwise not appropriate, to be considered judicially cognizable? Is the line of causation between the illegal conduct and injury too attenuated? Is the prospect of obtaining relief from the injury as a result of a favorable ruling too speculative? These questions and any others relevant to the standing inquiry must be answered by reference to the Art. III notion that federal courts may exercise power only "in the last resort, and as a necessity," and only when adjudication is "consistent with a system of separated powers and [the dispute is one] traditionally thought to be capable of resolution through the judicial process. . . . "

B

Respondents allege two injuries in their complaint to support their standing to bring this lawsuit. First, they say that they are harmed directly by the mere fact of Government financial aid to discriminatory private schools. Second, they say that the federal tax exemptions to racially discriminatory private schools in their communities impair their ability to have their public schools desegregated. . . .

1

Respondents' first claim of injury can be interpreted in two ways. It might be a claim simply to have the Government avoid the violation of law alleged in respondents' complaint. Alternatively, it might be a claim of stigmatic injury, or denigration, suffered by all members of a racial group when the Government discriminates on the basis of race. Under neither interpretation is this claim of injury judicially cognizable.

This Court has repeatedly held that an asserted right to have the Government act in accordance with law is not sufficient, standing alone, to confer jurisdiction on a federal court. In Schlesinger v. Reservists Committee to Stop the War, 418 U.S. 208 (1974), for example, the Court rejected a claim of citizen standing to challenge Armed Forces Reserve commissions held by Members of Congress as violating the Incompatibility Clause of Art. I, § 6, of the Constitution. As citizens, the Court held, plaintiffs alleged nothing but "the abstract injury in nonobservance of the Constitution. . . . " More recently, in *Valley Forge*, we rejected a claim of standing to challenge a Government conveyance of property to a religious institution. Insofar as the plaintiffs relied simply on " 'their shared individuated right' " to a Government that made no law respecting an establishment of religion, . . . we held that plaintiffs had not alleged a judicially cognizable injury. "[Assertion] of a right to a particular kind of Government conduct, which the Government has violated by acting differently, cannot alone satisfy the requirement of Art. III without draining those requirements of meaning." Respondents here have no standing to complain simply that their Government is violating the law.

Neither do they have standing to litigate their claims based on the stigmatizing injury often caused by racial discrimination. There can be no doubt that this sort of noneconomic injury is one of the most serious consequences of discriminatory government action and is sufficient in some circumstances to support standing. See Heckler v. Mathews, 465 U.S. 728, 739–740 (1984). Our cases make clear, however, that such injury accords a basis for standing only to "those persons who are personally denied equal treatment" by the challenged discriminatory conduct.

In Moose Lodge No. 107 v. Irvis, 407 U.S. 163 (1972), the Court held that the plaintiff had no standing to challenge a club's racially discriminatory membership policies because he had never applied for membership. . . . Insofar as their first claim of injury is concerned, respondents are in exactly the same position: . . . they do not allege a stigmatic injury suffered as a direct result of having personally been denied equal treatment.

. . . If the abstract stigmatic injury were cognizable, standing would extend nationwide to all members of the particular racial groups against which the Government was alleged to be discriminating by its grant of a tax exemption to a racially discriminatory school, regardless of the location of that school. All such persons could claim the same sort of abstract stigmatic injury respondents assert in their first claim of injury. A black person in Hawaii could challenge the grant of a tax exemption to a racially discriminatory school in Maine. Recognition of standing in such circumstances would transform the federal courts into "no more than a vehicle for the vindication of the value interests of concerned bystanders." Constitutional limits on the role of the federal courts preclude such a transformation.

2

It is in their complaint's second claim of injury that respondents allege harm to a concrete, personal interest that can support standing in some circumstances. The injury they identify—their children's diminished ability to receive an education in a racially integrated school—is, beyond any doubt, not only judicially cognizable but, as shown by cases from Brown v. Board of Education, 347 U.S. 483 (1954), to Bob Jones University v. United States, 461 U.S. 574 (1983), one of the most serious injuries recognized in our legal system. Despite the constitutional importance of curing the injury alleged by respondents, however, the federal judiciary may not redress it unless standing requirements are met. In this case, respondents' second claim of injury cannot support standing because the injury alleged is not fairly traceable to the Government conduct respondents challenge as unlawful.

The illegal conduct challenged by respondents is the IRS's grant of tax exemptions to some racially discriminatory schools. The line of causation between that conduct and desegregation of respondents' schools is attenuated at best. From the perspective of the IRS, the injury to respondents is highly indirect and "results from the independent action of some third party not before the court," Simon v. Eastern Kentucky Welfare Rights Org., 426 U.S., at 42 . . . .

The diminished ability of respondents' children to receive a desegregated education would be fairly traceable to unlawful IRS grants of tax exemptions only if there were enough racially discriminatory private schools receiving tax exemptions in respondents' communities for withdrawal of those exemptions to make an appreciable difference in public school integration. Respondents have made no such allegation. It is, first, uncertain how many racially discriminatory private schools are in fact receiving tax exemptions. Moreover, it is entirely speculative, as respondents themselves conceded in the Court of Appeals, . . . whether withdrawal of a tax exemption from any particular school would lead the school to change its policies. . . . It is just as speculative whether any given parent of a child attending such a private school would decide to transfer the child to public school as a result of any changes in educational or financial policy made by the private school once it was threatened with loss of tax-exempt status. It is also pure speculation whether, in a particular community, a large enough number of the numerous relevant school officials and parents would reach decisions that collectively would have a significant impact on the racial composition of the public schools.

The links in the chain of causation between the challenged Government conduct and the asserted injury are far too weak for the chain as a whole to sustain respondents' standing. In Simon v. Eastern Kentucky Welfare Rights Org. the Court held that standing to challenge a Government grant of a tax exemption to hospitals could not be founded on the asserted connection between the grant of tax-exempt status and the hospitals' policy concerning the provision of medical services to indigents. The causal connection depended on the decisions hospitals would make in response to withdrawal of tax-exempt status, and those decisions were sufficiently uncertain to break the chain of causation between the plaintiffs' injury and the challenged Government action. . . . The chain of causation is even weaker in this case. It involves numerous third parties (officials of racially discriminatory schools receiving tax exemptions and the parents of children attending such schools) who may not even exist in respondents' communities and whose independent decisions may not collectively have a significant effect on the ability of public school students to receive a desegregated education.

The idea of separation of powers that underlies standing doctrine explains why our cases preclude the conclusion that respondents' alleged injury "fairly can be traced to the challenged action" of the IRS. Simon v. Eastern Kentucky Welfare Rights Org., at 41. That conclusion would pave the way generally for suits challenging, not specifically identifiable Government violations of law, but the particular programs agencies establish to carry out their legal obligations. Such suits, even when premised on allegations of several instances of violations of law, are rarely if ever appropriate for federal-court adjudication. . . .

[T]he idea of separation of powers ... counsels against recognizing standing in a case brought, not to enforce specific legal obligations whose violation works a direct harm, but to seek a restructuring of the apparatus established by the Executive Branch to fulfill its legal duties. The Constitution, after all, assigns to the Executive Branch, and not to the Judicial Branch, the duty to "take Care that the Laws be faithfully executed." U.S. Const., Art. II, § 3. We could not recognize respondents' standing in this case without running afoul of that structural principle. ...

[The dissenting opinion by JUSTICE BRENNAN is omitted.]

JUSTICE STEVENS, with whom JUSTICE BLACKMUN joins, dissenting.

Three propositions are clear to me: (1) respondents have adequately alleged "injury in fact"; (2) their injury is fairly traceable to the conduct that they claim to be unlawful; and (3) the "separation of powers" principle does not create a jurisdictional obstacle to the consideration of the merits of their claim.

I

Respondents, the parents of black school-children, have alleged that their children are unable to attend fully desegregated schools because large numbers of white children in the areas in which respondents reside attend private schools which do not admit minority children. The Court, Justice Brennan, and I all agree that this is an adequate allegation of "injury in fact." The Court is quite correct when it writes:

> "The injury they identify—their children's diminished ability to receive an education in a racially integrated school—is, beyond any doubt, not only judicially cognizable but, as shown by cases from Brown v. Board of Education, to Bob Jones University v. United States, one of the most serious injuries recognized in our legal system."

This kind of injury may be actionable whether it is caused by the exclusion of black children from public schools or by an official policy of encouraging white children to attend nonpublic schools. A subsidy for the withdrawal of a white child can have the same effect as a penalty for admitting a black child.

II

In final analysis, the wrong respondents allege that the Government has committed is to subsidize the exodus of white children from schools that would otherwise be racially integrated. The critical question in these cases, therefore, is whether respondents have alleged that the Government has created that kind of subsidy. ...

An organization that qualifies for preferential treatment under § 501(c)(3) of the Internal Revenue Code, because it is "operated exclusively for ... charitable ... purposes," is exempt from paying federal income taxes, and under § 170 of the Code, persons who contribute to such organizations may deduct the amount of their contributions when calculating their taxable income. Only last Term we explained the effect of this preferential treatment:

> "Both tax exemptions and tax deductibility are a form of subsidy that is administered through the tax system. A tax exemption has much the same effect as a cash grant to the organization of the amount of tax it would have to pay on its income. Deductible contributions are similar to cash grants of the amount of a portion of the individual's contributions." Regan v. Taxation With Representation of Washington, 461 U.S. 540, 544 (1983) (footnote omitted).

The purpose of this scheme, like the purpose of any subsidy, is to promote the activity subsidized; the statutes "seek to achieve the same basic goal of encouraging the development of certain organizations through the grant of tax benefits." Bob Jones University v. United States. If the granting of preferential tax treatment would "encourage" private segregated schools to conduct their "charitable" activities, it must follow that the withdrawal of the treatment would "discourage" them, and hence promote the process of desegregation....

This causation analysis is nothing more than a restatement of elementary economics: when something becomes more expensive, less of it will be purchased. Sections 170 and 501(c)(3) are premised on that recognition. If racially discriminatory private schools lose the "cash grants" that flow from the operation of the statutes, the education they provide will become more expensive and hence less of their services will be purchased. Conversely, maintenance of these tax benefits makes an education in segregated private schools relatively more attractive, by decreasing its cost. Accordingly, without tax-exempt status, private schools will either not be competitive in terms of cost, or have to change their admissions policies, hence reducing their competitiveness for parents seeking "a racially segregated alternative" to public schools, which is what respondents have alleged many white parents in desegregating school districts seek. In either event the process of desegregation will be advanced ... [because] the withdrawal of the subsidy for segregated schools means the incentive structure facing white parents who seek such schools for their children will be altered. Thus, the laws of economics, not to mention the laws of Congress embodied in §§ 170 and 501(c)(3), compel the conclusion that the injury respondents have alleged—the increased segregation of their children's schools because of the ready availability of private schools that admit whites only—will be redressed if these schools' operations are inhibited through the denial of preferential tax treatment.

III

Considerations of tax policy, economics, and pure logic all confirm the conclusion that respondents' injury in fact is fairly traceable to the Government's allegedly wrongful conduct. The Court therefore is forced to introduce the concept of "separation of powers" into its analysis. The Court writes that the separation of powers "explains why our cases preclude the conclusion" that respondents' injury is fairly traceable to the conduct they challenge.

The Court could mean one of three things by its invocation of the separation of powers. First, it could simply be expressing the idea that if the plaintiff lacks Art. III standing to bring a lawsuit, then there is no "case or controversy" within the meaning of Art. III and hence the matter is not within the area of responsibility assigned to the Judiciary by the Constitution.... While there can be no quarrel with this proposition, in itself it provides no guidance for determining if the injury respondents have alleged is fairly traceable to the conduct they have challenged.

Second, the Court could be saying that it will require a more direct causal connection when it is troubled by the separation of powers implications of the case before it. That approach confuses the standing doctrine with the justiciability of the issues that respondents seek to raise. The purpose of the standing inquiry is to measure the plaintiff's stake in the outcome, not whether a court has the authority to provide it with the outcome it seeks....

Thus, the " 'fundamental aspect of standing' is that it focuses primarily on the party seeking to get his complaint before the federal court rather than 'on the issues he wishes to have adjudicated,' " United States v. Richardson. The strength of the plaintiff's interest in the outcome has nothing to do with whether the relief it seeks would intrude upon the prerogatives of other branches of government; the possibility that the relief might be inappropriate does not lessen the plaintiff's stake in obtaining that relief.... Imposing an undefined but clearly more rigorous standard for redressability for reasons unrelated to the causal nexus between the injury and the challenged conduct can only encourage undisciplined, ad hoc litigation, a result that would be avoided if the Court straight-forwardly considered the justiciability of the issues respondents seek to raise, rather than using those issues to obfuscate standing analysis.

Third, the Court could be saying that it will not treat as legally cognizable injuries that stem from an administrative decision concerning how enforcement resources will be allocated. This surely is an important point. Respondents do seek to restructure the IRS's mechanisms for enforcing the legal requirement that discriminatory institutions not receive tax-exempt status. Such restructuring would dramatically affect the way in which the IRS exercises its prosecutorial discretion. The Executive requires latitude to decide how best to enforce the law, and in general the Court may well be correct that the exercise of that discretion, especially in the tax context, is unchallengeable.

However, as the Court also recognizes, this principle does not apply when suit is brought "to enforce specific legal obligations whose violation works a direct harm." For example, despite the fact that they were challenging the methods used by the Executive to enforce the law, citizens were accorded standing to challenge a pattern of police misconduct that violated the constitutional constraints on law enforcement activities in Allee v. Medrano, 416 U.S. 802 (1974). Here, respondents contend that the

IRS is violating a specific constitutional limitation on its enforcement discretion. There is a solid basis for that contention. . . .

Respondents contend that [under past court decisions] . . . the IRS cannot provide "cash grants" to discriminatory schools through preferential tax treatment without running afoul of a constitutional duty to refrain from "giving significant aid" to these institutions. Similarly, respondents claim that the Internal Revenue Code itself, as construed in *Bob Jones*, constrains enforcement discretion.[2] It has been clear since Marbury v. Madison, that "[i]t is emphatically the province and duty of the judicial department to say what the law is." Deciding whether the Treasury has violated a specific legal limitation on its enforcement discretion does not intrude upon the prerogatives of the Executive, for in so deciding we are merely saying "what the law is." Surely the question whether the Constitution or the Code limits enforcement discretion is one within the Judiciary's competence, and I do not believe that the question whether the law, as enunciated in [earlier cases], imposes such an obligation upon the IRS is so insubstantial that respondents' attempt to raise it should be defeated for lack of subject-matter jurisdiction on the ground that it infringes the Executive's prerogatives.

In short, I would deal with the question of the legal limitations on the IRS's enforcement discretion on its merits, rather than by making the untenable assumption that the granting of preferential tax treatment to segregated schools does not make those schools more attractive to white students and hence does not inhibit the process of desegregation. I respectfully dissent.

———————

Questions and Comments

1. In what ways could standing doctrine help identify the best plaintiffs, from among a variety of people whose interests are affected by a challenged government policy, or protect the interests of those not before the Court but likely to be affected by its decisions? In what respect does standing

2. In *Bob Jones* we clearly indicated that the Internal Revenue Code not only permits but in fact requires the denial of tax-exempt status to racially discriminatory private schools:

"Few social or political issues in our history have been more vigorously debated and more extensively ventilated than the issue of racial discrimination, particularly in education. Given the stress and anguish of the history of efforts to escape from the shackles of the 'separate but equal' doctrine of Plessy v. Ferguson, 163 U.S. 537 (1896), it cannot be said

that educational institutions that, for whatever reasons, practice racial discrimination, are institutions exercising 'beneficial and stabilizing influences in community life,' Walz v. Tax Comm'n, 397 U.S. 664, 673 (1970), or should be encouraged by having all taxpayers share in their support by way of special tax status.

"There can thus be no question that the interpretation of § 170 and § 501(c)(3) announced by the IRS in 1970 was correct. . . ."

doctrine simply prevent the Court from reviewing the acts, or omissions, of other branches of government? To what extent is this appropriate?

2. Under U.S. standing doctrine, it is far easier to challenge government action when you are the object of government enforcement than where you are complaining of government's failure to act. See Linda R.S. v. Richard D., 410 U.S. 614 (1973) (unwed mother of an illegitimate child lacked standing to enjoin state's discriminatory failure to prosecute fathers of illegitimate children for support); United States v. Richardson, 418 U.S. 166 (1974) (taxpayer lacked standing to challenge section of Central Intelligence Agency Act of 1949, providing that CIA expenditures not be made public, as inconsistent with Article I, Section 9 of the Constitution which requires a "regular statement of the Receipts and Expenditures of all public Money [to] be published from time to time;" plaintiff's claim was a mere "generalized grievance," "common to all members of the public ... he [the plaintiff taxpayer] is in [no] danger of suffering any particular concrete injury as a result of the operation of this statute.")[ak] Compare the German Abortion decisions ruling on minority legislators' views that laws did not go far enough in condemning abortion.

3. The U.S. Supreme Court has not been receptive to "congressional standing" to challenge the enactment or nonenactment of laws. See, e.g., Raines v. Byrd, 117 S.Ct. 1489 (1997). Legislative standing is commonplace in abstract review systems. Are there differences between the U.S. and European systems that make it "necessary" in the U.S. to avoid legislative standing? Is this a falsely felt sense of necessity? How to tell?

4. What is the effect (if any) of the Court's standing doctrine on the legitimacy of judicial review?

---

2. FRANCE AND THE CONSEIL CONSTITUTIONNEL

John Bell, FRENCH CONSTITUTIONAL LAW (1992) (excerpts from pp. 41–56)

Procedure and Methods of Working in the Conseil constitutionnel. Since the Conseil is not formally a court, its procedures are not fully judicial, and in many ways they resemble those of an administrative inquiry. There is no set of procedural rules, other than the exiguous organic law contained in the *ordonnance* of 7 November 1958. The fact that members of the Conseil are bound to secrecy about their deliberations has led to an air of secrecy about the way in which it functions. The following description of the

ak. In *Richardson*, the Court further commented that if its conclusion meant that no one would suffer such injury, and thus that no one could challenge the statute in court, this would not be troubling. It would simply mean that

> "the subject matter is committed to the surveillance of Congress, and ultimately to the political process. Any other conclusion would mean that the Founding Fathers intended to set up something in the

nature of an Athenian democracy or a New England town meeting to oversee the conduct of the National Government by means of lawsuits in federal courts. The Constitution created a representative Government with the representatives directly responsible to their constituents at stated periods of two, four and six years ... Lack of standing ... does not impair the right to assert ... views in the political forum or at the polls."

procedure draws on a number of disparate remarks in the literature, and on discussions with members of the Conseil and especially of its legal service.

The procedure before the Conseil varies significantly depending on the task in hand. It is most judicial when dealing with electoral disputes, and least judicial when dealing with the declassification of *lois* under article 37 § 2.

Acting as an election court for parliamentary elections, the Conseil operates very much like the Conseil d'Etat when it deals with disputed local elections. Here the *ordonnance* of 7 November 1958 is at its fullest, providing fourteen detailed articles on the procedure to be adopted.

Within ten days of the election result, any candidate or elector for the constituency concerned may present a petition by way of a letter to the Conseil, or to the local prefect, or to his or her equivalent, setting out the grounds of complaint. For election matters, the Conseil then divides into sections of three members, chosen by lot, who are assisted by associate reporters selected from the Conseil d'État or the Cour des comptes on an annual basis. One of the associate reporters is appointed to act as reporter *(rapporteur)* on the particular petition. His task is to provide the analysis of facts and rules on which the section can prepare a report for discussion by the whole Conseil. This process of *instruction* is closely modelled on the procedure of the Conseil d'État.* Petitions that are inadmissible for some reason—because the petitioner is not an elector of that constituency, for example—or that clearly cannot affect the result of the election can be rejected without *instruction*. In other cases the reporter will collate the allegations and any observations from the elected deputy or senator. The section can conduct hearings under oath, and can require the communication of any official document relating to the election. A member of the Conseil or the reporter may be sent to conduct a site inspection. The results of these enquiries are provided to the parties concerned, who then make their observations (with or without the help of lawyers). Once the *instruction* is complete, the report is presented to the Conseil. Only members of the Conseil have a vote, though the reporter may present cases to the meeting.

It is clear that here the Conseil is operating much as any administrative court, with all the safeguards of hearing both sides.

---

* [Editors' Note: The Conseil d'État is the highest court in France for review of administrative or executive action. Dating back to the 1799 constitution (though conceived originally as an administrative organ, not a court), it is now a court of specialized jurisdiction to review the legality of the acts of public officials and employees (other than the constitutionality of enacted laws). The Conseil d'État also provides advice to the Government on the constitutionality of bills before they are submitted to parliament, in which capacity it studies the decisions of the Conseil Constitutionnel. The Conseil d'État has also evolved "general principles of law" that it applies to constrain interpretation of statutes that trench on fundamental rights, and to assure the validity of decrees enacted by executive order. See Mauro Cappelletti & William Cohen, Comparative Constitutional Law 29–45 (1979); L. Neville Brown & John S. Bell, French Administrative Law (4th ed. 1993).]

The rules on the procedure for referring legislative texts are more exiguous. The *ordonnance* of 7 November 1958 merely states who should transmit the text, who should be notified in the case of a reference made by members of Parliament, and that decisions should be reasoned. For the rest, it is a matter of practice and personalities, both of which have changed over time.

... [Notification of a reference] is only formally required where a reference is made by sixty senators or deputies, so that the office-holders— the President of the Republic, the Prime Minister, the President of the National Assembly, and the President of the Senate—are aware of this and can make observations.

The Conseil must reach its decision within a short period of time. This is normally one month, though it can be reduced to eight days where the Government claims that it is a matter of urgency. The issue of who is to judge "urgency" has never been put to the test, and is left obscure by both the Constitution and by the *ordonnance*. In practice, there is a *gentleman's agreement* not to use this procedure, and it was only officially requested in one case between 1981 and 1986 (the second decision on *nationalizations* in 1982). Usually, the Secretary–General of the Conseil and the Secretary–General of the Government come to an arrangement about the time-scale for decision. It is notable that the urgency procedure was not invoked in the case of the *Urgency Law for New Caledonia* in January 1985, when the Conseil took barely twenty-four hours to make its decision. Equally, at the Government's request, the Conseil published its first decision on *Nationalizations* on a Saturday, when the Stock Exchange was closed, since the decision was bound to affect dealings in the companies in question.

There is no requirement that the President should wait to see whether there will be a reference before promulgating the *loi*. This can lead to nervousness on the part of members of Parliament that the text will be promulgated before a reference can be made, and this results in a number of stratagems. The most extreme came with the *Urgency Law for New Caledonia*, where a courier was stationed outside the Conseil with a reference already signed. When the final vote on the text had been taken in Parliament, he was contacted on citizens' band radio and promptly marched in to present the reference. It is more usual for the text of the reference to be discussed in the parliamentary group of the party wishing to make a reference, and then signed by the requisite number of deputies or senators, before the final vote is taken on the text. Because the reference has been drawn up before the bill has been approved by Parliament, it can happen that it complains about articles that are not in the final text of the *loi*.

The reference can take the form of a single letter or several letters from individual deputies or senators; the Conseil only counts the first sixty, to reach the requisite number. It is usually reasoned, setting out grounds for challenging particular articles of the *loi,* but, as in the case of the *Associations Law* of 1971, the letter may simply request the Conseil to examine the constitutionality of the whole text. In addition, the party leader may submit a memorandum containing more detailed arguments; this occurred in the *Vehicle Searches* case of 1977, for instance. These days the references are usually well reasoned, and are often based on legal arguments drawn up by consultants (frequently professors of constitutional law). They may, at times, be excessively inventive in argumentation. Since 1983, the text of the reference has often been published in the *Journal officiel.* . . .

The Conseil considers itself free to examine any part of the text, not merely the specific articles contained in the reference. Since the decision certifies the constitutionality of the *loi,* the Conseil considers that it has the right to raise issues ex officio. This was done, for example, in the *Feminine Quotas* case of 1982, where the article of the electoral law providing for a minimum of 25 per cent of candidates of each sex on the lists for local elections was struck down as unconstitutional, even though this point was not discussed in the reference. On the whole, issues are only raised ex officio where there is an obvious and serious question of unconstitutionality. This practice has become more frequent in recent years, rising from one decision in twenty, between 1974 and 1981, to one in ten between 1981 and 1986, one in three in 1986–7, and one in five from 1987 to 1989, and there were twelve such arguments raised by the Conseil ex officio in 1989–90.

The short time-scale for deliberation, and the limited scope of the argumentation in the reference may require the Conseil to do a lot of work very quickly. Quite sensibly, the Conseil has developed a practice of jumping the gun. When a bill is presented to Parliament, opponents will usually move a motion that it or some of its articles are unconstitutional, and are thus out of order, and will set out the reasons for this view. The Government will provide a reasoned reply to the motion, thereby making sure that the basic issues have been aired. Such motions put the Conseil on alert, and the President may well then decide to appoint a reporter to start work, building up the file on the potential reference. The choice of reporter is at the discretion of the President. Attention will be paid to a reasonable distribution of the work-load, but also to the expertise of particular members. Although the identity of the reporter is not officially made public, it is known that Chatenet and Lecourt acted as reporters on European Community matters, Segalat on finance bills, Gros on broadcasting laws, and Vedel on nationalizations (1982), university professors (1984), privatizations (1986), the Competition Council (1987), and the press (1984 and 1986).

The file will be built up by the reporter, acting usually with the help of the Secretary–General (an expert lawyer) and the small legal service under him. This will consist initially of three elements. First, there are the legal texts (constitutional and otherwise) on this particular area, to show the context and scope of the contested provisions. Secondly, there are the parliamentary debates, with special attention to the arguments on constitutionality developed at different stages in the parliamentary proceedings (the Conseil is equipped to listen into parliamentary debates at any time). Thirdly, there will be other materials, such as case-law in the public or private law courts, doctrinal legal writings, or memorandums produced by the legal service to help the reporter (which can be more or less detailed). The advice that the Conseil d'État gives on a Government bill is not published, and there is no formal mechanism for it to be transmitted to the Conseil constitutionnel. Nevertheless, since a member of the Conseil d'État is likely to be on either the Conseil constitutionnel or its legal staff, no difficulty is usually encountered in obtaining the text of the advice. Depending on the personality and legal expertise of the reporter, the Secretary–General and the legal service may well have an important role in the preparation of the file and in the drafting of the text of the decision presented to the Conseil. (It is not, however, unknown for a reporter to seek legal advice from outside the Conseil's staff.)

Once a formal reference has been made, the reporter will have a precise set of grounds to work from, though they will be almost identical to points made earlier. The text of the reference is sent to the Secretary-General of the Government, who will usually provide observations on it or on the *loi* in general. These observations do not represent a full defence. As a recent Secretary–General has written: "The written observations presented by the Secretary–General of the Government in no way constitute a memorandum in defence. Most often, they remain limited to replying to questions asked by the member of the Conseil constitutionnel designated as reporter during a working meeting held at the Conseil constitutionnel." Since 1986, this memorandum has been sent to the authors of the reference, so that they can make comments. All the same, there is not the same kind of hearing of each side that occurs in disputes over electoral matters.

The reporter remains master of the procedure. He may consult or listen to whomsoever he likes, and take note of whatever he wishes. It is up to him how much of what he learns in this way is communicated to his colleagues when the Conseil meets. He may often confer with the reporters of the parliamentary committees that examined the bill. On 3 June 1986 Badinter suggested that this might be formalized, and that the reporters might be consulted officially. This proposal was rejected by the Presidents of both chambers on the ground that the committee reporters had no standing to speak on behalf of the whole chamber. All the same, the practice is of some importance. The authors of the reference and the Secretary–General of the Government may well be called to meetings with the reporter, so that he can clarify issues. In addition, others may be invited to attend or may seek an audience. Pressure groups may telephone the reporter at home or invite him out to lunch. For example, in the *Nationalizations* case some of the directors of the affected companies were seen by the reporter. Interested persons may write letters to the reporter, and he makes such use of them as he considers fit. These are not necessarily referred to in the *visas* (the introductory phrases beginning "Vu ...") of the decision.[80] The point is that, like an administrator compiling a

---

80. See the letter of the Green party (*Les Verts*) to the Conseil constitutionnel concerning a provision in a *loi* submitted to it that permitted new tourist developments in mountain regions: *Le Monde*, 17 July 1990. Although the Conseil constitutionnel annulled the provision criticized by *Les Verts* (art. 16) ex officio. and even though it was

dossier, the reporter follows up all interesting leads until he considers that he has seen all sides of the question.

Reporters work in different ways: some very much on their own, others discussing matters with the legal service, and others discussing with colleagues. Since not all of them are in Paris, this last may be difficult to arrange much before the decision-making meetings. The President of the Conseil may play an important part. He may keep in touch with a reporter to see how things are going, and may suggest meetings of a few members from time to time. (Unlike members of the Conseil d'État, members of the Conseil constitutionnel have their own individual offices, and may well thus work on site.) The President may prefer just to have an occasional lunch with the reporter or with other members of the Conseil. Other Presidents have left reporters very much on their own. Although he does not act as a reporter himself, the President may well secure a good sense of how the draft judgment is going to look, and may seek to influence its content. But he is not typically a dominant figure among so many authoritative individuals. One former member of the Conseil, [F. Goguel] wrote:

> In truth, important though the role of its President is in the functioning of the Conseil constitutionnel, this is only through the climate that he creates between its members, by the tone that he contributes to deliberations, and by the way in which he conducts these. This role includes no interference with the judgment of each of the Conseil's members. It would be altogether wrong to contrast the Gaston Palewski case-law or the Roger Frey case-law with the case-law of Léon Noël: there is only a case-law of the Conseil constitutionnel, the development of which is explained essentially by the widening of the grounds on which references are made.

The reporter produces a draft judgment, which is circulated to all members of the Conseil at least one day before the decision-making meeting. These other members may also receive a general file from the Secretary–General setting out the legal texts, the parliamentary debates, and other matters that the reporter considers would be useful.

The actual decision-making occurs in the meeting-room of the Conseil, part of the Palais–Royal fitted out for Napoleon III's sister. Only members of the Conseil attend, and no minutes are kept. The report is discussed, and votes, if necessary, are taken after that. No time-limit is set on discussion, and some cases take more than one day (hence they have two dates in their official reference). It is not generally known how people vote. It is known that the Conseil split 6 to 4 on the *Referendum Law* decision, and that it split 4 to 4 on the *Séguin Amendment*. However, it is reliably said that unanimous decisions are common, and that members do not necessarily vote in the way that their party allegiances might suggest. Once they are in the Conseil, with no political future ahead of them, they can act as free

---

not challenged by the authors of the formal reference, commentators are skeptical of any link between the letter of *Les Verts* and the willingness of the Conseil to challenge the provision of its own motion: see Favoreu and Renoux, *RFDC* 1990, 730, and J.-C. Douence, *RFDA* 1991, 346 . . . .

agents. In any case, the dynamics of collective decision-making, free from the public gaze, may produce different pressures from those in a politicized forum.

When the Government wishes to legislate by way of decree, using its powers under article 37, it may need to ask the Conseil to declassify a provision contained in a *loi* enacted after 1958. (It does not have to follow the declassification procedure for earlier *lois*.) The procedure is entirely *ex parte*, in that nobody other than the Government and the Conseil is involved. The Government will submit a list of texts that it wishes to amend or repeal by decree, together with drafts of the provisions that it proposes to enact. This last part of the procedure is not necessary, but it helps the Government to obtain a useful ruling from the Conseil, in that the latter will try to frame its decision in such a way as to provide guidance to the Government on what it has specifically in mind.

Authority of Decisions of the Conseil constitutionnel. Article 62 states that a provision that the Conseil has declared unconstitutional cannot be promulgated or implemented. That aspect of the decision effectively binds the President on *loi* and treaties, the Government on proposed *règlements*, or Parliament in respect of proposed bills, amendments, or standing orders. More widely, the same article states that its decisions "are binding . . . on all administrative and judicial authorities". In the case of the administration, a circular of the Prime Minister of 25 May 1988 reminded civil servants of the need not only to respect decisions of the Conseil constitutionnel, but also to anticipate potential breaches of the Constitution. If the purpose of this kind of constitutional review is to obtain early and authoritative rulings on all aspects of a *loi*, then it is important that the decisions are adhered to by the courts. But French courts do not have a formal doctrine of *stare decisis,* and were initially reluctant to treat rulings on abstract points of law as authoritative when they come from what is, formally at least, a non-judicial body, though attitudes have changed in more recent years.

The normal policy for French courts, set out by article 5 of the Civil Code, is that they cannot lay down general rules for the future. The formal authority of the decision is thus confined to the case itself, and appeal to previous judgments is not, as such, a sufficient reason for a judicial decision. All the same, in practice, courts will follow earlier judicial decisions, especially those of the highest courts. *La jurisprudence* has thus a real authority, even if there is no rigid, formal rule of *stare decisis.*

Unlike the ordinary courts, the Conseil is not solving particular disputes between parties, but ruling in abstract on the validity of a *loi* that will affect a variety of future cases. It is said to judge a text, not litigants. In addition, the Conseil recognizes its responsibility for creating constitutional doctrine, a doctrine far more unsettled than private, criminal, or administrative law. In its decisions the Conseil has tried, therefore, to set out general principles of constitutional law, rather than simply to make specific rulings relating only to the particular *loi* under discussion. In this way general guidance can be offered to the Government, the Parliament, and the courts.

The Conseil takes a wide view of the binding force of its decisions. In the *Agricultural Orientation Law* of 1962, the Conseil stated "that the authority of the decisions [of the Conseil constitutionnel] mentioned [by article 62 of the Constitution] attaches not only to their result *(dispostif)*, but also to the reasons that are its necessary support and constitute its very foundation". The Conseil had already ruled in two decisions of 1961 that certain parliamentary amendments to an agricultural bill that sought to fix prices fell within the legislative competence of the Government under article 37. When asked the same question by the Government in relation to a *loi* of 1960, the Conseil merely replied that it did not require an answer since it had already ruled on that matter.

The scope of such binding authority extends to any provision with the same effect as one on which the Conseil has already ruled. Thus, in the case of the *Amnesty Law of 1989* a provision was introduced both to amnesty and to make eligible for reinstatement those who had been guilty of serious fault during industrial disputes. A clause to this effect had already been struck down in the case of the *Amnesty Law of 1988* because it would impose an excessive burden on the victims of the fault. Although the legislature had tried to modify the 1988 provision by making an exception for employers thus affected, on the Conseil did not consider that this had cured the problem, particularly in relation to the burdens that reinstatement would place on fellow employees. Relying on its previous decision, the Conseil struck down the new provision because it "violates the authority that attaches, by virtue of article 62 of the Constitution, to the decision of the Conseil constitutionnel of 20 July 1988".

The private and administrative courts have used techniques similar to those known in common law to distinguish decisions of the Conseil constitutionnel that they have not wished to follow. The first technique is to confine the decision to the text that was before the Conseil. This is often combined with a second technique of restrictive interpretation of the reasoning. Thus, in a decision of 1977 the Conseil held as unconstitutional a *loi* that intended to confer on the police an unlimited power to search vehicles on the highway even where no crime had been committed and there was no threat to public order, on the ground that the imprecise nature of the grounds of intervention by the police threatened individual liberty. In 1979 the Chambre criminelle of the Cour de cassation held that the police could search vehicles belonging to any person under the general provisions relating to the investigation of "flagrant offences". While formally consistent, the latter decision did much to undermine the effect of the decision of the Conseil constitutionnel.

The third technique is to draw a distinction between the necessary reasons for the decision and other points that may be raised (in other words, between the *ratio decidendi* and mere *obiter dicta*). . . .

Although the formal *ratio* of the Conseil decisions may be understood narrowly, their practical importance reflects its function of giving authoritative rulings on the meaning of the Constitution upon which a variety of public authorities can rely.

Article 62 states that the decisions of the Conseil constitutionnel bind public powers and administrative and judicial authorities. In the first group are included the President, the Government, and the Parliament. The President is not permitted to promulgate a *loi* or any provisions of it that have been declared unconstitutional by the Conseil, nor can he promulgate a text where the unconstitutional provisions have not been declared to be severable from the *loi* as a whole. It is up to the President to decide whether to promulgate a text without the severable, unconstitutional provisions, to require a new deliberation by Parliament on the whole text submitted to the Conseil, or merely on those articles that were declared unconstitutional, or to require a new *loi* to be presented to Parliament. Decisions on declassification restrict matters on which the Government can legislate by way of decree. Similarly, decisions on the admissibility of amendments bind the parliamentary chambers as to the proposals that can be discussed or adopted. In each case, the binding effect of the decision is very firmly limited to the text considered by the Conseil.

As far as the Conseil itself is concerned, it is in no way bound by its previous decisions. All the same, to ensure its authority and effectiveness, these "must be marked with the seal of continuity and coherence". From the earliest days, the Conseil has sometimes referred to its previous decisions either in the *visas* or in its actual reasons. But such citations are confined to instances where these do have binding force, as in the *Amnesty Law of 1989,* and the Conseil does not explicitly discuss how the current decision fits into the pattern of previous case-law, even though the precedents are frequently cited in the letter of reference to it. Where it intends to follow earlier rulings, it adopts the practice of the higher French courts of repeating the wording of the previously declared principle verbatim, but without attribution. As with these courts also, changes in the case-law can be noticed by attending to the formulations adopted. In some areas the Conseil has departed from its previous decisions. For example, on the matter of whether a decree can alter the constituent elements of a criminal offence, the Conseil constitutionnel has aligned itself with the Conseil d'État.

The possibility that the Conseil will overrule its previous decisions to some extent justifies the narrow view of binding judgments taken by the ordinary courts. All the same, although these courts may have been wary of, or even hostile to, the Conseil in the 1960s and the early part of the 1970s, more recently they have accorded more authority to the Conseil decisions. This happens in two ways, reflecting the different levels of authority that these enjoy.

Where a decision of the Conseil constitutionnel has binding force, this will provide a sufficient reason for the judgment of a subsequent court. This has been clearly recognized by the Conseil d'État, which applied a decision of the Conseil constitutionnel that certain "pollution payments" made to water authorities constituted taxes, thereby reversing its own previous decisions on the matter.... [T]he decision of the Conseil constitutionnel was cited as the reason in the judgment itself. ...

Beyond this, the Conseil constitutionnel frequently provides the inspiration for decisions of the courts. For example, the Cour de cassation held that criminal judges were competent to judge the legality of identity checks made by the administrative police.* The justification for the decision was that article 66 of the Constitution confers the protection of civil liberties on (private law) judges. As the conclusions of the *avocat général* make clear, this was taken directly from the case-law of the Conseil constitutionnel. Currently, the civil and criminal courts do pay attention to developments in the case-law of the Conseil, but this merely aids the discovery of principles leading to a solution, rather than providing the solution itself. Like lower courts faced with rulings by the Cour de cassation or the Conseil d'État, they prefer to use their own judgment in deciding what the Constitution requires....

All the same, there have been significant divergences of opinion. ... Such a situation is not at all unusual for a supreme court in France. The highest courts of each judicial system meet resistance from below, and this may well cause them to reverse their original opinions. Uniformity is not as highly valued as correctness in the legal system as a whole, and the Conseil constitutionnel cannot expect any special treatment if it is to act as a court.

It must not be forgotten that the Conseil d'État also acts as adviser to the Government, vetting all bills before they are presented to Parliament. A significant part of its advice consists of deciding whether provisions, as drafted, are constitutional or not. In doing this, the Conseil d'État is inevitably driven to study carefully the case-law of the Conseil constitutionnel and to predict its likely reactions. This advice will, as we have seen, find its way unofficially to the Conseil constitutionnel, so that there is an indirect dialogue between the two institutions over the scope and content of legislation. All the same, there may be differences of opinion. The most famous one was over the law on nationalizations passed in 1982. The Conseil d'État considered that certain changes had to be made to the indemnity provisions proposed by the Government in their draft bill. The Government followed this advice, only to find that the changes were condemned as unconstitutional by the Conseil constitutionnel. While such a pre-emptive control may not be infallible, it does reduce the litigation before the Conseil constitutionnel and increase its influence over the whole legislative process.

Techniques of the Conseil constitutionnel. The influence of the Conseil is also extended by the character of its judgments. It is not content simply to answer the straightforward question of whether a particular provision is constitutional or not. Because it is deciding the issue once and for all and in abstract, it tries to anticipate the various situations that may arise and to provide guidance as to the *manner* in which the provision can be constitu-

---

* [Editors' Note: The Cour de Cassation is the highest court reviewing lower court judgments in private civil cases and in criminal litigation.]

tionally valid. The guidance comes in the form of "reservations of interpretation" that condition the constitutionality of the clauses considered, so that the judgment may state that "subject strictly to the reservations of interpretation" set out in the decision, the *loi* is not contrary to the Constitution. This technique dates from one of the earliest decisions of the Conseil.

Three different forms of such reservations can be identified, and they can be illustrated from the important decision on *Security and Liberty* of 1981. The first is *interpretation*, whereby the Conseil offers a reading of the text that will be consistent with the Constitution. Thus, in that case a provision made it an offence, *inter alia,* to use any means to hinder or obstruct the passage of vehicles on the highway. It was objected that this might interfere with picketing or demonstrations connected with the right to strike. The Conseil simply stated in paragraph 14 of its decision that "there is no possibility that the application of these provisions might, in whatever way, prevent or interfere with the lawful exercise of the right to strike or union action." The text was "emptied of its venom" so that it could not be applied in an unconstitutional way. The second technique is that of *addition*, whereby the provision is filled out in such a way as to make it constitutional. Thus, article 39 of the *loi* simply provided that an extension of detention before being charged could be authorized by the investigating magistrate or by the President of the local criminal court. It was objected that, in the latter case, the detention would be extended without the judge having read the file. The Conseil replied in paragraph 19 that the judge authorizing the extension "will necessarily have to examine the file to authorize the extension of the detention before charge". A third technique is to address *injunctions* to the administration about how the law should be administered. Thus, in relation to identity checks, the Conseil remarked in paragraph 64 that:

> with a view to preventing abuses, the legislature has surrounded the procedure for controlling and checking identity that it has created with numerous precautions; that it is up to the judicial and administrative authorities to ensure that they are fully respected, as well as to the competent courts to punish, where necessary, illegalities that are committed and to provide compensation for their harmful consequences.

This was a strong encouragement to the courts, who are normally loath to provide damages for illegal acts by the police.

The use of such techniques depends on both the nature of the *loi* in question and on the body charged with its implementation. Where the *loi* is very general and really is no more than a framework for future Government discretion or for legislation that will not be subject to control by the Conseil, then there is good reason for the Conseil constitutionnel to be expansive in the reservations of interpretation that it lays down. This was noticeable in the range of *ordonnances* issued in 1986. In the context of privatization, there were detailed reservations on the way in which the price was to be calculated and on the protection of national independence. On more specific *lois,* the extent of reservations may be more limited.

The other consideration is the body that has to implement the *loi.* In *Security and Liberty* the body in question was the police. The guidance provided in the decision was adopted by the *Garde des Sceaux* (Minister of Justice) and incorporated in a circular on the application of the *loi.* In many cases judges will control the implementation, and it will be relevant to consider their normal principles of interpretation (and, indeed, their attitude to the decisions of the Conseil). The more the interpretation put forward departs from established principles within the relevant jurisdiction, or the more there is resistance to the Conseil, the more the reservations will have to be set out. In an extreme case the Conseil may prefer to quash the *loi,* if it is not likely that these reservations will be adopted.

On the whole, however, the Conseil will prefer to uphold a text as constitutional rather than strike it down. The inconvenience of a ruling of unconstitutionality against a text is significant. The Conseil's decision will usually come after the end of the parliamentary session, with perhaps three months until the next session is due to commence. Unless a provision is minor and severable, the Government may be forced to convene an extraordinary session of Parliament just to get the bill passed. Interpretation may well be a kindness in preference to nullity. Total unconstitutionalities are very rare. In part this is because severance is used to a significant extent, though this itself will require some interpretation of the text.

The scope and procedure of the constitutional review now operated by the Conseil constitutionnel is very much like that of a constitutional court, but with substantial differences from the kinds of court that exist in the United States and Germany. The Conseil constitutionnel is a court in all but name, though its procedure for reviewing legislation lacks significant attributes of a judicial process, even when compared just to ordinary French courts. Its jurisdiction is limited to reviewing *loi* before they are promulgated; once promulgated, a *loi* becomes immune from challenge in the ordinary courts. At the time of the bicentenary, proposals were made by the President of the Republic and the President of the Conseil constitutionnel that the ordinary courts should be allowed to refer to the Conseil constitutionnel the issue of the constitutionality of *loi* as they affected the fundamental rights of the citizen, even after they had been promulgated. But the proposed constitutional amendment to this effect met with resistance and was blocked in Parliament in autumn 1990. The system depends heavily on the willingness of the opposition to refer *loi* to Parliament. For example, the penalty imposed by the *loi* of 13 July 1990 on racism, anti-Semitism, and xenophobia was to deprive convicted persons of their civic rights. Although this was of obvious constitutional significance, no political party with sufficient members was willing to refer the matter to the Conseil constitutionnel before it was promulgated.

Within the balance of political institutions, the development of constitutional review places obvious limits on the sovereignty of Parliament, already reduced by the "rationalized parliamentarianism" of the Fifth

Republic. But since in political reality Parliament is now dominated by the Government (or even, arguably, by the President of the Republic), the growth of constitutional review may be seen as part of the process of redressing the balance between political institutions within the Fifth Republic. All the same, its emergence is a significant departure in terms of constitutional principle from previous Constitutions, especially in relation to conceptions of the separation of powers and parliamentary sovereignty. On the other hand, there is substantial continuity with concepts of the rule of law and with elements in the French State tradition. If Parliament and the executive are merely organs of the nation, then they must be kept within the powers that they have been given by the nation in the Constitution. . . .

---

3. GERMANY'S CONSTITUTIONAL COURT

Donald Kommers, THE CONSTITUTIONAL JURISPRUDENCE OF THE FEDERAL REPUBLIC OF GERMANY (1989) (pp. 16–27)

[Procedure for Filing Constitutional Complaints]

The procedure for filing complaints in the Constitutional Court is relatively easy and inexpensive. No filing fee or formal papers are required. Most complaints are handwritten and prepared without the aid of a lawyer. (About a third are prepared by counsel.) Nor is legal assistance required at any stage of the complaint proceeding. As a consequence of these rather permissive "standing" rules, the court has been flooded with complaints, swelling in number from well under 1,000 per year in the 1950s to around 3,500 per year in the mid-1980s, when constitutional complaints rivaled the bulk of the appellate docket of the U.S. Supreme Court. And while the court grants full dress review to barely more than 1 percent of all complaints, these cases are among its most significant decisions and make up about 55 percent of its published opinions.

Constitutional complaints had nevertheless become so burdensome and time-consuming that the court was statutorily authorized early on to adopt specified procedures for dispatching its work load. With the new changes, and under current law, each senate has established three screening committees, each consisting of three justices, to filter out frivolous complaints. (Until 1957 the full senate acted on all constitutional complaints.) These three-judge committees now dispose of 95 percent of all complaints, relieving the full senates of what otherwise would have been an impossible work load. In 1963, in order to cut down on the hundreds of trivial complaints filed each year, the court was authorized by law to impose a nominal fine upon petitioners who "abuse" the constitutional complaint procedure. The court initially used this power sparingly; more recently, however, the signs have pointed to a harsher policy. The court has not only used the FCCA's* "abuse" provision more frequently than in the past, but a 1985 change in

---

* [Editors' Note: The FCCA is the statute relating to the Constitutional Court.]

the law allows it to impose a maximum fine of DM 5,000 (ca. $2,800) upon a frivolous petitioner. In addition, filing a constitutional complaint is no longer a cost-free procedure. As of 1986, a three-judge committee may impose a fee of up to DM 1,000 (ca. $600) upon any petitioner whose complaint it refuses to accept. . . .

Intra-Senate Chamber System

A major change in the structure of the two senates accompanied the jurisdictional change that took place in 1956. Because the court was awash in constitutional complaints, the federal parliament permitted each senate to establish three committees, each consisting of three justices, to screen these complaints. The three-judge committees, as they were then called, could dismiss a complaint by unanimous agreement if they considered it to be "inadmissible or to offer no prospect of success for other reasons." Under current procedure, if one justice on a three-member committee votes to accept a complaint—that is, if he thinks it has some chance of success— it is forwarded to the full senate. At this stage the "rule of two" controls the result: If at least two justices in the full senate hold the view that the complaint raises a question of constitutional law likely to be clarified by a judicial decision or that the complainant will suffer serious harm in the absence of a decision, the complaint will be held "acceptable." Thereafter, and on the basis of more detailed inspection, a senate majority could still reject the complaint as "trivial" or "inadmissible."

In 1986 the federal parliament, on the Constitutional Court's recommendation, enhanced the power of the three-judge committees to further alleviate the burden of the full senates. The FCCA renamed the committees "chambers" and, in addition to their other functions, empowered them to rule on the merits of an accepted complaint if the decision is unanimous and clearly within the standards already laid down in a prior case by a full senate. This authority applies to those well-founded complaints—mainly procedural complaints against lower courts—rather easily disposed of and deemed unworthy of the attention of the parent senate.

As noted earlier, the chambers dispose of 95 percent of all complaints. A chamber is under no obligation to offer reasons for the dismissal of a complaint if court officials notify the complainant at the outset "that doubt exists as to the admissibility or foundation of the application." In practice, however, the chambers do notify, often in formal statements of one to ten typewritten pages, close to 75 percent of all complainants of their reasons for declining their petitions.[77] These decisions, like chamber opinions

---

77. The source of the 75 percent figure is Justice Helmut Steinberger, interview with author, October 22, 1986. An example of such a rejected petition is the complaint brought by the Academic Council of Oldenburg University's social science faculty. The Federal Office of Political Education had denied the faculty permission to inspect its records under a rule requiring such documents to remain classified for a period of thirty years. The complaint challenged the constitutional validity of the ruling and several administrative court decisions sustaining it. On January 30, 1986, a chamber consisting of Justices

addressing the merits of a given complaint, are not published in the court's official reports. They are, however, released to legal periodicals at the chambers' discretion and are often reprinted in full by these journals.[78] These decisions serve mainly to clarify points of law already laid down in the court's reported decisions.

The chamber system has been the subject of several constitutional challenges, the complainant having argued in each case that a chamber's dismissal of his complaint denied him the right to "the jurisdiction of his lawful judge" under Article 101 of the Basic Law, because the Constitution provides for one constitutional court, all of whose members are to be elected by the *Bundestag* and *Bundesrat*. Accordingly, the complainants argued, nothing less than full senate treatment would be constitutionally valid. In the *Three-Justice Committee* cases, involving decisions by both senates, the court ruled against the complainant on the basis of its statutory authority to create internal committees in one instance; seemingly piqued by the audacity of the complainant who challenged its decision-making procedures, the Second Senate even slapped a nominal fine on the complainant for "abusing the constitutional complaint procedure." These decisions, all rendered before the right to file a constitutional complaint was entrenched in the Basic Law, underscored the finality of a committee decision unanimously rejecting a complaint. In short, no "appeal" lay to the full senate, its sister senate, or the Plenum.

The constitutionalization of the complaint procedure in 1969 appeared to erode the foundation of the *Three-Justice Committee* cases. So far, however, no challenge has been hurled against the chamber system on constitutional grounds, "and in any event it is rather hard to imagine the court undermining its own protective ramparts." Clearly, some kind of gatekeeping procedure involving less than full senate membership is necessary as a practical matter if the court is to cope with a system that "entitles [anyone] to complain to it about virtually anything." On the other hand, the system could permit hidden criteria to influence the summary disposi-

Herzog, Katzenstein, and Henschel dismissed the complaint over the objection that the federal office had interfered with the freedom of information and the freedom of research and teaching secured, respectively, by paragraphs 1 and 3 of Article 5 of the Basic Law. Citing precedent as well as authoritative commentary, the committee explained in detail why the full senate would not decide the case on its merits. Chamber Judgment of January 30, 1986 (1 BvR 1352/85 [typescript]).

78. These "unofficial" opinions constitute a large and growing body of constitutional decisions. The original complaints from which these published opinions emerge are often prepared by legal counsel and arguably raise issues of constitutional significance. The justices feel obligated to respond to such ar-

guments notwithstanding their dismissal of the complaint on the ground of its probable lack of success. An illustration is the judgment of October 11, 1985, by Justices Zeidler, Steinberger, and Böckenförde involving a constitutional complaint against a procedural ruling of a Stuttgart court allegedly incompatible with a decision of the European Court of Human Rights and thus in conflict with a general rule of international law within the meaning of the Basic Law's Article 25. In a rather detailed nine-page opinion the committee cited several decisions of the European Human Rights Court to sustain its conclusion that the complaint would not succeed if accepted and decided by the full senate. Chamber Judgment of October 11, 1985 (2 BvR 336/85 [typescript]).

tion process and thus, perhaps, to "resolve" matters rightfully within the full senate's competence. There is also the problem of different standards that may exist from chamber to chamber, potentially invading the right of the Plenum to ensure the uniformity of judgments across senates. To some extent these problems are mitigated by the requirement that chamber memberships be changed every three years. . . .

PROCESS

Internal Administration

The Federal Constitutional Court achieved a major victory when it won the authority early on to administer its own internal affairs. Administrative autonomy had two notable consequences for the court's institutional development. First, armed with the power to prepare its own budget in direct consultation with parliament and the Ministry of Finance, the court was able to plan its own future. In 1964 it even won approval for an ultramodern building designed by its own architects and engineers. Second, the president's administrative authority was substantially enlarged. While only *primus inter pares* in the judicial conference room, he was *primus* on all other matters of internal administration, a situation that aggravated relations between the president and many of the associate justices.

In 1975, after years of discord between the president and individual justices over their respective duties and powers, parliament enacted a set of standing rules of procedure governing the court's internal operations. These new rules charge the Plenum, over which the president presides, with preparing the budget, deciding all questions pertaining to the justices' duties, and formulating general principles of judicial administration. . . . [T]he rules entitle each senate to an administrative director who is responsible to its presiding "chief" justice. The Constitutional Court's overall administration is in the hands of the director, who answers only to the president. Finally, each justice is entitled to three research assistants or clerks of his own choosing. Law clerks are not recent law school graduates as in the United States. They are usually in their thirties or early forties and already embarked upon legal careers as judges, civil servants, or professors of law. Most serve for two or three years, although some clerks have stayed on for longer periods.

Adjudication

The courts judicial procedures are prescribed by statute. They are laid down in the FCCA and in the court's own rules of procedure. The FCCA, for its part, includes general and special provisions governing each category of jurisdiction (e.g., party prohibition cases, federal-state conflicts, collateral judicial-review references, etc.). The general provisions deal with (1) conditions under which a justice may be excluded from a case, (2) rules incident to the various proceedings, (3) rights of the parties involved in litigation before the court, including the qualifications of those legally entitled to represent them, (4) obligations of public officials and courts to cooperate with the court in disposing of certain cases, (5) special rules accompanying the issuance of temporary orders, and (6) the manner in which decisions are made and announced.

The first of these procedures requires a justice to recuse himself from a case if he has a personal interest in it or is related to one of the participants. Recusation, however, is not left to a justice's own discretion. If, pursuant to a challenge of bias by one of the parties, he fails to remove himself voluntarily, the full senate decides the matter in his absence. A decision to recuse must be supported in writing and is included among the court's published opinions. So far, two justices have been excluded under these procedures: Justice Gerhard Leibholz in the *Party Finance Case I* of 1966 and Justice Joachim Rottmann in the *Inter-German Basic Treaty Case* of 1973, both moments of high tension on the court. In each instance petitioners complained that the justice compromised his impartiality by making off-the-bench—and admittedly indiscreet—public comments on the merits of the pending litigation.

The Constitutional Court's deliberations are secret, and the justices render their decisions on the basis of the official record. The rules require written opinions justified by supporting arguments and signed by all participating justices. Public hearings seldom take place, because the court limits oral argument to cases of major political importance. A decision handed down on the basis of oral proceedings is known as a judgment (*Urteil),* while a decision without oral argument is labeled an order, or a ruling *(Beschluss).* The distinction is a mere formality, for Constitutional Court decisions, whether *Urteile* or *Beschlüsse,* bind all state authorities. But certain decisions, according to the FCAA, "have the force of [general] law." (As a result, the *Federal Law Gazette [Bundesgesetzblatt]* publishes all such decisions.) These include rulings handed down in abstract and collateral review cases as well as those arising out of constitutional complaints where the court declares a law compatible or incompatible with the Constitution.

Assignment. Cases arriving at the court go directly to the Office of the Director. Once classified and numbered, the director forwards them, along with their accompanying records and briefs, to the administrative office of the senate with jurisdiction over their subject matter. A special committee of six justices—consisting of the president, vice president, and two justices from each senate—resolves jurisdictional disputes between the senates. The president casts a second and deciding vote in the event of a deadlock.

When a senate receives a case, its presiding officer (president or vice president), assisted by his chief clerk, forwards the file to a particular justice in accordance with an assignment plan worked out at the beginning of each calendar year. The annual assignment schedule is an in-house system of allocation not generally known or revealed to outsiders. A particular justice may preside over as many as seven categories of cases. A representative list might include (1) all disputes in international public law, (2) claims to asylum and citizenship, (3) cases arising under Article 100(2) of the Basic Law (determining whether a rule of public international law is an integral part of federal law), (4) cases involving European community law, and (5) administrative law cases not already assigned to another justice.

As this list shows, there is some interrelationship among the assigned categories, often consistent with the expertise a particular justice brings to the court, but a justice also carries his share of work outside his immediate specialization. Just as the special committee of six decides jurisdictional disputes between the senates, the full senate resolves any conflict between two justices over an assignment. The justice in charge of a case—i.e., the *Berichterstatter,* or reporter specialized in the area of law involved in the constitutional dispute—is responsible for preparing a report known as a *votum,* which constitutes the basis of discussion and deliberation by the full senate. Each justice also receives an equal share of constitutional complaints. Assisted by his law clerks, he prepares a short memorandum—a mini-*votum*—on each complaint for the benefit of his two colleagues on the three-justice chambers. Law clerks, incidentally, are also chosen for their expertise in selected areas of public and private law.

Vota. The preparation of a *votum* represents a crucial stage in the decisional process. The *votum* is a detailed report on all aspects of a case: The reporting justice prepares a statement of the facts and issues, including a summary of the arguments on both sides of the dispute, with full citation to judicial decisions and published commentary, and concludes with his recommendation as to how to decide the case. A *votum* in a complex case may take weeks, even months, to prepare. Often it turns out to be a weighty document, 50 to 250 pages or more, and often it forms the basis of the first draft of the final opinion. Assisted by their law clerks, the justices work at their own pace. The full senate could, if it wanted, set a deadline for the consideration of a *votum* or, if necessary, reassign the case to another justice, but this rarely happens. The justices are expected to keep up with their work, meet conference schedules, and enhance the court's collegial atmosphere. In any one calendar year each justice prepares major *vota* in three to six cases, drafts mini-*vota* on constitutional complaints in about two hundred cases for chamber consideration, studies thirty to forty *vota* of other justices, writes final opinions in cases assigned to him, and prepares for the weekly conference.

Oral Argument. As already indicated, formal hearings before the court are rare. Each senate hears oral argument in three or four cases annually, usually in *Organstreit* and abstract judicial-review cases where oral argument is mandatory, unless waived by the litigants. The reporter, who by this time has neared the completion of his *votum,* usually dominates the questioning, the main function of which at this stage is less to refine legal issues than to uncover, if possible, additional facts bearing on them. The public hearing also adds legitimacy to the decision-making process in cases of major political importance, particularly when minority political parties allege that the established parties have treated them unconstitutionally. The absence of any time limit on an oral presentation, and the court's readiness to hear the full gamut of argumentation on both sides of a disputed question, are intended to generate goodwill and convey a sense of fairness and openness to winners and losers alike.

Conference. The presiding officer of each senate schedules weekly—occasionally semi-weekly—meetings to decide cases and dispose of other judicial business. Except for August and September, when the court is not in session, meetings are normally held every Tuesday, frequently spilling over into Wednesday and Thursday. *Vota* and draft opinions of cases already decided dominate the agenda. In considering a *votum*, the "chief" calls upon the reporter to summarize the case and state the reasons for his recommendation. The reporter's role is crucial here, for a carefully drafted and well-organized *votum* usually carries the day in conference. In addition, the pressure of time often prompts justices to defer to the reporter's expertise and judgment.

Still, the reporter has to win the consent of his colleagues. It is his responsibility, along with that of the "chief," to marshal a majority or "find" a broad basis of agreement. Skill and personality matter here. The reporter who does his homework, solicits the views of colleagues, and negotiates artfully is likely to prevail in conference. Justices who lack these gifts or the full confidence of their colleagues are unlikely to prevail. If, on the other hand, the reporter is in the minority—and even the most influential justices occasionally find themselves in this position—he does not necessarily lose his influence over the case, for he still has the task of writing the court's opinion. If he combines political sagacity with a deft literary hand, he may leave his imprint on the finished product. A reporter with strong dissenting views may request that the writing of the opinion be assigned to another justice, but this rarely occurs. If he knows the requisites of judicial statesmanship, he will draft an opinion broadly reflective of a wide common denominator of agreement, often representing a compromise among conflicting constitutional arguments.

The production of such opinions—that is, opinions which reduce discord on the bench and preserve its moral authority in the public mind—is likely to be a function of the presiding officer's capacity for leadership. His task is to guide discussion, frame the questions to be voted upon, and marshal the largest majority possible behind judicial decisions. His leadership is particularly important in sessions where opinions undergo final and often meticulous editing. Despite the introduction of signed dissenting opinions in 1971, the court continues unanimously to decide well over 90 percent of its reported cases. Although these reports disclose the identities of the justices participating in a case, majority opinions remain unsigned. It is common knowledge among informed observers, however, that the reporter in a unanimous decision is the principal author of the final opinion. The institutional bias against personalized judicial opinions has tended to minimize published dissents. Dissenting justices—even if they have circulated written dissents inside the court—more often than not, and partly out of a sense of institutional loyalty, choose not to publish their dissents or even to be identified as dissenters. The prevailing norm seems to hold that personalized dissenting opinions are proper only when prompted by deep convictions.

Questions and Comments

1. In both Germany and France the jurisdiction of the Constitutional Court can be invoked by legislators in the parliamentary minority under circumstances that would not satisfy the U.S. Supreme Court's standing requirements. Reconsider in light of these practices the U.S. Court's conclusion that its standing doctrine is based on concern for "the proper— and properly limited—role of the courts in a democratic society." Are there features of the U.S. constitutional system, including the diffuse and decentralized system of constitutional review, that would support a standing requirement here more than in other democratic, constitutional societies?

2. How would the absence or presence of dissenting opinions affect the legitimacy or reception of a constitutional court's decisions?

3. In the U.S. Supreme Court oral argument is now ordinarily restricted to one hour per case, a half hour per side. In its early days, the Supreme Court heard arguments that extended over days in major cases. The German and French courts rarely or never hear oral argument. Will the U.S. Supreme Court follow suit? Should it?

E.   JUSTICIABILITY, JUDICIAL ACTIVISM, AND THE EFFECTS OF DIFFERENT FORMS OF JUDICIAL REVIEW ON LEGISLATIVE ROLES

This section will introduce some comparative perspective on the functions of "justiciability" doctrines in constitutional adjudication, and on the effects of the "constitutionalization" of public or legislative debate on substantive policy and ensuing effects on commitments to democratic political processes. This section draws on experiences in France, India, the U.S. and Russia, and materials in the next chapter shed light on justiciability doctrines in both Canada and Germany.

As has been suggested before, comparative study "has the liberating effect of unsettling our own presuppositions, revealing the contingency of legal forms and exposing vast ranges of what is legally possible." Jamie Cassels, *Bitter Knowledge, Vibrant Action: Reflections of Law and Society in Modern India,* 1991 Wis. L. Rev. 109 (reviewing Marc Galanter, Law and Society in Modern India (1989)). Does India's experience suggest that procedural aspects of U.S. law, and justiciability limitations on the Court's jurisdiction, are "false necessities"? Does the Russian court's experience with judicial activism between 1991–93 suggest that they (or some of them) may be "true" necessities? Or is each of these experiences so entwined in the particular histories of the respective nations that they shed little light on U.S. approaches?

As you read the next set of materials, recall Professor Tushnet's elaboration of the argument that judicial review will result in "democratic debilitation." Recall also Thayer's claim that when "the correction of legislative mistakes comes from the outside, . . . the people . . . lose the political experience, and the moral education and stimulus that come from fighting the question out in the ordinary way, and correcting their own errors. [The] tendency of a common and easy resort to [judicial review is] to dwarf the political capacity of the people and to deaden its sense of moral responsibility." J. Thayer, John Marshall 103–07 (1901). Consider in this regard Alec Stone's study of the effects of the Conseil Constitutionnel in France which, he argues, has had an unhealthy effect of "judicializing" discourse in the legislative branch. Is this an example of such "debilitation," or is it a counterexample of constitutional invigoration of legislative discourse?

Consider, as well, whether decisions of the U.S. Supreme Court had such an effect. Is it unhealthy for the legislative body to incorporate considerations of what will pass constitutional muster in its legislative decisionmaking? Is it unhealthy for a constitutional court to provide detailed guidance to legislatures of how to avoid constitutional difficulties?

---

1.   INDIA AND PUBLIC INTEREST LITIGATION

India became an object of European conquest and colonization in the 16th century; by mid-nineteenth century, most of India was under British rule. British governors were appointed for the Indian provinces,[al] and established court systems which used an amalgam of local and British law. In the late 19th century, the Indian National Congress was established, with representatives from all over India, which began to demand self-governance. The Muslim League was organized soon after, partially out of fear that the Hindu-dominated National Congress would not protect the position of Muslims. For most of the period after World War I until 1947, India's peoples struggled for independence from Britain. Mohandas Gandhi (trained as a lawyer) persuaded the Indian National Congress to adopt a program of nonviolent disobedience and resistance against British rule.[am] In 1947, British and Indian leaders agreed on a partition of the country (establishing the separate nation of Pakistan to protect Muslim interests) and a plan for independence. Following independence, violence between Hindus and Muslims continued.[an] India continued to acquire control over

al. Outside of "British India," Indian princes ruled in the separate "Indian states", whose external relations were under British control.

am. In response to increasing agitation, the British created a new constitution for India in 1935 which increased Indian self-

rule but under which, however, the British viceroys and governors retained veto power over legislation.

an. Large numbers of Muslims left India for Pakistan and of Hindus left Pakistan for India; fighting continued over the status independent princely states, and over areas under the control of Portugal, into the 1960s. For useful historical accounts of the pre-independence period, see Judith M. Brown, Modern India: The Origins of an Asian Democracy (2d ed. 1994); D.A. Low, Britain and Indian Nationalism: The Imprint of Ambiguity 1929–42 (1997).

Under its post-independence Constitution of 1950, India is a federal republic of more than 700 million religiously and ethnically diverse people, most of them very poor. The Constitution establishes a strong central government on a parliamentary model. There is a two house parliament, a lower house (House of the People) and an upper house (House of Elders or Council of States). The lower house is popularly elected at least every 5 years, and the upper house is elected for staggered, 6–year terms, largely by the various state legislatures; each state is allotted a number of seats based primarily on its population. If the two houses do not agree on a measure, the measure is put before a joint meeting of both houses and can be passed by a simple majority, thus giving more power to the larger lower house than is enjoyed by the U.S. House of Representatives. A largely titular President exists, but most executive power is exercised by the Prime Minister and his or her council of ministers.

The Constitution establishes both fundamental rights (e.g., freedom of the press, equality before law) and "Directive Principles" that are not justiciable but which encourage the government to pursue social and economic welfare measures, including, e.g. to secure "the right to an adequate means of livelihood." India Const. art. 39. The Supreme Court of India, like the U.S. Supreme Court, functions as a final court of appeals for civil and criminal matters, and also has the power of constitutional review over the actions of the Parliament, of executive officers and of the state governments. The court system is unitary, with most judges of the Supreme Court having previously served on a lower court. Justices are appointed by the President, upon consultation with the Chief Justice; they serve until the mandatory retirement age of 65 (after which they are prohibited from practicing law). See M.V. Pylee, India's Constitution 202 (1994).

Between 1950 and 1975, the Court established itself as a fairly activist Supreme Court, but one that was at least on occasion "accused of obstructing social reform" particularly for its invocation of private property rights to strike down socialist programs, an effort that "led Prime Minister Indira Gandhi to make changes in the courts that became part of the background of the 1975–77 Emergency." Jeremy Cooper, *Poverty and Constitutional Justice: The Indian Experience*, 44 Mercer L. Rev. 611, 613 (1993). During this emergency period, Indira Gandhi was convicted by a lower court of illegal campaign practices but refused to resign, and instead declared a state of emergency in which many of her political opponents were arrested, the press was censored, Parliament passed legislation retroactively purporting to legalize her actions, and amendments were passed increasing Parlia-

of Kashmir until 1949, and intermittently since.

mentary power and decreasing the powers of the courts. Various law reform committees in India in the 1970s, including one in 1977 on which two Supreme Court justices served, recommended modifications of litigation rules and procedures in order to permit litigation to enforce the legal rights and improve the lives of the poor. By the early 1980s, the activism of the Indian Supreme Court looked in a different direction, as described in the following excerpts.

Carl Baar, *Social Action Litigation in India: The Operation and Limits of the World's Most Active Judiciary*, in Comparative Judicial Review and Public Policy (Donald W. Jackson & C. Neal Tate eds., 1992)

Judicial review is not only used more extensively in Indian than American courts, but also quite differently. The Indian judiciary has adapted the wide discretion characteristic of English practice, principally via interim orders, to support its interventionist approach. Its distinctive techniques, partly a response to massive arrears and delay, have allowed the delays themselves to reinforce judicial activism and fundamental rights. At the same time, the real impact of judicial activism remains problematic, since it occurs in an activist state capable of marginalizing even the most courageous and controversial interventions by the courts.

JUDICIAL ACTIVISM IN INDIA

. . . [Since 1977] judges have become outspoken supporters of the political, social, and economic rights of oppressed peoples. The vehicle for this new form of judicial activism is usually termed public interest litigation (PIL) or social action litigation (SAL), the term preferred by some of its leading advocates.

Public interest litigation had its origins not in a popular or even a professional movement. It began in the Supreme Court of India itself, initially in two-judge panels of reform-minded judges who sought new ways to bring issues affecting unrepresented Indian people before the courts. By the mid–1980s, public interest litigation "would comprehend any legal wrong or injury or illegal burden, caused or threatened" (Agrawala, 1985: 9). It would extend beyond individual rights to collective or social rights that "require active intervention by the State and other public authorities for their realization, including freedom from indigency, ignorance and discrimination as well as the right to a healthy environment, to social security and to protection for massive financial, commercial and corporate oppression" (Bhagwati, 1987: 21). "[A] determinate class of persons . . . threatened . . . by reason of poverty, helplessness or disability or socially or economically disadvantaged position" would be covered even when that class was "unable to approach the court for relief." [Justice Bhagwati] . . .

ELEMENTS OF SOCIAL ACTION LITIGATION

Judicial activism is built into the very procedures of social action litigation, in some cases extending the activism of Indian courts well beyond that of its American counterparts. SAL's key procedural elements (summarized in Bhagwati, 1987) include:

1. *Epistolary jurisdiction.* The Supreme Court of India, as well as the High Courts in the various states, can convert a letter from a member of the public into a writ petition. Thus access to judicial redress may be obtained without a lawyer or even the filing of formal papers. The earliest epistles were addressed to individual members of the Supreme Court, and reports abound of individual judges soliciting petitions. The number of letters has remained high enough to justify the creation and continuation of a "PIL cell" within the Supreme Court to process the paperwork—and perhaps to place administrative controls on individual judges. No similar procedure exists in the United States or Canada: prisoners can gain access in some circumstances by letter, but not members of the public.

2. *Broadened roles of standing (locus standi).* "[A]ny member of the public or social action group acting bona fide" can apply on behalf of an individual or class unable to do so on its own (Bhagwati, 1987: 24). Social activists filed "a preponderant number" of some 75 SAL writs in 1980–82; among the petitioners have been law professors, a third-year law student. a social worker, and journalist. This is a dramatic change from strict English-style rules of standing; even a critic of PIL found "virtual unanimity" for liberalization (Agrawala, 1985: 14).

3. *Sociolegal commissions of inquiry.* Once a litigant group was given standing and its petition accepted, a lack of resources would likely make the development of a case extremely difficult. A "passive approach" by the Court would mean "fundamental rights would remain merely an illusion," wrote Justice P. N. Bhagwati, requiring a "departure from the adversarial procedure without in any way sacrificing the principle of fair play." The result was the creation of sociolegal commissions of inquiry:

> The Supreme Court started appointing social activists, teachers, researchers, journalists, government officers and judicial officers as Court Commissioners to visit particular locations for fact-finding. The Commissioners were required to submit a quick and detailed report setting out their findings and also their suggestions and recommendations.

While there is precedent for commissioners of inquiry in British administrative regulation dating back to the Public Health Act of 1848, no American court of last resort uses this approach to fact-finding, and American trial courts would do so in a much more modified and limited form.

4. *New remedies and monitoring.* Finally, social action litigation has resulted in a wide variety of remedial court orders. Many would have a familiar ring to American public interest litigators, but they represent radical departures from British legal practice all within a short time period. A particularly important element is the establishment of a monitoring agency, by which social activism or judicial officers check on compliance. In practice, District Court Judges are frequently designated inquiry commis-

sioners or monitors, although they are state-appointed judges of limited jurisdiction.

A review of the major cases and substantive principles enunciated through social action litigation will not be attempted here. It is sufficient to note that cases have involved not only the prison conditions and pretrial detention rights (for example, *Hussainara Khatoon v. State of Bihar,* 1979) familiar in America litigation, but have extended to bonded laborers *(Bandhua Mukti Morcha,* 1984), pavement dwellers *(Olga Tellis v. State of Maharastra,* 1979), rickshaw pullers, construction workers, and thousands of *adivasis* and *dalits*[2].

In this process, Indian judges have rendered interpretations of constitutional language that are much broader than comparable American interpretations: antislavery provisions of the constitution have been extended to a setting in which workers were paid below the minimum wage; the state has been given a positive obligation to protect the environment; and a commuter was able to sue the state railway for failing in its constitutional obligation to guarantee freedom of movement.

JUDICIAL ACTIVISM IN CROWDED COURTS

Overcrowded dockets in Indian Courts have been a subject of scholarly concern within the country and amazement outside. But what is important to our current analysis is how arrears and delay, by reinforcing an English-style approach to judicial discretion, have promoted judicial activism by facilitating selective judicial intervention.

The Supreme Court of India's caseload is staggering by any calculation. The Court's own monthly statement for January 1988 showed a total of 39,454 "regular hearing matters" pending, plus 137,622 "admission and miscellaneous matters"—a combined total of 177,076. In January alone, over 4,000 matters had been disposed of, but over 5,000 matters had come in. While the bulk of the pending cases are not constitutional, the Court shows a total of 7,611 constitutional matters pending on February 1, 1988, including 104 civil writ petitions from 1978 that are listed as ready for hearing.

These gigantic numbers suggest that the very concept of litigation and readiness for hearing must be treated differently in India than in other common-law countries. Thus an advocate who had recently completed a Supreme Court appeal in a nonconstitutional matter that had commenced 52 years earlier brushed aside my concerned questions, referring to the case as "luxury litigation." If a matter is important, it will come on for hearing; what the Court considers a priority is handled expeditiously.

And so it is. When a controversial television miniseries on partition led to protests and riots, the Bombay High Court "stayed further screening of

2. *Adivasis* are aboriginals (literally, "original inhabitants"), usually members of scheduled tribes designated for protection under Part XVI of the Constitution, sections 330ff. *Dalits* refer broadly to the depressed or downtrodden, members of "backward classes" [including so-called "untouchables"].

the serial on the basis of a writ petition filed by a Bombay businessman" (Tripathi, 1988: 75). Two days later (January 23, 1988), a two-judge panel had viewed the six-part film and lifted the interim order. The petitioner appealed to the Supreme Court, but the Court dismissed the petition on February 1. The entire matter was resolved within the short life of the series and without an episode being missed. To do otherwise would have prevented the judiciary from bringing its own distinctive approach and concerns to bear at a time of major national debate. While the American or Canadian Supreme Courts would have waited for an opportunity for sober second thought and for the quieting of public debate, the Supreme Court of India heard arguments and delivered a 23-page judgment within two weeks after the first action in a lower court.

What is happening is quite simple: the Indian courts are operating on interim orders. In contrast, the U.S. Supreme Court uses doctrines of ripeness and exhaustion of remedies to ensure that lower court action is complete. This is done not just because of that court's delicate constitutional position, but because American courts have generally rejected the use of interlocutory appeals (appeals from the decisions of trial judges on preliminary motions). In contrast, British courts (and their Canadian and Australian counterparts) make extensive use of interlocutory appeals, usually through a single superior court judge hearing an appeal from the ruling of an inferior trial judge. The Indian courts, following British practice, also make extensive use of interim orders—so that even when there is no time to complete a case, steps can be taken to control state action.

The use of interim orders is a key to the success of social action litigation. Even by the early 1980s, Baxi (1987: 42) noted that "not a single leading SAL matter has yet resulted in a final verdict. . . . In the meantime, the Court rules through interim directions and orders. Bit by bit, it seeks improvement in the administration, making it more responsive than before to the constitutional ethic and law." When a letter came to the Supreme Court on behalf of adivasis and dalits claiming harassment by forest and revenue authorities, a two-judge bench not only accepted the letter as a writ petition, but issued a restraining order against the authorities— shifting the burden of court delays from the petitioners to the state.

The use of interim orders allows the Indian judiciary to cope with delay. At the same time, extensive delays can be used and not merely coped with. Delays legitimate the need to reset priorities for hearing, giving the judiciary wide discretion to pick and choose from among those demanding a hearing. Jumping the queue is no longer deemed unfair when the queue is ten years long. Thus a court committed to an agenda of social justice could advance matters on its docket whose resolution would promote that goal, and avoid cases that are either marginal or detrimental to the goal. . . . [C]onstitutional petitioners may not lose in great numbers, but neither is a high proportion successful. Numerous cases simply fall by the wayside, never reached by the courts. In this process, however. the Indian judiciary does hear a wide range of matters that provide opportunities to teach symbolic lessons to the state and the society. And those lessons are given at the very moment when the attention of that audience is most intense.

CONSTITUTIONAL CONDITIONS FOR SOCIAL ACTION LITIGATION

Social action litigation did not develop out of a history of judicial restraint and institutional weakness. It has flourished because of the judiciary's original constitutional position and subsequent constitutional role. Consider four constitutional factors that have facilitated the development of social action litigation:

1.   There is the tradition of judicial activism going back to the beginning of the constitution in 1950, culminating in the two great cases of *Golak Nath* in 1967 and *Kesavananda Bharati* in 1973. In the former, the Supreme Court effectively declared a constitutional amendment unconstitutional, by holding that Parliament could not amend the constitution in a manner that would abridge the Fundamental Rights in Part III. An 11-judge bench heard the case for two months: its four separate opinions took 173 pages. In *Kesavananda,* the Court modified its earlier holding, allowing Parliament to amend the constitution, including Part III, but only as long as the "basic structure" of the constitution was preserved. That decision followed a six-month hearing before a 13-judge bench, and resulted in 11 opinions running a total of 701 pages.

The Court in both cases was reviewing land reform legislation in the name of property rights, thus arraying itself as a conservative institution challenging the authority of a redistributive regime in a highly visible political event. If *Kesavananda* could be India's *Marbury. v. Madison* (because, as argued by the Rudolphs [1987:110], it "establish[ed] an acceptable ground for judicial review"), it could also be India's *Schechter Poultry* case (the most newsworthy of the U.S. Supreme Court's decisions invalidating New Deal legislation in the 1930s). For just as President Franklin Roosevelt responded to *Schechter* by appointing a number of Supreme Court judges more sympathetic to his social and economic reforms, and saw those judges go on to become judicial activists when individual rights were violated by government action, so it was that the Indira Gandhi government, in the years following *Golak Nath,* appointed a number of more left-wing judges, including Bhagwati, V. R. Krisna Iyer, and O. Chinnappa Reddy, who accepted an active state role in socioeconomic policy, but supported judicial activism in cases of government infringement of civil liberties.

2.   There is a constitution that includes not only fundamental rights but also "Directive Principles of State Policy." Sections 12–35 of the Indian constitution entrench a full range of fundamental rights, enforceable in the Supreme Court (s.32). Sections 36–51 go in a different direction, enunciating a set of directive principles that are not judicially enforceable (s.37). Derived from the Irish constitution, these positive obligations extend to a variety of areas of economic and social policy, providing a context for the application of fundamental rights. ... [F]ear that a doctrine of substantive due process would be read into ... [the Constitution] to promote a

conservative economic agenda, in the style of the *Lochner*-era U.S. Supreme Court, would be mitigated by the understanding that fundamental rights gain meaning from their relationship to directive principles.... [T]he Supreme Court of India saw the two as "complementary to each other," with directive principles "prescrib[ing] the goal" and fundamental rights "lay[ing] down the means" (*Minerva Mills,* 1980).

3. There is an administratively independent judiciary. Section 50 of the Indian Constitution provides that "the State shall take steps to separate the judiciary from the executive in the public services of the State." While this language is part of the nonenforceable "Directive Principles of State Policy," the goal it enunciates has been achieved in India to an extent greater than in any other common law parliamentary system. Thus Indian courts are administered under the direction of the judiciary, as in the United States, and not by the executive, as in Canada, Australia, and the United Kingdom.... As in the United States, the Indian courts are still subject to external budget constraints: however, the Indian judiciary has control over internal allocation of resources—an authority that would be condemned as contrary to principles of parliamentary government in Canada, Australia, or the United Kingdom....

...[C]ontrol over its own administrative apparatus has allowed the judiciary to shift to an empowerment strategy. As a result. the administrative infrastructure needed to support social action litigation (the Supreme Court's PIL cell, the sociolegal commissions of inquiry) is within the judiciary's control; a chief justice, for example, need not go to an executive official to request that a unit be created to handle a new wave of court-encouraged letters and writ petitions.

4. There is a Supreme Court with broad jurisdiction. The Supreme Court of India has a wide range of both original and appellate jurisdiction entrenched in the constitution itself. Section 32 gives access to the Supreme Court to anyone who claims their fundamental rights are violated. While the Court has urged public interest litigants to start in their state High Courts, original petitions continue to be filed, and continue to be admitted for hearing. The Supreme Court, consistent with its surrounding political culture, has emphasized the need to maintain access rather than move to the kind of tight docket control that has been used in the courts of last resort in the United States and Canada. One of the trade-offs has been the growth of the Court (18 members by the mid–1980s. and more recently up to 25) and the use of the "double bench"—two-judge panels that hear the overwhelming majority of constitutional arguments in PIL cases. Participants are aware of the cost of these steps in potentially reducing doctrinal coherence, but there has been no move to reduce Supreme Court jurisdiction.

The Supreme Court's original jurisdiction reinforces its activist character in comparison with other national courts of last resort. One of the reasons why India's Supreme Court is so much more active than the U.S. Supreme Court is that a large number of the matters before the Indian Court would be handled in the United States by federal district courts. It is these federal trial courts that have been in the forefront of institutional reform litigation, which bears the closest resemblance to Indian social action litigation in its use of interim orders and designation of officials to monitor enforcement of court orders. Thus the contrast between the Indian and American judiciaries may not be as great as the contrast between the two countries' highest courts.

THE LIMITATIONS OF JUDICIAL ACTIVISM

[Baar explains some reasons for what he sees as the limited practical impact of social action litigation in India.]

Part of the judiciary's limited impact may be a product of the absence of other checks on government power in general and national political power in particular. For example, the states are relatively weak units in the Indian federal system. Constitutional amendments, even changes to provisions for fundamental rights, require only approval in the union parliament. It is no wonder that the Supreme Court developed the "basic structure" doctrine; no other institution outside the government in power at the center could check so fundamental an exercise of authority.

Nor is there an independent upper house to challenge judicial appointments in the style of the U.S. Senate. In practice, it is the Supreme Court again that has provided a check. No justice has been appointed to the Supreme Court of India since independence without the consent of the chief justice, and the veto has gained strength as its conventional use has continued. The chief justice's pivotal role has made his appointment all the more sensitive. The chief justiceship normally goes by seniority, and attempts by government to move past the most senior justices have given rise to supercession controversies. It is also rare for a Supreme Court appointee not to have had extensive experience on a state High Court, further constraining the central government appointing authorities.

Balanced against these constraints, however, is the provision for compulsory retirement of Supreme Court justices at age 65 (High Court justices retire at 62). The retirement age, reflecting the shorter life spans at the time the constitution was written 40 years ago, produces an enormous turnover, with the resulting opportunity for a new government to remake the Court in short order. For example, 14 of the 18 Supreme Court justices sitting on May 1, 1985, had retired by the end of 1988. The longest period of service among those 18 was a term of 13 years, 5 months.

The impact of social action litigation is mitigated by the absence of a bar with sufficient independent resources to support litigation challenging the legitimacy of government action. In the United States, public interest law grew through the public and private financial support of a network of law firms with the resources and expertise to vindicate new and expanded rights for their clientele. In India, no similar structure exists for perfecting challenges to state authority through the courts. Once again, the initiative fell to the Supreme Court; the PIL procedures that originated within the judiciary were in this sense a matter of necessity.

In summary, judicial activism in India is in a very real sense a constitutional imperative. The underdevelopment of other checks on a powerful central government has widened the scope and use of accountability mechanisms in the hands of the judiciary. India has neither the strong provincial governments that operate in Canada, the separation of powers that operates in the United States, nor the referenda used in Australia. As a result, the judiciary has become both a first and a last resort. It has responded to its role with a vigor and creativity that are breathtaking to outside observers. Yet, whether additional checks can develop to relieve some of the pressures on the Indian polity remains to be seen.

Questions and Comments

1. Consider whether, as Baar suggests, "arrears and delay" can promote "judicial activism by facilitating selective judicial intervention." Compare the certiorari jurisdiction of the U.S. Supreme Court, which in recent years has granted certiorari in about 80–130 of the more than 6,000 cases in which petitions are filed each year. To what extent does the U.S. Supreme Court's certiorari jurisdiction resemble the uses of overcrowding and delay that Baar describes in India? To what extent is the use of 2–judge panels in India analogous to the 3–judge screening panels for constitutional complaints used in Germany?

2. Baar suggests that certain conditions—including the presence of both fundamental rights and Directive Principles, a Supreme Court of broad jurisdiction, an independent judiciary, and traditions of judicial activism—can facilitate a socially progressive, activist court. Which of these are present in the U.S.? What explanatory power do these have? Do they cause you to rethink Professor Tushnet's skepticism about judicial review?

3. The epistolary jurisdiction may be "more important for its symbolic reaching out to the common man and its confirmation that access to justice is upheld as a fundamental right by the Indian Supreme Court than for its extensive practical uses." Cooper at 624. As Cooper goes on to note, it has been "particularly welcomed and used by investigative journalists who have written articles about social injustices they have uncovered, which when issues of fundamental rights have been involved have subsequently been translated by social action groups into direct writs to the Indian Supreme Court. One of the first uses of this jurisdiction was by a Supreme Court advocate, who filed a writ in 1980, based on a series of journalistic articles in a national daily, the Indian Express, exposing certain nefarious practices in Bihar involving pretrial prisoners. In the same year, two professors of law wrote a letter to the same newspaper, exposing barbaric conditions in a protective home for women, which the Indian Supreme Court translated into a writ petition. . . . Following this, a law student and a social worker adopted a similar strategy to expose barbarism in a woman's home in Delhi, and three journalists exposed and filed a writ concerning a market in which women were bought and sold as chattel." Cooper suggests that the "symbolic function" of the Indian Supreme Court "in replacing, and thereby diverting the threat of direct action," is key, insofar as it allows for a process of participation in government decisionmaking for the politically disempowered that no other government branch or agency can achieve. Should this diversion be regarded as a positive or negative feature of PIL in India?

———————

Jamie Cassels, *Judicial Activism and Public Interest Litigation in India: Attempting the Impossible?*, 37 Am. J. Comp. L. 495 (1989)

[Professor Cassels' article provides some greater detail on the procedural aspects of PIL noted in Baar's piece, and considers objections to the fairness, legitimacy, and efficacy of PIL]

* * *

Painfully aware of the limitations of legalism, the judiciary of India has struggled over the last decade to bring law into the service of the poor and oppressed. Under the banner of Public Interest (or Social Action) Litigation (PIL) and the enforcement of fundamental rights under the Constitution, the courts have sought to rebalance the distribution of legal resources, increase access to justice for the disadvantaged, and imbue formal legal guarantees with substantive and positive content. Originally aimed at combatting inhumane prison conditions and the horrors of bonded labor, public interest actions have now established the right to a speedy trial, the right to legal aid, the right to a livelihood, a right against pollution, a right to be protected from industrial hazards, and the right to human dignity.

A number of distinctive characteristics of PIL can be identified, each of which is novel and in some cases contrary to the traditional legalist understanding of the judicial function. Unlike the case of public interest litigation in Canada or the United States, the legal aid/public interest movement in India has been almost entirely initiated and led by the judiciary. The movement has been widely discussed by judges in the popular press and academic literature, and it is clearly informed by strong socio-political views and commitments. Its distinctive characteristics include: a) liberalization of the rules of standing; b) procedural flexibility; c) a creative and activist interpretation of legal and fundamental rights; d) remedial flexibility and ongoing judicial participation and supervision.

A. Access and Standing...

Anticipating later innovations, the Indian Supreme Court declared in 1976 that: "Where a wrong against community interest is done, 'no *locus standi*' will not always be a plea to non-suit an interested public body chasing the wrong doer in court ... *Locus standi* has a larger ambit in current legal semantics than the accepted, individualist jurisprudence of old.' Since that time the Indian approach to PIL has extended the rules of standing to the point that they may be said to have ceased to present any real obstacle to the public interest litigant. Public interest litigation has been initiated by individuals on behalf of other individuals and groups, by academics, journalists and by many social action organizations. As Krishna Iyer J. explained in *Mumbai Kangar Sabhha v. Abdulbhai*"

> Test litigations, representative actions, pro bono publico and like broadened forms of legal proceedings are in keeping with the current accent on justice to the common man and a necessary disincentive to those who wish to bypass the real issues on the merits by suspect reliance on peripheral, procedural shortcomings. . . . Public interest is promoted by a spacious construction of *locus standi* in our socio-economic circumstances and conceptual latitudinarianism permits taking liberties with individualization of the right to invoke the higher courts where the remedy is shared by a considerable number, particularly when they are weaker.

In *S.P. Gupta v. Union of India* Bhagwati C.J. (as he then was) was even more explicit:

> Where a legal wrong or a legal injury is caused to a person or to a determinate class of persons . . . and such a person or determinate class of persons is by reason of poverty, helplessness or disability or socially or economically disadvantaged position, unable to approach the court for relief, any member of the public can maintain an application for appropriate direction . . .

B. *Procedural Flexibility*

The Indian judiciary has shown a willingness to alter the rules of the game where necessary. Actions may be commenced not only by way of formal petition, but also by way of letters addressed to the court or a judge who may choose to treat it as a petition. There are reports of actions begun by postcard, and even of one judge converting a letter to the editor in a newspaper into a PIL writ. Judges have been known to invite and encourage public interest actions.

Legal aid has been established as a fundamental right in criminal cases and in others the courts will often waive fees, award costs and provide other forms of litigation assistance to public interest advocates. The court frequently appoints commissions of enquiry or socio-legal committees to investigate and collect the necessary facts, thus relieving the petitioner of the financial burden of proof. These commissions not only investigate the facts, but may also be directed to recommend appropriate remedies. The court will often order that they receive expenses and an honorarium from the defendant.

Just as the court has sought to enhance access, so has it sought to increase impact. So, for example, where there are a wide variety of offenders, the court may choose to treat a particular case as a representative action and issue orders binding on the entire class. In one case concerning massive pollution of the river Ganga, the court published notices in the newspaper drawing the litigation to the attention of all concerned industries and municipal authorities inviting them to enter an appearance. The final order, closing a large number of industries and prohibiting the discharge of untreated effluent, was directed to scores of enterprises *ex parte*. . . .

C.   *Creative Adjudication and the Elaboration of Rights* . . .

The fundamental rights of Indian citizens are specified in Articles 12–35 of the Indian Constitution. Article 21 declares that "No person shall be deprived of his life or personal liberty except according to procedure established by law'. The earliest understanding of this provision was a narrow procedural one: that the state had to demonstrate only that the interference with the individual accorded with the procedure laid down by properly enacted law. Moreover, inconvenient Supreme Court decisions on the constitutionality of state action were simply overturned by amending the constitution until the 'basic structure' of the constitution was declared unalterable."

It was not until 1978 that the Supreme Court breathed substantive life into Article 21 by subjecting state action interfering with life or liberty to a test of reasonableness; requiring not only that the procedures be authorized by law, but that they are "right, just and fair."[35] This transformation paved the way for a substantive reinterpretation of constitutional and legal guarantees and positive judicial intervention.

The former Chief Justice of the Supreme Court, writing in both the popular press and the academic journals, made quite clear his rejection of the "bureaucratic tradition" of mechanical and rule-bound adjudication.[36] He suggested that positivism is a myth, "deliberately constructed to insulate judges against vulnerability to public criticism, and to preserve their image of neutrality. . . . It also helps judges to escape accountability for what they decide, because they can always plead helplessness." In interpreting the Constitution, the Supreme Court is neither bound by doctrines of literal meaning or original intent, nor constrained to read into it only formal rights and liberties. Instead, the text can be read as one which is "vibrant with a socio-economic ideology geared to the goal of social justice" and can be infused with principles that transcend mere formal equality, and transform legal rights into positive social entitlements.

> The judges in India have asked themselves the question: can judges really escape addressing themselves to substantial questions of social justice? Can they . . . simply follow the legal text when they are aware that their actions will perpetuate inequality and injustice? Can they restrict their inquiry into law and life within the narrow confines of a narrowly defined rule of law?

35. Maneka Ghandi v. Union of India, (1978) 2 S.C.R. 621, A.I.R. 1978 S.C. 597. This was a particularly dramatic achievement given that Art. 21 contains no equivalent of a 'due process' requirement. . . .

36. Bhagwati, "Bureaucrats? Phonographers? Creators?," The *Times of India*, 21–23 September 1986. Reproduced and discussed in Agarwala, "The Legal Philosophy of P.N. Bhagwati," 14 *Indian Bar Rev.* 136 (1987).

Most constitutionally-based public interest litigation in India is aimed not at challenging the validity of legislative measures, but rather at enforcing existing laws and forcing public agencies to take steps to enhance the welfare of the citizens. As the Supreme Court declared in one case (concerning the displacement of slum dwellers in Bombay), positive action is required "if the theory of equal protection of laws has to take its place in the struggle for equality. . . . "

> In these matters, the demand is not so much for less Governmental interference as for positive Governmental action to provide equal treatment to the neglected segments of society. The profound rhetoric of socialism must be translated into practice. . . .

Through an expansive reading of fundamental rights, informed by a commitment to the (non-enforceable) social welfare objectives of the Directive Principles, the courts have sought to read substance into otherwise formal guarantees.[40]

. . . A few examples . . . will illustrate this tendency. In *Olga Tellis*, the court affirmed that "the sweep of the right to life contained in Article 21 is wide and far reaching" and includes the right to a livelihood.[41] In *Francis Coralie Mullin*, the court stated that

> the right to life includes the right to life with human dignity and all that goes along with it and . . . must in any view of the matter, include the right to the basic necessities of life and also the right to carry on such functions and activities as constitute the bare minimum expression of the human self.

40. Art. 37 states that the provisions contained in Part IV are "not enforceable by any court, but the principles therein laid down are fundamental in the governance of the country." Though the Directive Principles are not enforceable, the courts consistently use them to interpret enforceable fundamental rights (to the extent of reading them into fundamental rights), to ground their assumption of jurisdiction over "regulatory" matters, and to support the remedial strategies they adopt. The reliance on Directive Principles is particularly apparent in legal aid, prison and environmental litigation. The relevant Directive Principles are 39–A (state to provide free legal aid) and 48–A (environmental protection). In *Hussainara Khatoon*, the court relied on Art. 39–A to support its finding that legal aid was a fundamental right under Art. 21 and suggested, even in the absence of legislation, that if legal aid was not provided by the state criminal trials might be void: "This constitutional obligation cannot wait any longer for its fulfillment . . . . [N]o state Government can possibly have any alibi for not carrying out this command of the Constitution" (at 1381). For the use of the Directive Principles in environmental litigation, see M.C. Mehta v. Union of India (1987) 4 S.C.C. 463, (1987) 2 Scale 611, continued in (1988) 1 Scale 54 (pollution of the river Ganga); Sachidanand Pandey v. State of West Bengal (1987) 2 S.C.J. 70 (reliance on Art. 48–A to review municipal decision to locate hotel in Calcutta zoological garden).

41. S.C.C., 572, A.I.R., 193. This case concerned the eviction of pavement and slum dwellers from the streets in Bombay. The "right" established may have been somewhat hollow since the court held in the end that the law authorizing their eviction was reasonable if read down to provide for a hearing. Some protection was provided. The court ordered that established communities could not be removed where they did not interfere with the public way unless the land was needed for a proper public purpose, that others could not be removed until after the monsoon, and that alternate accommodation should be found (though this was not a precondition).

In *Bandhua Mukti Morcha,* Article 21 was said to include the right to be "free from exploitation" and

> at the least, therefore, it must include protection of the health and strength of workers, men and women, and of the tender age of children against abuse, opportunities and facilities for children to develop in a healthy manner and in conditions of freedom and dignity, educational facilities, just and humane conditions of work and maternity relief. These are the minimum requirements which must exist in order to enable a person to live with human dignity.

In cases dealing with the treatment of prisoners awaiting trial, the court has found support in the Constitution for orders requiring the state to take active steps to ensure effective legal aid. In one such case it ordered that assistance be funded by the state, that information on prisoners be provided immediately to Legal Aid Committees, that prisoners be educated about their legal rights, and that compliance be monitored by surprise visits to the jail by a local judge. The court reasoned that, absent positive measures, prisoners would be priced out of their rights.

In *M.C. Mehta v. Union of India,* the Supreme Court accepted that environmental pollution and industrial hazards were not only potential civil torts, but also violations of fundamental rights, redressable directly by the Supreme Court through a public interest petition. It took the opportunity in this case to forge a doctrine of absolute liability with respect to hazardous operations, unrestricted by the traditional qualifications and exceptions that have grown about the common law rule in *Rylands v. Fletcher.* The Court reasoned that injuries to workers and others caused even by necessary industries are part of the social cost of development and should not be borne by the victims.

As one observer has concluded, through their interpretation of Article 21 the courts have sought to convert formal guarantees into positive human rights....

If left unqualified, this is an overstatement. While interpretations of fundamental rights may be informed by a commitment to the welfare objectives contained in the Directive Principles, these are specifically declared to be non-justiciable. And while the court may attempt to improve the administration of various welfare laws (in some cases almost rewriting them) it has said consistently that it cannot force the state to enact legislation to enhance fundamental rights or to pursue the Directive Principles.[50] The true measure of judicial activism in India, therefore, is found less in the rhetoric of rights definition than in the remedial strategies deployed and actual outcomes in PIL cases.

---

50. [Citations omitted] The Supreme Court has, however, ruled that where a fundamental right applies against private action as well as government, the government is constitutionally obligated to take steps to enforce that right. See People's Union for Democratic Rights v. Union of India (the Asiad Worker's Case), A.I.R. 1982 S.C. 1473.

D. Remedial Flexibility

The usual understanding of judicial remedies requires that the rights of the parties be determined with finality and that the court avoid prolonged or multiple suits and, at all costs, resist involving itself in any ongoing supervision of the matter. The institutional limitations of courts and the doctrine of the separation of powers are thought to exclude the judiciary from interfering with the operation of the administration and to prohibit second-guessing discretionary decisions requiring the delicate balancing of material and policy factors. In the name of efficiency, the courts will often require that the applicant exhaust all other forms of redress before seeking a judicial remedy.

In this area too, the Indian courts have demonstrated an ability to press against the boundaries of the traditional understanding....

By way of example, in environmental litigation the court has shown itself willing to assume wide powers that might otherwise be left to other rule-making authorities and regulatory agencies. In the *Shiriam Fertilizer* case[54] the court permitted a chemical plant to reopen after a gas leak only upon satisfying a set of stringent conditions. On the basis of recommendations of four separate court-appointed technical teams the court ordered specific technical, safety and training improvements. It required the allocation of trained staff to defined safety functions. To monitor the plant the court set up an independent committee to visit the plant every two weeks, and also ordered the government inspector to make surprise visits once a week. In addition, noting the increasing frequency of environmental litigation, and the technical difficulties which the court experienced in acquiring competent independent technical information and advice, it "suggested" that the government establish an Ecological Sciences Resource Group to assist the court. The court also required the company and its managers to deposit security to guarantee compensation to any who might be injured as a result of the enterprise's activity.

Similarly, in the *Bonded Labour Case* the court instructed local officials to identify oppressed workers, and to effect their release and physical, economic and psychological rehabilitation. To this end the court directed the authorities to accept the assistance of social action groups, to carry out surprise checks on local quarries, to set up labour camps to educate workers about their legal rights, and to ensure a pollution-free environment with adequate sanitary, medical and legal facilities. In a case dealing with the conditions in children's homes, the court ordered the public

---

54. M.C. Mehta v. Union of India, (1986) 2 S.C.C. 176. 1987 A.I.R.S.C. 965; conditions modified (1986) 2 S.C.C. 325, 1987 A.I.R.S.C. 982. See also, M.C. Mehta v. Union of India, (1988) 1 Scale 54, concerning the pollution of the river Ganga. In this case the court ordered the public authorities to complete proposed work on sewage treatment in a timely fashion, to remove dairies from the proximity of the river or provide facilities for waste removal and to refuse new industrial licenses in the absence of proof of adequate waste management facilities. Also, relying on Directive Principle 51–A(g) (specifying the duty of government to educate about pollution) it ordered that schools would teach environmental awareness one hour per week and that the central government would have texts written and distributed free of cost.

broadcasting authorities to provide publicity for the effort to rehabilitate destitute children.

III. PROBLEMS, CRITICS AND THEMES...

A. *Procedure and Practical Difficulties*

...[T]he non-adversarial nature of the proceedings is a matter of concern to many. Unfounded allegations may be made that cannot be subjected to rigorous tests of proof; defendants may not know the full case against them; and over-extensive reliance on socio-legal commissions of enquiry may give the court a partial and possibly biased view of the facts. These concerns are, perhaps, exaggerated. The facts upon which the courts rely are made available to the concerned parties and an opportunity is given to them to respond. Affidavits may be challenged, additional reports commissioned and new evidence entered.

Both the manner in which litigation may be initiated and the activism of the judiciary in prosecuting such cases raise the spectre that litigants are shopping for particular judges and that judges are shopping for particular issues and causes. Increased formalization, however, would block access to less sophisticated petitioners....

The expansive approach to standing puts pressure on the court to develop theories of justiciability by which issues that are unsuitable to resolution by litigation can be winnowed out.... [O]f more immediate consequence, the relaxed test of standing and the expedited fashion in which cases can be brought in public interest matters put enormous strains on already extremely scarce judicial resources.[58] Some High Courts are reported to receive 50 to 60 public interest letters per day. In the fifteen months from 1 January 1987 to 31 March 1988, the Supreme Court received 23,772 letters.[59]

Permanent PIL cells have now been established at some courts to act as an initial filter for applications. These enable judges to pass communications through a screening process[60] and from there on to the Chief Justice for assignment in the ordinary way. Resources permitting, these bodies, along with the various legal aid organizations, might also serve a more active investigatory role. The PIL cells cull through the letters, winnowing out frivolous and inappropriate matters and prepare files for the Chief Justice.[61] Nevertheless, the problem of backlogs and delays remains a

---

58. By Canadian and American standards, Indian courts are dramatically understaffed and poorly equipped. For an account of some of the problems, see Rajeev Dhavan, *Litigation Explosion in India* (1985).

59. Of these, 110 were automatically posted as writ petitions in the Supreme Court. 938 were referred to the Supreme Court Legal Aid Committee, and 5,857 to various state Legal Aid and Advice boards for action. 4,745 were referred directly to various government departments for direct action,

and the remaining 10,746 were either lodged or otherwise disposed of. Figures provided by the PIL cell, Supreme Court of India, New Delhi, 15 April 1988.

60. The Chief Justice issues general guidelines to the cells which broadly categorize classes of complaints and sets down procedures for their disposal.

61. Informally the workers at these cells estimate that they receive 60–65 letters per day. While the Chief Justice has provided

serious concern and appears to underlie a recent retrenchment in PIL matters. As Khalid J. said in a recent case, PIL is now a firmly established part of Indian law, but "one is led to believe that it poses a threat to courts and public alike. Such cases are now filed without any rhyme or reason." He expressed fear that the courts were becoming swamped with PIL matters and that other areas of judicial operation were suffering. Calling for clear guidelines, he suggested that PIL might be limited to cases of 'gross violations' where the conscience of the court was shocked. Several months later, as if to confirm the reversing tide, the court dismissed an Article 32 petition (though not strictly a PIL matter) on the grounds that the Supreme Court was stretched beyond capacity and the High Court could provide the appropriate remedy. The Court said, "even if no new case is filed in this Court hereafter, with the present strength of judges it may take more than 15 years to dispose of all the pending cases."

B.   Legitimacy: The Politics of Judicial Activism

The dominant understanding of the judicial function in the common law world is that it can be rendered compatible with liberal democratic principles only if adjudication remains distinct from legislation. . . .

It should come as no surprise, then, that some of the fiercest criticism of judicial innovation in public interest litigation has drawn on these traditional conceptions of the judicial role. . . .

The question of legitimacy is a highly problematic one. To suggest that the way in which an institution functions is illegitimate may be a way of saying that it is deviating from preferred practices in a way that is inconsistent with the theory of institutional relations underlying the Constitution. Alternatively, it may be to make a statement of fact that for some reason the *de facto* authority of the institution is in jeopardy. . . .

The power struggle between the courts and the legislature is as old as independent India; no one institution is the unequivocal historical champion of the poor and oppressed. Judges are drawn from the elite and propertied classes in Indian society and have demonstrated their willingness to deploy the Constitution to serve the interests of those classes. The battle between the courts and legislatures over land reform began virtually on day one of the Constitution, and since that time the courts have vigorously scrutinized redistributive measures. In *Golak Nath,* the Supreme Court declared that fundamental rights, including the right to property, were unamendable. In the early 1970s it protected the privileges and pensions of princes from the government, and invalidated bank nationalization legislation—moves hardly likely to engender the support of social activists. Indira G[handi]'s substantial victory in the election of 1971 was achieved on issues of economic and social reform and was a popular rebuke to the courts.

broad guidelines, there is obviously a great
deal of discretion involved in assessing these
letters.

During the years leading up to the 1975–77 Emergency the courts became increasingly subordinate to the executive and legislature. Their pro-property decisions were increasingly neutralized by constitutional amendments; political appointments, transfers of 'uncommitted judges' to undesirable posts, and the practice of supersession served to erode further the autonomy of judges[75] The courts' failure to assert fundamental rights during the Emergency made their marginal position painfully clear to the Indian public, and the process culminated in the 42nd amendment to the Constitution (1977), which sought all but to eliminate the power of judicial review.[77]

The new judicial activism may thus be understood as part of the courts' effort to retrieve a degree of legitimacy following the Emergency. The courts had been politicized and marginalized. PIL represents a strategic reversal of previous judicial priorities in order to win popular support and achieve a more prominent role in Indian society. The question is whether there is room in the Indian political system for such an enterprise.

Indian political institutions are dominated by competing elite groups (capitalists, wealthy farmers, professional classes). Public institutions, including the bureaucracy, social agencies and the police have, through patronage, political pressure and corruption, become partly privatized by these elites, whose interests are often adverse to social reform. . . . Liberal ideals of equality clash with traditional social arrangements and the most well-intentioned formal laws run into the impasse posed by relatively autonomous structures of traditional power, authority and social organization. The experience of the Emergency and the increasing centralization of government power under the domination of a single party threatens to engender a crisis of confidence in democratic institutions.

It is in response to these factors that in the last two decades social action groups have begun mobilizing outside the mainstream of Indian politics and have sought other arenas of social struggle. And it is in this context that the courts have risked asserting for themselves a more high profile role in India's socio-political life.

The judges have been accused of illegitimately 'politicizing' constitutional adjudication. This criticism assumes the coherence of a distinction between legislation and adjudication, and the possibility of neutral constitutional interpretation. Without wishing to enter the debate, it must be said that the activist members of the judiciary are certainly not alone when they

75. Supersession is the promotion of junior judges over their senior colleagues. The government also transferred large numbers of anti-government High Court judges to hardship posts. Both of these moves were seen as attacks on the independence of the judiciary. For a brief account of these developments see, Richard Nyrop (ed.), *India, A Country Study* 396–400 (1985).

77. Park & Mesquita, supra n. 63 at 71–72. The 42nd amendment which sought among other things to override the 'basic structure' doctrine, has since been tempered by the 43rd and 44th amendments, enacted by the post-emergency Janata government.

suggest that the issue is not *whether,* but *what type* of, political values should enter into adjudication....

There can be little doubt that the Indian courts have penetrated policy formulation and administrative operations to a much greater extent—or at least in a more open fashion—than Western court-watchers are used to seeing. The judiciary is, of course, aware of the danger of taking on a policy role "to a degree characteristic of political authority" and indeed, "running the risk of being mistaken for one." However, the doctrine of separation of powers, while suggesting good reasons why such lines must be drawn (judicial non-accountability, institutional competence, etc.), does not of itself indicate precisely where they should be placed. As one Supreme Court judge said, when a citizen seeks vindication of a fundamental right or Directive Principle the court cannot simply "shrug its shoulders and say priorities are a matter of policy and so it is a matter for the policy-making authority." Whenever a court is called upon to scrutinize an official decision or operation it is immediately and inevitably engaged in both policy analysis and the political exercise of determining its own jurisdiction. Principles of standing, justiciability, and judicial deference do not remove so much as disguise this dimension. Where the lines may be drawn is as much a matter of institutional capacity, practical politics and popular support as of constitutional theory....

The question of practical politics brings us once again to the more general issue of political viability and popular support. The effectiveness of general and intrusive judicial remedies depends almost entirely upon good faith compliance efforts. In the absence of such efforts many fear that there is little the court can do except watch its own authority erode. As one Supreme Court Justice said of the 'politicization' of the judiciary:

> Since the court possesses the sanction neither of the sword nor [of] the purse and ... its strength lies basically in public confidence and support, consequently the legitimacy of its acts and decisions must remain beyond all doubt. ... Indeed, both certainty of substance and certainty of direction are indispensible requirements in the development of law, and invest it with the credibility which commands public confidence in its legitimacy.

There is a recognized need to ensure that the remedies are clear and feasible, to monitor and assess the extent of compliance, and also to determine the degree to which PIL orders have actually contributed to improving the lives of the disadvantaged.

Whether the popular legitimacy of the courts has been enhanced or diminished as a result of its PIL activism is another empirical question that awaits systematic study. The informal evidence is, however, instructive. There seems to be no doubt that the courts' public profile has been raised considerably. The popular press, social action newsletters and magazines and scholarly literature are replete with reports, by and large favorable, of PIL matters. The sheer volume of PIL petitions attests to the demand for the new forum. One of the foremost observers of PIL has claimed that by transcending received liberal notions of the judicial function courts are retrieving a degree of popular moral support at the *same* time that other social and political institutions are facing a legitimation crisis. He suggests that the "transition from a traditional captured agency with a low social visibility into a liberated agency with a high socio-political visibility is a remarkable development." The principle of separation of powers and the distinction between legislation and adjudication presuppose that the executive and legislature are themselves vested with legitimacy and popular support. Where this is not entirely the case, the assumption of a political role beyond that traditionally ascribed to the judiciary may not undermine, but indeed enhance its credibility and support.

The final question is whether such claims are an over-enthusiastic response to the early experience of PIL; whether they underestimate the nature of India's social problems and ignore the inherent limitations of the judicial process. As noted above, there has been some retrenchment, foreshadowing a more restricted and regulated approach to PIL matters. Moreover, there is not as yet any significant data on the actual impact of PIL on the lives of the groups that it is supposed to serve.

C. *Efficacy*

To the foreign observer, one of the most striking aspects of the Indian legal system is the extent to which formal legal arrangements exist in almost metaphysical isolation from social reality. It is hardly surprising, therefore, that while public interest litigation may have secured a better life for some individuals, it has not ended bonded labor nor found homes for the Bombay pavement dwellers. . . .

Critics and social activists alike question the utility of expending scarce human and financial resources on litigative strategies. . . . As [Upendra Baxi, a] PIL activist, suggested: . . . We must link up with social activists who alone can provide them with ground support.

To admit the limitations of PIL is not necessarily to dismiss it. . . .

. . . The experience of both the social activists and the beneficiaries of PIL is no doubt a contradictory one. For example, after a drawn out effort to improve the practices prevailing in children's homes, one prominent social activist stated, "I shall not [again] enter the courts as a petitioner or as a respondent . . . I have no respect for the courts." Of public interest litigation she said, "Does it work for the commoners *sans* silk gown? The thousands of children in jails throughout India testify to the fact that it does not." Four months later, the Supreme Court again had occasion to decide a petition filed by this same individual. This time she was more successful. The issue concerned the denial of public access for journalists to prisons in order to assess conditions and ensure the welfare of the detainees. The Court took note of the fact that through public interest litigation and the intervention of the courts, prison conditions had substantially improved over the years. But the court also reasoned that, until the attitudes of administrators changed, the ongoing efforts of social activists on the ground remained the crucial link in ensuring the fundamental rights of citizens.

IV. CONCLUSION

In the final analysis, the fate of PIL in India may therefore hinge on the concrete experience and continued faith and effort of social activists and their constituent groups; and, notwithstanding some successes, this experience is a contradictory one. The Indian legal system suffers exponentially from all the same defects as that in the developed countries of the West. Ordinary litigation is expensive and well beyond the means of disadvantaged groups in society. Delays of *Bleak House* proportions are notorious. Stories of corruption, bias, and political interference can frequently be found in the national press. The Indian legal system was designed to further the goals and policies of colonial control and exploitation, and today a lively literature questions the extent to which it has emerged from this role. More recently, the bar and bench have proved their willingness to serve the needs of modern corporate capitalism; they have extended to the powerful segments of society constitutional guarantees which to many observers simply obstruct socially progressive measures.

Judges, lawyers and politicians of the left, from which many PIL activists are drawn, are vividly aware of their inheritance. Many perceive law in straightforward Marxist terms: a system organized around formal individual rights and private property, designed by and for the ruling class, to preserve the maldistribution of wealth and power in society. As one judge of the Supreme Court said even of the constitutional guarantees of equality and social welfare: "It is obvious that the provision for socialism and the high-ringing Directive Principles are a facade and that to the ruling classes equality has never meant more than 'formal equality' and socialism has never been more than a verbal mask."

Even the immediate future of PIL remains uncertain.... [I]t remains dependent on the personal commitment of individual judges.... Simple non-compliance can effectively derail judicial reforms and the ultimate power of easy constitutional amendment allows inconvenient decisions to be legislatively overruled....

Nevertheless, critical legal activists also believe that to the extent that law does have a degree of autonomy from the immediate requirements of the political and economic elite it might be harnessed for the cause of the less advantaged. Enhanced access of such groups to law, and increased support might give the formal promises of law some, albeit, limited, value. By exploiting the limited autonomy of law, the courts become an arena of social struggle wherein the stakes may be largely ideological and only incrementally material.... The crucial question remains whether this ideological function will serve to expose and alter pathological social arrangements, or simply paper over the abyss which separates formal legal promises from Indian social reality.

———————

Questions and Comments

1. Of what relevance is the Emergency Period in explaining the new direction of India's judicial activism? Consider Cassels' suggestion that the

Court's new activism should be seen as an effort to retrieve a judicial legitimacy lost in the events leading up to and in the course of the Emergency Period. For an interesting speculation on why the Supreme Court held that the legislature, using constitutionally provided for procedures, nonetheless lacked power to amend the Constitution in certain respects, see Upendra Baxi,The Indian Supreme Court and Politics 19–20 (1980) (suggesting that the 1967 Golak Nath decision—that Parliament could not amend the fundamental rights provisions of the Constitution—came from the justices' fear of the new group of leaders then standing for election to replace Nehru; the Court "intervened to ensure that second-generation politicians would not make fundamental rights into playthings.")

2.   For another comparative perspective, see Douglas L. Parker, *Standing to Litigate 'Abstract Social Interests' in the United states and Italy: Reexamining the 'Injury in Fact'*, 33 Colum. J. Transnational L. 259 (1995). As Parker describes, while individual plaintiffs have to meet requirements of having particularized interests in the adjudication, Italian legislation also permits challenges to be brought by certain designated groups, including labor unions, the Italian Red Cross, and

> "environmental protection organizations of a national character, present in at least five regions, to be identified as such by the Minister of the Environment. The minister bases her decision on the programmatic goals of the organization and a determination of its 'internal democratic character,' as well as on the demonstrated 'continuity of its actions' and its . . . 'external importance or consequences.' "

Compare Lujan v. Defenders of Wildlife, 504 U.S. 555 (1992) (federal statute, authorizing "any person" to sue to enjoin the United States or its agencies from alleged violation of environmental laws requiring consultation to assure that federally financed projects not jeopardize the continued existence of endangered species, held unconstitutional to the extent it authorized an environmental organization or its members to bring such action where they could not show injury in fact, causation and redressability; Court emphasizes that "when the plaintiff is not himself the object of the government action or inaction he challenges, standing is . . . substantially more difficult to establish").

---

2.   On "Intermediate Societies" and Public Interest Litigation

Mauro Cappelletti, The Judicial Process in Comparative Perspective (1989) (pp. 295–99)

[In his discussion of barriers to the development of public interest/social justice litigation in civil law countries in Europe (including the "orientation of civil law judges" as less well-suited to litigation that "reaches beyond the parties 'present' in" an adjudication, and their wariness of "too evident manifestations of lawmaking through the courts"), Mauro Cappelletti identifies the absence of strong traditions of "intermediate societies" as a further obstacle.]

* * *

B. THE REVOLUTIONARY TRADITION AGAINST 'INTERMEDIATE SOCIETIES'

There is another obstacle which is of extraordinary importance, even though there are now signs that it is being gradually overcome in civil law nations. This obstacle consists of a traditional reluctance to accept groups united to further a common interest.

Many class and public interest actions in America have been brought by private groups and spontaneous organizations created to represent otherwise unorganized interests: civil rights associations, environmentalists' and consumers' organizations, and last, but not least, public interest lawyers organized in larger or smaller groups. Similarly, relator actions in England, Australia, and other common law countries have been brought by private groups and organizations acting for the general public interest or for the interest of one sector of the public, rather than by isolated individuals or aggregates of non-organized individuals. The fact is that even the most liberal granting of standing to individuals would be an insufficient solution to the problem of asserting diffuse rights if the 'private Attorneys–General' were not allowed to associate and fight as an organized group.

This very fact, however, constitutes an additional obstacle for the representation of meta-individual interests in civil law courts. It should be recalled that among the principal targets of the great bourgeois revolution initiated in France in 1789, which later spread over much of Continental Europe, were the *corps intermédiaires*—the organizations intermediate between the individual and the state, which were identified with the feudal structure of the *ancien régime*. As Max Rheinstein put it: 'With eighteenth century, Enlightenment the individualizing view of society began to be preponderant. In the French Revolution the new ideology became official. . . . The state was now clearly conceived to be composed of individual citizens. The intermediate groups of manor, guild, estate, province were swept away.'

Of course, this initial attitude of hostility and distrust *vis-à-vis* 'intermediate societies' soon had to come to grips with the very profound changes of European societies in the post-Revolutionary epoch. Industrialization, in particular, brought about the need for articulate organization of both capital and the emerging labour class. Yet the resistance against the new was strong. In France, for instance, it was only in 1884 that labour unions were definitively recognized as legitimate entities.

Legal fictions were frequently used to adapt the existing law to the new social needs. A 'legal personality', for instance, was fictitiously attributed to partnerships, corporations, and professional associations; thus, the principle that only individual 'persons'—natural or legal—can be participants in the legal and judicial processes was preserved.

At least two problems, however, still remain largely unsolved: first, the problem of the legal status of non-personalized, unincorporated, *de facto* associations and other organizations; second, the problem of organizations (incorporated or not) seeking access to court not to protect their own rights, as in the case of a trade union or a political party claiming damages for the pillage of its own premises, but rather to protect the rights of their members or the collective rights of classes or groups that the organizations purport to represent. The first problem cannot be dealt with here. The second, however, must be discussed, since it is central to any study of modern public interest advocacy in the courts.

C. THE PROLIFERATION OF 'INTERMEDIATE SOCIETIES' ACTING AS 'ORGANIZATIONAL PRIVATE ATTORNEYS–GENERAL': IDEO-LOGICAL PARTIES AND THE DANGER OF A 'RETURN TO FEU-DALISM'

New groups have been rising and proliferating in recent times to fight the new menaces of our epoch—the tyranny of racial, religious, and political majorities, the oppressions of the modern corporate society, the red tape of bureaucracies, the blind selfishness of producers and polluters. The essential aim of these groups is not to protect rights 'belonging' to them, but rather to represent the aggregate of many 'small rights' and the diffuse 'rights without a holder'—the 'newer property'. Their very essence is—to borrow from a widely accepted definition by Louis Jaffe—to act as 'ideological', not as 'Hohfeldian', plaintiffs; in other words, to act for the public good as 'organized private Attorneys–General'. Should they not be allowed to so act, their very reason for being would disappear.

Of course, this development, unprecedented in its size and impact, is not itself without dangers. Opponents have described it as a dreadful 'return to feudalism', and undoubtedly new abuses and tyrannies can grow out of it. Labour unions, political parties, national and transnational corporations, and professional organizations can themselves become fearful centres of oppression against both their members and third parties… [L]egal instruments valuable *per se*, such as class actions, have sometimes been used as tools of blackmail.

This is the reason why public checks and controls … are particularly vital. Recall that such controls are entrusted to the Attorney–General in the English relator action, to the judge in the American class action, and to the *ministère public* in the action brought in France by consumer associations.

Neither the dangers of abuse nor the tenacity of traditionalism, however, seem able to stop the grand movement. … As early as 1913, a landmark decision by the French Cour de Cassation, confirmed in 1920 by legislation, recognized the power of labour unions and other *syndicats professionnels* to represent in court the 'collective interest of the association';… recent French and German statutes have granted standing to private organizations to sue for the diffuse interests of consumers and racial minorities. In Italy, a 1973 decision by the Supreme Administrative

Court, breaking an uninterrupted 'Hohfeldian' tradition of that court, granted standing to a private environmental association called Italia Nostra—an Italian analogue of the Sierra Club—to bring suit against the government for the diffuse interests of environmental conservation. Since the 1973 decision allowed Italia Nostra to litigate *as an organization* rather than as a representative of injured individuals, it went an important step beyond the 1972 doctrine of the U.S. Supreme Court in Sierra Club v. Morton [405 U.S. 727 (1972)]....[I]n Germany, where the 'Hohfeldian' doctrine still prevails ... an important departure ... though not yet at the Supreme Court level, also occurred in 1973 ... [when] the administrative court of Bavaria granted standing to an environmental association that requested a court order to stay the construction of a hotel....

Questions and Comments

1. In India, could one say that the judges, acting in the "common law" tradition, are trying to create the conditions for "intermediary societies" that can focus on litigation as a tool for social justice?

2. If so, is this appropriate for courts to do? Is it likely to be as effective as other organizing and political strategies?

3.   EASTERN EUROPE AND RUSSIA

In *Allen v. Wright*, the Court wrote that U.S. conceptions of standing and justiciability relate to the "article III notion that federal courts may exercise power 'only as a last resort, and as a necessity', and only when adjudication is 'consistent with a system of separated powers and the [dispute is one] traditionally thought to be capable of resolution through the judicial process.'" Herman Schwartz notes that in the U.S., justiciability requirements "enable the federal courts to avoid deciding many questions of major constitutional significance—a goal frequently invoked in American constitutional jurisprudence"; in Europe, he points out, constitutional courts were "created for the express purpose of *deciding* constitutional issues, not evading them." Herman Schwartz, *The New East European Constitutional Courts*, 13 Mich. J. Intl L. 741, 752–53 (1992) As he summarizes the situation at the time in Europe (especially in Eastern Europe).

> "standing is not based solely on the adversary process; abstract judicial review is welcomed, rather than avoided; questions may be considered both before the question arises as well as after it has been rendered moot; and finally, political questions lie well within the European court's judicial authority."

For example, he notes that in Hungary, anyone was permitted to challenge existing legal rules and statutes, though more limited parties could challenge bills or treaties not yet enacted or implemented. (Note that at the time of his writing in 1992, Romania and Hungary allowed review of unimplemented laws, and the Russian Constitutional Court act specifically provided that a court proceeding should be completed even if the challenged act had been repealed or had expired.) At that time, moreover, the Russian, Romanian and Hungarian courts could in some cases begin a proceeding *sua sponte*, without a complaint being filed.

While we will consider the political question doctrine in the U.S. and in Germany in a later section, here we examine the Russian Constitutional Court, particularly in its initial period of activism between 1991–93. Its experience may be taken to stand as a caution about the risks to constitutional courts of having, or exercising, some of the powers with which they were initially provided.

The Lawyers Committee for Human Rights describes the Soviet constitutional tradition as one that "rejected genuine control over legislative powers . . . as an unnecessary reflection of the bourgeois idea of separation of powers." Lawyers Committee for Human Rights, Justice Delayed: the Russian Constitutional Court and Human Rights 1 (March 1995). The USSR's Constitution of 1977 provided for political review of constitutional issues by the Presidium of the Supreme Soviet. In 1989, this was changed to provide for a Committee for Constitutional Supervision. While the Lawyers Committee regarded establishment of the Committee for Constitutional Supervision as a step forward for the enforcement of human rights, several shortcomings were noted: the Committee for Constitutional Supervision could not receive individual petitions, and its decisions on human rights norms were often ignored.

When the Russian Federation emerged from the fall of the Soviet Union, it established a Constitutional Court, along the lines of the European model of centralized review but which permitted individuals to file petitions. Although it received hundreds of petitions dealing with human rights issues under the Russian Constitution, this first Constitutional Court spent more of its time dealing with questions of separation of powers, a course which, according to the Lawyers Committee "eventually led to its destruction." Consider, as you read the following materials, how much the demise of the first court was the responsibility of the justices (or of the Chief Justice's extrajudicial activities); how much of the elected officials; and how much of a Constitution that, in the Lawyers' Committee's words, was "inherited from the Soviet era . . . [and] so heavily amended . . . that it was filled with internal contradictions that the court was unable to resolve [including for example, that] the Constitution stressed the principle of separation of powers but went on to guarantee parliamentary supremacy."

Robert Sharlet, *Chief Justice as Judicial Politician*, 2 East European Constitutional Review 32 (Spring 1993)

[This essay was written during the brief existence of the first Russian Constitutional Court.]

Since December 1992, Russia's newest democratic institution, the Constitutional Court, and especially its Chief Justice, Valery Zorkin, have been at the center of the country's ongoing constitutional crisis. In the space of four months. Chief Justice Zorkin's reputation has fluctuated as he has led the Court, judicially and extrajudicially, in an effort to arbitrate the profound political dispute between the legislative and executive branches. Zorkin, a consummate judicial activist, has over the past year and a half consistently carried his activism off the bench and into the political arena. By the Spring of 1993, however, friends and foes of the Court alike were asking whether the Chief Justice's extrajudicial activity had not, by impairing his judicial reputation, damaged the credibility the Court needs if it is to carry out judicial review of executive and legislative acts....

Zorkin was a Communist Party member until he resigned in the fall of 1991. His public career as an active reformer did not get underway until he became a senior consultant to the Russian Constitutional Commission in 1990. On the Commission, Zorkin strongly advocated a presidential republic within a separation of powers doctrine, a position he continues to hold, notwithstanding the widespread canard that he is trying to undermine the presidency on behalf of the parliament. When elevated to the Court, Zorkin was considered one of its most distinguished jurists, but reportedly was not the President's first choice for Chief Justice, despite his support for Yeltsin.

What kind of Chief Justice has Zorkin been during the early history of the Court? Created by the Fourth Congress of Russian People's Deputies and President Yeltsin in the summer of 1991, the Court, coincidentally, convened for the first time just a few days after the collapse of the USSR in late December 1991. During the Court's first term in 1992, Zorkin and his twelve judicial brethren issued "rulings" on nine cases, not all of which were well received by the affected parties.... It was in these instances that Zorkin began to display his penchant for extrajudicial comment.

Strictly speaking, the statute on Russia's Constitutional Court does not prohibit extrajudicial comment on a case *after* a ruling has been adopted, but to the American legal ear, Zorkin's remarks will sound discordant. Scholars may recall that Chief Justice John Marshall commented extrajudicially on *McCulloch v. Maryland*, but did so under a pseudonym. Recently, in a similar spirit, Justice Byron White, upon announcing retirement, replied to a journalist that he had not advised Presidents nor had they advised him. At the same time, the reader should note that not all American high judges maintained such standards. The Nixon tapes reveal, for example, that former Chief Justice Warren Burger frequently briefed the President on cases pending before the Supreme Court *(The New Yorker,* December 14, 1992, p. 81).

Extrajudicial case commentary

In its first decision, on the Internal Security case, the Constitutional Court ruled unconstitutional Yeltsin's executive order merging the police and security ministries into a single superministry. The President was taken aback, and Zorkin reportedly spent an hour in private cajoling

Yeltsin into accepting the decision. Yeltsin's lawyer in the case, Deputy Prime Minister Sergei Shakhrai, was less restrained, criticizing the Court for deciding the case on political rather than legal grounds. The Chief Justice reacted immediately, and in a manner that surprised Western legal observers. He spoke from the podium of the Russian Supreme Soviet, appeared on TV and gave interviews to the print media, all in defense of the judicial character of the Court's first ruling. To deter further criticism from the President's entourage, Zorkin publicly threatened to review the constitutionality of Shakhrai's actions "in accordance with impeachment procedures," and led the Court as it fined a prominent editor whose newspaper was obliged to publish the ruling, but had instead printed misleading comments on the case.

A few months later, in early spring of 1992, the Court took up its third case, the Tatarstan Referendum case, the most frustrating of the first term. The Tatar Autonomous Republic of the Russian Federation, a large and populous territory on the middle Volga, had announced its intention to hold a referendum on whether it should become a separate associate state within the federation. The Russian Federation Constitutional Commission petitioned the Court to assess the constitutionality of Tatarstan's plans. The Court promptly *did* so, ordering the referendum canceled. Tatarstan, defying the Court, continued to plan for the ballot. The Chief Justice, particularly concerned over the secessionist implications of the move, strove hard from both on and off the bench to obtain Tatarstan's compliance, mixing court pronouncements with personal threats. Zorkin even went on nationwide television, darkly forecasting that Tatarstan's defiance could lead to a situation "a hundred times worse than Yugoslavia." It was all to no avail. Chief Justice Zorkin had overreached himself by speechifying extrajudicially, and the Court suffered a setback. The referendum was held, in the teeth of the judicial ban, and 82% of eligible voters turned out; 61% of them opted for sovereignty.

In the Constitutional Court's final case of 1992, the Communist Party case, Zorkin became embroiled in a series of increasingly sharp public exchanges with former Soviet President Mikhail Gorbachev. At issue in the case was the constitutionality of Russian President Yeltsin's 1991 post-coup decrees, initially suspending and then banning the all-union and Russian Republic Communist parties and seizing their property. The Court issued a summons for the ex-President to appear which Gorbachev steadfastly refused to obey, arguing in the press that both parties to the trial, the former Communists and Yeltsin's legal team, would attempt to use him as a scapegoat. The Chief Justice tried private persuasion at first, and then, becoming exasperated with Gorbachev, began to address him through the press. As their public colloquy escalated, Zorkin became more intemperate, finally declaring that Gorbachev had "signed his own death sentence as a politician." While Gorbachev was legally wrong to refuse the summons (he was fined a nominal sum by the Court and temporarily stripped of his exit visa), he had the last word, rightly calling into question the propriety of Zorkin's public remarks. Since, in this instance, the Chief Justice had made off-the-bench comments on a case then under review, he was unequivocally in violation of the Law on the RSFSR Constitutional Court (Art. 20, Sec. 3).

Zorkin's political rhetoric

The Chief Justice has by no means confined himself to commentary on cases either decided or under review. He has actually commented more frequently and in far greater volume on public matters not immediately or specifically related to court business. Zorkin's political broadsides usually concern highly general constitutional questions. Presumably he feels this course of action appropriate on two counts. First, he chairs the institution charged with constitutional control in Russia. Second, he undoubtedly believes he is additionally qualified as a former professor of constitutional law, as well as a former head of the expert panel on the Constitutional Commission.

In his speeches, interviews and occasional writings since becoming Chief Justice, Zorkin has been preoccupied with three constitutional themes: the nature of the extant constitution, the development of the separation of powers, and the stabilization of the federal system.

While agreeing that Russia needs a new constitution and acknowledging that the extant document contains inconsistencies and flaws, Zorkin has insisted that a bad constitution is better than none at all. He recognizes that the present constitution dates from 1978, but quickly adds that it has been extensively amended since the demise of the Soviet Union, beginning in April 1992 at the Sixth Congress of People's Deputies. Hence, he rejects labelling the document a "Brezhnev Constitution" since the great bulk of its now 340 amendments have been passed during Yeltsin's tenure, including the amendments on the Presidency and the Constitutional Court. Zorkin has repeatedly said that the task of the leaders and people of the Russian Federation is to learn to conduct their public affairs within the revised constitution until a viable political consensus emerges to support a new fundamental law. In promoting constitutionalism, Zorkin has adopted a pedagogical approach, patiently lecturing his sometimes fractious listeners on the virtues of not straying from the path of the law.

While the Chief Justice's remarks on cultivating a constitutional culture are addressed to the broad public, his more specific comments on the separation of powers in Russia are directed primarily at the feuding political leaders in Moscow. Though he personally favors a presidential republic, Zorkin sees himself and the Court as impartial arbiters in the intense conflict between Ruslan Khasbulatov and Boris Yeltsin, leaders of the legislative and executive branches, in their often zero-sum struggle for either parliamentary or Presidential supremacy. For Zorkin, the point is not to choose between the combatants but to foster the development of a system of power-sharing over policymaking and policy implementation, both of which are now institutionally vested in the cabinet. The Constitutional Court is the third player in the emerging dynamic, ideally serving as a balance wheel between the behemoth political branches while checking their excesses when necessary through the medium of judicial review. In its first year, the Court weighed in against both presidential decrees and parliamentary acts, overturning what it considered unconstitutional decisions in seven instances (to the relative neglect, incidentally, of individual rights cases). In both his judicial and his political role, Zorkin has struggled to soften the edges of the power conflict, to keep open the lines of communication between the principal players, and to convince elite groups of the utility and necessity of an independent high court as an active participant in fashioning and consolidating a functional separation of powers doctrine in Russia.

The third constitutional theme, the problems of federalism in Russia, is the one which Zorkin apparently views with the most alarm. In theory, he has written, the Court is charged with protecting the constitutional integrity of the Russian Federation, but he recognizes that in reality centrifugal forces are pulling the country apart. His fear that Russia may follow the path of the Soviet Union to disintegration and possible civil war often inspires him to come forth with apocalyptic scenarios. The terms "abyss," "catastrophe," "chaos," and "disaster" appear with regularity in his political Jeremiads about the future of the federation. This accounts for the intensity of Zorkin's reaction to the Tatars, his periodic admonitions to the Moscow leadership to quit feuding and fulfill their constitutional duties lest the country slip into disunion, and his concern that a fair and reasonable division of powers between the center and the constituent republics be implemented to stabilize the federation and preserve the country's cohesion. In this role Zorkin, who seems to be a deeply religious man, often sounds prophetic, warning his flock to heed his call and avert the collapse of civilization in Russia.

The Chief Justice as crisis manager

By the end of 1992, Russia was engulfed in multiple crises—economic, political and constitutional. The question "Who shall govern Russia?" remained unresolved as the respective partisans of parliamentary and presidential government defined the political universe in mutually exclusive rather than complementary terms. From late spring through the fall as economic shock therapy went awry, eroding Yeltsin's support and inciting parliamentary rebellion, Zorkin and the Court were mired in the complexities of the Party-banning case. As the Seventh Congress approached in December, political tensions mounted. Parliamentary conservatives threatened to impeach the President, while Yeltsin's men broadly hinted at emergency powers and suspension of the Congress. Both sides were bluffing; neither had the means to carry out their threats. Meanwhile, the Chief Justice, mindful of the menacing atmosphere, finally steered the divided Court to a verdict in the Party case, released the day before the Congress opened. Issuing a solomonic judgment, a ruling that was bad law but perhaps good politics, Zorkin and the justices then hurried across town to take their special seats at the parliament. (The third branch is permitted to attend the Congress, although the Court Law is silent on participation.)

Undaunted by the law's lacunae, the Chief Justice made his first of several speeches to the Congress at its opening session. Casting his remarks as a report on the Court's first term, Zorkin disavowed any intention of interfering in politics and proceeded to describe the confrontation between the political branches as the main source of the constitutional crisis. Reiterating the familiar themes of his first year in office, Zorkin poured scorn on the inapposite phrase "Brezhnev Constitution," and reminded the legislators and executive officials of the grave threat to "Russia's unity" from rebellious republics such as Chechnya (which declared its independence in 1991), and Tatarstan. Throwing down the gauntlet, Zorkin ominously warned the assemblage that if they did nothing to "save Russia" from the abyss of disintegration, the Court, despite the law, would have no choice but to intervene in politics.

Ten days later, with the legislative and executive with leaders at loggerheads and the Congress in shambles, Zorkin plunged headlong into the political arena, summoning Yeltsin and Khasbulatov to a meeting which he chaired. On behalf of the Court, the Chief Justice advised the leaders that if the meeting did not produce a resolution of the crisis, the Constitutional Court would begin proceedings against both for failure to fulfill their constitutional obligations. The meeting yielded an agreement to hold a referendum on April 11, 1993, which was approved in a hasty and irregular fashion by the Congress. The crisis averted, Zorkin was fêted by both sides, awarded a prestigious prize, and declared "Man of the Year." Loyally supporting their leader, other justices found statutory support for the Chief Justice's extraordinary political involvement by broadly construing an obscure part of the Court Law (Art. 80, Sec. 1). Nonetheless, Zorkin had stepped vigorously across the invisible line between law and politics, potentially putting at risk the Court's accrued moral and judicial capital.

Zorkin as politician

The Constitutional Court began its second term with a docket of 40 cases awaiting review. Given the hampering requirement of *seriatim* deliberation, this was a substantial caseload, although priority would be given to individual rights cases. However, by mid-January 1993, the political deal Zorkin had brokered began to unravel and both the Chief Justice and the Court soon found themselves swept back into the swirling waters of mainstream politics. For the next several months, the Court's judicial routine would be regularly interrupted by political negotiations, crisis petitions and public vilification.

The constitutional referendum that had promised a way out of the political gridlock soon encountered unanticipated problems. A number of constituent regions of the Russian Federation threatened not to conduct the referendum or to use it for their own ends. Fearing that the plebiscite might exacerbate secessionist trends, Speaker Khasbulatov began to back out of the agreement. As chairman of the supra constitutional Reconciliation Commission he had created at the December Congress, Zorkin was called upon by Yeltsin to broker a new deal. Unable to reconcile the two political adversaries and having serious doubts himself about the wisdom of a spring referendum, Zorkin seems to have concluded that he had now gotten involved beyond his political depth, and withdrew as a personal mediator.... Yeltsin still wanted a referendum, and accused Zorkin of reneging on the plan which he himself had proposed. A now presumably more politically cautious Chief Justice began to confine his political commentary to press conferences at the courthouse in the company of other justices.

By March 1993, the Yeltsin–Khasbulatov conflict grew more bitter, a vengeful parliament convened two emergency Congresses in quick succession, and Zorkin, abandoning his short-lived restraint, found himself caught in the crossfire. In mid-March, Khasbulatov convened the Eighth Extraordinary Congress which expeditiously abrogated the Seventh Congress's resolution on the referendum deal reached by the heads of the three branches of government, and tried to humiliate Yeltsin by stripping him of certain presidential powers. Furious at this outcome, the President's parliamentary supporters turned to the Constitutional Court for relief, challenging the constitutionality of the Congress's latest decisions.

Zorkin, meanwhile, had left for the United States on an official visit to the U.S. Supreme Court....

The Chief Justice returned on March 18 and immediately called the Court into session. Sensitive to the perception that he had tilted too far in Khasbulatov's direction at the Eighth Congress, Zorkin opened deliberations on a case which had been on the docket since the summer of 1992, a petition from liberal parliamentary deputies challenging over two dozen decrees issued by Speaker Khasbulatov. The next day, Friday, the Chief Justice, presiding at a hastily called press conference, announced the Court's decision nullifying twenty-seven of the Speaker's decrees, and expressed concern that Yeltsin might attempt to impose "Presidential Rule" on the basis of emergency powers. Holding a copy of the constitution up for the TV cameras, the Chief Justice somberly commented that he was "alarmed ... as are all the justices of the Constitutional Court ... because the constitution does not mention this phrase."

Reacting to the President's address

The following day, Saturday, March 20, tensions were running high in political circles as the President's address to the nation that evening was awaited. The Court met twice during the day in closed session to discuss the political situation and the impending address. Zorkin tried to reach Yeltsin by phone, telegram and messenger, with the hope of dissuading him from any unconstitutional action, but to no avail—the President was not taking his calls. That night, Yeltsin went on the air and announced what Martin Malia has called a "soft coup," including the proviso that any ruling by the Constitutional Court would be invalid prior to a constitutional referendum set for April 25. Zorkin reacted an hour later, joining Khasbulatov, Vice President Rutskoi and Procurator–General Stepankov at a press conference to denounce the President's actions. In his most explicit political intervention of his tenure as Chief Justice, Zorkin aptly called the President's proclamation a "coup d'état." Having been unable to deter Yeltsin juridically, Zorkin shed judicial restraint and confronted the errant chief executive politically.

During the next ten eventful days of Russia's constitutional crisis, Zorkin moved with lightning speed back and forth, and in and out of his multiple roles—as Chief Justice, extrajudicial commentator, and freelance politician. He could be sighted at all points on the political compass, at the Court, in the media, seated at the Supreme Soviet, speaking before the Congress, and meeting in the Kremlin. Following the President's dramatic speech, the Court, on its own initiative—and in the absence of any formal decree from the President—had begun deliberations on the constitutionality of its content. After an all-night and possibly rancorous session, a 9–3 "Opinion" was released, with Zorkin leading the majority, declaring most of Yeltsin's as-yet-unpublished proposals unconstitutional, but allowing for a referendum. On possible grounds for impeachment, however, the Court was silent.

Nonetheless, the Supreme Soviet summoned the full complement of deputies back to Moscow for a Ninth Extraordinary Congress to consider impeachment of the President. In the midst of preparations for the Congress, the President's Office finally published the text of the decree on which his Saturday night address had been based. It bore only a slight resemblance to his rhetoric, most of the offending parts cited by the Court having been deleted. Yeltsin's modified decree, though a notable victory for the Court in the informal system of checks and balances and a partial concession to the parliament, did not quiet passions. The impeachment juggernaut rolled on, narrowly failing short of the two-thirds majority needed....

...Nonetheless, Zorkin's commingling of law and politics provoked a torrent of personal criticism and even abuse from the President, his advisors, pro-Yeltsin deputies, the liberal press, fellow justices, former colleagues, Russian lawyers, and even foreign observers. He was called a demagogue, hypocrite, and a Judas; addressed as "Comrade Zorkin" and the "former Chief Justice," and called upon to resign. Zorkin defended his actions legally and politically, arguing that Yeltsin's "coup" required instant reaction to save the constitutional realm, but his professional reputation had taken a nosedive. As jurists as well as politicians soon come to learn, appearances often count as much as reality.

Can the Court survive Zorkin's politicization?

The short answer for the near term appears to be yes.... After the close of the raucous Ninth Congress, virtually all parties in Russia's ongoing crisis—the Presidency, liberal and conservative legislative factions, and the press—turned to the Court with fresh petitions, including one on the April 25 referendum, to peacefully resolve in the near and longer term. On April 21, the Court correctly settled one of these complaints, the referendum case, finding for Yeltsin against the Congress, declaring that only a majority of the turnout was necessary to win the first two questions, namely, confidence in the President and approval of his economic policy. On the third and fourth questions, which could have led to legally binding calls for early elections of the parliament and President, the Court found that the Law on Referenda required the approval of a majority of eligible voters....

———————

The next essay by Professor Hausmaninger offers an assessment of the causes for the downfall of the first Constitutional Court, and identifies some of the obstacles facing the new Russian Constitutional Court.

Herbert Hausmaninger, *Towards a "New" Russian Constitutional Court*, 28 Cornell Int'l L. J. 349 (1995)

Introduction

On September 21, 1993, when President Boris Yeltsin issued the Decree on Step-by-Step Constitutional Reform in the Russian Federation dismissing the Russian Parliament and calling for new elections, the Supreme Soviet, under the leadership of Speaker Ruslan Khasbulatov, immediately countered with a resolution which declared the powers of the President terminated under Article 121.6 of the Constitution. At the Parliament's request, Constitutional Court Chairman Valerii Zorkin called an emergency session of the Court, although the President's decree had "instructed" the Court not to convene any sessions. On the night of September 21, the Constitutional Court decided by a majority of nine to four that the President's violations of the Constitution provided grounds for his removal from office under either Constitution Article 121.10 (impeachment proceedings) or 121.6 (automatic termination).

As the power struggle continued, the parliamentary leadership, under Speaker Khasbulatov, and Vice–President Aleksandr Rutskoi, who had joined them in their confrontation with President Yeltsin, found themselves on September 28 isolated in the "White House" (the Russian parliament building) by police and army forces loyal to President Yeltsin and his government. On October 3, anti-Yeltsin demonstrators, encouraged by Vice–President Rutskoi, attacked the Moscow mayor's office and the Ostankino television station. In the course of this raid, sixty-two people were killed. On October 4, Yeltsin's troops stormed the White House and arrested Khasbulatov and Rutskoi.

On October 6, Constitutional Court Chairman Zorkin, under pressure from the President's office, resigned his chairmanship but remained a Court member. On October 7, President Yeltsin signed the Decree on the Constitutional Court of the Russian Federation, accusing the Court of flagrant violations of its duties and suspending its decisionmaking process until the adoption of the new Constitution. However, the President charged the Court, under the leadership of Acting Chairman Nikolai Vitruk, with preparing proposals for submission to the future federal assembly concerning "forms of implementing constitutional justice in the Russian Federation, including the possibility of creating a constitutional collegium within the Supreme Court of the Russian Federation." . . .

. . . In preparing the Draft Constitution, which was published on November 10, 1993, and adopted by popular referendum on December 12, 1993, President Yeltsin chose not to abolish the Constitutional Court. On the basis of Article 125 of this new Constitution, the Russian Parliament promulgated the Federal Constitutional Law on the Constitutional Court and by February 7, 1995, six additional justices had been appointed. Now that the last vacancy has been filled and the Court has thus become operational, one hopes that at least some lessons of the past have been learned and that the new Court will be able to make a more substantial and enduring contribution to legal culture and the rule of law than its predecessor. . . .

I. *The Zorkin Court (1991–1993): An Obituary*

In June 1988, Mikhail Gorbachev persuaded the Communist Party of the Soviet Union (CPSU) that *perestroika*, to be successful, required the development of a "Socialist state committed to the rule of law." Among the various measures taken to attain this goal, a Committee of Constitutional Supervision of the USSR was established to review and ensure the observance of constitutionality and legality in the Soviet political system. The member republics of the USSR were authorized to create their own institutions of constitutional review. Rather than following the federal example of setting up a committee with predominantly advisory and suspensive functions that would recognize the supremacy of parliament, the Russian Republic, after its declaration of sovereignty on June 12, 1991, chose to establish a genuine Constitutional Court. The Russian Law on the Constitutional Court was adopted in July 1991, and Parliament elected the first thirteen Court members in October 1991. The constitutional number of justices on the Court was fifteen, but the Parliament could not agree on whom to elect to fill the two remaining vacancies. However, the law permitted the Court to be operative in the presence of ten members. The justices elected Professor Valerii D. Zorkin as Chairman and Professor Nikolai V. Vitruk as Vice-Chairman of the Court.

A. Jurisdiction of the Constitutional Court

Article 165 of the Russian Constitution, as amended on April 21, 1992, defined the Constitutional Court as "the highest organ of judicial power in the protection of the constitutional order." Under Article 165.1, the Court's jurisdiction encompassed judicial as well as non-judicial functions. Among the former, the two major areas were undoubtedly the adjudication of the constitutionality of legal norms at the request of various state organs and the adjudication of complaints of individual citizens against violations of their constitutional rights.

1.   Citizens' Complaints

Like the German constitutional complaint, after which the Russian instrument was modelled, the adjudication of citizens' complaints was an extraordinary remedy to secure the protection of civil rights. The Russian complaint—as opposed to the German—could not be directed against a statute, but only against the application of the law by courts or administrative organs when all other remedies had been exhausted. It was available to persons claiming that their fundamental rights or other constitutionally protected interests had been violated by an established pattern of administrative action or constant adjudicative practice (in particular such practice as based on "guiding explanations" of the highest courts). As the law empowered the Constitutional Court to examine legal acts even if they were only capable of creating an unconstitutional practice, and also gave it the right to reject a complaint if it considered such examination "inadvisable" (*netselesoobraznym*), the Court enjoyed great latitude in accepting or rejecting individual complaints.

In the course of 1992, the Court received no fewer than 1700 citizens' complaints, most of them without merit but a good number seeming to have deserved more attention than the Court was able or willing to devote. Individual complaints were examined by the Registry of the Court, occasionally returned for improvement, but most frequently rejected at this point. Justices did not participate in these decisions. Constitutional questions recognized as such by the Registry staff were submitted to the Chairman, the Vice–Chairman, or the Secretary of the Court, who sent them to one of several specialized divisions of the Secretariat. On the basis of a report prepared by the staff of legal specialists, the Court would then vote whether to accept the case, and if accepted, the Chairman would assign it to a justice as reporter, who was responsible for preparing the case for oral hearing.

2.   Court Practice in Civil Rights Cases

[Only] six individual complaints [were] heard and decided by the Court in the first sixteen months of its activity (between January 1992 and April 1993).... In the months leading up to the suspension of the Court on October 6, 1993, the justices did little to improve the skimpy record in this area. Instead, they handed down only one opinion based on an individual complaint. Only a minority of the justices were critical of the fact that the Court did not devote sufficient attention to human rights questions.... But the Court majority, led by Chairman Zorkin, rejected this criticism and insisted that the role of the Court in the ongoing constitutional crisis, produced by the confrontation between the President and the Parliament, should be to focus its attention on arrogation of jurisdiction and unconstitutional enactments by state organs.

B.   Review of Constitutionality of Legal Enactments

[The Constitutional Court had jurisdiction to consider the constitutionality of statutes and other legal acts of, inter alia, the Congress of People's

Deputies, the Supreme Soviet, the President, or the republics, and to decide jurisdictional conflicts between all organs of government, federal and republic, and to rule on the constitutionality of political parties.]

. . .

Through the end of April 1993, the Court handed down eleven opinions on the constitutionality of legal enactments, all of which declared the examined legal enactments (or parts of such) unconstitutional. One of these decisions was directed against a republic (Tatarstan), one against an ordinance of the Council of Ministers, one against a resolution of the Congress of People's Deputies, two against the Supreme Soviet and two against its Presidium, and four against decrees of President Yeltsin. In May, June, and September 1993, the Court added eight more cases to this list. . . .

3. The Referendum Case

One of the most interesting and fateful decisions of the Court was undoubtedly its opinion of April 21, 1993, concerning the constitutionality of the Referendum Resolution passed by the Congress of People's Deputies on March 29.

In the preceding months, several attempts had been made by President Yeltsin to come to an accord with Parliament concerning a new Constitution or at least a joint procedure for submitting its basic provisions to a popular referendum. After these attempts had failed, the President submitted to the Congress on March 7, 1993, the following questions for a referendum to be held on April 11, 1993:

1. Do you agree that the Russian Federation should be a presidential republic?

2. Do you agree that the supreme legislative body of the Russian Federation should be a bicameral parliament?

3. Do you agree that the new Constitution of the Russian Federation should be adopted by a Constitutional Assembly representing the multinational people of the Russian Federation?

4. Do you agree that every citizen of the Russian Federation should have the right to own, use, and dispose of land as its owner?

On March 13, the Congress of People's Deputies rejected the President's proposal and forbade the referendum. In a radio and television address on March 20, the President announced a referendum for April 25 on the people's confidence in the President and Vice–President, the basic provisions of a new Constitution, a new electoral law, and the election of a new bicameral parliament. Yeltsin announced that until the resolution of the state crisis a "special administrative regime" would be in force, under which all orders of the President would be unchallengeable.

The first reaction of the Congress was an impeachment proceeding against the President on March 28 which failed by a narrow margin. The vote was 617 to 268. A successful impeachment would have required 689 votes, two-thirds of the 1033 total deputies. The Congress then decided to order a referendum with a different set of questions that were clearly designed to hurt the President:

1.   Do you trust the President of the Russian Federation?

2.   Do you approve of the social-economic policy carried out by the President and government of the Russian Federation since 1992?

3.   Do you deem it necessary to hold early presidential elections?

4.   Do you deem it necessary to hold early elections for people's deputies?

The Congressional Resolution decreed that a referendum on these questions would be conducted on the basis of the RSFSR Law on the Referendum of October 16, 1990. The resolution went on to state that "decisions . . . are considered to have been adopted, if more than one half of the citizens *entitled to be registered* have voted in favor of them."

On April 8, the constitutionality of this resolution was challenged in a petition to the Constitutional Court by ten deputies belonging to the parliamentary caucus "Democratic Russia," which usually supported the President. They argued that the resolution violated the Referendum Law, which ordinarily required a majority of the citizens who participated in the referendum. Under the Referendum Law, a majority of those registered is required only for questions concerning the adoption or amendment of the Constitution of the Russian Federation. The petitioners claimed that none of the referendum questions concerned a change of the Constitution. Thus, insofar as the resolution deviated from the Law on the Referendum, it violated Article 5 of the Constitution, which required referenda to be held on the basis of the Constitution and the laws of the Russian Federation. It did not provide for regulation by resolution. The resolution also violated Article 4 of the Constitution which required all state organs (including the Congress) to observe the Constitution and laws.

In the Constitutional Court's oral proceedings of April 20, two professors of constitutional law testified as experts and were extensively questioned by the judges. . . .

A key issue was the hierarchy of sources of the law: Does a resolution of the Congress rank above a statute of the Supreme Soviet, or, in other words, do all legal acts of the Congress enjoy supreme force, regardless of their labels? This view had been undisputed under Soviet constitutional doctrine and practice. Another fundamental issue was whether referendum questions three and four concerning early elections implied a change of the Constitution, as the latter did not envisage a resignation of the President or a dissolution of Parliament before the expiration of their respective terms of office.

In its opinion announced on April 21, the Court affirmed the constitutionality of the Congress' resolution on the vote-counting procedure issue in questions three and four with five of the thirteen justices dissenting. . . . Concerning questions one and two, the Court unanimously found a violation of Constitutional Articles 4 and 5. Thus the Court for the first time invalidated parts of a normative act of the Congress as unconstitutional. The Court found these violations even though Article 104 of the Constitution refers to the Congress as the supreme organ of state power which may decide any question and may repeal any act of the Supreme Soviet, and even though Article 109 of the Constitution expressly states that laws and resolutions of the Supreme Soviet must not contradict laws and resolutions of the Congress.*

This ruling of the Constitutional Court, as one Moscow newspaper wrote, offered the President a lifesaver: Yeltsin could not have won the vote of confidence in the referendum but for the Court's decision concerning the vote count. But the Court's opinion also expressed an important legal doctrine: a statute ranks as superior to other legal enactments. It thus wrote a chapter of constitutional law that moved Russia closer to the West European rule of law model.

The five dissenting justices who denied that referendum questions three and four had constitutional quality, pointed, with good reason, to technical arguments supporting their position. These include the fact that the questions contained no specific proposal for constitutional change and no specific time for early elections. In reaching its decision, the Court majority probably reflected on the unconstitutional measures a referendum victory of the President might entail, in particular the scheduling of parliamentary elections against the will of Parliament. Such reflections had already guided the Court in its March 23 finding concerning Yeltsin's March 20 television address.

C.   Nonjudicial Functions of the 1991 Constitutional Court

In a manner unprecedented in Western legal traditions, the Law on the Russian Constitutional Court assigned no fewer than five types of nonjudicial functions to the Court. One of these, the finding (*zakliuchenie*), merits a closer look at this point. Among the several types of findings to be issued by the Court, the most important was the one concerning the constitution-

---

* [Editors' Note: The Russian Federation Constitution as of late 1992 can be found in an English translation in Albert P. Blaustein & Gisbert H. Flanz, Constitutions of the Countries of the World (1993). The Congress of People's Deputies was a very large representative assembly, with more than 1,000 elected deputies. The Supreme Soviet was a body "formed by the Congress of People's Deputies ... from among the people's deputies, and will be accountable to the Congress." Both entities formally possessed powers to enact laws: the Congress "by a vote supported by the majority of people's deputies," Art. 104, and the Supreme Soviet by a majority vote of its two chambers, Art. 111. As Hausmaninger noted, Art. 109 also provides that "The laws and decrees passed by the Supreme Soviet of the Russian Federation may not contradict laws and other instruments adopted by the Congress of People's Deputies. ..." Though not an intuitively obvious reading based on these translations, the Constitutional Court's decision— that a Resolution of the Congress was unconstitutional, because inconsistent with a statute passed by the Supreme Soviet—was unanimous. Consider whether there are interpretations, e.g., a "temporal" view of Article 109 as constraining the Supreme Soviet only from enacting laws inconsistent with pre-existing decrees of the Congress, that could account for the result.]

ality of actions and decisions of the President in the context of an impeachment procedure. Surprisingly, the Court could issue such findings on its own initiative and thus become an important political player in its own right.

Prior to September 21, 1993, the Constitutional Court had issued only one finding, which, however, had a spectacular quality and effect. It deeply divided the Court and had a profound impact on the future political development of the country. The finding concerned President Yeltsin's March 20, 1993, television address. In that speech the President explained his decision to order a referendum concerning the question of confidence in the President and Vice–President. The main reason for the political crisis in the country, he said, was not a conflict between the Congress and the President, but a conflict between the people and the Bolshevik system. The Congress, Yeltsin claimed, had manipulated the Constitution and blocked the referendum on land ownership and constitutional principles. Yeltsin argued that as the possibility of agreement with the conservative majority in Parliament had been exhausted, the President would assume direct responsibility for the fate of the country. It was his duty to guarantee the observation of fundamental constitutional principles such as popular government, federalism, separation of powers, human rights, and basic freedoms. Yeltsin continued:

> Today I have signed a decree on a special administrative regime until the resolution of the crisis of power. On the basis of this decree a referendum is ordered for April 25 concerning confidence in the President and Vice President of the RF. . . . The people must decide . . . who should rule the country: the President and Vice President or the Congress of People's Deputies.

> Together with the vote of confidence in the President a vote on the draft of a new constitution and on the draft of the law on elections to Parliament will be held. These drafts will be submitted by the President and will become effective when the people support the President and Vice President.

> Under the Constitution and the new electoral law which you will approve there will be no elections to Congress but to a new Russian parliament. Under the new Constitution there will be no Congress. Until new elections can be held, Congress and the Supreme Soviet will not be dissolved, their work will not be suspended. The people's deputies will retain their mandates. But on the basis of the decree all decisions of organs or functionaries that aim at abolishing or suspending decrees and orders of the President or ordinances of the government will be without legal effect.

Constitutional Court Chairman Zorkin considered this television statement an attempted coup d'etat. The Court, on its own initiative (which was subsequently endorsed by a request from the Supreme Soviet), examined the television clip in an emergency session. President Yeltsin refused to attend this session or to submit documents requested by the Court, including the text of his decree.

In its nine-to-three opinion of March 23 ..., the Court found seven violations of the Constitution and the Union Treaty in the President's address. The Court, however, remained silent on the question of impeachment. Justices Ametistov and Morshchakova wrote dissenting opinions which considered the speech a mere declaration of political intent that was not subject to legal evaluation.[86] In article 1(3), the Law on the Constitutional Court forbids the Court to examine political questions. Under article 32(6), the Court does not have the right to review unadopted enforceable enactments. Also, under article 74(3), it is forbidden to pass findings on questions which may later be subject to review of an enforceable enactment. Justice Ametistov also correctly criticized as illegal the various public statements made by Chairman Zorkin in a press conference, on television, and in the Supreme Soviet prior to the Court's deliberations. Article 20(3) of the Law on the Constitutional Court expressly states that:

> A judge on the RSFSR Constitutional Court does not have the right anywhere except at a session of the RSFSR Constitutional Court to voice publicly his opinion on a question under review or accepted for review by the RSFSR Constitutional Court before the adoption of a ruling by it on this question.

Further, article 18(1)(4) provides that a judge may be suspended by the Court for this behavior.

D. Critique of the Zorkin Court's Judicial Activity

In the first sixteen months of its activity, from November 1991 to April 1993, the Court issued seventeen decisions. This output represents a modest achievement by any standard, especially in view of the large number of highly qualified legal personnel working for the Court. From May to September of 1993, the Court added eight more opinions to its record, thereby barely exceeding the meager record of its predecessor, the Committee of Constitutional Supervision of the USSR. A partial explanation of this limited accomplishment may be found in the Court's rules of procedure. These rules, written into the Law by an inexperienced draftsman, ... forced the Court to: 1) take all decisions in plenary meetings; 2) decide all cases after extensive trial-type public oral hearings; and 3) abstain from dealing with other cases as long as an ongoing proceeding was not finished. Thus, these rules blocked the Court from deciding other cases during the hearings and recesses of the Communist Party case between May 25 and November 30, 1992.

Yet perhaps the focus should be less on the number of cases decided than on the vision projected by the Court, its public image, and its power of legal and political persuasion. Given the lack of enforcement of the Court's opinions, the decision to refrain from publishing a great number of ineffec-

---

86. President Yeltsin's subsequently published Decree of March 24 makes no reference to a "special administration" and [is] an obvious attempt to avoid all conflict with the Constitution. *On the Activity of Executive* *Bodies Pending the Resolution of the Crisis,* Izvestiia, Mar. 25, 1993, at 1, *translated in* 45 Current Dig. of the Post–Soviet Press No. 12, at 11–12 (1993).

tual decisions may have been wise. But one could certainly argue that the Court should have made its legal points more guardedly and selectively, and that it could have built a more impressive record in the field of civil rights protection.

There was certainly legitimate frustration on the part of the Court over the widespread neglect of its decisions. This frustration may help explain Chairman Zorkin's excessive language and public posturing, which included giving apocalyptic speeches in the Supreme Soviet, imposing fines for contempt of court, and threatening impeachment against the highest public officials. However, more restraint might have preserved a higher degree of Court authority.[97]

Initially, the substance of the Court's opinions reflected a fair amount of solid legal work, political sensitivity, and capacity for compromise on the part of the justices. However, since the Communist Party case, the growing politicization of the Court's judicial decisionmaking became increasingly troubling.[98]

E.   Critical Remarks Concerning the Court's Nonjudicial Activities

There is no doubt that the Court's exercise of nonjudicial functions led to excessive political involvement outside the Court's core function of judicial review. This development certainly did not add to the Constitutional Court's legal authority and prestige....

...Zorkin increasingly confirmed my fears by developing a kind of political activism that was at times clearly in violation of the law and at least improper for a neutral arbiter of constitutional conflict. But there is also a caveat to be considered in view of the Court's role in an emerging constitutional crisis. Is it really permissible in an extraordinary situation of this type to evaluate the Russian Constitutional Court on the basis of those standards that apply to Western Constitutional Courts in normal times?

Many observers agree that in December 1992 the Chairman of the Constitutional Court justifiably received ample public praise for assuming the role of referee in a dramatic struggle between the legislature and the President and for substantially contributing to the finding of a compromise. However, it appears that Zorkin extensively enjoyed the limelight and the power involved in playing this active role. He did not abide by the agreement, formalized in a resolution adopted by the Congress on December 13, 1992. As early as January, Zorkin was among the first to join

97. For example, Zorkin's handling of the Tatarstan case had the unfortunate consequence that other state organs ignored Court decisions. In the Communist Party case, the Court was unable to force Gorbachev to appear as a witness. As a result, the public image of the Court suffered serious damage.

98. This politicization especially occurred in the National Salvation Front case of Feb. 12, 1993. Vedomosti RF, Issue No. 9, Item No. 344 (1993). In this case, the court majority ignored the unconstitutional contents of the Front's program, and focused exclusively on the unconstitutional character of the presidential decree outlawing the Front....

Speaker Khasbulatov in voicing doubts and criticism concerning the constitutional referendum scheduled for April 11, 1993.

In the eyes of a critical and liberal Russian intelligentsia, this support for Speaker Khasbulatov was an unforgivable betrayal. In their view, Zorkin had clearly aligned himself politically with a reactionary parliament in its struggle against a reform-minded President. A more neutral observer would agree that Zorkin not only assumed a partisan political role inappropriate for the country's highest judge, but also undermined the Court's prestige as signatory to a solemn constitutional agreement.... But any censure directed at the Chairman should be mindful of the fact that Zorkin, for most of his activities, enjoyed the support of a solid Court majority.

In their struggle with Parliament, President Yeltsin and his supporters frequently insisted that without radical economic reform a stable democratic society cannot develop, and that without a democratic society no functioning rule of law can exist. Did this perspective give legitimacy to the President's revolutionary transformation that disregarded the existing Constitution, the elected Parliament, and a lawfully appointed and functioning Constitutional Court?

Although it could be claimed that the President's actions were subsequently endorsed by the popular referendum on his draft of a new Constitution, an impartial observer could give his endorsement only with great reluctance. He would at the same time deplore the lack of political culture and place blame on all three major players in the power struggle: the Parliament, the President, and the Constitutional Court....

2. The President

President Yeltsin's supporters have argued that the Constitutional Court majority employed legal formalism to aid an illegitimate parliament to the detriment of a reformist executive. There is some truth in this charge. It may be explained in part by the formalist tradition in Soviet jurisprudence, in part by the political preferences of the justices, and also as a reaction to the arrogant behavior of Yeltsin and his team. The brusque and frequently insulting style of the President and his advisers, the improvisation and shortsightedness of some of Yeltsin's previous political actions, his personal lack of appreciation of law and legality, and the poor legal quality of many of his decrees increasingly alienated Yeltsin from the Russian legal community, including the justices of the Constitutional Court....

II. [The New Constitution]

The New Constitution increases the number of justices from fifteen, only thirteen of whom were actually appointed, to nineteen. It also enumerates the state organs and persons that have access to the Court, and lists the competencies of the Court. The language of Article 125 ... restricts the powers of the Court in several instances.[119] However, it also provides a

---

119. For example, the Court may no longer determine the constitutionality of actions and decisions of the highest officials of the Russian federation and its members, nor

foundation for new avenues of access and a broader civil rights jurisdiction for the Constitutional Court.[120]

According to Article 128 of the New Constitution, justices of the Constitutional Court are nominated by the President and appointed by the upper house of Parliament, the Council of the Federation. Under the provisions of this article, a federal constitutional law is to define the powers and to prescribe procedures for the formation and activity of the Court. Under Item 2 of Article 108, a federal constitutional law requires the approval of three-fourths of the deputies in the Council of the Federation and two-thirds in the State Duma, the lower house of Parliament. The law then must be signed and promulgated by the President within fourteen days.

Part II of the Constitution, Concluding and Transitional Provisions, invalidates all preconstitutional legislation to the extent that it contradicts the New Constitution. However, it confirms the office terms of all previously elected judges, including the thirteen justices serving on the Constitutional Court.

III. The Constitutional Law On the Constitutional Court of the Russian Federation

On February 1, 1994, responding to the President's request as well as exercising its constitutional right of legislative initiative, the Constitutional Court submitted the Draft Law on the Constitutional Court to the State Duma (Draft Law).... The Council of the Federation approved the New Law on July 12, and President Yeltsin signed it on July 21. The New Law became effective on the day of its official publication....

A.   Court Structure and Status of Justices

Chapter I of the New Law contains general provisions, including a list of no fewer than twelve competencies of the Court. The Court needs a quorum of three-quarters, i.e., fifteen justices, in order to function. Five fundamental principles should guide the Court's activities: independence, collegiality, *glasnost*, adversarial procedure, and equality of the parties. Article 7 emphasizes the organizational and financial independence of the Court from all other state organs.

---

may it issue findings concerning the presence of grounds for their removal from office. In addition, the Court lost the right to examine the constitutionality of political parties and public associations. Also, deputies of parliament and public associations may no longer contest the constitutionality of statutes and other normative acts. The drafters probably imposed most of these restrictions in reaction to the Court's excessive politicization and, in particular, the Chairman's activities during the preceding two years....

120. The Constitution envisions a role for the Court as protector of constitutional rights. It foresees a Court which will hear not only citizens' complaints, but also constitutional questions certified by the ordinary courts. New Const., art. 125(4). However, this authority depends upon enactment of specific procedures by federal law.

Chapter II contains provisions concerning the status of justices. Article 8 increases the minimum age from thirty-five to forty and raises the required previous legal work experience from ten to fifteen years. According to article 9, the Council of the Federation must examine the candidates nominated by the President within fourteen days. They are elected by simple majority in a secret ballot. When a vacancy occurs, the President must nominate a candidate within one month. Justices serve single twelve-year terms of office and must retire at age seventy. This provision has obviously been inspired by the German model, except that justices on the German Constitutional Court must retire at age sixty-eight.... [150]

... Whereas the old Constitutional Court, like most other Constitutional Courts, worked as a single body, the new Court functions either in plenary session or in panels.... [155] [156] [160] [161] The Chairman and Deputy-Chairman belong to different panels while the other justices are assigned by lot. The panels may not remain unchanged for more than three years, and the members are to take turns as presiding justices....

The Plenum of the Russian Constitutional Court [is provided certain exclusive authority].... In addition, the Plenum elects the Chairman, Deputy-Chairman, and Secretary of the Court by secret ballot for three-year terms with the right to be re-elected. It assigns personnel and cases to

150. The average age of the 13 Russian justices when they were elected in 1991 was 50. Thus, on average they would have served for 15 years. More rapid turnover in the Court's membership is not only likely to make it more responsive to social and political development, but also to prevent legal petrification at a time when all sitting justices received their training under the Communist system. From this perspective, raising the minimum age to 40 may not have been a wise decision.

155. Article 11 forbids justices to be deputies to representative organs or to hold other public office; they must refrain from any other paid activity except teaching or other academic functions that do not interfere with their work on the Court. Justices may not belong to political parties or movements or engage in any political activities. Before the Court delivers its decision, justices may not publicly state their views on matters that could become cases, or are subject to judicial examination. [eds.—relocated footnote]

156. Article 13 of the New Constitutional Law expressly mentions "material guarantees" of independence such as pay, annual leave, housing, social and consumer services, and health insurance. Whereas the Draft Law submitted by the Court proposed elaborate special provisions concerning the material and social security of the justices, the New Law puts Constitutional Court justices on the same footing as other top federal judges. [eds.—relocated footnote]

160. Article 18 lists 12 reasons for removal ranging from procedural error in the justice's appointment (Item 1) to the justice's death (Item 12). Other reasons include voluntary resignation, criminal conviction, declaration of incapacity by a final court ruling, "the commission ... of an act that brings the honor and dignity of justices into disrepute" (Item 6), "the continuation by the justice, despite warnings from the Russian Federation Constitutional Court, of occupations or actions incompatible with his position" (Item 7), and "failure ... to take part in ...sessions, or failure to vote more than twice in succession without a valid reason" (Item 8). As an afterthought to this list, article 18 adds termination on account of disability for health reasons lasting for more than 10 consecutive months. The Council of the Federation may terminate a justice's tenure under Items 1 and 6 on the basis of a recommendation by the Court. In other cases the Court itself may adopt the appropriate decision by simple majority. [eds.—relocated footnote]

161. Article 19 provides for generous retirement benefits. [eds.—relocated footnote]

the panels, schedules the work of the Plenary meetings, adopts Rules of Procedure, and may suspend or dismiss a justice or remove the Chairman, Deputy–Chairman, or Secretary from their functions. The previous law had not provided for a limitation of terms of the Chairman and the other Court officers. The present provisions are obviously a reaction to Chairman Zorkin's much criticized political activism.

The jurisdiction of panels includes all competencies of the Court that have not been expressly assigned to or assumed by the Plenum. Specifically, these include: a) ruling upon the constitutionality of federal statutes; normative acts of the President, the Council of the Federation, the State Duma, and the Government; statutes and other normative acts of members of the Russian Federation affecting matters of federal or joint jurisdiction; treaties between organs of state power of the Russian Federation and organs of state power of members of the Russian Federation; treaties among members of the Russian Federation; and international treaties that have not yet entered into force; b) settling jurisdictional disputes between federal organs of state power; between organs of state power of the Federation and organs of state power of its members; or among the highest state organs of members of the Federation; c) examining the constitutionality of laws applied or to be applied to specific cases on the basis of citizens' complaints alleging the violation of constitutional rights and freedoms and at the request of the courts.

B. General Procedural Provisions

The general rules of procedure provide for trial-type oral hearings in open session and explanations by parties as well as testimony from experts and witnesses. Sessions in each case are to be held without interruption. The New Law surprisingly retains the provision of the previous constitutional law that the Constitutional Court may not decide other questions while the pending case remains unresolved. The Court is merely allowed to work concurrently in panels and in plenary session. . . .

The Bulletin of the Constitutional Court is to publish dissenting and concurring opinions of individual justices alongside the majority decision. Decisions are also to be published in other official publications of the state organs concerned. They become effective when announced by the Court; unconstitutional acts become immediately invalid. If this nullification creates a gap in legal regulation, the Constitution applies directly. Article 80 does, however, leave the door open for the Court to set a later date for its decision to take effect.

C. Special Procedures

. . . [T]he constitutionality of normative acts of organs of state power or treaties between them may be examined at the request of a number of high state organs. . . . The same state organs may ask the Constitutional Court to determine the constitutionality of an international treaty that has not yet entered into force but is subject to ratification by the State Duma or the approval of another federal organ of state power. The review of constitutionality may be "abstract," i.e., the challenge may be brought without a specific case or controversy having arisen. This is typical of the Austrian (and West European) model of constitutional review....

Citizens or their organizations may lodge complaints concerning the violation of their constitutional rights and freedoms. If the Constitutional Court accepts the complaint for examination, it has to notify the state organ concerned, but this notification does not automatically suspend pending proceedings. If the Court considers the contested act or provision unconstitutional, the organs concerned are to decide the pending case accordingly.

At first sight, these provisions appear to broaden considerably access to the Court, in so far as they do not require citizens to exhaust all possibilities of appeal or even await a decision of the trial court. Whereas the previous law granted the Constitutional Court discretion to reject a petition if it considered a review "inadvisable," the New Law appears to allow an appeal as of right with no discretion of the Court and no screening standards whatsoever. A careful reading of the Constitution, however, shows that this chapter is not self-executing. It requires enabling legislation to become effective. At least that is how Russian legal scholars understand the qualifying clause in Article 125 of the New Constitution which reads: "The Constitutional Court ... shall review the constitutionality ... *in accordance with procedures established by federal law.*" This federal law has not been passed as of this writing.

When a court determines that a law to be applied to a case before it is unconstitutional, it shall suspend proceedings and submit the question to the Constitutional Court....

Concerning the problem of impeachment by a hostile parliament, a situation which President Yeltsin confronted more than once, Article 93 of the New Constitution curtails the powers of both the legislature and the Constitutional Court. The State Duma may, with a two-thirds majority of its total membership, indict the President for treason or other serious crimes. The Supreme Court must then determine whether any such crime has indeed been committed. The Constitutional Court is restricted to issuing a finding that the proper constitutional procedure has been observed. The Council of the Federation may then remove the President from office, provided that two-thirds of its total membership agree to do so within three months from the date the charge was brought by the Duma.

IV.   Forming the "New" Constitutional Court

...The New Law went into effect on July 23, 1994.

On October 6, 1994, President Yeltsin submitted to the Council of the Federation a list of six candidates for appointment to the Constitutional Court. On October 24, voting by secret ballot, the Council elected only three justices from Yeltsin's list....

On November 15, 1994, the Council of the Federation voted on a list of five candidates for the remaining three openings on the Court.... Only one of the five candidates … passed scrutiny and brought the membership of the Court to seventeen.

On December 1, 1994, President Yeltsin nominated two more candidates to fill the remaining vacancies on the Court. On December 6, the Council of the Federation elected Vladimir Strekozov (fifty-four years old, Doctor of Law, Deputy Head of the Military Academy of Economics, Finance and Law, and a major general) with a comfortable majority of 100 votes. President Yeltsin's other candidate, Sergei Vitsin (Doctor of Law, Department Head at the Moscow Higher Police Academy, and also a major general), received only seventy-eight votes and thus was not elected.

For the last remaining vacancy on the Court, President Yeltsin nominated Robert Tsivilev, who was a legal aide to his Chief of Staff Sergei Filatov. On December 16, 1994, the Council of the Federation cast eighty-six votes (of the required ninety) in favor and forty-five against him, falling short of appointment by merely four votes.

Assuming he had mustered the necessary votes, President Yeltsin again presented Robert Tsivilev to the Council of the Federation on January 13, 1995. On January 17, Tsivilev was defeated for the second time, garnering only sixty-one votes. One reason for this defeat may have been President Yeltsin's refusal to nominate Issa Kostoev, chairman of the Federation Council Committee for Constitutional Legislation, Judicial and Legal Matters, and a popular choice among Council Members.

The unfortunate effect of this political maneuvering between the President and the Council of the Federation was that more than one year after the adoption of the new Constitution the Constitutional Court was still inoperative. This delay was due to the Transitional Provisions of the New Constitutional Law which required the election of the Chairman and other officers of the Court as well as the formation of the two chambers to take place "following the formation of [the Court's] full membership." Meanwhile, Court members grew restive because so many important issues awaited resolution. On December 30, 1994, Acting Court Chairman Nikolai Vitruk openly aired his disappointment, pointing out more than sixty open cases on which the Court would have to act. Justice Ernest Ametistov even accused the Council of the Federation of "sabotage" and suggested that the Court resume its work without waiting for the last member to be elected.

On February 2, 1995, President Yeltsin presented to the Council two law professors as candidates for the last vacant seat on the Constitutional Court: Anatolii Vengerov, a prominent specialist in legal theory and constitutional law, and Marat Baglai, an expert in constitutional and labor law. On February 7, the Council elected Marat Baglai (sixty-four years old, and First Pro–Rector of the Academy of Labor and Social Relations) by a vote of 101 to thirty.

On February 13, 1995, the Constitutional Court elected Professor Vladimir Tumanov as Chairman by a vote of eleven to eight, and Professor Tamara Morshchakova as Vice–Chairman, while reelecting Yurii Rudkin as Secretary of the Court. On February 15, the Court formed two panels of nine and ten justices, respectively. After more than sixteen months of suspension, there was again a functional Constitutional Court ready to assume an active role in the Russian legal and political system.

V. Evaluation of the New Legislation on the Constitutional Court

An analysis of the provisions of the new Constitution and the new Constitutional Law on the Constitutional Court yields a number of surprising observations. First, the Constitutional Court survived its serious political confrontation with the President virtually unscathed. Second, the New Law does not profoundly reflect the lessons that should have been learned from flaws in the previous law and from the Court's own mistakes in applying that law. Third, the Court and other constitutional law specialists were not able to make better use of time-tested foreign models in drafting the New Law.

A. Continuity of Personnel and Functions

After Valerii Zorkin's reluctant resignation as Chairman on October 6, 1993, the Court, under Acting Chairman Nikolai Vitruk, kept a low profile and apparently came to terms with the President in such a way as to emerge relatively unharmed in the revised (November 10, 1993) Draft of the Constitution. Threats and fears that the Court might be dissolved, and that some of its major functions would be abolished or transferred proved to be unfounded.

All thirteen justices from the Old Court retained their "life tenure" (until age sixty-five) and benefits. These thirteen had been nominated by the Chairman of the Supreme Soviet (Ruslan Khasbulatov) and appointed by secret election in the Congress of People's Deputies on October 29,- 1991. . . . With one exception . . . all thirteen justices had been members of the CPSU.**

Given the fact that nine of these justices consistently opposed President Yeltsin in the past, the constitutional provision for the election of six additional justices by the Council of the Federation can hardly be considered a court-packing bill. It does not automatically assure the President of a solid majority on the Court, although the right of nomination would appear to enable him to alter the balance in his favor. Surprisingly, in the course of constitutional reform the President did not demand the right to nominate the Chairman and Deputy–Chairman of the Court. The absence of this nomination right seems to further reduce the influence of the President and enhance the independence of the Court . . .

Of the six new appointees, four possess the highest academic qualification (the doctorate of law), and two are former judges. Some observers may consider these appointments a correction of a weakness of the old Court. One of the six new appointees is a woman and none represent an ethnic minority, while at least two (the two former judges) come from cities other

** [Editors' Note: The CPSU is the Communist party of the Soviet Union.]

than Moscow. Their average age is fifty-four, very close to that of the original justices. . . .

Russian Constitutional Court justices are products of the Communist *nomenklatura* system. They would not have reached their positions without the political loyalty and adaptability required by that system. Some of them may have retained more conservative political beliefs, while others may have developed progressive views. As long as it appeared possible, or even likely, that the Parliament would emerge victorious from its struggle with the President, the conservatives on the Court could well afford to challenge the President in the name of "constitutional legality." Once the President had consolidated his power, political opposition became self-destructive. In a system that continues to be based on quasi-feudal alliances and opportunism, it will not be surprising to find a more cooperative attitude on the part of the President's former opponents on the Court as long as the President appears to have firm control of the vast powers allocated to his office under the new Constitution. In light of his first appointments, President Yeltsin seemed reasonably certain that the future Court would respond to his political needs. However, the subsequent brutal and incredibly clumsy handling of the Chechnya situation has raised grave doubts about the course of Russian politics in the minds of many Russians, including President Yeltsin's most loyal supporters. A political crisis of enormous magnitude may again engulf all Russian institutions, including the Constitutional Court. From this perspective, much will depend on the signals which the Court sends in its first decisions.

B. Learning from the Past

The New Law unquestionably intends to correct technical shortcomings of the Old Law and to redefine and strengthen the Court's role in an emerging legal system characterized by separation of powers and the rule of law. It makes several promising attempts to reinforce the independence of the justices and to depoliticize the activities of the Court. The most obvious step in the direction of depoliticization is the elimination of the Court's right to take the initiative in impeachment proceedings. A similar depoliticization will result from the Court's new standing requirements for presenting the Court with a constitutional question. Previously, the Court granted standing to any deputy. The New Law, however, requires at least one-fifth of the total membership of either house of Parliament to present a constitutional question. It also abolishes standing for social associations in matters of abstract review. Despite these restrictions, the standing requirements are still extremely vague and undifferentiated; they provide little safeguard against the Court's involuntary involvement in political conflicts. . . .

Unfortunately, the Russian legal and political establishment retained a major obstacle to efficient constitutional review: the obligatory public hearing, which involves elaborate and immensely time-consuming adversarial fact finding and pleading procedures, from which the Law contains no escape clause. No potential argument turning on *"glasnost"* or "legitimacy" justifies the incredible waste of time and energy which these procedures require, and the resulting inability to deal swiftly and effectively with the many serious issues confronting the Court. The inexplicable retention of the provision that prohibits the Court from treating other, potentially urgent, cases before resolving pending cases aggravates this situation.

C.   Learning from Foreign Experience...

Arguably, the introduction of twelve-year terms and two panels, as in Germany, may enhance quality and speed in the Court's work. However, the reservation of important functions to a nineteen-member plenum—including the adoption and assignment of every individual case for examination—shows that profound political distrust overwhelms considerations of professional efficiency. Despite this manifest distrust, reformers could have adopted safeguards to secure the jurisdiction of the full court while also utilizing the positive experiences of the countries (e.g., Germany and Austria) with smaller screening panels and screening standards. A positive development may be seen in the authorization of the Court to extend the life of legislative acts judged unconstitutional so as to avoid regulatory vacuums (as is the case in Austria). In addition, an especially noteworthy feature of the new Russian legislation is to obligate judges in the ordinary court system to certify constitutional questions to the Constitutional Court. This judicial referral is an important part of the German and Austrian systems of constitutional adjudication, and raises the constitution-consciousness of the ordinary judiciary. Unfortunately, the same provision in the Constitution that declares the right to bring a citizen's complaint to the Constitutional Court as non-self-executing also applies to judicial referral. It will be practically impossible to implement this process without concurrent structural and procedural reform, which would profoundly affect the work of the Court. Such change would include the development of screening panels with clear standards and expedited procedures designed to avoid unacceptable delays.

A negative development is that the Court no longer has the right to examine the constitutionality of political parties. It is with good reason that the German Constitution assigns this politically sensitive task to the Constitutional Court rather than the regular court system. The same observation applies to electoral disputes.

Conclusion

I have attempted a first—and necessarily selective—evaluation of the technical aspects of the new Russian Constitutional Court such as structure, functions, and procedures. The real test will be the quality of opinions rendered by the Court and the acceptance and enforcement of these opinions by the other branches of government, particularly the President and his government. The Constitutional Court has a new, although this time more limited, opportunity to promote the establishment of the rule of law. To achieve this end, patient persuasion may be more helpful than overt confrontation. The Court must refrain from political involvement, and individual justices must avoid public posturing if the Court hopes to affect and protect an emerging Russian legal culture. Since its suspension on October 7, 1993, the Constitutional Court has had ample time to ponder past mistakes and reflect on a future course of action. . . . [I]t should both signal and practice judicial restraint as its guiding principle until by solid legal work it will have earned that level of respect and legitimacy which will enable it to move forward to the sort of legal activism exhibited by other constitutional courts in other political systems. The Russian Court has yet to learn the skills and become aware of the responsibilities of a judicial activism practiced in the public interest, as well as the art of interacting with other governmental organs in a functioning democratic society. . . . Russian legislative and executive bodies . . . will have to undergo even more profound learning processes. While Russia's road to a flourishing democratic society under the rule of law will be long and arduous, there is clearly no alternative.

Questions and Comments

1. In the report described earlier, the Lawyers Committee for Human Rights complained of the two-year delay in establishing a functioning constitutional court to replace Russia's first one which, notwithstanding its concentrating on separation of powers issues, had made some contributions on human rights decisions. It reported that 8 of the 29 decisions of the first Constitutional Court were on human rights complaints, including rulings that a dismissal of an employee "in order to avoid pension payments was unconstitutional age discrimination, and a judgment that housing evictions were unconstitutional in the absence of judicial review. . . . [as well as] some important interpretations of constitutional human rights norms [such as its conclusion that Yeltsin's] decree banning the hard line National Salvation Front violated the freedom of association. . . . " (Compare Hausmaninger's more critical assessment of the National Salvation Front case.) During this same time, the Lawyers Committee complained of repeated violations of the human rights provisions of the new constitution of 1993, including a presidential decree issued in June 1994 on fighting crime that assertedly conflicted with several articles of the new constitution, and the continued practice of requiring residence permits. Note that, consistent with Professor Hausmaninger's predictions of a "more cooperative" and less confrontational attitude toward the president, in July, 1995 the Russian Constitutional Court upheld President Yeltsin's invasion of the Republic of Chechnya as constitutional. For analysis see Elliot Stanton Berke, *The Chechnya Inquiry: Constitutional Commitment or Abandonment*, 10 Emory Intl Law Rev. 879 (1996).

2. Following the reconstitution of the Constitutional Court, Russia has evolved a more decentralized system of constitutional review in which the all courts, including the Supreme Court, have authority to engage in constitutional review (though only the Constitutional Court has jurisdiction over abstract review of the "normative acts" of the President and Government). See Peter Krug, *Departure from the Centralized Model: The Russian Supreme Court and Constitutional Control of Legislation*, 37 Va. J. Intl Law 725 (1997); see also Peter B. Maggs, *The Russian Courts and the Russian Constitution*, 8 Ind. Intl & Comp. Law Rev. 99 (1997). Krug suggests that that Russia's departure from the centralized model is explained in part by the "assertiveness" of the Supreme Court, the absence of deep support in Russia for principles of legislative or parliamentary supremacy, and "the fact that so much Russian legislation remains that was enacted either during the Soviet era or at least prior to adoption of the 1993 Constitution." He suggests that the Russian diffusion of judicial review may be a symptom of the distrust of representative decisionmaking that Stephen Holmes and Cass Sunstein have identified as a key problem in making transitions to constitutionalism in former communist states. See Chapter IV above.

3. The Lawyers' Committee's 1995 Report was particularly critical of the provisions of the new law on the Constitutional Court which prohibits it from ruling on the constitutionality of the *application* of legal norms. Dismissing concerns that entertaining such applications would have overwhelmed the court, the Committee was not optimistic about the capacity of the ordinary courts to respond to such challenges. While it found occasional instances of the ordinary courts invalidating government action based on unconstitutionality, the Committee concluded that "the ordinary courts are not yet strong or independent enough to be the primary guardian of the new Constitution against attacks from other branches ... [a situation that will continue] as long as ordinary courts with no expertise in constitutional law are expected to implement general constitutional norms without the help of authoritative interpretations by the Constitutional Court."

Recall Professor Favoreu's suggestion at the beginning of this chapter that the centralized system of review may produce better decisions, while the diffuse system was more efficacious at spreading constitutional norms: is there an argument that, at least in theory, the new division of jurisdiction is an effort to have the benefits of both systems?

4. Professor Hausmaninger expresses concern over the failure to change certain procedures of the Russian constitutional court, such as the requirement for seriatim consideration of cases. Why might such a requirement be adopted in the first place? What role do such procedural rules play in the legitimation of a constitutional court?

5. Consider whether the ban on deciding "political questions," found in article 1(3) of the 1991 Law on the Constitutional Court, was in tension with provisions permitting members of parliament to bring cases before the court challenging the constitutionality of normative acts, or the more dramatic provisions authorizing the Constitutional Court, on its own initiative, to make "findings" (such as those made concerning President Yeltsin's speech in March 1993)? Reconsider what purposes justiciability limitations might serve.

6. Does the experience in Russia raise questions about the ability of courts (or of new courts), to decide "landmark" cases—at least if they themselves think of the cases as landmarks?

7. The Lawyers Committee for Human Rights concluded that while the first Russian Constitutional Court was not a wholly "innocent victim of the power struggle between parliament and the president," its experience "shows that it is extremely hard to establish an independent body exercising judicial review in a country where the principle of separation of powers has traditionally been mocked .... [T]he termination of the court's power with an unconstitutional *ukaz* sets a dangerous precedent and indicates how difficult it will be to insulate the future court from pressures that emanate from the other branches of power." This comment assumes that the basic problem was the court's lack of insulation from the political branches. Can the story of Russia's constitutional court be read instead to suggest the disadvantages of judicial review in transitions to democracy?

In thinking about this last question, compare the experience of Russia's first Constitutional Court with the following account, found in *Constitution Watch*, 5 East European Constitutional Review 8 (Fall 1996), of the nature and effect of judicial rulings on presidential elections in Bulgaria:

> Judicial rulings have also had in impact on the presidential elections, the most important instance being the elimination of Georgi Pirinski, principal candidate of the ruling party, from the race. Article 93.2 of the Constitution declares that "eligible for president shall be persons who are Bulgarian citizens by birth," and Art. 25.1 provides that "A Bulgarian citizen by birth shall be anyone born of at least one parent holding Bulgarian citizenship, or 'born on the territory of the Republic of Bulgaria, should he not be entitled to any other citizenship by virtue of origin.'" Pirinski was born in New York in 1948 of a Bulgarian father and an American mother, and he subsequently became an American citizen. In 1952, the family resettled in Bulgaria, whereupon he obtained Bulgarian citizenship. The question which was legitimately raised in this context is whether he is a Bulgarian citizen "by birth" or "by naturalization." Anticipating problems with Pirinski's citizenship, Parliament amended the citizenship law, which now provides that, "A Bulgarian citizen by birth is anyone born of at least one parent holding Bulgarian citizenship, regardless of the place and time of his or her birth."

> In response to this act of the parliamentary majority, opposition deputies appealed to the Constitutional Court, asking for a binding interpretation of the constitutional provision defining the eligibility requirements governing the citizenship of the president. The Court decided that the amendment to the citizenship law does not have retroactive force and that the citizenship of each candidate for president should be determined by the citizenship laws in effect at the time of his birth. Even though the Court did not mention Pirinski explicitly, its decision had a direct bearing upon his candidacy. According to the communist citizenship law passed in 1948 (several months before

Pirinski's birth), children of Bulgarian citizens born abroad were denied Bulgarian citizenship whenever they acquired automatically the citizenship of the country of their birth. This arrangement was designed to deprive of Bulgarian citizenship the offspring of Bulgarian political emigrants.

When Pirinski attempted to register as a candidate with the Central Electoral Commission, the commission—which was composed of 11 members appointed by BSP and 10 members representing the opposition and which took all decisions about registration by a two-thirds vote—turned him down. In retaliation for the refusal of the opposition to register Pirinski BSP members blocked the registration of the UDF candidate, Petar Stoyanov, citing "procedural irregularities."

The electoral law allows candidates who have been refused registration to seek redress before the Supreme Court, which both Pirinski and Stoyanov promptly did. In two unanimous decisions (5:0), a panel of the Supreme Court affirmed the decision of the commission in the Pirinski case, and reversed it in the Stoyanov case. Thus, the ruling party's candidate was juridically forced to bow out of the presidential race, and BSP subsequently nominated Minister of Culture Ivan Marazov to take Pirinski's place.

At the first round of the presidential elections, held on October 27, none of the candidates drew more than 50 percent of the votes. When the results were announced, it was clear that public support for BSP had plummeted. Stoyanov received almost 44 percent of the vote, Marazov came in a distant second with 27 percent and, in many electoral districts, the latter was beaten by the third major candidate, maverick politician George Ganchev, who received 22 percent of the vote. In accord with the law, a second round was then scheduled, with Stoyanov and Marazov competing. On November 3, BSP suffered a crushing electoral rebuff when Stoyanov won by a 20 percent margin (60 percent of the votes, against 40 percent for his opponent). This reversal of the political fortunes of BSP will certainly have an impact on the party and the political situation in the country as a whole. Virtually all opposition parties, seconded by dissident factions within BSP, are trying to put the issue of pre-term parliamentary elections onto the agenda (the official term of the present Parliament will not expire until December 1998). In addition to a bleak winter, Bulgarian society now has to cope with an intensified political crisis.

Does this suggest how interpretations of a Constitution that are arguably legally reasonable can provoke a political crisis, particularly in transitional regimes?

---

4.   THE QUESTION OF "JURIDIFICATION"

What effect on political discourse and decisionmaking does "constitutionalization", or "juridicization" of issues have? Alec Stone has argued in his book on France, and again in the short essay excerpted below, that the presence of the constitutional court has been to "juridicize" legislative discourse, making primary in legislators minds the question whether a proposal is constitutional (instead of good policy). (Michael Mandel makes a similar claim with respect to Canada in an essay included in Chapter VII, below). Can activist constitutional courts, unconstrained by jurisdictional or justiciability limits, weaken commitments to democratic political processes?[ao] Consider whether such "juridification" of the political branches is a bad, or good, result.

Alec Stone, *Abstract Constitutional Review and Policy Making in Western Europe,* in Comparative Judicial Review and Public Policy (Donald W. Jackson & C. Neal Tate eds., 1992).

Constitutional review has exploded into prominence in Western Europe.... Yet before 1950, the power of European courts to control the constitutionality of legislation was nearly unknown. Comparative political scientists have all but ignored this development and constitutional courts generally (Sigelman and Gadbois, 1983). The French case, where *no major book or article on the Constitutional Council has yet been produced by native social scientists,* is a telling, if extraordinary, example. But in all European countries, academic discourse on law and courts is the privileged domain of law professors, the vast majority of whom are exercised exclusively by traditional, jurisprudential concerns. In this discourse, there is a fierce resistance to the notion that constitutional courts are political actors at all; a radical dissociation between legal and policy-making processes is propagated; and the impact of courts on macro politics is obscured or altogether ignored.

This chapter is an overview and assessment of the establishment and subsequent development of abstract review in Europe, focusing on the interaction between constitutional courts, governments, and parliaments in the making of public policy. First, I examine the creation of constitutional jurisdictions set apart from the ordinary and administrative court systems in Austria, Germany, France, and Spain. This creation had the particular advantage of allowing for the *constitutional review* of legislation by special judges while preserving the main tenets of European separation of powers doctrines, tenets that had long enshrined an uncompromising hostility to *judicial review.* In the second section I describe aspects of the structure, mandate, and activity of European courts that exercise abstract review—in Austria. France, West Germany, and Spain. Abstract review differs from American judicial review in that it is not dependent on, or incidental to, concrete litigation or controversy involving a statute. The abstract review process results in a decision on the *prima facie* constitutionality of a legislative text: a concrete tort is not a requisite condition; the process is a

---

ao. This is a more specialized version of an argument made long ago by Thayer about the effects of any judicial invalidation of legislative acts, in the context of U.S. constitutional law. See J. Thayer, John Marshall 103–07 (1901).

purely exegetical exercise. In the third section, I examine the impact of abstract review on legislative processes, focusing on the cases we know the most about—France and Germany. In both of these countries, policy making has been transformed and in remarkably similar ways. . . .

STRUCTURE AND ACTIVITY

There is significant variation in the constitutional mandate and activity of the European courts that exercise abstract review authority. . . . [A] constitutional court may possess abstract review powers alone, or in combination with powers of concrete review. Further, there exist two modes of abstract review:

a posteriori (Austria, Portugal, Spain, West Germany), and *a priori* (France, Spain until 1985, Portugal). In the former, laws are referred to the constitutional court after promulgation; in the latter, laws are referred after final adoption by parliament, but *before* promulgation. In all cases, abstract review is initiated by politicians, who refer legislation directly to the court. Courts cannot refuse to rule, and governments and legislative majorities cannot avoid having their legislation examined. *Abstract review therefore functions to extend what would otherwise be a concluded legislative process*—referrals in effect require the court to undertake a final "reading" of a disputed bill or law.

The highly partisan nature of this process places constitutional courts in delicate situations, and the possibility of explosive judicial-political confrontation might appear to be virtually permanent. However, *for every European court excepting the French, abstract review processes do not constitute a major source of case-load or of public perceptions about their role in the political system*. Whatever impact abstract review might have on debates and controversies about a court's institutional legitimacy is counterbalanced by routine lower profile tasks. That is, in countries other than France, what constitutional courts do most of the time is not salient to partisan politics: political parties are not involved directly in these processes, and they do not actively question and debate the legitimacy of the work being performed.

Statistics show the extent to which abstract review constitutes only a small fraction of total activity outside of France. . . .

In Austria, concrete review of cases originating in the administrative court system comprises well over 90 percent of the Vienna court's caseload. The court has dealt with over 1,000 such cases per year during the 1980's. . . . The court, which also receives approximately 25 individual referrals each year, is motivated above all else by its desire or responsibility to harmonize the legal order, and not by politically initiated reviews. *Abstract review is exceedingly rare in Austria, and, indeed, is politically insignificant*. In 1975, the right of referral was granted to one-third of the deputies in the federal and state lower houses—that is, to the minority party. Whether due to the consensual nature of Austrian politics, to a belief that referrals are not altogether legitimate, or to both, the court has received only five referrals to date, resulting in only one ruling of unconstitutionality. In consequence, the legislative process has not been significantly altered by the existence of such review.

The work of the Spanish court, like that of its German counterpart, is dominated by individual referrals (90 percent of all cases that reach the court). These referrals *(amparos)* may not attack a law directly, but instead are requests that the court defend against alleged administrative infringement those fundamental rights enumerated in Articles 14 and 30 of the constitution. From 1981, when the court began its work, through 1985, it has handed down 422 decisions on nearly 4,000 individual referrals. Moreover, the court has clearly signaled that it considers the protection of individual rights to be its top priority. *As in Germany, this is largely due to the court's wish to contribute to the stability of a democratic regime created in the wake of fascist rule . . . .* Abstract review referrals for *a posteriori* control have averaged 8 per year, while the court received a total of 13 petitions for *a priori* control until 1985. In 1985, the *a priori* power was rescinded because it was considered to be an illegitimate affront to parliamentary sovereignty.

The French Constitutional Council exercises *a priori* abstract review exclusively, and solely upon referral by political authorities. Once promulgated, laws are immune from scrutiny by the Council or by any other jurisdiction. Further, not only is the Council detached from the greater judicial system (any influence it may exercise upon ordinary or administrative courts is neither systematic nor formal), it is also cut off from direct popular contact with the citizenry . . . : Unable to claim that it performs a function of harmonizing legal decisions or administrative activity with the exigencies of the constitution, and bereft of a stable constituency, the Council may be said to possess relatively fewer resources with which to counter criticisms of its activities. These occur with greater frequency and are much more public and vitriolic than those directed at other European courts. At the same time, the Council's role has vastly expanded: from 1974, when the power of referral was granted to any 60 deputies or senators, through 1987 the Council received 191 referrals—in the 1958–73 period, it received a total of 9 . . . .

THE "JURIDICIZATION" OF POLICY MAKING

The development of abstract constitutional review in France and Germany has transformed the customs and conduct of politicians and policymakers. Indeed, policy making can be described as "juridicized" to the extent that a constitutional court's decisions, the pedagogical authority of its past jurisprudence, and the threat of future censure alter legislative outcomes. When a constitutional court rules on the constitutionality of legislative provisions, this influence is direct but not always negative. The court may have an indirect influence to the extent that governments and their parliamentary majorities sacrifice policy preferences in order to avoid constitutional censure. This indirect impact also might be said to constitute a court's legislative behavior.

The juridicization of policy-making processes in France and Germany can be explained by four interrelated structural and behavioral factors: (1) the modes of constitutional review exercised by the respective constitutional courts over legislation; (2) the use by politicians of the courts' offices for political ends; (3) judicial activism and the attendant development by courts of creative techniques of controlling legislation; and (4) the strict application of decisions by legislators. The study of "juridicization" thus focuses empirical attention on the interaction between courts and legislative institutions in the making of public policy....

Mode of Control

In his pathbreaking, now classic essay on conceptualizing the U.S. Supreme Court as a "national policymaker," R. Dahl (1957) argued that "what is critical is the extent to which a court can or does make policy decisions by going outside established 'legal' criteria found in precedent, statute, and constitution." Creative judicial interpretation will have policy impact in any political system. But Dahl's focus is too limited for our purposes, reflecting strictly the realities of the American judicial review mechanism and a specifically American separation-of-powers tradition. Abstract control is typically justified as providing for a more complete, potentially systematic, and therefore efficacious defense of the supremacy of the constitution within a hierarchy of judicial norms (Weber, 1987: 50–57). *Abstract review is of interest to policy studies because it requires or enables constitutional courts to intervene in and alter legislative processes and outcomes.* This intervention is virtually immediate: in France, bills must be referred to the Council within 15 days after their adoption in Parliament, and may not be promulgated until a decision has been reached by the Council; in Germany, politicians have one month from the date of promulgation to refer legislation. Thus, it should not be surprising that the subsequent decision is viewed by politicians as the true final stage of the legislative process.

Juridicizing Legislative Politics

The remarkable development of abstract constitutional control in France and Germany is a result of, and a response to, the exploitation of the courts by politicians for partisan political ends. In France, successive oppositions in the 1980s correctly viewed petitions to the Council, or the mere threat of petition, to be their most effective means to obstruct or enforce changes in legislation proposed by the government and its parliamentary majority. Because governments can not prevent such petitions, they are obliged either to work on the assumption that the opposition will refer important projects to constitutional judges or to risk court censure, embarrassment, and lost time. Since 1981, such major reforms as the laws on decentralization (1982), press pluralism (1984), audiovisual communications (1986), and the Chirac government's penal code reforms (1986) were subject to massive autolimitation processes, as majorities sacrificed important policy objectives due to threats of referral and fear of censure. In West Germany, governments and their supporters are apparently even more willing to compromise with the opposition, so risk-averse have they become in constitutional matters, and in consequence policy making is "overloaded with legal arguments and considerations" (Landfried, 1988) as the "opposition in the Bundestag [works] to attain its political goals by judicial means" (Landfried, 1985: 541). The laws on codetermination (1976) and on military service for conscientious objectors (1978) are just two important reforms that were substantially altered by the juridicized process. Constitutional debate is therefore not limited to official judicial intervention, but may occur during all stages of the legislative process.

That said, juridicization is not a permanent state within ministries and parliament. The most important aspects of a great number of bills either raise no fundamental constitutional objections or are treated as though they do not by politicians. The opposition does not waste time and resources in threatening court intervention if compelling objections as to the constitutionality of legislation in question do not exist or can not be found. Moreover, even debates that can be empirically characterized as juridicized are not juridicized evenly or in the same way. Any given policy area has its own dynamic of constitutional possibility or constraint, conforming to jurisprudential development. Legislative debate is more or less juridicized as a function of this variation—that is, oppositions have a greater chance of juridicizing processes to the extent that constitutional courts have already laid the ground rules for legislating in that policy sector. The French Council's annulments of the Socialist's bills on nationalization (1982), press pluralism (1984), and electoral reform in New Caledonia (1985) thus structured the policy processes and debates on the Chirac government's privatization program (1986), press and audiovisual reform (1986) and the reform of the electoral system in metropolitan France (1986). In a similar manner, no West German government engaged in reforming party finance law (a pressing issue these days) can afford to ignore the court's rulings of 1966, 1967, and 1983.

In juridicized debates, the constitutional text is a site of partisan conflict. For the opposition, threats of referrals are useful weapons in the pursuance of its policy positions—but they will be credible threats only if jurisprudence is taken seriously. Accordingly, oppositions in both countries have come to employ outside constitutional specialists and court watchers to develop constitutional arguments for juridicized debate and to write petitions. For the government and its majority, the increased tendency for parliamentary debates to be juridicized poses even greater technical. practical. and political problems. They are forced to address a multitude of often contradictory claims of constitutional obligation or enjoinment emanating from opposition bancs, their own ranks. and from special experts. The opposition can proliferate constitutional arguments with impunity, but only the government can be punished for misunderstanding constitutional principles. As a result. the role of the Council of State, the French government's official legal advisor, has been enhanced, as ministers seek to insulate bills from future censure. In Germany, long Bundestag hearings have been organized during which selected legal experts, jurists, and former constitutional judges are asked to engage in what Landfried (1988) calls "Karlsruhe-astrology"—attempts to predict the future position which the court will adopt. In any event, the task of insulating a bill from constitutional censure is not a simple one, since official advisers, politicians, and private constitutional consultants may have radically differing conceptions of the legislator's legal obligations and predict different rulings. More problematic, governments usually set limits on how far they are willing to compromise, and these are largely determined by partisan and not judicial considerations.

Judicial Activism

Constitutional courts are intervening in legislative processes at an increasing rate, as statistics show. In France, in the 1958–80 period, the Council examined 45 laws referred to it by politicians; in the 1981–87 period, the number more than doubled—to 91. In the 1974–80 period, an average of 6.1 percent of the bills adopted by Parliament were referred: since 1981, the percentage is 13.8 percent, with a high of 24 percent in 1986. In the 1980s, therefore, nearly one in seven laws adopted by the French Parliament was subjected to constitutional review, a remarkably large fraction since a majority of laws are only of the narrowest technical interest and take up practically none of the time and resources of the average parliamentarian. Indeed, Council intervention in the legislative process can be said to be systematic: *All budgets since 1974 have been scrutinized by the Council as has virtually every major piece of legislation since 1981.*

In West Germany, the intervention is relatively limited: 71 laws were referred to the Constitutional Court between 1951 and 1981; in the 1981–87 period, 23 laws were referred. Several points should be made about the German statistics. First, in terms of the legislative process in the Bundestag, partisan battles over legislation occur—if they are to occur—at the committee stage, accounting for the fact that nearly nine of every ten laws are adopted by unanimity. The approximate three laws per year that are referred are those on which the parties were not able to achieve prior consensus. The impact of the court can therefore not be assessed or measured by examining referrals and decisions alone. The researcher must be willing to wade through committee debates in searches for autolimitation. Second, the power of the Lander governments to refer federal legislation has been used without reference to problems of federalism. Parties in opposition at the federal level but making up the governments of Lander have used the referral in service of the national party, in what are essentially national conflicts. Thus, the Social Democratic Party (SDP) used its control of state governments to refer federal legislation on rearmament (1950s) and social welfare policy (1961), and the Christian Democratic Union–Christian Social Union Lander governments did the same, after 1969. to refer to the Court the SDP legislation on abortion (1974), and the Ostpolitik treaties with East Germany (1973). Moreover, as in France since the first *alternance* in 1981, the number of referrals is highest after national elections yielding an alternation in power—that is, during a new government's so-called honeymoon period and when reform spirits are highest. . . .

These figures measure only the volition of politicians to use constitutional courts as a means of obtaining their political goals, and not "judicial activism." However, there is a structured complicity between politicians in opposition and constitutional courts. Referrals to courts act as a kind of jurisprudential transmission belt: the more petitions the court receives, the more opportunity they have to elaborate jurisprudential techniques of control; this elaboration, in turn, provides oppositions with a steady supply of issues, expanding the grounds of judicial debate in parliament and in future petitions. In addition, constitutional principles are most effectively enshrined when legislative choices are invalidated (or rewritten by the court)—a more acceptable raw measure of activism. Since 1981, substantially more than 50 percent of the laws referred to the French Council were judged to be unconstitutional, in whole or in part, as adopted, up from 24 percent in the 1958–74 period. In West Germany, where concrete control also exists, judicial invalidation rose dramatically in the 1980s: in the 1951–80 period, 85 federal laws were judged to be in whole or in part unconstitutional; since 1981, the number is 94.

As important, constitutional courts have developed a host of techniques of controlling the legislator other than through declarations of unconstitutionality. The most important of these are the declaration of "strict reserves of interpretation"—that is, a declaration "that one particular interpretation of the law is the only constitutional one" (Landfried, 1985:531–532)—and the acceptance of the *principle* of a reform but not of the *means* chosen by the legislator. These "weapons of limited warfare against constitutionality" (Cappelletti and Cohen, 1979: 94) were initially developed as means of judicial self-restraint. In both countries, the practical result has been to give positive law-making authority to constitutional judges because lawmakers have responded simply by copying the terms of the courts' decisions directly into subsequent laws on the same legislative subject.

Last, constitutional judges in both countries have aroused controversy in both political and academic milieux by "going outside of established 'legal' criteria found in precedent, statute, and constitution." In France, as noted above, the Council has willfully expanded its field of reference by incorporating into the constitution an ever-expanding bill of rights. In 1986, a number of government ministers and high parliamentary officials called the Council a "deviation," and "a new kind of legislator" exercising "discretionary, power over parliament," and called for a codification of constitutional obligations to eliminate "arbitrary" rulings. The German court, for its part, has been accused of "drawing conclusions from the basic law which one can hardly relate to the text of the constitution" (Landfried, 1988: 162). That judges are creatively building constitutional law is undeniable, if a natural response to the fact that many of the problems they are asked to solve are highly complex socially and politically, and do not fall into neat constitutionally fixed categories.

"Overdone Scrupulousness" and Corrective Revisions

The application of negative court decisions by legislators is best illustrated by in-depth case study. but some comments should be made here. Theoretically, legislators would have a range of options available to them in response to constitutional censure or control: they could, on one extreme, copy word-for-word relevant jurisprudence directly into new legislation, could seek creative ways to circumvent a court's dictates on the other, or strike balances between the two. What Landfried concludes with respect to West German legislators could also describe their French counterparts: "The problem is not so much the absence, but rather the excess of obedience ... towards the court"—there is an "overdone scrupulousness" (Landfried, 1988: 157–158). The practical effect of many of the most important decisions of unconstitutionality is to force a second legislative process, which I call a "corrective revision" process—the reelaboration of a censured text in conformity with judicial prescriptions in order to avoid a second censure. This conformity can be characterized as strict, and no legislative project has ever been censured twice, despite multiple referrals.

In cases such as these, legislators simply allow constitutional courts to dictate, often word-for-word, the terms of new legislation. Policy outcome may have no relation to initial policy preferences as expressed by the respective parliaments. Indeed, revised laws reflect the policy preferences of constitutional judges unambiguously overriding those of elected officials. A few examples will suffice. In 1982 the French Council struck down a nationalization bill on the grounds that its provision for compensation to expropriated stockholders violated property rights. It then went on to state how the government could save the bill, by employing different formulas for arriving at the valuation of the companies concerned. The government was obliged to write the formulas into the law; the bill survived a second referral, but the revision raised the cost of nationalizations by a full 25 percent. In 1986 the Chirac government was forced to revise both its press and audiovisual bills after they had been struck down because, the Council asserted, they did not adequately protect media "pluralism"—a concept that is not mentioned in any constitutional text (including in those incorporated by the Council). In both cases, the government simply copied word-for-word, comma-for-comma, long sections of the Council's decision directly into the law. In 1967, the German parliament all but unanimously passed an electoral finance law elaborated, or so it was thought, in accordance with a 1966 decision on the same topic. The court. however, struck down the law as unconstitutional because it provided for reimbursements of campaign expenses only for those parties that had received at least 2.5 percent of the vote. The Court ruled that the floor should be placed at .5 percent, though of course it could point to no constitutional text in support of such a judgment. The subsequent corrective revision process enshrined the court's solution. Again, this result is the rule not the exception; indeed,

Kommers (1976: 275) reports that strict compliance is more prevalent in cases of abstract review than for any other forms.

The macropolitical effect of the evolving "juridicization of policy-making processes" has been to close off reform routes that would otherwise be open to reform-minded governments. Said differently, because these courts have never reversed themselves, because politicians perceive the effects of judicial review as binding upon them forever, and because lawmakers choose to incorporate constitutional court jurisprudence directly into legal regimes. more and more political issues are no longer open to legislative activity, and the web of constitutional obligation and enjoinment becomes more and more "close-meshed." The situation has led some, including Landfried, to argue that the "juridicization of parliament [is] dangerous for democracy," and that abstract control mechanisms "should be abolished" (Landfried, 1988: 165: Landfried, 1985: 541). It is perhaps inevitable that normative debate attends any discussion of juridicization, for it is there that a complex set of political, academic, and ideological commitments intersect in the concrete world of policy making.

At times, abstract review itself is put on trial, as in France from 1981 to 1987 when a succession of ministers and parliamentarians from both the Left and the Right decried what they viewed as a dangerous development toward a "government of judges" and publicly threatened the Council with curtailing its powers. The case of Spain, where review has at times paralyzed the government since the Left came to power in 1983, provides another dramatic example (Bon and Modeerne, 1985). Until 1985, the Spanish court possessed *a priori* review authority over organic laws and those laws governing the status of the autonomous regions. Upon coming to power, the Socialist Workers embarked on a number of wide-ranging reforms of both legislative and constitutional regimes, and these required extensive organic legislation. In the 3–year period 1983–85, the opposition referred 6 laws (of a total of 27 that could have been referred) to the court according to the rules governing *a priori* review, 3 of which were judged to be in whole or in part unconstitutional. Unfortunately, these referrals delayed the reforms for ludicrous periods of time. In France, the Council is required to rule within one month, and in Germany referrals do not suspend the law's effect unless a negative decision has been rendered. The Spanish referrals suspended promulgation, but worse for the government, in five of these six cases the court took over one year to render a judgment. Two main arguments—both of which have been heard in France and West Germany—were most widely made for this suppression [of a priori review in Spain after 1985]. First, *a priori* control was considered—by the governing party, the major press, and significantly by the scholarly community—as manifestly "political," because its effect was to implicate the court directly in day-to-day politics. Second, it was judged that ... the *a priori* procedure was being used primarily as a means of parliamentary obstruction, as parliamentary politics by other methods.

CONCLUSION

From the perspective developed here, the constitutional politics of abstract review are legislative politics by another name. As a description of function, constitutional courts exercising politically initiated abstract review can be conceptualized profitably as third legislative chambers whose behavior is nothing more or less than the impact—direct and indirect—of constitutional review on legislative outcomes. This is not to imply that courts exercise legislative powers identical to those of governments and parliaments, or that judges behave as card-carrying members of political parties. It is to assert that abstract review requires these courts to participate in policy-making processes, and to the extent that *legislative* outcomes are substantively altered by such review, its function is easily and profitably assimilated into a legislative one. Some may protest that this confuses behavior with the effects of constitutional jurisprudence on policy output. If this is a confusion, it is willful and, I believe, necessary. Study of juridicization has the advantage of focusing empirical attention on how abstract review actually functions in political systems, and on how these courts are shaped by and in turn shape their political environments. It is thus a profitable approach for political scientists, especially those whose primary interests lie *beyond* the study of public law, courts, and judicial processes more narrowly conceived. Nevertheless, courts, unlike legislators, produce jurisprudence, and that aspect of their activity, judged to be central by academic lawyers, is admittedly deemphasized here with certain negative effects.

Still, it is crucial to note that when constitutional judges are engaged in abstract review, their decision-making processes are closer to legislative decision-making processes than when they are applying a code, or even the constitution, to decide disputes arising from concrete litigation. That is, in abstract review processes, the lawmaking function of these courts is far more important than is dispute-resolution. Moreover, the "dispute" at hand is primarily partisan-political, rather than judicial. Blair (1978: 354) reports that the German court readily understands this and is thus "far more cautious" when engaging in abstract review than for other activities. The French Council, on the other hand, can never engage in anything but abstract interpretation, and thus it is in a much more vulnerable institutional position than are other European constitutional courts. The implicit assumption here—borne out, I believe, in empirical studies—is that politically initiated, abstract review is inherently more destabilizing than is concrete review, precisely because it poses the "countermajoritarian difficulty" unambiguously, from the moment it is initiated.

. . . German jurist Carl Schmitt (1958) long opposed the establishment of an organ replete with the power of constitutional review on the grounds that it would lead either to the "judicialization of politics" or to a "politicization of justice." Of course, from a policy-making perspective, it led to both. In all cases, whether in Spain, France, Germany, or Austria, abstract review exists only to the extent that politicians seek to alter legislative outcomes, by having their policy choices ratified or the government's and parliamentary majority's choices watered down or vetoed. If politicians ceased to use referrals as political weapons, abstract review would disappear, and the countermajoritarian difficulty would no longer be posed.

Questions and Comments

1. Assuming judicial review is to take place, consider the comparative advantages of more directive, or less directive, judicial decisionmaking. Recall the earlier questions about whether *Roe v. Wade* suffered by the specificity of its trimester approach. Should it matter in thinking about this whether a court is reviewing an issue that will come before only a single national legislative body (e.g., Northern Pipeline Const. Co. v. Marathon Pipe Line Co., 458 U.S. 50 (1982)) or before multiple state and local decisionmakers (e.g., Miranda v. Arizona, 384 U.S. 436 (1966)).

In *Northern Pipeline*, the Court found unconstitutional the 1978 Bankruptcy Act because of its reliance on non-Article III bankruptcy judges to adjudicate state law claims asserted on behalf of the bankrupt against parties otherwise outside the bankruptcy proceedings. The Court stayed its judgment for several months in order to "afford Congress an opportunity to reconstitute the bankruptcy courts or to adopt other valid means of adjudication without impairing the interim administration of the bankruptcy laws." It declined simply to sever the power to adjudicate state law claims from the statute, since one of the purposes of the 1978 act had been to "ensure adjudication of all claims in a single forum and to avoid the delay and expense of jurisdictional disputes." The Court emphasized that it was "for Congress to determine the proper manner of restructuring the Bankruptcy Act of 1978 to conform to the requirements of Art. III, in the way that will best effectuate the legislative purpose."

In *Miranda*, the Court held that confessions by criminal defendants, if made in custodial interrogation (and absent waiver of their rights) would not be admissible in state or federal criminal prosecutions unless certain specific procedures were followed. The defendant must be warned of the right to remain silent, that any statements made could be used against him or her, that the defendant has a right to an attorney and that if the defendant cannot afford an attorney, one would be appointed for him or her. What purposes are served by rigid, bright line requirements such as these? Does *Miranda* unnecessarily "juridify" police interrogations?

2. Is there a difference between the juridification that Stone criticizes and the duty—if any—of legislators to consider the constitutionality of proposed legislation?

3. As described by Allan–Randolph Brewer–Carias, Judicial Review in Comparative Law 265–69 (1989), Portugal's 1982 Constitution creates a Constitutional Court, designed to function as a special constitutional organ "competent to judge whether acts are unconstitutional and illegal" under the Constitution, and to rule on matters relating to elections and presidential functions. All courts, however, are directed not to apply unconstitutional provisions. Decisions of the ordinary courts on constitutional issues may be appealed to the Constitutional Court. But in addition to this "diffuse" system of review, the Constitutional Court can review *proposed* treaties, laws, decrees, executive acts or regional decrees, upon the request of ministers of the republic. If the Court rules against the constitutionality of any such act, it must be vetoed by the president, or the concerned minister. Apart from this a priori review, abstract review of the constitutionality of an *enacted* law can be requested by a variety of government organs, including one-tenth of the legislature.

Of particular interest is the power assigned by the Constitution to the Constitutional Court to control "unconstitutionality by omission". As translated by Brewer–Carias, the Constitution provides that "at the request of the President of the Republic, the Ombudsman, or, on the grounds that the rights of the autonomous regions have been violated, the President of the regional assemblies, the Constitutional Court shall judge and verify failure to comply with the Constitution by omission on the part of the legislative acts necessary to implement the provisions of the Constitution." In other words, the Constitutional Court can find that the legislature violated the Constitution by failing to act.

The Constitution goes on to state that "When the Constitutional Court verifies the existence of unconstitutionality by omission, it shall communicate the fact to the competent legislative organ."

Between 1976 and 1982, Brewer–Carias reports, this power was used on two occasions by the predecessor to the Constitutional Court, the Council of the Revolution, first to recommend enactment of legislation banning fascist organizations, and second, to recommend enactment of legislation assuring domestic employees of workers' rights to rest, limited hours, and recreation.

In the U.S., such a power would probably be deemed an "advisory" opinion, prohibited to the federal courts. Consider whether such an "advisory" power to enforce positive obligations of the state would be a sensible way to enforce social and economic welfare rights embodied in many modern constitutions. Alternatively, consider whether such jurisdiction only compounds what Stone condemns as the juridicization of politics.

CHAPTER VII

SEPARATION OF POWERS: GOVERNMENTS, COURTS AND FOREIGN/MILITARY AFFAIRS

In this chapter, we introduce the range of structures by which representative democracies have organized their central government and reconsider the role of constitutional courts in policing or enforcing boundaries of power among those government organs. Although separation of powers issues are pervasive, these materials focus on the foreign affairs and military powers. One hallmark of constitutional democracies is that changes of power are accomplished through free elections, not military coups. Control of the military power of the state is an essential task of or prerequisite for constitutional governance in democracies. And in representative democracies, the tensions between judicial review and legislative primacy, as well as between the executive arm of government and legislative assemblies, often seem most acute in connection with the exercise of a nation's foreign affairs and military powers. (In the United States, the traditions of civilian control of the military and of the military's nonpolitical role appear extremely well-established. But because of justiciability limitations (or possibly a more general pattern of judicial deference to executive decisions to commit military power) the conflict between executive and legislative power over foreign and military affairs is often not resolved by the courts and remains a prominent feature of constitutional tension (and constitutional decisionmaking outside the courts) in the United States.)

In the first section below, we introduce some of the rudimentary differences in the structures of government power at the national level: what are the constitutional relationships between governments and their legislative branches? The next section asks: What functions would constitutionalists identify for the different branches of representative democracies in addressing foreign affairs and military matters? It presents the claim that legislatures should play the dominant role in committing forces to hostilities. The final section returns to the question of the courts' relationship to the exercise of powers by other branches and considers the justiciability of foreign affairs and military powers issues. Should judicial review extend to matters affecting directly the foreign affairs of the nation, or its military's preparedness or deployment?

A.   Comparative Structures of Representative Government: Parliamentary or Presidential Systems; Voting

Constitution-designers must make a number of fundamental structural decisions, which once made are sometimes reconsidered in crises and rarely otherwise.

1. *Parliamentary or Presidential?* One such choice is whether to put into place a presidential system (as in the United States and much of Latin America), a parliamentary system (as in much of western Europe), or what has been called a semi-presidential system, for which the Fifth French Republic is the model. These structural decisions have important implications for other aspects of constitutionalism. For example, a classic article by political scientist Juan Linz argues that presidential systems have tendencies toward political instability, as shown by experience in Latin America, and that the case of the U.S. presidential system is exceptional. The article, and some responses and reflections, is reprinted in Juan J. Linz & Arturo Valenzuela, The Failure of Presidential Democracy, vols. I and II (1994). In the United States, the Presidential system has been remarkably stable, but has drawn criticism for its tendency towards stalemate when the presidency and congress are controlled by different parties.

Many western democracies use a parliamentary system in which the executive officers of the government are selected by and accountable to an elected legislature, rather than a presidential system in which the chief executive officer is elected by the same constituency that chooses the legislative branch. In parliamentary systems, the executive and legislative branches are controlled by the same party or coalition of parties, and at the highest levels of executive officers of the government there may be interlocking membership with the legislature. In the U.K., for example, the prime minister and the cabinet ministers are chosen from and continue to serve in the Parliament. In the presidential system in the U.S., by contrast, members of Congress are prohibited from holding any other federal office while serving in Congress. See U.S. Const. Art I., Section 6. In parliamentary systems, moreover, if the prime minister loses the "confidence" of the legislature, a new election may result prior to the time otherwise dictated by law or convention. Note that in a purely parliamentary system, there is much less "separation" of the legislative and executive power than in the U.S.-style presidential system.

Many permutations between presidential and parliamentary governments exist. In Germany, for example, the Basic Law contemplates a form of parliamentary government designed to moderate the parliamentary model's capacity for frequent elections and changes in government. The chief officer of the government is the Chancellor, who is chosen by the Bundestag (the popularly elected and most important part of the legislature). A vote of no confidence initiated by the Bundestag will not result in new elections, however, unless it is accompanied by selection of the new chancellor, a provision designed to prevent too ready use of the no confidence vote. (This procedure is sometimes referred to as the constructive vote of no confidence.) See Art. 67, Basic Law. There is also a federal President, who is elected by a body called the Federal Convention, which consists of the members of the Bundestag and an equal number of electors chosen by the land parliaments on the basis of proportional representation. The President serves for five years, a term that extends beyond the Bundestag's terms of four years.[a]

In the Fifth French Republic, the President is a particularly powerful organ of government. In part this reflects the terms Charles de Gaulle insisted upon as a condition for returning to office at the time of the Algerian crisis and the adoption of the Constitution of the Fifth French Republic in 1958. The French President is directly elected, appoints the prime minister, and can appoint cabinet members (of whom the Prime Minister need not approve). Cabinet members cannot serve in Parliament at the same time. The President through the government has substantial powers to issue decrees, which have legal effect, and the government has substantial power to control the agenda of the Parliament.

The literature on the choice and effects of presidential as compared to parliamentary systems is large. For a recent comparative analysis of presidential and parliamentary structures, and an argument in favor of "alternating presidentialism" designed to "have a parliamentary system goaded or otherwise punished by a presidential displacement and replacement," see Giovanni Sartori, Comparative Constitutional Engineering: An Inquiry Into Structures, Incentives and Outcomes 153 (1994). For analysis of the choices facing South Africa, see Jonathan Zasloff, *The Tyranny of Madison*, 44 UCLA Law Rev. 795, 810–17 (1997) (discussing literature on presidential vs. parliamentary systems). Relevant readings that appear earlier in this book include Finer, Bogdanor, & Rudden, in Chapter V(A), and Nino, in Chapter III(B).

2. *Allocations of Powers.* The different structures of representative government are often accompanied by allocations of powers that differ markedly from the formal allocations of power to which U.S. students may be accustomed. For example, the Constitution of the Fifth French Republic has an entire Title captioned, "Relations Between the Parliament and the Government." Its provisions specify the substantive areas which must be dealt with by the legislature through "lois," but also state that matters apart from those within the domain of "loi" have a "regulatory character," and are thus within the power of the Government to formulate through by

---

a. In many parliamentary systems there are two "executive" officers—someone who serves as a "head of state," with limited substantive powers, and someone who serves as the head of government, like the Prime Minister or, in Germany, the chancellor, and who exercises more power. While the Presidency in Germany has been largely ceremonial, the role of such a head of state can be of real importance: For example, in the Czech Republic, Vaclav Havel, noted author and pre–1989 dissident, has held the office of President, and has been looked to for moral leadership, while the operational head of the government is the Prime Minister.

decrees ("règlements"). (In addition, the legislature can authorize executive rule-making in areas of "loi," through what are called "ordonnances"). If the legislature enacts a "loi" that is within the regulatory jurisdiction, those "lois" can be modified by decrees (provided the Constitutional Council declares that the laws are of a regulatory character).[b] Constitution of the Fifth French Republic (1958), Arts. 34, 37, 38; see John Bell, French Constitutional Law 14–19, 86–111 (1992).[c] Although U.S. "separation of powers" doctrine requires that laws be enacted by Congress, and that agency rule-making be authorized by Congress under appropriate delegations, under French constitutional law a question can arise whether the Parliament is intruding on an area reserved for executive law-making. See Conseil Constitutionnel Decision No. 59-1 FNR of 27 November 1959, reproduced in translation in Bell, at 282–84 (holding that a bill introduced in Parliament was "inadmissible," because it attempted to change a decree modifying the method by which the premium for agricultural leases was determined; the bill was outside the legislative power since it concerned not a change in fundamental principle but a modification of prior rules and was thus within the regulatory jurisdiction). Professor Bell, a leading scholar of the French constitution, concludes that while the powers of the government under earlier Republics to issue laws in the form of decrees were already broader than in Britain, the French Constitution of 1958 marked a significant change in constitutional theory: "Parliament was no longer to be sovereign over all potential areas of legislation," and "formal residuary power lies with the executive, not with Parliament." [Bell at 87, 18.][d]

In Germany, issues that in the U.S. might involve the separation of powers may instead arise as federalism questions, since under the German Basic Law, the default rule is that the länder administer federal law; in addition, the German Constitutional Court will adjudicate when the affirmative vote of the Bundesrat is required to enact federal laws (i.e., when they affect the interests of the länder). See Chapter VIII, below, for discussion. The parliamentary model itself generates a different set of constitutional questions having to do with when new elections should be held. For example, under the Basic Law's rules for no-confidence votes initiated by the Chancellor (see Basic Law, Art. 68), the German Constitu-

b. Laws enacted prior to 1958 may be modified by decree without advance clearance by the Constitutional Council.

c. Bell also concludes that the Conseil d'Etat's jurisprudence has imposed additional limits on the executive decree, consistent with the "general principles of law" which, the Conseil d'Etat has held, sometimes require legislation even where not specified in Art. 34. Moreover, while earlier Conseil Constitutionnel decisions upheld the exclusivity of the executive power over matters that fell within the regulatory jurisdiction of Art. 37, Bell found that more recent decisions in the 1980s concluded that Parliament was not barred from legislating in areas within the regulatory jurisdiction but only that if a "loi" were enacted within the regulatory jurisdiction it could be modified by decree, issued once the loi has been "declassified" by the Conseil Constitutionnel's agreement that the "loi" was of a regulatory character.

d. Bell concludes, however, that the formal revolution in constitutional theory has not been as revolutionary in practice, in part because expected confrontations between the parliament and President have not materialized and governments have made greater use of delegated powers under Art. 38 authority to enact ordonnances.

tional Court has been called on to decide whether a dissolution of Parliament and new election was valid, or was an inappropriate political manipulation of the rules by a government holding an actual majority who sought to increase that majority through a new election. See the Parliamentary Dissolution Case, 62 BverfGE 1 (1984), translated and discussed in Kommers, The Constitutional Jurisprudence of the Federal Republic of Germany 118–22 (1997).

3. *Electoral Systems*. Another structural choice, sometimes made in constitutions, is about the electoral system. The basic choices are between asystem in which representatives are elected by districts in which the winner must have either a plurality or a majority (often achieved only in a run-off election), or systems of proportional representation (PR). (Note that PR is possible only in multi-representative bodies and it therefore cannot be used to select a single person to serve as a chief executive.)[e] The plurality systems are often called "first past the post" systems; they have been adopted by the United States for national elections and nearly all state and local elections as well.

Proportional representation systems have many variants. (a) The threshold required for representation in the legislature is one variable: The lower the threshold, the more purely proportional the system is (and the more parties are likely to be represented in the legislature). Thresholds range from what political scientists regard as a very low 1% (Israel until 1992) to higher figures such as the 5% level in Germany. (b) The list from which voters choose is another important variable: A voter can be asked to rank his or her preferences, or the voter can be required to cast a vote for an entire party list, with the party determining the ranking of the candidates on the list. These design possibilities, and others, mean that proportional voting systems vary widely from one nation to another.

The French political scientist Maurice Duverger proposed two "laws" about electoral systems. (a) "First past the post" electoral systems tend to produce two-party political systems. (b) Proportional representation electoral systems (and majority systems with run offs) tend to produce multi-party systems. The logic of the laws is straightforward. To prevail in a "first past the post" system, a political party must appeal to more voters than its competitors. This drives parties to the center. (Why?) Parties in proportional representation systems can win seats in the legislature by appealing only to enough voters to satisfy the system's threshold requirement. But the precise degree to which these tendencies exist is controversial among political scientists. For example, Great Britain's "first past the post" system has produce a system in which three parties regularly contend for office (Labor, Conservative, and Liberal, the latter under a variety of names in different elections). The implications of the two systems for

e. Other mechanisms, however, are at least in theory available to achieve representation, over time, of members of different groups in filling a single office (and thus to achieve some of the purposes of proportional voting for representatives): for example, in the former Yugoslavia and for a time in Lebanon rules provided for rotating a single executive from one group to another.

political stability are also controversial. Proportional representation systems rarely produce majorities for a single party in a national government resulting in coalition governments. But although coalition governments in some nations change frequently, their core participants may be quite stable, with a fair degree of consistency in national policy across a rather wide range. And "first past the post" systems can involve "implicit" coalitions, in which bargaining over the participants' programs occurs before the election (in negotiations over party platforms, for example), rather than afterwards, as occurs in PR systems. Giovanni Sartori's book is a useful introduction to the controversies; Sartori is a political scientist who takes sides on many of the issues.

These choices matter for constitutionalism because the nature of a nation's party system, and the degree to which the electoral system promotes political stability or instability, affects the degree to which the nation can conform to the requirements of constitutionalism. The details of how these choices play themselves out are exceedingly complex, and are more frequently studied by political scientists than by law professors. (Why?)

B.   LEGISLATIVE AND EXECUTIVE POWER IN FOREIGN AND MILITARY AFFAIRS: REPRESENTATIVE DECISIONMAKING AND COMMITMENT TO HOSTILITIES

Constitutions vary in their provisions for executive and legislative power in the area of foreign and military affairs. The U.S. Constitution provides, as does the 1958 French Constitution, that the President is the Commander-in-Chief of the armed forces. Other powers in the area of foreign affairs in the U.S. are divided or, in Louis Henkin's phrase, "fissured," between the Congress and the President in hard to define ways: the Congress has the power to "declare war," and to regulate "foreign commerce," the President to "receive Ambassadors." See Louis Henkin, Foreign Affairs and the Constitution 32 (1972). The U.S. Constitution divides the treaty making power between the President and Senate, and does not advert to the established constitutional practice of "executive agreements" that have legal effects although they are signed only by the President. The French Constitution provides that certain kinds of treaties require parliamentary approval, while others do not, a dividing line struck by the German Basic Law and addressed in the Commercial Treaty case below. Questions about the need for involvement of the elected legislatures in foreign affairs and military decisions—ranging from approval of the Maastricht Treaty to commitments of troops to U.N. authorized actions—have arisen in the constitutional courts of Europe. Debate over the constitutional powers of the U.S. president and the Congress is reflected in the War Powers Resolution (enacted by Congress in 1973) that seeks to curtail the President's powers to commit troops to hostilities and to require notification to Congress of proposed actions; Presidents have ordinarily treated the War Powers Resolution as not constitutionally binding upon their actions.

In U.S. constitutional law, the arguments in favor of executive power tend to reach their height when issues of foreign relations or military action are at issue, invoking the need for expeditious action, the President's constitutional authority to speak for the nation, and his superior access to relevant information. See United States v. Curtiss–Wright, 299 U.S. 304 (1936) (upholding constitutionality of a Joint Resolution of Congress authorizing the President to prohibit arms sales to Bolivia or Paraguay, pursuant to which the President had issued a proclamation prohibiting such shipments, an alleged violation of which gave rise to a criminal indictment against the defendant company);[f] Dames & Moore v. Regan, 453 U.S. 654 (1981) (upholding Presidential power to suspend private claims against a foreign nation by concluding an executive agreement in order to secure the release of American hostages).[g] In Youngstown Sheet & Tube Co. v. Sawyer, 343 U.S. 579 (1952), the Court did reject President Truman's claim of inherent presidential power to seize industries, purportedly to advance the war efforts in Korea by averting a nationwide strike in the steel industry. Some justices were influenced by Congress' having recently failed to give the President authority to seize industries in order to prevent the disruptions of a strike, and some by their perception that the foreign relations or military threat was not so grave. Apart from *Youngstown*, the modern history of the Court's decisions is to uphold claims of presidential power in foreign and military affairs. *Loving*, excerpted below, is a recent example of the Court's upholding congressional delegation to the President of a power, there to prescribe rules governing life and death issues of punishment for offenses committed by members of the military.

In some tension with the U.S. caselaw are recent studies by political scientists that have identified a so-called "liberal peace"—the phenomenon

f. After concluding that external affairs powers would vest in the nation even without the Constitution, the Court wrote:

Not only, as we have shown, is the federal power over external affairs in origin and essential character different from that over internal affairs, but participation in the exercise of the power is significantly limited. In this vast external realm, with its important, complicated, delicate and manifold problems, the President alone has the power to speak or listen as a representative of the nation. He makes treaties with the advice and consent of the Senate, but he alone negotiates ... As Marshall said [in] the House of Representatives, "The President is the sole organ of the nation in its external relations, and its sole representative with foreign nations."

The President's power was supported by his superior opportunity to know the "conditions which prevail in foreign countries .... He has his confidential sources of information. He has his agents in the form of diplomatic, consular and other officials." Not only is he better informed, but he can act with "[s]ecrecy ... [that] may be highly necessary...." 299 U.S. at 319.

g. After describing patterns of congressional acquiescence to presidential claims settlements by executive agreements, the Court, while reserving whether the President had plenary power to settle claims, held that "where ...the settlement of claims has been determined to be a necessary incident of a major foreign policy dispute between our country and another," and where Congress has acquiesced in the President's action, no specific statutory authority was required for the President to settle claims.

that western liberal democracies, generally characterized by constitutional protection of human rights, representative democracy and market economies do not tend to go to war with each other.[h] While the causes for the so-called liberal peace are contested, one important hypothesis is that in liberal representative democracies, government structures require deliberation by representative bodies (and a concomitant passage of time) before commitments to war can occur.[i] The hypothesis, then, is that constitutional, governmental structures that require public deliberation by representative bodies facilitate peace. Consider whether the German cases discussed in Damrosch's essay and excerpted below are more congruent with these possible requirements for peace than the U.S. caselaw's emphasis on the need for Presidential flexibility, speed and secrecy. Professor Damrosch advances both empirical and normative arguments to support the claims that in representative constitutional democracies, there is, and should be, a trend to require the involvement of the most representative branch (the legislature) in decisions involving commitment to hostilities. Consider, in this regard, whether the question of presidential power to define aggravating circumstances justifying imposition of the death penalty in the system of U.S. military justice is distinct from that of commitment to hostilities.

German Commercial Treaty Case

12 BverfGE 372 (1952) (Federal Constitutional Court of Germany).

[Social Democratic members of the legislature challenged the German government's failure to submit to the legislature for approval through enactment of law a commercial treaty concluded with France. Under article 59[2] of the Basic Law, those treaties that "regulate the political relations of the Federation," or relate to matters of federal legislation, require the consent or participation of the appropriate legislative bodies in the form of a federal law. The Court agreed with the Government that the commercial treaty with France was not a "political treaty" and was thus valid without legislative approval.

The following excerpt, both describing and translating portions of the German Constitutional Court's decision is from Hersch Lauterpacht, ed., International Law Reports, year 1952 (London, Butterworth & Co., Ltd, 1957), v. 19, Case No. 99, at 462–63:]

h. See Bruce Russett, Grasping the Democratic Peace: Principles for a Post–Cold War World (1993); Michael W. Doyle, *Liberalism and World Politics*, 80 Am. Poli. Sci. Rev. 1151 (1986).

i. See Anne Marie Slaughter Burley, *Are Foreign Affairs Different?*, 106 Harv. L. Rev. 1980, 2003–04 (1993) (discussing Jefferson and Hamilton's views about "representation" as the best check on unnecessary war; by transferring the decision to go to war from the Executive to the Legislative, those who "bear the physical and financial burdens of war [are] represented in the decisionmaking process, and not by an elected Executive alone."); *id.* (discussing Bruce Russett's views of "deliberation", which creates a "drag effect" from the "need to ponder and debate . . . [which] provide[s] for critical 'cooling off periods' between . . . liberal states").

"A treaty does not become a political treaty within the meaning of Article 59 (2) of the Constitution merely by reason of the fact that it deals quite generally with public affairs, the good of the community, or affairs of State. If this were so, every treaty would be a political treaty, and the limitation contained in Article 59 (2) would be devoid of meaning. In addition to the matters here referred to, a treaty must directly affect the existence of the State, its territorial integrity, its independence and its position or relative weight within the community of States. Such are, above all, alliances, treaties of guarantee, treaties relating to political co-operation, peace treaties, non-aggression pacts, treaties of neutrality and disarmament, treaties of arbitration and similar international agreements. The history of Article 59 (2) of the Constitution indicates that there shall be room for an interpretation which will do justice to constantly changing conditions. In contradistinction to the Weimar Constitution (Article 45), the Constitution of the Federal Republic has adopted a wider terminology so as to extend beyond alliances the category of treaties requiring the approval of Parliament. . . . The contents and object of a treaty within the meaning of Article 59 (2) must be directed towards governing political relations with foreign States. The content or purpose of the treaty *itself* must be to govern political relations with foreign States; this purpose must not be secondary, or perhaps even unintentional or unexpected in its bearing on such relations. If, therefore, a treaty is of political significance for the Federal Republic merely because it has an important bearing on the internal political, economic or social conditions of the country, it does not thereby become a political Treaty within the meaning of Article 59 (2) of the Constitution. There was a time when the doctrine of international law generally did not regard commercial treaties as political treaties. This theory, however, does not in its generality correspond to the reality of present-day international relations. In special circumstances, a commercial treaty may be as much in the nature of a political treaty as an alliance. This might be so where the Contracting Parties, by concluding a commercial treaty, intend to strengthen their economic position in competition with other States generally. In a case of that kind non-political market relations may become power relations. It is possible nowadays for the power position of a State within the community of States to be influenced more strongly by the conclusion of a commercial treaty than by the conclusion of a treaty of neutrality, a non-aggression pact or a treaty of guarantee. In referring to power in this context we do not confine ourselves to the position of States in the struggle for political hegemony, but we refer generally to their relative weight within the community of States. Whether a treaty within the meaning of the foregoing considerations is a political treaty can only be determined *in each individual case* by reference to the special circumstances and the actual political situation of the Federal Republic and the other Contracting Parties."

The Court then examined the contents of the Treaty and pointed out that it dealt only with purely technical questions of a commercial nature. The Court added that in any event the Federal Republic of Germany was not at that time in a position to make political decisions, having regard to the occupation régime to which it was then subject. It stressed more particularly the following facts, namely, that the Treaty did not contain any provision indicating a desire on the part of the Federal Republic to support so-called European integration, nor an acknowledgement that the Saar Territory was no longer part of Germany. In the result, as indicated, the Court denied the political character of the Treaty.

Loving v. U. S.

517 U. S. 748 (1996).

JUSTICE KENNEDY delivered the opinion of the Court.

The case before us concerns the authority of the President, in our system of separated powers, to prescribe aggravating factors that permit a court-martial to impose the death penalty upon a member of the armed forces convicted of murder.

I

On December 12, 1988, petitioner Dwight Loving, an Army private stationed at Fort Hood, Texas, murdered two taxicab drivers from the nearby town of Killeen. He attempted to murder a third, but the driver disarmed him and escaped. Civilian and Army authorities arrested Loving the next afternoon. He confessed.

After a trial, an eight-member general court-martial found Loving guilty of, among other offenses, premeditated murder and felony murder under Article 118 of the Uniform Code of Military Justice (UCMJ), 10 U.S.C. §§ 918(1), (4). In the sentencing phase of the trial, the court-martial found three aggravating factors: (1) that the premeditated murder of the second driver was committed during the course of a robbery, Rule for Courts–Martial (RCM) 1004(c)(7)(B); (2) that Loving acted as the trigger-man in the felony murder of the first driver, RCM 1004(c)(8); and (3) that Loving, having been found guilty of the premeditated murder, had committed a second murder . . . [and] sentenced Loving to death. . . .

II

Although American courts-martial from their inception have had the power to decree capital punishment, they have not long had the authority to try and to sentence members of the armed forces for capital murder committed in the United States in peacetime. In the early days of the Republic the powers of courts-martial were fixed in the Articles of War. Congress enacted the first Articles in 1789 by adopting in full the Articles promulgated in 1775 (and revised in 1776) by the Continental Congress. (Congress reenacted the Articles in 1790 "as far as the same may be applicable to the constitution of the United States." The Articles adopted by the First Congress placed significant restrictions on court-martial jurisdiction over capital offenses. Although the death penalty was authorized for 14 military offenses, the Articles followed the British example of ensuring the supremacy of civil court jurisdiction over ordinary capital crimes that were punishable by the law of the land and were not special military offenses. 1776 Articles, § 10, Art. 1 (requiring commanders, upon application, to exert utmost effort to turn offender over to civil authorities)....

Over the next two centuries, Congress expanded court-martial jurisdiction. In 1863, concerned that civil courts could not function in all places during hostilities, Congress granted courts-martial jurisdiction of common-law capital crimes and the authority to impose the death penalty in wartime. In 1916, Congress granted to the military courts a general jurisdiction over common-law felonies committed by service members, except for murder and rape committed within the continental United States during peacetime. Persons accused of the latter two crimes were to be turned over to the civilian authorities. In 1950, with the passage of the UCMJ, Congress lifted even this restriction. Article 118 of the UCMJ describes four types of murder subject to court-martial jurisdiction, two of which are punishable by death:

"Any person subject to this chapter who, without justification or excuse, unlawfully kills a human being, when he—

"(1) has a premeditated design to kill;

"(2) intends to kill or inflict great bodily harm;

"(3) is engaged in an act which is inherently dangerous to another and evinces a wanton disregard of human life; or

"(4) is engaged in the perpetration or attempted perpetration of burglary, sodomy, rape, robbery, or aggravated arson;

"is guilty of murder, and shall suffer such punishment as a court-martial may direct, except that if found guilty under clause (1) or (4), he shall suffer death or imprisonment for life as a court-martial may direct." 10 U.S.C. § 918.

So matters stood until 1983, when the CMA* confronted a challenge to the constitutionality of the military capital punishment scheme in light of Furman v. Georgia, 408 U.S. 238 (1972), and our ensuing death penalty jurisprudence. Although it held valid most of the death penalty procedures followed in courts-martial, the court found one fundamental defect: the failure of either the UCMJ or the RCM to require that court-martial members "specifically identify the aggravating factors upon which they have relied in choosing to impose the death penalty." United States v. Matthews, 16 M.J. 354, 379. The Court reversed Matthews' death sentence, but ruled that either Congress or the President could remedy the defect and that the new procedures could be applied retroactively.

The President responded to *Matthews* in 1984 with an Executive Order promulgating RCM 1004. In conformity with 10 U.S.C. § 852(a)(1), the Rule, as amended, requires a unanimous finding that the accused was guilty of a capital offense before a death sentence may be imposed, RCM 1004(a)(2). The Rule also requires unanimous findings (1) that at least one

* [Editors' Note: U.S. Court of Military Appeals].

aggravating factor is present and (2) that any extenuating or mitigating circumstances are substantially outweighed by any admissible aggravating circumstances, 1004(b). RCM 1004(c) enumerates 11 categories of aggravating factors sufficient for imposition of the death penalty. The Rule also provides that the accused is to have "broad latitude to present evidence in extenuation and mitigation," 1004(b)(3), and is entitled to have the members of the court-martial instructed to consider all such evidence before deciding upon a death sentence, 1004(b)(6).

This is the scheme Loving attacks as unconstitutional. He contends that the Eighth Amendment and the doctrine of separation of powers require that Congress, and not the President, make the fundamental policy determination respecting the factors that warrant the death penalty.

III

A preliminary question in this case is whether the Constitution requires the aggravating factors that Loving challenges. The Government does not contest the application of our death penalty jurisprudence to courts-martial, at least in the context of a conviction under Article 118 for murder committed in peacetime within the United States, and we shall assume that *Furman* and the case law resulting from it are applicable to the crime and sentence in question. . . .

Although the Government suggests the contrary, we agree with Loving, on the assumption that *Furman* applies to this case, that aggravating factors are necessary to the constitutional validity of the military capital-punishment scheme as now enacted. Article 118 authorizes the death penalty for but two of the four types of murder specified: premeditated and felony murder are punishable by death, 10 U.S.C. §§ 918(1), (4), whereas intentional murder without premeditation and murder resulting from wanton and dangerous conduct are not, §§ 918(2), (3). The statute's selection of the two types of murder for the death penalty, however, does not narrow the death-eligible class in a way consistent with our cases. Article 118(4) by its terms permits death to be imposed for felony murder even if the accused had no intent to kill and even if he did not do the killing himself. The Eighth Amendment does not permit the death penalty to be imposed in those circumstances. As a result, additional aggravating factors establishing a higher culpability are necessary to save Article 118. We turn to the question whether it violated the principle of separation of powers for the President to prescribe the aggravating factors required by the Eighth Amendment.

IV

Even before the birth of this country, separation of powers was known to be a defense against tyranny. Montesquieu, The Spirit of the Laws 151–152 (T. Nugent trans.1949); 1 W. Blackstone, Commentaries *146–*147, *269–*270. Though faithful to the precept that freedom is imperiled if the whole of legislative, executive, and judicial power is in the same hands, the Framers understood that a "hermetic sealing off of the three branches of

Government from one another would preclude the establishment of a Nation capable of governing itself effectively," Buckley v. Valeo, 424 U.S. 1, 120–121 (1976).

> "While the Constitution diffuses power the better to secure liberty, it also contemplates that practice will integrate the dispersed powers into a workable government. It enjoins upon its branches separateness but interdependence, autonomy but reciprocity." Youngstown Sheet & Tube Co. v. Sawyer, 343 U.S. 579, 635 (1952) (Jackson, J., concurring).

Although separation of powers " 'd[oes] not mean that these [three] departments ought to have no partial agency in, or no controul over the acts of each other,' " it remains a basic principle of our constitutional scheme that one branch of the Government may not intrude upon the central prerogatives of another. See Bowsher v. Synar, 478 U.S. 714, 726 (1986) (Congress may not remove executive officers except by impeachment); INS v. Chadha, 462 U.S. 919, 954–955 (1983) (Congress may not enact laws without bicameral passage and presentment of the bill to the President); United States v. Klein, 13 Wall. 128, 147 (1872) (Congress may not deprive court of jurisdiction based on the outcome of a case or undo a Presidential pardon). Even when a branch does not arrogate power to itself, moreover, the separation-of-powers doctrine requires that a branch not impair another in the performance of its constitutional duties. Mistretta v. United States, [488 U.S. 361, 397–408 (1989)] (examining whether statute requiring participation of Article III judges in the United States Sentencing Commission threatened the integrity of the Judicial Branch).

Deterrence of arbitrary or tyrannical rule is not the sole reason for dispersing the federal power among three branches, however. By allocating specific powers and responsibilities to a branch fitted to the task, the Framers created a National Government that is both effective and accountable. Article I's precise rules of representation, member qualifications, bicameralism, and voting procedure make Congress the branch most capable of responsive and deliberative lawmaking. See Chadha, at 951. Ill suited to that task are the Presidency, designed for the prompt and faithful execution of the laws and its own legitimate powers, and the Judiciary, a branch with tenure and authority independent of direct electoral control. The clear assignment of power to a branch, furthermore, allows the citizen to know who may be called to answer for making, or not making, those delicate and necessary decisions essential to governance.

Another strand of our separation-of-powers jurisprudence, the delegation doctrine, has developed to prevent Congress from forsaking its duties. Loving invokes this doctrine to question the authority of the President to promulgate RCM 1004. The fundamental precept of the delegation doctrine is that the lawmaking function belongs to Congress, U.S. Const., Art. I, § 1, and may not be conveyed to another branch or entity. This principle does not mean, however, that only Congress can make a rule of prospective force. To burden Congress with all federal rulemaking would divert that branch from more pressing issues, and defeat the Framers' design of a workable National Government. Thomas Jefferson observed, "Nothing is so embarrassing nor so mischievous in a great assembly as the details of execution." See also A.L.A. Schechter Poultry Corp. v. United States, 295 U.S. 495, 529–530 (1935) (recognizing "the necessity of adapting legislation to complex conditions involving a host of details with which the national legislature cannot deal directly"). This Court established long ago that Congress must be permitted to delegate to others at least some authority that it could exercise itself.

" 'The true distinction . . . is between the delegation of power to make the law, which necessarily involves a discretion as to what it shall be, and conferring authority or discretion as to its execution, to be exercised under and in pursuance of the law. The first cannot be done; to the latter no valid objection can be made.' " [Field v. Clark, 143 U.S. 649, 693–94 (1892).]

Loving contends that the military death penalty scheme of Article 118 and RCM 1004 does not observe the limits of the delegation doctrine. He presses his constitutional challenge on three fronts. First, . . . that Congress cannot delegate to the President the authority to prescribe aggravating factors in capital murder cases. Second, . . . that, even if it can, Congress did not delegate the authority by implicit or explicit action. Third, . . . that even if certain statutory provisions can be construed as delegations, they lack an intelligible principle to guide the President's discretion. Were Loving's premises to be accepted, the President would lack authority to prescribe aggravating factors in RCM 1004, and the death sentence imposed upon him would be unconstitutional.

A

Loving's first argument is that Congress lacks power to allow the President to prescribe aggravating factors in military capital cases because any delegation would be inconsistent with the Framers' decision to vest in Congress the power "To make Rules for the Government and Regulation of the land and naval forces." U.S. Const., Art. I, § 8, cl. 14. At least in the context of capital punishment for peacetime crimes, which implicates the Eighth Amendment, this power must be deemed exclusive, Loving contends. In his view, not only is the determination of aggravating factors a quintessential policy judgment for the legislature, but the history of military capital punishment in England and America refutes a contrary interpretation. He asserts that his offense was not tried in a military court throughout most of English and American history. It is this historical exclusion of common-law capital crimes from military jurisdiction, he urges, which must inform our understanding of whether Clause 14 reserves to Congress the power to prescribe what conduct warrants a death sentence, even if it permits Congress to authorize courts-martial to try such crimes. Mindful of the historical dangers of autocratic military justice and of the limits Parliament set on the peacetime jurisdiction of courts-martial over capital crimes in the first Mutiny Act, 1 Wm. & Mary, ch. 5 (1689), and having experienced the military excesses of the Crown in colonial America, the Framers harbored a deep distrust of executive military power and military tribunals. It follows, Loving says, that the Framers intended that

Congress alone should possess the power to decide what aggravating factors justify sentencing a member of the armed forces to death.

We have undertaken before, in resolving other issues, the difficult task of interpreting Clause 14 by drawing upon English constitutional history. Doing so here, we find that, although there is a grain of truth in Loving's historical arguments, the struggle of Parliament to control military tribunals and the lessons the Framers drew from it are more complex than he suggests. The history does not require us to read Clause 14 as granting to Congress an exclusive, nondelegable power to determine military punishments. If anything, it appears that England found security in divided authority, with Parliament at times ceding to the Crown the task of fixing military punishments. From the English experience the Framers understood the necessity of balancing efficient military discipline, popular control of a standing army, and the rights of soldiers; they perceived the risks inherent in assigning the task to one part of the government to the exclusion of another; and they knew the resulting parliamentary practice of delegation. The Framers' choice in Clause 14 was to give Congress the same flexibility to exercise or share power as times might demand.

In England after the Norman Conquest, military justice was a matter of royal prerogative. The rudiments of law in English military justice can first be seen in the written orders issued by the King for various expeditions. For example, in 1190 Richard I issued an ordinance outlining six offenses to which the crusaders would be subject, including two punishable by death: "Whoever shall slay a man on ship-board, he shall be bound to the dead man and thrown into the sea. If he shall slay him on land he shall be bound to the dead man and buried in the earth." Ordinance of Richard I—A.D. 1190. The first comprehensive articles of war were those declared by Richard II at Durham in 1385 and Henry V at Nantes in 1419, which decreed capital offenses that not only served military discipline but also protected foreign noncombatants from the ravages of war. . . .

Thus, royal ordinances governed the conduct of war, but the common law did not countenance the enforcement of military law in times of peace "when the king's courts [were] open for all persons to receive justice according to the laws of the land." . . .

"The Common Law made no distinction between the crimes of soldiers and those of civilians in time of peace. All subjects were tried alike by the same civil courts, so 'if a life-guardsman deserted, he could only be sued for breach of contract, and if he struck his officer he was only liable to an indictment or action of battery.'" [Reid v. Covert, 354 U.S. 1, 24 n. 44 (1957)] (quoting 2 J. Campbell, Lives of the Chief Justices of England 91 (1849)).

The triumph of civil jurisdiction was not absolute, however. The political disorders of the 17th century ushered in periods of harsh military justice, with soldiers and at times civilian rebels punished, even put to death, under the summary decrees of courts-martial. Cf. Petition of Right of 1627, 3 Car. I, ch. 1 (protesting court-martial abuses). Military justice was brought under the rule of parliamentary law in 1689, when William and Mary accepted the Bill of Rights requiring Parliament's consent to the raising and keeping of armies. In the Mutiny Act of 1689, Parliament declared the general principle that "noe Man may be forejudged of Life or Limbe or subjected to any kinde of punishment by Martiall Law or in any other manner then by the Judgment of his Peeres and according to the knowne and Established Laws of this Realme," but decreed that "Soldiers who shall Mutiny or stirr up Sedition or shall desert Their Majestyes Service be brought to a more Exemplary and speedy Punishment than the usuall Forms of Law will allow," and "shall suffer Death or such other Punishment as by a Court–Martiall shall be Inflicted." 1 Wm. & Mary, ch. 5.

In one sense, as Loving wants to suggest, the Mutiny Act was a sparing exercise of parliamentary authority, since only the most serious domestic offenses of soldiers were made capital, and the militia was exempted. He misunderstands the Mutiny Act of 1689, however, in arguing that it bespeaks ... a desire of Parliament to exclude Executive power over military capital punishment.

The Mutiny Act, as its name suggests, came on the heels of the mutiny of Scottish troops loyal to James II. The mutiny occurred at a watershed time. Menaced by great continental powers, England had come to a grudging recognition that a standing army, long decried as an instrument of despotism, had to be maintained on its soil. The mutiny cast in high relief the dangers to the polity of a standing army turned bad. Macaulay describes the sentiment of the time:

> "There must then be regular soldiers; and, if there were to be regular soldiers, it must be indispensable, both to their efficiency, and to the security of every other class, that they should be kept under a strict discipline.... A strong line of demarcation must therefore be drawn between the soldiers and the rest of the community. For the sake of public freedom, they must, in the midst of freedom, be placed under a despotic rule. They must be subject to a sharper penal code, and to a more stringent code of procedure, than are administered by the ordinary tribunals." [3 T. Macaulay, History of England 50]

The Mutiny Act, then, was no measure of leniency for soldiers. With its passage, "the Army of William III was governed under a severer Code than that made by his predecessors under the Prerogative authority of the Crown. The Mutiny Act, without displacing the Articles of War and those Military Tribunals under which the Army had hitherto been governed, gave statutory sanction to the infliction of Capital Punishments for offences rather Political than Military, and which had rarely been so punished under Prerogative authority." [C.] Clode, [Administration of Justice Under Military and Martial Law 9–10 (1872)]. Indeed, it was the Crown which later tempered the excesses of courts-martial wielding the power of capital punishment. It did so by stipulating in the Articles of War (which remained a matter of royal prerogative) that all capital sentences be sent to it for revision or approval.

Popular suspicion of the standing army persisted, and Parliament authorized the Mutiny Acts only for periods of six months and then a year. But renewed they were time and again, and Parliament would alter the power of courts-martial to impose the death penalty for peacetime offenses throughout the next century.... The third of the Mutiny Acts of 1715 subjected the soldier to capital punishment for a wide array of peacetime offenses related to political disorder and troop discipline. And, for a short time in the 18th century, Parliament allowed the Crown to invest courts-martial with a general criminal jurisdiction over soldiers even at home, placing no substantive limit on the penalties that could be imposed.... The propriety of that general jurisdiction within the kingdom was questioned, and the jurisdiction was withdrawn in 1749. Nevertheless, even as it continued to adjust the scope of military jurisdiction at home, Parliament entrusted broad powers to the Crown to define and punish military crimes abroad. In 1713, it gave statutory sanction to the Crown's longstanding practice of issuing Articles of War without limiting the kind of punishments that might be imposed.... Cf. Duke & Vogel, [*The Constitution and The Standing Army*, 13 Vand. L. Rev. 435 (1960)] at 444 (noting that Parliament in 1803 gave statutory authority to the Crown to promulgate Articles of War applicable to troops stationed in England as well).

... [T]he Framers well knew this history, and had encountered firsthand the abuses of military law in the colonies. See Reid, 354 U.S., at 27–28, 77 S.Ct., at 1236. As many were themselves veterans of the Revolutionary War, however, they also knew the imperatives of military discipline. What they distrusted were not courts-martial per se, but military justice dispensed by a commander unchecked by the civil power in proceedings so summary as to be lawless. The latter was the evil that caused Blackstone to declare that "martial law"—by which he ... meant decrees of courts-martial disciplining soldiers in wartime—"is built upon no settled principles, but is entirely arbitrary in its decisions...." ... The partial security Englishmen won against such abuse in 1689 was to give Parliament, preeminent guardian of the British constitution, primacy in matters of military law. This fact does not suggest, however, that a legislature's power must be exclusive. It was for Parliament, as it did in the various Mutiny Acts, to designate as the times required what peacetime offenses by soldiers deserved the punishment of death; and it was for Parliament, as it did in 1713, to delegate the authority to define wartime offenses and devise their punishments, including death. The Crown received the delegated power and the concomitant responsibility for its prudent exercise. The lesson from the English constitutional experience was that Parliament must have the primary power to regulate the armed forces and to determine the punishments that could be imposed upon soldiers by courts-martial. That was not inconsistent, however, with the further power to divide authority between it and the Crown as conditions might warrant.

Far from attempting to replicate the English system, of course, the Framers separated the powers of the Federal Government into three branches to avoid dangers they thought latent or inevitable in the parliamentary structure.... [W]ith [the English] experience to consult they elected not to "freeze court-martial usage at a particular time" for all ages following, Solorio, 483 U.S., at 446, nor did they deprive Congress of the services of the Executive in establishing rules for the governance of the military, including rules for capital punishment. In the words of Alexander Hamilton, the power to regulate the armed forces, like other powers related to the common defense, was given to Congress

> "without limitation: Because it is impossible to foresee or define the extent and variety of national exigencies, or the corresponding extent & variety of the means which may be necessary to satisfy them. The circumstances that endanger the safety of nations are infinite, and for this reason no constitutional shackles can wisely be imposed on the power to which the care of it is committed. This power ought to be co-extensive with all the possible combinations of such circumstances; and ought to be under the direction of the same councils, which are appointed to preside over the common defence." The Federalist, No. 23, at 147 (emphasis omitted).

. . .

Under Clause 14, Congress, like Parliament, exercises a power of precedence over, not exclusion of, Executive authority. This power is no less plenary than other Article I powers, and we discern no reasons why Congress should have less capacity to make measured and appropriate delegations of this power than of any other. Indeed, it would be contrary to precedent and tradition for us to impose a special limitation on this particular Article I power, for we give Congress the highest deference in ordering military affairs. And it would be contrary to the respect owed the President as Commander in Chief to hold that he may not be given wide discretion and authority. We decline to import into Clause 14 a restrictive nondelegation principle that the Framers left out.

There is no absolute rule, furthermore, against Congress' delegation of authority to define criminal punishments. We have upheld delegations whereby the Executive or an independent agency defines by regulation what conduct will be criminal, so long as Congress makes the violation of regulations a criminal offense and fixes the punishment, and the regulations "confin[e] themselves within the field covered by the statute." United States v. Grimaud, 220 U.S. 506, 518 (1911) .... In the circumstances presented here, so too may Congress delegate authority to the President to define the aggravating factors that permit imposition of a statutory penalty, with the regulations providing the narrowing of the death-eligible class that the Eighth Amendment requires.

In 1950, Congress confronted the problem of what criminal jurisdiction would be appropriate for armed forces of colossal size, stationed on bases that in many instances were small societies unto themselves. Congress, confident in the procedural protections of the UCMJ, gave to courts-martial jurisdiction of the crime of murder. Cf. Solorio, at 450–451 (Congress may extend court-martial jurisdiction to any criminal offense committed by a service member during his period of service). It further declared the law that service members who commit premeditated and felony murder may be sentenced to death by a court-martial. There is nothing in the constitutional scheme or our traditions to prohibit Congress from delegating the prudent and proper implementation of the capital murder statute to the President acting as Commander in Chief.

B

Having held that Congress has the power of delegation, we further hold that it exercised the power in Articles 18 and 56 of the UCMJ. Article 56 specifies that "[t]he punishment which a court-martial may direct for an offense may not exceed such limits as the President may prescribe for that offense." 10 U.S.C. § 856. Article 18 states that a court-martial "may, under such limitations as the President may prescribe, adjudge any punishment not forbidden by [the UCMJ], including the penalty of death when specifically authorized by" the Code, § 818.... Articles 18 and 56 support ... an authority in the President to restrict the death sentence to murders in which certain aggravating circumstances have been established.

There is yet a third provision of the UCMJ indicative of congressional intent to delegate this authority to the President. Article 36 of the UCMJ, which gives the President the power to make procedural rules for courts-martial, provides:

"Pretrial, trial, and post-trial procedures, including modes of proof, for [courts martial] ... may be prescribed by the President by regulations which shall, so far as he considers practicable, apply the principles of law and the rules of evidence generally recognized in the trial of criminal cases in the United States district courts, but which may not be contrary to or inconsistent with this chapter." 10 U.S.C. § 836(a).

Although the language of Article 36 seems further afield from capital aggravating factors than that of Article 18 or 56, it is the provision that a later Congress identified as the source of Presidential authority to prescribe these factors. In 1985, Congress enacted Article 106(a) of the UCMJ, 10 U.S.C. § 906a, which authorized the death penalty for espionage. The Article requires a finding of an aggravating factor if the accused is to be sentenced to death; it enumerates three such factors, but allows death to be decreed on "[a]ny other factor that may be prescribed by the President by regulations under section 836 of this title (article 36)." § 906(a)(c)(4). Article 106a itself, then, is premised on the President's having authority under Article 36 to prescribe capital aggravating factors, and " '[s]ubsequent legislation declaring the intent of an earlier statute is entitled to great weight in statutory construction.' " Whether or not Article 36 would stand on its own as the source of the delegated power, we hold that Articles 18, 36, and 56 together give clear authority to the President for the promulgation of RCM 1004.

Loving points out that the Articles were enacted in 1950, well before the need for eliminating absolute discretion in capital sentencing was established in Furman v. Georgia. In 1950, he argues, Congress could not have understood that it was giving the President the authority to bring an otherwise invalid capital murder statute in line with Eighth Amendment strictures. Perhaps so, but *Furman* did not somehow undo the prior delegation. What would have been an act of leniency by the President prior to *Furman* may have become a constitutional necessity thereafter, but the fact remains the power to prescribe aggravating circumstances has resided with the President since 1950.

C

... Congress as a general rule must also "lay down by legislative act an intelligible principle to which the person or body authorized to [act] is directed to conform." J. W. Hampton, Jr. Co. v. United States, 276 U.S. 394, 409 (1928). The intelligible-principle rule seeks to enforce the understanding that Congress may not delegate the power to make laws and so may delegate no more than the authority to make policies and rules that implement its statutes.... Had the delegations here called for the exercise of judgment or discretion that lies beyond the traditional authority of the President, Loving's last argument that Congress failed to provide guiding principles to the President might have more weight. We find no fault, however, with the delegation in this case.

... [T]he question to be asked is not whether there was any explicit principle telling the President how to select aggravating factors, but whether any such guidance was needed, given the nature of the delegation and the officer who is to exercise the delegated authority. First, the delegation is set within boundaries the President may not exceed. Second, the delegation here was to the President in his role as Commander in Chief. Perhaps more explicit guidance as to how to select aggravating factors would be necessary if delegation were made to a newly created entity without independent authority in the area. Cf. Mistretta. The President's duties as Commander in Chief, however, require him to take responsible and continuing action to superintend the military, including the courts-martial. The delegated duty, then, is interlinked with duties already assigned to the President by express terms of the Constitution, and the same limitations on delegation do not apply "where the entity exercising the delegated authority itself possesses independent authority over the subject matter," See also United States v. Curtiss–Wright Export Corp., 299 U.S. 304, 319–322 (1936). Cf. Swaim v. United States, 165 U.S. 553, 557–558 (1897) (President has inherent authority to convene courts-martial).... [W]e need not decide whether the President would have inherent power as Commander in Chief to prescribe aggravating factors in capital cases. Once delegated that power by Congress, the President, acting in his constitutional office of Commander in Chief, had undoubted competency to prescribe those factors without further guidance. "The military constitutes a specialized community governed by a separate discipline from that of the civilian," Orloff v. Willoughby, 345 U.S. 83, 94 (1953), and the President can be entrusted to determine what limitations and conditions on punishments are best suited to preserve that special discipline.

...From the early days of the Republic, the President has had congressional authorization to intervene in cases where courts-martial decreed death.... It would be contradictory to say that Congress cannot further empower him to limit by prospective regulation the circumstances in which courts-martial can impose a death sentence. Specific authority to make rules for the limitation of capital punishment contributes more towards principled and uniform military sentencing regimes than does case-by-case intervention, and it provides greater opportunity for congressional oversight and revision.

Separation-of-powers principles are vindicated, not disserved, by measured cooperation between the two political branches of the Government, each contributing to a lawful objective through its own processes. The delegation to the President as Commander in Chief of the authority to prescribe aggravating factors was in all respects consistent with these precepts, and the promulgation of RCM 1004 was well within the delegated authority. Loving's sentence was lawful, and the judgment of the Court of Appeals for the Armed Forces is affirmed.

It is so ordered.

Justice Stevens, with whom Justice Souter, Justice Ginsburg, and Justice Breyer join, concurring. [Omitted]

Justice Scalia, with whom Justice O'Connor joins, concurring in part and concurring in the judgment.

I join the Court's opinion, except that with respect to Part IV thereof I join only subparts B and C.

The discussion of English history that features so prominently in the Court's discussion of Congress's power to grant the authority at issue to the President is in my view irrelevant. To be sure, there is ample precedent in our cases for looking to the history of English courts-martial—but not where the question is of the sort before us today. We have surveyed that history for the purpose of establishing the permissible scope of the jurisdiction of military tribunals over certain classes of defendants and offenses. This case does not present such a question. Petitioner does not assert that tradition establishes his offense to be, in its nature, beyond the jurisdiction of military courts, or that courts-martial are historically incapable of adjudicating capital offenses. His arguments are altogether different: that Congress cannot authorize the President to establish "aggravating factors" designed to carry out the narrowing function that (we assume) is necessary for imposition of a capital sentence; and that, even if Congress can give the President authority to perform this function, such authorization has not been effected by the statutes upon which the Government relies.

I do not see how consideration of those arguments profits from analysis of the historical sharing of power between Parliament and the English throne. William and Mary's acceptance of the Bill of Rights, and Parliament's enactment of the Mutiny Act of 1689, are presumably significant occurrences for students of the unwritten English constitution. Our written Constitution does not require us to trace out that history; it provides, in straightforward fashion, that "The Congress shall have Power ... To make Rules for the Government and Regulation of the land and naval forces,"

U.S. Const., Art. I, § 8, cl. 14, and as the Court notes, it does not set forth any special limitation on Congress's assigning to the President the task of implementing the laws enacted pursuant to that power....

In drafting the Constitution, the Framers were not seeking to replicate in America the government of England; indeed, they set their plan of government out in writing in part to make clear the ways in which it was different from the one it replaced. The Court acknowledges this, but nonetheless goes on to treat the form of English government as relevant to determining the limitations upon Clause 14's grant of power to Congress. I would leave this historical discussion aside. While it is true, as the Court demonstrates, that the scheme of assigned responsibility here conforms to English practices, that is so not because Clause 14 requires such conformity, but simply because what seemed like a good arrangement to Parliament has seemed like a good arrangement to Congress as well....

Justice Thomas, concurring in the judgment.

...There is abundant authority for according Congress and the President sufficient deference in the regulation of military affairs to uphold the delegation here, and I see no need to resort to our nonmilitary separation-of-powers and "delegation doctrine" cases in reaching this conclusion. I write separately to explain that by concurring in the judgment in this case, I take no position with respect to Congress' power to delegate authority or otherwise alter the traditional separation of powers outside the military context.

In light of Congress' express constitutional authority to regulate the Armed Forces, see U.S. Const., Art. I, § 8, cl. 14, and the unique nature of the military's mission, we have afforded an unparalleled degree of deference to congressional action governing the military. "[I]t is the primary business of armies and navies to fight or be ready to fight wars should the occasion arise," and this Court has recognized the limits on its own competence in advancing this core national interest, see Gilligan v. Morgan, 413 U.S. 1, 10 (1973). Mindful of the factors that "differentiate military society from civilian society," we have concluded that the Constitution permits Congress "to legislate both with greater breadth and with greater flexibility when prescribing the rules by which the former shall be governed than it is when prescribing rules for the latter." This heightened deference extends not only to congressional action but also to executive action by the President, who by virtue of his constitutional role as Commander in Chief, see U.S. Const., Art. II, § 2, cl. 1, possesses shared authority over military discipline. See Schlesinger v. Ballard, 419 U.S. 498, 510 (1975) ("The responsibility for determining how best our Armed Forces shall attend to th[e] business [of fighting or preparing to fight wars] rests with Congress and with the President"); See also Brown v. Glines, 444 U.S. 348, 360 (1980) ("Both Congress and this Court have found that the special character of the military requires civilian authorities to accord military commanders some flexibility in dealing with matters that affect internal discipline and morale. In construing a statute that touches on such matters, therefore, courts must be careful not to 'circumscribe the authority of military commanders to an extent never intended by Congress' ' '). Under these and many similar cases reviewing legislative and executive control of the military, the sentencing scheme at issue in this case, and the manner in which it was created, are constitutionally unassailable.

. . . I agree with Justice Scalia that the majority's extended analysis of the division of authority between the English Parliament and the Crown with regard to regulation of the military, has no relevance to this case. It is true that we frequently consult English history and common law in attempting to determine the content of constitutional provisions, but the majority fails to cite a single separation-of-powers case in which we have relied on the structure of the English Government in attempting to understand the governmental structure erected by the Framers of the Constitution. Nor does the majority cite any historical evidence, whether from the constitutional debates, the Federalist Papers, or some other source, that demonstrates that the Framers sought to embrace, or at least actively considered, the English system of shared power over the military. If the majority pointed to some basis for conducting the inquiry that it does, I might be willing to accept its analysis. . . . [I]t is too simplistic for purposes of constitutional analysis to draw conclusions about the allocation of constitutional authority among the branches of the United States Government from mere speculation about the Framers' familiarity with English military history and the significance that they attached to it.

Questions and Comments

1. Recall the earlier discussion by Stone of juridicization. Does *Loving* mean that Congress can make valid delegations of life and death authority without knowing of, much less considering, the constitutional limits on the scope of the power it has delegated?

2. Why does the opinion of the U.S. Supreme Court discuss English legal history? Why does it not consider the practices of other contemporary liberal democracies in administering military justice?

Lori Fisler Damrosch, *Constitutional Control Over War Powers: A Common Core of Accountability in Democratic Societies?* 50 U. Miami L. Rev. 181 (1995).

. . . There is reason to explore the possibility that the American experiment of constitutional control over war power, even while remaining controversial in concept and implementation with respect to contemporary U.S. military involvements, has generated trends outside the United States toward subordinating executive warmaking to constitutional control. In places where this American constitutional idea did fall on fertile soil, significant advances have been made toward constraining the initiation of military conflict.

The argument I propose to make—and I would like to enlist Professor Ely[5] in the effort both to make it and to strengthen the empirical basis for it—is that around the world, in constitutional democracies everywhere, we see a borrowing of what was an American innovation in 1787. That idea is the Madisonian one (elaborated upon as well by other eighteenth-century thinkers and leaders) of committing the most solemn national decision, the decision to go to war, not to one person or even one body of persons, but rather to the shared judgment of two branches, with the Legislative branch having the ultimate say.

All constitutional democracies have had to grapple with the fundamental problem of determining when national military power should be committed to situations of actual or potential conflict. To date, however, legal scholarship on war powers—Professor Ely's and everyone else's—has addressed only single national systems. The present symposium is no exception, for the only mention of other countries' legal systems has come in Professor Bernard Oxman's comments addressed to the problem of fashioning a United Nations security system that can function efficiently (and in that context, parliamentary involvement was portrayed as a potential impediment to collective decisionmaking).[7] . . .

My central argument is that the body of experience of the mature democracies in their war-and-peace decisions reflects a common core of commitment to democratic accountability. The techniques of accountability surely do vary—some techniques are embodied in written constitutions and other formal instruments, while others are unwritten or informal; some entail greater and others lesser degrees of legislative supervision; some are before-the-fact and others after-the-fact; some do and some do not include control through constitutional courts or other judicial bodies. For all their differences, however, constitutional democracies share certain basic values as well as a common interest in transplanting those values to other polities where they are not yet entrenched.

My project seeks to understand what is common among the democracies and what is not, as well as what is transferable and what is not. Thus, while I proceed from the assumption (already validated by considerable literature) that expansion of communities committed to democratic governance correlates with expansion of domestic and international peace, I do not argue that the details of the American form of constitutionalism are

---

5. See John H. Ely, War and Responsibility: Constitutional Lessons of Vietnam and Its Aftermath, 47–67 (1993).

7. Professor Oxman is concerned that a second level of deliberations in national legislatures could delay and possibly derail or prevent collective action. Bernard H. Oxman, *The Relevance of the International Order to the Allocation of Internal Powers to Use Force*, 50 U. Miami L. Rev. 129, 139–41 (1995). This concern deserves serious consideration, going beyond what is feasible in the scope of this comment. In some constitutional systems (including in the United States, although Professor Ely might not agree, cf. Ely, note 5, at 54–60), the difficulty could be addressed by conferring advance authorization through standing legislation. In other constitutional systems, however, such as the German and Japanese systems, a fresh legislative decision is required to validate each specific commitment to participate in international peacekeeping.

necessarily the best model for polities in transition to adopt. A major objective of the research is to understand what aspects of the American experience are unique and what aspects are generalizable.

What can we in the United States learn from the experience of other constitutional democracies? With typically American missionary fervor, we have often sought to impose our own vision of constitutionalism on others; some "transplants" took, but others did not. Too often, however, Americans deny or fail to perceive the possibility that the legal systems of other countries could have any relevance for our own. The American experience is in many respects unique. However, through a better understanding of what is common to and what is different among constitutional democracies, we may not only be able to make wiser choices within our own constitutional system, but also be able to reach some generalizations about the transferability of our successes to other polities that are going through constitutional transformation.

II.   Why a Comparative Constitutional Study of War Power?

The intrinsic interest of a comparative study of constitutionalism and war perhaps needs no further defense or apology. However, in view of widespread skepticism about the effectiveness of law in regulating the use of force, I would like to make several claims about the value of a comparative legal study of this subject, not only for its own sake but also in the service of widely shared objectives. The international community does indeed have a major stake in the constitutional evolution of member states as regards the authority to decide to go to war. That stake, or rather those multiple interests, are to:

(1) Strengthen trends toward constitutionalism generally, by which I mean the concept of governance based on law;

(2) Strengthen trends toward civilian control over military forces;

(3) Support the adoption of constitutional safeguards governing war powers, so as to reduce the possibility of international conflict;

(4) Ensure that states are in a position to fulfill their responsibilities under international treaties, including those concerning collective defense and collective security;

(5) Ensure that decisions concerning the use of force within an international system of collective security are made on a rational and responsible basis.[10]

---

10.   . . .An understanding of the decision-making processes of potential nondemocratic adversaries could also have instrumental value in conflict prevention (for example, it was essential during the Cold War to have as accurate an appreciation as possible of military decisionmaking within the Kremlin); but those processes fall outside the scope of the present study.

Contributors to the democracy-and-peace literature have speculated that the relative transparency of military decisionmaking in democratic societies could be one of the factors decreasing the possibility of initiation or escalation of conflicts against those societies, because misperception of their actual intentions is reduced. If this speculation has merit, then dissemination of a deeper

I will not pause here to defend the assertion of a shared interest in strengthening constitutionalism in general, but rather will move to the specific applications of constitutionalism to war powers—a sphere of inquiry almost entirely ignored in comparative legal scholarship. This vacuum is unfortunate. Although the "market" for comparative analysis of domestic legal systems should and does include a demand for comparative understanding of the bodies of public law reflecting political organization, governance structures, and relationships between government and polity, the supply of research in these areas is quite limited. While excellent comparative legal studies exist in certain areas of public law (for example, judicial review of legislative or executive action, and protection of human rights), this literature leaves essentially unexplored the problem of war-and-peace decisionmaking.

The absence of any significant comparative examination of constitutional control of war power may well reflect conventional wisdom that laws on war are to be disregarded—or so one might infer if one's horizons are limited to American experiences of the past few decades, and indeed so one might conclude from much of the discussion at this symposium. If American constitutionalism has proved less than fully successful in the war powers field, then must one despair of the efficacy of constitutional constraint of war across the board? Not at all. A principal purpose of the research agenda I have in mind is to ask whether and how constitutional control of war power can work in any democratic society, with our own democratic society being just one example, and perhaps a less-than-optimal one.

My hypothesis is that constitutional control of war power is not only conceivable as an ideal, but is in fact operational and effective in many diverse countries. In a variety of different democracies, constitutionalism works to ensure that representative organs, and ultimately the people, participate in the processes for deciding on the polity's military commitments. Where constitutionalism works, we should both recognize that fact and learn from it. What makes it work? Can it be made to work in other countries, or in a wider range of circumstances? How can its workings be improved within polities with established traditions of constitutional control and in other polities that may draw on them as models?

Not the least of the possible values of such an inquiry is as a source of ideas for the constitutional reforms now underway in Eastern Europe, the Americas, and elsewhere. Attention to constitutional control over war power should be an important component of the strengthening of democracy in Argentina and Turkey, which under previous regimes resorted to war in an attempt to settle longrunning disputes (over the Falklands/Malvinas and Cyprus, respectively). A balanced appreciation of the limitations as well

understanding of the workings of military decisionmaking within constitutional democracies could contribute to this conflict-avoidance potential. Indeed, a fuller appreciation of parliamentary participation in defining the interests worth fighting for could strengthen deterrence by enhancing the credibility of the military commitments of democratic states.

as the possibility of constitutional transplants should inform any discussion of whether, for example, the U.S.-led multinational coalition (composed largely of forces from democratic countries) should have pursued more activist policies of attempting to impose Western-style governance on Iraqi society after the Persian Gulf War of 1990—91.[12]

Above all, we must be attentive to the conditions that make constitutionalism, and constitutional transplants, take root and flourish in new contexts, as well as to the factors tending toward the opposite effect. If, for example, the renunciation-of-war clauses in the U.S.-imposed German and Japanese constitutions have worked and continue to structure decisionmaking and political debate over those countries' military undertakings even half a century later, then it is important to understand both why the roots of the exotic plant took hold and whether the circumstances of success were so unusual as to preclude the possibility of a further grafting onto other constitutional cultures. Similar questions can be asked about other apparent success stories, such as the constitutionalization of neutrality in postwar Austria.

Covert action is another sphere in which comparative constitutional law can supply relevant insights. A decade ago, Stansfield Turner pointed out that virtually all Western democracies (with the notable isolated exception of the United Kingdom) had moved toward legislative supervision of intelligence activities.[14] Former CIA directors, including Turner, are among the most effective advocates for parliamentary oversight of intelligence activities. The efficacy of legislative oversight obviously varies quite dramatically, both between different democracies and within one democracy over time, as our own Iran–Contra affair shows. Rudimentary oversight did not prevent France's Rainbow Warrior affair, for example. But these difficulties in implementing the concept of democratic control over secret services do not undercut the value of scholarly comparative analysis, or indeed of interparliamentary dialogue aimed at sharing experiences and learning from them. The important point is to identify and understand the common trend across democratic societies to subject covert paramilitary activities to parliamentary control.

The efforts of the post-Cold War period to redesign systems of collective defense and collective security in light of contemporary needs show further applications for the comparative law of war powers. The Persian Gulf War marks the start of the current phase of such efforts; the Bosnian conflict (which continues as of this writing) illustrates the perplexities faced by democratic states that try to use multilateral military force while their electorates remain deeply skeptical about being drawn into a foreign

---

12. Such an argument is made in Robert W. Tucker & David C. Hendrickson, The Imperial Temptation 142–151 (1992) (arguing that the coalition should have pursued a military occupation of Iraq, with a view toward reconstructing its political institutions as was done with Germany and Japan in the aftermath of World War II).

14. Stansfield Turner, Secrecy and Democracy 179 (1985) (citing West Germany, France, Italy, Australia, and Canada as countries that have all "taken steps to bring their intelligence organizations under closer control of their political authorities," and predicting that British intelligence would soon be similarly brought under oversight).

quagmire. Constitutional democracies likewise have had to wrestle with whether to participate in U.N.-authorized operations in Somalia, Rwanda, Haiti, and elsewhere. The problem of constitutional control over collective military action has been central to each of these conflicts and has figured prominently in attention being given in the 1990s to devising new systems (which could be prepared in advance rather than on an ad hoc basis for each new emergency) for collective response to future crises.

The drafters of the U.N. Charter were aware that domestic constitutional requirements would affect the extent to which states could commit national military forces to a collective security endeavor. In deference to both constitutional and political sensitivities, Article 43 of the Charter contemplates that national military units would be placed at the Security Council's disposal on the basis of agreements to be negotiated between states and the United Nations; such agreements would be subject to ratification by member states "in accordance with their respective constitutional processes." When the U.S. Senate gave advice and consent to ratification of the Charter, and when the U.S. Congress enacted the U.N. Participation Act to implement the Charter, it was clearly understood that the legislative organ with constitutional responsibility for deciding to go to war—the Congress—would approve any agreement under Article 43; after such approval, the Executive branch could execute the agreement. Although Article 43 fell victim to the Cold War and was never activated, a revival of interest following the end of the Cold War has led to several proposals for establishing the terms under which the United Nations could draw on military forces committed to it in advance by member states. For democratic states, a key issue in the consideration of any such proposals is the mechanism for ensuring a constitutionally sufficient decision to participate in such a system and in particular uses of military force thereunder.

A comparative study of constitutional aspects of participation in collective security arrangements shows that democratic states attach a high value to preserving constitutional control over military action within any multilateral framework, whether under the auspices of the United Nations, the North Atlantic Treaty Organization, or other body. Far from being a hindrance, fidelity to national constitutional requirements is essential to the success of such arrangements. In particular, the participation of the Legislative branch, to the extent required by national constitutional law, should strengthen rather than undermine collective military action.

III.   Constitutionalism and Conflict: Domestic Foundations of International Peace

The correlation between international peace and internal political organization was developed as a philosophical and constitutional proposition more than two centuries ago. Immanuel Kant commonly receives credit for the intellectual paternity of the philosophical linkage between the two concepts in his essay To Perpetual Peace, published in 1795. James Madison and other American constitutionalists had already expounded the notion that republics under popular control would be less likely than kings to take their countries into war,[21] and that view found juridical expression in the Constitution drafted at Philadelphia in 1787. The eighteenth-century argument stood in contradistinction to then-prevalent tyrannical-monarchical forms of political organization, which were seen as more likely to drag the people into unwarranted, unwanted hostilities.

Kant's insight has been the object of intensive research by twentieth-century political scientists, who in recent years have analyzed almost two centuries' worth of wars between and among countries of differing political structures, with the objective of understanding whether democratization promotes peace. The accumulated data and analysis provide a starting point for moving beyond the effort to understand observable phenomena toward a more explicit articulation of implications for constitutional decisionmaking.

The proposition is now firmly established that democracies virtually never go to war with each other; thus we now have empirical proof of Kant's philosophical speculation about peaceful relations within a league of democratic states—what some contemporary political scientists call the theory of the "interdemocratic peace."[23] Yet the hypothesis that democracies are inherently more pacific than nondemocracies has not been empirically validated. To the contrary, the conventional wisdom is that the evidence tends to show that in their relations with nondemocracies, democracies are just as violence-prone and perhaps even just as likely to initiate conflict as other regimes.[24] The evidence on conflicts between democracies and nondemocracies, and especially on democracies as initiators of conflicts against nondemocracies, requires further consideration in order to arrive at a fair assessment of the Madisonian claims of the war-restraining characteristics of the American model of constitutional democracy.

The political science literature on the democracy-peace linkage is not always attentive to questions of greatest interest to legal consumers of this research. Political scientists have adopted different definitions of "democracy" in their methodologies but have rarely attempted to ascertain whether, within the overall category of "democracies," there are subtypes that have been more successful than others in avoiding violent conflict. Although

21. Madison wrote, for example, that the Constitution "supposes, what the History of all Govts demonstrates, that the Ex. is the branch of power most interested in war, & most prone to it. It has accordingly with studied care, vested the question of war in the Legisl." Letter from James Madison to Thomas Jefferson (Apr. 2, 1798), in 6 The Writings of James Madison 312 (Gaillard Hunt ed., 1906); see also Michael W. Doyle, Kant, Liberal Legacies, and Foreign Affairs, 12 Phil. & Pub. Aff. 205, 225 n.23 (citing Thomas Paine for the assertion that democracy and war are incompatible).

23. Cf. Bruce Russett, Grasping the Democratic Peace (1993) (exploring the peaceful relationships among democracies).

24. See, e.g., Doyle, note 21, at 225 ("Liberal states are as aggressive and war prone as any other form of government or society in their relations with nonliberal states."). But see James L. Ray, R.J. Rummel's Understanding Conflict and War 8–10 (Feb. 1995) (on file with the author) (discussing literature tending to show that democracies may indeed be less conflict-prone than other types of regimes); see also James L. Ray, Democracy and International Conflict (1995).

researchers have introduced some refinements of arguable relevance to legal concerns, the information bearing on a comparative assessment of differing forms of democratic control of warmaking is not easy to tease out. Interdisciplinary dialogue between lawyers and political scientists may help shed light on this question.

Michael W. Doyle (whose article set the tone for much of the research of the past decade) erects a dichotomy between "liberal" and "illiberal" regimes, with the former defined in terms of four basic attributes. One attribute is representative government, including "the requirement that the legislative branch have an effective role in public policy" and that "representative government is internally sovereign (. . . especially over military and foreign affairs)." Doyle takes some account of the legislative role in formulating foreign policy. For example, he excludes pre-World War I Germany from his catalogue of liberal states, largely on the ground that the Kaiser's control of military policy was unchecked by a legislature that otherwise had substantial policy-making authority. Doyle, however, does not make a separate investigation of the criterion of legislative constraint on the executive, apart from its use to assign states to either the "liberal" or "illiberal" category.

While Doyle analyzes the democratic variable as a dichotomy, other commentators use three or more categories. Still others rank states in terms of scores assigned to various democratic attributes (such as the percentage of the adults enjoying suffrage, or the extent of freedoms of speech or press). Other researchers, while examining whether polities that undergo transformation from nondemocratic to democratic regime-types (or vice versa) are more or less likely to get involved in conflict during periods of democratization, have drawn attention to the destabilizing potential of turbulent transitions. Like Doyle's work, much of this literature treats substantial constraints over the executive in the foreign policy field (whether emanating from the legislature or otherwise) as among the factors relevant to ascertaining and/or ranking a state's "democratic" credentials; the extent of judicial independence is also sometimes factored in. Yet none of these inquiries gets very far in analyzing the extent to which structural features of different democratic types correlate with lesser levels of violence, especially with the initiation of violence. In particular, there is little explicit discussion of the constraining role of different modalities of controls on the war-initiating powers of the executive branch.

Looking at the problem through the lens of comparative constitutional law challenges us to test the hypothesis that the phenomenon of democracies initiating violence against nondemocracies might be explained partly in terms of imperfect subordination of executive war powers to constitutional controls. To the extent that executive warmaking is constitutionally constrained and made subject to prior legislative approval, democracies might become more pacific, not only in their relations with other democracies but with any type of regime. Although this hypothesis remains untested and unproved, important normative implications would flow from its being proved. Among those would be that it is not enough to favor democratization in the sense of periodic electoral validation of the government, or liberalization in the sense of respect for human rights and individual autonomy; rather, attention must also be given to whether particular political structures and systems of constitutional control might be more effective than others in checking the war-making potential of the executive branch.

The role of the American President as initiator of several conflicts during the 1980s suggests some of the issues to be explored in attempting to understand conflicts between democracies and nondemocracies. U.S. involvement in Central America in the mid–1980s, and U.S. interventions in Grenada in 1983 and Panama in 1989, are examples of imperfect constitutional control on the part of a democratic state that initiated conflict with nondemocratic states. As for the Central American controversy, the Reagan Administration (or at least some of its key figures) found ways to circumvent explicit congressional prohibitions on U.S. attempts to overthrow the Nicaraguan government or to provoke a military exchange with Nicaragua, and in this way (among others) undermined the proper functioning of our constitutional system of government. The Reagan and Bush Administrations acted without congressional authorization in undertaking the invasions of Grenada and Panama, even though the nature of the operations and the likelihood of combat implicated the constitutional prerogatives of Congress. The courts declined to articulate the boundaries of lawful executive action and left the President essentially free to implement an expansive view of his own constitutional powers.[31]

Whether the U.S. constitutional system ultimately worked in each instance to implement a commitment to constitutional control of war powers is a matter for fair debate. My purpose in this brief comment is to identify the issues rather than resolve them and to suggest the importance of exploring different modalities of constitutional governance as they succeeded (or failed) to halt initiation of violence between democratic and nondemocratic states. This inquiry is especially pertinent regarding mature democracies, which have devised varying methods for controlling executive actions in the domestic and foreign spheres. Once these variations in constitutional control are identified and explained, with attention to successes as well as failures, we will have a better understanding of the relationship between democracy and peace. We may also be able to confine the proposition that "democracies are not inherently more pacific than nondemocracies" to a subset of democratic countries with identifiable anomalies or pathologies in their constitutional control structures.

IV.   The Gulf War Coalition and the Cases of Germany and Japan

Americans are well aware that in January 1991, Congress conducted a historic debate that resulted in legislation authorizing the President to use military force against Iraq, in accordance with resolutions of the U.N.

---

31.   See, e.g., Crockett v. Reagan, 558 F.Supp. 893 (D.D.C.1982), aff'd, 720 F.2d 1355 (D.C.Cir.1983).

Security Council. Less well known in this country are the corresponding deliberations that occurred in democratic parliaments in London, Paris, Ottawa, Rome, Madrid, Canberra, and elsewhere that also produced support for multinational military action. The constitutional significance of these decisions varies considerably from country to country, with some of the parliamentary actions largely reflecting political endorsement of decisions already put into operation by the executive, and others signaling a greater potential for legislative control over military decisionmaking.

The parliamentary deliberations in Bonn and Tokyo were not at all of the rubberstamp sort. Although Chancellor Kohl and Prime Minister Kaifu had staked considerable political capital on policies entailing a not insignificant degree of tangible support for the multinational coalition, they were reined in by parliaments with rather different interpretations of constitutional limits on military participation. These events led to developments of import for the present project: In Japan in 1992, the legislature passed a peace-keeping operations law that both enabled and constrained Japanese involvement in U.N. peacekeeping in Cambodia; and in Germany, the Federal Constitutional Court in a landmark decision delineated the conditions under which participation in U.N.-authorized interventions could proceed.

In Japan, the fundamental war powers principle is expressed in Article 9 of the 1946 constitution, which provides as follows under the heading "Renunciation of War":

> Aspiring sincerely to an international peace based on justice and order, the Japanese people forever renounce war as a sovereign right of the nation and the threat or use of force as a means of settling international disputes.

> In order to accomplish the aim of the preceding paragraph, land, sea, and air forces, as well as other war potential, will never be maintained. The right of belligerency of the state will not be recognized.

American occupation authorities wrote the Japanese constitution to further the plan sketched by Allied leaders at Potsdam for a thorough demilitarization and pacification of Japan. A literal reading of the constitution, which was drafted in English and then translated into Japanese, seems to preclude maintenance of any military capability whatsoever. But at several points in Japanese postwar history, decisions have been taken and understandings reached that have allowed Japan to remain a substantial military power, albeit in a passive posture; recently, however, active involvement in collective military efforts has become possible. The pivotal points have included: (1) the creation of the Self–Defense Forces in the early 1950s, (2) the ratification and subsequent renewal of the Mutual Security Treaty with the United States, and (3) the reassessment of Japanese war powers precipitated by U.N.-related developments of the 1990s, including the Persian Gulf War (in which Japanese involvement was minimal),[38] and

---

38. Two months after the end of the war, Japan dispatched a minesweeper to the Gulf. This was the first extra-regional deployment of the Japanese military since World War II.

the U.N. transitional authority in Cambodia (in which Japanese peacekeepers had a tangible presence).[39]

With respect to judicial interpretation of ambiguous constitutional provisions concerning war powers, the Japanese experience has been more like the American experience than like the German experience, which will be discussed below. Except for two lower court decisions that were later reversed,[40] Japanese courts have avoided ruling on constitutional challenges to sensitive security policies. Using a version of the "political question doctrine" and related techniques similar to those applied by U.S. courts, the Japanese Supreme Court (like its American counterpart) has refrained from articulating limits on the government's military powers.[41] By deferring to the political organs of government and expressing a reluctance to interfere with the decisions of those organs in the security sphere, Japanese courts have given the political branches broad discretion in carrying out military functions.

This is not to say that constitutional control mechanisms are absent in Japan, but rather that they have taken a largely nonjudicial form. With respect to Article 9, as with other constitutional questions, the Japanese judiciary is not in any essential sense the "last resort," but merely one forum among several in which to make constitutional arguments. The role of Japanese courts may be merely incidental with respect to important political questions. The real constitutional debate occurs in the legislature, in newspapers, and in gathering places.

Seen in this light, the Japanese Legislature, or Diet, is the forum in which Article 9 has acquired most of its contemporary meaning. The Diet, in the 1950s, decided that the creation of the Self–Defense Forces could be reconciled with a view of the constitution which was within the realm of plausibility. Since then the Diet has engaged in a continual reassessment of what contemporary constitutional consciousness requires. In the 1990s, the Diet has acted as a substantial check on executive power, as the history of the government's proposals for action during the Gulf War shows. The enactment in 1992 of a statutory framework to govern cooperation with

39. Japanese contributions included a ground unit of 600 troops and several hundred troops in other capacities, including naval and air transport and civilian monitoring.

40. See John M. Maki, Court and Constitution in Japan 298–361 (1964) (discussing the Sunakawa case, of 1959, in which a Tokyo trial judge ruled that the presence of U.S. forces in Japan was unconstitutional); James E. Auer, Article Nine of Japan's Constitution, 53 Law & Contemp. Probs. 171, 182 (1990) (discussing the Naganuma case, of 1973, in which a trial judge ruled that the Self–Defense Forces were unconstitutional).

41. See Maki, note 40, at 348. Summarizing the Japanese Supreme Court majority's decision in the Sunakawa case, one judge wrote:

> the Security Treaty possesses a highly political nature of great importance to the very existence of our country; that a decision as to the unconstitutionality of such treaty, as a matter of principle, does not involve a decision of the judicial courts; and that, accordingly, the constitutional review of such a treaty, unless it is recognized as being "clearly and obviously unconstitutional or invalid," lies outside the scope of constitutional review....

U.N. peace-keeping operations reflects another legislative act of constitutional interpretation. In my work-in-progress, I am examining the very real constraints rooted in Article 9, as interpreted by the Japanese Diet, as an important instance of legislative control over executive war powers.

The German example illustrates the role of a judicial organ exercising constitutional control and the democratic theory of legislative control of war powers. For purposes of comparative constitutional analysis, a recent decision of the German Federal Constitutional Court is highly instructive. That decision interprets the relevant provisions of the German constitution as applied to German participation in military actions under the auspices of the United Nations. The German form of judicial constitutional supervision is quite different from the American model in many respects. It shows, inter alia, that judicial organs can play a constructive role in giving contemporary meaning to constitutional war powers provisions. As Thomas Franck cogently documented in his book criticizing the U.S. political question doctrine, German courts, and the German Federal Constitutional Court in particular, do not shrink from addressing war-and-peace decisions, but rather confront them on the merits.* The results are laudable: The polity as a whole benefits from understanding the legitimacy of the actions of the political branches (or, where relevant, the constitutional limits applicable to such actions), and the political branches themselves draw strength from that process of legitimation.

The reasoning of the German decision on U.N. peacekeeping is perhaps even more pertinent to this essay than the fact that a decision was rendered on the merits. The German constitution embodies a renunciation of the power to initiate war but preserves the power to engage in self-defense of German territory and the territory of its allies, and to enter into collective security arrangements. Previous judicial decisions in Germany had dealt with German participation in collective security efforts under NATO, such as through military bases and the emplacement of certain controversial weapons on German territory. But as of the time of the Persian Gulf War, the question of the constitutionality of participation in U.N.-authorized military actions had not been authoritatively resolved.

The 1994 judicial decision arose from divisions within Germany over the constitutional permissibility of German participation in the multinational peace-keeping (or peace enforcement) actions in the former Yugoslavia and Somalia. The substance of the decision allows Germany to play a significant role in certain collective efforts, subject to advance authorization by the parliament, or Bundestag. The Federal Constitutional Court wrote, "The Constitution obliges the Federal Government to seek enabling agreement by the German Bundestag, as a rule in advance, before committing the armed forces to action." The court thus gave particular application in the military sphere to the "democracy principle" of German constitutional law. The court in previous decisions stated that that principle required parliamentary endorsement of certain international commitments. The

---

* [Editors' Note. See below for Franck's views.]

democracy principle is an "unassailable" core element of German constitutionalism: It cannot be altered even by constitutional amendment. Significantly, the court stressed that only a legitimizing decision by the Bundestag could satisfy the democracy principle with respect to military engagements.

The court's insistence on legislative endorsement of the constitutional validity of German participation in U.N.-authorized military actions warrants close comparison to the corresponding question in constitutional discourse elsewhere. This is one of many pieces of evidence showing a worldwide trend toward subordinating executive war power to advance legislative authorization.

V.   Conclusion

A comparative study will, I hope, generate new insight for the ongoing controversy in the United States about the roles of the President and the Congress in war-and-peace decisionmaking.... Judicial resolution is unlikely, at least for as long as U.S. courts continue their course of eschewing decision on the merits when presidential war powers are challenged.

The framers' choices made for the Constitution of 1787 reflect their convictions that no one person, or body of persons, should have sole responsibility for deciding to go to war; that the person who would be crowned with the laurel of victory has the greatest temptation toward war and therefore should be denied the decision-making prerogative; that those who hold the purse strings should determine at the outset whether to incur the costs of conflict; and that the war power should rest with the most representative organ. Those choices may indeed embody the height of wisdom for the framers' time; but if the framers' insights are to command respect in a world dramatically changed, they must be validated anew for our own generation and for the generations to follow.

A comparative examination of war powers across a variety of democratic societies can contribute a new dimension to the U.S. constitutional debate. If worldwide trends are toward greater constitutional control over executive war powers, as manifested through legislative supervision and some measure of judicial review for validity, then the U.S. experience must be reinterpreted. Undoubtedly, the framers' insights of 1787 helped set those trends in motion and provided a model that many other democracies have emulated. It is ironic that post-World War II American presidents have advanced sweeping claims for their own military prerogatives, even while working to instill notions of constitutional control over executive power in other polities. A global comparative study can put the American experience in perspective and help us understand what aspects of that experience are (and arguably should remain) unique.

I invite Professor Ely to join me on the quest to understand and strengthen these crossnational trends. Perhaps our next symposium can be held in Moscow, where the image of a strong executive ordering a military assault on the stronghold of the legislature (there known as the White House) gives new meaning to Edward Corwin's famous image of an "invitation to struggle" for the privilege of control over foreign policy.

Several years ago I was in Moscow at a time of optimism that the then-ascendant elites of the Gorbachev period had come to understand that the worst misadventures of Soviet rule (including the invasions of Czechoslovakia and Afghanistan) had come about precisely because of the centralization of war-making power in too few hands. The recent events in Chechnya indicate that, in present-day Russia, structural guarantees against excessive concentration of war powers in one person's hands are nonexistent or at least nonfunctioning. The same events also illustrate the broader relevance of one of the propositions Harold Koh has offered at this symposium, which I reformulate as follows: Presidents who are weak in their domestic political posture, but who believe themselves to possess very potent and essentially unchecked war powers, are the most dangerous of all.

Questions and Comments

1. If Prof. Damrosch's hypothesis proves to be correct, what are the implications for U.S. constitutionalism? Will judicial enforcement be effective if Congress has not seized for itself the obligation to participate in troop commitment decisions?

2. Compare Prof. Damrosch's hypothesis concerning the effect of representative decisionmaking on decisions to go to war with the suggestion that, in liberal western representative democracies, the internal effects of international treaties are likely to be strongest where the most representative branch of the government is involved in the approval of the treaty. See S.E. Finer, Vernon Bogdanor and Bernard Rudden, Comparing Constitutions 35 (1995) (asserting that in the U.K., treaties are ratified by the executive and have no internal effect on the legal positions of citizens, without further legislation; that the U.S., which requires Senate approval of treaties, sometimes gives them internal effect like legislation; and that France, which requires parliamentary approval of treaties that will change French law, gives such treaties status superior to that of national legislation). While this characterization of the effects of treaties in these three states may be contestable,[j] assuming arguendo it is correct, does this suggest that courts in the U.S. should be more aggressive in policing the use of executive agreements? In more generally requiring explicit congressional action authorizing or ratifying presidential acts in foreign affairs?

C. FOREIGN AFFAIRS, MILITARY DECISIONS AND THE COURTS: OF JUSTICIABILITY AND POLITICAL QUESTIONS

In the United States, the Court has on many occasions decided questions concerning the foreign affairs and military powers of the government.

---

j. Recall, in this regard, the effects of international decisions concerning treaty obligations of the U.K. in the materials on reproductive freedom in Ireland in Chapter II.

It has, for example, upheld Congress' power to enact legislation to enforce treaties untrammelled by "invisible radiation[s]" from the Tenth Amendment, Missouri v. Holland, 252 U.S. 416 (1920), and rejected as unconstitutional federal laws authorizing military trials of civilians, Reid v. Covert, 354 U.S. 1 (1957); see also Ex parte Milligan, 71 U.S. (4 Wall.) 2 (1867). It has upheld legislation controlling rental prices of housing under the war power, Woods v. Cloyd W. Miller Co., 333 U.S. 138 (1948), but rejected a President's assertion that presidential powers over the military and conduct of foreign affairs authorize a presidential seizure of U.S. businesses. *Youngstown*. It has upheld military induction laws that substantially limit the draftees' opportunity to challenge the validity of induction, see Falbo v. United States, 320 U.S. 549 (1944), while suggesting that some opportunity to challenge the validity of draft classifications must be provided. See Estep v. United States, 327 U.S. 114 (1946). It has, in older cases, rejected assertions that the sovereign immunity of the United States prevents the Court from adjudicating claims by private persons of title to land used by U.S. military forces. United States v. Lee, 106 U.S. 196 (1882) (U.S. army officers held land, now Arlington Cemetery, found still to belong to Robert E. Lee's family).[k] And it has upheld the validity of an executive agreement entered into between the President and a foreign government, to secure the release of U.S. hostages, in extinguishing claims held by U.S. companies against the foreign government, Dames & Moore v. Regan, 453 U.S. 654 (1981).

In more recent years, the U.S. Supreme Court has indicated that it may be inappropriate for it to rule on issues involving governmental powers in the realm of foreign affairs. See Baker v. Carr, 369 U.S. 186, 211–13 (1962) (noting that "[t]here are sweeping statements to the effect that all questions touching foreign relations are political questions," but arguing that whether a matter touching on foreign relations is nonjusticiable requires a more "discriminating analysis"). The final question of this chapter is whether foreign affairs and military issues, or some of them, are "political" questions which constitutional courts cannot, or should not, address. Consider, as you read the materials, whether Germany's approach is really as different as Professor Franck suggests it to be from the U.S. approach. Does it advance the rule of law more to apply very deferential review to government action in foreign affairs than it would to hold such cases to be nonjusticiable? In addition to "rule of law" and "checks and balances" arguments about judicial review in these areas, reconsider Stone's thesis that judicial review can cause not necessarily benign "juridicization" of politics, a thesis similarly advanced in Michael Mandel's article about the Canadian cruise missile litigation.

Although the U.S. Supreme Court has decided many cases that touch— in some cases very directly—on the foreign relations of the U.S., in Goldwater v. Carter, 444 U.S. 996 (1979) the Supreme Court summarily,

---

k. See also Meigs v. McClung's Lessee, 13 U.S. (9 Cranch) 11 (1815) (upholding judgment for private plaintiff, in ejectment, against U.S. Army officers who had built garrison on land erroneously believed to belong to US).

but without an opinion from the Court as a whole, vacated a lower court decision that had held, on the merits, that the President had authority to act unilaterally to terminate a mutual defense treaty with Taiwan. Reprinted below are Justice Rehnquist's opinion for four justices, concurring in the judgment, Justice Powell's opinion concurring in the judgment but disagreeing with Justice Rehnquist's "political question" analysis, and Justice Brennan's dissent.

1. "POLITICAL QUESTIONS" AND FOREIGN AFFAIRS IN THE U.S.

Goldwater v. Carter

444 U.S. 996 (1979).

Certiorari granted, judgment is vacated and case remanded with directions to dismiss the complaint.

MR. JUSTICE MARSHALL concurs in the result. . . . MR. JUSTICE WHITE and MR. JUSTICE BLACKMUN join in the grant of the petition for a writ of certiorari but would set the case for argument and give it plenary consideration. MR. JUSTICE BLACKMUN filed a statement in which MR. JUSTICE WHITE joins. . . .

MR. JUSTICE POWELL, concurring in the judgment.

Although I agree with the result reached by the Court, I would dismiss the complaint as not ripe for judicial review.

I

This Court has recognized that an issue should not be decided if it is not ripe for judicial review. Buckley v. Valeo, 424 U.S. 1, 113–114 (1976). Prudential considerations persuade me that a dispute between Congress and the President is not ready for judicial review unless and until each branch has taken action asserting its constitutional authority. Differences between the President and the Congress are commonplace under our system. The differences should, and almost invariably do, turn on political rather than legal considerations. The Judicial Branch should not decide issues affecting the allocation of power between the President and Congress until the political branches reach a constitutional impasse. Otherwise, we would encourage small groups or even individual Members of Congress to seek judicial resolution of issues before the normal political process has the opportunity to resolve the conflict.

In this case, a few Members of Congress claim that the President's action in terminating the treaty with Taiwan has deprived them of their constitutional role with respect to a change in the supreme law of the land. Congress has taken no official action. In the present posture of this case, we do not know whether there ever will be an actual confrontation between the Legislative and Executive Branches. Although the Senate has considered a resolution declaring that Senate approval is necessary for the termination of any mutual defense treaty, see 125 Cong.Rec. S7015, S7038–S7039 (June 6, 1979), no final vote has been taken on the resolution. See id., at S16683–S16692 (Nov. 15, 1979). Moreover, it is unclear whether the resolution would have retroactive effect. See id., at S7054–S7064 (June 6, 1979); id., at S7862 (June 18, 1979). It cannot be said that either the Senate or the House has rejected the President's claim. If the Congress chooses not to confront the President, it is not our task to do so. I therefore concur in the dismissal of this case.

II

Mr. Justice Rehnquist suggests, however, that the issue presented by this case is a nonjusticiable political question which can never be considered by this Court. I cannot agree. In my view, reliance upon the political-question doctrine is inconsistent with our precedents. As set forth in the seminal case of Baker v. Carr, 369 U.S. 186, 217 (1962), the doctrine incorporates three inquiries: (i) Does the issue involve resolution of questions committed by the text of the Constitution to a coordinate branch of Government? (ii) Would resolution of the question demand that a court move beyond areas of judicial expertise? (iii) Do prudential considerations counsel against judicial intervention? In my opinion the answer to each of these inquiries would require us to decide this case if it were ready for review.

First, the existence of "a textually demonstrable constitutional commitment of the issue to a coordinate political department" turns on an examination of the constitutional provisions governing the exercise of the power in question. Powell v. McCormack, 395 U.S. 486, 519 (1969). No constitutional provision explicitly confers upon the President the power to terminate treaties. Further, Art. II, § 2, of the Constitution authorizes the President to make treaties with the advice and consent of the Senate. Article VI provides that treaties shall be a part of the supreme law of the land. These provisions add support to the view that the text of the Constitution does not unquestionably commit the power to terminate treaties to the President alone. Cf. Gilligan v. Morgan, 413 U.S. 1, 6 (1973); Luther v. Borden, 7 How. 1, 42 (1849).

Second, there is no "lack of judicially discoverable and manageable standards for resolving" this case; nor is a decision impossible "without an initial policy determination of a kind clearly for nonjudicial discretion." Baker v. Carr. We are asked to decide whether the President may terminate a treaty under the Constitution without congressional approval. Resolution of the question may not be easy, but it only requires us to apply normal principles of interpretation to the constitutional provisions at issue. See Powell v. McCormack, 395 U.S., at 548–549. The present case involves neither review of the President's activities as Commander in Chief nor impermissible interference in the field of foreign affairs. Such a case would arise if we were asked to decide, for example, whether a treaty required the President to order troops into a foreign country. But "it is error to suppose that every case or controversy which touches foreign relations lies beyond judicial cognizance." This case "touches" foreign relations, but the question presented to us concerns only the constitutional division of power between Congress and the President.

A simple hypothetical demonstrates the confusion that I find inherent in Mr. Justice Rehnquist's opinion concurring in the judgment. Assume that the President signed a mutual defense treaty with a foreign country and announced that it would go into effect despite its rejection by the Senate. Under Mr. Justice Rehnquist's analysis that situation would present a political question even though Art. II, § 2, clearly would resolve the dispute. Although the answer to the hypothetical case seems self-evident because it demands textual rather than interstitial analysis, the nature of the legal issue presented is no different from the issue presented in the case before us. In both cases, the Court would interpret the Constitution to decide whether congressional approval is necessary to give a Presidential decision on the validity of a treaty the force of law. Such an inquiry demands no special competence or information beyond the reach of the Judiciary.[1]

Finally, the political-question doctrine rests in part on prudential concerns calling for mutual respect among the three branches of Government. Thus, the Judicial Branch should avoid "the potentiality of embarrassment [that would result] from multifarious pronouncements by various departments on one question." Similarly, the doctrine restrains judicial action where there is an "unusual need for unquestioning adherence to a political decision already made." Baker v. Carr, 369 U.S., at 217.

If this case were ripe for judicial review, none of these prudential considerations would be present. Interpretation of the Constitution does not imply lack of respect for a coordinate branch. If the President and the Congress had reached irreconcilable positions, final disposition of the question presented by this case would eliminate, rather than create, multiple constitutional interpretations. The specter of the Federal Government brought to a halt because of the mutual intransigence of the President and the Congress would require this Court to provide a resolution pursuant to our duty " 'to say what the law is.' " United States v. Nixon, 418 U.S. 683, 703, quoting Marbury v. Madison.

III

In my view, the suggestion that this case presents a political question is incompatible with this Court's willingness on previous occasions to decide whether one branch of our Government has impinged upon the power of another. See Buckley v. Valeo, 424 U.S., at 138; United States v.

---

1. The Court has recognized that, in the area of foreign policy, Congress may leave the President with wide discretion that otherwise might run afoul of the nondelegation doctrine. United States v. Curtiss-Wright Export Corp., 299 U.S. 304 (1936). As stated in that case, "the President alone has the power to speak or listen as a representative of the Nation. He makes treaties with the advice and consent of the Senate; but he alone negotiates." Resolution of this case would interfere with neither the President's ability to negotiate treaties nor his duty to execute their provisions. We are merely being asked to decide whether a treaty, which cannot be ratified without Senate approval, continues in effect until the Senate or perhaps the Congress take further action.

Nixon, supra, 418 U.S., at 707; The Pocket Veto Case, 279 U.S. 655, 676–678 (1929); Myers v. United States (1926).[2] Under the criteria enunciated in Baker v. Carr, we have the responsibility to decide whether both the Executive and Legislative Branches have constitutional roles to play in termination of a treaty. If the Congress, by appropriate formal action, had challenged the President's authority to terminate the treaty with Taiwan, the resulting uncertainty could have serious consequences for our country. In that situation, it would be the duty of this Court to resolve the issue.

MR. JUSTICE REHNQUIST, with whom THE CHIEF JUSTICE, MR. JUSTICE STEWART and MR. JUSTICE STEVENS join, concurring in the judgment.

I am of the view that the basic question presented by the petitioners in this case is "political" and therefore nonjusticiable because it involves the authority of the President in the conduct of our country's foreign relations and the extent to which the Senate or the Congress is authorized to negate the action of the President. In Coleman v. Miller, a case in which members of the Kansas Legislature brought an action attacking a vote of the State Senate in favor of the ratification of the Child Labor Amendment, Mr. Chief Justice Hughes wrote in what is referred to as the "Opinion of the Court":

> "We think that . . . the question of the efficacy of ratifications by state legislatures, in the light of previous rejection or attempted withdrawal, should be regarded as a political question pertaining to the political departments, with the ultimate authority in the Congress in the exercise of its control over the promulgation of the adoption of the Amendment.

> "The precise question as now raised is whether, when the legislature of the State, as we have found, has actually ratified the proposed amendment, the Court should restrain the state officers from certifying the ratification to the Secretary of State, because of an earlier rejection, and thus prevent the question from coming before the political departments. We find no basis in either Constitution or statute for such judicial action. Article V, speaking solely of ratification, contains no provision as to rejection. . . . " Id., at 450.

---

2. Coleman v. Miller, 307 U.S. 433 (1939), is not relevant here. In that case, the Court was asked to review the legitimacy of a State's ratification of a constitutional amendment. Four Members of the Court stated that Congress has exclusive power over the ratification process. Id., at 456–460 (Black, J., concurring, joined by Roberts, Frankfurter, and Douglas, JJ.). Three Members of the Court concluded more narrowly that the Court could not pass upon the efficacy of state ratification. They also found no standards by which the Court could fix a reasonable time for the ratification of a proposed amendment. Id., at 452–454.

The proposed constitutional amendment at issue in *Coleman* would have overruled decisions of this Court. Thus, judicial review of the legitimacy of a State's ratification would have compelled this Court to oversee the very constitutional process used to reverse Supreme Court decisions. In such circumstances it may be entirely appropriate for the Judicial Branch of Government to step aside. The present case involves no similar principle of judicial nonintervention.

Thus, Mr. Chief Justice Hughes' opinion concluded that "Congress in controlling the promulgation of the adoption of a constitutional amendment has the final determination of the question whether by lapse of time its proposal of the amendment had lost its vitality prior to the required ratifications."

I believe it follows *a fortiori* from Coleman that the controversy in the instant case is a nonjusticiable political dispute that should be left for resolution by the Executive and Legislative Branches of the Government. Here, while the Constitution is express as to the manner in which the Senate shall participate in the ratification of a treaty, it is silent as to that body's participation in the abrogation of a treaty. In this respect the case is directly analogous to *Coleman*. As stated in Dyer v. Blair, 390 F.Supp. 1291, 1302 (N.D.Ill.1975) (three-judge court):

> "A question that might be answered in different ways for different amendments must surely be controlled by political standards rather than standards easily characterized as judicially manageable."

In light of the absence of any constitutional provision governing the termination of a treaty, and the fact that different termination procedures may be appropriate for different treaties (see, e. g., n. 1, infra), the instant case in my view also "must surely be controlled by political standards."

I think that the justifications for concluding that the question here is political in nature are even more compelling than in *Coleman* because it involves foreign relations—specifically a treaty commitment to use military force in the defense of a foreign government if attacked. In United States v. Curtiss–Wright Corp., 299 U.S. 304 (1936), this Court said:

> "Whether, if the Joint Resolution had related solely to internal affairs it would be open to the challenge that it constituted an unlawful delegation of legislative power to the Executive, we find it unnecessary to determine. The whole aim of the resolution is to affect a situation entirely external to the United States, and falling within the category of foreign affairs.... "

The present case differs in several important respects from Youngstown Sheet & Tube Co. v. Sawyer, 343 U.S. 579 (1952), cited by petitioners as authority both for reaching the merits of this dispute and for reversing the Court of Appeals. In *Youngstown*, private litigants brought a suit contesting the President's authority under his war powers to seize the Nation's steel industry, an action of profound and demonstrable domestic impact. Here, by contrast, we are asked to settle a dispute between coequal branches of our Government, each of which has resources available to protect and assert its interests, resources not available to private litigants outside the judicial forum.[1] Moreover, as in *Curtiss–Wright*, the effect of

---

1. As observed by Chief Judge Wright in his concurring opinion below:

> "Congress has initiated the termination of treaties by directing or requiring the

President to give notice of termination, without any prior presidential request. Congress has annulled treaties without any presidential notice. It has conferred

this action, as far as we can tell, is "entirely external to the United States, and [falls] within the category of foreign affairs." Finally, as already noted, the situation presented here is closely akin to that presented in *Coleman*, where the Constitution spoke only to the procedure for ratification of an amendment, not to its rejection.

Having decided that the question presented in this action is nonjusticiable, I believe that the appropriate disposition is for this Court to vacate the decision of the Court of Appeals and remand with instructions for the District Court to dismiss the complaint. . . .

Mr. Justice Brennan, dissenting.

I respectfully dissent from the order directing the District Court to dismiss this case, and would affirm the judgment of the Court of Appeals insofar as it rests upon the President's well-established authority to recognize, and withdraw recognition from, foreign governments.

In stating that this case presents a nonjusticiable "political question," Mr. Justice Rehnquist, in my view, profoundly misapprehends the political-question principle as it applies to matters of foreign relations. Properly understood, the political-question doctrine restrains courts from reviewing an exercise of foreign policy judgment by the coordinate political branch to which authority to make that judgment has been "constitutional[ly] commit[ted]." Baker v. Carr, 369 U.S. 186, 211–213, 217 (1962). But the doctrine does not pertain when a court is faced with the antecedent question whether a particular branch has been constitutionally designated as the repository of political decisionmaking power. Cf. Powell v. McCormack, 395 U.S. 486, 519–521 (1969). The issue of decisionmaking authority must be resolved as a matter of constitutional law, not political discretion; accordingly, it falls within the competence of the courts.

The constitutional question raised here is prudently answered in narrow terms. Abrogation of the defense treaty with Taiwan was a necessary incident to Executive recognition of the Peking Government, because the defense treaty was predicated upon the now-abandoned view that the Taiwan Government was the only legitimate political authority in China. Our cases firmly establish that the Constitution commits to the President alone the power to recognize, and withdraw recognition from, foreign

---

on the President the power to terminate a particular treaty, and it has enacted statutes practically nullifying the domestic effects of a treaty and thus caused the President to carry out termination. . . .

"Moreover, Congress has a variety of powerful tools for influencing foreign policy decisions that bear on treaty matters. Under Article I, Section 8 of the Constitution, it can regulate commerce with foreign nations, raise and support armies, and declare war. It has power over the appointment of ambassadors and the funding of embassies and consu-

lates. Congress thus retains a strong influence over the President's conduct in treaty matters.

"As our political history demonstrates, treaty creation and termination are complex phenomena rooted in the dynamic relationship between the two political branches of our government. We thus should decline the invitation to set in concrete a particular constitutionally acceptable arrangement by which the President and Congress are to share treaty termination."

regimes. See Banco Nacional de Cuba v. Sabbatino, 376 U.S. 398, 410 (1964). That mandate being clear, our judicial inquiry into the treaty rupture can go no further.

***

Questions and Comments

1. The reported opinion of the lower federal court indicates that the President gave notice in December 1978 of intent to terminate the treaty effective January 1, 1980. See 617 F.2d 697, 700–02 & n. 7 (D.C.Cir.1979) (en banc) (per curiam). On June 6, 1979 the District Court dismissed the complaint for lack of standing, observing that several resolutions were then pending in the Senate that might resolve the controversy without need for judicial intervention. "Within hours" of the district court's order being entered, the Senate called up for debate Senate Resolution 15 which would have recognized 14 grounds justifying unilateral presidential action to terminate treaty obligations. By a vote of 59 to 35, the Senate substituted for its consideration an amendment providing that "it is the sense of the Senate that approval of the United States Senate is required to terminate any mutual defense treaty between the United States and another nation." 125 Cong. Rec. S7015, S7038–S7039 (daily ed. June 6, 1979). Later that day, a dispute arose in the Senate over the retroactive application of the resolution. As the Senate parliamentarian opined and the courts found, "no final action [was] taken" on the Resolution.

2. Had the final vote been taken and had it been made clear that the sense of the Senate was that prior terminations of treaties without its approval were invalid, would the Supreme Court have resolved the merits of Sen. Goldwater's claim?

***

2. Is there a "political question" doctrine in Germany?

The formal answer to this question is probably no. See Donald P. Kommers, The Constitutional Jurisprudence of the Federal Republic of Germany 153 (2d ed. 1997) (stating that "[a]ll questions arising under the Basic Law are amenable to judicial resolution" if properly raised, including foreign affairs questions). Professor Franck agrees that there is no political question doctrine of nonjusticiability in Germany and argues that, while outcomes in German cases involving sensitive foreign affairs matters are similar to those that courts in the U.S. would reach, possibly under the 'political question' doctrine, the difference in conceptualization is significant and the German approach superior. Professor Burley takes issue with this claim.

In his 1989 book, Professor Kommers described the formal absence of a political question doctrine "as such" in Germany:

"*All* questions arising under the Basic Law are amenable to judicial resolution if properly initiated under one of eighteen different procedures ... for the adjudication of constitutional issues. These issues include the highly politicized field of foreign affairs. The court cannot avoid deciding a case in this field, especially when brought by a state or members of the *Bundestag* in the form of an abstract review proceeding."

Donald P. Kommers, The Constitutional Jurisprudence of the Federal Republic of Germany 163 (1989). After noting that in a very controversial case involving the Inter–German Basic Treaty (1973) the Constitutional Court had upheld the treaty on its merits, with a warning to "the federal government that it must always be faithful to the ultimate goal of national unification," he continues (at 164),

> In recent years, however, as the *Rudolf Hess Case* illustrates, the court has exhibited considerable caution in reviewing the political judgment of the executive branch in the sensitive areas of foreign relations and political terrorism. Hess's son filed a constitutional complaint in 1980 charging the federal government with failure to take the steps necessary for securing the release of his father from the Berlin–Spandau Military Prison in which he had been incarcerated, alone, since 1967. (Hess had been sentenced to life imprisonment in 1945 by the Nürnberg War Crimes Tribunal.) The complaint charged that the federal government's reluctance to undertake negotiations with the Allied governments for the purpose of liberating Hess from his isolated imprisonment violated several provisions of the Basic Law, including the right to human dignity and the European Convention on Human Rights. The court accepted the complaint, implying that it was justiciable, but then wrote an opinion that sounded as if it was not justiciable.

> *Hess* underscored the broad discretion enjoyed by governmental organs in dealing with political matters: "The breadth of this discretion in foreign affairs has its basis in the nature of foreign relations," said the Second Senate. "Such events are not governed solely by the will of the federation," the Senate continued, "but rather are dependent on many circumstances over which it has little control. In order to facilitate the realization of the federation's political goals within the framework of what is constitutionally permissible, ... the Constitution confers considerable discretion on foreign affairs agencies in assessing the practicality and feasibility of certain policies or actions." The First Senate reached a similar conclusion in the *Schleyer Kidnapping Case* (1977). Whether the federation should negotiate for the release of a hostage out of respect for the right to life secured by Article 2 (2) of the Basic Law or resort to other actions in dealing with terrorists, held the Senate, is wholly within the discretion of the politically responsible organs of government. Some constitutional scholars have detected the emergence of a political-question doctrine in these cases.

Consider the German Constitutional Court's 1983 decision involving constitutional complaints by citizens against the upcoming deployment of the U.S . Pershing II and Cruise missiles equipped with nuclear warheads in West Germany.

The Cruise Missile Case

66 BVerfGf 39 (1983) (Federal Constitutional Court of Germany)

[The following material has been excerpted from *Case Translation, Pershing II and Cruise Missile Case*, Federal Constitutional Court of West Germany (Bundesverfassungsgericht), Second Senate, Decision of December 16, 1983, translated by Christopher B. Kuner, in 2 Notre Dame Int'l & Comp. L. J. 193 (1984)]:

[In 1979 the foreign ministers of the NATO countries, including West Germany, agreed to install U.S. nuclear-equipped missiles in several locations in Europe (including West Germany). This was discussed in the Bundestag on more than one occasion, and in 1983 the Bundestag adopted a resolution (by a vote of 286–225) regretting the absence of an accord on medium range missiles with the Soviet Union and agreeing that "in order to ensure the military security and political freedom of Western Europe we need [in accord with the NATO resolution of 1979] ... a counterweight to the Soviet SS 20 missiles which threaten us. For these reasons, the Bundestag supports the Federal Government's decision to commence the stationing process in a timely fashion and in accordance with the Government's duty" under the NATO resolution.

Appellants made a number of challenges. They argued that installation of the weapons would violate their constitutional rights to life and bodily integrity under Article 2 of the Basic Law, because the missiles would not be an effective deterrent and were not necessary for Germany's defense; rather they would increase the uncertainties of the situation and thus create incentives for a Soviet first strike, disproportionately increasing the risks of war and unnecessarily endangering their lives. They further argued that the deployment required formal legislative approval through an enacted law; that it violated international law and the U.N. Charter prohibition against threatening the first use of nuclear weapons; and that it violated the constitutional principle limiting Germany to defensive military force only because the weapons were not necessary for Germany's defense and had offensive potential. A further claim was that having the missiles under U.S. command violated the constitutional sovereignty of West Germany. The complainants sought injunctive relief against permitting the installation. The Court dismissed the complaint, without reaching the question whether, if the complaint were substantively well founded, injunctive relief would have been available. It reasoned in part as follows:]

* * *

The constitutional complaints are inadmissable.

1.   As far as the appellants can be interpreted as assailing the conduct of non-German public power in connection with installing Pershing II and Cruise missiles, their constitutional complaint is inadmissible. It is true that the protected sphere of human rights including the basic rights and freedoms recognized in the Grundgesetz* applies against every form of

---

* [Editors' Note: Grundgesetz means the Basic Law.]

sovereign power. However, Article 93, Paragraph 1, Number 4a of the Grundgesetz and § 90 of the Law Concerning the Bundesvefassungsgericht (BVerfGG) grant the constitutional complaint as a legal remedy only against German state public power which derives from the Grundgesetz. . . .

2. As far as they attack the conduct of German sovereign power, it follows neither from the appellants' allegations nor from other circumstances that the asserted endangering was caused by German public power and therefore falls within the protected realm of basic rights claimed to have been injured by German public power.

a) The appellants claim that installing medium-range Pershing II and Cruise missiles equipped with nuclear warheads in the sovereign realm of the Federal Republic increases the danger for its inhabitants to be killed or injured by a nuclear preemptive strike against the missile sites by the Soviet Union, or by a nuclear "counter-strike" mistakenly caused by a technical failure. The appellants do not claim that the purpose of stationing Pershing II and Cruise missiles in the territory of the Federal Republic is to bring about this danger or to lead to a war of aggression. Therefore, it has not been shown that there can be a possible injury to their lives and their health by the conduct of German public power, against which the constitutional complaints are directed.

The violation of Article 2, Paragraph 2, Sentence 1 of the Grundgesetz which appellants claim is not ruled out as a possible violation just because they claim only an endangering (or imminent injury) of legal values protected by Article 2, Paragraph 2, Sentence 1 of the Grundgesetz. Although mere threats to basic rights in general lie on the perimeter of constitutionally significant impairments of basic rights, they may under certain conditions be considered identical to injuries to basic rights. . . .

Even if one accepts the appellants' assumptions that installing Pershing II and Cruise missiles increases the danger of a Soviet nuclear attack against targets in the Federal Republic and, therefore, the risk to legal rights protected by Article 2, Paragraph 2, Sentence I of the Grundgesetz, it is nevertheless questionable whether this injury to appellants' life and limb by the conduct of German public power which they assail is similar to a violation. . . . In the present case, . . . there is no suitable, reliable process by which the degree of increase in the danger to appellant's life and limb could be ascertained judicially. The controlling sources of this endangerment are the decisions of a foreign, sovereign state in relation to the general world political situation and changing political and military relations. Judicially verifiable findings concerning such things cannot be taken in advance under these circumstances. Moreover a possible impairment of the basic rights which they complain were violated does not fall into the protected sphere of basic rights directed against the conduct of *German* public power. . . .

b) By the very facts which appellants assume, there can be no question of either an intended or a direct endangerment of the right to life and bodily inviolability as a result of the Federal Government's agreement to install and deploy Pershing II and Cruise missiles in the territory of the Federal Republic. Appellants do not contend that the goal of these acts is to create the danger they allege. By the very facts they assume, the direct threat to their protected legal rights under Article 2, Paragraph 2, Sentence 1 of the Grundgesetz arises from the nuclear potential of a third state which is not a member of the NATO alliance, not from the weapons to be installed in the Federal Republic.

It is true that there might be a question of an indirect consequence of the conduct of German state power in regard to the danger the appellants allege; such danger might come within the protected sphere of Article 2, Paragraph 2, Sentence 1 of the Grundgesetz as an actual impairment. However, only if at least two requirements existed would there be a consequent impairment by German public power affecting the protected sphere of the right to life and bodily inviolability. First of all, the conduct which appellants assail must have caused this danger: secondly, the creation of this danger must be attributed to public power in the sense of § 90, Paragraph 1 of the Law Concerning the Bundesverfassungsgericht (BVerfGG) and Article 93, Paragraph 1, Number 4a of the Grundgesetz....

As legally controlling criteria are lacking, it cannot be established by a constitutional court whether or not the conduct of German public power which appellants assail will have any influence on those decisions of the Soviet Union which might or might not bring about the military measures (a preventive or responsive nuclear strike) appellants fear. Such estimates are the duty of the federal organs responsible for the foreign and defense policy of the Federal Republic. Within the intended goals of the Grundgesetz, ... and within the scope of what is permissible under international law, the constitutional competence of such organs for foreign and defense policy includes the competence to defend the Federal Republic effectively. It rests on their political decision and responsibility to decide what measures are promising for this purpose. In so far as areas of risk which cannot be estimated remain, as is often the case, they must be included in the deliberations of constitutionally responsible political organs of the Federation and answered politically. It is not the function of the Bundesverfassungsgericht beyond legally standard intentions in this area to substitute its opinions for the opinions and deliberations of the competent political organs of the Federation. This also applies to the question of in what manner the State's objective legal *(objektivrechtlichen)* duty of protection regarding basic rights in the sphere of foreign and defense policy in relation to foreign states is satisfied. In light of the fact that the dangerous state of affairs which appellants presume depends significantly on the political volition of a foreign sovereign state in connection with the entire global political situation, the Bundesverfassungsgericht cannot judge by legally controlling criteria whether the conduct of German public power which appellants have assailed is to be judged decisive for the creation of this dangerous state of affairs, or whether it is at least contributory and therefore causal. It is quite possible that the danger of a Soviet nuclear attack, as the appellants fear it, existed already before the Federal Government's agreement to station or before the deployment itself, or will come into being independent of the deployment. It can also not be judged by legal standards whether it is correct to say that the development of the danger of a Soviet nuclear attack represents a change of existing circumstances "legally" connected according to empirical knowledge with the conduct that appellants censure.

But even if one assumes such an empirical legal connection, the new dangerous state of affairs which appellants assume cannot be constitutionally attributed to the Federal Republic. This is so because this feared state of affairs was decisively brought about by an independent decision of organs of a foreign sovereign state which are not subject to German sovereign power, ... The danger by which appellants see themselves threatened cannot be attributed to German sovereign power, ... [T]he most efficacious cause of the endangering of life and limb which appellants assume must be judged to be the decision of the Soviet Union to launch a nuclear preventive strike in time of crisis against Pershing II and Cruise missile sites, and, as appellants say, to rely on a technical system prone to failure in deciding whether to launch a nuclear "counterstrike." The acts of German sovereign power which appellants assail would appear to be one of the prerequisites of an assumed dangerous state of affairs for which the constitutional responsibility of German sovereign power cannot be founded. Its essential cause would be the independent action of a foreign state in the domain of German sovereign power....

e) It can also not be established that the agreement to install missiles equipped with nuclear warheads, or the placement itself, for defensive purposes and especially to deter a potential opponent who also has atomic weapons at its disposal from attacking the Federal Republic or an ally, violates a general principle of international law in the sense of Article 25 of the Grundgesetz.... The actual conduct of nations with nuclear weapons at their disposal, such as the Soviet Union, the United States of America, France, or Great Britain, does not substantiate a general practice and legal conviction that it is forbidden by general international law to keep on hand missiles equipped with nuclear warheads for defensive purposes, especially in order to deter a possible enemy already possessing nuclear weapons from using them.

. . .

This decision is issued unanimously as to the result, with one vote dissenting as to the grounds of judgment.

————————

Thomas M. Franck, POLITICAL QUESTIONS/JUDICIAL ANSWERS: DOES THE RULE OF LAW APPLY TO FOREIGN AFFAIRS? (1992).

Abolishing Judicial Abdication: The German Model

GERMAN JUDGES ON WHETHER TO DECIDE

If our judges were to embark on a new approach to cases dealing with sensitive foreign-relations and national-security issues, they could be guided by the experience of their German brethren. While our legal culture is based on the common-law tradition of Great Britain, the British model is misleading ... [because] The object of the colonies' revolutionary enterprise had been to sever their tie to the mother country's system of executive prerogatives and parliamentary supremacy. These notions continue to hold sway at Westminster, making it profoundly different from our traditions of constitutionalism, limited and divided powers, and judicial umpiring. It is in the constitutional development of the German Federal Republic, designed after World War II to emulate our system of checks and balances, that useful analogies may be sought.

The German Constitutional Court, the final interpreter of the Federal Republic's constitution, operates in a system of separated powers, protected rights, and federalism readily comparable to our own. Like our Constitution, the German Basic Law neither requires nor precludes judicial reticence in foreign relations. The judges are thus left free to steer their own course. Unlike American courts, however, they have chosen a path of activism, rejecting invitations to imitate the abdicationist U.S. practice. Moreover, they have developed a coherent theory applicable to the adjudication of foreign-affairs cases that is reasonable, works adequately, and provides a thread of jurisprudence that is pursued with far greater consistency than in the American practice. This judge-made German jurisprudence has staked out a middle course between judicial abdication and rampant judicial interference in the making and execution of foreign and security policy, one that satisfies systemic imperatives of the rule of law and political flexibility....

The German theory begins at the opposite doctrinal pole from ours, then moves in practical increments toward a pragmatic middle position. In theory, the German courts are logically consistent: Everything is adjudicable....

... Even though, as Justice Kondrad Hesse has observed, "separation of powers constitutes the basic organizing principle of the [German] Constitution," this has not been translated by the German judiciary to require abstention from questions raising political questions. Specifically, German judges have been careful to avoid creating any theoretical basis for exempting from the scope of their authority to review legislation and executive initiatives the broad category of legal disputes arising out of the conduct of foreign relations or efforts to protect the national security. In German jurisprudence, such cases are as amenable to adjudication as any other.

This can be illustrated by a few leading examples from German constitutional litigation. In 1954, the Constitutional Court decided the *Status of the Saar* case, an action brought by one-third of the members of the Bundestag (lower house)....

The legislators' complaint focused on a recently signed treaty between the German Federal Republic and France concerning the status of the Saar, or more precisely on the law purporting to implement that agreement in Germany. Plaintiffs argued that this treaty and law would derogate from several of the Basic Law's guarantees to German citizens by instituting a special status for the Saar that would differentiate between its inhabitants and those of other German *Länder* (states of the federation). They pointed out that the purport of the agreement was to "Europeanize" the Saar and in particular that the German federal government had struck an unconstitutional deal with France by which Paris, in return for renouncing annexation, received Bonn's acquiescence in a regime imposing mandatory political constraints on that particular state.

These restrictions, the plaintiffs argued, violated numerous articles of the Federal Republic's Basic Law. For example, one provision of the treaty reserved certain external-affairs functions to an unelected Saarland Commissioner, who was to be appointed by the Western European Union, an intergovernmental regional organization. In the complainants' view, the Basic Law did not permit such derogations from sovereignty, nor did it allow invidious derogations from citizens' entrenched rights, including a constitutional right to equality. In particular, the treaty was alleged to violate article 146, which provides for popular participation in the eventual transformation of the Basic Law into a constitution for a unified Germany. By vesting external affairs powers in a commissioner, it was urged, the Saarlanders could be deprived of the right to participate in the legal rites of eventual reunification.

The federal government initially saw no reason even to answer these allegations, preferring to urge the court to dismiss them as "essentially political ... and ... thus nonjusticiable." The court flatly rejected this maneuver. Although the judges ultimately did conclude that the treaty, was constitutional, they were careful to emphasize that exercises of the treaty-making power are never immune per se to judicial review. On the contrary, treaties, like legislation, are circumscribed by constitutional limitations enforceable in litigation....

... [A]fter the court upheld the treaty, it was not ratified by the requisite pleb[i]scite. Somewhat later, the Saar was able to join the Federal Republic on terms of complete equality with the other *Länder*. Nevertheless, the *Status of the Saar* case set the jurisprudential direction of the German Federal Constitutional Court, one to which it consistently adhered thereafter. Essentially, the court regards itself as charged by the Basic Law with responsibility for saying what the law is in any case properly brought before it by parties with standing....

The constitutionality of a law implementing a treaty was again considered by the court in the *Inter-German Basic Treaty Case*. In this instance, the challenge was to Chancellor Willi Brandt's *Ostpolitik*, which had led to an agreement between the two Germanies normalizing aspects of their relations. The constitutionality of the law was questioned by the state of Bavaria, ruled by a branch of the conservative opposition to the federal government led by Brandt's Social Democrats. The federal authorities once again sought to induce the Constitutional Court to adopt the political-question doctrine. As before, the judges refused. "There is no question that the constitutional order cannot be altered by a treaty," they said, carefully reserving for themselves the duty to determine whether a conflict between constitution and a treaty had arisen. The limits imposed by the constitution on the exercise of political power are equally applicable to the conduct of international relations, they added, because that is the very essence of the *Rechtsstaat,* a "state under law." In a *Rechtsstaat,* the final responsibility for the protection of this constitutional order must rest squarely with the court. Nothing done by government is beyond judicial review. That is what the rule of law means in Germany.

Addressing the merits of the complaint, the judges reiterated that the entrenched rights of Germans and the constitutionally established goals of governance, such as the reunification of Germany, cannot be renounced or restricted by any action of the political organs. Although the court found that the treaty did not transgress these basic norms, its decision made clear the central role the judiciary intended to play in ensuring that international agreements, or any exercise of political authority, fully comported with the national values and purposes entrenched in the Basic Law.

In 1975, a number of German nationals mounted a somewhat similar constitutional challenge to certain agreements concluded by the Federal Republic normalizing relations with Poland and the Soviet Union. They alleged that those agreements failed to carry out the requirements of the Basic Law "to protect German nationals and their interests as against other nations." ... Once again the court upheld the government, but only after testing the agreements against the normative standards established by the constitution and its framework of civil rights.

Although the expansive rhetoric that accompanies the taking of jurisdiction by the Constitutional Court in these cases is in marked contrast with that found in some U.S. courts, the actual outcome in both systems would probably have been the same. In a flat confrontation between the terms of a treaty and a claim based on the Constitution, American judges nowadays are unlikely to refuse to rule. The German treaty cases, however, establish a far more expansive basis for judicial review, one that has equal application to nontreaty cases. For example, the Constitutional Court has taken jurisdiction over disputes involving the exercise of tactical discretion in the conduct of foreign affairs. In the *Rudolph Hess* case of 1980, the court was petitioned by the son of that well-known prisoner then still serving a life sentence for war crimes in Berlin's Spandau jail under the authority of the occupying Allied powers. Rudolph Hess had been committed by a judgment of the Nuremberg Tribunal in 1946. The petitioner sought the court's help in compelling the German federal government to make a more active diplomatic effort to free him, the only remaining such prisoner, in accordance with the alleged "constitutional tradition" that the state owes its citizens a duty of protection against other states.

The Constitutional Court agreed that this general duty is judicially enforceable by individuals, that the judges could review the officials' policy to determine "whether they went beyond the limits of their allotted discretion, or whether in their action they were guided by an erroneous belief about the legal constraints on their discretion." The court also asserted its right to determine whether genuine steps had been taken to seek Hess's release and whether the authorities were committed to further efforts on his behalf. Moreover, the court added, in choosing the means to carry out their constitutional mandate, the authorities must be seen not to have acted arbitrarily *(mit Willkur)*, and the judges assumed responsibility. for reviewing the government's actions to ensure that this due-process-like standard had been met in practice. The case offers a striking contrast, for example, to the summary, refusal of the Fourth Circuit to consider whether the president was making sufficient effort to locate American soldiers missing in action in Indochina, as ordained by the Hostage Act.[23]

An especially expansive rejection by the German judiciary of the abdicationist doctrines favored by some American judges is found in a peculiar flurry of suits brought during 1983, collectively called the *Tabatabai* litigation. Here, the Düsseldorf Regional Court and Appellate State Court were called upon to decide the weight to be given to an intervention by the Foreign Ministry declaring that it recognized the diplomatic immunity of Dr. Tabatabai, an Iranian professing to be a special envoy on a negotiating mission to the Federal Republic. Upon entering Germany, Tabatabai had been apprehended by customs officials while in possession of 1.7 kilograms of "smoke opium."

In America, even after passage of the Foreign Sovereign Immunities Act . . ., the courts almost certainly would treat such government intervention as dispositive of the diplomat's status. The German lower court, however, rejected the Foreign Office's intercession in Tabatabai's favor, proceeding instead with a criminal indictment. Although it was twice reversed by the appellate courts, the trial court sentenced Tabatabai to three years' imprisonment, an outcome he evaded by leaving the country after being declared persona non grata by the authorities.

In the final stage of this litigation, the criminal panel of the Federal Court of Justice took the position that it was "not bound by the legal view of the Foreign Office [that] . . . established the immunity of the accused. Regardless of the competence of the Foreign Office to shape the relations of the Federal Republic of Germany with foreign countries," the judges said, "the courts have to examine, within their own competence, whether immunity has been established in a specific case: here, whether the accused is exempted from German jurisdiction according to the general rules of international law (Section 20, Judicative Act)." Having thus given itself the final word, however, the court agreed with the government's view of the matter and, reversing the verdict of the lower court, ordered the conviction quashed.

It will be evident from this selection of German cases that many of the courts' bold assertions of broad jurisdiction are found in litigation the government has won. It would be wrong, however, to conclude from this that the taking of jurisdiction is illusory. That the courts will not permit otherwise valid foreign-relations objectives to be pursued by means that violate explicit (or even implicit) constitutional norms has been further

---

23. [citing Smith v. Reagan. 844 F.2d 195 (1988)].

demonstrated by several recent decisions of the Constitutional Court where the government has lost on the merits. These have held, for example, that treaties may not retroactively impose duties or illegalize previously legal activities since such provisions would violate the *Rechtsstaatsprinzip* of the Basic Law. Most recently, the Constitutional Court held unconstitutional the German electoral law by which the voters of the merged German Democratic Republic would have participated in the first postunification election of the German Federal Republic, a move with the most serious potential foreign-policy implications. As a result, the law had to be revised before the reunification election could be held.

A particularly dramatic example of German judicial review reversing a government policy despite foreign affairs and national security implications is found in the controversial *Citizenship* case. This was a naturalization claim brought by Tiso, a person born in East Germany of an Italian father and East–German-born (but at the time of the son's birth expatriated) mother. Plaintiff had acquired a certification of citizenship from the authorities of the German Democratic Republic. In 1969 he escaped to the West with a passport obtained from the Italian consulate general in East Berlin after satisfying those authorities of his Italian nationality. Once in West Germany, however, Tiso claimed recognition by the Federal Republic of his status as a naturalized German citizen. The Bonn government rejected this claim on the ground that his East German naturalization had not made him a German in the sense of being a citizen of the nation designated "Germany" by the German federal constitution. Petitioner asserted that this decision violated at least twelve articles of the Basic Law.

The court ruled the complaint not only justiciable but justified. In an extraordinarily long and thorough opinion, the court reversed the federal government's contention in a matter of considerable importance to foreign relations and national security. In effect, the judges decided that persons naturalized by the East German regime were constitutionally entitled to recognition of their status as German citizens in the Federal Republic. In the circumstances of a divided Germany, one democratic, the other Communist, this decision raised the specter of an ever more unpopular East German regime compensating for the flight of its nationals by recruiting large numbers of Eastern European, Asian, and African immigrants to staff its depleted infrastructure, then granting those persons citizenship. To some, including the ministries concerned with such matters, this seemed to pose the danger of an uncontrollable flood of ethnic non-Germans becoming entitled to automatic citizenship in the Federal Republic.

The court reached its conclusion by making its own findings based on the Basic Law and relevant international law. Those findings significantly contradicted the views of the federal government. The basic laws of both East and West Germany, the judges held, confirm the concept of the juristic unity of the German nation. Moreover, in such actions as its payment of reparations to German victims of nazism and to Israel, as well as in treaty negotiations, the German federal government's actions and rhetoric were held to have been based on the indivisibility of German nationhood, despite its de facto partition.

German indivisibility, the court continued, has also been the consistent legal policy espoused by the three western occupying powers, who continued to have residual responsibility for the status of Germany. This, the judges said, rather than the position taken by Bonn authorities in connection with Tiso's application, was the proper definition of the status of Germany, one that could be altered only in accordance with the Basic Law through an act of popular self-determination. The court added further ballast to its conclusion by pointing out that the Basic Law's self-determination provision is supported by the UN Charter, the international Human Rights Covenants, and various agreements between the Federal Republic and Eastern European nations....

Only once, in passing, does the Court mention the right of the government, in the name of "public order," to exercise broad political discretion over immigration and citizenship. The executive had argued that international law prohibits the automatic extension of citizenship by West Germany to someone like Tiso with whom the Federal Republic had no real nexus. Moreover, the authorities had urged that the court should avoid "multifarious pronouncements" by heeding the ministerial interpretation of applicable international law. Rejecting this, the judges interpreted their obligation differently. They agreed that the court should follow the government's lead in interpreting international law, but not if that interpretation is "obviously contrary to international law." They were able to conclude that the federal government's interpretation of international law was correct by purporting to apply not the version of that law set out in the government's brief but rather the different positions previously taken consistently by the authorities. Again, citing the many instances in which the federal government had expressed its adherence to a "one-Germany" legal theory, the court declared its readiness to conform to that pattern of interpretation rather than to the ministerial views expressed for the purpose of prevailing in a specific suit involving the rights of one claimant.

That the highest constitutional court of the German Federal Republic felt itself free to override a policy decision of the government in a matter of such political importance, unmistakably asserting its power as the ultimate guardian of constitutional legality, is the result of its having long rejected the political-question doctrine as a matter of formal conceptual jurisprudence even while deciding the substance of various cases in the government's favor....

Another example of judicial independence is the 1989 decision of the German Federal Constitutional Court in the *Asylum Case,* which proceeded from the government's refusal to grant asylum to several Sri Lankan Tamils. The lower court had upheld the federal authorities' judgment that applicants were not such "victims of political persecution" as were entitled to political refuge in Germany by operation of article 16(2)(2) of the Basic Law. In overturning this decision, the Constitutional Court refused to apply a standard of proof weighted in favor of the ministerial determination.

Instead, it considered in great detail evidence of current and historical conditions in Sri Lanka as well as evidence of the political activities of the applicants. On this evidence, the court concluded that petitioners were constitutionally entitled to asylum.

There is good reason why the German courts should have decided to weigh the evidence in such a case themselves rather than deferring to the ministerial evaluation. Since it is the government that is seeking to exclude, deport, or extradite, its evidence should be as rebuttable as that of any other self-interested party.

The German judges seem to have understood, as some American counterparts have not, that rules pertaining to evidentiary weight and onus of proof need to take into account the degree of disinterested expertise, or self-interest, of political authorities' assertions about disputed questions of fact that are crucial to the outcome of a case. They also understand that a distinction should be made between evidence presented by the foreign ministry, and by other ministries (Justice, or the attorney general) that can lay less claim to foreign-relations expertise. Finally, as in the *Citizenship Case,* they have understood the distinction between evidence of a consistent pattern of governmental conduct and legal rhetoric as opposed to a mere opportunistic ministerial statement supporting a particular litigious interest.

GERMAN JUDGES ON HOW TO DECIDE

In effect, the German courts have redefined the issue. It is not *whether* but *how* judges should decide: what evidentiary credence courts should give to the government's assessment of the facts; how much room they should leave the policymakers to choose among options; on what terms constitutionally protected yet conflicting public and private interests are to be reconciled.

The focus, in other words, has shifted in German courts from the issue of jurisdiction to the task of creating rules governing the weight and probity of government evidence in foreign-affairs litigation. Even while asserting its unlimited right of review, the German judiciary has developed evidentiary presumptions that favor the political organs. In the *Inter-German Basic Treaty Case,* for example, the Constitutional Court, while firmly asserting its jurisdiction, applied a presumption of constitutionality. In interpreting the agreement, it ruled that "in the event several interpretations are possible the Court should choose the one which is congruent with the strictures of the Constitution."

In assessing disputed facts, the German judiciary has also developed a presumption that favors the government's "story," its account of why it chose to pursue one among several available courses of action or why it used one rather than another means. The judges, having satisfied themselves that the government's foreign-policy objectives are lawful, will disallow the means chosen only upon a showing of bad faith or arbitrariness *(Willkur).* This is illustrated by the *Schleyer Kidnapping Case* where the Constitutional Court said that the tactical question of whether to negotiate with terrorists for the release of a hostage, plaintiff having urged that this was required by the constitutional guarantee of respect for "life" (article 2(2) of the Basic Law), was within the discretion of the politically responsible organs of government unless the discretion was demonstrably being exercised in bad faith.

While the German courts are willing to enter the political thicket at the behest of parties challenging the constitutionality of a foreign-policy, objective or the means employed to attain it, in effect they give the government the benefit of any reasonable doubt. To put it another way: The complainant must discharge the onus of proving the essential ingredients of unconstitutionality or illegality in the challenged actions of the government. This is a difficult onus to discharge in an area—foreign affairs and national security—where conjecture reigns but does not constitute proof and some or even most of the facts are uniquely within the purview of the foreign office.

This is demonstrated in the *Pershing 2 and Cruise Missile I Case,* decided in 1983 by the Constitutional Court. Several persons had complained that the Federal Republic's agreement allowing Allied forces to deploy a new generation of weapons with nuclear warheads on its territory significantly increased the chances of a Soviet nuclear strike against Germany. They contended that this violated the government's duty, prescribed by article 2(2) of the Basic Law, to protect its nationals' "life." The court responded that the injury forming the basis of the complaint must be shown to be both actually foreseeable and also caused by or attributable to the federal government's decision to deploy these weapons. Neither foreseeability, nor causality could be demonstrated to the court's satisfaction.

Nevertheless, the court treated the petitioners' allegations with great seriousness before concluding that it would be impossible for the judges to ascertain, "because there are no relevant criteria," the probable effect on the Soviet Union of the German government's decision to permit the weapons' deployment. Assessments of this sort, the judges concluded, are within the jurisdiction of the appropriate organs of the federal government. It is their responsibility under the Basic Law to make the determinations necessary to secure the defense of the Federal Republic. What steps are required to achieve this is "within the ambit of political decision and responsibility," and the Basic Law does not permit the judges to substitute their assessment of the political risks for that of the appropriate political organs.

While this test superficially resembles the one stated by Justice Brennan in *Baker v. Cart,* which allows U.S. courts to abstain from adjudicating cases in which there is a lack of judicially ascertainable standards for deciding the issues, the similarity is misleading. The German judges' position is not that there is a category. of cases beyond their power to decide but that where the applicable standards for making a judgment are highly subjective, they will decide, but may also give greater leeway than otherwise to the policymakers. In Germany it is not difficult to be heard in a case purporting to hold the government to a vaguely defined legal standard, but it is quite hard to win. The judges will reverse the political decision only where the petitioner can demonstrate that the government was acting in bad faith: if, for example, it can be shown that an action purportedly taken to pursue a lawful objective (to strengthen NATO defenses) was actually motivated by an unlawful one (to enrich the minister of defense or one of his constituents).

While the German court thus recognized the enforceable constitutional obligation of the state not to endanger the lives or well-being of its citizens, it pointed out that the dangers of deploying the missiles, if such there were, would proximately arise not from the deployment itself but from the reaction of foreign states. The Basic Law could not be interpreted to have accorded a foreign government the power to determine by threats and demands the constitutionality of actions that in themselves posed no danger to the lives or health of German citizens. . . .

The judicial presumption in favor of the government's story is augmented by what is tantamount to a presumption in favor of the government's account of the content of international law. In the aforementioned *Hess* case, for example, petitioner argued that the federal government was misconstruing the limit that article 107 of the UN Charter, dealing with the special status of the former Axis powers, placed on Germany's legal options in seeking Hess's release from prison. To this the court responded that a truly conclusive or definitive interpretation of the relevant international law could be given only by the International Court of Justice and that in the absence of such clarification, a national court must recognize that "it is of great importance to the interests of the German Federal Republic that it speak in international forums with a single voice." For this reason the court must "exercise the greatest measure of restraint" before finding the government's interpretations of its rights and duties under international law in error. The court could contradict the policymakers on such a matter only "if the Government's interpretation of an international law were shown to be willfully wrong so as to affect directly the rights of a citizen." It must be demonstrated, in other words, that the government's interpretation "is not comprehensible."

The judges defined the test to be applied—*arbitrariness (Willkur)*—and concluded that the onus of proving it rested with the plaintiff, who had failed to discharge it to their satisfaction. "It is not the place of courts to replace the views of the competent organs of foreign policy with their own," the court reiterated. When it is asked to assess the effectiveness of various foreign-policy options, the court must accept the government's view unless it has been shown that the policy chosen cannot be justified "by any sensible view of the matter."

This should be set against the previously noted refusal of the Constitutional Court in the *Citizenship Case* to accept the argument of the federal authorities that their denial of plaintiff's claim to German citizenship was mandated by international customary law. There, however, the court was able to point to wide discrepancies between the government's contentions and quite different accounts of the law given by the government on other occasions.

Besides developing evidentiary. presumptions favoring the government, the German courts in taking jurisdiction over foreign affairs cases have interpreted the Basic Law to give the political organs *Spielraum:* wide, but judicially reviewable and not unlimited, policy discretion. In the *Saar* case, for example, the Constitutional Court held that in interpreting the validity, of that treaty and the legislation enacting it, the judges "above all ... should not lose sight of ... the political realities which are the starting point from which the treaty emerges, as well as the political realities which the agreement seeks to establish or to alter." The Basic Law, said the court, must be read in the political context in which it was operating, such as the military occupation of the Federal Republic by the three western Allied powers. "While all exercises of state power in the German Federal Republic must be limited by the terms of the Basic Law," the judges added, "it is nevertheless necessary to imagine whether, in these circumstances, only agreements are to be held constitutional which give full effect to the Basic Law, or whether it is not more satisfactory, that the steps contemplated by the agreement have been taken with the intent, and have the tendency, to advance [the nation] towards a full realization of the prescribed constitutional conditions at least to such an extent as these are politically achievable. The Federal Constitutional Court considers itself obliged to answer this question by adopting the latter position."

In effect, the judges applied a half-a-loaf theory that justified their conclusion that the political settlement envisaged by the Saar agreement was "well within the ambit" of political discretion because it tended to launch the step-by-step dismantling of the Saar's status as a French-occupied territory, one that legally severed it from the rest of the German Federal Republic but also envisioned the gradual restoration of the Saar's constitutional legitimacy within the German state. "Within such boundaries [of their discretion] the treaty-making organs of the Federal Government are only politically accountable for their content and agreed measures."

Specifically, a judicial finding of unconstitutionality is excluded if the effect of the agreement, as interpreted by the judges on a full review of the record, is to create conditions more nearly in accord with the constitution than would otherwise exist. "The bad," the court intoned, "must not be allowed to defeat the better merely because the best is ... unattainable. This the Basic Law cannot intend." The question whether the agreement will advance or retard the prospects of the Saar rejoining the greater part of the Federal Republic that already enjoys all the rights established by the Basic Law in the period before the conclusion of a final peace treaty "is a question of political judgment" beyond the Constitutional Court's competence. Beyond the judges' competence, however, not *inherently* but only because it is an issue on which reasonable persons might differ.... [T]his is no carte blanche. "A finding of unconstitutionality," the judges cautioned, "could be made if it were evident that the effect of the agreement were to retard those prospects. That is not here the case." In effect, the judges asserted their inalienable right to make the call, but where it is close, they agree to give the benefit of the doubt to the government.

The *Saar* case demonstrates that in discharging its responsibility for judicial review, the court will (1) take into account the circumstances and where appropriate interpret the meaning of the constitutional requisites in the light of existential reality and the range of options available to the political authorities, and moreover, (2) where the constitutionality of an agreement depends upon an informed judgment of its likely future operational effect, the judicial, will substitute its prognosis for that of the political organs only in extraordinary cases.

A similar reading of the constitution to give the government broad discretion in the shaping of foreign policy was enunciated by the Constitutional Court in the *Inter-German Treaty Case*. There the judges specified that the Basic Law must be read to give the authorities the leeway to decide which policies are most likely to serve the national interest in matters concerning foreign relations and agreements with foreign states. However, the principle of "judicial self-restraint" (rendered in English by the German court) does not imply the fore-shortening or weakening of judicial competence to decide. It does require the judges to "refuse to play politics" by "trenching upon the area created and circumscribed by the Basic Law as appropriate for the unrestricted operation of the political institutions." What those areas are is for judges to say. . . .

Thus the court in the *Inter-German Treaty Case* managed to uphold the constitutionality of the treaty while asserting its right fully to review the constitutionality of its terms and objectives. . . .

The *Hess* case makes this duality particularly clear: The court's broad power of review coexists with the political organs' broad discretion in questions of policy. In holding justiciable the suit brought by Hess's son, the lower court had also declared that the Federal Republic has "a wide discretion" as to "whether and how they will provide this external protection" to which Hess was entitled under the constitution. That discretion, said the court, was necessary because the duty of protection imposed on the government by the Basic Law, while real and judicially enforceable, is owed by the political authorities not only to the imprisoned Hess but also to the nation as a whole. Where relations with other states are concerned, it is thus for the government to balance its duty toward the individual German against the interests of the entire community. "The Government's political judgment applicable to this balancing," the judge concluded, "is not reviewable by a court." On the other hand, he said, the courts will review whether the authorities have violated a requirement of law, exceeded their allotted discretion, or misunderstood "the legal constraints on their discretion."

When the case reached the Constitution Court, it endorsed this summary of the standard of review. Although the case was plainly justiciable, the Constitutional Court's judges held that the government's "breadth of discretion in foreign affairs is justified in that foreign relations and events are not solely within the [political] control of the German Federal authorities, but are frequently beyond its control. In order to pursue the political objectives of the Federal Republic within the limits of what is permissible by international and constitutional law, the Constitution accords the organs of foreign policy, a very wide discretion in assessing the practicality, and feasibility, of various policy options."

It suffices if the federal authorities have demonstrated to the court's satisfaction that various steps have been taken to secure the liberty of the subject of the petition and that it is intended to take further measures. The mere fact that initiatives taken so far have failed does not demonstrate that other steps would have been more successful. For example, the complainant failed in his contention that the authorities should have used more arguments based on errors of law in Hess's conviction and should have raised the matter publicly in the forum of the United Nations because he cannot demonstrate that such tactics would have been more successful than those chosen, in their discretion, by the authorities. The onus of proof, in other words, is with those challenging the government. . . .

This summary of key cases makes clear that the German judiciary has reserved for itself the right to decide but that the judges tend to listen (sympathetically) to the policymakers. In practice, there has been little serious conflict between the political and judicial organs. It is also evident from the jurisprudence that foreign-policy cases are not litigated on an entirely level playing field. The German judiciary applies a rather narrow standard of review in foreign-relations questions that explicitly gives the political organs sufficient latitude to make policy choices without judicial second-guessing.

This achieves results that have not seriously discomfited the political branches while reassuring litigants with claims against the government that they will have their day in court. Measured by outcomes, the German judiciary, taking jurisdiction in virtually every instance, has upheld the contested foreign-policy and security initiatives of the political branches in roughly the same proportion (which is to say equally often) as the U.S. federal courts have by practicing abdication. The judicial results in the two systems are about as similar as the judges' conceptual formulations are different. In its theoretical pronouncements, neither judiciary is entirely candid about what it is doing. The German judges sound more assertive, just as their American counterparts, sometimes by practicing double-entry bookkeeping, have tended to sound more reticent, than they really are.

Nevertheless, the German Constitutional Court has at least managed to develop a seamless theory and by and large has given it a consistent application. That theory is consonant with the rule of law. No litigant in the German courts will be refused a hearing because the issue is too political, the interests too important, the facts too difficult, or the law too inscrutable.

Closer to home, the experience of Canada became a relevant standard of comparison once its federal system (in place since 1867) was augmented in 1982 by a constitutionally entrenched Charter of Rights and Freedoms. . . . [In a challenge to] a Canadian–U.S. agreement to permit U.S. cruise-missile testing in Canada, ... [the Court rejected the political question doctrine.] "I have no doubt," wrote Justice Dickson, "that disputes of a political or foreign policy nature may properly be cognizable by the courts." The Canadian Supreme Court's approach to the missile-testing case corresponds closely to the approach developed by the German Constitutional Court.

Courts do not merely decide cases. They speak, by word and example, as teachers. One should not underestimate the salutary effects of this approach on the legal culture of a society, manifesting that in government none are omnipotent and that the last word belongs to the least dangerous branch.

Questions and Comments

1. Recall Professor Kommers' description of the *Rudolf Hess* case earlier in this chapter, and compare it with Professor Franck's. Note the difficulty in doing research in comparative law when one is dependent on the translations, interpretations and descriptions of others.

2. Are you persuaded that in Germany there is no "political question" doctrine, or do you agree with those scholars, referred to by Professor Kommers at the end of his discussion of the *Rudolph Hess* case, who see the possible emergence of such a doctrine?

3. Consider again the question of audience. For what audience(s) are the distinctions between the German and U.S. approaches, as described by Franck significant? Power elites? The general citizenry?

3. POLITICAL QUESTIONS, LAW AND LEGITAMATION

Anne–Marie Slaughter Burley, *Are Foreign Affairs Different?* (reviewing Thomas M. Franck, POLITICAL QUESTIONS/JUDICIAL ANSWERS), 106 Harv.L. Rev. 1980 (1993)

. . .

I. TRANSFORMING POLITICAL QUESTIONS INTO LEGAL QUESTIONS

The core of Franck's argument is quickly summarized. The rule of law in the U.S. system is coextensive with judicial review. Judicial review should extend equally to foreign and domestic affairs. To the extent that the political question doctrine functions in foreign affairs cases as a mechanism that allows judges to abdicate their obligation of judicial review, it should be abolished. In its place, the United States should follow the German federal constitutional court in recognizing that distinctions between "political" and "legal" questions are inchoate and irrelevant as guides to judicial decisionmaking, and should hence adopt a presumption that all questions are justiciable. To take account of constitutionally granted discretion to the political branches in foreign affairs, courts should replace the political question doctrine with a "rule of evidence" designed to permit "due deference" to the political branches. On Franck's logic, upholding the principle of judicial review in all cases extends the rule of law to foreign affairs, even if the practice of deferring to the Executive in its conduct of foreign affairs is left largely undisturbed....

... Franck identifies three components that ultimately merged to form the present-day doctrine. First is a historical "Faustian pact," "the giveback practice of judges who enlarge their jurisdiction over domestic political conflicts but then seek to pacify the enraged political beast by making a grand gesture of jettisoning judicial review of disputes touching foreign affairs." [15] Second is the unreflective adoption of a British precedent that affirmed an absolute and unreviewable royal foreign affairs power and accepted a monarchic tradition that the Court steadily rejected in domestic affairs. Third is the practice of "double-entry bookkeeping," cases in which courts purport to abstain from judicial review in one part of the decision, but in fact proceed to reach the same result via a full legal analysis of the merits in another. Cases in this last category can be cited both in support of the political question doctrine and of the contrary proposition that courts are perfectly capable of adjudicating foreign affairs cases.

This account suggests that the political question doctrine in foreign affairs cases developed almost by default, with judges either performing their normal function or airily giving away their review powers in cases that had little to do with foreign affairs. It is the history of "How Abdication Crept In." Yet if these are the origins of the political question doctrine in foreign affairs cases, they do not explain its continuing application to such cases. Franck instead emphasizes a pervasive judicial sense that foreign affairs are "different," "that 'it's a jungle out there' and that the conduct of foreign relations therefore requires Americans to tolerate a degree of concentrated power that would be wholly unacceptable domestically." This entrenched belief that foreign affairs are "different" informs three contemporary justifications for reliance on the political question doctrine to avoid decision of any issue with foreign affairs implications. Franck's presentation and rebuttal of each of these rationales yields three of the book's main themes.

The first rationale is itself grounded in the Constitution, the claim that the political question doctrine reflects "constitutionally mandated limits." The critical question here is who shall determine these limits, the courts or

---

15. The initial bargain was struck in Marbury v. Madison itself, 5 U.S. (1 Cranch) 137 (1803), when the Supreme Court was still weak. Chief Justice Marshall used a foreign affairs example to illustrate the proposition that:

> [T]he President is invested with certain important political powers, in the exercise of which he is to use his own discretion, and is accountable only to his country in his political character, and to his own conscience.... The application of this remark will be perceived by adverting to the act of congress for establishing the department of foreign affairs.... The acts of such an officer, as an officer, can never be examinable by the courts.

the political branches? Franck deems it a "self-evident proposition" that the courts should opine on the scope of the constitutional allotments of political discretion and thereby preserve their exclusive function of constitutional interpretation. He firmly rejects the alternative position, that the Executive itself should determine the scope of its discretionary foreign affairs power and that this determination should be unreviewable. Such a claim, he argues, makes a mockery of the very notion of constitutional limits. [Franck] traces this more expansive constitutional rationale back to its roots in British parliamentary practice, charts its definitive rejection by the Supreme Court in the 1950s, and laments its irrational and unsupported persistence in the lower courts.

A second rationale for the political question doctrine in foreign affairs cases does not deny courts the constitutional power to decide such cases, but argues that they should refrain because of "prudential concerns." These come in four flavors: the unavailability and unsuitability of factual evidence in foreign affairs cases; the lack of judicially manageable standards to resolve policy issues; the inadequacy of judges to decide matters that potentially affect the survival of the nation; and the potential undermining of judicial legitimacy through noncompliance with judicial decisions in this area. In response, Franck first argues that the evidentiary question either requires courts merely to "decide complex issues of fact the loci of which are wholly or partially outside the United States" or "relates to evidentiary probity and onuses of proof," both of which are quite manageable problems. Second, the articulation of manageable legal standards is a court's job; "only in international matters is a claim of 'no law' thought an acceptable judicial response to legal ambiguity." Third, courts do far greater damage to the national interest by disabling the safeguards afforded by judicial review in an entire class of cases than they could ever do by issuing rulings even in the midst of foreign affairs crises. They do not make foreign policy thereby, but rather judicial policy, and thus speak with their own voice in a necessarily multivocal system. Finally, Franck insists that concerns about the enforceability of judicial decisions are far more pertinent to the nineteenth century judicial system than to the twentieth, because the modern public has clearly accepted the necessity of "a nondemocratic body of decision makers deliberately insulated from popular political fashion and consciously protected from majoritarian will."

The third rationale for the political question doctrine is an outgrowth of part of the second: the "technical" objection that courts are untrained and hence unable to decide foreign affairs cases. Franck meets this objection by first setting forth the parade of horribles invoked by courts as reasons not to decide foreign affairs cases. He then systematically highlights the insubstantiality of such fears by examining all the cases in which courts have had the courage to adjudicate. When judges refuse to abdicate, he argues, "they demonstrate, though rarely expound, a conscious competence that reproves and rebuts the abdicationist judicial proclivity". In the process, they analyze and dismiss governmental assertions of foreign policy and national security interests as insufficient to justify the trampling of individual property rights and civil rights.[18] Moreover, in two subject areas, Congress and the Executive have actually combined to mandate adjudication of such delicate questions as the scope of foreign sovereign immunity and the legality of foreign expropriations.[19] The rationale here, ironically enough, is the desire to depoliticize political questions by subjecting them to nondiscretionary judicial review bounded by relatively clear legislative standards. . . .

The final two chapters of Political Questions, Judicial Answers are devoted to an elaboration of Franck's German-inspired approach to the political question doctrine. He would replace the doctrine with a "rule of evidence" and would condition judicial review in all foreign affairs cases on the adoption of an evidentiary standard designed to permit the political branches wide latitude and flexibility in the conduct of foreign policy. Even if U.S. courts can be convinced to recognize the distinction between deciding to engage in judicial review and deciding the substantive foreign policy questions at issue in these cases, they will still have "to confront the prudential problems posed by foreign-relations cases," first and foremost "the evidentiary one." From this perspective, the problem becomes how a court is to assess evidence that the political branches transgressed the constitutional boundaries of their discretion both to determine the nation's foreign policy goals and to choose the means to achieve them. . . .

II. BEGGING THE (POLITICAL) QUESTION

A. The Limits of Legal Alchemy

Franck's solution is seductive. He appears to transform political questions into legal questions through skilled legal alchemy: conceptual translation from one doctrinal vocabulary to another. Questions of justiciability can certainly be recast as standards of evidentiary review, just as questions of abstention can be recast as questions of conflicts of law, or questions of privacy as questions of equal protection. From the perspective of the disputants in any particular case, the outcome may be exactly the same,

---

18. The necessity of reaching a comprehensive claims settlement with Iran to resolve the hostage crisis did not prevent the Supreme Court from examining the takings claims of individual litigants. See Dames & Moore v. Regan, 453 U.S. 654, 674 & n. 6, 688, 689–90 (1981). The Court ultimately sided with the Executive, but not on political question grounds. See id. at 688. In Kent v. Dulles, 357 U.S. 116 (1958), charges of communist infiltration proved unavailing against Mr. Kent's right to travel, see id. at 130. Similarly, in cases such as I.N.S. v. Chadha, 462 U.S. 919 (1983), and United States v. American Tel. & Tel. Co., 567 F.2d 121 (D.C.Cir.1977), the courts have proved perfectly capable of umpiring separation of powers disputes between the executive and legislative branches, notwithstanding such foreign policy implications as the control of immigration and wiretapping for "national security" purposes [according to Franck].

19. The examples here are the passage of the Second Hickenlooper Amendment, Pub. L. No. 88–633, § 301(d)(4), 78 Stat. 1009, 1013 (1964) (codified at 22 U.S.C. § 2370(e)(2) (1988)) (requiring courts to adjudicate the validity of takings alleged to violate international law), and the Foreign Sovereign Immunities Act of 1976, Pub. L. No. 94–583, 90 Stat. 2891, 2891 (1976) (codified at 28 U.S.C. §§ 1330, 1332(a)(2)-(4), 1391(f), 1441(d), 1602–1611 (1988)) (setting forth the conditions under which suits may be brought against foreign sovereigns).

but a different and arguably more desirable principle is upheld. This reshaping of the legal landscape bypasses old obstacles and links previously isolated and separated areas, even if it inevitably highlights the contours of new problems.

Moreover, pondering the standard of review would seem to focus the attention of courts and commentators on the canon of foreign policy needs—secrecy, dispatch, flexibility—in the context of specific cases. On these facts, from war to wiretapping, what should be the scope of political discretion? Franck's point here is less the transformation from political to legal questions, but from abstract to concrete questions. Once a court is seized of the merits of a particular dispute, it is less likely to be swayed by the "mystique" of foreign affairs and the siren song of national interest. On the contrary, he would argue, the government will have to fill those empty concepts with specific content and pinpoint the precise differences between foreign and domestic affairs that would justify a particularly lenient standard of review. . . .

On closer examination, however, Franck's formula for converting political questions into "evidentiary questions" is not a universal solution. "Evidentiary" has a reassuringly technical sound, associated with core judicial functions such as fact-finding and assigning burdens of proof. Therein lies its appeal to courts unsure of their footing in foreign affairs. Yet if so construed, the category of "evidentiary questions" can encompass only a fraction of the political questions Franck seems to transform. He actually relies on a much broader definition of "evidentiary," one that ultimately undermines its initial attraction.

Assume that a group of Congressional plaintiffs sues the Administration in an effort to enforce the War Powers Resolution.[23] They claim that U.S. troops acting as "advisors" to a Central American government fighting a civil war are in fact engaged in "hostilities" within the meaning of the Resolution, and thus that the sixty-day time clock established by the Resolution has begun to run.[24] Assuming that the court finds the plaintiffs to have standing, it would face several distinct questions. First, a determination of the facts about the actual conditions faced by U.S. soldiers in the region. Were they under fire? How frequently? With what intensity and duration? To make this determination, the court would hear evidence from a variety of sources: eyewitness testimony, evidence about the level of pay received by troops in recognition of hostile conditions, evidence from intelligence sources.

---

23.   50 U.S.C. §§ 1541–1548 (1988). The text presents the facts of Crockett v. Reagan, 558 F.Supp. 893 (D.D.C.1982), aff'd, 720 F.2d 1355 (D.C.Cir.1983) (per curiam), cert. denied, 467 U.S. 1251 (1984), a case dismissed in part on political question grounds.

24.   Section 4(a)(1) of the War Powers Resolution, Pub. L. No. 93–148, § 4(a)(1), 87 Stat. 555–56 (1973) (codified at 50 U.S.C. § 1543(a) (1988)), requires the President to submit a report to the Speaker of the House and the President of the Senate when U.S. armed forces are introduced "into hostilities or into situations where imminent involvement in hostilities is clearly indicated by the circumstances." Id. Under § 5(b), any such forces must be withdrawn within sixty days after a report is submitted or is required to be submitted, unless Congress has taken further action. See 50 U.S.C. § 1544(b) (1988).

Second, having found the facts, the court would have to interpret them. Even if U.S. troops are subject to enemy fire of a certain duration and intensity, what is the legal significance of these conditions? Specifically, do they constitute "hostilities" in the sense meant by the War Powers Resolution? This question cannot be resolved by the presentation of evidence. On the contrary, it requires the application of a particular provision of law, an exercise that, in turn, requires the interpretation of both law and fact. It is a question not of evidence but of judgment, the very judgment courts seek to avoid when they invoke the political question doctrine.

A third question encountered by this hypothetical court would concern the constitutionality of the War Powers Resolution itself. Thus, even if the court found that the facts qualified as "hostilities" within the meaning of the statute, it could determine that Congress does not have the constitutional power to limit the Executive's discretion to deploy troops in the national defense by imposing a sixty-day time limit. Again, this question is not an "evidentiary question," but rather a question of constitutional interpretation.

For Franck, however, all three of these questions could be subsumed under the German approach. "[T]he German courts have redefined the issue," he writes.

> It is not *whether* but *how* judges should decide: what evidentiary credence courts should give the government's assessment of the facts; how much room they should leave the policymakers to choose among options; on what term constitutionally protected yet conflicting public and private interests are to be reconciled.

Are these evidentiary questions? Yes, according to Franck, in the following sense: they shift the focus "from the issue of jurisdiction to the task of creating rules governing the weight and probity of government evidence in foreign-affairs litigation" . . . .

. . . Yet this analysis begs a fundamental legal, indeed constitutional, question. Even if the technical manipulation of the standard of review is a matter of "onus and evidentiary weight," the determination of how strict or lax that standard of review should be rests on a prior determination of the statutory or constitutional division of power in foreign affairs, a decision to tilt the balance toward the Executive or Congress or individuals affected by foreign policy decisions. This question is precisely what plaintiffs in the majority of foreign affairs cases would have the courts decide. Courts in Franck's scheme would decide it not "in evidentiary terms," but on the basis of a general presumption of deference to the Executive.

B.   The Limitations of Judicial Review

If Franck cannot transform all questions of legal and political judgment into questions of trial technique, he has at least ensured that courts will exercise that judgment. Yet what substantive outcomes will judicial review of these questions yield? The answer to that question and the palatability of that answer, ignites an old debate.

1. Bickel Redux: The Virtues of Passivity in Foreign Affairs.—By raising the flag of judicial review and denying the difference between foreign and domestic affairs, Franck rejoins the great debates of the 1950s and 1960s about the role of the courts in a democratic society. He assumes Herbert Wechsler's mantle, arguing for an unqualified duty of judicial review.[28] In this guise, however, he must contend with Alexander Bickel,[29] who defends the political question doctrine as the queen of the "passive virtues" that enable a court to decide when not to decide. . . .

[Bickel's argument is] that the legitimate exercise of judicial review in a democracy rests on a court's ability to articulate the "enduring values" of a society. Thus legitimated, courts performing judicial review also perform a larger "legitimating function," both by rallying support for particular legal positions and by symbolizing the power and continuity of the Constitution itself.

Thus, courts must weigh their words. Equally important, they must know when to hold their peace as they wait for principle to ripen in the face of necessary political compromise. The political question doctrine is just one of a number of "techniques that allow leeway to expediency without abandoning principle." More specifically, political questions are questions about which we believe " 'that even though there are applicable rules, these rules should be only among the numerous relevant considerations.' " The possibility of a decision on principle exists, but it must bow to necessity: the necessity of national security needs or the limits of domestic political consensus.

From this perspective, little is to be gained by conditioning a guarantee of judicial review of foreign affairs cases only on the proviso that the courts give the political branches virtually free rein. Franck's German example is instructive here. Although it is true that the German Constitutional Court has on occasion been willing to give real teeth to its foreign affairs decisions, it has overwhelmingly tended to favor the Executive. Moreover, as Franck himself points out in arguing for special in camera proceedings and declaratory judgments, the German Court need not contend with the weighty responsibilities of superpower status. The temptation to rubber-stamp the Executive's foreign policy decisions is likely to be even greater in this country.

But if there is little to gain, there is much to lose. Justice Jackson spelled out Bickel's position with anguish and urgency in his dissent in Korematsu v. United States, condemning his brethren for stretching the due process clause to permit the internment of Japanese–Americans on military orders. He acknowledged the inherent difficulty of reviewing military orders. "But if we cannot confine military expedients by the Constitution," he argued, "neither would I distort the Constitution to

---

28. [See Herbert Wechsler, Toward Neutral Principles of Constitutional Law, 73 Harv. L. Rev. 1, 2–3 (1959).]

29. [See Alexander M. Bickel, The Least Dangerous Branch: The Supreme Court at the Bar of Politics 183–97 (2d ed. 1986).]

approve all that the military may deem expedient." Commenting on the nature of the legal process, he continued:

> [A] judicial construction of the due process clause that will sustain this order is a far more subtle blow to liberty than the promulgation of the order itself. A military order, however unconstitutional, is not apt to last longer than the military emergency. . . . But once a judicial opinion rationalizes such an order to show that it conforms to the Constitution, or rather rationalizes the Constitution to show that the Constitution sanctions such an order, the Court for all time has validated the principle of racial discrimination in criminal procedure and of transplanting American citizens. The principle then lies about like a loaded weapon ready for the hand of any authority that can bring forward a plausible claim of an urgent need.

Justice Jackson argued for a decision on the merits, on the principle that civil courts could not be required to enforce unconstitutional military orders. A majority of the Court was not persuaded, however. At such a pass, would not the political question doctrine have offered a second-best solution? The effective outcome would have been the same, but no principle could have been adduced " 'to expand itself to the limit of its logic.' " Conversely, would it not have been worse for courts to have legitimized Executive foreign policy decisions in the various cases in which they did invoke the political question doctrine? To have affirmed the use of the Tonkin Gulf Resolution as a legal basis for the war in Vietnam? Or the President's failure to consult Congress on the use of force in El Salvador, Nicaragua, and the Persian Gulf? To have sanctioned the Cuban expropriation of U.S. property? To have endorsed the President's unilateral termination of a treaty? To have authorized the U.S. government's blithe bypass of the arbitration provisions in the U.N. Headquarters Agreement? Indeed, a cynical view would suggest that courts are perfectly capable of rejecting the political question doctrine when they have made up their minds to decide against the government, whether the U.S. government or a foreign power. They are more likely to invoke it as an alternative to deciding in favor of that government.

Questions and Comments

1. Professor Burley asks whether, "[i]f courts *must* decide, are we willing to risk the resulting legitimation of a range of foreign affairs outcomes that currently remain contested?" Does her question assume that a dismissal on justiciability grounds is understood to leave foreign affairs outcomes as "contested" in a way that a determination of constitutionality does not? If so, do you agree? Compare her argument to Professor Tushnet's argument in chapter V concerning adverse legitimation effects of judicial review.

2. Note that Justice Jackson's *Korematsu* dissent argued, not for a holding of nonjusticiability, but for a decision on the merits against the validity of the courts' enforcing the exclusion orders. Recall also that Jackson wrote one of the concurring opinions in *Youngstown Steel*, rejecting President Truman's claims of authority under war-related powers to seize the steel industry. Yet neither Franck, nor Burley, seem to contemplate that abandoning the political question doctrine would significantly change outcomes in U.S. cases involving foreign affairs. Are there reasons to think that foreign affairs are different enough from domestic affairs to expect that courts will (should?) be highly deferential to other branches, whether through the political question doctrine or through evidentiary deference?

3. Under Professor Burley's views have the German Court's decisions legitimated outcomes that should not have been legitimated?

---

4.   POLITICAL QUESTIONS AND THE "LEGALIZATION" OF POLITICS

Michael Mandel, THE CHARTER OF RIGHTS AND THE LEGALIZATION OF POLITICS IN CANADA (1989)

Legalized Politics Beyond the Courtroom

The Charter means that more. and more political issues will be subjected to this peculiarly legal form of resolution. But it signifies an even more general ascendancy of the legal approach to politics. because the Charter*s impact goes far beyond the courtroom. As Chief Justice Dickson said in a 1986 television interview:

> The coming years will undoubtedly see the Supreme Court playing a major role in shaping the legal. moral and social contours of our country

Of course, politicians must now seek to fit their actions into forms that will pass muster according to judicial values, but that is not even the half of it. Earlier, we talked of the (carefully cultivated) broad public appeal of the Charter and that, too, will tend to enhance the spread of judicial ideas. But this new form of politics also has a great appeal for political actors themselves, be they professional or amateur, or on the left or the right. The beauty of the Charter from all these points of view is that it appears to *depoliticize* politics. In form, it replaces "conflicts of interest" with "matters of principle." It is easy to understand why this appeals to actors on the right, because it allows power to disguise itself in the abstraction of claims about rights. The National Citizens' Coalition's mortal struggle against all interferences in the marketplace are made, as we shall see, not on behalf of the big business interests it actually serves, but in defence of the "individual rights" of abstract classless "citizens." And the NCC's courtroom victories under the Charter are proudly displayed to lend credibility to its claims (*The Globe and Mail*, July 15, 1987: A3). In similar fashion, the multibillion dollar tobacco industry has tried to portray its all-out battle to protect its interests in "the most profitable consumer product ever sold legally" (Stoffman 1987: 20) as a battle being fought on behalf of the individual rights of all Canadians. A recent full-page advertisement against government regulation of tobacco advertising began with a picture of the Parliament buildings and the flag over this caption:

> *Many Canadians believe that banning advertising for a legal product is in violation of Canada's Charter of Rights and Freedoms.*

In chilling terms, the ad asked:

> If the rights inherent in the Charter of Rights and Freedoms can be conveniently trampled upon in the tobacco advertising issue, whose rights will be denied next? (*The Globe and Mail,* July 9, 1987: A11)

The Charter's appeal for professional politicians is only slightly more difficult to understand. One might be forgiven for thinking that politicians would be as jealous of their powers and jurisdictions as they are when they come into conflict with one another. But it turns out that they are often quite relieved to have controversial and unpredictable issues transformed into "non-partisan" questions about rights and about the correct interpretation of the constitution so they can be taken off their hands and resolved by the courts. In fact, politicians are increasingly orchestrating such resolutions themselves by use of the reference procedure. In the short life of the Charter, the Ontario government has already used this device twice. In 1984, it invoked the aid of the Ontario Court of Appeal in extending French language education rights by the ingenious device of referring to the Court the question of the constitutionality of both its current law (which it wanted to change) and its proposed changes. The Court then conducted its own public hearings and obligingly declared the current law unconstitutional *and* the amendments an appropriate cure for the unconstitutionality (*Re Education Act,* 1984). In other words, the Court helped the government defend its amendments by saying they were not only consistent with the constitution but were actually *required* by it. Naturally, the government did not appeal this "loss."

But this case was merely a warmup for the Catholic School Funding reference. The extension of full funding in 1984–85 to Catholic high schools, a bombshell dropped by retiring Premier William Davis, was an issue that divided Ontario right down the middle by religion and by ethnicity—but not by political party! For political reasons of their own, all three parties came out in favour of the $80 million per year enterprise that would cause mass transfers of school populations and weaken the public school system, even though the plan was opposed by slightly more than half the voters.... Consequently, it was by mutual agreement left out of all debates during the 1985 election. Instead, it was referred to the Ontario Court of Appeal. Once again the Court acted like a legislative committee, hearing submissions from 32 groups and individuals and deciding by the narrow margin of three judges to two that the law was constitutional and not inconsistent with the equality provisions of the Charter (*Re Education Act,* 1986). The expressions of doubt did not deter the government from going ahead with its plans, but they encouraged opponents, headed by the Toronto Board of Education, to pursue the case in the Supreme Court of Canada. That Court was ultimately unanimous in its approval of full funding—not that the answer was all that obvious in legal terms (see page

242)—with a majority holding not only that the law was *consistent* with the constitution, but that it was actually *required* by it. The law, said the majority, "returns rights constitutionally guaranteed to separate schools by s.93(*l*) of the *Constitution Act, 1867*" (*Re Education Act,* 1987: 59). The decision put an end to the organized opposition. Immediately upon the release of the decision, the Metropolitan Toronto School Board Chairperson said the Board was giving up a fight that had cost three years and $500,000:

> While we regret the (court) decision, we acknowledge the jurisdiction and accept the decision ... and we are anxious to continue our responsibility in providing a first-rate system of public education for the people of Metropolitan Toronto (*The Toronto Star,* June 26, 1987: A10).

Naturally, if the politicians were not going to debate the question before the Supreme Court decision, they were not going to debate it after. The 1987 election campaign was another one that avoided the funding issue. And it did so with relative ease. The Supreme Court decision was described as having taken "much of the wind out of the sails of full-financing opponents ... [T]here isn't something people can sink their teeth into any more" (*The Globe and Mail,* August 29, 1987: A2). And following the election, when flare-ups occurred over the mass student transfers, the Minister of Education could defend it against charges of "apartheid" by the fact that it had all been approved by the Supreme Court of Canada.

According to Professor Morton the reference procedure provides Canadian governments with "interesting political options in their game of Charter politics":

> ... there seems to be a growing trend of "issue avoidance" by elected political leaders ... the increasing political role of the courts under the Charter may come not only because judges arrogate to themselves the policy-making function, but also because politicians abdicate this responsibility (Morton, 1987: 51).

So it is a serious error to see the threat of invalidation under the Charter as placing the government and the courts in opposition. Nor is this an entirely new development. During the Depression, the courts rescued an unenthusiastic federal government from having to bring in an unemployment insurance scheme. During the constitutional negotiations of 1981, the courts provided a means of legitimating a constitutional accord which excluded Quebec and which avoided the necessity of a "divisive" referendum. The Charter and the courts will continue to provide politicians with a means of avoiding going directly to the people when there is no political profit to be made, or when the likely results are unpalatable.

So the attraction of legalized politics for the political Right and for governments is easy to understand. But what could it be for the Left? We cannot discount entirely the personal attraction of the Charter for politically conscious lawyers. Their jobs are considerably enriched when courts are made the locus of major political confrontations. No doubt some of them genuinely, if briefly, entertain the misconception we noted earlier, that Charter concepts are open-ended enough to be hijacked for progressive purposes. Just maybe, with enough ingenuity, preparation, and so on, important political victories can be won in the courts that cannot be won in the more familiar political arenas, dominated as they are by established interests. But the most important reason is the idea that there is something to be gained by going, to court even if you know you are going to lose.

Organizing political campaigns is a difficult and expensive business. Much of it is occupied with getting publicity. The press, dominated by big business, always seems reluctant to give publicity to left wing movements even when they have broad popular support, but especially when they do not. Politicians will always be counting votes. Legal action has seemed a way around these problems. You are guaranteed a day in court and the opportunity to make your case. Furthermore, the *form* of legal discourse, treating each side impartially and professing to be as blind as the Statue of Justice to political clout, appears open-ended enough to allow even the weak and unpopular to win. In court, the David and Goliath scenario always seems possible. Most lawyers can make almost any political case, no matter how weak, sound like a strong legal case and can do so in terms sufficiently removed from the predictability of everyday politics to make the press attentive. This is very hard to resist for groups on the Left. Whether they win or lose in legal terms, legalized politics affords them a platform to make their case to the world.

Operation Dismantle v. The Queen

One such group was Operation Dismantle, the Ottawa peace group that tried to stop the cruise missile with the Charter. This bizarre and ironic case is a vivid illustration of just how wrong things can go when the Left tries to appropriate legalized politics. In July 1983, the federal government announced that it would allow the American government to conduct a series of Cruise missile tests in Canada. Opinion polls indicated that most Canadians who had an opinion on the matter opposed the tests.... However, this popular opposition did not find a proportionate expression in Parliament where the two major parties combined to defeat a New Democratic Party motion against the tests 213 to 34.

Immediately following the government's announcement, Operation Dismantle commenced an action to have the tests declared unconstitutional as contrary to section 7 of the *Charter,* which guarantees

> the right to life, liberty and security of the person and the right not to be deprived thereof except in accordance with the principles of fundamental justice.

As one of the first overtly political Charter actions in English Canada on a matter of great importance and controversy, the action received an extraordinary amount of publicity. It started with the carefully staged filmclip of the footsteps of Operation Dismantle's lawyer heading into the Federal Court building to file the papers and it ended, almost two years later, with many filmclips and headlines in between, on the steps of the

Supreme Court of Canada building, with a speech to reporters by Operation Dismantle's president when the action was finally lost. The publicity was encouraged by Operation Dismantle's rather surprising victory on a preliminary motion soon after the action was launched. The government had applied to have the suit thrown out before trial on legal (as opposed to factual) grounds. Indeed, Operation Dismantle's legal case was weak. It came as a surprise, therefore, when Judge Alexander Cattanach, something of a maverick (the oldest judge in the trial division and the only Diefenbaker appointment) threw the motion out and held that the case had to go to trial *(Operation Dismantle, 1983)*. Cattanach's decision was very poorly reasoned; his major concern at the hearing seems to have been about the unarmed cruise missile "failing on somebody's head" during a test and despite opposition howling, the government promptly appealed.

With all the publicity, it was hardly noticed that the Charter action was only one of two initiatives spearheaded by Operation Dismantle against the cruise missile. The other was a proposal for a binding national referendum, launched right after the action, following Prime Minister Trudeau's statement that he would "reconsider" the tests if it could be demonstrated to him that a majority of Canadians were opposed to them. Trudeau said he "could not imagine" how this could be done outside of a general election fought on the issue of membership in NATO. Operation Dismantle thought that a referendum would suffice, with the simple question: "Are you in favour of the cruise missile being tested in Canada? Yes or No," and expressed its willingness to include a separate question on NATO membership. This was not its first venture in the referendum business; Operation Dismantle had previously arranged 132 municipal referenda on general disarmament questions. In fact, the organization's main goal for its seven years of existence was to have a worldwide referendum on balanced disarmament sponsored and organized by the United Nations General Assembly.

The proposal for a referendum on the cruise tests was announced at a press conference on August 2, 1983, in Toronto, chaired by Mayor Arthur Eggleton, who announced himself in favour of the idea, saying he would vote against the cruise tests but for membership in NATO. But a curious thing happened. The media, while salivating over the court case, was supremely uninterested in the referendum. Why? Because this was politics not law, and there was an almost complete lack of political support for the initiative. When Operation Dismantle polled all 282 Members of Parliament, only 18 replied. Of these, fifteen were opposed and only three were in favour. One MP wrote on his questionnaire: "This is pure NDP." He could not have been more wrong. One of the biggest blows to the referendum proposal was that it was opposed by NDP members on the recommendation of their disarmament spokesperson, Pauline Jewett. She had written to the NDP caucus warning of the "divisiveness" of binding referenda and the dangers of putting questions like bilingualism, capital punishment, abortion, and foreign aid to the people. Where the cruise missile was concerned, the electoral process was definitely to be preferred even to a nonbinding referendum:

Canadians at the next federal election can make political choices that will reflect their views and concerns about the cruise missile ... Canadians can, in fact, put a government in place, the NDP, that will refuse the cruise in Canada ... Elected politicians need a good shaking up and the government of Canada should be changed for the fight (Jewett, 1983: 3).

It was obvious to everyone that the NDP had no hope of forming the next government of Canada or of stopping the cruise missile tests in a Parliamentary forum against the combined opposition of the Liberals and the Tories. As the only party to oppose cruise testing, the NDP's self-interest in making a federal election the only means of expressing opposition to the tests should also be obvious. The principled nature of its support for the electoral process is also rendered suspect by its vigorous support for Operation Dismantle's court action, even to the extent of protesting the government's appeal of the original ruling. A victory in the court case would, of course, have bound Parliament to the decision of a few judges. When challenged on this point during a speech at Osgoode Hall Law School, Jewett's feeble reply was that "judicial decisions are part of our democratic tradition" (*Obiter Dicta*, February 10, 1984: 15). This sentiment appears to have been shared by the Prime Minister, who rejected outright a direct offer by the President of Operation Dismantle to drop the court action if the government would agree to the referendum. Trudeau, too, was happier to face the courts than the people.

Without institutional or press support, and embroiled in the increasingly expensive court battle, Operation Dismantle lacked both the resources and enthusiasm for pursuing the referendum, which it put on the back burner, never to take it off again. As for the court action, it quickly turned sour. The Federal Court of Appeal held hearings on the government's appeal in record time (less than a month after the original decision), and unanimously reversed Judge Cattanach six weeks later (*Operation Dismantle*, 1984). Each judge wrote a separate opinion, and numerous legal grounds were cited, including the lack of any alleged violation of "principles of fundamental justice" as required by the words of section 7 of the Charter, and the defence policy nature of the cruise tests which made them, as a question of "policy," a subject unfit for judicial determination.

A minor irony occurred when Operation Dismantle was granted leave by the Supreme Court to appeal the ruling of the Federal Court of Appeal in December 1983. This happened within one day of the group's announcement that its seven-year quest for a UN sponsor for the worldwide referendum had ended in success. Operation Dismantle's newspaper, *The Dismantler* (1983, Vol. 5, No. 4.), carried the large headline, "WE DID IT," to announce the event. The press completely ignored this announcement but made the Supreme Court's granting of leave to appeal front page news.

Operation Dismantle spent the next year and a half throwing good money after bad, in and out of court, while two sets of cruise missile tests took place in Alberta. The organization put all of its eggs in one legal basket—the Supreme Court of Canada. In January 1985, when the massive protest marches against the cruise missile had dwindled from the tens of thousands to the hundreds, Operation Dismantle's President, Jim Stark, announced:

> We made our decision a year and a half ago, that protest in the streets, letter-writing campaigns, telephone campaigns were not going to stop the cruise missile tests. The only chance of stopping those tests, short of the government seeing the light, was a decision by the Supreme Court of Canada. So we have put our eggs in that basket. (*The Toronto Star,* January 20, 1985: A3).

In May, when the Supreme Court of Canada put the action out of its misery and unanimously decided against Operation Dismantle, the group was reduced to trying to salvage something from its near two-year quest by proclaiming that the decision was "a victory for the strength of the Charter and the civil rights and liberties of Canadians" *(The Toronto Star,* May 9, 1985: Al). Why? Because the Supreme Court of Canada had recognized (though of course had not exercised) a judicial power to review Cabinet decisions on Charter grounds. This from a group that had alleged in its Statement of Claim that testing the cruise missile was a foot in the grave for all humanity! Similar congratulatory remarks were made by Liberal and NDP members in the House of Commons when requesting the government not to insist on its right to legal costs. A Liberal member characterized the decision as the "finest hour" of the Charter. An NDP member called it "a very important court action ... which established the fundamental principle that Cabinet decisions are subject to the Charter of Rights." The Prime Minister, in his response, agreed that the courts' new role made this "the kind of a democracy for which we are all thankful." Though the Government did ultimately forgive its costs, Operation Dismantle's lawyers were apparently not so generous with their fees.

Professor F. L. Morton recently wrote of the Operation Dismantle episode:

> While ultimately unsuccessful in stopping the testing, the litigation did achieve considerable publicity for the "peace movement." Such publicity and the legitimacy that it can confer was probably the objective of Operation Dismantle all along, and in this sense the case was a victory of sorts for the coalition (Morton, 1987: 40).

It is true that Operation Dismantle had hoped that its case, *win or lose,* would have an educative effect. And clearly Operation Dismantle got a lot of publicity from it (the peace movement hardly needed any). But what did it teach Canadians about nuclear weapons? If anything, that the cruise missile was not the catastrophe that it had been cracked up to be and that peace groups were not all that serious in their claims about the dangers of nuclear weapons. What else could Canadians learn from this newly famous anti-nuclear group that was now telling us that the power of the Supreme Court to review Cabinet decisions outweighed the threat from the cruise tests?

Certainly the Supreme Court of Canada's own reasoning did nothing to dispel this general feeling of security. A motion of the sort involved in the case, since it is meant to preempt a trial of the facts by showing it to be unnecessary. is always disposed of by accepting the plaintiff's (Operation Dismantle's) allegations of fact as true. The only question is whether, assuming the allegations are true, there is a case in law. But in *Operation Dismantle* the majority of the Supreme Court disregarded the rules and took the extraordinary step of expressing an opinion on the facts—naturally, without hearing evidence. Speaking for five of the six judges, Chief Justice Dickson ruled that the facts alleged by Operation Dismantle, and, as several opinion polls showed, accepted by millions of Canadians, "could never be proven." *(Operation Dismantle*, 1985: 488). The unverifiability of the cruise missile, which Operation Dismantle wanted to prove would render arms control agreements unenforceable, met with this response:

> [I]t is just as plausible that lack of verification would have the effect of enhancing enforceability than of undermining it, since an inability on the part of nuclear powers to verify systems like the cruise missile could precipitate a system of enforcement based on co-operation rather than surveillance

To the claim that deploying the cruise missile could lead to a "preemptive strike or an accidental firing," the majority argued:

> It would be just as plausible to argue that foreign states would improve their technology with respect to detection of missiles, thereby decreasing the likelihood of accidental firing or a preemptive strike

These conclusions were reached without hearing a shred of evidence, let alone any of the experts Operation Dismantle wanted to parade in court. Nor did Justice Dickson hint at any hitherto unknown personal expertise in the art of nuclear war or politics. Instead, he seems to have decided this as a matter of *principle* flowing from the juridical sovereignty and theoretical freedom of foreign states. No matter how predictable their actions might be in fact, no matter how many livings might be earned advising governments how other governments could be expected to react, in *law* they were completely unpredictable:

> Since the foreign policy decisions of independent and sovereign nations are not capable of prediction, on the basis of evidence, to any degree of certainty approaching probability, the nature of such reactions can only be a matter of speculation. . . .

Why would the Court take such an extraordinary approach? One answer might be that any other approach to dismissing the action would have limited the authority of the Court to intervene in political questions in the future. It was better from the point of view of the Court to decide the case on the merits than on any limitations on its jurisdiction. In fact, the majority took the opportunity to stress how wide its jurisdiction was, even going beyond the self-imposed limits of the United States Supreme Court under the so-called "political questions" doctrine:

> Cabinet decisions fall under § 32(1)(a) of the Charter and are therefore reviewable in the courts and subject to judicial scrutiny for compatibili-

ty with the Constitution. I have no doubt that the executive branch of the Canadian Government is duty bound to act in accordance with the dictates of the Charter.

I have no doubt that disputes of a political or foreign policy nature may be properly cognizable by the courts

Nor was there any difference between the majority and Justice Wilson in this regard. Like most of the Court of Appeal, she seems to have rested her decision on the failure of Operation Dismantle to allege the violation of some legally recognizable *principle,* such as equal treatment before the law, in their disagreement with government policy:

I do not see how one can distinguish *in a principled way* between this particular risk and any other danger to which the government's action vis-a-vis other states might incidentally subject its citizens

As for judicial competence in political questions, her opinion was an ardent, if unconvincing defence:

[T]he courts should not be too eager to relinquish their judicial review function simply because they are called upon to exercise it in relation to weighty matters of State. Equally, however, it is important to realize that judicial review is not the same thing as substitution of the court's opinion on the merits for the opinion of the person or body to whom a discretionary decision-making power has been committed....

Because the *effect* of the appellants' action is to challenge the wisdom of the government's defence policy, it is tempting to say that the court should in the same way refuse to involve itself. However, I think this would be to miss the point, to fail to focus on the question which is before us. The question before us is not whether the government's defence policy is sound but whether or not it violates the appellants' rights under § 7 of the *Charter of Rights and Freedoms.* This is a totally different question. I do not think there can be any doubt that this is a question for the courts *(Operation Dismantle,* 1985: 503–504; emphasis in original).

Justice Wilson can call what she's doing whatever she likes, but when the constitution is as open-ended as the Charter of Rights, the difference between determining whether it has been "violated" and substituting her opinion for the government's is just words.

To summarize: a group formed to fight for popular democracy on disarmament, in search of a quick legal fix for a complex political question, is swallowed up by the legal monster and spat out two years later, not only having been denied the day in court it sought, but also having its own case turned against it with no opportunity to respond except by praising the monster for increasing its swallowing capacity. This is legalized politics *par excellence.*[1]

Operation Dismantle was not the last group to use the courts to try to short-circuit the difficulties and complexities of ordinary mass politics. We

---

1. Almost needless to say, the Americans have conducted cruise missile tests in Canada each year since March 1984. Organized protests have been invisible during the last two.

will see many more examples.... And we can expect this phenomenon to increase, if only because, as we noted earlier, the various governments, obviously less than threatened by Charter politics, have expanded the funding of Charter challenges. Nor is engaging in legalized politics always a matter of choice. As Petter points out, a lot of the money being raised by groups such as the women's action group LEAF, both privately and publicly, "is being used to defend from Charter challenge legislation that is beneficial to women." But whether for purposes of defence or offence, the "money, time and energy devoted by such groups to the Charter are money, time and energy that will be taken away from lobbying and other forms of political action." (Petter, 1987a: 859). Russell, too, fears the "judicialization of politics":

> ... excessive reliance on litigation and the judicial process for settling contentious policy issues can weaken the sinews of our democracy. The danger here is not so much that non-elected judges will impose their will on a democratic majority, but that questions of social and political justice will be transformed into technical legal questions and the great bulk of the citizenry who are not judges and lawyers will abdicate their responsibility for working out reasonable and mutually acceptable resolutions of the issues which divide them (Russell, 1983: 52).

However harmful it is to Canadian democracy, it is clear that the legalization of politics has not "technicalized" political issues. As we have seen, the courts have taken their public relations tasks very seriously. Yet if their style has changed, the basic nature of what they have to offer has not. And if the world outside the courtroom is more receptive, it is not because of a spontaneous change in judicial style, but in the world outside the courtroom itself.

What has been missing from the discussion of technicalization and similar fears—for example, of judicial incompetence for the new tasks—is an appreciation of the extent to which the legalization of politics is not merely a phenomenon of changing forums but a change in the form of politics *whatever the forum*. What is missing is an explanation of why all this is taking place and why it is taking place now.

Understanding the Legalization of Politics

The Charter of Rights, in its substitution of judicial for representative for forums and of abstract/principle for concrete/policy forms of argument

In the aftermath of the Charter action, Operation Dismantle all but folded. After laying off all of its staff and moving to cheaper offices, it says it has re-oriented itself to less ambitious projects: "We are not trying to be all things to all people anymore" *(Fundraising letter,* January 1988). The peace movement has not given up on the Charter yet, though. World Federalists of Canada are co-ordinating a "Nuclear Weapons Legal Action," that will rely partly on the interventionist reasoning of the Supreme Court in *Operation Dismantle,* to have nuclear weapons declared illegal under the Charter and international law. No longer at the top of the list of plaintiffs, but supporting it nevertheless, is Operation Dismantle itself.

for the resolution of political controversy, represents a fundamental change in the structure of Canadian political life, a "legalization of politics." [Earlier] we reviewed the circumstances that brought us to this point: the overwhelming influence of the United States on Canadian life, and the solution the general formula provided the federalist forces for the specifically Canadian problem of Quebec independentism. But the phenomenon of legalized politics has spread far beyond the shores of North America and seems to be sweeping the Western industrialized world. It has even spread to the home of Parliamentary sovereignty, the UK, where a movement for an entrenched Charter has been gathering momentum for some time. So it seems reasonable to suppose that there are deeper reasons for the rise of this political form. In fact, the legalization of politics can be tied to important societal changes stretching back to the end of the last century which have picked up considerable steam since the end of the Second World War. Specifically, it is possible to understand the legalization of politics in the context of three interconnected contemporaneous phenomena: the expansion of the suffrage, the deep involvement of the state in the economy, and the increasing tendency to malfunction of Western industrial economies. Legalized politics can be seen as a defence mechanism developed to preserve the status quo of social power from the threats posed to it by these phenomena. . . .

Questions and Comments

1. Mandel's critique suggests that the Canadian Court's purported willingness to decide the cruise missile issue on the merits, albeit with the same outcome that the political question doctrine might require in the U.S., fosters the "legalization" of politics by encouraging relatively less powerful groups to focus on court litigation rather than political mobilization. Would *expansion* of the "political question" doctrine slow down what he sees as a tendency towards "legalized" or juridicized politics?

2. Consider as an alternative whether Mandel's underlying critique is that western liberal constitutionalism focuses on "abstract rights," rather than "concrete interests"? If so, would it follow that what the courts do matters only at the bottom line result?

3. Had there been no Charter in Canada, nor judicial review under the Charter, is Mandel suggesting that Operation Dismantle would have had a better chance for a national referendum on the cruise missile and NATO membership issues? Does this seem right? plausible?

CHAPTER VIII

FEDERALISM: POWER SHARING AND MINORITY PROTECTION

Federal systems are a subset of constitutional systems. Our examination of comparative constitutional federalism will focus on three main issues: the relationship between federalist structures and the exercise of political power, the possible uses of federalism to protect individual or minority group rights, and the role of constitutions, and constitutional courts, in maintaining balances of power, or promoting individual rights, through federal structures. What is the relation between federalism and the actual exercise of political power? What, if anything, does federalism contribute to protecting individual rights? And to what extent can constitutions, and constitutional courts, enforce or promote the power-sharing and/or individual-protecting goals of federalism?

The U.S. federal structure is regarded by many as an important contribution to political theory and comparative constitutional law. Justice Kennedy in U.S. Term Limits v. Thornton, 514 U.S. 779 (1995) described the Constitution as having "split the atom of sovereignty," creating a nation in which people saw themselves as citizens of both their state and of the larger nation of which the state was a part. The passage from confederation[a] to federation was a significant innovation of the U.S. experience. For European scholars, notable as well was the combination of a "federal system ... with republicanism, implying political rights for individual citizens." Thomas Fleiner–Gerster, *Federalism, Decentralization and Rights*, in Constitutionalism and Rights: The Influence of the United States Constitution Abroad 20 (Louis Henkin and Albert J. Rosenthal eds., 1990), (noting Art. IV of the U.S. Constitution, guaranteeing a republican form of government in the states, together with protections of liberty found in state constitutions as well as the federal Bill of Rights).

The federal form of the U.S. government is often contrasted with the highly centralized government that followed the other major revolutionary movement in the late 18th century, that of France. European thought emphasized the idea of "indivisible sovereignty," with a legislative power that essentially reflects the sovereign will and thus must control exercise of other powers. The French Revolution's emphasis on equality was conceived to require a national, and uniform, concept of citizenship, incompatible

---

a. A confederation is a union of states that join together and assume mutual obligations towards each other but in which the central government does not have a direct relationship to the citizens of its component parts.

with the internal differences associated with strongly decentralized federal unions.[b]

The federal form is one that many nations in the world use, including Canada, Australia, India, Germany, Switzerland, Belgium, Russia, South Africa, Nigeria and Venezuela. All federal governments involve some allocation of power between a national (or central) level government and governments of subnational units (states, länder, provinces). Typically, the national or central government has substantial powers in foreign affairs and military matters, but in other areas distributions of power can vary widely, as Professor Field's discussion below of Canadian federalism suggests.

Consider, as you read the materials in this chapter, the following questions (some drawn from arguments advanced by Fleiner–Gerster):

(1) Is the vibrancy of federalism related to the degree of democracy in each nation's internal structures? Fleiner–Gerster, at 22–23, argues that "only states with democratic internal structures can develop true federal structures of government. If one compares different federal states, it seems that the more power such states recognize for, or grant to, the people, the more decentralized they are. Switzerland, with its strong direct democracy on the national, cantonal and local levels, is much more decentralized than Canada or even Germany." (Recall the arguments of Justice Powell in Garcia v. SAMTA, 469 U.S. 528 (1985), and of Justice O'Connor in New York v. United States, 505 U.S. 144 (1992).)

(2) How is federalism connected to the separation of powers? Is parliamentary democracy less well-suited to a federal structure than systems where executive power is more distinct from legislative power? Can strong opposition parties in a parliamentary system provide a check on powers compatible with federalism? Consider in this regard the problems of instability in the former Soviet Union and the former Yugoslavia. Consider, as well, that both Canada and Germany are federal states with modified parliamentary democracies.

(3) Do federalist arrangements result more from pragmatic and historical considerations than from political theory? If so, of what value is the comparative study of federal arrangements? Tushnet's article below attempts to connect history and theory. Do you find it persuasive?

(4) Are federal structures, to the extent that they involve decentralized decisionmaking, in tension with the modern social welfare state, which some believe demands centralized decisionmaking? Does the social welfare state demand more than a national government with the power to (a) make interregional transfers to equalize wealth and (b) prescribe minimum social welfare requirements? Influenced by the social teachings of the Roman Catholic Church, the designers of the European Union have stressed the importance of the principle of subsidiarity, which prescribes that decisions

b. For a related discussion, see Guy Scoffoni, *Constitutional Equality and the Anti-discrimination Principle in France: The French System in Comparative Perspective*, in Citizenship and Rights in Multicultural Societies 127–40 (eds. Michael Dunne and Tiziano Bonazzi 1995).

be made at the smallest, most local levels compatible with accomplishing the Union's goals. What is the relation between federalism and subsidiarity?

(5) Does federalism prevent governmental tyranny and thus advance individual liberty? See New York v. United States, 505 U.S. 144 (1992). Or does federalism suppress liberty by adding to the number of governments with regulatory authority?

(6) Can federalism usefully address questions of minority rights? If so, what is the relation between federal decisionmaking structures for the protection of minority rights, and substantive provisions directly protecting minority rights (e.g., guaranteeing language rights)? Are there particular characteristics of minorities that can be protected through federal structures? Territorially organized federalism can protect territorially concentrated minorities. Political scientists have described what they call "consociational" government structures in which interest groups are represented in the national government. See, e.g., Arend Lijphart, Democracy in Plural Societies (1977). Do federal states provide useful models for consociational states?

(7) What do we mean when we speak of successful "federalism"? How would one define a "successful" polity? Does your definition require stability in the existence of the federal union? stability in the existence of the same nation, regardless of the degree of centralization or decentralization? Consider, in this regard, whether Canada's debate over the inclusion and status of Quebec is a sign of the failure, or the success, of Canadian federalism.

A. FEDERAL STRUCTURE AND POLITICAL POWER: U.S., CANADA, GERMANY, SWITZERLAND AND EUROPE

1. THE UNITED STATES

In the United States, Congress is given certain enumerated powers, e.g., Article I, Section 8 ("[t]o borrow money ... [t]o regulate Commerce with foreign Nations, and among the several States ... [t]o establish an uniform Rule of Naturalization ... "), while the 10th Amendment provides that "[t]he powers not delegated to the United States by the Constitution, nor prohibited by it to the States, are reserved to the States respectively, or to the people." As its Article I power to regulate interstate and foreign commerce has been interpreted in recent decades, Congress has power to regulate the wages and hours of workers engaged in manufacturing and production activities, United States v. Darby, 312 U.S. 100 (1941); the amount of wheat grown for home consumption on a farm, Wickard v. Filburn, 317 U.S. 111 (1942); extortionate credit transactions (both intrastate and interstate), Perez v. United States, 402 U.S. 146 (1971); and the salaries and working conditions of state and local government employees, Garcia v. San Antonio Metropolitan Transit Authority, 469 U.S. 528 (1985).

Congress also may attach substantial conditions to the receipt of federal revenues by the States.

Several recent decisions signal a halt in the Court's willingness to uphold federal regulation claimed to intrude on state government competences. In New York v. United States, 505 U.S. 144 (1992) the Court struck down a federal hazardous waste disposal law's requirement that states assume liability for privately owned waste in their states if they did not provide for a facility or other arrangement, meeting federal standards, for disposal of the waste. The Court found that this amounted to a "commandeering" of the state's governmental capacities, which power the Congress did not possess, and asserted that the Constitution of 1787 did not contemplate state administration of federal law (other than in state courts). In United States v. Lopez, 514 U.S. 549 (1995), the Court struck down as beyond the "commerce" power a federal law outlawing possession of guns near schools. The Court found no nexus to commercial or economic activity sufficient to sustain the law. In Printz v. United States, 521 U.S. 98 (1997), the Court held unconstitutional a federal law requiring local sheriffs to conduct background checks on gun purchasers, because the original Constitution did not permit federal "commandeering" of state executive officers. And in City of Boerne v. Flores, 521 U.S. 507 (1997), the Court held that Congress exceeded its powers under the 14th amendment in requiring, in the Religious Freedom Restoration Act, state and local governments to go beyond what the Constitution required in accommodating religious practices.

One strand in the U.S. Court's early approach to federalism that has been largely ignored in recent decades is the question of the motive or purpose of federal legislation. Cf. McCulloch v. Maryland, 17 U.S. 316, 423 (1819) (suggesting that if Congress was acting under the pretext of an enumerated power to achieve some other goal, Court would strike down the statute in question). Consider as you read the next set of materials whether Canada's "pith and substance" test is similar to the "pretext" inquiry contemplated by *McCulloch*.

---

2. CANADIAN FEDERALISM

Canada, unlike the U.S., combines a federal system (having 10 provinces and two territories) with a parliamentary system for the central government. Executive power is exercised by a Prime Minister and Cabinet, who hold power with the confidence of the House of Commons. The Parliament is bicameral, including the Commons and Senate. While the House of Commons is elected from single-member districts distributed fairly evenly based on population, the Senators are appointed, essentially on the recommendation of the *federal* Prime Minister.[c] While Senate assent

c. The two most populous provinces (Ontario and Quebec) each have 24 seats in the Senate, while the remaining provinces have between 10 and six seats and the two territories each have one seat.

to bills passed by Commons is required, its power is regarded as more nominal than real by some observers.

The distribution of powers between the federal and provincial governments is largely governed by the Constitution Act, 1867 (formerly called the British North America Act of 1867). When Canada adopted the Charter in 1982, in the same package of enactments it sought and received permission from Britain to fully "patriate" its basic laws; Britain formally ceded its vestigial authority to legislate for Canada in approving the so-called Canada Act in 1982.

For discussion of the status of Quebec, a central issue in Canada's constitutional history, and of the aboriginal peoples' claims to self-government, see below at Section B (1).

In the following article, Professor Field gives an overview of Canadian federalism from the perspective of a U.S. scholar. Her article focusses on three particular aspects of federalism: the scope of the national government's legislative power; the relationship between national and subnational sources of law; and the nature of the national judicial power.[d] She particularly emphasizes the apparent paradox that the Canadian Constitution enumerates the powers of the nation and the provinces, and purports to give the national government residual authority over everything not specified, yet the courts have been much more protective of provincial authority than has the United States Supreme Court in interpreting a constitution that purports to give the states (or the people) residual authority.

Martha Field, *The Differing Federalisms of Canada and the United States,* 55 Law and Contemporary Problems 107 (1992).

INTRODUCTION

There are some remarkable differences in the ways that Canada and the United States have structured their federalisms—differences that teach us not only about the two systems involved but also about the possibilities of federalism generally. The aim of this article is to provide an overview of this subject for the reader who is new to it. It will compare the role of the provinces and the role of the states in the federal schemes of Canada and the United States and will survey three main subjects:

    1. the scope of the central government's legislative power in the United States and Canadian systems;

    2. the relationship between federal and provincial or state law; and

---

d. In evaluating the legal forms of federalism, one could consider several questions, including (1) the allocations of legislative subject matter powers as between the national and subnational units, (2) the distribution of power to administer or execute laws, (3) distribution of judicial powers, (4) the role of the subnational units in amending the national constitution, (5) the degree to which the forms of self-governance of the subnational units are constrained by national law, (6) the role of the subnational units in elections or appointments of the national government, and (7) the financial autonomy vel non of the subnational and national governments (i.e., ability to tax, and spend). In a single chapter, only some of these questions can be explored.

3. some of the differences in national judicial power between our systems. This topic illustrates, among other things, the Canadian approach of negotiation between the branches—and between central and provincial spheres—in comparison with the United States's more legalistic approach and somewhat clearer separation of powers and functions.

II

THE DISTRIBUTION OF LEGISLATIVE POWER BETWEEN THE TWO LEVELS OF GOVERNMENT

One remarkable truth of the Canadian and United States federalisms is that each country has departed from the original understanding of the distribution of federal power as expressed in the Constitution. In both cases, the departure has been accomplished primarily by judicial interpretation by the nation's highest court. An irony, however, is that each system has evolved to be more like the plan for the other: In Canada, the intent, clearly reflected in the Constitution of 1867, was for the central government to predominate, but the Judicial Committee of the Privy Council (which was the ultimate judicial authority until 1949, when that position was inherited by the Supreme Court of Canada) interpreted provincial powers generously and federal powers with restraint, giving the provinces a much greater share in the balance of power than had been contemplated.[1]

---

1. The result was so counter to the original intention that an apochryphal story about the Attorney General of the Southern Confederacy, after its defeat, going to England and there winning the ear of the Privy Council for the "states' rights" cause, is a familiar way of explaining it. It is true that Judah Benjamin, who had been Attorney General of the Confederacy, went to London after the fall of the Confederacy and became prominent in the London Bar, but it is not certain that during the last 20 years of the nineteenth century he really exercised the influence over the Privy Council that is claimed for him.

For whatever reason, however, the Privy Council did depart from the Framers' conception of the proper balance between the center and the provinces. The Canadian Constitution of 1867 profited from its southern neighbor's example of a federal system and also, adopted in the aftermath of the U.S. Civil War, sought to avoid what was perceived as the mistakes of strong states' rights and the centrifugal force that had led to the U.S. Civil War. As Chief Justice Ritchie said,

[by] the constitution of the Dominion . . . the legislative power of the Local Assemblies, is limited and confined to the subjects specifically assigned to them, while all other legislative powers, including what is specially assigned to the Dominion Parliament, is conferred on that Parliament; differing in this respect entirely from the constitution of the United States of America, under which the State Legislatures retained all the powers of legislation which were not expressly taken away.

Valin v. Langlois, [1880] 3 SCR 1, 14 (Ritchie) (emphasis in original). Despite this intent, the Privy Council interpreted national power narrowly:

[T]he exercise of legislative power by the Parliament of Canada, in regard to all matters not enumerated in section 91, ought to be strictly confined to such matters as are unquestionably of Canadian interest and importance, and ought not to trench upon provincial legislation with respect to any of the classes of subjects enumerated in section 92. To attach any other construction to the general power which, in supplement of its enumerated powers, is conferred upon the Parliament of Canada by section 91, would, in their

The United States has moved in the opposite direction; here the constitutional plan was one of states' rights, but the result has been strong central government.

The degree of central government power is not the only difference between the systems. If anyone ever entertained the notion that there was a "normal" way for federalism to be structured, a comparison of the distribution of legislative power in the United States and Canada would dispel that notion. On one level, there are noticeable differences in where particular powers are lodged. Marriage and divorce and criminal law, for example, are governed by the central government in Canada but the state governments in the United States, while labor law, nationalized in the United States, is an area jealously guarded by Canada's provincial governments. Moreover, Canadian provinces have much more exclusive power over local commerce than U.S. states do. The central government in Canada does not have effective power to impose economic plans and solutions without the participation and assent of the provinces. The U.S. Congress, by comparison, has authority to regulate essentially all economic activity.

Even more basic than the different distribution of particular powers are the structural differences between the systems. In Canada, the federal and provincial governments are each assigned certain categories of legislation, to the exclusion of the other.[2] If the government to which the subject has been entrusted does not act, therefore, the subject goes unregulated.*

Lordships' opinion, not only be contrary to the intendment of the Act, but would practically destroy the autonomy of the provinces. Local Prohibition Case, [1896] AC 348, 360–61 (PC).

2. The central government in Canada was given important enumerated powers as well as the residuary power (unlike the U.S. states, which was given only residuary power). In § 91—the main section giving legislative power to the Parliament—29 enumerated powers are listed, and it is then provided that "any Matter coming within any of the Classes of Subjects enumerated in this Section shall not be deemed to come within the Class of Matters of a local or private Nature . . . assigned exclusively to the Legislatures of the Provinces [set out in § 92]." The residuary clause provides,

> It shall be lawful for the Queen, by and with the Advice and Consent of the Senate and House of Commons, to make Laws for the Peace, Order, and good Government of Canada, in relation to all Matters not coming within the Classes of Subjects by this Act assigned exclusively

to the Legislatures of the Provinces . . . . Id.

Section 91 also spells out that the enumerated powers should not be deemed to limit or detract from this broad power. The grant of residuary power—known as the peace, order, and good government provision ("POGG")—appears to grant the central government something like what is called the "police power" in the United States—the power to legislate generally for the public health, safety, welfare, and morals, a power associated with the *states* in the United States.

* [Editors' Note: For a discussion of how sections 91 and 92 of the Constitution Act, 1867, distributing powers "exclusively" either to the provinces or the federal government, have been interpreted to permit, in effect, areas of overlapping jurisdiction, see Peter W. Hogg, Constitutional Law of Canada 377–91 (3d ed. 1992) (discussing, *inter alia*, the "double aspect" doctrine acknowledging "that some kinds of laws have both a federal and a provincial 'matter' and are therefore competent to both the Dominion and the provinces").]

In the United States, by contrast, the norm is that the nonexercise of federal power to regulate increases the area for state regulation; there are few if any separate spheres in which it is constitutionally permissible only for states to regulate.

This situation of no separate sphere for state lawmaking evolved in part because the states were not given specific powers in the U.S. Constitution, but were left the residuary power. The scheme was that the federal government would have limited and specified powers and all the other powers would belong to the states. In the Canadian Constitution, the scheme was the opposite: the central government would have the residuary as well as specific powers, and the provincial governments' power was to be limited and specified.

In both countries the intent was that the government with the residual power would play the stronger role. The framers of the U.S. Constitution intended federal law to be supreme, but they also assumed that the subject matter of federal law would be limited, so that the residuary clause—"The powers not delegated to the United States by the Constitution, nor prohibited by it to the States, are reserved to the States respectively, or to the people"[3]—would have some content. The general lawmaking power thus retained by states, including the basic police power functions of government, were thought to have some significant scope. But because in the U.S. governmental structure the tenth amendment was only a truism,[4] granting to states only whatever power was not possessed by the federal government, expansions of federal power *ipso facto* cut down on what was reserved to the states. Eventually, federal powers in the United States were interpreted so broadly that little or nothing remained of the residuum.**

The obvious example of broad interpretation of a federal power having this effect is the commerce clause, giving Congress power to regulate interstate commerce. The clause has been read to allow Congress to regulate any activity that could have any impact at all on interstate commerce, leaving Congress free to regulate any economic activity it wishes and displacing any separate sphere for state legislative control of the economy. The framers could not have foreseen the extent to which Congress would be empowered to control the economy.

In Canada, by contrast, the clause giving the central government control over trade and commerce has been interpreted to allow regulation of only international or interprovincial trade. That narrow interpretation of the commerce power is part of a more general cutback on the powers of the central government.[5] Other legislative powers, most notably the power of

---

3. US Const, Amend X.

4. See United States v. Darby, 312 U.S. 100, 124 (1941) ("The [tenth] amendment states but a truism that all is retained which has not been surrendered.").

** [Editors' Note: Professor Field's article appeared just as the U.S. Court's revival of federalism was beginning.]

5. The Canadian provinces have much more control over local commerce as part of their broadly-interpreted exclusive legislative powers over "Property and Civil Rights in the Province" and "Generally all Matters of a merely local or private Nature in the Province." § 92 (13), (16). This local control has been found to exist even though one of the

the central government "to make laws for the Peace, Order and good Government of Canada" ("POGG"), were also narrowly read—artificially narrowly, and certainly more narrowly than the original framers had intended.[6] Indeed, the experiences of both nations attest to the relative unimportance of both constitutional language and framers' intent in determining results. . . .

The perceived problem is that in the United States it is only by default of Congress that states are left with areas in which state laws can operate. In retrospect, a structure like that of the Canadian government, which reserves explicit powers at both the central and provincial levels, might have better protected the states' rights that the framers envisioned. . . .

[T]he absence of any constitutionally mandated separate sphere for state lawmaking makes the U.S. states look significantly less powerful than their provincial counterparts. Although that is the popular view of this subject, a further comparison of Canadian and United States federalism may cast light upon whether this view is entirely accurate.

III

THE RELATIONSHIP BETWEEN FEDERAL AND PROVINCIAL OR STATE LAW

In the United States, the Constitution does not define the areas in which state law can operate; instead, it leaves that decision to be made primarily by Congress. While in comparison to the Canadian provinces the states are weak [vis-a-vis] the national legislature (except for their representation there), they are more insulated from national control in other ways. There is no predefined area in which state law can operate in the United States, but when it does operate, it is more autonomous and has more independent force than provincial law does in Canada.

In the United States, national courts sometimes apply state law, but they never claim to be its interpreter. State law is, by definition, what that state's supreme court says it is. However unreasonable a state's reading of its own law may appear to the U.S. Supreme Court, that law nonetheless

enumerated powers of the central legislature set out in § 91 is "The Regulation of Trade and Commerce" and despite the rules of liberal construction of central government powers set out in § 91 and described in note 2.

6. Of course, the central government is by no means powerless. Not all provisions have been read as narrowly as the commerce power and the POGG clause have. The spending clause in Canada, as in the United States, has been an avenue for centralization, and cost-sharing programs have allowed for central government influence even over areas the Constitution leaves exclusively to the provinces. Moreover, as Katherine Swinton discusses in her interesting article, the courts have accepted an emergency theory of the POGG provision, allowing the national legislature to use that provision broadly when enacting temporary legislation that might be thought necessitated by an emergency or crisis. See Katherine Swinton, *Federalism under Fire: The Role of the Supreme Court of Canada*, 55 L & Contemp Probs 121, 126 (Winter 1992). Nonetheless, the general situation in Canada remains one of strong provincial legislatures and, accordingly, dual sovereignty.

governs unless the U.S. Supreme Court holds that the law, so interpreted, violates the U.S. Constitution.

The position that state courts are the final arbiters of the meaning of state law was adopted in this country in *Memphis v. Murdock,* decided in 1875. Although the result was not required by the Constitution, and also flew in the face of the intent Congress appeared to express in the statute granting jurisdiction to the Supreme Court, *Murdock's* approach has remained in effect to the present and indeed is deemed one of the cornerstones of the federal system. Each year I discuss with law students whether the Supreme Court was warranted in imposing this system despite the apparent lack of legal justification, and the consensus often is that the rule that state courts are the arbiters of the meaning of state law seems necessary. Otherwise, how could the states have any control over the development of their own law? Indeed, what would the phrase "state law" even mean if the states were not to have the last word on what the law of the state is?

Here again the Canadian system illustrates that the United States's ways of doing things are not the inevitable ones. Nor are they the only workable ones. Canada has a system of provincial courts, which are in fact the primary courts in Canada. When it reviews their decisions, however, the Canadian Supreme Court has the final word in deciding issues of common law and also in interpreting provincial enactments. Provincial law is not separated from national law or from the input of national judicial decisionmakers in the same way state law is in the United States.

The United States system goes even beyond *Murdock.* In the even more famous *Erie R.R. v. Tompkins,* the Supreme Court ruled that lower federal court judges faced with state common law issues should not fathom their own solutions but should follow decisions of the supreme court of the relevant state. The concept behind Erie was the same as *Murdock's*—that to have control over their own law, state courts, and not federal, must be the authority concerning the law's meaning.

The Canadian system of allowing federal judicial input into the meaning of provincial law is something like the system that *Erie* overruled, the system we associate with *Swift v. Tyson. Swift* set out the pre-*Erie* system wherein federal judges decided for themselves state common law issues, partly because common law was seen as a brooding omnipresence containing one right answer to any question that each judge, state or federal, could independently strive to discover. Even under Swift v. Tyson, however, state statutes were exempt from federal judicial input, and state common law relating to real estate and other immovables was also exempt.

In short, while the Canadian model recognizes much more of a separate and exclusive legislative sphere for provincial lawmaking than the U.S. model does for the states, it does not grant as much independence to the provincial law that is thus made; Canada has more centralized judicial control of provincial law, and provincial courts have less of a separate sphere than provincial legislatures do, or than the state judicial system does in the United States.

This may tell us something about federalism. It certainly suggests that there are varied ways for the different levels of government, which are the essence of federalism, to maintain their significance. It may be that one reason Canada does not need a separate, more independent provincial law is that the Canadian Constitution leaves for provinces important spheres of activity in which only provincial law can operate. Maybe as long as a nation has one of these forms of strong state or provincial power, it does not need others for there to be a strong intergovernmental relationship—strong enough to satisfy the demands of a viable federalism. Even powers as basic as a separate sphere of legislative competence or the ability to interpret one's own laws are not necessary in order for governments to retain significance if governments have other important powers.

The U.S. states and the Canadian provinces achieve their power through different mechanisms. In the United States, states remain significant units of government because they have the significant power of a separate and independent state law over which the state has the final word.[18] Moreover, there is a large area in which state law operates, although the area is not predefined or protected from possible future congressional encroachment.

IV

SOME COMPARISONS BETWEEN THE CANADIAN AND U.S. JUDICIAL SYSTEMS

I want to compare the experience of our two nations concerning the judicial branch of government, and then to examine a few of the themes that pervade the Canadian system and that seem to distinguish it from that of the United States.

There are many levels on which to compare our court systems. In both systems, the Supreme Court has jurisdiction to review decisions coming from both state and federal courts, and has the power and duty—unusual even in countries that have constitutions—to depart from legislation that does not conform to the national constitution. Although the federal courts in Canada have been increasing in number and importance, they are not as important as the U.S. federal courts, and they also are not nearly as important as the provincial courts, which are empowered to decide all legal questions. Canada's federal courts, by contrast, do not have pendent and ancillary jurisdiction over issues governed by provincial law, so a litigant who wants a controversy decided in one tribunal instead of two must present the controversy to a provincial rather than a federal court.

Distinctions are often drawn between the Canadian and U.S. judicial systems on the basis of judicial activism; the U.S. system is said to be significantly more activist than the Canadian. It is worth noting, however,

---

18. State law is subject to federal constitutional law, and in that sense is within the control of the federal judiciary, but unless the state law is held unconstitutional, the state, through its legislature, courts, or other agencies, can define what the law is and what it means.

that there are ways in which the Canadian judicial system is more assertive than the United States's.... [Apart from the Canadian Supreme Court's power to interpret provincial laws,] [t]here are other examples as well. For one, Canadian courts reviewing the constitutionality of a challenged legislative enactment have the duty to examine the purpose and effect of the law and to uphold it only if "the pith and substance" of the enactment is within the jurisdiction of the enacting legislature. U.S. courts, by contrast, in most instances must accept legislation at face value and not question its legitimacy if there is any reasonable basis for upholding it. In this respect, at least, Canadian doctrine is more encouraging of courts' second-guessing legislatures. In some other ways, the Canadian Constitution gives the judiciary broad powers of decisionmaking (for example, the 1982 Charter's endorsement of affirmative action). Moreover, the enactment of the Charter, authorizing for the first time judicial review of legislation for violation of constitutionally protected individual rights, represents a relatively recent but extremely significant increase in the scope of judicial review, which formerly had been exercised chiefly in cases reviewing issues of federalism.

A more interesting comparison than the degree of activism in the respective judiciaries is the difference in the way the judicial function is perceived. Some precepts accepted in the United States as essential to the judicial function are not applicable at all to the Canadian judiciary. For example, the judiciary in Canada is explicitly given reference jurisdiction and the ability to render advisory opinions. Reference of questions can be made by the federal cabinet (which also appoints the judges). By contrast, advisory opinions are prohibited by the U.S. Constitution's limitation of "the judicial power of the United States" to "cases and controversies." Moreover, the opinions of the judiciary are not invariably final in Canada— they may be but one step in a decisionmaking process that also involves other branches of the central government, or even the provinces; in the United States, by contrast, courts are constitutionally incapacitated from deciding cases unless their decisions will be final. When a Supreme Court pronouncement is subject to veto by the executive and legislative branches, or merely expresses an opinion not necessary to decision of a concrete case, it is not within the judicial power and is an unconstitutional advisory opinion.

The most extreme example of the opposite doctrine in Canada is the override clause in the 1982 Canadian Charter adopting an approach that is contrary to anything in the U.S. constitutional scheme or experience. The Canadian Charter allows provincial legislatures to override constitutional decisions. They can provide that a particular law applies for a five-year period notwithstanding the Charter. There is a sunset clause, but the legislature can renew its override at the end of the five-year period. A province can insulate its law from a finding of unconstitutionality by providing in the law's preamble that it applies notwithstanding the Charter. It can also reenact the provision and override five years later.

The override applies in areas of fundamental freedoms, legal rights, and antidiscrimination.[27] The override procedure was adopted to resolve a political impasse over the adoption of the Charter. It was thought it would be politically costly for provinces to use the override, and thus its use would be minimal. In this spirit, Manitoba early said it would not use the override. The principal user has been Quebec, which has used the clause to back off the Charter, saying Quebec is subject only to the Quebec Charter of Rights and not to the 1982 Charter, to which Quebec did not consent.

In the United States, such an override scheme would be contrary both to rules about the finality of judicial decisions and to federal supremacy. In *Martin v. Hunter's Lessee,* the state of Virginia sought independence from U.S. Supreme Court rulings, and that position was seen as a fundamental challenge to our federal scheme [and rejected]. In Canada, however, this override scheme, combined with Supreme Court review of provincial law, carries some elements of giving the provinces the last word on national law, while giving the national system the last word on provincial!

Canada has no separation of powers doctrine as we know it . . . . In Canada, courts can perform "nonjudicial functions" . . . . Indeed, in Canada, the courts are part of the negotiating process and seem less separate from other branches of government than U.S. courts are.

The override scheme that Canada has adopted can be seen as an example of various branches and levels of government working out solutions through compromise rather than principle. Similarly, the Canadian Supreme Court can be seen as playing a negotiating role in the decisions in the early 1980s about how the Constitution could be amended, decisions resulting in the adoption of the 1982 Charter. In 1981, the Supreme Court ruled in response to references made by three provinces that a "substantial degree" of provincial consent was required to amend the Constitution. Subsequently the federal-provincial agreement of November 1981 was passed by the provincial legislatures, signed by all premiers except the Premier of Quebec, then passed by both houses of Parliament, and transmitted to the U.K. Parliament, which enacted it. In the meantime, Quebec directed a second reference, asking directly whether its consent was necessary for the proposed amendments. The Quebec Court of Appeal and the Supreme Court of Canada both answered that Quebec's consent was unnecessary.[32]

In many ways, the *most* basic theme about Canadian governmental structure, including federalism, in relation to that of the United States, is that there is a less-felt need in Canada for separation of functions or clear definition of boundaries. While Canada's provinces do have a separate legislative sphere, in contrast to the states in the U.S. system, in all other ways the Canadian system has significantly less separation of functions

---

27. The following subjects are not, however, subject to override: democratic rights, mobility rights, language rights, the enforcement provision of the Charter, and the sexual equality clause (even though other substantive equality rights, such as freedoms of conscience and religion, expression, association, and the media are subject to override). Canadian Charter § 33.

32. Re: Objection to a Resolution to Amend the Constitution, [1982] 2 SCR 793.

than our own. Not only do national courts review provincial laws, but the central government participates in the appointment and compensation of most provincial judges. Provincial governors also are appointed by the national executive and are removable for cause by him or her. The Senate is also controlled by the Governor General through appointment of each senator and one speaker, a process that may affect the Senate's concern with national issues more than regional ones. . . .

In short, both the law and the institutions of the Canadian provinces are less separate and independent than the law and institutions of the U.S. states. Indeed, the only separation in the Canadian system is in the legislative spheres of power of the national government and the provinces— the one type of separation that the U.S. Constitution, as interpreted, fails to create.

Moreover, the Canadian style of decisionmaking is more one of working things out through negotiation and compromise than one of finding the "right answer" to each problem or having one authoritative decisionmaker. Negotiation is a dominant form of the exercise of power in Canada, including negotiation between the central and the provincial governments. This practice in some ways treats the provinces like separate sovereigns whose consent must be obtained. Indeed, a primary forum for governmental decisionmaking in Canada is "executive federalism," whereby disputed issues are resolved through meetings and negotiations between the different levels of government.[33] Instead of dealing with economic problems on a nationwide basis through federal legislation, as the U.S. Congress does, Canada deals with these and other important and sensitive matters through negotiation, principally at federal-provincial conferences. This may be accomplished at special ad hoc conferences, or at conferences between the prime minister and the premiers, or at a departmental or ministerial level. The aim of each conference is to achieve mutual agreement— sometimes only between one of the provinces and the national government, or sometimes more broadly—on some problem(s) that gave rise to the conference. Negotiated agreement is what the conference must produce to be successful, but no agreement on theoretical underpinnings is required.

The Canadian attitude was well summed up by Pierre Trudeau when he congratulated the framers of the Canadian Constitution for "its absence of principles, ideas, or other frills . . . . "[34] In general, the Canadian attitude is that legalisms and legal analysis are less important than political flexibility, "cooperative federalism," negotiation and adjustment, and shar-

---

33. In the United States, there is nothing comparable to Canada's executive federalism. It may be that the existence of an executive that is responsible to the legislature (the parliamentary system), in contrast to the U.S. separation of powers between executive and legislature, makes executive federalism possible and helpful for Canada but impossible in the United States. After all, even if all the U.S. governors did agree on a position, or negotiated with the White House a particular compromise arrangement, who is to say their agreement would be accepted by state legislatures or by Congress?

34. Pierre Trudeau, *Federalism, Nationalism and Reason,* in Paul-Andre Crepeau & C.B. Macpherson, eds, The Future of Canadian Federalism 16, 29 (U Toronto Press, 1965).

ing of power. The United States resembles Canada in that it is not bound by the original understanding of its Constitution's composers. But unlike Canada, the U.S. power structure is based on legalisms, on a carefully worked-out hierarchy of rights, and not on practical stances like bargaining and compromise, to work out the bounds of central and state/provincial power.

V

CONCLUSION

In both the United States and the Canadian systems (unlike many other constitutional systems), there is judicial supremacy, but the systems are organized in different ways. Canada recognizes far more legislative power in the provinces, as a matter of constitutional law, than the United States does in its states (although through congressional inaction the states are in fact allowed to exercise many powers of government). There is no provincial law in Canada that is protected in the sense that state law is protected in the United States, because in Canada common law is national, the only provincial law is statutory, and the statutes are subject to interpretation by the Canadian Supreme Court.... In some senses, then, the provinces seem less supreme than the U.S. states. We next find, however, that after Canada's Supreme Court finds a law unconstitutional, that decision is subject to override by popular vote in any province. The judiciary is not accepted as the final arbiter, nor is the federal system. Several aspects of the Canadian system, such as the lack of independent state law and the existence of nonbinding judicial constitutional pronouncements, would be unthinkable in the United States federal system, yet seem to work successfully in Canada.

Enough has been said to show that the Canadian experience raises some questions about many of our suppositions in the United States about what a federal system necessarily entails. Federalism has many forms; moreover, the form a government adopts is not much controlled by its constitution's language or intent. Comparison of the U.S. system with Canada's also shows the United States does have strong states' rights, in some respects, stronger than those of its neighbor to the north....

The Labatt Case:

(Introduction by Peter H. Russell, Rainer Knopff and Ted Morton eds., FEDERALISM AND THE CHARTER 243–52 (1989))

In the Labatt case the Supreme Court rejected the trade and commerce power as a basis for federal consumer protection legislation. This decision indicated that the Court's majority was inclined to set very tight limits on exercises of federal regulatory power not aimed primarily at interprovincial or international trade.

Back in 1881 in the *Parsons* case, Sir Montague Smith referred to "general regulation of trade affecting the whole Dominion" as another possible application of the trade and commerce power in addition to the regulation of interprovincial and international activities. The modern Supreme Court's reluctance to give much scope to this "general regulation of trade" dimension of trade and commerce first became evident in the Court's 1977 decision in MacDonald v. Vapor Canada Ltd. There the Court unanimously ruled that a part of the federal Trade Marks Act establishing a national code of fair business practice was ultra vires. The application of the legislation to business throughout the Dominion did not, in the Court's view, justify federal legislation which, by embracing civil wrongs covered by the law of torts, encroached on provincial jurisdiction over property and civil rights. This was the first time since the abolition of Privy Council appeals in 1949 that the Supreme Court had found federal legislation unconstitutional. . . .

At issue in the *Labatt* case were regulations passed under the federal Food and Drugs Act requiring brewers using the generic term "light beer" to meet certain prescribed standards (e.g., an alcoholic content of 1.2 to 2.5 per cent). The Court decided, six to three, that the legislation was unconstitutional. None of the judges considered that the legislation could be based on the criminal law or the peace, order and good government powers. Justice Estey's majority opinion focused on his finding that the legislation did not in its pith and substance apply to international and interprovincial trade but to a particular industry which appeared to be essentially local in character. Justice Pigeon's dissent, concurred in by Justice McIntyre, was based primarily on the Privy Council's decision in one of the 1937 New Deal references which upheld federal legislation permitting the use of a national trademark for products meeting the requirements of a Canada Standard. Chief Justice Laskin's dissent went further. He defended Parliament's power to equalize competitive advantages in the national market by enforcing commodity standards. In his view section 121's prohibition of interprovincial trade barriers provided a constitutional "reinforcement" of such a power by indicating a constitutional intention "marking Canada as a whole as an economic union." . . .

. . . Observers originally thought this decision, along with *Dominion Stores*. would undermine a coherent system of national product standards to the detriment of the consumer, but this has not happened. The food industry has an interest in maintaining such standards because common standards facilitate a differential price structure for degrees of quality that are not evident to visual inspection. The industry has thus continued to support the standards. In addition, the impulse to cheat has been kept in check by alternative enforcement possibilities. *Labatt* struck down section 6 of the Act, which enforced the product standards directly, but left in place prohibitions of false, misleading or deceptive packaging and labelling. The latter prohibitions have been used to enforce the standards indirectly.

Labatt v. Attorney General of Canada

[1980] 1 S.C.R. 914 (Supreme Court of Canada)

The judgment of MARTLAND, DICKSON, BEETZ and ESTEY JJ. was delivered by

ESTEY J.: . . .

. . . The appellant challenges the constitutional validity of § 6 and § 25(1)(c) of the Food and Drugs Act and the regulations promulgated thereunder with reference to the production and sale of beer. Before embarking on a discussion of the constitutional considerations, let us examine the form and thrust of the Act and its regulations.

Part I of the Act is entitled "Foods, Drugs, Cosmetics and Devices." Under the heading "Food" we find four sections creating, offences such as the sale of harmful substances, adulterated food and food unfit for human consumption and food manufactured under unsanitary conditions. There is a prohibition against the labelling, packaging, selling or advertising of food in any manner that is false and misleading or deceptive; and there is a general provision applicable to the whole of Part I making it an offence to advertise food, drugs, cosmetics or devices to the general public as a treatment, preventative or cure for any disease. Then we come to § 6 in the "Food" portion of Part I of the Act . . . .

. . . In Part II of the statute, provision is made for the "administration and enforcement" of the Act, including the powers of inspectors, the power of forfeiture, the right to make analysis of substances. Section 25(1)(c) appears in this part and establishes the authority in the Governor-in-Council to pass regulations under the statute

. . . for carrying the purposes and provisions of this Act into effect, and, in particular, but not so as to restrict the generally of the foregoing . . .

(c) prescribing standards of composition, strength, potency, purity, quality or other property, of any article of food, drug, cosmetic or device;

The regulatory authority under subs. (c) appears to extend to the four classes of goods or articles regulated under Part I which include "foods" with which we are here concerned.

Under the authority of § 25(1)(c), there has been produced an elaborate set of regulations dealing with the preparation, manufacture and sale of the four articles or commodities dealt with in Part I of the Act . . . . The part of the regulations pertaining to alcoholic beverages with which this proceeding is concerned commences under the heading "Malt Liquors" with regulation B.02.130, . . . which prescribes the nature of "beer," its alcoholic content, and permitted additives. The other malt liquors described by these regulations are ale, stout, porter, light beer, and malt liquor. The only difference between these various malt liquors appears to be the alcoholic content, and "the aroma, taste and character commonly attributed to" them. As we have seen, the alcoholic content for beer shall be not less than 2.6 per cent and not more than 5.5 per cent by volume, and in the case of light beer shall be not less than 1.2 per cent and not more than 2.5 per cent alcohol by volume. It may be observed that § 6 was introduced into the Act in 1953 and § 25(1)(c) was expanded at the same time to its present form . . . .

What then is the constitutional basis for the enactment of the contested portions of this statute by Parliament? The possible origins of this sovereign power include the federal authority under § 91 of the British North America Act in respect of criminal law, trade and commerce, and peace, order and good government. I turn first to the criminal jurisdiction . . .

That there are limits to the extent of the criminal authority is obvious and these limits were pointed out by this Court in *The Reference as to the Validity of Section 5(a) of the Dairy Industry Act (Margarine Reference)*, where Rand J. looked to the object of the statute to find whether or not it related to the traditional field of criminal law, namely public peace, order, security, health and morality. In that case, the Court found that the object of the statute was economic:

> . . . to give trade protection to the dairy industry in the production and sale of butter; to benefit one group of persons as against competitors in business in which, in the absence of the legislation, the latter would be free to engage in the province. To forbid manufacture and sale for such an end is *prima facie* to deal directly with the civil rights of individuals in relation to particular trade within the provinces,

(*per* Rand J.)

The test is one of substance, not form, and excludes from the criminal jurisdiction legislative activity not having the prescribed characteristics of criminal law.

A crime is an act which the law, with appropriate penal sanctions, forbids; but as prohibitions are not enacted in a vacuum, we can properly look for some evil or injurious or undesirable effect upon the public against which the law is directed. That effect may be in relation to social, economic or political interests; and the legislature has had in mind to suppress the evil or to safeguard the interests threatened.

(*per* Rand, J.)

This approach to the federal authority in the field of criminal law was relied upon by this Court in *Dominion Stores v. The Queen* (judgment rendered December 13, 1979). That there is an area of legitimate regulations in respect of trade practices contrary to the interest of the community such as misleading, false or deceptive advertising and misbranding, is not under debate. In the statute now before us, the question of mislabelling arises only after the category of "light beer" is created and the specifications for its production are assigned. When all this has been obtained, the use of the words "Special Lite" by the appellant may be said to be misleading to the beer buying public. The contest, however, is not in respect of this second stage, but rather the first stage, that is the right in the federal Parliament and the federal government to establish the standards of production and content of this product. In any case, the first stage of the process does not come within the criminal law reach as traditionally described in the authorities. I can find no basis therefore, for this detailed regulation of the brewing industry in the production and sale of its product as a proper exercise of the federal authority in criminal law.

The jurisdiction of Parliament in matters related to health similarly has no application here. Parliament may make laws in relation to health for the peace, order and good government of Canada: quarantine laws come to mind as one example. The Privy Council hinted that legislation enacted by Parliament to deal with an "epidemic of pestilence" would be valid in *Toronto Electric Commissioners v. Snider*. But we are not concerned with such matters here. Where health is an aspect of criminal law, as in the case of adulteration provisions in the statute, the answer is clear but here not helpful. The appellant discussed succinctly in its submission to this Court another aspect of the "health" jurisdiction.

Furthermore the regulations under consideration do not on their face purport to be, nor can they be, connected or related to the protection of health since any such beverage regardless of its name having an alcoholic content by volume of not less than 1.2% and not more than 8.5% and otherwise brewed in accordance with the process common to all "Malt Liquors" is presumptively not a hazard to health.

One cannot successfully ground the contested elements of this legislation in the field of the federal health power.

By § 91(2) of the British North America Act, authority with reference to "the regulation of Trade and Commerce" was assigned without qualification or explanation to Parliament. Without judicial restraint in the interpretation of this provision, the provincial areas of jurisdiction would be seriously truncated. It is not surprising, therefore, to find the Privy Council stating within fifteen years of Confederation:

> The words "regulation of trade and commerce," in their unlimited sense are sufficiently wide, *if uncontrolled by the context and other parts of the Act, to include every regulation of trade ranging from political arrangements in regard to trade with foreign governments, requiring the sanction of parliament, down to minute rules for regulating particular trades*. But a consideration of the Act shews that the words were not used in this unlimited sense. In the first place the collocation of No. 2 with classes of subjects of national and general concern affords an indication that regulations relating to general trade and commerce were in the mind of the legislature, when conferring this power on the dominion parliament. If the words had been intended to have the full scope of which in their literal meaning they are susceptible, the specific mention of several of the other classes of subjects enumerated in sect. 91 would have been unnecessary; as, 15, banking; 17, weights and measures; 18, bills of exchange and promissory notes; 19, interest; and even 21, bankruptcy and insolvency.

per Sir Montague Smith at p. 112 in *Citizens Insurance Company of Canada v. Parsons*. (Emphasis added.)

Thus it is clear that "minute rules for regulating particular trades" are not within the trade and commerce competence. The statute and regulation with which we are here concerned purport to establish such a detailed single industry regulatory pattern. The judgment of the Privy Council continues:

Construing therefore the words "regulation of trade and commerce" by the various aids to their interpretation above suggested, they would include political arrangements in regard to trade requiring the sanction of parliament, regulation of trade in matters of interprovincial concern, and *it may be that they would include general regulation of trade affecting the whole dominion.* Their Lordships abstain on the present occasion from any attempt to define the limits of the authority of the dominion parliament in this direction. It is enough for the decision of the present case to say that, in their view, its authority to legislate for the regulation of trade and commerce does not comprehend the power to regulate by legislation the contracts of a particular business or trade, such as the business of fire insurance in a single province, and therefore that its legislative authority does not in the present case conflict or compete with the power over property and civil rights assigned to the legislature of Ontario by No. 13 of sect. 92. . . .

Reverting to the *Parsons* case, the trade and commerce head was there described as consisting of two branches. The first in the words of the judgment includes "political arrangements in regard to trade requiring the sanction of Parliament, regulation of trade in matters of interprovincial concern. . . ." The second branch is said to ". . . include general regulation of trade affecting the whole Dominion." The first branch is illustrated in the succession of cases dealing with the marketing of natural products commencing with *R. v. Eastern Terminal Elevator Co.* ([1925] S.C.R. 434), and continuing to the recent egg marketing judgment in *Reference Re Agricultural Products Marketing Act* ([1978] 2 S.C.R. 1198). . . .

The principles developed in the natural products marketing judgments only obliquely deal with the second branch of the *Parsons* description of trade and commerce, and hence are not of direct application here. The impugned regulations in and under the Food and Drugs Act are not concerned with the control and guidance of the flow of articles of commerce through the distribution channels, but rather with the production and local sale of the specified products of the brewing industry. There is no demonstration by the proponent of these isolated provisions in the Food and Drugs Act and its regulations of any interprovincial aspect of this industry. The labels in the record reveal that the appellant produces these beverages in all provinces but Quebec and Prince Edward Island. From the nature of the beverage, it is apparent, without demonstration, that transportation to distant markets would be expensive, and hence the local nature of the production operation . . . .

The first successful attempt to breathe life into the second branch of the *Parsons* trade and commerce description, is found in *John Deere Plow Co. v. Wharton* ([1915] A.C. 330). The provincial legislature had attempted to establish regulation in a limited sense of federally incorporated companies within the provincial boundaries. The Court determined that such provincial action was *ultra vires* as being an invasion of the power of

Parliament to regulate the exercise by federal companies of their powers throughout the Dominion. This subject should not be left without adding that the Court there found the constitutional basis for legislation authorizing the establishment of federal incorporations in the peace, order and good government clause while the regulation of their activities fell into the trade and commerce category. Viscount Haldane speaking in the *Wharton* case, *supra*, stated at p. 340:

> ... the power to regulate trade and commerce at all events enables the Parliament of Canada to prescribe to what extent the powers of companies the objects of which extend to the entire Dominion should be exercisable, and what limitations should be placed on such powers. For if it be established that the Dominion Parliament can create such companies, then it becomes *a question of general interest throughout the Dominion* in what fashion they should be permitted to trade. (Emphasis Added.)

To this date this is still the test in determining whether the second branch of the trade and commerce power applies; *vide* Laskin C.J. in *Reference re the Anti-Inflation Act*, at p. 426.

What clearly is not of general national concern is the regulation of a single trade or industry.

The section of the Act before the Court in *In Re Insurance Act 1910* provided:

> 3. The provisions of this Act shall not apply—
>
> . . .
>
> > (b) to any company incorporated by an Act of the legislature of the late province of Canada, or by an Act of the legislature of any province now forming part of Canada, which carries on the business of insurance wholly within the limits of the province by the legislature of which it was incorporated, and which is within the exclusive control of the legislature of such province.

Nevertheless the statute was struck down as an attempt to regulate a trade within a particular province whether or not the trade was also carried on in all the provinces. The businesses before the Court were national concerns operating in several provinces under a statute which exempted from its application wholly intraprovincial businesses. Thus it is clear that neither national ownership of a trade or undertaking or even national advertising of its products will alone suffice to authorize the imposition of federal trade and commerce regulation.

In more modern times, this Court in *MacDonald v. Vapor Canada Ltd.* struck down that part of the Trade Marks Act of Canada purporting to create a cause of action in connection with "any business practice contrary to honest industrial or commercial usage in Canada." Unrestricted geographic play of the provision was not sufficient to find legislative authority under the trade and commerce heading. . . .

> . . . As we have seen, the trade and commerce head cannot be applied to the regulation of a single trade, even though it be on a national basis,

and in the *Board of Commerce* disposition, the invocation of the trade and commerce head of federal jurisdiction is forbidden in the regulation of elements of commerce such as contracts, in an individual trade or concern even though the control was imposed in a series of separate regulatory codes each purporting to regulate a separate trade or industry....

In the result, the trade and commerce power has been rescued from near oblivion following the *Citizens Insurance* case, by the extension or development of the *obiter* or afterthought of Sir Montague Smith in that case. The application of the power to this stage in our constitutional development finds illustration firstly in general regulation of an element of trade such as the regulation of federal incorporations. With respect to legislation relating to the support, control or regulation of the various levels or components in the marketing cycle of natural products, the provincial authority is *prima facie* qualified to legislate with reference to production and the federal Parliament with reference to marketing in the international and interprovincial levels of trade. In between, the success or failure of the legislator depends upon whether the pith and substance or primary objective of the statute or regulation is related to the heads of power of the legislative authority in question. Incidental effect on the other legislative sphere will no longer necessarily doom the statute to failure. Several indicia of the proper tests have evolved. For example, if contractual rights within the province are the object of the proposed regulation, the province has the authority. On the other hand, if regulation of the flow in extraprovincial channels of trade is the object, then the federal statute will be valid. Between these spectrum ends, the shadings cannot be foretold in anything approaching a constitutional formula. The majority of the illustrated tests thus far encountered are largely in the distribution, and not the production, of farm products. Here, however, we are concerned with the proper regulatory authority in connection with the production process of a single industry and, to some extent, with the sale of its products, the latter being concerned largely with the use of labels or identification. Nowhere are the impugned statutory regulations or provisions concerned with the control or regulation of the extraprovincial distribution of these products or their movement through any channels of trade. On the contrary, their main purpose is the regulation of the brewing process itself by means of a "legal recipe," as counsel for the appellant put it. Indeed, if the industry is substantially local in character, as seems to be the case from the sparse record before the court, the regulations are, in fact, confined to the regulation of a trade within a province.

In the end, the effort of the respondent here is simply to build into these regulations a validity essentially founded upon the embryonic definition of the application of the trade and commerce heading in the *Citizens Insurance* case. That observation and the subsequent references thereto are all predicated upon the requirement that the purported trade and commerce legislation affected industry and commerce at large or in a sweeping, general sense. In the context of the Food and Drugs Act, it follows that even if this statute were to cover a substantial portion of Canadian economic activity, one industry or trade at a time, by a varying array of regulations or trade codes applicable to each individual sector, there would not, in the result, be at law a regulation of trade and commerce in the sweeping general sense contemplated in the *Citizens Insurance* case. That, in my view, is the heart and core of the problem confronting the respondent in this appeal. Thus the provisions regulating malt liquors relate either to a single industry or a sector thereof, while other regulations appear to concern themselves in a similar way with other individual industries; the former being condemned by the *Citizens Insurance* case, and the latter does not rescue the malt liquor regulations by reason of the *Board of Commerce* case.

I conclude, therefore, in this part, that the impugned sections as they relate to malt liquors cannot be founded in the trade and commerce head of jurisdiction.

There remains to be examined the peace, order and good government clause in § 91 as the basis for these federal regulations. This subject has already been adverted to above in connection with the health aspect of this statute. The principal authorities dealing with the range of the federal jurisdiction under this heading are illustrated by:

(1) *Fort Frances Pulp and Paper Co. v. Manitoba Free Press*, basing the federal competence on the existence of a national emergency;

(2) The *Radio Reference* and the *Aeronautics Reference*, wherein the federal competence arose because the subject matter did not exist at the time of Confederation and clearly cannot be put into the class of matters of merely local or private nature; and

(3) Where the subject matter "goes beyond local or provincial concern or interest and must, from its inherent nature, be the concern of the Dominion as a whole." *Attorney General of Ontario v. Canada Temperance Federation per* Viscount Simon, at p. 205.

The brewing and labelling of beer and light beer has not been said to have given rise either to a national emergency or a new problem not existing at the time of Confederation, nor to a matter of national concern transcending the local authorities' power to meet and solve it by legislation. This latter concept is the subject of analysis and review by P. W. Hogg, *Constitutional Law of Canada*, 1977 at pp. 259–261. That learned author concludes at p. 261:

These cases suggest that the most important element of national dimension or national concern is a need for one national law which cannot realistically be satisfied by cooperative provincial action because the failure of one province to cooperate would carry with it grave consequences for the residents of other provinces. A subject matter of legislation which has this characteristic has the necessary national dimension or concern to justify invocation of the p.o.g.g. [peace, order and good government] power.

I see no basis for advancing the proposition that the impugned statutory provisions and regulations as they relate to malt liquor find their basis in law in the peace, order and good government clause of § 91. . . .

For these reasons, I would therefore answer the following question in the negative:

Is it within the competence of the Parliament of Canada to enact sections 6 and 25(1)(c) of the Food and Drugs Act R.S.C. 1970, c. F–27, and are regulations B.02–130 to B.02–135 inclusive thereunder validly made? . . .

THE CHIEF JUSTICE (*dissenting*): . . .

The matter therefore comes down to whether this Court views the federal trade and commerce power as a sufficient support for the legislation and Regulations which are attacked in the present case. I would hold that it does, and, in so doing I would adopt the statement in the *Parsons* case, at p. 113, which envisages competent federal legislation by way of "general regulation of trade affecting the whole Dominion." . . .

In the *Board of Commerce* case the Privy Council indicated that it might be open to Parliament "to call . . . for statistical and other information which may be valuable for guidance in questions affecting Canada as a whole. Such information may be required before any power to regulate trade and commerce can be properly exercised. . . ." I do not press any perfect analogy to the prescription of common standards for an article of food which is produced throughout the country and which is also imported from abroad, but it does appear to me that if Parliament can set up standards for required returns for statistical purposes, it should be able to fix standards that are common to all manufacturers of foods, including beer, drugs, cosmetics and therapeutic devices, at least to equalize competitive advantages in the carrying on of businesses concerned with such products. I find some reinforcement in this view of the scope of the federal trade and commerce power in § 121 of the British North America Act which precluded interprovincial tariffs, marking Canada as a whole as an economic union.

The operations of Labatt Breweries and of other brewers of beer extend throughout Canada, and I would not attenuate the federal trade and commerce power any further than has already been manifested in judicial decisions by denying Parliament authority to address itself to uniform prescriptions for the manufacture of food, drugs, cosmetics, therapeutic devices in the way, in the case of beer, of standards for its production and distribution according to various alcoholic strengths under labels appropriate to the governing regulations. . . .

The Crown Zellerbach Case:

Introduction by Peter H. Russell, Rainer Knopff, and Ted Morton eds., FEDERALISM AND THE CHARTER 273–88 (1989)

Constitutional interpretation never stands still—for long. In the *Anti-Inflation Reference* the Court's majority supported Justice Beetz's view that the peace, order and good government power could serve as a constitutional basis only for (i) temporary legislation dealing with a national emergency, or (ii) legislation dealing with "distinct subject matters which do not fall within any of the enumerated heads of § 92 and which, by nature, are of national concern". Subsequent decisions indicated that this second use of peace, order and good government might be wide enough to accommodate a "provincial inability" test which would justify federal legislation if it could be established that a particular problem required national treatment unobtainable through provincial co-operation. In *Crown Zellerbach*, the Court, for the first time, used this test to uphold federal legislation.

The issue in the case was whether federal legislation regulating dumping in the sea could apply to waters well within provincial territory. In defending this application of the legislation the federal government relied primarily not on specific heads of power dealing with matters such as navigation and fisheries but on its general power to legislate for the peace, order and good government of Canada. The federal government was successful in persuading a plurality of judges (four out of seven) that controlling marine pollution is one of those problems which from a functional point of view is indivisible and therefore a justifiable use of the peace, order and good government power. The dissenting judges saw no evidence that in order to deal effectively with ocean pollution Parliament had to claim a plenary power to control the dumping of any substance in provincial waters. They are clearly much more cautious about employing a functional test to justify the use of peace, order and good government in areas normally under provincial jurisdiction. . . .

Regina v. Crown Zellerbach Canada Ltd.

[1988] 1 S.C.R. 401 (Supreme Court of Canada)

SUMMARY: The accused was charged with breach of § 4(1) of the Ocean Dumping Control Act, S.C. 1974–75–76, c. 55, which provides that no person shall dump except in accordance with the terms and conditions of a permit. Dumping is defined by § 2 of the Act as any deliberate disposal from any manmade structure at sea of any substance, and sea is defined by § 2 of the Act to include the internal waters of Canada other than inland waters. The evidence indicated that the accused had caused woodwaste to be dumped into the waters of Beaver Cove, a place within the Province of British Columbia. There was no evidence that the dumping had affected any marine life. The trial judge dismissed the charges on the ground that § 4(1) was ultra vires Parliament. An appeal by the Crown from this decision was dismissed by the British Columbia Court of Appeal....

LE DAIN J. [joined by DICKSON C.J., McINTYRE, and WILSON, JJ.]:—The question raised by this appeal is whether federal legislative jurisdiction to regulate the dumping of substances at sea, as a measure for the prevention of marine pollution, extends to the regulation of dumping in provincial marine waters. In issue is the validity of § 4(1) of the Ocean Dumping

Control Act, S.C. 1974–75–76, c. 55, which prohibits the dumping of any substance at sea except in accordance with the terms and conditions of a permit, the sea being defined for the purposes of the Act as including the internal waters of Canada other than fresh waters. . . .

. . . The respondent carries on logging operations on Vancouver Island in connection with its forest products business in British Columbia and maintains a log dump on a water lot leased from the provincial Crown for the purpose of log booming and storage in Beaver Cove, off Johnstone Strait, on the north-east side of Vancouver Island. The waters of Beaver Cove are *inter fauces terrae*, or as put in the stated case, "Beaver Cove is of such size that a person standing on the shoreline of either side of Beaver Cove can easily and reasonably discern between shore and shore of Beaver Cove." On August 16 and 17, 1980, the respondent, using an 80-foot crane operating from a moored scow, dredged woodwaste from the ocean floor immediately adjacent to the shoreline at the site of its log dump in Beaver Cove and deposited it in the deeper waters of the cove approximately 60 to 80 feet seaward of where the woodwaste had been dredged. The purpose of the dredging and dumping was to allow a new A-frame structure for log dumping to be floated on a barge to the shoreline for installation there and to give clearance for the dumping of bundled logs from the A-frame structure into the waters of the log dump area. The woodwaste consisted of waterlogged logging debris such as bark, wood and slabs. There is no evidence of any dispersal of the woodwaste or any effect on navigation or marine life. . . .

. . . [T]he Attorney-General of Canada [contended] that the control of dumping in provincial marine waters, for the reasons indicated in the Act, was part of a single matter of national concern or dimension which fell within the federal peace, order and good government power. He characterized this matter as the prevention of ocean or marine pollution. His reliance on the specific heads of federal jurisdiction with respect to navigation and shipping and seacoast and inland fisheries, as well as others of a maritime nature, was rather as indicating, in his submission, the scope that should be assigned to federal jurisdiction under the peace, order and good government power to regulate the dumping of substances for the prevention of marine pollution. . . .

It is necessary then to consider the national dimensions or national concern doctrine (as it is now generally referred to) of the federal peace, order and good government power as a possible basis for the constitutional validity of § 4(1) of the Act, as applied to the control of dumping in provincial marine waters.

The national concern doctrine was suggested by Lord Watson in the *Local Prohibition* case (A.-G. Ont. v. A.-G. Can., [1896] A.C. 348) and given its modern formulation by Viscount Simon in *A.-G. Ont. v. Canada Temperance Federation* [1946], 85 C.C.C. 225. In Local Prohibition, Lord Watson said at p. 361:

> Their Lordships do not doubt that some matters, in their origin local and provincial, might attain such dimensions as to affect the body

politic of the Dominion, and to justify the Canadian Parliament in passing laws for their regulation or abolition in the interest of the Dominion. But great caution must be observed in distinguishing between that which is local or provincial and therefore within the jurisdiction of the provincial legislatures, and that which has ceased to be merely local or provincial, and has become matter of national concern, in such sense as to bring it within the jurisdiction of the Parliament of Canada.

In *Canada Temperance Federation*, Viscount Simon said at pp. 230–1 C.C.C.

> In their Lordships' opinion, the true test must be found in the real subject-matter of the legislation: if it is such that it goes beyond local or provincial concern or interests and must from its inherent nature be the concern of the Dominion as a whole (as for example in the *Aeronautics* case [*Re Aerial Navigation, A.-G. Can. v. A.-G. Ont.,* [1932]], 1 D.L.R. 58, and the *Radio* case [*Re Regulation & Control of Radio Communication, A.-G. Que. v. A.-G. Can.,* [1932]], 2 D.L.R. 81, A.C. 304, 39 C.R.C. 49), then it will fall within the competence of the Dominion Parliament as a matter affecting the peace, order and good government of Canada, though it may in another aspect touch upon matters specially reserved to the provincial legislatures. War and pestilence, no doubt, are instances; so too may be the drink or drug traffic, or the carrying of arms. In *Russell v. The Queen*, Sir Montague Smith gave as an instance of valid Dominion legislation a law which prohibited or restricted the sale or exposure of cattle having a contagious disease. Nor is the validity of the legislation, when due to its inherent nature, affected because there may still be room for enactments by a provincial legislature dealing with an aspect of the same subject in so far as it specially affects that province....

In *Labatt Breweries*, in which a majority of the full court held that certain provisions of the Food and Drugs Act and regulations thereunder were ultra vires, Estey J., with whom Martland, Dickson and Beetz JJ. concurred, had occasion to consider the peace, order and good government power as a possible basis of validity. He summed up the doctrine with respect to that basis of federal legislative jurisdiction as falling into three categories: (a) the cases "basing the federal competence on the existence of a national emergency"; (b) the cases in which "federal competence arose because the subject matter did not exist at the time of Confederation and clearly cannot be put into the class of matters of a merely local or private nature", of which aeronautics and radio were cited as examples; and (c) the cases in which "the subject matter 'goes beyond local or provincial concern or interest and must, from its inherent nature, be the concern of the Dominion as a whole' ", citing *Canada Temperance Federation*. Thus Estey J. saw the national concern doctrine enunciated in *Canada Temperance Federation* as covering the case, not of a new subject-matter which did not exist at Confederation, but of one that may have begun as a matter of a local or provincial concern but had become one of national concern. He referred to that category as "a matter of national concern transcending the local authorities' power to meet and solve it by legislation", and quoted in support of this statement of the test a passage from Professor Hogg's Constitutional Law of Canada (1977), p. 261, in which it was said that "the most important element of national dimension or national concern is a need for one national law which cannot realistically be satisfied by cooperative provincial action because the failure of one province to cooperate would carry with it grave consequences for the residents of other provinces". . . .

From this survey of the opinion expressed in this court concerning the national concern doctrine of the federal peace, order and good government power I draw the following conclusions as to what now appears to be firmly established:

> 1. The national concern doctrine is separate and distinct from the national emergency doctrine of the peace, order and good government power, which is chiefly distinguishable by the fact that it provides a constitutional basis for what is necessarily legislation of a temporary nature.

> 2. The national concern doctrine applies to both new matters which did not exist at Confederation and to matters which, although originally matters of a local or private nature in a province, have since, in the absence of national emergency, become matters of national concern.

> 3. For a matter to qualify as a matter of national concern in either sense it must have a singleness, distinctiveness and indivisibility that clearly distinguishes it from matters of provincial concern and a scale of impact on provincial jurisdiction that is reconcilable with the fundamental distribution of legislative power under the Constitution.

> 4. In determining whether a matter has attained the required degree of singleness, distinctiveness and indivisibility that clearly distinguishes it from matters of provincial concern it is relevant to consider what would be the effect on extra-provincial interests of a provincial failure to deal effectively with the control or regulation of the intraprovincial aspects of the matter.

This last factor, generally referred to as the "provincial inability" test and noted with apparent approval in this court in *Labatt*, *Schneider* and *Wetmore*, was suggested, as Professor Hogg acknowledges, by Professor Gibson in his article, "Measuring 'National Dimensions'", (1976) 7 Man. L.J. 15, as the most satisfactory rationale of the cases in which the national concern doctrine of the peace, order and good government power has been applied as a basis of federal jurisdiction. As expounded by Professor Gibson, the test would appear to involve a limited or qualified application of federal jurisdiction. As put by Professor Gibson at pp. 34–5, "By this approach, a national dimension would exist whenever a significant aspect of a problem is beyond provincial reach because it falls within the jurisdiction of another province or of the federal Parliament. It is important to emphasize however that the entire problem would not fall within federal competence in such circumstances. Only that aspect of the problem that is beyond provincial control would do so. Since the "P.O. & G.G." clause bestows only residual powers, the existence of a national dimension justifies no more federal legislation than is necessary to fill the gap in provincial powers. For example, federal jurisdiction to legislate for pollution of interprovincial waterways or to control "pollution price-wars" would (in the absence of other independent sources of federal competence) extend only to measures to reduce the risk that citizens of one province would be harmed by the non co-operation of another province or provinces"....

As expressed by Professor Hogg in the first and second editions of his *Constitutional Law of Canada*, the "provincial inability" test would appear to be adopted simply as a reason for finding that a particular matter is one of national concern falling within the peace, order and good government power: that provincial failure to deal effectively with the intraprovincial aspects of the matter could have an adverse effect on extra-provincial interests. In this sense, the "provincial inability" test is one of the indicia for determining whether a matter has that character of singleness or indivisibility required to bring it within the national concern doctrine. It is because of the interrelatedness of the intraprovincial and extra-provincial aspects of the matter that it requires a single or uniform legislative treatment. The "provincial inability" test must not, however, go so far as to provide a rationale for the general notion, hitherto rejected in the cases, that there must be a plenary jurisdiction in one order of government or the other to deal with any legislative problem. In the context of the national concern doctrine of the peace, order and good government power, its utility lies, in my opinion, in assisting in the determination whether a matter has the requisite singleness or indivisibility from a functional as well as a conceptual point of view....

Marine pollution, because of its predominantly extra-provincial as well as international character and implications, is clearly a matter of concern to Canada as a whole. The question is whether the control of pollution by the dumping of substances in marine waters, including provincial marine waters, is a single, indivisible matter, distinct from the control of pollution by the dumping of substances in other provincial waters. The Ocean Dumping Control Act reflects a distinction between the pollution of salt water and the pollution of fresh water. The question, as I conceive it, is whether that distinction is sufficient to make the control of marine pollution by the dumping of substances a single, indivisible matter falling within the national concern doctrine of the peace, order and good government power....

There remains the question whether the pollution of marine waters by the dumping of substances is sufficiently distinguishable from the pollution of fresh waters by such dumping to meet the requirement of singleness or indivisibility. In many cases the pollution of fresh waters will have a pollutant effect in the marine waters into which they flow, and this is noted by the United Nations Report, but that report, as I have suggested, emphasizes that marine pollution, because of the differences in the composition and action of marine waters and fresh waters, has its own character-istics and scientific considerations that distinguish it from fresh water pollution. Moreover, the distinction between salt water and fresh water as limiting the application of the Ocean Dumping Control Act meets the consideration emphasized by a majority of this court in the *Anti-Inflation Act* reference—that in order for a matter to qualify as one of national concern falling within the federal peace, order and good government power it must have ascertainable and reasonable limits, in so far as its impact on provincial jurisdiction is concerned.

For these reasons I am of the opinion that § 4(1) of the Ocean Dumping Control Act is constitutionally valid as enacted in relation to a matter falling within the national concern doctrine of the peace, order and good government power of the Parliament of Canada, and, in particular, that it is constitutional in its application to the dumping of waste in the waters of Beaver Cove. . . .

LA FOREST J. (dissenting) [joined by Beetz and Lamer, JJ.] The issue raised in this appeal involves the extent to which the federal Parliament may constitutionally prohibit the disposal of substances not shown to have a pollutant effect in marine waters beyond the coast but within the limits of a province. . . .

I start with the proposition that what is sought to be regulated in the present case is an activity wholly within the province, taking place on provincially owned land. Only local works and undertakings are involved, and there is no evidence that the substance made subject to the prohibition in § 4(1) is either deleterious in any way or has any impact beyond the limits of the province. It is not difficult, on this basis, to conclude that the matter is one that falls within provincial legislative power unless it can somehow be established that it falls within Parliament's general power to legislate for the peace, order and good government of Canada.

There are several applications of the peace, order and good government power that may have relevance to the control of ocean pollution. One is its application in times of emergency. The federal Parliament clearly has power to deal with a grave emergency without regard to the ordinary division of legislative power under the Constitution. The most obvious manifestation of this power is in times of war or civil insurrection, but it has in recent years also been applied in peacetime to justify the control of rampant inflation: see *Reference re Anti-Inflation Act*. But while there can be no doubt that the control of ocean pollution poses a serious problem, no one has argued that it has reached such grave proportions as to require the displacement of the ordinary division of legislative power under the Constitution.

A second manner in which the power to legislate respecting peace, order and good government may be invoked in the present context is to control that area of the sea lying beyond the limits of the provinces. The federal government may not only regulate the territorial sea and other areas over which Canada exercises sovereignty, either under its power to legislate respecting its public property, or under the general power respecting peace, order and good government under § 91 (*Reference re Ownership of Off-shore Mineral Rights*, [1967] S.C.R. 792) or under § 4 of the Constitution Act, 1871 (U.K.), c. 28. I have no doubt that it may also, as an aspect of its international sovereignty, exercise legislative jurisdiction for the control of pollution beyond its borders: see *Reference re Seabed and Subsoil of Offshore Newfoundland*, [1984] 1 S.C.R. 86.

In legislating under its general power for the control of pollution in areas of the ocean falling outside provincial jurisdiction, the federal Parliament is not confined to regulating activities taking place within those areas. It may take steps to prevent activities in a province, such as dumping substances in provincial waters that pollute or have the potential to pollute the sea outside the province. Indeed, the exercise of such jurisdiction, it would seem to me, is not limited to coastal and internal waters but extends to the control of deposits in fresh water that have the effect of polluting outside a province. Reference may be made here to *Interprovincial Co-operatives Ltd. v. The Queen in right of Manitoba*, [1976] 1 S.C.R. 477, where a majority of this court upheld the view that the federal Parliament had exclusive legislative jurisdiction to deal with a problem that resulted from the depositing of a pollutant in a river in one province that had injurious effects in another province. This is but an application of the doctrine of national dimensions triggering the operation of the peace, order and good government clause. . . .

In fact, as I see it, the potential breadth of federal power to control pollution by use of its general power is so great that, even without resort to the specific argument made by the appellant, the constitutional challenge in the end may be the development of judicial strategies to confine its ambit. It must be remembered that the peace, order and good government clause may comprise not only prohibitions, like criminal law, but regulation. Regulation to control pollution, which is incidentally only part of the even larger global problem of managing the environment, could arguably include not only emission standards but the control of the substances used in manufacture, as well as the techniques of production generally, in so far as these may have an impact on pollution. This has profound implications for the federal-provincial balance mandated by the Constitution. The challenge for the courts, as in the past, will be to allow the federal Parliament sufficient scope to acquit itself of its duties to deal with national and international problems while respecting the scheme of federalism provided by the Constitution. . . .

However widely one interprets the federal power to control ocean pollution along the preceding line of analysis, it will not serve to support the provision impugned here, one that, as in the *Fowler* case, is a blanket prohibition against depositing any substance in waters without regard to its nature or amount, and one moreover where there is, in Martland J.'s words, at p. 226 S.C.R. of that case, "no attempt to link the proscribed conduct to actual or potential harm" to what is sought to be protected; in

Fowler, the fisheries, here, the ocean. As in *Fowler*, too, there is no evidence to indicate that the full range of activities caught by the provision cause the harm sought to be prevented....

Le Dain J. has in the course of his judgment discussed the cases relating to the development of the "national concern or dimension" aspect of the peace, order and good government clause. ... [T]his development has since the 1930's particularly been resorted to from time to time to bring into the ambit of federal power a number of matters, such as radio, aeronautics, and the national capital region that are clearly of national importance. They do not fit comfortably within provincial power. Both in their workings and in their practical implications they have predominantly national dimensions. Many of these subjects are new and are obviously of extra-provincial concern. They are thus appropriate for assignment to the general federal legislative power. They are often related to matters intimately tied to federal jurisdiction. Radio (which is relevant to the power to regulate interprovincial undertakings) is an example. The closely contested issue of narcotics control is intimately related to criminal law and international trade.

The need to make such characterizations from time to time is readily apparent. From this necessary function, however, it is easy but, I say it with respect, fallacious to go further, and, taking a number of quite separate areas of activity, some under accepted constitutional values within federal, and some within provincial legislative capacity, consider them to be a single indivisible matter of national interest and concern lying outside the specific heads of power assigned under the Constitution. By conceptualizing broad social, economic and political issues in that way, one can effectively invent new heads of federal power under the national dimensions doctrine, thereby incidentally removing them from provincial jurisdiction or at least abridging the provinces' freedom of operation. This, as I see it, is the implication of the statement made by my colleague, then Professor Le Dain, in his article, "Sir Lyman Duff and the Constitution", 12 Osgoode Hall L.J. 261 (1974). He states, at p. 293:

> As reflected in the *Munro* case, the issue with respect to the general power, where reliance cannot be placed on the notion of emergency, is to determine what are to be considered to be single, indivisible matters of national interest and concern lying outside the specific heads of jurisdiction in sections 91 and 92. It is possible to invent such matters by applying new names to old legislative purposes. There is an increasing tendency to sum up a wide variety of legislative purposes in single, comprehensive designations. Control of inflation, environmental protection, and preservation of the national identity or independence are examples.

Professor Le Dain was there merely posing the problem; he did not attempt to answer it. It seems to me, however, that some of the examples he gives, notably the control of inflation and environmental protection, are all-pervasive, and if accepted as items falling within the general power of Parliament, would radically alter the division of legislative power in Canada. The attempt to include them in the federal general power seems to me to involve fighting on another plane the war that was lost on the economic plane in the Canadian new deal cases....

. . . All physical activities have some environmental impact. Possible legislative responses to such activities cover a large number of the enumerated legislative powers, federal and provincial. To allocate the broad subject-matter of environmental control to the federal government under its general power would effectively gut provincial legislative jurisdiction. As I mentioned before, environment protection, of course, encompasses far more than environmental pollution, which is what we are principally concerned with here. To take an example from the present context, woodwaste in some circumstances undoubtedly pollutes the environment, but the very depletion of forests itself affects the ecological balance and, as such, constitutes an environmental problem. But environmental pollution alone is itself all-pervasive. It is a by-product of everything we do. In man's relationship with his environment, waste is unavoidable. The problem is thus not new, although it is only recently that the vast amount of waste products emitted into the atmosphere or dumped in water has begun to exceed the ability of the atmosphere and water to absorb and assimilate it on a global scale. There is thus cause for concern and governments of every level have begun to deal with the many activities giving rise to problems of pollution. In Canada, both federal and provincial levels of government have extensive powers to deal with these matters. Both have enacted comprehensive and specific schemes for the control of pollution and the protection of the environment. Some environmental pollution problems are of more direct concern to the federal government, some to the provincial government. But a vast number are interrelated, and all levels of government actively cooperate to deal with problems of mutual concern; for an example of this, see the Great Lakes study in I.J.C. Report.

To allocate environmental pollution exclusively to the federal Parliament would, it seems to me, involve sacrificing the principles of federalism enshrined in the Constitution.... Indeed, as Beetz J. in *Reference re Anti-Inflation Act*, at p. 458 S.C.R., stated of the proposed power over inflation, there would not be much left of the distribution of power if Parliament had exclusive jurisdiction over this subject. For similar views that the protection of environmental pollution cannot be attributed to a single head of legislative power, see P.W. Hogg, *Constitutional Law of Canada*, 2nd ed. (1985), pp. 392, 598 . . . .

It is true, of course, that we are not invited to create a general environmental pollution power but one restricted to ocean pollution. But it seems to me that the same considerations apply.... [S]ubjects that have been held to fall within the peace, order and good government clause as being matters of national concern . . . must be marked by a singleness, distinctiveness and indivisibility that clearly distinguishes it from matters of provincial concern. In my view, ocean pollution fails to meet this test for a variety of reasons. In addition to those applicable to environmental pollution generally, the following specific difficulties may be noted. First of all, marine waters are not wholly bounded by the coast; in many areas, they extend upstream into rivers for many miles. The application of the Act appears to be restricted to waters beyond the mouths of rivers (and so intrude less on provincial powers), but this is not entirely clear, and if it is so restricted, it is not clear whether this distinction is based on convenience or constitutional imperative. Apart from this, the line between salt and fresh water cannot be demarcated clearly; it is different at different depths of water, changes with the season and shifts constantly; see U.N. Report, p. 12. In any event, it is not so much the waters, whether fresh or salt, with which we are concerned, but their pollution. And the pollution of marine water is contributed to by the vast amounts of effluents that are poured or seep into fresh waters everywhere (ibid., p. 13). There is a constant intermixture of waters; fresh waters flow into the sea and marine waters penetrate deeply inland at high tide only to return to the sea laden with pollutants collected during their incursion inland. Nor is the pollution of the ocean confined to pollution emanating from substances deposited in water. In important respects, the pollution of the sea results from emissions into the air, which are then transported over many miles and deposited into the sea; see U.N. Report, p. 15; I.J.C. Report, p. 22. I cannot, therefore, see ocean pollution as a sufficiently discrete subject upon which to found the kind of legislative power sought here. It is an attempt to create a federal pollution control power on unclear geographical grounds and limited to part only of the causes of ocean pollution. Such a power then simply amounts to a truncated federal pollution control power only partially effective to meet its supposed necessary purpose, unless of course one is willing to extend it to pollution emanating from fresh water and the air, when for reasons already given such an extension could completely swallow up provincial power, no link being necessary to establish the federal purpose.

This leads me to another factor considered in identifying a subject as falling within the general federal power as a matter of national domain: its impact on provincial legislative power. Here, it must be remembered that in its supposed application within the province the provision virtually prevents a province from dealing with certain of its own public property without federal consent. A wide variety of activities along the coast or in the adjoining sea involves the deposit of some substances in the sea. In fact, where large cities like Vancouver are situated by the sea, this has substantial relevance to recreational, industrial and municipal concerns of all kinds. As a matter of fact, the most polluted areas of the sea adjoin the coast; see U.N. Report, pp. 3–4. Among the major causes of this are various types of construction, such as hotels and harbours, the development of mineral resources and recreational activities (ibid., p. 3). These are matters of immediate concern to the province. They necessarily affect activities over which the provinces have exercised some kind of jurisdiction over the years. Whether or not the "newness" of the subject is a necessary criterion for inventing new areas of jurisdiction under the peace, order and good government clause, it is certainly a relevant consideration if it means removing from the provinces areas of jurisdiction which they previously exercised. As I mentioned, pollution, including coastal pollution, is no new phenomenon, and neither are many of the kinds of activities that result in pollution.

A further relevant matter, it is said, is the effect on extra-provincial interests of a provincial failure to deal effectively with the control of intraprovincial aspects of the matter. I have some difficulty following all the implications of this, but taking it at face value, we are dealing here with a situation where, as we saw earlier, Parliament has extensive powers to deal with conditions that lead to ocean pollution wherever they occur. The difficulty with the impugned provision is that it seeks to deal with activities that cannot be demonstrated either to pollute or to have a reasonable potential of polluting the ocean. The prohibition applies to an inert substance regarding which there is no proof that it either moves or pollutes. The prohibition in fact would apply to the moving of rock from one area of provincial property to another. I cannot accept that the federal Parliament has such wide legislative power over local matters having local import taking place on provincially owned property. The prohibition in essence constitutes an impermissible attempt to control activities on property held to be provincial in *Reference re Ownership of Bed of Strait of Georgia*. It may well be that the motive for enacting the provision is to prevent ocean pollution, but as Beetz J. underlines in *Reference re Anti-Inflation Act*. Parliament cannot do this by attempting to regulate a local industry, although it can, of course, regulate the activities of such an industry that fall within federal power, whether such activities are expressly encompassed within a specific head of power, e.g., navigation, or affect areas of federal concern, e.g., health under the criminal law power, or cause pollution to those parts of the sea under federal jurisdiction. But here the provision simply overreaches. In its terms, it encompasses activities—depositing innocuous substances into provincial waters by local undertakings on provincial lands—that fall within the exclusive legislative jurisdiction of the province. . . .

Questions and Comments

1. Why is the national consumer protection statute in *Labatt* not a proper exercise of the national power over trade and commerce? Why is it not a proper exercise of any other national powers? Note that uniform national labelling apparently persists in Canada, because of industry pressures and the availability of "alternative enforcement possibilities." Can you draw any—admittedly speculative—conclusions from that outcome?

2. Compare the Canadian cases with Hodel v. Virginia Surface Mining & Reclamation Association, 452 U.S. 264 (1981) (upholding federal regulation of strip mining operations). Exemplary of the highly deferential review that characterized the U.S. Court's decisions on federalism limits on congressional power from the late New Deal through the early 1990s is the majority opinion: "when Congress has determined that an activity affects

interstate commerce the court need inquire only whether the finding is rational." That "rational basis" standard was easily met, in the Court's view, by findings in the legislative history, discussed by the Court, of widespread environmental damage from stripmining, including reduced recreational values, killing of fish, impaired water supply, increased floods, and higher operating costs for commercial waterway users. 452 U.S. at 280. Given those findings, the Court could not "say that Congress did not have a rational basis for concluding that surface coal mining has substantial effects on interstate commerce." The Court also noted Congress' finding that nationwide standards for surface mining were needed " 'to insure that competition in interstate commerce among sellers of coal produced in different states will not be used to undermine the ability of the several states to improve and maintain adequate standards on coal mining operations within their borders.' The prevention of this sort of destructive interstate competition is a traditional role for congressional action under the commerce clause."

Justice Rehnquist wrote separately, though he concurred in the Court's judgment. Asserting a more limited view of Congress' power, he wrote,

> [It] would be a mistake to conclude that Congress' power to regulate ... [is] unlimited. Some activities may be so private or local in nature that they simply may not be *in* commerce. Nor is it sufficient that the person or activity reached have *some* nexus with interstate commerce. Our cases have consistently held that the regulated activity must have a *substantial* effect on interstate commerce. E.g. [*NLRB v. Jones & Laughlin Steel Corp.*, 301 U.S. 1, 37 (1937)]. Moreover, simply because Congress may conclude that a particular activity substantially affects interstate commerce does not necessarily make it so. Congress' findings must be supported by a "rational basis" and are reviewable by the courts. Cf. [*Perez v. United States*, 402 U.S. 146, 157 (1971)] (Stewart, J., dissenting)....

> [T]he Court asserts that regulation will be upheld if Congress had a rational basis for finding that the regulated activity affects interstate commerce .... [But] it has long been established that the commerce power does not reach activity which merely "affects" interstate commerce. There must be instead be a showing that regulated activity has a *substantial effect* on that commerce. As recently as Maryland v. Wirtz, 392 U.S. 183, 197, n. 27 (1968), Justice Harlan stressed that "[n]either here nor in *Wickard* has the Court declared that Congress may use a relatively trivial impact on commerce as as excuse for broad general regulation of state or private activities." ...

And in United States v. Lopez, 514 U.S. 549 (1995), the "substantial effects" test advocated in Justice Rehnquist's *Hodel* concurrence was adopted by the Court in an opinion striking down a federal law banning gun possession near schools. How would the U.S. Supreme Court today address the question of Congress' power to regulate private dumping in intrastate waters?

3. Do judicial review, or constitutional texts, serve as predictable and reliable constraints on federal allocations of power? Was Canada's residuary power clause (the "peace, order and good government" provision) any more effective in assuring the flow of power to the national government than the 10th Amendment to the U.S. Constitution was in assuring that power remained with the states?

4. An aspect of Canadian federalism that bears mention is "executive federalism." Since the 1960s, a federal-provincial ministers' conference has regularly met and has "become a major instrument for the resolution of intergovernmental relations. In recent years these federal-provincial conferences have become the basic mechanism for attempts at reforming Canadian federalism. To a very large extent, the conferences, an expression of 'executive federalism,' have superseded the Canadian parliament as the primary focus for constitutional deliberation." Daniel J. Elazar, Federal Systems of the World 50 (2d ed. 1994). Would a comparable structure serve a useful role in the U.S.? Are the recent consultations in the United States between the President and the state Governors on education reform indicative of a developing "executive federalism" in the U.S.? Why or why not? Compare "executive federalism" in Canada with the German idea of "Bundestreue" discussed below.

---

3. GERMAN FEDERALISM

Germany is a federal state with, since reunification, 16 länder. (The länder are the federal subunits of Germany.) The länder have representatives in the federal Bundesrat, (Council of States) who are members of the land governments which appoint and may recall them. Each land has between three and six voting representatives; länder must cast their votes in a block. While the Bundestag is the primary legislative organ for Germany, the Bundesrat exercises a suspensive veto over all federal legislation.[e] The Bundesrat's consent, moreover, is required for legislation that vitally affects the interests of the länder.

In Germany, the federal government has extensive legislative powers, but the länder are ordinarily charged with administration of federal law. While the länder have residuary legislative authority in areas not delegated to the federal government, the federation is given exclusive jurisdiction over a number of areas in which länder cannot legislate without specific federal permission.[f] In areas of concurrent jurisdiction,[g] the länder may

---

e. If the Bundesrat disapproves a bill by a simple majority, the Bundestag may reenact it with a simple majority; if the Bundesrat disapproves by a two-third majority, the Bundestag can reenact only with a two-thirds majority. Basic Law Art. 77.

f. Article 73 lists, inter alia, foreign affairs and defense, citizenship, freedom of movement and immigration, currency, money and coinage, air transport, operation of railways, postal services and telecommunications, industrial property rights, and copyright.

g. Article 74 identifies as areas of concurrent legislative jurisdiction, inter alia, civil and criminal law, court organization and the legal profession, public welfare, economic af-

legislate unless the federal government has done so. The federal government has authority to enact framework legislation for the länder to apply in further detail concerning, e.g, general principles of education, the legal status of the press, and land distribution and regional planning. Other than with respect to some exclusively federal areas, länder are generally responsible under Art. 83 of the Basic Law for the administration of the federal laws.[h]

The following materials introduce some of the distinctive features of the Constitutional Court's federalism jurisprudence: the principle of "Bundestreue", or what has been called "pro-federal loyalty," see David P. Currie, The Constitution of the Federal Republic of Germany 77–79 (1994); the protection of the relatively small areas of exclusively länder competence to legislate; and the effect of länder administration of federal law, or what Professor Kommers calls "administrative federalism," on expanding the circumstances in which consent of the Bundesrat (not merely suspensive veto) is required.

---

a.   *"Bundestreue" and the Legislative Competence of the Länder*

Professor Kommers, in his book, on The Constitutional Jurisprudence of the Federal Republic of Germany 79 (1989), refers to "Bundestreue" as a doctrine of federal comity, a "principle that obligates federal and state governments to work toward a common understanding in their relations with each other." First invoked by the Constitutional Court in 1952, Professor Kommers says,

> "[t]he doctrine of comity . . . had no warrant in express constitutional language. It was rather an unwritten constitutional principle inferred by the court from the various structures and relationships created by the Constitution. German federalism, said the court, is essentially a relationship of trust between state and national governments. Each has a constitutional duty to keep 'faith' (*Treue*) with the other and to respect the rightful prerogatives of the other."

Professor Currie's book describes "Bundestreue" less as a form of comity than as an implication from the constitutional requirement of a federal system: "the very existence of a federal system implies a duty of fidelity to the principles of federalism . . . [I]n exercising their authority the Länder are bound to respect one another's interests and those of the Federation, and the Bund [the federal government] is required to respect the interests of the Länder." According to Currie, the principle of Bundestreue was considered an essential element of federalism by the Herrenchiemsee

fairs, labor relations, educational and training grants, economic viability of hospitals, road traffic, waste disposal and pollution control.

h. The German Basic Law also addresses finances in some detail, setting forth basic principles requiring federal subsidies for länder administration of federal law. It also provides a mechanism for some equalization of financial resources between the länder. See below in this chapter, Note on Federalism and Finances.

Committee that drafted the Basic Law, and the idea is found in German legal literature as early as 1916. See David P. Currie, The Constitution of the Federal Republic of Germany 77–80 (1994)

In the following materials, consider the role played by the "Bundestreue" principle, as well as the Court's willingness narrowly to construe grants of exclusive power to the federal government in order to preserve legislative competency to the länder.

The First Television Case (1961)

12 BVerfGE 205 (Federal Constitutional Court of Germany).

[Articles 86 and 73 of the Basic Law confer exclusive authority on the federation to regulate "postal and telecommunications services." Claiming to act under this authority, Chancellor Adenaur's Christian Democratic (CDU) government issued a decree establishing a second television network, which would compete with a major television network established under authority of some länder. Prior to issuing the decree, the government had consulted with the head of only a single land, and had ignored a counterproposal by several of the länder who believed that negotiations with the federal government were ongoing. The new federal television network was challenged by four länder. The challenge relied on Article 30 of the Basic Law ("except as otherwise provided or permitted by this Basic Law the exercise of government power and the discharge of government function shall be incumbent on the Länder") and Article 70(1) ("The Länder shall have the right to legislate in so far as this Basic Law does not confer legislative power on the Federation").

The following translation and edit of the case is a shorter version of what appears in Walter F. Murphy and Joseph Tanenhaus, COMPARATIVE CONSTITUTIONAL LAW: CASES AND MATERIALS 212–15 (1977).]

* * *

Judgment of the Second Senate. . . .

The Basic Law regulates legislative competencies of Federation and Laender on the basis of a principle that favors the competency of the Laender. . . . The Federation has legislative competencies only insofar as the Basic Law confers them on it (Art. 70, par. 1). Thus, as a rule, federal legislative powers can be derived only from an express statement to that effect in the Basic Law. In cases of doubt, nothing speaks in favor of the Federation's competency. Rather, the systematic order of the Basic Law demands a strict interpretation of Articles 73ff. [conferring power on the Federation].

In addition, broadcasting is in any case a cultural matter. As far as cultural affairs are subject to governmental regulation at all, the Basic Law exercises a fundamental decision (Art. 30, 70ff., and Art. 83ff.) that they come within the scope of the Laender. . . . Exceptions occur only when special provisions of the Basic Law provide that the Federation has authority. This fundamental decision of the Constitution, a decision in favor of the federal structure of the nation in the interest of an effective division of powers, precisely prohibits the assumption that the Federation is competent in the field of cultural matters. The Federation has authority only when there is a clear exception spelled out in the Basic Law. This sort of provision is lacking here.

Art. 87, par. 1, determines that the federal postal service shall be conducted as a matter of direct federal administration. No conclusions as to the extent of the Federation's legislative competency can be drawn from this.... Moreover, "postal and telecommunication services" in Art. 73, no. 7, and "federal postal administration" in Art. 87, par. 1, refer to the same subject. The scope of "federal postal administration" follows from what is to be understood by "postal and telecommunication services."

The interests of the public demand a regulation of wireless traffic that can be effectively made only by the Federation. This is also true of broadcasting. Allocation and delimitation of frequency ranges of stations, determination of their locations and transmitting powers[,] ... control of wireless traffic, protection from widespread and local disturbances, and implementation of international agreements must be subject to uniform regulations to prevent chaos.

Art. 73, no. 7, makes it possible to enact uniform regulations that are indispensable to these and similar matters. But implementation of this objective does not require that, in addition to technical questions of wireless transmission, federal law also regulate production of broadcasts....

A historical interpretation of the term telecommunication services does not lead to any different results....

The Federation, on substantive grounds, is not entitled to any further legislative competencies for broadcasting.... It is true neither for studio technology nor for production of programs that their regulation ... is an indispensable requisite for regulating technical matters relating to broadcasting.... Transmission and production of programs are fields that can be treated separately. In this respect, "broadcasting" is not a whole that must be treated in a uniform manner and thus can be regulated by the Federation.

As far as, pursuant to Art. 73, no. 7, the Federation can regulate broadcasting, it can also lay down in law their "organization." The Federation is thus competent to issue regulations concerning the organization (the responsible body) operating facilities for transmitting broadcasts....

The Federation, however, can issue organizational rules only for institutions that are limited to the establishment and technical operation of transmitting facilities.... Organizational regulations for producers and for production of programs are matters for the Land legislator....

The Federation does not have any authority to regulate broadcasting beyond technical aspects of transmission....

The Federation must . . . observe the principle of pro-federal behavior. . . . This principle would be violated if the Federation today made use of its authority to regulate the telecommunication system so as to withhold from existing broadcasting companies the right to dispose of transmitting facilities owned and operated by them. The same would be true if the Federation took away from these companies the frequency ranges used by them, and in distributing frequencies to be used now or in the future did not duly consider the companies in light of Land regulations concerning producers of programs. . . .

By founding the Deutschland-Fernsehen Co., the Federation has violated Art. 30. . . . In the development of German legal history, production of programs has become a public function. If the government deals with this function in any way, it becomes a "governmental function" whose discharge under Art. 30 is incumbent upon the Laender insofar as the Basic Law does not otherwise prescribe or permit. With respect to production of programs, the Basic Law has not prescribed or permitted otherwise in favor of the Federation. . . .

In the German federal state all constitutional relationships between the whole state and its members and the constitutional relationships among members are governed by the unwritten constitutional principle of the reciprocal obligation of the Federation and Laender to behave in a pro-federal manner. . . . From this principle, the Federal Constitution has developed a number of concrete legal obligations. In considering the constitutionality of the so-called horizontal financial adjustment, this Court said: "The federal principle by its nature creates not only rights, but also obligations. One of these obligations consists in financially strong Laender having to give assistance within certain limits to financially weaker Laender. . . ." Furthermore, in cases where a law demands an understanding between the Federation and the Laender, this constitutional principle can create an increased obligation of cooperation by all parties concerned. . . . In the decision on granting Christmas allowances to public employees, this Court held that Laender must maintain *Bundestreue* (loyalty to the Union) and therefore show consideration for the overall financial structure of Federation and Laender. . . . This legal restraint, derived from the concept of loyalty to the Union, becomes even more evident in the exercise of legislative powers: "If the effects of a law are not limited to the territory of a Land, the Land legislator must show consideration for the interests of the Federation and other Laender. . . ." . . . In the execution of federal competencies in the field of broadcasting, the principle of pro-federal behavior is also of fundamental importance. . . .

Previous decisions show that additional concrete obligations of the Laender can be developed from this principle, obligations that surpass constitutional obligations explicitly laid down in the Basic Law. . . .

The case at hand offers an occasion to further develop in a different direction the constitutional principle of the obligation to act in a pro-federal manner: The procedure and style of the negotiations required in constitutional life between the Federation and its members and among Laender are also governed by the rule of pro-federal behavior. In the Federal Republic of Germany all Laender have the same constitutional status; they are states entitled to equal treatment when dealing with the Federation. Whenever the Federation tries to achieve a constitutionally relevant agreement in a matter in which all Laender are interested and participating, the obligation to act in a pro-federal manner prohibits the Federation from trying to "divide and conquer," that is, from attempting to divide the Laender, to seek an agreement with only some of them, and then force the others to join. In negotiations that concern *all* Laender, that principle also prohibits the federal Government from treating Land Governments in a different manner according to their party orientation, and in particular from inviting to politically decisive discussions only representatives from Land Governments that are politically close to the federal Government and excluding Land Governments that are close to opposition parties in the federal Parliament. . . .

The year-long efforts to reorganize the broadcasting system entered a new phase in early 1958 when the federal Government considered drafting a federal law. After the draft of a federal law had been discussed several times during 1959 with Land representatives, the Laender in January 1960 agreed to set up a commission, consisting of two Christian-Democratic and two Social-Democratic members of Land Governments, to represent the Land Governments in negotiations with the Federation. The federal Government, however, never let this commission participate in negotiations. Only one of its members, the Christian-Democratic prime minister of the Rhineland-Palatinate, participated—not in this role, but as a member of his party—in a number of debates between politicians and deputies of the Christian-Democratic and Christian-Social Union. . . . The fact that Land Governments led by Social-Democratic prime ministers were informed of these plans by the prime minister of the Rhineland-Palatinate in a letter of July 16, 1960, and at the same time were invited by him together with the other prime ministers to a discussion of these plans on July 22, 1960, did not release the federal Government from its obligation to confer directly with all Land Governments concerning the plan it had drafted. That it neglected to do so violated the obligation to act in a pro-federal manner.

The manner in which the federal Government treated Laender in the last few days before the foundation of the company was also incompatible with this obligation. The federal Government knew that on July 22, 1960, the prime ministers of the Laender . . . were given their first opportunity to discuss the plan to have a second television network established by a company founded by the Federation and the Laender. The prime ministers, including those of the Christian-Democratic and Christian-Social Union, did not fully accept the federal Government's proposal, but made counterproposals by a letter of July 22, 1960; the federal Government was informed of the result of these discussions. Nevertheless, the federal Government insisted that the corporate contract that it alone had drafted be signed on July 25, 1960. The letter of the federal Government dated July 23, 1960, was mailed in Bonn on July 24, 1960, 5 p.m., and reached the addressee, the prime minister of the Rhineland-Palatinate, on July 25,

1960, 4:15 p.m., that is, at a time when the corporate contract had already been notarized.... Such a proceeding is blatantly incompatible with the obligation to act in a pro-federal manner, even if the federal Government had reason to be displeased with the delaying opposition of the Laender or some Land Governments. At issue here is not the question whether the federal Government could consider negotiations with the Laender as having failed and follow a course it considered constitutionally admissible ... but the fact that each Land Government as the constitutional body of a member-state of the Federal Republic of Germany could expect the federal Government to answer the counter-proposals of the Laender which dealt with a *new* plan not with a *fait accompli*—and that with inappropriately short notice....

---

b. *The Reserved Powers of the German Länder and the Concordat Case (1957)*

The areas of reserved legislative competence of the länder under the Basic Law are quite limited, including "cultural matters, education, hospitals and various social services," powers which, Kommers suggests, "the court has tended to guard ... closely, probably because they are so few." Kommers (1997) at 79. The Concordat Case is often cited to illustrate the Court's willingness to preserve an area reserved to the länder from federal intrusion. It involved the federal government's challenge to the failure of Lower Saxony to provide state-supported confessional schools for Catholic children, as required by a Concordat that Hitler's regime entered into in 1933 with the Vatican. Although the Concordat was found valid under international law, the Court held that the confessional schools requirement could not be enforced against the länder.

The following translation of the case is excerpted from Murphy & Tanenhaus, at 226–29.

The Concordat Case

6 BVerfGE 309 (1957) (Federal Constitutional Court of Germany)

[Enforcing the Concordat's educational provisions against the Laender] would encroach deeply upon the Laender's cultural authority, contrary to the federal structure of the nation, in which cultural authority, in particular educational authority, is the kernel of the Laender's independent existence.

These considerations have far-reaching importance inasmuch as Art. 123 did not ordain continued validity of transformed treaty law ... except insofar as previous treaty law did not contradict the Basic Law. Pars. 1 and 2 of Art. 123 subordinate treaty law to the Basic Law. It follows from this general consideration that the Basic Law's provisions concerning distribution of authority between Federation and Laender must also be weighed in determining whether Laender are obligated toward the Federation to observe the content of treaties....

III

We need not here examine the extent of the Laender's obligation towards the Federation to honor treaties internationally binding upon the Federal Republic of Germany. In no case could the Laender's obligation toward the Federation to honor the Concordat's educational provisions ... be derived from the constitutional order created by the Basic Law. Arts. 7, 30, and 70ff. of the Basic Law have made certain fundamental choices that shape the relationship between Federation and Laender.... These choices reject such an obligation. In contrast to the Weimar Constitution, these provisions establish the Laender as exclusive custodians of cultural leadership. In the area of denominational organization of the school system, this exclusive authority is limited only by provisions of Arts. 7 and 141. This allocation is an important element of the federal structure of the Federal Republic of Germany.

1. We must proceed from the view that, where Laender possess exclusive legislative competence, they alone are entitled to make law. In Arts. 30 and 70ff., the Basic Law very clearly expresses this principle. Legislative freedom of the Laender in this area is limited only by obligations arising from federal constitutional law, since no federal law can be passed where Laender have exclusive legislative competence.

It must therefore be considered as an important principle of federal constitutional law that, in their legislative authority, Laender are subject to no limitation other than that imposed by the Basic Law. This principle is valid also for the legislation of Laender in relation to law which continues to be valid under Art. 123, pars. 1 and 2....

Constitutionally binding Laender to the educational provisions of the Concordat would flatly contradict their authority freely to make educational law within the limits of the Constitution.

2. As for organization of the school system along denominational lines, the Basic Law made a specific choice which rejected constitutionally binding the Laender to the educational provisions of the Concordat. Based upon the Laender's freedom of action, Arts. 7 and 141 of the Basic Law establish the limits within which the Land legislator should be confined in this particular area.... This choice is not reconcilable with the educational provisions of the Concordat....

3. The meaning of Art. 7 ... can be correctly understood only in relation to the entire situation encountered by the Basic Law in the matter of educational law.

From 1933 to 1945 the educational provisions of the Concordat were not fulfilled and in many cases were violated.

After the collapse of the Reich in 1945, the civil reconstruction of Germany was achieved with the help of the Laender. It was in the Laender that civil life was reconstituted, during a period when the entire German state was not yet capable of action. As a result, during this time the Laender could alter previous laws of the Reich. Thus the Basic Law also expressly recognized changes in earlier laws of the Reich made by the Laender during this period (Art. 125, no. 2).

In the civil structure of the Laender, the educational question had particular importance and was the subject of lively dispute; the Laender often deviated from the educational provisions of the Concordat....

The constitution framer thus had to start from the fact that the new educational law of a large part of the territory under the Basic Law contradicted the educational provisions of the Concordat. ... This legal situation ... would have made it necessary that the Basic Law spell out any intention to constitutionally obligate the Laender to fulfill the educational provisions of the Concordat. In view of the diversified legal situation in education among Laender and the Basic Law's own choices in this area (Arts. 7 and 141), the Basic Law, if it wished to oblige Laender to observe the educational provisions of the Concordat, could not have been silent on that matter. Moreover, the Basic Law could not have been content merely to ordain in general the continued validity of domestic law corresponding to international treaties of the German Reich. This choice did not remove contradictory Land laws; nor was the Land legislator bound by continuingly valid law....

5. To understand correctly the constitutional order of the Federal Republic of Germany, one must realize that the Basic Law's division of authority between Federation and Laender was not a matter of apportioning the power of a totalitarian state.... The events from 1945 to 1949 constituted more than a change in the form of the state.... Rather, an entirely new order and form was given to German state power in Federation and Laender, by a fundamental reconstruction, in place of the state organization which in 1945 completely collapsed and was entirely removed [citing a case]. The fact that this reconstruction took place during a time lag between development of governmental power in the Laender and reorganization of the entire German state confronted the Basic Law maker with two *faits accomplis*. On the one hand, to a large extent law in the Laender had developed independently and to such a degree ... that the Basic Law could not ignore it.... On the other hand, the authority of the Laender, if only because of their political influence, could not be arbitrarily curbed: to become effective, the Basic Law had to be accepted by the parliaments of two-thirds of the Laender.... In this constitutional-political situation, the federal constitution could not guarantee the Laender's acceptance of obligations contracted by the Reich government to the same extent it might perhaps have been able ... had it had as its task distribution between Federation and Laender of the unlimited power of a totalitarian state.

In interpreting the Basic Law, one must proceed from the inner harmony of constitutional structure which gave the German state a new federal and democratic order in place of a totalitarian dictatorship. The supposition that Laender are obligated to the Federation to observe the Concordat's educational provisions is irreconcilable with the basic decisions of this constitutional structure, including assignment to the Laender of supremacy in educational law.

IV

The constitutional principle of *Bundestreue* (federal loyalty) belongs among the constitutional standards immanent in the Basic Law. *Bundestreue* can be correctly understood only in comparison with all other constitutional standards that regulate relationships between Federation and Laender. Both Laender and Federation have the constitutional obligation to cooperate in accordance with the substance of the constitutional "bond" connecting them, and to contribute to strengthening that tie and to preserving the well-understood structure of the Federation and its members [citing cases]. From this source, a limitation on the Land legislator arises. If the effects of a legal measure are not restricted to a Land's territory, that Land legislator must take into consideration interests of the Federation and other Laender. If a Land legislator has clearly abused his discretion by violating this obligation of considerateness, his behavior is unconstitutional [citing a case].

... *Bundestreue* demands that each part take into consideration situations of interest and tension which arise in the Federation, in particular outside interests of the Federation. Thus one must conclude that the Laender's obligation of loyalty toward the Federation is to be taken particularly seriously in foreign relations, where the Federation alone is competent.

Nonetheless, no obligation of Laender to the Federation to observe the Concordat's educational provisions can be derived from the principle of *Bundestreue:*

1. The Basic Law's choice constitutionally to limit Laender in the denominational orientation of education only by Art. 7 excludes any further obligation of the Laender toward the Federation in this area.

2. Concordats do not come under the provisions of Arts. 32 and 59. Thus competence to conclude concordats is governed by legislative competence in domestic affairs.... It is up to the Federation and the Laender to negotiate, on an equal basis, a suitable compromise when their interests are in tension....

Editors' Note [From Murphy and Tanenhaus]: In 1969 Arts. 74, 75, and 91 of the Basic Law were amended to allow federal participation in regulating and funding "higher education" and research institutions.

Questions and Comments

1. Writing in 1989, Professor Kommers observed that "the vast scope of federal legislation [in Germany] has prompted a special vigilance on the part of the Constitutional Court over what little authority remains with the states under the Basic Law. In this sense, the residual-powers clause of Article 30 is a greater limitation on federal power than the reserved-powers clause of the American Constitution's Tenth Amendment." Kommers (1989) at 95. In light of the recent renewal of federalism as a basis for invalidating national action in the U.S., e.g., United States v. Lopez, 514 U.S. 549 (1995); Printz v. United States, 521 U.S. 98 (1997), consider how much influence on the U.S. Court's decisions should be attributed to the nature of the 10th Amendment "reserved powers" clause and how much to such other factors as the perceived growth of federal legislation.

2. Leading scholars of German constitutional law comment on the capacities of the system to resolve federal-länder conflicts through nonjudicial mechanisms, while at the same time concluding that the decision of a substantial number of federalism cases by the Constitutional Court has had significant effects on the relationship between the federal government and the länder. In addition to the work of Professors Kommers and Currie, see Phil M. Blair, Federalism and Judicial Review in West Germany (1981). Notwithstanding the possibility that members of the Bundesrat could raise many challenges to federal legislation, Kommers implies that they do not do so, relying instead on informal cooperative mechanisms of resolving conflict even when different parties control the Bundesrat and Bundestag.

Compare the argument made by prominent U.S. scholars that that the U.S. Supreme Court is, compared to the political branches, less well situated to enforce federalism limits against the national government (and better situated to resolve individual rights claims) and thus should take a very deferential, or even a hands-off, approach to resolving federalism challenges to national legislation. See Herbert Wechsler, *The Political Safeguards of Federalism: The Role of States in the Composition and Selection of the National Government*, 54 Colum L. Rev.543, 559–60 (1954); Jesse H. Choper, Judicial Review and the National Political Process 175–258 (1980). Does the German experience cast any light on the accuracy, or generalizability, of these arguments? (Bear in mind that the Bundesrat is made up of officials of the länder governments and that the Bundesrat has a full right of participation only in some federal legislation, both in contrast to the U.S. Senate.) Are there other features of the German and U.S. constitutional systems you would want to know about to analyze these questions?

---

c. *Länder Authority Over Government Structure and Employees*

In the United States since the 1960s, constitutional attention has focussed on federal control (direct and indirect) of the structure of state and local governments, and the relations between state governments and their employees. Control over state and local governments is an important issue in Germany as well. The German Constitutional Court has ruled that, notwithstanding the Basic Law's requirement that länder governments "must conform to the principles of republican, democratic and social government based on the rule of law," the länder have considerable discretion over the form of their own governments. See Startbahn West Case, 60 BfVerfGE 175 (1982) (upholding decision, under land law, by land of Hesse not to hold referendum on its planned airport expansion). The Court emphasized that

> "[T]he *Länder* are states vested with their own sovereign powers— even though limited as to subject matter—derived not from but rather recognized by the federation (*Bund*) . . . The Basic Law requires only a certain degree of identity between federal and state constitutions. To the extent that the Basic Law [does not provide otherwise] the states are free to construct their own constitutional orders . . . [and may determine] whether the legislature should reserve to itself the passage of a law or provide for [its approval] in a popular referendum." Kommers (1989) at 89 (translating decision).

With respect to treatment of their own employees, the länder benefit from the requirement that, with respect to matters covered by the authorization for the federal government to pass *framework* laws, the federation may enact only the framework, and must leave details to the länder. Article 75 authorizes the Federation to enact "framework legislation for legislation of the Länder on the legal status of persons in the public service of the länder . . ." In 1954, the Constitutional Court held that a federal statute forbidding länder to pay their civil servants more than their federal counterparts was unconstitutional. In response, article 74a was added to the Basic Law, providing concurrent legislative authority over the pay scales and pensions of members of the public service, thereby authorizing the federal government to enact such legislation.

---

d. *Bundestreue as A Constraint on the Länder: The Hesse Atomic Weapons Referendum Case*

In cases arising out of a political dispute between the Social Democratic Party and the Bundestag over atomic weapons, the Constitutional Court asserted the Bundestreue principle against three länder. In one case, the Court held that länder had violated federal authority over the national defense by providing for the holding of referenda on the question whether to permit nuclear weapons in Germany. These referenda were found to be inconsistent with the federal government's exclusive authority because their purpose was to influence, and thus interfere with, the "free exercise of" that exclusive authority, according to Professor Currie. In the companion case (Atomic Weapons Referenda II), the Court invoked the Bundestreue principle to hold that Hesse, by permitting local referenda within its borders, violated the requirement of fidelity to the federal system. Emphasizing that it was not accusing Hesse of malice, the Court said that the Bundestreue principle was " 'exclusively an objective idea of constitutional law, and it assumes that the participants, with respect to a given subject matter, are convinced [subjectively] of the constitutionality of their mutual dealings.' " (Kommers translation, (1989) at 88). It held that Hesse had the obligation to prevent localities within its jurisdiction from holding the referendum.

---

e. *"Administrative Federalism," the Role of the Bundesrat and the Bundesrat Case*

One of the most important of the powers of the länder is the power of administration of federal law. After discussing the willingness of the Constitutional Court to protect the few reserved legislative powers of the länder, Professor Kommers (1989) at 90–91, comments:

> An equally important linchpin in the structure of German federalism is the night of the states "to execute federal law as matters of their own concern" unless the Constitution specifies otherwise (Article 83). State governments in turn delegate the actual implementation of most laws (federal and state) to still-lower levels of administration. State and local governments are therefore predominant in the field of public administration, for they organize and operate, outside of those few areas in which the Basic Law provides for direct federal administration, nearly all of the country's administrative agencies. As a consequence, the states are primarily responsible for putting into force most rules and regulations pertaining to the training and employment of civil servants. Federal law, on the other hand, controls the general legal status of civil servants, including their classification, educational qualifications, pay scales, and retirement benefits—a legal status that the states must respect in enacting laws to fill gaps in federal policy.

> Federal administrative substructures, on the other hand, exist only in those limited areas of the federation's exclusive legislative competence (Article 73) and in matters where the Basic Law expressly provides for direct federal administration. These matters include the foreign affairs, railroad and postal services, federal waterways, certain police functions and, of course, the armed services. [Professor Kommers' discussion of complications concerning federal administration of certain insurance programs is omitted.] The prevailing view among constitutional commentators ... is that the spheres of federal and state administration are to remain organizationally separate and independent. . . .

And as he has explained earlier, (Kommers (1989) at 85),

> The German states are autonomous governments with their own legislative, executive, and judicial institutions. Like the American states, they share power with the federal government within the same territory and over the same people. But the comparison between the two federal systems ends here. In ... Germany the bulk of legislative

power is vested in the federal government, while the administration of federal law is the main responsibility of the states. This system of 'legislative-executive,' or 'administrative' federalism, as it is sometimes called, encourages flexibility in adjusting general policy to local conditions. But the system is also very complex. At least forty-three articles of the Constitution deal with relations between state and national governments. . . .

In addition to enforcement through Constitutional Court review of laws claimed to be inconsistent with the requirement for länder administration, the interests of the länder in the administration of federal law combines with the veto authority of the Bundesrat to provide substantial power to the länder in influencing federal legislation. As noted at the outset, while the Bundestag must send all bills that it adopts to the Bundesrat, the Bundesrat only has the power to delay the enactment of bills that do not require its consent, and its objections may be overridden in the Bundestag.

In some instances, however, the consent of the Bundesrat is required. Kommers says that Bundesrat consent is required for all "laws affecting the vital interests of the state." Among the specific constitutional provisions requiring Bundesrat consent to legislation are declarations of states of emergency, (art. 81), proposed constitutional amendments (art. 79), legislation concerning compensation of civil servants (art. 74a), legislation relating to länder boundaries (art. 29), and perhaps most importantly, federal laws that regulate how the states carry out their responsibility for the administration of federal law. See article 84(1), (2), (5).[j] A number of Constitutional Court decisions address when Bundesrat consent is required, as discussed in the following excerpt.

―――――――

Donald P. Kommers, THE CONSTITUTIONAL JURISPRUDENCE OF THE FEDERAL REPUBLIC OF GERMANY *107–08 (1989)*:

. . . The upshot of these and related constitutional provisions is that over half the legislation passed by the *Bundestag* now requires the *Bundesrat's* consent. There is, however, a major twilight zone in which the *Bundesrat* encounters opposition from the *Bundestag* over the scope of its power to consent. The five cases summarized in table 3.1 are examples of these situations.

j. Article 84 of the German Basic Law provides, inter alia:

(1) Where the Länder implement federal legislation in their own right they shall establish the authorities and administrative procedures in so far as federal legislation with Bundesrat consent does not provide otherwise

(2) The Federal Government may, with the consent of the Bundesrat, issue general administrative rules.

. . .

(5) With a view to implementing federal legislation the Federal Government may be empowered by a federal law requiring the consent of the Bundesrat to issue directives in special cases . . . .

In addition, article 85 provides, inter alia, that

[w]here the länder implement federal legislation for the Federation the establishment of authorities shall remain their concern except in so far as federal legislation with the consent of the Bundesrat provide otherwise.

(2) The federal government may, with the consent of the Bundesrat, issue general administrative rules. . . .

Table 3.1 Early Examples of Twilight-Zone Situations

Case	Judgment
Income and Corporation Tax Administration Case (1951)	Consent required when federal law sets forth procedures to be used by a state in collecting federal revenue.
Price Law Case (1958)	Consent required for the mere extension of a law originally requiring *Bundesrat* consent where the prolongation of a state administrative procedure established by federal law was involved.
Prussian Cultural Property Case (1959)	Consent not required for federal law creating a special foundation to oversee cultural property in the former state of Prussia.
Bank Lending Case (1962)	Consent not required for the passage of Federal Bank Lending Act because state judicial agencies entrusted with partial enforcement of law were not "administrative authorities" within the meaning of Article 84(1).
Telephone Charges Case (1970)	Consent required for issuances of federal ordinances pertaining to fares and charges for postal and telecommunications services.

By the mid-1970s, when Christian Democrats prevailed in the *Bundesrat*, they began to wield their authority against the government coalition (SPD-FDP) in a manner that virtually asserted the *Bundesrat's* equality with the *Bundestag* in the legislative process. The theory of coresponsibility, as several state governments called it, was a central issue in the well-known *"Bundesrat Case."*

Pension Insurance Amendment Case ("*Bundesrat Case*") (1975)

37 BVerfGE 363 (Federal Constitutional Court of Germany)

[(translation and commentary by Kommers, (1989) at 108–13)] [The question in this case is whether a later amendment of a law requiring the original consent of the *Bundesrat* is also subject to an absolute veto, even if the amendment itself does not affect a matter requiring its assent. In 1972 the *Bundestag* passed the Pension Reform Act. Since the act regulated the procedures of state administration, it required and received the *Bundesrat's* approval. The *Bundestag* amended the act one year later, but the amendment did not change its essential content, and thus the *Bundestag* maintained that the amendment did not require the *Bundesrat's* consent. Rhineland-Pfalz and Bavaria petitioned the Constitutional Court to vindicate the *Bundesrat's* claim to its veto right and to a position of coresponsibility with the *Bundestag* in West Germany's parliamentary system.]

Judgment of the Second Senate ...

C. II. 1.... [The fact] that the Pension Reform Act required the consent of the *Bundesrat* ... does not establish that the ... amending act also requires such consent. Not every statute amending a law requiring consent is for this reason alone subject to the consent requirement. The Basic Law contains no provisions from which to deduce such a principle....

(a) The distribution of authority between the federation and the states, as provided by the Basic Law, demands protective measures against the danger that ordinary legislation may produce distortions of the system that are not within the purview of the Basic Law. The provisions in the Basic Law requiring consent of the *Bundesrat*—including Article 84 (1)—serve this purpose in the interest of the states. Consequently, this article requires that a law containing provisions which regulate the state administrative process obtain the consent of the *Bundesrat*—as the federal body through which the states participate in the making of federal laws. By approving the Pension Reform Act in its entirety, the *Bundesrat* also gave its approval to [those parts of the act] regulating the administrative procedure of the states. The *Bundesrat* has by its consent to the [original] Reform Bill approved this "penetration" into the sphere of administrative execution of federal laws which Article 83 guarantees to the states. If, in a later amending act, no new "penetration" into the sphere reserved to the states occurs and no renewed distortion of the system results, then this amending act does not require the consent of the *Bundesrat*....

(b) ... The *Bundestag* adopts federal laws pursuant to Article 77 (1). The *Bundesrat* merely participates in the legislative process (Article 50).... In this connection it is important [to realize] that the requirement of consent to a statute under the Basic Law represents an *exception* to the rule. Only in certain explicitly enumerated cases in which the states' field of interest will be affected in a *particularly intensive* way does the Basic Law require consent.... The *Bundesrat* has no general right of control which may be derived from this principle....

(c) It is true that the *Bundesrat* examines the entire content of every law requiring its consent, not only those provisions which bring the consent requirement into play. It therefore may refuse its consent to a law containing substantive norms as well as provisions respecting states' administrative procedures because it disagrees with the substantive provisions....

(d) But it does not follow from the fact that the consent of the *Bundesrat* applies to the entire statute as a legislative unit that every amendment itself requires the *Bundesrat*'s consent. Rather, the view that a law requiring consent is a legislative unit speaks against a consent requirement for amending statutes....

The amending statute is also a technical legislative unit. The court must independently and renewedly examine all prerequisites for its legislative adoption just as in the case of any other law: It must determine whether the federal legislature has the authority to enact a law of this content and whether the law requires consent by virtue of its content. If the law does not itself contain provisions requiring consent, and if it also amends no such provisions, then it does not require consent. . . .

(e) A further consideration supports this result: Nothing precludes the *Bundestag*, in exercising its legislative discretion, from using several laws to regulate a subject. It can, for example, put the substantive provisions in one law, as to which the *Bundesrat* has only a suspensive veto [see Article 77], and can enact provisions respecting administrative procedures of the states in another law requiring *Bundesrat* consent—as not infrequently happens in practice. If one accepted the argument of the *Bundesrat* [that every amendment of a law requiring its consent in turn requires consent], then a later amendment of the original statute containing only substantive law would not require consent; but if substantive and procedural provisions were in one statute (requiring consent), then every later amendment of this law would similarly require consent. But it would be absurd to decide these two cases differently. . . .

2. Nonetheless, there are a number of cases in which the *Bundesrat*'s consent is necessary for the amendment of a law that itself requires such consent. This is apparent when the amending law contains new provisions which in their own right require consent. The same is true when the amendment affects those provisions of the amended statute that caused that statute to require *Bundesrat* consent. Also included is the case in which a statute amends another statute requiring consent and containing substantive norms as well as provisions respecting states' administration. To be sure, [the amending statute may be] confined to substantive matters but nevertheless make such changes in this realm as to give an essentially different meaning and scope to the administrative provisions it does not expressly amend. . . . [The court went on to find that the amending law in this case did not regulate state procedure and thus held that the *Bundesrat*'s consent was not required.]

JUSTICES V. SCHLABRENDORFF, GEIGER, and RINCK, dissenting . . .

Everyone agrees that the Basic Law contains no express provision requiring the *Bundesrat*'s consent for the amendment of every statute that itself requires such consent. It cannot in the least be deduced from this that an amendment would only require consent when it falls within the rule of Article 84 (1) or another express provision of the Basic Law—especially since, according to our decision of February 24, 1970 [citing the *Telephone Charges Case*], the Basic Law does not exhaustively list the cases in which a law requires consent.

3. (a). . . The assumption that requiring *Bundesrat* consent for every law amending a statute which itself requires consent would lead to an imbalance between federal legislative bodies to the detriment of the *Bundestag* assumes what is to be proved. . . . The argument . . . that the exception would become the rule and the rule the exception is just as unconvincing. . . .

(b) For the instant case ... it is quite irrelevant how [we should] generally determine the relationship between *Bundestag* and *Bundesrat* in the legislative process.... When a statute requires consent, the position of the *Bundesrat* is no weaker than that of the *Bundestag*.... Everyone agrees that consent to a statute means consent to the entire statute as a legislative unit....

... The amending law is, to be sure, a new legislative unit, ... [but] not an ... independent, enforceable regulation in itself; [it] derives its meaning only in connection with the law it amends.... The essential content of the amending statute necessarily becomes a part of a statute that undoubtedly required consent because of its content and continues to require consent so long as it exists....

Finally, the consent requirement ... follows from the further consideration that legislation is a political process that demands compromise.... The addition of new material by an amending law ... alters the content of that compromise, and one cannot preclude the possibility—indeed it is quite likely—that the *Bundesrat* would not have agreed to this new compromise....

4. In addition, this conclusion is consistent with what the Federal Constitutional Court has already decided ... [citing *inter alia* the *Legalization of Documents Case* (24 BVerfGE 184), which held that the *Bundesrat* must approve all regulations issued under a statute requiring consent pursuant to Article 80 (2)]. It would hardly be comprehensible to assume that regulations implementing such a law ... required *Bundesrat* consent, whereas amendments did not.

* * *

Note [by Professor Kommers]: Expansion of the Bundesrat's Power. The *"Bundesrat Case"* was a defeat for the council of state governments. Its role over the years, however, has grown increasingly important. As David Conradt remarked:

> Originally, the framers of the Basic Law anticipated that only about 10 percent of all federal legislation would require Bundesrat approval and hence be subject to Bundesrat veto. In practice, however, through bargaining in the legal committees in each house, and judicial interpretation, the scope of the Bundesrat's absolute veto power has been enlarged to the point where it can now veto roughly 60 percent of all federal legislation. This unforeseen development occurred largely because many federal laws which refer to matters not subject to Bundesrat veto nonetheless contain provisions that set forth how the states are to administer and implement the legislation. Citing Article 84 of the Basic Law, the states have argued that, since they are instructed as to how the federal legislation is to be administered, the legislation, in both its substantive and procedural aspects, requires Bundesrat approval.

The [1975] *Abortion* and *Conscientious Objection Reform Act* cases are two examples of other instances where the *Bundesrat*'s authority came into question. When the *Bundesrat* returned the original abortion bill to the *Bundestag* without its consent, the latter in turn voted to override the objection, holding that the *Bundesrat*'s consent was unnecessary. The dispute resolved itself into a disagreement over the nature of the statute. Was it a substantive change in public policy, where consent would not be required, or was it a matter affecting the administration of federal law, where consent would be required? The *Bundesrat* argued that its consent was necessary because the substantive legal change vitally affected the meaning and scope of the states' administrative procedures. The court rejected this claim on the authority of the rule set forth in the *Bundesrat Case*, holding, in addition, that the states enjoyed even wider latitude than previously to structure the administration of the statute.

In the *Conscientious Objector Case*, however, the Constitutional Court ruled in favor of the *Bundesrat*. In 1977 the *Bundestag* enacted a law substantially modifying the procedure for determining whether a prospective draftee is entitled to be exempt from military service on the ground of conscience. Instead of submitting to a hearing on the sincerity of his claim—a process administered in different ways in the various states—an applicant could now simply declare in writing that he is a conscientious objector, in which case he would automatically receive the exemption. The statute did not receive nor did the *Bundestag* seek the consent of the *Bundesrat*. Article 87b (2), however, declares: "Federal laws concerning defense, including recruitment for military service and protection of the civilian population, may, with the consent of the *Bundesrat*, provide for their implementation by the federation itself ... or by the states on behalf of the federation...." The court held that this provision requires the *Bundesrat*'s consent whenever an amendment to a statute modifies or expands an administrative responsibility—i.e., one transferred to the states with the *Bundesrat*'s consent—if the amendment in the light of Article 83 is equivalent to a new transfer of responsibility. The newly liberalized rule on conscientious objection "fundamentally transformed civilian alternative service into a second form of community service," thus imposing upon the states a much enlarged responsibility for finding community service jobs for conscientious objectors. Such a large shift of responsibility, said the court, is permissible only with the consent of the *Bundesrat*.

---

4. Swiss Federalism

For helpful sources, see Otto Kaufman, *Swiss Federalism*, in Forging Unity Out of Diversity: The Approaches of Eight Nations (Robert Goldwin, Art Kaufman and William Schambra eds., 1985) and Daniel J. Elazar, Federal Systems of the World 246–50 (2d ed. 1994) on which this opening background discussion relies.

Switzerland's history dates back to the 13th century when a treaty, the "Everlasting Alliance," was created amongst the "men of the valleys." This was essentially a defense treaty that gradually extended to include cities (Lucerne, Zurich and Berne) and other rural communities by the mid–14th century. Additional members of the confederation were admitted over the next centuries, following wars against the Hapsburgs, Charles the Bold, and the German Emperor Maximilian. During the Reformation, many in this confederation became Protestant, but the confederation stayed neutral during the Thirty Years war (a time to which Swiss neutrality traditions date). This confederation of 13 member entities, all German-speaking, met as a "diet," and lasted from the 16th century until after the French Revolution when Napoleon conquered Switzerland.

After initial difficulty with attempts to impose a unitary government, Napoleon constituted Switzerland as a new confederation with additional cantons, some French-speaking. After Napoleon's defeat, the European powers gave recognition to Swiss neutrality and added further cantons (including Geneva and Neuchatel). Beginning in about 1830, liberal Protestant cantons sought to enact a constitution and finally, after a short civil war against the more conservative catholic cantons, a constitution was accepted in 1848, and a revised constitution adopted in 1874.

The Swiss Confederation today has 26 full and half cantons, whose history, in the words of Professor Kaufman, shows that *"the federal structure of the Swiss confederation is very old, and the desire of the people to belong to their particular cantons is very much alive today....* [T]here is ... a feeling that Swiss democracy is not a construction but a living organism."[k] Switzerland's population includes two major religious groups (Protestant and Catholic) and several major language groups: German, French and Italian are all "official languages" in which Swiss national laws are published. Cantons vary in their official language(s): there are several cantons whose official language is German; four in which French is the official language; three in which German and French are the official languages; one in which Italian is the official language, and one in which German, Romansch and Italian are official languages. French, Italian and Romansch speakers are regarded as "minority groups": about 63% of Swiss speak German, 20% speak French, 7% Italian, and less than 1% Romansch; in addition, the Swiss population of about 7 million includes about 1 million foreigners (mostly guest workers, but also including refugees). See Peter Sager, *Federalism in the Post–Cold War Era: Swiss Federalism: A Model for Russia?*, 1995 St. Louis–Warsaw Transatl. L. J. 163, 164. Kaufman emphasizes sociological as well as language and religious differences among cantons.

There is no single executive head of state: the Federal Council, composed of 7 members elected by both houses of parliament every four years, is the chief executive. Each year, the Chair rotates among the members the

---

k. According to Otto Kaufman, the history of the half cantons illustrates salient features of Swiss federalism, with its emphasis on decentralized local autonomy. For example, the canton of Appenzell was divided, after the Reformation, into Protestant and Catholic half-cantons; and the nineteenth century division of Basel resulted when citizens of the city refused to allow equal rights to rural citizens who then insisted on their own half-canton.

the Council; Parliament selects the Chair, referred to as President of the Confederation, for a one year term; the outgoing "President" cannot serve as Chair or Vice–Chair in the following year. According to Kaufman, "[m]ost Swiss citizens do not know who is president in any given year."

The legislative body is bicameral, and both houses participate equally in law-initiation and approval. Enactment of a law requires agreement of the two houses, the Council of States and the National Council. The Council of States has 2 members from each of the 20 full cantons and 1 from each of the six half cantons. The National Council has 200 members directly elected, and distributed among the cantons based on population; but each half canton and canton has at least one member. Laws enacted by the national legislature must be submitted to referendum when 50,000 citizens or 8 cantons request. The Constitution is amended by referendum (a majority of voters and cantons), or by initiative (sought by 100,000 citizens). Due to large variations in the size of the cantons (the two largest containing one-third of the population); the twelve smallest cantons, which contain only about one-fifth the population, can, by refusing their consent block amendments to the Constitution that have passed both houses and been approved by enormous popular majorities. As explained in readings that follow, the people also participate substantially in the law making functions at both the federal and cantonal levels.

The Federal Court engages in constitutional review of cantonal action, but not of federal laws or the decisions of the Federal Council.

The next two readings provide differing perspectives on the nature and role of democracy in Swiss federalism.

Otto Kaufman, *Swiss Federalism*, in Forging Unity Out of Diversity: The Approaches of Eight Nations (Robert Goldwin, Art Kaufman, and William Schambra eds., 1985) (excerpts)

. . .

Present Tensions in Switzerland: Is Federalism a Calming or an Aggravating Factor?

Switzerland is a peaceful country, and internal tensions have not become dramatic in the past fifty years.... The peace agreement between the trade unions and the employers' associations in the metal and watch industries has been renewed several times. Swiss farmers receive better prices than farmers in other European countries. Although everyone criticizes the government, the critics finally cancel one another out. Therefore, one should not dramatize the tensions to be discussed next. They exist; they are in the center of political disputes; but they are not perilous to Swiss democracy. To this day, there has been no polarization either in the linguistic and cultural areas, as in Belgium, or between right and left, as in France. The opposing groups vary according to the subject in dispute....

... [T]ensions do exist

- between industrial, urban areas and rural areas

- between the French-speaking and the German-speaking parts of Switzerland
- between the working class and the so-called bourgeois groups in the population
- between Swiss citizens and foreigners
- among the political parties

Tensions between Cities and Rural Areas. There are typical urban cantons, like Basel-City, Geneva, and (more and more) Zurich, and typical rural cantons, like the small cantons of central Switzerland and Appenzell. But most of the cantons do not fit in either group because industry, handicrafts, and small businesses are widespread throughout the country. Tourism has created many places of work in nonindustrialized areas....

Nevertheless, the old tension between rural states and cities that for centuries troubled the old Swiss confederation, persists; it is a problem of mentality, a feeling that the cities may acquire too much influence and democratic power. The rural population feels a permanent threat that the "too modern" moral and cultural views of the cities may conquer the whole country. They especially fear that Zurich will become too big and have too much weight. Certainly social ideas and new life styles do not stop at cantonal frontiers, but strong cantonal autonomy is a safeguard against the imposition by federal law of views not yet generally accepted. The big cities may have very liberal nightclubs that are tolerated by their own cantonal regulations of restaurants, but the cantons of central Switzerland dislike this kind of "progress"; they want their own rules for restaurants and dancing, their own school systems, and so on. These examples show why rural cantons are strong federalists and why they try to fight many proposals to broaden the federal power.

Tensions between French- and German-speaking Areas. Some tensions between the French- and German-speaking parts of Switzerland have existed since the admission of French-speaking cantons. In recent years this tension has grown because the Romands (the French-speaking Swiss) think that economic development is faster in some parts of German-speaking Switzerland than in the Romandie. The Romands maintain careful watch over the federal administration to protect their share, and they want at all costs to safeguard their cultural identity, asking for federal financial help in this effort. Four French-speaking cantons have their own universities (Fribourg, Vaud, Neuchatel, Geneva); these universities depend to a large extent on federal subsidies, but they are centers of cultural life in their cantons.

The Romands fight more often than their German-speaking compatriots against new federal laws. A few years ago the legal requirement to wear safety belts while driving in a car became a political issue; the majority of the German-speaking Swiss emphasized security, the Romands, liberty: liberty not to use a safety belt. The Romands lost the battle in the voting, but this was not a national catastrophe. A linguistic limitation is a frontier of culture, but the differences between German and French culture in our time cannot be easily defined. To moderate tensions, the cantons have very broad authority to establish and organize schools. . . .

After the Second World War the English language was increasingly taught in Switzerland. The second language of many Swiss is not another national language but English. The consequence is that people read more English publications and fewer books or periodicals of other cultural areas of Switzerland.

The Italian- and the Romansch-speaking parts of Switzerland have also had to fight to maintain their cultural identity. They have the sympathy of the rest of the Swiss, but the people of Ticino in Lugano, Locarno, and Ascona especially feel submerged by German-speaking immigrants from the north. . . .

Legally, German, French, Italian, and Romansch are the national languages of Switzerland; the first three are official languages (Article 116), which means that all laws are published in those three languages. When there is a difference in meaning, the Federal Court finds a solution most appropriate to the aims of the law. In the Federal Assembly, in federal commissions, in the Federal Council, and in the Federal Court, everyone speaks his own language. . . . Judges in the Federal Court must be able to read papers in all three official languages. Federalism is the key enabling peoples of different languages and cultures to live together.

Tensions between the Working Class and the Bourgeoisie. Social tensions are not as strong in Switzerland as in other European countries. The Socialist party has always been a minority party; in many areas federal social security laws came later than in other European countries. But there is some truth to the saying that the Socialists point out the social aims to be realized and the so-called bourgeois parties find the ways and means to solve the problems. Trade unions know that Swiss industry must be competitive in the world market, and employers know best how to deal with their personnel. Swiss Socialists are very pragmatic. Some democratic feeling is not only a political but a social fact. Many managers participate in the general cultural and sporting activities of the people. They "hear how the mind is turning." Extensive strikes, therefore, have been infrequent, and inflation is kept down fairly well. Wage agreements are common. In the metal and watch industry, a so-called peace agreement has survived all difficulties; it provides that all collective labor disputes must be resolved by arbiters without strikes or lockouts. The federal pattern may have influence even in this field: the cantonal sections of professional groups want to keep their autonomy; in this way they are influenced by the federal pattern of the state.

Tensions among Political Parties. Tensions among political parties are normal and necessary in a democracy; everything depends on fair fighting. In Switzerland this fairness is widely respected. It is even said that the programs of some parties are so similar to one another that elections for the Federal Assembly are no great national event. The main parties' percentages of votes in the latest election for the National Council (the lower house) were as follows:

Radical Democratic party	23
Christian Democratic party	21
Socialists	23
People's party	11
Independents party	4
Liberal party	3
Evangelical party	2
National Action party	3
Workers party (Communists)	1
Others	9

The first four parties together have formed the government for some forty years; they have more than three-fourths of all the votes, and their strength does not vary much from one election to the next. The opposition, therefore, is left to small groups with limited weight. But there is no 5 percent minimum quota for small groups as in ... Germany.... Within the cantons, however, the strengths of the parties may be quite different, and the political battles are often more vigorous there than in federal elections. The parties are organized on a cantonal basis. Once an election is over, the winners and losers of all parties begin to work together again.

Tensions between Citizens and Foreigners. The strongest tensions in Switzerland exist between Swiss citizens and some groups of foreigners. The very fact that one-seventh of the population is foreign creates a strong feeling that Switzerland may be overwhelmed by aliens. Application of the alien policy is to a large extent left to the cantons....

Differences of Religion. For centuries the tensions caused by the division of Christianity into Catholics and Protestants were of primary importance. There were and are Catholic cantons, Protestant cantons, and mixed cantons. In the census (taken every ten years) most people declare the denomination to which they belong, and most also pay public church taxes....[S]tatistics ... still reveal Protestant cantons (for instance, Berne, which is 77 percent Protestant) and Catholic cantons (for instance, the cantons of central Switzerland, which are 86–91 percent Catholic); but religion does not have the same weight as in the past, and fortunately religious tensions have diminished significantly. Nevertheless, religion has its political impact; the Christian Democratic party, composed mostly of Catholics (90 percent), is a very federalist party.

The Influence of Federalism. Swiss federalism is at the same time an aggravating and a calming factor. On the one hand, the cantons are places of experiment where new ideas may be put into practice before they are given a chance on the federal level. For instance, voting rights for women were introduced in some French-speaking cantons twelve years before the victory in the confederation as a whole. On the other hand, new ideas will not inundate the whole country because it is hard to take over a confederation of twenty-six member states—even though they are very small. Nothing is eaten when it is too hot—that is Swiss wisdom....

The Federal Constitution in Its Substantive and Formal Aspects ...

... The written Federal Constitution of 1874 is full of gaps on the one hand and of secondary rules on the other. This ought to be explained.

The authors of the Constitutions of 1848 and 1874 were practical politicians, not professors of constitutional law. They were solving problems of their own day. Afterward, each of the more than 100 amendments to the Federal Constitution addressed one specific item, and each new rule was introduced between any two already existing paragraphs; for instance, after the paragraph about freedom of commerce (Article 31) there are now seven articles (Article 31b, 31c, ... 31g) about federal regulation of the economy. Many articles are the result of long-discussed compromises and therefore are sometimes very detailed. There are, for instance, three long articles on distilled spirits (Articles 32b, 32c, 32d), but there is not one line about the separation of powers.

Therefore, the problem of unwritten, but generally accepted, constitutional law is very important for the Swiss confederation. The Swiss Federal Court has "deduced" from the provision in Article 4 "All Swiss citizens are equal before the law" a great number of specific constitutional rights, such as the right to due process of law, the right not to be harmed by "arbitrary decisions" *(Willkürverbot)*, the protection of good faith in the relations between administration and citizens, and so on. Furthermore, the Federal Court has admitted the existence of "fundamental unwritten rights" that are generally recognized in Western democracies, such as freedom of opinion, personal liberty, and guarantee of property. Some of these unwritten freedoms are now guaranteed by the European Convention on Human Rights. These guarantees of civil liberty are binding on the central power and on the cantons; every law must respect the Federal Constitution as interpreted by the Federal Court. Further, the limitations on cantonal autonomy mean that all federal statutory law prevails over cantonal law (Article 2). . . .

Many articles in the first part of the Constitution go into greater detail than, for instance, the U.S. Constitution. There are no broad articles like the interstate commerce clause of the U.S. Constitution. Therefore, the jurisdiction of the federal power cannot be broadened by a new interpretation by the Federal Court; the Constitution must be adapted to new needs practically every year.

The Organization of the Federal Power *(Bund)*

The main constitutional organs of the federal power are the people, (the Federal Assembly with two houses), the Federal Council (the head of the executive), and the Federal Court. The function of the people is discussed in the next section; what follows is a short outline of the other organs.

The Federal Assembly. In 1848 the Swiss confederation copied the American idea of a bicameral legislature. . . .

[In the National Council, each] canton or half-canton forms an electoral district, and elections are based on a sophisticated system of proportional representation.

The Council of States is composed of forty-six representatives of the cantons, two for every canton and one for every half-canton. The Council of States is more to the right than the National Council [including a smaller percentage of socialist representatives].

... The two councils assemble for a joint meeting for the election of the members of the Federal Council and the Federal Court.

Because members in both houses have previously been active in cantonal politics, both houses have a strong tendency to safeguard cantonal autonomy. The Socialists are most in favor of strengthening the federal power.

The Federal Council. The supreme executive and governing authority is called the Federal Council. It is composed of seven members, elected by the Federal Assembly for a four-year term (Articles 95 and 96). The chairman of the Federal Council is called president of the confederation (Bundespräsident), but he has no more power than the six other members; each of the seven becomes president for one year in rotation....

This system is unique. For about forty years the political composition of the Federal Council has been based on the so-called magic formula: two Radical Democrats, two Christian Democrats, two Socialists, one member of the People's party. The election of the Federal Council takes place after the election of the National Council every four years; a federal councilor who has been "satisfying" will be reelected. His higher officers will help him do the job. There are four or five German-speaking councilors and two or three French- or Italian-speaking councilors. The first woman was elected in 1984.

The members of the Federal Council become independent of their own party when they are elected....

Every federal councilor is the head of a department, but all important decisions are made by the Federal Council as a body (Article 103). Every federal councilor must therefore look into the work of the others. They are all overburdened, but they have secretaries to develop their positions on issues. This shared responsibility is essential to the Swiss system.

The Federal Court. Justice is a matter for the cantons. There are no lower federal courts, just the Federal Court at Lausanne and its autonomous branch, the Federal Court for social insurance at Lucerne. The Federal Court is composed of thirty judges from all parts of the country and is a multifaceted court [hearing civil, criminal, administrative, and constitutional cases]....

The means to bring a case on a constitutional matter before the Federal Court is called *staatsrechtliche Beschwerde*, or *recours de droit public*. It can be directed only against cantonal laws and cantonal decisions. The Federal Court is bound by federal laws (Article 113), and it cannot review decisions of the Federal Council.

The plaintiff before the court must show that the cantonal law or the cantonal decision violates one of his constitutional rights or a right guaranteed by an international treaty. . . .

The Organization of the Cantons

The organization of all the cantons is very similar. All have unicameral parliaments, most of which are elected on a proportional basis.

The executive is elected by the people on the day they elect the parliament. In all cantons every change in a cantonal constitution and almost every new law is submitted to a referendum. . . .

In all cantons the local communities (*Gemeinden*, or communes) are very important, and in most cantons voting rights are well established in the local communities. Even the schoolteachers or the parish priest may be elected by popular vote. Local officers very often execute federal and cantonal law. The local communities insist on autonomy. If their autonomy is restricted illegally through cantonal decisions, they may accuse the canton before the Federal Court.

The judiciary varies widely from one canton to another. In cities the judges are mostly lawyers trained in the law faculty of a university; in the countryside laymen-judges elected by the people are common . . . .

The Specific Tools of Swiss Democracy: Referendums and Popular Initiatives

Swiss federalism is deeply entwined with the specific form of Swiss democracy; the special tools of this form of direct or semidirect democracy used by the central power and the cantons are the referendum and the popular initiative. The referendum is an instrument used to overturn laws and (in the cantons) large expenses already accepted by parliament but opposed by a group of citizens. The popular initiative is a "prodding instrument." A sufficiently large group of citizens, by collecting signatures, may force the government and the parliament to discuss acts with which they disagree. They have the right to a popular vote on their proposition, even if the government and the parliament recommend that the citizens reject it.

The Referendum. In the second half of the nineteenth century, the so-called democratic movement . . . marshaled public opinion behind the idea that all new laws should be ratified by the people. The assent of the people may take two forms: (1) every law must be submitted to a popular vote (required referendum), as in the majority of the cantons; or (2) a popular vote takes place if a specified number of citizens, by their signatures on referendum forms, request it (an optional referendum), as in the Bund and in some cantons. In the Bund 50,000 signatures are needed, and they must be submitted within ninety days after publication of the act of the Federal Assembly. In the cantons and in the local communities, required or optional referendums are even more important for large expenses.

The optional referendum is used for only a minority of federal statutes, but it is used whenever there is clear-cut opposition. In Switzerland it is said, "The people are the opposition." To reduce the opposition, all groups of the population (and in federal matters all the cantons) are asked to submit their views about a bill before it is introduced in the parliament. Switzerland has thus become a "democracy of compromise." The threat of a referendum strongly influences discussion in the Federal Assembly. If the opposition collects its 50,000 signatures in time (and for some large organizations that is easy), a debate about the strong and weak points of the new law begins; the government sends more or less neutral information to all voters. The political parties recommend acceptance or rejection of the law. In this way some important laws, such as the penal code and the Agricultural Act, have been accepted; others, such as the Alien Act, have been rejected.

For the acceptance of normal laws, a simple majority of votes is sufficient. But a broader majority is needed for a change in the Federal Constitution. *Every change in the Constitution must be approved through a required referendum and must be accepted by a majority of both the people and the cantons*; without this double majority no change in the Constitution, especially no broadening of the central power, is possible. Since the Swiss people vote every year on one or more amendments to the Constitution, this double majority is the principal stronghold of the cantons.

In Switzerland, therefore, the parliament and the people together constitute the legislature, and the people and the states (cantons) together constitute the constitutional power. This rule gives to all laws a higher authority than in countries where the majority of the parliament is sufficient to create new laws.

Even important parts of international treaties are submitted to the optional referendum. Parliamentary decisions to enter "an organization of collective security" (such as the United Nations) or "a supranational community" (such as the European Economic Community) are submitted to the obligatory referendum; they must be approved by a majority of the people and a majority of the cantons. In 1985 the Federal Assembly decided to join the United Nations; but in the vote of March 1986 the people (by a majority of 3:1) and all twenty-six cantons and half-cantons voted against joining—a very rare unanimous opposition to the federal government and the Federal Assembly.

The Popular Initiative. The popular initiative in the cantons is a tool for requesting a popular vote for a change in the constitution, for a new law, or for a change in a law despite opposition from the government and the parliament. In the Bund the only aim of a popular initiative is to change the Constitution; it therefore needs a double majority of both the people and the cantons. On the federal level a group of citizens must collect, within six months, at least 100,000 signatures for a "formulated" or an "unformulated" initiative. The formulated initiative contains a fixed text for a new article (or a changed article) of the Federal Constitution; the unformulated initiative contains only an order for the Federal Assembly to change a portion of the constitutional text on a certain topic (Article 121). The text of the unformulated popular initiative is completely open, provided that it deals with just one topic.

The Federal Assembly has a strong weapon against popular initiatives: the *counterproposition* (Article 121, paragraph 6), which normally has less reach than the initiative. The people must vote on both the popular initiative and the counterproposition the same day. A citizen may reject both, accept one and reject the other, or vote primarily for the popular initiative and eventually (if the initiative does not gain the required double majority) for the counterproposition. This is a very recent solution in order to favor the acceptance of the counterproposition and to avoid a completely negative result. The popular initiative is a very original weapon for minorities to introduce new ideas in the political debate, to force the government and the parliament to enter in the discussion, and eventually to win the majority of the people and the cantons in spite of the opposition of the government and the parliament.

Popular initiatives must be voted on within four years after submission. During this time the government and the Federal Assembly must decide what recommendation and eventually what counterproposition they will issue for the popular vote. The counterproposition may include a change in an article of the Federal Constitution and a law based on the new article (as was the case with the counterproposition for the protection of tenants against excessive rents and other abuses in rental housing in 1985).

Most popular initiatives are rejected, but there have been exceptions. The most spectacular acceptance was in 1949. After the years of war a popular initiative requested a quick restoration of the constitutional order and elimination of all "war laws." The government, the Federal Assembly, and all the political parties recommended rejection of the proposal, but the majority of the people and the states accepted it and in this way restored the traditional constitutional order in a very short time.

Between January 1, 1979, and July 1, 1985, the Swiss people voted on forty matters. They

- accepted fourteen changes in the Constitution proposed by the Federal Assembly

- rejected six changes in the Constitution proposed by the Federal Assembly

- accepted one popular initiative (against abusive prices)

- rejected twelve popular initiatives

- accepted three counterpropositions of the Federal Assembly to popular initiatives

- accepted three federal laws on which referendums were requested

- rejected one federal law on which a referendum was requested (Alien Act)

Between 1875 and 1983, 103 amendments to the Constitution were accepted, and 102 were rejected....

... In recent years 30 to 53 percent of the people with voting rights have voted, but the voters speak, one may say, for the whole people.

The Swiss system of semidirect democracy increases the power of pressure groups of all kinds. With the threat to use the optional referendum or the popular initiative, they influence members of the government and the Federal Assembly. There is widespread debate, for instance, about whether it is necessary to limit speed on the national highways to 100 kilometers per hour (60 miles per hour) to reduce air pollution and to protect the woods. The automobile clubs are planning to launch a popular initiative to set the limit at 130 km/h (80 mph) if the Federal Council proposes that it fall below 120 km/h (75 mph)....

The price paid for the Swiss form of democracy is *slowness*. It is much easier to pass a bill through a parliament by a clear majority of its members, as in other countries, than to win the majority of the people, as is necessary in Switzerland. "A truth needs a generation to enter into the mind and the heart of the population." Sometimes two battles must be won: first, to create a federal power in the Federal Constitution; and second, to establish a federal law based on this power.... The constitutional basis for old age and survivors' insurance and disability insurance was created in 1925, but the Old Age Insurance Act dates only from 1947 and the Disability Insurance Act from 1959. Voting rights for women were rejected in 1959 and accepted in 1971. Swiss family law was made uniform in 1907, but its modernization, based on the equality of husband and wife, was only recently accepted (after referendum). The Swiss confederation goes on, however, even with old laws....

... A Swiss citizen has both his assault rifle (with ammunition) and his voting card in his home. His voting right has ... greatest weight in the local community, less in the canton, and even less in the confederation, but it always has more weight than in a mere parliamentary democracy where citizens elect only members of parliament. In Switzerland federalism and direct democracy are closely bound together.

The Division of Powers between the Central Power and the Cantons

Article 3 states: "The cantons are sovereign insofar as their sovereignty is not limited by the Federal Constitution and, as such, exercise all rights not entrusted to the federal power." The idea is clear: sovereignty may be divided into federal and cantonal sectors. Some areas are exclusively under federal jurisdiction and others under cantonal jurisdiction. For instance, the federal railroads and the federal postal and telecommunications systems are exclusively under the jurisdiction of the federal power. All personnel are federal officers or federal employees; profits and losses concern the federal treasury. The relationship between church and state, however (subject to the constitutional protection of freedom of religion), is left entirely to the cantons and varies widely from one canton to another. Geneva has a separation of church and state; in neighboring Vaud the ministers of the Protestant and Catholic churches are paid by the canton out of taxpayers' money. In other cantons the members of the recognized churches pay a special public church tax.

In most fields, however, no clear division exists between the powers of the federal government and those of the cantons. Sometimes a confusing collaboration prevails between them. On the one hand, most federal laws must be executed by the cantonal authority; on the other hand, the cantons may receive federal subsidies in the area of their own exclusive tasks (for example, the federal government partly finances the cantonal universities)....

The cantons insist most strongly on their autonomy in the area of schools and education. Every canton has its own school system; each freely chooses its schoolbooks, and in many cantons, local communities select their own schoolteachers. A long-fought change in the Federal Constitution was needed to impose on all cantons a common beginning of the school year in all "obligatory schools" (Article 27). But the confederation regulates access to the study of human and veterinary medicine, pharmacology, and all studies in the two federal technical universities of Zurich and Lausanne. The confederation therefore regulates access to the universities in general. Examinations are prepared by cantonal professors under the control of federal experts. Unlike the primary and secondary schools, the vocational schools are under the control of the federal Department of Economics, but they are still cantonal schools.

In the German-speaking part of Switzerland only the cantons of Zurich, Berne, and Basel have complete universities.... In the French-speaking part of Switzerland, four cantons—Geneva, Vaud, Neuchatel, and Fribourg—have their own universities....

In the field of economics the Federal Constitution (Article 31) emphasizes that "freedom of trade and industry is guaranteed throughout the territory of the confederation subject to such limitations as contained in the Federal Constitution and legislation enacted under its authority" (Article 31, paragraph 1). The limitations must be regulated by federal laws and federal decrees on which a popular vote can be requested (Article 32), and they must have constitutional bases. Federal laws restricting economic freedom have been enacted to maintain good agriculture (Article 31b, paragraph 3b), but the general approach is not to reduce free enterprise; it is to promote economic activity. The cantons have no right to limit economic freedom, except insofar as necessary for the protection of health or good faith in business (police power, Article 31, paragraph 2). There is one exception: the canton may restrict the number of establishments serving food or drink so that there are no more than needed.

Today the confederation and the cantons must work together to stabilize economic development. Therefore, in 1978 the people and the states accepted Article 31e of the Federal Constitution, with the following text:

1. The confederation shall take measures to ensure balanced economic development and, in particular, to prevent and combat unemployment and price inflation. It shall collaborate with the cantons and private enterprises.

2. In the case of measures taken in the monetary and banking spheres, public finances, and foreign trade, the confederation may depart, if necessary, from the principle of freedom of trade and industry. It may require firms to form tax-privileged employment creation reserves. After their release, the firms shall decide freely how to use them within the purposes laid down by law.

3. When drawing up their budgets, the confederation, the cantons, and the communes shall take into consideration the requirements of the economic situation. The confederation may temporarily levy surcharges or grant rebates on federal taxes to stabilize the economy. The money withdrawn from circulation is to be frozen for as long as the economic situation requires. Direct taxes shall then be refunded individually, and indirect ones shall be used for the granting of rebates or for work creation.

4. The confederation shall take into consideration the varying economic development of the individual regions of the country.

5. The confederation shall conduct the necessary economic policy surveys.

This article shows the meshing of the confederation and the cantons in the area of economic policy.

There are no federal police in Switzerland. The attorney general of the confederation looks to cooperation among the cantonal police troops....

The Financial Order ...

The financial strength of the cantons and of the local communities varies widely. Laws on fiscal equalization look to better distribution of revenues among financially strong and financially weak cantons and communities. But important differences in the amounts of income taxes cannot be avoided. A married man without children and a salary income of SFr 100,000 in 1983 paid SFr 10,500 in cantonal and communal income tax in Zug; SFr 18,800 in Berne; and SFr 21,100 in Sion (a ratio between Zug and Sion of 1:2). This inequality of the tax burden (in spite of fiscal equalization) is the price paid for the fiscal autonomy of the cantons and local communities. The same taxes for all citizens in the country cannot coexist with wide autonomy of the cantons and the local communities.

Although most people do not realize the great differences, they generally accept the fiscal autonomy of the cantons and local communities and the inequality of the tax burden....

Obviously the confederation has expenses different from those of the cantons and local communities. It has the main burden of providing military defense, financing of social insurance, protecting agriculture, and covering the deficit of the federal railroads. The cantons and local communities need funds primarily for schools, health expenses, roads, protection of the natural environment (water and air), and the administration of justice. New, larger expenses of the cantons and local communities must be accepted by popular vote. This financial order, with all its problems, is a keystone of Swiss federalism.

Civil Liberties and Cantonal Autonomy

The federal legislature and the federal government as well as the cantonal legislatures and governments, have to respect the civil liberties defined in the Federal Constitution and the European Convention on Human Rights. The Federal Court, however, cannot decide whether federal laws (submitted to a referendum) are in conformity with the Constitution (Article 113, paragraph 3); it does decide the constitutionality of cantonal laws and all kinds of cantonal decisions. This power to decide is very important because the Federal Court may annul laws and decisions as violating equality under law or as being "arbitrary." An act is arbitrary if it has no legal basis or cannot be sustained by reasonable means (Article 4). In 1984, 1,663 citizens attacked cantonal laws or cantonal decisions by a *recours de droit public* for violating the Constitution; 209 appeals were allowed. A citizen can go to the Federal Court only if he has tried in vain to invoke the protections provided by cantonal law. This control over the protection of civil liberties by the cantons is an important wheel in the "gearing" of Swiss democracy.

A Test Case for Swiss Federalism: The Birth of the Canton of Jura, 1978

The most critical situation of the Swiss confederation in recent years was the tension surrounding the separatist movement in the northern, French-speaking part of the canton of Berne; it was finally solved in a democratic way through the creation of a new Swiss canton (by amendment of Article 1). The procedure, not foreseen in the Constitution, reveals in an interesting way the persistence, and also the difficulties, of decision making in Swiss federal democracy.

Berne, a mostly German-speaking canton, was reorganized at the Congress of Vienna in 1815 and at the "Long Diet" thereafter. It received "in compensation for lost territories, the Cantons Aargau and Vaud," the French-speaking territories of the prince-bishop of Basel in the Jura, in the northwestern part of the canton. The people became Bernese citizens, and the French-speaking parts of the new canton held equal rights with the German-speaking majority of "the old canton." The French-speaking minority was itself split into two parts. The Protestant, industrialized southern part wanted to be closer to the Protestant German-speaking part of the canton of Berne rather than the northern Catholic part "behind the mountains." This northern, French-speaking part of the canton was always somewhat isolated, and some tensions always existed.

In 1943 they requested some degree of autonomy, and in 1951 they created a political movement, the Jurassian Rally (Rassemblement Jurassien), which held that the whole French-speaking part (north *and* south) should leave the canton of Berne and form a separate new canton, Jura. They wanted to be free from Berne, as Vaud had been "liberated" from Berne by Napoleon. In 1957 the so-called separatists first chose the democratic procedure of a cantonal popular initiative for the creation of this canton. But they lost the battle by 87,000 no votes to 23,130 yes votes because the old German-speaking Bernese saw no reason for dividing their canton. The north of the Jura voted for separation; the French-speaking south voted against it. But the determined minority in the north did not accept the decision of the Bernese people. In 1963–1964 the Front for the Liberation of Jura (Front de Liberation Jurassien) began acts of terrorism, and rejected every idea of limited autonomy for Jura inside the canton and Berne. Dialogue between the Bernese government and the leaders of the separatists became impossible. The fighting group of the separatists were the *beliers* (the books), the fighting group of the antiseparatists the *sangliers* (wild boars); many families were deeply divided by this political fight.

Finally the Federal Council intervened; in 1970 a constitutional complement was accepted by the old Bernese voters and the Jura voters, and they settled on a democratic procedure. The people of north and south Jura had to decide together first whether a canton of Jura should be created and then what French-speaking districts of Jura should belong to the new canton.

This procedure allowed some southerners to vote yes the first time and no the second time; on June 23, 1974, therefore, 52 percent of the Jura voters voted for a new canton, 48 percent against it; in the second vote, of March 16, 1975, only the three northern districts chose to become part of the new canton. A third vote provided the local communities on the borderline an opportunity to choose. The tension during the vote was very high, but the votes were free and secret, and they were accepted—though with anger—by the population.

After the third vote the voters of the northern district elected a constitutional council; within one year this council drafted a constitution for the new canton, which had to be ratified by the Federal Assembly. Once the new cantonal constitution was established, the Federal Constitution had to be changed to include the new canton in the confederation. On September 24, 1978, this change was accepted by more than 80 percent of the Swiss voters and by all the cantons, and on January 1, 1979, the new canton was born—twenty-eight years after the beginning of the Jurassian Rally. The governments of the old and the new cantons agreed on the details of the separation. The extremists among the separatists still do not want peace; they think that sooner or later the south must be "conquered." But peace has returned, and the story shows that ways and means can be found to overcome even very serious tensions by a prudent use of democratic means....

Thomas O. Hueglin, *New Wine in Old Bottles? Federalism and Nation States in the Twenty-First Century: A Conceptual Overview*, in Rethinking Federalism: Citizens, Markets and Governments in a Changing World 206–09 (Karen Knop, Sylvia Ostry, Richard Simeon and Katherine Swinton eds., 1995)

[Hueglin, a Professor at Wilfrid Laurier University educated in Switzerland and Germany, in an earlier portion of the essay argues that federalism has no necessary connection with democracy. At the same time, he asserts that federalism has made Germany more democratic by giving "new social movements regional springboards to political authority and responsibility," and has given Canada "regional social stability through regional equalization," and has helped "curtail imperial power aspirations of American presidents." Hueglin then raises concern about the overlapping of public and corporate leadership in Switzerland:]

* * *

A number of peculiarities suggest that Swiss federalism is unique.... First, there is a strong plebiscitarian component to political decision-making, including both a legislative *referendum* and *initiative*. As a consequence, Swiss citizens are asked to go to the polls more frequently than citizens elsewhere. Between 1970 and 1986, for example, some 120 decisions were put before them in this way. Second, there is a more recent trend of pragmatic decentralization. As Kloeti reports, most of the tasks constitutionally assigned to federal government have in fact been at least partially 'delegated' back to the cantonal level. Third, there is a regime of strict proportionality. Its most visible and important manifestation is the composition of the federal government which includes the four major parties according to the famous 2:2:2:1 formula and which also takes account of regional and cultural-linguistic differences. As a consequence of this *grand coalition* arrangement, there is for all practical purposes no opposition to which the government would be formally accountable.

At first glance, then, it appears that Swiss federalism has found various antidotes to the traditionally recognized weaknesses of federalism elsewhere: the plebiscitarian component serves as a corrective to the heavy-handed routine of executive bargaining among intergovernmental elites, ensuring that the people's voice is not lost and even breaking deadlocks resulting from irreconcilable self-interest at the two levels of government; the practice of delegating competency from the federal to the lower government levels helps to satisfy such self-interest and enhances local flexibility in administering policies which, at the same time, remain under the control of a centrally regulated universality; the adherence to strict proportionality dampens divisive partisanship, and especially so when such partisanship appears reinforced by regional conflicts. However, this conventional picture of Swiss federalism as a nearly perfect model ready for imitation elsewhere is alarmingly deceiving.

The plebiscitarian component is more often characterized by manipulation from above than by popular input from below. The frequency of referenda and initiatives has resulted in one of the lowest voter turnouts in the Western industrialized world. Therefore, the outcome of plebiscites mostly depends on massive mobilization campaigns requiring money and media influence. With regard to both, organized business dominates all other interest-groups. This domination is facilitated by the exceptionally high degree of centralization of organized business. The most influential *Vorort*, for example, represents 108 sections of more than twenty different branches of the Swiss secondary and tertiary economy.

Organized business also controls the media to a considerable extent. The control mechanism here is advertising money in a small national media market. When the left-liberal *Tages-Anzeiger* published an analysis of the influence the corporate sector had exercised in the defeat of a 1977 popular initiative concerning air pollution control, for example, car importers collectively withdrew advertisements worth millions of Swiss francs. Similar concerted actions have frequently accompanied the plebiscitarian process.

Plebiscitarian manipulation is ultimately facilitated by the country's demographic composition, as well as by constitutional provisions. Constitutional changes, for example, subject to a mandatory popular referendum, require a double majority of the population at large and of the population in at least half of the cantons. Thus, a majority in fourteen of the smallest cantons can block a constitutional amendment, or, in other words, 20 per cent of the population can in theory block a decision supported by 80 per cent. Add the notoriously low general degree of voter participation, and referendum campaigns inevitably come down to a battle among a few crucial groups affected by the decision.

The plebiscitarian component in Swiss federalism can hardly serve as an encouraging model of how to leaven the executive elitism embedded in the intergovernmental process with popular input. The delegation of central powers back to lower levels of government, on the other hand, appears to be a promising corrective to the inefficiencies and inflexibilities of the federal duplication of government and administration. In Germany, for example, most general legislation is made at the federal level, but its detailed specification, administration, and implementation is left to the Länder. Citizens are spared expensive dual layers of federal *and* provincial administration, but the division of powers—between central legislation and local administration—is maintained.

In Switzerland, this division of powers is crucially undermined by the overlapping accumulation of public office between the three levels of government. About 10 per cent of the members in the two chambers of the Swiss national legislature are members of cantonal or city governments, and local government presidents routinely sit in cantonal legislatures. The suspicion inevitably arises that the process of power delegation is largely driven by personal-interest collusion at all levels of government, and that this collusion will, in Hobbes' words, 'no whit advantage the liberty of the subject.'

The full extent of power and office collusion in Switzerland only emerges when what the Swiss themselves refer to as 'militia democracy' is taken into consideration. What 'militia' stands for is an old and venerable concept of honorary participation in public office. Swiss parliamentarians are not paid a salary. Compensated for their expenses only, they are considered part-time politicians on an honorary basis.

In practice, of course, they have long since been turned into 'semi-professionals.' Reimbursement comes in the form of multiple board memberships. Of the 244 deputies in both houses, 82 per cent at one point occupied a collective 'total of over 1,000 directors' jobs,' representing some 15 billion Swiss francs, or one-third of 'all the social capital of all the limited companies registered in Switzerland.' In other words, they receive remuneration from the private sector they come to represent. They do their business mainly in the 400 or so hearing commissions that dominate the policy process, and it is perfectly normal that a hearing, say, on banking law will be stacked with representatives of the large banks, or on nuclear reactors with the board members of the energy sector. This is why Hans Tschaeni, one of the country's leading journalists, speaks of the Swiss legislature as a 'cartelized fortress' deformed by 'militia entanglement.'

The better known military militia system also makes it a male fortress. With voluntary military activity the inevitable price of a political and economic career, the militia army provides the bonding glue for a political system of 'male societies' of power and influence. A typical member of the ruling cartel may hold office at both levels of government, he will be a president or board member of one or several of the country's leading industries, and he will hold the rank of reserve officer in the militia army. Typically, his soldiers will be his employees. It is not surprising, therefore, that women gained the national vote only in 1971. Gender-*apartheid* in Switzerland is not an accidental Alpine anachronism, routinely acknowledged with a wink and a chuckle by the world's predominantly male political-science community.

The system of strict proportionality also ensures that the influence of organized labour remains limited. Tied into an accord for industrial peace or 'voluntary restraint' with business since 1937 and coopted into the ruling cartel of the multiparty Federal Council since 1943, unions and socialists have traded the independent representation of working class interests for a share of political power as well as (more modest) access to the pecuniary sinecure of multiple board memberships. One consequence of that cooption is their complicity in Switzerland's labour policy of sustaining near full employment via the 'flexible' regulation of a large and nearly rightless migrant work-force. Simply put, Swiss unions acquiesce in a policy that imports and exports workers according to the fluctuations of the business cycle, because that policy exports unemployment to the migrant workers' countries of origin and thus sustains the employment and income stability of their Swiss members.

Add to this the overlapping memberships in public office, and a pattern of power collusion emerges that eclipses the formal provisions of federalist power separation. Moreover, adherence to principles of strict proportionality appears far less as a device for subordinating partisanship to the principles of federalism than a mechanism to intensify the grip of a small ruling elite on the overall system. Because the Swiss appear increasingly uninterested in honorary public office, no longer do the many take turns in administering the few functions of a minimal state, but rather the few share among themselves a multitude of functions through the channels of an 'incestuous interlocking of political, economic and military hierarchies.'

Swiss federalism does play a significant role in the spatial allocation of fiscal resources and in the proportional accommodation of cultural diversity. But other than from a rather narrow institutionalist perspective, there is little that could serve as a federalist model for the empowerment of more people and groups of people. The growing distemper of Swiss citizens over environmental scandals, military expenditure, and gender discrimination, and the continuing divisiveness over the inevitable prospects of European integration indicate that Switzerland, rather than providing such a model, must finally develop one.

Questions and Comments

1. *Separated Executive and Legislative Power and Federalism.* Thomas Fleiner observes that the structure of the Executive Power in Switzerland is modelled on the "directory" of the French Revolution, as well as on a collegial model of "town government". Thomas Fleiner, *Commentary on Swiss Federalism*, in Forging Unity Out of Diversity: The Approaches of Eight Nations 244 (Robert A. Goldwin, Art Kaufman, and William A. Schambra eds., 1985). He emphasizes the difference between the Federal Council (the Executive) and a parliamentary system—the members of the Council are "not at the same time the leaders of their political parties. Thus, the Swiss government is by no means a coalition ... but is a government composed of seven members with seven independent opinions." This independence of the government from the parliament is, according to Fleiner, recognized by political parties and members of parliament.

He then argues that the independence of the executive and legislative power facilitates cantonal influence in the decisionmaking of the legislature. He suggests that it does so better than in a system of parliamentary democracy: "Such direct influence [of the cantons] is possible only in a system that establishes an independent executive power and allows equal powers to the two chambers of the parliament—the chamber representing the people and the chamber representing the cantons." He argues that these structures of Swiss governance make it easier for the cantons to exercise influence in parliament than for the provinces or länder in Canada and Germany.

Consider how, or whether, an independent executive is related to federal power. Are subnational units more likely to be influential if they can appeal to competing power structures (i.e., independent executive and legislative powers)?

2. *Federalism and Bicameralism.* The relation between a bicameral legislature and cantonal power is perhaps more obvious. Some researchers in the U.S. have suggested that federal spending is disproportionately greater than population would suggest in smaller states, possibly due to the influence of the Senate's structure. Compare the debate in Canada over the relative weakness of the upper house.

3. *"Packages" of Federalism.* Is Fleiner correct in suggesting that the two structures of separation of executive from legislative power and bicameralism are particularly important for successful federalism? Consider, instead, whether different "packages" of arrangements might be utilized to reinforce desired power balances between central governments and their federal units. There are a variety of politically structured "checks" on the allocation of powers in a federalist system:

(a) judicial review of allocation of powers,

(i) by many, or just one, federal court, and

(ii) in abstract, or concrete, review (or both);

(b) representation of states in federal legislature,

(i) in a system of divided power (i.e. presidential system), or

(ii) in a parliamentary system;

(c) proportional voting for representation in a system in which particular political parties represent particular regional interests;

(d) representation of states in process of selecting chief executive or through rotational holding of executive offices;

(e) participation of states in the constitutional amending process;

(f) state-level administration of federal-level law;

(g) participation of states in law-enacting processes;

(h) rights of subnational units not to be bound by particular federal laws, or rights of secession.

4. *Federalism, Government Structure and Culture.* Consider further whether the vitality of federalism flows from broader questions like these or flows from broader questions of "federal culture" which are in turn reflected in legal/political structures.

5. *Compromise, Decentralized Administration and Diversity.* Consider Fleiner's comments on the role of compromise, the implementation of federal law by the cantons, and problems of diversity:

> *Federal Government by Compromise.* The independence of the executive from the parliament, proportional representation in the parliament, the power of the cantons in the decision-making process, and the obligation to consult various interest groups have had a great effect on the political culture of Switzerland. Important decisions are based on compromise since every authority must seek such a compromise between groups. It thus takes a long time to prepare statutes and make governmental decisions, but once adopted they are usually implemented and adhered to by the citizens. The system of proportional influence of interest groups has also had the consequence that not only

the government but every cantonal, federal, or judicial authority is composed of officials representing different political parties or groups. Even the administration reflects differing political ideas and groups, and this "proportionalism" gives rise to a stability of the government and a due respect for diverse political interests.

Implementation of Federal Law in the Cantons

We have already seen that many laws are made by the cantons autonomously. The federal government issues federal laws, but most of them are implemented by the cantons—in most cantons by the local authorities. Thus a federal law usually requires a cantonal law or at least an ordinance. The consequence is that federal laws are not always implemented in the same way in all the cantons.

Civil law or penal law (implemented by cantonal courts under the control of the Federal Court) can be interpreted differently by cantonal authorities. Abortion and divorce decisions are not made in the same way in a Catholic canton as in a Protestant canton. This aspect of diversity appears even more important if we take into account the implementation of other federal laws that need additional cantonal statutes to be implemented in the cantonal territories. The cantonal executive and especially the cantonal administration must execute federal laws, and the way they fulfill this obligation depends on the political opinions and structures of the cantons.

For the same reason, even individual liberties and rights can be implemented in different ways. For a long time religious liberty has been interpreted in Catholic and Protestant cantons according to their different political histories. In some cantons schools have long been integrated into the religious culture, although the Constitution clearly provides that freedom of religion cannot be infringed by cantonal schools.

An amendment of Article 4 of the Constitution provides "equal rights for men and women," but the canton of Appenzell still does not allow women to vote. Even though a large majority of the Swiss people and the cantons adopted the equal rights amendment, the parliament is not willing to impose on two small cantons women's right to vote.**

For a long time the Federal Court has allowed constitutional rights to be interpreted in different ways in the various cantons. The political culture of Switzerland, the political institutions, and the Constitution have developed over a long period, and it is certainly only this long historical development that enables political institutions to cope with the great diversity in Switzerland. It has never been possible to impose the will of a majority on a minority through democracy because no clear-cut line exists between a majority and a minority. . . .

** [Editors' Note: It was not until 1989 (Ausserhoden) and 1990 (Innerhoden) that these two cantons changed their laws disenfranchising women. See Lee Ann Banaszak, Why Movements Succeed or Fail: Opportunity, Culture and The Struggle for Woman Suffrage 19 (1996).]

Problems of Diversity and Federalism in Switzerland

Switzerland can certainly be considered a country that strongly respects the interests of minorities. But it has many problems concerning diversity.

Liberty of Commerce. That the state does not intervene in economic affairs has had the consequence that the country's economic structure has become more and more centralized. Most important economic decisions are made at the headquarters of banks and industries in Zurich, Basel, or Berne. All those towns are German-speaking, and none of the headquarters of large economic enterprises has been located in Geneva or Lausanne, both French-speaking. Thus, as Switzerland has become more and more economically centralized, the French-speaking part has felt more and more marginal in commerce and industry. That is because most citizens living in French-speaking Switzerland are not willing to give up a lower position and move to join a headquarters in Zurich or Basel. They prefer to stay in the lower position and remain integrated within their social group. Of course, some leading industries have realized these problems and strive to consider the interests of minorities.

Linguistic Minorities within the Cantons. Four of the Swiss cantons have to cope with two to four languages. In those cantons the problems of diversity can be solved only by giving more autonomy—especially in cultural and educational affairs—to the local communities. Minority problems still exist in those cantons, however. A strict territorial concept cannot be the solution, because people do not choose their homes only according to linguistic borderlines; they also consider economic and other reasons. For instance, one problem in bilingual or multilingual cantons is that parents may want to send their children not to schools in their local community but to neighboring schools that speak their language....

6. *Public participation.* Kaufman and Hueglin present different views on the significance of public participation in Swiss governance. Who do you find more persuasive?

7. *Public Participation and Constrained Judicial Review.* Are the opportunities in Switzerland for public participation justifiably related to the constrained role of the Court in not being able to review federal laws for constitutionality?

8. *Federalism and Equality Rights.* Is the slowness of all of Switzerland to accept full political equality for women related to its federal character?

Note on Federalism and Finances

Allocations of powers to tax, to incur public debt, and to spend, vary substantially among federal systems. What is the relationship between the allocation of revenue raising and spending powers and the idea(s) of constitutionalism? Between allocations of these economic powers and federalism?

In the U.S., both the federal and state governments have independent and concurrent powers of taxation—for example, typically states as well as the federal government impose a tax on income. These taxes are independently collected and administered. By contrast, in other systems, national powers to tax may be exclusive and preclude identical forms of state taxation. Australia provides an example of more centralized economic powers—state governments do not levy or collect their own income taxes, their authority to levy sales taxes is constitutionally limited; they rely heavily on revenues disbursed from taxes collected by the central government; and states' power to incur public debt has been regulated by a national Loan Council. See Jon Craig, *Australia*, in Fiscal Federalism in Theory and Practice (Teresa Ter–Minassian, International Monetary Fund ed. 1997) [hereafter "Fiscal Federalism"]; Richard E. Johnston, The Effect of Judicial Review on Federal–State Relations in Australia, Canada and the United States 137 (1969). Still other possibilities are represented by fiscal federalism in Canada, in which, for example, all provinces other than Quebec participate in a tax collection agreement under which the federal government collects both federal and provincial income taxes. See Russell Krelove, Janet G. Stotsky, and Charles L. Vehorn, *Canada*, in Fiscal Federalism, 204. And in Germany, the Basic Law provides most important tax powers to the federal government, and specifies what kinds of taxes the länder can impose. It also provides that the länder administer the collection of both federal and land taxes, specifies how both land taxes and federal taxes are to be divided and shared according to principles of "equalization," and establishes principles of budgeting for both the federal and land governments.

1. *Government Structure*: Consider possible relationships of government structure and fiscal powers. In the U.S., unlike in Germany, each state has authority to determine its method of budgeting and taxing, although the federal income tax imposes some practical limits on amounts available for state income taxation. U.S. states administer their own tax systems separately from the federal government. See also Janet G. Stotsky and Emil M. Sunley, *The United States*, in Fiscal Federalism 359–62 (commenting inter alia that "subnational governments play a much larger role in American political life than in most other countries ... "). Stotskey and Sunley also report that from 1972 to 1990, states in the U.S. had the option of electing to have the Internal Revenue Service collect state income taxes, piggybacked on the federal form, though at a rate set by each state, but that no state ever elected to do so. They suggest that states were unwilling to conform their own provisions closely enough to the federal provisions to meet the law's requirements, had concerns over changes in the federal tax base affecting state revenues, and interests in retaining state jobs both for employment and for enforcement reasons.

In Germany, the länder lack many of the concurrent powers of taxation that U.S. states preserve; länder cannot impose income taxes because those would be prohibited as "identical" to federal taxes. Their budget principles, and authority to borrow, are constrained by the Basic Law as well. Yet länder participation in the Bundesrat affords those subnational units bargaining authority over budgetary issues and in ways that differ from the role of state governments in the U.S. legislative process.

2. *Equalization.* Many federal constitutional systems have explicit commitments to "equalization," that is, redistribution from richer to poorer subnational units of the nation. Germany and Canada provide examples. See German Basic Law Art. 107 (1) (authorizing the federal government, with consent of the Bundesrat, to provide that up to 25% of the land share of taxes be granted to other länder whose per capita revenue from land taxes and from federal income and corporation tax is below the average of all the länder combined); id. 107(2) (providing that such laws "shall ensure a reasonable equalization of the financial disparity of the Länder, due account being taken of the financial capacity and requirements of the municipalities," and also authorizing grants of tax monies otherwise allocated to the federal government to the "financially weak Länder in order to complement the coverage of their general financial requirements"); Canadian Constitution Act of 1982, Section 36(2) (affirming federal government commitment to the "principle of making equalization payments to ensure that provincial governments have sufficient revenues to provide reasonably comparable levels of public services at reasonably comparable levels of taxation"). The United States, by contrast, has no formal or explicit commitment to geographic equalization, and some data suggest that the structure of the federal government in according equal senatorial representation to all states may create a systemic movement of resources at the federal level from larger population states to smaller population states. See Lynn A. Baker and Samuel H. Dinkin, The *Senate: An Institution Whose Time Has Gone?*, 13 J. Law & Politics 21, 23 (1997) (arguing that Senate systematically "redistributes wealth from the large population states to the small ones"). For a thoughtful argument that the U.S. consider "horizontal fiscal equalization among states and localities," as a means of restoring "decisional choice to states and localities while honoring national concerns about distributional equity" and protecting states from some adverse consequences of jurisdictional mobility, see Richard Stewart, *Federalism and Rights*, 19 Ga. L. Rev. 917, 972, 975–979 (1985).

Equalization, or a norm that economic variations among regions should not be too large, is in tension with those values of federalism associated with the benefits of local government competition and maintenance of diversity. In Germany equalization is constrained in an effort to maintain economic incentives for subnational units to improve themselves. See David P. Currie, The Constitution of the Federal Republic of Germany 59 (1994) (describing Constitutional Court decision holding that equalization, while constitutionally required, could not constitutionally result in a leveling of state finances, which would be inconsistent with state autonomy). How does the idea of equalization relate to the maintenance of constitutional order in a federal system? Even in systems without any explicit constitutional commitment to equalization, will a stable federal nation tend to produce some equalization of resources?[1]

3. *Constitutional culture.* Recall the principle of "Bundestreue," or mutual trust, in Germany, discussed earlier, and the emphasis in Canadian constitutional discourse on pluralism, pragmatism and compromise. Both of these are federal nations whose basic constitutional laws embrace a principle of some equalization between provinces or länder. In the U.S., by contrast, there is neither any explicit constitutional commitment to such equalization transfers nor is there any widely accepted political convention that this is, as a general rule, a desirable norm. What is the relationship between redistributive aspects of constitutional fiscal federalism and constitutional culture?

4. *Judicial review.* To what extent are constitutional provisions concerning fiscal powers judicially enforceable? The German Constitutional Court has, according to one of its leading U.S. scholars, resolved several major cases dealing with the constitutionality under the Basic Law of federal equalization statutes. See Currie, at 52–60 & n. 143 (describing decision in 1986 invalidating certain provisions as involving miscalculations of the financial status of the länder, and interpreting other provisions narrowly to avoid "excessive equalizing," yet also noting earlier decision that how far equalization should go is a question of " 'financial policy and not of constitutional law' "). In the U.S., constitutional decisions about the federal government's fiscal powers impose few restraints on taxing, spending, or borrowing powers. See United States v. Doremus, 249 U.S. 86 (1919) (upholding federal tax); Steward Machine Co. v. Davis, 301 U.S. 548 (1937) (upholding tax and spend scheme); South Dakota v. Dole, 483 U.S. 203 (1987) (upholding condition on receipt of federal funds); Smith v. Kansas City Title & Trust Cop., 255 U.S. 180 (1921) (upholding creation of federal agency authorized to issue bonds); see also Smyth v. United States, 302 U.S. 329 (1937) (upholding redemption of federal bonds in disregard of original gold clause). Moreover, U.S. justiciability rules may preclude resolution of the merits of challenges to federal spending. See e.g. Frothingham v. Mellon, 262 U.S. 447 (1923) (denying taxpayer standing to enjoin expenditures as violation of 10th amendment). In Australia, the High Court upheld federal preemption of state income taxes during World War II as a war-time measure. The system continued after the war, but its provision giving automatic priority to the payment of federal over state income taxes was held unconstitutional in 1957; nonetheless, no state income taxes were passed, the states preferring not to exercise tax authority and instead to receive federal grants, essentially the approach adopted during the war. Johnston, at 150–54; Craig, *Australia,* in Fiscal Federalism, at 178 (noting exclusive federal control of income taxes).

---

1. The difficult problem of defining equalization is beyond the scope of this note. For a brief description of the literature and of different approaches to defining equalization, see Ehtisham Ahmad and Jon Craig, *Intergovernmental Transfers,* in Fiscal Federalism, at 78–81.

5. *Spending Powers and Centralization?* Substantial attention in recent year in U.S. scholarship has focussed on spending powers—both on the growth of conditions on federal spending to the claimed detriment of state autonomy, see e.g.,Thomas R. McCoy and Barry Friedman, *Conditional Spending: Federalism's Trojan Horse*, 1988 Supreme Court Review 85; David Engdahl, *The Spending Power*, 44 Duke L. J. 200 (1994), and on the inefficiencies that result from the federal government forcing state expenditures through mandates, see Roderick M. Hills, Jr., *The Political Economy of Cooperative Federalism*, 97 Mich. L. Rev. 813 (1998). In both Canada and Germany, revenue sharing (in Germany mandated by Article 106 of the Basic Law, though at rates to be set by the legislature) is sometimes said to substitute for conditional federal grants in aid, permitting greater subnational unit autonomy over spending decisions. Yet early on scholars noted the development of conditional federal spending programs to influence länder choices in Germany, notwithstanding that the länder had "sacrificed the legal right to levy any major taxes or determine tax levels, in return for a greater assurance of obtaining through tax-sharing an adequate share of total financial resources and thereby avoiding financial domination by the centre." Phil M. Blair, Federalism and Judicial Review in West Germany 226–27 (1981). Blair also notes the role of the Court in influencing the scope and nature of federal conditional grants. See Blair at 231 (describing Constitutional Court decision of 1975 which, while upholding a particular grant program for urban renewal, emphasized that "a federal order must guarantee in principle that financial subsidies from the federal budget to the länder remain the exception ... [so that] they do not become means of exerting influence over the freedom of decision of the member states in fulfillment of the tasks incumbent on them"). After the 1975 decision, the Court in 1976 invalidated a grant program at the behest of Bavaria, on the grounds that a condition for federal approval of particular grants violated the principle of länder administration, and that the federal government could not make the grants directly to municipalities. Blair at 236–37. These decisions did not eliminate federal power to make conditional grants in aid, but limited the conditions that could be imposed, in ways that can be contrasted with decisions in the United States. See North Carolina v. Califano, 435 U.S. 962 (1978).

While noting these developments, Blair concludes that as of 1981, West Germany had experienced a substantial growth of "co-operative federalism" which increased the power of the central government and eluded control by the constitutional court. Blair suggests that "in developing this system of grants-in-aid, West Germany was merely following the same path as most federal systems, in which the extension of the power of the center has come principally via the superior financial power of the Federal authorities who by offers of subsidies can often ensure that their policy preferences prevail and indeed reduce the weaker members of the federal to a state of dependence." Blair at 225. Does Blair's description suggest that even strong judicial review cannot constrain centralizing fiscal tendencies of a successful federation?

Note that in the United States, federal grants as a percentage of state and local general expenditures peaked in the 1980 at 27.6%, and then declined by 1991 to 17.6%. See Advisory Commission on Intergovernmental

Relations, Significant Features of Fiscal Federalism vol. 2 at 30 (1994). Given the Supreme Court's jurisprudence, this development must be attributed primarily to political structures' response to political and economic (rather than legal) developments. How does this bear on your thinking about the role of judicial review in fiscal federalism? About the force of centralizing tendencies?

5. FEDERALISM, CENTRALIZATION AND DECENTRALIZATION: THE EUROPEAN UNION AND SUBSIDIARITY

What is the relationship between federalism, as a political form, and the centralization or decentralization of policy making and law administration? Consider this question as you read the following excerpt.

George A. Bermann, *Taking Subsidiarity Seriously: Federalism in the European Community and the United States*, 94 Colum. L. Rev. 331 (1994).

... [S]ubsidiarity enjoins the institutions of the Community to act in areas of concurrent competence "only if and insofar as the objectives of the proposed action cannot be sufficiently achieved by the Member States." ...

I. Subsidiarity and the European Community

The notion that action should be taken at the lowest level of government at which particular objectives can adequately be achieved can be applied in any polity in which governmental authority is lodged at different vertical levels ...

Advocates of subsidiarity in the European Community trace the concept to twentieth-century Catholic social philosophy, citing a 1931 Papal Encyclical of Pius XI entitled Quadragesimo anno. According to that document, subsidiarity requires that "[s]maller social units ... not be deprived of the possibility and the means for realizing that of which they are capable [and] [l]arger units ... restrict their activities to spheres which surpass the powers and abilities of the smaller units." For reasons that will become clear in the next section, Community leaders were content to distill from the ecclesiastical literature on subsidiarity a very rudimentary but quite suggestive concept ....

B. Subsidiarity and the European Community Treaties

...[The 1986 Single Europe Act, or SEA] created the conditions that would soon make subsidiarity one of the Community's most prominent concerns. Under the system of qualified majority voting, a Commission proposal could ripen into Council legislation over the opposition of several Member States.* This change made it easier for the Council to pass

---

* [Editors Note: Until the SEA, any member country could block proposals because of the former requirement of unanimous voting in the Council of Ministers of the EC.]

legislation, which in turn made the Commission bolder in its legislative initiatives and more determined in advancing them. The Member States were left in need of new instruments for controlling the Community institutions, especially since the SEA had also extended the Community's sphere of action to new areas (worker health and safety, research and technology, and regional development, as well as environmental protection)
. . . .

It is no coincidence then that the 1992 Maastricht Treaty on European Union (TEU)—which emerged from two 1990 intergovernmental conferences, one on economic and monetary union and the other on European political union—put subsidiarity in plain view, making it a central principle of Community law. Article A of the TEU proclaims that in the new European Union, "decisions are [to be] taken as closely as possible to the citizen." Article B of the TEU requires the Community institutions, in pursuing their objectives under the TEU, to "respect . . . the principle of subsidiarity," a principle spelled out as such in a new Article 3b added to the EC Treaty:

> In areas which do not fall within its exclusive competence, the Community shall take action, in accordance with the principle of subsidiarity, only if and in so far as the objectives of the proposed action cannot be sufficiently achieved by the Member States and can therefore, by reason of the scale or effects of the proposed action, be better achieved by the Community . . .

C.   Subsidiarity and the Evolution of Community Federalism

What accounts for the urgency with which subsidiarity has been pressed upon the European Community? The answer to this question lies in the magnitude of constitutional change that the Community has experienced over its brief history . . . [whose] cumulative effect was to alter profoundly the balance of power between the Community and the Member States, and eventually generate pressures for a doctrine like subsidiarity.

1.   The Court of Justice and its Supranationalist Creation.—The Court's fundamental doctrines concerning the relationship between Community law and the law of the Member States—notably the doctrines of direct applicability, direct effect, and supremacy, expounded by the Court in a series of rulings of the early 1960s—are by now well known . . . .

The principle of direct applicability posits that the adoption of legal norms by the Community institutions is sufficient to integrate them in to the legal orders of the Member States as well. In other words, whatever a State's ordinary treatment of international agreements might be, Community enactments do not need to be transposed, incorporated, or otherwise formally received into a Member State's law in order to become law within that State. The direct effects doctrine makes the further claim that Community law norms, if expressed clearly and unconditionally enough, confer on private parties rights that are legally enforceable against the Member States and that the institutions of those States, administrative and judicial alike, are required to protect. Put differently, a directly effective Community norm imposes obligations on the governments of the Member States in favor of private parties, which the latter may invoke directly, if need be, in national courts.

Lastly, the principle of supremacy mandates that Member State officials give precedence to Community law over national law in the event of a conflict between them. That the drafters failed to include an express Supremacy Clause in the EEC Treaty did not prevent the Court of Justice from inferring one, basing it on the necessity that the Community possess legal unity and that Community law be effective throughout the territory of the Member States . . . .

The doctrines of direct applicability, direct effect, and supremacy are by their nature expansive of Community law in relation to national law, and were readily seen as such, particularly as against the background of traditional attitudes toward the force and effect of international law in the national legal orders. Their claims have accordingly been described as "supranationalist." . . .

If the Member States largely accepted the Court's supranationalist claims, this is because they originally retained ultimate control over the Community's legislative process. The framers of the EC Treaty had entrusted the Community's legislative powers chiefly to a Council of Ministers in which representatives of the Member States could unapologetically express and vote the political interests of the States they represented. Moreover, by virtue of a combination of Treaty provisions and legislative tradition, the determined opposition of any one Member State to a measure would cause the measure to fail. Thus, while advocates of European integration drew satisfaction from the normative aspects of Community federalism (notably direct applicability, direct effect, and supremacy), advocates of Member State sovereignty took comfort in the special composition and voting procedures of the Council of Ministers. In fact the Court's heightening of the normative stakes of Community action probably caused the States to guard their political prerogatives all the more jealously.

2. New Elements in Community Federalism.—While the Court's federalist doctrines, on the one hand, and the States' preponderance in the Community legislative process, on the other, had produced something of a balance of power, other forces were working to disturb that balance . . . .

. . . [T]he advent in the SEA of qualified majority voting in the Council of Ministers threatened to deprive Member States of the political and legislative leverage to which they had become accustomed. . . . [T]he impact of qualified majority voting on the Community's federalism balance did not come in for very close examination at the time. . . . [T]he Commission**

** [Editors' Note: The Commission is an administrative arm of the Community with responsibilities *inter alia*, for drafting and proposing legislation for the Council to act on.]

believed, and very largely succeeded in convincing the Member States, that completion of the internal market by the end of 1992 was the Community's paramount objective and that substituting qualified majority voting for unanimous voting in the Council was vital to achieving it. . . .

The Maastricht Environment.—If further inducements toward subsidiarity were needed, the political and economic climate in which the Member State conferees were gathering in 1990 . . . supplied them. For the first time since the "Europessimism" of the 1970s and very early 1980s, the Member States governments found themselves in deep anxiety over the condition of their economies . . . .

In addition to an obstinate economic recession, the Member States also faced the prospect of a significant enlargement of the Community. Although the most imminent widening stood to bring relatively prosperous States—Austria, Finland, Norway, Sweden, and Switzerland—into the Community, the very increase in membership suggested that political agreement on common solutions would in the future only become more difficult to produce . . . .

At a constitutional moment like this—with the supranationalist stakes long since established, the terrain for Community action widened and still widening, and the rules of decision-making relaxed—subsidiarity was at its most beguiling. Other factors—the influx of immigrants, the loss of confidence in an effective common European foreign policy, and regional demands within the Member States themselves—only heightened the subsidiarity impulse. But, although it is the constitution-makers' task to shape political impulses like subsidiarity into workable and durable instruments, the established instruments of federalism all missed the point.

The principle of subsidiarity does not, for example, seek to challenge the direct applicability, direct effect, or supremacy of Community law, or any of the prerogatives of the Court of Justice. It does not quarrel with the notion of implied powers or with Community preemption, provided the use is fair. Since subsidiarity deals with the exercise of legislative self-restraint within the constitutional sphere of federal power, enumerating federal powers as such does not help; the Maastricht Treaty predictably reaffirmed the enumeration principle, requiring the Community to "act within the limits of the powers conferred upon it by this Treaty and of the objectives assigned to it therein." Subsidiarity asks a quite different question, namely whether the powers that do fall within the Community sphere should in fact be exercised. By the same token, expressly reserving to the States all powers not delegated to the federal government, as does the U.S. Tenth Amendment, simply begs the question. Subsidiarity challenges none of these notions, but it is not satisfied by any of them either. It starts off precisely where the conventional tools of constitutional federalism leave off and where legislative politics is ordinarily thought to begin.

II.   Putting Subsidiary into Practice

Subsidiarity may function in at least four different ways. Its ... most important function is legislative. Arguably, each participant in the legislative process of the Community—the Commission in proposing (and in some cases issuing) a rule, the Parliament and other bodies in expressing an opinion on a proposed rule, and the Council in adopting a rule—can determine whether the measure comports with the principle of subsidiarity. ... Second, any legislative doctrine can also perform an interpretive function. If the Council or Commission may be presumed to observe the principle of subsidiarity in adopting legislation, then those who are called on to interpret that legislation—including the Court of Justice but more commonly the various Member State officials who administer and enforce it—should, in case of doubt, favor the interpretation that most respects that principle. Third, compliance with the principle of subsidiarity may be regarded as an element of the legality of Community action. Thus, any measure infringing upon the principle would be invalid on that ground alone. However, even if subsidiarity is justiciable, its enforcement is reserved to the Community judiciary, since Member State courts cannot themselves rule on the validity of a Community measure.

Finally, the principle of subsidiarity can perform a confidence-building function by reassuring the constituent states, and notably the regions and other subcommunities within the states, that their distinctiveness will be respected at the European Community level. As shown by the evolution of Community federalism ... subsidiarity is ... being asked to play[] this role today. . . .

D.   Subsidiarity and the Court of Justice

... [T]he drafters at Maastricht sidestepped the question of whether and to what extent the principle of subsidiarity would be justiciable. When the European Council finally addressed the question at Edinburgh in 1992, ... [it decided that] while individual litigants in national courts might not be permitted to invoke the principle of subsidiarity to avoid the application of otherwise valid Community measures, legal challenges to Community measures could be brought on subsidiarity grounds directly in the Court of Justice ... by a Community institution or by one or more of the Member States politically opposed to it.

1.   Subsidiarity as a Procedural and Substantive Norm.—Assuming justiciability, ... casting subsidiarity in procedural rather than substantive terms will best allow the Court of Justice to promote respect for the values of localism without enmeshing itself in profoundly political judgments that it is ill-equipped to make and ultimately not responsible for making. The same characteristics that make the inquiry difficult for the political branches to conduct—namely, uncertainty about how much localism really matters on a given issue, the heavy reliance on prediction and the probabilities of competing scenarios, the possibility of discretionary tradeoffs between subsidiarity and proportionality, and the sheer exercise of political judgment entailed—make the inquiry even more problematic for the Court. . . .

[H]owever, the Court can seek to verify whether the institutions them-selves examined the possibility of alternative remedies at or below the Member State level. That very inquiry should encourage the political institutions to structure their discussion and focus their debate on the most central legislative task. ... Moreover, a decisional process which demon-strates that the institutions genuinely considered the available Member State alternatives before resolving to act is likely to win measurably greater trust and thus enjoy greater support among the Member States and European public opinion than one that does not ....

The efficacy of a procedural review of this sort should not, of course, be exaggerated, particularly since there are limits to the resources that the Court of Justice can or should expend in verifying whether the political branches actually inquired into subsidiarity and whether the inquiry was a genuine one.... The Court should not attempt to police closely the performance of such analyses; one can hope that the mere prospect of the Court policing their performance will cause the political branches to per-form the required examinations more seriously. If the values that the subsidiarity inquiry can be expected to serve—self-determination and ac-countability, personal liberty, flexibility, preservation of local identities, diversity, and respect for the internal divisions of component states—are important enough ... and if the costs of the inquiry are not too great (as I believe they are not), then the Court of Justice should require that it be made ....

... The German Constitutional Court has in effect determined that the largely comparable provisions on federal subsidiarity in the German Constitution are nonjusticiable, with the result that the "necessity" for federal government legislation in areas of concurrent competence is essen-tially a political question to be decided by the political branches without judicial interference. But deference to the political branches on subsidiarity does not require that the principle be made wholly nonjusticiable. ... The mere possibility that the Court will find the Community to have egregious-ly overstated the risks of leaving a matter in Member State hands, and will annul its exercise of power, should induce the Community's political branches to exercise sound judgment in this respect....

2. The Strength of the Political Safeguards of Subsidiarity.—The decision whether to assign the judiciary a role in policing legislative respect for subsidiarity ... is ... highly problematic .... [In the United States there is] the theory that the structure and composition of the federal government itself furnish adequate political safeguards for federalism .... [W]hatever the strengths of the theory of political safeguards in the United States, the theory fits the Community rather poorly.

Superficially, the Council of Ministers exhibits precisely the kind of structure that should enable it to safeguard the political interests of the States. Each Member State is separately represented in the Council by the government minister responsible for the field in which the Council is considering action. The minister's acknowledged responsibility is to look after the State's interests in the matter before the Council and to cast a vote accordingly.

The fact that a minister represents the interests of a Member State does not, however, mean that he or she will necessarily vote in a manner consistent with the principle of subsidiarity or the purposes underlying it, that is, the notion that policymaking discretion should be left in the most local hands possible.... [Rather,] Member State representatives will vote in the Council in accordance with their State's economic and political advantage as they see it in the context of the issue at hand. A particular policy may be so economically or politically favorable to a Member State that it wins the State's support in the Council, despite the fact that the policy's underlying objective could adequately be accomplished by action taken at or below the Member State level. In this respect, subnational regions may be among those most disadvantaged by the transfer of national regulatory authority to the Community institutions ....

The weakness of the Council in terms of domestic political accountability has ... become a preoccupation in certain Member States, particularly as the Community's powers of governance have grown. Denmark, for example, has pioneered techniques of national parliamentary oversight of the Government's voting patterns in the Council of Ministers. The French Constitution was amended in 1992 in contemplation of the Maastricht Treaty to ensure that the French Parliament would be consulted on the exercise of legislative powers by the Council. As a federal state itself, Germany recently amended its Constitution to guarantee that the Länder would actually have a decisive role in at least some of the votes that Germany casts in the Council; and the German Constitutional Court's recent affirmance of the constitutionality of the Maastricht Treaty seems to be conditional on the Länder having effective opportunities to participate in Council decision-making. These various strategies for heightening the responsiveness and accountability of Member State representatives in the Council, however, are still poorly developed and have yet to prove their efficacy.

The claim that the structure and composition of the Community institutions guarantee respect for subsidiarity is not much stronger in the case of the Commission or the European Parliament. The Commission, whose role in drafting and proposing Community legislation is paramount, does not even purport to act in the interests of the States ....

The European Parliament offers greater institutional promise in this respect. Its members are popularly elected by territorially-defined constituencies from among the Member States. As such, they are or should be in closer touch with the local populations and their aspirations for self-governance. ... On the other hand, seats in the European Parliament have chiefly attracted persons in search of a platform for the advancement of more or less well-defined political views or philosophies rather than the representation of local interests as such. Significantly, parliamentarians sit, and vote, according to broad cross-national party affiliations, not according to national or subnational geographic criteria . . . *

All in all, the institutional support for a theory of political safeguards of subsidiarity in the European Community is not very impressive . . . Arguably, the real institutional safeguard of subsidiarity in the Community is that, in most areas, the implementation of Community policy ultimately lies in the hands of Member State and local officials. Thus, states and localities have it within their power to influence the ways in which, and the efficacy with which, Community policy is actually administered. Unless the Community acquires much greater fiscal independence from the Member States than it now has, which is not in the offing, this situation is unlikely to change.

The argument that the decentralized administration of Community law favors subsidiarity is, however, deeply flawed. . . . [The argument confuses policy-making and policy-execution, and] only suggests that States and localities may weaken the enforcement of policies made at an inappropriately high level of government, not that they will do so, and certainly not that they will do so with any consistency. . . . . [T]he U.S. Supreme Court has come to view federalism as being ultimately impaired when the public cannot hold its elected officials politically responsible for the policy decisions they carry out. . . . Yet this is precisely the situation in the Community law system: Member State officials regularly implement policies they had little or no role in making . . . .

III. Subsidiarity and U.S. Federalism

. . .[T]he term federalism suggests a state of affairs in which political authority is both in law and in fact allocated between two or more levels of government. However, although federalism conveys a general sense of a vertical distribution . . . of power, it is not generally understood as expressing a preference for any particular distribution of that power, much less dictating any particular inquiry into the implications of specific governmental action for that distribution. In this respect, federalism and subsidiarity, though of course closely related, are quite different.

To inquire into the role of subsidiarity in U.S. federalism is to ask whether the federal government's exercise of legislative or regulatory authority over a field lying within the constitutional limits of federal jurisdiction is limited in any significant way out of respect for the states' capacity to accomplish the federal government's general objectives within that field. The traditional response to this question has been that whether and to what extent federal legislative or regulatory authorities refrain from exercising powers that are properly theirs to exercise under our Constitution is a political question for the political branches to resolve. A powerful school of thought, associated with Herbert Wechsler, claims that restraints on intervention by the federal government flow chiefly from "the sheer

* [Editors' Note: The European parliament's powers are still quite limited.]

existence of the states and [from] their political power to influence the action of the national authority." . . .

. . . [L]ike its foreign-sounding name, subsidiarity is foreign to the law and practice of federal legislation. The working assumption in the United States seems in fact to be that Congress, by virtue of its composition and mode of operation, will not act with needless disregard for the states' interest in regulatory autonomy. The courts accordingly have declined to enforce against Congress a specific legislative precept such as subsidiarity even though there is little evidence to suggest that Congress systematically follows any such precept of its own accord.

The situation is at least partially different when we turn to the exercise of authority by the federal agencies. On the one hand, . . . Congress . . . has not exerted pressure on the agencies to act in ways that demonstrate a high degree of respect for the states' own capacity to govern. . . . The Executive, on the other hand, has attempted to introduce into the regulatory process certain considerations that bear directly on federalism and that at least in part reflect subsidiarity. Thus, a series of executive orders calls upon the federal agencies not only to minimize the regulatory burdens imposed on the private sector, but also to refrain from regulating at all if action at the state or local level would satisfactorily accomplish the federal government's objectives. These executive orders evoke, respectively, the Community law notions of proportionality and subsidiarity[;] their effectiveness with respect to subsidiarity, in particular is, however, very doubtful. . . .

. . . Certainly Congress as an institution does not systematically evaluate the capacity or will of the states to deal with particular problems before seeking to address them at the federal level.[303] . . .

Nevertheless, one can readily imagine ways in which the federal legislative process might be structured to promote consideration of federalism issues, and even subsidiarity, as a regular feature of that process. For example, the Rules of the House or Senate could require the committee report on a bill to assess the states' capacity to deal with the problem that the bill addresses and to demonstrate the need for federal intervention in their place. Alternately, a standing body within the House and Senate . . . might be asked to review bills, at some point prior to a final vote, specifically from a subsidiary point of view. . . .

In the absence of any institutional mechanism of federalism review within Congress itself, advocates of greater state autonomy in political affairs strive to have their message heard by [particular congressional committees and subcommittees] . . . .

One source of support . . . [in] mounting a political claim based on subsidiarity is state and local officialdom itself. For example, state highway

---

303.   . . . The National Governors' Association (NGA) has recommended that Congress make a specific determination of the compelling need for federal action before enacting legislation and that it actively involve the States before doing so. See NGA, Permanent Policy on Federalism, § 1.6.1 (1993) . . . .

officials, opposed to the conditioning of federal highway aid on a state's conformity to federal standards on the control of drunken driving, can provide key Senators and Representatives (perhaps most readily those of their own states) with material demonstrating the State Highway Department's successes in controlling drunken driving or their fresh and promising initiatives in that direction. ... Still, at the end of the day, those who would complain about the federalism implications of a bill enjoy no greater or different opportunities to influence its fate than those adversely affected by the bill's other aspects ....

... [N]either *National League of Cities* (prior to its overruling by *Garcia*) nor New York v. United States is directly responsive to subsidiarity as the Europeans conceive of it. Subsidiarity is not served by carving out a privileged zone of "traditional governmental functions," as under *National League of Cities*, and sheltering it from federal governance; subsidiarity calls for the practice of legislative self-restraint across the full range of substantive lawmaking power. Nor is subsidiarity secured by the New York v. United States remedy of "offer[ing] States the choice of regulating [an] activity according to federal standards or having state law pre-empted by federal regulation." It seeks to preserve the states' authority to prescribe rules of law and not merely to decide whether to lend their resources to the administration of federal law.

The language of the Tenth Amendment contributes to its awkwardness as an anchor for subsidiarity. ... It is quite difficult to see how a principle of enumeration of federal powers can even begin to address the political allocation of power where power is constitutionally shared. Yet that is precisely subsidiarity's province.

We thus find that, although federalism lies at the heart of the United States constitutional system, neither the text of the Constitution nor the Court's federalism jurisprudence offers very strong legal guarantees that a proper political balance between the federal government and the states will be maintained ....

The principle of subsidiarity is in fact poorly adapted to the particular challenges to federal regulation now being mounted in state and local governmental circles in the United States. Subsidiarity expresses an elementary and abstract principle of regulatory power-sharing, one designed to reassure a polity experiencing sudden and dramatic centralization in the exercise of regulatory power. By contrast, regulatory patterns in the United States, although always subject to change, are well established, and a strong federal regulatory presence in the lives of Americans is not in itself something new. In some respects, state and local officials actually prefer a strong federal presence. What they often seek is not so much a broad federal regulatory retreat of the sort conjured by subsidiarity as a series of specific operational remedies in the workings of federalism: greater flexibility in the administration of federal programs, less "red tape," fewer conditions on federal grants in aid, few if any "unfunded mandates," and much more generous federal financial support to state and local governments. Thus, although the leading organizations of state and local government are almost certainly sympathetic to subsidiarity as a general proposition, they have shown greater interest in targeting particular federal legislative and regulatory practices than in re-delineating federal and state spheres of authority as such . . . .

. . .[T]he Supreme Court has . . . thought in terms of a categorical "core of State sovereignty" that Congress may not invade. That "core" has been defined as the states' right to organize themselves freely in the performance of their functions, or as their right not to be conscripted in the enforcement of federal law. But never has it been translated into an express and judicially enforceable statement of preference for state over federal action in areas of concurrent jurisdiction . . . .

This is not to suggest that organizations that speak for the interests of state and local government as such in the United States have never subscribed to a general principle of federalism along the lines of subsidiarity; in fact they have, especially recently. Even in those quarters, however, the notion that the purposes of federalism will be served by systematically favoring state over federal initiatives still tends to take a back seat to more pragmatic concerns over such issues as the fiscal and administrative costs of federal regulation to state and local governments.

IV.   EC Subsidiarity and U.S. Federalism

The elevation of subsidiary to a first principle of Community constitutional law contrasts sharply with the apparent indifference to subsidiarity both as an abstract tenet and a working instrument of U.S. federalism. . . . The point of the comparison is . . . not to have the United States join the subsidiarity band-wagon—far from it; it is, rather, to ask whether the tepid embrace of subsidiarity in U.S. federalism signals that subsidiarity has indeed been oversold in the Community, and if not, why not. If subsidiarity is not equal to federalism's task in the United States, it is certainly fair to ask why it should be considered fit for those purposes in Europe. The comparison, in short, may help us assess the virtues of subsidiarity for the Community and, in the process, may allow us to better understand the respective natures of EC and U.S. federalism.

. . . [T]he United States, although it takes federalism seriously, behaves as if it can afford to take subsidiarity rather lightly. The comparison with the United States helps clarify the basic distinction . . . between the concepts of subsidiarity and federalism. Reexamining institutional relationships within the Community in light of the United States situation and experience, I conclude that the Community does not have the same luxury of indifference toward subsidiarity . . . [and] that the Court of Justice should undertake the delicate policing functions that I also described there.

A.   The U.S. and EC Settings

Any comparison between the United States and the Community today must of course acknowledge the fundamental difference between, on the one hand, maintaining a semblance of balance in the power relations between the federal government and the states in a system designed along federal lines from its very beginning, and, on the other hand, consciously imposing a new multi-layered legal system on a continent historically dominated by sovereign Nation-States, themselves mostly unitary in structure. The mere fact that the United States has endured as a federal system over as long a period as it has, on the basis of a largely stable set of federalism ground rules, has afforded it a sense of both continuity and security. That sense of continuity and security in turn helps to explain the reluctance to designate any single legislative principle, be it subsidiarity or anything else, as the watchword of federalism, or to ask the judiciary to enforce that principle against the political branches.

The escalating debates over regulatory federalism in the United States tell us that at least some participants in the U.S. political process, and some observers, consider this sense of continuity and security to be basically false . . . .

It is interesting that, while critics in the United States commonly allege and deplore a growing imbalance of power between the federal government and the states, to the detriment of the states, the means of redress that they most vigorously advance are ones that sidestep the central issue raised by subsidiarity. . . . [T]he most common prescriptions include a reduction in the detail of federal legislation and regulation, an increase in flexibility in the choice of means by which state and local governments carry out federal policies, an abandonment of particularly objectionable federal legislative techniques, and, above all, the provision of full federal funding to the states for implementing programs that are essentially imposed on them from above. It is tempting to explain away the difference between the debates in the United States and Europe in terms of a supposed American penchant for the pragmatic and particularized and an aversion to the abstract. The fact is that . . . the advocates of federalism in the United States may simply be more concerned with the specifics of the relationship between the federal government and the states than with the relative scale on which those governments exercise political power. This in turn may reflect an assumption that, while certain patterns or techniques of federal governance are especially objectionable to state and local governments . . . the American system of federalism nevertheless tolerates . . . a wide range of differences in the distribution of policymaking authority between the federal government and the states.

A further factor shaping the qualitative difference between U.S. and EC federalism relates to the political and cultural stakes in the integration process. While regional differences in the United States are not to be underestimated, it is idle to suppose that geography as such plays nearly as big a role in federalism debates in the United States today as it does in Europe. In Europe, geography still brings along with it differences in culture, language, and social and political values that are far more pronounced than the generally prevailing differences in the United States. These differences obtain not only among Member States, but also among regions within them. Because the reservation of political authority to more local units, at the expense of the federal government, brings greater opportunities for the assertion of distinctive cultural, linguistic, and social and political values, subsidiarity is a particularly apt instrument for a polity determined not merely to maintain a decent equilibrium in power between the federal government and the states, but to minimize the loss of political autonomy at the more local levels.

B.   Subsidiarity and Federalism Revisited

For these and doubtless other reasons, U.S. federalism places greater emphasis on the presence of an overall balance of power between the federal government and the states than on respect for any single rule for allocating competences among the different levels of government. Federal and state-level decision-making each have at least some natural advantages that nearly all would concede and that Congress and the federal agencies have often sought to combine in creative ways. Beneath the well-worn generalities about the virtues of centralism and localism lies a recognition that the choice of the governmental level at which a given problem is best addressed, or a given policy best established, should in principle turn on a number of different considerations. The European Community doctrine of subsidiarity certainly points to one such consideration—the relative capacities of federal and state government to deal effectively or adequately with the problem or policy at hand . . . .

However, one may, in assigning political authority in a democratic society, legitimately ask other, perhaps more focused, questions. One may ask, for example, whose interests are likely to be affected by a given policy, and seek to vest the power to establish that policy in the body that most effectively represents those interests. It is likewise fitting, in a market that would be "common," to inquire into the importance on any given issue of having a common regulatory standard, and to set that value off against the value of allowing standards on that particular issue to be set locally. (Some matters may strike us as of "naturally" local interest; others may not, but a wide disparity in local needs or conditions might nevertheless argue in favor of local governance.) Economists remind us to look also at the risk that communities may regulate in ways that impose costs unfairly on neighboring communities, . . . that they will engage in destructive competition in an effort to attract and keep industry, or that they may fail to capture important economies of scale. Conversely, governance at the state or local level may be a way to ensure, if we deem it appropriate to do so, that communities bear the burdens of remedying a problem that they may have had a unique hand in causing. . . . As the range of considerations deemed relevant to the allocation of power among levels of government widens, the number of criteria and the incidence of conflict among them inevitably increase. It is no wonder that discussions of federalism in the United States so rarely produce general outcome-decisive formulas.

Subsidiarity, on the other hand, entails approaching federalism with the distinctive attitude that federal action should be taken in areas of shared competence only if the goal in question cannot adequately be achieved by action at the state level or below. Unless the term "adequately" is, as seems quite possible, simply a cover for something else (including the specific factors I have mentioned above, but possibly others as well), the choice between state and federal action under the principle of subsidiarity could turn on some diffuse assessment of whether action at the state level will satisfactorily meet the purposes that seem chiefly to underlie a proposed course of action. In other words, subsidiarity could displace a variety of specific considerations that are actually highly pertinent to choosing the most appropriate level of government for action. In a seasoned federalism like that of the United States, accustomed to taking this variety of considerations into account, the notion of subsidiarity may, in the end, have a somewhat hollow, even foolish, ring to it . . . .

. . . [Moreover] if, due to subsidiarity, we foreclose federal regulation of an activity on the ground that the states can adequately regulate it, while wholly disregarding the indirect effects of disparate state regulations on the functioning of a common market, we run the risk of causing substantial harm to interstate commerce. Prevailing attitudes toward federalism in the United States avert this risk because they allow the political branches, if they choose to do so, to entertain the tradeoff squarely. The Office of Management and Budget summarizes the exercise as deciding "whether the burdens on interstate commerce arising from divergent State and local regulations are so great that they outweigh the advantages of diversity and local political choice."

The difference between subsidiarity, as the Community understands it, and federalism, as commonly understood in this country, is therefore not simply one of emphasis. As expressed in the Maastricht Treaty, subsidiarity states a generic preference for state over federal action when either would in some generalized sense do. Put differently, subsidiarity systematically places the burden of proof on the proponents of Community action. How strong this preference for state action turns out to be will ultimately depend on what it takes and, especially, how much it takes to establish the states' inadequacy in this regard. My purpose in contrasting the notion of subsidiarity with federalism is not to discredit it, but . . . to show that an equation of subsidiarity with federalism . . . is misleading and possibly false.

C. The Political Safeguards of Federalism and "Commandeering" in the Community

. . . [T]he basic notion that the Council of Ministers directly represents the peoples of Europe has never been seriously advanced, even by the Community's strongest advocates.

The Council's unique structure thus forces recognition of the distinction between representing the states and representing the people that Congress (at least since the direct election of U.S. Senators) has managed to obscure. The Council represents, and claims to represent, only the states themselves. . . . The Council simply has sufficient incentives and opportunities—including a strong sense of Community "mission" and a relative insulation from the ordinary national mechanisms of accountability, to name just two—to offset any natural calling to protect the Member States' interests and to help preserve their identities and the identities of their various subcommunities . . . .

The direct institutional relations between the Community and the Member States also differ substantially from those that obtain in U.S. federalism, and they too argue in favor of taking subsidiarity especially seriously. From its beginnings, the Community has relied pervasively on the Member State legislatures, executives, and courts for the enforcement of Community law, and this is unlikely to change in the near future. One consequence of this arrangement . . . is that the resources of all the branches of government in the Member States, and thus the resources of their populations, are harnessed . . . to the implementation of policy that has effectively been made in Brussels, at an altogether different level of government. Moreover, as we have seen, the makers of that policy are neither politically accountable in any verifiable way to the people of those states, nor necessarily even politically representative of them. This "accountability deficit" is all the more pronounced where the Member States are themselves divided among culturally or linguistically distinctive subcommunities that are even further removed from the Community decisional process than the national constituencies that the Member States purport to represent.

What we observe in the workings of the Community is thus the very pattern of intergovernmental relations—specifically, commandeering of Member State apparatus and resources in the service of federally-established policies—that has generated constitutional disquiet in the United States in recent years. To the extent that a disjunction between the freedom to make policy and the burdens of implementing it compromises democratic values, the European Community finds itself in a very precarious situation indeed. Subsidiarity has a special calling in the Community precisely because it may help reduce the field over which this unavoidable disjunction occurs.

D. Conclusion

The European Community (or . . . after Maastricht, the European Union) is basically a young federal system still in search of enduring constitutional foundations. Memories easily reach back to a period when the Community did not exist, or existed but was barely taken seriously. . . . Precisely because the Community institutions have come so far so fast in securing their place in European governance, they have awakened intense fears in the Member States, their subcommunities, and their populations over a loss of control of their political future.

. . . Community institutions have very largely behaved, at least since 1985, as if the mere prospect of strengthening the commonness of the internal market justified establishing Community-wide standards in business and trade even in otherwise purely intrastate situations . . . . [D]espite the impressive arsenal of doctrinal limits on Community action, a political decision to regulate a matter on a Community-wide basis was unlikely to be questioned by the Court of Justice. More recently, the institutions have shown their readiness to regulate in essentially non-economic spheres as well.... The conditions in the Community are thus decidedly ripe for the kind of federal legislative self-discipline that subsidiarity implies ....

...[S]ubsidiarity even on its own terms seems quite crude, certainly as compared to prevailing attitudes toward federalism in the United States. A salient feature of United States federalism is its capacity to accommodate a wide assortment of considerations in the decision to allocate political responsibility over a given issue to a certain level of government. Another feature is its close attention to the operational aspects of federalism.... As against this combination of breadth in identifying the factors relevant to federalism, on the one hand, and attentiveness to specificity in the workings of federalism, on the other, the European Community's absorption with subsidiarity may appear to be immature. However, for a polity that is still seeking to establish its basic federal-state equilibrium, rather than merely to preserve it, the search for a guiding principle of regulatory federalism, and the designation of subsidiarity as that principle, are entirely appropriate.

Questions and Comments

1. Professor Bermann suggests that subsidiarity developed as a substitute for the unanimous voting requirement that used to exist in the Council. How does this work functionally? The unanimous voting requirement permitted a member state to block a measure, even if it promoted a policy that could only be pursued at the transnational level, because it would have severe disadvantageous effects in that state. Would the principle of subsidiarity provide protection from this? In arguing for judicial review of subsidiarity issues, Bermann critiques the "political safeguards" of voting in council to preserve the subsidiarity principle, because countries will tend to vote in accord with their particular interests on discrete issues rather than in accord with the "neutral principle" of subsidiarity. If this is so, does the substitution of the standard of subsidiarity for the rule of unanimous voting reflect a substantial step towards the E.U. becoming a nation? Cf. J.H.H. Weiler, *The Transformation of Europe*, 100 Yale L. J. 2403, 2458–61 (1991) (emphasizing constitutional importance of abandonment of unanimity in Council voting).

2. Professor Bermann advocates procedural, rather than substantive, review of the subsidiarity norms. Consider whether U.S. v. Lopez, 514 U.S. 549 (1995) (holding unconstitutional federal guns near schools law) could be reconceptualized as a form of such procedural review in the United States, in which Congress' failure to provide reasons for federal, in addition to state, regulation and its failure to explain how the law related to a source of federal power suggested a failure seriously to consider these issues. See Vicki C. Jackson, *Federalism and the Uses and Limits of Law: Printz and Principle*, 111 Harv L. Rev. 2180, 2234–46 (1998). For an argument that a principle something like subsidiarity can and should inform U.S. constitutional analysis of the scope of federal preemption of state laws, see Stephen Gardbaum, *Rethinking Constitutional Federalism*, 74 Tex. L. Rev. 795, 831–37 (1996)

3. To what extent does the "procedural safeguards of federalism" argument depend on whose interests are being protected—those of the subnational governments, or those of the people in the subnational governments? Are there other possibilities?

4. A prominent European scholar and judge, Koen Lenaerts, suggests that there are at least two kinds of federalisms: "integrative," or centralizing federalism, and "devolutionary," or decentralizing federalism. See Koen Lenaerts, *Constitutionalism and the Many Faces of Federalism*, 38 Am. J. Comp. L. 205 (1990). Does the nearly simultaneous creation of the European Union and the adoption of the principle of subsidiarity suggest that one polity can move in both directions at once? See also Michael C. Dorf and Charles F. Sabel, *A Constitution of Democratic Experimentalism*, 98 Colum. L. Rev. 267 (1998) (arguing for more "experimentation and power sharing between the federal and state governments and within the federal government").

5. Professor Bermann characterizes the U.S. and the E.U. as being at very different stages in the development of federalism, with the basic structure in the U.S. being more or less set. Consider whether in the U.S. there is a process of constitutional change via interpretation that is in fact quite active at the moment, giving rise to renewed debate over constitutional fundamentals.

6. Professor Weiler has raised a number of questions about the European Union. First, he has asked how to solve the so-called "Democratic Deficit," of the E.U.'s institutions, a deficit reflected in the very limited influence of the elected European parliament; he distinguishes between the "formal" legitimacy of the E.U. and its "social legitimacy," which, he has argued, remains to be established. He has also raised cautions about a future of European "unity," which he sees as entailing possibilities for European nationalism writ large, and has urged instead a conception of a European community that does not involve eliminating the sovereignty of the nation states that make it up, thus maintaining an ongoing tension between and among member states and the Community. See Weiler, at 2480; J.H.H. Weiler, *Parliamentary Democracy in Europe 1992: Tentative Questions and Answers,* in Constitutionalism and Democracy: Transitions in the Contemporary World (Douglas Greenberg, Stanley N. Katz, Melanie Beth Oliviero, and Steven C. Wheatley eds. 1993).

Note on Federalism and Constitutionalism Beyond National Borders

Widespread discussion of constitutional change in the E.U. illustrates the degree to which versions of both federalism and constitutionalism exist that are not linked to traditional sovereign states. If Belgium (discussed below) suggests that federalism does not necessarily require government structures that are always territorially defined, the E.U. and the experience of the European Court of Justice suggest that federalism and constitutionalism can exist in an institutional regime lacking traditional indicia of sovereignty (such as control over military defense and foreign affairs). International human rights law is another important instance in which aspects of what might be thought of as constitutionalism is reflected in governmental mechanisms for investigating (e.g., the U.N. Human Rights Committee) or adjudicating (e.g., the European Court on Human Rights) compliance with human rights standards found in international law. For a useful explication of the argument that the emergence of international law concerning the treatment owed individuals and minority groups, as well as the increased development of international agreements and organizations, threaten traditional concepts of state sovereignty, see Neil MacCormick, *Beyond the Sovereign State,* 56 Mod. L. Rev. 1 (1993).

1.   How do such supranational mechanisms become established, legitimate and constraining? As discussed earlier in Chapter II, one important feature of late 20th century developments has been the increasing recognition in international law that states owe enforceable duties to individuals. Consider in this regard the effects of assigning rights, under international law, to individuals, in "constitutionalizing" international relationships, as well as the effects of national courts' participation in the declaration and application of developing transnational constitutional norms. See Laurence R. Helfer and Anne–Marie Slaughter, *Toward a Theory of Effective Supranational Adjudication,* 107 Yale L. J. 273 (1997) (arguing that the success of the European Court of Justice and European Court of Human Rights is "linked to their power to hear claims brought by private parties directly against national governments or against other private parties," which allows the European courts to "penetrate the surface of the state," forging direct relationships with individual citizens and with national courts); Jeffrey C. Cohen, *The European Preliminary Reference Jurisdiction and U.S. Supreme Court Review of State Court Judgments: A Study in Comparative Judicial Federalism,* 44 Am. J. Comp. L. 421 (1996). International norms can become "constitutionalized" as well by being incorporated into the domestic constitutional law of nation states. See Eric Stein, *International Law in Internal Law: Towards Internationalization of Central–Eastern European Constitutions?,* 88 Am. J. Int'l Law 427 (1994); see also John H. Jackson, *Status of Treaties in Domestic Legal Systems: A Policy Analysis,* 86 Am. J. Int'l Law 310 (1992).

2.   Does focus on legal instruments and decisions obscure the effects of transnational developments? For a discussion of globalization as a threat to constitutionalism (because globalization is characterized by the development of multinational economic forces that are not linked to or constrained by traditional nation states) see Phil G. Cerny, *Globalization and the Residual State: The Challenge to Viable Constitutionalism,* in Abdo I. Baaklini & Helen Desfosses, eds., Designs for Democratic Stability: Studies in Viable Constitutionalism (1997). For a different set of concerns, see John

O. McGinnis, *The Decline of the Western Nation State and the Rise of the Regime of International Federalism,* 18 Cardozo L. Rev. 903 (1996) (raising concern for the future that new international mechanisms of governance might issue redistributive orders and thus interfere with markets' capacity to increase wealth).

3.   Consider whether the growth of transnational legal organs may contribute to or facilitate the growth of regional and local autonomy movements within existing nation states. To the extent that one of the benefits provided by the nation state is the material advantage that comes from economic centralization and large free trade areas, and to the extent that supranational agreements assure a broader and more efficient common market, the costs to subnational communities compared to the benefits of seeking greater autonomy within their nation states may be diminished. Should one expect that if the E.U. continues to grow in importance and power, there will be increased demand for devolution of power to subnational, or cross-national, regions and communities? For a different perspective on the effects of the E.U. on the development of regional autonomy movements, see Naomi Roht–Arriaza, *The Committee on the Regions and the Role of Regional Governments in the European Union,* 1997 Hast. Int'l & Comp. L. Rev. 413 (1997). Exploring the simultaneous centralization of the European Union and the decentralization of government functions in a number of its member states, she describes the growth of both formal and informal mechanisms by which subnational governments influence E.U. institutions, attributing some of this growth to concerns that E.U. developments not impede the devolutionary effects of decentralization within member states.

4.   How might these developments bear on what is the appropriate "unit" of comparison in thinking about comparative constitutional federalism?

B.   FEDERALISM AND THE PROTECTION/ACCOMMODATION OF MINORITIES: CANADA, BELGIUM, ETHIOPIA AND THE U.S.

A second set of questions about comparative constitutional federalism concerns what federalism can contribute to the protection of individual rights, particularly those of members of identifiable minorities. Under what, if any, conditions is federalism a helpful way to deal with protecting and accommodating the interests of minorities?

In thinking about federalist solutions to the treatment of minority groups and their interests, consider the degree to which having subnational units of governance that correspond to ethnic, linguistic, religious or racial groupings may reinforce differences and exacerbate conflict rather than facilitate cooperation. Consider, in this regard, the claim that nationalism can have a "domino" effect, and that certain federalist solutions can be destabilizing in encouraging competing nationalisms. See John Meisel,

Multinationalism and the Federal Idea, in Rethinking Federalism: Citizens, Markets and Governments in a Changing World 342 (Karen Knop, Sylvia Ostry, Richard Simeon, and Katherine Swinton eds. 1995). Note, moreover, that in precisely those circumstances where geographic federalism might be seen as a solution to demands of a territorially compact minority in a larger union, the situation of other "minorities" within a minority is likely to arise. To avoid such tragic responses as "ethnic cleansing," federalist solutions to minority concerns may need to be coupled with some form of universal human rights protection.

1. CANADA

Consider Canada, which since its founding has been confronted with the linguistic distinctiveness and francophonic attitudes of its French-speaking province of Quebec. Currently both English and French are official languages in Canada; while there is no official state religion, there are guarantees of tax support for certain religious schools for Catholics and for Protestants in some provinces where those groups are in a minority. Of Canada's population of 29 million, about 40% are of British origin, 27% of French origin, another 20% from other European countries, about 11% of other national origin (mostly Asian) and about 1.5–2% of aboriginal origin. According to Barry Strayer, in 1981, about 61% of the population had English as their "mother tongue" and 25% French; but of the population of Quebec, 82% were of French mother tongue. In 1996, official Canadian statistics show 59% reporting English and 23% reporting French as the mother tongue; in Quebec in 1996, 81% reported French as the mother tongue and only 8% reported English as the mother tongue. Canada Year Book 1999 99 (Table 3.16). Strayer reports that French speakers outside of Quebec are far more likely to be bilingual than English speakers; within Quebec, English speakers were more likely to be bilingual (in French) than French speakers were in English. In the essay excerpted below, Strayer observes that this distribution "demonstrate[s] the importance of a critical mass in the daily use and maintenance of language," noting as well that the majority of aboriginal peoples used English in their homes, while smaller numbers used aboriginal languages or French.

Quebec did not approve the 1982 Charter, and has sought recognition as a "distinct society" within Canada. After the failure of the Meech Lake accord (discussed above in Chapter V) the federal government sponsored further intergovernmental consideration of the form of Canadian federalism, leading to the Charlottetown Consensus Report that would have effected several changes, including recognition of Quebec as a "distinct society" within Canada. These proposals, however, were rejected in a national referendum held in 1992.

A referendum in Quebec on independence in October 1995 was defeated by a very narrow margin—50.6% against, 49.4% in favor. As advocates of independence for Quebec continue to push for a future referendum, talk has emerged about the possible partition of Quebec, in order to permit

Montreal (which voted more strongly against independence than the rest of Quebec) to remain part of Canada.

As you read the materials in this section, consider competing visions of multiculturalism in Canada: Trudeau's "pan-Canadian" vision of a bilingual Canada, in which a French or English speaker could obtain services in and deal with the government in their own tongue across the country; "asymmetric" federalism, in which Quebec is seen as a "distinct society," and as the special place for the French language and culture in Canada; and a more multi-ethnic federalism, which extends the idea of special recognition to a multitude of language groups and the aboriginal peoples. How have constitutional developments reflected, and affected, these visions?

History: Canada's struggle with the multiple identities of its inhabitants goes back hundreds of years in its history as a colony. France was the first of the European powers to colonize large areas of Canada (called "New France"), imposing French law and a semi-feudal landholding system. The Catholic Church played an important role, a Catholic bishop sitting as a member of the nonrepresentative governing council; the Church controlled education.

After years of fighting with the French, Britain gained control over Canada in the 1763 Treaty of Paris. Well before the 1867 British North America Act (regarded as the creation of the modern nation of Canada), Great Britain had struggled with how to approach the French-speaking population of Quebec. Its policies ranged over the years from assimilationist to accommodating of the language and customs of its French-speaking colonists: For example, according to Barry Strayer, despite provisions of the Treaty of Paris to protect freedom to practice Catholicism, the British made it a condition to serve in the elected assembly of Quebec to take an oath inconsistent with Catholicism, leading to the absence of a general assembly during the first years of British control.

Yet as the American colonies became more confrontational in the 1770s, Britain modulated its approach towards the Quebecois in order to cement their loyalties, for example, restoring in part use of the French law of property and civil rights. In 1791, the British adopted a Constitution Act dividing its Canadian holdings into two parts: Upper Canada (the southern part of what is now Ontario) and Lower Canada (the southern part of Quebec). Each separate province had its own government, an arrangement permitting the French in Quebec to preserve French language and legal institutions. After armed uprisings in both provinces in the 1830s, the British passed a new Union Act, of 1840, combining the two provinces into a single unit, with a single government in which English was the only official language. Representation rules advantaged the English-speaking settlers in Upper Canada. The assimilative goals of the Act, however, were defeated by the development of a political practice within the unitary legislature not to enact major legislation without a majority vote from the members of each of the two regions. Within 8 years, moreover, the restrictions on the use of French as an official language had been repealed.

The 1867 British North America Act, now called the Constitution Act, 1867, formally united four provinces: Quebec, Ontario, Nova Scotia and New Brunswick. Each had a provincial government, and a new federal government was established.

In the first excerpt, Barry Strayer (on whose work some of this summary relied) takes up the story line.

Barry Strayer, *The Canadian Constitution and Diversity* (1985), in Forging Unity Out of Diversity: The Approaches of Eight Nations (Robert A. Goldwin, Art Kaufman, and William A. Schambra eds., 1985)

Constitutional Protection of Diversity. Canadians generally regard July 1, 1867, as the date their country was born. On that day occurred what is generally referred to as confederation, the coming into force of what was then called the British North America Act, 1867 (now known as the Constitution Act, 1867), which federally united the provinces of Canada, Nova Scotia, and New Brunswick. The new entity thus created was entitled the Dominion of Canada; it had a central government in Ottawa and four provinces—Quebec, Ontario, Nova Scotia, and New Brunswick—each with its own provincial government. The act distributed powers between the provincial and federal governments and established a number of other institutions.

Although the Constitution Act did not complete the process of nation building, it provided a vehicle by which this has been accomplished. It included means by which other British territories in North America could be added to the nucleus, and this has been done, the process being completed in 1949 with the union of Newfoundland as the tenth province of Canada. Although the act confirmed and enlarged the area of self-government enjoyed by British North Americans, it did not make the Dominion of Canada fully independent. Control over Canada's external relations and initially much of its defense policy was retained by British authorities. Full independence came about as an evolutionary process that was not completed until after the First World War, in which Canada played an important role. For some sixty years Canada has been, for all practical purposes, an independent nation. . . .

. . . [T]he Constitution Act, 1867, which we have long regarded as our basic Constitution, contained nothing by way of a comprehensive declaration or guarantee of individual rights. Its preamble, in expressing the desire of the provinces concerned to be federally united "with a constitution similar in principle to that of the United Kingdom," was generally understood to adopt by reference the principles of parliamentary supremacy. Nevertheless, confederation, with its benefits of maintaining a separate British North American identity, was possible only on terms that would preserve the diversity of its two main languages and religions.

The adoption of a federal system was itself a means of preserving the diversity existing among the previously separate colonies. In no respect was this more important than in gaining the adherence of Quebec to the scheme: federation, with its distribution of powers, detached the governance of the new province of Quebec from the old province of Canada and put it in the hands of a new provincial government elected by a majority of French-speaking Roman Catholics. Given the wide scope of provincial powers, including education and "property and civil rights," this was thought to put in the hands of Quebeckers the power to preserve and shape their own culture.

Apart from the federal system itself, the Constitution provided two specific forms of protection for diversity: one with respect to language and the other with respect to religion. French speakers would be in the majority in one province, Quebec, although that province would continue to have a substantial English-speaking minority. In the dominion as a whole, however, the French would be in a minority. Section 133 of the Constitution Act, 1867, guaranteed the right of individuals to use either English or French in the federal parliament, the legislature of Quebec, federally created courts, and the courts of Quebec. An additional requirement was that the bills and statutes and other records of the two legislative bodies be published in both languages, which has been interpreted to mean that laws must be enacted in both languages, not merely translated later from one language to the other. In 1870, when the province of Manitoba was established, a similar guarantee was provided with respect to its legislature and courts. These guarantees created individual rights—freedom to choose either English or French as a means of expressing oneself in the courts or legislatures concerned, as well as the right to use the records of those legislatures in either language and to be governed by laws enacted in both languages.

The religious guarantees are found in section 93 of the Constitution Act, 1867, and counterparts adopted in respect of provinces later joining the confederation. Although the Constitution did not establish a religion, it tried to protect the established rights of certain religious minorities to public funding of their denominational schools. Section 93 assumed that the population could be divided into two categories—Protestants and Roman Catholics—and provided that where at the time of confederation a system of publicly funded denominational schools existed in any province for either of those religious minorities, the province was obliged to continue that system. Apart from opening an avenue to judicial review when any province denied such rights, the section provided that when a province denied such rights as existed at union or as may have been granted since union, an appeal would lie to the federal cabinet, which could require the province to take remedial action. If the province failed to comply with such a directive, Parliament could enact the necessary remedial laws.

Because these guarantees were designed to protect the status quo at the time of union, they are generally thought to apply in only six of the ten provinces. Certain modifications of section 93 have been adopted with respect to provinces that came in after 1867. One of these provinces, Newfoundland, has in effect no system of public schools, and therefore a comparable guarantee protects the funding of a variety of denominational schools in that province.

For present purposes there are a few salient points to note. First, section 93 appears to be a protection of collective rights since it refers to rights or privileges "with respect to denominational schools which any class of persons have by law in the province at the Union." Obviously, the assertion of the right to establish a school requires a collective effort by a large number of like-minded people, and this is not a right that attaches to an individual.

Second, and as a corollary of the preceding point, these guarantees have occasionally worked to the detriment of the individual right of choice. They have sometimes, for example, been held to preclude children not of the minority faith from attending its schools, and vice versa.

Third, in spite of several efforts through the courts to do so, it has not been possible to use these guarantees to protect the use of a minority language as the medium of instruction in denominational schools run by religious minorities. Over the years both the French-speaking Roman Catholics of Ontario and the English-speaking Protestants of Quebec have unsuccessfully sought to invoke section 93 for this purpose.

Fourth, this is the only clear assignment by the [1867] Canadian Constitution of authority to the federal government and Parliament to protect individual or collective rights, through appeal to the federal cabinet and, if necessary, remedial federal legislation. In this respect it is somewhat analogous to the provisions in the Thirteenth, Fourteenth, and Fifteenth amendments to the United States Constitution, which authorize Congress to enforce by legislation the guarantees in those amendments. It must be noted, however, that these powers have never been successfully used, because of the political difficulties, and at least one federal government has been defeated largely as a result of trying to adopt remedial legislation. It seems unlikely that we will see direct federal intervention under section 93.

The only other provisions of the 1867 Constitution that have come to be seen as devices for protecting individual and collective rights in the face of provincial legislative majorities are the power given to the federal cabinet to "reserve assent" to provincial bills (that is, through the lieutenant governor of the province, to have a bill referred to the federal cabinet for a decision whether royal assent, normally a matter for the lieutenant governor, should be given to the bill) and the federal cabinet's power to disallow provincial laws already enacted and assented to. These federal powers were extensively used in the earlier days of the dominion, but their use came to be thought appropriate only in limited circumstances, one of which would be a flagrant denial of collective or individual rights. The political feasibility of using these powers now appears much in doubt: the power of reservation has not been used since 1960 and the power of disallowance not since 1943.

The guarantees of specific forms of diversity provided by the original Constitution of 1867, then, were limited in many respects. The language guarantees, while giving some protection to the individual at the federal level and in the provinces of Quebec and Manitoba, did nothing in the provinces of New Brunswick and Ontario, where there were, and still are, large French-speaking minorities. In jurisdictions where the guarantees did apply, they gave protection to the use of the minority language only in the legislative and judicial branches of government. They did not address the use of the minority language in the executive branch, the branch with which the average citizen would most frequently come into contact. Nor did they in any way recognize or protect the use of indigenous languages employed by native peoples long before either the English or the French came to Canada.

The religious guarantees protected collective, not individual, rights. They did not protect freedom of religion and tended to be a negation of freedom of conscience insofar as that embraces freedom from religion.

Position in Law and Fact.

1867–1960. . . . Up to 1960 legal and administrative developments more often reinforced assimilation. During that time, it is estimated, some 10 percent of Canadians of French ethic origin adopted English as their mother tongue. By far the largest portion of them would have lived outside Quebec, the only province where French speakers have always formed a majority.

French speakers have been in the minority in each of the other provinces since confederation. In certain provinces, such as Ontario and New Brunswick, persons whose mother tongue is French have formed a substantial minority: today they make up approximately 33.6 percent (234,000) of the population of New Brunswick and some 5.5 percent (over 475,000) of the population of Ontario. In these provinces of greater concentration, the critical mass was sufficient to sustain the popular use of the French language, although it had no official status in government and a limited use in business and education.

Legal developments during this period outside Quebec did little to preserve or enhance the French language. In the English-speaking provinces to which the denominational-schools guarantees of section 93 or its equivalent applied, the protection of minority denominational education did not embrace the use of the minority language as a medium of instruction. In both Manitoba and Ontario schools the use of French as a medium of instruction was almost eliminated at one point, and the Constitution was held to be no bar.

In 1870 Manitoba had a non-native population almost equally divided between French and English speakers. It was for this reason that the language guarantees concerning the use of French and English in the legislature and courts were included in its constitution. In the next two decades the province experienced a wave of English-speaking immigration, and by 1890 its legislature abolished the use of French in those institutions. Not until the 1970s was that abolition successfully attacked in the higher courts, and not until 1985 did the Supreme Court of Canada finally rule that the use of both languages in the legislation of that province was mandatory, with the consequence that all laws passed in the English language only are invalid.

These direct measures to curtail the use of French outside Quebec are salient examples of a general assimilative trend. Most provinces had from the outset an overwhelmingly English-speaking population that paid scant regard to the use of French in government, schools, business, or social affairs. The federal government, while recognizing its obligations under section 133 to use both languages in its laws and to permit the use of both languages in debates and in its courts, did little to enhance the role of French in government institutions. Even in the federally created courts of that period the use of French was not always practicable for a litigant. The executive branch of the federal government was operated predominantly in English, and outside certain parts of Quebec a French speaker could not assume that he would be able to deal with that government in his own language. Certainly the executive branch had no constitutional or legal obligation to provide such service.

This situation may be contrasted to that in the province of Quebec, where members of the English-speaking minority, at least in the areas where they were concentrated, were able to live their lives in English with little pressure for assimilation. Schools using English as a medium of instruction were readily available, federal and provincial government services were available in English, and Quebec courts were able and willing to conduct cases in either language. This practical recognition of the needs of the English-speaking minority, which in 1971 amounted to no more than 15 percent of the population of Quebec, largely reflected the fact that English was and is the language of the majority of Canadians and of North Americans and that all manner of governmental, commercial, professional, and social communications in North America will inevitably occur in English. The negative side of this situation was that the use of French tended to be diluted in Quebec, even for the French-speaking majority, particularly in commercial affairs. The position of French in Quebec was somewhat static, the language being preserved and used within the family, the church, and the school but having practical limits in the world of government and business, limits that were generally accepted in fact and not challenged by law.

1960–1982. . . . The year 1960 was the approximate point in our political development when a resurgence of French Canadian nationalism focused on the use of government, particularly the government of the province of Quebec, as a vehicle for enhancing the French language and French Canadian social and cultural values. This was the beginning of what has come to be called the quiet revolution in Quebec. It included a revamping of the provincial government and an expansion of its role into both traditional and nontraditional areas. One faction of nationalist opinion has taken the position that only the independence of Quebec would suffice to preserve and enhance the French culture and language in North America: the party in power in Quebec when this paper was written still has sovereignty for the province as its stated ultimate goal. In a referendum held in Quebec in 1980 seeking approval for the provincial government to negotiate some different form of association between Quebec and the rest of Canada, some 60 percent of the voters voted against such an initiative.

This is not the appropriate place to detail such developments, but they reflect a change from a defensive preservation of the status quo for French Canadians, particularly in Quebec, to a dynamic and expansive view of their role. The date with which I close my discussion of this period, 1982, marks the coming into force of the Canadian Charter of Rights and Freedoms, which was a significant event in relation to the subject of diversity and constitutionalism.

Two broad and often conflicting approaches to the development of French Canadian society must be seen as running through the latter half of the twentieth century. One view, held in varying degrees by successive governments of the province of Quebec and their supporters, is a form of what might be called Quebec nationalism, that is, the identification of the welfare of French Canadians with that of Quebec and the government of the province of Quebec. Notwithstanding that (in 1981) some 11 percent of the Quebec population claimed English as their mother tongue and that outside Quebec some 5.3 percent of the population claimed French as theirs, Quebec is viewed in this school of thought as more or less coterminous with French Canadian society. It follows that Quebec should, to the greatest extent possible, be unilingually French, and it is a matter of no great consequence whether the rest of the country is unilingually English. The government of Quebec is seen as the representative of French Canadian society dealing with "Ottawa," which is largely seen as the representative of English-speaking Canada. This approach emphasizes the rights of the French Canadian collectivity in Quebec and the importance of provincial powers to protect that collectivity. It logically leads to a form of territorial linguistic rights, in which the right to use French would be essentially confined to Quebec and the right to use English to the other provinces and territories.

The other polar view might be called pan-Canadianism. This view has been embraced in varying degrees, explicitly or implicitly, by the government of Canada and many of its supporters. In this view both French Canadian and Anglo-Canadian society exist throughout the country, and neither is identified with a particular government. Consequently, Canadians of either group should be able to move freely about the country and wherever at all practicable have access to essential services and education in their own language. This approach emphasizes the mobility of individuals and thus more readily finds legal expression in the form of individual rights. A corollary of pan-Canadianism is that each government, whether federal, provincial, or territorial, should so regulate matters within its jurisdiction as to protect the interests of official language minorities, be they the English-speaking minority in Quebec, the French-speaking minority of the Canadian population as a whole, or the French-speaking minorities in the nine provinces other than Quebec and in the two territories.

This dichotomy of approach has had serious implications for the federal system in Canada. Quebec nationalists, in identifying the position of French Canadians with that of the government of Quebec, have naturally pressed for more powers for that government to achieve the flowering of

French language and culture. Taken to its logical conclusion, this approach leads at the least to special status for Quebec, with powers greater than those of other provinces, and at most to independence for Quebec. Pan-Canadianism suggests that each government in Canada, federal or provincial, has a role in protecting linguistic minorities in respect of those matters otherwise coming within its jurisdiction. Since the French-speaking minorities outside Quebec have no vote in Quebec, they must be protected by their federal and provincial governments. And since our history has demonstrated that electoral majorities have too often ignored or curtailed the interests of minorities, it is also important that basic linguistic rights be constitutionally protected.

Much of the constitutional turmoil in Canada in the past two and a half decades has flowed from the tension between the adherents of these views. This controversy has been reflected in legal and administrative measures taken by various governments.

One of the first major responses of the federal government to the revival of Quebec nationalism and growing support for separation was the establishment in 1963 of the Royal Commission on Bilingualism and Biculturalism. In 1967 the commission recommended a number of reforms to establish an equal status for English and French in Canada. It recommended that at the federal level of government the two languages be declared official, with equal status in all matters, executive, legislative, and judicial, rather than the somewhat limited status that French then enjoyed in the legislative and judicial areas. The commission also called for equality of the two languages for legislative and judicial purposes in Ontario and New Brunswick comparable to that already constitutionally established in Quebec. Further, it called for a kind of territorial bilingualism in provinces or areas with a substantial linguistic minority. In this it appears to have borrowed from the Finnish model. Part of this report was implemented in the Official Languages Act adopted by the Parliament of Canada in 1969, such reforms being spurred by growing nationalist pressures in Quebec.

The Official Languages Act was of dramatic importance, both for its symbolism and for its content. Symbolically it was important because it declared English and French equal in status as the official languages of the government and Parliament of Canada. This went well beyond the rather limited 1867 constitutional provision for the use of both languages in Parliament and federally created courts.

Its practical requirements included the publication in both languages not only of the statutes but also of regulations and other delegated legislation, public notices and information provided by the executive branch of government to the public, and judgments or orders of federal courts and tribunals. It required that federal departments and agencies be equipped to provide services in both languages in the National Capital Region, at their head offices wherever they might be, and at other offices where there was a sufficient demand to warrant it. Corporations owned and directly controlled by the federal government were made subject to the requirements of the act. Services to the traveling public provided by the federal government or its agencies, directly or indirectly, were required to be available in both languages. The office of commissioner of official languages was established as a language ombudsman to receive complaints and oversee the observance of the spirit as well as the letter of the act.

The impact of the act has been dramatic since its adoption. French, which had had no legal status in the operations of the executive branch of the federal government, now enjoys equal status. This is not to say that old habits have died easily or that the legal requirements of the act are always met, but the effects have been very visible. Signs on federal institutions from one end of the country to the other are now in both languages, and most government forms and publications are bilingual or are readily available in either language.

In the federal public service all positions have been categorized as requiring knowledge of English, knowledge of French, or knowledge of both languages. In 1974 some 40,000 bilingual positions were identified, but by 1984 there were 63,000, or 28 percent of all positions in the public service. A massive language training program has been used to enable public servants to meet linguistic requirements: 80,000 have been provided with language training in the past twenty years.

Three objectives have been identified by Parliament for official language policy in the public service: first, and most important, providing service to members of the public in the official language chosen by them; second, enabling public servants to work to the greatest degree possible in their own language; and third, ensuring "full participation" by persons of both language groups (meaning that the composition of the public service should more or less reflect the linguistic composition of the Canadian population). Before the Official Languages Act French speakers were underrepresented in the federal public service and very substantially underrepresented in its senior levels. Although this situation has not been completely eliminated, it has much improved. Those whose mother tongue was French constituted approximately 26 percent of the population in 1981; in 1984 they made up 27.8 percent of federal public servants, an increase of three and one-half percentage points in a decade, and 19.9 percent in the management category, an increase of approximately one and one-half percentage points in a decade.

Outside the public service the direct and indirect effects of the Official Languages Act have also been important. Two decades ago broadcasting services in the French language were very limited outside central Canada, but today services of the state-owned Canadian Broadcasting Corporation (Radio-Canada) are available in both languages coast to coast. Services are available in the minority official language wherever there are communities of 500 or more members of that language minority. Federally owned transportation systems and facilities such as airports strive, not always with complete success, to provide service in both languages throughout the country. These measures are all typical of the thrust of the languages policy of successive federal governments: to maximize the mobility and equalize the opportunities of individual Canadians of both official language groups.

Consistent with these measures respecting the apparatus of the federal government, the legislature of the Northwest Territories has recently adopted an ordinance making English and French the official languages of the territorial government and legislature. Also consistent with this approach are legislative and administrative measures in the province of New Brunswick. Although New Brunswick has a large French-speaking population, now some 33 percent, with its origins going back to the French colony of Acadia, no provision was made in the 1867 Constitution for the protection of the French language in that province. Nevertheless, in 1969 the legislature of New Brunswick adopted the Official Languages of New Brunswick Act, which has subsequently been amended and enlarged upon. The act generally parallels the federal law in declaring both languages official for all provincial purposes and specifically provides for their use in the legislature and in the enactment and publication of legislation. It requires that services of the executive branch of government be available in the official language of choice, and it makes certain provisions guaranteeing education in both languages and the use of both languages in provincial courts.

Also consistent with the concept of bilingualism, though without establishing formal legal equality, are the legislative and administrative measures taken by Ontario and to a lesser extent by other English-speaking provinces to enhance the use of French. Ontario has no doubt gone the furthest in assuring the availability of trials in both languages and rapidly expanding governmental services available in French. The publicly funded school system has been extensively adjusted to provide education using French as the medium of instruction for children whose parents wish them to be so educated. While this development has been more dramatic in Ontario, with its large French-speaking minority (some 475,000), parallel developments have occurred in most English-speaking provinces, where public funding is provided by one means or another for a growing number of schools or school programs using French as the medium of instruction. The federal government shares in the costs of minority language education in all provinces, transferring over $200 million to the provinces for this purpose in fiscal year 1984–1985.

These developments in the predominantly English-speaking provinces have largely been a response to Quebec nationalism. At the very least that movement has made English-speaking Canadians far more conscious of the legitimate concerns of French Canadians about the preservation of their culture and language. At another level the implicit threat of the separation of Quebec to achieve this goal has induced other provinces to recognize and encourage the use of the French language within their borders in the interests of national unity. Bilingualism has obtained ever wider acceptance in these provinces as a condition of our nationhood, although there is still far from a general consensus on the matter.

The legislative and administrative trends in Quebec have been, in form at least, in somewhat the opposite direction. The percentage of the Quebec population whose mother tongue was English was 13.3 percent in 1961 but only 11 percent in 1981. During this time successive governments in Quebec have consistently moved to give legal and practical priority to the French language. The Charter of the French Language, adopted by the National Assembly (legislature) of Quebec in 1977, though by no means the first such law, is now the most notable.

The charter declares that "French is the official language of Quebec." It guarantees, as far as is within provincial powers, that every person in Quebec has the right to communicate with both public and private institutions and agencies in the province in French. It seeks to limit in various ways the use of English in the courts, although this has been held to be unconstitutional as contrary to section 133 of the Constitution Act, 1867. It attempts to ensure that French will become the predominant language of business. It requires a knowledge of French for those seeking a career in public administration or the professions. It seeks to prevent the use of English in commercial signs, although this prohibition has also been successfully attacked in the courts.

One of the most controversial provisions of the charter essentially restricts entrance to schools using English as the medium of instruction to children of parents who have themselves been educated in English in Quebec. Apart from certain exceptions, this prevented recent immigrants to Quebec, whether from non-English-speaking countries or from the United States, the United Kingdom, Australia, New Zealand, or other parts of the English-speaking world (including the nine other provinces of Canada), from having their children educated in English in Quebec. This provision has been held invalid because it conflicts with the Canadian Charter of Rights and Freedoms, adopted in 1982.

Although the Quebec law and the administration by which it has been implemented have been attacked as Draconian and destructive of support for French minority language rights in other provinces, the situation in which the Quebec National Assembly thought it necessary to legislate priority for French in its own territory was very different from that obtaining in the English-speaking provinces, where the priority of the majority language had never been in doubt. French as the language of some 5 million persons in Quebec is under very great pressure in a country of some 20 million English speakers and in a continent with over 250 million English speakers. It is only fair to remember that the English-speaking minority in Quebec, which once numbered some 1 million, traditionally enjoyed services and education in its own language comparable to those available in other parts of the country. In business English tended to dominate as the language of management, and it was widely acceptable in government. The consequence was that, rightly or wrongly, many of the majority language in Quebec felt threatened by English, the language of a group that was provincially a minority but nationally a majority. Nevertheless, the effect of Quebec measures on language and associated matters has been a net emigration of English speakers from Quebec in the past twenty years, sometimes estimated to number in the hundreds of thousands. This has contributed to a trend toward unilingualism in Quebec that is consistent with Quebec nationalism.

I would be remiss in leaving this critical period of our national life without observing that in all the attention and controversy concerning the role of English and French, the languages of what are often referred to as our "two founding peoples," little has been said or done about the preservation of aboriginal languages. They have no legal protection except in the Northwest Territories, where seven of them have been declared the "official aboriginal languages" of the territory. The trends have mostly been in the direction of assimilation of our native peoples insofar as language is concerned, and that assimilation has been predominantly in favor of the English language, even in Quebec. Presumably, on the arrival of Europeans, all of the 220,000 aboriginal peoples spoke their own language. Of the half-million descendants of those people, according to a study made in 1981, only 22.1 percent spoke an aboriginal language at home; 71.7 percent spoke English, and 3.9 percent spoke French. Many governments have been giving more attention to education in aboriginal languages: in 1981–1982 some 34,000 students were enrolled in schools where an aboriginal language was used as a medium of instruction or taught as a language.

Canadian Charter of Rights and Freedoms, 1982. The adoption of the charter was the culmination of a long and contentious constitutional debate in Canada. Apart from some of its more formal aspects (such as the termination of the authority of the British Parliament, exercisable with our consent, to amend our Constitution), basic issues going to the preservation of our nation were involved. Underlying the debate for many years were the conflicting themes that I have discussed: Quebec nationalism, with its emphasis on collective rights preserved by the French Canadian collectivity in Quebec through the government of that province; and pan-Canadianism, to be fostered by the legal recognition of both official languages and the guarantee of individual rights of Canadians to live to the greatest extent practicable in their own language anywhere in Canada. While this debate is by no means off our national agenda and the legitimacy of the charter is not universally recognized, it embodies in a constitutional instrument the elements of pan-Canadian bilingualism and individual rights. In this sense it reflects priorities asserted by the federal government and ultimately accepted by the nine English-speaking provinces.

Most of the charter came into operation as part of a constitutional package on April 17, 1982. It constitutes an amendment to the Canadian Constitution of pervasive importance. Our basic Constitution of 1867 was a positivist document that unquestioningly recognized the supremacy of Parliament and paid little heed to declaring the rights of individuals, which were thought to be best secured through the wisdom of duly elected legislators. In contrast, the charter guarantees a variety of individual rights and perhaps at least one that is collective. It thus limits in important ways the powers of legislators and leaves many decisions to the courts by recognizing their power of judicial review over governmental activities and laws thought to contravene those rights.

... [S]ection 1... states: "The Canadian Charter of Rights and Freedoms guarantees the rights and freedoms set out in it subject only to such reasonable limits prescribed by law as can be demonstrably justified in a free and democratic society." This provision reflects a compromise between the interests of the individual on the one hand and those of the public as represented by elected governments on the other. It means that the rights set out in the charter cannot be abrogated without a law purporting to have that effect, and even then the onus is on those who rely on such a law to show that it is "justified in a free and democratic society."

The charter guarantees a number of individual rights typical of democratic pluralistic societies. These include freedom of conscience and religion, protection from arbitrary use of the legal system, the right to vote and to hold public office, the right to enter and leave Canada and to move about in it, freedom from arbitrary state action, and the right to be treated equally under the law without discrimination. Such rights protect diversity in whatever form it may be found.

Other provisions in the charter, however, give priority to certain forms of diversity individually or collectively. The charter makes it clear that the guarantees of equal rights for all are not to be taken to interfere with the rights to publicly supported schools of certain denominations or to abridge treaty or aboriginal rights of our native people (particularly aboriginal claims to the traditional use and enjoyment of land). The charter must be interpreted "in a manner consistent with the preservation and enhancement of the multicultural heritage of Canadians." So, while the charter endorses the freedom of choice of the individual, it tempers that freedom with respect for certain collective interests.

In this same vein—and more germane to the focus of this paper—the charter gives clear constitutional priority to only two languages, English and French. It continues, in effect, the existing constitutional guarantees with respect to English and French in the Parliament of Canada, the legislature of Quebec, and the federal and Quebec courts. But it provides important new constitutional language guarantees. For the first time the Constitution guarantees the use of both languages in the legislature, the laws, and the courts of New Brunswick. It also guarantees the right of any member of the public to receive services in either English or French from the executive branch of the federal government and from the executive branch of the New Brunswick government. For the first time English and French are constitutionally the official languages of Canada in all federal institutions and the official languages of New Brunswick in all its institutions of government. These language provisions essentially give rise to individual rights.

The other kind of linguistic right provided for in the charter, though framed as an individual right, is more a collective right. That is the right given to members of English- or French-speaking minorities, wherever they may be found in the country, to have their children educated at public expense in their language. This right applies when they belong to the minority language group in the province in which they reside or when, although the children's mother tongue is that of the majority of the province, the parents were educated somewhere in Canada in the other official language. For example, if a person whose mother tongue is English was nevertheless educated in French in Quebec, he could insist, in moving to Ontario, that his children be educated in French. This provision has been held by the courts to override the "Quebec clause" in the Quebec Charter of the French Language, which purported to limit the right to an education in English in Quebec to children of parents who had been educated in English in Quebec.

There is an important qualification to the minority language educational rights: such rights cannot be asserted except where the number of children entitled to benefit "is sufficient to warrant the provision to them out of public funds of minority language instruction." In effect, then, an individual cannot assert these rights unless there are enough persons in similar circumstances to warrant the provision of minority language education in that area. In this sense minority language educational rights are collective.

The thrust of these language guarantees in the charter is that to the greatest extent possible every Canadian should be able to move about his or her country and use his or her own language, provided it is one of the two official languages. Of course, most of the language guarantees apply to the federal and New Brunswick governments, while other limited constitutional guarantees apply to the use of either language in respect to the governments of Quebec and Manitoba. The extent to which a French speaker may find provincial governmental services available in other provinces will vary greatly and will depend on legal and administrative measures other than constitutional guarantees.

Nevertheless, the uniform provision in section 23 of the charter concerning minority language education is of fundamental importance. Applying in every province, it means that Canadians with school-age children moving to a province of a different majority language need not accept as inevitable the abandonment by their children of their mother tongue. That all the provinces with an English-speaking majority were able to agree to this constitutional amendment in 1982 reflects the fact that, with federal financial aid, much progress has been made outside Quebec in strengthening the facilities for offering primary and secondary education using French as the medium of instruction.

One important effect of the constitutionalization of language guarantees in the charter is that language disputes are moving more and more from the legislatures to the courts. Since the adoption of the charter, important decisions have been handed down in Quebec and Ontario concerning the validity of provincial minority language education laws in relation to the charter. The "Quebec clause" was held invalid in the face of the "Canada clause" of the charter, by which persons educated in English anywhere in Canada had the right to have their children educated in English in Quebec. And section 23 of the charter was held to require that the French linguistic minority in Ontario be entitled to manage and control the facilities for the provision of education in French. Other cases will no doubt follow as it becomes necessary to interpret the charter.

Conclusion . . .

   . . . At the time of confederation in 1867, while there was some recognition of linguistic rights, constitutional guarantees for Protestant or Roman Catholic minorities concerning education were regarded as an important condition for federation. The national understanding was revised and updated by the adoption of the Canadian Charter of Rights and Freedoms in 1982, in which mutual respect for, and preservation of, the two official languages were seen by the governments endorsing the charter as more relevant for the continuation of our nation. The government of Quebec did not subscribe to that view or to the charter, although the charter nevertheless applies in Quebec.

   In looking at the ways in which assimilation has been countered and the two languages have been protected, one sees many devices at work in Canada. In part, diversity as between English and French has been fostered by the federal system, in which each government responds to its particular constituency, with the English-speaking majorities in nine provinces giving priority in their institutions to the English language and the French-speaking majority in Quebec giving priority to French in its institutions. In this sense we have an element of territorial language rights. The federal government has sought to be responsive to both language groups, both of them being electorally important within the political structures of the national government. In exercising its responsibility to preserve the Canadian nation, the rights of Canadian citizenship, and the political and economic integration of the country, it has sought to enhance the use of both languages throughout Canada.

   Diversity has also been maintained in Canada through constitutional guarantees of collective rights. These were found in section 93 of the original Constitution Act, 1867, with respect to denominational schools. More recently new collective rights have been established with respect to minority language education by means of section 23 of the Canadian Charter of Rights and Freedoms.

   Most recently Canada has entrenched in its Constitution a series of individual rights. These, apart from basic equality and freedom of choice, include rights to the use of the language of choice as long as that choice is either English or French.

   We thus see no consistent pattern or logic in the means adopted in the governance of Canada during the past two centuries to accommodate linguistic or other forms of diversity. Any consistency that exists is with respect to ends rather than means: the desire to accommodate such diversity within one political unit on the principle that Canadians still believe they have more in common with one another than they have with the outside world, even their closest neighbor.

Excerpts from Canadian Constitutional Provisions

Constitution Act, 1867, 30 & 31 Vict. c. 3 (excerpts)

93. In and for each Province the Legislature may exclusively make Laws in relation to Education, subject and according to the following Provisions:

(1) Nothing in any such Law shall prejudicially affect any Right or Privilege with respect to Denominational Schools which any Class of Persons have by Law in the Province at the Union:

(2) All the Powers, Privileges, and Duties at the Union by Law conferred and imposed in Upper Canada on the Separate Schools and School Trustees of the Queen's Roman Catholic Subjects shall be and the same are hereby extended to the Dissentient Schools of the Queen's Protestant and Roman Catholic Subjects in Quebec:

(3) Where in any Province a System of Separate or Dissentient Schools exists by Law at the Union or is thereafter established by the Legislature of the Province, an Appeal shall lie to the Governor General in Council from any Act or Decision of any Provincial Authority affecting any Right or Privilege of the Protestant or Roman Catholic Minority of the Queen's Subjects in relation to Education . . .

133. Either the English or the French Language may be used by any Person in the Debates of the Houses of the Parliament of Canada and of the Houses of the Legislature of Quebec; and both those Languages shall be used in the respective Records and Journals of those Houses; and either of those Languages may be used by any Person or in any Pleading or Process in or issuing from any Court of Canada established under this Act, and in or from all or any of the Courts of Quebec.

The Acts of the Parliament of Canada and of the Legislature of Quebec shall be printed and published in both those languages.

* * *

Canadian Charter of Rights and Freedoms, enacted by the Canada Act, 1982 (U.K.) 1982 c.11 (excerpts)

Official Languages of Canada

16. (1) English and French are the official languages of Canada and have equality of status and equal rights and privileges as to their use in all institutions of the Parliament and government of Canada.

(2) English and French are the official languages of New Brunswick and have equality of status and equal rights and privileges as to their use in all institutions of the legislature and government of New Brunswick.

(3) Nothing in this Charter limits the authority of Parliament or a legislature to advance the equality of status or use of English and French.

17. (1) Everyone has the right to use English or French in any debates and other proceedings of Parliament.

(2) Everyone has the right to use English or French in any debates and other proceedings of the legislature of New Brunswick.

18. (1) The statutes, records and journals of Parliament shall be printed and published in English and French and both language versions are equally authoritative.

(2) The statutes, records and journals of the legislature of New Brunswick shall be printed and published in English and French and both language versions are equally authoritative.

19. (1) Either English or French may be used by any person in, or in any pleading in or process issuing from, any court established by Parliament.

(2) Either English or French may be used by any person in, or in any pleading in or process issuing from, any court of New Brunswick.

20. (1) Any member of the public in Canada has the right to communicate with, and to receive available services from, any head or central office of an institution of the Parliament or government of Canada in English or French, and has the same right with respect to any other office of any such institution where

(a) there is a significant demand for communications with and services from that office in such language; or

(b) due to the nature of the office, it is reasonable that communications with and services from that office be available in both English and French.

(2) Any member of the public in New Brunswick has the right to communicate with, and to receive available services from, any office of an institution of the legislature or government of New Brunswick in English or French.

21. Nothing in sections 16 to 20 abrogates or derogates from any right, privilege or obligation with respect to the English and French languages, or either of them, that exists or is continued by virtue of any other provision of the Constitution of Canada.

22. Nothing in sections 16 to 20 abrogates or derogates from any legal or customary right or privilege acquired or enjoyed either before or after the coming into force of this Charter with respect to any language that is not English or French.

Minority Language Educational Rights

23. (1) Citizens of Canada

(a) whose first language learned and still understood is that of the English or French linguistic minority population of the province in which they reside, or

(b) who have received their primary school instruction in Canada in English or French and reside in a province where the language in which they received that instruction is the language of the English or French linguistic minority population of the province,

have the right to have their children receive primary and secondary school instruction in that language in that province.

(2) Citizens of Canada of whom any child has received or is receiving primary or secondary school instruction in English or French in Canada, have the right to have all their children receive primary and secondary school instruction in the same language.

(3) The right of citizens of Canada under subsections (1) and (2) to have their children receive primary and secondary school instruction in the language of the English or French linguistic minority population of a province

(a) applies wherever in the province the number of children of citizens who have such a right is sufficient to warrant the provision to them out of public funds of minority language instruction; and

(b) includes, where the number of those children so warrants, the right to have them receive that instruction in minority language educational facilities provided out of public funds.

The Ford v. Quebec Case:

Introduction by Peter Russell, Rainer Knopf, and Tom Norton eds., Federalism and the Charter 557-59 (1989)

The decision which the Supreme Court of Canada rendered on December 15, 1988 striking down Quebec's French only sign law is one of the Court's most important Charter decisions. The decision moves constitutional jurisprudence in two different directions simultaneously: while it embraces a very wide interpretation of "freedom of expression" as a constitutional right, it also establishes a very broad basis for legislatures to use the power they have under section 33 of the Charter to override constitutional rights and freedoms. In addition to these important developments in the interpretation of the Charter, the decision had a major impact on constitutional politics in Canada.

This was by no means the first Supreme Court decision overturning sections of Bill 101, the Charter of The French Language introduced by the PQ [Parti Québécois] Government in 1977. In 1979 the Court struck down provisions of Bill 101 making French the official language of the province's legislature and courts. Another decision in 1984 forced Quebec to open its English schools to Canadians moving to Quebec from other provinces. Both of these decisions were based on entrenched constitutional language rights to which the legislative override in [section 33 of] the Charter did not apply. But the attack on sections of Bill 101 making French the exclusive language for commercial signs and firm names was based not on specific language rights but on the right to freedom of expression—a right found in section 2(b) of the Canadian Charter (a section to which the override does apply) as well as in Quebec's Charter of Human Rights and Freedoms.

In June 1982, just two months after the Charter was proclaimed, Quebec's National Assembly, in a defiant gesture against the constitutional settlement of 1982 to which Quebec had not consented, passed a law re-enacting all laws passed prior to the Charter but adding to each a section invoking the override. After five years, in 1987, this omnibus use of the override lapsed and was not renewed. However, Quebec had used the override a second time: in February 1984 a law came into force applying the override just to the French only sign provision of Bill 101. This override, if valid, was still in force when the Supreme Court was deciding the sign case. But the section of Bill 101 requiring French only firm names had not been protected from judicial review by the override clause. Also the Quebec Charter of Rights contained a right to freedom of expression and it had not been overridden. Thus, whether or not an override was still in force, the Supreme Court had to consider the compatibility of French only commercial regulations with the right to freedom of expression.

In the 1985 election campaign in which the Liberals led by Robert Bourassa threw the Parti Quebecois out of office, the Liberals indicated that they would lift restrictions on the use of bilingual commercial signs. This promise was important in attracting some outstanding representatives of the Quebec's English-speaking minority to the Liberal team. On the other hand it threatened to alienate many Quebec Francophones who regarded the French only sign policy as essential for insuring that the public face of Quebec would be French.

After the election, Premier Bourassa decided not to act on this controversial issue until the constitutional litigation under way had run its course. A number of firms had challenged provisions of Bill 101 requiring French only commercial signs and firm names. A challenge had also been brought by Alan Singer, the owner of a stationary shop in an English-speaking district of Montreal, against provisions of Bill 101 which for some commercial activities—for instance the publication of catalogues and the signs of firms employing less than four persons or specializing in foreign products—required the use of French but also permitted the use of another language. Like other politicians in Charterland, Bourassa hoped that the Court might take a deeply divisive issue off his hands.

The litigation may have given the Premier a temporary reprieve but when the Court's decision finally came down it did not make his political burden any lighter. On the contrary, the Supreme Court's finding that laws prohibiting the use of any language other than French violated the right to freedom of expression in both the Canadian Charter and the Quebec Charter deepened the resentment of the English-speaking community. The right to advertise in the language of one's choice could now be referred to as "a fundamental right". On the other hand, the Court's argument that a

French only policy was not necessary to preserve the French face of Quebec failed to make much impression on the Francophone majority.

The Court took a remarkably liberal approach to the concept of "freedom of expression". It built into this freedom a new, universal language right—a right to communicate in one's own language, a right, it argued, which is essential to personal identity. The Court rejected arguments that commercial speech should be excluded from freedom of expression. It recognized that when consumer-protection regulations of advertising are under review consideration would have to be given to competing policy interests. But the Court took the position that this kind of balancing was to be done not by narrowly defining freedom of expression but by considering the justification for limits on the right under section 1 of the Charter. Applying section 1 to the cases at hand, the Court felt that the objective of maintaining the predominantly French character of Quebec could justify requiring the use of French on a joint use basis and even a law requiring the "marked predominance" of the French language. However, it saw no evidence justifying the exclusive use of French. Hence it struck down the French only provisions attacked in *Ford* but upheld bilingual requirements attacked by Singer.

While the Court's expansive interpretation of freedom of expression expanded the basis for judicial review, the Court in this same decision made it easier for legislatures to use section 33 of the Charter, the override clause, to immunize their laws from judicial review. Quebec's Court of Appeal had found Quebec's broad-brush use of the override to be unconstitutional, insisting that to fulfill its democratic purpose the override must be used in an accountable way with the legislature indicating precisely which rights and freedoms it was overriding. But here in *Ford* the Supreme Court rejected this argument: it would come too close to requiring "a prima facie justification of the decision to exercise the override". The Supreme Court made it clear that it wished to minimize judicial review of the use of the override.

And use the override is exactly what Premier Bourassa did in response to the Court's decision. After agonizing for 48 hours, Bourassa announced his decision to bring in legislation permitting bilingual signs indoors but requiring French only signs outside. To fend off a court challenge the override clause was applied to this legislation. The new law, Bill 178, cost Bourassa the services of three of his Anglophone Ministers and aroused the ire of English-speaking Quebecers. From the other side it was attacked by the opposition PQ Party and by many Quebec francophones who resented compromising the French-only program of Bill 101.

In the arena of constitutional politics Bourassa's action was a bombshell. By December 1988, there remained only two provinces, Manitoba and New Brunswick, whose legislatures had not approved the Meech Lake package of constitutional amendments. On the day after the Supreme Court decision, the Premier of Manitoba, Gary Filmon, introduced the Meech Lake Accord in the Manitoba legislature. But a few days later, following Premier Bourassa's decision to use the override and restore a unilingual French policy for outdoor signs, Filmon announced that he was suspending legislative consideration of the Meech Lake Accord. Legislative hearings, he said, "may invite a very negative anti-Quebec backlash."

So at this stage the Meech Lake Accord, with its controversial clause recognizing Quebec as a "distinct society", was stalled if not dead. Although this meant that the prospects of a constitutional reconciliation with Quebec were dimmed, the French majority in Quebec learned through these events that the 1982 constitutional changes had left them with considerable power to protect their distinctive culture. For all Canadians the really ominous implication of these events was that they pointed to a deep gulf between the French majority in Quebec and the non-French majority in Canada over what should be regarded as fundamental in Canadian constitutionalism.

Ford v. Quebec (Attorney General)

[1988] 2 S.C.R. 712 (Supreme Court of Canada)

BY THE COURT—The principal issue in this appeal is whether ss. 58 and 69 of the Quebec Charter of the French Language, R.S.Q., c. C-11, which require that public signs and posters and commercial advertising shall be in the French language only and that only the French version of a firm name may be used, infringe the freedom of expression guaranteed by s. 2(b) of the Canadian Charter of Rights and Freedoms and s. 3 of the Quebec Charter of Human Rights and Freedoms, R.S.Q., c. C-12....

... The commercial advertising and signs displayed by the five respondents are described in paragraphs 1 to 5 of their petition as follows:

1. La Chaussure Brown's Inc. ("Brown's") operates a business of retail shoe stores throughout the Province of Quebec, and since at least September 1, 1981, it has used and displayed within and on its premises of its store situated in the Fairview Shopping Centre, 6801 Trans-Canada Highway, Pointe-Claire, commercial advertising containing the following words:

BRAVO   BRAVO
"Brown's quality.   "La qualité
Bravo! price."   à tout prix"

2. Valerie Ford, carrying on business under the firm name and style of Les Lainages du Petit Mouton Enr. ("Ford"), operates a retail store selling, inter alia, wool, and since at least September 1, 1981, she has used and displayed on her premises at 311 St. Johns Boulevard, Pointe-Claire, an exterior sign containing the following words:

"LAINE   WOOL"

3. Nettoyeur et Tailleur Masson Inc. ("Nettoyeur Masson") carries on the business of a tailor and dry cleaner, and since at least September 1,

1981, it has used and displayed on its premises at 3259 Masson Street, Montreal an exterior sign containing the following words:

NETTOYEURS	Masson	CLEANERS
TAILLEUR	inc.	TAILOR
SERVICE		ALTERATIONS
1 HEURE		REPAIRS
HOUR		

4. McKenna Inc. ("McKenna") carries on business as a florist in the City of Montreal and since at least September 1, 1981, it has used and displayed on its premises at 4509 Côte Des Neiges Road, Montreal, an exterior sign containing the following words: "Fleurs McKENNA Flowers"

5. La Compagnie de Fromage Nationale Ltée ("Fromage Nationale") carries on the business of a cheese distributor and since at least September 1, 1981, it has used and displayed on its premises at 9001 Salley Street, Ville LaSalle, exterior signs containing the following words:

| "NATIONAL CHEESE | La Cie de FROMAGE |
| Co Ltd Ltée" | NATIONALE |

The petition further alleges that the respondents La Chaussure Brown's Inc., Valerie Ford and La Compagnie de Fromage Nationale Ltée received a mise en demeure from the Commission de surveillance de la langue française advising them that their signs were not in conformity with the provisions of the Charter of the French Language and calling on them to conform to such provisions and that the respondents McKenna Inc. and Nettoyeur et Tailleur Masson Inc. were charged with violation of the Charter of the French Language....

Sections 1, 58 [and] 69 ... of the Charter of the French Language, R.S.Q., c. C-11, provide:

1. French is the official language of Québec.

58. Public signs and posters and commercial advertising shall be solely in the official language.

Notwithstanding the foregoing, in the cases and under the conditions or circumstances prescribed by regulation of the Office de la langue française, public signs and posters and commercial advertising may be both in French and in another language or solely in another language.

69. Subject to section 68, only the French version of a firm name may be used in Québec....

Sections 1 and 2(b) of the Canadian Charter of Rights and Freedoms and s. 52(1) of the Constitution Act, 1982 provide:

1. The Canadian Charter of Rights and Freedoms guarantees the rights and freedoms set out in it subject only to such reasonable limits prescribed by law as can be demonstrably justified in a free and democratic society.

2. Everyone has the following fundamental freedoms: ...

(b) freedom of thought, belief, opinion and expression, including freedom of the press and other media of communication. . . .

[B]oth the Superior Court and the Court of Appeal held that freedom of expression includes the freedom to express oneself in the language of one's choice. After indicating the essential relationship between expression and language by reference to dictionary definitions of both, Boudreault J. in the Superior Court said that in the ordinary or general form of expression there cannot be expression without language. Bisson J.A. in the Court of Appeal said that he agreed with the reasons of Boudreault J. on this issue and expressed his own view in the form of the following question: "Is there a purer form of freedom of expression than the spoken language and written language?" He supported his conclusion by quotation of the following statement of this Court in *Reference re Manitoba Language Rights*, [1985] 1 S.C.R. 721, at p. 744:

> "The importance of language rights is grounded in the essential role that language plays in human existence, development and dignity. It is through language that we are able to form concepts; to structure and order the world around us. Language bridges the gap between isolation and community, allowing humans to delineate the rights and duties they hold in respect of one another, and thus to live in society."

The conclusion of the Superior Court and the Court of Appeal on this issue is correct. Language is so intimately related to the form and content of expression that there cannot be true freedom of expression by means of language if one is prohibited from using the language of one's choice. Language is not merely a means or medium of expression; it colours the content and meaning of expression. It is, as the preamble of the Charter of the French Language itself indicates, a means by which a people may express its cultural identity. It is also the means by which the individual expresses his or her personal identity and sense of individuality. That the concept of "expression" in s. 2(b) of the Canadian Charter and s. 3 of the Quebec Charter goes beyond mere content is indicated by the specific protection accorded to "freedom of thought, belief [and] opinion" in s. 2 and to "freedom of conscience" and "freedom of opinion" in s. 3. That suggests that "freedom of expression" is intended to extend to more than the content of expression in its narrow sense.

The Attorney General of Quebec made several submissions against the conclusion reached by the Superior Court and the Court of Appeal on this issue, the most important of which may be summarized as follows: (a) in determining the meaning of freedom of expression the Court should apply the distinction between the message and the medium which must have been known to the framers of the Canadian and Quebec Charters; (b) the express provision for the guarantee of language rights in ss. 16 to 23 of the Canadian Charter indicate that it was not intended that a language freedom should result incidentally from the guarantee of freedom of expression in s. 2(b); (c) the recognition of a freedom to express oneself in the language of one's choice under s. 2(b) of the Canadian Charter and s. 3 of the Quebec Charter would undermine the special and limited constitutional position of the specific guarantees of language rights in s. 133 of the Constitution Act, 1867 and ss. 16 to 23 of the Canadian Charter that was emphasized by the Court in *MacDonald v. City of Montreal*, [1986] 1 S.C.R. 460, and *Société des Acadiens du Nouveau-Brunswick Inc. v. Association of Parents for Fairness in Education*, [1986] 1 S.C.R. 549; and (d) the recognition that freedom of expression includes the freedom to express oneself in the language of one's choice would be contrary to the views expressed on this issue by the European Commission of Human Rights and the European Court of Human Rights.

The distinction between the message and the medium was applied by Dugas J. of the Superior Court in *Devine v. Procureur général du Québec*, in holding that freedom of expression does not include freedom to express oneself in the language of one's choice. It has already been indicated why that distinction is inappropriate as applied to language as a means of expression because of the intimate relationship between language and meaning. As one of the authorities on language quoted by the appellant Singer in the *Devine* appeal, J. Fishman, The Sociology of Language (1972), at p. 4, puts it: "... language is not merely a means of interpersonal communication and influence. It is not merely a carrier of content, whether latent or manifest. Language itself is content, a reference for loyalties and animosities, an indicator of social statuses and personal relationships, a marker of situations and topics as well as of the societal goals and the large-scale value-laden arenas of interaction that typify every speech community." As has been noted this quality or characteristic of language is acknowledged by the Charter of the French Language itself where, in the first paragraph of its preamble, it states: "Whereas the French language, the distinctive language of a people that is in the majority French-speaking, is the instrument by which that people has articulated its identity."

The second and third of the submissions of the Attorney General of Quebec which have been summarized above, with reference to the implications for this issue of the express or specific guarantees of language rights in s. 133 of the Constitution Act, 1867, and ss. 16 to 23 of the Canadian Charter of Rights and Freedoms, are closely related and may be addressed together. These special guarantees of language rights do not, by implication, preclude a construction of freedom of expression that includes the freedom to express oneself in the language of one's choice. A general freedom to express oneself in the language of one's choice and the special guarantees of language rights in certain areas of governmental activity or jurisdiction—the legislature and administration, the courts and education— are quite different things. The latter have... their own special historical, political and constitutional basis. The central unifying feature of all of the language rights given explicit recognition in the Constitution of Canada is that they pertain to governmental institutions and for the most part they oblige the government to provide for, or at least tolerate, the use of both official languages. In this sense they are more akin to rights, properly understood, than freedoms. They grant entitlement to a specific benefit from the government or in relation to one's dealing with the government. Correspondingly, the government is obliged to provide certain services or benefits in both languages or at least permit use of either language by persons conducting certain affairs with the government. They do not ensure, as does a guaranteed freedom, that within a given broad range of private conduct, an individual will be free to choose his or her own course of activity. The language rights in the Constitution impose obligations on government and governmental institutions that are in the words of Beetz J. in *MacDonald*, a "precise scheme", providing specific opportunities to use English or French, or to receive services in English or French, in concrete, readily ascertainable and limited circumstances. In contrast, what the respondents seek in this case is a freedom as that term was explained by Dickson J. (as he then was) in *R. v. Big M Drug Mart Ltd.*, [1985] 1 S.C.R. 295, at p. 336: "Freedom can primarily be characterized by the absence of coercion or constraint. If a person is compelled by the state or the will of another to a course of action or inaction which he would not otherwise have chosen, he is not acting of his own volition and he cannot be said to be truly free. One of the major purposes of the Charter is to protect, within reason, from compulsion or restraint." The respondents seek to be free of the state imposed requirement that their commercial signs and advertising be in French only, and seek the freedom, in the entirely private or non-governmental realm of commercial activity, to display signs and advertising in the language of their choice as well as that of French. Manifestly the respondents are not seeking to use the language of their choice in any form of direct relations with any branch of government and are not seeking to oblige government to provide them any services or other benefits in the language of their choice. In this sense the respondents are asserting a freedom, the freedom to express oneself in the language of one's choice in an area of non-governmental activity, as opposed to a language right of the kind guaranteed in the Constitution. The recognition that freedom of expression includes the freedom to express oneself in the language of one's choice does not undermine or run counter to the special guarantees of official language rights in areas of governmental jurisdiction or responsibility. The legal structure, function and obligations of government institutions with respect to the English and French languages are in no way affected by the recognition that freedom of expression includes the freedom to express oneself in the language of one's choice in areas outside of those for which the special guarantees of language have been provided.

The decisions of the European Commission of Human Rights and the European Court of Human Rights on which the Attorney General of Quebec relied are all distinguishable on the same basis, apart from the fact that, as Bisson J.A. observed in the Court of Appeal, they arose in an entirely different constitutional context. They all involved claims to language rights in relations with government that would have imposed some obligation on government. . . .

. . . The Attorney General of Quebec contended that if the guarantee of freedom of expression included the freedom to express oneself in the language of one's choice the respondents must still show that the guarantee extends to commercial expression. The respondents disputed this on the ground that the challenged provisions are directed to the language used and not to regulation of the substantive content of the expression. At the same time they made alternative submissions that the guarantee extended to commercial expression. The Attorney General of Quebec is correct on this issue: there cannot be a guaranteed freedom to express oneself in the language of one's choice in respect of a form or kind of expression that is not covered by the guarantee of freedom of expression. . . .

It was not disputed that the public signs and posters, the commercial advertising, and the firm name referred to in ss. 58 and 69 of the Charter of the French Language are forms of expression, and it was also assumed or accepted in argument that the expression contemplated by these provisions may be conveniently characterized or referred to as commercial expression Sections 58 and 69 appear in Chapter VII of the Charter of the French Language, entitled "The Language of Commerce and Business". It must be kept in mind, however, that while the words "commercial expression" are a convenient reference to the kind of expression contemplated by the provisions in issue, they do not have any particular meaning or significance in Canadian constitutional law, unlike the corresponding expression "commercial speech", which in the United States has been recognized as a particular category of speech entitled to First Amendment protection of a more limited character than that enjoyed by other kinds of speech. The issue in the appeal is not whether the guarantee of freedom of expression in s. 2(b) of the Canadian Charter and s. 3 of the Quebec Charter should be construed as extending to particular categories of expression, giving rise to difficult definitional problems, but whether there is any reason why the guarantee should not extend to a particular kind of expression, in this case the expression contemplated by ss. 58 and 69 of the Charter of the French Language. Because, however, the American experience with the First Amendment protection of "commercial speech" was invoked in argument, as it has been in other cases, both for and against the recognition in Canada that the guarantee of freedom of expression extends to the kinds of expression that may be described as commercial expression, it is convenient to make brief reference to it at this point. [The Court's discussion of U.S. "commercial speech" cases is omitted.] . . .

It is apparent to this Court that the guarantee of freedom of expression in s. 2(b) of the Canadian Charter and s. 3 of the Quebec Charter cannot be confined to political expression, important as that form of expression is in a free and democratic society. The pre-Charter jurisprudence emphasized the importance of political expression because it was a challenge to that form of expression that most often arose under the division of powers and the "implied bill of rights", where freedom of political expression could be related to the maintenance and operation of the institutions of democratic government. But political expression is only one form of the great range of expression that is deserving of constitutional protection because it serves individual and societal values in a free and democratic society. . . .

While . . . attempts to identify and define the values which justify the constitutional protection of freedom of expression are helpful in emphasizing the most important of them, they tend to be formulated in a philosophical context which fuses the separate questions of whether a particular form or act of expression is within the ambit of the interests protected by the value of freedom of expression and the question whether that form or act of expression, in the final analysis, deserves protection from interference under the structure of the Canadian Charter and the Quebec Charter. These are two distinct questions and call for two distinct analytical processes. The first, at least for the Canadian Charter, is to be determined by the purposive approach to interpretation set out by this Court in *Hunter v. Southam Inc.*, [1984] 2 S.C.R. 145, and *Big M Drug Mart Ltd.* The second, the question of the limitation on the protected values, is to be determined under s. 1 of the Charter as interpreted in *Oakes*, and *R. v. Edwards Books and Art Ltd.*, [1986] 2 S.C.R. 713. The division between the two analytical processes has been established by this Court in the above decisions. First, consideration will be given to the interests and purposes that are meant to be protected by the particular right or freedom in order to determine whether the right or freedom has been infringed in the context presented to the court. If the particular right or freedom is found to have been infringed, the second step is to determine whether the infringement can be justified by the state within the constraints of s. 1. It is within the perimeters of s. 1 that courts will in most instances weigh competing 12 values in order to determine which should prevail.

In order to address the issues presented by this case it is not necessary for the Court to delineate the boundaries of the broad range of expression deserving of protection under s. 2(b) of the Canadian Charter or s. 3 of the Quebec Charter. It is necessary only to decide if the respondents have a constitutionally protected right to use the English language in the signs they display, or more precisely, whether the fact that such signs have a commercial purpose removes the expression contained therein from the scope of protected freedom.

In our view, the commercial element does not have this effect. Given the earlier pronouncements of this Court to the effect that the rights and freedoms guaranteed in the Canadian Charter should be given a large and liberal interpretation, there is no sound basis on which commercial expression can be excluded from the protection of s. 2(b) of the Charter. It is worth noting that the courts below applied a similar generous and broad interpretation to include commercial expression within the protection of freedom of expression contained in s. 3 of the Quebec Charter. Over and above its intrinsic value as expression, commercial expression which, as has been pointed out, protects listeners as well as speakers plays a significant role in enabling individuals to make informed economic choices, an important aspect of individual self-fulfillment and personal autonomy. The Court accordingly rejects the view that commercial expression serves no individual or societal value in a free and democratic society and for this reason is undeserving of any constitutional protection.

Rather, the expression contemplated by ss. 58 and 69 of the Charter of the French Language is expression within the meaning of both s. 2(b) of the Canadian Charter and s. 3 of the Quebec Charter. This leads to the conclusion that s. 58 infringes the freedom of expression guaranteed by s. 3 of the Quebec Charter and s. 69 infringes the guaranteed freedom of expression under both s. 2(b) of the Canadian Charter and s. 3 of the Quebec Charter. Although the expression in this case has a commercial element, it should be noted that the focus here is on choice of language and on a law which prohibits the use of a language. We are not asked in this case to deal with the distinct issue of the permissible scope of regulation of advertising (for example to protect consumers) where different governmental interests come into play, particularly when assessing the reasonableness of limits on such commercial expression pursuant to s. 1 of the Canadian Charter or to s. 9.1 of the Quebec Charter. It remains to be considered whether the limit imposed on freedom of expression by ss. 58 and 69 is justified....

The test under s. 1 of the Canadian Charter was laid down by this Court in *R. v. Oakes*, and restated by the Chief Justice in *R. v. Edwards Books and Art Ltd.*, as follows at pp. 768–69:

> Two requirements must be satisfied to establish that a limit is reasonable and demonstrably justified in a free and democratic society. First, the legislative objective which the limitation is designed to promote must be of sufficient importance to warrant overriding a constitutional right. It must bear on a "pressing and substantial concern". Second, the means chosen to attain those objectives must be proportional or appropriate to the ends. The proportionality requirement, in turn, normally has three aspects: the limiting measures must be carefully designed, or rationally connected, to the objective; they must impair the right as little as possible; and their effects must not so severely trench on individual or group rights that the legislative objective, albeit important, is nevertheless outweighed by the abridgment of rights. The Court stated that the nature of the proportionality test would vary depending on the circumstances. Both in articulating the standard of proof and in describing the criteria comprising the proportionality requirement the Court has been careful to avoid rigid and inflexible standards....

The section 1 and s. 9.1 materials consist of some fourteen items ranging in nature from the general theory of language policy and planning to statistical analysis of the position of the French language in Quebec and Canada. The material deals with two matters of particular relevance to the issue in the appeal: (a) the vulnerable position of the French language in Quebec and Canada, which is the reason for the language policy reflected in the Charter of the French Language; and (b) the importance attached by language planning theory to the role of language in the public domain, including the communication or expression by language contemplated by the challenged provisions of the Charter of the French Language. As to the first, the material amply establishes the importance of the legislative purpose reflected in the Charter of the French Language and that it is a response to a substantial and pressing need. Indeed, this was conceded by the respondents both in the Court of Appeal and in this Court. The vulnerable position of the French language in Quebec and Canada was described in a series of reports by commissions of inquiry beginning with the Report of the Royal Commission on Bilingualism and Biculturalism in 1969 and continuing with the Parent Commission and the Gendron Commission. It is reflected in statistics referred to in these reports and in later studies forming part of the materials, with due adjustment made in the light of the submissions of the appellant Singer in *Devine* with respect to some of the later statistical material. The causal factors for the threatened position of the French language that have generally been identified are: (a) the declining birth rate of Quebec francophones resulting in a decline in the Quebec francophone proportion of the Canadian population as a whole; (b) the decline of the francophone population outside Quebec as a result of assimilation; (c) the greater rate of assimilation of immigrants to Quebec by the anglophone community of Quebec; and (d) the continuing dominance of English at the higher levels of the economic sector. These factors have favoured the use of the English language despite the predominance in Quebec of a francophone population. Thus, in the period prior to the enactment of the legislation at issue, the "visage linguistique" of Quebec often gave the impression that English had become as significant as French. This "visage linguistique" reinforced the concern among francophones that English was gaining in importance, that the French language was threatened and that it would ultimately disappear. It strongly suggested to young and ambitious francophones that the language of success was almost exclusively English. It confirmed to anglophones that there was no great need to learn the majority language. And it suggested to immigrants that the prudent course lay in joining the anglophone community. The aim of such provisions as ss. 58 and 69 of the Charter of the French Language was, in the words of its preamble, "to see the quality and influence of the French language assured". The threat to the French language demonstrated to the government that it should, in particular, take steps to assure that the "visage linguistique" of Quebec would reflect the predominance of the French language.

The section 1 and s. 9.1 materials establish that the aim of the language policy underlying the Charter of the French Language was a serious and legitimate one. They indicate the concern about the survival of the French language and the perceived need for an adequate legislative response to the problem. Moreover, they indicate a rational connection between protecting the French language and assuring that the reality of Quebec society is communicated through the "visage linguistique". The section 1 and s. 9.1 materials do not, however, demonstrate that the

requirement of the use of French only is either necessary for the achievement of the legislative objective or proportionate to it. That specific
question is simply not addressed by the materials. Indeed, in his factum
and oral argument the Attorney General of Quebec did not attempt to
justify the requirement of the exclusive use of French. He concentrated on
the reasons for the adoption of the Charter of the French Language and the
earlier language legislation, which, as was noted above, were conceded by
the respondents. The Attorney General of Quebec relied on what he
referred to as the general democratic legitimacy of Quebec language policy
without referring explicitly to the requirement of the exclusive use of
French. In so far as proportionality is concerned, the Attorney General of
Quebec referred to the American jurisprudence with respect to commercial
speech, presumably as indicating the judicial deference that should be paid
to the legislative choice of means to serve an admittedly legitimate legislative purpose, at least in the area of commercial expression. He did,
however, refer in justification of the requirement of the exclusive use of
French to the attenuation of this requirement reflected in ss. 59 to 62 of
the Charter of the French Language and the regulations. He submitted
that these exceptions to the requirement of the exclusive use of French
indicate the concern for carefully designed measures and for interfering as
little as possible with commercial expression. The qualifications of the
requirement of the exclusive use of French in other provisions of the
Charter of the French Language and the regulations do not make ss. 58
and 69 any less prohibitions of the use of any language other than French
as applied to the respondents. The issue is whether any such prohibition is
justified. In the opinion of this Court it has not been demonstrated that the
prohibition of the use of any language other than French in ss. 58 and 69 of
the Charter of the French Language is necessary to the defence and
enhancement of the status of the French language in Quebec or that it is
proportionate to that legislative purpose. Since the evidence put to us by
the government showed that the predominance of the French language was
not reflected in the "visage linguistique" of Quebec, the governmental
response could well have been tailored to meet that specific problem and to
impair freedom of expression minimally. Thus, whereas requiring the
predominant display of the French language, even its marked predominance, would be proportional to the goal of promoting and maintaining a
French "visage linguistique" in Quebec and therefore justified under the
Quebec Charter and the Canadian Charter, requiring the exclusive use of
French has not been so justified. French could be required in addition to
any other language or it could be required to have greater visibility than
that accorded to other languages. Such measures would ensure that the
"visage linguistique" reflected the demography of Quebec: the predominant
language is French. This reality should be communicated to all citizens and
non-citizens alike, irrespective of their mother tongue. But exclusivity for
the French language has not survived the scrutiny of a proportionality test
and does not reflect the reality of Quebec society. Accordingly, we are of the
view that the limit imposed on freedom of expression by s. 58 of the
Charter of the French Language respecting the exclusive use of French on

public signs and posters and in commercial advertising is not justified under s. 9.1 of the Quebec Charter. In like measure, the limit imposed on freedom of expression by s. 69 of the Charter of the French Language respecting the exclusive use of the French version of a firm name is not justified under either s. 9.1 of the Quebec Charter or s. 1 of the Canadian Charter. . . .

James Tully, Strange Multiplicity: Constitutionalism in an Age of Diversity 169–76 (1995)

[p]oliticians and commentators immediately hailed or condemned the case as a great conflict between individual and group rights, or between individual and community. Scholars unhesitatingly and habitually interpret it in these terms, thereby proving the captivity that the language of modern constitutionalism continues to exert over the way we look at constitutional issues.

However, as Avigail Eisenberg demonstrates in her careful survey of this and related cases, the federal court justices did not take up the case in these terms, but, rather, in the language of cultural recognition. They reasoned over the value of 'identity related differences'. The 'notion of difference', she explains, 'denotes differences between people that play a constitutive role in shaping their identities. Culture, religion, language and gender are amongst the central differences that distinguish and help to determine the identities of people in Canadian society'. That is, the sovereign people come already constituted in diverse ways by their 'identity related' or, in my terms, 'cultural' differences of language, religion and gender. If a valuable cultural difference is constitutive of the ways a person speaks and acts, then, like custom in ancient constitutionalism, not to recognise and accommodate it is the injustice of cultural imperialism, for it is to assimilate that person to different ways of speaking and acting without consent.

In their decision, the justices begin with the plaintiffs' side. They give full recognition to individual freedom of expression in public in the language of one's choice. 'Language is so intimately related to the form and content of expression', they write, 'that there cannot be true freedom of expression by means of language if one is prohibited from using the language of one's choice.' They then draw attention to a connection between the two sides. Language is not only 'a means by which a people may express its cultural identity', as the Québec charter of the French language indicates and the defendants submit, but also 'the means by which the individual expresses his or her personal identity and sense of individuality'.

Once language is shown to fit expression in the way form-line sculpture fits Haida myth creatures, they argue that freedom of expression in one's own language is essential to participation in a democratic society. It is necessary to individual 'development' and 'dignity', as well as to 'participation by the members of the society in social, including political, decision-making'. Once the value of the cultural difference in question is established by these criteria drawn from John Stuart Mill and shared by both sides, the only remaining question is whether the use of one's language in commercial signage is an area of free expression protected by the Charter. In a ground-breaking section, the justices conclude that it is, giving the English-speaking shopkeepers the most sympathetic hearing they could have imagined.

The justices then turn to listen to the other side, asking what could justify placing limits on such a valuable identity-related difference in a free and democratic society. The answer they gave is that if it threatens the preservation and enhancement of the French language. For, as we have seen in the above quotation, the French language is reciprocally recognised as the constitutive means in which the 'people' of Québec express their cultural identity. Hence, the French *visage linguistique* is a valuable cultural difference worthy of protection, especially in light of its vulnerability in the context of North America.

After the two claims for cultural continuity are mutually recognised in these terms, the justices ask if there is a mode of accommodation suitable to the circumstances of the case. They answer that a commercial sign policy of French 'always' rather than French 'only' resolves the conflict. As long as the overall 'predominance' of the French language is ensured, bilingual signs should be permitted. The resolution, much like the later decision in France overturning the French only sections of the Toubon law, accommodates each claim for recognition. Moreover, the linguistic minorities in Québec, by expressing themselves on their signs in French and their first language, affirm the predominance of French language and give proportional public expression to the diverse languages that constitute aspects of the linguistic character of the society as a whole.

In coming to their decision, the justices explained that they used a heuristic test which can be applied in many cases of cultural recognition. It is not a set of universal rules and a calculus for its application in every instance. The heuristic test is more like Wittgenstein's 'object of comparison' which brings to light the cultural differences and similarities in a case and furnishes criteria for their mutual accommodation. It might be called the 'even-handed' test for mutual cultural recognition. Two requirements must be satisfied to establish that a legislative limit to a constitutional right, such as the freedom of expression, is justified in a free and democratic society. First the legislative objective, such as the preservation and promotion of the French language, must be 'of sufficient importance' and 'a pressing and substantial concern' to 'warrant' overriding the right. Second, the legislative means employed must be 'proportional to the ends'. The proportionality requirement, in turn has three aspects. The 'limiting measures must be carefully designed, or rationally connected, to the objective; they must impair the right as little as possible; and their effects must not so severely trench on individual or group rights that the legislative objective, albeit important, is nevertheless outweighed by the abridgement of rights'. The court adds that the proportionality test varies 'with circumstances' and that 'rigid and inflexible standards' should be avoided....

I would like to emphasise that in each of these cases rights are taken seriously. The question the justices ask is how to apply rights even-handedly so they do not discriminate against citizens' identity-related differences that can be shown to be worthy of protection. If rights were applied without taking these cultural differences into account, the result would not be impartial. The dominant culture would in fact be imposed in each case. Therefore, there are no grounds for complaint from a defender of rights, for rights are rescued from being a tool of cultural domination. Conversely, a critic of rights has no reason to complain, for the alleged blindness to cultural differences has been corrected, yet without abandoning rights....

To resume, the government of Québec overrode the court's decision and continued to enforce the French only sign law. To protect the balance between the sovereignty of the people in their provincial parliaments and the unelected federal court, whose justices are appointed by the prime minister, the constitution allows a provincial parliament to override an unpopular federal court interpretation of the Charter for a period of up to five years. This balancing device of diverse federalism provides an opportunity to bring hot-headed democratic sentiment in line with the court's reasonable interpretation or, alternatively, to bring a biased court to see that its interpretation overlooked the respect-worthy regional circumstances that should have been taken into account. In this case, Québec parliamentarians considered themselves justified in invoking override not only because the sovereignty of the Québec parliament had been at the heart of Québec's struggle for recognition for over two hundred years, but also because the federal court's interpretation was based on the very Charter Québec had not consented to in 1981.

Notwithstanding any of these points, the sign legislation itself violates the conventions of mutual recognition and continuity, for it unilaterally recognises the French language to the exclusion of the minority English language, and this was confirmed by Québec's own provincial court. One might conclude that this proves the poverty of diverse federalism. A strong Hobbesian sovereign is needed to enforce unilaterally the federal court's rulings. This is to misunderstand how enforcement works in a culturally diverse society. Unilateral attempts of enforcement by the federal government are ineffective and they provoke disunity and secession. There will always be conflicts over mutual recognition in any free and diverse society. There is no final solution. The mutual checks and balances of the diverse members are a more effective and democratic method of enforcement than a central sovereign.

At the same time as the government of Québec overrode the court's decision, they were also negotiating a constitutional amendment to regain powers from the federal government. Even though their amendment, the

Meech Lake agreement, contained a clause protecting the English-speaking minority, a majority of the citizens of the rest of Canada were sceptical. They rejected the proposed amendment on the express ground that the Québec government had failed to abide by the court decision. This expression of democratic will played a decisive role in defeating the amendment. Further pressure was applied by an English-speaking citizen of Québec who referred the offensive law to the United Nations.

These pressures helped citizens in Québec who were in favour of revising the sign legislation. The government of Québec initiated a public discussion and pluralistic nationalists published a *pacte linguistique* calling for the official recognition of the English language and the eleven Aboriginal languages as constituents of the linguistic character of Québec. As a result of public deliberation, the majority expressed themselves in favour of bringing the sign legislation in line with the court ruling and the law was changed. This illustrates the democratic and dialogical way in which mutual recognition can be enforced in diverse societies without recourse to a Hobbesian sovereign or any other unilateral device.

Questions and Comments

1.   Consider the following perspectives, most less optimistic than Tully's, on the success of Canadian federalism in managing its different linguistic communities:

(a) Max Nemni, *Ethnic Nationalism and the Destabilization of the Canadian Federation* in Evaluating Federal Systems 143 (Bertus deVilliers ed. 1994): "The case of Quebec ... illustrates how ethnicity, through powerful symbolic appeals to cultural survival, can be politicized to the extent of seriously threatening the very existence of an otherwise stable and prosperous federation."

(b) Richard Simeon, *Canada and the United States: Lessons from the North American Experience*, in Rethinking Federalism: Citizens, Markets and Governments in a Changing World 256–60 (Karen Knop, Sylvia Ostrey, Richard Simeon, and Katherine Swinton eds. 1995):

> [The failed history of the Meech Lake and Charlottetown accords] suggests that the answer to the question of whether federalism has facilitated the management of linguistic cleavages in Canada should be 'no.' Throughout Canadian history, and especially since the 1960s, the country has been in the throes of almost continual constitutional crisis. The independence movement has grown; the Parti Québécois now forms the government in Quebec, and is committed to [another] early referendum....
>
> At another level, however, the answer might be more positive. After all, the federation has managed to survive over a long period. Quebec has been the central force for ensuring that the Canadian federal system is in some ways the most decentralized federation in the world. Quebec has been able to use the institutional, political and financial resources which federal provides to build a powerful national soci-

ety.... It has been able to develop distinctive economic, linguistic and social policies ... to erase the economic inequality between francophone and anglophone citizens in Quebec. ... Arguably, Quebec's economic, social and linguistic security as a small minority on the North American continent has been stronger within the Canadian federation that it would have been as a small independent state....

Nevertheless ... federalism entrenches, perpetuates and institutionalizes the very divisions it is designed to manage. It is Janus-faced; its virtues are also its vices....

Second, federalism ... does not address the problems of minorities within minorities....

The most difficult barrier to reconciling Quebec with the rest of Canada ... is the fundamental clash between the dualist, or 'two founding peoples' conception of the country, and rival conceptions ... [including] the view of Canada as a collection of at least ten distinct societies ... [and] a third set of conceptions of community in Canada. The adoption of the Charter was a fundamental constitutional change which embodied an attack on the premises of both federalism and parliamentarism. It explicitly conferred rights on individual citizens against governments. Since the Charter, Canadian constitutional politics have been as much about citizens and governments as they have been about the relationships between governments. The Charter also gave recognition and status to collectivities which cut across provincial lines—women, multicultural groups, the disabled and the Aboriginal peoples. Many of these groups have argued that federalism is a direct barrier to their political effectiveness.

Their mobilization was a decisive factor in the defeat of the Meech Lake Accord ...[m] Many saw it as a potential threat to the rights which they had gained in the Charter....

In sum, we see a bewildering kaleidoscope of competing identities played out on the constitutional stage....

(c) Colin H. Williams, *A Requiem for Canada*, in Federalism: The Multiethnic Challenge 66 (Graham Smith ed. 1995):

It is evident that the status quo, which includes Québec within the Confederation, is the preferred option for most Canadians. And yet within English Canada, of late, there has been a double backlash, both against multiculturalism and against the 'special pleading' of a dissenting Québec.... [T]he farther away one is from the border with Québec the less active support there may be for maintaining Québec within Canada at any price. There are good grounds for predicting the eclipse of the myth of the two founding European peoples....

---

m. See also Max Nemni, at 143–54 (noting Alain Cairns' argument that the Charter created its own constituencies of "Charter Canadians," permitting the Charter to act as "a powerful counterweight to the centrifugal pulls of regionalism and ethnic nationalism") Nemni points out that it was an aboriginal member of the Manitoba legislature who was instrumental in the defeat of the Meech Lake accords in 1990. Elijah Har-

per refused to waive internal rules requiring two days before consideration of a motion, which prevented the Meech Lake accord from being considered. Nemni comments: "His gesture symbolized the political coming-of-age of the aboriginal people. Meech had committed the fatal mistake of leaving them completely out. If Quebec is 'distinct,' claimed these 'First Nations,' we are even more so."

It may be assumed that most people in English Canada would accept the result if the majority of Québécois citizens were to opt for independence outside Canada.... What they appear not to be able to accept is 'special status and treatment' for Québec inside Canada.

If Quebec is given "special treatment," what implications would this have for the more than 600 groups of aboriginal peoples in Canada? for new immigrant groups?

(d) Finally, for a competing vision in favor of "asymmetrical federalism," see Alain–G Gagnon, *Manufacturing Antagonisms: The Move Toward Uniform Federalism in Canada* in Evaluating Federal Systems 138 (Bertus deVilliers ed. (1994)):

> Canada is essentially formed of three nations—each constituted differently.... [English Canadians confuse these nations, with the state of Canada, a view which makes the future of Canada seem bleak given the desire of Quebeckers and aboriginal nations to express their nationhood] ... [W]e should face the reality as it presents itself and not as it was reconstructed by Trudeau.... Asymmetrical federalism proposes an alternative that could accommodate Quebeckers and aboriginal nations within a reimagined 'tripartite state', and more equal federalism with powers commensurate with the desire of the nations to express themselves.

Nemni notes the impact of immigration on Canada, asserting that 50% of Toronto's population of immigrants, the majority of whom are from Asia. For immigrant groups not members of the two "founding" language communities, the Charter offers an appealing concept of citizenship. If, as Nemni argues, Canada is increasingly a nation of immigrants from outside the two or three "founding nations," how would "asymmetrical federalism" affect the interests of those newer immigrants?

2. There is some evidence that the English-speaking population of Quebec has declined in recent years. If unilingualism is the goal of Quebec's language and cultural policies, is achievement of that goal a victory for federalism?

---

2. Belgium

Note the creativity (or desperation?) of a system like that in Belgium, which uses both geographic and linguistic lines to create its subunits and in which power even in foreign affairs is shared with the constituent parts.

Richard Cullen, *Adaptive Federalism in Belgium*, 13 University of New South Wales Law Journal 346 (1990)

I. INTRODUCTION

... [M]ajor constitutional changes ... have been occurring in Belgium recently....

In fact, Belgium is the newest federal state in the western world.[1] It is a federal state in an adaptive phase. Less than twenty years ago, it still had

---

1. Some may argue that the new Belgian constitutional structure fails to measure up as "truly" federal, that is, it fails to accord with classical definitions of what is feda highly centralized political structure, a legacy, more than anything else, of the twenty year period of French occupancy which ended with Napoleon's defeat at the Battle of Waterloo (located in present day Belgium) in 1815. How then, has Belgium come to this constitutional crossroads and what has been the outcome of this process of change? . . .

II.   PRELIMINARY CONSIDERATIONS

A.   The Historical Political Setting

Belgium has a population of just under 10 million. It covers an area of approximately 31,000 square kilometres. It has the highest population density of all the major European nations. It is a nation sharply divided along language and ethnic lines. Like Switzerland, it is a nation which straddles the intersection of the two great (Latin and Germanic) western European cultures. Belgium is now becoming even more like Switzerland in that a federal structure is being used to help deal with this reality.

Belgium, historically, has been relatively prosperous, at least when it has not been being used as a convenient battlefield by its more powerful neighbours. It continues to enjoy significant prosperity today. Like most of Europe, its per capita income exceeds that of Australia. The social service infra-structure is comprehensive and, although the national debt is huge (about BF 7000 billion . . .) it seems most of it comprises funds lent by Belgians to themselves. The currency is stable, incomes are high and prices and inflation are moderate. Moreover, with Brussels clearly establishing itself as the capital of Europe and a buoyant local economy, future prospects appear propitious.

Visitors are often surprised to discover that there are three official language communities in Belgium (Dutch, French and German) and three distinct geographic regions in which each language predominates. The German speaking part of Belgium (which was added to the country in 1919 pursuant to the Treaty of Versailles and which briefly reverted to Germany during the Second World War) is in the extreme east of the country. It covers only a small area and accounts for less than 1% of the total population. The balance of the population is approximately 60% Dutch speaking and 40% French speaking. The geographic divide which separates these two major linguistic groups runs, roughly, horizontally across the country. The regional names for these two *geographic* regions are Flanders (for the Dutch speaking northern region) and Wallonia (for the French speaking southern region). The capital, Brussels, is an 80% French speaking enclave, just north of the divide, in Flanders.

eral. My own view is that the new structure, as proposed, is clearly federal. . . .

But where lie the linguistic origins of Belgium? The Romans had invaded the Low Countries, by the first century BC. The resistance of the competing Germanic tribes was too strong to permit their complete permanent conquest, however. The Franks were the most successful of these tribes. Ultimately, they ended the Roman occupation in the Low Countries (and the Roman occupation further south). Their cultural influence was, however, never sufficient to oust the Roman languages. Thus, the linguistic frontier between Romance and Germanic languages was fixed at the point of maximum (stable) Roman conquest. It remains at this point, essentially, today. That is, the linguistic dividing line, which separates Flanders and Wallonia in modern Belgium has been in place for some 2,000 years.

The modern political entity Belgium dates from 1830. In that year, the historical fact of continuous foreign domination finally ended with the Belgian Revolution against their ultimate colonial masters, the Dutch.[7] The immediately previous period of French occupation (from 1794 until 1815) was far more important in shaping the political framework of modern Belgium, however. The Napoleonic era left Belgium with a highly organized and *centralized* political structure, modelled on that of France.

B. The Constitution of 1831

The new Belgian State was established with a written constitution (from 1831) which survives to this day. It established Belgium as a unitary state with a bicameral legislature and a constitutional monarchy.[8]

The constitution is laid out, in the accepted way, under a number of major headings. . . .

Title 1 deals with the territorial division of Belgium. Title 2 contains the Belgian Bill of Rights. It includes over 20 articles which stipulate an extensive agenda of guaranteed individual rights. These include equality rights, rights to education, religious and press freedom, restraints on the operation of the criminal law and a right to peaceful assembly. Until very recently, the application of the Bill of Rights was not subject to judicial review. It is now partly so subject. Historically it thus has acted as a non-judicially enforceable constitutional constraint on legislative and administrative excess.

Title 3, "The Powers" is the most extensive in the constitution. Article 25 stipulates that all powers emanate from the nation, thus neither the people nor the King are the ultimate repository of sovereignty, apparently. Article 26 then vests legislative authority in the King, the House of Representatives and the Senate. Chapter 1 of Title 3 sets down the structure, procedures and powers of the two Chambers of the National Parliament in articles 32 to 59. Chapter 2 of Title 3 provides a striking contrast with the Australian Constitution for, in it, the role and powers of

7. Following the defeat of Napoleon in 1815, the Congress of Vienna, in the same year, reunified Belgium Holland and Luxembourg under King Willem of the Netherlands.

8. The bicameral National Parliament remains, as does the constitutional monarchy but, as we shall see, Belgium is no longer a unitary State.

the King are set out in great detail. Article 60 provides, inter alia, that all women are perpetually excluded from exercising royal authority in Belgium. Chapter 3 of Title 3 prescribes the manner in which judicial power is to be exercised and the institutions which are to exercise it. Title 4, entitled Finances, establishes Parliamentary control of public revenue raising and expenditure in articles 110 to 117. Title 5 regulates the constitutional position of the Belgian military. Titles 6 and 8 govern a number of miscellaneous matters, including the nomination of Brussels as the national capital. Also, article 130, in Title 6, prohibits any suspension of the constitution in whole or in part.

Title 7 contains, in article 131, the mechanism for changing the Belgian constitution. Initiatives for change need to come, by way of a declaration, from the National Legislature. When such a declaration of the need for change is made, both Chambers of the National Parliament are dissolved. A national election ensues and the new Parliament debates the proposed changes and votes on them. The quorum for such a debate is two-thirds in each Chamber and no change may be adopted unless it secures at least two-thirds of the total votes cast.

C.   Resolution of the Language Issue

Although the new constitution of 1831 provided for freedom in the use of language, in article 23, French remained Belgium's sole official language for many years.[12] Economically, Wallonia was the dominant region. It had major coal deposits and it developed a thriving iron and steel industry. This economic power led to political domination of the country, notwithstanding that the Flemish were the majority group.[13] The educated classes in Flanders all were bilingual as a matter of practical necessity. This, of course, tended to reinforce the dominance of French language and culture.

Not surprisingly, political agitation for improvement of the language rights of the Flemish was an aspect of early Belgian political life. Energetic campaigning produced a number of gradual changes. In the 1870s, approval was given for the use of Dutch in criminal courts. In 1883, Dutch was finally approved as a language of instruction in *Flemish* secondary schools and in 1898 laws began to be published, at last, in both Dutch and French. During the First World War, the occupying Germans tried to capitalize on the internal antagonism by supporting demands for Flemish autonomy. The Germans established a Council of Flanders and a Flemish University. Most Flemings were hostile to the occupying forces and refused to recognize either institution, however. The next period of major change was during the 1930s. The University of Ghent became a Dutch speaking university and Dutch was adopted as the sole and compulsory language for many official purposes throughout Flanders.

---

12.   This was, in part, another legacy of the French occupation prior to 1815. During that time, French was made the sole official language.

13.   They have become more so with the passage of time....

A number of forces were driving these changes. First, there was the gradual extension of voting rights (by 1949 universal suffrage was achieved)[18] which, of course, tended to shift political power towards the numerically stronger Flemish. Secondly, the economic strength of Wallonia began to decline as its heavy industries lost out to more efficient international competitors. At the same time, rapid industrialization of the north was taking place. Thus the Flemish were swiftly catching up in terms of economic prosperity and their ascendency in sheer numbers continued to grow.

Major reform of language laws followed in 1962–63. These laws brought about a high degree of unilingualism in Flanders in education, the civil service and the army.[20] These reforms were driven by Flemish demands. It is important to note that the thrust for language rights was pervaded by a demand for a *unilingual* structure for Flanders. That is, the Flemish were not prepared to accept bilingualism in Flanders. They reasoned that, because of its dominance *internationally* (vis a vis Dutch), if French were allowed to enjoy any official status, Dutch would not be able to compete and thus would continue to languish as a subsidiary language. The same problem did not confront Wallonia. The historical political-economy of language in Belgium has meant that there has been little need for the French speaking region to speak other than French. Despite the relative economic and numerical decline of Wallonia, French language and culture have yet to experience any serious threat to their continued vitality.

III.   THE NEW FEDERAL SYSTEM

A.   Preamble

The momentum developed in the quest for language reform has now led to a series of major constitutional reforms over the last two decades. Further reform is envisaged. It is important to stress that this process of reform has been characterized by an absence of serious violence, notwithstanding the long-running nature of the language dispute and the antagonism which has flourished across the community divide.[21] The most signifi-

---

18. Article 47 of the Belgian Constitution now guarantees universal suffrage to all citizens over 18 years of age. The extension of the franchise was extraordinarily delayed by Australian standards. Interestingly, Belgium ... [has] compulsory voting. (In the European Community, voting is also compulsory in Italy and Luxembourg.) Article 48 provides that elections are to be based on a system of proportional representation, although the Senate is partly composed of members elected under a collegiate system (see article 53).

20. Previously, French retained an influence in these domains. In Wallonia, Dutch has never provided any competition to French ...

21. Probably the most divisive incident incident of this century came during the resolution of the so called, "Royal Question" shortly after the Second World War. It was indirectly related to the language question. King Leopold III, unlike his government and other royal brethren in occupied Europe, refused to leave the country as the Germans approached. The King was incarcerated in Germany for the duration. His return to the throne after the war was delayed whilst a referendum on his suitability was held. He received a comfortable overall majority, but there was a strong majority *against* his return in Wallonia. When he returned to take the throne in July 1950 a wave of demonstra-

cant legacy of community cleavage in Belgium has thus not been a Northern Ireland style, deeply violent impasse but, rather, continual political and constitutional development riven with political compromise.

The modern reform of the 1831 Belgian Constitution proper is generally regarded as having taken place in three stages. The First Reform was in 1970; the Second Reform in 1980 and we are currently in the midst of the Third Reform, which began in 1988. It must be said that the Belgians have created a most complex federal structure with this series of reforms. Still greater complexity is promised for the future.

It was the movement for language rights which provided the momentum for much of what has happened since. The Flemish community has been pushing for greater Flemish autonomy in all areas, since the major problems with language were addressed. Since the 1960s, Walloon leaders, such as Andre Renard, have also favoured federal style reform as a mechanism to protect their cultural, political and *economic* interests as a diminishing minority group.

Throughout the recent period of constitutional reform, the governance and control of Brussels has presented singular difficulties. This moderately sized and attractive city of 1.3 million is not only the capital of Belgium, it is also the capital of Europe. And as the European Community moves closer to some sort of federal political form, Brussels's status as a centre of power is steadily being enhanced. In the battle across the linguistic divide, it is a major prize. The city itself is predominantly French speaking[26] but it is located within Flanders. Devising an acceptable system to devolve power to the Brussels region has proved very difficult indeed, for all concerned.[27]

B.   The First Reform (1970)

The First Reform, of 1970, recognised that there were four language regions in Belgium; the unilingual Dutch, French and German language regions and the bilingual Brussels region. These then were *geographical* areas of the country which were divided on a territorial basis according to the language predominant in each geographic area. This was, ultimately, the least important of the *three* divisions at the regional level which make Belgian federalism so remarkable. The same reform *also* recognised that there were three *Communities* in Belgium; the French, the Dutch and the German. The emphasis here was on divisions according to *persons* not *geography*; rather after the fashion in which we speak of the Italian community in Australia. Councils of the Communities were established *but* the members of the Councils were drawn from the National Parliament. That is, the members of the National Parliament also got to wear hats as

---

tions and protest strikes ensued. The King abdicated very shortly after this.

26. Approximately 80% of the population speak French and 20% Dutch. Many French speakers are of Flemish origin, however. These families have, simply, over the years, taken on the principal tongue of the city in which they live for practical reasons.

Also, there are many non-Belgians living in Brussels and these tend to swell the numbers for the dominant language.

27. The small German speaking region has not been a serious cause of concern in this regard.

regional politicians. If that wasn't confusing enough, the 1970 Reform also recognized three *Socio-Economic Regions*, in addition to the four *Language Regions*. These were the Walloon Region (which encompassed the German speaking region in *this* carve-up), the Flemish Region and the Brussels Region. The important divisions, then, are the *Communities* (hereinafter, the Communities) and the *Socio–Economic Regions* (hereinafter, the Regions).

This remarkable system of overlapping divisions did not come into existence in its entirety in 1970, though the ground work was all laid at that time. Important powers over linguistic matters were devolved to the Communities in 1970 but little else. A protracted political debate prevented the Regions from operating until 1980. The First Reform, thus, did not greatly change the centralized system of Government.

C. The Second and Third Reforms (1980–1991)

All the institutions of the second tier of government are now in place. And many more powers have been devolved to these regional entities. Although still legally separate, the Community and Region are merged, for management purposes, in Flanders (outside of Brussels). There is thus, effectively, a single Flemish Council (the regional law[32] making body) with its own Executive (or government). In Wallonia, however, there is both a *Community* Council and a *Regional* Council (with their respective Executives).

The governance of the Brussels area is now[33] controlled by an *elected* Council plus three other Commissions which draw their membership from the two language groups. The Council of the German Community is also elected.

Rather simply put, it is the Flemish, with their superior numbers who have pushed for *Community* Councils and the Walloons who have pushed, as a minority protective measure, for the *Regional* Councils.

In the process of devolving powers to this plenitude of regional entities, some powers have gone (in the Second and Third Reforms) to the Communities and some to the Regions. Basically, the Communities have powers over what are termed cultural matters. These include language and most educational matters, health care, and a wide range of social welfare issues. The Regions have substantial economic management powers (subject to National override in certain cases), planning powers, environment protection responsibilities and energy management powers. They also are responsible for major public works and roadworks, housing and have parallel power with respect to initiating scientific research. Perhaps even more remarkable, from an Australian view point, is the power being given to

---

32. Regional laws are actually known as *decrees* to distinguish them from the *laws* of the National Parliament. Laws in the Brussels region are known as *ordinances*.

33. Since mid-1989.

Regions to construct their own international export policies and to grant work (though not residence) permits to foreign workers.

Thus far, the Communities and Regions are almost completely fiscally reliant on a share of National taxes. Regional taxes, such as those on lotteries, distilleries and electronic games, are of minor importance. A reducing fiscal equalization program (known as the *national solidarity contribution*) will take effect over the ten year period from 1990. Initially, it will assist Wallonia by maintaining the old (National Government) expenditure bias towards that region, although assistance will gradually be reduced over this term.

It must be remembered that the politicians of the principal regional entities (of Flanders and Wallonia) are *not* elected *as politicians of those regional governments*; they are chosen from within the ranks of the National Parliament. However, this system of double office holding is scheduled for abolition in the third *phase* of the current Third Reform of the constitution. The respective Councils would then be elected. It is also proposed that the Regions would take over greater responsibility for international relations.

D.   The Court of Arbitration

The creation of this component in the new Belgian political order is the major *judicial* change to have emerged in the political restructuring of the country. The Second Reform of 1980 provided for the establishment of Court of Arbitration. This is something of a misnomer as the court is, essentially, a constitutional court. The title "Constitutional Court" was rejected, however, apparently because the name evoked the possibility of control of the legislature by the court. In the event, the court was not established, fully, until 1985. Initially, standing was only provided to the political institutions in the system, that is, there was no individual standing. Moreover, the orthodoxy is that there is no "hierarchy of laws" (as the Belgians describe it) or paramountcy rule to cover conflicts between laws of the National Parliament and those of the regional Councils. The court *is*, however, able to strike down laws which are ultra vires, that is beyond the constitutionally stipulated power of the particular legislature.

The Third Reform (phases one and two of 1988 and 1989) has widened the standing rules substantially and also the court's jurisdiction. Now any person "interested" in a relevant matter can seek to bring it before the court. Furthermore the court can review both national and regional laws to ensure that they comply with a *selection* of sections in the Bill of Rights. Thus far, the court is only able to apply articles 6, 6bis and 17 from the Bill of Rights. The first two guarantee equality of treatment before the law and prohibit discrimination. Article 17 sets out important education rights.

The membership of the court is carefully controlled to maintain a balance between the two major linguistic groups. There are two Chief Justices, one from each region and they serve for twelve months each on an alternate basis. The court has twelve members, six French speaking and six Dutch speaking. Half its members have to be judicial or academic lawyers of long standing and the other half, former politicians. The court simply hands down decisions; it does not give written reasoned judgments. It seems that the political sensitivities involved in making judicial decisions preclude this.

The Court of Arbitration potentially has the power to be a serious force indeed in the new political structure. It has been given significant powers and can widen its brief by interpretation of what is a division of powers issue and by a wide reading of the Bill of Rights provisions it is authorized to apply. There are powerful political constraints in place, however. The judges are acutely aware of the political sensitivity of their decisions. The omnipresent Germanic - Roman divide runs right through the court itself, after all. Nevertheless, given the wide range of its authority, it is very difficult to see the court side-stepping significant controversy in the longer term.

IV. CONCLUSION

It must be said that the Belgians have shown energy, skill and resourcefulness in crafting, in stages, their new political structure. The constitution is being moulded and shaped to meet the demands facing the country as it approaches the 21st century.

The result of all these labours is highly complex, however. Certainly, working from an English translation of the Belgian Constitution, as I have, has possibly heightened this apparent complexity. Nevertheless one can reasonably describe the federal political structure emerging in Belgium as being not a little byzantine. Apart from the structural complexities, the wording of some of the new provisions is quite tortuous. I doubt they would have passed a plain Dutch or plain French drafting protocol. They certainly do not translate into plain English. Article 26bis provides a good example:

> The Laws enacted in the implementation of Art. 107quater determine the judicial force of the rules, which are enacted by organs created by them in matters which they determine.

> They may confer upon these organs the power to enact decrees having the force of law in the area and the manner which they establish.

One must not, however, underestimate the political-constitutional achievements of the Belgians. The makings for significant civil violence have always been at hand, yet this menace has, for the most part, been avoided. There has been, on both sides it would seem, a real commitment to the politics of negotiation. The changes achieved are often riven with compromise but change *is* being accomplished and in the face of some extraordinary obstacles. Perhaps there is a collective recognition by the two sides that, unless they ultimately strike a deal when in dispute, the option is a stand-off which could fracture the nation, with France and Holland happy to pick up the pieces. Or, to put it another way, Flanders and Wallonia, despite their differences, ultimately have far more in common with each other than with either of their respective language-related neighbours.

Some of the more difficult obstacles have been dealt with, it must be admitted, by collective acts of political neglect. The failure to implement a formal paramountcy rule falls, plausibly, into this category. The inexactness surrounding the jurisdiction and procedures of the awkwardly named Court of Arbitration is also a product, I suspect, of an implicit agreement to put off some hard decisions. Likely this approach is simply storing up difficulties for the future. For instance, the apparently not deeply thought-out way in which the Court of Arbitration has been given power to give effect to certain sections of the Bill of Rights would ring alarm bells with many constitutional lawyers, especially in Canada where the political impact of the Charter of Rights has embroiled that document in continuous controversy. The nub of the problem is the appropriateness of allowing unelected judges to second-guess legislative policy on the basis of the judges' interpretation of certain, generally expressed protections of individual rights. My impression is that, so far, this concern has not gained much currency in Belgium. It may be that, in a country so accultured to perpetual political negotiation, constitutional loose ends hold far fewer terrors than in other jurisdictions. Doubtless the shapers of the new order are *aware* of the loose ends but perhaps they reason (based on much past experience) that they will be able to deal with them when they have to. In the mean time, the thing to do is get done what can be done now....

... [W]hat has determined these cultural predilections? ... [V]enturing a preliminary conjecture on the issue of cultural leanings, ... Belgium's position as a small *continental* nation abutting large, powerful and aggressive adjacent societies has had a potent influence on national perspectives. Notwithstanding an essentially conservative political tradition, Belgium has developed a noteworthy capacity for intelligent collective judgment on the timing of and need for constitutional change. Conversely, Australia's political culture has been deeply influenced by its 200 year, uninterrupted, isolated island status. We draw many strengths from that but it also has incubated inward looking and fairly unsophisticated (and highly abrasive) political habits. Our political culture appears confined to generating ever more strident political stand-offs as the sole response to the growing neuroses in the Australian political-economy. The resilience of this phenomenon normally is egregiously verified whenever we attempt formal constitutional change.

Alexander Murphy, *Belgium's Regional Divergence: Along the Road to Federation*, in Federalism: The Multiethnic Challenge 73–100 (Graham Smith ed. 1995).

... What has it meant for Belgium to adopt a federal structure in which the territories of the most important administrative units are close reflections of underlying language patterns? Were there alternative territorial configurations on which the federal system could have been built? Do such alternatives still exist?

... During the mid-1980s, a time when the country was already committed to a linguistically-based system of internal governance, Belgians from across the political and economic spectrum were arguing that tensions between the language communities had been essentially diffused; the real problems were economic and social, it was said, and these had little to do with the language problem. Yet the early 1990s saw mounting calls for Flemish autonomy, volatile disputes among the representatives of the language regions over the allocation of resources, and the collapse of the national government over an intense disagreement concerning the differential regional impacts of a telecommunications contract. Any serious analysis of these developments cannot ignore the structural features of political life that may be contributing to polarization along language lines. One of the most important of these features is the concrete political geography of Belgian federalism.

To question the role of Belgium's internal territorial structure in the expression of ethnolinguistic differences is not to argue against federalism, nor is it to suggest that the country had other good options at certain crucial junctures in its historical development. Rather, it is to focus attention on a critical issue both for Belgium and for our understanding of federalism. In the Belgian case, the political-territorial structure of federalism has had a profound effect on ethnolinguistic relations....

The Territorial Dimension of Federalism

... Although increasingly forceful arguments have been made about the implications of spatial structures for social, political, cultural, and economic processes, such arguments have received little attention in the theoretical literature on federalism....

... The importance of inquiries of this sort becomes immediately apparent if we pose a series of counterfactual questions. Would ethnolinguistic identity and intergroup conflict in Canada be different if Québec had developed as three separate provinces instead of one? Would Armenian-Azerbaijani relations be any different if Stalin had not created an Armenian enclave within Azerbaijan? ... The obvious 'yes' that each of these questions commands indicates the importance of going beyond questions that take the territorial status quo for granted.

That we have not made much progress in this direction is revealed by the literature on politics and the language problem in Belgium.... [T]here has been little consideration of the ways in which the political geography of Belgian federalism plays a role in identity and conflict. Yet the importance of this issue is clearly revealed in the controversies that have been taking place over such issues as funding for scientific research and surface water management. Although these matters are not inherently ethnic in character, they have invoked considerable tensions along language lines because the regions that control them are self-conscious territorial manifestations of the language groups of Belgium. Hence, every issue that is dealt with at the regional level has the potential of being interpreted as an ethnolinguistic issue as well. . . .

The Rise of Ethnoregionalism in Belgium . . .

The nationalism of early nineteenth century Belgium was focused on a territory that was linguistically complex. . . . Over the centuries, standardized French made significant inroads in southern Belgium, and by 1830 a significant proportion of the population of southern Belgium used French. In the north, variants of Dutch became widely used, but by 1830 standardized Dutch had made less progress in northern Belgium than had French in southern Belgium.

Further complicating the linguistic picture in the north was the presence of a numerically small, but socially significant coterie of French speakers in a few of the larger Flemish cities, particularly Ghent, Antwerp, and Brussels. These were generally people of Flemish ancestry who had started using the French language during the eighteenth century when French was the language of education, culture, and government . . . [A]t the time of the Belgian Revolution the number of French speakers in northern Belgium remained small. Their economic and political power, however, was far greater than their numbers.

The Belgian Revolution thus took place in a country that was decidedly heterogeneous from the standpoint of language. Language was one of many issues at stake in the movement for Belgian independence—the Francophone elite objected to William I's insistence on the use of Dutch in northern Belgium—but the Revolution was not perpetrated in the name of linguistic nationalism. At its heart was a desire to be free from outside control.

Newly independent Belgium was established as a parliamentary democracy with a constitutional monarch. There was no widespread sense at the time that Belgium was made up of two ethnolinguistic regions; dialectical differences precluded the development of any indigenous sense of linguistic homogeneity in either northern or southern Belgium and almost no one thought of the Romance or Germanic parts of Belgium as social or political unities (Murphy, 1988). Indeed, the terms Flanders and Wallonia were not even used to refer to northern and southern Belgium, respectively. . . . [A] highly centralised government structure was put into place along with a constitution that called for freedom of choice in language use.

Despite this constitutional guarantee, French was the language of public affairs in nineteenth-century Belgium. Political and economic life was dominated by French speakers who came from the South—the economic heartland of the country at the time—or who were members of the Francophone elite in Ghent, Antwerp, and Brussels. . . . [F]igures from the 1846 census show that 57% of the population used Dutch/Flemish most frequently, whereas only 42.1% used French/Walloon most of the time, continued Francophone dominance was ensured, however, by a system that limited the right to vote to large property owners . . . Indeed, there was an assumption among many that Belgium would gradually evolve into a French-speaking state.

A reactionary movement to this state of affairs developed among a small group of Flemish intellectuals who were influenced by romantic nationalist ideas sweeping Europe at the time and who objected to the privileged position of French in public life.... Throughout the nineteenth century, Flemish movement leaders were fundamentally concerned with the unequal position of the major languages in Belgium; they promoted the right of the Flemish people to use Dutch in government, education, commerce, and the military. Their efforts were largely frustrated, however, by an entrenched Francophone élite who resisted any changes in the linguistic status quo....

Frustrated by the intransigence of the Francophone elite and galvanised by the increasingly obvious inequities in the structure of language use in Belgium, the Flemish movement began to adopt a more radical stance by the turn of the twentieth century. Flemish radicalism in turn helped to fuel the growth of a Walloon movement that had started in the 1880s to promote Walloon culture and oppose 'excessive' Flemish demands. In the middle of everything was the city of Brussels, the capital of the country and historically a Flemish city.... [But] the city's French-speaking population grew rapidly during the nineteenth century because of the concentration of public functions in the Belgian capital. By 1910 the French speakers were in the majority[;] ... many were of Flemish ancestry. Hence, Brussels was neither a Walloon city from the standpoint of ancestry nor a Flemish city from the standpoint of language. Not surprisingly, the linguistic status of the capital became a matter of contention for both the Flemish and Walloon movements....

In the years leading up to World War I, a number of prominent Flemish leaders abandoned an emphasis on individual language rights in favor of a territorial approach to the language problem. The rapid growth of French in Brussels and a string of legislative defeats in the language arena led them to conclude that the cultural rights of the Flemish people could only be protected by defining a Flemish territory and insisting on the exclusive use of Dutch or Flemish dialects therein. Nevertheless, no one seriously called into question the political unity of the Belgian state. Flemish leaders were simply searching for a means of guaranteeing cultural and linguistic equality in Belgium.

A significant change occurred during and after World War I that set Belgium firmly on the road to federalism. A growing number of Belgians began to think of their country as an entity composed not just of two peoples but of two distinct ethnolinguistic regions as well. A variety of factors encouraged this development, including: (1) growing recognition of the disadvantaged position of non-French speakers in Belgium resulting from the sociolinguistic structure of the Belgian army; (2) associations that developed among soldiers from all parts of northern Belgium who shared a common experience of discrimination because of their language; (3) an administrative partition along language lines imposed by the occupying

Germans during the war, which was designed to curry the favour of Flemish activists; and (4) the acceptance of universal male suffrage after the war, which gradually translated into greater political power for the numerically superior Flemish population.... These developments culminated in the ... territorially based language law[s] in 1921 [and 1932 calling] ... for the use of Dutch in most aspects of public life in northern Belgium. With [their] adoption 'Belgium accepted [a] principle ... of territorial, rather than personal, choice....' (Lorwin 1970:13)

At the heart of the language legislation of the 1920s and 1930s was a territorial vision of Belgium as a state divided into two main language regions, Flanders and Wallonia, and a capital city combining elements of both. This was the vision that eventually became the basis for the political structure of the Belgian state. The language regions were not part of the political structure of Belgium at the time, however, and their territorial extent was subject to change if the decennial census showed a changed majority in any commune. Moreover, violations of the laws were frequent and many institutions in Flanders, including the famous Catholic University of Louvain, did not abandon the use of French. The adoption of the 1932 language laws, however, both signalled and helped to further the view of Belgium as a country made up of two distinct ethnic regions.

In light of the significance of this view for the later turn towards federalism, it is worth pausing for a moment to consider other views that might have developed. If there had been true equality for the Dutch language from the beginning, or if the Francophone elite had been more responsive to the Flemish call for individual language rights, Flanders and Wallonia might not have taken on such perceptual significance.... Alternatively, a territorial approach to cultural rights might have developed that was focused on [Belgium's eleven] provinces, the most important administrative subdivisions in Belgium prior to the 1970s.... Such an approach might have grown out of a desire to acknowledge local differences, including linguistic differences within Flanders and Wallonia.... This approach would have had the added advantage of opening up the possibility for territorial coalitions to develop across language regions. History, however, cannot be undone....

Ethnoregional opposition intensified through the 1930s as violations of the language laws became more apparent. Capitalising on this state of affairs, the Germans once again divided the country along language lines during World War II.... [T]he already ingrained tendency to frame issues in regional terms meant that such post-war issues as state funding for Catholic schools and the king's alleged collaboration with the Germans became ethnoregional issues as well. Moreover, concerns over the spread of French into traditionally Flemish territory, both along the language border and around Brussels, led to controversies over the post-war censuses. The eventual refusal of many Flemish mayors even to distribute the 1960 census forms because of

concerns over their political-territorial implications led ultimately to a demand that the boundaries of the language regions be permanently fixed.

Two bills were passed in the early 1960s ... [calling] for strict unilingualism in Flanders and Wallonia, and establish[ing] the nineteen communes of Brussels as a bilingual area. In addition, special Dutch-language facilities and rights were guaranteed in four communes just to the south of the language line, and special French-language facilities and rights were guaranteed in twelve communes, six just to the north of the language line and six others immediately adjacent to Brussels. Stabilizing the language boundary did not lead to a relaxation in ethnoregional tensions, however.... [E]fforts to retain French language programmes and facilities at the Catholic University of Louvain in Flanders sparked a national debate over language and regionalism that ended in the transfer of the French-speaking part of the university to a new campus south of the language line. With both Flemings and Walloons feeling victimised and with so many issues being cast in ethnoregional terms, it is not surprising that, by the late 1960s, pressure was mounting for a change in Belgium's unitary state structure.

The Institutionalisation of Federalism ...

As the centrifugal tendencies of regionalism deepened, some modification in the unitary structure of the state became necessary. The first major step was taken in 1970 with the adoption of amendments to the Constitution that started Belgium down the road to federation. At the core of the 1970 constitutional revisions was the official recognition of (1) four linguistic regions—a Walloon region, a Flemish region, a bilingual Brussels region, and a German region, the last encompassing a small area in southeastern Belgium that had been acquired from Germany after World War I, and (2) three cultural communities—French-speaking, Dutch-speaking, and German-speaking. In the aftermath of these revisions, councils were established for the French, Dutch, and German cultural communities, as well as for the Walloon and Flemish regions. In each case, the councils were made up of members of the national Parliament with the appropriate linguistic or regional affiliations. No agreement could be reached on forming a Brussels regional council, however; the Flemings thought Brussels should not have the same regional status as Flanders, whereas the Walloons and the French-speaking inhabitants of Brussels wanted the capital to be a third official region in Belgium.

... [C]ompetence over a some aspects of cultural and educational affairs was vested in the French- and Dutch-speaking cultural councils (the German cultural council had more limited powers), whereas the regional councils were given control over specified social and economic matters. The powers of the cultural and regional councils were narrowly circumscribed, however, and fiscal allocations from the national government were small.

. . . [E]ach of the established councils was endowed with its own executive. The autonomy of the latter was often in question, however, since the chief executive could be a national government minister as well. Getting this cumbersome administrative structure off the ground proved to be difficult . . . but by the late 1970s it was more or less in place, paving the way for the next round of constitutional revisions in 1980.

The 1980 revisions grew out of the need to deal with problems that had emerged with the institutionalization of the 1970 revisions, as well as with continued centrifugal tendencies along ethnolinguistic and ethnoregional lines. The new constitutional provisions, together with associated legislative enactments, converted the cultural councils into 'community' councils and expanded their competence over such matters as broadcasting, tourism, health care, social welfare, and scientific research. The authority of the Walloon and Flanders regional councils was also enlarged to encompass such issues as urban planning, environmental affairs, housing, water use, regional economic development, energy, and employment. In addition, Parliament approved the merging of the Flanders regional council and the Dutch community council into the 'Flemish Council' to reflect the commonality of interest between region and language community in northern Belgium. The delegates from Brussels, however, were given only advisory powers when the merged council met to consider regional issues. A Court of Arbitration was also set up to deal with conflicts between the various governmental institutions. Finally, the executives of the Walloon regional council, the French community council, and the Flemish council were separated from the central government ministry. . . .

The most recent, and most definitive, steps toward federation have taken place during a three-phase revision of the Constitution between 1988 and 1993. The first two phases, completed in 1988 and 1989, widened the competencies of the regional and community institutions still further, established regional institutions for Brussels, and significantly expanded the budgets of the regional and community institutions. . . . Important new powers over education were transferred to the community level, and the regions acquired complete responsibility over infrastructure, public transportation, employment, and the use and conservation of natural resources (Senelle, 1990). Budget allocations to the five subnational governments grew from 8.4 per cent of the total national budget to 33 per cent. . . . The Brussels problem was resolved by establishing a council and an executive for the capital region with somewhat more limited powers than their Flemish and Walloon counterparts; the national government retained significant control over regional issues that have national and international ramifications.

The institutions of the region of Brussels reflect a commitment to the dual representation of Flemish and Francophone inhabitants. The Brussels executive has two Dutch-speaking and two French-speaking ministers elected by the regional council, plus a president similarly elected. Members of the council itself are divided into two language groups in proportion to the percentage of votes cast for Dutch- and French-speaking 'lists', and special protection mechanisms can be invoked when minority interests are threatened. In addition, there are French and Dutch community commissions for Brussels ... composed of the French- and Dutch-speaking members of the regional council plus two members of the appropriate language group within the regional executive. They meet both separately and jointly. When meeting separately, they make decisions on matters affecting 'uni-community' educational institutions, rest homes, cultural programmes, and the like. When meeting jointly, they make decisions about 'bi-community' institutions and affairs. Brussels community commissions are necessary because control over such matters by the French and Flemish community councils would be difficult and divisive in a city in which there is no easy means of identifying which inhabitants belong to which language group.

In the third phase of the most recent round of state reforms (1992–1993), the final steps were taken towards the establishment of what Article 1 of the Belgian Constitution now describes as a federal state. The key ingredients of this phase were (1) the transfer of all residual powers to the regional and community governments, (2) a restructuring of the Senate to make it the body of regional and community representation (directly elected Senators became the regional/community representatives), and (3) the devolution of substantial new responsibilities over agriculture, scientific research, and foreign trade to the regions. In addition, the substate governments were given treaty-making rights with foreign governments for matters within their competencies. The federal government retained substantial control in the fiscal arena, however, as it did in the realms of defence, diplomacy, and social security.

By almost any reckoning, then, Belgium is now a federal state. Its particular form of federalism is unique and not entirely territorial; the existence of community as well as regional institutions provides a different twist on the classical federal model. At the same time, the regions are the bedrock of the federal system. The regional councils possess significant powers and, in the Flemish case, the regional and community councils have merged. . . .

Federal Form and Social Consequence

As we have already seen, the ideological roots of linguistic regionalism were established well before the 1970 constitutional reforms. Consequently, issues ranging from the status of Brussels to funding for Catholic schools were already being understood and debated in ethnoregional terms. The tendency to view issues in these terms intensified as the move toward a linguistically based federal system gained momentum in the 1960s. With the institutionalization of that system over the past twenty-five years, an array of political and social interests have been cast in the mould of

Belgium's tripartite regional structure. In the process, interaction patterns have come increasingly to mirror regional patterns, identities have been crystallised along regional lines, and cross-cutting cleavages have been weakened.

... [D]espite the dramatic headlines that have appeared in a number of foreign papers over the past year, Belgium is probably not on the brink of a Czechoslovak-style breakup. Most surveys show a substantial majority of the Belgian population opposed to a complete parting of the ways between Flanders and Wallonia, and the peculiar status of Brussels precludes any neat partitioning of the country. Moreover, much of the financial and political elite in Brussels is concerned about the negative economic and political ramifications of separatist tendencies. At the same time, regionalism has strengthened over the past several decades, and it is not inconceivable that it could strengthen still further. It is thus important to understand the ways in which the structure of the system itself may be implicated in these developments.

At the heart of the matter is the particular territorial structure of Belgian federalism itself. The theoretical literature on multiethnic states tells us that those dominated by two distinct ethnic groups—so-called bicommunal polities—are the most likely to fail. The potential instability of bicommunal polities derives from the lack of opportunity for the communities to alter their relationship through shifting alliances or coalitions; in particular, the inability of a minority group to strengthen its position by sharing power with a third group can lead to serious resentment. Although Belgium is not a classic bicommunal polity because of the Brussels situation, the regionalization process has brought the country closer to this model by structuring so many interests in terms of the opposition between French-speaking Wallonia and Dutch-speaking Flanders. This, in turn, has produced polarities that, typical of bicommunal systems, have both taken on a life of their own and overridden other potential polarities.

The territorial structure of Belgian federalism has promoted social polarisation along ethnoregional lines in at least two mutually reinforcing ways: (1) it has led to a restructuring of key social and economic arrangements to reflect underlying ethnoregional divisions, and (2) it has bestowed ethnoregional significance on a variety of issues, including many that have nothing to do with language or culture....

Social and economic restructuring. The imposition of a limited regime of regional unilingualism in the 1930s initiated a process of linguistic segmentation that made it increasingly difficult for Francophones to live and work in Flanders and for Dutch speakers to do the same in Wallonia. Hence, with the exception of a few communes around Brussels and along the language border where minority language rights were eventually guaranteed, Flanders and Wallonia have become more linguistically homogenous. The trend towards linguistic homogeneity can be attributed in part to language shift, but migration has played a role as well. Whatever the cause, daily life in Flanders and Wallonia is increasingly carried out in an essentially unilingual context.

Accelerated movement toward a linguistically based federal system not only furthered regional unilingualism; it precipitated the division of a host of social and economic institutions along language lines as well. An early example of the latter was the division of the Belgian broadcasting services into Dutch- and French-language wings, which eventually were completely separated. With this split, news and entertainment programs were generated by distinct entities that had 'no explicit mandate ... to promote integrative values, or even mutual understanding, across linguistic lines'. (McRae, 1986:249) ...

Other institutional divisions followed that helped to focus attention at the regional level. Once again, these were prompted in significant part by the evolving structure of Belgian federalism. One of the most important was the division of the major political parties (Christian, Socialist, and Liberal) along language lines. Regionalist political parties sprang up in Flanders, Brussels, and Wallonia in the 1950s and early 1960s in response to demands for greater regional autonomy. As these demands intensified in the late 1960s, the regionalist parties gained considerable ground. Moreover, the major parties had to take stands on regional issues. The pressure eventually became too great, forcing the parties to split into separate Dutch- and French-language wings. Although the newly divided parties managed to recapture some of the votes they had lost to the regionalist parties, the division of the political parties blunted one of the major cross-cutting cleavages that had existed in Belgian society. ...

The broadcasting services and the political parties are but two of a host of institutions that have been divided along linguistic and regional lines. Organisations ranging from trade unions to the Belgian Bar Association to the national water regulatory board have been so divided. Even the Roman Catholic Church has adjusted the boundaries of its dioceses so that they will correspond to the division between language regions (Beaufays, 1988:69). Many of these divisions were necessitated by the structure of a system in which political power was organised along language community and language region lines. At the same time, their net effect has been to reinforce regional structures and identities. They have done so by diminishing opportunities for interregional interaction and communication, by weakening cross-cutting cleavages, and by providing regionally grounded institutional frameworks within which interests can be articulated and goals can be pursued. ...

Political polarization along ethnoregional lines. Polarisation over language issues is nothing new in Belgium, and continued controversies surrounding such issues as the right of French speakers to use their language in the communes surrounding Brussels is hardly surprising. More remarkable, however, is the extent to which issues su[pe]rficially unrelated to language and culture have become points of contention between Flemings and Walloons. This too is a product of the particular territorial form of Belgian federalism. Because primary powers are vested in territorial units that correspond closely to language divisions, almost every issue with differential regional impact has the potential of sparking ethnoregional polarisation.

This tendency is particularly evident in the economic sphere.... After World War II, ... the older industrial areas fell into decline and the centre of gravity moved [from Wallonia] to the Brussels–Antwerp corridor. This transformation accompanied the growing perceptual significance of the language regions in Belgium, and it consequently was understood in ethnoregional terms: Wallonia was losing out to Flanders....

With the institutionalisation of a linguistically based federal structure, the comparative economic status of Flanders and Wallonia has taken on new significance. Now practically every issue of economic aid to a particular industry, neighbourhood, commune, or province carries with it larger questions of interregional equity. In addition, many national programmes that benefit one region more than another are questioned. Consequently, debates over regional fiscal issues have been one of the greatest sources of instability over the past several years.

A recurrent theme in interregional fiscal debates is the Flemish concern that national fiscal policies effectively put the inhabitants of Flanders in the position of subsidising Wallonia. They point particularly to social security, a matter that has remained under national government control. The disproportionate share of national benefits that Walloons receive under the social security programme has become something of a rallying point for Flemish nationalists....

From the Walloon perspective, fiscal allocations that are made in proportion to regional wealth have created unacceptable imbalances in, for example, funding for schools. In 1990 Walloon teachers went on strike for some weeks to protest their salary and benefit packages. Their woes were a direct consequence of a French-speaking community budgetary allocation that was insufficient to provide support packages equivalent to those being received by Flemish teachers....

The tendency to interpret most issues in regional terms extends beyond the fiscal arena to such issues as the routing of the high speed train through Belgium and funding for research and development When it was revealed that more than three-quarters of the Belgian budget of the European Space Agency was spent on contracts with firms in Brussels and Wallonia, for example, loud protests were lodged about the unfair treatment of Flanders. A more dramatic controversy unfolded in 1991 when a decision was made by the national government to permit two financially ailing arms makers in Wallonia to sell weapons to the Middle East. The Flemish parties objected, ostensibly on moral and geopolitical grounds. In response, the French-language parties sought to block the approval of a large telecommunications contract that would have benefited Flemish firms disproportionately. Flemish leaders responded by opposing an agreement that would have allowed the proceeds from television licences to be used to help pay the salaries of French-language teachers. The ensuing controversy eventually prompted the collapse of the governing coalition and new elections had to be called.

In each of these instances issues that would not necessarily pit north against south were interpreted in that way because of the particular configuration of Belgian federalism. Under other circumstances one could imagine debates over fiscal policy focused on competition between the industrial heartland of central Belgium and the agricultural periphery of the northeast and the far south. One could image controversies over school funding between richer cities and poorer towns. One could imagine high-profile competitions between communes or districts within Flanders and Wallonia for telecommunication contracts. Or one could imagine disputes over arms sales between pacifist university communities and industrial centres where jobs were dependent on continued arms production. But the structure of federalism imposes a different geographical logic on these matters—a logic in which linguistic identity, institutional politics, and social interest are largely spatially coincident and mutually reinforcing.

Assessment and Conclusion . . .

. . . [T]here can be little doubt that a sense of Flemish distinctiveness has heightened over the past several decades. A public opinion poll taken by the Dutch-language newspaper *De Standaard* in September 1992 showed 30.9 per cent of Flemings in favour of outright independence for Flanders. This was far from a majority, but it was a much stronger statement of regionalist thinking than was evident in surveys taken a decade earlier. Moreover, the increasing willingness of Flemish political leaders to speak openly over the past several years about regional autono-my and even independence provides evidence of the growth of ethnoregion-alist sentiment.

Ethnoregional identity is weaker in Wallonia than it is in Flanders, but it is developing among Walloons as well. . . .

Against this backdrop, it is doubtful that settlement of the remaining ambiguities in Belgium's institutional structure will resolve the language problem once and for all. Instead, divisiveness is likely to continue both because the system encourages interregional comparison and because there are limited possibilities for the development of cross-cutting cleavages. If Belgians are to move beyond the polarities of the present system, some rethinking of the territorial structure of federalism will be required. Most obviously, consideration must be given to the possibility of devolving greater powers to the provinces. With the exception of Brabant, the provinces are unilingual and would thus be in a position to guarantee the linguistic status quo. At the same time, with greater say in economic and social matters, the provinces could enter into shifting coalitions that would help to disentangle language community issues from many economic and social issues. Thus, Limbourg and Luxembourg could find themselves on the same side of certain agricultural and social issues, just as East Flanders could be aligned with Hainaut on certain industrial and labour issues.

The possible advantages to such an arrangement are suggested by reference to the Swiss case. Switzerland is a federal system made up of twenty-six cantons. There also four major language groups found in the country. The cantons of Switzerland are, for the most part, homogeneous from a linguistic standpoint. At the same time, each major linguistic region comprises multiple cantons. Since primary powers are vested in the cantons, the territorial structure of Swiss federalism discourages the development of ethnonationalism across language community lines. Political parties do not correspond to language regions and the press rarely refers to language regions when discussing economic and political affairs. Moreover, crosscutting cleavages are easily expressed in the cantonal system. Language regions stand out only occasionally in maps of post-World War II voting patterns in Switzerland and the voting behaviour of cantons on constitutional issues is associated far more with sociopolitical patterns than with language.

There are, of course, issues in Switzerland that break down along language lines, most notably the recent vote on participation in the developing European Economic Area.... [D]ivision between Protestants and Catholics also functions as a strong cross-cutting cleavage in Switzerland.... The likelihood of the development of Belgian-style linguistic polarisation is small, however, since the territorial structure of Swiss federalism ensures that cross-cutting cleavages will remain strong.

The Swiss case highlights the potential advantages of a system in which federal territories are not derivatives of the spatial structure of large-scale cultural divisions. For Belgium, it suggests a possible avenue for mitigating ethnoregional polarisation ... [through] the potential role of the provinces....

The larger lesson of the Belgian and Swiss cases is that the actual geographical configuration of federalism matters. We simply cannot afford to discuss the nature and tendencies of federalism without reference to the underlying spatial configuration of federal territories themselves. If Belgium had sought to retain a unitary state structure in the face of the pressures of the past few decades, conflict would arguably be worse than it is today. At the same time, the particular political geography of Belgian federalism has generated its own set of conflicts. Recognition of this point highlights a critically important qualification to the common generalisation that federalism reduces conflict.

Questions and Comments

1. As residuary powers in Belgium shift to the communities and regions, it is contemplated that a list of express federal powers will be provided. See Patrick Peeters, *Federalism: A Comparative Perspective—Belgium Transforms from a Unitary to a Federal State*, in Evaluating Federal Systems 194–207 (Bertus deVilliers ed. 1994). Would it be fair to say that in Belgium the Constitution is being rewritten to reflect ongoing political changes in structure, rather than to constrain them?

2. Peeters describes an "alarm bell" mechanism which was

"introduced to protect the French speaking minority in both Houses of Parliament. [With certain exceptions] [w]henever the French linguistic group is of the opinion that a ... [bill] is likely to seriously impair relations between the [French and Flemish] communities, it can start the "Alarm–Bell Procedure," by means of a reasoned motion signed by at least three-quarters of the members of this linguistic group. This motion results in the immediate suspension of the parliamentary procedure. Within a period of thirty days, the Council of Ministers must prepared its wellreasoned findings on the motion and invite the House concerned to reach a decision either on those findings or on the Bill as it may have been amended.

Peeters goes on to state that "[t]he fact that, since 1970, the protective mechanism of the 'Alarm Bell' was used only once . . . obviously points to the preventive, dissuasive character of the procedure. Any dispute between the communities is either solved in the Cabinet, where the Communities are equally represented, or the motion results in the resignation of the government." Peeters, at 204–05. Compare this "alarm bell" procedure with mechanisms such as the U.S. Supreme Court's "clear statement" requirements for finding federal statutes to have displaced state authority. See Gregory v. Ashcroft, 501 U.S. 452 (1991).

3.   Murphy argues that bipolar federations are likely to be unstable, and urges devolution of power to the level of the eleven provinces in Belgium, most of which are unilingual. Bipolarity may have contributed to the peaceful breakup of Czechoslovakia. A number of other factors have been identified in the break-up of Czechoslovakia, as well: (1) the influence of elites who, in both the Czech and Slovak Republics, were more inclined to separate than were the people as a whole, (2) the absence of a tradition of mass mobilization because of the abruptness of the formation and success of the anticommunist movement, (3) the absence of significant impact of the federal structures in contributing to the regime change of the Velvet Revolution, (4) absence of significant experience in bargaining, and (5) the impact of ethnic nationalism in reinforcing suspicion. See Jim Seroka, *The Dissolution of Federalism in East and Central Europe*, in Evaluating Federal Systems (Bertus de Villiers ed., 1994). Many Slovaks perceived the Czechs to be unfairly dominating and sought parity in legislative and other governmental bodies, while many Czechs perceived the Slovaks unfairly to have been beneficiaries of wealth redistribution subsidized by the Czech lands and preferred greater use of population measures in the allocation of government power at the federal level. Neither side's elite was convinced enough of the benefits of remaining federated to work out necessary arrangements.

Are differences in elite and mass opinion on federalist issues (in the direction of having elites more interested in separation) to be anticipated where elites perceive that they will have greater opportunities for personal power in smaller units?

4.   Consider as an alternative the suggestion that in central and eastern Europe, including Czechoslovakia and Yugoslovia, the "smaller and weaker nations—the Slovaks, the Croats and the Slovenes—only pretended to struggle for federalism; for them, federalism was only a way station on the road to their own independent nation state." Mihailo Markovic, *The*

Federal Experience in Yugoslovia, in Rethinking Federalism: Citizens, Markets and Governments in a Changing World 77 (Karen Knop, Sylvia Ostrey, Richard Simeon and Katherine Swinton eds. 1995). Markovic argues that "historical time is not the same for all nations," and that the peoples of eastern and central Europe have not fully experienced "romantic nationalism" which western Europe went through in the 19th century. According to this developmental model, "federalism is only possible for multinational societies where the constituent nations have already passed through the stage of national statehood and where a plurality of spheres [of] organizations and levels has already been clearly differentiated." What makes a society "multinational"? Is (was?) Canada? Was the U.S. at its founding? Is it now? Did either the U.S. colonies or the Canadian provinces experience "national statehood" prior to confederating?

Note on Northern Ireland

In 1998 the Republic of Ireland, the United Kingdom and the political parties in Northern Ireland reached an accord that used novel constitutional arrangements in an effort to resolve the long-standing conflict over the status of Northern Ireland, a conflict that originated with the creation of the Republic of Ireland in the early part of the twentieth century and that claimed over 3,200 lives in the 30 years preceding the agreements. The new constitutional arrangements may be a unique product of the specific conflict. Consider, however, whether these arrangements might be treated, along with the developing constitutional order in Belgium, as part of an emerging trend towards constitutional arrangements that do not depend on traditional notions of unitary sovereignty.

The peace agreement was signed on April 10, 1998, and was approved by public referenda in the Republic of Ireland and the six counties of Northern Ireland on May 22, 1998. It establishes several cross-border political bodies. A new North–South Council composed of ministers from both Northern Ireland and the Republic of Ireland gives the two governments joint responsibilities in policy areas that affect the entire island, including tourism, transportation, and the environment. A new consultative Council of the Isles will meet twice a year to foster discussion among representatives from the Irish and British Parliaments and the local assemblies in Northern Ireland, Scotland, and Wales on issues affecting Ireland and the United Kingdom.

The agreement also provides for the creation of a democratically elected 108–seat Northern Ireland Assembly to govern the province. Elections in June 1998 divided the seats by proportional representation, with 80 seats going to proponents of the peace agreement from Protestant, Catholic, and non-sectarian parties. Legislation in the Assembly must be passed by at least 70 percent, which ensures (under current demographics) that a Protestant bloc cannot consistently outvote the Catholic parties.

Together, the new institutions are designed to satisfy the desire of Northern Ireland's Catholic minority for a closer relationship with the Republic of Ireland, while guaranteeing to its Protestant majority that Northern Ireland will remain part of the United Kingdom until the people of Northern Ireland decide otherwise. The peace agreement affirmed the parties' "commitment to exclusively democratic and peaceful means of resolving differences," as well as to "partnership, equality and mutual respect as the basis of relationships within Northern Ireland, between North and South, and between these islands." Consider what extra-constitutional developments might be required for the hopes and goals of the new institutions established by the peace agreement to be realized.

---

3.   ETHIOPIA

For another, more skeptical, view of the utility of federalism as a solution to ethnic or tribal divisions, this time in the Ethiopian context, consider the next excerpt.

Minasse Haile, *The New Ethiopian Constitution: Its Impact Upon Unity, Human Rights and Development*, 20 Suffolk Transnational L. Rev. 1, 10–43 (1996).

. . .

III.   An Overview of Ethnic Federations

The "classic federations" which have been historic successes, such as those in the United States, Australia, and Canada (except for Quebec), have not been primarily based on ethnicity. These federations have held the nations together because of the nature of the federations as well as because of certain historical, economic, and social factors prevailing in each country. It would be a "superficial analogy" to take the successful experiences of these countries with federations and apply them blindly to new nations. This "false analogy" is likely to be [misleading] . . . . Part of the success of the classical federal system is due to the general homogeneity of the population. For example, in regard to the American colonists, John Jay made the observation "Providence has been pleased to give this one connected country, to one united people, a people descended from the same ancestors, speaking the same language, professing the same religion, attached to the same principles of government, very similar in their manners and customs."

The fact that the classical federations had a great frontier land to conquer may have helped their respective peoples "to join together in realizing the great vision" and thereby forge greater unity. In addition, the fact that Canadians had faced a common enemy in the form of "manifest destiny from the South" has helped to keep Canadians united.

A.   Reason for the Failure of Ethnic Federations

Ethnic federations have not been generally successful in large polities except, perhaps, when they have been supplemented by other institutional arrangements, by peculiar societal facts, or by threat or use of force, to constrain the centrifugal forces inherent in such federations. This is the case essentially because when a country is divided into ethnically based regions for the purpose of establishing a federal system of government, certain serious problems are thereby generated within each region as well as on the national level. First, particularly in Africa, the act of drawing regional boundaries based on major ethnic groups, ipso facto, creates minority ethnic groups in each region which are condemned to be permanent minorities without any hope of obtaining political power. This situation will produce intensified tribal conflicts, which may have been regarded as benign before, because the minorities within each region would now resent with increasing vehemence the fact that a local tribe has, in effect, been given a perpetual mandate to rule them. Furthermore, since minorities within each region cannot successfully challenge the dominant tribe for political power in elections, the latter tends to be arrogant in power and may also neglect the welfare of the minorities, whose political support and vote it does not need either to be elected or to remain in office. This situation is a prescription for anarchy and political instability within each tribal homeland.

Second, on the national level, dangerous problems are caused by a federation based on the dominant tribal group in a region. The existence of such a federation provides added reason for the political parties to form along ethnic territorial units, as has already happened in Ethiopia, and to begin to advocate the exclusive concerns of their respective constituencies regardless of the consequences upon the national interest.

In this predicament it would be naive to speak of the national interest. It is difficult to see how the fifty nine mainly ethnically based "Ethiopian Political Parties That Have Made Their Existence Known to the Election Board as of April 14, 1995," as announced by the TGE [Transitional Government of Ethiopia], could effectively work in the interest of the country. Speaking on the First Nigerian Independence Constitution of 1960, which established a tribal based federation similar to that of Ethiopia, Professor Nwabueze, in effect, foretold what awaits Ethiopia when he observed that federalism in Nigeria:

> ... [e]nabled the parties in control of the regional governments to use institutionalized power to champion, at both the regional and federal levels, the interest of the tribes which they represented. The effect of this at the federal level was particularly unfortunate. It caused the federal government to be regarded as a single huge cake, already baked, of which it was the duty of each tribal party to secure for its tribe as a large a share as possible.... [T]he resulting situation was one of continued inter-tribal enmity and hostility.

Furthermore, in a territorially based ethnic federation coalitions are likely to form on the national level among certain regions, particularly, among the larger ones or between a large region and several smaller ones in order to confront and undermine the interests of the other members of the federation. This is bound to generate fear of domination by a tribal coalition in the minds of those groups that are outside the coalition. Obviously, this byproduct of ethnic federation is inconsistent with the aim of nation-building in peace and tranquility. It sets the stage for political instability which subverts all democratic institutions. The Ethiopian Constitution reflects this danger when it provides that the number of the members of the Council of People's Representatives (CPR), a parliamentary body, "shall not exceed 550" and that "among these minority nationalities shall have at least 20 seats." Discounting the minority seats, the number of members of the CPR would not exceed 530.... [T]he percentages the

Oromo ethnic groups and the Amhara in Ethiopia constitute are 29.1% and 28.3% respectively. In the CPR, the two ethnic groups together could have about 304 members in the CPR—a clear majority of the total membership of the CPR. In accordance with the constitution, unless otherwise provided, "all decisions of the Council shall be by a majority vote of members present and voting" and the quorum requirement is the "presence of more than half" of the members of CPR. Therefore, the combined vote of the Oromos and the Amharas would more than suffice for most of the business of the Council. This amalgamated vote would also enable the CPR to fulfill one of the three constitutional requirements to amend the civil rights provisions of the constitution if 2/3 of the quorum (a little more than 176 affirmative votes) agree to do so. This is not to imply that the two groups would forge a united front, but it is merely an example of the danger an ethnic federation faces from tribal coalitions in the central government. Since there are more than eighty ethnic groups in Ethiopia the essential harmony needed to advance the national interest would simply not be available.

B. Some Examples of Ethnic (Tribal) Federations

The experiences gained under federal systems based on ethnicity in other countries should have sufficed to dissuade the TGE from using tribes as the foundation of the constitution of Ethiopia. Why is it that ethnic federation failed in Nigeria, lasted for a long time in the Soviet Union, and succeeded in India?

1. The Failure of the Nigerian Constitution

The first Independence Constitution of Nigeria which took effect on October 1, 1960, the date of the independence of Nigeria, divided the country into three regions structured "upon the nucleus of a major tribe" and, as in Ethiopia, "[n]ot one of the existing Regions ... approaches the ideal of an ethnic or linguistic unity." [citing Nwabueze] The three tribal regions are the Hausa in the North, Yoruba in the West, and Ibo in the East. This arrangement caused serious tension to arise within each region between the majority and minority tribes because it "entrenched the permanent control of the regional government by the majority tribe." The hostility between the majority and the disadvantaged minority within each region "continued, creating instability in the government and in the community."

The tribal enmity was also reflected on the national level in the conduct of the affairs of Nigeria. Since the political parties were based on tribal affiliations,

> [E]very question, whether it be the award of scholarships or contracts, ... economic development or the siting of an industrial project, was viewed from the viewpoint of tribal advantage, and support or opposition to it depended upon whether or not it advanced the interest of one's tribe. In the civil service, the tribe was always the pervading influence, intruding into questions of appointments and promotions

and undermining efficiency.[60]

The focus of loyalty went not to Nigeria as a whole but "to the region and then to the tribe." Regionalism and tribalism, the "greatest ills" of the Nigerian Constitution, were the main reasons for the collapse of the government.

The fact that the number of the constituent units of the Nigerian federation were only three created the fear that two of them could gang up against the third. This fear helped make the federation unstable. In fact, the threat materialized when the Northern and Eastern regions formed a coalition against the Western Region from 1959 to 1964. The consequence of all this was that, ". . . leadership on the national scene was fickle and sick: It condoned compromise after compromise, even of crucial fundamental issues . . . ."[64]

This tribal constitution, which fractured the Nigerian society and rendered the government an impotent institution of unceasing ethnic squabbles, opened the way for a military coup under the leadership of Major-General Johnson Aguiyi-Ironsi on January 15, 1966. This military take-over was " overwhelmingly acclaimed" by Nigerians as a relief from the tribal federation. The new military regime suspended the constitution and announced that a new constitution for Nigeria should provide for a greater centralized authority by transferring legislative competence to the central government and for ending regionalism and tribalism. Subsequently, in a May 24, 1966 decree, General Ironsi abolished the federation and changed the former regions to provinces. Since then, democratic rule has merely been an interlude in changing and unstable military regimes.

In sum, the Nigerian federation turned out to be nonviable essentially because of the divisive, unmanageable, and destabilizing elements generated by its tribal foundation. A similar fate is likely to await the tribal federation of Ethiopia.

2.   The Longevity and Final Collapse of the Soviet Federation

The government of the Soviet Union was ostensibly based on the principle of ethnic or tribal federation. The country was divided into fifteen union republics "whose boundaries and names correspond to the dominant ethnic nationality historically residing in each." In addition, within some of these republics there "were a number of smaller autonomous enclaves . . . named after the minority nationality residing in each." Although the republics and the ethnic enclaves were given certain rights of self-administration, like all other "rights" of all Soviet citizens, they existed only on paper. The fact was that the tribal groups "were in effect colonized." The ethnic groups in the Soviet Union were held together by an ideology that permitted no divergence from the dictates of the rulers under the so-called "democratic centralism," and the existence of the omnipresent Communist

---

60. [B.O. Nwabueze, Constitutionalism in the Emergent States 126 (1973)]

64. [Kalu Ezera, The Failure of Nigerian Federalism and Proposed Constitutional Changes, African Forum 19 (1966)]

Party which controlled all levels of government, and enforced conformity throughout the Soviet society.

Since the Soviet tribal federation was held together by threat or use of force, as soon as communism collapsed, the cementing force of the dictatorship that kept the various ethnic groups within the fold collapsed with it and the Soviet Union broke-up into fifteen independent states. Rasmussen and Moses made this pointed observation:

> [D]uring the Soviet era, federalism in Russia was a sham. The heads of the local Communist parties appointed by Moscow in effect ruled all jurisdictions as a de facto unitary republic.

3. The Success of the Indian Federation

The existence of a tribal based federal system of government in India, which includes twenty-two linguistic states and nine union territories under a central administrator, does not help to justify the peculiar Ethiopian tribal federation. Although the Indian Constitution of 1950 has been thought to have served as a model emulated by the drafters of the Ethiopian Constitution, the similarity between the two constitutions is superficial. There are certain conditions ... that obtain in India which favor the viability of the specific type of the federal system adopted in India, which do not obtain in Ethiopia. More than eighty percent of the population of India has "some form of Hindu religion" and share Hindu culture. The Muslims constitute only eleven to twelve percent of the population. In addition, the existence of foreign enemies such as China and Pakistan has helped keep the Indian people together. An even more important factor that preserved the ethnic federation of India has been the constitution itself. The constitution provides safeguards to facilitate the continued existence of the country as a united entity. . . .

Another very important factor that preserves the unity of India, in spite of the ethnic federation, is the judicial system. In India, the constitution is supreme and this supremacy is assured because "what the judges say the constitution is ... prevails."[83] The judiciary, including the Supreme Court, has a "centrist bias." Whenever cases involving conflict between the Union and the States come before the courts "the center has always come out on the top because the judges genuinely believe that a strong center is important." This favorable situation for the unity of India is essentially due to the fact that the judges of the Supreme Court of India are independent and are appointed by the president of India "after consultation with such judges of the Supreme Court and the High Courts in the States, as the President may deem necessary." The Supreme Court, however, has ruled that "consultation" does not imply concurrence.

In fact, it has even been suggested [by Edward McWhinney] that the Indian Constitution establishes in substance not a federal system but rather a unitary system of government:

> ... the Indian republican constitution ... in spite of its being expressed to be federal in structure ... is really the most strongly

83. [Fali Sam Nariman, *The Indian Constitution: An Experiment in Unity and Diversity*, reprinted in Forging Unity Amid Diversity: The Approach of Eight Nations 58 (Robert A. Goldwin et al. eds. 1989)].

centralised of all the federal systems, with no substantial deference at all to the principle of ethnic-culturally based minority interests. In form the Indian constitution ... may seem federal, but in substance and as law-in- action it appears to be essentially unitary."

It is thus clear that from the point of view of using a constitution to bind a people in a common destiny there is no resemblance between the Indian and the Ethiopian constitutions. The approach of the Indian constitution in envisaging a common language in the future, and in establishing an independent national supreme court—in whose composition the central government plays a decisive role—with the power to interpret the constitution, is diametrically opposed to what is contained in the Ethiopian Constitution.

IV. The Tribal "Federation" of Ethiopia: The Distribution of Constitutional Power

The particular form of federation established by the new Ethiopian Constitution not only lacks the essential attributes of successful federations, it is riddled with those undesirable features that will doom the federation as still born and perhaps trigger the disintegration of Ethiopia into mini-tribal entities in perpetual warfare against one another.

The dangerous nature of the Ethiopian federation is found mainly in the near total transfer of sovereignty from the center to tribal regions, in the disproportionate powers allocated to the tribal subunits collectively and individually, and in the creation of a government of unlimited powers.

A. The Nine Near-Sovereign Tribes

1. Sovereignty Resides in the State

The new Constitution of Ethiopia does not in reality establish a national federal government for Ethiopia. On the contrary, it almost renders Ethiopia an extinct legal entity and creates in its place nine virtually sovereign ethnic "states" in to which the country is divided. The constitution accomplishes this outrageous feat by creating nine "states" or regional units whose boundaries and names are conterminous with the major tribal groups of each area, and by providing for a lopsided distribution of powers in favor of the regional units thereby raising questions as to juridical existence of the central or the "federal" government for the whole country.

The nine "states" are based on the "settlement patterns, identity, language and consent of the people concerned," in other words, the "states" are established in accordance with ethnic affiliation. The nine "states" division of the country is not final. Further fragmentation is envisaged, indeed encouraged, by providing for minorities within each of the "states" to establish their own additional "states," without setting any limit to the number of claimants to the status of statehood. When it is recalled that the TGE itself had legislated in 1992 that about 65 " nations, nationalities and people" of Ethiopia "shall establish National Regional Self-Government," the prospect of a total constitutionally mandated disintegration of the country becomes more than a mere possibility.

... Again, when it is provided that "[e]very nation, nationality and people in Ethiopia" has the right to secession, it can hardly be taken to mean that the whole people of the country can secede; it merely means the tribes have rights of secession. Therefore, when Article 8(1) provides that sovereignty resides "in the nations, nationalities, and peoples," it means sovereignty henceforth lies in those tribal entities rather than in the state of Ethiopia as it existed prior to the constitution or in the people of Ethiopia as a whole. It is in this sense that the constitution can be said to have juridically extinguished Ethiopia as a sovereign entity and created nine sovereign tribal entities in its place in the same territory.

Startling as this tribalization of Ethiopia may be, it is not an accidental notion in the constitution. There is an all-pervasive and relentless preoccupation with the mantra of "nations, nationalities, and peoples" throughout the constitution. Professor Vestal has observed that the fundamental principles of the constitution in Chapter 2 begin "with the credo of the EPRDF"* that "sovereign power emanates from ethnic groups" and the "disposition to 'nations, nationalities, and peoples' is stated forthrightly as the first principle and its echoes are explicit and implicit throughout the remainder of the document."

2.   Common Characteristics of Ethiopians

Instead of uniting the Ethiopian people (as is the primordial task of governments) by stressing the values, culture, and history the people share and creating means for even further stronger ties, the constitution written under the authority of the government purports to hold the country together, if indeed that is the real intention, by emphasizing and institutionalizing tribalism, and by glorifying parochialism. The web of interests, values, and culture that identified Ethiopians as a distinct people will now be put asunder by a vindictive constitution of the TPLF.** The nation that the constitution is about to destroy is an ancient land that has preserved its nationhood and independence for more than 2,000 years.... The peoples of Greater Ethiopia have homogeneous traits in many respects: "belief about supernatural beings; ritual practices; food taboos; the cult of masculinity; aspects of social organization; insignia of rank; and custom regarding personal status and the home."[108]

According to population statistics published by TGE in 1991, the majority of the population of Ethiopia is Christian. Excluding the rural areas of Tigray and Eritrea, about "61 percent of the total population ...

---

* [Editors' Note: EPRDF stands for the Ethiopian People Revolutionary Democratic Front.]

** [Editors' Note: TPLF stands for the Tigre Peoples Liberation Front.]

108.   [Donald N. Levine, Greater Ethiopia: The Evolution of a Multiethnic Society 47 (1974).]

were Christian and about 33 percent were Muslims." In urban areas, however, the proportion of Christians were "81.4 percent" and those of Muslims were only "17.7 percent." The Amharic language is used much more widely than revealed by the TGE's policy as reflected in the constitution. . . .

B. Disproportionate Distribution of Powers

The hostility of the framers of the constitution toward Ethiopia as a united legal entity is further illustrated by the distribution of powers between the central government and the subunits. The tribal homelands, or the "states" in the language of the document, have been given such a disproportionately large measure of competence that it can reasonably be questioned whether the "federal government" the constitution purports to establish in fact exists at all. . .

1. Powers given to the State collectively through the Federal Council. . .

a. What is the FC?

The FC [Federal Council] is a political body representing solely the states or the tribal homelands and its membership consists only of those persons elected by the nine major tribes into which the country is divided. The federal government is neither represented in the Council nor plays any part in its creation. This is made clear by the constitutional provisions that "(t)he Federal Council is composed of the representatives of nations, nationalities and peoples" and that its members are "elected by the State Councils."

Clearly, the FC is not a second legislative chamber sharing general law-making power with the Council of Peoples' Representatives (CPR), an elected legislative body. . . .

Although the FC does not primarily function as a legislative chamber, the constitution makes it a repository of the most potent and decisive powers, a system incompatible with the rudimentary character of a federal system of government. The FC, a mere representative of the nine tribal homelands, holds the power to destroy all by itself the constitution that established it. The following are some of the unusual powers given by the constitution to the FC.

b. The FC has the exclusive authority to make the final interpretation of the constitution . . .

The constitution, after stating that the FC "has the power to interpret the constitution" and that "(a)ll constitutional disputes shall be decided by the Federal Council," authorizes the FC to "organize" another body entitled "the Council of Constitutional Inquiry."

The Council of Constitutional Inquiry has been incongruously designated as a "Constitutional Court" and as a body having "judicial powers," while at the same time the constitution makes quite clear that it lacks the power to make final decisions by requiring it to submit its findings "to the Federal Council for a final decision." Although from a strictly compositional point of view the Council of Constitutional Inquiry could perhaps have been some kind of a Constitutional Court, the denial to it of the power to make final decisions and its subordination to the FC make it, in effect, a mere fact-finding body of the FC. It is thus not a judicial body with a final authority to interpret the constitution.

2.   Federalism

    a.   Federal power depends on the States

When the power of interpreting the constitution with finality is lodged in a political body elected only by the constituent subunits of the federation, the whole elaborate constitutional structure pretending to found a federal government is rendered a sham. The reach of both federal and state power depends on what the subunits determine to be a proper exercise of constitutional authority . . . .

On the one hand, the CPR is designated as the "highest authority of the Federal Government" and is presumably given the power to legislate in matters delegated to the federal government. It also has redundant enumerated powers of its own. On the other hand, the extent and nature of the real power the CPR can exercise depends on what the FC with its power to interpret the constitution is prepared to concede to it.

    b.   State Powers

Second, the nature and reach of the power of the states is unilaterally determined by the states themselves acting through the FC. Its composition and its political attributes foretell that its propensity is likely to favor the augmentation of the power of the state at the expense of federal power.

The power of the FC to interpret what the constitution says and does not say and the fact that it represents only the nine tribal homelands is a further confirmation of the view that there is no genuine federalism under the constitution and that the subunits are the real sovereigns.

    c.   Compassion with other countries

In most other countries that have adopted a system of judicial review or political review of the constitutionality of legislation, the members of the bodies that are assigned to perform the task are normally appointed under schemes in which the organs of the central government play crucial roles. The selection of members of such reviewing bodies are not left exclusively to the discretion of the subunits as in the case of Ethiopia where the members of the FC, the reviewing body, are selected solely by the constituent subunits of the federation. A cursory look at how other countries approach the appointment of the reviewing bodies helps show the meaninglessness and the absurdity of the Ethiopian method. For example, in the United States members of the Supreme Court of the United States, which has the power of judicial review, are appointed to the Court by the president of the country " with the Advise and Consent of the Senate." . . . [Professor Haile's description of the French, Austrian, and Italian courts is omitted.] In Germany, the Constitutional Court is composed of sixteen judges "half being elected by the Bundestag and half by the Bundesrat."
. . .

Similarly, in the developing world, the members of the body assigned to oversee constitutionality are appointed by processes where the central government plays a decisive role rather than leaving the matter to the exclusive discretion of subunits as is done in the Ethiopian Constitution.

c. The FC Decides on Secession

. . . Since the constitution grants to every "nation, nationality and people in Ethiopia" the "right to secession" to establish their own independent state, the FC is empowered to "decide on claims based upon" the right to secession. This means that the FC, a body exclusively selected by the nine tribal homelands and representing only them, has the constitutional authority to validate the claims of the minority tribes within each of the homelands to a separate existence as independent states. This FC power is likely to further undermine the continued existence of Ethiopia as a legal entity.

d. The FC Decides Whether the Federal Government can Intervene in the States

The FC has the power to "order Federal intervention if any State . . . endangers the constitutional order." Presumably the "order" is to be given by the FC after it finds that "constitutional order" is, in fact, "endangered" by a state. Since the FC is the only body to interpret the constitution with finality, the federal government would have no possibility of intervening in the states to preserve the "constitutional order" without the consent of the states represented in the FC. Again, the tribal homelands, operating through the FC, hold the key to whether or not the federal government can even order intervention in a state when the state is engaged in a violation of the constitutional order. . . .

2. Powers Given to the States Individually

Not only has the constitution given to the states extensive powers collectively through the instrumentality of the FC, other unusual powers have also been entrusted to them severally. All this is done again in conformity with the proclivity of the framers of the constitution to make the tribal homelands the bearers of the ultimate powers of the federation, rather than the central government. . . .

a. States have the Right to Secede

The constitution provides "[e]very nation, nationality and people in Ethiopia has the unconditional right to self-determination, including the right to secession." . . . Not only the states, but also all minorities within each state have a right of secession. The Soviet constitutions, from which the idea of secession appears to have been taken, do provide for the right of secession but under entirely different circumstances than those prevailing in Ethiopia. First, the Soviet Constitution of 1936 (the "Stalin Constitution") gave a right of secession to "(e)very Union Republic" and the 1977 constitution gave the same right to "each Union Republic." The Union Republics numbered only fifteen. No such rights, however, have been given to more than fifty other ethnic or tribal groups found within each Republic and elsewhere. By contrast, the Ethiopian Constitution grants the right of secession to more than eighty ethnic groups. Second, the Soviet Constitution of 1977 establishes the principle of "democratic centralism" which affirms "the obligation of lower bodies (of state authority) to observe the decision of higher ones." Thus, the requirement that all Union Republics "must fulfill the decisions of the Union government," is, in effect, to take back the right of secession granted affirmatively under Article 72....

The very fact of providing for a right to secede in the constitution even when the actual exercise of the right is not very easy has several consequences which reduce the prospect of a viable federalism and democracy. Unless the leaders of the TPLF are intending to adopt the Soviet's "democratic centralism," a euphemism for dictatorship, the constitutional right to secede is likely to submerge Ethiopia into the abyss of warring tribal factions. It should not be forgotten that "democratic centralism" has not saved the Soviet Union from disintegration. Neither democracy nor a federal system can survive in a constitutional system that is subject to constant preoccupation with threats and blackmail emanating from tribal groups armed with the power to secede.... Sunstein has summarized why constitutions should not provide for a right of secession as follows:

> ... constitutions ought not to include a right to secede. To place such a right in a founding document would increase the risks of ethnic and factional struggle; reduce the prospect for compromise and deliberation in government; raise dramatically the stakes of day-to-day political decisions; introduce irrelevant and illegitimate considerations into those decisions; create dangers of blackmail, strategic behavior, and exploitation; and, most generally, endanger the prospects of a long-term self-governance.

If the principal reason for the insertion of a right to secede in the constitution is to deter tribal oppression and discrimination, it is important to realize that those dangers can be more effectively resolved by other constitutional devices such as those that are designed genuinely to protect the civil liberties of citizens. But the policy of attempting to prevent injustice against ethnic groups by recognizing secession increases problems for societies, particularly for those with less than full national cohesion, without ending the discrimination and the injustice. The very survival of the constitution will be "at issue in every case in which a subunit's interests are seriously at stake." The subunits can "raise the stakes in ordinary political and economic decisions simply by threatening to leave" and hence be able to veto proposals that may benefit the nation as a whole....

b. Each Tribal Homeland can Determine its Own Language; Comparison with the Approaches of the Soviet Union, the Russian Federation and India

In addition to the right of secession, each tribal state has the authority to determine the language it will use. The constitution provides that "(e)ach member of the Federation shall determine its own working language." This would allow the nine members of the Federation to function on the basis of at least nine different languages. Of course, when other minorities within each tribal homeland establish their own state, the number of the languages in use in the federation may increase further. The only concession to unity of language was that Amharic "shall be the working language of the Federal Democratic Republic of the Ethiopia."

Even this friendly nod to a common language appears to be qualified by the provision that all "Ethiopian languages shall enjoy equal state recognition."

If the framers of the constitution had any interest in not creating the biblical Tower of Babel in Ethiopia, they would not have failed to look at the possibility of encouraging the use of Amharic with the eventual purpose of making it the national language, without, at the same time infringing upon the right of the ethnic group to use their own languages.

The population statistic published by the TGE confirms that "Amarigna [Amharic] was the most dominant language" and that it "was usually spoken at home by 32 percent of the total population." Furthermore, in the "urban areas, the majority (67.4%) of the population speaks Amarigna at home." Since the attainment of educational level in most age groups in Ethiopia "is higher in urban than in rural areas," and they are also the most politicized elements in developing countries, a language spoken by 67.4% of the urban Ethiopians at home, i.e. Amharic, should not have been dismissed by the framers of the constitution as an important instrument for the eventual creation of greater cohesion among Ethiopians in language and in a sense of common national destiny as one people. The Economist summarized the current language situation in the country as follows: "(t)he official use of local languages was ... encouraged, and Amharic, the language of the large group in central Ethiopia, declared no longer the national tongue. Everyone had to be registered according to his ethnic group."

Even in earlier times (about 400 years ago) Amharic was a widely spoken language in Ethiopia. Professor Levine wrote that even "[a]s early as the 1620s it was observed that in spite of the enormous linguistic complexity of the land anyone who knew Amharic could find in all parts of the country people with whom he could converse intelligently."

Furthermore, when it is recalled that Amharic and Ge'ez, from which Amharic is derived, "have a written form that dates back to at least 250 B.C.," that both languages have "extensive traditional literature," that the first Amharic grammar was written by foreigners "250 years ago," and that Amharic has made "tremendous strides as a language of national unity" in the 20th century, it is puzzling that the drafters of the constitution should overlook one important basis for strengthening the cohesion among Ethiopians....

The provision of the Ethiopian Constitution concerning languages seems to have been inspired by a literal reading of the Soviet Constitution of 1977 which provided that the exercise of the right of equality of different races and nationalities is "ensured by a policy of all-round development and drawing together of all the nations and nationalities of the U.S.S.R., by educating citizens in the spirit of Soviet patriotism ... and by the possibility to use their own native language ...."

In practice, however, this meant that the "Union republics and ethnic enclaves were allowed to instruct their children and to publish in their own languages, *but only if they simultaneously encouraged the mastery of Russian as the universal language* of discourse in the Soviet Union." [quoting Rasmussen and Moses] Clearly then, it is a superficial view that the Soviet Constitution and the practice under it regarding languages created linguistic disunity in the country. However, the Ethiopian Constitution appears to have been designed to produce a permanent linguistic division of the country. This points to the danger of slavishly copying the provisions of other countries' constitutions without first examining the practice-a matter regarding which the guilt of the drafters of the Ethiopian Constitution is evident throughout the text, particularly in their subservience to the defunct Soviet constitutions.

In contrast to the position of the Soviet Constitution with respect to languages, the attitude of the new Constitution of Russian Federation is more specific and emphatic in the need to create linguistic unity without depriving ethnic groups of the use of their own languages. The Constitution of Russia provides outright that the "state language of the Russian Federation throughout its territory shall be the Russian language" and that although the republics have a right to institute their own languages, the languages of the republics "shall be used alongside the state language of the Russian Federation in bodies of state power, bodies of local self-government and state institutions of the republics." Although Russia has about thirty ethnic enclaves containing twenty-six million people these constitutional provisions are likely to help in forging a linguistically close-knit Russia.

Insofar as languages are concerned, the Constitution of India provides that "(t)he official language of the Union shall be Hindi in Devanagri script" and for a period of fifteen years from the commencement of the constitution "the English language shall continue to be used for all the official purpose of the Union . . . ." The period for the use of English was extended indefinitely by parliament in the Official Languages Act in 1963. While a state may adopt "any one or more of the languages in use in the State or Hindi as the language or languages to be used for all or any official purposes of that state," until the state otherwise decides, "the English language shall continue to be used for those official purposes within the state for which it was being used" before the constitution took effect.

English and Hindi are not only the languages for the Union purposes; they are also required to be the official languages for "communication between one state and another state and between a state and the Union." Thus, "since 1950 both Hindi and English have been official languages of the union of India," as both "are used to transact business in the houses of Parliament . . . and for all official communications between the union government and the government of a state that has not adapted Hindi as a national language." [quoting Nariman] . . .

c. Other Provisions which Diminish the Federation

In addition to empowering the states to secede and to use any language of their choice, the constitution grants certain other rights to each tribal homeland that are potentially destructive of the federal system itself. . . [including]:

1) Federal Judicial Power Delegated to the States

The constitution provides that "[u]nless and until . . . lower Federal Courts are established, federal high and first-instance judicial powers are delegated to the State Courts." This sounds like a reasonable provisional measure. However, when one thinks of the outstanding position such subunits occupy in the federal system as a whole, the expenses involved in establishing a parallel system of federal courts, and the shortage of trained personnel to staff them, however, it becomes quite doubtful that the federal government will create the high and first-instance federal courts to obviate the exercise by states of the entire federal judicial power in the foreseeable future. Under the circumstances, the delegation of federal judicial power to the tribal homelands may well turn out to be, in effect, close to being permanent.

Furthermore, certain other provisions of the constitution . . . see[m] to create a permanent state jurisdiction over federal matters independently from the "unless and until" clause. For example, it is stated in the constitution that the state supreme courts "shall also exercise Federal High Court jurisdiction," and "State High Courts, in addition to State jurisdiction, exercise federal first-instance court jurisdiction."

2) The Federal and State Governments can Delegate Power to Each Other

Although the constitutional division of powers gives the appearance of being a permanent arrangement, that image is destroyed by the provision that the federal government "may delegate to the States powers and functions granted to it by Article 51 of this Constitution." Article 51 details in twenty-one clauses the powers of the federal government. Similarly, states "may likewise, delegate to the federal government State powers and functions granted to them by the Constitution." In the peculiar system of federation established by the constitution where the tribal homelands are supreme, the likely direction of the flow of power would be one that would further emasculate the already dwarfed federal government. . . .

Questions and Comments

1. Professor Haile praises efforts to require a common language, yet notes that Amharic is used at home by less than 40% of the population. Do you agree with him that it would have been unifying to have required Amharic to a greater extent than the 1994 Constitution did?

2. Professor Haile opposes constitutionalizing rights of secession, as has Professor Cass Sunstein. Are there circumstances where preserving such a right might promote stability rather than lead to dissolution, anarchy or blackmail? Should Quebec be permitted to secede from Canada if a majority of its inhabitants so desire? If a majority of both its inhabitants and those of the rest of Canada agree? For the recent Canadian Supreme Court advisory opinion on this question, see Reference re Secession of Quebec, 1998 Can. Sup. Ct. LEXIS 1539 (Aug. 20. 1998)

3. Consider how the FC described by Professor Haile differs from other structures to represent the interests of subnational units in the national government. How substantially does it differ from such practices as assuring that some members of the Supreme Court of Canada are from Quebec?

4. Professor Haile suggests that one of the motivations of the drafters of this constitution in Ethiopia may have been to provide for the independence of Eritrea after its secession, since the dominant party that came to power and drafted the 1994 Constitution had been assisted by the Eritrean People's Liberation Front. Haile, at 45. Does this chronology, if correct, raise doubts about the significance of the 1994 constitution in promoting tribal or ethnic dissolution?

5. To what extent does assessment of a constitution's "failure" or "success" in maintaining a consolidated national government turn on the premise that the nation's initial boundaries ought to be preserved? Why might people be concerned about the redefinition of boundaries that secession or national "disintegration" entails?

6. The provisions of the Ethiopian Constitution criticized by Professor Haile can be seen as a strong effort to implement the "right of self-determination" recognized in international law. The scope and meaning of such a right is highly contested. What factors should be considered in recognizing, and resolving, claims of self-determination rights, whether expressed in secessionist movements or movements for greater autonomy in self-governance? For a more positive assessment of Ethiopia's constitution, see Bereket Habte selassie, *Self-Determination in Principle and Practice: The Ethiopian-Eritean Experiment*, 29 Colum. Human Rights L. Rev. 1 (1997).

Note on the United States

Many commenters note that in the United States, unlike in Canada or Belgium with respect to language differences, the essential problem of racial division is one that cuts broadly across geographic state lines. It is thus argued by some that the federal nature of the union does not afford opportunities in the U.S. for using differences between states as a way of addressing the most profound social cleavages in the nation.

Federalism as a National Neurosis? How much has U.S. state-based federalism permitted or preserved widely divergent cultures that are geographically and politically identifiable? Consider Edward L. Rubin and Malcolm Feeley, *Federalism: Some Notes on a National Neurosis*, 41 U.C.L.A. L. Rev. 903, 907–09 (1994):

> [F]ederalism in American achieves none of the beneficial goals that the Court claims for it.... [F]ederalism is America's neurosis. We have a federal system because we began with a federal system.... We carry

this system with us, like any neurosis, because it is part of our collective psychology, and we proclaim its virtues out of the universal desire for self-justification. But our political culture is essentially healthy, and we do not let our neuroses control us. Instead, we have been trying to extricate ourselves from federalism for at least the last 130 years. When federalism is raised as an argument against some national policy, we generally reject it by whatever means are necessary....

[While states] fulfill the important governmental function of facilitating decentralization..., [t]he Supreme Court should never invoke federalism as a reason for invalidating a federal statute or as a principle for interpreting it [because] there is no normative principle involved that is worthy of protection.

Indian Tribes: In thinking about federalism in the United States, consider also the position of Indian tribes. Described by one scholar as "dependent sovereigns,'"[n] the tribes constitute separate political communities, whose membership is defined in part by self-identification and in part by family origin, and which are treated in many respects "asymmetrically" as compared with the states.[o] While federal policy for decades was to encourage assimilation of the tribes, in more recent years the policy has changed to one of encouraging tribal-self government and some measure of cultural autonomy.[p] The Court has explained that "tribes remain quasi-sovereign nations which, by government structure, culture and source of sovereignty are in many ways foreign to the constitutional institutions of the federal and state governments." Santa Clara Pueblo v. Martinez, 436 U.S. 49, 71 (1978). Yet the "constitutional institutions" of those governments maintain legal relationships with and exercise regulatory authority over the tribes. The federal government's relationship with the Indian tribes (e.g., in unilaterally abrogating treaties) has been unconstrained by many of the constitutional protections that apply to state governments. Despite this, and many years of assimilationism, many tribes survive— albeit often in poverty. Indian tribes may today rival or exceed states as political bodies that are integral to maintaining a separate way of life, but they are often absent from discussions of U.S. federalism.

---

n. Judith Resnik, *Dependent Sovereigns: Indian Tribes, States and the Federal Courts*, 56 U. Chi. L. Rev. 671 (1989); Oklahoma Tax Commn. v. Citizen Band Potawatomi Indian Tribe of Oklahoma, 498 U.S. 505 (1991) ("domestic dependent nations").

o. See, e.g., Mountain States Tel. & Tel. Co. v. Pueblo of Santa Ana, 472 U.S. 237 (1985) (federal law prohibits application of state law in connection with real estate transactions concerning Pueblo Indian lands after 1924); California v. Cabazon Band of Mission Indians, 480 U.S. 202 (1987) (federal law prohibits enforcement of state gambling laws on Indian reservation). Compare, e.g.,

Santa Clara Pueblo v. Martinez, 436 U.S. 49 (1978) (refusing to adjudicate claim that tribe's requirements that members have a father who was a member of the tribe violated equal protection rights of female tribal members on grounds that there was no cause of action against the tribe in federal court under the Indian Civil Rights Act) with Loving v. Virginia, 388 U.S. 1 (1967) (holding unconstitutional Virginia's anti-miscegenation statute making it a crime for people of different races to marry.

p. See, e.g., Indian Child Welfare Act, 25 U.S.C. § 1911.

4. Tolerance, Federalism and Liberalism

One of the paradoxes of liberal societies arises from their commitment to tolerance. A society committed to respecting the viewpoints and customs of diverse people within a pluralistic society inevitably encounters the challenge posed by those who themselves do not agree to respect the viewpoints or customs of others. Does the liberal commitment to tolerance require, at some point, intolerance for those who would reject that very commitment? The next two articles offer different perspectives on this question.

Mark Tushnet, *Federalism and Liberalism*, 4 Cardozo J. Int'l & Comp. L. 329 (1996)

Today's political theories, most notably those of John Rawls, are universal in the sense that they attempt to define the principles that would regulate any good polity in which the populace is characterized by a wide divergence in the views of the good they possess—a morally pluralist polity. Of course, Rawls leaves room for more particular specifications, which will depend on the circumstances in which people find themselves. Here, I want to reflect on the characteristics of one of those specifications—federalism conceived in a particular way.

Federalism is an interesting topic in the Rawlsian context.... Rawls' theory is ... universal in the sense that it leaves no room for variation anywhere on earth in the principles it commends. In [this] sens[e], universalism seems more attractive in the face of a pluralism whose paradigm example is the struggle between the Serbs and the Croats in the former Yugoslavia, and less attractive where pluralism's paradigms are the Amish and the First Nations in Canada. Despite efforts to sustain and even expand the scope of such cultures, they are likely to remain provocative reminders of historical paths that have not been followed.

Federalism is a system in which pluralism is accommodated because governing principles vary from place to place. My basic argument is this: while it will almost certainly be difficult to sustain a truly federal political system over the long run, some institutional designs, coupled with a particular legal culture (which I call formalist), can retard the speed at which a federal system is converted into a centralized one. The delay may be what such systems require for a non-Rawlsian modus vivendi to be converted into a Rawlsian overlapping consensus.[1]

I begin my argument with definitions of federalism and of a certain type of pluralism for which federal systems seem particularly well-suited. Then, I identify what a national government will almost inevitably be authorized to do in a federal system and briefly discuss pressures, which I characterize as economic, on the national government to exercise its powers expansively. With these definitions in hand, my principal argument is that

---

1. The long run I am concerned with is the very long run, similar to the period with which Rawls deals: decades rather than years and centuries rather than decades.

no constitutional arrangement is likely to preserve a federal system against these pressures but that some arrangements may be more resistant to change than others.

To begin my argument, I should distinguish between [federalism and subsidiarity]. [F]ederalism [is] a system in which a constitution or other basic agreement defines the powers that central, national, or subnational governments possess, [and] the allocation of authority can only be changed by constitutional amendment. Although the methods of constitutional amendment may vary, they cannot include change at the sole option of the ordinary, typically majoritarian political processes of national decision-making.... [S]ubsidiarity is ordinarily not referred to as an institutional form but as a principle. According to the principle of subsidiarity, power over a subject matter ought to be exercised by the level of government that can most "appropriately" or efficiently exercise it, subject to adequate majority control.

Although subsidiarity is in itself an uncontroversial principle, identifying which subjects are most "appropriately" controlled by which level of government may be controversial. Federalism is an embodiment of the principle of subsidiarity in which the constitution controls that allocation. The principle of subsidiarity, however, can be endorsed by a fully central-ized government. Such a government may decide that certain subjects should be regulated by a subnational unit. In contrast to a federal system, adjustments of the allocation of power could occur through the exercise of central legislative power.

My argument is restricted to ... federal systems of a specific sort. Societies may be pluralist in two ways. In one, differences among groups are, as political scientists have called them, cross-cutting. A person who shares one interest with forty other people discovers that he or she disagrees with thirty of them on another issue, with a different set of thirty on a third, and so on. A pluralist society with cross-cutting differences will rapidly settle on liberal political institutions. Its members quickly discover that cooperation on one issue requires that they put aside their disagree-ments on other issues, which are equally important to them but are not relevant to the issue at hand. They will quickly generalize the many modus vivendi they arrive at into principles of political liberalism.

The other type of pluralist society is characterized by reinforcing rather than cross-cutting differences. It is quite likely that if one disagrees with a person about one important issue, one will disagree with him or her about many other important issues. Federalism is initially attractive as a solution to the obvious problems of organizing a national government in a polity characterized by reinforcing differences. The constitution allocates powers to different groups, so that one group's resolution of the issues that divide it from the others has no implications for the resolution of those same issues by any other group. Consider, for example, the issue of religious establishment. In a federal system, some subnational units may choose to establish the Reformed Church, others choose the Church of England, and still others choose no church at all. Because differences are reinforcing rather than cross-cutting, it is unlikely that anyone who disagrees with the establishment of the Reformed Church will be subject to the authority of the unit that establishes that church. As a result, even militant secularists can tolerate the establishment of churches in other units. . . .

The pacific picture of mutual toleration of differences in federal systems rests on the proposition that the resolution of problems within one subnational unit has no effect on people living in other such units. Federal systems are designed to deal with the problems that arise when spill-overs occur by allocating power to address such problems to the central government. Some obvious examples of spill-overs between two or more subnational units are the economic spill-overs that characterize many environmental issues.

One final assumption, regarding an important effect that could be characterized as a spill-over, is built into my analysis. I assume that each subnational unit desires for its members the highest level of material well-being compatible with the preservation of the unit without substantial change in the short term, and that few, if any, subnational units can achieve that level of material well-being without exchanges with members of other subnational units. The central government will have the power to assure the conditions under which these exchanges maximize the level of material well-being achievable in the short run.[5] These conditions include the provision of a material infra-structure of exchange, such as roads and bridges. In addition, they include the provision of a legal infra-structure or national legal system that will develop the law and decide particular cases without favoring one subnational unit over another.

In the long run, extra-constitutional bargaining structures might emerge to coordinate exchange. Meanwhile, however, federalism offers a constitutionally protected sphere in which diverse groups can at least survive and possibly flourish, while offering a national unit that can coordinate exchange and secure the conditions for economic prosperity. Furthermore, the evolution of federalism may well preempt the development of other bargaining structures. To solve the problems of coordinating and securing the conditions of economic exchange, national governments in a good federalist polity will almost certainly have the power to engage in some important activities. These will include defense, regulation of the national economy to ensure an achievable level of material well-being, and the use of a national tax system in adjusting the relative wealth positions of the subnational governments.[7]

5. I state this assumption in terms of the short run because the dynamics of a federal system are such that achieving a high level of material well-being may preserve the subnational unit in the short run, while eroding it over time.

7. This is particularly important if the subnational governments are defined territorially, because natural resources will certainly be unevenly distributed, even in the aggregate. The issue may arise, however, even if the subnational governments are defined in

Thus far I have proceeded largely ahistorically. [H]owever, a fact of modern life needs to be addressed. The organization of economic systems proceeds on a larger than national scale. Such globalization of economic relations places pressure on national governments to assert their power to coordinate economic matters in response.

Now consider a federalist polity in which the constitution allocates important powers over the economy to the national government and allocates other important powers, such as the power to develop a distinctive subnational culture through an established church and a subnational educational system, to the subnational governments. Notwithstanding the constitutional allocation of powers, federal systems drift toward centralization. Subsidiarity becomes at most a political principle guiding the central government, not a constitutional principle constraining it.

I begin with an illustration from the United States' experience, although similar examples could be drawn from nations with temporarily more vigorous federal systems such as Canada or Germany.

Certainly in the 1950's and probably today, most students of the United States Constitution would assert that the national government has no general power over education. No provision in Article I and none of the amendments to the Constitution confer such a power on the national government. Yet in the 1950's, when concern about the Soviet Union's scientific achievements arose, Congress and the President found no constitutional barrier to enacting educational programs. The vehicle they used to enact these programs was the spending power for the national defense, a power clearly lodged in the national government. By making funds available for education programs purportedly connected to the national defense, the central government came to play a large role in education throughout the country.

Today the national government in the United States has and exercises a general legislative power. It relies on a number of its specified constitutional powers, the most notable being the power to offer funds to subnational governments on the condition that they adhere to nationally prescribed norms. This power is closely analogous to making transfers among subnational units.

These examples illustrate the general path upon which centralization occurs. The national government relies on its rather expansive powers, such as the power to provide for national defense or to make inter-unit transfers, as the basis for exercising power over areas that had previously been under subnational units' control. For reasons I will discuss shortly, the constitutional allocation of that latter power to the subnational units does not prevent centralization.

Why, however, does the national government seek to assert its powers in this way? The main reason is economic. Economic expansion, and

some other way, particularly if differences in material wealth are among the reinforcing differences in the polity.

ultimately globalization, frequently make possible increases in the levels of material well-being that can be achieved in subnational units, without serious short-term disruptions of those units. The central government's role in securing conditions for expansion results in its continued efforts to extend its power over areas previously reserved to the subnational units.

Once the national government does expand its range, for whatever reason, something like a ratchet is in place. The national government can invoke an expansive national power to justify expanding its range. It is far more difficult to devise mechanisms by which subnational governments can retake from the national government powers the constitution allocated to the national government.[12] When the national government wants to exercise new powers, it may be able to do so; when subnational governments want to do so, they cannot. By specifying that the national government has important powers, federal constitutions create a one-way ratchet.

Various institutional mechanisms, however, can retard the drift toward centralization. James Madison's famous argument to that effect relied on the direct participation of state governments in the national political system to allay concerns that the United States Constitution created a centralized government. The states were represented in the Senate through the selection of senators by state legislatures, and they were represented in the electoral college for the selection of the president. In addition, if, as Madison and the framers believed would happen often, the votes in the electoral college were not decisive, the states would be represented as units in the House of Representatives' decision to select a president. Although these particular mechanisms have been altered by constitutional amendment or atrophy, Madison's insight was correct. If the subnational units are built into the national political process, either through representation, as Madison argued, or through a formal requirement of subnational consent to national legislation, the rate at which centralization occurs will be slower than if the national government is independent of the subnational governments.[13]

A judiciary can also be structured to retard centralization. Consider, for example, the choice between allowing abstract and a priori judicial review, common in continental constitutional systems, and allowing only

12. Judicial review is one mechanism by which subnational units can resist assertions of national power. However, judicial review cannot return to the subnational units any powers the constitution previously granted the national government.

13. It may be worth noting, in light of recent Canadian experience, that requiring unanimous subnational consent for exercises of national power, or giving only one or a few subnational units the power to veto exercises of national power, is a prescription for constitutional crisis. The vetoing unit may correctly believe that allowing the national government to exercise the power at issue will seriously erode that unit's ability to sustain itself, while large majorities in the other units may desire the program and insist on its implementation. The Canadian experience to this point suggests, perhaps not incidentally, that the benefits of national economic integration are so great that they can overcome subnational concern over the erosion of its coherence. Specifically, the people of Quebec still seem more reluctant to begin the process of secession than they are to vote for the secessionist Parti Quebecois, largely because they appreciate the high economic cost of secession.

concrete and a posteriori review as in the United States. The "case or controversy" requirement of Article III of the United States Constitution has been interpreted to mean that, in general, people can challenge new assertions of national power only after they have gone into effect and have adversely affected them. This allows a shift in power from subnational units to the national government some time to adjust before it becomes subject to judicial review. By the time judicial review occurs, the shift may seem natural or plainly constitutional. In contrast, a system allowing constitutional courts to render advisory opinions will make it easier to cut off institutional innovations at their inception.

Another element of institutional design that can retard the drift to centralization is the creation of a dual judicial system. In a dual judicial system, some judges authorized to exercise the power of judicial review are employees of subnational units, while others are employees of the national government. Of course, any sensible constitutional system will make the national court decisions supreme over those of subnational courts. However, in a system with a dual judiciary, the judges in the subnational system are likely to resist aggressive exercises of national power. This resistance may be substantial enough to retard the drift toward centralization, even though ultimately a national court will resolve the controversy.[15]

Finally, there is the language of the constitution itself as a constraint on the drift toward centralization. A constitution which lists the powers of the national government, and states that it may exercise only those powers, may make centralization more difficult than other constitutional forms. However, it would be incorrect to say anything stronger than "may make centralization more difficult." The Tenth Amendment to the United States Constitution was designed to emphasize the nation's lack of a centralized government. It provides that "[t]he powers not delegated to the United States by the Constitution . . . are reserved to the States respectively, or to the people. "As a textual matter, this "states but a truism that all is retained which has not been surrendered." It provides no guidance on the question of whether a specific exercise of power falls within an enumerated grant, which is of course the question that the courts facing a claim of improper centralization must decide.

Could anything more be done through constitutional language enforced by constitutional courts? Recall that the general mechanism for centralization involves the use of some conceded expansive power as a vehicle. United States constitutional history suggests that, over the long run, courts will be unable to sustain doctrines that constrain that mechanism. Faced with centralizing legislation, the United States Supreme Court developed two doctrines. First, it purported to require that such legislation "really" be an exercise of an enumerated power. The enumerated power invoked to justify the legislation must not be a mere "pretext" for the exercise of a power not

---

15. An even stronger mechanism would be a unitary judiciary in which all judges, other than those of the nation"s highest court, were employees of the subnational units. The ultimate controlling power of national judges is likely to cause resistance on lower levels that will only slow down, but not stop, nationalizing tendencies.

delegated to the national government. Second, the Court purported to require that such legislation "directly" promote the goals of the enumerated power.

Neither doctrine proved sustainable. The "pretext" constraint fell under the weight of [related] concerns. The Court invoked the constraint erratically, upholding a national ban on the interstate shipment of lottery tickets and mislabeled products while invalidating a similar ban on the interstate shipment of goods made by child workers. The distinctions the Court offered were analytically unpersuasive, ... [in distinguishing] between one statute that was a pretext and another that accomplished what it purported to do....

The "directness" requirement also succumbed to concerns about judicial capacity. Critics argued that directness had to be treated as an economic or social matter. They asked how the courts were able to determine that regulating coal prices was not directly related to ensuring an uninterrupted supply of coal throughout the country. At the same time, in a globally interconnected economy, it made no economic sense to contend that even the most local activity did not have some significant connection to interstate and international trade, subjects over which the national government concededly has power.

These examples suggest ... that constitutional language enforced by judicial review cannot stand in the way of a long-term drift toward centralization. However, they also suggest that constitutional language, coupled with a certain kind of legal culture, can retard that drift. The examples are drawn from a constitutional conflict that has persisted in the United States for several generations. Although proponents of centralization now appear to have won the analytic points, they did not always find the legal victories falling into their hands.

It is important to distinguish between two ideal types of legal cultures. In a formalist legal culture, legal documents are believed to have reasonably clear meanings that can be discerned by examining the words of the documents in light of some relatively abstract general constitutional and interpretive principles. In contrast, in a legal realist legal culture, such documents are taken to have no fixed meaning but must be interpreted in light of their purposes and, more importantly, the purposes to which they can be turned to resolve contemporary policy problems.

How will these different legal cultures respond to centralizing initiatives where the constitution purports to specify a limited domain for national power? A formalist culture or judge is likely to greet these initiatives skeptically, seeing them as departures from the plain meaning of the constitution's allocation of power, or from the clear intentions of the constitution's designers, no matter how pressing the national concerns in favor of the legislation appear to be. They will be reluctant to entertain arguments that the centralizing initiative is consistent with the constitution's basic purposes. Like the United States judges in the early twentieth century, formalist judges will find it relatively easy to decide whether legislation really rests on an assertion of constitutionally granted power. If they are concerned about the direct connection between an enumerated national power and the centralizing initiative, they will take "directness" to identify a conceptual category rather than a practical one.

Legal realist judges, on the other hand, will view the constitution as designed to promote some real-world goals and will examine whether the centralizing initiative actually does so. Some judges will become concerned that they lack the information available to the national legislature and will tend to defer to the legislature's choices. At the least, the legal realist approach opens up the possibility that sometimes the answer to the question, "does this law really advance a national purpose?" must be "yes." The formalist judge would find the question irrelevant.[23]

Why might a legal culture be formalist or legal realist? To some extent, the answer is that one or the other theory is simply a better account of law-making. For example, the historical trend in the United States from formalism to legal realism is understood (by legal realists) as a trend from error to truth. The persistence of formalism in other legal cultures is understood as a simple phenomenon of historical lag. In this view, eventually all legal cultures will become substantially legal realist.

There is another more historical element to the answer. In contemporary elite legal circles, particularly in the United States, a legal realist culture clearly predominates. To the extent that judges are members of elite legal circles, or seek to have good reputations in those circles, they will tend to become legal realists rather than formalists. To reiterate, a legal realist culture is more likely than a formalist one to accommodate centralizing initiatives no matter how specific the constitution's language.

Federal systems in the modern world drift toward centralization because of globalization and the dominance of a legal realist legal culture. The rate of drift, however, is affected by elements in the design of federal institutions. A constitutional specification of powers to be exercised solely by national units, a priori judicial review, a dual judiciary, and judges trained in formalist traditions all retard the drift toward centralization. Furthermore, the drift toward centralization could be retarded by courts interpreting a constitution with a clearly specified allocation of power, if those courts participated in a vigorous non-legal realist legal culture. For historical and analytic reasons, however, even such a culture will gradually erode. Ultimately, centralization will prevail. By the time that occurs, however, the problems of reinforcing the differences that make federalism an attractive interim solution to the problems of political organization may also have disappeared.

---

23. Historically, formalism has frequently been associated with the positivist claim that the law is simply what the authorized lawmakers say it is. Positivism is a difficult position for judges to sustain in a government with constitutional judicial review. If the authorized decision-maker is the legislature, judges should defer to its decisions. If the authorized decision-makers are the constitution-makers, judges should defer to their decisions. Unfortunately, the issue in constitutional cases is precisely the decisions of the constitution-makers. Positivism cannot help decide that issue.

Slowing the pace of centralization may be particularly important in systems that choose the federal form, because federalism alleviates problems caused by reinforcing pluralist differences. Here I return to Rawls, or at least to one interpretation of the argument Rawls presents in Political Liberalism.[24] As is well-known, Rawls distinguishes between systems characterized by a mere modus vivendi and those characterized by an overlapping consensus. The distinction matters, Rawls argues, because the latter systems are more stable than the former. In systems characterized by a modus vivendi, groups with different views of the good cooperate only because they acknowledge that conflict would not advance their own views of the good. Nevertheless, Rawls argues, in such a system any group would seize the opportunity to impose its view of the good if it believed that it could get away with it. One might say that groups are always on the lookout for opportunities to seize power. This makes for instability. In contrast, where there is an overlapping consensus, each group finds the principles of political liberalism to be the only principles of political organization compatible with their own views of the good. They are committed to those principles in principle, so to speak, and not merely strategically. As a result, even if the opportunity to seize power presented itself, no group would want to do so. Seizing power would be incompatible with its view of the good.

Rawls argues that stable liberal political institutions have historically emerged through a process in which a modus vivendi was converted into an overlapping consensus. It is not entirely clear to me what weight Rawls himself intends to place on this historical proposition, but I will make the process central to my argument. Once groups understand the benefits that flow from political stability, they gradually modify their views of the good so that, ultimately, the liberal political institutions that promote stability can be derived from the views of the good they have come to hold.

Almost as well known as Rawls's distinction, though, is that this construction works only if the society's pluralist groups differ in their views of the good. A modus vivendi will be converted into an overlapping consensus only if the groups in the society have what Rawls calls "reasonable" views of the good. As the construction indicates, the key to reasonableness is that the views are revisable. They can be changed as their adherents come to appreciate the value of political stability under liberal institutions.

What if the differing views are, as some might put it, fundamentalist? Adherents to fundamentalist views of the good do not admit, even in principle, that such views might be revised. In societies with important segments committed to fundamentalist views, there seems to be little prospect that an overlapping consensus will emerge. Although there is no conceptual connection, societies characterized by reinforcing differences are likely to have important groups with fundamentalist views. The reason is that within each group, particularly within those regularly subordinated to

---

24.   John   Rawls,   Political   Liberalism (1993).

others in many dimensions of life and those that regularly subordinate others, a sense develops that everything about the world is closely tied to each person's sense of being a member of the group. Where there are reinforcing differences, if a person changes his or her view of the good with respect to only one or two of the issues that matter, and retains the old view with respect to everything else, that person will discover him or herself quite isolated. In such a society, views of the good come in a few large and discrete packages. If someone does not accept one of the available packages, then there is nowhere to turn. Piecemeal revisions in one's beliefs are likely to threaten one's deepest sense of identity. Views of the good, therefore, will be resistant to revision, like fundamentalist views.

In societies with reinforcing pluralist differences, a centralized government could only be based on a modus vivendi....[26] As one group captured centralized power, it would impose its view of the good and subordinate other groups. How, then, could federalism be a solution for these societies when even federal systems drift toward centralization?

Fundamentalist views, though not in principle revisable, are likely to be revisable in actuality, although revisions in fundamentalist views will occur more slowly than revisions in reasonable views of the good. More narrowly, political liberalism, to the extent that it can deal with fundamentalist views,[27] must be committed to the proposition that fundamentalist views are in fact revisable....

The idea is simple enough. Recall that each group in the reinforcing-pluralism society wants to achieve the highest level of material well-being compatible with the preservation of the group's identity. Achieving that goal requires that the group engage in exchanges with other groups.[28] Each such exchange places modest cultural pressure on the group's identity because the process of exchange brings information to the group about how the other groups live.[29] The most sensitive in the group may believe that this modest pressure threatens the group's identity and will urge their compatriots to resist the material exchanges. They describe the changes as diminishing them from their own point of view. Most people, however, are likely to think that the threat to their way of life posed by the modest material exchange is small and that even their own point of view allows them to see themselves as fundamentally unchanged after such modest alterations. They will prefer the concrete material benefits to the more

---

26. Perhaps, parochially, I have in mind the United States experience, in which the drift toward centralization in a society with reinforcing differences provoked a civil war.

27. The qualification is important because, as I have suggested, it is not clear that Rawls' construction is concerned with fundamentalist views. Revising Rawls' construction may be useful nonetheless, to the extent that fundamentalisms or reinforcing pluralisms are an important feature of modern politics.

28. See, e.g., John Tomasi, *Kymlicka, Liberalism, and Respect for Cultural Minorities*, 105 Ethics 580, 588 (1995)(describing an "Inuit girl ... who from age two to eighteen experienced the rapid and disorienting transition of her culture from Inuit to white ways.").

29. The pressure placed on fundamentalist views, such as the Amish in the United States, by the availability of television are well-known.

abstract satisfaction of knowing that they have resisted a small threat to their group's identity. Generations later, those who identify themselves as historically continuous with the earlier group will see that major changes have occurred, though none will seem transformative.

Over time, cultural pressures are likely to accumulate in ways that make sustaining the fundamentalist view extremely difficult. Although no one believes that the view is in principle revisable, many people will come to believe that some modifications are merely adjustments to the facts of life. Because the process I have described results from the accumulation of small pressures occasioned by many material exchanges, it is likely to take a long time to occur.

That is why a federal system drifting gradually toward centralization seems an appropriate solution to the problems of organizing a society characterized by reinforcing differences.[30] Rawls, and proponents of other universalistic theories of liberal society, may be correct in thinking that, in the end, only a centralized government regulated by the universalistic principles of liberalism is consistent with liberal stability. Such theories, however, may have difficulty dealing with various fundamentalisms. An indirect strategy such as [federalism] may be more effective.

Questions and Comments

1. Professor Tushnet's essay can be seen as one kind of response to Rubin and Feeley. The normative value of federalism in Tushnet's scheme is to promote the gradual emergence of a "cross-cutting" consensus sufficient to sustain liberal, morally pluralistic societies. If one were to agree with Tushnet's argument, what implications would that have for judicial review? Would the scope of judicial review of federalism issues need to change over time if federalism succeeds in the gradual creation of a cross-cutting consensus? See Vicki C. Jackson, *Federalism and the Uses and Limits of Law: Printz and Principle*, 111 Harv. L. Rev. 2180, 2223 (1998)

2. Some scholars might answer by saying that in order to maintain stability, whether or not a polity moves in the direction of a liberal, cross-cutting consensus, the basic "deal" of federalism must be understood to be enforceable. Cf. Jenna Bednar & William N. Eskridge, Jr., *Steadying the Court's "Unsteady Path": A Theory of Judicial Enforcement of Federalism*, 68 S.Cal.L.Rev. 1447 (1995) (all participants in federal system must be discouraged from cheating on their commitment and must believe that all other participants are also discouraged from cheating). Consider whether, if courts are the basic agency for enforcement of legal obligations, a blanket refusal to enforce federalism limits could be destabilizing. See Jackson, at

----

30. Participants in the Symposium on the Good Polity Today raised one important qualification to this argument. When cross-cutting differences evolve into reinforcing ones, a previously stable system, whether fed-eral or centralized, may experience unaccustomed instability. There is reason to think that this describes the experience of Canada with respect to Quebec.

2223–26 (arguing that declared nonenforcement of federalism-based limits is potentially destabilizing to the rule of law).

3. Consider Professor Jackson's comments (at 2219–20) on whether federalism necessarily requires that subordinate units enjoy areas of exclusive lawmaking jurisdiction:

> [Such a view] ignores the independent value of [other aspects] of a federal system: the existence of two ongoing levels of government, each with leadership independently chosen by the people. A federal system might simply provide for the existence of two levels of government, with independently elected leaderships, in which the national level government had plenary legislative jurisdiction and the subnational level had principal administrative responsibilities [a model approached by German federalism]. Even if no areas of substantive legislative jurisdiction were reserved exclusively for a subnational-level government, it is at least in theory possible that having independently elected and accountable subnational leadership would provide a structural check on the actions and policies of the national government.

If a subnational unit has no lawmaking power, however, how in a constitutional system can it check national power?

4. If the subnational units are not sharply divided from one another by, e.g., language, religion, or race and ethnicity, does this suggest that there is no reason for judicial invalidation, on federalism grounds, of national laws, as Rubin and Feeley have argued with respect to the U.S.? For a contrary view on U.S. federalism, given the U.S. court-oriented legal culture, see Jackson, at 2221–22:

> Enforcing federalism may help maintain the significance of state and local governments as organizing features of identity and participation in public life, and thereby promote structures of tolerance, at least given current demographic distributions. In part because state lines do not necessarily correspond to lines of ethnic, racial or religious identity, which can be more deeply divisive, maintaining the significance of state governments may help foster civic identities that overlap with more deeply felt identities in ways that create cross-cutting allegiances. These allegiances, in turn, could increase the prospects for toleration and accommodation in the face of profound disagreements. In other words, states ... may be useful loci toward which to direct political activism and organizing, because their borders differ from other divisions that more profoundly divide.

Martha Minow, *Putting Up and Putting Down: Tolerance Reconsidered*, in Comparative Constitutional Federalism, Europe and America (Mark Tushnet ed. 1990)

[In the following essay, Minow raises profound questions about the values of tolerance and self-governance in a diverse society. The question of whether a liberal, tolerant society should "not tolerate" those who do not believe in tolerance is further considered in Chapters X and XI. Here, consider to what extent a diverse society must centralize control over its subunits in order to protect smaller minorities within those units. Consider

Minow's argument that minority groups benefit from overlapping authorities, and how well this idea works for different minorities.]

* * *

One of the paradoxes of liberal societies arises from their commitment to tolerance. A society committed to respecting the viewpoints and customs of diverse people within a pluralistic society inevitably encounters the challenge posed by those who themselves do not agree to respect the viewpoints or customs of others. Paradoxically, the liberal commitment to tolerance required, at some point, intolerance for those who would reject that very commitment.

Imagine this paradox, however, from the perspective of the member of a group who rejects the liberal commitment to respect the viewpoints or customs of others yet lives in a liberal society. This person may see toleration for variety a threat to the integrity and coherence of his or her community's way of life. This perspective is perhaps made even more understandable when a further assumption of liberal societies is brought to view. Liberalism treats the proper unit for concern as the separate and distinct individual, who bears rights to develop and express viewpoints that then deserve tolerance, and who is obliged to tolerate others. A contrasting assumption, however, identifies the individual as importantly located within a group of shared traditions. Someone proceeding with this contrasting assumption could argue that true tolerance requires recognition and respect for this contrasting mode of group identity. A diverse society would include some subcommunities that do not embrace the attitudes of liberal society and instead make commitments contrary to tolerance. Tolerance then would require respect even for a subcommunity that inculcates attitudes that are inconsistent with—indeed, intolerant of—the liberal commitments to individual rights and to obligations of tolerance. Unless the larger society respects such a subcommunity, it threatens the latter"s very viability and existence. Paradoxically, perhaps, this subcommunity views liberal tolerance as intolerance. Indeed, to the subcommunity, tolerance that stops short of accommodation is in effect intolerance, and tolerance that imposes routes of access to the larger society for each individual inside the subcommunity represents an invasion of the subcommunity's values and ways of life.

Tolerance without accommodation perpetuates assumptions that those who put up with others are actually superior to those others. Yet from another perspective, the very injunction to put up with others may be experienced as putting down some ways of life.

Now consider the debate between these two perspectives on tolerance in the context of another debate—the debate over allocating political and legal authority among local, state, national, and international levels of government. One might suppose that allocation of primary political power to local authorities would preserve cultural diversity and increasing grants or concessions of authority to centralized or coordinated authorities would risk interference with the cultural diversity. A closer look at the actual worldwide experience of cultural diversity demonstrates many contrary patterns. Often, increased centralization affords new protection for minority subgroups that otherwise face intolerance by local authorities.

Centralized rather than decentralized authority may be more protective of subgroups because local governmental units seldom correspond to homogeneous communities. Thus, even with the most decentralized form of official authority, potential conflicts among cultural groups and tensions between majorities and minorities arise and persist. Centralized authorities may be more likely to pursue norms of tolerance because of pressures to solicit respect and maintain legitimacy among a broader array of interest groups and communities.

Perhaps the only conclusion to be drawn is that the content of the norms adopted by a government, at whatever level, will be more relevant to the question of tolerance for diverse cultures than will the actual level of government entrusted with final authority on the question. A local, state, national, or transnational authority could embrace a policy of respect for the practices adopted by a minority subcommunity. Similarly, any level of governmental authority could adopt a rule that is intolerant of cultural practices of deviations from the rules applicable to the majority.

In sum, like the paradox of tolerance itself, a related paradox arises in the choices from among competing models of relationships between and among local, regional, national, and international political units—and even nongovernmental units, such as designated religious institutions. A commitment to respect diversity may seem to support respect for the more immediate levels of government through which policies tailored to particular communities may be developed. Yet minority groups in any given community may find greater support for their different needs and interests in a strong political authority that announces protections for minorities and restricts the prerogatives of local authorities. A political commitment to diversity may require, at some point, regulation of the self-determination processes of local authorities in order to protect subgroups within their midst, even though the local authorities themselves may assert the goal of diversity in order to preserve their own autonomy.

There is still another twist to the problem. Development of centralized authority structures that recognize and implement rights contrary to the preferences of local authorities may create avenues for individuals to challenge practices of subgroups and may thereby pose a threat to the autonomy and vitality of distinctive cultures. Cultural subcommunities thus may clash with the prerogatives of local authorities, the preferences of centralized authorities, and the commitments of any governmental authority to respect rights of individuals to leave or reject aspects of a subcommunity. The creation of centralized authorities empowered to protect subgroups may itself threaten the viability of subgroups by elaborating rights for individuals to escape subgroups. Centralized authority may challenge cultural diversity in other ways as well, especially in pursuing goals that are insensitive to, or disruptive of, some forms of cultural practice and identity.

These issues are vital as various nations and continents struggle with relationships among subgroups in their midst. Will adoption of national and international conceptions of individual rights promote the ideals of tolerance or impose one from among competing perspectives about individuality, group identity, and fundamental values? As the European Community heads toward ... harmonization of economic and regulatory arrangements, the treatment of ethnic and religious subgroups will surface even if not intended as a subject for concern. As the United States and Canada struggle with new waves of immigrants, old issues about the treatment of subgroups will be posed in the context of evolving legal rights. Similar issues in India, Sri Lanka, the Soviet Union, and other parts of the world have inspired scholarly and political attention.

The disparity between solutions that emphasize the rights of each distinct individual and solutions that recognize a realm of self-governance for subgroups becomes especially salient when women's rights, pronounced by central governments, conflict with deference to distinctive cultural groupings that operate on contrary assumptions about women, families, and communities. With the potential conflict between women's rights and respect for cultural differences as a recurring concern, this [essay] examines the issues of tolerance, first by discussing definitions and assumptions, then by exploring the challenges to cultural diversity that arise across a range of contemporary societies. The final section turns to the potential threats to cultural diversity posed by varied relationships among levels of government through a contrast between the United States and Canada. The discussion offers a distinction between threats to cultural diversity posed by failures of respect and threats posed by the creation of individual rights reaching within the traditional cultural subgroups, although this distinction may not be meaningful to members of subgroups confronting a challenge to their self-determination. The chapter also develops arguments for maintaining cultural diversity while articulating a conception of oppression to set the boundaries of tolerance. Consequences of these arguments for models of governmental authority are suggested, with special attention to developments emerging in Europe. Finally, the presentation recommends, and attempts to exemplify, a recognition of the long-standing tensions and paradoxes of tolerance, centralization, and decentralization, and respect for individuals and groups....

FEDERALISM AND CULTURAL DIVERSITY

[T]he viability of a federal society depends upon the capacity of citizens to have recourse to principles of constitutional choice in organizing concurrent communities of interest for solving problems arising from the inconveniences that neighborhood brings.

— Vincent Ostrom

Lo and behold, here in our midst is dissimilarity that simply could not be squelched, and that now is insisting on its right to flourish.

— Jane Jacobs

The problems of tolerance and intolerance are familiar and enduring. . . . [The] problems of tolerance and intolerance increase with the lack of coincidence between territorial boundaries and cultural boundaries. Geographical boundaries fail to match up with cultural boundaries as nation states form and reform with boundaries that encompass members of many different cultural groups, and as members of different cultural groups move to nation-states where they have not previously lived. One observer commented that "[t]here are thousands of ethnic, tribal, racial, lingual and ethno-religious communities" while "there are only about 150 'nation' states, within which heterogeneous groups coexist."

Given this diversity of cultural groupings within nation-states, there are historic and persistent demands for self-governance by local and regional authorities that claim greater identification with, and responsiveness to, their particular cultural groups. Some groups remain minorities even at the local and regional levels. They may find more protection for their interests—more promise of tolerance—if a centralized national government retains control. Still other groups may believe that international accords better ensure tolerance, perhaps because they represent cultures that are minorities in their own country of residence but majorities elsewhere, or perhaps because the norms developed in international accords better recognize their rights or needs. Some groups may discover that no particular form of official policy within a nation provides protection for cultural autonomy, self-governance, or basic human rights; they may find more promising assistance in the sphere of international human rights. The experience of Native Americans in the United States may provide such an example. . . . [F]rom coordinate sovereigns, to dependent nations, to wards protected by the nation-state, to individuals with some special claims, Native Americans have seen the range of legal statuses and witnessed the inventive interpretation of these statuses by administrators and judges to repeatedly deny the power and entitlements of these culturally distinctive groups. . . .

. . . In the abstract, it is not obvious that any particular allocation of responsibility among levels of government will ensure more tolerance for cultural diversity than any other. Contextual, historical inquiries can provide some illumination of the consequences of varied patterns of relationships among local, regional, national, and international authorities for the preservation of cultural diversity. . . . The intersection of pluralism and federalism problems appears in two historical examples in the United States. These examples help to explain the support for centralized, national governance in the United States as part of the campaign to protect cultural diversity. Yet a contrasting set of examples, drawn from the Canadian experience, identifies a context in which decentralized control has been more effectively linked to the preservation of distinctive cultures and highlights particular traits of the United States experience that warrant caution before emulation.

Two Stories from the United States

The first story arises from the presence, in the United States, of minority groups that have sought a refuge. Such groups sought space within which to construct their own community and preserve their own culture. What chance do such groups have, given the overlapping and concurrent sovereign authorities of local, state, and national governments? The facts behind the United States Supreme Court decision in *Wisconsin v. Yoder** illuminate the problem and demonstrate the intersection between issues of tolerance for cultural differences and choices among levels of governmental control. A law adopted by the state of Wisconsin required all children to attend school until they reached the age of sixteen; otherwise, their parents would be subject to a fine. Members of the Amish community, who opposed schooling for their children past the eighth grade, challenged this law as an intrusion on their rights to exercise their religion freely, as guaranteed by the First Amendment to the Constitution. They argued that their religion called for a way of life tied to the local farming activities and deliberately shielding community members from the industrial and hetero-geneous world. They demonstrated, to the satisfaction of the Court, that these beliefs were religiously motivated and thus protected under the Constitution.

Wisconsin maintained, however, that it represented the interests of the broader community and the children themselves in ensuring that all of its children received the same minimum amount of educational instruction. As pursued in a separate opinion by one Supreme Court justice, concern for the children's interests should include a commitment to the future and preserve options for individual children who might wish to leave the Amish community as adults—and who then could well need the extra years of school instruction required by the state. The majority on the Court con-cluded that the burdens placed on the religious freedoms of the Amish could not be justified by the state's espoused interests, especially because, in the Court's view, the Amish already fulfilled many of the state's purposes by ensuring that its children become self-sufficient and productive individuals.

The case presents in sharp relief the potential conflict between and among subcommunity cultural traditions, state-level public demands, and federal constitutional guarantees of toleration for religious diversity. The case also presents the tension between a conception of the group, in which adults speak for children, and the individual as the focus for concerns about tolerance. A critic of the decision could argue that the Court failed to protect the rights of individual Amish children to develop the abilities and experiences that would enable free choice about how to live; a defender could celebrate the Court's willingness to sacrifice a liberal value of individual choice through respect for the subcommunity's choice about how to raise their children.

For yet another layer of complexity, the enforcement of a commitment to diversity by a tribunal or legal structure that is maintained by the state, national, or transnational authority, itself already represents a considerable

---

* [406 U.S. 205 (1972)]

intrusion on the cultural practices of a subgroup forced to try to persuade people outside of itself. From the subgroup's perspective, complete tolerance may require recognition of that group's own right to self-determination and self-governance, beyond the control or even direct permission of state, national, or international authorities. This concept involves a recognition of the plurality of sources of legal authority, rather than an assumption that all sources of legal authority fit together in one united whole. The spheres of authority, in this view, are not nested in a hierarchy, with each successive level subsuming the more local and intimate ones, but instead, the subcommunity provides a reference point for its members that sets them outside the structures of governmental authority. It is quite plausible that if the Amish had lost in the Supreme Court, they would have left Wisconsin, and indeed, left the United States, for their allegiance to these sovereign political authorities remains overshadowed by their religious and cultural identities.

For individuals and subgroups, then, the choice from among competing levels of authority includes options outside the scheme of a coordinated federal structure devised within one constitutional framework, or even within one international federation. Decisions reached within such structures do not end the matter for members of subgroups who are themselves tolerating the secular political arrangement only as long as it remains compatible with their own sense of alternative authorities. The pilgrim groups who helped to settle America, and lent their stories to the myths of America's founding, represent just this sort of migration to the new locale due to conscientious objection to the political choices in their home state.

For groups that have migrated to the United States from another country, persistent conflicts among levels of government in governing their affairs etch the results of interest-group politics and of larger political tides in the country. Here is a second story about United States federalism and pluralism: the story of bilingual education. A local community may decide to provide within its schools classes conducted in the language spoken by a majority of its students, even though that is not the official language of the state within which the local community exists. The state may argue that this local decision violates the state's own commitment to promote literacy in the official language and mobility for individuals who seek success beyond their local communities. The nation-state may, in turn, articulate basic rights for each student to receive an education that accommodates his or her own language background. . . .

A federal agency took the lead in developing the acceptable forms of education for children whose primary language is not English. Those forms are designed to foster proficiency in English on a transitional basis. . . . Shifting political tides, however, produced a federal administration that disagreed with this approach and instead decided to return discretion to state and local authorities in the selection of programs for students lacking proficiency in English. This shift of authority to state and local officials allows the adoption of programs such as "structured immersion" in which teachers primarily use English while structuring the curriculum to ease assimilation for students lacking extensive familiarity with English.... Many advocates for the rights of language-minority students fear that increased state and local discretion will produce programs that are unresponsive to those students' needs and disrespectful of the goal of preserving their native languages and cultures.

Which level of government should be entrusted with making the final decision about the language to be used in school instruction or the form of instruction? Recognition of cultural diversity may require greater authority at the national level to check the state-level effort to override local choices. The minority group's interest in national authority may be even more pronounced where it lacks the political power to secure control of the school programs at the local level—or to require self-governance powers— and finds only in the national government's intervention an ability to challenge local, as well as state, decision-making. Yet this preference for centralized authority depends on substantive commitments at that level to respond to the minority cultures' needs and preferences. Absent those commitments, the choice of federal authority may provide no greater protection for the minority groups than would state or local authorities. Perhaps, for this reason, advocates of cultural diversity have argued in favor of multiple and overlapping jurisdictions and governmental authorities. The very presence of more than one authority provides some chance for minority groups to seek a second opinion, some free space in the tension and gaps between layers and competing sovereigns, and some opportunity to correct errors made by one through recourse to another. Most important will be the room to develop nonpublic norms—subcommunity values that may then be advocated at any favorable level of government.

Contrasts Between Canada and the United States

The very example of linguistic subcultures in the United States highlights an important contrast with Canada, a contrast that many observers link to differences in the two nations' experiences with federalism. Although the United States is a nation composed of people who are members of numerous linguistic communities, the United States primarily employs English, and public and private authorities are authorized to implement a preference for English. In contrast, Canada reflects its historical settlement by primarily two linguistic groups: English and French. Despite British rule for the early part of the Canadian history, the French communities remained powerful....

Yet an imbalance between the two language groups exists, both in terms of the numbers of people originally involved in each group and in the preferences of new immigrants to learn English and send their children to English-speaking schools, as most perceive English as the language of mobility. This pattern has in some senses strengthened the Francophone resolve to pursue a separate political base in order to ensure a future for the French culture in Canada. As a result, Quebec has adopted rules forcing non-Anglophone immigrant children to attend the French language schools within the province. And many Canadians expressly oppose the notion of "the melting pot" that for so long dominated American attitudes toward cultural diversity. These conflicts over bicultural and multiculturalism have largely been fought, in Canada, in the arena of federal-provincial relations. Some have identified the preoccupation with federalism as pivotal to Canadian identity.

Ronald Watts, a professor of political studies at Queen's University in Ontario, Canada, has developed an intriguing comparison of federalism in the United States and Canada. He noted first that Canada is moving from centralization toward greater regionalism, while the United States has moved from regionalism (with a constrained central government) toward greater national governmental powers....

Watts also observes the contrasting "territorial concentration" of the most significant minority groups in each country. In Canada the French-speakers are a minority of 26 percent across the country, but their concentration in Quebec gives them an 80 percent majority in that province. In contrast, the blacks in the United States constitute 11 percent of the total population and have no majority in any state. While the Francophones in Quebec push for regional power to enable greater self-governance, blacks have pursued centralized federal protection to guard against local and intolerant majorities. Actually, even more may be made of this contrast than Watts affords. The unique circumstance of blacks in the United States due to the history of slavery means that blacks have for the most part lacked the political or economic power to articulate and preserve a distinctive culture, although much that is original in United States music and oratory is directly traceable to the contributions of blacks. The Francophones may have lacked a dominant economic position during many periods of Canadian history, yet historically, they had considerably more power to create their own cultural institutions than did African Americans in the United States.

Watts offers several other suggestions for the contrasting development of intergovernmental relations in Canada and the United States. He notes that the United States economy since World War II has become largely national while the Canadian economy remains largely organized at the regional level....

Unlike the United States system, Canadian federalism has been characterized as a community of communities, the centralized, federal government is simply one of these communities, albeit a big one. Perhaps, as some suggest, the significance of "a sense of place" to Canadians accompanies a self-consciousness about hyphenated (or multiple) identities, unlike the United States cultivation of outside identities.

As Canada struggles to interpret its Charter of Rights and Freedoms, these hypotheses about Canadian federalism will have practical tests and challenges. The decision by the Supreme Court of Canada in *Ford v. Quebec* and the response of Quebec to that decision provide evidence of an experiment still unfolding. The case posed the question whether the Quebec Charter of French Language, which required all public signs and commercial advertising to use only French, infringes upon the freedom of expression guaranteed by the Canadian Charter.... The court interpreted the guarantee of freedom of expression to extend beyond political expression to commercial speech, or, more precisely, held that the right of individuals to use the English language persists even when exercised through signs that have a commercial purpose. This decision could be characterized as the imposition by the central government of a conception of individual rights on a province that sought to protect a group against cultural domination; it could also be characterized as the search for a national common denominator of basic respect through the concept of individual freedoms despite regional differences.

If this decision were reached by the United States Supreme Court, and premised on the federal Constitution, it would be the last word, absent, that is, a constitutional amendment or a reversal by the Supreme Court itself. But ... in Canada, the decision in *Ford v. Quebec* simply served as a volley in a continuing process of centralized/provincial struggle. Quebec responded by exercising its right to override a Supreme Court decision.

This array of factors differentiating Canada and the United States helps to portray how complicated are the relationships between alternate federalist structures and cultural diversity. The particular appeal of decentralized versus centralized governmental control within a generally federalist system depends upon particular historical circumstances and the relative power and geographic concentration of cultural minorities....

CONCLUDING A BEGINNING...

This [essay] began by advocating commitments to preserve distinctive cultures. This means reconceiving tolerance to include the vantage point of members of traditional subgroups that do not share the dominant liberal commitments to individual choice, experimentation, and value relativism. An argument has also been made in favor of gender equality, although in many instances, this runs counter to the practices of traditional cultures and religious groups. Together, these arguments pose a question: What mix of concerns for group rights or cultural preservation, on the one hand, and individual rights and freedoms, on the other, should a given society pursue if it hopes to respect cultural diversity without colluding in the domination or oppression of some of its own members?

Even this question makes the problem look too simple.... The allocation of governmental powers between levels and among branches of governments, and between nations and continents, poses a difficult enough question when economic and military concerns are most salient. When combined with the paradoxes and dilemmas of tolerance, these central questions of political design are enormously complicated, and comparisons of historical experiences suggest no determinate mix of powers is particularly better than another to preserve distinctive cultures or to enforce individual rights.

In short, the tensions and paradoxes explored [here] do not suggest solutions. Indeed, one purpose here is to argue that solutions are likely to neglect the multiple perspectives on issues of tolerance, cultural diversity, and allocation of governmental power. The search for an answer is often stymied by the faulty assumption that the right question has been asked. What questions are right profoundly reflects the point of view of the inquirer, and this fact can bedevil efforts to get beyond the acknowledged limits of one point of view. "How can a society promote tolerance?" is an inadequate question, not only because tolerance leads to passive acquiescence in existing power arrangements rather than accommodating or respecting differences, but also because tolerance risks undermining subgroups committed to particular values inconsistent with majority practices. Yet there are comparable faults in a question such as, "how can a society respect and preserve cultural diversity?" for that formulation obscures the potential tension between preserving some subcultures and promoting individual rights that may be undermined by those very groups. It is also no solution, for a complex society, simply to embrace an existing point of view in order to address questions about tolerance and cultural diversity. The challenge is to formulate an inquiry from a point of view that can be attentive to other points of view, that can acknowledge them and their differences. Once pursued, such an inquiry cannot be neutral. It is for that reason that I advocate explicit attention to the concept of oppression, even though that concept will inevitably draw debates over its meaning and its application. I suggest that respecting cultural diversity while pursuing basic liberal freedoms and individual rights must be an ongoing struggle among people who disagree about many things. In the spirit of such a struggle, scholarly and political efforts to define the notion of oppression must be pursued by people coming from different points of view. . . .

. . . [T]here is nothing peculiar to a federal system that exacerbates or eases problems of preserving cultural diversity. Within particular historical moments, within particular constellations of relationships among levels of government and between cultural groups, arguments for and arguments against greater centralization or greater decentralization provide avenues for both protecting and undermining cultural diversity. Centralized governmental authority, historically, has been linked to the development and articulation of individual rights that may become corrosive to particular cultural traditions while advancing the freedom and self-realization of each person. There may be ways, however, that centralized governments can protect subgroups from intolerant policies of local authorities. But whatever level of government retains control on any given issue, there will persist a tension between basic rights of individuals to be free from discrimination on the basis of immutable traits and respect for subgroups so that cultural traditions may be preserved.

What may be most important is simply the existence of multiple levels of governmental authority. For it is the presence of multiple authorities that, paradoxically, gives minority groups the opportunity to seek alternatives to a singular answer. Robert Cover's work on the values of jurisdictional redundancy provides an eloquent defense of the multiple court systems in the United States as increasing the chances that errors will be corrected, and then less powerful voices will ultimately have a chance to be heard. Thus, governmental powers should be allocated to multiple sources of authority in an effort to enhance the avenues for challenging public and private intolerance.

The challenge, from this vantage point, is to devise modes of inquiry that can solicit multiple perspectives rather than suppress them. . . .

CHAPTER IX

PLURALISM, RIGHTS AND DEMOCRACY

Federalism, which we looked at in the last chapter, might be understood as a method for structural accommodation of pluralism and democracy. Both territorial units based on geography, and consociational systems in which the national governing structures take account of groups dispersed through the nation, are methods that can be employed (as in Belgium) to provide forms of structural accommodation. We now look at what might be called substantive efforts to accommodate pluralism and democracy through constitutional rules concerning rights for members of particular groups to equality of treatment and/or social advancement.

In addition to the problems associated with linguistic communities, a pervasive set of questions in diverse societies concern the establishment, protection and/or accommodation of religious freedom and diversity. This set of problems emerges with frequency in part because religion and religious practices are often importantly self-constituting and group-constituting; resolution is often difficult because of the complex interactions between individual self-definition and the relationship of claims about religion to group beliefs and practices. Federal structures may, but need not, provide a form in which controversies over the relationship between states and religion are contested.[a] Chapter X will explore problems of religious accommodation.

Differences of race and ethnicity provide another set of pluralism issues for many polities, including the United States and India. This chapter's readings explore the evolving U.S. constitutional law on whether, and how, government can take race into account in the design of such government functions as higher education, government contracts, and creation of voting districts. We will compare the U.S. experience with the experience of India in trying to break down the in part religious, in part ethnic, distinctions among different "castes". Both involve possible deployments of constitutional law to encourage, or prevent, affirmative govern-

---

a. For example, in the U.S. state or local governments have frequently asserted rights to have school prayer or public displays of religious symbols in conflict or tension with Supreme Court doctrine; see, e.g., James v. ACLU, 711 So.2d 952 (Ala. 1998) (dismissing as nonjusticiable action brought by state governor, state attorney general and state court judge seeking to vindicate judge's practice of organizing prayer sessions in court and displaying a plaque with the Ten Commandments behind his seat); Suhre v. Haywood Co., 131 F.3d 1083 (4th Cir. 1997) (upholding plaintiff's standing to challenge display of Ten Commandments in North Carolina county courthouse). In Germany, the Land of Bavaria has resisted compliance with German Constitutional Court decisions prohibiting requirements for displays of crucifixes in public classrooms. For further discussion, see Chapter X below.

mental steps to remedy perceived substantive social and economic disadvantages of particular racial, ethnic or religious groups.

A. The United States

As you read the excerpts of the cases below, consider what role constitutional text, constitutional history, and the justices' evaluation of the social consequences of race conscious government decisionmaking play in their decisions. Recall the words of the 13th, 14th and 15th amendments:

Amendment 13 (1865)

Section 1. Neither slavery nor involuntary servitude, except as a punishment for crime whereof the party shall have been duly convicted, shall exist within the United States, or any place subject to their jurisdiction.

Section 2. Congress shall have power to enforce this article by appropriate legislation.

Amendment 14 (1868)

Section 1. All persons born or naturalized in the United States and subject to the jurisdiction thereof, are citizens of the United States and of the State wherein they reside. No State shall make or enforce any law which shall abridge the privileges or immunities of citizens of the United States; nor shall any State deprive any person of life, liberty, or property, without due process of law; nor deny to any person within its jurisdiction the equal protection of the laws.

Section 5. The Congress shall have power to enforce, by appropriate legislation, the provisions of this article.

Amendment 15 (1870)

Section 1. The right of citizens of the United states to vote shall not be denied or abridged by the United States or by any State on account of race, color or previous condition of servitude.

Section 2. The Congress shall have power to enforce this article by appropriate legislation.

Regents of University of California v. Bakke

438 U.S. 265 (1978).[b]

Mr. Justice Powell announced the judgment of the Court [and filed an opinion expressing his views of the case, in Parts I, III-A and V-C of which

---

b. Note: In the opinions that follow the Justices are engaged in several debates, including one over the appropriate standard of review for "benign" racial classifications. In equal protection doctrine, most government classifications will be upheld if they have a "rational" basis. Classifications based on race or other "suspect" characteristics can be upheld only if they meet "strict" scrutiny, that is, a showing that the classification is neces-

WHITE, J., joined and in Parts I and V-C of which BRENNAN, MARSHALL and BLACKMUN, JJ., joined].

This case presents a challenge to the special admissions program of the petitioner, the Medical School of the University of California at Davis, which is designed to assure the admission of a specified number of students from certain minority groups. The Superior Court of California sustained respondent's challenge, holding that petitioner's program violated the California Constitution, Title VI of the Civil Rights Act of 1964, 42 U.S.C. § 2000d et seq., and the Equal Protection Clause of the Fourteenth Amendment. The court enjoined petitioner from considering respondent's race or the race of any other applicant in making admissions decisions. It refused, however, to order respondent's admission to the Medical School, holding that he had not carried his burden of proving that he would have been admitted but for the constitutional and statutory violations. The Supreme Court of California affirmed those portions of the trial court's judgment declaring the special admissions program unlawful and enjoining petitioner from considering the race of any applicant. It modified that portion of the judgment denying respondent's requested injunction and directed the trial court to order his admission.

For the reasons stated in the following opinion, I believe that so much of the judgment of the California court as holds petitioner's special admissions program unlawful and directs that respondent be admitted to the Medical School must be affirmed. For the reasons expressed in a separate opinion, my Brothers The Chief Justice, Mr. Justice Stewart, Mr. Justice Rehnquist and Mr. Justice Stevens concur in this judgment. [These four justices concluded that a federal statute, Title VI of the Civil Rights Act of 1964, applied to preclude Davis' plan. Accordingly, they did not reach the constitutional question, but joined the Court's judgment insofar as it affirmed the order that Bakke be admitted to the medical school.]

I also conclude for the reasons stated in the following opinion that the portion of the court's judgment enjoining petitioner from according any consideration to race in its admissions process must be reversed. For reasons expressed in separate opinions, my Brothers Mr. Justice Brennan, Mr. Justice White, Mr. Justice Marshall, and Mr. Justice Blackmun concur in this judgment. [These four justices concluded that Title VI's prohibition were the same as those of the Equal Protection Clause and therefore went on to decide the constitutional question. They argued that under the Equal Protection Clause, benign remedial use of racial classifications can be justified to overcome substantial, chronic underrepresentations in the profession, and would have upheld the Davis plan and reversed the judgement below.]

sary and narrowly tailored to meet a compelling government interest. At the time of most of the following cases, gender-based classifications were reviewed under so-called "intermediate" scrutiny, variously formulated, but requiring a strong connection between the classification and some important government purpose.

[Justice Powell wrote only for himself but provided the dispositive vote for each part of the Court's judgment. Agreeing that the case had to be resolved on constitutional grounds, he emphasized the need for strict scrutiny of any racial classification, and concluded that achieving a diverse student body was a compelling interest for a public university and that race under some circumstances could be used as a factor in admissions to achieve that goal. The special admissions program at Davis, he concluded, could not be justified under a compelling interest standard, and the order that Bakke be admitted should be affirmed, but the portion of the judgment below precluding the university from any consideration of race in admissions must be reversed.]

Affirmed in part and reversed in part.

I

The Medical School of the University of California at Davis opened in 1968 with an entering class of 50 students. In 1971, the size of the entering class was increased to 100 students, a level at which it remains. No admissions program for disadvantaged or minority students existed when the school opened, and the first class contained three Asians but no blacks, no Mexican-Americans, and no American Indians. Over the next two years, the faculty devised a special admissions program to increase the representation of "disadvantaged" students in each Medical School class. The special program consisted of a separate admissions system operating in coordination with the regular admissions process.

Under the regular admissions procedure, a candidate could submit his application to the Medical School beginning in July of the year preceding the academic year for which admission was sought. Because of the large number of applications[2], the admissions committee screened each one to select candidates for further consideration. Candidates whose overall undergraduate grade point averages fell below 2.5 on a scale of 4.0 were summarily rejected. About one out of six applicants was invited for a personal interview. Following the interviews, each candidate was rated on a scale of 1 to 100 by his interviewers and four other members of the admissions committee. The rating embraced the interviewers' summaries, the candidate's overall grade point average, grade point average in science courses, scores on the Medical College Admissions Test (MCAT), letters of recommendation, extracurricular activities, and other biographical data. The ratings were added together to arrive at each candidate's "benchmark" score. Since five committee members rated each candidate in 1973, a perfect score was 500; in 1974, six members rated each candidate, so that a perfect score was 600. The full committee then reviewed the file and scores of each applicant and made offers of admission on a "rolling" basis. The chairman was responsible for placing names on the waiting list. They were not placed in strict numerical order; instead, the chairman had discretion to include persons with "special skills."

2. For the 1973 entering class of 100 seats, the Davis Medical School received 2,464 applications. For the 1974 entering class, 3,737 applications were submitted.

The special admissions program operated with a separate committee, a majority of whom were members of minority groups. On the 1973 application form, candidates were asked to indicate whether they wished to be considered as "economically and/or educationally disadvantaged" applicants; on the 1974 form the question was whether they wished to be considered as members of a "minority group," which the Medical School apparently viewed as "Blacks," "Chicanos," "Asians," and "American Indians." If these questions were answered affirmatively, the application was forwarded to the special admissions committee. No formal definition of "disadvantaged" was ever produced, but the chairman of the special committee screened each application to see whether it reflected economic or educational deprivation. Having passed this initial hurdle, the applications then were rated by the special committee in a fashion similar to that used by the general admissions committee, except that special candidates did not have to meet the 2.5 grade point average cutoff applied to regular applicants. About one-fifth of the total number of special applicants were invited for interviews in 1973 and 1974. Following each interview, the special committee assigned each special applicant a benchmark score. The special committee then presented its top choices to the general admissions committee. The latter did not rate or compare the special candidates against the general applicants, but could reject recommended special candidates for failure to meet course requirements or other specific deficiencies. The special committee continued to recommend special applicants until a number prescribed by faculty vote were admitted. While the overall class size was still 50, the prescribed number was 8; in 1973 and 1974, when the class size had doubled to 100, the prescribed number of special admissions also doubled, to 16.

From the year of the increase in class size—1971—through 1974, the special program resulted in the admission of 21 black students, 30 Mexican-Americans, and 12 Asians, for a total of 63 minority students. Over the same period, the regular admissions program produced 1 black, 6 Mexican-Americans, and 37 Asians, for a total of 44 minority students. Although disadvantaged whites applied to the special program in large numbers, none received an offer of admission through that process. Indeed, in 1974, at least, the special committee explicitly considered only "disadvantaged" special applicants who were members of one of the designated minority groups.

Allan Bakke is a white male who applied to the Davis Medical School in both 1973 and 1974. In both years Bakke's application was considered under the general admissions program, and he received an interview. His 1973 interview was with Dr. Theodore C. West, who considered Bakke "a very desirable applicant to [the] medical school." Despite a strong benchmark score of 468 out of 500, Bakke was rejected. His application had come late in the year, and no applicants in the general admissions process with scores below 470 were accepted after Bakke's application was completed. There were four special admissions slots unfilled at that time however, for which Bakke was not considered. After his 1973 rejection, Bakke wrote to Dr. George H. Lowrey, Associate Dean and Chairman of the Admissions

Committee, protesting that the special admissions program operated as a racial and ethnic quota.

Bakke's 1974 application was completed early in the year. His student interviewer gave him an overall rating of 94, finding him "friendly, well tempered, conscientious and delightful to speak with." His faculty interviewer was, by coincidence, the same Dr. Lowrey to whom he had written in protest of the special admissions program. Dr. Lowrey found Bakke "rather limited in his approach" to the problems of the medical profession and found disturbing Bakke's "very definite opinions which were based more on his personal viewpoints than upon a study of the total problem." Dr. Lowrey gave Bakke the lowest of his six ratings, an 86; his total was 549 out of 600. Again, Bakke's application was rejected. In neither year did the chairman of the admissions committee, Dr. Lowrey, exercise his discretion to place Bakke on the waiting list. In both years, applicants were admitted under the special program with grade point averages, MCAT scores, and benchmark scores significantly lower than Bakke's.[7]

After the second rejection, Bakke filed the instant suit in the Superior Court of California. He sought mandatory, injunctive, and declaratory relief compelling his admission to the Medical School. He alleged that the Medical School's special admissions program operated to exclude him from the school on the basis of his race, in violation of his rights under the Equal Protection Clause of the Fourteenth Amendment, Art. I, § 21, of the California Constitution, and § 601 of Title VI of the Civil Rights Act of 1964, 78 Stat. 252, 42 U.S.C. § 2000d. The University cross-complained for a declaration that its special admissions program was lawful....

III

A

Petitioner does not deny that decisions based on race or ethnic origin by faculties and administrations of state universities are reviewable under

7. The following table compares Bakke's science grade point average, overall grade point average, and MCAT scores with the average scores of regular admittees and of special admittees in both 1973 and 1974[:]

Class Entering in 1973 MCAT (Percentiles)

	SGPA	OGPA	Verbal	Quantitative	Science	Gen. Infor.
Bakke	3.44	3.46	96	94	97	72
Average of regular admittees	3.51	3.49	81	76	83	69
Average of special admittees	2.62	2.88	46	24	35	33

Class Entering in 1974 MCAT (Percentiles)

	SGPA	OGPA	Verbal	Quantitative	Science	Gen. Infor.
Bakke	3.44	3.46	96	94	97	72
Average of regular admittees	3.36	3.29	69	67	82	72
Average of special admittees	2.42	2.62	34	30	37	18

Applicants admitted under the special program also had benchmark scores significantly lower than many students, including Bakke, rejected under the general admissions program....

the Fourteenth Amendment. For his part, respondent does not argue that all racial or ethnic classifications are per se invalid. See, e. g., *Hirabayashi v. United States*, 320 U.S. 81 (1943); *Korematsu v. United States*, 323 U.S. 214 (1944); *Lee v. Washington*, 390 U.S. 333 (1968) (Black, Harlan, and Stewart, JJ., concurring); *United Jewish Organizations v. Carey*, 430 U.S. 144 (1977). The parties do disagree as to the level of judicial scrutiny to be applied to the special admissions program. Petitioner argues that the court below erred in applying strict scrutiny, as this inexact term has been applied in our cases. That level of review, petitioner asserts, should be reserved for classifications that disadvantage "discrete and insular minorities." See *United States v. Carolene Products Co.*, 304 U.S. 144, 152 n. 4 (1938). Respondent, on the other hand, contends that the California court correctly rejected the notion that the degree of judicial scrutiny accorded a particular racial or ethnic classification hinges upon membership in a discrete and insular minority and duly recognized that the "rights established [by the Fourteenth Amendment] are personal rights." *Shelley v. Kraemer*, 334 U.S. 1, 22 (1948).

En route to this crucial battle over the scope of judicial review, the parties fight a sharp preliminary action over the proper characterization of the special admissions program. Petitioner prefers to view it as establishing a "goal" of minority representation in the Medical School. Respondent, echoing the courts below, labels it a racial quota.

This semantic distinction is beside the point: The special admissions program is undeniably a classification based on race and ethnic background. To the extent that there existed a pool of at least minimally qualified minority applicants to fill the 16 special admissions seats, white applicants could compete only for 84 seats in the entering class, rather than the 100 open to minority applicants. Whether this limitation is described as a quota or a goal, it is a line drawn on the basis of race and ethnic status.

The guarantees of the Fourteenth Amendment extend to all persons. Its language is explicit: "No State shall . . . deny to any person within its jurisdiction the equal protection of the laws." It is settled beyond question that the "rights created by the first section of the Fourteenth Amendment are, by its terms, guaranteed to the individual. The rights established are personal rights." *Shelley v. Kraemer*, at 22. The guarantee of equal protection cannot mean one thing when applied to one individual and something else when applied to a person of another color. If both are not accorded the same protection, then it is not equal. . . .

. . . Racial and ethnic distinctions of any sort are inherently suspect and thus call for the most exacting judicial examination.

B

This perception of racial and ethnic distinctions is rooted in our Nation's constitutional and demographic history. The Court's initial view of the Fourteenth Amendment was that its "one pervading purpose" was "the freedom of the slave race, the security and firm establishment of that freedom, and the protection of the newly-made freeman and citizen from the oppressions of those who had formerly exercised dominion over him." *Slaughter-House Cases*, 16 Wall. 36, 71 (1873). The Equal Protection Clause, however, was "[v]irtually strangled in infancy by post-civil-war judicial reactionism." It was relegated to decades of relative desuetude while the Due Process Clause of the Fourteenth Amendment, after a short germinal period, flourished as a cornerstone in the Court's defense of property and liberty of contract. See, e. g., *Lochner v. New York*, 198 U.S. 45 (1905). In that cause, the Fourteenth Amendment's "one pervading purpose" was displaced. See, e. g., *Plessy v. Ferguson*, 163 U.S. 537 (1896). It was only as the era of substantive due process came to a close, see, e. g., *Nebbia v. New York*, 291 U.S. 502 (1934); *West Coast Hotel Co. v. Parrish*, 300 U.S. 379 (1937), that the Equal Protection Clause began to attain a genuine measure of vitality, see, e. g., *United States v. Carolene Products*, 304 U.S. 144 (1938); *Skinner v. Oklahoma ex rel. Williamson*.

By that time it was no longer possible to peg the guarantees of the Fourteenth Amendment to the struggle for equality of one racial minority. During the dormancy of the Equal Protection Clause, the United States had become a Nation of minorities. Each had to struggle—and to some extent struggles still—to overcome the prejudices not of a monolithic majority, but of a "majority" composed of various minority groups of whom it was said—perhaps unfairly in many cases—that a shared characteristic was a willingness to disadvantage other groups. As the Nation filled with the stock of many lands, the reach of the Clause was gradually extended to all ethnic groups seeking protection from official discrimination. See *Strauder v. West Virginia*, 100 U.S. 303 (1880) (Celtic Irishmen) (dictum); *Yick Wo v. Hopkins*, 118 U.S. 356 (1886) (Chinese); *Truax v. Raich*, 239 U.S. 33, 41 (1915) (Austrian resident aliens); *Korematsu*, (Japanese); *Hernandez v. Texas*, 347 U.S. 475 (1954) (Mexican-Americans). The guarantees of equal protection, said the Court in *Yick Wo*, "are universal in their application, to all persons within the territorial jurisdiction, without regard to any differences of race, of color, or of nationality; and the equal protection of the laws is a pledge of the protection of equal laws." 118 U.S., at 369.

Although many of the Framers of the Fourteenth Amendment conceived of its primary function as bridging the vast distance between members of the Negro race and the white "majority," *Slaughter-House Cases*, the Amendment itself was framed in universal terms, without reference to color, ethnic origin, or condition of prior servitude. As this Court recently remarked in interpreting the 1866 Civil Rights Act to extend to claims of racial discrimination against white persons, "the 39th Congress was intent upon establishing in the federal law a broader principle than would have been necessary simply to meet the particular and immediate plight of the newly freed Negro slaves." And that legislation was specifically broadened in 1870 to ensure that "all persons," not merely "citizens," would enjoy equal rights under the law. Indeed, it is not unlikely that among the Framers were many who would have applauded a reading of the Equal Protection Clause that states a principle of universal application and is responsive to the racial, ethnic, and cultural diversity of the Nation. See, e. g., . . . [Cong. Globe,] 40th Cong., 2d Sess., 883 (1868) (remarks of Sen. Howe) (Fourteenth Amendment "protect[s] classes from class legislation"). See also Bickel, The Original Understanding and the Segregation Decision, 69 Harv.L.Rev. 1, 60–63 (1955).

Over the past 30 years, this Court has embarked upon the crucial mission of interpreting the Equal Protection Clause with the view of assuring to all persons "the protection of equal laws," *Yick Wo*, 118 U.S., at 369, in a Nation confronting a legacy of slavery and racial discrimination. See, e. g., *Shelley v. Kraemer*, 334 U.S. 1 (1948); *Brown v. Board of Education*, 347 U.S. 483 (1954). Because the landmark decisions in this area arose in response to the continued exclusion of Negroes from the mainstream of American society, they could be characterized as involving discrimination by the "majority" white race against the Negro minority. But they need not be read as depending upon that characterization for their results. It suffices to say that "[o]ver the years, this Court has consistently repudiated '[d]istinctions between citizens solely because of their ancestry' as being 'odious to a free people whose institutions are founded upon the doctrine of equality.'" *Loving v. Virginia*, 388 U.S. 1, 11 (1967), quoting *Hirabayashi*, 320 U.S., at 100.

Petitioner urges us to adopt for the first time a more restrictive view of the Equal Protection Clause and hold that discrimination against members of the white "majority" cannot be suspect if its purpose can be characterized as "benign." The clock of our liberties, however, cannot be turned back to 1868. *Brown v. Board of Education*, 347 U.S., at 492; accord, *Loving v. Virginia*, 388 U.S., at 9. It is far too late to argue that the guarantee of equal protection to all persons permits the recognition of special wards entitled to a degree of protection greater than that accorded others. "The Fourteenth Amendment is not directed solely against discrimination due to a 'two-class theory'—that is, based upon differences between 'white' and Negro." *Hernandez*, 347 U.S., at 478.

Once the artificial line of a "two-class theory" of the Fourteenth Amendment is put aside, the difficulties entailed in varying the level of judicial review according to a perceived "preferred" status of a particular racial or ethnic minority are intractable. The concepts of "majority" and "minority" necessarily reflect temporary arrangements and political judgments. As observed above, the white "majority" itself is composed of various minority groups, most of which can lay claim to a history of prior discrimination at the hands of the State and private individuals. Not all of these groups can receive preferential treatment and corresponding judicial tolerance of distinctions drawn in terms of race and nationality, for then the only "majority" left would be a new minority of white Anglo-Saxon Protestants. There is no principled basis for deciding which groups would merit "heightened judicial solicitude" and which would not.[36] Courts would

---

36. As I am in agreement with the view that race may be taken into account as a factor in an admissions program, I agree with my Brothers Brennan, White, Marshall, and

be asked to evaluate the extent of the prejudice and consequent harm suffered by various minority groups. Those whose societal injury is thought to exceed some arbitrary level of tolerability then would be entitled to preferential classifications at the expense of individuals belonging to other groups. Those classifications would be free from exacting judicial scrutiny. As these preferences began to have their desired effect, and the consequences of past discrimination were undone, new judicial rankings would be necessary. The kind of variable sociological and political analysis necessary to produce such rankings simply does not lie within the judicial competence—even if they otherwise were politically feasible and socially desirable.[37]

Blackmun that the portion of the judgment that would proscribe all consideration of race must be reversed. See Part V, infra. But I disagree with much that is said in their opinion. They would require as a justification for a program such as petitioner's, only two findings: (i) that there has been some form of discrimination against the preferred minority groups by "society at large," and (ii) that "there is reason to believe" that the disparate impact sought to be rectified by the program is the "product" of such discrimination:

"If it was reasonable to conclude—as we hold that it was—that the failure of minorities to qualify for admission at Davis under regular procedures was due principally to the effects of past discrimination, then there is a reasonable likelihood that, but for pervasive racial discrimination, respondent would have failed to qualify for admission even in the absence of Davis' special admissions program." Post.

The breadth of this hypothesis is unprecedented in our constitutional system. The first step is easily taken. No one denies the regrettable fact that there has been societal discrimination in this country against various racial and ethnic groups. The second step, however, involves a speculative leap: but for this discrimination by society at large, Bakke "would have failed to qualify for admission" because Negro applicants—nothing is said about Asians, cf., e. g., post, at n. 57—would have made better scores. Not one word in the record supports this conclusion, and the authors of the opinion offer no standard for courts to use in applying such a presumption of causation to other racial or ethnic classifications. This failure is a grave one, since if it may be concluded on this record that each of the minority groups preferred by the peti-

tioner's special program is entitled to the benefit of the presumption, it would seem difficult to determine that any of the dozens of minority groups that have suffered "societal discrimination" cannot also claim it, in any area of social intercourse. See Part IV-B, infra.

37. Mr. Justice Douglas has noted the problems associated with such inquiries:

"The reservation of a proportion of the law school class for members of selected minority groups is fraught with ... dangers, for one must immediately determine which groups are to receive such favored treatment and which are to be excluded, the proportions of the class that are to be allocated to each, and even the criteria by which to determine whether an individual is a member of a favored group. [Cf. Plessy v. Ferguson, 163 U.S. 537, 549, 552 (1896).] There is no assurance that a common agreement can be reached, and first the schools, and then the courts, will be buffeted with the competing claims. The University of Washington included Filipinos, but excluded Chinese and Japanese; another school may limit its program to blacks, or to blacks and Chicanos. Once the Court sanctioned racial preferences such as these, it could not then wash its hands of the matter, leaving it entirely in the discretion of the school, for then we would have effectively overruled Sweatt v. Painter, 339 U.S. 629, and allowed imposition of a 'zero' allocation. But what standard is the Court to apply when a rejected applicant of Japanese ancestry brings suit to require the University of Washington to extend the same privileges to his group? The Committee might conclude that the population of

Moreover, there are serious problems of justice connected with the idea of preference itself. First, it may not always be clear that a so-called preference is in fact benign. Courts may be asked to validate burdens imposed upon individual members of a particular group in order to advance the group's general interest. See *United Jewish Organizations v. Carey*, 430 U.S., at 172–173 (Brennan, J., concurring in part). Nothing in the Constitution supports the notion that individuals may be asked to suffer otherwise impermissible burdens in order to enhance the societal standing of their ethnic groups. Second, preferential programs may only reinforce common stereotypes holding that certain groups are unable to achieve success without special protection based on a factor having no relationship to individual worth. Third, there is a measure of inequity in forcing innocent persons in respondent's position to bear the burdens of redressing grievances not of their making.

By hitching the meaning of the Equal Protection Clause to these transitory considerations, we would be holding, as a constitutional principle, that judicial scrutiny of classifications touching on racial and ethnic background may vary with the ebb and flow of political forces. Disparate constitutional tolerance of such classifications well may serve to exacerbate racial and ethnic antagonisms rather than alleviate them. Also, the mutability of a constitutional principle, based upon shifting political and social judgments, undermines the chances for consistent application of the Constitution from one generation to the next, a critical feature of its coherent interpretation. In expounding the Constitution, the Court's role is to discern "principles sufficiently absolute to give them roots throughout the community and continuity over significant periods of time, and to lift them above the level of the pragmatic political judgments of a particular time and place." A. Cox, The Role of the Supreme Court in American Government 114 (1976).

If it is the individual who is entitled to judicial protection against classifications based upon his racial or ethnic background because such distinctions impinge upon personal rights, rather than the individual only

Washington is now 2% Japanese, and that Japanese also constitute 2% of the Bar, but that had they not been handicapped by a history of discrimination, Japanese would now constitute 5% of the Bar, or 20%. Or, alternatively, the Court could attempt to assess how grievously each group has suffered from discrimination, and allocate proportions accordingly; if that were the standard the current University of Washington policy would almost surely fall, for there is no Western State which can claim that it has always treated Japanese and Chinese in a fair and evenhanded manner. See, e. g., Yick Wo v. Hopkins, 118 U.S. 356; Terrace v. Thompson, 263 U.S. 197; Oyama v. California, 332 U.S. 633. This Court has not sustained a racial classification since the wartime cases of Korematsu v. United States, 323 U.S. 214, and Hirabayashi v. United States, 320 U.S. 81, involving curfews and relocations imposed upon Japanese-Americans.

"Nor obviously will the problem be solved if next year the Law School included only Japanese and Chinese, for then Norwegians and Swedes, Poles and Italians, Puerto Ricans and Hungarians, and all other groups which form this diverse Nation would have just complaints." DeFunis v. Odegaard, 416 U.S. 312, 337–340 (1974) (dissenting opinion) (footnotes omitted).

because of his membership in a particular group, then constitutional standards may be applied consistently. Political judgments regarding the necessity for the particular classification may be weighed in the constitutional balance, *Korematsu v. United States*, 323 U.S. 214 (1944), but the standard of justification will remain constant. This is as it should be, since those political judgments are the product of rough compromise struck by contending groups within the democratic process. When they touch upon an individual's race or ethnic background, he is entitled to a judicial determination that the burden he is asked to bear on that basis is precisely tailored to serve a compelling governmental interest. The Constitution guarantees that right to every person regardless of his background. *Shelley v. Kraemer*, 334 U.S., at 22; *Missouri ex rel. Gaines v. Canada*, 305 U.S., at 351.

C

Petitioner contends that on several occasions this Court has approved preferential classifications without applying the most exacting scrutiny. Most of the cases upon which petitioner relies are drawn from three areas: school desegregation, employment discrimination, and sex discrimination. Each of the cases cited presented a situation materially different from the facts of this case.

The school desegregation cases are inapposite. Each involved remedies for clearly determined constitutional violations. Racial classifications thus were designed as remedies for the vindication of constitutional entitlement. Moreover, the scope of the remedies was not permitted to exceed the extent of the violations. Here, there was no judicial determination of constitutional violation as a predicate for the formulation of a remedial classification.

The employment discrimination cases also do not advance petitioner's cause. For example, in *Franks v. Bowman Transportation Co.*, 424 U.S. 747 (1976), we approved a retroactive award of seniority to a class of Negro truckdrivers who had been the victims of discrimination—not just by society at large, but by the respondent in that case.... [W]e have never approved preferential classifications in the absence of proved constitutional or statutory violations.

Nor is petitioner's view as to the applicable standard supported by the fact that gender-based classifications are not subjected to this level of scrutiny. Gender-based distinctions are less likely to create the analytical and practical problems present in preferential programs premised on racial or ethnic criteria. With respect to gender there are only two possible classifications. The incidence of the burdens imposed by preferential classifications is clear. There are no rival groups which can claim that they, too, are entitled to preferential treatment. Classwide questions as to the group suffering previous injury and groups which fairly can be burdened are relatively manageable for reviewing courts. The resolution of these same questions in the context of racial and ethnic preferences presents far more complex and intractable problems than gender-based classifications. More importantly, the perception of racial classifications as inherently odious stems from a lengthy and tragic history that gender-based classifications do not share. In sum, the Court has never viewed such classification as inherently suspect or as comparable to racial or ethnic classifications for the purpose of equal protection analysis.

Petitioner also cites *Lau v. Nichols*, 414 U.S. 563 (1974), in support of the proposition that discrimination favoring racial or ethnic minorities has received judicial approval without the exacting inquiry ordinarily accorded "suspect" classifications. In *Lau*, we held that the failure of the San Francisco school system to provide remedial English instruction for some 1,800 students of oriental ancestry who spoke no English amounted to a violation of Title VI of the Civil Rights Act of 1964, 42 U.S.C. § 2000d, and the regulations promulgated thereunder. Those regulations required remedial instruction where inability to understand English excluded children of foreign ancestry from participation in educational programs. 414 U.S., at 568. Because we found that the students in *Lau* were denied "a meaningful opportunity to participate in the educational program," we remanded for the fashioning of a remedial order.

Lau provides little support for petitioner's argument. The decision rested solely on the statute, which had been construed by the responsible administrative agency to reach educational practices "which have the effect of subjecting individuals to discrimination." We stated: "Under these state-imposed standards there is no equality of treatment merely by providing students with the same facilities, textbooks, teachers, and curriculum; for students who do not understand English are effectively foreclosed from any meaningful education." Moreover, the "preference" approved did not result in the denial of the relevant benefit—"meaningful opportunity to participate in the educational program"—to anyone else. No other student was deprived by that preference of the ability to participate in San Francisco's school system, and the applicable regulations required similar assistance for all students who suffered similar linguistic deficiencies. Id., at 570–571 (Stewart, J., concurring in result).

In a similar vein,[42] petitioner contends that our recent decision in *United Jewish Organizations v. Carey*, 430 U.S. 144 (1977), indicates a willingness to approve racial classifications designed to benefit certain minorities, without denominating the classifications as "suspect." The State of New York had redrawn its reapportionment plan to meet objections of the Department of Justice under § 5 of the Voting Rights Act of 1965, 42 U.S.C. § 1973c (1970 ed., Supp. V). Specifically, voting districts were redrawn to enhance the electoral power of certain "nonwhite" voters

---

42. Petitioner also cites our decision in Morton v. Mancari, 417 U.S. 535 (1974), for the proposition that the State may prefer members of traditionally disadvantaged groups. In *Mancari*, we approved a hiring preference for qualified Indians in the Bureau of Indian Affairs of the Department of the Interior (BIA). We observed in that case, however, that the legal status of the BIA is sui generis. Indeed, we found that the preference was not racial at all, but "an employment criterion reasonably designed to further the cause of Indian self-government and to make the BIA more responsive to the needs of its constituent ... groups ... whose lives and activities are governed by the BIA in a unique fashion."

found to have been the victims of unlawful "dilution" under the original reapportionment plan. *United Jewish Organizations*, like *Lau*, properly is viewed as a case in which the remedy for an administrative finding of discrimination encompassed measures to improve the previously disadvantaged group's ability to participate, without excluding individuals belonging to any other group from enjoyment of the relevant opportunity—meaningful participation in the electoral process.

In this case, unlike *Lau* and *United Jewish Organizations*, there has been no determination by the legislature or a responsible administrative agency that the University engaged in a discriminatory practice requiring remedial efforts. Moreover, the operation of petitioner's special admissions program is quite different from the remedial measures approved in those cases. It prefers the designated minority groups at the expense of other individuals who are totally foreclosed from competition for the 16 special admissions seats in every Medical School class. Because of that foreclosure, some individuals are excluded from enjoyment of a state-provided benefit—admission to the Medical School—they otherwise would receive. When a classification denies an individual opportunities or benefits enjoyed by others solely because of his race or ethnic background, it must be regarded as suspect. E. g., *McLaurin v. Oklahoma State Regents*, 339 U.S., at 641–642.

IV

We have held that in "order to justify the use of a suspect classification, a State must show that its purpose or interest is both constitutionally permissible and substantial, and that its use of the classification is 'necessary . . . to the accomplishment' of its purpose or the safeguarding of its interest." The special admissions program purports to serve the purposes of: (i) "reducing the historic deficit of traditionally disfavored minorities in medical schools and in the medical profession," Brief for Petitioner 32; (ii) countering the effects of societal discrimination;[43] (iii) increasing the num-

---

43. A number of distinct subgoals have been advanced as falling under the rubric of "compensation for past discrimination." For example, it is said that preferences for Negro applicants may compensate for harm done them personally, or serve to place them at economic levels they might have attained but for discrimination against their forebears. Another view of the "compensation" goal is that it serves as a form of reparation by the "majority" to a victimized group as a whole. That justification for racial or ethnic preference has been subjected to much criticism. Finally, it has been argued that ethnic preferences "compensate" the group by providing examples of success whom other members of the group will emulate, thereby advancing the group's interest and society's interest in encouraging new generations to overcome the barriers and frustrations of the past. For purposes of analysis these subgoals need not be considered separately. Racial classifications in admissions conceivably could serve a fifth purpose, one which petitioner does not articulate: fair appraisal of each individual's academic promise in the light of some cultural bias in grading or testing procedures. To the extent that race and ethnic background were considered only to the extent of curing established inaccuracies in predicting academic performance, it might be argued that there is no "preference" at all. Nothing in this record, however, suggests either that any of the quantitative factors considered by the Medical School were culturally biased or that petitioner's special admissions program was formulated to correct for any such biases.

ber of physicians who will practice in communities currently underserved; and (iv) obtaining the educational benefits that flow from an ethnically diverse student body. It is necessary to decide which, if any, of these purposes is substantial enough to support the use of a suspect classification.

A

If petitioner's purpose is to assure within its student body some specified percentage of a particular group merely because of its race or ethnic origin, such a preferential purpose must be rejected not as insubstantial but as facially invalid. Preferring members of any one group for no reason other than race or ethnic origin is discrimination for its own sake. This the Constitution forbids. E. g., *Loving v. Virginia*, 388 U.S., at 11.

B

The State certainly has a legitimate and substantial interest in ameliorating, or eliminating where feasible, the disabling effects of identified discrimination. The line of school desegregation cases, commencing with *Brown*, attests to the importance of this state goal and the commitment of the judiciary to affirm all lawful means toward its attainment. In the school cases, the States were required by court order to redress the wrongs worked by specific instances of racial discrimination. That goal was far more focused than the remedying of the effects of "societal discrimination," an amorphous concept of injury that may be ageless in its reach into the past.

We have never approved a classification that aids persons perceived as members of relatively victimized groups at the expense of other innocent individuals in the absence of judicial, legislative, or administrative findings of constitutional or statutory violations. After such findings have been made, the governmental interest in preferring members of the injured groups at the expense of others is substantial, since the legal rights of the victims must be vindicated. In such a case, the extent of the injury and the consequent remedy will have been judicially, legislatively, or administratively defined. Also, the remedial action usually remains subject to continuing oversight to assure that it will work the least harm possible to other innocent persons competing for the benefit. Without such findings of constitutional or statutory violations, it cannot be said that the government has any greater interest in helping one individual than in refraining from harming another. Thus, the government has no compelling justification for inflicting such harm.

Petitioner does not purport to have made, and is in no position to make, such findings. Its broad mission is education, not the formulation of any legislative policy or the adjudication of particular claims of illegality. For reasons similar to those stated in Part III of this opinion, isolated

---

Furthermore, if race or ethnic background were used solely to arrive at an unbiased prediction of academic success, the reserva-tion of fixed numbers of seats would be inexplicable.

segments of our vast governmental structures are not competent to make those decisions, at least in the absence of legislative mandates and legislatively determined criteria.[45] Before relying upon these sorts of findings in establishing a racial classification, a governmental body must have the authority and capability to establish, in the record, that the classification is responsive to identified discrimination. . . .

Hence, the purpose of helping certain groups whom the faculty of the Davis Medical School perceived as victims of "societal discrimination" does not justify a classification that imposes disadvantages upon persons like respondent, who bear no responsibility for whatever harm the beneficiaries of the special admissions program are thought to have suffered. To hold otherwise would be to convert a remedy heretofore reserved for violations of legal rights into a privilege that all institutions throughout the Nation could grant at their pleasure to whatever groups are perceived as victims of societal discrimination. That is a step we have never approved.

C

Petitioner identifies, as another purpose of its program, improving the delivery of health-care services to communities currently underserved. It may be assumed that in some situations a State's interest in facilitating the health care of its citizens is sufficiently compelling to support the use of a suspect classification. But there is virtually no evidence in the record indicating that petitioner's special admissions program is either needed or geared to promote that goal. The court below addressed this failure of proof:

> "The University concedes it cannot assure that minority doctors who entered under the program, all of whom expressed an 'interest' in practicing in a disadvantaged community, will actually do so. . . . [T]here are more precise and reliable ways to identify applicants who are genuinely interested in the medical problems of minorities than by race. An applicant of whatever race who has demonstrated his concern for disadvantaged minorities in the past and who declares that practice in such a community is his primary professional goal would be more likely to contribute to alleviation of the medical shortage than one who is chosen entirely on the basis of race and disadvantage . . . ."[47]

45. For example, the University is unable to explain its selection of only the four favored groups—Negroes, Mexican-Americans, American-Indians, and Asians—for preferential treatment. The inclusion of the last group is especially curious in light of the substantial numbers of Asians admitted through the regular admissions process. See also n. 37, supra.

47. It is not clear that petitioner's two-track system, even if adopted throughout the country, would substantially increase representation of blacks in the medical profession.

That is the finding of a recent study by Sleeth & Mishell, Black Under-Representation in United States Medical Schools, 297 New England J. of Med. 1146 (1977). Those authors maintain that the cause of black underrepresentation lies in the small size of the national pool of qualified black applicants. In their view, this problem is traceable to the poor premedical experiences of black undergraduates, and can be remedied effectively only by developing remedial programs for black students before they enter college.

D

The fourth goal asserted by petitioner is the attainment of a diverse student body. This clearly is a constitutionally permissible goal for an institution of higher education. Academic freedom, though not a specifically enumerated constitutional right, long has been viewed as a special concern of the First Amendment. The freedom of a university to make its own judgments as to education includes the selection of its student body. Mr. Justice Frankfurter summarized the "four essential freedoms" that constitute academic freedom:

> "It is the business of a university to provide that atmosphere which is most conducive to speculation, experiment and creation. It is an atmosphere in which there prevail 'the four essential freedoms' of a university—to determine for itself on academic grounds who may teach, what may be taught, how it shall be taught, and who may be admitted to study." *Sweezy v. New Hampshire*, 354 U.S. 234, 263 (1957) (concurring in result).

Our national commitment to the safeguarding of these freedoms within university communities was emphasized in *Keyishian v. Board of Regents*, 385 U.S. 589, 603 (1967):

> "Our Nation is deeply committed to safeguarding academic freedom which is of transcendent value to all of us and not merely to the teachers concerned. That freedom is therefore a special concern of the First Amendment .... The Nation's future depends upon leaders trained through wide exposure to that robust exchange of ideas which discovers truth 'out of a multitude of tongues, [rather] than through any kind of authoritative selection.' *United States v. Associated Press*, D.C., 52 F.Supp. 362, 372."

The atmosphere of "speculation, experiment and creation"—so essential to the quality of higher education—is widely believed to be promoted by a diverse student body.[48] As the Court noted in *Keyishian*, it is not too much to say that the "nation's future depends upon leaders trained

---

48. The president of Princeton University has described some of the benefits derived from a diverse student body:

"[A] great deal of learning occurs informally. It occurs through interactions among students of both sexes; of different races, religions, and backgrounds; who come from cities and rural areas, from various states and countries; who have a wide variety of interests, talents, and perspectives; and who are able, directly or indirectly, to learn from their differences and to stimulate one another to reexamine even their most deeply held assumptions about themselves and their world. As a wise graduate of ours observed in commenting on this aspect of the educational process, 'People do not learn very much when they are surrounded only by the likes of themselves.'

"In the nature of things, it is hard to know how, and when, and even if, this informal 'learning through diversity' actually occurs. It does not occur for everyone. For many, however, the unplanned, casual encounters with roommates, fellow sufferers in an organic chemistry class, student workers in the library, teammates on a basketball squad, or other participants in class affairs or student government can be subtle and yet powerful sources of improved understanding and personal growth." Bowen, Admissions and the Relevance of Race, Princeton Alumni Weekly 7, 9 (Sept. 26, 1977).

through wide exposure" to the ideas and mores of students as diverse as this Nation of many peoples.

Thus, in arguing that its universities must be accorded the right to select those students who will contribute the most to the "robust exchange of ideas," petitioner invokes a countervailing constitutional interest, that of the First Amendment. In this light, petitioner must be viewed as seeking to achieve a goal that is of paramount importance in the fulfillment of its mission.

It may be argued that there is greater force to these views at the undergraduate level than in a medical school where the training is centered primarily on professional competency. But even at the graduate level, our tradition and experience lend support to the view that the contribution of diversity is substantial. In *Sweatt v. Painter*, 339 U.S., at 634, the Court made a similar point with specific reference to legal education:

> "The law school, the proving ground for legal learning and practice, cannot be effective in isolation from the individuals and institutions with which the law interacts. Few students and no one who has practiced law would choose to study in an academic vacuum, removed from the interplay of ideas and the exchange of views with which the law is concerned."

Physicians serve a heterogeneous population. An otherwise qualified medical student with a particular background—whether it be ethnic, geographic, culturally advantaged or disadvantaged—may bring to a professional school of medicine experiences, outlooks, and ideas that enrich the training of its student body and better equip its graduates to render with understanding their vital service to humanity.

Ethnic diversity, however, is only one element in a range of factors a university properly may consider in attaining the goal of a heterogeneous student body. Although a university must have wide discretion in making the sensitive judgments as to who should be admitted, constitutional limitations protecting individual rights may not be disregarded.... [T]he question remains whether the program's racial classification is necessary to promote this interest. *In re Griffiths*, 413 U.S., at 721–722.

V

A

It may be assumed that the reservation of a specified number of seats in each class for individuals from the preferred ethnic groups would contribute to the attainment of considerable ethnic diversity in the student body. But petitioner's argument that this is the only effective means of serving the interest of diversity is seriously flawed. In a most fundamental sense the argument misconceives the nature of the state interest that would justify consideration of race or ethnic background. It is not an interest in simple ethnic diversity, in which a specified percentage of the student body is in effect guaranteed to be members of selected ethnic groups, with the remaining percentage an undifferentiated aggregation of students. The diversity that furthers a compelling state interest encompasses a far broader array of qualifications and characteristics of which racial or ethnic origin is but a single though important element. Petitioner's special admissions program, focused solely on ethnic diversity, would hinder rather than further attainment of genuine diversity.

Nor would the state interest in genuine diversity be served by expanding petitioner's two-track system into a multitrack program with a prescribed number of seats set aside for each identifiable category of applicants. Indeed, it is inconceivable that a university would thus pursue the logic of petitioner's two-track program to the illogical end of insulating each category of applicants with certain desired qualifications from competition with all other applicants.

The experience of other university admissions programs, which take race into account in achieving the educational diversity valued by the First Amendment, demonstrates that the assignment of a fixed number of places to a minority group is not a necessary means toward that end. An illuminating example is found in the Harvard College program:

"In recent years Harvard College has expanded the concept of diversity to include students from disadvantaged economic, racial and ethnic groups. Harvard College now recruits not only Californians or Louisianans but also blacks and Chicanos and other minority students. . . .

"In practice, this new definition of diversity has meant that race has been a factor in some admission decisions. When the Committee on Admissions reviews the large middle group of applicants who are 'admissible' and deemed capable of doing good work in their courses, the race of an applicant may tip the balance in his favor just as geographic origin or a life spent on a farm may tip the balance in other candidates' cases. A farm boy from Idaho can bring something to Harvard College that a Bostonian cannot offer. Similarly, a black student can usually bring something that a white person cannot offer. [See Appendix hereto.] . . .

"In Harvard College admissions the Committee has not set target-quotas for the number of blacks, or of musicians, football players, physicists or Californians to be admitted in a given year. . . . [A]wareness [of the necessity of including more than a token number of black students] does not mean that the Committee sets a minimum number of blacks or of people from west of the Mississippi who are to be admitted. It means only that in choosing among thousands of applicants who are not only 'admissible' academically but have other strong qualities, the Committee, with a number of criteria in mind, pays some attention to distribution among many types and categories of students." App. to Brief for Columbia University, Harvard University, Stanford University, and the University of Pennsylvania, as Amici Curiae 2–3.

In such an admissions program, race or ethnic background may be deemed a "plus" in a particular applicant's file, yet it does not insulate the individual from comparison with all other candidates for the available seats. The file of a particular black applicant may be examined for his potential contribution to diversity without the factor of race being decisive when compared, for example, with that of an applicant identified as an Italian-American if the latter is thought to exhibit qualities more likely to promote beneficial educational pluralism. Such qualities could include exceptional personal talents, unique work or service experience, leadership potential, maturity, demonstrated compassion, a history of overcoming disadvantage, ability to communicate with the poor, or other qualifications deemed important. In short, an admissions program operated in this way is flexible enough to consider all pertinent elements of diversity in light of the particular qualifications of each applicant, and to place them on the same footing for consideration, although not necessarily according them the same weight. Indeed, the weight attributed to a particular quality may vary from year to year depending upon the "mix" both of the student body and the applicants for the incoming class.

This kind of program treats each applicant as an individual in the admissions process. The applicant who loses out on the last available seat to another candidate receiving a "plus" on the basis of ethnic background will not have been foreclosed from all consideration for that seat simply because he was not the right color or had the wrong surname. It would mean only that his combined qualifications, which may have included similar nonobjective factors, did not outweigh those of the other applicant. His qualifications would have been weighed fairly and competitively, and he would have no basis to complain of unequal treatment under the Fourteenth Amendment.[52]

It has been suggested that an admissions program which considers race only as one factor is simply a subtle and more sophisticated—but no less effective—means of according racial preference than the Davis program. A facial intent to discriminate, however, is evident in petitioner's preference program and not denied in this case. No such facial infirmity exists in an admissions program where race or ethnic background is simply one element—to be weighed fairly against other elements—in the selection process. "A boundary line," as Mr. Justice Frankfurter remarked in another connection, "is none the worse for being narrow." And a court would not assume that a university, professing to employ a facially nondiscriminatory admissions policy, would operate it as a cover for the functional equivalent of a quota system. In short, good faith would be presumed in the absence of a showing to the contrary in the manner permitted by our cases.[53]

52. The denial to respondent of this right to individualized consideration without regard to his race is the principal evil of petitioner's special admissions program. Nowhere in the opinion of Mr. Justice Brennan, Mr. Justice White, Mr. Justice Marshall, and Mr. Justice Blackmun is this denial even addressed.

53. Universities, like the prosecutor in Swain [v. Alabama, 380 U.S. 202 (1965), upholding prosecutor's use of race-based peremptory challenges, overruled in Batson v.

B

In summary, it is evident that the Davis special admissions program involves the use of an explicit racial classification never before countenanced by this Court. It tells applicants who are not Negro, Asian, or Chicano that they are totally excluded from a specific percentage of the seats in an entering class. No matter how strong their qualifications, quantitative and extracurricular, including their own potential for contribution to educational diversity, they are never afforded the chance to compete with applicants from the preferred groups for the special admissions seats. At the same time, the preferred applicants have the opportunity to compete for every seat in the class.

The fatal flaw in petitioner's preferential program is its disregard of individual rights as guaranteed by the Fourteenth Amendment. Such rights are not absolute. But when a State's distribution of benefits or imposition of burdens hinges on ancestry or the color of a person's skin, that individual is entitled to a demonstration that the challenged classification is necessary to promote a substantial state interest. Petitioner has failed to carry this burden. For this reason, that portion of the California court's judgment holding petitioner's special admissions program invalid under the Fourteenth Amendment must be affirmed.

C

In enjoining petitioner from ever considering the race of any applicant, however, the courts below failed to recognize that the State has a substantial interest that legitimately may be served by a properly devised admissions program involving the competitive consideration of race and ethnic origin. For this reason, so much of the California court's judgment as enjoins petitioner from any consideration of the race of any applicant must be reversed....

Opinion of Mr. Justice Brennan, Mr. Justice White, Mr. Justice Marshall, and Mr. Justice Blackmun, concurring in the judgment in part and dissenting in part.

Kentucky, 476 U.S. 79 (1986)], may make individualized decisions, in which ethnic background plays a part, under a presumption of legality and legitimate educational purpose. So long as the university proceeds on an individualized, case-by-case basis, there is no warrant for judicial interference in the academic process. If an applicant can establish that the institution does not adhere to a policy of individual comparisons, or can show that a systematic exclusion of certain groups results, the presumption of legality might be overcome, creating the necessity of proving legitimate educational purpose.

There also are strong policy reasons that correspond to the constitutional distinction between petitioner's preference program and one that assures a measure of competition among all applicants. Petitioner's program will be viewed as inherently unfair by the public generally as well as by applicants for admission to state universities. Fairness in individual competition for opportunities, especially those provided by the State, is a widely cherished American ethic. Indeed, in a broader sense, an underlying assumption of the rule of law is the worthiness of a system of justice based on fairness to the individual. As Mr. Justice Frankfurter declared in another connection, "[j]ustice must satisfy the appearance of justice." Offutt v. United States, 348 U.S. 11, 14 (1954).

The Court today, in reversing in part the judgment of the Supreme Court of California, affirms the constitutional power of Federal and State Governments to act affirmatively to achieve equal opportunity for all. The difficulty of the issue presented—whether government may use race-conscious programs to redress the continuing effects of past discrimination—and the mature consideration which each of our Brethren has brought to it have resulted in many opinions, no single one speaking for the Court. But this should not and must not mask the central meaning of today's opinions: Government may take race into account when it acts not to demean or insult any racial group, but to remedy disadvantages cast on minorities by past racial prejudice, at least when appropriate findings have been made by judicial, legislative, or administrative bodies with competence to act in this area. . . .

I

Our Nation was founded on the principle that "all Men are created equal." Yet candor requires acknowledgment that the Framers of our Constitution, to forge the 13 Colonies into one Nation, openly compromised this principle of equality with its antithesis: slavery. The consequences of this compromise are well known and have aptly been called our "American Dilemma." Still, it is well to recount how recent the time has been, if it has yet come, when the promise of our principles has flowered into the actuality of equal opportunity for all regardless of race or color.

The Fourteenth Amendment, the embodiment in the Constitution of our abiding belief in human equality, has been the law of our land for only slightly more than half its 200 years. And for half of that half, the Equal Protection Clause of the Amendment was largely moribund so that, as late as 1927, Mr. Justice Holmes could sum up the importance of that Clause by remarking that it was the "last resort of constitutional arguments." *Buck v. Bell*, 274 U.S. 200, 208 (1927). Worse than desuetude, the Clause was early turned against those whom it was intended to set free, condemning them to a "separate but equal"[2] status before the law, a status always separate but seldom equal. Not until 1954—only 24 years ago—was this odious doctrine interred by our decision in Brown v. Board of Education, 347 U.S. 483 (*Brown I*), and its progeny, which proclaimed that separate schools and public facilities of all sorts were inherently unequal and forbidden under our Constitution. Even then inequality was not eliminated with "all deliberate speed." *Brown v. Board of Education*, 349 U.S. 294, 301 (1955). In 1968 and again in 1971, for example, we were forced to remind school boards of their obligation to eliminate racial discrimination root and branch. And a glance at our docket and at dockets of lower courts will show that even today officially sanctioned discrimination is not a thing of the past.

Against this background, claims that law must be "color-blind" or that the datum of race is no longer relevant to public policy must be seen as aspiration rather than as description of reality. . . . [W]e cannot . . . let

---

2. See *Plessy v. Ferguson*, 163 U.S. 537 (1896).

color blindness become myopia which masks the reality that many "created equal" have been treated within our lifetimes as inferior both by the law and by their fellow citizens. . . .

III

A

The assertion of human equality is closely associated with the proposition that differences in color or creed, birth or status, are neither significant nor relevant to the way in which persons should be treated. Nonetheless, the position that such factors must be "constitutionally an irrelevance," *Edwards v. California*, 314 U.S. 160 (1941) (Jackson, J., concurring), summed up by the shorthand phrase "[o]ur Constitution is color-blind," *Plessy v. Ferguson*, 163 U.S. 537 (1896) (Harlan, J., dissenting), has never been adopted by this Court as the proper meaning of the Equal Protection Clause. Indeed, we have expressly rejected this proposition on a number of occasions.

Our cases have always implied that an "overriding statutory purpose," *McLaughlin v. Florida*, 379 U.S. 184, 192 (1964), could be found that would justify racial classifications. See, e. g., ibid.; *Loving v. Virginia*, 388 U.S. 1, 11 (1967); *Korematsu v. United States*, 323 U.S. 214 (1944); *Hirabayashi v. United States*, 320 U.S. 81, 100–101 (1943). More recently, in *McDaniel v. Barresi*, 402 U.S. 39 (1971), this Court unanimously reversed the Georgia Supreme Court which had held that a desegregation plan voluntarily adopted by a local school board, which assigned students on the basis of race, was per se invalid because it was not color-blind. And in *North Carolina Board of Education v. Swann* we held, again unanimously, that a statute mandating color-blind school-assignment plans could not stand "against the background of segregation," since such a limit on remedies would "render illusory the promise of *Brown* [I]." 402 U.S., at 45–46.

We conclude, therefore, that racial classifications are not per se invalid under the Fourteenth Amendment. Accordingly, we turn to the problem of articulating what our role should be in reviewing state action that expressly classifies by race.

B

Respondent argues that racial classifications are always suspect and, consequently, that this Court should weigh the importance of the objectives served by Davis' special admissions program to see if they are compelling. In addition, he asserts that this Court must inquire whether, in its judgment, there are alternatives to racial classifications which would suit Davis' purposes. Petitioner, on the other hand, states that our proper role is simply to accept petitioner's determination that the racial classifications used by its program are reasonably related to what it tells us are its benign purposes. We reject petitioner's view, but, because our prior cases are in many respects inapposite to that before us now, we find it necessary to define with precision the meaning of that inexact term, "strict scrutiny."

Unquestionably we have held that a government practice or statute which restricts "fundamental rights" or which contains "suspect classifications" is to be subjected to "strict scrutiny" and can be justified only if it furthers a compelling government purpose and, even then, only if no less restrictive alternative is available. But no fundamental right is involved here. Nor do whites as a class have any of the "traditional indicia of suspectness: the class is not saddled with such disabilities, or subjected to such a history of purposeful unequal treatment, or relegated to such a position of political powerlessness as to command extraordinary protection from the majoritarian political process." [S]ee *United States v. Carolene Products Co.*, 304 U.S. 144, 152 n. 4 (1938).[31]

Moreover, if the University's representations are credited, this is not a case where racial classifications are "irrelevant and therefore prohibited." *Hirabayashi*, supra, 320 U.S., at 100. Nor has anyone suggested that the University's purposes contravene the cardinal principle that racial classifications that stigmatize—because they are drawn on the presumption that one race is inferior to another or because they put the weight of government behind racial hatred and separatism—are invalid without more. See *Yick Wo v. Hopkins*, 118 U.S. 356, 374 (1886).

On the other hand, the fact that this case does not fit neatly into our prior analytic framework for race cases does not mean that it should be analyzed by applying the very loose rational-basis standard of review that is the very least that is always applied in equal protection cases. "[T]he mere recitation of a benign, compensatory purpose is not an automatic shield which protects against any inquiry into the actual purposes underlying a statutory scheme." [Weinberger v. Weisenfeld, 420 U.S. 636, 648 (1975)] Instead, a number of considerations—developed in gender-discrimination cases but which carry even more force when applied to racial classifications—lead us to conclude that racial classifications designed to further remedial purposes "must serve important governmental objectives and must be substantially related to achievement of those objectives."[35] Craig v. Boren, 429 U.S. 190, 197 (1976).

---

31. Of course, the fact that whites constitute a political majority in our Nation does not necessarily mean that active judicial scrutiny of racial classifications that disadvantage whites is inappropriate.

35. We disagree with our Brother Powell's suggestion, that the presence of "rival groups which can claim that they, too, are entitled to preferential treatment" distinguishes the gender cases or is relevant to the question of scope of judicial review of race classifications....

[W]ere we asked to decide whether any given rival group—German-Americans for example—must constitutionally be accorded preferential treatment, we do have a "principled basis," for deciding this question, one

that is well established in our cases: The Davis program expressly sets out four classes which receive preferred status. The program clearly distinguishes whites, but one cannot reason from this a conclusion that German-Americans, as a national group, are singled out for invidious treatment. And even if the Davis program had a differential impact on German-Americans, they would have no constitutional claim unless they could prove that Davis intended invidiously to discriminate against German-Americans. See *Arlington Heights v. Metropolitan Housing Dev. Corp.*, 429 U.S. 252, 264–265. If this could not be shown, then "the principle that calls for the closest scrutiny of distinctions in laws denying fundamental rights ... is inapplicable,"

First, race, like, "gender-based classifications too often [has] been inexcusably utilized to stereotype and stigmatize politically powerless segments of society." Kahn v. Shevin, 416 U.S. 351, 357 (1974) While a carefully tailored statute designed to remedy past discrimination could avoid these vices, we nonetheless have recognized that the line between honest and thoughtful appraisal of the effects of past discrimination and paternalistic stereotyping is not so clear and that a statute based on the latter is patently capable of stigmatizing all women with a badge of inferiority. State programs designed ostensibly to ameliorate the effects of past racial discrimination obviously create the same hazard of stigma, since they may promote racial separatism and reinforce the views of those who believe that members of racial minorities are inherently incapable of succeeding on their own.

Second, race, like gender and illegitimacy, is an immutable characteristic which its possessors are powerless to escape or set aside. While a classification is not per se invalid because it divides classes on the basis of an immutable characteristic, it is nevertheless true that such divisions are contrary to our deep belief that "legal burdens should bear some relationship to individual responsibility or wrongdoing," [Weber v. Aetna Casualty & Surety Co., 406 U.S. 164, 175 (1972)], and that advancement sanctioned, sponsored, or approved by the State should ideally be based on individual merit or achievement, or at the least on factors within the control of an individual.

Because this principle is so deeply rooted it might be supposed that it would be considered in the legislative process and weighed against the benefits of programs preferring individuals because of their race. But this is not necessarily so: The "natural consequence of our governing process [may well be] that the most 'discrete and insular' of whites ... will be called upon to bear the immediate, direct costs of benign discrimination." Moreover, it is clear from our cases that there are limits beyond which majorities may not go when they classify on the basis of immutable characteristics. Thus, even if the concern for individualism is weighed by the political process, that weighing cannot waive the personal rights of individuals under the Fourteenth Amendment.

In sum, because of the significant risk that racial classifications established for ostensibly benign purposes can be misused, causing effects not unlike those created by invidious classifications, it is inappropriate to inquire only whether there is any conceivable basis that might sustain such a classification. Instead, to justify such a classification an important and articulated purpose for its use must be shown. In addition, any statute must be stricken that stigmatizes any group or that singles out those least well represented in the political process to bear the brunt of a benign program. Thus, our review under the Fourteenth Amendment should be

and the only question is whether it was rational for Davis to conclude that the groups it preferred had a greater claim to compensation than the groups it excluded. Thus, claims of rival groups, although they may create thorny political problems, create relatively simple problems for the courts.

strict—not " 'strict' in theory and fatal in fact," [36] because it is stigma that causes fatality—but strict and searching nonetheless.

IV

Davis' articulated purpose of remedying the effects of past societal discrimination is, under our cases, sufficiently important to justify the use of race-conscious admissions programs where there is a sound basis for concluding that minority underrepresentation is substantial and chronic, and that the handicap of past discrimination is impeding access of minorities to the Medical School.

A

At least since *Green v. County School Board*, 391 U.S. 430 (1968), it has been clear that a public body which has itself been adjudged to have engaged in racial discrimination cannot bring itself into compliance with the Equal Protection Clause simply by ending its unlawful acts and adopting a neutral stance. Three years later, *Swann v. Charlotte-Mecklenburg Board of Education*, 402 U.S. 1 (1971), ... reiterated that racially neutral remedies for past discrimination were inadequate where consequences of past discriminatory acts influence or control present decisions. And the Court further held both that courts could enter desegregation orders which assigned students and faculty by reference to race, and that local school boards could voluntarily adopt desegregation plans which made express reference to race if this was necessary to remedy the effects of past discrimination. Moreover, we stated that school boards, even in the absence of a judicial finding of past discrimination, could voluntarily adopt plans which assigned students with the end of creating racial pluralism by establishing fixed ratios of black and white students in each school. *Charlotte-Mecklenburg*, 402 U.S., at 16. In each instance, the creation of unitary school systems, in which the effects of past discrimination had been "eliminated root and branch," *Green*, 391 U.S., at 438, was recognized as a compelling social goal justifying the overt use of race.

Finally, the conclusion that state educational institutions may constitutionally adopt admissions programs designed to avoid exclusion of historically disadvantaged minorities, even when such programs explicitly take race into account, finds direct support in our cases construing congressional legislation designed to overcome the present effects of past discrimination. Congress can and has outlawed actions which have a disproportionately adverse and unjustified impact upon members of racial minorities and has required or authorized race-conscious action to put individuals disadvantaged by such impact in the position they otherwise might have enjoyed. See *Franks v. Bowman Transportation Co.*, 424 U.S. 747 (1976); *Teamsters v. United States*, 431 U.S. 324 (1977). Such relief does not require as a predicate proof that recipients of preferential advancement have been

---

36. Gunther, The Supreme Court, 1971 Term—Foreword: In Search of Evolving Doctrine in a Changing Court: A Model for a Newer Equal Protection, 86 Harv.L.Rev. 1, 8 (1972).

individually discriminated against; it is enough that each recipient is within a general class of persons likely to have been the victims of discrimination. Nor is it an objection to such relief that preference for minorities will upset the settled expectations of nonminorities. See *Franks*. In addition, we have held that Congress, to remove barriers to equal opportunity, can and has required employers to use test criteria that fairly reflect the qualifications of minority applicants vis-a-vis nonminority applicants, even if this means interpreting the qualifications of an applicant in light of his race. See *Albemarle Paper Co. v. Moody*, 422 U.S. 405, 435 (1975).[37]

These cases cannot be distinguished simply by the presence of judicial findings of discrimination, for race-conscious remedies have been approved where such findings have not been made. *McDaniel v. Barresi*; *UJO*. Indeed, the requirement of a judicial determination of a constitutional or statutory violation as a predicate for race-conscious remedial actions would be self-defeating. Such a requirement would severely undermine efforts to achieve voluntary compliance with the requirements of law. . . .

B

Properly construed, therefore, our prior cases unequivocally show that a state government may adopt race-conscious programs if the purpose of such programs is to remove the disparate racial impact its actions might otherwise have and if there is reason to believe that the disparate impact is itself the product of past discrimination, whether its own or that of society at large. There is no question that Davis' program is valid under this test. . . .

Moreover, Davis had very good reason to believe that the national pattern of underrepresentation of minorities in medicine would be perpetuated if it retained a single admissions standard. For example, the entering classes in 1968 and 1969, the years in which such a standard was used, included only 1 Chicano and 2 Negroes out of the 50 admittees for each year. Nor is there any relief from this pattern of underrepresentation in the statistics for the regular admissions program in later years.

Davis clearly could conclude that the serious and persistent underrepresentation of minorities in medicine depicted by these statistics is the result of handicaps under which minority applicants labor as a consequence of a background of deliberate, purposeful discrimination against minorities in education and in society generally, as well as in the medical profession. From the inception of our national life, Negroes have been subjected to unique legal disabilities impairing access to equal educational opportunity.

---

37. In *Albemarle*, we approved "differential validation" of employment tests. See 422 U.S., at 435. That procedure requires that an employer must ensure that a test score of, for example, 50 for a minority job applicant means the same thing as a score of 50 for a nonminority applicant. By implication, were it determined that a test score of 50 for a minority corresponded in "potential for employment" to a 60 for whites, the test could not be used consistently with Title VII unless the employer hired minorities with scores of 50 even though he might not hire nonminority applicants with scores above 50 but below 60. Thus, it is clear that employers, to ensure equal opportunity, may have to adopt race-conscious hiring practices.

Under slavery, penal sanctions were imposed upon anyone attempting to educate Negroes. After enactment of the Fourteenth Amendment the States continued to deny Negroes equal educational opportunity, enforcing a strict policy of segregation that itself stamped Negroes as inferior, that relegated minorities to inferior educational institutions, and that denied them intercourse in the mainstream of professional life necessary to advancement. See *Sweatt v. Painter*, 339 U.S. 629 (1950). Segregation was not limited to public facilities, moreover, but was enforced by criminal penalties against private action as well. Thus, as late as 1908, this Court enforced a state criminal conviction against a private college for teaching Negroes together with whites. *Berea College v. Kentucky*, 211 U.S. 45.

Green v. County School Board, 391 U.S. 430 (1968), gave explicit recognition to the fact that the habit of discrimination and the cultural tradition of race prejudice cultivated by centuries of legal slavery and segregation were not immediately dissipated when *Brown I*, announced the constitutional principle that equal educational opportunity and participation in all aspects of American life could not be denied on the basis of race. Rather, massive official and private resistance prevented, and to a lesser extent still prevents, attainment of equal opportunity in education at all levels and in the professions. The generation of minority students applying to Davis Medical School since it opened in 1968—most of whom were born before or about the time *Brown I* was decided—clearly have been victims of this discrimination. Judicial decrees recognizing discrimination in public education in California testify to the fact of widespread discrimination suffered by California-born minority applicants; many minority group members living in California, moreover, were born and reared in school districts in Southern States segregated by law.[54] Since separation of school-children by race "generates a feeling of inferiority as to their status in the community that may affect their hearts and minds in a way unlikely ever to be undone," *Brown I*, 347 U.S., at 494, the conclusion is inescapable that applicants to medical school must be few indeed who endured the effects of de jure segregation, the resistance to *Brown I*, or the equally debilitating pervasive private discrimination fostered by our long history of official discrimination, and yet come to the starting line with an education equal to whites. . . .

C

The second prong of our test—whether the Davis program stigmatizes any discrete group or individual and whether race is reasonably used in light of the program's objectives—is clearly satisfied by the Davis program.

It is not even claimed that Davis' program in any way operates to stigmatize or single out any discrete and insular, or even any identifiable, nonminority group. Nor will harm comparable to that imposed upon racial minorities by exclusion or separation on grounds of race be the likely result

---

54. For example, over 40% of American-born Negro males aged 20 to 24 residing in California in 1970 were born in the South, and the statistic for females was over 48%. . . .

of the program. It does not, for example, establish an exclusive preserve for minority students apart from and exclusive of whites. Rather, its purpose is to overcome the effects of segregation by bringing the races together. True, whites are excluded from participation in the special admissions program, but this fact only operates to reduce the number of whites to be admitted in the regular admissions program in order to permit admission of a reasonable percentage—less than their proportion of the California population—of otherwise underrepresented qualified minority applicants.[58]

Nor was Bakke in any sense stamped as inferior by the Medical School's rejection of him. Indeed, it is conceded by all that he satisfied those criteria regarded by the school as generally relevant to academic performance better than most of the minority members who were admitted. Moreover, there is absolutely no basis for concluding that Bakke's rejection as a result of Davis' use of racial preference will affect him throughout his life in the same way as the segregation of the Negro schoolchildren in *Brown I* would have affected them. Unlike discrimination against racial minorities, the use of racial preferences for remedial purposes does not inflict a pervasive injury upon individual whites in the sense that wherever they go or whatever they do there is a significant likelihood that they will be treated as second-class citizens because of their color. . . . [T]he injury inflicted by such a policy is not distinguishable from disadvantages caused by a wide range of government actions, none of which has ever been thought impermissible for that reason alone. . . .

. . . The program does not establish a quota in the invidious sense of a ceiling on the number of minority applicants to be admitted. . . .

E

Finally, Davis' special admissions program cannot be said to violate the Constitution simply because it has set aside a predetermined number of places for qualified minority applicants rather than using minority status as a positive factor to be considered in evaluating the applications of disadvantaged minority applicants. For purposes of constitutional adjudication, there is no difference between the two approaches. In any admissions program which accords special consideration to disadvantaged racial minorities, a determination of the degree of preference to be given is unavoidable, and any given preference that results in the exclusion of a white candidate

---

58. The constitutionality of the special admissions program is buttressed by its restriction to only 16% of the positions in the Medical School, a percentage less than that of the minority population in California, and to those minority applicants deemed qualified for admission and deemed likely to contribute to the Medical School and the medical profession. This is consistent with the goal of putting minority applicants in the position they would have been in if not for the evil of racial discrimination. Accordingly, this case does not raise the question whether even a remedial use of race would be unconstitutional if it admitted unqualified minority applicants in preference to qualified applicants or admitted, as a result of preferential consideration, racial minorities in numbers significantly in excess of their proportional representation in the relevant population. Such programs might well be inadequately justified by the legitimate remedial objectives. . . .

is no more or less constitutionally acceptable than a program such as that at Davis....

The "Harvard" program, as those employing it readily concede, openly and successfully employs a racial criterion for the purpose of ensuring that some of the scarce places in institutions of higher education are allocated to disadvantaged minority students. That the Harvard approach does not also make public the extent of the preference and the precise workings of the system while the Davis program employs a specific, openly stated number, does not condemn the latter plan for purposes of Fourteenth Amendment adjudication. It may be that the Harvard plan is more acceptable to the public than is the Davis "quota." If it is, any State, including California, is free to adopt it in preference to a less acceptable alternative, just as it is generally free, as far as the Constitution is concerned, to abjure granting any racial preferences in its admissions program. But there is no basis for preferring a particular preference program simply because in achieving the same goals that the Davis Medical School is pursuing, it proceeds in a manner that is not immediately apparent to the public.

V

Accordingly, we would reverse the judgment of the Supreme Court of California holding the Medical School's special admissions program unconstitutional....

MR. JUSTICE MARSHALL.

I agree with the judgment of the Court only insofar as it permits a university to consider the race of an applicant in making admissions decisions. I do not agree that petitioner's admissions program violates the Constitution. For it must be remembered that, during most of the past 200 years, the Constitution as interpreted by this Court did not prohibit the most ingenious and pervasive forms of discrimination against the Negro. Now, when a State acts to remedy the effects of that legacy of discrimination, I cannot believe that this same Constitution stands as a barrier.

I

A

Three hundred and fifty years ago, the Negro was dragged to this country in chains to be sold into slavery. Uprooted from his homeland and thrust into bondage for forced labor, the slave was deprived of all legal rights. It was unlawful to teach him to read; he could be sold away from his family and friends at the whim of his master; and killing or maiming him was not a crime. The system of slavery brutalized and dehumanized both master and slave.

The denial of human rights was etched into the American Colonies' first attempts at establishing self-government. When the colonists determined to seek their independence from England, they drafted a unique document cataloguing their grievances against the King and proclaiming as "self-evident" that "all men are created equal" and are endowed "with certain unalienable Rights," including those to "Life, Liberty and the pursuit of Happiness." The self-evident truths and the unalienable rights were intended, however, to apply only to white men. An earlier draft of the Declaration of Independence, submitted by Thomas Jefferson to the Continental Congress, had included among the charges against the King that

> "[h]e has waged cruel war against human nature itself, violating its most sacred rights of life and liberty in the persons of a distant people who never offended him, captivating and carrying them into slavery in another hemisphere, or to incur miserable death in their transportation thither." [John Hope Franklin, From Slavery to Freedom (4th ed. 1974)], 88.

The Southern delegation insisted that the charge be deleted; the colonists themselves were implicated in the slave trade, and inclusion of this claim might have made it more difficult to justify the continuation of slavery once the ties to England were severed. Thus, even as the colonists embarked on a course to secure their own freedom and equality, they ensured perpetuation of the system that deprived a whole race of those rights.

The implicit protection of slavery embodied in the Declaration of Independence was made explicit in the Constitution, which treated a slave as being equivalent to three-fifths of a person for purposes of apportioning representatives and taxes among the States[,] Art. I, § 2, [and which protected the slave trade and provided for return of fugitive slaves, Art. I, § 9, Art IV, § 2.]... In their declaration of the principles that were to provide the cornerstone of the new Nation, therefore, the Framers made it plain that "we the people" for whose protection the Constitution was designed, did not include those whose skins were the wrong color. As Professor John Hope Franklin has observed, Americans "proudly accepted the challenge and responsibility of their new political freedom by establishing the machinery and safeguards that insured the continued enslavement of blacks."

The individual States likewise established the machinery to protect the system of slavery through the promulgation of the Slave Codes, which were designed primarily to defend the property interest of the owner in his slave. The position of the Negro slave as mere property was confirmed by this Court in *Dred Scott v. Sandford*, 19 How. 393 (1857), holding that the Missouri Compromise—which prohibited slavery in the portion of the Louisiana Purchase Territory north of Missouri—was unconstitutional because it deprived slave owners of their property without due process. The Court declared that under the Constitution a slave was property, and "[t]he right to traffic in it, like an ordinary article of merchandise and property, was guaranteed to the citizens of the United States ...." The Court further concluded that Negroes were not intended to be included as citizens under the Constitution but were "regarded as beings of an inferior order ... altogether unfit to associate with the white race, either in social or political relations; and so far inferior, that they had no rights which the white man was bound to respect ...."

B

The status of the Negro as property was officially erased by his emancipation at the end of the Civil War. But the long-awaited emancipation, while freeing the Negro from slavery, did not bring him citizenship or equality in any meaningful way. Slavery was replaced by a system of "laws which imposed upon the colored race onerous disabilities and burdens, and curtailed their rights in the pursuit of life, liberty, and property to such an extent that their freedom was of little value." *Slaughter-House Cases*, 16 Wall. 36, 70 (1873). Despite the passage of the Thirteenth, Fourteenth, and Fifteenth Amendments, the Negro was systematically denied the rights those Amendments were supposed to secure. The combined actions and inactions of the State and Federal Governments maintained Negroes in a position of legal inferiority for another century after the Civil War.

The Southern States took the first steps to re-enslave the Negroes. Immediately following the end of the Civil War, many of the provisional legislatures passed Black Codes, similar to the Slave Codes, which, among other things, limited the rights of Negroes to own or rent property and permitted imprisonment for breach of employment contracts. Over the next several decades, the South managed to disenfranchise the Negroes in spite of the Fifteenth Amendment by various techniques, including poll taxes, deliberately complicated balloting processes, property and literacy qualifications, and finally the white primary.

Congress responded to the legal disabilities being imposed in the Southern States by passing the Reconstruction Acts and the Civil Rights Acts. Congress also responded to the needs of the Negroes at the end of the Civil War by establishing the Bureau of Refugees, Freedmen, and Abandoned Lands, better known as the Freedmen's Bureau, to supply food, hospitals, land, and education to the newly freed slaves. Thus, for a time it seemed as if the Negro might be protected from the continued denial of his civil rights and might be relieved of the disabilities that prevented him from taking his place as a free and equal citizen.

That time, however, was short-lived. Reconstruction came to a close, and, with the assistance of this Court, the Negro was rapidly stripped of his new civil rights. In the words of C. Vann Woodward: "By narrow and ingenious interpretation [the Supreme Court's] decisions over a period of years had whittled away a great part of the authority presumably given the government for protection of civil rights."

The Court began by interpreting the Civil War Amendments in a manner that sharply curtailed their substantive protections. See, e. g., *Slaughter-House Cases*. Then in the notorious *Civil Rights Cases*, 109 U.S. 3(1883), the Court strangled Congress' efforts to use its power to promote racial equality. In those cases the Court invalidated sections of the Civil Rights Act of 1875 that made it a crime to deny equal access to "inns, public conveyances, theatres and other places of public amusement." According to the Court, the Fourteenth Amendment gave Congress the power to proscribe only discriminatory action by the State. The Court ruled that the Negroes who were excluded from public places suffered only an invasion of their social rights at the hands of private individuals, and Congress had no power to remedy that. "When a man has emerged from slavery, and by the aid of beneficent legislation has shaken off the inseparable concomitants of that state," the Court concluded, "there must be some stage in the progress of his elevation when he takes the rank of a mere citizen, and ceases to be the special favorite of the laws . . . ." As Mr. Justice Harlan noted in dissent, however, the Civil War Amendments and Civil Rights Acts did not make the Negroes the "special favorite" of the laws but instead "sought to accomplish in reference to that race . . .—what had already been done in every State of the Union for the white race—to secure and protect rights belonging to them as freemen and citizens; nothing more."

The Court's ultimate blow to the Civil War Amendments and to the equality of Negroes came in *Plessy v. Ferguson*, 163 U.S. 537 (1896). In upholding a Louisiana law that required railway companies to provide "equal but separate" accommodations for whites and Negroes, the Court held that the Fourteenth Amendment was not intended "to abolish distinctions based upon color, or to enforce social, as distinguished from political equality, or a commingling of the two races upon terms unsatisfactory to either." Ignoring totally the realities of the positions of the two races, the Court remarked:

> "We consider the underlying fallacy of the plaintiff's argument to consist in the assumption that the enforced separation of the two races stamps the colored race with a badge of inferiority. If this be so, it is not by reason of anything found in the act, but solely because the colored race chooses to put that construction upon it."

Mr. Justice Harlan's dissenting opinion recognized the bankruptcy of the Court's reasoning. He noted that the "real meaning" of the legislation was "that colored citizens are so inferior and degraded that they cannot be allowed to sit in public coaches occupied by white citizens." He expressed his fear that if like laws were enacted in other States, "the effect would be in the highest degree mischievous." Although slavery would have disappeared, the States would retain the power "to interfere with the full enjoyment of the blessings of freedom; to regulate civil rights, common to all citizens, upon the basis of race; and to place in a condition of legal inferiority a large body of American citizens . . . ."

The fears of Mr. Justice Harlan were soon to be realized. In the wake of *Plessy*, many States expanded their Jim Crow laws, which had up until that time been limited primarily to passenger trains and schools. The segregation of the races was extended to residential areas, parks, hospitals, theaters, waiting rooms, and bathrooms. There were even statutes and ordinances which authorized separate phone booths for Negroes and whites, which required that textbooks used by children of one race be kept separate from those used by the other, and which required that Negro and white prostitutes be kept in separate districts. . . .

Nor were the laws restricting the rights of Negroes limited solely to the Southern States. In many of the Northern States, the Negro was denied the right to vote, prevented from serving on juries, and excluded from theaters, restaurants, hotels, and inns. Under President Wilson, the Federal Government began to require segregation in Government buildings; desks of Negro employees were curtained off; separate bathrooms and separate tables in the cafeterias were provided; and even the galleries of the Congress were segregated. When his segregationist policies were attacked, President Wilson responded that segregation was "not humiliating but a benefit" and that he was " 'rendering [the Negroes] more safe in their possession of office and less likely to be discriminated against.' " [Richard Kluger, Simple Justice (1975)], 91.

The enforced segregation of the races continued into the middle of the 20th century. In both World Wars, Negroes were for the most part confined to separate military units; it was not until 1948 that an end to segregation in the military was ordered by President Truman. And the history of the exclusion of Negro children from white public schools is too well known and recent to require repeating here. That Negroes were deliberately excluded from public graduate and professional schools—and thereby denied the opportunity to become doctors, lawyers, engineers, and the like—is also well established....

II

The position of the Negro today in America is the tragic but inevitable consequence of centuries of unequal treatment. Measured by any benchmark of comfort or achievement, meaningful equality remains a distant dream for the Negro.

A Negro child today has a life expectancy which is shorter by more than five years than that of a white child.[2] The Negro child's mother is over three times more likely to die of complications in childbirth, and the infant mortality rate for Negroes is nearly twice that for whites. The median income of the Negro family is only 60% that of the median of a white family,[5] and the percentage of Negroes who live in families with incomes below the poverty line is nearly four times greater than that of whites.

When the Negro child reaches working age, he finds that America offers him significantly less than it offers his white counterpart. For Negro adults, the unemployment rate is twice that of whites,[7] and the unemployment rate for Negro teenagers is nearly three times that of white teenagers. A Negro male who completes four years of college can expect a median annual income of merely $110 more than a white male who has only a high school diploma.[9] Although Negroes represent 11.5% of the population,[10]

2. U. S. Dept. of Commerce, Bureau of the Census, Statistical Abstract of the United States 65 (1977) (Table 94).

5. U. S. Dept. of Commerce, Bureau of the Census, Current Population Reports, Series P–60, No. 107, p. 7 (1977) (Table 1).

7. U. S. Dept. of Labor, Bureau of Labor Statistics, Employment and Earnings, January 1978, p. 170 (Table 44).

9. U. S. Dept. of Commerce, Bureau of the Census, Current Population Reports, Series P-60, No. 105, p. 198 (1977) (Table 47).

10. U. S. Dept. of Commerce, Bureau of the Census, Statistical Abstract, supra, at 25 (Table 24).

they are only 1.2% of the lawyers, and judges, 2% of the physicians, 2.3% of the dentists, 1.1% of the engineers and 2.6% of the college and university professors.

The relationship between those figures and the history of unequal treatment afforded to the Negro cannot be denied. At every point from birth to death the impact of the past is reflected in the still disfavored position of the Negro.

In light of the sorry history of discrimination and its devastating impact on the lives of Negroes, bringing the Negro into the mainstream of American life should be a state interest of the highest order. To fail to do so is to ensure that America will forever remain a divided society.

III

I do not believe that the Fourteenth Amendment requires us to accept that fate. Neither its history nor our past cases lend any support to the conclusion that a university may not remedy the cumulative effects of society's discrimination by giving consideration to race in an effort to increase the number and percentage of Negro doctors.

A

This Court long ago remarked that

> "in any fair and just construction of any section or phrase of these [Civil War] amendments, it is necessary to look to the purpose which we have said was the pervading spirit of them all, the evil which they were designed to remedy ...." *Slaughter-House Cases*, 16 Wall., at 72.

It is plain that the Fourteenth Amendment was not intended to prohibit measures designed to remedy the effects of the Nation's past treatment of Negroes. The Congress that passed the Fourteenth Amendment is the same Congress that passed the 1866 Freedmen's Bureau Act, an Act that provided many of its benefits only to Negroes. Act of July 16, 1866, ch. 200, 14 Stat. 173. Although the Freedmen's Bureau legislation provided aid for refugees, thereby including white persons within some of the relief measures, 14 Stat. 174; see also Act of Mar. 3, 1865, ch. 90, 13 Stat. 507, the bill was regarded, to the dismay of many Congressmen, as "solely and entirely for the freedmen, and to the exclusion of all other persons ...." Cong.Globe, 39th Cong., 1st Sess., 544 (1866) (remarks of Rep. Taylor). See also id., at 634–635 (remarks of Rep. Ritter); id., at App. 78, 80–81 (remarks of Rep. Chanler). Indeed, the bill was bitterly opposed on the ground that it "undertakes to make the negro in some respects ... superior ... and gives them favors that the poor white boy in the North cannot get." Id., at 401 (remarks of Sen. McDougall). The bill's supporters defended it—not by rebutting the claim of special treatment—but by pointing to the need for such treatment:

> "The very discrimination it makes between 'destitute and suffering' negroes, and destitute and suffering white paupers, proceeds upon the distinction that, in the omitted case, civil rights and immunities

are already sufficiently protected by the possession of political power, the absence of which in the case provided for necessitates governmental protection." Id., at App. 75 (remarks of Rep. Phelps).

Despite the objection to the special treatment the bill would provide for Negroes, it was passed by Congress. President Johnson vetoed this bill and also a subsequent bill that contained some modifications; one of his principal objections to both bills was that they gave special benefits to Negroes. Rejecting the concerns of the President and the bill's opponents, Congress overrode the President's second veto.

Since the Congress that considered and rejected the objections to the 1866 Freedmen's Bureau Act concerning special relief to Negroes also proposed the Fourteenth Amendment, it is inconceivable that the Fourteenth Amendment was intended to prohibit all race-conscious relief measures. It "would be a distortion of the policy manifested in that amendment, which was adopted to prevent state legislation designed to perpetuate discrimination on the basis of race or color," to hold that it barred state action to remedy the effects of that discrimination. Such a result would pervert the intent of the Framers by substituting abstract equality for the genuine equality the Amendment was intended to achieve.

B . . .

Only last Term, in *United Jewish Organizations v. Carey*, 430 U.S. 144 (1977), we upheld a New York reapportionment plan that was deliberately drawn on the basis of race to enhance the electoral power of Negroes and Puerto Ricans; the plan had the effect of diluting the electoral strength of the Hasidic Jewish community. We were willing in *UJO* to sanction the remedial use of a racial classification even though it disadvantaged otherwise "innocent" individuals. In another case last Term, *Califano v. Webster*, 430 U.S. 313 (1977), the Court upheld a provision in the Social Security laws that discriminated against men because its purpose was "the permissible one of redressing our society's longstanding disparate treatment of women.' " We thus recognized the permissibility of remedying past societal discrimination through the use of otherwise disfavored classifications.

Nothing in those cases suggests that a university cannot similarly act to remedy past discrimination. It is true that in both *UJO* and *Webster* the use of the disfavored classification was predicated on legislative or administrative action, but in neither case had those bodies made findings that there had been constitutional violations or that the specific individuals to be benefited had actually been the victims of discrimination. Rather, the classification in each of those cases was based on a determination that the group was in need of the remedy because of some type of past discrimination. There is thus ample support for the conclusion that a university can employ race-conscious measures to remedy past societal discrimination, without the need for a finding that those benefited were actually victims of that discrimination.

IV

While I applaud the judgment of the Court that a university may consider race in its admissions process, it is more than a little ironic that, after several hundred years of class-based discrimination against Negroes, the Court is unwilling to hold that a class-based remedy for that discrimination is permissible.... It is unnecessary in 20th-century America to have individual Negroes demonstrate that they have been victims of racial discrimination; the racism of our society has been so pervasive that none, regardless of wealth or position, has managed to escape its impact. The experience of Negroes in America has been different in kind, not just in degree, from that of other ethnic groups. It is not merely the history of slavery alone but also that a whole people were marked as inferior by the law. And that mark has endured. The dream of America as the great melting pot has not been realized for the Negro; because of his skin color he never even made it into the pot.

These differences in the experience of the Negro make it difficult for me to accept that Negroes cannot be afforded greater protection under the Fourteenth Amendment where it is necessary to remedy the effects of past discrimination. In the *Civil Rights Cases*, the Court wrote that the Negro emerging from slavery must cease "to be the special favorite of the laws." We cannot in light of the history of the last century yield to that view. Had the Court in that decision and others been willing to "do for human liberty and the fundamental rights of American citizenship, what it did ... for the protection of slavery and the rights of the masters of fugitive slaves," 109 U.S., at 53 (Harlan, J., dissenting), we would not need now to permit the recognition of any "special wards."

Most importantly, had the Court been willing in 1896, in *Plessy v. Ferguson*, to hold that the Equal Protection Clause forbids differences in treatment based on race, we would not be faced with this dilemma in 1978. We must remember, however, that the principle that the "Constitution is color-blind" appeared only in the opinion of the lone dissenter. The majority of the Court rejected the principle of color-blindness, and for the next 58 years, from *Plessy* to *Brown v. Board of Education*, ours was a Nation where, by law, an individual could be given "special" treatment based on the color of his skin.

It is because of a legacy of unequal treatment that we now must permit the institutions of this society to give consideration to race in making decisions about who will hold the positions of influence, affluence, and prestige in America. For far too long, the doors to those positions have been shut to Negroes. If we are ever to become a fully integrated society, one in which the color of a person's skin will not determine the opportunities available to him or her, we must be willing to take steps to open those doors. I do not believe that anyone can truly look into America's past and still find that a remedy for the effects of that past is impermissible....

I fear that we have come full circle. After the Civil War our Government started several "affirmative action" programs. This Court in the *Civil Rights Cases* and *Plessy v. Ferguson* destroyed the movement toward complete equality. For almost a century no action was taken, and this nonaction was with the tacit approval of the courts. Then we had *Brown v. Board of Education* and the Civil Rights Acts of Congress, followed by numerous affirmative-action programs. Now, we have this Court again stepping in, this time to stop affirmative-action programs of the type used by the University of California.

[The separate opinions of Mr. Justice White and Mr. Justice Blackmun are omitted, as is the opinion of Mr. Justice Stevens, with whom the Chief Justice, Mr. Justice Stewart, and Mr. Justice Rehnquist joined.]

Notes on Fullilove v. Klutznick, 448 U.S. 448 (1980) and City of Richmond v. Croson, 488 U.S. 469 (1989)

In *Fullilove*, the Court upheld provisions of the federal Public Works Employment Act of 1977 which generally required that 10% of federal construction funds given to state and local governments be used to obtain services from "minority business enterprises" (MBEs). An MBE was defined as a business owned or controlled by "citizens of the United States who are Negroes, Spanish-speaking, Orientals, Indians, Eskimos and Aleuts." There was no opinion in which five or more justices joined. Chief Justice Burger, announcing the judgment of the Court and joined by Justices White and Powell, concluded that use of racial or ethnic criteria for remedial purposes required "close examination" but was constitutional in view of Congress' constitutional authority to create remedies for discrimination, the limited duration of the statutory provision, the availability of waivers from the 10% requirement, and the absence of substantial injury to nonminority businesses. Justice Marshall, joined by Justices Brennan and Blackmun, concurred, arguing that there was ample evidence for a congressional finding that minority-owned firms were suffering continuing effects of past unlawful discrimination and that the program chosen was "substantially related" to remedying those continuing effects. Justice Stewart, joined by then-Justice Rehnquist, dissented, arguing that "the government may never act to the detriment of a person solely because of that person's race," referring to the treatment of the nonminority contractors. Justice Stevens also dissented on the grounds that Congress had not done enough to establish the need for this particular scheme which, accordingly, could not be upheld as a "narrowly tailored" use of race.

In *Croson*, the Court held unconstitutional a subcontracting requirement, modeled on the federal program upheld in *Fullilove*. The City of Richmond, whose population was 50% black but which had less than 1% of its city construction contracts or subcontracts going to minority businesses, adopted a requirement that 30% of municipal subcontracts go to MBEs. The plan adopted the definition of MBEs provided by the federal statute in *Fullilove*, and had some provisions for waivers. (Five of the City Council's nine members were black.) Once again, there was no opinion for the Court. Justice O'Connor announced the judgment of the Court in an opinion, joined in part by Justices White and Kennedy and Chief Justice Rehnquist. She first distinguished Congress' powers to enforce the Reconstruction Amendments from those of state and local governments; the "mere recitation of a benign or compensatory purpose for the use of a racial classification [does not] entitle the States to exercise the full power of Congress under Section 5 of the Fourteenth Amendment ...." Because the Equal Protection clause provided guarantees of equal treatment to individuals, "strict scrutiny" was called for in order to screen out illegitimate uses of race, because "[c]lassifications based on race carry a danger of stigmatic harm [and] [u]nless they are strictly reserved for remedial settings, they may in fact promote notions of racial inferiority and lead to a politics of racial hostility." While state and local governments may remedy past violations of section 1 of the 14th amendment, Richmond did not have an adequate basis to conclude that there had been prior discrimination in the construction industry in Richmond; the O'Connor opinion rejected as inadequate reliance on national data, "societal discrimination," or generalized testimony the City Council heard about Richmond's history.[c] Justice Marshall, with Justices Brennan and Blackmun, dissented, sharply criticizing the majority for second-guessing Richmond in its finding that past discrimination had impeded minorities from participating fully in its construction contracting industry.

Adarand Constructors, Inc. v. Pena

515 U.S. 200 (1995).

JUSTICE O'CONNOR announced the judgment of the Court and delivered an opinion with respect to Parts I, II, III-A, III-B, III-D, and IV, which is for the Court except insofar as it might be inconsistent with the views expressed in JUSTICE SCALIA's concurrence, and an opinion with respect to Part III–C in which JUSTICE KENNEDY joins.

Petitioner Adarand Constructors, Inc., claims that the Federal Government's practice of giving general contractors on government projects a financial incentive to hire subcontractors controlled by "socially and economically disadvantaged individuals," and in particular, the Government's use of race-based presumptions in identifying such individuals, violates the equal protection component of the Fifth Amendment's Due Process Clause.

---

c. Justice Stevens concurred in the judgment, in part because a city legislature, rather than a court, had designed the remedial program and in part because of the lack of fit between the ordinance and findings about past discrimination against particular groups of contractors. Justice Scalia concurred in the judgment, arguing that "the benign purpose of compensating for social disadvantages, whether they have been acquired by reason of prior discrimination or otherwise," can not be pursued by "the illegitimate means of racial discrimination ...." Nothing short of an impending prison riot, he argued "can justify an exception to the principle embodied in the Fourteenth Amendment that" the Constitution is color-blind. Moreover, he urged, "a sound distinction between and federal and state (or local) action based on race" exists in light of James Madison's observations about the dangers of faction in smaller, rather than larger, units of society.

The Court of Appeals rejected Adarand's claim. We conclude, however, that courts should analyze cases of this kind under a different standard of review than the one the Court of Appeals applied. We therefore vacate the Court of Appeals' judgment and remand the case for further proceedings.

I

In 1989, the Central Federal Lands Highway Division (CFLHD), which is part of the United States Department of Transportation (DOT), awarded the prime contract for a highway construction project in Colorado to Mountain Gravel & Construction Company. Mountain Gravel then solicited bids from subcontractors for the guardrail portion of the contract. Adarand, a Colorado-based highway construction company specializing in guardrail work, submitted the low bid. Gonzales Construction Company also submitted a bid.

The prime contract's terms provide that Mountain Gravel would receive additional compensation if it hired subcontractors certified as small businesses controlled by "socially and economically disadvantaged individuals," Gonzales is certified as such a business; Adarand is not. Mountain Gravel awarded the subcontract to Gonzales, despite Adarand's low bid, and Mountain Gravel's Chief Estimator has submitted an affidavit stating that Mountain Gravel would have accepted Adarand's bid, had it not been for the additional payment it received by hiring Gonzales instead. Federal law requires that a subcontracting clause similar to the one used here must appear in most federal agency contracts, and it also requires the clause to state that "[t]he contractor shall presume that socially and economically disadvantaged individuals include Black Americans, Hispanic Americans, Native Americans, Asian Pacific Americans, and other minorities, or any other individual found to be disadvantaged by the [Small Business] Administration pursuant to section 8(a) of the Small Business Act." 15 U.S.C. §§ 637(d)(2), (3). Adarand claims that the presumption set forth in that statute discriminates on the basis of race in violation of the Federal Government's Fifth Amendment obligation not to deny anyone equal protection of the laws....

III ...

Adarand's claim arises under the Fifth Amendment to the Constitution, which provides that "No person shall ... be deprived of life, liberty, or property, without due process of law." Although this Court has always understood that Clause to provide some measure of protection against arbitrary treatment by the Federal Government, it is not as explicit a guarantee of equal treatment as the Fourteenth Amendment, which provides that "No State shall ... deny to any person within its jurisdiction the equal protection of the laws". Our cases have accorded varying degrees of significance to the difference in the language of those two Clauses. We think it necessary to revisit the issue here.

A

Through the 1940s, this Court had routinely taken the view in non-race-related cases that, "[u]nlike the Fourteenth Amendment, the Fifth contains no equal protection clause and it provides no guaranty against discriminatory legislation by Congress." When the Court first faced a Fifth Amendment equal protection challenge to a federal racial classification, it adopted a similar approach, with most unfortunate results. In *Hirabayashi v. United States*, 320 U.S. 81 (1943), the Court considered a curfew applicable only to persons of Japanese ancestry. The Court observed—correctly—that "[d]istinctions between citizens solely because of their ancestry are by their very nature odious to a free people whose institutions are founded upon the doctrine of equality," and that "racial discriminations are in most circumstances irrelevant and therefore prohibited." But it also cited *Detroit Bank* [317 U.S. 329 (1943)] for the proposition that the Fifth Amendment "restrains only such discriminatory legislation by Congress as amounts to a denial of due process," and upheld the curfew because "circumstances within the knowledge of those charged with the responsibility for maintaining the national defense afforded a rational basis for the decision which they made."

Eighteen months later, the Court again approved wartime measures directed at persons of Japanese ancestry. *Korematsu* [v. United States, 323 U.S. 214 (1944)], concerned an order that completely excluded such persons from particular areas. The Court ... began by noting that "all legal restrictions which curtail the civil rights of a single racial group are immediately suspect ... [and] courts must subject them to the most rigid scrutiny." That promising dictum might be read to undermine the view that the Federal Government is under a lesser obligation to avoid injurious racial classifications than are the States. But in spite of the "most rigid scrutiny" standard it had just set forth, the Court then inexplicably relied on "the principles we announced in the *Hirabayashi* case," to conclude that, although "exclusion from the area in which one's home is located is a far greater deprivation than constant confinement to the home from 8 p.m. to 6 a.m.," the racially discriminatory order was nonetheless within the Federal Government's power.*

In *Bolling v. Sharpe*, 347 U.S. 497 (1954), the Court for the first time explicitly questioned the existence of any difference between the obligations of the Federal Government and the States to avoid racial classifications. *Bolling* did note that "[t]he 'equal protection of the laws' is a more explicit safeguard of prohibited unfairness than 'due process of law.'" But *Bolling* then concluded that, "[i]n view of [the] decision that the Constitution

---

* [Asterisked footnote in original] Justices Roberts, Murphy, and Jackson filed vigorous dissents; Justice Murphy argued that the challenged order "falls into the ugly abyss of racism." Korematsu, 323 U.S., at 233. Congress has recently agreed with the dissenters' position, and has attempted to make amends. See Pub.L. 100–383, § 2(a), 102 Stat. 903 ("The Congress recognizes that ... a grave injustice was done to both citizens and permanent resident aliens of Japanese ancestry by the evacuation, relocation, and internment of civilians during World War II").

prohibits the states from maintaining racially segregated public schools, it would be unthinkable that the same Constitution would impose a lesser duty on the Federal Government."

Bolling's facts concerned school desegregation, but its reasoning was not so limited. The Court's observations that "[d]istinctions between citizens solely because of their ancestry are by their very nature odious," *Hirabayashi*, and that "all legal restrictions which curtail the civil rights of a single racial group are immediately suspect," *Korematsu*, carry no less force in the context of federal action than in the context of action by the States.... *Bolling* relied on those observations, and reiterated " 'that the Constitution of the United States, in its present form, forbids, so far as civil and political rights are concerned, discrimination by the General Government, or by the States, against any citizen because of his race,' ". The Court's application of that general principle to the case before it, and the resulting imposition on the Federal Government of an obligation equivalent to that of the States, followed as a matter of course.

Later cases in contexts other than school desegregation did not distinguish between the duties of the States and the Federal Government to avoid racial classifications....

... *Loving v. Virginia*, which struck down a race-based state law, cited *Korematsu* for the proposition that "the Equal Protection Clause demands that racial classifications ... be subjected to the 'most rigid scrutiny.' " 388 U.S. 1, 11 (1967). The various opinions in *Frontiero v. Richardson*, 411 U.S. 677 (1973), which concerned sex discrimination by the Federal Government, took their equal protection standard of review from *Reed v. Reed*, 404 U.S. 71 (1971), a case that invalidated sex discrimination by a State, without mentioning any possibility of a difference between the standards applicable to state and federal action. Thus, in 1975, the Court stated explicitly that "[t]his Court's approach to Fifth Amendment equal protection claims has always been precisely the same as to equal protection claims under the Fourteenth Amendment." We do not understand a few contrary suggestions appearing in cases in which we found special deference to the political branches of the Federal Government to be appropriate, e.g., *Hampton v. Mow Sun Wong*, 426 U.S. 88, 100, 101–02 n. 21 (1976) (federal power over immigration), to detract from this general rule.

B

Most of the cases discussed above involved classifications burdening groups that have suffered discrimination in our society. In 1978, the Court confronted the question whether race-based governmental action designed to benefit such groups should also be subject to "the most rigid scrutiny." ... *Bakke* did not produce an opinion for the Court, but Justice Powell's opinion announcing the Court's judgment ... [i]n a passage joined by Justice White ... [stated] that "[t]he guarantee of equal protection cannot mean one thing when applied to one individual and something else when applied to a person of another color." He concluded that "[r]acial and ethnic distinctions of any sort are inherently suspect and thus call for the most exacting judicial examination." On the other hand, four Justices in *Bakke* would have applied a less stringent standard of review to racial classifications "designed to further remedial purposes." And four Justices thought the case should be decided on statutory grounds.

Two years after *Bakke*, the Court faced another challenge to remedial race-based action, this time involving action undertaken by the Federal Government. In *Fullilove*, the Court upheld Congress' inclusion of a 10% set-aside for minority-owned businesses in the Public Works Employment Act of 1977. As in *Bakke*, there was no opinion for the Court. Chief Justice Burger, in an opinion joined by Justices White and Powell, observed that "[a]ny preference based on racial or ethnic criteria must necessarily receive a most searching examination to make sure that it does not conflict with constitutional guarantees." ... That opinion, however, "d[id] not adopt, either expressly or implicitly, the formulas of analysis articulated in such cases as [*Bakke*]." It employed instead a two-part test which asked, first, "whether the *objectives* of th[e] legislation are within the power of Congress," and second, "whether the limited use of racial and ethnic criteria, in the context presented, is a constitutionally permissible *means* for achieving the congressional objectives." It then upheld the program under that test, adding at the end of the opinion that the program also "would survive judicial review under either 'test' articulated in the several *Bakke* opinions." Justice Powell wrote separately to express his view that the plurality opinion had essentially applied "strict scrutiny" as described in his *Bakke* opinion—i.e., it had determined that the set-aside was "a necessary means of advancing a compelling governmental interest"—and had done so correctly. Justice Stewart (joined by then-Justice Rehnquist) dissented, arguing that the Constitution required the Federal Government to meet the same strict standard as the States when enacting racial classifications, and that the program before the Court failed that standard....

In *Wygant v. Jackson Board of Ed.*, 476 U.S. 267 (1986), the Court considered a Fourteenth Amendment challenge to another form of remedial racial classification. The issue in *Wygant* was whether a school board could adopt race-based preferences in determining which teachers to lay off. Justice Powell's plurality opinion observed that "the level of scrutiny does not change merely because the challenged classification operates against a group that historically has not been subject to governmental discrimination,".... In other words, "racial classifications of any sort must be subjected to 'strict scrutiny.'" Id., at 285 (O'Connor, J., concurring in part and concurring in judgment). The plurality then concluded that the school board's interest in "providing minority role models for its minority students, as an attempt to alleviate the effects of societal discrimination," was not a compelling interest that could justify the use of a racial classification.... Justice White concurred only in the judgment, although he agreed that the school board's asserted interests could not, "singly or together, justify this racially discriminatory layoff policy." Four Justices dissented, three of whom again argued for intermediate scrutiny of remedial race-based government action.

The Court's failure to produce a majority opinion in *Bakke, Fullilove*, and *Wygant* left unresolved the proper analysis for remedial race-based governmental action.

The Court resolved the issue, at least in part, in 1989. *Richmond v. J.A. Croson Co.*, concerned a city's determination that 30% of its contracting work should go to minority-owned businesses. A majority of the Court in *Croson* held that "the standard of review under the Equal Protection Clause is not dependent on the race of those burdened or benefited by a particular classification," and that the single standard of review for racial classifications should be "strict scrutiny." *Id.*, at 493–494 (opinion of O'Connor, J., joined by Rehnquist, C.J., White, and Kennedy, JJ.); *id.*, at 520 (Scalia, J., concurring in judgment) ("I agree . . . with Justice O'Connor's conclusion that strict scrutiny must be applied to all governmental classification by race"). As to the classification before the Court, the plurality agreed that "a state or local subdivision . . . has the authority to eradicate the effects of private discrimination within its own legislative jurisdiction," but the Court thought that the city had not acted with "a 'strong basis in evidence for its conclusion that remedial action was necessary,'" The Court also thought it "obvious that [the] program is not narrowly tailored to remedy the effects of prior discrimination."

With *Croson*, the Court finally agreed that the Fourteenth Amendment requires strict scrutiny of all race-based action by state and local governments. But *Croson* . . . had no occasion to declare what standard of review the Fifth Amendment requires for such action taken by the Federal Government. . . .

Despite lingering uncertainty in the details, however, the Court's cases through *Croson* had established three general propositions with respect to governmental racial classifications. First, skepticism: " '[a]ny preference based on racial or ethnic criteria must necessarily receive a most searching examination.' " Second, consistency: "the standard of review under the Equal Protection Clause is not dependent on the race of those burdened or benefited by a particular classification," *Croson*, 488 U.S., at 494 (plurality opinion); *id.*, at 520 (Scalia, J., concurring in judgment); see also *Bakke*, 438 U.S., at 289–290 (opinion of Powell, J.), i.e., all racial classifications reviewable under the Equal Protection Clause must be strictly scrutinized. And third, congruence: "[e]qual protection analysis in the Fifth Amendment area is the same as that under the Fourteenth Amendment," *Buckley v. Valeo*, 424 U.S., at 93. Taken together, these three propositions lead to the conclusion that any person, of whatever race, has the right to demand that any governmental actor subject to the Constitution justify any racial classification subjecting that person to unequal treatment under the strictest judicial scrutiny. . . .

A year later, however, the Court took a surprising turn. *Metro Broadcasting, Inc. v. FCC*, 497 U.S. 547 (1990), involved a Fifth Amendment challenge to two race-based policies of the Federal Communications Commission. In *Metro Broadcasting*, the Court repudiated the long-held notion that "it would be unthinkable that the same Constitution would impose a lesser duty on the Federal Government" than it does on a State to afford equal protection of the laws, *Bolling*, at 500. It did so by holding that "benign" federal racial classifications need only satisfy intermediate scrutiny, even though *Croson* had recently concluded that such classifications enacted by a State must satisfy strict scrutiny. "[B]enign" federal racial classifications, the Court said, "—even if those measures are not 'remedial' in the sense of being designed to compensate victims of past governmental or societal discrimination—are constitutionally permissible to the extent that they serve *important* governmental objectives within the power of Congress and are *substantially related* to achievement of those objectives." *Metro Broadcasting*, 497 U.S., at 564–565 (emphasis added). The Court did not explain how to tell whether a racial classification should be deemed "benign," other than to express "confiden[ce] that an 'examination of the legislative scheme and its history' will separate benign measures from other types of racial classifications."

Applying this test, the Court first noted that the FCC policies at issue did not serve as a remedy for past discrimination. Proceeding on the assumption that the policies were nonetheless "benign," it concluded that they served the "important governmental objective" of "enhancing broadcast diversity," and that they were "substantially related" to that objective. It therefore upheld the policies.

By adopting intermediate scrutiny as the standard of review for congressionally mandated "benign" racial classifications, *Metro Broadcasting* departed from prior cases in two significant respects. First, it turned its back on *Croson's* explanation of why strict scrutiny of all governmental racial classifications is essential:

> "Absent searching judicial inquiry into the justification for such race-based measures, there is simply no way of determining what classifications are 'benign' or 'remedial' and what classifications are in fact motivated by illegitimate notions of racial inferiority or simple racial politics. Indeed, the purpose of strict scrutiny is to 'smoke out' illegitimate uses of race by assuring that the legislative body is pursuing a goal important enough to warrant use of a highly suspect tool. The test also ensures that the means chosen 'fit' this compelling goal so closely that there is little or no possibility that the motive for the classification was illegitimate racial prejudice or stereotype." *Croson*, at 493 (plurality opinion of O'Connor, J.).

We adhere to that view today, despite the surface appeal of holding "benign" racial classifications to a lower standard, because "it may not always be clear that a so-called preference is in fact benign" . . . .

Second, *Metro Broadcasting* squarely rejected one of the three propositions established by the Court's earlier equal protection cases, namely, congruence between the standards applicable to federal and state racial classifications, and in so doing also undermined the other two—skepticism of all racial classifications, and consistency of treatment irrespective of the race of the burdened or benefited group. Under *Metro Broadcasting*, certain racial classifications ("benign" ones enacted by the Federal Government) should be treated less skeptically than others; and the race of the benefited group is critical to the determination of which standard of review to apply. *Metro Broadcasting* was thus a significant departure from much of what had come before it.

The three propositions undermined by *Metro Broadcasting* all derive from the basic principle that the Fifth and Fourteenth Amendments to the Constitution protect persons, not groups. It follows from that principle that all governmental action based on race—a group classification long recognized as "in most circumstances irrelevant and therefore prohibited," *Hirabayashi*—should be subjected to detailed judicial inquiry to ensure that the *personal* right to equal protection of the laws has not been infringed. These ideas have long been central to this Court's understanding of equal protection, and holding "benign" state and federal racial classifications to different standards does not square with them. "[A] free people whose institutions are founded upon the doctrine of equality," should tolerate no retreat from the principle that government may treat people differently because of their race only for the most compelling reasons. Accordingly, we hold today that all racial classifications, imposed by whatever federal, state, or local governmental actor, must be analyzed by a reviewing court under strict scrutiny. In other words, such classifications are constitutional only if they are narrowly tailored measures that further compelling governmental interests. To the extent that *Metro Broadcasting* is inconsistent with that holding, it is overruled. . . .

. . . According to Justice Stevens, our view of consistency "equate[s] remedial preferences with invidious discrimination," and ignores the difference between "an engine of oppression" and an effort "to foster equality in society," or, more colorfully, "between a 'No Trespassing' sign and a welcome mat." It does nothing of the kind. The principle of consistency simply means that whenever the government treats any person unequally because of his or her race, that person has suffered an injury that falls squarely within the language and spirit of the Constitution's guarantee of equal protection. It says nothing about the ultimate validity of any particular law; that determination is the job of the court applying strict scrutiny. The principle of consistency explains the circumstances in which the injury requiring strict scrutiny occurs. The application of strict scrutiny, in turn, determines whether a compelling governmental interest justifies the infliction of that injury.

Consistency *does* recognize that any individual suffers an injury when he or she is disadvantaged by the government because of his or her race, whatever that race may be. . . . Justice Stevens does not explain how his views square with *Croson*, or with the long line of cases understanding equal protection as a personal right.

Justice Stevens also claims that we have ignored any difference between federal and state legislatures. But requiring that Congress, like the States, enact racial classifications only when doing so is necessary to further a "compelling interest" does not contravene any principle of appropriate respect for a co-equal Branch of the Government. . . .

C

"Although adherence to precedent is not rigidly required in constitutional cases, any departure from the doctrine of stare decisis demands special justification." *Arizona v. Rumsey,* 467 U.S. 203, 212 (1984). In deciding whether this case presents such justification, we recall Justice Frankfurter's admonition that "stare decisis is a principle of policy and not a mechanical formula of adherence to the latest decision, however recent and questionable, when such adherence involves collision with a prior doctrine more embracing in its scope, intrinsically sounder, and verified by experience." . . .

It is worth pointing out the difference between the applications of stare decisis in this case and in *Planned Parenthood of Southeastern Pa. v. Casey,* 505 U.S. 833 (1992). *Casey* explained how considerations of stare decisis inform the decision whether to overrule a long-established precedent that has become integrated into the fabric of the law. Overruling precedent of that kind naturally may have consequences for "the ideal of the rule of law." In addition, such precedent is likely to have engendered substantial reliance, as was true in *Casey* itself. ("[F]or two decades of economic and social developments, people have organized intimate relationships and made choices that define their views of themselves and their places in society, in reliance on the availability of abortion in the event that contraception should fail"). But in this case, as we have explained, we do not face a precedent of that kind, because *Metro Broadcasting* itself departed from our prior cases—and did so quite recently. By refusing to follow *Metro Broadcasting,* then, we do not depart from the fabric of the law; we restore it. . . .

. . . *Metro Broadcasting's* untenable distinction between state and federal racial classifications lacks support in our precedent, and undermines the fundamental principle of equal protection as a personal right. In this case, as between that principle and "its later misapplications," the principle must prevail.

D

Our action today makes explicit what Justice Powell thought implicit in the *Fullilove* lead opinion: federal racial classifications, like those of a State, must serve a compelling governmental interest, and must be narrowly tailored to further that interest. . . .

[R]equiring strict scrutiny is the best way to ensure that courts will consistently give racial classifications that kind of detailed examination, both as to ends and as to means. *Korematsu* demonstrates vividly that even "the most rigid scrutiny" can sometimes fail to detect an illegitimate racial classification. . . . Any retreat from the most searching judicial inquiry can only increase the risk of another such error occurring in the future.

Finally, we wish to dispel the notion that strict scrutiny is "strict in theory, but fatal in fact." *Fullilove,* at 519 (Marshall, J., concurring in judgment). The unhappy persistence of both the practice and the lingering effects of racial discrimination against minority groups in this country is an unfortunate reality, and government is not disqualified from acting in response to it. As recently as 1987, for example, every Justice of this Court agreed that the Alabama Department of Public Safety's "pervasive, systematic, and obstinate discriminatory conduct" justified a narrowly tailored race-based remedy. See *United States v. Paradise*, 480 U.S., at 167 (plurality opinion of Brennan, J.); *id.*, at 190 (Stevens, J., concurring in judgment); *id.*, at 196 (O'Connor, J., dissenting). When race-based action is necessary to further a compelling interest, such action is within constitutional constraints if it satisfies the "narrow tailoring" test this Court has set out in previous cases.

IV

Because our decision today alters the playing field in some important respects, we think it best to remand the case to the lower courts for further consideration in light of the principles we have announced. . . .

Moreover, unresolved questions remain concerning the details of the complex regulatory regimes implicated by the use of subcontractor compensation clauses. For example, the SBA's 8(a) program requires an individualized inquiry into the economic disadvantage of every participant, whereas the DOT's regulations ... do not require certifying authorities to make such individualized inquiries [instead presuming both social and economic disadvantage for members of the designated minority groups.] We also note an apparent discrepancy between the definitions of which socially disadvantaged individuals qualify as economically disadvantaged for the 8(a) and 8(d) programs; the former requires a showing that such individuals' ability to compete has been impaired "as compared to others in the same or similar line of business *who are not socially disadvantaged*," while the latter requires that showing only "as compared to others in the same or similar line of business." The question whether any of the ways in which the Government uses subcontractor compensation clauses can survive strict scrutiny, and any relevance distinctions such as these may have to that question, should be addressed in the first instance by the lower courts. . . .

Justice Scalia, concurring in part and concurring in the judgment.

I join the opinion of the Court, except Part III-C, and except insofar as it may be inconsistent with the following: In my view, government can never have a "compelling interest" in discriminating on the basis of race in order to "make up" for past racial discrimination in the opposite direction. Individuals who have been wronged by unlawful racial discrimination should be made whole; but under our Constitution there can be no such thing as either a creditor or a debtor race. That concept is alien to the Constitution's focus upon the individual, see Amdt. 14, § 1 ("[N]or shall any State ... deny *to any person*" the equal protection of the laws) (emphasis added), and its rejection of dispositions based on race, see Amdt. 15, § 1 (prohibiting abridgment of the right to vote "on account of race") or based on blood, see Art. III, § 3 ("[N]o Attainder of Treason shall work

Corruption of Blood"); Art. I, § 9 ("No Title of Nobility shall be granted by the United States"). To pursue the concept of racial entitlement—even for the most admirable and benign of purposes—is to reinforce and preserve for future mischief the way of thinking that produced race slavery, race privilege and race hatred. In the eyes of government, we are just one race here. It is American.

It is unlikely, if not impossible, that the challenged program would survive under this understanding of strict scrutiny, but I am content to leave that to be decided on remand.

JUSTICE THOMAS, concurring in part and concurring in the judgment.

I agree with the majority's conclusion that strict scrutiny applies to *all* government classifications based on race. I write separately, however, to express my disagreement with the premise underlying Justice Stevens' and Justice Ginsburg's dissents: that there is a racial paternalism exception to the principle of equal protection. I believe that there is a "moral [and] constitutional equivalence" between laws designed to subjugate a race and those that distribute benefits on the basis of race in order to foster some current notion of equality. Government cannot make us equal; it can only recognize, respect, and protect us as equal before the law.

That these programs may have been motivated, in part, by good intentions cannot provide refuge from the principle that under our Constitution, the government may not make distinctions on the basis of race. As far as the Constitution is concerned, it is irrelevant whether a government's racial classifications are drawn by those who wish to oppress a race or by those who have a sincere desire to help those thought to be disadvantaged. There can be no doubt that the paternalism that appears to lie at the heart of this program is at war with the principle of inherent equality that underlies and infuses our Constitution. See Declaration of Independence ("We hold these truths to be self-evident, that all men are created equal, that they are endowed by their Creator with certain unalienable Rights, that among these are Life, Liberty, and the pursuit of Happiness").

These programs not only raise grave constitutional questions, they also undermine the moral basis of the equal protection principle.... [T]here can be no doubt that racial paternalism and its unintended consequences can be as poisonous and pernicious as any other form of discrimination. So-called "benign" discrimination teaches many that because of chronic and apparently immutable handicaps, minorities cannot compete with them without their patronizing indulgence. Inevitably, such programs engender attitudes of superiority or, alternatively, provoke resentment among those who believe that they have been wronged by the government's use of race. These programs stamp minorities with a badge of inferiority and may cause them to develop dependencies or to adopt an attitude that they are "entitled" to preferences. Indeed, Justice Stevens once recognized the real harms stemming from seemingly "benign" discrimination. See *Fullilove v. Klutznick*, 448 U.S. 448, 545 (1980) (Stevens, J., dissenting) (noting that "remedial" race legislation "is perceived by many as resting on an assumption that those who are granted this special preference are less qualified in some respect that is identified purely by their race").

In my mind, government-sponsored racial discrimination based on benign prejudice is just as noxious as discrimination inspired by malicious prejudice.* In each instance, it is racial discrimination, plain and simple.

Justice Stevens, with whom Justice Ginsburg joins, dissenting. . . .

II

The Court's concept of "consistency" assumes that there is no significant difference between a decision by the majority to impose a special burden on the members of a minority race and a decision by the majority to provide a benefit to certain members of that minority notwithstanding its incidental burden on some members of the majority. In my opinion that assumption is untenable. There is no moral or constitutional equivalence between a policy that is designed to perpetuate a caste system and one that seeks to eradicate racial subordination. Invidious discrimination is an engine of oppression, subjugating a disfavored group to enhance or maintain the power of the majority. Remedial race-based preferences reflect the opposite impulse: a desire to foster equality in society. No sensible conception of the Government's constitutional obligation to "govern impartially," should ignore this distinction.

To illustrate the point, consider our cases addressing the Federal Government's discrimination against Japanese Americans during World War II. The discrimination at issue in those cases was invidious because the Government imposed special burdens—a curfew and exclusion from certain areas on the West Coast—on the members of a minority class defined by racial and ethnic characteristics. Members of the same racially defined class exhibited exceptional heroism in the service of our country during that War. Now suppose Congress decided to reward that service with a federal program that gave all Japanese-American veterans an extraordinary preference in Government employment. Cf. *Personnel Administrator of Mass. v. Feeney*, 442 U.S. 256 (1979). If Congress had done so, the same racial characteristics that motivated the discriminatory burdens in *Hirabayashi* and *Korematsu* would have defined the preferred class of veterans. Nevertheless, "consistency" surely would not require us to describe the incidental burden on everyone else in the country as "odious" or "invidious" as those terms were used in those cases. We should reject a concept of "consistency" that would view the special preferences that the National Government has provided to Native Americans since 1834[3] as comparable

---

* [Asterisked footnote in original] It should be obvious that every racial classification helps, in a narrow sense, some races and hurts others. As to the races benefitted, the classification could surely be called "benign." Accordingly, whether a law relying upon racial taxonomy is "benign" or "malign," ante (Ginsburg, J., dissenting); see also, ante (Ste-vens, J., dissenting) (addressing differences between "invidious" and "benign" discrimination), either turns on "whose ox is gored," or on distinctions found only in the eye of the beholder.

3. See Morton v. Mancari, 417 U.S. 535, 541 (1974). To be eligible for the preference in 1974, an individual had to "be one fourth

to the official discrimination against African Americans that was prevalent for much of our history.

The consistency that the Court espouses would disregard the difference between a "No Trespassing" sign and a welcome mat. It would treat a Dixiecrat Senator's decision to vote against Thurgood Marshall's confirmation in order to keep African Americans off the Supreme Court as on a par with President Johnson's evaluation of his nominee's race as a positive factor. It would equate a law that made black citizens ineligible for military service with a program aimed at recruiting black soldiers. An attempt by the majority to exclude members of a minority race from a regulated market is fundamentally different from a subsidy that enables a relatively small group of newcomers to enter that market. An interest in "consistency" does not justify treating differences as though they were similarities....

... As with any legal concept, some cases may be difficult to classify,[4] but our equal protection jurisprudence has identified a critical difference between state action that imposes burdens on a disfavored few and state action that benefits the few "in spite of" its adverse effects on the many. *Feeney*, 442 U.S., at 279....

[T]he Court may find that its new "consistency" approach to race-based classifications is difficult to square with its insistence upon rigidly separate categories for discrimination against different classes of individuals. For example, as the law currently stands, the Court will apply "intermediate scrutiny" to cases of invidious gender discrimination and "strict scrutiny" to cases of invidious race discrimination, while applying the same standard for benign classifications as for invidious ones. If this remains the law, then today's lecture about "consistency" will produce the anomalous result that the Government can more easily enact affirmative-action programs to remedy discrimination against women than it can enact affirmative-action programs to remedy discrimination against African Americans— even though the primary purpose of the Equal Protection Clause was to end discrimination against the former slaves. When a court becomes preoccupied with abstract standards, it risks sacrificing common sense at the altar of formal consistency.

As a matter of constitutional and democratic principle, a decision by representatives of the majority to discriminate against the members of a minority race is fundamentally different from those same representatives' decision to impose incidental costs on the majority of their constituents in

or more degree Indian blood and be a member of a Federally-recognized tribe." We concluded that the classification was not "racial" because it did not encompass all Native Americans. In upholding it, we relied in part on the plenary power of Congress to legislate on behalf of Indian tribes. In this case the Government relies, in part, on the fact that not all members of the preferred minority groups are eligible for the preference, and on the special power to legislate on behalf of minorities granted to Congress by § 5 of the 14th Amendment.

4. For example, in *Richmond v. J.A. Croson Co.*, 488 U.S. 469 (1989), a majority of the members of the city council that enacted the race-based set-aside were of the same race as its beneficiaries.

order to provide a benefit to a disadvantaged minority.[5] Indeed, as I have previously argued, the former is virtually always repugnant to the principles of a free and democratic society, whereas the latter is, in some circumstances, entirely consistent with the ideal of equality. By insisting on a doctrinaire notion of "consistency" in the standard applicable to all race-based governmental actions, the Court obscures this essential dichotomy.

III

The Court's concept of "congruence" assumes that there is no significant difference between a decision by the Congress of the United States to adopt an affirmative-action program and such a decision by a State or a municipality. In my opinion that assumption is untenable. It ignores important practical and legal differences between federal and state or local decisionmakers.

These differences have been identified repeatedly and consistently both in opinions of the Court and in separate opinions authored by members of today's majority. Thus, in *Metro Broadcasting, Inc. v. FCC*, 497 U.S. 547 (1990), in which we upheld a federal program designed to foster racial diversity in broadcasting, we identified the special "institutional competence" of our National Legislature. "It is of overriding significance in these cases," we were careful to emphasize, "that the FCC's minority ownership programs have been specifically approved—indeed, mandated—by Congress." ... We recalled that the opinions of Chief Justice Burger and Justice Powell in *Fullilove* had "explained that deference was appropriate in light of Congress' institutional competence as the National Legislature, as well as Congress' powers under the Commerce Clause, the Spending Clause, and the Civil War Amendments." ...

... In his separate opinion in *Richmond v. J.A. Croson Co.*, 488 U.S. 469 (1989), Justice Scalia discussed the basis for this distinction. He observed that "it is one thing to permit racially based conduct by the

---

5. In his concurrence, Justice Thomas argues that the most significant cost associated with an affirmative-action program is its adverse stigmatic effect on its intended beneficiaries. Although I agree that this cost may be more significant than many people realize, see *Fullilove*, 448 U.S., at 545 (Stevens, J., dissenting), I do not think it applies to the facts of this case. First, this is not an argument that petitioner Adarand, a white-owned business, has standing to advance.... Second, even if the petitioner in this case were a minority-owned business challenging the stigmatizing effect of this program, I would not find Justice Thomas' extreme proposition—that there is a moral and constitutional equivalence between an attempt to subjugate and an attempt to redress the effects of a caste system—at all persuasive. It is one thing to question the wisdom of affirmative-action programs: there are many responsible arguments against them, including the one based upon stigma, that Congress might find persuasive when it decides whether to enact or retain race-based preferences. It is another thing altogether to equate the many well-meaning and intelligent lawmakers and their constituents—whether members of majority or minority races—who have supported affirmative action over the years, to segregationists and bigots.

Finally, ... I am not persuaded that the psychological damage brought on by affirmative action is as severe as that engendered by racial subordination. That, in any event, is a judgment the political branches can be trusted to make....

Federal Government—whose legislative powers concerning matters of race were explicitly enhanced by the Fourteenth Amendment, see U.S. Const., Amdt. 14, § 5—and quite another to permit it by the precise entities against whose conduct in matters of race that Amendment was specifically directed, see Amdt. 14, § 1.'' Continuing, Justice Scalia explained why a "sound distinction between federal and state (or local) action based on race rests not only upon the substance of the Civil War Amendments, but upon social reality and governmental theory."

> "What the record shows, in other words, is that racial discrimination against any group finds a more ready expression at the state and local than at the federal level. To the children of the Founding Fathers, this should come as no surprise. An acute awareness of the heightened danger of oppression from political factions in small, rather than large, political units dates to the very beginning of our national history. See G. Wood, The Creation of the American Republic, 1776–1787, pp. 499–506 (1969). As James Madison observed in support of the proposed Constitution's enhancement of national powers:

> " 'The smaller the society, the fewer probably will be the distinct parties and interests composing it; the fewer the distinct parties and interests, the more frequently will a majority be found of the same party; and the smaller the number of individuals composing a majority, and the smaller the compass within which they are placed, the more easily will they concert and execute their plan of oppression. Extend the sphere and you take in a greater variety of parties and interests; you make it less probable that a majority of the whole will have a common motive to invade the rights of other citizens; or if such a common motive exists, it will be more difficult for all who feel it to discover their own strength and to act in unison with each other.' The Federalist No. 10, pp. 82–84 (C. Rossiter ed. 1961)."

In her plurality opinion in *Croson*, Justice O'Connor also emphasized the importance of this distinction when she responded to the City's argument that *Fullilove* was controlling. She wrote:

> "What appellant ignores is that Congress, unlike any State or political subdivision, has a specific constitutional mandate to enforce the dictates of the Fourteenth Amendment. The power to 'enforce' may at times also include the power to define situations which Congress determines threaten principles of equality and to adopt prophylactic rules to deal with those situations. The Civil War Amendments themselves worked a dramatic change in the balance between congressional and state power over matters of race."

An additional reason for giving greater deference to the National Legislature than to a local lawmaking body is that federal affirmative-action programs represent the will of our entire Nation's elected representatives, whereas a state or local program may have an impact on nonresident entities who played no part in the decision to enact it. Thus, in the state or local context, individuals who were unable to vote for the local representatives who enacted a race-conscious program may nonetheless feel the effects of that program. . . .

. . . [The Court] provides not a word of direct explanation for its sudden and enormous departure from the reasoning in past cases. Such silence, however, cannot erase the difference between Congress' institutional competence and constitutional authority to overcome historic racial subjugation and the States' lesser power to do so.

. . . [I]t is one thing to say (as no one seems to dispute) that the Fifth Amendment encompasses a general guarantee of equal protection as broad as that contained within the Fourteenth Amendment. It is another thing entirely to say that Congress' institutional competence and constitutional authority entitles it to no greater deference when it enacts a program designed to foster equality than the deference due a State legislature. The latter is an extraordinary proposition; and, as the foregoing discussion demonstrates, our precedents have rejected it explicitly and repeatedly. . . .[11]

In my judgment, the Court's novel doctrine of "congruence" is seriously misguided. Congressional deliberations about a matter as important as affirmative action should be accorded far greater deference than those of a State or municipality. . . .

JUSTICE SOUTER, with whom JUSTICE GINSBURG and JUSTICE BREYER join, dissenting. . . .

When the extirpation of lingering discriminatory effects is thought to require a catch-up mechanism, like the racially preferential inducement under the statutes considered here, the result may be that some members of the historically favored race are hurt by that remedial mechanism, however innocent they may be of any personal responsibility for any discriminatory conduct. When this price is considered reasonable, it is in part because it is a price to be paid only temporarily; if the justification for the preference is eliminating the effects of a past practice, the assumption is that the effects will themselves recede into the past, becoming attenuated and finally disappearing. Thus, Justice Powell wrote in his concurring opinion in *Fullilove* that the "temporary nature of this remedy ensures that a race-conscious program will not last longer than the discriminatory effects it is designed to eliminate." . . .

JUSTICE GINSBURG, with whom JUSTICE BREYER joins, dissenting. . . .

---

11. We have read § 5 as a positive grant of authority to Congress, not just to punish violations, but also to define and expand the scope of the Equal Protection Clause. Katzenbach v. Morgan, 384 U.S. 641 (1966). In *Katzenbach*, this meant that Congress under § 5 could require the States to allow non-English-speaking citizens to vote, even if denying such citizens a vote would not have been an independent violation of § 1. Congress, then, can expand the coverage of § 1 by exercising its power under § 5 when it acts to foster equality. Congress has done just that here; it has decided that granting certain preferences to minorities best serves the goals of equal protection.

I

The statutes and regulations at issue, as the Court indicates, were adopted by the political branches in response to an "unfortunate reality": "[t]he unhappy persistence of both the practice and the lingering effects of racial discrimination against minority groups in this country." The United States suffers from those lingering effects because, for most of our Nation's history, the idea that "we are just one race" (Scalia, J., concurring in part and concurring in judgment), was not embraced. For generations, our lawmakers and judges were unprepared to say that there is in this land no superior race, no race inferior to any other. In *Plessy v. Ferguson*, 163 U.S. 537 (1896), not only did this Court endorse the oppressive practice of race segregation, but even Justice Harlan, the advocate of a "color-blind" Constitution, stated:

> "The white race deems itself to be the dominant race in this country. And so it is, in prestige, in achievements, in education, in wealth and in power. So, I doubt not, it will continue to be for all time, if it remains true to its great heritage and holds fast to the principles of constitutional liberty." Id., at 559 (Harlan, J., dissenting).

Not until *Loving v. Virginia*, 388 U.S. 1 (1967), which held unconstitutional Virginia's ban on interracial marriages, could one say with security that the Constitution and this Court would abide no measure "designed to maintain White Supremacy." [2]

The divisions in this difficult case should not obscure the Court's recognition of the persistence of racial inequality and a majority's acknowledgement of Congress' authority to act affirmatively, not only to end discrimination, but also to counteract discrimination's lingering effects. Those effects, reflective of a system of racial caste only recently ended, are evident in our workplaces, markets, and neighborhoods. Job applicants with identical resumes, qualifications, and interview styles still experience different receptions, depending on their race.[3] White and African-American

---

2. The Court, in 1955 and 1956, refused to rule on the constitutionality of antimiscegenation laws; it twice declined to accept appeals from the decree on which the Virginia Supreme Court of Appeals relied in *Loving*. See *Naim v. Naim*, 197 Va. 80, 87 S.E.2d 749, vacated and remanded, 350 U.S. 891 (1955), reinstated and aff'd, 197 Va. 734, 90 S.E.2d 849, appeal dism'd, 350 U.S. 985 (1956). *Naim* expressed the state court's view of the legislative purpose served by the Virginia law: "to preserve the racial integrity of [Virginia's] citizens"; to prevent "the corruption of blood," "a mongrel breed of citizens," and "the obliteration of racial pride."

3. See, e.g., H. Cross, et al., Employer Hiring Practices: Differential Treatment of Hispanic and Anglo Job Seekers 42 (Urban Institute Report 90–4, 1990) (e.g., Anglo applicants sent out by investigators received 52% more job offers than matched Hispanics); M. Turner, et al., Opportunities Denied, Opportunities Diminished: Racial Discrimination in Hiring xi (Urban Institute Report 91–9, 1991) ("In one out of five audits, the white applicant was able to advance farther through the hiring process than his black counterpart. In one out of eight audits, the white was offered a job although his equally qualified black partner was not. In contrast, black auditors advanced farther than their white counterparts only 7 percent of the time, and received job offers while their white partners did not in 5 percent of the audits.").

consumers still encounter different deals.[4] People of color looking for housing still face discriminatory treatment by landlords, real estate agents, and mortgage lenders.[5] Minority entrepreneurs sometimes fail to gain contracts though they are the low bidders, and they are sometimes refused work even after winning contracts.[6] Bias both conscious and unconscious, reflecting traditional and unexamined habits of thought, keeps up barriers that must come down if equal opportunity and nondiscrimination are ever genuinely to become this country's law and practice.

Given this history and its practical consequences, Congress surely can conclude that a carefully designed affirmative action program may help to realize, finally, the "equal protection of the laws" the Fourteenth Amendment has promised since 1868.

II

The lead opinion uses one term, "strict scrutiny," to describe the standard of judicial review for all governmental classifications by race. But that opinion's elaboration strongly suggests that the strict standard announced is indeed "fatal" for classifications burdening groups that have suffered discrimination in our society. That seems to me ... the enduring lesson one should draw from Korematsu v. United States, 323 U.S. 214 (1944).... A *Korematsu*-type classification, as I read the opinion in this case, will never again survive scrutiny: Such a classification, history and precedent instruct, properly ranks as prohibited ....

For a classification made to hasten the day when "we are just one race," however, the lead opinion has dispelled the notion that "strict scrutiny" is "fatal in fact." Properly, a majority of the Court calls for review that is searching, in order to ferret out classifications in reality malign, but masquerading as benign. The Court's once lax review of sex-based classifications demonstrates the need for such suspicion. See, e.g., *Hoyt v. Florida*, 368 U.S. 57, 60 (1961) (upholding women's "privilege" of

---

4. See, e.g., Ayres, Fair Driving: Gender and Race Discrimination in Retail Car Negotiations, 104 Harv.L.Rev. 817, 821–822, 819, 828 (1991) ("blacks and women simply cannot buy the same car for the same price as can white men using identical bargaining strategies"; the final offers given white female testers reflected 40 percent higher markups than those given white male testers; final offer markups for black male testers were twice as high, and for black female testers three times as high as for white male testers).

5. See, e.g., A Common Destiny: Blacks and American Society 50 (G. Jaynes & R. Williams eds., 1989) ("[I]n many metropolitan areas one-quarter to one-half of all [housing] inquiries by blacks are met by clearly discriminatory responses."); M. Turner, et al., U.S. Department of Housing and Urban Development, Housing Discrimination Study: Synthesis i-vii (1991) (1989 audit study of housing searches in 25 metropolitan areas; over half of African-American and Hispanic testers seeking to rent or buy experienced some form of unfavorable treatment compared to paired white testers); Leahy, Are Racial Factors Important for the Allocation of Mortgage Money?, 44 Am.J.Econ. & Soc. 185, 193 (1985) (controlling for socioeconomic factors, and concluding that "even when neighborhoods appear to be similar on every major mortgage-lending criterion except race, mortgage-lending outcomes are still unequal").

6. See, e.g., *Associated General Contractors v. Coalition for Economic Equity*, 950 F.2d 1401, 1415 (C.A.9 1991) (detailing examples in San Francisco).

automatic exemption from jury service); *Goesaert v. Cleary*, 335 U.S. 464 (1948) (upholding Michigan law barring women from employment as bartenders). Today's decision thus usefully reiterates that the purpose of strict scrutiny "is precisely to distinguish legitimate from illegitimate uses of race in governmental decisionmaking," "to 'differentiate between' permissible and impermissible governmental use of race," to distinguish " 'between a "No Trespassing" sign and a welcome mat.' " *Id.*

Close review also is in order for this further reason. As Justice Souter points out and as this very case shows, some members of the historically favored race can be hurt by catch-up mechanisms designed to cope with the lingering effects of entrenched racial subjugation. Court review can ensure that preferences are not so large as to trammel unduly upon the opportunities of others or interfere too harshly with legitimate expectations of persons in once-preferred groups.

* * *

While I would not disturb the programs challenged in this case, and would leave their improvement to the political branches, I see today's decision as one that allows our precedent to evolve, still to be informed by and responsive to changing conditions.

Note on the Use of Race in Drawing Voting Districts

In Shaw v. Reno, 509 U.S. 630 (1993) the Court held that redistricting legislation "that is so extremely irregular on its face that it rationally can be viewed only as an effort to segregate the races for purposes of voting" was suspect under the Equal Protection Clause, and could be upheld only if it met the standards for strict scrutiny (i.e., that it was necessary to serve a compelling state interest). Designing districts based on race was a form of "political apartheid," wrote the Court, reinforcing "the perception that members of the same racial group—regardless of their age, education, economic status or community in which they live—think alike, share the same political interests, and will prefer the same candidates at the polls, ... perceptions [rejected] elsewhere as impermissible racial stereotypes." In addition, reasoned the Court, "[w]hen a district is obviously created solely to effectuate the perceived common interests of one racial group, elected officials are more likely to believe that their primary obligation is to represent only members of that group, rather than their constituency as a whole ...." The Court expressed its strong preference for color-blindness, arguing that

> "[racial] classifications of any sort pose the risk of lasting harm to our society. They reinforce the belief, held by too many for too much of our history, that individuals should be judged by the color of their skin. Racial classifications with respect to voting carry particular dangers ... [of] balkan[izing] us into competing racial factions, ... [carrying] us further from the goal of a political system in which race no longer

matters—a goal that the Fourteenth and Fifteenth Amendments embody, and to which the Nation continues to aspire."

Justices White, Blackmun and Stevens dissented, arguing that redistricting always involves considerations of race, political affiliation, religion, and other factors reflecting group interests that should only be subject to judicial review on a showing that members of a particular group had less opportunity than other residents to participate in the political process and elect legislators of their choice, a showing they argued was not made simply by the bizarre, serpentine shape of the district at issue.

In Miller v. Johnson, 515 U.S. 900 (1995), the Court suggested that there was a distinction between being "aware" of race and being "motivated" by race in drawing district lines, and said that it was only where race was the predominant motive for drawing district lines that the Equal Protection clause would demand strict scrutiny. Agreeing with the lower courts that the proposed districts were predominantly motivated by race, the Court held that the state's justification—to meet the Justice Department's views of what the Voting Rights Act required—did not sustain the plans under the compelling interest standard because the Justice Department had exceeded its statutory authority under the Voting Rights Act.

Justices Ginsburg, Stevens, Breyer and Souter dissented, arguing that race was only one consideration and that the Georgia district at issue in *Miller* was not bizarre or extremely irregular in shape as had been the North Carolina district at issue in *Shaw*. The dissenters argued that "ethnicity can tie people together," that "[o]ur Nation's cities are full of districts identified by their ethnic character—Chinese, Irish, Italian, Jewish, Polish, Russian" and that "creation of ethnic districts reflecting felt identity is not ordinarily viewed as offensive or demeaning to those included in the delineation . . . ." Unlike other government decisions, the dissent suggests, districting plans "do not treat people as individuals" but as groups, and thus, caselaw focussed on racial classifications and individuals in fields of employment, or education, was not apposite.

Questions and Comments

1. Consider whether the distinctions in the U.S. decisions concerning the "affirmative" use of race in the design of remedial measures based on (a) court-adjudicated past discrimination, (b) legislatively-found past discrimination and (c) findings by administrative units of government, correspond with constitutional text or purposes.

2. Justice Ginsburg's dissent in *Miller* can be taken to suggest that some government decisions are necessarily about groups, as she argues is the case in legislative districting, while others are about individuals, as in the case of employment discrimination. How persuasive is the dissent's proposed distinction? How does it relate to constitutional text or purposes?

3. In Metrobroadcasting v. FCC, 497 U.S. 547 (1990) the Court had upheld preferences for minority firms in the award of broadcast licenses by the FCC, under an intermediate level of scrutiny. *Metrobroadcasting* had distinguished *Croson* primarily on the grounds that "race conscious decisions by Congress to address racial and ethnic discrimination are subject to a different standard than such classifications prescribed by state and local governments." In overruling *Metrobroadcasting*, the *Adarand* Court relies on an interpretation of the Fifth Amendment to the U.S. Constitution as imposing the same "equal protection obligations" on the federal government as the Fourteenth Amendment imposes on states.

Recall that the Fifth Amendment was ratified as part of the Constitution in 1791, at a time when slavery was practiced in several of the states and when the Constitution itself prohibited Congress from enacting any law prohibiting "the migration or importation of such persons as any of the States now existing shall think proper to admit..." Art. I, Sec. 9, clause 1 (prohibition up until 1808). As *Adarand* notes, up through the 1940s the Court had repeatedly asserted that the Fifth Amendment contained no equal protection guarantee protecting against discrimination by Congress. See Detroit Bank v. United States, 317 U.S. 329, 337 (1943); LaBelle Iron Works v. United States, 256 U.S. 377, 392 (1921) (cases decided under 14th amendment equal protection clause are "clearly ... not in point. The Fifth Amendment has no equal protection clause."). As you read the next set of materials on India, consider how the age of, and the ease of amending, a constitution may affect judicial interpretation of that constitution.

B. PLURALISM AND DEMOCRACY: THE POSITIVE STATE AND AFFIRMATIVE ACTION IN INDIA

To what extent do U.S. approaches to the affirmative consideration of race in government decisionmaking reflect the silence of the constitutional text on the question of "affirmative action"? In India, the constitutional text itself addresses affirmative action, e.g., in articles 15[4], and 16[4], which permit the government to make special provisions for members of the "Scheduled Castes" (formerly referred to as "untouchables"), Scheduled Tribes and other "socially and educationally Backward Classes" in government employment, and for elected offices as well. Some of these provisions were enacted as amendments to the Indian Constitution following a 1951 decision by the Indian Supreme Court finding unconstitutional a state government program allocating places in medical and engineering schools based on caste and religion.[d]

d. State of Madras v. Champakam Dorairajan, A.I.R. 1951 S.C. 226. According to the leading U.S. scholar on the subject, the decision not only invalidated the educational reservations but by implication "barred all preferential treatment outside the area of government employment," in which reservations had been authorized by article 16(4); in response to this decision, the Constitution was amended to include Article 15(4). Marc Galanter, Competing Equalities 164–65 (1984).

In 1975, the Indian Supreme Court held that affirmative action was in some circumstances required by the equality provisions in the Indian constitution.[e] As the following readings describe, the government has adopted substantial set-asides of positions in education and government hiring for members of the "scheduled castes and scheduled Tribes" and other "socially and educationally backward classes." As a result, judicial decisions in India often involve questions of identifying the appropriate group membership for a citizen seeking a preference, rather than the underlying question of the permissibility of affirmative action.

In order to assist you in thinking about the context of affirmative action in India, we have included one essay broadly surveying the background of the Indian Constitution and another assessing India's political and constitutional culture which appear below, before the materials more focussed on affirmative action (or "compensatory discrimination"). Consider whether the problems giving rise to affirmative action in India are similar to or different from those in the U.S. And how, if at all, does the constitutional status of affirmative action affect evaluation of its social consequences?

1.   SELECTED PROVISIONS, CONSTITUTION OF INDIA

Part III, Fundamental Rights . . .

Right to Equality

Article 14   Equality before law

The State shall not deny to any person equality before the law or the equal protection of the laws within the territory of India.

Article 15   Prohibition of discrimination on grounds of religion, race, caste, sex or place of birth

(1) The State shall not discriminate against any citizen on grounds only of religion, race, caste, sex, place of birth or any of them.

(2) No citizen shall, on grounds only of religion, race, caste, sex, place of birth or any of them, be subject to any disability, liability, restriction or condition with regard to—

(a) access to shops, public restaurants, hotels and places of public entertainment; or

(b) the use of wells, tanks, bathing ghats, roads and places of public resort maintained whole or partly out of State funds or dedicated to the use of general public.

(3) Nothing in this article shall prevent the State from making any special provision for women and children.

---

e. State of Kerala v. N.M. Thomas, A.I.R. 1976 S.C. 490. For further discussion, see below for excerpts from (Galanter, Law and Society in Modern India (1989)).

(4) Nothing in this article or in clause (2) of article 29 shall prevent the State from making any special provision for the advancement of any socially and educationally backward classes of citizens or for the Scheduled Castes and the Scheduled Tribes. [Added by amendment in 1951]

Article 16 *Equality of opportunity in matters of public employment*

(1) There shall be equality of opportunity for all citizens in matters relating to employment or appointment to any office under the State.

(2) No citizen shall, on grounds only of religion, race, caste, sex, descent, place of birth, residence or any of them, be ineligible for, or discriminated against in respect of, any employment or office under the State. . . .

(4) Nothing in this article shall prevent the State from making any provision for the reservation of appointments or posts in favour of any backward class of citizens which, in the opinion of the State, is not adequately represented in the services under the State. . . .

(4A) Nothing in this article shall prevent the State from making any provision for reservation in matters of promotion to any class or classes of persons in the service under the State in favour of the Scheduled Castes and the Scheduled Tribes which in the opinion of the State are not adequately represented in the services under the State. [Added by amendment effective 1995; see Sharal D. Abhyankar, *India*, in Constitutions of the Countries of the World (Gisbert H. Flanz, ed. 1997)]

Article 17 *Abolition of Untouchability*

"Untouchability" is abolished and its practice in any form is forbidden. The enforcement of any disability arising out of "Untouchability" shall be an offence punishable in accordance with law.

Article 29 *Protection of interests of minorities*

(1) Any section of the citizens residing in the territory of India or any part thereof having a distinct language, script or culture of its own shall have the right to conserve the same.

(2) No citizen shall be denied admission into any educational institution maintained by the State or receiving aid out of State funds on grounds only of religion, race, caste, language or any of them.

Article 30 *Right of minorities to establish and administer educational institutions*

(1) All minorities, whether based on religion or language, shall have the right to establish and administer educational institutions of their choice. . . .

(2) The State shall not, in granting aid to educational institutions, discriminate against any educational institution on the ground that it is under the management of a minority, whether based on religion or language. . . .

Part VI, Directive Principles of State Policy . . .

Article 37

The provisions contained in this part shall not be enforced by any court, but the principles therein laid down are nonetheless fundamental in the governance of the country and it shall be the duty of the State to apply these principles in making laws. . . .

Article 46   Promotion of educational and economic interests of Scheduled Castes, Scheduled Tribes and other weaker sections

The State shall promote with special care the educational and economic interests of the weaker sections of the people, and in particular, of the Scheduled Castes and the Scheduled Tribes, and shall protect them from social injustice and all forms of exploitation. . . .

Part XVI Special Provisions Relating to Certain Classes

Article 330   Reservation of seats for Scheduled Castes and Scheduled Tribes in the House of the People

(1) Seats shall be reserved in the House of the People for—

(a) the Scheduled Castes;

(b) the Scheduled Tribes . . .

(2) The number of seats reserved in any State or Union territory for the Scheduled Castes or the Scheduled Tribes under clause (1) shall bear, as nearly as may be, the same proportion to the total number of seats allotted to that State or Union territory in the House of the People as the population of the Scheduled Castes in the State or Union territory or of the Scheduled Tribes in the State or Union territory or part of the State or Union territory, as the case may be, in respect of which seats are so reserved, bears to the total population of the State or Union territory. . . .

Article 331   Representation of the Anglo-Indian community in the House of the People

Notwithstanding anything in article 81, the President may, if he is of opinion that the Anglo-Indian community is not adequately represented in the House of the People, nominate not more than two members of that community to the House of the People.

Article 332   Reservation of seats for Scheduled Castes and Scheduled Tribes in the Legislative Assemblies of the States

(1) Seats shall be reserved for the Scheduled Castes and the Scheduled Tribes, . . . in the Legislative Assembly of every State. . . .

(3) The number of seats reserved for the Scheduled Castes or the Scheduled Tribes in the Legislative Assembly of any State under clause (1) shall bear, as nearly as may be, the same proportion to the total number of seats in the Assembly as the population of the Scheduled Castes in the State or of the Scheduled Tribes in the State or part of the State, as the case may be, in respect of which seats are so reserved, bears to the total population of the State....

Article 333   Representation of the Anglo-Indian community in the Legislative Assemblies of the States

Notwithstanding anything in article 170, the Governor of a State may, if he is of opinion that the Anglo-Indian community needs representation in the Legislative Assembly of the State and is not adequately represented therein, nominate one member of that community to the Assembly.

Article 334   Reservation of seats and special representation to cease after fifty years*

Notwithstanding anything in the foregoing provisions of this Part, the provisions of this Constitution relating to—

(a) the reservation of seats for the Scheduled Castes and the Scheduled Tribes in the House of the People and in the Legislative Assemblies of the States; and

(b) the representation of the Anglo-Indian community in the House of the People and in the Legislative Assemblies of the States by nomination,

shall cease to have effect on the expiration of a period of fifty years from the commencement of this Constitution:

Provided that nothing in this article shall affect any representation in the House of the People or in the Legislative Assembly of a State until the dissolution of the then existing House or Assembly, as the case may be.

Article 335   Claims of Scheduled Castes and Scheduled Tribes to services and posts

The claims of the members of the Scheduled Castes and the Scheduled Tribes shall be taken into consideration, consistently with the maintenance of efficiency of administration, in the making of appointments to services and posts in connection with the affairs of the Union or of a State.

* * *

[Article 338 now provides for a National Commission for the Scheduled Castes and Tribes, to perform investigations, provide information, and recommend policies for the advancement of the Scheduled Castes and

---

* [Editors' Note: This time period was originally shorter and was (as of 1997) most recently extended by the Constitution (62d amendment) Act of 1989, according to Abhyankar, at 128].

Tribes. Articles 341 and 342 provide for the President to specify the castes, races, or tribes, or parts thereof, which for purposes of the Constitution are deemed Scheduled Castes and Tribes in particular States or Union territories, and further provides that Parliament may by law include or exclude others from such lists, which cannot be varied other than by such parliamentary action.]**

---

2. Background Readings on India

Fali Sam Nariman, *The Indian Constitution: An Experiment in Unity Amid Diversity*, in Forging Unity Out of Diversity: The Approaches of Eight Nations (Robert A. Goldwin, Art Kaufman, and William A. Schambra eds., 1985)

. . .

Writing in the quiet seclusion of a British prison in 1944 (during his ninth term of imprisonment for revolting against the British), Jawaharlal Nehru contemplated "the variety and unity" of India:

> The diversity of India is tremendous; it is obvious: it lies on the surface and anybody can see it. It concerns itself with physical appearances as well as with certain mental habits and traits. There is little in common, to outward seeming, between the Pathan of the Northwest and the Tamil in the far South. Their racial stocks are not the same, though there may be common strands running through them; they differ in face and figure, food and clothing, and, of course, language.... The Pathan and Tamil are two extreme examples; the others lie somewhere in between. All of them have still more the distinguishing mark of India. It is fascinating to find how the Bengalis, the Marathas, the Gujaratis, the Tamils, the Andhras, the Oriyas, the Assamese, the Canarese, the Malayalis, the Sindhis, the Punjabis, the Pathans, the Kashmiris, the Rajputs, and the great central block comprising the Hindustani-speaking people, have retained their peculiar characteristics for hundreds of years, have still more or less the same virtues and failings of which old tradition or record tells us, and yet have been throughout these ages distinctively Indian, with the same national heritage and the same set of moral and mental qualities. There was something living and dynamic about this heritage which showed itself in ways of living and a philosophical attitude to life and its problems. Ancient India, like ancient China, was a world in itself, a culture and a civilization which gave shape to all things. Foreign influences poured in and often influenced that culture and were absorbed. Disruptive tendencies gave rise immediately to an attempt to

** [Editors' Note: In 1989 this period was extended another 10 years (or a total of 50 years) to the year 2000.]

find a synthesis. Some kind of a dream of unity has occupied the mind of India since the dawn of civilization. That unity was not conceived as something imposed from outside, a standardization of externals or even of beliefs. It was something deeper and, within its fold, the widest tolerance of beliefs and customs was practiced and every variety acknowledged and even encouraged. . . .

In ancient and medieval times, the idea of the modern nation was non-existent, and feudal, religious, racial, and cultural bonds had more importance. Yet I think that at almost any time in recorded history an Indian would have felt more or less at home in any part of India, and would have felt as a stranger and alien in any other country. He would certainly have felt less of a stranger in countries which had partly adopted his culture or religion. Those, such as Christians, Jews, Parsees, or Moslems, who professed a religion of non-Indian origin or, coming to India, settled down there, became distinctively Indian in the course of a few generations. Indian converts to some of these religions never ceased to be Indians on account of a change of their faith. They were looked upon in other countries as Indians and foreigners, even though there might have been a community of faith between them.

Drafting a Constitution for Independent India. Nehru was the main architect of the Constitution of independent India and its first prime minister. But when he wrote the quoted passage, he was speaking of undivided India, of British India—the home of more than fourteen major languages (and thirty-three main dialects) belonging to four language families wholly unrelated to one another. The Indian National Congress, of which he was president, regarded India as a single country and its diverse inhabitants as one people. The rival political organization, the Muslim League, considered India to be occupied by two nations, the Hindus and the Muslims; in the late 1940s, the league pressed its demands for territorial adjustments to establish what later became the Islamic State of Pakistan.

Eventually, in June 1947, a scheme was devised that enabled the Muslims to have Pakistan if they wanted; since this was ultimately acceptable to the Indian National Congress, the Indian Independence Act of 1947 was passed by the British Parliament. . . .

Competing Claims of Diversity and Unity

The Constitution of India of 1950—one of the longest ever fashioned for an independent country—was proclaimed on January 26, 1950. It contained 395 articles and eight schedules occupying, in the official edition, 251 pages. "Too long, too detailed and too rigid" was the laconic comment of Sir Ivor Jennings, the constitutional historian of the Commonwealth. Its length was due not merely to the size of the country but also to the problems of accommodating, in a federal parliamentary constitution, the points of view of representatives of peoples speaking different languages and observing varied faiths, all striving at the same time to transform a rigid, hierarchical social order into an egalitarian society. The Chapter on Fundamental Rights (Part III) owed much to the standard-setting Charter of the United Nations and the almost contemporaneous Universal Declaration of Human Rights of 1948.

The Constitution ... is replete with incongruities.

- With more than thirty main indigenous languages and dialects from which to choose, the Constitution recognized English as one of two official languages.

- Among the fourteen regional languages listed in the Eighth Schedule was Sanskrit, which, like Latin, is a dead language, spoken only in prayer.

- The Preamble to the Constitution proclaimed India a secular republic; yet the Chapter on Fundamental Rights recognized and protected India's six main religions and nearly 200 "religious persuasions."

- The right to equality was guaranteed, and the state was prohibited from discriminating against any citizen on grounds of race, religion, caste, or place of birth, but the Constitution recognized and encouraged compensatory discrimination in favor of socially and educationally backward classes of citizens; however, economic backwardness arising out of dire poverty was not recognized as a basis for preferential treatment in educational institutions or in employment by the state.

- While adopting adult suffrage as the basis for periodic elections to Parliament and state assemblies and abolishing special electoral rolls based on race, religion, caste, or sex, the Constitution provided for the reservation of seats in the House of the People and in the legislative assembly of every state for Scheduled Castes and Scheduled Tribes (for centuries the outcastes of Hindu society).

Despite these seemingly disparate and contradictory provisions necessitated by social, historical and political considerations, if there is one overriding concept discernible in the Indian Constitution, it is the concern for the unity of the nation.

Common Citizenship as a Bond of Unity

The ideal of a unified, independent India mentioned in the Preamble to the Constitution, which inspired the provisions for common citizenship, posed few problems. British India was already politically one unit. With the lapse of paramountcy and the loss of protection by the British Crown, the inhabitants of the Indian states became virtually stateless. This condition contributed directly to the relatively smooth absorption of almost all the Indian states into the union of India. The Constitution provided a common citizenship not only for the former inhabitants of British India but also for those of the former Indian states. With their accession to India, the territory of these states became a part of the territory of India. Every person domiciled in India who was born (or either of whose parents was born) in India or who had ordinarily been a resident in India since 1945 was deemed to be a citizen of India (Part II, Article 5). The Constitution guaranteed to every citizen the right to move freely throughout India and to reside and settle in any part of India (Article 19[1][d] and [e]).

Common citizenship meant nondiscriminatory participation in the political life and affairs of the country. Communal representation in legislative bodies and separate electorates for separate communities (introduced by the British in 1909) were abolished. There was to be one general electoral roll for every territorial constituency (Article 325), and every adult citizen of India was entitled to be registered as a voter at every election of the House of the People (the lower house of Parliament) and of the assembly of the state in which he or she resided (Article 326). Anyone—Hindu, Muslim, Sikh, Christian, Buddhist, Jain, Parsee—who was a citizen could be elected to any office in the land, including the highest. Each decennial census (after 1951) has found that more than 80 percent of the Indian people profess some form of the Hindu religion; the Muslims constitute about 11 to 12 percent of the population and the Sikhs less than 2 percent. Since 1950 there have been seven presidents of India; three have been Muslims (one of them acting president), and the present incumbent is a Sikh.

Problems of Language, the Growth of Linguistic States, and Special Provisions for Linguistic Groups

If the provision of a common citizenship raised few or no problems, the next step—that of a common language—presented manifold difficulties and occasioned acrimonious debates in the Constituent Assembly. The languages spoken by the majority of the people of India fell into two major, unrelated language families: in the north the Sanskrit-based Indo-Aryan languages (Assamese, Bengali, Gujarati, Hindi, Marathi, Oriya, Pahari, and Punjabi); in the south the Dravidian languages (Kannada, Malayalam, Telugu, and Tamil).

Then there was the language of the conquerors. Under the Moghul rule (which preceded the British), Persian was the court language, but with the fall of the Moghul Empire, Persian was replaced by Urdu. With the establishment and consolidation of British rule, English came to be adopted as the language in which official correspondence was carried on at higher levels throughout the country. Higher education was also imparted in English, and English became increasingly the language linking the intelligentsia of the country. It was also the language of the superior courts (the high courts and the Federal Court of India). It served as a force for national unity and for the development of a national consciousness.

Competing claims were made in the Constituent Assembly for recognition of one or another language as the official language. Feelings ran high. To assuage them Gandhiji suggested the adoption of Hindustani—a mixture of Hindi and Urdu—as the common language, its use being recognized in both the Devnagari and the Urdu scripts. But Hindustani was not acceptable to the people of the south. The Constituent Assembly commenced its debate on the official language and on recognition of regional languages in a tense atmosphere; more than 300 amendments to the

Language Resolution were offered. Language, which contributed to the diversity and cultural richness of India, was now threatening to divide it. Statesmanship compelled a compromise, and this compromise is reflected in the language clauses of the Constitution.

The official language of India was declared to be Hindi in the Devnagari script, but English was to continue in use for all official purposes for an initial period of fifteen years, extendable by Parliament (Article 343). This period for the concurrent use of English was extended indefinitely with the enactment by Parliament of the Official Languages Act of 1963. Accordingly, since 1950 both Hindi and English have been official languages of the union of India. Both are used to transact business in the houses of Parliament (the House of the People and the Council of States) and for all official communications between the union government and the government of a state that has not adopted Hindi as its national language (see Article 346). The official language in each state was left to be decided by the state legislatures—each could adopt the regional language or Hindi (Article 345). In 1950 the states were multilingual; several languages were spoken in different regions of each state. Therefore, the Constitution provided that the president be empowered to direct that a language be recognized officially throughout a state when a substantial portion of that state's population who spoke the language so demanded (Article 347).

The territorial division of states in 1950 was a legacy from the past, a result of historical accident; the demarcation was determined partly by the sporadic growth of British power in India and partly by the process of integration of 550 princely states into India. Shortly after the Constitution came into effect, a demand arose for a rational reorganization of states on linguistic and cultural bases . . . . It was first conceded (in 1953) in the case of the Telugu-speaking areas of Madras and Mysore states, which in 1956 were merged with the Telugu-speaking areas of the former state of Hyderabad to form India's first and largest linguistic state, Andhra Pradesh, in the south.

This new state had to contend with many growing pains. Shortly after its formation, people of the same stock, united by a common language, again threatened to divide. There were demands—and violent demonstrations—for the formation of a separate state for the Telangaha region, which was economically and culturally more backward than the rest of Andhra. Happily, the problems were contained, and disruption of the state was averted, but only after a constitutional guarantee that in matters of public employment and education equitable opportunities would be provided for the people of the Telangaha region (Article 371-D, introduced in 1973). Andhra is a reminder that a feeling of being oppressed and outflanked by the more fortunate can transcend, and even disrupt, bonds of racial and linguistic affinity.

On the recommendation of a distinguished commission presided over by a sitting judge of the Supreme Court of India, the territories of other existing states were readjusted by law, and the readjustment of territorial boundaries to fit the linguistic and cultural similarities of inhabitants of various areas has continued. In northeastern India an attempt was made to enforce a regional language. The composite state of Assam, as defined by the Constitution, included the hill and tribal areas. In their zeal to promote unity among diverse elements in the state, the Assamese insisted that theirs should be the only recognized regional language. This alienated the people of the hill area. "Nothing gives rise to so much anger, hostility and even hatred," writes [Nari Rustumjee,] a distinguished civil servant with firsthand experience in the northeastern region, "as the apprehension of cultural aggression and it is this apprehension that has been at the root of unrest in India's Northeastern frontiers since British withdrawal." The result was the formation of smaller, nonviable northeastern states and union territories—the new state of Meghalaya and the Union territories of Mizoram and Arunachal Pradesh—which were once part of Assam. Today India (which is described in the opening article of the Constitution as "a Union of States") includes twenty-two linguistic states and nine union territories directly administered by the central government.

Each linguistic unit has adopted its own regional language—at times more than one. Hindi is the regional language in the five northern states (Bihar, Haryana, Madhya Pradesh, Rajasthan, and Uttar Pradesh); Urdu in Jammu and Kashmir; Punjabi in Punjab; Hindi and Gujarati in Gujarat; Pahari in Himachal Pradesh (a hill state carved out of the former state of East Punjab); Marathi in Maharashtra (whose principal city is Bombay); Oriya in Orissa; Assamese in Assam; Bengali in Tripura and West Bengal; Manipuri in Manipur; English (along with Lepcha, Bhutia, and Nepali) in the eastern hill state of Sikkim; English and Khasi in Meghalaya and in the tribal and mountainous state of Nagaland; and English and Mizo in the union territories of Mizoram and Arunachal Pradesh.

In the south the regional language is Telugu in Andhra Pradesh; Kannada in Karnataka (the former state of Mysore); Malayalam in Kerala and in the offshore union territory of Lakshadweep (the Laccadive Islands); and Tamil—the oldest Dravidian language—in Tamil Nadu (originally, the state of Madras). In the former Portuguese possession of Goa on the west coast, the languages of administration are Konkani and Marathi; and in the former French enclaves of Pondicherry and Mahe on the east coast, French, English, Tamil, Telugu, and Malayalam are used for official purposes.

This proliferation of regional languages has prompted India's constitutional historian to remind its citizens of the biblical story of the Tower of Babel and why it was never built. The reminder is timely. But the Founding Fathers anticipated this trend and laid the constitutional groundwork for strengthening the official language of the union. Article 351 imposes a duty on both Parliament and the central government to promote and strengthen the Hindi language, drawing sustenance from, but not interfering with, the fourteen other main languages specified in the Eighth Schedule. It also directs that a commission be constituted every ten years to make recommendations for the progressive use of the Hindi language for the official purposes of the union (Article 344).

Because of a desire not to disturb the broad pattern of the judicial system introduced by the British, all proceedings in the Supreme Court of India (the highest court) and in the high courts located in the states were to be (and are) conducted in English. Bills introduced in, and all acts passed by, the Parliament and state legislatures were also to continue to be in English (Article 348). A provision authorizing the use of Hindi in the high courts when the state legislature so decides and the president concurs has been availed of in two high courts (the High Court of Uttar Pradesh and the High Court of Rajasthan), where proceedings are now conducted both in English and in Hindi.

In providing for the principal languages spoken in India, the constitutional draftsman apparently overlooked the innumerable "mother tongues," languages spoken in homes in various parts of India. By a constitutional amendment in 1956, special obligations were imposed on states and local authorities throughout India to provide adequate facilities for instruction in the mother tongue at the primary stage of education for children belonging to linguistic minorities (Article 350-A).

Safeguards for Linguistic Groups and the Problems of Regionalism and
    Linguistic States

The constitutional safeguards for linguistic groups are found in Articles 29 and 30. Any group of citizens having a distinct language, script, or culture has a fundamental right to conserve it (Article 29[1]) and thus maintain its cultural identity. Likewise, no citizen can be denied admission on grounds of language, religion, race, or caste into any educational institution maintained by the state or receiving aid out of state funds (Article 29[2]). Since language, script, and culture can only be preserved and promoted through education, Article 30 guarantees to linguistic minorities "the right to establish and maintain educational institutions of their choice." These rights are absolute and, like all other fundamental rights, are enforceable through the established superior courts.

In 1952 a small linguistic minority known as Anglo-Indians, who managed many reputable schools in Bombay, were adversely affected when the state government passed an order forbidding state-aided schools that used English as a medium of instruction to admit pupils other than Anglo-Indians or citizens of non-Asian descent. Anglo-Indians could maintain and administer their schools and teach in English but only to Anglo-Indians; if they admitted other Indians, they forfeited state aid unless, of course, they switched to Hindi as the medium of instruction. The object was laudable—to encourage the use of the official language (itself a constitutional prescription under Article 351)—nonetheless, the order was struck down as violating Article 29(1) and 29(2) because Anglo-Indians had a distinct language (English) that they had the right to conserve and because the direct effect of the order was to prevent Indians from entering Anglo-Indian schools, on grounds of race and language.

The Supreme Court of India has also emphasized that included in Article 29(1) is the right to agitate, even politically, for the protection and preservation of a particular language and for one that is not necessarily a regional or a state-recognized language. With the reorganization of states into linguistic units, a constitutional amendment in 1956 provided for the appointment of a special officer for linguistic minorities. His duty is to investigate all matters relating to constitutional safeguards for linguistic minorities and to report to the Parliament and to concerned state governments (Article 350-B).

Differing views have been held on the utility and effect of the regrouping of states on linguistic and cultural bases and on ensuring separate educational and cultural opportunities to linguistic groups. They have led in recent years to regional, fissiparous, and at times secessionist tendencies. To counteract them, the Constitution was amended in 1963 to introduce the overriding concept of the sovereignty and integrity of India. Basic individual freedoms guaranteed under Article 19 (of free speech, peaceful assembly, forming associations or unions, moving freely throughout India, residing and settling in any part of India, and practicing any profession, occupation, trade, or business) are now subject to laws imposing reasonable restrictions on the exercise of these rights in the interests *(inter alia)* of "the sovereignty and integrity of India"—in other words, in the wider interests of the unity of India.

Then, in accordance with recommendations of the National Integration Council, amendments were introduced in the general penal law to make it an offense for anyone to promote or attempt to promote feelings of enmity or hatred among religious, social, or language groups or communities. The divisive force of language has also been contained by the Supreme Court of India in its role as interpreter of the Constitution. States had plenary power over education until 1976. When the state of Gujarati enacted a law prescribing Gujarati as the exclusive language of instruction in the universities in the state, the Supreme Court invalidated the law. It held that although the subject matter of education was within the exclusive jurisdiction of the state, legislation respecting "co-ordination and determination of standards in the institutions for higher education" included prescription of the language of instruction in Indian universities. The substance of the state law touched on a matter reserved exclusively for legislation by Parliament and was therefore beyond the competence of the state legislature.

Despite judicial and constitutional attempts at containment, linguistic factionalism has fostered a pervading spirit of regionalism. Language differences are the most significant aspect of the diversity of India. They are part of regional identity, but they help to perpetuate regional distinctiveness and encourage regional loyalty. . . .

Accommodating Religions in a Secular Republic

India is also a religiously pluralistic society. The majority of its people (82.6 percent in the census of 1981) profess the Hindu religion; almost the same percentage did so when Europeans (the French, the Portuguese, and the British) first came to India. Within its borders are also found followers of all the major religions of the world. From the matrix of Hinduism have emerged three other great world religions—Jainism, Buddhism, and Sikhism. Christianity came to India many centuries before it reached Europe. One of the twelve original apostles of Jesus, St. Thomas, visited India in A.D. 56, converted a large number of Hindus, was martyred in Mylapore, and lies buried in Madras. Judaism and its adherents (though very few) also found a home and refuge in India. The ancient synagogue in Cochin, in the state of Kerala, built in 1568, bears testimony to the Indian rulers' tolerance of those of alien faiths.

Next to the several cults of Hinduism, however, the main religion is Islam. It has been on Indian soil since A.D. 650, a few years after the Prophet's death, when Arab traders settled on the western seacoast of Malabar (now part of the state of Kerala). Their descendants are so Indianized that they speak the same language as their Hindu brethren and read the Koran only in Malayalam. Forced conversion in Europe and Central Asia in the Middle Ages effectively destroyed the identity of religious minorities. Not so in India. The Ismaili Khojas (followers of the Aga Khan), the Cutchi Memons, and the Bohras were all originally Hindus; they were converted to Islam about 500 years ago during the invasions of Mohamed of Gazni and his successors. Devout Muslims, they practice the religion of Islam but for centuries have retained part of their original identity. Until statutory law intervened in 1938, they were governed by Hindu law in matters of inheritance and succession.

Religion in India not only means the profession of faith but also encompasses places—temples, gurudwaras, mosques, churches, and synagogues. It includes idols and deities and offerings to them, bathing places, graves, tombs, and properties attached to and owned by religious institutions. All this—faith, worship, ritual, and the secular activities of religious groups—had to be provided for in the Constitution, in the Chapter on Fundamental Rights, beyond the reach of legislative or executive interference.

There is no provision similar to the First Amendment of the Constitution of the United States of America, prohibiting the establishment of religion by law, but there is no state religion. That was clarified in 1976 by a constitutional amendment that added the word "Secular" to the Preamble. In the "Sovereign, Socialist, Secular Democratic Republic of India" no religious instruction can be provided in any educational institution wholly maintained out of state funds (Article 28[1]), nor can any person be compelled to pay taxes to be used for the promotion or maintenance of any particular religion or religious denomination (Article 27). Similarly, no person attending any educational institution recognized by the state or receiving aid out of state funds can be compelled to take part in any religious instruction imparted in that institution or to attend any religious worship conducted in it without his or his guardian's consent (Article 26[3]).

At the same time all persons (not merely citizens) are equally entitled to freedom of conscience and the right freely to profess, practice, and propagate their religion (Article 25). All religious denominations (there were 183 of them in the 1981 census) and even particular sects have the fundamental right to establish and maintain institutions for religious and charitable purposes, to manage their own affairs in matters of religion, and to own, acquire, and administer their properties in accordance with law (Article 26).

The freedom to practice religion and the freedom to manage religious affairs are not, however, absolute; they are subject to public order, morality, and health. The clauses on freedom of religion were modeled on Article 44 of the Constitution of Ireland. The Supreme Court of India has repeatedly stressed the breadth and the limits of this freedom. Religion includes forms of worship and all religious practices that are (or are believed by the faithful to be) an integral part of the religion; even the right of the head of a religious denomination to excommunicate any of its members on religious grounds has been upheld.... Although every religious denomination enjoys complete autonomy in deciding what rites and ceremonies are essential according to its tenets, the right to manage the properties of a religious institution has always been regarded as a secular matter that can be regulated by law.

Protection of Minority Rights by the Constitution and the Courts

The Objectives Resolution, moved by Jawaharlal Nehru at the first sitting of the Constituent Assembly on December 13, 1946, contained a pledge that in the Constitution "adequate safeguards shall be provided for minorities, backward and tribal areas and other backward classes." Accordingly, Article 30(1) of the Constitution guaranteed to all minorities, whether based on religion or on language, the right to establish and administer educational institutions; the state was prohibited from discriminating against any educational institution on the ground that it was under the management of a religious or linguistic minority (Article 30 [2]). When the right to acquire and hold property was deleted from the Chapter on Fundamental Rights by a constitutional amendment in 1978, an exception was made for minority educational institutions. Under Article 30(1A) their property could be compulsorily acquired for public purposes only if the state ensured that the amount fixed or determined by law for the acquisition was such as would not restrict or abrogate the right guaranteed under Article 30(1).

When Sikkim became a part of India in 1975, special provisions had to be made for the protection of its original inhabitants. With the waves of immigration of the Nepalese into Sikkim over the course of a hundred years, the Bhutia-Lepchas (the indigenous population) had become a minority in their own country. This ethnic group was ensured equal representation in the Sikkim assembly.

Despite declarations of constitutional rights, minorities in society cannot find adequate protection in the normal political process; they need the protection of courts. The courts in India, when dealing with minority rights, have tended to conceptualize their role as that of a political party in opposition. Almost every time that minorities have approached the Supreme Court complaining of infraction by state or central legislation, the challenge has been upheld. In 1958 the court thwarted an attempt by the Communist-controlled government of Kerala to take over the management of Christian schools. In an advisory opinion given by the Supreme Court (on a reference by the president under Article 143 of the Constitution), large parts of the Kerala Education Bill were declared unconstitutional.

Since the state governments found it increasingly difficult to regulate educational standards, the highest court was asked in 1974 to constitute a larger bench to reconsider its previous decisions. Certain provisions of the Gujarat University Act of 1949 laid down conditions for affiliation of colleges in Gujarat with the Gujarat University. They applied to all educational institutions, including those run by minorities, and they provided that teaching and training in all colleges affiliated with the university would be conducted and imparted by teachers appointed only by the university. Since the provisions interfered with the right of minorities "to establish and administer educational institutions of their choice"—a right guaranteed under Article 30—they were challenged by the Ahmedabad St. Xavier's College Society (managed by Jesuits).

The court, sitting *en banc* (nine judges participating), struck down the offending provisions as inapplicable to colleges run by minorities. Mr. Justice K. K. Mathew read into the article the right of parents to determine which school their children should be sent to for study: "The fundamental postulate of personal liberty excludes any power of the State to standardize and socialize its children by forcing them to attend public schools only." Mr. Justice Khanna gave the reason why minority interests were so zealously protected by the courts:

> The safeguarding of the interest of the minorities amongst sections of the population is as important as the protection of the interest amongst individuals of persons who are below the age of majority or are otherwise suffering from some kind of infirmity. The Constitution and the laws made by civilized nations, therefore, generally contain provisions for the protection of those interests. It can, indeed, be said to be an index of the level of civilization and catholicity of a nation as to how far their minorities feel secure and are not subject to any discrimination or suppression.

The ambit of the constitutional protection for minorities has been considerably extended by the judicial interpretation given to the term "minorities." Members of a reformed Hindu sect (Arya Samaj) were held to be entitled, under Article 30(1), to the fundamental right to establish and administer educational institutions in the state of Punjab (where Sikhs and not Hindus are in a majority). In India, because of its size, minority status is determined by state, not by country.

Accommodating Equality in a Sea of Untouchability and Backwardness

The Legacy of the Past. The provisions relating to "the Right of Equality" in the Constitution (Articles 14 to 18) reflect the grim reality of a developing country, slowly emerging out of a rigid, caste-bound social system. "The spirit of the Age," Nehru once wrote, "is in favor of equality, but practice denies it almost everywhere." In keeping with the spirit of the age, the Constitution guarantees to all persons the equal protection of the laws and prohibits the state (which includes all lawmaking and law enforcement bodies) from denying to any person equality before the law (Article 14). Equality of opportunity is ensured to all citizens in matters relating to employment or appointment to any office under the state (Article 16[1]); the state cannot discriminate (either generally or in matters relating to public employment) against any citizen on grounds of religion, race, caste, sex, or place of birth (Articles 15[2] and 16[2]); and no citizen can be denied admission into any educational institution maintained by the state or receiving aid out of state funds on grounds of religion, race, caste, or language (Article 29[2]).

Nothing in these provisions, however, prevents the state from making special provisions for what the Constitution regards as "weaker sections of Society": for them protective discrimination is recognized and encouraged as a fundamental duty of the state. Article 46 (in Part IV, Directive Principles of State Policy) enjoins the state to "promote with special care the educational and economic interest of the weaker sections of the people and in particular of the Scheduled Castes and the Scheduled Tribes"; it directs the state to "protect them from social injustice and all forms of exploitation." The beneficiaries of preferential treatment are indicated clearly in the Constitution:

- Women and children are exceptions to the general rule against any form of discrimination (Article 15[3]).

- Scheduled Castes, Scheduled Tribes, and socially and educationally backward classes of citizens are also exceptions to the general rule against discrimination (Articles 15[4] and 16[4]). The Scheduled Castes (or "untouchables") are the largest of these groups. The Constitution enables the state to make special reservations in educational institutions and in public services for backward classes of citizens and to ensure that they are adequately represented insofar as is consistent with maintaining efficient administration (Article 335). It also provides for representation in Parliament and in state assemblies for Scheduled Castes and Scheduled Tribes and a proportional reservation of seats for them in the lawmaking bodies of the nation (Articles 330 and 331). These provisions for representation were initially intended to operate for ten years but have been extended periodically by constitutional amendments. As the Constitution now stands, they will be in effect until 1990.*

Preferential treatment for women and children is easily explained. In every society children are treated differently from adults. Women consti-

---

* [Editors' Note: In 1989 this period was   years) to the year 2000.]
extended another 10 years (or a total of 50

tute nearly 50 percent of India's population; the majority of them have been an oppressed class. The personal and customary laws of the Hindus and Muslims imposed special disabilities and constraints on them. *"Na stree swatjamtramarhati,"* said Manu the lawgiver: The woman does not deserve independence. In a male-dominated society women were looked on as chattels, useful only for marriage and the bearing of children. The institution known in Roman law as the perpetual tutelage of women was, as Sir Henry Maine pointed out, carried to its logical conclusion in India.

Why have safeguards and special provisions for "Scheduled Castes," "Scheduled Tribes," and "Backward Classes"? For treating adult male citizens differently there must be a reason, for, as Isaiah Berlin said in a famous essay on the subject, "the assumption is that equality needs no reason, only inequality does." The answer lies in our history. The reason for the unequal and preferential treatment of these categories in the Constitution is that these groups have been disadvantaged for centuries, many of them beyond the pale of law—Scheduled Castes and Scheduled Tribes even beyond human compassion. For more than 2,000 years, "untouchables" and "tribals" were treated as if they were less than human beings, a treatment rationalized by the argument that they and their children were inherently inferior in ability to those born into superior stations in life. As Marc Galanter says in his excellent treatise on the subject: "India embraced equality as a cardinal value against a background of elaborate, valued and clearly perceived inequalities." In other words, when drafting the Constitution, we were atoning for the past.

What was the past? We must go back over two milleniums. The Aryans were the first invaders of the land inhabited by the serpent-worshiping Nagas and other ancient tribes in the north and by the Dravidians in the south. The Aryans subjugated India without pretending to elevate it. They wanted land and pasture for their cattle; slowly they made their way eastward along the Indus and the Ganges until all Hindustan was under their control. Outnumbered by a subject people whom they considered inferior, the Vedic Aryans sought to preserve their racial identity. In a couple of centuries, however, they were assimilated and absorbed. The first caste division was not by status but by color (as Will Durant reminds us). It separated the fair Aryans with long noses from the dark, broad-nosed Dravidians: "It was merely the marriage regulation of an endogamous group." But that was only how it started.

As the India pictured in the Vedas (2000–1000 B.C.) changed to the conditions described in the great Hindu epics of the Mahabarata and the Ramayana (1000–400 B.C.), occupations became hereditary and more specialized, and caste divisions were more rigidly defined. First were the Kshatriyas (or fighters), who considered it a sin to die in bed. But as conditions of war gave way to peace and as religion and ritual (largely an aid to agriculture in the face of incalculable elements) grew in importance and complexity, requiring proficient intermediaries between men and gods, the Brahmins consolidated their position. They alone knew the ancient Sanskrit (the oldest in the European group of languages); they alone could recite the Vedas. They were able to recreate the past and form the future in their own image, molding each generation into one with greater reverence for the priests, building for their caste a prestige that in later centuries gave them the supreme place in Hindu society.

Below the Brahmins and Kshatriyas were the Vaishyas—farmers and traders. These three castes (or varnas) were regarded as twice born, the second birth (or regeneration) consisting in the study of the Vedas and in the performance of sacraments. The twice-born status was denied to the fourth varna, the Shudras—or the working class—who made up most of the population. Over the years a fifth category long unrecognized in theory, the outcastes, emerged—unconverted native tribes, captives of war, and men reduced to slavery as punishment. This small group of the casteless formed the nucleus of what has become the world's largest minority: the untouchables (euphemistically described as "the Scheduled Castes").

It was not as if the caste principles on which Hindu society was organized were never questioned from within. The religious hegemony of the Brahmins was contested by the Kshatriya nobleman who founded Buddhism. This new religion rejected the predetermination of status by birth and the hierarchical ranking of castes. It became the religion of the kings who ruled India for nearly 900 years. Embraced by the Emperor Ashoka (273–232 B.C.), Buddhism gained a foothold in the subcontinent. For more than 200 years it posed a real threat to Hinduism. But then it became riddled with schisms and sects and was influenced by Hindu pantheistic beliefs.... Hindu culture proved too much for this ascetic, nontheistic religion. Buddha was slowly absorbed into the Hindu pantheon as one of the incarnations of the God Vishnu. During the reign of Harsh-Vardhan (A.D. 606–648)—the last Buddhist king—the great casteless religion was stamped out in the land of its birth. The oriental scholar Sir Charles Eliot has described the denouement in an expressive phrase: "Brahmins killed Buddhism by a fraternal embrace."

The Hinduism that replaced Buddhism was an amalgam of faiths and ceremonies that had four common characteristics; it recognized the caste system; it reaffirmed the leadership of the Brahmins; it accepted the law of karma (destiny) and the transmigration of souls; and it replaced with new gods the deities of the Vedas. Caste came back into its own and with it the antithesis of "pure" versus "impure." The untouchables—Hindu outcastes—grew in number, particularly with the introduction of new occupations. By the latter part of the Middle Ages India was more advanced in agriculture, handicrafts, and commerce than many other countries. To the traditional division of society into four main castes (Brahmins, Kshatriyas, Vaishyas, and Shudras) were added an almost indefinite number of occupational castes (in the thousands). The criteria for the hierarchical status of high or low multiplied a thousand-fold with new occupations. For each new activity it was the Brahmins who determined which aspects were low or impure, and the number of outcastes increased even further.

Muslim rule brought some changes into Indian society, but neither the new language of the courts (Persian) nor the religion of the new rulers

(Islam) made any difference to the traditional division of labor organized through specialized groups ranked in hierarchical order. Caste and untouchability flourished during Muslim rule.

Only during British rule were the first attempts made at emancipation. The new economic order brought in by the conquerors from the West altered the design of a social system that had retained a remarkable continuity for centuries. Moreover, with English education more people became acquainted with modern European and American history, with their concepts of equality and fraternity. The beneficiaries of the British system of education, mainly the children of high-caste Hindu families, grew up questioning the principles on which their society was organized. A few cosmetic changes were introduced, such as the Caste Disabilities Removal Act of 1850, but it was a dead letter. Social consciousness had not yet been aroused.

Then, at the beginning of this century, Gandhi introduced into the independence movement two new concepts: peaceful noncooperation with the British (nonviolent Satyagraha) and a plea for a better deal for the outcastes. Gandhi lived among them and described them as Harijans (children of God). In the liberal spirit of the age, the name stuck. It brought an increasing awareness to the Indian mind of the shame of untouchability. Among the more enlightened of the higher castes a movement started to do something to relieve the lot of the depressed classes. To uplift them was regarded as an act of compassion, a voluntary righting of the wrongs of many years. But as the benefits of Western-style education permeated downward, the bright young men in the society of outcastes also spearheaded a movement that was based not on compassion but on right. The leader of this movement—and its most eloquent member—was Dr. B. R. Ambedkar, a Harijan; he was, along with Nehru, one of the principal architects of the Constitution of India.

Atonement for the Past. This, then, was the legacy that we inherited with independence. Aware of the generations of accumulated and accentuated group inequalities, the Constituent Assembly adopted a constitutional policy of deliberate preferential treatment for the historically disadvantaged peoples. First untouchability was abolished and its practice in any form forbidden (Article 17). The Untouchability Offences Act of 1955 (renamed in 1967 the Civil Rights Act) adopted legal sanctions in aid of the constitutional prohibition. All temples and religious institutions were constitutionally "thrown open" to the untouchables (Article 25[1][b]). A form of apartheid, long practiced by the twice-born classes against the untouchables, was abolished, and all citizens became entitled to equal access to shops, restaurants, hotels, and places of entertainment and to the use of wells, tanks, bathing places, roads, and places of public resort (Article 15[2]).

Untouchability was not merely a stigma, however; it was an attitude of mind. Mere constitutional declarations were not enough. It was against this background that the Constitution recognized, promoted, and encouraged special treatment in educational and employment opportunities for the

Harijans and the less fortunate classes. It enabled Parliament and the states to make special provisions through ordinary law for the advancement of Scheduled Castes, Scheduled Tribes, and other backward classes—those who by reason of their occupational background were socially and educationally backward. Provisions could be made, without infringing the equality clauses, for reservation of seats in educational institutions and of posts at almost all levels of public services. Although the Constitution does not prescribe the number, reservations up to (and at times exceeding) 50 percent have always been upheld by the Supreme Court of India as not violating the clauses guaranteeing equality to all (Articles 14, 15[1], and 15[2]) or the meritocratic principles they embody.*

The Constitution prescribed an agency and a method for designating Scheduled Castes and Scheduled Tribes. The president (that is, the central government, since all executive action of the government of India is taken in the name of the president) was empowered to specify the castes, races, or tribes that, for the purposes of the Constitution, would be deemed to be Scheduled Castes or Scheduled Tribes within any particular state or union territory (Articles 341 and 342). Once promulgated, these lists could be changed only by an act of Parliament.

The Scheduled Castes Order promulgated by the president in 1950 (with amendments introduced over the years) proceeded primarily on the basis of untouchability, measured by the incidence of social disability combined with economic, occupational, educational, residential, and religious tests. The Scheduled Tribes Order of 1950—amended over the years—listed backward tribes in need of preferential treatment.

The scheme of Scheduled and Tribal Areas (under the Government of India Act of 1935) was adopted in the Constitution (Part X, Article 244 and 244[A], and the Fifth and Sixth schedules). These designated areas were to be administered as a special responsibility of the governor of the state in consultation with tribal committees and councils.

The provisions for Scheduled Tribes in the Constitution were intended to preserve their separate identities. The aim was a balanced improvement of their condition with such a degree of assimilation as would preserve their distinctiveness and give them a measure of autonomy. Primitive cultures react sharply to alien interference. Experience has shown that indigenous tribal communities are prepared to adapt themselves to change only on their own terms and in their own time. The constitutional policy for Scheduled Castes has been to overcome their disabilities and disadvantages by preferential treatment, to eliminate their distinctiveness by enabling them to share the advantages for lack of which they are still a class apart from other, advantaged citizens of Hindu society.

While the categories of Scheduled Castes and Scheduled Tribes have been constitutionally determined, the "other backward classes" (OBCs)

* [Editors' Note: See discussion below in   49.5% rule and of the *Indra Sawhney* case.]
Questions and Comments, paragraph 1, of

also designated for preferential treatment (Articles 15[4] and 16[4]) were left undefined. They are therefore to be determined by the states and by government agencies. The absence of any identifiable and constitutionally prescribed test has led to much bitterness and dissatisfaction, especially in recent years. Although commissions appointed under Article 340 to investigate and report on the socially and educationally backward classes have made recommendations, they have not always been uniform, nor have they been accepted. The first Backward Classes Commission submitted its report in 1955, listing 2,939 castes as "socially and educationally backward." The report was not accepted by the central government since no objective tests were laid down for identifying OBCs. The government was opposed to the adoption of caste as a criterion for backwardness; it would have preferred the application of an economic or means test.

The second Backward Classes Commission (better known as the Mandal commission), in its report submitted in 1980, rejected the application of a means test in view of the language of Article 340; that article and the reservations envisaged in Article 15(4) applied only, it said, to "socially and educationally backward classes," not to economically backward classes. The commission concluded that, in view of the permanent stratification of society in a hierarchical caste order, low ritual caste status had a direct bearing on a person's social backwardness.

The commission produced some startling figures. It estimated, from census data, that socially and educationally backward classes (both Hindu and non-Hindu) constituted as much as 52 percent of the population of India, excluding the Scheduled Castes and Scheduled Tribes, which accounted for an additional 22.5 percent. It also reported that the representation of other backward classes in government services and public employment was only 13 percent and their representation in "plum" jobs (Class I posts) a meager 4.7 percent. Statistics, when skillfully presented, dispel complacency. The backward classes were agitated.

Meanwhile, the state of Karnataka set up its own commission to investigate and report on backward classes in the state. This commission (named, after its chairman, the Havanur commission) ignored the principle of caste in the concept of social backwardness and devised a new test, that of poverty coupled with isolation. This test cut across the caste system and included as backward classes several groups of temple functionaries (who belonged to higher castes) as well as some Kshatriyas. At the same time it excluded some groups in the traditionally low castes on the grounds of their economic advancement. The state of Karnataka accepted the report and made reservations in accordance with it. As expected, the state action was challenged in the High Court of Karnataka and later in the Supreme Court of India.

Meanwhile a commission in Gujarat, appointed to recommend identifying tests for the socially and educationally backward classes in the state, submitted its report to the government of Gujarat. This commission (known as the Rane commission) also ignored castes and subcastes in listing the socially and educationally backward classes. It concluded that, for an initial period of ten years, it should be assumed that those who belonged to the lower castes or subcastes but who were individually and financially well off did not suffer from any social and educational backwardness. The financial criterion adopted was an annual family income over Rs. 10,000; those with family incomes less than that figure would become beneficiaries of Articles 15(4) and 16(4) of the Constitution. The government's acceptance of this recommendation and its decision to increase the percentage of reservations from about 30 percent to nearly 50 percent sparked a series of riots in the state in the summer of 1985. The decision has generated a new conflict over reservation that threatens to spread beyond Gujarat. The swelling numbers of the backward classes ... have further aggravated the problem.

Against this background the decision of the Indian Supreme Court in the Karnataka case (*K.C. Vasanth Kumar v. State of Karnataka*, [2 A.I.R. (S.C.) 1495 [1985]], was disappointing. Called on to give guidelines for determining other backward classes (for purposes of the state's reservation policy), the five justices spoke in different voices, responding without any unanimity on the main points of contention. The justices were divided on whether reservation of more than 50 percent was permissible; on whether castes should form the basis—or at least an important element—for determining social and educational backwardness; and on whether in jobs requiring high expertise and skill a policy of reservation, detracting from merit, was possible.

On one point, however, they were all agreed. They were agreed and alarmed about a new trend, that of privileged groups among underprivileged classes monopolizing for themselves the preferential benefits intended for the class. Mr. Justice Chinnappa Reddy dwelt on the degrading spectacle:

> The paradox of the system of reservation is that it has engendered a spirit of self-denigration among the people. Nowhere else in the world do castes, classes or communities queue up for the sake of gaining the backward status. Nowhere else in the world is there competition to assert backwardness and to claim "we are more backward than you." This is an unhappy and disquieting situation, but it is stark reality.

Mr. Justice D. A. Desai, who made a fervent plea for the recognition of poverty as a true criterion for backwardness, said that if a survey were made about the benefits of preferred treatment among the undefined economically and socially backward classes, "it would unmistakably show that the benefits of reservations are snatched away by the top creamy layer of the backward castes."

This consideration prompted the chief justice of India, C. J. Chandrachud, to recommend that a test of economic backwardness be applied not only to the other backward classes but also to Scheduled Castes and Scheduled Tribes. He stated that the policy of reservations in public employment, in education, and in legislative bodies should be reviewed once every five years. That would help the state to rectify the distortions arising out of the implementation of the reservations policy; it would also help the people (backward and other) to vent their views in a continuing public debate on the practical effects of that policy.

Conclusion

... [T]he Indian experiment of unity amid diversity has so far succeeded only partially.

The difficulty of language was almost insurmountable in the early years; it has not been resolved. It has been contained through a spirit of accommodation, by constant attempts at a synthesis; consensus has been the distinguishing feature of Indian culture.

We have achieved greater success in our treatment of minorities. Thirty-five years under the Constitution have ensured for religious and linguistic minorities and for religious denominations of every kind a freedom from state interference that is truly remarkable. The freedom these groups enjoy in the Indian polity is unsurpassed among developing, pluralistic societies.

We have not yet solved our main problem, however. We have not resolved the complexities that lie buried in the great but elusive doctrine of equality. To what extent should the claim based on merit and on the fundamental right of equality be ignored? How far does the Constitution, truly interpreted, direct us to go? How soon are we to atone for the oppression of centuries? Should we go on equalizing downward? and for how long? These questions surface periodically. The underrepresentation of the underprivileged in public employment remains highly disproportionate, and, as Ralph Bunche once said, "Inalienable rights cannot be enjoyed posthumously."

Still, we cannot ignore the groundswell of public opinion: an increasing resistance to the view that the sins of generations of forefathers in the higher castes should be expiated here and now—in a couple of generations. Even the Hindu law's theory of "pious obligation" requires the Hindu son to meet the financial obligations only of his father, not of the forebears of his father. The judges, who have the final word in all constitutional matters, have not been very helpful. They have interpreted the compensatory discrimination clauses differently at different times. They have on occasion prodded and energized governments to live up to the constitutional commitment to alleviate the lot of the downtrodden, but the ground rules have kept fluctuating. Marc Galanter, a sympathetic critic, has explained why:

> In an area of law founded on the constitutional embrace of conflicting principles, it should not be expected that courts would provide an enduring synthesis that transcends and encompasses them and settles disputed issues with finality. Rather, we would expect—if the courts are at all representative of the larger society—some ambiguity and vacillation.

Amid all the controversy and vacillation one thing is certain: as long as poverty continues to stalk the land and gross disparities between the rich and poor remain, the ideal of an egalitarian society envisaged in our basic document of governance will remain a dream. Whatever the nation's karma, the founding fathers cannot be faulted for a lack of idealism. . . . It is not because of our Constitution but despite its provisions that we have failed to achieve what were naively assumed (in 1950) to be achievable goals.

We have abolished untouchability and outlawed backwardness in the Constitution of India. Alas, many of us have not eliminated it from our hearts.

————

Sankaran Krishna, *Constitutionalism, Democracy and Political Culture in India*, Political Culture and Constitutionalism (Daniel P. Franklin and Michael J. Baun eds., 1994)

. . . [I]n India, there exists a strong mutual relationship between the institutions of democratic governance and the culture of politics. . . . What is paradoxical about this dialectic between political institutions and political culture is that today, with the pronounced erosion of the institutions of democracy, it is really in civil society, with its pluralist and tolerant culture, that the foundations of democracy lie. How long India can sustain the democratic way of life, given the reality of eroding institutions, is an open question. . . .

At independence, there was a small industrial sector, an overwhelmingly stagnant and backward agrarian sector, and one of the largest and poorest populations in the world. Colonialism did, however, bequeath an impressive political and administrative legacy. Prominent among these was the Indian National Congress Party, formed in 1885, that led the drive for independence. By the 1930s, the Congress had built up a far-reaching organizational structure that penetrated the hinterland. While the leadership remained urban and middle class (consisting of lawyers, journalists, teachers, professionals, and the like), the party's ability to mobilize the people in the struggle against colonialism (primarily via the still somewhat inexplicable persona of Mohandas Gandhi) had been amply demonstrated.

The national movement had eschewed extremism for moderation. In this stand, it was favored by the colonial regime that lent legitimacy to such bourgeois-liberal politics and came down heavily on both left-wing and "terrorist" movements calling for an armed struggle against colonialism. . . . The first serious attempt at devolving any power came with the passage of the Government of India Act of 1935. This act expanded the voting population to one-sixth of the adult population and conceded limited self-rule at the provincial level. In the elections to the provincial councils held in 1937 and 1938, Congress secured comfortable majorities in eight of the eleven provinces and formed governments in these areas. Although this experiment proved short-lived (with all the Congress regimes resigning in protest over Britain's unilateral decision in 1939 to "enter" India in the war against Germany), it provided Congress with some experience in government. At the same time, the leadership of the Congress Party (prominently Mohandas Gandhi, Jawaharlal Nehru, Vallabhbhai Patel, Maulana Abul Kalam Azad, and Subhas Chandra Bose) had very different visions of the postindependent future.

This tolerance for diversity in forging a nationalist movement would prove to be an important legacy of this period. However, this inclusiveness imparted a certain character to the Congress Party that would later on become more of a liability. Simply put, the Congress was a party ideally suited for conducting a broad-based political struggle against colonialism. Once independence was achieved, the lack of a coherent ideology of social change and a committed cadre for its implementation rendered the Congress a party that was long on reformist rhetoric but short on the organizational ability to deliver on its promises.

The other great holdover from this period was the Indian Civil Service. At independence, the British members resigned, but the Indians remained and, over-night, were transformed into the administrative arm of the new government. The civil service proved to be especially crucial in the new government's establishing control in the five-hundred-odd former princely states, ... which controlled nearly 40 percent of the country.

The foundations of the new state were debated in the Constituent Assembly (elected indirectly from the various provinces in 1946) in the years 1947–50. The result was the Constitution of India, adopted on January 26, 1950, proclaiming India a democratic republic with a parliamentary system of government. The real locus of power is the prime minister (who heads a Council of Ministers) and the other important institutions of governance at the Centre are the lower house of the legislature (the Lok Sabha, or the House of the People), the Supreme Court, and the civil service. The Fundamental Rights guarantees each citizen the right to equality, freedom, nonexploitation, freedom of religion, cultural and educational development, property, and constitutional redress. The separately listed Directive Principles of State Policy (in Part 4 of the Constitution) move theoretically further along the direction of a welfarist state by enjoining the state actively to promote a "social order in which justice, social, economic and political, shall inform all the institutions of public life." The Directive Principles, however, are nonjusticiable. Notwithstanding the egalitarian sentiments expressed in this section of the Constitution, state policy has, in the main, been unable to implement them....

In terms of its division of responsibility between the Centre and the states (which have a parallel political structure), most would agree that the form of federalism in India is highly centralized.... The summary by Robert L. Hardgrave Jr. and Stanley Kochanek should suffice:

> Several things impart to Indian federalism a highly centralized
> form: the constitutional right of the central government to invade the
> legislative and executive domain of the states; the power of the Centre
> to intervene in state affairs and exercise supervisory powers over the

states; and the heavy dependence of the states on central financial assistance, both for their regular budgetary needs as well as for capital expenditures. Moreover, the existence of a dominant party that controlled both the central government and almost all of the state governments [until 1967] reinforced these constitutional provisions at the political level for some time....

Despite the domination of the Congress Party (five of the nine prime ministers were from the Congress; Congress regimes have been in power for forty-one of the forty-six years since independence, thirty of those continuously from 1947 to 1977), it has never secured more than 48.1 percent of the popular vote in any election to the legislature, and, more often than not, its share of the popular vote has hovered in the high-30s to the mid-40s as a percentage. At the level of the district, Congress has been dominant in less than one-quarter of the country as a whole. In the elections of 1967, non-Congress governments were voted to power in eight of the then-sixteen states. In the middle of 1987, well over half the Indian states were ruled by non-Congress opposition parties even as the Congress had its largest majority ever in the central legislature under Rajiv Gandhi.

Voter turnouts have steadily increased from about 45 percent of the eligible electorate in the first general elections of 1952 to a high of 64 percent in the elections of 1984. In 1989, the turnout was 61.9 percent of a total electorate of close to half a billion, with 308.3 million people casting their ballots.... Since 1967 at the state level, voters have ensured the emergence of a two-party system in most of the twenty-five states that constitute the union as voters in all but two of these states have elected non-Congress parties to power in the state legislatures. Since 1977, voters have defeated incumbent regimes in four of five elections to the central legislature ....

In summary, the institutions of democracy were primarily inherited from the colonial period in India, and the available evidence indicates that in the first decades after independence they have operated with vigor and energy. The relatively protracted and democratic nature of the anti-imperialist movement, the gradual transfer of power, the establishment of the Congress Party, and, finally, the genuine commitment to a liberal-democratic polity by the first generation of leaders, especially the first prime minister, Jawaharlal Nehru (1947–64), must be regarded as the key factors in the emergence and persistence of democracy in India. We now turn to the numerous stresses and strains that seriously threaten this democracy....

[Krishna explores the "erosion of democracy" in the period after 1967, in which the more "personalized politics" of Indira Gandhi played an important role in the decline of important political institutions.]

Perhaps the most important change introduced by Mrs. Gandhi is often described as a shift to a "plebiscitary" form of politics. The Congress Party, and indeed the nation, became in her rhetoric (and, probably, in her mind) inseparable from herself.... [A]fter winning the general elections of 1971 and then cementing this victory with victories in various state assembly elections in 1972 (greatly assisted by the conclusive defeat and bifurcation of Pakistan in the war of 1971), Mrs. Gandhi seemed at the pinnacle of power. Within the next three years, however, the country was plunged into anarchy. Movements based on a variety of proximate political causes erupted all across the country, most prominently in Bihar and Gujarat.

Mrs. Gandhi's reaction to these, typically, was to portray them as personal attacks and to delegitimize them as irresponsible. Her shrill repetition of this theme had begun to lose its credibility when, on June 12, 1975, a Supreme Court judgment overturned her 1971 election to the central legislature on a rather innocuous count (misuse of some government property for electioneering). The judgment, coming as it did alongside a crescendo of political protest in various states and an electoral defeat in the assembly elections in Gujarat, seemed to Mrs. Gandhi an orchestrated plot to overthrow her. She reacted by declaring an emergency on grounds of internal threat to the country. She suspended the Constitution, imprisoned all key opposition leaders and Congress dissidents, and promulgated ordinances that, in the name of internal security, ran roughshod over the democratic rights of citizens....

... [T]hrough the Thirty-eighth and Thirty-ninth Amendments, the proclamation of the emergency and electoral matters involving the prime minister and other important leaders were made nonjusticiable.... [T]hrough the comprehensive Forty-second Amendment (which affected as many as fifty-nine clauses in the Constitution), the balance of power between the legislature and the judiciary was shifted decisively in favor of the former. Notably, (legislative) amendments to the Constitution were no longer to be subject to judicial review. At its height, independent India's only experiment with nondemocratic rule had resulted in the arbitrary arrest and imprisonment of more than a hundred thousand citizens and had witnessed a campaign of forced sterilization of the poor and the weak in many villages in northern India. It was marked by the imposition of very strict censorship on the press, resulted in the disappearance of hundreds of individuals, and produced the complete demoralization of the bureaucracy, as officials were arbitrarily transferred and political factors decided promotions. Symbolizing the gap between the populist rhetoric of the emergency and its actual results was the incredibly cruel demolition of the shanties in Delhi's poorest sections (predominantly Muslim) during the freezing winter of 1975–76. At the level of the executive, this period marked the elevation of Sanjay Gandhi to a position of virtually *de facto* deputy prime minister.

The point worth stressing about the emergency is this: its proximate causes were overwhelmingly political. The decision to go for authoritarian rule emerged because of the mind-set of Mrs. Gandhi (and her main adviser at this time, Sanjay Gandhi). In other words, democracy was briefly suspended due to a failure in political leadership, not because of forces in civil society or other structural socioeconomic factors. The emergency lasted from June 1975 until March 1977, when the Congress was routed in the legislative elections. Inexplicably, Mrs. Gandhi had called for elections on January 24, 1977. The precise reasons for her decision are hard to fathom. Certainly, the evidence seems to indicate that she badly miscalculated the degree of alienation from her regime and to the "excesses" of the emergency. The extent of her miscalculation can be gleaned from the fact that both she and Sanjay Gandhi lost their own seats in the central legislature by wide margins.

While India's first national non-Congress government (the coalition of opposition parties, the Janata Party) rapidly dissipated its goodwill and squandered the opportunity it had worked so hard to get, three important aspects from this period stand out: First, the democratic impulse had been thoroughly ingrained in the people. Anyone who thought that fundamental rights and democratic freedoms did not matter in a poor and illiterate country got their comeuppance in the elections of 1977. Second, in its brief tenure the Janata Party managed to reverse most of the damage done to the Constitution through the various amendments under Mrs. Gandhi's emergency regime. And, third, although the non-Congress regime was brief, it brought home the fact that there was, and always would be, an alternative to the Congress Party (and, indeed, the Nehru family) in India's governance....

[Krishna describes the return to power in the 1980s of Mrs. Ghandi and her son Rajiv Ghandi, as a period in which "the deinstitutionalization and corruption of the bureaucracy, the judiciary, the party system, the state legislatures and the giant public sector have all proceeded apace," including a rise in religious, ethnic and regional movements accompanied by "state and societal violence," riots between Hindus and Moslems and "violent confrontations between the so-called backward and forward castes on the issue of reservations (India's version of affirmative action programs)" in several states.]

Culture and Institutions ...

... [Distinguishing between the initial emergence and subsequent sustenance of democracy, Krishna explores whether Indian democracy will survive.]

...The closest any argument connecting democracy to class has come to finding acceptance is Pranab Bardhan's thesis wherein he argued that

> the Indian experience suggests that the very nature of class balance and heterogeneity may make the proprietary classes somewhat more interested in the maintenance of democratic processes.... The cause of democracy in India certainly owes a lot to the liberal professional elite at the helm of the freedom struggle, but its general persistence and the form that it has taken has much to do with the political exigencies of bargaining within its heterogeneous dominant coalition....

... [T]he broader idea (implicit in Bardhan's argument above) that Indian democracy is in part a product of crosscutting and enduring social cleavages is one that finds agreement from many writers. Echoing Arend Lijphart's seminal work, Myron Weiner argues that the sheer diversity and heterogeneous character of society within most of the country's electoral constituencies and the federal structure together operate in such a way as to penalize political parties that try exclusively to represent a single ethnic or religious group and to reward parties that are aggregationist and inclusive.

More important, the segmented character of society, while making it difficult to mobilize groups and classes across the nation, allows the Centre literally to quarantine struggles and deal with them piecemeal. Together these factors operate to produce a polity that is in a state of perpetual crisis (perhaps the perfect oxymoron to describe India) but is in no real danger of self-destructing.

The common thread running through all the above is the emphasis on institutional factors for the emergence and the difficult sustenance of democracy: leadership, party structure, colonial inheritance, social cleavages, federalism. These authors regard democracy as something akin to a game in that the more societies play the game, the better they become at it. In the process, democratic ideals and that way of life permeate society and become routinized and, interestingly enough, a part of the political culture of the society itself. Certainly the survey research evidence cited above and everyday life in India will convince most that a commitment to electoral democracy has become deep and abiding.

To sum up the argument, although these theorists emphasize institutional factors, they are sensitive to the strong mutual relationship between these factors and the culture of politics. Indeed, the latter has now become the bedrock of democracy, even as institutions have, in recent years, decayed. Yet it is obvious that the decaying of political institutions has reached levels that make the sustenance of even the limited notion of electoral democracy difficult in the long run. At the same time, it is unclear what the alternatives are. Certainly the military (with its long tradition of staying within the barracks) and class-based revolutionary parties do not loom as possibilities on the horizon. Paradoxical as it may sound (except perhaps to Indians), this may well be one of the first societies to internalize crises as a way of life.

The most prominent analyst highlighting cultural factors in analyzing democracy in India might be Ashis Nandy. Nandy's argument, however, is marvelously counterintuitive. He extols civil society (especially rural peoples, whom he quaintly describes as "premodern") as the reservoir of tolerance and pluralism, while he regards the elites, especially the Westernized and urbanized middle classes, with their messianic convictions regarding the virtues of modernity, science, rationalism, and secularism, as the real threat to democracy. Skeptical of projects of social engineering, Nandy points out that far more have been killed in the name of unquestioned virtues such as development, science, and democracy in this century than in all previous centuries combined. Similarly, it is not the supposedly superstitious, backward, and parochial rural villager who has fomented the incredible degree of communal and ethnic violence in India, but it is rather the modern politician, the criminalized sections of business elites, and the urban lower-middle classes who are mainly responsible.

While most of the educated classes in India would regard modernity as the solution to the various ethnic and communal crises, Nandy regards these problems as themselves reflecting the pathology of modern society. Far from being the vestiges of primordial identities in a developing society, Nandy argues these new identities are crafted for and by the modern world of party politics and find fertile soil in the urbanized, secularized, and anomic classes of the cities and small towns. In a brilliant analysis of Indian political culture and Mrs. Gandhi, Nandy makes the point that, in many ways, educated Indian middle classes were complicitous with the emergency and the authoritarian streak in Mrs. Gandhi. Like her, they, too, held India's main problem to be "softness," an inability to exercise social discipline in the single-minded pursuit of economic and political goals.

In a classic instance of the victim ingesting the value system and structures of the aggressor, postcolonial middle-class Indians have defined the national project to be emulating the erstwhile imperial "successes"—countries such as Britain, the United States, and Japan. The desire that emerges is one that favors the disciplining of all ambiguity, the obliteration of diversity, and the elevation of one narrative script of history to "the truth." The physical and epistemic violence that this desire produces, Nandy argues, is writ all over contemporary India. Redemption, if found anywhere at all, may come from the reservoirs of tolerance and pluralism that exist in nonmodern Indian society, a society that is deeply religious in the sense of faith, not ideology.

... Nandy ... would regard Indian political culture as inherently democratic if by that is meant tolerance and pluralism. Paradoxically, this unself-conscious democracy is under threat precisely from those "modernizers" who would force their parochial notions of democracy, secularism, development, and science down the throats of a people who are probably least in need of such instruction. Finally, if India remains a democratic country today, Nandy would aver, it is not because of its modern institutions and elites, but despite them.

... [M]ost analysts would hold that a dialectic between institutional and cultural factors underlies Indian democracy. The longer democratic institutions have survived, the more ingrained they have become in the political culture of the country and the more secure democracy itself has become in the long run. There is here a virtuous cycle, if you will, in that nothing strengthens democracy more than the continuance of democratic politics.... [W]hether one traces the sustenance of India's democracy to its political institutions or to its political culture of tolerance and pluralism, one would have to agree that the continued survival of this way of life is a deeply problematic question....

This study of India ought to raise a few points regarding constitutionalism and democracy in the modern world. By any yardstick, this is an incredibly diverse and multicultural society. Yet democracy has not only persisted here but in fact has, in many ways, been strengthened by this diversity. The most salient feature of India's ongoing experiment with democracy is perhaps the growing realization that the more a country persists with democracy, the stronger democracy becomes. . . .

The emergence of democratic politics, as we have seen, was in large part a colonial legacy. Certainly there appear to have been aspects to the political culture of traditional Indian society that facilitated the consolidation of democracy. More important, political culture and institutions seem to have a dialectical relationship that has resulted in their mutual reinforcement of democracy. Paradoxically, especially since the mid-1960s, the main threats to Indian democracy have emerged not from civil society, but from state and party elites who have, at various points, favored authoritarian and personalized rule and technocratic solutions that would further polarize society. These elites have played loose and fast with the institutions of governance and put into play ideologies that are chauvinistic and divisive. Against all odds, the ballot box has survived as the great equalizer in this context, and the Indian voter has used it, time and again, to reassert the sanity of the body politic. . . .

---

3.   COMPENSATORY DISCRIMINATION IN INDIA

Marc Galanter, LAW AND SOCIETY IN MODERN INDIA (1989)

SYMBOLIC ACTIVISM: A JUDICIAL ENCOUNTER WITH THE COUNTERS OF INDIA'S COMPENSATORY DISCRIMINATION POLICY.

Pursuing Substantive Equality: The Classic Compromise.

In the text of the Constitution, the general principle of compensatory discrimination is established as a Directive Principle, but the specific provisions authorizing it are framed as exceptions to general Fundamental Right. This arrangement expresses the basic tension between the broad purposes to be achieved and the commitment to confine the device and make it comport with other constitutional commitments, especially that to formal equality.

The exceptional character of compensatory discrimination has frequently been noted by the courts. That Article 15(4) 'has to be read as a proviso or an exception to Articles 15(1) and 29(2)' was evident from its history, according to the Supreme Court in *Balaji v. State of Mysore*. This has been the received characterization of Article 15(4). Thus in *State of Andhra Pradesh v. Sagar* the Supreme Court emphasizes that as an exception, Article 15(4) cannot be extended so as in effect to destroy the guarantee of equality in Article 15(1).

In *Devadasan v. Union of India* the Supreme Court emphasized that Article 16(4) 'is by way of a proviso or an exception' to Article 16(1) and 'cannot be so interpreted to nullify or destroy the main provision.' Thus its 'over-riding effect' is only to permit a 'reasonable number of reservations ... in certain circumstances. That is all.' The characterization as an exception was challenged by Subba Rao, J., dissenting in *Devadasan*. In his view, Article 16(4) 'has not really carved out an exception, but has preserved a power untrammeled by the other provisions of the Article.' An extension of this argument was put forward in *C.A. Rajendran v. Union of India*, where it was urged that Article 16(4) was not merely an exception engrafted on Article 16, but was itself a Fundamental Right granted to the Scheduled Castes and Tribes and untrammeled by any other provision of the Constitution. The Supreme Court's response was that Article 16(4) imposed no duty on the government to make reservations for these classes but 'Article 16(4) is an enabling provision and confers a discretionary power on the State to make a reservation'. . . .

But if the particular means are discretionary, the object is not: the Constitution explicitly declares it 'the duty of the state' to promote the interests of the 'weaker sections' and to protect them. And if these provisions are exceptions, they are exceptions of a peculiar sort. They do not merely carve out an area in which the general principle of equality is inapplicable. Rather, they are specifically designed to implement and fulfill the general principle.

Article 15(4) and 16(4) are undoubtedly exceptions to the constitutional prohibition of State employment of the otherwise forbidden criteria of caste, religion and so forth. But it does not follow that they are exceptions to the policy of equal treatment mandated by Articles 14, 15, and 16. In respect to the general policy of equality they represent an empowerment of the State to pursue substantive equality in respect to the disparities between the backward classes and others. It might be argued that in a state generally committed to formal equality this commitment to reduce these disparities is an exception. . . .

It was the realization that mere provision of formal equality would not suffice to bring about the desired 'EQUALITY of status and of opportunity' that led to the adoption of these provisions. As a Full Bench of the Kerala High Court observed:

> . . . [I]n a country like India where large sections of the people are backward socially, economically, educationally and politically, these declarations and guarantees [of equality] would be meaningless unless provision is also made for the uplift of such backward classes who are in no position to compete with the more advanced classes. Thus to give meaning and content to the equality guaranteed by Articles 14, 15, 16, and 29, provision has been made in Articles 15(4) and 16(4) enabling preferential treatment in favour of the 'weaker sections.'

Indeed, as the Supreme Court has observed, guarantees of equality might by themselves aggravate existing inequalities. If taken literally,

> instead of giving equality of opportunity to all citizens, it will lead to glaring inequalities. . . . In order to give a real opportunity to [the backward to] compete with the better placed people . . . [Article 16(4)

is included in the Constitution.] The predominant concept underlying [Article 16] is equality of opportunity in the matter of employment; and, without detriment to said concept, the State is enabled to make reservations in favour of backward classes to give a practical content to the concept of equality. [Triloki Nath Tiku v. State of Jammu and Kashmir, A.I.R. 1967 S.C. 1283]

The tension between these commitments to non-discrimination and to substantive equalization was poignantly expressed by Prime Minister Nehru when he remarked in the course of the First Amendment debate that '... we arrive at a peculiar tangle. We cannot have equality because in trying to attain equality we come up against some principles of equality.' The textual juxtaposition of guarantees of equality and authorization of compensatory discrimination reflects a deeper conflict between different views of equality and divergent notions of the goal and scope of protective discrimination. While in practice these views tend to merge and overlap, it may be helpful here to isolate in pure form what we may conveniently label the horizontal and the vertical perspectives on equality and compensatory discrimination.

In the horizontal view, the relevant time is the present. Equality is visualized as identical opportunities to compete for existing values among those differently endowed, regardless of structural determinants of the chances of success or of the consequences for the distribution of values. One of the dissenting judges in the *Thomas* case sums it up neatly when he cautions that Article 16(1) 'speaks of equality of opportunity, not opportunity to seek equality'. In this view, preferential treatment is accepted as a marginal adjustment to be made where results of complete equality are unacceptable. Compensatory discrimination detracts from equality: it amounts to a kind of social handicapping to insure fair present distribution among relevant units. Thus in *Devasan v. Union of India* the Supreme Court emphasized that in combining these provisions it might strike a fair balance between the claims of the backward and the claims of other communities.

The relation of equality and compensatory discrimination is viewed very differently in what we may call the vertical perspective. In this view the present is seen as a transition from a past of inequality to a desired future of substantive equality; the purpose of compensatory discrimination is to promote equalization by offsetting historically accumulated inequalities. Thus, compensatory discrimination does not detract from equality in the interest of present fairness; rather, it is seen as a requisite to the fulfilment of the nation's long-run goal of substantial redistribution and equalization. Not only present claims but historical deprivations and national aspirations are relevant. Such a view was given its most clear judicial expression in *Viswanath v. State of Mysore*, where Hegde J. repulsed the argument that reservations should be confined with the observation that counsel

> did not appear to be very much alive to the fact that there can be neither stability nor real progress if predominant sections of an awak-

ened Nation live in primitive conditions, confined to unremunerative occupations and having no share in the good things of life, while power and wealth are confined in the hands of only a few and the same is used for the benefit of the sections of the community to which they belong.... Unaided many sections of the people, who constitute the majority in this State cannot compete with the advanced sections of the people, who today have a monopoly of education and consequently have predominant representation in the Government services as well as in other important walks of life. It is cynical to suggest that the interest of the Nation is best served if the barber's son continues to be a barber and a shepherd's son continues to be a shepherd.... We have pledged ourselves to establish a welfare State. Social justice is an important ingredient of that concept. That goal cannot be reached if we overemphasize the 'merit theory'.

Advantages secured due to historical reasons cannot be considered a fundamental right guaranteed by the Constitution. The nation's interest will be best served—taking a long-range view—if the backward classes are helped to march forward and take their places in a line with the advanced sections of the people.

From this 'long-range' perspective, Justice Hegde later elaborated, the 'immediate advantages of the Nation [in the effective utilization of talent] have to be harmonized with its long-range interests.'

Rarely do these contrasting views of equality and compensatory discrimination appear with such purity and clarity; more common is the attempt to harmonize them in what we might call 'the classic compromise': advancement of the backward permits exceptional means and enjoys special priority, but these means and priorities must be balanced against other rights and other interests. Thus in *Balaji v. State of Mysore*, Gajendragadkar, J. observes that:

It is obvious that unless the educational and economic interests of the weaker sections of the people are promoted quickly and liberally, the ideal of establishing social and economic equality will not be attained....

Surely the State is authorized to take 'adequate steps' toward that objective, but these special, exceptional provisions do not override the Fundamental Rights of others. Furthermore, there are other crucial national interests which have to be taken into account:

The interests of weaker sections of society which are a first charge on the States and the Centre have to be adjusted with the interests of the community as a whole.

The inevitable weighing and balancing is rendered particularly difficult because the constitutional provisions set up another tension as to the relevant units whose interests are to be balanced or who are ultimately to be equalized, as the case may be. The Constitution confers Fundamental Rights on individual citizens in their personal capacity, not as members of communal groups. All citizens have a fundamental right that another, excepting a member of a backward class, shall not be preferred by the State on the basis of his membership in a particular group. However the government is obliged to advance the weaker sections of backward classes. Therefore the scope of compensatory discrimination involves tension between individuals or groups as objects of State policy.

The constitutional embrace of the antagonistic principles of equal treatment and compensatory discrimination, individual rights and group rights, confronts both government and courts with the problem of reconciling them in specific settings. The sweeping language of Articles 15(4) and 16(4) indicates that their framers relied primarily on the discretion of the politicians and administrators of the future, rather than on the courts, to effect such a reconciliation. But while these provisions give the executive and the legislatures broad discretion in their application, judicial intervention is not entirely excluded. Leverage for judicial oversight is supplied by the placement of these provisions as exceptions to the judicially enforceable Fundamental Rights. These rights can only be vindicated to the extent that the courts scrutinize the government's designation of beneficiaries to see that only the backward are included, that the extent or method of operation does not prejudice others unduly, that the schemes are designed and administered to work in favour of the intended beneficiaries and not to their detriment. Such review is necessary not only to vindicate individual rights but to effectuate the policy of these provisions—by preventing unwarranted dilution of benefits (for the more unrestrained the inclusion of beneficiaries, the less the assistance the intended beneficiaries will receive) and abuses that undermine public support for these measures.

The courts have indeed played a major role in shaping policy in this area by defining the constitutional boundaries of preferential treatment. Recent developments in the constitutional doctrine of equality indirectly raise the question of whether courts might play an even more central role in the design and implementation of compensatory policies.

A New Constitutional Vista: the Thomas Case

For the first quarter-century of constitutional development, the approaches discussed in the previous section bounded the discourse about the way in which competing commitments to formal equality and compensatory discrimination might be combined. But much of the earlier understanding of constitutional policies of compensatory is cast into doubt by a remarkable 1975 decision of the Supreme Court in *State of Kerala v. N. M. Thomas*.

Employees of the Registration Department of the State of Kerala were divided into Lower Division Clerks and Upper Division Clerks. The former could be promoted to the higher position on a 'Seniority-cum-merit' basis. To qualify for promotion it was necessary to pass some tests . . .—this was the merit requirement. Among those who satisfied this prerequisite, the promotions went to the most senior Lower Division Clerks. The rules allowed for temporary appointments to the higher posts for a two-year period during which the clerk would have to pass the required tests; the two years was extended to four years in the case of Scheduled Caste and

Scheduled Tribe clerks. Nevertheless a number of Scheduled Caste clerks had not satisfied the test qualifications within the extended period and were facing reversion to the lower posts.

In 1972 the Government promulgated a new rule:

> 13AA. Notwithstanding anything contained in these rules, the Government may, by order, exempt for a specific period, any member or members, belonging to a Scheduled Caste or a Scheduled Tribe, and already in service, from passing the tests....

On the same day the State promulgated an Order granting Scheduled Castes and Scheduled Tribes already in service 'temporary exemption ... from passing all tests ... for a period of two years'. In 1974 this was extended for a further period to ensure each employee two chances to appear for the required tests. This time the government ordered that 'these categories of employees will not be given any further extension of time to acquire the test qualifications.' Because of earlier difficulties with the test barrier, there was a heavy concentration of Scheduled Caste lower division clerks with high seniority. When the test barrier was removed temporarily, many of them were promoted to the higher posts. Thus in 1972, of 51 vacancies in the category of Upper Division Clerks, 34 were filled by Scheduled Castes who had not passed the tests and only 17 were filled by persons who had passed the tests. A writ petition was filed by N. M. Thomas, a lower division clerk who did pass the test and would have been promoted but for the extensions authorized by Rule 13AA.

A Division Bench of the Kerala High Court concluded that: 'What has been done is not to reserve ... posts ... [R]eservations had already been made.... What has been attempted by Rule 13AA is to exempt persons from possessing the necessary qualifications.' Such exemption lies beyond the scope of Article 16(4)'s authorization of reservations, and on the scale it is done here, directly violates Article 335's directive that claims of Scheduled Castes and Tribes may be taken into account in government employment 'consistently with the maintenance of efficiency of administration....' On appeal to the Supreme Court, counsel for the State took an innovative tack and argued that the extension need not be subsumed under Article 16(4)'s provision for reservations, but could be justified as a reasonable classification under Article 16(1). A seven judge bench decided five to two to reverse, issuing seven separate opinions. One of the majority judges thought that Article 16(4) rightly interpreted would authorize the State's provision; the other four accepted some version of the broad classification argument advanced by the State.

Chief Justice Ray's opinion for the majority sketches the outline of the classification argument: providing equal opportunity in government employment is a legitimate objective; Article 46 directs the State to promote the economic interests of Scheduled Castes and Tribes with special care; Article 335 directs the State to take into its consideration their claims regarding service under the State. Thus the classification of employees belonging to these groups to afford them an extended period to pass tests for promotion is 'a just and reasonable classification having rational nexus to the object of promoting equal opportunity ... relating to [public] employment....' The difference in condition of these groups justifies differential treatment; just as rational classification is permissible under the general equal protection provision of Article 14, so it is permissible to treat unequals unequally under Article 16.

The extent of the doctrinal innovation here can be appreciated by considering the opinion of Justice Beg, the only member of the majority who does not participate in the reconceptualization of Article 16. He helpfully restates a conventional understanding of the constitutional provisions. In this view 'the guarantee contained in Article 16(1) is not by itself aimed at removal of social backwardness due to socio-economic and educational disparities produced by past history of social oppression, exploitation, or degradation of a class of persons.' Instead 'it was in fact intended to protect the claims of merit and efficiency ... against incursions of extraneous considerations.' And efficiency tests, in turn, 'bring out and measure ... existing inequalities in competency and capacity or potentialities so as to provide a fair and rational basis for justifiable discrimination between candidates.' Thus provisions for equality of opportunity are meant to insure 'fair competition' in securing government jobs; they are not directed to 'removal of causes for unequal performances....' But such provisions do not stand alone: they are juxtaposed with Articles 46 and 335 which imply 'preferential treatment for the backward classes' to mitigate the rigour of equality in the sense of strict application of uniform tests of competence.

> Article 16(4) was designed to reconcile the conflicting pulls of Article 16(1), representing ... justice conceived of as equality (in the conditions of competition) and of Articles 46 and 335, embodying the duties of the State to promote the interests of the economically, educationally and socially backward, so as to release them from the clutches of social injustice.

Thus Article 16(4) may be thought to 'exhaust all exceptions made in favour of backward classes'. Yet the effect of the Kerala promotion rules here is 'a kind of reservation', for it is a temporary promotion that would be confirmed only if the appointee satisfied specified tests within a given time. These rules may be viewed as 'implementation of a policy of qualified [or] partial [or] conditional reservations' which could be justified under Article 16(4)....'

Dismissing the interpretation of Article 16(4) as an exception to Article 16(1), Justice Mathew articulates the view of equality that implies the doctrinal shift. The equality of opportunity guaranteed by the Constitution is not only formal equality with fair competition, but 'equality of result'. In order to assure the disadvantaged 'their due share of representation in public services' the Constitutional equality of opportunity was fashioned 'wide enough to include ... compensatory measures....' Thus the guarantee of equality 'implies differential treatment of persons who are unequal'. Article 16(1) is 'only a part of a comprehensive scheme to ensure equality in all spheres'. It implies 'affirmative action' by government to achieve equality—that is, 'compensatory State action to make people who are really unequal in their wealth, education or social environment ... equal'.

> If equality of opportunity guaranteed under Article 16(1) means effective material equality, then Article 16(4) is not an exception to Article 16(1). It is only an emphatic way of putting the extent to which equality of opportunity could be carried *viz*, even up to the point of making reservation.

Thus 'the state can adopt any measure which would ensure the adequate representation in public service of the members of the Scheduled Castes and Scheduled Tribes and justify it as a compensatory measure to ensure equality of opportunity provided the measure does not dispense with the acquisition of the minimum basic qualification necessary for the efficiency'.

Justice Krishna Iyer propounds a complex vision of the constitutional commitment to equality. Interpreting the Constitution by 'a spacious, social science approach, not by pedantic, traditional legalism', he proposes to erect a 'general doctrine of backward classification' to pursue 'real, not formal, equality'. According to the doctrine of backward classification, the State may, for purposes of securing genuine equality of opportunity, treat unequals equally. Thus Article 16(4)

> serves not as an exception [to the strictures of Article 16(1) and (2)] but as an emphatic statement, one mode of reconciling the claims of backward people and the opportunity for free competition the forward sections are ordinarily entitled to.... Closely examined it is an illustration of a constitutionally sanctified classification.

So, in addition to reservations provided by Article 16(4), the State may also confer 'lesser order(s) of advantage' on the principle of classification under Article 16(1).

At this point in the argument there is a crucial divergence between the views of Justice Krishna Iyer and those of Justice Mathew. For the latter, the compensatory measures authorized by Article 16(1) might be extended to 'all members of the backward classes', not only to the Scheduled Castes and Scheduled Tribes. But Justice Krishna Iyer's more complex vision of Article 16 contains a second layer: the power of classification outside the boundaries of Article 16(4) for purposes of overcoming inequality may be used only on behalf of Scheduled Castes and Tribes.

> Article 16(4) covers all backward classes, but to earn the benefit of grouping under Article 16(1) based on Articles 46 and 335 ... the twin considerations of terrible backwardness of the type Harijans have to endure and maintenance of administrative efficiency must be satisfied.

'Not all caste backwardness is recognized' as a basis for differential treatment under Article 16(1).

> The differentia ... is the dismal social milieu of harijans.... The social disparity must be so grim and substantial as to serve as a foundation for benign discrimination. If we search ... we cannot find any large segment other than the Scheduled Castes and Scheduled

Tribes ... no class other than harijans can jump the gauntlet of 'equal opportunity' guarantee. Their only hope is in Article 16(4).

This is perplexing, for it appears that the stronger measures of reservation may be taken on behalf of all the backward, yet those who suffer the most terrible backwardness are the only ones entitled to measures which confer 'a lesser order of advantage'.

Later he suggests that to allow the Other Backward Classes to participate in these benefits may be detrimental to those who are most deserving:

> ... no caste, however seemingly backward ... can be allowed to breach the dykes of equality of opportunity guaranteed to all citizens. To them the answer is that ... equality is equality.... The heady upper berth occupants from backward classes do double injury. They beguile the broad community into believing that backwardness is being banished. They rob the need based bulk of the backward of the ... advantages the nation proffers.

This distinction is justified because 'the Constitution itself makes a super-classification between harijans and others, grounded on the fundamental disparity in our society and the imperative social urgency of raising the former's sunken status'. From the provision of Articles 330, 332, 335, 338 and others, we may deduce that 'the Constitution itself demarcates Harijans from others.... This is based on the stark backwardness of this bottom layer of the community'. This constitutional differentiation of Harijans is specifically extended to the area of government employment as part of the State's obligation to 'promote the economic interests of harijans and like backward classes'. Articles 14 and 16 are, according to Justice Krishna Iyer 'the tool kit' to carry out the 'testament' of Articles 46 and 335.

An attenuated form of this 'super classification' argument is found in each of the four majority opinions that embrace the classification argument. That argument posits a general authorization flowing from Article 16(1) to adopt reasonable classifications for purposes of securing equality of opportunity. But it is conceded that this does not include a power to employ those classifications specifically forbidden in Article 16(2). Therefore each of these four 'classification' opinions argues that the Scheduled Castes and Tribes do not comprise a classification on the basis of 'caste'.

Thus Justice Krishna Iyer argues that the ban of 16(2) doesn't arise in connection with measures for the Scheduled Caste and Scheduled Tribes for they are 'no[t] castes in the Hindu fold but an amalgam of castes, races, groups, tribes, communities or parts thereof found ... to be the lowliest and in need of massive State aid and notified as such by the President'. Article 16(4) allows use of these forbidden grounds to identify the Backward Classes that may be recipients of reservation. The four judgements imply that the other kinds of compensatory treatment justified directly by Article 16(1) are available only to classes which avoid the classification forbidden by Article 16(2), including Scheduled Castes and Tribes since they are not castes. But if the idea is to confine compensatory classification under Article 16(1) to Scheduled Castes and Tribes, this argument proves too much. For there are innumerable categories—e.g., on the basis of income, occupation, physical handicap, etc.—that are not based on the classifications forbidden in Article 16(2). The argument for Scheduled Castes and Tribes as a 'super-classification' cannot be sustained on the basis of the structure of Article 16, but only on the basis of their special recognition in the Constitution. But if that is the argument for their distinctiveness, the fact that they are not 'castes' within Article 16(2) is a distracting irrelevance.

In this and other matters, the *Thomas* opinions leave open many perplexing questions. Are equalizing measures permissible even if they employ the categories forbidden by Article 16(2)? Or, conversely, is the power to adopt equalizing classifications under Article 16(1) to be used exclusively to address disparities along the dimensions listed in Article 16(2)? How about differences in class? Income? Is the doctrine of classification merely permissive, so that government may make such compensatory classifications, but need not? Suppose it fails to do so? Do classifications that do not take account of inequalities violate the Article 16(1) guarantee of equality of opportunity?

Yet *Thomas* is welcome because it makes unavoidable reflection on compensatory treatment. By revealing the constitutional indeterminacy and doctrinal disarray in this field, it poses new challenges for jurisprudence and policy. Where courts could rely without much thought on quotations from *Balaji* or *Sagar*, they must now articulate their choices. Actors, governmental and private, can no longer assume that the categories of compensatory policy are immutable.

A Symbolic Breakthrough, but ... Who Gets What, When, How?

In terms of doctrinal housekeeping, there was little need for the *Thomas* reconceptualization of Article 16.... Article 16 arrives on the agenda at the cost of an unimaginatively narrow reading of what common sense would regard as the most relevant constitutional provision, Article 16(4).

A generous construction of Article 16(4) would not only have addressed the problem in *Thomas*, but would have been readily comprehensible to all the different groups concerned with reservations in government posts—officials in charge of appointments and promotions, government servants and aspirants to government posts. *Thomas* reaches the same immediate outcome by elaboration of ambiguous ... doctrine that is not readily accessible to officials who must design and manage programmes of preference, or to the beneficiaries of such programmes, or to disappointed non-beneficiaries—or in large measure even to lawyers and judges.

Perhaps, though, the accomplishment of *Thomas* lies in its providing government with more ample means to pursue compensatory policies. The doctrinal obstacles that might have impeded governmental policies in this area stood for the most part on weak ground, unlikely to withstand sustained conceptual attack. Openings for favourable reinterpretation were plentiful. To bestow on government more ample authority to do something does not automatically mean that more of it will get done. Was the critical shortage one of doctrine favourable to such policies? Or, the will, energy and competence to implement them?

Consider the situation of the Kerala Registration clerks in *Thomas*. The State's scheme here seems less a carefully calculated modification of job requirements than a desperate improvization amounting to a confession of failure of its earlier policies. Extensions hadn't worked before, so another one is tried. There is no indication that any thought was given to (1) some way of helping the Scheduled Caste lower division clerks prepare to pass these tests; nor to (2) modifying the tests to eliminate cultural biases or extraneous matters and measure qualities genuinely needed for the job; or (3) modifying the job to make it suitable to candidates with the qualifications of these applicants. The immediate thrust of the decision is to enlarge the State's authority to confer preferential treatment. But the failure of the earlier measures was not due mainly—perhaps even at all—to lack of State authority, but to lack of will or capability to make its schemes work. Enlarging State authority will not necessarily supply the lack. Indeed, it may allow the State to substitute easy shortcuts (like the one here) for thinking about how to do the job effectively. Since it may now in effect decree the result of keeping these clerks in the higher posts, it may have less incentive to devise ways of motivating or enabling them to grasp these opportunities and improve their performance, thus prolonging their lack of qualification and reinforcing their dependence. And, as the State's authority is more broadly defined, there will be fewer occasions for the courts to observe State programmes and to monitor and energize government performance.

Of course, it is not only a question of the capability of the State, but also of the recipients of preferential treatment. The argument in favour of the extension of the Scheduled Caste clerks in the upper division posts is that it will somehow motivate or equip them to pass the test eventually. And unless they are motivated and enabled to take the initiative and improve their own capacity to perform the extension (and any compensatory measure for that matter) is only a temporary palliative. There is no indication that the State of Kerala in any way enhanced its ability to elicit a satisfactory performance from these clerks.

Thus *Thomas* does not offer any hope of breaking out of the pattern of patronage and dependence. Both majority and minority judgements visualize the Scheduled Castes as the passive recipients of governmental largesse, rather than as active participants in their own improvement. And for all its apparent radicalism, *Thomas* enlarges State power in a way that may jeopardize the future of compensatory preference for the Backward Classes. In two senses this enlargement is a false victory for the Scheduled Castes.

First, the court passed up the chance to make the modest contribution of usefully expanding the meaning of reservations to align doctrine with existing practice about age waivers, coaching schemes, etc. In taking the more radical course, the court attempts to make legal doctrine yield up benefits that it cannot yield.... [T]he crucial shortage was not of State authority, but of the will and capacity of the State to deliver benefits (and of the recipients to utilize those opportunities to enlarge their capabilities). The result is a symbolic breakthrough in which Scheduled Castes, their well-wishers and wider publics are beguiled into thinking that much (or too much) is being done for Scheduled Castes.

Second, the new reading of equality may detract from the attention and priority accorded to the Backward Classes. The new equality doctrine is so ample that it sweeps in its path all that confines the commitment to compensatory treatment to specific historic groups. If Articles 14–16 proclaim a regime of substantive equality and if the State may employ classification to remedy any falling short of the equality thus mandated, the government's responsibility to confer compensatory preference is vastly larger than it has hitherto been understood. It is a responsibility that runs not only to Scheduled Castes and Tribes and to Backward Classes more widely conceived, either in terms of social groups or the poor. It also includes those who suffer difficulties as a result of personal misfortune (disaster victims), accidents of personal history (the physically handicapped) or as a result of meritorious service to the nation (ex-servicemen or dislocated children of diplomats).

In a setting of chronic shortage, an enlarged commitment to remedy all undeserved difficulties betokens a commendable generosity of spirit. But it also raises the question of priorities and of allocation of scarce resources, including attention. The Government's authorization to pursue substantive equality is vastly greater than the resources that will conceivably be available to it. Among the claimants on its compensatory powers will be many who are better placed to press their claims on the attention and sympathies of government. Will not the commitment to the lowest social groups—especially where these are perceived to receive massive benefits—be overwhelmed by governmental response to better-placed claimants on its compensatory attention?

Of course, the State could always take account of these difficulties under Article 14 in terms of reasonable classification. But the notion that the State has a general obligation to produce substantive equality means that the kinds of disadvantage that afflict the better off—diplomats, central government employees, retired army officers, physically handicapped children in well-to-do, educated families—are now elevated, as far as compensatory responsibilities go, to parity with the government's commitment to overcome disparities associated with the traditional social hierarchy. The earlier sense of a regime of formal equality qualified by a singular exception, to alleviate disparities derived from position in the traditional social hierarchy, is now liquidated or dissolved into a general and unfulfillable commitment to substantive equality.

The distributive potential of this new dispensation is dramatically realized in *Jagdish Rai v. State of Haryana* where the State reserved a substantial portion of government posts for ex-servicemen on the ground that they were handicapped because 'over the years [they] have lost opportunities for entering government service and have also lost contact with ordinary civilian life'. The Full Bench sweeps aside the notion that reservations have to be justified by Article 16(4) as 'a relic of the old way of thinking. . . . The old idea has now given way to the idea that [Article 15(4) and Article 16(4)] . . . are themselves aimed at achieving the very equality proclaimed and guaranteed by Article 14 and other clauses of Articles 15 and 16'. After extensive citation from *Thomas*, the Court observes that '[i]t is no longer necessary to "apologetically" explain laws aimed at achieving equality as permissible exceptions. It can now be boldly claimed that such laws are necessary incidents of equality'. Reservation of posts for ex-servicemen is justified for they suffer difficulties in competing with civilians for civilian job and the State has an obligation to provide them employment. Thus the State is justified in classifying them separately as a source of recruitment. To secure a just proportion of posts to those who suffer a peculiar handicap in competition is 'an extension of the principle of Article 16(4) to those that do not fall under Article 16(4)'.

In effect, other deserving groups are now entitled to reservations along with the Backward Classes specified by Article 16(4) and in effect, all the kinds of preferential treatment which seemed to be allowed exclusively to the Backward Classes may now be bestowed on other groups regarded as deserving by the State. It is a fitting symbol that the losing petitioner in *Jagdish Rai* was herself a Scheduled Caste.

Thus *Thomas* opens Pandora's box: compensatory classification is available—perhaps incumbent—to succour all the disadvantaged. The earlier notion that 'the interests of the weaker sections are a first charge' on government is dissolved into a diffuse, and in the nature of things, largely symbolic, generalized egalitarianism. Justice Krishna Iyer's doctrine of super-classification may be understood as an attempt to close the lid again, confining compensatory classification to Scheduled Castes and Tribes. Were this doctrine to gain acceptance, state authorization to confer benefits on these groups might end up not very far from where liberal reading of Article 15(4) and 16(4) would have left it. Superclassification would re-establish the priority of Scheduled Caste claims by emphasizing a picture of Indian society as riven by an unbridgeable dichotomy between Scheduled Castes and Tribes and the rest of the population. This dichotomous picture, by drawing a rigid line between Scheduled Castes and Other Backward Classes, could impede programme administration and obstruct the eventual dismantling of preferential treatment by preventing merger of these categories. More immediately, it would further stigmatize Scheduled Castes and Tribes by portraying them as uniquely hapless and helpless specimens, a potential demonstrated in the overtones of condescension found in some of the *Thomas* opinions.

But it would be shortsighted to judge *Thomas* only in terms of what it does to governmental power in this area. There is another side to the coin and one that is potentially of even greater significance. If Articles 14, 15, and 16 are read as mandating the pursuit of substantive equality, then to what extent is substantive equality—or at least governmental efforts to promote it—an enforceable Fundamental Right? Since those denied Fundamental Rights may resort to the courts to enforce them, would the potential beneficiaries of such equalizing measures have a right to resort to the courts to secure governmental compliance with this right of equalization?

It would not be surprising if the courts would shrink from affirmative enforcement of these reconceptualized rights to equality. But imagine for a moment that they were willing to do so. Scheduled Castes and others would not have to wait for government preference on their behalf, but could take the initiative in the courts to secure the 'enforcement' or implementation of their rights to substantively equalizing measures. Scheduled Castes movements could mobilize around these issues, generating the kind of political movement that would make government responsive to judicial proddings. . . .

. . . [I]n this reading the ultimate significance of *Thomas* is not the enlargement of State authority to confer preferential treatment, but the acknowledgement of a Fundamental Right to substantive equality and the possibilities for affirmative litigation by disadvantaged groups to force the State to fulfil its responsibilities. This would amount to an ironic reversal of the meaning of *Thomas*. We started with the obvious view that *Thomas* loosened judicially-imposed restraints on government, allowing it to patronize the least advantaged; we end by viewing *Thomas* as suggesting the imposition on government of a new and onerous accountability to these disadvantaged, an accountability mediated through the courts.

This scenario is subject to a number of contingencies. . . . [A]re the judges likely to be responsive to such claims, claims that ask them to depart from deeply held notions about the judicial role? They would have not only to innovate original standards of what is appropriate movement towards equality, they would have to undertake a sustained activist monitoring of government that they may find both ideologically uncongenial and institutionally discomfiting. (Were they to shrink from this, while maintaining an interpretation of equality rights as substantive, *Thomas* would, in the guise of exalting the Directive Principles, have helped to demote these Fundamental Rights to the non-enforceable status that led to the disdain of the Directive Principles.) . . . [E]ven if claimants come forward and courts are responsive, do the realities of litigation in India, the delay and manoeuver and cost, make it possible for groups to improve their position through litigation against powerful adversaries? . . . [A]re the real barriers to improvement of the conditions of these groups reachable by even the most well-disposed and capable judiciary? To what extent is the notion of remedying these problems through litigation yet a further tempting illusion?

Conclusion

It is not clear yet in what ways and how deeply *Thomas* will transform earlier doctrine and practice. It was pronounced by a divided court; it expresses the heated symbolic egalitarianism that was both institutionalized and discredited during the Emergency Rule. It liberates the courts conceptually from what we tagged the 'classic compromise' on compensatory discrimination, but it does so at the cost of obscuring and diffusing the commitment to remedy the historical plight of the lowest groups in Indian society. But if it provides no satisfying answers, its presence invites and requires some fresh thought about the principles underlying compensatory discrimination policies and about the role of courts, lawyers, and citizens in effectuating them.

———

State of Kerala v. N.M. Thomas

A.I.R. 1976 S.C. 490 (Supreme Court of India)

[This case was summarized and discussed in the Galanter above. We include brief portions of these very long opinions for you to review, on the assumption that you will first have already read Galanter's summary.]

* * *

The following Judgments of the Court were delivered by

RAY, C.J. (Majority Judgment):— ...

27. There is no denial of equality of opportunity unless the person who complains of discrimination is equally situated with the person or persons who are alleged to have been favoured. Article 16 (1) does not bar a reasonable classification of employees or reasonable tests for their selection (State of Mysore v. V. P. Narasinga Rao, (1968) 1 SCR 407 (AIR 1968 SC 349)).

28. This equality of opportunity need not be confused with absolute equality. Article 16 (1) does not prohibit the prescription of reasonable rules for selection to any employment or appointment to any office. In regard to employment, like other terms and conditions associated with and incidental to it, the promotion to a selection post is also included in the matters relating to employment and even in regard to such a promotion to a selection post all that Article 16 (1) guarantees is equality of opportunity to all citizens. Article 16 (1) and (2) gives effect to equality before law guaranteed by Article 14 and to the prohibition of discrimination guaranteed by Article 15 (1). Promotion to selection post is covered by Article 16 (1) and (2)....

31. The rule of parity is the equal treatment of equals in equal circumstances. The rule of differentiation is enacting laws differentiating between different persons or things in different circumstances. The circumstances which govern one set of persons or objects may not necessarily be the same as those governing another set of persons or objects so that the question of unequal treatment does not really arise between persons governed by different conditions and different sets of circumstances. The principle of equality does not mean that every law must have universal application for all persons who are not by nature, attainment or circum-

stances in the same position and the varying needs of different classes of persons require special treatment. The legislature understands and appreciates the need of its own people, that its laws are directed to problems made manifest by experience and that its discriminations are based upon adequate grounds. The rule of classification is not a natural and logical corollary of the rule of equality, but the rule of differentiation is inherent in the concept of equality. Equality means parity of treatment under parity of conditions. Equality does not connote absolute equality. A classification in order to be constitutional must rest upon distinctions that are substantial and not merely illusory. The test is whether it has a reasonable basis free from artificiality and arbitrariness embracing all and omitting none naturally falling into that category....

38.   The principle of equality is applicable to employment at all stages and in all respects, namely, initial recruitment, promotion, retirement, payment of pension and gratuity. With regard to promotion the normal principles are either merit-cum-seniority or seniority-cum-merit. Seniority-cum-merit means that given the minimum necessary merit requisite for efficiency of administration, the senior though the less meritorious shall have priority. This will not violate Articles 14, 16 (1) and 16 (2). A rule which provides that given the necessary requisite merit, a member of the backward class shall get priority to ensure adequate representation will not similarly violate Article 14 or Article 16 (1) and (2). The relevant touchstone of validity is to find out whether the rule of preference secures adequate representation for the unrepresented backward community or goes beyond it.

39.   The classification of employees belonging to Scheduled Castes and Scheduled Tribes for allowing them an extended period of two years for passing the special tests for promotion is a just and reasonable classification having rational nexus to the object of providing equal opportunity for all citizens in matters relating to employment or appointment to public office. Granting of temporary exemptions from special tests to the personnel belonging to Scheduled Castes and Scheduled Tribes by executive orders has been an integral feature of the service conditions in Kerala from its very inception on 1 November, 1956. That was the pattern in Travancore-Cochin State. The special treatment accorded to the Scheduled Castes and Scheduled Tribes in Government service which had become part and parcel of the conditions of service over these long periods amply justify the classification of the members of the Scheduled Castes and Scheduled Tribes as a whole by the impugned rule and orders challenged. What was achieved by the Government orders is now given a statutory basis by Rule 13AA. The historical background of these rules justifies the classification of the personnel of the Scheduled Castes and Scheduled Tribes in service for the purpose of granting them exemption from special tests with a view to ensuring them the equality of treatment and equal opportunity in matters of employment having regard to their backwardness and under representation in the employment of the State.

40. The Constitution makes a classification of Scheduled Castes and Scheduled Tribes in numerous provisions and gives a mandate to the State to accord special or favoured treatment to them. Article 46 contains a Directive Principle of State policy—fundamental in the governance of the country enjoining the State to promote with special care educational and economic interests of the Scheduled Castes and Scheduled Tribes and to protect them from any social injustice and exploitation. Article 335 enjoins that the claims of the members of the Scheduled Castes and Scheduled Tribes to the services and posts in the Union and the States shall be taken into consideration. Article 338 provides for appointment by the President of a Special Officer for the Scheduled Castes and Scheduled Tribes to investigate all matters relating to the safeguards provided for them under the Constitution. Article 341 enables the President by public notification to specify castes, races or tribes which shall be deemed to be Scheduled Castes in the States and the Union Territories. Article 342 contains provision for similar notification in respect of Scheduled Tribes. Article 366 (24) and (25) defines Scheduled Castes and Scheduled Tribes. The classification by the impugned rule and the orders is with a view to securing adequate representation to Scheduled Castes and Scheduled Tribes in the services of the State as otherwise they would stagnate in the lowest rung of the State services.

41. Article 335 of the Constitution states that claims of members of the Scheduled Castes and Scheduled Tribes shall be taken into consideration in the making of appointments to the services and posts in connection with affairs of the State consistent with the maintenance of efficiency of administration. The impugned rule and the impugned orders, are related to this constitutional mandate. Without providing for relaxation of special tests for a temporary period it would not have been possible to give adequate promotion to the Lower Division Clerks belonging to Scheduled Castes and Scheduled Tribes to the posts of Upper Division Clerks. Only those Lower Division Clerks who were senior in service will get the benefit of the relaxation contemplated by Rule 13AA and the impeached orders. Promotion to Upper Division from Lower Division is governed by the rule of seniority subject only to passing of the qualified test. The temporary relaxation of test qualification made in favour of Scheduled Castes and Scheduled Tribes is warranted by their inadequate representation in the services and their overall backwardness. The classification of the members of the Scheduled Castes and Scheduled Tribes already in service made under Rule 13AA and the challenged orders for exempting them for a temporary period from passing special tests are within the purview of constitutional mandate under Article 335 in consideration of their claims to redress imbalance in public service and to bring about parity in all communities in public services. . . .

44. Our Constitution aims at equality of status and opportunity for all citizens including those who are socially, economically and educationally backward. The claims of members of backward classes require adequate representation in legislative and executive bodies. If members of Scheduled Castes and Tribes, who are said by this Court to be backward classes, can

maintain minimum necessary requirement of administrative efficiency, not only representation but also preference may be given to them to enforce equality and to eliminate inequality. Articles 15 (4) and 16 (4) bring out the position of backward classes to merit equality. Special provisions are made for the advancement of backward classes and reservations of appointments and posts for them to secure adequate representation. These provisions will bring out the content of equality guaranteed by Articles 14, 15 (1) and 16 (1). The basic concept of equality is equality of opportunity for appointment. Preferential treatment for members of backward classes with due regard to administrative efficiency alone can mean equality of opportunity for all citizens. Equality under Article 16 could not have a different content from equality under Article 14. Equality of opportunity for unequals can only mean aggravation of inequality. Equality of opportunity admits discrimination with reason and prohibits discrimination without reason. Discrimination with reasons means rational classification for differential treatment having nexus to the constitutionally permissible object. Preferential representation for the backward classes in services with due regard to administrative efficiency is a permissible object and backward classes are a rational classification recognised by our Constitution. Therefore, differential treatment in standards of selection are within the concept of equality.

45. A rule in favour of an under-represented backward community specifying the basic needs of efficiency of administration will not contravene Articles 14, 16 (1) and 16 (2). The rule in the present case does not impair the test of efficiency in administration inasmuch as members of Scheduled Castes and Tribes who are promoted have to acquire the qualification of passing the test. The only relaxation which is done in their case is that they are granted two years more time than others to acquire the qualification. Scheduled Castes and Tribes are descriptive of backwardness. It is the aim of our Constitution to bring them up from handicapped position to improvement. If classification is permissible under Article 14, it is equally permissible under Article 16, because both the Articles lay down equality. The quality and concept of equality is that if persons are dissimilarly placed they cannot be made equal by having the same treatment. Promotion of members of Scheduled Castes and Tribes under the impeached rules and orders is based on the classification with the object of securing representation to members of Scheduled Castes and Tribes. Efficiency has been kept in view and not sacrificed.

46. All legitimate methods are available for equality of opportunity in services under Article 16 (1). Article 16 (1) is affirmative whereas Art. 14 is negative in language. Art. 16 (4) indicates one of the methods of achieving equality embodied in Art. 16 (1). Article 16 (1) using the expression "equality" makes it relatable to all matters of employment from appointment through promotion and termination to payment of pension and gratuity. Article 16 (1) permits classification on the basis of object and purpose of law or State action except classification involving discrimination prohibited by Art. 16 (2). Equal protection of laws necessarily involves classification. The validity of the classification must be adjudged with reference to the purpose of law. The classification in the present case is

justified because the purpose of classification is to enable members of Scheduled Castes and Tribes to find representation by promotion to a limited extent. From the point of view of time a differential treatment is given to members of Scheduled Castes and Tribes, for the purpose of giving them equality consistent with efficiency. . . .

KHANNA, J. (Minority view): . . .

56. [T]he reservation of posts for a section of population has the effect of conferring a special benefit on that section of the population because it would enable members belonging to that section to get employment or office under the State which otherwise in the absence of reservation they could not have got. Such preferential treatment is plainly a negation of the equality of opportunity for all citizens in matters relating to employment or appointment to an office under the State. Clause (4) of Article 16 has, therefore, been construed as a proviso or exception to Clause (1) of that article (see The General Manager, Southern Rly. v. Rangachari, (AIR 1962 SC 36) and T. Devadasan v. Union of India. (AIR 1964 SC 179)).

57. It has been argued on behalf of the appellants that equality of treatment does not forbid reasonable classification. Reference in this context is made to the well accepted principle that Article 14 of the Constitution forbids class legislation but does not forbid classification. Permissible classification, it is equally well established, must be founded on an intelligible differentia which distinguishes persons or things that are grouped together from others left out of the group and the differentia must have a rational relation to the object sought to be achieved by the statute in question. It is urged that the same principle should apply when the court is concerned with the equality of opportunity for all citizens in matters relating to employment or appointment to any office under the State. In this respect I may observe that this Court has recognised the principle of classification in the context of Clause (1) of Article 16 in matters where appointments are from two different sources, e.g., guards and station masters, promotees and direct recruits, degree holder and diploma holder engineers . . . . The question with which we are concerned, however, is whether we can extend the above principle of classification so as to allow preferential treatment to employees on the ground that they are members of the scheduled castes and scheduled tribes. So far as this question is concerned. I am of the view that the provision of preferential treatment for members of backward classes, including scheduled castes and scheduled tribes, is that contained in Clause (4) of Art. 16 which permits reservation of posts for them. There is no scope for spelling out such preferential treatment from the language of Clause (1) of Article 16 because the language of that clause does not warrant any preference to any citizen against another citizen. The opening words of Clause (4) of Article 16 that "nothing in this article shall prevent the State from making any provision for the reservation of appointments or posts in favour of backward class of citizens" indicate that but for Clause (4) it would not have been permissible

to make any reservation of appointments or posts in favour of any backward class of citizens. . . .

63.   In construing the provisions of the Constitution we should avoid a doctrinaire approach. A Constitution is the vehicle of the life of a nation and deals with practical problems of the government. It is, therefore, imperative that the approach to be adopted by the courts while construing the provisions of the Constitution should be pragmatic and not one as a result of which the court is likely to get lost in a maze of abstract theories. Indeed, so far as theories are concerned, human thinking in its full efflorescence, free from constraints and inhibitions, can take such diverse forms that views and reasons apparently logical and plausible can be found both in favour of and against a particular theory. If one eminent thinker supports one view, support for the opposite view can be found in the writings of another equally eminent thinker. Whatever indeed may be the conclusion, arguments not lacking in logic can be found in support of such conclusion. The important task of construing the articles of a Constitution is not an exercise in mere syllogism. It necessitates an effort to find the true purpose and object which underlies that article. The historical background, the felt necessities of the time, the balancing of the conflicting interests must all enter into the crucible when the court is engaged in the delicate task of construing the provisions of a Constitution. The words of Holmes that [the] life of law is not logic but experience have a direct relevance in the above context. . . .

65.   The liberal approach that may sometimes have been adopted in upholding classification under Article 14 would in the very nature of things be not apt in the context of Article 16 when we keep in view the object underlying Article 16. Article 14 covers a very wide and general field of equality before the law and the equal protection of the laws. It is, therefore, permissible to cover within its ambit manifold classifications as long as they are reasonable and have a rational connection with the object thereof. As against that, Article 16 operates in the limited area of equality of opportunity for all citizens in matters relating to employment or appointment to an office under the State. Carving out classes of citizens for favoured treatment in matters of public employment, except in cases for which there is an express provision contained in Clause (4) of Article 16, would as already pointed out above in the very nature of things run counter to the concept underlying Clause (1) of Article 16.

66.   The matter can also be looked at from another angle. If it was permissible to accord favoured treatment to members of backward classes under Clause (1) of Article 16, there would have been no necessity of inserting Clause (4) in Article 16. Clause (4) in Article 16 in such an event would have to be treated as wholly superfluous and redundant. The normal rule of interpretation is that no provision of the Constitution is to be treated as redundant and superfluous. . . .

67.   This Court in the case of State of Madras v. Smt. Champakam Dorairajan, 1951 SCR 525 (AIR 1951 SC 226) unequivocally repelled the argument the effect of which would have been to treat clause (4) of Article

16 to be wholly unnecessary and redundant. Question which arose for consideration in that case was whether a Communal G. O. fixing percentage of seats for different sections of population for admission in the engineering and medical colleges of the State of Madras contravened the fundamental rights. It was held that the Communal G. O. by which percentage of seats was apportioned contravened Article 29 (2) of the Constitution. A seven Judge Bench of this Court in that case referred to Clause (4) of Art. 16 of the Constitution and observed:

> "If the argument founded on Article 46 were sound then Clause (4) of Article 16 would have been wholly unnecessary and redundant. Seeing, however, that Clause (4) was inserted in Article 16, the omission of such an express provision from Article 29 cannot but be regarded as significant.... The protection of backward classes of citizens may require appointment of members of backward classes in State services and the reason why power has been given to the State to provide for reservation of such appointments for backward classes may under those circumstances be understood. That consideration, however, was not obviously considered necessary in the case of admission into an educational-institution and that may well be the reason for the omission from Art. 29 of a clause similar to Clause (4) of Art. 16."

After the above decision of this Court, Clause (4) of Article 15 was added in the Constitution by the Constitution (First Amendment) Act, 1951 and the same reads as under:

> "Nothing in this article or in Clause (2) of Article 29 shall prevent the State from making any special provision for the advancement of any socially and educationally backward classes of citizens or for the Scheduled Castes and the Scheduled Tribes."

68. If the power of reservation of seats for backward classes was already contained in Clause (1) of Art. 15, the decision in the above-mentioned case would in the very nature of things have been different and there would have been no necessity for the introduction of Clause (4) in Article 15 by means of the Constitution (First Amendment) Act....

MATHEW, J. (Majority view): . . .

77. Justice Brandeis has said that knowledge must precede understanding and that understanding must precede judgment. It will therefore be in the interest of clarity of thought to begin with an understanding of just what equality of opportunity means. Article 16 (1) provides for equality of opportunity for all citizens in the matter of employment and there can be no doubt that the equality guaranteed is an individual right. The concept of equality of opportunity is an aspect of the more comprehensive notion of equality. The idea of equality has different shades of meaning and connotations. It has many facets and implications. Plato's remark about law is equally applicable to the concept of equality "a perfectly simple principle can never be applied to a state of things which is the reverse of simple"....

83.   The notion of equality of opportunity is a notion that a limited good shall in fact be allocated on the grounds which do not a priori exclude any section of those that desire it. All sections of people desire and claim representation in the public service of the country, but the available number of posts are limited and therefore, even though all sections of people might desire to get posts, it is practically impossible to satisfy the desire. The question therefore is: On what basis can any citizen or class of citizens be excluded from his or their fair share of representation? Article 335 postulates that members of Scheduled Castes and Scheduled Tribes have a claim to representation in the public service both of the Union and the States and that the claim has to be taken into consideration consistently with the maintenance of efficiency of administration in the making of appointments to services of the Union and the States. As I said, the notion of equality of opportunity has meaning only when a limited good or, in the present context, a limited number of posts, should be allocated on grounds which do not a priori exclude any section of citizens of those that desire it. . . .

87.   It is clear that one is not really offering equality of opportunity to X and Y if one contents oneself with applying the same criteria to X and Y. What one is doing there is to apply the same criteria to X as affected by favourable conditions and to Y as affected by unfavourable but curable conditions. Here there is a necessary pressure to equal up the conditions. . . .

90.   Equality of opportunity is not simply a matter of legal equality. Its existence depends, not merely on the absence of disabilities, but on the presence of abilities. It obtains in so far as, and only in so far as, each member of a community, whatever his birth or occupation or social position, possesses in fact, and not merely in form, equal chances of using to the full his natural endowments of physique, of character, and of intelligence.

91.   The guarantee of equality before the law or the equal opportunity in matters of employment is a guarantee of something more than what is required by formal equality. It implies differential treatment of persons who are unequal. Egalitarian principle has therefore enhanced the growing belief that government has an affirmative duty to eliminate inequalities and to provide opportunities for the exercise of human rights and claims. Fundamental rights as enacted in Part III of the Constitution are, by and large, essentially negative in character. They mark off a world in which the government should have no jurisdiction. In this realm, it was assumed that a citizen has no claim upon government except to be let alone. But the language of Article 16 (1) is in marked contrast with that of Article 14. Whereas the accent in Article 14 is on the injunction that the State shall not deny to any person equality before the law or the equal protection of the laws, that is, on the negative character of the duty of the State, the emphasis in Article 16 (1) is on the mandatory aspect, namely, that there shall be equality of opportunity for all citizens in matters relating to employment or appointment to any office under the State implying thereby

that affirmative action by Government would be consistent with the Article if it is calculated to achieve it. If we are to achieve equality, we can never afford to relax. . . .

92. Today, the political theory which acknowledges the obligation of government under Part IV of the Constitution to provide jobs, medical care, old age pension, etc., extends to human rights and imposes an affirmative obligation to promote equality and liberty. The force of the idea of a state with obligation to help the weaker sections of its members seems to have increasing influence in constitutional law. The idea finds expression in a number of cases in America involving racial discrimination and also in the decisions requiring the state to offset the effects of poverty by providing counsel, transcript of appeal, expert witnesses, etc. Today, the sense that government has affirmative responsibility for elimination of inequalities, social, economic or otherwise, is one of the dominant forces in constitutional law. While special concessions for the under-privileged have been easily permitted, they have not traditionally been required. Decisions in the areas of criminal procedure, voting rights and education in America suggest that the traditional approach may not be completely adequate. In these areas, the inquiry whether equality has been achieved no longer ends with numerical equality; rather the equality clause has been held to require resort to a standard of proportional equality which requires the state, in framing legislation, to take into account the private inequalities of wealth, of education and other circumstances.

93. The idea of compensatory state action to make people who are really unequal in their wealth, education or social environment, equal, in specified areas, was developed by the Supreme Court of the United States. Rousse[a]u has said:

"It is precisely because the force of circumstances tends to destroy equality that force of legislation must always tend to maintain it"

94. In Griffin v. Illinois, (1956) 351 U.S. 12 an indigent defendant was unable to take advantage of the one appeal of right granted by Illinois law because he could not afford to buy the necessary transcript. Such transcripts were made available to all defendants on payment of a similar fee; but in practice only non-indigents were able to purchase the transcript and take the appeal. The Court said that "there can be no equal justice where the kind of trial a man gets depends on the amount of money he has" and held that the Illinois procedure violated the equal protection clause. The state did not have to make appellate review available at all; but if it did, it could not do so in a way which operated to deny access to review to defendants solely because of their indigency. A similar theory underlies the requirement that counsel be provided for indigents on appeal. In Douglas v. California, (1963) 372 U.S. 353 the case involved the California procedure which guaranteed one appeal of right for criminal defendants convicted at trial. . . . In the case of indigents the appellate court checked over the record to see whether it would be of advantage to the defendant or helpful to the appellate court to have counsel appointed for the appeal. A negative answer meant that the indigent had to appeal pro se if at all. The

Court held that this procedure denied defendant the equal protection of the laws. Even though the state was pursuing an otherwise legitimate objective of providing counsel only for non-frivolous claims, it had created a situation in which the well-to-do could always have a lawyer—even for frivolous appeals—whereas the indigent could not.

95.   Justice Harlan, dissenting in both (1955) 351 U.S. 12 Griffin and (1963) 372 U.S. 353 Douglas cases said that they represented a new departure from the traditional view that numerically equal treatment cannot violate the equal protection clause. He concluded that the effect of the decisions was to require state discrimination. He said:

> "The Court thus holds that, at least in this area of criminal appeals, the Equal Protection Clause imposes on the States an affirmative duty to lift the handicaps flowing from differences in economic circumstances. That holding produces the anomalous result that a constitutional admonition to the States to treat all persons equally means in this instance that Illinois must give to some [what] it requires others to pay for...... It may accurately be said that the real issue in this case is not whether Illinois has discriminated but whether it has a duty to discriminate."

96.   Though in one sense Justice Harlan is correct, when one comes to think of the real effect of his view, one is inclined to think that the opinion failed to recognise that there are several ways of looking at equality, and treating people equally in one respect always results in unequal treatment in some other respects. For Mr. Justice Harlan, the only type of equality that mattered was numerical equality in the terms upon which transcripts were offered to defendants. The majority, on the other hand, took a view which would bring about equality in fact, requiring similar availability to all of criminal appeals in Griffin's case and counsel-attended criminal appeals in Douglas' case. To achieve this result, the legislature had to resort to a proportional standard of equality. These cases are remarkable in that they show that the kind of equality which is considered important in the particular context and hence of the respect in which it is necessary to treat people equally.

97.   Look at the approach of the Supreme Court of United States of America in Harper v. Virginia Board of Elections, (1966) 383 U.S. 663. The Court there declared, as unconstitutional a Virginia poll tax of $ 1.50 per person which had been applied to all indiscriminately. As in Griffin and Douglas, the state had treated everyone numerically alike with respect to the fee. Whatever discrimination existed was the result of the state's failure to proportion the fee on the basis of need or, what is the same thing, to employ a numerically equal distribution with respect to the vote itself. The result again is a requirement that the legislature should take note of difference in private circumstances in formulating its policies.

98.   There is no reason why this Court should not also require the state to adopt a standard of proportional equality which takes account of the differing conditions and circumstances of a class of citizens whenever

those conditions and circumstances stand in the way of their equal access to the enjoyment of basic rights or claims.

99. The concept of equality of opportunity in matters of employment is wide enough to include within it compensatory measures to put the members of the Scheduled Castes and Scheduled Tribes on par with the members of other communities which would enable them to get their share of representation in public service. How can any member of the so-called forward communities complain of a compensatory measure made by government to ensure the members of Scheduled Castes and Scheduled Tribes their due share of representation in public services? . . .

104. The State can adopt any measure which would ensure the adequate representation in public service of the members of the Scheduled Castes and Scheduled Tribes and justify it as a compensatory measure to ensure equality of opportunity provided the measure does not dispense with the acquisition of the minimum basic qualification necessary for the efficiency of administration. . . .

Krishna Iyer, J. (Majority view):— . . .

131. Law, including constitutional law, can no longer 'go it alone' but must be illumined in the interpretative process by sociology and allied fields of knowledge. Indeed, the term 'constitutional law' symbolizes an intersection of law and politics, wherein issues of political power are acted on by persons trained in the legal tradition, working in judicial institutions, following the procedures of law, thinking as lawyers think. So much so, a wider perspective is needed to resolve issues of constitutional law. May be, one cannot agree with the view of an eminent jurist and former Chief Justice of India: 'the judiciary as a whole is not interested in the policy underlying a legislative measure' (Mr. Hidayatullah—'Democracy in India and the Judicial Process'—1965—p. 70). Moreover, the Indian Constitution is a great social document, almost revolutionary in its aim of transforming a medieval, hierarchical society into a modern egalitarian democracy. Its provisions can be comprehended only by a spacious, social-science approach, not by pedantic, traditional legalism. Here we are called upon to delimit the amplitude and decode the implications of Art. 16 (1) in the context of certain special concessions relating to employment, under the Kerala State (the appellant), given to Scheduled Castes and Scheduled Tribes (for short, hereinafter referred to as harijans) whose social lot and economic indigence are an Indian reality recognized by many Articles of the Constitution. An overview of the decided cases suggests the need to reinterpret the dynamic import of the 'equality clauses' and, to stress again, beyond reasonable doubt, that the paramount law, which is organic and regulates our nation's growing life, must take in its sweep 'ethics, economics, politics and sociology'. . . .

132. Naturally surges the interrogation, what are the challenges of changing values to which the guarantee of equality must respond and how? To pose the problem with particular reference to our case, does the impugned rule violate the constitutional creed of equal opportunity in Art. 16 by resort to a suspect classification or revivify it by making the less

equal more equal by a legitimate differentiation? Chief Justice Marshall's classic statement in McCulloch v. Maryland, (1816–19) 17 U.S. (4 Wheat) 316, 421 quoted in (1966) 384 U.S. 650 followed by Justice Brennan in Katzenbach v. Morgan, (1966) 384 U.S. 641 remains a beacon light:

> "Let the end be legitimate, let it be within the scope of the constitution, and all means which are appropriate, which are plainly adapted to that end, which are not prohibited, but consist with the letter and spirit of the constitution, are constitutional." ...

136.   Back now to the rule of exemption and its vires. Frankly, here the respondents who have passed the 'tests' are stalled in their promotion because of the new rule of harijan exemption. As individuals, their rights vis a vis their harijan brethren are regarded unequally. In a strictly competitive context or narrowly performance-oriented standard, Rule 13AA discriminates between a harijan and a non-harijan. The question is whether a perceptive sensitivity sees on 'equal opportunity' a critical distinction between distribution according to 'merit' of individuals and distribution according to 'need' of depressed groups, subject to broad efficiency criteria. We enter here 'a conceptual disaster area'. . . .

142.   Let us proceed to assess the constitutional merit of the State's ex facie 'unequal' service rule favouring in-service harijan employees in a realist socio-legal perspective. But before that, some memorable facts must be stated. The Father of the Nation adopted, as his fighting faith, the uplift of the bhangi and his assimilation, on equal footing, into Hindu society, and the Constitution, whose principal architect was himself a militant mahar, made social justice a founding faith and built into it humanist provisions to lift the level of the lowly scheduled castes and tribes to make democracy viable and equal for all. Studies in social anthropology tell us how cultural and material suppression has, over the ages, crippled their personality, and current demography says that nearly every fifth Indian is a harijan and his social milieu is steeped in squalour. The conscience of the Constitution found adequate expression on this theme in Dr. Ambedkar's words of caution and premonition in the Constituent Assembly:

> "We must begin by acknowledging first that there is complete absence of two things in Indian society. One of these is equality. On the social plane, we have in India a society based on privilege of graded inequality which means elevation for some and degradation of others. On the economic plane, we have a society in which there are some who have immense wealth as against the many who are living in abject poverty. On the 26th of January, 1950, we are going to enter into a life of contradictions. In politics we will have equality and in social and economic life we will have inequality .... We must remove this contradiction at the earliest possible moment, or else those who suffer from inequality will blow up the structure of political democracy which this Assembly has so laboriously built up." (Speeches, Vol. II, pp. 184–187).

Judges may differ in constitutional construction but, without peril of distorting the substance, cannot discard the activism of the equal justice concept in the setting of deep concern for the weaker sections of the community. What I endeavour to emphasize, as I will elaborate later, is that equal justice is an aspect of social justice, the salvation of the very weak and down-trodden, and the methodology for levelling them up to *a real*, not formal, equality, being the accent.

143. The Kerala State, the appellant, has statistically shown the yawning gap between what number of posts in Government service harijans are entitled to, population-ratiowise, and the actual number of posts occupied by them. Their 'official' fate is no less ominous elsewhere in India and would have been poorer on the competitive market method of selection unaided by 'reservation'. The case for social equality and economic balance, in terms of employment under the State, cries for more energised administrative effort and a Government that fails to repair this depressed lot, fools the public on harijan welfare. Indeed, an *aware* mass of humanity, denied justice, for generations, will not take it lying down too long but may explode into Dalit Panthers, as did the Black Panthers in another country,—a theme on which Sri Gajendragadkar, a former Chief Justice of India, has laid disturbing stress in two Memorial Lectures delivered recently. Jurists must listen to real life and, theory apart, must be alert enough to read the writing on the wall! Where the rule of law bars the doors of collective justice, the crushed class will seek hope in the streets! The architects of our Constitution were not unfamiliar with direct action where basic justice was long withheld and conceived of 'equal opportunity' as inclusive of equalising opportunity. Only a clinical study of organic law will yield correct diagnostic results....

147. ... However, we are under a Constitution and mere social anthropology cannot override the real words used in the Constitution. For, Judges may read, not reconstruct. Plainly, harijans enjoy a temporary *advantage* over their non-harijan brethren by virtue of Rule 13AA and this, it is plausibly urged by counsel for the contestants, is violative of the merciless mandate of equality 'enshrined' dually in Art. 16 (1) and (2). It discriminates without constitutional justification and imports the caste differentia in the face of a contrary provision. The learned Advocate General seeks to meet it more by a legal realist's approach and, in a sense, by resort to functional jurisprudence. What is the constitutional core of equality? What social philosophy animates it? What luminous connotation does the pregnant, though terse, phrase 'equality of opportunity for all citizens in matters of employment' bear? What excesses of discrimination are banned and what equalitarian implications invite administrative exploration? Finally, what light do we derive from precedents of this Court on these facets of Art. 16? I will examine these contentious issues presently....

149. A word of sociological caution. In the light of experience, here and elsewhere, the danger of 'reservation', it seems to me, is three-fold. Its benefits, by and large, are snatched away by the top creamy layer of the

'backward' caste or class, thus keeping the weakest among the weak always weak and leaving the fortunate layers to consume the whole cake. Secondly, this claim is over-played extravagantly in democracy by large and vocal groups whose burden of backwardness has been substantially lightened by the march of time and measures of better education and more opportunities of employment, but wish to wear the 'weaker section' label as a means to score over their near-equals formally categorised as the upper brackets. Lastly, a lasting solution to the problem comes only from improvement of social environment, added educational facilities and cross-fertilisation of castes by inter-caste and inter-class marriages sponsored as a massive State programme, and this solution is calculatedly hidden from view by the higher 'backward' groups with a vested interest in the plums of backwardism. But social science research, not judicial impressionism, will alone tell the whole truth and a constant process of objective re-evaluation of progress registered by the 'under-dog' categories is essential lest a once deserving 'reservation' should be degraded into 'reverse discrimination'. Innovations in administrative strategy to help the really untouched, most backward classes also emerge from such socio-legal studies and audit exercises, if dispassionately made. In fact, research conducted by the A. N. Sinha Institute of Social Studies, Patna, has revealed a dual society among harijans, a tiny elite gobbling up the benefits and the darker layers sleeping distances away from the special concessions. For them, Arts. 46 and 335 remain a 'noble romance', the bonanza going to the 'higher' harijans. I mention this in the present case because lower division clerks are likely to be drawn from the lowest levels of harijan humanity and promotion prospects being accelerated by withdrawing, for a time, 'test' qualifications for this category may perhaps delve deeper. An equalitarian break-through in a hierarchical structure has to use many weapons and Rule 13AA perhaps is one . . . .

153. The Constitution itself makes a super-classification between harijans and others, grounded on the fundamental disparity in our society and the imperative social urgency of raising the former's sunken status. Apart from reservation of seats in the Legislatures for harijans, which is a deliberate departure, taking note of their utter backwardness (Arts. 330 and 332), a special officer to investigate and report to the President upon the working of special constitutional safeguards made to protect harijans has to be appointed under Art. 338. Gross inadequacy of representation in public services is obviously one subject for investigation and report. More importantly, Art. 335, which Shri Garg relied on to hammer home his point, reads:

> "335.   Claims of Scheduled Castes and Scheduled Tribes to services and posts.—The claims of the members of the Scheduled Castes and the Scheduled Tribes shall be taken into consideration, consistently with the maintenance of efficiency of administration, in the making of appointments to services and posts in connection with the affairs of the Union or of a State."

This provision directs pointedly to (a) the claims of—not compassion towards—harijans to be given special consideration in the making of appointments to public services; and (b) lest this extra-attention should run riot and ruin administrative efficiency, a caution is uttered that maintenance of efficiency in administration should not suffer mayhem. . . .

160.   We may clear the clog of Art. 16 (2) as it stems from a confusion about *caste* in the terminology of Scheduled Castes and Scheduled Tribes. This latter expression has been defined in Arts. 341 and 342. A bare reading brings out the quintessential concept that they are no castes in the Hindu fold but an amalgam of castes, races, groups, tribes, communities or parts thereof found on investigation to be the lowliest and in need of massive State aid and notified as such by the President. To confuse this backward-most social composition with *castes* is to commit a constitutional error, misled by a compendious appellation. So that to protect harijans is not to prejudice any caste but to promote citizen solidarity. Art. 16 (2) is out of the way and to extend protective discrimination to this mixed bag of tribes, races, groups, communities and non-castes outside the four-fold Hindu division is not to compromise with the acceleration of castelessness enshrined in the sub-article. The discerning sense of the Indian Corpus Juris has generally regarded Scheduled Castes and Scheduled Tribes, not as caste but as a large backward group deserving of societal compassion. The following provisions of the Income-tax Act, 1961 are illustrative of this principle:

> "13.   Section 11 not to apply in certain cases: (1) (b) Nothing contained in Section 11 or Section 12 shall operate so as to exclude from the total income of the previous year of the person in receipt thereof
>
> (a) . . . .
>
> (b) in the case of a trust for charitable purposes or a charitable institution created or established after the commencement of this Act, any income thereof if the trust or institution is created or established for the benefit of any particular religious community or caste;
>
> xxx
>
> Explanation 2.—A trust or institution created or established for the benefit of Scheduled Castes backward classes, Scheduled Tribes or women and children shall not be deemed to be a trust or institution created or established for the benefit of a religious community or caste within the meaning of Cl. (b) of subsection (1)."

161.   The next hurdle in the appellant's path relates to Art. 16 (4). To my mind, this sub-article serves not as an exception but as an emphatic statement, one mode of reconciling the claims of backward people and the opportunity for free competition the forward sections are ordinarily entitled to. In the language of Subba Rao J. (as he then was), in Devadasan, (1964) 4 SCR 680, 700 (AIR 1964 SC 179 at p. 190):

"The expression 'nothing in this article' is a legislative device to express its intention in a most emphatic way that the power conferred thereunder is not limited in any way by the main provision but falls outside it. It has not really carved out an exception, but has preserved a power untrammelled by the other provisions of the Article."

True, it may be loosely said that Art. 16 (4) is an exception but, closely examined, it is an illustration of constitutionally sanctified classification. Public services have been a fascination for Indians even in British days, being a symbol of State power and so a special Article has been devoted to it. Art. 16 (4) need not be a saving clause but put in due to the over-anxiety of the draftsman to make matters clear beyond possibility of doubt.

162. 'Reservation' based on classification of backward and forward classes, without detriment to administrative standards (as this Court has underscored) is but an application of the principle of equality within a class and grouping based on a rational differentia, the object being advancement of backward classes consistently with efficiency. Arts. 16 (1) and (4) are concordant. This Court has viewed Art. 16(4) as an exception to Art. 16(1). Does classification based on desperate backwardness render Art. 16 (4) redundant? No. Reservation confers pro tanto monopoly, but classification grants under Art. 16 (1) ordinarily a lesser order of advantage. The former is more rigid, the latter more flexible, although they may overlap sometimes. Art. 16 (4) covers all backward classes, but to earn the benefit of grouping under Art. 16 (1) based on Arts. 46 and 335 as I have explained, the twin considerations of terrible backwardness of the type harijans endure and maintenance of administrative efficiency must be satisfied. . . .

166. The basic question thus is one of social dynamics implied in Art. 16 (1). . . . In a spacious sense, 'equal opportunity' for members of a hierarchical society makes sense only if there exists a strategy by which the underprivileged have environmental facilities for developing their full human potential. This consummation is accomplished only when the utterly depressed groups can claim a fair share in public life and economic activity, including employment under the State, or when a classless and casteless society blossoms as a result of positive State action. To help the lagging social segments, by special care, is a step towards and not against a larger and stabler equality. I had occasion to observe . . .

"In this unequal world the proposition that all men are equal has working limitations, since absolute equality leads to Procrustean cruelty or sanctions indolent inefficiency. Necessarily, therefore, an imaginative and constructive modus vivendi between commonness and excellence must be forged to make the equality clauses viable. This pragmatism produced the judicial gloss of 'classification' and 'differentia', with the byproducts of equality among equals and dissimilar things having to be treated differently. The social meaning of Arts. 14 to 16 is neither dull uniformity nor specious 'talentism'. It is a process of producing quality out of larger areas of equality extending better facilities to the latent capabilities of the lowly. It is not a methodology of substitution of pervasive and slovenly mediocrity for activist and intelligent—but not snobbish and uncommitted—cadres. However: if the State uses classification casuistically for salvaging status and elitism, the point of no return is reached for Arts. 14 to 16 and the Court's jurisdiction awakens to deaden such manoeuvres. The soul of Art. 16 is the promotion of the common man's capabilities, over-powering environmental adversities and opening up full opportunities to develop in official life without succumbing to the sophistic argument of the elite that talent is the privilege of the few and they must rule, wriggling out of the democratic imperative of Arts. 14 and 16 by the theory of classified equality which at its worst degenerates into class domination."

————

Marc Galanter, LAW AND SOCIETY IN MODERN INDIA (1989)

PURSUING EQUALITY IN THE LAND OF HIERARCHY: AN ASSESSMENY OF INDIA'S POLICIES OF COMPENSATORY DISCRIMINATION FOR HISTORICALLY DISADVANTAGED GROUPS

Independent India embraced equality as a cardinal value against a background of elaborate, valued and clearly perceived inequalities. Her constitutional policies to offset these proceeded from an awareness of the entrenched and cumulative nature of group inequalities. The result has been an array of programmes that I call, collectively, a policy of compensatory discrimination. If one reflects on the propensity of nations to neglect the claims of those at the bottom, I think it is fair to say that this policy of compensatory discrimination has been pursued with remarkable persistence and generosity (if not always with vigour and effectiveness) for the past thirty years.

These compensatory discrimination policies entail systematic departure from norms of equality (such as merit, evenhandedness, and indifference to ascriptive characteristics). These departures are justified in several ways: first, preferential treatment may be viewed as needed assurance of personal fairness, a guarantee against the persistence of discrimination in subtle and indirect forms. Second, such policies are justified in terms of beneficial results that they will presumably promote: integration, use of neglected talent, more equitable distribution, etc. With these two—the anti-discrimination theme and the general welfare theme—is entwined a notion of historical restitution or reparation to offset the systematic and cumulative deprivations suffered by lower castes in the past. These multiple justifications point to the complexities of pursuing such a policy and of assessing its performance.

India's policy of compensatory discrimination is composed of an array of preferential schemes. These programmes are authorized by Constitutional provisions that permit departure from formal equality for the purpose of favouring specified groups.

The benefits of 'compensatory discrimination' are extended to a wide array of groups. There are three major classes. First, there are those castes designated as Scheduled Castes on the basis of their 'untouchability'. They number nearly 80 million (14.6 per cent of population) according to the 1971 Census. Second, there are the Scheduled Tribes who are distinguished by their tribal culture and physical isolation and many of whom are residents of specially-protected Scheduled Areas. They number more than 38 million (6.9 per cent of the population in 1971). Third, there are the 'Backward Classes' (or, as they are sometimes called, 'Other Backward Classes',) a heterogeneous category, varying greatly from state to state, comprised for the most part of castes (and some non-Hindu communities) low in the traditional social hierarchy, but not as low as the Scheduled Castes.... It has been estimated that there were approximately 60 million persons under the Other Backward Classes heading in 1961—roughly the magnitude of the Scheduled Caste population at that time (64 millions). (Today the portion of the population designated under this heading is probably larger)....

Preferences are of three basic types: first, there are reservations, which allot or facilitate access to valued positions or resources. The most important instances of this type are reserved seats in legislatures, reservation of posts in government service, and reservation of places in academic institutions (especially the coveted higher technical and professional colleges). To a lesser extent, the reservation device is also used in the distribution of land allotments, housing and other scarce resources. Second, there are programmes involving expenditure or provision of services—e.g., scholarships, grants, loans, land allotments, health care, legal aid—to a beneficiary group beyond comparable expenditure for others. Third, there are special protections. These distributive schemes are accompanied by efforts to protect the backward classes from being exploited and victimized. Forced labour is prohibited by the Constitution (Art. 23 (2)) and in recent years there have been strenuous efforts to release the victims of debt bondage, who are mostly from Scheduled Castes and Tribes. Legislation regulating money lending, providing debt relief, and restricting land transfers attempt to protect Scheduled Castes and Tribes from economic oppression by their more sophisticated neighbours. Anti-untouchability propaganda and the Protection of Civil Rights Act attempt to relieve Untouchables from the social disabilities under which they have suffered. This legislation is not 'compensatory discrimination' in the formal sense of departing from equal treatment to favour these groups; it enjoins equal treatment rather than confers preferential treatment. But in substance it is a special undertaking to remedy the disadvantaged position of the Untouchables.

The Array of (Alleged) Costs and Benefits

Few in independent India have voiced disagreement with the proposition that the disadvantaged sections of the population deserve and need 'special help'. But there has been considerable disagreement about exactly who is deserving of such help, about the form this help ought to take, and about the efficacy and propriety of what the government has done under this head.

There is no open public defence of the *ancien regime*. Everyone is against untouchability and against caste. Public debate takes the form of argument among competing views of what is really good for the lowest castes and for the country. These views involve a host of assertions about the effects—beneficial and deleterious—of compensatory discrimination policies. . . .

A Costly Success

Have these policies 'worked'? What results have they produced? And at what costs? Our tabulation of alleged costs and benefits suggests the complexity hidden in these apparently simple questions. Performance is difficult to measure: effects ramify in complex interaction with other factors. . . .

What I want to do here is draw a crude sketch of the effects of the compensatory discrimination policy in their largest outline. What has the commitment to compensatory discrimination done to the shape of Indian society and of lives lived within it? . . .

. . . The following summary focuses on programmes for Scheduled Castes and Tribes and adds some qualifications in the light of experience with schemes for the Other Backward Classes.

Undeniably compensatory discrimination policies have produced substantial redistributive effects. Reserved seats provide a substantial legislative presence and swell the flow of patronage, attention and favourable policy to Scheduled Castes and Scheduled Tribes. The reservation of jobs has given to a sizable portion of the beneficiary groups earnings, and the security, information, patronage and prestige that goes with government employment. At the cost of enormous wastage, there has been a major redistribution of educational opportunities to these groups. (Of course not all of this redistribution can be credited to preferential policies, for some fraction would presumably have occurred without them.)

Such redistribution is not spread evenly throughout the beneficiary group. There is evidence for substantial clustering in the utilization of these opportunities. The clustering appears to reflect structural factors (e.g., the greater urbanization of some groups) more than deliberate group aggrandizement, as often charged. The better situated among the beneficiaries enjoy a disproportionate share of programme benefits. This tendency, inherent in all government programmes—quite independently of compensatory discrimination—is aggravated here by passive administration and by the concentration on higher echelon benefits. Where the list of beneficiaries spans groups of very disparate condition—as with the most expansive lists of other Backward Classes—the 'creaming' effect is probably even more pronounced.

The vast majority are not directly benefitted, but reserved jobs bring a manyfold increase in the number of families liberated from circumscribing subservient roles, able to utilize expanding opportunities and support high educational attainments. Although such families comprise only a tiny fraction—an optimistic guess might be 6 per cent—of all Scheduled Caste families, they provide the crucial leaven from which effective leadership might emerge.

Reserved seats afford a measure of representation in legislative settings, though the use of joint electorates deliberately muffles the assertiveness and single-mindedness of that representation. The presence of SC and ST in legislative settings locks in place the other programmes for their benefit and assures that their concerns are not dismissed or ignored. Job reservations promote their presence in other influential roles and educational preferences provide the basis for such participation. Of course these positions are used to promote narrower interests—although we should not assume automatically that those they displace would bestow the benefits of their influence more broadly. If, for example, reserved seat legislators are disproportionately attentive to the concerns of those of their fellows who already have something, it is not clear that this is more the case with them than with legislators in general seats.

Legislative seats are occupied by members of national political parties. They must aggregate broad multi-group support in order to get elected and, once elected, must participate in multi-group coalitions in order to be effective. In the office setting, too, there are relations of reciprocity and interdependence. The broad participation afforded by reserved seats and reserved jobs is for many others a source of pride and warrant of security.

If the separate and special treatment entailed by preferential programmes wounds and alienates the members of beneficiary groups, this is amplified by the hostility experienced on being identified as a recipient. As sources of alienation, these experiences must be placed against the background of more devastating manifestations of hostility, such as the much publicized assaults and atrocities perpetrated on Scheduled Castes.

At the policy-making level, reserved seats have secured the acceptance of Scheduled Castes and Tribes as groups whose interests and views must be taken into account. In every legislative setting they are present in sufficient numbers so that issues affecting these groups remain on the agenda. Anything less than respectful attention to their problems, even if only lip service, is virtually unknown. Overt hostility to these groups is taboo in legislative and many other public forums. But there is evidence that Scheduled Castes and Tribes are not accepted politically. Very few members of these groups are nominated for non-reserved seats and only a tiny number are elected. There is massive withdrawal by voters from participation in election for reserved seats in the legislative assemblies. Apparently large numbers of people do not feel represented by these legislators and do not care to participate in choosing them.

In the long term, education and jobs help weaken the stigmatizing association of Scheduled Castes and Tribes with ignorance and incompetence, but in the short run they experience rejection in the offices, hostels and other settings into which they are introduced by preferential treatment. Resentment of preferences may magnify hostility to these groups, but rejection of them obviously exists independently of compensatory programmes.

Compensatory programmes provide the basis for personal achievement and enlarge the beneficiaries' capacity to shape their own lives. But in other ways the programmes curtail their autonomy. The design of the legislative reservations, the dependence on outside parties for funds and organizations and the need to appeal to constituencies made up overwhelmingly of others—tends to produce compliant and accommodating leaders rather than forceful articulators of the interests of these groups. The promise of good positions offers a powerful incentive for individual effort. But reservations in government service—and educational programmes designed to provide the requisite qualifications—deflect the most able to paths of individual mobility that remove them from leadership roles in the community.... [E]ligibility requirements ... penalize those who would solve the problem of degraded identity by conversion to a non-Hindu religion.

Although preferential treatment has kept the beneficiary groups and their problems visible to the educated public, it has not stimulated widespread concern to provide for their inclusion apart from what is mandated by government policy. (This lack of concern is manifest in the record of private sector employment—as it was in public undertaking employment before the introduction of reservations.) Against a long history of such lack of concern, it is difficult to attribute its current absence to compensatory discrimination policy. But this policy has encouraged a tendency to absolve others of any responsibility for the betterment of Scheduled Castes and Scheduled Tribes on the ground that it is a responsibility of the government. The pervasive overestimation of the amount and effectiveness of preferential treatment reinforces the notion that enough (or too much) is already being done and nothing more is called for....

Reserved seats in legislatures are self-perpetuating in the literal sense that their holders can help to produce their extension, but extension requires support from others. The periodic necessity of renewal provides an occasion for assessment and curtailment. Programmes for Scheduled Castes and Scheduled Tribes are for a delimited minority and pose no danger that the compensatory principle will expand into a comprehensive and self-perpetuating system of communal quotas. Although restrained by the courts, the provisions for the Other Backward Classes are open-ended: a majority may be the beneficiaries and the dangers of self-perpetuation cannot be dismissed.

The diversion of resources by compensatory discrimination programmes entails costs in the failure to develop and utilize other talents. The exact extent of this is unclear. It seems mistaken, for example, to consider compensatory discrimination a major factor in the lowering of standards that has accompanied the vast expansion of educational facilities since independence. The pattern in education has been less one of excluding others than of diluting educational services while extending them nominally to all. Similarly the effect of Scheduled Castes and Tribes on the effectiveness of a much enlarged government bureaucracy is overshadowed by a general lowering of standards combined with the assumption of a wide array of new and more complex tasks.

The most disturbing costs of preferential programmes may flow not from their exclusion of others but from their impact on the beneficiaries. What do the programmes do to the morale and initiative of those they purport to help? The numbers who fall by the educational wayside are legion. How rewarding is the educational experience of those who survive? Compensatory discrimination policies are not the source of the deficiencies of Indian education which impinge with special force on the beneficiaries.

As a forced draft programme of inclusion of Scheduled Castes and Scheduled Tribes within national life, compensatory discrimination has been a partial and costly success. Although few direct benefits have reached the vast mass of landless labourers in the villages, it has undeniably succeeded in accelerating the growth of a middle class within these groups—urban, educated, largely in government service. Members of these groups have been brought into central roles in the society to an extent unimaginable a few decades ago. There has been a significant redistribution of educational and employment opportunities to them; there is a sizable section of these groups who can utilize these opportunities and confer advantages on their children; their concerns are firmly placed on the political agenda and cannot readily be dislodged. But if compensatory discrimination can be credited with producing this self-sustaining dynamic of inclusion, there is at the same time a lesser counter-dynamic of resentment, rejection, manipulation and low self-esteem. And these gains are an island of hope in a vast sea of neglect and oppression. This mixed pattern of inclusion and rejection, characteristic of urban India and of the 'organized' sector, is echoed in the villages by a pattern of increasing assertion and increasing repression.

Since independence India has undergone what might crudely be summarized as development at the upper end and stagnation at the bottom. With the boost given by compensatory discrimination a section of the Scheduled Castes and Scheduled Tribes has secured entry into the 'modern' class manning the organized sector. What does this portend for the bulk of untouchables and tribals who remain excluded and oppressed? Are they better or worse off by virtue of the fact that some members of their descent groups have a share in the benefits of modern India? . . .

. . . [I]n dealing with measures for Other Backward Classes[, p]olicies diverge from state to state, and very different groups of people are involved. In some states the Other Backward Classes category is used to address the problems of a stratum of lowly groups who are roughly comparable in circumstance to the Scheduled Castes and Tribes. In other places this category has been used to tilt the distribution of government benefits in favour of a major section of the politically dominant middle castes. The latter doubtless produce substantial redistributive effects, if less in the way of including the most deprived. But these expensive preferences for Other Backward Classes are of immense consequence for the Scheduled Castes and Tribes. They borrow legitimacy from the national commitment to ameliorate the condition of the lowest. At the same time they undermine that commitment by broadcasting a picture of unrestrained preference for those who are not distinctly worse off than non-beneficiaries, which attaches indiscriminately to all preferential treatment. And because the Other Backward Class categories are less bounded and are determined at the state rather than at the Centre, they carry the threat of expanding into a general regime of communal allotments. . . .

We arrive then at an ironic tension that lies at the heart of the compensatory discrimination policy. Since the conditions that invite compensatory treatment are matters of degree, special treatment generates plausible claims to extend coverage to more groups. The range of variation among beneficiaries invites gradation to make benefits proportionate to need. Those preferential policies create new discontinuities and it is inviting to smooth them out by a continuous modulated system of preferences articulated to the entire range of need and/or desert. But to do so is to establish a general system of group allotments.

Compensatory discrimination replaces the arbitrariness of formal equality with the arbitrariness of a line between formal equality and compensatory treatment. The principles that justify the preference policy counsel flexibility and modulation, We may shave away the arbitrary features of the policy in many ways. But we may dissolve the arbitrary line separating formal equality and preferential treatment only at the risk of abandoning the preference policy for something very different.

If there is to be preferential treatment for a distinct set of historically victimized groups, who is to bear the cost? Whose resources and life-chances should be diminished to increase those of the beneficiaries of this policy? In some cases, the costs are spread widely among the taxpayers, for example, or among consumers of a 'diluted' public service. But in some cases major costs impinge on specific individuals like the applicant who is bumped to fill a reservation. Differences in public acceptance may reflect this distinction. Indians have been broadly supportive of preferential programmes—e.g. the granting of educational facilities and sharing of political power—where the 'cost' of inclusion is diffused broadly. Resentment has been focussed on settings where the life chances of specific others are diminished in a palpable way, as in reservations of jobs and medical college places.

There is no reason to suppose that those who are bumped from valued opportunities are more responsible for past invidious deprivations than are those whose well-being is undisturbed. Nor that they were disproportionately benefitted by invidious discrimination the past. Reserved seats or posts may thus be seen as the conscription of an arbitrarily selected group of citizens to discharge an obligation from which equally culpable debtors are excused. The incidence of reservations and the effectiveness with which they are implemented tends to vary from one setting to another. Reservations impinge heavily on some careers and leave others virtually untouched. The administration of compensatory discrimination measures seems to involve considerable unfairness of this kind. If some concentration of benefits is required by the aims of the preference policy, it seems clear that more could be done to distribute the burden among non-beneficiaries more widely and more evenly.

Secularism and Continuity

Fairness apart, to many Indian intellectuals compensatory discrimination policies seem to undermine progress toward the crucial national goal of a secular society. Secularism in this setting implies more than the separation of religion and state .... It refers to the elimination (or minimization) of caste and religious groups as categories of public policy and as actors in public life. In th[e] 1950s and 1960s this was frequently expressed as pursuit of a 'casteless' society. Proponents of such a transformation were not always clear whether they meant the disestablishment of social hierarchy or the actual dissolution of caste units. But at the minimum what was referred to was a severe reduction in the salience of caste in all spheres of life.

The Constitution envisages a new order as to the place of caste in Indian life. There is a clear commitment to eliminate inequality of status and invidious treatment and to have a society in which government takes minimal account of ascriptive ties. But beyond this the posture of the legal system toward caste is not as singleminded as the notion of a casteless society might imply. If the law discourages some assertions of caste precedence and caste solidarity, in other respects the prerogatives previously enjoyed by the caste group remain unimpaired. The law befriends castes by giving recognition and protection to the new social forms through which caste concerns can be expressed (caste associations, educational societies, political parties, religious sects)....

The use of caste groups to identify the beneficiaries of compensatory discrimination has been blamed for perpetuation the caste system, accentuating caste consciousness, injecting caste into politics and generally impeding the development of a secular society in which communal affiliation is ignored in public life. This indictment should be regarded with some scepticism. Caste ties and caste-based political mobilization are not exclusive to the backward classes. The political life within these groups is not necessarily more intensely communal in orientation: nor are the caste politics of greatest political impact found among these groups. Communal considerations are not confined to settings which are subject to compensatory discrimination policies but flourish even where they are eschewed. Although it has to some extent legitimated and encouraged caste politics, it is not clear that the use of caste to designate beneficiaries has played a preponderant role in the marriage of caste and politics. Surely it is greatly overshadowed by the franchise itself, with its invitation to mobilize support by appeal to existing loyalties. But the avowed and official recognition of caste in compensatory discrimination policy combines with the overestimation of its effects to provide a convenient target for those offended and dismayed by the continuing salience of caste in Indian life.

The amount of preference afforded to the Scheduled Castes and Tribes is widely overestimated. The widespread perception of ubiquitous and unrestrained preferment for these groups derives from several sources. First, there is the chronic overstatement of the effects of reservation: large portions of reservations (especially for cherished higher positions) are not filled; of those that are filled, some would have been gained on merit; diversion of benefits to a few may be perceived as a deprivation by a much larger number. The net effect is often considerably less than popularly perceived. Second, ambiguous nomenclature and public inattention combine to blur the distinction between measures for Scheduled Castes and Tribes and those for Other Backward Classes. The resentment and dismay engendered by use of the Other Backward Classes category to stake out massive claims on behalf of peasant-middle groups (particularly in some southern states) are readily transferred to discredit the more modest measures for Scheduled Castes and Tribes.

If caste has displayed unforeseen durability it has not remained unchanged. Relations between castes are increasingly independent and competitive, less interdependent and co-operative. 'Horizontal' solidarity and organization within caste groups have grown at the expense of 'vertical' integration among the castes of a region. . . .

If secularism is defined in terms of the elimination of India's compartmental group structure in favour of a compact and unitary society, then the compensatory discrimination policy may indeed have impeded secularism. But one may instead visualize not the disappearance of communal groups but their transformation into components of a pluralistic society in which invidious hierarchy is discarded while diversity is accommodated. In this view compensatory discrimination policy contributes to secularism by reducing group disparities and blunting hierarchic distinctions.

The development of a secular society in which the hierarchic ordering of groups is not recognized and confirmed in the public realm is a departure from older Indian patterns. The compensatory discrimination policy is a major component in the disestablishment of a central part of the traditional way of ordering the society. But this break with the past, itself is conducted in a familiar cultural and institutional style. The administration of preference programmes reflects older patterns in the fecund proliferation of overlapping schemes, the fragmentation of responsibility and the broad decentralization of authority under the aegis of unifying symbols. When these policies encounter the judiciary, what purports to be a pyramidal hierarchy establishing fixed doctrine turns out to be a loose collegium presiding over an open textured body of learning within which conflicting tendencies can be accommodated and elaborated.

The compensatory principle of substantive equality is added to the constitutional scheme of formal equality but it does not displace it. This juxtaposition of conflicting principles is an instance of what Glanville Austin admiringly describes as one of

India's original contributions to constitution-making [that is] accommodation . . . the ability to reconcile, to harmonize, and to make work without changing their content, apparently incompatible concepts—at least concepts that appear conflicting to the non-Indian, and especially to the European or American observer. Indians can accommodate such apparently conflicting principles by seeing them at different levels of value, or, if you will, in compartments not watertight, but sufficiently separate so that a concept can operate freely within its own sphere and not conflict with another operating in a separate sphere....

> With accommodation, concepts and viewpoints, although seemingly incompatible, stand intact. They are not whittled away by compromise but are worked simultaneously.

The expectation that these principles could co-exist has been fulfilled. The compensatory principle has been implemented but it has not been allowed to overshadow or swallow up opposing commitments to merit and to formal equality.

The compensatory discrimination policy is not to be judged only for its instrumental qualities. It is also expressive: through it Indians tell themselves what kind of people they are and what kind of nation. These policies express a sense of connection and shared destiny. The groups that occupy the stage today are the repositories and transmitters of older patterns. Advantaged and disadvantaged are indissolubly bound to one another. There is a continuity between past and future that allows past injustices to be rectified. Independence and nationhood are an epochal event in Indian civilization which make possible a controlled transformation of central social and cultural arrangements. Compensatory discrimination embodies the brave hopes of India reborn that animated the freedom movement and was crystallized in the Constitution. If the reality has disappointed many fond hopes, the turn away from the older hierarchic model to a pluralistic participatory society has proved vigorous and enduring.

Marc Galanter, COMPETING EQUALITIES: LAW AND THE BACKWARD CLASSES IN INDIA 562–67 (1984)

The Indian experience has obvious resonances with the contemporary American encounter with "affirmative action" and/or "reverse discrimination." India and the United States are two of a number of democratic countries which employ policies of formal preference for members of disadvantaged groups for the purpose of erasing group disparities.[15] I have tried to portray the Indian policies in the setting of Indian society and in its distinct political and legal culture. It would be inappropriate to assume that patterns found there would accompany cognate measures in very different settings. But Indian policies are more than expressions of unique and

---

15. Others are programs for Oriental Jews in Israel and programs for the Burakumin in Japan. Cf. Malaysia's extension of similar preferential devices into a comprehensive scheme of communal quotas favoring its politically dominant but economically backward Malay majority.

peculiar Indian conditions. The government that conducts them shares basic architectural features that are found elsewhere (constitutionalism, the rule of law, a "neutral" civil service, an independent judiciary, etc.,); these policies are oriented to values that are widely shared.

India and the United States are both large, complex, democratic societies with heterogeneous populations in which sizable descent groups were in the past systematically suppressed, deliberately deprived of resources, skills, and opportunities, and branded as socially inferior. Each is embarked on an attempt to offset this heritage of invidious distinction by policies of preferential treatment for these historically disadvantaged groups. In both of these countries preferential policies are framed by a commitment to formally equal treatment of individuals. In India as in the United States courts occupy an extraordinarily prominent position as forums for individual grievances, monitors of governmental policy, and producers of political symbols. In both societies courts are called upon to play a key role in resolving the tensions between commitments to formal equality and to compensatory preference. Notwithstanding the colossal differences in history, culture, and wealth that separate the two countries, there are enough parallels and affinities to suggest that India's encounter with the perplexities of these policies may illuminate our own.

At the least the Indian experience should make us wary of hasty and tendentious inferences about the necessary characteristics of compensatory discrimination policies. It displays a range of options that are open. If it alerts us to some general tendencies in such policies, it suggests ways of tempering or counteracting these features. It cautions us about the difficulties of assessing such programs.

Perhaps the most important lesson is that there is no single big lesson. That is, there is no large general consequence that flows inexorably from embrace of a principle of compensatory preference. Compensatory discrimination does not necessarily extinguish commitments to merit and evenhandedness, and it does not necessarily metastasize into a comprehensive system of communal quotas. On the other hand, it does not automatically produce the sought-after redistribution and it is not costless.

The Indian experience demonstrates that the compensatory commitment can co-exist with commitments to formal equality. Tensions at the level of principle can be contained; conflicting principles can be accommodated in a relatively stable pattern. The effects of the compensatory policy cannot be predicted from analysis of the principles that animate it. Nor can the performance of the policy be judged by the legal doctrine or public discourse that accompanies it. The symbolic dimensions of the policy are important in their own right, but they do not necessarily reflect crucial successes and failures in the design and implementation of programs.

The Indian experience indicates that recognition of group identity in public life does not inevitably erode evenhandedness, generate invidious exclusions, or justify oppression. This instance of a relatively benign jurisprudence of group identity should remind us that South Africa and Nazi Germany are not the most relevant examples of the use of group membership as a category for policy. But it should also be clear that the development of authoritative official learning on the question of group identity is an unavoidable concomitant of compensatory preference policies. However commonsensical the categories may appear at first blush, programs which turn on descent or ethnic categories inevitably encounter questions of who is included within these categories. Where descent, affiliation, avowal, and public regard coincide, such questions are easy to answer; where they diverge, we are drawn into a small forest of less tractable puzzles. These puzzles reflect the overlap and indeterminacy of social identities; their malleability is stimulated by the incentive offered by such programs to align identities with official categories. These tendencies appear in India, where these policies could address bounded corporate groups; surely they are no less present in the United States, where identities such as Black or Hispanic are less bounded and more diffuse.

The development of such a jurisprudence reflects in miniature the irony of employing group identity in the service of reducing disparities among groups. To the extent that the policy aims to dissolve or diffuse the boundaries between groups, application of rigid categories based on "objective" criteria should be eschewed in favor of determinations that recognize movement, overlap, and voluntarism. It requires more resources to administer flexible standards than mechanical ones; and the administration of flexible standards broadcasts the problematic quality of group identity and points to the relative character of the selection of beneficiaries.

Questions about which individuals are within the beneficiary groups flow into the problem of selection—why these groups and not others? —and thus into the justification of the programs. If justification is logically prior to group selection, in practice it is likely to be the other way around. Some group is widely acknowledged to require or deserve special treatment. The emergent response to that paradigm case—"untouchables" in India or Blacks in the United States—is summarized and codified in a set of justifications which present both barriers and precedents for other claimants. Once some group histories or conditions are accepted as justifying preferential treatment, there are inevitable questions of comparison. Are the deprivations of forced migration or peonage or religious persecution comparable to those of slavery? How should incidents of personal misfortune—family handicap, disease, accident, disaster, victimization—compare with those inflicted on whole groups? Should preference be triggered by the need of the victims? or by the accountability of others for their deprivations? or by the potential for promotion of general well-being? Is there to be a single line separating those deserving of preferential treatment? Or should it be modulated by degrees?

Once deserving beneficiaries are selected and levels of benefits set, the system is attended by other ironies that can be displayed with a simple numerical example. Let us take as a paradigm case a selection for some coveted benefit in limited supply—e.g., medical college admission. Let us suppose that there is an uncontroverted way of measuring ability to perform as a medical student and that there is general agreement that it is good to choose medical students on the basis of this test. Suppose that there are twenty available places and that two of them are reserved for members of "backward class" X. Hundreds of students take the test, including dozens of Xs. Suppose that the highest ranking X is number 6 and the next highest is number 46. In accordance with the reservation, number 20 is deprived of the twentieth seat and it is given to number 46 instead.

(This example presents the basic preferential mechanism in the starkest form. The edges may be softened in various ways: there may be less than full agreement about the suitability of the test; the selection may involve a summing of incommensurables; and student performance may not be unambiguously ranked; who the Xs are may be open-ended; the reservation may be merely a guideline; and number 46 might be included without excluding number 20, presumably diluting ever so slightly the training given to each student.)

This example points to some of the salient features of many compensatory discrimination schemes. First, there is the tendency of the program to cast a symbolic shadow much longer than the program itself, producing demoralization and resentment far disproportionate to the benefits delivered. In our example, not only is number 20 displaced, but numbers 21 to 45 are "passed over" and someone with a lower score is chosen before them. Those below 46 may come away feeling that their failure to gain the prize was due to unfair preference for the Xs. Even the successful non-Xs may resent the additional jeopardy to which their ambitions were exposed.

Second, it is likely that all of the Xs are stigmatized as the recipients of preferential treatment, even though in our example 50% of the Xs won their place on "merit." Third, in contrast to the non-Xs who see ubiquitous and unrestrained preference, to the dozens of Xs who didn't make it the amount of preference may seem paltry. Fourth, anyone who seeks admission to a medical college may be deprived in the select company of his fellow applicants, but ranks high in education and advantages compared with the whole society and especially with the Xs.

Ironically, benefits justified by the need and deprivation of the Xs tend to flow to those Xs who are least needful and deprived. Number 46 is elevated because his selection will benefit the Xs—by a percolation of tangible benefits, by representation, by their vicarious participation in his success, or in some other way. In India, where programs deal with endogamous corporate groups, the diffusion of benefits throughout the group is problematic; in the United States, where beneficiary classes are less bounded and cohesive, the diffusion of benefits is even more problematic.

Similarly, there is the converse of this problem. In our example, the direct cost of the preference was borne by number 20, who lost his opportunity to attend medical college. To the extent that the compensatory discrimination policy is based upon promotion of social benefit or recompense for historic wrongs, the transfer from number 20 to number 46 is a payment for a collective good. These costs should be spread to the whole society (or some appropriate segment) rather than being borne by those individuals who happen to be located in the path of the policy.

Like all remedial redistributions, compensatory discrimination imposes its own arbitrariness and unfairness. This is amplified to the extent that benefits are large and non-decomposable higher-echelon benefits (i.e., open only to those who have acquired demanding preliminary qualifications). They can be diminished by concentrating on benefits that can be spread more generally (like early educational opportunities) and the cost of which can be monetized and spread widely. Such widespread costs and benefits impinge less dramatically on individual expectations and are far less provocative of resentment and resistance.

While benefits and costs should be spread, they must also be bounded. Compensatory discrimination not only creates resentment of particular redistributions, but arouses fears that, by broadening the categories and modulating benefits, it will gravitate into a comprehensive system of group allotments. To prevent such a slide it is important that boundaries be clearly established—for what groups and for what amount of time—with self-liquidating devices built into preference programs.

Insight into the cumulative structural character of inequality has taught us that a regime of formal equality tends to perpetuate disparities we find intolerable. But if we find formal equality an insufficient remedy, we shrink from the uncharted plunge into comprehensive individualized substantive justice. Compensatory discrimination offers a way to leaven our formalism without entirely abandoning its comforts. The Indian example is instructive: India has managed to pursue a commitment to substantive justice without allowing that commitment to dissolve competing commitments to formal equality that make law viable in a diverse society with limited consensus. The Indian experience displays a principled eclecticism that avoids suppressing the altruistic fraternal impulse that animates compensatory policies, but that also avoids being enslaved by it. From afar it reflects to us a tempered legalism—one which we find more congenial in practice than in theory.

Questions and Comments

1. In his 1989 book, Galanter wrote that while programs for "scheduled Castes and Scheduled Tribes are for a delimited minority and pose no danger that the compensatory principle will expand into a comprehensive and self-perpetuating system of communal quotes ... the provisions for the Other Backwards Classes are open-ended: a majority may be beneficiaries and the dangers of self-perpetuation cannot be dismissed." Consider Galanter's concern in light of subsequent events, described by E.J. Prior, *Constitutional Fairness or Fraud on the Constitution? Compensatory Discrimination in India*, 28 Case W. Res. J. Int'l L. 63 (1996): In 1990, then Prime Minister Singh proposed to implement the Mandal Commission Report, which had recommended that in addition to the guarantee of 22.5% of

government jobs reserved for Scheduled Castes and Tribes, an additional 27% be reserved for the Other Backwards Classes.[f] In other words, the proposal was to set aside 49.5% of all federal government jobs, and university openings, for these groups. The proposal to implement these recommendations led to student protests (including rioting and self-immolations) and contributed to the downfall of the Singh government.

In Indra Sawhney v. Union of India, 80 A.I.R. 1993 S.C. 477, the Court affirmed the view expressed by some justices in Kerala v. Thomas that Art. 16(4) should not be read as an exception to Art 16(1); that the reservations and classifications permitted in Art 16(4) were exemplary of the approach demanded by 16(1). It concluded that for purposes of Art 16(4), the concept of backwardness turned on social backwardness (which could not be determined solely on economic criteria). Caste, the Court held, could be used as a criterion for determining backwardness, though it was not required to be used, and for non-Hindus other measures would have to be used. The Court also held that the government *must* adopt an additional test (which could be an economic means test) to exclude from the definition of the other backward classes the "creamy layer" who had sufficient social advancement not to need government assistance. The court disapproved a reservation of 10% for poorer members of the upper classes.[g] The decision occasioned further violence and rioting, though then Prime Minister Narsimha Rao announced plans immediately to implement the larger federal job set aside.

2.   For a recent argument in favor of the Indian approach for use in the U.S. in the aftermath of *Adarand* and Hopwood v. Texas, 78 F.3d 932 (5th Cir.1996) (invalidating race conscious admission program at University of Texas law school), see Clark D. Cunningham & N.R. Madhava A. Menon, *An Empirical Model for Designing Affirmative Action Programs: Transcending Categories of Race and Class*, at http://ls.wustl.edu/Conferences/Equality (still posted April 1999) (prepared for Conference, Rethinking Equality in the Global Society, 75 Wash U. L. Q. (1997); for later versions, see Michigan Law Review (forthcoming 1999). Cunningham and Menon argue that the *Sawhney* "methodology offers a way to more narrowly tailor group designation to evidence of societal discrimination," and, with some "creamy layer" criteria, also to address "the overinclusion of individual group members who are not disadvantaged to the degree of most group members." *Sawhney* largely endorsed the Mandal Commission approach, which relied on eleven factors to determine the "backward classes," but

f. The Mandal Commission found that the Other Backward Classes made up 52% of India's population; observing a 50% limit articulated by past Supreme Court judgments, the Mandal Commission recommended a set aside up to the 50% ceiling.

g. The Court in *Sawhney* also held that reservations in promotions could not be upheld under Article 16(4) (a conclusion in some tension with *Thomas v. Kerala*, which *Sawhney* distinguished as involving only a relaxation of requirements, not a reservation of promotional positions)). But in 1995 a constitutional amendment was enacted, adding Section 4A to Article 16 (see Section 1 above). Section 4(A) to Article 16 permits reservations of promotions for members of Scheduled Castes and Tribes, but apparently not for members of the Other Backward Classes.

also ruled that the government had to exclude, either through an economic means test or otherwise, particularly socially advanced individuals who were members of a "backwards class." Cunningham and Menon propose use of the following criteria to determine groups whose "social and educational" backwardness warrant special admissions treatment in Texas: degree of endogamy; degree of residential segregation; degree of educational segregation in high school; percentage completing high school; and percentage completing four year college, with possible supplemental criteria (considered by the Mandal Commission in India) including median household income, percentage receiving various forms of public assistance, and percentage owning their own home. They suggest that under these criteria, it is likely that

> black Texas residents as a group would "jump out" of the data in terms of every criteria, and that an admission program that treated black applicants differently as the result of [such] analysis would be based on evidence about social structure not skin color. If Mexican-Americans were the only other group ... that emerged from the analysis as [a socially and educationally backward class], then the law school's decision to provide those two groups only with preferential treatment might be "narrowly tailored." It is also possible, though, that [such] analysis might point toward a differently designed admissions program. Native Americans in Texas, for example, might turn out to be more endogamous, segregated and educationally deprived than either African-Americans or Mexican-Americans, prompting re-examination of the decision to exclude them from the affirmative action program.

This approach, they argue, would show that "societal discrimination' may not be so 'amorphous' as to lead inevitably to haphazard or politically motivated selection of beneficiary groups," and thus might survive constitutional scrutiny in the U.S.

Consider whether U.S. constitutional law would require that a group-based affirmative action program, such as that proposed by Cunningham and Menon, provide for some means of excluding the "creamy layer" of the group in question?

3. Galanter described India's affirmative action programs as a "costly success." For a considerably more negative assessment of affirmative action in India (and the U.S., and elsewhere), see the next excerpt.

Thomas Sowell, PREFERENTIAL POLICIES: AN INTERNATIONAL PERSPECTIVE 90–95 (1990)

. . .

India's "untouchables" are perhaps the world's classic pariah class. Even today—long after untouchability has been officially outlawed—government reports still distinguish "caste Hindus" from "scheduled castes,"

"Harijans" (children of God, a name given them by Gandhi), and other euphemisms for untouchables. Historically, severe restrictions against touching caste Hindus (and vice versa) were only one of many oppressions against untouchables. In some places, untouchables were not even to let their shadow fall upon a caste Hindu and had to beat drums upon entering a caste Hindu community, to warn others to keep their distance. They could not take water from a well where caste Hindus drank, and in some places still cannot in practice, whatever their legal rights may be. In 1978, an untouchable girl who drew water from a well reserved for caste Hindus had her ears cut off.

Even where they are allowed to take water from the same source, strict caste taboos may still persist. "While taking water from a tap, a Scheduled Caste woman put her water pot on the pot of a caste Hindu woman" is the way an official report describes the beginning of a 1979 riot in which police had to be called in, and in which an untouchable received fatal injuries. The same year, a 15-year-old untouchable boy went to his employer's home to work and drank a cup of coffee that he found there. According to the official report, this "enraged the employer who beat him black and blue" with a stick, until the boy fell unconscious—and later died, having been refused medical treatment by the local doctor. In some cases, police have stood by passively while violence was unleashed against untouchables, and in still other cases the police have themselves initiated the violence, including both murder and rape. Incidents of this sort still occurred in the 1980s. The government regularly collects statistics on officially defined "atrocities" against untouchables. In 1981, these included 493 murders and 1,245 cases of arson, among 14,306 total atrocities. The incidence of such behavior varies greatly from state to state, and especially from rural to urban communities. There are what the government calls "untouchability-prone areas." On the other hand, in some places untouchable students are roommates of caste Hindus in college without incident. A recent survey of 1,155 villages in India found that wells and laundries were accessible to untouchables in just under half the villages. Most temples were not accessible but most hotels, restaurants, and barbers were.

There is not a uniform national pattern, either in behavior or in the definition of an untouchable. Moreover, untouchables are by no means a single homogeneous group, any more than the other castes are. In India, there are literally thousands of local castes, of whom more than 1,000 were placed on the schedule or list of untouchables drawn up by the colonial government for purposes of ameliorative policies. Some groups are considered untouchable in some parts of the country but not in others and some groups of untouchables observe untouchability toward other groups of untouchables. In addition to the various untouchables, the schedule of groups to receive ameliorative benefits included tribal groups deemed backward. Scheduled castes and scheduled tribes are thus often mentioned together and ultimately there developed a government agency called the Commission for the Scheduled Castes and Scheduled Tribes.

Among the social disabilities still suffered by untouchables in some places are restrictions on their "wearing sandals, riding horses, and leading a marriage procession through certain caste-Hindu localities"—in short, dressing or behaving in a way suggesting a dignity above what others are prepared to concede to them. In one wedding procession incident in 1980, 14 untouchables were killed, including 6 burned alive.

The concept and practice of untouchability go back for untold centuries in India. Untouchables performed many tasks that were physically dirty and others that were ritually "unclean" in terms of the tenets of the Hindu religion. Untouchables were—and are—typically the poorest and most powerless group in their respective communities and numerically are nowhere a majority. Whatever the historical origins of their pariah status in their occupations and way of life, that stigma has acquired a life of its own, independent of the occupation or lifestyle of any given individual untouchable. Thus, the most famous of the untouchables, Dr. B. R. Ambedkar, was ousted from a hotel in India when he returned home after receiving his Ph.D. from Columbia University, once it became known that he was an untouchable. To some extent, the caste system followed Indians to other countries, usually varying in its intensity with the distance from India. In nearby Ceylon in the early 1930s, at a time when blacks in the southern United States were supposed to be seated in the back of buses, untouchables were not supposed to be seated at all:

> ... there was the refusal to concede to *harijans* the right to a seat in buses. Eventually it required government intervention to enforce this right, but attempts to enforce it led to outbreaks of violence in 1930–31, and to a strike of bus drivers and conductors. Previously, *harijans* were expected to stand at the back of the bus, or to sit, or squat, on the floor of the bus even though they were required to pay the normal fare. It took decades before *vellalas* accepted this change, and most of them did so with undisguised reluctance. Discrimination against *harijans* extended to restrictions on entry into cafes and "eating houses," access to village amenities like wells and cemeteries, and on the clothes they wore—their right to wear shoes was a frequent point of contention. [K. M. de Silva]

Clearly, if any group can claim to be an historically oppressed minority it is the untouchables. Concern for their plight has come relatively recently in history, and has been by no means wholly humanitarian in origin. At one time, there was a question as to whether untouchables could be considered Hindus at all, since some of their occupations involved making products from animals slaughtered in violation of Hindu tenets. But the struggle for independence in India raised the more pragmatic question of the relative balance of power between Hindus and Moslems after independence. Hindu leaders of the independence movement therefore chose to count the untouchables as part of the Hindu population. Untouchable leader Dr. B. R. Ambedkar maneuvered to gain whatever concessions he could for his people under these circumstances and Mahatma Gandhi took up the untouchable cause as a moral issue....

Education . . .

Unused reservations or quotas have been common, and are especially striking at the university or post-graduate level. A 1977–78 survey showed that less than half the university places reserved for members of the scheduled castes or scheduled tribes were in fact filled. A 1969 survey of 42 medical and engineering schools in India showed that scheduled caste students filled much less than half of the 11 percent of all places reserved for them. A later survey of medical schools in 1979–80 and in 1980–81 showed that only 23 out of 77 institutions had full utilization of their quotas for scheduled caste and scheduled tribe students while 10 did not have a single student in either category.

Under-utilization of benefits in fact extends well beyond education to housing subsidies, health programs, maternity and other benefits—so much so that governmental expenditures on these programs have repeatedly fallen short of the funds available. Government jobs reserved for scheduled castes and scheduled tribes likewise often are not all taken, due to a lack of qualified candidates. In their very different ways, these facts all reflect the same need for complementary inputs—whether money or educational performance or job skills—as a prerequisite for taking advantage of the benefits reserved for particular groups.

The failure of students from untouchable backgrounds to fill the available educational openings has been by no means due to a rigid adherence to entrance standards by the institutions concerned. In the Bombay medical schools, for example, lower standards are officially prescribed for untouchables. Even so, in 1974, 40 percent of the untouchable candidates passed the qualifying examination only on the second attempt and another 20 percent only on the third attempt, compared to 97 percent of the non-preferred candidates who passed on their first attempt. By 1978, a new system was used, and in this system the vast majority of all categories of candidates passed. Clearly, the standards were being brought down to the students, rather than raising the students to the standards.

At a medical college in the state of Madhya Pradesh, when the scheduled caste and scheduled tribe candidates "failed to attain even the barest minimum of 35 percent, the qualifying requirement was pushed down to a meager 15 percent so that reserved seats could be filled up." Six highly selective engineering schools in India likewise lowered their admissions requirements for scheduled caste and scheduled tribe students. Normally they select about 1,200 students from among 30,000 who take their joint nationwide examination. Although the normal range of scores of those admitted is from 70 percent to 90 percent on the examination, scheduled caste or scheduled tribe students with scores as low as 10 percent were admitted. Even so, the quota of 54 was never filled, though a high of 42 such students was admitted in 1977. Of 106 preferentially admitted students over a six-year period, only 15 were able to maintain the minimum grade average needed to continue in school—and none of these 15 kept up with the schedule appropriate for a student with his own number of years in attendance.

The need for complementary resources is demonstrated by the fact that, among those who do use the quotas, the more prosperous of the scheduled castes use a disproportionate share. For example, the Chamars of Maharashtra are among the most prosperous of the scheduled castes in that state. They are 17 percent of that state's population and 35 percent of the medical students. In the state of Haryana, only 18 of the 37 scheduled castes officially entitled to preferential scholarships actually received any and one caste—the Chamars—received 65 percent of these scholarships at the graduate level and 80 percent at the undergraduate level. Similar patterns of large disparities within the preferred groups have been found in other parts of India and for scheduled tribes as well as scheduled castes.

The academic performance of scheduled caste students has been substandard in a number of ways. In general, they attend inferior and less prestigious universities and, within these institutions, are concentrated in courses that do not lead to remunerative or high-status occupations. Even so, only 8 percent of scheduled caste and scheduled tribe students received their degrees in the prescribed four years and 85 percent left college without a degree. Moreover, even those few who graduated tended to receive low grades.

At the Bombay medical schools, untouchable students entered nearly three years older than the other students, suggesting a slower pace in finishing college. They entered with generally lower grades, fewer courses in higher mathematics and lower performance even in elementary mathematics, as well as in general science and in English—the language in which students are taught at the Bombay medical colleges.

Against this background, it is hardly surprising that only 22 percent of the untouchable students finished medical school on time, compared to 78 percent of students who entered without preferences. Similar patterns are found among untouchable students studying engineering in Bombay. At Nehru Medical College in Raipur, the results were still worse. Over a period of a decade, 42 untouchable students entered but only 4 completed the medical college within four and a half years and only 23 within eight years. A study of second-year college students at 10 Bombay colleges found that no more than one-fourth of the scheduled caste students passed the examinations required to advance to the third year, during a three-year period surveyed.

The unfilled quotas and high attrition rates among untouchable students are especially (and tragically) ironic in view of the violent backlash against the preferential policies—and against the untouchables. In the state of Gujarat, for example, less than 5 percent of the medical school places reserved for untouchables over a period of five years were actually filled. Yet bloody riots have broken out again and again in Gujarat over medical school preferences for untouchables. In 1981, 42 people died in extensive riots—over 7 places reserved for untouchables.

For India, as a whole, violence against untouchables has been generally rising over the years, amid generally adverse reactions against preferential policies. So are other forms of intergroup violence. In 1976 there were 169 incidents of intergroup violence, with 39 people killed. By 1980, there were 421 incidents of intergroup violence, with 372 people killed. Not all of these began over educational issues, and even some that did were fueled by other issues as well. Gujarat was again the scene of one of the more widespread and prolonged of these intergroup outbursts of violence. A plan to increase the reserved places for "other backward classes" in the medical and engineering schools of Gujarat in 1985 led to months of rioting in various parts of the state, with the estimated deaths exceeding 200 people. Widespread riots have been provoked, not only where substantive benefits were at issue, but also where purely symbolic benefits were involved. A decision to rename the Marathwada University for the late untouchable leader, Dr. B. R. Ambedkar, set off riots in 1978 that spread to more than 300 villages, with 1,725 homes destroyed. Several people lost their lives over this purely symbolic issue.

Government

Preferential policies within government include reserved seats in the lower houses of both the national and state legislatures and preferential employment opportunities in the civil service. These reservations were originally scheduled to expire in ten years, but in 1959 they were extended for another ten years. In 1969 they were again extended for another ten years and in 1980 for yet another decade. Reserved legislative seats, like other preferential benefits, tend to go disproportionately to those already more fortunate. Those untouchables serving in India's lower house of parliament are generally less representative of their constituency—in education, occupation, or urbanization—than other members of parliament *vis-à-vis* their own respective constituencies. Nor are the various untouchable sub-castes evenly represented among the untouchable political elite. In the state of Andhra Pradesh, for example, it was found that only 5 of the 65 untouchable sub-castes were represented among this elite. In the state of Rajasthan, 16 of the 28 state legislators holding seats reserved for untouchables had acquired certificates of untouchability by being adopted. The adoption strategy has also been used by students to gain admission to medical schools and engineering schools.

India's national government has reserved jobs for members of the scheduled castes since 1943 and for members of the scheduled tribes since 1950. The percentage of jobs reserved has increased slightly at the national level and state governments have instituted similar job reservations. Official preferences take various forms, from simple reservations or quotas to waivers of some requirements that other job applicants must meet, to subsidies for travel. Untouchables are most represented in the lowest level of government employment—as sweepers and in other tasks characterized as "menial." They are successively less well represented in clerical, lower administrative, and higher administrative positions. However, their share of the latter three kinds of occupations has increased substantially over the years, though only at the lowest level does their representation approximate their share of the population.

By and large, whether at the state or the national level, the jobs actually held by officially preferred groups have tended to fall short of those reserved for them. In obtaining jobs, as in education and reserved seats, the benefits have favored those already more fortunate. A massive study of preferential policies in India reports "a severe clustering" of "some of the larger and more advanced groups" of untouchables in the jobs reserved for scheduled caste members. In the state of Andhra Pradesh, where 37 percent of the untouchables are Malas, more than half of all fellowships awarded to untouchable students went to Malas. A slightly larger group of untouchables, the Madiga, constituting 44 percent of the untouchable population of the state, trailed far behind the Malas in government jobs, all the way up to the highest echelons.

Preferences have spread from the hiring stage to the promotions stage after 1957 at the national level and state governments have subsequently followed suit. The preferences took the form of both quota reservations and of differential weighting of performance recommendations. The backlash from non-preferred individuals has been especially strong on this issue. The bulk of litigation over reserved jobs has been over promotions. The backlash has also taken the form of supervisors' deliberately neglecting to impart their knowledge to untouchable subordinates, for fear of having them preferentially promoted to—or above—the supervisor's own level.

Land disputes have been one of the major sources of violence against untouchables. Often squatters on government land or on land declared "surplus" by the government launch violence against untouchables who receive such land under government auspices. In one case which occurred only 15 miles from Delhi, untouchables whose right to the land awarded them by the government had been upheld by the High Court were harassed by attackers who set their hay stacks on fire, held untouchable women as hostages, and blocked sales of essential commodities to the untouchable. . . .

The *apparent* losses to one group under preferential policies may also far exceed the real losses, thereby further raising the indirect social costs of backlash and turmoil. For example, an observer of India's preferential policies has commented:

> . . . we hear innumerable tales of persons being deprived of appointments in favour of people who ranked lower than they did in the relevant examinations. No doubt this does happen, but if all these people were, in fact, paying the price for appointments to Scheduled Castes, there would be many more SC persons appointed than there actually are. To illustrate: supposing that 300 people qualify for ten posts available. The top nine are appointed on merit but the tenth is reserved, so the authorities go down the list to find an SC applicant. They find one at 140 and he is appointed. Whereupon all 131 between him and the merit list feel aggrieved. He has not taken 131 posts; he has taken one, yet 131 people believe they have paid the price for it.

Moreover, the remaining 159 often also resent the situation, believing that their chances were, somehow, lessened by the existence of SC reservations. [Lelah Duskin]

Where certain opportunities are rigidly "set aside" for particular groups, in the sense that members of other groups cannot have them, even if these opportunities remain unused, then there is the potential for a maximum of grievance for a minimum of benefit transfer. Admission to medical school in India's state of Gujarat operates on this principle—and has led repeatedly to bloody riots in which many people have died. Reservations or "set-asides" in general tend to provoke strong objections. The first major set-back for "affirmative action" in the U.S. Supreme Court was based on objections to reserved admissions places for minority applicants in the 1978 *Bakke* case. A later major set-back occurred in *City of Richmond* v. *Croson* (1989), where minority business set-asides were struck down by the Supreme Court. Similarly, in India, an exhaustive scholarly legal study of preferential policies [Galanter, Competing Equalities], found: "Virtually all of the litigation about compensatory discrimination has involved reservations, even though preferences in the form of provisions of facilities, resources, and protections directly affect a much larger number of recipients." This litigation has been initiated mostly by non-preferred individuals who complain of being adversely affected. In some ultimate sense, non-preferred individuals are just as much adversely affected by preferences in other forms that direct resources away from them and toward preferred groups. But it is preference in the specific form of "reservation" or "set-aside" that seems most to provoke both violence and litigation.

By contrast, resource transfers designed to enable disadvantaged groups to meet standards are accepted while attempts to bring the standards down to them are overwhelmingly rejected. In the United States, preferential policies have repeatedly been rejected in public opinion polls. However, the same American public has strongly supported "special educational or vocational courses, free of charge, to enable members of minority groups to do better on tests." More than three-fifths of all whites even support "requiring large companies to set up special training programs for members of minority groups." The issue is not simply whether one is for or against the advancement of particular groups or is willing to see transfers of resources for their betterment. The method by which their betterment is attempted matters greatly in terms of whether such efforts have the support or the opposition of others.

————————

Questions and Comments

1. Sowell describes attacks in the 1970s and 1980s against "untouchables," e.g., by squatters against untouchables who receive surplus government land, or by persons offended at "untouchables" touching food or cooking items of higher caste members. To what extent might the backlash against "affirmative action" (like reserved places or quotas) that Sowell described fueled by longstanding prejudice against "untouchables" as a "pariah caste"?

2.   India prohibits the promotion of religious hatred and certain appeals to religion to gain votes. In evaluating the next commentary on India, note the rise in the 1990s of "Hindu Right" parties, dedicated to "Hindutva" as a way of life and to establishment of a Hindu State, which assert that accommodations of religious minorities (especially the Muslim) constitute prejudice against the Hindu majority. See Brenda Cossman and Ratna Kapur, *Secularism's Last Sigh?: The Hindu Right, The Courts, and India's Struggle for Democracy*, 38 Harv. Int'l L. J. 113 (1997) (critically describing rise of Hindu Right and Court decisions in prosecutions of Hindu Right leaders, which upheld some convictions for appealing to religion to gain votes and fomenting religious hatred, but which also recognized Hindu Right claim that "Hindutva" was a way of life and not a religion within the meaning of the prohibitions on appeals to religion and religious hatred.). See also the discussion of these cases in Ch. X below. Consider the following argument, suggesting that India's policies for managing its diversity have worked well in the past but may need to be changed.

––––––––––

Bhikku Parekh, *India's Diversity*, in Dissent 145–48 (Summer 1996)

No country in the world matches India in its diversity. It has more than six hundred eighty-seven million Hindus, more than one hundred million Muslims, more than nineteen million Christians, more than sixteen million Sikhs, more than nine million Buddhists and Jains, and just under a half million Zoroastrians. Although the religious minorities are spread throughout the country, most of them are concentrated in a small number of states and constitute powerful political presences.

India also has over sixty million tribal people who live in government-designated "reserved" areas scattered over most of India. They form majorities in three states. India has thirty-five languages spoken by more than a million people each, and more than twenty-two thousand dialects.

The ethnic diversity is as broad as it is deep. Tribal people in the northeast are ethnically different from those in Gujarat, and both again from their counterparts in the south. North India has been exposed to waves of foreigners since the time of Alexander the Great, and especially from the eighth century, when Muslims came to India from Persia, Afghanistan, and Central Asia. Gujarati merchants, mainly Muslim, financed Arab slave traders, with the result that some coastal areas of Gujarat contain descendants of black slaves and their racially mixed progeny.

None of these communities is cohesive. Speakers of local languages belong to different religious, ethnic, and cultural communities, and almost all the religious communities speak the local languages. Although Urdu is supposed to be the community language of many Muslims, large sections of them in many parts of the country have no knowledge of it. This is equally true of the Christians, most of whom are far more at home in local languages than in English, which is generally regarded as their community language. By and large the Sikhs have stuck to their language wherever they have settled in India.

Cultural beliefs and practices also cut across linguistic and religious boundaries. Because many of the religious minorities are Hindu converts, they retain many Hindu beliefs and practices. Islam in India is quite different from its counterparts elsewhere, and even in India it varies from one region to another. Hindu castes or caste-like divisions are common among Muslims, Sikhs, and Christians. Indeed, in several churches in south India recent converts sit separately from the rest. For their part, the Hindus have absorbed Muslim and Christian practices, and some of them see nothing wrong in worshiping at the shrines of all three religions.

Although the Hindus formally constitute the majority of the population, that number can be misleading. What is clumsily called Hinduism is in fact a family of sects, each with its own deities, theology, scripture, temple, and rituals. Although broadly aware of sharing a religious heritage, they cherish their distinct histories and identities. Hindus never developed the sharp and exclusive collective self-consciousness characteristic of such credal religions as Christianity and Islam, and do not have a single name for their religion: the term Hindu itself is a Muslim corruption of an original Greek word. Hindus are also divided into castes along with all their regional variations. Brahmins are regarded as the highest caste in many parts of India, but they are looked down upon in several parts of the south, where some even avoid social contacts with them. The "scheduled castes" (once called "untouchables") constitute nearly 16 percent of the population. Their relationship with the mainstream of Hindu society is deeply ambiguous, for they both are and are not a part of it. As for the so-called Caste Hindus, they are further divided into subgroups, some of whom have little contact with each other.

With India made up of so many criss-crossing communities, every Indian is the bearer of several identities. An average Indian has multiple affections and loyalties: while Muslims in one part of India, for example, share their religion with their counterparts elsewhere, they share their language, customs, and even religious practices with local Hindus. These bonds are often stronger than ties with Muslims elsewhere.

All this means that the concept of majority and minority explain little in India. Because individuals belong to several different communities, one might be in the majority of one community, in the minority of another. Or one might be in the majority within one's state, while a minority again nationally. In such a situation individuals have neither the conceptual resources nor the need to identify themselves as belonging to majority and minority communities. The concepts of majority and minority become central to a community's self-understanding when, for some reason, one of its several identities is abstracted and privileged. That identity then becomes the basis for classifying and enumerating people.

The idea of *national* majorities and minorities does not arise unless two further conditions are met. First, the country as a whole must become the primary point of orientation; second, there must be an identity with a national reach. In India languages and ethnicities are mostly regional and lack national reach. Only religion provides the latter, and it is only when religion becomes the politically significant basis of self-identification that the concepts of national majority and minority acquire currency. This is precisely what began to happen in India for the first time during the last three decades of the nineteenth century. Thanks to the enthusiastic Hindu response to westernization, the rise of a westernized Hindu middle class, the decline of the Muslim aristocracy, and the consolidation of colonial rule, Muslims began to feel left out and to ask for special protection. . . . The result was much Hindu-Muslim violence, and the eventual partition of the country in 1947.

The partition had a traumatic effect on Indian self-understanding. It made the ideas of majority and minority the dominant currency of political discourse. For the first time non-Hindus began to see themselves as cohesive minorities and Hindus to see themselves as an actual or potential majority. The ideas of majority and minority soon traveled to many other areas of life, giving rise to ideas of collective or group rights. At the national level, religion became an extremely sensitive issue and an easily mobilizable basis of political identity; at regional levels, language and ethnicity took its place.

Independent India had three possible ways of dealing with its minorities. It could have opted for a strictly liberal strategy. . . . The concepts of majority and minority would thereby have had no more than numerical significance. Alternately, India could have pursued a corporatist strategy, in which different communities had autonomous status and ran the state as a partnership. The third possibility was to combine liberalism and pluralism, superimposing a liberal state on self-governing religious communities. The Constitution of India institutionalized the third strategy, and its authors clearly hoped that in time minorities would have enough confidence in the Indian state to enable it to progress on liberal individualistic principles alone.

The combined liberal-pluralist strategy included a commitment by the Indian state to respect minority cultures and religions. The state funds minority schools and cultural institutions, and in some parts of the country it even pays the salaries of Muslim religious officials and subsidizes their pilgrimages to Mecca. More important, the state leaves the religious communities free to govern themselves in personal matters like marriage, divorce, succession, and inheritance. In other domains—criminal law, laws relating to the economy, and so forth—the state makes all laws it deems necessary. The original hope was that all Indian citizens would one day be governed by a single personal law or civil code, but the Constitution didn't say how or when this would come about. . . . The Constitution also conferred a special status on the Muslim-majority state of Kashmir, giving it powers denied to other states. Subsequently created "tribal states" also enjoy considerable autonomy, and Indians from elsewhere are not at liberty to settle and buy land in them. In important respects, then, the Indian state resembles the asymmetrical federation that the Québécois are pressing for in Canada.

The Indian state also follows a policy of preferential treatment for "untouchables" and less-developed tribes in education, the civil service, and in publicly owned companies. India's founders believed affirmative action was justified to redress past wrongs and to integrate previously disadvantaged communities into the national mainstream, giving them a stake in the country and thereby broadening the state's legitimacy.

Finally, although the framers of the Constitution did not—it would seem deliberately—mention the word, they clearly wanted a secular state, and this is what, despite occasional aberrations, India has remained. This does not mean that religion is kept out of politics altogether. There is no ban on religious parties or the political use of religious idioms. Nor does it mean that religion is kept entirely out of the state.... The Indian state is secular in four ways: it does not favor any particular religion; it respects all religions equally; in all secular matters its authority is final; and although its leaders may have religious preferences, their decisions are guided in principle solely by the moral and material well-being of its citizens.

Although successive Indian governments have introduced variations in the liberal-pluralist strategy, the basic design has remained intact, a political compass in the murky waters of Indian politics. Respect for the personal laws of minority communities has gone a long way to reassure them that the state honors their cultural identities. This has sometimes come at the expense of desirable internal reforms.... While a uniform civil code clearly has something to be said for it, it cannot be developed in the absence of a broad consensus, a shared culture, and mutual trust.

The protective policy toward the religious and cultural minorities, however, has a negative side. The country's fragmented educational system has hindered the emergence of a sense of common citizenship. Because minority status secures certain privileges, it has provoked resentments among the majority Hindu community. This became clear a few years ago when Ramkrishna Mission, a much admired reformist Hindu cultural organization, asked to be classified not as a "Hindu" but as a "minority" organization! It would seem that everyone wants to be in a political majority and a cultural minority.

As for affirmative action, government programs have realized many of its symbolic objectives, but it remains necessary. It has, however, several serious problems. First, the mere set-aside of places for the disadvantaged hardly begins to tackle the consequences of centuries-old inequalities. The government needs to allocate greater resources to primary education, to provide much more start-up capital and to develop commercial skills among the target populations. Second, because the state thought preferential treatment was sufficient, it did nothing to combat the widespread discrimination against the lower castes and tribes, not to mention Muslims, in the private sector, which has over twenty times more jobs than the state. (India has some of the weakest anti-discrimination laws among the liberal democracies.)

The secular dimension of the liberal-pluralist strategy has served the country reasonably well. It has made the state legitimate in the eyes of religious minorities, and enabled it to tackle evils perpetrated in the name of religion. On the other hand, the state has felt free to reform Hindu personal law, partly with the hope that this would encourage corresponding reforms in the minority communities. In so doing, however, it implicitly acted as the state of the Hindus (though not a Hindu state); this encouraged the Hindus to use the state to promote their interests and compromised its secular character. Since Indian secularism largely comes from the fear of politicized religion, it is essentially negative and lacks self-confidence, consistency, and a clear sense of direction. Religious parties have found it easy to manipulate the Indian state; the government alternately placated and resists them, depending on political expediency. Not surprisingly, secularism is today one of the most contentious issues in Indian politics. Many Hindus think that it is mainly meant to regulate and restrain them; the minorities fear it is weak, timid, and likely to disintegrate under Hindu pressures.

The liberal-pluralist strategy has had complex consequences. It has generally stood India well for nearly half a century and helped to hold the country together. It stabilized the country after the birth-trauma of partition, reassured the minorities, and created a secure framework within which the different communities are able to form alliances, and fight for shared goals. However, its weaknesses are increasingly coming to the fore. New Delhi is facing an increasingly angry Hindu majority on the one hand and increasingly discontented minorities on the other. Without some new thinking, the country is headed for dangerous times.

Questions and Comments

1. As Galanter elsewhere describes, India's affirmative action programs for Scheduled Castes and other "socially and economically backward peoples" has required its courts to be able to adjudicate the membership of individuals in particular castes. In the Jasami case, 1954 S.C.R. 817, as he describes it, an "Election Tribunal had rejected the nomination papers for a reserved seat submitted by a Mahar who had joined the Mahanublava Panth, a Hindu sect which repudiated the multiplicity of gods and the caste system." Galanter, Law and Society in Modern India 105. The Supreme Court found that he remained a Mahar (and was thus allowed to run for the reserved seat), based on its consideration of three factors: (1) the reactions or rules of the old sect, (2) the intentions of the candidate, and (3) the rules of the new sect of which he had become a member. Applying these, the court found that he had been allowed to marry (twice) within the Mahar community, and had continued to identify himself as a Mahar. On the third criterion the Court found that the Panth sect had not penalized him for his allegiance to the Mahar caste. Relying primarily on the individual's own intentions, the Court concluded that his "conversion to this sect imports little beyond ... intellectual acceptance of [its] ideological tenets and does not alter the convert's caste status." Id. at 106. Also of importance, Galanter emphasizes, are the views of the old caste, which is the group entitled to special representation.

In a similar case involving a Scheduled Tribe, the Court found that the challenged candidate's family's conversion to Christianity two generations earlier did not deprive him of eligibility to run for a seat reserved for a Scheduled Tribe on the ground that he had abandoned its animistic faith. Rather, the court found, the candidate's active participation in the civic life of the tribe rebutted the claim of lack of common interest. Christian tribals, moreover, retained some of the ceremonial observances of the tribe, including harvest rites. The court emphasized that "the most important thing ...is that the non-Christian tribals treat the converted Oraons as tribals ...." [Kartik Oraon v. David Munzni, A.I.R. 1964 S.C. 201]

Finally, Galanter discusses the Court's somewhat different treatment of claimed conversions from a Scheduled Tribe to a high-caste status. In the Dora case, the Court dealt with an election challenge to a seat reserved for a Scheduled Tribe and sought by a man born a "Moka Dura" (an eligible Scheduled Tribe) but whose family had since the 1880s described themselves as Kshatriyas (a high caste) and adopted Kshatriya customs, married into Kshatriya families, and used Brahmin priests. In this case, the Court focussed on the third of the Jasani factors—the reactions of the new group. The Court found that despite evidence of the candidate's desire to be regarded as a Kshatriya, there was inadequate evidence that the Kshatriyas recognized him as a member. The Court concluded that since he had not become a Kshatriya, he therefore remained a Moka Dura and was thus eligible.

Galanter is critical of the Court's reasoning. First, he argues it is inconsistent with the earlier cases: "Had the courts in these cases seriously considered acceptance by the non-privileged [in terms of eligibility for the reserved seats] group as incompatible with membership in the privileged group, the cases would most probably have had different outcomes." Id. at 112–13.

Moreover, he argues, the court's notion that there was a "logical incompatibility between membership in the two groups" represents a visualization of society "as consisting of groups with unique corporate ranks in some definite rank ordering." Id. at 114. This concept, he suggests, may come from the need, for purposes of applying the personal laws of marriage, divorce, and inheritance, to assign a person to a particular religious group to determine the appropriate choice of law. But in defining eligibility for reserved seats, Galanter suggests, there is no reason to think a person can be a member of only one group. The Court's apparently contrary assumption, he argues, suggests that the Court believes it very difficult for someone who belongs by birth to a lower caste or tribe to obtain the status of a higher caste, suggesting that "Hindu society is not only hierarchic but inflexible as well." Id. at 117.

[B]y making membership in the old group dependent on failure to achieve the purported membership in the new group, the majority's theory may disincline the courts from giving legal recognition to existing patterns of mobility, which ordinarily involve a period of conflicting claims and overlapping identifications. Successful separation from the old group may be overlooked, with the result of imposing on a privileged group a candidate who is not an accepted member of it. More generally existing channels of mobility may be discredited. For if acceptance by a new group removes one from the old, the Hinduization of tribals and the formation of new sects would be accompanied by the danger of disqualification for receipt of preference. Since the system of preferences is designed to increase flexibility and mobility within Indian society, there seems little reason to make abandonment of older and slower methods of mobility a condition for the utilization of the new ones. Id. at 117–18.

Is it inevitable that a system of preferences be accompanied by this kind of litigation over who is entitled to the preference?

2. Retired Indian Supreme Court Justice Reddy has described more recent affirmative action litigation in India. B.P. Jeevan Reddy, *Equality and Social Justice: Rethinking Equality in the Global Society*, available at http://ls.wustl.edu/Conferences/Equality (discussion paper prepared for Conference, Rethinking Equality in the Global Society, 75 Wash. U. L. Q. 1561 (1997)). According to Justice Reddy, some states have tried to ignore the 50% limit on reservations, hiking reservations for Scheduled Castes, Scheduled Tribes and OBCs to 69%; others have made reservations for women, the physically handicapped, children of veterans and other types of reservations in addition to the 50% permitted for "social" reservations for the Scheduled Castes and Tribes and the other backward classes (again, Justice Reddy says, in violation of the 50% rule and the *Sawhney* requirement that reservations for reasons other than social backwardness, e.g., for women, or the handicapped, must "cut across" the categories for "social" reservation); and another state eliminated any minimal passing requirement on an entrance exam to post graduate medical school for Scheduled Caste/Scheduled Tribe members in an effort to fill a reserved percentage (which, Justice Reddy says, was struck down as an impermissible and irrational exercise of power since it permitted reserved seats to be filled by those scoring 1% on the exam while some scoring 80% could be excluded).

3. Is India's constitutional experience with affirmative action of any relevance to questions of the constitutionality, or desirability, of affirmative action in the United States? Why or why not?

Note on Pluralism, Federalism, Group-Based Rights and Gender Equality

Claims of gender equality—whether conceived of as resting on liberal values of individual equality, on principles of anti-subordination, or on postmodern assertions of the contingency and constructedness of gendered identities[h]—often come into conflict with claims of groups seeking cultural recognition or autonomous self-governance. Sociocultural claims of group distinctiveness are often bound up with particular practices of gender roles, family membership and hierarchies. See, e.g., Santa Clara Pueblo v. Martinez, 436 U.S. 49 (1978) (tribe asserting right of self-governance and freedom from review of its practice discriminating against female tribe members in denying them capacity to pass on tribal membership to their children); Wisconsin v. Yoder, 406 U.S. 205 (1972) (Amish community asserting right to limit their children's education in ways designed to promote their community by, inter alia, making it less likely that children will develop desire, and tools, to leave the community); see also Reynolds v. U.S., 98 U.S. 145 (1879) (Mormon asserting a religiously based claim of right to polygamy in defense of criminal prosecution).

The conflict between claims of self-governing autonomy for authentic communities, on the one hand, and for equality for women who argue that they are subordinated by the practices of such community, is widespread. For example, in Native Women's Association of Canada v. Canada [1994], 3 S.C.R. 627 the Canadian Supreme Court rejected the claim of the Native Women's Association that the government's failure to invite it to join negotiations or to fund it equally with that of certain other representatives of the aboriginal peoples violated the Charter. The plaintiff organization had not been invited to join the negotiating process between the Canadian government and certain representatives of the aboriginal people concerning aboriginal claims for self governance; the women's group sought to assure that Charter rights—especially those of gender equality—be made applicable to aboriginal self government. Women's groups in Canada have been important advocates of the Charter, and have been concerned that the possible secession of Quebec would impair gender equality and have sought the extension of the Charter's equality provisions to aboriginal self-government. These positions have been opposed by some advocates of secession and by some advocates of aboriginal self-government.

Questions about what constitutes gender equality are important in understanding constitutionalism. Should particular practices be understood as undesirable forms of gender subordination or as authentic and empowering cultural practices? Consider the question of what some call female circumcision and others call female genital mutilation. See, e.g., L. Amede Obiora, *Bridges and Barricades: Rethinking Polemics and Intransigence in the Campaign Against Female Circumcision*, 47 Case Western L. Rev. 275 (1997) and responses in the *Colloquium: Bridging Society, Culture and Law: The Issue of Female Circumcision*, 47 Case Western L. Rev. (Winter 1997). As increasing numbers of constitutions condemn inequality based on sex, questions proliferate about what constitutes such inequality—whether

---

h. For a thoughtful recent treatment and collection of works, see William N. Eskridge Jr. and Nan D. Hunter, Sexuality, Gender and the Law 229–320 (1997).

sexual orientation discrimination violates norms of gender equality;[i] wheth-er differential treatment of women and men in the military is inconsistent with gender equality;[j] whether affirmative action for women (e.g., "quotas" for minimum numbers of female participation) violate abstract norms of gender equality or (at least in the short run) are necessary tools to achieving real equality of opportunity.[k]

Positive and negative conceptions of states' obligations to equality are important poles of difference among constitutional systems that accept at an abstract level equality of the sexes as a constitutional norm. In the U.S., the predominant understanding of the constitutional norm of equality is an anti-discrimination norm of formal equality of treatment and anti-discrimi-nation. But see Robin West, Progressive Constitutionalism (1994) (arguing that 14th amendment should be understood to impose affirmative duty on states to advance and protect equality). The absence of support in the constitutional caselaw for an understanding that governments owe duties affirmatively to protect and advance gender equality could result in efforts to use the Constitution to invalidate affirmative programs for the recruit-ment, hiring and retention of women. In recent years most important decisions on gender equality from the U.S. Supreme Court have rested on statutes, rather than on the Constitution, (with some notable exceptions, for example, United States v. Virginia, 518 U.S. 515 (1996)). In some western constitutional democracies, however, constitutions impose positive

i. Compare Bowers v. Hardwick, 478 U.S. 186 (1986) (rejecting constitutional claim of privacy right to engage in consensual homosexual conduct) with Toonen v. Austra-lia, Case No. 488–1992, U.N. Hum. Rts. Comm., 50th Sess., U.N. Doc. CCPR/C/50/D/488/1992 (1994) (finding that criminal prohi-bition of homosexual sodomy by Tasmania, an Australian state, violated international human rights covenant to which Australia was a party); cf. P v. S and Cornwall County Council, European Court of Justice, Case C-13/94, 1996 E.C.R. 397, [1996] 2 C.M.L.R. 247 (1996) (equality principle of EU directive prohibits job discrimination against transsex-uals).

j. Compare Rostker v. Goldberg, 453 U.S. 57 (1981) (rejecting equal protection challenge to U.S. law that subjected men, but not women, to draft) with Miller v. Minister of Defense, H.C.4541/94 (Israel, Nov. 8 1995) (holding according to Menachem Hofnung, *The Unintended Consequences of Unplanned Constitutional Reform: Constitutional Politics in Israel*, 44 Am. J. Comp. L. 585, 596 & n. 45 (1996)), that administrative rules exclud-ing women from training as combat jet fight-ers violated equality principles in the Basic Law: Human Dignity and Liberty).

k. Compare the Feminine Quotas Case, No. 82–146 (Nov. 18, 1982), French Constitu-

tional Council (invalidating an enactment re-quiring that lists of candidates have no more than 75% of persons of the same sex) (dis-cussed in John Bell, French Constitutional Law 349–50) with Marschall v. Land Nor-drheim-Westfalen, European Court of Jus-tice, Case C-409/95, 1997 E.C.R. 865 (uphold-ing German rule that, if woman and man were equally qualified, woman should be ap-pointed or promoted if position sought was one in which women were underrepresented, unless there were reasons specific to the man to prefer him). The European Court of Jus-tice found the German rule in *Marschall* to be an appropriate effort to advance equality of women under Directive 76/207 Art 2(4)—authorizing national measures to give advan-tages to women to improve their ability to compete in the labor market and pursue ca-reers on equal footing with men—and thus not barred by general equality principle of Art. 2(1). The ECJ distinguished its earlier decision in Kalanke v. Bremen, Case C-450/93, 1996 E.C.R. 66, [1996] 1 C.M.L.R. 175 (1996) which found a violation of the equality principle of Art. 2(1) in a German rule giving equally qualified women an abso-lute and unconditional preference in hiring for positions in which women were underrep-resented. (i.e., fewer than 50%).

duties on governments to seek to promote substantive equality between women and men, e.g., by facilitating combining career with family obligations. See Anita Grandke, *Equal Rights—Compatibility of Family and Career—Legal Comparison: East Germany and the Federal Republic of Germany Today*, 3 Card. Wom. L. J. 287, 305 (1996) (describing change in Basic Law Art 3–2 after reunification to state that "The government promotes the actual implementation of equal rights for men and women and works to eliminate existing disadvantages."). Such constitutions can provide a basis for a court to support affirmative programs designed to promote equality if they are challenged, even if the provisions do not establish justiciable obligations. Cf. Canadian Charter, Section (15)(2) (preserving affirmative action programs from attack under charter equality principle); see ch. XII below (social welfare rights).

Reflect critically on the categories through which these materials have been presented. Developments in domestic constitutional law in western democracies and in international human rights law concerning gender equality could have been expanded into a whole section in a book on comparative constitutional law. Consider whether the attention we have devoted to compensatory discrimination or affirmative action for racial minorities in the United States and for disadvantaged castes in India should be regarded as a reflection of gendered hierarchies in U.S. constitutional law. But cf. Adarand Constructors v. Pena, 515 U.S. 200 (1995) (holding that race-based "benign" classifications must be subject to compelling interest scrutiny, in reasoning that seems to imply that affirmative action programs based on gender would be easier to sustain than those based on race). For an interesting discussion of the relative absence of feminist discourse on constitutionalism, see Tracy E. Higgins, *Democracy and Feminism*, 110 Harv. L. Rev. 1657 (1997).

Note on Citizenship

All polities need to define who counts as a member. Whether for purposes of defining the electorate, who can be drafted into the military, who is entitled to certain civil benefits, or for purposes of knowing who can invoke the protections of that jurisdiction in international disputes, identifying who counts as a member of the nation is a familiar aspect of public law. The United States has a constitutional rule that persons born in the United States are, by virtue of that birthplace, citizens, a form of the principle of "jus soli." Amend XIV (defining as citizens "[a]ll persons born or naturalized in the United States and subject to the jurisdiction thereof"); Peter H. Schuck and Rogers M. Smith, Citizenship Without Consent: Illegal Aliens in the American Polity (1985); see also Rogers Brubaker, Citizenship and Nationhood in France and Germany 21–34 (1992). Some nations, including France and the U.K., have accorded citizenship to those born within the country only if, in addition, their parents have some established connection with the country. See Schuck and Smith at 119 &

nn. 6, 7. (Reliance on the national affiliation of one or both parents to establish a child's citizenship is referred to as "jus sanguinis".) Still other nations, such as Germany until recently, have relied almost entirely on concepts of citizenship by descent. Definitions of citizenship can be used as a means of addressing questions raised by the presence of minority groups, e.g., by refusing to extend citizenship to linguistic or ethnic minorities so as to exclude them from the benefits, protection and participation rights of citizens,[1] or by extending citizenship to disadvantaged minority groups living within the territory (as arguably was the case in the Fourteenth Amendment).

The domain of constitutional law addresses not only the relation between a state and its citizens but between a state and persons subject to its jurisdiction. In the United States, for example, "persons" are entitled to the protection of the laws even if they are not "citizens," and there is a substantial body of law addressing questions of when noncitizens may be treated differently from citizens. See, e.g., Graham v. Richardson, 403 U.S. 365 (1971); Foley v. Connelie, 435 U.S. 291 (1975); Bernal v. Fainter, 467 U.S. 216 (1984); T. Alexander Aleinikoff, David Martin and Hiroshi Motomura, Immigration and Citizenship: Law and Policy 516–35 (4th ed. 1998). The emergence of multiple, effective mechanisms for transnational decisionmaking, the evolution of cross-national, regional or linguistic communities seeking forms of international recognition, and the increased demands by minority groups for autonomous self-determination within existing nations, cause some to question single-nation citizenship as the appropriate norm. See Andre Liebich, *Citizenship in its International Dimension*, in Citizenship, East and West 25–39 (Andre Liebich and Daniel Warner eds., 1995) (arguing that "it is time to praise multiple citizenships"); see also Ursula Vogel and Michael Moran, The Frontiers of Citizenship (1991); Joseph H. Carens, *Aliens and Citizens: The Case for Open Borders*, 49 Rev. Pol. 251 (1987). For an extended argument in favor of relaxed standards for dual national citizenships, see Peter J. Spiro, *Dual Nationality and the Meaning of Citizenship*, 46 Emory L.J. 1411 (1997). Questions about whether dual citizenship should be discouraged or welcomed are part of a broader debate over the meaning and role of citizenship, including whether national citizenship will remain the dominant form of identification with polities or whether parts of the world have entered a "post-national" period in which international human rights norms define the rights and status of persons, see, e.g., Jasemin Soysal, Limits to Citizenship: Migrants and Post-

---

1. See, e.g., Commission on Security and Cooperation in Europe, Human Rights and Democratization in Estonia 8–12 (September 1993) (describing barriers to ethnic Russians acquiring Estonian citizenship) and Report on the March 5, 1995 Parliamentary Election in Estonia and the Status of Non-Citizens 3–4 (May 1995) (describing continuing efforts to discourage Russians from seeking Estonian citizenship); Human Rights Watch/Helsinki, Roma in the Czech Republic: Foreigners in their own Land 16–29 (June 1996) (describing changes in law for acquiring citizenship believed to be designed to discourage Roma applications); Commission on Security and Cooperation in Europe, Human Rights and Democratization in the Czech Republic 23–27 (Sept. 1994) (noting that relative to other ethnic groups new requirements for citizenship served to exclude almost exclusively Roma).

National Membership in Europe (1994), and whether any rights of persons should turn on whether they are citizens or long-time resident alien "denizens," see e.g., Tomas Hammar, Democracy and the Nation-State: Aliens, Denizens and Citizens in a World of International Migration (1990). For a useful collection of essays on these and related topics, see Christian Joppke, ed., Challenge to the Nation-State: Immigration in Western Europe and the United States (1998).

Consider these questions about constitutions and citizenship.

a. Entrenched Definitions? Should constitutional norms govern who is a citizen or should the qualifications for citizenship be determined solely by statute? On what should the answer to this question depend? Is citizenship so fundamental an issue, and one so prone to divisiveness, that it should be "taken off the table" by entrenchment in a difficult-to-amend constitution? Or is it a concept that, as understandings of the nation state and sovereignty in an increasingly interconnected world change, must remain fluid and responsive to changes in migration, in foreign relations, in international law and regimes—and hence statutory?

b. Treatment of Noncitizens: To what extent should constitutional norms govern the treatment of noncitizens? Consider prohibitions, e.g., on cruel or unusual punishments, on infringing freedom of speech, or on takings of property; consider rights to social welfare benefits, to hold public employment, or to vote. (Note that noncitizens (as well as citizens) hold some rights against nation-states that are considered "human rights" protected by and derived from international law.) For a sampling of scholarly views in addition to sources already cited, see, e.g., Jamin B. Raskin, *Legal Aliens, Local Citizens: The Historical Constitutional and Theoretical Meaning of Alien Suffrage*, 141 U. Pa. L. Rev. 1391 (1993) (favoring voting rights for resident aliens in local elections); Stephen H. Legomsky, *Why Citizenship?* 35 Va. J. Int'l L. 279 (1994) (arguing that citizenship as a concept is justified primarily by facts of international life but that it need not serve as the basis for voting rights, military service or other domestic rights and duties); Peter H. Schuck, Citizens, Strangers and In-Betweens: Essays on Immigration and Citizenship 163-75, 186-93 (1998) (raising questions about the "devaluation" of citizenship as a distinctive status).

c. *Admission of Noncitizens*: To what extent should constitutional norms govern the admission of noncitizens into a nation's territory? Many nations have versions of the "plenary powers" doctrine under which an attribute of sovereignty is to exercise political discretion through statutes dealing with the admission of aliens. Should this be a subject for constitutional law, or only for international law?

d. National Minorities: National minorities within one country may have their rights or interests asserted, or protected, by another country. Hungarians living in the Slovak Republic, for example, or Albanians living in Kosovo, may look to their felt country of national origin for support. Persons of Mexican origin living in the United States likewise may look to Mexico to advance their claims, and rising interest in dual or multiple nationalities reflect the increased opportunities for migration modern transportation and commerce present. Does this phenomenon bear on whether to constitutionalize questions of citizenship? Ethnic or national minority group rights? In thinking about this question, would you need to consider what other mechanisms, e.g., in international law and fora, exist for securing rights of persons against governments?

CHAPTER X

RELIGIOUS PLURALISM AND CONSTITUTIONAL LAW

The emergence of the idea of constitutionalism in both the United States and in Europe was associated with efforts to address persistent conflicts arising from religious differences. Early bills of rights included provisions designed to protect individual liberties associated with religious belief and practice. Conflicts over religion were sometimes resolved through structures of governance; for example, some of the cantons or half-cantons in Switzerland exist to accommodate particular religious groups. Classic liberal arguments for religious toleration combined a concern to protect individual liberty with the claim that toleration helped stabilize government, as potential dissenters find their interests accommodated in the government.

This chapter examines the ways in which some constitutions address issues of religious pluralism. Many nations today have populations in which a majority of the people, sometimes a substantial majority, adheres to one religion (sometimes with varying degrees of attachment), and a minority adheres to a number of other religions. The first can be called the majority religion, but you should be alert to the different ways in which people who are associated with that religion can be attached to it. The materials address question like these: How do different constitutions allow religious majorities to seek public support? Does public support for religious majorities necessarily imply that the liberty of religious minorities is restricted? Do limitations on public support for religion disfavor the religious interests of adherents of a majority religion? (In U.S. constitutional law, the First Amendment's establishment clause is often invoked in challenges to laws (such as those providing support to private schools, including religious schools) enacted to accommodate majority religions or religious groups important to major political coalitions, while concerns about the practices of small minority religions are more typically associated with questions arising under the free exercise clause.) In thinking about these and related questions, you should also consider the varying ways in which constitutions address other forms of pluralism.

A. INTRODUCTION

Governments around the world supervise religions and religious practices in a range of ways. We introduce this topic through four examples of different ways in which governments support or regulate religion or religious organizations, followed by Professor Durham's analytic framework for considering the relationship between religious liberty and government support or regulation of religion. Professor Durham argues that moderate to substantial levels of government support of religion can be consistent with substantial levels of religious liberty, and that extreme forms of government "separation" from religion can amount to hostility inconsistent with acceptable levels of religious liberty. The examples of state involvement in religions provided in this introductory section are intended to provide an inductive background for evaluation of Professor Durham's thesis.

1. STATE SUPPORT OR SUPERVISION: EXAMPLES

a. Israel

In the first excerpt, Asher Maoz describes the system of government financial support for religion in Israel. In the second excerpt, Professor Lapidoth provides additional background on some of the elements of the relationship of government regulation to both the establishment of religion and the exercise of religious freedom in Israel.

Asher Maoz, *Religious Human Rights in the State of Israel*, in Religious Human Rights in Global Perspective: Legal Perspectives (Johan D. van der Vyver and John Witte, Jr., eds., 1996)

. . .

Religious institutions in Israel enjoy wide state financial support—in the form of both direct funding and tax exemptions. Both forms of state support are not uniform with regard to the various religious communities and lack clear criteria to ensure equal support for all religions. State funding for religious institutions has not developed on a systematic legal basis. It should be noted that, to some extent, discrimination in one area of state funding for religion may be offset by preferential treatment in another. Thus, though Christian churches seem to enjoy less direct state funding, they enjoy tax exemptions to a substantially larger degree than other communities, including Jews and Muslims.

Direct State Funding. Religious institutions are supported by the state. Jewish, Muslim, and Druze religious courts, which are established under state law and constitute state organs, are fully financed by the state as are other courts of law. The judges of these courts are paid salaries on a par with the judges of other states courts of law.

Jewish religious needs are furnished by the Jewish Religious Services Law, 1971, which states that the entire budget of the Religious Councils, as approved by the local council or by the Ministry of Religious Affairs, shall be funded by the government and by the local council. The state also pays the salaries of the Chief Rabbis of the state and of local rabbis who are elected according to law. The Ministry of Religious Affairs provides specific funding for various needs of religious life, such as participation in the construction of synagogues, cemeteries, and ritual baths, or the supplying of praying books and other ritual articles. The Ministry allocates special funding for religious instruction and education, maintenance of cemeteries, cultivation of ties with Jews in the Diaspora, and care for the religious needs of new immigrants.

Within the Ministry of Religious Affairs, special departments deal with Christian, Muslim, Karaite, Druze, and Samarite communities. This arrangement is apparently designed to enable the Ministry to tailor its services to the distinct needs of each minority communities—though some consider this to be a form of preferential treatment of the Jewish community. Since none of the religious services of these minority religious communities operate according to law, . . . their budgets are not fully funded by the state.

The Druze community enjoys full financing of its religious courts as well as state funding for other communal activities. This includes state subsidies for the salaries of clergy, operating expenses, building and maintenance of places of worship.

Muslim religious courts are state courts, and are likewise fully financed by the government. The Ministry of Religious Affairs pays the salaries of some 300 clergy connected with mosques, notably imams and muezzin. The Ministry also allocates funds for Muslim religious services as well as for the construction, renovation, and maintenance of mosques and cemeteries. Another important source of income for the Muslim community is the revenue derived from various *wakfs*,* now administered by the Custodian of Absentee Property. Representatives of the Muslim community have criticized this arrangement and demanded that the *wakf's* assets be placed in the control of the Muslim community. They have further criticized the seemingly preferential treatment accorded Christians, whose assets are exempt from the Absentee Property Law. The state has replied that Christian properties, unlike Muslim properties, are exempt since they were in 1948 and are now still registered not in the corporate name of the Church but in the individual names of the Archbishop and clergymen who are not absentees. Moreover, they had an organized church structure within recognized Christian communities, which could administer these properties. This explanation has not satisfied the Muslim Leadership. Present government guidelines indicate that a special committee of Muslims will be established to administer the *wakf* for and within the Muslim communities.

As mentioned, Christian institutions, which are not state institutions, receive little direct funding, but ample tax exemptions. Christian communities do, however, benefit directly from the funding of several important

---

* [Editors' Note: A wakf is a form of trust in which the income from specified property is used for charitable or family purposes.]

historical sites in Israel. These include the two million dollar renovation of the *Via Delaros* in the old city of Jerusalem—the last journey of Jesus crossing fourteen stations, from his trial until his crucifixion—as well as the construction of a modern facility for baptizing in the Jordan River near the lake of Galilee and the construction of a special road to an isolated monastery in the Judea Desert. The Israeli administration in Judea and Samaria is also participating in the reformation and construction of other Christian holy sites. The Ministry of Religious Affairs announced [its] intention to prepare festive celebrations for the second millennium of the birth of Jesus.

Besides the direct funding of religious courts and religious services, the State of Israel supports various religious institutions. These allocations were, at earlier times, openly partisan, and not according to legal provisions. The Supreme Court has had to criticize more than one such allocation scheme, leading to reforms and interventions by the State Comptroller. In recent years, such state funding has been more fairly distributed, though Israel still lacks a comprehensive clear scheme of equal distribution of state funding among the various religious communities and the different sects within each community.

In the past, such state funding came from the general budgets of the different ministries, not from designated resources. This practice was challenged in a 1971 petition to the Supreme Court, when organizers of a music festival where church music was to be played were denied financial support by the Ministry of Education. The Ministry stated that it was not its duty to support the performances of church music. The majority of the court, though expressing discontent with the ministry's decision, ruled that courts are not authorized to intervene in the distribution of funds, which are not regulated by law. The minority opinion by Justice Cohn, however, paved the way for later reform. Justice Cohn disqualified the ministry's considerations, although he was sympathetic to its reservations about funding a performance of *St. John's Passion*, which treats the Jews as responsible for Jesus Christ's crucifixion. Such considerations, he said, illegitimately discriminate against the art work of minority religions. Although the law provided no criteria for allocation of funds, content-based discrimination was illegitimate, Justice Cohn concluded, and the ministry's decision should be overruled.

Such decisions notwithstanding, Jewish religious institutions generally enjoy substantially more state funding than do other religions, and most of that funding goes to Orthodox institutions. This is not only a function of demography, that is, the vast preponderance of (Orthodox) Jews in Israel. National, historical and political factors have all contributed to this disparity as well. Israel, as the homeland of the Jewish people, has assumed as one of its major tasks the maintenance and development of Jewish culture and tradition, which naturally have religious dimensions. Moreover, following the Holocaust which destroyed the world center of Jewish learning, Israel assumed the task of replacing those centers in Israel, and rebuilding the institutions of learning destroyed in Europe. Israel continually strives to maintain the chain of Torah learning and to establish a Torah center in place of the one destroyed. The state thus allocates substantial financial support to Yeshivoth (Jewish religious academies). This policy has won the approval of the Supreme Court in the 1984 case of *Watad v. Ministry of Finance.* In upholding this policy, the Court stressed "the unique and special place of Torah studying among the Jewish people and the place of Yeshivoth and of the Torah students." Students pursuing traditional study of the Torah were thus worthy of state support. The Court stated, however, that similar allocations should be granted to non-Jewish religious educational institutions, which are parallel to the Yeshivoth when established.

Debates over state funding for religious institutions has brought on several rounds of rulings. In a 1983 Supreme Court case, *Central Tomchei Tmimim v. The State of Israel*, the Lubavich movement argued that a state scheme of funding educational institutions discriminated against the movement. In response, the Knesset made allocations of funds to specific religious institutions. Due to parliamentary sovereignty, the Court could not enjoin this Knesset policy, but it did sharply criticize the practice of allocating funds to favored institutions and without objective criteria. It did not regard the remedial proceedings pending in the Knesset as an obstacle to trying the case, and ordered that thereafter no funds could be allocated without "clear, relevant and equal criteria."

Following the Court's decision, the Attorney General issued directives for governmental support of public institutions. According to the new policy, state money may be allocated to public institutions only in accordance with just and equal criteria. Direct allocation of funds to named institutions on an unequal basis is strictly forbidden. The Foundations of Budget Law was also amended to provide that annual budget laws must specify the state subsidy for each category of public institution, and promulgate in the official Gazette the objective criteria and application procedures used for its distributions. Various ministries have, in response, published detailed criteria for the allocation of State funding on an objective and equal basis. Funding for Jewish institutions, as a consequence, is no longer automatic. For example, a recent application by a religious Zionist institution for grants allocated for Orthodox cultural activities was denied by the Ministry of Religious Affairs, and the applicant's appeal was dismissed by the Supreme Court.

The debate on the issue of state funding for religious institutions is far from closed, however. Not only has it been difficult to set objective guidelines, but state funding has remained subject to constant political pressure and preferences. Orthodox and Ultra-Orthodox movements traditionally take part in Israeli political life and were usually part of its coalition governments. Representatives of these movements sponsor allocations that support their own institutions, and that discriminate against various non-Orthodox groups in Judaism or against unfavored sects within Orthodoxy. Non-Orthodox Jewish groups, in particular, have often not qualified for funding according to the criteria published by the Minister of Religious Affairs. This has led to further litigation before the Supreme

Court. In response, the Ministry of Religious Affairs included a category of "support for other Jewish religious institutions," which provides allocations to institutions affiliated with the Reform and the Conservative movements.

Muslim and Druze religious institutions are allocated even fewer funds by the Ministry—even though Muslim groups receive additional distributions from *wakfs*. Recently, high officials within the Ministry have admitted to discrimination against these groups, and special funds have been distributed in an attempt to bridge the gap. The present Government has declared its intention to rectify the funding of these communities, and to treat them equally henceforth. It also made a commitment to integrate the Arab and Druze communities in Israel into areas of state life, to shore up their support for education, welfare, industry, housing and health services in these communities, and to absorb Arabs and Druze holding academic degrees into the civil service. A progress report published recently by a non-political association for the advancement of equality of opportunity shows considerable progress in this area in recent years. Thus, the state funding of Muslim religious sites in 1994 exceeded 20 times the funding in 1993. The newly appointed Minister of Religious Affairs published a platform in which he pledges commitment to full equalization of financial support for all religions. This reform includes the establishment of a center for the development of religious services and structures for the Muslim community which will be duly financed and will take care of the existing Muslim holy sites as well as building new mosques and cemeteries. Within this program all existing buildings of the Shari'a Courts will move into new buildings by the end of 1996.

An administration for Muslim religious services will be established which will take care of the entire religious services for Muslims, will administer the Muslim clergy, and will take care of Muslim shrines. Ample independence will be conferred upon this administration which will promote religious services for the Muslim community. Specific care will be taken for the appointment of sufficient Muslim clergymen and in their status and conditions.

This entire policy of state funding of religious organizations is the subject of a special report by the State Comptroller on the Ministry of Religious Affairs. In her report, the State Controller sharply criticized both the criteria and their implementation. Following the report, the incoming Minister of Religious Affairs established a public committee which examined the entire matter and offered its recommendations. The Minister adopted these recommendations, and in July 1995 published new criteria for allocation of funds. Those criteria were formulated on objective considerations to ensure that no preference may be conferred upon certain institutions. Moreover, the new criteria establish a tight inspection mechanism to insure the equal allocation of funds and their spending in accordance with the criteria.

Besides direct funding by the Ministry of Religious Affairs, religious institutions are eligible for funding from bequests made in favor of the

State of Israel, according to the Ministry's recommendations. According to the guidelines published by the Ministry, equal criteria will be applied to Jewish and to non-Jewish institutions and projects. Moreover, funding will be made available to assist the pilgrimages of Muslims to Mecca and Christians to the Holy Land. Special funds will be made available for the encouragement of the understanding among Jews, Christians, and Muslims and other religions. The Ministry is also contemplating the establishment of public committees for the advancement of inter-religious understanding and of religious tolerance.

Ruth Lapidoth, *Freedom Of Religion and Of Conscience in Israel*, 47 Cath. U. L. Rev. 441 (1998)

... Israel has a rather heterogeneous population ... The country is not only inhabited by adherents of various religions, but it is also holy to four major faiths: Judaism, Christianity, Islam, and Baha'i..... About eighty percent of the population is Jewish, but the Jews are rather divided on matters of religion....

Due to the system of government that prevails in Israel, a multi-party parliamentary democracy, Jewish orthodox religious parties have a considerable influence on the political life of the country....

III. The Jewish Character of the State

Although there is a Jewish majority in the country, Judaism has not been proclaimed the official religion of the State. Neither is Jewish law the applicable legal system, except in certain matters of personal status of Jews.

... [But] the 1948 Declaration on the Establishment of the State of Israel proclaimed "the establishment of a Jewish State in Eretz-Israel [the Land of Israel]...the State of Israel." Similarly, the Basic Law: The Knesset, provides that:

[a] candidates' list shall not participate in elections to the Knesset if its objects or actions, expressly or by implication ... negat[e] the existence of the State of Israel as the State of the Jewish people ...

The Jewishness of the State is also reflected in the fact that the Sabbath and the Jewish holidays have been declared to be the official days of rest for the majority of the population, that the flag and emblem express Jewish tradition, and that the army has to provide only Kosher food to its soldiers....

Another relevant provision has been included in the two 1992 Basic Laws on human rights. ... [T]heir purpose is to protect the rights dealt with by these laws, namely, human dignity, liberty, as well as freedom of occupation, "in order to establish in a Basic Law the values of the State of Israel as a Jewish and democratic state." ...

[Despite the Jewishness of the State, the] basic attitude of the State toward religious freedom and pluralism is reflected in the 1948 Declaration on the Establishment of the State of Israel: "[The State] will guarantee freedom of religion, conscience, language, education and culture; it will safeguard the Holy Places of all religions . . . ." The Declaration is neither a constitution nor a statute, but the Supreme Court has decided that it "expresses the nation's vision and its credo," and should be taken into consideration "when we attempt to interpret or clarify the laws of the State." ...

In this context one should also refer to a legislative text enacted in 1922 at the time of the British Mandate, and which is still in force in Israel:

> All persons in Palestine [now Israel] shall enjoy full liberty of conscience, and the free exercise of their forms of worship subject only to the maintenance of public order and morals. Each religious community...shall enjoy autonomy for the internal affairs of the community subject to the provisions of any Ordinance or Order issued by the High Commissioner. ...

Israel has also committed herself to freedom of belief and religion in various international instruments ... [including] the 1966 International Covenant on Civil and Political Rights which provides for religious freedom....

Compliance with freedom of religion in Israel has been assured by the criminal law which made it a punishable offence to outrage religious sentiments, to disturb worship, or to desecrate places of worship.... [a] protection ... granted to "all religions," without distinction....

V.   The Holy Places

... The Holy Places have often been a source of conflicts. In the nineteenth century a bitter controversy arose when certain European countries extended their protection over the various Christian churches in Palestine, and over the places which were holy to them. In order to regulate the status of the different churches at the Holy Places, the Ottoman government promulgated a number of firmans, the most important one being that of 1852. That firman dealt with certain Holy Places and determined the powers and rights of the various denominations in those places. That arrangement became known as the historical status quo. The status quo has been applied to the Church of the Holy Sepulcher and its dependencies, the Convent of Deir al-Sultan, the Sanctuary of the Ascension on the Mount of Olives, and the Tomb of the Virgin Mary near Gethsemane, all four in Jerusalem, as well as to the Church of the Nativity, the Milk Grotto, and the Shepherds' Field near Bethlehem....

The 1922 Terms of the British Mandate for Palestine, drafted by the Council of the League of Nations, also dealt with the Holy Places. The Mandatory power was requested to preserve existing rights in those places and to ensure free access and worship, subject to requirements of public order and decorum....

The 1936 Criminal Law Ordinance by which the Mandatory codified the penal law in Palestine, includes several provisions on the protection of Places of Worship against desecration. These provisions are today included in Israel's Penal Law. In 1948 the State of Israel was established, and, as mentioned earlier, the Declaration signed at that time by the leaders of the Jewish community included a provision on the safeguarding of the Holy Places of all religions.

Until 1967, most of the Holy Places in the territory of former mandatory Palestine were under Jordanian control. However, as a result of the 1967 Six-Day War, they came under the administration of Israel. Immediately after the fighting ended, Prime Minister Levi Eshkol convened the spiritual leaders of the various communities and reassured them of Israel's intention to protect all the Holy Places and to permit free worship. Soon the Knesset adopted the Protection of the Holy Places Law, which ensures protection of the Holy Places against desecration as well as freedom of access thereto. These principles were reconfirmed with regard to Holy Places situated in Jerusalem by the 1980 Basic Law: Jerusalem Capital of Israel....

... [O]ne should [also] mention certain international texts related to the Holy Places.... [T]he 1993 Fundamental Agreement between the Holy See and Israel ...[calls for] both ... the preservation of the historical status quo in those Christian Holy Places to which it applies, and ... the protection of freedom of Catholic worship at others. In the 1994 Treaty of Peace between Israel and Jordan, Israel promised to "[respect] the present special role of ... Jordan in Muslim Holy Shrines in Jerusalem." ...

With regard to the Palestinians, one should mention a letter sent by then Foreign Minister of Israel Shimon Peres to the Foreign Minister of Norway in October 1993.... [according to which] "all the Palestinian institutions of East Jerusalem, including the economic, social, educational, cultural, and the holy Christian and Moslem places, are performing an essential task for the Palestinian population ..." and "will be preserved ...."

Freedom of access and of worship at the Holy Sites in the West Bank and Gaza Strip, as well as the protection of those sites, have been dealt with by the 1994 Agreement on the Gaza Strip and the Jericho Area, [and other agreements].... How do courts in Israel deal with disputes in which Holy Places are involved? ... [T]he principles of freedom of religion and of worship are generally recognized.... However, in recent years, disputes, sometimes accompanied by violence, have erupted among various Jewish denominations, in particular with regard to prayer at the Western Wall.... [I]n principle, courts do not consider themselves authorized to adjudicate on matters related to the implementation of the right to worship at Holy Places. It is the government [that is, the prime minister and cabinet] that has to deal both with disputes about rights to Holy Places and with the modalities of worship. Thus, the Supreme Court has so far refused to intervene in order to ensure the right of Jews to pray in groups on the

Temple Mount, which is holy to both Jews and Muslims, and is under the administrative control of the Muslim Waqf.

On the other hand, the courts consider themselves authorized to deal with all matters mentioned in the Protection of the Holy Places Law, namely, protection against desecration, against violation of freedom of access, and against violations of the feelings of the members of a community with regard to the place which is sacred for them. The courts are also authorized to deal with criminal offences in order to preserve public order at the Holy Places. Even where a dispute actually relates to claims or rights to a Holy Site, the courts may intervene in order to restore possession to a community if it had been deprived of this possession by a recent act. The reason for this rule is that the courts have an obligation to preserve law and order.

... [I]n some cases the Supreme Court has even refused to override a decision of the police to deny freedom of mere access (independent of worship) because of the fear that such access would jeopardize law and order. Thus, in certain cases individual Jews were denied access to the Temple Mount for reasons of public order. Moreover, even a temporary complete prohibition for all Jews to ascend the Mount may be lawful if needed for reasons of safety.

An interesting question concerns the distinction between the right to worship at Holy Places, which according to the courts is not within their jurisdiction, and the right to access with which the courts are authorized to deal. The request of Jews for permission to pray in a group on the Temple Mount was considered a matter of worship, but it seems that according to the Supreme Court the right of an individual to pray by himself is part of his right of access. . . .

The Holy Places in Israel are administered by members of the faith for whom those places are holy. In practice, Israel has been very careful to carry out the policy of respect for the Holy Places of all religions. At the entrance of each Holy Place the Ministry of Religious Affairs has posted an announcement in several languages requesting visitors not to desecrate the place, to be properly dressed, and to behave becomingly. In the few cases of violations of the sanctity of Holy Places, the police have acted diligently to apprehend the offenders and bring them to justice. . . .

... Respect for religious pluralism is at the base of various laws which reject automatic equality in order to preserve the identity and tradition of a religious community. Thus, the Adoption of Children Law prescribes that the adopting persons be of the same religion as the adoptee. In the matter of weekly rest, it is provided that non-Jews may choose Sunday or Friday instead of Saturday, which is the Jewish Sabbath. . . .

VII. The Right to Change One's Religion

... [T]he possibility to change one's religion... has been the subject of a special enactment adopted during the mandatory period, the Religious Community (Change) Ordinance, of 1927, which is still in force. Since—as will be seen later—belonging to a religious community has important consequences in matters of personal status and the jurisdiction of the courts, it was laid down that a change of religion has to be registered. Thus, everyone is free to change his religion, but in order for that conversion to have legal consequences, and only for that purpose, he needs the consent of the new religious community which he joins. The head of this religious community will provide him with an appropriate certificate, and he has to notify the Ministry of Religious Affairs of the change. The consent of the community which he leaves is not needed. The religion of a minor shall not be changed unless both of his parents consent or with a court's approval, and if the minor is above the age of ten, his consent is also required.

VIII.   Proselytizing . . .

Proselytizing is legal in Israel, but since 1977 it has been prohibited to promise money or other material advantages in order to induce someone to change his religion. Similarly, it is prohibited to receive material advantages in exchange for a promise to change one's religion. . . .

. . . [M]issionary activity is allowed, but the buying of souls for money has been prohibited. It has also been condemned by various religions. This law applies equally to all religions. According to an instruction issued by the Attorney General, no one shall be prosecuted under this law without prior authorization by the State Attorney. In fact, the law has never been applied. . . .

As a reaction to the mailing of Christian literature to one-half million Israeli homes by an American evangelical organization in San Diego, some members of the Knesset proposed bills in 1997 that would limit missionary activity in Israel. At the time this article was written, it was unknown whether (and if so in what terms) these bills would ever be adopted. The government of Israel has declared that it strongly objects to them.

IX.   The Right to a Religious Education

The right to religious education is guaranteed by law. It is essentially based on governmental support, while recognizing the autonomy of the various religious communities. The parents of a child may choose to send him to a secular state school, to a religious state school, or to a private religious school. . . .

X.   Matters of Personal Status

. . . Under Ottoman rule (1517–1917), the recognized religious communities (Millets) were granted autonomy in matters of personal status. This system was taken over with some modifications by the Mandatory authorities and later by the State of Israel. Today there are, besides the Jewish community, thirteen Recognized Religious Communities in Israel: the Muslim, Eastern Orthodox, Latin Catholic, Gregorian Armenian, Armenian Catholic, Syrian Catholic, Chaldean Uniate, Greek Catholic-Melkite, Maronite, Syrian Orthodox, Druze (since 1962), Episcopal-Evangelical (since

1970) and Baha'i (since 1971) communities. The last two do not have their own religious tribunals. The list of Recognized Religious Communities does not include several Christian communities, such as Christian Monophysite, like the Copts and the Ethiopian Orthodox Church, the Protestant-Lutheran, the Baptist and the Quaker, nor certain other religious communities within or outside the bounds of the Jewish community. Priests of the various religious communities are in charge of conducting marriages and notifying the authorities for the purpose of registration, and the tribunals of recognized communities have jurisdiction in certain matters of personal status, sometimes to the exclusion of the jurisdiction of civil courts. There are differences in the scope of jurisdiction among the various communities. The Muslim tribunal has the broadest powers. In certain matters the jurisdiction of the religious tribunals is exclusive, while in others it is concurrent and depends on the consent of all the parties involved.

Both the religious tribunals and the civil courts primarily apply the religious laws of the relevant parties to questions of personal status, in addition to relevant laws enacted by the Knesset. The difference between the application of religious law by the civil courts on the one hand and the religious tribunals on the other hand is apparent in two matters: first, each of these jurisdictions applies its own rules of procedure and evidence, and second, the civil courts take into consideration rules of private international law (conflict of laws) whereas the religious tribunals disregard them. Due to the jurisdiction and autonomy of the religious tribunals, Israel had to add to its 1991 ratification of the 1966 International Covenant on Civil and Political Rights a reservation that "to the extent that such law [the religious law of the relevant parties] is inconsistent with its obligations under the Covenant, Israel reserves its right to apply that law."

Although, as mentioned, the religious tribunals are in principle autonomous and may apply their respective legal system, Israel's Supreme Court has decided that these tribunals have to comply with certain laws of the State, such as the Succession Law. Moreover, they also have to apply general legal principles derived from the basic values of Israel's legal system, including human rights. Thus, in view of the right to freedom of movement, the Supreme Court has limited the power of a Jewish religious tribunal to prohibit a party to leave the country. Similarly, the Court has ruled that the tribunal must judge in conformity with the presumption of equal partnership of spouses in the property acquired by one of them.

Although the jurisdiction of the Rabbinical tribunals is not broader than that of some of the other communities, it has given rise to special problems and considerable opposition from many Jews, while it seems that no such resentment with regard to tribunals of other religious communities has been recorded. . . .

. . . [T]he opposition to the Jewish religious tribunals stems from three reasons. First, many non-religious Jews resent the exclusive authority of the religious institutions and consider it a case of religious coercion. Second, although Jewish law is quite liberal on certain matters, such as divorce by consent, it nevertheless includes some rather strict rules and restrictions, as well as discrimination between the genders, which may be considered outdated and may create unnecessary hardship.* Third, while other religious communities in Israel are rather homogeneous, the Jewish population is very heterogeneous, but so far the State has in fact given the Orthodox movement a monopoly over official activities, namely, the registration of marriages and jurisdiction in matters of personal status. This has engendered resentment from members of other movements, including the Conservative, Reform, Kara'ites, and Falashas (the Ethiopian Jews).

... [N]on-believers and members of an unrecognized religious group are at a disadvantage in matters of personal status. There are no lay officials authorized to celebrate and register marriages, there is no secular law on marriages, and civil courts have no jurisdiction in matters of marriage and divorce. However, in order to alleviate the situation, in those matters of dissolution of marriage which are not within the exclusive jurisdiction of a religious tribunal, the civil courts do have jurisdiction in certain circumstance. ...

Questions and Comments

1. Is Israel's policy of protecting the feelings of members of different religious communities from offense by prohibiting desecration of their holy places an instance of religious freedom, religious establishment, or both? What about the "right to a religious education"?

2. Given the presence of the "Holy Places" in Israel, is there any "neutral" posture the government of Israel could take with respect to the regulation or protection of those places?

b. Greece

Greece has a Ministry of National Education and Cults, which supervises all religions in Greece through a General Secretariat of Cults. The Secretariat has departments of Ecclesiastical Administration, of Ecclesiastical Education and Religious Instruction, and of Persons of a Different Cult and a Different Religion. The Department of Ecclesiastical Administration deals with the administration of the Orthodox Church, including the status of bishops, and such matters as the operation of churches and monasteries, including the acquisition of land for building or enlarging churches. The Department of Ecclesiastical Education is responsible for personnel decisions about religious teachers and for the operation of religious schools. The Department of Persons of a Different Cult deals with proselytism,

---

* [Editors' Note: For example, under Jewish law only the husband can grant a divorce to his wife; without the husband's agreement, then, even abused spouses cannot receive a divorce that will permit them later marriage under the Orthodox Jewish religious laws.]

admission of foreign clergy into Greece, and the procedures for operating places of worship of the non-Orthodox churches. In addition, many acts by the Orthodox Church, implementing public laws, are reviewable in administrative courts. These acts including transferring or dismissing a parish priest, and electing an abbot. For a complete description, see Charalambos K. Papastathis, *The Hellenic Republic and the Prevailing Religion*, 1996 Brigham Young U. L. Rev. 815.

----

c.   Germany

Germany imposes a "church tax" on the wages of salaried members of churches. The tax is administered through the regular wage withholding system, in the form of an 8–10% surcharge on the regular withholding. Everyone who appears in a church registry is subject to the tax. About 175,000 people per year resign from churches and are thereby exempted from the church tax. In addition, the "mixed marriage" case, 19 BVerfGE 226 (1965), held that the tax could not be imposed on the income of a non-church member whose spouse was a church-member: "[In a mixed marriage, the] marital community is not based upon mutual recognition of religious articles of faith, values, and obligations. Consequently, it would be unreasonable and would contradict the libertarian constitutional system of the Basic Law if one wished to force the nonmember spouse to establish direct relations—even if only financial ones—to a religious community by imposing unavoidable legal sanctions.... Marriage may be linked with economic legal consequences only if these consequences are related to the sphere of life being regulated. This is not the case here. The liability for church tax is the economic equivalent and consequence of church membership; that is, it results from a strictly personal relationship. However, the tax relationship to be regulated is, by its nature, an individual one." Translation from Donald Kommers, The Constitutional Jurisprudence of the Federal Republic of Germany 487–88 (2d ed. 1997).

----

d.   United States

The Establishment Clause of the U.S. Constitution has been interpreted to bar direct government financial support of religion as such. See Everson v. Board of Education, 330 U.S. 1 (1947). But not all government support of activities conducted by religious organizations is barred. For example, Rosenberger v. Rector & Visitors of the University of Virginia, 515 U.S. 819 (1995), held that the Establishment Clause did not require the University to bar the use of money from a fund created by a student activity fee to support the publication costs of a student publication that "promote[d]... a particular belief in or about a deity or an ultimate reality." The Court's opinion mentioned that the money was paid not to the student group but to the printer, and that the money came from a special student fee rather than from general state revenues. The precise scope of the Establishment Clause's barrier to financial assistance to religious institutions remains in dispute.

---

2. AN ANALYTIC FRAMEWORK

The following reading provides one taxonomy and "map" of the ways in which constitutions deal with religious pluralism. Professor Durham frames his presentation around questions of religious liberty primarily for minority religions, but his map describes the ways in which majority religions assert themselves in public and political life. Consider Durham's claims about the relation, if any, between public protection of majority religions and religious liberty.

W. Cole Durham, *Perspectives on Religious Liberty: A Comparative Framework*, from Religious Human Rights in Global Perspective: Legal Perspectives (Johan D. van der Vyver and John Witte, Jr., eds., 1996)

A Comparative Model for Analyzing Religious Liberty

Threshold Conditions for Religious Liberty.

An initial consideration in any generalized reflection on religious liberty is the recognition that there are certain threshold conditions that must be met before religious liberty can emerge. Briefly stated, there must be some measure of (1) pluralism, (2) economic stability, and (3) political legitimacy within the society in question. In addition, (4) there must be some willingness on the part of differing religious groups and their adherents to live with each other. Each of these threshold conditions deserves fuller analysis, but only a few comments are possible here.

Minimal Pluralism. Until some measure of divergence in fundamental belief systems emerges in a society, the question of religious liberty does not even arise. One can imagine a primitive society, for example, in which all the members of the community share assumptions about the nature of the physical and moral cosmos and in which agreement is so pervasive that questions of religious liberty and dissent would not arise.

Given human propensities to disagree and struggle with each other concerning fundamental issues, it seems difficult to imagine such pristine social homogeneity enduring for long. This difficulty is evident even within nuclear families, and is all the more likely to emerge in societies of any complexity. On the other hand, one can imagine societies enduring for substantial periods in which dominant religious views achieve effective consensus. Some medieval Christian communities no doubt functioned in this manner.

Similarly, one can imagine a society maintaining a sense of its own homogeneity by conceptualizing dissenters as strangers or foreigners. That is, group differentiation may obscure the emergence of incipient pluralism. Each group is committed to its own understanding of the world. Struggles between rival groups are understood as battles for the dominance of one outlook over another. Particularly if exit (or expulsion) from one group is easy, the home group remains homogeneous and the need for religious liberty is not perceived. Dissent appears as treason, betrayal, or at a minimum, as the mark of an outsider. Issues of religious liberty only begin to arise when differences between outlooks must be taken seriously as an unavoidable part of the relevant community.

Cultural blindness can play an analogous role in obscuring the need for religious liberty protections. Dominant European groups have often failed to show adequate respect for the belief systems of indigenous groups during periods of colonization. Similarly, even well-intended secular bureaucrats often fail to see how a seemingly routine regulation can have serious adverse consequences for a particular religious community. The distance between outsiders and marginalized insiders is very short.

Economic Stability. In situations of dire necessity, religious liberty concerns appear to have lower priority than meeting basic economic needs. In Eastern Europe, for example, resolution of the economic crisis appears to be a more urgent concern than enhancing religious liberty. The fact that religious liberty can exist in countries with very weak economies suggests that this threshold is not very high. And it may simply be that when economic crisis is sufficiently acute, no regime is sufficiently stable to afford effective religious liberty guarantees. If differing religious orientations take differing views as to how the economic crisis can be resolved, this can exacerbate the problem of political instability and reduce the extent to which a regime is inclined to foster religious liberty. On the other hand, religious belief may help people to weather economic hardship (a partial truth behind Marx's notion of religion as "the opiate of the people") and may contribute to economic productivity (e.g., Weber's notion that the Protestant ethic contributed to the productivity of capitalism). Nonetheless, there appears to be some correlation between the level of economic productivity and effective religious liberty protections.

Political Legitimacy. Since religion can be a powerful legitimizing (or delegitimizing) force in a society, the likelihood of achieving religious liberty is reduced to the extent that a regime's political legitimacy is weak. Such a regime is likely either to exploit the legitimizing power of a dominant religion (with concomitant risks of oppression for dissenting groups) or to view religion in general as a threat. In either case, religious liberty suffers.

Public emergency situations can result either from economic or political instability or from natural or foreign threats (or any combination of the foregoing), but in any event, it is not surprising to find derogations of religious liberty rights during periods of emergency. I am not suggesting that this state of affairs is good—just that it is not surprising.

Religious Respect for Rights of Those with Differing Beliefs. Religious liberty for all is not possible in a context in which one religious group not only rejects the beliefs of another group but is unwilling to live with that group. If the intolerant group is dominant, it will persecute adherents of other groups. If not, it is likely to attract persecution itself because of efforts to actualize its religious views. In either event, religious liberty will not be fully actualized in the community because there will be at least one group that feels inhibited in actualizing its religious beliefs.

This problem can only be solved if there are grounds within a religious tradition calling for toleration of or respect for the rights of others to have divergent beliefs. Fortunately, there are resources within most religious traditions that support according others such respect. Within the Roman Catholic tradition, there is the pronouncement from Vatican II in *De Libertate Religiosa*. Within Islam, there is the doctrine of toleration of the "People of the Book." Numerous pronouncements on religious liberty have been promulgated by the World Council of Churches.

Religious teachings such as the foregoing which encourage toleration and respect are not always as expansive as one might wish, and are not always lived up to in practice. But they at least provide a starting point for making religious liberty possible.

The Relationship Between Religious Freedom Rights and Church–State Separation.

With the foregoing analysis of threshold conditions for religious freedom in mind, we can turn to a comparative analysis of different types of church-state systems. The degree of religious liberty in a particular society can be assessed along two dimensions—one involving the degree to which state action burdens religious belief and conduct and another involving the degree of identification between governmental and religious institutions.[32] In the United States, because of the wording of the religion clause of the First Amendment of the U.S. Constitution, these two dimensions are thought of respectively as the "free exercise" and "establishment" aspects of religious liberty. But for comparative purposes, it is useful to think more broadly in terms of varying degrees of religious freedom and church-state identification.

At least in lay thought, there is a tendency to assume that there is a straightforward linear correlation between these two values that could be represented as shown in Figure 1 [below].

This picture considerably oversimplifies matters. The primary difficulties arise in connection with the church-state identification gradient and its correlation to the religious freedom continuum. Few religious establishments have ever been so totalistic as to achieve complete identification of church and state. To the extent that extreme situation is reached or

---

32. For the basic features of the model I described in this section, I am indebted to the insights of a former student, George R. Ryskamp. For his description of the basic features of the model, see George R. Ryskamp, "The Spanish Experience in Church– State Relations: A Comparative Study of the Interrelationship Between Church–State Identification and Religious Liberty," *Brigham Young University Law Review* (1980): 616. . . .

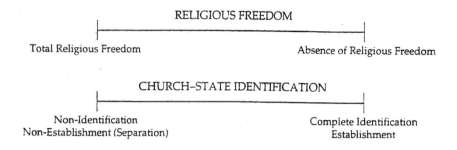

Figure 1

approached, there is clearly an absence of religious freedom. This is obviously true for adherents of minority religions, and even the majority religion is likely to suffer because of extensive state involvement in or regulation of its affairs or due to the enervation that results from excessive dependence of religious institutions on the state.

At the other end of the church-state identification continuum, things seem more confused. The mere fact that a state does not have a formally established church does not necessarily mean that it has a separationist regime characterized by rigorous non-identification with religion. Moreover, there is considerable disagreement about the exact configuration of relationships between church and state that maximizes religious liberty, and it may well be that the optimal configuration for one culture may be different than that for another. Further, it is not clear whether "non-identification" accurately marks the end of this particular continuum. Non-establishment and separation may mark intermediate points along a longer continuum that actually ends with "negative" identification: i.e., overt hostility or persecution. But if persecution lies at both ends of the church-state identification continuum, it is not at all clear how this continuum correlates with the religious liberty continuum.

The degree of confusion becomes evident when one considers [Ryskamp's] attempt to plot countries along these two continues as shown in Figure 2 [below.]

One can challenge several aspects of the [second] diagram. For example, with respect to the identification continuum, it is not ... clear ... why the United States should be located between France and Luxemburg. Lumping all Islamic regimes together is unfair in that it fails to take account of variance across such regimes. It is also important to remember that through much of history, Islamic regimes were in fact more tolerant than their Christian counterparts.... In short, the rankings in the diagram with respect to degree of identification are oversimplified.... Many of the religious freedom rankings seem equally arbitrary. But minor reshuffling of ... these rankings fails to remove more fundamental puzzles, such

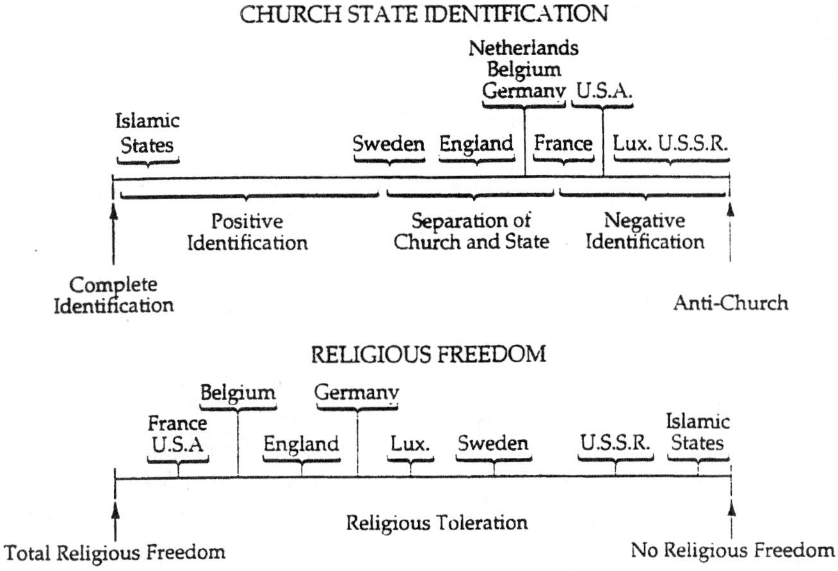

CHURCH STATE IDENTIFICATION

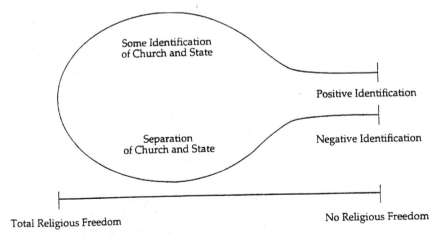

Figure 2

as why states located at opposite ends of the identification gradient should be located so close to each other on the religious freedom gradient.

The answer to this seeming puzzle lies in reconceptualizing the church-state identification continuum as a loop that correlates with the religious freedom continuum as shown in Figure 3:

Figure 3

This model accurately reflects the fact that both strong positive and strong negative identification of church and state correlate with low levels of religious freedom. In both situations, the state adopts a sharply defined attitude toward one or more religions, leaving little room for dissenting views.

The model also captures a related but less obvious reality. Changes in political regimes often move back and forth between extreme positions near the ends of the identification gradients, skipping more moderate intermediate positions. Thus, the history of church-state experience in Spain reflects radical shifts from regimes strongly supportive of an established church to secularist, anti-clerical regimes. In other settings, fundamentalist regimes may be replaced by radically secularist regimes, and vice versa.

Another significant aspect of religious liberty clarified by the model is that one cannot simply assume that the more rigidly one separates church and state, the more religious liberty will be enhanced. At some point, aggressive separationism becomes hostility toward religion. Mechanical insistence on separation at all costs may accordingly push a system toward inadvertent insensitivity and ultimately intentional persecution. Stalinist constitutions generally had very strong church-state separation provisions, but these can hardly be said to have maximized religious liberty. Rather, they were construed as a demand that religion should be excluded from any domain where the state was present. But in a totalitarian state, this became a demand in practice that religion be marginalized to the vanishing point. Secularist insistence in other countries that religion be confined to the ever-diminishing "private sphere," though typically less extreme, can have similar results in marginalizing religious life and reducing religious liberty.

Once one recognizes the foregoing general features of the religious freedom and identification gradients, one can begin to introduce refinements that help describe significant subfeatures along the two continua. These subfeatures in turn help identify salient differences among national religious liberty systems.

Turning first to the identification continuum, one can conceive it as a representation of a series of types of church-state regimes. Beginning at the positive identification end of the continuum, one first encounters *absolute theocracies* of the type one associates with stereotypical views of Islamic fundamentalism. In fact, a range of regimes is possible in Muslim theory, depending on the scope given to internal Muslim beliefs about toleration and also depending on the extent to which flexible interpretation of Shari'a law creates normative space for modernization.

Established Churches. The notion of an "established church" is vague, and can in fact cover a range of possible church-state configurations with very different implications for the religious freedom of minority groups. At one extreme, a regime with an established church that is granted a strictly enforced monopoly in religious affairs is closely related to one with theocratic rule. Spain or Italy at some periods are classical exemplars. The next position is held by countries that have an established religion that tolerates a restricted set of divergent beliefs. An Islamic country that tolerates "people of the Book" (but not others) would be one example; a country with an established Christian church that tolerates a number of major faiths, but disparages others would be another. The next position is a country that maintains an established church, but guarantees equal treatment for all other religious beliefs. Great Britain would be a fitting example.

Endorsed Churches. The next category consists of regimes that fall just short of formally affirming that one particular church is the official church of a nation, but acknowledge that one particular church has a special place in the country's traditions. This is quite typical in countries where Roman Catholicism is predominant and a new constitution has been adopted relatively recently (at least since Vatican II). The endorsed church is specially acknowledged, but the country's constitution asserts that other groups are entitled to equal protection. Sometimes the endorsement is relatively innocuous, and remains strictly limited to recognition that a particular religious tradition has played an important role in a country's history and culture. In other cases, endorsement operates in fact as a thinly disguised method of preserving the prerogatives of establishment while maintaining the formal appearance of a more liberal regime.

Cooperationist Regimes. The next category of regime grants no special status to dominant churches, but the state continues to cooperate closely with churches in a variety of ways. Germany provides the prototypical example of this type of regime, though it is certainly not alone in this regard. Most notably, the cooperationist state may provide significant funding to various church-related activities, such as religious education or maintenance of churches, payment of clergy, and so forth. Very often in such regimes, relations with churches are managed through special agreements, concordats, and the like. Spain, Italy and Poland as well as several Latin American countries follow this pattern. The state may also cooperate in helping with the gathering of contributions (e.g., the withholding of "church tax" in Germany). Cooperationist countries frequently have patterns of aid or assistance that benefit larger denominations in particular. However, they do not specifically endorse any religion, and they are committed to affording equal treatment to all religious organizations. Since different religious communities have different needs, cooperationist programs can raise more complex interdenominational problems of equal treatment. It is all too easy to slip from cooperation into patterns of state preference. Also, vis-à-vis more separationist regimes, more complex questions of protecting the self-determination and internal autonomy of religious organizations arise.

Note that in some cases, a cooperationist approach may be necessary for a transition period. For example, because of the devastated condition of churches after communism in East Central Europe and the former U.S.S.R., corrective justice seems to require return of extensive properties wrongfully taken from various churches. This process of restoration will necessarily entail heavy cooperation on the part of the state with churches, but it is not completely clear whether this process should be handled in a way that will aim at restoration of patterns of cooperation, or whether the required cooperation will be merely transitional, while the long term policy is to establish a more voluntarist regime.

Accommodationist Regimes. A regime may insist on separation of church and state, yet retain a posture of benevolent neutrality toward religion. Accommodationism might be thought of as cooperationism without the provision of any direct financial subsidies to religion or religious education. An accommodationist regime would have no qualms about recognizing the importance of religion as part of national or local culture, accommodating religious symbols in public settings, allowing tax, dietary, holiday, Sabbath, and other kinds of exemptions, and so forth. Many scholars in the United States argue that the United States religion clause should be construed to allow a more accommodationist approach to religious liberty. Note that the growth of the state intensifies the need for accommodation. As state influence becomes more pervasive and regulatory burdens expand, refusal to exempt or accommodate shades into hostility.

Separationist Regimes. As suggested by the earlier comments on Stalinist church-state separation, the slogan "separation of church and state" can be used to cover a fairly broad and diverse range of regimes. At the benign end, separationism differs relatively little from accommodationism. The major difference is that separationism, as it names suggests, insists on more rigid separation of church and state. Any suggestion of public support for religion is deemed inappropriate. Religious symbols in public displays such as Christmas creches are not allowed. Even indirect subsidies to religion through tax deductions or tax exemptions are either suspect or proscribed. Granting religiously-based exemptions from general public laws is viewed as impermissible favoritism for religion. No religious teaching or indoctrination of any kind is permitted in public schools (although some teaching about religion from an objective standpoint may be permitted). The mere reliance on religious premises in public argument is deemed to run afoul of the church-state separation principle. Members of the clergy are not permitted to hold public office.

More extreme forms of separationism make stronger attempts to cordon off religion from public life. One form this can take is through tightening the state monopoly on certain forms of educational or social services. In the educational realm, the state can ban home schooling altogether, can proscribe private schools, or can submit either of the foregoing to such extensive accreditation requirements that it is virtually impossible for independent religious education to function. Different regimes make differing judgments about the extent to which religious marriages will be recognized. A range of social or charitable services (including health care) may be regulated in ways that make it difficult for religious organizations to carry out their perceived ministries in this area. "Separation" in its most objectionable guise demands that religion retreat from any domain that the state desires to occupy, but is untroubled by intrusive state regulation and intervention in religious affairs.

Inadvertent Insensitivity. Overlapping with some forms of separationism is a recurrent pattern of legislative or bureaucratic insensitivity to distinctive religious needs. Bureaucrats often fail to distinguish between conduct regulated in secular settings (e.g., regulating land use planning, labor discrimination, taxation with respect to secular business activities) and regulating similar conduct in religious settings. In many cases, fairly simple accommodations can satisfactorily solve religious concerns. Regulations as initially formulated often lack any anti-religious animus; those drafting the regulations were simply unaware of the religious implications of their regulations. At some point, those afflicted by the unintended burden bring the problem to the attention of government officials. At this point, a reasonable accommodation can be worked out, or inadvertent insensitivity shades into conscious persecution. The flip side of inadvertent insensitivity is subtle or not-so-subtle privileging of main-line or dominant groups. It is altogether too easy for state officials who work with major religious groups to be less concerned with the needs of smaller groups and to speak of them in disparaging ways.

Hostility and Overt Persecution. The test in this area is how smaller religious groups are treated. Government officials seldom persecute larger religious groups (though this was certainly not unheard of in communist lands). Persecution can take the form of imprisonment of those who insist on acting in accordance with divergent religious beliefs. In its most egregious forms, it involves "ethnic cleansing" or most extreme, genocide. More typical problems involve less dramatic forms of bureaucratic roadblocks which cumulatively have the effect of significantly impairing religious liberty. These can take the form of denying or delaying registration (granting entity status) and obstructing land use approvals.

With the foregoing categories in mind, the relationship between the more refined identification gradient and the religious freedom gradient can be modeled as shown in *Figure 4:*

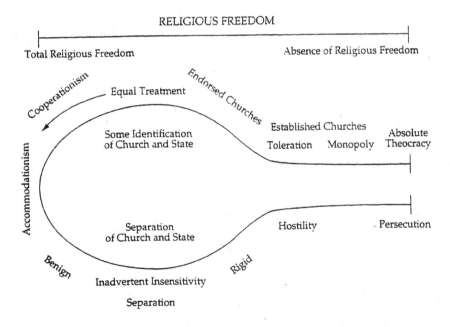

[*Figure 4*]

. . .

The church-state identification loop is useful not only in comparing types of institutional configurations, but also in keeping institutional issues in perspective. It is useful to note, for example, that the often highly polarized constitutional debates in the United States are in fact debates about which of a fairly narrow range of institutional options is optimal. Seeing the different possible configurations as a continuum helps to alert one to risks of ways that one type of regime can gradually slip into another. Unfortunately, because religious and governmental institutions are striving for influence and prestige, and because accommodation is not necessarily the bureaucratic path of least resistance, the natural tendency in the system is in directions that drift away from optimal respect for religious freedom. This means that vigilance is necessary, and that legal remedies that can counter this drift are vital. . . .

Questions and Comments

1. *The utility of the analytical framework*: Professor Durham's primary argument is that religious liberty is in some sense independent of the separation of church and state, or that the relationship between religious liberty and formal separation of church and state is not unidirectional. In light of Professor Durham's essay, consider whether there is *any* relation between "establishments of religion" and the religious liberty of minority religions, at least once we eliminate the extreme cases of fully theocratic constitutions on one end and regimes dedicated to ensuring secularism in every social domain on the other?

The "loop" Professor Durham offers suggests that for any given degree of religious liberty, there are two possible forms of identification or separation of church and state. Consider whether his examples show instead that for any degree of religious liberty there can be any type of relation between majority religion and the state (and conversely, that for any type of relation there can be any degree of religious liberty). Consider also whether his "loop" is subject to some of the same objections he raised to Ryskamp's linear model: for example, Figure 4 might suggest that there would be less religious freedom in England, which has an established church, than in the U.S., which does not (and thus might fall somewhere between "benign accommodationism" and "inadvertent insensitivity" on the loop)—a result that is at least controversial.

2. *The Effects of Transition:* Consider proposals in the United States to amend the Constitution to allow some forms of publicly organized prayer. If Durham's analysis is correct, a constitutional system allowing such prayers might have precisely the same amount of religious liberty as one that does not allow them. But consider whether there might be some impact from the *transition* from one system to another: Adopting an amendment might express the majority's view about the proper relation between religion and the state in a way that would indirectly affect religious liberty.

3. *Religion and Citizenship?* Professor Durham suggests that some systems might treat religious "dissenters" as strangers or foreigners. In such a system, the religious majority would take adherence to the majority religion as an essential for full affiliation with the nation. Consider whether the system might treat dissenters as something like permanent resident aliens, and whether doing so would necessarily impair their religious liberty. How would this differ from being a practicing member of a tolerated but not officially established religion in a nation that has an established church?

---

3.   TENSION BETWEEN CONSTITUTIONALISM AND RELIGIOUS FREEDOM?

Are there situations in which constitutionalism would be better developed by not protecting religion? Consider the following argument, that protection of religious freedoms—particularly freedom to evangelize—is inconsistent with rights of self-determination.

Makau Wa Mutua, *Limitations on Religious Rights: Problematizing Religious Freedom in the African Context*, in Religious Human Rights in Global Perspective: Legal Perspectives (Johan D. van der Vyver and John Witte, Jr., eds., 1996).

[After observing that African constitutions typically "make no mention of indigenous religions choosing instead to provide the generic protection of religious freedom contained in international human rights instruments," the author continues:]

Although human rights law amply protects the right to proselytize through the principles of free speech, assembly, and association, the "pecking" order of rights problematizes the right to evangelize where the result is the destruction of other cultures or the closure of avenues for other religions. It is my argument that the most fundamental of all human rights is that of self-determination and that no other right overrides it. Without this fundamental group or individual right, no other human right could be secured, since the group would be unable to determine for its individual members under what political, social, cultural, economic, and legal order they would live. Any right which directly conflicts with this right ought to be void to the extent of that conflict. Traditionally, the self-determination principle has been employed to advance the cause of decolonization or to overcome other forms of external occupation. The principle was indispensable to the decolonization process. This usage of the principle—as a tool for advancing demands for external self-determination—could be expanded to disallow cultural and religious imperialism or imposition by external agencies through acculturation, especially where the express intent of the "invading" culture or religion, as was the case in Africa, is to destroy its indigenous counterparts and seal off the entry or growth of other traditions. Furthermore, the principle could also be read to empower internal self-determination, that is, the right of a people to "cultural survival." This usage of self-determination is advanced by the Draft Declaration on the Rights of Indigenous Peoples. It is also an argument against cultural genocide. It is one of the ideas advanced by advocates of autonomy regimes for minorities: unless groups are given protection against invasion and control by others, their cultural and ethnic identities could be quashed by more powerful cultures and political systems. The violent advocacy of the messianic religions in Africa could be seen as a negation of this right particularly because religion is often the first point of attack in the process of acculturation.

Christianity and Islam forcibly entered Africa not as guests but as masters. The two traditions came either as conquerors or on the backs of conquerors. As they had done elsewhere, they were driven by the belief and conviction of their own innate superiority—and conversely what they saw as barbaric African religions and cultures. This belief was not a function of an objective assessment and reflection about African religions and cultures. It was born of the contempt and ignorance of that which was different and the exaggerated importance of the messianic faiths. The messianic religions—Christianity to be precise—came to Africa at a time of great technological and scientific imbalance between the West and the continent. Already the beneficiaries of the industrial revolution, the colonial church and state commanded superior resources in the areas of the military, economic organization and finance, the media, and other social and political spheres. Africa was no match, and the successful imposition of colonialism is proof of that fact. The West was able through coercion, intimidation, trickery, and force to impose a new political, social, cultural, and thanks to the missionaries, religious order in Africa. African political, social, and religious traditions were delegitimized virtually overnight.

Thus begun the process of de-Africanization through large-scale cash-crop farming for European industries, industrialization, urbanization, and the wholesale subversion of traditional values and structures. Africa—from top to bottom—was re-made in the image of Europe complete with Euro-centric modern states. Christianity played a crucial role in this process: weaning Africans from their roots and pacifying them for the new order. Utilizing superior resources, it occupied most political space and practically killed local religious traditions and then closed off society from other persuasions. It is in this sense that the practice of colonial Christian advocacy constituted a violation of the fundamental freedoms of Africans. Islam, which had invaded Africa at an earlier date, was equally insidious and destructive of local religions. Its forceful conversions and wars of conquest together with its prohibition of its repudiation, were violative of the rights of Africans as well. . . .

... I share with other scholars and activists in the human rights movement the importance of protecting religious human rights and enjoining governments from unduly burdening or prohibiting the free exercise of religion. But I am concerned by those dimensions of messianic religions that claim a right not merely to persuade individuals or groups of peoples of the "truth" as they see it but rather actively demonize, systematically discredit, and forcibly destroy and eventually replace non-universalist, non-competitive, indigenous religions. Quite often, indigenous religions anchor a total worldview and their destruction usually entails a fundamental distortion of ethnic identities and history.

Perhaps there is nothing that can be done today to reverse the negative effects of forced or coerced religious proselytization during the era of colonialism in Africa. Nor is it possible to reclaim wholly the African past as though history has stood still. This does not mean, however, that we should simply forget the past and go on as if nothing happened. The anguish and deprivation caused by that historical experience is with me— and millions of other Africans—today. We bear the marks of that terrible period. For those Africans who choose not to be Christians or Muslims, the past is not really an option: it was so effectively destroyed and delegitimized that it is practically impossible to retrieve. It is this loss that I mourn and for which I blame Christianity and Islam. The human rights corpus should outlaw those forms of proselytization used in Africa, because their purpose and effect have been the dehumanization of an entire race of people. It could do so by elaborating a treaty that addresses religious human rights but provides for the protection and mechanisms of redress for forms of proselytization that seek to unfairly assimilate or impose dominant cultures on indigenous religion.

B. PROBLEMS OF "ESTABLISHMENT"

1. RELIGION AND THE SCHOOLS

German School Prayer Case

52 BVerfGE 223 (1979) (Federal Constitutional Court of Germany).

[Excerpted from Donald Kommers, The Constitutional Jurisprudence of the Federal Republic of Germany (2d ed. 1997)]

[The German Constitutional Court consolidated two cases. In one a parent objected that the school's *ban* on prayer in a state-run, nondenominational school violated his constitutional rights. The lower court held that a student's objection to school prayer required that prayer be barred from the school entirely. Students had a right to abstain from religious worship, and, the court said, could not be put in a position where they had to remove themselves from the classroom to protect their "negative freedom of confession." The other case involved a state-supported denominational school. There the lower court held that "positive religious freedom"—the right of religious adherents to express themselves through prayer—prevailed over the right to remain silent, at least to the extent that the fact that a student objected to participating in the prayer did not require that prayers be prohibited completely. (Some of the bracketed material below is by Professor Kommers)]

* * *

Judgment of the First Senate....

A. The two decisions, combined into one constitutional complaint, touch upon the issue of whether school prayer outside religion class should be permitted in compulsory state schools when a pupil's parents object to the prayer.

C. I. 1. The standards for judging the constitutional questions raised by the issue of school prayer are set forth primarily in Article 6 (2) [1] of the Basic Law [the parent's right of control concerning the care and custody of minors], Articles 4 (1) and 4 (2) of the Basic Law [freedom of religion and the right to practice one's faith without harassment], as well as Article 7 (1) of the Basic Law [the state's mandate to establish educational systems].

Article 6 (2) [1] of the Basic Law accords parents the right and duty to freely determine the care and education of their children. This right has precedence over the rights of other educational institutions but is subject to the limitations of Article 7 of the Basic Law. This [parental right] also includes the right to educate one's child in religious and ideological respects. Paragraphs 1 and 2 of Article 4 encompass parents' right to teach their children those religious and ideological convictions which they believe to be true.

On the other hand, Article 7 (1) of the Basic Law confers a constitutional mandate upon the state to establish schools. The state's power to shape the school system, vested in the eleven German states, includes not only the power to organize the school structure but also [the power] to determine course content and objectives. Consequently, the state can pursue its own educational goals in the classroom, goals which may be fundamentally independent of parental aims. The state's mandate to establish a school system is autonomous and stands on the same footing as parents' right to control the education and upbringing of their children; neither has an absolute priority over the other.

2. The problem of school prayer must first be seen in the broader framework of whether religious references are ever permissible in (compulsory) interdenominational state schools, or whether the state within its authority to structure the school system is confined to making religious or

ideological references in religion classes, which are expressly guaranteed in Article 7 (3) of the Basic Law. . . .

Pursuant to [this Court's 1975 decisions concerning Baden's and Bavaria's interdenominational schools] the incorporation of Christian references is not absolutely forbidden when establishing public schools, even though a minority of parents may not desire religious instruction for their children and may have no choice but to send their children to the school in question. However, the school may not be a missionary school and may not demand commitment to articles of Christian faith. [State] schools also must be open to other ideological and religious ideas and values. They may not limit their educational goals to those belonging to a Christian denomination except in religion classes, which no one can be forced to attend. Affirming Christianity within the context of secular disciplines refers primarily to the recognition of Christianity as a formative cultural and educational factor which has developed in Western history. It does not refer to the truth of the belief. With respect to non-Christians, this affirmation obtains legitimacy as a progression of historical fact. Christianity's educational and cultural aspects include not insignificantly the notion of tolerance for those holding other beliefs. . . .

3. If religious references are permissible in compulsory state schools within the principles and guidelines developed by the Federal Constitutional Court, then praying in school is not fundamentally and constitutionally objectionable. However, the performance of the prayer also must comply with the limits of the states' right to establish school systems under Article 7 (1) of the Basic Law and not violate other constitutional precepts, in particular the individual rights of participants derived from Article 4 of the Basic Law.

(a) School prayer . . . represents a supradenominational (ecumenical) invocation of God based upon Christian beliefs. . . .

As an act of religious avowal made outside religion class, school prayer is not part of the general school curriculum taught within the framework of the states' mandate to establish an educational system for children. It is neither instruction typical of teaching a course nor the imparting of knowledge to pupils. Nor is it a goal-oriented, pedagogical exercise of influence on the part of the school and teacher upon the children. Rather, it is a religious activity undertaken, as a rule, in concert with the teacher. Thus it does not fall into the category of conveying Christian cultural and educational values, which the Federal Constitutional Court has deemed permissible within the framework of general instruction in Christian interdenominational schools. The constitutional permissibility of school prayer does not necessarily follow from the permissibility of these schools.

(b) Because school prayer is not a part of teaching a class in the sense of scholastic instruction, it cannot be a component of a binding lesson plan. Its performance must be completely voluntary. This is universally undisputed in view of the provisions of Articles 4 (1) and 4 (2) of the Basic Law as well as Article 140 of the Basic Law in conjunction with Article 136 (4) of the Weimar Constitution. [Voluntary participation] applies not only to pupils but also to teachers of every class in which a school prayer takes place (compare Article 7 (3) [3] of the Basic Law)....

Even if school prayer is not and cannot be part of the mandatory, regulated class instruction, it remains a school event attributable to the state in each of the forms named—especially when school prayer takes place upon the teacher's instigation during class time. To be sure, the state's role is limited to creating the organizational setting for school prayer and permitting the prayer at the request of the parents or pupils or on its own initiative. The state does not issue an order in this case; it makes an offer which the school class may accept.

(c) If the state, in the sense described, permits school prayer outside religion classes as a religious exercise and as a "school event," then certainly it is encouraging belief in Christianity and thus encouraging a religious element in the school which exceeds religious references flowing from the recognition of the formative factor of Christianity upon culture and education. Even in its transdenominational form, prayer is connected to the truth of a belief; specifically, that God can grant that which is requested. Nonetheless, permitting this religious element in (compulsory) interdenominational schools with the safeguard of voluntary participation still remains within the scope of creative freedom granted to the states as bearers of supreme authority in school matters pursuant to Article 7 (1) of the Basic Law....

Article 4 of the Basic Law grants not only freedom of belief but also the external freedom publicly to acknowledge one's belief. In this sense Articles 4 (1) and 4 (2) of the Basic Law guarantee a sphere in which to express these convictions actively. If the state permits school prayer in interdenominational state schools, then it does nothing more than exercise its right to establish a school system pursuant to Article 7 (1) of the Basic Law, so that pupils who wish to do so may acknowledge their religious beliefs, even if only in the limited form of a universal and transdenominational appeal to God....

To be sure, the state must balance this affirmative freedom to worship as expressed by permitting school prayer with the negative freedom of confession of other parents and pupils opposed to school prayer. Basically, [schools]may achieve this balance by guaranteeing that participation be voluntary for pupils and teachers....

4.   Although the states are free to allow school prayer in the sense discussed here within their authority for the establishment of the educational system, they are not always compelled to permit prayer in public schools.

Under the Constitution, the states are bound to provide religious instruction as a regular subject of instruction in all state schools (except strictly secular schools). But parents have neither an affirmative right to demand that schools allow prayers nor a right to demand that the state establish schools of a particular religious or ideological character....

II.   Although in principle [we] see no constitutional impediments to school prayer, [we] could reach a different conclusion if, in a specific case, a pupil or his parents object to praying at school. Both the Hesse Constitutional Court and the Münster Administrative Appeals Court ... took this view, but for different reasons. The deliberations of neither court may be upheld.

1.   The Hesse Constitutional Court believes that [schools] must forbid school prayer upon the objection of a pupil because the pupil may not be placed in the position of having to proclaim to the world his religiously or ideologically motivated rejection of the prayer through his nonparticipation. . . .

3.   The objection of a pupil holding other beliefs or of his parents or guardians could lead to the prohibition of school prayer only if the [school] did not guarantee the dissenting pupil's right to decide freely and without compulsion whether to participate in the prayer. As a rule, however, a pupil can find an acceptable way to avoid participating in the prayer so as to decide with complete freedom not to participate.

(a) Pupils can avoid praying in the following ways. The pupil can stay out of the classroom while the prayer is being said; for example, he or she can enter the room only after the end of the prayer or leave the room at the end of class, before the closing prayer is spoken. The pupil holding other beliefs may also remain in the classroom during the prayer but not say the prayer along with the others; he may then remain seated at his desk, unlike his fellow pupils saying the prayer.

(b) Admittedly, whenever the class prays, each of these alternatives will have the effect of distinguishing the pupil in question from the praying pupils—especially if only one pupil professes other beliefs. His behavior is visibly different from that of the other pupils. This distinction could be unbearable for the person concerned if it should place him in the role of an outsider and serve to discriminate against him as opposed to the rest of the class. Indeed, the pupil in a classroom is in a different, much more difficult position than an adult who publicly discloses his dissenting conviction by not participating in certain events. This is especially true of the younger schoolchild, who is hardly capable of critically asserting himself against his environment. With respect to the issue of school prayer, the child will generally be involved in a conflict not of his own choosing, but rather one carried on by his parents, on the one hand, and the parents of the other schoolchildren or teachers, on the other hand.

4.   Nonetheless, one cannot assume that abstaining from school prayer will generally or even in a substantial number of cases force a dissenting pupil into an unbearable position as an outsider. An assessment of the conditions under which the prayer is to occur, the function that the teacher has in connection with this exercise, and the actual conditions in the school leads us to conclude that we need not fear discrimination against a pupil who does not participate in the prayer. . . .

Questions and Comments

1.   Compare the U.S. Supreme Court's decision in Engel v. Vitale, 370 U.S. 421 (1962): The New York State Board of Regents composed the following prayer: "Almighty God, we acknowledge our dependence upon Thee, and we beg Thy blessings upon us, our parents, our teachers, and our Country." The Regents recommended that school boards require that this prayer be said aloud by each class in the presence of a teacher at the start of each school day. Justice Black, writing for the Court, said that this practice was "wholly inconsistent with the Establishment Clause.... [I]t is no part of the business of government to compose official prayers for any group of the American people to recite as part of a religious program carried on by government.... Neither the fact that the prayer may be denominationally neutral nor the fact that its observance on the part of the students is voluntary can serve to free it from the limitations of the Establishment Clause, as it might from the Free Exercise Clause...." Justice Black's opinion noted that "laws officially prescribing a particular form of religious worship [might]involve coercion," but said that finding that coercion existed was not a prerequisite to finding an establishment clause violation. Justice Stewart, the sole dissenter, wrote, "I think that to deny the wish of these school children to join in reciting this prayer is to deny them the opportunity of sharing in the spiritual heritage of our Nation." Abington School District v. Schempp, 374 U.S. 203 (1963), held unconstitutional the practice of beginning each school day with readings from the Bible.

Could a U.S. public school allow its teachers to oversee a prayer activity conducted in the five minutes preceding the official opening of the school day? Would that be a "school event" as you understand the German court to use the term?

2.   Note that Germany provides public support to denominational schools. Doing so may be prohibited in the United States, although it is unclear in early 1999 whether states may provide parents with vouchers that they may use to pay tuition at private denominational schools. In any event the school prayer decisions in the U.S. involved prayers at public schools. Consider whether the mere fact that public support of denominational schools is permitted might affect the analysis of the prayer issue, both in nondenominational and denominational schools.

German Classroom Crucifix Case II

93 BVerfGE 1 (1995) (Federal Constitutional Court of Germany)

[Excerpted from and based upon Donald Kommers, The Constitutional Jurisprudence of the Federal Republic of Germany (2d ed. 1997)]

[Bavaria is the most heavily Roman Catholic state in Germany. It required the display of a crucifix in every elementary school classroom. Prior decisions had held that the Basic Law was not violated by education systems in which the only public school available to some parents and their children was a denominational school. Parents, adherents of a humanistic philosophy or religion known as anthroposophy, objected to the display as an offense to their children's religious beliefs. A short-term compromise was worked out, in which the large crucifix on display in the children's classroom was replaced by a smaller cross without the figure of Jesus. The compromise fell apart in the next year, and the parents filed suit. The case attracted a great deal of public attention.]

* * *

Judgment of the First Senate

C.   The constitutional complaint is well founded. The rejection of the plaintiff's claim is incompatible with Article 4(1) ["Freedom of faith, of conscience, and freedom to profess a religion or a particular philosophy shall be inviolable"] and Article 6 (2) ["The care and upbringing of children shall be a natural right of an a duty primarily incumbent on the parents"]. . . .

[The court first addressed the claim that delays in dealing with the parents' objections violated the Basic Law. It said that the Bavarian authorities had erroneously placed the burden on the parents to work out an acceptable compromise. It noted that the parents appeared willing to compromise, but that the school authorities refused to work out a final arrangement. Under these circumstances, the court said, the lower courts should have acted more promptly to protect the children and their parents. (Some of the bracketed material below is by Professor Kommers).]

II.   The decisions also violate the basic rights of complainants under Article 4 (1) in tandem with Article 6 (2) of the Basic Law. . . . [These decisions] are based on section 13 (1.3) of Bavaria's Elementary School Ordinance, which in turn is incompatible with the Basic Law and thus void.

1.   Article 4 (1) of the Basic Law protects freedom of belief. Whether under this provision one is for or against a particular belief is an affair of the individual, not the state. The state must neither prescribe nor forbid a religion or a religious belief. Freedom of belief includes not only the freedom to uphold a faith but also the freedom to live and act according to one's own religious convictions. In particular, freedom of faith guarantees the right to participate in cultish activities which a specific belief prescribes or in which it expresses itself. It likewise guarantees the right to refrain from participating in such activities. Article 4 also applies to symbols that incorporate a belief or a religion. It allows individuals to decide for themselves which religious symbols they wish to acknowledge or venerate and which they wish to reject. To be sure, in a society that tolerates a wide variety of faith commitments, the individual clearly has no right to be spared exposure to quaint religious manifestations, cultish activities, or religious symbols. However, a different situation arises when the state itself exposes an individual to the influence of a given faith, without giving the child a chance to avoid such influence, or to the symbols through which such a faith represents itself. Article 4 (1) safeguards precisely those areas of life which enjoy the special protection of the state, . . . a safeguard

reinforced by Article 140 of the Basic Law in tandem with Article 136 (4) of the Weimar Constitution. These provisions prohibit the state from forcing anyone to participate in religious practices.

Article 4 (1) does not simply command the state to refrain from interfering in the faith commitments of individuals or religious communities. It also obliges the state to secure for them a realm of freedom in which they can realize their personalities within an ideological and religious context. The state is thus committed to protect the individual from attacks or obstructions by adherents of different beliefs or competing religious groups. Article 4 (1), however, grants neither to the individual nor to religious communities the right to have their faith commitments supported by the state. On the contrary, freedom of faith as guaranteed by Article 4 (1) of the Basic Law requires the state to remain neutral in matters of faith and religion. A state in which members of various or even conflicting religious and ideological convictions must live together can guarantee peaceful coexistence only if it remains neutral in matters of religious belief. Therefore, the state must be wary of independently endangering religious peace in society. This mandate finds its basis not only in Article 4 (1) of the Basic Law, but also in Article 3 (3), Article 33 (1), and Article 140, which incorporates into the Basic Law Articles 136 (1) and (4) and 137 (1) of the Weimar Constitution. These articles prohibit the establishment of official churches and forbid the state from granting special privileges to members of certain faiths. The numerical strength or social importance [of a religious community] has no relevance. Rather, the state is obligated to treat various religious and ideological communities with an even hand. And when the state supports or works together with [these religious communities], it must take care not to identify itself with a particular community.

Article 4 (1), when considered in relation to Article 6 (2) of the Basic Law, which confers on parents the natural right to take care of and to raise their children, also embraces the right of parents to educate their children in accord with their religious and ideological convictions. It is up to the parents to transmit to their children those commitments of faith and ideology which they accept as true. Similarly, they have the right to shield their children from religious beliefs they consider false or harmful.

2.   Section 13 (1.3) of the Bavarian Elementary School Ordinance and the disputed [judicial] decisions based on this provision encroach on this basic right.

(a) Section 13 (1.3) of the Bavarian Elementary School Ordinance prescribes the display of the crucifix in all elementary school classrooms in Bavaria. According to the interpretation of the courts involved in the initial proceedings, the term "cross" represents both a simple cross and one adorned with the figure of Christ. Our examination of the ordinance, therefore, must consider the significance of both the cross and the crucifix. In their action before the administrative court, the complainants had requested that only the crucifixes be removed; the court below, however, insisted that the motion might also include [a simple] cross without the figure of Christ. . . .

Given the context of compulsory education, the presence of crosses in classrooms amounts to state-enforced "learning under the cross," with no possibility to avoid seeing it. This constitutes the crucial difference between the display of the cross in a classroom and the religious symbols people frequently encounter in their daily lives. Encounters of the latter type are not the result of any state action but are merely a consequence of the pervasive presence of various faith commitments and religious communities in society. In addition, the latter situation does not admit to the same degree of compulsion. Admittedly, persons who walk the streets, use public transportation, or enter buildings have no control over such encounters with religious symbols and manifestations. But as a rule, these encounters are fleeting, and even if they are not, they are still not the result of any state preference backed by sanctions. . . .

(b) The cross is the symbol of a particular religious conviction, and not merely an expression of cultural values that have been influenced by Christianity.

Admittedly, numerous Christian traditions have found their way into the general culture of our society over the centuries, and these traditions cannot be denied even by the adversaries of Christianity and its historical heritage. However, these traditions must be distinguished from the particular tenets of the Christian religion, and especially from a particular Christian faith together with its ritual and symbolic representations. Any support of these faith tenets by the state would undermine freedom of religion, a matter already determined by the Federal Constitutional Court in its ruling on the constitutionality of so-called biconfessional public elementary schools [*Simultanschulen*] (citing 41 BVerfGE 29, 52). In affirming the Christian character of these schools, the court ruled that the state may legitimately recognize Christianity's imprint on culture and education over the course of Western history, but not the particular tenets of the Christian religion. Only if the parameters of its continued historical impact are delineated can the affirmation of Christianity be legally justified in the eyes of non-Christians.

The cross now as before represents a specific tenet of Christianity; it constitutes its most significant faith symbol. It symbolizes man's redemption from original sin through Christ's sacrifice just as it represents Christ's victory over Satan and death and his power over the world. Accordingly, the cross symbolizes both suffering and triumph. For believing Christians, it is the object of veneration and practiced piety. To this day, the presence of a cross in a home or room is understood as an expression of the dweller's Christian faith. On the other hand, because of the significance Christianity attributes to the cross, non-Christians and atheists perceive it to be the symbolic expression of certain faith convictions and a symbol of missionary zeal. To see the cross as nothing more than a cultural artifact of the Western tradition without any particular religious meaning would amount to a profanation contrary to the self-understanding of Christians and the Christian church. Section 13 (1) of the Bavarian ordinance also makes clear the religious significance of the cross.

(c) One cannot deny, as do the challenged decisions of the administrative courts, that the cross also has an effect on students.

Needless to say, the presence of the cross in classrooms does not force children to identify with or to venerate the cross, or to conduct themselves in certain ways. Similarly, the cross has no influence on the teaching of secular subjects, and no religious belief or practice is required in learning these subjects. But the cross does exert influence in other ways. Education is more than just transmitting fundamental cultural values and developing cognitive facilities. It also involves the development of pupils' emotional and affective abilities. The mission of the school is to develop and promote a pupil's personality and to influence his or her social behavior. In this context, the display of the cross in classrooms takes on critical significance. Its presence constitutes a deeply moving appeal; it underscores the faith commitment it symbolizes, thus making that faith exemplary and worthy of being followed. This is particularly true with young and impressionable people who are still learning to develop their critical capacities and principles of right conduct.

While the decisions below acknowledge the appeal of the cross, they do not suggest that it has a specific Christian meaning for students of different faiths. According to the lower courts it is an essential expression of faith only for the Christian pupils. Similarly, although the Bavarian prime minister was of the opinion that the cross has no distinctive religious meaning during periods of ordinary instruction, he conceded that the cross transforms itself into a distinct symbol of faith when students are engaged in reciting prayer and during periods of religious instruction.

3.   The basic right to religious freedom is unconditionally guaranteed, but this guarantee does not imply that there is no limitation on this right. Any limitation, however, must be rooted in the Constitution. Legislatures are not free to restrict [religious] liberty in the absence of such limiting provisions in the Basic Law itself. In short, there is no constitutional justification for the limitation imposed here....

... [T]he state need not abandon all references to religion or ideology in meeting the educational mission mandated by Article 7 (1) of the Basic Law. No state, even one that universally guarantees freedom of religion and is committed to religious and ideological neutrality, is in a position completely to divest itself of the cultural and historical values on which social cohesion and the attainment of public goals depend. The Christian religion and the Christian churches have always exerted a tremendous influence in our society, regardless of how this influence is evaluated today. The intellectual traditions rooted in their heritage, the meaning of life and the patterns of behavior transmitted by them cannot simply be dismissed by the state as irrelevant. This applies particularly to education since it constitutes a unique setting for perpetuating our traditions and renewing the cultural foundations of society. Furthermore, any state that requires children to attend state schools must respect the religious freedom of those parents who want their children to receive a religiously based education. Article 7 (5) of the Basic Law acknowledges this parental right by permitting the establishment of public ideological and confessional schools and by making religious instruction a regular part of the curriculum in state schools (Article 7 [3]). Additionally, the Basic Law also leaves room for the exercise of a student's faith commitment.

In a pluralistic society, needless to say, the state, in setting up a system of compulsory public school instruction, cannot possibly satisfy all educational goals or needs. Problems will always arise, and it will be particularly difficult to implement the negative as well as the positive aspects of religious freedom in one and the same public institution. So far as education is concerned, no one can claim an absolute right under Article 4 (1) of the Basic Law.

In resolving the inevitable tension between the negative and positive aspects of religious freedom, and in seeking to promote the tolerance that the Basic Law mandates, the state, in forming the public will, must strive to bring about an acceptable compromise. On the one hand, Article 7 of the Basic Law acknowledges the role of religious and ideological influences in education; on the other hand, Article 4 of the Basic Law mandates—to the extent possible—that religious and ideological pressures be removed from decisions favoring a certain type of school. Each article must be interpreted in the light of the other, and the two must be harmonized in such a way as to protect the interests that they were originally designed to safeguard.

The Federal Constitutional Court has concluded [in its previous case law] that the state legislature is not forbidden to introduce Christian values into the organization of public elementary schools, even if parents who cannot avoid sending their children to this type of school reject all forms of religious education. This presupposes, however, that coercion is to be reduced to an indispensable minimum. In particular, the school must not proselytize on behalf of a particular religious doctrine or actively promote the tenets of the Christian faith. Christianity's influence on culture and education may be affirmed and recognized, but not particular articles of faith. Christianity as a cultural force incorporates in particular the idea of tolerance toward people of different persuasions. Confrontation with a Christian worldview will not lead to discrimination or devaluation of a non-Christian ideology so long as the state does not impose the values of the Christian faith on non-Christians; indeed, the state must foster the autonomous thinking that Article 4 of the Basic Law secures within the religious and ideological realms. In the light of these principles we have already sustained the validity of the establishment of Christian community schools under Article 135 (2) of the Bavarian Constitution; the court has likewise upheld the constitutionality of the biconfessional public elementary schools of Baden-Württemberg. These schools were based on traditions prevailing in the region of Baden [and were designed to serve the needs of the major denominations without interfering with the religious liberty of any student or parent].

The display of crosses in classrooms, however, exceeds [these guidelines and constitutional limits]. As noted earlier, the cross cannot be separated from its reference to a particular tenet of Christianity; far from being a mere symbol of Western culture, it symbolizes the core of the Christian faith, one that has admittedly shaped the Western world in multiple ways but which is not commonly shared by all members of society.... The display of the cross in public compulsory school thus violates Article 4 (1) of the Basic Law. This rule, of course, does not apply to [state-supported] Christian confessional schools.

(b) Parents and pupils who adhere to the Christian faith cannot justify the display of the cross by invoking their positive freedom of religious liberty. All parents and pupils are equally entitled to the positive freedom of faith, not just Christian parents and pupils. The resulting conflict cannot be resolved on the basis of majority rule since the constitutional right to freedom of faith is particularly designed to protect the rights of religious minorities. Moreover, Article 4 (1) does not provide the holders of the constitutional right with an unrestricted right to affirm their faith commitments within the framework of public institutions. Inasmuch as schools heed the Constitution, leaving room for religious instruction, school prayer, and other religious events, all of these activities must be conducted on a voluntary basis and the school must ensure that students who do not wish to participate in these activities are excused from them and suffer no discrimination because of their decision not to participate. The situation is different with respect to the display of the cross. Students who do not share the same faith are unable to remove themselves from its presence and message. Finally, it would be incompatible with the principle of practical concordance to suppress completely the feelings of people of different beliefs in order to enable the pupils of Christian belief not only to have religious instruction and voluntary prayer in the public schools, but also to learn under the symbol of their faith even when instructed in secular subjects.

D.   The provision of section 13 (1.3) of the Bavarian Community School Ordinance, which is the subject of this opinion, is incompatible with the Basic Law and therefore unconstitutional.

JUSTICES OTTO SEIDL, ALFRED SÖLLNER, and EVELYN HAAS, dissenting.

We do not share the senate majority's opinion that section 13 (1.3) of the Bavarian Elementary School Ordinance, which mandates the display of crosses in all classrooms, violates the Basic Law....

I.   1.   According to Article 7 (1) of the Basic Law, ... the right to establish schools is conferred exclusively on the individual states.... The right to establish and operate schools is unlisted among the powers [conferred exclusively on the national government]. In contrast to the Weimar Constitution, which assigned legislative authority in educational matters to the Reich, the Basic Law confers no legislative or administrative authority on the federal government in the field of education. The history of Article 7 shows that the individual states were to enjoy extensive power over the ideological and religious character of public schools. This was one manifestation of the federal principle.... The founders repeatedly said that educational policy would remain in the hands of the [individual] states.

2. Therefore, the constitutional issue raised by the complaints must be considered in the light of the special situation in the *Land* of Bavaria....

[Article 131 (2) of] the Bavarian Constitution of December 2, 1946, defines the state's educational objectives as follows:

(2) The highest goals of the educational system are: Fear of God; respect for the religious convictions of all; the dignity of the human person; self-control; willingness to accept responsibility; readiness to assist others; an open mind in matters of truth, goodness, and beauty; and a sense of responsibility for nature and the environment.

The last clause on environmental responsibility was added to the Constitution on June 20, 1984. The other objectives listed in Article 131 have remained unchanged since the Constitution entered into force in 1946.

As for elementary education, Article 135 of the Bavarian Constitution initially provided for confessional and community schools, with some degree of preference given to confessional schools. In the course of time, however, the people of Bavaria changed this policy. On July 22, 1968, they voted—in a plebiscite—to amend Article 135 of the state constitution. [Article 135] now reads as follows:

All children subject to compulsory elementary education shall attend common public schools. These schools shall instruct and educate their pupils in accordance with the principles of the Christian faith. Details shall be regulated by law.

According to Article 135 (2) of the amended Bavarian Constitution, Christianity is not to be understood in a confessional sense. Rather, the principles of the Christian faith within the meaning of this provision encompass those values common to all Christian denominations as well as the ethical norms on which they are based. These values and norms are characteristically Christian and are widely recognized as such. Instruction in these principles is intended to lead pupils toward the educational goals described in Article 131 (2) of the Bavarian Constitution. Bavaria's constitution, however, does not mandate a specific Christian faith commitment. In affirming Christianity, the state is merely acknowledging the West's cultural and educational indebtedness to Christianity. [This acknowledgment], as borne out by the history of Western civilization, is warranted even in the eyes of non-Christians.

Given these considerations, there can be no constitutional objection to the type of Christian community school provided for under Article 135 (2) of the Bavarian Constitution.

3. Under Article 7 (1) and (5) of the Basic Law, individual states enjoy a large measure of discretion in determining the [nature] and organization of elementary schools.... The rule that mandates the display of a cross in

every classroom does not exceed that discretion. Since the state legislature is permitted to establish a Christian community school, it cannot be prevented from expressing, through the symbol of the cross, the values and ideals which characterize this type of school.

(a) Section 13 (1.3) of the Bavarian Elementary School Ordinance implements the organization of the Christian community school. For teachers and students alike, the display of the cross in classrooms symbolizes Western values and ethical norms that transcend confessional considerations and are to be taught in this type of school. In enacting this law, the state legislature was permitted to consider the fact that the majority of citizens residing in Bavaria belong to one or another form of the Christian church. Furthermore, the state legislature was permitted to assume that the display of a cross would be welcomed, or at least respected, by the majority of persons unaffiliated with any of the aforementioned churches; [it could legitimately be assumed that the] cross's symbolic character— representing nondenominational Western values and norms—would be accepted by all. Indeed, the majority of the population approved the Bavarian Constitution's provisions on Christian community schools. . . .

4. The state has a constitutional mandate to remain neutral in religious and ideological matters. But the principle of neutrality must not be construed as indifference toward such matters. The church-state articles of the Weimar Constitution, which have been incorporated into Article 140 of the Basic Law, envision neutrality in the sense of cooperation between the state, churches, and religious communities. These articles [may even require the state] to support churches and religious communities.

In its decisions regarding the constitutional admissibility of Christian community schools, the Federal Constitutional Court, following the constitutional command of neutrality [in religious affairs], declared that the school may exercise only minimal influence in those areas where it is in a position to influence children in matters of faith and conscience. Furthermore, a public school must not be missionary in nature, nor is the school permitted to demand the obligatory acceptance of Christian faith commitments; schools must remain open to influences from other ideological and religious ideas and values (citing 41 BVerfGE 29, 51).

The provisions of section 13 (1.3) of the Bavarian Elementary School Ordinance that the senate struck down as unconstitutional meet every one of these criteria. The mere presence of the cross demands no particular mode of conduct and does not convert the school into a missionary enterprise. Nor does the cross change the character of the Christian community school; rather, as a symbol shared by all Christian faiths, the cross is uniquely suited to illustrate the constitutionally permitted educational subject matter of this type of school. The display of the cross does not exclude consideration of other ideological or religious norms and values. In addition, Article 136 (1) of the Bavarian Constitution requires the schools to respect the religious sensibilities of all persons.

II. Contrary to the view of the senate majority, the display of the cross in school classrooms does not interfere with religious freedom. . . .

The undisturbed *practice* of religion secured by Article 4 (2) reinforces and accentuates the religious freedom that Article 4 (1) guarantees, a fact that the senate majority entirely overlooks. Together these two paragraphs provide the individual with a space in which actively to practice his or her faith. If therefore one cannot object constitutionally to participation in voluntary nondenominational prayer, then surely this holds equally true of the display of the cross in school classrooms. Thus the state provides space for positive freedom of creed in areas for which it has assumed complete responsibility and in which religious and ideological views have traditionally been relevant. . . .

2. Thus there has been no violation of religious freedom.

(a) The complainants have not invoked the freedom to practice their religion under Article 4 (2) of the Basic Law, nor have they claimed that the state has violated their positive freedom of faith under Article 4 (1); they merely assert a violation of their negative freedom of religion, a freedom Article 4 (1) also guarantees. In fact, they do not demand the display of a symbol of their own faith or ideology next to or in place of the cross. Rather, they request the removal of crucifixes, which they perceive to be symbols of a religious doctrine to which they do not adhere. In our ruling of November 5, 1991 . . . which rejected the complainants' request for a temporary injunction, we formulated the constitutional issue—even more pointedly than in the present ruling—as follows: "Under what circumstances does the display of religious symbols in schools implicate the negative right to freedom of religion and to what extent must a minority be expected to tolerate [such a display] in the interest of the majority's right to practice its religion?"

This issue . . . deals with the question of how the positive and negative freedoms of religion of pupils and their parents can be generally reconciled in the public compulsory school arena. To find a solution to the inevitable tension between the negative and positive freedoms of religion is the task of the democratic state legislature; the legislature is required to work out a compromise that honors the various opinions and values present during the formation of the public will. . . . In the process, the negative freedom of religion must not be allowed to negate the positive right to manifest one's religious freedom in the event that the two conflict. The principle of religious liberty implies no right to have religious expression banned altogether. The key principle here is tolerance. This principle requires the reconciliation of opposing views on religious freedom.

(b) Section 13 (3) of the Bavarian Elementary School Ordinance satisfies these principles and requirements. The recommended balancing [that has taken place here] fully complies with the Basic Law.

(aa) In evaluating and assessing the concerns of the parties to this case, the senate majority has mistakenly identified the cross with a Christian theological view. What matters instead is the effect that the sight of the cross has on individual pupils. Admittedly, the Christian pupil may see the cross in the religious light suggested by the majority. The nonbelieving pupil, however, cannot be assumed to share the same view. From his or her point of view, the cross is less a symbol of the Christian faith than of the values reflected in the Christian community school, namely, those values associated with a Western culture deeply rooted in Christian ideas. . . .

(bb) In view of the cross's symbolic character, non-Christian pupils and their parents are obligated to accept its presence in the classroom. The principle of tolerance requires as much, and the display of the cross does not constitute an unacceptable burden [on the religious conscience of non-Christian pupils].

The psychological effect that exposure to the cross has on non-Christian pupils is relatively mild. The mental burden here is minimal, for pupils are not required to behave in a given way or to participate in religious practices before the cross. In contrast to [compulsory] school prayer, pupils are not forced to reveal their ideological or religious convictions through nonparticipation. This precludes any discrimination against them.

In addition, the cross does not imply any kind of missionary activity. As noted above, its [narrow] religious significance has no impact on the course of instruction. Moreover, the particular situation in Bavaria must be considered. Even outside the narrow confines of the church, pupils are exposed daily to the sight of crosses in many areas of life. We need only mention the presence of crosses along roadways, their exhibition on secular buildings (such as hospitals, nursing homes, and even hotels and restaurants), and their display in private homes. Under these circumstances, the presence of the cross in schoolrooms is nothing unusual; it has nothing to do with anything [that could remotely be regarded as] missionary.

Questions and Comments

1. How can the German Crucifix case be distinguished from the school prayer case? Is there less "coercion" in the school prayer case?

The court says that the Basic Law "requires the state to remain neutral in matters of faith and religion." The U.S. Supreme Court has made a similar statement: "Neither a state nor the Federal Government can set up a church. Neither can pass laws which aid one religion, aid all religions, or prefer one religion to another." Everson v. Board of Education, 330 U.S. 1 (1947). *Everson* found constitutional a state law authorizing school districts to reimburse parents for their costs of transporting their children to school on buses, even when the parents were sending their children to Catholic parochial schools.

How can a government that provides support for denominational schools be "neutral in matters of faith and religion"? How can a government that provides support for non-denominational schools but not for denominational ones be "neutral"? Does a government that permits denominational schools to meet requirements for education of children depart from concepts of neutrality? Would a government that prohibits denominational schools from fulfilling such requirements also depart from neutrality? Cf. Pierce v. Society of Sisters, 268 U.S. 510 (1925) (holding unconstitutional a state law that would have prevented parents from sending their children to nonpublic denominational schools). The concept of neutrality requires that we identify some baseline from which we can identify non-neutral departures. But can we set a baseline in a neutral way?

2. Stone v. Graham, 449 U.S. 39 (1980), held unconstitutional a state statute requiring the posting of the Ten Commandments in public school classrooms. The Court found that this requirement had "no secular legislative purpose.... [I]f the posted copies [are] to have any effect at all, it will be to induce the school children to read, meditate upon, perhaps to venerate and obey, the Commandments." Justice Rehnquist dissented, saying that the statute's purpose was secular because the Commandments "have had a significant secular impact on the development of secular legal codes of the Western World." Litigation has recently occurred in lower federal courts in different circuits involving challenges to the display of the Ten Commandments in public courthouses and courtrooms. See Chapter IX, above at note a.

3. Note the dissenters' emphasis on federalism. What are the special circumstances in Bavaria on which the dissenters rely? Are they sufficient to overcome what the majority describes as the fundamental rights of all Germans?

4. Note the dissenters' discussion of the psychological impact of the display of crucifixes on Christians and non-Christians. What evidence do you think judges should have to support such discussions? In Brown v. Board of Education, 347 U.S. 483 (1954), the Supreme Court said, "To separate [children in elementary and secondary schools] from others of similar age and qualifications solely because of their race generates a feeling of inferiority as to their status in the community that may affect their hearts and minds in a way unlikely ever to be undone." It quoted the lower court's finding that "[s]egregation with the sanction of law ... has a tendency to [retard] the educational and mental development of [N]egro children," and then said, "[T]his finding is amply supported by modern authority." The accompanying footnote 11 cited several studies by social psychologists summarizing their conclusions.

5. The German crucifix decision was highly controversial. The Bavarian state government responded to the decision by developing legislation that would require removal of crucifixes if an objector gave "sufficiently valid" reasons for the objection. One objector stated, "I told the school that a religious symbol has no place in a classroom, especially if it represents a church that is antidemocratic in nature and practices sex discrimination by refusing equal rights to women, such as the opportunity to become priests." He also said that "the Church has no place in school because the Catholic hierarchy appeared to be anti-science in the way it once treated Galileo." School authorities rejected these objections as "too polemical and not sufficiently personal." They defended their decision by saying, "This is not just a question of religion. It's all about cultural traditions going back more than a thousand years, and the crucifix is one of our most cherished historical symbols.... [I]n a peaceful democracy, the minority must consent to go along with the majority view." (Quotations are taken from William Drozdiak, "Crucifix in Classroom Sparks German Debate," *Washington Post*, Aug. 17, 1997, p. A17.)

The U.S. school prayer decisions were also controversial. Particularly in rural school districts, various prayer practices continued after the Supreme Court's decisions. For an early study, see William Muir, Prayer in the Public Schools: Law and Attitude Change (1967). Among the efforts to continue some form of religious practice in the public schools have been courses in "The Bible as Literature" and, more controversially, "The Bible as History," and student-organized prayer sessions, sometimes announced over school public announcement systems. The federal Equal Access Act of 1984 requires that any public school receiving federal financial assistance that allows noncurriculum-related student groups to meet on campus outside regular school hours cannot deny access to other student groups based on the religious, political, or philosophical content of their speech. The U.S. Supreme Court upheld the Act in Board of Education v. Mergens, 496 U.S. 226 (1990).

Does the degree of resistance to the school prayer and Bavarian crucifix decisions signal that they were mistaken because they were too far out of line with public belief? Because they invoked a notion of neutrality that cannot be implemented in a way that the public viewed as fair? Is the degree of resistance different in kind—and is it more or less justifiable—than resistance to other controversial constitutional decisions?

6. According to Donald Kommers, the *Crucifix* and other controversial decisions "have tarnished the court's reputation in the eyes of many Germans and raised questions ... about the legitimacy of judicial review...." Kommers points out that such reactions are "not uncommon in the United States," but were previously "a rare occurrence in Germany." Donald Kommers, The Constitutional Jurisprudence of the Federal Republic of Germany xiv (2d ed. 1997).

Responding to the controversy in Germany over the Bavarian Crucifix decision, Justice Dieter Grimm, one of the judges in the majority, wrote a letter published in the nation's leading newspaper. As translated by Kommers (2d ed. at 483–84), the letter reads:

> In a system that sets forth its political social order in a constitution and establishes a constitutional court to protect that document, political and social conflicts are bound to arise in the form of constitutional disputes. Unlike the political arena, the court is unable to sidestep such disputes by refusing to decide them. It has to decide the conflicts, yet not on its own initiative and according to the justices' individual preferences or the supposed wishes of a popular majority, but according to the preestablished provisions of the Basic Law. Not everyone will be satisfied with the court's decision, but that is in the nature of the judicial resolution of conflicts; and, at times the majority will be the disappointed party. This is what constitutionalism is all

about; its purpose is to safeguard the rights of minorities against encroachment by the majority.

Under these circumstances constitutional Court decisions cannot always be greeted with universal approval. Criticism of such decisions is normal and in the interest of the court's own reflections about its role as the final arbiter of the Constitution; indeed, such criticism is necessary. Disagreement with a decision, however, does not relieve the critic of the duty to comply with it. This is the basic premise of the entire system of constitutional governance. The process of decision making must be established in a way that gives room to the different viewpoints. The result of the process is valid notwithstanding one's disagreement with it. If in the light of the *Crucifix* case, state or church officials create the impression that this is not so, they threaten to disrupt the Federal Republic's generally stable history of postwar constitutional governance and are likely to shake the foundations of social peace.

Those who insist on disobeying the court's decision or encouraging resistance to it act on the maxim that the law is to be respected only if we agree with it. At risk here is nothing less than the unitary force of the law. This binding force constitutes the foundation of the rule of law and political order, at least within the constitutional state. Anyone who encourages others to defy a judicial ruling today because he or she fails to approve of it will be unable to explain tomorrow why others should obey laws or administrative orders of which they disapprove. If politicians continue on their chosen path, they will not only undermine the foundation of the constitutional state, they will also make it impossible to conduct their own affairs [of state]. This is meanwhile the issue of the Federal Constitutional Court's crucifix ruling.

In light of the processes by which the judges on Germany's Constitutional Court are chosen, the centralization of judicial review, and other aspects of German constitutionalism, do you think it was appropriate for a judge to respond to public criticism in this manner?

7. Can the preceding problems be understood as presenting conflicts between a majority's view about what or how religion ought to be presented in public schools, and a constitutional commitment—originating perhaps in some other majority's view—to some degree of separation between government and religion? Consider whether they might be understood as conflicts *within* a majority, over the proper relation between religion and government. In this connection, recall the discussion in Jacobsohn, ch. VII above, of the efforts in Israel to work out a national understanding of the sense in which Israel is a Jewish state. To what extent is federalism an adequate response to these controversies? Note that the principal material presented here comes from Germany and the United States, both with reasonably robust federal systems.

8. Sometimes, although not universally, governments respond to challenges to their religious practices by insisting that they are non-denominational. The actions, the governments assert, may favor religion in general, but do not favor any particular religion over another. In reading the material that follows, consider whether the practices are in fact nondenominational, and if so whether they respect or water down the population's religious beliefs.

2. OTHER PUBLIC ENDORSEMENT OF (ARGUABLY) RELIGIOUS PRACTICES: JAPAN AND THE UNITED STATES

a. Japan

To understand the Japanese constitutional case included below, some knowledge of the history of Shinto in Japan is helpful. The following account draws heavily from David M. O'Brien, To Dream of Dreams: Religious Freedom and Constitutional Politics in Postwar Japan 16–25, 32–62 (1996).

Shinto developed as an indigenous, Japanese religion or set of folkways, described as a "religion of Japaneseness" that lacks a founder or an organized theology. Shinto includes a range of folk rituals relating to worship of many "kami", or gods, found everywhere in nature, and rituals performed at shrines devoted to the honoring of ancestors, forces of nature, and particular skills or crafts. According to O'Brien, "[t]hrough purification rituals, according to Shinto tradition, the body and soul are cleansed and connections with the kami are magically restored in an aesthetic sense, not a moral or metaphysical one." In the view of some, Shinto is not an organized religion but a loose conglomeration of cults and attitudes.

Buddhism was introduced to Japan from China and Korea in the 6th century A.D., after Shinto had developed as the indigenous tradition. O'Brien describes Buddhism in Japan as both reinforcing "traditional Shinto customs governing the worship of ancestral deities" and as being itself "transformed by Shinto's preoccupation with this-worldliness," resulting in a "pragmatic overlay and interweaving of Shinto and Buddhism." He reports that in the early 1980s, 60% of households in Japan had Shinto "kami shelfs" honoring ancestors as deities, and another 61% had Buddhist alters memorializing family ancestors; 45% of households had both and only 24% had neither. Public opinion polls indicate that while 51% indicated that they believed in God or Buddha, 71% went to a shrine or temple on New Year's to pray; 31% explained this practice as a matter of custom.

Shinto had various relationships to the governments of Japan over time. One of the conditions imposed by the Allies for Japanese reconstruction after World War II was that the Emperor's divinity be disavowed, thus ending a relatively brief period of the state's relationship to Shinto known as the "emperor system." During this period, school children's participation in Shinto ceremonies at shrines for war dead was mandatory; Shinto rituals were invoked to instruct students that "dying for their country and the emperor would result in deification." During the earlier

Tokugawa period of Japan's isolation (roughly 1603–1868) power was wielded mostly by shoguns (governing in the name of the Emperor) who practiced Buddhism. Shinto and its shrines remained alive as folkways but Buddhism dominated as an organized religion. Near the end of this period and at the beginning of the Meiji Restoration, a movement to "purify" or emphasize Shinto, to separate it from Buddhism and other foreign influences, occurred. Central features of the Meiji reforms were separation of Shinto from Buddhism, and the emphasis on a unity between Shinto and the State embodied in the Emperor. Shinto priests replaced Buddhists priests as those responsible for registering births, deaths and marriages. Government support for Buddhism ended, and Shinto received state support; yet Shinto practices remained highly decentralized, tied in to small communities with local kamis and with rituals and shrines integrated into every day life. From about 1928 until the end of World War II, other religions were suppressed, and compliance with "state shinto" became mandatory (and closely associated with rising tolls of war dead).

One of the principal efforts of the Allied Occupation was to dismantle State Shinto, which, General MacArthur was convinced, reinforced Japanese militarism. The General Headquarters staff of the Supreme Commander for Allied Forces (SCAP) in 1945 issued a "Shinto Directive," designed to "separate religion from the state, to prevent the misuse of religion for political ends, and to put all religions, faiths and creeds upon exactly the same legal basis" and forbidding "affiliation with the government and the propagation and dissemination of militaristic and ultra nationalist ideology not only to Shinto but to the followers of all religions, faiths, sects, creeds or philosophies." The four page directive prohibited all public financial support for Shinto shrines. According to O'Brien, interpretation and application of this directive was a point of some contention between Japanese constitution-drafters and the SCAP offices, which ended up rejecting a Japanese draft of religious freedom clauses and insisting on Japanese acceptance of SCAP-drafted provisions.[a]

Selected provisions of Japan's Constitution

Article 20 of the Japanese Constitution provides

"[1] Freedom of religion is guaranteed to all. No religious organization shall receive any privileges from the State, nor exercise any political authority.

"[2] No person shall be compelled to take part in any religious act, celebration, rite or practice."

a. Notwithstanding these provisions, Class A war criminals are buried in the national shrine for the war dead in Tokyo, a shrine regularly visited by government ministers, which, according to Professor James Feinerman, is a major irritant in Japan's relations with other Asian nations.

"[3] The State and its organs shall refrain from religious education or any other religious activity."

Article 89 states, "No public money or other property shall be expended or appropriated for the use, benefit or maintenance of any religious institution or association, or for any charitable, education or benevolent enterprises not under the control of public authority."

Kakunaga v. Sekiguchi

31 Minshū 4 at p. 533 (1977) (Supreme Court of Japan, Grand Bench)

[Excerpted from Lawrence W. Beer and Hiroshi Itoh, The Constitutional Case Law of Japan, 1970 through 1990 (1996)]

[Tsu City held a Shinto groundbreaking ceremony conducted by four Shinto priests, for a city gymnasium. Two tents were erected, one for an altar and one for spectators. Each spectator performed a Shinto purification ritual aided by one of the priests. The ceremony started at 10 AM, and included rituals and prayers for the project's safe construction; it ended forty minutes later. The city appropriated funds as stipends for the priests and to cover the ritual's expenses. The plaintiff was a city assemblyman who attended the ceremony at the mayor's invitation, and then sued for return of the funds spent on the program, and for damages for mental suffering caused by his attendance.]

[Students may want to glance first at the dissenting opinions in the case that follows, which provide more background material. Bracketed insertions below are by Professors Beer and Itoh.]

* * *

This Court's Judgment is as follows. . . .

A.   The Constitutional Principle of Separation of Religion and the State.

Generally, the principle of separation of religion and the State has been understood to mean that problems of religion and belief have been considered matters of individual conscience that transcend the dimension of politics and are separated from the State, which, as the holder of secular authority, is not to interfere with religion. The relationship between religion and the State has differed in various countries in response to various historical and social conditions. Previously in Japan, Article 28 of the *Meiji* Constitution (1889) ostensibly guaranteed the freedom of religion, but actually restricted freedom of worship unless "(it was) not prejudicial to peace and order, and not antagonistic to the people's duties as subjects." Moreover, State *Shinto* was virtually established as the national religion, with belief therein made compulsory; other religious groups were subject to severe persecution.

[The Court then noted that … Article 20 of the Constitution, promulgated on November 3, 1946, provides unconditionally for freedom of worship and established the principle of separation of religion and the State.]

Our country, unlike Christian or Moslem countries, has been living basically with religions developing one on top of the other and coming [over time] to co-exist. In these circumstances, an unconditional guarantee of religious freedom alone has not been enough to guarantee fully the freedom of worship. So as to eliminate all ties between the State and religion, it has also been necessary to enact rules providing for the separation of religion and the State. Thus, the Constitution can be interpreted as striving for a secular and religiously neutral State by taking as its ideal the total separation of religion and the State.

The separation of religion and the State, however, is only a systematic and indirect guarantee of religious freedom. It does not directly guarantee freedom of religion *per se*, it attempts to guarantee it indirectly by securing a system that separates religion and the State. On the other hand, the phenomenon of religion does not end with the phenomenon of individual belief; religion also has a multifaceted social side that brings it into contact with many aspects of social life including education, culture, social welfare, and folk customs. As a natural result of this contact, connections with the State become unavoidable as the State regulates social life or implements various policies to promote or subsidize education, social welfare, or culture. Thus, an actual system of government that attempts a total separation of religion and the State is virtually impossible.

Furthermore, to attempt total separation would inevitably lead to anomalous situations such as, for example, questioning the propriety of extending to religiously affiliated schools the financial assistance given to private schools in general, and of the assistance provided for the maintenance of architectural or artistic treasures owned by religious groups. Ironically, to deny such subsidies would impose a disadvantage on these entities simply because of their religious nature and would inevitably result in invidious discrimination because of religion. Similarly, in prisons, a policy of forbidding all religious activity would result in a severe deprivation of inmates' religious freedom. Thus, from these examples, it follows that there are inevitable and natural limits to the separation of religion and the State. A State must, according to its own societal and cultural characteristics, accept some degree of actual relationship with religion, and what remains open to question is the extent to which such a relationship will be tolerated. From this perspective, the principle as enunciated in the Constitution demands the neutrality of the State, but does not prohibit all connection with religion. Rather, it should be interpreted as prohibiting conduct which leads to collusion between the State and a religion only when such activity exceeds reasonable bounds as determined with reference to the conduct's purpose and effects.

B.   Religious Activity Prohibited by Article 20, Paragraph 3.

Article 20, paragraph 3 of the Constitution provides that "The State and its organs shall refrain from religious education or any other religious activity." If this language is interpreted in the light of the above discussion on separation of religion and the State, it should not be taken to prohibit all contact with religion, but rather that which exceeds reasonable limits and which has as its purpose some religious meaning, or the effect of which is to promote, subsidize, or, conversely, to interfere with or oppose religion. The prime example is religious education which is explicitly prohibited in Article 20, paragraph 3, as are missionary work, proselytizing, propaganda, and so forth. Other religious activities like celebrations, rites, and functions which purport to propagate or suppress any religion are also proscribed, and should be viewed from the standpoint of their purpose and effect to determine if they too are prohibited. In determining whether or not a given religious act constitutes proscribed "religious activity", the external aspects of the conduct, whether the procedure is set by religion, and so on, should not be the only factors considered. The place of the conduct, the average person's reaction to it, the actor's purpose in holding the ceremony, the existence and extent of religious significance, and the effect on the average person, are all circumstances that should be considered to reach an objective judgment based on socially accepted ideas.

Furthermore, if one thinks of the relationships between paragraphs 2 and 3 of Article 20, both are provisions for religious freedom in its broad sense, but paragraph 2 means that no one can be compelled to participate in religious activity against his will. It therefore guarantees directly freedom of religion in the narrow sense as well; i.e., against deprivation of that freedom by the majority religion. Paragraph 3, on the other hand, directly prohibits a certain area of activity by the State and establishes a system of separation while only indirectly guaranteeing freedom of religion.... Not all of the activities forbidden in Article 20, paragraph 2 are necessarily included in Article 20, paragraph 3. Even ceremonies and rituals that are religious in nature but would not be forbidden under paragraph 3 could be found violative of paragraph 2 if the State violated by coercion the freedom of worship of those who chose not to take part in activities they might consider alien to their religious beliefs. For that reason, the above interpretation of prohibited activities under Article 20, paragraph 3 does not immediately lead to fears for the freedom of belief of religious minorities.

C.   The Nature of the Groundbreaking Ceremony in This Case.

From this perspective, let us determine whether the groundbreaking ceremony in this case constitutes a religious activity as proscribed in Article 20, paragraph 3 of the Constitution.

It is clear from the trial court that the groundbreaking was a ceremony to pray for a stable foundation and accident-free construction. The form of the ceremony was religious. A professional *Shinto* priest in religious robes and following specific *Shinto* rituals prepared a particular place for the ceremony and used particular ceremonial equipment. Moreover, the priest who performed the service did so, one can assume, out of religious conviction and belief. This was undoubtedly a ceremony of religious nature.

However, although it is true that a *Shinto* groundbreaking ceremony has its origin in a religious ceremony intended to pacify the earth god (*tochi no kami*), and thereby to ensure a firm foundation for the building and safe construction, there can be no doubt that this religious significance has weakened gradually over time. Even though a present-day groundbreaking ceremony might feature some prayer-like behavior, generally these affairs have become nothing more than ritual formalities in the construction industry almost completely devoid of religious significance. Most people would evaluate the ceremony, even when conducted in accord with established religious practice, as a secularized ritual without religious meaning. The groundbreaking in the case was conducted as a *Shinto* religious ceremony, but for most citizens and the mayor of Tsu City and others involved in sponsoring the groundbreaking, this was a secular event inasmuch as the function in question was no different from the standard ritual practiced over many years.

Furthermore, it is general practice today in the construction industry for the contractor to sponsor and attend a ceremony like the one in this case; those involved in the building, moreover, regard the ritual as indispensable for safety. Taking industry custom and public consciousness into account, the motive of the contractor in holding this ceremony is merely an extremely secular response to the demands for a customary groundbreaking ceremony from those involved in the building process. It is reasonable to assume that the motive of the mayor of Tsu City, the sponsor of the ceremony in question, was no different from that of those contractors who seek to ensure the safety of the building.

It is not unreasonable to say that the average Japanese has little interest in and consciousness of religion. Many people are believers in *Shinto* as members of the community and in Buddhism as individuals. Their religious consciousness is somewhat jumbled, and they feel no sense of contradiction even while using different religions on different occasions. Furthermore, one of the salient characteristics of *Shinto* is its close attention to ceremonial form and its converse lack of interest in external activities such as the proselytizing seen in other religions. With these factors in mind, it is unlikely that a *Shinto* groundbreaking, even when performed by a *Shinto* priest, would raise the religious consciousness of those attending or of people in general or lead in any way to the encouragement or promotion of *Shinto*. So the State in performing such a ceremony stands in the same position as a private citizen doing so. It is absolutely inconceivable that such a practice threatens to lead to the development of a special relationship between the State and *Shinto*, or the reestablishment of *Shinto* as a State religion, or to the loss of religious freedom.

Considering all the factors discussed above, we reach the following judgment. While it is incontrovertible that the groundbreaking in the present case is connected with religion, the purpose of conducting the ceremony was to ensure a stable foundation and safe construction. It was thus chiefly secular. It will not have the effect of promoting or encouraging *Shinto* or of oppressing or interfering with other religions. It therefore should not be considered as falling within the category of religious activities prohibited by Article 20, paragraph 3. [The concluding portion reversing the high court holding is omitted.] . . .

. . .

The dissenting opinion of JUSTICES YUTAKA YOSHIDA, SHIGEMITSU DANDO, TAKAAKI HATTORI, SHOICHI TAMAKI, and EKIZO FUJIBAYASHI is as follows:

1.   The Constitutional Principle of Separation of Religion and the State.

Freedom of religion is the origin of the spiritual freedom of modern mankind. As such, it is universally guaranteed as the fundamental principle of the life of the spirit. In Japan too, the Constitution attempts to guarantee religious freedom fully. Along with the first section of Article 20, paragraph 1, which provides an unconditional guarantee of religious freedom for all, the second section of paragraph 1 prohibits the granting of any special privileges to or the exercise of any political authority by religious groups. Paragraph 2 prohibits compulsory participation in religious activities; paragraph 3 prohibits the State or its organs from engaging in religious activity; and Article 89 prohibits any financial aid to religious groups or organizations.

The declaration of unconditional religious freedom in itself is insufficient to guarantee freedom of belief. To accomplish that, the elimination of all ties between the State and religion is absolutely essential in that, in the long run, any connection between religion and State will most likely result either in religious influence over the State or, conversely, the interference in or suppression of religious freedom by the State. The history of Japan since the *Meiji* Restoration (1868) gives ample evidence of the potential for collusion between religion and the State and the latter's deprivation of the freedom of belief.

In the first year of the *Meiji* regime (1868), the new government proclaimed the unity of religion and the State. *Shinto* priests were reinstated, and all the shrines and priests in Japan were put under government control, thus suggesting the subsequent establishment of *Shinto* as a State religion. The separation of *Shinto* and Buddhism was ordered. Moreover, the authorities launched a campaign for the purification and independence of *Shinto* and simultaneously attacked Buddhism. Meanwhile, the Tokuugawa policy [of unmitigated intolerance] toward Christianity was essentially maintained and suppression continued.

[The Justices then detailed the process by which the government took total control of the *Shinto* religion by nationalizing its shrines, making its priests public officials, separating it from Buddhism and giving it special privileges, and in many ways turning Japan into a theocracy. They then described the limited freedom of religion under Article 29 of the *Meiji* Constitution and pointed out that, despite the legal equality accorded to all religions, State Shintoism had actually been established as the national religion and all citizens were expected to conform to *Shinto* religious practice as a civil duty. The dissenting judges then described the arrangements that made *Shinto* shrines financially dependent on either the State or local administrative bodies. This was also a period of persecution of other religions. Eventually, all religions were forced to accept the basic concept of *kokutai*, the fundamental nationalist ideology of State Shintoism, or forfeit their status as officially sanctioned religions. The abolition of these institutional arrangements by the Allied Occupation in 1945 and the inclusion in the new Constitution of the separation of religion and State are then described.]

Reviewing the above history, a correct interpretation of the principle of separation of religion and the State embodied in Article 20, paragraphs 1 and 3 and Article 89 would require absolute separation, that is, that religion and the State should be mutually independent with no connecting ties and that the State should allow no interference by religion in its affairs and conversely no interference in religious affairs.

The majority opinion claims that religion-State separation is merely an ideal, impossible of actual realization. It argues that attempting a perfect separation will lead to anomalous social results and that the principle is best understood as requiring only the neutrality of the State since some connection with religion is inevitable. The question of what contact should be permissible would be decided by reference to a reasonableness standard based on Japanese social and cultural conditions. The problem with this approach, however, is not only that the meaning of religion-State contact in the majority opinion is ambiguous, but it is also unclear when such contact would exceed reasonable limits. The majority's interpretation of the separation principle makes it easy to allow ties between religion and the State and, in our opinion, raises the fear that the guarantee of religious freedom itself will be weakened. Furthermore, from our perspective of an absolute separation of the State and religion, the majority's contention that an attempt at complete separation would inevitably lead to social anomalies is unfounded, insofar as the majority's examples of such social "anomalies" resulting from permissible religion-State ties are perfectly reasonable when interpreted from the standpoint of equality and other constitutional principles.

2. Religious Activity Prohibited by Article 20, Paragraph 3 of the Constitution.

Given the significance of the separation of religion and the State described above, the definition of prohibited religious activity in Article 20, paragraph 3 should not be limited to the propagation of religious doctrine or the cultivation of converts, as the majority contends. It should include as a matter of course the sponsoring of religious ceremonies, functions, and festivals. Such activities are the expression of religious belief. A public entity undertaking to sponsor such activities is fundamentally at odds with the religious neutrality of the State. One should not, as the majority would require, look to the concrete effects of the activity. This does not mean, however, that there will not be instances where the State may undertake religious activities, because to fail to do so would violate citizens' religious freedom or the guarantee of equality before the law.

Even given the above interpretation, it is true that Article 20, paragraph 3 would not prohibit the performance of a ceremony or event originally religious in nature but that had completely lost its religious significance and had become a purely secular convention. However, custom or convention that retains its religious nature, that is, a religious custom or convention, should naturally be included in a definition of prohibited religious activity. (Further, whether an event is a secular custom is to be determined by the interpretation of the foregoing provisions, not by testing whether the event in question meets certain ethnological requirements).

3.   The Nature of the Groundbreaking in this Case.

Based on the above interpretation we now turn to whether the groundbreaking in this case was prohibited religious activity....

It is clear from the above that this groundbreaking was a religious ceremony performed by a *Shinto* priest according to distinctively *Shinto* rituals. It is true that such ceremonies have been performed for many years and have become secularized over time, but this groundbreaking was profoundly religious in atmosphere. It is inconceivable that it could be considered non-religious. Furthermore, even if we look to the concrete effect of the ceremony as the majority did, it is obvious that Tsu City's sponsorship of this ceremony constitutes special treatment and the subsidization of *Shinto*. It also invites the prospect of the establishment of a close tie between Tsu City and the *Shinto* religion. The majority admitted the religious connection but treated its significance lightly and considered its effects trivial. We simply cannot in any sense agree with this appraisal. From our point of view, this groundbreaking clearly constitutes religious activity as prohibited by Article 20, paragraph 3. Moreover, there are absolutely no grounds for allowing such activity in this case. The groundbreaking, therefore, violates Article 20, paragraph 3 of the Constitution and should not be allowed . . .

* * *

The supplementary dissenting opinion of CHIEF JUSTICE EKIZO FUJIBAYASHI is as follows.

1.   The State and Religion

The freedom of religion is a great principle of contemporary democratic States. This [principle] represents a crystallization of the victorious spirit of tolerance emerging from centuries of political and intellectual conflict. The principle of separation of religion and the State has come to be considered the indispensable presupposition in the historical process of confirming freedom of religion. It includes the following two principal points.

a.   The State does not bestow special financial or institutional support and does not impose any special restrictions on any religion. In other words, the State should adopt an equally neutral attitude towards all religions.

b.   The State should not intrude at all upon the religious beliefs of the individual person. Religious belief should be left to the freedom of each individual. It is a private matter for each citizen whether or not to believe in a religion, and if one believes, what sort of religion to choose.

With the confirmation of these principles, the conjoining of the State with a specific religion is negated. It is understood that the state should concern itself only with secular matters, but with that problems between the State and religion are not completely eliminated. Since all States have a spiritual or conceptual foundation for their existence, and since religions are also a product of the human spirit, at the same time that the State recognizes the principle of religious freedom, the State itself must not be uninterested or insensible towards religion. The principle of freedom of belief must not be marked by State indifference to religion, but on the contrary must result in respect for religion.

The existence of the State must be based on truth, and the truth must be protected. However, it is not the State which decides what the truth is, nor is it the people. Even in the age of democracy, no one would consider the truth something to be determined by a majority vote of the people. That which determines what the truth is is the truth itself, what has been proven true with the passage of history, in other words, in the course of the long experience of humankind. Truth is its own proof. However, that truth is not confirmed simply by an assertion that it is true. Only with the passage of history does something become confirmed [as true] for humankind. Even regarding religion, we must say that the truth is its own proof. Consequently, religious truth is something which can stand and should stand without the support of the State or other secular power. That independence of religion itself should be respected.

2.   The Democratization of Religion

The so-called "*Shinto* Directive" of the General Headquarters of SCAP [during the Allied Occupation] concerning State *Shinto* and shrine *Shinto* included three points, and these became the foundation for Article 20 of the Constitution.

a.   Shrines are recognized as religious in nature. This does not mean there was no room for doubt about whether these [shrines] fit perfectly with the national sentiments of the Japanese people. As a religion, the shrines have a very limited thought system, and at many points express simple folk feelings about life. However, the acts of *Shinto* priests and the annual functions of the shrines include matters recognized as religious functions, and these are the problem in the present case.

b.   Besides recognizing shrine *Shinto* as a religion, [the Directive] ordered that administrative and financial protection of shrines by the State be abolished in keeping with the principle of separation of religion and the State.

c. It was understood that the people were free to believe in shrine *Shinto*, thus separated from the State, as a religion.

In constructing a new Japan after the *Meiji* Restoration (1868), the government imported institutions and culture from the West, but for a spiritual foundation they relied on the way of the gods of ancient Japan; in this limping condition, they opened up Japan's modernization movement. In this way, while recognizing in fact shrine *Shinto* as in the position of the State religion, to avoid conflict with the principle of freedom of religion in dealing with international and domestic circumstances, [the government] handed down the interpretation that shrine *Shinto* was not a religion. After that, Japan's politics and education were conducted according to that line. Without asking what religion an individual believed in, it became the custom for newly appointed State Ministers to worship at the Ise Shrine, and local officials were ordered to worship as Imperial *Shinto* messengers at the major festivals of official national shrines.

School students led by teachers worshipped at shrines as a group, and local citizens, as people under the protection of the shrine [gods], were required to make contributions to pay for ceremonies. For the following reasons, these functions were generally conducted peacefully as customs.

a. The religious nature of shrines was uncomplicated. In shrine *Shinto* there is no organizational theology, and the sense of deity is very elemental. There is virtually no element of the supernatural or miraculous. As a rule, all is nature and the human. Thus, with the simplicity of the religious nature of shrine *Shinto*, shrine worship was easily received by the general populace as something not in conflict with the principle of freedom of religion.

b. In historical fact, Japanese Buddhism had few struggles and conflicts with shrine *Shinto*, regarding both theory and practice; they cooperated and flowed together and came to coexist side by side. In other words, regarding Japan's gods the sutras of Buddhism were chanted, and it was theorized that the various Buddhas of Buddhism and the gods of Japan coexisted in harmony and unity. Within some Buddhist temples (grounds), prayers were offered at protective shrines. In great part, the Japanese people are at the same time believers in Buddhism and followers of shrine *Shinto*. Put otherwise, as individuals they believe in Buddhism and as a people they offer prayers at *Shinto* shrines, and without agonizing about it, they have come to enjoy a peaceful life. This was because of policies (adopted) when propagating Buddhism and, on the other hand, as already noted, because of the simple nature of shrine *Shinto* as a religion. In any case, over the past thousand years, this dual life of Buddhism and shrine *Shinto* has been carried on.

c. The religious consciousness of the Japanese people nurtured in the past by shrine *Shinto* and Buddhism was not sufficiently sensitive with respect to freedom of religion. However, both shrine *Shinto* and Buddhism are polytheistic and pantheistic, not monotheistic like Christianity with its personal God. They did not stimulate (awareness of) the concept of the individual person and further the development of the conception of fundamental human rights. Consequently, there was also little awareness of the importance of freedom of religion. These factors are a major reason why the issue of *Shinto* shrine visits [by officials] has not been taken to be important as touching upon the principles of freedom of religion.

3.   Religious Activities Prohibited under Article 20, Paragraph 3 of the Constitution

The First Amendment of the United States Constitution is considered the greatest influence on the establishment of Article 20, paragraph 3, proclaiming the principles of religious freedom and separation of religion and the State. . . .

Paragraph 3 provides, "The State and its organs shall refrain from religious education or any other religious activity." When one considers the significance of the principle of separation of religion and the State as the natural guiding standard for interpreting that (provision), then the provision should be interpreted as forbidding the State and its organs from engaging in any act which has religious significance, not just positive activities with a religious purpose such as propagation, dissemination of material about religion and the nurturing and education of believers, but also such (acts) as religious festivals, ceremonies and processions. The substantive reasons for broadly construing the meaning of religious activities are as follows.

It is said that perhaps no people known in history has been without a religion. Of course the meaning of "religion" in theology and the study of religious history should not always be taken to be the same as that in the study of law. Concerning religion, theologians, philosophers and those in scientific religious studies have for long presented various definitions of religion, and their diversity is such that there are said to be as many definitions as there are scholars. For that reason, it can be thought natural that in our country no definition of religion is presented anywhere in the laws. In the United States Constitution as well, not only can be found no definitions of the words religious and religion, but the American Supreme Court when dealing with every sort of religion and religion-like (phenomenon) does not define the terms religion and religious. When asking what these words mean, they are satisfied with saying the First Amendment means that the government must not be prohibited from actions "which interfere with acts destructive of good moral order or in opposition to duties to society." In other words, since laws are made to control acts, laws cannot interfere with religious views and beliefs but can control religious activities. . . .

In our Constitution as well, the words religion and religious should be interpreted as broadly as possible. When these terms are given strict definition or narrow interpretation, then Article 20 guarantees do not extend to other acts of religion or of a religious type outside their [purview]; and this not only results in a marked limitation on the freedom of religion but also, on the other hand, opens the way to allowing a tight bond between the State and a religion.

4.   The Nature of the Groundbreaking Ceremony at Issue

The majority opinion recognizes that the groundbreaking ceremony is a ceremony to ask for safety without incident during construction and even that it includes acts of "praying." (They hold that) its meaning these days to the general public and the sponsors is that it is considered a customary function as a matter of the etiquette surrounding construction. In its origins, of course, it developed as a religious matter; but today it is not unreasonable to recognize it as among those functions which have no religious significance .... These days it is performed for good luck. It is enough to understand it as similar to the Girls' Doll Festival or Christmas trees, as ways parents bring pleasure to the home for children .... Nowadays we may say that such matters do not have religious significance. However, as in the circumstances recognized by the court below, as with the groundbreaking ceremony, can we say it is nothing more than a pleasantry? As the majority opinion also recognizes, the performance of a groundbreaking involving a ceremony as in the present case is understood to be an indispensable event, especially for the construction people who pray for a safe building (process). Whatever the will of the sponsors may be, [the function] takes place in response to the request of people related to the construction to assure the smooth progress of the construction.

The ceremony carried out in this case cannot possibly be considered to be intended as the traditional feast after a groundbreaking ceremony. Here, something exists which cannot be understood as only a habitual practice. If the only consideration was what was necessary for safe and trouble-free construction, then as long as there was adequate supervision based on present advanced construction technology, scientifically, there was nothing more to add. However, since they sought something beyond human powers in relations to construction safety, it come to relying on something there beyond human works. If we do not call this religious, then what should we call religious? Even though the mayor of Tsu City who sponsored the groundbreaking ceremony in this case does not believe in a religion, since the groundbreaking ceremony at issue was performed as something essential for the construction people seeking something beyond human powers, it did not lose its [character] as a religious function. When a child who is the chief mourner and who sponsors a religious funeral for a parent is without religious sentiment, that does not change the fact that it is a religious function. It is the same thing with this case.

In the present case ... as the court below recognized [the ceremonies involved] were central expressions for shrine *Shinto* and were what has the greatest significance for shrine *Shinto*. This is strongly argued by all *Shinto* scholars .... [These] were religious acts of the highest order.

5.   The Human Rights of Those in Minority Religions

The majority opinion is that even if these [ceremonies were religious]... to specialized religious persons, they are not something that particularly heightens the religious interest of those in attendance and the general public. Since shrine *Shinto* is said to be weak in educative power, that becomes the argument. But even if that is so, it is also a fact that there are people who feel excluded at such ceremonies. From the start, an individual or a private legal person is free to conduct a groundbreaking ceremony according to shrine *Shinto* or some other religion. This is precisely what freedom of religion is about; but the groundbreaking ceremony in this case took place under the sponsorship of a local public entity, and this must not be taken lightly. That is, when there exists in the background of a particular religion support in the way of the authority, prestige and financial resources of the State or a local public entity, this gives rise to strong indirect pressure on those of minority religions to submit to the religion which has received public recognition.

Even if the necessary costs of the ceremony are modest, and even if the general citizenry is not forced to participate, that is not the issue. (At the ceremony in this case, 150 local influentials and others were in attendance as guests, those responsible for the construction were present, Tsu City employees were involved, and the public funds expended came to 174,000 yen, including 7,663 yen for the ceremony, which became the target of the petition of the appellees.)

When all is said and done, the State and local public entities should withdraw from such circumstances. Even if it is seen as an opinion based on hypersensitive feelings on the part of minorities, [this ceremony] was an impermissible violation by majority decision of their freedoms of conscience and religion. It is there in the existence of the human rights to freedoms of the spirit that [we find] the ultimate minimum which must be protected as indispensable for the maintenance of democracy . . . [Jefferson is quoted on freedom of belief.]

The State and local public entities should avoid circumstances related to conscience and belief such as give rise to social conflicts and confrontations in public sentiment. Here lies the significance of the principle of separation of religion and the State. . . .

Ekizo Fujibayashi (presiding) Masao Okahara, Buichi Amano, Yasuo Kishigami, Kiyo Eriguchi, Kiichiro Otsuka, Masami Takatsuji, Yutaka Yoshida, Shigemitsu Dando, Yuzuru Motobayashi, Takaaki Hattori, Shoichi Tamaki, and Kazuo Kurimoto.

(Translated by Frank K. Upham. Chief Justice Fujibayashi's opinion translated by Lawrence Beer.)

---

b. United States

The background of the two religion clauses of the First Amendment may be well known to U.S. students. The First Amendment prohibits Congress from making laws "respecting an establishment of religion, or prohibiting the free exercise thereof." In Everson v. Board of Education,

330 U.S. 1 (1947), the Court described how, notwithstanding that many came to the colonies to escape religious persecution in Europe, dissenting religious groups were persecuted in the colonies, sometimes by preachers for whose support they had to pay taxes. The Court went on to say:

> "These practices became so commonplace as to shock the freedom loving colonials into a feeling of abhorrence. The imposition of taxes to pay ministers' salaries and to build and maintain churches and church property aroused their indignation. It was these feelings which found expression in the First Amendment. . . . The people . . . reached the conviction that religious liberty could be achieved best under a government which was stripped of all power to tax, to support, or otherwise to assist any or all religions, or to interfere with the beliefs of any religious individual or group. . . .

> [The Court then described Madison's and Jefferson's resistance in 1785–86 to Virginia's effort to renew a tax levy to support the established church:] Madison wrote his great Memorial and Remonstrance against the law. In it he eloquently argued that a true religion did not need the support of law; that no person, either believer or non-believer, should be taxed to support a religious institution of any kind; that the best interests of a society required that the minds of men always be wholly free; and that cruel persecutions were the inevitable result of government-established religion." . . . [This led to Virginia's adoption of the Bill for Religious Liberty, and then to the First Amendment]. . . .

> [The establishment clause] means at least this: Neither a state nor the Federal government can set up a church. Neither can pass laws which aid one religion, aid all religions, or prefer one religion over another. Neither can force nor influence a person to go to or remain away from church against his will or force him to profess a belief or disbelief in any religion. No person can be punished for entertaining or professing religious beliefs or disbeliefs, for church attendance or non-attendance. No tax in any amount, large or small, can be levied to support any religious activities or institutions, whatever they may be called, or whatever form they may adopt to teach or practice religion. Neither a state nor the Federal Government can, openly or secretly, participate in the affairs of any religious organizations or groups and vice versa. In the words of Jefferson, the clause was intended to erect "a wall of separation between Church and State."

This view of the history of the U.S. religion clauses is not uncontroversial. There is evidence, for example, that the ban on establishment of churches may have applied only to the federal government, and not to the state governments. Application of these clauses to religiously derived rituals or symbols in public life remains controversial, as seen in the *Lynch* case below.

Lynch v. Donnelly

465 U.S. 668 (1984)

The CHIEF JUSTICE [BURGER] delivered the opinion of the Court. . . .

Each year, in cooperation with the downtown retail merchants' association, the City of Pawtucket, Rhode Island, erects a Christmas display as part of its observance of the Christmas holiday season. The display is situated in a park owned by a nonprofit organization and located in the heart of the shopping district. The display is essentially like those to be found in hundreds of towns or cities across the Nation—often on public grounds—during the Christmas season. The Pawtucket display comprises many of the figures and decorations traditionally associated with Christmas, including, among other things, a Santa Claus house, reindeer pulling Santa's sleigh, candy-striped poles, a Christmas tree, carolers, cutout figures representing such characters as a clown, an elephant, and a teddy bear, hundreds of colored lights, a large banner that reads "SEASONS GREETINGS," and the crèche at issue here. All components of this display are owned by the City.

The crèche, which has been included in the display for 40 or more years, consists of the traditional figures, including the Infant Jesus, Mary and Joseph, angels, shepherds, kings, and animals, all ranging in height from 5″ to 5′. In 1973, when the present crèche was acquired, it cost the City $1365; it now is valued at $200. The erection and dismantling of the crèche costs the City about $20 per year; nominal expenses are incurred in lighting the crèche. No money has been expended on its maintenance for the past 10 years. . . .

This Court has explained that the purpose of the Establishment and Free Exercise Clauses of the First Amendment is

> "to prevent, as far as possible, the intrusion of either [the church or the state] into the precincts of the other." Lemon v. Kurtzman, 403 U.S. 602, 614 (1971).

At the same time, however, the Court has recognized that

> "total separation is not possible in an absolute sense. Some relationship between government and religious organizations is inevitable." Ibid.

In every Establishment Clause case, we must reconcile the inescapable tension between the objective of preventing unnecessary intrusion of either the church or the state upon the other, and the reality that, as the Court has so often noted, total separation of the two is not possible.

The Court has sometimes described the Religion Clauses as erecting a "wall" between church and state, see, e.g., Everson v. Board of Education, 330 U.S. 1, 18 (1947). The concept of a "wall" of separation is a useful figure of speech probably deriving from views of Thomas Jefferson. The metaphor has served as a reminder that the Establishment Clause forbids an established church or anything approaching it. But the metaphor itself is not a wholly accurate description of the practical aspects of the relationship that in fact exists between church and state.

No significant segment of our society and no institution within it can exist in a vacuum or in total or absolute isolation from all the other parts, much less from government. "It has never been thought either possible or desirable to enforce a regime of total separation...." Committee for Public Education & Religious Liberty v. Nyquist, 413 U.S. 756, 760 (1973). Nor does the Constitution require complete separation of church and state; it affirmatively mandates accommodation, not merely tolerance, of all religions, and forbids hostility toward any. See, e.g., Zorach v. Clauson, 343 U.S. 306, 314, 315 (1952). Anything less would require the "callous indifference" we have said was never intended by the Establishment Clause. Zorach, at 314....

Our history is replete with official references to the value and invocation of Divine guidance in deliberations and pronouncements of the Founding Fathers and contemporary leaders. Beginning in the early colonial period long before Independence, a day of Thanksgiving was celebrated as a religious holiday to give thanks for the bounties of Nature as gifts from God. President Washington and his successors proclaimed Thanksgiving, with all its religious overtones, a day of national celebration and Congress made it a National Holiday more than a century ago. That holiday has not lost its theme of expressing thanks for Divine aid any more than has Christmas lost its religious significance....

There are countless other illustrations of the Government's acknowledgment of our religious heritage and governmental sponsorship of graphic manifestations of that heritage. Congress has directed the President to proclaim a National Day of Prayer each year "on which [day] the people of the United States may turn to God in prayer and meditation at churches, in groups, and as individuals." Our Presidents have repeatedly issued such Proclamations. Presidential Proclamations and messages have also issued to commemorate Jewish Heritage Week and the Jewish High Holy Days. One cannot look at even this brief resume without finding that our history is pervaded by expressions of religious beliefs such as are found in *Zorach*. Equally pervasive is the evidence of accommodation of all faiths and all forms of religious expression, and hostility toward none. Through this accommodation, as Justice Douglas observed, governmental action has "follow[ed] the best of our traditions" and "respect[ed] the religious nature of our people." 343 U.S., at 314....

In each case, the inquiry calls for line drawing; no fixed, per se rule can be framed. The Establishment Clause like the Due Process Clauses is not a precise, detailed provision in a legal code capable of ready application.... The line between permissible relationships and those barred by the Clause can no more be straight and unwavering than due process can be defined in a single stroke or phrase or test....

In this case, the focus of our inquiry must be on the crèche in the context of the Christmas season. See, e.g., Stone v. Graham, 449 U.S. 39 (1980) (per curiam); Abington School District v. Schempp. In *Stone*, for example, we invalidated a state statute requiring the posting of a copy of the Ten Commandments on public classroom walls. But the Court carefully pointed out that the Commandments were posted purely as a religious admonition, not "integrated into the school curriculum, where the Bible may constitutionally be used in an appropriate study of history, civilization, ethics, comparative religion, or the like." 449 U.S., at 42. Similarly, in *Abington*, although the Court struck down the practices in two States requiring daily Bible readings in public schools, it specifically noted that nothing in the Court's holding was intended to "indicat[e] that such study of the Bible or of religion, when presented objectively as part of a secular program of education, may not be effected consistently with the First Amendment." 374 U.S., at 225. Focus exclusively on the religious component of any activity would inevitably lead to its invalidation under the Establishment Clause. . . .

The District Court inferred from the religious nature of the crèche that the City has no secular purpose for the display. In so doing, it rejected the City's claim that its reasons for including the crèche are essentially the same as its reasons for sponsoring the display as a whole. The District Court plainly erred by focusing almost exclusively on the crèche. When viewed in the proper context of the Christmas Holiday season, it is apparent that, on this record, there is insufficient evidence to establish that the inclusion of the crèche is a purposeful or surreptitious effort to express some kind of subtle governmental advocacy of a particular religious message. In a pluralistic society a variety of motives and purposes are implicated. The City, like the Congresses and Presidents, however, has principally taken note of a significant historical religious event long celebrated in the Western World. The crèche in the display depicts the historical origins of this traditional event long recognized as a National Holiday.

The narrow question is whether there is a secular purpose for Pawtucket's display of the crèche. The display is sponsored by the City to celebrate the Holiday and to depict the origins of that Holiday. These are legitimate secular purposes. The District Court's inference, drawn from the religious nature of the crèche, that the City has no secular purpose was, on this record, clearly erroneous. . . .

The dissent asserts some observers may perceive that the City has aligned itself with the Christian faith by including a Christian symbol in its display and that this serves to advance religion. We can assume, *arguendo*, that the display advances religion in a sense; but our precedents plainly contemplate that on occasion some advancement of religion will result from governmental action. . . . Here, whatever benefit to one faith or religion or to all religions, is indirect, remote and incidental; display of the crèche is no more an advancement or endorsement of religion than the Congressional and Executive recognition of the origins of the Holiday itself as "Christ's Mass," or the exhibition of literally hundreds of religious paintings in governmentally supported museums. . . .

We are satisfied that the City has a secular purpose for including the crèche, that the City has not impermissibly advanced religion, and that including the crèche does not create excessive entanglement between religion and government.

Justice Brennan [in dissent] describes the crèche as a "re-creation of an event that lies at the heart of Christian faith." The crèche, like a painting, is passive; admittedly it is a reminder of the origins of Christmas. Even the traditional, purely secular displays extant at Christmas, with or without a crèche, would inevitably recall the religious nature of the Holiday. The display engenders a friendly community spirit of good will in keeping with the season. The crèche may well have special meaning to those whose faith includes the celebration of religious masses, but none who sense the origins of the Christmas celebration would fail to be aware of its religious implications. That the display brings people into the central city, and serves commercial interests and benefits merchants and their employees, does not, as the dissent points out, determine the character of the display. That a prayer invoking Divine guidance in Congress is preceded and followed by debate and partisan conflict over taxes, budgets, national defense, and myriad mundane subjects, for example, has never been thought to demean or taint the sacredness of the invocation.[12]

Of course the crèche is identified with one religious faith but no more so than the examples we have set out from prior cases in which we found no conflict with the Establishment Clause. It would be ironic, however, if the inclusion of a single symbol of a particular historic religious event, as part of a celebration acknowledged in the Western World for 20 centuries, and in this country by the people, by the Executive Branch, by the Congress, and the courts for two centuries, would so "taint" the City's exhibit as to render it violative of the Establishment Clause. To forbid the use of this one passive symbol—the crèche—at the very time people are taking note of the season with Christmas hymns and carols in public schools and other public places, and while the Congress and Legislatures open sessions with prayers by paid chaplains would be a stilted overreaction contrary to our history and to our holdings. If the presence of the crèche in this display violates the Establishment Clause, a host of other forms of taking official note of Christmas, and of our religious heritage, are equally offensive to the Constitution.

... The Court has acknowledged that the "fears and political problems" that gave rise to the Religion Clauses in the 18th century are of far less concern today. We are unable to perceive the Archbishop of Canterbury, the Bishop of Rome, or other powerful religious leaders behind every public acknowledgment of the religious heritage long officially recognized by the three constitutional branches of government. Any notion that these symbols pose a real danger of establishment of a state church is far-fetched indeed....

12. Justice Brennan states that "by focusing on the holiday 'context' in which the crèche appear[s]," the Court seeks to "explain away the clear religious import of the crèche," and that it has equated the crèche with a Santa's house or a talking wishing well. Of course this is not true.

We hold that, notwithstanding the religious significance of the crèche, the City of Pawtucket has not violated the Establishment Clause of the First Amendment....

[A concurring opinion by Justice O'Connor is omitted.]

Justice Brennan, with whom Justice Marshall, Justice Blackmun and Justice Stevens join, dissenting....

The "primary effect" of including a nativity scene in the City's display is, as the District Court found, to place the government's imprimatur of approval on the particular religious beliefs exemplified by the crèche. Those who believe in the message of the nativity receive the unique and exclusive benefit of public recognition and approval of their views. For many, the City's decision to include the crèche as part of its extensive and costly efforts to celebrate Christmas can only mean that the prestige of the government has been conferred on the beliefs associated with the crèche, thereby providing "a significant symbolic benefit to religion...." The effect on minority religious groups, as well as on those who may reject all religion, is to convey the message that their views are not similarly worthy of public recognition nor entitled to public support....

... The Court, by focusing on the holiday "context" in which the nativity scene appeared, seeks to explain away the clear religious import of the crèche and the findings of the District Court that most observers understood the crèche as both a symbol of Christian beliefs and a symbol of the City's support for those beliefs....

The Court's struggle to ignore the clear religious effect of the crèche seems to me misguided for several reasons. In the first place, the City has positioned the crèche in a central and highly visible location within the Hodgson Park display....

Moreover, the City has done nothing to disclaim government approval of the religious significance of the crèche, to suggest that the crèche represents only one religious symbol among many others that might be included in a seasonal display truly aimed at providing a wide catalogue of ethnic and religious celebrations, or to disassociate itself from the religious content of the crèche. In Abington School Dist. v. Schempp, we noted that reading aloud from the Bible would be a permissible schoolroom exercise only if it was "presented objectively as part of a secular program of education" that would remove any message of governmental endorsement of religion....

Finally, and most importantly, even in the context of Pawtucket's seasonal celebration, the crèche retains a specifically Christian religious meaning. I refuse to accept the notion implicit in today's decision that non-Christians would find that the religious content of the crèche is eliminated by the fact that it appears as part of the City's otherwise secular celebration of the Christmas holiday. The nativity scene is clearly distinct in its purpose and effect from the rest of the Hodgson Park display for the simple reason that it is the only one rooted in a biblical account of Christ's birth. It is the chief symbol of the characteristically Christian belief that a divine Savior was brought into the world and that the purpose of this miraculous birth was to illuminate a path toward salvation and redemption. For Christians, that path is exclusive, precious and holy. But for those who do not share these beliefs, the symbolic re-enactment of the birth of a divine being who has been miraculously incarnated as a man stands as a dramatic reminder of their differences with Christian faith....

[W]e have noted that government cannot be completely prohibited from recognizing in its public actions the religious beliefs and practices of the American people as an aspect of our national history and culture. While I remain uncertain about these questions, I would suggest that such practices as the designation of "In God We Trust" as our national motto, or the references to God contained in the Pledge of Allegiance can best be understood, in Dean Rostow's apt phrase, as a form a "ceremonial deism," protected from Establishment Clause scrutiny chiefly because they have lost through rote repetition any significant religious content. Moreover, these references are uniquely suited to serve such wholly secular purposes as solemnizing public occasions, or inspiring commitment to meet some national challenge in a manner that simply could not be fully served in our culture if government were limited to purely non-religious phrases. The practices by which the government has long acknowledged religion are therefore probably necessary to serve certain secular functions, and that necessity, coupled with their long history, gives those practices an essentially secular meaning....

Questions and Comments

1. *"Not very" religious?* Is it fair to say that both courts in these cases uphold the challenged practices because the practices, though religious, are "not very" religious? What might account for the pull toward such a characterization? Consider the following observations, from Winnifred Fallers Sullivan, Paying the Words Extra: Religious Discourse in the Supreme Court of the United States 109–12 (1994). (Sullivan's discussion of Japan focuses on a later and more complex case than the Shinto dedication ceremony case, but her observations seem applicable to the earlier case as well.)

> Why do American and Japanese justices publicly affirm traditional religious forms, even if they do so by calling them secular? The problem for these courts is how to acknowledge, support, and celebrate the whole—"the inherent sacredness of secular authority," in Geertz's words—in the context of a religiously pluralistic but highly secular society....
>
> In modern societies what [some assert] ... to be the necessarily close coincidence between complete integration and religion is impossi-

ble. Edward Shils seems to see it as characteristic of modern society (probably this is true of all societies) that there is a constant tension among "competing conceptions about the ultimate locus of charisma." This tension is revealed in the strain these courts put on the language they use to talk about religion. How to represent and celebrate the unity when the diversity is so apparent and so constitutionally protected? ...

... Justice Burger, in his "accommodation" theory, attempts the solution that Americans are "a religious people," in some general way, and that that very religiousness can be constitutionally expressed through the appropriation of sectarian religious—here Christian—symbols. The Japanese justices express the position that the use of religious symbols is permissible by emphasizing that the Japanese *are not* a religious people. While reserving "religious" as an epithet for those who are excessively "scrupulous," they affirm the Japaneseness of Shinto deification, as a symbol of national unity, in a generalized way. The religious nature of the Japanese people is to be not religious!

Neither Burger not the Japanese justices intend to establish a majority religion, in the traditional, coercive, and exclusive sense. Both would vehemently object to such a characterization of their opinions. They seem to be seeking a way to have their cake and eat it too: a way to acknowledge, even accommodate, religious unity, while endorsing religious tolerance at the same time....

Both American and Japanese majority solutions ... invite, no doubt unintentionally, manipulation from the right. Whereas Burger and the Japanese majority may wish to endorse a benign celebration of civic spirit, accommodation of nonsectarian religion or nonreligion may be appropriated as a battle cry for those whose purpose is more particular and divisive....

What Burger and the Japanese Court are insisting on, however, with the Lewis Carroll-like language, is that writing separation into the Constitution is not enough. We have to work together to create a new public language and practice about religion that will acknowledge the religiousness of people in a new way.... If the center is defined as secular and religion is by definition excluded from the center, religion will be defined by the extremes and will be limited to the prophetic voice.

If Sullivan is right in accounting for the desire to create a new language about religion and the nation, can you describe a way of talking about the religiousness of the people that would acknowledge both religiosity and religious diversity without forcing the words in the two constitutions to mean whatever the justices say they mean. (Sullivan's allusion to Lewis Carroll is to a passage in which Humpty Dumpty says that he uses words to mean "just what I choose [them] to mean," and "When I make a word do a lot of work like that, I always pay it extra.")

2. *India and Defining Religion*: Several Indian cases raise questions about a court's ability to distinguish between "real" religion and "ceremonial" observances. An Indian statute, the Representation of Peoples Act (1952, as amended in 1961), defines as a "corrupt practice" "[t]he appeal by a candidate ... to vote or refrain from voting for any person on the ground of his religion ... or the use or appeal to religious symbols ... for the furtherance of the prospects of election of that candidate or for prejudicially affecting the election of any candidate." Shubh Nath v. Ram Narain, A.I.R. 1960 S.C. 148, involved a candidate in an Adivasi dominated area whose party had been given a rooster as its election symbol. The rooster is not a religious symbol among the Adivasis, but roosters are used as sacrificial birds for curing diseases. Election literature had the rooster saying, "Give me food in the shape of votes, I am victorious. Do not forget me, otherwise I tell ye the sons of man will suffer eternal miseries." The Indian Supreme Court held that this was an unlawful appeal in the name of religion. A dissenting justice distinguished between appealing to religion and using myths.

A later case, Raman Bhai v. Dabhi, A.I.R. 1965 S.C. 669, involved an upper-caste candidate associated with a conservative party that had been given the star as an electoral symbol. The candidate's pamphlets employed the star in a way evoking the traditional Hindu meaning of Dhruva, a mythic figure associated with the pole star, as a symbol of eternity and permanence. The pamphlets said that "Dhruva means eternal ... firm ... guide ... determined ... one devoted to religion." The Supreme Court treated Dhruva as a myth, not a religious figure, distinguishing among reverence, worship, and religion. Dhruva was revered but not worshiped as a god; he was a symbol of devotion to God. In addition, the Court said, the qualities associated with Dhruva were qualities given to good "persons professing other religions or systems of belief."

Kultar Singh v. Muktiar Singh, A.I.R. 1965 S.C. 141, held that the statement, "This is not the time to criticize the weaknesses of the leaders of the Panth," referred to Sikh politics, not Sikh religion, even though "etymologically" the word *Panth* could indicate Sikh religion.

The candidate in Ebrahim Sulaiman Sait v. M.C. Mohammed, A.I.R. 1980 S.C. 354, made speeches asserting that another party "caused the killing of Muslims," while a third was anti-religious. The Court held that these speeches did not appeal to religion, but were rather "communal" in nature. Its opinion suggested that direct appeals to religion were prohibited, but indirect ones were not.

Five years later, the Court decided another case involving Sikhs, S. Harcharan Singh v. S. Sajjan Singh, A.I.R. 1985 S.C. 236. It wrote, "It would not be an appeal to religion if a candidate is put up by saying 'vote for him' because he is a good Sikh or he is a good Christian or he is a good Muslim, but would be an appeal to religion if it is publicised that not to vote for him would be against Sikh religion or against Christian religion or against Hindu religion—or to vote for other candidate would be an act against a particular religion. It is the total effect of such an appeal that has to be borne in mind whether there was an appeal to religion as such or not."

Consider these comments, from V.S. Rekhi, *Religion, Politics and Law in Contemporary India: Judicial Doctrine in Critical Perspective*, in Robert S. Baird, Religion and Law in Independent India, p. 196 (1993): "These observations ... do not disclose any realization of the identity building function of religion even though they travel beyond the formal distinction between religion and community. The link between religion and community has become the bone of contention in recent past. The identity and community building function of religion became the crux of the problem when the BJP [a prominent party of Hindu nationalists]... unleashed their election propaganda appealing to the element of *hindutva*. Their principal argument has been that under the Congress rule[b] a particular variety of pseudo-secularism consisting of unabashed appeasement of minority groups had been practiced at the cost of the national identity of India." What is the alternative to distinguishing between direct and indirect appeals to religion, as long as party appeals to a community's interests are allowed and communities are substantially defined along religious lines? Note that the fact of deep division among social groups has been one of the central issues in India's constitutional history.

Consider that the provision at issue in these cases would almost certainly be held to violate the First Amendment in the United States— although you should consider what social conditions would have to emerge before a legislature in the United States would think it *politically* appropriate to adopt such a provision, and then whether under *those* conditions it would be obvious that the provision violated the First Amendment.

3. *Religion and Ethnicity.* As the materials on India in the preceding note show, religious pluralism is sometimes closely connected to ethnic pluralism. This is illustrated, in the United States, by Employment Division, Department of Human Resources v. Smith, 494 U.S. 872 (1990) which involved a claim for exemption from a state's law prohibiting the use of peyote, a mind-altering drug, made by a Native American who wanted to use the drug in the rituals of the Native American Church with which he had become affiliated.

The overlap between ethnicity and religion sometimes requires courts to determine the basis for exclusions or claims of right. Mandla v. Dowell Lee, [1983] 1 All E.R. 1062, is a decision by the British House of Lords interpreting England's statutory ban on discrimination against a "racial group" or on the basis of "ethnic or national origins." The headmaster of a private school refused to admit as a pupil an orthodox Sikh who wore long hair under a turban, unless the boy removed the turban and cut his hair. The headmaster said that wearing the turban would accentuate religious distinctions that the school wanted to minimize. Finding that the Sikhs,

b. [Editors' Note: The Congress Party controlled the national government for many years after India's independence.]

though originally a religious group, "were no longer a purely religious group but were a separate community with distinctive customs," the House of Lords held that discrimination against Sikhs was discrimination against an ethnic group. The applicable statute did not prohibit discrimination on the basis of religion. An ethnic group "had to regard itself, and be regarded by others, as a distinct community ... [with] a long shared history, of which the group was conscious as distinguishing it from other groups, and the memory of which it kept alive, and ... it had to have a cultural tradition of its own, including family and social customs and manners, often but not necessarily associated with religious observance." The U.S. Supreme Court held that discrimination against persons of Arab ancestry and against Jews was made unlawful by an 1870 statute that the Court had previously held to bar discrimination on the basis of race. Saint Francis College v. Al-Khazraji, 481 U.S. 604 (1987); Shaare Tefila Congregation v. Cobb, 481 U.S. 615 (1987).

C. PROBLEMS OF RELIGIOUS LIBERTY AND CULTURAL PRESERVATION

Durham, excerpted above, at 27–30 describes a range of regimes of religious liberty. The most restrictive "permits *only internal freedom of religion,* and limits religious freedom to its ineradicable-psychological minimum: the freedom to think and believe as one will, so long as absolutely no external manifestation of such belief occurs.... A slightly enlarged version of religious freedom can be described as *freedom of the hearth* ... [where] internal beliefs can at least be externalized within the walls of the home, so long as they are not disclosed outside that setting.... Closely related ... is the *freedom to change religion or belief....* The next enlargement of religious liberty ... is protection of *freedom of worship,* narrowly construed.... [This] might be construed to permit group services in churches or other edifices, without allowing any manifestation of belief outside of such "private" buildings.... [Further extensions would allow communal and private conduct, and public conduct.] Finally, ... [religious liberty could] protect *"teaching, practice and observance."* ... It is also vital that religious organizations and families have the right to teach the rising generation and new converts or potential converts. The independent right to freedom of speech will protect many of these practices, but the notion of freedom of religion more clearly implies the need to protect institutional structures needed to carry out processes of teaching and transmitting religious heritage and beliefs."

Why might political or religious majorities seek to limit practices by minority religions? The two principal cases in this section involve efforts by majorities to preserve or extend their cultures—or to suppress minority religious practices. In both the courts use human rights arguments to defeat those efforts. Consider whether the case for the majorities' efforts might be stronger than the courts suggest.

Wisconsin v. Yoder

406 U.S. 205 (1972)

[Jonas Yoder was a member of the Old Order Amish religion. He refused to send his 15-year-old daughter to school, in violation of Wisconsin's compulsory school attendance law, which required attendance of children through their sixteenth birthdays. Yoder defended his refusal by citing his religious beliefs. Sending children to high school, he believed, would endanger their spiritual salvation. Other facts are detailed in the Court's opinion.]

MR. CHIEF JUSTICE BURGER delivered the opinion of the Court. . . .

. . . The history of the Amish sect . . . [began] with the Swiss Anabaptists of the 16th century who rejected institutionalized churches and sought to return to the early, simple, Christian life de-emphasizing material success, rejecting the competitive spirit, and seeking to insulate themselves from the modern world. As a result of their common heritage, Old Order Amish communities today are characterized by a fundamental belief that salvation requires life in a church community separate and apart from the world and worldly influence. This concept of life aloof from the world and its values is central to their faith.

A related feature of Old Order Amish communities is their devotion to a life in harmony with nature and the soil, as exemplified by the simple life of the early Christian era that continued in America during much of our early national life. Amish beliefs require members of the community to make their living by farming or closely related activities. Broadly speaking, the Old Order Amish religion pervades and determines the entire mode of life of its adherents. Their conduct is regulated in great detail by the Ordnung, or rules, of the church community. Adult baptism, which occurs in late adolescence, is the time at which Amish young people voluntarily undertake heavy obligations, not unlike the Bar Mitzvah of the Jews, to abide by the rules of the church community.

Amish objection to formal education beyond the eighth grade is firmly grounded in these central religious concepts. They object to the high school, and higher education generally, because the values they teach are in marked variance with Amish values and the Amish way of life; they view secondary school education as an impermissible exposure of their children to a "worldly" influence in conflict with their beliefs. The high school tends to emphasize intellectual and scientific accomplishments, self-distinction, competitiveness, worldly success, and social life with other students. Amish society emphasizes informal learning-through-doing; a life of "goodness," rather than a life of intellect; wisdom, rather than technical knowledge;

community welfare, rather than competition; and separation from, rather than integration with, contemporary worldly society.

Formal high school education beyond the eighth grade is contrary to Amish beliefs, not only because it places Amish children in an environment hostile to Amish beliefs with increasing emphasis on competition in class work and sports and with pressure to conform to the styles, manners, and ways of the peer group, but also because it takes them away from their community, physically and emotionally, during the crucial and formative adolescent period of life. During this period, the children must acquire Amish attitudes favoring manual work and self-reliance and the specific skills needed to perform the adult role of an Amish farmer or housewife. They must learn to enjoy physical labor. Once a child has learned basic reading, writing, and elementary mathematics, these traits, skills, and attitudes admittedly fall within the category of those best learned through example and "doing" rather than in a classroom. And, at this time in life, the Amish child must also grow in his faith and his relationship to the Amish community if he is to be prepared to accept the heavy obligations imposed by adult baptism. In short, high school attendance with teachers who are not of the Amish faith—and may even be hostile to it—interposes a serious barrier to the integration of the Amish child into the Amish religious community. Dr. John Hostetler, one of the experts on Amish society, testified that the modern high school is not equipped, in curriculum or social environment, to impart the values promoted by Amish society.

The Amish do not object to elementary education through the first eight grades as a general proposition because they agree that their children must have basic skills in the "three R's" in order to read the Bible, to be good farmers and citizens, and to be able to deal with non-Amish people when necessary in the course of daily affairs. They view such a basic education as acceptable because it does not significantly expose their children to worldly values or interfere with their development in the Amish community during the crucial adolescent period. While Amish accept compulsory elementary education generally, wherever possible they have established their own elementary schools in many respects like the small local schools of the past. In the Amish belief higher learning tends to develop values they reject as influences that alienate man from God.

On the basis of such considerations, Dr. Hostetler testified that compulsory high school attendance could not only result in great psychological harm to Amish children, because of the conflicts it would produce, but would also, in his opinion, ultimately result in the destruction of the Old Order Amish church community as it exists in the United States today. The testimony of Dr. Donald A. Erickson, an expert witness on education, also showed that the Amish succeed in preparing their high school age children to be productive members of the Amish community. He described their system of learning through doing the skills directly relevant to their adult roles in the Amish community as 'ideal' and perhaps superior to ordinary high school education. The evidence also showed that the Amish have an excellent record as law-abiding and generally self-sufficient members of society. . . .

There is no doubt as to the power of a State, having a high responsibility for education of its citizens, to impose reasonable regulations for the control and duration of basic education. Providing public schools ranks at the very apex of the function of a State. . . . [A] State's interest in universal education, however highly we rank it, is not totally free from a balancing process when it impinges on fundamental rights and interests, such as those specifically protected by the Free Exercise Clause of the First Amendment, and the traditional interest of parents with respect to the religious upbringing of their children so long as they, in the words of Pierce [v. Society of Sisters], "prepare (them) for additional obligations." 268 U.S., at 535.

It follows that in order for Wisconsin to compel school attendance beyond the eighth grade against a claim that such attendance interferes with the practice of a legitimate religious belief, it must appear either that the State does not deny the free exercise of religious belief by its requirement, or that there is a state interest of sufficient magnitude to override the interest claiming protection under the Free Exercise Clause. Long before there was general acknowledgment of the need for universal formal education, the Religion Clauses had specifically and firmly fixed the right to free exercise of religious beliefs, and buttressing this fundamental right was an equally firm, even if less explicit, prohibition against the establishment of any religion by government. The values underlying these two provisions relating to religion have been zealously protected, sometimes even at the expense of other interests of admittedly high social importance. . . .

We come then to the quality of the claims of the respondents concerning the alleged encroachment of Wisconsin's compulsory school-attendance statute on their rights and the rights of their children to the free exercise of the religious beliefs they and their forebears have adhered to for almost three centuries. In evaluating those claims we must be careful to determine whether the Amish religious faith and their mode of life are, as they claim, inseparable and interdependent. A way of life, however virtuous and admirable, may not be interposed as a barrier to reasonable state regulation of education if it is based on purely secular considerations; to have the protection of the Religion Clauses, the claims must be rooted in religious belief. Although a determination of what is a 'religious' belief or practice entitled to constitutional protection may present a most delicate question, the very concept of ordered liberty precludes allowing every person to make his own standards on matters of conduct in which society as a whole has important interests. Thus, if the Amish asserted their claims because of their subjective evaluation and rejection of the contemporary secular values accepted by the majority, much as Thoreau rejected the social values of his time and isolated himself at Walden Pond, their claims would not rest on a religious basis. Thoreau's choice was philosophical and personal rather than religious, and such belief does not rise to the demands of the Religion Clauses.

Giving no weight to such secular considerations, however, we see that the record in this case abundantly supports the claim that the traditional way of life of the Amish is not merely a matter of personal preference, but one of deep religious conviction, shared by an organized group, and intimately related to daily living. That the Old Order Amish daily life and religious practice stem from their faith is shown by the fact that it is in response to their literal interpretation of the Biblical injunction from the Epistle of Paul to the Romans, "be not conformed to this world . . . ." This command is fundamental to the Amish faith. Moreover, for the Old Order Amish, religion is not simply a matter of theocratic belief. As the expert witnesses explained, the Old Order Amish religion pervades and determines virtually their entire way of life, regulating it with the detail of the Talmudic diet through the strictly enforced rules of the church community.

The record shows that the respondents' religious beliefs and attitude toward life, family, and home have remained constant—perhaps some would say static—in a period of unparalleled progress in human knowledge generally and great changes in education. The respondents freely concede, and indeed assert as an article of faith, that their religious beliefs and what we would today call "life style" have not altered in fundamentals for centuries. Their way of life in a church-oriented community, separated from the outside world and "worldly" influences, their attachment to nature and the soil, is a way inherently simple and uncomplicated, albeit difficult to preserve against the pressure to conform. Their rejection of telephones, automobiles, radios, and television, their mode of dress, of speech, their habits of manual work do indeed set them apart from much of contemporary society; these customs are both symbolic and practical.

As the society around the Amish has become more populous, urban, industrialized, and complex, particularly in this century, government regulation of human affairs has correspondingly become more detailed and pervasive. The Amish mode of life has thus come into conflict increasingly with requirements of contemporary society exerting a hydraulic insistence on conformity to majoritarian standards. So long as compulsory education laws were confined to eight grades of elementary basic education imparted in a nearby rural schoolhouse, with a large proportion of students of the Amish faith, the Old Order Amish had little basis to fear that school attendance would expose their children to the worldly influence they reject. But modern compulsory secondary education in rural areas is now largely carried on in a consolidated school, often remote from the student's home and alien to his daily home life. As the record so strongly shows, the values and programs of the modern secondary school are in sharp conflict with the fundamental mode of life mandated by the Amish religion; modern laws requiring compulsory secondary education have accordingly engendered great concern and conflict. The conclusion is inescapable that secondary schooling, by exposing Amish children to worldly influences in terms of attitudes, goals, and values contrary to beliefs, and by substantially interfering with the religious development of the Amish child and his integration into the way of life of the Amish faith community at the crucial adolescent stage of development, contravenes the basic religious tenets and practice of the Amish faith, both as to the parent and the child.

The impact of the compulsory-attendance law on respondents' practice of the Amish religion is not only severe, but inescapable, for the Wisconsin law affirmatively compels them, under threat of criminal sanction, to perform acts undeniably at odds with fundamental tenets of their religious beliefs. Nor is the impact of the compulsory-attendance law confined to grave interference with important Amish religious tenets from a subjective point of view. It carries with it precisely the kind of objective danger to the free exercise of religion that the First Amendment was designed to prevent. As the record shows, compulsory school attendance to age 16 for Amish children carries with it a very real threat of undermining the Amish community and religious practice as they exist today; they must either abandon belief and be assimilated into society at large, or be forced to migrate to some other and more tolerant region. . . .

Wisconsin concedes that under the Religion Clauses religious beliefs are absolutely free from the State's control, but it argues that "actions," even though religiously grounded, are outside the protection of the First Amendment. But our decisions have rejected the idea that religiously grounded conduct is always outside the protection of the Free Exercise Clause. It is true that activities of individuals, even when religiously based, are often subject to regulation by the States in the exercise of their undoubted power to promote the health, safety, and general welfare, or the Federal Government in the exercise of its delegated powers. But to agree that religiously grounded conduct must often be subject to the broad police power of the State is not to deny that there are areas of conduct protected by the Free Exercise Clause of the First Amendment and thus beyond the power of the State to control, even under regulations of general applicability. This case, therefore, does not become easier because respondents were convicted for their "actions" in refusing to send their children to the public high school; in this context belief and action cannot be neatly confined in logic-tight compartments.

Nor can this case be disposed of on the grounds that Wisconsin's requirement for school attendance to age 16 applies uniformly to all citizens of the State and does not, on its face, discriminate against religions or a particular religion, or that it is motivated by legitimate secular concerns. A regulation neutral on its face may, in its application, nonetheless offend the constitutional requirement for governmental neutrality if it unduly burdens the free exercise of religion. The Court must not ignore the danger that an exception from a general obligation of citizenship on religious grounds may run afoul of the Establishment Clause, but that danger cannot be allowed to prevent any exception no matter how vital it may be to the protection of values promoted by the right of free exercise. . . .

We turn, then, to the State's broader contention that its interest in its system of compulsory education is so compelling that even the established religious practices of the Amish must give way. Where fundamental claims of religious freedom are at stake, however, we cannot accept such a sweeping claim; despite its admitted validity in the generality of cases, we must searchingly examine the interests that the State seeks to promote by its requirement for compulsory education to age 16, and the impediment to those objectives that would flow from recognizing the claimed Amish exemption.

The State advances two primary arguments in support of its system of compulsory education. It notes, as Thomas Jefferson pointed out early in our history, that some degree of education is necessary to prepare citizens to participate effectively and intelligently in our open political system if we are to preserve freedom and independence. Further, education prepares individuals to be self-reliant and self-sufficient participants in society. We accept these propositions.

However, the evidence adduced by the Amish in this case is persuasively to the effect that an additional one or two years of formal high school for Amish children in place of their long-established program of informal vocational education would do little to serve those interests. Respondents' experts testified at trial, without challenge, that the value of all education must be assessed in terms of its capacity to prepare the child for life. It is one thing to say that compulsory education for a year or two beyond the eighth grade may be necessary when its goal is the preparation of the child for life in modern society as the majority live, but it is quite another if the goal of education be viewed as the preparation of the child for life in the separated agrarian community that is the keystone of the Amish faith.

The State attacks respondents' position as one fostering "ignorance" from which the child must be protected by the State. No one can question the State's duty to protect children from ignorance but this argument does not square with the facts disclosed in the record. Whatever their idiosyncrasies as seen by the majority, this record strongly shows that the Amish community has been a highly successful social unit within our society, even if apart from the conventional "mainstream." Its members are productive and very law-abiding members of society; they reject public welfare in any of its usual modern forms. . . .

It is neither fair nor correct to suggests that the Amish are opposed to education beyond the eighth grade level. What this record shows is that they are opposed to conventional formal education of the type provided by a certified high school because it comes at the child's crucial adolescent period of religious development. Dr. Donald Erickson, for example, testified that their system of learning-by-doing was an "ideal system" of education in terms of preparing Amish children for life as adults in the Amish community, and that "I would be inclined to say they do a better job in this than most of the rest of us do." As he put it, "These people aren't purporting to be learned people, and it seems to me the self-sufficiency of the community is the best evidence I can point to—whatever is being done seems to function well."

We must not forget that in the Middle Ages important values of the civilization of the Western World were preserved by members of religious orders who isolated themselves from all worldly influences against great obstacles. There can be no assumption that today's majority is "right" and the Amish and others like them are "wrong." A way of life that is odd or even erratic but interferes with no rights or interests of others is not to be condemned because it is different.

The State, however, supports its interest in providing an additional one or two years of compulsory high school education to Amish children because of the possibility that some such children will choose to leave the Amish community, and that if this occurs they will be ill-equipped for life. The State argues that if Amish children leave their church they should not be in the position of making their way in the world without the education available in the one or two additional years the State requires. However, on this record, that argument is highly speculative. There is no specific evidence of the loss of Amish adherents by attrition, nor is there any showing that upon leaving the Amish community Amish children, with their practical agricultural training and habits of industry and self-reliance, would become burdens on society because of educational shortcomings. Indeed, this argument of the State appears to rest primarily on the State's mistaken assumption, already noted, that the Amish do not provide any education for their children beyond the eighth grade, but allow them to grow in "ignorance." To the contrary, not only do the Amish accept the necessity for formal schooling through the eighth grade level, but continue to provide what has been characterized by the undisputed testimony of expert educators as an "ideal" vocational education for their children in the adolescent years.

There is nothing in this record to suggest that the Amish qualities of reliability, self-reliance, and dedication to work would fail to find ready markets in today's society. Absent some contrary evidence supporting the State's position, we are unwilling to assume that persons possessing such valuable vocational skills and habits are doomed to become burdens on society should they determine to leave the Amish faith, nor is there any basis in the record to warrant a finding that an additional one or two years of formal school education beyond the eighth grade would serve to eliminate any such problem that might exist.

Insofar as the State's claim rests on the view that a brief additional period of formal education is imperative to enable the Amish to participate effectively and intelligently in our democratic process, it must fall. The Amish alternative to formal secondary school education has enabled them to function effectively in their day-to-day life under self-imposed limitations on relations with the world, and to survive and prosper in contemporary society as a separate, sharply identifiable and highly self-sufficient community for more than 200 years in this country. In itself this is strong evidence that they are capable of fulfilling the social and political responsibilities of citizenship without compelled attendance beyond the eighth grade at the price of jeopardizing their free exercise of religious belief. When Thomas Jefferson emphasized the need for education as a bulwark of a free people against tyranny, there is nothing to indicate he had in mind compulsory education through any fixed age beyond a basic education. Indeed, the Amish communities singularly parallel and reflect many of the virtues of Jefferson's ideal of the "sturdy yeoman" who would form the basis of what he considered as the ideal of a democratic society. Even their idiosyncratic separateness exemplifies the diversity we profess to admire and encourage.

The requirement for compulsory education beyond the eighth grade is a relatively recent development in our history. Less than 60 years ago, the educational requirements of almost all of the States were satisfied by completion of the elementary grades, at least where the child was regularly and lawfully employed. The independence and successful social functioning of the Amish community for a period approaching almost three centuries and more than 200 years in this country are strong evidence that there is at best a speculative gain, in terms of meeting the duties of citizenship, from an additional one or two years of compulsory formal education. Against this background it would require a more particularized showing from the State on this point to justify the severe interference with religious freedom such additional compulsory attendance would entail. . . .

Contrary to the suggestion of the dissenting opinion of Mr. Justice Douglas, our holding today in no degree depends on the assertion of the religious interest of the child as contrasted with that of the parents. It is the parents who are subject to prosecution here for failing to cause their children to attend school, and it is their right of free exercise, not that of their children, that must determine Wisconsin's power to impose criminal penalties on the parent. The dissent argues that a child who expresses a desire to attend public high school in conflict with the wishes of his parents should not be prevented from doing so. There is no reason for the Court to consider that point since it is not an issue in the case. The children are not parties to this litigation. . . .

Our holding in no way determines the proper resolution of possible competing interests of parents, children, and the State in an appropriate state court proceeding in which the power of the State is asserted on the theory that Amish parents are preventing their minor children from attending high school despite their expressed desires to the contrary. Recognition of the claim of the State in such a proceeding would, of course, call into question traditional concepts of parental control over the religious upbringing and education of their minor children recognized in this Court's past decisions. It is clear that such an intrusion by a State into family decisions in the area of religious training would give rise to grave questions of religious freedom comparable to those raised here and those presented in Pierce v. Society of Sisters, 268 U.S. 510 (1925). On this record we neither reach nor decide those issues. . . .

However read, the Court's holding in *Pierce* stands as a charter of the rights of parents to direct the religious upbringing of their children. And, when the interests of parenthood are combined with a free exercise claim of the nature revealed by this record, more than merely a "reasonable relation to some purpose within the competency of the State" is required to sustain the validity of the State's requirement under the First Amendment.... [I]n this case, the Amish have introduced persuasive evidence undermining the arguments the State has advanced to support its claims in terms of the welfare of the child and society as a whole. The record strongly indicates that accommodating the religious objections of the Amish by forgoing one, or at most two, additional years of compulsory education will not impair the physical or mental health of the child, or result in an inability to be self-supporting or to discharge the duties and responsibilities of citizenship, or in any other way materially detract from the welfare of society....

Aided by a history of three centuries as an identifiable religious sect and a long history as a successful and self-sufficient segment of American society, the Amish in this case have convincingly demonstrated the sincerity of their religious beliefs, the interrelationship of belief with their mode of life, the vital role that belief and daily conduct play in the continued survival of Old Order Amish communities and their religious organization, and the hazards presented by the State's enforcement of a statute generally valid as to others. Beyond this, they have carried the even more difficult burden of demonstrating the adequacy of their alternative mode of continuing informal vocational education in terms of precisely those overall interests that the State advances in support of its program of compulsory high school education. In light of this convincing showing, one that probably few other religious groups or sects could make, and weighing the minimal difference between what the State would require and what the Amish already accept, it was incumbent on the State to show with more particularity how its admittedly strong interest in compulsory education would be adversely affected by granting an exemption to the Amish.

Nothing we hold is intended to undermine the general applicability of the State's compulsory school-attendance statutes or to limit the power of the State to promulgate reasonable standards that, while not impairing the free exercise of religion, provide for continuing agricultural vocational education under parental and church guidance by the Old Order Amish or others similarly situated. The States have had a long history of amicable and effective relationships with church-sponsored schools, and there is no basis for assuming that, in this related context, reasonable standards cannot be established concerning the content of the continuing vocational education of Amish children under parental guidance, provided always that state regulations are not inconsistent with what we have said in this opinion.

[Concurring opinions by JUSTICE STEWART, joined by JUSTICE BRENNAN, and by JUSTICE WHITE, joined by JUSTICES BRENNAN and STEWART, are omitted. JUSTICES POWELL and REHNQUIST did not participate in the decision.]

MR. JUSTICE DOUGLAS, dissenting in part....

Religion is an individual experience. It is not necessary, nor even appropriate, for every Amish child to express his views on the subject in a prosecution of a single adult. Crucial, however, are the views of the child whose parent is the subject of the suit. . . .

On this important and vital matter of education, I think the children should be entitled to be heard. While the parents, absent dissent, normally speak for the entire family, the education of the child is a matter on which the child will often have decided views. He may want to be a pianist or an astronaut or an oceanographer. To do so he will have to break from the Amish tradition.

It is the future of the student, not the future of the parents, that is imperiled by today's decision. If a parent keeps his child out of school beyond the grade school, then the child will be forever barred from entry into the new and amazing world of diversity that we have today. The child may decide that that is the preferred course, or he may rebel. It is the student's judgment, not his parents', that is essential if we are to give full meaning to what we have said about the Bill of Rights and of the right of students to be masters of their own destiny. If he is harnessed to the Amish way of life by those in authority over him and if his education is truncated, his entire life may be stunted and deformed. The child, therefore, should be given an opportunity to be heard before the State gives the exemption which we honor today. . . .

I think the emphasis of the Court on the "law and order" record of this Amish group of people is quite irrelevant. A religion is a religion irrespective of what the misdemeanor or felony records of its members might be. I am not at all sure how the Catholics, Episcopalians, the Baptists, Jehovah's Witnesses, the Unitarians, and my own Presbyterians would make out if subjected to such a test. . . .

Questions and Comments

1. The U.S. Supreme Court modified the general standard articulated in *Yoder* in Employment Division, Department of Human Resources v. Smith, 494 U.S. 872 (1990), which held that states were not required to accommodate religious beliefs in implementing "neutral laws of general applicability." It reaffirmed the result in *Yoder*, however, because that case involved a "hybrid" claim, blending a claim of religious liberty with a claim by parents of their constitutional right to control their children's upbringing.

2. According to *Yoder*, sometimes state law must accommodate the religious beliefs of minority religions. One reason for such a requirement might be that such an accommodation is an important or even essential means by which the minority religion is able to preserve and perpetuate itself. (The questions after the next principal case ask whether or why a constitutional system ought to be concerned about the preservation or perpetuation of minority religions.) In the United States, some forms of accommodation might conflict with the non-establishment principle.

Consider in this connection Board of Education of Kiryas Joel Village School District v. Grumet, 512 U.S. 687 (1994). The village was an enclave inhabited almost entirely by Satmar Hasidim, Orthodox Jews "who make few concessions to the modern world and go to great lengths to avoid assimilation." Most of the group's children attended private religious schools, but providing education for the handicapped in such schools was quite expensive, and the village residents initially arranged to have a public school system provide education for the handicapped children. A court decision ended that arrangement, after which the children were sent to schools in the neighboring public school system. The village residents found that unsatisfactory in part because the children were suffering "fear and trauma" from "leaving their own community and being with people whose ways were so different." The New York state legislature then enacted a statute designating the village as a separate school district. The Supreme Court held that this statute violated the Establishment Clause: "The anomalously case-specific nature of the legislature's exercise of state authority in creating this district for a religious community leaves the Court without any direct way to review such state action for the purpose of safeguarding a principle at the heart of the Establishment Clause, that government should not prefer one religion to another." As the Court saw it, the village had not received its educational authority "simply as one of many communities eligible for treatment under a general law," and the Court could not be certain "that the next similarly situated group seeking a school district of its own will receive one." Why was the Court not concerned in *Yoder* with whether similarly situated groups could demand exemption from school attendance laws? How can the state accommodate the religious needs of the residents of Kiryas Joel after this decision?[c]

Kokkinakis v. Greece

European Court of Human Rights (Judgment of 25 May 1993), publication of the European Court of Human Rights, Series A, Vol. 260, *reprinted in* 17 E.H.R.R. 397 (1993)

[The excerpt here begins with a statement of the case from the Judgment of the European Court of Human Rights. This portion is followed by excerpts from the report of the European Commission on Human Rights, which at the time this case was decided screened cases for the European Court and recommended a disposition. This excerpt in turn is followed by the Court's decision, which is labeled as such.]

---

c. Note that Aguilar v. Felton, 473 U.S. 402 (1985), which had held that New York's provision of remedial educational services to parochial school students in their schools violated the Establishment Clause, was overruled shortly after *Kiryas Joel* was decided. Agostini v. Felton, 521 U.S. 203 (1997) (granting motion for relief from judgment entered in *Aguilar* and describing that case as "no longer good law"). To the extent that Aguilar v. Felton had prevented New York from providing special services to the Hasidic children in their sectarian schools, that barrier has now been removed.

As to the facts

I.   The circumstances of the case

6.   Mr Minos Kokkinakis, a retired businessman of Greek nationality, was born into an Orthodox family at Sitia (Crete) in 1919. After becoming a Jehovah's Witness in 1936, he was arrested more than 60 times for proselytism. He was also interned and imprisoned on several occasions.

The periods of internment, which were ordered by the administrative authorities on the grounds of his activities in religious matters, were spent on various islands in the Aegean. (13 months in Amorgos in 1938, six in Milos in 1940 and 12 in Makronisos in 1949.)

The periods of imprisonment, to which he was sentenced by the courts, were for acts of proselytism (three sentences of two and a half months in 1939—he was the first Jehovah's Witness to be convicted under the Laws of the Metaxas Government—and four and a half months in 1949, and two months in 1962), conscientious objection (18 and a half months in 1941) and holding a religious meeting in a private house (six months in 1952).

Between 1960 and 1970 the applicant was arrested four times and prosecuted but not convicted.

7.   On 2 March 1986 he and his wife called at the home of Mrs Kyriakaki in Sitia and engaged in a discussion with her. Mrs Kyriakaki's husband, who was the cantor at a local Orthodox church, informed the police, who arrested Mr and Mrs Kokkinakis and took them to the local police station, where they spent the night of 2–3 March 1986.

A.   Proceedings in the Lasithi Criminal Court

8.   The applicant and his wife were prosecuted under section 4 of Law no. 1363/1938 making proselytism an offence and were committed for trial at the Lasithi Criminal Court (*trimeles plimmeliodikio*), which heard the case on 20 March 1986.

9.   After dismissing an objection that section 4 of that Law was unconstitutional, the Criminal Court heard evidence from Mr and Mrs Kyriakaki, a defence witness and the two defendants and gave judgment on the same day:

> "[The defendants], who belong to the Jehovah's Witnesses sect, at-tempted to proselytise and, directly or indirectly, to intrude on the religious beliefs of Orthodox Christians, with the intention of under-mining those beliefs, by taking advantage of their inexperience, their low intellect and their naïvety. In particular, they went to the home of [Mrs Kyriakaki]... and told her that they brought good news; by insisting in a pressing manner, they gained admittance to the house and began to read from a book on the Scriptures which they interpret-ed with reference to a king of heaven, to events which had not yet occurred but would occur, etc, encouraging her by means of their judicious, skilful explanations ... to change her Orthodox Christian beliefs."

The court found Mr and Mrs Kokkinakis guilty of proselytism and sentenced each of them to four months' imprisonment, convertible (under Article 82 of the Criminal Code) into a pecuniary penalty of 400 drachmas per day's imprisonment, and a fine of 10,000 drachmas. Under Article 76 of the Criminal Code, it also ordered the confiscation and destruction of four booklets which they had been hoping to sell to Mrs Kyriakaki.

B.   The proceedings in the Crete Court of Appeal

10.   Mr and Mrs Kokkinakis appealed against this judgment to the Crete Court of Appeal (*Efetio*). The Court of Appeal quashed Mrs Kokkinakis's conviction and upheld her husband's but reduced his prison sentence to three months and converted it into a pecuniary penalty of 400 drachmas per day. The following reasons were given for its judgment, which was delivered on 17 March 1987:

"... it was proved that, with the aim of disseminating the articles of faith of the Jehovah's Witnesses sect (*airesi*), to which the defendant adheres, he attempted, directly and indirectly, to intrude on the religious beliefs of a person of a different religious persuasion from his own, [namely] the Orthodox Christian faith, with the intention of changing those beliefs, by taking advantage of her inexperience, her low intellect and her naïvety. More specifically, at the time and place indicated in the operative provision, he visited Mrs Georgia Kyriakaki and after telling her he brought good news, pressed her to let him into the house, where he began by telling her about the politician Olof Palme and by expounding pacifist views. He then took out a little book containing professions of faith by adherents of the aforementioned sect and began to read out passages from Holy Scripture, which he skilfully analysed in a manner that the Christian woman, for want of adequate grounding in doctrine, could not challenge, and at the same time offered her various similar books and importunately tried, directly and indirectly, to undermine her religious beliefs. He must consequently be declared guilty of the above mentioned offence, in accordance with the operative provision hereinafter, while the other defendant, his wife Elissavet, must be acquitted, seeing that there is no evidence that she participated in the offence committed by her husband, whom she merely accompanied ..."

One of the appeal judges dissented, and his opinion, which was appended to the judgment, read as follows:

"... the first defendant should also have been acquitted, as none of the evidence shows that Georgia Kyriakaki ... was particularly inexperienced in Orthodox Christian doctrine, being married to a cantor, or of particularly low intellect or particularly naïve, such that the defendant was able to take advantage and ... [thus] induce her to become a member of the Jehovah's Witnesses sect."

According to the record of the hearing of 17 March 1987, Mrs Kyriakaki had given the following evidence:

"They immediately talked to me about Olof Palme, whether he was a pacifist or not, and other subjects that I can't remember. They talked to me about things I did not understand very well. It was not a discussion but a constant monologue by them.... If they had told me they were Jehovah's Witnesses, I would not have let them in. I don't recall whether they spoke to me about the Kingdom of Heaven. They stayed in the house about 10 minutes or a quarter of an hour. What they told me was religious in nature, but I don't know why they told it to me. I could not know at the outset what the purpose of their visit was. They may have said something to me at the time with a view to undermining my religious beliefs ... [However,] the discussion did not influence my beliefs ..." ...

II. Relevant domestic law and practice

A. Statutory provisions

1. The Constitution

13. The relevant Articles of the 1975 Constitution read as follows:

Article 3

1. The dominant religion in Greece is that of the Christian Eastern Orthodox Church. The Greek Orthodox Church, which recognises as its head Our Lord Jesus Christ, is indissolubly united, doctrinally, with the Great Church of Constantinople and with any other Christian Church in communion with it (*omodoxi*), immutably observing, like the other Churches, the holy apostolic and synodical canons and the holy traditions. It is autocephalous and is administered by the Holy Synod, composed of all the bishops in office, and by the standing Holy Synod, which is an emanation of it constituted as laid down in the Charter of the Church and in accordance with the provisions of the Patriarchal Tome of 29 June 1850 and the Synodical Act of 4 September 1928.

2. The ecclesiastical regime in certain regions of the State shall not be deemed contrary to the provisions of the foregoing paragraph.

3. The text of the Holy Scriptures is unalterable. No official translation into any other form of language may be made without the prior consent of the autocephalous Greek Church and the Greek Christian Church at Constantinople.

Article 13

1. Freedom of conscience in religious matters is inviolable. The enjoyment of personal and political rights shall not depend on an individual's religious beliefs.

2. There shall be freedom to practise any known religion; individuals shall be free to perform their rites of worship without hindrance and under the protection of the law. The performance of rites of worship must not prejudice public order or public morals. Proselytism is prohibited.

3. The ministers of all known religions shall be subject to the same supervision by the State and to the same obligations to it as those of the dominant religion.

4. No one may be exempted from discharging his obligations to the State or refuse to comply with the law by reason of his religious convictions.

5. No oath may be required other than under a law which also determines the form of it."

14. The Christian Eastern Orthodox Church, which during nearly four centuries of foreign occupation symbolised the maintenance of Greek culture and the Greek language, took an active part in the Greek people's struggle for emancipation, to such an extent that Hellenism is to some extent identified with the Orthodox faith.

A royal decree of 23 July 1833 entitled 'Proclamation of the Independence of the Greek Church' described the Orthodox Church as 'autocephalous.' Greece's successive Constitutions have referred to the Church as being 'dominant.' The overwhelming majority of the population are members of it, and, according to Greek conceptions, it represents *de jure* and *de facto* the religion of the State itself, a good number of whose administrative and educational functions (marriage and family law, compulsory religious instruction, oaths sworn by members of the Government, etc.) it moreover carries out. Its role in public life is reflected by, among other things, the presence of the Minister of Education and Religious Affairs at the sessions of the Church hierarchy at which the Archbishop of Athens is elected and by the participation of the Church authorities in all official State events; the President of the Republic takes his oath of office according to Orthodox ritual (Art. 33 § 2 of the Constitution); and the official calendar follows that of the Christian Eastern Orthodox Church.

15. Under the reign of Otto I (1832–62), the Orthodox Church, which had long complained of a Bible society's propaganda directed at young Orthodox schoolchildren on behalf of the Evangelical Church, managed to get a clause added to the first Constitution (1844) forbidding "proselytism and any other action against the dominant religion." The Constitutions of 1864, 1911 and 1952 reproduced the same clause. The 1975 Constitution prohibits proselytism in general (Art. 13 § 2) in fine); the ban covers all "known religions," meaning those whose doctrines are not apocryphal and in which no secret initiation is required of neophytes.

2. Law nos. 1363/1938 and 1672/1939

16. During the dictatorship of Metaxas (1936–1940), proselytism was made a criminal offence for the first time by section 4 of Law (*anagastikos nomos*) 1363/1938. The following year that section was amended by section 2 of Law no. 1672/1939, in which the meaning of the term "proselytism" was clarified:

1. Anyone engaging in proselytism shall be liable to imprisonment and a fine of between 1,000 and 50,000 drachmas; he shall, moreover, be

subject to police supervision for a period of between six months and one year to be fixed by the court when convicting the offender.

The term of imprisonment may not be commuted to a fine.

2.   By "proselytism" is meant, in particular, any direct or indirect attempt to intrude on the religious beliefs of a person of a different religious persuasion (*eterodoxos*), with the aim of undermining those beliefs, either by any kind of inducement or promise of an inducement or moral support or material assistance, or by fraudulent means or by taking advantage of his inexperience, trust, need, low intellect or naïvety.

3.   The commission of such an offence in a school or other educational establishment or a philanthropic institution shall constitute a particularly aggravating circumstance."

B.   Caselaw

17.   In a judgment numbered 2276/1953 a full court of the Supreme Administrative Court (*Symvoulio tis Epikratias*) gave the following definition of proselytism:

"Article 1 of the Constitution, which establishes the freedom to practise any known religion and to perform rites of worship without hindrance and prohibits proselytism and all other activities directed against the dominant religion, that of the Christian Eastern Orthodox Church, means that purely spiritual teaching does not amount to proselytism, even if it demonstrates the errors of other religions and entices possible disciples away from them, who abandon their original religions of their own free will; this is because spiritual teaching is in the nature of a rite of worship performed freely and without hindrance. Outside such spiritual teaching, which may be freely given, any determined, importunate attempt to entice disciples away from the dominant religion by means that are unlawful or morally reprehensible constitutes proselytism as prohibited by the aforementioned provision of the Constitution."

18.   The Greek courts have held that persons were guilty of proselytism who had: likened the saints to "figures adorning the wall," St Gerasimos to "a body stuffed with cotton" and the Church to "a theatre, a market, a cinema"; preached, while displaying a painting showing a crowd of wretched people in rags, that "such are all those who do not embrace my faith"; promised Orthodox refugees housing on specially favourable terms if they adhered to the Uniate faith; offered a scholarship for study abroad; sent Orthodox priests booklets with the recommendation that they should study them and apply their content; distributed "so-called religious" books and booklets free to "illiterate peasants" or to "young schoolchildren"; or promised a young seamstress an improvement in her position if she left the Orthodox Church, whose priests were alleged to be "exploiters of society."

The Court of Cassation has ruled that the definition of proselytism in section 4 of Law no. 1363/1938 does not contravene the principle that only the law can define a crime and prescribe a penalty. The Piraeus Criminal

Court followed it in an order numbered 36/1962, adding that the expression "in particular" in section 4 of Law no. 1363/1938 referred to the means used by the person committing the offence and not to the description of the *actus reus*.

19.   Until 1975 the Court of Cassation held that the list in section 4 was not exhaustive. In a judgment numbered 997/1975 it added the following clarification:

"... it follows from the provisions of section 4 ... that proselytism consists in a direct or indirect attempt to impinge on religious beliefs by any of the means separately listed in the Law."

20.   More recently courts have convicted Jehovah's Witnesses for professing the sect's doctrine "importunately" and accusing the Orthodox Church of being a "source of suffering for the world": for entering other people's homes in the guise of Christians wishing to spread the New Testament; and for attempting to give books and booklets to an Orthodox priest at the wheel of his car after stopping him.

In a judgment numbered 1304/1982, on the other hand, the Court of Cassation quashed a judgment of the Athens Court of Appeal as having no basis in law because, when convicting a Jehovah's Witness, the Court of Appeal had merely reiterated the words of the indictment and had thus not explained how "the importunate teaching of the doctrines of the Jehovah's Witnesses sect" or "distribution of the sect's booklets at a minimal price" had amounted to an attempt to intrude on the complainants' religious beliefs, or shown how the defendant had taken advantage of their inexperience' and "low intellect." The Court of Cassation remitted the case to a differently constituted bench of the Court of Appeal, which acquitted the defendant.

Similarly, it has been held in several court decisions that the offence of proselytism was not made out where there had merely been a discussion about the beliefs of the Jehovah's Witnesses, where booklets had been distributed from door to door or in the street or where the tenets of the sect had been explained without any deception to an Orthodox Christian. Lastly, it has been held that being an "illiterate peasant" is not sufficient to establish the "naïvety," referred to in section 4, of the person whom the alleged proselytiser is addressing.

21.   After the revision of the Constitution in 1975, the Jehovah's Witnesses brought legal proceedings to challenge the constitutionality of section 4 of Law no. 1363/1938. They complained that the description of the offence was vague, but above all they objected to the actual title of the Act, which indicated that the Act was designed to preserve Articles 1 and 2 of the Constitution in force at the time (The 1911 Constitution), which prohibited proselytism directed against the dominant religion. In the current Constitution this prohibition is extended to all religions and furthermore is no longer included in the chapter concerning religion but in the one dealing with civil and social rights, and more particularly in Article 13, which guarantees freedom of conscience in religious matters.

The courts have always dismissed such objections of unconstitutionality, although they have been widely supported in legal literature.

III. The Jehovah's Witnesses in Greece

22. The Jehovah's Witnesses movement appeared in Greece at the beginning of the twentieth century. Estimates of its membership today vary between 25,000 and 70,000. Members belong to one of 338 congregations, the first of which was formed in Athens in 1922.

23. Since the revision of the Constitution in 1975 the Supreme Administrative Court has held on several occasions that the Jehovah's Witnesses come within the definition of a "known religion." Some first-instance courts, however, continue to rule to the contrary. In 1986 the Supreme Administrative Court held that a ministerial decision refusing the appointment of a Jehovah's Witness as a literature teacher was contrary to freedom of conscience in religious matters and hence to the Greek Constitution.

24. According to statistics provided by the applicant, 4,400 Jehovah's Witnesses were arrested between 1975 (when democracy was restored) and 1992, and 1,233 of these were committed for trial and 208 convicted. Earlier, several Jehovah's Witnesses had been convicted under Act 117/1936 for the prevention of communism and its effects and Act 1075/1938 on preserving the social order.

The Government has not challenged the applicant's figures. It has, however, pointed out that there have been signs of a decline in the frequency of convictions of Jehovah's Witnesses, only 7 out of a total of 260 people arrested having been convicted in 1991 and 1992....

OPINION OF THE EUROPEAN HUMAN RIGHTS COMMISSION (Report of 3 Dec. 1991) ...

D. Compliance with Article 9 of the Convention

52. Article 9 of the [European] Convention [on Human Rights and Fundamental Freedoms] provides as follows:

"1. Everyone has the right to freedom of thought, conscience and religion; this right includes freedom to change his religion or belief and freedom, either alone or in community with others and in public or in private, to manifest his religion or belief, in worship, teaching, practice and observance.

2. Freedom to manifest one's religion or beliefs shall be subject only to such limitations as are prescribed by law and are necessary in a democratic society in the interests of public safety, for the protection of public order, health or morals, or for the protection of the rights and freedoms of others"...

1. "Prescribed by law"...

2. Legitimate aim...

65. The Government observes that proselytism was prohibited in 1844, in response to the energetic propagation of Protestant beliefs to the detriment of Orthodox schoolchildren. The aim of the prohibition of proselytism, as enunciated in the 1844 and 1952 Constitutions, was to protect the Orthodox religion, in so far as it concerned only proselytism practised to the latter's detriment. On the other hand, Article 13 § 2 of the 1975 Constitution instituted a general prohibition of proselytism. As the Court of Cassation stated in the judgment it gave in the applicant's case, proselytism is prohibited in respect of every known religion.

66. The Government also asserts that the regulations in question do not prohibit the proclamation of a belief or religious teaching, but rather abuse of the right to proclaim one's religion, manifested by the use of fraudulent means and stratagems with intent to undermine another person's religious beliefs. The prohibition of proselytism protects freedom of religion inasmuch as every change of religion must be the result of a decision free of any moral or material constraint, rather than the result of fraud or deception.

67. The Commission does not see in the judgments given by the Greek courts in this case any reason to believe that the applicant's conviction under section 4 of Law no. 1363/1938 pursued any objective other than the protection of Mrs [K.]'s freedom of religion. Consequently, it considers that the measure complained of was adopted in pursuit of a legitimate aim for the purpose of the Convention, namely protection of the rights of others.

(3) "Necessary in a democratic society"

68. The applicant maintains that criminal penalties for inoffensive remarks made during a private visit cannot be held to be "necessary in a" "democratic society." On the other hand, the Government maintains that such a penalty was necessary in the light of the circumstances of the case as found by the Greek courts. The applicant took advantage of Mrs K.'s inexperience, feebleness of mind and irresponsibility and, after importuning her until she let him into her home, attempted to undermine her religious beliefs by devious means.

69. The Commission points out that the adjective "necessary" in the phrase "necessary in a democratic society" implies the existence of a pressing social need. (See, *mutatis mutandis*, Eur. Court H.R., Lingens v. Austria Judgment of 8 July 1986, Series A, no. 103, p. 25, § 39 [A/103]: (1986) 8 E.H.R.R. 103, para 39.] Admittedly, Contracting States enjoy a wide margin of appreciation in assessing the existence of such a necessity, but this margin is subject to European supervision, embracing both the legislation and the decisions applying it, even those given by an independent court. (See Eur. Court H.R., Barfod v. Denmark judgment of 22 February 1989, Series A, no. 149, p. 12, § 28 [(1989) 13 E.H.R.R. 493, para 28.)] Moreover, punishment of the exercise of a right guaranteed by the Convention cannot be justified thereunder unless it is proportionate to the legitimate aim pursued.

70. The Commission observes that, according to the judgment of the Crete Court of Appeal, the conduct held against the applicant consisted in talking his way into the house of Mr and Mrs [K], beginning a discussion about the politician O Palme and pacifism, reading passages from a book containing professions of faith by Jehovah's Witnesses, analysing certain passage in Holy Scripture and offering similar books to Mrs. K. with intent to undermine her religious beliefs.

71. The reasons put forward by the national courts to justify the applicant's conviction, and consequently for the infringement of his freedom to manifest his religion, cannot be deemed sufficient in themselves. It is hard to see how the words and opinions attributed to the applicant, whose inoffensive nature seems obvious, could have encroached on Mrs [K]'s freedom of conscience in religious matters.

72. In particular, the Commission does not see on what evidence the national courts could have based their finding that the applicant had taken advantage of the "inexperienced," "feebleness of mind" and "ingenuousness" of Mrs [K], none of which, in any event, have been established.

73. Even taking into account the margin of appreciation enjoyed by Contracting States with regard to the protection of the population's religious sensibilities, the Commission cannot accept that, having regard to the circumstances of this case, the applicant's conviction was justified by a pressing social need. One particular fact appeared decisive to the Commission, namely the lack of proportion between the conduct held against the applicant and the criminal penalty for that conduct, which seriously infringes the applicant's fundamental freedom to manifest his religion. In addition, that penalty is incompatible with the spirit of tolerance and broadmindedness which should obtain in contemporary democratic society. (See *mutatis mutandis*, Eur. Court H.R. Handyside v. United Kingdom judgment of 7 December 1976, Series A, no. 24, p. 23, § 49 [(A/24): (1976) 1 E.H.R.R. 737, para 49.])

74. Consequently, the measure complained of was not "necessary in a democratic society" within the meaning of Article 9 § 2 of the Convention.

Conclusion

75. The Commission concludes unanimously that in this case there has been a violation of Article 9 of the Convention....

JUDGMENT [of the European Court of Human Rights] AS TO THE LAW

27. Mr Kokkinakis complained of his conviction for proselytism; he considered it contrary to Articles 7, 9 and 10 of the Convention, and to Article 14 taken together with Article 9.

I. Alleged violation of Article 9

28. The applicant's complaints mainly concerned a restriction on the exercise of his freedom of religion. The Court will accordingly begin by looking at the issues relating to Article 9, which provides:

"(1) Everyone has the right to freedom of thought, conscience and religion; this right includes freedom to change his religion or belief and freedom, either alone or in community with others and in public or private, to manifest his religion or belief, in worship, teaching, practice and observance.

"(2) Freedom to manifest one's religion or beliefs shall be subject only to such limitations as are prescribed by law and are necessary in a democratic society in the interests of public safety, for the protection of public order, health or morals, or for the protection of the rights and freedoms of others."

29.   The applicant did not only challenge what he claimed to be the wrongful application to him of section 4 of Act 1363/1938. His submission concentrated on the broader problem of whether that enactment was compatible with the right enshrined in Article 9 of the Convention, which, he argued, having been part of Greek law since 1953, took precedence under the Constitution over any contrary statute. He pointed to the logical and legal difficulty of drawing any even remotely clear dividing-line between proselytism and freedom to change one's religion or belief and, either alone or in community with others, in public and in private, to manifest it, which encompassed all forms of teaching, publication and preaching between people. . . .

30.   In the Government's submission, there was freedom to practise all religions in Greece; religious adherents enjoyed the right both to express their beliefs freely and to try to influence the beliefs of others, Christian witness being a duty of all churches and all Christians. There was, however, a radical difference between bearing witness and 'proselytism that is not respectable,' the kind that consists in using deceitful, unworthy and immoral means, such as exploiting the destitution, low intellect and inexperience of one's fellow beings. Section 4 prohibited this kind of proselytism—the 'misplaced' proselytism to which the European Court referred in its Kjeldsen, Busk Madsen and Pedersen v. Denmark judgment of 7 December 1976 (Series A no. 23, p. 28 § 54 [1 E.H.R.R. 711, para 54])—and not straightforward religious teaching. Furthermore, it was precisely this definition of proselytism that had been adopted by the Greek courts.

A.   General principles

31.   As enshrined in Article 9, freedom of thought, conscience and religion is one of the foundations of a "democratic society" within the meaning of the Convention. It is, in its religious dimension, one of the most vital elements that go to make up the identity of believers and of their conception of life, but it is also a precious asset for atheists, agnostics, sceptics and the unconcerned. The pluralism indissociable from a democratic society, which has been dearly won over the centuries, depends on it.

While religious freedom is primarily a matter of individual conscience, it also implies, *inter alia*, freedom to "manifest [one's] religion." Bearing witness in words and deeds is bound up with the existence of religious convictions.

According to Article 9, freedom to manifest one's religion is not only exercisable in community with others, "in public" and within the circle of those whose faith one shares, but can also be asserted "alone" and "in private"; furthermore, it includes in principle the right to try to convince one's neighbour, for example through "teaching," failing which, moreover, "freedom to change [one's] religion or belief," enshrined in Article 9, would be likely to remain a dead letter. . . .

33. The fundamental nature of the rights guaranteed in Article 9(1) is also reflected in the wording of the paragraph providing for limitations on them. Unlike the second paragraphs of Articles 8, 10 and 11, which cover all the rights mentioned in the first paragraphs of those Articles, that of Article 9 refers only to "freedom to manifest one's religion or belief." In so doing, it recognises that in democratic societies, in which several religions coexist within one and the same population, it may be necessary to place restrictions on this freedom in order to reconcile the interests of the various groups and ensure that everyone's beliefs are respected.

34. According to the Government, such restrictions were to be found in the Greek legal system. Article 13 of the 1975 Constitution forbade proselytism in respect of all religions without distinction; and section 4 of Act 1363/1938, which attached a criminal penalty to this prohibition, had been upheld by several successive democratic governments notwithstanding its historical and political origins. The sole aim of section 4 was to protect the beliefs of others from activities which undermined their dignity and personality. . . .

B. Application of the principles

36. The sentence passed by the Lasithi Criminal Court and subsequently reduced by the Crete Court of Appeal amounts to an interference with the exercise of Mr Kokkinakis's right to "freedom to manifest [his] religion or belief." Such an interference is contrary to Article 9 unless it was "prescribed by law," directed at one or more of the legitimate aims in paragraph 2 and "necessary in a democratic society" for achieving them. . . .

1. "Prescribed by law" . . .

2. Legitimate aim

42. The Government contended that a democratic State had to ensure the peaceful enjoyment of the personal freedoms of all those living on its territory. If, in particular, it was not vigilant to protect a person's religious beliefs and dignity from attempts to influence them by immoral and deceitful means, Article 9(2) would in practice be rendered wholly nugatory.

43. In the applicant's submission, religion was part of the "constantly renewable flow of human thought" and it was impossible to conceive of its being excluded from public debate. A fair balance of personal rights made it necessary to accept that others' thought should be subject to a minimum of influence, otherwise the result would be a "strange society of silent animals

that [would] think but ... not express themselves, that [would] talk but ... not communicate, and that [would] exist but ... not coexist."

44. Having regard to the circumstances of the case and the actual terms of the relevant courts' decisions, the Court considers that the impugned measure was in pursuit of a legitimate aim under Article 9(2), namely the protection of the rights and freedoms of others, relied on by the Government.

3. "Necessary in a democratic society"

45. Mr Kokkinakis did not consider it necessary in a democratic society to prohibit a fellow citizen's right to speak when he came to discuss religion with his neighbour. He was curious to know how a disclosure delivered with conviction and based on holy books common to all Christians could infringe the rights of others. Mrs Kyriakaki was an experienced adult woman with intellectual abilities; it was not possible, without flouting fundamental human rights, to make it a criminal offence for a Jehovah's Witness to have a conversation with a cantor's wife. Moreover, the Crete Court of Appeal, although the facts before it were precise and absolutely clear, had not managed to determine the direct or indirect nature of the applicant's attempt to intrude on the complainant's religious beliefs; its reasoning showed that it had convicted the applicant "not for something he had done but for what he was."

The Commission accepted this argument in substance.

46. The Government maintained, on the contrary, that the Greek courts had based themselves on plain facts which amounted to the offence of proselytism: Mr Kokkinakis's insistence on entering Mrs Kyriakaki's home on a false pretext; the way in which he had approached her in order to gain her trust; and his "skilful" analysis of the Holy Scriptures calculated to "delude" the complainant, who did not possess any "adequate grounding in doctrine." They pointed out that if the State remained indifferent to attacks on freedom of religious belief, major unrest would be caused that would probably disturb the social peace.

47. The Court has consistently held that a certain margin of appreciation is to be left to the Contracting States in assessing the existence and extent of the necessity of an interference, but this margin is subject to European supervision, embracing both the legislation and the decisions applying it, even those given by an independent court. The Court's task is to determine whether the measures taken at national level were justified in principle and proportionate.

In order to rule on this latter point, the Court must weigh the requirements of the protection of the rights and liberties of others against the conduct of which the applicant stood accused. In exercising its supervisory jurisdiction, the Court must look at the impugned judicial decisions against the background of the case as a whole. (See, inter alia and mutatis mutandis, Barford v. Denmark, judgment of 22 February 1989, Series A, no. 149, p. 12, § 28 [(1989) 13 E.H.R.R. 493, para 28.])

48. First of all, a distinction has to be made between bearing Christian witness and improper proselytism. The former corresponds to true evangelism, which a report drawn up in 1956 under the auspices of the World Council of Churches describes as an essential mission and a responsibility of every Christian and every Church. The latter represents a corruption or deformation of it. It may, according to the same report, take the form of activities offering material or social advantages with a view to gaining new members for a Church or exerting improper pressure on people in distress or in need; it may even entail the use of violence or brainwashing; more generally, it is not compatible with respect for the freedom of thought, conscience and religion of others.

Scrutiny of section 4 of Law no. 1363/1938 shows that the relevant criteria adopted by the Greek legislature are reconcilable with the foregoing if and in so far as they are designed only to punish improper proselytism, which the Court does not have to define in the abstract in the present case.

49. The Court notes, however, that in their reasoning the Greek courts established the applicant's liability by merely reproducing the wording of section 4 and did not sufficiently specify in what way the accused had attempted to convince his neighbour by improper means. None of the facts they set out warrants that finding.

That being so, it has not been shown that the applicant's conviction was justified in the circumstances of the case by a pressing social need. The contested measure therefore does not appear to have been proportionate to the legitimate aim pursued or, consequently, "necessary in a democratic society ... for the protection of the rights and freedoms of others."

50. In conclusion, there has been a breach of Article 9 of the Convention....

[The Court rejected a claim based on a separate section of the Convention that the challenged statute was impermissibly vague.]

FOR THESE REASONS, THE COURT

1. *Holds* by six votes to three that there has been a breach of Article 9....

Partly Concurring Opinion of JUDGE PETTITI

I was in the majority which voted that there had been a breach of Article 9, but I considered that it would have been instructive to establish the motives behind this judgment....

The expression "proselytism that is not respectable", which is ia criterion used by the Greek courts when applying the Law, is sufficient for the enactment and the case-law applying it to be regarded as contrary to Article 9.

The Government themselves recognised that the applicant had been prosecuted because he had tried to influence the person he was talking to by taking advantage of her inexperience in matters of doctrine and by exploiting her low intellect. It was therefore not a question of protecting others against physical or psychological coercion but of giving the State the possibility of arrogating to itself the right to assess a person's weakness in order to punish a proselytiser, an interference that could become dangerous if resorted to by an authoritarian State.

The vagueness of the charge and the lack of any clear definition of proselytism increase the misgivings to which the Greek Law gives rise. Even if it is accepted that the foreseeability of the law in Greece as it might apply to proselytes was sufficient, the fact remains that the haziness of the definition leaves too wide a margin of interpretation for determining criminal penalties. . . .

Interpretation criteria in relation to proselytism that are as unverifiable as "respectable or not respectable" and "misplaced" cannot guarantee legal certainty.

Proselytism is linked to freedom of religion; a believer must be able to communicate his faith and his beliefs in the religious sphere as in the philosophical sphere. Freedom of religion and conscience is a fundamental right and this freedom must be able to be exercised for the benefit of all religions and not for the benefit of a single Church, even if this has traditionally been the established Church or "dominant religion".

Freedom of religion and conscience certainly entails accepting proselytism, even where it is "not respectable". Believers and agnostic philosophers have a right to expound their beliefs, to try to get other people to share them and even to try to convert those whom they are addressing.

The only limits on the exercise of this right are those dictated by respect for the rights of others where there is an attempt to coerce the person into consenting or to use manipulative techniques.

The other types of unacceptable behaviour—such as brainwashing, breaches of labour law, endangering of public health and incitement to immorality, which are found in the practices of certain pseudo-religious groups—must be punished in positive law as ordinary criminal offences. Proselytism cannot be forbidden under cover of punishing such activities. . . .

The forms of words used by the World Council of Churches, the Second Vatican Council, philosophers and sociologists when referring to coercion, abuse of one's own rights which infringes the rights of others and the manipulation of people by methods which lead to a violation of conscience, all make it possible to define any permissible limits of proselytism. They can provide the member States with positive material for giving effect to the Court's judgment in future and fully implementing the principle and standards of religious freedom under Article 9 of the European Convention.

Concurring Opinion of JUDGE DE MEYER

Proselytism, defined as "zeal in spreading the faith," [1] cannot be punishable as such: it is a way—perfectly legitimate in itself—of "manifesting one's religion."

1. (Le Petit Robert, vol 1, 1992 ed, p 1552).

In the instant case the applicant was convicted only for having shown such zeal, without any impropriety on his part.

All that he could be accused of was that he had tried to get Mrs Kyriakaki to share his religious beliefs. Mrs Kyriakaki had let him into her house and there is nothing to show that she asked him at any point to leave; she preferred to listen to what he had to say while awaiting the arrival of the police, who had been alerted by her husband, the cantor.

Dissenting Opinion of JUDGE VALTICOS

I regret that I cannot share the opinion of the majority of the Court and I regret just as much that they could not accept my view. My disagreement concerns both the scope of Article 9 and the assessment of the facts in this case.

As regards the scope of Article 9, I am unable to interpret the words "freedom, either alone or in community with others and in public or private, to manifest [one's] religion or belief, in worship, teaching, practice, and observance" as broadly as the majority do. As with all freedoms, everyone's freedom of religion must end where another person's begins. Freedom "either alone or in community with others and in public or private, to manifest [one's] religion," certainly means freedom to practise and manifest it, but not to attempt persistently to combat and alter the religion of others, to influence minds by active and often unreasonable propaganda. It is designed to ensure religious peace and tolerance, not to permit religious clashes and even wars, particularly at a time when many sects manage to entice simple, naive souls by doubtful means. But even if the Chamber considers that such is not its purpose, that is, at all events, the direction in which its conception may lead.

At this stage a misunderstanding must be removed: it has been maintained that conversations during which a person merely sets out his religious beliefs cannot constitute an attack on the religion of others. In reality, the position in the instant case is quite different. In another case being heard by another Chamber (the Hoffman case) the Commission states in its report that the complainant, who is also a Jehovah's Witness, made visits *once a week* to spread her faith. In the case of this sect, therefore, what is involved is indeed a systematic attempt at conversion, and consequently an attack on the religious beliefs of others. That has nothing to do with Article 9, which is designed solely to protect the religion of individuals and not their right to attack that of others.

I may add that the term "teaching" in Article 9 undoubtedly refers to religious teaching in school curricula or in religious institutions, and not to personal door-to-door canvassing as in the present case.

This brings me to the present case.

There are three aspects to it: national law, the facts properly speaking and the court decisions.

First of all, the Law: is it precise or does it contain an element of ambiguity, of excessive generality, which might allow of arbitrariness in the application of it as a criminal statute? In my view, there is no room for doubt. The law deals with, as an offence, "proselytism," which is of course a Greek word and, like so many others, has passed into English and also into French, and which the *Petit Robert* dictionary defines as "zeal in spreading the faith, and *by extension* in making converts, winning adherents." This is a far cry from merely manifesting one's belief, as covered by Article 9. Someone who proselytises seeks to convert others; he does not confine himself to affirming his faith but seeks to change that of others to his own. And the *Petit Robert* clarifies its explanation by giving the following quotation from Paul Valéry: "I consider it unworthy to want others to be of one's own opinion. Proselytism astonishes me."

Whereas the term "proselytism" would, in my view, have sufficed to define the offence and to satisfy the principle that an offence must be defined in law, Greek criminal law, for the avoidance of any ambiguity, gives an illustration of it which, while intended as an explanation and an example (no doubt the commonest one), nonetheless constitutes a meaningful definition, and that is: By "proselytism" is meant, in particular, any direct or indirect attempt to intrude on the religious beliefs of a person of a different religious persuasion, with the aim of undermining those beliefs, either by any kind of inducement or promise of an inducement or moral support or material assistance, or by fraudulent means or by taking advantage of his inexperience, trust, need, low intellect or naivety."

This definition of, if one may so term it, rape of the beliefs of others cannot in any way be regarded as contrary to Article 9 of the Convention. On the contrary, it is such as to protect individuals' freedom of religious belief.

Let us look now at the facts of the case. On the one hand, we have a militant Jehovah's Witness, a hardbitten adept of proselytism, a specialist in conversion, a martyr of the criminal courts whose earlier convictions have served only to harden him in his militancy, and, on the other hand, the ideal victim, a naive woman, the wife of a cantor in the Orthodox Church (if he manages to convert her, what a triumph!). He swoops on her, trumpets that he has good news for her (the play on words is obvious, but no doubt not to her), manages to get himself let in and, as an experienced commercial traveller and cunning purveyor of a faith he wants to spread, expounds to her his intellectual wares cunningly wrapped up in a mantle of universal peace and radiant happiness. Who, indeed, would not like peace and happiness? But is this the mere exposition of Mr Kokkinakis's beliefs or is it not rather an attempt to beguile the simple soul of the cantor's wife? Does the Convention afford its protection to such undertakings? Certainly not.

One further detail must be provided. The Greek Law does not in any way restrict the concept of proselytism to attempts at the intellectual corruption of Orthodox Christians but applies irrespective of the religion concerned. Admittedly, the Government's representative was not able to give concrete examples concerning other religions, but that is not surprising since the Orthodox religion is the religion of nearly the whole population and sects are going to fish for followers in the best-stocked waters.

Probably in recent years there have been rather too many prosecutions and the police have been rather too active, but more recently there has been a substantial drop in the number of such prosecutions, and in the present case there was no official prosecution—it was the victim's husband who, on returning home and discovering what the home preacher was up to, raised his voice, which was a strong one, to call the police.

I should certainly be inclined to recommend the Government to give instructions that prosecutions should be avoided where harmless conversations are involved, but not in the case of systematic, persistent campaigns entailing actions bordering on unlawful entry.

That having been said, I do not consider in any way that there has been a breach of the Convention.

PS. Having read certain separate opinions annexed to the judgment, I must express my regret at a number of exaggerations which go so far as to make reference to totalitarian regimes.

I should also like to sound a note of caution with regard to the opinion that "attempting to make converts is not in itself an attack on the freedom and beliefs of others or an infringement of their rights." Certainly that is an expression of moderation and common sense and the Chamber (perhaps even the plenary Court should have dealt with it) very rightly warned against abuses where proselytism is concerned. But faith can sometimes be blind and attempts to spread it can be overzealous. Acts of faith have sometimes culminated in *autos-da-fé* and questioning on the subject has lead to inquisitions, while the names of certain saints have remained associated with excesses committed on their feast days. In matters of faith, as in so many other matters, respect for the human person must always be upheld.

At a time when sects enjoying varying degrees of recognition and, sometimes, even adherents of recognised religions resort, under the influence of fanaticism, to all kinds of tactics to obtain conversions, sometimes with tragic results, as has been seen again recently, it is regrettable that the above judgment should allow proselytising activities on condition only that they should not be "improper." Can a convention on human rights really authorise such an intrusion on people's beliefs, even where it is not a forceful one?

Partly Dissenting Opinion of Judge Martens

Introduction

1. I concur with the Court that there has been a breach of Article 9, but for reasons other than those relied on by the Court. . . .

3.   ... [A]lthough both parties have—rightly—elevated the debate to the plane of important principle, it should not be forgotten that what occasioned this debate was a normal and perfectly inoffensive call by two elderly Jehovah's Witnesses (the applicant was 77 at the time) trying to sell some of the sect's booklets to a lady who, instead of closing the door, allowed the old couple entry, either because she was no match for their insistence or because she believed them to be bringing tidings from relatives on the mainland. There is no trace of violence or of anything that could properly be styled "coercion"; at the worst there was a trivial lie. If resort to criminal law was at all warranted, a prosecution for disturbance of domestic peace would seem the severest possible response....

Has Article 9 been violated?

13.   The Court's judgment touches only incidentally on the question which, in my opinion, is the crucial one in this case: does Article 9 allow member States to make it a *criminal offence* to attempt to induce somebody to change his religion? From what it said in paragraphs [42] and 46 it is clear that the Court answers this question in the affirmative. My answer is in the negative.

14.   The basic principle in human rights is respect for human dignity and human freedom. Essential for that dignity and that freedom are the freedoms of thought, conscience and religion enshrined in Article 9 § 1. Accordingly, they are absolute. The Convention leaves no room whatsoever for interference by the State.

These absolute freedoms explicitly include freedom to change one's religion and beliefs. Whether or not somebody intends to change religion is no concern of the State's and, consequently, neither in principle should it be the State's concern if somebody attempts to induce another to change his religion.

15.   There were good reasons for laying down in Article 9 that freedom of religion includes freedom to teach one's religion: many religious faiths count teaching the faith amongst the principal duties of believers. Admittedly, such teaching may gradually shade off into proselytising. It is true, furthermore, that proselytising creates a possible "conflict" between two subjects of the right to freedom of religion: it sets the rights of those whose religious faith encourages or requires such activity against the rights of those targeted to maintain their beliefs.

In principle, however, it is not within the province of the State to interfere in this "conflict" between proselytiser and proselytised. Firstly, because—since respect for human dignity and human freedom implies that the State is bound to accept that in principle everybody is capable of determining his fate in the way that he deems best—there is no justification for the State to use its power "to protect" the proselytised (it may be otherwise in very special situations in which the State has a particular duty of care, but such situations fall outside the present issue). Secondly, because even the "public order" argument cannot justify use of coercive State power in a field where tolerance demands that "free argument and debate" should be decisive. And thirdly, because under the Convention all religions and beliefs should, as far as the State is concerned, be equal.

That is also true in a State where, as in the present case, one particular religion has a dominant position: as the drafting history of Article 9 confirms, the fact of one religion having a special position under national law is immaterial to the State's obligation under that Article.

To allow States to interfere in the "conflict" implied in proselytising by making proselytising a *criminal offence* would not only run counter to the strict neutrality which the State is required to maintain in this field but also create the danger of discrimination when there is one dominant religion. The latter point is tellingly illustrated by the file that was before the Court.

16.   In this context the Court suggests that some forms of proselytism are "proper" while others are "improper" and therefore may be criminalised.

Admittedly, the freedom to proselytise may be abused, but the crucial question is whether that justifies enacting a criminal-law provision generally making punishable what the State considers improper proselytism. There are at least two reasons for answering that question in the negative. The first is that the State, being bound to strict neutrality in religious matters, lacks the necessary touchstone and therefore should not set itself up as the arbiter for assessing whether particular religious behaviour is "proper" or "improper." The absence of such a touchstone cannot be made good (as the Court attempts to do) by resorting to the quasi-neutral test whether or not the proselytism in question is "compatible with respect for the freedom of thought, conscience and religion of others." This is because that very absence implies that the State is lacking intrinsic justification for attributing greater value to the freedom not to be proselytised than to the right to proselytise and, consequently, for introducing a criminal-law provision protecting the former at the cost of the latter. The second reason is that the rising tide of religious intolerance makes it imperative to keep the State's powers in this field within the strictest possible boundaries. However, the Court achieves quite the reverse in attempting to settle those boundaries by means of so elusive a notion as "improper proselytism," a definition of which the Court does not even attempt to give.

17.   Should the judgment be otherwise where proselytism is combined with "coercion"? I do not think so.

Coercion in the present context does not refer to conversion by coercion, for people who truly believe do not change their beliefs as a result of coercion; what we are really contemplating is coercion in order to make somebody join a denomination and its counterpart, coercion to prevent somebody from leaving a denomination. Even in such a case of "coercion for religious purposes" it is in principle for those concerned to help themselves. Accordingly, if there is to be a legal remedy, it should be a civil-law remedy. The strict neutrality which the State is bound to observe in religious matters excludes interference in this conflict by means of criminal law. Unless, of course, the coercion, *apart from its purpose*, constitutes an ordinary crime, such as physical assault. In such cases the State may, of course, prosecute under the applicable provision of (ordinary) criminal law and a defence based on freedom to proselytise may properly be rejected if that freedom is clearly abused. There is, however, no justification for making coercion in religious matters a criminal offence *per se*.

18.   Is there no such justification even for making proselytism practised by means of serious forms of *spiritual* coercion a criminal offence? Cannot such justification be found in the methods of conversion used by some of the numerous new sects which have emerged these last decades, methods which are often said to be akin to brainwashing? Should not the State be entitled to protect its citizens—and especially its minors—against such methods?

Even if the use of such objectionable methods of proselytising had been established, I would have hesitated to answer this question in the affirmative, since it is evidently difficult to establish where spiritual means of conversion cross the borderline between insistent and intensive teaching, which should be allowed, and spiritual coercion akin to brainwashing. I am not satisfied, however, that the existence of such offensive methods has been established. In 1984 the author of a study on these new sects, made at the request of the Netherlands Parliament, concluded after extensive research that, as far as the Netherlands were concerned, there was no such evidence. The author stressed that everywhere the new sects had provoked violent reactions including persistent allegations about such methods, but that Governments had up till then declined to take measures.

I would add that there probably are methods of spiritual coercion akin to brainwashing which arguably fall within the ambit of Article 3 of the Convention and should therefore be prohibited by making their use an offence under ordinary criminal law. But in this context also I would stress that there is no justification for making a special provision in the law for cases where such methods are used for the purpose of proselytising....

20.   For these reasons I find that Greece, which, as far as I have been able to ascertain, is the only member-State to have made proselytism a criminal offence *per se*, in so doing has violated Article 9 of the Convention.

Joint Dissenting Opinion of JUDGES FOIGHEL and LOIZOU

We regret that we are unable to agree with the opinion of the majority of the Court as we take a different approach to the issues raised in this case. Article 9 § 1 guarantees to everyone the right to freedom of thought, conscience and religion; this right includes freedom to change one's religion or belief and freedom, either alone or in community with others and in public or private, to manifest one's religion or belief, in worship, teaching, practice and observance. We are concerned here with the freedom one has to teach one's own religion....

The term "teach" entails openness and uprightness and the avoidance of the use of devious or improper means or false pretexts as in this case in order to gain access to a person's home and, once there, by abusing the courtesy and hospitality extended, take advantage of the ignorance or inexperience in theological doctrine of someone who has no specialist training and try to get that person to change his or her religion.

This is all the more so as the term "teach" has to be read in the context of the whole Article and in conjunction with the limitations prescribed by paragraph 2, in particular that of the protection of the rights and freedoms of others, which no doubt includes a duty imposed on those who are engaged in teaching their religion to respect that of others. Religious tolerance implies respect for the religious beliefs of others.

One cannot be deemed to show respect for the rights and freedoms of others if one employs means that are intended to entrap someone and dominate his mind in order to convert him. This is impermissible in the civilised societies of the Contracting States. The persistent efforts of some fanatics to convert others to their own beliefs by using unacceptable psychological techniques on people, which amount in effect to coercion, cannot in our view come within the ambit of the natural meaning of the term "teach" to be found in paragraph 1 of this Article.

For the above reasons we find in the circumstances of this case that there has been no breach of Article 9.

Questions and Comments

1. *Defending Wisconsin and Greece?* The best defense of Wisconsin's application of its mandatory attendance rule may be that the state sought to preserve the option for children of becoming more completely integrated into non-Amish society. The best defense of Greece's application of its anti-proselytization statute may be that the nation sought to preserve its current cultural-religious make-up. Are these policies that a constitutional order ought to be allowed to pursue? If efforts to do so characterize many constitutional orders, what limits should there be to such efforts? Note that statutes banning proselytizing raise free expression as well as freedom of religion concerns. The Court in *Kokkinakis* found it unnecessary to address Kokkinakis's free expression claim in light of its disposition of the freedom of religion claim.

2. *Representation, Majorities and Minorities, and Judicial Review:* John Hart Ely, Democracy and Distrust (1980), argues that courts should intervene on behalf of minorities whose interests the majority is likely to discount systematically. Such a theory might justify the decisions in *Yoder* and *Kokkinakis*. Does it overestimate the majority's ability to protect *its* perceived interests through non-legal means, such as the general culture's commitment to the majority's religion? Recall Makau Wa Mutua's argument earlier in this Chapter, against rights to proselytize, as you read the following defenses of efforts by religious majorities in Russia and eastern Europe to preserve their religious position in the face of different kinds of challenges. If you find such arguments persuasive, do they shed light on the problem addressed in the principal cases?

3. *Russia, Religious Preferences and Constitutional Transition*: In 1997 the Russian parliament adopted a law "On Freedom of Conscience and on Religious Associations." The law's preamble stated, "Confirming the right of equal to freedom of conscience and freedom of creed, and also to equality before the law regardless of his attitudes to religion and his convictions; basing itself on the fact that the Russian Federation is a secular state; recognizing the special contribution of Orthodoxy to the history of Russia and to the establishment and development of Russia's spirituality and culture; respecting Christianity, Islam, Buddhism, Judaism and other religions which constitute an inseparable part of the historical heritage of Russia's peoples; considering it important to promote the achievement of mutual understanding, tolerance and respect in questions of freedom of conscience and freedom of creed." The statute's most controversial provisions in the law distinguished between religious groups and religious organizations. Religious groups were defined as voluntary associations "formed for the goals of joint confession and dissemination of their faith, carrying out [their] activities without state registration and without obtaining the legal capabilities of a legal personality" such as property ownership. Religious groups have the right "to carry out worship services, religious rituals, and ceremonies, and also the teaching of religion and religious upbringing of their followers."

Religious organizations have more rights, including the rights to own property and to carry out religious activities in hospitals and prisons, and to distribute literature. They have "the exclusive right to institute enterprises for producing liturgical literature." The statute sets up procedures for registering religious organizations. The key provision allows the registration of religious organizations only if they have "existed over the course of no less than fifteen years on the relevant territory." Such organizations would therefore have to have been in existence during the period of Soviet rule, when the government was officially hostile to religion. The statute would have the effect of giving long-standing religions such as Orthodoxy a favored place in the law.

Consider these comments made in 1994 by a representative of the Moscow Orthodox Patriarchate, and reported in Harold J. Berman, *Religious Rights in Russia at a Time of Tumultuous Transition: A Historical Theory,* in Religious Human Rights in Global Perspective: Legal Perspectives 302–03 (Johan D. van der Vyver and John Witte, Jr., eds. 1996):

> [In response to the observation that foreign missionaries were attracting atheistic or agnostic Russians, not those who were members of the Orthodox Church]: It is our task to return them to Orthodoxy.... [I]t would be better if at the end of the sermon your preachers would tell the Russians in the congregation that they can also find these same truths in their own Russian Orthodox Church....
>
> The changes now taking place in Russia, ... including especially the economic reforms, require a new post-Soviet psychology among the

people. For three generations the people has been brought up on a simple monolithic ideology that is now repudiated. The belief in Soviet superiority is gone. The belief in progress toward a bright future is gone. The people feels lost.

The foreign evangelical missionaries ... know that there is a spiritual crisis but they do not understand it. In fact, they are offering to the people another simple solution. Like the Communists, they offer salvation in return for a commitment which requires little efforts. "Just believe, and you will be saved." This reinforces the old psychology, in which simple slogans were offered in return for immediate minimum rewards but great rewards in the future. Russian Orthodoxy is more complex and more difficult. It teaches not rewards but sacrifice. It teaches the positive value of suffering. Its spiritual demands are great....

In the past, ... whenever there has been a spiritual crisis of this intensity, the people has turned to the Russian Church.... Moreover, both the extreme nationalists on the right and the radical democrats on the left can be reconciled on this point, namely, that to meet our spiritual crisis it is important that a strong role be played not only by the Russian Orthodox Church but also by other traditional Russian confessions, confessions that have been tested by repression for seventy-five years and that have forged a fraternal relationship with each other....

Russia needs time to recover her health before [foreign missionaries]descend on us. The Russian Orthodox Church is like a very sick person that is only beginning to recover her health.

Moreover, ... we lack both the material and the human resources needed to compete on an equal basis. The foreign missionaries are pouring huge sums of money into evangelization, paying for billboard advertisements and for television programs featuring American preachers and hiring huge stadiums for spreading their message.... For 75 years we were permitted to talk only to the faithful in our congregations. We are only beginning now to educate clergy in how to speak to non-believers....

In the United States, ... you can tolerate and assimilate these groups. You have had 200 years of democracy. We are only beginning our democracy. Today your pluralism would destroy us.

Is this defense of preference for the Orthodox Church persuasive? Is it a rationalization of a self-serving position by a member of that church's hierarchy? Note that the defense relies heavily on the special circumstances of transition. Can a similar defense be mounted for the Greek anti-proselytization statute?

4. *Civil and Criminal Penalties; State Action and Proportionality:* Note the suggestion of Judge Martens that a civil law remedy for unwanted proseltyzing might be appropriate but not a criminal penalty, which might compromise the "strict neutrality" of the state. Does Judge Martens' view

rest on the assumption that when a court gives a judgment in a civil case it is not compromising the state's neutrality? Consider here the Note on State Action, Chapter XI below. Note also Judge Martens' suggestion that, in the absence of any "trace of violence," proportionality should have limited criminal sanctions to charges of disturbing the peace.

5. *Transitions, Religious Establishment and Compensatory Justice in Eastern Europe*: For descriptions of church-state relations in Poland, Hungary, and the Czech Republic, see Ruti Teitel, *Partial Establishments of Religion/Post-Communist Transitions*, in The Law of Religious Identity: Models for Post-Communism (Andras Sajo and Shlomo Avineri eds., 1998). Teitel argues that partial establishments in those nations—including favoritism to older churches—may serve compensatory justice goals, including the restoration of church property seized under Nazi and Communist rule. She concludes, "as the transition wears on, state support of and connection to institutionalized religion will occasion the inevitable entanglement and political divisiveness." Consider whether partial establishments may nonetheless be stable elements in a liberal constitutional state, along lines suggested in the introductory reading from Durham.

6. *Historical Specificity vs. Universality:* You have now seen several defenses of systems of partial establishments, preferences for certain religions, and hostility to other religions, which rest on the identification of historically specific circumstances said to be unique to each system. Consider whether the U.S. system of non-establishment and free exercise is similarly historically specific to the circumstances in the United States, or alternatively whether there are some systems of relations between religion and government that can fairly be defended as implementing universal human rights.

CHAPTER XI

FREEDOMS OF EXPRESSION AND ASSOCIATION AND THE STATE ACTION PROBLEM

The First Amendment in the U.S. Bill of Rights provides that "Congress shall make no law ... abridging the freedom of speech, or of the press; or the right of the people peaceably to assemble, and to petition the Government for a redress of grievances." While most western democracies enjoy greater freedom of speech and political activity than exists in authoritarian or dictatorial regimes, some do so through nonconstitutional means, and in many the constitutional approaches to such issues as regulation of hate speech or libel laws differ substantially from U.S. doctrine.

In this chapter, we return to some of the questions raised in Chapter I concerning reproductive rights, this time in the context of freedom of speech and association, particularly in the political context. First, to what extent are freedoms of speech and political association normatively embraced in concepts of constitutionalism? Second, to the extent that these rights are, in some sense, necessary to constitutional democracies, how broad a sphere of protection, or conversely, how much government prohibition/regulation, is consistent with or required by such a commitment? Can these questions be answered across different constitutional cultures or not? Third, what is the relationship between majoritarian institutions and "constitutional rules" in this area? And finally, what significance does constitutional text play in the decisions of the Canadian, German and U.S. courts?

Last, we turn to a particularly difficult question in constitutional law, in the U.S. called the "state action" question and elsewhere referred to as the question of "horizontal effect." Do constitutions constrain only governments or private parties as well? Even if constitutions constrain only, or primarily, governments and those acting on their behalf, difficult questions of line drawing are posed. For example, when private disputes are adjudicated, when do the courts' decisions constitute "state action" for purposes of constitutional constraints?

A. A EUROPEAN PERSPECTIVE ON U.S. AND EUROPEAN FREE SPEECH/FREE PRESS FREEDOMS

As the following excerpt suggests, Europeans (and some U.S. scholars) have found both much to admire and much to criticize in various aspects of U.S. free speech/free press doctrine. Errera describes the developing European Union law on freedom of speech, discusses the constitutional and philosophical development of free speech theories in France and the United States, and compares U.S. and French law in three areas: commercial speech, libel, and regulation of hate speech. While praising the more systematic development of theories of the First Amendment in the United States, he is critical of the U.S. posture on regulation of hate speech.

Roger Errera, *The Freedom of the Press: The United States, France, and Other European Countries,* in Constitutionalism and Rights: The Influence of the United States Constitution Abroad (Louis Henkin and Albert J. Rosenthal eds., 1990)

. . .

[W]e are witnessing not a convergence but a limited rapprochement of concepts and social attitudes on both sides of the Atlantic, as illustrated in three areas: commercial speech; the libel of public officials; and the protection of journalists' sources of information. On the other hand, there remain deep differences regarding general principles—and, in particular, extremist forms of political expression and prior restraints.

THE FIRST CENTURY OF FREEDOM OF EXPRESSION: THE UNITED STATES AND FRANCE

The reciprocal influences of United States and French constitutional ideas in the last quarter of the eighteenth century have been the subject of a substantial volume of literature. The history of those ideas in the United States and in France during what may be called the "first century" is less known and less adequately appreciated. In the United States this period extends from the adoption of the First Amendment to the 1920s, when the Supreme Court began to extend the protection of the Fourteenth Amendment to freedom of speech and to develop a philosophy of the First Amendment. In France, a comparable significant period covers almost exactly one hundred years, from the Declaration of the Rights of Man and of the Citizen (1789) to the enactment of the 1881 statute on freedom of the press.

The United States: The Modest Beginnings of the First Amendment

The present importance of the First Amendment in United States law and in its legal and social philosophy was not prefigured in the circumstances that surrounded its inclusion in the Bill of Rights. It seems certain that the text that was adopted was meant to protect freedom of speech and of the press against Congress and not against the states. Alexander Hamilton was of the opinion that a prohibition against Congress was superfluous. He asked, "Why, for instance, should it be said that the liberty of the press shall not be restrained, when no power is given by which restrictions may be imposed?" For this reason, when the text of the Constitution was being discussed, Charles Pinckney's proposal, aiming at the addition of a clause relating to freedom of expression, was rejected as serving no purpose.

These circumstances explain the minor role attributed to the First Amendment in United States history during the nineteenth century. The only measures affecting freedom of the press came either from the states or, during the Civil War, from the President. As one commentator puts it:

> There was no realistic way for the press to claim federal First Amendment protection until after the Civil War for a variety of reasons. Notions of the autonomy and sovereignty of each individual state, for example, permitted Southern states to exclude antislavery speakers, newspapers, pamphlets, and books from their jurisdiction. [A. Soifer]

The First Amendment was barely referred to in litigation concerning freedom of expression, such as cases involving libel or obscenity. Even where freedom of expression was mentioned, as in regard to public speeches or the punishment of the press for contempt of court, the freedom was weighed against the needs of public order, and subordinated to the police powers of state and local officials and authorities.

French authors of the nineteenth century had varied comments. Alexis de Tocqueville did not even mention the First Amendment. He maintains that the press's "power is certainly much greater in France than in the United States." He noted what he called the "excessive dissemination of its power" and concluded that "in the United States each separate journal exercises but little authority; but the power of the periodical press is second only to that of the people."

When French liberal authors commented on American legal and political institutions half a century later, they placed special emphasis on the First Amendment. Edouard Laboulaye, in his valuable *Histoire des Etats-Unis,* commenting on the scope of the First Amendment, writes that should a state or Congress take measures restricting the freedom of the press (such as imposing stamp duties, requiring authorization, or providing for warning or censorship), the Supreme Court would invalidate such a statute as unconstitutional. Emile Boutmy, on the other hand, believes that the Supreme Court should, in such a case, deny its own jurisdiction. For him, "the content and substance of the first eight amendments are essentially precautions taken by the States against invasions coming from an external source of sovereignty, represented by the president and by Congress.... They did so to protect their autonomy and not for the sake of abstract rights." It is now evident that Laboulaye had anticipated, by fifty-five years, the case law inaugurated in 1925 by the Supreme Court in *Gitlow v. New York.**

* [Editors' Note: In Gitlow v. New York, 268 U.S. 652 (1925), the Court "assume[d] that freedom of speech and of the press—which are protected by the First Amendment from abridgement by Congress—are among the fundamental personal rights and 'liberties' protected by the due process clause of the Fourteenth Amendment from impair-ment by the States," but held that First Amendment principles did not prevent a state from punishing speech that advocated overthrow of the government by unlawful means. For the modern approach, distinguishing between advocacy and incitement to imminent lawlessness see below this chapter p. 1273 (editors' note) (discussing Branden-

France: 1780–1881

Almost one hundred years separate the Declaration of the Rights of Man and of the Citizen from the 1881 statute on freedom of the press. There are three main features of that century that are relevant to this discussion:

(1) Most French constitutions of the period incorporated the 1789 declaration and thereby its clauses on the freedom of the press. It is important to recall these clauses, because throughout the last century they shaped the minds and actions of those who wrote and acted in favor of freedom of speech and of the press in France.

Article 11 of the 1789 declaration states that "the free communication of thought and of opinion is one of the most precious rights of man; every citizen then may speak, write, and publish freely, but he is responsible for the abuse of that freedom in cases determined by law." This provision was echoed in later constitutions.... For example, Article 8 of the 1848 Constitution declared that

> Citizens have the right to associate, to assemble peacefully and without weapons, to send petitions and to express their thoughts through the press or by other means. The only limit to the exercise of such rights is the rights or the freedoms of others and public security. The press may not, in any case, be subjected to censorship.

Many of the clauses emphasized freedom of *expression* before mentioning freedom of the press. This is a fact of salient importance in modern France. The resemblance between Article 8 in the Constitution of 1848 and the U.S. Constitution's First Amendment is evident. Such formulations could have been the basis of a *general* law on freedom of speech, of which freedom of the press would have been a special category. This, however, was not the case. The law relating to the press, to demonstrations, to public meetings, or to associations was contained in different instruments. That is one of the main differences between United States and French law today.

(2) These constitutional declarations did not provide effective constitutional protection. There was no judicial review. More important, perhaps, the constitutional clauses themselves provided that the relevant statute (*la loi*) could define the scope of freedom of the press. Worse, the existence of authoritarian or illiberal regimes or tendencies resulted in unchecked restrictions on the freedom of the press. Even in 1881, the guarantee then afforded was no more than a very liberal and comprehensive statute; the law continued to define the freedom of expression....

(3)   ... The trial of press crimes by the jury was deemed of great importance throughout the nineteenth century. Tocqueville and Pierre Royer-Collard, a leading liberal author, saw a direct link between the legal status of an essential freedom, such as of the press, and political institu-

burg v. Ohio). *Gitlow* is often cited for Justice Holmes' dissenting opinion (urging application of the "clear and present danger" standard and arguing that mere advocacy should not be the basis for punishment). See below in this essay for further discussion of Holmes' *Gitlow* dissent.]

tions in general. In an 1835 speech Royer-Collard mentioned "the great achievement, the national achievement, by which press trials go before a jury," and stated that "the members of the jury are those entitled to vote.... Like you, they are repositories of sovereignty. If you do not trust them today, they might in their turn not trust you." He added:

> The jury is not one of those everyday courts of law, that depend entirely on what the legislator will decide and what he may place in a very high or in a very low position. The jury is not, in fact, a court of law [Ce n'est même pas une juridiction]; it is a political institution. It represents, like you and in the same degree, the sovereignty of the country itself.

A generation later another liberal author, A. Prévost-Paradol, maintained that "to discover whether the press is free in such or such a country, we never think first of the relevant statute that applies to it. Without hesitation, at once, ask: Who tries?" Prévost-Paradol also thought that the jury was the "logical and natural judge of the press."

The second point of focus in the debates concerned the role of the press in a liberal society. According to Chateaubriand there could be "no representative government without freedom of the press." Benjamin Constant, when attempting to separate what today would be called "speech" from "conduct," declared: "Writings, like speech, like the most simple movements, can become part of an action. They must be considered, or tried, as parts of that action if it is a criminal one. But if they are not part of any action, they must, like speech [la parole] be left entirely free." Constant used the same arguments as John Stuart Mill to justify freedom of the press. To him such freedom was "the only safeguard of the citizens."

This parallel history (or prehistory) of the United States and France offers many contrasts. In France the political and legal debate during the nineteenth century was intense and of high quality; it was almost nonexistent in the United States. Also, in France there was a sharp contrast between the continued repetition of constitutional proclamations and the absence of effective constitutional protection for freedom of speech or of the press. Both countries, however, shared a common element, which ultimately proved to be of great importance. Each country had an authoritative text from the beginning—the First Amendment in the United States, and Article 11 of the 1789 Declaration in France. Lawyers, the courts, and politicians might have been slow to discover the full legal implication of those texts. After *Gitlow* in the United States and, much more recently, the 1984 decision of the French *Conseil constitutionnel*, the full import of those texts has been recognized.

FREEDOM OF EXPRESSION IN FRANCE: CONSTITUTIONAL STATUS, WITH A LIMITED GUARANTEE

Today freedom of expression has constitutional status in France as in the United States, but in France it provides only a limited guarantee.

The constitutional status of the freedom of the press is based not only on Article 11 of the 1789 Declaration but also on the fact that such freedom constitutes, in French constitutional law, one of the "fundamental principles recognized by the laws of the Republic." This is declared in the Preamble of the 1946 Constitution (recognized as an integral part of that Constitution) and has been adopted by the Constitution of 1958 which is in effect today.

. . . The Constitutional Council's decisions concerning freedom of expression can be summed up as follows. As stated in Article 11 of the 1789 Declaration, the communication of ideas and information was a basic freedom. Consequently, under Article 34 of the Constitution, which defines the legislative jurisdiction of Parliament, Parliament (and not the executive) has exclusive jurisdiction to enunciate the rules relating to the fundamental guarantee of the exercise of such a freedom. In doing so, Parliament may not go beyond what is deemed necessary—an important affirmation of the principle of necessity and proportionality. Therefore, decisions relating to the monopoly of the state over broadcasting, and the authorization needed by private broadcasters granted by the government or by an independent authority had to take account of the freedom of communication, technical constraints, and three objectives, each of constitutional character: the needs of public order *(ordre public);* respect for the freedoms of others; and the preservation of what the Constitutional Council called "pluralism," taking into full consideration the special character of broadcasting in this respect.

On October 10–11, 1984 the Constitutional Council rendered a landmark decision. A new statute on the press had just been passed by Parliament. The statute required newspapers and press companies to make public certain information on ownership. The statute also sought to limit economic concentration. The discussion of the bill in Parliament and in the press itself had been the occasion of a long and sometimes heated debate, and the opposition in Parliament did not conceal its intention to refer the bill to the Constitutional Council, whose decision set forth many elements of a general concept of the freedom of the press.

First, the obligation to make public certain information on ownership (referred to as *transparence* in France) is not inconsistent with, and does not limit, freedom of the press. On the contrary, such information tends to reinforce an effective exercise of the freedom of the press. By informing the public about the identity of the real proprietors *(dirigeants)* of press companies, about financial transactions relating to them, and about related economic interests, readers will be in a position to decide freely among newspapers. Public opinion will be fully informed of what the press offers.

Political parties posed a special problem under the new statute. According to Article 4 of the Constitution, "Political parties and associations are a vital part of the expression of suffrage. They may be created and may operate freely. They must, however, respect the principles of national sovereignty and of democracy." The Constitutional Council's decision here set forth two principles: First, in matters pertaining to the press, political parties do not enjoy rights superior to those of ordinary citizens. Second, in applying the new statute, there must be special care taken not to hinder the activity of political parties as protected under Article 4 of the Constitution.

As regards the dispositions of the statute limiting economic concentration in the press *(pluralisme)*, the Constitutional Council quoted Article 11 of the 1789 Declaration: "The free communication of thought and of opinion is one of the most precious rights of man; every citizen then may speak, write and publish freely, but he is responsible for the abuse of that freedom in cases determined by law." The Council used this article not only to assign limits to the 1984 statute, but also to assign them to *any* future statute on the subject. The Council affirmed that Parliament has exclusive jurisdiction to legislate with respect to the exercise of a fundamental freedom, such as the freedom of communication (Art. 34 of the Constitution). But there are limits to the powers of Parliament. Legislation may have only two legitimate purposes: to facilitate the exercise of freedom of expression and to reconcile it with other constitutional rules or principles.

The Council noted that the exercise of freedom of expression "is one of the essential guarantees of the respect for other rights and freedoms and for national sovereignty." The reference to national sovereignty apart, these words echo those used by Justice Cardozo in 1937 when he justified the freedom of speech as a fundamental liberty. Freedom of expression was "the indispensable condition of nearly every other form of freedom." That passage in the Constitutional Council's decision did not go unnoticed and we may anticipate its influence in the coming years.

The Constitutional Council declared the protection of "pluralism"—that is, the prevention of excessive economic concentration—in the newspapers a constitutional objective: "The objective is that readers, who form an essential part of the beneficiaries of freedom of expression proclaimed by Article 11 of the 1789 Declaration, be in such a position as to choose freely without any interference from private interests or from the government and this cannot be made a business matter." The 1984 statute imposed a limit of 15 percent of the total national circulation as the maximum that any newspaper can control. The Constitutional Council construed this limitation narrowly, as applying only to growth due to takeovers and mergers, not to growth due to success in the market. The [C]ouncil also stated that the statute applied only to future acquisitions. As an English commentator wrote, "It considered that upsetting existing arrangements could only be constitutionally appropriate where the situation had been illegally created, or where calling it into question was 'really necessary to ensure the realization of the constitutional objective pursued,' neither of which applied to the present case."

It is important to recognize the legal and political significance of the Constitutional Council's statement on freedom of expression in general. When the statute of 1881 was passed it covered essentially the printing profession and newspapers; it made no reference to press companies and readers. What may seem surprising to us today was entirely understandable then. After generations of battles for freedom to publish, forgetting the economics of the press and the interests of readers was natural. Such an oversight would not occur today.

A Limited Protection

Constitutional protection of freedom of expression in France is limited by certain features of the French legal system:

(1) Under Article 61 of the Constitution, statutes may be referred to the Constitutional Council only after their adoption by Parliament but before their promulgation. . . .

(2) The ordinary courts have no power to declare statutes unconstitutional or even to refer a question about the validity of a statute to the Constitutional Council. The Conseil d'Etat and other administrative courts can annul an action by the government that is within its autonomous regulatory power—the *pouvoir réglementaire autonome*—if they find that it is invalid under the Constitution.

(3) For reasons rooted in French legal and political history, the law governing freedom of the (written) press and freedom of association and assembly and the law relating to marches and demonstrations do not form a unified law. The different freedoms are governed by different statutes passed at different times, and in some respects they are very different in their content and construction. A unifying principle such as that of the U.S. constitution's First Amendment is absent.

(4) A comparison of court decisions and the legal literature of freedom of the press and of expression in the United States and in France yields one major difference. On the European side there is not the range of reflection and discussion on the philosophical, political, and social foundations of such freedoms and on the related social values that are found in American writings and court decisions. In the French judicial tradition, court decisions are extremely concise. They usually shun philosophical or social arguments of the kind familiar to United States court decisions. The publication of concurring or dissenting individual opinions would be considered a breach of both law and precedent.

Recent decisions of the Constitutional Council provide a welcome and much-needed departure from earlier habit. But whereas the body of important U.S. Supreme Court decisions on freedom of speech is more than half a century old, French constitutional case law is recent. The general courts are not yet fully accustomed to using, in their judgments, such texts as Article 11 of the 1789 Declaration. But there is change in the air, and United States legal ideas are likely to have increasing influence.

In most treatises on information law or on civil liberties the exposition of the law is preceded by historical developments or by a few general considerations. Until recently constitutional law tended to be considered in French law schools as a kind of poor relation of law teaching. Jurisprudence is not generally taught, and where it does exist, it is not compulsory. Such items of the curriculum as constitutional and administrative law and civil liberties are taught separately, and the link between them is not always highlighted. A rather sterile form of legal positivism has dominated. Which French general legal journal, for instance, has ever offered its readers a debate like that found in the *Harvard Law Review* in 1958 between H. L. A. Hart and Lon Fuller? Which French philosopher has given lawyers the kind of intellectual stimulus provided by A. Meiklejohn? Perhaps, however, things are beginning to change: the creation in 1985 of a new legal journal, *Droits: Revue française de théorie juridique,* is cause for some hope.

TOWARD A GENERAL EUROPEAN CONCEPT OF FREEDOM OF EXPRESSION

A proposal for a general concept of expression might address, first, the philosophical foundations of such a freedom, and then the scope of the concept. . . .

Toward the end of the twentieth century the central elements for a European concept of freedom of expression are Article 10 of the European Convention on Human Rights and the case law of the European Human Rights Commission and the European Court of Human Rights in Strasbourg on the enforcement of that article. That case law is not impervious to United States influence and can provide a basis for comparison with the philosophy and the case law of the First Amendment.

The European Convention requires the high contracting parties to "secure to everyone within their jurisdiction" the rights and freedoms defined in the Convention. Most of the rights defined are not absolute. Every article enunciates a basic freedom as well as the legitimate restrictions that may be placed on it.

Article 10 of the Convention provides:

1. Everyone has the right to freedom of expression. This right shall include freedom to hold opinions and to receive and impart information and ideas without interference by public authority and regardless of frontiers. This Article shall not prevent States from requiring the licensing of broadcasting, television or cinema enterprises.

2. The exercise of these freedoms, since it carries with it duties and responsibilities, may be subject to such formalities, conditions, restrictions or penalties as are prescribed by law and are necessary in a democratic society, in the interests of national security, territorial integrity or public safety, for the prevention of disorder or crime, for the protection of health or morals, for the protection of the reputation of rights of others, for preventing the disclosure of information received in confidence, or for maintaining the authority and impartiality of the judiciary.

The cases applying Article 10 have articulated several considerations for a philosophy of free expression. An important element in such a theory is the concept of a "democratic society" invoked in Article 10: "The court's supervisory function obliges it to pay the utmost attention to the principles characterizing a 'democratic society.' Freedom of expression constitutes one of the essential foundations of such a society, one of the basic conditions for its progress and for the development of any man."

The Court referred to the phrase "in a democratic society" as contemplating "the demands of that pluralism, tolerance, and of that broadmindedness without which there is no 'democratic society.'" Article 10 is "applicable not only to 'information' or 'ideas' that are favorably received or regarded as inoffensive or as a matter of indifference, but also to those that offend, shock or disturb the State or any sector of the population." In a democratic society, "every 'formality', 'condition', 'restriction' or 'penalty' imposed in this sphere must be proportionate to the legitimate aim pursued."

The notions of pluralism and tolerance are indeed essential. I would suggest, however, that pluralism is a *necessary* condition of a democratic society; it is not a *sufficient* condition. Without consensus on the kind of society in which we want to live and on certain basic values that must be respected and protected, pluralism is nothing more than a confederation of tendencies or interests, and tolerance becomes a kind of indifference and moral relativism.

According to Article 10(2), in a democratic society the exercise of freedom of expression "carries with it duties and responsibilities" that depend on all of the circumstances including the means used for the exercise of the freedom. Therefore the exercise of freedom is subject to "formalities, conditions, restrictions or penalties" imposed by public authority, irrespective of their nature (administrative, civil, or criminal) or their source (administrative, legislative, or judicial).

These restrictions and their elaboration by the European Human Rights Commission and the European Human Rights Court have also contributed elements to a general concept of freedom of expression:

(1) Restrictions on freedom of expression must be "prescribed by law":

First, the law must be adequately accessible. The citizen must be able to have an indication that is adequate in the circumstances of the legal rules applicable to a given case. Secondly, a norm cannot be regarded as a "law" unless it is formulated with sufficient precision to enable the citizen to regulate his conduct. He must be able—if need be with appropriate advice—to foresee, to a degree that is reasonable in the circumstances, the consequences a given action may entail. Those consequences need not be foreseeable with absolute certainty.... [Sunday Times v. U.K., April 6, 1979, Series A, No. 30, 2 EARR 245]

(2) The only legitimate restrictions on the freedom of expression are those enunciated in Article 10(2): the interests of national security; territorial integrity or public safety; the prevention of disorder or crime; the protection of health or morals; the protection of the reputation or rights of others; the protection of confidential information; and the authority and impartiality of the judiciary. This article must, however, be read in conjunction with other articles of the Convention, such as the provisions permit-

ting derogation from rights in a time of public emergency (Art. 15) and the permissible limitations on the political activities of aliens (Art. 16).

(3) The Court seems to resist the notion of "balancing" the freedom of expression against the public good, a principle familiar in the jurisprudence of the United States. The Court "is faced not with a choice between two conflicting principles, but with a principle of freedom of expression that is subject to a number of exceptions which must be narrowly interpreted."

(4) In judging restrictions, the Court has been alert to its own role:

> It is not sufficient that the interference involved belongs to that class of the exceptions listed in Article 10(2) which has been invoked. Neither is it sufficient that the interference was imposed because its subject-matter fell within a particular category or was caught by a legal rule formulated in general or absolute terms. The Court has to be satisfied that the interference was necessary with regard to the facts and circumstances prevailing in the specific case before it. [*Sunday Times*]

The general theory of the freedom of expression has been applied in a number of cases involving restrictions claimed to be justified under Article 10(2):

(a) The protection of morals. The *Handyside* case involved the seizure, forfeiture, and later destruction, as obscene, of copies of the *Little Red Book for Schoolchildren,* which a British company had proposed to publish. The Court found the interference with the publisher's freedom of expression to be "prescribed by law" (i.e., the Obscene Publication Act, 1959 and 1964) and "necessary in a democratic society" for the protection of morals.

(b) The prevention of the disclosure of information received in confidence. The editor of a Swiss daily was sentenced and fined for publishing part of a classified report by the Swiss secret services regarding espionage. The European Human Rights Commission held that under the circumstances this was not a violation of the Convention.

(c) The protection of the reputation or rights of others. The law of blasphemous libel—an historical curiosity in most countries today—led, in Great Britain, to the conviction of applicants to a fine and to a suspended sentence of imprisonment for publishing a poem on Christ's alleged homosexuality. The Commission concluded that Article 10 of the Convention had not been violated.

Two Austrian cases of libel led to important decisions contributing to the theory of freedom of expression. In the first case the European Human Rights Commission held that the Austrian law obliging the press to publish only what can be proven true did not go beyond what is reasonably necessary in a democratic society. The full measure of the law was to be brought into play only when allegations of an *objectively* defamatory character had been made against a particular person. In the *Lingens* case, the Commission held that Article 10 had been violated. Bruno Kreisky, the former chancellor of Austria, initiated criminal proceedings against a journalist who was subsequently convicted of public defamation. The journalist had criticized Kreisky's political behavior and some of his statements, in particular his relations with Peter, a leader of the Austrian Liberal party, and Peter's alleged past involvement with the Nazi movement; there was no reference to any conduct within Kreisky's private life. The journalist was convicted on the grounds that he had described Kreisky's behavior as coming close to the "ugliest opportunism," and as "immoral" and "undignified." ... [T]he Court ... [found] that the interference with the journalist was not "necessary in a democratic society ... for the protection of the reputation ... of others."

The Commission rejected the application in a case involving the conviction of applicants for possessing racist pamphlets. Quoting Article 17 of the European convention, the Commission said that its general purpose was "to prevent totalitarian groups from exploiting, in their own interests, the principles enunciated in the Convention." In another case, the Commission upheld German defamation laws prohibiting the display of literature denying the genocide of the Jews.

Maintaining the Authority and Impartiality of the Judiciary

This was the issue in the *Sunday Times* case decided by the European Court of Human Rights in 1979. In that case,

distillers had marketed a drug, "thalidomide," which had been taken by a number of pregnant women who later gave birth to deformed children. Writs were issued by the parents and a lengthy period of negotiations followed without the cases proceeding to trial. A weekly newspaper, *The Sunday Times,* began a series of articles with the aim of assisting the parents in obtaining a more generous settlement of their actions. One proposed article was to deal with the history of the testing, manufacturing and marketing of the drug, but the Attorney-General obtained an injunction restraining publication of the article on the ground that it would constitute a contempt of court. The injunction had been granted in the High House of Lords. The publisher, editor, and a group of journalists of the *Sunday Times* filed an application ... claiming that the injunction infringed on their right to freedom of expression.

The Court held that Article 10 of the Convention had been violated. After examining at length the English law of contempt, the Court found that the interference with the applicants' freedom of expression was prescribed by law within the meaning of Article 10(2). But was the law, as applied to this case, "necessary in a democratic society"? Did it respond to a pressing social need? Was it proportionate to the legitimate end pursued? Under the circumstances the Court found that the law did not meet those standards. The proposed article was couched in moderate terms and did not present just one side of the evidence. Its publication would not have had adverse consequences for the "authority of the judiciary." The Court added:

There is general recognition of the fact that the Courts cannot operate in a vacuum. Whilst the mass-media must not overstep the bounds imposed in the interests of the proper administration of justice, it is incumbent on them to impart information and ideas concerning matters that come before the courts just as in other areas of public interest. Not only do the media have the task of imparting such information and ideas but the public also has a right to receive them.

The Court underlined the fact that "the thalidomide disaster was a matter of undisputed public concern.... Fundamental issues concerning protection against and compensation for injuries resulting from scientific developments were raised and many facets of the existing law on these subjects called into action."

The theory that emerges from Article 10, as illustrated in these cases, cannot be articulated in a single phrase, like that in the First Amendment to the United States Constitution—a phrase that has also required and continues to require definition and interpretation. The emerging European concept, as articulated in the paragraphs of Article 10 of the European Convention on Human Rights, is also being defined and refined. In that process, the earlier United States jurisprudence makes itself felt....

COMMERCIAL SPEECH: A COMMON HESITATION

The degree of protection, if any, afforded to commercial speech by the First Amendment or by Article 10 of the European Convention on Human Rights has been debated in the United States and in Europe during the last ten years, without conclusion. One may detect a degree of convergence of the two societies in the form of a common hesitation. On both sides of the Atlantic the ... courts have refused to exclude commercial speech altogether from the protection extended to "speech." This was the ruling in the United States in 1976 in *Virginia State Board of Pharmacy v. Virginia Consumer Council,* and the new tendency was confirmed a year later in the *Linmark* case. These two cases, however, did not relate to commercial advertising generally. The first involved a prohibition against pharmacists advertising the price of prescription drugs. In the second case the Supreme Court had to pronounce on the validity of a local ordinance banning "sold" or "for sale" signs in front of houses. In a series of later cases, the Court drew various lines in upholding some but invalidating other restrictions on the soliciting of clients by lawyers. There have been sharp differences among members of the Court regarding what is properly to be considered "commercial speech."

Things are not much clearer in Europe. The European Human Rights Commission has twice declared that commercial speech as such is not beyond the protection afforded by Article 10(1) of the European Convention on Human Rights; but these decisions were exclusively on admissibility. More recently, in the Barthold case, the European Court explicitly refused to take sides on the compatibility of the restriction of advertising by veterinarians with Article 10. Barthold, a German veterinarian, had given an interview to a newspaper in which he had been critical of the lack of emergency services at night in Hamburg. Within the interview he made mention of his own night practice. Proceedings were subsequently brought against him for breaking rules of professional conduct forbidding advertisement and publicity and for unfair competition. According to the Court:

> The restrictions imposed related to the inclusion, in any statement, of Dr. Barthold's views as to the need for a night veterinary service in Hamburg, and of certain factual data and assertions regarding in particular his person and the running of his clinic. . . . All these various components overlap to make up a whole, the gist of which is the expression of "opinions" and the imparting of "information" on a topic of general interest. It is not possible to dissociate from this whole those elements which go more to manner of presentation than to substance and which, according to the German courts, have a publicity-like effect. This is specially so since the publication prompting the restriction was an article written by a journalist and not a commercial advertisement.

The Court found that Article 10 was applicable "without needing to inquire in the present case whether or not advertising as such comes within the scope of the guarantee under this provision." It found that there had been a breach of Article 10. In his concurring opinion, Judge Pettiti briefly mentioned the evolution in standards of professional conduct. "Commercial speech," he added, is "directly connected with freedom of expression." He mentioned the United States case law on the subject and seemed to regret that the Court did not go further.

In Europe, as in the United States, a number of issues will have to be settled in order to determine what kind of protection commercial speech can be afforded *qua* speech. First, within the broad category of commercial speech it seems feasible to isolate at least two subcategories—commercial advertising and advertising by members of liberal professions (in particular, physicians and lawyers). In most countries members of these professions are subject to more or less strict rules of professional behavior, but the forms of practice are changing. Second . . . [o]ne of the main issues here is *whom* the law seeks to protect and to what degree. . . .

[Consider four groups: advertisers, broadcasters, those who use advertisements to increase their profits and consumers.]

Does our general theory of freedom of expression afford any guidelines as to how competing claims should be resolved? . . . Some Supreme Court decisions, especially *Virginia State Board of Pharmacy* and *Linmark,* can be read as indicating that consumer interests deserve greater consideration than others. The "balancing" that will have to be practiced in the United States here remains imprecise. European jurisprudence is a few steps behind. The rationale for less protection for commercial advertising than for other speech seems self-evident, and in most countries false, misleading, or inaccurate advertisement is not allowed. . . .

In a number of Western European countries television advertising is regulated by strict and detailed rules and practices relating to length and content; advertising certain products or activities is completely prohibited. With the development of national and international cable and satellite television systems, these restrictions and regulations are likely to be challenged, first before national courts, then before the European Human Rights Commission and the European Court of Human Rights in Strasbourg, or before the European Court of Justice in Luxembourg. . . .

LIBEL OF PUBLIC OFFICIALS

Whether public officials should enjoy less protection against libel than other people has been an issue in both the United States and Europe. More than twenty years after the Supreme Court decision in *New York Times v. Sullivan,* United States and European case law suggests that, in practice as well as in law, there may be a degree of convergence.

New York Times v. Sullivan involved a libel action brought by a public official against critics of his official conduct. The Court laid down the principle that, in relation to the defamation of a public official, the freedom of the press required greater protection for the press and less protection for the official. . . .

The Court concluded that "the constitutional guarantees require . . . a federal rule that prohibits a public official from recovering damages for a defamatory falsehood relating to his official conduct unless he proves that the statement was made with 'actual malice'—that is, with knowledge that it was false or with reckless disregard of whether it was false or not." . . .

New York Times v. Sullivan had far-reaching effects. Following what for some was a slippery slope but for others the logic of the *Sullivan* case, the Court applied the same standard to "public figures," then to all matters of "public or general interest." It was high time to call for a halt, if not a retreat, but there was more to come. Another fruit of *Sullivan* appeared in *Herbert v. Lando.* Here a "public figure" was trying to recover damages for defamation; the *Sullivan* test applied. To prove "actual malice" he sought to interrogate the defendants and their colleagues about their beliefs and knowledge. The defense that such interrogation cast a heavy financial burden on the defendant and would have a "chilling effect" on the willingness of the media to criticize public officials was not accepted by the Court. Professor Archibald Cox wrote: "The affront felt by editors and reporters when sharply questioned about their thoughts and emotions while preparing a story is readily understandable, but it too appears to be a consequence of the substantive law that attaches significance to an actor's state of mind." . . .

The law and practice in Europe were not very different. Some countries provide a statutory defense of "justified interest" to an action for defamation. Others, like Great Britain, have the common law defense of fair comment on matters of public interest. In the United Kingdom, the Committee on Defamation studied a proposal to establish, by statute, qualified privilege for newspapers. . . .

The committee rejected such a reform for a number of reasons. The proposed privilege "would place newspapers and broadcasting and television authorities in a special position. We are," the committee stated, "against creating such a position." Second, the committee found no evidence that the press was handicapped in its proper function by the absence of this extra protection. Such a change in the law would seriously alter the balance of the law against the plaintiff. This the committee found "intrinsically undesirable." It also thought that in many instances the proposed privilege would be ineffective as long as the press held to its principle of nondisclosure of confidential sources. Finally, the committee thought that qualified privilege in general law was available to newspapers, television, and broadcasting authorities as much as to any other person.

The committee's report twice mentioned United States case law [citing] dissenting opinions of Justices Harlan and Marshall in *Rosenbloom v. Metromedia*. . . .

French libel law applies only to a statement of fact, as distinct from opinion. In France, libel is both an offense and a tort. The same court, for example, can sentence a journalist or an editor to pay a fine and to pay damages to the person defamed. The 1881 statute on the press makes it a special offense, distinct from ordinary libel, to defame a civil servant, a member of the cabinet or of Parliament, any public official in relation to his or her duties or his or her character, or any person discharging a public service (even temporarily), such as a member of a jury or a witness before the court. The penalty incurred is more severe than in ordinary cases.

On its face, French law might seem to be much harsher on the press than United States law. In fact, it is not. In France the press has the advantage of a narrower definition of what constitutes libel as well as a narrower definition of who is a public figure. Also, the press has the benefit of strict procedure. Notably, the plaintiff must state the ground on which he/she is suing; that is, whether he/she thinks that he/she has been defamed in the capacity of public official or as a private person. He/she may not allege both, and if he/she fails in his/her suit as an official he/she cannot proceed in the same lawsuit to sue as a private citizen (this condition is contained in the 1881 statute itself, in Articles 50 and 53).

In the end, it is difficult for public officials to recover, and there is not much incentive for officials listed in Article 31 of the French law to sue for libel. The press also enjoys the additional protection of a defense of fair comment on a matter of public interest. . . .

WHERE UNITED STATES AND EUROPEAN VIEWS DIFFER

There are three important differences in legal and social attitudes between the United States and European countries regarding freedom of the press and of expression generally. The first, already mentioned, is the existence in the United States of the First Amendment—its text on freedom of speech and of the press, and its unifying power. There is a *system* of freedom of expression in the United States which contrasts with the dispersion of the law on expression in European countries. In Europe, the press, marches, demonstrations, public meetings, associations, and other forms of speech are subject to different regulations, enacted separately and often with different inspiration. Article 10 of the European Convention on Human Rights and its case law are an important step toward a unified European theory of expression, but its influence cannot be but slow.

Judicial review of statutes by national courts, where it exists, will have a more direct influence.

A second difference involves the strong resistance of the United States legal system to prior restraints in whatever form. The law of many European countries allows, under certain circumstances, the suppression of writings either by way of a court injunction or by a decision of the executive; in the United States such measures are usually held invalid under the First Amendment.... In the *Pentagon Papers* case, the Government sought to enjoin newspapers from publishing the contents of a classified study of United States policy in Vietnam. The Supreme Court declared that the Government had failed to meet its burden of justifying such prior restraint. Even court orders forbidding the press to report on confessions by a murder defendant or other facts "strongly implicative" of the accused must be based on a specific finding that other available measures would not adequately protect the defendant's right to a fair trial.

ON THE LIMITS OF TOLERANCE

A third area of difference concerns the limits of freedom of expression in relation to extreme forms of political speech. In this respect, the United States and European scenes reveal strong cultural and legal differences; yet these were not always present. Like the law of European countries today, from 1917 until the late 1920s and again in the 1950s United States law permitted various regulations and restrictions affecting the content of speech; the Supreme Court did not then consider them invalid under the principles of the First Amendment. Today United States law allows virtually a free course to any kind of political expression. In the "Skokie case," the court of appeals held that a ban on Nazi demonstrations, even in a village whose inhabitants included survivors of the Holocaust, violated the First Amendment.[120]

The philosophy behind the prevailing United States attitude today to extreme forms of political expression is twofold. There is the stated analogy between economic liberalism and total freedom of expression. In *Abrams,* Holmes said:

> When men have realized that time has upset many fighting faiths, they may come to believe even more than they believe the very foundations of their own conduct that the ultimate good desired is better reached by *free trade in ideas*—that the best test of truth is the power of the thought to get itself accepted in *the competition of the market,* and that truth is the only ground upon which their wishes safely can be carried out. That at any rate is the theory of our Constitution.

---

120. *Collin v. Smith,* 578 F.2d 1197 (7th Cir. 1978); *cert. denied,* 439 U.S. 916 (1978). See A. Neier, *Defending My Enemy: American Nazis, the Skokie Case and the Risks of Freedom* (New York: Dutton, 1979); Donald A. Downs, "Skokie Revisited: Hate Group Speech and the First Amendment," *Notre Dame L. Rev.* (1985), 60:628; and Donald A. Downs, *Nazis in Skokie: Freedom, Community and the First Amendment* (Notre Dame, Ind.: University of Notre Dame Press, 1986).

This led Justice Powell to write, half a century later, that "under the First Amendment there is no such thing as a false idea. However pernicious an opinion may seem, we depend for its correction not on the conscience of judges and juries but on the *competition* of other ideas." One might conclude that a second element in United States thinking, linked to the first, is an inveterate social and historical optimism.

I suggest that a liberal society should not tolerate simply *any* form of expression; freedom of expression has limits; and these and their rationale should be stated and justified. The European philosophy and attitude are very different from those that have prevailed in the United States. Our societies, I think, rest ultimately on essential moral values. Among them preeminence must be given to respect for the dignity of the individual and concern for the rights of minorities. Throughout this century, these values have been pitted against currents of thought whose aim has been their outright destruction. Even when Europeans disagree on today's policies or on the future of their societies (as they do), they know what they do not want to see, what they refuse, and who and what are their enemies.

Indeed, we owe a great deal to Alexander Bickel, a great United States lawyer and thinker, for one of the best criticisms of what passes for the main United States creed with respect to moral values. In commenting on the advocacy of genocide or speech urging the segregation and the expulsion of certain minorities, Bickel said:

> One may allow such speech on one of two premises; either the cynical premise that words don't matter, that they make nothing happen and are too trivial to bother with; or else the premise taken by Justice Brandeis in *Whitney v. California* that "discussion affords ordinarily adequate protection against dissemination of noxious doctrine." The first premise is inconsistent with the idea of the First Amendment. If speech does not matter we might as well suppress it, because it is sometimes a nuisance. As to the second, *we have lived through too much to believe it.*

He continued:

> Disastrously, unacceptably noxious doctrine can prevail, and can be made to prevail by the most innocent sort of advocacy. Holmes recognized as much in the passage in the *Gitlow* dissent in which he said that "eloquence may set fire to reason." ... According to him, "If in the long run the beliefs expressed in proletarian dictatorship are destined to be accepted by the dominant forces of the community, the *only* meaning of free speech is that they should be given their chance and have their way."

Bickel disagrees:

> If in the long run the belief, let us say, in genocide is destined to be accepted by the dominant forces of the community, the only meaning of free speech is that it should be given its chance to have its way. Do we believe that? Do we accept it?

I agree with Bickel that:

There is such a thing as verbal violence, a kind of cursing, assaultive speech that amounts to almost physical aggression, bullying that is no less punishing because it is simulated.... This sort of speech constitutes an assault. More, and equally important, it may create a climate, an environment in which conduct and actions that were not possible before become possible.... *Where nothing is unspeakable, nothing is undoable.*

These insights reveal a deep understanding of the nature of speech and its effects in our societies. Reflecting experience during this century and a somewhat different social philosophy, these insights can be taken as representing the dominant state of mind in today's Europe. That is why there are group libel laws in many countries, sometimes the banning of extremist groups or of some of their activities, while the Supreme Court's acceptance of group libel laws in *Beauharnais v. Illinois* is now deemed questionable and its refusal to review the Skokie case has been deemed to reflect current law in the United States.

No doubt the *Skokie* case would have been decided differently in Europe and on different grounds. What is striking to a European reader about the court's decision is that the village did not invoke the needs of public order and relied mainly, in its argument, on the "falsity" of Nazism and on the issues of *Beauharnais*. When we in Europe read the famous Holmes dictum in *Gitlow,* cited by Bickel ("they should be given their chance and have their way") and Meiklejohn's comment in 1948 ("That is Americanism"), our response is that that, at any rate, is not the theory or practice in Europe. And indeed Article 17 of the European Convention on Human Rights embodies Europeans' attitudes in law....

B.   FREE SPEECH, HATE SPEECH AND COMMERCIAL SPEECH

As Errera's essay suggests, a particularly difficult issue in both the United States and in other liberal constitutional democracies is the degree to which society should, or is required to, allow (or even protect) speech that is inconsistent with liberal norms of equality and tolerance. Does a system of free expression have to tolerate hate speech? Does it have to prohibit hate speech?[a] The following materials on the constitutionality of regulating hate speech in Canada and the U.S. provide an introduction to these difficulties. A note on commercial speech is included as well, to permit further evaluation of Professor Greenawalt's claims about the

---

a. Similar questions arise with respect to tolerance or prohibition of political parties   committed to nondemocratic principles.

differences between the balancing called for by Canada's Charter Section 1 and the more "categorical" approach he sees U.S. courts using.

1. CANADA

Professor Greenawalt focuses on textual and doctrinal differences between the U.S. and Canada in explaining differences in outcome.[b] He argues that the U.S. Constitution has tended to result in "categorical" forms of analysis, in which the critical distinction is in the classification of an act as "speech" or not, whereas the Canadian Charter permits a balancing approach in which acts can be more broadly recognized as speech and then regulated or not depending on the nature of the reasons for regulation.

The *Keegstra* opinion, which both Greenawalt and Mahoney comment upon, is a leading Canadian decision analyzing criminal prohibitions of "hate speech" under the Charter. Later in this chapter, after reading R.A.V. v. City of St. Paul, 505 U.S. 377 (1992), reflect on the convergences and divergences in the approaches of both majority and dissents in these two cases.

Professor Kathleen Mahoney places greater weight on differences in the overall purposes of the Canadian Charter reflecting cultural differences between Canada and the United States. She emphasizes Canada's provisions on equality, as well as the constitutional status given to protection of multiculturalism, as a reflection of Canada's emphasis on society as a "mosaic," as opposed to the U.S. view of society as a "melting pot." She argues that the *Keegstra* case can be understood as a reflection of a more positive approach to the assurance of multicultural equality in Canada. She condemns the reasoning in *Keegstra*, however, as unduly "categorical" in insisting on seeing hate speech as a form of speech rather than of violence.

Kent Greenawalt, *Free Speech in the United States and Canada,* 55 Law & Contemp. Probs. 5 (1992)

I . . .

In both countries, a major premise of modern adjudication is that freedom of expression is a central feature of liberal democracy. Government "by the people," even in the extended sense of government by representatives, requires that citizens openly debate the merits of candidates and policies. Under prevailing liberal democratic theory, open discourse is more conducive to discovering truth than is government selection of what the public hears. Free statement of personal beliefs and feelings is an important aspect of individual autonomy.

In recent years, some critics of the liberal democratic theory have claimed that existing liberty of speech reinforces false consciousness, social

b. He notes, for example, that content neutrality and rules against prior restraints are less significant in Canada than in the U.S., while the distinction in whether the context is civil or criminal may be of greater importance in Canada than in the U.S.

inequality, and domination by protecting the expression of those already in power and failing to open channels for the dispossessed.[2] The particular areas I consider are significant ones in response to that critique.

The United States and Canada are at different stages in the development of constitutional free speech doctrines. American principles, based on the 200 year-old Bill of Rights, have grown over the last seventy years with very limited attention to documents and judicial rulings of other countries. Although preceded by some judicial elaboration of ideals of free expression, the Canadian Charter of Rights and Freedoms drastically altered Canada's constitutional landscape in 1982. Canadian courts have drawn extensively from the legal materials of other countries, including the United States, and from sources in international law. They have regarded themselves, to a degree so far uncharacteristic in the United States, as giving meaning to liberties that transcend national boundaries.

II

CONSTITUTIONAL LANGUAGE AND GENERAL APPROACHES

One critical inquiry in free speech cases asks what falls within the definition of speech. Another critical inquiry asks what constitutes interference with speech. How stringently courts will review government actions that interfere with speech is also a central concern. In respect to each question, judicial approaches may be expansive or modest, and they may be balancing or conceptual.

An expansive approach understands speech broadly, to include virtually all written and oral communication, fine arts and music, demonstrations, and symbolic acts such as flag burning. An expansive approach treats indirect threats to speech as well as focused interference as raising constitutional questions. A modest approach defines the limits of constitutional speech more closely, perhaps not including private communications about private subjects, demonstrations, or physical acts such as flag burning. Under a modest approach, it is assumed that no constitutional issue is raised by a government practice that is not aimed at speech. An expansive approach to the scope of judicial review of allegedly impermissible interference regards impairments of speech with skepticism and requires a heavy burden to justify them. A modest approach permits impairments under fairly relaxed standards of review.

Balancing approaches to decision openly weigh crucial factors; conceptual approaches employ categorical analysis. A rule that a practice is invalid unless sustained by a compelling interest relies on balancing. A rule that defamation of public officials is protected unless there is knowledge or reckless disregard of falsity is categorical.[3] Of course, conceptual ap-

---

2. It is one of the ironies of the recent past that while neo-Marxists in Western democracies have challenged the liberal vision of freedom of speech, citizens of countries with official Marxist ideologies have put their lives on the line to achieve some form of liberal free speech.

3. But note that, to a degree, recklessness itself is a balancing concept, because the

proaches typically reflect some underlying balance of rights and interests. In addition, many applicable standards employ a combination of conceptual and balancing approaches. For instance, if "content distinctions" can be upheld only upon an extremely strong showing of government need, then content distinction operates as an important category that triggers highly stringent balancing review.

Constitutional language and broader traditions concerning review of legislative and executive action will largely determine the approaches a country's judiciary takes. The language of the U.S. Constitution is rather unrevealing. The first amendment states "Congress shall make no law . . . abridging the freedom of speech, or of the press . . . ." The "the" preceding "freedom of speech" might have been taken to mean whatever freedom of speech then existed at common law, but courts have declined this limiting perspective. Despite the specific language about "Congress," the clause as construed covers any abridgement of free speech by any officer of the federal government. The fourteenth amendment, with its requirements that states not deprive persons of due process of law or abridge the privileges or immunities of citizens, has been held to make the first amendment applicable to the states. Since the American Constitution does not provide for government justifications of violations of guaranteed individual rights,[5] a court's formal determination that free speech has been abridged is necessarily a formal decision that the government action was impermissible.

The Canadian Charter of Rights and Freedoms is strikingly different in important respects. Section 2 provides that everyone has the fundamental freedoms of "thought, belief, opinion and expression, including freedom of the press and other media of communication."[6] The Charter explicitly applies to the national and the provincial governments. Under section 1 of the Charter, fundamental freedoms are subject "to such reasonable limits prescribed by law as can be demonstrably justified in a free and democratic society." According to section 33(1), Parliament or a provincial legislature may, by making an express declaration that its action complies with section 1, adopt legislation notwithstanding the protections of section 2. A Canadian court may thus decide that an act limits freedom of expression under section 2 but is nonetheless effective because it satisfies the standard of section 1 or has been shielded by an express legislative declaration.

These differences in constitutional language might be expected to yield variances in judicial approach. The basic American constitutional standard of "abridging the freedom of speech" seems to call for conceptual categorization to play the central role in judicial decision, although courts may need

---

benefit of action is weighed against the risk of harm.

5. The Constitution does, however, allow suspension of the writ of habeas corpus "when in Cases of Rebellion or Invasion the public Safety may require it." U.S. Const. Art. I, § 9.

6. The Charter also includes freedom of conscience as a part of "freedom of conscience and religion." Can Const. (Constitution Act, 1982) pt. I (Canadian Charter of Rights and Freedoms), § 2(a).

some explicit balancing to avoid unacceptable results. In discerning the fundamental freedoms of section 2, Canadian courts might rely even more exclusively on conceptual approaches, because the explicit balancing standard of section 1 allows courts to balance when they believe they must.

Since section 1 permits government justification of action that infringes section 2 freedoms, Canadian courts can find a violation of section 2's freedoms more easily than an American court would find a violation of the first amendment. But one would expect the flexibility that section 1 introduces to lead Canadian courts to invalidate fewer laws and practices as finally unconstitutional than their American counterparts. This is partly because the section 1 justification for regulation appears by its terms to grant more latitude to the political branches of government than does the language of the first amendment. It is also because most balancing tests tend to induce deference to legislative or executive wisdom. A court that is "balancing" considerations that were before the legislature may be more hesitant to conclude that the legislature made a mistake than a court inquiring whether the legislature ran afoul of some conceptual barrier.

Another reason we might expect Canadian courts to be less activist than American courts has to do not with constitutional language but with a long tradition of treating legislative judgments (at least ones that do not arguably violate principles governing division of powers) as finally authoritative. The Charter's novel principle of direct judicial invalidation based on individual rights could not be expected to alter drastically and swiftly engrained habits of deference to the political branches. . . .

Both American and Canadian courts have accepted broad rationales for freedom of speech and an accompanying expansive view of the speech that raises constitutional questions. In the United States, nonpolitical speech is protected as well as speech related to public affairs, while commercial communication for profit enjoys some lesser protection. Music and art count as speech. Forms of expression that indicate emotional intensity or capture attention are also protected even if less offensive words or methods could convey the same substance. The law of defamation is largely constitutionalized, and other private law doctrines impinging on expression receive constitutional scrutiny. Controversially, the U.S. Supreme Court continues to leave obscene expression unprotected. Drawing the line between what is obscene and what is not remains a perplexing inquiry.

In pre-Charter days, when freedom of speech was invoked mainly in connection with issues concerning the division of authority between the national and provincial governments, Canadian decisions suggested that only expression about political affairs was protected. But the advent of the Charter has led to coverage roughly similar to that of the American first amendment jurisprudence. One important exception concerns the common law of defamation and other common law bases of liability. According to present interpretation, common law rules enforcing private rights do not present Charter issues.* An American's initial reaction is to wonder if all

---

* [Editors' Note: See the discussion of Canada's Dolphin Delivery case and the state action problem below in Section E.]

such judicial actions can continue to be beyond the scope of section 2. If a provincial court held that ordinary political comment constituted defamation, would the Canadian Supreme Court conclude that no fundamental freedom had been violated?

In comprehending the present status of common law and Charter rights, one needs to recognize a crucial difference between common law in the United States and in Canada. In the United States, common law is generally state law; if common law doctrines do not infringe the federal Constitution or federal statutes, they are not a matter of federal concern and they are unreviewable by the Supreme Court. In Canada, Supreme Court powers are different. The Supreme Court is the court of last resort in a unitary system and may revise common law decisions of any lower court. Whether in some theoretical sense parts of the common law might be viewed as "federal law" or "provincial law," the Supreme Court can overturn what it regards as a bad common law judgment. Thus, in my example, the Supreme Court could develop the common law of defamation in light of Charter values. This structure reduces the practical significance of a rule that common law doctrines never directly infringe Charter rights. . . .

American law entertains a strong presumption against the validity of prior restraints. Only the very strongest reasons can justify government censorship of speech before it is made. This principle precluded government interference with the publication of highly classified material about the Vietnam conflict in the "Pentagon Papers."[18] In addition, it has made restricting pretrial publicity of criminal cases virtually impossible.[19]

In the last two decades, a principle prohibiting "content regulation" has emerged as a central doctrine of first amendment law. The fundamental idea is that some messages should not be favored over others. Certain differences in content are permissible bases of distinction; a message urging the commission of a crime may be treated differently from a message urging law obedience. But, in general, differences in viewpoint are not a permissible basis for distinction. Differences among categories in speech, for example, political as opposed to sexual speech, are also treated with suspicion. When the government interferes with speech in a manner that would normally be impermissible, its action will be sustained only if it is necessary to serve a compelling need and is narrowly drawn to achieve that end.[20] In free speech cases using the "compelling interest" test, judges rarely sustain what the government has done.

Within the boundaries of speech that enjoys some protection, certain limited categories of speech are considered to have lower value, most notably commercial advertising and sexually explicit speech that falls short

18. New York Times v. United States, 403 U.S. 713 (1971).

19. See Nebraska Press Ass'n v. Stuart, 427 U.S. 539 (1976).

20. Perry Education Ass'n v. Perry Local Educators' Ass'n, 460 U.S. 37 (1983).

of obscenity. Regulation of these types of speech is subject to less stringent standards of review.

Less stringent standards also apply to government regulation that serves a purpose independent of the communication's substance. Thus, the government may restrict the size of billboards or limit the volume of sound trucks without satisfying a stringent compelling interest test.

Canadian constitutional doctrine, up to the present, is less complicated than that of the United States. There is both an expansive approach to what counts as freedom of speech and a developed balancing test under section 1 of the Charter. I will describe these features more fully when I consider recent Canadian Supreme Court decisions. For most troublesome cases, the section 1 balancing test raises the critical inquiry. In time, Canadian courts may develop various subsidiary doctrines similar in character if not in substance to those of the United States; but the contextualized standard under section 1 will probably limit such doctrinal proliferation by making much of it unnecessary. The following treatment of specific substantive areas illustrates the general remarks I have made thus far. . . .

IV

FIGHTING WORDS AND HATE SPEECH: RESPONSIVE VIOLENCE AND INDEPENDENT HARMS

Among the most controversial modern questions about freedom of speech is the proper treatment of strong insults and "hate speech." Many strong insults use coarse language in a highly derogatory way ("You are a fucking bastard"), but others avoid any single shocking word. Many strong insults are cast in terms of race, religion, ethnic origin, gender, or sexual preference. Some language that is contemptuous or hateful toward members of such groups occurs in contexts other than individual insults.

The leading American case on direct insults remains *Chaplinsky v. New Hampshire*,[45] decided half a century ago. A Jehovah's Witness who had been warned about his proselytizing by a city marshal responded by calling the marshal "a God damned racketeer" and "a damned Fascist." The defendant was convicted under a law that prohibited calling someone an offensive or derisive name. The state supreme court had construed the statute to cover only words that "men of common intelligence would understand [to be] likely to cause an average addressee to fight." The Supreme Court, affirming the conviction, said:

> There are certain well-defined and narrowly limited classes of speech, the prevention and punishment of which have never been thought to raise any Constitutional problem. These include the lewd and obscene, the profane, the libelous, and the insulting or "fighting" words—those which by their very utterance inflict injury or tend to incite an immediate breach of the peace . . . . [S]uch utterances are no essential part of any exposition of ideas, and are of such slight social

45. 315 U.S. 568 (1942).

value as a step to truth that any benefit that may be derived from them is clearly outweighed by the social interest in order and morality.

Two developments since *Chaplinsky* have substantially undercut its rationale and its permissive attitude toward punishment of fighting words.... The opinion says "such utterances are no essential part of any exposition of ideas ...." Fighting words cannot, unfortunately, be dismissed as lacking any expressive value. In meaning, they attribute negative characteristics to their object. Group epithets, such as "kike" or "wop" or "nigger," call to mind negative qualities that some people associate with a group, such as laziness, greed, dishonesty, stupidity, and vulgarity, and make a strongly negative evaluation of the group.

Is the expressive value of such utterances negligible because the same ideas could be stated in less troubling language? In one of the first developments since *Chaplinsky*, the Court rejected this approach in a 1971 case, overturning a conviction for wearing a jacket that said "Fuck the Draft." Justice Harlan's opinion for the Court in *Cohen v. California* indicated that people are free to choose the words that best reflect their feelings, and strong words may better convey to listeners the intensity of feeling than more conventional language.[48]

The second important development since *Chaplinsky* has been the Court's invalidation of statutes directed at offensive language, on grounds of overbreadth and vagueness. Provisions have been found too vague to guide conduct and overbroad in reaching too much speech that is protected. Under Supreme Court doctrine, when a statute suffers the defect of substantial overbreadth, it improperly chills free speech, and it may not be used even against those whose own speech otherwise might properly be punished.

The basic idea that likely responsive violence can be the basis for punishing insulting words remains from *Chaplinsky* and lies close to the subject covered by the *Brandenburg* principle.* It would be odd to say that

---

48. 403 U.S. 15, 25–26 (1971). The Court also distinguished *Chaplinsky* on the ground that the defendant in *Cohen* had spoken to the world at large, rather than a specific individual or group, and thus his speech was less likely to provoke a violent response.

* [Editors' Note: Brandenburg v. Ohio, 395 U.S. 444 (1969) invalidated an Ohio "criminal syndicalism" statute making criminal the advocacy of the propriety of crime or violence as a means of accomplishing industrial or political reform, and reversed the conviction of a Ku Klux Klan member based on videotape of a Klan meeting at which derogatory references to African-Americans and Jews were made and at which the defendant said, "We're not a revengent organization but if our President, our Congress, our

Supreme Court continues to suppress the white, Caucasian race it's possible that there might have to be some revengence taken," and then announced plans for a march on Congress and in Florida and Mississippi. *Brandenberg* reversed an earlier decision, Whitney v. California, 274 U.S. 357 (1927) which had upheld a similar California Law. The *Brandenberg* court explained that more recent decisions had "fashioned a principle that constitutional guarantees of free speech and free press do not permit a State to forbid or proscribe advocacy of the use of force or of law violation except where such advocacy is directed to inciting or producing imminent lawless action and is likely to incite or produce such action." The distinction *Brandenberg* draws between "mere advocacy" of illegal action, which is constitutionally pro-public insults can be punished on a lower probability of violence than actual urgings of illegal violent acts. Under *Brandenburg*, imminent lawless action must be likely; something similar should be needed if fighting words are punished for their propensity to cause immediate violence. *Chaplinsky's* suggestion that an "average addressee" must be likely to fight, however, is inappropriate or misleading, and almost certainly reflects the implicit sense that actors are male. When one takes women, children, and older people of both sexes into account, it is doubtful whether any words are likely to cause the "average addressee" to fight. The focus on groups of addressees other than young males raises a more deeply troubling question as to whether likely violence in the particular instance should be the standard for punishment. In otherwise similar circumstances, a white male of twenty-five calls an Afro-American male of twenty-five a "nigger," and six white males of twenty-five call an Afro-American female of sixty a "nigger." Can it really be that the first male is constitutionally punishable and the other six males are not? ...

Abusive words can wound their targets deeply, offending them and a much broader audience as well. Perhaps they may have a negative effect on public communication by endangering the civility of discourse. Group epithets can reinforce feelings of prejudice, inferiority, and hostility among groups, thus contributing to social patterns of domination. Which, if any, of these bases underlie punishment of insulting words in the United States?

Perhaps the Supreme Court has not completely rejected the idea that offensiveness of expression could underlie conviction, but in *Cohen v. California* and other cases striking down criminal provisions for overbreadth and vagueness, it has strongly suggested that in our society people must be hardy enough to tolerate very strong expression if they do not avoid it. The Court has permitted a ban on some words on daytime radio,[49] regulation of the location of theaters specializing in adult movies,[50] and discipline of a high school student who used "vulgar and offensive" language at a school assembly,[51] but it has not sustained any absolute prohibition of forms of speech because they are thought to be offensive....

When focusing on long-term harms, one encounters problems that are among the most difficult for any democratic legal order. In the first instance, the relevant domain of utterances expands significantly. The harm from group epithets can occur not only when words are directed toward members of the group but also when members are not present. For example, men who use denigrating expressions about women in conversations with each other may impair gender equality just as much as men who address denigrating expressions toward women. Moreover, the harm can

tected, and "incitement to imminent lawless action" has been adhered to in several later decisions. See, e.g., Hess v. Indiana, 414 U.S. 105 (1973); NAACP v. Claiborne Hardware Co., 458 U.S. 886 (1982).]

49. FCC v. Pacifica Foundation, 438 U.S. 726, 748–51 (1978).

50. Young v. American Mini Theatres, 427 U.S. 50 (1976); City of Renton v. Playtime Theatres, 475 U.S. 41 (1986).

51. Bethel School District v. Fraser, 478 U.S. 675, 683 (1986).

occur whether or not the speaker chooses particularly crude or offensive language. Even neutral-sounding scientific language can be deeply worrisome, as we see when people deny that many Jews were killed during World War II or claim that Afro-Americans possess less intelligence on the average than whites.

. . . [I]f concern is with the long-term effect of language that denigrates members of groups, even polite language can cause much of the same harm. To admit that such language can be punished is to strike much more severely at traditional concepts of free speech, and certainly flies in the face of a principle of "no content regulation." Yet allowing such speech may perpetuate or cause unjust inequalities. For liberal democracies committed to equality and to liberty of speech, the dilemma is painful.

The leading U.S. Supreme Court case on the subject, now nearly forty years old, vividly portrays the problem.[56] An Illinois law forbade publications portraying "depravity, criminality, unchastity, or lack of virtue of a class of citizens, of any race, color, creed or religion [in a way that exposes those citizens] to contempt, derision, or obloquy or which is productive of breach of the peace or riots." Beauharnais had organized distribution of a leaflet asking city officials to resist the invasion of the Negro and warning that if "the need to prevent the white race from becoming mongrelized by the negro will not unite us, then the aggressions, . . . rapes, robberies, knives, guns and marijuana of the negro, surely will." The Court upheld the conviction, assimilating the publication to group libel, instances in which a small group is defamed in such a way that the damaging remark falls on all group members. The Court mentioned the danger of racial riots, which a legislature might reasonably think is increased by racist speech.

The leaflet's collection of claimed facts and opinions certainly did not contribute to a healthy racial climate. Yet, under ordinary free speech standards, the opinions, for example, about the undesirability of whites having children with blacks, would be protected. The asserted facts are either too vague to be shown to be false or are subject to an interpretation that would allow them to be defended as true. For example, Beauharnais could argue that talk about the aggressions of the Negro obviously did not mean that all blacks committed aggression but only that a higher percentage of blacks than whites did so.

Developments since Beauharnais have led most commentators to suppose that the decision, itself by a 5–4 margin, is no longer authoritative. [See R.A.V. below]

[Professor Greenawalt then discusses *Keegstra*, which follows below.]

---

56. See Beauharnais v. Illinois, 343 U.S. 250 (1952). [Editors' Note: This article was written prior to R.A.V. v. St. Paul, 505 U.S. 377 (1992), discussed below in Section 2.]

Regina v. Keegstra et al.

[1990] 3 S.C.R. 697 (Supreme Court of Canada)

Prior-History: Appeal by the Crown from a judgement of the Alberta Court of Appeal, 43 C.C.C. 3d 150 [1988] allowing the accused's appeal from his conviction on a change of wilfully promoting hatred contrary to § 319 of the Criminal Code. . . .

Judges: Dickson C.J.C., *Wilson, La Forest, L'Heureux-Dube, Sopinka, Gonthier and McLauchlin JJ. [*Chief Justice at the time of the hearing.]

Opinion: Dickson C.J.C.—This appeal . . . raises a delicate and highly controversial issue as to the constitutional validity of s. 319(2) of the Criminal Code, R.S.C., 1985, c. C–46, a legislative provision which prohibits the wilful promotion of hatred, other than in private conversation, towards any section of the public distinguished by colour, race, religion or ethnic origin. In particular, the Court must decide whether this section infringes the guarantee of freedom of expression found in s. 2(b) of the Canadian Charter of Rights and Freedoms in a manner that cannot be justified under s. 1 of the Charter. . . .

I. Facts

Mr. James Keegstra was a high school teacher in Eckville, Alberta from the early 1970s until his dismissal in 1982. In 1984 Mr. Keegstra was charged under s. 319(2) of the Criminal Code with unlawfully promoting hatred against an identifiable group by communicating anti-Semitic statements to his students. He was convicted by a jury in a trial before McKenzie J. of the Alberta Court of Queen's Bench.

Mr. Keegstra's teachings attributed various evil qualities to Jews. He thus described Jews to his pupils as "treacherous", "subversive", "sadistic", "money-loving", "power hungry" and "child killers". He taught his classes that Jewish people seek to destroy Christianity and are responsible for depressions, anarchy, chaos, wars and revolution. According to Mr. Keegstra, Jews "created the Holocaust to gain sympathy" and, in contrast to the open and honest Christians, were said to be deceptive, secretive and inherently evil. Mr. Keegstra expected his students to reproduce his teachings in class and on exams. If they failed to do so, their marks suffered. . . .

The Attorneys General of Canada, Quebec, Ontario, Manitoba and New Brunswick, the Canadian Jewish Congress, Interamicus, the League for Human Rights of B'nai Brith, Canada, and the Women's Legal Education and Action Fund (L.E.A.F.) have intervened in this appeal in support of the Crown. The Canadian Civil Liberties Association has intervened in support of striking down the impugned legislation. . . .

III. Relevant Statutory and Constitutional Provisions

The relevant legislative and Charter provisions are set out below:

Criminal Code 319

(2) Every one who, by communicating statements, other than in private conversation, wilfully promotes hatred against any identifiable group is guilty of

(a) an indictable offence and is liable to imprisonment for a term not exceeding two years; or

(b) an offence punishable on summary conviction.

(3) No person shall be convicted of an offence under subsection (2)(a) if he establishes that the statements communicated were true;

(b) if, in good faith, he expressed or attempted to establish by argument an opinion on a religious subject;

(c) if the statements were relevant to any subject of public interest, the discussion of which was for the public benefit, and if on reasonable grounds he believed them to be true; or

(d) if, in good faith, he intended to point out, for the purpose of removal, matters producing or tending to produce feelings of hatred towards an identifiable group in Canada....

(6) No proceeding for an offence under subsection (2) shall be instituted without the consent of the Attorney General.

(7) In this section ... "identifiable group" [means any section of the public distinguished by colour, race, religion or ethnic origin.] ...

Canadian Charter of Rights and Freedoms

1. The Canadian Charter of Rights and Freedoms guarantees the rights and freedoms set out in it subject only to such reasonable limits prescribed by law as can be demonstrably justified in a free and democratic society.

2. Everyone has the following fundamental freedoms: ...

(b) freedom of thought, belief, opinion and expression, including freedom of the press and other media of communication; ...

15. (1) Every individual is equal before and under the law and has the right to the equal protection and equal benefit of the law without discrimination and, in particular, without discrimination based on race, national and ethnic origin, colour, religion, sex, age or mental or physical disability.

27. This Charter shall be interpreted in a manner consistent with the preservation and enhancement of the multicultural heritage of Canadians....

V. The History of Hate Propaganda Crimes in Canada ...

While the history of attempts to prosecute criminally the libel of groups is lengthy, the [early] Criminal Code provisions [did] ... not focus specifically upon expression propagated with the intent of causing hatred against racial, ethnic or religious groups. Even before the Second World War, however, fears began to surface concerning the inadequacy of Canadian criminal law in this regard. In the 1930s, for example, Manitoba passed a statute combatting a perceived rise in the dissemination of Nazi propaganda. Following the Second World War and revelation of the Holocaust, in Canada and throughout the world a desire grew to protect human rights, and especially to guard against discrimination. Internationally, this desire led to the landmark Universal Declaration of Human Rights in 1948, and, with reference to hate propaganda, was eventually manifested in two international human rights instruments. In Canada, the post-war mood saw an attempt to include anti-hate propaganda provisions in the 1953 revision of the Criminal Code, but most influential in changing the criminal law in order to prohibit hate propaganda was the appointment by Justice Minister Guy Favreau of a special committee to study problems associated with the spread of hate propaganda in Canada.

The Special Committee on Hate Propaganda in Canada, usually referred to as the Cohen Committee, was composed of the following members: Dean Maxwell Cohen, Q.C., Dean of the Faculty of Law, McGill University, chair; Dr. J.A. Corry, Principal, Queen's University; L'Abbé Gérard Dion, Faculty of Social Sciences, Laval University; Mr. Saul Hayes, Q.C., Executive Vice-President, Canadian Jewish Congress; Professor Mark R. MacGuigan, Associate Professor of Law, University of Toronto; Mr. Shane MacKay, Executive Editor, Winnipeg Free Press; and Professor Pierre-E. Trudeau, Associate Professor of Law, University of Montreal. This was a particularly strong Committee, and in 1966 it released the unanimous Report of the Special Committee on Hate Propaganda in Canada.

The tenor of the Report is reflected in the opening paragraph of its Preface, which reads:

> This Report is a study in the power of words to maim, and what it is that a civilized society can do about it. Not every abuse of human communication can or should be controlled by law or custom. But every society from time to time draws lines at the point where the intolerable and the impermissible coincide. In a free society such as our own, where the privilege of speech can induce ideas that may change the very order itself, there is a bias weighted heavily in favour of the maximum of rhetoric whatever the cost and consequences. But that bias stops this side of injury to the community itself and to individual members or identifiable groups innocently caught in verbal cross-fire that goes beyond legitimate debate.

In keeping with these remarks, the recurrent theme running throughout the Report is the need to prevent the dissemination of hate propaganda without unduly infringing the freedom of expression, a theme which led the Committee to recommend a number of amendments to the Criminal Code. These amendments were made, essentially along the lines suggested by the Committee, and covered the advocation of genocide (s. 318), the public incitement of hatred likely to lead to a breach of peace (s. 319(1)) and the provision challenged in this appeal and presently found in s. 319(2) of the Code, namely, the wilful promotion of hatred.

VI.   Section 2(b) of the Charter—Freedom of Expression

[After quoting *Ford v. Quebec:*] . . . [T]he reach of § 2(b) is potentially very wide, expression being deserving of constitutional protection if "it serves individual and societal values in a free and democratic society". . . . [T]he Court has attempted to articulate more precisely some of the convictions fueling the freedom of expression, these being summarized in *Irwin Toy* [[1989] 1 S.C.R. 927] as follows: (1) seeking and attaining truth is an inherently good activity; (2) participation in social and political decision-making is to be fostered and encouraged; and (3) diversity in forms of individual self-fulfillment and human flourishing ought to be cultivated in a tolerant and welcoming environment for the sake of both those who convey a meaning and those to whom meaning is conveyed.

Although *Ford* commented upon the values generally seen to support the freedom of expression, the decision was also sensitive of the need to consider these values within the textual framework of the Charter. . . . It is the presence of s. 1 which makes necessary this bifurcated approach to Canadian freedom of expression cases. Indeed, the application of this approach in *Ford* in part permitted the Court to give a large and liberal interpretation to s. 2(b), on the facts of the case leading to the inclusion of commercial expression within its ambit, and to state that the weighing of competing values would "in most instances" take place in s. 1. . . .

. . . Apart from rare cases where expression is communicated in a physically violent form, the Court [has] viewed the fundamental nature of the freedom of expression as ensuring that "if the activity conveys or attempts to convey a meaning, it has expressive content and *prima facie* falls within the scope of the guarantee". In other words, the term "expression" as used in s. 2(b) of the Charter embraces all content of expression irrespective of the particular meaning or message sought to be conveyed.

The second step in the analysis . . . is to determine whether the purpose of the impugned government action is to restrict freedom of expression. The guarantee of freedom of expression will necessarily be infringed by government action having such a purpose. If, however, it is the effect of the action, rather than the purpose, that restricts an activity, s. 2(b) is not brought into play unless it can be demonstrated by the party alleging an infringement that the activity supports rather than undermines the principles and values upon which freedom of expression is based. . . .

. . . Communications which wilfully promote hatred against an identifiable group without doubt convey a meaning, and are intended to do so by those who make them. Because . . . the type of meaning conveyed is irrelevant to the question of whether s. 2(b) is infringed, that the expression covered by s. 319(2) is invidious and obnoxious is beside the point. It is enough that those who publicly and wilfully promote hatred convey or attempt to convey a meaning, and it must therefore be concluded that the first step of [the] . . . test is satisfied.

Moving to the second stage of the s. 2(b) inquiry, one notes that the prohibition in s. 319(2) aims directly at words—in this appeal, Mr. Keegstra's teachings—that have as their content and objective the promotion of racial or religious hatred. The purpose of s. 319(2) can consequently be formulated as follows: to restrict the content of expression by singling out particular meanings that are not to be conveyed. Section 319(2) therefore overtly seeks to prevent the communication of expression, and hence meets the second requirement of the *Irwin Toy* test.

In my view, through s. 319(2) Parliament seeks to prohibit communications which convey meaning, namely, those communications which are intended to promote hatred against identifiable groups. I thus find s. 319(2) to constitute an infringement of the freedom of expression guaranteed by s. 2(b) of the Charter. . . .

. . . [I]t was argued before this Court that the wilful promotion of hatred is an activity the form and consequences of which are analogous to those associated with violence or threats of violence. This argument contends that Supreme Court of Canada precedent excludes violence and threats of violence from the ambit of s. 2(b), and that the reason for such exclusion must lie in the fact that these forms of expression are inimical to the values supporting freedom of speech. . . . [W]e were urged to find that hate propaganda of the type caught by s. 319(2), insofar as it imperils the ability of target group members themselves to convey thoughts and feelings in non-violent ways without fear of censure, is analogous to violence and threats of violence and hence does not fall within s. 2(b). . . .

. . . [T]he communications restricted by s. 319(2) cannot be considered as violence, which . . . refer[s] to expression communicated directly through physical harm. . . . [H]ate propaganda is to be categorized as expression so as to bring it within the coverage of s. 2(b). . . .

The second matter which I wish to address before leaving the s. 2(b) inquiry concerns the relevance of other Charter provisions and international agreements to which Canada is a party in interpreting the coverage of the freedom of expression guarantee. It has been argued in support of excluding hate propaganda from the coverage of s. 2(b) that the use of ss. 15 and 27 of the Charter—dealing respectively with equality and multiculturalism—and Canada's acceptance of international agreements requiring the prohibition of racist statements make s. 319(2) incompatible with even a large and liberal definition of the freedom. . . .

. . . I believe, however, that s. 1 of the Charter is especially well suited to the task of balancing, and consider this Court's previous freedom of expression decisions to support this belief. It is, in my opinion, inappropriate to attenuate the s. 2(b) freedom on the grounds that a particular context requires such; the large and liberal interpretation given the freedom of expression in *Irwin Toy* indicates that the preferable course is to weigh the various contextual values and factors in s. 1.

I thus conclude on the issue of s. 2(b) by finding that s. 319(2) of the Criminal Code constitutes an infringement of the Charter guarantee of freedom of expression, and turn to examine whether such an infringement is justifiable under s. 1 as a reasonable limit in a free and democratic society.

VII.   Section 1 Analysis of Section 319(2) . . .

In the words of s. 1 are brought together the fundamental values and aspirations of Canadian society. As this Court has said before, the premier article of the Charter has a dual function, operating both to activate Charter rights and freedoms and to permit such reasonable limits as a free and democratic society may have occasion to place upon them. What seems to me to be of significance in this dual function is the commonality that links the guarantee of rights and freedoms to their limitation. This commonality lies in the phrase "free and democratic society". . . . "The underlying values of a free and democratic society both guarantee the rights in the Charter and, in appropriate circumstances, justify limitations upon those rights." [Slaight Communications Inc. v. Davidson, [1987] 1 S.C.R. 1038]

. . . To a large extent, a free and democratic society embraces the very values and principles which Canadians have sought to protect and further by entrenching specific rights and freedoms in the Constitution, although the balancing exercise in s. 1 is not restricted to values expressly set out in the Charter. With this guideline in mind, in *Oakes* I commented upon some of the ideals that inform our understanding of a free and democratic society, saying:

> The Court must be guided by the values and principles essential to a free and democratic society which I believe embody, to name but a few, respect for the inherent dignity of the human person, commitment to social justice and equality, accommodation of a wide variety of beliefs, respect for cultural and group identity, and faith in social and political institutions which enhance the participation of individuals and groups in society. The underlying values and principles of a free and democratic society are the genesis of the rights and freedoms guaranteed by the Charter and the ultimate standard against which a limit on a right or freedom must be shown, despite its effect, to be reasonable and demonstrably justified. . . . [R. v. Dalces, [1986] 1 S.C.R. 103]

It is important not to lose sight of factual circumstances in undertaking a s. 1 analysis, for these shape a court's view of both the right or freedom at stake and the limit proposed by the state; neither can be surveyed in the abstract. As Wilson J. said in Edmonton Journal [v. Alberta (Attorney General), [1989] 2 S.C.R. 1326] referring to what she termed the "contextual approach" to Charter interpretation:

> . . . a particular right or freedom may have a different value depending on the context. It may be, for example, that freedom of expression has greater value in a political context than it does in the context of disclosure of the details of a matrimonial dispute. The contextual approach attempts to bring into sharp relief the aspect of the right or freedom which is truly at stake in the case as well as the relevant aspects of any values in competition with it. It

seems to be more sensitive to the reality of the dilemma posed by the particular facts and therefore more conducive to finding a fair and just compromise between the two competing values under s. 1. . . .

B. The Use of American Constitutional Jurisprudence

Having discussed the unique and unifying role of s. 1, I think it appropriate to address a tangential matter, yet one nonetheless crucial to the disposition of this appeal: the relationship between Canadian and American approaches to the constitutional protection of free expression, most notably in the realm of hate propaganda. Those who attack the constitutionality of s. 319(2) draw heavily on the tenor of First Amendment jurisprudence in weighing the competing freedoms and interests in this appeal, a reliance which is understandable given the prevalent opinion that the criminalization of hate propaganda violates the Bill of Rights . . . .

A myriad of sources—both judicial and academic—offer reviews of First Amendment jurisprudence as it pertains to hate propaganda. Central to most discussions is the 1952 case of Beauharnais v. Illinois, 343 U.S. 250, where the Supreme Court of the United States upheld as constitutional a criminal statute forbidding certain types of group defamation. Though never overruled, *Beauharnais* appears to have been weakened by later pronouncements of the Supreme Court (see, e.g., Garrison v. Louisiana, 379 U.S. 64 (1964); Ashton v. Kentucky, 384 U.S. 195 (1966); New York Times Co. v. Sullivan, 376 U.S. 254 (1964); Brandenburg v. Ohio, 395 U.S. 444 (1969); and Cohen v. California, 403 U.S. 15 (1971)). The trend reflected in many of these pronouncements is to protect offensive, public invective as long as the speaker has not knowingly lied and there exists no clear and present danger of violence or insurrection.

In the wake of subsequent developments in the Supreme Court, on several occasions *Beauharnais* has been distinguished and doubted by lower courts. Of the judgments expressing a shaken faith in *Beauharnais*, Collin v. Smith, 578 F.2d 1197 (7th Cir.1978), certiorari denied, 439 U.S. 916 (1978), is of greatest relevance to this appeal. In *Collin*, the Court of Appeal for the Seventh Circuit invalidated a municipal ordinance prohibiting public demonstrations inciting "violence, hatred, abuse or hostility toward a person or group of persons by reason of reference to religious, racial, ethnic, national or regional affiliation" (p. 1199), and thereby allowed members of the American Nazi Party to march through Skokie, Illinois, home to a large number of Jewish Holocaust survivors. . . .

The question that concerns us in this appeal is not, of course, what the law is or should be in the United States. But it is important to be explicit as to the reasons why or why not American experience may be useful in the s. 1 analysis of s. 319(2) of the Criminal Code. In the United States, a collection of fundamental rights has been constitutionally protected for over two hundred years. The resulting practical and theoretical experience is immense, and should not be overlooked by Canadian courts. On the other

hand, we must examine American constitutional law with a critical eye
. . . .

> While it is natural and even desirable for Canadian courts to
> refer to American constitutional jurisprudence in seeking to eluci-
> date the meaning of Charter guarantees that have counterparts in
> the United States Constitution, they should be wary of drawing
> too ready a parallel between constitutions born to different coun-
> tries in different ages and in very different circumstances . . . . [R.
> v. Rahey, [1987] 1 S.C.R. 588]

Canada and the United States are not alike in every way, nor have the
documents entrenching human rights in our two countries arisen in the
same context. It is only common sense to recognize that, just as similarities
will justify borrowing from the American experience, differences may
require that Canada's constitutional vision depart from that endorsed in
the United States.

Having examined the American cases relevant to First Amendment
jurisprudence and legislation criminalizing hate propaganda, I would be
adverse to following too closely the line of argument that would overrule
Beauharnais on the ground that incursions placed upon free expression are
only justified where there is a clear and present danger of imminent breach
of peace. Equally, I am unwilling to embrace various categorizations and
guiding rules generated by American law without careful consideration of
their appropriateness to Canadian constitutional theory. Though I have
found the American experience tremendously helpful in coming to my own
conclusions regarding this appeal, and by no means reject the whole of the
First Amendment doctrine, in a number of respects I am thus dubious as to
the applicability of this doctrine in the context of a challenge to hate
propaganda legislation.

First, it is not entirely clear that *Beauharnais* must conflict with
existing First Amendment doctrine. . . . Indeed, there exists a growing body
of academic writing in the United States which evinces a stronger focus
upon the way in which hate propaganda can undermine the very values
which free speech is said to protect. . . . [and suggests that] First Amendment doctrine might be able to accommodate statutes prohibiting hate
propaganda (see, e.g., R. Delgado, "Words That Wound: A Tort Action for
Racial Insults, Epithets, and Name-Calling" (1982), 17 Harv. C.R.-C.L. L.
Rev. 133; M. Matsuda, "Public Response to Racist Speech: Considering the
Victim's Story" (1989), 87 Mich. L. Rev. 2320, at p. 2348.)

Second, the aspect of First Amendment doctrine most incompatible
with s. 319(2), at least as that doctrine is described by those who would
strike down the legislation, is its strong aversion to content-based regulation of expression. I am somewhat skeptical, however, as to whether this
view of free speech in the United States is entirely accurate. Rather, in
rejecting the extreme position that would provide an absolute guarantee of
free speech in the Bill of Rights, the Supreme Court has developed a
number of tests and theories by which . . . the legitimacy of government
regulation [can be] assessed. Often required is a content-based categoriza-

tion of the expression under examination. As an example, obscenity is not protected because of its content and laws proscribing child pornography have been scrutinized under a less than strict First Amendment standard even where they extend to expression beyond the realm of the obscene (see New York v. Ferber, 458 U.S. 747 (1982)). Similarly, the vigorous protection of free speech relaxes significantly when commercial expression is scrutinized (see, e.g., Posadas de Puerto Rico Associates v. Tourism Co. of Puerto Rico, 478 U.S. 328 (1986)), and it is permissible to restrict government employees in their exercise of the right to engage in political activity (Cornelius v. NAACP Legal Defense and Educational Fund, Inc., 473 U.S. 788 (1985)).

In short, a decision to place expressive activity in a category which either merits reduced protection or falls entirely outside of the First Amendment's ambit at least impliedly involves assessing the content of the activity in light of free speech values.... [E]ven in the United States it is sometimes thought justifiable to restrict a particular message because of its meaning.

Third, applying the Charter to the legislation challenged in this appeal reveals important differences between Canadian and American constitutional perspectives. I have already discussed in some detail the special role of s. 1 in determining the protective scope of Charter rights and freedoms. Section 1 has no equivalent in the United States, a fact previously alluded to by this Court in selectively utilizing American constitutional jurisprudence. Of course, American experience should never be rejected simply because the Charter contains a balancing provision, for it is well known that American courts have fashioned compromises between conflicting interests despite what appears to be the absolute guarantee of constitutional rights. Where s. 1 operates to accentuate a uniquely Canadian vision of a free and democratic society, however, we must not hesitate to depart from the path taken in the United States. Far from requiring a less solicitous protection of Charter rights and freedoms, such independence of vision protects these rights and freedoms in a different way. As will be seen below, in my view the international commitment to eradicate hate propaganda and, most importantly, the special role given equality and multiculturalism in the Canadian Constitution necessitate a departure from the view, reasonably prevalent in America at present, that the suppression of hate propaganda is incompatible with the guarantee of free expression....

... Most importantly, the nature of the s. 1 test as applied in the context of a challenge to s. 319(2) may well demand a perspective particular to Canadian constitutional jurisprudence when weighing competing interests. If values fundamental to the Canadian conception of a free and democratic society suggest an approach that denies hate propaganda the highest degree of constitutional protection, it is this approach which must be employed.

C. Objective of Section 319(2)

I now turn to the specific requirements of the *Oakes* approach in deciding whether the infringement of s. 2(b) occasioned by s. 319(2) is justifiable in a free and democratic society. According to *Oakes*, the first aspect of the s. 1 analysis is to examine the objective of the impugned legislation. Only if the objective relates to concerns which are pressing and substantial in a free and democratic society can the legislative limit on a right or freedom hope to be permissible under the Charter....

(i) Harm Caused by Expression Promoting the Hatred of Identifiable Groups

Looking to the legislation challenged in this appeal, one must ask whether the amount of hate propaganda in Canada causes sufficient harm to justify legislative intervention of some type. The Cohen Committee, speaking in 1965, found that . . .:

> . . . there exists in Canada a small number of persons and a somewhat larger number of organizations, extremist in outlook and dedicated to the preaching and spreading of hatred and contempt against certain identifiable minority groups in Canada. It is easy to conclude that because the number of persons and organizations is not very large, they should not be taken too seriously. The Committee is of the opinion that this line of analysis is no longer tenable after what is known to have been the result of hate propaganda in other countries, particularly in the 1930's when such material and ideas played a significant role in the creation of a climate of malice, destructive to the central values of Judaic-Christian society, the values of our civilization. The Committee believes, therefore, that the actual and potential danger caused by present hate activities in Canada cannot be measured by statistics alone.

> Even the statistics, however, are not unimpressive, because while activities have centered heavily in Ontario, they nevertheless have extended from Nova Scotia to British Columbia and minority groups in at least eight Provinces have been subjected to these vicious attacks.

In 1984, the House of Commons Special Committee on Participation of Visible Minorities in Canadian Society in its report, entitled Equality Now!, observed that increased immigration and periods of economic difficulty "have produced an atmosphere that may be ripe for racially motivated incidents". With regard to the dissemination of hate propaganda, the Special Committee found that the prevalence and scope of such material had risen since the Cohen Committee made its report, stating:

> There has been a recent upsurge in hate propaganda. It has been found in virtually every part of Canada. Not only is it anti-semitic and anti-black, as in the 1960s, but it is also now anti-Roman Catholic, anti-East Indian, anti-aboriginal people and anti-French. Some of this material is imported from the United States but much of it is produced in Canada. Most worrisome of all is that in recent years Canada has become a major source of supply of hate propaganda that finds its way to Europe, and especially to West Germany.

As the quotations above indicate, the presence of hate propaganda in Canada is sufficiently substantial to warrant concern.... Essentially, there are two sorts of injury caused by hate propaganda. First, there is harm done to members of the target group. It is indisputable that the emotional damage caused by words may be of grave psychological and social consequence. In the context of sexual harassment, for example, this Court has found that words can in themselves constitute harassment. In a similar manner, words and writings that wilfully promote hatred can constitute a serious attack on persons belonging to a racial or religious group, and in this regard the Cohen Committee noted that these persons are humiliated and degraded.

In my opinion, a response of humiliation and degradation from an individual targeted by hate propaganda is to be expected. A person's sense of human dignity and belonging to the community at large is closely linked to the concern and respect accorded the groups to which he or she belongs. The derision, hostility and abuse encouraged by hate propaganda therefore have a severely negative impact on the individual's sense of self-worth and acceptance. This impact may cause target group members to take drastic measures in reaction, perhaps avoiding activities which bring them into contact with non-group members or adopting attitudes and postures directed towards blending in with the majority. Such consequences bear heavily in a nation that prides itself on tolerance and the fostering of human dignity through, among other things, respect for the many racial, religious and cultural groups in our society.

A second harmful effect of hate propaganda which is of pressing and substantial concern is its influence upon society at large. The Cohen Committee noted that individuals can be persuaded to believe "almost anything" if information or ideas are communicated using the right technique and in the proper circumstances:

> ... we are less confident in the 20th century that the critical faculties of individuals will be brought to bear on the speech and writing which is directed at them. In the 18th and 19th centuries, there was a widespread belief that man was a rational creature, and that if his mind was trained and liberated from superstition by education, he would always distinguish truth from falsehood, good from evil. So Milton, who said "let truth and falsehood grapple: who ever knew truth put to the worse in a free and open encounter".
>
> We cannot share this faith today in such a simple form. While holding that over the long run, the human mind is repelled by blatant falsehood and seeks the good, it is too often true, in the short run, that emotion displaces reason and individuals perversely reject the demonstrations of truth put before them and forsake the good they know. The successes of modern advertising, the triumphs of impudent propaganda such as Hitler's, have qualified sharply our belief in the rationality of man. We know that under strain and pressure in times of irritation and frustration, the individual is swayed and even swept

away by hysterical, emotional appeals. We act irresponsibly if we ignore the way in which emotion can drive reason from the field.

It is thus not inconceivable that the active dissemination of hate propaganda can attract individuals to its cause, and in the process create serious discord between various cultural groups in society. Moreover, the alteration of views held by the recipients of hate propaganda may occur subtlely, and is not always attendant upon conscious acceptance of the communicated ideas. Even if the message of hate propaganda is outwardly rejected, there is evidence that its premise of racial or religious inferiority may persist in a recipient's mind as an idea that holds some truth, an incipient effect not to be entirely discounted....

[The Cohen Committee wrote:]

The amount of hate propaganda presently being disseminated and its measurable effects probably are not sufficient to justify a description of the problem as one of crisis or near crisis proportions. Nevertheless the problem is a serious one. We believe that, given a certain set of socio-economic circumstances, such as a deepening of the emotional tensions or the setting in of a severe business recession, public susceptibility might well increase significantly. Moreover, the potential psychological and social damage of hate propaganda, both to a desensitized majority and to sensitive minority target groups, is incalculable. As Mr. Justice Jackson of the United States Supreme Court wrote in Beauharnais v. Illinois, such "sinister abuses of our freedom of expression ... can tear apart a society, brutalize its dominant elements, and persecute even to extermination, its minorities"....

The close connection between the recommendations of the Cohen Committee and the hate propaganda amendments to the Criminal Code made in 1970 indicates that in enacting s. 319(2) Parliament's purpose was to prevent the harm identified by the Committee as being caused by hate-promoting expression....

(ii) International Human Rights Instruments ...

Generally speaking, the international human rights obligations taken on by Canada reflect the values and principles of a free and democratic society, and thus those values and principles that underlie the Charter itself ....

No aspect of international human rights has been given attention greater than that focused upon discrimination....

In 1966, the United Nations adopted the International Convention on the Elimination of All Forms of Racial Discrimination, Can. T.S. 1970 No. 28 (hereinafter "CERD"). The Convention, in force since 1969 and including Canada among its signatory members, contains a resolution that States Parties agree to:

... adopt all necessary measures for speedily eliminating racial discrimination in all its forms and manifestations, and to prevent and combat racist doctrines and practices in order to promote understanding between races and to build an international community free from all forms of racial segregation and racial discrimination.

Article 4 of the CERD is of special interest, providing that: . . .

States Parties condemn all propaganda and all organizations which are based on ideas or theories of superiority of one race or group of persons of one colour or other ethnic origin, or which attempt to justify or promote racial hatred and discrimination in any form, and undertake to adopt immediate and positive measures designed to eradicate all incitement to, or acts of, such discrimination and, to this end, with due regard to the principles embodied in the Universal Declaration of Human Rights and the rights expressly set forth in article 5 of this Convention, inter alia:

(a) Shall declare an offence punishable by law all dissemination of ideas based on racial superiority or hatred, incitement to racial discrimination, as well as all acts of violence or incitement to such acts against any race or group of persons of another colour or ethnic origin, and also the provision of any assistance to racist activities, including the financing thereof; . . .

Further, the International Covenant on Civil and Political Rights, 999 U.N.T.S. 171 (1966) (hereinafter "ICCPR"), adopted by the United Nations in 1966 and in force in Canada since 1976, in the following two articles guarantees the freedom of expression while simultaneously prohibiting the advocacy of hatred:

Article 19. . . .

2. Everyone shall have the right to freedom of expression; this right shall include freedom to seek, receive and impart information and ideas of all kinds, regardless of frontiers, either orally, in writing or in print, in the form of art, or through any other media of his choice.

3. The exercise of the rights provided for in paragraph 2 of this article carries with it special duties and responsibilities. It may therefore be subject to certain restrictions, but these shall only be such as are provided by law and are necessary:

(a) For respect of the rights or reputations of others;

(b) For the protection of national security or of public order (*ordre public*), or of public health or morals.

Article 20. 1. Any propaganda for war shall be prohibited by law.

2. Any advocacy of national, racial or religious hatred that constitutes incitement to discrimination, hostility or violence shall be prohibited by law.

It appears that the protection provided freedom of expression by CERD and ICCPR does not extend to cover communications advocating racial or religious hatred. . . .

In discussing the stance taken toward hate propaganda in international law, it is also worth mentioning the European Convention for the Protection of Human Rights and Fundamental Freedoms, 213 U.N.T.S. 221 (1950), to which twenty-one states are parties. The Convention contains a qualified guarantee of free expression in Article 10. . . .

Article 10(2), the language of which bears significant resemblance to that of s. 1 of the Charter, has been interpreted by the European Commission of Human Rights so as to permit the prohibition of racist communications as a valid derogation from the protection of free expression . . .

CERD and ICCPR demonstrate that the prohibition of hate-promoting expression is considered to be not only compatible with a signatory nation's guarantee of human rights, but is as well an obligatory aspect of this guarantee. Decisions under the European Convention for the Protection of Human Rights and Fundamental Freedoms are also of aid in illustrating the tenor of the international community's approach to hate propaganda and free expression. . . .

(iii) Other Provisions of the Charter . . .

. . . Most importantly for the purposes of this appeal, ss. 15 and 27 represent a strong commitment to the values of equality and multiculturalism, and hence underline the great importance of Parliament's objective in prohibiting hate propaganda. . . .

> It is clear that the purpose of s. 15 is to ensure equality in the formulation and application of the law. The promotion of equality entails the promotion of a society in which all are secure in the knowledge that they are recognized at law as human beings equally deserving of concern, respect and consideration. It has a large remedial component. . . . [Andrews v. Law Society, [1989] 1 S.C.R. 143]

The value expressed in s. 27 cannot be casually dismissed in assessing the validity of s. 319(2) under s. 1, and I am of the belief that s. 27 and the commitment to a multicultural vision of our nation bear notice in emphasizing the acute importance of the objective of eradicating hate propaganda from society. . . . [T]he sense that an individual can be affected by treatment of a group to which he or she belongs is clearly evident in a number of other Charter provisions not yet mentioned, including ss. 16 to 23 (language rights), s. 25 (aboriginal rights), s. 28 (gender equality) and s. 29 (denominational schools).

Hate propaganda seriously threatens both the enthusiasm with which the value of equality is accepted and acted upon by society and the connection of target group members to their community. . . . When the prohibition of expressive activity that promotes hatred of groups identifiable on the basis of colour, race, religion, or ethnic origin is considered in light of s. 27, the legitimacy and substantial nature of the government objective is therefore considerably strengthened. . . .

D.   Proportionality

The second branch of the *Oakes* test—proportionality—poses the most challenging questions with respect to the validity of § 319(2) as a reasonable limit on freedom of expression in a free and democratic society....

(i) Relation of the Expression at Stake to Free Expression Values ...

... One must ask whether the expression prohibited by s. 319(2) is tenuously connected to the values underlying s. 2(b) so as to make the restriction "easier to justify than other infringements." In this regard, let me begin by saying that, in my opinion, there can be no real disagreement about the subject matter of the messages and teachings communicated by the respondent, Mr. Keegstra: it is deeply offensive, hurtful and damaging to target group members, misleading to his listeners, and antithetical to the furtherance of tolerance and understanding in society. Furthermore, as will be clear when I come to discuss in detail the interpretation of s. 319(2), there is no doubt that all expression fitting within the terms of the offence can be similarly described. To say merely that expression is offensive and disturbing, however, fails to address satisfactorily the question of whether, and to what extent, the expressive activity prohibited by s. 319(2) promotes the values underlying the freedom of expression. It is to this difficult and complex question that I now turn.

From the outset, I wish to make clear that in my opinion the expression prohibited by s. 319(2) is not closely linked to the rationale underlying s. 2(b). Examining the values identified in *Ford* and *Irwin Toy* as fundamental to the protection of free expression, arguments can be made for the proposition that each of these values is diminished by the suppression of hate propaganda.... [E]xpression intended to promote the hatred of identifiable groups is of limited importance when measured against free expression values.

At the core of freedom of expression lies the need to ensure that truth and the common good are attained, whether in scientific and artistic endeavors or in the process of determining the best course to take in our political affairs. Since truth and the ideal form of political and social organization can rarely, if at all, be identified with absolute certainty, it is difficult to prohibit expression without impeding the free exchange of potentially valuable information. Nevertheless, the argument from truth does not provide convincing support for the protection of hate propaganda. Taken to its extreme, this argument would require us to permit the communication of all expression, it being impossible to know with absolute certainty which factual statements are true, or which ideas obtain the greatest good. The problem with this extreme position, however, is that the greater the degree of certainty that a statement is erroneous or mendacious, the less its value in the quest for truth. Indeed, expression can be used to the detriment of our search for truth; the state should not be the sole arbiter of truth, but neither should we overplay the view that rationality will overcome all falsehoods in the unregulated marketplace of ideas. There is very little chance that statements intended to promote hatred against an identifiable group are true, or that their vision of society will lead to a better world. To portray such statements as crucial to truth and the betterment of the political and social milieu is therefore misguided.

Another component central to the rationale underlying s. 2(b) concerns the vital role of free expression as a means of ensuring individuals the ability to gain self-fulfillment by developing and articulating thoughts and ideas as they see fit. It is true that s. 319(2) inhibits this process among those individuals whose expression it limits, and hence arguably works against freedom of expression values. On the other hand, such self-autonomy stems in large part from one's ability to articulate and nurture an identity derived from membership in a cultural or religious group. The message put forth by individuals who fall within the ambit of s. 319(2) represents a most extreme opposition to the idea that members of identifiable groups should enjoy this aspect of the s. 2(b) benefit. The extent to which the unhindered promotion of this message furthers free expression values must therefore be tempered insofar as it advocates with inordinate vitriol an intolerance and prejudice which view as execrable the process of individual self-development and human flourishing among all members of society.

Moving on to a third strain of thought said to justify the protection of free expression, one's attention is brought specifically to the political realm. The connection between freedom of expression and the political process is perhaps the linchpin of the s. 2(b) guarantee, and the nature of this connection is largely derived from the Canadian commitment to democracy. Freedom of expression is a crucial aspect of the democratic commitment, not merely because it permits the best policies to be chosen from among a wide array of proffered options, but additionally because it helps to ensure that participation in the political process is open to all persons. Such open participation must involve to a substantial degree the notion that all persons are equally deserving of respect and dignity. The state therefore cannot act to hinder or condemn a political view without to some extent harming the openness of Canadian democracy and its associated tenet of equality for all.

The suppression of hate propaganda undeniably muzzles the participation of a few individuals in the democratic process, and hence detracts somewhat from free expression values, but the degree of this limitation is not substantial. I am aware that the use of strong language in political and social debate—indeed, perhaps even language intended to promote hatred—is an unavoidable part of the democratic process. Moreover, I recognize that hate propaganda is expression of a type which would generally be categorized as "political", thus putatively placing it at the very heart of the principle extolling freedom of expression as vital to the democratic process. Nonetheless, expression can work to undermine our commitment to democracy where employed to propagate ideas anathemic to democratic values. Hate propaganda works in just such a way, arguing as it does for a society in which the democratic process is subverted and individuals are denied respect and dignity simply because of racial or religious characteristics.

This brand of expressive activity is thus wholly inimical to the democratic aspirations of the free expression guarantee.

Indeed, one may quite plausibly contend that it is through rejecting hate propaganda that the state can best encourage the protection of values central to freedom of expression, while simultaneously demonstrating dislike for the vision forwarded by hate-mongers. . . .

. . . [G]iven the unparalleled vigour with which hate propaganda repudiates and undermines democratic values, and in particular its condemnation of the view that all citizens need be treated with equal respect and dignity so as to make participation in the political process meaningful, I am unable to see the protection of such expression as integral to the democratic ideal so central to the s. 2(b) rationale. . . .

(ii) Rational Connection . . .

Doubts have been raised, however, as to whether the actual effect of s. 319(2) is to undermine any rational connection between it and Parliament's objective. As stated in the reasons of McLachlin J., there are three primary ways in which the effect of the impugned legislation might be seen as an irrational means of carrying out the Parliamentary purpose. First, it is argued that the provision may actually promote the cause of hate-mongers by earning them extensive media attention. . . . Second, the public may view the suppression of expression by the government with suspicion, making it possible that such expression—even if it be hate propaganda—is perceived as containing an element of truth. Finally, it is often noted, citing the writings of A. Neier, Defending My Enemy: American Nazis, the Skokie Case, and the Risks of Freedom (1979), that Germany of the 1920s and 1930s possessed and used hate propaganda laws similar to those existing in Canada, and yet these laws did nothing to stop the triumph of a racist philosophy under the Nazis.

If s. 319(2) can be said to have no impact in the quest to achieve Parliament's admirable objectives, or in fact works in opposition to these objectives, then I agree that the provision could be described as "arbitrary, unfair or based on irrational considerations."

. . . [F]rom my perspective, s. 319(2) serves to illustrate to the public the severe reprobation with which society holds messages of hate directed towards racial and religious groups. The existence of a particular criminal law, and the process of holding a trial when that law is used, is thus itself a form of expression, and the message sent out is that hate propaganda is harmful to target group members and threatening to a harmonious society. As I stated in my reasons in *R. v. Morgentaler,* "The criminal law is a very special form of governmental regulation, for it seeks to express our society's collective disapprobation of certain acts and omissions." The many, many Canadians who belong to identifiable groups surely gain a great deal of comfort from the knowledge that the hate-monger is criminally prosecuted and his or her ideas rejected. Equally, the community as a whole is reminded of the importance of diversity and multiculturalism in Canada, the value of equality and the worth and dignity of each human person being particularly emphasized.

In this context, it can also be said that government suppression of hate propaganda will not make the expression attractive and hence increase acceptance of its content. Similarly, it is very doubtful that Canadians will have sympathy for either propagators of hatred or their ideas. Governmental disapproval of hate propaganda does not invariably result in dignifying the suppressed ideology. Pornography is not dignified by its suppression, nor are defamatory statements against individuals seen as meritorious because the common law lends its support to their prohibition. Again, I stress my belief that hate propaganda legislation and trials are a means by which the values beneficial to a free and democratic society can be publicized....

As for the use of hate propaganda laws in pre-World War Two Germany, I am skeptical as to the relevance of the observation that legislation similar to s. 319(2) proved ineffective in curbing the racism of the Nazis. No one is contending that hate propaganda laws can in themselves prevent the tragedy of a Holocaust.... Rather, hate propaganda laws are one part of a free and democratic society's bid to prevent the spread of racism, and their rational connection to this objective must be seen in such a context. Certainly West Germany has not reacted to the failure of pre-war laws by seeking their removal, a new set of criminal offences having been implemented as recently as 1985 (see E. Stein, "History Against Free Speech: The New German Law Against the 'Auschwitz'—and other—'Lies'" (1987), 85 Mich. L. Rev. 277). Nor, as has been discussed, has the international community regarded the promulgation of laws suppressing hate propaganda as futile or counter-productive. Indeed, this Court's attention has been drawn to the fact that a great many countries possess legislation similar to that found in Canada (see, e.g., England and Wales, Public Order Act 1986 (U.K.), 1986, c. 64, ss. 17 to 23; New Zealand, Race Relations Act 1971 (N.Z.), No. 150, s. 25; Sweden, Penal Code, c. 16, s. 8; Netherlands, Penal Code, ss. 137c, 137d and 137e; India, Penal Code, ss. 153-A and 153-B, and generally, the United Nation's Study on the Implementation of Article 4 of the International Convention on the Elimination of All Forms of Racial Discrimination). The experience of Germany represents an awful nadir in the history of racism, and demonstrates the extent to which flawed and brutal ideas can capture the acceptance of a significant number of people. One aspect of this experience is not, however, determinative in deciding whether or not hate propaganda laws are effective.

In sum, having found that the purpose of the challenged legislation is valid, I also find that the means chosen to further this purpose are rational....

(iii) Minimal Impairment of the Section 2(b) Freedom

The criminal nature of the impugned provision, involving the associated risks of prejudice through prosecution, conviction and the imposition of up to two years imprisonment, indicates that the means embodied in hate propaganda legislation should be carefully tailored so as to minimize impairment of the freedom of expression. It therefore must be shown that s. 319(2) is a measured and appropriate response to the phenomenon of hate propaganda, and that it does not overly circumscribe the s. 2(b) guarantee.

The main argument of those who would strike down s. 319(2) is that it creates a real possibility of punishing expression that is not hate propaganda. It is thus submitted that the legislation is overbroad, its terms so wide as to include expression which does not relate to Parliament's objective, and also unduly vague, in that a lack of clarity and precision in its words prevents individuals from discerning its meaning with any accuracy. . . .

a.   Terms of Section 319(2)

In assessing the constitutionality of s. 319(2), especially as concerns arguments of overbreadth and vagueness, an immediate observation is that statements made "in private conversation" are not included in the criminalized expression . . . indicating Parliament's concern not to intrude upon the privacy of the individual. . . . [T]hat the legislation excludes private conversation . . . suggests that the expression of hatred in a place accessible to the public is not sufficient to activate the legislation. . . .

Is s. 319(2) nevertheless overbroad because it captures all public expression intended to promote hatred? It would appear not, for the harm which the government seeks to prevent is not restricted to certain mediums and/or locations. To attempt to distinguish between various forms and fora would therefore be incongruent with Parliament's legitimate objective.

A second important element of s. 319(2) is its requirement that the promotion of hatred be "wilful". . . .

> The principle of restraint requires lawmakers to concern themselves not just with whom they want to catch, but also with whom they do not want to catch. For example, removing an intent or purpose requirement could well result in successful prosecutions of cases similar to *Buzzanga*, [(1979), 49 C.C.C. (2d) 369 (Ont. C.A.)] where members of a minority group publish hate propaganda against their own group in order to create controversy or to agitate for reform. This crime should not be used to prosecute such individuals [quoting Law Reform Commission, Working Paper on Hate Propaganda].

I agree with the interpretation of "wilfully" in *Buzzanga*, and wholeheartedly endorse the view of the Law Reform Commission Working Paper that this stringent standard of mens rea is an invaluable means of limiting the incursion of s. 319(2) into the realm of acceptable (though perhaps offensive and controversial) expression. It is clear that the word "wilfully" imports a difficult burden for the Crown to meet and, in so doing, serves to minimize the impairment of freedom of expression.

It has been argued, however, that even a demanding *mens rea* component fails to give s. 319(2) a constitutionally acceptable breadth. The problem is said to lie in the failure of the offence to require proof of actual hatred resulting from a communication, the assumption being that only such proof can demonstrate a harm serious enough to justify limiting the freedom of expression under s. 1....

While mindful of the dangers ... I do not find them sufficiently grave to compel striking down s. 319(2). First, to predicate the limitation of free expression upon proof of actual hatred gives insufficient attention to the severe psychological trauma suffered by members of those identifiable groups targeted by hate propaganda. Second, it is clearly difficult to prove a causative link between a specific statement and hatred of an identifiable group. In fact, to require direct proof of hatred in listeners would severely debilitate the effectiveness of s. 319(2) in achieving Parliament's aim. It is well accepted that Parliament can use the criminal law to prevent the risk of serious harms, a leading example being the drinking and driving provisions in the Criminal Code. The conclusions of the Cohen Committee and subsequent study groups show that the risk of hatred caused by hate propaganda is very real, and in view of the grievous harm to be avoided in the context of this appeal, I conclude that proof of actual hatred is not required in order to justify a limit under s. 1....

c. Alternative Modes of Furthering Parliament's Objective

One of the strongest arguments supporting the contention that s. 319(2) unacceptably impairs the s. 2(b) guarantee posits that a criminal sanction is not necessary to meet Parliament's objective.... Most generally, it is said that discriminatory ideas can best be met with information and education programmes extolling the merits of tolerance and cooperation between racial and religious groups. As for the prohibition of hate propaganda, human rights statutes are pointed to as being a less severe and more effective response than the criminal law. Such statutes not only subject the disseminator of hate propaganda to reduced stigma and punishment, but also take a less confrontational approach to the suppression of such expression. This conciliatory tack is said to be preferable to penal sanction because an incentive is offered the disseminator to cooperate with human rights tribunals and thus to amend his or her conduct.

Given the stigma and punishment associated with a criminal conviction and the presence of other modes of government response in the fight against intolerance, it is proper to ask whether s. 319(2) can be said to impair minimally the freedom of expression....

In assessing the proportionality of a legislative enactment to a valid governmental objective, however, s. 1 should not operate in every instance so as to force the government to rely upon only the mode of intervention least intrusive of a Charter right or freedom. It may be that a number of courses of action are available in the furtherance of a pressing and substantial objective, each imposing a varying degree of restriction upon a right or freedom. In such circumstances, the government may legitimately employ a more restrictive measure, either alone or as part of a larger programme of action, if that measure is not redundant, furthering the objective in ways that alternative responses could not, and is in all other respects proportionate to a valid s. 1 aim.

Though the fostering of tolerant attitudes among Canadians will be best achieved through a combination of diverse measures, the harm done through hate propaganda may require that especially stringent responses be taken to suppress and prohibit a modicum of expressive activity. At the moment, for example, the state has the option of responding to hate propaganda by acting under either the Criminal Code or human rights provisions. In my view, having both avenues of redress at the state's disposal is justified in a free and democratic society....

d.   Conclusion as to Minimal Impairment

To summarize the above discussion, in light of the great importance of Parliament's objective and the discounted value of the expression at issue I find that the terms of s. 319(2) create a narrowly confined offence which suffers from neither overbreadth nor vagueness. This interpretation stems largely from my view that the provision possesses a stringent mens rea requirement, necessitating either an intent to promote hatred or knowledge of the substantial certainty of such, and is also strongly supported by the conclusion that the meaning of the word "hatred" is restricted to the most severe and deeply-felt form of opprobrium. Additionally, however, the conclusion that s. 319(2) represents a minimal impairment of the freedom of expression gains credence through the exclusion of private conversation from its scope, the need for the promotion of hatred to focus upon an identifiable group and the presence of the s. 319(3) defences. As for the argument that other modes of combatting hate propaganda eclipse the need for a criminal provision, it is eminently reasonable to utilize more than one type of legislative tool in working to prevent the spread of racist expression and its resultant harm. It will indeed be more difficult to justify a criminal statute under s. 1, but in my opinion the necessary justificatory arguments have been made out with respect to s. 319(2)....

(iv)   Effects of the Limitation

The third branch of the proportionality test entails a weighing of the importance of the state objective against the effect of limits imposed upon a Charter right or guarantee....

... I have little trouble in finding that its effects, involving as they do the restriction of expression largely removed from the heart of free expression values, are not of such a deleterious nature as to outweigh any advantage gleaned from the limitation of s. 2(b)....

McLACHLIN J. (dissenting)—

Introduction

The issue on this appeal is whether ss. 319(2) and 319(3) of the Criminal Code, R.S.C., 1985, c. C-46, creating the offence of unlawfully promoting hatred, should be struck down on the ground that they infringe the guarantees of free expression and the presumption of innocence embodied in the Canadian Charter of Rights and Freedoms.

Mr. Keegstra, a secondary school teacher in Eckville, a small town in Alberta, was convicted of unlawfully promoting hatred under s. 319(2). The evidence established that he had systematically denigrated Jews and Judaism in his classes.... He maintained that anyone Jewish must be evil and that anyone evil must be Jewish. Not only did he maintain these things; he advised the students that they must accept his views as true unless they were able to contradict them. Moreover, he expected his students to regurgitate these notions in essays and examinations. If they did so, they received good marks. If they did not, their marks were poor....

Salient among the justifications for free expression ... is the postulate that the freedom is instrumental in promoting the free flow of ideas essential to political democracy and the functioning of democratic institutions. This is sometimes referred to as the political process rationale. The locus classicus of this rationale is A. Meiklejohn, Free Speech and its Relation to Self-Government (1948).

A corollary of the view that expression must be free because of its role in the political process is that only expression relating to the political process is worthy of constitutional protection. However, within these limits protection for expression is said to be absolute. The political process rationale has played a significant role in the development of First Amendment doctrine in the United States, and various justices of the U.S. Supreme Court (though never a majority) have embraced its theory that protection of speech is absolute within these restricted bounds. Its importance has also been affirmed by Canadian courts, both before and since the advent of the Charter....

Another venerable rationale for freedom of expression (dating at least to Milton's Areopagitica in 1644) is that it is an essential precondition of the search for truth. Like the political process model, this model is instrumental in outlook. Freedom of expression is seen as a means of promoting a "marketplace of ideas", in which competing ideas vie for supremacy to the end of attaining the truth. The "marketplace of ideas" metaphor was coined by Justice Oliver Wendell Holmes, in his famous dissent in Abrams v. United States, 250 U.S. 616 (1919). This approach, however, has been criticized on the ground that there is no guarantee that the free expression of ideas will in fact lead to the truth. Indeed, as history attests, it is quite possible that dangerous, destructive and inherently untrue ideas may prevail, at least in the short run.

Notwithstanding the cogency of this critique, it does not negate the essential validity of the notion of the value of the marketplace of ideas. While freedom of expression provides no guarantee that the truth will always prevail, it still can be argued that it assists in promoting the truth in ways which would be impossible without the freedom....

But freedom of expression may be viewed as more than a means to other ends. Many assert that free expression is an end in itself, a value essential to the sort of society we wish to preserve. This view holds that freedom of expression "derives from the widely accepted premise of Western thought that the proper end of man is the realization of his character and potentialities as a human being". It follows from this premise that all persons have the right to form their own beliefs and opinions, and to express them. "For expression is an integral part of the development of ideas, of mental exploration and of the affirmation of self": T. I. Emerson, "Toward a General Theory of the First Amendment" (1963), 72 Yale L.J. 877, at p. 879.... Freedom of expression is seen as worth preserving for its own intrinsic value....

... [A]n emphasis on the intrinsic value of freedom of expression provides a useful supplement to the more utilitarian rationales, justifying, for example, forms of artistic expression which some might otherwise be tempted to exclude.

Arguments based on intrinsic value and practical consequences are married in the thought of F. Schauer (Free Speech: A Philosophical Enquiry (1982)). Rather than evaluating expression to see why it might be worthy of protection, Schauer evaluates the reasons why a government might attempt to limit expression. Schauer points out that throughout history, attempts to restrict expression have accounted for a disproportionate share of governmental blunders—from the condemnation of Galileo for suggesting the earth is round to the suppression as "obscene" of many great works of art. Professor Schauer explains this peculiar inability of censoring governments to avoid mistakes by the fact that, in limiting expression, governments often act as judge in their own cause. They have an interest in stilling criticism of themselves, or even in enhancing their own popularity by silencing unpopular expression. These motives may render them unable to carefully weigh the advantages and disadvantages of suppression in many instances. That is not to say that it is always illegitimate for governments to curtail expression, but government attempts to do so must prima facie be viewed with suspicion....

How do these diverse justifications of freedom of expression relate to s. 2(b) of the Charter? First, it may be noted that the broad wording of s. 2(b) of the Charter is arguably inconsistent with a justification based on a single facet of free expression. This suggests that there is no need to adopt any one definitive justification for freedom of expression. Different justifications for freedom of expression may assume varying degrees of importance in different fact situations....

The interpretation which has been placed on s. 2(b) of the Charter confirms the relevance of both instrumental and intrinsic justifications for free expression. This Court has adopted a purposive approach in construing the rights and freedoms guaranteed by the Charter. When placed in the context of the judicial history of freedom of expression in Canada, it suggests that it is appropriate to consider the ends which freedom of speech may serve in determining its scope and the justifiability of infringements upon it. These ends include the maintenance of our democratic rights and the benefits to be gained from the pursuit of truth and creativity in science, art, industry and other endeavours. At the same time, the emphasis which this Court has placed upon the inherent dignity of the individual in interpreting Charter guarantees suggests that the rationale of self-actualization should also play an important part in decisions under s. 2(b) of the Charter. . . .

B.   The Historical Perspective

Freedom of speech and the press had acquired quasi-constitutional status well before the adoption of the Charter in 1982. In a series of cases dealing with legislation passed by repressive provincial regimes, the Supreme Court endorsed the proposition that the right to express political ideas could not be trammelled by the legislatures.

The focus of these decisions was the division of powers between the provinces and the federal government. The Alberta Press reference (Reference re Alberta Statutes, [1938] S.C.R. 100) provides a good example. At issue was a bill introduced by the Alberta Legislature to compel newspapers to disclose their sources of news information and to print government statements correcting previous articles. The bill was struck down on the basis that the province had no jurisdiction over the free working of the political institutions of the state. Political expression, vital to the country as a whole, could not be limited by provincial legislation. . . .

These decisions confirmed the fundamental importance of freedom of speech and the press in Canada. The conception of freedom of speech embodied in these cases, however, was largely limited to the political process model. . . .

Nevertheless, one thing has remained constant through all the decisions. That is the recognition that freedom of speech is a fundamental Canadian value. . . .

The enactment of s. 2(b) of the Charter represented both the continuity of these traditions, and a new flourishing of the importance of freedom of expression in Canadian society. . . .

C.   Hate Propaganda and Freedom of Speech—An Overview . . .

Hate literature presents a great challenge to our conceptions about the value of free expression. Its offensive content often constitutes a direct attack on many of the other principles which are cherished by our society. Tolerance, the dignity and equality of all individuals; these and other values are all adversely affected by the propagation of hateful sentiment. The problem is not peculiarly Canadian; it is universal. Wherever racially or culturally distinct groups of people live together, one finds people, usually a small minority of the population, who take it upon themselves to denigrate members of a group other than theirs. Canada is no stranger to this conduct. Our history is replete with examples of discriminatory communications. In their time, Canadians of Asian and East Indian descent, black, and native people have been the objects of communications tending to foster hate. In the case at bar it is the Jewish people who have been singled out as objects of calumny.

The evil of hate propaganda is beyond doubt. It inflicts pain and indignity upon individuals who are members of the group in question. Insofar as it may persuade others to the same point of view, it may threaten social stability. And it is intrinsically offensive to people—the majority in most democratic countries—who believe in the equality of all people regardless of race or creed.

For these reasons, governments have legislated against the dissemination of propaganda directed against racial groups, and in some cases this legislation has been tested in the courts. Perhaps the experience most relevant to Canada is that of the United States, since its Constitution, like ours, places a high value on free expression, raising starkly the conflict between freedom of speech and the countervailing values of individual dignity and social harmony. Like s. 2(b), the First Amendment guarantee is conveyed in broad, unrestricted language, stating that "Congress shall make no law ... abridging the freedom of speech, or of the press". The relevance of aspects of the American experience to this case is underlined by the factums and submissions, which borrowed heavily from ideas which may be traced to the United States.

The protections of the First Amendment to the U.S. Constitution, and in particular free speech, have always assumed a particular importance within the U.S. constitutional scheme, being regarded as the cornerstone of all other democratic freedoms. As expressed by Jackson J., in West Virginia State Board of Education v. Barnette, 319 U.S. 624 (1943), "[i]f there is any fixed star in our constitutional constellation, it is that no official, high or petty, can prescribe what shall be orthodox in politics, nationalism, religion, or other matters of opinion or force citizens to confess by word or act their faith therein." ...

Nevertheless, tolerance for unpopular speech, especially speech which was perceived as a threat to vital security interests, was not initially a hallmark of the U.S. Supreme Court. When the socialist labour leader Eugene Debs made a speech critical of United States involvement in the First World War, the court was content to uphold his conviction for "wilfully caus[ing] or attempt[ing] to cause ... insubordination, disloyalty, mutiny, or refusal of duty, in the military or naval forces ... or ... wilfully obstruct[ing] ... the recruiting or enlistment service": Debs v. United States, 249 U.S. 211 (1919). A companion case set out the classic test for the justifiability of an abridgement of free speech:

> The question in every case is whether the words used are used in such circumstances and are of such a nature as to create a clear and present danger that they will bring about the substantive evils that Congress has a right to prevent. (Schenck v. United States, 249 U.S. 47 (1919), at p. 52.)

The test was stiffened in the famous dissents of Holmes J. in Abrams v. United States, supra, at p. 628 ("present danger of immediate evil or an intent to bring it about") and Brandeis J. (Holmes J. concurring) in Whitney v. California, 274 U.S. 357 (1927):

... If there be time to expose through discussion the falsehood and fallacies, to avert the evil by the processes of education, the remedy to be applied is more speech, not enforced silence....

Moreover, even imminent danger cannot justify resort to prohibition of these functions essential to effective democracy, unless the evil apprehended is relatively serious .... There must be the probability of serious injury to the State.

This stricter formulation of the "clear and present danger" test came to be accepted as the standard for a justified infringement of the free speech guarantee, but it too was subject to varying interpretation. In the crisis atmosphere of the cold war, the court upheld convictions of communists for conspiring to advocate the overthrow of the United States government in Dennis v. United States, 341 U.S. 494 (1951). Purporting to apply the above test, the court endorsed the following formulation: "In each case [courts] must ask whether the gravity of the 'evil', discounted by its improbability, justifies such invasion of free speech as is necessary to avoid the danger." This is how matters stood when hate propaganda first came to the attention of the court.

[Justice McLachlin's discussion of *Beauharnais* is omitted.] ...

But the full flowering of First Amendment doctrine came after the *Beauharnais* case. Later cases have weakened its authority to the extent that many regard it as overruled.... The test that emerges from *Brandenburg* is much stricter than the earlier formulations—advocacy of the use of force or violation of the law cannot be proscribed "except where such advocacy is directed to inciting or producing imminent lawless action and is likely to incite or produce such action." ...

It is worth describing a few doctrines associated with free speech that form part of the reasoning in the U.S. cases, and which are cited in the factums. One is a hierarchy of possible abridgements on free speech. Legislation against the content of speech has been distinguished from legislation restricting speech in other ways, with the former attracting stricter judicial scrutiny. For example, while "time, place and manner" regulation of speech has traditionally been given some latitude, an ordinance preventing picketing other than labour picketing near schools has been struck down because it draws a distinction based on content of the speech: Police Department of the City of Chicago v. Mosley, 408 U.S. 92 (1972). Viewpoint-based abridgements of speech, in which the Government selects between viewpoints, will very rarely be justifiable. Section 319(2) of the Criminal Code is probably best described as content-based rather than viewpoint-based, because the Government itself does not choose between viewpoints directly. For example, a statement declaring the superiority of a particular race is not preferred over a declaration suggesting the reverse hierarchy. Rather, all discussion of the superiority of a particular race over another is potentially suspect. This content-based provision is similar in this regard to the statute forbidding demonstrations critical of foreign governments within 500 feet of embassies that was struck down as an impermissible content-based restriction on speech in Boos v. Barry, 108 S.

Ct. 1157 (1988). Although not as offensive as viewpoint-based restrictions, content-based restrictions on speech have attracted "most exacting scrutiny" from the U.S. Supreme Court, being upheld only if "necessary to serve a compelling state interest and ... narrowly drawn to achieve that end": Perry Education Ass'n v. Perry Local Educators' Ass'n, 460 U.S. 37 (1983)....

... [I]nternational instruments embody quite a different conception of freedom of expression than the case law under the U.S. First Amendment. The international decisions reflect the much more explicit priorities of the relevant documents regarding the relationship between freedom of expression and the objective of eradicating speech which advocates racial and cultural hatred. The approach seems to be to read down freedom of expression to the extent necessary to accommodate the legislation prohibiting the speech in question.

Both the American and international approach recognize that freedom of expression is not absolute, and must yield in some circumstances to other values. The divergence lies in the way the limits are determined. On the international approach, the objective of suppressing hatred appears to be sufficient to override freedom of expression. In the United States, it is necessary to go much further and show clear and present danger before free speech can be overridden.

The Charter follows the American approach in method, affirming freedom of expression as a broadly defined and fundamental right, and contemplating balancing the values protected by and inherent in freedom of expression against the benefit conferred by the legislation limiting that freedom under s. 1 of the Charter. This is in keeping with the strong liberal tradition favouring free speech in this country—a tradition which had led to conferring quasi-constitutional status on free expression in this country prior to any bill of rights or Charter. At the same time, the tests are not necessarily the same as in the United States....

[On the relevance of s. 27:] Different people may have different ideas about what undermines multiculturalism. The issue is inherently vague and to some extent a matter of personal opinion. For example, it might be suggested that a statement that Canada should not permit immigration from a certain part of the world is inconsistent with the preservation and enhancement of multiculturalism. Is s. 2(b) to be cut back to eliminate protection for such a statement, given the differing opinions one might expect on such a matter? It may be argued, moreover, that a certain latitude for expression of derogatory opinion about other groups is a necessary correlative of a multicultural society, where different groups compete for limited resources....

IV.   The Analysis under Section 1

A.   Section 1 and the Infringement of Freedom of Expression ...

The task which judges are required to perform under s. 1 is essentially one of balancing. On the one hand lies a violation or limitation of a fundamental right or freedom. On the other lies a conflicting objective which the state asserts is of greater importance than the full exercise of the right or freedom, of sufficient importance that it is reasonable and "demonstrably justified" that the limitation should be imposed. The exercise is one of great difficulty, requiring the judge to make value judgments. In this task logic and precedent are but of limited assistance. What must be determinative in the end is the court's judgment, based on an understanding of the values our society is built on and the interests at stake in the particular case. As Wilson J. has pointed out in *Edmonton Journal*, this judgment cannot be made in the abstract. Rather than speak of values as though they were Platonic ideals, the judge must situate the analysis in the facts of the particular case, weighing the different values represented in that context. Thus it cannot be said that freedom of expression will always prevail over the objective of individual dignity and social harmony, or vice versa. The result in a particular case will depend on weighing the significance of the infringement on freedom of expression represented by the law in question, against the importance of the countervailing objectives, the likelihood the law will achieve those objectives, and the proportionality of the scope of the law to those objectives....

(1) The Objective of Section 319(2) of the Criminal Code

In *Oakes* Dickson C.J., speaking for the majority, stated that the first consideration in an analysis under s. 1 is that the objective be "of sufficient importance to warrant overriding a constitutionally protected right or freedom" ... [H]e observed that the standard must be high in order to ensure that objectives of a trivial nature do not gain s. 1 protection. The objective must be of a pressing and substantial nature before it can be characterized as sufficiently important to override a Charter right.

The objective of s. 319(2) of the Criminal Code is to prevent the promotion of hatred toward identifiable groups within our society....

These are laudable goals and serious ones. The objectives are clearly of a substantial nature. Given the history of racial and religious conflict in the world in the past fifty years, they may be said to be pressing, even though it is not asserted that an emergency exists in Canada....

The continued existence of hateful communication in Canada is symptomatic of an unfortunate reality that while Canadians often pride themselves for maintaining a tolerant and welcoming society, it is undermined by the persistence of racial and religious division. The conflict is harmful both to the individuals and groups who are the target of prejudice, and to society as a whole. Members of minority groups are inclined to consider themselves outsiders in their country, and may be inhibited from contributing to the extent of their desire and ability. The loss of this potential talent and ability threatens to deprive Canada of the skills and talents of those who feel excluded and unwelcome. Moreover, the animosity created by ignorance and hatred further exacerbates the divisions of a nation.

The problem is not new, but neither is it quickly disappearing. As the Annual Report 1989 (1990) of the Canadian Human Rights Commission strongly remarked, intolerance among Canadians towards members of different groups remains a serious problem:

> The demons of racial and cultural prejudice have never been either officially or unofficially exorcised from Canadian society. We may, on occasion, have been marginally more enlightened than our southern neighbours, but instances of racism and intolerance are deeply etched in the historical record and, for that matter, not hard to find in the daily newspapers.

Given the problem of racial and religious prejudice in this country, I am satisfied that the objective of the legislation is of sufficient gravity to be capable of justifying limitations on constitutionally protected rights and freedoms.

(2) Proportionality

(a) General Considerations

The real question in this case, as I see it, is whether the means—the criminal prohibition of wilfully promoting hatred—are proportional and appropriate to the ends of suppressing hate propaganda in order to maintain social harmony and individual dignity. The objective of the legislation is one of great significance, such significance that it is capable of outweighing the fundamental values protected by the Charter. The ultimate question is whether this objective is of sufficient importance to justify the limitation on free expression effected by s. 319(2) of the Criminal Code....

... In approaching the difficult task of determining where the balance lies in the context of this case, it is important not to be diverted by the offensive content of much of the speech in question. As this Court has repeatedly stated, even the most reprehensible or disagreeable comments are prima facie entitled to the protection of s. 2(b). It is not the statements of Mr. Keegstra which are at issue in this case, but rather the constitutionality of s. 319(2) of the Criminal Code....

Another general consideration relevant to the balancing of values involved in the proportionality test in this case relates peculiarly to the nature of freedom of expression. Freedom of expression is unique among the rights and freedoms guaranteed by the Charter in two ways.

The first way in which freedom of expression may be unique [is that t]he right to fully and openly express one's views on social and political issues is fundamental to our democracy and hence to all the other rights and freedoms guaranteed by the Charter. Without free expression, the vigourous debate on policies and values that underlies participatory government is lacking. Without free expression, rights may be trammelled with no recourse in the court of public opinion....

A second characteristic peculiar to freedom of expression is that limitations on expression tend to have an effect on expression other than that which is their target. In the United States this is referred to as the chilling effect.... This chilling effect must be taken into account in performing the balancing required by the analysis under s. 1. It mandates that in weighing the intrusiveness of a limitation on freedom of expression our consideration cannot be confined to those who may ultimately be convicted under the limit, but must extend to those who may be deterred from legitimate expression by uncertainty as to whether they might be convicted.

I make one final point before entering on the specific tests for proportionality proposed in *Oakes*. In determining whether the particular limitation of a right or freedom is justified under s. 1, it is important to consider not only the proportionality and effectiveness of the particular law in question, but alternative ways of furthering the objective. This is particularly important at stages two (minimum impairment) and three (balancing the infringement against the objective) of the proportionality analysis proposed in *Oakes*. . . .

(b) Rational Connection

. . . [I]t is clear that the legislation does, at least at one level, further Parliament's objectives. Prosecutions of individuals for offensive material directed at a particular group may bolster its members' beliefs that they are valued and respected in their community, and that the views of a malicious few do not reflect those of the population as a whole. Such a use of the criminal law may well affirm certain values and priorities which are of a pressing and substantial nature.

It is necessary, however, to go further, and consider not only Parliament's intention, but whether, given the actual effect of the legislation, a rational connection exists between it and its objectives. Legislation designed to promote an objective may in fact impede that objective. In *R. v. Morgentaler* this Court considered the actual effect of abortion legislation designed to preserve women's life and health and found that it had the opposite effect of the legislative goals by imposing unreasonable procedural requirements and delays. This Court was particularly mindful of the effects that these requirements had in practice of substantially increasing the risks to the health of pregnant women, especially in certain locations. Dickson C.J. treated this in the context of rational connection, stating, "to the extent that s. 251(4) is designed to protect the life and health of women, the procedures it establishes may actually defeat that objective."

This approach recognizes that s. 1 of the Charter could easily become diluted if an intention on the part of government to act on behalf of a disadvantaged group sufficed in all cases to establish the necessary rational connection between the legislation and its objective. In some cases the link between the intention of the legislators and the achievement of the goal may be self-evident. In others, there may be doubt about whether the legislation will in fact achieve its ends; in resolving that doubt deference must be paid to the Parliament and the legislatures. But in cases such as *Morgentaler*, where it appears that the legislation not only may fail to achieve its goal but may have a contrary effect, the Court is justified in finding that the rational connection between the measure and the objective is absent. This is only a matter of common sense. How can a measure which takes away a measure of one's constitutional freedom be reasonably and demonstrably justified unless there is some likelihood that it will further the objective upon which its justification rests? . . .

In my view, s. 319(2) of the Criminal Code falls in this class of case. Section 319(2) may well have a chilling effect on defensible expression by law-abiding citizens. At the same time, it is far from clear that it provides an effective way of curbing hate-mongers. Indeed, many have suggested it may promote their cause. Prosecutions under the Criminal Code for racist expression have attracted extensive media coverage. . . . There is an unmistakable hint of the joy of martyrdom in some of the literature for which Andrews, in the companion appeal, was prosecuted:

> "The Holocaust Hoax has been so ingrained in the minds of the hated 'goyim' by now that in some countries . . . challenging its validity can land you in jail." (R. v. Andrews (1988), 65 O.R. (2d) 161, at p. 165 (C.A.).)

Not only does the criminal process confer on the accused publicity for his dubious causes—it may even bring him sympathy. . . .

The argument that criminal prosecutions for this kind of expression will reduce racism and foster multiculturalism depends on the assumption that some listeners are gullible enough to believe the expression if exposed to it. But if this assumption is valid, these listeners might be just as likely to believe that there must be some truth in the racist expression because the government is trying to suppress it. Theories of a grand conspiracy between government and elements of society wrongly perceived as malevolent can become all too appealing if government dignifies them by completely suppressing their utterance. It is therefore not surprising that the criminalization of hate propaganda and prosecutions under such legislation have been subject to so much controversy in this country.

Historical evidence also gives reason to be suspicious of the claim that hate propaganda laws contribute to the cause of multiculturalism and equality. . . .

> Remarkably, pre-Hitler Germany had laws very much like the Canadian anti-hate law. Moreover, those laws were enforced with some vigour. During the fifteen years before Hitler came to power, there were more than two hundred prosecutions based on anti-semitic speech. And, in the opinion of the leading Jewish organization of that era, no more than 10 per cent of the cases were mishandled by the authorities. As subsequent history so painfully testifies, this type of legislation proved ineffectual on the one occasion when there was a real argument for it. Indeed, there is some indication that the Nazis of pre-Hitler Germany shrewdly exploited their criminal trials in order to increase the size of their constituency. They used the trials as platforms to propagate their message. [A.A. Borovoy, When Freedoms Collide (1988)]

Viewed from the point of view of actual effect, the rational connection between s. 319(2) and the goals it promotes may be argued to be tenuous.

Certainly it cannot be said that there is a strong and evident connection between the criminalization of hate propaganda and its suppression.

(c) Minimum Impairment . . .

Despite the limitations found in s. 319(2), a strong case can be made that it is overbroad in that its definition of offending speech may catch many expressions which should be protected.

The first difficulty lies in the different interpretations which may be placed on the word "hatred." . . .

. . . "Hatred" is proved by inference—the inference of the jury or the judge who sits as trier of fact—and inferences are more likely to be drawn when the speech is unpopular. The subjective and emotional nature of the concept of promoting hatred compounds the difficulty of ensuring that only cases meriting prosecution are pursued and that only those whose conduct is calculated to dissolve the social bonds of society are convicted.

But "hatred" does not stand alone. To convict, it must have been "wilfully promote[d]". Does this requirement sufficiently constrain the term to meet the claim that s. 319(2) is overbroad? . . .

The real answer to the debate about whether § 319(2) is overbroad is provided by the section's track record. Although the section is of relatively recent origin, it has provoked many questionable actions on the part of the authorities. There have been no reported convictions, other than the instant appeals. But the record amply demonstrates that intemperate statements about identifiable groups, particularly if they represent an unpopular viewpoint, may attract state involvement or calls for police action. Novels such as Leon Uris' pro-Zionist novel, The Haj (1984), face calls for banning: Toronto Star, September 26, 1984, p. A6. Other works, such as Salman Rushdie's Satanic Verses (1988), are stopped at the border on the ground that they violate s. 319(2). Films may be temporarily kept out, as happened to a film entitled "Nelson Mandela", ordered as an educational film by Ryerson Polytechnical Institute in 1986: Globe and Mail, December 24, 1986, p. A14. Arrests are even made for distributing pamphlets containing the words "Yankee Go Home": Globe and Mail, July 4, 1975, p. 1. Experience shows that many cases are winnowed out due to prosecutorial discretion and other factors. It shows equally, however, that initially quite a lot of speech is caught by s. 319(2).

Even where investigations are not initiated or prosecutions pursued, the vagueness and subjectivity inherent in s. 319(2) of the Criminal Code give ground for concern that the chilling effect of the law may be substantial. . . .

This brings me to the second aspect of minimum impairment. The examples I have just given suggest that the very fact of criminalization itself may be argued to represent an excessive response to the problem of hate propagation. . . .

(d) Importance of the Right versus Benefit Conferred

The third consideration in determining whether the infringement represented by the legislation is proportionate to the ends is the balance between the importance of the infringement of the right in question and the benefit conferred by the legislation. The analysis is essentially a cost-benefit analysis. On the one hand, how significant is the infringement of the fundamental right or freedom in question? . . .

I deal first with the significance of the infringement of the constitutionally guaranteed freedom at issue in this case. Viewed from the perspective of our society as a whole, the infringement of the guarantee of freedom of expression before this Court is a serious one. Section 319(2) of the Criminal Code does not merely regulate the form or tone of expression—it strikes directly at its content and at the viewpoints of individuals. It strikes, moreover, at viewpoints in widely diverse domains, whether artistic, social or political. It is capable of catching not only statements like those at issue in this case, but works of art and the intemperate statement made in the heat of social controversy. While few may actually be prosecuted to conviction under s. 319(2), many fall within the shadow of its broad prohibition. These dangers are exacerbated by the fact that s. 319(2) applies to all public expression. In short, the limitation on freedom of expression created by s. 319(2) of the Criminal Code invokes all of the values upon which s. 2(b) of the Charter rests—the value of fostering a vibrant and creative society through the marketplace of ideas; the value of the vigourous and open debate essential to democratic government and preservation of our rights and freedoms; and the value of a society which fosters the self-actualization and freedom of its members. . . .

I turn then to the other side of the scale and the benefit to be gained by maintenance of the limitation on freedom of expression effected by s. 319(2) of the Criminal Code. As indicated earlier, there is no question but that the objectives which underlie this legislation are of a most worthy nature. Unfortunately, the claims of gains to be achieved at the cost of the infringement of free speech represented by s. 319(2) are tenuous. It is far from clear that the legislation does not promote the cause of hate-mongering extremists and hinder the possibility of voluntary amendment of conduct more than it discourages the spread of hate propaganda. Accepting the importance to our society of the goals of social harmony and individual dignity, of multiculturalism and equality, it remains difficult to see how s. 319(2) fosters them.

In my opinion, the result is clear. Any questionable benefit of the legislation is outweighed by the significant infringement on the constitutional guarantee of free expression effected by § 319(2) of the Criminal Code. . . .

Note on Attis v. Board of School Trustees, [1996] 1 S.C.R. 825 (Supreme Court of Canada)

In *Attis*, the Court applied the reasoning of *Keegstra* in a somewhat different setting. Parents of Jewish students at a public school in New

Brunswick filed a complaint with the Human Rights Commission against the local school board for its failure to respond to a schoolteacher's public circulation of anti-semitic statements during his off-duty hours. Given the publicity attending his statements, the parents claimed the teacher's conduct had an adverse effect on their children's comfort and security in school. The schoolteacher had made "racist and discriminatory statements" in published writings (including four books or pamphlets and three letters to local newspapers) as well as in public television appearances, arguing that "Christian civilization was being undermined and destroyed by an international Jewish conspiracy."

In response to the complaint the Commission found (and the courts agreed) that the school board, in not affirmatively responding to and disciplining the teacher, had discriminated against its Jewish students in violation of the provincial Human Rights Law. The Commission ordered, *inter alia*, that the school board (1) transfer the teacher into a nonteaching, administrative position and (2) permanently prohibit him from circulating any such material as long as he was a school employee. The Supreme Court upheld the disciplinary order transferring the teacher into a nonteaching position. But, finding a violation of the teacher's Charter Section 2 rights of freedom of expression and religious belief, it concluded that the Charter Section 1 requirement of proportionality (particularly of minimal impairment) was violated by the order permanently barring the school teacher from communicating these ideas.

Attis is in some ways an extension of *Keegstra,* since it upholds adverse government action against a teacher for making anti-semitic remarks on his off-duty time, whereas *Keegstra* involved criminal prosecution of a teacher for anti-semitic comments made in class. But *Attis* also suggests that the Section 1 analysis of proportionality can be calibrated to achieve protection of the equality-related interests of others without prohibiting expressions of unpopular or prejudiced views, perhaps to a greater degree than the majority opinion in *Keegstra* suggested.

————————

Kathleen Mahoney, *The Canadian Constitutional Approach to Freedom of Expression in Hate Propaganda and Pornography*, 55 Law & Contemp. Probs. 77 (1992)

[In reading this article about the regulation of hate speech and pornography by a well-known Canadian scholar, note how a Canadian observer characterizes Canadian and U.S. free speech cases. In particular, note Mahoney's critique of *Keegstra* as, in some respects, too generous in its definition and protection of speech as compared with equality rights. Note, as well, Mahoney's agreement with Justice Dickson on the distinctiveness of Canadian and U.S. free speech law in discussing *Keegstra*.]

* * *

I

INTRODUCTION

Constitutional law can be many things, but most of all it can be an agent of change. Ultimately, it determines the way we organize our lives, socially and politically. It provides us with insights to help us understand and define our society and where it is heading. It is intimately concerned with giving meaning to ourselves and our relations with others. . . .

Recently, a series of decisions by the Supreme Court of Canada has articulated some alternative perspectives on freedom of expression that are more inclusive than exclusive, more communitarian than individualistic, and more aware of the actual impacts of speech on the disadvantaged members of society than have ever before been articulated in a freedom of expression case. It is an approach that redistributes speech rights between unequal groups. I am calling this series of decisions an equality approach to freedom of expression. The approach is particularly evident in a recent trilogy of cases dealing with hate propaganda; it is also evident in a strong line of cases dealing with the definition of obscenity. This article discusses the Supreme Court's treatment of extremist speech in light of the freedom of expression guaranteed by the 1982 Charter of Rights and Freedoms, and laws prohibiting the public, wilful promotion of hatred and obscenity. . . . [and] argue[s] that the equality, harm-based rationale developed by the Court for the regulation of hate propaganda even more strongly supports the regulation of pornography as a practice of inequality. I will further argue that the competing constitutional values as weighed and evaluated by the Supreme Court point the way to a more inclusive, democratic, and egalitarian society, avoiding the more limited view of freedoms that in past decisions have emphasized the autonomy of individuals, weighed their competing claims as though they were equal, and ignored the social realities in which they operated.

The argument that hate propaganda and pornography may be constitutionally regulated on an equality theory engages sections 1, 2(b), 15, 27, and 28 of the Charter.

Section 1 of the Charter is the central, preeminent provision. It states that the Charter "guarantees the rights and freedoms set out in it subject only to such reasonable limits prescribed by law as can be demonstratively justified in a free and democratic society." This is an unusual section if one compares it with other national or international rights-protecting instruments. The American Bill of Rights, for example, has no similar section. At first glance, section 1 may appear to be inconsistent or contradictory. On the one hand, it guarantees rights, yet, on the other, it authorizes limits on those rights in certain circumstances. . . . This double function embodies the idea that constitutional rights in the Charter are not absolute.

The freedom of expression guarantee is found in section 2(b) of the Charter, which provides that "[e]veryone has the following fundamental freedoms: . . . freedom of thought, belief, opinion and expression, including freedom of the press and other media of communication." The most important substantive provision relevant to the egalitarian approach to freedom of expression is section 15, the equality section. It, like section 1, is distinctive compared to other national and international instruments that exist to prohibit discrimination. It actually contains four equality guarantees, an open-ended list of prohibited grounds, and an affirmative action provision to allow for beneficial programs for disadvantaged groups or individuals. It reads:

> (1) Every individual is equal before and under the law and has the right to the equal protection and equal benefit of the law without discrimination and, in particular, without discrimination based on race, national or ethnic origin, colour, religion, sex, age or physical or mental disability.

> (2) Subsection (1) does not preclude any law, program or activity that has as its object the amelioration of conditions of disadvantaged individuals or groups including those that are disadvantaged because of race, national or ethnic origin, colour, religion, sex, age or mental or physical disability.

Section 27, a multicultural section, and section 28, a gender equality section, are meant to assist in the interpretation of the Charter. They emphasize that multiculturalism and gender equality are important Canadian goals. Section 27 provides that the Charter "shall be interpreted in a manner consistent with the preservation and enhancement of the multicultural heritage of Canadians." Section 28 further states that, "[n]otwithstanding anything in this Charter, the rights and freedoms referred to in it are guaranteed equally to male and female persons."

II

HATE PROPAGANDA AND FREEDOM OF EXPRESSION: THE *KEEGSTRA* CASE ...

A. *Keegstra*'s Section 2(b) Analysis

To determine whether or not the hate propaganda prohibition violated the Charter, Chief Justice Dickson, writing for the majority, first examined the scope of the freedom of expression section. He did so by looking at the underlying values supporting the freedom of expression guarantee. Those values, he said, are seeking and attaining the truth, encouraging and fostering participation in social and political decisionmaking, and cultivating diversity in forms of individual self-fulfilment and human flourishing.

After finding the scope of section 2(b) to be both large and liberal, the Court adopted a strict categorical test, permitting content-based restrictions only if the speech is communicated in a physically violent form.[16]

---

16. In RWDSU v Dolphin Delivery Ltd., [1986] 2 SCR 573, 588, the Supreme Court ruled that the freedom of expression guarantee does not extend to acts of violence and threats of violence. In *Keegstra*, the Chief Justice, writing for the majority, clarified this exception, ruling that only meanings communicated through the medium of violence will be excluded from § 2(b) protection. R. v *Keegstra*, [1990] 3 SCR at 731. The minority

Otherwise, as long as an expressive activity conveys a meaning, it is protected by section 2(b), regardless of the meaning or message conveyed. The Court held that even threats of violence are within the scope of the section's protection. Governments may restrict expressive activity only when their purpose is other than to restrict the content of the activity. Even if the purpose is directed solely at the effect rather than the content of the expression, section 2(b) can still be brought into play if the affected party can demonstrate that the activity in question supports rather than undermines the principles and values upon which freedom of expression is based.

Applying this categorical test to the hate propaganda provision, Chief Justice Dickson found that the legislation prohibiting the public, wilful promotion of group hatred did indeed infringe section 2(b) of the Charter. He said the hate propaganda provision was an attempt by Parliament to prohibit communication conveying meaning. . . .

At this point, the Court rejected the argument that hate propaganda is a form of violence in and of itself, and, as an integral link in systemic discrimination, should be excluded from section 2(b) protection. It is unfortunate that the Court significantly deviated from the purposive approach to adopt a rigid form/content distinction in its interpretation of section 2(b). While it is true that hate propaganda combines content and form (colour, race, religion, or national origin are the content), when it takes the form of wilful, public promotion of group hatred on the enumerated grounds, it should be seen as a practice of inequality similar to racial segregation.

In Regina v. Andrews & Smith [65 O.R. (2d) 161 (Ont. CA 1988)], Justice Cory (as he then was) identified the connection between hate propaganda and discrimination: "When expression does instill detestation it . . . lays the foundation for the mistreatment of members of the victimized group." Viewed this way, it can be said that the wilful, public promotion of group hatred is an act, an injury, and a consequence itself. It is not a mere intention to act in the future. To promote group hatred is to practice discrimination, and discrimination is an act that contradicts one of the core values underlying freedom of expression, individual self-fulfilment and human flourishing—the very value we are told defines the environment in which all the goals of freedom of expression should be pursued. Under this view, regulation of hate propaganda should not be invalidated by the doctrine of free speech any more than legal regulation of racial segregation is invalidated by the same doctrine. Enforcement of inequality results in injury just as violence does. Its violent nature ranges from immediate psychic wounding and attack to well-documented consequent physical aggression.

opinion, authored by Justice McLachlin, maintained that threats of violence fall outside § 2(b) protection.

At the very least, the Court should have viewed hate propaganda as harassment on the basis of group membership. The courts in both Canada and the United States have accepted that harassment is a practice of inequality resulting in legally recognized harm and loss, even when it consists solely of words. It is a form of discrimination, even if the action is words. When legislatures regulate harassment, they do not regulate the content of expression, although the expression has content. The Court treats harassment as a practice of inequality. Hate propaganda, which is a particularly virulent form of harassment, should be treated similarly.

A purposive approach, if applied as it was in earlier Supreme Court decisions, would lead to the conclusion that hate propaganda is an abuse of freedom of expression beyond the contemplation of the Charter. At this stage of the analysis, the Supreme Court incorporated a strict categorical approach for the Canadian constitutional context without providing convincing reasons for doing so. The purposive approach to rights protection under the Charter developed prior to *Irwin Toy*, which said the judiciary evolves the content of the right from the nature of the interests it is meant to protect, would seem to require more. For example, the majority of the Court says violence in the form of murder or rape would not be protected under section 2(b), but it fails to tell us why. Surely the reason is that such expression does not recognize or respect human dignity and autonomy and is inimical to the rule of law. While the Court acknowledges that some wordless human activity can have meaning and must be protected under section 2(b), it does not seem to recognize that the corollary is also true. That is, activity that takes the form of expression can also be devoid of meaning in the constitutional sense. The denial of equality rights through the discriminatory practice of promoting hatred arguably deserves the same constitutional consideration under section 2(b) as does violence. Because the text of the Charter focuses on expression as the medium of thought that manifests the individuality and common humanity of right holders, the wilful promotion of hatred should have no constitutional significance.

Had the Court viewed the content/form distinction as points on a continuum rather than as discernibly distinct categories, it could have taken a more nuanced, sensitive, and practical approach to forms of speech that should not be dignified or legitimized by Charter protection. Speech activity such as pornography, racist signs, sexual and racial harassment, as well as hate propaganda fall on this continuum.

Social-psychologist Gordon Allport's analysis of the harms of prejudice is convincing. His analysis supports a continuum approach rather than the categorical approach and appeals to common sense and historical experience. According to Allport, there are five stages of racial prejudice: expression of prejudicial attitudes, avoidance, discrimination, physical attack, and extermination. Each stage depends on and is connected to the preceding one. Allport uses as an example the history of the Third Reich:

> It was Hitler's antilocution that led Germans to avoid their Jewish neighbours and erstwhile friends. This preparation made it easier to enact the Nuremburg laws of discrimination which, in turn, made the

subsequent burning of synagogues and street attacks upon Jews seem natural. The final step in the macabre progression was the ovens at Auschwitz.

It is this progressive, interdependent connection of hate propaganda and violence that cannot be contemplated within the "violent form" limitation on content regulation as articulated in *Irwin Toy*. The category of "violent form" is thus unhelpful and even misleading. Without more convincing reasons, the deviation from the purposive approach introduces unnecessary rigidity into section 2(b) interpretation. The effect of the narrow exclusion not only dignifies vicious, harmful speech activity, it progressively erodes expression rights by increasing the frequency of policy-oriented decisions performed in section 1. Ultimately, using section 1 in this way may soften the stringency of its requirements, deny meaningful content to section 2(b), and trivialize the Charter guarantee of freedom of expression.

B. *Keegstra*'s Section 1 Analysis

Having determined that the public, wilful promotion of group hatred as a category falls within the protection of section 2(b) and that the criminal prohibition infringed James Keegstra's freedom of expression, the Court turned to consider whether under section 1 the infringement was a reasonable limit demonstrably justifiable in a free and democratic society. The Court split four to three in finding that the burden of section 1 was satisfied and that the legislation could be upheld.

... Chief Justice Dickson stressed that extremist hate speech is not merely offensive; it causes "real" and "grave" harm to both its target groups and society at large. Like sexual harassment, hate propaganda constitutes a serious attack on psychological and emotional health. Members of the target groups are humiliated and degraded, their self worth is undermined, and they are encouraged to withdraw from the community and deny their own personal identity. The majority described hate propaganda's societal harm as causing serious discord between cultural groups and creating an atmosphere conducive to discrimination and violence.

It is worth noting that the majority rejected the American "clear and present danger" test of harm, saying it and other categorizations generated by American law may be inappropriate to Canadian constitutional theory. This is a welcome clarification in the law.... The harms caused by hate propaganda are often difficult to detect, either immediately or ever. Hate propaganda has subtle effects. It relies on fear and ignorance to engender indoctrination over time.... Any requirement to prove "clear and present danger" or scientifically verifiable harm not only ignores the realities of the crime, it ensures that very few, if any, convictions will ever be obtained....

A second, related reason the provisions were found by the majority to be of pressing and substantial concern was the importance of the Canadian commitment to equality and multiculturalism reflected in sections 15 and 27 of the Charter. The majority situated section 27 in an equality context, saying that attacks on groups need to be prevented because group discrimination can adversely affect its individual members. According to the Court, in restricting hate propaganda, Parliament seeks "to bolster the notion of mutual respect necessary in a nation which venerates the equality of all persons." This reasoning is not dissimilar to that of the United States Supreme Court in *Beauharnais v. Illinois*, to which the Chief Justice referred in *Keegstra*, suggesting that the *Beauharnais* decision is closer to the Canadian approach to freedom of expression than the line of cases that subsequently undermined it. The Chief Justice cautioned that even though current American free speech doctrine may be helpful in many respects, it is of dubious applicability in the context of a challenge to hate propaganda legislation.

The Chief Justice is entirely correct on this point.... Although both countries share a democratic ideal, they do not share the same view of social and political life. In sociological terms, Canada and the United States experience some of the same realities of heterogeneity of population, of language differences, and of original native population. In this dimension, definition and reconciliation of minority rights have been central to civil liberties politics in both countries. But a major ideological difference is Canada's rejection of the melting pot approach to cultural diversity adopted in the United States in favour of a mosaic approach. One of the objectives of the drafters of the Charter was to develop a bilingual, multicultural country and a pluralistic mosaic.

As a result, Charter commitments are different in many respects from the commitments of the American Bill of Rights. The multicultural section is a case in point. Section 27 states that the Charter shall be interpreted in a manner consistent with the preservation and enhancement of the multi-cultural heritage of Canadians. This provision is particularly important when courts are required to balance the freedom of expression of hate propagandists against the multiculturalism ideal and the powerful equality provision. It is thus much broader in scope than the fourteenth amend-ment, containing wider substantive protections as well as more prohibited grounds of discrimination. Section 15(2) of the Charter expressly adds a clause that legitimizes affirmative action in the constitutional definition of equality rights. Reading section 15 together with the multiculturalism section creates a formidable obstacle for those who would use the freedom of expression guarantee to promote hatred against identifiable groups.

The other minority interests protected in the Charter—including lan-guage and education rights, aboriginal rights, and rights for denomination-ally separate dissentient schools—underline the strong commitment to collective rights in the Charter that is not evident in the American Constitution. Against this background, it is not surprising the Court found the prohibition of the public, wilful promotion of group hatred is a matter of pressing and substantial concern sufficient to meet the section 1require-ments.

To further emphasize the point that hate propaganda laws relate to pressing and substantial concerns, the Court took note of international human rights obligations that require Canada to suppress hate propaganda criminally to protect identifiable and vulnerable groups. The Court said that when values such as equality and freedom from racism enjoy status as international human rights, they are generally ascribed a high degree of importance under section 1. The United States has not ratified this or similar conventions.

The connections the Canadian Supreme Court makes between institutional arrangements, collective and individual harms, human relations, and equality are very important elements in its equality approach to freedom of expression. The centrality of equality to the enjoyment of individual as well as group rights emphasizes that the main constitutional consideration surrounding extremist speech is the harm it causes to equality interests. The Court is clear that if we are to live in a society without discrimination, the harm of hate speech must be redressed.

The majority again referred to harm in applying proportionality, the second portion of the *Oakes* test. The Court made the point that hate propaganda is only tenuously connected to the values underlying section 2(b), because the harm of hate speech is significant and the truth value marginal. . . .

The minority, on the other hand, believed some hate speech could be important. It feared that regulations on hate propaganda could start a "slippery slope" of encroachment on valuable political speech or could catch angry speech by members of disadvantaged minority groups against dominant majorities. The Chief Justice was of the view that the mens rea requirement would restrict the reach of the provision to only those groups meant to be caught by it. Perhaps a stronger argument is that the contextualized approach serves as a sufficient safeguard to isolate extremist hate speech from legitimate political speech. Constitutional equality as interpreted by the Court in *Andrews v. The Law Society of British Columbia* [[1989] 1 S.C.R. 143], is essentially designed to protect the groups that suffer social, political, and legal disadvantage. If hate propaganda were directed against historically dominant group members, a contextual approach would constitutionally protect it even in the section 1 balance. This is appropriate because the attack would not be linked to the perpetuation of disadvantage. It would be tied to the structural domination of the group attacked. If the groups were equal, presumably any special protection would be removed.

Finally, the Court examined the relationship between the equality rights in the Charter and the freedom of expression guarantee. While acknowledging that section 15 of the Charter does not itself guarantee social equality, the Court nevertheless made it clear that equal law is seen as a means to an equal society, as well as an end in itself. The Court's statement that "the principles underlying section 15 of the Charter are . . . integral to the section 1 analysis" requires section 15 to have a broader constitutional function than protecting individuals from state-imposed discrimination. The *Keegstra* Court clearly established that just as Charter rights can be used to challenge legislation, they can be used to uphold existing legislation that furthers section 15 values. In the words of Chief

Justice Dickson, "[i]nsofar as it indicates our society's dedication to promoting equality, section 15 is also relevant in assessing the aims of section 319(2) of the Criminal Code under section 1." ... Similarly, the Court took account of section 27 and its recognition that Canada possesses a multicultural society in which the diversity and richness of various cultural groups is a value to be protected and enhanced....

The approach established by the *Keegstra* decision in the section 1 balancing stage legitimated group rights to the extent that they outweighed the competing individual right of freedom of expression. This was due to the influence of section 15. The recognition that the harm of discrimination can outweigh the free speech interest marks a major new development in freedom of expression jurisprudence. The connections the Court made between institutional arrangements, collective and individual harms, human relations, and equality are unique. The Court's recognition that boundaries between individual and collective rights must be confronted demonstrates the Charter's potential to propose new relationships.

Canada's departure from American free speech doctrine is clear. Under the first amendment, social reality is not considered when legislation regulating extremist speech is challenged. This is a critical difference from the Canadian practice because, depending on the facts of the case, a contextual analysis can result in a right or freedom having a different value. In *Keegstra*, when assessing the value of challenged expression, the Court looked at the reality of the situation at hand, including the nature of the interests at stake. The centrality of equality to the enjoyment of individual as well as group rights in the decision demonstrates a firm acceptance of the view that equality is a positive right, that the Charter's equality provision has a large remedial component, and that legislatures should take positive measures to improve the status of disadvantaged groups. Most importantly, *Keegstra* identifies a transformation potential in the Charter, a potential to achieve social change toward the creation of a society based on an ethic that responds to needs, honours difference, and rejects abstractions....

CONCLUSION

Canadian judges are in the process of challenging existing thought about the constitutional protection of freedom of expression. The assumption that human behaviour can be generalized into natural universal laws is being challenged by the analytical approach which favours context rather than detached objectivity. It rebels against linearity and inevitability. It does not accept that certain truths exist and that it is futile to try and change them. By expanding the perimeters of the discussion, previously hidden underlying facts and issues are being exposed. As a result, decisions as to which facts are relevant, how the issues are framed, and which legal principles are binding are changing. Obscenity and hate propaganda laws are being reframed in equality terms and defended as such in constitutional litigation. The question of harm is starting to be addressed in a way that recognizes the experience of inequality and subordination.

In the United States, on the other hand, the contextual approach has not been incorporated into first amendment doctrine as it applies to extremist speech to the extent that it has in Canada. Furthermore, equality, particularly sex equality, does not appear to carry the same constitutional weight.

Earlier in the article, I discussed the different civil liberties politics in Canada and the United States. Both countries' traditions for civil liberties grow from the thoughts of Locke, Hobbes, Rousseau, and Mill. The tradition has centered on individualism and the individual's relationship to the state. The state was to interfere only when one individual violated the rights of another. The law, as neutral arbiter, was to apply rules equally.

But the commitment to civil liberties, while a good start, is only the beginning. Human rights start where civil liberties end. Human rights go beyond the relationship of the individual to the state and emphasize the relationship of individuals to one another. They invoke the state's intervention and assistance because individuals in their capacity as members of groups are disadvantaged for arbitrary reasons. Human rights principles allow for different treatment because not all individuals have suffered historic, generic exclusion because of their group membership. Where barriers impede fairness for some individuals they should be removed, even if this means treating some people differently. Intellectual pluralism does not and cannot mean that racism or sexism will be given the same deference as tolerance.

Where we can make common cause with civil liberties, we should. But when the debate involves the clash of interests presented by hate propaganda and pornography, eighteenth- and nineteenth-century theories that served a need that modern democracies have outgrown do not seem to be the best way to solve the problem. No democracy should be embarrassed or uncomfortable prioritizing the needs of the impoverished, disempowered, and disadvantaged over those who are more privileged.

Equality is an emerging right. Establishing it requires reciprocity of respect and parity of regard for physical dignity and personal integrity. Legal interpretation must be guided by these values and goals if the constitutional mandate of equality is to be met. Problems of the future cannot always be solved using the intellectual frameworks of the past. The goal of a more humane and egalitarian society requires new ways of talking about the problems of free expression; otherwise we will find the progressive tools of an earlier era turned against progress. I hope that Canadian and American judges will continue along the path that has been mapped by a few in deciding what is and is not obscene, and what limits can be set on the public, wilful promotion of group hatred based on a context-driven, harm-based equality analysis. If they do, rights and duties will be allocated equitably, not simply on the basis of abstract, doctrinally stagnant grand principles of formal equality that thwart rather than achieve substantive liberty and substantive equality.

Regina v. Butler

[1992] 1 S.C.R. 452 (Supreme Court of Canada)

[Section 163 of the Canadian criminal code prohibits *inter alia* the sale or distribution of obscene material. Subsection (8) provides that "For the purposes of this Act, any publication a dominant characteristic of which is the undue exploitation of sex, or of sex and any one or more of the following subjects, namely, crime, horror, cruelty and violence, shall be deemed to be obscene." In reviewing convictions of adult bookstore operators for violations of the Act, the Court upheld its constitutionality. Excerpts from the majority opinion (joined by Justice MacLachlin, author of the *Keegstra* dissent) follow, beginning with a portion of the Court's discussion of the meaning of "obscenity" in Canada, and including longer excerpts of its discussion of the Charter question.]

* * *

... In order for the work or material to qualify as "obscene", the exploitation of sex must not only be its dominant characteristic, but such exploitation must be "undue". In determining when the exploitation of sex will be considered "undue", the courts have attempted to formulate workable tests. The most important of these is the "community standard of tolerance" test....

> "The cases all emphasize that it is a standard of tolerance, not taste, that is relevant. What matters is not what Canadians think is right for themselves to see. What matters is what Canadians would not abide other Canadians seeing because it would be beyond the contemporary Canadian standard of tolerance to allow them to see it." [Towne Cinema Theatres Ltd. v. The Queen, [1985] 1 S.C.R. 494] ...

Therefore, the community standards test is concerned not with what Canadians would not tolerate being exposed to themselves, but what they would not tolerate <u>other</u> Canadians being exposed....

There has been a growing recognition in recent cases that material which may be said to exploit sex in a "degrading or dehumanizing" manner will necessarily fail the community standards test....

Among other things, degrading or dehumanizing materials place women (and sometimes men) in positions of subordination, servile submission or humiliation. They run against the principles of equality and dignity of all human beings. In the appreciation of whether material is degrading or dehumanizing, the appearance of consent is not necessarily determinative. Consent cannot save materials that otherwise contain degrading or dehumanizing scenes. Sometimes the very appearance of consent makes the depicted acts even more degrading or dehumanizing.

This type of material would, apparently, fail the community standards test not because it offends against morals but because it is perceived by public opinion to be harmful to society, particularly to women. While the accuracy of this perception is not susceptible of exact proof, there is a substantial body of opinion that holds that the portrayal of persons being subjected to degrading or dehumanizing sexual treatment results in harm, particularly to women and therefore to society as a whole. . . .

Pornography can be usefully divided into three categories: (1) explicit sex with violence, (2) explicit sex without violence but which subjects people to treatment that is degrading or dehumanizing, and (3) explicit sex without violence that is neither degrading nor dehumanizing. Violence in this context includes both actual physical violence and threats of physical violence. Relating these three categories to the terms of s. 163(8) of the Code, the first, explicit sex coupled with violence, is expressly mentioned. Sex coupled with crime, horror or cruelty will sometimes involve violence. Cruelty, for instance, will usually do so. But, even in the absence of violence, sex coupled with crime, horror or cruelty may fall within the second category. As for category (3), subject to the exception referred to below, it is not covered.

Some segments of society would consider that all three categories of pornography cause harm to society because they tend to undermine its moral fibre. Others would contend that none of the categories cause harm. Furthermore there is a range of opinion as to what is degrading or dehumanizing. . . . Because this is not a matter that is susceptible of proof in the traditional way and because we do not wish to leave it to the individual tastes of judges, we must have a norm that will serve as an arbiter in determining what amounts to an undue exploitation of sex. That arbiter is the community as a whole.

The courts must determine as best they can what the community would tolerate others being exposed to on the basis of the degree of harm that may flow from such exposure. Harm in this context means that it predisposes persons to act in an antisocial manner as, for example, the physical or mental mistreatment of women by men, or, what is perhaps debatable, the reverse. Antisocial conduct for this purpose is conduct which society formally recognizes as incompatible with its proper functioning. The stronger the inference of a risk of harm the lesser the likelihood of tolerance. The inference may be drawn from the material itself or from the material and other evidence. Similarly evidence as to the community standards is desirable but not essential.

In making this determination with respect to the three categories of pornography referred to above, the portrayal of sex coupled with violence will almost always constitute the undue exploitation of sex. Explicit sex which is degrading or dehumanizing may be undue if the risk of harm is substantial. Finally, explicit sex that is not violent and neither degrading nor dehumanizing is generally tolerated in our society and will not qualify as the undue exploitation of sex unless it employs children in its production. . . .

C.   Does s. 163 Violate s. 2(b) of the Charter?

[The Court rejected the conclusion of the court of appeals that pornography was not speech within the protection of Section 2 of the Charter.] Meaning sought to be expressed need not be "redeeming" in the eyes of the court to merit the protection of s. 2(b) whose purpose is to ensure that thoughts and feelings may be conveyed freely in non-violent ways without fear of censure.

In this case, both the purpose and effect of s. 163 is specifically to restrict the communication of certain types of materials based on their content.... [T]here is no doubt that s. 163 seeks to prohibit certain types of expressive activity and thereby infringes s. 2(b) of the Charter....

D.   Is s. 163 Justified Under s. 1 of the Charter? ...

The respondent argues that there are several pressing and substantial objectives which justify overriding the freedom to distribute obscene materials. Essentially, these objectives are the avoidance of harm resulting from antisocial attitudinal changes that exposure to obscene material causes and the public interest in maintaining a "decent society". On the other hand, the appellant argues that the objective of s. 163 is to have the state act as "moral custodian" in sexual matters and to impose subjective standards of morality.

The obscenity legislation and jurisprudence prior to the enactment of s. 163 were evidently concerned with prohibiting the "immoral influences" of obscene publications and safeguarding the morals of individuals into whose hands such works could fall....

I agree with Twaddle J.A. of the Court of Appeal that this particular objective is no longer defensible in view of the Charter. To impose a certain standard of public and sexual morality, solely because it reflects the conventions of a given community, is inimical to the exercise and enjoyment of individual freedoms, which form the basis of our social contract.... The prevention of "dirt for dirt's sake" is not a legitimate objective which would justify the violation of one of the most fundamental freedoms enshrined in the Charter.

On the other hand, I cannot agree with the suggestion of the appellant that Parliament does not have the right to legislate on the basis of some fundamental conception of morality for the purposes of safeguarding the values which are integral to a free and democratic society. As Dyzenhaus writes: "Moral disapprobation is recognized as an appropriate response when it has its basis in Charter values."

As the respondent and many of the interveners have pointed out, much of the criminal law is based on moral conceptions of right and wrong and the mere fact that a law is grounded in morality does not automatically render it illegitimate. In this regard, criminalizing the proliferation of materials which undermine another basic Charter right may indeed be a legitimate objective.

In my view, however, the overriding objective of s. 163 is not moral disapprobation but the avoidance of harm to society. In *Towne Cinema*, Dickson C.J.C. stated: "It is harm to society from undue exploitation that is aimed at by the section, not simply lapses in propriety or good taste."

The harm was described in the following way in the Report on Pornography by the Standing Committee on Justice and Legal Affairs (MacGuigan Report) (1978) (at p. 18:4):

> The clear and unquestionable danger of this type of material is that it reinforces some unhealthy tendencies in Canadian society. The effect of this type of material is to reinforce male-female stereotypes to the detriment of both sexes. It attempts to make degradation, humiliation, victimization, and violence in human relationships appear normal and acceptable. A society which holds that egalitarianism, non-violence, consensualism, and mutuality are basic to any human interaction, whether sexual or other, is clearly justified in controlling and prohibiting any medium of depiction, description or advocacy which violates these principles....

[Referring to *Keegstra*]: This court has thus recognized that the harm caused by the proliferation of materials which seriously offend the values fundamental to our society is a substantial concern which justifies restricting the otherwise full exercise of the freedom of expression. In my view, the harm sought to be avoided in the case of the dissemination of obscene materials is similar.... [T]here is a growing concern that the exploitation of women and children, depicted in publications and films can, in certain circumstances, lead to "abject and servile victimization".... [I]f true equality between male and female persons is to be achieved, we cannot ignore the threat to equality resulting from exposure to audiences of certain types of violent and degrading material. Materials portraying women as a class as objects for sexual exploitation and abuse have a negative impact on "the individual's sense of self-worth and acceptance".

In reaching the conclusion that legislation proscribing obscenity is a valid objective which justifies some encroachment of the right to freedom of expression, I am persuaded in part [by the fact] that such legislation may be found in most free and democratic societies....

The advent of the Charter did not have the effect of dramatically depriving Parliament of a power which it has historically enjoyed. It is also noteworthy that the criminalization of obscenity was considered to be compatible with the [statutory] Canadian Bill of Rights....

Finally, it should be noted that the burgeoning pornography industry renders the concern even more pressing and substantial than when the impugned provisions were first enacted....

(c) Proportionality ...

(i) General

The proportionality requirement has three aspects:

(1) the existence of a rational connection between the impugned measures and the objective;

(2) minimal impairment of the right or freedom, and

(3) a proper balance between the effects of the limiting measures and the legislative objective.

In assessing whether the proportionality test is met, it is important to keep in mind the nature of expression which has been infringed. In the *Prostitution Reference** Dickson C.J.C. wrote:

> When a Charter freedom has been infringed by state action that takes the form of criminalization, the Crown bears the heavy burden of justifying that infringement. Yet, the expressive activity, as with any infringed Charter right, should also be analysed in the particular context of the case. Here, the activity to which the impugned legislation is directed is expression with an economic purpose. It can hardly be said that communications regarding an economic transaction of sex for money lie at, or even near, the core of the guarantee of freedom of expression.

The values which underlie the protection of freedom of expression relate to the search for truth, participation in the political process, and individual self-fulfilment. The Attorney-General for Ontario argues that of these, only "individual self-fulfilment", and only in its most base aspect, that of physical arousal, is engaged by pornography. On the other hand, the civil liberties groups argue that pornography forces us to question conventional notions of sexuality and thereby launches us into an inherently political discourse. In their factum, the B.C. Civil Liberties Association adopts a passage from R. West, "The Feminist-Conservative Anti-Pornography Alliance and the 1986 Attorney General's Commission on Pornography Report", 4 Am. Bar Found. Res. J. 68 (1987), at p. 696:

> Good pornography has value because it validates women's will to pleasure. It celebrates female nature. It validates a range of female sexuality that is wider and truer than that legitimated by the non-pornographic culture. Pornography when it is good celebrates both female pleasure and male rationality.

A proper application of the test should not suppress what West refers to as "good pornography". The objective of the impugned provision is not to inhibit the celebration of human sexuality. However, it cannot be ignored that the realities of the pornography industry are far from the picture which the B.C. Civil Liberties Association would have us paint. Shannon J., in R. v. Wagner, described the materials more accurately when he observed:

> Women, particularly, are deprived of unique human character or identity and are depicted as sexual playthings, hysterically and instantly responsive to male sexual demands. They worship male genitals and their own value depends upon the quality of their genitals and breasts.

---

* [Editors' Note: In this case, [1990] 1 S.C.R. 1123, the Supreme Court held that solicitation of prostitution is an exercise of free expression protected by Charter § 2(b), but that the infringement of this right by a criminal prohibition was justified and valid under Charter § 1.]

In my view, the kind of expression which is sought to be advanced does not stand on equal footing with other kinds of expression which directly engage the "core" of the freedom of expression values.

This conclusion is further buttressed by the fact that the targeted material is expression which is motivated, in the overwhelming majority of cases, by economic profit. This court held in Rocket v. Royal College of Dental Surgeons of Ontario (1990), 71 D.L.R. (4th) 68 at p. 79, [1990] that an economic motive for expression means that restrictions on the expression might "be easier to justify than other infringements".

I will now turn to an examination of the three basic aspects of the proportionality test.

(ii) Rational connection

The message of obscenity which degrades and dehumanizes is analogous to that of hate propaganda. As the Attorney-General of Ontario has argued in its factum, obscenity wields the power to wreak social damage in that a significant portion of the population is humiliated by its gross misrepresentations.

Accordingly, the rational link between s. 163 and the objective of Parliament relates to the actual causal relationship between obscenity and the risk of harm to society at large. On this point, it is clear that the literature of the social sciences remains subject to controversy....

While a direct link between obscenity and harm to society may be difficult, if not impossible, to establish, it is reasonable to presume that exposure to images bears a causal relationship to changes in attitudes and beliefs. The Meese Commission Report [U.S] concluded in respect of sexually violent material:

> ... the available evidence strongly supports the hypothesis that substantial exposure to sexually violent materials as described here bears a causal relationship to antisocial acts of sexual violence and, for some subgroups, possibly to unlawful acts of sexual violence.

> Although we rely for this conclusion on significant scientific empirical evidence, we feel it worthwhile to note the underlying logic of the conclusion. The evidence says simply that the images that people are exposed to bear a causal relationship to their behavior. This is hardly surprising. What would be surprising would be to find otherwise, and we have not so found. We have not, of course, found that the images people are exposed to are a greater cause of sexual violence than all or even many other possible causes the investigation of which has been beyond our mandate. Nevertheless, it would be strange indeed if graphic representations of a form of behavior, especially in a form that almost exclusively portrays such behavior as desirable, did not have at least some effect on patterns of behavior.

In the face of inconclusive social science evidence, the approach adopted by our court in *Irwin Toy* is instructive. In that case, the basis for the legislation was that television advertising directed at young children is per se manipulative. The court made it clear that in choosing its mode of intervention, it is sufficient that Parliament had a <u>reasonable basis</u>:

> In the instant case, the court is called upon to assess competing social science evidence respecting the appropriate means for addressing the problem of children's advertising. The question is whether the government had a reasonable basis, on the evidence tendered, for concluding that the ban on all advertising directed at children impaired freedom of expression as little as possible given the government's pressing and substantial objective. . . .
>
> . . . [T]he Court also recognized that the government was afforded a margin of appreciation to form legitimate objectives based on somewhat inconclusive social science evidence.

Similarly, in *Keegstra*, the absence of proof of a causative link between hate propaganda and hatred of an identifiable group was discounted as a determinative factor in assessing the constitutionality of the hate literature provisions of the Criminal Code. . . .

Accordingly, I am of the view that there is a sufficiently rational link between the criminal sanction, which demonstrates our community's disapproval of the dissemination of materials which potentially victimize women and which restricts the negative influence which such materials have on changes in attitudes and behaviour, and the objective.

Finally, I wish to distinguish this case from *Keegstra*, in which the minority adopted the view that there was no rational connection between the criminalization of hate propaganda and its suppression. As McLachlin J. noted, prosecutions under the Criminal Code for racist expression have attracted extensive media coverage. The criminal process confers on the accused publicity for his or her causes and succeeds even in generating sympathy. The same cannot be said of the kinds of expression sought to be suppressed in the present case. The general availability of the subject materials and the rampant pornography industry are such that, in the words of Dickson C.J.C. in *Keegstra*, "pornography is not dignified by its suppression". In contrast to the hate-monger who may succeed, by the sudden media attention, in gaining an audience, the prohibition of obscene materials does nothing to promote the pornographer's cause.

(iii) Minimal impairment

In determining whether less intrusive legislation may be imagined, this court stressed in the *Prostitution Reference* that it is not necessary that the legislative scheme be the "perfect" scheme, but that it be appropriately tailored in the context of the infringed right. Furthermore, in *Irwin Toy* Dickson C.J.C., Lamer and Wilson JJ. stated:

> While evidence exists that other less intrusive options reflecting more modest objectives were available to the government, there is evidence establishing the necessity of a ban to meet the objectives the govern-

ment had reasonably set. This court will not, in the name of minimal impairment, take a restrictive approach to social science evidence and require legislatures to choose the least ambitious means to protect vulnerable groups.

There are several factors which contribute to the finding that the provision minimally impairs the freedom which is infringed.

First, the impugned provision does not proscribe sexually explicit erotica without violence that is not degrading or dehumanizing. It is designed to catch material that creates a risk of harm to society. It might be suggested that proof of actual harm should be required. It is apparent from what I have said above that it is sufficient in this regard for Parliament to have a reasonable basis for concluding that harm will result and this requirement does not demand actual proof of harm.

Secondly, materials which have scientific, artistic or literary merit are not captured by the provision. As discussed above, the court must be generous in its application of the "artistic defence". . . .

Thirdly, in considering whether the provision minimally impairs the freedom in question, it is legitimate for the court to take into account Parliament's past abortive attempts to replace the definition with one that is more explicit. In *Irwin Toy*, our court recognized that it is legitimate to take into account the fact that earlier laws and proposed alternatives were thought to be less effective than the legislation that is presently being challenged. The attempt to provide exhaustive instances of obscenity has been shown to be destined to fail (Bill C-54, 2nd Sess., 33rd Parl.). It seems that the only practicable alternative is to strive towards a more abstract definition of obscenity which is contextually sensitive and responsive to progress in the knowledge and understanding of the phenomenon to which the legislation is directed. In my view, the standard of "undue exploitation" is therefore appropriate. The intractable nature of the problem and the impossibility of precisely defining a notion which is inherently elusive makes the possibility of a more explicit provision remote. In this light, it is appropriate to question whether, and at what cost, greater legislative precision can be demanded.

Fourthly, . . . the impugned section . . . has been held by this court not to extend its reach to the private use or viewing of obscene materials. . . .

Accordingly, it is only the public distribution and exhibition of obscene materials which is in issue here.

Finally, I wish to address the arguments of the interveners, Canadian Civil Liberties Association and Manitoba Association for Rights and Liberties, that the objectives of this kind of legislation may be met by alternative, less intrusive measures. First, it is submitted that reasonable time, manner and place restrictions would be preferable to outright prohibition. I am of the view that this argument should be rejected. Once it has been established that the objective is the avoidance of harm caused by the degradation which many women feel as "victims" of the message of obscenity, and of the negative impact exposure to such material has on perceptions and attitudes towards women, it is untenable to argue that these harms could be avoided by placing restrictions on access to such material. Making the materials more difficult to obtain by increasing their cost and reducing their availability does not achieve the same objective. Once Parliament has reasonably concluded that certain acts are harmful to certain groups in society and to society in general, it would be inconsistent, if not hypocritical, to argue that such acts could be committed in more restrictive conditions. The harm sought to be avoided would remain the same in either case.

It is also submitted that there are more effective techniques to promote the objectives of Parliament. For example, if pornography is seen as encouraging violence against women, there are certain activities which discourage it—counselling rape victims to charge their assailants, provision of shelter and assistance for battered women, campaigns for laws against discrimination on the grounds of sex, education to increase the sensitivity of law enforcement agencies and other governmental authorities. In addition, it is submitted that education is an under-used response.

It is noteworthy that many of the above suggested alternatives are in the form of responses to the harm engendered by negative attitudes against women. The role of the impugned provision is to control the dissemination of the very images that contribute to such attitudes. Moreover, it is true that there are additional measures which could alleviate the problem of violence against women. However, given the gravity of the harm, and the threat to the values at stake, I do not believe that the measure chosen by Parliament is equalled by the alternatives which have been suggested. Education, too, may offer a means of combating negative attitudes to women, just as it is currently used as a means of addressing other problems dealt with in the Code. However, there is no reason to rely on education alone. It should be emphasized that this is in no way intended to deny the value of other educational and counselling measures to deal with the roots and effects of negative attitudes. Rather, it is only to stress the arbitrariness and unacceptability of the claim that such measures represent the sole legitimate means of addressing the phenomenon. Serious social problems such as violence against women require multi-pronged approaches by government. Education and legislation are not alternatives but complements in addressing such problems. There is nothing in the Charter which requires Parliament to choose between such complementary measures.

(iv) Balance between effects of limiting measures and legislative objective

The final question to be answered in the proportionality test is whether the effects of the law so severely trench on a protected right that the legislative objective is outweighed by the infringement. The infringement on freedom of expression is confined to a measure designed to prohibit the distribution of sexually explicit materials accompanied by violence, and those without violence that are degrading or dehumanizing. As I have already concluded, this kind of expression lies far from the core of the guarantee of freedom of expression. It appeals only to the most base aspect of individual fulfilment, and it is primarily economically motivated.

The objective of the legislation, on the other hand, is of fundamental importance in a free and democratic society. It is aimed at avoiding harm, which Parliament has reasonably concluded will be caused directly or indirectly, to individuals, groups such as women and children, and consequently to society as a whole, by the distribution of these materials. It thus seeks to enhance respect for all members of society, and non-violence and equality in their relations with each other.

I therefore conclude that the restriction on freedom of expression does not outweigh the importance of the legislative objective.

5.   Conclusion

I conclude that while s. 163(8) infringes s. 2(b) of the Charter, freedom of expression, it constitutes a reasonable limit and is saved by virtue of the provisions of s. 1....

[The concurring opinions are omitted.]

Questions and Comments

1. *Durability of Canada's Proportionality Doctrine*: Note the continued agreement of members of the Court on a broad definition of what constitutes free expression protected by Section 2, and on the *Oakes* proportionality test as the proper measure of the Section 1 question. Does Canada's commitment to this kind of flexible balancing test have any implications for other constitutional systems? See generally Nicholas Emiliou, The Principle of Proportionality in European Law (1996).

2. *Balancing Tests in the U.S.*? Consider use of such a test in the U.S. Although Professor Greenawalt accurately describes contemporary U.S. free speech law as more categorical than current Canadian law, balancing approaches to free speech issues have been attractive to U.S. justices in the past, and to some today. Dennis v. United States, 341 U.S. 494 (1951), upheld convictions of the major leaders of the U.S. Communist Party for conspiracy to advocate the overthrow of the government by force or violence. The Court's plurality opinion endorsed the lower court's interpretation of the "clear and present danger" test, which was this: "In each case [courts] must ask whether the gravity of the 'evil,' discounted by its improbability, justifies such invasion of free speech as is necessary to avoid the danger." In NAACP v. Alabama, 357 U.S. 449 (1958), invalidating the state's demand for membership lists from the NAACP, the Court asked whether the state had "demonstrated an interest in obtaining the disclosures it seeks ... which is sufficient to justify the deterrent effect ... these disclosures may well have on the free exercise by [the NAACP's] members of their constitutionally protected right of free association." How different are these approaches from the Canadian Supreme Court's?

Balancing approaches to free speech issues were later advocated by Justice Lewis F. Powell. See, for example, Healy v. James, 408 U.S. 169 (1972). For a critique of balancing approaches, see T. Alexander Aleinikoff, *Constitutional Law in the Age of Balancing*, 96 Yale L. J. 943 (1987). Critics of balancing approaches argue that they leave too much discretion in judges' hands, allowing them to uphold repressive legislation where they think it a "good idea" and to invalidate laws with which they disagree on policy grounds. Proponents of balancing argue that such tests promote candor in judicial decisionmaking and can constrain adjudication if appropriate deference is accorded decisions by politically accountable bodies in striking the balance. See arguments noted in Kathleen M. Sullivan, *Foreword, The Justice of Rules and Standards*, 106 Harv. L. Rev. 22 (1992). Do the materials about Canada that you have read help you assess the defense and critiques of balancing approaches?

Recall Professor Tribe's argument, in Chapter I, against compromise solutions that mediate among competing principles and in favor of clear rights-based decisions in a rights-oriented legal culture. Are balancing approaches in tension with the "rights" culture Professor Tribe notes in ways that would too greatly undermine judicial legitimacy if used in the U.S.? If so, what accounts for the sometime use of balancing approaches by the Supreme Court and by individual justices?

Do the comparative materials you have studied help you assess the following argument: The contrast between balancing approaches and categorical rule approaches is overdrawn. The real issue is the extent to which judges defer to judgments made by other institutions. A judge suspicious of those institutions can employ a balancing approach, overturning their decisions by placing greater weight on certain considerations than the other institutions had. A judge who thought deference appropriate could use a categorical approach with categorical exceptions to a a particular categorical rule, or could define the rule's scope so that it did not cover the problem at hand. A weaker version of this argument is that the stance of deference taken by the courts to decisions of other institutions is at least as important as whether a balancing or categorical test is employed.

3. Note the role of the Charter's commitments to equality and multiculturalism in the opinions in *Keegstra* and *Butler*. Is there a difference between relying on those commitments to uphold, rather than to invalidate, legislation?

4. Advancing arguments similar to those of some U.S. feminists, Professor Mahoney has argued that pornography should be treated as outside the protections of Section 2 of the Charter, and should be treated as a form of violence; the *Butler* court rejected this argument. How, under Canadian constitutional law, would it matter whether the constitutional question was analysed under Section 1 or Section 2 of the Charter?

Note on Commercial Speech and RJR-MacDonald Inc. v. Attorney General, [1995] 3 S.C.R. 199

In the Canadian tobacco regulation case discussed below, note the parallels to the kind of analysis called for in such U.S. commercial speech cases as Central Hudson Gas & Elec. Corp. v. Public Service Comm'n. of N.Y., 447 U.S. 557 (1980)(commercial speech entitled to less protection from state control than noncommercial speech, but government regulation permissible only if it directly advances substantial government interest and the regulation is no more extensive than necessary to serve that interest). In light of *RJR-MacDonald*, how persuasive is the argument that the Canadian constitutional approach to evaluating governmental action affecting the exercise of speech rights is significantly different from that in the United States?

RJR-MacDonald Inc. v. Attorney General

[1995] 3 S.C.R. 199 (Supreme Court of Canada)

[Editors' Summary:] In this case the Supreme Court of Canada held that federal legislation prohibiting advertising for tobacco products and requiring unattributed health warnings on tobacco packages violated the Charter's protection of expression rights.

The Court, voting seven to two, first rejected a federalism challenge to the legislation, finding it a valid exercise of federal criminal power under section 91 (27) of the Constitution Act of 1867. The criminal power was appropriate because, the Court found, the legislation was directed at a clear public health evil, and protection of health is one of the ordinary aims of the criminal law. Two justices dissented from this ruling as to the advertising prohibition. They would have held that prohibiting advertising was a regulatory measure, and that tobacco advertising did not of itself pose such a grave danger to public health as to fall within the federal criminal power. They would have held that legislation prohibiting all advertising of a product which is legal for sale throughout Canada lacks a typically criminal purpose and thus was outside the federal criminal power.

On the Charter rights question, the Court was more closely divided, striking down the advertising ban and the requirement to place unattributed health warnings on tobacco packages by a vote of five to four.[c] On the most important issue—the ban on advertising and promotion of tobacco products—the government had conceded a violation of Section 2(b) freedom of expression rights.[d] The parties thus agreed that the question was whether the ban could be upheld under Section 1 of the Charter.

---

c. The law had been struck down by the trial court, but upheld by the Court of Appeals whose judgment was in turn reversed by the Supreme Court.

d. The Attorney General did not concede that the requirement for unattributed health warnings on tobacco packages was an infringement of Section 2. Justice LaForest agreed with the Attorney General but the five justice majority disagreed, finding the unattributed warning requirement an in-

The appellants conceded that the objective of protecting Canadians from the health risks associated with tobacco use and informing them of those risks is sufficiently substantial to meet the first criterion of Section 1 analysis, but argued that the measures were not proportional to these objectives.

The opinion of Justice LaForest, which would have upheld the laws,[e] emphasized flexibility of analysis and deference to the Parliament's finding of "legislative facts" concerning the criteria for proportionality. The "guidelines" provided by *Oakes*

> should not be interpreted as a substitute for s. 1 itself. It is implicit in the wording of s.1 that the courts must, in every application of that provision, strike a delicate balance between individual rights and community needs. Such a balance cannot be achieved in the abstract, with reference solely to a formalistic test uniformly applied in all circumstances. The s. 1 inquiry is an unavoidably normative inquiry, requiring the courts to take into account both the nature of the infringed right and the specific values and principles upon which the state seeks to justify the infringement.

The gap in scientifically rigorous evidence on the relationship between advertising and tobacco consumption raises a "fundamental institutional problem" in Section 1 balancing, because too strict an application of proportionality standards would place an impossible burden on Parliament thus paralyzing the government to act in the sphere of socio-economic predictions requiring balancing the interests of different social groups (such as smokers, nonsmokers, tobacco producers).

Applying this standard, the LaForest opinion relied on *Keegstra* and *Butler*, arguing that the harms engendered by tobacco and the profit motive underlying its promotion made tobacco advertising a form of expression as far from the core values of promoting political, scientific or artistic ends, as prostitution, hate mongering or pornography, and thus entitled to a low degree of protection under Section 1. It also argued that the power differential between advertiser and consumer is relevant to evaluating the Section 1 justification, and that, in light of the low value of the speech an "attenuated Section 1 justification" is appropriate. The laws should be upheld if the government showed that they had a rational basis.

On the three specific criteria for proportionality, the LaForest opinion argued that there is a rational connection between advertising and consumption *inter alia* because tobacco companies spend a great deal of money on advertising; moreover, internal marketing documents reflected the view that advertising influences consumption. In finding a rational connection

---

fringement of Section 2 rights and unsustainable under Section 1.

   e.   The LaForest opinion is the principal opinion of the majority on the federalism issue. Even though its treatment of the Charter issue is in dissent from the decision of the Court, it is treated by the other opinion writers as the principal, organizing opinion on this issue. Thus, the opinions of those justices who constitute the majority on the Charter issue organize themselves in a sense as responses to the LaForest opinion.

between the prohibition on advertising and consumption of tobacco, the LaForest opinion relied on U.S. cases such as Central Hudson Gas & Electric v. Public Service Commn., 447 U.S. 557 (1980) (finding advertising likely to affect electrical consumption but invalidating regulation nonetheless); Metromedia v. San Diego, 453 U.S. 490 (1981) (finding billboards to be related to highway safety despite lack of evidence in the record demonstrating the connection but invalidating the regulation at issue); Posadas de Puerto Rico Association v. Tourism Co. of Puerto Rico, 478 U.S. 328 (1986) (upholding prohibition of advertising for gambling). According to Justice LaForest, the connection between advertising and future consumption is the kind of fact involving causal predictions about the effect of a rule on future behavior that is peculiarly within the legislative province.

Justice LaForest's minimal impairment analysis turned on identifying the law's objective as reducing consumption of tobacco. In analyzing whether the legislative means impair the right of freedom of expression as little as possible, Justice LaForest rejected the argument that there is no reason to prohibit brand preference or informational advertising (as distinct from lifestyle advertising)[f] because all interfere with the substantial interest in reducing smoking. "It must be kept in mind that the infringed right at issue is the right ... to advertise the only legal product sold in Canada which, when used precisely as directed, harms and often kills those who use it." A ban on advertising, the opinion argued, is less intrusive than simply banning all tobacco products. And consistent with the opening analysis, the opinion asserted that it is not for the Court to decide that a lesser prohibition on advertising would serve those purposes as well. A similar analysis was applied to the balance of harmful and beneficial effects from the ban.

With respect to the required display of an unattributed health message on tobacco packages, LaForest concluded that in this context the unattributed message would not be attributed to the tobacco company, in part because of "common knowledge" that the government requires it. Thus, the opinion suggested, it is possible that this portion of the law involves no infringement on expression, but is rather simply "a requirement imposed by the government as a condition of participating in a regulated activity." Even if it were an infringement of Section 2, Justice LaForest found it fully justifiable under Section 1. "[B]old, unattributed messages on a tobacco package," the opinion argued, "are more striking to the eye than messages

---

f. "The appellants ... suggest that Parliament could have established a partial prohibition [with equal effectiveness] by forbidding 'lifestyle advertising' (which seeks to promote an image by associating the consumption of the product with a particular lifestyle) or advertising directed at children, without at the same time prohibiting 'brand preference' advertising (which seeks to promote one brand over another based on the colour and design of the package) or 'informational advertising' (which seeks to inform the consumer about product content, taste and strength and the availability of different new brands) ...[and argue] there is no need to prohibit brand preference or informational advertising because both are targeted solely at smokers and serve a beneficial function by promoting consumer choice."

cluttered by subtitles and attributions," and thus met the rational connection, minimal impairment and balance of effects tests.

Justice McLachlin's opinion for herself and two others concluded that the unattributed warning requirement infringes free expression as a burden on the right to say nothing. Moreover, it found that neither the unattributed warning nor the complete ban on advertising and promotion could be justified under Section 1. While agreeing with much of Justice LaForest's discussion of the need for reasonable flexibility in Section 1 analysis, Justice McLachlin sounded a different note:

> While remaining sensitive to the social and political context of the impugned law and allowing for difficulties of proof inherent in the context, the courts must nevertheless insist that before the state can override constitutional rights, there be a reasoned demonstration of the good which the law may achieve in relation to the seriousness of the infringement. It is the task of the courts to maintain this bottom line if the rights conferred by our constitution are to have force and meaning. The task is not easily discharged, and may require the courts to confront the tide of popular public opinion. But that has always been the price of maintaining constitutional rights. No matter how important Parliament's goal may seem, if the state has not demonstrated that the means by which it seeks to achieve its goals are reasonable and proportionate to the infringement of rights, then the law must perforce fail.

Accordingly, the opinion emphasized that while context, deference to the Parliament, and a flexible and realistic standard of proof are important to Section 1 analysis, "these concepts ... must not be attenuated to the point that they relieve the state of the burden the Charter imposes of demonstrating that the limits imposed on our constitutional rights and freedoms are reasonable and justifiable in a free and democratic society."

The McLachlin opinion made its key analytical move in defining the "objectives" of the law. After stating that "care must be taken not to overstate the objective," the opinion construed the objective of these parts of the law more narrowly than did the LaForest opinion. While the Act is "but one facet of a complex legislative ... scheme to protect Canadians from the health risks of tobacco use[,]" the advertising and promotion ban have the more narrow objective to "prevent people in Canada from being persuaded by advertising and promotion to use tobacco products." Likewise, the "objective of the mandatory package warning must be to discourage people who see the package from tobacco use." The evil, then, is not that of tobacco generally, but the evil which the legislation addresses—use of advertising and promotion to persuade people to smoke. While the McLachlin opinion agreed that these are both important objectives for purposes of the first part of Section 1 analysis,[g] the more narrow definition

---

g. These limited objectives meet the first part of the Section 1 test with respect to the ban on advertising and the mandatory package warnings, though not, Justice McLachlin concluded, the ban on display of tobacco logos.

of the objectives supported the different result reached in the proportionality analysis.

While agreeing with LaForest that the "rational connection" test was met, Justice McLachlin agreed with the trial judge that the "minimal impairment" test was not. The government had adduced no evidence to show that less intrusive regulation would not achieve its goal as effectively as an outright ban. The prohibition on advertising extended to informational advertising, brand advertising, and lifestyle advertising. While as a matter of logic lifestyle advertising is designed to increase consumption and thus presumably could be regulated given the objective of reducing increased consumption that results from advertising, there was no evidence that purely informational or brand preference advertising would increase consumption. The justices were especially concerned that the government had done a study on alternatives to a complete ban, prior to enactment of the legislation, which the government refused to produce for the court during the litigation.

The McLachlin opinion disagreed with Justice LaForest's minimal valuation of commercial speech, and what it saw as an excessive emphasis by Justice LaForest on the profit motive. According to Justice McLachlin, commercial speech undertaken for profit is still protected and its infringement can only be justified under proper standards.

As to the requirement for unattributed health warnings, the McLachlin opinion asserted that the government would clearly be justified in requiring warnings, but could not justify the requirement that the warnings be "unattributed" as a minimal impairment. The McLachlin opinion found the advertising ban and the unattributed warnings requirement invalid because they were not minimal impairments; the opinion therefore did not go on to consider the third step in proportionality analysis, concerning the balance of effects.

Justice Iacobucci, joined by one other justice, also disagreed with Justice LaForest, particularly on the question whether the Act met the minimal impairment requirement. For Justice Iacobucci, "[m]inimal impairment analysis requires this court to consider whether the legislature turned its mind to alternative and less rights-impairing means to promote the legislative goal in question"; the Attorney General's refusal to disclose the prior study of alternatives to the total advertising ban was deeply troubling. Contrary to Justice LaForest's view, the fact that government could prohibit tobacco use entirely is not relevant to the minimal impairments analysis, since the government itself agreed that such a ban was not feasible. Where the evidence is unclear whether a partial prohibition would be as effective as a full prohibition, the Charter requires that legislature enact only the partial denial of charter rights.

Justice Iacobucci disagreed with Justice McLachlin as to the disposition. McLachlin, joined on this point by three other justices, would have declared the statute invalid, while Iacobucci, joined on this point by one other justice, would have suspended the declaration of invalidity for one year; given the adverse effects of tobacco on public health, they would have allowed Parliament a year in which to come up with a new scheme while the former law still was in place. Justice Cory, who agreed with Justice LaForest's reasoning, agreed with Justice Iacobucci's proposed disposition. Justice Lamer, who agreed with Justice Iacobucci's opinion, agreed with Justice McLachlin (and Justices Sopinka and Major) as to the disposition. Thus, while the vote was 5–4 against the validity of the challenged tobacco laws, the vote on the remedy was 4 for a declaration of invalidity, and 2 for a declaration of invalidity "suspended" for one year.

Questions and Comments

1. How would this case be decided under current U.S. First Amendment law? In 44 Liquormart Inc. v. Rhode Island, 517 U.S. 484 (1996), the Court invalidated a state law prohibiting advertisements of the prices of alcoholic beverages other than inside liquor stores. The Court unanimously found the law unconstitutional but could not agree on the standard for review of regulation of commercial advertising. All agreed that the ban on price advertising could not be sustained as a measure to advance the state's legitimate interest in temperance. Under one plurality opinion by Justice Stevens, regulations of truthful advertising for lawful products would be subject to nearly the same scrutiny as regulation of political speech. Under the other major opinion, by Justice O'Connor, the criteria for evaluating regulation of commercial speech would differ from those for regulation of political speech, but would still require that the ban be no more extensive than necessary to serve the state's interest, under the test of Central Hudson Gas & Elec. Corp. v. Public Serv. Comm'n of N.Y., 447 U.S. 557 (1980), a test that was not met in the case. Since the state's stated purpose was to reduce consumption, there were more direct ways of doing so (for example, a sales tax) that would impinge less on truthful speech about prices. Justice Thomas expressed the view that truthful advertising of lawful products could never be prohibited under the First Amendment.

2. What are the relationships between commercial free speech and political free speech? Between free markets and free elections? Between citizenship and consumerism?

3. There has apparently been no systematic effort to invoke the Section 33 override clause to reinstate the scheme of regulation invalidated in *RJR–MacDonald*. Does this support the claim that there is a "convention" against use of the override? See also Vriend v. Alberta, [1998] 1 S.C.R. 493, a Canadian Supreme Court decision holding that a provincial antidiscrimination law had to include sexual orientation as a protected ground. Notwithstanding intense public reaction, and calls to invoke the override, it has been reported that the head of the provincial government announced that his government would accept the decision.

---

2. THE UNITED STATES

R.A.V. v. City of St. Paul

505 U.S. 377 (1992)

[Two years after Canada's *Keegstra* decision, the U.S. Supreme Court, closely divided on this point, held that prohibition of hate speech directed at groups based on their race, color, creed, religion or gender, was an impermissible "content" and "viewpoint-discrimination" prohibited by the First Amendment. Four of the justices did not join in this conclusion, but found that the particular statute was invalid because it was overbroad and regulated some speech that the First Amendment protected.

The Court held that the defendant, who with his friends had burned a cross inside the fenced yard of a black family that lived across the street, could not constitutionally be prosecuted under the local "Bias-Motivated Crime Ordinance," which provided:

> Whoever places on public or private property a symbol, object, appellation, characterization or graffiti, including, but not limited to, a burning cross or Nazi swastika, which one knows or has reasonable grounds to know arouses anger, alarm or resentment in others on the basis of race, color, creed, religion or gender commits disorderly conduct and shall be guilty of a misdemeanor."

The Supreme Court, in an opinion by Justice Scalia, began by noting that the defendant had been charged under this bias ordinance although "the conduct might have violated [other] Minnesota statutes carrying significant penalties," citing statutes prohibiting terrorist threats (up to five year penalty), arson (up to five years) and criminal damage to property (up to one year), and that the petitioner had also been indicted for violating a statute prohibiting racially motivated assaults, which was not challenged. Accepting the state court's interpretation of the statute as reaching only "fighting words," the majority concluded that while the state could prohibit all "fighting words," it could not single out speech designed to arouse anger in others on the basis of the enumerated categories. Justice Scalia's opinion for the Court reasoned as follows:]

SCALIA, J. . . .

. . . Assuming, *arguendo*, that all of the expression reached by the ordinance is proscribable under the "fighting words" doctrine, we nonetheless conclude that the ordinance is facially unconstitutional in that it prohibits otherwise permitted speech solely on the basis of the subjects the speech addresses.

The First Amendment generally prevents government from proscribing speech, or even expressive conduct, see, e. g., Texas v. Johnson, 491 U.S. 397, 406 (1989), because of disapproval of the ideas expressed. Content-based regulations are presumptively invalid. Simon & Schuster, Inc. v. Members of N. Y. State Crime Victims Bd., 502 U.S. 105, 115 (1991);

Consolidated Edison Co. of N. Y. v. Public Serv. Comm'n of N. Y., 447 U.S. 530, 536 (1980); Police Dept. of Chicago v. Mosley, 408 U.S. 92, 95 (1972). From 1791 to the present, however, our society, like other free but civilized societies, has permitted restrictions upon the content of speech in a few limited areas, which are "of such slight social value as a step to truth that any benefit that may be derived from them is clearly outweighed by the social interest in order and morality." *Chaplinsky*, [315 U.S]. at 572. We have recognized that "the freedom of speech" referred to by the First Amendment does not include a freedom to disregard these traditional limitations. See, e. g., Roth v. United States, 354 U.S. 476 (1957) (obscenity); Beauharnais v. Illinois, 343 U.S. 250 (1952) (defamation); Chaplinsky v. New Hampshire (" 'fighting' words").... Our decisions since the 1960's have narrowed the scope of the traditional categorical exceptions for defamation, see New York Times Co. v. Sullivan, 376 U.S. 254 (1964); Gertz v. Robert Welch, Inc., 418 U.S. 323 (1974), and for obscenity, see Miller v. California, 413 U.S. 15 (1973), but a limited categorical approach has remained an important part of our First Amendment jurisprudence.

We have sometimes said that these categories of expression are "not within the area of constitutionally protected speech," *Roth*, 352 U.S. at 483; Beauharnais, at 266; *Chaplinsky*, at 571–572, or that the "protection of the First Amendment does not extend" to them, Bose Corp. v. Consumers Union of United States, Inc., 466 U.S. 485, 504 (1984); Sable Communications of Cal., Inc. v. FCC, 492 U.S. 115, 124 (1989). Such statements must be taken in context, however, and are no more literally true than is the occasionally repeated shorthand characterizing obscenity "as not being speech at all" .... What they mean is that these areas of speech can, consistently with the First Amendment, be regulated *because of their constitutionally proscribable content* (obscenity, defamation, etc.)—not that they are categories of speech entirely invisible to the Constitution, so that they may be made the vehicles for content discrimination unrelated to their distinctively proscribable content. Thus, the government may proscribe libel; but it may not make the further content discrimination of proscribing *only* libel critical of the government....

Our cases surely do not establish the proposition that the First Amendment imposes no obstacle whatsoever to regulation of particular instances of such proscribable expression, so that the government "may regulate [them] freely," post, (White, J., concurring in judgment). That would mean that a city council could enact an ordinance prohibiting only those legally obscene works that contain criticism of the city government or, indeed, that do not include endorsement of the city government. Such a simplistic, all-or-nothing-at-all approach to First Amendment protection is at odds with common sense and with our jurisprudence as well. It is not true that "fighting words" have at most a *"de minimis"* expressive content, or that their content is *in all respects* "worthless and undeserving of constitutional protection"; sometimes they are quite expressive indeed. We have not said that they constitute "no part of the expression of ideas," but only that they constitute "no *essential* part of any exposition of ideas." *Chaplinsky*, 315 U.S. at 572 (emphasis added).

The proposition that a particular instance of speech can be proscribable on the basis of one feature (*e.g.*, obscenity) but not on the basis of another (*e.g.*, opposition to the city government) is commonplace and has found application in many contexts. We have long held, for example, that nonverbal expressive activity can be banned because of the action it entails, but not because of the ideas it expresses—so that burning a flag in violation of an ordinance against outdoor fires could be punishable, whereas burning a flag in violation of an ordinance against dishonoring the flag is not. See *Johnson*, 491 U.S. at 406–407. Similarly, we have upheld reasonable "time, place, or manner" restrictions, but only if they are "justified without reference to the content of the regulated speech." And just as the power to proscribe particular speech on the basis of a noncontent element (*e.g.*, noise) does not entail the power to proscribe the same speech on the basis of a content element; so also, the power to proscribe it on the basis of *one* content element (*e.g.*, obscenity) does not entail the power to proscribe it on the basis of *other* content elements.

In other words, the exclusion of "fighting words" from the scope of the First Amendment simply means that, for purposes of that Amendment, the unprotected features of the words are, despite their verbal character, essentially a "nonspeech" element of communication. Fighting words are thus analogous to a noisy sound truck: Each is, as Justice Frankfurter recognized, a "mode of speech," Niemotko v. Maryland, 340 U.S. 268, 282 (1951) (opinion concurring in result); both can be used to convey an idea; but neither has, in and of itself, a claim upon the First Amendment. As with the sound truck, however, so also with fighting words: The government may not regulate use based on hostility—or favoritism—towards the underlying message expressed. Compare Frisby v. Schultz, 487 U.S. 474 (1988) (upholding, against facial challenge, a content-neutral ban on targeted residential picketing), with Carey v. Brown, 447 U.S. 455 (1980) (invalidating a ban on residential picketing that exempted labor picketing).

The concurrences describe us as setting forth a new First Amendment principle that prohibition of constitutionally proscribable speech cannot be "underinclusive." .... In our view, the First Amendment imposes not an "underinclusiveness" limitation but a "content discrimination" limitation upon a State's prohibition of proscribable speech. There is no problem whatever, for example, with a State's prohibiting obscenity (and other forms of proscribable expression) only in certain media or markets, for although that prohibition would be "underinclusive," it would not discriminate on the basis of content. See, e. g., *Sable Communications*, 492 U.S. at 124–126 (upholding 47 U. S. C. § 223(b)(1), which prohibits obscene *telephone* communications).

Even the prohibition against content discrimination that we assert the First Amendment requires is not absolute. It applies differently in the context of proscribable speech than in the area of fully protected speech. The rationale of the general prohibition, after all, is that content discrimination "raises the specter that the Government may effectively drive certain ideas or viewpoints from the marketplace." [Simon & Schuster, 502

U.S. at 116] But content discrimination among various instances of a class of proscribable speech often does not pose this threat.

When the basis for the content discrimination consists entirely of the very reason the entire class of speech at issue is proscribable, no significant danger of idea or viewpoint discrimination exists. Such a reason, having been adjudged neutral enough to support exclusion of the entire class of speech from First Amendment protection, is also neutral enough to form the basis of distinction within the class. To illustrate: A State might choose to prohibit only that obscenity which is the most patently offensive *in its prurience*—i.e., that which involves the most lascivious displays of sexual activity. But it may not prohibit, for example, only that obscenity which includes offensive *political* messages. And the Federal Government can criminalize only those threats of violence that are directed against the President, see 18 U. S. C. § 871—since the reasons why threats of violence are outside the First Amendment (protecting individuals from the fear of violence, from the disruption that fear engenders, and from the possibility that the threatened violence will occur) have special force when applied to the person of the President. See Watts v. United States, 394 U.S. 705, 707 (1969) (upholding the facial validity of § 871 because of the "overwhelming interest in protecting the safety of [the] Chief Executive and in allowing him to perform his duties without interference from threats of physical violence"). But the Federal Government may not criminalize only those threats against the President that mention his policy on aid to inner cities....

Another valid basis for according differential treatment to even a content-defined subclass of proscribable speech is that the subclass happens to be associated with particular "secondary effects" of the speech, so that the regulation is *"justified* without reference to the content of the ... speech." A State could, for example, permit all obscene live performances except those involving minors. Moreover, since words can in some circumstances violate laws directed not against speech but against conduct (a law against treason, for example, is violated by telling the enemy the Nation's defense secrets), a particular content-based subcategory of a proscribable class of speech can be swept up incidentally within the reach of a statute directed at conduct rather than speech. Thus, for example, sexually derogatory "fighting words," among other words, may produce a violation of Title VII's general prohibition against sexual discrimination in employment practices, 42 U. S. C. § 2000e-2; 29 CFR § 1604.11 (1991). See also 18 U.S.C. § 242.... Where the government does not target conduct on the basis of its expressive content, acts are not shielded from regulation merely because they express a discriminatory idea or philosophy.

... [T]o validate such selectivity (where totally proscribable speech is at issue) it may not even be necessary to identify any particular "neutral" basis, so long as the nature of the content discrimination is such that there is no realistic possibility that official suppression of ideas is afoot. (We cannot think of any First Amendment interest that would stand in the way of a State's prohibiting only those obscene motion pictures with blue-eyed actresses.) Save for that limitation, the regulation of "fighting words," like the regulation of noisy speech, may address some offensive instances and leave other, equally offensive, instances alone.

II

Applying these principles to the St. Paul ordinance, we conclude that . . . the ordinance is facially unconstitutional. Although the phrase in the ordinance, "arouses anger, alarm or resentment in others," has been limited by the Minnesota Supreme Court's construction to reach only those symbols or displays that amount to "fighting words," the remaining, unmodified terms make clear that the ordinance applies only to "fighting words" that insult, or provoke violence, "on the basis of race, color, creed, religion or gender." Displays containing abusive invective, no matter how vicious or severe, are permissible unless they are addressed to one of the specified disfavored topics. Those who wish to use "fighting words" in connection with other ideas—to express hostility, for example, on the basis of political affiliation, union membership, or homosexuality—are not covered. The First Amendment does not permit St. Paul to impose special prohibitions on those speakers who express views on disfavored subjects.

In its practical operation, moreover, the ordinance goes even beyond mere content discrimination, to actual viewpoint discrimination. Displays containing some words—odious racial epithets, for example—would be prohibited to proponents of all views. But "fighting words" that do not themselves invoke race, color, creed, religion, or gender—aspersions upon a person's mother, for example—would seemingly be usable ad libitum in the placards of those arguing in favor of racial, color, etc., tolerance and equality, but could not be used by those speakers' opponents. One could hold up a sign saying, for example, that all "anti-Catholic bigots" are misbegotten; but not that all "papists" are, for that would insult and provoke violence "on the basis of religion." St. Paul has no such authority to license one side of a debate to fight freestyle, while requiring the other to follow Marquis of Queensberry rules.

What we have here, it must be emphasized, is not a prohibition of fighting words that are directed at certain persons or groups (which would be facially valid if it met the requirements of the Equal Protection Clause); but rather, a prohibition of fighting words that contain (as the Minnesota Supreme Court repeatedly emphasized) messages of "bias-motivated" hatred and in particular, as applied to this case, messages "based on virulent notions of racial supremacy." One must wholeheartedly agree with the Minnesota Supreme Court that "it is the responsibility, even the obligation, of diverse communities to confront such notions in whatever form they appear," but the manner of that confrontation cannot consist of selective limitations upon speech. St. Paul's brief asserts that a general "fighting words" law would not meet the city's needs because only a content-specific measure can communicate to minority groups that the "group hatred" aspect of such speech "is not condoned by the majority." The point of the

First Amendment is that majority preferences must be expressed in some fashion other than silencing speech on the basis of its content. . . .

. . . St. Paul has not singled out an especially offensive mode of expression—it has not, for example, selected for prohibition only those fighting words that communicate ideas in a threatening (as opposed to a merely obnoxious) manner. Rather, it has proscribed fighting words of whatever manner that communicate messages of racial, gender, or religious intolerance. Selectivity of this sort creates the possibility that the city is seeking to handicap the expression of particular ideas. That possibility would alone be enough to render the ordinance presumptively invalid, but St. Paul's comments and concessions in this case elevate the possibility to a certainty.

St. Paul argues that the ordinance comes within another of the specific exceptions we mentioned, the one that allows content discrimination aimed only at the "secondary effects" of the speech. . . . [But a]s we said in Boos v. Barry, 485 U.S. 312 (1988), "Listeners' reactions to speech are not the type of 'secondary effects' we referred to in *Renton*." . . .[7]

It hardly needs discussion that the ordinance does not fall within some more general exception permitting *all* selectivity that for any reason is beyond the suspicion of official suppression of ideas. The statements of St. Paul in this very case afford ample basis for, if not full confirmation of, that suspicion.

Finally, St. Paul and its amici defend the conclusion of the Minnesota Supreme Court that, even if the ordinance regulates expression based on hostility towards its protected ideological content, this discrimination is nonetheless justified because it is narrowly tailored to serve compelling state interests. Specifically, they assert that the ordinance helps to ensure the basic human rights of members of groups that have historically been subjected to discrimination, including the right of such group members to live in peace where they wish. We do not doubt that these interests are compelling, and that the ordinance can be said to promote them. But the "danger of censorship" presented by a facially content-based statute, Leathers v. Medlock, 499 U.S. at 448, requires that that weapon be employed only where it is "necessary to serve the asserted [compelling] interest." . . . The existence of adequate content-neutral alternatives thus "undercuts significantly" any defense of such a statute, . . . casting considerable doubt on the government's protestations that "the asserted justification is in fact an accurate description of the purpose and effect of the law." . . . The dispositive question in this case, therefore, is whether content

---

7. St. Paul has not argued in this case that the ordinance merely regulates that subclass of fighting words which is most likely to provoke a violent response. But even if one assumes (as appears unlikely) that the categories selected may be so described, that would not justify selective regulation under a "secondary effects" theory. The only reason why such expressive conduct would be especially correlated with violence is that it conveys a particularly odious message . . . . [I]t is clear that the St. Paul ordinance regulates on the basis of the "primary" effect of the speech—*i.e.*, its persuasive (or repellant) force.

discrimination is reasonably necessary to achieve St. Paul's compelling interests; it plainly is not. An ordinance not limited to the favored topics, for example, would have precisely the same beneficial effect. In fact the only interest distinctively served by the content limitation is that of displaying the city council's special hostility towards the particular biases thus singled out.[8] That is precisely what the First Amendment forbids. The politicians of St. Paul are entitled to express that hostility—but not through the means of imposing unique limitations upon speakers who (however benightedly) disagree.

* * *

Let there be no mistake about our belief that burning a cross in someone's front yard is reprehensible. But St. Paul has sufficient means at its disposal to prevent such behavior without adding the First Amendment to the fire.

The judgment of the Minnesota Supreme Court is reversed, and the case is remanded for proceedings not inconsistent with this opinion.

It is so ordered.

JUSTICE WHITE, with whom JUSTICE BLACKMUN and JUSTICE O'CONNOR join, and with whom JUSTICE STEVENS joins except as to Part I-A, concurring in the judgment.

I agree with the majority that the judgment of the Minnesota Supreme Court should be reversed. However, our agreement ends there.

This case could easily be decided within the contours of established First Amendment law by holding, as petitioner argues, that the St. Paul ordinance is fatally overbroad because it criminalizes not only unprotected expression but expression protected by the First Amendment. . . .

I

A

This Court's decisions have plainly stated that expression falling within certain limited categories so lacks the values the First Amendment was designed to protect that the Constitution affords no protection to that

---

8. A plurality of the Court reached a different conclusion with regard to the Tennessee antielectioneering statute considered earlier this Term in Burson v. Freeman, 504 U.S. 191 (1992). In light of the "logical connection" between electioneering and the State's compelling interest in preventing voter intimidation and election fraud—an inherent connection borne out by a "long history" and a "widespread and time-tested consensus"—the plurality concluded that it was faced with one of those "rare cases" in which the use of a facially content-based restriction was justified by interests unrelated to the suppression of ideas. Justice White and Justice Stevens are therefore quite mistaken when they seek to convert the *Burson* plurality's passing comment that "the First Amendment does not require States to regulate for problems that do not exist," into endorsement of the revolutionary proposition that the suppression of particular ideas can be justified when only those ideas have been a source of trouble in the past.

expression. Chaplinsky v. New Hampshire, 315 U.S. 568 (1942), made the point in the clearest possible terms:

> "There are certain well-defined and narrowly limited classes of speech, the prevention and punishment of which have never been thought to raise any Constitutional problem.... It has been well observed that such utterances are no essential part of any exposition of ideas, and are of such slight social value as a step to truth that any benefit that may be derived from them is clearly outweighed by the social interest in order and morality."

Thus, as the majority concedes, this Court has long held certain discrete categories of expression to be proscribable on the basis of their content. For instance, the Court has held that the individual who falsely shouts "fire" in a crowded theater may not claim the protection of the First Amendment. Schenck v. United States, 249 U.S. 47, 52 (1919). The Court has concluded that neither child pornography nor obscenity is protected by the First Amendment. New York v. Ferber, 458 U.S. 747, 764 (1982).... And the Court has observed that, "leaving aside the special considerations when public officials [and public figures] are the target, a libelous publication is not protected by the Constitution."

All of these categories are content based. But the Court has held that the First Amendment does not apply to them because their expressive content is worthless or of *de minimis* value to society. *Chaplinsky*, at 571–572. We have not departed from this principle, emphasizing repeatedly that, "within the confines of [these] given classifications, the evil to be restricted so overwhelmingly outweighs the expressive interests, if any, at stake, that no process of case-by-case adjudication is required." *Ferber*, [458 U.S.] at 763–764. This categorical approach has provided a principled and narrowly focused means for distinguishing between expression that the government may regulate freely and that which it may regulate on the basis of content only upon a showing of compelling need.

Today, however, the Court announces that earlier Courts did not mean their repeated statements that certain categories of expression are "not within the area of constitutionally protected speech." The present Court submits that such clear statements "must be taken in context" and are not "literally true."

To the contrary, those statements meant precisely what they said: The categorical approach is a firmly entrenched part of our First Amendment jurisprudence. Indeed, the Court in *Roth* reviewed the guarantees of freedom of expression in effect at the time of the ratification of the Constitution and concluded, "In light of this history, it is apparent that the unconditional phrasing of the First Amendment was not intended to protect every utterance." ...

... It is inconsistent to hold that the government may proscribe an entire category of speech because the content of that speech is evil, *Ferber*, at 763–764; but that the government may not treat a subset of that category differently without violating the First Amendment; the content of the subset is by definition worthless and undeserving of constitutional protection.

The majority's observation that fighting words are "quite expressive indeed," is no answer. Fighting words are not a means of exchanging views, rallying supporters, or registering a protest; they are directed against individuals to provoke violence or to inflict injury. *Chaplinsky*, 315 U.S., at 572. Therefore, a ban on all fighting words or on a subset of the fighting words category would restrict only the social evil of hate speech, without creating the danger of driving viewpoints from the marketplace. . . .

Any contribution of this holding to First Amendment jurisprudence is surely a negative one, since it necessarily signals that expressions of violence, such as the message of intimidation and racial hatred conveyed by burning a cross on someone's lawn, are of sufficient value to outweigh the social interest in order and morality that has traditionally placed such fighting words outside the First Amendment.[4] Indeed, by characterizing fighting words as a form of "debate," the majority legitimates hate speech as a form of public discussion.

Furthermore, the Court obscures the line between speech that could be regulated freely on the basis of content (i. e., the narrow categories of expression falling outside the First Amendment) and that which could be regulated on the basis of content only upon a showing of a compelling state interest (i. e., all remaining expression). By placing fighting words, which the Court has long held to be valueless, on at least equal constitutional footing with political discourse and other forms of speech that we have deemed to have the greatest social value, the majority devalues the latter category.

B

In a second break with precedent, the Court refuses to sustain the ordinance even though it would survive under the strict scrutiny applicable to other protected expression. Assuming, arguendo, that the St. Paul ordinance is a content-based regulation of protected expression, it nevertheless would pass First Amendment review under settled law upon a showing that the regulation "is necessary to serve a compelling state interest and is narrowly drawn to achieve that end." Simon & Schuster, at 118. . . . Nevertheless, the Court treats strict scrutiny analysis as irrelevant to the constitutionality of the legislation:

> "The dispositive question . . . is whether content discrimination is reasonably necessary to achieve St. Paul's compelling interests; it plainly is not. An ordinance not limited to the favored topics, for example, would have precisely the same beneficial effect."

---

4. This does not suggest, of course, that cross burning is always unprotected. Burning a cross at a political rally would almost certainly be protected expression. Cf. Brandenburg v. Ohio, 395 U.S. 444, 445 (1969). But in such a context, the cross burning would not be characterized as a "direct personal insult or an invitation to exchange fisticuffs," Texas v. Johnson 491 U.S. 397, 409 (1989), to which the fighting words doctrine applies.

Under the majority's view, a narrowly drawn, content-based ordinance could never pass constitutional muster if the object of that legislation could be accomplished by banning a wider category of speech. This appears to be a general renunciation of strict scrutiny review, a fundamental tool of First Amendment analysis.

This abandonment of the doctrine is inexplicable in light of our decision in Burson v. Freeman, which was handed down just a month ago.[6] In *Burson*, seven of the eight participating Members of the Court agreed that the strict scrutiny standard applied in a case involving a First Amendment challenge to a content-based statute. The statute at issue prohibited the solicitation of votes and the display or distribution of campaign materials within 100 feet of the entrance to a polling place. The plurality concluded that the legislation survived strict scrutiny because the State had asserted a compelling interest in regulating electioneering near polling places and because the statute at issue was narrowly tailored to accomplish that goal.

Significantly, the statute in *Burson* did not proscribe all speech near polling places; it restricted only political speech. . . . [The plurality] squarely rejected the proposition that the legislation failed First Amendment review because it could have been drafted in broader, content-neutral terms:

> "States adopt laws to address the problems that confront them. *The First Amendment does not require States to regulate for problems that do not exist.*" [*Burson*] at 207 (emphasis added)

This reasoning is in direct conflict with the majority's analysis in the present case, which leaves two options to lawmakers attempting to regulate expressions of violence: (1) enact a sweeping prohibition on an entire class of speech (thereby requiring "regulation for problems that do not exist"); or (2) not legislate at all.

Had the analysis adopted by the majority in the present case been applied in *Burson*, the challenged election law would have failed constitutional review, for its content-based distinction between political and nonpolitical speech could not have been characterized as "reasonably necessary," to achieve the State's interest in regulating polling place premises. . . .

Although the First Amendment does not apply to categories of unprotected speech, such as fighting words, the Equal Protection Clause requires that the regulation of unprotected speech be rationally related to a legitimate government interest. A defamation statute that drew distinctions on the basis of political affiliation or "an ordinance prohibiting only those legally obscene works that contain criticism of the city government," would unquestionably fail rational-basis review. . . .

---

6. Earlier this Term, seven of the eight participating Members of the Court agreed that strict scrutiny analysis applied in Simon & Schuster, Inc. v. Members of N. Y. State Crime Victims Bd., 502 U.S. 105 (1991), in which we struck down New York's "Son of Sam" law, which required "that an accused or convicted criminal's income from works describing his crime be deposited in an escrow account."

C

The Court has patched up its argument with an apparently nonexhaustive list of ad hoc exceptions, in what can be viewed either as an attempt to confine the effects of its decision to the facts of this case, or as an effort to anticipate some of the questions that will arise from its radical revision of First Amendment law.

For instance, if the majority were to give general application to the rule on which it decides this case, today's decision would call into question the constitutionality of the statute making it illegal to threaten the life of the President. 18 U. S. C. § 871.... [T]his statute, by singling out certain threats, incorporates a content-based distinction; it indicates that the Government especially disfavors threats against the President as opposed to threats against all others. But because the Government could prohibit all threats and not just those directed against the President, under the Court's theory, the compelling reasons justifying the enactment of special legislation to safeguard the President would be irrelevant, and the statute would fail First Amendment review.

To save the statute, the majority has engrafted the following exception onto its newly announced First Amendment rule: Content-based distinctions may be drawn within an unprotected category of speech if the basis for the distinctions is "the very reason the entire class of speech at issue is proscribable." Thus, the argument goes, the statute making it illegal to threaten the life of the President is constitutional, "since the reasons why threats of violence are outside the First Amendment (protecting individuals from the fear of violence, from the disruption that fear engenders, and from the possibility that the threatened violence will occur) have special force when applied to the person of the President."

The exception swallows the majority's rule. Certainly, it should apply to the St. Paul ordinance, since "the reasons why [fighting words] are outside the First Amendment ... have special force when applied to [groups that have historically been subjected to discrimination]."

To avoid the result of its own analysis, the Court suggests that fighting words are simply a mode of communication, rather than a content-based category, and that the St. Paul ordinance has not singled out a particularly objectionable mode of communication. Again, the majority confuses the issue. A prohibition on fighting words is not a time, place, or manner restriction; it is a ban on a class of speech that conveys an overriding message of personal injury and imminent violence, *Chaplinsky*, 315 U.S. at 572, a message that is at its ugliest when directed against groups that have long been the targets of discrimination. Accordingly, the ordinance falls within the first exception to the majority's theory.

As its second exception, the Court posits that certain content-based regulations will survive under the new regime if the regulated subclass "happens to be associated with particular 'secondary effects' of the speech ...," which the majority treats as encompassing instances in which "words can ... violate laws directed not against speech but against conduct ...."

Again, there is a simple explanation for the Court's eagerness to craft an exception to its new First Amendment rule: Under the general rule the Court applies in this case, Title VII hostile work environment claims would suddenly be unconstitutional.

Title VII of the Civil Rights Act of 1964 makes it unlawful to discriminate "because of [an] individual's race, color, religion, sex, or national origin," 42 U. S. C.§ 2000e-2(a)(1), and the regulations covering hostile workplace claims forbid "sexual harassment," which includes "unwelcome sexual advances, requests for sexual favors, and other verbal or physical conduct of a sexual nature" that create "an intimidating, hostile, or offensive working environment," 29 CFR § 1604.11(a) (1991). The regulation does not prohibit workplace harassment generally; it focuses on what the majority would characterize as the "disfavored topic" of sexual harassment. In this way, Title VII is similar to the St. Paul ordinance that the majority condemns because it "imposes special prohibitions on those speakers who express views on disfavored subjects." Under the broad principle the Court uses to decide the present case, hostile work environment claims based on sexual harassment should fail First Amendment review; because a general ban on harassment in the workplace would cover the problem of sexual harassment, any attempt to proscribe the subcategory of sexually harassing expression would violate the First Amendment.

Hence, the majority's second exception, which the Court indicates would insulate a Title VII hostile work environment claim from an under-inclusiveness challenge because "sexually derogatory 'fighting words' . . . may produce a violation of Title VII's general prohibition against sexual discrimination in employment practices." But application of this exception to a hostile work environment claim does not hold up under close examination.

. . . [T]he hostile work environment regulation is not keyed to the presence or absence of an economic quid pro quo, but to the impact of the speech on the victimized worker. Consequently, the regulation would no more fall within a secondary effects exception than does the St. Paul ordinance.

II

Although I disagree with the Court's analysis, I do agree with its conclusion: The St. Paul ordinance is unconstitutional. However, I would decide the case on overbreadth grounds. . . .

In construing the St. Paul ordinance, the Minnesota Supreme Court drew upon the definition of fighting words that appears in *Chaplinsky*—words "which by their very utterance inflict injury or tend to incite an immediate breach of the peace." However, the Minnesota court was far from clear in identifying the "injuries" inflicted by the expression that St. Paul sought to regulate. Indeed, the Minnesota court emphasized (tracking the language of the ordinance) that "the ordinance censors only those displays that one knows or should know will create anger, alarm or resentment based on racial, ethnic, gender or religious bias.". I therefore understand the court to have ruled that St. Paul may constitutionally prohibit expression that "by its very utterance" causes "anger, alarm or resentment."

Our fighting words cases have made clear, however, that such generalized reactions are not sufficient to strip expression of its constitutional protection. The mere fact that expressive activity causes hurt feelings, offense, or resentment does not render the expression unprotected.

In the First Amendment context, "criminal statutes must be scrutinized with particular care; those that make unlawful a substantial amount of constitutionally protected conduct may be held facially invalid even if they also have legitimate application." . . . The St. Paul antibias ordinance is such a law. Although the ordinance reaches conduct that is unprotected, it also makes criminal expressive conduct that causes only hurt feelings, offense, or resentment, and is protected by the First Amendment. The ordinance is therefore fatally overbroad and invalid on its face. . . .

JUSTICE BLACKMUN, concurring in the judgment.

. . . [B]y deciding that a State cannot regulate speech that causes great harm unless it also regulates speech that does not (setting law and logic on their heads), the Court seems to abandon the categorical approach, and inevitably to relax the level of scrutiny applicable to content-based laws. As Justice White points out, this weakens the traditional protections of speech. If all expressive activity must be accorded the same protection, that protection will be scant. The simple reality is that the Court will never provide child pornography or cigarette advertising the level of protection customarily granted political speech. If we are forbidden to categorize, as the Court has done here, we shall reduce protection across the board. It is sad that in its effort to reach a satisfying result in this case, the Court is willing to weaken First Amendment protections. . . .

I see no First Amendment values that are compromised by a law that prohibits hoodlums from driving minorities out of their homes by burning crosses on their lawns, but I see great harm in preventing the people of Saint Paul from specifically punishing the race-based fighting words that so prejudice their community.

I concur in the judgment, however, because I agree with Justice White that this particular ordinance reaches beyond fighting words to speech protected by the First Amendment.

JUSTICE STEVENS, with whom JUSTICE WHITE and JUSTICE BLACKMUN join as to Part I, concurring in the judgment. . . .

[W]hile I agree that the St. Paul ordinance is unconstitutionally overbroad . . ., I write separately to suggest how the allure of absolute principles has skewed the analysis of both the majority and Justice White's opinions.

I

. . . Drawing on broadly worded dicta, the Court establishes a near-absolute ban on content-based regulations of expression and holds that the

First Amendment prohibits the regulation of fighting words by subject matter. Thus, while the Court rejects the "all-or-nothing-at-all" nature of the categorical approach, it promptly embraces an absolutism of its own: Within a particular "proscribable" category of expression, the Court holds, a government must either proscribe *all* speech or no speech at all. This aspect of the Court's ruling fundamentally misunderstands the role and constitutional status of content-based regulations on speech, conflicts with the very nature of First Amendment jurisprudence, and disrupts well-settled principles of First Amendment law.

Although the Court has, on occasion, declared that content-based regulations of speech are "never permitted," Police Dep't of Chicago v. Mosley, 408 U.S. 92, 99 (1972), such claims are overstated.... [O]ur decisions demonstrate that content-based distinctions, far from being presumptively invalid, are an inevitable and indispensable aspect of a coherent understanding of the First Amendment.

... Although the First Amendment broadly protects "speech," it does not protect the right to "fix prices, breach contracts, make false warranties, place bets with bookies, threaten, [or] extort." Whether an agreement among competitors is a violation of the Sherman Act or protected activity under the *Noerr-Pennington* doctrine hinges upon the content of the agreement. Similarly, "the line between permissible advocacy and impermissible incitation to crime or violence depends, not merely on the setting in which the speech occurs, but also on exactly what the speaker had to say." [Young v. American Mini Theatres, Inc., 427 U.S. 50, 66 (1976)].

Likewise, whether speech falls within one of the categories of "unprotected" or "proscribable" expression is determined, in part, by its content. Whether a magazine is obscene, a gesture a fighting word, or a photograph child pornography is determined, in part, by its content. Even within categories of protected expression, the First Amendment status of speech is fixed by its content. New York Times Co. v. Sullivan, 376 U.S. 254 (1964), and Dun & Bradstreet, Inc. v. Greenmoss Builders, Inc., 472 U.S. 749 (1985), establish that the level of protection given to speech depends upon its subject matter: Speech about public officials or matters of public concern receives greater protection than speech about other topics. It can, therefore, scarcely be said that the regulation of expressive activity cannot be predicated on its content: Much of our First Amendment jurisprudence is premised on the assumption that content makes a difference.

Consistent with this general premise, we have frequently upheld content-based regulations of speech. For example, in Young v. American Mini Theatres, the Court upheld zoning ordinances that regulated movie theaters based on the content of the films shown. In FCC v. Pacifica Foundation, 438 U.S. 726 (1978) (plurality opinion), we upheld a restriction on the broadcast of specific indecent words. In Lehman v. Shaker Heights, 418 U.S. 298 (1974) (plurality opinion), we upheld a city law that permitted commercial advertising, but prohibited political advertising, on city buses. In Broadrick v. Oklahoma, 413 U.S. 601 (1973), we upheld a state law that restricted the speech of state employees, but only as concerned partisan political matters. We have long recognized the power of the Federal Trade Commission to regulate misleading advertising and labeling, see, e. g., Jacob Siegel Co. v. FTC, 327 U.S. 608 (1946)....

All of these cases involved the selective regulation of speech based on content—precisely the sort of regulation the Court invalidates today. Such selective regulations are unavoidably content based, but they are not, in my opinion, "presumptively invalid." As these many decisions and examples demonstrate, the prohibition on content-based regulations is not nearly as total as the *Mosley* dictum suggests.

Disregarding this vast body of case law, the Court today goes beyond even the overstatement in *Mosley* and applies the prohibition on content-based regulation to speech that the Court had until today considered wholly "unprotected" by the First Amendment—namely, fighting words. This new absolutism in the prohibition of content-based regulations severely contorts the fabric of settled First Amendment law.

Our First Amendment decisions have created a rough hierarchy in the constitutional protection of speech. Core political speech occupies the highest, most protected position; commercial speech and nonobscene, sexually explicit speech are regarded as a sort of second-class expression; obscenity and fighting words receive the least protection of all. Assuming that the Court is correct that this last class of speech is not wholly "unprotected," it certainly does not follow that fighting words and obscenity receive the *same* sort of protection afforded core political speech. Yet in ruling that proscribable speech cannot be regulated based on subject matter, the Court does just that. Perversely, this gives fighting words *greater* protection than is afforded commercial speech. If Congress can prohibit false advertising directed at airline passengers without also prohibiting false advertising directed at bus passengers and if a city can prohibit political advertisements in its buses while allowing other advertisements, it is ironic to hold that a city cannot regulate fighting words based on "race, color, creed, religion or gender" while leaving unregulated fighting words based on "union membership ... or homosexuality." The Court today turns First Amendment law on its head: Communication that was once entirely unprotected (and that still can be wholly proscribed) is now entitled to greater protection than commercial speech....

... Just as Congress may determine that threats against the President entail more severe consequences than other threats, so St. Paul's City Council may determine that threats based on the target's race, religion, or gender cause more severe harm to both the target and to society than other threats. This latter judgment—that harms caused by racial, religious, and gender-based invective are qualitatively different from that caused by other fighting words—seems to me eminently reasonable and realistic....

Similarly, it is impossible to reconcile the Court's analysis of the St. Paul ordinance with its recognition that "a prohibition of fighting words that are directed at certain persons or groups ... would be facially valid." A selective proscription of unprotected expression designed to protect "certain persons or groups" (for example, a law proscribing threats directed at the elderly) would be constitutional if it were based on a legitimate determination that the harm created by the regulated expression differs from that created by the unregulated expression (that is, if the elderly are more severely injured by threats than are the nonelderly). Such selective protection is no different from a law prohibiting minors (and only minors) from obtaining obscene publications. See Ginsberg v. New York, 390 U.S. 629 (1968). St. Paul has determined—reasonably in my judgment—that fighting-word injuries "based on race, color, creed, religion or gender" are qualitatively different and more severe than fighting-word injuries based on other characteristics. Whether the selective proscription of proscribable speech is defined by the protected target ("certain persons or groups") or the basis of the harm (injuries "based on race, color, creed, religion or gender") makes no constitutional difference: What matters is whether the legislature's selection is based on a legitimate, neutral, and reasonable distinction.

In sum, the central premise of the Court's ruling—that "content-based regulations are presumptively invalid"—has simplistic appeal, but lacks support in our First Amendment jurisprudence. . . .

II

Although I agree with much of Justice White's analysis, I do not join Part I-A of his opinion because I have reservations about the "categorical approach" to the First Amendment. . . .

Admittedly, the categorical approach to the First Amendment has some appeal: Either expression is protected or it is not—the categories create safe harbors for governments and speakers alike. But this approach sacrifices subtlety for clarity and is, I am convinced, ultimately unsound. As an initial matter, the concept of "categories" fits poorly with the complex reality of expression. Few dividing lines in First Amendment law are straight and unwavering, and efforts at categorization inevitably give rise only to fuzzy boundaries. Our definitions of "obscenity" and "public forum" illustrate this all too well. The quest for doctrinal certainty through the definition of categories and subcategories is, in my opinion, destined to fail.

Moreover, the categorical approach does not take seriously the importance of context. The meaning of any expression and the legitimacy of its regulation can only be determined in context. Whether, for example, a picture or a sentence is obscene cannot be judged in the abstract, but rather only in the context of its setting, its use, and its audience. Similarly, although legislatures may freely regulate most nonobscene child pornography, such pornography that is part of "a serious work of art, a documentary on behavioral problems, or a medical or psychiatric teaching device" may be entitled to constitutional protection; the "question whether a specific act of communication is protected by the First Amendment always requires some consideration of both its content and its context." [*Ferber* at 778 (Stevens, J., concurring)]. The categorical approach sweeps too broadly when it declares that all such expression is beyond the protection of the First Amendment.

[Justice Stevens develops the argument that the nature of constitutional protection depends on the content and context of both the speech, and the contested restriction of speech, continuing into Part III of his separate opinion.]

III ...

In applying this analysis to the St. Paul ordinance, I assume, *arguendo*—as the Court does—that the ordinance regulates *only* fighting words and therefore is *not* overbroad. Looking to the content and character of the regulated activity, two things are clear. First, by hypothesis the ordinance bars only low-value speech, namely, fighting words. By definition such expression constitutes "no essential part of any exposition of ideas, and [is] of such slight social value as a step to truth that any benefit that may be derived from [it] is clearly outweighed by the social interest in order and morality." *Chaplinsky*, 315 U.S. at 572. Second, the ordinance regulates "expressive conduct [rather] than ... the written or spoken word." Texas v. Johnson, 491 U.S. at 406.

Looking to the context of the regulated activity, it is again significant that the ordinance (by hypothesis) regulates only fighting words. Whether words are fighting words is determined in part by their context. Fighting words are not words that merely cause offense; fighting words must be directed at individuals so as to "by their very utterance inflict injury." By hypothesis, then, the St. Paul ordinance restricts speech in confrontational and potentially violent situations. The case at hand is illustrative. The cross burning in this case—directed as it was to a single African-American family trapped in their home—was nothing more than a crude form of physical intimidation. That this cross burning sends a message of racial hostility does not automatically endow it with complete constitutional protection.

Significantly, the St. Paul ordinance regulates speech not on the basis of its subject matter or the viewpoint expressed, but rather on the basis of the harm the speech causes. In this regard, the Court fundamentally misreads the St. Paul ordinance.... Contrary to the Court's suggestion, the ordinance regulates only a subcategory of expression that causes injuries based on "race, color, creed, religion or gender," not a subcategory that involves discussions that concern those characteristics.[9] The ordinance, as construed by the Court, criminalizes expression that "one knows

9. ... One need look no further than the recent social unrest in the Nation's cities to see that race-based threats may cause more harm to society and to individuals than other threats. Just as the statute prohibiting threats against the President is justifiable because of the place of the President in our social and political order, so a statute prohibiting race-based threats is justifiable because of the place of race in our social and political order. Although it is regrettable that race occupies such a place and is so incendiary an issue, until the Nation matures beyond that condition, laws such as St. Paul's ordinance will remain reasonable and justifiable.

... [by its very utterance inflicts injury on] others on the basis of race, color, creed, religion or gender." In this regard, the ordinance resembles the child pornography law at issue in *Ferber*, which in effect singled out child pornography because those publications caused far greater harms than pornography involving adults.

Moreover, even if the St. Paul ordinance did regulate fighting words based on its subject matter, such a regulation would, in my opinion, be constitutional. As noted above, subject-matter-based regulations on commercial speech are widespread and largely unproblematic. As we have long recognized, subject-matter regulations generally do not raise the same concerns of government censorship and the distortion of public discourse presented by viewpoint regulations....

Contrary to the suggestion of the majority, the St. Paul ordinance does *not* regulate expression based on viewpoint. The Court contends that the ordinance requires proponents of racial intolerance to "follow the Marquis of Queensberry rules" while allowing advocates of racial tolerance to "fight freestyle." The law does no such thing.

The Court writes:

"One could hold up a sign saying, for example, that all 'anti-Catholic bigots' are misbegotten; but not that all 'papists' are, for that would insult and provoke violence 'on the basis of religion.'"

This may be true, but it hardly proves the Court's point. The Court's reasoning is asymmetrical. The response to a sign saying that "all [religious] bigots are misbegotten" is a sign saying that "all advocates of religious tolerance are misbegotten." Assuming such signs could be fighting words (which seems to me extremely unlikely), neither sign would be banned by the ordinance for the attacks were not "based on ... religion" but rather on one's beliefs about tolerance. Conversely (and again assuming such signs are fighting words), just as the ordinance would prohibit a Muslim from hoisting a sign claiming that all Catholics were misbegotten, so the ordinance would bar a Catholic from hoisting a similar sign attacking Muslims.

The St. Paul ordinance is evenhanded. In a battle between advocates of tolerance and advocates of intolerance, the ordinance does not prevent either side from hurling fighting words at the other on the basis of their conflicting ideas, but it does bar both sides from hurling such words on the basis of the target's "race, color, creed, religion or gender." To extend the Court's pugilistic metaphor, the St. Paul ordinance simply bans punches "below the belt"—*by either party*. It does not, therefore, favor one side of any debate.

Finally, it is noteworthy that the St. Paul ordinance is, as construed by the Court today, quite narrow. The St. Paul ordinance does not ban all "hate speech," nor does it ban, say, all cross burnings or all swastika displays. Rather it only bans a subcategory of the already narrow category of fighting words. Such a limited ordinance leaves open and protected a vast range of expression on the subjects of racial, religious, and gender equality. As construed by the Court today, the ordinance certainly does not "'raise the specter that the Government may effectively drive certain ideas or viewpoints from the marketplace.'" Petitioner is free to burn a cross to announce a rally or to express his views about racial supremacy, he may do so on private property or public land, at day or at night, so long as the burning is not so threatening and so directed at an individual as to "by its very [execution] inflict injury." Such a limited proscription scarcely offends the First Amendment. . . .

Thus, were the ordinance not overbroad, I would vote to uphold it.

Questions and Comments

1. In Beauharnais v. Illinois, 343 U.S. 250 (1952) the Court had upheld a conviction for violation of an Illinois "group libel" statute making it an offense to publish anything that "portrays depravity, criminality . . . or lack of virtue of a class of citizens, of any race, color, creed or religion, which exposes [such] citizens to contempt, derision or obloquy or which is productive of breach of the peace or riots." Justice Frankfurter for the Court began by observing that libel of an individual was a common law crime, to which truth or good motive was no defense. Since the murder of the abolitionist Elijah Lovejoy in 1837 to the Cicero riots of 1951, the Court noted, Illinois had been the "scene of exacerbated tension between races, often flaring into violence and destruction. In many of these outbreaks, utterances of the character here in question, so the Illinois legislature could conclude, played a significant part . . . In the face of this history . . . , we would deny experience to say that the Illinois legislature was without reason in seeking ways to curb false or malicious defamation of racial and religious groups, made in public places and by means calculated to have a powerful emotional impact on those to whom it was presented." Recognizing the argument that this kind of statute might not help, the Court wrote that "[i]t is not within our competence to confirm or deny claims of social scientists as to the dependence of the individual on the position of his racial or religious group in the community . . . . [W]e are [thus] precluded from saying that speech concededly punishable when immediately directed at individuals cannot be outlawed if directed at groups with whose position and esteem in society the affiliated individual may be inextricably involved."

Addressing concerns about viewpoint or content discrimination, and that "prohibiting libel of a creed or of a racial group . . . is but a step from prohibiting libel of a political party," the Court wrote, "[e]very power may be abused, but the possibility of abuse is a poor reason for denying Illinois the power to adopt measures against criminal libels sanctioned by centuries of Anglo-American law." After upholding Illinois' requirement that the truth defense show not only the accuracy of the facts but that the publication was made for good motives, the Court concluded that it need not reach application of the "clear and present" danger test because "[l]ibelous utterances [are not] within the area of constitutionally protected speech . . ."

To the extent that *Beauharnais* treats libelous speech as completely unprotected, and permits libel actions for other than false statements of facts, it has been either disavowed or substantially undermined by later cases, including N.Y. Times v. Sullivan, below. But in considering claims about difference in the form and substance of U.S. approaches to government regulation of free speech and those of other nations, is Beauharnais helpful?

2. *Keegstra* mentioned other constitutional provisions in determining whether the speech regulation there survived Section 1 analysis. Are there any other portions of the U.S. Constitution that might be invoked to analyze free speech issues here? Cf. Charles Lawrence, *If He Hollers, Let Him Go: Regulating Racist Speech on Campus*, 1990 Duke L. J. 431, 439–40 (arguing that *Brown v. Board of Education* involved a condemnation of speech, because segregation was condemned for the message of inferiority it gave to black children and thus *Brown* can be read to uphold regulation of the content of racist speech).

3. The history of the Nazis' rise to power in Weimar Germany played a role in both the majority and dissent in *Keegstra*. It has played a powerful role in the design and interpretation of the German Basic Law as well. See, e.g., Article 9[2] (prohibiting organizations "whose purposes or activities . . . are directed against the constitutional order or the concept of international understanding"); Article 21[2] ("Parties which, by reason of their aims or the behavior of their adherents, seek to impair or abolish the free democratic basic order or endanger the existence of the Federal Republic of Germany, shall be unconstitutional"). These provisions are sometimes referred to as providing for "militant democracy." In two decisions in the 1950s the Constitutional Court found a Nazi party and a Communist party to be unconstitutional under this provision. (Similar provisions are found in other European constitutions, e.g., Italy's constitution, which bans "fascist" political groups. Constitution of Italy, Art XII.) German law has been designed to be particularly restrictive of antisemitic speech, such as Holocaust denial. See generally Eric Stein, *History Against Free Speech: The New German Law Against the "Auschwitz"—and other—"Lies"*, 85 Mich. L. Rev. 277 (1986). The recent "Auschwitz Lie" case, 90 BVerfGE 241 (1994), in which the Court upheld an injunction against a demonstration designed to publicize the view that the Holocaust never occurred, demonstrates a continuing divide between European and U.S. approaches. See Edward J. Eberle, *Public Discourse in Contemporary Germany*, 47 Case W. Res. L. Rev. 797 (1997) (concluding that in U.S. preeminent value is individualistic freedom of discourse while in Germany preeminent value is human dignity); Kommers (1997) at 382–87.

Should the history of Hitler's rise to power play a more prominent role in U.S. free speech law than it has until now? In thinking about this question, consider competing perspectives on the role of law in discouraging hate speech in the Weimar Republic. summarized by Cyril Levitt in *Racial*

Incitement and the Law: The Case of the Weimar Republic, in Freedom of Expression and the Charter (David Schneiderman ed. 1991). Levitt describes the Weimar Republic's laws against religious insults, incitement to class struggle, and insult invoked to prosecute anti-semitic behavior, trials and court decisions thereunder, and identifies views ranging from Udo Beer's conclusion that the Weimar legal system generally provided equal and effective protection under law of the Jews to Leo Strauss's view that the Weimar Republic was too weak in its use of law to defeat the anti-semites that led to Hitler's rise. Agreeing with other scholars that "the overwhelming majority of cases which went to trial were adjudicated fairly," Levitt concludes that there were enough "clearly biased verdicts" that, though atypical, encouraged antisemites and thwarted efforts by Jewish organizations to use the tools of law to combat such behavior; he also notes that some of the trials were sought by the racist defendants as showcases for their views. While not arguing for Canada to abandon its prohibition of hate speech, his emphasis is that law "should not be seen as a first, or even prominent, line of defence."

For further discussion of the problem of tolerance of the intolerant, particularly in regimes that are in transition to democracy, see Gregory F. Fox and Georg Nolte, *Intolerant Democracies*, 36 Harv. Intl L. J. 1 (1995). Fox and Nolte argue that "national and international practice favor a substantive [rather than procedural] model of democracy, which holds that the long-term survival of democratic institutions outweighs short-term deprivation of political rights to anti-democratic actors," and further argue that international human rights treaties may require states to exclude anti-democratic actors from the political process if they threaten the integrity of democratic institutions.

4. U.S. discussions of free speech, and of government power to regulate or prohibit hate speech, often invoke "McCarthyism" and concerns over government censorship. See Mark A. Graber, *Old Wine in New Bottles: The Conditional Status of Unconstitutional Speech*, 48 Van. L. Rev. 349 (1995):

> [Advocates of hate speech regulation fail to realize] ... that in every age the leading opponents of various bans on certain ideas have insisted that the First Amendment does not fully protect the right to deny or criticize what their generation regards as fundamental constitutional values.... [The leading] proponents of restrictions on speech during World War I [for example argued] that persons had no constitutional right to attack what they believed to be essential principles of republican government.... [Similarly], proponents of the freedom of contract [argued] that the First Amendment did not protect overly strident attacks on private property because such advocacy was also unconstitutional ... speech [who would restrict the speech of communists argued that] "no democratic or constitutional principle is violated ...when a democracy acts to exclude those groups from entering the struggle for political power which, if victorious, will not permit that struggle to continue in accordance with the democratic way" [quoting Carl Auerbach]...."

See also Charles Fried, *The New First Amendment Jurisprudence: A Threat to Liberty*, 59 U. Chi. L. Rev. 225 (1992):

> The ideas the [hate speech rules] condemn are false and offensive, but the universities do not condemn all false and offensive ideas. For example, an invective condemning the United States as an oppressor nation or condemning capitalism as a form of exploitation may be repeated with impunity.... Individuals within the community may not espouse some forms of gender and race superiority but may espouse others .... This discrimination make clear that those who promulgate these regulations assign to themselves the authority to determine which ideas are false and which false ideas people may not express as they choose .... Thus the holders of [some] noxious ideas are suppressed and the rest of the community is ... intimidated by this display of political might."

Does the history of censorship and speech in the U.S. support the Court's decision in *R.A.V.*?

5. *R.A.V.* seems to hold that content-based and viewpoint-based distinctions, within a category of speech that could be constitutionally prohibited, violate the First Amendment. What dangers does this approach seek to avoid? Justice Stevens' dissent challenged Justice Scalia's argument that the St. Paul ordinance involved viewpoint discrimination because, the dissent argued, it permits both anti-tolerance and anti-intolerance expressions even-handedly. See also Sunstein, Democracy and the Problem of Free Speech (1993) (ordinance prohibits both anti-white and anti-black sentiments, and regulates on the basis of the subjects of discussion, not on the basis of viewpoint). Who has the better of this argument?

6. Under *R.A.V.* are employment discrimination laws that prohibit employers from firing employees because of their race or gender a prohibited "content-based" regulation of the employer's views? What about laws prohibiting public cross-burning, or the public display of swastikas? Compare Wisconsin v. Mitchell, 508 U.S. 476 (1993) (unanimously upholding conviction and sentence of black defendant for assaulting a young white boy because he was white, where sentence for crime of assault was enhanced upon special finding, under enhancement statute, that the defendant had intentionally chosen the victim because of his race). In *Mitchell* the Court said that physical assaults are not expressive conduct protected by the First Amendment, and that a state can permissibly make a discriminatory motive for such conduct a basis for sentence enhancement. The Court distinguished *R.A.V.* because, while the "ordinance struck down in R.A.V. was explicitly directed at expression (i.e. speeches or messages) the statute in this case is aimed at conduct unprotected by the First Amendment ... [and] singles out for enhancement bias-inspired conduct because this conduct is thought to inflict greater individual and societal harms ..."

7. Professor Greenawalt's article, 55 Law & Contemp. Probs. at 23–24, described the decision in a companion case to *Keegstra*, and raised the following questions:

In [Canada Human Rights Comm'n v.] Taylor, [[1990], 3 S.C.R. 892] the majority sustained the provision of the Canadian Human Rights Act that forbids using the telephone to expose a person or a group to hatred or contempt, as it applies to race and religion. Because the provision is civil rather than criminal, the majority of the Court accepted the absence of a requirement that the defendant intend to discriminate and the lack of any defense for truth. The majority's easy approval of a cease and desist order, which underlay a contempt judgment, indicated a much more comfortable attitude toward prior restraints than one would find in American courts.

The same three justices dissented. Emphasizing the broad range of communications that might be covered, Justice McLachlin found the provision wanting on all three prongs of the proportionality requirement.

One peculiar aspect of broad application was not noted by either opinion. Religions usually consist of views as well as traditions and practices. If anything warrants hatred or contempt, some actual or potential religious views do, because religious views may support the most contemptible attitudes and practices. Suppose, for example, that right wing members of the South African Dutch Reformed Church moved to Canada and preached that colored peoples of various sorts are inferior to whites and that apartheid should be established in Canada. A citizen telephones neighbors and warns them against this hateful religion then being established in their town. Saying the doctrines are hateful is likely to expose members and the group to hatred or contempt, so it seems the citizen would have violated the provision, which recognizes no defense for honest religious disagreement (or any disagreement, religious or otherwise). Unless Canadian courts are willing to swallow the principle that vigorous religious disagreement is always inappropriate over the telephone, this kind of case seems one in which the impairment of legitimate expression is very great.

... A problem of more general concern is "hate speech" directed at the dominant white majority. This problem is hardly fanciful; in Great Britain a substantial percentage of "hate speech" prosecutions have been against members of minorities. Much of what the Court says about the pressing concern to suppress hate speech does not apply to hate speech of small minorities against dominant groups. Presumably, whether such speech can constitutionally be punished remains an open question.

How do you think the Canadian justices would respond to these questions? Justice Scalia? Justice Stevens?

8. Professor Greenawalt, at 24–35, 32–33 also drew the following comparisons between U.S. and Canadian approaches:

In contrast to the vast bulk of free speech cases in the United States, the majority and the dissenters agree on the formulation of standards applicable to the problems. The careful and fairly elaborate criteria for section 1 turn out to be less stringent than the rigorous compelling interest test, under which legislation rarely survives, and more stringent than most other American balancing formulas, under which legislation rarely fails. One may expect a paradoxical effect on the stability of doctrine and on results. Because the section 1 approach of Regina v. Oakes, and especially its proportionality components, permit so much to be taken into account, it seems unlikely that justices will find a need to discard the formula, although nuances of difference in the significance of the approach have emerged. However, since future justices will probably feel relatively free to emphasize factors they regard as appropriate, not believing precedent constrains them greatly on the status and weight to be given particular factors, the Court's declaration of the status of some provisions will not be a very sure guide about what a changed Court some years later will decide about other provisions. Particular categories such as prior restraint and content discrimination carry much less importance in Canada than in the United States. The nuanced, contextualized approach encouraged by section 1 can yield relative flexibility of result under relatively stable, open-ended criteria of evaluation....

Free speech law in the United States and Canada is characterized by strong similarities and significant differences. In the free speech cases it has decided under the Charter, the Canadian Supreme Court has mainly put questions in terms of statutory provisions' facial constitutionality. It has not focused on individual situations in the way the U.S. Supreme Court commonly does when deciding whether laws are unconstitutional in their applications to particular facts.... The Canadian Supreme Court is developing a distinctive balancing approach under section 1 and avoids relying as much upon categorical analysis as do U.S. courts. That approach leads it to sustain some measures that would probably be held unconstitutional in the United States.

Both Supreme Courts have an expansive sense of free speech that is based on the centrality of speech for liberal democracy. Typically, Canadian opinions have discussed American cases and commentary, but they decline to import American doctrines as they stand. American decisions have yet to pay much attention to what is happening in Canada, but that time may come.

Professor Greenawalt's comments precede *Butler* and *RJR*. Do those cases confirm or cast doubt on his predictions as to the durability and flexibility of the proportionality test? For other discussions of proportionality tests in comparative public law settings, see Jeffrey Jowell and Anthony Lester, *Proportionality: Neither Novel Nor Dangerous*, in New Directions in Judicial Review 51–72 (J.L. Jowell and Dawn Oliver, eds. 1988); Jeremy Kirk, *Constitutional Guarantees, Characterisation and the Concept of Proportionality*, 21 Melbourne U. L. Rev. 1 (1997); see also Nicholas Emiliou, The Principle of Proportionality in European Law (1996).

C.   FREE SPEECH AND ASSOCIATION WITHOUT A CONSTITUTION? A QUICK LOOK AT THE U.K. AND ISRAEL

Sharfman recounts the Israeli experience with prohibiting organizations. Note the degree to which the arguments and decisions about permitting the existence of organizations that imperil the existence of the state parallel those described in Germany, notwithstanding the absence of a written constitution controlling these questions in Israel at the time. Courtney's description of British hate laws can be read to suggest that courts are invoking quasi-constitutional norms in narrowly construing those provisions, and to raise questions about the efficacy of hate laws in achieving their purposes. Professor Krotoszynski's essay, finally, questions the significance of a written constitution in explaining judicial (or legislative) decisions in the regulation of unpopular speech. (Recall the earlier discussion in Chapter IV of constitutionalism without a constitution, and especially of the Australian campaign law decision.)

1.   ISRAEL

Daphna Sharfman, LIVING WITHOUT A CONSTITUTION: CIVIL RIGHTS IN ISRAEL (1993) (excerpts from ch. 7)

In the period following the establishment of the state, voluntary organizations were perceived as having criminal or dangerous political potential, and the tendency was to exercise tight control over them. However, when these associations no longer appeared to present much danger to state security, control was slackened until it became little more than bureaucratic routine.

The Law of Ottoman Societies

In Israel, noncommercial associations are governed by the Law of Ottoman Societies and the Law of Voluntary Associations that superseded it in 1980. Most of the important cases cited in the present chapter are based on Ottoman law, adopted first by the British mandatory government, and later by Israel under Article 11 of the Government and Courts Ordinance of 1948. With a few minor exceptions, this law is what determines the contemporary approach to freedom of association.

The law prohibits organizations created on the basis of nationality or race (Article 4) and secret associations; the founders of new organizations are obliged to register them with the Israel Ministry of Internal Affairs (Article 6). Associations failing to give notification of their founding are outlawed (Article 12)....

Associations organized by Arab citizens were subjected to closer scrutiny, against the background of the fear of nationalistic organizing; their notifications of new organizations were also submitted to the attorney general for approval. There are very few cases in which the freedom to organize was curtailed for security reasons. Most of them occurred during the 1950s and 1960s. The reference is mainly to limited efforts to organize in various Arab villages, some of which were approved and others rejected.

The most important legal and public debate regarding the freedom to organize occurred in connection with the Al Ard affair. In June 1964, an Arab organization calling itself Al Ard (in Arabic, the land) notified the district commissioner that its organizers wished to register it as an Ottoman society. In enumerating the aims of the association, the founders mentioned the desire to find a just solution to the problem of Palestine, one that would involve maintaining it as a single, undivided entity, in keeping with the desire of the Arab nation, and respecting its interests and aspirations. They called for a return of the independent status of the Palestinian nation, which would ensure its legal right to self-determination.

At the end of June 1964, the Haifa district commissioner wrote to Sabri Jiryis, one of the founders of the association, that since one of its aims endangered the existence of the state of Israel and its integrity, the organization calling itself "Al Ard" was outlawed by Article 3 of the Law of Ottoman Societies, and if the organization was to function despite the prohibition, steps would be taken against its members in accordance with the law.

In his reply to the deputy district commissioner, Jiryis wrote that part 13 of the notification stated a list of general principles according to which the association intended to act to find a solution to the problem of Palestine. In his opinion, this list did not include any declaration or proclamation from which one could deduce that it intended to pose a threat to the existence of the state of Israel or its integrity, and that the founders had no such intentions. The purpose of the statement in question was to find a general solution to the problems between Israel and the Arab world. The founders had not gone into any detail, knowing that the specifics would be determined by the parties involved.

The letter was followed by a petition to the High Court for an *order nisi* against the Haifa district commissioner. The Court rejected the petition. It held that the decision regarding the legality of the aims of the association depended on what was written [in] its charter, and not on explanations and interpretations later offered by the founders. In its judgment, the Court stated that if the government was of the opinion that the lofty language of the Al Ard charter served to conceal subversive aims, it should bring evidence of such aims. Finally, it held that while the freedom to organize was one of the fundamental principles of democracy, no government could provide a remedy to a movement that intended to subvert it. Shortly after the verdict was handed down, the association was declared unlawful by an order of the defense minister. Membership in it was prohibited, and anyone found belonging to it was to be punished.

A few months after the Al Ard judgment, a party calling itself "The Socialist List" attempted to register for the elections to the Sixth Knesset.

Of the ten candidates on the list, five had been members of Al Ard. The Elections Commission refused to approve the list. In his explanation, the chairman, Justice Landau, made the following statement:

> I have no difficulty drawing the line between this list, whose aims were defined in its charter, parts of which were cited in the High Court judgment, and other parties that wish to change the internal workings of constitutional government in the state.

> I see an enormous difference between the two, like the distance between East and West, between a group of persons wishing to subvert the very existence of the state, or at any rate its territorial integrity, and a party recognizing the political integrity of the state but wishing to make internal changes.

The list petitioned the High Court of Justice, but once again, the judgment went against the petitioners. Justices Zussman and Agranat concurred with the decision of the chairman of the Central Elections Commission, and Justice Cohen dissented. The majority opinion stated that it was incumbent on the Knesset to safeguard the existence and integrity of the state of Israel, and that a list of candidates opposing it had no right to take part in Knesset elections. Candidates on the list or its supporters had the right to be elected to the Knesset as individuals, but not as members of a subversive list. The Court could not give a remedy to those who sought the demise of the state.

In a dissenting opinion, Justice Cohen held that the Elections Commission should have approved the list, since it had been submitted in accordance with all the regulations (Article 23 of the Elections to the Knesset Law). Since the Elections Commission was composed of representatives of the existing parties, a situation could arise in which, given a free hand, they might refuse to approve any party that desired a change in the government or the abolition of certain laws. Furthermore, Justice Cohen objected to the application of Article 3 of the Law of Ottoman Societies to the Knesset Elections Law, since the initiators of the list did not constitute an association according to Ottoman law, and the unlawfulness of another association to which the initiators of the list or its candidates had belonged did not give the Commission the authority to reject the list.

Justice Cohen added that the fundamental law of the land offered no directives: the Knesset permitted discrimination of every kind, and there were also Jews who denied the right of the state to exist. In his opinion, it was not likely that the members of Al Ard were acting on the instructions of the enemy. Examining the petition in light of the test of "clear and imminent danger," Justice Cohen was unable to discern any clear or imminent danger to the state or its institutions that might derive from the participation of the list in elections to the Knesset. If there were such a danger, it was obvious only to the security services. The evidence presented to the Court did not justify the assumption that any real danger was involved.

Looking through thousands of files on voluntary associations, one gets the distinct impression that there were very few cases of attempts to organize that appeared to the authorities as problematic from a political point of view. The aims of the great majority of associations appear to be cultural or charitable.

The Law of Voluntary Associations

The Law of Voluntary Associations differs from its predecessor, the Law of Ottoman Societies, mainly with regard to founding procedures. Under the Ottoman law, an association came into being by virtue of agreement, and no permit was required in order to organize. A new association received legal status when its founders notified the district commissioner of its existence. In contrast, the newer law states that an association is not recognized unless it is registered; it becomes a legal entity only if it receives a certificate of registration. At the same time, the law does not prohibit the functioning of associations that have not been duly registered, as the Ottoman law did. Voluntary associations that are not registered with the Ministry of Internal Affairs have no legal status, but their members may appear in court on their behalf, and they may acquire property through the agency of their trustees.

The new law also provides that the Registrar of Voluntary Associations has, under certain conditions, the authority to refuse to register an association (Article 5). Associations must follow certain rules with regard to the administration of their financial affairs.

It should be noted that the desire to retain a free hand when it came to the internal functioning of political parties and labor and employees' unions led legislators to refrain from passing a Political Parties Law that would govern party institutions. Thus party organizations fall under the jurisdiction of the Law of Voluntary Associations. During the Knesset debate on the Law of Voluntary Associations, the large parties joined forces in supporting it, while representatives of the smaller parties opposed the law or parts of it, fearing that it could be utilized to restrict their freedom to organize.

David Glass, former chairman of the Knesset Constitution, Law, and Courts Committee, described the debate that had ensued in committee regarding Article 3 of the proposed law. Some of the members feared that the wording might lead to restraints on the freedom to organize. In order to allay such fears, Minister of Justice Shmuel Tamir suggested changing the wording. The original version read: "A voluntary association shall not be registered if one of its *explicit or implied* aims opposes the basis of the existence of the state of Israel, its security or its democratic nature, or if there is reasonable cause to suspect that the association will serve as a subterfuge for unlawful actions." The proposed version was: "A voluntary association shall not be registered if one of its aims opposes the existence of the state of Israel, or if there is a reasonable basis from which it can be concluded that the association will serve as a subterfuge for unlawful actions or aims."

In a personal interview, Glass stated that the members of the committee had entertained the suspicion that the term "democratic nature" might allow associations to be ruled out for reasons not intended by the legislators. His own position with regard to two organizations whose legality had been challenged in 1984—Meir Kahane's "Kach" on the Right, and the Progressive Peace List on the Left—was unequivocal: both had the right to run:

> Kahane makes my blood boil. In my view, he is the incarnation of all the evil to be found among the Jewish people, a distortion. But at the same time, as long as he does not go beyond expressing opinions and stays within the limits of the law, one has to grit his teeth and [bear] with him. I am not in favor of placing restrictions on the "Kach" movement, because if you start with Kahane, tomorrow it's someone else for another reason ... you start with Kahane and the Progressive List, and tomorrow it will be the Communist party, and day after tomorrow, the Tchia party. It depends on the situation, and then why not Neturei Karta, which openly denies the existence of the state. There's an association that opposes the very existence of the state of Israel.

Dov Shilansky, a member of the Likkud, opposed the new version of the law, suggesting that the words "explicit or implicit" be retained. During the Knesset debate, he argued that no state could afford to register an association that even indirectly opposed its own existence.

In contrast, Mordechai Virshuvsky of the Citizens' Rights party agreed with Glass:

> The administration of a democracy cannot X-ray the heart and kidneys. I say that an association that makes an explicit declaration can be outlawed. If it does not make such a declaration, but rather commits unlawful actions under the guise of the law, there are ways of countering it, if one succeeds in proving the case. Of course, this can cause certain difficulties for the state police and security services, but I believe that the greater these difficulties are, the stronger the democracy.

Minister of Justice Shmuel Tamir, who was strongly opposed to the activities of radical parties, stated in an interview with the writer that in his opinion, such activities should be restricted by a Political Parties Law, but he did not succeed in getting such a law passed.

The Elections Commission refused to allow Kach and the Progressive List for Peace to run in the elections to the Eleventh Knesset in 1984, and the two parties petitioned the High Court of Justice. The Court handed down a judgment in favor of the petitioners, stating that unless a list declared it wished to destroy the state or harm the integrity of its borders, the Court could not reject its pleas on the basis of the test of "bad intent." During the hearing, the Court stated that the decision to reject the lists had been taken by a political body. If that body was to be granted the authority to determine which list was subversive, without legislation to guide it, future lists might be rejected because they represented different interests. (This situation changed when the Knesset passed Amendment 12 to the Knesset Law [Article 7A], which stipulated that a list could not take part in Knesset elections if it denied that Israel was the state of the Jewish people, negated the democratic nature of its regime, incited to racism, or was liable to serve as a subterfuge for unlawful actions.)

The question of the freedom of association of Rabbi Kahane's Kach movement changed the situation with regard to this civil right. Prior to the Kach case, restriction efforts had been limited to leftist organizations, mostly those of Arab citizens.

In April 1981, the minister of defense, using the authority invested in him by the Emergency Regulations, outlawed the National Coordinating Committee, an umbrella organization for nine Arab groups. One of the founders was Mansour Kardosh, who had been a member of Al Ard. The nine organizations themselves were not outlawed. In the 1984 elections, the Progressive List for Peace was supported by some of the same elements that had organized the National Coordinating Committee, as was the Arab Democratic Movement of Abed Alwahab Darawshe in 1988.

It is my opinion that the present liberal stance taken toward organizing efforts on the part of Arab citizens is mainly the result of the fact that the issue has come to be viewed as a political and ideological one rather than as a security matter.

---

2. Britain

Nathan Courtney, *British and United States Hate Speech Legislation: A Comparison*, 19 Brook. J. Int'l L. 727 (1993)

I. Introduction

In both the United States and Great Britain, the last few years have been marked by an increase in the number of racist and anti-Semitic incidents in the workplace, on college campuses, and on the streets. These incidents have been coined instances of "hate speech." The term refers to a broad category of speech which degrades a person or class of people based on a person's race, religion, gender, sexual orientation, or other distinguishing status. Within this larger category, hate speech can be divided into two subdivisions: "speech addressed to the public" and "speech directed at individuals."

Legislatures in both Great Britain and the United States are struggling for ways to address these repugnant episodes while not infringing on cherished notions of free speech. In the Race Relations Act of 1965,[5] Great

---

5. Race Relations Act, 1965, ch. 73, § 6(1) (Eng.). Penalties for a conviction are steep: a maximum of two years' imprison- ment or a fine of £1000, or both. Id. § 6(3). While hatred based upon religion is notice- ably missing from the law, the Public Order

Britain targeted racist hate speech of the first subdivision: "speech addressed to the public." Partly to fulfill its obligations under the United Nations International Convention on the Elimination of All Forms of Racial Discrimination, the British made it illegal for a speaker or a publisher to incite people to racial hatred. Premised on the notion that such public and persuasive speech enabled Nazism to flourish in the 1930s, this law aimed to curtail racist and anti-Semitic propaganda.

More recently, the British targeted hate speech of the second subdivision: "speech directed at individuals." In the Public Order Act, 1986 (POA 1986), Parliament made it illegal to use "threatening, abusive, or insulting words" that cause another "harassment, alarm, or distress." While this law was designed to cover abusive speech in general, it is viewed by the British as another weapon in the fight against racist speech.

The United States has never ratified the International Convention on the Elimination of All Forms of Racial Discrimination and does not have laws which prohibit incitement to racial hatred. Generally, the United States is much more tolerant of racist and other harassing speech than is Great Britain. Unlike the British, the approach in the United States is to deny government the power to "decide what is 'legitimate' speech and what is not." Nonetheless, there have been several recent attempts to legislate in the area of racist speech. . . .

II. Great Britain's Incitement and Harassment Laws

The history of the British incitement and harassment laws can be traced back to the seventeenth-century offense of seditious libel. This law embodied the concept that those who spread hatred of individuals and groups threaten not only those groups but the security of the government itself. As the incitement and harassment laws developed, the protection of government security became less of a goal, but the emphasis remained on those who incited hatred of other groups.

A. Seditious Libel

All of Great Britain's hate speech regulations are premised upon the common law offense of seditious libel. This offense punished the publication of, or the articulation of, words with "an intention to bring into hatred or contempt or to excite disaffection against the person of Her Majesty ..., or to promote feelings of ill-will and hostility between different classes of [her] subjects." Since the law punished "bring[ing] into hatred" or "promot[ing] feelings of ill-will," it targeted the speaker who was persuasive enough to convince others of his contempt for the monarchy or of his hatred of a class of its subjects. This law was not, therefore, directly concerned with the harmful effect that words might have on the Queen or one of her subjects.

Act, 1936 (POA 1936) and its progeny were all used to punish anti-Semitic propaganda.

Patricia M. Leopold, *Incitement to Racial Hatred*, 1977 PUB.L. 389, 392.

Although the law was used primarily to punish those who posed a threat to the monarchy, on several occasions it was also used to punish what would today be recognized as hate speech. R. v. Osborne [1732] concerned the publishers of a pamphlet which asserted that certain Jewish immigrants living in London had killed a woman and her child because the father of the child was a Christian. Following the distribution of the pamphlet, several of the Jews named were beaten and were threatened with death if they did not depart London. The publishers of the anti-Semitic pamphlet were found guilty of seditious libel.

Since the turn of the century, prosecutions for seditious libel have rarely succeeded. One of the reasons for the law's ineffectiveness is that, under the common law, the defendant was only guilty if his or her speech led to a direct incitement to violence or public disorder. . . .

B. The Public Order Act, 1936

In order to address the inadequacies of the sedition laws, in 1936 Parliament passed section 5 of the Public Order Act, 1936 (POA 1936). Like the sedition laws, punishment under the POA 1936 required a nexus between speech and violence. The law provided the following:

> Any person in any public place or at a public meeting to use threatening, abusive or insulting words or behaviour with intent to provoke a breach of the peace or whereby a breach of the peace is likely to be occasioned shall be guilty of an offense.

A plain reading of the POA 1936 reveals two notable changes from the sedition laws. First, speech could be punished even if it did not provoke actual violence as long as it was "likely" to provoke such violence. Second, mere intent to provoke violence could be punished.

Section 5 proved useful in controlling the rise of British fascism prior to and during World War II. Police, in disguise, would attend meetings of the British Union of Fascists where they recorded insulting words that were later used in the prosecution of the group's prominent leaders. "The result was a definite modification of [f]ascist propaganda with less provocation to Jews and other anti-[f]ascists."

In *Jordan v. Burgoyne* [2 All E.R. 225 (Q.B. 1963)] a leader of the National Socialist Movement was charged with violating section 5 after making various anti-Semitic remarks while addressing a meeting in Trafalgar Square. Addressing a sizeable crowd of both supporters and hecklers, he proclaimed that, "Hitler was right, . . . our real enemies, the people we should have fought, were not Hitler and the national socialists of Germany but world Jewry and its associates in this country." At trial, a "reasonable man" argument was used to acquit Jordan: the judge held that his words "were not likely to lead ordinary reasonable persons attending the meeting . . . to commit breaches of the peace. . . ." On appeal, however, Lord Parker, C.J. of the Divisional Court, rejected the "reasonable man" approach and concluded that Jordan "must take his audience as he finds them." Since Jordan's speech resulted in "complete disorder" among his audience, he was convicted of violating section 5 of the POA 1936.

As time went on, British officials found the incitement laws to be an insufficient obstacle to racist speech making. In the mid-1960s the ultra right wing National Front (NF) began achieving widespread support among the British lower and middle class. The group's popularity can be traced to the widespread resentment over the immigration of people of color from Commonwealth countries. In their efforts to gain further support, many NF leaders who campaigned for seats in Parliament made insulting comments about the new immigrants.

Since the NF had shifted its focus from disturbing the peace to gaining electoral support, it abandoned its usual calls to violence. The group was primarily concerned with persuading others of its particular brand of racism in order to win votes. Since section 5 of the POA 1936 did not address speech that lacked threats of violence or resulted in violence, many of the members' speeches went unpunished.

In the face of increasing numbers of racist and fascist speeches, elected officials came under pressure to legislate against these types of less virulent hate speech. Thus, in order to curtail racist speech that did not directly incite people to violence, Britain's laws under the Race Relations Acts of 1965 and 1976 prohibited speech that merely incited people to hatred of racial groups. Like seditious libel and section 5 of the POA 1936, these laws did not directly protect the individual who was the victim of abusive racist speech; rather, they focused on the speaker who was likely to persuade others of his or her racist views.

C.   The Race Relations Act, 1965

Great Britain was not alone in its call for laws that punished racist propaganda. In 1963 the General Assembly of the United Nations adopted the Declaration on the Elimination of All Forms of Racial Discrimination to respond to an increase in the appearance of swastikas around the world. As a party to the ensuing International Convention on the Elimination of All Forms of Racial Discrimination, Great Britain agreed to "declare an offense punishable by law all dissemination of ideas based on racial superiority or hatred...."[33]

In 1965 Parliament passed section 6 of The Race Relations Act, 1965 (RRA 1965). Under section 6, a person is guilty of incitement to racial hatred if

> with intent to stir up hatred against any section of the public in Great Britain distinguished by colour, race or ethnic or national origins: (a) he publishes or distributes written matter which is threatening, abusive or insulting; or (b) he uses in any public place or at any public

---

33.   ... Under article 20 of the International Covenant on Civil and Political Rights, Dec. 19, 1966, art. 20, 999 U.N.T.S. 171, 178, Great Britain was already obligated to under-take the necessary steps to prohibit "any advocacy of national, racial or religious hatred that constitutes incitement to discrimination, hostility or violence."

meeting words which are threatening, abusive or insulting, being matter or words likely to stir up hatred against that section on grounds of colour, race or ethnic or national origin.

Section 6 of RRA 1965 is notable in several respects: first, it reverts back to the seditious libel standard in that it requires that the speaker have the "intent" to stir up hatred; second, it punishes only the cruder forms of speech; third, it targets only public racist commentary; and, finally, the use of the law to combat racist speech requires the consent of the Attorney General.

1. Intent to Stir Up Hatred

The new intent requirement made it very difficult for the Crown to win convictions under the RRA 1965. The inherent difficulty in proving that someone intends to stir up racial hatred was illustrated in a case involving the prosecution of four members of the Racial Preservation Society for their publishing of a newspaper entitled *Southern News*. The newspaper declared as its goal the "return of people of other races from this 'overcrowded island' to 'their own countries.'" In defending against the claim that they intended to incite racial hatred, the authors argued that their newspaper had educational value as a means for addressing important social issues. Because the prosecutors were unable to prove that the defendants had the intention to instill in the populace any hatred of immigrants, the authors were acquitted.

The failure to convict the publishers of the *Southern News* highlights one of the dangers lurking behind the incitement laws. The failed prosecution gave "a measure of respectability to racialists and their organisations.... After the unsuccessful prosecution in the Southern News case, there was an increase in that type of quasi-educational racialist literature." [citing Patricia M. Leopold] Moreover, the case gave immense news coverage to an otherwise insignificant newspaper. Indeed, upon acquittal, the authors reprinted the issue of *Southern News* that was the subject of the case and sold it as a "Souvenir Edition—The Paper the Government Tried to Suppress."

2. Cruder Forms of Speech

Section 6(a) of the RRA 1965 targets the same type of speech ("threatening, abusive or insulting") that was proscribed under the POA 1936. Thus, the law applies only to the cruder forms of racist expression. As the cases bear out, the "crudeness" of particular words varies over time.[42] The

---

42. John Kingsley Read was tried in January 1978 for telling an audience that he was under a court injunction prohibiting slurs against colored immigrants and, therefore, would talk about "niggers, wogs, and coons." [Aryeh Neier, Defending My Enemy 155 (1979)]. Read also spoke of the death of a young Asian, saying, "[o]ne down one million to go." Read was acquitted by an all-white jury after the judge instructed the jury that the term "nigger" was harmless. When he attended schools in Australia, the judge explained, he was nicknamed "nigger" because "he sang songs in an aboriginal language. Spectators in the courtroom greeted the acquittal with applause." Neier, [at 155.] Geof-

first conviction under section 6 came in 1967 against Colin Jordan, the aforementioned leader of the National Socialist Movement who had been convicted under the POA 1936. Jordan had been arrested after publishing and distributing a pamphlet entitled *The Coloured Invasion* in which he asserted that "[t]he presence of this [c]oloured million in our midst is a menace to our nation." Jordan was sentenced to eighteen months imprisonment.

Racist groups have been able to avoid operation of the incitement laws by "expressing their views without overt threats, abuse or insults."... In 1967 Colin Jordan served eighteen months for publishing *The Coloured Invasion*; whereas, in 1968, the authors of *Southern News* went unpunished for calling for the "return of people of other races from this 'overcrowded island' to 'their own countries.'" Both of these editorials conveyed the same message, yet the publishers of the more recent publication went unpunished.

3. Public Occasions

Section 6 of the RRA 1965 maintains the same focus on public hate speech that was established in the original common law offense of seditious libel. Thus the law applies only to written materials or words spoken on a public occasion. One-on-one instances of racial harassment, therefore, are not covered by the law. The emphasis on public speech shows that the goal of the statute is not to protect the feelings of those against whom racism is directed. Instead, the focus is on the "speech's likely effect on its presumed consumers—those most likely to be persuaded by it."

This emphasis is consistent with the UN's attempt to deal with Nazi-like propaganda.[50] Indeed, when proposing the bill to the House of Commons, the Home Secretary explained that section 6 was "designed to deal with more dangerous, persistent and insidious forms of propaganda campaigns—the campaign which, over a period of time, engenders hate which

---

frey Bindman, What Happened to Racial Incitement, 87 LAW SOC'Y GAZETTE 25 (1990).

In a modern example of the same type of speech, Bill Galbraith, a Cheltenham businessman who called a black Conservative parliamentary candidate, John Taylor, a "bloody nigger," "is to face prosecution for alleged incitement to racial hatred." Peter Vidor, Race Hatred Case Filed Against Cheltenham Tory, THE TIMES (London), Apr. 13, 1991, at 3.

50. See R. v. Relf & Cole, 1 Crim.App. (S) 111, 114 (1979) (Eng.). In this case, Relf and Cole were sentenced to prison for having published leaflets containing derogatory comments made toward members of the West Indian London community. One such leaflet was entitled "Notice Wog Nuisance" and read, "[o]wing to an increase in the nuisance caused by unsupervised wogs on this estate, a wog warden has been engaged, and wogs not wearing a collar bearing the owner's name and address, will be taken to Leamington Police Station." Another leaflet was entitled "Jungle News" and stated that London had suffered "400 crimes a month by a gang of muggers." To justify the prison sentence, Judge Lawton compared Relf and Cole's pamphlets to Nazi propaganda. While comparing the "lies" found in "Jungle News" to the repetition of lies concerning Jews in Nazi Germany, he remarked that, "the constant repetition of lies might in the end lead some people into thinking that the lies are true."

begets violence." Congruous with this emphasis, the prosecution of seventeen-year-old Christopher Britton failed. Britton, a "wretched little youth," had placed racialist bulletins ("Blacks Not Wanted Here") at the front door of a member of Parliament, and wrapped one of them around a beer bottle which he then hurled through the official's glass front door. The Court of Appeal, Criminal Division, held that a member of Parliament did not constitute a member of the "public at large" as described in section 6(a). Lord Parker, C.J. went on to note that he did not believe that Parliament envisioned the prosecution of such small scale offenders, even if Britton's actions were technically violative of section 6.

While the emphasis in section 6 on speech addressed to the public prevents prosecutors from wasting time on insignificant cases,[56] this emphasis also has its detrimental aspects. For instance, several section 6 prosecutions have involved speeches made at Speakers' Corner in Hyde Park. This part of the park is world-renowned as a place to hear soapbox orators speak on a wide variety of issues of public interest. Because of the importance of Speakers' Corner as a symbol of free speech, it is a momentous occasion when someone is arrested there simply for speaking.

4. Consent of the Attorney General

To counter criticisms that section 6 would constitute an unjust infringement on free speech, the law requires that no prosecution be brought without the Attorney General's consent. This requirement was thought to serve two functions. First, in order to avoid biased prosecutions, section 6(3) takes the matter out of the jurisdiction of the local police. Second, the law rules out potentially frivolous private civil claims of incitement.

In some cases, the Attorney General has failed in its charge to prevent biased prosecutions. In the late 1960s, for instance, there were several notable prosecutions of leaders of the Black Liberation Movement. In one case, Michael Abdul Malik (Michael X) was sentenced to twelve months in prison for having asserted that whites are "vicious and nasty people."[62] At trial Michael X agreed that his speech was offensive to whites, but claimed

---

56. In the first year after the 1976 amendment, many of the defendants facing charges of incitement were youths. Roger Cotterrell, Prosecuting Incitement to Racial Hatred, 1982 PUB.L 378, (citing Paul Gordon, Incitement to Racial Hatred (1982)). Many of the defendants are young first-time offenders for whom it is difficult to distinguish "determined political action from mere delinquency."

62. ... During his speech, Michael X went on to say,

> Killing is a strange thing. Before I killed for the first time I wondered if I would have a conscience. But I slept well. And now I am no longer afraid.

I saw in this country in 1952 white savages kicking black women. If ever you see a white man lay hands on a black woman, kill him immediately. If you love our brothers and sisters you will be willing to die for them.

Bitter Attack on Whites, The Times (London), July 25, 1986, at 1. By calling on his followers to kill, Michael X's speech bordered on incitement to violence. Under U.S. law, such speech would not be punishable unless it was intended to incite imminent lawless action and the advocacy was likely to result in such action.

that he should have the right to respond to "certain things that have happened to us as a people."

In another case, four prominent members of the Universal Coloured People's Association who made speeches at Speakers' Corner, Hyde Park were also convicted of incitement to racial hatred. The defendants had called on black nurses to give white patients the wrong injections.[65] In his defense at trial, one of the defendants claimed that "[h]e was merely expressing the frustration of coloured people and was not contravening the Race Relations Act." It would appear, therefore, that some political speech has been suppressed under the guise of incitement to racial hatred.

The consent requirement has also resulted in the underuse of the law. From 1965 to 1976, the Attorney General gave his consent to prosecute only twenty-one people for alleged offenses under section 6 of the Race Relations Act. Considering that 106 complaints were sent to the office, it would appear that the Attorney General did not consider the incitement laws to be a top priority.

D.   The Race Relations Act, 1976

In an effort to make prosecutions for incitement easier, section 70 of the Race Relations Act, 1976 (RRA 1976) discarded the intent requirement. Thus, convictions could be based upon the mere proof that the speech or publication of "threatening, abusive, or insulting" words was likely to stir up hatred against "any racial group in Great Britain." This change in the law was designed, in part, to address the difficulty in gaining a conviction in the *Southern News* case.

With the passage of RRA 1976, the prosecution no longer had to prove that the defendant had the intent to stir up hatred. Rather, the defendant's intent was inferred from the fact that he had used insulting speech. In *R. v. Knight* the defendant admitted to having published a racist pamphlet, but stated that he had abandoned any plans to distribute it. Even though the pamphlets remained boxed up in Knight's apartment, the trial judge obviously inferred Knight's intent to incite to racial hatred. Faced with such a certain outcome, Knight pleaded guilty to a charge of publishing a racist pamphlet in violation of RRA 1976.

The liberalization of the law proved useful in helping prosecutors to win most of the cases that went to trial under the incitement laws. Many of these involved the publishing of similar types of racist pamphlets. In *R. v. Edwards*, an editor was convicted of violating the RRA 1976 for having published *The Stormer*, which contained several comic strips including

---

65. *Sentences Today on Four Coloured Men*, The Times (London), Nov. 29, 1967, at 3. In the United States, in Watts v. United States, a black draft resister asserted that "[i]f they ever make me carry a rifle, the first man I want to get in my sights is L.B.J." 394 U.S. 705, 706 (1969). Considering the context of the speech (made at an anti-war rally) and the laughter that followed the statement, the Supreme Court rejected the contention that the speaker's words posed a true threat. Rather, the Court held that the speech was "a kind of very crude offensive method of stating a political opposition to the President."

"Billy the Yid," and "Ali the Paki." The former described the alleged "ritualistic practice of Jews in crucifying Christian boys in order to use their blood for their meals." Convinced that the pamphlet was "clearly one which incited readers to racial hatred," the trial judge sentenced Edwards to twelve months imprisonment.

Despite the new ease with which convictions could be won, the Attorney General consent requirement still hampered the realization of the incitement law's potential. In the period between 1976 and 1981, only twenty-one defendants faced trial on charges of racial incitement. Even with the relaxation of the government's burden, there were few prosecutions considering the rise in racial strife and violence during that period.

E. Public Order Act, 1986

1. Incitement to Racial Hatred

In a further effort to strengthen the incitement laws, Parliament passed Part III of the Public Order Act 1986 (POA 1986). Most importantly, the law invokes standards originally introduced in the POA 1936. Under section 18, the "use of threatening, abusive, or insulting words" is an offense if the speaker: a) intends thereby to stir up racial hatred, or b) having regard to all the circumstances racial hatred is likely to be stirred up thereby. Now, a person can be punished for either the intent to stir up racial hatred or for using words likely to stir up hatred.

. . . [A] compromise measure created new procedures for investigating instances of racial incitement. Under the old measures, an initial police determination was sent directly to the Attorney General for consideration. Under the POA of 1986, the local police send their determination up through the hierarchy of the Crown Prosecution Service where further investigations may be undertaken. Perhaps it was thought that with these further investigations, a stronger case would be presented to the Attorney General and, therefore, there would be a greater likelihood that the case would get the Attorney General's consent. One danger of the new procedures, however, is that they create more levels at which the police may decide to forego prosecution before the case even reaches the Attorney General.

For unknown reasons, there have been only three prosecutions for incitement to racial hatred since passage of the POA 1986. The first prosecution took place in 1988 and resulted in a suspended sentence for a "soapbox orator" who had made a racist speech and had distributed racist literature. The second prosecution, also in 1988, resulted in the conviction of a neo-Nazi who posted anti-Semitic stickers on lamp-posts. As of the end of 1990, sixteen more cases were being investigated by the police for possible prosecution. . . .

2. Harassment

With a completely different focus, Parliament, in 1986, also made punishable verbal or symbolic speech that was intended and likely to harass another person. Under the POA 1986 section 5,

(1) [a] person is guilty of an offense if he

(a) uses threatening, abusive or insulting words or behaviour, or disorderly behaviour, or

(b) displays any writing, sign or other visible representation which is threatening, abusive or insulting within the hearing or sight of a person likely to be caused harassment, alarm, or distress thereby.

And section 6 provides:

(4) A conviction under this section requires that the accused is aware that [the speech or conduct] may be threatening, abusive, or insulting.

Although the new law prohibits the same type of speech as the incitement laws (threatening, abusive or insulting), the law addresses hateful speech used in a very different context. Unlike the bans on incitement to hatred, which seek to reduce persuasive speech, this new law targets hate speech that is directed at a particular individual. Thus, the law focuses on the effect that speech has on the individual victim of abusive speech. . . .

In *DPP v. Clarke*, Lord Justice Nolan refused to convict Michael Edward Clarke of harassment because it was not proven that he subjectively intended to harass the complainants. Clarke was accused of harassment for having carried a picture of an aborted fetus while protesting outside of a licensed abortion clinic. The prosecution argued that Clarke must have been aware that his conduct would harass the clients at the clinic. The judge rejected an objective test that would have inferred Clarke's intent to harass from the circumstances of the protest. According to Lord Justice Nolan, the words "is aware that it may be threatening, abusive, or insulting" in section 6(4) demanded nothing less than an inquiry into the subjective intent of the defendant.

To date, the harassment statute has only been used to prosecute persons who assault traditional standards of public decency. In one case, the defendant was convicted for harassment of a police officer during an arrest. Other cases have been brought against men for kissing in the street and against abortion activists who display fetuses at demonstrations.

Section 5 has the potential for punishing racist speech that is not covered by the incitement laws. It is hard to predict at this early stage what types of conduct or speech will be the focus of the Crown's prosecutions. However, Lord Justice Taylor has expressed a willingness to convict soccer spectators who subject non-white players to "obscenities." . . .

III.   Regulation of Hate Speech in the United States

Legislative bodies and courts in the United States are much more tolerant of hate speech than their counterparts in Great Britain. In fact, the First Amendment was created in direct response to the British sedition laws which made criticism of the government illegal. While a few categories of speech including obscenity, defamation, and fighting words may be regulated because of their constitutionally proscribable content, the United States Supreme Court has used the First Amendment to strike a number of federal and state restrictions on speech that would fall under the definition of "hate speech."

Given the current state of First Amendment law, therefore, it is unlikely that the United States Senate will ratify the UN Convention on the Elimination of all Forms of Racial Discrimination. Although the United States signed the Convention, it did so with the following caveat:

> The Constitution of the United States contains provisions for the protection of individual rights, such as the right of free speech, and nothing in the Convention shall be deemed to require or to authorize legislation or other action by the United States of America incompatible with the provisions of the Constitution of the United State of America.

Congress has never ratified the Convention because of article 4 of the Convention. As described above, article 4 would require the United States to "declare an offense punishable by law all dissemination of ideas based on racial superiority or hatred." . . .

IV. Applicability of British Laws in the United States

Much of the debate on United States hate speech legislation is argued in the abstract. Judges, scholars, and legislators involved in this subject spend considerable time predicting the consequences of such legislation in order to determine whether any law marks the top of the "slippery slope." Fortunately, we have the opportunity to learn from the mistakes of the British as we decide whether to adopt a given measure. The following sections will address the overall benefits and disadvantages of the incitement and the harassment laws and their individual constitutionality were they adopted in the United States.

A. Incitement to Racial Hatred

1. *Value of the Law in Great Britain*

The incitement laws have had a marginal effect on racism in Great Britain. According to Robert Moore, a professor at Liverpool University, "Blacks continue to be the victims of prejudice in housing and employment, and threatened by racially motivated violence. . . . Black people remain just as trapped in the lowest-paid, most unpleasant jobs, and the least desirable homes and areas as were their immigrant parents and grandparents." Similar conclusions for the continued prevalence of anti-Semitism have been made. For instance, one study notes that racist motivated violence increased by twenty-five percent from 1989 to 1990; for the same period, anti-Semitic incidents rose by fifty percent.

On the other hand, one development over the last ten years in Great Britain is that "organised [sic] British fascist politics have all but collapsed." Arguably, the incitement laws are partially responsible for the demise of these groups. Certainly, the law kept leaders of the National

Socialist Movement and the British Nationalist Party in prison at the peak of their careers.

However, these groups flourished during much of the twenty-five year period that these laws have been in effect. During the first ten years immediately after the inception of the RRA 1965, Great Britain actually saw an increase in the "number of National Front outdoor meetings." In the Greater London council elections of 1977, the "National Front won 119,000 votes, or 5.5 percent of the total votes cast."

Although the old fascist parties may be virtually non-existent, there are signs that organized neo-Nazism is on the rise both in Great Britain and in the rest of Europe. According to Geoffrey Alderman, a University of London Professor of History, sporadic incidents of fascism and the popularity of more organized groups have been increasing in Great Britain in the last few years. Moreover, "there has been a clear increase in the amount of anti-semitic literature in circulation."

Many weaknesses of the incitement laws may have been responsible for the continued existence of racist and fascist activity since the laws were developed in 1965. As discussed above, for instance, many racist speakers and publishers were able to elude prosecution by avoiding the "threatening, abusive, or insulting" words proscribed in the incitement laws. By referring to the problems of immigration rather than the "Coloured Invasion," some speakers were able to continue to spread their racist views. Indeed, "[c]ode words are easily substituted for explicit references to race."

Other factors surrounding the cases that went to trial may have actually benefited the defendants. For instance, the trials produced publicity for little known groups and publications that might have otherwise gone unnoticed. In addition, the prosecutions that resulted in convictions also created martyrs for the cause of national socialism.

At a time when incidents of racism are on the rise, it is interesting to note that some black leaders are calling for a repeal of the incitement laws. Nigel Fraser, a member of the Society for Black Lawyers, describe the incitement and other Race Relations laws as "cosmetic" and ineffective in fighting the root causes of racism. He and his colleagues argue that "prejudice is a disease too deep-seated to be eradicated by statute."

Considering the marginal success that the incitement laws have had in Great Britain, there is no reason to introduce them in the United States. If the laws have achieved anything, they may have helped reduce the popularity of organized fascist and racist groups and they may have reduced the prevalence of racist newspapers and pamphlets. However, in the United States, the National Socialist Party and the KKK have not been major forces since the 1960s and racist newsletters are not nearly as prevalent in the United States as they are in Great Britain.

2.   *Problems of Enforcement*

The consent of the Attorney General requirement has created two problems that have prevented the incitement laws from realizing their potential in fighting racism. The first problem may be described as a slippery slope dilemma: the incitement laws have been used on occasions that arguably hinder their original goals. Second, the Attorney General has failed to give his consent to prosecute what, to many, seem to be blatant examples of racist speech. . . .

Great Britain's incitement laws, though enacted for laudable reasons, have been used to silence those they were seeking to protect. As described above, the prosecution of Michael Abdul Malik put a prominent leader of black nationalism in prison for eighteen months. Though he was arguably preaching hatred of white people, he also was expressing the fundamentally political message that blacks were not being treated fairly in British society. Because Great Britain claims to be a democracy, his speech was owed more protection. Yet, in a society which has not yet gained a consensus on whether it is possible to be black and British, it seems inevitable that a law as broadly written as the incitement law would be used to prosecute minority group members.

The second problem with the Attorney General consent requirement may also have political overtones: the government has foregone the prosecution of incidents of racist speech. Both the Board of Deputies of British Jews and the Commission for Racial Equality have repeatedly criticized the Attorney General's office for refusing to prosecute certain cases. While these groups sometimes have been able to pressure the government to increase the number of prosecutions for incitement, groups which are not typically served by these organizations have no redress. . . .

Considering the problems the British have had in enforcing these laws, the United States should forego adopting them. Consider, for the moment, if such a law were on the books in Louisiana and David Duke had been elected its governor. The broad terms "hatred" and "incite" have the potential of being used against what most people of the United States would consider to be valid political protest, but someone such as David Duke would consider un-American. . . .

Ronald J. Krotoszynski, Jr., *Brind and Rust v. Sullivan: Free Speech and the Limits of a Written Constitution*, 22 Fl. St. U. L. Rev. 1 (1994)

I. Introduction

The existence of a written constitution is thought by some to place certain rights, obligations, and duties in a preferred place within a nation's legal constellation. Thus, the existence of the First Amendment, with an express guarantee of speech and press rights, should provide (at least nominally) greater protection for those liberties than would otherwise exist in the absence of such a provision. Quite often, this seemingly unobjectionable proposition holds true.

However, the proposition is not as self-evident as one might assume. Counter examples do exist. The presence of a written constitutional guarantee of a particular right does not automatically mean that courts will afford the right greater solicitude, and the absence of a written constitutional provision does not preclude the protection of a particular liberty.

This is not to suggest that the absence of a specific textual provision protecting freedom of speech and the press has no affect on the disposition of cases raising such claims. The point is more limited—the presence or absence of a textual guarantee of speech and press rights is not as sure a predictor of actual outcomes as one might expect....

In February 1991, in *Regina v. Secretary of State for the Home Dep't, Ex parte Brind*, the British House of Lords[18] upheld a ban on broadcasts featuring in-person appearances by representatives of several designated political affiliates of allegedly terrorist organizations. The ban went into effect in 1988, pursuant to an administrative order issued by then-Home Secretary Douglas Hurd....

In *Brind*, the House of Lords, sitting as a court of law in a nation with no written constitution, appeared to import a "compelling state interest" test into a routine review of an administrative regulation, all in the name of protecting the "fundamental right" of free speech. More or less concurrently, the United States Supreme Court, hearing an appeal challenging the legality of a federal regulation, declined to apply seemingly well-settled First Amendment law, and in the process weakened both the scope and strength of the First Amendment.[17] Given these developments, one could reasonably challenge the proposition that written foundational documents are either a prerequisite to or a guarantor of personal liberties in general, or free speech in particular....

II.   *Brind* and *Rust*: Similar Cases, Similar Results ...

A.   *Brind*: Incorporating Free Speech Values Absent a Constitutional Mandate

England, unlike the United States, has no written constitution. Consequently, the English courts do not possess a direct textual command to consider free speech claims. The absence of a written constitution containing a guarantee of free speech no doubt is in part responsible for the English judiciary's failure to vindicate free speech and free press claims routinely. However, this explanation may be a bit too facile.

1.   Free Speech as a Canon of Statutory Interpretation and as a Restraint on Administrative Discretion

In Great Britain, the citizen's interest in free speech stems from community tradition rather than legal fiat. Although there is no written

---

18. [relocated] A "law lord" is a member of the House of Lords who is appointed for life (he or she is not necessarily a member of the peerage) and who sits in decision over the appeals taken from the lower British courts. The House of Lords, as a whole, does not sit to decide cases. Rather, the small cadre of law lords discharge this function. P.S. ATIYAH & ROBERT S. SUMMERS, FORM AND SUBSTANCE IN ANGLO-AMERICAN LAW 269 (1987).

17. See *Rust v. Sullivan*, 111 S.Ct. 1759, 1771–76 (1991).

provision of law securing a "right" of free speech in British domestic law, the English judiciary has demonstrated a willingness to address free speech claims substantively. Thus, the casual observer would be mistaken if, upon discovering the absence of a written guarantee of free speech, he immediately drew the conclusion that freedom of speech as an autonomy interest lacks currency.

The absence of a textual provision undoubtedly circumscribes the British judiciary's ability to vindicate speech interests. Historically the British courts have deferred to Parliamentary acts regardless of the judiciary's appraisal of the wisdom of Parliament's action. Consistent with the doctrine of Parliamentary supremacy, the British judiciary does not possess the constitutional authority to reject an act of Parliament, so long as Parliament promulgated the act properly. Judicial review, in the strong United States form, simply does not exist in Britain. Thus, the British judiciary, in the absence of a Parliamentary command to vindicate speech rights, is limited to considering the tradition of favoring speech rights only at the margins—for example, as a consideration in issues involving statutory interpretation.

Any analysis of the strength of free speech interests in English law must begin with the frank recognition that if Parliament acts clearly and unambiguously, a claim of privilege under some notion of free speech will fail in the British domestic courts. This illustrates the most obvious effect of a textual speech clause: such provisions legitimate—and often necessitate—judicial review of legislative enactments for consistency with the asserted speech right. At the outset, then, this Article concedes that the absence of an analog to the First Amendment in British domestic law substantially restricts the ability of the British judiciary to consider free speech claims on the merits. In the vast majority of cases, any claim that an act of Parliament unduly infringes legitimate speech rights must be heard (if at all) by the European Court of Human Rights in Strasborg, France.

However, there are exceptions to this general proposition. First, if an act of Parliament is ambiguous, the British courts are free to interpret the act consistently with the European Convention on Human Rights and Fundamental Freedoms (ECHR). The ECHR contains a free speech provision, which may be raised in the British domestic courts as a textual basis for the vindication of free speech claims. Thus, when a statutory provision is ambiguous, British courts will have recourse to Article 10 of the ECHR to help determine the proper meaning of the provision. . . .

The British judiciary possesses the power to consider speech claims in another context: review of administrative regulations. Parliamentary acts sometimes require implementing regulations, and those regulations are subject to judicial review. . . .

When reviewing the exercise of administrative discretion, recourse to the ECHR is not mandatory. Thus, unlike cases in which a court engages in statutory interpretation—in such circumstances the British domestic courts must have recourse to the ECHR to resolve statutory ambiguities—recourse to the ECHR is entirely within the discretion of the administrative decisionmaker. In consequence, when a British court reviews an administrative regulation, there is no textual source for the protection of speech rights on which the reviewing court may rely. Nevertheless, the British judiciary has seemingly incorporated free speech values into its review of administrative regulations.

2. *Brind and Judicially Created Speech Interests*

In *Brind*, the British judiciary had to decide whether an administrative regulation proscribing the in-person broadcast of any message by an official representative of certain allegedly terrorist political organizations[48] exceeded the lawful authority of the government minister who promulgated the regulations. . . .

Consistent with the terms of the directive, the broadcast media can report the words of an official representative of a proscribed organization; indeed, using actors, they may even recreate the statement. The directive thus erects a prior restraint against the broadcasting of statements by certain persons, unless the statements were made incident to an election or are part of a fictional work.

The House of Lords' standard of review for the Home Secretary's action was quite modest: the sole question before the court was whether a reasonable administrator could reasonably have promulgated the regulation at issue. The House of Lords does not exercise plenary review of an administrator's choice among policy options; rather, the Lords are limited to reviewing a decision to ensure that it was not wholly arbitrary. Lord Ackner explained that unlike run-of-the-mill legal cases in which the courts exercise "appellate" jurisdiction, that is, the power to review a trial court's decision on the merits without regard to the lower court's disposition of the legal issues, the court's review of an administrator's exercise of discretion is merely "supervisory."

Despite the court's admittedly modest scope of review, four of the five law lords hearing the case strongly suggested in dicta that they would reject a regulation regulating speech more aggressively; a more stringent regulation of speech would be sufficiently "perverse" to fail the "reasonableness" test.

Among the law lords, Lord Bridge is the strongest proponent of free speech as a normative value in the process of judicial review of the exercise of discretionary administrative authority. After noting that the court lacked authority to consider whether the regulation was consistent with Article 10

---

48. Including Sinn Fein, Republican Sinn Fein, and the Ulster Defence Association, *Brind*, [1991] 1 App.Cas. at 755. Sinn Fein and Republican Sinn Fein are organizations committed to the reunification of Ireland, and historically have not proven averse to the use of force in their attempts to further this objective. The Ulster Defence Association is committed to the continued unification of Northern Ireland with the United Kingdom, and has proven itself equally receptive to the use of force. See generally David Remnick, *A Reporter At Large: Belfast Confetti*, NEW YORKER, Apr. 25, 1994, at 58 (discussing the shared propensity for terrorist violence on the part of republican and unionist paramilitary groups in Northern Ireland).

of the ECHR, Lord Bridge explained that "[I] do not accept that this conclusion means that the courts are powerless to prevent the exercise by the executive of administrative discretions, even when conferred, as in the instant case, in terms which are on their face unlimited, in a way which infringes fundamental human rights." He continued:

> In exercising the power of judicial review we have neither the advantages nor the disadvantages of any comparable code [referring to the ECHR] to which we may refer or by which we are bound. But again, this surely does not mean that in deciding whether the Secretary of State, in the exercise of his discretion, could reasonably impose the restriction he has imposed on the broadcasting organisations, *we are not perfectly entitled to start from the premise that any restriction of the right to freedom of expression requires to be justified and that nothing less than an important competing public interest will be sufficient to justify it.*

Lord Bridge observed that the "primary judgment as to whether the particular competing public interest justifies the particular restriction imposed" is within the administrative decisionmaker's province. However, the British courts "are entitled to exercise a secondary judgment by asking whether a reasonable Secretary of State, on the material before him, could reasonably make that primary judgment." Applying the test he proposed, Lord Bridge, joined by Lord Roskill, concluded that the restriction at issue furthered an important public interest, and that a reasonable administrator therefore could adopt the regulation.

Although ostensibly cabined within the confines of the "reasonable administrator/reasonable conclusion" test, Lord Bridge's opinion promulgates a relatively stout framework for applying that test: "an important competing public interest" is necessary to justify "any restriction" on "the right to freedom of expression." This test sounds somewhat like the Supreme Court's "compelling state interest" test, used in cases such as Boos v. Barry. To be sure, Lord Bridge's "important competing public interest" test appears to be at least marginally less protective than the "compelling state interest" test, insofar as "compelling" connotes a sense of urgency not inherent in the words "important competing." Regardless of the relative strength of the test, Lord Bridge's opinion is significant because it demonstrates that absent any written document providing a textual basis for the protection of speech interests, a law lord is prepared to promulgate de novo a standard for the protection of speech interests, and moreover, a standard with potential bite.

Lord Bridge and Lord Roskill were not the only members of the *Brind* panel who gave voice to concerns over the protection of free speech. Lord Templeman expressed what Lord Bridge merely implied: "My Lords, freedom of expression is a principle of every written and unwritten democratic constitution." Lord Templeman ultimately concluded that "the interference with freedom of expression" caused by the regulation was "minimal" and that "the reasons given by the Home Secretary [were] compelling." Like Lord Bridge, Lord Templeman decried engaging in judicial review beyond ensuring that the "reasonable administrator/reasonable decision" standard has been satisfied. However, according to Lord Templeman, the context in which the reasonableness analysis occurs must take account of the value British society places on free expression.

Lord Lowry's opinion also reflected concern for the protection of free expression:

> [T]he inspiration for the applicants' argument, if not perhaps the facts on which the argument is based, is closely linked with the principle of freedom of speech in a democratic society, so far as compatible with the safety of the state and the well-being of its citizens, which may provide a reason for me to say something.

Lord Lowry concluded that the restrictions at issue imposed at most a "modest" burden on freedom of expression. However, he emphasized that "administrative acts" which severely burdened free expression "might well be justified, but they would certainly deserve the closest scrutiny."

The remaining panel member, Lord Ackner, noted that "[i]n a field which concerns a fundamental human right—namely that of free speech— close scrutiny must be given to the reasons provided as justification for interference with that right." Lord Ackner found that "the extent of the interference with the right to freedom of speech is a very modest one," and concluded that it was therefore reasonable.

Significantly, Lord Ackner appeared to place considerable reliance on Parliament's subsequent affirmation of the Home Secretary's regulation. Thus, for Lord Ackner, Parliament's overt approval of the directive counted heavily against finding that the regulation was unreasonable. However, Lord Ackner's ultimate conclusion probably stems as much from his conclusion that the directive's interference with the right to free expression was minimal as from his respect for Parliament's imprimatur.

3. *Brind* and the Limits of Unwritten Protections of Civil Liberties

Brind demonstrates that the absence of a written provision protecting free expression does not bar consideration of speech interests as either a "right" or a decisional "principle." In *Brind*, three of the five law lords view free expression as a fundamental "right." All five lords believe that when an administrator promulgates a regulation which impinges on free expression, the regulation must receive "close" or the "closest scrutiny" and/or further an "important public interest." Although one may quibble with the result that the lords reach, the language they use along the way closely parallels the language of Supreme Court cases interpreting the First Amendment....

Brind is significant not because it represents a "strong" free expression case, but rather because it shows that the British judiciary, left to its own devices, will embrace free expression as a decisional norm without any prodding from Parliament. Community tradition, rather than legal fiat, provides the British judiciary with sufficient justification to create and police barriers against enforcement of restrictions on free expression absent overt approval by Parliament. The strong and longstanding British community tradition in favor of permitting any citizen to speak his piece constitutes, at least in the abstract, a viable partial alternative to a legal right stemming from a textual source.

B. *Rust* and Limits of the First Amendment

[Professor Krotosaynski argues that in *Rust v. Sullivan*, 500 U.S. 173 (1991), the U.S. Supreme Court subjected the government's regulation of abortion-related speech by publicly funded clinics to virtually no burden of justification under the First Amendment, in contrast to the British approach, in *Brind*.] . . .

IV. Conclusion . . .

Brind and *Rust* together help to show the limits of a written constitution and the possibilities of an unwritten constitution. Along the way, they also help highlight the importance of principled decision making by judges if there is to be determinacy in the law. To the extent that *Rust* is disturbing for its lack of principled decision making, *Brind* is to the same degree a cause for hope.

Questions and Comments

1. Courtney's discussion suggests that Britain's hate speech laws, unconstrained by constitutional protections of freedom of speech (and possibly required by international human rights instruments), were nonetheless narrowly construed, infrequently invoked, and at times counterproductive to goals of fostering tolerance and fighting racism. Krotoszynski's paper suggests that written constitutions matter less than might have been thought in judicial decisions on free speech issues—at least when comparing the U.S. and Britain. These conclusions are controversial, and many would disagree. Do their conclusions cast doubt on the usefulness or scope of the enterprise of comparative constitutional law?

2. How does one measure freedom of political expression and association? And what is the relationship between legal measures of protection and the amount of expression that occurs? For an interesting essay concerning the degree to which political development of freedoms in Hungary antedated legal protections, see Gabor Kardos, *Freedom of Speech in the Time of Transition*, 8 Conn. J. Int'l L. 529 (1993) (implying that the development of greater freedom of political association came at a time when legal restrictions on association were increasing).

3. Reflect on the role of the enforcement structure for how hate speech violations are prosecuted—who has the power to invoke the law, whether the power is centralized or not, and what (if any) limits exist on discretion whether to invoke the law.

4. A caution about purposive theories of free expression, based on concerns that some forms of free expression are dangerous for democracies, is raised by Frances H. Foster, *Information and the Problem of Democracy: The Russian Experience*, 44 Am. J. Comp. L. 243 (1996). Foster describes how post-Soviet Russia tried different theories for regulating information flow in democracies, including (1) an "informed citizenry theory [that] posits that the citizenry should receive the information it needs to monitor, check and correct governing authorities ... [which] failed ... because it lacked definition, [led to fighting over what information the citizenry needs,] and [b]y negative implication ... became an excuse for regulating information rights and asserting official control over the channels of distribution of information..." and (2) a "popular mandate theory" under which the public was bombarded with "raw unanalyzed political information to encourage public interest in ... the political arena, [but which entailed] extensive government regulation to ensure proper format and conditions for information transmission, to override audience preferences [i.e. for nonpolitical entertainment] and to prevent media interference ...[which failed also because it] bored the public and only intensified popular political apathy, alienation and nonparticipation ..."

Note on Campaign Finance and Freedoms of Speech and Expression

The financing of political campaigns involves both money and archetypal political speech and political associative activity. See Buckley v. Valeo, 424 U.S. 1 (1976) (upholding requirements limiting amount of individual campaign contributions and requiring disclosure of donors; upholding optional public financing of presidential campaigns; invalidating limits on campaign expenditures); Federal Election Commission v. National Conservative Political Action Committee, 470 U.S. 480 (1985) (holding unconstitutional limits on expenditures by independent political action committee in connection with publicly financed presidential candidate). U.S. constitutional law and practice raise issues that have been addressed in many other constitutional democracies.

The German Constitutional Court has issued a number of opinions on the status and financing of political parties (as well as access by small parties and independent candidates), enforcing principles of equality of access and opportunity in some ways to a greater extent than analogous caselaw in the United States. It has held, for example, that permitting donations to political parties to be deductible without limit from income taxes violated principles of equality because it offered greater benefits to the wealthy who made such contributions, thus favoring parties whose programs and activities appealed to the wealthy.[h] A series of decisions from

---

h. The Party Tax Deduction Case [1958], 8 BVerfGE 51, whose core holding was, according to Professor Kommers, reaffirmed by the Court in 1992 in 85 BVerfgGE

the 1960s to the 1990s have invalidated aspects of legislation providing for public funding of political parties while upholding others that were tailored to promote political parties' constitutional role in helping to form and express the popular will at elections. For example, in the Party Finance Case [1966], 20 BVerfGE 56, the Court held that the finance laws' exclusion of parties outside of the parliament was unconstitutional and that those parties were also entitled to be reimbursed for their campaign expenses; the "5%" rule for representation in the Parliament could not be used to deny reimbursements to smaller parties, though a lower minimum percentage for public financing could be used. For more detailed treatment of the German constitutional approach to the role of political parties, see Donald P. Kommers, The Constitutional Jurisprudence of the Federal Republic of Germany 200–15 (2d ed. 1997) (arguing that the court's constitutional doctrine in recent years has been designed to "send the parties back into society, where they would have to depend much more than in the past on their own resources and fund-raising capabilities," in order to assure that political parties serve as agents of the constitution in helping to form the will of the people in elections but not as state controlled agencies or as monopolists of influences upon the state).

In contrast with the German emphasis on the positive role of parties in maintaining democracy, and on the need for the law to mitigate the potential effects of wealth in the distribution of the power of the political parties, the United States' caselaw on regulation of campaign finance, while complex, places greater emphasis on the relationship between expenditures of money and protected political speech and thus on the need to avoid undue restrictions on the freedom of individual donors to expend funds for political purposes. See Buckley v. Valeo ("A restriction on the amount of money a person or group can spend on political communication during a campaign necessarily reduces the quantity of expression by restricting the number of issues discussed, the depth of their exploration, and the size of the audience reached.") Moving from doctrine to practice, U.S. regulation of political campaigns differs markedly from that of many other democracies. For example, many countries provide free broadcast time for political parties or candidates: in 21 of 24 countries surveyed (including Australia, Canada, Germany, Great Britain, India, Israel, Italy) free broadcast time was provided; but not in the U.S., Taiwan, or Mexico. See Law Library of Congress, Campaign Financing of National Elections in Foreign Countries at Table 3 (1991). For further discussion of the complex issues posed by campaign finance and regulation, see Herbert Alexander, with the assistance of Joel Federman, eds., Comparative Political Finance in the 1980s (1989).

---

264. In the United States by statute contributions to political parties or campaigns are not tax deductible, and the Court has had no occasion to address the constitutionality of an alternative approach.

Note on Pre-constitutional Traditions and Freedom of Speech in Botswana

Botswana represents a particular kind of African perspective on the interplay between formal structures and societal traditions in fostering freedom of expression. Its constitution was adopted in 1966, and has been amended a number of times. Botswana's constitutional experience combines formal constitutional protection of abstract rights of conscience, expression, assembly and association in Sections 11–13 of the 1966 Constitution with an ongoing tradition of institutional assemblies grounded in both tribal custom and in the southern African anti-colonial experience.

Notwithstanding constitutionally specified rights and the availability of judicial review, the Botswanan courts have largely restrained themselves from broadly construing the constitutional protections, which are subject to such restrictions as can be "reasonably justified in a democratic society." (Recall Section 1 of the Canadian Charter of Freedoms, adopted in 1982). The Botswanan courts have, however, protected political speech in some specific instances by finding that particular speech could not be sanctioned as likely to provoke breach of the peace, or as seditious or defamatory.[i] On the other hand, some requirements that would violate freedom of speech or association in other systems have been upheld, e.g., requirements that students agree not to participate in demonstrations that lack university approval as a condition for attending a state university.

The tradition of relatively formal tribal assemblies, the Kglota, has survived the colonial experience. These assemblies, which incorporate both elements of status-based hierarchy (e.g., the chief and his advisers have much control over the agenda; seating arrangements are based on status as is the amount of time given speakers) and consensus decision-making (e.g., at least theoretically everyone who is entitled to participate may speak, though criticism is generally couched in stylized poems or songs; ultimately, the chief summarizes debate and announces the consensus) are still used at the village level and above, functioning as a form of self-governance (e.g., with respect to public works projects). Traditionally open only to adult males, women are now recognized as having the right to attend; while attendance by women is high, active participation by women is low. Political parties in Botswana also use rallies, called Freedom Squares, to disseminate party information and to offer opportunities for informal debate where heckling and vigorous questioning often occur.[j] Freedom Squares developed in the anti-colonial period as a means to circumvent the formalist and conservative Kglota, providing a forum for more straightforward criticism particularly, by younger men with less tribal status. Free-

i. See Athaliah Maalokomme, *Political Rights in Botswana: Regression or Development?*, in Democracy in Botswana 163, 165, 168–69 (John Holm & Patrick Mokitsi eds. 1989) (discussing constitutional protections and particular court cases). We gratefully acknowledge the research assistance of Elaine Combs, Georgetown J.D. 1998, in preparing this section.

j. See Mogopodi H. Lekorwe, *The Kgotla and the Freedom Square: One-Way or Two-Way Communication?*, in Democracy in Botswana, at 216.

dom of expression is also found in academic debate and dialogue regarding the roles these institutions and other communications media (including radio and the written press) play in fostering democracy in Botswana.[k]

Botswana, a country 95% of whose population are Tswana and use the Setswanan language, has maintained civilian government since 1966, with 7 changes of government by elections held under the 1966 constitution, as amended. While the Botswana Democratic Party (BDP) has headed the government during this period, a major opposition party, the Botswana National Front (BFP), exists, which won the vice-presidency in 1984 (in a reelection following annulment of an election by the High Court) and in 1994 won 13 seats to the BDP's 26 in the National Assembly. The National Assembly selects up to 7 members in addition to the 40 who stand for election; in 1997, the BDP held 31 seats while the BNF held 13. Consider the relation between the structures of free expression and the political makeup of the national assembly.

D.   DEFAMATION AND THE CONSTITUTIONAL PROTECTION OF EXPRESSION

Recall the questions which opened this chapter. Is some version of freedom of speech essential to constitutionalism?[1] If so, what are its contours? What criteria should we use to evaluate the differing constitutional rules we have seen on such issues as regulation of hate speech? Likewise, does a democratic system have to tolerate defamatory speech about public officials; if so, to what extent?

1.   THE UNITED STATES

New York Times Co. v. Sullivan

376 U.S. 254 (1964)

MR. JUSTICE BRENNAN delivered the opinion of the Court.

We are required in this case to determine for the first time the extent to which the constitutional protections for speech and press limit a State's power to award damages in a libel action brought by a public official against critics of his official conduct.

---

k. See generally Democracy in Botswana (collecting papers and discussions from a 1988 symposium sponsored by the University of Botswana and the Botswana Society); see also James J. Zaffiro, *The Press and Political Opposition in an African Democracy: The Case of Botswana*, 27 J. of Commonwealth and Comparative Politics 51–73 (1989) (analyzing role of press in the political process)

1. To answer this one might need to identify the degree to which constitutionalism reflects theories of human nature and/or of the good society.

Respondent L. B. Sullivan is one of the three elected Commissioners of the City of Montgomery, Alabama. He testified that he was "Commissioner of Public Affairs and the duties are supervision of the Police Department, Fire Department, Department of Cemetery and Department of Scales." He brought this civil libel action against the four individual petitioners, who are Negroes and Alabama clergymen, and against petitioner the New York Times Company, a New York corporation which publishes the New York Times, a daily newspaper. A jury in the Circuit Court of Montgomery County awarded him damages of $500,000, the full amount claimed, against all the petitioners, and the Supreme Court of Alabama affirmed.

Respondent's complaint alleged that he had been libeled by statements in a full-page advertisement that was carried in the New York Times on March 29, 1960. Entitled "Heed Their Rising Voices," the advertisement began by stating that "As the whole world knows by now, thousands of Southern Negro students are engaged in widespread non-violent demonstrations in positive affirmation of the right to live in human dignity as guaranteed by the U.S. Constitution and the Bill of Rights." It went on to charge that "in their efforts to uphold these guarantees, they are being met by an unprecedented wave of terror by those who would deny and negate that document which the whole world looks upon as setting the pattern for modern freedom...." Succeeding paragraphs purported to illustrate the "wave of terror" by describing certain alleged events. The text concluded with an appeal for funds for three purposes: support of the student movement, "the struggle for the right-to-vote," and the legal defense of Dr. Martin Luther King, Jr., leader of the movement, against a perjury indictment then pending in Montgomery.

The text appeared over the names of 64 persons, many widely known for their activities in public affairs, religion, trade unions, and the performing arts. Below these names, and under a line reading "We in the south who are struggling daily for dignity and freedom warmly endorse this appeal," appeared the names of the four individual petitioners and of 16 other persons, all but two of whom were identified as clergymen in various Southern cities. The advertisement was signed at the bottom of the page by the "Committee to Defend Martin Luther King and the Struggle for Freedom in the South," and the officers of the Committee were listed.

Of the 10 paragraphs of text in the advertisement, the third and a portion of the sixth were the basis of respondent's claim of libel. They read as follows:

Third paragraph:

"In Montgomery, Alabama, after students sang 'My Country, 'Tis of Thee' on the State Capitol steps, their leaders were expelled from school, and truckloads of police armed with shotguns and tear-gas ringed the Alabama State College Campus. When the entire student body protested to state authorities by refusing to re-register, their dining hall was padlocked in an attempt to starve them into submission."

Sixth paragraph:

"Again and again the Southern violators have answered Dr. King's peaceful protests with intimidation and violence. They have bombed his home almost killing his wife and child. They have assaulted his person. They have arrested him seven times—for 'speeding,' 'loitering' and similar 'offenses.' And now they have charged him with 'perjury'— a felony under which they could imprison him for ten years...."

Although neither of these statements mentions respondent by name, he contended that the word "police" in the third paragraph referred to him as the Montgomery Commissioner who supervised the Police Department, so that he was being accused of "ringing" the campus with police. He further claimed that the paragraph would be read as imputing to the police, and hence to him, the padlocking of the dining hall in order to starve the students into submission. As to the sixth paragraph, he contended that since arrests are ordinarily made by the police, the statement "They have arrested (Dr. King) seven times" would be read as referring to him; he further contended that the "They" who did the arresting would be equated with the "They" who committed the other described acts and with the "Southern violators." Thus, he argued, the paragraph would be read as accusing the Montgomery police, and hence him, of answering Dr. King's protests with "intimidation and violence," bombing his home, assaulting his person, and charging him with perjury. Respondent and six other Montgomery residents testified that they read some or all of the statements as referring to him in his capacity as Commissioner.

It is uncontroverted that some of the statements contained in the two paragraphs were not accurate descriptions of events which occurred in Montgomery. Although Negro students staged a demonstration on the State Capital steps, they sang the National Anthem and not "My Country, 'Tis of Thee." Although nine students were expelled by the State Board of Education, this was not for leading the demonstration at the Capitol, but for demanding service at a lunch counter in the Montgomery County Courthouse on another day. Not the entire student body, but most of it, had protested the expulsion, not by refusing to register, but by boycotting classes on a single day; virtually all the students did register for the ensuing semester. The campus dining hall was not padlocked on any occasion, and the only students who may have been barred from eating there were the few who had neither signed a preregistration application nor requested temporary meal tickets. Although the police were deployed near the campus in large numbers on three occasions, they did not at any time "ring" the campus, and they were not called to the campus in connection with the demonstration on the State Capitol steps, as the third paragraph implied. Dr. King had not been arrested seven times, but only four; and although he claimed to have been assaulted some years earlier in connection with his arrest for loitering outside a courtroom, one of the officers who made the arrest denied that there was such an assault.

On the premise that the charges in the sixth paragraph could be read as referring to him, respondent was allowed to prove that he had not participated in the events described. Although Dr. King's home had in fact been bombed twice when his wife and child were there, both of these occasions antedated respondent's tenure as Commissioner, and the police were not only not implicated in the bombings, but had made every effort to apprehend those who were. Three of Dr. King's four arrests took place before respondent became Commissioner. Although Dr. King had in fact been indicted (he was subsequently acquitted) on two counts of perjury, each of which carried a possible five-year sentence, respondent had nothing to do with procuring the indictment.

Respondent made no effort to prove that he suffered actual pecuniary loss as a result of the alleged libel.[3] . . .

The cost of the advertisement was approximately $4800, and it was published by the Times upon an order from a New York advertising agency acting for the signatory Committee. The agency submitted the advertisement with a letter from A. Philip Randolph, Chairman of the Committee, certifying that the persons whose names appeared on the advertisement had given their permission. Mr. Randolph was known to the Times' Advertising Acceptability Department as a responsible person, and in accepting the letter as sufficient proof of authorization it followed its established practice. . . . The manager of the Advertising Acceptability Department testified that he had approved the advertisement for publication because he knew nothing to cause him to believe that anything in it was false, and because it bore the endorsement of "a number of people who are well known and whose reputation" he "had no reason to question." Neither he nor anyone else at the Times made an effort to confirm the accuracy of the advertisement. . . .

The trial judge submitted the case to the jury under instructions that the statements in the advertisement were "libelous per se" and were not privileged, so that petitioners might be held liable if the jury found that they had published the advertisement and that the statements were made "of and concerning" respondent. The jury was instructed that, because the statements were libelous per se, "the law . . . implies legal injury from the bare fact of publication itself," "falsity and malice are presumed," "general damages need not be alleged or proved but are presumed," and "punitive damages may be awarded by the jury even though the amount of actual damages is neither found nor shown." . . . He refused to charge, however, that the jury must be "convinced" of malice, in the sense of "actual intent" to harm or "gross negligence and recklessness," to make such an award, and he also refused to require that a verdict for respondent differentiate between compensatory and punitive damages. The judge rejected petitioners' contention that his rulings abridged the freedoms of speech and of the press that are guaranteed by the First and Fourteenth Amendments.

[The judgment was affirmed by the state supreme court.] . . .

---

3. Approximately 394 copies of the edition of the Times containing the advertisement were circulated in Alabama. Of these, about 35 copies were distributed in Montgomery County. The total circulation of the Times for that day was approximately 650,000 copies.

... We reverse the judgment. We hold that the rule of law applied by the Alabama courts is constitutionally deficient for failure to provide the safeguards for freedom of speech and of the press that are required by the First and Fourteenth Amendments in a libel action brought by a public official against critics of his official conduct.[4] We further hold that under the proper safeguards the evidence presented in this case is constitutionally insufficient to support the judgment for respondent.

I

We may dispose at the outset of two grounds asserted to insulate the judgment of the Alabama courts from constitutional scrutiny. The first is the proposition relied on by the State Supreme Court—that "The Fourteenth Amendment is directed against State action and not private action." That proposition has no application to this case. Although this is a civil lawsuit between private parties, the Alabama courts have applied a state rule of law which petitioners claim to impose invalid restrictions on their constitutional freedoms of speech and press.... The test is not the form in which state power has been applied but, whatever the form, whether such power has in fact been exercised.

The second contention is that the constitutional guarantees of freedom of speech and of the press are inapplicable here, at least so far as the Times is concerned, because the allegedly libelous statements were published as part of a paid, "commercial" advertisement....

The publication here ... communicated information, expressed opinion, recited grievances, protested claimed abuses, and sought financial support on behalf of a movement whose existence and objectives are matters of the highest public interest and concern. That the Times was paid for publishing the advertisement is as immaterial in this connection as is the fact that newspapers and books are sold. Any other conclusion would discourage newspapers from carrying "editorial advertisements" of this type, and so might shut off an important outlet for the promulgation of information and ideas by persons who do not themselves have access to publishing facilities.... To avoid placing such a handicap upon the freedoms of expression, we hold that if the allegedly libelous statements would otherwise be constitutionally protected from the present judgment, they do not forfeit that protection because they were published in the form of a paid advertisement.

II

Under Alabama law as applied in this case, a publication is "libelous per se" if the words "tend to injure a person ... in his reputation" or to "bring (him) into public contempt".... Once "libel per se" has been established, the defendant has no defense as to stated facts unless he can

---

4. Since we sustain the contentions of all the petitioners under the First Amendment ... we do not decide the questions presented by ... individual petitioners' [contention] ... that the Due Process and Equal Protection Clauses were violated by racial segregation and racial bias in the courtroom.

persuade the jury that they were true in all their particulars. His privilege of "fair comment" for expressions of opinion depends on the truth of the facts upon which the comment is based. Unless he can discharge the burden of proving truth, general damages are presumed, and may be awarded without proof of pecuniary injury. A showing of actual malice is apparently a prerequisite to recovery of punitive damages, and the defendant may in any event forestall a punitive award by a retraction meeting the statutory requirements. Good motives and belief in truth do not negate an inference of malice, but are relevant only in mitigation of punitive damages if the jury chooses to accord them weight.

The question before us is whether this rule of liability, as applied to an action brought by a public official against critics of his official conduct, abridges the freedom of speech and of the press that is guaranteed by the First and Fourteenth Amendments.

Respondent relies heavily, as did the Alabama courts, on statements of this Court to the effect that the Constitution does not protect libelous publications. Those statements do not foreclose our inquiry here. None of the cases sustained the use of libel laws to impose sanctions upon expression critical of the official conduct of public officials.... In Beauharnais v. Illinois, 343 U.S. 250, the Court sustained an Illinois criminal libel statute as applied to a publication held to be both defamatory of a racial group and "liable to cause violence and disorder." But the Court was careful to note that it "retains and exercises authority to nullify action which encroaches on freedom of utterance under the guise of punishing libel"; for "public men, are, as it were, public property," and "discussion cannot be denied and the right, as well as the duty, of criticism must not be stifled." ... Like insurrection, contempt, advocacy of unlawful acts, breach of the peace, obscenity, solicitation of legal business, and the various other formulae for the repression of expression that have been challenged in this Court, libel can claim no talismanic immunity from constitutional limitations. It must be measured by standards that satisfy the First Amendment.

The general proposition that freedom of expression upon public questions is secured by the First Amendment has long been settled by our decisions. The constitutional safeguard, we have said, "was fashioned to assure unfettered interchange of ideas for the bringing about of political and social changes desired by the people." Roth v. United, 354 U.S. 476, 484. "The maintenance of the opportunity for free political discussion to the end that government may be responsive to the will of the people and that changes may be obtained by lawful means, an opportunity essential to the security of the Republic, is a fundamental principle of our constitutional system." Stromberg v. California, 283 U.S. 359, 369. "[I]t is a prized American privilege to speak one's mind, although not always with perfect good taste, on all public institutions," Bridges v. California, 314 U.S. 252, 270, and this opportunity is to be afforded for "vigorous advocacy" no less than "abstract discussion." NAACP v. Button, 371 U.S. 415, 429. The First Amendment, said Judge Learned Hand, "presupposes that right conclusions are more likely to be gathered out of a multitude of tongues, than through any kind of authoritative selection. To many this is, and always will be, folly; but we have staked upon it our all." United States v. Associated Press, 52 F.Supp. 362, 372 (D.C.S.D.N.Y. 1943). Mr. Justice Brandeis, in his concurring opinion in Whitney v. California, 274 U.S. 357, 375–376, gave the principle its classic formulation:

> "Those who won our independence believed ... that public discussion is a political duty; and that this should be a fundamental principle of the American government. They recognized the risks to which all human institutions are subject. But they knew that order cannot be secured merely through fear of punishment for its infraction; that it is hazardous to discourage thought, hope and imagination; that fear breeds repression; that repression breeds hate; that hate menaces stable government; that the path of safety lies in the opportunity to discuss freely supposed grievances and proposed remedies; and that the fitting remedy for evil counsels is good ones. Believing in the power of reason as applied through public discussion, they eschewed silence coerced by law—the argument of force in its worst form. Recognizing the occasional tyrannies of governing majorities, they amended the Constitution so that free speech and assembly should be guaranteed."

Thus we consider this case against the background of a profound national commitment to the principle that debate on public issues should be uninhibited, robust, and wide-open, and that it may well include vehement, caustic, and sometimes unpleasantly sharp attacks on government and public officials. The present advertisement, as an expression of grievance and protest on one of the major public issues of our time, would seem clearly to qualify for the constitutional protection. The question is whether it forfeits that protection by the falsity of some of its factual statements and by its alleged defamation of respondent.

Authoritative interpretations of the First Amendment guarantees have consistently refused to recognize an exception for any test of truth—whether administered by judges, juries, or administrative officials—and especially one that puts the burden of proving truth on the speaker. The constitutional protection does not turn upon "the truth, popularity, or social utility of the ideas and beliefs which are offered." NAACP V. Button, 371 U.S. 415, 445. As Madison said, "Some degree of abuse is inseparable from the proper use of every thing; and in no instance is this more true than in that of the press." In Cantwell v. Connecticut, 310 U.S. 296, 310 the Court declared:

> "In the realm of religious faith, and in that of political belief, sharp differences arise. In both fields the tenets of one man may seem the rankest error to his neighbor. To persuade others to his own point of view, the pleader, as we know, at times, resorts to exaggeration, to vilification of men who have been, or are, prominent in church or state, and even to false statement. But the people of this nation have ordained in the light of history, that, in spite of the probability of excesses and abuses, these liberties are, in the long view, essential to

enlightened opinion and right conduct on the part of the citizens of a democracy."

[E]rroneous statement is inevitable in free debate, and ... it must be protected if the freedoms of expression are to have the "breathing space" that they "need ... to survive" ....

Injury to official reputation affords no more warrant for repressing speech that would otherwise be free than does factual error. Where judicial officers are involved, this Court has held that concern for the dignity and reputation of the courts does not justify the punishment as criminal contempt of criticism of the judge or his decision. Bridges v. California, 314 U.S. 252. This is true even though the utterance contains "half-truths" and "misinformation." Such repression can be justified, if at all, only by a clear and present danger of the obstruction of justice. If judges are to be treated as "men of fortitude, able to thrive in a hardy climate," surely the same must be true of other government officials, such as elected city commissioners. Criticism of their official conduct does not lose its constitutional protection merely because it is effective criticism and hence diminishes their official reputations.

If neither factual error nor defamatory content suffices to remove the constitutional shield from criticism of official conduct, the combination of the two elements is no less inadequate. This is the lesson to be drawn from the great controversy over the Sedition Act of 1798, 1 Stat. 596, which first crystallized a national awareness of the central meaning of the First Amendment. That statute made it a crime, punishable by a $5,000 fine and five years in prison, "if any person shall write, print, utter or publish ... any false, scandalous and malicious writing or writings against the government of the United States, or either house of the Congress ..., or the President ..., with intent to defame ... or to bring them, or either of them, into contempt or disrepute; or to excite against them, or either or any of them, the hatred of the good people of the United States." The Act allowed the defendant the defense of truth, and provided that the jury were to be judges both of the law and the facts. Despite these qualifications, the Act was vigorously condemned as unconstitutional in an attack joined in by Jefferson and Madison. In the famous Virginia Resolutions of 1798, the General Assembly of Virginia resolved that it

> "doth particularly protest against the palpable and alarming infractions of the Constitution, in the two late cases of the 'Alien and Sedition Acts,' passed at the last session of Congress.... [The Sedition Act] exercises ... a power not delegated by the Constitution, but, on the contrary, expressly and positively forbidden by one of the amendments thereto—a power which, more than any other, ought to produce universal alarm, because it is levelled against the right of freely examining public characters and measures, and of free communication among the people thereon, which has ever been justly deemed the only effectual guardian of every other right."

Madison prepared the Report in support of the protest. His premise was that the Constitution created a form of government under which "The people, not the government, possess the absolute sovereignty." The structure of the government dispersed power in reflection of the people's distrust of concentrated power, and of power itself at all levels. This form of government was "altogether different" from the British form, under which the Crown was sovereign and the people were subjects. "Is it not natural and necessary, under such different circumstances," he asked, "that a different degree of freedom in the use of the press should be contemplated?" Earlier, in a debate in the House of Representatives, Madison had said: ". . . the censorial power is in the people over the Government, and not in the Government over the people." . . . The right of free public discussion of the stewardship of public officials was thus, in Madison's view, a fundamental principle of the American form of government.[15]

Although the Sedition Act was never tested in this Court,[16] the attack upon its validity has carried the day in the court of history. Fines levied in its prosecution were repaid by Act of Congress on the ground that it was unconstitutional. . . . Jefferson, as President, pardoned those who had been convicted and sentenced under the Act and remitted their fines, stating: "I discharged every person under punishment or prosecution under the sedition law, because I considered, and now consider, that law to be a nullity, as absolute and as palpable as if Congress had ordered us to fall down and worship a golden image." The invalidity of the Act has also been assumed by Justices of this Court. See Holmes, J., dissenting and joined by Brandeis, J., in Abrams v. United States, 250 U.S. 616; Jackson, J., dissenting in Beauharnais v. Illinois, 343 U.S. 250, 288–289. These views reflect a broad consensus that the Act, because of the restraint it imposed upon criticism of government and public officials, was inconsistent with the First Amendment. . . .

What a State may not constitutionally bring about by means of a criminal statute is likewise beyond the reach of its civil law of libel. The fear of damage awards under a rule such as that invoked by the Alabama courts here may be markedly more inhibiting than the fear of prosecution under a criminal statute. . . . [C]riminal-law safeguards such as the requirements of an indictment and of proof beyond a reasonable doubt . . . are not

---

15. The Report on the Virginia Resolutions further stated:

"[I]t is manifestly impossible to punish the intent to bring those who administer the government into disrepute or contempt, without striking at the right of freely discussing public characters and measures; . . . which, again, is equivalent to a protection of those who administer the government, if they should at any time deserve the contempt or hatred of the people, against being exposed to it, by free animadversions on their characters and conduct. Nor can there be a doubt . . . that a government thus intrenched in penal statutes against the just and natural effects of a culpable administration, will easily evade the responsibility which is essential to a faithful discharge of its duty.

"Let it be recollected, lastly, that the right of electing the members of the government constitutes more particularly the essence of a free and responsible government. The value and efficacy of this right depends on the knowledge of the comparative merits and demerits of the candidates for public trust, and on the equal freedom, consequently, of examining and discussing these merits and demerits of the candidates respectively." [4 Elliot's Debates at 575]

16. The Act expired by its terms in 1801.

available to the defendant in a civil action. The judgment awarded in this case—without the need for any proof of actual pecuniary loss—was one thousand times greater than the maximum fine provided by the Alabama criminal statute, and one hundred times greater than that provided by the Sedition Act. And since there is no double-jeopardy limitation applicable to civil lawsuits, this is not the only judgment that may be awarded against petitioners for the same publication.[18] Whether or not a newspaper can survive a succession of such judgments, the pall of fear and timidity imposed upon those who would give voice to public criticism is an atmosphere in which the First Amendment freedoms cannot survive....

The state rule of law is not saved by its allowance of the defense of truth. A defense for erroneous statements honestly made is no less essential here than was the requirement of proof of guilty knowledge which, in Smith v. California, we held indispensable to a valid conviction of a bookseller for possessing obscene writings for sale. We said:

> "For if the bookseller is criminally liable without knowledge of the contents, . . . he will tend to restrict the books he sells to those he has inspected; and thus the State will have imposed a restriction upon the distribution of constitutionally protected as well as obscene litera-ture.... And the bookseller's burden would become the public's bur-den, for by restricting him the public's access to reading matter would be restricted.... [H]is timidity in the face of his absolute criminal liability, thus would tend to restrict the public's access to forms of the printed word which the State could not constitutionally suppress directly. The bookseller's self-censorship, compelled by the State, would be a censorship affecting the whole public, hardly less virulent for being privately administered. Through it, the distribution of all books, both obscene and not obscene, would be impeded." (361 U.S. 147, 153–154.)

A rule compelling the critic of official conduct to guarantee the truth of all his factual assertions—and to do so on pain of libel judgments virtually unlimited in amount—leads to a comparable "self-censorship." Allowance of the defense of truth, with the burden of proving it on the defendant, does not mean that only false speech will be deterred.[19] ... Under such a rule, would-be critics of official conduct may be deterred from voicing their criticism, even though it is believed to be true and even though it is in fact true, because of doubt whether it can be proved in court or fear of the expense of having to do so.... The rule thus dampens the vigor and limits

---

18. The Times states that four other libel suits based on the advertisement have been filed against it by others who have served as Montgomery City Commissioners and by the Governor of Alabama; that anoth-er $500,000 verdict has been awarded in the only one of these cases that has yet gone to trial; and that the damages sought in the other three total $2,000,000.

19. Even a false statement may be deemed to make a valuable contribution to public debate, since it brings about "the clearer perception and livelier impression of truth, produced by its collision with error." Mill, On Liberty (Oxford: Blackwell, 1947), at 15; see also Milton, Areopagitica, in Prose Works (Yale, 1959), Vol. II, at 561.

the variety of public debate. It is inconsistent with the First and Four-teenth Amendments.

The constitutional guarantees require, we think, a federal rule that prohibits a public official from recovering damages for a defamatory false-hood relating to his official conduct unless he proves that the statement was made with "actual malice"—that is, with knowledge that it was false or with reckless disregard of whether it was false or not. An oft-cited statement of a like rule, which has been adopted by a number of state courts, is found in the Kansas case of Coleman v. MacLennan, 78 Kan. 711, 98 P. 281 (1908). The State Attorney General, a candidate for re-election and a member of the commission charged with the management and control of the state school fund, sued a newspaper publisher for alleged libel in an article purporting to state facts relating to his official conduct in connection with a school-fund transaction. The defendant pleaded privilege and the trial judge, over the plaintiff's objection, instructed the jury that

> "where an article is published and circulated among voters for the sole purpose of giving what the defendant believes to be truthful informa-tion concerning a candidate for public office and for the purpose of enabling such voters to cast their ballot more intelligently, and the whole thing is done in good faith and without malice, the article is privileged, although the principal matters contained in the article may be untrue in fact and derogatory to the character of the plaintiff; and in such a case the burden is on the plaintiff to show actual malice in the publication of the article."

... On appeal the Supreme Court of Kansas, in an opinion by Justice Burch, reasoned as follows:

> "It is of the utmost consequence that the people should discuss the character and qualifications of candidates for their suffrages. The importance to the state and to society of such discussions is so vast, and the advantages derived are so great that they more than counter-balance the inconvenience of private persons whose conduct may be involved, and occasional injury to the reputations of individuals must yield to the public welfare, although at times such injury may be great. The public benefit from publicity is so great and the chance of injury to private character so small that such discussion must be privileged."

The court thus sustained the trial court's instruction as a correct statement of the law, saying:

> "In such a case the occasion gives rise to a privilege qualified to this extent. Any one claiming to be defamed by the communication must show actual malice, or go remediless. This privilege extends to a great variety of subjects and includes matters of public concern, public men, and candidates for office." ...

III

We hold today that the Constitution delimits a State's power to award damages for libel in actions brought by public officials against critics of their official conduct. Since this is such an action, the rule requiring proof of actual malice is applicable. While Alabama law apparently requires proof of actual malice for an award of punitive damages, where general damages are concerned malice is "presumed." Such a presumption is inconsistent with the federal rule.... Since the trial judge did not instruct the jury to differentiate between general and punitive damages, it may be that the verdict was wholly an award of one or the other. But it is impossible to know, in view of the general verdict returned. Because of this uncertainty, the judgment must be reversed and the case remanded.

Since respondent may seek a new trial, we deem that considerations of effective judicial administration require us to review the evidence in the present record to determine whether it could constitutionally support a judgment for respondent. This Court's duty is not limited to the elaboration of constitutional principles; we must also in proper cases review the evidence to make certain that those principles have been constitutionally applied. This is such a case, particularly since the question is one of alleged trespass across "the line between speech unconditionally guaranteed and speech which may legitimately be regulated." ... We must "make an independent examination of the whole record," so as to assure ourselves that the judgment does not constitute a forbidden intrusion on the field of free expression.

Applying these standards, we consider that the proof presented to show actual malice lacks the convincing clarity which the constitutional standard demands, and hence that it would not constitutionally sustain the judgment for respondent under the proper rule of law....

As to the Times, we ... conclude that the facts do not support a finding of actual malice. The statement by the Times' Secretary that, apart from the padlocking allegation, he thought the advertisement was "substantially correct," affords no constitutional warrant for the Alabama Supreme Court's conclusion that it was a "cavalier ignoring of the falsity of the advertisement [from which], the jury could not have but been impressed with the bad faith of The Times, and its maliciousness inferable therefrom." The statement does not indicate malice at the time of the publication; even if the advertisement was not "substantially correct"— although respondent's own proofs tend to show that it was—that opinion was at least a reasonable one, and there was no evidence to impeach the witness' good faith in holding it. The Times' failure to retract upon respondent's demand, although it later retracted upon the demand of Governor Patterson, is likewise not adequate evidence of malice for constitutional purposes. Whether or not a failure to retract may ever constitute such evidence, there are two reasons why it does not here. *First*, the letter written by the Times reflected a reasonable doubt on its part as to whether the advertisement could reasonably be taken to refer to respondent at all. *Second*, it was not a final refusal, since it asked for an explanation on this point—a request that respondent chose to ignore....

. . . We think the evidence against the Times supports at most a finding of negligence . . . and is constitutionally insufficient to show the recklessness . . . required for a finding of actual malice. . . .

We also think the evidence was constitutionally defective in another respect: it was incapable of supporting the jury's finding that the allegedly libelous statements were made "of and concerning" respondent. . . . There was no reference to respondent in the advertisement, either by name or official position. A number of the allegedly libelous statements—the charges that the dining hall was padlocked and that Dr. King's home was bombed, his person assaulted, and a perjury prosecution instituted against him—did not even concern the police; despite the ingenuity of the arguments which would attach this significance to the word "They," it is plain that these statements could not reasonably be read as accusing respondent of personal involvement in the acts in question. The statements upon which respondent principally relies as referring to him are the two allegations that did concern the police or police functions: that "truckloads of police . . . ringed the Alabama State College Campus" after the demonstration on the State Capitol steps, and that Dr. King had been "arrested . . . seven times." These statements were false only in that the police had been "deployed near" the campus but had not actually "ringed" it and had not gone there in connection with the State Capitol demonstration, and in that Dr. King had been arrested only four times. The ruling that these discrepancies between what was true and what was asserted were sufficient to injure respondent's reputation may itself raise constitutional problems, but we need not consider them here. Although the statements may be taken as referring to the police, they did not on their face make even an oblique reference to respondent as an individual. . . .

. . . For good reason, "no court of last resort in this country has ever held, or even suggested, that prosecutions for libel on government have any place in the American system of jurisprudence." City of Chicago v. Tribune Co., 307 Ill. 595, 601. The [decision below] would sidestep this obstacle by transmuting criticism of government, however impersonal it may seem on its face, into personal criticism, and hence potential libel, of the officials of whom the government is composed. There is no legal alchemy by which a State may thus create the cause of action that would otherwise be denied for a publication which, as respondent himself said of the advertisement, "reflects not only on me but on the other Commissioners and the community." Raising as it does the possibility that a good-faith critic of government will be penalized for his criticism, the proposition relied on by the Alabama courts strikes at the very center of the constitutionally protected area of free expression. We hold that such a proposition may not constitutionally be utilized to establish that an otherwise impersonal attack on governmental operations was a libel of an official responsible for those operations. . . .

The judgment of the Supreme Court of Alabama is reversed and the case is remanded to that court for further proceedings not inconsistent with this opinion.

Reversed and remanded.

MR. JUSTICE BLACK, with whom MR. JUSTICE DOUGLAS joins, concurring.

I concur in reversing this half-million-dollar judgment against the New York Times Company and the four individual defendants.... I base my vote to reverse on the belief that the First and Fourteenth Amendments not merely "delimit" a State's power to award damages to "public officials against critics of their official conduct" but completely prohibit a State from exercising such a power.... Unlike the Court, therefore, I vote to reverse exclusively on the ground that the Times and the individual defendants had an absolute, unconditional constitutional right to publish in the Times advertisement their criticisms of the Montgomery agencies and officials....

In my opinion the Federal Constitution has dealt with this deadly danger to the press in the only way possible without leaving the free press open to destruction—by granting the press an absolute immunity for criticism of the way public officials do their public duty. Stopgap measures like those the Court adopts are in my judgment not enough. This record certainly does not indicate that any different verdict would have been rendered here whatever the Court had charged the jury about "malice," "truth," "good motives," "justifiable ends," or any other legal formulas which in theory would protect the press. Nor does the record indicate that any of these legalistic words would have caused the courts below to set aside or to reduce the half-million-dollar verdict in any amount....

We would, I think, more faithfully interpret the First Amendment by holding that at the very least it leaves the people and the press free to criticize officials and discuss public affairs with impunity. This Nation of our elects many of its important officials; so do the States, the municipalities, the counties, and even many precincts. These officials are responsible to the people for the way they perform their duties. While our Court has held that some kinds of speech and writings, such as "obscenity," are not expression within the protection of the First Amendment, freedom to discuss public affairs and public officials is unquestionably, as the Court today holds, the kind of speech the First Amendment was primarily designed to keep within the area of free discussion. To punish the exercise of this right to discuss public affairs or to penalize it through libel judgments is to abridge or shut off discussion of the very kind most needed. This Nation, I suspect, can live in peace without libel suits based on public discussions of public affairs and public officials. But I doubt that a country can live in freedom where its people can be made to suffer physically or financially for criticizing their government, its actions, or its officials.... An unconditional right to say what one pleases about public affairs is what I consider to be the minimum guarantee of the First Amendment....

MR. JUSTICE GOLDBERG, with whom MR. JUSTICE DOUGLAS joins, concurring in the result.

The Court today announces a constitutional standard which prohibits "a public official from recovering damages for a defamatory falsehood relating to his official conduct unless he proves that the statement was made with 'actual malice'—that is, with knowledge that it was false or with reckless disregard of whether it was false or not." The Court thus rules that the Constitution gives citizens and newspapers a "conditional privilege" immunizing nonmalicious misstatements of fact regarding the official conduct of a government officer. The impressive array of history and precedent marshaled by the Court, however, confirms my belief that the Constitution affords greater protection than that provided by the Court's standard to citizen and press in exercising the right of public criticism.

In my view, the First and Fourteenth Amendments to the Constitution afford to the citizen and to the press an absolute, unconditional privilege to criticize official conduct despite the harm which may flow from excesses and abuses. The prized American right "to speak one's mind," about public officials and affairs needs "breathing space to survive." The right should not depend upon a probing by the jury of the motivation of the citizen or press. The theory of our Constitution is that every citizen may speak his mind and every newspaper express its view on matters of public concern and may not be barred from speaking or publishing because those in control of government think that what is said or written is unwise, unfair, false, or malicious. In a democratic society, one who assumes to act for the citizens in an executive, legislative, or judicial capacity must expect that his official acts will be commented upon and criticized. Such criticism cannot, in my opinion, be muzzled or deterred by the courts at the instance of public officials under the label of libel....

We must recognize that we are writing upon a clean slate.[3] As the Court notes, although there have been "statements of this Court to the effect that the Constitution does not protect libelous publications ... [n]one of the cases sustained the use of libel laws to impose sanctions upon expression critical of the official conduct of public officials." We should be particularly careful, therefore, adequately to protect the liberties which are embodied in the First and Fourteenth Amendments. It may be urged that deliberately and maliciously false statements have no conceivable value as free speech. That argument, however, is not responsive to the real issue presented by this case, which is whether that freedom of speech which all agree is constitutionally protected can be effectively safeguarded by a rule allowing the imposition of liability upon a jury's evaluation of the speaker's state of mind. If individual citizens may be held liable in damages for strong words, which a jury finds false and maliciously motivated, there can be little doubt that public debate and advocacy will be constrained. And if newspapers, publishing advertisements dealing with public issues, thereby risk liability, there can also be little doubt that the ability of minority groups to secure publication of their views on public affairs and to seek

3. It was not until Gitlow v. New York, 268 U.S. 652 decided in 1925, that it was intimated that the freedom of speech guaranteed by the First Amendment was applicable to the States by reason of the Fourteenth Amendment.

support for their causes will be greatly diminished. The opinion of the Court conclusively demonstrates the chilling effect of the Alabama libel laws on First Amendment freedoms in the area of race relations. The American Colonists were not willing, nor should we be, to take the risk that "[m]en who injure and oppress the people under their administration [and] provoke them to cry out and complain" will also be empowered to "make that very complaint the foundation for new oppressions and prosecutions." The Trial of John Peter Zenger, 17 Howell's St. Tr. 675, 721–722 (1735) (argument of counsel to the jury)....

Our national experience teaches that repressions breed hate and "that hate menaces stable government." Whitney v. California, 274 U.S. 357, 375 (Brandeis, J., concurring). We should be ever mindful of the wise counsel of Chief Justice Hughes:

> "[I]mperative is the need to preserve inviolate the constitutional rights of free speech, free press and free assembly in order to maintain the opportunity for free political discussion, to the end that government may be responsive to the will of the people and that changes, if desired, may be obtained by peaceful means. Therein lies the security of the Republic, the very foundation of constitutional government." De Jonge v. Oregon, 299 U.S. 353, 365.

This is not to say that the Constitution protects defamatory statements directed against the private conduct of a public official or private citizen.... Purely private defamation has little to do with the political ends of a self-governing society. The imposition of liability for private defamation does not abridge the freedom of public speech or any other freedom protected by the First Amendment. This, of course, cannot be said "where public officials are concerned or where public matters are involved.". . .

The conclusion that the Constitution affords the citizen and the press an absolute privilege for criticism of official conduct does not leave the public official without defenses against unsubstantiated opinions or deliberate misstatements. "Under our system of government, counterargument and education are the weapons available to expose these matters, not abridgment ... of free speech ...." Wood v. Georgia, 370 U.S. 375, 389. The public official certainly has equal if not greater access than most private citizens to media of communication....

For these reasons, I strongly believe that the Constitution accords citizens and press an unconditional freedom to criticize official conduct. It necessarily follows that in a case such as this, where all agree that the allegedly defamatory statements related to official conduct, the judgments for libel cannot constitutionally be sustained.

---

2. GERMANY: THE LÜTH AND BÖLL CASES

The *Lüth* and *Böll* cases illustrate some of the distinctive features of German constitutional law encountered in other areas. Note the positive conception of state obligations in *Lüth*, which in some respects mirrors the positive conception of the state's obligation to protect life that we saw in the German abortion cases. In *Böll*, note that a constitutional violation of Böll's rights to a protected intimate sphere (privacy?) was found to have occurred through a lower court's *failure* to award him damages for having been misquoted. In the U.S., it is possible that the commentary would have been protected by the *New York Times v. Sullivan* doctrine. In any event, even under Masson v. New Yorker, 501 U.S. 496 (1991) (holding that actual malice standard of *Sullivan* could be met by publication of false quotations but only if the quotations were materially different in meaning), the injured party's right to a damage judgment would not have been conceived of as an individual constitutional right to be balanced against free speech rights.

As you read the German materials, revisit the questions asked earlier in this Section and this Chapter about the relationship between freedom of speech (and the regulation or prohibition of that speech where, e.g., it is likely to arouse group hatreds, or is defamatory of public officials) and successful constitutionalism.

The Lüth Case (1958)

7 BVerfGe 198
(Federal Constitutional Court of German)

(Translation from Donald Kommers, The Constitutional Jurisprudence of the Federal Republic of Germany (1989))

[The *Lüth* case is a major decision in German constitutional law, referred to by Professor Currie, at 181 as "groundbreaking." It arose from public efforts by Erich Luth, press minister of the Hamburg government, to influence movie theaters and the general public to boycott showings of a movie made by a director (Veit Harlan) who had, under the Nazi regime, produced a notorious anti-semitic film. An injunction was obtained from the Hamburg courts against Lüth who, in addition to heading the information ministry was also the head of the Hamburg Press Club and an active participant in a group seeking to promote religious tolerance. Lüth was essentially enjoined from his efforts to influence the public not to see the movie and theaters not to show it, on the grounds that his conduct violated an article in the general civil law that one who intentionally causes damage to another "in a manner offensive to good morals" must compensate the other for the damage.

After exhausting his remedies in the Hamburg courts, Lüth filed a constitutional complaint before the Court, asserting violations of his free speech rights under article 5 of the Basic Law.[m] As you read, note the

---

m.   German Basic Law, Article 5 [Freedom of expression]:

(1) Everybody has the right freely to express and disseminate their opinions orally, in writing or visually and to obtain information from generally accessible sources with- out hindrance. Freedom of the press and freedom of reporting through audiovisual media shall be guaranteed. There shall be no censorship.

(2) These rights are subject to limitations embodied in the provisions of general legisla-

Court's argument that, in deciding the case between the two private parties, the courts were constitutionally required to consider free speech rights, as well as its assertion of the Basic Law as an "objective order of values." (Bracketed material in the following excerpt is by Kommers)]

* * *

Judgment of the First Senate . . .

B. II. The complainant claims that the superior court has violated his basic right to free speech as safeguarded by Article 5 (1) [1] of the Constitution.

1. The decision of the superior court is an act of public authority in the special form of a judicial decision. It can violate a basic right of the complainant only if the court was required to take the right in question into consideration when deciding the case.

The decision prohibits the complainant from making statements that could influence others to adhere to his opinion regarding Harlan's reappearance [as a film director]. . . . Seen objectively, this limits the complainant's freedom of expression. . . . [But] such a ruling can violate the complainant's basic right under Article 5 (1) only if [a] provision of the Civil Code [Article 826] would be so affected by a basic right as to render it an impossible basis for a decision. . . .

Whether and to what extent basic rights affect private law is controversial [citing legal literature]. The extreme positions in this dispute are, on the one hand, that basic rights are exclusively directed against the state and, on the other hand, that the basic rights as such, or at least some and in any case the more important of them, also apply in civil [i.e., private] law matters against everybody. Neither of these extremes finds support in the Constitutional Court's existing jurisprudence. . . . Nor is there any need here to resolve fully the dispute over the so-called effect of the basic rights on third persons [*Drittwirkung*]. The following discussion is sufficient to resolve this case.

. . . [T]he primary purpose of the basic rights is to safeguard the liberties of the individual against interferences by public authority. They are defensive rights of the individual against the state. This [purpose] follows from the historical development of the concept of basic rights and from historical developments leading to the inclusion of basic rights in the constitutions of various countries. This also corresponds to the meaning of the basic rights contained in the Basic Law and is underscored by the enumeration of basic rights in the first section of the Constitution, thereby stressing the primacy of the human being and his dignity over the power of the state. This is why the legislature allowed the extraordinary remedy . . .

tion, statutory provisions for the protection of young persons and the citizen's right to personal respect.

(3) Art and scholarship, research and teaching shall be free. Freedom of teaching shall not absolve anybody from loyalty to the constitution.

of the constitutional complaint to be brought only against acts of public authority.

[An Objective Order of Values]

It is equally true, however, that the Basic Law is not a value-neutral document [citations from numerous decisions]. Its section on basic rights establishes an objective order of values, and this order strongly reinforces the effective power of basic rights. This value system, which centers upon dignity of the human personality developing freely within the social community, must be looked upon as a fundamental constitutional decision affecting all spheres of law [public and private]. It serves as a yardstick for measuring and assessing all actions in the areas of legislation, public administration, and adjudication. Thus it is clear that basic rights also influence [the development of] private law. Every provision of private law must be compatible with this system of values, and every such provision must be interpreted in its spirit.

The legal content of basic rights as objective norms is developed within private law through the medium of the legal provisions directly applicable to this area of the law. Newly enacted statutes must conform to the system of values of the basic rights. The content of existing law also must be brought into harmony with this system of values. This system infuses specific constitutional content into private law, which from that point on determines its interpretation. A dispute between private individuals concerning rights and duties emanating from provisions of private law—provisions influenced by the basic rights—remains substantively and procedurally a private-law dispute. [Courts] apply and interpret private law, but the interpretation must conform to the Constitution.

The influence of the scale of values of the basic rights affects particularly those provisions of private law that contain mandatory rules of law and thus form part of the *ordre public*—in the broad sense of the term—that is, rules which for reasons of the general welfare also are binding on private legal relationships and are removed from the domination of private intent. Because of their purpose these provisions are closely related to the public law they supplement. Consequently, they are substantially exposed to the influence of constitutional law. In bringing this influence to bear, the courts may invoke the general clauses which, like Article 826 of the Civil Code, refer to standards outside private law. "Good morals" is one such standard. In order to determine what is required by social norms such as these, one has to consider first the ensemble of value concepts that a nation has developed at a certain point in its intellectual and cultural history and laid down in its constitution. That is why the general clauses have rightly been called the points where basic rights have breached the [domain of] private law [citation to Dürig, in Neumann, Nipperdey, and Scheuner, Die Grundrechte, 2:525].

[Function of Lower Courts]

The Constitution requires the judge to determine whether the basic rights have influenced the substantive rules of private law in the manner described. [If this influence is present] he must then, in interpreting and applying these provisions, heed the resulting modification of private law. This follows from Article 1 (3) of the Basic Law [requiring the legislature, judiciary, and executive to enforce basic rights "as directly applicable law"]. If he does not apply these standards and ignores the influence of constitutional law on the rules of private law, he violates objective constitutional law by misunderstanding the content of the basic right (as an objective norm); as a public official, he also violates the basic right whose observance by the courts the citizen can demand on the basis of the Constitution. Apart from remedies available under private law, [citizens] can bring such a judicial decision before the Federal Constitutional Court by means of a constitutional complaint.

The Constitutional Court must ascertain whether an ordinary court has properly evaluated the scope and impact of the basic rights in the field of private law. But this task is strictly limited: It is not up to the Constitutional Court to examine decisions of the private-law judge for any legal error that he might have committed. Rather, the Constitutional Court must confine its inquiry to the "radiating effect" of the basic rights on private law and make sure that the [judge below] has correctly understood the constitutional principle [involved] in the area of law under review. . . .

[Freedom of Speech and General Laws]

2. With regard to the basic right of free speech (Article 5), the problem of the relationship between basic rights and private law is somewhat different. As under the Weimar Constitution (Article 118), this basic right is guaranteed only within the framework of the "general laws" (Article 5 (2)). [O]ne might take the view that the Constitution itself, by referring to limits imposed by the general laws, has restricted the legitimate scope of the basic right to that area left open to it by courts in their interpretation of these laws. Such an approach would mean that any general law restricting a basic right would never constitute a violation of that right.

However, this is not the meaning of the reference to "general laws." The basic right to freedom of opinion is the most immediate expression of the human personality [living] in society and, as such, one of the noblest of human rights. . . . It is absolutely basic to a liberal-democratic constitutional order because it alone makes possible the constant intellectual exchange and the contest among opinions that form the lifeblood of such an order; [indeed,] it is "the matrix, the indispensable condition of nearly every other form of freedom" [Cardozo, quoted in English].

Because of the fundamental importance of freedom of speech in the liberal-democratic state, it would be inconsistent to allow the substance of this basic right to be limited by an ordinary law (and thus necessarily by judicial decisions interpreting the law). Rather, the same principle applies here that was discussed above in general terms with regard to the relationship between the basic rights and private law. [Courts] must evaluate the effect of general laws which would limit the basic right in the light of the importance of the basic right. [They] must interpret these laws so as to preserve the significance of the basic right; in a free democracy this process [of interpretation] must assume the fundamentality of freedom of speech in all spheres, particularly in public life. [Courts] may not construe the mutual relationship between basic rights and "general laws" as a unilateral restriction on the applicability of the basic rights by the "general laws"; rather, there is a mutual effect. According to the wording of Article 5, the "general laws" set bounds to the basic right but, in turn, those laws must be interpreted in light of the value-establishing significance of this basic right in a free democratic state, and so any limiting effect on the basic right must itself be restricted.

The Federal Constitutional Court is the court of last resort for constitutional complaints relating to the preservation of basic rights. Therefore it must have the legal right to control the decisions of the courts where, in applying a general law, they enter the sphere shaped by basic rights.... The Federal Constitutional Court must have the right to enforce a specific value found in the basic rights. [Its authority to exercise such control] extends to all organs of public authority, including the courts. It can thus create an equilibrium, as desired by the Constitution, between the mutually contradictory and restricted tendencies of the basic rights and the "general laws."

[Meaning of General Laws as Applied to Speech]

3.   The concept of "general laws" was controversial from the very beginning.... In any event, ... the phrase was interpreted as referring not only to laws that "do not prohibit an opinion or the expression of an opinion as such" but also to those that "are directed toward the protection of legal rights which need such protection regardless of any specific opinion"; in other words, laws that are directed toward the protection of a community value that takes precedence over the exercise of free speech [citations to legal literature]....

If the term "general laws" is construed in this way, then we can say the following with regard to the purpose and scope of the protection of the basic right: [We] must reject the view that the basic right protects only the expression of an opinion but not the inherent or intended effect on other persons. It is precisely the purpose of an *opinion* to produce an "intellectual effect on the public, to help form an opinion and a conviction in the community" [citation to a commentary on the Basic Law]. Article 5 (1) of the Basic Law protects value judgments, which are always aimed at having an intellectual impact, namely, at convincing others. Indeed, the protection of the basic right is aimed primarily at the personal opinion of the speaker as expressed in the value judgment. To protect the expression itself but not its effect would make no sense.

If understood in this way, the expression of an opinion in its purely intellectual effect is free. However, if someone else's legal rights are violated [and] the protection of these rights should take precedence over the protection of freedom of opinion, then this violation does not become permissible simply because it was committed through the expression of an opinion. [Courts] must weigh the values to be protected against each other. [They] must deny the right to express an opinion if the exercise of this right would violate a more important interest protected [by private law]. [Courts] must decide whether such interests are present on the basis of the facts of each individual case.

[In the light of this discussion the court noted that "there is no reason why norms of private law should not also be recognized as 'general laws' within the meaning of Article 5 (2)." The court thus rejected the prevailing view, cited in the literature, that "general laws" embrace only public laws regulating the relations between individuals and the state.]

4. ... The complainant fears that any restriction upon freedom of speech might excessively limit a citizen's chance to influence public opinion and thus no longer guarantee the indispensable freedom to discuss important issues publicly.... This danger is indeed present.... To counter the danger, however, it is unnecessary to exclude private law from the category of "general laws." Rather, we must strictly adhere to the character of the basic right as a personal freedom. This is especially important when the speaker is exercising his basic right not within the framework of a private dispute but for the purpose of influencing public opinion. Thus his opinion may possibly have an impact upon another's private rights even though this is not his intention. Here the relationship between ends and means is important. The protection of speech is entitled to less protection where exercised to defend a private interest—particularly when the individual pursues a selfish goal within the economic sector—than speech that contributes to the intellectual struggle of opinions.... Here the assumption is in favor of free speech.

To conclude: Decisions of ordinary civil courts that restrict freedom of opinion on the basis of the "general laws" in the field of private law can violate the basic right of Article 5 (1). The private-law judge also is required to weigh the importance of the basic right against the value to the person allegedly injured by [the utterance of an opinion] of the interest protected by the "general laws." A decision in this respect requires the judge to consider all the circumstances of the individual case. An incorrect balancing of the factors can violate the basic right and provide the basis for a constitutional complaint to the Federal Constitutional Court.

[In section III of its opinion the Constitutional Court examined closely the facts of the case and the judgment of the lower court. In noting that the advocacy of a boycott is not always contrary to "good morals" within the meaning of Article 826 of the Civil Code, the court said: "'Good morals' are not unchangeable principles of pure morality; they are rather defined by the views of 'decent people' about what is 'proper' in social intercourse among legal partners." The court then proceeded on its own to weigh Lüth's interests against those of Harlan and the film companies, holding that the district court had given insufficient attention to the motives of the complainant and the historical context of his remarks. The court's concerns are captured in the following extracts.]

2. (b)... The complainant's statements must be seen within the context of his general political and cultural efforts. He was moved by the apprehension that Harlan's reappearance might—especially in foreign countries—be interpreted to mean that nothing had changed in German cultural life since the National Socialist period.... These apprehensions concerned a very important issue for the German people.... Nothing has damaged the German reputation as much as the cruel Nazi persecution of the Jews. A crucial interest exists, therefore, in assuring the world that the German people have abandoned this attitude and condemn it not for reasons of political opportunism but because through an inner conversion they have come to realize its evil....

Because of his especially close personal relation to all that concerned the German-Jewish relationship, the complainant was within his rights to state his view in public. Even at that time he was already known for his efforts toward reestablishing a true inner peace with the Jewish people.... It is understandable that he feared all these efforts might be disturbed and thwarted by Harlan's reappearance....

The demand that under these circumstances the complainant should nevertheless have refrained from expressing his opinion out of regard for Harlan's professional interests and the economic interests of the film companies employing him ... is unjustified.... Where the formation of public opinion on a matter important to the general welfare is concerned, private and especially individual economic interests must, in principle, yield. This does not mean that these interests are without protection; after all, the basic right's value is underscored by the fact that it is enjoyed by *everyone*. Whoever feels injured by the public statements of someone else can make a public reply. Public opinion is formed, like the formation of a personal opinion, only through conflicts of opinion freely expressed....

IV. On the basis of these considerations, the Federal Constitutional Court holds that the superior court, in assessing the behavior of the complainant, has misjudged the special significance of the basic right to freedom of opinion. [Courts] must consider [the significance of this right] when it comes into conflict with the private interests of others. The decision below is thus based on an incorrect application of the standards applying to basic rights and violates the basic right of the complainant under Article 5 (1) of the Basic Law. It must therefore be quashed.

The Böll Case (1980)

54 BVerfGe 208
(Federal Constitutional Court of Germany)

(Introduction and translation from Donald Kommers, The Constitutional
    Jurisprudence of the Federal Republic of Germany (1989))

[Heinrich Böll, a renowned author, brought suit against a well-known commentator for remarks made about him in a television editorial on the occasion of the funeral of the president of the Berlin Court of Appeals, who had been murdered by terrorists. The commentator lamented the political climate in Germany and complained about the attitude of intellectuals and politicians toward the problem of terrorism. In the course of his remarks he singled out Böll, accusing him of having laid the groundwork of political terrorism. He quoted Böll as having characterized the state against which the terrorists were fighting as a "dung heap defended by ratlike rage by the remnants of rotten power," whereupon the author sued for damages in the civil courts, alleging a violation of his honor. Böll argued that the quotations were false or so ripped from context as to give them a meaning he had never intended. He won his damage suit in a lower court, but the judgment was quashed by the Federal High Court of Justice. The court concluded that while the quotation was incorrect, the commentary was justified as a reasonable interpretation of the author's past statements and thus within the protection of the free-speech provisions of Article 5. Invoking his right to personal integrity guaranteed by the dignity and personality clauses of the Basic Law, Böll brought this constitutional complaint against the High Court's denial of his claim.]

Judgment of the First Senate . . .

B.   The constitutional complaint is valid.

II.   The challenged decision violates Article 2 (1) in tandem with Article 1 (1) of the Basic Law; the form and manner in which the controversial statement of the complainant was reproduced in the [television] commentary is not protected by the free-speech provisions of Article 5.

1.   (a) The attacks upon the complainant in the commentary were of such a nature as to impair his constitutionally guaranteed general right to an intimate sphere. Among other things this right includes personal honor and the right to one's own words; it also protects the bearer of these rights against having statements attributed to him which he did not make and which impair his self-defined claim to social recognition.

The individual may also invoke his right to personality to the extent that his statements are falsified, distorted, or rendered inaccurate. . . . As the Federal High Court of Justice explained, a quotation does not involve the discussion of the critic's subjective opinion but rather a fact for which the person being criticized must be held accountable. For this reason a quotation used as evidence of criticism is an especially potent weapon in the battle of opinions: Unlike the easily recognizable expression of an opinion, this particular quotation is perceived as a fact, with the same power [of a fact] to convince and persuade. If the quotation is incorrect, distorted, or false, then it encroaches that much more upon the speaker's right to an intimate sphere, because he is thus led onto the battlefield as a witness against himself.

(b) The [news] commentator's opinion that the complainant sympathized with those who perpetrated terrorist acts is a public disparagement of the complainant and an attack on his personal honor. The attack is particularly serious because it is based on a direct quotation. If the defendant falsely claimed, as charged, that the complainant described the state as a "dung heap," then he violated [the author's] general right to an intimate sphere as well as assaulted his personal honor. The same is true if the complainant's statements were presented in an altered form. The Federal High Court rightly states that one may not allow criticism to seep into one's citation so as to distort the content of what the speaker actually said. To do so is a violation of the speaker's right to his own words and the [correlative] right to determine how he will present himself to another person or to the public. . . .

2. (a). . . Because value judgments are so much at issue in public discussion, freedom of speech must be allowed in the interest of furthering the formation of public opinion and without regard to the content of individual judgments [citing the *Lüth Case*]. But this protection does not extend to false statements of fact. Incorrect information does not merit protection under the rubric of freedom of opinion because it does not contribute to the constitutionally guaranteed process of forming public opinion [citing the *Schmid-Spiegel Case*]; [on the other hand], the duty to tell the truth cannot be enforced in such a way as to jeopardize the process of forming public opinion: An exaggerated emphasis upon the duty to tell the truth, with the consequent levying of burdensome sanctions, could restrict and even cripple the media by preventing them, because of the unreasonable risks involved, from fulfilling their function, particularly in serving as a public check against government abuses. But neither democracy nor the task of forming public opinion will suffer if the media is required to quote [someone] correctly. Indeed, the task of providing information in the interest of forming public opinion will not be fulfilled in the absence of the duty to report correctly and accurately. The pressures of time and the difficulties of proof do not play the significant role here [where quotations are concerned] as might be the case with other statements of fact. One who transmits a statement is not substantially or unreasonably burdened by the obligation to quote someone correctly. Thus, if by a misquotation one impairs another's general right to personality, this misdeed is not protected under Article 5 (1) of the Basic Law. Otherwise the media would have a license to treat the truth lightly and to ignore without cause or necessity the rights of the party involved.

(b) To be sure, the courts may find it difficult in particular cases to be certain whether a [quoted] statement is properly rendered. The test applied by the Federal High Court is constitutionally doubtful; i.e., how the average reader or listener understands both the statement of the person criticized and the quotation, and whether he also judges as "correct" a quotation that follows some other plausible meaning of the statement within the standard of evaluation used [by the commentator]. This standard would protect a broad spectrum of possible meanings even though they do not correspond to the actual intent of the speaker. Thus [the media] could present to the reader or listener statements clearly objectionable by the customary principles of correct quotation as statements of the person being criticized with the corresponding appearance of truth and objectivity. . . . In any event, the constitutional right of free speech does not justify presenting one interpretation of a complex statement made by the person criticized as if it were a direct quotation without making it clear that this is only the critic's interpretation.

[The court next turned to a brief discussion of the relationship between the freedoms of expression and an intimate sphere.] The use of a direct quotation as proof of a critical evaluation is, as indicated, a particularly sharp weapon in the battle of opinions and very effective in undermining the personality right of the person being criticized. This is especially true with regard to criticism in the press, radio, and television, for the effects here are far-reaching. To rule out any possibility of invading the personality right in these situations, the person quoting someone else is duty-bound to make clear that he is employing his own interpretation of a statement open to several interpretations. The statement would then be placed in proper context; namely, out of the realm of fact and into that of opinion, where it belongs. The listener or reader would then be able to recognize that what is quoted is a statement of opinion and not the communication of a fact. He will then be accurately informed and have a reliable basis for making up his own mind.

Article 5 (1) does not alter the duty to protect the right of personality. [Further], there is no evidence that requiring a journalist to state clearly when he is presenting an exact repetition of an interpretation will restrict the flow of public information or impair the process of freely forming public opinion, or that the freedom to make public criticism would be unduly hampered. . . . To this extent the commentator was required to make clear that he was only giving his interpretation. Instead, he conveyed the impression that he reproduced the complainant's unequivocal statement. Article 5 (1) does not protect either the form or manner of this reproduction. . . .

Questions and Comments

1. What is the rule of law provided by Lüth? What result if Lüth had urged a boycott of a film to protest the film production company's cruelty to animals used in the film, or anti-environmental activities?

2. What role did the text of the constitutional document play in these decisions? Recall the Australian High Court's invalidation of a statute on "freedom of political speech" grounds derived from a constitutional requirement of elections, see Chapter IV above, and note its recent modification of the common law of defamation in order to protect free speech interests. See Theophanous v. Herald & Weekly Times Ltd. (1994), 182 C.L.R. 104 (finding a constitutional right to criticize government officials to be implicit in representative government and to require a new constitutional defense in defamation actions involving criticism of government officials); for further discussion of implicit "freedoms of political communication" in Australia, see Jeremy Kirk, *Constitutional Guarantees, Characterisation and the Concept of Proportionality*, 21 Melbourne U. L. Rev. 1 (1997); A.R. Blackshield, *The Implied Freedom of Communication*, in Future Directions in Australian Constitutional Law: Essays in Honour of Professor Leslie Zines (Geoffrey Lindell ed. 1994)

3. Note that in *Lüth* the challenge was by the defendants and to an injunction issued by a court, while in *Böll* the challenge was by the plaintiff and to the failure of the lower court to impose a penalty on the defendant. Both cases involve litigation between private parties in which the party plaintiff sought vindication of rights of reputation and/or personal autonomy, arrayed against which were claims of freedom of expression. In both cases the German Court saw constitutional interests on both sides of the litigation. Should the interests of the sheriff in New York Times v. Sullivan have been regarded as being of a constitutional magnitude?

In Shelley v. Kraemer, 334 U.S. 1 (1948) the Court held that judicial enforcement of private, racially restrictive covenants, pursuant to a seemingly neutral rule of property law, violates the Fourteenth Amendment's equal protection clause. Yet, as the authors of a leading constitutional law casebook say, *Shelley* is "widely regarded as one of the most controversial decisions in all of constitutional law," Geoffrey Stone, L. Michael Seidman, Cass Sunstein, & Mark Tushnet, Constitutional Law 1717 (3d ed. 1996); they ask why the "state action" question would be controversial in *Shelley* but not in *New York Times v. Sullivan.* Id. at 1718. Compare Canadian Charter Art. 32 (Charter applies to "parliament and government of Canada" and to "the legislature and government of each province") and Art. 24 ("anyone whose rights or freedoms as guaranteed by this Charter have been infringed or denied may apply to a court of competent jurisdiction to obtain" a remedy), which provisions, taken together, have raised questions whether and to what extent the Charter applies to private relations and whether judicial orders in private litigation implicate Charter values. These issues, and related questions, are explored in Section E below.

E.   State Action, Nongovernment Conduct and Rights

Constitutional bills of rights state norms of appropriate conduct. Two closely related and important questions are: Who must comply with those norms? And if norms apply only to governments, when do particular actions count as "governmental"? Constitutional systems have struggled with these questions, particularly the latter, described variously as the "state action" question (U.S.), the question of the constitution's horizontal effect (Canada), or *drittwirkung*, the term used in German constitutional law.

One position is that constitutional restrictions limit the powers of governments, the primary sources of threats to the freedoms protected by bills of rights. Even on this view, categorizing judicial action in private litigation poses definitional issues. For example, the German court believes that a judicial decision refusing to provide a remedy for defamatory statements might violate constitutional rights; the courts, as part of the government, could thus threaten freedom. Another position challenges the claim that a legal system can coherently distinguish between public and private entities or action. Still another position is that in the modern world, some private entities can engage in conduct as subversive of freedom as any legislation might be. Consider the relative threat to liberty of a democratically elected government's suppression of speech (remember that such a suppression must pass through the ordinary legislative processes and survive non-constitutional judicial consideration) and a large private employer's policy of discharging workers who take political positions with which the employer disagrees (remember that such an employer may have to bargain with a union, and in any event must hire workers from somewhere). Consider the relative threat to equality of government employment or housing policies that discriminate on the basis of race and equally discriminatory employment or housing decisions in the private sector (where such policies are not reached by anti-discrimination legislation).

In reading the materials that follow, note the extent to which the words of particular constitutions appear to affect the legal analysis.

Retail, Wholesale & Department Store Union, Local 580 v. Dolphin Delivery Ltd.

[1986] 2 S.C.R. 573 (Supreme Court of Canada)

[The union represented striking workers at Purolator, which continued to operate by using Supercourier, a related company. Before the strike began, Dolphin Delivery performed delivery services for Purolator. Afterwards, it performed the same services for Supercourier. The union threatened to picket Dolphin Delivery's operations if it continued to perform services for Supercourier during the Purolator strike. The trial court enjoined the union from carrying out this threat, invoking the general common law rule in Canada against secondary picketing, that is, picketing of one business because of a strike at another. The common law rule treats secondary picketing as a tort because it is intended to induce a breach of contract—here, Dolphin Delivery's contract with Supercourier. The union appealed to the provincial court of appeal, arguing that common-law standards for injunctions were not satisfied, and that the common law's restrictions on picketing were inconsistent with the Charter's guarantees of free expression and association. Dolphin Delivery responded, in part, that the Charter did not apply to the common law. One justice at the court of appeal suggested to Dolphin Delivery that it withdraw that contention, in exchange for which the union would withdraw its contention that common-law standards were not satisfied. The parties agreed with that suggestion, thereby narrowing the issue to whether the picketing was protected by the Charter. The provincial court of appeal then held that picketing was not an exercise of a right protected by the Charter and, alternatively, that the injunction's provisions were a reasonable restriction on the rights of expression and association and therefore did not violate the Charter. The union appealed to the Supreme Court. The parties' briefs dealt solely with the question of whether the common-law restrictions on secondary picketing violated the Charter. Shortly after the union's representative began arguing, the justices informed the parties that the Court wanted to hear argument on the question of whether the Charter applied to the common law. The parties prepared their positions overnight. Both the union and Dolphin Delivery took the position that the Charter did apply to the common law.]

* * *

McINTYRE J.: . . .

Does the Charter apply to the common law?

In my view, there can be no doubt that it does apply. Section 52(1) of the Constitution Act, 1982 provides . . . that "any law that is inconsistent with the provisions of the Constitution is, to the extent of the inconsistency, of no force or effect". . . . To adopt a construction of s. 52(1) which would exclude from Charter application the whole body of the common law which in great part governs the rights and obligations of the individuals in society, would be wholly unrealistic and contrary to the clear language employed in s. 52(1) of the Act.

Does the Charter apply to private litigation? . . .

[The opinion presents a substantial review of academic commentary and case law from other Canadian courts.]

I am in agreement with the view that the Charter does not apply to private litigation. It is evident from the authorities and articles cited above that that approach has been adopted by most judges and commentators who have dealt with this question. In my view, s. 32 of the Charter, specifically dealing with the question of Charter application, is conclusive on this issue. [Section 32 states: "This Charter applies (a) to the Parliament and government of Canada . . . and (b) to the legislature and government of each province. . . ."] Section 32(1) refers to the Parliament and Government of Canada and to the legislatures and governments of the provinces in respect of all matters within their respective authorities. In this, it may be seen that Parliament and the legislatures are treated as separate or specific branches of government, distinct from the executive branch of government, and therefore where the word "government" is used in s. 32 it refers not to government in its generic sense—meaning the whole of the governmental apparatus of the State—but to a branch of government. The word 'government', following as it does the words 'Parliament' and 'legislature', must then, it would seem, refer to the executive or administrative branch of government. This is the sense in which one generally speaks of the Government of Canada or of a province. I am of the opinion that the word 'government' is used in s. 32 of the Charter in the sense of the executive government of Canada and the provinces. This is the sense in which the words 'Government of Canada' are ordinarily employed in other sections of the Constitution Act, 1867. Sections 12, 16, and 132 all refer to the Parliament and the Government of Canada as separate entities. The words 'Government of Canada', particularly where they follow a reference to the word 'Parliament', almost always refer to the executive government.

It is my view that s. 32 of the Charter specifies the actors to whom the Charter will apply. They are the legislative, executive and administrative branches of government. It will apply to those branches of government whether or not their action is invoked in public or private litigation. It would seem that legislation is the only way in which a legislature may infringe a guaranteed right or freedom. Action by the executive or administrative branches of government will generally depend upon legislation, that is, statutory authority. Such action may also depend, however, on the common law, as in the case of the prerogative. To the extent that it relies on statutory authority which constitutes or results in an infringement of a guaranteed right or freedom, the Charter will apply and it will be unconstitutional. The action will also be unconstitutional to the extent that it relies for authority or justification on a rule of the common law which constitutes or creates an infringement of a Charter right or freedom. In this way the Charter will apply to the common law, whether in public or private litigation. It will apply to the common law, however, only in so far as the common law is the basis of some governmental action which, it is alleged, infringes a guaranteed right or freedom.

The element of a governmental intervention necessary to make the Charter applicable in an otherwise private action is difficult to define. We have concluded that the Charter applies to the common law but not between private parties. The problem here is that this is an action between private parties in which the appellant resists the common law claim of the respondent on the basis of a Charter infringement. The argument is made that the common law, which is itself subject to the Charter, creates the tort of civil conspiracy and that of inducing a breach of contract. The respondent has sued and has procured the injunction which has enjoined the picketing on the basis of the commission of these torts. The appellants say the injunction infringes their Charter right of freedom of expression under s. 2(b). . . .

I find [this] position . . . troublesome and, in my view, it should not be accepted as an approach to this problem. While in political science terms it is probably acceptable to treat the courts as one of the three fundamental branches of government, that is, legislative, executive, and judicial, I cannot equate for the purposes of Charter application the order of a court with an element of governmental action. This is not to say that the courts are not bound by the Charter. The courts are, of course, bound by the Charter as they are bound by all law. It is their duty to apply the law, but in doing so they act as neutral arbiters, not as contending parties involved in a dispute. To regard a court order as an element of governmental intervention necessary to invoke the Charter would, it seems to me, widen the scope of Charter application to virtually all private litigation. All cases must end, if carried to completion, with an enforcement order and if the Charter precludes the making of the order, where a Charter right would be infringed, it would seem that all private litigation would be subject to the Charter. In my view, this approach will not provide the answer to the question. A more direct and a more precisely-defined connection between the element of government action and the claim advanced must be present before the Charter applies.

An example of such a direct and close connection is to be found in Re Blainey and Ontario Hockey Ass'n, [(1986) 26 D.L.R.(4th) 728 (Ontario Court of Appeal)]. In that case, proceedings were brought against the hockey association in the Supreme Court of Ontario on behalf of a 12-year-old girl who had been refused permission to play hockey as a member of a boys' team competing under the auspices of the Association. A complaint against the exclusion of the girl on the basis of her sex alone had been made under the provisions of the Human Rights Code, 1981 (Ont.), c. 53, to the Ontario Human Rights Commission. It was argued that the hockey association provided a service ordinarily available to members of the public without discrimination because of sex, and therefore that the discrimination against the girl contravened this legislation. The commission considered that it could not act in the matter because of the provisions of s. 19(2) of the Human Rights Code, which are set out hereunder:

> 19(2) The right under section 1 to equal treatment with respect to services and facilities is not infringed where membership in an athletic organization or participation in an athletic activity is restricted to persons of the same sex.

In the Supreme Court of Ontario it was claimed that s. 19(2) of the Human Rights Code, 1981 was contrary to s. 15(1) of the Charter and that it was accordingly void. The application was dismissed. In the Court of Appeal, the appeal was allowed [three judges dissenting]. Dubin J.A., writing for the majority, stated the issue in these terms:

> Indeed, it was on the premise that the ruling of the Ontario Human Rights Commission was correct that these proceedings were launched and which afforded the status to the applicant to complain now that, by reason of s. 19(2) of the Human Rights Code, she is being denied the equal protection and equal benefit of the Human Rights Code by reason of her sex, contrary to the provisions of s. 15(1) of the Canadian Charter of Rights and Freedoms (the "Charter").

He concluded that the provisions of s. 19(2) were in contradiction of the Charter and hence of no force or effect. In the *Blainey* case, a lawsuit between private parties, the Charter was applied because one of the parties acted on the authority of a statute, i.e., s. 19(2) of the Ontario Human Rights Code, 1981, which infringed the Charter rights of another. *Blainey* then affords an illustration of the manner in which Charter rights of private individuals may be enforced and protected by the courts, that is, by measuring legislation—government action—against the Charter. . . .

... Where such exercise of, or reliance upon, governmental action is present and where one private party invokes or relies upon it to produce an infringement of the Charter rights of another, the Charter will be applicable. Where, however, private party "A" sues private party "B" relying on the common law and where no act of government is relied upon to support the action, the Charter will not apply. I should make it clear, however, that this is a distinct issue from the question whether the judiciary ought to apply and develop the principles of the common law in a manner consistent with the fundamental values enshrined in the Constitution. The answer to this question must be in the affirmative. In this sense, then, the Charter is far from irrelevant to private litigants whose disputes fall to be decided at common law. But this is different from the proposition that one private party owes a constitutional duty to another, which proposition underlies the purported assertion of Charter causes of action or Charter defences between individuals.

Can it be said in the case at bar that the required element of government intervention or intrusion may be found? In *Blainey*, s. 19(2) of the Ontario Human Rights Code, 1981, an Act of a legislature, was the factor which removed the case from the private sphere. If in our case one could point to a statutory provision specifically outlawing secondary picketing of the nature contemplated by the appellants, the case—assuming for the moment an infringement of the Charter—would be on all fours with *Blainey* and, subject to s. 1 of the Charter, the statutory provision could be struck down. In neither case, would it be ... the order of a court which would remove the case from the private sphere. It would be the result of one party's reliance on a statutory provision violative of the Charter.

In the case at bar, however, we have no offending statute. We have a rule of the common law which renders secondary picketing tortious and subject to injunctive restraint, on the basis that it induces a breach of contract. While, as we have found, the Charter applies to the common law, we do not have in this litigation between purely private parties any exercise of or reliance upon governmental action which would invoke the Charter. It follows then that the appeal must fail. The appeal is dismissed....

Notes on the State Action Problem

a. *Scope Note*: *Dolphin Delivery* illustrates some of the main problems associated with the state action issue. The following notes begin by examining the doctrine articulated in the case; subsequent notes describe the issue as it is dealt with in some other constitutional systems, and identify recurring problems.

b. *The Charter and the common law*: *Dolphin Delivery* holds that the Charter "applies" to the common law, but not in litigation between private parties where the claim for relief rests on common law. This appears to mean that the Charter applies to *executive* (and legislative) actions justified by common law; these might include what are described as the prerogative

powers of the executive—its power to act without legislative authorization—and perhaps such legislative activities as summary punishment for
contempt of the legislature.

Justice McIntyre's discussion of the *Blainey* case is more puzzling.
There a statute generally prohibited discrimination but excluded some
discriminatory acts from its coverage. The complainant sued the athletic
club, and the court held the exclusion a violation of the Charter. Why is
this not simply "private" litigation as described by *Dolphin Delivery*, in
which the athletic club relies on its common-law right to determine who
may use its property? Is the implicit argument that in changing the
common law in many but not all respects, and by preserving the private
club's power to discriminate on the basis of gender, the legislation endorsed
that sort of discrimination?

A related question is raised in Brian Slattery, *The* Charter*'s Relevance
to Private Litigation: Does* Dolphin *Deliver*, 32 McGill L.J. 905, 919 (1987):
"Suppose that the common law holds that a private person should not do
act A to another person in situation X and probably also in situation Y,
although in the latter case the judicial precedents are unclear. However,
the common law clearly permits a person to do act A in situation Z.... The
legislature, in its wisdom, judges this result undesirable and passes a
statute providing that no person shall do act A to others in situations Y and
Z, on pain of the normal civil remedies. The statute does not mention
situation X. It *assumes* the existence of the basic common law rule, and
effectively *extends* it to contexts where its application was hitherto doubtful
or nonexistent. Does it make sense to hold that the rule barring act A is
subject to *Charter* review in contexts Y and Z but not in context X?"

Dolphin Delivery holds that the Charter applies to private rights that
arise from statutory grants. Many commentators assert that this creates an
anomaly, in that all private rights in Quebec arise from the Civil Code, a
statute. On this view, private litigation in Quebec is regulated by the
Charter while private litigation elsewhere in Canada is not. Note, however,
that Germany, which has a similar code-based system of private law, deals
with the state action issue without subjecting all private claims to full
constitutional scrutiny. See note d below.

c. *United States*: The Fourteenth Amendment provides, "No State
shall make or enforce any law which shall abridge the privileges or
immunities of citizens of the United States; nor shall any State deprive any
person of life, liberty, or property, without due process of law; nor deny to
any person within its jurisdiction the equal protection of the laws." The
Civil Rights Cases, 109 U.S. 3 (1883), held unconstitutional a federal
statute, enacted pursuant to Congress's power to enforce the foregoing
provision, making unlawful discrimination on the basis of race in places of
public accommodation. The Court said that the Amendment was "prohibi-
tory upon the states.... Individual invasion of individual rights is not the
subject matter of the amendment.... An individual cannot deprive a man
of his right to vote, to hold property, to buy and sell ...; he may, by force
and fraud, interfere with the enjoyment of the right in a particular case;

... but unless protected in these wrongful acts by some shield of State law or State authority, he cannot destroy or injure the right."

The following notes provide only a sketchy introduction to the complex body of U.S. state action doctrine.

(i) *Common-law rules*: *New York Times v. Sullivan*, held that Alabama's courts violated the First Amendment by imposing liability for a false statement made in a newspaper publication about a public official, without requiring that the plaintiff show that the statement was made with knowledge that it was false or with reckless disregard of whether it was false or not. The Alabama rule was a common-law rule.

More controversial is Shelley v. Kraemer, 334 U.S. 1 (1948), finding state action in a state court's enforcement, by an injunction, of a covenant contained in a private deed barring the sale of the property to African Americans. The Court said, "So long as the purposes of those agreements are effectuated by voluntary adherence to their terms, it would appear clear that there has been no action by the State.... But here there was more. These are cases in which the purposes of the agreement were secured only by judicial enforcement by state courts of the restrictive terms of the agreements.... It is clear that but for the active intervention of the state courts, supported by the full panoply of state power, petitioners would have been free to occupy the properties in question without restraint. These are not cases ... in which the States have merely abstained from action, leaving private individuals free to impose such discriminations as they see fit. Rather, these are cases in which the States have made available to such individuals the full coercive power of government to deny to petitioners, on the grounds of race or color, the enjoyment of property rights...." It was irrelevant, the Court said, whether the state courts would have enforced "restrictive covenants excluding white persons from the ownership or occupancy of property covered by such agreements."[n]

Flagg Brothers v. Brooks, 436 U.S. 149 (1978), involved a challenge to the constitutionality of a state law (a provision in the Uniform Commercial Code), allowing a warehouseman to sell goods entrusted to it for storage to satisfy a lien on those goods, without a prior judicial hearing on such questions as whether the property owner had justifiably refused to pay storage fees. The Court held that the sale of the goods did not involve state action. It described the statute as "a State's mere acquiescence in a private action." "If New York had no commercial statutes at all, its courts would still be faced with the decision whether to prohibit or permit the sort of sale

---

n. The Court asserted that because equal protection rights are "personal rights," "[i]t is...no answer to these petitioners to say that the courts may also be induced to deny white persons rights of ownership and occupancy on grounds of race or color. Equal protection of the laws is not achieved through indiscriminate imposition of inequalities." The Court also noted, however, that it was aware of no case, in either state or federal court, "to enforce a covenant excluding members of the white majority from ownership or occupancy of real property on grounds of race or color," and that it was aware of restrictive agreements used to exclude "Negroes" and "Indians, Jews, Chinese, Japanese, Mexicans, Hawaiians, Puerto Ricans, and Filipinos, among others." See id. at 21–22 & n. 26.

threatened here the first time an aggrieved bailor came before them for relief.... If the mere denial of judicial relief is considered sufficient encouragement to make the State responsible for those private acts, all private deprivations of property would be converted into public acts whenever the State, for whatever reasons, denies relief sought by the putative property owner."

One way of understanding these cases is that the Court is testing the constitutionality of the rule of law directing courts to act as they did. In *New York Times v. Sullivan*, the rule of law directed the courts to award damages when a public figure was libeled by a false statement. That rule was inconsistent with the First Amendment. In *Flagg Brothers*, the rule of law directed the courts to deny relief to the bailor when a bailee sold property in its possession. The Constitution's due process clause did not invalidate that rule. *Shelley v. Kraemer* can be understood in these terms if the rule of law at issue directed the courts to enforce racially restrictive covenants. That would have been a law expressly cast in racial terms, and, on one view of the equal protection clause, unconstitutional. The difficulty with that interpretation is that the rule of law appears to have been more general. Most state courts in 1948 would enforce *all* restrictive covenants, racial or otherwise, as long as they made it possible to sell the property to a sufficiently large number of people. That rule is not cast in racial terms, and may not be unconstitutional under today's interpretations of the equal protection clause.° Other understandings of *Shelley* might invoke the particularly widespread effect racially-restrictive covenants had on housing opportunities for African-Americans.

An exchange in Du Plessis v. De Klerk, 1996 (5) BCLR 658 (South African Constitutional Court), which is discussed in more detail below, illuminates some problems with *Shelley v. Kraemer*. Justice Kriegler would have followed *Shelley* in holding that South Africa's interim constitution applied to common law rules invoked in private litigation. He wrote:

> The [constitution] has nothing to do with the ordinary relationships between private persons or associations. What it does govern, however, is all law, including that applicable to private relationships. Unless and until there is a resort to law, private individuals are at liberty to conduct their private affairs exactly as they please as far as the fundamental rights and freedoms are concerned. As far as the [constitution] is concerned a landlord is free to refuse to let a flat to someone because of race, gender or whatever; a white bigot may refuse to sell property to a person of colour; a social club may black-ball Jews,

---

o. A "neutral" rule enforcing restrictive covenants as long as they did not exclude large numbers of potential buyers would probably have had a highly disproportionate impact on blacks, Jews and other disfavored minorities of the time, since a restrictive covenant prohibiting sale to "whites" would probably not have been enforced because it would exclude too many; given patterns of residential segregation the effect of enforcing racially restrictive covenants was to reinforce substantial limits on where disfavored minorities could live. Subsequent decisions cast doubt on whether the U.S. Supreme Court would recognize such disproportionate effects, alone, as sufficient to demonstrate a violation of the Constitution. See Washington v. Davis, 426 U.S. 229 (1976).

Catholics or Afrikaners if it so wishes. . . . But none of them can invoke the law to enforce or protect their bigotry.

Justice Mahomed found "force in this approach but [had] difficulties with it."

> The premise is and must be that private persons falling within the examples . . . who perform acts otherwise inconsistent with the rights specified in [the constitution], are not doing so in terms of law. I think this is an incorrect premise. All the acts performed by such private persons are acts performed in terms of what the common law would allow. A landlord who refused to let to someone because of his race is exercising a right which is incidental to the rights of the owner of property at common law; this applies equally to the white bigot who refuses to sell property to a person of colour. . . . I am not persuaded that there is, in the modern State, any right which exists which is not ultimately sourced in some law, even if it be no more than an unarticulated premise of the common law and even if that common law is constitutionally immunized from legislative invasion. Whatever be the historical origins of the common law and the evolutionary path it has taken, its continued existence and efficacy in the modern State depends, in the last instance, in the power of the State to enforce its sanction and its duty to do so when its protection is invoked by the citizen who seeks to rely on it. . . . Freedom is a fundamental ingredient of a defensible and durable civilization, but it is ultimately secured in modern conditions, only through the power, the sovereignty and the majesty of the law activated by the State's instruments of authority in the protection of those prejudiced through its invasion by others. Inherently there can be no "right" governing relations between individuals inter se or between individuals and the State the protection of which is not legally enforceable and if it is legally enforceable it must be part of law.

(ii) *Who is the government?*: Lebron v. National Railroad Passenger Corp., 513 U.S. 374 (1995), found state action when the Corporation (Amtrak) refused to lease advertising space to someone who wanted to display a political advertisement. Amtrak, the Court held, was "the Government itself": the United States owned all of Amtrak's preferred stock, and the President appointed a majority of its board of directors. In contrast, there was no state action in Rendell-Baker v. Kohn, 457 U.S. 830 (1982). A school fired employees for making statements critical of the school's policies. The school was a facility for "problem" students, and nearly all of its students were referred to it by public institutions. It was heavily regulated, and over 90% of its operating budget came from public funds. According to the Court, "Acts of . . . private contractors do not become acts of the government by reason of their significant or even total engagement in performing public contracts."

These cases can be compared with McKinney v. University of Guelph, [1990] 3 S.C.R. 229 (Supreme Court of Canada), where a majority of the Canadian Supreme Court held that the university was a private entity even though it was incorporated and largely funded by the government, and could therefore impose a mandatory retirement age for its professors. A minority of the University's governing body were appointed by the government, "and their duty is not to act at the direction of the government but in the interests of the university.... The government thus has no legal power to control the universities even if it wished to do so." Similarly, the actions of a hospital board in terminating physicians' privileges were not covered by the Charter, in Vancouver General Hospital v. Stoffman, [1990] 3 S.C.R. 483 (Supreme Court of Canada). There fourteen of the sixteen members of the hospital's board of trustees were appointed by a public official. Seven were to be appointed "from the community at large," and seven from lists of nominees submitted by educational, medical, and health groups. The Court relied on *McKinney* in Harrison v. University of British Columbia, [1990] 3 S.C.R. 451 (Supreme Court of Canada), where a majority of the board was appointed by a public official. A community college, in contrast, was found to be part of the government in Lavigne v. Ontario Public Service Employees Union, [1991] 2 S.C.R. 211 (Supreme Court of Canada), finding unconstitutional the use of union funds for political purposes over the objection of someone who was required to pay union fees pursuant to a collective bargaining agreement. The community college's board was appointed by a public official, and had the statutory duty of assisting the province's Minister of Colleges and Universities in planning educational programs.

(iii) *Balancing*: Burton v. Wilmington Parking Authority, 365 U.S. 715 (1961), was an action for an injunction against racial segregation at the Eagle Coffee Shop. Eagle had a twenty-year lease on space in a public parking garage, which had signs indicating the building's public character. Eagle was located on the street and had no marked public entrance directly into the garage. The Court held that Eagle's race discrimination could be imputed to the state. "Only by sifting facts and weighing circumstances can the nonobvious involvement of the State in private conduct be attributed its true significance." Here, "[t]he State has so far insinuated itself into a position of interdependence with Eagle that it must be recognized as a joint participant in the challenged activity."

Burton and other state action cases are sometimes explained as involving a balancing of competing rights. See, for example, Robert J. Glennon Jr. and John E. Nowak, *A Functional Analysis of the Fourteenth Amendment "State Action" Requirement*, 1976 Sup. Ct. Rev. 221, 231–32: "The court must balance the relative merits of permitting the challenged practice to continue against the limitation which it imposed on the asserted right.... If the importance of the right is not clearly greater than that of the challenged practice, the effect of the practice on the right does not violate the Amendment. The impact of the practice on the asserted right is in accordance with the Amendment, not because state action is missing, but because it is permissible for the state to prefer the challenged practice rather than the asserted right." Are there any ways of structuring this balancing?

d. *Germany*: Germany's Constitutional Court confronted the state action issue in its first major free speech case, the *Lüth* case excerpted above. In the movie distributor's suit against Lüth, the plaintiff invoked a general provision in the Civil Code providing a remedy against anyone who "causes damage to another person intentionally and in a manner offensive to good morals." The trial court issued an injunction against Lüth, who filed a constitutional complaint in the Constitutional Court, contending that the injunction violated Lüth's constitutional "right freely to express and disseminate his opinion." Recall the Court's discussion of the relationship of the Basic Law to the Civil Code (as translated by Kommers (1989) at 370–71):

> ... the Basic Law is not a value neutral document.... Its section on basic rights establishes an objective order of values, and this order strongly reinforces the effective power of basic rights. This value system ... must be looked upon as a fundamental constitutional decision affecting all spheres of law.... Thus it is clear that basic rights also influence [the development of] private law. Every provision of private law must be compatible with this system of values, and every such provision must be interpreted in its spirit.

> ... This system infuses specific constitutional content into private law, which from that point on determines its interpretation. A dispute between private individuals concerning rights and duties emanating from provisions of private law—provisions influenced by the basic rights—remains substantively and procedurally a private-law dispute....

> The influence of the scale of values of the basic rights affects particularly those provisions of private law that contain mandatory rules of law ..., that is, rules which for reasons of the general welfare also are binding on private legal relationships and are removed from the domination of private intent. Because of their purpose these provisions are closely related to the public law they supplement. Consequently, they are substantially exposed to the influence of constitutional law.... In order to determine what is required by social norms such as ["good morals"], one has to consider first the ensemble of value concepts that a nation has developed at a certain point in its intellectual and cultural history and laid down in its constitution....

> The Constitution requires the judge to determine whether the basic rights have influenced the substantive rules of private law in the manner described.... [H]e must then, in interpreting and applying these provisions, heed the resulting modification of private law. This follows from Article 1 (3) of the Basic Law [stating, "The following basic rights shall bind the legislature, the executive and the judiciary as directly enforceable law"]. If he does not apply these standards and ignores the influence of constitutional law on the rules of private law, he violates objective constitutional law by misunderstanding the content of the basic right (as an objective norm); as a public official, he

also violates the basic right whose observance by the courts the citizen can demand on the basis of the Constitution.

The opinion describes the effect of the Basic Law on private law rights as its "radiating effect." The Court stated that the "basic right to freedom of opinion ... is absolutely basic to a liberal-democratic constitutional order because it alone makes possible the constant intellectual exchange and the contest among opinions that form the lifeblood of such an order...."

> Because of the fundamental importance of freedom of speech in the liberal-democratic state, it would be inconsistent to allow the substance of this basic right to be limited by an ordinary law (and thus necessarily by judicial decisions interpreting the law).... [Courts] must evaluate the effect of general laws which would limit the basic right in the light of the importance of the basic right. [They] must interpret these laws so as to preserve the significance of the basic right....

> ... [Courts] must weigh the values to be protected against each other. [They] must deny the right to express an opinion if the exercise of this right would violate a more important interest protected [by private law]....

> To conclude: Decisions of ordinary civil courts that restrict freedom of opinion on the basis of the "general laws" in the field of private law can violate the basic right of [free speech]. The private-law judge also is required to weigh the importance of the basic right against the value to the person allegedly injured by [the utterance of an opinion] of the interest protected by the "general laws." A decision in this respect requires the judge to consider all the circumstances of the individual case. An incorrect balancing of the factors can violate the basic right and provide the basis for a constitutional complaint to the Federal Constitutional Court. [Kommers' translation (1989) at 372–74]

After considering the facts of the case, the Court found that the trial court had "misjudged the special significance of the basic right to freedom of opinion." Commentators sometimes describe the German approach as one involving the *indirect* horizontal effects of the Basic Law.

Peter Quint, *Free Speech and Private Law in German Constitutional Theory*, 48 Maryland L. Rev. 247 (1989), explains that, prior to *Lüth* German legal theory sharply distinguished between public law and private law, and held that the state was "excluded from private law, except to the extent necessary for the judiciary to allocate the private rights recognized by the Civil Code." The idea was that private law arrangements reflected the individuals wills of private parties, not any public judgment: "[T]he rules of private law were thought to enhance a more general freedom of individuals not to be interfered with by the state—particularly in commercial relationships but also in other areas of everyday life." The "mandatory laws" in private law referred to in *Lüth* cannot be changed by private agreement. As Quint puts it, mandatory laws "refer to extra-legal values such as 'good morals' and thus expressly take into account the broader interests and values of society, including constitutional values."

Do all basic rights have the same "radiating effect" on private law? If not, how can one determine which rights do? The idea of an objective order of values appears to be crucial to the *Lüth* opinion. Does its discussion help courts, lawyers, and citizens to determine what that objective order of values is?

Consider that question in this comparative context: How would a U.S. court analyze the constitutional issue presented in *Lüth*? In NAACP v. Claiborne Hardware Co., 458 U.S. 886 (1982), the Court overturned a state court award for damages incurred by the targets of a commercial boycott designed to secure compliance with demands for equality and racial justice. The state court had found that statements made by boycott leaders caused some people to withhold their business. Noting that "[g]overnmental regulation that has an incidental effect on First Amendment freedoms may be justified in certain narrowly defined instances," the Court held that when a court relied on the causal impact of speech on listeners, the stringent standards established in Brandenburg v. Ohio, 395 U.S. 444 (1969), had to be satisfied. Does the context—in *Lüth* of a noneconomically motivated boycott over a matter raising questions about Germany's rejection of Nazism and in *Claiborne* the importance of a noneconomically motivated boycott with respect to race discrimination by the boycott's targets—play an important role? Consider Edmonson v. Leesville Concrete Co., 500 U.S. 614 (1991), which found that a private litigant's use of peremptory challenges in a civil action to exclude jurors based on race amounted to state action; the Court relied in part on the "overt, significant participation of the government" in establishing the peremptory challenge and in conducting civil litigation and on the judge's involvement in jury voir dire. The Court also noted that "the injury caused by the discrimination is made more severe because the government permits it to occur within the courthouse itself. . . . [which] compounds the racial insult inherent in judging a citizen by the color of his or her skin." Could it be said that, given the particular salience of rejecting racism in the U.S. and the governmental context of the courthouse and the jury selection, this was a contextualized decision based on an objective order of values?

e. *South Africa*: The "state action" issue arose under South Africa's interim constitution in Du Plessis v. De Klerk, 1996 (5) BCLR 658 (South African Constitutional Court): Gert de Klerk operated an air supply service. Du Plessis's newspaper, the Pretoria News, published a series of stories dealing with the supply of arms to Angolan rebels, which violated South African air control regulations. De Klerk sued Du Plessis for libel. A majority of the court held that the defendants could not invoke the protections of the interim constitution's free speech provisions as a defense because those provisions were not "capable of application to any relationship other than that between persons and legislative or executive organs of government."

The principal opinion by Justice Kentridge canvassed the experience in other constitutional systems, and drew "one positive lesson from the Canadian and German approaches.... Both Canada and Germany have developed a strong culture of individual human rights, which finds expression in the decisions of their courts. Yet, after long debate, both judicial and academic, in those countries, the highest courts have rejected the doctrine of direct horizontal application of their Bill of Rights."

The opinion then turned to the interim constitution's language. By its terms, the constitution applied "to all law in force and all administrative decisions taken and acts performed." Justice Kentridge said that the Afrikaans version made it clear that this referred to both statutory and common law. Another provision, § 7 (1), stated that the constitution "shall bind all legislative and executive organs of state at all levels of government." Justice Kentridge said that this clearly excluded the courts from coverage. Finally, he asked why § 35 (3) (which states that "[i]n the interpretation of any law and the application and development of the common law and customary law, a court shall have due regard to the spirit, purport and objects" of the constitution), would be needed if the constitution directly applied to common law disputes between private litigants.

Justice Kentridge argued that applying the constitution to common law rules would lead to anomalies. Suppose the courts held unconstitutional a common law rule barring the widow in a common law marriage from recovering from the estate for loss of support. "[W]hat specific rights are to be accorded the widow? ... This Court would have ... no power to fill the gap. Defendants point out that if this is so, striking down a statute may leave an even worse common law regime in place. The lesson is to be circumspect in attacking statutes. The radical amelioration of the common law has hitherto been a function of Parliament; there is no reason to believe that Parliament will not continue to exercise that function." He also noted that only the Constitutional Court had power to adjudicate constitutional questions, and that applying the constitution to common law rules would mean that a wide range of ordinary cases would raise questions that would have to be referred to the Constitutional Court for resolution. (South Africa's final Constitution gave the high court of appeal in ordinary cases the power to consider constitutional questions, with review of such decisions in the Constitutional Court.)

According to Justice Kentridge, it would be better for the courts to develop the common law with reference to constitutional values, in the usual common law incremental manner, than to strike down common law rules as unconstitutional. After enumerating questions that had arisen in the United States and elsewhere about the proper scope of a defamation action, Justice Kentridge argued that resolving those questions entailed choices that "are not choices which this Court can or ought to make. They are choices which require consideration perhaps on a case by case basis by the common law courts. The common law, it is often said, is developed on incremental lines. Certainly it has not been developed by the process of 'striking down.'" Section 35 (3) authorized the "indirect horizontal application" of the constitution by directing courts to take constitutional values into account in formulating common law rules. "The model of indirect application or, if you will indirect horizontality, seems peculiarly appropriate to a judicial system which, as in Germany, separates constitutional jurisdiction from ordinary jurisdiction." Note how Justice Kentridge combines an argument—perhaps weak standing alone—about the difference between common law and constitutional adjudication with an argument relying on the specific jurisdictional allocations in South African law. See also Note f. below.

Justice Kriegler wrote the principal dissent in *Du Plessis*. He described "a pervading misconception held by some and, I suspect, an egregious caricature propagated by others. That is that so-called direct horizontality will result in an Orwellian society in which the all-powerful State will control all private relationships. The tentacles of government will, so it is said, reach into the marketplace, the home, the very bedroom.... That is nonsense. What is more, it is malicious nonsense preying on the fears of privileged whites, cosseted in the past by laissez faire capitalism thriving in an environment where the black underclass had limited opportunity to share in the bounty."

> Our past is not merely one of repressive use of State power. It is one of persistent, institutionalized subjugation and exploitation of a voiceless and largely defenceless majority by a determined and privileged minority.... The [interim constitution's] Postscript mentions "a divided society characterised by strife [and] conflict." That is not a reference to governmental action only, or even primarily. The "reconciliation and reconstruction" mentioned in the last paragraph relate not so much, if at all, to the oppressed and the oppressive government, but to reconciliation of whites and blacks, to reconstruction of a skewed society....

> It is therefore no spirit of isolationism which leads me to say that our Constitution is unique in its origins, concepts and aspirations. Nor am I a chauvinist when I describe the negotiation process which gave birth to that Constitution as unique.... Nowhere in the world that I am aware of have enemies agreed on a transitional coalition and a controlled two-stage process of constitution building. Therefore, although it is always instructive to see how other countries have arranged their constitutional affairs, I do not start there. And when I do conduct comparative study, I do so with great caution.

Justice Kriegler read the constitution "to expand its scope to the widest limit [its] language could express."

> The internal logic and cohesion of [the bill of rights] is manifest. All organs of State in all their decisions and actions are bound by the terms of the rights. So too are any resorts to law by anybody....

> My reading of [the bill of rights] gives to the Constitution a simple integrity. It says what it means and means what it says. There is no room for the subtleties and nice distinctions so dear to the hearts of mediaeval theologians and modern constitutional lawyers. The Consti-

tution promises an "open and democratic society based on freedom and equality," a radical break with the "untold suffering and injustice" of the past.... No one familiar with the stark reality of South Africa and the power relationships in its society can believe that protection of the individual only against the State can possibly bring those benefits. The fine line drawn [in *Dolphin Delivery* and *Shelley v. Kraemer*] ... ha[s] no place in our constitutional jurisprudence....

What is more, my reading of the Constitution avoids jurisprudential and practical conundrums inherent in the vertical-but-indirectly-horizontally-irradiating interpretation. One does not need to ascertain whether a question is one of public or private law ...; one is not confronted with knotty problems where a private relationship is, wholly or partially, governed by statute....

... We do not operate under a constitution in which the avowed purpose of the drafters was to place limitations on governmental control. Our Constitution aims at establishing freedom and equality in a grossly disparate society....

Also in dissent in *Du Plessis*, Justice Madala observed: "Ours is a multi-racial, multi-cultural, multi-lingual society in which the ravages of apartheid, disadvantage and inequality are just immeasurable. The extent of the oppressive measures in South Africa was not confined to government/individual relations but equally to individual/individual relations. In its effort to create a new order, our constitution must have been intended to address these oppressive and undemocratic practices at all levels. In my view our Constitution starts at the lowest level and attempts to reach the furthest in its endeavours to restructure the dynamics in a previously racist society." In a separate concurring opinion Justice Mogkoro added, "Indeed, in practical terms, the average South African may now be more likely on a day-to-day basis to have her or his human dignity and other fundamental rights threatened by the actions of entities and individuals who are not in any sense organs of the State, than by agents clothed with public power." Even so, Justice Mogkoro was persuaded by the textual analysis in Justice Kentridge's opinion. Justice Mogkoro's opinion emphasized the delicacy of the task of accommodating customary law to constitutional values.

Consider whether the dissenters' position in *Du Plessis* might be consistent with the idea that U.S. courts find state action more readily when the underlying legal issue deals with race. If so, are the dissenters correct in articulating a *general* standard for the horizontal application of constitutional limitations, or should they articulate a standard applicable only to cases connected in some sense to the apartheid regime? If the latter, is *Du Plessis* itself so connected? And if so, would a doctrine attempting to limit horizontal applicability be one that courts could administer?

Note Justice Kriegler's discussion of the limits of the utility of comparative constitutional law.

Section 8 (2) of South Africa's final constitution provides: "A provision of the Bill of Rights binds a natural or a juristic person if, and to the extent that, it is applicable, taking into account the nature of the right and the nature of any duty imposed by the right."

Does this provision create the kind of balancing test that some critics of the U.S. state action doctrine have advocated? Suppose a group of white parents in South Africa decide to create a private school that restricts enrollment to whites, believing that their "traditions" do not receive sufficient attention or respect in the state-run or in non-discriminatory private schools. How should a South African court think about a challenge to this policy based on the final constitution's non-discrimination provision? (a) Is the "nature" of the right against racial discrimination "applicable" to a natural person or corporate entity? (b) Does the "duty" to accept application without regard to race impose impermissible burdens on the private school? (c) Should the legal regime be such that experiments with respect to racially discriminatory policies are allowed?

South Africa's constitutional arrangements required the Constitutional Court to certify that the final constitution was consistent with a series of fundamental principles. It rejected objections to § 8 (2) based on separation of powers principles:

> [Para. 54] The argument was that the effect of horizontality is to permit the courts to encroach upon the proper terrain of the legislature, in that it permits the courts to alter legislation and, in particular, the common law. However, that argument has two flaws. First, it fails to acknowledge that courts have always been the sole arm of government responsible for the development of the common law.... Second, the objectors also fail to recognize that the courts have no power to "alter" legislation.... [E]ven where a bill of rights does not bind private persons, it will generally bind a legislature. In such circumstances all legislation is subject to review. The argument, then, that a "horizontal" application of the Bill of Rights will inevitably involve the courts in the business of the legislature to an extent that they would not be involved were the Bill of Rights to operate only "vertically" is misconceived.

> [Para. 55] A further argument ... was that [§ 8 (2)] would bestow upon courts the task of balancing competing rights which ... is not a proper judicial role. This argument once again fails to recognise that even where a bill of rights binds only organs of state, courts are often required to balance competing rights. For example, in a case concerning a challenge to legislation regulating the publication and distribution of sexually explicit material, the court may have to balance freedom of speech with the rights of dignity and equality. It cannot be gainsaid that this is a difficult task, but it is one fully within the competence of courts.

In re Certification of the Constitution of the Republic of South Africa, 1996 (Constitutional Court of South Africa, Sept. 6, 1996), 10 BCLR 1253 (cc).

    f. *Interpretation in light of a constitution*: *Dolphin Delivery* asserts that the Canadian courts should interpret the common law in light of the

Charter.[p] For example, in M. (A.) v. Ryan, [1997] 1 S.C.R. 157 (Supreme Court of Canada), M. sued Dr. Ryan, her first psychiatrist who, she alleged, had engaged in sexual relations with her. Dr. Ryan sought the records and notes from Dr. Parfitt, M.'s second psychiatrist. Dr. Parfitt asserted a common law privilege against disclosure. The lower courts held that he had to disclose the notes, and the Supreme Court, while recognizing a privilege, agreed:

> [T]he law of privilege may evolve to reflect the social and legal realities of our time. One such reality is the law's increasing concern with the wrongs perpetrated by sexual abuse and the serious effect such abuse has on the health and productivity of the many members of our society it victimizes. Another modern reality is the extension of medical assistance from the treatment of its physical effects to treatment of its mental and emotional aftermath through techniques such as psychiatric counselling. Yet another development of recent vintage which may be considered in connection with new claims for privilege is the Canadian Charter.... [But the] most that the private litigant can do is argue that the common law is inconsistent with Charter values. It is very important to draw this distinction between Charter rights and Charter values. ... [E]nsuring that the common law of privilege develops in accordance with "Charter values" requires that the existing rules be scrutinized to ensure that they reflect the values the Charter enshrines.

Privileges could be justified when the communications involved originated under an assumption of confidentiality, and when confidentiality was essential to the underlying relationship. The "relevant Charter values" included the interest in privacy and the right to equal treatment and benefit of the law:

> A rule of privilege which fails to protect confidential doctor/patient communications in the context of an action arising out of sexual assault perpetuates the disadvantage felt by victims of sexual assault, often women. The intimate nature of sexual assault heightens the privacy concerns of the victim and may increase, if automatic disclosure is the rule, the difficulty of obtaining redress for the wrong. The victim of a sexual assault is thus placed in a disadvantaged position as compared with the victim of a different wrong. The result may be that the victim of a sexual assault does not obtain the equal benefit of the law to which s. 15 of the Charter entitles her. She is doubly victimized, initially by the sexual assault and later by the price she must pay to claim redress—redress which in some cases may be part of her program of therapy. These are factors which may properly be considered in determining the interests served by an order for protection from disclosure of confidential patient-psychiatrist communications in sexual assault cases.

p. *Lüth* likewise suggests that the German Civil Code must be interpreted in light of the objective values of the Basic Law.

These considerations led the Court to recognize a psychiatrist-patient privilege. But it rejected the U.S. Supreme Court's holding that an absolute psychiatrist-patient privilege should be recognized (Jaffee v. Redmond, 518 U.S. 1 (1996)), and endorsed a partial privilege that could be overcome on a sufficient showing and with adequate protections for confidentiality, for example, disclosure only to "trustworthy professionals" such as the defendant's lawyers and expert witnesses.

Is there any difference between this approach and one that would hold the Charter applicable to judicially developed rules of common law? In R. v. Robinson, [1996] 1 S.C.R. 683 (Supreme Court of Canada), the majority rejected a common law rule regarding the availability of intoxication as a defense to a criminal charge. An opinion concurring with this outcome asserted that only the fact that the common law rule was inconsistent with the Charter gave the Court sufficient reason to overrule its prior decisions.

In Du Plessis v. De Klerk, above, Justice Mahomed thought that dispute over the horizontal application of the constitution was almost entirely theoretical because the directive to interpret the common law in light of constitutional values reduced the issue to "whether or not such 'horizontality' is to arise in consequence of the direct application of the relevant [constitutional] right or through the mechanism of interpreting, applying and developing the common law by having regard to the spirit, purport and objects" of the constitution. The latter mechanism would, according to Justice Mahomed, avoid the "distressing" conclusion that "the unfair gains of Apartheid" might be "fossilized and protected by courts.... The common law is not to be trapped within the limitations of its past. It needs not to be interpreted in conditions of social and constitutional ossification. It needs to be revisited and revitalized with the spirit of the constitutional values defined in [the constitution]."

Concurring in Du Plessis, Justice Sachs argued that interpretation in light of constitutional values had the advantage of allowing the courts to develop common law, subject to revision by the legislature. After the legislature acted, the Constitutional Court would "weigh up the matter ... and make an appropriate ruling.... If ... we reformulated the common law ourselves in the manner we thought most consonant with the Constitution, we would ... tie the hands of Parliament until death or a constitutional amendment did us part. There would be little or no scope for Law Commission enquiry, little chance for subsequent amendments in the light of experience and public opinion."

Are the processes of constitutional and common law adjudication as distinct as these excerpts suggest?q Justice Sachs's argument was preceded

---

q. Consider an even sharper formulation:

Judges, in common-law countries, are bound by the doctrine of precedent. They do, however, have some latitude in restricting or expanding the applicab[ility] of a common law rule. Ambiguity in the content of a rule ... gives judges some flexibility in interpreting what the law requires. And the long-recognised need for judges to uphold the values of the community ... in making their deci-

by his statement, "The judicial function simply does not lend itself to the kinds of factual enquiries, cost-benefit analyses, political compromises, investigations of administrative/enforcement capacities, implementation strategies and budgetary priority decisions, which appropriate decision-making on social, economic, and political questions requires. Nor does it permit the kinds of pluralistic public interventions, press scrutiny, periods for reflection and the possibility of later amendments, which are part and parcel of Parliamentary procedures." Is this a general criticism of constitutional judicial review?

Consider Justice Sachs's observations about mechanisms for addressing race discrimination in private employment: "The appropriate manner for such issues to be dealt with would be through legislation pioneered perhaps by the Human Rights Commission. Litigation is a clumsy, expensive and time-consuming way of responding to the multitudinous problems of racist behaviour. Mediation and education could produce results far more satisfactory for the injured person, and considerably more transformatory for the perpetrator. Widespread research and consultation would be needed to decide precisely where to establish the cut-off point in each situation. . . . The problems of sex discrimination might be considerably different from those related to race discrimination, or discrimination on grounds of disability. It is Parliament, and not the courts, that investigates these matters and decides on appropriate interventions and remedies." Is Parliament better suited to resolve remedial issues affecting discrimination in private employment than in public employment?

Note that "interpretation in light of a constitution" is possible only where the constitutional court has authority to determine the substantive law. Recall the South African Constitutional Court's concerns about the division of jurisdiction between the Constitutional Court and the ordinary courts. The Canadian Supreme Court is authorized to determine the common law applied in all provincial courts. The U.S. Supreme Court, in contrast, must accept state law as it is determined by state courts. For an interesting example of the problems created by the U.S. federal system, see Novosel v. Nationwide Insurance Co., 721 F.2d 894 (3d Cir. 1983), in which a federal court guessed that Pennsylvania courts would rely on the First Amendment's free speech provision to create a common law cause of action for wrongful discharge based on an employee's political views. The Pennsyl-

sions, gives the courts, in some circumstances, a margin of discretion in both the application and the interpretation of existing rules.

Judges have never been free, however, to "strike down" the common law and replace it with new rules of their own devising. . . .

Direct horizontal application of guaranteed rights, however, is premised on giving judges the power to remake and remould the law—to reformulate it until it is considered sufficiently consistent with the hierarchy of rights established by the courts through the balancing process. To give judges this wide-ranging power marks a *radical* departure from existing principle.

Anthea J. Jeffrey, *The Danger of Direct Horizontal Application: A Cautionary Comment on the 1996 Bill of Rights*, The Human Rights and Constitutional Law Journal of Southern Africa, vol. 1, no. 4 (Feb. 1997), p. 13.

vania courts subsequently restated the traditional rule allowing discharges at will unless there are the strongest reasons of public policy supporting a limitation on the rule, Paul v. Lankenau Hosp., 569 A.2d 346 (Pa. 1990). Consider the proposition that the U.S. system places more pressure on the Supreme Court to develop an expansive theory of state action than would a system allowing the Supreme Court to resolve controversies on non-constitutional "state law" grounds. See also the discussion of the allocation of common law and constitutional jurisdiction in Du Plessis v. De Klerk, above.

g. *State action and affirmative duties*: State action doctrines are intimately connected to theories about the affirmative duties of government. Consider a claim that a private employer discriminated against an employee on the basis of sexual orientation, in a jurisdiction with an anti-discrimination statute that does not include sexual orientation as a prohibited basis but with a general anti-discrimination clause in its constitution. The employee can claim either that the employer should be bound by the horizontal effect of the general anti-discrimination clause (an approach that does not treat the constitutional clause as requiring "state action," or at least gives the constitutional clause indirect effect), or that the legislature's failure to include sexual orientation in the anti-discrimination statute violates the constitutional anti-discrimination clause (an approach that identifies an assertedly unconstitutional state action in the enactment of the anti-discrimination statute). Recall the treatment of the *Blainey* case in *Dolphin Delivery*.

The connection is brought out by Eldridge v. British Columbia (Attorney General), [1997] 3 S.C.R. 624 (Supreme Court of Canada): Three plaintiffs, who were born deaf, claimed that the province's health care act violated the Charter's anti-discrimination provision guaranteeing "the right to equal protection and equal benefit of the law ... without discrimination based on ... physical disability," because it failed to provide public funding for sign language interpreters for the deaf when they received medical services. The Supreme Court agreed that the "failure to provide sign language interpreters constitutes discrimination in the provision of a benefit." Note that the Court might have conceptualized the claim as follows: The plaintiffs are seeking medical services provided by doctors who act in their private capacities and are reimbursed by the provincial government. The government's refusal to reimburse for sign interpreters' services simply leaves the plaintiffs where they would have been without any governmental intervention, where they would have to pay the interpreters themselves.

Compare Maher v. Roe, 432 U.S. 464 (1977), refusing to find unconstitutional a state regulation granting benefits for childbirth but denying such benefits for abortions that are not medically necessary: The regulation "places no obstacles—absolute or otherwise—in the pregnant woman's path to an abortion. An indigent woman who desires an abortion suffers no disadvantage as a consequence of [the state's] decision to fund childbirth; she continues as before to be dependent on private sources for the service she desires." Is it more helpful to think of these cases as "state action" cases or as cases deciding what the constitution's substantive provisions require?

h. *Conclusion*: A noted U.S. constitutional scholar called the U.S. state action doctrine a "conceptual disaster area." Charles Black, *The Supreme Court, 1966 Term—Foreword: "State Action," Equal Protection, and California's Proposition 14*, 81 Harv. L. Rev. 69, 95 (1967). Do other constitutional courts treat the problem in a more satisfactory way? Consider Louis Michael Seidman and Mark V. Tushnet, Remnants of Belief: Contemporary Constitutional Issues, 70–71 (1996):

> State action problems are authentically hard. The New Deal revolution has left us unable to believe in the naturalness of the public-private distinction, yet also unable to reconceive a system of individual rights without it. We want to repudiate state action rhetoric because we know that it blinds us to human suffering that the state might otherwise ameliorate. Yet we also want to embrace that it preserves a space for individual flourishing that the state might otherwise destroy.
>
> In the face of this ambivalence, it is no wonder that the Supreme Court's state action opinions are confused. The confusion is not the product of sloppy reasoning or unprincipled manipulation of doctrine. It is rooted in the fundamental difficulty in thinking about constitutional law in the legal culture we have inherited from the legal realists and the New Deal.

Does the material in this section cast doubt on that argument? Or does it suggest that the "legal culture" Seidman and Tushnet describe is a more general late twentieth century legal consciousness rather than something unique to the U.S. constitutional experience? Recall the discussion of the "objective order of values" in the *Lüth* and other German cases.

CHAPTER XII

SOCIAL WELFARE RIGHTS

What approaches do constitutions take towards guarantees of social welfare rights, such as rights to subsistence, housing, jobs, or health care? The first generation of modern constitutions contained what we now think of as protections for political and civil rights: guarantees of free expression, freedom of religion, and non-discrimination. Starting in the late nineteenth century, constitutional designers began to consider whether to include second generation social welfare rights in constitutions. They were influenced by the rise of social democratic parties, which sought to advance workers' social welfare, by the conservative response to such parties, exemplified by German Chancellor Otto Von Bismarck's preemptive establishment of some social welfare institutions, and by Catholic social thought, stated most prominently in the 1891 papal encyclical *Rerum Novarum*. Contemporary constitutions sometimes include "third generation" rights as well: guarantees of cultural rights, particularly of minority communities, and environmental protections.

The United States Constitution is a product of a different era and ideology.[a] It contains no textual provisions clearly identifying constitutional social welfare rights, although some modern lawyers and academics have attempted to infuse such rights in the document through the due process and equal protection clauses. In addition, politicians, most prominently President Franklin D. Roosevelt, have articulated accounts of American ideals in which the provision of social welfare rights is a natural complement to, and completion of, the project expressly laid out in the Constitution. After identifying the so-called "Four Freedoms" in early 1941,[b] Roosevelt's State of the Union Address in 1944 called for implementation of what he described as a "Second Bill of Rights" that "[w]e have accepted." These rights, according to Roosevelt, included "the right to earn enough to provide adequate food and clothing and recreation," the right to "adequate

---

a. For discussion, see, e.g., Gerhard Casper, *Changing Concepts of Constitutionalism: 18th to 20th Century*, 1989 Sup. Ct. Rev. 311, 318–21 (suggesting that differences in constitutional approaches are products of differing conceptions of the state, and that even in the 18th and 19th century European conceptions of the state embraced more positive duties than did that in the U.S.); Mary Ann Glendon, *Rights in Twentieth-Century Constitutions*, 59 U. Chi. L. Rev. 519, 525–26 (1992) (noting distinctiveness of the United States'

constitutional approach to welfare rights, including its "dubious distinction" of being the "only liberal democracy that has not ratified ... the two United Nations Covenants on Civil and Political Rights, and on Economic, Social and Cultural Rights").

b. In his 1941 State of the Union Address, President Roosevelt urged that all people were entitled to "four freedoms": freedom of speech and expression, freedom of worship, freedom from want, and freedom from fear.

medical care," "a decent home," and "a good education," and "the right to adequate protection from the economic fears of old age, sickness, accident and unemployment."

The readings that follow raise questions about social welfare rights: Are there conflicts between social welfare rights and first generation political and civil rights? Can courts effectively enforce social welfare rights? Why might constitution designers include social welfare rights in constitutions even if such rights are not judicially enforceable? Does including social welfare rights in a constitution make a difference in the nature of legislative or administrative action? in the material conditions of people's lives?

A. INTRODUCTION: SELECTED CONSTITUTIONAL PROVISIONS

Because the U.S. Constitution does not contain anything resembling modern constitutional social welfare provisions, we begin by providing examples from the Irish and Italian Constitutions. Why these? The Irish Constitution of 1937 has been influential in the development of constitutions by other former members of the British Commonwealth, most notably India. (See chapter IX above.) Including Ireland's and Italy's formulation of the social welfare rights illustrates how two predominantly Catholic countries differently formulate the rights. These two constitutions thus suggest some of the possibilities that can emerge from the various strands of thought identified above.

1. IRISH CONSTITUTION (1937) (SELECTED PROVISIONS)

Article 45. Directive Principles of Social Policy

The principles of social policy set forth in this Article are intended for the general guidance of the Oireachtas [the parliament]. The application of those principles in the making of laws shall be the care of the Oireachtas exclusively, and shall not be cognisable by any Court under any of the provisions of this Constitution.

1. The State shall strive to promote the welfare of the whole people by securing and protecting as effectively as it may a social order in which justice and charity shall inform all the institutions of the national life.

2. The State shall, in particular, direct its policy towards securing:—

i. That the citizens (all of whom, men and women equally, have the right to an adequate means of livelihood) may through their occupations find the means of making reasonable provision for their domestic needs.

ii. That the ownership and control of the material resources of the community may be so distributed amongst private individuals and the various classes as best to subserve the common good.

iii.   That, especially, the operation of free competition shall not be allowed so to develop as to result in the concentration of the ownership or control of essential commodities in a few individuals to the common detriment.

iv.   That in what pertains to the control of credit the constant and predominant aim shall be the welfare of the people as a whole.

v.   That there may be established on the land in economic security as many families as in the circumstances shall be practicable.

3.   (1) The State shall favour and, where necessary, supplement private initiative in industry and commerce.

(2) The State shall endeavour to secure that private enterprise shall be so conducted as to ensure reasonable efficiency in the production and distribution of goods and as to protect the public against unjust exploitation.

4.   (1) The State pledges itself to safeguard with especial care the economic interests of the weaker sections of the community, and, where necessary, to contribute to the support of the infirm, the widow, the orphan, and the aged.

(2) The State shall endeavour to ensure that the strength and health of workers, men and women, and the tender age of children shall not be abused and that citizens shall not be forced by economic necessity to enter avocations unsuited to their sex, age or strength.

---

2.   ITALIAN CONSTITUTION (1948) (SELECTED PROVISIONS)

(Translation from Albert P. Blaustein and Gisbert H. Flanz, Constitutions of the Countries of the World (Italy) (1987, 1994))

Article 2:   The Republic recognizes and guarantees the inviolable rights of man, both as an individual and as a member of the social groups in which his personality finds expression, and imposes the performance of unalterable duties of a political, economic, and social nature.

Article 3:   ... It is the responsibility of the Republic to remove all obstacles of an economic and social nature which, by limiting the freedom and equality of citizens, prevent the full development of the individual and the participation of all workers in the political, economic, and social organization of the country.

Article 4:   The Republic recognizes the right of all citizens to work and promotes such conditions as will make this right effective.

Every citizen shall undertake, according to his possibilities and his own choice, an activity or a function contributing to the material and moral progress of society.

Article 32:   The Republic provides health safeguards as a basic right of the individual and in the interests of the community, and grants medical assistance to the indigent free of charge. . . .

Article 36:   An employed person is entitled to wages in proportion to the quantity and quality of his work, and in any case sufficient to provide him and his family with a free and dignified existence. . . .

Article 38:   Every private citizen unable to work and unprovided with the resources necessary for existence is entitled to private and social assistance.

Workers are entitled to adequate insurance for their requirements in case of accident, illness, disability, old age, and involuntary unemployment. . . .

Questions and Comments

1.   What is accomplished by the Irish Constitution's inclusion of directive principles of social policy that are explicitly made unenforceable in the courts? Consider (a) the extent to which such principles might influence the courts in interpreting statutes or developing the common law (or in implementing the nation's obligations under international agreements); (b) the extent to which such principles might weigh against claims that social welfare statutes are unconstitutional redistributions of private property in violation of provisions such as the Due Process or Takings Clauses in the United States Constitution; and (c) the extent to which such principles might influence the legislature's deliberations. As to the first, the High Court of Ireland held that directive principle (2)(i) created a constitutional right to equality in employment, which in turn meant that picketing aimed at inducing an employer to fire women employees was illegal. *Murtagh Properties Ltd. v. Cleary*, [1972] 1 I.R. 330 (High Court). As to the second, consider how the presence of a social welfare clause in the U.S. Constitution would affect analysis of the attack on limits on employees' hours in cases like *Lochner*.[c] As to the third, would the effect of including the principles in the constitution be different from the effect of including them in a party platform or a speech by a respected national leader?

2.   The post-war Indian Constitution drew on the pre-war Irish Constitution for its enumeration of "directive principles of social policy." Its parallel to section 45 (1) reads "justice, social, economic, and political,"

---

c.   More generally, the presence of non-justiciable social welfare rights provisions might in theory support a presumption in favor of the constitutionality of social welfare schemes enacted by legislatures. See Mary Ann Glendon, *Rights in Twentieth-Century Constitutions*, 59 U. Chi. L. Rev. 519, 530 (1992). As Glendon suggests, some modern constitutions with social welfare rights may not include the same kind of explicit protection for private property rights as exists in the U.S. Constitution. See id. at 529 & n.34 (describing the Constitution of Japan as not including specific protection of property rights but as including social welfare rights that are not, in terms, "programmatic," i.e. aspirational in character).

rather than "justice and charity." There are minor wording differences between section 45 (2) and the Indian equivalent, section 39 of the Indian Constitution. The Indian Constitution's "Directive Principles" also include provisions dealing with village government, the right to work, maternity relief, education, and the protection of monuments and places of national importance and Article 46, providing: "The State shall promote with special care the educational and economic interests of the weaker sections of the people, and, in particular, of the Scheduled Castes and the Scheduled Tribes, and shall protect them from social injustice and all forms of exploitation."

(a) What is the significance of the differences in the texts of Section 45 of the Irish Constitution and Section 39 of the Indian Constitution? To what extent do the differences in wording reflect the substantial social, economic, cultural, and political differences between India and Ireland? Is it possible to evaluate particular texts without also considering the constitutions as a structural whole?

(b) If the idea of including directive principles in a constitution is attractive, how extensive should the list be? Would an extensive list "water down" the directive principles? If the principles are not judicially enforceable, what does it mean to say that they might be watered down if the list were extensive? Does this question ignore the three possible uses of such directive principles noted in paragraph 1 above?

3. Are the above-quoted provisions of the Italian Constitution effectively enforceable in the courts? Note that Article 4 appears to impose a duty on individuals. Consider the possibility that imposing such duties may be necessary if a constitution guarantees social welfare rights. Should constitution designers be concerned about the implications of imposing duties on individuals rather than—or as well as—imposing duties on governments and limitations on government power? Would this be an added reason to regard such provisions as nonjusticiable?

4. Recall Justice Kriegler's suggestion that eliminating the state action requirement in South Africa was a necessary response to the problem of reordering a society structured on an unjust prior regime. See Chapter XI above at 1429 ("No one familiar with the stark reality of South Africa and the power relationships in its society can believe that protection of the individual only against the State can possibly..." create the desired constitutional changes). As you read these materials, consider possible relationships between constitutionalizing social welfare rights and the scope of any "state action" requirement.

B. JUDICIAL ENFORCEMENT OF SOCIAL WELFARE RIGHTS

To what extent does the inclusion of social welfare rights in a constitution make a difference in constitutional adjudication? In the cases that follow the highest courts in Japan and the United States both hold that non-judicial officials have substantial discretion in determining appropriate social welfare policy, even though Japan has a constitutional guarantee of social welfare rights and the United States does not. In reading the cases, note that the doctrine applied by the United States Supreme Court implicates the Equal Protection clause: Those seeking higher levels of public assistance argued that the legislature violated the Constitution by distinguishing between two types of families eligible by statute for public assistance. The Japanese Supreme Court examines the constitutional guarantee of social welfare directly. Does this difference in doctrinal form make a difference in the outcome? In the implications of the holdings?

Asahi v. Japan (1967)

21 Minshū 5 at p. 1043 (1967) (Supreme Court of Japan)

(Introduction and translation from Hiroshi Itoh and Lawrence Ward Beer, The Constitutional Case Law of Japan: Selected Supreme Court Decisions, 1961–1970 (1978))

Shigeru Asahi was a tuberculosis patient at the Okavama National Sanitarium where he was receiving 600 yen (ca. $1.75) from the government, the highest monthly allowance set by the Minister of Welfare, in addition to free meals and free medical treatment. However, when his brother began to send him 1,500 yen each month, the director of the Social Welfare Office not only stopped payment of the 600 yen, but also ordered Asahi to pay 900 yen out of the amount sent by his brother to cover part of his medical expenses. Asahi sought and received a court order restoring the 600 yen payments in full, on grounds that the allowance was unreasonably inadequate for a patient to maintain the minimum standards of healthy and cultured living guaranteed by the Livelihood Protection Law (Article 3 and Article 8, paragraph 2) and Article 25 of the Constitution. However, the Tokyo High Court overturned the first instance decision and held that the minister has the discretionary power under the law to determine the level of payment necessary pursuant to Article 3 of the Livelihood Protection Law. The monthly allowance was found to be low, but not unlawfully low; the monthly cost of daily necessities was computed to be 670 yen for such a patient at that time. The plaintiff's executors appealed the case to the Supreme Court.

[The Court held that the suit was terminated by Asahi's death, because any rights at stake were personal and not inheritable. "For reference," it then discussed the underlying constitutional issue.]

1. Article 25, paragraph 1 of the Constitution provides that "All the people shall enjoy the right to maintain the minimum standards of wholesome and cultured living." This provision merely proclaims that it is a duty of the state to administer national policy in such a manner as to enable all the people to enjoy at least the minimum standards of wholesome and

cultured living, and it does not grant the people as individuals any concrete rights. [citation omitted] A concrete right is secured only through the provisions of the Livelihood Protection Law enacted to realize the objectives prescribed in the provisions of the Constitution. The Livelihood Protection Law provides that any person who satisfies "the requirements under this law" is entitled to "receive assistance under this law" (. . . and such protection is to be given according to the schedule set by the Minister of Health and Welfare). . . . Therefore, the concrete right consists of a right to receive such assistance as is stipulated in the schedule that the minister of Health and Welfare establishes on the belief that the schedule is sufficient to maintain minimum standards of living. Such standards should be set in accordance with the requirements enumerated in Article 8, paragraph 2 of the law and thereby be appropriate to maintain the minimum standards of wholesome and cultured living guaranteed by the Constitution. The concept of minimum standards of wholesome and cultured living, however, is rather abstract and relative. Its substance changes in relation to the development of culture and the national economy and can be determined only after taking into consideration all these and other uncertain factors. Consequently, the authority to determine what constitutes the minimum standards of wholesome and cultured living is usually vested in the discretionary power of the minister of Health and Welfare. His decision may not directly create an issue of illegality, although it might lead to political debate on an issue of propriety and governmental responsibility. Only in cases where such a decision is so made as to exceed or abuse the power bestowed by the law in violation of the objectives of the Constitution and the Livelihood Protection Law, by ignoring the real conditions of life and establishing extremely low standards for the schedule, would such a decision be subject to judicial review as an illegal action.

The judgment below interpreted the act of establishing the standards for aid as a limited administrative action. It was also of the opinion that it is left to the expert discretion of the minister of Health and Welfare to determine what are the minimum standards of wholesome and cultured living and that a mistake made in such judgment is merely a question of propriety as long as it does not deviate from the aims and purposes of the law. Even restricted discretionary action undeniably allows some room for the administrative office to exercise its discretionary power. The judgment below, therefore, was not involved in any illegal contradictory reasoning when regarding the act of establishing standards for aid as an exercise of limited discretion on the one hand, and on the other hand admitting some room for expert discretion of the minister of Health and Welfare. Moreover, the judgment below allegedly took into consideration elements not directly involved in life maintenance when judging the propriety of the aid schedule in this case. These elements would include such factors as the existing national income or the national financial condition as reflected by such income, general standards of living, differences in urban and rural living standards, living standards of the lower income bracket, and the percentage of the population belonging to this class, sentiment among some people that it is unjust to allow better living conditions to those who receive livelihood protection than to the mass of people who do not receive protection, and the priorities of the national budget. It falls within the discretionary power of the minister of Health and Welfare to take these elements into consideration, so his decision does not raise any issues of illegality, but of propriety, as long as it does not deviate from the aims and purposes of the law.

2. As for the livelihood aid schedule under consideration in the present case, the standard was established in July 1953, and the items, quantities, and unit costs that were used as bases for the calculation of 600 yen a month are, as shown in the appendix, attached to the first instance judgment.

The minimum standard of living guaranteed by the Livelihood Protection Law should be of such a level as to make it possible to maintain standards of wholesome and cultured living (Article 3), and the substance of the assistance offered should be determined efficiently and properly with due consideration given to the actual needs of the beneficiary himself and of his family (Article 9); but at the same time, it should not be more than what is required to satisfy the minimum requirements of living (Article 8, paragraph 2). Concerning a beneficiary who is an in-patient like the appellant in this case, there are certain restrictions arising from special factors, such as long-term hospitalization and other medical reasons. In such instances, there is undeniably a certain relationship between the cost of commodities and the effective cure of a disease; and a shortage may have a grave bearing upon the patient. As a means to satisfy the minimum needs of patients, the law prescribes the kind and scope of aid for meeting their needs as well as for providing appropriate aid; the law divides the protective scheme into single and double benefits, and enables in-patients to receive medical aid, including meals, in addition to general livelihood assistance. There is, of course, a difference between the medical and livelihood benefits, both in nature and in manner of disbursal: there is also a system for rehabilitation aid. Therefore, attacks on the livelihood aid schedule as illegal must not be allowed on grounds that no expenditures are made for daily expenses to effect cures or to fill gaps in the present medical and nursing systems, or that it is necessary to maintain one's livelihood after he has left the hospital.

The quantity of daily necessities used by patients naturally depends on the degrees of their individual frugality and the quality of articles concerned. The type of articles needed also differs from patient to patient depending upon the seriousness of the illness; and among certain categories of patients, articles may be used interchangeably. Consequently, in examining whether or not the general and abstract yardstick, called the livelihood aid schedule, for measuring the degree of daily needs of patients is appropriate in actual practice, the answer cannot be determined by analyzing the quantity or unit cost of each individual item. It must be determined with a grasp of the overall picture. Furthermore, daily articles for in-patients can be divided into those for ordinary needs and those for extraordinary need; it is left to the discretion of the minister of Health and

Welfare to determine whether to put such an expenditure under the ordinary schedule, a special schedule, contingency benefits, or a loan system.

Thus construed, the livelihood aid schedule that was determined by the minister of Health and Welfare to be sufficient to meet the minimum daily needs of the in-patient under the facts found by the court below, cannot be said to have exceeded the discretionary power granted him under the law, or to be an abuse of such power, and therefore illegal.

Therefore, this Court, by the opinion of all the justices on the bench, except for the supplementary opinion of Justice Ken'ichi Okuno and the dissenting opinions of Justices Asanosuke Kusaka, Jirō Tanaka, Jirō Matsuda and Makoto Iwata, renders judgment as stated in the Formal Judgment in accordance with the provisions of Articles 95 and 89 of the Code of Civil Procedure.

[All other opinions are omitted.]

Dandridge v. Williams

397 U.S. 471 (1970)

[Maryland's Aid to Families with Dependent Children (AFDC) program computed a "standard of need." It then imposed a maximum monthly grant of $250 per family without regard to family size or the family's needs as determined by its own computation. The Supreme Court held that the Maryland program did not violate the equal protection clause.]

JUSTICE STEWART delivered the opinion of the Court.

... [H]ere we deal with state regulation in the social and economic field, not affecting freedoms guaranteed by the Bill of Rights, and claimed to violate the Fourteenth Amendment only because the regulation results in some disparity in grants of welfare payments to the largest AFDC families. For this Court to approve the invalidation of state economic or social regulation [here] would be far too reminiscent of an era when the Court thought the Fourteenth Amendment gave it power to strike down state laws "because they may be unwise, improvident, or out of harmony with a particular school of thought." Williamson v. Lee Optical Co., 348 U.S. 483, 488. That era long ago passed into history.

In the area of economics and social welfare, a State does not violate the Equal Protection Clause merely because the classifications made by its laws are imperfect. If the classification has some "reasonable basis," it does not offend the Constitution simply because the classification "is not made with mathematical nicety or because in practice it results in some inequality." Lindsley v. Natural Carbonic Gas, 220 U.S. 61, 78 ...

To be sure, the cases ... enunciating this fundamental standard have in the main involved state regulation of business or industry. The administration of public assistance, by contrast, involves the most basic economic needs of impoverished human beings. We recognize the dramatically real factual difference between the cited cases and this one, but we can find no basis for applying a different constitutional standard.... [I]t is a standard that is true to the principle that the Fourteenth Amendment gives the federal courts no power to impose upon the States their views of what constitutes wise economic or social policy....

[T]he maximum grant regulation is constitutionally valid.... It is enough that a solid foundation for the regulation can be found in the State's legitimate interest in encouraging employment and in avoiding discrimination between welfare families and the families of the working poor. By combining a limit on the recipient's grant with permission to retain money earned, without reduction in the amount of the grant, Maryland provides an incentive to seek gainful employment. And by keying the maximum family AFDC grants to the minimum wage a steadily employed head of a household receives, the State maintains some semblance of an equitable balance between families on welfare and those supported by an employed breadwinner.

It is true that in some AFDC families there may be no person who is employable. It is also true that with respect to AFDC families whose determined standard of need is below the regulatory maximum, and who therefore receive grants equal to the determined standard, the employment incentive is absent. But the Equal Protection Clause does not require that a State must choose between attacking every aspect of a problem or not attacking the problem at all. It is enough that the State's action be rationally based and free from invidious discrimination. The regulation before us meets that test.

We do not decide today that the Maryland regulation is wise, that it best fulfills the relevant social and economic objectives that Maryland might ideally espouse, or that a more just and humane system could not be devised. Conflicting claims of morality and intelligence are raised by opponents and proponents of almost every measure, certainly including the one before us. But the intractable economic, social, and even philosophical problems presented by public welfare assistance program are not the business of this Court.... [T]he Constitution does not empower this Court to second-guess state officials charged with the difficult responsibility of allocating limited public welfare funds among the myriad of potential recipients....

[Justice Marshall, joined by Justice Brennan, dissented. They would have applied the following test: "[C]oncentration must be placed upon the character of the classification in question, the relative importance to individuals in the class discriminated against of the governmental benefits that they do not receive, and the asserted state interests in support of the classification." Justice Douglas dissented on statutory grounds.]

Questions and Comments

1. Would the result in *Dandridge* necessarily differ under Justice Marshall's test? His test is often described as requiring a balancing of interests. To what extent can (must) a balancing test incorporate deference to administrators or legislators?

2. The U.S. Supreme Court uses the language of federalism: "the Fourteenth Amendment gives the federal courts no power to impose upon the States their views of what constitutes wise economic or social policy." Is federalism really an issue in *Dandridge*? Assume that Congress *could* develop a national system of public assistance. Would the Court have a larger role if the program at issue had been adopted by Congress? Should federalism concerns play a role in interpreting the Constitution if Congress chooses a policy in which states have substantial leeway in implementing public assistance programs? Are constitutional guarantees of social welfare rights easier to implement in unitary nations than in federal ones?

3. Both Supreme Courts appear to emphasize the complex social and economic questions that public assistance statutes implicate. The Japanese Supreme Court mentions "such factors as the existing national income or the national financial condition," and the U.S. Supreme Court mentions "limited public assistance funds." Harvard law professor Lon Fuller contrasts "bipolar" and "polycentric" disputes. Lon L. Fuller, *The Forms and Limits of Adjudication*, 92 Harv. L.Rev. 353 (1978). (This article was widely circulated among academics many years before it was published, and influenced constitutional scholarship in the United States in the 1960s.) The central form of bi-polar disputes is a dispute involving two parties, whose rights could be adjusted without substantially affecting anyone else. Polycentric disputes, in contrast, resembled "a spider web. A pull on one strand will distribute tensions after a complicated pattern throughout the web as a whole.... [E]ach crossing of strands is a distinct center for distributing tensions." Fuller acknowledged that "the distinction involved is often a matter of degree. There are polycentric elements in almost all problems submitted to adjudication. A decision may act as a precedent...." But, as Fuller saw it, "[w]hen an attempt is made to deal by adjudicative forms with a problem that is essentially polycentric, ... three things can happen, sometimes all at once. *First*, the adjudicative solution may fail. Unexpected repercussions make the decision unworkable: it is ignored, withdrawn, or modified, sometimes repeatedly. *Second*, the purported arbiter ignores judicial proprieties—he 'tries out' various solutions in posthearing conferences, consults parties not represented at the hearings, guesses at facts not proved and not properly matters for anything like judicial notice. *Third*, instead of accommodating his procedures to the nature of the problem he confronts, he may reformulate the problem so as to make it amenable to solution through adjudicative procedures."

Do constitutional provisions creating social welfare rights present the courts with polycentric problems that they are unsuited to adjudicate? Are social welfare rights different from political or civil rights along the dimension Fuller identifies? Consider, for example, constitutional questions about affirmative action, or free expression rights in political campaign financing. Do such questions differ from those in more traditional free speech controversies, where the government seeks to suppress speech either because it disapproves of its message or because it contends that the speech will lead to law-breaking, including violence?

4. The person seeking to obtain a constitutionally guaranteed social welfare right loses in both principal cases. Does this suggest that the inclusion of such rights in the Japanese constitution has no effects?.[d] Compare the discussion of the application of the political question concept in the United States and Germany, Chapter VII above, which questioned whether nominal differences in doctrinal formulations actually produced differing results.

5. Consider the argument of David Beatty, *The Last Generation: When Rights Lose their Meaning*, in Human Rights and Judicial Review: A Comparative Perspective (David Beatty, ed., 1994). Beatty begins by observing that constitutional courts have frequently recognized rights to education through enforcement of equality and other constitutional provisions (in the United States, see Brown v. Board of Education, 347 U.S. 483 (1954), and Wisconsin v. Yoder, Chapter X below), and rights to employment through enforcement of provisions requiring procedural regularity and non-discrimination. In Beatty's view, constitutional courts generally enforce requirements of fairness and proportionality, without regard to whether the underlying interest is social, economic, or something else. He then addresses the argument that constitutional courts ought not make decisions that have significant effects on social and economic policy:

> In terms of the everyday world of politics and policy formulation, it is easy to identify the line from which the courts have consistently recoiled. In functional terms the line is drawn around the power to fix a community's political priorities and to control the fisc or the purse. The fact is that no matter how much encouragement the words of a constitution may seem to provide, no court has ever stood up to the other two, elected branches of government and told them that the actual amounts or levels of financial or cultural support they have provided are inadequate as a matter of constitutional law. Except in cases when a finding of discrimination or unequal treatment has been made out, whenever claimants have asked a court to second guess the

d. For thoughtful discussion, see Mary Ann Glendon, *Rights in Twentieth-Century Constitutions*, 59 U. Chi. L. Rev. 519, 529–30 (1992). While arguing that the constitutional status of social and economic rights reinforces welfare commitments by influencing the tenor of public, legislative and judicial deliberations, Glendon is quite cautious in her evaluation of the extent to which constitutional social welfare rights matter in the actual level of material services provided. She notes that Japan's Constitution, unlike the constitutions of most liberal democracies in Europe, did not identify social welfare rights as "programmatic," nonjusticiable aspirational goals, but textually treated social rights as other enforceable rights. Nonetheless, she concludes, "In Japan ...as in the countries whose constitutional welfare rights are explicitly programmatic, and as in countries like our own without any constitutional welfare rights at all, the welfare state has been constituted through ordinary political processes." Id. at 529.

amount of money a Government has decided to spend on particular social or cultural programmes, they have, without exception, gone away empty-handed.[72]

In legal parlance, the courts have consistently and without exception held that claims of this kind—which ask them to establish basic levels of economic and cultural well-being beyond those fixed by the elected representatives of the people—are "non-justiciable". In lay terms, all of the courts recognize that the elected branches of government have the ultimate authority to decide how much of a community's resources will be spent educating, housing and healing its people and how much will be set aside to alleviate the suffering of those facing conditions of poverty and extreme privation. Even when a constitution explicitly guarantees people a sweeping right to a minimum standard of "wholesome and cultural living" or provides very specific entitlements to social assistance, pensions and health care programmes, as in Japan and Italy, the courts have acknowledged that legislators possess the final discretion to settle, as a matter of hard currency, what meaning these constitutional entitlements will have.[73] Even the Supreme Court of India, which has been especially vocal in urging governments to be responsive to the plight of those forced to live at the margins of human existence, has stopped short of ordering the central or one of the regional Governments to provide work or higher levels of social assistance....

... From the decisions they have made about people's economic and group rights, we have seen that the role of the third branch of government is to guarantee that all laws and official action taken in the name of the state must meet what are, in effect two very basic measures of distributive justice or formal equality. For the most part, the principles of rationality and proportionality impose duties on how those elected to govern must "act" in translating their political platforms into law; not on what the content of their policies and programmes should be.

To borrow a phrase Ronald Dworkin has popularized, one could say the role of the court is to ensure that those who are entrusted with the powers of the state show equal concern and respect for those whose lives they can affect. The principle of rationality guarantees everyone a measure of equal respect by ruling unconstitutional laws which restrict their freedom unnecessarily or gratuitously. The principle of proportionality ensures Governments will show the same concern for everyone's life by insisting that there is some consistency in how burdens and benefits which are contained in the law are distributed.

So long as the courts restrict their role to the impartial application of these broad precepts of equality and personal autonomy, they can with good reason be called "the least dangerous branch" of government. Indeed, the duties and obligations which these principles impose

---

72. See, e.g. *Asahi v Japan.*   **73.** *Asahi v Japan.*

on the "will of the people" and on the powers of the other two, elected branches of government are not only consistent with, they actually promote the same values and ideals which underlie democracy and popular sovereignty as well. By contrast, it would constitute a serious setback for the forces of democracy and the sovereignty of the people if judges ever did assume that, in addition to being guardians of the constitution, they held ultimate power over the purse. The juxtaposition of such sweeping powers in the branch of government least representative of and accountable to the people would be to signal a regression to the kind of oligarchic institutions which distinguished (and ultimately discredited) colonial ideas of 'responsible' government. . . .

. . . [H]uman rights activists . . . will say the protection of human rights will be only partial and incomplete until the courts take up the task of ensuring that Governments guarantee every person a satisfactory level of physical and spiritual well-being. For them, talk of economic and group rights would be a charade if it did not guarantee substantial social and economic entitlements.

To the separation of powers argument advanced by the courts, they will reply that the jurisprudence shows that the line which is supposed to divide the judiciary from the other two branches of government is crossed all the time. . . . To support their claim, reference is often made to those cases in which courts have ordered the state to provide free legal aid or appoint more judges to satisfy the guarantees, common to all constitutions, that everyone has a right to be tried fairly and fairly expeditiously. As well, they commonly cite those judgments, which we have already noted, in which the courts have extended the benefits of various social assistance programmes to individuals and groups which the Governments who designed them meant to exclude.

Human rights activists argue that judgments such as these undermine the force of the separation of powers argument. They will say that if it is appropriate for the courts to order Governments to guarantee a basic level of legal and social services in cases such as these, there can be nothing wrong [in] also insisting that politicians respect whatever minimum standards of housing, health care, education, income etc. are pre-conditions for enjoying a "wholesome and cultured" life. Without guarantees of this kind, they will say, ideas of formal equality and personal freedom can be used to legitimate living conditions of extreme inequality and deprivation.

Both in spirit and as a matter of empirical observation, the case of the human rights activist pulls hard on most people's sympathies. The cause of the dispossessed and the disadvantaged is a compelling one and the fact is, as we have seen for ourselves, on many occasions judges have been very strong and direct in their dealings with the elected branches of government and have insisted that initiatives be taken and social programmes extended at considerable cost to the state.

But however appealing the claim of the human rights activists may first appear, neither the justice of their cause nor the past jurisprudence of the courts warrants assigning the third branch of government ultimate power over the purse. . . .

The decisions to which human rights activists point in support of their case do not really involve the judiciary laying claim to the power of the purse. In fact, they are of a quite different kind. For the most part they follow logically from a straightforward application of the principle of formal equality. Rather than take issue with the level of assistance a programme may guarantee, the courts have simply required legislatures and Governments to make whatever services they do provide available to everyone in a non-discriminatory way. There is no attempt to tell the elected representatives of the people how rich such programmes have to be. Rather than question the practical goals and objectives (the levels of assistance) the people and their representatives set for themselves, in these cases the focus of the courts is strictly on the means—the criteria of distribution—that are chosen to identify who the beneficiaries of these programmes will be.

Even the cases in which the effect of the court's decision has meant that Governments had to spend considerable sums of money on legal aid schemes or in the construction and staffing of more courts, the idea of equality has done much of the work. Essentially, the reasoning of the courts in cases of this kind has been that Governments should set up legal aid schemes in those proceedings when one of the parties (including the state in criminal trials) will have counsel to represent them. Even the decision of the Supreme Court of Canada, ordering one of its regional Governments to provide more facilities and staff for the courts so that people could have their cases decided within a reasonable time, was based on a gross inequality in how those charged with similar offences in different parts of the country were brought to trial.

Those judgments in which courts have ordered a state to pay a person's legal costs are like those in which the judges have insisted that there must be some social, economic, environmental etc. programme or policy in place but have stopped short of asking whether in substance and in detail what has been done is good enough. In all of these cases the courts have recognized that Governments may have different options, with different price tags, available to them to ensure that the legal process is equal and fair, and they have respected the sovereignty of the people and their elected representatives to choose the policy that best suits their needs. Indeed, the Constitutional Court of Italy, regarded by some as the most active court in the field of social and economic rights, upheld the constitutionality of a system of legal aid which provided no compensation for the lawyers involved in part on the ground that questions concerning the adequacy of social programmes like the provision of legal aid do not raise issues within the domain of constitutional law.

6. Beatty argues that constitutional courts can enforce principles of fairness and proportionality, even if they have substantial fiscal implications, but should not enforce social welfare guarantees directly. Would it be fair to reply that the impropriety of the decisions Beatty approves is demonstrated by the fact that they have the same troubling fiscal implications as would enforcement of social welfare guarantees?

Note on the Polish Family Allowance Case and the German "Sozialstaat"

In 1997 the Polish Constitutional Tribunal held that a statute similar to the one at issue in *Dandridge* violated constitutional principles of social justice and equality. The statute provided a subsidy to people who spent a large portion of their income on rent. The subsidy depended on the family's income, the number of family members, and the size of the rental housing. But the subsidy was capped, no matter how large the family, once the housing space exceeded 91 square meters (about 900 square feet). The eight person family whose case resulted in the referral to the Tribunal was living in an apartment of 114 square meters (about 1140 square feet) and was entitled to no housing subsidy. In addition to finding an unconstitutional inequality in the treatment of families of similar incomes, the Tribunal found a violation of the constitutional principle directing the government to provide special protection to families with many children. See 4 East Eur. Case Rep. 69 (1997) (reporting on case POL-1997-1-003).

Recall the discussion of the role of the Catholic Church in the development of the Polish Constitution, Chapter IV above. After reading the materials on Hungary that follow, consider what you would want to know in order to be able to assess the Polish court's decision. Would Beatty consider the Polish Family Allowance case as one involving discrimination and equality principles, or as a resource allocation and redistribution case?

The Weimar Constitution of 1919 in Germany provided for a list of social and economic rights, which could not be implemented. Some, like Professor Osiatynksi, have argued that the failure to implement those rights, due to economic crises between the two World Wars, contributed to undermining respect for constitutionalism and the rule of law. The German Basic Law adopted after World War II did not include a similar list, but does provide that Germany is a "Sozialstaat"—a social state, meaning one that "stands for social justice" and has positive duties to provide for the welfare and basic needs of its citizens. David P. Currie, The Constitution of the Federal Republic of Germany 24–25 (1994). Whether particular polices, like family allowances, are required is disputed in Germany, but the influence of the Sozialstaat concept can be seen in the Numerus Clausus case, where the Constitutional Court invalidated certain restrictions on university admission. See Donald P. Kommers, The Constitutional Jurisprudence of the Federal Republic of Germany 35–36 (2d ed. 1997). Recall, as well, the German Court's emphasis, in the abortion decisions in chapter

I, on the positive obligation of the state to provide support for pregnancy and for the care and upbringing of children, and the recent amendment of the Basic Law on equality to articulate a state duty to take affirmative steps to promote the equality of women and men, described above in Chapter IX. How would Professor Beatty account for these provisions and decisions?

C.   THE DEBATE OVER INCLUDING SOCIAL WELFARE RIGHTS IN EASTERN EUROPEAN CONSTITUTIONS

1.   HUNGARY AS A CASE STUDY

The following case, and the commentary by Professor Sajo, raise additional questions about the judicial capacity to enforce social welfare rights. The Hungarian Supreme Court invalidated adjustments in the nation's social welfare statutes that the legislature thought necessary to speed the transition to a market economy. It allowed the legislature to alter the system, but required a transition period so that those already receiving benefits could adjust to the new system. Professor Sajo, an important participant who takes one side in on-going debates in Hungary (and is generally skeptical about the performance of the Hungarian Supreme Court and its head László Sólyom), criticizes the decision, and related later ones, for interfering with the transition to a market economy.

Hungarian Benefits Case

43/1995 (VI.30) AB Decision (Constitutional Court of Hungary), 4 E. Eur. Case Rep. Const. L. 64 (1997)
(English translation)

IN THE NAME OF THE REPUBLIC OF HUNGARY!

In a procedure aimed at the subsequent examination of the unconstitutionality of legal regulations, the Constitutional Court—with the concurring opinion of Zlinszky, J.—rendered the following

DECISION

1.   The Constitutional Court declares that legal certainty as the most substantial conceptual element and theoretical foundation of the protection of acquired rights is of particular significance from the viewpoint of the stability of welfare systems.

In the interest of the protection of acquired rights, legal certainty requires that benefits provided for a relatively short and determined period under the framework of maternity and child welfare benefits—the pregnancy allowance, the maternity benefit, the child care benefit, the child care fee and the child care allowance—be guaranteed under conditions not less favourable than those specified in legal regulations in force with respect to children already born and children to be born within 300 days as of 15 June 1995.

In the case of the form of subsidy within the maternity and child welfare benefits pertaining to a long period—particularly if it does not include an element of insurance—the legislator is entitled to amend the entire legal regulation of the subsidy so as also to affect the legal grounds of entitlement and its preconditions so that the amendment affects those who had already acquired a right to the subsidy. In such cases, however, the legal certainty related constitutional requirement pertaining to the shift to the new system is to guarantee a period of preparation for those concerned that is needed for adjustment to the amended provisions and for the organization of the finances of a family adjusted to the new conditions.

2. In consideration of the above, the Constitutional Court declares that s. 68, s. 79(4) and (5), s. 92(1)(d) and (2) and, further, s. 93(1) in the part referring to s. 25(1) and (2) of the Social Security Act, s. 25(3) thereof, s. 159(1) and (2) with respect to the sections, subsections and paragraphs listed item by item and, further, s. 83 of Act XLVIII of 1995 on the Amendment of Certain Laws to promote Economic Stabilisation (hereinafter referred to as the "Economic Stabilisation Act") are unconstitutional. . . .

REASONING

I

The Constitutional Court received a number of petitions against Chapters Two and Three of the Economic Stabilisation Act entitled "Amendments to the laws related to the welfare benefit systems." Thus petitions were submitted on the subsequent evaluation of the unconstitutionality and annulment of certain provisions on the family allowance in Chapter Two, Part I, child care benefit and maternity benefit in Chapter Two, Part II, the amendment of Act II of 1975 on Social Security in Chapter Three and, moreover, on the pregnancy benefit and the child care allowance.

Several petitioners regard the fact that the Economic Stabilisation Act virtually overnight annuls or alters the conditions of the benefits, which have played a substantial role in the livelihood of families, as a violation of acquired rights, constitutionality and, within this, legal certainty. As a result of the Law, a portion of the families bringing up children will no longer be eligible in the system. The benefits according to the new system can be planned at most a year in advance.

The family allowance, the child care benefit, the child care fee, the pregnancy allowance, the maternity benefit and, finally, the child care allowance, constituted a calculable, continuous system of benefits; hence, according to the views of the petitioners, the Economic Stabilisation Act violates Art. 70/E of the Constitution* and, furthermore, as a result of its

---

* [Editors' Note: Article 70E provides:

(1) Citizens of the Republic of Hungary have the right to social security; they are entitled to the support required to live in old age, and in the case of sickness, disability, being widowed or orphaned and in the case of unemployment through no fault of their own.

(2) The Republic of Hungary shall implement the right to social support through the social security system and the system of so-

provisions, the rights guaranteed to families, children and mothers in Arts. 66 and 67 of the Constitution would also be violated....

II

The Constitutional Court found this part of the petitions under consideration to be well grounded.

In Hungary, the so-called mixed system of social security has been in operation for decades, in which, in addition to elements of insurance, welfare elements are also present based on the principle of solidarity.

Certain welfare benefits, however, are closely linked to social security benefits ensuring subjective rights for those eligible to the benefit.

The benefits granted in view of the existence of a child, support the families raising children through the intertwined system of several different interrelated institutions.

The mother is eligible to the pregnancy allowance from the fourth month of pregnancy, to a family allowance from the date of delivery, to the maternity benefit for the period of the maternity leave and thereafter, until the child reaches the age of two, to the child care fee;

the woman who received a child care fee or was otherwise eligible to the child care fee is also eligible to claim the child care benefit until the third year of the child; whereas

the State granted the child care allowance, provided that the conditions obtained, to those raising three or more children from the third year to the eighth year of the youngest child.

Apart from the child care allowance, the payment of the established benefits took place automatically within the social security disbursement system.

The provisions of the Economic Stabilisation Act pertaining to the welfare benefit system altered this system in such a way that they transformed it into a so-called "aid system" based on the principle of need, not affecting, however, the family allowance of families and single-parent families raising three or more children; and simultaneously terminated a few institutions, namely, the entire child care fee and the pregnancy benefit.

The pregnancy benefit due as a subjective right for the six months preceding delivery is replaced by the non-recurrent maternity grant following delivery. The child care fee is replaced by a new-system child care benefit.

Eligibility for family allowance, child care benefit and child care allowance will be based on the principle of need.

The benefits to those already eligible according to the conditions of the former system can be disbursed until 31 December 1995 if they do not

cial institutions. See http://www.uni-wuerz-burg.de/law/hu00000_.html.

apply for the version according to the new conditions within the given due date or can no longer do so because of the change in conditions.

The onus probandi of need is to be borne by the applicant or rather his/her *per capita* income must be calculated pursuant to the principles applied to the income tax return (and according to its form).

Benefits are to be determined for a year at most. Need must be proved by the applicant annually, changes within the benefit period, promptly. If this condition does not obtain, the benefit is terminated.

As a result of the Economic Stabilisation Act, the changes taking place in the welfare benefit system are highly substantial because they replace a well-known and calculable benefit system maintained for decades that families have become used to and these changes affect acquired rights already acknowledged according to this former system.

In the course of the interpretation of Art. 70/E of the Constitution, the Constitutional Court has pointed out several times that the State meets its obligation specified in this Article if it organises and operates the system of social security and welfare benefits to ensure welfare provisions. Within this, the legislature can itself determine the means whereby it wishes to achieve the objectives of social policy.

In relation to Art. 70/E(1) of the Constitution, the Constitutional Court also declared that "social security means neither guaranteed income, nor that the achieved living standard of citizens could not deteriorate as a result of the unfavourable development of economic conditions" [citing earlier constitutional court decisions].

It follows that the State has wide-ranging rights with respect to changes, regroupings and transformations within welfare benefits depending on economic conditions. The right of the State to change, however, is not unlimited |citing another constitutional court decision].

The Constitutional Court points out that the constitutional criteria of changing welfare benefits by force of law are partially independent of the question of what benefits those eligible would be entitled to pursuant to Art. 70/E of the Constitution. In judging which of the benefits actually enjoyed and how they can be withdrawn constitutionally, social rights have a role insofar that, as a result of such withdrawals, the extent of welfare benefits may not be reduced to below a minimal level which may be required according to Art. 70/E. The constitutionality of the individual changes, however, also depends on whether or not they clash with other constitutional principles and rights, thus whether or not they are contrary to the principle of legal certainty, the ban on negative discrimination and, if it is also a benefit including elements of insurance, to the protection of property.

The legislature therefore does have a constitutional possibility to transform welfare benefits due as a citizen's right into a benefit based on the principle of need within the above limitations.

This change laid down in the Economic Stabilisation Act, however, constitutes a substantial change in comparison to the former system which has an impact on the acquired rights and expectations affecting the existence and livelihood of families, and the education of children and also has an impact on additional family decisions pertaining to livelihood.

Hence the rights due to the State—the legislature—pertaining to changes, can be constitutionally exercised only within the very stringent restrictions of constitutionality.

The Constitutional Court had already pointed out with the force of a principle that Art. 2(1) of the Constitution declares that "constitutionality includes the honouring of acquired rights" [citing earlier decision].

The protection of acquired rights is enforced as a law in a constitutional state. It is not, however, of absolute force that would not allow for exceptions. The judging of exceptions, however, is only possible on an ad hoc basis. The Constitutional Court must be the ultimate forum to decide whether the conditions of an exceptional intervention obtain.

Legal certainty—which, according to the Constitutional Court, is the most substantial conceptual element of a constitutional state and the theoretical basis of the protection of acquired rights—is therefore of exceptional significance from the viewpoint of the stability of the welfare benefit systems.

The benefits and the related expectations cannot be substantially altered constitutionally without sufficient reason or overnight. Special reasons are required for changes without a transition.

In the case of a mandatory insurance system, the insured may expect a greater stability in the system against the mandatory payment of contributions, that is, against this type of "expropriation."

According to the Constitutional Court, the objectives of Art. 70/E of the Constitution can be equally implemented through mandatory or voluntary insurance. [citing earlier decision]. The two systems, however, also imply different obligations for the State.

The mandatory payment of contributions ordained by law—which, in substance, differs from the sharing of the public burden (Constitution Art. 70/I) because it gives rise to a personal and predetermined claim—can be legitimised only by a high degree of state guarantee (from another aspect: confidence protection).

Mandatory insurance draws off the assets which the person concerned could have used to take care of himself/herself and his/her family at his/her own risk and puts these assets in the service of social security so that the insured will also be able to take care of others based on solidarity.

By turning the coverage into social property, the state collectivises a typical ownership behaviour.

Within the mandatory insurance system, the protection of the welfare benefits that had evolved in relation to this system is therefore particularly warranted.

The expectations enjoy the greater protection the nearer they are to "fulfilment," that is, to the opening of the subjective right to the benefit. The benefit acquired and already enjoyed should be protected even more.

This is also related to the bearing of risk inherent in long-term continuous legal relationships to which the Constitutional Court had already referred to several times [in an earlier opinion].

The beneficiary must attach particular importance to the historically evolved situation and operation of social security in the sense that it manages its finances not out of capitalised assets or other assets the value of which can be maintained over time, but it consumes the current payments of the active generations (who can only pin their hopes on the future). That is to say, this type of financing makes the system even more high-risk. The further away the due date of the benefits, the less calculable it is as to what social security will be able to provide them with.

Hence, the period of the benefit promised must make a difference from the viewpoint of the protection of acquired rights.

Benefits for a short and determined period such as the child care benefit, the child care fee and the child care allowance enjoy priority protection not only because of their subject but also because the short, foreseeable period of confidence.

Because of this, their termination before maturity violates the acquired rights constituting legal certainty, hence it is unconstitutional.

Protection has a different mode and extent in the case of the family allowance for the period of a generation where, in view of the long period of performance, a change in the economic situation may constitute a better grounded reason for the interim change planned by the State.

The protection of expectations and benefits is stronger depending on whether or not they are matched by the financial contributions of the beneficiaries. The withdrawal of the benefit due against the contribution or the unfavourable change of its legal basis can be evaluated according to the criteria of the impairment of basic rights.

This the Constitutional Court has professed to as to the priority of the insurance element within the mixed system of social security. The pension must be disbursed for the period covered by the contribution unconditionally, otherwise the beneficiary would be deprived of an acquired right; the nominal pension calculated according to the rules of insurance is inviolate, the arbitrary changing of the ratios of insurance and solidarity is constitutionally excluded.

Changing a benefit without a transition or "allowing it to slide down" from an insurance to a form of aid also brings about an essential change in the legal position in the sense that the person concerned falls into a weaker category from the viewpoint of confidence protection (the protection of property ceases) and this is commensurate with an intervention in basic rights.

The constitutionality of such a change should also be evaluated accordingly. The unconstitutionality of an arbitrary change in the ratios of the insurance and solidarity elements can be interpreted in this context. In itself, it is difficult to separate the part of the contribution that will be turned into one's own benefit and the part that will be spent on others. It is against the Constitution if the ratios shift to the extent that the level of the protection enjoyed to date deteriorates to a qualitatively weaker one and this is not constitutionally grounded.

The legal relations of social security must be addressed in their entirety.

The employers (principals, *etc.*) paying the contribution also constitute part of the system. According to the technical structure of financing, a part of the contribution is paid by the employer but based on the personal income disbursed. The direct deduction is like the advance on tax, in principle, it could be disbursed and the beneficiary could be required to have it paid immediately. Therefore, the beneficiary is entitled to all the guarantees concomitant with the insurance element irrespective of who actually pays the contribution in his favour.

According to the present system, the greater part of the payment constitutes an obligation of the employer, it is the employer who has to manage his assets in such a way as to be able to meet this obligation. Confidence protection—also as part of the protection of property as a basic right—extends to the employer as well.

In the case of social security benefits where the insurance element has a role to play, the constitutionality of the reduction or termination of the benefits should be evaluated according to the criteria of the protection of property.

The extension of the protection of property as a basic right to social security benefits and expectations fits into the conception of the Constitutional Court expounded on the function of property. "The Constitution protects the right to property as the traditional material base of individual autonomy in action. Constitutional protection must follow the changes in the social role of property so as to be able to perform this protective task in the meantime.... The protection of property as a basic right extends to rights and titles and rights based on public law taking over the former such role of property (for instance, claims against social security)." [citing earlier decision]. It was in that spirit that the Constitutional Court protected the assets of the churches, public bodies and primarily municipalities on the grounds that that is the basis of their autonomy. The change that has taken place in the protection of property has been discussed many times in literature and is generally accepted.

The vast majority of the people today are not "self-pensioners," it is not their own material goods that constitute social and economic security in their inactive age; ab ovo, they live in a way that they invest a part of the result of their work in social security and it is its benefits that perform the function of guaranteeing security of property taken *stricto sensu* according to the Civil Code. If their goods are withdrawn for this purpose by law, it is the law that must provide for a security comparable to that of property. The same applies to the benefit due in case of loss of income arising because of illness or other reasons and, further, to the part of the coverage of the additional burden arising from the raising of children, which the insured compensates for by the payment of contributions. (From the viewpoint of protection, there is no significance in the fact of whether or not the benefit was due after or during the period of contribution payment.)

The protection of property does not lose its link to one's own property or value generating work in the field of social security either. That is why we distinguish the more full protection of "insurance" services paid for by our own contribution from the lesser protection of grants of an aid type. Property protection may extend until the service or benefit performs the same function which the material property would serve, from which it follows that this one of its attributes cannot be terminated. At the same time, an exact matching between one's own payments and the benefits received is excluded by the mode of operation of social security (non-capitalised assets), the built-in solidarity element and the risk also borne by the contribution payer in the long term.

The Constitutional Court expounded its views on the protection of property as a basic right and the social limitedness of property in *Dec. 64 of 1993 (XII.22) AB*(9). It declared, *inter alia*, that the extent of the constitutional protection of property is always concrete: it depends on the subject of the property, its object and function as well as the mode of restriction. On the other hand, the Constitutional Court also declared that, simultaneously with the extension of the protected range:

"the socially limited nature of property makes the far-reaching restriction of the owner's autonomy constitutionally possible.... The issue of constitutionality has turned out to be the question of what are the cases when the owner must suffer restriction by public powers without any compensation and when he or she may lay claim to compensation.... The focus of the evaluation of the constitutionality of State intervention, the actual sphere of evaluation by the Constitutional Court has now become the judgement of whether ends and means, public interest and the restriction of property are proportionate."

According to Art. 13(2), "public interest" is sufficient to allow for restriction. The establishment thereof is the task of the legislature. The Constitutional Court does not examine the absolute necessity of the choice of the legislature. Instead, it examines the grounds for the reference to the public interest and whether the solution "in the public interest" does or does not violate another constitutional right....

Within these frameworks of the examination of proportionality, we obtain an instrument that also takes into account the specific features of the legal relationship of social security in order to match the objective and means of the change in the course of the constitutional investigation into the changes. The "public interest" justifying the reduction in benefits, the operating capability and survival of the entire social security system, the increased difficulties in the fulfilment of the commitments of the State due to external reasons and those inherent in social security (also including the impossibility of collecting contributions from the employers) that can be appraised in terms of the categories of constitutional law.

In the cases, however, where the insurance element does not have a role or this role has been ultimately terminated, the constitutionality of intervention in welfare benefits must be decided not on the basis of the protection of property as a basic right, but on the basis of the requirements of legal certainty which is the most important constituent of a constitutional state. The Constitutional Court has expounded the content of legal certainty in a number of Decisions. The judgments which specify a period of preparation for the implementation of the new provisions in relation to the coming into force of a legal regulation as a constitutional requirement, represent a substantial portion among these [citing cases].

In the case of the family allowance, the constitutional problem consists not of the changing of the former system but of the fact that already acquired rights are to be replaced by a system with a different base without any transition. In developing the provisions of the Economic Stabilisation Act, the legislature neglected the fact that the regularly received benefit already received and the promised expectation played an important role in the long-term decisions pertaining to the livelihood of the family in making the decision to have a child or children as well as their schooling and education. Although the family allowance by itself has never covered the financial obligations of the families raising children, by virtue of its calculability, it guaranteed a relative stability in taking care of them.

The State intervenes in this system with its decisions appearing in the Economic Stabilisation Act, taken because of the detrimental economic position of the country so that the impact of such intervention is not known. Nor is there an opportunity for the family to prepare for the decisions related to the sustenance of the family, establishing a family or schooling required which it has to bear because of the changed system of the family allowance and the other burdens appearing in parallel (lack of subsidies on children's clothing, textbook prices, tuition fees, other burdens related to the livelihood of the family).

As the Economic Stabilisation Act ordained the implementation of the withdrawal or transformation of already acquired rights with respect to the family allowance virtually with immediate effect, this gave rise to an unconstitutional situation. In view of this, the Constitutional Court rendered its Decision on the unconstitutionality of the termination of the family allowance acquired in accordance with earlier provisions and the provisions entering the Economic Stabilisation Act into force as specified in the purview.

III

Children and mothers are particularly protected by the Constitution [Arts. 15, 16, 66(2) and 67(1) of the Constitution]. Therefore, in judging whether the intervention in already acquired rights has been constitutional or arbitrary, the Constitutional Court is of the view that it is not sufficient to refer to the economic reasons for the intervention. It is also necessary to examine whether the constitutional provisions referred to are also asserted. Society also has an elementary right linked to having an active population in the future, able to realize the commitments of the State....

Although the maternity benefit, the pregnancy allowance and other benefits or even the concrete regulation or extent of the family allowance cannot be directly derived from the provisions of the Constitution, in order to decide whether the actual formulation of a benefit is contrary to another constitutional right, the provisions of the Constitution pertaining to the right to live [Art. 54(1)] must also be taken into account.

The far-reaching consideration of the mother's right to self-determination according to the law in force requires appropriate positive counter-measures that will facilitate the willingness to bear children. The institutions of the child care fee and of the pregnancy benefit introduced in 1993 were expressly such encouraging institutions. Their immediate termination—as the new rules of the child care allowance, similarly, the non-recurrent maternity grant available upon delivery which replaces the pregnancy benefit guaranteed from the fourth month of pregnancy, cannot constitute a comparable compensation—upset the balance between the obligation of the State to protect life and the acknowledgement of the right of the mother to self-determination. Through this, an unconstitutional situation may arise.

The Constitutional Court annulled the rules which gave force to the provisions pertaining to the termination of the pregnancy benefit due from the fourth month of the mother's pregnancy and of the child care fee due until the child is two years old as well. In addition to specifying a new date for the coming into force of these provisions, the legislature must also take care that the forms of benefit replacing these institutions be harmonised with the obligation of the State to protect life arising from the Constitution and guarantee the exercise of the mother's right to self-determination....

With this Decision, the Constitutional Court also points out that before bringing and implementing decisions pertaining to the transformation of the entire welfare benefit system, the State must, in addition to the aspects related to the financial-economic situation of the country, also take into account its obligations to protect the mother, the family and the child as expressly assigned to it by the Constitution.

In implementing and putting into force the legal regulations aimed at the transformation of the welfare benefit system affecting a substantial portion of society, it is a requirement adequate to the constitutional state according to Art. 2 of the Constitution, that the behaviour of the State be calculable, so that both natural and legal persons be able to plan with good grounds in making their economic- or family- or livelihood-related decisions and that they be able to infer the will of the State incorporated into legal regulations.

The Constitutional Court found that the entry into force of the Economic Stabilisation Act through the fact of having ordained the implementation of the provisions terminating certain benefits and transforming the entire welfare benefit system as of 1 July 1995, even if certain benefits were to continue to be disbursed until 31 December 1995, failed to meet this requirement, hence it is unconstitutional.

Because of this, the Constitutional Court annulled the sections of the Economic Stabilisation Act which pertain to the implementation and entry into force of provisions related to the welfare benefits of mothers and families raising children and to the annulment of certain former provisions in accordance with the provisions of the purview. The related rules of the state decrees issued in execution of the Economic Stabilisation Act share in the fate of these provisions.

ZLINSZKY, J., concurring: I agree with both the purview and the reasoning of the Decision. Yet I [prefer]...a more comprehensive theoretical analysis of the constitutionality of the interrelated reform plan of legislation .... The introductory part of the Constitution prescribes the peaceful transition to a constitutional state realising a social market economy as a constitutional goal. In the course of the transition to a market economy, the State withdraws from significant areas of the economy transferring them to private owners, whereby private interest, private business and initiative take over the role hitherto played by state planning and control. In the interest of improving social production, living standards and personal dignity, society must take on the disadvantages that appear in the course of this process because all in all, the process equally serves the interests of the individual and of the community. Nevertheless, it is a requirement of the transition to a social market economy that, in the course of the transition, the constitutional state guarantee the social protective net for all those who have not been able to prepare in time for the new order, for those who disproportionately suffer the free assertion of market conditions or who, because of their age, condition of health or other reasons, are no longer capable of adjusting to the new conditions. If those having landed in a disadvantageous situation have acquired a state promise under the former social system to guarantee their social security, this is guaranteed for them in the first [paragraph] of Art. 70/E of the Constitution harmonised with the constitutional requirements of the protection of property. If they lose the basis of their livelihood through no fault of their own as a result of the transition, but do not have guarantees of this kind, the second turn of Art. 70/E of the Constitution obliges the State pursuant to the principle set forth in Art. 17 to guarantee the benefits (supplements) needed to live.

In the course of the transition to a market economy, the withdrawal of the State from the economy and from the area of administering public tasks transferred to within the sphere of other private autonomy is *ab ovo* concomitant with a decrease in the burden on general state and the downsizing of state administration to expedient and efficient dimensions.

In the course of this, care must be taken that the utilisation of the material assets of the State be effected so as to serve the public interest in a proportionate manner: the market economy brings about a situation whereby the individuals better able to adjust to the market may have outstanding advantages in the enforcement of their financial interests but it is the requirement of a constitutional state that the utilisation of funds covered by the common sharing of the public burden, that is, the funds of the State, be legal and serve the interest not of individuals, but of the public. The constitutional requirement of sharing the public burden (Art. 70/I) prescribes both the proportionate sharing of the public burden and their expedient, transparent and conscientious, responsible utilisation within the framework of a constitutional state.

Factors covering direct state tasks as well as constitutional cost factors to be put to guaranteeing social interests protected by the Constitution, by the State, or the equalisation of society-level additional burdens undertaken by individual strata, play a role in the development of the public burden. Although the objective is to reduce the secondary distributive role of the State to a minimum in a market economy, nevertheless, this cannot be fully disregarded in a social market economy, although the more efficient distribution of state funds according to new methods, the support of current and rightful claims exclusively and the elimination of superfluous expenditure obviously constitute important public interests.

Beside the development of industry, the establishment of the market, the efficient and environmentally-friendly management of natural resources, the "reproduction" of the human factor of society appears as a factor among the tasks ensuring the sources of the social burden. The Decision of the Constitutional Court also points out that, under the existing system, social security is, and will also be in the future, ensured not through the capitalisation of the accumulated goods the value of which can be maintained over time but through the burden undertaken by the current productive population. Not even accumulated capital can produce without human collaboration. That is why Arts. 15, 16, 66(2), 67(1) and (3) of the Constitution prescribe the priority protection of families, parents and the young by the Constitution entrusting the legislature with the task of developing and regulating the system of this support and protection. Article 70(2) of the Constitution makes express reference to the fact that the legislature must take measures aimed at the elimination of inequality of chances, whereas Art. 70/B sets forth the right of those participating in production to an adequate income and rest (and indirectly forbids their disproportionate use for public objectives and their withdrawal).

If all these constitutional measures are regarded in harmony with the fact that our present legal order obliges the parents to maintain, educate and raise their children and that the strictly material part of this burden serves expressly social objectives and if we take into consideration that the various strata of society take an unequal part in maintaining and providing for the future generation and that this burden causes the more inequality of chances to the detriment of those raising children, the better and more expediently they meet their obligations as parents, then it must be established that the package presently under discussion serving economic stabilisation as a correct and necessary social objective, is far from being in harmony with the constitutional principles and provisions referred to from the viewpoint of family protection and equality of chances and the proportionate bearing of the burden of social reproduction.

The Constitutional Court does not wish to tie the hands of the legislature in the search for the appropriate solutions, but in a form more express than that incorporated in the Decision, the Court must call [to] the attention of the legislature that it can expect the agreement and cooperation of society, which is the necessary precondition of the success of the reforms, only if it chooses and requires restrictive solutions which meet the moral perceptions and sense of social justice of society. It may well be that the existing welfare benefit system is obsolete, it contains deficiencies, it occasionally provides superfluous support and overall, even to date, is far from guaranteeing the equal sharing of the burden of social reproduction. In perspective it continues to assist in the continuous deterioration of the social equilibrium also, in the long run, reducing the quality of society. Rather than providing excessive benefits to the strata which, on the whole, undertakes the reproduction of the population, it provides them with less support than that which could be expected constitutionally.

It seems that the present "package" rather than facilitating stabilisation as it promised will further increase these differences as it makes the conditions of raising children much more difficult. Its provisions that have appeared to date are expressly contrary to the requirement and objective of social and economic stabilisation in the long run. The legislature should present at least an acceptable plan for long-term settlement to society in order to be able to justify even the maintenance of the existing negative discrimination. Their aggravation, especially for the sake of the apparent advantage of savings, which are of negligible importance in quantitative terms from the viewpoint of the entire budget can hardly be harmonised with the word and the spirit of the Constitution. The decision of the Constitutional Court provides an opportunity for the legislature to create the missing harmony. There are good reasons to call attention separately to this opportunity as well as a necessity.

Questions and Comments

1. To what extent does the Hungarian Supreme Court treat social welfare provisions as a form of property, protected by the principle that legislation must respect settled expectations to justify its holding? For a parallel argument in the U.S. context, see Charles Reich, *The New Property*, 73 Yale L.J. 733 (1964). To what extent does the court rely on the fact that beneficiaries made required contributions to state-sponsored social assistance systems? What do the court's references to the "solidarity element" of such systems mean? Note that the court distinguishes between constitutional protections for property as such and the constitutional principle of "legal certainty." What is the legal effect of such a distinction?

2. Does the court's decision provide guidance to a legislator who seeks to revise the statutes held unconstitutional in a way that would simultaneously satisfy the court and continue the transition to a market economy? Consider the possibility that it would be sufficient to include some schedule for phasing out benefits due under the prior system. How much discretion would the legislature have in developing such a schedule, according to your reading of the court's decision? Does the court's decision leave you with the impression that it would give substantial deference—or any deference—to legislation phasing out the benefits due?

3. With respect to the benefits that, in theory, the legislature can phase out with a long enough transition period, consider how persuasive are the Court's arguments for why the transition provided by the law was inadequate.

––––––––––

Andras Sajo, *How the Rule of Law Killed Hungarian Welfare Reform*, East European Constitutional Review, vol. 5, no. 1 (Winter 1996), p. 31

Recent decisions of the Hungarian Constitutional Court have slowed the restructuring of the Hungarian welfare system and dramatically raised fundamental questions concerning society's post-communist welfare dependence. In order to understand what is at stake in these decisions, one must look at the role of welfare rights before and after 1989. . . . [A] broader view reveals some perverse effects of the rule of law in a poorly designed separation of powers system. Against this background, moreover, the tension between constitutional rights protection and economic modernization, under the specific circumstances of postcommunism, becomes visible. Contrary to the pattern commonly observed in less developed countries making the transition to market economies, in a number of East European countries legal institutions introduce a new dimension to the process. The rule of law, generally associated with both democratization and support for emerging markets, produces unexpected outcomes.

Welfare rights and welfare service provisions, as used in this article, refer to all social services and monetary support provided by the government to individuals according to their social status. It includes pensions for the retired and the handicapped, sickness benefits (including the universal and free health care system), child, maternity and family support (both monetary supplements and special care), unemployment benefits, and free or subsidized housing—including low-interest loans. (Free education, subsidized cultural activities, and even communications are or were provided as free or heavily subsidized ["social"] government services; but they are not included here, although they too were intended to promote the general welfare.) All of this is generally referred to as the social insurance scheme. The scheme is administered with government-underwritten, non-voluntary "social insurance funds," governed by the 1975 Social Security Act which is used as a reference law in special benefits schemes (e.g., unemployment benefits). . . .

Recent decisions of the Constitutional Court, which reflect its social welfare theories, represent the most elaborate effort so far to protect welfare rights and institutional services inherited from state socialism. The social and political consequences of its 1995 social welfare decisions indicate that the rule of law and constitutional arrangements indeed play an obstructionist role, preventing changes to the inherited welfare system. In the current stage of the transition process, the constitutional social-rights provisions help to perpetuate the inherited status quo, including state socialist institutional and organizational arrangements.

Welfare rights and transition (to what?): Hungary as an example

An important debate is taking place in the West concerning (a) the affordability of maintaining welfare services, such as those provided under state-socialism, and the efficiency of the structures and institutions that provided these services; and (b) the wisdom of writing into the new constitutions these welfare entitlements as enforceable or vested rights, state goals, state promises or, for that matter, in any other form.

. . . [Some] authors emphasize the importance of local East European political realities and pragmatically invoke the political impossibility of omitting such rights. They argue that the majority will never endorse a constitution or support any political leadership that does not offer the social services and social security enjoyed under state socialism, or at least does not promise most of the traditional forms of social security. Without an adequate safety net, or simply because of growing economic inequality, increasing social discontent may permit populist or totalitarian groups to win the day. Others assert that social and economic rights are indeed fundamental human rights, heralded in the United Nations Universal Declaration of Human Rights. Socialists claim that such social rights were indeed provided under state socialism: they belong to the people, and therefore the people cannot be deprived of these services or of social security in general.

The counterargument is that, by constitutionalizing welfare rights and thus obliging the state to provide welfare services, the relatively poor countries of East Europe are destined either to stagnation and eventual economic collapse, or to a cavalier disregard of constitutional provisions. Such disregard will undermine the constitution's credibility. Actually, most East European constitutions promise a fair number of social rights that are unenforceable in court, mandating that the government maintain welfare institutions, particularly a social insurance scheme. Despite constitutional promises and political pledges, there has been a steady deterioration in the quality and quantity of these services.

The actual impact of constitutionalized social welfare provisions on society is not easy to determine. The welfare provisions of the East European constitutions force governments in their region to offer at least a minimum of services. Under conditions of early capitalist accumulation, a constitutionally required safety net may play a humane and even politically stabilizing role, tempering a system of unlimited exploitation and rampant theft. After all, in these societies, private charity is ridiculed, social solidarity at the interpersonal level is on the verge of collapse, and a considerable percentage of the GNP escapes taxation (20 to 30 percent of the market in Hungary is "black," and thus unreachable by the authorities).

. . . Everywhere in postsocialism, pensioners are the victims, paying an excessive price for having lived under state socialism. They are now at the mercy of state socialist pension schemes. And do not forget that it was prohibited during the communist period to accumulate personal wealth. With such a legacy, state welfare remains the only major form of compensation for lived injustices and, for many employees, particularly those with many children, the only chance to retrieve at least the crumbs of their earlier contributions to national wealth.

On the other hand, both the inherited bureaucracy and the clients or recipients of the welfare system insist on welfare spending that is excessive given deficit-riddled budgets and scant public resources. In 1993, for example, welfare spending in Hungary was 27.7 percent of GDP, compared to 23.3 percent in France (which the Juppé government in 1995 believed to be inhibiting growth even in France.) Welfare spending in Hungary is much higher than in most other countries with a comparable level of economic development.

Losers in the market transition, in any case, may find that constitutional courts are ready to spring to their support. This help is somewhat unexpected, as constitutional courts are not designed to respond to special group interests. Nevertheless, some of these courts, notably the Hungarian and the Polish ones, seem prepared to give more protection to welfare entitlements than any political party in power. Of course, political parties in power are subject to relatively less pressure from welfare recipients than from fiscal bureaucracies, private entrepreneurs, and government employees. One cannot expect much social responsiveness from governments, unless it is extorted by strong trade unions or the direct action of powerful groups (e.g., railway engineers), especially before elections (consider Yeltsin's sudden preelection attentiveness to pensions and wages). Constitutional courts, by contrast, are well-insulated from both pro- and anti-welfarist influences. The justices are therefore free to follow the ideological platform of the parties that elected them. Since Christian and social democratic parties played a crucial role in appointing these justices, they usually sympathize with the values of social solidarity and are less acutely concerned with fiscal responsibility. Justices are inclined to justify their decisions by invoking timeless values rather than economic calculations. Moreover, the language of the constitutions in Eastern Europe mandates (although not imperatively) the protection of social rights, while market development and deficit reduction are not constitutionalized aims. Creating market economies is an aspiration, while welfare is a requirement.

As a consequence, constitutional courts will assume the role of defending the poor, and even more, of the "respectable" impoverished classes, whatever the social costs. This attitude may result in a kind of judicial activism that destabilizes the constitutionally mandated, although imperfect, separation of powers. To assume the role of "protector of ordinary people" is undoubtedly tempting. By defending entitlements against budget cutting measures, constitutional courts may gain popularity and public authority, as happened after the Hungarian Court overturned certain legal amendments that would have reduced welfare spending.

The inherited welfare system . . .

Due to the current shortfall in services (shortages of heating and electricity, inadequate health care, nonavailability of prescription drugs, absence of affordable housing, etc.), the state socialist welfare system, in hindsight, looks attractive to most citizens, notwithstanding all the inadequacies and hidden inequalities in that system.

What nostalgic citizens seem to forget is that the former welfare system hampered genuine economic modernization. There is probably no "iron law" concerning the relationship between the level of economic development and welfare expenditure, but the costs of social welfare services provided under late state socialism clearly exceeded available resources. Welfare overspending and non-productive incentives hampered economic reforms aimed at growth and social modernization. The welfare system was based on the assumption of full employment. Social services quite often included free or below-cost in-kind benefits. In Russia, for example, food was heavily subsidized at the workplace canteen or in school meal programs. Childcare, housing, vacations, and many other services were provided by the employer. Most healthcare services were provided free of charge at the workplace. As long as the government welfare sector survives the collapse of communism, strong pressure to maintain these elements of "local welfare" will persist. . . .

The costs of reforming the welfare system are inhibiting the transformation. Restructuring the welfare system is expensive. It involves enormous economic losses, and generates substantial material and human sources of resistance. In addition, certain services were provided in a manner that is impossible to reproduce. (What can one do with social welfare provided at the workplace when the workplace has been shut down? Who would like to take over a factory-based kindergarten, especially if, say, heating at the kindergarten was provided by the factory's now defunct power station?) The inherited pension service is incapable of coping administratively with the problem of fund management, even if governments were to transfer assets to pension funds and if new contributions were allocated directly to those funds. Inefficient service providers, delivering now unaffordable services, resist changes and insist on continuing services. Hospitals and schools resist scaling down even where alternative, and more cost-effective, methods are available. Traditional welfare bureaucracies continue with their previous managerial practices. . . .

Only against this background can we understand the "mystery" of the socialist electoral victories and resistance to welfare reform in general. It also helps us understand why, even where and when nonsocialist parties were in power, inherited welfare services were not formally discontinued. Both Catholicism and nationalist solidarity favored the perpetuation of welfare provisions. In Hungary, during the center-right coalition government (1990 to 1994), social service entitlements were actually extended to new groups and made available to all citizens, and means-testing was not used. In most socialist countries, welfare spending was further increased as part of the effort to compensate for past (communist) injustices....

In at least two respects, privatization has contributed to increased reliance on government services and welfare spending. First, private owners are reluctant to bear the costs of social welfare for those they employ. Second, competitiveness requires new owners to undertake massive layoffs. After 1989, therefore, governments had to subsidize welfare recipients more directly. The pensioners and the unemployed (including the temporarily unemployed, such as the sick) needed more money to cover food, rent, and utility expenses. The free health-care system faced increased expenditures for pharmaceuticals and personnel.

To the extent that the state tried to meet the above requirements, at least where economic stagnation or depression did not allow high taxes, governments had to *increase budget deficits*. The financing of the public debt contributed to inflation, which then further contributed to an increase in the deficit and additionally undermined the position of the socially most vulnerable welfare-dependent groups. The initial underfinancing of public services was further aggravated by inflation and these two factors resulted in a deterioration of the social services provided.

The social gospel according to the Court

After 1989, having added to an already enormous internal and foreign debt, Hungary was particularly vulnerable to (since dependent on) foreign lending institutions. It had no choice but [to] give serious consideration to the demands of Western lending organizations and to foreign and domestic investors. The conservative Antall government continued state socialist welfare spending practices, thereby increasing the budget deficit, which was financed in part by foreign loans. In 1995, servicing the debt risked plunging the country into bankruptcy. After considerable delay and numerous failed attempts, in February 1995, the socialist government agreed to an austerity package that included reduced welfare spending. These measures primarily affected higher education (layoffs and a $18-a-month tuition fee), health-care (contributions were required for certain services), family and child support (restricting child support and maternity support to the needy), and social insurance (limiting sick-leave benefits and apparently imposing more sick-leave costs on employers). The government also introduced measures to reduce tax evasion and other forms of cheating.

Although the austerity package was watered down to some extent in Parliament, the "Act on Economic Stabilization" was adopted in May and promulgated in June 1995. The president of the Constitutional Court declared (while the act was still being debated prior to the president's promulgation) that the Court had received many complaints on this matter and that it would review the case with exceptional urgency. According to Court precedent, such speedy review of unsigned bills should have been granted only upon a presidential request.

On June 30, 1995, the Constitutional Court ruled: (a) that the welfare changes could not enter into force as of July 1, 1995 because there was no "adequate adjustment period" granted; (b) that some of these restrictions were unconstitutional and therefore void per se, irrespective of their date of entry into force; and (c) that the Court would continue to examine the legislation after its summer recess.

In a series of additional decisions rendered during fall 1995, the Court refused a number of complaints challenging the bill but continued to strike down a number of its provisions not meeting the test established in the June decision. In response, cabinet members criticized the Court for exceeding its constitutional mandate. In the opinion of the minister of finance, half of the expected savings from the legislation were lost because of the Court's decisions. In order to maintain most of the social services and benefits, without further increasing the budget deficit, the socialist majority in Parliament increased the personal income tax for the highest income bracket (48 percent in the above $4000 bracket, which represents about 10 percent of the taxpayers). . . .

The doctrinal position of the Court . . .

In order to provide substantive social security, in the name of formal legal certainty, the Court relies on a number of doctrines.

(1) *Purchased rights.* In earlier pension cases, the Court emphasized that a pension is, at least partly, a purchased right because employees actually contribute to their pension funds. As late as 1993, however, the Court recognized that the Hungarian pension system did not operate as an actual pension fund. Contributions were not managed separately, the actuarial principle did not apply, the pension benefit provided to a person was largely unrelated to actual contributions and was paid out of the current budget. Before 1995, the Court recognized that social and insurance considerations were mixed in the pension system. In this regard, only the "arbitrary disregard" of the insurance element would be unconstitutional (ABH, 1993. 203).

In Hungarian law, the pension fund and pension claims are called *tarsadalombiztosites* (social security) and the 1975 Social Security Act regulates, among other benefits, pensions of the handicapped, sick leave, and work related benefits. The 1995 "stabilization" legislation was concerned with sick leave which was financed from a Sickness Insurance Fund and is separate from the Pension Fund and was based on ongoing employer and employee contributions. The employer contribution was in the range of 45 percent of the employee's salary, while the employee contributed only about 1.5 percent. The austerity legislation provided that the first five days of sick leave would not be paid, while an additional 20 days would be paid directly by the employer and not by the fund. (Previously, between 1990 and 1995, three days were unpaid and the employer had to cover the sixth to the fifteenth day of an illness.)

The Court ruled that sick-leave compensation was a social insurance service. The right to benefits under the law was a purchased right based on pension contributions. The Court stated that disregarding employer and employee contributions in determining the amount of services and benefits under the scheme was arbitrarily excessive and therefore unconstitutional. The insured employer receives less than half his contribution's value and a reduction that exceeds 50 percent is arbitrary, according to the classic legal notion of laesio aenormis. . . .

(2) *New Property.* The identification of sick leave compensation with insurance-based social security allows the Court to grant it property-like protection. In order to do so, the Court developed its own "new property" theory of social security services.

The idea of a property-like protection of welfare rights was developed by Charles Reich. The US Supreme Court granted property-like protection to welfare recipients (Goldberg v. Kelly, 397 U.S. 254 [1970]). Given the fundamental textual differences between the US and the Hungarian constitutions, "property likeness" means opposite things in the two countries. In the United States, property-like protection in this context means due-process protection. Accordingly, an individual cannot be deprived of a welfare service without due process, meaning that the beneficiary is entitled to some kind of hearing. In the Hungarian constitutional context, property protection means a flat prohibition on takings. The purely procedural-individual new property of the Supreme Court has thus been transformed in Hungary into a substantive property protection against legislation. The Hungarian Court considers the non-contribution-related pension benefits (and as mentioned above, by extension, all contributions presupposing social security benefits) to be constitutionally secured against legislative alteration. Today's legislation cannot change in a fundamental way social benefits promised by earlier legislation, unless the legislature can prove to the Court that the taking serves the public interest and only if there is full and immediate compensation. Such compensation is highly unlikely, although the ongoing reform contains an element of institutional compensation, namely, the government is supposed to transfer assets to the funds in order to guarantee their independence.

In a 1993 concurring opinion, Chief Justice Laszlo Solyom argued that the communists took away private property, which is an important guarantee of personal autonomy. In order to assure the autonomy-granting function of property, the functional equivalent of property, namely, welfare entitlement, should also receive property-like protection. In other words, the autonomous citizen of postcommunism will be independent of government if government cannot deprive him of government-provided services and benefits. If citizens take for granted that they will receive benefits irrespective of their contributions, their decisions will not depend on the attitude of the state in this or any other matter. This is not socialism. This is communism, pure and simple. It presupposes that the communist abundance of goods will satisfy all needs. It also presupposes that the social welfare status quo is financially affordable.

But what if the Hungarian welfare system is bankrupt and administratively incapable or corrupt? What kind of autonomy do we have if the beneficiaries, as political (voting) actors, depend on the survival of the status quo ante? They will insist, by democratic means, on channeling more and more resources into the system (or the "system" itself will do so, following its autopoetic-Solyomian program). Autonomy has become dependency in this brave new postcommunist world. In the end, the noble attempt to create autonomy by tying the state to social rights and constitutional promises has obstructed the dismantling of the socialist-bureaucratic, red-tape state.

(3) *Acquired Rights*. The Hungarian Court has extended the legislative irrevocability of property-like social rights (in case of contributions) to other welfare rights, even where there is no contributory element. It carried out this extension on the basis of the theory of acquired rights. It has granted constitutional protection to various forms of status-related family support (child and maternity support) against legislative attempts to turn these supports into means-tested allowances....

It should be noted that the Hungarian Court has avoided the simple language of constitutional welfare rights. To have struck down the Stabilization Act's provision on the grounds that it directly violates social rights granted by the Constitution, would have been inconsistent with the majority's view. In the earlier cases, the Constitutional Court ruled (in conformity with the text of the Constitution) that, without further legislative steps, social security rights guarantee only subsistence-level care. Subsistence-level protection was not challenged under the Stabilization Act. In order to protect entitlements above the level of subsistence, the Court had to rely on non-subsistence based rights. Some of these rights are not even in the Constitution, such as a mother's right to self-determination, a concept developed in the context of the Court's abortion decision.

According to the theory of positive (affirmative) rights protection, the material conditions guaranteed by the state should enable such self-determination. Restrictions on these entitlements would therefore undermine those claims apparently related to civil status, such as the protection of motherhood, which are directly related to human dignity, the core value of the constitutional system.

The key concept is that there are legitimate expectations, based on constitutional promises made good by legislation. But legitimate expectations of welfare support are based on personal contribution or sacrifice. But what kind of personal contribution can there be in a welfare system that is *not* based on need? What are the personal contribution-generating expectations in the case of maternity benefits and child support (and here the beneficiaries include the unborn fetus)? Is procrastination a sacrifice, generating legitimate expectations? The last time that people were rewarded by the state for procreating was when the Romans granted benefits to the mob because they were providing *proles*. Is the Court saying or intending to say that people should be rewarded for reproduction simply because they expected the state to give financial support once they produced babies? Is there an implicit contract between parents and the state where the baby is delivered in consideration of a welfare package? The Court's reasoning implies that, wherever there is a constitutional task for the state, legislation cannot deprive rights-holding beneficiaries of what was once promised by law because, in the case of constitutional welfare tasks, the legislatively generated expectations of the beneficiaries result in acquired rights. . . .

In order to balance the government's powers, the Court holds up constitutional rights that need protection. The more fundamental rights citizens have, the more there is to be protected and, therefore, the regulatory domain becomes increasingly constitutionalized, i.e., subject to constitutional review. Every time the Court is perceived to be the protector of additional rights, it gains additional power of review over both legislative and executive branches.

This nondeferentialism has serious doctrinal consequences. In order to maintain its permanent control over legislation, the Court may undermine the very value it claims to be upholding, namely, the predictability and stability of legal relations. While the Hungarian Court strongly emphasizes its reliance on earlier decisions in politically sensitive cases, unfortunately, these precedents are often only two weeks old. The Court, as was predicted by Max Weber, has to disregard the binding power of its own precedents. With more rigid rules, the Court's power to manipulate would disappear.

Deference to the legislative branch, in any case, is not the Constitutional Court's guiding consideration. The Court recognized in principle that the welfare system can be, and even should be, transformed. These changes cannot, however, have a destabilizing or expectation-annihilating effect on the actual beneficiaries of the system and a "sufficient" transition period is needed. It is not clear from the Court's decision how long expectations are to be respected. The six months expressly provided for in the Stabilization Act was not enough time in the justices' eyes, although those who would qualify under a subsistence-income test for support were still to receive benefits at a slightly lower level.

As for the maternity-leave system (270 days plus three years after birth), it seems that everyone who has a claim will receive all actual or comparable benefits. In the case of child support, the Court allows adjustments, although only after a non-specified period of preparation. The Court stated that, with respect to immutability, child support is different. In this case, the service is provided for a very long period of time (up to age 18 and 25 for students). It is therefore legitimate or reasonable to expect that there will be changes in the benefits. There can be no legitimate expectation that the benefit will be provided without significant changes throughout the whole period. It is not clear whether a significant reduction in the amount of support or its restriction in time (for example, child support only until the age of 14) will be held constitutional.

From the formal rationality of the market to populist material justice

The Hungarian Court attempted to ground its decisions on strictly neutral and formal rule-of-law concepts. But it usually employs these formal rule-of-law criteria without heeding their generally held meaning, and in a way that ... systematically extends the review powers of the Court over legislation. As the Court tried to argue on neutral grounds, it could afford not to look at the socioeconomic consequences of its decisions. In practical terms, the social and economic consequences of the Constitutional Court's Stabilization Act decisions support the social status quo. The effects are in line with populist reasoning, which claims that "ordinary people" are entitled to currently enjoyed gratuities. The people deserve it, simply because they are the people. Or, as was openly stated in a concurring opinion by Justice Janos Zlinszky, the state should support those groups that undertake the reproduction of society. Such support shall be granted by the whole society. In practical terms, this means a redistribution at the expense of those whom the state can most easily tax. As mentioned above, the government was constrained to increase further taxes on the highest income bracket.

Moreover, as most people feel that they have a vested interest in the current system, and because this feeling received constitutional status in the Court's reasoning, the Hungarian social welfare system will continue to deteriorate and offer deteriorating services to all. The inflation of social services (as well as the inflation generated by an unrestricted financing of these services) is the least efficient and, in terms of its distributive effects, probably the most unfair way to reshape and streamline the social service and welfare systems. The price will be paid even by those now believed to be the principal beneficiaries of welfare services.

The Court's formalistic approach is based on a series of doctrines and notions, all interpreted in a singular and dogmatically distorted way. The interpretation is systematically biased towards the status quo. What was intended to be a formal doctrine of the rule of law turns out to be a series of non-neutral concepts with a clear material (substantive) or natural law orientation (acquired rights, legitimate expectations without contribution, new property and the injustice of laesio aenormis). These concepts help give formal support to specific non-positive claims that belong to natural law (substantive conditions or material guarantees of the right to self-determination).

It is tempting to see a certain parallel between the disguised aspirations of the Court to material justice (in the Weberian sense) and the prevailing populist attitude of the welfare-dependent masses under post-communism. Many Hungarians believe that the state should take care of them irrespective of their efforts, as was customary under state socialism. People expected that, in exchange for their political loyalty and docility, the government would provide services. The welfare provided by the state as a monopoly provider developed a *dependency* on the state. If they were noncompliant or disloyal, people deprived of their means of independent subsistence could be brought "into line" under this system of dependency.

To receive housing or housing support from your employer was a matter of discretionary choice, based on micro-loyalty (loyalty within the workplace or party cell). Of course both the oppressors and the oppressed cheated. People thought that they were exploited, and many felt that they were robbed (by nationalization, lack of opportunities, censorship, etc.), and therefore whatever they got back surreptitiously was less than what they deserved. People believed they were entitled to all free social services regardless of their performance and contribution. Their loyalty was limited. In those days, the social compact was based on the assumption that there could be no open resistance or challenge to the regime while a certain amount of cheating, black market activity etc., was more or less "legitimate" in everyday thinking. "One has to make a living under hardship." This is the mentality of *petty survivalism*. It is reproduced today in the general welfare expectancy of the public. People feel that formal restrictions concerning these services are unfair, irrespective of their needs, and access to those services by mass cheating is legitimate. . . .

The Hungarian Constitutional Court, in its earlier decisions, declared that its mission was to restore the rule of law. Ironically, it ended up propounding a concept of material justice, the sworn enemy of the formal rationality of the rule of law. Material justice will undermine the market economy and limit freedom of contract. In our case, the anti-market effects of material justice are exacerbated because of the existence of the inherited, premature welfare state. Material justice in Hungary jeopardizes the efficiency of the social, formal rationality of the budget, hence it threatens the financing of state activities and even macro-economic stability itself.

Questions and Comments

1. Consider the possibility that the Hungarian Supreme Court regarded its decision as a statesmanlike way of easing the transition to a market economy. The concurring opinion hints that abrupt changes could produce social resentment that would in turn undermine the nation's ability to make the transition. On what basis could we assess the comparative ability of a court and a legislature to make such a judgment accurately? How much would you have to know about the partisan composition of the legislature that enacted the social welfare provisions at issue? About the training and ideology of the judges on the supreme court?

2. More generally, consider the role of courts in protecting reliance interests. The Hungarian Court suggests that "legal certainty" is the "most substantial conceptual element of a constitutional state," which limits how quickly the legislature may change welfare laws. Compare this with the discussion in *Casey*, Chapter I, of *stare decisis* concerns regarding women's expectations of the availability of abortion as they made decisions about work and family. Is the Hungarian Court's invocation of reliance here any less a countermajoritarian exercise than the plurality in *Casey*? Consider also the Hungarian court's decision applying the principle of "legal certainty" to preclude prosecutions for offenses committed under a prior regime. See Chapter IV above. Would Sajo say that the Hungarian court has chosen the wrong virtues (consistency and continuity) for the moment?

3. Why does Sajo say that "material justice is the sworn enemy of the formal rationality of the rule of law"? Is the rule of law concept limited to formal rationality, or are there ways of thinking about the rule of law that are more compatible with material justice? (Note that Professor Currie, at 24, has concluded that under Germany's conception of the Sozialstaat, the Court may be willing to limit the legislature's capacity to withdraw certain levels of existing benefits provided.)

---

2.   GENERAL CONSIDERATIONS

The next reading offers a general introduction to the idea of social welfare rights and its relation to other civil and political rights. Professor Tushnet draws on the U.S. experience to argue that we cannot sharply distinguish between traditional political and civil rights on the one hand and social welfare rights on the other: Protecting property rights in certain ways may make it difficult to guarantee constitutional protection of other political and civil rights, and may impede the development of legislation to protect social welfare rights. The reading raises one of the recurring questions in this book: To what extent can one generalize about constitutions and constitutionalism, and to what extent must one confine one's statements to the circumstances of specific societies at particular points in their historical development?[e]

Mark Tushnet, *Civil Rights and Social Rights: The Future of the Reconstruction Amendments*, 25 Loyola of Los Angeles L. Rev. 1207 (1992)

In speaking of civil rights, as defined in today's legal culture, many have been influenced by Dworkin's idea that rights are "trumps," that is, considerations that absolutely override competing factors. Further, many appear to believe that, at least in advanced constitutional systems, civil rights must be enforceable through some sort of judicial proceeding.

It has been contended that social rights are different. They often seem to require social provision; governments cannot simply stand aside, but must take positive steps to assure that rights to shelter, food and work are honored. Yet, although courts are well positioned to protect civil rights, they are ill-suited to enforce social rights; courts cannot devise effective methods of ensuring that shelter, food or jobs are available to citizens. The

e. For an earlier formulation, consider Mauro Cappelletti, *The 'Mighty Problem' of Judicial Review and the Contribution of Comparative Analysis*, 53 S. Cal. L. Rev. 409, 412 (1980) (raising and responding to attacks on comparative study based on existence of contingent variables, e.g., of history and tradition).

latter point is reflected in international human rights documents, which typically declare that social rights are to be provided to the degree compatible with the state of economic development of each society; no such qualifications attach to the description of civil rights.

I believe the foregoing claims are wrong.[21] First, civil rights are not in fact absolute in any interesting sense; that social rights cannot be absolute, therefore, does not distinguish them from civil rights. Second, enforcing both civil and social rights requires the same degree of judicial action, whether the action be a lot or a little.

A. Non-Absolute Rights: Civil and Social

Legal philosophers in the United States may have been beguiled by Dworkin's treatment of rights as trumps in part because they are familiar with the so-called absolutist tradition in free speech adjudication. The absolutist tradition, associated with Justice Hugo Black, took the language of the First Amendment to mean what it said: Congress shall pass no law abridging the freedom of speech means that Congress shall pass *no law*. In closely aligned constitutional traditions, however, the formulations are somewhat different. These traditions reflect a balancing of competing interests.

The preface to the Canadian Charter of Rights and Freedoms, for example, provides that rights are "subject only to such reasonable limits prescribed by law as can be demonstrably justified in a free and democratic society." One can imagine a constitution that protects social and economic rights with an analogous preface. Indeed, the standard formulation that the rights are to be provided to the degree compatible with the society's level of economic development seems a suitable transformation. This formulation is an expression of the underlying idea that rights are qualified by the social setting—the values of a free and democratic society in one case, the level of economic development in the other—in which they are exercised or guaranteed....

---

21. In one dimension that is sometimes overlooked, the claims may well be pernicious. Given the historical legacy of the regimes in Eastern and Central Europe, the people there have become accustomed to the idea that they are entitled to second generation rights (that is, economic and social rights). Further, the role of international norms in assisting successor regimes in attaining legitimacy means that those regimes can (strategically) defend their adherence to prerevolutionary modes of social and economic organization by referring to the international guarantees of second-generation rights. As a result, abjuring second-generation rights would amount to a historical regression.

If we examine how civil and social rights emerged, however, we might be troubled by one aspect of such a regression. Typically guarantees of rights to women lagged behind guarantees to men. To oversimplify, when men had civil rights, women had no rights; when men had political rights, women had civil rights; when men had social and economic rights, women had political rights. As intermittent news reports suggest, it seems likely that women will be the first victims of a regression in the protection of social rights. (There is, I should stress, no analytic connection between abjuring protection of social rights and increasing discrimination against women.)

B. Negative and Affirmative Obligations

Requiring governments to promote social rights, however, immediately suggests that social rights differ from civil rights, because governments must only protect civil rights. Affirmative governmental action seems to be required to promote social rights; someone, and legislatures are the obvious candidates, must establish programs for public provision of housing, food and work in order to implement social rights. In contrast, civil rights seem to be largely negative; all governments must do to promote them is to stand aside, not interfere with free speech or voting rights, and the like.

The contrast is heightened when the idea of rights is coupled with the thought that, to deserve to be called a right, an interest must be protected by an enforcement mechanism that can compel compliance with the right. Thus, courts stand ready to invalidate laws that interfere with free speech. But, if social rights are the same as civil rights, then courts would have to stand ready to say, for example, that the legislature's public housing program falls short of what the Constitution requires. Therefore, it would seem that the courts could force the legislature to raise taxes and devise a more adequate program. Yet there is little reason to think that judges would be adept at figuring out how to move from an unconstitutionally deficient housing policy to a constitutionally acceptable one. Moreover, the vision of judges compelling the imposition of taxes, or otherwise severely constraining the legislature in an area of difficult policy choices, troubles many.

I believe criticisms of the idea that social rights are analytically the same as civil rights are wrong. Civil rights implicate positive governmental action no less than social rights do. The argument has several components.

First, immediately after the domain of civil rights was expanded to encompass the right to vote and the right to be free from discrimination in the job market, protecting civil rights entailed positive action by the United States government. The government must establish voting schemes in which everyone's vote counts. When nongovernmental actors prevent someone from voting, the present legal culture finds a violation of the right to vote. Thus, protecting the right to vote means that the government must act positively to eliminate such interferences. Similarly, governments must establish mechanisms to enforce the civil rights limitation on discrimination by private employers, which also require positive steps by the government.

Second, we need to specify more precisely what is meant by "protecting a right." Some rights are purely formal in the sense that we demand only that the laws refer to those rights in the correct way but are unconcerned about associated social consequences. For example, a formal right to equality based on race would be satisfied by laws—such as laws dealing with housing—that made no reference to race, even though as a practical matter the quality of the housing available to people varied significantly based on race.

Other rights are more concerned with the actual distribution of social benefits and burdens. In the jargon of the constitutional lawyer, these rights deal with "effects" or "disparate impact." . . .

. . . [J]udicial enforcement of formal rights is quite limited. Formal constitutional rights provide statements of constitutional aspiration; that is, they identify values to which everyone ought to be sensitive. Therefore, legislatures ought to strive to devise programs that accommodate values inherent in formal rights. Moreover, courts ought to interpret statutes with an eye to those values.

The important point is that many civil rights are, to a substantial degree, formal rights. Social rights may be similarly formal. A right to housing, for example, may be satisfied when the legislature adopts a program aimed at assuring housing for all, even if the program falls short of the mark. To the extent that civil rights are simply formal rights (which I believe considerable) and that they serve as statements of aspiration rather than as enforceable legal norms, they may not differ substantially from many social rights.

Third, consider the idea of "effects." Suppose that when we call something a right, we mean that we would be concerned if people in the society could not, as a practical matter, exercise the right. So, for example, a society might protect a purely formal right to free speech, and yet the means of communication might be so concentrated that policies opposed by those who controlled the media could not be effectively put before the public. Similarly, as to the right of racial equality: many people believe that such a right is violated when, despite a regime in which law makes no reference to race, social benefits and burdens are in fact distributed differentially according to race.

If this is our conception of rights, or of some particular rights, then a right will be protected only when adequate provision is made for the effective exercise of that right. Thus, to protect rights, people must have access to the means of communication; social benefits and burdens must be "re"-distributed. This subset of civil rights, then, like social rights, would require positive government action.

Fourth, the objection to social rights is that they require governmental distribution of important social goods, either by legislatures or by courts. Yet civil rights involve similar questions of distribution. The point has been put most forcefully by proponents of restrictions on the availability of pornography. Proponents of these restrictions argue that women's liberty is restricted—their ability to walk on the streets without fear is limited—when pornography is freely available. The manner in which free speech rights are distributed affects the distribution of other societal goods, such as freedom of action. Thus, when a society defines free speech or other civil rights, it is defining what it regards as an acceptable distribution of important social rights.

The pornography example does not quite bring us to social rights, because the claim is that defining one civil right, free speech, in one way rather than another affects the distribution of another civil right. Consider, however, the problem of campaign financing. To the extent that free speech principles restrict a nation's ability to regulate campaign financing, substantive political outcomes regarding social rights are affected. Put crudely, making it difficult to regulate campaign financing helps preserve the status quo with respect to the distribution of shelter, food and jobs. The point is quite general: the definition of civil rights affects the degree to which social rights will be promoted. It therefore cannot be a distinctive criticism of social rights that defining what they are involves determining the distribution of social benefits and burdens, for the same is true when civil rights are defined.

Another way of making this point is that those who distinguish between civil and social rights assume that the distribution of housing, jobs and food results from private ordering—market processes—with which the government is uninvolved. Yet, as the current experience in Central and Eastern Europe abundantly shows, government is essentially implicated in structuring markets. The choices open to system designers are, in a sense, transparent, while the choices that have been made in more established systems are opaque.

Finally, consider the objection that "government in the large" may perhaps determine the distribution of food, jobs and housing by structuring markets, but courts should not. Courts may be appropriate institutions to define civil rights, but they are inappropriate institutions to define social rights. Yet the distinction between civil and social rights is thinner than its proponents claim. Civil rights include the right to own property, to act freely subject to ordinary liability rules and to enter into contracts. The manner in which those rights are defined determines how the interests protected by social rights are distributed.

For example, if a society defines the right to dispose of property to include a factory owner's power to shut down the plant whenever he or she wants, jobs may be more at risk than if the property right is defined so as to permit a shutdown only if certain conditions are met. There is nothing in the nature of the concept of property, or other civil rights, that forecloses the second definition of property. Yet, of course, the two definitions have quite different implications for the protection that society accords work. If we want to assure a certain distribution of jobs, shelter and food, we can reach that goal by a careful definition of property rights.

Undoubtedly, the distribution of investment between plants covered by plant-closing laws and other economic opportunities will vary depending on the property and contract regimes a society has; if plant-closing laws define property rights only with respect to what used to be called the commanding heights of the economy, there will be more investment in "non-peak" industries than there would be if such laws applied to every enterprise. As a result, the forms of material well-being will also differ: less steel, more computers, perhaps. These differences, while arguably relevant to the question of how wealthy a society is, have essentially no connection to the more important question of what the society's level of social welfare is.

Social welfare takes into account all of society's values in a way that money wealth does not.

In this way the distinction between civil and social rights collapses: by defining the civil right to property in a specified way, we can accomplish whatever we want regarding social rights.

Arguably, the preceding point may be correct when considering the initial distribution of property, but transactions between freely contracting parties will undo whatever provision of social rights we accomplish through the initial definition of property rights. The next step though should be obvious: nothing in the nature of civil rights determines what definition of "freedom with respect to contract" the society should adopt. Any system will have exceptions or conditions under which it may be said that a party was not freely contracting. One manner in which society may limit freedom of contract is through the law of incapacity. The system could have a quite narrow definition of incapacity, limiting it to lunatics and children, and it could invalidate only contracts procured by fraud narrowly defined. But, again, nothing inherent in the notion of civil rights bars a broader definition of incapacity. A system could, without violating any accepted notions of civil rights, hold that a person who lacked knowledge or appreciation of some important characteristics associated with a transaction—including the transaction's impact on the long- term distribution of power—lacked capacity to enter into a binding contract. Instead of taking intellectual capability as the measure of capacity, it could recognize cognitive impairments that make it unlikely that the party accepting the short end of the deal truly understood what was at stake.

By coupling a careful definition of initial property rights with an equally careful definition of the conditions of "free contract," then, we arrive at whatever specification of social rights we want. Notice, too, that this regime involves only the traditional categories of property and contract, that is, legal categories whose definition is ordinarily remitted to the courts. In short, if we think that courts have the ability to define civil rights, we must think that they have the ability to determine social rights. The only question is whether they will be sufficiently aware of that ability.

None of this is to say, of course, what choices societies should make as they define civil or social rights. My only point is that people involved in the process should not attempt to distinguish between civil and social rights in the way many have suggested. . . .

Questions and Comments

1. Professor Tushnet suggests several ways in which first and later generation rights might be related. Consider the following suggestion that second generation social welfare rights might conflict with third generation rights to cultural community: "[M]any defenders of the Scandinavian welfare state view efforts to preserve the linguistic and cultural patterns of minorities as a *threat* to the welfare state. Immigrant men, especially from Turkey and other countries in the Middle East, tend to view the female-friendly aspects of the Scandinavian welfare states with great suspicion: day care, child allowances, and public health services, in their view, represent attempts by the authorities to impose secular and egalitarian values upon their religious, traditional, and usually patriarchal beliefs. By insisting that the language of the welfare state is, and can only be, Swedish, welfare authorities try to reach around immigrant men and establish direct contact with the women for whom services are designed— or, in some cases, to reach around both parents in an effort to target the children." Alan Wolfe and Jytte Klausen, *Identity Politics and the Welfare State*, Social Philosophy & Policy, vol. 15, no. 1, at p. 244 (Summer, 1997).

2. Is it correct that "[t]here is ... no analytic connection between abjuring social rights and increasing discrimination against women"? If one regarded women as a class that was subordinated in the family and the market, could one conclude, analytically, that positive government conduct was required to prevent further subordination?

3. Professor Tushnet argues that careful definitions of civil and political rights can yield any desired set of social welfare rights. Are constitution writers likely to be able to develop definitions that produce such results?

4. In the following article, Professor Sunstein argues that constitutions should "work against" the "most threatening tendencies" in a country. Based on your reading of the Hungarian Supreme Court decision and Professor Sajó's article, what are those tendencies in Hungary? Wiktor Osiatinski responds with a defense of including social welfare rights in the Polish Constitution, but with the important qualification that such rights should not in general be enforceable in the courts. Professor Sunstein argues that it is unwise to include unenforceable rights in Eastern European constitutions. Whose arguments do you find more persuasive?

Cass R. Sunstein, *Against Positive Rights*, in Western Rights? Post-Communist Application (András Sajó ed., 1996)

If we look at the actual and proposed constitutions for Eastern Europe, we will find a truly dazzling array of social and economic rights. The Hungarian Constitution, for example, protects not merely the right to equal pay for equal work, but also the right to an income conforming with the quantity and quality of work performed. (Pause for a moment over what it would mean for the Hungarian Constitutional Court to take these provisions seriously.) The Slovak Constitution [includes a] right to a standard of living commensurate to each citizen's potential and that of society as a whole. It also includes the right to just pay. Almost all of the actual documents and proposed drafts include the rights to recreation, to paid holidays, to food and shelter, to a minimum wage, and to much more. A chaotic catalogue of abstractions from the social welfare state coexists with the traditional rights to private property, free speech, and so on.

I think that this is a large mistake, possibly a disaster. It seems clear that Eastern European countries should use their constitutions principally to produce two things: (i) firm liberal rights—free speech, voting rights, protection against abuse of the criminal justice system, religious liberty, protection from and prevention of invidious discrimination, property and contract rights; (ii) and the preconditions for some kind of market economy. The endless catalogue of what I will be calling "positive rights," many of them absurd, threatens to undermine both of these important tasks....

... [T]he argument against positive rights applies with distinctive force to countries in the unique position of transition from communism to a market economy. Other countries, especially in the West, are in a different situation, and it is by no means clear that social and economic rights would be futile or harmful for them. Some such countries—which have market economies, are doing well economically and sometimes neglect the poor— might benefit from a constitutional culture that makes a commitment to (for example) decent medical care and adequate nourishment. Eastern European countries are in a quite different position.

We may draw an important and general conclusion from this suggestion. It is often said that a constitution, as a form of higher law, must be compatible with the culture and mores of those whom it regulates. Of course there is much truth in this. But in one sense, the opposite is true. Constitutions can be understood as *precommitment strategies*, being used as a founding document for practical and concrete purposes, including the provision of protection against the most likely problems in the usual political processes. If this is so, constitutions should be designed to work against those aspects of a country's culture and traditions that will predictably produce harm through that country's ordinary politics. Constitutions should therefore work *against* each particular country's own most threatening tendencies. We might think of good constitutions as counter-cultural in this respect. Because of their practical goals, constitutions might work against current tendencies, and leave out rights that are likely to be safeguarded in any case, or that are likely to create damage to a particular national project....

... Under imaginable social circumstances, a good constitution might omit certain rights that a "just" society would ultimately furnish. The omission might be justified on various grounds, including the difficulty of obtaining agreement on the relevant rights at the constitutional stage and the likelihood that those rights will be adequately guaranteed through ordinary political processes. In the United States, this argument might apply with respect to (say) freedom of contract or environmental protection; it is reasonable to think that these are important goods that should not be recognized in the U.S. Constitution. In Eastern Europe, we might believe that there is no special reason to constitutionalize the welfare state, even if its guarantees are properly part of a decent society; perhaps there is no risk that the welfare state will be jeopardized by the new regimes, and perhaps the specification of welfare rights would jeopardize the urgent project of creating a system of legally enforceable guarantees. If one of a constitution's distinctive roles—especially in the realm of rights—is to counteract predictable problems in the ordinary politics of particular nations, the constitution might not guarantee rights that, while a part of a good society, are not at particular risk in the politics of the country for which the constitution is designed. . . .

. . . [N]ot all positive rights are the same. The right to education, for example, is more readily subject to judicial enforcement than the right to a clean environment. Some of the relevant rights pose especially severe risks. Others are relatively harmless. A fine-tuned analysis would distinguish among different rights in terms of the threat they pose to the establishment of judicial review, free markets, and civil society.

Nonetheless, I believe that few positive rights belong in Eastern European constitutions, at least as a presumption. There are several reasons for this conclusion.

Governments in post-communist nations should not be compelled to interfere with free markets. Some positive rights establish government interference with free markets as a constitutional obligation. For countries that are trying to create market economies, this is perverse. A constitution that prevents the operation of free labor markets may defeat current aspirations in Eastern Europe.

Recall that the Hungarian Constitution protects not merely the right to equal pay for equal work, but also the right to an income conforming with the quantity and quality of work performed. This provision will have one of two consequences: (a) If the provision is to mean something, courts will have to oversee labor markets very closely, to make sure that every bargain produces the right wage. We know enough to know that government is ill-equipped to undertake this task. Courts are in an even worse position to do so. And if courts are going to oversee the labor market, it will be impossible to have a labor market. (b) The relevant provisions will be ignored—treated as goals or aspirations not subject to legal enforcement. This is a better outcome than (a), and courts in Eastern Europe should be encouraged to reach this conclusion. But it is hardly desirable to have a system in which many constitutional rights are ignored.

The Hungarian provision referred to above is an extreme example, but similar problems are raised by provisions calling for specified maximum hours, for paid parental leave, for paid holiday, and much else. Many of these provisions may make sense if they are placed in ordinary legislation. . . .

Constitutions should not hobble the creation of civil society. It is important to distinguish between the constitutional duties of government and the constitutional duties of the private sphere. This is especially true in post-communist nations, which are trying to establish civil society in the first instance. The post-communist constitutions pervasively fail to make this distinction, and instead impose their duties on everyone, and create rights which are good against everyone. This step perpetuates, if in a small way, the failure of communist societies to create and protect a civil sphere....

Wiktor Osiatynski, *Social and Economic Rights in a New Constitution for Poland*, in Western Rights? Post-Communist Application (András Sajó ed., 1996)

[Professor Osiatynski surveys the protection of social welfare rights in the constitutions of Western democracies, and summarizes the conclusions he draws]:

4. ... There are two general rules about the constitutionalization of social and economic rights: 1) the more rights of this type in the constitution, the less enforceable those rights and, sometimes, all rights; and 2) the constitutionalization of social and economic rights does not result in their automatic protection, while their absence from the constitution does not prevent some countries from instituting fairly generous welfare policies.

5. The inclusion of social and economic rights in communist constitutions created expectations and set standards which continue to be approved by a majority of people in post-communist countries. It is only a tiny minority of economic liberals who would do away with constitutional social and economic rights. A simultaneous transition to constitutionalism and democracy implies that social and economic rights cannot be neglected in new constitutions, especially if a constitution is to be approved by popular referendum as is the case in Poland.

6. The real problem is not the inclusion or even the scope of social and economic rights but the manner in which these rights are constitutionalized, as well as the mechanisms of protection granted to such rights. The constitutional provisions should distinguish between enforceable rights and mere social tasks of the state. While only the rights could be offered means of individual enforcement, other constitutional mechanisms should be designed to prevent the state from neglecting social tasks.

7. Social and economic rights should be accorded, in the constitution itself, different protections from those accorded to civil liberties and political rights, so that the budgetary and welfare policies of the state remain in the domain of the legislature, relatively free from adjudication by constitutional courts. One means toward this end would be to grant the legislature the authority to define in a separate statute the detailed content of particular social and economic rights as well as the scope of their protection by the courts....

... [S]ocial and economic rights should be given different constitutional protection from that accorded to civil liberties and political rights. While the latter should be directly enforceable in courts, the enforceability and the scope of social and economic rights should be left to the decision of the legislature.

This idea was first reflected in the draft Bill of Rights and Freedoms submitted by President Lech Walesa to Poland's Parliament in 1992. The draft bill divided traditional social and economic rights into two separate categories. The first category included five enforceable rights: the right to education, freedom of employment, the right to safe working conditions, the right to medical care, and the right to social security.[1]

The other category of social and economic "rights" included those benefits which cannot be enforced by courts: the betterment of the conditions of work, full employment, aid to families, health care beyond the basic level, education beyond the elementary level, the protection of cultural heritage, and protection of the natural environment. The draft stated expressly that these tasks of public authorities do not imply individual rights which can be claimed in court. The emphasis in the chapter was on the active role of the state, which is held responsible by political rather than legal means for the fulfillment of these tasks. The Bill of Rights differed from all other draft constitutions submitted in Poland between 1989 and 1993 in that it distinguished clearly between enforceable rights and the social, economic and cultural tasks of the state.

The National Assembly (elected in October 1993) selected a new Constitutional Committee. The Subcommittee on Individual Rights and Freedoms submitted to the Committee its draft of the chapter on individual rights, which went a step further than the draft Bill of Rights. It upheld the distinction between social and economic rights and social tasks of the state, and retained the political protections for the latter. It changed, however, the character of the social and economic rights. First, it increased the number of provisions formulated in terms of rights. Second, rights necessitating government spending were limited to Polish citizens rather than granted to "everyone." . . .

3.   Social and Economic Rights as Human Rights . . .

One commonly emphasized characteristic of social and economic rights (perhaps with the exception of property rights and the right to free enterprise) is that they require "positive" action by the state. Classical liberal rights are primarily defensive, *i.e.*, they protect the individual from intrusion by the state. Social and economic rights, by contrast, create positive claims against the state. While civil liberties and political rights are perceived as rights "from" interference, social and economic rights are often seen as rights "to" something; rights which are to be realized through the action of the state. Another characteristic of social and economic rights is that their implementation requires expenditures from the state budget.

On a closer look, however, one can see that these two features are also characteristic of many civil and political rights. Due process rights involve a

---

1.   Chapter III of the draft bill was entitled "Social and Economic Rights and Freedoms" (Arts. 29–33). This category of social and economic rights was kept to a minimum. All of the enumerated rights were to be, however, directly enforceable in the courts by instruments provided for in the Bill of Civil and Political Rights.

claim against the state for protection of the right to a fair trial. They put on the state a "positive" obligation to create and sustain a system of rather costly institutions through which individuals can enforce their rights. Political rights imply the state's duty to create mechanisms such as elections and representative institutions which enable the citizens to participate in politics; in some countries, the state is obliged to subsidize political parties. Thus, the belief that social and economic rights cost the state money while civil liberties and political rights do not is simply not true.

There exists, however, a more subtle difference between "old" and "new" rights. In the case of civil and political rights, the claim against the state is limited to the creation of a general mechanism which facilitates the implementation of rights. Social and economic rights, by contrast, imply an entitlement to a specific benefit. Moreover, civil and political rights serve all people living in a community, while social and economic rights provide benefits for some people at the expense of others.

To put it differently, civil liberties and political rights are designed to achieve the essential goals of the state, while social and economic rights pursue more subsidiary goals. Protection of individual liberties is the main goal of the state; no one is expected to provide court services for himself. Social rights, by contrast, imply that a state will provide for some people the kinds of goods and services that others, usually the majority, provide for themselves, buy on the market, or receive through charities. Since a modern state does not have independent sources of income other than direct or indirect taxation, social and economic rights involve a transfer of resources from taxpayers to rights claimants. The word "transfer" is perhaps the key to understanding the peculiarities of social and economic rights.

This feature of social and economic rights has influenced attitudes toward them. Many people see them as a matter of social policy rather than rights. For them, social and economic rights belong to the same category as equality and justice—they are legitimate aims of social policy, but not rights which society owes automatically to its members without discussion and bargaining among competing values....

4. Social and Economic Rights as Legal and Constitutional Rights

To call social and economic rights "human rights" is not to make them automatically enforceable. Human rights should set standards and provide justification for moral claims to decent treatment, and should guide legislators in the implementation of legal rights. In the last two hundred years there has been a steady trend toward legal implementation—and often constitutionalization—of numerous human rights, especially civil and political rights.

When human rights are constitutionalized, they are taken out of the realm of political debate. In short, in the case of civil liberties and political rights, constitutional polities have made a precommitment that such rights will not be violated, ignored or suspended in the absence of extremely compelling circumstances, and some of them will not be violated under any circumstances. Constitutional rights are also protected from abridgement by statute. . . .

In choosing how to influence the operation of market forces, a community should always weigh its needs and resources, values and priorities. Since such important elements of the decision-making process as the availability of resources, the sense of urgency, the feeling of deprivation, and the ability to find political support for demands are unpredictable, the decisions are usually left to the relatively short-term realm of politics. In a majority of democratic systems, such decisions are usually made by legislatures (or by a cabinet which claims democratic legitimacy, as in France) in the form of budgets and specific statutes and regulations. All governments avoid long-term pre-commitments in this domain. . . .

[Professor Osiatynski surveys the protection of social welfare rights in the constitutions of Western democracies, and summarizes the conclusions he draws]:

1.   Social and economic rights are usually given different protection from that given to civil liberties and political rights, even when social and economic rights are included in the constitution. The exception is the declaratory constitutions which do not provide for the direct enforcement of any constitutional rights.

2.   In those constitutions which do not distinguish between social and economic rights and other rights and liberties, the rule is relatively simple: the more social and economic rights in the constitution, the fewer enforcement mechanisms in the entire chapter on rights.

3.   The most developed "welfare state" social programs have been created in countries where the constitution either neglects social and economic rights altogether (Sweden, the United States) or declares as a general goal the implementation of social policy by the state (Federal Republic of Germany, France).

4.   Western democracies have gradually implemented social and economic rights; the main instruments of this implementation have been legislation and the decisions of constitutional courts.

5.   It seems more than plausible that the economic well-being of a society is a more important factor in the implementation of social and economic rights than any constitutional provisions. Constitutions, however, are extremely important for they help to justify inclusion of social policies in legislation and form the basis for the decisions of constitutional courts.

The experience of Western democracies can be helpful in thinking about the constitutionalization of social and economic rights in Eastern Europe today. The experience of the countries that launched the transition to democracy in the 1970s is especially revealing. The similarity lies in the fact that for a great majority of people in these countries, social and economic welfare similar to that which had been achieved by older democracies, was an obvious goal of a decent government. Thus a draft constitution which hoped for popular support could not neglect the social and economic aspirations of the people. On the other hand, by the 1970s,

Western European democracies realized that a constitution cannot be treated simply as a programmatic declaration of aims and values but has to be an enforceable instrument of protection of individual rights via courts and other remedies. This forced the authors of the constitutions of Spain and Portugal to adopt more realistic solutions than the drafters of the Italian Constitution of 1947.

The constitution makers of Eastern Europe face a similar problem. They must balance popular expectations for social security, an economic reality which cannot sustain these expectations, and the need to treat constitutions seriously. The problems of Eastern European transition, however, are even more difficult than those of Spain and Portugal in the 1970s. East European countries face a much more acute economic crisis and cannot count on such immense Western help as the nascent democracies of the 1970s. Moreover, they must undergo a double transition—to constitutional democracy and to the free market—simultaneously....

6. The Debate on the Inclusion of Social and Economic Rights in Post-Communist Constitutions

Such is the background against which the debate over social and economic rights in post-communist constitutions is framed. In fact, the role of social and economic rights in post-communist constitutions is one of most important controversies in current constitutional theory.

Many arguments have been voiced against the inclusion of social and economic rights in post-communist constitutions. The most important of them are the following:

1. The economics argument emphasizes the idea that "governments should not be compelled to interfere with free markets." Although many social provisions, including maximum work hours, paid vacations and maternal leave, are appropriate subjects for ordinary legislation, control of private markets should not be the task of a constitution. "These issues should be subject to democratic debate, not constitutional foreclosure." [Sunstein].

Other economic arguments against the inclusion of positive rights emphasize the fact that post-communist economies cannot afford such rights. Their inclusion in constitutions will either be a meaningless promise or will result in an unbalanced budget, growing debt and the ultimate bankruptcy of the state. Some economists emphasize the fact that government spending for social purposes increases purchasing power without balancing it with production, thus ever increasing the inflationary spiral. Inflation, in turn, is perceived as the main obstacle to successful economic reform and private investment.

2. The legal argument emphasizes the fact that many positive rights cannot be enforced by courts. Courts cannot enforce a right to the highest level of physical health, or to healthy environment or to vocational training for disabled persons. Court-ordered remedies are not the proper vehicle to

create positive government programs needed for the implementation of such rights.

3.   Moral and psychological arguments emphasize the fact that the inclusion of positive rights into constitutions could undermine the efforts to encourage individual initiative and the sense of responsibility for one's own life, both of which are very much needed in Eastern Europe. The constitutionalization of social rights would perpetuate the sense of entitlement and powerlessness which have characterized the people of the region.....

4.   Other authors have presented additional arguments against the inclusion of social and economic rights in constitutions. One argument concerns the potential adverse impact of such rights on traditional negative rights. Jon Elster warns that "the inclusion of symbolic rights in the constitution creates a danger that other, more traditional rights might also be interpreted as mere symbols or aspirations." In short, the inclusion of nonenforceable positive rights in constitutions may destroy negative rights.

The most important arguments in favor of the constitutionalization of social and economic rights are:

1.   Historical arguments point to the fact that social rights are not a Soviet invention but are, in fact, common throughout the world. They are espoused by international human rights documents and in many constitutions of the Western world, including France, Japan and Switzerland. Moreover, historical arguments also highlight the predominant ideological traditions in Eastern Europe. The exclusion of social and economic rights from constitutions is characteristic of a liberal tradition which has always been relatively weak in this part of the world. Two more influential ideologies, socialism (or social-democracy) and various currents of Christian thought, share a conviction about the paramount importance of the social goals of the state. The teaching of the Catholic Church has always put much more emphasis on social rights than on political freedoms.

2.   These ideological traditions feed into "constitutional arguments" for the inclusion of social rights. According to advocates of this view, a constitution is not only a legal document; it is also a founding document that assures national and individual survival. "Everything that a nation believes to be indispensable to their general welfare, belongs in the constitution." Thus "social and economic rights belong to the constitution because functionally a constitution removes such indispensables from the vicissitudes of majority rule." [Herman Schwartz].

3.   The claim that social rights lack judicial enforceability is not convincing for the advocates of the inclusion of such rights. First of all, some social rights—such as the rights to strike, to equal pay, to minimum wage, to a safe workplace—are enforceable. Second, even if other rights may be unenforceable and involve the enaction of new programs, such programs can be ordered by the courts.

4.   Even if many social rights are unenforceable, they can give rise to an obligation on the part of the state to act toward the fulfillment of an implied promise. According to Gomien, if some rights appear non-justicia-

ble, a constitution may simply note that they have only programmatic character and are not enforceable in courts. She also suggests that some social rights which cannot be immediately guaranteed can be included in a separate transitional chapter.

5. There is no empirical evidence that the inclusion of some judicially unenforceable rights in the constitution will tend to undermine negative rights.

6. Similarly, there is no evidence that the presence of such rights in a constitution strengthens a sense of entitlement and discourages individual initiative and self-reliance. Schwartz points here to the fact that the existence of positive rights in the Czech Charter of Rights and Fundamental Freedoms did not threaten the conservative policies of the Klaus government. Similarly, the existence of positive rights in the constitution of the Hungary has not slowed the trend toward a market economy in that country.

7. Thus, it has not been proven that social and economic rights impede the emergence of a free market. Moreover, the argument against such intervention would imply the ban on such rights anywhere in a legal system, not just in the constitution, for even a statutory program will interfere with the working of the market. Thus the free market argument is not an argument against the constitutionalization of social rights but against the very existence of redistributive social programs. "And that is a matter not of constitutional theory, but of political philosophy," concludes Schwartz.

8. Historical arguments also play a role in support of social and economic rights. First, some argue that many Western countries instituted social policies before they had amassed enough resources to be shared. Conversely, others claim that the experience of Western democracies proves that, in the process of economic growth, the social and political structure drastically changes. As a result, the groups which benefit from economic growth have a bigger say about the distribution of resources, and naturally resist the implementation of social rights. A great crisis—a wave of strikes or a revolution—may then be necessary to press the elites to share resources. The same may happen in post-communist countries, where ruling elites now insist that there is a need to wait on social rights until the countries can afford them. Therefore, if there is a commitment to social rights, it would be worthwhile to adopt a pre-commitment strategy which will automatically devote, for example, a fraction of a growing GNP to social policies.

9. Finally, the constitutionalization of social and economic rights may be required by the fact that constitutions need legitimacy. If a constitution is to become a reflection of democratic consensus, it has to include what people want to be included in it. There is no doubt that a majority of people in post-communist societies want social and economic rights to be included in their constitutions.

All of these arguments advocate the inclusion of social and economic rights in the constitution but they do not dictate the form which such rights should take. ...

7.   The consequences of the constitutionalization of Social and Economic Rights

In a truly constitutional culture, the constitutionalization of social and economic rights will have the following consequences:

1.   Citizens will have a constitutional claim in court to certain benefits and entitlements; such a claim will be disconnected from the actual state of the economy and will be protected from the political process and the decisions of the parliament.

2.   Since the resources needed for the implementation of social rights will have to be set aside on the basis of constitututional provisions, this will pre-determine a significant part of the state budget, further limiting political debate about social, economic and other goals of the society and state.

3.   The ultimate decision about a significant part of the budget will be transferred from the legislature to the judiciary, for a great majority of the decisions by the constitutional court on social and economic rights will have grave consequences for the budget. Thus, the principle of the separation of powers, according to which the legislature has the "power of the purse," would be distorted.

4.   There will be a more or less permanent conflict between the legislature and the Constitutional Tribunal over competencies, policies and decisions in view of scarce resources.

5.   Existing social and economic legislation will be petrified and the much-needed reform of the system of social insurance and social welfare will become harder to achieve. Constitutionalization of social and economic rights will freeze in place most of the old statutes that granted individuals some rights.

The alternative to constitutionalization would be to leave social and economic rights outside the constitution and leave them for the legislature, which would be permitted to abridge those entitlements which are outdated or unrealistic. This approach would not prevent the state from implementing social and economic policies according to the needs and possibilities of the time. Moreover, the constitution can place a positive obligation on the state to undertake such social programs. Such an obligation could be formulated as a number of state tasks specified in the constitution or one general provision similar to the "social state" clause of the German Basic Law.

Although such a solution seems very attractive, economically and legally, it is highly improbable in today's Poland. A constitution without provisions on social and economic rights would be seen as an attempt by the ruling elite to deprive the people of their acquired rights. Such a constitution will have little chance of support in the popular referendum by which the constitution must ultimately be adopted. Therefore, very few democratic politicians would have the courage to submit such a constitution to the referendum.

These are compelling practical arguments. Moreover, in the view of this author, social and economic rights should not be discarded from the constitution. They should be stated as an important goal during the dual transition. They are an ingredient of the transition to constitutionalism, for without them the constitution will not receive wide legitimacy. They are also an ingredient of the transition to democracy, for there is little doubt that a majority of Poles would want constitutional guarantees of social and economic rights.

8.   Protecting Social and Economic Rights: A Two-Tier Scheme

Thus, social and economic rights should be a part of post-communist constitutions. They should be formulated, however, in a different manner from provisions on civil liberties and political rights. First of all, some social and economic matters should be put in the constitution as tasks of the state rather than individual rights enforceable by courts. To avoid empty promises, such tasks should be given some form of political enforcement. Other social and economic matters can be formulated in the language of rights, however, with limited direct enforceability. As we have seen, most of the theoretical and legal problems with social and economic rights arise when they are afforded full constitutional protections, placing them above the legislature, in the hands of constitutional courts. The solution is to put them in the constitution but make it very clear that they remain within the domain of the legislature.

Taking into consideration all the arguments mentioned above, we can formulate the following recommendations for the drafters of a new constitution:

1.   Some rather limited number of social and economic rights should be included in the constitution. They should be formulated in a legalistic manner with no baroque programmatic formulations and with sensitivity to the fact that all promises need to be kept. These rights must therefore be enforceable against the state through the established legal remedies duly indicated in the constitution.

2.   The constitution should spell out the possibility of introducing, via legislation, an enforcement mechanism for social and economic rights different from that for civil liberties and political rights. A clause stating that social and economic rights can be claimed only within the limits set by statute can achieve this aim. In any case, there should be a provision that the scope and enforcement of social and economic rights are within the competence of the legislature.

3.   The social, economic and cultural "tasks of the state" can be included in the constitution, either in a separate chapter (as suggested in the draft Bill of Rights) or in the chapter on social and economic rights. In

any case, a separate article which clearly spells out that the social tasks of the state are not enforceable through the courts is indispensable. It would be desirable, however, to write into the constitution some nonjudicial mechanisms that would help in the implementation of these tasks.

4. The drafters should be extremely cautious in formulating any general clauses which may become the basis for social and economic claims to be adjudicated by the Constitutional Tribunal. Such provisions should be as concrete and clear as possible and should not create expectations that cannot be met.

5. This solution will require the re-evaluation of the traditional catalogue of social and economic rights. Many of them should be put in parts of the constitution other than the section on social and economic rights.

The following rights should be treated as civil liberties or political rights and awarded full constitutional protection:

1. The right of parents to bring up children according to their convictions; this right is more related to the freedom of thought and belief than to social and economic rights.

2. The right to private property, freedom of inheritance and the freedom of enterprise—these are classical personal freedoms.

3. The right to education, which is closer to a political right (for one can claim that there can be no participation in the affairs of a community without education); freedom of religious instruction in the schools (which is closer to the freedom of conscience than social rights); and the right of citizens and institutions to create schools (which is closer to freedom of enterprise).

4. Freedom of creative activities and scientific research, including the publication of results as well as the autonomy of the academia, belong to freedom of thought and expression.

5. The rights of the family, as well as the protection of the family from violence, are classical personal freedoms.

6. The rights of children to receive proper care; the protection of their personal goods and privacy; the right of children to be listened to and the right to claim protection from violence and abuse—these also belong in a section on personal freedoms.

This would leave the following rights in the section on social, cultural, and economic rights:

—the freedom of work;

—the right to safe conditions of work;

—the freedom to form unions, including the rights to collective bargaining and to strike;[74]

---

74. This freedom, however, could be ation.
moved to the article on the freedom of associ-

—the right to social welfare, including the right to financial help in the case of inability to work due to old age, illness or disability;

—the right to health care;

—the right to information about the state of the environment;

—the right to participate in culture;

—the rights of consumers.

Some of the articles that will include these rights will also contain separate provisions about related tasks of the state.

This solution makes sense for several reasons. First, it solves a great majority of the difficulties analyzed in this article. It gives social and economic rights constitutional status and pronounces them as important goals of the state. It permits, indeed obligates, the state to initiate social policies and makes the government accountable for them. On the other hand, it does not promise impossible things and it takes into consideration the limited resources of the state. It makes social programs a matter of democratic policy rather than a limitation on democratic choices. It respects the separation of powers, leaving social spending in the hands of the legislature. It gives everyone basic security without promoting an excessive sense of entitlement. It also permits the legislature to rationalize and reform the extremely inefficient system of social insurance, welfare and assistance grounded in existing statutory law.

Second, such a solution is in agreement with international human rights conventions. In fact, it is far in excess of the requirements imposed on the signatory states by the Covenant on Social, Economic and Cultural Rights and by the European Social Charter. It places on the state an obligation to protect such rights by statute and by developing policies which will fulfill the social goals of the state.

Third, such a solution follows the pattern of other countries such as Spain and Portugal. It gives stronger constitutional protection to social and economic rights than the constitutions of such democratic welfare states as the United States, Germany, Sweden or France. It also resembles the pattern adopted in other countries of East Central Europe that have already made a constitutional transition to democracy, notably the Czech Republic, the Slovak Republic, and Hungary.

Fourth, this solution is logically embedded in the history of human rights. For it can be claimed that while civil liberties limited the state by protecting the individual against the state, social and economic rights have arisen from the obligation of the community and later, the state, to care for its members. This obligation was originally formulated in terms of the tasks of the state power and only relatively recently re-formulated into the language of rights. The proposal defended in this paper makes a distinction between social policies which reflect the tasks of the state and social rights, which can become claims against the state, not by themselves but only by an additional decision of the democratic community. . . .

Questions and Comments

1. To what extent are Sunstein's arguments specific to the situation in eastern Europe in the 1990s? Note that the Italian Constitution contains provisions similar to those cited from the Hungarian and Slovak Constitutions. What information would you need to determine whether Sunstein's arguments are equally applicable to Hungary and Italy? Consider Professor Herman Schwartz' argument, in favor of constitutionalizing social and economic rights, that a constitution is "a political, social and moral foundation instrument that reflects the triumphs and sorrows of a nation's past and its hopes for the future." Herman Schwartz, *In Defense of Aiming High*, 1 East. Eur. Const. Rev. issue 3, 25–28 (1992). Are aspirational constitutions inconsistent with the rule of law?

2. Are there implications for constitutional provisions regarding the difficulty or ease of amendment of Sunstein's claim that his argument "applies with distinctive force to countries in the unique position of transition"? Consider, for example, whether on his arguments it would be appropriate for the United States Constitution today to contain some guarantees of social welfare rights, and whether Article V's amendment process obstructs that potentially useful development.

3. *Who* should be allocated initial property rights? In Eastern Europe many "holders" of property in 1989 and shortly thereafter were members of the Communist party bureaucracies. Their entitlement to the property was surely questionable. State enterprises were successors to private property holders. But some of those property holders had themselves received the property by government takings, particularly from Jews during the Nazi period. How can a constitution designer decide who should receive the initial property right: the present holders (who might have received the property through unjust transactions), their immediate predecessors (who might similarly have received the property unjustly), or remote holders? See Chapter IV above. Is there a relationship between this question and the question of social welfare rights? Is constitutionalization of welfare rights an appropriate response to regimes that restricted the accumulation and transfer of private wealth?

4. Should all constitutional rights in Eastern European constitutions be judicially enforceable, while some constitutional provisions in other constitutions need not be? Consider the possible ethnocentricity in such an analysis. Would the aims of Eastern European constitutions be undermined by treating social welfare rights as the Irish Constitution does?

5. Note the relation between the arguments here and constitutional provisions dealing with the difficulty or ease of amending the constitution. But note as well that, to the extent that Sunstein believes that constitutional protections of property rights are important to encourage investment in transitional economies, those protections must be hard to amend. Sunstein is explicitly concerned only with encouraging initial investment in transitional economies. Is it possible to write a constitution that is hard to amend in the short run, easier to amend in the longer run? Consider the provision in the New York State Constitution requiring a popular referendum to be held every twenty years on the question of whether to convene a convention to revise the state constitution.

7.   Osiatynski argues that social welfare rights should be included in a constitution in the form of unenforceable state duties. Is this a pragmatic and workable accommodation of the disagreements identified in the Sunstein and Tushnet readings? Or is it likely to reinforce the negative aspects of including unenforceable rights in a constitution, identified by Sunstein, while reinforcing a distinction between social welfare rights and other rights that Tushnet criticizes as untenable?

INDEX

1-56662-728-1

90000

9 781566 627283